GW01607904

THE IRISH CONSTITUTION

BUTTERWORTHS
1994

THE IRISH CONSTITUTION

J.M. KELLY

(THIRD EDITION)

BY

GERARD HOGAN

B.C.L., LL.M. (N.U.I.), LL.M. (PENN.), M.A., Barrister,
Fellow of Trinity College, Dublin

and

GERRY WHYTE

B.C.L., LL.M. (N.U.I.), M.A., Barrister, Fellow of Trinity College, Dublin,
Senior Lecturer in Law, Trinity College, Dublin.

BUTTERWORTHS
1994

Republic of Ireland	Butterworth (Ireland) Ltd, 26 Upper Ormond Quay, DUBLIN 7
United Kingdom	Butterworth & Co (Publishers) Ltd, Halsbury House, 35 Chancery Lane, London WC2A IEL and 4 Hill Street, EDINBURGH EH2 3JZ
Australia	Butterworths Pty Ltd, SYDNEY, MELBOURNE, BRISBANE, ADELAIDE, PERTH, CANBERRA and HOBART
Canada	Butterworths Canada, TORONTO and VANCOUVER
Malaysia	Malayan Law Journal Sdn Bhd, KUALA LUMPUR
New Zealand	Butterworths of New Zealand Ltd, WELLINGTON and AUCKLAND
Puerto Rico	Equity de Puerto Rico, Inc, HATO REY
Singapore	Malayan Law Journal Pte Ltd, SINGAPORE
USA	Butterworth Legal Publishers, AUSTIN, Texas; BOSTON, Massachusetts; CLEARWATER, Florida (D & S Publishers); ORFORD, New Hampshire (Equity Publishing); ST PAUL, Minnesota; and SEATTLE, Washington

First Published 1994
Reprinted 1995

A CIP Catalogue record for this book is available from the British Library.

ISBN 1 85475 1506

Typeset in Ireland by Compuscript Ltd

Printed in Ireland by SciPrint Ltd

TABLE OF CONTENTS

THE GOVERNMENT

OTHER CONSTITUTIONAL ORGANS

THE COURTS

FUNDAMENTAL RIGHTS

DIRECTIVE PRINCIPLES

CONSTITUTIONAL CHANGE; AND TRANSITION

TABLE OF STATUTES

ACTS OF THE OIREACHTAS OF SAORSTÁT ÉIREANN (IRISH FREE STATE) AND THE OIREACHTAS (POST 1922 ACTS)

ACTS OF THE PARLIAMENTS OF GREAT BRITAIN, IRELAND, THE UNITED KINGDOM OF GREAT BRITAIN AND IRELAND (PRE-1922) AND OF THE PARLIAMENTS OF THE UNITED KINGDOM AND OF NORTHERN IRELAND (POST-1922)

STATUTORY INSTRUMENTS

INTERNATIONAL TREATIES AND CONVENTIONS

TABLE OF CASES

DECISIONS OF THE IRISH COURTS

DECISIONS OF THE COURTS OF NORTHERN IRELAND, ENGLAND AND WALES, AND OF THE PRIVY COUNCIL

DECISIONS OF THE COURT OF JUSTICE OF THE EUROPEAN COMMUNITIES

DECISIONS OF THE EUROPEAN COURT AND EUROPEAN COMMISSION OF HUMAN RIGHTS

DECISIONS OF THE COURTS OF THE UNITED STATES OF AMERICA

DECISIONS OF THE COURTS FROM THE COMMONWEALTH (AUSTRALIA, CANADA, INDIA, JAMAICA AND NEW ZEALAND)

DECISIONS OF THE GERMAN COURTS

DECISIONS OF THE ITALIAN COURTS

FOREWORD

John Maurice Kelly (31 August 1931 – 24 January 1991), educated Glenstal Abbey, University College, Dublin, Heidelberg and Oxford. Barrister (later Senior Counsel), King's Inns. Fellow (later Honorary Fellow), Trinity College, Oxford. Professor of Jurisprudence and Roman Law, U.C.D., 1965-91. Editor, *The Irish Jurist*, 1966-73. Senator, 1969-73; T.D., 1973-89. At various times Parliamentary Secretary to the Taoiseach, the Minister for Defence, and the Minister for Foreign Affairs. Attorney-General, 1977; Minister for Industry and Commerce 1981-2. Author of *Princeps Iudex* (Weimar, 1957); *Fundamental Rights in The Irish Law and Constitution* (Figgis Dublin, 1961); *Roman Litigation* (Oxford, 1966); *Studies in the Civil Judicature of the Roman Republic* (Oxford, 1976); *The Irish Constitution* (1980); *A Short History of Western Legal Theory* (Oxford,1992), and many articles in learned periodicals.

Cassell's *English Dictionary* defines a foreword as "an introductory statement to a book." It has always seemed a rather dubious art-form to me, being, I thought, a response by some senior person to a call for aid by a young author fearful lest his frail craft should be overwhelmed on launching by hostile currents. The resultant puff from above would, hopefully, restore the equilibrium. As this book is the third edition of a textbook with a European reputation such a foreword is especially inappropriate. Nor are facile compliments from me required to bolster the self-confidence of the two editors, for they already enjoy an established reputation as legal authors. In John Kelly's noble and distinguished book the reader will be able to admire that "union of high speculative power with exact and comprehensive knowledge of detail" which H.A.L. Fisher found in F.W. Maitland. The work of the editors – and it has been a huge task to incorporate the legislative, judicial and academic achievements of the past decade – is fully worthy of such an author. In their introduction they explain fully the scope and nature of this new edition.

Before the reader turns eagerly to it, a few words of personal recollection may be in order, for my acquaintance with John Kelly went back to 1956, when, with my (very nominal) supervision he produced the Oxford graduate thesis which became the germ of this book. Before the outburst of judicial creativity in the 1960s, there really was no constitutional law in Ireland – just a few shreds and patches. John Kelly was almost the first person to identify and analyse the main problems. His intellectual powers matured noticeably as the years went by. If I had to point to one single example of his scholarly achievements, apart from this text book and the wonderful posthumous history of legal theory, I would cite the lecture on the Derrynaflan treasure trove case (*Webb v Ireland* [1988] IR 353), published in (1988) 10 DULJ 5. This covers no less than 16 different concepts, in depth, with comparative illustration from Roman and other legal systems, and with perceptive and sardonic asides drawn from his knowledge of human behaviour in the National Parliament.

Some were surprised that such a pure scholar should have held with evident enjoyment the position of Chief Whip in the Fine Gael party. In fact this post enabled him to develop on the national scene two gifts which had first been displayed at U.C.D. As Dean of the Law Faculty he showed much administrative skill in setting up a first class Law School within a decade and as Editor of *The Irish Jurist* he had a masterly personal touch in keeping contributors up to the mark. The most testy *savant* or *gelehrten* would respond favourably to one of John's beautifully written letters in fluent French or German. (Italian was also on call if needed). I vividly recall a brief visit to Leinster House years ago which showed these two gifts in action. One of his chores was settling the order of business for the coming week – he disposed of this task with brisk self-confidence, and he then took me to the bar, where he was soon the centre of a group of back-slapping professional politicians. (It was noticeable that they also treated him with cautious respect: his power of withering repartee was legendary). Oddly, for a Chief Whip he was the least biddable of men, at least when questions of principle were concerned. This may have hindered his rise to the summit of political life.

It was a very full life, but he always seemed to have time for long continental holidays or the exchange of Dublin gossip with one of his many friends. We feel proud to have been given the friendship of such a person.

R.F.V. Heuston

1 August 1993

PREFACE

This book is arranged around the text of the Constitution of Ireland of 1937. Its more informal, more general title, *The Irish Constitution*, is intended to reflect the fact that the general characteristics of the State were substantially formed before 1937; and while all the branches of our law depend for their formal validity on the 1937 Constitution, this enactment was very largely a re-bottling of wine most of which was by then quite old and of familiar vintages.

In the course of the re-bottling operation - to stick for a moment to that metaphor - there is no doubt that some elements of the emerging national legal system which formerly had been delicate and unstable - notably the principle of judicial review of legislation on constitutional criteria - were given a new security; and no doubt also that the very extended recitals of fundamental rights (by comparison with the Constitution of 1922) have yielded most important results.

Yet even in these two points it is quite possible that the State might have developed, within the 1922 framework, in much the same way as it ultimately did within that of 1937. More settled political conditions would have probably have led a Government to allow the transitional period (within which the Constitution could be amended without a referendum, by ordinary legislation) to expire, thus letting judicial review become a reality: though even under the rigid 1937 Constitution it is doubtful if the part which judicial review ultimately played was what its framers envisaged; and likely that it would have been much slower to reach that point if it had not been for the enterprise of one particular judge, George Gavan Duffy, to whom almost all the assertive interpretation of the Constitution in the first fifteen years after its enactment can be attributed. With regard to the fundamental rights recitals, too, the large edifice of judge-made law which has been erected on Articles 40-44 (and on Articles 34 and 38) might, apart from the newly entrenched rights in the field of the family and education, have arisen on the less elaborate statements of the old Articles 6-10 and 64-72, just as the US Supreme Court has constructed a great corpus of jurisprudence on the fairly brief statements of the early amendments.

These reflections are not intended to diminish the existing Constitution by comparison with its predecessor, but merely to show that the basic law of 1937 can be fairly presented as a stabilising and reforming continuation of that of 1922; indeed, that it would be misleading to present it in any other way. A great number of articles and sections of the later document are copied virtually, and often literally, word for word from the earlier one; and the case-law of the years 1922-37 in the constitutional field has often been relevant to the interpretation of the 1937 Constitution. It seems to me, accordingly, that in attempting a statement of Irish constitutional law, arranged for simplicity of presentation around the successive provisions of the present Constitution, the right approach is to regard the State as one which has been substantially the same polity since 1922.

In one respect, indeed, the Irish State has moved far away from its 1922 origins, namely in its status in the law of nations and its relationship to the British Crown, which occupied a formal place in the Constitution of Saorstát Éireann. This place had been expressly stipulated in the Treaty of 1921; and Dáil Éireann, sitting in the Autumn of 1922 as a constituent (i.e. constitution-making) assembly, had respected the treaty by entrenching it in the Constitution and putting it outside the amending power. It was this act of the constituent assembly, and not the Treaty or any British Legislation, which the

Irish courts thereafter regarded as the "root of title" of the Irish Constitution; while the English courts saw the Irish Constitution as the creation of the British parliament (through the Irish Free State Constitution Act 1922). The curious result was that, while in Britain the passage of the 1931 Statute of Westminster freed Dominion legislatures from the constraints of British constituent acts, and thus (from the British point of view) left the Oireachtas perfectly free to do what it liked with the 1921 Treaty (which was scheduled to another British Act of 1922), in Ireland the courts, denying that British legislation had conferred validity on the Saorstát Éireann Constitution and seeing its source of validity only in pre-Constitution Dáil Éireann, regarded the Statute of Westminster as equally irrelevant to what the Oireachtas might or might lawfully do. Accordingly, in their eyes the Treaty remained unalterable, whatever the British said, because the constituent Dáil had made it so.

In the first decade of the State, under W.T. Cosgrave, the nationalist background and inclinations of the Government's members ensured that while the Treaty was respected to the letter, the Crown enjoyed no more official recognition than the letter absolutely enjoined. In strong contrast to other self-governing Dominions, to which the Treaty assimilated Saorstát Éireann, the Crown was here kept on a shelf, scarcely visible behind an apparatus of State symbolism and practice which was entirely republican. There were no royal visits. The Army was the Army of the Irish Free State, and its officers held their commissions from the Government of the Irish Free State. The State's flag was the republican tricolour for which that of France had served as a model.

In 1932 the first Government was succeeded by an administration led by Mr de Valera whose whole programme was rooted in opposition to the Treaty and whose adherents had pushed their resistance to it to the length of civil war in 1922-23. Once in power, they proceeded to dismantle the Crown's positions, disregarding the judicial view that the treaty was beyond the amending power of the Oireachtas. In 1933 the reservation "within the terms of the Scheduled treaty" was removed from Article 50, and the oath of allegiance provided for in Article 17 was scrapped by the same Act. Further Acts of the same year abolished the appeal to the Privy Council from decisions of the Supreme Court, and reduced the functions of the Representative of the Crown. In 1936 the Representative of the Crown himself was eliminated, and with him every other reference to the British sovereign which the Constitution contained. However, by a separate Act passed the next day, the Executive Authority (External Relations) Act, the Crown survived with the sole practical function of accrediting Irish diplomatic representatives. In 1948 the first Inter-Party government, led by John A. Costello (who had been Attorney General under the First Government from 1926-32) repealed this Act; the repealing measure provided that executive authority in external relations might thenceforth be exercised by the President on the advice of the Government, and formally declared the State a republic (a designation which the 1937 Constitution had mysteriously avoided). Thus the royal and British theme descended between 1922 and 1948 in a chromatic scale until it ran off the constitutional keyboard; and the full republican chord, which might have been struck together in 1916 if the Easter Rising had succeeded, sounded (for twenty-six counties) in an arpeggio gradually formed over a quarter of a century.

During this period the State was part of the British Commonwealth, though the quality of its membership and the motive for keeping it up (the desire to retain some formal link with the North) were idiosyncratic. Up to the end of 1937 this membership had a formal place in the law, as it was stated in Article 1 of the old Constitution; but when the new Constitution came into force, membership became informal, the only surviving institutional link with Britain being the Executive Authority (External Relations) Act, which referred vaguely to Saorstát Éireann's "association" with other nations. Such a link, in the case of a sovereign State, was a unique anomaly; and it meant that the precise status of Ireland, and the category of nations to which the country was to be assigned, were impossible to state in clear terms. In 1947 Mr de Valera was received with derision when he resorted to a dictionary to prove that in spite of this link Ireland was a republic; and only since 1949, when even informal Commonwealth membership was discontinued, has it been arguable that the State bears the same character internationally as the French or the Italian Republic.

So far as concerns the internal structure of the State, a foreign lawyer looking over the Constitution will find very little that he has not seen before elsewhere- except, indeed, the dimensions attributable to the Catholic faith which come through especially in Article 41 and 42. The most conspicuous elements of the Constitution - a bicameral parliament whose lower House is elected from constituencies, a Government dependent on a parliamentary majority and consisting of Ministers all themselves members of that parliament, periodical elections, an independent judiciary, a head of State with functions largely ceremonial - are pretty much the same as the corresponding features of the British Constitution were in 1922 and still are: except that the British Constitution was and is alterable by parliament and that the judiciary, though independent, may not invalidate Acts of Parliament by reference to the principle of the constitution. The Irish Constitution has therefore the un-British features of rigidity of a written document containing a comprehensive bill of rights and interpreted by a judiciary with power to invalidate measures which conflict with it; this dimension of the Irish polity must be ascribed to the American example.

While the Constitution itself contains very little that is either original or specifically and characteristically Irish, the role it has played as a factor in the judicial department of the State has been of interest, particularly since about the year 1960.

The older generation of judges consisted of cautious men with a modest view of their own status *vis-à-vis* the legislature, and slow either to invalidate what the legislature had done or to take it on themselves to supply what it had left undone. This judicial attitude was perhaps natural in men most of whom had been born not long after the Franco-Prussian war. The world which formed their successors was radically different: the present Supreme Court and High Court consist of men (and one woman) who were students during or soon after the Second World War, who can remember the ruin of the European dictatorships of the right and the rise of the dictatorships of the left, who were able to observe both McCarthyism and the Soviet repression of Hungary, the influence of the institutional Catholic Church still at its height in the Irish Republic in the time of Pius XII, and the still unchallenged smooth rock-face of Orangeism in the Ulster of Sir Basil Brooke. Of the twenty-one judges who now sit in those courts, seventeen learned constitutional law from Patrick McGilligan (professor at University College, Dublin, from 1934 to 1959 simultaneously with a brilliant political career), who believed strongly in vigorous judicial review. Thus the judicial arm of the Irish State contained within the short stretch of sixty years both judges who were willing to assent to the doctrine of automatic implicit amendment of the Constitution by ordinary legislation; and judges who, a few years ago, evoked from a Taoiseach (Mr Jack Lynch) the comment that "it would be a brave man who would predict, these days, what was or was not contrary to the Constitution", so adventurous have the courts become.

If the judgment of the average liberal observer were asked for, he would probably say the overall impact of the courts on modern Irish life, in their handling of constitutional issues, had been beneficial, rational, progressive, and fair: as witness the decisions in *O'Donovan's*, *Ryan's*, *Macauley's*, *Byrne's*, *McGee's* and *de Búrca's* cases (the list could be much extended). That is my own view. But even an admiring and respectful eye can see certain strands in the texture of recent constitutional jurisprudence which invite a certain amount of doubt.

First, the minute word-by-word interpretation of the Constitution which the last decade has seen bears no relation to the realities of the process by which it was drafted and enacted. While it is true that the text was not treated with enough attention in the 1940s and 1950s, the sort of parsing and analysis - in two languages - which has become standard since about 1965 may go too far in the other direction. Article 34.1 clearly contemplated a fresh establishment of the courts. But must it follow that the Supreme Court mentioned in Article 26 was therefore not meant to cover the Supreme Court which existed in 1937, and that the three Article 26 referrals which took place before the courts were nominally reconstituted were all a mistake - even though Mr de Valera, who was in the best position to point out the mistake, headed the Government whose voice was available to the President, through the Council of State and otherwise, at the time of the former two of these (1940 and 1943), and was himself the referring President in the case of the third (in 1961)? The principle of equality of citizens before the law was a shibboleth long before Article 40.1 put it in a constitutional text. But did anyone in 1937 really intend that the phrase "as human persons" was to be used to whittle down its significance, rather than as a piece of pious padding? "Laws" is a word used in the Constitution in several contexts which require it to be understood *in those contexts* as statutes. Does it follow that the continuance provisions of Article 50 do not carry non-statutory law? or that such a conclusion is warranted by the use of the words "repealed or amended", when the purpose of drawing such a distinction between these categories of law is not apparent? May we not simply say that the intent of the Article is plain, but its drafting awkward? The Irish text being the authoritative one (however absurd the background of this rule) it is used as an elucidatory aid in construing the English. But does anyone believe that the nameless translators of 1937 (whose work was left virtually without debate in a Dáil most of whose members knew very little Irish anyway) deliberately used the Irish future tense rather than the Irish present (where English grammar would make no distinction) in order to convey that only post-1937 events were contemplated, or that the Government (let alone the Dáil or people) understood the results of such a technique? Such things have however been said or implied by the courts in recent times, and require from the observer an act of good faith of the kind which is normally accorded only to theological propositions.

Secondly, there is a tendency towards what seems a needless proliferation of concepts: some of them, one may suspect, inspired by the need to justify a result which instinctive common sense suggests, some of them redundant and looking like familiar, root concepts run to seed. An example of the former is the distinction, first surfacing in *Conroy v Attorney General*, between "primary" and "secondary" punishment (for the purpose of Article 38.5); of the latter, the notion of "constitutional justice", the coining of which implies that it has dimensions not in any case implicit in natural justice, or explicit elsewhere.

Thirdly, there is - as is perhaps unavoidable in a case-by case system, such as judicial as distinct from academic jurisprudence must be - not always a firm dogmatic groundwork for the structures into which the courts must fit some of the situations they are called on to adjudicate. One instance is the rather confused relationship between the "personal rights" of Article 40.3 and the "fundamental rights" of Articles 40-44 in general: do the these phrases mean different things? Have these rights different sources? Is any conclusion to be drawn from the fact that some rights, e.g. private property, figure in both settings in somewhat different verbal dress? Again, the position of natural law and natural rights is unclear; there are plenty of *dicta* which derive various written rights from a higher source "antecedent to positive law"; but if a clear conflict emerged between the Constitution itself and some principle of natural law - e.g. if an Act with the protection of Article 28.3.3 purported to deprive an accused person of the right to be heard - would the courts assert jurisdiction to override the plain words of the Constitution (seeing that the Constitution is itself an item of positive law)? Again, in the very important area of equality and its converse, discrimination, although there have been about thirty cases in which the matter was of greater or lesser relevance, no firm criteria seem to have emerged. It must be admitted that these problems are largely the consequence of the loose and vague language of the Constitution itself, whose drafters never intended it to pass through the analytical machine which the post-1960 Supreme Court has become.

****

The foregoing pages formed the main part of the Preface to the first edition of this book, which appeared in February, 1980. The last thirteen years have seen such an explosion of constitutional litigation that many topics (such as the principles of judicial review and the right to trial in due course of law) scarcely admit of the possibility of coherent thematic treatment and, indeed, the very format of this book may well have to be reviewed in advance of any subsequent edition. Nevertheless, the following general observations might be made about the progress and development of Irish constitutional law in the thirteen years which have intervened since the first edition was published.

First, respect for precedent and earlier authority has been weakened. Not only has the overruling of settled doctrine become more frequent (indeed, in the space of a few weeks in March 1990 the Supreme Court overruled three earlier decisions of its own concerning respectively Articles 2 and 3, the operation of the exclusionary rule following a breach of constitutional rights and whether paramilitaries engaging in unlawful violence outside of the State could be said to be engaging in unconstitutional behaviour), but it is also evident in an increasing inconsistency of approach and results as between major constitutional decisions. In this regard, one only has to compare *Quilligan (No.2)* (1988) with *O'Shea* (1982); *Crotty* (1987) with *McGimpsey* (1990); the *Well-Woman* case (1988) with the *X.* case (1992) and, not least, the decision in *Ambiorix* (1991) with the subsequent *Cabinet Confidentiality* case (1992). Not least because all of these judgments were of major constitutional, political and social importance, it behoves the judiciary to draw on a consistent seam of constitutional doctrine. If such important and far-reaching decisions as these cannot be rationalised in conventional legal terms - by reference to objective legal principles such as precedent and other accepted sources of law - this may well lead to the politicisation of constitutional law and adjudication.

Secondly, at the same time there has been an element of constitutional dogmatism in some areas which has, perhaps, left the Supreme Court defending intellectually unenviable positions. *Conroy's* case (1965) is a good example of this from an earlier judicial era, but the judicial attitude to the disappearance of the prerogative (as witnessed in *Byrne* (1972), *Webb* (1988) and *Howard* (1993)) is not easy to defend. This trilogy of cases rests on assumptions about the role of the Crown in the 1922 Constitution which were not shared by our legal and political forefathers of that era. These decisions effectively render redundant Article 49 of the Constitution, yet it can scarcely have been the intention of the drafters of the Constitution that an Article of the Constitution would effectively be set at nought by reason of a series of judicial decisions.

Thirdly, it may be possible to detect changing trends in the pattern of constitutional litigation. This seems especially true with regard to Article 40.3, since the courts' enthusiasm for new unspecified personal rights has clearly waned. Indeed, it may be significant that there appears to be only one recent decision of any significance (*Cox*, 1991) where the Supreme Court invalidated legislation by reference to Article 40.3. In contrast, one might tentatively suggest that the concept of equality - derived mainly, though not exclusively, from Article 40.1 - may feature more prominently in the future. Certainly recent cases like *MhicMathúna* (1989), *McKinley* (1992) and *Howard* (1993) invest the concept with some vitality, unlike earlier Supreme Court decisions, derided in previous editions of this work, which employed the idea of the essence of the human personality to keep Article 40.1 in a state of suspended animation. Moving on, the era of the constitutional test case - where, typically, litigants challenged (often successfully) rather restrictive social legislation reflecting the social values of earlier generations - would seem to be passing. Decisions such as *McGee* (1973) (family planning); *de Búrca* (1975) (womens' right to sit on juries) and *Murphy* (1980) (married couples' taxation) might be said to be characteristic of this particular era. Nowadays, such test-cases seem to be rarer, a trend which is probably explained by the fact that the Oireachtas is now in the process of finally completing a programme of social reform which was first initiated by the Supreme Court in the *McGee* case. At the same time, we must not underestimate the ever-increasing significance of the role of the courts in constitutional adjudication, since many issues of political controversy nowadays provide the spur for major constitutional litigation. Thus, within the last twelve months or so, we have seen five major constitutional cases arising from the Beef Tribunal; two such cases arising from the Telecom Inquiry and one arising from the Mullaghmore interpretative centre. In addition, the Beef Tribunal cases served to highlight important areas dealing with the machinery of Government (such as parliamentary privilege and cabinet confidentiality) which had hitherto received scarcely any scrutiny.

Fourthly, one cannot help observing that despite all the signal advances in many areas of constitutional law, some topics remain almost stubbornly underdeveloped. This seems especially true of both Article 40.6.1 and Article 44. With the possible exception of O'Hanlon J's judgment in *Desmond v Glackin* (1992), it would be difficult to point to a single case where more than lip service has been paid to the rights of free speech and free expression. In the case of freedom of religion, almost nothing has happened since the seminal decision in *Quinn's Supermarket* (1972). This is only partially explained by the fact that formal discrimination or even differentiation on grounds of religion is almost completely absent from Irish society, since there is a variety of administrative practices (ranging from the State's endorsement of the fact that certain publicly-funded hospitals avowedly follow the "ethos" of a particular religious denomination to the practice of requiring school pupils to follow an "integrated" curriculum in a manner that apparently subverts the right to parents to insist that their children receive separate religious instruction) which raise interesting questions concerning the proper interpretation of Article 44.

Fifthly, the increasing secularisation of Irish society is gradually bringing to the surface the ideological tension within the Constitution itself between precepts of liberal democracy on the one hand and aspects of Roman Catholic social teaching on the other. This is very marked in some areas such as education. Now that the Oireachtas has to some degree fallen under the sway of liberal democracy - as witnessed by recent family planning legislation and legislation providing for the decriminalisation of homosexual acts between consenting adults - we may perhaps come to expect litigation in which more traditionally minded plaintiffs will seek to assert the primacy of the "family values" in Articles 41 and 42 in order to attack the constitutionality of social legislation in areas such as education and child sexual abuse: indeed, the *MhicMathúna* (1989) case provides a good example of just such a challenge. There are already some indications that this conflict has affected some judicial views. One consequence of this may be - especially in the light of such controversial cases as the *X.* case - that we will have closer political scrutiny of judicial appointments in the future. Certainly, there is growing academic interest in the political role of the judiciary as interpreters of the Constitution.

Sixthly, we have seen the importance of European Community law and the decisions of the European Court of Human Rights grow apace. With regard to Community law, the most important issue that needs to be addressed in this context is the precise inter-action between Community law (as a species of federal law) and the Constitution itself. This question has manifested itself in a number of ways in recent years. Important decisions of the Court of Justice - such as *Simmenthal* (1978), *Factortame* (1990) and *Marleasing* (1990) - have re-inforced the operation of the Community's supremacy doctrine; yet the Supreme Court has hinted in *Grogan* (1989) that it may have the last word in this area. Perhaps what is really needed is a good single judgment on the meaning of the "necessitated" clause in Article 29.4.5 and, at the time of writing, it appeared that the Supreme Court had availed of this opportunity with its judgment in *Meagher v Minister for Agriculture and Food.* (While this judgment was delivered after this edition had gone to press, it is noted (together with a few other recent decisions) in an Addendum at pp. 1182-1183). The jurisprudence of the European Court of Human Rights has also greatly expanded in recent years and its importance for areas of domestic constitutional law (such as police powers and freedom of speech) can scarcely be over-stated.

One practical point must also be mentioned in this context. The decision of the German Constitutional Court - upholding the constitutionality of the ratification by Germany of the Maastricht treaty - in October 1993 removed the final obstacle to the ratification of the Maastricht Treaty on European Union. This particular court decision - with its obvious affinity to the issues raised with regard to the Single European Act in *Crotty* - only serves to remind us of the rich seam of jurisprudence that awaits any comparative constitutional lawyer who is minded to draw parallels between the decisions of the Spanish, Italian and German Constitutional Courts and those of our own High and Supreme Courts. We have endeavoured to address this question to a very limited degree by including passing references to continental decisions - in particular to those of the German and Italian Constitutional Courts.

The preparation of this edition has taken about eighteen months. We have endeavoured to remain faithful to the format and layout used by Professor Kelly in the earlier editions and supplement, save in two respects. First, we now treat of constitutional interpretation as a separate and distinct topic in an introductory chapter, rather than as an aspect of Article 34.3.2. Second, considerations of expense have compelled us to replace the distinctive marginal notes of previous editions with sub-headings in the body of the page. This decision was not lightly taken, though we feel sure that the new arrangement will serve equally as well to highlight the points under discussion in the text.

It only remains to thank those who have assisted us in the completion of this book. In the first place we must thank Mrs Delphine Kelly who at all times has given us every possible encouragement and assistance. Professor Robert Heuston was kind enough to write the Foreword. A number of our colleagues at the Law School, Trinity College, Dublin were also most supportive. In particular, Anthony Whelan read virtually the entirety of the book in draft, making many corrections and helpful suggestions, while Professor William Duncan and Eoin O'Dell gave similar assistance in relation to the chapters on the family and freedom of expression respectively. We would also like to express our thanks to Ms Geraldine Skinner of the Department of Foreign Affairs and Dr Clive Symmons for their assistance with the section on the law of the sea at pp. 17-20 and to Mr Sheamus Smith, the Film Censor, for supplying some information on the operation of his office. We must particularly acknowledge our indebtedness, once more, to Eoin O'Dell for converting our computer discs to suit the printer's specifications.

Paul Coughlan kept us supplied with a constant stream of recent judgments as soon as they appeared. Des Mulherne and Paul Moloney of the Law Library responded to every request with courtesy and exemplary diligence. We are also indebted to Jennifer Aston and her colleagues of the Law Library, Margaret Byrne of the Incorporated Law Society; Hilary Delany, Barrister; Dervla Browne, Barrister; Niamh Hyland; Michael McDowell S.C.; Desmond O'Malley T.D.; Bryan Sheridan, Solicitor; Peter Ward, Barrister and Seamus Woulfe, Barrister, all of whom supplied us with material which was otherwise difficult to trace; and we apologise if through inadvertence we have omitted from this list anyone who was kind enough to help us. As ever, we would be glad to hear from readers who notice mistakes or omissions.

We must also thank Julitta Clancy for preparing an exemplary Index which will, no doubt, be greatly appreciated by the reader, and Gráinne McDermott and Clodagh Fitzpatrick, for administrative assistance at various stages during this project. Our publishers were at all times very supportive of our efforts. We owe a particular debt of gratitude to Thérèse Carrick on a number of counts - for the highly efficient and ever courteous manner in which she liaised between the typesetter, printer and ourselves, and also for the many tedious hours she spent preparing the table of cases and table of statutes. We have endeavoured to state the law on the basis of materials available to us as of 1 November 1993, the date on which the Maastricht Treaty on European Union came into force. We have, however, managed to squeeze in brief references to some significant subsequent developments.

Penultimately, we must also thank our respective families, Karen and Niall, Mary and Audrey, for their unfailing support, encouragement and patience in the completion of a task which, in the end, proved to be more difficult and complex than we had anticipated.

Finally, as the reader will be only too painfully aware, the third edition of this book will be the first which has not been written by the late John Kelly. We can only here acknowledge the Herculean task involved in the conception, writing and production of the first two editions of this book. Sadly, we will miss the inspiration derived from his incisive intellect and breadth of knowledge and this edition will be all the poorer as a result.

Gerard Hogan
Gerry Whyte

Law School,
Trinity College, Dublin

20 December 1993.

CONSTITUTIONAL INTERPRETATION

Since the theme of constitutional interpretation[1] is probably best described as "adjectival" rather than "substantive" in character (in the sense that it informs every provision in the Constitution) it seems appropriate to begin our examination of the Irish Constitution with a consideration of the different approaches to constitutional interpretation adopted by the Irish judiciary.

No fewer than five different approaches to the interpretation of the Constitution may be found in the extensive case-law on this subject, although it is true that these approaches sometimes overlap. The approaches in question may be characterised as follows: literal interpretation; the "broad" approach; the doctrine of harmonious interpretation ; the historical approach and the natural law approach. These separate approaches will be examined in due course. One needs to emphasise, however, that the courts have shown no consistency with regard to any particular approach and this gives rise to the suspicion that individual judges are willing to rely on any such approach as will offer adventitious support for a conclusion which they have already reached. At present, however, the "broad" and "harmonious interpretation" approaches are probably in the ascendancy, although contemporary examples may be found in respect of all these distinct approaches.

THE LITERAL APPROACH

Two particularly good examples of this approach may be found in two judgments of the Supreme Court which concern the appellate jurisdiction of that Court: *The State (Browne) v Feran*[2] and *The People (Director of Public Prosecutions) v O'Shea*.[3] In both cases, the Supreme Court interpreted Article 34.4.3 literally so as to permit (in the *Browne* case) an appeal against a decision to order the release of a prisoner by way of *habeas corpus* and (in the *O'Shea* case) an appeal by the prosecution against an acquittal in the Central Criminal Court. In the latter case, O'Higgins CJ gave a useful exposition of the interpretative process employed in both cases:

> "The Constitution, as the fundamental law of the State, must be accepted, interpreted and construed according to the words which are used; and these words, where the meaning is plain and unambiguous, must be given their literal meaning. Of course, the Constitution must be construed as a whole and not merely in parts and, where doubts or ambiguity exists, regard may be had to other provisions of the Constitution and to the situation which obtained and the laws which were in force when it was enacted. Plain words must, however, be given their plain meaning unless qualified or restricted by the Constitution itself."[4]

This approach undoubtedly has its merits, chief among them the fact that it enables the courts to follow closely the actual language of the text of the Constitution itself. This in

[1] See generally, Gwynn Morgan, "*Constitutional Interpretation: Three Cautionary Tales*" (1988) 10 DULJ 24; Hogan, " *Constitutional Interpretation*" in Litton ed., "*The Constitution of Ireland, 1937-1987*" (Dublin, 1987) and Barrington, " *Some Problems of Constitutional Interpretation*" in Curtin and O'Keeffe eds., "*Constitutional Adjudication in European Community Law and National Law*" (Dublin, 1992).

[2] [1967] IR 147.

[3] [1982] IR 384.

[4] These examples are by no means exclusive: see, e.g., *per* Henchy J in *The State (Nicolaou) v An Bord Uchtála* [1966] IR 567; (1968) 102 ILTR 1 (holding that since the applicant was not a "citizen" he had no standing to rely on Article 40.3); *McGimpsey v Ireland* [1990] 1 IR 110; [1990] ILRM 440, (treaty not a "law" for the purposes of Article 40.3). See also discussion of the literalist interpretation of Article 40.1 at pp. 722-723.

turn militates against the high degree of judicial subjectivity, inherent in other approaches to constitutional interpretation, such as that of harmonious interpretation. Its chief disadvantages are essentially two-fold. First, it obliges the courts to fall back on standard common law principles of statutory interpretation. These principles are designed as an aid to the interpretation of legislation which, following the common law tradition, has been carefully drawn with these principles in mind. For this reason these principles may not be appropriate in the case of a Constitution, which in the nature of things tends to lay down general principles. And as both Gavan Duffy J and Costello J have each separately remarked, it seems wrong to parse the Constitution as if it were a Finance Act.[5] The second disadvantage is related to the first, namely, that it is plain that the drafters of the Constitution never intended that it should be so construed. One example suffices to make this point. If it had ever been foreseen that such an approach would be adopted, steps would have been taken to harmonise the drafting of Articles 40 to 44 so as to provide for uniformity as regards the State's duty to vindicate and protect the individual rights protected by these provisions.

THE "BROAD" APPROACH

The essence of the "broad" approach is that, while it favours a process of interpretation which is guided by the actual language of the text of the Constitution, it rejects the excessive literalism of cases such as *O'Shea*. In other words judges employing this method are likely to construe the text of the Constitution in a broad, purposeful manner which best advances the "intentions of the people as embodied therein" and which identifies the Constitution's "purpose and objective in protecting human rights." This in turn means that such judges are less likely to have recourse to standard common law methods of interpretation such as the *expressio unius* rule or a construction which would tend to construe certain terms in the Constitution as terms of art.

Evidence of such an approach can be seen in a number of decisions. We may commence with *N.U.R. v Sullivan*,[6] where, in discussing the sense of Article 40.6.2 which envisages laws "regulating" the exercise of the right of association, Gavan Duffy J said:

> "Regulation" has been the subject of much discussion in other jurisdictions, but an organic law is emphatically not to be parsed as if it were an Income Tax Act; the elaborate details, absolutely requisite in a fiscal enactment, would be out of place in a fundamental law... the text of a Constitution ought to attempt no more than to mark its great outlines."

A similar view was expressed by Costello J in *Attorney General v Paperlink Ltd.*:[7]

> "The Constitution is a political instrument as well as a legal document and in its interpretation the courts should not place the same significance on differences of language used in two succeeding sub-paragraphs as would, for example, be placed on differently drafted subsections of a Finance Act. A purposive, rather than a strictly literal approach to the interpretation of the sub-paragraphs is appropriate."[8]

[5] See *per* Gavan Duffy J in *N.U.R. v Sullivan* [1947] IR 77; (1947) 81 ILTR 55 and *per* Costello J in *Attorney General v Paperlink Ltd* [1984] ILRM 348.

[6] [1947] IR 77; (1947) 81 ILTR 55.

[7] [1984] ILRM 348.

[8] See also the extra-judicial comments of Costello J in "*The Irish Judge as Law-Maker*" in Curtin and O'Keeffe eds., " *Constitutional Adjudication in European Community Law and National Law*" (Dublin, 1992):

> "it should be remembered that the Court is not construing a badly drafted statue - it is construing the Constitution which is both a political as well as a legal document. That means that it is designed to be inspirational as well as normative and that its language approaches rhetoric which would be out of place in a modern statute. This means that a minute textual analysis of the constitutional texts is not the correct approach and that it would be wrong to infer a legal significance in every drafting difference which may be found."

In *O'Byrne v Minister for Finance*[9] Lavery J said that the Constitution of 1922 was:

> "to be construed as a statute would be, subject to the proviso that being properly expressed in general words having regard to its character as the fundamental law, a broader meaning might be legitimately given to its provisions than might be given to an Act of parliament;"

though later in his judgment he said a Constitution should be construed according to its words and not according to any supposed intent. In the same case Dixon J had said in the High Court that:

> "it may be that the literal meaning rather than the intention should prevail, although, in the case of a Constitution, which is a unique, fundamental document, concerned primarily with the statement of broad principles in general language, I am inclined to the view that it is not to be parsed with the particularity appropriate to ordinary legislation, and that the intention, if it can reasonably be gathered, should prevail."

In *Sullivan v Robinson*[10] O'Byrne J said, in giving the judgment of the Supreme Court:

> "A Constitution is to be liberally construed so as to carry into effect the intentions of the people as embodied therein;"

and in *Melling v Ó Mathghamhna*[11] Ó Dálaigh CJ, rejecting the argument based on the verbal difference between the phrases "criminal charge" and "criminal offence" (in the context of the right to trial by jury as against summary trial) said:

> "If there be some difference, which I do not discern, let it suffice to say that the Constitution is to be read not as dealing with words but rather with the substance of liberty."

The doctrine was applied by Costello J in both *Attorney General v Paperlink Ltd.*[12] and *Murray v Ireland.*[13] In the *Paperlink* case, the judge said it must be borne in mind that the Constitution was a political as well as a legal document, and thought that the difference of phraseology as between Article 40.3.1 and Article 40.3.2 was not of significance:

> "The courts should not place the same significance on differences of language used in two succeeding sub-paragraphs as would, for example, be placed on differently drafted sub-sections of a Finance Act. A purposive, rather than a strictly literal, approach to the interpretation of the sub-paragraphs is appropriate. I do not, therefore, think that any significance should attach to the fact that the State's duty towards the citizens' unspecified personal rights in Article 40.3.1 is phrased in somewhat different language to its duty towards the citizens' specific personal rights as set out in Article 40.3.2.

The plaintiffs in the *Murray* case were husband and wife, who were serving life sentences for the murder of a policeman. They claimed that the right to procreate was one

[9] [1959] IR 1; (1960) 94 ILTR 11.
[10] [1954] IR 151; (1954) 88 ILTR 169.
[11] [1962] IR 1.
[12] [1984] ILRM 348.

of the "inalienable and imprescriptible" rights guaranteed to them by Article 41; and that as, unlike the other fundamental rights clauses, Article 41 contains no qualifying language, it followed that the State had no power to interfere with the exercise of the rights secured by it. Costello J took the view that the right to procreate derived from Article 40.3 rather than Article 41; but even if he was wrong on this, it did not follow that the plaintiffs' contention was correct:

> "The power of the State to delimit the exercise of constitutionally protected rights is expressly given in some Articles and not referred to at all in others, but this cannot mean that, where absent, the power does not exist. For example, no reference is made in Article 41 to any restrictive power, but it is clear that the exercise by the Family of its imprescriptible and inalienable right to integrity as a unit group can be severely and validly restricted by the State when, for example, its laws permit a father to be banned from a family home or allow for the imprisonment of both parents of young children."

An approach to interpretation "which would look at the whole text of the Constitution and identify its purpose and objective in protecting human rights" was thus the correct one; and as the reasonable requirements of prison security and administration justified the restrictions of which the plaintiffs were complaining, there was no infringement of their constitutional rights.

THE DOCTRINE OF "HARMONIOUS INTERPRETATION"

What should, in logic, probably be the first canon of interpretation of the Constitution itself - the doctrine of "harmonious" interpretation - has been articulated only very recently. This is the principle that constitutional provisions should not be construed in isolation from all the other parts of the Constitution among which they are embedded, but should be so construed as to harmonise with the other parts. This doctrine is no more than a presumption that the people who enacted the Constitution had a single scale of values, and wished those values to permeate their charter evenly and without internal discordance. It is, however, first expressed in 1980, in *Dillane v Ireland,*[14] in which the plaintiff was arguing the validity of a rule of court which prevented him from being awarded costs against a policeman who had unsuccessfully prosecuted him: this, he said, was an attack on his property rights and was an unjustified discrimination (in favour of the police). The Supreme Court held that the special position of the police in the context of the rule about costs could be justified on the basis of their difference in "social function" from others, and so did not offend Article 40.1 (which acknowledges such differences as justifying varying statutory treatment); and that, since it was warranted by Article 40.1, it could not be considered an "unjust" attack on property rights for the purposes of Article 40.3. Henchy J said:

> "Under the doctrine of harmonious interpretation, which requires, where possible, the relevant constitutional provisions to be construed and applied so that each will be given due weight in the circumstances of the case, it would not be a valid form of constitutional interpretation to rule that the immunity given to a Garda by Rule 67 is necessarily permitted by Article 40.1, and in the same breath to hold that it is

[13] [1985] IR 532; [1985] ILRM 542.
[14] [1980] ILRM 167.

proscribed by [Article 40.3.2]...What happened when the plaintiff was denied his costs... was categorically permitted by Article 40.1, so it cannot be part of the injustice which Article 40.3.2 was designed to prevent."[15]

In the following year, in *The State (Director of Public Prosecutions) v Walsh*[16] the Supreme Court had to reconcile Article 38.5, which prescribes trial by jury for all offences other than minor ones, with the needs of the courts to be able to protect their own process and independence directly and effectively, in other words summarily, against threats taking the form of criminal contempt. The Court upheld the right to punish even serious contempts summarily, saying that this right was a necessary consequence of the position and functions attributed to courts and judges by Articles 34 and 35, even though this exceptional treatment of a non-minor offence was not expressly provided for in the Constitution. O'Higgins CJ said that, were it otherwise, the courts could not control their own enforcement of respect for them (as normal prosecution on indictment would be in the hands of an executive authority, the Director of Public Prosecutions):

> "This result seems to me to follow logically and inevitably from a consideration of Article 38.5 in isolation and apart from the other Articles and the general scheme of the Constitution. However, to do so is erroneous. Article 38.5 may not be so considered. It must be construed and considered as part of the Constitution and it should be given, if possible, a meaning and an application which does not lead to conflict with other Articles and which conforms with the Constitution's general scheme."

He went on to show that the objects of Articles 34 and 35 would be defeated if they were not allowed to modify the absoluteness of Article 38.5. Henchy J also spoke trenchantly to the same effect.

Here, at least, it was possible to point to one part of the Constitution's text as requiring a modified understanding of another part. But a year later, in *The People (Director of Public Prosecutions) v O'Shea*,[17] the Court declined (by a 3-2 decision) to treat a clear constitutional provision as modified by a traditional principle of constitutional weight, though one not given expression in the Constitution's text, when it took literally the provision of Article 34.4.3, which says that "all" decisions of the High Court may be appealed to the Supreme Court, save such decisions as may be excluded from the Supreme Court's appellate jurisdiction by post-1937 legislation; and refused to admit that acquittals in the High Court on a criminal charge, in consequence of a jury's *Not Guilty* verdict, were "inherently" unappealable. However, Henchy J, who was one of the dissenters, based his view on the immunity of jury acquittals on the idea of harmonious interpretation:

> "I agree that if the relevant sub-section of the Constitution is looked at in isolation and is given a literal reading, it would lend itself to that interpretation. But I do not agree that such an approach is a correct method of constitutional interpretation. Any single constitutional right or power is but a component in an ensemble of interconnected and interacting provisions which must be brought into play as part of a larger

[15] And yet it might argued that the doctrine of harmonious interpretation was improperly applied in this case. The fact that a rule might not be formally discriminatory in its operation surely provides little guide to the quite separate question of whether the plaintiff had suffered an injustice by the infringement of his substantive property rights.

[16] [1981] IR 412.

[17] [1982] IR 384.

composition, and which must be given such an integrated interpretation as will fit it harmoniously into the general constitutional order and modulation. It may be said of a constitution, more than of any other legal instrument, that "the letter killeth, but the spirit giveth life". No single constitutional provision (particularly one designed to safeguard personal liberty or social order) may be isolated and construed with undeviating literalness. [He cited words used by Black J in *The People (Attorney General) v Kennedy*[18] in interpreting not the Constitution but the Courts of Justice Act 1924.] The Supreme Court held [in that case] that, on the true, rather than the literal, construction of s 29 [of that Act] such appeal did not lie. The letter gave way to the spirit, the spirit being the paramount principle of *autrefois acquit.*"

Another - and, perhaps, more easily defensible - example of where the courts declined to modify a clear provision of the Constitution in order to safeguard other (and, in this case, express) constitutional values is supplied by the judgment of Geoghegan J in *Attorney General v Hamilton (No.2).*[19] Here the issue was whether three Deputies - who had relied on information supplied to them by confidants and who had used this information to make allegations concerning a particular individual and his company - could be coerced by a Tribunal of Inquiry to supply the names of their informants. Geoghegan J held that the Deputies were entitled, pursuant to Article 15.13 of the Constitution, to claim privilege with regard to their sources. It was then argued that the rights of privilege and non-amenability which the Deputies enjoyed had to give way, in the circumstances, to the necessity to vindicate the good name of the individual and company concerned under Article 40.3. But Geoghegan J refused to construe Article 15.13 in this manner, since, in his view, the rights of:

> "privilege and non-amenability [are] absolute and intended by the Constitution to be absolute in the sense that [they] cannot be sacrificed to protect other constitutional rights."

An earlier - and possibly more sweeping - example of the harmonious interpretation doctrine is to be found in *Tormey v Ireland*,[20] which concerned the constitutionality of ss 31 and 32 of the Courts Act 1981, which had the combined effect of withdrawing a large category of indictable offences (including offences under the Larceny Act 1916) from the jurisdiction of the High Court. The plaintiff, charged with offences under that Act and returned for trial before the Circuit Court, complained that this statutory withholding of jurisdiction from the High Court was contrary to Article 34.3.1. Henchy J, speaking for the Supreme Court, agreed that on a literal interpretation of that sub-section, the plaintiff might be right. But such an interpretation would produce absurdity and bring Article 34.3.1 into conflict with other constitutional provisions:[21]

[18] [1946] IR 517; (1947) 81 ILTR 73. Black J said: "A small section of a picture, if looked at close up, may indicate something quite clearly; but when one stands back and views the whole canvas, the close-up view of the small section is often found to have given a wholly wrong view of what it really represented. If one could pick out a single word or phrase and. finding it perfectly clear in itself, refuse to check its apparent meaning in the light thrown upon it by the context or by other provisions, the result would be to render the principle of *eiusdem generis* and *noscitur a sociis* utterly meaningless: for this principle requires frequently that a word or phrase or even a whole provision which, standing alone, has a clear meaning must be given a quite different meaning when viewed in the light of its context."

[19] [1993] ILRM 821. This view was confirmed by the Supreme Court on appeal.

[20] [1985] IR 532; [1985] ILRM 542. For another - somewhat questionable - example of the doctrine of harmonious interpretation, see the judgment of Walsh J in *Campus Oil Ltd. v Minister for Industry and Energy* [1983] IR 82 described at pp. 284-285, 515.

[21] Henchy J said that a literal reading of Article 34.1 would bring it into conflict with Articles 34.3.4, 37, 38.2, 38.3 and 39.4.1, all of which, in his view, demonstrated that an original jurisdiction in certain justifiable matters "shall, or may be, exercised by other courts, tribunals, persons or bodies."

> "The rule of literal interpretation, which is generally relied on in the absence of ambiguity or absurdity in the context, must here give way to the more fundamental rule of constitutional interpretation, that the Constitution must be read as a whole and that its several provisions must not be looked at in isolation, but be treated as interlocking parts of the general constitutional scheme. This means that where two constructions of a provision are open in the light of the Constitution as a whole, despite the apparent unambiguity of the provision itself, the court should adopt the construction which will achieve the smooth and harmonious operation of the Constitution. A judicial attitude of strict construction should be avoided when it would allow the imperfection or inadequacy of the words used to defeat or pervert any of the fundamental purposes of the Constitution. It follows from such global approach that, save where the Constitution itself otherwise provides, all its provisions should be given due weight and not be subordinated one to the other... The true purpose and range of a Constitution would not be achieved if it were treated as no more than the sum of its parts."[22]

The doctrine of harmonious interpretation seems highly rational and useful in contexts like *Walsh's* and *Tormey's* cases. In contexts like *O'Shea's* case, too, it would have operated to prevent the Constitution being interpreted in a way which (as Henchy J said) those who drafted and approved it in 1937 most certainly never intended or foresaw; but the problem of harmonious interpretation by reference not to another Article but to some tacitly understood principle, or the spirit of the Constitution, is that it must incur the criticism which Johnston J expressed in 1939 in *Burke's* case[23] and which was afterwards vindicated in *The State (Browne) v Feran*:[24] he said he "did not think that a further Constitution - an unwritten one was intended by the people of Éire to exist side by side with this written Constitution or even - perhaps it would be more correct to say - outside and beyond the present Constitution". The admission of a doctrine of harmonious interpretation, unless related to other parts of the express text of the Constitution, seems to open the door widely to judicial policy-making.

Are some Articles more important than others?

Side by side with the doctrine of harmonious interpretation, and needing to be reconciled with it, there has lately emerged the judicial view that some Articles of the Constitution are more important than others, and must, in a case of conflict, take priority over them. Under the old Constitution and in the early life of the present Constitution, the courts tended to reject any such notion; thus in *The State (Ryan) v Lennon*[25]- in which this point was raised against Article 2A, which derogated drastically from several Articles of fundamental importance to liberty - Murnaghan J said in the Supreme Court:

> "In this argument it is sought to be established that many Articles of the Constitution are so fundamental as to be incapable of alteration, and that the true meaning of the word "amendment" in Article 50...does not authorise any change in these fundamental Articles or doctrines. It has to be admitted that the Constitution itself does not segregate as fundamental specified Articles or doctrines, nor does it in terms make any distinction between the different classes of Articles."

22 See also the judgment of Walsh J in *Dreher v Irish Land Commission* [1984] ILRM 94 (legislation regulating property rights which is justified by the "exigencies of the common good" under Article 43 cannot by definition be an "unjust attack" within the meaning of Article 40.3 on the same property rights.)
23 [1940] IR 136; (1940) 74 ILTR 36.
24 [1967] IR 147.
25 [1935] IR 170; (1935) 69 ILTR 125.

A few years later in *The State (Burke) v Lennon*[26] Meredith J said:

> "I do not accept [counsel's] contention that the heading placed over certain Articles... describing certain rights as "fundamental", meant that those Articles were to be interpreted as of more fundamental importance than any other Article... - for instance, that the Articles conferring and preserving the liberty of the subject had any more importance than those Articles which provide for a constitutional change in the law, or for a change in the Constitution, or for the will of the people being carried out by constitutional means and not by unconstitutional means. The heading in question is perfectly plain in its meaning - it is a division and classification, not of Articles, but of the rights conferred by the Constitution."

However, occasional judicial expressions, even when rhetorical, could be seen as reflecting some kind of acceptance that a certain hierarchy of values, a certain order of rank, existed among the Constitution's provisions: see the emphasis laid by Ó Dálaigh J in *The State (O'Flaherty) v Ó Floinn*[27] on the seriousness of any encroachment on personal liberty; and the question asked by Kenny J in *Ryan v Attorney General*:[28] "What can be more important in a democratic State than the personal rights of the citizens?" In two cases decided in 1971, *Quinn's Supermarket v Attorney General*[29] and *McMahon v Attorney General,*[30] the Supreme Court found something like a collision or conflict between different constitutional rights, and had to resolve these conflicts by treating one provision (respectively, the prohibition of religious discrimination and the requirement of a secret ballot in Dáil elections) as subsidiary to the other (respectively, the general guarantee of religious freedom and the general right to vote); again, in *Draper v Attorney General,*[31] the Supreme Court held that the Oireachtas was entitled to refrain from providing for a postal vote for persons physically unable to attend a polling station, having to weigh, against the individual elector's rights, the overriding value of an election free from the risk of abuses or loss of secrecy. These functional subsidiaries, if they may be so called, did not however amount to the acknowledgement of a genuine order of rank or importance as between competing constitutional rules or rights.

Something like this had, however, begun to emerge in 1974, in *Dillon-Leetch v Calleary (No.1)*[32] the Court (*per* Henchy J) held that, even though the constitutional requirement of secrecy of the Dáil ballot had not been perfectly respected in a particular election count, this breach could not justify invalidating the whole election in that constituency (which had not been affected by the breach) as this would defeat the paramount interest of the electors in having representatives elected:

> "Where the Court is confronted with the inescapable necessity of giving effect to one or other of two constitutional principles or rights, it should opt for the one that is more essential to the smooth and harmonious operation of the Constitution in the light of its basic assumptions and primary aims [he mentioned the *Quinn's Supermarket* case.]"

[26] [1940] IR 136; (1940) 74 ILTR 36.
[27] [1954] IR 295; (1956) 90 ILTR 179.
[28] [1965] IR 294.
[29] [1972] IR 1.
[30] [1972] IR 69; (1972) 106 ILTR 89.
[31] [1984] IR 277; [1984] ILRM 539.
[32] Supreme Court, 31 July 1974.

Hierarchy of constitutional rights

A full and express acknowledgement of a hierarchy of constitutional rules and rights was finally made by the Supreme Court in *The People v Shaw*.[33] Here the issue turned on the lawfulness of the continued detention of a murder suspect - with consequences for the admissibility of evidence obtained during the period of the possibly unjustifiable detention - where the police had some faint hope that a girl, whom the suspect had in fact already killed, might be still alive and that the suspect, by leading them to her, would enable them to save her life. Four of the five judges based their ruling - that the evidence was admissible - on the notion of allowing the higher constitutional value to prevail. Kenny J said:

> "There is a hierarchy of constitutional rights and, when a conflict arises between them, that which ranks higher must prevail. This is the law for the exercise of all three powers of government and flows from the conception that all three powers must be exercised to promote the common good: see the Preamble to the Constitution. The decision on the priority of constitutional rights is to be made by the High Court and, on appeal, by this Court. When a conflict of constitutional rights arises, it must be resolved by having regard to (a) the terms of the Constitution, (b) the ethical values which all Christians living in the State acknowledge and accept and (c) the main tenets of our system of constitutional parliamentary democracy."

Griffin J, with whom Henchy and Parke JJ agreed, expressed the same idea in a more muted tone:

> "[Where a harmonious application of constitutional rules is not possible] the hierarchy or priority of the conflicting rights must be examined, both as between themselves and in relation to the general welfare of society. This may involve the toning down or even the putting into temporary abeyance of a particular guaranteed right so that, in a fair and objective way, the more pertinent and important right in a given set of circumstances may be preferred and given application."

Express acknowledgments of the existence of a hierarchy of constitutional values is to be found in a series of recent cases. In *Murray v Ireland*,[34] the plaintiff prisoners had argued that the right to procreate was an "inalienable and imprescriptible" right protected by Article 41, and that, accordingly, this must be one of the "core" constitutional rights retained by prisoners (along with such rights as the right to life and to fair procedures). Costello J said:

> "It does not follow...that because the Constitution ascribes to only some human rights characteristics of inalienability and imprescriptibility, [it] should be construed as implying that other fundamental rights lack these qualities, or that only those rights are superior to positive law which are expressly so declared...[The right to life and freedom from torture] must surely be reckoned amongst the most basic human rights, and the Constitution should be interpreted to give effect to this view, even though neither is expressly declared as being inalienable and imprescriptible or as being superior to all positive law. So if a court is required to make an evaluation as between two constitutionally protected human rights, it should have particular regard to the intrinsic nature of the rights concerned."

[33] [1982] IR 1.
[34] [1985] IR 532; [1985] ILRM 542.

Later he said that the right to life "was clearly superior to the right to liberty, but the right to fair procedures clearly is not".[35] A similar evaluation of the merits of competing rights was made by Hamilton P in *Attorney General (S.P.U.C. Ltd.) v Open-Door Counselling Ltd.*[36] Holding that the defendants' pregnancy counselling activities were in conflict with Article 40.3.3 which guarantees the right to life of the unborn, he said the latter right should take precedence over the constitutional rights of the defendants:

> "The qualified right to privacy, the rights of association and freedom of expression and the right to disseminate information cannot be invoked to interfere with such a fundamental right."

The question of the ranking of fundamental rights figured prominently in *Attorney General v X*,[37] a decision which was to highlight the possible shortcomings in any doctrine which attempted to construct an abstract, *a priori* ranking of constitutional rights. Here the Attorney General had sought an injunction restraining a fourteen-year old alleged rape victim - who had exhibited suicidal tendencies - from seeking an abortion in the United Kingdom. This case thus illustrated a whole panoply of potentially conflicting constitutional rights, ranging form the right to life of the unborn, the mother's right to life and the right to travel. A majority of the Supreme Court resolved these questions in favour of the defendant's right to life and her ancillary right to travel abroad.[38] While the very text of Article 40.3.3 had sought to rank equally the right to life of the mother and that of the unborn child, the Supreme Court pointed out that this was simply impossible on the facts of the case. McCarthy J observed that if a balancing test were to be applied, it would almost always have to be resolved in favour of the right to life of the unborn, since termination of pregnancy will always result in the death of the foetus, whereas the continuation of pregnancy will not always - no matter how high the probability - result in the death of the mother. He, therefore, concluded that, having regard to other provisions of the Constitution (such as Articles 40 and 41) which might be thought implicitly to favour the mother's rights, termination of pregnancy was possible where there was "a real and substantial risk" to the life of the mother throughout her pregnancy. In these special circumstances where an equal ranking of constitutional rights was not possible, the decision of the Court's was, in effect, to give preference to the right to life of the mother.

In relation to the second potential conflict presented by the facts of the case - between that of the right to life and the right to travel - Finlay CJ and Egan J both accepted that where such reconciliation of rights was not possible, it was necessary, as the Chief Justice said, "to apply a priority of rights."

Finlay CJ and Egan J both accepted - in admittedly *obiter* remarks - that in such circumstances the right to life of the unborn would have to take priority over the mother's right to travel. This case graphically illustrates one potential shortcoming of the hierarchy of rights approach, since such *a priori* ranking of such rights (e.g., life over liberty, liberty over free speech etc.) focuses on philosophical abstractions which, if inflexibly employed, would tend to lead to the pre-determination of the outcome of particular litigation, at the expense of the flexibility which is desirable in any judicial appraisal of the relevant facts of each case and the competing merits of particular arguments.

[35] On appeal ([1991] ILRM 465) the Supreme Court accepted (*per* McCarthy J) that there was a hierarchy of constitutional norms but held that it was unnecessary and, indeed, undesirable, to identify such a hierarchy in the instant case.

[36] [1988] IR 593; [1987] ILRM 477.

[37] [1992] 1 IR 1; [1992] ILRM 401; [1992] 2 CMLR 277. This important decision - perhaps the most celebrated in the whole history of Irish constitutional law - is considered more fully at pp. 796-803.

Is there a constitutional "abuse of rights" doctrine?

A related question is whether there is an "abuse of rights" doctrine such as might inform constitutional interpretation. Such a doctrine might take several forms. The first category of potential "abuse of rights" cases would seem to embrace instances of where the Constitution cannot be construed as giving immunity to protection to activities or acts which are essentially subversive of the Constitution itself.[39] There is more than a hint of such an approach in the (now overruled) decision of the Supreme Court in *Russell v Fanning*[40] where the Supreme Court said that it could not interpret the political offence exception as granting "immunity from extradition to a person charged with an offences the purpose of which is to subvert the Constitution." While it is true that far-reaching nature of this decisions was curtailed somewhat by *Finucane v McMahon*,[41] the underlying principles would appear to remain intact, even if its application to particular categories of cases remains somewhat uncertain.

The second potential category of "abuse of rights" case has not yet been judicially admitted, even if the principles underlying some of the case-law can best be explained on this basis. The principle would appear to be this: that the courts will not entertain a constitutional action (or, at least, will do so only with reluctance) where it appears that the plaintiff is employing the litigation as a stratagem or a device to obtain an ulterior objective. There is a hint of this in the judgment of Finlay CJ in *McGimpsey v Ireland*[42] (where the plaintiffs contended for an interpretation of Articles 2 and 3 which to them personally was an anathema) where he observed that:

> "one would have to entertain considerable doubt as to whether any citizen would have the *locus standi* to challenge the constitutional validity of an act of the executive or of a statute of the Oireachtas for the sole and specific purpose of achieving an objective directly contrary to the purpose of the constitutional provision invoked."

Indeed, one may wonder whether this sort of consideration really lay at the heart of the Supreme Court's concerns about *locus standi* in *Cahill v Sutton*,[43] since the Court appears to have regarded the case as essentially presenting a form of stratagem to achieve an ulterior result (i.e., the right to sue her doctor following an invalidation of the statute). While one must urge caution on this front - since, as McCarthy J noted in *McGimpsey*, it is a commonplace for litigants "to invoke the law for the worst of

[38] See pp. 882-883.

[39] In this regard, the position in German constitutional law is especially interesting. Article 18 of the Basic Law provides, *inter alia*, that: "Whoever abuses freedom of expression...in order to combat the free democratic basic order, shall forfeit these basic rights." This has given rise to the concept of the State as a "militant democracy" ("streitbare demokratie"), a doctrine thus explained by the Constitutional Court in the *Klass* case (1970) 30 BVerfGE 1: "Constitutional provisions must not be interpreted in isolation, but rather in a manner consistent with the Basic Law's fundamental principles and its system of values...In the context of this case it is especially significant that the Constitution...has decided in favour of 'militant democracy' that does not submit to abuse of basic rights or an attack on the liberal order of the State."

[40] [1988] IR 505. Cf. the statement by Finlay CJ in *Cox v Ireland* [1992] 2 IR 503: "The State is entitled, for the protection of public peace and order, and for the maintenance and stability of its own authority, by its laws to provide onerous and far-reaching penalties and forfeitures imposed as a major deterrent to the commission of crimes threatening such peace and order and State security." See also *Quinn v Wren* [1985] IR 322, where what amounts to this variant of "abuse of rights" doctrine was first judicially announced.

[41] [1990] 1 IR 156.

[42] [1990] 1 IR 110.

[43] [1980] IR 269.

motives" - yet it would not be surprising if this embryonic case-law were to ripen into a firm constitutional doctrine, possibly linked to the rule that the plaintiff may not generally plead a *jus tertii* to advance his own constitutional arguments.[44]

The third category is where the holder of a constitutional right has exercised that right with a view to defeating the constitutional rights of others. This occurred in *Crowley v Ireland*[45] where McMahon J found on the facts that the teachers who had gone on strike at a particular primary school had done so with the object of depriving the children at the school of primary education and thus coercing the authorities into settling their grievance. As McMahon J put it:

> "The character of an act depends on the circumstances in which it is done and the exercise of a constitutional right for the purpose of infringing the constitutional rights of others is an abuse of that right which...can be restrained by the courts. The teachers who refused to enrol the Drimoleague schoolchildren in adjoining schools did not act primarily for the purpose of exercising a right to work or not to work, or to choose the conditions under which they would work. In my view, their purpose was to deprive the Drimoleague children of primary education in order to exact pressure...what was done amounted to the use of unlawful means to deprive the...children of their constitutional rights."

This is a good example of "abuse of rights" (in the sense that this term would be understood by civilian lawyers) which turns on the fact that the persons exercising such rights were actuated by improper motives in doing so.

THE HISTORICAL APPROACH

State of the law

An important element in the construction of the Constitution is the state of affairs, legal as well as extra-legal, at the time of the Constitution's enactment. The relevance of this consideration was first asserted in *In re Article 26 and the Offences Against the State (Amendment) Bill 1940*,[46] when the Supreme Court was being asked (by counsel assigned to attack the Bill) to find its internment provisions unconstitutional. The Court said:

> "Before dealing [with the relevant Articles] we desire to point out that several Acts authorising the detention of persons had been passed by the Oireachtas of the Irish Free State prior to the enactment of the Constitution which we are now considering. The existence and effect of these Acts must have been within the knowledge of the framers of the Constitution and, nevertheless, there is no express prohibition in the Constitution against such legislation. This is a matter to which we are bound to attach considerable weight in view of the fact that many Articles of the Constitution prohibit the Oireachtas, in plain and unambiguous language, from passing certain laws therein specified."

[44] See pp. 443-444. In this regard, one wonders how the courts would now react to the facts of *Quinns Supermarket v Attorney General* [1972] IR 1? This was a case where the constitutional argument was essentially a stratagem to permit longer opening hours for a supermarket, but yet to achieve this purpose the plaintiff supermarket was permitted to advance an argument based on Article 44 which did not directly concern it.
[45] [1990] IR 102.
[46] [1940] IR 470; (1940) 74 ILTR 161.

However, the Court, in upholding the Bill, did not expand this very general implication that the Constitution was not against internment. In *O'Donovan v Attorney General*[47] this passage was cited to Budd J; its relevance here was the alleged parallel between internment laws and electoral laws. Just as statutes authorising internment had been enacted under the pre-1937 Constitution and were part of the legal landscape, so to speak, so as to permit the assumption that the framers of the Constitution took the occasional necessity for such laws for granted, so too (it was argued) two Electoral Acts passed under the 1922 Constitution had effected divergencies in ratio of population to Dáil seats just as clear as those effected by the Electoral (Amendment) Act 1959, and, since the earlier Acts had been generally accepted as not conflicting with the provisions of Article 26 of the old Constitution (very similar to the material parts of the existing Article l 6), that range of tolerance should be now accepted as within the contemplation of those who framed the 1937 Constitution. However, Budd J drew a sharp distinction:

> "I have to point out...that these two Electoral Acts were never challenged or tested. Moreover, it seems to me that there is no analogy, because, whereas the existence of laws providing for the detention of persons during the existence of the former Constitution was well known, it could scarcely be contended that the statistical information necessary to comprehend the result of these Electoral Acts was ever in the mind of those that enacted the Constitution. It appears nowhere in these Acts and it has involved considerable work and research to produce it now. While I respectfully agree that regard may be had to the background in which the Constitution was passed, I do not feel that any inference that can be drawn from the existence of these two Acts can justify a departure from the clear directive contained in Article 16.2.3. Moreover, the disparity now existing in ratio is far greater than ever was the case under the two Acts in question."

The following year the admissibility of this canon of construction was asserted again in *Melling v Ó Mathghamhna*.[48] Lavery J assented to the proposition "that in construing a provision of a statute or of the Constitution it is proper to consider how the law stood when the statute was passed."[49] And - decisive for this particular case - Ó Dálaigh J said:

> "One can have little doubt that the framers of the Constitution of Ireland, when in Article 38 they spoke of a minor offence, meant the kind of thing that had been generally understood to be such under the laws of Saorstát Éireann. Here, truly, is the kind of situation which it may be thought Stone J had in mind when he spoke of looking to the standard which prevailed at the time of the adoption of the Constitution. And since one may assume that "minor offence" in both Constitutions was intended to mean the same thing, an examination of the statute roll of Saorstát Éireann will throw a flood of light on where the line is to be fixed between minor and non-minor offences, so far at least as imprisonment is a factor which operates to change what at first and *prima facie* might be the one into the other."

It may be noted that Lavery J spoke of "a statute or the Constitution", and that the cases which he mentioned involved, respectively, interpretation of the 1922 Constitution and interpretation of the Courts of Justice Act 1924. In *Melling's* case, Lavery J himself had

[47] [1961] IR 114; [1962] 96 ILTR 121.

[48] [1962] IR 1; (1962) 96 ILTR 29.

[49] Lavery J referred to *O'Byrne v Minister for Finance* [1959] IR 1; (1960) 94 ILTR 11 as an illustration of the doctrine. In that case a majority of the Court had noted that payment of income tax by judges was normal and familiar at the time of the drafting of the 1922 Constitution.

cited Maxwell's *Interpretation of Statutes*, which in turn had cited Coke's classical summary of what must be considered in interpreting an Act including "what was the law before the Act was passed". It is clear, therefore, that the principle of admitting consideration of the state of the law in 1937 in order to gather the scope and intent of a constitutional provision rests at least in part on a long-established canon of ordinary interpretation of statute law.[50]

In 1965 the Supreme Court was again considering the question of what was a "minor" offence triable summarily under Article 38.2 - this time in the context of drunken driving - and the Court said that, while it proposed to consider "the state of the law when the Constitution was enacted and public opinion at the time of that enactment", these were "but secondary considerations" (the Court's judgment rested principally on the consideration of punishment applicable to such offences). However, the Court (*per* Walsh J) did add this further dimension to its judgment (*Conroy v Attorney General*[51]):

> "Article 71 of the Constitution of Saorstát Éireann was similar in essentials to the provisions of Article 38 of the Constitution. In the year 1922 the existing law for the trial of offences authorised the summary trial of a wide range of offences which were not trivial either by their nature or by the punishments they attracted. After the enactment of that Constitution the Courts of Justice Act 1924, recognised that many of such offences should be tried summarily and the Act also recognised the obvious fact that a particular offence might be considered to be minor or non-minor according to the circumstances of the particular case. After the enactment of the present Constitution the same fact was recognised by the Criminal Justice Act 1951. The Constitution of Saorstát Éireann may be considered to have accepted the existing pattern of distinction between offences to be tried in a court of summary jurisdiction and offences to be tried on indictment by a jury. In 1937 the people with full knowledge of the existing structure of the courts and the modes of trial gave themselves the present Constitution...The procedure for prosecuting offences of drunken driving prescribed by the Road Traffic Act 1933, was part of the procedural pattern in existence and was widely known in 1937. Its creation by Act of the Oireachtas sufficiently indicates that it reflected public opinion. The procedure prescribed by the provision under challenge, s 49 of the Act of 1961, in form corresponds to the pattern in existence in 1937 and the offence thereby created does not, by reason of the punishment prescribed, differ in character from the corresponding offence in the Act of 1933."

The constitutional validity of the 1961 Act was upheld. In 1970 the statutory provisions about ballot papers for Dáil elections were under attack (on the ground that they did not

[50] Note, however, that in *Melling's* case, Ó Dálaigh J declined to use the pre 1922 norm as a necessarily obvious guide in the interpretation of the 1922 Constitution: "The framers of the Constitution of Saorstát Éireann had no particular reason to look with reverence or respect to the British statute roll in Ireland as affording them an example of standards which they would wish to enshrine in their new Constitution... Mr. Justice Stone's test ["look to the standard which prevailed at the time of the adoption of the Constitution": *District of Columbia v Clawans* 300 US 617,625 (1937)] is, in my opinion, unsuitable to be applied in the case of the undoing of a conquest." On the other hand, in *Webb v Ireland* [1988] IR 353 Walsh J was prepared to rely on the democratic Programme of the First Dáil (from which, he said, Article 10 was ultimately derived) as a guide to the construction of that constitutional provision.

[51] [1965] IR 411. Note that in *Ryan v Attorney General* [1965] IR 294, where the statute authorising the fluoridation of water was under attack as being, *inter alia*, an interference with the family rights of Article 41, Kenny J had been also willing to apply this principle:

> "At the time when the Constitution was enacted, there were a number of Acts of Parliament in force which prescribed minimum standards and contents for food and drink and I am entitled to take this legal background into consideration when interpreting the Constitution."

ensure a "secret ballot" as the Constitution required) in *McMahon v Attorney General.*[52] It was contended for the defendant that when the 1937 Constitution used the words "secret ballot", being the words which had also been used in the 1922 Constitution, the state of the law and of public opinion was that a system which involved only a limited secrecy of voting had operated without question for fifteen years, so that the 1937 Constitution should be taken to have tacitly approved it. But Pringle J refused to accept this:

> "If...the procedure which had been allowed to operate unquestioned for these fifteen years was itself unconstitutional, I do not consider that this argument can be valid...I should also point out that *Melling's* case and *Conroy's* case were both cases which were concerned more with questions in regard to the structure of the courts and the modes of trial than with a fundamental right of a citizen under the Constitution. I do not think that a consideration of the state of law or of public opinion at the time of the enactment of the Constitution leads to the conclusion that the words "secret ballot" must be interpreted in the limited sense that has been suggested."

The Supreme Court also rejected this contention for the defendant.

In summary, therefore, the judicial practice with regard to the relevance of the state of affairs at enactment of the Constitution is, it must be said, uneven, a point illustrated by *The State (Rollinson) v Kelly*.[53] Here the question was whether a penalty of £500 created in 1926 for certain betting offences indicated a minor offence. O'Higgins CJ thought that regard should be had to monetary values in 1937 in order to assess whether the punishment was sufficiently serious to take the case out of that category; but the rest of the Supreme Court disagreed with him, Henchy J saying:

> "With due respect to dicta to the contrary in some of the decided cases, I do not consider that the state of the law when the Constitution was enacted in 1937, or public opinion at the time of that enactment, are crucial considerations."

Nevertheless, two recent cases provide a particularly good illustration of how the state of the law at the time of the enactment of the Constitution can provide a useful guide to its interpretation. In *Attorney General v Hamilton (No.1)*[54] Finlay CJ readily demonstrated by reference to historical circumstances the manner by which the "one judgment" rule in Article 34.4.5 came to be drafted,[55] so that it could not be properly inferred that the absence of a similar express clause in Article 28.4.2 defeated the State's claim that discussion at a Government meeting were absolutely privileged from disclosure. In *Attorney General v Hamilton (No.2)*[56] - where the ambit of the parliamentary privilege provisions of Article 15.12 and Article 15.13 was at issue - Geoghegan J traced the provenance of these provisions back to Article 9 of the Bill of Rights 1689 and said that he accepted that the "historic case law in relation to parliamentary privilege in the various common law jurisdictions" was "highly relevant" to the matters at issue. This meant that it would be wrong for him of assume "that the historical reasons underlying parlia-

[52] [1972] IR 69.
[53] [1984] IR 248; [1984] ILRM 625. In *The State (D.P.P.) v Walsh* [1981] IR 412, O'Higgins CJ, in a partially dissenting judgment, had declared himself in favour of admitting the state of law in 1937 with regard to summary trial for criminal contempt as an important consideration when interpreting Article 38.5.
[54] [1993] 2 IR 250; [1993] ILRM 81.
[55] See pp. 527-528.
[56] [1993] ILRM 821.

mentary privilege would have been completely redundant in the new state" and that some "completely novel basis" for the privilege arose. This historic background was very helpful to the construction of the relevant constitutional provisions, since the drafters of the Constitution must be intended in this respect to have followed both the English and American constitutional practice, although this did not mean that they "did not intend to apply to the Oireachtas some adaptations and improvements on the legal position under the Bill of Rights."

These cases cumulatively give the impression that the principle of interpretation which admits as a consideration - even a "secondary" one, as Walsh J said in *Conroy's* case - the state of law and public opinion at the enactment of the Constitution is peculiarly liable to subjective application. The unreliable nature of this principle was admitted in *Brennan v Attorney General*,[57] when Barrington J, while admitting the relevance of 1937 conditions, said these could not be decisive, and drew attention to what had been in 1937 well established systems (of jury service and of taxation of married couples) which were nevertheless later found unconstitutional. Nevertheless, the process of historical interpretation is of some utility, especially where some law-based system is issue, such as the interpretation of the provisions concerning parliamentary privilege or the guarantee of jury trial in Article 38.5. This need not mean that the shape of such systems must be fixed permanently by reference to "the permafrost of 1937":

> "The courts ought to have some leeway for considering which dimensions of a system are secondary,[58] and which are so material to traditional constitutional values that a willingness to see them diluted or substantially abolished without a referendum could not be imputed to the enacting electorate."[59]

Thus, it may be said that where the Constitution carefully defines certain powers, rights, privileges and procedures (as is the case, for example, of the powers of the President, the scope of parliamentary privilege, the regulation of Dáil and Seanad elections and definition of a money bill) the courts must follow the text carefully, aided, where necessary, by a historical understanding of what the framers sought to achieve. But it would equally seem that many fundamental concepts - trial in due course of law, equality before the law, personal liberty, property rights - were left deliberately vague and imprecise. One can only assume that the drafters intended that the ambit of these clauses would become clearer in the light of experience as they were applied to novel and ever-changing facts and circumstances. Indeed, as the Irish example has clearly shown, it is through the accretion of case-law alone that such general clauses gather depth and meaning. Indeed, the method of interpretation of these general clauses - with frequent judicial warnings about the undesirability of a strict construction "which would allow the imperfection or inadequacy of the words used to defeat or pervert any of the fundamental purposes of the Constitution"[60] - tends to resemble a traditional common law method of adjudication (with its reliance on emerging doctrine from the case-law) in contradistinction to any strict exegesis of the actual text of the Constitution.

[57] [1983] ILRM 449.

[58] Thus, *O'Callaghan v Attorney General* [1993] 2 IR 17; [1993] ILRM 764 (where the constitutionality of the provisions of s 25 of the Criminal Justice Act 1984 allowing for majority jury verdicts was upheld) may be regarded as an example of a significant change from 1937 practice which was nonetheless regarded as "secondary" in this sense.

[59] Kelly, "*Law and Manifesto*" in Litton ed., *The Constitution of Ireland, 1937-1987* (Dublin, 1988).

[60] See *per* Henchy J in *Tormey v Ireland* [1985] IR 289 and see pp. ciii-civ.

Public opinion and mores

Not only the state of legal affairs in 1937 has been admitted by the courts as relevant in construing the sense of the Constitution (albeit, as has been seen, with very uncertain effect) but the state of public opinion, and the values of society in 1937, have been used in order to determine whether a pre-1937 law can be said to have been carried over by Article 50 into the post-1937 era. Here there is as much uncertainty, and as much room for suspecting that we are dealing less with hard criteria than with what may or may not offer adventitious support for what a court really wants to do anyway, as in the case of the 1937 state of legal affairs.

This is well illustrated by *McGee v Attorney General.*[61] Here O'Keeffe P heard at first instance a challenge to s 17 of the Criminal Law (Amendment) Act 1935 (which prohibited the importation of contraceptives, even for the personal use of the person importing them); and, in grounding his decision that the section had not been inconsistent, in 1937, with the Constitution, considered contemporary public opinion as mirrored (he assumed) in the parliamentary proceedings on the Bill for that Act:

> "The section impugned was barely two years on the statute book when the Constitution was adopted. If the submission of the plaintiff is correct, then public opinion as to what were fundamental rights must have been such as to require that the rights guaranteed to individuals by the Constitution were inconsistent with the continued legality of the section. I consider that the best test of the position is to be found in the views expressed when the section was being passed into law since, in point of time, this was so close to the enactment of the Constitution by the people. I find that the section was adopted without a division, although it was technically opposed. I cannot think that this reflects a public opinion in favour of the existence of such a right of privacy as is alleged by the plaintiff to be guaranteed under the Constitution."

Yet in that very case, the judgments of the Supreme Court which reversed his decision disclose the view that it is the public opinion or *mores* of today, not of 1937, which ought to be looked at in measuring a pre-1937 law (and the same reasoning would hold good for a post-1937 law as well) against the Constitution. Walsh J said, with reference to the values declared in the Preamble:

> "It is but natural that from time to time the prevailing ideas of [prudence, justice and charity] may be conditioned by the passage of time; no interpretation of the Constitution is intended to be final for all time."

A few years later, in *The State (Healy) v Donoghue,*[62] O'Higgins CJ likewise said that:

> "the rights given by the Constitution must be considered in accordance with concepts of prudence, justice and charity which may gradually change or develop as society changes and develops, and which fall to be interpreted from time to time in accordance with prevailing ideas...The Constitution did not seek to impose for all time the ideas prevalent or accepted with regard to these virtues at the time of its enactment."

[61] [1974] IR 287.
[62] [1976] IR 325; (1976) 110 ILTR 9.

In *Norris v Attorney General*[63] McCarthy J (in a dissenting judgment) was for abandoning all attempt to re-establish, as a usable measure for judicial review under Article 50, the public opinion of 1937:

> "It would plainly be impossible to identify with the necessary degree of accuracy of description the standards or mores of the Irish people in 1937 - indeed, it is no easy task to do so today [sc. in regard to today's mores?]. If one had to seek, in testing the consistency or otherwise of a pre-1922 statute or a statute of Saorstát Éireann with the Constitution, to do so by reference to the presumed attitude of the Irish people in 1937, however difficult that might be forty-five years after the enactment of the Constitution, one must postulate the concept of doing so 145 years after its enactment... In my view, it passes from the realm of legal fiction into the world of unreality if the test sought to be applied is one based on some such question as "Did the people of Saorstát Éireann in 1937 consider that the offence created by some Victorian statute should no longer be in force?"

And yet it must be conceded that there are contexts in which the exercise would seem not unreal, but an antidote to unreality: for instance, in trying to decide whether the kind of literal interpretation of the Constitution which has now become common produces a sense which can really be imputed to the people (or the Dáil, or the draftsmen) of 1937. A good instance of this kind of case is *The People (Director of Public Prosecutions) v O'Shea*.[64] Here Henchy J, in his dissenting judgment on the question whether the general words of Article 34.4.3 meant that appeals could be brought to the Supreme Court against a verdict of acquittal in the High Court (in its Central Criminal Court *persona)*, invoked the putative public and political opinion of 1937 to support his view:

> "I venture to think that if one were to scrutinise the debates in parliament and the records of the written and spoken arguments for and against the draft Constitution in 1937, one would not find the hint of an opinion, either from the proponents or the opponents of the Constitution, that a verdict of not guilty emanating from a jury trial as mandated by Article 38.5 could be reopened by appeal or otherwise. Indeed, it is to be arguably contended that if such opinion had been expressed by any reputable person or body, the Constitution would never have been enacted by the people."

Whether the public opinion of nearly half a century ago, if it can be discovered at all, ought to be gauged from sources *other than* the law itself, or the Constitution itself, of that date, is a question which must present itself on a reading of *Conroy v Attorney General*,[65] which decided that drunken driving is, for the purposes of Article 38, a minor offence which can be tried summarily. The Supreme Court, speaking by Walsh J, said that the enactment by the Oireachtas of the Road Traffic Act 1933, which made the offence summarily triable, "sufficiently indicates that it reflected public opinion"; and noted that "in 1937 the people with full knowledge of the existing structure of the courts and the modes of trial gave themselves the present Constitution". To read public opinion out of the fact of enactment of the very statute which is under challenge seems a dubious method of interpretation. *Conroy's* case illustrates the difficulty of relying on outside sources as a guide to public opinion in 1937. But the case of the interpretation of the contemporary constitutional amendments by reference to this criterion - where the state

[63] [1984] IR 36.
[64] [1982] IR 384.
[65] [1965] IR 411.

of public opinion at the date of the relevant referenda might be thought to be more objectively ascertainable - presents its own problems. Would it have been relevant to the construction of Article 40.3.3 if, for example, it could have been demonstrated in *Attorney General v X* that the majority of the electorate in 1983 had not intended to interfere with a woman's right to travel? Likewise, in a case involving the Fourteenth Amendment of the Constitution Act 1992, would it be relevant for the courts to bear in mind that in an official Government publication circulated in advance of the referendum in November 1992 the electorate had been assured that the passage of that amendment would secure the right to abortion information, but not to assistance or referral?

Is there an "original understanding" of the Constitution?

This brings us directly to the question of whether there exists any so-called "original understanding" of the Constitution which may guide - or even determine - the courts' approach to constitutional interpretation. We have just seen how an historical approach which relies on the imputed state of the law, public opinion and mores in 1937 has been judicially employed as a guide - even if an uneven one - to constitutional interpretation. An "original understanding" doctrine would, however, require the courts to go a step further and ask highly specific questions such as "did the framers of the Constitution intend Article 34.4.3 to permit the prosecution to appeal against an acquittal?" or "was it intended that Article 40.3.3 could be employed to prevent a pregnant woman travelling abroad?"

While there have been occasional (essentially rhetorical) judicial references to this doctrine or something like it - such as Henchy J's comments in *O'Shea* case, quoted above - there are several reasons why this approach - which has proved to be enormously influential in contemporary American constitutional jurisprudence[66] - is unlikely to find favour with the Irish courts. First, documentary material which might assist with an objective assessment of the framers' intentions is not generally available. Unlike the United States - where the courts have available to them the detailed workings of the Constitutional Convention of 1787[67] - the drafting of the 1937 Constitution took place in secret and the subsequent Dáil Debates were more often marred by partisan squabbling rather than attempt to ascertain the objective intention of the framers. Secondly, the intentionalist approach would be at odds with a legal tradition which has focused on the words of the text under consideration rather than the supposed intentions of the

[66] See generally, Bork, *The Tempting of America: The Political Seduction of the Law* (New York, 1990). Bork summarises thus the "original understanding" doctrine:

> "The search is not for a subjective intention. If someone found a letter from George Washington to Martha telling her that what he meant by the power to lay taxes was not what other people meant, this would not change our reading of the Constitution in the slightest. Nor would the subjective intentions of all the members of a rectifying convention alter anything...All that counts is how the words used in the Constitution would have been understood at the time. The original understanding is thus manifested in the words used in secondary materials, such as the debates at the conventions, public discussion, newspaper, articles, dictionaries in use at the time, and the like."

[67] A contemporary example provides an excellent illustration of the US Supreme Court's methodology in cases of this kind. In *Nixon v United States* 122 L.Ed.2nd. 1 (1993) (which concerned the meaning of the words "sole" and "to try" in the following sentence of Article 1 of the US Constitution: "The Senate shall have sole Power to try all Impeachments"), the US Supreme Court referred to *inter alia*, drafts of this sentence which had been submitted to the Constitutional Convention, the published drafts prepared by the Convention's "Committee of Style" and contemporary commentary (A. Hamilton's, *The Federalist Papers*) in order to ascertain the framers' intentions with regard to this clause.

[68] The Supreme Court has recently affirmed this approach in the case of statutory interpretation: see *Howard v Commissioners of Public Works in Ireland* [1993] ILRM 665 and pp.472-474.

drafters.[68] Finally, the fact that the Constitution was enacted by plebiscite and subsequently amended through a series of referenda strongly suggests that it is the objective meaning of the text itself - rather than the supposed intention of the drafters - which should carry the most weight when it comes to constitutional interpretation.[69]

Pre-Constitution legislation and state of law in 1937

These unresolved questions about the role played by the year 1937 in applying a constitutional test to earlier but ostensibly surviving legislation lead naturally to the more general question: is a pre-1938 statute, even if it could be said to have survived the enactment of the Constitution (by according at that time with the text of the Constitution both literally and in the light of current legal and moral opinions) still at risk thereafter? The answer must be yes, if only because of the unacceptable result which would follow if, by reason only of momentary conformity with the Constitution on 29 December 1937, a pre-Constitution, perhaps even a British Act would enjoy an immunity from challenge which a post-1937 Act of the Oireachtas did not enjoy. In other words, consistency with the Constitution is a rolling standard; the notion of "continuance" in Article 50 means continuance through the moment of the Constitution's coming into force *and all time thereafter*; and "the Constitution" in Article 50 means the Constitution as interpreted by contemporary standards at *any time thereafter*. The only judicial authority in this area appears to be a passage from the judgment of Walsh J (the other judges did not mention the point) in *McGee's* case; and would seem to provide foundation for this view:

> "If a pre-Constitution statute was such that it was not in conflict with the Constitution when taken in conjunction with other statutory provisions then in existence and with a particular state of facts then existing, and if such other statutory provisions continued in effect after the coming into operation of the Constitution and the particular state of facts remained unaltered, the provisions of the first statute might not in any way be inconsistent with the provisions of the Constitution. If, however, subsequent to the coming into force of the Constitution the other statutory provisions were repealed and the state of facts was altered to a point where the joint effect of the repeal of the other statutes and the alteration of the facts was to give the original statute a completely different effect, then the question would arise of its continuing to be part of the law. In my view, Article 50 by its very clear terms (both in its Irish and English texts) make it clear that laws in force in Saorstát Éireann shall continue to be in force only to the extent to which they are not inconsistent with the Constitution; and that, if the inconsistency arises for the first time after the coming into force of the Constitution, the law carried forward thereupon ceases to be in force."[70]

[69] For further discussion of originalism in the context of the Irish Constitution, see Quinn, "*The Nature and Significance of Critical Legal Studies*" (1989) 7 ILT 282; by the same author, "*Reflections on the legitimacy of judicial activism in the field of constitutional law*" (Winter, 1991) Dlí 29; and Whyte, "*Constitutional Adjudication, Ideology and Access to the Courts*" in Whelan, ed. *Law and Liberty in Ireland* (1993).

[70] This might arise if a fixed statutory sum of money intended before 1937 to do justice, were since then rendered grossly unjust by the fall in the value of money: e.g. s 503 of the Merchant Shipping Act 1894, as amended by s 1 of the Merchant Shipping (Limitation of Liability) Act 1900, the effect of which is to limit the compensation liability of a ship-owner, where damage is caused without actual fault, to £8 per tonne of displacement of the vessel causing the damage? The comments of Murphy J in *Browne v Attorney General* [1991] 2 IR 58 seems to hint at a contrary view; but this view fails to take account of the fact that legislation can become unconstitutional by reason of the fact that legislation can become unconstitutional by reason of the failure of the Oireachtas to change its terms having regard to variable factors such as inflation, population movements: see e.g., *Blake v Attorney General* [1981] IR 117.

The Natural Law Approach

The use of natural law as a method of constitutional interpretation has always attracted varying degrees of support among the judiciary. This approach is more fully described elsewhere,[71] but we may here note some of its essential features. The influence of natural law may be noted in several contexts. First, there is the willingness of at least some judges to interpret the Constitution by reference to "extra-constitutional" principles. While the balance of judicial authority is against such an approach,[72] nevertheless this method of constitutional interpretation retains a stubborn vibrancy and may yet be used in future to reject a literalist interpretation of a particular constitutional provision which, if adopted, would lead to a result inconsistent with generally accepted principles of justice. Secondly, the development of the unenumerated personal rights doctrine has been largely influenced by natural law thinking, a fact which has been expressly recognised in a number of the leading cases.[73] But in this area, at least, the use of explicit natural law reasoning has waned somewhat over the last decade or so, probably as a result of an increasing judicial awareness that an express reliance on this approach is open to the objections that it permits reliance on standards which are often diffuse and subjective and thus provide less than firm guidance on concrete constitutional problems.[74] Finally, there is the suggestion that there are certain rights which are so fundamental that they cannot be immutable and cannot be changed even by constitutional amendment. There is some limited support for this (potentially) far-reaching analysis,[75] but it must suffer the criticism that it is virtually at odds with the very text of the Constitution itself (having regard to the deliberately wide manner in which Article 46 was drafted) and the twin concepts of democratic government and popular sovereignty which under-pin it. Perhaps in conclusion we may say that the natural law approach will continue to be employed as a mechanism of avoiding an unpalatable result in any case where this might be produced by a stark, literalist interpretation of the Constitution; but as far as the day to day routine of constitutional adjudication is concerned, the natural law method will prove to have only a limited application.

Miscellaneous matters

It is now proposed to consider some miscellaneous matters touching on the question of constitutional interpretation.

Does mention in the Constitution entrench the existence of anything?

A question which arises naturally from the foregoing discussion is whether, apart from the conditions of 1937 being used as an interpretative implement in applying the Constitution, the fact that the Constitution mentions some institution - in itself quite contingent - gives it any status of entrenchment, so as to prevent its abolition or substantial transformation? The question is easily, or fairly easily, answered so far as concerns the reference to "a jury" in Article 38.5, because this is itself the subject of a guarantee which (as suggested below) must prevent any serious dilution of the jury role. or a jury's composition, as understood in 1937. But what of the system of taking a census (adverted

[71] See pp. 676-682.
[72] See *The People (Director of Public Prosecutions v O'Shea* [1982] IR 384 and pp. cii-ciii, above.
[73] See e.g., *The State (Nicolaou) v An Bord Uchtála* [1966] IR 567; *McGee v Attorney General* [1974] IR 284; *The State (Healy) v Donoghue* [1976] IR 325.
[74] See generally, Kelly, "*Fundamental Rights in the Irish Law and Constitution*" (Dublin, 1967), pp.62-73; Clarke, "*The Role of Natural Law in Irish Constitutional Law*" (1982) 17 Ir Jur 187.
[75] See generally at pp. 682-684.

to in Article 16.2.3)? Would it be permissible to compute the population by applying some demographic calculus to a piece of cheaply available data (numbers of school-children enrolled, or voters on the latest register, or old age pensioners) and calling the result a "census" for the purpose of Article 16.2.3? Or what of the Defence Forces, alluded to in Articles 13.4-5, 13.4-2 and 40.4.6 (and contemplated by Article 15.6)? Would it be constitutionally competent for a pacifist Oireachtas to disband them and to repeal the legislation establishing them? What of the concept of "felony" mentioned in Article 15.13? Might it be abolished? Does the reference in Article 47.2 to the "register" of voters absolutely require a register to be kept? Do the references to the death penalty in Articles 13.6 and 40.4.5 preclude the Oireachtas from enacting its general and total abolition, even though this has now taken place with the enactment of the Criminal Justice Act 1990? Must there always be an official gazette, carrying the title *Iris Oifigiúil*, because Article 25.4.2 mentions it as such? This range of problems seems never to have been judicially considered. In case, however, it may be suggested that mere mention in the Constitution could not operate to entrench existence, it is worth noting that on the enactment of the Seventh Amendment in 1979 a subsection was expressly added in Article 18 (as sub-s 4.3) reading:

> "Nothing in this Article shall be invoked to prohibit the dissolution by law of a university mentioned in sub-section 1 of this section."

Evidently therefore the specific references to the National University of Ireland and the University of Dublin were felt to give those institutions (unless this sub-section were inserted) a certain security of existence.

Expressio unius rule and the residual legislative power

The question to what extent the mention of a particular right, facility, category etc. in the Constitution leaves the Oireachtas free, without specific constitutional authority, to extend such right, facility, category etc. to persons or areas not contemplated by the Constitution is only now receiving judicial consideration. On the one hand there is the view of Finlay P in *The State (Walshe) v Murphy*[76] that the Oireachtas possesses a residual legislative power subject only to not *conflicting* with what the Constitution prescribes:

> "It was contended that the effect of the provisions of Article 36(ii) so construed, is to confine the Legislature to regulating by law (i.e. by statute) the terms of appointment and the number of the judges of the District Court and thus to prohibit the Legislature from making any other provision with regard to such appointment, such as the qualifications for appointment. I cannot accept that contention. It involves, as I understand it, a basic misconception of the entire scheme provided in the Constitution for the exercise of the legislative power. The sole and exclusive power of making laws for the State is vested in the Oireachtas by Article 15.2.1. *Prima facie*, such power of legislation is absolute and all-embracing, subject to the qualifications imposed upon it by the Constitution."

But the validity of this proposition must depend on the character, context and purpose of the constitutional provision which this residual legislative power is invoked to add to or to qualify. Clearly, to some constitutional statements the principle *expressio unius exclusio alterius* must apply. Thus, in connection with Article 34.1 which reads: "Justice

[76] [1981] IR 275.

shall be administered in courts established by law by judges appointed in the manner provided by this Constitution, etc.", the old Supreme Court said in *In re Solicitors Act 1954*,[77] that:

> "The corollary must be that justice is not to be administered by persons who are not judges appointed in the manner provided by the Constitution, save in those cases specially excluded by other provisions of the Constitution."

The old Supreme Court had earlier employed a variant of the *expressio unius* rule in *Buckley v Attorney General*[78] when, in the course of rejecting the State's contention that the interpretation of Article 43 was peculiarly a matter for the Legislature, O'Byrne J said that if it had been intended to remove this matter entirely form the cognisance of the courts, "we are of opinion that it would have been done in express terms as it was done in Article 45 with reference to the directive principles of social policy."

Similarly, in *Byrne v Ireland*[79] - though here not a statute, but a supposed rule or prerogative of common law was under challenge - Budd J drew attention to the immunity from suit enjoyed by the President under Article 13.8.1; this showed that the framers of the Constitution had had immunity from suit in their minds, but "in sharp contrast" they had not provided for an immunity in favour of the State, which seemed to him to "carry an implication of some weight that it was not intended to confer any such immunity on the State"; if this is so (and two of the other judges of the Court agreed with him), an Act of the Oireachtas could not validly do so. Relevant also is the view of Walsh J in *The State (Aherne) v Cotter*[80] that Article 40.4 sets out the "whole procedure" relative to the habeas corpus remedy, and that it is "outside the competence of any rule-making authority to make any rules whatever to regulate this procedure", a view which must be equally applicable to a regulation undertaken by the Oireachtas to add to this procedure.

This question became acutely topical in *In re Article 26 and the Electoral (Amendment) Bill 1983*,[81] in which the Bill passed by both Houses of the Oireachtas purported to entitle resident British citizens "to be registered as Dáil electors", whereas Article 16.1.2 gives the right to vote at Dáil elections to "every citizen (of Ireland]" who fulfils the conditions laid down by the subsection. The President referred the Bill to the Supreme Court, the central question being whether it was competent for the Oireachtas to extend to category *b* a right given by the Constitution only to category *a* (though without words denoting expressly the exclusivity of the attribution). The Court, having noted that the principle of the Bill might by analogy also be invoked to justify legislation making a non-citizen eligible to be elected President or a member of the Dáil, decided that the Oireachtas could not extend a category which the Court judged to be implicitly exclusive; and distinguished this franchise, exclusive to citizens, from other constitutional rights (such as those of Articles 40-42) which, though expressed to belong to "citizens", it was constitutionally permissible to treat as available also to persons who were not citizens.[82] This analysis has implications for other areas of the Constitution as well. Thus, when Article 44.2.4 speaks of "Legislation providing state aid for schools shall not dis-

[77] [1960] IR 239. See also the comments of Kenny J in *Deaton v Attorney General* [1963] IR 170; (1964) 98 ILTR 99.

[78] [1950] IR 67. Kingsmill Moore J made a similar point in *Comyn v Attorney General* [1950] IR 142; (1949) 83 ILTR 146. Kenny J employed a similar approach in *Ryan v Attorney General* [1965] IR 294 in contrasting the different language of Article 40.3.1 with Article 40.3.2.

[79] [1972] IR 241.

[80] [1982] IR 188.

[81] [1984] IR 268; [1984] ILRM 539.

criminate between schools under the management of different religious denominations..." this by implication only allows the provision of state aid in a manner prescribed by an Act of the Oireachtas.

Limits of the expressio unius rule as an aid to construction

There, of course, limits to this doctrine as a useful rule of construction. Thus, in *Attorney General v Hamilton (No.1)*[83] the Supreme Court engaged in a historical analysis of the background to the one-judgment rule in Article 34.4.5.[84] By demonstrating that, historically, the rule was enacted to meet a particular and special contingency, Finlay CJ demonstrated that one could not extrapolate from this express rule so as to infer that, in the absence of any similar express rule in the context of Government meetings, there could be no principle of absolute confidentiality of discussions at Government meetings.[85] But a comprehensive, theoretical exposition of the criteria on which the *expressio unius* principle will be seen as governing constitutional provisions has not yet been undertaken.

No review by reference to "extra-constitutional" principles

There have been occasions when the courts have been asked to apply, by the route of judicial review of legislation, not the express terms of the Constitution, but what were said to be principles latent in it, or outside it but co-ordinate with it; these solicitations have mostly been rejected. Thus Fitzgibbon J in *The State (Ryan) v Lennon*[86] cited this passage from the American case of *Walker v Cincinnati*:[87]

> "Courts cannot nullify an Act of the State legislature on the vague ground that they think it opposed to a general latent spirit supposed to pervade or underlie the Constitution where neither the terms nor the implications of the instrument disclose any such restriction."

In *The State (McCarthy) v Lennon*[88] the suggestion was repeated that the drastic provisions of Article 2A (imported into the old Constitution by an amending Act[89]) infringed latent but basic principles; Murnaghan J said simply: "It is... impossible for a court to hold that the Constitution is contrary to natural justice."

The words of Fitzgibbon J in *Ryan's* case were cited with approval by Dixon J in *Foley v Irish Land Commission*;[90] he added that, so far as he knew, the dictum had not been

[82] The *Electoral (Amendment) Bill* case was one in which an obvious criterion for *expressio unius* existed. The franchise has always been seen as a privilege (if only to judge by the grudging stages by which the universal adult suffrage was established, quite apart from the assertion in Article 6 of the people's *right to designate the rulers of the State*, reflecting the rejection of any such pretension on behalf of non-nationals); whereas most, if not all, of the rights of Articles 40-44, even where declared for the benefit of citizens, are now acknowledged to be natural human rights, so that their protection must necessarily transcend the mere citizen category.

[83] [1993] 2 IR 250; [1993] ILRM 81.

[84] See pp. 527-528.

[85] See also the judgment of Barrington J in *The State (Whelan) v Government of Mountjoy Prison* [1983] ILRM 52 (see p. 905-906) where he seemed to hint at a similar approach with regard to the construction of Article 40.4.3, which - just as with Article 34.4.5 - had been inserted into the Constitution by the Second Amendment of the Constitution Act 1941 in response to a special necessity.

[86] [1935] IR 170; (1935) 69 ILTR 125.

[87] 21 Ohio 41.

[88] [1936] IR 485.

[89] By the Constitution (Amendment No. 17) Act 1931.

[90] [1952] IR 118; (1952) 86 ILTR 44.

dissented or departed from in any subsequent decision. Sullivan CJ giving the judgment of the Supreme Court in *In re Article 26 and the Offences Against the State (Amendment) Bill 1940*,[91] said that a clear infringement or repugnancy has to be established in order to invalidate an Act on the ground of supposed conflict with a rule implied by the Constitution even if not expressly stated by it. And in *The State (Burke) v Lennon*[92] Johnston J (who dissented from the majority of the Supreme Court on the concrete issue) said:

> "The Constitution of 1937 represents a fresh start in respect of the fundamental principles that are to be the guide of this country for the future, and I do not think that a further Constitution - an unwritten one - was intended by the people of Éire to exist side by side with this written Constitution or even perhaps it would be more correct to say - outside and beyond the present Constitution."

Yet the other point of view has had, and still has, judicial adherents. There is the famous dissent of Kennedy CJ in *The State (Ryan) v Lennon*[93] a passionate denunciation of the novel principles admitted by Article 2A, and an assertion of the Court's right to declare them void by reference to immutable, fundamental principles outside but superior to the Constitution. In *The State (Burke) v Lennon*[94] - decided by the identical Court that decided the *Offences Against the State (Amendment) Bill* reference a few weeks later - four of the five judges had held that the old judicial rule which excluded appeals against the granting of an order of *habeas corpus* must be taken to have survived into the post-1937 era so as to qualify the express words of Article 34.4.3; Murnaghan J based his view on the constitutional value of personal freedom (as expressed in the old Constitution) and the maxim *generalia specialibus non derogant*). In more recent times the dissenting opinion of Henchy J delivered in *The People (Director of Public Prosecutions) v O'Shea*,[95] which would allow the traditional non-appealability of jury acquittals to prevail over the same general words of Article 34.4.3, is in the same category.

[91] [1940] IR 470; (1940) 76 ILTR 61.
[92] [1940] IR 136; (1940) 76 ILTR 36, 131.
[93] [1935] IR 170; (1935) 69 ILTR 125
[94] [1940] IR 136; (1940) 76 ILTR 36, 131.
[95] [1982] IR 384. See pp. 684-686.

PREAMBLE

Preamble

BUNREACHT NA hÉIREANN

In the Name of the Most Holy Trinity, from Whom is all authority and to Whom, as our final end, all actions both of men and States must be referred,

We, the people of Éire,
Humbly acknowledging all our obligations to our Divine Lord, Jesus Christ, Who sustained our fathers through centuries of trial,

Gratefully remembering their heroic and unremitting struggle to regain the rightful independence of our Nation,

And seeking to promote the common good, with due observance of Prudence, Justice and Charity, so that the dignity and freedom of the individual may be assured, true social order attained, the unity of our country restored, and concord established with other nations,

Do hereby adopt, enact, and give to ourselves this Constitution.

Brollach

BUNREACHT NA hÉIREANN

In Ainm na Tríonóide Ró-Naofa is tobar don uile údarás agus gur chuici, ós í is críoch dheireanach dúinn, is dírithe ní amháin gníomhartha daoine ach gníomhartha Stát,
Ar mbeith dúinne, muintir na hÉireann, ag admháil go huiríseal a mhéid atáimid faoi chomaoin ag Íosa Críost, ár dTiarna Dia, a thug comhfhurtacht dár sinsir i ngach cruatan ina rabhadar ar feadh na gcéadta bliain,
Agus ar mbeith dúinn ag cuimhneamh go buíoch ar a chalmacht a rinneadarsan troid gan staonadh chun an neamhspleáchas is dual dár Naisiún a bhaint amach,
Agus ar mbeith dúinn á chur romhainn an mhaitheas phoiblí a chur ar aghaidh maille le Críonnacht agus le hIonracas agus le Carthanacht de réir mar is cuí, ionas go dtiocfaidh linn a uaisleacht agus a shaoirse a chur in áirithe do gach aon duine, saol ceart comhdhaonnach a bhunú, aiseag a haontachta a thabhairt dár dtír, agus comhcharadra a dhéanamh le náisiúin eile,
Atáimid leis seo ag gabháil an Bhunreachta seo chugainn, agus á achtú agus á thíolacadh dúinn féin.

Mode of enactment of the Constitution

This Preamble[1] incorporates the words of enactment of the Constitution and identifies the enacting authority as "the people of Éire".[2] This popular enactment contrasts - and was designed to contrast - with the mode of enactment of the 1922 Constitution, which

[1] The opening invocation of the Most Holy Trinity recalls the similar preface to the decrees which formed the basis of the constitution of the Confederation of Kilkenny in 1642 - see Grogan, 8 *Christus Rex*, p.202. The 1922 Constitution itself had contained no Preamble, but the opening words of the Constitution of the Irish Free State (Saorstát Éireann) Act performed a similar function; they read: "Dáil Éireann sitting as a Constituent Assembly in this Provisional Parliament, acknowledging that all lawful authority comes from God to the people and in the confidence that the National life and unity of Ireland shall thus be restored, hereby proclaims the establishment of the Irish Free State (otherwise called Saorstát Éireann) and in the exercise of undoubted right, decrees and enacts as follows:" (the Constitution followed as a Schedule).

[2] The logical problem of using this expression when, in fact, only the electors of the twenty-six county Irish Free State were going to take part in the plebiscite to enact the Constitution was adverted to in the Dáil on 4 June 1937(67 *Dáil Debates* 1911ff.). Mr. de Valera said: "If we in a part of this document say that, pending reintegration, the laws of the Parliament and the Government set up here cannot effectively operate in a certain part of the national territory, it is quite obvious that the people in that part of the national territory are unable to participate in this declaration, and therefore, the declaration on behalf of the whole nation, on behalf of the State, can only be by the people in that part of it whose voice can effectively be heard or made to be heard."
A further difficulty with this expression is that it is at odds with Article 4 which requires that the State be referred to, in the English language, as "Ireland". As to how this might be corrected, see below, p. 9.

was scheduled to the Constitution of the Irish Free State (Saorstát Éireann) Act passed by Dáil Éireann "sitting as a constituent assembly" on 25 October of that year.

In the eyes of the Irish courts, the act of the constituent assembly was the "one and all-sufficient root of title" for the Constitution, as Meredith J put it in *Cahill v Attorney General*;[3] a view previously expressed by Murnaghan J in *Fogarty v O''Donoghue*[4] ("the source of all authority [is] derived through the people of Ireland"), and later stated, with canonical force, by Kennedy CJ and Fitzgibbon J in the Supreme Court in *The State (Ryan) v Lennon*.[5] (It was stated yet again by the new Supreme Court in *In re Article 26 and the Criminal Law (Jurisdiction) Bill, 1975*.[6]) The result of this view was a curious paradox: since the Dáil *as a constituent assembly* had limited the Constitution-amending power of its creation, the Oireachtas, to such amendments as were "within the terms of the scheduled Treaty" (i.e. the 1921 Anglo-Irish Treaty), it was not competent for the Oireachtas to dismantle any elements of the Constitution - such as the controversial oath - which the Treaty had expressly stipulated; whereas seen from the point of view of the British courts[7] - which regarded the Constitution as deriving its validity from an Act of the United Kingdom Parliament, the Irish Free State Constitution Act 1922 - the amending power of the Oireachtas was subject to no such limitation, once the 1931 Statute of Westminster had entitled the Dominion legislatures, including that of the Irish Free State, to repeal or amend any United Kingdom Act applying to them, and hence had empowered the Oireachtas to amend the Irish Free State (Agreement) Act 1922, the Act which gave legal force to the Treaty.[8]

Opposition to the Treaty was central to the programme of Mr. de Valera's party; and it was this posture of the Irish courts that led him, in 1937, to promote a fundamental break with the 1922 Constitution rather than merely to amend it.[9] By securing the adoption of the draft Constitution at a popular plebiscite which was expressed to "enact" it,[10]

[3] [1925] IR 70; (1925) 59 ILTR 2.

[4] [1926] IR 531.

[5] [1935] IR 170; (1935) 69 ILTR 125.

[6] [1977] IR 129; (1976) 110 ILTR 69. See also the words of Kennedy CJ in *Lynham v Butler (No. 2)* [1933] IR 74; (1933) 67 ILTR 75; [1932] LJ Ir 172; and of Kingsmill Moore J in *In re Irish Employers' Mutual Insurance Association* [1955] IR 176.

[7] *Moore v Attorney General* [1935] IR 472; (1935) 69 ILTR 159. An American court took the same view - that "Saorstát Éireann had succeeded to the United Kingdom by a British Act" - in *Irish Free State v Guaranty Safe Deposit Co.*, 222 N.Y.S 182 (1927).

[8] The terms of the Treaty - although this document, having been concluded between representatives of the British Government, on the one hand, and representatives of what in the strict British eye was an illegal assembly of rebels, on the other, was *sui generis* - echoed in some respects the legislation underlying the constitutions of the self-governing Dominions, to which the new Irish State was to be assimilated: thus the Treaty said in its first Article that there was to be a parliament with power to make "laws for the peace, order and good government" of Ireland, a phrase previously used in s 91 of the British North America Act 1867 (with reference to Canada), and in s 59 of the South Africa Act 1909.

[9] He said (67 *Dáil Debates* 416): "The courts here have expressed certain opinions in dealing with certain cases and made certain suggestions as to their views about the powers here to pass Acts in relation to the terms of the Treaty. We were not going to risk a Constitution like this... being enacted here and being operated with such possible views held by the courts. What we are doing is, we are going back to the sovereign authority, to the Irish people, or that section of the Irish people whom we can consult on the matter. We go back to them and ask them to enact it. It is they who will enact it and... when they enact it, there is a provision that any judge, or anybody else, who is not prepared to function under it can resign and get out" (on the last matter, see below, n. 16).

[10] The 1922 Constitution contained no provision conferring such a legislative role on a plebiscite. The necessary legal provision for holding a plebiscite was made by the Plebiscite (Draft Constitution) Act 1937; which was, however, not expressed to be an amendment of the existing Constitution, or to confer the force of law on what it determined (this, under the "implicit amendment" doctrine, would have been just as good: see below, under Article 51). The Act merely provided (s 2(1)) that: "The Draft Constitution shall be submitted to a plebiscite of the people in accordance with this Act". The vote was: 685,105 in favour, 526,945 against. The date of the plebiscite was 1 July 1937.

while confining the Dáil[11] to the role of merely "approving" the draft before it was submitted to plebiscite, he by-passed the Constitution of 1922 and made irrelevant, for the future, the question whether its validity depended on the act of the Irish constituent assembly (which kept it shackled by the Treaty) or on that of the United Kingdom Parliament (which, though it had loosed those shackles, represented an emotionally unacceptable "root of title" for the national Constitution).[12] Naturally it was arguable, whether one stood on either an Irish or a United Kingdom *Grundnorm* of 1922, that the new Constitution of 1937, not having been enacted according to the mode of amendment prescribed by its predecessor, and not having respected the limits which at any rate the Irish courts saw as restraining that amending power, was invalid; but although the point was mentioned during the Dáil debate on the draft,[13] it was never afterwards raised in a court: the possibility that a court might entertain it was anticipated by providing[14] that the judges in office at the moment when the new Constitution came into force would continue in office only subject to taking an oath to uphold the Constitution (none of them declined the oath), and the same oath was required[15] in the case of all subsequent judicial appointments.[16]

The whole proceeding amounted to a break in legal continuity;[17] to a supplanting of one *Grundnorm* (albeit a disputed one) by another; and thus, legally speaking, to a revolution.

The Preamble has been adverted to judicially in several cases of importance. On no occasion has a decision been based solely upon it, but it has been used to lay the ground for the deployment of later parts of the Constitution, or to underpin judgements rhetorically and emotionally.

General significance of the Preamble: underlying spirit of the Constitution

General references to its place in constitutional interpretation are found in a few cases.[18] In *Attorney General v Southern Industrial Trust*[19] the Supreme Court, *per* Lavery J, said:

[11] The Dáil was at that time the sole house of the Oireachtas (and so the two terms were coextensive), the Seanad having been abolished in 1936 by the Constitution (Amendment No. 24) Act. See Donal O'Sullivan, *The Irish Free State and its Senate*, pp. 446ff.

[12] Though the resolution of this issue may be important in determining the ultimate fate of the royal prerogative under the present Constitution - see the discussion by Lenihan, *"Royal Prerogative and the Constitution"* (1989) 24 Ir Jur (*n.s.*) 1, pp. 7 - 11.

[13] By Deputy James Fitzgerald-Kenney, a former Minister for Justice: 67 *Dáil Debates* 351-3.

[14] Article 58.

[15] Article 34.5.

[16] But would the judgment of a judge who found against the validity of the Constitution's enactment be invalid by reason simply of his having defied his oath? Such a defiance would presumably be misbehaviour justifying his removal (Article 35.4); and moreover a pronouncement of invalidity against the Constitution would logically vitiate his own status as a judge appointed thereunder - see comment of Barrington J in *Crotty v An Taoiseach* [1987] IR 715; [1987] ILRM 400, wherein he said, "It would not be open to the Court [of Justice] to question the validity of the Treaty [of Rome] to which it owed its existence any more than it would be open to this Court to question the validity of the Irish Constitution" - but this might not end the question. Problems from this kind of area arose in Rhodesia after the 1965 unilateral declaration of independence: see Honore, "*Reflections on Revolutions*", (1967) 2 Ir Jur (n.s.)268; also, with a list of the literature on the subject, Eekelaar, "*Principles of Revolutionary Legality*", *Oxford Essays in Jurisprudence* (Second Series), 22.

[17] This is the phrase of K. C. Wheare, in *The Constitutional Structure of the Commonwealth* (1960), p. 94. His treatment of the differing judicial views on the source of validity of the 1922 Constitution, and of the transformation of the Irish State's Constitution from being "autonomous" to being "autochthonous" [=indigenous] as well (via the "revolution" of 1937), is excellent: pp. 89ff. See also pp. 72ff. of that work.

[18] In *Lawlor v Minister for Agriculture* [1990] 1 IR 356, Murphy J referred to the various occasions on which the Preamble has been invoked as an example of the teleological approach to constitutional interpretation.

[19] (1960) 94 ILTR 161.

> "The declaration in the Preamble, made in general terms, may add little to the more precise terms of the relevant Articles. Nevertheless, the words of the Preamble declaring the purpose of the people in adopting, enacting, and giving to themselves the Constitution may help in determining the meaning of and the effect to be given to particular provisions."

Davitt P had previously said in his judgment in the High Court, in regard to the guarantees for property in Article 40.3, that:

> "the justice or otherwise of any legislative interference with the right has to be considered in relation, *inter alia*, to the proclaimed objects with which the Constitution was enacted, including the promotion of the common good."

In this particular case, however, the Supreme Court did not use the Preamble for analysing later provisions, saying merely that:

> "so far as the Court can see, it is the fact that the Constitution does adequately declare and define the essential property rights which the Irish people regard as proper so that, in the words of the Preamble, "the dignity and freedom of the individual may be assured and true social order attained"."

In *Buckley v Attorney General*[20] the Court said, *per* O'Byrne J, that:

> "These most laudable objects [expressed in the Preamble] seem to us to inform the various Articles of the Constitution, and we are of opinion that, so far as possible, the Constitution should be so construed as to give them life and reality."

Changing and developing values

In a number of cases, the Preamble has been invoked to justify judicial activism in the construction of the Constitution. Thus in *McGee v Attorney General*[21] Walsh J said:

> "According to the Preamble, the people gave themselves the Constitution to promote the common good with due observance of prudence, justice and charity so that the dignity and freedom of the individual might be assured. The judges must, therefore, as best they can from their training and their experience interpret these rights in accordance with their ideas of prudence, justice and charity. It is but natural that from time to time the prevailing ideas of these virtues may be conditioned by the passage of time; no interpretation of the Constitution is intended to be final for all time."

This approach was endorsed by O'Higgins CJ in *The State (Healy) v Donoghue*[22] when

[20] [1950] IR 67. A *dictum* similar to this and to the foregoing one is that of Budd J in *McGee v Attorney General* [1974] IR 284; (1975) 109 ILTR 29: "When the Preamble to the Constitution speaks of seeking to promote the common good by the observance of prudence, justice and charity so that the dignity and freedom of the individual may be assured, it must surely inform those charged with its construction as to the mode of application of its Articles."

[21] [1974] IR 284; (1975) 109 ILTR 29.

[22] [1976] IR 325. It was followed also by McWilliam J in the High Court in considering whether "the Legislature could now, under current social conditions, having regard to the prevailing ideas and concepts of morality and the current knowledge of matters affecting public health, reasonably come to the conclusion that the homosexual acts declared unlawful by the statutes under challenge were such as ought to be prohibited for the attainment of true social order as mentioned in the Preamble to the Constitution [and the objects of Articles 40 and 45]": *Norris v Attorney General* [1984] IR 36. See also *King v Attorney General* [1981] IR 233, in which McWilliam J referred to the Preamble in laying the ground for his finding that part of s 4 of the Vagrancy Act 1824, was inconsistent with the Constitution; and a brief reference by Henchy J in *Garvey v Ireland* [1981] IR 75.

he used the Preamble in support of the Court's view of "fair procedures" in a criminal trial as being a concept that could develop and expand in content:

> "In my view, [the] Preamble makes it clear that rights given by the Constitution must be considered in accordance with concepts of prudence, justice and charity which may gradually change or develop as society changes and develops, and which fall to be interpreted from time to time in accordance with prevailing ideas. The Preamble envisages a Constitution which can absorb or be adapted to such changes. In other words, the Constitution did not seek to impose for all time the ideas prevalent or accepted with regard to these virtues at the time of its enactment."[23]

That this dynamism in the interpretation of the Constitution extends even to the right to life was accepted by Finlay CJ in *Attorney General v X* [24] wherein he cited both of the above passages with approval and continued:

> "I find [the passages cited] particularly and peculiarly appropriate and illuminating in the interpretation of a sub-section of the Constitution which deals with the intimate human problem of the right of the unborn to life and its relationship to the right of the mother of an unborn child to her life."

Such an approach to the interpretation of the Constitution certainly has the potential to produce a more liberal abortion policy by way of judicial innovation.[25]

Preamble as a dubious forensic weapon

That the Preamble is a dubious forensic weapon is evident from those cases in which it has been retorted upon the side invoking it in argument. Thus in *In re Article 26 and the Offences Against the State (Amendment) Bill, 1940*[26] the Supreme Court adverted to two objectives expressed in the Preamble, and saw one as depending on the other:

> "It seems to us difficult to understand how the dignity and freedom of the individual member of a State can be attained unless social order is maintained in that State."

And in *In re Philip Clarke*,[27] where the issue was the constitutionality of provisions of the Mental Treatment Act 1945, which empowered members of the Garda Síochána to take mentally disturbed persons into charge, the Supreme Court said:

> "We do not see how the common good would be promoted or the dignity and freedom of the individual assured by allowing persons, alleged to be suffering from such infirmity, to remain at large to the possible danger of themselves and others."

In spite of its general terms which can be as easily used against them as in their favour, litigants now regularly plead the Preamble in addition to Articles - see, for example, *The*

[23] In *McKinley v The Minister for Defence* [1992] 2 IR 333, Hederman J referred to the statement in the Preamble that the Constitution sought, *inter alia*, to assure the "dignity and freedom of the individual" as a reason for construing Articles 40 and 41 so as to extend the common law action for loss of consortium to plaintiff wives.

[24] [1992] 1 IR; [1992] ILRM 401.

[25] Cp. the remarks of McCarthy J in *Norris v Attorney General* [1984] IR 36, made prior to the enactment of Article 40.3.3, that he regarded the Preamble as "leaning heavily against any view other than that the right to life of the unborn is a sacred trust to which all organs of government must lend support."

[26] [1940] IR 470: (1940) 74 ILTR 61.

[27] [1950] IR 235: (1951) 85 ILTR 119.

State (McMorrow) v Barry;[28] *Blake v Attorney General*,[29] *Norris v Attorney General*.[30] In none of these, however, did the Preamble play a part in the court's decision.

The Preamble in judicial rhetoric

Purely rhetorical, but still forceful judicial invocations of the Preamble may be found in *The State (Burke) v Lennon*,[31] in which Gavan Duffy J said: "The Constitution, with its most impressive Preamble, is the Charter of the Irish people, and I will not whittle it away"; and in *McGee v Attorney General*,[32] in which Henchy J mobilised the Preamble against the practical effect of a law prohibiting the importation or sale of contraceptives. This had the effect of:

> "condemning the plaintiff and her husband to a way of life which, at best, will be fraught with worry, tension and uncertainty... And this in the context of a Constitution which in its Preamble proclaims as one of its aims the dignity and freedom of the individual."

The Preamble and binding norms

That the Preamble might, on occasion, give rise to binding constitutional norms was recognised by Hederman J in his dissenting judgment in *Russell v Fanning*[33] wherein he said that the re-unification of the national territory is:

> "by the provisions of the Preamble to the Constitution and of Article 3 of the Constitution a constitutional imperative and not one the pursuit or non-pursuit of which is within the discretion of the government or any other organ of State."

This viewpoint was subsequently endorsed by the Supreme Court in *McGimpsey v Ireland*.[34]

Religion in the Preamble

The religious dimension of the Preamble has been referred to in a number of cases. In *Quinn's Supermarket v Attorney General*[35] Walsh J said the Constitution "reflects a firm conviction that we are a religious people", because, *inter alia*, "the Preamble acknowledges that we are a Christian people". In *McGee v Attorney General*[36] the same judge associated "natural human rights" with natural law and the law of God in reliance jointly on the Preamble and Article 6:

> "Both in its Preamble and in Article 6, the Constitution acknowledges God as the ultimate source of all authority... In view of the acknowledgement of Christianity in the Preamble and in view of the reference to God in Article 6, it must be accepted that the Constitution intended the natural human rights I have mentioned as being in the category of natural law derived from God's law."

Thirty years previously Gavan Duffy J had built a reference to the Preamble into a judgment of more specifically Catholic import. In *Maguire v Attorney General*[37] he turned

[28] Unreported: High Court (Barrington J), 17 July 1980.
[29] [1982] IR 117.
[30] [1984] IR 36.
[31] [1940] IR 136; (1940) 74 ILTR 36, 131.
[32] [1974] IR 284; (1975) 109 IITR 29.
[33] [1988] IR 505; [1988] ILRM 333.
[34] [1990] 1 IR 110; [1990] ILRM 440.
[35] [1972] IR 1.
[36] [1974] IR 284; (1975) 109 IITR 29.
[37] [1943] IR 238.

his back on post-Reformation English authority, and held that a testamentary gift to found a convent for the perpetual adoration of the Blessed Sacrament was a valid charitable gift. He said:

> "And that conclusion is in harmony with the Constitution enacted by the Irish people "in the Name of the Most Holy Trinity...to Whom, as our final end, all actions both of men and States must be referred"."

In *Norris v Attorney General*[38] O'Higgins CJ said:

> "It cannot be doubted that the people, so asserting and acknowledging [in the Preamble] their obligations to Our Divine Lord Jesus Christ, were proclaiming a deeply religious conviction and faith and an intention to adopt a Constitution consistent with that conviction and faith and with Christian beliefs."

a proposition later endorsed by Hamilton P in *Attorney General (Society for the Protection of the Unborn Child (Ireland) Ltd.) v Open-Door Counselling Ltd.*[39]

The Preamble and the sovereign people

A conclusion of material importance was deduced from the wording of the Preamble, in connection with the supposed "sovereignty" of the State, in *Byrne v Ireland.*[40] Walsh J, with whom Ó Dálaigh CJ concurred, based his view that the State is the creation of the People not only on three Articles but also on the Preamble; it was, he emphasised, "a preamble by the People formally adopting, enacting and giving themselves a Constitution".[41] In *Webb v Ireland* [42] the same judge referred to the sovereign People as having rights and duties, in this instance, the right and duty, acting through the State, to exercise dominion over all objects forming part of the national heritage.

Private property

In *O'Callaghan v Commissioners of Public Works*[43] the Supreme Court invoked the Preamble in support of its decision upholding the validity of s 8 of the National Monuments Act 1930 (as amended by s 3 of the National Monuments (Amendment) Act 1954), which provides for the making of preservation orders in respect of national monuments, with consequent restrictions on the rights of the landowner. The Court noted that:

> "the State, through s 8, delimits by law, not the right of private ownership or the general right to transfer etc. but the exercise of those rights - in this instance the user of land - so that that user will be reconciled with the exigencies of the common good - here, the national aspirations as set out in the Preamble and Article 1 of the Constitution."

38 [1984] IR 36.
39 [1988]; IR 593; [1987] ILRM 477.
40 [1972] IR 241.
41 This distinction between the State and the People has been criticised by Gwynn Morgan on the ground that since they are both "artificial entities, with no clear demarcation of purpose between them, it was merely complicating the issue, to no advantage, to analyse them as legally distinct bodies." *Constitutional Law of Ireland*, p.28.
42 [1988] IR 353; [1988] ILRM 565.
43 [1985] ILRM 364.

The criminal appellate jurisdiction

In *The People (Director of Public Prosecutions) v Mulligan*[44] the Preamble was invoked by counsel in support of the proposition that the Court of Criminal Appeal should, having considered the evidence disclosed in the transcript in an appeal against conviction, consider its own reaction in a subjective manner, not merely from the evidence as such, but from the "feel of the case" as experienced by the Court, and that if the Court should have "any lurking doubt" as to whether justice had been done, or should feel that in all the circumstances of the case the verdict of the trial court was unsafe or unsatisfactory, the conviction should be quashed. The Court rejected this suggestion.

The power to deport

In *Osheku v Ireland*[45] Gannon J cited the Preamble in support of the State's right to deport aliens. He said:

> "The integrity of the State, constituted as it is of the collective body of its citizens within the national territory, must be defended and vindicated by the organs of the State and by the citizens so that there may be true social order within the territory and concord maintained with other nations in accordance with the objectives declared in the Preamble to the Constitution. It seems to me to follow that personal rights guaranteed under the Constitution are not so absolute as to be capable of being considered entirely independently of the provisions overall of the Constitution."

Extradition

In *The State (Trimbole) v Governor of Mountjoy Prison*[46] McCarthy J cited, *inter alia*, the objective of establishing concord with other nations, stated in the Preamble, in support of the proposition that where a friendly state seeks the extradition of a person alleged to have committed serious crimes within that state, this State should co-operate in effecting that extradition.

The consequences of judicial invalidation of legislation

The word "order" in the Preamble was interpreted by O'Higgins CJ in *Murphy v Ireland*[47] in the sense of "orderliness, dependable regularity", when he said, in rejecting the view that a declaration of invalidity meant the Act had been at all times void from the moment of enactment (a view which in this case would have entailed the refunding of huge sums collected under a taxation statute now found invalid):

> "It would appear to me to be unthinkable that a people who adopted a Constitution in the interest (*inter alia*) of achieving "a true social order" (see Preamble) should have intended that, under that Constitution, laws, formally passed, which went into operation and which were respected and obeyed, could, years after their enactment, be declared never to have had the force of law. Such an interpretation of the Constitution would provide for our people the very antithesis of a true social order - an uneasy existence fraught with legal and constitutional uncertainty."

[44] (1980) 2 Frewen 164.

[45] [1986] IR 733; [1986] ILRM 330. Though see now *Fajujonu v The Minister for Justice* [1990] 2 IR 151; [1990] ILRM 234, discussed below, pp 66-67, 1001-3.

[46] [1985] IR 550; [1985] ILRM 465.

[47] [1982] IR 241.

Sentencing policy

In *The People (Director of Public Prosecutions) v W.C.*,[48] Flood J considered that the principle of selecting a punishment which was appropriate, not only to the crime, but also to the criminal, was an application of the concept of justice referred to in the Preamble.

Amendment of the Preamble

The question whether the Preamble can be amended arises because the amending power of Article 46 relates to a "provision" ("forálleamh") of the Constitution. Is the Preamble a "provision"? This point has occurred in connection with the suggested desirability of changing the phrase "people of Éire" to "people of Ireland" and the view has been expressed that if the people by referendum approved an amendment to the Preamble it would be "unreal" to say the amendment was *ultra vires* the people. This point of view seems unsound, since if the Preamble is not a "provision", a referendum purporting to amend it would achieve nothing, and there would be nothing to stop a court from saying so. The problem would disappear if Article 46 were itself amended so as expressly to subject the Preamble to the amending power.

[48]High Court, 14 July 1993.

Articles 1-3

THE NATION

THE NATION

Article 1

The Irish nation hereby affirms its inalienable, indefeasible, and sovereign right to choose its own form of Government, to determine its relations with other nations, and to develop its life, political, economic and cultural, in accordance with its own genius and traditions.

Article 2

The national territory consists of the whole island of Ireland, its islands and the territorial seas.

Article 3

Pending the re-integration of the national territory, and without prejudice to the right of the Parliament and Government established by this Constitution to exercise jurisdiction over the whole of that territory, the laws enacted by that Parliament shall have the like area and extent of application as the laws of Saorstát Éireann and the like extra-territorial effect.

AN NÁISIÚN

Airteagal 1

Deimhníonn náisiún na hÉireann leis seo a gceart doshannta, dochloíte, ceannasach chun cibé cineál Rialtais is rogha leo féin a bhunú, chun a gcaidreamh le náisiún eile a chinneadh, agus chun a saol polaitíochta is geilleagair is saíochta a chur ar aghaidh de réir dhúchais is gnás a sinsear.

Airteagal 2

Is é oileán na hÉireann go hiomlán, maille lena oileáin agus a fharraigí teorann, na críocha náisiúnta.

Airteagal 3

Go dtí go ndéantar athchomhlánú ar na críocha náisiúnta, agus gan dochar do cheart na Parlaiminte is an Rialtais a bhunaítear leis an mBunreacht seo chun dlínse a oibriú sna críocha náisiúnta uile, bainfidh na dlíthe a achtófar ag an bParlaimint sin leis an limistéar céanna lenar bhain dlíthe Shaorstát Éireann, agus beidh an éifeacht chéanna acu taobh amuigh den limistéar sin a bhí ag dlíthe Shaorstát Éireann.

Mixed legal and political content

This group of Articles, which had no counterpart in the Constitution of 1922, is of mixed legal and political content: and although the next group, Articles 4 - 11, is collectively entitled "The State", so as to suggest a distinction between nation and State, it is clear that part of the subject-matter of Articles 1-3 is referable to the State rather than to the nation. The mixed character of this part of the Constitution (and of some other Articles also) led the Supreme Court, in *In re Article 26 and the Criminal Law (Jurisdiction) Bill 1975*[1] to say:

> "It is true that the Constitution is a legal document, but it is a fundamental one which establishes the State and it expresses not only legal norms but basic doctrines of political and social theory... The Constitution contains more than legal rules: it

[1] [1977] IR 129; (1976) 110 ILTR 69.

reflects, in part, aspirations and aims and expresses the political theories on which the people acted when they enacted the Constitution."[2]

The Court went on to summarise an important area of theory or aspiration:

> "One of the theories held in 1937 by a substantial number of citizens was that a nation, as distinct from a State, had rights; that the Irish people living in what is now called the Republic of Ireland and in Northern Ireland together formed the Irish nation; that a nation has a right to unity of territory in some form, be it as a unitary or federal state; and that the Government of Ireland Act 1920,[3] though legally binding, was a violation of that national right to unity which was superior to positive law."

These ideas come through in Articles 1- 3, and on the political plane, so far as they imply the illegitimacy of the separate constitutional existence of Northern Ireland, are naturally contentious. On the legal plane they have played a certain secondary role in reinforcing conclusions which might have been arrived at anyway.

Judicial references to Article 1

Article 1 has been used in argument in conjunction with several other Articles in a few cases in which the courts formulated their judgments without specifically considering it.[4] In *Attorney General v Crawford*[5] it was sought to identify the Revenue Commissioners with, or as successors to, the Crown; in rejecting this submission Maguire J said:

> "The matter has been put beyond doubt by the Constitution of Éire, Articles l, 6, 11, 12, 15, 25, 28, 30 and 49 of which are all clearly repugnant to the continued existence of "The Crown" as an expression designating any function of Government in this State."

In *The State (Duggan) v Tapley*[6] Article 1 was one of a number of Articles relied on in challenging the survival into the post-1937 era of the provisions of the Petty Sessions (Ireland) Act 1851, regulating the transfer, by a sort of quasi-extradition between different parts of the United Kingdom, of accused persons from Ireland to Britain and vice-

[2] It also echoes earlier documents significant in Irish political history: in particular the 1916 Proclamation, which declared "the right of the people of Ireland to the ownership of Ireland, and to the unfettered control of Irish destinies, to be sovereign and indefeasible": the Sinn Féin Manifesto for the 1918 General Election, which declared Sinn Féin's acceptance of that Proclamation and its "[reassertion of] the inalienable right of the Irish nation to sovereign independence"; and the Message from Dáil Éireann to the Free Nations of the World in 1919, asserting Ireland's "inalienable right of nationhood"; these documents are reproduced in Dorothy Macardle, *The Irish Republic*, pp. 168, 919, 925 respectively. See also in the same book early statements of Mr. de Valera laying emphasis not on a "republican" form of government as such, but on the Irish people's right to choose their own form of government (whether republican or anything else): pp. 917, 929, 932. In his Dáil speech on the Republic of Ireland Bill in 1948, while in Opposition, he came back to the same theme: "It was not to fall into a category of States our people have fought through the centuries. Our people have fought for independence, and the point about the republic was that it was in that form that our independence was crystallised in our time... not that we might be classed by some jurists as this type of State" (113 *Dáil Debates* 422). The 1937 Dáil debate on this draft Article largely revolved around the same point of logic as that raised by the Preamble. Deputy Frank MacDermot also contradicted the notion that Article 1 contained anything that was not just as effectively present under the 1922 Constitution: "This right of sovereignty, this right to choose our own form of government, to determine our relations with other nations, and to develop our life, political, economic and cultural, in accordance with our own genius and traditions, is a right that has been claimed and exercised by the Irish Free State since its foundation" (67 *Dáil Debates* 950).

[3] The Act which created a separate Northern Ireland and was thus the basis of partition: see below, p. 14-15.

[4] *The State (Hully) v Hynes* (1966) 100 ILTR 145, mentions Article 1 in the headnote but it is not clear what bearing it can have had on the case.

[5] [1940] IR 335; (1940) 74 ILTR 140.

[6] [1952] IR 62; (1951) 85 ILTR 22.

versa; the Supreme Court disregarded the Article for the purpose of its judgment. In *Boland v An Taoiseach*,[7] the Article was relied on by the plaintiff in seeking to impeach the constitutionality of the Government's Sunningdale declaration, but the Supreme Court judgments do not refer to it.

A somewhat more substantial role was played by Article 1 in *Byrne v Ireland*,[8] in which the Supreme Court rejected the notion that the State enjoyed an internal sovereignty so as to give it immunity from suit. The case turned mainly on Articles 5 and 49; but both Walsh and Budd JJ used Article 1 in asserting that the sovereign entity, superior to the State, is the People. The latter judge said:

> "Article l of the Constitution itself underlines that it is the nation, which can only be a reference to the People, which has the sovereign right to choose its form of government; it has in fact done this by the enactment of the Constitution... Both [Article 1 and Article 6] indicate that it is recognised in the Constitution itself that there is a higher authority than the State, and this again is incompatible with any theory that the State is sovereign as regards internal affairs of government..."

In *O'Callaghan v Commissioners of Public Works*[9] the Supreme Court referred to the "national aspirations" expressed in the Preamble and Article 1 as identifying the common good in whose interest s 8 of the National Monuments Act 1930, as amended, legitimately prevented landowners from damaging national monuments.

In *Crotty v An Taoiseach*[10] Henchy J deduced from the affirmation, in Article 1, of the Nation's right to determine its relations with other nations that

> "the State's right to conduct its external relations is part of what is inalienable and indefeasible in what is described in Article 5 as "a sovereign, independent, democratic State".

Consequently he held that ratification of Title III of the Single European Act which obliged Ireland to consult with the other member states of the European Communities in matters of foreign policy, was contrary to the Constitution.[11]

National unity: implicit claim on the North

Prior to the Supreme Court decision in *McGimpsey v Ireland*[12] two schools of thought existed as to the nature of the national claim to unity of territory. According to the Supreme Court in the *Criminal Law (Jurisdiction) Bill* case,[13] this claim "exists not in the legal but in the political order".[14] That this was a claim *as of right* had been asserted, however, two years earlier by O'Keeffe P in *Boland v An Taoiseach.*[15] In this case the plaintiff relied on the assertion in Article 3 of "the right of the Parliament and Government established by this Constitution to exercise jurisdiction over the whole of

[7] [1974] IR 338; (1975) 109 ILTR 13.
[8] [1972] IR 241.
[9] [1985] ILRM 364.
[10] [1987] IR 731; [1987] ILRM 400.
[11] Following a referendum held on 26 May 1987, Article 29 of the Constitution was amended to permit Ireland to ratify the Single European Act.
[12] [1990] 1 IR 110; [1990] ILRM 440.
[13] [1977] IR 129; (1976) 110 ILTR 69.
[14] A view endorsed by Costello J in *McGlinchey v Ireland (No.2)* [1990] 2 IR 220. See also the extra-judicial comments of Kenny J in "*The Advantage of a Written Constitution Incorporating a Bill of Rights*", (1975) 30 NILQ 189, at 203-206.
[15] [1974] IR 338; (1975) 109 ILTR 13.

[the national] territory" in attempting to impeach the agreement reached in December 1973 between representatives of the Irish and British Governments and of both unionist and nationalist interests in Northern Ireland (the Sunningdale Agreement). What he objected to was the statement, expressing the position of the Irish Government, incorporated in paragraph 5 of the agreement and printed side by side with a statement expressing that of the British Government; the Irish statement read:

> "The Irish Government fully accepted and solemnly declared that there could be no change in the status of Northern Ireland until a majority of the people of Northern Ireland desired a change in that status."

The plaintiff sought, *inter alia*, a declaration that "the signing of any agreement, formal or otherwise", in the terms (essentially) of this paragraph was an unconstitutional act on the Government's part having regard to several Articles but essentially Articles 2 and 3; and an injunction to restrain the Government from entering into any agreement "which would have the effect of limiting the exercise of sovereignty over any portion of the national territory or of prejudicing the right of the Parliament and Government of Ireland to exercise jurisdiction over the whole of the national territory". He failed, as the Supreme Court would not agree that the Government's statement of its position or policy on a *de facto* situation breached its constitutional obligations, and refused to interfere with an activity which it thought exclusively confined to the Government under Article 28:[16] but O'Keeffe P showed that Article 3 might nevertheless impose limits on what a Government could lawfully do. He said:

> "An acknowledgement by the Government that the State does not claim to be entitled *as of right* to jurisdiction over Northern Ireland would in my opinion be clearly not within the competence of the Government having regard to the terms of the Constitution. I cannot presume that the Government would consciously make an acknowledgement of that kind, and accordingly I accept the view of the Chief Justice that clause 5 represents no more than a reference to the *de facto* position of Northern Ireland coupled with a statement of policy in regard thereto."

In a similar vein, Hederman J, in *Russell v Fanning,*[17] referred to the re-unification of the national territory as a "constitutional imperative", imposed by the terms of the Preamble and Article 3.

This position was ultimately endorsed by the Supreme Court in *McGimpsey v Ireland.*[18] In a case of some irony, the plaintiffs, members of the Official Unionist party of Northern Ireland, sought a declaration that the Anglo-Irish Agreement was unconstitutional because, *inter alia*, Article 1 of the Agreement,[19] which recognised the legitimacy of the present status of Northern Ireland, allegedly violated Articles 2 and 3 of the Constitution. This argument was rejected by an unanimous Supreme Court on the ground that article 1 of the Agreement, read together with the denial of derogation from sovereignty contained in Article 2(b), constituted a recognition of the *de facto* situation

[16] See below, p. 227.

[17] [1988] IR 505; [1988] ILRM 333.

[18] [1990] 1 IR 110; [1990] ILRM 440. *McGimpsey* is an important authority on the matter of judicial review of the executive's treaty-making powers and this is examined below at pp.299-300. On this issue, see Symmons, "*International Treaty Obligations and the Irish Constitution: the McGimpsey case*" (1992) 41 ICLQ 311.

[19] Article 1 reads: "The two Governments (a) affirm that any change in the status of Northern Ireland would only come about with the consent of a majority of the people of Northern Ireland; (b) recognise that the present wish of a majority of the people of Northern Ireland is for no change in the status of Northern Ireland; (c) declare that, if in the future a majority of the people of Northern Ireland clearly wish for and formally consent to the establishment of a united Ireland, they will introduce and support in the respective Parliaments legislation to give effect to that wish."

in Northern Ireland without abandoning the claim to the re-integration of the national territory. On the nature of this latter claim, counsel for both parties had argued that Article 2 constituted a claim of a legal right and, further, that the Oireachtas was entitled, at any time it wished, to enact laws applicable in the counties of Northern Ireland. Finlay CJ, with whom, on this issue, all members of the Court agreed, rejected this view of the extent of the legislative powers of the Oireachtas but agreed with the classification of the claim to unity.[20] He said:

> "With Articles 2 and 3 of the Constitution should be read the Preamble and I am satisfied that the true interpretation of these constitutional provisions is as follows:
>
> 1. The re-integration of the national territory is a constitutional imperative (cf. Hederman J in *Russell v Fanning* [1988] IR 505).
>
> 2. Article 2 of the Constitution consists of a declaration of the extent of the national territory as a claim of legal right.
>
> 3. Article 3 of the Constitution prohibits, pending the re-integration of the national territory, the enactment of laws with any greater area or extent of application or extra-territorial effect than the laws of Saorstát Éireann and this prohibits the enactment of laws applicable in the counties of Northern Ireland.
>
> 4. The restriction imposed by Article 3 pending the re-integration of the national territory in no way derogates from the claim as a legal right to the entire national territory."
>
> The provision in Article 3 of the Constitution contained in the words "and without prejudice to the right of the Parliament and Government established by this Constitution to exercise jurisdiction over the whole of that territory" is an express denial and disclaimer made to the community of nations of acquiescence to any claim that, pending the re-integration of the national territory, the frontier at present existing between the State is or can be accepted as conclusive of the matter or that there can be any prescriptive title thereby created and an assertion that there can be no estoppel created by the restriction in Article 3 on the application of the laws of the State in Northern Ireland. This is of course quite distinct from the extra-territorial effect of the laws of the State in respect of matters occurring outside the State for which persons are made answerable in the courts of the State."

Extent of the State

The physical extent of the State, in the sense of the area in which its laws apply, is described by Article 3 not only provisionally ("pending reintegration etc.") but also indirectly, by reference to the extent of the State's predecessor, Saorstát Éireann. The Constitution of 1922, however, contained no statement of the State's extent, so that the area of its jurisdiction has to be gathered elsewhere, as follows: (l) The Government of Ireland Act 1920, provided for Parliaments for both Northern and Southern Ireland. The Parliament of Northern Ireland, which in fact came into being and functioned until 1972,[21] had by s 1(2) a limited jurisdiction over "the parliamentary counties of Antrim, Armagh, Down, Fermanagh, Londonderry and Tyrone and the parliamentary boroughs

[20] This clarification of Article 2 as constituting a claim of legal right has given rise to the argument that the State is in breach of its international obligations under the Helsinki Final Act of the CSCE, pursuant to which frontiers may be changed only by peaceful means and by agreement - *The Irish Times,* 29 October 1990.

[21] It was "prorogued" on 30 March of that year by s 1(3) of the Northern Ireland (Temporary Provisions) Act and abolished the following year by s 31 of the Northern Ireland Constitution Act 1973.

of Belfast and Londonderry"; the Parliament of Southern Ireland was to have jurisdiction over the rest of Ireland. (2) The Southern Parliament never functioned after its first abortive meeting;[22] and the 1921 Treaty envisaged instead an Irish Free State, ostensibly comprising the whole of Ireland, from which however by Article 12 the Northern Parliament could opt out. (3) The Constitution of that Irish Free State (Saorstát Éireann) came into force on 6 December 1922, and on the following day the Parliament of Northern Ireland exercised its opting-out power. (4) By the Treaty (Confirmation of Amending Agreement) Act 1925, Saorstát Éireann confirmed that "the extent of Northern Ireland for the purposes of the Government of Ireland Act 1920, and of the [Treaty] shall be such as was fixed by subsection (2) of section one of that Act". Accordingly the jurisdiction of Saorstát Éireann, and thus the present jurisdiction of the State in virtue of Article 3, is gathered by regarding it as Ireland minus Northern Ireland as defined by s 1(2) of the Government of Ireland Act 1920.[23]

But does this recital conclude the question of the State's extent? It must be admitted that the peculiar formulation of Articles 1-3 leaves some room for ambiguity, if only in theory. While it is easily seen that "Ireland", as the name of the State (Article 4), may be a term of art, not necessarily implying a claim that the State comprehends *de jure* all of "Ireland" in the geographical sense, the structure of Article 3 does leave open the possibility of arguing that the State, and the area of application of its laws, are not coextensive. This point has not arisen in litigation; but it may be noted that, in *The People v Ruttledge*,[24] O'Byrne J interpreted Articles 2 - 4 as follows:

> "The effect of these Articles is to proclaim that the whole of Ireland is included in the national territory *of the State*[25] but that, for the time being, the laws enacted by the national parliament (i.e. the Oireachtas) are to have the same area and extent of application as the laws of Saorstát Éireann."

In practice, however, the courts - like the Legislature[26] - have recognised the limitation of the State to the area of the former Saorstát Éireann, and the lawful existence of Northern Ireland in the remaining part of the island. In *In re Article 26 and the Criminal Law (Jurisdiction) Bill 1975*[27] the Supreme Court held that the Oireachtas was not free to legislate for Northern Ireland as though it were part of the State. In *The State*

[22] See Dorothy Macardle, *The Irish Republic,* 472 - 3.

[23] Section 7 of the Air Navigation and Transport (Preinspection) Act 1986, constitutes, for a special purpose, a notional or fictitious diminution in the extent of the State inasmuch as it provides that a person, arriving in transit at an airport in the State and presenting himself at a preinspection facility, shall not be deemed to have arrived in the State, for the purposes of the Aliens Act 1935, or the European Communities (Aliens) Orders, 1977 to 1985, unless he has been refused permission by the US Immigration and Naturalization Service to travel onwards to the U.S.A.

[24] [1978] IR 376. This case was decided in 1947, but was not reported until after it had been unearthed during the hearing of *The State (Gilsenan) v McMorrow* [1978] IR 360.

[25] Emphasis added.

[26] For some legislative examples of the "working" level of legality on which the separate existence of Northern Ireland is recognised, see Part III of the Extradition Act 1965, ss 9 and 17 of the Trade Union Act 1975, the Criminal Law (Jurisdiction) Act 1975, s 8 of the Juries Act 1976, s 238 of the Social Welfare (Consolidation) Act 1993, and S.I. No.213/1964 made thereunder, and s 5 of the Domicile and Recognition of Foreign Divorces Act 1986.

[27] [1977] IR 129; (1976) 110 ILTR 69. See also *McGlinchey v Ireland (No.2)* [1990] 2 IR 220 and *McGimpsey v Ireland* [1990] 1 IR 110; [1990] ILRM 440. In *Donegal Fuel and Supply Co. Ltd. v The Londonderry Port and Harbour Commissioners*, High Court, 6 May 1992, Costello J reached the same conclusion in relation to the Irish Free State based on principles of international law - in particular, the concepts of sovereignty and equality of states.

(Gilsenan) v McMorrow[28] both the High Court and the Supreme Court rejected the contention that Northern Ireland is not a geographical expression known to the law of this State. Henchy J said in the Supreme Court:

> "It is true that since 1937 there has been no general statutory interpretation or adaptation of the expression "Northern Ireland", but the frequency with which it occurs in our statutes, the unambiguous way in which it has been so used to identify the six counties over which this State does not exercise jurisdiction, and the clear intention of the Legislature in such use that the courts of this State should give judicial recognition to the identity of the territory comprehended by the expression (apart from any other considerations) would make it impossible for our courts to say that "Northern Ireland" is other than an officially recognised and clear appellation for the part of this island which has remained within the United Kingdom of Great Britain and Northern Ireland....
>
> In my opinion the courts are bound to take judicial notice of the expression "Northern Ireland" as connoting the part of this island which is outside the functioning jurisdiction of the State, which State has been given the statutory description of "the Republic of Ireland".[29]

In *McGlinchey v Ireland (No.2)*[30] Costello J held that there was no constitutional restriction on the Oireachtas prohibiting it from recognising the legal efficacy of laws enacted for Northern Ireland by the Parliaments of Northern Ireland or of the United Kingdom or by ministerial order pursuant to delegated powers.

In summation, it would seem that Articles 2 and 3 constitute a legal claim to the entire national territory which denies the legitimacy of Northern Ireland as an entity withdrawn from the jurisdiction of the Oireachtas and Government established by the Constitution and prohibits an acknowledgement, by any authority (such as the Oireachtas or the Government) subject to control on constitutional criteria, amounting to an admission of any *de jure* status for the dispensation under which Northern Ireland exists. Concomitantly, they may even leave open some room for asserting that the State in theory comprehends all of Ireland, notwithstanding that it exercises no jurisdiction in Northern Ireland; but that - so to speak, on a less fundamentalist, "working" level of legality - they allow both Oireachtas and courts to treat Northern Ireland as lawfully existing.

Delineation of the State's land boundaries

The courts, as Henchy J said, will take judicial notice of the existence of Northern Ireland; and - since the extent of the State (assuming this is the same as the extent of the application of its laws) is to be gathered by subtracting Northern Ireland from the whole island - the courts also, as Walsh J said in *The People v McGeough*,[31] "have judicial knowledge of the extent of the State and, for example, of the administrative counties which are comprised in the State and of the cities and towns which are in the State". But he added that "the courts have not judicial knowledge that any particular farmhouse or

[28] [1978] IR 360. The courts constantly recognise the validity of the courts in Northern Ireland - see, for example, *MacB. v MacB.* High Court, 6 June 1984, in which Barron J said that, in exercising jurisdiction in a matrimonial case in which the children of the marriage were resident in Northern Ireland, he did not intend or wish the Court in Northern Ireland, which also had seisin of the issue, to be in any way fettered in its jurisdiction.

[29] In *Moyne v The Londonderry Port and Harbour Commissioners* [1986] IR 299, Costello J took judicial notice of the fact that the city of Londonderry was outside the jurisdiction of the State.

[30] [1990] 2 IR 220.

[31] [1978] IR 384.

yard, as such, is within or without the State"; when, as sometimes happens, a question arises as to the precise delineation of the State's boundary, the matter must be proved with a scale map. In *Brown v Donegal County Council*[32] - a malicious injuries case not concerned with the State's boundary as such - Henchy J extracted from a consideration of several nineteenth-century Acts the conclusion that "the true definition or delineation of a county boundary is to be found in the relevant ordnance map"; and since some county boundaries coincided with the State's boundary, an ordnance map might be relied on to prove whether a particular place is within the State or not.

Adjacent waters and seabed[33]

Unlike the State's land frontier, the extent of the territorial seas - and in general the State's rights in water adjacent to it and in the seabed underlying the adjacent water - is partly derived from international law and practice. Several different features of this area may be briefly mentioned.

(a) The "territorial seas" - The phrase "territorial seas" is part of international usage, and in default of domestic legislation would have to be interpreted according to "the generally recognised principles of international law" which the State (by Article 29.3) is declared to accept. However, the Maritime Jurisdiction Act 1959, provides by s 2 that:

> "For the purposes of this Act the territorial seas of the State shall be that portion of the sea which lies between the baseline and the outer limit of the territorial seas."

By s 3, as amended by s 2(1) of the Maritime Jurisdiction (Amendment) Act 1988:

> "For the purposes of this Act the outer limit of the territorial seas is the line every point of which is at a distance of 12 nautical miles from the nearest point of the baseline."[34]

By s 4 the "baseline" is low-water mark, except that by sub-s 2:

> "The Government may by order prescribe straight baselines in relation to any part of the national territory and the closing line of any bay or mouth of a river, and any line so prescribed shall be taken as the baseline."

Such baselines have in fact been so prescribed, by the Maritime Jurisdiction Act 1959 (Straight Baselines) Order 1959; this gives the south and west coasts, from Carnsore Point around to Malin Head, a configuration resulting from a chain of straight lines; according to the Explanatory Note to the Order, these are the lines "from which the territorial seas are to be measured in relation to certain parts of the national territory".[35] By s 5 of the Act, sea areas to the landward side of a baseline are "internal or inland waters" which:

> "shall be subject to the jurisdiction of the State to the same extent in all respects as its ports and harbours, bays, lakes and rivers, subject to any right of innocent passage for foreign ships in those sea areas which previously had been considered as part of the territorial seas or of the high seas."[36]

[32] [1980] IR 132

[33] See generally C.R. Symmons, *Ireland and the Law of the Sea* (Dublin 1993).

[34] A claim that Directive 80/181/EEC on the approximation of the laws of Member States relating to units of measurement prohibited the use of the concept of the "nautical mile", thereby invalidating s 3, was dismissed by the Court of Criminal Appeal in *The People (D.P.P) v Ferris* (1985) 3 Frewen 114. According to the Court, the Directive did not prohibit the use of traditional units of measurement but rather required the additional use of the units set out in the Directive.

[35] No baselines are prescribed for the east coast, or for any part of the north coast east of Malin Head. The straight baselines join up the extremities of large inlets in the coast, such as Donegal Bay, where the baseline is about thirty miles from point to point, and elsewhere are strung around the outermost islets and rocks.

[36] By s 10(1): "Every offence committed within the territorial seas or internal waters is an offence within the jurisdiction of the State and may be dealt with by a court of competent jurisdiction although committed on

The very surprising question has occasionally been canvassed whether the State's jurisdiction might extend to a belt of water, corresponding to "territorial seas" as understood by domestic or international law at any given time, surrounding the Northern Ireland coast, on the grounds that the State's jurisdiction is Ireland plus territorial seas, minus a number of parliamentary counties and boroughs, and that parliamentary counties and boroughs themselves cannot have territorial seas. The point has not yet been judicially discussed here,[37] but was raised in Northern Ireland in *Director of Public Prosecutions v McNeill*[38] on a case stated by a Resident Magistrate (who had himself taken the point). The Northern Ireland Court of Appeal rejected it on several grounds, but chiefly on the general ground (*per* Lowry LCJ) that it was:

> "inconceivable [once Northern Ireland had opted out of the Irish Free State] that waters adjacent to County Antrim could be regarded as the territorial waters of a State the powers of whose Parliament and Government no longer extended to... Northern Ireland as a whole."

It is possible to regard the point as one of small merit or reality and yet to feel that the Northern Ireland Court of Appeal did not satisfactorily answer it.[39]

(b) *The "contiguous zone"*. The 1958 Geneva Convention on the Territorial Sea and Contiguous Zone[40] recognised a so-called "contiguous zone", or belt contiguous with the territorial sea, but of no greater extent than twelve miles from low-water mark or baselines, within which there is no sovereignty, but a degree of control is permitted to the State for the purpose of securing compliance with its laws regarding its territory and territorial sea. The Law of the Sea Convention 1982 now proposes to recognise a contiguous zone extending to a maximum of 24 miles from baselines.[41] Ireland, however, has not laid claim to any contiguous zone.

(c) *Fishery limits*.[42] The State's fishery limits are much more substantial than its territorial seas; formerly extending for 12 miles, they were fixed, by the Maritime Jurisdiction (Exclusive Fishery Limits) Order, 1976, at 200 miles or, where a line so drawn would

board or by means of a foreign ship and a person who commits such offence may be arrested, tried and punished accordingly." But by s 11 proceedings beyond the preliminary investigation require, in the case of an alien and of an offence other than a fishery offence, "the certificate of the Minister for Foreign Affairs that the institution of the proceedings is in his opinion expedient".

[37] However in 1987, the Government of the day formally objected to the British Territorial Sea Act 1987, which purported to extend British territorial waters across the entire width of the North Channel. This objection would appear to have been based on Articles 2 and 3 of the Constitution - *The Irish Times* 22- May 1987.

[38] [1975] NI 177. For a detailed discussion of this case, see Symmons, "*Who owns the territorial waters of Northern Ireland?*" (1976) 27 NILQ 48; Towey, "*Who owns the territorial waters of Northern Ireland? The McNeill case: another view*" (1983) 32 ICLQ 1013, and Symmons' subsequent reply in (1984) 33 ICLQ 1064. For earlier Dáil comments on this matter, see 212 *Dáil Debates* 439-50 (5 November 1964).

[39] Lowry LCJ cited the European Fisheries Convention, 1964, which had been signed for Ireland by the then Taoiseach and whose terms were inconsistent with the Resident Magistrate's point: the Government of Ireland Act 1920, itself, which contained provisions envisaging that the Northern Parliament would legislate for some purposes with offshore effect; and the developments culminating in the 1925 settlement, saying it would be "surprising" if the Irish Free State had "conceded for no tangible consideration an exclusive right of fishery" which (on the Magistrate's argument) it would still then have possessed in the waters surrounding Northern Ireland. All this, together with the obvious absence of intention on anyone's part that the independent Irish State should contain the water off Derry, Antrim and Down, does not seem to alter the fact that there was here a *casus omissus*, which it should have been the business of legislatures to rectify. The Northern Ireland Court of Appeal would scarcely assert that, had the Resident Magistrate's point occurred to the British Government at the turn of 1921 - 22, it would not have been expressly met when the 1922 legislation was being drafted.

[40] Ireland signed but did not ratify this Convention.

[41] See Article 33. This Convention has not yet come into force as it has not yet been ratified by the requisite number of states.

[42] See Symmons, "*The Sea Fishery Regime of the Irish Sea*" (1989) 4 International Journal of Estuarine and Coastal Law 192.

cross a similar line drawn by Britain or France, at the "equitable equidistant line between the State and the other state" (s 4 of the Order). Within that area, however, the fishery must be shared with the other member States of the European Communities up to a point six miles from the baselines.[43] Special transitional arrangements, expiring in 1996, have been made for Spain and Portugal, following their accession to the E.C.[44]

(d) *The "exclusive economic zone"*. This concept results from the claim of many States to rights in regard to exploitation of the sea and seabed adjacent to their coasts but far exceeding the limits of the "contiguous zone". The concept of the "exclusive economic zone" competes, in a sense, with that of the "continental shelf", namely the part of the seabed shelving down and away from the general land-mass of which the resources of in respect of which the coastal States exercise sovereign rights. The 1958 Geneva Convention on the Continental Shelf defines "continental shelf" as the "seabed and subsoil of the submarine areas adjacent to the coast outside the area of the territorial sea, to a depth of 200 meters or, beyond that limit, to where the depth of the superjacent waters admits of the exploitation of the natural resources of the said areas". Article 2 of the Convention gives the coastal State sovereign rights of an exclusive nature for the purpose of exploring and exploiting the natural resources of the shelf: but the status of the waters and air above the shelf remains unchanged; and while necessary installations and devices with surrounding safety zones to a distance of 500 metres may be established, these may not have the status of islands or have territorial seas of their own. Article 76 of the Law of the Sea Convention 1982 now proposes to define "continental shelf" as "the sea-bed and subsoil of the submarine areas that extend beyond its territorial sea throughout the natural prolongation of its land territory to the outer edge of the continental margin, to a distance of 200 nautical miles from the baselines from which the breadth of the territorial sea is measured where the outer edge of the continental margins does not extend up to that distance." This Convention has not yet entered into force: moreover Article 76 cannot be regarded as reflecting customary law. However it has been predicted that this Article will influence State practice.[45] Article 57 of the same Convention provides that the exclusive economic zone shall not extend beyond 200 nautical miles from the baselines from which the breadth of the territorial sea is measured, while Article 56 confers on coastal States sovereign rights for the purpose of exploring, exploiting, conserving and managing the natural resources in such zones. The exclusive economic zone is now generally regarded as an established institution as detailed in the 1982 Convention,[46] though to date, Ireland has not made any formal claim to such a zone.

The Continental Shelf Act 1968, provides by s 2(l) that:

> "Any rights of the State outside territorial waters over the seabed and subsoil for the purpose of exploring such seabed and subsoil and exploiting their natural resources are, subject to sub-section (2) of this section, hereby vested in the Minister [for Transport, Energy and Communication and shall be exercisable by the Minister."

(Sub-section 2 merely provides that the Government may re-vest these rights in another Minister if it thinks fit.) Section 3 provides for the application of the State's criminal law and law of torts to acts on or near installations situated in a "designated area" of continental shelf.

[43] See EEC Regulation No.101/76, OJ 1976 L 20/19, on the common fisheries policy; and Article 100 of the Treaty of Accession (22 January 1972).

[44] See the Act of Spanish and Portuguese Accession, OJ 1987 L 302/23, Articles 154 - 168, 347 - 355.

[45] U. Klemm, "*Continental Shelf*" in R. Bernhardt, *Encyclopaedia of International Public Law*, Instalment 11, (1989), 101.

[46] S. Oda, "*Exclusive Economic Zone*" in *Bernhardt, op.cit.*

Extra-territorial effect of laws

The special question of the extra-territorial effect of the State's laws arose in acute form in *In re Article 26 and the Criminal Law (Jurisdiction) Bill 1975*.[47] This legislation arose ultimately from the political necessity, recognised at the Sunningdale conference in 1973 between the Irish Government, the British Government, and the Northern Ireland Executive, to provide a substitute for extradition between the two parts of Ireland,[48] so that neither part could be used as a refuge by offenders who had committed crimes in the other; the device envisaged was a system for trying and punishing such offenders in whichever jurisdiction they might be apprehended in, in respect of offences committed in either jurisdiction; reciprocating British legislation was enacted at the same time.[49] The Bill was entitled "An Act to extend the criminal law of the State to certain acts done in Northern Ireland, to provide for the admission of evidence obtained by the examination of witnesses in Northern Ireland at trials for offences in respect of these acts, to enable evidence to be obtained by the examination of witnesses in the State for trials in Northern Ireland for corresponding acts done in the State [etc.]"; on its passage by both Houses the President referred it to the Supreme Court under Article 26.

Counsel assigned to argue against the Bill attacked it on several grounds; the ground here relevant was that Articles 2 and 3 constituted a prohibition on the Oireachtas legislating in relation to matters occurring in Northern Ireland, whether such legislation was to have territorial or extra-territorial effect. The Court agreed that the Oireachtas was not free to legislate for Northern Ireland with territorial effect there as though it were part of the State; its reasoning, expressed with less than total clarity, rested in part on the observation that Article 10 states that "all natural resources... within the jurisdiction of the Parliament and Government established by this Constitution" - the same formula as used in Article 3 - "belong to the State", and that the Constitution in general distinguishes clearly between the Nation and the State:

> "If the saver contained in Article 3 [i.e. the "without prejudice" clause] were to be interpreted as entitling the Parliament established by the Constitution to legislate at any time it so decided for the parliamentary counties and boroughs set out in subsection (2) of section 1 of the Government of Ireland Act 1920, then the effect of Article 10 would be that it would apply to the natural resources of the national territory and [that Article] would have been so expressed."

In regard to Oireachtas legislation with extra-territorial effect in Northern Ireland, this possibility depended on whether the Parliament of Saorstát Éireann had had power to legislate with extra-territorial effect. The Supreme Court said it had:

> "no doubt that in 1937 Saorstát Éireann had power to legislate with extra-territorial effect. This view was not contested by [counsel assigned to argue against the Bill]. The 1929 Report of the Conference on the operation of Dominion legislation noted that the question whether the Dominions had power to legislate with extra-territorial effect was "full of obscurity". However, there was the all-important distinction that

[47] [1977] IR 129; (1976) 110 ILTR 69. See Redmond, *The Criminal Law (Jurisdiction) Act 1976 and the Constitution* (1978) 13 Ir Jur (n.s.) 1.
[48] See the Agreed Communiqué issued on 9 December 1973; and the *Report of the Law Enforcement Commission*, signed 25 April 1974 (Prl.3832).
[49] Criminal Jurisdiction Act 1975.

> the Constitution of Saorstát Éireann derived its authority, not from any Act of the Imperial Parliament but from an Act of the Dáil, while the Constitutions of the other Dominions derived their authority from Acts of the Imperial Parliament. If there was any doubt about the position of the other Dominions it was dispelled by s 3 of the Statute of Westminster, 1931, which declared and enacted that the Parliament of a Dominion had full powers to make laws having extra territorial operation."

(The last sentence of this passage might appear to have nothing to do with Saorstát Éireann as it refers to "the other Dominions". The 1922 Constitution was however regarded by the British courts as deriving its validity not from the Act of Dáil Éireann but from the (British) Irish Free State Constitution Act 1922,[50] so that even from a British point of view - the Supreme Court probably wished delicately to hint in this way - the Statute of Westminster would have put the extra-territorial legislative capacity of the pre-1937 Oireachtas beyond question.) The Court continued:

> "The Court is satisfied that Saorstát Éireann had full power to legislate with extra-territorial effect from 1922. This was the view of Mr. Justice Fitzgibbon in *R. (Alexander) v Circuit Court Judge for Cork*,[51] and, therefore, the Statute of Westminster, 1931, should be regarded as declaratory of the law and not as making any change in it."

In regard to the international law on legislation with extra-territorial effect, the Court said it was:

> "established... by the decision of the Permanent Court of International Justice in the *Lotus* case[52] that every sovereign State has power to legislate with extra-territorial effect in the sense that it may enact that acts or omissions done outside its borders are criminal offences which may be successfully prosecuted within its borders - this is sometimes called the jurisdiction to prescribe - provided that the events, acts or persons to which its enactment applies bear upon the peace, order and good government of the legislating State: see O'Connell on *International Law* (2nd ed., vol. 2, p. 602). The Court has no doubt that the offences described in the Schedule to the Bill bear upon the peace, order and good government of the State, particularly as they are committed within the national territory."

The Court accordingly rejected:

> "the contention that Articles 2 and 3 of the Constitution constitute a prohibition on the Oireachtas legislating with extra-territorial effect in relation to matters occurring in Northern Ireland so long as the island is divided. The Bill is not repugnant to the Constitution on this ground."[53]

It may be noted that in *In re Reilly, a Bankrupt*[54] Sullivan CJ had said in 1942 that if pre-1922 bankruptcy legislation vesting property in Ireland in the Trustee in Bankruptcy in

[50] See *Moore v Attorney General* [1935] IR 472; (1935) 69 ILTR 159.

[51] [1925] 2 IR 165, 193.

[52] (1927) PCIJ Ser. A, No.10.

[53] Possible repugnances to Articles 38 and 40 were also considered by the Court. For comment on the Act and on the Supreme Court's decision, see Redmond, *The Criminal Law (Jurisdiction) Act 1976, and the Constitution*; and Symmons, "*The Criminal Law (Jurisdiction) Act 1976, and International Law*", both in (1978) 13 Ir Jur pp.1 and 36 respectively. In *McGimpsey v Ireland* [1990] 1 IR 110; [1990] ILRM 440 Finlay CJ, with whom the other members of the Court agreed, re-affirmed, at p.119, that Article 3 did not adversely affect the State's power to legislate with extra-territorial effect.

[54] [1942] IR 416.

England (and vice versa) were inconsistent with the 1922 Constitution (so as not to have been continued in force) it followed that then:

> "the Oireachtas would have had no jurisdiction to enact a law providing that upon an adjudication of bankruptcy in England the bankrupt's property in the Irish Free State should vest in the Trustee. I can see no reason to justify such a limitation upon the legislative powers conferred upon the Oireachtas by that Constitution. The desirability of such legislation would be a matter to be determined by the Oireachtas alone, but the jurisdiction to enact it would, in my opinion, be unquestionable."

Meredith, Geoghegan and O'Byrne JJ took the same view.

In late 1975, a few months before the *Criminal Law (Jurisdiction) Bill* reference, McMahon J heard in the High Court the case of *The State (Devine) v Larkin*[55] which arose out of a fishery prosecution, under the Foyle Fisheries Act 1952, for offences some of which were alleged to have been committed in Co. Derry, i.e. outside the State. The applicant argued, *inter alia*, that the reference in Article 3 to "the laws of Saorstát Éireann" meant the laws actually in force in 1937; and that, since in 1937 there was no legislation corresponding to the Act of 1952, it was not competent for the Oireachtas to give the latter an extra-territorial effect. McMahon J, having held that the Oireachtas of Saorstát Éireann had power to legislate with extra-territorial effect, said:

> "It would be a strange anomaly if the sovereign independent State constituted in 1937 did not have as ample a power of making laws as was vested in Saorstat Éireann more than forty years ago...In my opinion Article 3...in providing that the laws enacted by Parliament shall have the like extra-territorial effect as the laws of Saorstát Éireann, means that the laws of the Oireachtas shall have the like extra-territorial effect as the laws of Saorstát Éireann were capable of having."

A general provision giving the State extra-territorial jurisdiction is contained in s 38(l) of the Extradition Act 1965:

"Where any citizen of Ireland does any act outside the State which constitutes an offence for which he would be liable to extradition but for the fact that he is a citizen of Ireland he shall be guilty of the like offence and be liable on conviction to the like punishment as if the act were done within the State."

Sub-section 2 makes proceedings under sub-s 1 conditional on the direction of the Attorney General[56] in response to a request to that effect made by the country where the alleged offence was committed; and by sub-s 4, for the purpose of the exercise of jurisdiction the offence is deemed to have been committed within the area of the Dublin Metropolitan District. By sub-s 3 the section applies only to acts committed after the commencement of the Act. The section is in Part II of the Act which applies (by s 8(1)) only to cases where an extradition agreement exists with the other country, or where the Government is satisfied that "reciprocal facilities to that effect will be afforded" by that other country.

[55] [1977] IR 24. An attempt was made to take the point of the unconstitutionality of the Foyle Fisheries Act 1952, in *Foyle Fisheries Commission v Gallen* (1960) Ir Jur Rep 35; see below, pp. 424-425.

[56] Or of the Director of Public Prosecutions, by virtue of s 3 of the Prosecution of Offences Act 1974.

Re-integration of national territory and extradition

In *Russell v Fanning* [57] a majority of the Supreme Court took the view that decisions as to how the re-integration of the national territory is to be achieved are matters for the Government, subject to the control of the Dáil, and that the implementation of such decisions could only be carried out by or on the authority of the organs of State established by the Constitution. The majority reasoned further that individuals who sought to take over the carrying out of a policy of re-integration decided without the authority of the organs of State were subverting the Constitution and that, in particular, they could not obtain the benefit of the "political offence" defence to a request for extradition. Strong dissenting judgements were delivered by Hederman and McCarthy JJ on the grounds that insurrectional activity taking place outside the jurisdiction does not constitute an attack upon the State (Hederman J) or that taking action in furtherance of an opinion which differs from Government policy cannot always be regarded as subverting the Constitution (McCarthy J).

Both strands of the dissenting judgments were endorsed by a differently constituted majority[58] of the Supreme Court in *Finucane v McMahon.*[59] Following a review of the political and historical background to the extradition legislation, Walsh J concluded that:

> "the Court cannot draw the inference that it was the intention of the Oireachtas that the provisions relating to the political exemption in the Act of 1965 should not apply to persons charged with politically motivated offences of violence when the objective of such offences was to secure the ultimate unity of the country."

He also remarked that:

> "[t]he fact that the policy or activities followed by persons acting outside the jurisdiction of the State is opposed to or contrary to the policy adopted by the Government of Ireland in relation to the unity of the country is not...sufficient to equate it to a policy to overthrow this State or to subvert the Constitution of this State."[60]

[57] [1988] IR 505; [1988] ILRM 333.

[58] Walsh, Hederman and McCarthy JJ. Griffin J dissented on this point, but both he and Finlay CJ, who were part of the majority in *Russell*, accepted this overruling of their views in the interests of providing a degree of certainty in the law on extradition - *ibid.* pp.206 - 7, 218.

[59] [1990] 1 IR 165, at 217; [1990] ILRM 505 at 522, where Walsh J endorsed the analysis and conclusions of the two dissenting judges in *Russell*. See also *Carron v McMahon* [1990] 1 IR 239; [1990] ILRM 802.

[60] In *Sloan v Culligan* [1992] 1 IR 223; [1992] ILRM 194, Lynch J applying this test, concluded that offences of possession of firearms and ammunition with intent to endanger life in Northern Ireland and false imprisonment of a Northern Ireland citizen did not tend to subvert the Constitution or institutions of State so as to disqualify the plaintiff form relying on the political offence exemption to extradition. (This subsequent Supreme Court appeal focused primarily on the effect of the Extradition (European Convention on the Suppression of Terrorism) 1987 on this defence.)

Article 4

THE STATE

THE STATE	AN STÁT
Article 4	**Airteagal 4**
The name of the State is Éire, or in the English language, *Ireland*.	**Éire is ainm don Stát nó, sa Sacs-Bhéarla, *Ireland*.**

The State can be sued as "Ireland"

This Article appears to have been first mentioned in the case of that of *Byrne v Ireland*[1] which established that the State enjoys no inherited or other prerogative immunity from suit. The plaintiff's proceedings had originally been issued against "The People of Ireland"; this was amended before the hearing when O'Keeffe P ordered by consent "that 'Ireland' be substituted as defendant for the above-named 'The People of Ireland'". In the Supreme Court Walsh J said:

> "Under Article 4 the name of the State in the English language is "Ireland". If the State can be sued, then in my opinion it can be sued by its official name which is "Ireland" in the English language."

Budd J also observed:

> "Throughout the arguments "Ireland" as an entity was equated with the State. Under the heading of "The State" the Constitution in Article 4 deals with the State in these words: "The name of the State is Éire, or in the English language, Ireland". By suing "Ireland" the plaintiff is doing no more than suing the State."

(In the High Court Murnaghan J had observed the indiscriminate use of "Ireland" and "the State" throughout the Constitution, one expression being used in some places, the other expression in others, on no principle that is apparent.)

The Republic of Ireland

It may be noted that the designation "Republic of Ireland" is not the name of the State, and could not be in view of the express words of Article 4 confining this to "Éire" or "Ireland". The statutory basis for "Republic of Ireland" in official usage is s 2 of the Republic of Ireland Act 1948, which reads:

> "It is hereby declared that the description of the State shall be the Republic of Ireland."[2]

This distinction between the official name of the State and its description in the 1948 Act was forcefully drawn by Walsh J in *Ellis v O'Dea*[3] when he condemned the practice of courts in the United Kingdom in referring to the State, in extradition warrants, as "the

[1] [1972] IR 241.

[2] As this Act is one of the very rare Acts enacted in both official languages, and as (by Article 25.4.6 of the Constitution) the Irish version will prevail in case of conflict, the Irish version of this section should be cited: "Dearbhaítear leis seo gur Poblacht na hÉireann is gné-thuairisc ar an Stát".

[3] [1989] IR 530. See also his comments in *Kutchera v Buckingham International Holdings Ltd.* [1988] IR 61, at 67 where he described a reference in a contract to the "Republic of Ireland" as an "error in the English language version of the name of the State."

Republic of Ireland". He observed that while foreign courts are at liberty to issue such warrants in the Irish language, if they choose to use the English language, they must refer to the State as "Ireland", in accordance with Article 4. Furthermore, in accordance with the duty imposed on every court in the State and every member of the Garda Síochána to uphold the Constitution and not to condone or acquiesce in any refusal to recognise the Constitution or any part thereof, warrants which did not comply with this requirement should be returned to the courts of the requesting country for appropriate rectification.

CHARACTER OF THE STATE

Article 5
Ireland is a sovereign, independent, democratic state.

Airteagal 5
Is Stát ceannasach, neamhspleách, daonlathach Éire.

Juristic nature of the State

Perhaps the most elementary question that could be asked about the Irish State is whether it is, or is not, a legal person; to this question the Constitution gives no express answer, nor to questions about the State's possible legal capacities or privileges. These answers must be elaborated from the narrow base of Article 5, with the help of some other indications. Similarly, the implications of the State's characterisation as "sovereign", "independent" and "democratic" must all be worked out in the absence of detail in the Constitution itself.

(a) *The State*. The question of the juristic nature of Saorstát Éireann did not, apparently, arise during the lifetime of the 1922 Constitution; that State was given no particular character by its Constitution (except that Article 1 declared it to be "a co-equal member of the Community of Nations forming the British Commonwealth of Nations"[1]). The situation was perhaps complicated by the survival of the British Crown as part of the Constitution, the Crown being in British constitutional law the bearer of the legal personality which elsewhere would normally be the State's.

The State as a juristic person

In the early years of the 1937 Constitution the nature of the State also escaped exploration, until in 1949 in the case of *Comyn v Attorney General*[2] the question arose in the context of a dispute as to whether compensation for compulsorily acquired mining rights should be assessed under the Acquisition of Land (Assessment of Compensation) Act 1919 (as the Government, which had effected the acquisition, claimed), or by a judge of the High Court (as the plaintiff demanded). The case turned on whether the acquisition was by a "Government Department" (s 1(1) of the 1919 Act), in which case the special statutory assessment provisions would have applied; in fact the rights had been taken over by an Order made by the Government itself under s 2(2)(*g*) of the Emergency Powers Act 1939, which empowered it to "authorise... the acquisition... by or on behalf of the State of any land or other property whatsoever". Here the State, by the instrumentality of the Government, was the acquiring entity. Was "the State" the same as a "Government Department"? If not, what was it? The issue was argued before Kingsmill Moore J. He rejected the submission that the acquisition was effectively one by a "Government Department" (that of Industry and Commerce); this submission had rested on the proposition, put forward by the Attorney General, that acquisition "by the State", as the phrase appeared in s 2(2)(*g*) of the Emergency Powers Act 1939, was "a mere *façon de parler*" as the State, as such, was incapable of holding property. He said:

[1] This Commonwealth membership, although discontinued after the entry into force of the Republic of Ireland Act 1948, was regarded by one English authority as incapable of being unilaterally shed, even after the Statute of Westminster, 1931, had empowered Dominion legislatures to override the Imperial legislation which previously bound them. In *Murray v Parkes* [1942] 2 KB 123, Viscount Caldecote CJ said the Statute of Westminster "did not either expressly or by implication provide for any separation, described sometimes as the right to secede, from the British Commonwealth of Nations."
[2] [1950] IR 142; (1949) 83 ILTR 146.

"English law avoided the necessity of considering the juristic nature of the State by the expedient of regarding the King (or Crown) as a corporation sole... but the King has now disappeared from our Constitution, and, for all internal matters, he disappeared after the passing of the Constitution (Amendment No. 27) Act 1936... Irish lawyers can no longer shut their eyes to the problems involved in the conception of a State...

Ultimately, the nature and attributes of the State must be found in the wording of the Constitution. It is, however, not unreasonable to assume that those who framed, and those who debated, the Constitution were familiar with current opinions as to the nature of the State. The King had been removed from the Constitution, the King formerly so omnipresent in every branch of political activity, the King whose nature as corporation sole had provided the necessary element of continuity... This Protean conception had disappeared. Into the vacuum so left some new political conception had to be inserted. The new conception - in reality, a very old conception - was the State. Nowhere in the Constitution is the legal or philosophical nature of the State explained or defined. We are told, indeed, that Ireland is a sovereign, independent, democratic State. We are not told what a State is, but are left to discover this indirectly from the various Articles."

He went on to cite a large number of different Articles which expressed various rights, capacities, obligations, and incidents of the State, and concluded:

"The Constitution has told us a great deal about the State, its organisation its rights, its obligations and its attributes; but still it has not attempted to define its juristic nature. Is it a corporation? Is it, as has been suggested, an unincorporated association? Is it neither of these, but a legal *persona* of a new type and *sui generis?* These questions may provide much food for discussion in future cases. It is not necessary, and it would be dangerous, to attempt a full or final answer. For the purposes of this case, all that is necessary is to find that the State is conceived of as a juristic person or entity having as one of its legal attributes the capacity to hold property. It may, or may not, be a corporation. It may be a conception entirely new to English and Irish law; but I hold that it is a juristic person and that it can hold property."

He added that he thought this conclusion had been implicit in the judgment of O'Byrne J in *Cork County Council and Burke v Commissioners of Public Works,*[3] though the attribute of the State's capacity to own property - as distinct from the question of its own nature - seems expressly conceded by Article 10 and perhaps Article 11 also, both of which Articles he had included in his review.

The Supreme Court, to which the Attorney General appealed, gave a short judgment affirming Kingsmill Moore J. Maguire CJ said on this point:

"Under our Constitution the State is a juristic person with a capacity to hold property. In the opinion of this Court the State cannot be regarded as a Government Department."

The decision in *Comyn's* case was reinforced by the judgment of Kingsmill Moore J in *In re Irish Employers Mutual Insurance Association*;[4] and by *Commissioners of Public Works v Kavanagh,*[5] which was an application by the plaintiffs for a new tenancy under

[3] [1946] IR 561: see below, under Article 49. The case concerned an attempt to charge rates on what O'Byrne J called "property vested in the State as such".
[4] [1955] IR 176; see below, under Article 49.
[5] [1962] IR 216; (1963) 97 ILTR 180.

the Landlord and Tenant Act 1931; on a case stated it reached the Supreme Court, which had to settle several questions including the question whether the plaintiffs, who as tenants had been agents of the State, were "tenants" for the purpose of getting the benefit of the 1931 Act; the point was essentially the prior question whether the State was a "person", as this word was used in the relevant part of the Act. Ó Dálaigh J, with whom the other judges agreed, said:

> "I have said the Commissioners took as agents for the State. The first lease was made in 1927. The State then was Saorstát Éireann. *Comyn's* case... is a decision under the Constitution of Ireland. By parity of reasoning I am prepared to hold that Saorstát Éireann was a juristic person capable of holding land. It is enough to refer to Article 11 of the Constitution of Saorstát Éireann and to Article 10.2 of the Constitution of Ireland. When in 1937 Saorstát Éireann was supplanted by the new State under the Constitution of Ireland the Commissioners continued to hold the then current lease as agents for the State...
>
> In my opinion the word "person" should... be construed as not being limited to human persons, and the word is general enough to include the concept, new to our law, of the State as a juristic person...
>
> It is not necessary for me to say whether the State as a juristic person is to be looked upon as an abstract concept or viewed rather as the body of the citizens in a corporate capacity."

The State is capable of enjoying rights

That the State enjoys rights has been asserted by Gannon J on two occasions. In *Osheku v Ireland*[6] he referred in a general way to the "fundamental rights" of the State, saying:

> "There are fundamental rights of the State itself as well as fundamental rights of the individual citizens, and the protection of the former may involve restrictions in circumstances of necessity on the latter."

He went on to identify the maintenance of social order, by imposing the sanctions of the law in the administration of justice, as one such right of the State.[7]

Similarly, in *McGlinchey v Governor of Mountjoy Prison*,[8] he spoke of the State being "entitled to the benefit of fair procedures and due processes", from which he concluded that an application under Article 40.4.2 could not be used as an informal means of obtaining the resolution of disputed questions of fact or law previously ruled upon or pending determination under regular court procedure.

More recently, in *Cox v Ireland*[9] the Supreme Court accepted that the State had a right, for the protection of public peace and order and its own authority, to provide for the imposition of onerous penalties and forfeitures in order to deter the commission of crimes threatening public order and State authority. Furthermore, it was also entitled to ensure, as far as practicable, that persons who commit such crimes were not included

[6] [1986] IR 733; [1987] ILRM 330.

[7] It is arguable that this concept is in fact a "power" in the sense of the analysis offered by Costello J in *Murray v Ireland* [1985] IR 532; [1985] ILRM 542. See below, pp. 697-8. In this context, it is worth noting that in both *Comyn* and *Kavanagh*, the Supreme Court referred to the State's *capacity* to hold property.

[8] [1988] IR 671, Lynch J, delivering a concurring judgment, expressly agreed with Gannon J.

[9] [1992] 2 IR 503.

among those involved in carrying out the functions of the State. However, the State also had a continuing obligation to protect the constitutional rights of the citizens and the indiscriminate and overbroad nature of s 34 of the Offences Against the State Act 1939 - which provided for automatic forfeiture of State pensions and automatic disqualification for holding an office or employment remunerated form public funds for a period of seven years in the case of a person convicted of a scheduled offence before the Special Criminal Court - failed to meet this obligation.

The State is capable of being sued[10]

In *Macauley v Minister for Posts and Telegraphs*;[11] Kenny J relied on *Comyn* and *Kavanagh* as a step for the further conclusion that the State could be sued:

> "[These two cases have] established an entirely new concept which is more in accord with modern thought than the ideas which inspired the decision in *Carolan v Minister for Defence*[12]... [They] establish that the Republic of Ireland (or the People)[13] is, and that Saorstát Éireann was, a legally recognised juristic person capable of holding property. In my view, the State may now be sued in the courts whenever this is necessary to vindicate or assert the rights of a citizen."

As this was not material to the issue before him - the constitutionality of the fiat requirement before a Minister could be sued - this opinion is in itself only a *dictum*; but it turned out to be the opinion also of the Supreme Court majority in a later case, *Byrne v Ireland*,[14] where the position of the State in litigation was directly in issue. Walsh J saw the State's capacity to be sued as resulting from its proprietary capacity:

> "It has already been established that the State is a juristic person capable of holding property; [he cited *Comyn's* and *Kavanagh's* cases]. It was implicit in the judgments in those cases that the State could have been sued as such. Drummond's famous dictum that property has its duties as well as its rights is no less true in this context."

Budd J took a slightly different route to the same conclusion: he thought that a litigious capacity, both active and passive, resulted already from the State's character as a juristic person,[15] and laid no particular emphasis on its property owning character as implying such a capacity:

> "Once it is established that the State is a juristic person, then *prima facie* there would not seem to be any reason why in the eyes of the law the State should not be in the same position as any other legal *persona* and be thus capable of being sued, unless some particular reason can be shown to the contrary."

The capacity of the State to be sued as such (i.e. as "Ireland") is now beyond doubt, and in actions against Ministers or other responsible heads of State agencies, the State itself

[10] See ch.14 of Hogan and Morgan, *Administrative Law in Ireland* (2nd ed., 1991).

[11] [1966] IR 345.

[12] [1927] IR 62; (1925) 59 ILTR 115, (1927) 61 ILTR 27.

[13] It was established later, in *Byrne v Ireland* [1972] IR 241, that the People and the State are different entities, the latter being the creation of the former.

[14] [1972] IR 241.

[15] Hanna J had said in *Carolan v Minister for Defence* [1927] IR 62; (1925) 59 ILTR 115; (1927) 61 ILTR 27, that the capacity to sue, and to be sued, is inherent in legal personality.

is regularly also named as a defendant.[16] In *Kearney v Minister for Justice*[17] Costello J held that the State may be vicariously liable for a breach of constitutional rights on a principle analogous to vicarious liability in tort. He said:

> "The State may be liable for the acts of a servant of the State which amount to an infringement of a constitutionally protected right even though done outside the scope of the State's servant's employment - but I need express no view on that point now. That is because the State is clearly liable for such a wrong when it can be shown that had the wrong been a tort, vicarious liability would attach to the State."

Thus the plaintiff was able to recover damages for an unlawful interference by prison staff with his right to communicate, though in the particular circumstances of this case, nominal damages only were awarded.

The right to sue the State even extends to serving members of the Defence Forces. In *Ryan v Ireland*[18] the Supreme Court rejected the view that the State enjoyed an immunity from a claim of negligence brought by a serving soldier in respect of operations consisting of armed conflict or hostilities. Delivering the unanimous decision of the Court, Finlay CJ denied that the common law provided for such an immunity and, in the alternative, ruled that if such immunity did exist at common law, it was inconsistent with the guarantees by the State to respect, defend and vindicate the rights of the citizen contained in sub-sections 1 and 2 of Article 40.3.

While there is now no doubt that the State may be sued, it has been suggested that it can never be injuncted. In *Pesca Valentia Ltd. v Minister for Fisheries and Forestry, Ireland and the Attorney General*[19] the Supreme Court rejected the contention that the Courts should never grant an interlocutory injunction which in effect prohibited, even for a temporary period, the exercise of a statutory power contained in a post-Constitution statute;[20] but also ruled that, whereas Ireland might be an appropriate defendant in the substantive action, "it does not appear to be appropriate that any injunction should ever be given against Ireland."[21]

The State is capable of suing

The State may also sue as plaintiff in its own right. Thus, in *Ireland v Mulvey*[22] the State brought proceedings against the defendants asserting title to an eight century cross by virtue of Article 5. Hamilton P granted Ireland an injunction restraining the defendants from removing the cross from the jurisdiction.

[16] See, e.g. *McHugh v Commissioner of the Garda Síochána, Ireland and the Attorney General* [1986] IR 228, [1987] ILRM 181; *Pine Valley Developments Ltd. v Minister for the Environment, Ireland and the Attorney General* [1987] IR 23, [1987] ILRM 620; *Pesca Valentia Ltd. v Minister for Fisheries and Forestry, Ireland and the Attorney General* [1985] IR 193, [1986] ILRM 68. For examples of actions brought against Ireland for wrongs committed by State servants, see *Dowman v Ireland* [1986] ILRM 111, *McKevitt v Ireland* [1987] ILRM 541

[17] [1986] IR 116; [1987] ILRM 52.

[18] [1989] IR 177; [1989] ILRM 544.

[19] [1985] IR 193; [1986] ILRM 68. See *Casey*, (1985) 7 DULJ 123.

[20] Followed in *Grange Development Ltd v Dublin Co Co (No. 1)* [1989] IR 377.

[21] This statement may be contrasted with the view of Budd J in *Byrne v Ireland* [1972] IR 241, that "*Prima facie* the ordinary procedure of execution by way of levy or enforcement by mandamus would both seem to be appropriate" [for enforcing a decree against the State]. However, in *Beara Fisheries and Shipping Ltd. v Minister for the Marine, Ireland* [1987] IR 413, the plaintiff sought (and obtained) interlocutory injunctions against the first and third defendants only.

[22] *The Irish Times*, 11 November 1989.

State sovereignty

(b) *A "sovereign" State.* A preliminary point worth noting here is the relationship between the sovereignty of the State and the sovereignty of the People. The creation of a distinction between the concepts of the People and the State has been criticised.[23] Nonetheless it seems that the sovereign authority within the Constitution is the People,[24] from whom is derived the sovereignty of the State, identified by Article 5. [25]

State sovereignty would appear to have two spheres of operation - it has consequences for both domestic law and the State's international relations with other countries.

That State sovereignty could have implications for domestic law is a recent discovery for in *Byrne's* case, a majority of the Supreme Court took the view that the "sovereign" nature of the State, while unimpeachable *vis-á-vis* other States, did not operate *internally* so as to put the State, as a juristic person, above the law.[26] Walsh J made the distinction thus:

> "I think that the learned trial judge misconstrued the intent of Article 5 if he construed it as a constitutional declaration that the State is above the law. Article 1... affirms that the Irish nation has the "sovereign right to choose its own form of government". Our constitutional history, and in particular the events leading up to the enactment of the Constitution, indicate beyond doubt, to my mind, that the declaration as to sovereignty in Article 5 means that the State is not subject to any power of government save those designated by the People in the Constitution itself, and that the State is not amenable to any external authority for its conduct. To hold that the State is immune from suit for wrong because it is a sovereign State is to beg the question."

He went on to review the position in several other countries, which, he found, provided "ample support" for his view that "immunity from suit for wrong is not a necessary ingredient of State sovereignty".

Budd J reached a similar conclusion; his reading of the Constitution was to the effect that:

> "it is the People who are paramount and not the State. Such a conclusion is inconsistent with any suggestion that the State is sovereign internally... The State is not internally sovereign but, in internal affairs, subject to the Constitution which limits, confines and restricts its power. In the result, any contention that the State enjoys immunity from suit by reason of its sovereignty falls to the ground... What I have said, however, is not to be taken as in any way derogating from the external sovereignty of the State in so far as the rest of the world is concerned."

While these remarks, particularly those of Budd J, could reasonably be understood to mean that the concept of State sovereignty had no internal operation, the more recent decision in *Webb v Ireland*[27] suggests otherwise. The constitutional issue in this case

[23] See Gwynn Morgan, *Constitutional Law of Ireland*, (2nd ed.) p.28.
[24] See, e.g. the remarks of Walsh and Budd JJ in *Byrne v Ireland* [1972] IR 241; the decisions of the Supreme Court in *In re Article 26 and the Electoral (Amendment) Bill 1983* [1984] IR 268; [1984] ILRM 539 and *Crotty v An Taoiseach* [1987] IR 713; [1988] ILRM 565; [1987] ILRM 400.
[25] See remarks of Walsh and McCarthy JJ in *Webb v Ireland* [1988] IR 353. See also the comments of Denham J in *Howard v Commissioners of Public Works in Ireland* [1993] ILRM 665.
[26] See also *The State (King) v Minister for Justice* [1984] IR 169 where Doyle J noted that the rejection of the theory of internal State sovereignty had been observed as early as 1932 by Dr. Leo Kohn in his book, *The Constitution of the Irish Free State* (1932).
[27] [1988] IR 353; [1988] ILRM 565.

was whether the royal prerogative of treasure trove had survived the enactment of the Constitution of Saorstát Éireann so as to be covered by the terms of Article 49.1 of the Constitution and thus available to the State as a defence to a claim, by the finders, for the return of extremely valuable historical artefacts, known collectively as the "Derrynaflan Hoard".[28]

The five members of the Supreme Court were unanimous in holding that no royal prerogative had vested in the Irish Free State.[29] However a right to treasure trove, comparable to the royal prerogative, was found in the provisions of Article 10.1, by Finlay CJ, Henchy and Griffin JJ, and in those of Article 5, by Walsh and McCarthy JJ. Speaking for the majority, and after citing Articles 5, 10.1 and 10.3, Finlay CJ said:

> "I am satisfied that the phrase "all royalties" contained in Article 10, s 1 of the Constitution, construed in the light of Article 5, must be widely construed and must include one of the definitions of royalty to be found in the Shorter Oxford English Dictionary, namely, the sovereignty or sovereign rule of a State.
>
> It would, I think, now be universally accepted, certainly by the people of Ireland, and by the people of most modern states, that one of the most important national assets belonging to the people is their heritage and knowledge of its true origins and the buildings and objects which constitute keys to their ancient history. If this be so, then it would appear to me to follow that a necessary ingredient of sovereignty in a modern state, and certainly in this State, having regard to the terms of the Constitution, with an emphasis on its historical origins and a constant concern for the common good is and should be an ownership by the State of objects which constitute antiquities of importance which are discovered and which have no known owner. It would appear to me to be inconsistent with the framework of the society sought to be created and sought to be protected by the Constitution that such objects should become the exclusive property of those who by chance may find them.
>
> The existence of such a general ingredient of the sovereignty of the State, does, however, seem to me to lead to the conclusion that the much more limited right of the prerogative of treasure trove known to the common law should be upheld not as a right derived from the Crown but rather as an inherent attribute of the sovereignty of the State which was recognised and declared by article 11 of the 1922 Constitution."[30]

Walsh and McCarthy JJ reached the same conclusion though by a different route, eschewing all reliance on Article 10[31] and grounding themselves solely on the sovereignty of the State, derived from the People. Thus Walsh J said:

> "I am satisfied that the People as the sovereign authority having by the Constitution created the State, and by Article 5 declared it to be a sovereign State, have the right and duty, acting by the State which is the juristic person capable of holding property by virtue of the Constitution, to exercise dominion over all objects forming part

[28] The plaintiffs' alternative claim was for a reward for finding these artefacts, entitlement to which, they argued, was a constituent part of the royal prerogative.

[29] For incisive, and characteristically entertaining, criticism of this view, grounded on what one might call an originalist interpretation of the Constitution, see Kelly, "*Hidden Treasure and the Constitution*" (1988) 10 DULJ 5. See also Gwynn Morgan, "*Constitutional Interpretation*" (1988) 10 DULJ 24, at pp.26 - 35 and Lenihan, *Royal Prerogatives and the Constitution* (1989) 24 Ir Jur (n.s.) 1.

[30] The forerunner to Article10.

[31] As to which, see below, p. 72.

of the national heritage, whether they be found or not, subject always to the lawful title of a true owner if and when the true owner is discovered and to exercise full rights of ownership when no true owner can be ascertained."

In all of this, however, the notion of sovereignty was invoked as a self-evident source for the modern claim to treasure trove, without any further elaboration.

Byrne and *Webb* are not easily reconciled on the matter of sovereignty. If one understands "sovereignty" to mean supreme power, then clearly the State is not sovereign internally in the light of *Byrne.* Unfortunately the resurrection, in a domestic context, of State sovereignty in *Webb* was unaccompanied by any explanation of the concept, let alone any attempt to accommodate the earlier remarks in *Byrne.* One senses that it is being used as a type of political magnet to attract to the State powers and privileges which are not explicitly regulated by the Constitution itself, an analogue, as it were, to Article 34.3.1 dealing with the jurisdiction of the courts.[32]

External sovereignty

The operation of the State's "external sovereignty" was dramatically illustrated in *Crotty v An Taoiseach*[33] where a majority of the Supreme Court held that it prevented the State from fettering its right to determine foreign policy by concluding international agreements requiring consultation with other countries on such policy and, in particular, from ratifying Title III of the Single European Act. Henchy J said:

> "It appears to me that this affirmation [in Article 1] means that the State's right to conduct its external relations is part of what is inalienable and indefeasible in what is described in Article 5 as "a sovereign, independent, democratic state". It follows...that any attempt by the Government to make a binding commitment to alienate in whole or in part to other States the conduct of foreign relations would be inconsistent with the Government's duty to conduct those relations in accordance with the Constitution."

Walsh J said:

> "The powers of external sovereignty on the part of the State do not depend on the affirmative grant of this in the Constitution. They are implicit in the provisions of Article 5. The State would not be completely sovereign if it did not have in common with other members of the family of nations the right and power in the field of international relations equal to the right and power of other States. These powers of the State include the power to declare war or to participate in a war, to conclude peace, to make treaties, and to maintain diplomatic relations with other States."

Later, quoting from the single-judgment decision in the first part of the case, he said that "the essential nature of sovereignty is the right to say yes or to say no." Because the Single European Act materially qualified that right,[34] he held that it could not be ratified by the State.[35]

[32] However, this amorphous concept does not, apparently, encompass the former common law presumption, derived form the royal prerogative, that the State is not bound by legislation unless referred to either expressly or by necessary implication - see *Howard v Commissioners of Public Works in Ireland* [1993] ILRM 665. O'Flaherty J was alone among the members of the Court in holding that such a presumption did exist, though perhaps significantly not even he invoked the concept of State sovereignty, preferring instead to justify the rule as one which would serve well the workings of a parliamentary democracy.

[33] [1987] IR 713; [1987] ILRM 400.

[34] For criticism of this premise, see Hogan, "*The Supreme Court and the Single European Act*" (1987) 22 Ir Jur (n.s) 55, especially pp.64 - 67.

[35] The Tenth Amendment to the Constitution Act 1987 subsequently enabled Ireland to ratify the Single European Act.

The breadth of the majority's reasoning is such, however, that it could plausibly be regarded as casting doubt on the State's general treaty-making powers. Consequently it may be appropriate to take a less than sanguine view of its prospects for survival.[36]

Prior to the decision in *Crotty,* the implications of the concept of "external" sovereignty had occasionally surfaced in cases where it itself was not in issue. In *In re Reilly, a Bankrupt*[37] the High Court and Supreme Court admitted the constitutionality of the survival of pre-1922 legislation which provided for the reciprocal effect, as between the Irish State and Britain, of bankruptcy adjudications. Black J agreed entirely with counsel's submission that "a provision in a British statute purporting to vest land in Éire in an English official was inconsistent with the sovereign status of this State", adding however that the Irish people were free to ratify such an arrangement as part of a reciprocal system. In the Supreme Court Sullivan CJ recalled (while distinguishing the present issue from the former case) the words of Kennedy CJ in *In re Corballis*:[38]

> "It would be wholly inconsistent with the constitutional status of the Saorstát to hold that the order of an English court could automatically transfer land situate in the Saorstát from a citizen of the Saorstát to an official of the English court."

Again, in *The State (Devine) v Larkin,*[39] where McMahon J upheld the validity of an arrangement whereby regulations made by the Foyle Fisheries Commission (set up by an Act of the Oireachtas) required the approval of the Northern Ireland Ministry of Commerce, he held that a transfer of functions made in Northern Ireland whereby a different Ministry approved the regulations was ineffective to validate them here; it needed a separate Act of the Oireachtas to give this transfer validity.

Any significance in "independence" as distinct from (external) sovereignty?

(c) *An "independent" State*. There appears to be no case in which attention has been focused on the "independent" character of the State; in view of the positive sense given so emphatically to the word "sovereign" (in the external sense) by the Supreme Court majority in *Byrne v Ireland*, as well as of the emphatic language of Article l, it might seem that the specific attribution of independence to the State is redundant.

Implications of "democratic" character of the State

(d) *A "democratic" State*. As might be expected in connection with so porous an epithet, this attribution in Article 5 has not received much active interpretation by the courts. Essentially it has been used in a marginal way, to set the scene for, or to lend some colour to, judicial statements which would have been made anyway. In *The State (Burke) v Lennon,*[40] virtually the first serious civil rights issue that arose under the Constitution, Gavan Duffy J laid down ponderous foundations for his judgment on internment without trial, including a passage beginning:

[36] Thus in *McGimpsey v Ireland* [1990] 1 IR 110; [1990] ILRM 440 the Supreme Court distinguished the Anglo-Irish Agreement from the Single European Act in a manner which was less than convincing. For comment on this, see Symmons, "International Treaty Obligations and the Irish Constitution: the *McGimpsey* case" (1992) 41 ICLQ 311 at 317-318. Cp. the decision of the Queen's Bench Divisional Court in *R v Secretary of State for Foreign and Commonwealth Affairs, ex parte Rees-Mogg* [1993] 3 CMLR 101, holding *inter alia*, that ratification of Title V of the Treaty on European Union, far from involving a transfer of prerogative powers to conduct foreign and security policy, was actually an exercise of those powers.

[37] [1942] IR 416; (1943) 77 ILTR 38. In *In re Gibbonss* (1960) Ir Jur Rep 60, Walsh J held that the discretionary powers conferred on the Irish courts by pre-1922 legislation to act as auxiliary to the English bankruptcy court must be exercised in accordance with the general convention whereby the courts of any State will refuse to assist the enforcement of revenue claims of a foreign State.

[38] [1929] IR 266.

[39] [1977] IR 24.

[40] [1940] IR 136; (1940) 74 ILTR 36, 131.

"The architects of the Constitution were alive to the need for protecting the rights declared in the Constitution; accordingly, in Article 5, they characterised the State as a democratic State."

In *Ryan v Attorney General*,[41] the case in which the courts first declared that the Constitution might contain, latent in Article 40.3, fundamental "personal rights" additional to those specifically enumerated, Kenny J said that many of such rights followed "from the Christian and democratic nature of the State", though he did not mention Article 5 specifically. But in another passage in his judgment he referred to Article 5, saying "Ireland is a democratic State, and what can be more important in such a State than the personal rights of the citizens?"

Slightly more concrete standards were extracted from the designation of the State as "democratic" in *de Búrca v Attorney General*,[42] in which Pringle J said *obiter*:

"A democracy, as I understand it, is a form of government in which the sovereign power resides in the people as a whole and is exercised by the people either directly or through their elected representatives. This obviously does not mean that every citizen has a right to take part personally in the government of the country."

More concrete still were the conclusions of Budd J in *O'Donovan v Attorney General*,[43] in which he plainly derived from the word "democratic" a standard which is characteristic of, and perhaps only of, western parliamentary democracies:

"Article 5 provides, *inter alia*, that Ireland is a democratic State... A "democratic State" is one where government by the people prevails. In modern usage of the words I believe it to be correct to say a "democratic State" denotes one in which all citizens have equal political rights. That the words should be given such a meaning in our Constitution seems to be supported by [Articles 16.1.4 and 40. 1] as to the restriction of voting power to one vote per person and the equality of all before the law."

In *The State (M.) v Attorney General*[44] Finlay P, (as he then was) in establishing for the first time the general right of a citizen to a passport, adverted to the characteristics of democracies of the type that he took the Irish State to be one of. After saying that the right to travel and to hold a passport had been recognised, as intertwined together, by the law of the United States, he added:

"Furthermore, one of the hallmarks commonly accepted as dividing States which are categorised as authoritarian from those which are categorised as free and democratic is the inability of citizens or residents in the former to travel outside their country except at what is usually considered to be the whim of the executive power. I have no doubt therefore that a right to travel outside the State... is a personal right of each citizen..."

More recently, in *Howard v Commissioners of Public Works in Ireland*[45] Denham J invoked the description of the State as democratic in rejecting the presumption that the executive is not bound by legislation. She said:

"The Constitution does not create expressly or by implication any presumption in favour of the executive in legislation, and the Oireachtas may legislate including or

[41] [1965] IR 294.
[42] [1976] IR 38; (1977) 111 ILTR 37. Article 5 and the democratic State were fleetingly mentioned also in the Supreme Court judgments in this case.
[43] [1961] IR 114; (1962) 96 ILTR 121.
[44] [1979] IR 73
[45] [1993] ILRM 665.

excluding the application of an Act to the executive in accordance with constitutional parameters. The absence of a presumption in favour of the executive is a natural corollary of a democratic state."

Constitution does not describe the State as a republic

It will be noticed that the Constitution does not describe the State as a republic. The official description of the State as "the Republic of Ireland" results from the Republic of Ireland Act 1948.[46]

[46] See above, p. 24.

Article 6

THE POWERS OF GOVERNMENT

Article 6

1 All powers of government, legislative, executive and judicial, derive, under God, from the people, whose right it is to designate the rulers of the State and, in final appeal, to decide all questions of national policy, according to the requirements of the common good.

2. These powers of government are exercisable only by or on the authority of the organs of State established by this Constitution.

Airteagal 6

1. Is ón bpobal, faoi Dhia, a thagas gach cumhacht riala, idir reachtaíocht is comhallacht is breithiúnas, agus is ag an bpobal atá sé de cheart rialtóirí an Stáit a cheapadh, agus is faoin bpobal faoi dheoidh atá gach ceist i dtaobh beartas an Náisiúin a shocrú de réir mar is gá chun leasa an phobail.

2. Is leis na horgain Stáit a chuirtear ar bun leis an mBunreacht seo, agus leo sin amháin nó lena n-údarás, is féidir na cumhachtaí riala sin a oibriú.

Source of the powers of government: 1922 provision

Article 6.1 recalls both the Preamble of the Constitution of the Irish Free State (Saorstát Éireann) Act 1922, and Article 2 of the 1922 Constitution itself: the former acknowledged "that all lawful authority comes from God to the people", and the latter declared that "All powers of government and all authority legislative, executive and judicial in Ireland, are derived from the people of Ireland..."[1] Article 6.2 corresponds to the words with which the old Article 2 continued:"... and the same shall be exercisable in the Irish Free State (Saorstát Éireann) through the organisations established by or under, and in accord with, this Constitution". The second part of Article 6.1 had no analogue in the old Constitution, and seems to be a gloss on the State's democratic character declared by Article 5.

Ideology of the Constitution

Article 6 offers some rather general insights into the ideological foundations of the Constitution. In *Murphy v Attorney General*[2] Henchy J pointed to the dominant role of the people, as expressed by this section, as being "a central feature of the ideological rationale and political philosophy underlying the Constitution", emphasising that the role of the legislature was, in consequence, one of limited delegation only. Subsequently, in *Crotty v An Taoiseach*[3] the Article was one of a number cited by Barrington J as constituting part of the general framework of the institutions of a sovereign, independent, constitutional and democratic State.

The ideological perspective underpinning the judicial understanding of Article 6 itself would appear to be that of liberal democracy. However the Constitution also embraces

[1] Hugh Kennedy, KC, later Chief Justice, wrote on 5 August 1922 that "the great principle upon which Dáil Éireann was founded was that all legislative, executive, administrative and judicial power had its source in and was derived from the sovereign people of Ireland": see Brian Farrell, "*The Drafting of the Irish Free State Constitution*" (1975) 10 Ir Jur (n.s.) 112.
[2] [1982] IR 241.
[3] [1987] IR 713; [1987] ILRM 400.

a more communitarian ideology which, if applied to the doctrine of separation of powers, could produce a different perspective on that doctrine.[4]

The right of the people to designate the State's rulers

The right of the people to designate the rulers of the State was invoked by the Supreme Court in *In re Article 26 and the Electoral (Amendment) Bill, 1983*,[5] in finding repugnant the proposed extension of the Dáil franchise to non-citizens (resident British nationals). According to the Court, the phrase "the people" or, in Irish, "an pobal", in Articles 12 and 47, had the same meaning as in Article 6, and did not refer to the general public. Furthermore, the Court took the view that:

> "it is not possible to regard [Article 6] as contemplating the sharing of such powers [of government] with persons who do not come within the constitutional concept of the Irish people in Article 6."[6]

The right of the people to decide all questions of national policy

The people's right, under Article 6, to decide all questions of national policy, according to the requirements of the common good, would appear to have been cited for the first time by O'Hanlon J in *Russell v Fanning*[7] when holding that the campaign of the I.R.A. to "reintegrate the national territory, by force of arms, if necessary" was in direct conflict with that Article. In *Attorney General (Society for the Protection of the Unborn Child (Ireland) Ltd.) v Open-Door Counselling Ltd.*[8] Hamilton P. described the enactment of the Eighth Amendment to the Constitution as the exercise of this right by the people so as to ensure that there could be no doubt that abortion was contrary to national policy and public morality.

Perhaps the most dramatic affirmation of the right of the people under Article 6 to decide all questions of national policy occurred in *Crotty v An Taoiseach,*[9] in which the plaintiff sought an injunction to prevent the State from ratifying the Single European Act. The Supreme Court held, by a 3-2 majority, that Title III of the S.E.A., which obliged Ireland to consult with the other member states of the European Communities in relation to foreign policy, was contrary to the Constitution to the extent to which it made the national interests of the State subservient to the national interests of other member states in the area of foreign policy and that its adoption would require the consent of the people.[10] Walsh J said:

[4] For further discussion of this point, see two articles by Quinn, "*The Nature and Significance of Critical Legal Studies*" (1989) 7 ILT 282 and "*Reflections on the Legitimacy of Judicial Activism in the Field of Constitutional Law*" (1991) Dlí 29. See also Whyte, "*Constitutional Adjudication, Ideology and Access to the Courts*" in Whelan (ed.) *Law and Liberty in Ireland* (1993) at 149.

[5] [1984] IR 268; [1984] ILRM 539.

[6] Writing extra-judicially, Walsh J noted that, unlike the 1916 Proclamation and the Constitution of the Irish Free State, the present Constitution refers only to "the people", not "the people of Ireland". Nonetheless he deduces from the Preamble and Articles 1 and 2 that "the people" referred to in Article 6 are the people of Ireland - see "*The Judicial Power, Justice and the Constitution of Ireland*" in Curtin and O'Keeffe, *Constitutional Adjudication in European Community and National Law* (1992) at p.146.

[7] [1988] IR 505; [1986] ILRM 401.

[8] [1988] IR 593; [1987] ILRM 477.

[9] [1987] IR 713; [1987] ILRM 400. The outcome of this case was subsequently reversed, following a referendum held on 26 May 1987 which enabled Ireland to accede to the S.E.A.

[10] *Crotty* was distinguished in *McGimpsey v Ireland* [1990] 1 IR 110; [1990] ILRM 440 on the ground that the Anglo-Irish Agreement did not involve such a fettering of the State's power to conduct foreign policy - see pp. 299-80. Cp. the recent decision of the Queen's Bench Divisional Court in *R. v Secretary of State for Foreign and Commonwealth Affairs, ex parte Rees-Mogg* [1993] 3 CMLR 101, holding, *inter alia*, that ratification of Title V of the Treaty on European Union constituted an exercise of prerogative powers to conduct foreign and security policy, rather than their transfer.

> "The foreign policy organ of the State cannot, within the terms of the Constitution, agree to impose upon itself, the State or the people the contemplated restrictions upon freedom of action. To acquire the power to do so would, in my opinion, require a recourse to the People "whose right it is", in the words of Article 6, "...in final appeal, to decide all questions of national policy, according to the requirements of the common good". In the last analysis it is the People themselves who are the guardians of the Constitution."

In his judgment, Henchy J noted that the ultimate source and limits of the Government's powers in the conduct of foreign relations are to be found in Article 6.1 and, after citing that provision, continued:

> "It follows that the common good of the Irish People is the ultimate standard by which the constitutional validity of the conduct of foreign affairs by the Government is to be judged. In this and in a number of other respects throughout the Constitution the central position of the common good of the Irish people is stressed as one of the most fundamental characteristics of Ireland as a sovereign, independent, democratic State...In regard to Ireland, while under the Constitution the point of reference for the determination of a final position on any issue of foreign relations is the common good of the Irish people, under Title III the point of reference is required to be the common position determined by member states."

In *Russell v Fanning*[11] a strong disagreement emerged among members of the Supreme Court as to how this right could be exercised by the people in relation to the re-integration of the national territory. According to the majority, (Finlay CJ, Henchy and Griffin JJ), the Constitution, in particular, Article 6, made it clear that decisions as to the method of re-integration were matters for the government, subject to the control of Dáil Éireann[12] and that the carrying out of such decisions was exercisable only by or on the authority of the organs of State established by the Constitution. Accordingly anyone seeking to carry out a policy of re-integration other than that determined by the government was subverting the Constitution by usurping the function of government. The immediate consequence of this position was that members of subversive groups such as the I.R.A. were, irrespective of the specific circumstances of the offence in respect of which their extradition was sought, automatically denied the benefit of s 50 of the Extradition Act 1965, excluding political offences from the scope of that legislation.

Strong dissents were recorded by both Hederman and McCarthy JJ, the latter in particular questioning whether the right of the people to decide all questions of national policy "means that individuals who differ from the people on such decisions are thought to be subverting the Constitution, even when such individuals seek, in another jurisdiction, by different means to achieve the same or a different end."[13] According to McCarthy J, Article 6 should be read as "merely defining the separation of powers into legislative, executive and judicial and their derivation under God, from the people...". He did not accept that an act committed for the purpose of pursuing a particular policy which might be opposed to that expressed by the government of the day, whether or not endorsed by the legislature, could, by virtue of Article 6, be deprived of the protection of s 50. Later

[11] [1988] IR 505; [1988] ILRM 333.

[12] This reference to Dáil Éireann is somewhat problematic. By virtue of Article 29.5.1 every international agreement to which the State becomes a party must be laid before the Dáil. However it is only in relation to international agreements involving a charge on public funds that the Dáil has any power to reverse the government's decision to ratify - Article 29.5.2 - while the power to incorporate international agreements is conferred on the Oireachtas, rather than on the Dáil - Article 29.6.

[13] [1988] IR 505 at 547; [1988] ILRM 333 at 356-7. In particular situations, such activity could amount to an attempt to subvert the organs of State or to overthrow the Constitution but this would be dealt with in accordance with statutory law, rather than Article 6 - see Hederman J at p.538.

in his judgment, he suggested that the exercise of the people's power to determine questions of national policy was not exclusively delegated to the legislature.

> "The people, in final appeal, must decide all questions of national policy and decide them according to the requirements of the common good. The Constitution provides but one means of ascertaining the will of the people on such a question. I question how a court determines (a) a question of national policy; (b) what is the decision on it; (c) whether or not that decision is that of the people; (d) how did the people decide such a question; (e) how the requirements of the common good were taken into account. It seems clear that the legislature has no power to decide on questions of national policy to the exclusion of the people's power."[14]

These dissents were subsequently vindicated by a majority of the Supreme Court in *Finucane v McMahon.*[15] Delivering the leading judgment, Walsh J concluded from a review of the historical and political background to the extradition legislation that it could not have been the intention of the Oireachtas that s 50 of the 1965 Act should not apply to persons charged with politically motivated acts of violence designed to secure the ultimate unity of the country. He went on to agree expressly with the analysis and conclusions of the dissenting judges in *Russell.*

The "separation of powers"

Both the 1922 and the 1937 Constitutions enumerate the powers of government as of three distinct *types*, legislative, executive and judicial, but neither of them actually *prescribes* a "separation of powers".[16] Nonetheless in *In re Haughey*[17] the Supreme Court said, *per* Ó Dálaigh CJ, that "the Constitution of Ireland is founded on the doctrine of the tripartite division of the powers of government"; he had previously, speaking for himself, used similar words in *The State (C.) v Minister for Justice,*[18] and in *Melling v Ó Mathghamhna*[19] he offered a rationalisation of the principle in specifically Irish terms:

> "If our Constitution and the Constitution of Saorstát Éireann both have adopted the theory of the tripartite separation of the powers of government with express limitations on the powers alike of Legislature and Executive over the citizen, the reason is not unconnected with our previous experience under an alien government whose parliament was omnipotent and in whose executive lay wide reserves of prerogative power."[20]

A number of Articles, principally Articles 15, 28 and 34, do in fact entrench the different arms of government in varying degrees and prescribe their sovereignty in their own areas, without, however, hermetically insulating the different powers from one another in all respects; as Lavery J said of the old Article 2 in *O'Byrne v Minister for Finance,*[21] the "separation of powers" was "imperfect" so far as the executive and legislative powers were concerned, and "definite" only in respect of the judicial power, though Walsh J said in *Murphy v Dublin Corporation*[22] that the division of powers "does not give para-

[14] Presumably the will of the people on questions of national policy would be ascertained in accordance with the procedures contained in Articles 27 and 47.2.

[15] [1990] 1 IR 165; [1990] ILRM 505. See also *Clarke v McMahon* [1990] 1 IR 228; [1990] ILRM 648, and *Carron v McMahon* [1990] 1 IR 239; [1990] ILRM 802.

[16] In *Attorney General v Hamilton (No. 1)* [1993] 2 IR 250; [1993] ILRM 81, however, Finlay CJ said that the doctrine of separation of powers "undoubtedly flows" from Article 6, while O'Flaherty J described it as "inherent in Article 6".

[17] [1971] IR 217.

[18] [1967] IR 106.

[19] [1962] IR 1.

[20] In *Howard v Commissioners of Public Works in Ireland* [1993] ILRM 665, Denham J described the separation of the powers of the State as "the kernel of the democratic state set up under the Constitution," implicitly associating it with Article 5.

[21] [1959] IR 1; (1960) 94 ILTR 11.

[22] [1972] IR 215; (1973) 107 ILTR 65.

mountcy in all circumstances to any one of the organs exercising the powers of government over the other"; and the Supreme Court acknowledged in *Abbey Films Ltd. v Attorney General*[23] that "the framers of the Constitution did not adopt a rigid separation between the legislative, executive and judicial powers". The same view was expressed again by McMahon J in *Madden v Ireland*.[24]

The best Irish statement on the necessarily incomplete nature of the separation of powers is, however, the sixty-year old judgment of Johnston J in *Lynham v Butler (No. 2)*,[25] a case about the much disputed frontier between judicial and administrative powers. He traced the ancestry of the old Article 64 (on the judicial power) through Article 3 of the United States Constitution back to the *Commentaries* of Blackstone,[26] and said:

> "I do not think that *Sir William Blackstone*, writing in the middle of the eighteenth century, foresaw the enormous increase in the administrative work of the executive power which was to come in the nineteenth and twentieth centuries; but at the same time it must be noted that his statement as to the necessity for the separation of governmental powers is couched in very guarded language as if he had some vision of what was to happen in the future. It will be observed that he deals with the exercise of judicial power in relation to "causes between party and party" and to "the fundamental laws of the Kingdom"; and it is "the administration of common justice" that is to be kept separate and distinct from the business of legislation and the exercise of administrative power."

Johnston J was thus crediting Blackstone with leaving a certain manoeuvring room free for the later assertion that administrative justice, as distinct from common justice; or causes between an ordinary party and an administrative body executing a statutory policy, as distinct from causes between party and party, might be carried on by bodies other than courts, without wrecking the basic value represented by the separation of powers theory. That theory, he said, ought not to be pressed with excessive rigour and consistency into practice:

> "It has been found through universal experience that this division of governmental functions cannot, as a matter of practical polity, be carried out to its logical conclusion and can only take place as an approximation. In no system of which I have any knowledge has it been found to be possible to confine the legislative, the executive and the judicial power each in what I may call its own water tight compartment; and, if such a thing were to be attempted, the result, I fear, would be so much the worse for the compartment."

More recently, in *Crotty v An Taoiseach*[27] Finlay CJ referred to the separation of powers as fundamental to all of the provisions of the Constitution. He then provided a description of this doctrine as it applies to the judiciary which is worth setting out in full:

> "[The separation of powers] involves for each of the three constitutional organs not only rights but duties also; not only areas of activity and function, but boundaries to them as well. With regard to the legislature, the right and duty of the courts to intervene is clear and express.
>
> 1 Articles 15.4, 34.3.2 and 34.4.4 vest in the High Court and, on appeal, in this Court the right and duty to examine the validity of any impugned enactment of the Oireachtas, and if it be found inconsistent with the Constitution, to condemn it in whole or in part.

[23] [1981] IR 158.
[24] Unreported; High Court, 22 May 1980.
[25] [1933] IR 74; (1933) 67 ILTR 75; (1932) LJ Ir 172.
[26] He cited a passage from the Dublin edition (1769), vol. 1, p.267.
[27] [1987] IR 713; [1987] ILRM 400.

2. Article 26 confers on this Court the duty upon the reference to it by the President of a Bill passed or deemed to have been passed by both Houses of the Oireachtas, to decide whether such Bill or any specified provision or provisions of such Bill is or are repugnant to the Constitution or to any provision thereof.

3. The Courts do not, in my opinion, have any other right to intervene in the enactment of legislation by the Oireachtas.

With regard to the executive, the position would appear to be as follows: This Court has on appeal from the High Court a right and duty to interfere with the activities of the executive in order to protect or secure the constitutional rights of individual litigants where such rights have been or are being invaded by those activities or where activities of the executive threaten an invasion of such rights. This right of intervention is expressly vested in the High Court and Supreme Court by the provisions of Articles 34.3.1 and 34.4.3 and impliedly arises from the form of the judicial oath contained in Article 34.5.1."

Separation of powers used to determine the extent of judicial power

The doctrine of separation of powers has been invoked in a number of cases to determine the extent of the judicial power. In some cases, this is achieved in a positive manner, by invoking the doctrine in order to reinforce Article 34, in other words, in defence of the integrity of the judicial arm. But in other cases, perhaps arising from the tendency of interest groups to resort increasingly to the courts, the extent of the judicial power has been determined more negatively, by identifying those tasks which are not justiciable.[28]

The use of the doctrine of separation of powers in defence of the independence of the courts[29] may be seen in *Fisher v Irish Land Commission*,[30] where Gavan Duffy J spoke of the legislature's freedom to entrust administrative tasks - even ones entailing quasi-judicial functions - "provided only that it respects the essentials of the distribution of powers, required by the written charter". In *Buckley v Attorney General*[31] the same judge struck down the Sinn Féin Funds Act for failing to do this, and was powerfully upheld by the Supreme Court, speaking by O'Byrne J:

> "The manifest object of [Article 6] was to recognise and ordain that, in this State, all powers of government should be exercised in accordance with the well-recognised principle of the distribution of powers between the legislative, executive and judicial organs of the State and to require that these powers should not be exercised otherwise. The subsequent Articles are designed to carry into effect this distribution of powers."

In somewhat similar fashion, Article 6 was cited by O'Higgins CJ, in conjunction with Article 34, in *The State (Director of Public Prosecutions) v Walsh*[32] in support of the proposition that the Constitution authorises the courts to take any action that is necessary for the due administration of justice, including the summary trial of persons charged with criminal contempt, while in *Ambiorix Ltd. v Minister for the Environment,*[33] the doctrine of separation of powers was relied on by the Supreme Court

[28] As Casey points out - *Constitutional Law in Ireland* (2nd ed.,1992) at p.277 - no test for identifying non-justiciable issues has ever been laid down by the Supreme Court. *Cp.* Costello J's decision in *O'Reilly v Limerick Corporation* [1989] ILRM 181, discussed below, pp. 44-46.
[29] On the independence of the courts, see below, pp. 360 *et seq.*
[30] [1948] IR 3; (1948) 82 ILTR 50.
[31] [1950] IR 67.
[32] [1981] IR 412.
[33] [1992] 1 IR 277; [1992] ILRM 209.

in asserting the exclusive rights of the courts to determine whether or not, in the administration of justice, information should be afforded by one litigant to another.[34]

In *Attorney General (Society for the Protection of the Unborn Child (Ireland) Ltd.) v Open-Door Counselling Ltd.*[35] the doctrine of separation of powers was invoked by Hamilton P to justify judicial intervention to protect the life of the unborn in the absence of any legislation on the point.

Other cases in which Article 6 was touched on to introduce or to reinforce Article 34 are *The State (Burke) v Lennon,*[36] *Foley v Irish Land Commission,*[37] *The State (Duggan) v Tapley,*[38] *In re Solicitors Act 1954,*[39] and *The State (Commins) v McRann.*[40]

Defence of the legislature

In a number of other cases, the courts have sought to identify the limits of judicial power with a view to preventing judicial encroachment on the legislative functions of government.[41] Very predictably, the legislative process itself has been identified as being beyond the scope of judicial review, other than in accordance with Article 26 - *Wireless Dealers' Association v Fair Trade Commission.*[42] *A fortiori*, the courts cannot interfere in the process of amending the Constitution.[43]

The courts have also considered the extent of their powers to interpret legislation, either with specific regard to its compatibility with the Constitution or more generally, in the light of the doctrine of separation of powers. In relation to the former type of case, the courts only apply the principle of severability to save part of a statutory provision which is otherwise unconstitutional where such an exercise will not render the provision futile or turn it into something which the legislature had never envisaged.[44] In relation to the interpretation of legislation generally, the courts have indicated that they cannot add to or delete from express statutory provisions so as to achieve objectives which appear desirable to the courts or which are significantly different from those originally intended by the legislature.[45] This approach is especially manifest where the courts are invited to fill what is alleged to be a lacuna in a piece of legislation. Thus in *McGrath v McDermott*[46] where the Supreme Court was asked to read Irish taxation legislation in the

[34] Re-affirming *Murphy v Dublin Corporation* [1972] IR 215 - see below, pp. 229, 377-9.
[35] [1988] IR 593; [1987] ILRM 477.
[36] [1940] IR 136; (1940) 74 ILTR 36, 131.
[37] [1952] IR 118; (1952) 86 ILTR 44.
[38] [1952] IR 62; (1951) 85 ILTR 22.
[39] [1960] IR 239.
[40] [1977] IR 78.
[41] On the legislative function, see below, pp. 104-122.
[42] Supreme Court, 14 March 1956.
[43] See *Roche v Ireland*, High Court, 17 June 1983; *Finn v Minister for the Environment* [1983] IR 154; *MacMathúna v Ireland*, *The Irish Times*, 10 June 1986; *Murphy v Minister for the Environment*, The Irish Times, 10 June 1992.
[44] For cases on the principle of severability, see below, pp. 474-8.
[45] Nor can they correct any error in the legislation. In *Howard v Commissioners of Public Works in Ireland* [1993] ILRM 665, Finlay CJ said:

> "If...a court were satisfied upon the terms of a statute itself, that it was based upon a misapprehension as to legal principles which would be applicable to the subject matter outside of any statutory provision, the error thus arising and the consequence arising from such an error could not properly, having regard to the separation of powers, be corrected by a court but could only be corrected if it wished to do so, by the legislature itself."

See also *The State (Murphy) v Johnson* [1983] IR 235.
[46] [1988] IR 258; [1988] ILRM 647. Though *cp.* the decision of Murphy J in *Grange Developments Ltd. v Dublin Co. Co. (No.3)* [1989] IR 367, where he purported to remedy an omission in the Local Government (Planning and Development) Act 1963, by requiring the defendant to give an undertaking to pay a specified sum of money to the plaintiff in the event of an application for planning permission made pursuant to an earlier undertaking being refused.

light of the doctrine of "fiscal nullity" developed by the courts in the UK, Finlay CJ said:

> "The function of the courts in interpreting a statute of the Oireachtas is ... strictly confined to ascertaining the true meaning of each statutory provision, resorting in cases of doubt or ambiguity to a consideration of the purpose and intention of the legislature to be inferred from the provisions of the statute involved, or even of statutes expressed to be construed with it. The courts have not got a function to add to or delete from express statutory provisions so as to achieve objectives which to the courts appear desirable. In rare and limited circumstances words or phrases may be implied into statutory provisions solely for the purpose of making them effective to achieve their expressly avowed objective."

Accordingly, he concluded that:

> "for this Court to avoid the application of the provisions of the [Capital Gains Tax Act 1975] to these transactions [by the application of the doctrine of "fiscal nullity"] could only constitute the invasion by the judiciary of the powers and functions of the legislature, in plain breach of the constitutional separation of powers."

Other earlier cases in which the courts were invited to remedy alleged legislative omissions include *O'Shaughnessy v Attorney General,*[47] where O'Keeffe P held that it was for the legislature to determine how the personal rights of the citizen are to be vindicated and accordingly refused to invalidate the Criminal Justice (Legal Aid) Act 1962, because it made no provision for civil legal aid; *Reynolds v Attorney General,*[48] where Kenny J indicated, *inter alia*, that he had no power to legislate for the registration of the new electors entitled to vote as a result of the Fourth Amendment to the Constitution Act 1972, which lowered the voting age to 18; and *Somjee v Minister for Justice.*[49] In this last case, Keane J rejected a constitutional challenge to the Irish Nationality and Citizenship Act 1956, based on the fact that it failed to treat alien men married to Irish women in the same way as alien women married to Irish men for the purposes of acquiring citizenship. The judge said that, even if he held in the plaintiff's favour as to the alleged discrimination by way of omission, a declaration to that effect would be futile as it could only have the immediate effect of invalidating the beneficent part of the statutory scheme. Significantly, however, he did accept that plaintiffs complaining of legislative omissions might be entitled to a declaration that their rights had not been vindicated by the Oireachtas, in the expectation that the Oireachtas would then take the appropriate steps to remedy the situation.

A number of miscellaneous cases exist in which the plaintiff's assertion of a right, independent of any statutory framework, has been rejected by the courts on the ground that the claim should more properly be addressed to the Oireachtas. In *O'Reilly v Limerick Corporation*[50] Costello J dismissed a claim that the plaintiff had a constitutionally protected right to be provided by the State with certain physical resources and services, specifically in this case, serviced halting sites. In *L. v L.*[51] the Supreme Court dismissed the respondent's claim that she was entitled to a share in the matrimonial property by virtue of Article 41.2 of the Constitution on the ground that judicial identification of such a right would take the court into the legislative realm. According to Finlay CJ:

[47] High Court, 16 February 1971.
[48] High Court, 16 February 1973.
[49] [1981] ILRM 324. See also *MhicMathúna v Ireland* [1989] IR 504.
[50] [1989] ILRM 181. See *Whyte* in (1988) 10 DULJ (n.s.) 189.
[51] [1992] 2 IR 77; [1992] ILRM 115. The same point was made in a companion case, *N. v N.*, decided the same day - [1992] IR 116; [1992] ILRM 127. But *cp. F. v C.* [1991] 2 IR 300; [1991] ILRM 65, where the Supreme Court upheld what could fairly be regarded as significant judicial developments of the law of nullity.

> "to identify this right in the circumstances set out in this case is not to develop any known principle of common law, but is rather to identify a brand new right and to secure it to the plaintiff. Unless that is something clearly and unambiguously warranted by the Constitution or made necessary for the protection of either a specified or unspecified right under it, it must constitute legislation and be a usurpation by the courts of the function of the legislature."[52]

In *A.D. v Ireland*[53] Carroll J rejected the plaintiff's claim that she should be compensated by the State for certain criminal injuries which she sustained, again on the ground that the question of compensation was a matter for the government and the Oireachtas, while the same argument was invoked by Henchy J in *Hynes-O'Sullivan v O'Driscoll*[54] to defeat the defendant's claim that the defence of privilege to a defamation action should be extended to protect a defendant who had an honest, but mistaken, belief that the party addressed had an interest or duty in receiving the publication.

Of these cases, however, only Costello J's judgment in *O'Reilly* offers any general guidelines as to how to identify matters which, as he put it, "should, to comply with the Constitution, be advanced in Leinster House rather than in the Four Courts."[55] For Costello J, the dividing line between the judicial and legislative spheres of operation is marked out by the Aristotelian distinction between commutative and distributive justice, i.e. between the relationships which arise in dealings between individuals (a term which includes dealings between individuals and servants of the State and public authorities) and the relationship which arises between the individual and those in authority in a political community when goods held in common for the benefit of the entire community fall to be distributed and allocated. On reviewing the constitutional design for the governing of the State, Costello J concluded that the judicial function was restricted to matters of commutative justice only. He continued:

> "What could be involved in the exercise of the [jurisdiction suggested by the plaintiff] would be the imposition by the Court of its view that there had been an unfair distribution of national resources. To arrive at such a conclusion, it would have to make an assessment of the validity of the many competing claims on those resources, the correct priority to be given to them and the financial implications of the plaintiffs' claim. As the present case demonstrates, it may also be required to decide whether a correct allocation of physical resources available for public purposes has been made. In administering this function the Court would not be administering justice as it does when determining an issue relating to commutative justice but it would be engaged in an entirely different exercise, namely, an adjudication on the fairness or otherwise of the manner in which other organs of State had administered public resources. Apart from the fact that members of the judiciary have no special qualification to undertake such a function, the manner in which justice is administered in the Courts, that is on a case by case basis, make them a wholly inappropriate institution for the fulfilment of the suggested role. I cannot construe the Constitution as conferring it on them."

[52] However McCarthy J's concurring judgment was clearly influenced by the particular facts of the case and he appeared open to the possibility that, in another case, the courts might accord proprietary rights to the mother on the basis of Article 41.2. Admittedly there is a passage in Finlay CJ's judgment, with which McCarthy J concurred, in the subsequent case of *N. v N.* [1992] 2 IR 116 at 122; [1992] ILRM 127, at 131, which restates the legal position as understood by the Chief Justice in *L.* However in *N*, the wife succeeded in establishing a claim to the matrimonial home on the basis of the traditional equitable principles, so that the remarks in this case on the Constitution might be regarded as *obiter*.

[53] High Court, 20 July 1992.

[54] [1988] IR 436.

[55] [1989] ILRM at 195. His judgment has been described as "the beginning of an increased sophistication in the manner by which the judiciary view their relationship with the other branches of government." - Byrne and Binchy, *Annual Review of Irish Law 1988*, (1989), p.115.

While this is a valuable contribution to the search for the dividing line between judicial and legislative spheres of operation, it is not conclusive of the matter. In the first place, the distinction between distributive and commutative justice is of no assistance in relation to matters which do not necessarily involve public expenditure, for example, whether the right of privacy protects homosexual behaviour. Second, the rather bold nature of the claim in *O'Reilly* permitted Costello J to invoke the distinction between distributive and commutative justice to great effect in that case. However this distinction is not as watertight as might appear from that judgment. Claims on commutative justice may have implications for public expenditure[56] and cannot be discounted by the courts simply for that reason.[57] Third, and most radical of all, one might question whether the Constitution does erect an impenetrable barrier between the courts and issues of distributive justice. If, for example, the Government was to decide to withdraw all funding from primary education in the interests of curbing public expenditure, would an aggrieved parent have no right to sue on foot of Article 42.4 of the Constitution?[58]

Penultimately, the relevance of Article 6 to the legislature's primary competence to interpret the "requirements of the common good" was stated, not very lucidly, by the Supreme Court in *Attorney General v Southern Industrial Trust*,[59] while in *Ormsby v Ormsby*[60] the Article was used - by the unsuccessful party - in making the point that "the People declare the public policy of the State" through the appropriate organs. That the old Article 2 entrenched the legislative power in such a way that a price-fixing function (alleged to be legislative in nature) could not be delegated to a subordinate body was argued in *Pigs Marketing Board v Donnelly*[61] but the point received short shrift from Hanna J.

Finally, among the many important contributions of the Beef Tribunal saga to constitutional law was the affirmation by the Supreme Court, in *Goodman International v Hamilton*,[62] that a resolution passed by both Dáil and Seanad Éireann providing for the establishment of a tribunal of inquiry into allegations of illegal activities, fraud and malpractice in and in connection with the beef processing industry did not amount to a usurpation of judicial functions. The various members of the Court held, *inter alia*, that the inquiry did not amount to either a criminal trial or an administration of justice.[63] Citing US authorities,[64] both Hederman and McCarthy JJ viewed the power to initiate inquiries as an inherent power of the Houses of the Oireachtas.[65] The contention that a tribunal of inquiry, established pursuant to such power, could not investigate facts within its remit merely on the ground that some of them were the subject of civil litigation

[56] See, *e.g.*, *State (Healy) v Donoghue* [1976] IR 325; *Murphy v Attorney General* [1982] IR 241; *Blake v Attorney General* [1982] IR 117.

[57] Though the courts may impose a more onerous burden of proof on the plaintiff wherever the claim affects the public finances - see the remarks of Barrington J in *Brennan v Attorney General* [1983] ILRM 449 at 478.

[58] The recent decision of O'Hanlon J in *O'Donoghue v The Minister for Health*, High Court, 27 May 1993 - discussed below, at pp. 1058-9 - suggests that such a grievance is justiciable.

[59] (1960) 94 ILTR 161.

[60] (1945) 79 ILTR 97.

[61] [1939] IR 413.

[62] [1992] 2 IR 542; [1992] ILRM 145. Separate judgments were delivered by Finlay CJ, Hederman and McCarthy JJ O'Flaherty and Egan JJ concurred with all three judgments.

[63] See further on these points at p. 572 and pp. 331-347 below respectively. See Ní Raifeartaigh, "*Goodman v The Beef Tribunal*" (1992) 2 IJCL 141.

[64] *Watkins v United States* 345 US 178 (1956). McCarthy J additionally cited *Kilbourn v Thompson* 103 US 169 (1880).

[65] In the High Court, Costello J indicated that the government or any minister may inquire into matters of public interest as part of the exercise of its executive powers. In *Attorney General v Hamilton (No. 1)* [1993] 2 IR 250; [1993] ILRM 81, Finlay CJ described the establishment of the inquiry as an exercise of one of the legislative powers of the State.

was unanimously rejected by the members of the Court. Nor could the tribunal be prevented from investigating matter which were the subject of disputes between private persons once the Houses of the Oireachtas had properly concluded that they were also matters of public importance. Furthermore the tribunal was also entitled to inquire into whether criminal acts had been committed by specific individuals. This power to inquire is not completely unfettered, however. Most obviously, the Houses of the Oireachtas cannot, in the exercise of this power, attempt to interfere in the administration of justice or to replace the right to a criminal trial with due process of law.

Defence of the executive

An additional fetter on the Beef Tribunal's power of inquiry, necessitated by the collective responsibility of the executive,[66] was identified by a majority of the Supreme Court in *Attorney General v Hamilton (No. 1).*[67] In the High Court, O'Hanlon J had refused the application of the Attorney General for a declaration that the Tribunal was not entitled to inquire into or consider the discussions occurring during a course of a meeting of the government or to inquire into or go beyond the terms of a formal or informal decision of the government. On appeal, however, a majority of the Supreme Court - Finlay CJ, Hederman and O'Flaherty JJ - took the view that the constitutional obligation on members of the government to act collectively involved, as a necessity, an obligation not to disclose different or dissenting views held by member of the government prior to the making of decisions. According to Finlay CJ:

> "the development of the doctrine of the separation of powers, without any express provision in the words contained in Article 6, or in any other provision of the Constitution to designate it, seems to me to justify a development of the claimed confidentiality for discussions at Government meetings from the provisions dealing with collective responsibility and collective activity."[68]

Other recent cases have affirmed some of the boundaries between executive and judicial functions in relation to the trial of offences. In *Director of Public Prosecutions v Ó Suilleabhain*[69] Carroll J cited *Attorney General (McDonnell) v Higgins*[70] in support of the proposition that a judge is not entitled to prefer charges. At the other end of this legal process, the protective effect of Article 6 on the executive power to determine duration of imprisonment or detention has also been considered by the courts on a number of occasions.[71] In *Director of Public Prosecutions v Tiernan*,[72] Finlay CJ, delivering the majority judgment of the Supreme Court, held, *inter alia*, that it was for the executive to decide the conventional period which a person sentenced to life imprisonment might expect to serve, and, accordingly, the courts could not take that period into account in imposing sentence in a rape case.[73] *A fortiori*, a decision as to whether a prisoner should obtain temporary release prior to final discharge is also a matter for the executive - *Murray v Ireland.*[74] (In contrast, whether a judicial policy of imposing suspended sentences is compatible with the executive power of remission cannot yet be regarded as finally settled - see below, p. 93.)

[66] On the executive function, see below, pp. 228-235, 277-280.
[67] [1993] 2 IR 250; [1993] ILRM 81.
[68] The majority position is not without its difficulties, however, and is examined in more detail below, pp. 250-257.
[69] High Court, 5 May 1992.
[70] [1964] IR 374.
[71] On the executive's power of commutation or remission of sentence, see, pp. 91-94.
[72] [1980] IR 250; [1989] ILRM 149.
[73] A decision to transfer a prisoner to military detention also comes within the remit of the executive - see the *ex tempore* decision of the Supreme Court in *The State (Boyle) v The Governor of the Curragh Military Detention Barracks* [1980] ILRM 242.
[74] [1991] ILRM 465.

A recent series of cases has focused attention on the constitutionality of the power given to the executive, pursuant to s 2(2) of the Trial of Lunatics Act 1883, to determine the duration of detention of an accused person who had been found guilty but insane. Doubts about the constitutionality of this arrangement arose because of the decision in *The State (O) v O'Brien*[75] in which a majority of the Supreme Court ruled that the power to determine the duration of imprisonment of a young person convicted of murder - originally conferred on the Crown pursuant to s 103 of the Children's Act 1908 - was a judicial power which now vested in the courts rather than in the executive. In *Application of Ellis,*[76] O'Hanlon J distinguished *O'Brien* from cases proceeding pursuant to s 2(2) of the 1883 Act on the ground that that legislation dealt with a situation in which a person had been acquitted of a charge brought against him[77] but concurrently, the jury had found that he was insane at the time he committed the act which led to the charge being brought. Accordingly there was no question of imposing a sentence and thus the power to determine the duration of detention of such a person could lawfully be conferred on the executive.[78] In *Application of Neilan,*[79] however, Keane J refused to follow *Ellis,* concluding instead that an order for the release of a person found guilty but insane constituted part of the administration of justice and that the making of such an order could not, therefore, be assigned to the executive.

The matter was ultimately resolved by the Supreme Court in *Application of Gallagher*[80] in favour of the approach taken in *Ellis.*[81] Delivering the unanimous decision of the Court, McCarthy J held that the special verdict was a verdict of acquittal after which the trial was concluded. At that point:

> "the role of the court is to order the detention of...the former accused until the executive, armed with both the knowledge and resources to deal with the problem, decides on the future disposition of the person... The result of the prosecution has been an acquittal but the statute which permits the special verdict requires that the former accused be detained at least for some minimum time."

The exercise of the power conferred by s 2(2) of the 1883 Act was not, therefore, an administration of justice but rather was "the carrying out of the executive's role in caring for society and the protection of the common good." In this, the power resembled that conferred on the executive by s 165 of the Mental Treatment Act 1945, the constitutional validity of which had been upheld in *In re Clarke.*[82]

The quest for the dividing line between judicial and executive functions has been pursued in relation to matters other than those ancillary to the trial of offences. In a series of cases dealing with the process of amending the Constitution, the courts have ruled that

[75] [1973] IR 50.
[76] [1990] 2 IR 291; [1991] ILRM 225.
[77] According to *R v Felstead* [1914] AC 534, a verdict of guilty but insane constitutes an acquittal in law.
[78] An appeal against O'Hanlon J's order directing that the defendant be kept in custody "till the pleasure of the Government shall be known" was allowed by the Supreme Court on the ground, *inter alia*, that the defendant had not been afforded any opportunity to be heard on the issue of the validity of an order made pursuant to the 1883 Act. Thus on this occasion the Supreme Court did not have to rule on the substantive issue. But see also footnote 81 below.
[79] [1990] 2 IR 267; [1991] ILRM 184.
[80] [1991] 1 IR 31; [1991] ILRM 339. For criticism of this decision, see Byrne and Binchy, *Annual Review of Irish Law 1990*, (1991) at pp.166-168.
[81] Following on the Supreme Court's decision in *Gallagher,* O'Hanlon J ruled, on 19 July 1991, that Ellis should return to the Central Mental Hospital until the pleasure of the Government became known. An appeal against this decision was dismissed by the Supreme Court which re-affirmed that the matter of his continued detention had to be determined by the executive, though there was an obligation on the executive to inquire, "without any possible delay", into the relevant circumstances of the case - *The Irish Times,* 26 July 1991.
[82] [1950] IR 235.

they have no jurisdiction to grant injunctions restraining the executive from holding a referendum without having previously fully explained its effect - *Slattery v An Taoiseach*[83] and *Murphy v Minister for the Environment*[84] - or from spending public money and campaigning exclusively in favour of a proposed constitutional amendment - *McKenna v An Taoiseach.*[85] However if the procedures adopted by the government for amending the Constitution were not those stipulated in the Constitution itself, no doubt the courts could intervene.[86] The conduct of foreign affairs is another area which is primarily entrusted to the executive. In the context of a constitutional challenge to an aspect of the State's foreign policy, FitzGerald CJ said, in *Boland v An Taoiseach,*[87] that Article 6:

> "established beyond question the separation of the executive, legislative and judicial powers of Government... Consequently, in my opinion, the courts have no power, either express or implied, to supervise or interfere with the exercise by the Government of its executive functions, unless the circumstances are such as to amount to a clear disregard by the Government of the powers and duties conferred upon it by the Constitution."

Thus in *Macken v An Taoiseach*[88] Lynch J refused to grant the plaintiff an injunction restraining the government from permitting President Reagan to bring into the State any equipment necessary to launch nuclear weapons on the ground, *inter alia*, that the conduct of foreign affairs was a matter for the government rather than the courts. However the significance of the rider in Finlay CJ's comment can be seen in *Crotty v An Taoiseach*[89] in which the executive was held to have transgressed constitutional principles on the conduct of foreign affairs.

Apart from these cases, the courts would appear to have considered the protective effect of Article 6 on the executive power in only two cases. One of these contains mere judicial speculation, as the point was not directly in issue: *Central Dublin Development Association v Attorney General*[90] in which Kenny J thought it possible that the separation of powers expressed in the Article might "[preclude] the High Court from enquiring whether a Minister of State has an opinion". The second was *Pine Valley Developments Ltd. v Minister for the Environment*[91] where Henchy J considered that the exemption of the State from liability in damages in connection with an invalid planning permission granted by the Minister was not alone not unconstitutional, but "in harmony with the due operation of the organs of government established under the Constitution."

The principle of separation has been much modified in practice

The separation of powers, as has been said, is imperfect - even on the face of the Constitution - and if such a principle exists, it must be understood as heavily modified, and in its practice not comparable with the rigid consistency with which in some other jurisdictions a "separation of powers" is maintained. The most conspicuous example of one arm of government exercising a supervisory control over another is present in the jurisdiction of the High and Supreme Courts to invalidate legislation on constitutional

[83] [1993] 1 IR 286.
[84] *The Irish Times*, 10 June 1992.
[85] High Court, 8 June 1992.
[86] In *Slattery*, McCarthy J allowed for the possibility that circumstances could arise in which judicial intervention in the amendment process would be appropriate and in *McKenna,* Costello J accepted that a citizen has the right to seek relief from the courts should a government act unconstitutionally.
[87] [1974] IR 338; (1975) 109 ILTR 13.
[88] *The Irish Times,* 26 May 1984.
[89] [1987] IR 713; [1987] ILRM 400. See below, pp. 231-2.
[90] (1975) 109 ILTR 69.
[91] [1987] IR 23; [1987] ILRM 137.

criteria; this function is not known in France, for example, the home of the "separation of powers" doctrine, as to permit the ordinary courts to strike down acts of the legislature would appear to be an encroachment on the sphere of the latter.

Other ways in which the arms of government are vulnerable to one another, or operate in some cases outside their own sphere, will show the degree to which the separation of powers - whether it is properly called a "principle" or not - is in practice not rigid.

Complete insulation is not a feature of the Legislature

(a) *The legislative power*. Apart from the power of the superior courts to review Acts of the Oireachtas on constitutional criteria, the courts may also - in consequence of an ordinary doctrine of the rule of law - review subordinate legislation on criteria of *vires* both substantive and procedural. Moreover, legislative functions are in practice often exercised by organs - such as Ministers - whose activity is principally executive, in making regulations and orders of general application, though of course under the authority of the Oireachtas: and again, though no specific notice is taken of the fact in the Constitution, the initiation of legislation is for practical purposes entirely in the hands of the executive.[92]

Complete insulation is not a feature of the Executive

(b) *The executive power*. This, by Article 28.2. is exercised by or on the authority of the Government; the Government however is subject to the Dáil, being dependent on its support and so on part of the legislature. Both the Government in the strict constitutional sense, and all of its members, and every part of the administration over which governmental powers in the broader sense are diffused, are subject to the intervention of the courts to ensure that in their actions they keep within the boundary of lawful authority; and of course, except for the Government (in the strict sense) itself, the whole executive machinery can be dismantled or re-arranged or deprived of functions by enactment of the legislature.

Complete insulation is not a feature even of the courts

(c) *The judicial power*. This power, though entrenched more carefully than the others, and in more detail, must administer a law which, except for the parts deriving from the Constitution, can be changed by the legislature - even if such change is deliberately intended to nullify the effect of a particular judgment of a court.[93] In some departments, notably the administration of criminal justice, the operation of the judicial power requires an executive initiative;[94] at the other end, executive discretion can remit penalties imposed by the courts.[95] The organisation of court business, and the assignment of judges, are matters which, as a matter of fact at this moment, the courts themselves control: but the legislature could transfer much of this to itself or to an executive authority if it wished. On the other hand, some courts exercise some traditional functions - e.g. in the licensing of premises for the sale of alcohol or for amusement - which are more naturally classifiable as executive than as judicial. The question of the legislative transfer of traditionally justiciable classes of issues away from the judicial domain is considered below.[96]

[92] The standing orders of both Dáil and Seanad provide for the initiation of Bills by any member, not necessarily by the Government or a Minister, but in practice private members' Bills are rare and regularly voted down by the Governmental majority.
[93] See below, pp. 348-9.
[94] See below, pp. 307-316.
[95] See above, pp. 91-94.
[96] See pp. 348-9.

Miscellaneous implications of Article 6: natural human rights

The reference in Article 6 to the powers of government being derived ultimately from God was adverted to by Walsh J in *McGee v Attorney General*[97] in connection with the right of matrimonial privacy on which the case turned:

> "In view of the acknowledgement of Christianity in the Preamble and in view of the reference to God in Article 6... it must be accepted that the Constitution intended the natural human rights I have mentioned as being in the latter category [the law of God promulgated by reason] rather than simply an acknowledgement of the ethical content of law in its ideal of justice."

The end of the old regime

In *Attorney General v Crawford*[98] Article 6 was one of a number of Articles which Hanna and Maguire JJ listed as demonstrating that the Crown did not survive in any form in the 1937 Constitution.

The organs of State

In *McLoughlin v Minister for Social Welfare*,[99] Kingsmill Moore J noted that, although Article 6 did not list the "organs of State established by this Constitution", they would include the President, the Oireachtas, the Government, the Council of State, the Courts, the Comptroller and Auditor General and the Attorney General.

In *Moyne v Londonderry Port and Harbour Commissioners*[100] Costello J held that the defendants could not be regarded as an organ or agent of the State as they were incorporated and constituted outside the jurisdiction of the State.

The Offences Against the State Act 1939

In *The People (Director of Public Prosecutions) v Quilligan*,[101] Walsh J referred to the Offences against the State Act 1939, as a legislative intervention designed, *inter alia*, to deal with breaches of the Constitution envisaged in a number of specified Articles, including Article 6.

[97] [1974] IR 284; (1975) 109 ILTR 29.
[98] [1940] IR 335; (1940) 74 ILTR 140.
[99] [1958] IR 1.
[100] [1986] IR 299.
[101] [1986] IR 495; [1987] ILRM 606.

Article 7

THE NATIONAL FLAG

Article 7
The national flag is the tricolour of green, white and orange.

Airteagal 7
An bhratach trí dhath .i. uaine, bán, agus flannbhui, an suaitheantas náisiúnta.

Origin of the national flag

The Irish tricolour, symbolising the union of the "green" and "orange" traditions, is said to have originated in roughly its present form in 1848 and the Young Ireland movement, its association at that time with France suggesting that it was modelled on the French tricolour.

Official usage

Between 1922 and 1937, while the tricolour carried no statutory patent, it was recognised by official usage as the national and State flag. The current official usage, in regard to the proper design and modes of display of the flag - a code of official protocol, without basis in statute - is contained in a booklet published by the Stationery Office.[1]

In statutory legislation the national flag appears to figure only in the Mercantile Marine Act 1955, which lays down in s 10 that, apart from certain exceptions:

> "the proper national colours to be worn by Irish ships shall be the national flag or that flag with a white border."

Section 11 prohibits in general the hoisting of any national flag on an Irish ship other than the proper national colours; and s 12 makes the hoisting of these colours obligatory in certain specified cases.

Specification of flag: Defence Force Regulations

Part V, s I, reg 1(1) of the Defence Force Regulations (A.2: Ceremonial), made in 1954, prescribes in regard to the national flag that:

> "the three coloured parts are of equal size and vertically disposed, the green being next to the staff, the white in the middle and the orange farthest from the staff."[2]

Naval ensign

The same regulation says the flag "may not be defaced by any inscription or device". Regulation 35 of these Regulations lays down that "the Ensign to be used by the Naval Service shall be the National flag". Provision is also made, by reg 42, for a "Jack" for Naval Ships (this is a small flag, denoting nationality, flown from the vessel's bow): the Jack is "a green flag with a yellow harp", specified more fully in an Appendix.

The President's standard

There is a special Presidential standard - a gold harp on a blue ground - authorised not by statute or regulation but by a Government decision of 29 December 1944.[3]

[1] "An Bhratach Náisiúnta": the name of the author does not appear, but it is understood to have been compiled by the late Professor G. A. Hayes-McCoy.

[2] A similar regulation was contained in the Defence Forces Regulations of 15 March 1929 (Part I, Regulation 1).

[3] Information informally supplied from an official source. There is no record of this decision in *Iris Oifigiúil.*

Article 8

THE NATIONAL LANGUAGE: THE OFFICIAL LANGUAGES

Article 8

1. **The Irish language as the national language is the first official language.**
2. **The English language is recognised as a second official language.**
3. **Provision may, however, be made by law for the exclusive use of either of the said languages for any one or more official purposes, either throughout the State or in any part thereof.**

Airteagal 8

1. **Ós í an Ghaeilge an teanga náisiúnta is í an phríomhtheanga oifigiúil í.**
2. **Glactar leis an Sacs-Bhéarla mar theanga oifigiúil eile.**
3. **Ach féadfar socrú a dhéanamh le dlí d'fhonn ceachtar den dá theanga sin a bheith ina haonteanga le haghaidh aon ghnó nó gnóthaí oifigiúla ar fud an Stáit ar fad nó in aon chuid de.**

1922 provision

This Article replaced Article 4 of the 1922 Constitution, which read:

> "The national language of the Irish Free State... is the Irish language, but the English language shall be equally recognised as an official language. Nothing in this Article shall prevent special provisions being made by the [Oireachtas] for districts or areas in which only one language is in general use."

The effect of this provision had been considered in three cases, the *ratio* of each of which is relevant to the present Article 8.

A number of issues have arisen in relation to that latter article - to what extent may Irish be used in court proceedings? What is the significance of describing Irish as "the national language"? Is the State obliged to translate official forms which are used other than in the context of court proceedings? Finally, may the State make knowledge of Irish a necessary qualification for obtaining employment in the public sector?

The use of Irish in court proceedings[1]

The basic principle here is that a litigant is entitled to use his native language when presenting his side of the case to the court, but, considerations of natural justice apart, he cannot impose his choice of language on the other parties to the litigation. This right arguably exists as an aspect of natural justice but in the case of either of the official languages, it derives additional force from the terms of Article 8.[2]

The use of Irish in court proceedings was considered on two occasions by the courts of the Irish Free State. In *R. (Ó Coileáin) v Crotty*[3] a defendant had asked in Irish to be allowed to give his evidence and cross-examine in Irish, saying that Article 4 gave him the right to do so. The District Judge would not permit this, as the complainant knew no Irish, and, in effect, convicted and fined the defendant without his having had an oppor-

[1] See Andrews and Henshaw, "*The Irish and Welsh Languages in the Courts: A Comparative Study*" (1983) 18 Ir Jur (n.s.) 1.

[2] Note also Article 6(3) of the European Convention on Human Rights which provides that a defendant in criminal proceedings is entitled, *inter alia*, to be informed promptly, in a language which he understands and in detail, of the nature and cause of the accusation against him, and to have the free assistance of an interpreter if he cannot understand or speak the language used in Court.

tunity to offer a defence. On certiorari the District Judge's order was quashed, though the brief judgment of Sullivan P does not make it plain that Article 4 gave the case a dimension which it would not in any case have had on simple considerations of natural justice (in other words, assuming that the defendant did not understand English, the proceeding was clearly defective in natural justice quite apart from the official status of Irish recognised by Article 4. Had the defendant's native language been any foreign language, and had he been denied interpreter facilities for making his case, the same considerations must have applied).

The matter became clearer a few years later with the judgment of the Court of Criminal Appeal delivered by Kennedy CJ in *Attorney General v Joyce and Walsh*,[4] in which Article 4 was seen as redoubling the right which an Irish-speaking party must have to make his case through Irish:

> "It would seem to me to be a requisite of natural justice, particularly in a criminal trial, that a witness should be allowed to give evidence in the language which is his or her vernacular language, whether that language be Irish or English, or any foreign language; and it would follow, if the language used should not be a language known to the members of the court, that means of interpreting the language to the court (judge and jury), and also, in the case of evidence against a prisoner, that means of interpreting it to the prisoner, should be provided. The Irish language, however, is not merely the vernacular language of most, if not all, of the witnesses in question in the present case, but it holds a special position by virtue of the Constitution of the Saorstát, in which its status is recognised and established as the national language of the Saorstát, from which it follows that, whether it be the vernacular language of a particular citizen or not, if he is competent to use the language, he is entitled to do so. Therefore, it may be said that all those who gave their evidence in the Irish language in the present case had, as it were, a double right to do so: first on general principles of natural justice as their vernacular language; and, secondly, as a matter of constitutional right."

The Court held, however, that there was no objection to the Court stenographer at the trial making a note, not of the original Irish evidence, but of the interpreter's English rendering of it.

Since the enactment of the Constitution, the use of Irish in the conduct of court proceedings has been considered in two cases. *Ó Monacháin v An Taoiseach* [5] confirms that, although a party to such proceedings is entitled to give his evidence in Irish, even in parts of the country where English is the vernacular, he is not entitled to demand that the entire proceedings should be conducted in Irish, even in districts where it is generally spoken. The plaintiff, who had been prosecuted for alleged planning offences at Bunbeg in the Donegal Gaeltacht, sought to establish that the Government and the Minister for Justice had failed in what he said was their duty to ensure that the District Justice who heard the summonses against him was a person competent to understand evidence given in Irish without the aid of an interpreter. He relied on s 71 of the Courts of Justice Act 1924, which provides:

> "so far as may be practicable having regard to all relevant circumstances the Justice of the District Court assigned to a District which includes an area where the Irish

[3] (1927) 61 ILTR 81.
[4] [1929] IR 526.
[5] [1986] ILRM 660.

language is in general use shall possess such a knowledge of the Irish language as would enable him to dispense with the assistance of an interpreter when evidence is given in that language."

The Supreme Court, affirming Hamilton J in the High Court, held against the plaintiff. Henchy J, with whom Griffin J agreed, said that:

> "although any witness may give evidence in his native language, no authority can be found in s 71 or any other provision for compelling the judge to hear the case without the assistance of an interpreter to make the evidence intelligible to those who need to understand it."[6]

Although it appears from the judgment of Hamilton J in the High Court that the plaintiff's case consisted partly of the contention that Article 8 intensified the duty laid on the Government by s 71 of the 1924 Act, this point does not emerge from the Supreme Court judgments. It will be observed, also, that the words of Henchy J bear on the rights of a person to give evidence in his native language, not on the right to use (or require that others should use) Irish as such, whether one's native language or not, merely because of the status given to it by Article 8.

The case of *An Stát (Mac Fhearraigh) v Mac Gamhnia*[7] affirms that the right of a litigant to use Irish in the conduct of his case covers his cross-examination of witnesses. It arose from a proceeding before an employment appeals tribunal, in which the applicant demanded not only the right to give his own evidence in Irish, but also the right to cross-examine other witnesses in Irish. The tribunal turned down his request on the ground that, as he understood English perfectly well, it was wasting the tribunal's time to insist on Irish cross-examination (presumably because of the resulting need to interpret for the benefit of others involved in the hearing). He sought an order of mandamus against the tribunal to order it to conduct the hearing in the way he wished; and his view was upheld in the High Court by O'Hanlon J, who said that:

> "whenever any party wishes to put his side of a case to a court or tribunal, whether by argument, the giving of evidence, or the examination or cross-examination of witnesses, I am of opinion that he has a constitutional right to do all of this through Irish if he wishes."[8]

Moreover, the court or tribunal had no business to enquire of such a person whether he understood English; and, even if the consequence was additional expenditure of time and money, this had to be accepted in order to fulfil the Constitution's precept in Article 8. This, he said, by its terms accorded a higher status to the language than the old Article 4 had accorded it; it was, of course, open to the Oireachtas to prescribe limitations of the kind envisaged by Article 8.3, but until this had been done in any particular case, the primacy of the Irish language had to be respected.

[6] This part of the judgment reads in the original: "Cé go bhfuil ag finné ar bith a chuid fianaise a thabhairt ina theanga dhúchais, ní féidir údarás a fháil ó alt 71 ná ó aon fhoráil dlí eile le iachall a chur ar an mBreitheamh an cás a éisteacht gan cabhair a fháil ó ateangaire chun tuiscint na fianaise sin a thabhairt do na daoine gur gá an tuiscint sin bheith acu."

[7] Unreported, High Court, 1 June 1983.

[8] This part of the judgment reads in the original: "Aon uair gur mian le páirtí ar bith a thaobh fhéin den scéal do bhrú ar an gcúirt nó ar an bhínse, pé'cu tré aighneacht, tré fianaise do thabhairt, tré finnéithe do cheistiú nó do chros-cheistiú, táim den bhárúil go bhfuil sé de cheart aige fén mBunreacht an t-iomlán do dhéanamh tré mheán na Gaeilge, más toil leis."

In ancillary notices

As *Ó Monacháin* makes clear, a litigant cannot determine which language must be used by the other parties to the proceedings. This principle extends to the furnishing of legal notices in connection with such proceedings, unless the failure to translate such notices would lead to a breach of natural justice. In *Attorney General v Coyne and Wallace,*[9] which arose out of two prosecutions under the Road Traffic Act 1933, notices of intention to prosecute, as required by s 55 of that Act were served in each case, but the notices were in Irish (as was normally the case in the district concerned) and the defendants did not know enough Irish to understand them. However, a member of the Garda Síochána had explained their effect at the time of serving them: but it was contended that, if this explanation was to be viewed as the verbal notice which s 55(2)(*b*) contemplated, it was late in time. On the issue whether the written notice in an uncomprehended language satisfied s 55, the case reached the Supreme Court, which held that the written notice, as it had been interpreted at the moment of service, was adequate.[10] Kingsmill Moore J, with whom on this point Walsh J agreed, considered the bearing of Article 8 on the matter:

> "I was at first inclined to the view that Article 8.3 meant that an official document to be operative must be both in Irish and English, unless provision had been made by law sanctioning the use of only one of the languages. It was argued for the Attorney General that the true meaning of the Article was that either language might be used unless provision had been made by law that one language only was to be used for some one or more official purposes. On consideration I consider this construction to be correct.
>
> I hope that nothing in this judgment will be construed as reflecting on the desirability of ensuring that a person receives any official notice in the language with which he is most familiar, either by framing the notice originally in both Irish and English or by furnishing a translation if the recipient indicates that he is not familiar with the language in which it is couched."

Similarly, where a defendant is equally familiar with both languages, he cannot insist on being served with an Irish version of a summons. In *An Stát (Mac Fhearraigh) v Neilan*[11] the applicant sought an order of certiorari quashing his conviction in the District Court for not possessing a television licence, on the ground that the summons served on him was in English, notwithstanding the fact that he had made repeated requests for an Irish language version of the document. O'Hanlon J noted that, by virtue of Article 8.3, provision may be made by law for the exclusive use of either of the two official languages for any one or more official purposes, either throughout the State or in any part thereof. Both the Rules of the Superior Courts[12] and the Rules of the Circuit Court[13] made provision for the use of Irish (by requiring the translation or interpretation of documents) in relation to certain legal proceedings, but no comparable provision existed in relation to the District Court. On that basis, the judge concluded that:

[9] (1967) 101 ILTR 17.

[10] However this may not satisfy the requirements of Article 6(3)(a) of the European Convention on Human Rights which requires that a defendant in criminal proceedings must be "informed promptly, in a language which he understands and in detail, of the nature and cause of the accusation against him." In that context it has been suggested that "an oral elucidation by the person who serves the writ of summons upon [the defendant] or by an interpreter would seem to be an insufficient basis for the preparation of his defence" - Van Dijk and Van Hoof, *Theory and Practice of the European Convention on Human Rights* (2nd ed., 1990), p.346.

[11] Unreported, High Court, 1 June 1984.

[12] RSC, O 106. See now the 1986 Rules, O 120.

[13] Order 1 r 5.

"any prosecutor instituting proceedings in the District Court, whether in the Gaeltacht or otherwise, has a legal right to use an English language version of the summons if he wishes and...there is no obligation on him, either under the ordinary law or the Constitution, to provide an Irish version for the defendant, even where so requested."[14]

The judge expressly reserved his opinion in relation to a case where the defendant did not understand the language in which the summons was drafted; but in such a case the general principle of fairness adverted to by Kingsmill Moore J in *Attorney General v Coyne and Wallace*[15] must apply.

While, considerations of natural justice apart, the litigant cannot impose his choice of language on the other participants in the proceedings, he may be entitled to oblige the State to translate public documents where failure to do so would impede his right to conduct the case through Irish. This obligation would appear to be derived from the litigant's right to use Irish in the presentation of his case, rather than from the terms of Article 8. In *Delap v An tAire Dlí agus Cirt, Éire agus an tArd Aighne*[16] the applicant sought, *inter alia,* declarations that the respondents were constitutionally obliged to provide an Irish language version of the Rules of the Superior Courts, which determine the procedures to be followed when bringing litigation before the High and Supreme Court. Insofar as the case was grounded on Article 8, O'Hanlon J considered that he was bound by the decision in *Attorney General v Coyne and Wallace*[17] to the effect that either of the official languages may be employed for official purposes unless legislation makes provision for the exclusive use of one or the other. Accordingly, there was no breach of Article 8 when the Superior Courts Rules Committee and the Minister for Justice decided to publish the Rules of the Superior Courts in English only. Nor did this amount to an infringement of Article 25.4.4 as that provision only applies to Acts of the Oireachtas and not, as in this case, to secondary legislation. However this did not dispose of the case for, according to the judge, the citizen has a constitutional right of access to the courts; in exercising this right in relation to the High and Supreme Courts, he must abide by the provisions of the Rules of the Superior Courts; however the citizen who exercises his constitutional right to present his case in Irish faces a considerable obstacle because of the absence of an Irish language version of the Rules of the Superior Courts and, to that extent, is not treated fairly by comparison with other litigants who are happy to use English. It followed that the State had an obligation to provide a translation of the Rules within a reasonable period after their adoption by the Committee and the Minister.[18]

Legal significance of Irish as the national and first official language

There appears to have been only one case decided under the Constitution of 1922 on the question of the status of the Irish language itself as distinct from the rights of parties to court proceedings. This was *Ó Foghludha v McClean,*[19] in which a rule of court[20] was in issue; it provided that all summonses and notice to be served:

[14] This part of the judgment reads in the original: "Da réir sin, táim den bhárúil go bhfuil ceart do réir dlí ag aon inchúisitheoir a thionscnaíonn imeachta ós comhair na Cúirte Dóiche, pé 'cu sa Ghaeltacht nó sa Ghalltacht, feidhm do bhaint as toghairm i mBéarla má's mian leis, agus nach bhfuil iachall air fén ghnath-dlí nó fén Bhunreacht leagan Gaeilge a chur ar fáil don chosantóir, fiú má iarrtar air sin do dhéanamh."

[15] (1967) 101 ILTR 17.

[16] Unreported, High Court, 13 July 1990.

[17] (1967) 101 ILTR 17.

[18] The judge declined to grant an order of mandamus as the evidence before the court indicated that a translation of the Rules of the Superior Courts was in the process of being prepared.

[19] [1934] IR 469.

[20] Rules of the High Court and Supreme Court, 1926; O XXIX r 3.

> "in any part of Saorstát Éireann, if in Irish, may be accompanied by a translation thereof in English, and, if not so accompanied, shall be translated into English by one of the interpreters attached to the Central Office and the party serving such summons or notice shall be bound to serve the English version along with the Irish original."

The plaintiffs[21] served proceedings on the defendant wholly in Irish and unaccompanied by a translation; and then, as the defendant did not enter an appearance, sought judgment in default of appearance under one of the same Rules that had elsewhere prescribed an English translation; on the point that they had not complied with the latter Rule, they argued that this, inasmuch as it made no provision for a mandatory Irish translation where proceedings were served in English, discriminated against the national language and was thus an infringement of Article 4. In the High Court one of the judges, O'Byrne J, agreed with them and was for holding the rule invalid for contravening Article 4; but he was outvoted by the other members of the Court. Sullivan P interpreted Article 4 as follows:

> "Article 4...declares that the national language of the Irish Free State is the Irish language, but that the English language shall be equally recognised as an official language. This can only mean that both languages are official languages, and, as such, entitled to equal recognition. What does such equal recognition involve? To my mind no more than this so far as the administration of justice in the courts is concerned that every person shall be entitled at his option to use either language in transacting legal business, and that he shall not suffer any impediment or incur any liability or disability by reason of the language he uses...[From the distinction made in Order XXIX r 3] it does not follow that the rule is inconsistent with the Constitution if the opinion I have expressed as to the meaning of Article 4 is correct.
>
> The rule does not impose upon the parties affected by it any additional expense or burden, it facilitates the progress of litigation, and it does not place any obstacle in the way of those who desire to conduct their legal business in the Irish language. I am, therefore, of opinion that the rule is not inconsistent with the Constitution and is valid and operative."

The judgment of the High Court was affirmed by the Supreme Court. Kennedy CJ, while agreeing that the rule did not breach Article 4, gave an interpretation of the Article which conceded a potentially important effect to the word "national":

> "The declaration by the Constitution that the national language of the Saorstát is the Irish language does not mean that the Irish language is, or was at that historical moment, universally spoken by the people of the Saorstát, which would be untrue in fact, but it did mean that it is the historic distinctive speech of the Irish people, that it is to rank as such in the nation, and, by implication, that the State is bound to do everything within its sphere of action (as for instance in State-provided education) to establish and maintain it in its status as the national language and to recognise it for all official purposes as the national language. There is no doubt in my mind but that the term "national" in the Article is wider than, but includes, "official", in which respect only the English language is accorded constitutional equality. None of the organs of the State, legislative, executive or judicial, may derogate from the pre-eminent status of the Irish language as the national language of the State without offending against the constitutional provisions of Article 4. If the rule of court in question so offends then it is in my opinion unconstitutional and invalid."

[21] They were the trustees of Conradh na Gaeilge. The defendant was their tenant.

Obligation to translate official documents used other than in the context of legal proceedings?

These comments were subsequently relied on by O'Hanlon J in support of the conclusion that the recognition of Irish as the first official language obliged the State to provide dual language versions of official forms where the completion of such forms, or their equivalent, was necessary for citizens to carry on their lawful activities. In *Ó Murchú* (sic)[22] *v Cláraitheoir na gCuideachtaí agus an tAire Tionscail agus Tráchtála*[23] the applicant had instituted proceedings seeking an order of mandamus directing the respondents to furnish her with an Irish language version of the forms set out in S.I. No.147 of 1987, used for the incorporation of companies. Such forms eventually having been produced, the issue before the High Court was whether she could recover the costs of having instituted the earlier proceedings. This was opposed by the respondents on the ground that they were not obliged to produce a translation of the forms and that they had done so only as a matter of favour to the applicant. This argument was rejected by O'Hanlon J. Citing the remarks of O'Sullivan P and O'Kennedy CJ in *Ó Foghludha v McClean* [24] in reference to Article 4 of the Constitution of the Irish Free State, he said:

> "I am of the opinion that the provisions of Article 8 of the Constitution are more forceful with regard to the recognition to be given to Irish as the first official language of the State than was Article 4 of the Constitution of the Free State. I accept what the applicant says with regard to the delay and difficulty imposed on her when she wished to discharge her obligations under the Companies Acts and I am of the opinion that her rights under the Constitution were infringed and that it was reasonable to institute proceedings seeking relief from the High Court."[25]

Accordingly, he awarded her the costs of the proceedings.

However, the imposition of such a broad obligation on the State appeared to be at variance with Article 8.3 as that provision was construed by Kingsmill Moore J in *Attorney General v Coyne and Wallace* [26] and when this was brought to the attention of O'Hanlon J in *Delap v An tAire Dlí agus Cirt, Éire agus an tArd Aighne*[27] he resiled from his earlier position.[28]

The same judge again rejected his earlier decision in *Ó Murchú*, on this occasion implicitly, in the most recent case on this point - *Ní Cheallaigh v An tAire Comhshaoil.*[29] The applicant contended that the Road Vehicles (Index Marks) (Amendment) (No.2) Regulations 1986 were unconstitutional because they obliged car owners to affix registration plates to their cars but only provided for the use of English language version of such plates.[30] She had been convicted in the District Court for using an Irish language version of the Co. Dublin plate. O'Hanlon J distinguished this case from *Delap* on the

[22] The applicant was, in fact, a woman.
[23] Unreported, High Court, 20 June 1988.
[24] [1934] IR 469.
[25] This part of the judgment reads in the original: "Táim den bharúil go bhfuil forálacha Airteagal 8 de Bhunreacht na hÉireann níos treise maidir leis anaitheantas a tugtar don Ghaeilge mar phríomhtheanga oifigiúil an Stáit, ná mar abhí Airteagal 4 de Bhunreacht an tSaorstáit. Glaicaim leis an méid a deireann an tIarratasóir maidir leis an moill agus an dua a chuireadh uirthi."
[26] (1967) 101 ILTR 17.
[27] Unreported, High Court, 13 July 1990.
[28] Though, in the event, he was still able to rule in favour of the applicant, who was seeking to compel the State to provide an Irish translation of the Rules of the Superior Courts, on other grounds. See above, p. 57.
[29] Unreported, High Court, 4 June 1992.
[30] Each county (for this purpose Tipperary is divided into Tipperary North Riding and Tipperary South Riding) has a distinctive registration plate, the letters for which are derived from the English name of the county.

grounds that it did not involve the right of citizens to have access to the courts in order to vindicate and defend their rights and held that he was bound by *Attorney General v Coyne and Wallace*.

Competence in Irish as a necessary qualification for public sector employment.

The status of Irish as the national and first official language also featured in *Groener v Minister for Education and the CDVEC*[31] in which the European Court of Justice considered whether, and if so, under what conditions, the State may insist on competence in Irish as a necessary qualification for public sector employment. The plaintiff, a Dutch woman, who had been refused a full time position as an art lecturer at a Dublin college because she failed an oral Irish test, sought a declaration that the requirement of qualification in Irish for appointment to certain posts in the vocational education service was invalid, having regard to Article 3 of Council Regulation 1612/68 on free movement of workers within the EC. This article provides, in relevant part, that national provisions or administrative practices of a member state are not to apply where "though applicable irrespective of nationality, their exclusive or principal aim or effect is to keep nationals of other member states away from the employment offered." However the last subparagraph of Article 3(1) goes on to provide that that provision is not to "apply to conditions relating to linguistic knowledge required by reason of the nature of the post to be filled." The Court accepted that, in furtherance of a policy for the protection and promotion of a language which is both the national language and the first official language of a member state, teachers could be required to have some knowledge of that language. However the implementation of such a policy could not encroach upon the fundamental freedom of movement of workers and consequently the specific requirements derived from such a policy would only be acceptable where they were not disproportionate in relation to the aim pursued and where the manner of their application did not discriminate against nationals of other member states. In the instant case, the Court ruled that a permanent full-time post of lecturer in public education institutions did come within the meaning of the last subparagraph of Article 3(1), provided that the linguistic requirement in question was imposed as part of a policy for the promotion of Irish and provided that that requirement was applied in a proportionate and non-discriminatory manner.

Worth mentioning, finally, is the dictum of Henchy J in *The State (Cussen) v Brennan*[32] - in which the Supreme Court held that the Local Appointments Commissioners had acted *ultra vires* in purporting to introduce a knowledge of Irish as a qualification for a particular appointment, where this had not been approved by the relevant Minister - that:

> "it is incontestable that under a Constitution which recognises Irish as the first official language (Article 8) and which empowers the State in its enactments to have due regard to differences of capacity, physical and moral, and of social function (Article 40. 1), a law may provide that proficiency in Irish is relevant to the discharge of the duties of that office."

[31] (Case 87/379), [1990] ILRM 335; [1989] ECR 3967.
[32] [1981] IR 181.

CITIZENSHIP

Article 9

1. 1° On the coming into operation of this Constitution any person who was a citizen of Saorstát Éireann immediately before the coming into operation of this Constitution shall become and be a citizen of Ireland.

2° The future acquisition and loss of Irish nationality and citizenship shall be determined in accordance with law.

3° No person may be excluded from Irish nationality and citizenship by reason of the sex of such person.

2. Fidelity to the nation and loyalty to the State are fundamental political duties of all citizens.

Airteagal 9

1. 1° Ar theacht i ngníomh don Bhunreacht seo is saoránach d'Éirinn aon duine ba shaoránach de Shaorstát Éireann díreach roimh theacht i ngníomh don Bhunreacht seo.

2° Is de réir dlí a chinnfear fáil agus cailleadh náisiúntacht agus saoránacht Éireann feasta.

3° Ní cead náisiúntacht agus saoránacht Éireann a cheilt ar dhuine ar bith toisc gur fireann nó toisc gur baineann an duine sin.

2. Is bundualgas polaitiúil ar gach saoránach bheith dílis don náisiún agus tairiseach don Stát.

Saorstát Éireann citizenship

Section 1(1) of this Article involves referring back to the citizenship law of Saorstát Éireann. Article 3 of the 1922 Constitution read:

> "Every person, without distinction of sex, domiciled in the area of the jurisdiction of the Irish Free State (Saorstát Éireann) at the time of the coming into operation of this Constitution, who was born in Ireland or either of whose parents was born in Ireland or who has been ordinarily resident in the area of the jurisdiction of the Irish Free State (Saorstát Éireann) for not less than seven years, is a citizen of the Irish Free State (Saorstát Éireann) and shall [within the limits of the jurisdiction of the Irish Free State (Saorstát Éireann)][1] enjoy the privileges and be subject to the obligations of such citizenship: Provided that any such person being a citizen of another State may elect not to accept the citizenship hereby conferred; and the conditions governing the future acquisition and termination of citizenship [in[2]] of the Irish Free State (Saorstát Éireann) shall be determined by law."[3]

In addition, s 2 of the Irish Nationality and Citizenship Act 1935, conferred citizenship on persons thereafter born whose father was a citizen of Saorstát Éireann. Accordingly, Article 9 of the 1937 Constitution gave automatic citizenship to persons within the cate-

[1] The words in square brackets were deleted by the Constitution (Amendment No.26) Act 1935.

[2] "In" was replaced by "of" by the Constitution (Amendment No.26) Act 1935.

[3] The Irish Free State's "citizenship" was at that time unique in the Commonwealth. The countries to which it was constitutionally assimilated by the Treaty - Canada, Australia, New Zealand and South Africa - did not then possess "citizenships" of their own. See Clive Parry, *Nationality and Citizenship Laws of the Commonwealth and of the Republic of Ireland* (London, 1957), p. 925. In *Murray v Parkes* [1942] 2 KB 123, Viscount Caldecote CJ said that the Constitution of 1922 "did no more than confer upon [the appellant] a national character as an Irish citizen within the wider British nationality. The same is true in my opinion of the Constitution of 1937".

gories of the old Article 3 and s 2 of the 1935 Act. The old Article 3, which made original citizenship depend on domicile, was in issue in only two reported cases, both of which turned on domicile: *Iveagh v Revenue Commissioners*[4] (involving a revenue liability) and *Bradfield v Swanton*[5] (involving compliance with the law of Massachusetts on testamentary disposition).

The 1956 Act

The ambit of citizenship was extended by the Irish Nationality and Citizenship Act 1956, which provides by s 2 that "Ireland" for the purposes of the Act means "The national territory as defined in Article 2 of the Constitution", i.e. the thirty-two counties of the entire island; and by s 6 as follows:

> (1) Every person born in Ireland is an Irish citizen from birth.
>
> (2) Every person is an Irish citizen if his father or mother was an Irish citizen at the time of that person's birth or becomes an Irish citizen under subsection (1) or would be an Irish citizen under that subsection if alive at the passing of this Act.
>
> (3) In the case of a person born before the passing of this Act subsection (2) applies from the date of its passing. In every other case, it applies from birth.
>
> (4) A person born before the passing of this Act whose father or mother is an Irish citizen under subsection (2), or would be if alive at its passing, shall be an Irish citizen from the date of its passing.
>
> (5) Subsection (1) shall not confer Irish citizenship on the child of an alien who, at the time of the child's birth, is entitled to diplomatic immunity in the State.[6]

To these provisions must be added s 7(1):

> "Pending the reintegration of the national territory, subsection (1) of section 6 shall not apply to a person, not otherwise an Irish citizen, born in Northern Ireland on or after the 6th December, 1922, unless, in the prescribed manner, that person, if of full age, declares himself to be an Irish citizen or, if he is not of full age, his parent or guardian declares him to be an Irish citizen. In any such case, the subsection shall be deemed to apply to him from birth."

The Northern population

The sensational effect of these provisions (in which the opening words of s 7(1) were adopted from Article 3 of the Constitution) was to confer, in the eyes of Irish law, citizenship on the vast majority of the Northern Ireland population; the modifying effect of s 7(1) was aimed at people "of entirely alien parentage"[7] born in Northern Ireland, who

[4] [1930] IR 386; (1929) 63 ILTR 89.
[5] [1931] IR 446.
[6] This provision featured in *Gomaa v Minister for Foreign Affairs*, High Court, 24 July 1992, where Barr J held that a former employee of the Egyptian embassy in Dublin, who had left Ireland for Egypt but who had to return to Dublin because of the poor health of his pregnant wife, continued to enjoy diplomatic immunity within the meaning of s 6(5) with the result that his child did not acquire Irish citizenship on being born in this country.
[7] See speech by the Minister for Justice (Deputy James Everett) on the Second Stage of the Bill: 154 *Dáil Debates* 1000.

were to have Irish citizenship only if they expressly opted for it. The bulk of the northern population escaped this option because of the words "not otherwise an Irish citizen", i.e. not an Irish citizen by operation of provisions other than s 6(1). To take the extreme instance, the combination of sub-ss (2) and (4) of s 6 would result in automatic citizenship for "every living person who is the grandchild of a person born in any part of the thirty-two counties prior to 6th December, 1922".[8]

These provisions featured tangentially in *McGimpsey v Ireland*[9] in which the plaintiffs, who were born and resident in Northern Ireland, challenged the constitutionality of the Anglo-Irish Agreement of 1985. In the High Court, Barrington J simply stated that, as both plaintiffs were born in Ireland, they were, in contemplation of Irish law, citizens of Ireland. A clear implication of this ruling was that citizenship was a necessary, though not sufficient, condition which had to be satisfied before one could have *locus standi* to challenge the constitutionality of the Agreement. Both Finlay CJ and McCarthy J in the Supreme Court showed some unease with Barrington J's conclusion on the matter of citizenship, McCarthy J going so far as to say that, in his opinion, the plaintiffs were not shown to be citizens. Both judges pointed out that neither plaintiff had claimed to be a citizen in the statement of claim, nor had any evidence been adduced as to the plaintiffs having made the declaration prescribed by s 7(1) of the 1956 Act or as to any facts which would indicate that the plaintiffs were otherwise Irish citizens. However as no arguments had been put to the Supreme Court on this point, the Court proceeded to deal with the case on its merits.[10]

Loss of citizenship

Loss of citizenship is provided for in ss 21-25; citizenship may be "renounced" by a citizen about to become a citizen of another State by "lodging with the Minister [for Justice] a declaration of alienage", but it may not be renounced in "time of war as defined in Article 28.3.3 of the Constitution" except with the Minister's consent (s 21). There is no other provision for loss of citizenship, or of a citizen's rights, whether as a penal measure[11] or otherwise; except that in the case of naturalised citizens, the certificate of naturalisation may be revoked in certain conditions including the case where the Minister for Justice:

> "is satisfied...that the person to whom it has been granted has, by any overt Act shown himself to have failed in his duty of fidelity to the nation and loyalty to the State."[12]

The constitutionality of this provision seems highly questionable, partly because of the drastic nature of revocation of citizenship and the consequent question whether anyone other than a judge in a court could order it[13] and partly because the criterion here set up is so vague that it invites an unpredictable, subjective application of a kind hostile to the

[8] Minister for Justice on the Third (Committee) Stage of the Bill: 155 *Dáil Debates* 1056. This dispensation is subject only to registration in the case of a person who, with both of his parents, was born outside the thirty-two counties, unless either parent was at the time of the birth resident abroad in the public service: s 7(2).
[9] [1990] 1 IR 110; [1990] ILRM 440.
[10] See below, pp. 279-86.
[11] An international attempt to outlaw deprivation of citizenship is embodied in the Draft Conventions on the Elimination and Reduction of Future Statelessness adopted by the International Law Commission in 1944: U.N. Doc. A/2693. O'Connell, *International Law,* p.743, n. 59, says: "There is now a tendency to deduce a rule against denationalisation from the conception of human rights."
[12] Section 19(1)(*b*). The section provides for a quasi-judicial enquiry before such revocation. The duty mentioned here is that declared to exist by Article 9.2.
[13] See below, p. 564 *et seq.*

concept of "due process" or "due course of law".[14] In *Eastern Health Board, T.M. and A.M. v An Bord Uchtála*[15] Carroll J did suggest, *obiter,* that a certificate of naturalisation granted in that case to a foundling born abroad might be revoked by the Minister because the Irish putative adoptive parent had innocently misrepresented himself as parent, rather than guardian, on the application form. However the judge gave no consideration to the possible constitutional difficulties attaching to s 19.

Acquisition of citizenship on marriage

Article 9.1.3 is not a general prohibition of sex discrimination in all citizenship laws. So held Keane J in *Somjee v Minister for Justice,*[16] when he upheld the original s 8 of the Irish Nationality and Citizenship Act 1956, which allowed women to acquire citizenship on marriage to Irish men but made no similar provision for men who married Irish women. So far as Article 9.1.3 was concerned, the act of the Oireachtas in providing for *acquisition* of citizenship on marriage for women did not amount to an *exclusion* from citizenship for men. Section 8 has since been replaced by a new provision set out in s 3 of the Irish Nationality and Citizenship Act 1986, which provides for the conferring of post-nuptial citizenship on any alien, irrespective of sex, who marries an Irish citizen and who satisfies other prescribed conditions.

Other grounds

Other provisions of the Act are ss 9 - 11 dealing with citizenship of posthumous children, of foundlings, and of adopted children; ss 14-20 on naturalisation; and ss 7(2) and 13 on citizenship of persons born outside Ireland or on ships or aircraft.[17]

By virtue of s 12(1) of the Irish Nationality and Citizenship Act 1956, the President is empowered to grant Irish citizenship as a token of honour to a person or to the child or grandchild of a person who, in the opinion of the Government has done "signal honour or rendered distinguished service to the nation".[18]

Duty of citizenship

By virtue of Article 9.2, fidelity to the nation and loyalty to the State are fundamental political duties of all citizens. Furthermore, as we have already noted, by virtue of s 19(1)(*b*) of the 1956 Act a certificate of naturalisation may be revoked where the Minister for Justice is satisfied that the person to whom it was granted has failed in these political duties. In *McGimpsey v Ireland*[19] McCarthy J stated that such fidelity and loyalty do not prohibit or restrict disagreement with the content of the Constitution nor with the actions of government. In the earlier case of *O'Callaghan v Commissioners of Public Works*[20] the Supreme Court, upholding the constitutionality of s 8 of the National Monuments Act 1930, which is part of a legislative scheme for the protection of national

[14] See below, 573 *et seq.*
[15] [1992] ILRM 568.
[16] [1981] ILRM 324.
[17] For a very full account of the history of Irish citizenship law, and discussion of the 1956 Act see *Clive Perry, op. cit.* pp.925ff.
[18] To date, honorary citizenship has been conferred on seven persons - Sir Chester Beatty, a benefactor who made a gift of a distinguished and valuable collection of art and manuscripts to the State; Dr. Tiede Herrema, a Dutch industrialist who was kidnapped and held for ransom for a number of weeks in 1975, and his wife; Mr. T.P. O'Neill, one-time Chairman of the U.S. House of Representatives, and his wife; and Sir Alfred and Lady Beit, who donated a valuable art collection to the State.
[19] [1990] 1 IR 110; [1990] ILRM 440.
[20] [1985] ILRM 364.

monuments, referred to the preservation of such monuments as "the common duty of all citizens", though without invoking Article 9.2.

Article 9 in litigation

Apart from *Somjee*, Article 9 has been adverted to judicially in only four cases. In *The State (Duggan) v Tapley*,[21] arguments based on it were addressed unsuccessfully to both High Court and Supreme Court; the judgments do not disclose the nature of the arguments, merely that they were thought of no weight.

In the other case, *The State (Burke) v Lennon*,[22] Gavan Duffy J said he accepted the submission of State counsel that the Offences against the State Act 1939, was an Act passed to:

> "deal with offenders against Article 9 of the Constitution, which lays down the citizen's fundamental duty of fidelity and loyalty."

He had previously said in the same judgment - an *obiter dictum*, and an objectionable one[23] - that there was:

> "much to be said for the view that the citizen engaged in activities conflicting with that fidelity and loyalty commits a misdemeanour, for which he is liable to prosecution under the criminal law."

In 1986, Article 9 was cited in two challenges to the Irish Nationality and Citizenship Act 1956. In *Pok Sun Shum v Ireland*[24] the first-named plaintiff, an alien, had had his application for a certificate of naturalisation refused and was informed that he must leave the country. He argued, *inter alia*, that ss 15 and 16 of the 1956 Act were repugnant to Article 9 in that they discriminated against the exercise of the rights of his wife, the second-named plaintiff, who was an Irish citizen. Costello J rejected this, saying:

> "The rights given by Article 9 are rights given to all persons, so that no person can be excluded from Irish nationality by reason of the sex of such person. No right of the [second-named] plaintiff herself is being infringed by ss 15 or 16 of the Act. And, assuming that the first-named plaintiff can claim rights under the Constitution, no rights conferred by Article 9 on him are infringed by ss 15 and 16. These sections do not require or permit the Minister to exclude the plaintiff from Irish citizenship by reason of his sex."

The judge noted that under the 1956 Act the Minister for Justice was *empowered* to confer a benefit or privilege on an alien who had applied for a certificate of naturalisation, and that the granting of such a certificate was not a mandatory consequence once an alien had satisfied certain conditions. Consequently the Minister was not obliged to give reasons as to why an application for naturalisation was being refused. In a similar case, *Osheku v Ireland*,[25] Gannon J rejected the plaintiffs' contention that ss 8 and 16 were repugnant to Article 9 on the ground that the Minister had, at the time of the hearing, not yet made any ruling upon the first-named plaintiff's application for a certificate of natu-

[21] [1952] IR 62; (1951) 85 ILTR 22.

[22] [1940] IR 136; (1940) 74 ILTR 36, 131.

[23] Because of the vagueness and uncertainty of the standard. He did, however, add that he thought it would be "difficult or impossible, for a man to engage in activities calculated to prejudice the preservation of the peace, order or security of the State without offending the ordinary criminal law". The suggestion about a misdemeanour presumably refers to the notion that a breach of statute law is a misdemeanour even without the creation of a specific statutory offence.

[24] [1986] IR 733; [1986] ILRM 593.

[25] [1986] ILRM 330.

ralisation and that the court could not be asked to assume that the application would be refused, nor to speculate upon the grounds upon which a refusal might be based. The judge added that affording an opportunity to an alien to obtain the benefit of naturalised citizenship was no more than a privilege which need not be availed of.

In both cases, the respective judges rejected the argument that a male alien, who was otherwise liable to deportation, could acquire an immunity from such deportation if he married an Irish citizen. Costello J expressed the view that the Minister's power to order deportation in such circumstances was a permissible restriction on the rights of the family.

In relation to this last point, these cases must now be read in the light of the Supreme Court decision in *Fajujonu v Minister for Justice*[26] which, while it does not deny the Minister's power to deport aliens who are married to, or are parents of, Irish citizens, does stipulate somewhat demanding conditions which must be satisfied before that power may lawfully be exercised. The plaintiffs were a husband, wife and daughter, of whom only the latter had Irish citizenship.[27] They were appealing against Barrington J's dismissal of their claim in which they sought an order restraining the defendants from prohibiting them from continuing to reside in the State, a declaration that they were entitled to reside in the State, or alternatively, a declaration that the Aliens Act 1935 was inconsistent with the Constitution to the extent to which it authorised the defendants to deport the plaintiffs, and, finally, an order directing the Minister to grant the first two plaintiffs a visa entitling them to remain within the State for as long as they were members of the family unit, owing parental duties to care for and maintain the third plaintiff.

Judgments were delivered by both Finlay CJ and Walsh J, with both of whom the other three members of the Court concurred. Finlay CJ ruled that the children, as citizens, had a constitutional right to the company, care and parentage of their parents within the family unit and that while the first two plaintiffs could not themselves claim any constitutional right to remain in Ireland, they were entitled to assert a choice of residence on behalf, and in the interest, of their infant children. In view of these constitutional rights, the Minister could lawfully order the deportation of the family only where his decision was based on a "grave and substantial reason associated with the common good." As there was no basis for concluding that the Minister would exercise his discretion under the 1935 Act other than in accordance with fair procedures and having regard to the rights identified by the Court, the Chief Justice dismissed the appeal.

Walsh J reached a similar conclusion, though by a slightly different route. He held that the first two plaintiffs and their children constituted a family within the meaning of the Constitution and that the children were entitled to the care, protection and society of their parents within this family group which was resident in the State. Unlike Finlay CJ, therefore, Walsh J appears to leave open the possibility that the parents may be able to acquire constitutional rights themselves, rather than simply being allowed to assert such rights on behalf of their children. In the circumstances of the present case, to move to expel the parents would, according to Walsh J, be inconsistent with the provisions of Article 41 guaranteeing the integrity of the family. Before the Minister could lawfully deport the plaintiffs under the 1935 Act he would have to be satisfied:

[26] [1990] 2 IR 151; [1990] ILRM 234.

[27] After the institution of proceedings, two further children were born in Ireland to the first two plaintiffs.

> "for stated reasons, that the interests of the common good of the people of Ireland and of the protection of the State and its society are so predominant and so overwhelming in the circumstances of the case that an action which can have the effect of breaking up this family is not so disproportionate to the aim sought to be achieved as to be unsustainable."

Both judges emphasised in their respective judgments that the family in the instant case had been resident in the State for some time and had made its home here. However, given that citizens cannot be deported, it may be impossible to deny the benefits of this ruling in *Fajujonu* to a family which has not yet put down roots in the State but one of whose children is born here. Furthermore, though the bond between the aliens and the citizens in this family was especially strong because of the physical dependency of the young children on their parents, the reasoning in *Fajujonu* may also be applicable to the childless marriage of an alien and a citizen,[28] unless one is prepared to argue that one spouse is not constitutionally entitled to the society of his/her partner.[29]

On the basis of existing authority, the separation of the parents could affect the ability of the alien partner to resist deportation. In *Fajujonu,* Walsh J was careful to distinguish the facts of the instant case from those in *The State (Bouzagou) v The Station Sergeant, Fitzgibbon St. Garda Station*[30] in which Barrington J held that, because of the separation of the family - the wife had obtained a barring order against the prosecutor - the husband could not automatically claim the rights guaranteed to the family under Article 41. In that case, the alien did not have custody of any of the children and so the outcome would, no doubt, be quite different if the alien, though separated, had custody of one or more children of the marriage where such children were also citizens.

The right to a passport

The question of the entitlement of an Irish citizen to an Irish passport may be mentioned here. No Irish statute (and no pre-1922 statute remaining in force) defines a passport or regulates the granting of passports; as Finlay P said in *The State (M.) v Attorney General,*[31] "the granting or withholding of a passport does not appear to be of statutory origin but would appear to have originally derived from the Crown prerogative". The function is however noticed in the Ministers and Secretaries Act 1924, where the business of the Department of External Affairs (now Foreign Affairs) is stated by s 1(xi) to include "the granting of passports and of *visas* to passports".[32] Prior to *Webb v Ireland*[33] this function would have been regarded as a power derived from the old royal prerogative[34] but this analysis is no longer appropriate. Instead it is probably better to consider

[28] In *Murray v Ireland* [1985] IR 532; [1985] ILRM 533, Costello J accepted that such a family enjoyed the protection of Article 41 of the Constitution. This point was not addressed by the Supreme Court in the subsequent appeal - [1991] ILRM 465.

[29] The assumption here, of course, is that the marriage is bona fide and not one entered into simply in order to obtain citizenship or residency rights. Such a sham marriage would not satisfy the definition of marriage set down by Costello J in *Murray v Ireland* [1985] IR 532; [1985] ILRM 542, namely, a "partnership based on an irrevocable personal consent given by both spouses which establishes a unique and very special life-long relationship."

[30] [1986] ILRM 98.

[31] [1979] IR 73.

[32] The only statutory reference to passports, apart from this Act appears to be in the Spanish Civil War (Non-Intervention) Act 1937.

[33] [1988] IR 353; [1988] ILRM 565.

[34] Thus Kelly records that from the inception of the State up to 1936, Irish passports were issued in the name of the King. See "*Hidden Treasure and the Constitution*" (1988) 10 DULJ 5 (n.s.), at pp.12-13.

the function as an aspect either of the State's duty to respect the personal right to travel, or of State sovereignty or, finally, of the State's executive power which, pursuant to Article 28.1, is exercisable by or on the authority of the Government.

The practice observed in this matter is all of administrative origin; according to this administrative practice, Irish passports are never issued to non-citizens, so that citizenship is a precondition to the obtaining of a passport. While it may have been possible for the Department or Minister, in the days when the issuing of passports was regarded as a purely prerogative Act to exercise an arbitrary discretion in withholding them, this is certainly no longer so since *M.*'s case established that the right to travel outside the State - for which the holding of a valid passport is in practice indispensable - is one of the unenumerated personal rights of the citizen under Article 40.3. In that case what was at issue primarily was the constitutionality of a provision of the Adoption Act 1952, which effectively prevented a non-marital baby from being sent out of the country except in order to reside with its mother or one of its mother's relatives; and, secondarily, whether the Minister - in order to avoid abetting an infringement of this provision - was entitled to withhold a passport from the infant. Finlay P held the provision invalid. The child's rights, he held, were exercisable via its mother, who wished the baby to be sent abroad to be brought up in the environment of its natural father's home by the natural father's parents; and in the circumstances of the case the child's welfare seemed better assured by this course, so that no ground for the interference of the Court (in the interest of the infant's welfare) was apparent. Accordingly the question whether the child, as a citizen, had a personal right (in the sense of the latent, unenumerated rights of Article 40.3) to travel arose squarely. Finlay P held that the citizen had such a right; though one necessarily limited by the State's inability to guarantee that a travelling citizen would be admitted into any other State.

He concluded that, as a corollary to the right to travel:

> "a citizen has, subject to the obvious conditions which may be required by public order and the common good of the State, the right to a passport permitting him or her to avail of such facilities as international agreements, existing at any given time, afford to the holder of such a passport."

He gave an instance (see immediately below) of a case where the withholding of a passport could be justified; but said that, apart from such cases, the right to travel with a passport existed. In addition:

> "such a right to travel, inextricably intertwined with the right to obtain a passport, has been recognised by the constitutional law of the United States of America in such cases as *Kent v Dulles.*[35] Furthermore, one of the hallmarks commonly accepted as dividing States which are categorised as authoritarian from those which are categorised as free and democratic is the inability of citizens or residents in the former to travel outside the country except at what is usually considered to be the whim of the executive power. I have no doubt therefore that a right to travel outside the State in the limited form in which I have already defined it - that is to say, a right to avail of such facilities as applied to the holder of an Irish passport at any given time - is a personal right of each citizen..."

He accordingly quashed the record of the Minister's decision to refuse a passport to the infant.

[35] 357 US 1 (1957).

Withholding of passport

The case mentioned by Finlay P as an instance where the Minister had a "clearly justified" discretion to withhold a passport was:

> "the most common in practice [namely] the existence of some undischarged obligation, by the person seeking a passport or seeking to use his passport, to the State, such as his having entered into a recognisance to appear before a criminal court for the trial of an offence."

Such a case may indeed be clear, as warranting the curtailment of a personal right. In practice, however, the Department withholds passports also from persons in other categories, for reasons some of which - like the failure to repay money advanced by Irish diplomatic missions abroad - seem very frail justification for effectively frustrating the exercise of this personal right - the more so when, as here, the decision as to who is or is not fit to hold a passport and travel abroad is taken not by a court but as an act of administrative discretion.[36]

Withdrawal of passport

The status of the right to travel abroad as a constitutional right, with implications for the right to hold a passport and not have it arbitrarily withdrawn, was recognised subsequently in *Lennon v Ganly and Fitzgerald*,[37] an action brought by a plaintiff to stop an Irish Rugby Football Union touring party to South Africa from associating itself with Ireland. In support of his application, the plaintiff contended that the proposed tour amounted to a breach of the Constitution, and in particular, Article 29 thereof. O'Hanlon J, finding that there was no illegality in the proposed tour, said:

> "The defendants, and the players who are participating in the tour, have a prima facie constitutional right to travel abroad for the purpose of taking part in sporting fixtures in other countries as well as in Ireland if they wish to do so. They should only be restrained from exercising such right if it was in some way unlawful for them to act in the manner in which they seek to act."[38]

Irish passports carry the statement that "This passport remains the property of the Minister for Foreign Affairs and may be withdrawn at any time"; but as the substance of the passport resides not in its intrinsic value but in its being, for local considerations of security, indispensable for admission to virtually all other States, and as its physical

[36] The then Minister for Foreign Affairs (Deputy Michael O'Kennedy) said in answer to questions in the Dáil on 22 November 1978 that "successive Governments" had "regarded the right of Irish nationals to travel abroad as a personal right", but subject to certain limitations which he outlined rather vaguely. He said: "Passports are refused on legal grounds, such as a court order or refusal of parents' consent in the case of minors. A passport may also be refused to an applicant who, in the experience of the Passport Office arising out of passport facilities granted in the past, is an unfit person to hold another passport at the time of application." He gave instances of the latter category: persons who had not refunded money advanced to them by the Department while abroad, or who had already lost "three or four" passports. On 11 October 1978 he had already told the Dáil that passports were refused to Irish citizens resident in Rhodesia who "furthered or encouraged" the illegal regime there. See 309 *Dáil Debates* 1563; and 308 *Dáil Debates* 37-8.

[37] [1981] ILRM 84.

[38] The Minister for Foreign Affairs (Deputy Brian Lenihan) said around this time that although he deplored the tour, the passports of the players and officials would not be withdrawn: "In our democracy. there are limits to what the State or the Government can do, as the people have legal and constitutional rights" *(The Irish Times*, 30 March 1981). *The Irish Times*, 16 July 1977, contains a report of a case in which a petitioning creditor apparently requested the Department of Foreign Affairs to withdraw the bankrupt debtor's passport. Hamilton J asked the creditor's solicitor: "On what basis is anyone entitled to write to Foreign Affairs to withdraw the passport of an Irish citizen?" The solicitor replied that there were "precedents" and that "the passport would be handed in to the Official Assignee to ensure that a person did not leave the country without the consent of the court". The statutory authority for this proceeding is not apparent.

withdrawal in assertion of the Minister's property right thus effectively frustrates the citizen's right to travel abroad, it can hardly be - any more than in the case of refusing to issue a passport in the first instance - a matter of pure ministerial discretion to impose so drastic a sanction.

The power of the Minister to cancel a passport did feature in *P.I. v Ireland*[39] where the applicant sought an order of mandamus directing the Minister for Foreign Affairs to cancel his estranged wife's passport on which, he alleged, his child's name had been fraudulently entered. His wife had already left the jurisdiction for Canada and it was frankly admitted that these proceedings were taken in an attempt to improve the applicant's position with regard to custody proceedings which were pending before the Canadian courts. The Supreme Court refused to grant the order on the ground that the applicant had failed to show how this might improve his prospects of recovering custody and reserved its position as to whether the courts should in any circumstances direct the Minister to cancel a passport.

Summary of passport position

M.'s case appears to establish (a) that there is a personal, unenumerated right (in the sense of Article 40.3) of the citizen to travel outside the State; (b) that the exercise of this right is necessarily contingent on the willingness of other States to admit Irish citizens, which the Irish State is not obliged to ensure; (c) but that within the facilities actually available, the citizen is entitled to a passport if this is necessary in order to avail of them, though (d) that entitlement remains subject to an administrative discretion exercisable only in the interest of the common good and public order. The latter general standards must await another case for more concrete formulation in the context of the right to a passport.[40]

Children's passports

The issuing of passports for children is a special case. Section 40 of the Adoption Act 1952, provides that a child who is an Irish citizen under seven years of age may not be removed from the State without "the approval of a parent, guardian or relative of the child" (these alternatives being obviously applicable only in the sequence in which they are mentioned). Section 6(1) of the Guardianship of Infants Act 1964, however, constitutes the father and mother "guardians of the infant jointly"; so that (unless the High Court otherwise directs, in exercise of the jurisdiction created by s 11(10) of the Act) the removal of an infant under seven from the State will require the approval of both parents; and even in the case of older infants, the practice of the Department of Foreign Affairs - according to the evidence accepted by McWilliam J in *Cosgrave v Ireland*[41] - is to "require the written consent of both parents for the issue of passports to children under the age of sixteen years". In that case the plaintiff recovered damages from the State because, although he had indicated his objection to the issue of passports, the Department had issued them at the instance of his estranged wife, who had then taken his two small children to Holland and kept them there.

[39] [1989] IR 386; [1989] ILRM 810.

[40] As the practice surrounding passports has its origin in the royal prerogative, a modern British authority may be instructive: see Wade and Bradley, *Constitutional and Administrative Law,* (10th ed., 1985), p 444: "A passport merely provides *prima facie* evidence of status from which the duty of allegiance and possibly the protection of the Crown may flow... In the United Kingdom passports are issued... under the royal prerogative. A passport may be refused, withdrawn or revoked by the Crown at its absolute discretion." This statement could not be applied to Ireland without the radical qualification which constitutional values here would involve.

[41] [1982] ILRM 48.

Article 10

NATURAL RESOURCES AND STATE PROPERTY

Article 10.

1. **All natural resources, including the air and all forms of potential energy, within the jurisdiction of the Parliament and Government established by this Constitution and all royalties and franchises within that jurisdiction belong to the State subject to all estates and interests therein for the time being lawfully vested in any person or body.**
2. **All land and all mines, minerals and waters which belonged to Saorstát Éireann immediately before the coming into operation of this Constitution belong to the State to the same extent as they then belonged to Saorstát Éireann.**
3. **Provision may be made by law for the management of the property which belongs to the State by virtue of this Article and for the control of the alienation, whether temporary or permanent, of that property.**
4. **Provision may also be made by law for the management of land, mines, minerals and waters acquired by the State after the coming into operation of this Constitution and for the control of the alienation, whether temporary of permanent, of the land, mines, minerals and waters so acquired.**

Airteagal 10.

1. **Gach ábhar maoine nádúrtha, maraon leis an aer agus gach ábhar fuinnimh, dá bhfuil faoi dhlínse na Parlaiminte agus an Rialtais a bhunaítear leis an mBunreacht seo, maille le gach ríchíos agus díolúine dá bhfuil faoin dlínse sin, is leis an Stát iad uile, gan dochar do cibé eastáit agus leasanna is le haon duine nó le haon dream go dleathach in alt na huaire.**
2. **Gach talamh agus gach mianach, mianra, agus uisce ba le Saorstát Éireann díreach roimh theacht i ngníomh don Bhunreacht seo is leis an Stát iad uile sa mhéid go mba le Saorstát Éireann an uair sin iad.**
3. **Féadfar socrú a dhéanamh le dlí chun bainistí a dhéanamh ar an maoin is leis an Stát de bhua an Airteagail seo, agus chun sannadh buan nó sannadh sealadach na maoine sin a rialú.**
4. **Féadfar socrú a dhéanamh le dlí, fairis sin, chun bainistí a dhéanamh ar thalamh, ar mhianaigh, ar mhianraí agus ar uiscí a thiocfas seibh an Stáit d'éis teacht i ngníomh don Bhunreacht seo, agus chun sannadh buan nó sannadh sealadach na talún, na mianach, na mianraí agus na n-uiscí a thiocfas ina sheilbh amhlaidh a rialú.**

1922 provision

This replaced Article 11 of the 1922 Constitution, which read:

> "All the lands and waters, mines and minerals, within the territory of [Saorstát Éireann] hitherto vested in the State, or any department thereof, or held for the public use or benefit, and also all the natural resources of the same territory (including the air and all forms of potential energy), and also all royalties and franchises within that territory shall, from and after the date of the coming into operation of this Constitution, belong to [Saorstát Éireann], subject to any trusts, grants, leases or concessions then existing in respect thereof, or any valid private interest therein,

> and shall be controlled and administered by the Oireachtas, in accordance with such regulations and provisions as shall be from time to time approved by legislation, but the same shall not, nor shall any part thereof, be alienated, but may in the public interest be from time to time granted by way of lease or licence to be worked or enjoyed under the authority and subject to the control of the Oireachtas: Provided that no such lease or licence may be made for a term exceeding ninety-nine years, beginning from the date thereof, and no such lease or licence may be renewable by the terms thereof."

Reach of the Article: Mines, minerals, artefacts

Both the first section of Article 10, and the opening words of the old Article 11, echo the "Democratic Programme" of the First Dáil, which declared that "the Nation's sovereignty" extended "to all its material possessions, the Nation's soil and all its resources, all the wealth and all the wealth-producing processes". Even though the final phrases are not reproduced in the English text, they seem not far away from the Irish phrase "gach ábhar maoine nádúrtha" (literally, "every material of natural wealth").[1]

According to the majority of the Supreme Court in *Webb v Ireland,*[2] Article 10 embraces not only natural resources but artefacts as well. In this case, Article 10.1 was pressed in aid by the majority in order to salvage from the wreckage of the royal prerogative, which according to the court failed to survive the enactment of the Constitution of Saorstát Éireann,[3] a concept akin to the prerogative of treasure trove. Finlay CJ interpreted the phrase "all royalties" in Article 10.1 somewhat broadly, holding that it encompassed the notion of the sovereignty of the State. An inherent attribute of this concept in turn was the entitlement of the State to the ownership of antiquities of importance which have no known owner.[4] This reasoning does seem somewhat strained, almost metaphysical and both Walsh and McCarthy JJ dissented on this point.[5] After comparing Article 10 with Article 11 of the Free State Constitution and the Democratic Programme of 1919, Walsh J rejected the view that the phrase "all natural resources" in Article 10 included artefacts. As for the expression "royalties", that referred to the sums paid or payable for the use or exploitation of natural resources. He continued:

> "To equate the word "royalties" in the context in which it appears in Article 10 with the sovereignty or the sovereign authority of the State would be to say that the sovereignty of the State is conferred by Article 10 whereas it is asserted and declared by Article 5 of the Constitution."

[1] This probable inspiration of the old Article 11 was acknowledged by Kingsmill Moore J in *In re Irish Employers' Mutual Insurance Association* [1955] IR 176. See also the comments of Walsh J in *Webb v Ireland* [1988] IR 353 at 391; [1988] ILRM 565 at 602.

[2] [1988] IR 353; [1988] ILRM 565.

[3] On the face of it, this conclusion seems difficult to reconcile with the terms of Article 49.1 which vests in the people, *inter alia*, all prerogatives exercisable in or in respect of Saorstát Éireann immediately before December 11, 1936. On this point, Finlay CJ simply held that the royal prerogative was not captured by Article 49.1 but did not offer any interpretation of the term "prerogative" in that Article. For a critical comment on this, see Kelly, "*Hidden Treasure and the Constitution*" (1988) 10 DULJ (n.s.) 1, at p.14.

[4] The current legislative provision on the preservation of national monuments is contained in the National Monuments (Amendment) Act 1987. Kelly argued that, as a corollary of Finlay CJ's judgment, the concept of "national heritage" would limit the range of antiquities to which this entitlement would extend - *loc. cit.*, pp.17-19. *Pace* Kelly, however, the accuracy or otherwise of this prediction depends on how one understands "national heritage" and on this point the *Webb* case offers little guidance.

[5] John Kelly also preferred the minority viewpoint - *loc. cit.* at p.17. However, as Byrne and Binchy point out, the Chief Justice's analysis has the advantage over that of the minority of providing a continuity from 1922 to the present day - see *Annual Review of Irish Law 1987*, (1988) at p.105.

Article 10 speaks only of natural resources "within the jurisdiction, etc." and thus seems to forbear any claim to resources outside that limit as it was understood in 1937. However, provision in regard to the "continental shelf"[6] was in fact made by the Continental Shelf Act 1968, s 2, which vests the rights of the State in that matter of exploring and exploiting the continental shelf in the Minister for Transport, Energy and Communication.

Not a "conveyancing disposition"

The provisions of Article 11 of the old Constitution were said by Fitzgibbon J in *Commissioners of Public Works v Mackey*[7] not to be:

> "a conveyancing disposition of property at all. [The Article] is a simple statement or provision that all the property of the Crown within the territory of the Free State, whether vested in the Crown, or in any Department of State, or held for the public use or benefit, shall in future be appropriated to the Free State. In other words, that "public use or benefit" which theretofore included all citizens of the United Kingdom, is now limited to the use or benefit of the citizens of the newly constituted Free State; but there is no divesting of the property theretofore vested in the departments who were the legal owners empowered to administer it for the public benefit."

Effect of the 1922 declaration of inalienable State ownership

In *Attorney General v McIlwaine*[8] the defendant, in resisting a claim that a piece of foreshore belonged to the State, alleged that he had acquired a prescriptive title to it; the High Court held against him, one of the two judges (Gavan Duffy J) basing his decision on Article 11 of the 1922 Constitution; the defendant, he held, had not completed the necessary period of sixty years when the Constitution came into force (6 December 1922):

> "All he had was the prospect of such an interest at the expiry of the sixty years. Therefore this land vested in the State from and after that date and could never be alienated. In my opinion, the Nullum Tempus Acts cannot prevail against the emphatic assertion of inalienable State ownership contained in Article 11. Consequently the defendant cannot be entitled to this property."

The Supreme Court, however, while affirming the decision of the High Court, expressly refrained from basing its own decision on Article 11; and a few years later, in *Linnane v Nestor*,[9] another case about prescriptive title to foreshore, Maguire P disagreed with what Gavan Duffy J had said:

> "The effect of [Article 11 of the 1922 Constitution] has not been argued before me. I do not consider, however, that it is at all inconsistent with that Article to hold that time which was running in favour of the defendant in respect of acts of ownership before 1922 was not interrupted by the coming into force of the Constitution of which that Article forms a part."

State-owned property now not inalienable

Article 10 of the present Constitution differs conspicuously from the old Article 11 in expressly envisaging the alienation of State property; and in *The State (Devine) v*

[6] See above, pp. 19-20.
[7] [1941] IR 207.
[8] [1939] IR 437; (1939) 73 ILTR 104. On this general subject, see Edward J Smyth, "*The Seashores of Ireland: Public Rights and Restrictions*" (1935).
[9] [1943] IR 208.

Larkin,[10] where the defendants pleaded that s 8 of the Foyle Fisheries Act 1952, contravened Article 10 because it vested State property in a foreign authority, McMahon J held that even if the effect of s 8 could be so construed, it was not unconstitutional:

> "I see nothing in the Constitution to preclude the Oireachtas from enacting a law making direct provision for the alienation of any particular State property. It was... suggested that the fact that an interest in the property was vested in the Ministry of Commerce for Northern Ireland amounted to an unconstitutional transfer of national territory to a foreign State, but it is clear that no infringement of territorial sovereignty is involved, and no authority was cited to establish that property rights in the State may not be acquired by a foreign State."

In that case McMahon J also pointed out that the Article empowers the Oireachtas to make laws to regulate the alienation of State property, and that this had been done by the State Property Act 1954.[11] In addition, the Foreshore Act 1933, provides for the making of leases of foreshore, something which, when enacted, was evidently not felt to be in conflict with the old Article 11.[12]

Acquisition of property by the State

The acquisition of property by the State is envisaged by several statutes, notably by Part III of the Minerals Development Act 1940; and in *Mahony v Neenan*[13] it was recognised by the High Court that the State can acquire property by a natural mode of acquisition, such as by becoming entitled to foreshore newly formed by the encroachment of the sea. That the State can acquire by purchase or by gift or legacy, as well as by forfeiture and as "ultimate intestate successor",[14] is undoubted.

Article 10 supports the view that the State is a juristic person capable of holding property.

Article 10 was used by Kingsmill Moore J in his review of the State's attributes in *Comyn v Attorney General;*[15] and by Kingsmill Moore J in *In re Irish Employers Mutual Insurance Association*;[16] Ó Dálaigh J in *Commissioners of Public Works v Kavanagh*[17] and Murnaghan J in *Byrne v Ireland*[18] to demonstrate that the State is a juristic person capable of holding property.

[10] [1977] IR 24.

[11] For another example of statutory regulation of the alienation of state property, see s 105 of the Housing Act 1966, which provides that housing authorities cannot make purchase schemes in respect of cottages situated on state-owned land.

[12] Leases and Licences under the Foreshore Act must, by s 20 of the Act, be detailed annually in a statement laid before each House of the Oireachtas. A simple and important instance of such a lease would be that made on 2 October 1968 to Gulf Oil Terminals (Ireland) Ltd. for ninety-nine years for the construction of an oil terminal at Whiddy Island, Co. Cork. Leasing powers - specifically related to Article 11 of the old Constitution and to the "public interest" - were conferred on Ministers also by the State Lands Act 1924; the State Lands (Work-Houses) Act 1930; and the Mines and Minerals Act 1931. In *Shanley v Commissioner of Public Works in Ireland* [1992] 2 IR 449, Carroll J held that the Landlord and Tenant Act 1931 did not apply to State property, which was subject to a completely separate statutory regime under the State Lands Act 1924.

[13] [1966] IR 599.

[14] Escheat, which figured in Part III of the State Property Act 1954, was abolished by s 11(3) of the Succession Act 1965; and is, together with *bona vacantia* (see e.g. *In the Goods of Doherty* [1961] IR 219) replaced by the concept of the State as "ultimate intestate successor : Succession Act 1965, s 73.

[15] [1950] IR 142; (1949) 83 ILTR 146.

[16] [1955] IR 176.

[17] [1962] IR 216; (1963) 97 ILTR 180.

[18] [1972] IR 241.

While Article 10 speaks of "property which belongs to the State", and while the State has been judicially recognised as "a juristic person capable of holding property", the legal owner of State property - for ordinary private-law purposes and for purposes of litigation - is not the State, i.e. Ireland, but a State authority.[19] The position in this regard can be summarised thus:

(a) Property rights which by virtue of Article 49 belong to the people are exercised, by s 27 of the State Property Act 1954, "by the Government through and by the Minister [for Finance]". A difficulty here, of course, is that both Article 49 and s 27 appear to have been premised on the belief that the royal prerogative survived the enactment of the Constitution of Saorstát Éireann, a view now rejected by the Supreme Court in *Webb*. It is not at all clear, therefore, which property rights are now governed by these provisions.

(b) All land which is State land[20] is vested, by the joint operation of ss 2(1) and 5 of the 1954 Act either in a Minister or in the Commissioners of Public Works; land falling to the State, nation or people and not specifically vested in another Minister or in the Commissioners, vests in the Minister for Finance.

(c) Property other than land (as defined by s 2(1) of the 1954 Act) is not contemplated by the Act. If such property is appurtenant to the function of a Government Department, it is the property of the Department's Minister (who is, by s 2(1) of the Ministers and Secretaries Act 1924, a corporation sole with perpetual succession). The Department itself is a mere administrative structure into which the Minister and his fellow-servants[21] are organised, and of which he is the head,[22] but which, unlike the pre-1922 Departments of Government in Ireland, has no legal personality of its own and cannot own property.

(d) Gifts of property, whether real or personal, to the State, the Nation or the People, are regulated by s 19 of the State Property Act 1954. The Government may accept or refuse to accept the gift; if accepted, the property is to "vest in such State authority as the Government shall by warrant determine".

The State's interest in mines and minerals, adverted to by Article 10.2.4, arises mainly from the operation of the Land Purchase code; s 13(3) of the Land Act 1903, and s 45(5) of the Land Act 1923, respectively reserved to the Land Commission the mining rights in respect of land sold by the Land Commission, and vested such rights in Saorstát Éireann where land was vested under the Act. Doubts[23] as to the extent of the effect of these Acts were by-passed by the enactment of the Minerals Development Act 1979, which, with certain clear exceptions, vests in the Minister for Transport, Energy and Communication the exclusive right to work all mineral resources in the State.

[19] In *Webb v Ireland* [1988] IR 353; [1988] ILRM 565, Walsh J said that "the effect of the Article is that the State is the *ultimate* owner of all of the matters therein mentioned". (Emphasis added.)

[20] Defined in s 2(1) of the State Property Act 1954.

[21] See *Carolan v Minister for Defence* [1927] IR 62; (1925) 59 ILTR 115; (1927) 61 ILTR 27.

[22] Ministers and Secretaries Act 1924, s 1.

[23] See the speech of the Minister for Industry, Commerce and Energy (Deputy O'Malley) on the Second Stage of the Minerals Development Bill 1979: 311 *Dáil Debates* 1507.

Article 11

THE CENTRAL FUND

Article 11
All revenues of the State from whatever source arising shall, subject to such exceptions as may be provided by law, form one fund, and shall be appropriated for the purposes and in the manner and subject to the charges and liabilities determined and imposed by law.

Airteagal 11
Ní foláir cíos uile an Stáit cibé bunadh atá leis, ach amháin an chuid sin de ar a ndéantar eisceacht le dlí, a chur in aon chiste amháin agus é a leithghabháil chun na gcríocha agus ar an modh, a chinntear le dlí agus faoi chuimsiú na muirear agus na bhféichiúnas a ghearrtar le dlí.

1922 provision

This Article is substantially identical with Article 61 of the Constitution of Saorstát Éireann. The Adaptation of Enactments Act 1922 (passed two weeks after that Constitution came into force) provided by s 1 that the fund mentioned in Article 61 should be known as "The Central Fund of Saorstát Éireann" (or "The Central Fund" for short), and that references in earlier British statutes to the Consolidated Fund should be taken, in their surviving application to Saorstát Éireann, to be references to the Central Fund. The fund mentioned in Article 11 of the 1937 Constitution is, by s 6(1) of the Constitution (Consequential Provisions) Act 1937, likewise "called and known as the Central Fund"; and the remainder of s 6 and also s 7 of the Act provide for the transformation of the Central Fund of Saorstát Éireann into the Central Fund of Ireland, and for the succession of the latter to the entitlements and liabilities of the former. These steps are briefly listed by Gavan Duffy J in *In re Irish Aero Club.*[1]

Article 11 demonstrates the end of the old regime

Article 11 was included by Maguire J, in *Attorney General v Crawford,*[2] in the list of Articles which he thought "clearly repugnant to the continued existence of 'The Crown' as an expression designating any function of Government in this State".

The character of the State

Article 11 was also used by Kingsmill Moore J in *Comyn v Attorney General*[3] in his review of the State's attributes; and by Murnaghan J in *Byrne v Ireland*[4] as a sufficient indication, in conjunction with Article 10, that the State was a juristic person capable of holding property.

Function of the Central Fund

The status of revenue passing, on collection, into the Central Fund, and the special character of this fund in the context of claims for repayment of revenue collected under statutory powers subsequently found to be invalid, were subsidiary but important issues in *Murphy v Attorney General,*[5] a case in which taxation provisions which bore more heavily on a married couple than on an unmarried couple were successfully challenged.

[1] [1939] IR 204.
[2] [1940] IR 335; (1940) 74 ILTR 140.
[3] [1950] IR 142; (1949) 83 ILTR 146.
[4] [1972] IR 241.
[5] [1982] IR 241.

When the Supreme Court sat to rule on matters ancillary to its main judgment, Henchy J, with whom in this area Griffin J agreed, said that the plaintiffs' rights in regard to repayment, notwithstanding that the Act now held invalid had been in force when they first paid tax as a married couple, did not begin until "the first year for which they effectively objected to the flow of those taxes into the Central Fund". Up to that year, he said:

> "the State was entitled, in the absence of any claim of unconstitutionality, to act on the assumption that the taxes in question were validly imposed, that they were properly transmissible to the Central Fund, and that from there they were liable to be expended, according to the will of Parliament, for the multiplicity of purposes for which drawings are made on the Central Fund of the State. Equally, every taxpayer whose income tax was deducted from his earnings throughout a particular tax year, no matter how grudgingly or unwillingly he allowed the deductions to be made from his weekly or monthly income, could not avoid having imputed to him the knowledge that the tax he was paying was liable to be immediately spent by the State. As time went by, his right to complain of the State's unjust enrichment ran the risk of being extinguished by laches on his part."

O'Higgins CJ said the provisions of Article 11 "must be taken as a matter of general knowledge";

> "any citizen who accepts such taxation laws as are in operation and who pays his taxes without protest does so in the full knowledge that as a member of the community he will share in the expenditure and derive a benefit from the Central Fund."

Accordingly, while the Court is willing to see a sum invalidly collected in tax, and flowing into the Central Fund, as an unjust enrichment, access to the appropriate remedy is qualified by the presumption that the taxpayer who fails to challenge the tax law at once knows (as Henchy J put it) "that tax payments are liable to be quickly absorbed into the financial system of the State, and not to be amenable to extraction and repayment without considerable disruption and unfairness". O'Higgins CJ dealt more briefly with the "disruption" point, but regarded the plaintiffs as debarred, by a form of estoppel, from recovering tax paid without challenge.

In *The State (Gilliland) v Governor of Mountjoy Prison*[6] Barrington J equated the "public funds" referred to in Article 29.5.2 with the Central Fund. He also held that supply services, the monies for the payment of which are authorised by the Oireachtas annually (rather than by permanent Acts of the Oireachtas), constituted charges on the Central Fund. It followed that an Extradition Treaty between Ireland and the USA, which obliged Ireland to meet certain expenses arising in the course of extradition proceedings, did impose a charge upon public funds and consequently should have been approved by the Dáil pursuant to Article 29.5.2.

In *Howard v The Commissioners of Public Works in Ireland*,[7] Costello J held that the grant by an Appropriation Act to a statutory body of money from the Central Fund to defray the charges of the services it provides does not empower that body to provide services which are not otherwise within its statutory powers, as ascertained from the legislation relating specifically to the body in question.

[6] [1986] ILRM 381.

[7] High Court, 12 February 1993. This point was not adverted to by any member of the Supreme Court in the subsequent appeal: [1993] ILRM 665.

Statutory provisions

Statutory provision as to issues out of the Central Fund, and borrowing, is made by the Central Fund (Permanent Provisions) Act 1965. By s 38(2) of the Finance Act 1924, debts due to the Central Fund formerly enjoyed a right of prior payment but the sub-section was modified virtually to the point of repeal by s 99 of the Finance Act 1963. To the extent that that subsection also exempted the Central Fund from the Statutes of Limitation, it was repealed by s 9 and Part III of the Schedule of the Statute of Limitations, 1957.

Exception to the requirement that all State revenue should form one fund

The constitutionality of s 2 of the Appropriation Act 1969, which empowers the Minister for Finance to place foreign loans on deposit abroad, pending their transfer to the Central Fund, was defended by the Attorney General in an opinion summarised by the Committee of Public Accounts in its Interim and Final Reports (Appropriation Accounts) 1969 - 70,[8] on the ground that such a provision was a legislative exception, permitted by Article 11, to the requirement that all revenues of the State should form one fund.

[8] Prl. 3609. See Casey, *The Office of the Attorney General in Ireland*, at p.85ff.

Article 12

THE PRESIDENT

PRESIDENT

Article 12.

1. There shall be a President of Ireland (Uachtarán na hÉireann), hereinafter called the President, who shall take precedence over all other persons in the State and who shall exercise and perform the powers and functions conferred on the President by this Constitution and by law.

2. 1° The President shall be elected by direct vote of the people.

   2° Every citizen who has the right to vote at an election for members of Dáil Éireann shall have the right to vote at an election for President.

   3° The voting shall be by secret ballot and on the system of proportional representation by means of the single transferable vote.

3. 1° The President shall hold office for seven years from the date upon which he enters upon his office, unless before the expiration of that period he dies, or resigns, or is removed from office, or becomes permanently incapacitated, such incapacity being established to the satisfaction of the Supreme Court consisting of not less than five judges.

   2° A person who holds, or who has held, office as President, shall be eligible for re-election to that office once, but only once.

   3° An election for the office of President shall be held not later than, and not earlier than the sixtieth day before, the date of the expiration of the term of office of every President, but in the event of the removal from office of the President or of his

AN tUACHTARÁN

Airteagal 12.

1. Beidh Uachtarán ar Éirinn (.i. Uachtarán na hÉireann), ar a dtugtar an tUachtarán sa Bhunreacht seo feasta; beidh tosach aige ar gach uile dhuine sa Stát, agus ní foláir dó na cumhachtaí agus na feidhmeanna a bheirtear don Uachtarán leis an mBunreacht seo agus le dlí a oibriú agus a chomhlíonadh.

2. 1° Le vóta lomdíreach an phobail a thoghfar an tUachtarán.

   2° Gach saoránach ag a bhfuil ceart vótála i dtoghchán do chomhaltaí de Dháil Éireann, beidh ceart vótála aige i dtoghchán don Uachtarán.

   3° Is le rúnbhallóid agus de réir na hionadaíochta cionúire agus ar mhodh an aonghutha inaistrithe a dhéanfar an vótáil.

3. 1° Beidh an tUachtarán i seilbh oifige go ceann seacht mblian ón lá a rachaidh i gcúram a oifige mura dtarlaí roimh dheireadh an téarma sin go n-éagfaidh nó go n-éireoidh as oifig nó go gcuirfear as oifig é, nó go ngabhfaidh míthreoir bhuan é agus go suífear sin go sásamh na Cúirte Uachtaraí agus í comhdhéanta de chúigear breitheamh ar a laghad.

   2° Duine atá nó a bhí ina Uachtarán, is intofa chun na hoifige sin é aon uair amháin eile, ach sin a mbeidh.

   3° Ní foláir togchán d'oifig an Uachtaráin a dhéanamh lá nach déanaí ná dáta dheireadh théarma oifige gach Uachtaráin ar leith agus nach luaithe ná an seascadú lá roimh an data sin, ach má chuirtear an tUachtarán as oifig, nó má tharlaíonn dó

death, resignation, or permanent incapacity established as aforesaid (whether occurring before or after he enters upon his office), an election for the office of President shall be held within sixty days after such event.

(roimh é a dhul i gcúram a oifige nó dá éis sin) é d'éag nó é d'éirí as nó míthreoir bhuan arna suíomh mar a dúradh dá ghabháil, ní foláir toghchán d'oifig an Uachtaráin a dhéanamh taobh istigh de sheasca lá tar éis an ní sin a tharlú.

4. 1° Every citizen who has reached his thirty-fifth year of age is eligible for election to the office of President.

2° Every candidate for election, not a former or retiring President, must be nominated either

i. by not less than twenty persons, each of whom is at the time a member of one of the Houses of the Oireachtas, or

ii. by the Councils of not less than four administrative Counties (including County Boroughs) as defined by law.

3° No person and no such Council shall be entitled to subscribe to the nomination of more than one candidate in respect of the same election.

4° Former or retiring Presidents may become candidates on their own nomination.

5° Where only one candidate is nominated for the office of President it shall not be necessary to proceed to a ballot for his election.

4. 1° Gach saoránach ag a bhfuil cúig bliana triochad slán, is intofa chun oifig an Uachtaráin é.

2° Gach iarrthóir d'oifig an Uachtaráin, seachas duine atá nó a bhí ina Uachtarán cheana, is uathu seo a leanas nach foláir a ainmniú a theacht:

i. fiche duine ar a laghad agus gach duine faoi leith díobh sin ina chomhalta, in alt na huaire, de Theach de Thithe an Oireachtais, nó

ii. Comhairlí ceithre Chontae riaracháin ar a laghad (agus Contae-Bhuirgí a áireamh) mar a mhínítear le dlí.

3° Ní cead d'aon duine ná d'aon Chomhairle díobh sin bheith páirteach in ainmniú breis is aon iarrthóir amháin d'oifig an Uachtaráin san aontoghchán.

4° Tig le haon duine atá nó a bhí ina Uachtarán é féin a ainmniú d'oifig an Uachtaráin.

5° Nuair nach n-ainmnítear d'oifig an Uachtaráin ach aon iarrthóir amháin, ní gá vótáil chun é a thoghadh.

5. Subject to the provisions of this Article, elections for the office of President shall be regulated by law.

5. Faoi chuimsiú forálacha an Airteagail seo is le dlí a rialófar toghcháin d'oifig an Uachtaráin.

6. 1° The President shall not be a member of either House of the Oireachtas.

2° If a member of either House of the Oireachtas be elected President, he shall be deemed to have vacated his seat in that House.

6. 1° Ní cead an tUachtarán a bheith ina chomhalta de Dháil Éireann ná de Sheanad Éireann.

2° Má thoghtar comhalta de cheachtar de Thithe an Oireachtais chun bheith ina Uachtarán, ní foláir a mheas go bhfuil scartha aige le comhaltas an Tí sin.

3° The President shall not hold any other office or position of emolument.

7. The first President shall enter upon his office as soon as may be after his election, and every subsequent President shall enter upon his office on the day following the expiration of the term of office of his predecessor or as soon as may be thereafter or, in the event of his predecessor's removal from office, death, resignation, or permanent incapacity established as provided by section 3 hereof, as soon as may be after the election.

8. The President shall enter upon his office by taking and subscribing publicly, in the presence of members of both Houses of the Oireachtas, of Judges of the Supreme Court and of the High Court, and other public personages, the following declaration:

"In the presence of Almighty God I do solemnly and sincerely promise and declare that I will maintain the Constitution of Ireland and uphold its laws, that I will fulfil my duties faithfully and conscientiously in accordance with the Constitution and the law, and that I will dedicate my abilities to the service and welfare of the people of Ireland. May God direct and sustain me."

9. The President shall not leave the State during his term of office save with the consent of the Government.

10. 1° The President may be impeached for stated misbehaviour.

2° The charge shall be preferred by either of the Houses of

3° Ní cead don Uachtarán aon oifig ná post sochair a bheith aige seachas a oifig Uachtaráin.

7. Ní foláir don chéad Uachtarán dul i gcúram a oifige chomh luath agus is féidir é tar éis é a thoghadh, agus ní foláir do gach Uachtarán dá éis sin dul i gcúram a oifige an lá i ndiaidh deireadh théarma oifige a réamhtheachtaí nó chomh luath agus is féidir é dá éis sin nó, má tharlaíonn dá réamhtheachtaí go gcuirfear as oifig é nó go n-éagfaidh nó go n-éireoidh as oifig nó neachtar acu go ngabhfaidh mithreoir bhuan é agus go suífear sin mar a shocraítear le halt 3 den Airteagal seo, chomh luath agus is féidir é tar éis an toghcháin.

8. Is é slí a rachaidh an tUachtarán i gcúram a oifige ná leis an dearbhú seo a leanas a dhéanamh go poiblí agus a lámh a chur leis i bhfianaise chomhaltaí den dá Theach den Oireachtas, agus breithiúna den Chúirt Uachtarach agus den Ard-Chúirt agus maithe poiblí eile:-

"I láthair Dia na nUile-chumhacht, táimse á ghealladh agus á dhearbhú go sollúnta is go fírinneach bheith i mo thaca agus i mo dhídin do Bhunreacht Éireann, agus a dlíthe a chaomhnú, mo dhualgais a chomhlíonadh go dílís coinsiasach de réir an Bhunreachta is an dlí, agus mo lándícheall a dhéanamh ar son leasa is fón-aimh mhuintir na hÉireann. Dia do mo stiúradh agus do mo chumhdach".

9. Ní cead don Uachtarán imeacht ón Stát le linn é a bheith in oifig, ach amháin le toil an Rialtais.

10. 1° Féadfar an tUachtarán a tháinseamh as ucht mí-iompair a luafar.

2° Ceachtar de Thithe an Oireachtais a dhéanfas an

the Oireachtas, subject to and in accordance with the provisions of this section.

3° A proposal to either House of the Oireachtas to prefer a charge against the President under this section shall not be entertained unless upon a notice of motion in writing signed by not less than thirty members of that House.

4° No such proposal shall be adopted by either of the Houses of the Oireachtas save upon a resolution of that House supported by not less than two-thirds of the total membership thereof.

5° When a charge has been preferred by either House of the Oireachtas, the other House shall investigate the charge, or cause the charge to be investigated.

6° The President shall have the right to appear and to be represented at the investigation of the charge.

7° If, as a result of the investigation, a resolution be passed supported by not less than two-thirds of the total membership of the House of the Oireachtas by which the charge was investigated, or caused to be investigated declaring that the charge preferred against the President has been sustained and that the misbehaviour, the subject of the charge, was such as to render him unfit to continue in office, such resolution shall operate to remove the President from his office.

11. 1° The President shall have an official residence in or near the City of Dublin.

2° The President shall receive such emoluments and allowances as may be determined by law.

3° The emoluments and allowances of the President shall

cúiseamh agus is faoi chuimsiú agus de réir forálacha an ailt seo a dhéanfar é.

3° Má thairgtear do cheachtar de Thithe an Oireachtais cúis a thabhairt in aghaidh an Uachtaráin faoin alt seo ní cead aird a thabhairt ar an tairiscint sin ach amháin de bharr fógra tairisceana i scríbhinn faoi láimh tríocha comhalta ar a laghad den Teach sin.

4° Ní cead do cheachtar de Thithe an Oireachtais glacadh le haon tairiscint den sórt sin ach amháin de bharr rúin ón Teach sin lena mbeidh tacaíocht dhá thrian ar a laghad dá lán-chomhaltas.

5° Má dhéanann ceachtar de Thithe an Oireachtais cúiseamh faoin alt seo ní foláir don Teach eile an chúis a scrúdú nó an chúis a chur á scrúdú.

6° Beidh de cheart ag an Uachtarán bheith i láthair agus lucht tagartha a bheith aige ar an scrúdú sin.

7° Más é toradh an scrúdaithe sin go rithfear rún, le tacaíocht dhá thrian ar a laghad de lán-chomhaltas an Tí den Oireachtas a scrúdaigh an chúis nó a chuir an chúis á scrúdú, á dhearbhú gur suíodh an chúis a tugadh in aghaidh an Uachtaráin agus, an mí-iompar ba shiocair don chúiseamh, gur mí-iompar é a bhfuil an tUachtarán neamhoir-iúnach dá dheasca chun fanacht i seilbh oifige, is é is feidhm don rún sin an tUachtarán a chur as oifig.

11. 1° Beidh stát-áras ag an Uachtarán i gcathair Bhaile Átha Cliath nó ar a cóngar.

2° Gheobhaidh an tUachtarán sochair agus liúntais faoi mar a chinnfear le dlí.

3° Ní cead laghdú a dhéanamh ar shochair ná ar liúntais an

not be diminished during his term of office.

Uachtaráin le linn é a bheith in oifig.

The Presidency - an innovation

The creation of the office of President is one of the most conspicuous innovations of the 1937 Constitution by comparison with that of 1922; under the old Constitution, the British Crown, in an exiguous and ultimately vestigial form, and represented until 1936 by a Governor-General,[1] had provided the ceremonial apex of the State. In *Attorney General v Crawford*[2] Hanna J said that:

> "having regard to [... Articles] 6, 12, 15, 25, 28, 30, the Crown, as such, has no place in our Constitution, but has been replaced by the President..."

In earlier editions of this book, this statement of Hanna J was criticised for being inaccurate, on the ground, *inter alia,* that it failed to take account of the continued existence of the royal prerogative which was previously understood to have vested in the people by virtue of Article 49. However this must now be read in the light of *Webb v Ireland*[3] wherein the Supreme Court held that this prerogative did not survive the enactment of the Constitution of Saorstát Éireann.[4]

It may, incidentally, be noted that Article 12 does not attempt to explain, in terms facilitating comparison with other States, what the President *is;* though often colloquially referred to as "Head of State", the Constitution avoids paraphrasing the office in that way (contrast Article 28.5.1, which describes the Taoiseach as "the head of Government, or Prime Minister"). This diffidence about explaining the status of the Presidency may have been related to the perception that the British Crown had a vestigial, but still real status here even after 1937, not finally swept away until the coming into force of the Republic of Ireland Act in 1949.[5]

Apprehensions about the Presidency turned out to be unfounded

The establishment of the office of President was perhaps the most contentious aspect of the draft Constitution when it was debated in the Dáil in May and June 1937. The apprehensions of the Opposition at that time related to the possibility of the Presidency evolving into a dictatorship. In fact, the precedence accorded to the President by Article 12.1 is a purely ceremonial one;[6] and the powers conferred upon the President by law, additional to those specified in the Constitution, are few and insignificant.[7]

[1] The "Representative of the Crown": Article 60, deleted in 1936 by the Constitution (Amendment No.27) Act. Other references to this office had been previously removed. See above, in the Preface.

[2] [1940] IR 335; (1940) 74 ILTR 140.

[3] [1988] IR 353; [1988] ILRM 565.

[4] Though for criticism of this conclusion, see Kelly, "*Hidden Treasure and the Constitution*" (1988) 10 DULJ 5 (n.s.) at pp.7-141. See also Lenihan, "*Royal Prerogatives and the Constitution*" (1989) 24 Ir Jur (n.s.) 1.

[5] But see now *Webb v Ireland* [1988] IR 353; [1988] ILRM 565, considered above at pp. 31-33.

[6] It scarcely needs to be said that the flattering titles sometimes bestowed on the Presidency - "guardian of the Constitution", "guardian of the people's rights" and so on - are pure journalistic hyperbole. The Constitution nowhere describes the Presidency in such terms, and is extremely sparing in its attribution of any independent functions to the office at all. The only possible basis for describing the office in such a way - the rarely-used machinery of Article 26 - is in fact arguably inimical to the upholding of constitutional values, since a Bill, once cleared under the Article 26 procedure and passing into law, can by Article 34.3.3 never again be challenged, even though conditions (including the climate of public and judicial opinion) may have changed, or the working of the law may have disclosed objectionable results not foreseen at the time of the Article 26 reference. See below, p. 218.

[7] See below, p. 97.

Presidential elections

For the right to vote at a Dáil election (on which the right to vote at a Presidential election depends) see below, pp. 152-155. For the secret ballot, see below, pp. 155-158: and for the system of proportional representation by means of the single transferable vote, see below, p. 161. In the latter connection it may be noted that where, as here, an election is for a single seat or office the expression "proportional representation" is hardly apposite; the simplest comparison is with a by-election to fill a single vacant seat held in a constituency which, at a General Election, returns three or more members to Dáil Éireann.

In consequence of the amendment of Article 16,[8] which empowers the Oireachtas to confer the right to vote in Dáil elections on certain non-nationals resident in the State, s 4 of the Electoral (Amendment) Act 1985, now creates a new category of voter, known as a "presidential elector". This rather confusingly-named category really means all Irish citizens on the electoral register, and is so called because Irish citizens (unlike non-citizens, whose franchise is confined to Dáil elections, local elections, and elections to the European Parliament if they are citizens of member states of the European Community) can vote not only in these but in presidential elections and referenda as well.

The Presidency to date

Seven persons have so far occupied the office of President;[9] of the former Presidents, two served two terms, one served one term, one died in office, and one resigned.[10] Presidents were elected without a ballot (there being only one candidate) in 1938, 1952, 1974, 1976 and 1983. The impeachment procedure provided for by Article 12.10 has never been invoked; it may however be noted that it provides an exception, built into the Constitution itself and so invulnerable, from the general rules of Articles 34 to 38, which otherwise would certainly require a charge of stated misbehaviour - serious enough to warrant removing a President from office - to be tried by a court.[11]

Casus omissi in provisions on the Presidency

Unlike the specific provisions of the Constitution for the resignation of other holders of constitutional office, or of members of either House of the Oireachtas, there is no provision in Article 12 designating the mode of the President's resignation, though this step is expressly mentioned in Articles 12.3 and 12.7, so is evidently permissible.[12] The Constitution also does not provide for the *replacement* of the President in events other

[8] See below, p. 149.

[9] Dr. Douglas Hyde (Dubhghlas de hÍde), 1938-45; Seán T. O'Kelly, 1945-59; Éamon de Valera, 1959-73; Erskine Childers, 1973-74; Cearbhall Ó Dálaigh (former Chief Justice), 1974-76: Dr. Patrick Hillery, 1976-1990; and the present incumbent, Mary Robinson, who was elected in 1990.

[10] President Childers died after a year and a half in office; President Ó Dálaigh resigned after two years in office. For an account of the events leading up to the resignation of President Ó Dálaigh and the implications for constitutional conventions, see Gwynn Morgan, "*The Emergency Powers Bill Reference - I*" (1978) 13 Ir Jur (n.s.) 67, at 67-76.

[11] Another apparent exception, rather like the provision of Article 12.10, is that of Article 15.13, making a member of the Houses of the Oireachtas "amenable" only to his own House in respect of his utterances in the House.

[12] President Ó Dálaigh (who had formerly been Chief Justice) resigned on 22 October 1976 by "executing an instrument" (the press statement said "rinne sé gníomhas faoina láimh agus faoina shéala") to that effect. He transmitted copies to the Presidential Commission (see Article 14) which was to perform the President's duties until a successor was elected; and sent courtesy copies to the Taoiseach, the Tánaiste and the Leader of the Opposition.

than those specified in Article 12.7 (e.g. his disappearance or kidnapping); though his *functions*, in that event, would be discharged by the Presidential Commission which can act in the event of his mere absence.[13] These lacunae would not appear capable of being filled by the Council of State under Article 14.4, as the Council's contingency powers relate only to "the exercise and performance of the powers and functions conferred on the President by or under this Constitution".

Nomination process

The nomination requirement prescribed by Article 12.4.2 has the almost inevitable consequence of preventing the emergence of non-party candidates for election. In *Lennon v Minister for the Environment*[14] an injunction to prevent the 1990 presidential election from taking place was sought on the ground that this requirement was contrary to the common good. The action was dismissed by Egan J because of the plaintiff's delay in initiating it and no opinion was expressed on the substance of the argument. However, it would appear to have little merit.

"Own nomination"

The provision of Article 12.4.4 that former or retiring Presidents may become candidates (for re-election) on their own nomination was interpreted by one President[15] as being an optional facility rather than a direction.

Presidential oath

It is worth noting in passing that the Human Rights Committee of the United Nations recently indicated that the religious flavour of the Presidential oath violated Article 18 of the International Covenant on Civil and Political Rights on freedom of thought, conscience and religion.[16]

The President may hold other (honorary) office

The prohibition of Article 12.6.3 on the President's holding "any other office or position of emolument" has been interpreted in practice in a way which relates the phrase "of emolument" to "office" as well as to "position", as the Red Cross Act 1944, makes the President *ex officio* honorary President of the Irish Red Cross Society; no constitutional objection has been raised against this provision. The analogous provision of Article 35.3 about judges has been similarly interpreted in practice.[17]

Legal personality of the President: capacity in regard to holding property

The precise dimensions of the President's legal personality have not yet been explored. Unlike Ministers in charge of Departments, who by s 2 of the Ministers and Secretaries Act 1924, are corporations sole (thus having the capacity to hold property) and can sue and be sued as such, the President's civil capacity is nowhere defined. The President appears in current practice to hold, *qua* President, no property; the office is not mentioned in the State Property Act 1954; the official residence in Dublin, referred to in Article 12.11.1, is provided and maintained for the President by the Minister for Finance

[13] Article 14. See below, p. 99.

[14] *The Irish Times,* October 23, 1990.

[15] President de Valera, on standing for re-election in 1966, was nominated by twenty members of the Oireachtas.

[16] *The Irish Times*, 15 July 1993.

[17] See below, p. 550.

(Presidential Establishment Act 1938, s 2); gifts or bequests to the President, other than tokens of courtesy, seem to be appropriated by the same Minister.[18] But this does not seem to answer the fundamental question whether the President, as such, can hold property. Suppose a President devoted some part of the official allowance, other than that attributable to personal remuneration, to acquiring some permanent and substantial embellishment for the official residence, such as a statue or picture, would the President as such own it?

Litigation

For purposes of litigation the President is accorded a qualified personality by the Constitution, even if with partly negative effect, inasmuch as Article 13.8.1 confers immunity on the President from ordinary processes of law in respect of the exercise or purported exercise of the powers and functions of the Presidency (thus implying that, were it not for this special provision, the President has the capacity to be sued or prosecuted); while Article 12.10 creates the unique process of impeachment for stated misbehaviour, thus imputing to the office-holder a capacity for quasi-criminal purposes. The President's position as a potential civil plaintiff can only be conjectured; presumably, in the event that the allowances provided for by law (envisaged by Article 12.11.2) were not paid, he might bring proceedings *qua* President to recover them. Conceivably, if the President were obstructed in the performance of official functions (although this, if done by force or intimidation, is an offence under s 8 of the Offences against the State Act 1939), he might, *qua* President, bring proceedings for an injunction to restrain the interference.

Conflict of texts

As to an apparent conflict between the Irish and English texts of Article 12.4.1 relating to the age of qualifying to be a Presidential candidate, see below, p. 210.

Statutory provision

Statutory provision for Presidential elections is made by the Presidential Elections Acts, 1937 to 1973, and the Electoral Act 1963;[19] and for the President's emoluments and allowances by the Presidential Establishment Acts, 1938 to 1991.

German influence?

For the possible influence of the German Constitution of 1919 on the office of President, see below, pp. 97-98.

[18] An informal enquiry on this point proved difficult to pursue, encountering a delicate reticence in the Department of Finance.

[19] A possible *casus omissus* here is that Presidential elections do not appear to come within the scope of the Trade Union Act 1913, which places certain restrictions on the freedom of trade unions to engage in political activity. Thus a trade union can arguably contribute to the election campaign of a Presidential candidate without having to comply with the terms of that Act.

Article 13

THE FUNCTIONS OF THE PRESIDENT

Article 13.

1. 1° The President shall, on the nomination of Dáil Éireann, appoint the Taoiseach, that is, the head of the Government or Prime Minister.

   2° The President shall, on the nomination of the Taoiseach with the previous approval of Dáil Éireann, appoint the other members of the Government.

   3° The President shall, on the advice of the Taoiseach, accept the resignation or terminate the appointment of any member of the Government.

2. 1° Dáil Éireann shall be summoned and dissolved by the President on the advice of the Taoiseach.

   2° The President may in his absolute discretion refuse to dissolve Dáil Éireann on the advice of a Taoiseach who has ceased to retain the support of a majority in Dáil Éireann.

   3° The President may at any time, after consultation with the Council of State, convene a meeting of either or both of the Houses of the Oireachtas.

3. 1° Every Bill passed or deemed to have been passed by both Houses of the Oireachtas shall require the signature of the President for its enactment into law.

   2° The President shall promulgate every law made by the Oireachtas.

4. The supreme command of the Defence Forces is hereby vested in the President.

5. 1° The exercise of the supreme command of the Defence Forces shall be regulated by law.

   2° All commissioned officers of the Defence Forces shall hold their commissions from the President.

Airteagal 13.

1. 1° Ceapfaidh an tUachtarán an Taoiseach .i. an Ceann Rialtais nó an Príomh-Aire, arna ainmniú sin ag Dáil Éireann.

   2° Arna n-ainmniú ag an Taoiseach, le comhaontú Dháil Éireann roimh ré, ceapfaidh an tUachtarán na comhaltaí eile den Rialtas.

   3° Ar chomhairle an Taoisigh ní foláir don Uachtarán glacadh le haon chomhalta den Rialtas d'éirí as oifig, nó comhalta ar bith den Rialtas a chur as oifig.

2. 1° Is é an tUachtarán, ar chomhairle an Taoisigh, a chomórfas agus a lánscoirfeas Dáil Éireann.

   2° Tig leis an Uachtarán, as a chomhairle féin, diúltú do Dháil Éireann a lánscor ar chomhairle Taoisigh nach leanann tromlach i nDáil Éireann de bheith i dtacaíocht leis.

   3° Tig leis an Uachtarán uair ar bith, tar éis comhairle a ghlacadh leis an gComhairle Stáit, ceachtar de Thithe an Oireachtais, nó iad araon, a chomóradh.

3. 1° Gach Bille a ritear nó a mheastar a ritheadh ag dhá Theach an Oireachtais ní foláir lámh an Uachtaráin a bheith leis chun é a achtú ina dhlí.

   2° Gach dlí dá ndéanfaidh an tOireachtas ní foláir don Uachtarán é a fhógairt.

4. Leis seo cuirtear na Fórsaí Cosanta faoi ard-cheannas an Uachtaráin.

5. 1° An t-ardcheannas ar na Fórsaí Cosanta is le dlí a rialófar an modh ar a n-oibreofar é.

   2° Is ón Uachtarán a bheidh a ghairm ag gach oifigeach gairme de na Fórsaí Cosanta.

6. **The right of pardon and the power to commute or remit punishment imposed by any court exercising criminal jurisdiction are hereby vested in the President, but such power of commutation or remission may, except in capital cases, also be conferred by law on other authorities.**

6. **Bheirtear don Uachtarán leis seo ceart maithiúnais, agus cumhacht chun maolaithe nó loghtha pionóis a ghearrtar ar dhaoine in aon chúirt dlínse coire, ach, taobh amuigh de chásanna breithe báis, féadfar an chumhacht maolaithe nó loghtha sin a thabhairt le dlí d'údaráis eile freisin.**

7. **1° The President may, after consultation with the Council of State, communicate with the Houses of the Oireachtas by message or address on any matter of national or public importance.**

2° The President may, after consultation with the Council of State, address a message to the Nation at any time on any such matter.

3° Every such message or address must, however, have received the approval of the Government.

7. **1° Tig leis an Uachtarán, tar éis comhairle a ghlacadh leis an gComhairle Stáit, teachtaireacht nó aitheasc a chur faoi bhráid Tithe an Oireachtais i dtaobh aon ní a bhfuil tábhacht náisiúnta nó tábhacht phoiblí ann.**

2° Tig leis an Uachtarán uair ar bith, tar éis comhairle a ghlacadh leis an gComhairle Stáit, aitheasc a chur faoi bhráid an Náisiúin i dtaobh aon ní den sórt sin.

3° Ach i ngach cás díobh sin ní foláir an Rialtas a bheith sásta roimh ré leis an teachtaireacht nó leis an aitheasc.

8. **1° The President shall not be answerable to either House of the Oireachtas or to any court for the exercise and performance of the powers and functions of his office or for any act done or purporting to be done by him in the exercise and performance of these powers and functions.**

2° The behaviour of the President may, however, be brought under review in either of the Houses of the Oireachtas for the purposes of section 10 of Article 12 of this Constitution, or by any court, tribunal or body appointed or designated by either of the Houses of the Oireachtas for the investigation of a charge under section 10 of the said Article.

8. **1° Níl an tUachtarán freagrach d'aon Teach den Oireachtas ná d'aon chúirt in oibriú is i gcomhlíonadh cumhachtaí is feidhmeanna a oifige ná in aon ghníomh dá ndéanann sé nó a bheireann le tuiscint gur gníomh é a dhéanann sé in oibriú agus i gcomhlíonadh na gcumhachtaí is na bhfeidhmeanna sin.**

2° Ach féadfar iompar an Uachtaráin a chur faoi léirmheas i gceachtar de Thithe an Oireachtais chun críocha alt 10 d'Airteagal 12 den Bhunreacht seo, nó ag aon chúirt, binse nó comhlacht a cheapfar nó a ainmneofar ag ceachtar de Thithe an Oireachtais chun cúis faoi alt 10 den Airteagal sin a scrúdú.

9. **The powers and functions conferred on the President by this Constitution shall be exercisable and performable by him only on**

9. **Taobh amuigh de chás dá socraítear leis an mBunreacht seo go ngníomhóidh an tUachtarán as a chomhairle féin,**

the advice of the Government, save where it is provided by this Constitution that he shall act in his absolute discretion or after consultation with or in relation to the Council of State, or on the advice or nomination of, or on receipt of any other communication from, any other person or body.

nó tar éis comhairle a ghlacadh leis an gComhairle Stáit, nó go ngníomhóidh sé i dtaobh ní a bhaineas leis an gComhairle Stáit, nó ar chomhairle nó ainmniú aon duine nó aon dream eile, nó ar aon scéala eile a fháil ó aon duine nó aon dream eile, is ar chomhairle an Rialtais amháin is cead don Uachtarán na cumhachtaí agus na feidhmeanna a bheirtear dó leis an mBunreacht seo a oibriú is a chomhlíonadh.

10. Subject to this Constitution, additional powers and functions may be conferred on the President by law.

11. No power or function conferred on the President by law shall be exercisable or performable by him save only on the advice of the Government.

10. Faoi chuimsiú an Bhunreachta seo féadfar tuilleadh cumhachtaí agus feidhmeanna a thabhairt don Uachtarán le dlí.

11. Ní cead don Uachtarán aon chumhacht ná feidhm dá mbronntar air le dlí a oibriú ná a chomhlíonadh ach amháin ar chomhairle an Rialtais.

The President and the Government

The functions of the President in regard to the appointment of, or the acceptance of the resignation of the Taoiseach or other members of the Government, being purely formal and without scope for discretion, have given rise to no problems. These functions have been regularly performed from time to time; as has, on three occasions - in May 1970, October 1990, and November 1991[1] - the function of terminating the appointment of a member of the Government (under Article 28.9.4) who did not resign on being requested by the Taoiseach to do so.

Summoning and dissolution of the Dáil

The summoning and dissolution of Dáil Éireann by the President has equally produced no problems. In regard, however, to the potentially very important discretion accorded to the President by Article 13.2.2 - apart from Article 26, practically the only independent function of political importance which the President has - a serious uncertainty seems to lurk in the sub-section, which only the fact that it has never yet been invoked has prevented from emerging clearly, namely: what is the test of the Taoiseach's having "ceased to retain the support of a majority"? Does this require a vote of no confidence or the loss of a vote of confidence? Would defeat on a major issue such as a budget fulfil the condition? Or may the Taoiseach calculate his loss of majority support by counting probable heads, without a confrontation in the Dáil division lobbies? What is the posi-

[1] Mr Haughey (Minister for Finance) and Mr Blayney (Minister for Agriculture) were dismissed in 1970. Mr Lenihan (Minister for Defence) in 1990; and Mr Reynolds (Minister for Finance) and Mr Flynn (Minister for the Environment) in 1991.

tion under this subsection of a Taoiseach who has never enjoyed the support of a majority, but has been let in (through abstentions) to lead a minority Government?[2]

It is arguable that the exercise of the Presidential discretion under Article 13.2.2 to refuse to dissolve the Dáil should not be limited to cases in which a formal vote of no confidence in the Taoiseach has been taken, for otherwise a Taoiseach who had lost the support of a majority of the Dáil could pre-empt such a vote and insist the President grant a dissolution in accordance with Article 13.2.1.[3]

No role in forming an alternative Government without general election

A misconception of the President's role is occasionally[4] apparent when, as in January and November 1982, Governments were defeated on major issues - a budget and a vote of no confidence respectively - so as to appear to have "ceased to retain the support of a majority in Dáil Éireann". This is the notion that, instead of dissolving the Dáil, the President can "send for" some Deputy other than the defeated Taoiseach and "ask him to form a Government". This idea appears to have infiltrated the political and journalistic subconscious, having been suggested by observation of British practice. In fact the Constitution does not accord any such role of political initiative to the President. No doubt, if the President were to refuse a dissolution in the conditions of Article 13.2.2, and if the Taoiseach then resigned, as Article 28.10 requires him to do in this case, urgent consultations would follow, within and between parties in the Dáil, as to the formation of a new Government; and in this process it is possible to imagine a role for intermediaries not themselves members of the Dáil; and it might be argued that there is no reason why the President might not play such a part, even though the Constitution itself does not impute anything of the kind to the office.[5] On the other hand, if there is no basis in the Constitution for imputing such a power to the Presidency, an incumbent who sought to assist with the formation of a new Government might be exposed to a charge of having acted in excess of *vires*. In any event, as the Presidency is popularly supposed to be "above politics", a President might prudently calculate that intervention might appear invidious, and might prefer to stay aloof from the process.

Promulgation of laws

The President "promulgates" a law after signature in the way prescribed by Article 25.4.2.

Supreme Command of the Defence Forces

The supreme command of the Defence Forces vested in the President by s 4 of Article 13 replaced the provision of s 5 of the Defence Forces (Temporary Provisions) Act 1923, which (pursuant to the old Article 46, which made the Defence Forces "subject to

[2] *Casey* engages in interesting speculation as to how this discretion should be exercised. In particular, he contends that a dissolution should be refused only if an alternative government is feasible, can be assured of a working majority and can be expected to carry on for a reasonable period of time. Furthermore, he suggests that an outgoing Taoiseach who fails to secure renomination, following the reassembly of the Dáil, would receive an unsympathetic response if he immediately presented the President with a request for a dissolution of the new Dáil - *Constitutional Law in Ireland* (2nd ed.), pp.72-3. See also the discussion by Hogan, "*Legal and Constitutional Issues Arising from the 1989 General Election*" (1989) 24 Ir Jur (n.s.) 157 at pp.173-8.

[3] See *Hogan, loc.cit.* pp. 165-8.

[4] E.g. on 27 January 1982, when Mr. Haughey issued a statement saying that he was "available for consultation", if the President should wish it, after the Government led by Dr. FitzGerald had been defeated on a budget resolution. See *The Irish Times,* 28 January 1982.

[5] See discussion by *Hogan, loc. cit.* pp. 179-80.

the control of the Oireachtas") vested the "command in chief of and all executive and administrative powers in relation to the Forces" in the Executive Council, to be exercised however through the Minister for Defence (who was forbidden to "allocate to himself any executive military command" or to be "a member of the Forces on full pay"). The 1923 Act was repealed *in toto* by the Defence Act 1954, which makes the provision for the exercise of the supreme command envisaged by Article 13.5.1: s 17(1) of the 1954 Act provides:

> Under the direction of the President, and subject to the provisions of this Act the military command of, and all executive and administrative powers in relation to, the Defence Forces, including the power to delegate command and authority, shall be exercisable by the Government and, subject to such exceptions and limitations as the Government may from time to time determine, through and by the Minister for Defence.

Sub-s 3 empowers the Minister to make regulations in relation to the exercise of military command by officers. The position of the President in this setting - although the significance of the word "direction" in the subsection cited has not been judicially considered - appears to be a purely ceremonial one; and any role over and above the ceremonial would appear in any case to fall within Article 13.9 so as to be performable only on the advice of the Government. Certainly during the Dáil debate on the Constitution in 1937 it was expressly envisaged that the President's role in relation to the supreme command of the Defence Forces would be a purely nominal one.[6]

Power to pardon, commute or remit[7]

The power of commutation or remission contained in s.6 is "conferred by law on other authorities" by s 23 of the Criminal Justice Act 1951, which provides:

> (1) Except in capital cases, the Government may commute or remit, in whole or in part, any punishment imposed by a court exercising criminal jurisdiction, subject to such conditions as they may think proper.
>
> (2) The Government may remit, in whole or in part, any forfeiture or disqualification imposed by a court exercising criminal jurisdiction and restore or revive, in whole or in part, the subject of the forfeiture.
>
> (3) The Government may delegate to the Minister for Justice any power conferred by this section and may revoke any such delegation.
>
> (4) This section shall not affect any power conferred by law on other authorities.

It is clear from Article 13.6 (and indeed is reflected in s 23 of the 1951 Act) that the power to commute or remit punishment in capital cases can only be exercised by the President, acting on the advice of the Government. At the moment, however, this power is defunct, as s 1 of the Criminal Justice Act 1990 abolished the death penalty. By virtue of s 4 of the 1990 Act however, the courts must, in passing sentence, specify as the minimum period of imprisonment to be served a period of not less than 40 years where a person is convicted of, *inter alia*, murder which would previously have been classified

[6] Mr. De Valera said on 26 May 1937: "In regard to the position here that the supreme command of the Defence Forces should be vested in the President, it is quite clear that it is only nominal. It could only be nominal. Any powers that he might exercise there will have to be exercised under the Constitution, and, therefore, any powers that he might exercise in virtue of that vesting will have to be exercised on the direct advice of the Government" (67 *Dáil Debates* 1222).

as capital murder. That section also prescribes a minimum period of imprisonment of at least 20 years on conviction for attempt to commit such murder. Section 5(1) further provides that the power to commute or remit a punishment, conferred by s 23 of the 1951 Act shall not be exercisable before the expiration of the minimum period of imprisonment specified by s 4, less any reduction of that period for good conduct.

Section 23(5) of the 1951 Act dealt specially with disqualifications from holding driving licences; but s 124 of the Road Traffic Act 1961, provided that such a disqualification should "not be capable of being remitted under s 23 of the Criminal Justice Act 1951" - which would leave the power of remission, in this special category of cases, with the President to be exercised only on the advice of the Government. A special judicial power of remission in cases of driving licence disqualification is exercisable, in certain conditions, by the court that imposed the disqualification, under s 19 of the Road Traffic Act 1968.

The proposed Criminal Procedure Bill 1993 outlines a detailed procedure to be followed in the case of a person who seeks a Presidential pardon on the ground that new evidence shows that a miscarriage of justice has occurred. Section 7(2) obliges the Minister for Justice to make such enquiries as he considers necessary. If the Minister is of the opinion that the case may be dealt with more appropriately by the Court of Criminal Appeal under s 2 of the Bill or that a case has not been made out that a miscarriage of justice has occurred and that no useful purpose could be served by further investigation, the petition may be refused. In any other case, the Minister must recommend to the Government either that it should advise the President to grant the pardon or that it should appoint a committee to inquire into the case and report to the Government whether the President should be advised to grant a pardon. This committee will be a tribunal within the meaning of the Tribunals of Inquiry (Evidence) Acts 1921-1979 and it may receive such evidence and information as it sees fit, whether or not such material would be admissible in a court of law - s 8. Finally s 9 of the Bill obliges the Minister to pay compensation to, *inter alia*, a person who has been pardoned as a result of a petition under s 7, unless the non-disclosure of the fact supporting the conclusion that a miscarriage of justice had occurred was wholly or partly attributable to the petitioner.[8]

Unlike the power of commutation or remission, there is no provision for vesting the right of pardon in anyone other than the President. This right has been exercised on three occasions.[9]

Power essentially judicial but exceptionally conferred on non-judicial personages

The power of commutation and remission was considered by Walsh J in *The State (O.) v O'Brien.*[10] In his judgment, with which Budd J agreed, he said the power was essentially judicial in character - "the quality of the act is to be determined by the act itself, not by the person who is doing the act" - but it had been "nonetheless expressly conferred by

[7] See McDowell, "*Pardon: an adequate response to injustice?*" (1991) ICLJ 9.

[8] This obligation arises only where an application for compensation has been made to the Minister - s 9(2). By virtue of sub-ss (3) and (4), the amount of compensation payable is determined by the Minister though any person dissatisfied with the Minister's decision on this point may bring the issue before the High Court.

[9] The *Report of the Committee to enquire into Certain Aspects of Criminal Procedure* (1990) refers to two cases, in 1940 and 1943, while President Robinson granted a pardon to Eamon (Nicky) Kelly in April 1992.

[10] [1973] IR 50. According to the Committee, "Presidential pardons in our jurisdiction can negative guilt and blame. It seems to us that the effect of a pardon in such terms is to clear the pardoned person from all infamy". *Ibid*, at p.18.

provisions of the Constitution upon the President and, in certain instances, upon the Executive or members thereof":

> It was, of course, quite open to the people when enacting the Constitution to confer powers of a judicial character upon the Executive or to provide by the Constitution means whereby it could be done by Act of the Oireachtas; but that does not alter the nature of the power. The fact that this power can be exercised in such a way as to determine the length of a sentence by ending it or by reducing it, while in the nature of judicial power, does not mean that it amounts to a power which can be equated with determining in advance what the period of the sentence shall be, or determining from time to time how long it shall endure..."[11]

The remission power, whatever its essential character, once vested by the Constitution in an executive organ cannot be pre-empted by the order of a court. This appears from *The People v Cahill*,[12] a case in which a judge imposed a sentence of seven years' imprisonment but directed that after three years the prisoner should be brought back to the court so that the judge might consider, in the light of his behaviour under prison discipline, whether to suspend the rest of the sentence. The Court of Criminal Appeal quashed the sentence on several grounds, including the fact that it "impliedly [sought] to freeze the Executive discretion as to remission during that period, and then to vest in the court a power of review which is not readily compatible with the powers withheld from the courts and vested in the Executive by s 23 of the Act of 1951". This reasoning would equally apply to any judicial pre-emption of the remission function in such cases which may in the future rest with the President.

Doubt as to the correctness of *Cahill* was expressed by Walsh J in *The People (Director of Public Prosecutions) v Aylmer*.[13] The defendant had appealed from the Central Criminal Court to the Supreme Court against the decision of Finlay P to reactivate a partly suspended sentence for robbery which had been imposed by Butler J. The submission that this form of sentence was unconstitutional on the ground that it interfered with the executive power of government to commute a sentence under Article 13.6 was rejected by Walsh J. In his view, the partly suspended sentence postulated the continued existence of a sentence, but there was no way in which:

> "it could be construed as a direction, express or implied, to the executive not to exercise the powers of commuting the sentence. The sentence imposed by Mr. Justice Butler in no way involved an encroachment by the judicial arm of government upon the executive power. The sole power to impose a sentence is vested in the judicial arm of government and the sole arm to attach conditions to it is the judicial arm. The executive cannot impose a sentence of any description nor can it attach conditions to a sentence. Its power in respect of sentences is one of commuting or remitting sentences imposed by a court exercising criminal jurisdiction."

As all the other members of the Supreme Court reserved their position on this point, the question whether the imposition of a partly suspended sentence is actually unconstitutional or otherwise undesirable remains open.[14]

[11] In his dissenting judgment, however, McLoughlin J said he thought the right of pardon and the power to commute or remit punishments were "all functions corresponding to what formerly was the royal prerogative of mercy which, in my view, was an executive function."
[12] [1980] IR 8.
[13] Supreme Court, 18 December 1986.
[14] See Osborough, "*A Damocles' Sword Guaranteed Irish: The Suspended Sentence in the Republic of Ireland*" (1982) 17 Ir Jur (n.s.) 221.

An important limitation on the remission power under Article 13 exists, however, according to Walsh J, in the context of the indefinite imprisonment which a court can order for contempt; this, presumably being an order ancillary to the courts' civil jurisdiction (to compel obedience), is not a "punishment imposed by any court exercising criminal jurisdiction", and so "cannot be remitted or commuted by virtue of any of the powers granted by Article 13.6... It is a matter completely within the sphere of judicial power". Similarly, he thought, there was no reason why the Oireachtas might not enact that a person sentenced might be "detained during the pleasure of the court or until such time as the court thought fit to release such person"; this presumably could be construed as the "conferring by law on other authorities" (viz. the courts) of the commuting or remitting power.[15]

European Community judgments excluded

"Community judgments" (i.e. European Community judgments)[16] are, by regulation 8 of the European Communities (Enforcement of Community Judgments) Regulations, 1972, excluded from the remitting power of s 23 of the Criminal Justice Act 1951. And - although this does not concern punishments imposed in the course of criminal proceedings - it may be mentioned here that the power of the Minister for Justice under s 9 of the Enforcement of Court Orders Act 1940, to direct the release of persons imprisoned for failure to pay a sum of money (e.g. for disobedience to an instalment order)[17] is, by regulation 7 of the same Regulations, not exercisable in respect of the enforcement of Community judgments. (These Regulations are made under s 3 of the European Communities Act 1972, which empowers a Minister of State to make regulations to give effect to a range of Community instruments as part of the domestic law of the State.[18])

The President's right of expression

The question to what extent the President retains the ordinary rights of a citizen in regard to expressing his opinions or, in particular, replying to criticism, has been occasionally canvassed, especially in the light of Article 13.7 which contains an obvious inhibition on independent utterances of the kind which the section contemplates. Leaving aside the criterion of what may be proper or seemly, on which individuals' conceptions will vary, it does not appear that the law imposes total silence on the President except for whatever the Government may approve under Article 13.7. Inasmuch as the President has three important, independent and politically sensitive functions - that of referring Bills to the Supreme Court or to referendum under Article 26 or Article 27 respectively, and that of refusing a dissolution of the Dáil at his discretion in the conditions of Article 13.2.2 - the ordinary democratic axioms imply that he must submit to criticism for his exercise of them. The same axioms, and those of justice, equally require that he should be free to answer criticism. In such a context Article 13.7 scarcely comes

[15] Of interest is the view of Walsh J that under the 1922 Constitution "the power [of the Crown or its representative] to commute sentences or to remit sentences [had] ceased to be operative... The fact that there may have been many instances where such powers were purported to be exercised by the Crown on the advice of the Executive Council of Saorstát Éireann does not alter the matter as it must have been done under the mistaken belief that it was an executive function." See also *Keegan v de Búrca* [1973] IR 223.

[16] These are defined in the Regulations as "any decision, judgment or order which is enforceable under or in accordance with Article 187 or 192 of the EEC Treaty, Article 18, 159 or 164 of the Euratom Treaty or Article 44 or 92 of the ECSC Treaty."

[17] See below, pp. 850-7.

[18] See under Article 29.4.5, below, pp. 289-291.

into play; nor could it be said that "message to the Nation" or "aitheasc a chur faoi bhráid an Náisiúin" is a phrase which fits it.[19]

As for the President's right of expression under Article 13.7 itself, this has been exercised twice, on both occasions pursuant to sub-s 1. President de Valera addressed the Houses of the Oireachtas on the occasion of the fiftieth anniversary of the first meeting of Dáil Éireann, on 21 January 1969, while President Robinson exercised this right on 8 July 1992.

"Non-answerable" privilege of the President

In relation to Article 13.8, Gavan Duffy J said in *The State (Burke) v Lennon*[20] that the Constitution here "recognises... the exercise of his powers and functions by the President" as an "exception from the general jurisdiction of the High Court"; in *Byrne v Ireland*[21] Walsh J said that by sub-s 1 "an express immunity from suit is conferred on the President", and Budd J used the provision, on the principle *expressio unius exclusio alterius*, to bolster the case against any immunity from suit being enjoyed by the State.[22]

Purely formal Presidential functions are not protected from judicial review

The privilege of non-answerability enjoyed by the President under Article 13.8 evidently applies, however, only to the exercise of powers or functions which are within his own discretion; in other words, the section cannot be raised in order to prevent judicial review of a function which, as Finlay P put it in *The State (Walshe) v Murphy*[23] "require[s] his intervention for its effectiveness in law, [but is] in fact the decision and act of the Executive". In this case, in which a conviction was attacked on the ground that the convicting justice had not fulfilled the statutory requirements for appointment as

[19] The Dáil debate on the draft Constitution reveals (67 *Dáil Debates* 1277ff.) that Mr. de Valera intended Article 13.7 to work restrictively; it was put to him that the President should be able to explain a refusal to dissolve the Dáil, or to submit a Bill to referendum, but he disagreed emphatically. It emerges, however, clearly from these passages that what Mr. de Valera wished to avoid was a public clash between President and Government as such - "you would immediately have two authorities, and you cannot have that" - and the object of the section seems to be to prevent the President from raising an independent banner, so to speak, by addressing the nation in a sense hostile to the Government. It is a long way from this to the proposition that the President "cannot answer back" no matter what the source, form or content of the criticism, and that therefore the ordinary right of criticism ought to be forborne. These matters were much in public debate in the period immediately before and after the resignation of President Ó Dálaigh on 22 October 1976 after he had been abusively criticised by a Minister for submitting the Emergency Powers Bill, 1976, to the Supreme Court; and in connection with this particular case, it is relevant to observe that President Ó Dálaigh - who had formerly been Chief Justice and had played a leading role in the efflorescence of innovative constitutional jurisprudence in the 1960s and early 1970s - did in fact "answer back". On 19 October, in response to an apology from the Minister, the President wrote to him in terms of severe reproach, and elaborate justification of his own actions. He released the text of this letter after resigning (see *The Irish Times*, 23 October 1976); but there is no evident rule which would have prevented the Minister, or the Government, from doing so while the President was still in office, in which event his defence would have been effectively made in public. Equally, if the President was within his rights in defending himself, while still in office, in a letter to the person who had insulted him, he must be similarly entitled to do so in replying, for example, to an attack in the press or some other quarter. (Though, for a contrary view, see *Morgan* (1986) 21 Ir Jur (n.s.) 146 at 152-3.)

[20] [1940] IR 136; (1940) 74 ILTR 36,131.

[21] [1972] IR 241.

[22] The fact that the President is not answerable to any court for the exercise of the duty of dissolving the Dáil was cited by Hamilton P in *O'Malley v An Taoiseach* [1990] ILRM 460, as a reason for refusing to grant an injunction restraining the Taoiseach from advising the President to grant a dissolution.

[23] [1981] IR 275.

a justice,[24] the challenge was met by the contention, *inter alia*, that as the appointment had been made by the President (under Article 35.1), albeit on the advice of the Government, any attempt to have its validity judicially reviewed amounted to trying to make the President "answerable" in the sense precluded by Article 13.8. Finlay P said, firstly, that:

> "the ordinary meaning of a person being answerable to another person or to another institution is that he can be made or forced to answer for, or give account of his conduct to that institution. [These proceedings] do not in my view in any way involve the President in the sense that he could be made in any way to account for or explain his [function of appointing a justice]."

He went on to show the intolerable results of any other interpretation of the section, pointing to the fact that the immunity covered even acts "purporting" to be done by the President in exercise of his functions; on the respondents' reasoning, this could mean that any function in which the President's role was purely formal, such as the appointment of members of a Government, could be operated, by those to whose advice or nomination the President was tied, in a manner completely illegal or unconstitutional and in defiance of constitutional rights, yet with impunity once the function had, so to speak, been immunised (by interposition of the Presidential rubber stamp) against challenge. Such a proposition invited only one conclusion.

The President may not be impleaded

Earlier in the same year this judgment of Finlay P (against which no appeal was brought by the State) was foreshadowed by the Supreme Court in *Draper v The President*[25] a case where a woman, disabled by physical handicap from attending at a polling station, brought proceedings the purpose of which was to force the Oireachtas to introduce an alternative system of voting, such as a postal vote, at Dáil elections for persons in her category. However her proceedings took the form, *inter alia*, of seeking an injunction to restrain the Taoiseach from requesting, and the President from granting, the dissolution (then imminent) of the Dáil which was in being. In the High Court Hamilton J refused an application to discharge the President and Taoiseach from the proceedings; but the Supreme Court peremptorily removed the President from the proceedings (and subsequently the Taoiseach also). O'Higgins CJ said he:

> "wished to make it clear, without hearing any submissions from [State counsel], that the bringing of proceedings against the President of Ireland appeared prima facie to be in open defiance of the Constitution and appeared *prima facie* to be an abuse of the process of the Court...The removal of the President from the proceedings does not depend on any consent from [State counsel] or the plaintiff...The Court would not hear any address or submission in defence of that action [i.e. the bringing of proceedings against the President?] which was in open defiance of Article 13.8...The Court expresses condemnation of the action taken in that respect."

[24] See below, pp. 557-8.

[25] Unreported: the account of the case given here is taken from the reports in *The Irish Times* of 2, 13 and 14 May 1981. The citation from O'Higgins CJ is not from a written judgment, but from the newspaper account (14 May) of what the Chief Justice said from the bench. The report adds that the plaintiff's counsel said "the stricture of the Court was accepted". For her later substantive action, see below, p.154. For the striking of the Taoiseach out of the proceedings, see below, p. 263.

Powers conferred on the President by law

Additional powers and functions are occasionally conferred on the President by law under Article 13.10; as might be expected, having regard to the general subordination of the Presidential function to the advice of the Government (Article 13.9), these are purely formal. Instances[26] in chronological order of appearance are: the President's power to appoint Council members and Senior Professors of the Dublin Institute for Advanced Studies (under ss 8 and 9 of the Institute for Advanced Studies Act 1940);[27] to appoint the Governor of the Central Bank (under s 19 of the Central Bank Act 1942); to direct - in the conditions of the wartime emergency - that a Dáil general election should take place (by s 2 of the General Elections (Emergency Provisions) Act 1943);[28] his function as *ex officio* President of the Irish Red Cross Society (under s 1 of the Red Cross Act 1944); his exercise of executive power in external relations (under s 3 of the Republic of Ireland Act 1948);[29] various functions in relation to the Defence Forces, other than the mere appointment of commissioned officers envisaged by Article 13.5.2 (under the Defence Act 1954); the granting of Irish citizenship "as a token of honour" (under s 12(1) of the Irish Nationality and Citizenship Act 1956); the appointment of the chairman of An Foras Talúntais [The Agricultural Institute] (under s 5 of the Agriculture (An Foras Talúntais) Act 1958); the appointment of the Ombudsman (under s 2 of the Ombudsman Act 1980).[30]

Statutory exemptions in favour of the President

Further miscellaneous statutory provisions relating to the President may be found in Schedule 1, Part 1 of the Juries Act 1976 (President ineligible to sit on a jury); and s 5(1)(*e*) of the Ombudsman Act 1980 (discharge of official functions by the President may not be investigated by the Ombudsman).

Obstruction of the President

Section 8 of the Offences Against the State Act 1939, penalises the obstruction by force or intimidation of "the exercise or performance by the President of any of his functions, powers, or duties". By s 1(1)(*b*)(iii) of the Criminal Justice Act 1964, murder done "in course or furtherance" of this offence is capital.[31]

German model for the Presidency

The office and functions of the President, which had to be devised from scratch in 1937, exhibit so many secondary resemblances to the office and functions of the President of the Weimar Republic under the Constitution of 1919 that a direct importation must be suspected (the German Constitution was one of those collected and published by the Committee which drafted the Constitution of the Irish Free State, but its Articles on the

26 No catalogue of the President's statutory functions is available officially. The list here given may not be exhaustive.

27 As the Institute consisted originally of two constituent schools, of which the first mentioned was that of Celtic Studies, it may be that the earliest instance of a Presidential statutory function was intended as a compliment to the first President, Dr Douglas Hyde, a distinguished scholar in this field.

28 See below, p. 168.

29 See below, pp. 277-278.

30 Pursuant to this provision, the Ombudsman is appointed by the President on the recommendation of the Dáil and Seanad. *Casey* queries whether this arrangement is compatible with Article 13.11, which requires that statutory powers conferred on the President be exercisable only on the advice of the Government - *Constitutional Law in Ireland* (2nd ed.) at p.69.

31 By virtue of s 1 of the Criminal Justice Act 1990, this no longer attracts the death penalty. See above, pp.91-92.

Presidency were of course not serviceable for Irish purposes in 1922). The German President had a seven-year term (Article 43), it required a two-thirds majority of the Reichstag to remove him (Article 43), he might not be a member of the Reichstag himself (Article 44), he had the supreme command of the armed forces (Article 47) and the right of pardon (Article 49), and he appointed the Chancellor and, on his recommendation, the Ministers (Article 53). Every German citizen who had completed his thirty-fifth year was eligible for the office (Article 41).

Article 14

THE PRESIDENTIAL COMMISSION

Article 14.

1. In the event of the absence of the President, or his temporary incapacity, or his permanent incapacity established as provided by section 3 of Article 12 hereof, or in the event of his death, resignation, removal from office, or failure to exercise and perform the powers and functions of his office or any of them, or at any time at which the office of President may be vacant, the powers and functions conferred on the President by or under this Constitution shall be exercised and performed by a Commission constituted as provided in section 2 of this Article.

2. 1° The Commission shall consist of the following persons, namely, the Chief Justice, the Chairman of Dáil Éireann (An Ceann Comhairle), and the Chairman of Seanad Éireann.

   2° The President of the High Court shall act as a member of the Commission in the place of the Chief Justice on any occasion on which the office of Chief Justice is vacant or on which the Chief Justice is unable to act.

   3° The Deputy Chairman of Dáil Éireann shall act as a member of the Commission in the place of the Chairman of Dáil Éireann on any occasion on which the office of Chairman of Dáil Éireann is vacant or on which the said Chairman is unable to act.

   4° The Deputy Chairman of Seanad Éireann shall act as a member of the Commission in the place of the Chairman of Seanad Éireann on any occasion

Airteagal 14.

1. Má bhíonn an tUachtarán as láthair nó má bhíonn ar míthreoir go sealadach, nó má bhíonn ar míthreoir go buan agus go suífear sin mar a shocraítear le halt 3 d'Airteagal 12 den Bhunreacht seo, nó má tharlaíonn é d'éag nó é d'éirí as oifig nó é a chur as oifig, nó má theipeann air cumhachtaí is feidhmeanna a oifige nó aon cheann díobh a oibriú is a chomhlíonadh, nó má bhíonn oifig an Uachtaráin folamh, is Coimisiún a bheas comhdhéanta mar a shocraítear in alt 2 den Airteagal seo a oibreos is a chomhlíonfas na cumhachtaí is na feidhmeanna a bhronntar ar an Uachtarán leis an mBunreacht seo nó faoi.

2. 1° Is iad na daoine seo a leanas an Coimisiún, .i. an Príomh-Bhreitheamh, Cathaoirleach Dháil Éireann (An Ceann Comhairle) agus Cathaoirleach Sheanad Éireann.

   2° Gníomhóidh Uachtarán na hArd-Chúirte ina chomhalta den Choimisiún in ionad an Phríomh-Bhreithimh aon uair a bheas oifig an Phríomh-Bhreithimh folamh nó a bheas an Príomh-Bhreitheamh gan bheith i gcumas gníomhaithe.

   3° Gníomhóidh Leas-Chathaoirleach Dháil Éireann ina chomhalta den Choimisiún in ionad Chathaoirleach Dháil Éireann aon uair a bheas oifig Chathaoirleach Dháil Éireann folamh nó a bheas an Cathaoirleach sin gan bheith i gcumas gníomhaithe.

   4° Gníomhóidh Leas-Chathaoirleach Sheanad Éireann ina chomhalta den Choimisíun in ionad Chathaoirleach Sheanad

on which the office of Chairman of Seanad Éireann is vacant or on which the said Chairman is unable to act.

3. The Commission may act by any two of their number and may act notwithstanding a vacancy in their membership.

4. The Council of State may by a majority of its members make such provision as to them may seem meet for the exercise and performance of the powers and functions conferred on the President by or under this Constitution in any contingency which is not provided for by the foregoing provisions of this Article.

5. 1° The provisions of this Constitution which relate to the exercise and performance by the President of the powers and functions conferred on him by or under this Constitution shall subject to the subsequent provisions of this section apply to the exercise and performance of the said powers and functions under this Article.

2° In the event of the failure of the President to exercise or perform any power or function which the President is by or under this Constitution required to exercise or perform within a specified time, the said power or function shall be exercised or performed under this Article, as soon as may be after the expiration of the time so specified.

Éireann aon uair a bheas oifig Chathaoirleach Sheanad Éireann folamh nó a bheas an Cathaoirleach sin gan bheith i gcumas gníomhaithe.

3. Is dleathach don Choimisiún gníomhú trí bheirt ar bith dá líon agus gníomhú d'ainneoin folúntais ina gcomhaltas.

4. Féadfaidh an Chomhairle Stáit, le tromlach dá gcomhaltaí, cibé socrú is oircheas leo a dhéanamh chun na cumhachtaí agus na feidhmeanna a bhronntar ar an Uachtarán leis an mBunreacht seo nó faoi a oibriú is a chomhlíonadh in aon chás nach ndéantar socrú ina chomhair leis na forálacha sin romhainn den Airteagal seo.

5. 1° Na forálacha den Bhunreacht seo a bhaineas leis an Uachtarán d'oibriú is do chomhlíonadh na gcumhachtaí is na bhfeidhmeanna a bhronntar air leis an mBunreacht seo nó faoi bainfid, faoi chuimsiú na bhforálacha inár ndiaidh den alt seo, le hoibriú is le comhlíonadh na gcumhachtaí is na bhfeidhmeanna sin faoin Airteagal seo.

2° Má theipeann ar an Uachtarán aon chumhacht nó feidhm a oibriú nó a chomhlíonadh nach foláir dó, de réir an Bhunreachta seo nó faoi, í a oibriú nó a chomhlíonadh faoi cheann aimsire a luaitear, ní foláir í a oibriú nó a chomhlíonadh faoin Airteagal seo chomh luath agus is féidir é tar éis na haimsire a luaitear amhlaidh.

Article 14 makes no express provision for the Commission's failure to perform a function in place of the President. This would presumably be a "contingency" under Article 14.4, giving the Council of State power to prescribe substitute machinery. For the meaning of "majority of its members" in Article 14.4, see below, p. 326.

In *Loftus v Attorney General*[1] the Supreme Court held that, although strictly speaking on the dissolution of the Dáil there could be no Chairman or Deputy Chairman of Dáil

[1] [1979] IR 221.

Éireann, the outgoing holders of these offices must be taken to survive in office for the purposes of the Presidential Commission. The same must hold, by analogy, in the case of the Chairman or Deputy Chairman of Seanad Éireann in the interval between a Seanad general election and the first meeting of the new Seanad (the Seanad is not "dissolved"; its members remain such until the day before polling day, under Article 18.9). It will be noted that this means the Presidential Commission could contain even someone who had not been a candidate in, or had been defeated, in the Seanad general election, as the Seanad's outgoing Chairman - unlike the outgoing Chairman of the Dáil under Article 16.6 - is not automatically deemed to be a member of the freshly elected House.

The Presidential Commission has had to act on a number of occasions since 1937, in particular, after the death in office of President Childers in 1974 and following the resignation of President Ó Dálaigh in 1976. The first dissolution of Dáil Éireann ever granted by the Presidential Commission occurred in November 1992 while President Robinson was on a state visit to Australia.[2]

[2] *The Irish Times*, 5 November 1992.

THE NATIONAL PARLIAMENT

THE NATIONAL PARLIAMENT
Constitution and Powers

Article 15.

1. 1° The National Parliament shall be called and known, and is in the Constitution generally referred to as the Oireachtas.

2° The Oireachtas shall consist of the President and two Houses, viz: a House of Representatives to be called Dáil Éireann and a Senate to be called Seanad Éireann.

3° The Houses of the Oireachtas shall sit in or near the city of Dublin or in such other place as they may from to time determine.

AN PHARLAIMINT NÁISIÚNTA
Comhdhéanamh agus Cumhachtaí

Airteagal 15

1. 1° An tOireachtas is ainm don Pharlaimint Náisiúnta, agus sin é a bheirtear uirthi de ghnáth sa Bhunreacht seo.

2° An tUachtáran agus dhá Theach atá san Oireachtas: Teach Ionadóirí ar a dtugtar Dáil Éireann, agus Seanad ar a dtugtar Seanad Éireann.

3° Is i gcathair Bhaile Átha Cliath nó ar a cóngar, nó cibé áit eile ar a geinnfid ó am go ham, a shuífid Tithe an Oireachtas.

1922 Provision

The corresponding provisions of the 1922 Constitution were contained in its Articles 12 (first two sentences) and 13. Article 12 in its original form constituted a legislature of "the King and two Houses", but the King was removed in 1936 by the Constitution (Amendment No. 27) Act, and in the same year the Constitution (Amendment No. 24) Act abolished the Senate and reduced the Oireachtas to a single House, the Dáil. Numerous consequential amendments to the old Constitution's text were involved in these developments. The King's ceremonial functions under the old Constitution up to 1936 were exercised by "the Representation of the Crown".

The abolition of the old Senate, although a response to a particular situation (the defeat in the Senate of the Government's Bill to control the wearing of uniforms),[1] led to a debate about the merits of bicameral as against unicameral legislatures.[2] The new Senate constituted by the 1937 Constitution has somewhat lesser powers than the old.

"House of Representatives"

It may be observed that while the English description of Dáil Éireann in the 1922 Constitution was "Chamber of Deputies", in 1937 the American designation "House of Representatives" was preferred.

[1] See O'Sullivan, *The Irish Free State and its Senate* (London, 1940), pp. 359ff.
[2] *Id.*, pp. 363ff. and 62 *Dáil Debates*, Col. 1195ff.

Legal personality of the Oireachtas

While the Constitution affords some hints, and further conjecture is possible, as to the dimensions of the President's legal personality,[3] it does not appear that the other components of the Oireachtas - its two Houses - have any legal capacity beyond the exercise of the functions expressly attributed to them by the Constitution or by law. Neither House owns any property and there is but one inconclusive recorded instance[4] of where either House has sued or been sued and, on this analysis are probably best regarded as organs of public law, with defined functional spheres, but without civil capacity.

This view, however, may possibly be regarded as too conservative. There seems, for example, no reason why either House of the Oireachtas should not have the capacity to acquire or receive property. Moreover, it may be noted that with regard to both radio and television broadcasting of the Oireachtas, both Houses have separately and individually asserted copyright in the relevant broadcasts, e.g., "that copyright in the material be retained by Dáil Éireann". This formula would seem to involve an imputation that both the Dáil and Seanad can hold a form of property such as copyright; and, perhaps, also that it can assert its copyright, thus entailing a capacity for the purposes of litigation. But these isolated hints may be too tenuous for such a contention to rest on.

Resolution of both Houses is not equivalent to Act of the Oireachtas

The decision of Johnson J in *Meagher v. Minister for Agriculture*[5] appears to be the only case in which Article 15.1.2 was judicially considered. Here the question was whether legislation[6] enabling either House of the Oireachtas to nullify a statutory instrument made by a Minister could be equated with legislation independently confirming such a statutory instrument. Johnson J said that the two procedures could not be so equated, since in the latter case it was simply the action of the two Houses "without the President." This was not the same -as Johnson J pointed out- as legislation emanating from the Oireachtas which, by virtue of Article 15.1.2, includes the President and the both Houses.

The Houses of the Oireachtas have never sat elsewhere than in Dublin.[7]

[3] See above at pp. 85-86.

[4] In *Halliday v House of Oireachtas, The Irish Times,* 15 July 1993 Keane J rejected a claim which had been bought against the Houses of the Oireachtas by a former secretary of a former deputy. The case turned on whether certain assurances had been given to the applicant regarding her future employment and Keane J did not rule on the wider issue of whether the House of the Oireachtas had any legal personality.

[5] High Court, 1 April 1993.

[6] Section 1 of the European Communities (Amendment) Act 1973.

[7] The First Dáil met in the Mansion House, Dublin. The debate on the Anglo-Irish Treaty of 6 December 1921 was held in the Council Chamber of University College, Dublin (December 1921-January 1922).The debate on the draft Constitution of the Irish Free State was held in Leinster House (September-October 1922). Since December 1922 the Houses of the Oireachtas have sat in Leinster House, save that the First Seanad sat for a short time in the Furniture Hall of the National Museum next door until the Seanad Chamber in Leinster House was made ready. There was also, in 1969, a single special meeting of both Houses of the Oireachtas in the Mansion House to commemorate the fiftieth anniversary of the meeting of the First Dáil.

Article 15.2

EXCLUSIVE LEGISLATIVE POWER OF OIREACHTAS

2. 1° The sole and exclusive power of making laws for the State is hereby vested in the Oireachtas: no other legislative authority has power to make laws for the State.

2° Provision may however be made by law for the creation or recognition of subordinate legislatures and for the powers and functions of these legislatures.

2. 1° Bheirtear don Oireachtas amháin leis seo an t-aon chumhacht chun dlíthe a dhéanamh don Stát; níl cumhacht ag údarás reachtaíochta ar bith eile chun dlíthe a dhéanamh don Stát.

2° Ach féadfar socrú a dhéanamh le dlí chun fo-reachtais a chur ar bun nó chun glactha leo, agus chun cumhachtaí agus feidhmeanna na bhfo-reachtas sin a leagan amach.

1922 Provision

The provision of the 1922 Constitution which corresponded with the present Article 15.2.1 was Article 12; this however simply gave the Oireachtas exclusive power to make laws "for the peace, order and good government" of the State (a formula used in Article 1 of the Treaty)[1] and did not contain the emphatic tautology about "no other legislative authority" having such power.

"All-embracing" residual legislative power a consequence of Article 15.2.1

In *The State (Walshe) v Murphy*[2] Finlay P gave a very useful analysis of the nature of the legislative power conferred by Article 15.2.1 on the Oireachtas: this power was "absolute and all-embracing, subject to the qualifications imposed upon it by the Oireachtas." He identified these qualifications as follows: First, the Oireachtas may not, by virtue of Article 15.4.1, enact any law which is in any respect unconstitutional. Secondly, there are to be found throughout the Constitution "specific prohibitions against the enactment of laws with a particular effect or particular purpose."[3] Thirdly, there were several instances where the Oireachtas was "actively obliged" by the Constitution "to regulate certain matters by law; in other words, to enact statutory provisions to provide for them."[4] Finally, there was the residual general category consisting "of all other areas or topics or matters in respect of which legislation might be enacted", subject to the general obligation on the part of the Oireachtas not to enact legislation which might be unconstitutional.

[1] Article 12 appears to have been judicially considered in two cases only: *Pigs Marketing Board v Donnelly* [1939] IR 413 (see pp.105-106) and *Donegal Fuel and Supply Co. Ltd. v Londonderry Harbour Commissioners*, High Court, 6 May 1992 (Oireachtas may not impose statutory duties on foreign corporation where this would infringe on the sovereignty of a foreign state: see p. 1158).

[2] [1981] IR 275.

[3] Examples included Article 15.5 "The Oireachtas shall not declare acts to be infringements of the law which were not so at the date of their commission."

[4] Examples included Article 16.2.2, which provides that the number of members of Dáil Éireann shall from time to time by regulated by law. Finlay P explained that the effect of these provisions was that the Oireachtas: "while retaining a discretion as to the details of the legislation concerned and as to the precise regulations created thereby, has a constitutional obligation to make some regulations thereby."

Effect of membership of the European Community

An obvious qualification of the exclusive legislative power of the Oireachtas results from the State's membership of the European Community; the nature of Community Regulations, which apply here directly without needing to be re-cast in Irish legislation, clearly derogates from the absolute words "no other legislative authority has power to make laws for the State". A similar derogation, even if effected at one remove, lies in the status of domestic legislation which is "necessitated" by the obligations of Community membership, since this "necessity" pre-empts the discretion of the Oireachtas; such "necessitated" legislation has now been enacted in a vast number of areas ranging from agriculture and fisheries law to detailed regulations governing the Single Market to labour relations and sex discrimination etc. Constitutional cover for this situation is provided by Article 29.4.3, enacted in 1972 after a referendum.[5]

Conversely, while the Irish courts have not yet considered the status here of Irish legislation enacted in clear breach of a Community obligation, the Court of the Justice held in 1978 that:

> "Every national court must, in a case within its jurisdiction, apply Community law in its entirety and protect rights which the latter confers on individuals and must accordingly set aside any provision of national law which may conflict with it, whether prior to or subsequent to the community rule."[6]

In other words, the European Court will expect the Irish Courts to treat as inapplicable an item of Irish legislation which purports to overrule a Community provision applicable to Ireland. [7]

Attempts to deploy Article 15.2.1 against the regulatory power of Ministers and other subordinate authorities

The assertion in s 2 of this Article in regard to the "sole and exclusive" legislative power of the Oireachtas has been being increasingly used - with some degree of success - in order to attack an executive or ministerial function on the ground that it represents an unconstitutional usurpation of legislative power. The first such attempt was made on the defendants' behalf in *Pigs Marketing Board v Donnelly*[8] and was directed against the price-fixing function given to the Board by the Pigs and Bacon Acts 1935 and 1937 (enacted while the 1922 Constitution was still in force, so that the challenge was based on the old Article 12). In rejecting the argument that the Board's powers were essentially legislative, Hanna J gave a good analysis of the position:

> "It is axiomatic that powers conferred upon the Legislature to make laws cannot be delegated to any other body or authority. The Oireachtas is the only constitutional

[5] As amended by the 10th Amendment of the Constitutional Act 1987 (giving constitutional cover to the Single European Act) and the 11th Amendment of the Constitution Act 1992 (giving constitutional cover to the Maastricht Treaty on European Union).

[6] *Simmenthal v Ministero della Sanità* (Case 106/77) [1978] ECR 629. This judgment follows and expands on the earlier leading decision in *Costa v ENEL* (Case 6/64) [1964] ECR 585. See also *Marleasing SA v Commercial International de Alimentacion SA* (Case 106/89) [1992] 1 CMLR 305 (national law must be interpreted where at all possible in a manner which is in conformity with EC directives).

[7] This situation was foreshadowed by Keane J in *Murphy v Bord Telecom Éireann* [1988] ILRM 53 where he said:

> "Where such a conflict [between EC law and national law] exists, national law must yield primacy to Community law...The exclusive role of the making of laws assigned to the Oireachtas by Article 15 of the Constitution has been expressly modified by Article 29.4.3 so as to enable Community law to have the force of law in the State. Where such a conflict arises, the national law is, accordingly, inapplicable."

[8] [1939] IR 413.

> agency by which laws can be made. But the Legislature may, it has always been conceded, delegate to subordinate bodies or departments not only the making of administrative rules and regulations, but the power to exercise, within the principles laid down by the Legislature, the powers so delegated and the manner in which the statutory provisions shall be carried out. The functions of every government are now so numerous and complex that of necessity a wider sphere has been recognised for subordinate agencies, such as boards and commissions. This has been specially so in this State in matters of industry and commerce. Such bodies are not law makers; they put into execution the law as made by the governing authority and strictly in pursuance therewith, so as to bring about, not their own views, but the result directed by the Government...
>
> [Price-fixing] is a matter of such detail and upon which such expert knowledge is necessarily required, that the Legislature, being unable to fix such a price itself, is entitled to say: "We shall leave this to a body of experts in the trade who shall in the first place determine what the normal conditions in the trade would be apart from the abnormal conditions prescribed by the statute, and then form an opinion as to what the proper price in pounds, shillings and pence would be under such normal conditions." The Pigs Marketing Board, in doing so, is not making a new law; it is giving effect to the statutory provisions as to how they should determine that price."

In *N.U.R. v Sullivan*[9] one of the plaintiffs' arguments, though based primarily on Article 40.6.1.iii and 40.6.2, was associated also with Article 15.2.1, viz. that the regulatory laws envisaged by Article 40.6.2 were laws of the Oireachtas, whereas the regulation of which they were complaining would be carried out by a mere Trade Union Tribunal. They were ultimately successful, though on broader grounds, in the Supreme Court; but in the High Court Gavan Duffy J held against them on all points, saying in this regard:

> "The power of a sovereign Legislature to entrust its mandates to subordinate agencies is not challenged, and is generally unassailable...Here is a tribunal peculiarly constituted by statute to deal with a peculiar subject for which the Legislature must have deemed it to be peculiarly fitted..."

(He did not, however, advert to the then fairly recent *Pigs Marketing Board* case; a certain discordance remains between the "axiom" of Hanna J that legislative power cannot be delegated, and what Gavan Duffy J thought the unchallenged power of a legislature to "entrust its mandates" to subordinate agencies).

An objection of a similar kind was taken in *de Burca v Attorney General*[10] against the power of the Minister for Justice, under s 2 of the Juries Act 1927, to prescribe and vary rating qualifications for jurors; the argument was rejected in the High Court, and does not seem to have been pursued in the Supreme Court. In the High Court Pringle J adverted to the alleged:

> "[delegation] to the Minister [of] the legislative power which is vested solely and exclusively in the Oireachtas under Article 15.2. I do not consider that the Minister, in exercising the powers given to him by this section, can be said to be exercising in any sense the legislative powers of the Oireachtas. He is simply implementing the policy and provisions of the Act of 1927 as laid down by the Legislature."

[9] [1947] IR 77; (1947) 81 ILTR 55.
[10] [1976] IR 38.

Again, in *The State (Devine) v Larkin*[11] the prosecutors contended that s 13 of the Foyle Fisheries Act 1952, effectively constituted the Foyle Fisheries Commission a legislative body and so infringed Article 15.2 which gave the Oireachtas the sole power of making laws. McMahon J observed that:

> "The delegation of statutory powers was a well-established legislative procedure at the time the Constitution was enacted....."

"Principles and policies" test

The general trend of judicial opinion on this point was, finally, given a somewhat sharper dogmatic shape in *Cityview Press Ltd. v An Chomhairle Oiliúna.*[12] Here the plaintiffs challenged, as an unconstitutional delegation of legislative power, the provisions of the Industrial Training Act 1967, which empowered the defendants to make a levy order for the collection of a levy from each enterprise in a particular industry, to be used for the training of recruits to that industry. The Supreme Court rejected this challenge, noting that:

> "the giving of powers to a designated Minister or subordinate body to make regulations or orders under a particular statute has been a feature of legislation for many years. The practice has obvious attractions in view of the complex, intricate and ever-changing situations which confront both the Legislature and the Executive in a modern State. Sometimes, as in this instance, the Legislature, conscious of the danger of giving too much power in the regulating or order-making process, provides that any regulation or order made should be subject to annulment by either House...This retains a measure of control, if not in Parliament as such, at least in the two Houses. It is, therefore, a safeguard."

The Court continued:

> "Nevertheless, the ultimate responsibility rests with the courts to ensure that constitutional safeguards remain, and that the exclusive authority of the National Parliament in the field of law-making is not eroded by a delegation of power neither contemplated nor permitted by the Constitution."

The Court then formulated the general test it would apply to subordinate rule-making activities:

> "The test, in the view of this Court, is whether what is challenged as an unauthorised delegation of parliamentary power is more than a mere giving effect to principles and policies which are contained in the statute itself. If it be, then it is not authorised, for such would constitute a purported exercise of legislative power by an authority which is not permitted to do so under the Constitution. On the other hand, if it be within the permitted limits - if the law is laid down in the statute and details only filled in or completed by the designated Minister or subordinate body - there is no unauthorised delegation of legislative power.

In this instance, in the opinion of the Court, there has not been any unconstitutional delegation of authority. The Act in question contains clear declarations of policies and aims and it establishes machinery for the carrying out of these policies and the achievement of these aims. In particular, in s 21 the fact that there will be a levy is provided for, and

[11] [1977] IR 24.
[12] [1980] IR 381.

the obligation to pay it is laid down. The only matter left over for determination by AnCO is the manner of calculating this levy in relation to a particular industry.

Cityview Press criteria applied in subsequent cases

The criteria laid down in *Cityview Press* have been subsequently applied in a series of important decisions. In the first of these, *Cooke v Walsh*,[13] the infant plaintiff, who had been seriously injured in a road accident, would normally have been entitled, as a "fully eligible" person, to free medical care under s 45 of the Health Act 1970. However, the Minister for Health had purported, by virtue of a statutory instrument made under s 72 of the same Act to exclude fully eligible persons who had suffered personal injuries as a result of a road accident from the scope of free medical services unless it was established that the person concerned was not entitled to recover damages or compensation in respect of his injuries. Section 72(2) provides that:

> Regulations made under this section may provide for any service under this Act being made available only to a particular class of the persons who have eligibility for that service.

The Court noted that if s 72 authorised the Minister to make regulations which would have the effect of removing or altering the obligations imposed on health boards by s 45 of the same Act it would be an unconstitutional delegation of a law-making power, contrary to Article 15.2; and O'Higgins CJ said it was necessary to interpret s 72 in a manner which would absolve the Oireachtas "from any intention to delegate its exclusive power of making or changing the laws". He suggested that while s 72 might allow the Minister to make regulations permitting health boards not to provide certain kinds of services for patients with limited eligibility, he was satisfied that it did not empower the Minister effectively to amend s 45 by ministerial regulation. But while this narrow construction of s 72 preserved it from constitutional attack, it meant that the ministerial regulations - whose validity rested on a broader construction of the section - were condemned as *ultra vires*.

A similar point arose in *The State (Gallagher, Shatter & Co.) v de Valera*.[14] In the High Court, Costello J held that O 99 r 15(*e*) of the Rules of the Superior Courts, 1962, conferred jurisdiction on the Taxing Master to tax costs as between solicitor and client without the necessity for any court order. The Supreme Court did not share this view; McCarthy J said that Costello J had not taken into account the fact that:

> "the Rules Committee did not, and could not, constitutionally have power to confer the jurisdiction that would result from [such a construction of the rule]. Having regard to the canon of construction laid down by this Court in *East Donegal Co-Operative Ltd. v Attorney General* and the principles governing secondary or delegated legislation stated by this Court in *Cityview Press Ltd. v An Chomhairle Oiliúna*... the true construction of the relevant rule and statutes does not support the contention that [the Taxing Master] was accorded such a jurisdiction by O 99."

In effect, therefore, the Supreme Court held that the Rules Committee could not constitutionally have been given power either to create a new jurisdiction or to modify by Rules of Court the existing substantive law. Thus, both *Cityview Press* and *Gallagher, Shatter* would seem to put in doubt the constitutionality of s 36(ix) of the Courts of Justice Act 1924 (as applied to the present courts by s 48 of the Courts (Supplemental Provisions) Act 1961) which purports to confer the Superior Court Rules Committee

[13] [1984] IR 71.
[14] [1986] ILRM 3.

with power to secure the "adaptation or modification of any statute that may be requisite for any of the purposes of this Act."

The argument that s 8 of the Extradition Act 1965, had purported to invest the Minister for Justice with legislative power in relation to the making of extradition agreements was rejected in *The State (Gilliland) v Governor of Mountjoy Prison.*[15] Barrington J referred to the judgment of O'Higgins CJ in the *Cityview Press* case as authority for the proposition that if the Oireachtas lays down principles and policies in the statute, it may leave their application to an administrative authority. On this view, the powers conferred on the Minister by the section were not legislative in character:

> "In the Extradition Act 1965, the Oireachtas has laid down certain principles and policies which are incorporated in the law governing extradition in this country. It has also established certain machinery and procedures for controlling applications for extradition. But it has left to the Government the question of whether an extradition treaty should be entered into with a particular country and what additional safeguards should be incorporated in it."

This trend was continued with the judgment of the Supreme Court in *Harvey v Minister for Social Welfare*[16] where the applicant challenged the constitutionality of the Social Welfare Act 1952 on the ground that it empowered the Minister to make regulations which would have had the effect of overriding other statutory provisions. The Minister had in fact made regulations[17] which purported to withdraw certain welfare payments to which the applicant would otherwise have been entitled. The Supreme Court rejected the submission that s 75 amounted to an unconstitutional delegation of legislative power - but in a judgment which strongly paralleled its earlier reasoning in *Cooke v Walsh* - only did so on the narrow basis that the 1979 Regulations were *ultra vires*, since s 75 - as properly construed - did not in fact enable or empower the Minister to make regulations altering or amending the substantive law. As Finlay CJ observed:

> "[T]he terms of s 75 do not make it necessary or inevitable that a Minister for Social Welfare making regulations pursuant to the power therein created must invade the function of the Oireachtas in a manner which would constitute a breach of the provisions of Article 15.2. The wide scope and unfettered discretion contained in the section can clearly be exercised by a Minister making regulations so as to ensure that what is done is truly regulatory or administrative only and does not constitute the making, repealing or amending of the law in a manner which would be invalid having regard to the provisions of the Constitution."[18]

A significant feature of *Harvey* is that it demonstrates the fact that there are, in fact essentially two strands to the case-law on Article 15.2.1:

[15] [1987] IR 213.

[16] [1990] 2 IR 232. See also *McHugh v Minister for Social Welfare*, Supreme Court, 11 March 1992.

[17] Social Welfare (Overlapping Benefits) (Amendment) Regulations 1979.

[18] Note that in *Ambiorix Ltd. v Minister for Environment (No.2)* [1992] 1 IR 37, Lynch J upheld the constitutionality of s 6(2) of the Urban Renewal Act 1986 which provided that:

> "The Minister may....by order declare an area to be a designated area where he is satisfied that there is a special need to promote urban renewal therein, and may by such order describe such area in whatever manner he thinks fit."

Lynch J, rejecting the challenge based on Article 15.2.1, said that the "scheme or policy" of the legislation was clear and was quite similar to that upheld in *Cityview Press*: "The details are to be filled in by the Minister....and, in particular, the areas where having considered the factors for and against designation at any particular time and in relation to any particular area the Minister decided that the legislation should operate."

(i) the "principles and policies" criteria and

(ii) that the Oireachtas may not delegate the power to make, repeal or amend the law.[19]

While these strands are related, they are mutually exclusive criteria, in that, for example, a statute which contained clear principles and policies might yet fall to be condemned under Article 15.2.1 if it purported to give the relevant Minister power to amend its provisions by regulation.

Doubts as to the validity of the Imposition of Duties Act 1957

It was not, perhaps, until the judgment of Blayney J in *McDaid v Sheehy*[20] that the full significance and potential of the *Cityview Press* principles was realised. Here the applicant challenged the constitutionality of s 1 of the Imposition of Duties Act 1957, which empowers the Government power by order to impose, vary or terminate any excise, customs or stamp duty.[21] Such is the comprehensiveness of s 1, coupled with the absence of any principles or policies in the Act itself, it is scarcely surprising that Blayney J concluded that the section was inconsistent with Article 15.2:

> "The question to be answered is: Are the powers contained in these provisions more than a mere giving effect to principles and policies contained in the Act itself? In my opinion, they clearly are. There are no principles and policies contained in the Act. Section 1 states baldly that the 'Government may by order" do a number of things, one of which is to impose a customs duty or an excise duty of an amount as they think proper on any particular description of goods imported into the State. In my opinion, the power given to the Government here is a power to legislate. It is left to the Government to determine what imported goods are to have a customs or excise duty. And the Government is left totally free in exercising this power. It is far from a case of the Government filling in only the details. The fundamental question in regard to the imposition of customs or excise duties is, first, on what goods should a duty be imposed, and secondly, what should be the amount of the duty? The decision on both of these matters is left to the Government. In my opinion, it was a proper subject for legislation and could not be delegated by the Oireachtas. "

Although Blayney J declared that s 1 of the 1957 Act was unconstitutional, this did not avail the applicant, since the judge found that the 1975 Order (under which the applicant had been convicted) had been independently confirmed by the Oireachtas with the enactment of s 46 of the Finance Act 1976, and this served to cure the unconstitutionality which had originally attended the making of the Order in 1975. It was for this highly technical reason that the Supreme Court set aside the finding of Blayney J that s 1 was unconstitutional,[22] but this cannot take from the fact that the latter's impressive reason-

[19] Note that in *Meagher v Minister for Agriculture*, High Court, 1 April 1993, Johnson J observed that counsel for the Minister had "very properly" conceded that, were it not for the provisions of Article 29.4.3, legislation which purported to enable the Executive to amend the law by statutory instrument was unconstitutional. In any event, Johnson J found that Article 29.4.3 did not operate to confer constitutional immunity on this procedure: see pp. 290-291.

[20] [1991] 1 IR 1.

[21] The only check on the Government's powers in this regard is contained in s 2(1) which provides that any order will expire at the end of the year following that in which it is made unless confirmed by Act of the Oireachtas.

[22] Finlay CJ said that by reason of s 46 of the Finance Act 1976, "the applicant [had] not been prejudiced or damaged by the operation of any provision of the Act of 1957 or of any statutory order made pursuant it." In those circumstances, the Court held that it should decline to pronounce on the wider constitutional issue: see p. 451.

ing has effectively condemned the Act and it is now improbable that the Act would survive a challenge in an appropriate case.[23]

Doubts as to the validity of the European Communities (Amendment) Act 1973

These developments were taken a step further in *Meagher v Minister for Agriculture and Food.*[24] Here the applicant challenged the validity of 1988 and 1990 statutory instruments which had been by the Minister pursuant to s 3(2) of the European Communities Act 1972. This sub-section provides that:

> Regulations under this section may contain such incidental, supplementary and consequential provisions as appears to the Minister making the Regulations to be necessary for the purposes of the Regulations (including provisions repealing, amending or applying, without or without modification, other law, exclusive of this Act.

The statutory instruments in question[25] had purported to amend s 10(4) of the Petty Sessions (Ireland) Act 1851[26] and Johnson J noted that counsel for the Attorney General had conceded that, were it not "for the European law dimension", the applicant's case would have been unanswerable, inasmuch as the statutory instruments had purported to amend ordinary statute law. But Johnson J would not accept that Article 29.4.3[27] gave the Minister an unfettered discretion with regard to the implementation of directives, since he considered that:

> "where it is appropriate for the purposes of the directives and their implementation that, in regard to Article 15 of the Constitution, legislation be introduced and Acts enacted then they should be done and any power given to a Minister to make regulations for the purposes of amending or repealing laws is constitutional. "

Johnson J accordingly held that such portion of s 3(2) of the European Communities Act 1972 as gave the Minister power by regulation to repeal or amend other law was an unconstitutional contravention of Article 15.2.1.[28]

Other miscellaneous provisions open to challenge

There is a surprisingly large number of miscellaneous statutory provisions which would now seem open to challenge in the light of the *Cityview Press* criteria and some examples may be mentioned here. A good example is supplied by s 5 of the Aliens Act 1935 which enables the Minister for Justice to make orders regulating the conduct of aliens within the State. The generality of the powers thereby conferred, coupled with the absence of principles and policies in the section, would all seem to leave the section par-

[23] It may be significant that the Government has not made any orders pursuant to the 1957 Act since early 1989, the date of the judgment of Blayney J.

[24] High Court, 1 April 1993.

[25] European Communities (Control of Ostrogenic etc. Substances) Regulations, 1988 and European Communities (Control of Veterinary Medicinal Products and their Residues) Regulations 1990.

[26] Which provides that a complaint in summary matters must be made to the District Court within six months from the date of the alleged offence.

[27] Now Article 29.4.5.

[28] This analysis is borne out by Article 189 of the Treaty of Rome itself which clearly leaves the "choice and form of methods" of implementation to the member states, i.e., thereby suggesting that there is no particular *method of implementation* of directives which is "necessitated" by Community law.

ticularly vulnerable to constitutional challenge.[29] A more recent example is supplied by s 99(2A) of the Companies Act 1963 (as inserted by s 122 of the Companies Act 1990) which allows the Minister for Enterprise and Employment to make regulations amending s 99(2) (which prescribes a list of chattels and objects in respect of which charges must be registered with the Registrar of Companies) "so as to add any description of charge to, or remove any description of charge from, the charges requiring registration under this section." This would seem to involve the Minister engaging in impermissible legislative activity, since - in the words of Finlay CJ in *Harvey* - he would be thereby "making, amending or repealing the law."

A more difficult constitutional issue is presented by s 16(1) of the Courts Act 1991 which enables the Government to amend the monetary limits of civil jurisdiction in respect of the District and Circuit Courts, but which provides that any such variation order shall have regard "to changes in the value of money generally in the State since the said monetary amount was so specified." This sub-section plainly satisfies the "principles and policies" test[30] (since the Government are not "at large" in the making of any such order, but may only do so having regard to the inflation figures for the relevant years since the monetary limit was last statutorily adjusted), but it may nonetheless be objected to on the ground that it confers on the Government power to amend earlier enactments, something which *Harvey's* case would seem to prohibit.

Pursuit of secondary purpose does not necessarily vitiate exercise of delegated legislative power

It is well established that the Oireachtas may delegate the power to make rules etc. to a subordinate authority, in order to carry out the main purpose of the law which the Oireachtas has enacted; rules made in purported reliance on such a law can be successfully challenged only if their substance, or the motive of their making, are outside what the Oireachtas intended.[31] But it does not vitiate the exercise of a power thus conferred if the subordinate authority has a second motive concurrently in mind along with the one primarily related to the purpose of the Act. This appears from *Cassidy v Minister for Industry and Commerce*,[32] in which a Maximum Prices Order made under the Prices Act 1958, in respect of drink prices in the Dundalk area was challenged by the publicans affected. It was shown that the Minister had the purpose, not only of eliminating unwarranted price increases, but also of inducing the publicans to return to the voluntary practice, previously observed, of not making price increases without giving him notice. Henchy J, with whom O'Higgins CJ and Griffin J agreed, said:

[29] Thus, for example, s 5(2)(*b*) enables the Minister to make an order:

> "conferring on the Minister and on officers of the Minister, officers of customs and excise and the military and police forces of the State all such powers (including powers of arrest and detention) as are, in the opinion of the Minister, necessary for giving full effect to or enforcing compliance with such order."

The vagueness of these criteria, taken together with the absence of any guidance as to the length of detention, the circumstances in which the arrest might be effected etc., all suggests that this sub-section would not survive an attack based on *Cityview Press* criteria.

[30] On the other hand, s 2A of the Mergers, Take-Overs and Monopolies (Control) Act 1978 simply allows the Minister for Enterprise and Employment to amend the financial thresholds to which the Act applies. The threshold has been raised from the original turnover figure of £25m to £20m: see Mergers, Take-Overs and Monopolies (Control) Act 1978 (Section 2) Order 1993. This sub-section would seem to be constitutionally objectionable in that (i) it allows the Minister to amend the law by statutory order and (ii) the sub-section contains no adequate principles and policies.

[31] See generally, Hogan and Morgan, *Administrative Law in Ireland* (London, 1991) at 25-32.

[32] [1978] IR 297.

> "Where a power to legislate for a particular purpose is delegated and the power is exercised *bona fide* and primarily for that purpose, I consider that the exercise of the power is not vitiated if it is aimed also at the attainment of a subsidiary or consequential purpose which is not inconsistent with the permitted purpose. If the law were otherwise, many delegated powers would be unexercisable, for the permitted purpose frequently encompasses of necessity the attainment of other purposes."

A similar question was considered in unusual circumstances by Murphy J in *An Blascaoid Mór Teo. v Commissioners of Public Works*[33] where the plaintiffs had sought discovery of documents and material pertaining to the decision to enact a particular piece of legislation.[34] Murphy J held that such material was not relevant to the action and, hence, not discoverable. In his view, the motives of the legislators was irrelevant to the question of constitutional validity:

> "In legal terms an analysis of the motivation for legislation would be meaningless in practice...and wholly unjustified by the separation of powers The validity of the legislation must be tested by reference to the document ultimately enacted by the Oireachtas and not on the basis of motive, intention or purpose of the [legislators]."

It may be thought that this passage is too absolutist in its exclusion of motive in any consideration of the validity of legislation. Is it to be said, for example, that motive is wholly irrelevant in the case of legislation which is neutral on its face but which in reality is designed to disadvantage a particular group? Suppose, for example, that certain electoral legislation was designed to achieve a particular (impermissible) purpose, such as by, perhaps, unfairly assisting certain political parties through the revision of constituency boundaries, would not the question of motive and intention behind the sponsors of the legislation be a relevant issue? [35]

Intentions ascribed to Oireachtas in creating delegated legislation

The duty of administrative authorities not to exceed their powers and to observe fair procedures (or "natural and constitutional justice") is dealt with primarily in the context of Article 28 and Article 34. The relation of this duty to, and its derivation from, the presumed intent of the Oireachtas in enacting the legislation under which the authority functions was stated with peculiar clarity in *Burke v Minister for Labour*[36] where the functioning of a Joint Labour Committee under the Industrial Relations Act 1946, was under attack. Henchy J said:

> "Where Parliament has delegated functions of that nature, it is to be necessarily inferred as part of the legislative intention that the body which makes the orders

[33] High Court, 27 November 1992.

[34] The legislation in question was An Blascaoid Mór National Historic Park Act 1989. The plaintiffs contended that the 1989 Act conferred arbitrary powers of compulsory acquisition in respect of certain lands situate on the Blasket Islands, contrary to Articles 40.3 and 43.

[35] Consider in this context the difficult problem presented in *Palmer v Thompson* 403 US 217 (1971) where a municipality, having been ordered to de-segregate public swimming pools, decided to close them rather than avoid racial integration. A majority of the US Supreme Court held that mere legislative bad faith was not enough, with Black J saying that:

> "There was an element of futility in a judicial attempt to invalidate a law because of the bad motives of its supporters. If the law is struck down for this reason, rather than because of its facial content or effect, it would presumably be valid as soon as the legislature repassed it for different reasons."

On the other hand, it may be noted that in *Listowel UDC v McDonagh* [1968] IR 316 the Supreme Court that evidence as to the motives of the elected councillors was a relevant issue in considering the validity of local bye-laws.

[36] [1979] IR 354. Henchy J expressed similar views in a trenchant judgment in *McCord v ESB* [1980] ILRM 153.

will exercise its functions, not only with constitutional propriety and due regard to natural justice, but also within the framework of the terms and objects of the relevant Act and with basic fairness, reasonableness and good faith. The absoluteness of the delegation is susceptible of unjust and tyrannous abuse unless its operation is thus confined; so it is entirely proper to ascribe to the Oireachtas (being the Parliament of a State which is constitutionally bound to protect, by its laws, its citizens from unjust attack) an intention that the delegated functions must be exercised within those limitations."

Indispensable function of the Oireachtas in giving effect to international agreements

Article 15.2.1 has played a subsidiary role in enforcing the principle of Article 29.6 ("No international agreement shall be part of the domestic law of the State save as may be determined by the Oireachtas") and in refuting the argument that the State's acceptance of the generally recognised principles of international law Article 29.3) should give such principles primacy over domestic enactments. In *In re Ó Láighléis*,[37] in which the applicant unsuccessfully invoked the European Human Rights Convention against the internment provisions of the Offences against the State (Amendment) Act 1940, both Davitt P in the High Court and Maguire CJ in the Supreme Court cited Article 15.2.1 and Article 29.6 side by side; Maguire CJ described them as jointly representing an "insuperable obstacle" to the applicant's case. In *The State (Sumers Jennings) v Furlong*,[38] in which the applicant was raising, as a generally recognised principle of international law, the "rule of speciality" against Part III of the Extradition Act 1965, Davitt P cited his own words in *Ó Láighléis's* case:

> "Where there is an irreconcilable conflict between a domestic statute and the principles of international law or the provisions of an international convention, the courts administering the domestic law must give effect to the statute... If this principle were not to be observed it would follow that the Executive Government by means of an international agreement might, in certain circumstances, be able to exercise powers of legislation contrary to the letter and the spirit of the Constitution."

Henchy J added:

> "Section 3 of Article 29...was not enacted, and is not to be interpreted in these courts, as a statement of the absolute restriction of the legislative powers of the State by the generally recognised principles of international law."

This rather strict view has since been modified in part, for the courts will now presume that the law is in conformity with international agreements[39] and will also, in certain circumstances, give indirect effect to international agreements which have been ratified by the State, but which have not been incorporated into domestic law.[40]

The courts will not take on a legislative function

The courts have been careful in certain contexts to disclaim any exercise of their own jurisdiction that would encroach on the legislative function (as distinct from controlling

[37] [1960] IR 93; (1961) ILTR 92.

[38] [1966] IR 183.

[39] See the comments of Henchy J in *The State (DPP) v Walsh* [1981] IR 412 and *Ó Domhnaill v Merrick* [1984] IR 151 and those O'Hanlon J in *Desmond v Glackin (No.1)* [1992] ILRM 490.

[40] *Fakik v Minister for Justice* [1993] ILRM 274; *Gutrani v Minister for Justice*, Supreme Court, 2 July 1992; *Kajli v Minister for Justice*, High Court, 21 August 1992.

it on constitutional criteria). This has been frequently stated in a series of cases where the courts have been asked to interfere in the referendum process,[41] but similar statements of principle have also been made outside of this special context.

In *In re Green Dale Building Co.*[42] a claimant whose lands were the subject of a compulsory purchase order had, in reliance on a notice to treat served by the acquiring authority which turned out to be invalid, arranged for the appointment of a property arbitrator, and argued (because the value of the lands thereafter diminished) that by estoppel the acquiring authority had lost the right to rely on the invalidity of the notice. This original notice was invalid for failure to comply with the conditions prescribed by the Act under which it purported to have been issued; and the Supreme Court, *per* Henchy J, said that:

> "if the courts were to allow subsequent conduct to outweigh the requirements of the subsection, they would (in effect) be amending the subsection, which is something beyond the constitutional competence of the courts."

The incapacity of the courts to take on a legislative function has also been demonstrated in other contexts. In *The State (Murphy) v Johnston*[43] the Supreme Court refused to correct an obvious mistake in the provisions of the Road Traffic (Amendment) Act 1978. The prosecutor had been convicted of drunken driving under the provisions of s 49 of that Act but s 23 (which dealt with the taking of a blood or urine sample by a registered medical practitioner) erroneously referred to Part III, rather than to Part V of the Road Traffic Act 1968. The Court quashed the conviction, reaffirming the courts' incapacity to correct such an error.

Whether judicial development and extension of common law principles is a form of impermissible judicial legislation?

The extent to which the courts can take it upon themselves to extend and develop the law without infringing Article 15.2. has been considered in a series of cases involving aspects of family law. In the first of these decisions, *M.M. v P.M.*,[44] a nullity case, the High Court refused to invent a new ground for according a known remedy. Here McMahon J refused to recognise inability to inseminate as constituting impotence, on the grounds that this would amount:

> "to adding a new ground of nullity to those recognised in ecclesiastical law as administered before the Matrimonial Causes and Marriage Law (Ireland) Amendment Act 1870. That is a statutory requirement which governs the exercise of the jurisdiction of the High Court in nullity cases and...it is not open to the High Court to depart from the statute by admitting a new ground of nullity. Under the Constitution, the jurisdiction of the High Court extends to determining all questions of nullity of marriage, but that is a jurisdiction which clearly must be exercised upon grounds to be determined by the legislature. For the courts to add new grounds would be to engage in legislation."

This analysis was endorsed by Keane J in *U.F. v J.C.*[45], where he declined to sanction the extension of a new ground of nullity, namely, emotional disability or incapacity at the time of marriage. Noting that the Oireachtas had "studiously ... declined to imple-

[41] See, e.g., *Finn v Attorney General* [1983] IR 154; *Slattery v An Taoiseach* [1993] IR 286 and generally at pp. 1125-1128.
[42] [1977] IR 256.
[43] [1983] IR 235.
[44] [1986] ILRM 515.
[45] [1991] 2 IR 330.

ment in any way" either a report of the Attorney General[46] or previous policy suggests the Law Reform Commission[47] which had recommended such changes in the law, Keane J concluded that "to formulate new grounds for nullity in the manner suggested constitutes an impermissible assumption of the legislative power which Article 15.2.1 vests exclusively in the Oireachtas." Before the Supreme Court could hear the appeal from the judgment of Keane J, Lardner J had expressed a contrary view in *R.T. v V.P.*:[48]

> "Historically the common law has developed at least in part by the application of established principles to new cases - to novel facts and circumstances It has undoubtedly involved the development of the law and novel judicial decisions are not uncommonly referred to as judge-made law. It is a judicial activity which has occurred in Ireland for centuries and has continued in the superior courts prior to an since the enactment of the Constitution...It is not in its proper exercise an impermissible exercise of the legislative function."

The Supreme Court did not expressly deal with this point in allowing the appeal in *U.F.*, although it is implicit in the judgments of both Finlay CJ and McCarthy J that they were unpersuaded by the reasoning of Keane J. On the other hand, in *McGrath v McDermott*,[49] a revenue case, the Supreme Court rejected an invitation to apply the doctrine of "fiscal nullity", saying that in the absence of the courts being granted by statute a general power to deal with tax avoidance, for the courts now to avoid the application of tax legislation to the fiscal transactions under review in the case "could only constitute the invasion by the judiciary of the powers and functions of the legislature, in plain breach of the constitutional separation of powers." Another example of this approach is to be found in *L. v L.*,[50] where the Supreme Court was required to consider whether Article 41.2.2 could be construed as giving a wife a proprietary share in a family home even where no financial contribution had been made by her either to the purchase of the property or to any mortgage.[51] Finlay CJ reversing the decision of Barr J at first instance, concluded that this would not be permissible:

> "I conclude that to the identify this right in the circumstances...is not to develop any known principle of the common law, but is rather to identify a brand new right and to secure it to the plaintiff. Unless that is something clearly and unambiguously warranted by the Constitution or made necessary for the protection of either a specified or unspecified right under it, it must constitute legislation and be a usurpation by the courts of the function of the legislature."

Cases such as *McGrath* and *L.* show that it is widely acknowledged that there is a line beyond which the courts cannot or ought not to go under the guise of judicial development of the law,[52] but the difficulty arises in deciding where that line should be drawn.[53]

[46] *The Law of Nullity in Ireland* (Prl. 5626, 1976).
[47] *Report on Nullity in Marriage*, LRC-9, 1984.
[48] [1990] 1 IR 545.
[49] [1988] IR 258.
[50] [1992] 2 IR 77.
[51] See further at pp. 1010-1012.
[52] See, e.g., the comments of Henchy J in *Hynes-O'Sullivan v O'Driscoll* [1988] IR 436 where he said that: "the suggested radical change in the hitherto accepted law [of qualified privilege] should more properly be effected by statute. The public policy which a new formulation of the law would represent should more properly be found by the Law Reform Commission or by those others who are in a position to take a broad perspective as distinct from what is discernible in the tunnelled vision imposed by the facts of a single case."
[53] This issue was also visible in *W. v W.* [1993] ILRM 294 The Court was unanimous in its conclusion that the former dependent domicile rule infringed Article 40.1 (see p.998), but the Court divided on the question of whether it could substitute a new rule retroactively in respect of foreign divorces granted prior to 2 October

Courts have no role in law reform

In *Norris v Attorney General*,[54] which was an attack on nineteenth-century laws penalising male homosexual conduct, O'Higgins CJ was at pains to emphasise that law reform, as distinct from applying constitutional criteria to laws under challenge:

> "is not, and can never be a function of this Court. Judges may, and do share with other citizens, a concern and interest in desirable changes and reform in our laws, but, under the Constitution, they have no function in achieving such by judicial decision... The sole and exclusive power of altering the laws of Ireland is, by the Constitution, vested in the Oireachtas."

In *Attorney General (Society for the Protection of the Unborn Child (Ireland) Ltd.) v Open-Door Counselling Ltd.*[55] Hamilton P acknowledged that it was not ordinarily the function of the courts to extend the criminal law, but, although he was not required to decide the issue, he thought that in some cases:

> "where there is a breach of, or interference with, a fundamental personal or human right, [the courts] may be under a constitutional obligation to do so in order to respect, and, as far as practicable, to defend and vindicate that right.

But he also quoted with approval from the judgment of O'Higgins CJ in *Norris's* case,[56] and suggested that any extension of the criminal law in the context of abortion should best be left to the Oireachtas.

Similarly in *Attorney General v Paperlink Ltd.*,[57] where the defendants claimed that the post office monopoly infringed their rights to earn a livelihood (in this instance, by operating a courier service), and wanted to give evidence showing how the post office could be organised in a way which was both more efficient and not impaired by their separate operation, Costello J refused to permit this, saying that:

> "to carry out the inquiry which the defendants ask me to perform and, thereafter, make a determination on an alternative to the existing postal service, would amount to an unwarranted and unconstitutional interference with the powers of government exclusively conferred on the Executive and the Oireachtas."

The same judge also spoke to like effect in *O'Reilly v Limerick Corporation*[58] where, although sympathetic to the claim that the "personal freedom and dignity of which the Constitution speaks cannot adequately be achieved without the provision of certain basic services for the homeless and deprived young people", he nonetheless concluded that:

> "The courts' constitutional function is to administer justice, but I do not think that by exercising the suggested supervisory role it could be said that a court was admin-

1986 (i.e., the date on which the Domicile and Recognition of Foreign Divorces Act 1986 came into force). Blayney and Egan JJ delivered majority judgments in which they saw no such impediment; whereas Hederman J dissented on the ground that since the 1986 Act was not given retroactive effect, "this [issue] is solely a matter for the Oireachtas [and] it is not open to the Court to 'amend' [this Act] by giving it a retroactive effect expressly denied by the Oireachtas." See also the (somewhat rhetorical) comments of Denham J in *Howard v Commissioners of Public Works in Ireland* [1993] ILRM 665, where, in the course of rejecting a far-reaching interpretation of the Planning Acts which have resulted in the exemption of the Commissioners from its application, she declared that "so to construe the Act would, in fact, be to legislate which is not the function of this Court, but rather that of the Oireachtas."

[54] [1984] IR 36.

[55] [1988] IR 593.

[56] [1984] IR 36.

[57] [1984] ILRM 353.

[58] [1989] ILRM 181.

istering justice as contemplated in the Constitution. [Rather] it would be engaged in an entirely different exercise, namely, an adjudication on the fairness or otherwise of the manner in which other organs of State had administered public resources. Apart from the fact that members of the judiciary have no special qualification to undertake such a function, the manner in which justice is administered in the courts, that is on a case by case basis, make them a wholly inappropriate institution for the fulfilment of the suggested role. I cannot construe the Constitution as conferring it on them."[59]

Neither will the courts bend the application of a statutory scheme by reference to suggested standards of general justice. In *Heaney v Minister for Finance*[60] the plaintiff challenged the validity of the prize bond scheme established by the Finance (Miscellaneous Provisions) Act 1956, on the ground that inflation had rendered the competition unfair; he contended that, as Article 34 imposed upon judges an overriding duty to achieve justice by creating a new scheme, and as the issue of prize bonds in 1985 at the same nominal price as paid by him in 1961 - despite the steep fall in the value of money during that period - represented a serious injustice, judicial intervention was warranted. Murphy J said that to interpret Article 34 in this fashion:

"would be to vest in judges of the Superior Courts vast powers to substitute their view of what is fair and just for that of the Oireachtas, which has the right and duty of making the laws in accordance with which justice is to be achieved."[61]

Application of standards primarily legislative may be entrusted to the courts

But the Oireachtas need not be viewed as the sole constitutional arbiter of constitutional standards such as "the exigencies of the common good" recognised by the Preamble and by Article 43. In *Abbey Films Ltd. v Attorney General*,[62] in which the plaintiffs argued that s 15(3) of the Restrictive Practices Act 1972. which empowered the High Court to declare that "the exigencies of the common good did not warrant the exercise by the Examiner [of Restrictive Practices of the powers conferred on him by [the] section", infringed the sole discretion of the Oireachtas in the application of such a standard, the Supreme Court rejected the submission:

"The promotion of the common good is one of the aims (as stated in the Preamble) which the people wished to achieve by adopting the Constitution. While this promotion is primarily the function of the Legislature...there is nothing to prevent the Legislature from investing the courts with the sole jurisdiction to determine whether a particular act is or is not required by the exigencies of the common good."

[59] For a discussion of this important case, see Whyte, *Constitutional Adjudication, Ideology and Access to the Courts,* in Whelan ed., *Law and Liberty in Ireland* (Dublin 1993). See also *In re Article 26 and the Electoral (Amendment) Bill 1961* [1961] IR 169, where the Supreme Court refused - in the context of projected constituency revisions - to lay down a figure "above or below which a variation form what is called the national average is not permitted", saying that this was task for the Oireachtas.

[60] [1986] IR 164. See also *A.D. v Ireland,* High Court, 20 July 1992 (where Carroll J held that the plaintiff's claim that the State should compensate her for criminal injuries suffered was a matter for the Government and the Oireachtas and not for the Courts.)

[61] See also the comments by the same judge in *O'Reilly v Minister for Environment* [1986] IR 143 where, rejecting a claim that the alphabetical system of arranging ballot papers was discriminatory, he said that it was not his "duty or function", but that of the Oireachtas, to evaluate the competing merits of different method of compiling a ballot paper.

[62] [1979] IR 256.

Courts will not take it in themselves to "mend" legislation

A very important form taken by the disclaiming by the courts of any legislative function is the self-imposed limitation of the "mending" function in regard to legislation found partly constitutional. There have been instances[63] where the courts have treated sections of Acts as though certain words were deleted or added, where such deletions or additions appeared necessary in order to reconcile such sections with the Constitution; but in *Maher v Attorney General*[64] it was made clear that the constitutional flaw in an Act may be such that the courts will not undertake a patching operation more properly the business of the Legislature.[65]

Judicial role in filling constitutional lacuna

In the same way the courts will, generally speaking, not write a new provision into an Act in order to supply a gap which may have a constitutionally undesirable effect: this was made clear in a case in which the plaintiff complained of the state of the law on Dáil elections which left him unable to vote: *Reynolds v Attorney General.*[66] This approach was also manifest in *Somjee v Minister for Justice*[67] where the plaintiffs[68] had challenged the constitutionality of s 15 of the Irish Citizenship and Nationality Act 1956 which provided that foreign females marrying male citizens where automatically entitled to Irish citizenship, but the converse was not true in the case of foreign males marrying female citizens.[69] Keane J was of the view that this "diversity of arrangements" was not unconstitutional, but that even if he had been so minded, there was another "fatal obstacle" to the plaintiff's claim, since the court had jurisdiction only to invalidate the section (which in the circumstances would have conferred no benefit on the plaintiffs). The plaintiffs had urged the court to invalidate the section in the expectation that the Oireachtas would then be required to legislate in the light of that judgment, but this solution was firmly rejected:

> "The court has no jurisdiction to substitute for the impugned enactment a form of enactment which it considers desirable or to indicate to the Oireachtas the appropriate form of enactment which should be substituted for the impugned enactment." [70]

This reasoning is open to the objection that it would effectively allow the Oireachtas to evade its constitutional obligations by creating an under-inclusive statutory category for

[63] Examples include *Deaton v Attorney General* [1963] IR 170; (1964) 98 ILTR 99; *The State (Sheerin) v Kennedy* [1966] IR 379: *The State (C.) v Minister for Justice* [1967] IR 106; (1968) 102 ILTR 177: *In re McAllister* [1973] IR 238; *Desmond v Glackin*, Supreme Court, 30 July 1992.

[64] [1973] IR 140; (1974) 108 ILTR 41.

[65] See generally at pp. 473-477.

[66] *The Irish Times,* 18 February 1973. But c.f. the view of McMahon J in *Draper v Attorney General* [1984] IR 277 considered at FN 70 below.

[67] [1981] ILRM 324. Similar views were expressed by Carroll J in *Mhic Mathúna v Attorney General* [1989] IR 504 where she held that the plaintiffs lacked standing to challenge the validity of tax and social welfare benefits payable to other categories of persons in circumstances where "the best result the plaintiffs could hope to achieve would be the removal of such benefits" and "without achieving any benefits for themselves."

[68] The plaintiffs were husband and wife; the husband was a foreign national who sought Irish citizenship.

[69] This discriminatory regime has now been replaced by s 8 of the Irish Nationality and Citizenship Act 1986.

[70] But this reasoning was subsequently stated by McMahon J in *Draper v Attorney General* [1984] IR 277 not to apply where the Oireachtas is under a constitutional duty "to provide by law for the exercise of a constitutional right", since the duty so to provide "in accordance with the Constitution remains after the unconstitutional provisions are struck down." Examples of such constitutional duties to legislate would include Article 16.2.1 (duty to determine Dáil constituencies); Article 16.7 (regulation by law of Dáil elections); Article 36 (regulation by law constitution and organisation of the courts and the judiciary). Besides, the Supreme Court has subsequently indicated to the Oireachtas that certain forms of new legislation will be required following the invalidation of a statute: see, e.g., *Blake v Attorney General* [1981] IR 117.

which the courts could apparently provide no remedy. And yet there are hints from the Supreme Court that this approach may be regarded as too timorous. In *McKinley v Minister for Defence*[71] the Supreme Court condemned the common law rule whereby only husbands could sue in respect of loss of consortium as inconsistent with the guarantee of equality in Article 40.1. The Court was divided on the question of whether the rule should be extended (as contended for by the plaintiff) or whether the cause of action should simply be held to be unconstitutional. The minority judges - Finlay CJ and Egan J - favoured the latter solution, since to do otherwise would, in their view, involve the courts in legislating. The majority thought otherwise and argued that the rule should be extended, for, as McCarthy J explained:

> "Where a common law rule offends against the principle of equality in a marriage relationship, the solution is to identify and declare the equality by positive rather than negative action. Whatever the origin of a particular common law right, however artificial its base when viewed from a modern standpoint if, as here, such a right is so firmly established as part of the common law, equality amongst equals requires a Court declaration to that effect, rather than what would be judicial legislation by denying such a claim to the husband."

This, however, can scarcely be a universal test, even in the case of common law rules which offended against the doctrine of spousal equality. For example, the courts have invalidated the dependent domicile rule, rather than sanction its extension, since to do so would have led to bizarre results.[72] But while cases such as *McKinley* can be justified on the ground that the courts are merely developing the common law, different considerations may arise in cases where, as in *Somjee*, the rule has a legislative backing. How would the courts react, for example, to 0 75 r 47 of the Rules of the Superior Courts 1986, which allows a wife (but not a husband) to apply for alimony *pendente lite* in matrimonial proceedings? This rule would appear to offend against Article 40.1; but it is more difficult to say whether the courts would be empowered to read the rule in a gender-neutral way (by extending the ambit of the rule to include husbands) or whether the rule should simply be declared unconstitutional.[73]

Non-legislative functions of the Oireachtas

While Article 15 vests the Oireachtas with exclusive legislative power, this is not to suggest that other parliamentary functions - ranging from general supervision and review of the actions of the Government to powers of investigation - are not constitutionally sanctioned. This is borne out by other constitutional provisions Thus, Article 15.13 in declaring that utterances of members in either House are absolutely privileged may be taken as reflecting (in part) the desirability of protecting members who raise matters of contro-

[71] [1992] 2 IR 333. The plaintiff's husband had been injured in an explosion while training with the Defence Forces and had been rendered sterile and impotent. See generally, Hogan, "*Remedies for Inequality*" (1992) 10 DULJ (n.s.) 115.

[72] Such an extension would have meant that whereas a wife's domicile would have been dependent on that of her husband, the domicile of the husband would have been dependent on that of his wife!

[73] Note the approach of the German Constitutional Court in the *Judicial Salaries* case, BVerfGE 26,100 (1969). Here the Court was of opinion that the disparity in judicial salaries payable to judges of different courts infringed the equality provisions of Article 3 of the Basic Law. Having identified the presence of this unconstitutional norm, it left to the Bundestag the question of whether the higher salaries should be reduced or the lower salaries increased. On the other hand in (Case C - 377/89) *Cotter and McDermott v Minister for Social Welfare* [1991] 3 CMLR 507 the Court of Justice appeared to exclude any "levelling down" of welfare benefits in order to achieve equal treatment retrospectively under the Social Security Equality Directive - 79/7/EEC.

versy and concern, thus implicitly acknowledging that the proper role of parliamentarians goes beyond strictly legislative duties.[74] This is powerfully re-inforced by Article 28.4.1 (which requires that the Government is responsible to the Dáil) and by Article 28.4.3 (which requires the approval of the Dáil for Government estimates of expenditure). Finally, the Supreme Court has confirmed in *Goodman International v Hamilton (No.1)*[75] that the Oireachtas has power to conduct a fact-finding and investigative process - whether under its own aegis or that of an agent such as a Tribunal of Inquiry - thus providing further evidence that the Oireachtas is not to be confined to the manner or content of its deliberations to that which is strictly legislative in character.[76]

Usurping the legislative function

A special provision to penalise the usurpation of (*inter alia*) the function of the Oireachtas exists in s 6 of the Offences Against the State Act 1939. Subsection 1 makes it a felony, punishable with up to ten years' penal servitude, to:

> [usurp] or unlawfully [exercise] any function of government, whether by setting up, maintaining, or taking part in any way in a body of persons purporting to be a government or a legislature but not authorised in that behalf by or under the Constitution...

Subsection 2 makes it a misdemeanour punishable with up to two years' imprisonment to attempt, assist or conspire towards any such offence. These provisions replaced those of ss 4-6 of the Treasonable Offences Act 1925; s 5 of this Act was aimed at persons taking part in:

> any proceedings of any assembly or body (other than the Oireachtas or either House thereof) which claims, purports, proposes, or attempts to take upon itself, or does take upon itself, all or any of the powers and functions of the Oireachtas or of either House thereof.

"Subordinate legislatures": 1922 provision

The "subordinate legislatures" of Article 15.2.2 featured also in Article 44 of the old Constitution (though there the Oireachtas was empowered only to "create", not to recognise what would presumably be already existing legislatures). The provision in each Constitution was intended as a mechanism to facilitate new arrangements with Northern Ireland. No use was ever made of either the 1922 or the 1937 provision.

Rule-making agencies are not "subordinate legislatures"

Subordinate administrative agencies with rule-making functions are not within the intendment of the sub-section, or so it appears from *The State (Devine) v Larkin,*[77] where the regulatory functions of the Foyle Fisheries Commission were in issue; McMahon J said in the High Court that:

[74] As O'Flaherty J remarked in *Attorney General v Hamilton (No 2)* [1993] ILRM 821 when discussing the ambit of Article 15.13: "So while, undoubtedly, the essential function of deputies is to legislate it should be emphasised that it is not their only function. They are also *representatives* of those who elect them. Deputies have an obligation to air the concerns of the constituents and to draw attention to anything that is a matter of public unease or concern and they must be allowed to do so in freedom but each not neglecting to bring his individual judgment to bear on the issue in debate."

[75] [1992] 2 IR 542

[76] As Hederman J said in *Hamilton (No.1)*, the power to conduct investigations is "inherent in the legislative process", quoting with approval from the judgment of the US Supreme Court in *Watkins v United States* 354 US 178 (1957).

[77] [1977] IR 24.

> "No decision was cited in which the expression "subordinate legislatures" in Article 15.2...was considered, but it does not appear to be an appropriate description of a body which exercises a delegated statutory power to make regulations of the limited scope of fisheries regulations.. It is not necessary for the purpose of this judgment to decide upon the meaning of the expression "subordinate legislatures" as used in the Constitution."

The Executive may not suspend or refuse to enforce legislation

A corollary of the foregoing is that the executive may not take it upon itself to suspend or refuse to enforce Acts of the Oireachtas. This topic is considered elsewhere.[78]

[75] *Duggan v An Taoiseach* [1989] ILRM 710 and p. 228.

Article 15.3

FUNCTIONAL AND VOCATIONAL COUNCILS

3 1° The Oireachtas may provide for the establishment or recognition of functional or vocational councils representing branches of the social and economic life of the people.

2° A law establishing or recognising any such council shall determine its rights, powers and duties, and its relation to the Oireachtas and to the Government.

3 1° Tig leis an Oireachtas socrú a dhéanamh chun comhairlí feidhmeannais is gairme beatha, a ionadaíos ranna de shaol chomhdhaonnach agus de shaol gheilleagrach an phobail, a chur ar bun nó glacadh leo.

2° Dlí ar bith lena gcuirtear comhairle den sórt sin ar bun nó faoina nglactar léi ní foláir léiriú a bheith ann ar chearta, ar chumhachtaí agus ar dhualgais na comhairle sin, agus fós ar a comhbhaint leis an Oireachtais agus leis an Rialtas.

1922 provision

There was a substantially identical provision in Article 45 of the 1922 Constitution; possibly it may have been wished not to drop a provision which had proved harmless. Whether it has ever been relied on, in either the 1922 or the 1937 shape, is not apparent. Neither provision features in reported litigation.

No visible necessity for this section

In as much as the establishment of councils of the kind here envisaged must have been within the powers of the Oireachtas anyway, it is hard to see what purpose this section fulfills; it does not carry any suggestion that such councils might have powers or functions which would be unconstitutional unless they were specifically authorised in the Constitution itself.

Article 15.4

PROHIBITION OF UNCONSTITUTIONAL LEGISLATION

4. 1° The Oireachtas shall not enact any law which is in any respect repugnant to this Constitution or any provision thereof.

2° Every law enacted by the Oireachtas which is in any respect repugnant to this Constitution or to any provision thereof shall, but to the extent only of such repugnancy, be invalid.

4. 1° Ní cead don Oireachtas aon dlí a achtú a bheadh ar aon chuma in aghaidh an Bhunreachta seo nó in aghaidh aon fhorála den Bhunreacht seo.

2° I gcás aon dlí dá n-achtóidh an tOireachtas a bheith ar aon chuma in aghaidh an Bhunreachta seo nó in aghaidh aon fhorála den Bhunreacht seo beidh sé gan bhail sa mhéid go mbeidh sé in aghaidh an Bhunreachta seo agus sa mhéid sin amháin.

Article 15.4 is complementary to Article 34.3.2

The general prohibition on the enactment of unconstitutional legislation by the Oireachtas is given practical effect by Article 34.3.2, which empowers the High Court (and, on appeal, the Supreme Court: Article 34.4.4) to adjudicate on the constitutional validity of laws. Article 15.4 is occasionally expressly cited by court exercising this jurisdiction by way of laying the ground for it, e.g. in *N.U.R. v Sullivan;*[1] *Buckley v Attorney General.*[2] The presumption of constitutionality which operates in favour of an Act of the Oireachtas is based on the presumption an expression of the "respect which one great organ of State owes to another"[3] that the Oireachtas has obeyed the injunction of Article 15.4.1.[4] In *McMahon v Leahy*[5] Henchy J referred to Article 15.4.1 and said the fact that the Oireachtas was barred from enacting any law which is "in any respect" unconstitutional implied that legislation enacted by the Oireachtas not only enjoyed a presumption of constitutionality but also the presumption that the provisions of such laws will not be administered or applied in a way that will infringe constitutional rights.

Time from which invalidity of repugnant law is to date

Interpretation of Article 15.4.1 has an obvious role in the handling of the important and difficult question whether a finding of constitutional invalidity operates retrospectively to the moment of the enactment of the offending Act or provision - i.e. to the moment when the Oireachtas breached the prohibition of Article 15.4.1- or only from the moment of the finding. It seems more convenient to discuss this matter in the general context of judicial review, i.e. of Article 34.3.2[6].

[1] [1947] IR 77; (1947) 81 ILTR 55
[2] [1950] IR 67.
[3] O'Byrne J in *Buckley v Attorney General* [1950] IR 67, a dictum which has cited with approval in all the major separation of powers cases such as *Boland v An Taoiseach* [1974] IR 338; *Crotty v An Taoiseach* [1987] IR 713; [1987] ILRM.
[4] In *Goodman International v Hamilton* (No. 1) [1992] 2 IR 542; [1992] ILRM 145 Finlay CJ said, without actually mentioning Article 15.4.1, that the "necessary comity between the different organs of State" meant that a presumption of constitutional validity must apply in precisely the same way to a resolution of both Houses of the Oireachtas, even though it does not constitute legislation."
[5] [1984] IR 25: [1985] ILRM 423.
[6] See pp. 479-480.

No less strict test for pre-Constitution statute law

On the basis of the second subsection of this section Kingsmill Moore J constructed a rule of interpretation in regard to pre-1937 statutes, which seem worth citing, though it does not appear to have been afterwards taken up by other courts or judges. In *Educational Co. v Fitzpatrick (No. 2)*[7] he quoted the sub-section and said:

> "As I cannot conceive that the Constitution laid down a more stringent test for the validity of laws passed by the Oireachtas than it did for the continued validity of statutes or law carried forward into our *corpus iuris* by Article 50, I must interpret the words in Article 50, "Subject to this Constitution and to the extent to which they are not inconsistent therewith", as negativing the carrying forward of any statute or law which is "in any respect repugnant to the Constitution or to any provision thereof" to the extent of such repugnancy."

Does Article 15.4 apply to orders or measures not enacted by the Oireachtas?

The language of Article 15.4 ("the Oireachtas shall not enact any law...") strongly suggests that it only applies to primary legislation (i.e., Acts of the Oireachtas) and not delegated legislation (such as statutory instruments), still administrative schemes and circulars without any direct statutory provenance. This notwithstanding, the decision of the Supreme Court in *The State (Gilliland) v Governor of Mountjoy Prison*[8] appears to be authority for the proposition that a statutory instrument promulgated pursuant to a post - 1937 law constitutes a "law" for the purposes of Article 15.4. It is, however, otherwise in the case of administrative schemes and circulars. This emerges from the judgment of Murphy J in *Greene v Minister for Agriculture*[9] where the plaintiffs had challenged the validity of certain conditions attaching to an administrative circular on the ground that they effectively constituted a penalty on marriage.[10] In finding for the plaintiffs, the judge considered that since these schemes were not laws which were enacted by the Oireachtas, Article 15.4 had no application and could not provide any "direct assistance" in determining the extent to which the schemes would be invalidated or the date from which they would cease to have operative effect. The ministerial schemes were effective and had to be condemned because they failed to respect and vindicate express constitutional rights.

Greene's case shows that the courts will assume a power of judicial review in of respect of administrative schemes and circulars and will condemn them for constitutional frailty even in circumstances where the powers of judicial review of legislation contained in Article 15.4 and Article 34.3.2 do not apply.

Severability

The qualification "but to the extent only of such repugnancy" raises the question of "severability" of unconstitutional provisions and this is examined elsewhere.[11]

7 [1961] IR 345
8 [1987] IR 210; [1987] ILRM 278. See below at pp. 421-422, 528-530.
9 [1990] 1 IR 17.
10 They were ultimately to succeed on this point: see pp. 993-994.
11 See below at pp. 474-477 and see generally *Maher v Attorney General* [1973] IR 140 and *Desmond v Glackin, (No.2)*, Supreme Court, 30 July 1992.

McCarthy J drew attention in *The State (McLoughlin) v Eastern Health Board*[12] to the potential rescuing effect of Article 15.4.2 in the context of severability following a finding of unconstitutionality. In this case, part of a statutory instrument was found by the Supreme Court to be *ultra vires* the Social Welfare (Consolidation) Act 1981. McCarthy J said that as a statutory instrument found to be *ultra vires* on non-constitutional grounds did not enjoy the "restorative protection" of Article 15.4.2 (which, of course, only applies to Acts of the Oireachtas and (probably) statutory instruments found to be *ultra vires* on constitutional grounds[13]) he doubted whether any such statutory instrument can remain valid "when any material portion of it has been judicially condemned."[14] This implies that without the aid of Article 15.4.2 it would be impossible to operate the doctrine of severance enunciated in *Maher v Attorney General*[15] and subsequent cases.[16] Insofar as this suggests that the courts cannot sever the bad from the good in the context of a partially invalid statutory instrument in the absence of Article 15.4.2, this would seem to be incorrect. The common law doctrine of severance has always been employed by the courts and Article 15.4.2 has always been regarded as simply giving constitutional form and shape to a pre-existing doctrine: in other words, the courts would still be employing this doctrine or something like it, even if the Constitution did not contain any express provision along these lines.[17]

[12] [1986] IR 416.
[13] Above, pp. 528-530.
[14] This principle was applied by Murphy J to non-statutory schemes in *Greene v Minister for Agriculture* [1990 2 IR 17. See also *Howard v Minister for Agriculture* [1990] 2 IR 260.
[15] [1973] IR 140.
[16] See pp. 474-477.
[17] See Hogan & Morgan, *Administrative Law in Ireland* (London, 1991) at 388-390.

Article 15.5

PROHIBITION OF RETROACTIVE PENAL LEGISLATION

5. The Oireachtas shall not declare acts to be infringements of the law which were not so at the time of date of their commission.

5. Ní cead don Oireachtas a rá gur sárú dlí gníomhartha nár shárú dlí iad le linn a ndéanta.

1922 provision

This provision was a replacement of Article 43 of the 1922 Constitution, which was in substance identical.[1] The old Article 43 was relied on,[2] unsuccessfully, in *Attorney General v MacBride*,[3] where the Public Safety Act 1927,[4] was in issue; s 16(1) of this Act authorised the arrest of a person suspected by a superintendent of the Garda Síochána "of having been engaged or concerned in the commission of any [scheduled offence] and whose detention is in the opinion of such superintendent necessary or desirable for the proper investigation of such offence or any other like offence". Section 16(2) provided that, when such a person was brought before a Justice of the District Court and the superintendent stated that "in his opinion there was ground" for this suspicion and that his detention was necessary or desirable for this purpose, the Justice was to "order such person to be detained in custody for seven days". In this case the defendant had been arrested on suspicion of having been engaged in a conspiracy to murder a member of the Oireachtas (this was one of the scheduled offences), namely the late Minister for Justice; but the Minister had been murdered on 10 July, and the Act was passed on 1 August. It was argued for the defendant that to apply the special provisions of the Act to him in respect of an event which took place when no such statutory provisions existed amounted to a retrospective criminal sanction; also that the Act had created a new crime, namely murder of a member of the Oireachtas, and that proceedings in respect of this new crime could not take place in respect of an act committed before the new crime was created. Hanna J disposed of both arguments:

> "In my judgment, the operation of s 16 is to create the new, artificial, or statutory offence of "being a suspect"[5]...It is called preventive justice...I cannot gather, either from s 16 or from what has been called in argument "the intendment of the Acts", that the suspicion... which is to form the basis of this detention, must be confined to suspicion in connection with some crime committed after the passing of the Act."
>
> The acts so being investigated were crimes before the Act was passed; and, though the provisions of s 16 apply only to [murders]... of a particular class, I am still of opinion that the section extends to suspicion in respect of such, even though committed prior to the passing of the Act.

The description of the s 16 situation as an "artificial or statutory offence" seems unsatisfactory and questionable. It would have been better to regard the whole procedure as an almost discretionary ministerial internment or extended arrest, into which a minimal, cosmetic judicial dimension was interpolated, rather than attempt to analyse it in terms of sanctions applied to an "offence", however qualified. In *The State (Ryan) v Lennon*,[6]

[1] It was perhaps inspired by the similar provision of Article 115 of German (Weimar) Constitution of 1919.

[2] Tacitly; the principle, not the Article, was mentioned.

[3] [1928] IR 451.

[4] This Act, passed after the murder of the Minister for Justice, provided for an extended arrest on suspicion.

[5] Such an offence would nowadays almost certainly be regarded as unconstitutional: see, e.g., *King v Attorney General* [1981] IR 233 and p. 575.

[6] [1935] IR 170.

in which the powers of the Constitution (Special Powers) Tribunal created under Article 2A of the 1922 Constitution were in issue, the Supreme Court was asked by counsel for the applicants to say that some aspects of these powers were such as to offend against fundamental laws which it was outside the power of the Oireachtas to infringe, even by way of amending the Constitution. Two of the three judges rejected this submission; Kennedy CJ, in a celebrated dissenting judgment, was for upholding it. Among other features of the powers conferred by Article 2A was the power of a Minister to bring an offence within the jurisdiction of the Tribunal, and thus make it punishable by any sentence the Tribunal thought fit to impose, even where a statutory maximum was prescribed, if he certified that such offence "(whether committed before or after this Article was inserted in this Constitution...)" was, to the best of his belief, committed "with the object of impairing or impeding the machinery of government or the administration of justice". Kennedy CJ said this provision was in substance and practical effect repugnant to the principle and the almost universal practice which forbids retroactive penal legislation. It is within the application of the words of Alexander Hamilton, writing in *The Federalist,* No. LXXXIV:-

> "The creation of crimes after the commission of the fact or in other words, the subjecting of men to punishment for things which, when they were done, were breaches of no law, and the practice of arbitrary imprisonments, have been, in all ages, the favourite and most formidable instruments of tyranny."

It will be observed however that neither the Public Safety Act 1927, nor Article 2A, however they may have offended against the spirit, actually breached the letter of Article 43, which disabled the Oireachtas from "[declaring] acts to be infringements of the law which were not so at the date of their commission".

General interpretation of Article 15.5.

It has been only in recent years that Article 15.5 has received more extensive judicial consideration. In *Doyle* v *An Taoiseach* [7] the Supreme Court held that if the provisions of s 79 of the Finance Act 1980 (which purported to confirm the validity of certain levies on the sale of live cattle which had been introduced in 1979) were held to have retrospective effect, it would be to that extent unconstitutional, since, as Henchy J said, it would have the effect:

> "of making, *ex post facto*, non-payment of the levy in 1979 an infringement of the law. Such a result would make s 79 invalid having regard to Article 15.5 of the Constitution."

Since, however, there was nothing to indicate in the 1980 Act to suggest that the Oireachtas had intended it to apply retrospectively, the Court held that s 79 should be treated "as having only prospective effect" and therefore had no application to the present case.

In *Magee v Culligan*[8] the Supreme Court held that Article 15.5 constitutes:

> "an expressed and unambiguous prohibition against the enactment of retrospective laws declaring acts to be an infringement of the law, whether of the civil or the criminal law. It does not contain any general prohibition on retrospection of legislation, nor can it be by any means interpreted as a general prohibition of that description."

[7] [1986] ILRM 693. Note that in *R. v Kirk* [1984] 3 CMLR 522, the European Court of Justice said that the principle that penal provisions may not have retroactive effect was one "common to all legal orders of member states" and, consequently, it takes its place "among the general principles of law whose observance is ensured by the Court of Justice."

[8] [1992] 1 IR 233; [1992] ILRM 186.

Thus, while Article 15.5 is principally viewed as operating in the sphere of the criminal law, this judgment shows that the Oireachtas is similarly disabled from declaring acts to be infringements of the civil law. This means, for example, that the Oireachtas may not retroactively create a new civil wrong, or declare past acts to have been an infringement of some civil statutory prohibition. *Dublin Heating Co. Ltd. v Hefferon*[9] provides an example of the application of this latter principle. Section 33 of the Companies (Amendment) Act 1990 created what Murphy J described as new civil "wrongdoing of reckless trading" which "did not exist prior to the enactment of the 1990 Act." It followed that "reckless trading is now an infringement of the law and to declare retrospectively innocent actions as constituting that wrong would necessarily amount to a breach of Article 15." As Murphy J would not impute an intention on the part of the Oireachtas to act in an unconstitutional fashion, he construed the reckless trading provisions of the 1990 Act as having prospective effect only. This decision may be contrasted with the reasoning in the *Magee* case, where the Supreme Court refused to hold that s 1(4) of the Extradition (European Convention on the Suppression of Terrorism) Act 1987 (which expressly operated retroactively to deprive certain suspects of the benefit of the "political offence"[10] exception) was unconstitutional. Finlay CJ explained that the sub-section merely made a statutory amendment:

> "to what was a developing jurisdiction concerning the definition of a political offence for the purposes of the Extradition Act 1965, as amended. It does not create any offence or any infringement of the law in our jurisdiction."

This is doubtless so, but the fact remains that s 1(4) of the 1987 Act would seem to have offended against the spirit of Article 15.5, inasmuch as the sheer fortuity of when extradition proceedings were commenced in effect determined whether or not the suspect would be extradited.[11]

The relationship between Article 15.5 and Article 40.3

A number of recent cases have pointed to the relationship between Article 15.5 and Article 40.3 as far as the retrospective operation of legislation is concerned. This has emerged in cases where the plaintiff is clearly debarred from relying on Article 15.5, but where the potential unfairness of the retrospective operation of legislation is obvious, or, at least, discernible. An example here is *Hamilton v Hamilton*[12] in which the issue was whether the Family Home Protection Act 1976, could operate to defeat an action for specific performance of a contract entered into before the passage of the Act. O'Higgins CJ said that, quite apart from the constitutional dimension of the defendant's property rights, even at common law he:

> "would be bound to assume that the Legislature did not intend to affect contracts and transactions already entered into but, on the contrary, intended only to affect

[9] [1992] ILRM 51. See also *Dublin Heating Co. Ltd. v Hefferan (No. 2)* High Court, January 15, 1993.

[10] See generally at pp. 880-886.

[11] This may be illustrated in the following way. In *Finucane v McMahon* [1990] 1 IR 165 the Supreme Court held that attacks on the British security forces in Northern Ireland attracted the protection of the political offence exception contained in s 50 of the Extradition Act 1965. The extradition proceedings in *Finucane* had commenced *before* the Extradition (European Convention on the Suppression of Terrorism) Act 1987 (which greatly restricted the scope of the political offence exception) came into force on December 1, 1987. The actual result in *Finucane* would almost certainly have been different had the proceedings been started *after* December 1, 1987. Yet the offences in both *Finucane* and *Magee* had both been committed *before* the 1987 Act came into force. Why, therefore, should the fortuitous fact that the *Magee* proceedings were commenced after December 1, 1987 - as opposed to the *date* on which the offences were committed - have assumed such a crucial significance? cf. the requirement of "temporal equality" in extradition proceedings, see *McMahon v Leahy* [1984] IR 525 and p. 717.

[12] [1982] IR 466.

> such contracts and transactions as were entered into after the Act of 1976 came into operation...I can find nothing in the Act of 1976 which displaces the presumption of prospectivity."

The Chief Justice added, however, that, had the 1976 Act purported to a retrospective operation, it would to that extent have necessarily unfairly prejudiced the plaintiff's property rights.[13] Henchy J took a less maximalist approach, saying that in considering this issue, one would have been required to assess whether the Oireachtas had struck an unfair balance as between the plaintiff's property rights and its obligation to legislate to protect the family under Article 41.

This latter approach is evident in the judgment of Murphy J in *Chestvale Properties Ltd. v Glackin.*[14] Here Part II of the Companies Act 1990 (which extended the circumstances in which an inspector might be appointed to inquire into a company's affairs) was found by Murphy J to have retrospective effect and he rejected the contention that this necessarily constituted an unjust infringement of the plaintiff's property rights. But such a "marginal erosion" of the plaintiff's incorporeal rights (even if retrospective in nature) could not be regarded as unjust or unfair when balanced against the public interest in ensuring that an inspector had adequate powers to report and investigate the membership of a particular company.[15]

General leaning of the courts against injurious retrospection

It may also be appropriate to mention here in passing, even though Article 15.5 has no direct bearing on it, the general leaning of the courts against injurious retrospection. It must also be stressed that in the wake of the Supreme Court's decision in *Magee v Culligan,*[16] Article 15.5 cannot be regarded as containing "any general prohibition on retrospection of legislation." The judicial approach may be summarised as follows: it is presumed that legislation which affects substantive law or vested rights will not operate retrospectively unless there is a clear and unambiguous indication to the contrary.

This may be seen in a series of recent cases, of which the following are examples. In *Aer Lingus Teo. v Labour Court,*[17] the Supreme Court held that past discrimination prejudicing married women prior to the coming into force of the Employment Equality Act

[13] But cf. the decision of McWilliam J in *Condon v Minister for Labour (No.2)*, High Court, June 11, 1980 where legislation providing for the imposition of sanctions on bank officials who sought to collect wage increases negotiated by them pursuant to a collective agreement was upheld. McWilliam J accepted that the legislation interfered retrospectively with the plaintiffs' property rights, but felt that the Oireachtas was entitled to take the view that the general economic outlook required that workers in particular sectors be debarred from receiving unduly generous wage increases. See McCormack, "*Contractual Entitlements and the Constitution*" (1982) 17 Ir Jur (n.s.) 340.

[14] [1992] ILRM 221. The following passage from the judgment of Murphy J neatly summarises the inter-relationship of Article 15.5 and Article 40.3:

> "The plaintiffs did not and could not contend that Part II of the 1990 Act offended Article 15.5. In no sense does that part of the 1990 Act declare any act to be an infringement of the law which was not so at the date of its commission. What the plaintiffs say is that by enacting Part II aforesaid the Oireachtas contravened Article 40.3 of the Constitution in that it failed to protect and vindicate the property rights thereby guaranteed."

[15] See also *Magee v Culligan* [1992] 1 IR 223; [1992] ILRM 186, where the Supreme Court rejected arguments that the retrospective operation of the Extradition (European Convention on the Suppression of Terrorism) Act, 1987 deprived the applicant of a vested right or otherwise operated unjustly in a manner contrary to Article 40.3.

[16] [1992] 1 IR 223; [1992] ILRM 186.

[17] [1986] ILRM 693. On this question see generally Delany, "*Statutory Interpretation - Can Legislation have Retrospective Effect?*" (1992) 11 ILT (n.s.) 133.

could not be taken into, with Walsh J observing that, given the non-retroactive character of the legislation, "in effect the slate is wiped clean in respect of matters occurring before the Act." The presumption seems particularly strong with regard to vested rights, so thus in *Dublin C.C. v Grealy*[18] Blayney J held that s 25 of the Local Government (Planning and Development) Act 1963 (which enabled a planning authority to serve an acquisition notice when certain lands were not being maintained as open spaces) could not be given a retrospective operation. Barron J reached a similar conclusion in *O'H . v O'H.,*[19] holding that the power to make property transfer orders contained in s 29 of the Judicial Separation and Family Law Reform Act 1989 could not operate retrospectively. In doing so, Barron J drew the rather subtle distinction between applying new law to past events and taking past events into account when applying the new law. Only in the former case could the legislation be properly described as retrospective in character. This distinction also surfaced in *Chestvale Properties Ltd. v Glackin,*[20] where Murphy J held that Part II of the Companies Act 1990 (which extended the powers of company inspectors) was prospective in the sense that the inspectors could only be appointed after the relevant provisions of the Act came into force, but, contrariwise, the inspectors could take into account facts and documents prior to the coming into force of the Act. In addition it seems that the presumption against retrospection only applies to changes in the substantive law and does not apply to purely procedural matters.[21]

Finally this principle against injurious retrospection was given statutory endorsement in certain respects by ss 21 and 22 of the Interpretation Act 1937. For example, s 21(l)(*c*) provides that:

> Where an Act of the Oireachtas repeals the whole or a portion of a previous statute, then, unless the contrary intention appears, such repeal shall not... affect any right, privilege, obligation, or liability acquired, accrued, or incurred under the statute or portion of a statute so repealed.

[18] [1990] 1 IR 77. See also *Irish Land Commission v Dolan* [1930] IR 235 (new legislation allowing Land Commission sweeping powers to recover arrears held only to have prospective effect) and *Fitzpatrick v Minister for Industry & Commerce* [1931] IR 457 (new legislation imposing new conditions for registration as patent agent held to have no application to existing patent agents).

[19] [1990] 2 IR 558.

[20] [1992] ILRM 221.

[21] *Toss Ltd. v District Justice for Morgan Place*, High Court, November 24, 1987. But it is not always easy to draw a distinction between legislation affecting procedural - as opposed to substantive - matters.

Article 15.6

EXCLUSIVE RIGHT OF OIREACHTAS TO HAVE ARMED FORCES

6. 1° The right to raise and maintain military or armed forces is vested exclusively in the Oireachtas.
2° No military or armed force, other than a military or armed force raised and maintained by the Oireachtas, shall be raised or maintained for any purpose whatsoever.

6. 1° Is ag an Oireachtas amháin atá de cheart fórsaí mileata nó fórsaí armtha a bhunú agus a chothabháil.
2° Ní dleathach fórsa míleata nó fórsa armtha ar bith, seachas fórsa míleata nó fórsa armtha a bhunaítear agus a chothabháiltear ag an Oireachtas, a bhunú nó a chothabháil chun criche ar bith.

1922 provision

The 1922 Constitution's corresponding provision (Article 46) read:

> The Oireachtas has the exclusive right to regulate the raising and maintaining of such armed forces as are mentioned in the Scheduled Treaty in the territory of the Irish Free State (Saorstát Éireann) and every such force shall be subject to the control of the Oireachtas.

In *Conroy v Minister for Defence*[1] Kennedy CJ called this:

> "the very important [Article] by which the army is made the army of Parliament and not of the Crown."

Legal Character of the Defence Forces

The legal character of the Defence Forces was examined by Budd J in *In re Royal Kilmainham Hospital*,[2] a case in which the question arose whether the Defence Forces could be within the description of the object class in the Charter (of Charles II) which established the Hospital for old soldiers. He said:

> "The Defence Forces owe their origin and maintenance not to any Royal prerogative but to the provisions of the Constitution and the legislation of the Oireachtas relevant to their establishment. They are a statutory creation. These forces have their establishment within the territory of the Republic, depend for their maintenance upon the revenues of the Republic and are subject to the laws of the Republic...The members of the Defence Forces do not serve in any army of the successors of Charles II...
>
> It was suggested that during the period from 1922 to the coming into force of the Constitution the position might be different so that the soldiers of the Defence Forces during that period might answer the object class in the Charter...I find nothing in the Constitution of the Irish Free State or the Defence Forces (Temporary Provisions) Act 1923] which would warrant [that] submission..."

[1] [1934] IR 679; (1935) 69 ILTR 43.
[2] [1966] IR 451.

Statutory provisions

The Defence Forces' statutory basis until 1954 was the Defence Forces (Temporary Provisions) Act 1923, continued annually with amendments by further Defence Forces (Temporary Provisions) Acts. In 1954 these were all repealed and replaced by the Defence Act of that year. Overseas service with the United Nations was additionally authorised by the Defence (Amendment) (No. 2) Act 1960 and by the Defence (Amendment) Act 1993.[3] Section 16 of the Defence Act 1954, provides:

> It shall be lawful for the Government to raise, train, equip, arm, pay and maintain defence forces to be called and known as Óglaigh na hÉireann or (in English) the Defence Forces.

The Defence (Amendment) Act 1990 allows representative bodies to be established for members of the Defence Forces. Section 6 of the 1990 Act provides that a person who is subject to military law shall neither endeavour to persuade or conspire with any person to endeavour to persuade a member of the Defence Forces to join a trade union or other body other than an authorised association recognised under the terms of the 1990 Act.

Offences of raising etc. unauthorised armed force

The constitutional prohibition of other armed forces is reinforced by the Offences Against the State Act 1939, of which s 15 prohibits unauthorised military exercises, and s 18 makes unlawful, among others, any organisation which:

> (c) raises or maintains or attempts to raise or maintain a military or armed force in contravention of the Constitution or without constitutional authority.

Section 6 of the same Act replacing s 6 of the Treasonable Offences Act 1925, also penalises as felony punishable with up to twenty[4] years' penal servitude the:

> forming, maintaining, or being a member of an armed force or a purported police force not so authorised [by or under the Constitution].

Article 15.6 received some judicial attention in this context in *Quinn v Wren*,[5] where the plaintiff, claiming that he had engaged in fraudulent activities on behalf of the "Irish National Liberation Army" resisted extradition to England on the ground that these offences were "political offences" within the meaning of s 50 of the Extradition Act 1965.[6] This submission was rejected by the Supreme Court, where Finlay CJ said that, as the purposes of that organisation involved the overthrow of the institutions of the State by force of arms:

> "[its] attainment necessarily and inevitably involves the destruction and setting aside of the Constitution by means expressly or impliedly prohibited by it: see Article 15.6 and Article 39."

[3] The 1960 Act provides statutory authority for the participation by Irish troops in UN peace-keeping functions. The 1993 Act now provides authority for such participation in the context of the UN's newly emerging peace-enforcement role.

[4] As inserted by s 2 of the Criminal Law Act 1976

[5] [1985] IR 322; [1985] ILRM 411.

[6] The scope of this defence has, however, now been considerably modified by the provisions of the Extradition (European Convention on the Suppression of Terrorism) Act 1987: see pp. 883-886.

Hederman J was the sole dissenter on this point, saying that the mere fact that the organisation had used the word "army" in its title was not enough to bring it within the contemplation of Article 15.6. He admitted that there might be circumstances where an illegal organisation came within the terms of Article 15.6, but here there was "no evidence whatsoever as to where the self-styled army was raised and maintained, if at all".[7]

Use of the Defence Forces in aid of civil power

The question of the employment of the Defence Forces in a police capacity is occasionally canvassed. It appears that the classical view of the common law survives in Ireland, namely, that the Government is not only entitled but bound to maintain order, and to this end may require the service of citizens. If these are uniformed and disciplined in a special way, they still remain citizens and subject to the ordinary law. But there is no constitutional rule which rigidly separates the functions of one class of citizen, thus uniformed and disciplined, from another such class; and the fact that day-to-day keeping of the peace is conventionally attended to by a police force does not prevent any other part of the State's service from being called in to supplement it in need. This employment of soldiers "in aid of the civil power" is specifically recognised by statute, in ss 90-1 of the Defence Act 1954 (the special case of reservists) and in s 8 of the Criminal Law Act 1976, which gives - on police request - powers of arrest and search to the Defence Forces in certain cases.[8]

For military law, military tribunals, and courts-martial, see below, pp. 655-656. For supreme command of the Defence Forces, see above, pp. 90-91.

[7] The apparently open-ended language of *Quinn v Wren* has to be read with some circumspection in view of the subsequent decision of the Supreme Court in *Finucane v McMahon* [1990] 1 IR 165; [1990] ILRM 505. Here Walsh J stressed that mere membership of an organisation which was illegal under s 18 of the Offences Against the State Act 1939 did not of itself establish that either the organisation itself or an individual member following its general objectives was engaged in either treasonable activity or activity which was in contravention of Article 15.6.

[8] Section 2 of the Prisons Act 1972 also provided for the transfer of prisoners to military custody at times when regular prison accommodation or facilities were inadequate. This legislation lapsed in 1983.

Article 15.7-15

RULES, PROCEDURES AND PRIVILEGES OF HOUSES OF OIREACHTAS

7.	The Oireachtas shall hold at least one session every year.	7.	Ní foláir don Oireachtas suí uair sa bhliain ar a laghad.
8.	1° Sittings of each House of the Oireachtas shall be public.	8.	1° Is go poiblí a shuífidh gach Teach den Oireachtas.
	2° In cases of special emergency, however, either House may hold a private sitting with the assent of two-thirds of the members present.		2° Ach i gcás práinn speisialta a bheith ann, tig le ceachtar den dá Theach suí go príobháideach ach dhá thrian de na comhaltaí a bheas i láthair do thoiliú leis.
9.	l° Each House of the Oireachtas shall elect from its members its own Chairman and Deputy Chairman, and shall prescribe their powers and duties.	9	1° Toghfaidh gach Teach ar leith den Oireachtas a Chathaoirleach agus a Leas-Chathaoirleach féin as a chomhaltas féin, agus leagfaidh amach dóibh a gcumhachtaí agus a ndualgais.
	2° The remuneration of the Chairman and Deputy Chairman of each House shall be determined by law.		2° Is le dlí a chinnfear tuarastal Chathaoirieach is Leas-Chathaoirleach gach Tí ar leith.
10.	Each House shall make its own rules and standing orders, with power to attach penalties for their infringement, and shall have power to ensure freedom of debate, to protect its official documents and the private papers of its members, and to protect itself and its members against any person or persons interfering with, molesting or attempting to corrupt its members in the exercise of their duties.	10.	Déanfaidh gach Teach ar leith a rialacha agus a bhuan-orduithe féin, agus beidh sé de chumhacht ag gach Teach acu pionós a cheapadh do lucht a sáraithe sin; beidh sé de chumhacht aige fairis sin saoirse aighnis a chur in áirithe, agus a scríbhinní oifigiúla féin agus páipéir phríobháideacha a chomhaltaí a dhídean, agus fós é féin agus a chomhaltaí a dhídean ar aon duine nó ar aon dream daoine a dhéanfadh cur isteach nó toirmeasc ar a chomhaltaí nó a dhéanfadh iarracht ar iad a éilliú agus iad ag déanamh a ndualgas.
11	1° All questions in each House shall, save as otherwise provided by this Constitution, be determined by a majority of the votes of the members present and voting other than the Chairman or presiding member.	11.	1° Taobh amuigh de chás dá socraítear a mhalairt leis an mBunreacht seo is é slí a dtabharfar breith ar gach ceist i ngach Teach ar leith ná le formhór vótaí na gcomhaltaí a bheas i láthair agus a dhéanfas vótáil ach gan an Cathaoirleach nó an comhalta a bheas i gceannas a áireamh.
	2° The Chairman or presiding member shall have and exercise		2° Más ionann líon na votaí ar an dá thaobh beidh ag an

a casting vote in the case of an equality of votes.

3° The number of members necessary to constitute a meeting of either House for the exercise of its powers shall be determined by its standing orders.

12. All official reports and publications of the Oireachtas or of either House thereof and utterances made in either House wherever published shall be privileged.

13. The members of each House of the Oireachtas shall, except in case of treason as defined in this Constitution, felony or breach of the peace, be privileged from arrest in going to and returning from, and while within the precincts of, either House, and shall not, in respect of any utterance in either House, be amenable to any court or any authority other than the House itself.

14. No person may be at the same time a member of both Houses of the Oireachtas, and, if any person who is already a member of either House becomes a member of the other House, he shall forthwith be deemed to have vacated his first seat.

15. The Oireachtas may make provision by law for the payment of allowances to the members of each House thereof in respect of their duties as public representatives and for the grant to them of free travelling and such other facilities (if any) in connection with those duties as the Oireachtas may determine.

gCathaoirleach, nó ag an gcomhalta a bheas i gceannas, vóta cinniúna nach foláir dó a thabhairt.

3° Is lena bhuan-orduithe a chinnfear cén méid comhalta a bheas riachtanach do thionól de cheachtar den dá Theach chun é a bheith i gcumas feidhme.

12. Gach tuarascáil agus foilseachán oifigiúil ón Oireachtas agus ó gach Teach de, maille le caint ar bith dá ndéantar in aon Teach díobh, táid saor ar chúrsaí dlí cibé áit a bhfoilsítear.

13. Tá comhaltaí gach Tí den Oireachtas saor ar ghabháil le linn bheith i dtearmann ceachtar den dá Theach nó ag teacht chuige nó ag imeacht uaidh, ach amháin i gcás tréasa, mar a mhínítear sa Bhunreacht seo é, nó i gcás feileonachta nó briseadh síochána; agus cibé caint a dhéanfaidh comhalta in aon Teach díobh ní inchúisithe é mar gheall uirthi in aon chúirt ná ag údarás ar bith ach amháin an Teach féin.

14. Ní cead d'aon duine bheith ina chomhalta de dhá Theach an Oireachtais san am chéanna, agus aon duine a bheas ina chomhalta de Theach díobh agus go ndéanfar comhalta den Teach eile de, ní foláir a mheas láithreach go bhfuil éirithe aige as an gcéad ionad.

15. Tig leis an Oireachtas socrú a dhéanamh le dlí chun liúntais a íoc le comhaltaí gach Tí de as ucht a ndualgas i gcáil ionadóirí poiblí, agus chun go ndeonfaí dóibh, maidir lena ndualgais, saoráid chun taisteal in aisce agus cibé saoráid eile a chinnfidh an tOireachtas, má chinneann.

1922 position

These provisions substantially reproduce corresponding provisions of the old Constitution; Article 15.7 is identical with the first sentence of the old Article 24;

Article 15.8 virtually identical with the old Article 25; Article 15.9 with the old Article 21 (except that the latter permitted each House, rather than the whole Legislature, to fix the Chairman's remuneration); Article 15.10 with the old Article 20; and Article 15.11 with the old Article 22.

Removal of Chairman etc.

While Article 15.9 provides that each House is to elect its own Chairman and Deputy Chairman,[1] the Constitution is silent on whether such Chairmen or Deputy Chairmen can be removed. This is perhaps not so much an inadvertent lacuna, as a reflection of the inarticulate proposition that the power to elect must imply the power to remove. This proposition (which is by no means uniformly supported by analogies from within the Constitution) is at any rate given effect in practice by the Standing Orders of the Houses; Order 87.2 and Order 78.2 respectively provide that the Chairman or Deputy Chairman of the Dáil (called by tradition Ceann Comhairle or Leas-Cheann Comhairle) and the Chairman or Deputy Chairman of the Seanad (Cathaoirleach or Leas-Chathaoirleach) may be either appointed or removed by Resolution of the House concerned. No such officer of either House has ever been so removed.

Survival of Chairman after dissolution of the Dáil

While the dissolution of the Dáil, or the condition of the Seanad between a general election and a reassembly, ought in theory to mean that no such officer as Chairman or Deputy Chairman of either House is in existence, the strict application of this theory would have the obviously unintended effect that the Presidential Commission provided for by Article 14, which consists of the Chief Justice plus the Chairmen of both Houses, could not function during those periods. This anomaly surfaced incidentally in *Loftus v Attorney General*,[2] in which the composition of the appeal board for registration of political parties was in issue; this board, which included the Chairman of the Dáil, obviously could not be constituted after a dissolution if the person who had been Chairman of the outgoing Dáil (and who had, on the dissolution, ceased to be even a member, since there was no longer any assembly) must now be regarded as having no function. The Supreme Court, by strenuous exertion of the principle of construing an Act of the Oireachtas so as to reconcile it if at all possible with the Constitution,[3] managed to avoid the effect of this clear *casus omissus* in the 1963 Electoral Act by invoking the (equally clear) *casus omissus* in the Constitution. O'Higgins CJ reviewed the implications of Article 14 and concluded that they meant:

> "that, for constitutional purposes, when the Dáil has been dissolved and the new Dáil has not yet met, the Chairman of Dáil Éireann means the Chairman of the dissolved Dáil and the Deputy Chairman means the person who had been Deputy Chairman of the dissolved Dáil."

[1] The Constitution does not expressly provide for the non-election of a Ceann Comhairle. Following the (initially) inconclusive general election of November 1992 when it was anticipated that the Dáil might have difficulties in electing a Ceann Comhairle, the Clerk of the Dáil was reported to have taken legal advice on the matter from the Attorney General who, apparently, ruled out on constitutional grounds the election of temporary Ceann Comhairle (on the ground that the Ceann Comhairle was a constitutional officer elected for the term of the full Dáil). The Attorney General further advised that the Dáil would have to adjourn unless it could elect a Ceann Comhairle, apparently on the ground that the Dáil was constitutionally de-barred from conducting its business in the absence of a duly elected Ceann Comhairle of Leas-Ceann Comhairle: see *The Irish Times*, 9 December 1992.

[2] [1979] IR 221.

[3] See at p. 461.

The Court did not deal with the Seanad chairmanship, as this was not involved in the registration appeal board; but it must be that a similar conclusion would hold in relation to the Seanad for the period between a general election and assembly of the new Seanad.[4]

Powers of the Houses to enforce their rules and standing orders

The powers of the Houses in regard to infringements of their rules and standing orders are not clear, nor are their powers in regard to matters regarded as "breaches of privilege" which are not defined in Standing Orders. Firstly, is the determination of the question whether a member has infringed rules or standing orders, or been guilty of a breach of privilege, proper to be left to the House itself, or to strictly judicial decision? The latter possibility seems quite open, particularly since Article 15.13 specifically gives the House jurisdiction in respect of utterances within the House, thus perhaps impliedly excluding jurisdiction in other cases. On the one hand, the *dicta* of Ó Dálaigh J in *Wireless Dealers Association v Fair Trade Commission*[5] suggests that the courts have no such jurisdiction. Here the plaintiffs sought an injunction restraining the Minister for Industry and Commerce from introducing into the Seanad a Bill which they claimed was unconstitutional. Ó Dálaigh J referred generally to the provisions of Article 15.10, Article 26 and Article 34.3.2 and said:

> "This survey of the Constitution is adequate to demonstrate that the Constitution makes each of the two Houses of the Oireachtas complete master of its own deliberations and that the High Court, while granted a general jurisdiction to pronounce on the constitutional validity of laws, i.e., measures which have been passed by both Houses and duly signed and promulgated by the President, exercises no functions with regard to the deliberations of the Oireachtas."

A strict application of this principle might be thought to exempt from judicial scrutiny what might be described as the intra-mural proceedings of both Houses, such as, for example, the question of whether the Chairman of either House had been validly removed from his office.

On the other hand, in *Re Haughey*[6] the Supreme Court was prepared to supervise the procedures adopted by a Dáil committee, although an important consideration here must be that the plaintiff in that case was not a member of the Oireachtas. In early 1990, however, it seemed that these matters might at last be judicially considered when a member of the Seanad (Senator Norris) obtained leave to apply for judicial review in respect of a suspension imposed by the House. Senator Norris had made certain allegations against the Cathaoirleach of the Seanad and had been suspended for a week on the recommendation of the Committee of Procedures and Privileges. The meeting had been chaired (as was the usual practice) by the Cathaoirleach and it seems that Senator Norris was not allowed to be heard prior to the imposition of the suspension. This seemed, *prima facie*, a breach of both the *nemo iudex* and *audi alteram partem* rules and, it appears, for these reasons, Blayney J granted an interim order staying the suspension.[7] The case did not proceed further and, hence, the High Court was not required to choose between the competing values of Article 15.10 (suggesting that the Oireachtas is complete master of its

[4] See at p. 181.
[5] Supreme Court, 14 March 1956.
[6] [1971] IR 217.
[7] *The Irish Times*, 8 March 1990.

own procedures) and Article 40.3 (ensuring that fair procedures are observed even in the case of the intra-mural deliberations of the Oireachtas).

Secondly, can the disciplinary power of the Houses extend to suspending a member from the "service" of the House, i.e. excluding him from attendance and voting for a certain period?[8] And suppose that the member suspended is a member of the Government, how can his exclusion be reconciled with Article 28.8 which ordains that "every member of the Government shall have the right to attend and be heard in each House of the Oireachtas"? Standing Orders 52 of the Dáil and 42 of the Seanad provide for such a suspension in cases of "disregarding the authority of the Chair" or "grossly disorderly conduct" respectively; but of course the existence of such Standing Orders does not conclude the question whether it is compatible with the Constitution to exclude from either House, for whatever reason, a member duly elected, in particular a member of the Government; and to deprive him of his right to vote in that House. That the Constitution aims to protect those rights is plain from Article 15.10 itself, which speaks of "[ensuring] freedom of debate" and protecting members "against any person or persons interfering with [or] molesting" them; and also Article 15.13, which privileges members from arrest "in going to and returning from, and while within the precincts of, either House". It might seem that these doubts could be got out of the way only by positing that the constitutional provisions of the National Parliament must be understood against the background of pre-1937 and pre-1922 parliamentary practice - possibly capable of being regarded as part of the "law in force" so as to be carried over by Article 50 and the old Article 73 - which the Constitution ought to have expressly departed from if it was not intended to continue it tacitly.

"With power to attach penalties for their infringement...."

The language of Article 15.10 appears to suggest that each House retains a quasi-criminal jurisdiction to punish persons (not necessarily members) who have infringed rules and standing orders. This, in turn, echoes the British practice where traditionally both Houses enjoyed a power to punish for contempt those - whether strangers or members - who infringed parliamentary privilege,[9] but it would be certainly anomalous if a non-judicial body such as the Oireachtas enjoyed a power to impose the equivalent of a criminal sanction.[10]

Can the Houses by resolution change the substantive law?

By reason of what Finlay CJ described in *Goodman International v Hamilton (No.1)* [11] as the "necessary comity between the different organs of State", it is plain that resolutions of either House of the Oireachtas enjoy a presumption of constitutionality. In this case, the Supreme Court rejected suggestions to the effect that the resolutions of both Houses pursuant to s 1 of the Tribunal of Inquiry (Evidence) Act 1921 were an unconstitutional invasion of the judicial domain. The Tribunal was established to inquire into alleged malfeasance in the beef industry and it was said that the Tribunal would thereby

[8] For a discussion of whether a member of the Dáil who was serving a short prison sentence should have been released to allow him to attend a Budget debate, see 363 *Dáil Debates* 809-814 (28 January 1986). Note that in *Powell v McCormack* 395 US 486 (1969) the US Supreme Court held that Congress had no power to exclude a duly elected member from taking his seat.

[9] Hood Phillips, *Constitutional and Administrative Law* (London, 1987) at 244.

[10] This would not be readily compatible with other constitutional provisions (such as Article 38.1) and there is much in the reasoning of the Supreme Court in *Re Haughey* [1971] IR 217 which appears to negative this suggestion.

[11] [1992] 2 IR 542; [1992] ILRM 145.

necessarily have invaded the judicial domain. The Supreme Court explained that since it was not part of the judicial domain "to ascertain the truth or falsity of facts and report to them to parliament", the submission that the Tribunal would impermissibly exercise such judicial functions was misconceived.

However, it is plain that neither Houses of the Oireachtas may by resolution change the substantive law of the State, since, as Finlay CJ explained in the *Goodman* case, such a resolution "does not constitute legislation."[12] Relevant, perhaps, in this context are the various resolutions of the Dáil and Seanad asserting copyright in various radio and television broadcasts of Oireachtas proceedings and imposing conditions on their use. It seems questionable whether such resolutions come within the protection of Article 15.10, since the resolutions appear to represent an attempt to change the substantive law[13] and do not relate to purely intra-mural matters affecting either House.

Validity of pre-Constitution standing orders as amended

The status of the Standing Orders of Dáil Éireann arose in *In re Haughey*,[14] in which the appellant challenged their constitutional validity, on the ground that Article 15.10 envisaged the making of entirely fresh Standing Orders by the Houses of the Oireachtas established by the Constitution, whereas in fact it appeared that the Standing Orders in use in 1970, the material date, substantially represented the Standing Orders of the Dáil or Saorstát Éireann which had been merely occasionally amended by the post-1937 Dáil. The five judges of the Supreme Court, though not unanimous on other issues raised in the case, agreed that the Orders were still valid, for reasons stated by Ó Dálaigh CJ :

> "It is surprising that the new Dáil Éireann did not formally adopt a new body of standing orders when the Constitution came into force on the 29th December, 1937, and has not done so since. Article 15.10...contemplated that the new Dáil should make its own rules and standing orders. Instead, it appears that the new House has continued to operate under the standing orders of the old Dáil Éireann, subject to amendment. On the eve of the coming into force of the Constitution, the Committee of Procedure and Privileges met under the chairmanship of the Ceann Comhairle to consider the "amendment of Standing Orders relative to Public Business consequent on the coming into operation of the Constitution". The Committee's report... recommended certain amendments which were set out in a schedule to the report... The suggested amendments were adopted by the new Dáil on the 12th January, 1938. This, in my opinion, was a tacit adoption by the new Dáil Éireann of the standing orders of the former House, as amended, as the standing orders of the new House. It may indeed be that taciturnity is uncharacteristic of parliaments, but it seems to me that the action of Dáil Éireann on the 12th January, 1938, is susceptible of no other construction than that the new House was "making" its Standing Orders within the meaning and intention of Article 15."

[12] This point had been graphically made by Parker J in the context of the British Parliament in *Bowles v Bank of England* [1913] 1 Ch 57. Occasionally, legislation may purport to authorise amendments of the substantive law by resolution and the best example of this is, perhaps, s 1 of the Imposition of Duties Act 1957 which purports to allow the raise of taxation by Dáil resolution for a two year period. This section was held to be an unconstitutional delegation of legislative power (see p. 110) by Blayney J in *McDaid v Sheehy* [1991] 1 IR 1, save that the Supreme Court reversed him (without addressing the substantive issue) on the technical ground that it was not necessary on the facts for Blayney J to have addressed this wider constitutional question.

[13] It may be noted that s 51 of the Copyright Act 1963 only protects Government publications and broadcasts and thus would not seem to include publications and broadcasts of the Oireachtas.

[14] [1971] IR 217.

It will be noticed that this construction is quite different from that which the courts have applied to Article 34.1-4 in regard to the establishment of "new" courts. If the *Haughey* construction were applied in this area, it might be argued that mere amendment of the pre-Constitution legislation on which the courts were based would have sufficed to "tacitly adopt" them as the courts which the Constitution envisaged.

Houses can prescribe their own special rules on Bill procedure - but standing orders may not pre-empt legislative function

Two cases involving the Standing Orders of the pre-1937 Houses of the Oireachtas are of interest. In *Cane v Dublin Corporation*[15] it was held that the power of the Houses to make their own rules included the power to prescribe special rules as to the number, sequence etc. of Stages of Bills; also that the setting-up of a Joint Committee of both Houses to consider Private Bills did not represent a delegation of the legislative function, which would be impermissible. In *McM. v McM.*[16] Hanna J described the history of attempts in 1924-5 to promote Private Bills of divorce and of the efforts of the Houses to prevent their legislative function from being invoked in this area: he cited, with evident agreement, the Chairman of Seanad Éireann who had described a manoeuvre to adapt the Seanad's Standing Orders so as to forbid such Bills as an attempted usurpation of the legislative function.

Privilege of parliamentary utterance[17]

The question of privilege in regard to parliamentary utterances arose in 1975 in the context of a Tribunal of Inquiry appointed to investigate allegations made by two Deputies in the Dáil about the Minister for Local Government. When the Tribunal[18] held its first sitting, counsel for the two Deputies submitted, firstly, that Article 15.13, declaring the non-amenability of members to any outside authority in respect of utterances within the House, meant that they could not be required to attend or give evidence to the Tribunal; secondly, that the Tribunals of Inquiry (Evidence) Act 1921, was not intended to allow an extra-parliamentary inquiry into things said in Parliament. The latter point the Tribunal disposed of as follows:

> "The very first tribunal set up in 1921 under the Act was one to investigate allegations made in Parliament. The establishment of a tribunal under the 1921 Act is in no way inconsistent with the rights of members of Parliament. On the contrary, it is an exercise of those rights, for s 1(1) of the Act ensures that a tribunal cannot be set up unless and until both Houses of Parliament have resolved that "it is expedient that a tribunal be established for inquiring into a definite matter described in the resolution as of urgent public importance". The statute does not except from the scope of an inquiry an allegation made in Parliament. A tribunal set up under the Act to make an inquiry, so far from representing an intrusion into the affairs of Parliament, is the instrument chosen by Parliament itself to make the inquiry."

The former point the Tribunal did not rule on, holding that, as it felt able to make its investigation without taking evidence from the two Deputies, the question of compelling them did not arise.

[15] [1927] IR 582.
[16] [1936] IR 177. See also O'Sullivan, *The Irish Free State and its Senate* (London, 1940), pp. 162ff.
[17] For a very useful comparative study, see *Parliamentary Immunity in the Member States of the European Community and in the European Parliament* (European Parliament, Luxembourg, 1993).
[18] See *Report of the Tribunal appointed by the Taoiseach on the 4th day of July 1975*, Prl. 4745. The Tribunal consisted of Henchy, Parke and Conroy JJ.

In the following year another allegation by a Deputy against a Minister was taken up by the Committee of Procedure and Privileges of the Dáil, and the question then arose whether the privilege of Article 15.13 would attach to this Committee's proceedings so as to enable members to speak with the same immunity as in the House itself. In order to remove doubts on the matter, the Oireachtas enacted the Committees of the Houses of the Oireachtas (Privilege and Procedure) Act 1976[19], of which s 1 defines "a committee" as "a committee appointed by either House of the Oireachtas or jointly by both Houses of the Oireachtas"; and s 2 provides:

> (1) A member of either House of the Oireachtas shall not, in respect of any utterance in or before a committee, be amenable to any court or any authority other than the House or the Houses of the Oireachtas by which the committee was appointed.
>
> (2) (a) The documents of a committee and the documents of its members connected with the committee or its functions,
> (b) all official reports and publications of a committee, and
> (c) the utterances in a committee of the members, advisers, officials and agents of the committee, wherever published shall be privileged.

Even after the enactment of this Act a doubt survives as to whether the privilege which it creates would extend to *witnesses* summoned to give evidence before a committee (other than the Public Accounts Committee, where a witness has, under s 3(2) of the Committee of Public Accounts of Dáil Éireann (Privilege and Procedure) Act 1970, "the same immunities and privileges as if he were a witness before the High Court").[20]

These questions were considered in passing by some members of the Supreme Court in *Attorney General v Hamilton (No.1)*.[21] O'Flaherty J took the view that the effect of Article 15.13 was that:

> "If a Dáil Deputy is summoned before [a Tribunal of Inquiry] to explain utterances made by him in the House, he is no more amenable to it than he is to any court. Not only can he not be disciplined; he cannot be made to explain his utterances."

McCarthy J added that while the word "privileged" in Article 15.12 had the same meaning as in the law of defamation, Article 15.13 relieved the "members of the House from being answerable for what otherwise would be a contempt of Court." This latter observation might lead to some interesting results. It would seem to mean that a member of

[19] In *Attorney General v Hamilton (No.2)* [1993] ILRM 821, Geoghegan J agreed with counsel's submission that Article 15.13 was enacted *ex abundante cautela* and said that the 1976 Act would probably have covered utterances before Committees of Houses of the Oireachtas "irrespective of whether the 1976 Act had been passed or not."

[20] A related question is the extent to which the phrase "utterance" protects written statements (e.g., parliamentary questions) as well as verbal utterances. While the word "utterance" suggest that the protection was confined to the spoken word, this would seem unduly narrow, since the availability of the protection should scarcely turn on the fortuity of whether a questioner is actually called on by the Ceann Comhairle to pose the question orally or whether it happens to receive merely a written answer. (Note, however, that Article 9 of the English Bill of Rights 1688 might be thought to embrace a wider protection than Articles 15.12 and 15.13 in that it refers to "proceedings in Parliament.") As to whether this provision of the Bill of Rights has survived the enactment of the Constitution, see pp. 146-147. The full limits of the privilege have yet to be judicially explored, although it might be thought that it does not cover private defamatory communications between members (cf. *Coffin v Coffin* (1808) 4 Mass 1) or defamatory communications between a constituent and a member (cf. *Rivlin v Bilankin* [1953] 1 QB 485). See generally, McDonald, *Irish Law of Defamation* (Dublin, 1987) at 119-126.

[21] [1993] 2 IR 250; [1993] ILRM 81.

the Oireachtas was free, in the course of a speech within either House, to give out information which was specifically precluded by court order. In such circumstances, he could not be called to account for a contempt of court[22] and, presumably, persons who were not members of the Oireachtas would also be entitled to call attention and even re-publish that part of the record of either the Dáil or the Seanad where the offending words were spoken without committing a contempt of court.

Parliamentary privilege and the protection of confidants

The question of privilege was also raised before the Beef Tribunal in a particularly acute form: does Article 15.13, or for that matter, the common law, bestow on Deputies making allegations in the Dáil any privilege in regard to the non-disclosure of the identity of their sources. This matter was considered by Geoghegan J and the Supreme Court in *Attorney General v Hamilton (No.2).*[23] Here the Attorney General had sought judicial review of a ruling made by the Chairman of the Tribunal of Inquiry into the Beef Processing Industry to the effect that by virtue of Article 15 a member of either House of the Oireachtas could not be made to explain utterances made by him in that House and, furthermore, could not be required to furnish to the Tribunal the course of the information on which such utterances were based.

In a very elaborate judgment, Geoghegan J first accepted that while Article 15 had to be construed and understood by reference to the historic case-law, this did not mean that the framers of the Constitution "did not intend to apply to the Oireachtas some adaptations or improvements on the legal position in England under the Bill of Rights."[24] Next, having identified the purpose of Article 15 as being to ensure that "legislators are free to represent the interests of their constituents without fear that they will be later called to task in the Courts for that representation",[25] the judge went on to hold that:

> "having regard to the purpose behind the principle, he must be entitled to refuse to disclose the source of any information on foot of which any statement may have been made in a parliamentary institution without fear of sanction or penalty from an outside Court or authority."

Geoghegan J then proceeded to address the meaning of the word "amenable" as it appears in Article 15.13. It did not merely imply criminal penalties, but the word "probably does connote the rendering of a person to some liability or sanction." He continued:

> "If upon a refusal at a Tribunal...to answer a question certain legal consequences can flow adverse to a person so refusing - as indeed would be the case - it follows that a member of the Dáil questioned about utterances made by him in the Dáil cannot be made subject to those legal consequences."

It followed that a Deputy was entitled by virtue of Article 15.13 to claim privilege in respect of the confidentiality of his sources.

[22] Although the House in question might discipline him.
[23] [1993] ILRM 821.
[24] Geoghegan J added that: "While there might have been some doubts as to the detailed application of the principles, it would seem likely to me that the framers of the...Constitution would have broadly understood that parliamentary privilege in both England and the United States...involved the absolute non-amenability of members of Parliament to courts or other tribunals in respect of utterances made in Parliament [and] Article 15.12 and Article 15.13...must be read in that context."
[25] Quoting with approval from the judgment of Warren CJ in *Powell v McCormack* 395 US 486 (1969).

Privilege extends only to utterances made in the course of the legislative process

However, some limits had to be placed on the ambit of this privilege, since the exercise of that privilege had "serious implications...for the vindication of the good name of persons whose activities may be investigated by the Tribunal."[26] In the *Hamilton (No.2)* case, the deputies in question had expanded on and elaborated on their statements in the Dáil by providing written statements to the Tribunal of Inquiry. Geoghegan J held that the republication of such statements outside the physical confines of the Houses of the Oireachtas did not attract privilege under Article 15.12, as this provision was primarily dealing with privilege in a defamation context:[27]

> "the expression "wherever published" refers merely to the outside publication of actual utterances made in either House, as, for instance, reporting in a newspaper."

Nor was this republication protected by Article 15.13, since unless that was:

> "to be given an unnecessarily wide interpretation (which, in my view, would be unwarranted having regard to other rights protected by the Constitution and particularly by Article 40) , [Article 15.13] can only apply to utterances made in either House of the Oireachtas or at a meeting of a Committee of either House of the Oireachtas involved in the legislative process. I do not consider that the Tribunal itself is part of the legislative process and in my view [the Deputies] are not entitled to invoke either Article 15.12 or Article 15.13 to prevent questioning in respect of any matter contained in the statements delivered to the Tribunal."

The Supreme Court did not take issue with Geoghegan J's general analysis of the nature and purpose of Articles 15.12 and 15.13. A majority, however, saw the matter in a different light, since in their view the reality of the present case was that an attempt was being made to compel the Deputies in question to reveal the source of the information which supported the utterances which they had made in the Dáil. Finlay CJ drew attention to the fact that:

> "notwithstanding the submission of the statements which expand on or explain the utterances made in the Dáil by the three Deputies and notwithstanding the acceptance by the Tribunal at all times of the necessity to specify the allegations being made against the parties being investigated...we have been informed that no additional allegation of any description after the original book of allegations which was prepared on the basis of the Dáil debates has been filed as the result of the submission of statements by any of these three persons."

And, as Blayney J explained, it was not a case of the immunity in Article 15.13 being given an extended meaning so as to cover the "voluntary, conscious [and] deliberate repetitions" of the statements outside the House:

[26] For the related question of whether the exercise of parliamentary privilege might in some way violate another person's constitutional right to a good name, see *Goodman International v Hamilton (No.2)* High Court, 18 February 1993 and pp. 753-754.

[27] Geoghegan J thus agreed with the comments of McCarthy J in *Attorney General v Hamilton (No.1)* [1993] 2 IR 250; [1993] ILRM 81. On appeal the Supreme Court held that Article 15.12 applied to all forms of legal proceeding and not just defamation.

"The reason why the [Deputies] cannot be compelled to reveal the source of their allegations is because those allegations are identical with their utterances in the Dáil and so they would be being denied the immunity to which they are entitled in respect of the latter if they were compelled to reveal their sources."

The Supreme Court was, however, at one with Geoghegan J in holding that definite limits must be placed on the ambit of parliamentary privilege. Thus, Finlay CJ refused to give Articles 15.12 and 15.13 an extended interpretation so as to embrace statements made to the Tribunal itself, having regard to the fact that, those provisions were "explicit and definite in their terms." In addition, these Articles constituted "a very far-reaching privilege" which might in some cases amount to "a major invasion of personal rights of the individual, particularly with regard to his or her good name and property rights." For these reasons the Supreme Court concluded that the privilege thereby conferred should be confirmed in the manner indicated.

May a litigant rely on assurances, utterances etc. made in either House?

A related question was considered by Murphy J in *Garda Representative Association v Ireland.*[28] Did Article 15.13 have the effect of preventing the plaintiffs from relying on an assurance given by a Minister in the Dáil in order in support of a claim of promissory estoppel? Murphy J thought not, saying that it was desirable that Article 15.13 should be interpreted in such a way:

"as to permit and encourage members of the Oireachtas to engage in debate on matters of national interest without having to restrict their observations or edit their opinions because of the danger of being made "amenable to any court or authority" at the suit of some person who feel aggrieved by statements made in the course of debate. On the other hand, it is equally obvious that the official reports of Parliamentary debates contain a valuable record of the considered views of eminent politicians so that it would be absurd (as well as offensive to politicians) to proceed on the footing either that the statements were not made or that national organisations and concerned officials do not acquaint themselves with the statements and opinions expressed by politicians and more particularly Ministers in the forum designed for the purpose. In my view, the constitutional protection afforded by Article 15 would not in any way prevent the plaintiffs...from adverting to the statement [of the Minister for Justice.]"

Since, however, there was no evidence that the plaintiffs had actually relied on the Minister's assurances to the Dáil, it could not be invoked to found a promissory estoppel and the claim failed on the facts. Murphy J's views as to the effect of Article 15.13 may, however, no longer prevail in view of the *dicta* in *Attorney General v Hamilton (No.2)*, inasmuch as if a Minister could be bound by an assurance given in the Dáil, it could mean that - however indirectly - he would be held amenable to the courts, in the sense that his parliamentary utterances might affect his legal rights before a judicial forum.[29]

[28] [1989] IR 193.

[29] Note that in *Pepper v Hart* [1993] 1 All ER 42 the House of Lords held that Article 9 of the Bill of Rights did not preclude the courts examining the legislative history of an enactment, since, as Lord Browne-Wilkinson observed: "Relaxation of the rule will not involve the courts in criticising Parliament...Far from questioning the independence of Parliament and its debates, the courts would be giving effect to what is said and done there."

Privilege from arrest etc.

The question of the extent of the privilege from arrest conferred by Article 15.13 also surfaced in another case around this time which also involved a member of the Seanad. The Senator in question was said to have invoked this constitutional privilege when arrested on suspicion of drunk driving offences[30] and the D.P.P. decided not to take the matter any further. Of course, the privilege only extends to a privilege from *arrest* in respect of an alleged misdemeanour[31] and not from prosecution. Furthermore, the protection only extends when the member is "going to and returning from, and while within the precincts of, either House." The arrest in this case appears to have taken place some hours after the Seanad had concluded its business for the day and it is a moot point whether it could have been said that the Senator was actually "returning from" the House at the time when the arrest was purportedly effected.

Are the privileges referred to as parliamentary privileges properly so called?

What is not clear is whether the privileges referred to in Articles 15.12 and 15.13 are parliamentary privileges in the proper sense of the term[32] or whether the privileges are ones which exists for the benefit of the individual deputy or senator. The distinction is potentially an important one, since if the privilege exists for the benefit of the individual member of the Oireachtas, there seems no reason why it should not be waived by him should he see fit.[33] This might mean, for example, that if a Deputy were sued for defamation in respect of a utterance made in the Dáil, he might elect, if he saw fit, to defend the action on the merits rather than the raise the privilege conferred by Articles 15.12 and 15.13. On this view, the privilege would be personal to the Deputy or Senator concerned and he might claim the privilege or waive it as he saw fit in the circumstances.

The historical antecedents notwithstanding,[34] the phraseology of Article 15.13 suggests that the privilege is personal to the member ("The members of each House of the Oireachtas shall...be privileged etc."). And yet powerful arguments can be advanced to the contrary, for, if the privilege were a purely personal one, the member might be sub-

[30] *The Irish Times*, 30 March 1990.

[31] As it happens, s 49(4) of the Road Traffic Act 1978 is somewhat unusual in that it provides for a power of arrest in the case of drunk driving offences (which happen to be misdemeanours). Normally, misdemeanours are proceeded with by way of summons and not by way of arrest.

[32] Such privileges are, under British practice, regarded as parliamentary privileges in the proper sense of the term, i.e., that the privilege is regarded as attaching to each House of Parliament itself and not simply for the personal benefit of each member. As Hood Phillips observes (*Constitutional and Administrative Law* (London, 1987) at 234):

> "Each House exercises certain powers and privileges which are regarded as essential to the dignity and proper functioning of Parliament. The members also have certain privileges, although these exist for the benefit of the House and not for the personal benefit of the members."

The only Irish authority on this point is of pre-1922 vintage: *Dillon v Balfour* (1887) 20 LR Ir 600. Here Palles C.B. drew a distinction between the privilege of freedom from arrest and freedom of speech. The former privilege was "a matter of defence", whereas in the case of the latter privilege, once the Court had determined that the words were spoken in Parliament, then "the jurisdiction of the Court is ousted."

[33] The waiver - assuming it were possible at the instance of an individual member - would have to be "express and unequivocal": see *per* Geoghegan J in *Attorney General v Hamilton (No.2)* [1993] ILRM 821. Here neither the establishment of the Tribunal by resolutions of the Oireachtas nor the making of individual submissions to the Tribunal by the deputies was held to constitute waiver of parliamentary privilege.

[34] The question of the whether, and to what extent, the Bill of Rights 1688 can be said to have survived the enactment of the Constitution has never received serious judicial consideration. In *Attorney General v Hamilton (No.2)* [1993] ILRM 821, Finlay CJ excluded any extension of Articles 15.12 and 15.13 beyond their "explicit and definite terms." Accordingly, insofar as Article 9 of the Bill of Rights 1688 purports to

jected to unwelcome pressure to waive the privilege, something which in itself was not conducive to the effective functioning of the Oireachtas. [35]

However, in *Attorney General v Hamilton (No.2)*[36] all members of the Supreme Court majority envisaged the waiver by the individual member concerned of the privilege of non-amenability. Finlay CJ referred to the privilege as "an ouster of the jurisdiction of the Court or other authority", albeit a privilege which could be waived. In addition, both O'Flaherty and Blayney JJ envisaged what the latter described as a "voluntary, conscious [and] deliberate repetition outside the Dáil of utterances made in the Dáil", saying that in such a case the deputy in question "would have waived the right of immunity under Article 15.13." This, however, is a slightly different point, since this quotation from Blayney J does not address the issue of whether a Deputy or Senator (or, for that matter, either House) can waive immunity in respect of an utterance made in the House as such.[37] Clearly some privileges must be personal to the member concerned - the freedom from arrest, for example, - while the privilege contained in Article 15.12 in respect of "official reports and publications of the Oireachtas or of either House thereof" would seem to belong to either the Oireachtas or the individual House concerned (as the case may be).

Inhibitions imposed on free debate by practice of the Houses

The "freedom of debate" envisaged by Article 15.10 has been in practice subject to a body of restraining conventions developed over sixty years by the Chairmen (and doubtless to some extent, at any rate originally, under the influence of British practice). Some of these are obviously in the interest of order; others - particularly in view of the absolute privilege accorded by Article 15.13 - have led in the past to extremes of parliamentary self-denial. This rather restrictive regime has recently been modified in the interests of "striking a better balance"[38] between the right of Deputies and Senators to comment on matters of public importance on the one hand and the public interest in ensuring respect for the legal system and the avoidance of prejudicial pre-trial publicity on the other. The new *sub judice* rules now permit Deputies to raise matters "of general public importance" which are subject of litigation "even where court proceedings have been initiated", provided that the litigation concerned raises public policy issued and that notice of trial has not been served in a case involving a jury. The rules further state that any comments should not involve an "overt attempt" by members of the Oireachtas "to encroach on judicial proceedings" and members are enjoined to avoid comment "which might in effect prejudice the outcome" of any pending litigation.[39]

endow the Oireachtas or individual members thereof, with more extensive privileges that those conferred by Article 15 of the Constitution it would to that extent be unconstitutional. In any event, since Articles 15.12 and 15.13 would appear to have set out in full the extent and ambit of parliamentary privilege and prior legislative attempt to regulate this matter might be regarded as *pro tanto* unconstitutional. There is an obvious analogy here with the old Habeas Corpus Acts and Article 40.4, for which see pp. 897-899.

[35] Public policy issues of this kind seem latent in the judgment of Palles CB in *Dillon v Balfour* (1887) 20 LR Ir 600 where he held that the parliamentary privilege of freedom of speech meant that the courts had no jurisdiction to entertain defamation proceedings grounded on words spoken in Parliament. It may be noted that this issue has never received precise judicial consideration.

[36] [1993] ILRM 821.

[37] O'Flaherty J did say that the effect of Article 15.13 was that "an utterance made in either House of the Oireachtas cannot attract or be the subject matter of any form of legal proceeding, wherever it may be published." This tends to suggest that Article 15.13 constitutes an absolute ouster of jurisdiction which *as such* is not capable of waiver (one excludes here "voluntary, conscious, deliberate statements" made outside the House). But, perhaps, O'Flaherty J did not have this precise point in mind.

[38] These were the words of the Minister of State at the Department of the Taoiseach (Mr N Dempsey T.D. during statements in the Dáil on the relaxation of the rule: see 430 *Dáil Debates* at Cols. 353-369.

[39]The new *sub judice* rules are set out at 429 *Dáil Debates* at Col. 1034.

Pre-Constitution statute law

Pre-Constitution statute law relating to the old Oireachtas was continued in force with application to the Oireachtas of the present Constitution by s 4(1) of the Constitution (Consequential Provisions) Act 1937. This provides:

> Every mention or reference in any statute or statutory instrument in force immediately prior to the date of the coming into operation of the Constitution and continued in force thereafter by s 1 of Article 50 of the Constitution...of or to any official person or body or any governmental authority, whether legislative, judicial, or executive, established by or under or functioning under or by virtue of the Constitution of Saorstát Éireann shall...in relation to anything done or to be done or an event occurring after the coming into operation of the Constitution, be construed and have effect...as a mention of or reference to the official person or body or the governmental authority...who or which corresponds to or has the like functions as such official person or body or governmental authority [under the Constitution of Saorstát Éireann].

In *In re Haughey*[40] it was argued that "governmental authority" was not an expression which could convey a House of the Oireachtas (so as to warrant the continued application of the Oireachtas Witnesses Oaths Act 1924); but Ó Dálaigh CJ pointed out that the subsection envisages a "legislative governmental authority":

> "and this, it seems to me, points to the former Oireachtas and its committees. The corresponding legislative governmental authority under the new Constitution, in my opinion, can be none other than the new Oireachtas and its committees."

Free travel facilities

The provision of Article 15.15 for free travel facilities is also found in the old Article 23, and may have been suggested by the similar Article 40 of the German Constitution of 1919.

[40] [1971] IR 217.

Article 16.1

DÁIL ÉIREANN

DÁIL ÉIREANN

Article 16.

1. 1° Every citizen without distinction of sex who has reached the age of twenty-one years, and who is not placed under disability or incapacity by this Constitution or by law, shall be eligible for membership of Dáil Éireann.

2° i All citizens, and
ii such other persons in the State as may be determined by law,
without distinction of sex who have reached the age of eighteen years who are not disqualified by law and comply with the provisions of the law relating to the election of members of Dáil Éireann, shall have the right to vote at an election for members of Dáil Éireann.

3° No law shall be enacted placing any citizen under disability or incapacity for membership of Dáil Éireann on the ground of sex or disqualifying any citizen from voting at an election for members of Dáil Éireann on that ground.

4° No voter may exercise more than one vote at an election for Dáil Éireann, and the voting shall be by secret ballot.

DÁIL ÉIREANN

Airteagal 16.

1. 1° Gach saoránach, cibé acu fear nó bean, ag a bhfuil bliain agus fiche slán agus nach gcuirtear faoi mhíchumas nó faoi mhíthreoir leis an mBunreacht seo ná le dlí, tá sé intofa ar chomhaltas Dháil Éireann.

2° i. Gach uile shaoránach, agus
ii. cibé daoine eile sa Stát a cinnfear le dlí,
cibé acu fir nó mna, ag a bhfuil ocht mbliana déag slán agus ná cuirtear faoi dhícháilíocht le dlí, agus a chomhlíonann coinníollacha an dlí i dtaobh toghcháin comhaltaí do Dháil Éireann, tá ceart vótála acu i dtoghchán comhaltaí do Dháil Éireann.

3° Ní cead aon dlí a achtú a chuirfeadh saoránach ar bith, toisc gur fear nó toisc gur bean an saoránach sin, faoi mhíchumas nó faoi mhíthreoir maidir lena bheith ina chomhalta de Dháil Éireann nó ó bheith i dteideal vótála i dtoghchán comhaltaí do Dháil Éireann.

4° Ní cead do thoghthóir ar bith thar aon vóta amháin a thabhairt i dtoghchán do Dháil Éireann, agus is le rúnbhallóid a dhéanfar an vótáil.

1922 Position

This section reproduces in substance the provisions of Articles 14 and 15 of the 1922 Constitution. Article 16.1.2 has, in fact been amended by two separate constitutional amendments. The first amendment of sub-s 2 was effected by the Fourth Amendment of the Constitution Act 1972, which reduced to eighteen the qualifying age for voting in Dáil elections; previously it had been, as in the 1922 Constitution, twenty-one years. The second was effected by the Ninth Amendment of the Constitution Act 1984 which allowed for the extension by law of the Dáil[1] franchise. This amendment followed the earlier decision of the Supreme Court in *Re Article 26 and the Electoral (Amendment) Bill*[2] which had held that, given the self-contained nature of Article 16 and the fact that it prescribed a "total code" for Dáil elections, the Oireachtas could not extend the franchise through ordinary legislation alone.

[1] But not the franchise for either Presidential elections or referenda.

Incapacity for membership

Persons incapacitated by the Constitution from being members of either House of the Oireachtas are the President (Article 12.6), all judges (Article 35.3) and the Comptroller and Auditor General (Article 33.3). Categories disqualified by law are those specified in s 51(2) of the Electoral Act 1923. In addition, s 41 of the Electoral Act 1992 provides that the following categories of persons "shall not be eligible for election as a member of the Dáil:

> A person who -
> (a) is not a citizen of Ireland, or
> (b) who has not reached the age of 21 years, or
> (c) is a member of the Commission of the European Communities, or
> (d) is a Judge, Advocate General or Registrar of the Court of Justice of the European Communities, or
> (e) is a member of the Court of Auditors of the European Communities, or
> (f) is a member of the Garda Síochána, or
> (g) is a wholetime member of the Defence Forces ...or
> (h) is a civil servant who is not by the terms of his employment expressly permitted to be a member of the Dáil, or
> (i) is undergoing a sentence of imprisonment for any term exceeding six months, whether with or without hard labour, or of penal servitude for any term imposed by a court of competent jurisdiction in the State[3], or
> (k) is an undischarged bankrupt under an adjudication by a court of competent jurisdiction in the State[4].

In addition, s 42 provides that an *existing* member of the Dáil will lose his seat where he:

> (a) incurs an incapacity or disability referred to in section 41, or
> (b) is appointed to a post referred to in section 41, or
> (c) is appointed under the Constitution as a Judge or Comptroller and Auditor General.

Possible unconstitutionality of disqualifications imposed by 1992 Act?

Article 16.1.1 clearly allows the Oireachtas to prescribe that certain categories of persons will be ineligible for membership of the Dáil. By the same token, however, that latitude is not unlimited and, by analogy with the case-law as it has evolved in other areas of the Constitution[5] it may be said that the authority of the Oireachtas to impose a "disability or incapacity...by law" means that it must not stoop "to methods which ignore the fundamental norms of the legal order postulated by the Constitution".[6] Since the right of citizens to stand for election is one of those "fundamental norms", it would seem to follow that the Oireachtas must be able to present sound objective reasons to justify the disqualification of any particular category of persons. In some cases this may not prove

[2] [1984] IR 268; [1984] ILRM 539.

[3] Section 42(2) provides that the vacancy is to take effect either on the expiration of the time limit for any appeal or upon the confirmation of the sentence on appeal.

[4] Section 42(3) allows for a time period of six months within which if the bankruptcy adjudication is not annulled or the bankrupt has not obtained a discharge from bankruptcy under s 85(7) of the Bankruptcy Act 1988, a vacancy will then occur and the member of the Dáil will forfeit his seat.

[5] E.g., in the context of Article 40.4.1.

[6] See the comments of Henchy J in *King v Attorney General* [1981] IR 233 and those of Barr J in *Ryan v O'Callaghan*, High Court, 27 July 1987.

difficult. The disqualification of members of the Garda Síochána and the Defence Forces is probably justified if only on the basis that - as Barrington J said in a different context in *Aughey v Ireland*[7] - "because of their close connection with the security of the State" members of the Garda and the Defence Forces "may have to accept limitations on their [constitutional] rights which other citizens would not have to accept." Similar (if different) considerations would also apply in the case of senior civil servants, since it would be incongruous (if not destructive of the relationship of trust which must exist as between Minister and his civil servants advisers) if a senior civil servant could stand for election, even perhaps in the self-same constituency as his Minister. It may, however, be otherwise in the case of lower and even middle-ranking civil servants whose work is largely administrative and which rarely touches on policy questions.[8] Some other categories of disqualified persons - such as the exclusion of persons of unsound mind, prisoners and bankrupts - might also be vulnerable on constitutional grounds. It can scarcely be enough to justify the exclusion of prisoners on the ground that this constitutes some additional form of punishment, since the object of Article 16.1.1 in allowing for the imposition of such disabilities would seem to be designed to protect the integrity of the electoral process and not simply by way of punishment or penalty.[9] Nor can these exclusions be justified by reference to some wider concept of the public interest (in the sense that it would be generally undesirable if a member of the Dáil were either a prisoner or a bankrupt), since, again, the power to disqualify contained in Article 16.1.1 would not seem designed to protect the electorate from the consequences of its own foolishness

Can the Oireachtas impose conditions on candidature, e.g. a deposit?

In the context of the general eligibility of adult citizens "not placed under disability or incapacity by this Constitution or by law" (Article 16.1.1) it may be asked whether it is competent for the Oireachtas to impose any *condition* on candidature for the Dáil, such for instance as the requirement of a deposit. There has in fact always been such a requirement; the sum, £100, remained unchanged from 1923 until it was raised to £300 by s 47 of the Electoral Act 1992.[10] Given the meanings of "disability" and "incapacity" that may be gathered from the general contexts in which those terms are used in electoral law, it could hardly be said that a citizen who wished to be a Dáil candidate but refused to pay a deposit was "disabled" or "incapacitated"; and so the constitutional permissibility of the requirement must be in doubt. It does not seem capable of rescue by reliance on Article 16.7 (which says that subject to the Article as a whole "elections.. shall be regulated in accordance with law"), as the context is the *holding* of elections rather than eligibility; but if this view is wrong,[11] and Article 16.7 really does provide cover for the existing law, the question must then arise whether there is any limit to the power of the Oireachtas to increase the (at present, relatively small) amount of the

[7] [1986] ILRM 206. Barrington J was speaking in the context of a challenge to the statutory regulation of the right of Gardaí to join a professional association or trade union.

[8] Assuming, of course, that their contract of employment does not prevent them from standing as a candidate in an election for the Dáil.

[9] Note, however, that in *Murray v Ireland* [1991] ILRM 465 McCarthy J expressly included the loss of the right to vote as one of the consequences of imprisonment.

[10] Even with this increase to £300, the deposit now represents in real terms only a small fraction of its original value. The deposit is returned if the candidate withdraws his candidature; has not been validly nominated; dies before the poll is closed; is elected or, if not elected, has reached more than a quarter of the quota at the time of his elimination: see Electoral Act 1992, s 48.

[11] Some further support for this argument is also supplied by the decision of the Supreme Court in *Re Article 26 and the Electoral (Amendment) Bill 1983* [1984] IR 268; [1984] ILRM 539 where Article 16 was held to be a "total code" regulating, *inter alia*, "the eligibility of candidates" This seems to suggest that the Oireachtas may not interfere in this area (bar legislating for minor administrative details) by placing a new barrier - not otherwise contained in the Constitution - in the way of potential candidates for election.

deposit to the point where it would seriously inhibit the poorer would-be candidate; or indeed to create further conditions, of a kind not now known, for candidature. Either possibility seems repugnant to the general intent of Article 16.1.1 and indeed also to the general democratic character of the State.

The terms of Article 16 which define eligibility for Dáil membership can obviously be construed also as declaring the general right to citizens to seek election and to solicit votes. This right was asserted by the applicant in *The State (Lynch) v Cooney*,[12] who complained of the restraint placed by the operation of s 31 of the Broadcasting Authority Act 1960, on broadcasts which Provisional Sinn Fein wished to make during the February, 1982, general election. The Supreme Court held against him on grounds related to Article 40.6; but O'Higgins CJ referred to the argument based on Article 16 and appeared to accept that (unless interference with such rights could be otherwise justified) the right to seek votes was in general implied by the Article.

No disqualification from voting in Dáil elections

The right to vote, by contrast with the right to be a candidate, is not subject to any disqualifications at present, though disqualification is expressly envisaged as a possibility by Article 16.1.2.[13] The "provisions of the law relating to the election of members of Dáil Éireann", so far as these bear on the right to vote, are contained in s 8(1) of the Electoral Act 1992:

> A person shall be entitled to be registered as a Dáil elector in a constituency if he has reached the age of eighteen years[14] and he was, on the qualifying date -
> (a) a citizen of Ireland, and
> (b) ordinarily resident in that constituency.[15]

By s 8(2) it is provided that British citizens[16] and nationals of other European Community member States[17] who are ordinary resident in a particular constituency are also entitled to be registered as a Dáil elector.

[12] [1982] IR 337.

[13] Formerly there was provision, under s 6(3) of the Prevention of Electoral Abuses Act 1923, for the disqualification from voting of persons guilty of electoral offences, but this was repealed by s 3 of the Electoral Act 1963. Thus, the present law would seem to suggest that, theoretically at least, all prisoners are entitled to vote (in the sense that they are not placed under any disability by law) and could do so if they were at liberty (e.g., on temporary release) on election day. Indeed, this very possibility is contemplated by s 11(5) of which provides that where on the qualifying date "a person is detained in any premises in legal custody, he shall be deemed for the purposes of this section to be ordinarily resident in the place where he would have been residing but for his having been so detained in legal custody."

[14] The candidate must attain the age of 21 years by the date of the election, but not necessarily by the date on which he is nominated for election: see *Hall v Attorney General, The Irish Times*, 5 February 1987.

[15] In *Quinn v Waterford Corporation* [1990] 2 IR 507 McCarthy J said (in the context of the identical language of the now-repealed s 5 of the Electoral Act 1963) that an individual may be "ordinarily resident" in more than one constituency. He suggested that, for example, third-level students who had left their own constituency were ordinarily resident in their place of study for at least the whole of the academic year and that they were also "ordinarily resident" for this purpose in their family homes Note that there is a presumption that a person "shall not be deemed to have given up ordinary residence if he intends to resume residence within eighteen months after giving it up": see s 11(3). There are also special provisions governing residence in the case of members of the Defence Forces (s 11(4)) ; prisoners (s 11(5)) and patients or inmates of mental hospitals (s 11(6)).

[16] The phrase "a British citizen" is defined by s 8(7) as meaning a person who "under the Act of the British Parliament entitled the British Nationality Act 1981 is a British citizen."

[17] This is, however, contingent on the Minister for the Environment being of opinion that the laws of another EC State allow Irish citizens resident in that State to vote at elections to the national parliament of that State and that the Minister makes an order declaring that Member State to be a Member State to which s 8(2) applies. No such order has yet been made.

By s 111(1) it is provided that:

> Subject to the subsequent provisions of this section, every person whose name on the register of Dáil electors for the time being in force for a constituency, and no other person, shall be entitled to vote at the poll at a Dáil election in that constituency.

Register of electors

It will be observed that the ordinary statute law makes the exercise of the right to vote at a Dáil election conditional on one's name being on the register. The register in each constituency is revised once every year,[18] and members of the public are normally advised, by broadcast and printed advertisement, to make sure that their names are on the register if they are entitled to be registered; but it can and does happen that without neglect or default on an individual's part, his name is missing from the finalised register. He is now excluded from voting. The question whether such exclusion is constitutional evidently depends on the interpretation of the phrase "comply with" in Article 16.1.2. Does this phrase - or the Irish "choimhlíonann" - denote active behaviour on the citizen's part? If so, if he has duly applied for registration it can hardly be that an administrative or typographical oversight can constitutionally deprive him of his vote. The statute law could however be upheld if "comply with" and "choimhlíonann" were taken, not necessarily to denote active behaviour, but rather an overall objective situation, in the sense that one might be said to "comply" with some statutory condition attached to a burden or an entitlement if one's house had a certain rateable valuation, or one's income were in a certain bracket.

The question whether the objective issue - on the register, or not on the register? - can be expressed in terms of "compliance" with the law, even where it would have been impossible for the potential voter to have "complied" with it no matter how great his vigilance, arose in *Reynolds v Attorney General*,[19] a case in which a young man recently enfranchised by the constitutional amendment reducing the voting age to eighteen, but finding that a Dáil general election was being held before the next year's register could be compiled, sued for declarations aimed at giving himself (and about 140,000 other citizens in like case) the right to vote. Kenny J, although displaying great sympathy - he awarded the plaintiff his costs,[20] saying that "people who assert their constitutional rights were to be encouraged" - dismissed his action on the ground that the general right to vote given by Article 16.1.2 was "conditional upon the person complying with the provisions of the law relating to the election of members of Dáil Éireann" and that "attaining the age of eighteen did not of itself confer the right to vote at an election"; there was in any case "no way in which the Court could devise the machinery by which those between the ages of eighteen and twenty-one could vote". A doubt must however remain as to whether, where "non-compliance" with the law is both free of blame and inevitable, as in this case, the essential content of the subsection is being respected if the citizen is not allowed to vote.

As mentioned above, the Electoral Act 1992 contained some novel features which were designed to ameliorate the lot of the eligible - but as yet unregistered - voter. Section 15

[18] Electoral Act 1992, s 13. However, the 1992 Act makes provision for a special supplement to the electoral register in advance of any given election or referendum: see p. 154 below.
[19] High Court, 16 February 1973.
[20] He also incidentally declared constitutionally invalid some unchanged statutory provisions which presupposed the franchise at age twenty-one.

of that Act now allows such a voter to apply to the registration authority within twelve days of a particular election or referendum with a view to having his name entered on a supplementary register. A person thus entered on the supplementary register will thus be entitled to vote at that election or referendum, as the supplement is deemed "to form part of the register of electors."

Voting abroad by members of diplomatic missions

Section 12 of the Electoral Act 1992 allows Irish diplomats (together with their spouses) serving abroad to vote, since by virtue of s 15(2) such persons shall, for the purposes of this Part, be deemed to be ordinarily resident on the qualifying date in the premises in the State in which, but for the requirement of his duties, the qualified person would be resident.

Categories of postal voters and special voters

In addition to members of Irish diplomatic missions resident abroad, members of the Garda Síochána and the Defence Forces are entitled to vote by post: (see Electoral Act 1992, s 14). In addition, s 17 allows for a category of special voters, namely, persons who are unable to go in person to vote at the polling place "by reason of his physical illness or physical disability." Part XIV regulates the method of voting on the part of such special voters. This procedure was first introduced by the Electoral (Amendment)(No.2) Act 1986 which in turn followed the decision of the Supreme Court in *Draper v Attorney General.*[21] Here a disabled voter claimed that the then existing provisions of the electoral law was unconstitutional, inasmuch as she was prevented by physical infirmity was casting her vote in person. The Supreme Court dismissed her action, with O'Higgins CJ observing that the "present law...provides a reasonable regulation of elections to Dáil Éireann, having regard to the obligation of secrecy, the need to prevent abuses and other requirements of the common good." The Court did indicate, however, that the Oireachtas could constitutionally make special provision for the exercise of the franchise by disabled voters and this it has now done.

Constitutional infirmities with present voting system?

A clear possible discordance of existing electoral statute-law with the fundamental constitutional right of the citizen to vote arises from the present restrictions on the categories of postal voters and special voters, the improvements effected by the Electoral Act 1992 notwithstanding. These restrictions still have the result that several categories of citizens are effectively deprived of the possibility of voting since it is physically impossible for them to attend on polling-day the polling-station appropriate to the district in which they are registered electors: for example, citizens who are abroad, whether on the State service (e.g., civil servants[22] who are temporarily abroad at a meeting of some international body) or otherwise; citizens for whom public service duty, or private employment or other concerns, constrain to remain on polling-day in some distant part of the country, away from their local polling-station; persons who have recently moved

[21] [1984] IR 277; [1984] ILRM 539.

[22] But not, of course, diplomats on a permanent posting. It is interesting to note that in the *Second Non-resident Voting* Case (1981) 58 B Verf GE 202, a challenge was mounted to the validity of German legislation which confined the eligibility for postal votes to certain civil servants and soldiers. The German Constitutional Court suggested that the exclusion of other civil servants who happened to be working for the European Commission might be unconstitutional and the legislation was subsequently duly extended in time to cover those civil servants.

house and students who are enrolled at a third-level institution away from their own home constituency.[23]

Is the extension of franchise to emigrants unconstitutional?

The fact that members of Irish diplomatic missions serving abroad are allowed to vote while serving abroad through the expediency of a legislative fiction deeming such persons to be resident in the State raises the broader question of whether it would be constitutionally competent for the Oireachtas to extend the franchise to other Irish citizens who are temporarily resident abroad. This question was apparently considered by the Government in 1992, but it is understood that the Attorney General advised that such an extension would be unconstitutional on the ground that the entire tenor of Article 16 presupposed that only persons who were resident in the State would be eligible for the franchise.[24]

Statutory prohibition on double registration

The constitutional prohibition contained in Article 16.1.4 - according to McCarthy J in *Quinn v Waterford Corporation*[25] - "is on double voting, not double registration." This case concerned an application by students of the Waterford Regional Technical College. They claimed that they were "ordinarily resident" in Waterford during their academic year and in their home constituencies. The Supreme Court agreed with this contention and rejected the suggestion that, in order to give full effect to Article 16.1.4, it was necessary to prevent the double registration[26] of eligible voters.

Section 11(1)(*a*) of the 1992 Act now reverses *Quinn* inasmuch as it forbids double registration on the part of any particular voter. Section 11(1)(*b*) further augments this prohibition by providing that where any person is prima facie entitled to registration in more than one constituency, that constituency will - subject to any express choice on the part of the voter concerned - be determined by the registration authority. This effectively means that in the case of (say) the student living away from home, the registration authority will determine - in the absence of choice on the part of the student - whether he will be registered in his "home" constituency or in that of his own educational institution.

Secret Ballot

The only other portion of Article 16.1 that has been litigated is the requirement of sub-s 4 that "voting shall be by secret ballot"; in *McMahon v Attorney General*[27] the plaintiff succeeded in having the electoral law then operative in this regard declared unconstitutional. At that time (1970-71) the rules in regard to ballot papers, so far as here relevant, were as follows: (1) s 26 of the Electoral Act 1923 (as substituted by s 16(1) of the Electoral Act 1963, for the original s 26), provided that the "ballot of each voter

[23] This formed the background to *Quinn v Waterford Corporation* [1990] 2 IR 507. This practical problem tends to be compounded by the fact that elections and referenda are generally held on a weekday (usually a Thursday), a day on which many persons (such as students and sales representatives) happen to be away from their home constituency. Sunday has been suggested as an alternative voting day, but it is believed that this suggestion has encountered opposition from certain churches and other religious bodies.

[24] *The Irish Times*, August 14, 1992. Relevant, perhaps, in this context are the provisions of Article 16.2 which provide that the constituency ratios must be "so far as it is practicable, the same throughout the country." This, in turn, tends to suggest that only residents of the State will be eligible to vote, for why otherwise would the constituency ratios be based on the last census returns?

[25] [1990] 2 IR 507.

[26] I.e., the registration of voters in more than one constituency.

[27] [1972] IR 69; (1972) 106 ILTR 89.

[should] consist of a [ballot] paper... in form 5A in Part III of the Fifth Schedule to this Act". (2) One of the directions on this form 5A (with which the returning officer, who conducts the poll, is obliged by s 16(2) of the 1963 Act to comply) was that: "The back of each ballot paper shall be numbered consecutively and the front of the counterfoil attached to it shall bear the same number". (3) Rule 22 in Part I of the Fifth Schedule to the 1923 Act required that, immediately before a ballot paper was delivered to an elector for marking his vote on it, the elector's number on the electoral register should be marked on the counterfoil (the counterfoil remained with the returning officer's staff after the ballot paper was detached and given to the voter).

The plaintiff in *McMahon v Attorney General* alleged that the combined effect of these rules was to negative the secrecy of the ballot, as it would be possible to re-associate ballot and counterfoil through the identical serial number printed on each, and then, by identifying the voter whose number in the register had been noted on the counterfoil when his ballot paper was given to him, to see how he had voted. The case made by the Attorney General was that the possible breach of secrecy was a theoretical rather than a real one; and that unless there was some machinery, however seldom used and under safeguards however stringent, whereby a vote could be "traced", the elimination of irregularities such as spurious votes when an election was challenged would be impossible. The High Court and the Supreme Court successively held against him and made the declarations sought by the plaintiff. In the High Court Pringle J said that "the words 'secret ballot' in Article 16.1.4... mean a ballot in which there is complete and inviolable secrecy"; in consequence, he declared eight separate provisions of the 1923 and 1963 Acts and of the rules and forms authorised by them to be inconsistent with, or invalid having regard to the Constitution. On appeal Ó Dálaigh CJ spoke for the majority of the Supreme Court:[28]

> "Article 16.1.4 speaks of voting by secret ballot. The fundamental question is: *secret to whom?* In my opinion there can be only one plain and logical answer to that question. The answer is: *secret to the voter....* The acknowledged purpose of marking the voter's counterfoil is to disclose how he voted if that should be necessary in order to avoid the inconvenience of a re-poll. But this is what the Constitution says shall not be done; of course, the Constitution is speaking of the *bona fide* voter. Where votes cast at a particular polling-station are destroyed, the Oireachtas has authorised a re-poll limited to that station: see s 17 of the Act of 1963. This device could be made available wherever personation, to a significant degree, was proved to have occurred. In any event, inconvenience cannot prevail against the clear mandate of the Constitution...
>
> In my opinion a voting system which permits a State official to note the number of the ballot paper of every voter in the State, and which requires this information to be stored for a full year after the poll, of itself offends against the spirit and substance of the declaration that voting shall be by secret ballot.
> Under such a system, the fear of disclosure which secrecy is designed to drive away is ostentatiously retained.
>
> Constitutional rights are declared not alone because of bitter memories of the past but not less because of the improbable, but not-to-be-overlooked, perils of the future. I would affirm the order of Mr. Justice Pringle."

[28] Walsh and Budd JJ agreed with him; Fitzgerald and McLoughlin JJ dissented.

It may be added that it was argued also for the State that the right to secrecy could not in any case be an absolute one: if blind and incapacitated persons (for whom special provision was made by the legislation, authorising a companion to mark such a person's vote for him) were to exercise their right to vote. Pringle J saw such persons as waiving their right to secrecy; Ó Dálaigh CJ saw the situation in this regard as being rather a "reconciliation" of the incapacitated person's right to vote with the general right to vote by secret ballot: "willy-nilly and of necessity his vote cannot be cast otherwise... The fact that a few persons are, by natural privations, unable to vote secretly is not a valid reason for attempting to curtail the exercise of that right by the many".[29]

Legislative intervention securing the secrecy of the ballot

It may be noted that a variety of provisions of the Electoral Act 1992 are designed to give legislative effect to the underlying principles contained in *McMahon's* case. Sections 137 and 162 of the 1992 Act impose a duty of secrecy on persons present at the issue of a ballot paper or at the opening of ballot boxes. Section 137(3) provides, evidently with the problem in *McMahon* in mind:

> A person who is present in any capacity at the counting of the votes at a Dáil election shall be guilty of an offence if, except for some purpose authorised by law, he ascertains or attempts to ascertain at such counting the number on the back of a ballot paper or if at any time he communicates any information obtained at such count as to the candidate for whom any vote is given on any ballot paper.

Section 162 further provides that:

> A person who has voted at a Dáil election shall not in any legal proceedings be required to state for whom he has voted.

Breach of secrecy cannot defeat superior right of voters

In the election petition of *Dillon-Leetch v Calleary*[30] the petitioner complained of irregu-

[29] The statute law on ballot papers was regularised, in accordance with the declarations made in *McMahon*, by the Electoral (Amendment) Act 1972. See now Electoral Act 1992, s 101. In the *Mayen Absentee Ballot Case* (1981) 59 B Verf GE 119, the German Constitutional Court rejected a challenge to the constitutionality of legislation which allowed for absentee voting in certain limited circumstances. It had been argued that this undermined the secrecy of the ballot, but this view was rejected by the Court:

> "In providing for absentee balloting, the legislators attach special significance to the goal of [promoting] as much election participation as possible; in doing so, they entrust the freedom and secrecy of the ballot to the [absentee voter] himself. But from a constitutional point of view there is no objection to conferring more responsibility on the absentee voter [in this matter] than with [ordinary voting] in the polling place. The Federal Constitutional Court could take action against the regulation of the legislature only if it excessively endangered the principle of a direct, free, equal and secret election. This is not the case here."

[30] Supreme Court, 31 July 1974. For an example of a successful election petition (admittedly at local government level), see *Boyle v Allen* [1979] ILRM 281. Here the election had ended in a dead-heat and the returning officer had declared the candidate with the greatest first preference votes to be elected. The defeated candidate claimed that the returning officer (a) had incorrectly adjudged certain ballots to be spoiled and (b) had failed to order a re-count. Sheridan J referred with approval to the judgment of Henchy J in *Dillon-Leetch*, but concluded that, in the circumstances, the failure to provide a re-count could well have affected the result of the election:

> "....it is at least possible...that mistakes might well have occurred and it only required the slightest mistake....to have affected the result of the election. It seems to me that in a poll of 5,401 having regard to the intricacies of the proportional representation system, the court cannot rid itself of a possible or even probable inference that such a mistake might well have occurred and this view...forms an adequate basis for [ordering a re-count]."

larities in the custody of ballot papers. The Supreme Court held (*per* Henchy J) that it could overlook a breach of secrecy where the breach could not have affected the result:

> "the courts will not allow an electorally ineffective breach of that principle to be used to set aside the correctly exercised constitutional right of the rest of [the voters]; to hold otherwise would be as much an inversion of constitutional priorities as [to invalidate an election because of multiple voting which could not have affected the result]."

This principle now finds legislative expression in Article 4(3) of the Third Schedule to the Electoral Act 1992:

> No Dáil election shall be declared invalid by reason of a non-compliance with any provision contained in this Act or any mistake in the use of forms provided for in this Act or irregulations made thereunder, if it appears to the High Court that the election was conducted in accordance with principles laid down in this Act taken as a whole and that such non compliance or mistake did not affect the result of the election.

Order of candidates' names on ballot paper

Section 88(2)(*a*) of the Electoral Act 1992 (together with the Fourth Schedule) provides for a system of arranging the names of candidates on the ballot paper according to the alphabetical order of their surnames. This system was challenged in *O'Reilly v Minister for the Environment*[31] where it was argued that it operated unfairly in favour of those candidates whose names appeared on the top of a ballot paper and against those candidates whose names appear further down. He was able to show that in Dáil elections over a period that there had been significant over-representation, among successful candidates, of those whose names began with letters at or near the beginning of the alphabet and there was a body of expert evidence which suggested that a more randomised arrangement of the ballot paper would tend to reduce this in-built bias.

Murphy J accepted that the system advocated might constitute "a more perfect method of ascertaining the views of the electorate", but it did not follow that the existing system was "unreasonable or unconstitutional". In his view, the established bias in favour of candidates whose names appear at the top of the ballot paper was not so much a defect in the electoral system itself as a defect or want of care or want of interest by the electorate. Under the existing system the essential information is provided by the electorate and every voter is free to vote or not to vote at all, or to exercise his voting right fully or partially. In addition, it seems to me that the voter has "the right and the facility to mark his preferences between the candidates in a logical or careful fashion but that he is equally entitled, if he thinks fit, to choose some random procedure for selecting the candidates of his choice."

[31] [1986] IR 143; [1986] ILRM 290.

In any case, he said, it was not his duty or function to evaluate the competing merits of and, as the present system constituted a reasonable regulation of elections to Dáil Éireann, he could not different systems of compiling the ballot paper - that duty was placed on the Oireachtas by Article 16.7 - find it unconstitutional.

DÁIL CONSTITUENCIES AND PROPORTIONAL REPRESENTATION

2. 1° Dáil Éireann shall be composed of members who represent constituencies determined by law.

2° The number of members shall from time to time be fixed by law, but the total number of members of Dáil Éireann shall not be fixed at less than one member for each thirty thousand of the population, or at more than one member for each twenty thousand of the population.

3° The ratio between the number of members to be elected at any time for each constituency and the population of each constituency, as ascertained at the last preceding census, shall, so far as it is practicable, be the same throughout the country.

4° The Oireachtas shall revise the constituencies at least once in every twelve years, with due regard to changes in distribution of the population, but any alterations in the constituencies shall not take effect during the life of Dáil Éireann sitting when such revision is made.

5° The members shall be elected on the system of proportional representation by means of the single transferable vote.

6° No law shall be enacted whereby the number of members to be returned for any constituency shall be less than three.

2. 1° Ionadóirí do dháilcheantair a shocraítear le dlí comhaltas Dháil Éireann.

2° Socrófar líon comhaltaí Dháil Éireann le dlí ó am go ham ach ní cead a lánlíon a bheith faoi bhun comhalta in aghaidh gach tríocha míle den daonra, ná os cionn comhalta in aghaidh gach fiche míle den daonra.

3° An chomhréir a bheas idir an líon comhaltaí a bheas le toghadh aon tráth le haghaidh gach dáilcheantair ar leith agus daonra gach dáilcheantair ar leith, de réir an daonáirimh is déanaí dá ndearnadh roimhe sin, ní foláir í a bheith ar cothrom, sa mhéid gur féidir é, ar fud na dúiche uile.

4° Ní foláir don Oireachtas na dáilcheantair a athmheas uair ar a laghad sa dá bhliain déag ag féachaint go cuí d'aon athruithe ar shuíomh an daonra; ach athruithe ar bith dá ndéanfar ar na dáilcheantair ní thiocfaid i bhfeidhm i rith ré na Dála a bheas ina suí le linn an athmheasta sin.

5° Is de réir na hionadaíochta cionúire agus ar mhodh an aonghutha inaistrithe a thoghfar na comhaltaí.

6° Ní cead dlí a achtú a bhéarfadh faoi bhun triúir an líon comhaltaí a bheas le toghadh d'aon dáilcheantar.

1922 Position

This section of Article 16 substantially reproduces Article 26 of the 1922 Constitution, except that the old Article prescribed a revision of constituencies at least once every ten years, and did not specifically prescribe that no constituency should return less than three members.[1] The practice under the 1937 Constitution has been to do away with the very large constituencies once common - there has been since the Electoral (Amendment) Act 1947, no Dáil constituency returning more than five members - and, as under the 1922 Constitution, to adhere to the upper limit in fixing the number of members of the Dáil, i.e. to provide for one member per 20,000 people.

"Single Transferable vote"

The "system of proportional representation by means of the single transferable vote", prescribed for Dáil elections by sub-s 5, is given statutory expression by s 37(2) of the Electoral Act 1992, as follows:

> The expression "transferable vote" means a vote: -
> (a) capable of being given so as to indicate the voter's preference for the candidates in order; and
> (b) capable of being transferred to the next choice when the vote is not required to give a prior choice the necessary quota of votes, or when, owing to the deficiency in the number of votes given for a prior choice, that choice is eliminated from the list of candidates.

The detailed rules as to the operation of the system are contained in Part XIX of the Electoral Act 1992.[2]

Constituency revision

The revision of constituencies provided for in sub-s 4 of Article 16.2 was the subject of Electoral (Amendment) Acts in the years 1947, 1959, 1961, 1974, 1980,1983 and 1990.[3] The reason for the very short interval between the second and third of these Acts was that the Act of 1959 was successfully challenged on constitutional grounds and a fresh revision of constituencies by a further Act became necessary. This challenge - the case of *O'Donovan v Attorney General*[4] - related to the failure of the 1959 Act to respect the requirement of Article 16.2.3 that the ratio of members to population should, "so far as it is practicable, be the same throughout the country".

[1] There were, however, never constituencies with fewer than three members. Under the Electoral Act 1923 there were 6 constituencies with three seats each, 4 with four, 9 with five, 5 with seven, 3 with eight and one with nine. Under the Electoral (Revision of Constituencies) Act 1935, the pattern changed to 15 three-seat constituencies, 8 four-seaters and 3 seven-seaters.

[2] The crude essence - and, from the elector's point of view, central feature - of the system is that the voter marks the ballot-paper not with an "X" opposite a single meeting, but with *numbers* - "1", "2", "3" etc. - opposite the names of as many candidates as he likes, but in the *order of his preference*. (A party preference is not specifically indicated, but may of course be expressed by means of giving one's highest preferences to the candidates nominated for a particular party.) If a candidate receives more "No. 1" preferences than he needs - i.e., a number greater than the notional "quota" (see below) - he is declared elected and the excess votes are "transferred", i.e., redistributed among the remaining candidates according to the "No.2" preferences marked on the successful candidate's ballot-papers. At the other end of the poll, the candidate who has received the fewest "No.1" votes may be "eliminated" and his votes will be redistributed in the same way among the remaining candidates. This process - which has the merit of avoiding "wasted" votes - will ultimately result in the election of the appropriate number of candidates to fill the vacant seats as they successively reach the "quota". The quota is calculated by dividing the total valid poll by the number of seats to be filled *plus one* and adding one to the result. For example, in a three seat constituency, with a total valid poll of 30,724, the quota results from

$$\frac{30{,}724 + 1}{3 + 1} = 7{,}682$$

This is the smallest number of which it can be said that not more than three candidates can reach it. Four cannot: because 4 x 7,682 = 30,728, which is impossible, as it is more than the total valid poll. See further Chubb, *The Government and Politics of Ireland* (London, 1992) at 131-135.

[3] Constituencies had been revised previously under the old Constitution in 1935.

[4] [1961] IR 114; (1962) 96 ILTR 121.

Uneven spread of seats among population successfully challenged

The plaintiff in this case, who sued as an ordinary citizen,[5] was able to prove substantial disparities in the ratio of members to population as between different constituencies; in general, western constituencies, as designated by the Act tended to have fewer people per Deputy, and urban constituencies, particularly in the Dublin area, tended to have more people per Deputy. He was able to group and arrange the figures disclosed by the 1956 Census of Population in a variety of ways to illustrate this pattern; it will suffice here to mention the most extreme contrast: while the national average ratio was one Deputy per 20,127 people, the constituency of Dublin South (West) contained 23,128 people per Deputy, while the constituency of Galway South contained only 16,575 people per Deputy.[6]

It was contended for the State that the phrase "so far as it is practicable" should be interpreted so as to authorise the Oireachtas, in revising the constituency boundaries, to have regard to problems of contact and representation between Deputies and people, which would be of a quite different order in a built-up urban area on the one hand, and a thinly-populated, heavily indented area on the Atlantic coast on the other hand. This line of argument was rejected by Budd J in the High Court - he said there was "no direction whatsoever, in the Constitution that [such] matters...should be taken into consideration when the Legislature is performing its functions in enacting the electoral laws"; these were "important matters, and if those who enacted the Constitution had intended them to be taken into consideration... it is scarcely credible that they would not have said so" - and concentrated on the principle of political equality which, he said, was latent in Arts 5 and 40.1 as well as being express in the requirement of Article 16.1.4 that no voter may exercise more than one vote in a Dáil election. He said:

> "that equality is not maintained if the vote of a person in one part of the country has a greater effect in securing parliamentary representation than the vote of a person in another part of the country...There are thus contained in the Constitution other Articles the spirit of which demands equality of voting power and representation. The Articles I have just referred to admittedly have [no][7] reference to equality of voting power, but are relevant in construing Article 16.2.3 to this extent, that if it be established, as I believe it is, that the spirit and intendment of these other Articles is that the notion of equality in political matters is to be maintained, it would be illogical to find a different and inconsistent principle adumbrated elsewhere in the Constitution. If a departure from the principles to be implied from those Articles was intended, one would at least expect to find such form of words used as would clearly indicate a different principle. On examining Article 16.2.3, nothing of the kind is apparent. On the contrary, the whole object of the clause would seem to be designed to achieve the spirit of equality to be found in these other Articles. Thus, all of the relevant clauses harmonise. This all leads to the conclusion that any construction of Article 16.2.3 which would have the effect of destroying the dominant principle of equality should be rejected."

[5] The plaintiff was the first ordinary citizen to challenge the constitutionality of an Act which did not affect him in particular more than other citizens. He was in fact a member of the Seanad, but this could not have given him any *locus standi*, nor was such a thing mentioned in the case.

[6] The latent suggestion - not mentioned in the case - was that in the former constituency, an area where the Government party was weak, the Government wished to absorb as many votes in electing as few members as possible; while in the latter constituency, where it was strong, it wished to do the opposite.

[7] The judgment says 'have reference", but obviously "no" has dropped out through a typographical error.

The disparities under the 1959 Act he found substantial enough to regard as a breach of Article 16.2.3; he found against the State also on the subsidiary or related ground that the Oireachtas had not had "due regard to changes in distribution of the population" (these changes amounted, broadly speaking, to increases in the urban and eastern areas, declines in the rural and western areas). Budd J also suggested that deviations from of greater than 5% from the constituency average would probably be unconstitutional.

The State did not appeal against this judgment; instead, the Government introduced a new Electoral (Amendment) Bill in 1961, and, on its passing both Houses, the President referred it to the Supreme Court under Article 26 for a decision on its constitutionality. Under this Bill, while an exact mathematical parity of ratio had not been achieved - Budd J had himself recognised that such a parity would be impossible - there were no such large disparities as under the 1959 Act. In delivering the opinion of the Court Maguire CJ said:

> "Article 16.2.3] recognises that exact parity in the ratio between members and the population of each constituency is unlikely to be obtained and is not required. The decision as to what is practicable is within the jurisdiction of the Oireachtas...whose members have a knowledge of the problems and difficulties to be solved which this Court cannot have. Its decision should not be reviewed by this Court unless there is a manifest infringement of the Article. This Court cannot, as is suggested, lay down a figure above or below which a variation from what is called the national average is not permitted. This, of course, is not to say that a Court cannot be informed of the difficulties and may not pronounce on whether there has been such a serious divergence from uniformity as to violate the requirements of the Constitution...
>
> In the opinion of the Court the divergencies shown in the Bill are within reasonable limits."

The Court accordingly advised the President that the Bill was not repugnant.[8]

Level of deviation from the average which is constitutionally permissible?

The highest level of deviation from the average per constituency disclosed in *O'Donovan* was in the order of 25%[9] in the case of Dublin South West. However, in the light of Budd J's comments that deviations of greater than 5% from the national average might be unconstitutional, it may be noted that all the Electoral Acts between 1961 and 1974 adhered to a maximum limit of 5% from the national average.

Since 1977, a convention appears to have evolved whereby an independent commission would be assigned the task of recommending constituency revisions. This commission is usually presided over by a senior judicial figure and usually includes a senior civil servant in the Department of the Environment. The terms of reference can prove to be politically controversial.[10] In the latest set of recommendations[11] - to which effect was

[8] *In re Article 26 and the Electoral (Amendment) Bill 1961* [1961] IR 169.

[9] Remarkably, a similar deviation of 25% from the national average was also disclosed in the case of Dublin South West in *O'Malley v An Taoiseach* [1990] ILRM 461. Hamilton P had no difficulty in concluding that such a deviation was unconstitutional.

[10] For example, the recommendations of the 1988 Boundary Commission were not given legislative effect, since the terms of reference had proposed the elimination of virtually all urban five-seat constituencies. This was perceived by the opposition parties as being unduly favourable to the minority Fianna Fáil Government and had evoked the hostility of all the opposition parties. Following the 1989 General Election, the new Fianna Fáil/Progressive Democrats Government agreed to give the Commission terms of reference which preserved the traditional mix of three, four and five seat constituencies. The Commission duly reported in July 1990 and legislative effect was swiftly given to its recommendations: see Electoral (Amendment) Act 1990.

[11] Pl. 7520.

given by the Electoral (Amendment) Act 1990 - the greatest deviation from the constituency average is 7.6 per cent. What is interesting is that in its earlier recommendations in 1988, the Commission had suggested that such a deviation would be acceptable:

> "The Commission considered that a departure from the mathematical average of 8 per cent or over would be unacceptable and, in all probability, contrary to the provisions of the Constitution."

On the other hand, this view is not in harmony with the earlier *dictum* of Budd J in *O'Donovan* and, moreover, it is hard to see what special magic there is as far as this figure of 8% is concerned.

The census requirement: means census completed, with results known

It may be added that in the *Electoral (Amendment) Bill* reference one of the grounds advanced against the Bill (by counsel assigned to argue against it) was that at the date of the Supreme Court hearing (July 1961) a new census had actually been taken (in April of that year), and so the Bill, if made into an Act by the President's signature, would fall to conform with the condition of Article 16.2.3 about the "last preceding census" as, like the 1959 Act it was based on the census of 1956. In partial reliance on the Irish text - the Court drew attention to the autonomous past tense of "dearnadh" ("made", "effected") - this argument was rejected: "what is pointed to is the ascertainment of the figures of the census, not its mere taking". The Court said:

> "The duty of the Oireachtas, it is said, once a census is *taken,* is to stay its hand until the figures are counted. During this interval, the Oireachtas is, it was submitted, disabled from proceeding with a revision of the constituencies. If the idea of ascertainment of population were absent from the Irish text it would be somewhat surprising to find the Oireachtas in the position of having to await the publication of the figures of population before it could act under sub-s 4. It would be a more reasonable construction in such instance to construe the Irish text as pointing - and intended to point - to a completed census and not to a mere taking of census."

Does a census showing a population shift mean that a constituency revision must be undertaken before the next General Election?

A further serious question is whether, once a census has been completed and has disclosed substantial changes in the pattern of population distribution since the previous census (so as to indicate that an intervening redistribution of Dáil seats would no longer respect the requirement of Article 16.2.3), the Oireachtas is obliged to effect a fresh redistribution of seats although less than 12 years have elapsed since the last redistribution; or, to put it another way, whether in these circumstances a General Election can validly take place without such a redistribution. The sense and spirit of Article 16.2.3, and the plain words "to be elected at any time", suggest such a duty on the part of the Oireachtas, and suggest the invalidity of an election held in constituencies known from the census returns to have uneven representation in the sense of the sub-section. The 1983 revision, made only three years after that of 1980, was apparently actuated by this consideration in relation to the census of 1981: though in fact only minimal adjustments were made by the Act.

These views appear to be borne out by the judgment of Hamilton P. in *O'Malley v An Taoiseach.*[12] He drew attention to the language of Article 16.2.4:

[12] [1990] ILRM 461.

"The Oireachtas shall revise the constituencies at least once in every 2 years with due regard to changes in the distribution of the population."

He continued:

"The constitutional obligation placed on the Oireachtas is not discharged by revising the constituencies once in every 12 years. They are obliged to revise the constituencies with due regard to changes in distribution of the population and when a census return discloses major changes in the distribution of the population there is a constitutional obligation on the Oireachtas to revise the constituencies. No revision has taken place has taken place since the last census in 1986 and I am satisfied that the Oireachtas is in breach of its constitutional obligation, particularly when the census discloses a major change in the distribution of the population there is a constitutional obligation on the Oireachtas to revise the constituencies."[13]

While these views were strictly *obiter*, these comments have been accepted as binding by the Government.[14]

Consequences of General Elections held pursuant to unconstitutional legislation?

In the immediate aftermath of the *O'Malley* decision in May 1989, there was much speculation that the results of the ensuing general election might be upset if the provisions of the Electoral (Amendment) Act 1983 were found subsequently to have been unconstitutional. The failure on the part of the Oireachtas to revise the constituencies in the light of the preceding census and the resulting discrepancies in the constituency averages strongly suggested an unconstitutionality. In the event, no such challenge materialised, but what would have been the situation had the election been held pursuant to unconstitutional legislation?

This situation presents the courts with an awkward dilemma. The principles enunciated by the Supreme Court in *Dillon-Leetch v Calleary*[15] - namely, that the courts will only set aside an election result where the irregularity might have affected the result - can scarcely apply in this context, since the failure to effect a constituency revision would certainly affect the result. Yet other considerations of public policy and the need to prevent total electoral chaos[16] would seem to argue against this possibility.

Such has been the experience of other countries. In Germany, for example, the Constitutional Court refused - even in the face of a manifest unconstitutionality - to set aside the results of the 1961 federal elections.[17] These elections had taken place on foot of unrevised constituencies and the significant population shifts had taken place since the 1949 electoral law was first put in place. The Court side-stepped the problem by saying that the 1949 law "has become" unconstitutional because "it no longer corresponds

[13] He declined to grant the relief sought by the plaintiffs - an injunction restraining the Taoiseach from advising the President to dissolve the Dáil - on the ground that the Courts have no jurisdiction "to place any impediment between the President and his constitutional adviser in this important matter". The dissolution took place a few days later.

[14] See the comments of the Minister for the Environment (Mr. P. Flynn T.D.) 403 *Dáil Debates*, Col. 2655.

[15] Supreme Court, July 31, 1974.

[16] Cf. the comments of O'Higgins CJ in *de Búrca v Attorney General* [1976] IR 38 where, speaking in the context of the potential invalidation of thousands of jury verdicts which had been unconstitutionally arrived at, he said that "the overriding requirements of an ordered society" would prevent the courts invalidating such verdicts and see generally at pp. 479-484.

[17] *The Second Apportionment* Case (1963) 16 BVerfGE 130.

to up-to-date demographic figures". It warned that the 1949 law could not constitutionally be used for the next elections, but it refused to annul the 1961 elections on the ground that this unconstitutionality "was not so evident" as to invalidate the previous constituency apportionments. The Court thus, so to speak, had it both ways, so to speak: it avoided the chaos which an annulment of the 1961 elections results would have caused, while pointing the way for the future. Different reasons were given for arriving at the same result by Jacobs J in the High Court of Australia in *Western Australia v Commonwealth:*[18]

> "The procedure prescribed leads to the expression by the people of their preference of choice of elected representatives...and no court in the absence of a clearly conferred power has the right to thwart or interfere with the people's expression of their choice. The people's expression cures any formal defect which may previously have existed."

It would be surprising if the Irish courts were not prepared to fall back on similar reasoning to justify a similar result in such circumstances.

Unsuccessful attempts to amend Article 16.2

In 1959 and again in 1968 the Government of the day promoted, and secured the passage in Dáil and Seanad[19] of, Bills to amend the Constitution by substituting for proportional representation in multi-seat constituencies the British "first-past-the-post" system in single-seat constituencies; and in 1968 a second Bill proposed what was called by its advocates a "tolerance" in the operation of Article 16.2.3 so as to relax the requirement of an even spread of seats among the population. In both 1959 and 1968 the Bill to introduce the "first-past-the-post" system also proposed the establishment of a Commission to determine Dáil constituencies. On submission to referendum these Bills were rejected by the people; on the 1968 occasion by a much larger margin than in 1959.

[18] (1975) 134 CLR 81. This case concerned a challenge to the validity of the dissolution of both Houses of Parliament and the High Court held that, irrespective, of the legality of the dissolution what had happened could not now be undone. There is an element of similar thinking in *Simpson v Attorney General* [1955] NZLR 271 where the New Zealand Court of Appeal cited reasons of manifest public inconvenience in justifying its refusal to set aside a parliamentary dissolution (even though the formal procedures had not been complied with). See generally, Hogan, "*Legal and Constitutional Issues arising from the 1989 General Election*" (1989) 24 Ir Jur (n.s.) 157.

[19] On 19 March 1959 the Seanad actually rejected the Bill, but its rejection came to nothing because of the operation of Article 23.1: the Dáil passed the requisite resolution, "deeming" the Bill to have passed both Houses, on 13 May 1959.

DÁIL ELECTIONS

3. 1° Dáil Éireann shall be summoned and dissolved as provided by section 2 of Article 13 of this Constitution.

2° A general election for members of Dáil Éireann shall take place not later than thirty days after a dissolution of Dáil Éireann.

4. 1° Polling at every general election for Dáil Éireann shall as far as practicable take place on the same day throughout the country.

2° Dáil Éireann shall meet within thirty days from that polling day.

5. The same Dáil Éireann shall not continue for a longer period than seven years from the date of its first meeting: a shorter period may be fixed by law.

6. Provision shall be made by law to enable the member of Dáil Éireann who is the Chairman immediately before a dissolution of Dáil Éireann to be deemed without any actual election to be elected a member of Dáil Éireann at the ensuing general election.

7. Subject to the foregoing provisions of this Article, elections for membership of Dáil Éireann, including the filling of casual vacancies, shall be regulated in accordance with law.

3. 1° Ní foláir Dáil Éireann a chomóradh agus a lánscor mar a shocraítear le halt 2 d'Airteagal 13 den Bhunreacht seo.

2° Ní foláir olltoghchán do chomhaltaí do Dháil Éireann a bheith ann lá nach déanaí ná tríocha lá tar éis Dáil Éireann a lánscor.

4 1° An vótáil do gach olltoghchán ar leith do Dháil Éireann ní foláir í a dhéanamh, sa mhéid gur féidir é, an t-aon lá amháin ar fud na dúiche uile.

2° Ní foláir do Dháil Éireann teacht le chéile taobh istigh de thríocha lá ón lá vótála sin.

5 Ní bheidh de ré ag aon Dáil Éireann ach seacht mbliana ó lá a céad-tionóil; féadfar ré is giorra ná sin a shocrú le dlí.

6. An comhalta de Dháil Éireann a bheas ina Chathaoirleach díreach roimh lánscor do Dháil Éireann ní foláir socrú a dhéanamh le dlí chun go bhféadfar a mheas an comhalta sin a bheith tofa do Dháil Éireann sa chéad olltoghchán eile, gan é a dhul faoi thoghadh.

7. Faoi chuimsiú na bhforálacha sin romhainn den Airteagal seo is de réir dlí a rialófar toghcháin do chomhaltas Dháil Éireann, maraon le líonadh corrfholúntas.

1922 provision

Article 16.5 replaces the provisions of Article 28 of the old Constitution, under which the maximum term was originally four years but was increased to six years by the Constitution (Amendment No. 4) Act 1927. The shorter period which has been fixed by law under Article 16.5 is five years.[1] Article 16.4-5, 6 and 7 correspond with parts of Article 28, Article 21 and Article 29 of the old Constitution respectively.

[1] Electoral Act 1992 s 33. This replaced similar provisions which were contained in s 7 of the Electoral (Amendment) Act 1927 and s 10 of the Electoral Act 1963. Note that the five year period runs from the date of the first meeting of the new Dáil (which, by Article 16.4.2, must be within thirty days of the general election) and not, as is sometimes erroneously supposed, from the date of the dissolution of the old Dáil.

Article 16.4.1: exceptions

Exceptions from the generality of Article 16.4.1 exist in the cases of postal voting by members of the Garda Sichuan, Defence Forces and members of Irish diplomatic missions and their spouses who are resident abroad (Electoral Act 1992, s 14); special voters (Electoral Act 1992, s 17 and ss 79-82) advance polling on islands (Electoral Act 1992, s 85); and the death of a candidate (Electoral Act 1992, s 62).

Special position of Chairman of the Dáil

The provision contemplated by Article 16.6 is made by the Electoral Act 1992, s 36. The rationale of this special provision, which automatically returns the outgoing Chairman as a member of the new Dáil,[2] is that, while Chairman, convention demands of him an impartial behaviour which must inhibit much of the political activity on which a member may depend for his re-election.

Even after a dissolution, when no Dáil exists and consequently there are no members of Dáil Éireann until the new Dáil assembles after the general election, the outgoing Chairman retains a vestigial existence as such for certain purposes: *Loftus v Attorney General.*[3]

General statute law regulating Dáil elections

The general statute law on Dáil elections is now contained in the Electoral Acts, 1992. This was a much-needed consolidating measure which replaced a hotchpotch of earlier legislation. The filling of casual vacancies (i.e. bye-elections) is regulated by s 2(1) of the Electoral Act 1992 (definition of "bye-election") and s 39(2) and (3) of the same Act (issue and return of writs). The holding of a bye-election is superseded by the dissolution of the Dáil, so that no special election to fill that particular vacancy is then held: see Electoral Act 1992, s 40.

Emergency provisions: proclamation of election instead of dissolution

A special temporary provision for Dáil general elections was made by the General Elections (Emergency Provisions) Act 1943. This Act, which contained the recital envisaged by Article 28.3.3 and so was immune from attack on constitutional grounds, provided by s 2 that the Taoiseach might, "during the continuance of the present national emergency", advise the President to direct the holding of a general election for Dáil Éireann (instead of, as would be normal under Article 13.2, advising him to dissolve Dáil Éireann, after which a general election would follow within thirty days). The object of this was to leave no gap of time during which there was no Dáil in being; the old Dáil would be replaced by the new Dáil on the completion of the election (s 3). By s 2(2) the President had a discretion, analogous to that under Article 13.2.2, to refuse to proclaim a general election on the advice of a Taoiseach who had ceased to retain the support of a Dáil majority. The general election of 1944 was held under this Act.[4] The Act was repealed by the Electoral (Amendment) Act 1946.

[2] Provided that the outgoing Chairman "has not announced to the Dáil before the dissolution that he does not desire to become a member of the Dáil at the general election consequent on the dissolution: see Electoral Act 1992, s 36(1).

[3] [1979] IR 221: see pp. 137-138.

[4] See McDunphy, *The President of Ireland*, p. 53.

Role of the President in dissolution of the Dáil

In O'*Malley v An Taoiseach*[5] Hamilton P stressed that the constitutional duty of dissolving the Dáil is vested in the President and "he is not answerable to any court for the exercise and performance of his duty."

[5] [1990] ILRM 461.

Article 17

THE DÁIL'S FINANCIAL FUNCTIONS

Article 17

1 1° As soon as possible after the presentation to Dáil Éireann under Article 28 of this Constitution of the Estimates of receipts and the Estimates of expenditure of the State for any financial year, Dáil Éireann shall consider such Estimates.

2° Save in so far as may be provided by specific enactment in each case, the legislation required to give effect to the Financial Resolutions of each year shall be enacted within that year.

2. Dáil Éireann shall not pass any vote or resolution, and no law shall be enacted, for the appropriation of revenue or other public moneys unless the purpose of the appropriation shall have been recommended to Dáil Éireann by a message from the Government signed by the Taoiseach.

Airteagal 17

1. 1° Chomh luath agus is féidir é tar éis na Meastacháin ar fháltas an Stáit agus na Meastacháin ar chaitheamh airgid an Stáit i gcomhair aon bhliana airgeadais a chur faoi bhráid Dháil Éireann faoi Airteagal 28 den Bhunreacht seo, ní foláir do Dháil Éireann na Meastacháin sin a bhreithniú.

2° An reachtaíocht a bheas riachtanach chun feidhm dlí a thabhairt do Rúin Airgeadais gach bliana ar leith ní foláir í a achtú an bhliain sin féin ach amháin sa mhéid go mbeidh a mhalairt socair i dtaobh gach cás ar leith in achtachán chuige sin.

2. Ní dleathach do Dháil Éireann vóta ná rún a rith, ná ní dleathach aon dlí a achtú, chun leithghabháil a dhéanamh ar státchíos ná ar airgead poiblí ar bith eile, mura mbeidh teachtaireacht ag Dáil Éireann ón Rialtas faoi láimh an Taoisigh ag moladh críche na leithghabhála dóibh.

1922 provisions

These provisions substantially reproduce Articles 36 and 37 of the 1922 Constitution.

Primacy of the Dáil in the financial area

The combined effect of this Article and of Articles 21 - 22 (which restrict the powers of the Seanad, modest though these are, practically to zero in the case of Money Bills) is to give the Dáil, on the Government's activation, a constitutional primacy in the area of State finances; a primacy reflected also in the rule of Article 28.7.1 that, although the Government may contain up to two Senator members, the member who is in charge of the Department of Finance can be a member only of the Dáil, a requirement which exists in respect of no other member except the Taoiseach and the Tánaiste. These arrangements broadly reproduce British practice, which in its turn is the product of a long historical evolution resulting in the primacy of the popularly-elected House of Commons in raising taxation and appropriating public moneys; and in the rule that any specific proposal to do either of these things must originate with the Executive.[1]

[1] In *Howard v Commissioners for Public Works*, High Court, 17 February 1993, Costello J referred to the evolution of British practice and observed that upon the establishment of the State in 1922 "the constitutional importance and value of these procedures was signified by their enactment as part of the 1922 Constitution."

This is given expression by the Standing Orders of the Dáil, which provide that no private member - a term which includes the whole Opposition - may propose, whether by Bill or amendment, any measure involving the imposition of taxation or the appropriation of public moneys.[2] The Standing Orders also provide, in deference to Article 17.2, that the Committee Stage of a Bill involving the appropriation of public monies shall not be taken unless the purpose of the appropriation has been recommended to the Dáil by a message from the Government.[3]

Ordinary statute-law reinforces the Dáil's position of primacy in fiscal matters: the Provisional Collection of Taxes Act 1927, as amended, provides (s 2) that where the Dáil passes a resolution imposing or altering or renewing a tax, and declares it "expedient in the public interest that the resolution should have statutory effect", that resolution is to operate, immediately, "as if contained in an Act of the Oireachtas". This formula normally operates in the case of the financial resolutions which follow on a budget statement and express its new taxation proposals. Section 4A (inserted by s 250 of the Finance Act 1992) now provides that where Dáil Éireann is dissolved within four months of the date of a resolution under that Act then the period of dissolution shall be disregarded for the purposes of calculating the relevant time period. The constitutionality of this procedure is considered below.[4]

Another example of the primary role of the Dáil in relation to the public finances is provided by the decision of the Supreme Court in the *The State (Gilliland) v Governor of Mountjoy Prison*,[5] which involved a challenge to the validity of an extradition agreement with the United States. The Supreme Court held that the State was not bound by the agreement, as it created a charge of public funds, and its terms had not received the prior approval of the Dáil as required by Article 29.5.2.

In *Madigan v Attorney General*[6] the Supreme Court referred in passing to Article 17 in upholding the constitutionality of Part IV of the Finance Act 1983, which creates the residential property tax. O'Higgins CJ said that:

> "the decision to impose such a tax must be presumed to have been taken for the purpose of exacting that contribution from the better-off and well-to-do who can be presumed to occupy more valuable houses. This accords with the clear duty imposed on Dáil Éireann by Articles 28 and 17."[7]

Dáil Committee of Public Accounts

Standing Order 126 of the Standing Orders of Dáil Éireann relative to Public Business provides that at the beginning of each financial year a select committee of the Dáil, called the Committee of Public Accounts, is to be appointed "to examine and report to the Dáil upon the accounts showing the appropriation of the sums granted by the Dáil to meet the public expenditure, and to suggest alterations and improvements in the form of the Estimates submitted to the Dáil". This Committee - whose proceedings were the

[2] Orders 118-21. Orders 118-17 collectively contain the Dáil's rules on its financial functions.
[3] Order 119(2).
[4] At pp. 172-175.
[5] [1987] IR 213.
[6] [1986] ILRM 126.
[7] Note also *McGrath v McDermott* [1988] IR 258, where Finlay CJ referred in passing to "special constitutional rights vested in Dáil Éireann in regard to taxation legislation in their character as money bills." See in addition the judgment of Costello J in *O'Reilly v Limerick Corporation* [1989] ILRM 181.

subject of the litigation in *In re Haughey*[8] - discusses with the Comptroller and Auditor General his Report to the Dáil provided for by Article 33.4.

Imposition of taxation by executive order

Taxation which takes the form of customs duty, stamp duty or excise duty can be imposed without prior resort to the Dáil at all, under the Imposition of Duties Act 1957, as amended. Such duty can be imposed by Government order (s 1); any such order will expire at the end of the year following that in which it is made unless it is confirmed by Act of the Oireachtas (s 2(1)). An exceptional provision for raising taxation in circumstances of extreme emergency is contained in the Taxes and Duties (Special Circumstances) Act 1942, which is still in force. Under this Act whenever "enemy action" prevents the Dáil, or both Houses, from meeting to consider resolutions or Bills to impose taxation, or the Taoiseach from presenting such a Bill for the President's signature, such taxation may be imposed by declaration of the Taoiseach or "any person for the time being authorised by law to perform the functions of the Taoiseach".

Estimates

By Article 28.4.3 it is the duty of the Government to prepare and present the Estimates to which Article 17.1.1 refers. This presentation has up to lately taken place in the January of the year to which the Estimates related; but in 1991 the Estimates for 1992 were published in November.[9] The earlier publication of Estimates had already been advocated in order to facilitate a proper observance of the requirement of Article 17.1.1 (consideration by the Dáil "as soon as possible"), since previously, due to pressures of other business, including the budget and Finance Bill debates, the Dáil had regularly failed to get through the whole of the Departmental Estimates by the end of the year to which they related, and many had been discussed only in the latter part of the year, and then often only perfunctorily. The financial impasse which in theory this situation ought to have represented was met in two ways: firstly, by the agreed passing of Estimates without serious debate before the Dáil rose for the summer recess (as a rule about the beginning of July); and secondly by virtue of the Central Fund (Permanent Provisions) Act 1965, s 2 of which permits the Minister for Finance, even in advance of the Dáil's approval of the spending of funds on Departmental purposes, to authorise the issuing from the Central Fund of sums up to four-fifths of the amount of the preceding year's Estimate for any particular Department.[10] This state of affairs has been improved somewhat in recent years, with regular discussion of Estimates by the Dáil throughout the year.[11]

Constitutionality of present procedures and of the Central Fund (Permanent Provisions) Act 1965

It must be doubtful whether the practice of agreeing Estimates without anything but token "consideration" can be reconciled with the plain intent of Article 17.1.1. This issue has not been directly litigated, but the judgment of Blayney J in *Ahern v Kerry*

[8] [1971] IR 217.

[9] The estimates for 1993 were, in fact, published only in January 1993, but this delayed publication was probably caused by the (unexpected) General Election which had taken place in November 1992.

[10] Reform of this system has frequently been advocated in recent times: see, e.g., "*A Better Way to Plan the Nation's Finances*" (Pl. 299) which was published in 1981 on the initiative of the Minister for Finance (Deputy John Bruton).

[11] This consideration normally takes place without a vote on Fridays in which the Dáil is sitting.

County Council[12] does throw some light in a related area. In this case the question was whether a local authority had discharged its statutory duty to consider its estimates of expenses for the coming year. The councillors had in fact considered one set of estimates, but the other remaining estimates were approved *via* an omnibus resolution which did not admit a discussion by individuals. Blayney J held that, on the facts, the authority had failed to consider the estimates as required by statute. While he did not decide what would have amounted to sufficient consideration, he did add the following observations:

"Obviously it may not be asked that every single page of the estimate should be considered but, nonetheless, it seems to me that it would be at least necessary that each [set of estimates] should come up for consideration. It may be that on each consideration there would be very little discussion on them, but at least once every programme had been brought up for the Council's consideration then it would be possible to say the each [set] was considered. In this case, where each [set of estimates] was not considered, it cannot be said that the estimate of expenses was considered."

The constitutionality of the Central Fund (Permanent Provisions) Act 1965 must also be in doubt, inasmuch as the effect of this legislation is substantially to pre-empt, or to make redundant, the Dáil's "consideration" of annual estimates.

Constitutionality of the Imposition of Duties Act 1957

A related question is whether the imposition of Duties Act 1957 - which purports to give the executive power to raise or impose taxation by order - is compatible with Article 17, or, indeed, Articles 21-22 (which regulate the parliamentary procedure with regard to Money Bills).[13] These questions were touched on by Blayney J in *McDaid v Sheehy*[14] when he held that powers given to the Government by s 1 of the 1957 Act were legislative in character[15] and, hence, that s 1 was unconstitutional as infringing on the legislative power of the Oireachtas. While the Supreme Court set aside this decision on purely technical grounds,[16] the reasoning of Blayney J still stands (albeit only as an *obiter dictum*) and it is, perhaps, significant that no orders have in fact been made by the Government in the aftermath of this decision, presumably because of official fears as to the constitutional frailty of the 1957 Act. In any event, the very idea of raising taxation by executive order seems inconsistent with the primacy of the Dáil in financial matters, since if Money Bills can only be initiated in the Dáil[17] and that body alone has effective legislative competence in this area, the corollary would appear to be that taxation may only be raised with the consent of that body so that it would not seem competent for the Oireachtas to purport to vest this power in the Executive.[18]

Constitutionality of the Provisional Collection of Taxes Act 1927

Analogous considerations apply in the case of the 1927 Act which, as we have already seen, gives statutory effect to Dáil resolutions (which are normally passed immediately after the budget statement) imposing or altering or renewing a tax pending the enact-

[12] [1988] ILRM 392.
[13] See pp. 173-174.
[14] [1991] 1 IR 1.
[15] See pp. 110-111.
[16] On the basis that it was not necessary for Blayney J to have adjudicated on the wider constitutional issue: see p. 451.
[17] Article 21.1.1.
[18] See generally, Hogan, "*A Note on the Imposition of Duties Act 1957*" (1985) 7 DULJ (n.s.) 134.

ment of the Finance Act of that year. This procedure would seem at first sight to be of doubtful constitutionality, since a mere Dáil resolution is not a "law"[19] enacted by the Oireachtas and separation of power principles suggest that the Oireachtas may not devolve - even on a temporary or provisional basis - the power to amend or change the law - as is inevitably the case with taxation changes - to a lesser body, such as a single House of the Oireachtas. It is true that the 1927 Act simply gives effect to these resolutions for a temporary period pending the enactment of the Finance Act, but this still does not cater for the precise constitutional objection.

However, the validity of the 1927 Act might arguably be rescued by the provisions of Article 17.1.2 and its reference to legislation required "to give effect to the Financial resolutions of each year", thereby implying - it might be contended - that the Constitution was tacitly acknowledging a long-standing practice whereby taxation was provisionally levied and collected on the basis of financial resolutions of the Dáil (or, under pre-1922 practice, by the House of Commons) pending the enactment of the Finance Act for that year. In this context, the historical antecedents of the 1927 Act and, indeed, Article 17.1.2 itself, assume significance. As one noted commentator on the British Constitution has put it:[20]

> "For more than a century before the case of *Bowles v Bank of England*[21] it had been the practice to anticipate the passing of legislation by collecting certain taxes on the authority of the resolutions. In that case Parker J declared the practice of deducing tax without the authority of Parliament to be a violation of the Bill of Rights."

As Parker J himself explained in *Bowles'* case:

> "By the...Bill of Rights[22] it was finally settled that there could be no tax in this country except under the authority of an Act of Parliament. The Bill of Rights remains unrepealed and no practice or custom however prolonged or however acquiesced in on the part of the subject can be relied on by the Crown as justifying infringement of its provisions. It follows that with regard to the powers of the Crown to levy taxation no resolution either of the Committee for Ways and Means or the House itself has any legal effect whatever."[23]

The Provisional Collection of Taxes Act 1913 was enacted in the immediate aftermath of this decision and this legislation served as the model for the Provisional Collection of Taxes Act 1927, which repealed and replaced the earlier legislation.

This suggests that the drafters of the Constitution were aware of the fact that, under common law at least, the Financial Resolutions were deemed to have no legal standing.

[19] *Bowles v Bank of England* [1913] 1 Ch 57.

[20] O. Hood Phillips, *Constitutional and Administrative Law* (7th. ed., p.223).

[21] [1913] 1 Ch 57.

[22] Article 4 of which provides that "...levying of money for or to the use of the Crown without grant of Parliament is illegal." The elaborate provisions with regard to Money Bills contained in Articles 21 and 22 of the Constitution would seem to have superseded this particular provision of the Bill of Rights.

[23] The judgment of Costello J in *Howard v Commissioners for Public Works*, High Court, 17 February 1993 also leans in this direction. In this case it had been established that the Dáil had approved by resolution the expenditure of certain monies by the Commissioners on a Visitor's Centre in the Burren in County Clare, Costello J held that the Commissioners had no statutory authority to erect such a centre and rejected the argument that the approval of the Dáil of the estimates for the Centre's construction in some way validated this lack of *vires* on the Commissioners' part: "If...this expenditure is outside the Commissioners' statutory powers, then the resolution of approval [of the Dáil] cannot have the effect of bringing it within them."

This being so, the mere fact that Article 17.1.2 simply refers to Financial Resolutions[24] can scarcely confer on them a status which they would not otherwise have. In addition, the wording of the sub-section ("...legislation required *to give effect* to the Financial Resolutions of each year shall be enacted within that year"[25]) of itself suggest that the Resolutions of themselves cannot impose the tax and that legislation is required to give effect to them. As against this, it might be said that Article 17.1.2 was drafted with the 1913 and 1927 legislation in mind and that the sub-section provides tacit constitutional justification for the provisional collection of taxes system which had by then become an established feature of the State's budgetary and fiscal arrangements.

Authority for payments from public funds

This Article, particularly s 2, was evidently contemplated by Gannon J in *K Security v Ireland*,[26] which was a claim by the plaintiffs to be reimbursed out of public funds for the cost of their representation before a Tribunal of Inquiry. Gannon J held that:

"The fact that a Tribunal to which the [Tribunals of Inquiry (Evidence) Act 1921] may be applied is empowered by the Act to authorise interested parties to be represented before it is no basis for implying that the Act confers authority on such a Tribunal to award the costs of such representation to those parties at the expense of or as a charge upon the public funds. The public funds are entrusted by the Constitution to the care of the Government subject to the strict control and supervision of the Legislature upon whose resolutions in both Houses of the Oireachtas the constitution and authority of this Tribunal are founded. The very nature of the functions of the Legislature in relation to the control and disposition of public funds is such that any statutory authority for payment out of or a charge upon public funds must be clearly expressed and cannot be a matter merely of implication as contended for on behalf of the second-named plaintiff."

This case is, however, probably best viewed as authority for the narrower proposition that a charge on public funds cannot arise by mere implication and that the Oireachtas in its enactments must expressly specify and define the circumstances in which such a charge might arise.[27] But this is not to suggest that the courts may not make declarations, or even give judgments, against the State or Oireachtas for the benefit of the plaintiffs concerned, since this, in fact, is a very frequent occurrence in the courts. Thus in *Conroy v Minister for Defence*,[28] where the Supreme Court held the defendant liable to pay the plaintiff a military pension, Kennedy CJ said that the defendant, having got the sanction of the Minister for Finance (as the Act required) and having then granted the plaintiff his pension:

> "is bound to submit it to the Oireachtas for the purpose of having money for the payment of such military service pension voted by the Oireachtas."

In *Maunsell v Minister for Education*[29] Gavan Duffy J refused to accept that the plaintiff was precluded from having his right to payment judicially declared until an

[24] Note that in *Howard v Commissioners of Public Works*, High Court, 17 February 1993, Costello J seemed to regard the financial resolutions as a manifestation of the Dáil's political control of spending by the executive:

> "Dáil Éireann control[s] the revenue payable into the Central Fund by means of financial resolutions adopted annually after the Minister for Finance's budget statement followed by an annual Finance Act."

[25] Authors' emphasis.

[26] High Court, 15 July 1977.

[27] The converse proposition is also true as the grant of supply authorised by the Appropriation Act does not empower the recipient of the grant of moneys "to provide services which are not within its statutory powers as ascertained for the enactments relating to the statutory body": see *per* Costello J in *Howard v Commissioners of Public Works*, High Court, 17 February 1993.

[28] [1934] IR 679; (1935) 69 ILTR 43.

[29] [1940] IR 213; (1939) 73 ILTR 36.

Appropriation Act providing for payment had been passed, "however necessary it may be to prove that such an Act has been passed before an order for payment is made". In *Byrne v Ireland*,[30] both Walsh J and Budd J envisaged that it would be possible to compel a Minister by *mandamus* to apply to the Oireachtas for funds to meet the amount of a judgment.

In *Latchford v Minister for Industry and Commerce*[31] the Supreme Court construed the situation created (in respect of a bread subsidy) by the Appropriation Act 1944, as one of partial delegation:

> "in the appropriation of £4,126,124 for purposes including the payment of certain subsidies the amounts are not segregated, but it is clear that portion of the said sum is granted for the purpose of paying subsidies. If the Appropriation Act had prescribed the conditions under which persons would be entitled to such subsidies, a person who did in fact comply with the conditions prescribed by the Act would be entitled to some of the declarations sought in this case. Inasmuch as the Act itself has not prescribed the conditions, the Oireachtas has delegated to the Government, acting through the appropriate Minister and responsible to the Dáil, power to apply portion of the said sum in payment of such subsidies and to prescribe the conditions on which persons would be entitled to obtain subsidies."

[30] [1972] IR 241.
[31] [1950] IR 33.

SEANAD ÉIREANN

Seanad Éireann

Article 18

1. Seanad Éireann shall be composed of sixty members, of whom eleven shall be nominated members and forty-nine shall be elected members.
2. A person to be eligible for membership of Seanad Éireann must be eligible to become a member of Dáil Éireann.
3. The nominated members of Seanad Éireann shall be nominated, with their prior consent, by the Taoiseach who is appointed next after the re-assembly of Dáil Éireann following the dissolution thereof which occasions the nomination of the said members.
4. 1° The elected members of Seanad Éireann shall be elected as follows:-
   - i Three shall be elected by the National University of Ireland.
   - ii Three shall be elected by the University of Dublin.
   - iii Forty-three shall be elected from panels of candidates constituted as hereinafter provided.

   2° Provision may be made by law for the election, on a franchise and in the manner to be provided by law, by one or more of the following institutions, namely:

   - i. the universities mentioned in sub-section 1°of this section,
   - ii. any other institutions of higher education in the State,

   of so many members of Seanad Éireann as may be fixed by law

Seanad Éireann

Airteagal 18

1. Seasca comhalta líon Sheanad Éireann, .i. aon duine dhéag a ainmneofar agus naonúr is daichead a thoghfar.
2. Ionas go mbeadh duine inghlactha ar chomhaltas Sheanad Éireann ní foláir é a bheith inghlactha ar chomhaltas Dháil Éireann.
3. Na comhaltaí a ainmneofar do Sheanad Éireann ainmneofar iad le réamhchead uathu féin ag an Taoiseach a cheapfar ar Dháil Éireann d'ationól i ndiaidh an lánscoir ar Dháil Éireann is siocair leis na comhaltaí sin a ainmniú.
4. 1° Na comhaltaí a thoghfar do Sheanad Éireann, is ar an gcuma seo a leanas a thoghfar iad:-
   - i. Toghfaidh Ollscoil na hÉireann triúr.
   - ii. Toghfaidh Ollscoil Bhaile Atha Cliath triúr.
   - iii. Toghfar triúr is daichead as rollaí d'iarrthóirí a chóireofar ar an gcuma a shocraítear anseo inár ndiaidh.

   2° Féadfar foráileamh a dhéanamh le dlí chun go dtoghfar do réir togh-chórais, agus ar an modh, a socrófar le dlí ag ceann amháin nó níos mó de na forais seo a leanas, eadhon:

   - i. na hollscoileanna a luaitear i bhfo-alt 1° den alt so,
   - ii. aon fhorais eile ardoideachais sa Stát,

   an léon san comhaltaí de Sheanad Éireann a socrófar le dlí in ionad líon comhíonann de

in substitution for an equal number of the members to be elected pursuant to paragraphs i and ii of the said sub-section 1°.

A member or members of Seanad Éireann may be elected under this sub-section by institutions grouped together or by a single institution.

3° Nothing in this Article shall be invoked to prohibit the dissolution by law of a university mentioned in sub-section 1° of this section.

5. Every election of the elected members of Seanad Éireann shall be held on the system of proportional representation by means of the single transferable vote, and by secret postal ballot.

6. The members of Seanad Éireann to be elected by the Universities shall be elected on a franchise and in the manner to be provided by law.

7. 1° Before each general election of the members of Seanad Éireann to be elected from panels of candidates, five panels of candidates shall be formed in the manner provided by law containing respectively the names of persons having knowledge and practical experience of the following interests and services, namely:-

   i. National Language and Culture, Literature, Art, Education and such professional interests as may be defined by law for the purpose of this panel;
   ii. Agriculture and allied interests, and Fisheries;
   iii. Labour, whether organised or unorganised;
   iv. Industry and Commerce, including banking, finance,

na comhaltaí a bheas le toghadh do bhun míreanna i agus ii den fho-alt san 1°.

Féadfar comhalta nó comhaltaí de Sheanad Éireann a thoghadh fán bhfo-alt so ag forais a bheas tiomsaithe le chéile nó ag foras aonair.

3° Ní cead aon ní dá bhfuil san Airteagal so d'agairt chun toirmeasc a chur le hollscoil a luaitear i bhfo-alt 1° den alt so a lánscor do réir dlí.

5. Gach toghchán dá mbeidh ann do na comhaltaí a thoghfar do Sheanad Éireann is de réir na hionadaíochta cionúire a dhéanfar é agus ar mhodh an aonghutha inaistrithe, le rúnbhallóid phoist.

6. Na comhaltaí a thoghfar do Sheanad Éireann ag na hOllscoileanna is de réir toghchórais, agus ar an modh, a shocrófar le dlí a thoghfar iad.

7. 1° Roimh gach olltoghchán do na comhaltaí do Sheanad Éireann a thoghfar as rollaí d'iarrthóiri cóireofar ar an gcuma a shocrófar le dlí cúig rollaí d'iarrthóirí ar a mbeidh ainmneacha daoine ag a mbeidh eolas agus cleachtadh ar na gnóthaí agus na seirbhísí seo a leanas faoi seach:

   i. An Ghaeilge agus an tSaíocht Náisiúnta, Litríocht, Ealaíonacht, Oideachas agus cibé gairmeacha a léireofar le dlí chún críche an rolla seo;
   ii. Talmhaíocht, maille le gnóthaí a bhaineas léi, agus lascaireacht:
   iii. Oibreachas cibé comheagraithe é nó nach ea;
   iv. Tionscal is Tráchtáil ar a n-áirítear baincéireacht,

accountancy, engineering architecture;

v. Public Administration and social services, including voluntary social activities.

2° Not more than eleven and, subject to the provisions of Article 19 hereof, not less than five members of Seanad Éireann shall be elected from any one panel.

8. A general election for Seanad Éireann shall take place not later than ninety days after a dissolution of Dáil Éireann and the first meeting of Seanad Éireann after the general election shall take place on a day to be fixed by the President on the advice of the Taoiseach.

9. Every member of Seanad Éireann shall, unless he previously dies, resigns, or becomes disqualified, continue to hold office until the day before the polling day of the general election for Seanad Éireann next held after his election or nomination.

10. 1° Subject to the foregoing provisions of this Article elections of the elected members of Seanad Éireann shall be regulated by law.

2° Casual vacancies in the number of the nominated members of Seanad Éireann shall be filled by nomination by the Taoiseach with the prior consent of persons so nominated.

3° Casual vacancies in the number of the elected members of Seanad Éireann shall be filled in the manner provided by law.

Article 19

Provision may be made by law

airgeadas cuntasaíocht, innealtóireacht agus foirgníocht;

v. Riarachán Poiblí agus seirbhísí comhdhaonnacha agus obair chomhdhaonnach dheonach a áireamh.

2° Ní cead níos mó ná aon duine dhéag ná, faoi chuimsiú forálacha Airteagail 19 den Bhunreacht seo, níos lú ná cúigear de chomhaltaí Sheanad Éireann a thoghadh as aon rolla áirithe.

8. Ní foláir olltoghchán do Sheanad Éireann a bheith ann lá nach déanaí na nócha lá d'éis lánscor do Dháil Èireann, agus ní foláir do Sheanad Éireann teacht le chéile ar chéadtionól tar éis an olltoghcháin lá a chinnfidh an tUachtarán chuige ar chomhairle an Taoisigh.

9. Leanfaidh gach comhalta de Sheanad Éireann dá oifig, mura n-éaga nó mura n-éirí as oifig nó mura ndícháilítear é, go dtí an lá roimh lá na vótála don olltoghchán is túisce a bheas ann do Sheanad Éireann d'éis é a thoghadh nó é a ainmniú.

10. 1° Faoi chuimsiú na bhforálacha sin romhainn den Airteagal seo, is de réir dlí a rialófar gach toghchán do na comhaltaí a thoghfar do Sheanad Éireann.

2° Is le hainmniú ón Taoiseach a líonfar corrfholúntais i líon na gcomhaltaí a ainmnítear do Sheanad Éireann, le réamhchead na ndaoine a ainmneofar.

3° Is ar an gcuma a shocraítear le dlí a líonfar corrfholúntais i líon na gcomhaltaí a thoghtar do Sheanad Éireann.

Airteagal 19

Féadfar socrú a dhéanamh le dlí

for the direct election by any functional or vocational group or association or council of so many members of Seanad Éireann as may be fixed by such law in substitution for an equal number of the members to be elected from the corresponding panels of candidates constituted under Article 18 of this Constitution.

ionas go bhféadfadh aon dream feidhme nó gairme beatha, nó aon chomhlacht nó comhairle feidhme nó gairme beatha, an oiread comhaltaí do Sheanad Éireann a thoghadh go lomdíreach agus a chinnfear leis an dlí sin, in ionad an oiread chéanna de na comhaltaí a thoghfar as na comhrollaí d'iarrthóirí a chóireafar faoi Airteagal 18 den Bhunreacht seo.

The "new" and the "old" Senate

Article 18 is largely innovatory. There had been a Senate in the Constitution of 1922 (Articles 30-34 and *passim*), but it was abolished in 1936 by the Constitution (Amendment No. 24) Act so that for the last year of the old Constitution's life the Oireachtas contained only one House, Dáil Éireann.[1] The Senate reconstituted in 1937 by the new Constitution has somewhat different composition and powers from those of the old Senate;[2] in both Constitutions the Senate plays a very subordinate role compared with that of the Dáil.

Senate politically subservient to the Dáil

While under the old Constitution in its original form the Senate was so constructed as to ensure "representation for groups and parties not then adequately represented in Dáil Éireann" (Article 82) - which had the effect that almost half of the membership of the first Senate were not Catholics, and many belonged to what was called the "ex-Unionist" community - and while, despite amendments of the electoral system which whittled down this independent and minority interest in favour of growing representation of the big parties, the Senate never contained a permanent and reliable Government-controlled majority, the present Seanad Éireann is as nearly subservient to the current Dáil majority and Government as a second House well can be. This would not be the case if the option offered by Article 19 (direct election by functional or vocational groups or associations) were taken up: but this has never been done. At present the only Senate seats whose political complexion is unpredictable are the six university seats; and even here party politics has now begun to play a role.[3] Of the remaining fifty-four seats, forty-three are filled by an electorate consisting of about 900 persons, of whom the overwhelming majority are expressly representative of the large political parties: namely, all the members of the newly elected Dáil, plus all the outgoing Senators, plus all members of county councils or county borough councils (Seanad Electoral (Panel Members) Act 1947, s 44). The pattern of political party strength among the forty-three panel members thus will tend to reflect roughly the pattern seen in the last local elections, which will generally speaking not differ widely from the pattern seen in the recent Dáil general election. But even if, as often happens, the current Government does not control a majority of the forty-three panel members, nor of the six university members, any Government deficit is capable of being made up by way of the eleven members

[1] For a concise summary of the character and history of the old Senate, see Michael Nolan, "*The Influence of Catholic Nationalism on the Legislature of the Irish Free State*" (1975) 10 Ir Jur (n.s.) 128, 145ff.

[2] See Kohn, *The Constitution of the Irish Free State*, pp. 190ff.; O'Sullivan, *The Irish Free State and its Senate*, pp. 87ff., 235ff.: John McG. Smyth (former Clerk of the Seanad and Seanad Returning Officer), *The Theory and Practice of the Irish Senate* (Institute of Public Administration, Dublin, 1972).

[3] At the Seanad general election of January-February 1993, one of the six university members returned had explicit party associations, and is a member of his parliamentary party "taking the party whip".

whom it lies with the incoming Taoiseach to nominate. Accordingly, a Government reverse in the Seanad is exceedingly rare.[4]

University representation: potential extension

Sub-sections 2 and 3 of Article 18 were inserted in s 4 by the Seventh Amendment of the Constitution in 1979; the immediate object was to remove any possible constitutional objection[5] to the dissolution of the National University of Ireland (so that its constituent colleges could each be given independent university status); but the amendment serves also to permit Seanad representation to be given to new universities or other institutions of higher education. However, despite the creation of two new universities in 1989 - by the University of Limerick Act 1989 and the Dublin City University Act 1989 - the Oireachtas has not yet seen fit to extend the franchise in the manner envisaged by Article 18.4.2.

Seanad general elections linked to Dáil dissolutions: casus omissus?

Under s 8 of this Article the rhythm of Seanad general elections is linked to the dissolutions of successive Dála. Yet it will be observed that the Seanad itself is not dissolved, and can continue to meet and pass Bills even when a Dáil has been dissolved and a Dáil general election is in progress, and in the period between the Dáil general election and the assembly of the new Dáil. What the Constitution does not provide for is the situation which would arise if a newly-elected Dáil were to be dissolved (for instance, having failed to elect a new Taoiseach) before the Seanad general election necessitated by the dissolution of the previous Dáil had taken place. It would have been rational, had this possibility been foreseen, to provide that the originally-occasioned Seanad general election should be treated as aborted and discontinued, and that an election related to the second Dáil dissolution should be held instead. But as the letter of the Constitution stands, it would seem that there is no alternative to the absurdity of two Seanad elections in quick succession.[6] That the Oireachtas understands the position to be thus, appears from two amendments made by s 15 of the Seanad Electoral (Panel Members) Act 1954, to the Seanad Electoral (Panel Members) Act 1947.

Statutory provisions: Seanad franchise, candidature, elections

The "law" contemplated by ss 6 and 10 of this Article is contained in the Seanad Electoral (University Members) Act 1937; the Seanad Electoral (Panel Members) Acts, 1947 and 1954 and ss 166 and 169 of the Electoral Act 1992. By s 7 of the 1937 Act as amended by s 3 of the Electoral (Amendment) Act 1973, the franchise in elections to the university seats is confined to Irish citizens who have reached eighteen years of age and who have received a degree (other than an honorary degree) in one or other of the two universities or (in the case of the University of Dublin) have obtained certain scholarships. Candidature is not so confined; but by s 16(2) of the 1937 Act echoing Article 18.2, no one who is disqualified or incapacitated for Dáil membership may be a candidate.

[4] See above, p. 166 . and below p. 193.

[5] See above, pp. cxviii - cxvix.

[6] It might possibly be argued that in the event of a quick second dissolution of the Dáil, a second Seanad election need not take place, inasmuch as "a general election for Seanad Éireann" occasioned by a Dáil dissolution, albeit the former dissolution, would in fact be taking place within ninety days of "a dissolution of Dáil Éireann", albeit the second such dissolution. This view of the Constitution would, however, entail changes in the Seanad electoral legislation.

Distribution of seats among panels

The existing distribution of seats among the panels is, by s 52 of the 1947 Act as follows: five are filled from the cultural and educational panel, eleven from the agricultural panel, eleven from the labour panel, nine from the industrial and commercial panel, and seven from the administrative panel. Each panel is divided into two "sub-panels", the "Oireachtas sub-panel" and the "nominating bodies sub-panel" (ss 30, 35-37 of the 1947 Act), and s 52 provides that, within each panel, a minimum number must be elected from each sub-panel. Nomination to the Oireachtas sub-panel requires that a candidate be nominated by four members of the Oireachtas (i.e. of the incoming Dáil and outgoing Seanad - s 2 thus restricts the expression for the purposes of the Act the President being excluded although she is in the sense of the Constitution (Article 15.1.2) a part of the Oireachtas). Nomination to the nominating bodies sub-panel is by one of a long list of heterogeneous organisations, supposed to achieve in this way a vocationally organised voice in the Legislature - trade unions, farming organisations, professional and industrial or commercial associations, academies and learned societies, charitable bodies etc.- which list, or register, is maintained by the Seanad returning officer (s 8) and to which bodies desiring to be registered may be admitted on application (s 9). The electorate consists (s 44) of members of the outgoing Seanad, the incoming Dáil, plus the members of every council of a county or county borough - in all, about 900 persons. As these are mostly persons who are members of political parties, and as the nominating bodies play no part in the election after the nomination stage, the panel members tend to consist, despite the ostensibly vocational arrangement, simply of politicians, reflecting the same pattern of party strength as the most recent local elections exhibited.

Seanad elections, like Dáil elections, are conducted by proportional representation (ss 22-23 of the 1937 Act; ss 48 and 53 of the 1947 Act).

Measures consequential on the abolition of the "old" Senate in 1936 were reversed, so as to take account of the emergence of the "new" Senate, by ss 10 and 11 of the Constitution (Consequential Provisions) Act 1937.[7]

Duration of Senators' offices

Article 18.9 provides that Senators hold office "until the day before the polling-day of the general election for Seanad Éireann, etc." The expression "polling-day" is not defined in the legislation on Seanad elections; and its meaning is not obvious, as the forty-nine elected members are elected by a postal vote, the ballot papers for which are issued some weeks before the last day for voting. Seanad electors may complete their ballot paper at any time during this period. The informal practice is to interpret "the day before the polling-day" as meaning the day before the close of the poll (defined in s 2 of the Seanad Electoral (Panel Members) Act 1947, and s 12 of the Seanad Electoral (University Members) Act 1937).

Article 18 has been judicially considered - apart from references to the judicial referee of problems arising in the forming of panels - in only one case, *Ormonde and Dolan v Mac Gabhann*.[8] The plaintiffs sought a declaration that each of them had proper and appropriate qualifications for nomination on the Labour Panel; the Returning Officer, to whose judgment the question of qualification had first to be submitted under s 36(2)(*b*)(ii) of the Seanad Electoral (Panel Members) Act 1947, had decided against

[7] Amendments 8 and 11 in the Schedule to the 1954 Act.
[8] Unreported, High Court (Pringle J), 9 July 1969.

them, and for reasons of time they by-passed the procedure of s 38 of the Act whereby a judicial referee would have reviewed the Returning Officer's decision, and went straight to the High Court. Here it was argued on behalf of the Returning Officer that as Article 18.10.1 provided that elections were to be "regulated by law", and that as the 1947 Act provided by s 38 for the judicial referee procedure, this was the only course open to the plaintiffs; against this it was argued that if s 38 was intended by the Oireachtas to exclude the general jurisdiction of the High Court, it was unconstitutional. Pringle J said he was "satisfied that s 38 of the Act of 1947 does not bear the construction submitted [on the defendant's behalf]"; he held, in other words, that the plaintiffs were not prevented from having recourse to the High Court. This must in turn imply that Article 18.10.1 is not to be read as having the tacit addendum "such regulation to exclude any procedures, even such as the Constitution itself otherwise affords, that are not specifically provided for in such law". There may be further consequential implications by analogy for other parts of the Constitution.

In regard to the plaintiffs' claim to be qualified for nomination on the Labour Panel, Pringle J said:

"The word "Labour" in relation to the Labour Panel obviously cannot mean simply "work" nor can it mean manual labour only. I think the word "Labour" is intended to be read as labour with a capital L - in other words, that in order to qualify for nomination to this Panel a person should have knowledge and experience in the field of Labour Relations, as for instance an official of a trade union, whether of employees or employers. The only qualification required by the Constitution and the Act is that the person should have knowledge and practical experience *in the interest or services* of Labour whether organised or unorganised. The Constitution does not say he must have *special* knowledge and practical experience, nor does it indicate that he must have acquired this knowledge and experience in any particular manner or over any particular period. If he has knowledge and practical experience that is sufficient.

In the case of the Labour Panel I think that, if he has a reasonable amount of knowledge of the problems which arise in our society between employee and employer and if he has also had a reasonable amount of practical experience in dealing with these problems, that is sufficient to qualify him for the Labour Panel, even if he may have better qualifications for nomination to one or more of the other Panels. I do not however consider that mere membership of a trade union would, of itself, be sufficient, although an ordinary member of a trade union might conceivably have acquired sufficient knowledge and practical experience of labour relationships to qualify him, either from assiduous attendance at trade union meetings, which would give him knowledge and practical experience of trade union affairs and dealing with disputes between employers and employed or in some other way outside his membership of the union."[9]

Utility of the Seanad

The utility of the Seanad and its continued relevance to the modern political system are often questioned. Few items of legislation originate with the Seanad, although with the over-crowding in recent years of the Dáil's legislative programme, the percentage of less politically contentious but more technical legislation originating with the Seanad has tended to increase. Although Article 28.7.2 allows up to two members of the Government (apart from the Taoiseach, Tánaiste and Minister for Finance) to be members of the Government, this right has been exercised on only two occasions, so that, as

[9] On the Seanad generally. see *O'Sullivan, op. cit.* (above. fn. 2).

a rule, no senator is a member of the Government. The absence of parliamentary questions tends to stifle attempts by Senators to raise matters of public importance and, in addition, the Senate tends to sit rather infrequently and even then its sittings are largely determined by the need to consider Bills just passed by the Dáil. Finally, the practical operation of the Seanad electoral system seems to contribute to this political inertness. As that system is in the hands of politicians - members of the Oireachtas and councillors - it means that the Seanad itself is dominated by party politicians, thus negating to some degree the wider vocational element which the Constitution seems to contemplate.

For all of these reasons, the Seanad tends to lack political effectiveness. This has given rise to some political controversy on the question of whether the continued existence of the Seanad is necessary or even desirable. Perhaps a wider electoral body along the vocational lines already envisaged might tend to re-vitalise the Seanad, but no provision for direct election to the Seanad - such as is contemplated by Article 1.9 - has ever been made and no proposals for such change have been mooted in recent times.[10]

[10] See generally, Chubb, *The Government and Politics of Ireland* (London, 1992) , pp. 196-9.

Article 20

LEGISLATION

Legislation

Article 20

1. **Every Bill initiated in and passed by Dáil Éireann shall be sent to Seanad Éireann and may, unless it be a Money Bill, be amended in Seanad Éireann and Dáil Éireann shall consider any such amendment.**

2. **1° A Bill other than a Money Bill may be initiated in Seanad Éireann, and if passed by Seanad Éireann, shall be introduced in Dáil Éireann.**

   2° A Bill initiated in Seanad Éireann if amended in Dáil Éireann shall be considered as a Bill initiated in Dáil Éireann.

3. **A Bill passed by either House and accepted by the other House shall be deemed to have been passed by both Houses.**

Reachtaíocht

Airteagal 20

1. **Ní foláir gach Bille a thionscnaítear i nDáil Éireann agus a rítear ag Dáil Éireann a chur go Seanad Éireann agus, mura Bille Airgid é, tig le Seanad Éireann é a leasú, agus ní foláir do Dháil Éireann aon leasú den sórt sin a bhreithniú.**

2. **1° Is dleathach Bille nach Bille Airgid é a thionscnamh i Seanad Éireann, agus má ritheann Seanad Éireann é ní foláir é a thabhairt isteach i nDáil Éireann.**

   2° Má thionscnaítear Bille i Seanad Éireann agus go leasaíonn Dáil Éireann é, ní foláir a mheas é a bheith ina Bhille a thionscnaíodh i nDáil Éireann.

3. **Bille a ritear ag ceachtar den dá Theach agus lena nglacann an Teach eile ní foláir a mheas gur ritheadh é ag an dá Theach.**

1922 provision

The provisions of this Article reproduce material from Articles 38-40 of the 1922 Constitution as these Articles were before the Constitution (Amendment No. 24) Act 1936, deleted them from the Constitution as part of the general abolition of the Senate effected by that Act.

Article in litigation

Article 20 has not featured prominently in litigation, but it was considered by the former Supreme Court in *Wireless Dealers Association v Fair Trade Commission*[1] in which the plaintiffs unsuccessfully sought an injunction restraining the Minister for Industry and Commerce from introducing into the Seanad an allegedly unconstitutional Bill (which had already been passed by the Dáil). Maguire CJ said that the courts had no power "to prevent or stay the operation of Article 20":

> "The Constitution...entrusts to the two Houses of the Oireachtas the power and duty of considering and passing Bills which become law on being signed by the President. The consideration of proposed legislation is a matter which it entrusts to the Oireachtas alone, and in which the courts have no part."

[1] Supreme Court, 14 March 1956. Article 20 was also noted by O' Higgins CJ in *Murphy v Attorney General* [1982] IR 241, when paraphrasing the opening words of Article 26, he said that for the purposes of the Article, "a Bill is a legislative proposal which has gone through the procedure set out in Article 20."

He referred to the judicial review provided by Articles 26 and 34.3.2 in the point that:

> "If it had ever been intended that [in addition to these types of review] the question of whether a Bill was or was not repugnant to the Constitution could be determined by the Courts at any stage before it has been passed by both Houses, I feel certain that the Constitution would have so provided; and it has not done so...If the Court were to grant this application there would clearly be an interference with the process of legislation for which not only there is no warrant in the Constitution, but which would be, in my opinion, contrary to its plain intention."

Barrington J made a similar point in *Crotty v An Taoiseach,*[2] where, speaking of an earlier, unsuccessful application made to Carroll J to restrain the Minister for Foreign Affairs from introducing in the Dáil the European Communities (Amendment) Bill 1986 (intended to give effect to the Single European Act), he said that such an application:

> "was clearly misconceived because it is quite clear on the authorities that the Oireachtas is free to exercise its legislative powers without interference by the courts *in the course of* legislation."

Procedure

The Constitution does not prescribe any particular procedure e.g. the number or nature of the stages in the legislative process through which a Bill must pass in respect of either House. These matters are, in virtue of Article 15.10, regulated by the Standing Orders of each House.[3] The question arises, however, whether an attempt by a majority in either House to stifle or curtail debate on a particular Bill might justiciable by the courts on the ground that the imposition of such a guillotine on parliamentary debate infringed Article 20.[4] This seems unlikely, if for no other reason than that Article 15.10 seems to envisage that these are questions entirely for each House to decide. Yet this may not be necessarily true in all cases, since, for example, the curtailment of debate on individual estimates might be regarded as a breach of Article 17.12 and thereby justiciable by the courts.[5]

[2] [1987] IR 713.
[3] Dáil Standing Orders 88-103; Seanad Standing Orders 78-93.
[4] Such a claim was made by the opposition parties in July 1991 in respect of a guillotine imposed by the Government parties during the course of a Dáil debate.
[5] Cf. *Ahern v Kerry County Council* [1988] ILRM 392 and pp. 172-173.

MONEY BILLS

Money Bills

Article 21

1. 1° Money Bills shall be initiated in Dáil Éireann only.
2° Every Money Bill passed by Dáil Éireann shall be sent to Seanad Éireann for its recommendations.

2. 1° Every Money Bill sent to Seanad Éireann for its recommendations shall, at the expiration of a period not longer than twenty-one days after it shall have been sent to Seanad Éireann, be returned to Dáil Éireann, which may accept or reject all or any of the recommendations of Seanad Éireann.
2° If such Money Bill is not returned by Seanad Éireann to Dáil Éireann within such twenty-one days or is returned within such twenty-one days with recommendations which Dáil Éireann does not accept, it shall be deemed to have been passed by both Houses at the expiration of the said twenty one days.

Article 22

1. 1° A Money Bill means a Bill which contains only provisions dealing with all or any of the following matters, namely, the imposition, repeal, remission, alteration, or regulation of taxation: the imposition for the payment of debt or other financial purposes of charges on public moneys or the variation or repeal of any such charges; supply, the appropriation, receipt, custody, issue or audit of accounts of public money: the raising or guarantee of any loan or the repayment thereof, matters subordinate and incidental to these matters or any of them.
2° In this definition the expressions "taxation", "public money" and "loan" respectively do not

Billí Airgid

Airteagal 21

1. 1° Is i nDáil Éireann amháin is cead Billí Airgid a thionscnamh.
2° Ní foláir gach Bille Airgid a ritear ag Dáil Éireann a chur go Seanad Éireann d'iarraidh a moltaí ina thaobh.

2. 1° Gach Bille Airgid a chuirtear go Seanad Éireannn d'iarraidh a moltaí ina thaobh, ní foláir é a chur ar ais go Dáil Éireann i gcean tréimhse nach sia ná lá agus fiche tar éis an Bille a chur go Seanad Éireann, agus tig le Dáil Éireann iomlán na moltaí ó Sheanad Éireann nó aon chuid díobh a ghlacadh nó a dhiúltú.
2° Mura gcuirtear an Bille Airgid sin ar ais ó Sheanad Éireann go Dáil Éireann taobh istigh den lá agus fiche sin, nó má chuirtear ar ais é taobh istigh den lá agus fiche sin maraon le moltaí nach nglacann Dáil Éireann leo, ní foláir a mheas gur rith an dá Theach i gceann an lae agus fiche sin é.

Airteagal 22

1. 1° Is é is ciall do Bhille Airgid Bille nach mbíonn ann ach forálacha le haghaidh iomlán na n-ábhar seo a leanas nó aon chuid acu .i. cánachas a ghearradh, a aisghairm a loghadh, a athrú nó a rialú; muirir a leagan ar airgidí poiblí chun fiacha a íoc nó chun cuspóirí eile airgeadais, nó a leithéidí sin de mhuirir a athrú nó a aisghairm; soláthar; airgead poiblí a leithghabháil, a ghlacadh, a choinneáil nó a eisiúint nó cuntais air a iniúchadh; aon iasacht a chruinniú nó a ráthú nó a aisíoc; foábhair a bhfuil baint acu leis na nithe sin nó le haon chuid acu.
2° Sa mhiniú sin ní áirítear faoi na focail "cánachas", "airgead poiblí" agus "iasacht", faoi

include any taxation, money or loan raised by local authorities or bodies for local purposes.

seach, aon "chánachas", airgead ná iasacht a chruínníd údaráis nó comhlachtaí áitiúla chun críocha áitiúla.

2. 1° The Chairman of Dáil Éireann shall certify any Bill which, in his opinion. is a Money Bill to be a Money Bill, and his certificate shall, subject to the subsequent provisions of this section. be final and conclusive.

2. 1° Más é tuairim Chathaoirleach Dháil Éireann gur Bille Airgid aon Bhille faoi leith ní foláir dó a dheimhniú gur Bille Airgid é agus, faoi chuimsiú na bhforálacha inár ndiaidh den alt seo, ní bheidh dul thar an deimhniú sin.

2° Seanad Éireann, by a resolution, passed at a sitting at which not less than thirty members are present may request the President to refer the question whether the Bill is or is not a Money Bill to a Committee of Privileges.

2° Tig le Seanad Éireann rún a rith i dtionól nach mbeidh níos lú ná tríocha comhalta i láthair ann, á iarraidh ar an Uachtarán ceist a chur faoi bhráid Choiste Pribhléidí féachaint cé acu Bille Airgid an Bille nó nach ea.

3° If the President after consultation with the Council of State decides to accede to the request he shall appoint a Committee of Privileges consisting of an equal number of members of Dáil Éireann and of Seanad Éireann and a Chairman who shall be a Judge of the Supreme Court: these appointments shall be made after consultation with the Council of State. In the case of an equality of votes but not otherwise the Chairman shall be entitled to vote.

3° Má aontaíonn an tUachtarán leis an achainí tar éis comhairle a ghlacadh leis an gComhairle Stáit, ní foláir dó Coiste Pribhléidí a cheapadh. An líon céanna de chomhaltaí de Dháil Éireann agus de Sheanad Éireann a bheas ar an gCoiste sin, agus breitheamh den Chúirt Uachtarach ina Chathaoirleach orthu. Is tar éis comhairle a ghlacadh leis an Comhairle Stáit a dhéanfar na ceapacháin sin. Más ionann an líon vótaí ag an dá thaobh beidh vóta ag an gCathaoirleach, ach murab ionann ní bheidh.

4° The President shall refer the question to the Committee of Privileges so appointed and the Committee shall report its decision thereon to the President within twenty-one days after the day on which the Bill was sent to Seanad Éireann.

4° Ní foláir don Uachtarán an cheist a chur faoi bhráid an Choiste Pribhléidí a cheapfar mar sin, agus ní foláir don Choiste a mbreith ar an gceist a chur chun an Uachtaráin taobh istigh de lá agus fiche d'éis an lae a cuireadh an Bille go Seanad Éireann.

5° The decision of the Committee shall be final and conclusive.

5° Ní bheidh dul thar breith an Choiste.

6° If the President after consultation with the Council of State decides not to accede to the request of Seanad Éireann, or if

6° Má dhiúltaíonn an tUachtarán d'achainí Sheanad Éireann tar éis comhairle a ghlacadh leis an gComhairle Stáit, nó mura

the Committee of Privileges fails to report within the time herein before specified the certificate of the Chairman of Dáil Éireann shall stand confirmed.

gcuire an Coiste Pribhléidí a mbreith in iúl taobh istigh den tréimhse a luaitear anseo romhainn, seasfaidh deimhniú Chathaoirleach Dháil Éireann.

1922 provision

Article 21 reproduces in substance part of Article 38 of the 1922 Constitution as it was before the Constitution (Amendment No. 24) Act 1936, deleted it from the Constitution as part of the general abolition of the Senate effected by that Act. Article 22.1 is identical with the second sentence of the old Article 35. The first paragraph of the old Article 35 was a statement which, although absent from the Constitution of 1937, conveyed the essence of the situation in regard to Money Bills under both Constitutions:

> Dáil Éireann shall in relation to the subject matter of Money Bills as hereinafter defined have legislative authority exclusive of Seanad Éireann.

Court refused to investigate whether a Money Bill contained extraneous matter

While no Court since 1937 has had to consider the effect of the present Arts. 21 and 22, the old Article 35 arose indirectly in the case of *O'Crowley v Minister for Justice,*[1] in which the plaintiff raised pension claims in respect of his service as a judge of the Dáil Supreme Court[2] in the period 1920-1922. Payments by way of pension had, in fact been made to him by virtue of the Dáil Supreme Court (Pension) Act 1925; but he sought now to have this Act treated as invalid for reasons which Johnston J in the High Court set out in his judgment dismissing the plaintiff's claim:

> "But it is argued that the Act of 1925 was, in its origin, a "Money Bill" within the meaning of Article 35 of the Constitution, and it is suggested that an Act which was in its beginning a Money Bill can be scrutinised by the Courts and can be treated as of no effect in so far as it attempts to regulate matters which are outside the scope of the subjects referred to in Article 35. This is perhaps the most extraordinary of the points that have been raised in this extraordinary case. The Article defines a Money Bill as "a Bill which contains only provisions dealing with all or any of the following subjects", and these included "the appropriation, receipts, custody, issue or audit of accounts of public money", as well as "subordinate matters incidental to those subjects or any of them". The Chairman of the Dáil did, I understand, certify the Pensions Bill of 1925 to be a Money Bill, and I do not see how he could have done otherwise. The Bill was one for the "appropriation" of public money for pensions and for the "receipt" of such money by "any person who held office".
>
> The question of "tacking" extraneous matters to Bills dealing with finance and taxation has been the subject of acute difference between the two Houses for upwards of two hundred years... These matters have always been regarded as rais-

[1] [1935] IR 536; (1934) 68 ILTR 174.

[2] See Casey, "*Republican Courts in Ireland*, 1919-22", (1970) 5 Ir Jur (n.s.) pp. 321 ff., especially pp. 325-6.

> ing a question of privilege as between the Upper and the Lower House and have been fought out in Parliament. No one has ever yet had the courage to suggest that they could properly be the subject of a decision in a Court of law as to the validity of an Act of Parliament. In the present case the Bill was certified by the Chairman of the Dáil as a "Money Bill" and the Senate acquiesced in that view and did not exercise its rights to have the matter referred to the Committee of Privileges mentioned in Article 35. I must therefore receive, apply and construe the Act of 1925 in exactly the same way as I would any Act which did not originate as a Money Bill, and I have no authority to inquire how or by what process as a public Act it reached the statute book..."

Whether the Courts have jurisdiction under the 1937 Constitution to review legislation on the ground that some rule, whether itself constitutional or deriving from ordinary or subordinate legislation (or Standing Orders of one of the Houses), has not been complied with in the legislative process, has never been judicially discussed or decided. In a question such as that raised in *O'Crowley's* case - whether a Bill is properly a Money Bill or not, and, if not, it can be regarded as invalid if it has been wrongly treated as a Money Bill - it could be said that the Constitution, in Article 22.2, goes to great pains to prescribe a procedure for settling the matter, even building a judicial personage into this procedure (though entitled only to exercise a casting vote), and emphasising that the decision resulting from this procedure is to be "final and conclusive"; and that the intention here was plainly to exclude this question from any other settlement procedure, e.g. via the Courts. On the other hand, it has been held repeatedly[3] that a "final and conclusive" provision will not avail a procedure which has been faulty (e.g. where wrong considerations or incorrect constructions of law have influenced the outcome); and it seems perfectly conceivable that the High Court would, in a suitable case, assert its jurisdiction to review the process by which a particular Bill had passed the Houses, by contrast with the view of Johnston J under the old Constitution that he had "no authority to inquire how or by what process as a public Act [a Bill] reached the statute book". The matter seems however-at any rate in the context of the special rules about Money Bills-of slight potential importance, since the Seanad normally contains an easy Government majority, no more likely to pass unwelcome amendments to ordinary Bills than unwelcome recommendations on Money Bills; and in fact the Committee of Privileges procedure contained in Article 22.2 has never yet been invoked.

Consolidation Bill is not a Money Bill

Note that a purely consolidating Bill, such as was the Income Tax (Consolidation) Bill, 1966, although concerned with finance, is evidently not considered a Money Bill in the sense of Article 22.1.1, as the possible referral of the Bill to the Supreme Court was considered by the President and the Council of State notwithstanding that Article 26 excludes Money Bills from its application.

[3] See below, p. 416.

TIME FOR CONSIDERATION OF BILLS BY SEANAD

Time for Consideration of Bills

Article 23

1. This Article applies to every Bill passed by Dáil Éireann and sent to Seanad Éireann other than a Money Bill or a Bill the time for the consideration of which by Seanad Éireann shall have been abridged under Article 24 of this Constitution.

1° Whenever a Bill to which this Article applies is within the stated period defined in the next following subsection either rejected by Seanad Éireann or passed by Seanad Éireann with amendments to which Dáil Éireann does not agree or is neither passed (with or without amendment) nor rejected by Seanad Éireann within the stated period, the Bill shall, if Dáil Éireann so resolves within one hundred and eighty days after the expiration of the stated period be deemed to have been passed by both Houses of the Oireachtas on the day on which the resolution is passed.

2° The stated period is the period of ninety days commencing on the day on which the Bill is first sent, by Dáil Éireann to Seanad Éireann or any longer period agreed upon in respect of the Bill by both Houses of the Oireachtas.

2. 1° The preceding section of this Article shall apply to a Bill which is initiated in and passed by Seanad Éireann, amended by Dáil Éireann, and accordingly deemed to have been initiated in Dáil Éireann.

2° For the purpose of this application the stated period shall in

Tréimhse chun Billí a Bhreithniú

Airteagal 23

1. Baineann an tAirteagal seo le gach Bille a ritheann Dáil Éireann agus a sheoltar go Seanad Éireann, ach amháin Bille Airgid nó Bille a ndearnadh an tréimhse chun a bhreithnithe ag Seanad Éireann a ghiorrú faoi Airteagal 24 den Bhunreacht seo.

1° Má tharlaíonn, taobh istigh den tréimhse áirithe a luaitear sa chéad fho-alt eile, go ndiúltaíonn Seanad Éireann d'aon Bhille lena mbaineann an tAirteagal seo, nó go ritheann Seanad Éireann an Bille agus leasuithe air a ndiúltaíonn Dáil Éireann dóibh, nó mura ndéanann Seanad Éireann an Bille a rith (cibé acu leasaithe é nó gan leasú) nó diúltú dó taobh istigh den tréimhse áirithe, ansin má ritheann Dáil Éireann rún chuige sin taobh istigh de naoi bhfichid lá tar éis an tréimhse áirithe a bheith caite, ní foláir a mheas gur ritheadh an Bille sin ag dhá Theach an Oireachtais an lá a ritheadh an rún.

2° Nócha lá, nó aon tréimhse is sia ná sin a réitíd dhá Theach an Oireachtais le chéile maidir leis an mBille, an tréimhse áirithe, agus is é an lá a sheoltar an Bille ar dtús ó Dháil Éireann go Seanad Éireann tosach na tréimhse.

2. 1° Baineann an t-alt sin romhainn den Airteagal seo le gach Bille a thionscnaítear i Seanad Éireann agus a ritear ag Seanad Éireann, agus a leasaítear ag Dáil Éireann, agus go meastar dá bhíthin sin gur i nDáil Éireann a tionscnaíodh é.

2° Chuige sin is é an lá a sheoltar an Bille go Seanad Éireann

relation to such a Bill commence on the day on which the Bill is first sent to Seanad Éireann after having been amended by Dáil Éireann.

den chéad uair tar éis é a leasú ag Dáil Éireann a thosaíos an tréimhse áirithe i gcomhair an Bhille sin.

Article 24

1. If and whenever on the passage by Dáil Éireann of any Bill, other than a Bill expressed to be a Bill containing a proposal to amend the Constitution, the Taoiseach certifies by messages in writing addressed to the President and to the Chairman of each House of the Oireachtas that, in the opinion of the Government, the Bill is urgent and immediately necessary for the preservation of the public peace and security, or by reason of the existence of a public emergency, whether domestic or international, the time for the consideration of such Bill by Seanad Éireann shall, if Dáil Éireann so resolves and if the President, after consultation with the Council of State, concurs, be abridged to such period as shall be specified in the resolution.

2. Where a Bill, the time for the consideration of which by Seanad Éireann has been abridged under this Article,
(a) is, in the case of a Bill which is not a Money Bill, rejected by Seanad Éireann or passed by Seanad Éireann with amendments to which Dáil Éireann does not agree or neither passed nor rejected by Seanad Éireann, or

(b) is, in the case of a Money Bill, either returned by Seanad Éireann to Dáil Éireann with recommendations which Dáil Éireann does not accept or is not returned by Seanad Éireann to

Airteagal 24

1. Má ritheann Dáil Éireann Bille, seachas Bille a luaitear a bheith ina Bhille a bhfuil togra ann chun an Bunreacht a leasú, agus go seolann an Taoiseach teachtaireachtaí scríofa chun an Uachtaráin agus chun Cathaoirleach gach Tí den Oireachtas, á dheimhniú dóibh gurb é tuairim an Rialtais go bhfuil práinn agus riachtanas leis an mBille sin láithreach chun síocháin agus slándáil an phobail a chosaint, nó go bhfuil práinn agus riachtanas leis láithreach toisc éigeandáil phoiblí inmheánach nó idirnáisiúnta a bheith ann, ansin má bheartaíonn Dáil Éireann amhlaidh le rún, agus go n-aontaíonn an tUachtarán leis an rún tar éis comhairle a ghlacadh leis an gComhairle Stáit, ní foláir an tréimhse a fhágfar an Bille sin faoi bhreithniú Sheanad Éireann a ghiorrú agus a chur faoin teorainn a luaitear sa rún.

2. Bille ar bith a ndearnadh an tréimhse chun a bhreithnithe ag Seanad Éireann a ghiorrú faoin Airteagal seo, má tharlaíonn,
(a) i gcás Bille nach Bille Airgid, go ndiúltaíonn Seanad Éireann dó nó go ritheann Seanad Éireann é maille le leasuithe dá ndiúltaíonn Dáil Éireann nó ná déanann Seanad Éireann é a rith na diúltú dó, nó,

(b) i gcás Bille Airgid, go gcuireann Seanad Éireann ar ais go Dáil Éireann é maille le moltaí nach nglacann Dáil Éireann leo nó nach ndéanann Seanad Éireann é a chur ar ais

**Dáil Éireann,
within the period specified in the resolution, the Bill shall be deemed to have been passed by both Houses of the Oireachtas at the expiration of that period.**

**go Dáil Éireann,
taobh istigh den tréimhse a luaitear sa rún, ní foláir a mheas gur ritheadh an Bille ag dhá Theach an Oireachtas i gceann na tréimhse sin.**

3. **When a Bill the time for the consideration of which by Seanad Éireann has been abridged under this Article becomes law it shall remain in force for a period of ninety days from the date of its enactment and no longer unless, before the expiration of that period, both Houses shall have agreed that such law shall remain in force for a longer period and the longer period so agreed upon shall have been specified in resolutions passed by both Houses.**

3. **Ar dhéanamh dlí de Bhille a ndearnadh an tréimhse chun a bhreithnithe ag Seanad Éireann a ghiorrú faoin Airteagal seo, beidh sé i bhfeidhm ar feadh tréimhse nócha lá ó dháta a achtaithe, ach sin a mbeidh, mura n-aontaíd dhá Theach an Oireachtais roimh dheireadh na tréimhse sin an dlí sin a fhanacht i bhfeidhm ar feadh tréimhse is sia ná sin, agus go luaitear i rúin ón dá Theach an tréimhse a aontaítear amhlaidh.**

1922 Provision

Article 23 corresponds with, but in certain respects differs from Article 38 of the 1922 Constitution in the form which it had after amendment in 1928, together with Article 38A (inserted by the same amending Act). Article 24 is an innovation.

Article 23 invoked on only two occasions[1]

The provision of Article 23.1.1 has been resorted to only twice: in 1959, when the Seanad rejected the Third Amendment of the Constitution Bill, 1958; and in 1964, when the Seanad rejected the Pawnbrokers Bill, 1964; on each occasion the Dáil passed the requisite resolution "deeming" the Bill to have passed both Houses.[2]

Practice of "not insisting" masks a casus omissus

The position where the Seanad does not reject, but amends a Dáil Bill (in a sense unwelcome to the Dáil majority, i.e. the Government) was left unclear by the Constitution, perhaps by an oversight. Article 23.1.1 speaks of Seanad amendments "to which Dáil Éireann does not agree" in the same breath as it speaks of a Seanad rejection of a Bill; but whereas, in the latter case, the "deeming" resolution will rescue the Bill which the Seanad has thrown out in its entirety, in the former case the Constitution does not say in what form the Bill can be rescued. Presumably the intent is to override the Seanad in both cases, and so to disregard the Seanad amendments; but the Article does not say so, while it does speak of "amendments" as things perfected, which is in consonance with Article 20.1 which plainly says that a Bill passed by the Dáil may be amended in the Seanad, and that the Dáil is merely to "consider" any such amendment, but without specifying that it may disregard it. The question arose first in 1943, when the Seanad amended the Intoxicating Liquor Bill 1942, and the Dáil amended the Seanad amend-

[1] See above, p. 166.
[2] 174 *Dáil Debates* 1314ff.; 212 *Dáil Debates* 271ff. respectively.

ment whereupon the Seanad "disagreed" with the Dáil's amendment of its own one; an unprecedented "Conference" between members of both Houses was called, which recommended - though its Report[3] does not disclose either its statement of the problem or the reasoning behind its solution - that "the Seanad do not insist on its disagreement". The Seanad acquiesced.[4] In 1982 the Seanad[5] amended the Housing (Private Rented Dwellings) Bill of that year against Government opposition; the Dáil did not pass the resolution under Article 23.1.1, but resolved that it "did not agree with the Seanad" in its amendment, and the Ceann Comhairle said he took it that the Seanad should be informed "that the Dáil has disagreed its amendment and desires that the Seanad should not insist on it"; the Seanad then[6] agreed "not to insist". The concept of "not insisting" masks a constitutional *casus omissus.*[7]

Public emergency provision

Article 24 was adverted to by Gavan Duffy J in *The State (Burke) v Lennon*[8] by way of negativing any suggestion that the circumstances of the passing of the Offences Against the State Act 1939, entitled the Government to disregard the Constitution, as (he pointed out) the Constitution itself contained specific provision for different kinds of emergency or special situation:

> "The need to provide for times of emergency was clearly foreseen and the emergencies in contemplation were defined. Besides making the declaration of war subject to the assent of Dáil Éireann, the Constitution, where express amendment of the Constitution is not involved, facilitates the enactment of a Bill declared by the Government to be urgent and immediately necessary to preserve public peace and security or by reason of a public emergency (Article 24)...[he cited also Articles 28 and 38]. There is no provision enabling the Oireachtas or the Government to disregard the Constitution in any emergency short of war or armed rebellion."

This "public emergency, domestic or international", must include the "national emergency" of Article 28.3.3, but the different wording implies that they are not coextensive. A "public emergency" such as to bring Article 24 into play would exist in conditions, e.g. of localised or sectoral emergency, such as floods, epidemics, or breakdowns in essential services not necessarily involving the entire State.

Article 24 never yet invoked

Time for the consideration of a Bill by Seanad Éireann has not been abridged by Dáil Éireann under this Article on any occasion to date.

[3] The Report is printed as a Government Publication (by order of the Dáil, 7 April 1943; by order of the Seanad, 31 March 1943) with the reference T.108.
[4] 27 *Seanad Debates* 1754.
[5] The Seanad in question consisted of members elected or nominated in 1981, after the Dáil dissolution of that year. When the Dáil was again dissolved in early 1982 the ensuing Dáil general election produced a change of Government. But as the "old" Seanad was still in being (the Seanad election entailed by the 1982 Dáil dissolution not yet having taken place), it contained a majority reflecting the political interest of the outgoing, not of the incoming Taoiseach.
[6] By this time the "new" Seanad had been constituted, and contained a majority reflecting the interest of the new Government lately installed.
[7] See 333 *Dáil Debates* 1696, 1767: 98 *Seanad Debates* 1830. This process, and the formula of "not insisting", were evidently adopted from British practice. See Erskine May, *Parliamentary Practice,* 19th ed., pp. 547, 551. The last conference between the two Houses of Parliament over such a disagreement took place in 1836. The second last in 1740: Erskine May, *op. cit.*, p. 602.
[8] [1940] IR 136; (1940) 74 ILTR 36, 131.

SIGNATURE, PROMULGATION AND ENTRY INTO FORCE OF LAWS

Signing and Promulgation of Laws

Article 25

1. **As soon as any Bill, other than a Bill expressed to be a Bill containing a proposal for the amendment of this Constitution, shall have been passed or deemed to have been passed by both Houses of the Oireachtas, the Taoiseach shall present it to the President for his signature and for promulgation by him as a law in accordance with the provisions of this Article.**
2. **1° Save as otherwise provided by this Constitution, every Bill so presented to the President for his signature and for promulgation by him as a law shall be signed by the President not earlier than the fifth and not later than the seventh day after the date on which the Bill shall have been presented to him.**

   2° At the request of the Government, with the prior concurrence of Seanad Éireann, the President may sign any Bill the subject of such request on a date which is earlier than the fifth day after such date as aforesaid.
3. **Every Bill the time for the consideration of which by Seanad Éireann shall have been abridged under Article 24 of this Constitution shall be signed by the President on the day on which such Bill is presented to him for signature and promulgation as a law.**
4. **1° Every Bill shall become and be law as on and from the day on which it is signed by the President under this Constitution, and shall, unless the contrary intention appears, come into operation on that day.**

Dlíthe a Shíniú agus a Fhógairt

Airteagal 25

1. **Chomh luath agus a ritear Bille, seachas Bille a luaitear a bheith ina Bhille a bhfuil togra ann chun an Bunreacht seo a leasú, nó a mheastar é a bheith rite ag dhá Theach an Oireachtais, ní foláir don Taoiseach an Bille sin a thairiscint don Uachtarán chun a lámh a chur leis agus chun é a fhógairt ina dhlí de réir forálacha an Airteagail seo.**
2. **1° Taobh amuigh de chás dá socraítear a mhalairt leis an mBunreacht seo, gach Bille a thairgtear don Uachtaráran mar sin chun a lámh a chur leis agus chun é a fhógairt ina dhlí, ní foláir dó a lámh a chur leis lá nach luaithe ná an cúigiú lá agus nach déanaí ná an seachtú lá tar éis an lae a thairgtear an Bille dó.**

   2° Ar achainí an Rialtas, le comhtoil Sheanad Éireann roimh ré, tig leis an Uachtarán a lámh a chur le haon Bhille is siocair don achainí sin níos luaithe ná an cúigiú lá tar éis an dáta réamhráite.
3. **Gach Bille a ndearnadh an tréimhse chun a bhreithnithe ag Seanad Éireann a ghiorrú faoi Airteagal 24 den Bhunreacht seo, ní foláir don Uachtarán a lámh a chur leis an lá a thairgtear an Bille sin dó chun é a shíniú agus chun é a fhógairt ina dhlí.**
4. **1° Déanann dlí de gach Bille an lá a chuireann an tUachtarán a lámh leis faoin mBunreacht seo agus is dlí é an lá sin agus ón lá sin amach agus, mura léir a mhalairt d'intinn ina thaobh, is é an lá sin a thagann sé i ngníomh.**

2° Every Bill signed by the President under this Constitution shall be promulgated by him as a law by the publication by his direction of a notice in the *Iris Oifigiúil*, stating that the Bill has become law.

3° Every Bill shall be signed by the President in the text in which it was passed or deemed to have been passed by both Houses of the Oireachtas, and if a Bill is so passed or deemed to have been passed in both the official languages, the President shall sign the text of the Bill in each of those languages.

4° Where the President signs the text of a Bill in one only of the official languages, an official translation shall be issued in the other official language.

5° As soon as may be after the signature and promulgation of a Bill as a law, the text of such law which was signed by the President or, where the President has signed the text of such law in each of the official languages, both the signed texts shall be enrolled for record in the office of the Registrar of the Supreme Court, and the text, or both the texts, so enrolled shall be conclusive evidence of the provisions of such law.

6° In case of conflict between the texts of a law enrolled under this section in both the official languages, the text in the national language shall prevail.

2° Gach Bille a gcuireann an tUachtarán a lámh leis faoin mBunreacht seo ní foláir do é a fhógairt ina dhlí le fogra san *Iris Oifigiúil*, faoi ordú uaidh á rá go bhfuil an Bille ina dhlí.

3° Is é téacs de Bhille a gcuirfidh an tUachtarán a lámh leis ná an téacs a ritheadh nó a mheastar a ritheadh ag dhá Theach an Oireachtais agus, má ritear Bille nó má mheastar é a bheith rite amhlaidh sa dá theanga oifigiúla, cuirfidh an tUachtarán a lámh le téacs Gaeilge agus le téacs Sacs-Bhéarla an Bhille.

4° I gcás an tUachtarán do chur a láimhe le téacs Bille i dteanga de na teangacha oifigiúla agus sa teanga sin amháin, ní foláir tiontú oifigiúil a chur amach sa teanga oifigiúil eile.

5° Chomh luath agus is féidir é tar éis Bille a shíniú agus é a fhógairt ina dhlí, ní foláir an téacs den dlí sin lena mbeidh lámh an Uachtaráin nó, i gcás lámh an Uachtaráin a bheith le téacs Gaeilge agus le téacs Sacs-Bhéarla an dlí sin, an dá théacs sínithe sin a chur isteach ina iris nó ina n-iris in oifig Iriseoir na Cúirte Uachtaraí, agus is fianaise dhochloíte ar fhorálacha an dlí sin an téacs a chuirfear isteach ina iris, nó an dá théacs a chuirfear isteach ina n-iris, amhlaidh.

6° I gcás téacs Gaeilge agus téacs Sacs-Bhéarla de dhlí a chur isteach ina n-iris faoin alt seo agus gan an dá théacs sin a bheith de réir a chéile, is ag an téacs Gaeilge a bheidh an forlámhas.

1922 Provision

These sections correspond to, and in some respects resemble, Articles 41 and 42 of the 1922 Constitution.

Article 25 implies the end of the old regime

Article 25 - presumably in particular ss 1 and 2 of it - was cited by both Hanna J and Maguire J in *Attorney General v Crawford*[1] as one of a number of Articles which demonstrated that the Crown had no further place in the Constitution, its formal function in the legislative process having been taken over by the President in the 1937 Constitution.

Analogy to "signing and promulgating" law

The function of the President in signing and promulgating a law was said *obiter* by Davitt J in *The State (Taylor) v Circuit Court Judge of Wicklow*[2] to offer an analogy to the function of a Minister in making an order to bring an Act into force.

Bill "shall become and be law": unless constitutionally invalid

The wording of Article 25.4.1 was crucial to the (minority) opinion of O'Higgins CJ in *Murphy v Attorney General*[3] that, when a court finds an Act of the Oireachtas to be unconstitutional, the invalidity thus established relates not to the moment at which the Act was passed, but to the moment of the court's finding. He said the signing of the Bill by the President was:

> "the final "enactment" by the Oireachtas of the legislative proposal into a "law". This is made clear by Article 25.4.1 which declares: "Every Bill shall become and be law as on and from the day on which it is signed by the President, etc."...Irrespective of what repugnancy may exist, what has been signed, enacted and promulgated is by virtue of Article 25 immediately in force as a law of the State...If such invalidity is held to date back to the very enactment of the law then a clear conflict emerges between Article 15.4.2 and Article 25.4.1...Any interpretation of Article 15.4.2 which brings about such a conflict with the express provisions of Article 25.4.1 must be suspect. In my view, it is also erroneous."

As the remaining four judges of the Supreme Court took the other view, it seems best to read Article 25.4.1 ("shall become and be law") as containing the silent proviso or presumption that the Oireachtas has in fact respected the express prohibition of Article 15.4.1.

Time within which Bill must be signed

In *In re McGrath and Harte*[4] an attempt was made on the prisoners' behalf to have the First Amendment of the Constitution Act 1939 - which imported an artificial extension of the expression "time of war" into Article 28.3.3 - treated as invalid on the ground that in the case of the Bill for this Act the President did not wait for the requisite five days before signing it (it was in fact signed on the same day as it passed both Houses).[5] Gavan Duffy J rejected this argument in the High Court, saying, without going into reasons, that he thought it "quite clear that Article 25.2, dealing with the time-limit of five to seven days, does not apply to this constitutional amendment"; and in the Supreme Court Sullivan CJ, giving the Court's judgment, said that Article 25.2.1 was "clearly intended to apply to Bills, other than Bills expressed to be Bills containing proposals for

[1] [1940] IR 335; (1940) 74 ILTR 140.
[2] [1951] IR 311; (1953) 87 ILTR 105.
[3] [1982] IR 241.
[4] [1941] IR 38.
[5] It took from 3 p.m. to 4.05 p.m. to pass all stages in the Dáil, and from 4.15 p.m. to 5.50 p.m. to pass all stages in the Seanad.

the amendment of the Constitution, and [had], therefore, no application to the Bill in question in this case".

It is, however, not so absolutely clear, for the following reasons. (1) The First Amendment of the Constitution Bill was passed by both Houses of the Oireachtas on 2 September, 1939, which was within the period of three years after the date on which the first President entered upon his office (25 June, 1938); during this period, by virtue of Article 51 - one of the transitory provisions - the Constitution, except for Articles 46 and 51 itself, could be amended "by the Oireachtas", and this Bill was intended and taken to be an amendment under Article 51. (2) Article 51, by the terms of its own sub-ss 3 and 4, was to cease to have the force of law as soon as that three-year period expired, and was even to be "omitted from every official text of this Constitution published after [its] expiration". (3) Plainly, therefore, the provisions of Article 25, so far as they make any special provision for Bills to amend the Constitution, apply to Bills passing both Houses *after* 25 June, 1941; this indeed is plain from the wording of Article 25.1 which speaks of "a Bill containing a proposal for the amendment of this Constitution", a form of words appropriate to a Bill which is to be submitted to referendum but not appropriate to a Bill passed by two Houses during the transitional period when no referendum was necessary.[6] (4) The *ratio* of Article 25.1, in excluding from the fifth-to-seventh-days-signature rule a Bill to amend the Constitution, is patently related to the post-1941 necessity to submit such Bills to referendum. (5) Accordingly, the provisions of Article 51 on transitional amendment by the Oireachtas should be seen as envisaging the emergence of an ordinary Bill, to which the special exclusion in Article 25.1.1 would not apply. (6) To enable the President to sign such a Bill immediately on its passing, there should have been a request of the Government with prior concurrence of the Seanad (an "early signature motion"), to conform with Article 25.1.2. (7) But in the case of the First Amendment of the Constitution Bill 1939, no such request or concurrence took place.[7]

The fact however, that both High Court and Supreme Court listened to submissions on whether the machinery of Article 25, if applicable, had been properly operated, even though these submissions were summarily rejected, suggests that the courts will examine the procedure by which legislation emerges, as well as the content of legislation, on constitutional criteria.[8]

Whether anything less than the neglect of an express constitutional requirement would lead the courts to examine the history of an Act is doubtful. *R. (O'Brien) v Governor of the North Dublin Military Barracks*[9] appears to be the only case to date in this jurisdiction where something of the kind has happened. Here the old Court of Appeal held that the Public Safety (Emergency Powers) Act 1923 was invalid, since the Court found that the Act did not contain the recitation by both Houses that it was "necessary for the immediate preservation of public peace, health and safety" as was required by Article 47

[6] Compare the case of *R. (Murphy) v Military Governor, Mountjoy Prison* (1924) 58 ILTR 1 in which the prisoner challenged the Public Safety (Emergency Powers) (No. 2) Act 1923 (under which he was being held) on the ground that the Seanad which passed the Bill for this Act had not been summoned as the old Article 24 prescribed. It was, however, clear, the Court held, that Article 24 was meant to apply to each Seanad *after* the first Seanad, to which the transitory provision of Article 82 applied (although admittedly with a lacuna inasmuch as this Article did not specify who was to do the summoning.)

[7] The Taoiseach (Mr. de Valera) had said in the Dáil at about 4.00 p.m. that an early signature motion in the Seanad would be necessary; but in the Seanad at about 5.45 he said he had been mistaken and that no such motion was needed (77 *Dáil Debates* 19; 23 *Seanad Debates* 1043).

[8] Although it may that since this was a *habeas corpus* application brought by two prisoners who had been sentenced to death, the Supreme Court was willing to examine every argument, however tenuous, which had been advanced on their behalf.

[9] [1924] 1 IR 32.

of the 1922 Constitution. The net effect of the Court's finding was to rule the law was not really a "law" at all because of some fundamental defect of procedure in the mode of its enactment.

In the mid-thirties, however, more cautious sentiments were expressed. In *O'Crowley v Minister for Finance*[10] the plaintiff claimed a declaration that the Dáil Supreme Court (Pensions) Act 1925 was invalid insofar as the Act was a "Money Bill" (as defined by Article 35 of the 1922 Constitution) and that such an Act could be treated as a nullity inasmuch as it attempted to regulate matters which were outside the scope of Article 35. Johnston J dismissed this suggestion, saying that "he had no authority to inquire into how or by what process as a public Act it reached the statute book."[11] The same judge expressed similar views in *Halpin v Attorney General*[12] where the Land Act 1933, was challenged on the ground, among others, that it had passed through the Oireachtas and received the Governor-General's assent without having the necessary words of enactment attached to it; Johnston J rejected this ground, citing and adopting the words of a Canadian judge:[13]

"It is a matter of elementary law that when a statute appears on its face to have been duly passed by a competent legislature, the courts must assume that all things have been rightly done in respect of its passage through the legislature and cannot entertain any argument that there is a defect of parliamentary procedure lying behind the Act as a matter of fact."

This view surely overstates the position, inasmuch the powers of the legislature have been circumscribed by reference to a written Constitution which prescribes certain rules which must be observed prior to the enactment of legislation. For example, it could scarcely be suggested that, if the requirements of Article 24 were not complied with so that the time for the consideration by the Seanad was improperly abridged, the courts could not inquire into the non-compliance with the constitutional requirements.[14] On the other hand, the courts may well choose to ignore what may be described as "intramural" procedural requirements, e.g., technical non-compliance with the standing orders of the Dáil.

Deferral of coming into operation

The coming into operation of laws is generally deferred until a day named in the Bill, or until a day to be appointed by the Government or by the Minister who has sponsored the Bill: recent examples of the latter are the Liability for Defective Products Act 1991, s 14(2); Industrial Development (Amendment) Act 1991, s 13(3) and the Patents Act 1992, s 1(2). An example of the former is supplied by the Income Tax Act 1967; it was signed by the President on 8 March 1967 but it was provided by s 554(1) that it should

[10] [1935] IR 536.

[11] The full quotation is set out at pp. 189-190.

[12] [1936] IR 226; (1935) 69 ILTR 259.

[13] Audette J in *R. v Irwin* (1926) Exch., Canada 126.

[14] Commonwealth authority suggests that "the principle that the courts may not examine the way in which the law-making process has been performed has no application where a legislature is established under or governed by an instrument which prescribes that laws of a certain kind may only be passed if the legislature is constituted or exercises its functions in a particular manner...when the law requires a legislature to enact legislation in a particular manner, the courts may investigate whether the legislature has exercised its functions in the manner recognised": see *Cormack v Cope* (1974) 131 CLR 432 *per* Gibbs J. See also *Victoria v Commonwealth* (1975) 134 CLR 81; *Harris v Dönges* [1952] 1 TLR 1245 and *Bribery Commissioner v Ranasinghe* [1965] AC 172.

come into force on 6 April 1967. Occasionally, the commencement date is postponed to an indefinite date: thus, for example, s 7(2) of the Electoral (Amendment) Act 1990, provides that the Act "will come into force on the dissolution of the present Dáil."

Legislation enacted by the Oireachtas will occasionally be allowed to remain dormant. For example, s 2 of the Health (Mental Services) Act 1981 provides that the Minister for Health may make an order bringing the Act (or particular provisions thereof) into effect, but to date no such order has been made. Another example is supplied by s 60 of the Civil Liability Act 1961. Section 60(1) abolishes the rather anomalous non-feasance rule (which prevents users of the highway suing the relevant local authority in respect of loss and damage occasioned by failure to repair the highway), but s 60(7) provides that sub-s 1 "shall only come into operation on a day (not earlier than April 1, 1967) which may be fixed by the Government." No such commencement order has been made to date and in *The State (Sheehan) v Government of Ireland*[15] the question arose as to whether the Executive could be compelled by mandamus to make such an order.

In the High Court, Costello J agreed that s 60(7) vested the Government with a discretion as to the time in which the sub-section was brought into force. The discretion was, however, one which was not "open-ended", but was subject to review:

> "Whilst no time limit is imposed, and to that extent some discretion in the exercise of the powers is given to the Government, it seems to me that if Parliament intended (as I think it clearly did) that the law should be reformed, it did not intend to confer a discretion which would permit that intention to be frustrated. This means that the discretion given by s 60(7) is a limited one, and that it should be construed as requiring the Government to make an order within a reasonable time after the 1st April 1967. Obviously a reasonable time has long since passed and, in my opinion, the Government is shown to have failed to carry out its statutory duty."

The Supreme Court took a different view, with Henchy J holding that the sub-section conferred, in effect, an unreviewable discretionary power on the Government:

> "The important law reform to be effected by the section was not to take effect unless and until the Government became satisfied that, in the light of factors such as the necessary redeployment of financial and other resources, the postulated reform would come into effect. The discretion vested in the Government to bring the section into operation on a date after 1 April 1967 was not limited in any way as to time or otherwise."

Henchy J did, however, agree that if "on its true reading" s 60(7) were to the effect that the Government "was bound to bring the section into operation," it would, of course "be unconstitutional for the Government to achieve by their prolonged inactivity the virtual repeal of the section."

The Supreme Court judgment seems unduly timid in the circumstances, especially given that the Government had not advanced any reasons why no such order should have been made.[16] The practical effect of this decision - notwithstanding the protestations of Henchy J to the contrary - appears to allow the Government to violate the separation of

[15] [1987] IR 550. See generally, Hogan, "*Judicial Review of an Executive Discretion*" (1987) 9 DULJ (n.s.) 91.

[16] McCarthy J in dissent was willing to allow the Government to put forward evidence on this point, "no factual basis for it having been laid in the proceedings so far." He also observed that if the views of the majority were correct, it would follow "that much of the legislation of 1961, for instance, might never have been brought in force."

powers inasmuch as it has secured through its inaction the virtual repeal of a important piece of law reform.

This approach may be contrasted with the subsequent decision in *Rooney v Minister for Agriculture and Food*[17] where a farmer sought compensation in respect of diseased animals which had been slaughtered at the Minister's behest. The plaintiff claimed that had the appropriate regulations been made under s 58 of the Diseases of Animals Act 1966, he would be likely to benefit financially to a greater extent than would have been possible than under the existing non-statutory scheme and he sought an order compelling the Minister to implement the regulations as was envisaged by the section. The Supreme Court applied the principle in *Sheehan's case* and dismissed the plaintiff's claim. O'Flaherty J observed:

> "I need only look at the provisions as regards the various steps that would have to be taken if s 20 and s 58 were in operation to realise that it would be vastly more expensive than the scheme which is at present in operation and no one has ever suggested that that, itself, represented anything but a huge cost to the Exchequer. Therefore, this is, at the least, a plausible reason for the operation of such a scheme. The court would only be entitled to review such a decision and course of action (embodied in the scheme) if it were satisfied that the decision and course of conduct was *mala fides* - or, at the least that it involved an abuse of power...It may be that the Court has no power to enjoin the Minister to make orders under s 20 (cf. *The State (Sheehan) v Government of Ireland*) in any circumstances, but it certainly has no power to do so in the absence of proof of *mala fides* or abuse of power."

Here, at least, the Minister had put forward practical reasons justifying the failure to implement the relevant section. Indeed, there may well be other cases where by reason of the likely Exchequer costs or the absence of a suitable administrative support structure, it would not be practicable or even feasible to bring the section into operation[18]. But this seems a far cry from the facts of *Sheehan's* case where that failure appears to have prompted by official misgivings about the wisdom of effecting the reform envisaged by the section.

Text of Bills: Irish or bilingual Bills are very rare

Almost all Bills are introduced, passed and promulgated as Acts in English alone, with (as Article 25.4.4 requires) an official Irish translation. Such "official translation" enjoys no such preference, in case of conflict between texts, as would the Irish text of a law which had been passed in both official languages; such laws, however, are exceedingly rare, the only examples to date being the Second to the Fourteenth Amendments of the Constitution Acts 1941 to 1992, and the Republic of Ireland Act 1948. Legislation in Irish alone tends to be confined to Bills concerning the Gaeltacht or the Irish language.

Taoiseach's failure to present Bill for signature subject to review?

One question which has never actually arisen in practice is whether a failure by the Taoiseach to present a Bill for signature by the President following its passage though both Houses of the Oireachtas is subject to review. As the language of Article 25.1.1 is

[17] [1991] 2 IR 539.

[18] This may well explain the failure to bring into force any provisions of the Health (Mental Services) Act 1981.

mandatory, and as there could be no question here of interference with the processes of either House of the Oireachtas,[19] both of which would, on this hypothesis, have completed their function, there can be no reason to think that the Taoiseach might not be amenable to judicial compulsion.

[19] See pp. 185-186.

TEXT OF THE CONSTITUTION

5. 1° It shall be lawful for the Taoiseach, from time to time as occasion appears to him to require, to cause to be prepared under his supervision a text (in both the official languages) of this Constitution as then in force embodying all amendments theretofore made therein.

5 1° Is dleathach don Taoiseach a thabhairt, ó am go ham faoi mar a chífear dó gá a bheith leis, go ndéanfar téacs (sa Ghaeilge agus sa Sacs-Bhéarla) den Bhunreacht seo, mar a bheidh i bhfeidhm an tráth sin agus ina mbeidh na leasuithe uile a bheidh déanta air go dtí sin, a ullmhú faoina threorú.

2° A copy of every text so prepared, when authenticated by the signatures of the Taoiseach and the Chief Justice, shall be signed by the President and shall be enrolled for record in the office of the Registrar of the Supreme Court.

2° Gach téacs a ullmhófar amhlaidh ní foláir don Uachtarán a lámh a chur le cóip de ar bheith fíoraithe di le sínithe an Taoisigh agus an Phríomh-Bhreithimh, agus ní foláir an chóip sin a chur isteach ina hiris in oifig Iriseoir na Cúirte Uachtaraí.

3° The copy so signed and enrolled which is for the time being the latest text so prepared shall, upon such enrolment, be conclusive evidence of this Constitution as at the date of such enrolment and shall for that purpose supersede all texts of this Constitution of which copies were previously so enrolled.

3° An choip a bheidh sínithe agus curtha isteach ina hiris amhlaidh agus arb í an téacs is deireanaí, arna ullmhú amhlaidh, in alt na huaire í, beidh sí, ar bheith curtha isteach ina hiris dí amhlaidh, ina fianaise dhochloíte ar an mBunreacht seo mar a bheidh ar dháta an chóip sin a chur isteach ina hiris amhlaidh agus, chuige sin, gabhfaidh sí ionad na dtéacsanna uile den Bhunreacht seo a mbeidh cóipeanna díobh curtha isteach ina n-iris amhlaidh roimhe sin.

4° In case of conflict between the texts of any copy of this Constitution enrolled under this section, the text in the national language shall prevail.

4° I gcás gan na téacsanna d'aon chóip áirithe den Bhunreacht seo a bheidh curtha isteach ina hiris faoin alt seo a bheith de réir a chéile, is ag an téacs Gaeilge a bheidh an forlámhas.

Preparation of official texts of the Constitution

Texts of the Constitution have been from time to time prepared,[1] signed and enrolled under these sub-sections.[2] What may be called these successive editions of the Constitution have embodied not only the amendments of the Constitution to date, but also, in the case of the Irish text, a change to Roman type from the "Gaelic" type used in

[1] The latest version of the text enrolled pursuant to this provisions was enrolled on 23 March 1990.
[2] For the possible problems resulting from this and for a full consideration of related issues, see Humphreys, "*The Constitution of Ireland: The Forgotten Textual Quagmire*" (1987) 22 Ir Jur (n.s.) 169.

the draft originally enacted, and a standardisation of spelling, orthography and even in minor respects grammar. Whether changes of this kind are permissible - in view of the existence of sub-sections expressly dealing with editions of the Constitution but not mentioning such alterations as these - is uncertain.[3]

Conflict of texts: principle of approach

The principle upon which the courts will act in approaching the question of a possible discordance between the texts of the Constitution was first stated by Budd J in *O'Donovan v Attorney General*[4] in which it was argued that the Irish phrase "sa mhéid gur féidir é" imposed stricter limits on the latitude with which Dáil seats could be distributed throughout the country than did the corresponding English phrase "as far as practicable" ("féidir" means "possible" rather than "practicable" in ordinary speech). Budd J said:

> "Both texts of the Constitution are authoritative. It is not to be thought that those who framed or enacted the Constitution would knowingly do anything so absurd as to frame or enact texts with different meanings in parts. It could only happen by inadvertence. It would seem to follow as a matter of common-sense that one should not approach the elucidation of the meaning of either text with a view to seeking a conflict, but rather with a view to seeing if they can properly be reconciled. I say "properly" advisedly, because if in fact the words used are not in a form really found to correspond the Irish text must prevail...I have come to the conclusion that no material discordance exists between the English and Irish texts of Article 16.2.3."

The Supreme Court, in *In re Article 26 and the Electoral (Amendment) Bill 1961*,[5] took the same view, approving this statement of the principle of construing the parallel texts. There has been in fact no case so far in which what Budd J called a "material discordance", or a conflict, has been established between the Irish and the English versions; though in *Fisher v Irish Land Commission*[6] Gavan Duffy J remarked in passing and without explaining what he meant, that he thought the Irish version of Article 37 seemed "more favourable to the defendants" than the English version. A slightly different issue arose before Geoghegan J in *Attorney General v Hamilton (No.2)*[7] where the meaning of the word "amenable" as it appears in Article 15.13 was in dispute. The word "amenable" appears in both Article 15.13 and in Article 18 of the equivalent provision of the 1922 Constitution, but the expression "inchuisithe" in the Irish text of Article 15.13 had not been used in the former Article 18. In these circumstances Geoghegan J felt that he was entitled to have regard "to the near identical English text [as used in both the 1922 and 1937 Constitutions] in considering the true interpretation of Article 15.13" unless in doing so a conflict with the Irish text would thereby arise.[8] Finally, McCarthy J struck a realistic note on this issue in *Attorney General v X.*[9] when he said:

> "Despite the fact that there have been instances of the courts adverting to the Irish text in order to construe that in English, the debate on this being conducted in

[3] For the position in regard to the exclusion of the Transitory Provisions (Articles 51-63) from the text of editions subsequent to 25 June 1941, see below at p. 1171.

[4] [1961] IR 114; (1962) 96 ILTR 121.

[5] [1961] IR 169.

[6] [1948] IR 3; (1948) 82 ILTR 50.

[7] [1993] ILRM 821.

[8] He found that there was, in fact, no such conflict: see p. 206 below.

[9] [1992] 1 IR 1; [1992] ILRM 401; [1992] 2 CMLR 277.

English, I have some difficulty in identifying the conflict referred to in Article 25.5.4 as the circumstance under which the Irish text shall prevail. Historically, the Irish text is a translation of that in English."

Irish text used to elucidate English

It seems appropriate, however, to mention here that the courts have in recent years often looked at the Irish text of the Constitution (where the case in general has been conducted entirely in English) not in order to find a conflict, or because one of the parties alleged a conflict, but in order to elucidate the meaning of the corresponding English expression.[10] The instances are heterogeneous, and may be briefly listed here in order of the Articles involved.

Article 11

In *The State (Gilliland) v Governor of Mountjoy Prison*[11] Barrington J said that the "one fund" or "ciste" referred to Article 11 was the same as the "public funds" or "ciste poiblí" referred to in Article 29.5.2. In *The State (McCaud) v Governor of Mountjoy Prison*[12] Egan J said that there was "some merit" in the applicant's suggestion that the word "costas" (unlike the corresponding English expression "charge") included expenses incurred in the incidental administration of an international agreement. Barrington J encountered the same problem in *Gilliland's* case, where he said that while the term "costas" undoubtedly has the meaning "expense", it is wide enough to include the meaning "charge". The phrase "a charge upon public funds" is rendered in the Irish text as "costas ar an gciste poiblí". Literally this appears to mean "a charge on (or a cost or expense to) the public fund".

Article 15.4.2

In *Murphy v Attorney General*[13] Henchy J, in asserting that an unconstitutional measure was void from the moment of enactment and not merely voidable, said:

> "In its dictionary literary or colloquial connotation in modern Irish, "gan bhail" means "worthless, void, ineffective"...In this context "gan bhail" means "without legal effect", and not "voidable" or "liable to be deprived of legal effect"."

Article 15.10

In *In re Haughey*[14] Ó Dálaigh CJ cited, in addition to the English "Each House shall make its own rules and standing orders..." the Irish "Déanfaidh gach Tigh ar leith a

[10] Mr. de Valera had foreseen this. In the debate on the Second Amendment of the Constitution Bill in 1941 he said: "Where there is a slight ambiguity in one text, when you turn to the other text you find it is completely removed: that it quite clearly has one meaning and not another." (82 *Dáil Debates* at Col. 1259).

[11] [1987] IR 201. Barrington J also drew attention to the curious fact that while the English version of Article 11 is identical with the English version of Article 61 of the 1922 Constitution, the language used in the Irish versions differs in the two Constitutions. (The Irish version of the 1922 Constitution did not, however, have the same status as that of 1937. The old Constitution was enacted by the Dáil in English only, and an official translation into Irish was supplied later.)

[12] [1985] IR 68.

[13] [1982] IR 241.

[14] [1971] IR 217.

rialacha agus a bhuan-orduithe féin..." apparently in order to bring out the nature of the provision, equally imperative in both languages, which the Dáil had observed merely by way of carrying on with the Standing Orders of the Dáil of Saorstát Éireann, amending them as became necessary.

Article 15.12

In *Attorney General v Hamilton (No.1)*[15] McCarthy J referred to the Irish version of the concluding sentence of Article 15.12 ('táid saor ar chursaí dlí') and said that this emphasised that the word "privileged" had the same connotation in the law of defamation. This view was not, however, accepted by the Supreme Court in *Attorney General v Hamilton (No.2)*[16] where Finlay CJ stressed that the literal translation of the phrase - táid saor ar chursaí dlí - was "free from legal proceedings". This "very clearly indicate[d] that there are a great variety of legal proceedings which could follow upon the making of an utterance over and beyond a claim for damages for defamation, were it not for the privilege and immunity granted by Article 15.12.

Article 15.13

In *Attorney General v Hamilton (No.2)*[17] a case concerning the entitlement of a Dáil Deputy to refuse to disclose the source of the information on which utterances made by him in the Dáil Geoghegan J accepted that the Irish expression for "amenable" as used in Article 15.13 "inchuisithe" connoted "something like "'chargeable'". This did not necessarily lead to a conflict between the Irish and English texts, since he did not consider that the expression was not necessarily confined to a criminal context:

> "It seems clear that when used in the Constitution it is not so confined having regard to the wide scope of the expression "any court or any authority other than the House itself." But the word probably does connote the rendering of a person to some liability or sanction...If upon refusal at a Tribunal [of Inquiry] established [under the Tribunals of Inquiry Act 1921] to answer a question certain legal consequences can flow adverse to the person so refusing...it follows that, in my view, that a member of the Dáil questioned about utterances made by him in the Dáil cannot be made subject to those legal consequences. In the context of a Tribunal that is what is meant by "inchuisithe" and that is what is meant by "amenable." As I have already indicated, therefore. I do not believe that there is any conflict between the English and Irish versions."

Article 16.2.3

In *O'Donovan v Attorney General*[18] Budd J found "no material discordance" between "so far as it is practicable" and "sa mhéid gur féidir é"; the Supreme Court in *In re Article 26 and the Electoral (Amendment) Bill 1961*[19] agreed with him. In the same case, the Supreme Court attached no importance to the fact that in the Irish phrase "de réir an daonáirimh is déanaí dá ndearneadh roimhe sin" there was no word directly representing the word "ascertained" in the corresponding English phrase "as ascertained at the last preceding census". The Court said:

> "Daonáireamh" connotes not merely a census, but an ascertained census; the verb "dearnadh" strengthens this meaning."

[15] [1993] 2 IR 250; [1993] ILRM 81.
[16] [1993] ILRM 821.
[17] [1993] ILRM 821.
[18] [1961] IR 114; (1962) 96 ILTR 121.
[19] [1961] IR 169.

Article 28.4

In *Attorney General v Hamilton (No.1)*[20] McCarthy J said that the word "responsible" in Article 28.4.1 meant "answerable or accountable - a meaning borne out by the Irish text, 'freagrach'".

Article 29.3

In *The State (Sumers Jennings) v Furlong*[21] Henchy J said that the Irish version "makes clear" that Ireland accepts the generally recognised principles of international law "as a guide (ina dtreoir) in its relations with other states" - i.e. merely as a guide, not as a rule operating to restrict the powers of the Oireachtas.

Article 29.5

In *The State (Duggan) v Tapley*[22] Gavan Duffy P pointed to the Irish text as putting beyond doubt that only future international agreements were within the section's contemplation.

Article 30.3

In *The State (Ennis) v Farrell,*[23] where what was in issue was the question whether the right of a common informer had survived the constitutional provision restricting the bringing of prosecutions to the Attorney General "or some other person authorised in accordance with law to act for that purpose", Ó Dálaigh CJ (with whom the rest of the Supreme Court agreed) pointed out that the Irish counterpart of "authorised", namely "a udaraitear" was:

> "quite express as a present autonomous form in negativing the idea of the authorisation required being such only as might be made in the future."

He contrasted Article 34.4.3 (on the right of appeal to the Supreme Court from High Court decisions), where the clear future form of the Irish verb "ordofar" put the future sense of the phrase "as may be prescribed" beyond doubt. On the word "prosecuted" in the same section, he said this was to be understood in its widest sense; this was confirmed by the Irish text, where the equivalent used was "tugtar" = "brought".[24]

Article 34.3.1

In *The People (Attorney General) v Conmey*[25] O'Higgins CJ rejected a submission based on a supposed distinction between a "determination" of the Supreme Court (in the sense of its "power to determine" in Article 34.3.1) and a "decision" of the High Court (in the

[20] [1993] 2 IR 250; [1993] ILRM 81.
[21] [1966] IR 183.
[22] [1952] IR 62; (1951) 85 ILTR 22.
[23] [1966] IR 107.
[24] It must be seriously doubted whether the Constitution will stand up to such minute linguistic exegesis, or whether one's sense of reality - bearing in mind the history of the Irish version (see p.211 below) - can remain suspended in the face of it. If the words of Ó Dálaigh CJ mean, as they seem to, that the use of the present form imports a situation existing in 1937, it suggests - to remain with Article 30 - that the regulation of the Attorney General's office was to be contained in post-1937 legislation ("is de reir dlí a rialófar oifig an Ard-Aighne"), whereas the basic legislation on the office is contain in s 6 of the Ministers and Secretaries Act 1924 (see below at pp. 303-304). Another instance is Article 16.5: while the Irish version says, in regard to fixing a shorter period than seven year for the maximum duration of a Dáil, "feadfar ré is giorra na sin a shocrú le dlí," the actual five-year term observed from 1937 until the enactment of s 10 of the Electoral Act 1963, was that prescribed by s 7 of the Electoral (Amendment) Act 1927. These examples could be much extended.
[25] [1975] IR 341.

sense of its "decisions" in Article 34.4.3); he observed that the Irish text uses the word "breith" in both equivalent phrases, and said it followed "that no distinction or difference is indicated" between the functions envisaged by those two subsections.

Article 36.iii

In *The State (Walshe) v Murphy*[26] Finlay P used the Irish equivalent "comhdheanamh" in order to construe the English word "constitution" (of the courts), so as to make it include (via "comhdheanaim" = "I make up") the determination of qualifications for judicial appointment.

Article 38.5

In *The People (Attorney General) v Conmey*[27] Walsh J emphasised that the result of a trial on indictment was not a conviction or acquittal "by" the jury, but by the court; the wording of Article 38.5 referred not to trial "by" jury but to trial "with" a jury; this interpretation, he said, was "borne out by reference to the Irish language text of the Constitution" ("i láthair choiste tiomanta"). In *In re Haughey*[28] Ó Dálaigh CJ cited the Irish text of the section to reinforce the obviously mandatory meaning of the English text.

Article 40.1

In *In re Walker, decd; O'B. v S*,[29] Walsh J referred to the Irish version of the proviso to Article 40.1 and said this made it clear that:

> "the proviso refers to the difference of capacity, physical and moral, and of the social function of the citizens for whom, or in respect of whom, the State in its enactments has seen fit to have "due regard" to their differences under these headings."

Article 40.3.1

In *McGee v Attorney General*[30] Griffin J pointed out that the Irish version: "Ráthaionn an Stát gan cur isteach lena dhlithibh ar cheartaibh pearsanta aon tsaoránaigh" was a guarantee *not to interfere with* citizens' personal rights (thus adding depth to the guarantee to "respect" them in the English version). In the same case Walsh J used the Irish "féidir" so as to treat the English "practicable" as amounting to "possible"[31]. In *Pine Valley Developments Ltd. v Minister for Environment*[32] Henchy J referred to the Irish version of Article 40.3.2 ("chomh fada lena chumas" = "as best it may") in order to stress that the State's duty to respect and vindicate the citizens' constitutional rights was not an unqualified one.

Article 42.4

In *Crowley v Ireland*[33] Kenny J, speaking for the Supreme Court majority, pointed out that the Irish version "ní foláir don Stát socrú do dhéanamh chun bunoideachas do bhei-

[26] [1981] IR 275.
[27] [1975] IR 341.
[28] [1971] IR 217.
[29] [1984] IR 316; [1985] ILRM 86.
[30] [1974] IR 284.
[31] See also the comments of McCarthy J in *Attorney General v X* [1992] 1 IR 1; [1992] ILRM 401; [1992] 2 CMLR 277.
[32] [1987] IR 23.
[33] [1980] IR 102.

th ar fáil in aisce" brought out more clearly than the English the distinction between the duty to "provide *for*" free primary education, and a duty (alleged by the plaintiffs) actually to "provide" it.

Article 43

In *Central Dublin Development Association Ltd. v Attorney General*[34] Kenny J said, in regard to both Article 43.1.1 and Article 43.2.2, that "while there may not be a conflict" between the Irish and English versions, the English version seemed to him "to be a most unhappy attempt to reproduce the meaning of that in Irish":[35]

> "The phrase "de cheart nádúrtha aige maoin shaolta a bheith aige dá chuid féin go priobháideach"...means, I think, "a natural right to his own private share of worldly wealth" and not "the natural right to the private ownership of external goods"... Another source of confusion in the English text is the use in Article 43.2.2 of the word "delimit". The Irish phrase is "teorainn a chur" which would, I think, be more accurately translated as "restrict". In Professor de Bhaldraithe's standard English-Irish dictionary, the Irish equivalent of "restrict" is given as "cuirim teorainn le"."

Article 44.2.3

In *Quinn's Supermarket Ltd. v Attorney General*[36] Walsh J said it was quite clear from the Irish text ("ní cead don Stát neach a chur faoi mhi-chumas ar bith...") that this provision was "aimed at preventing the imposition of a personal, or perhaps even a corporate, disability". It was argued in this case that the discrimination forbidden by the sub-section should be construed as if it read "discrimination against", but Walsh J rejected this submission, pointing to the general formulation of the Irish version "ná aon idirdhealú" a dhéanamh" in confirmation of his view. In the High Court McLoughlin J had cited the Irish text for the same purpose. In *M. v An Bord Uchtála*[37] Pringle J cited from Walsh J in the *Quinn's Supermarket* case the passages just referred to. In *Mulloy v Minister for Education*,[38] where the plaintiff objected to a regulation which excluded him from an increment benefit because the service concerned had been given while he was not a layman (but a priest), Butler J considered the word "céim" in order to elucidate the word "status", and, in concluding that "status" was "something other than a question of religious profession or religious belief", observed that this difference is even more clearly stressed in the Irish text where the disjunctive "nó" is repeated, viz. "... ná aon idirdhealú do dhéanamh mar gheall ar chreideamh nó admháil chreidimh nó céim i gcúrsaibh creidimh".

Article 45

In *McGee v Attorney General*[39] O'Keeffe P said, in regard to the words "agus ní hintriailte ag cúirt ar bith ceist i dtaobh an fheidhmithe sin fá aon fhoráileamh d'fhoráiltíbh an Bhunreachta so", that this formulation:

[34] [1975] 109 ILTR 69.

[35] In view of the history of the Irish version (see p. 211), this phrase of Kenny J seems to be a mere judicial politeness.

[36] [1972] IR 1.

[37] [1975] IR 81; (1975) 109 ILTR 62.

[38] [1975] IR 88.

[39] [1974] IR 284; (1975) 109 ILTR 29. Pringle J however took the view, in *O'Brien v Manufacturing Engineering Co.* [1973] IR 334; (1974) 108 ILTR 105, that the first sentence of Article 45, "whether one looks at the Irish or the English version thereof", prevented the courts from enquiring whether the Oireachtas had implemented social policy as directed."

"appears to exclude from the cognisance of the courts only questions as to the attempts of the Oireachtas to have regard to the principles laid down in the course of framing legislation, and it may be argued that it does not preclude the consideration of these principles by the courts when a statute of the Oireachtas is not under review."

Article 45.2.i

In *Murtagh Properties v Cleary*[40] Kenny J used the Irish text to support his giving its full meaning to the provision that speaks of "men and women equally" having "the right to an adequate means of livelihood":

> "The phrase "all of whom, men and women equally" shows that the right is one conferred equally on men and women. The Irish text ("agus tá ceart acu uile, idir fhear is bean"), though it does not refer to "equally", also stresses that the right is one inherent in men and women. In Professor de Bhaldraithe's English-Irish dictionary the phrase "both women and children" is translated as "idir mhná is pháisti". If those who wrote the Constitution intended to refer to the right to an adequate means of livelihood only, it is impossible to understand why the phrase "all of whom, men and women equally" should have been inserted. Its purpose was to emphasise that [so far as that right was concerned] men and women were to be regarded as equal."

Article 46.1

In *Finn v Minister for the Environment*[41] Barrington J drew attention to the fact that the Irish equivalent for the phrase "whether by way of variation, addition, or repeal" contains no word corresponding to "whether", thus lending some (though he thought not enough) strength to the suggestion that the recital of these three modes of amendment was intended to be exhaustive rather than merely illustrative.

Article 50.1

In *The State (Sheerin) v Kennedy*[42] Walsh J pointed to the corresponding pairs of expressions (which were distinct in each text) "inconsistent/ina choinne", "validity/bail", "repugnant/in aghaidh" in order to fortify the practical distinction which he emphasised between "inconsistency" with the Constitution (under Article 50) and "invalidity" (under Article 34) or "repugnancy" (under Article 26).

Conflicts which have not yet surfaced

The Constitution seems to contain some possible conflicts which have not yet surfaced in litigation. The most obvious seems to be in Article 12.4.1, where the Irish text requires a Presidential candidate to have completed thirty-five years of age ("ag a bhfuil cúig bliana tríochad slán"), while the English text requires him only to have "reached his thirty-fifth year of age", which he would do on his thirty-fourth birthday. There may be another instance in Article 41.1, in which the rights of the family are called in English "imprescriptible", defined by Kenny J in *Ryan v Attorney General*[43] as "that which cannot be lost by the passage of time or abandoned by non-exercise". The corresponding Irish expression, "dochloíte", does not have this meaning, and conveys only something like "irrepressible", "indomitable" (in Article 1 it is used as the equivalent of "indefeasi-

[40] [1972] IR 330.
[41] [1983] IR 154.
[42] [1965] IR 379.
[43] [1965] IR 294.

ble", and in Articles 25.4.5, 25.5.3 and 63 as the equivalent of "conclusive" in the context of evidence). Another discordance appears to exist in Article 35.3, where the English text makes a judge "ineligible" to be a member of the Oireachtas (i.e. arguably, debarred from standing for election) while the Irish text merely says he may not be a member ("bheith ina chomhalta").

Amendment of the Constitution in one language only

A potentially far more serious matter arises in connection with Article 28.3.3. The First Amendment of the Constitution Act 1939, passed on the day after the German invasion of Poland in 1939, gave to the expression "time of war" an artificially extended meaning, and was regarded as the root of the immunity of the 1939-46 emergency legislation from challenge; it is equally seen as part of the armour of the Emergency Powers Act 1976.[44] The Bill for this amendment of the Constitution Act was passed *in English only*, and purported to alter *only the English version* of Article 28.3.3. Accordingly, in the period after the enactment of this amendment, there was a patent conflict between the Irish and English version of Article 28.3.3, inasmuch as the Irish version contained no reference to the artificially extended meaning of "time of war"; in applying Article 25.5.4 to this situation, therefore, and allowing the Irish version to prevail, that extended meaning ought not to have been allowed to operate. The Second Amendment of the Constitution Act 1941, was bilingual itself, and contained parallel bilingual amendments, except for this part of Article 28.3.3, where it purported merely to supply the Irish amendment previously missing. It remains, however, a question[45] whether a bilingual text can be effectively amended anyway by a purported amendment which is unilingual; and if on that ground the purported 1939 amendment was ineffective, the purported 1941 supplementary amendment was equally so.[46]

[44] See below at pp. 239-240.

[45] Apart from the other problem about the First Amendment of the Constitution Act 1939, related to the procedure by which it was signed: see above at pp. 197-198.

[46] The draft Constitution debated by Dáil Éireann in the summer of 1937 was in English and the Irish version arrived late on the scene and was barely even noticed (14 June; 68 *Dáil Debates* at Col. 334ff.) Deputy W.T. Cosgrave, former President of the Executive Council said at Col. 351:

> "The Irish text is being made operative in cases of dispute in a court of law. As a matter of fact the Irish text is a mere translation of the English. The Constitution was thought out and framed in English by the President [of the Executive Council, Mr. de Valera]. It was discussed in English by the Cabinet (if it was ever discussed by the Cabinet at all), and there are not two members of the Government capable of discussing it, or any part of it, in Irish.....It is unheard of and contrary to common sense that an imperfect translation, such as the Irish text of the Constitution, should be made the authoritative version for the courts."

Article 26

REFERENCE OF BILLS TO SUPREME COURT

Reference of Bills to the Supreme Court

Article 26

This Article applies to any Bill passed or deemed to have been passed by both Houses of the Oireachtas other than a Money Bill, or a Bill expressed to be a Bill containing a proposal to amend the Constitution, or a Bill the time for the consideration of which by Seanad Éireann shall have been abridged under Article 24 of this Constitution.

1. 1° The President may, after consultation with the Council of State, refer any Bill to which this Article applies to the Supreme Court for a decision on the question as to whether such Bill or any specified provision or provisions of such Bill is or are repugnant to this Constitution or to any provision thereof.

2° Every such reference shall be made not later than the seventh day after the date on which such Bill shall have been presented by the Taoiseach to the President for his signature.

3° The President shall not sign any Bill the subject of a reference to the Supreme Court under this Article pending the pronouncement of the decision of the Court.

2. 1° The Supreme Court consisting of not less than five judges shall consider every question referred to it by the President under this Article for a decision, and, having heard arguments by or on behalf of the Attorney General and by counsel

Billi a chur faoi bhreith na Cúirte Uachtaraí

Airteagal 26

Baineann an tAirteagal seo le gach Bille a ritear nó a mheastar a ritheadh ag dhá Theach an Oireachtais, ach amháin Bille Airgid, nó Bille a luaitear a bheith ina Bhille a bhfuil togra ann chun an Bunreacht a leasú, nó Bille a ndearnadh an tréimhse chun a bhreithnithe ag Seanad Éireann a ghiorrú faoi Airteagal 24 den Bhunreacht seo.

1. 1° Is cead don Uachtarán, tar éis comhairle a ghlacadh leis an gComhairle Stáit, aon Bhille lena mbaineann an tAirteagal seo a chur faoi bhreith na Cúirte Uachtaraí féachaint an bhfuil an Bille sin nó aon fhoráil nó fhorálacha áirithe de in aghaidh an Bhunreachta seo nó in aghaidh aon fhorála de.

2° I ngach cás den sórt sin ní foláir an Bille a chur faoi bhreith na Cúirte lá nach déanaí ná an seachtú lá tar éis an dáta a thairgeann an Taoiseach an Bille don Uachtarán chun a lámh a chur leis.

3° Bille ar bith a chuirtear faoi bhreith na Cúirte Uachtaraí faoin Airteagal seo, ní cead don Uachtarán a lámh a chur leis go dtí go dtugann an Chúirt a breith.

2. 1° Ní foláir don Chúirt Uachtarach, cúirt ina mbeidh cúigear breitheamh ar a laghad, gach ceist dá gcuireann an tUachtarán faoina breith faoin Airteagal seo a bhreithniú agus, tar éis éisteacht le hargóinti ón Ard-Aighne nó thar a cheann agus ó abhcóidí a thoghfar ag

assigned by the Court, shall pronounce its decision on such question in open court as soon as may be, and in any case not later than sixty days after the date of such reference.

2° The decision of the majority of the judges of the Supreme Court shall, for the purposes of this Article, be the decision of the Court and shall be pronounced by such one of those judges as the Court shall direct, and no other opinion, whether assenting or dissenting, shall be pronounced nor shall the existence of any such other opinion be disclosed.

3. 1° In every case in which the Supreme Court decides that any provision of a Bill the subject of a reference to the Supreme Court under this Article is repugnant to this Constitution or to any provision thereof, the President shall decline to sign such Bill.

2° If, in the case of a Bill to which Article 27 of this Constitution applies, a petition has been addressed to the President under that Article, that Article shall be complied with.

3° In every other case the President shall sign the Bill as soon as may be after the date on which the decision of the Supreme Court shall have been pronounced.

an gCúirt, ní foláir di a breith ar an gceist sin a thabhairt sa chúirt go poiblí chomh luath agus is féidir é agus, ar aon chuma, lá nach déanaí ná seasca lá tar éis an cheist a chur faoina breith.

2° An bhreith a bheireann an tromlach de bhreithiúna na Cúirte Uachtarai, sin í breith na Cúirte chun críocha an Airteagail seo agus is é a chraolfas an bhreith sin ná an duine sin de na breithiúna sin a cheapfaidh an Chúirt chuige sin, agus ní cead tuairim ar bith eile, ag aontú no ag easaontú leis an mbreith sin, a chraoladh ná ní cead a nochtadh tuairim ar bith eile den sórt sin a bheith ann.

3. 1° I gcás aon Bhille a chuirtear faoi bhreith na Cúirte Uachtaraí faoin Airteagal seo, más é breith na Cúirte go bhfuil aon fhoráil de in aghaidh an Bhunreachta seo nó in aghaidh aon fhorála de, ní foláir don Uachtarán diúltú dá lámh a chur leis an mBille sin.

2° I gcás achainí a bheith curtha chun an Uachtaráin faoi Airteagal 27 den Bhunreacht seo i dtaobh Bille lena mbaineann an tAirteagal sin, ní foláir an tAirteagal sin a chomhlíonadh.

3° I ngach cás eile ní foláir don Uachtarán a lámh a chur leis an mBille chomh luath agus is féidir é tar éis an lae a bheireann an Chúirt Uachtarach a breith.

Article 26 procedure a relative innovation

While Article 26 was a relative innovation in that there was no corresponding provision in the 1922 Constitution, the inspiration for its inclusion was nonetheless probably drawn from other pre-1922 legislative models. Thus, s 4 of the Judicial Committee Act 1833 allows for the reference of disputed points of law to the Privy Council and, since this procedure had already been used to settle one celebrated Anglo-Irish constitutional law issue in the late 1920s, the possible utility of such a procedure may have thereby commended itself to the Constitution's drafters.[1] In addition, s 51 of the Government of Ireland Act 1920 expressly provided for such a reference procedure.[2] It may also be of interest to note that some of the continental constitutional courts can entertain references in roughly similar circumstances[3] and the Court of Justice of the European Communities is also invested with a similar power under Article 228 of the Treaty of Rome.[4]

Use of Article 26 procedure

The procedure of Article 26, to which nothing in the 1922 Constitution corresponded, has been operated on eight occasions: in 1940, with the Offences Against the State (Amendment) Bill 1940;[5] in 1943, with the School Attendance Bill 1942;[6] in 1961, with the Electoral (Amendment) Bill 1961;[7] twice in 1976, with the Criminal Law (Jurisdiction) Bill 1975,[8] and the Emergency Powers Bill 1976;[9] in 1982 with the Housing (Private Rented Dwellings) Bill 1981;[10] in 1983-4 with the Electoral (Amendment) Bill 1983[11] and in 1988 with the Adoption (No.2) Bill 1987.[12] These cases are dealt with under the respective headings of the constitutional areas to which the Bills related: but certain general principles of the Article 26 procedure, and dicta in regard to it, may be outlined here; as well as a doubt in regard to whether the first three of these eight references should ever have taken place.

Presumption of constitutionality of a Bill

In the first reference - *In re Article 26 and the Offences Against the State (Amendment) Bill 1940* - the Supreme Court laid down a canon of construction somewhat similar to that already enunciated in regard to the challenging of an Act:

> "Where any particular law is not expressly prohibited and it is sought to establish that it is repugnant to the Constitution by reason of some implied prohibition or repugnancy, we are of opinion, as a matter of construction, that such repugnancy must be clearly established."[13]

[1] *In re Compensation to Civil Servants under Article X of the Treaty* [1929] IR 44.

[2] See Keane, "*Fundamental Rights in Irish Law; A Note on the Historical Background*" in O'Reilly ed., *Human Rights and Constitutional Law: Essays in Honour of Brian Walsh* (Dublin, 1992.)

[3] For example, Article 93 of the German Basic Law allows for what is described as the "abstract norm-control procedure" (*abstraktes Normkontolleverfahren)* whereby either the Federal Cabinet or one third of the *Bundestag* may refer the question of the constitutionality of a statute to the Constitutional Court. Article 61 of the French Constitution of 1958 gives the Conseil Constitutionel a similar role with regard to *lois organiques* (i.e., legislative measures giving effect to constitutional structures such as legislation regulating matters as diverse as presidential elections and the composition of the judiciary): see Pollard, "*France's Conseil Constitutionel - Not yet a Constitutional Court*" (1988) 23 Ir Jur (n.s.) 2.

[4] This allows the Court, at the request of either the Commission, Council or a Member State, to pronounce on the compatibility of an international agreement with the principles of Community law. Thus, in *Re the Draft Treaty on a European Economic Area* (Op.1/91) [1992] 1 CMLR 245 the Court of Justice held that the original European Economic Area Treaty was not compatible with Community law. The Treaty was then revised in the light of this opinion and its validity subsequently upheld by the Court of Justice: see *Re the Draft Treaty on a European Economic Area (No.2)* (Op.1/92) [1992] 2 CMLR 217. For an excellent comparative analysis, see Jaconelli, "*Reference of Bills to the Supreme Court - A Comparative Perspective*" (1983) 18 Ir Jur (n.s.) 322.

[5] [1940] IR 470; (1940) ILTR 61.

[6] [1943] IR 334; (1943) 74 ILTR 96.

[7] [1961] IR 169.

[8] [1977] IR 129; (1977) 110 ILTR 69.

[9] [1977] IR 129; (1978) 111 ILTR 29

[10] [1983] IR 181; [1983] ILRM 246.

[11] [1984] IR 268.

[12] [1989] IR 656.

[13] See p. 448.

(The word "law" in this passage must be taken as shorthand for "Bill which has passed both Houses of the Oireachtas" rather than as meaning literally "law" = Act of the Oireachtas). This test was adopted and reiterated in *In re Article 26 and the School Attendance Bill 1942*,[14] and in *In re Article 26 and the Electoral (Amendment) Bill 1961*.[15] In the fourth reference, *In re Article 26 and the Criminal Law (Jurisdiction) Bill 1975*,[16] the Court laid down the same principle as had been adopted by "the former Supreme Court", and adverted to a submission made by counsel assigned to argue against the Bill, to the effect that:

> "the same considerations should not be applied to a Bill referred by the President under Article 26 as are applied in the case of an Act which has been duly passed by both Houses of the Oireachtas and signed and promulgated by the President because the President has referred the Bill after consultation with the Council of State and because a question has been raised in relation to the constitutionality of such a Bill or some provision thereof. The Court does not accept that any distinction should be drawn in relation to the presumption of constitutionality between an Act of the Oireachtas and a Bill referred by the President under Article 26."

Reference of Bill designed to have protection of Article 28.3.3 possible but review of Bill is limited in scope

In the next reference - *In re Article 26 and the Emergency Powers Bill 1976*[17] - the Court did not mention the question of presumption of constitutionality. What was principally in issue here was whether a Bill designed to have the protection of Article 28.3.3 - i.e. expressed to be "for the purpose of securing the public safety and the preservation of the State" in the emergency conditions contemplated by that sub-section, and so to be incapable, when an Act of being invalidated by the invocation of anything in the Constitution - could be the subject of an Article 26 reference at all, since such a reference was for the very purpose of deploying constitutional criteria to test the Bill. The Court's judgment on this matter was to the effect that the Bill could be referred, but that - so to speak- only its carapace could be scrutinised, not its contents:

> "When a Bill is validly referred to the Court under Article 26 the test of its repugnancy or invalidity is what its force and effect will be if and when it becomes law. Thus in regard to a Bill which is to take effect as law under Article 28.3.3, if it is shown to the Court that the preliminary and procedural requirements for the passing of the Bill by both Houses of the Oireachtas have been complied with, it is *ipso facto,* because of the exemption granted by Article 28.3.3, incapable of being struck down on the ground of repugnancy to the Constitution or to any provision thereof."

Counsel assigned to argue against the Bill had submitted, however, not only that an Article 26 reference was possible in the case of an Article 28.3.3 Bill, but also that while the legislation was still only at Bill stage - in other words, before it had become a "law" through the President's signature - the immunity envisaged by Article 28.3.3 did not attach to it, as that sub-section specifically refers to any "law". This amounted to saying that if emergency legislation could be so to speak caught and challenged at Bill stage, *via* the Article 26 procedure, the same criteria could be deployed towards invalidating it

[14] [1943] IR 334; (1943) 77 ILTR 96.
[15] [1961] IR 169.
[16] [1977] IR 129; (1977) 110 ILTR 69.
[17] [1977] IR 159; (1978) 111 ILTR 29. The presumption was, however, mentioned *In re Article 26 and the Housing (Private Rented Dwellings) Bill 1981* [1983] IR 181; [1983] ILRM 246; in *In re Article 26 and the Electoral (Amendment) Bill 1983* [1984] IR 268 and *The Adoption (No.2) Bill 1987* [1989] IR 656.

as could be deployed against ordinary, non-emergency legislation at any time after it had become an Act or "law". The Court held that:

> "If Article 26 stood alone and could be construed without reference to Article 28.3.3, that submission would be correct and this Court might have to advise the President that the Bill would be repugnant to the Constitution...
>
> Every law enacted by the Oireachtas must initially have been a Bill passed by both Houses of the Oireachtas and is therefore capable of being referred to this Court by the President, unless it is a Bill of the kind expressly excluded by Article 26 from reference. The Bills which may be referred include Bills intended to be enactments in conformity with the provisions of Article 28.3.3. If such a Bill is not referred to this Court it must be signed by the President. Thereupon it becomes a law enacted by the Oireachtas and has the immunity conferred upon it by the sub-section in question. The Constitution therefore contemplates that laws which would otherwise be invalid may be validly enacted provided they conform with the requirements of Article 28.3.3."

The point here is that the intent of Article 28.3.3 would be frustrated if Article 26 were applied literally without regard to it.

Is the ratio decidendi of Article 26 a binding precedent?

While by Article 34.3.3 no court may question the validity of a law the Bill for which has been upheld by the Supreme Court in an Article 26 reference, the question arises whether the entire *ratio decidendi* of the Supreme Court's opinion binds the High Court and other courts in the same way as would a Supreme Court judgment on an issue between parties Here there are conflicting views, but by far the dominant view is that such advices are binding in the ordinary way. In *In re O Láighléis*[18] the High Court, *per* Davitt P, said the question whether a Minister's opinion[19] was well founded was "not one which this Court can consider" as it was "covered by authority", namely the view of the Supreme Court in *In re Article 26 and the Offences Against the State (Amendment) Bill 1940*[20] that "the validity of such opinions is not a matter which should be questioned in any court". In *The State (Lynch) v Cooney*[21] Henchy J said that "if that statement could be said to be part of the *ratio decidendi* of that judgment, he would agree that the doctrine of *stare decisis* would have obliged the judge to follow it", even though it had been pronounced by the "old" Supreme Court. But in *Ryan v Attorney General*[22] Kenny J said (with reference to the same Article 26 case) that his view was that "advice given by the Supreme Court to the President [does not bind] the High Court in the same way as does a decision of the Supreme Court in a case between parties".

[18] [1960] IR 93; (1961) 95 ILTR 92.

[19] That a person is "engaged in activities...prejudicial to the preservation of public peace and order or to the security of the State": Offences Against the State (Amendment) Act 1940, s 4(1).

[20] [1940] IR 470; (1940) 74 ILTR 61.

[21] [1982] IR 337; [1983] ILRM 89. Note also that in *McGimpsey v Ireland* [1990] 1 IR 110 Finlay CJ over-ruled a statement contained in *In re Article 26 and the Criminal Law (Jurisdiction) Bill 1975* [1977] IR 129 to the effect that Article 2 did not constitute a "claim of legal right" in respect of Northern Ireland. The point here is that there was no suggestion that the view of the Supreme Court in the *Criminal Law (Jurisdiction) Bill* reference was not binding (subject to over-ruling) on a later Supreme Court in the ordinary way.

[22] [1965] IR 294. Kenny J may have been influenced by the fact that the formal distinction between *obiter dicta* and *ratio decidendi* pre-supposed a finding of fact on the part of the trial judge, a feature which is - to date, at least - absent from the Article 26 reference procedure. But apart from this rather technical point, there seems little from the point of view of principle to support this *dictum*.

Should there have been reference to the "old' Supreme Court?

Whether the first three Article 26 references should ever have taken place, and, if not, what their status is (either in regard to the Bills referred, or to the *rationes decidendi*) must be a question after the Supreme Court's holding in *Sullivan v Robinson*[23] and *Eamonn Andrews Productions v Gaiety Theatre*[24] that references in Article 34.4.3 to the "Supreme Court" envisaged the "new" Supreme Court which was to be set up, but which was not, in fact set up until 1961 (subsequent to the Electoral (Amendment) Bill reference). While in the former case the "old" Supreme Court held itself entitled - though the point arose only obiter - to entertain Article 26 references, in the latter case the "new" Supreme Court held, in the words of Walsh. J, that "the provisions of Article 34.4.3...dealing with the appellate jurisdiction of the Supreme Court did not in any way relate to the courts carried on by virtue of Article 58", a view which seems based on reasoning which would equally exclude the "old" Supreme Court, transitionally carrying on under Article 58, from the intendment of Article 26, and would give it no function in regard to scrutinising Bills for constitutionality or advising the President on them.

Flexible procedure

A certain flexibility in procedure may be a feature of Article 26 references. The "old" Supreme Court noted, in its judgment in *In re Article 26 and the Electoral (Amendment) Bill 1961*,[25] that while in the two earlier references counsel for the Attorney General had opened the argument, in this case it was agreed by counsel that owing to the nature of the provisions contained in this Bill it would be more convenient if counsel assigned by the Court [to argue against the Bill] should open the argument and state the grounds on which it would be submitted that the Bill was repugnant to the Constitution. This course was approved by the Court and has been followed in all subsequent references.

Problems of Article 26 procedure: evidence?

In none of the Article 26 references which have so far taken place has the question arisen of the Supreme Court taking evidence; and in the *Housing (Private Rented Dwellings)* Bill reference[26] the Court specifically said it was "not necessary to decide whether evidence may or should be heard when considering a reference under Article 26". The Court, however, in the course of gently drawing attention to the defects and even disadvantages of the Article 26 procedure, emphasised that in all Article 26 cases to date the matters argued have had, in the absence of evidence, to be dealt with as abstract problems, to the extent that, unlike practically all other cases that come before the Court, there is an absence or shortage of concrete facts, proven, admitted or projected as a matter of probability. The Court, therefore, in a case such as this, has to act on abstract materials in order to cope with the social, economic, fiscal and other features that may be crucial to an understanding of the working and consequences of the referred Bill.

The Court mentioned also the obvious difficulty that could confront it in trying to reach "a unitary decision on the basis of conflicting evidence"; and pointed out that, in any case, if the evidence were of the complex technical character of that in *Ryan v Attorney General*,[27] it might be extremely hard for the Court to deliver advice to the President within the sixty days that Article 26.2.1 requires. Thus the Court expressed misgivings

[23] [1954] IR 161; (1954) 88 ILTR 169
[24] [1973] IR 295.
[25] [1961] IR 169.
[26] [1983] IR 181; [1983] ILRM 246.

both about having to decide an issue in the abstract without evidence, and about the practical difficulties it would be faced with if evidence were in fact offered and admitted.

Permanent immunity of Bill once cleared

The other aspect of the Article 26 procedure on which, on the same occasion, the Court commented, is its effect, by virtue of Article 34.3.3, of conferring permanent immunity on any Act or provision which has successfully passed an Article 26 reference at Bill stage. Referring to *Ryan v Attorney General* the Court said that, even where a challenge to an ordinary Act has been unsuccessful, "if in the future the scientific evidence available should be such as to warrant a different conclusion on the facts, the question of the validity of the Act could be re-opened". Presumably, depending on the type of legislation in issue, new evidence of a kind other than scientific could be used in bringing a new challenge. But as an Act once cleared under Article 26 as a Bill, can never again be challenged, no amount of new evidence - or indeed of new perceptions about the extent of constitutional rights - will avail to overturn it; this is why, although in the *Emergency Powers Bill* reference the State as much as admitted in 1976 that even a seven-day extended arrest would be constitutionally objectionable, the powers of unlimited detention contained in the Offences Against the State (Amendment) Act 1940, are immune from attack, because the Bill for that Act was cleared under Article 26 in 1940.[28]

The general feeling of the Court about the two questions of abstract adjudication and permanent immunity was expressed in the *Housing (Private Rented Dwellings) Bill* case thus:

> "Whether the constitutionality of a legislative measure...is better determined within a fixed and immutable period of time by means of reference under Article 26, in which case, if no repugnancy is found, the decision may never be questioned again in any court, rather than by means of an action in which specific imputations of unconstitutionality would fall to be determined primarily on proven or admitted facts, is a question on which we refrain from expressing an opinion."

Finding of repugnancy of one provision is not a "stamp of constitutionality for others"

One other practical problem of the Article 26 procedure was mentioned in the same case. If any provision of a Bill, or of a number of provisions, referred under Article 26 is found repugnant, the President may not sign the Bill at all. The Court's function extends only to detecting a repugnancy;

> "it is not the function of the Court to impress any part of a referred Bill with a stamp of constitutionality...There thus may be areas of a referred Bill or of referred provisions of a Bill which may be left untouched by the Court's decision. The authors of the Bill may therefore find the Court's decision less illuminating than they would wish it to be."

27 [1965] IR 294. Another potential difficulty which may yet arise (e.g., in the context of a future reference of a European Communities Bill) is where the Court might feel obliged to refer a question of Community law to the Court of Justice in the course of an Article 26 reference. This would scarcely be possible in the sixty day time limit, although it might be argued that this time limit would be inapplicable in such circumstances

28 Save, perhaps on the basis - canvassed below at p. 494 - that Article 34.3.3 had no application to this particular decision in that the Supreme Court which entertained that reference had no jurisdiction to do so.

Advantages of Article 26 procedure

As against this, there are clearly cases for which the Article 26 procedure is especially suited. These are cases presenting net points of law and in respect of which certainty is particularly important. This was certainly the case of the last two references - *Re Article 26 and the Electoral (Amendment) Bill 1983*[29] and *Re Article 26 and the Adoption (No.2) Bill 1987.*[30] Both cases presented net points of law - in the former case, whether the granting of the franchise to British citizens was compatible with Article 16 and in the latter, whether the adoption of certain legitimate children was compatible with Article 42 - and thus the courts' assessment of the constitutional issues was unlikely to vary even in the absence before the Supreme Court of a case with concrete facts. Moreover, one could well imagine the potential chaos that might have resulted had a general election been tainted with the votes of non-eligible voters or where certain adoption orders were declared unconstitutional.[31] In such circumstances, certainty is everything and there may well be advantages in having this type of legislation constitutionally vetted in advance by the Supreme Court.

Convocation by President of Council of State - but where no reference resulted

There have been some occasions on which the President consulted the Council of State with an eye to a possible reference but in which no reference ultimately took place. This occurred in 1947 with the Health Bill of that year, when the President summoned the Council at the instance of one of its members in order to consider Part III of the Bill, which contemplated the compulsory medical examination of children: he decided against referring the Bill to the Court.[32] Again, the President convoked the Council of State in 1967 to consider the Income Tax (Consolidation) Bill 1966, of which sections giving the revenue authorities powers of distraint and committal reappeared among the consolidated provisions although they had long been felt as objectionable (standing orders did not permit their deletion in the context of a consolidation Bill). The Government introduced a short, separate Bill to repeal these provisions and in the circumstances no reference took place.[33] Within the last few years, the President has twice convened the Council of State to consider possible references. In the case of the Criminal Justice Bill 1984, this controversial Bill regulated a variety of aspects of criminal procedure and some of its provisions were considered to have been of doubtful constitutionality. In the event, the President decided against referral and the Bill became law as the Criminal Justice Act 1984.[34] The President also decided against a reference in the case of the Fisheries (Amendment) Bill 1991, despite suggestions in certain quarters that the new licensing arrangements envisaged thereby might have infringed rights of association protected by Article 40.6.[35]

[29] [1984] IR 268.
[30] [1989] IR 656.
[31] For an analysis of these complicated questions, see pp. 165-166.
[32] *The Irish Times*, 15 August 1947.
[33] See 227 Dáil Debates 113.
[34] *The Irish Times*, 6, 7 December 1984.
[35] *The Irish Times*, 31 October 1991.

Article 27

REFERENCE OF BILLS TO THE PEOPLE

Reference of Bills to the People
Article 27

This Article applies to any Bill, other than a Bill expressed to be a Bill containing a proposal for the amendment of this Constitution, which shall have been deemed, by virtue of Article 23 hereof, to have been passed by both Houses of the Oireachtas.

1 A majority of the members of Seanad Éireann and not less than one-third of the members of Dáil Éireann may by a joint petition addressed to the President by them under this Article request the President to decline to sign and promulgate as a law any Bill to which this Article applies on the ground that the Bill contains a proposal of such national importance that the will of the people thereon ought to be ascertained.

2. Every such petition shall be in writing and shall be signed by the petitioners whose signatures shall be verified in the manner prescribed by law.

3. Every such petition shall contain a statement of the particular ground or grounds on which the request is based, and shall be presented to the President not later than four days after the date on which the Bill shall have been deemed to have been passed by both Houses of the Oireachtas.

4. 1° Upon receipt of a petition addressed to him under this Article, the President shall forthwith consider such petition and shall, after consultation with the Council of State, pronounce his decision thereon not later than ten days after the date on which the Bill to which such petition relates shall have been

Billí a chur faoi bhreith an Phobail
Airteagal 27

Baineann an tAirteagal seo le gach Bille, seachas Bille a luaitear a bheith ina Bhille a bhfuil togra ann chun an Bunreacht seo a leasú, a mheastar, de bhua Airteagal 23 den Bhunreacht seo, a ritheadh ag dhá Theach an Oireachtais.

1. Is cead do thromlach de chomhaltaí Sheanad Éireann, i bhfochair trian ar a laghad de chomhaltaí Dháil Éireann, comhachainí a chur chun an Uachtaráin faoin Airteagal seo, á iarraidh air diúltú dá lámh a chur le haon Bhille lena mbaineann an tAirteagal seo agus don Bhille sin a fhogairt ina dhlí, toisc togra a bheith ann ina bhfuil an oiread sin tábhacht náisiúnta gur cóir breith an phobail a fháil air.

2. Ní foláir gach achainí den sórt sin a bheith i scríbhinn agus í a bheith faoi láimh an lucht achainí agus ní foláir a sínithe sin a bheith fíoraithe ar an modh a ordaítear le dlí.

3. Ní foláir léirthuairisc a bheith i ngach achainí den sórt sin ar an ábhar nó ar na hábhair áirithe ar a bhfuil sí bunaithe, agus í a thairiscint don Uachtarán lá nach déanaí ná ceithre lá tar éis an data a mheastar a ritheadh an Bille ag dhá Theach an Oireachtais.

4. 1° Chomh luath agus a gheibheann an tUachtarán achainí faoin Airteagal seo ní foláir dó í a bhreithniú agus, tar eis comhairle a ghlacadh leis an Comhairle Stáit, a bhreith a thabhairt uirthi lá nach déanaí ná deich lá tar éis an lae a mheastar a ritheadh, ag dhá Theach an Oireachtais, an Bille

deemed to have been passed by both Houses of the Oireachtas.

2° If the Bill or any provision thereof is or has been referred to the Supreme Court under Article 26 of this Constitution, it shall not be obligatory on the President to consider the petition unless or until the Supreme Court has pronounced a decision on such reference to the effect that the said Bill or the said provision thereof is not repugnant to this Constitution or to any provision thereof, and, if a decision to that effect is pronounced by the Supreme Court, it shall not be obligatory on the President to pronounce his decision on the petition before the expiration of six days after the day on which the decision of the Supreme Court to the effect aforesaid is pronounced.

5. 1° In every case in which the President decides that a Bill the subject of a petition under this Article contains a proposal of such national importance that the will of the people thereon ought to be ascertained, he shall inform the Taoiseach and the Chairman of each House of the Oireachtas accordingly in writing under his hand and Seal, and shall decline to sign and promulgate such Bill as a law unless and until the proposal shall have been approved either—

(i) by the people at a Referendum in accordance with the provisions of section 2 of Article 47 of this Constitution within a period of eighteen months from the date of the President's decision, or

(ii) by a resolution of Dáil Éireann passed within the said period after a dissolution and reassembly of Dáil Éireann.

2° Whenever a proposal contained in a Bill the subject of a petition

sin lena mbaineann an achainí.

2° I gcás an Bille nó aon fhoráil de a chur faoi bhreith na Cúirte Uachtaraí faoi Airteagal 26 den Bhunreacht seo ní bheidh ar an Uachtarán an achainí a bhreithniú mura ndéana ná go dtí go ndéanfaidh an Chúirt Uachtarach, de dhroim an churtha faoi bhreith sin, breith a chraoladh á dhearbhú gan an Bille sin nó an fhoráil sin de a bheith in aghaidh an Bhunreachta seo ná in aghaidh aon fhorála de agus, i gcás an Chúirt Uachtarach do chraoladh breithe á dhearbhú sin, ní bheidh ar an Uachtarán a bhreith ar an achainí a chraoladh go ceann sé lá tar éis an lae a chraolfar breith na Cúirte Uachtaraí ag dearbhú mar a dúradh.

5. 1° I gcás gach Bille is siocair d'achainí faoin Airteagal seo, más é breith an Uachtaráin go bhfuil togra ann ina bhfuil an oiread sin tábhacht náisiúnta gur chóir breith an phobail a fháil air, ní foláir dó scríbhinn faoina láimh agus faoina Shéala a chur go dtí an Taoiseach agus go dtí Cathaoirleach gach Tí den Oireachtas á chur sin in iúl dóibh, agus diúltú dá lámh a chur leis an mBille sin agus dá fhógairt ina dhlí mura nglactar, agus go dtí go nglactar, an togra-

(i) le toil an phobail i Reifreann de réir forálacha alt 2 d'Airteagal 47 den Bhunreacht seo, taobh istigh d'ocht mí dhéag ón lá a bheireann an tUachtarán a bhreith, nó

(ii) le rún ó Dháil Éireann arna rith taobh istigh den tréimhse réamhráite i ndiaidh lánscor agus ationól do Dháil Éireann.

2° Cibé uair a dhéantar togra a bhíonn i mBille is siocair

under this Article shall have been approved either by the people or by a resolution of Dáil Éireann in accordance with the foregoing provisions of this section, such Bill shall as soon as may be after such approval be presented to the President for his signature and promulgation by him as a law and the President shall thereupon sign the Bill and duly promulgate it as a law.

6. In every case in which the President decides that a Bill the subject of a petition under this Article does not contain a proposal of such national importance that the will of the people thereon ought to be ascertained, he shall inform the Taoiseach and the Chairman of each House of the Oireachtas accordingly in writing under his hand and Seal, and such Bill shall be signed by the President not later than eleven days after the date on which the Bill shall have been deemed to have been passed by both Houses of the Oireachtas and shall be duly promulgated by him as a law.

d'achainí faoin Airteagal seo a ghlacadh le toil an phobail nó le rún ó Dháil Éireann de réir na bhforálacha sin romhainn den alt seo, ní foláir an Bille sin a thairiscint don Uachtarán chomh luath agus is féidir é tar éis a ghlactha, chun a lámh a chur leis agus é a fhógairt ina dhlí, agus air sin ní foláir don Uachtarán a lámh a chur leis an mBille agus é a fhógairt go cuí ina dhlí.

6. I gcás gach Bille is siocair d'achainí faoin Airteagal seo, más é breith an Uachtaráin nach bhfuil aon togra ann ina bhfuil an oiread sin tábhacht náisiúnta gur chóir breith an phobail a fháil air, ní foláir dó scríbhinn faoina láimh agus faoina Shéala a chur go dtí an Taoiseach agus go dtí Cathaoirleach gach Tí den Oireachtas á chur sin in iúl dóibh, agus a lámh a chur leis an mBille sin lá nach déanaí ná aon lá dhéag tar éis an lae a mheastar a ritheadh an Bille sin ag dhá Theach an Oireachtais, agus é a fhógairt go cuí ina dhlí.

1922 provisions

A similar provision was contained in Article 47 of the 1922 Constitution, but this Article was removed in 1928 by the Constitution (Amendment No. 10) Act. The procedure envisaged by Article 27 has never been used, no doubt in consequence of the political realities which virtually ensure that a Government majority in the Dáil will be reflected in a Government majority in the Seanad (so that the hypothesis of the Article - an anti-Government majority in the Seanad allied with an anti-Government minority in the Dáil - is virtually never in practice realised). The provision envisaged by Article 27.2 is made by the Constitution (Verification of Petition) Act 1944.

Article 27 referendum concentrates on vetoing rather than approving

Note that if the Article 27 procedure were ever used, the referendum it envisages would be subject to the special rule of Article 47.2.1 which, unlike the rule for referenda to amend the Constitution, provides for the negativing rather than the approving of the proposal submitted to the people. A proposal submitted under Article 47 is "vetoed if a majority of the votes at the referendum are cast against it and "if the votes so cast against its enactment into law shall have amounted to not less than thirty-three and one-third per cent, of the voters on the register". Thus if (for example) there were a sixty per cent. poll in which the votes against outnumbered the votes for the proposal in the proportion of 55 to 45, the proposal would not be considered vetoed and the Bill would become law.

THE GOVERNMENT

The Government

Article 28

1. **The Government shall consist of not less than seven and not more than fifteen members who shall be appointed by the President in accordance with the provisions of this Constitution.**
2. **The executive power of the State shall, subject to the provisions of this Constitution, be exercised by or on the authority of the Government.**

An Rialtas

Airteagal 28

1. **Mórsheisear ar a laghad, agus cúig dhuine dhéag ar a mhéid, líon comhaltaí an Rialtais, agus is é an tUachtarán a cheapfas na comhaltaí sin de réir forálacha an Bhunreachta seo.**
2. **Faoi chuimsiú forálacha an Bhunreachta seo, is é an Rialtas a oibreos, nó is le húdarás an Rialtais a oibreofar, cumhacht chomhallach an Stáit.**

Complements Article 6

The words of s 2 were relied on by Gavan Duffy J in *The State (Burke) v Lennon*[1] in his exposition of the "division of powers" in the State: the Government is here made the repository of the executive power. In *Crotty v An Taoiseach*,[2] Barrington J deduced from the doctrine of separation of powers that "the Government is free to formulate the external policy of the State [which is] a matter vested in the Government by the Constitution" while in *Attorney General v Hamilton (No.1)*[3] Finlay CJ invoked the doctrine of separation of powers in part justification for the conclusion that the Oireachtas could not inquire into the detail or contents of Government discussions.

Extent of executive power

Beyond noting that the conduct of foreign affairs[4] and the exercise of all powers, functions, rights and prerogatives formerly exercisable in respect of Saorstát Éireann[5] are matters within the remit of the executive, the Constitution is silent as to the extent of the power of the executive. One commentator has suggested that the notion of executive power is so indefinite that it must be considered to be that which is left when the legislative and judicial powers are subtracted.[6] For judicial consideration of the extent of executive power, see above, pp. 47-49.

Demonstrates end of old regime

In *Attorney General v Crawford*[7] Article 28 - presumably s 2 of the Article was principally in mind - was relied on among a number of Articles to demonstrate that no trace of the Crown remained in the Constitution; the relevance of Article 28 to this point arose from the original form of Article 51 of the 1922 Constitution, which had declared the executive authority of Saorstát Éireann to be vested in the King, to be exercised with the "aid and advice" of the Executive Council. In *Byrne v Ireland*[8] Walsh J cited Article 28.2 to the same effect.

[1] [1940] IR 136; (1940) 74 ILTR 36, 131.
[2] [1987] IR 713; [1987] ILRM 400.
[3] [1993] 2 IR 250; [1993] ILRM 81.
[4] Article 29.4.1.
[5] Article 49.2.
[6] Casey, *Constitutional Law in Ireland* (2nd ed., 1992), p.187.
[7] [1940] IR 335; (1940) 74 ILTR 140.
[8] [1972] IR 241.

1922 Executive Council had "like functions": legislation adapted

Apart from this purely formal[9] subordination, the Executive Council of the 1922 Constitution corresponded in function with the Government of the Constitution of 1937; and Article 56.1 provided that on the coming into operation of the 1937 Constitution "the Government[10] in office immediately before the coming into operation of this Constitution [should] become and be the Government for the purposes of this Constitution". Section 4 of the Constitution (Consequential Provisions) Act 1937, implicitly (by its reference to a body "with like functions" under the old Constitution) made possible the construction of pre-Constitution legislative references to the Executive Council as being references to the Government; ss 3, 8 and 9 of the Act made ancillary adaptations (the former Department of the President of the Executive Council was to become the Department of the Taoiseach; and the seals of the Executive Council and of the President of the Executive Council might, if necessary, be used temporarily as the seals of the Government and of the Taoiseach respectively).

Legal character of "the Government"

The precise legal dimensions of the constitutional organ called "the Government" have not yet been judicially measured though in *McLoughlin v Minister for Social Welfare*[11] Kingsmill Moore J referred briefly to the Government as "the executive organ of the State" and noted that under the Constitution the Government was set apart as an entity of its own, separate and distinct from the State, so that a distinction had to be drawn between the civil service of the Government and the civil service of the State, a distinction which did not exist in Saorstát Éireann. Pending an authoritative judicial survey, some observations on the apparent character of the Government may be offered.

First, it appears to have a less complete legal personality than its individual members, as Ministers, possess. By s 2(1) of the Ministers and Secretaries Act 1924, each Minister who is head of a Department (the original Departments are enumerated in the preceding section: the titles and functions have been continually altered by later legislation) is a corporation sole, with perpetual succession, and with power to sue and be sued, and to own land for his Department's purposes.[12] No such well-rounded *persona* is available to the Government itself. It has a seal to authenticate its acts and is capable of holding property.[13] On the other hand, its capacity to sue or to be sued is problematical. Its non-appearance as plaintiff may be explained by the existence of the Attorney General's function as representative of the State and of the public interest. In virtually all of the

[9] It corresponded with the British convention, whereby the Government's wishes, although politely labelled as mere "advice" to the monarch, were in fact paramount and left no room for independent action on the monarch's part.

[10] The "Government" of Saorstát Éireann, although colloquially so called, had the formal title of "Executive Council", the head of the Government being called "President of the Executive Council" in formal usage: Articles 51-2 of the 1922 Constitution.

[11] [1958] IR 1.

[12] The Departments have no legal personality. They are merely organisations with public purposes defined by statute. Any legal personality required for those public purposes is to be found in the Ministers in charge of them. Before 1922, however, the "Departments" operating here owned property as such: this is reflected in Articles 11 and 80 of the 1922 Constitution, and in the words of Fitzgibbon J, in expounding the old Article 11, in *Commissioners of Public Works v Mackey*: above, p. 73. The former Ministries in Northern Ireland had a similar personality.

[13] See s 51 of the Copyright Act 1963 which vests the copyright in certain publications in the Government. However the Government figures in the State Property Act 1954, only as the body which decides whether to accept a gift to the State, Nation or People, and which State authority such gift, if accepted, shall vest in - s 19.

actions substantially aimed at the Government as such[14] - *Boland v An Taoiseach,*[15] *Ó Monacháin v An Taoiseach,*[16] *Crotty v An Taoiseach,*[16a] *Duggan v An Taoiseach,*[17] *McGimpsey v Ireland,*[18] *McKenna v An Taoiseach*[19] and *Slattery v An Taoiseach,*[20] the defendants named in the proceedings were the Taoiseach, the Tánaiste and all the other members of the Government (named however as Ministers for this and that). The only exception to this appears to be *The State (Sheehan) v Government of Ireland*[21] where the Government was sued as such.

Secondly, while the spheres of individual Departments are precisely indicated by legislation, the sphere of the Government apart from its exercise of "the executive power of the State" is not clearly defined, nor perhaps could it be. In particular, and of special relevance to the "collective responsibility" prescribed by Article 28.4.2, there is no clear rule as to which matters positively require formal Government consideration and formal decision.[22]

The Government's domestic commitments

Thirdly, while the Government has a functional continuity, transcending changes in its political complexion and personnel on the occasions when power passes from one side to the other, it is hard to say clearly to what extent the Government is bound, in a legal sense, by former Government acts - in particular, by commitments entered into, domestically or internationally, by or on behalf of the Government when in the hands of a different political interest.

On the one hand, a statutory function attributed to "the Government" as such, like the making of some statutory Order, once exercised, will continue to have effect irrespective of "change of Government" in the political sense. Equally, an international agreement entered into on the State's behalf by or on the authority of the Government must be respected even when the Government is later formed from a political interest which disapproved the policy of entering into such an agreement.[23]

[14] An action aimed at the Government's predecessor, the Executive Council of Saorstát Éireann, was framed against the President of the Executive Council and all the other Ministers: *Leen v President of Executive Council and Others*, [1926] IR 456; [1928] IR 408, 594; (1928) 62 ILTR 69; (1929) 63 ILTR 24.

[15] [1974] IR 338.

[16] [1986] ILRM 660.

[16a] [1987] IR 713; [1987] ILRM 400.

[17] [1989] ILRM 710.

[18] [1990] 1 IR 110; [1990] ILRM 440.

[19] High Court, 8 June 1992.

[20] [1993] 1 IR 286.

[21] [1987] IR 550. See also *Lang* v *Government of Ireland*, High Court, 7 July 1993.

[22] In June 1982 the then Taoiseach (Deputy Haughey) was asked in the Dáil to say which decisions, advertised as "Government decisions" for political and publicistic purposes, were in fact the product of formal consideration by the Government meeting as a collective authority. Nothing concrete emerged from the exchange. The Taoiseach would go no further than to say that "in any instance where a Government decision is necessary, a Government decision is procured by this Government", though he acknowledged that "there are occasions when decisions not requiring formal Government decision can be taken by a Minister or group of Ministers with the Taoiseach" (336 *Dáil Debates* 1282). What this means is not clear. In practice it seems to be the case that, while items required *by law* to carry Government authority are formally dealt with at formal Government meetings, outside this area there is no invariable format for the Government's acting. It is apparently possible for the Government to become committed on the initiative of some one or more of its members, outside the framework of a formal meeting, perhaps in the expectation that their acts will be stood over by their colleagues. This, it may be noted, is *not* simply the operation of the doctrine of collective responsibility, as this applies only to what happens within the sphere of "the Departments of State administered by the members of the Government" (Article 28.4.2).

[23] "Change of government does not affect the personality of the State, and hence a successor government is required by international law to perform the obligations undertaken on behalf of the State by its predecessor": D. P. O'Connell, *International Law* (1965), Vol. I, p. 456.

On the other hand, there appears to be a category of Government acts which are the expression of current Government policy and which cannot be taken to preempt the Government's right (whether or not a political "change of Government" has supervened) to change its mind or to shape its policy differently. This seems to apply even where an expression of Government policy may take the form of a statement of intent, made with the purpose of inducing a certain course of conduct in others, and referred to officially as well as colloquially as a "commitment". Nothing more than hints can be offered on where this category of Government acts begins and ends, as the matter has not been authoritatively considered by an Irish court in recent times.

The Government's external commitments

So far as concerns Government undertakings in international relations not amounting to formal treaties, the only clue is afforded by *Boland v An Taoiseach.*[24] Here a number of members of the Government, including the Taoiseach, had joined in issuing, after four days of meetings with representatives of the British Government and of the parties involved in the Northern Ireland Executive (designate), an Agreed Communiqué containing a clause reading:

> "The Irish Government fully accepted and solemnly declared that there could be no change in the status of Northern Ireland until a majority of the people of Northern Ireland desired a change in that status."

That acceptance and declaration were intended to have a certain political effect, and to lay the ground for ultimate developments which would have clear legal dimensions. When the plaintiff challenged the constitutional right of the Government to give commitments which appeared to derogate from the effect of Article 3, the Supreme Court unanimously took the view that the acceptance and "solemn declaration" were no more than a "statement of policy" or of "the Government's position", and something therefore outside the jurisdiction of the Court to control.

Purported Government contracts

This would seem to assimilate such commitments given in the international area to analogous undertakings in the domestic area. Here too, however, there is a shortage of authority, particularly recent authority, in the specifically Irish context. The only clue seems to lie in the case of *Kenny v Cosgrave*[25] a case nearly sixty years old, in which the plaintiff complained that the defendant, President of the Executive Council, had urged him to resist strikers' demands and had undertaken, on behalf of the Executive Council, to indemnify him if this resistance should cause him loss. The Supreme Court, speaking by Fitzgibbon J, took the view that no contract to indemnify the plaintiff out of public funds would be enforceable against the Executive Council, partly because the payment of such an indemnity would have required a corresponding authorisation by the Oireachtas, whose rights in this regard could not be taken away by the Executive, but partly also because even a seriously meant undertaking of this kind was no more than a statement of the Executive's intent, and the Executive could not deprive itself in advance of the right to alter its policy. The Court adopted the principle stated by an English judge, Rowlatt J, in *Rederiaktiebolaget Amphitrite v The King*,[26] a case which arose out of the act of the British Government in promising certain neutral ship-owners immunity from wartime blockade regulations and then changing its mind, and cited his words:

[24] [1974] IR 338.
[25] [1926] IR 517.
[26] [1921] 3 KB 503.

"No doubt the Government can bind itself through its officers by a commercial contract, and if it does so it must perform it like anybody else or pay damages for the breach. But this was not a commercial contract; it was an arrangement whereby the Government purported to give an assurance as to what its executive action would be in the future in relation to a particular ship in the event of her coming to this country with a particular kind of cargo. And that is, to my mind, not a contract for the breach of which damages can be sued for in a court of law. It was merely an expression of intention to act in a particular way in a certain event. My main reason for so thinking is that it is not competent for the Government to fetter its future executive action, which must necessarily be determined by the needs of the community when the question arises It cannot by contract hamper its freedom of action in matters which concern the welfare of the State."

In *Duggan v An Taoiseach*[27] Hamilton P did award damages to the plaintiffs whose legitimate expectations had been frustrated by an unlawful act of the Government. However here the legitimate expectations were grounded on a representation of the Oireachtas - contained in the Farm Tax Act 1985 - rather than of the Government.

Executive power: status of the Government

In *Comyn v Attorney General*,[28] where the defendant sought to maintain that the expression "Government Department" in s 1(1) of the Acquisition of Land (Assessment of Compensation) Act 1919, would operate to cover "the Government" in the sense of the present Constitution, Kingsmill Moore J cited Article 28 and said of the Government:

"It is not a mere executive organ, it is *the* executive, exercising the supreme executive power of the State (Article 28.2). It is collectively responsible for all the Departments of State which are administered by individual members of the Government (Article 28.4.2). To equate the executive itself, which is responsible for all the Departments of State and whose individual members in their individual capacity administer such Departments, with a mere Department of State seems to me impossible. Even if I assume that a "Department of State" in our Constitution corresponds in popular language to a "Government Department" in 1919, the whole language of our Constitution shows that the Government and a Department of State are entirely different organs, and a power or right conferred on a Department of State, as such, is not thereby conferred on the Government, as such."

Statutory power conferred on members of executive not "the executive power of the State"

In *The State (C.) v Minister for Justice*[29] the applicant for *habeas corpus* challenged the Minister's power (purportedly derived by adaptation from the power of the Lord Lieutenant under the Lunatic Asylums (Ireland) Act 1875) to commit to an asylum a remand prisoner found to be insane. The point was taken that such a function was an exercise of executive power and, as such, could under Article 28.2 be exercised not by a Minister, but only by or on the authority of the Government. The argument failed in the Supreme Court, Walsh J saying:

"It is my opinion that the fact that a statutory power is conferred upon a member of the executive or a representative of the executive, as was the Lord Lieutenant, does not make that power an executive power within the meaning of that expression in

[27] [1989] ILRM 710. See below, pp. 232-3.
[28] [1950] IR 142; (1949) 83 ILTR 146.
[29] [1967] IR 106; (1968) 102 ILTR 177.

> the Constitution as the statute might just as easily have conferred the power on anybody else. The executive power of the State is not the same as a specific *ad hoc* power conferred by statute upon a Minister or some other member of the executive. In my opinion this statutory power, conferred upon the Lord Lieutenant, is not one which falls within Article 28.2."

The same judge carried the rest of the Court with him in making a not dissimilar point in *Murphy v Dublin Corporation*[30] five years later. Here the right of the Minister for Local Government to claim executive privilege in relation to the production of a document was in issue. The Court held against him on grounds arising from Article 34 and the judicial function;[31] but Walsh J went further:

> "Up to this I have been dealing with the case on the basis that the claim made was a claim of executive privilege not to produce a document. Such a claim is, of course, one made with reference to a document brought into being in the course of the carrying out of the executive functions of the State. It does not appear to me that this is such a document.
>
> The Housing Act 1966...constitutes the Minister...as the adjudicating authority upon the dispute which arises between the owner of the land which is made the subject of a compulsory purchase order and the local authority making such order. The executive powers of government of the State are vested in the Government: see Article 28.2. Different Departments of State are set up to deal with the business of executive government which are assigned to these Departments: see Article 28.12. The Government is collectively responsible for the Departments of State administered by the members of the Government assigned as Ministers over particular Departments (Article 28.4.2), and the powers, duties and functions of the Department are assigned to and administered by the Minister named.
>
> The function [in issue here] is not an executive power of the State assigned to his Department or a power which vested in the Government as an executive power from the State. He is *persona designata* in that the holder of the office of the Minister for Local Government is the person designated for that function. If the Oireachtas had so enacted, the Act could just as easily have assigned the function to [a quite different official]... The fact that the Minister for Local Government was the person chosen... does not *per se* confer upon the function the character of the exercise of the executive power of the State."

Executive power of the State exercisable by agencies other than the Government

That the Constitution envisages the exercise of the executive power of the State by agencies other than the Government was acknowledged by Ó Dálaigh J in *McLoughlin v Minister for Social Welfare*[32] when he said, in relation to the Attorney General, that "the exercise by the Attorney General of executive power, if in fact he exercises it, would not be a violation of Article 28.2 because the Article is expressed to be 'subject to the provi-

[30] [1972] IR 215; (1973) 107 ILTR 65.
[31] See below, pp. 377-9.
[32] [1958] IR 1.

sions of this Constitution'."[33] The functions conferred on the Comptroller and Auditor General by Article 33 afford us another possible example of this phenomenon.

In this context it is also worth noting the terms of Article 28.3.1 and Article 29.5.2 which make the exercise of certain executive powers - to declare war and to order participation in war and to enter into binding international obligations involving charges upon public funds - conditional on obtaining the assent of the Dáil.

Classification problem

The judgments in *C.'s* case and *Murphy's* case, inasmuch as they tend to interpret restrictively the "executive power of the State" in Article 28.2, open up the problem of how to classify, in terms of the "separation of powers", administrative functions (also often called "ministerial" or "executive") falling outside the boundaries of the "executive power of the State". Clearly they are incapable of being squeezed into the legislative or judicial categories. It seems that we must envisage a distinction, within the category of "executive power", between (a) the executive power *of* the State - exercisable by or on the authority of the Government; and (b) executive power *in* the State - not necessarily only so exercisable, but capable of being exercised also by other persons or bodies authorised by law. *McLoughlin* suggests a further classification, that of the executive power *of* the State conferred by the Constitution on agencies other than the Government, such as the Attorney General and the Comptroller and Auditor General. Finally, in certain instances noted above, the exercise of executive power by the Government is made conditional on obtaining the assent of the Dáil.

This classification raises the question of delimiting the type of executive power which, under the Constitution, is exercisable only by or on the authority of the Government. Does the reference to "the executive power of the State" in Article 28.2 mean those powers which, as a matter of fact, were customarily exercised in 1937 only by or on the authority of the Government or Executive Council, and that the object of the section is to entrench the prerogative of the Government in respect of those powers? Pending further judicial exploration, these questions must remain unanswered.

Judicial review of Government's acts only if there is "clear disregard" of Constitution

The question of the possible judicial review (on constitutional grounds) of an exercise of the executive power of the State first arose in *Boland v An Taoiseach.*[34] What was in issue was the conduct of the State's external relations and declarations of policy in this connection - clearly entrusted to the Government by Article 29.4.1 as part of the executive power of the State[35] - but the Supreme Court's approach would of course be relevant to other exercises of the "executive power of the State" as well. FitzGerald CJ said that in his opinion:

> "...the courts have no power, either express or implied, to supervise or interfere with the exercise by the Government 'of its executive functions, unless the circumstances are such as to amount to a clear disregard by the Government of the powers and duties conferred upon it by the Constitution."

[33] In *Crotty v An Taoiseach* [1987] IR 713; [1987] ILRM 400, however, Walsh J appeared to regard this phrase as referring to conditions imposed by the Constitution on the exercise of executive power by the Government in certain situations, rather than as authorising the exercise of executive power by agencies other than the Government - see p.777-8.

[34] [1974] IR 338; (1975) 109 ILTR 13. On the power of the courts to review ministerial decisions, see below, pp. 267-8.

[35] See below, p. 277.

The Court could find no such disregard in this instance; but O'Keeffe P did give an example of what he thought would be a disregard such as to justify the courts interference:

> "An acknowledgement by the Government that the State does not claim to be entitled *as of right* to jurisdiction over Northern Ireland would in my opinion be clearly not within the competence of the Government having regard to the terms of the Constitution.[36] I cannot presume that the Government would consciously make an acknowledgement of that kind and, accordingly, I accept the view of the Chief Justice that clause 5[37] represents no more than a reference to the *de facto* position of Northern Ireland coupled with a statement of policy in regard thereto."

Griffin J also asserted the "right and duty of the courts" to intervene if the Government were to act in contravention of the Constitution, but, like the other members of the Court, saw no such contravention in this case.

The very broad formulation of the courts' power to review the actions of the executive attracted little attention in the aftermath of *Boland,* no doubt because the Supreme Court declined to interfere with the decision of the executive in that case. However the implications of this approach became apparent in a most dramatic way in the subsequent case of *Crotty v An Taoiseach*[38] where a majority of the Supreme Court granted a declaration that the purported ratification of the Single European Act was unconstitutional. In response to the argument that in the case of treaties, the courts were not empowered to interfere unless the treaties were translated into domestic legislation, the majority reaffirmed the power of the courts to review the actions of the Government whenever it acted in clear disregard of the provisions of the Constitution. Walsh J said:

> "The Constitution confers upon the Government the whole executive power of the State, subject to certain qualifications.. and the Government is bound to take care that the laws of the State are faithfully executed...It is not within the competence of the Government, or indeed of the Oireachtas, to free themselves from the restraints of the Constitution or to transfer their powers to other bodies unless expressly empowered so to do by the Constitution. They are both creatures of the Constitution and are not empowered to act free from the restraints of the Constitution."

Henchy J said:

> "In the conduct of the State's external relations, as in the exercise of the executive power in other respects, the Government is not immune from judicial control if it acts in a manner or for a purpose which is inconsistent with the Constitution. Such control is necessary to give effect to the limiting words [in Article 28.2] "subject to the provisions of this Constitution".

The breadth of this basis for judicial review of executive action was such as to lead one commentator to describe *Crotty* as arguably the most significant decision in which

[36] What was in mind was Article 3.

[37] Clause 5 contained parallel declarations on the part of the Irish and British Governments. The Irish declaration is quoted under *Boland's* case, above, p. 13.

[38] [1987] IR 713; [1987] ILRM 400.

Walsh J participated, involving the recognition of a new constitutional right to have government conducted in accordance with the mandates of the Constitution.[39]

The dissenting judges, on the other hand, appeared to favour a narrower basis for judicial intervention, requiring the plaintiff to establish an actual or threatened invasion of his constitutional rights. Thus Finlay CJ said:

> "This Court has on appeal from the High Court a right and duty to interfere with the activities of the executive in order to protect or secure the constitutional rights of individual litigants where such rights have been or are being invaded by those activities or where activities of the executive threaten an invasion of such rights."

Griffin J put the matter even more forcefully when he said:

> "No express power is given by the Constitution to the courts to interfere in any way with the Government in exercising the executive power of the State. However, the Government, and all of its members and the administration in respect of which the members are responsible, are subject to the intervention of the Courts to ensure that in their actions they keep within the bounds of lawful authority. Where such actions infringe or threaten to infringe the rights of individual citizens or persons, the Courts not only have the right to interfere with the executive power but have the constitutional obligation and duty to do so. But that right to interfere arises only where the citizen or person who seeks the assistance of the Courts can show that there has been an actual or threatened invasion or infringement of such rights."[40]

A striking feature of *Crotty* is that none of the judges adverted to the "political question" doctrine which identifies certain issues as non-justiciable.[41] Furthermore the Court relaxed very significantly the rules on standing set out in *Cahill v Sutton*[42] to the point where the plaintiff was not required to prove the threat of any special injury or prejudice to him, as distinct from any other citizen.[43] However in two subsequent High Court cases, the judges appear to take a more restrictive attitude on both of these points. In *Duggan v An Taoiseach*[44] Hamilton P applied *Cahill v Sutton* to litigants challenging an act of the executive, saying:

> "A person or persons challenging an act of the executive must show that his or their interests have been adversely affected or stand in real or imminent danger of being adversely affected by the action of the executive."

On the facts of the case, the President held that the applicants did have l*ocus standi* to challenge an executive decision discontinuing the classification of land for the purposes

[39] See Casey, "*Crotty v An Taoiseach: A Comparative Perspective*" in O'Reilly ed., *Human Rights and Constitutional Law: Essays in Honour of Brian Walsh* (Dublin 1992) at p.189. In an earlier High Court case, *The State (Sheehan) v Government of Ireland* [1987] IR 550, Costello J took a similar approach when he asserted the right of the courts to ensure that the executive obey Acts of the Oireachtas, saying,

> "[I]f a statute imposes a duty on the Government it cannot claim immunity from the court's jurisdiction on the ground that in performing the duty it is carrying out an "executive function". There is no constitutional impropriety involved, in my view, if the courts require the Government to obey the requirements of an Act of the Oireachtas."

Though an appeal against his decision was subsequently upheld, none of the Supreme Court judges dissented from this proposition.

[40] Notwithstanding the somewhat broader language which he had used in *Boland,* Griffin J considered the decision in that case to be consistent with his dissenting view in *Crotty.*

[41] See, e.g. *Baker v Carr* 369 US 186 (1962) for a statement of this doctrine in the context of the US Constitution.

[42] [1980] IR 269.

[43] See also *McGimpsey v Ireland* [1990] 1 IR 110; [1990] ILRM 440 and pp. 441-2. For a general discussion on the rules of standing, see Hogan and Morgan, *Administrative Law in Ireland* (2nd ed.) pp.611-626.

[44] [1989] ILRM 710.

of the Farm Tax Act 1985 but he also held that they had no *locus standi* to challenge an unlawful decision of the Government to cease to charge and levy farm tax. On this last point, his decision would appear to be at odds with the approach taken in *Crotty*.

The "political question" doctrine, though not referred to as such in so many words, formed the basis for Costello J's decision in *McKenna v An Taoiseach*[45] to the effect that the courts had no jurisdiction to grant an injunction restraining the executive from spending public money, and campaigning, in support of a proposed constitutional amendment. The plaintiff had contended that the Constitution obliged the executive to ensure that the people were properly informed on the proposed amendment[46] and that where the executive was committed to a partisan campaign in support of the amendment, its failure to provide public funding to opponents of the proposal amounted to a breach of the Constitution. According to Costello J, however, this grievance did not give rise to a justiciable issue:

> "But not every grievance can be remedied by the courts. And judges must not allow themselves to be led, or indeed voluntarily wander, into areas calling for adjudication on political and non-justiciable issues...The merits or ratification or non-ratification of the Maastricht Treaty are, of course, not matters on which this Court should express a view. The extent of the role the Government feels called upon to play to ensure ratification is a matter of concern for the executive arm of government, not the judicial."

Costello J also rejected the proposition that the plaintiff had a constitutional right to oblige the Government to act in accordance with the Constitution:

> "No such express right exists in the Constitution and none can be inferred from the constitutional text. No such right can be said to be a personal right protected by Article 40.3.1. A citizen with *locus standi* has, of course, the right to seek relief from the courts should a government act unconstitutionally. Such a right is unaffected by the acts of which the plaintiff complains"

To the extent to which this passage appears to imply that a citizen must be able to point to some special injury or prejudice before he or she can challenge an act of the executive, it would appear to be inconsistent with the decision of the majority in *Crotty*, which was not cited in Costello J's judgment.

Deferral of law coming into operation - whether subject to judicial review

The question whether the courts can review the failure of the Government or a Minister to bring a particular item of legislation into operation was considered in *The State (Sheehan) v Government of Ireland*.[47] At issue in this case was the Government's failure to implement s 60(1) of the Civil Liability Act 1961, which abolishes the distinction between misfeasance and nonfeasance as far as the liability of highway authorities is concerned. However, s 60(7) provides that the section is to come into operation on such day, not earlier than 1 April 1967, as may be fixed by order of the Government. No such order had been made by the date of *Sheehan's* case, and the applicant sought an order of mandamus compelling the Government to bring the section into force. In the High Court, Costello J held that this matter was not beyond the reach of the courts' powers of review, and, rejecting arguments based on the separation of powers, he thought that

[45] High Court, 8 June 1992. Though formally an application for an interlocutory injunction, Costello J treated the motion as if it had been the trial of the action.

[46] The Eleventh Amendment to the Constitution, dealing with ratification of the Maastricht Treaty.

[47] [1987] IR 550; [1988] ILRM 437. See *Hogan*, (1987) 9 DULJ 91.

there was "no constitutional impropriety" involved if the courts were to "require the Government to obey the requirements of an Act of the Oireachtas". Turning to the question before him, he found that the discretion conferred on the Government was not an "open-ended" one; he thought the delay in this case was inexcusable and unreasonable, and granted the order of *mandamus* sought.

On appeal, however, a majority of the Supreme Court[48] held that s 60(7) did not impose any duty on the Government to bring the section into operation. Both Finlay CJ and Griffin J expressly reserved their opinion on the questions of whether the courts may direct the introduction into effect of legislation which the Oireachtas has provided should be introduced by executive order and whether the courts may make such an order in circumstances leading to the imposition of a significant burden on the Exchequer. However the fact that the Supreme Court refused to review the executive's discretionary power to bring the statutory provision into operation effectively resulted in frustration of the wishes of the Oireachtas in this instance.[49]

Presumption of constitutionality and "double construction" test in favour of Government

It may be noted that in *Boland*'s case something like a presumption of constitutionality and "double construction" test in favour of the Government's actions emerged, analogous to the long-established presumption and test in favour of Acts of the Oireachtas.[50] The words of O'Keeffe P cited above[51] virtually amount to this; and in the High Court Murnaghan J had said:

> "By reason of what O'Byrne J referred to in *Buckley v Attorney General*[52] "that respect which one great organ of State owes to another", this Court must assume, until it is clearly established to the contrary, that any declaration of policy by the Government is within the constitutional powers conferred on the Government."

In *Crotty v An Taoiseach*[53] Barrington J also held that a presumption of constitutionality attached to executive acts. In seeking an interlocutory injunction to restrain the Government from depositing any purported instrument of ratification of the Single European Act, the plaintiff had to establish that his claim gave rise to a "fair question of law"; the judge said a greater strictness was to be applied in admitting a "fair question of law" than would normally be applied in private litigation.

Usurping the Government's position, or obstructing Government, an offence

Section 6 of the Offences Against the State Act 1939, replacing s 4 of the Treasonable Offences Act 1925, penalises the "setting up, maintaining, or taking part in any way in a body of persons purporting to be a government... but not authorised in that behalf by or under the Constitution". Section 7 penalises the obstruction of government by violence or intimidation (and by s 1(1)(*b*)(iii) of the Criminal Justice Act 1964, murder done in the course of furtherance of an offence under either of those sections is capital). The

[48] McCarthy J dissented, holding to the same view as Costello J on the court's power to direct the executive to bring the section into operation.

[49] Another important piece of legislation affected by this ruling is the Health (Mental Services) Act 1981 which has not yet been brought into effect. (Nor, indeed, is it ever likely to be - see below, p. 867 FN 262.)

[50] See below, p. 448 *et seq.*

[51] See above, p. 13.

[52] [1950] IR 67.

[53] [1987] IR 713; [1987] ILRM 400.

sense of "government" in s 7 appears however to be much more general than the sense of Article 28: in *(The People) Director of Public Prosecutions v Kehoe* [54] (a case of a brutal attack on a police officer in the course of a demonstration which became a violent disturbance) the Court of Criminal Appeal *per* McCarthy J, said:

> "The section prohibits actions which prevent or obstruct the wide range of activities legislative, judicial or executive, which are involved in the government or governing of the State... To constitute an offence under s 7 it is necessary that the act complained of should constitute an attack on the State through one of its constitutional organs."

Confidentiality of Government deliberations

On the confidentiality of Government deliberations, see below, pp. 250-257.

[54] [1983] IR 136; [1983] ILRM 237.

Article 28.3

WAR AND NATIONAL EMERGENCY

3\. 1° War shall not be declared and the State shall not participate in any war save with the assent of Dáil Éireann.

2° In the case of actual invasion, however, the Government may take whatever steps they may consider necessary for the protection of the State, and Dáil Éireann if not sitting shall be summoned to meet at the earliest practicable date.

3° Nothing in this Constitution shall be invoked to invalidate any law enacted by the Oireachtas which is expressed to be for the purpose of securing the public safety and the preservation of the State in time of war or armed rebellion, or to nullify any act done or purporting to be done in time of war or armed rebellion in pursuance of any such law. In this sub-section "time of war" includes a time when there is taking place an armed conflict in which the State is not a participant but in respect of which each of the Houses of the Oireachtas shall have resolved that, arising out of such armed conflict, a national emergency exists affecting the vital interests of the State and "time of war or armed rebellion" includes such time after the termination of any war, or of any such armed conflict as aforesaid, or of an armed rebellion, as may elapse until each of the Houses of the Oireachtas shall have resolved that the national emergency occasioned by such war, armed conflict, or armed rebellion has ceased to exist.

3\. 1° Ní dleathach cogadh a fhógairt ná páirt a bheith ag an Stát in aon chogadh ach amháin le haontú Dháil Éireann.

2° Ach féadfaidh an Rialtas, i gcás ionraidh, aon ní a dhéanamh a mheasfaid a bheith riachtanach chun an Stát a chosaint, agus mura mbeidh Dáil Éireann ina suí ní foláir í a thionól chomh luath agus is féidir é.

3° Ní cead aon ní dá bhfuil sa Bhunreacht seo a agairt chun aon dlí dá n-achtaíonn an tOireachtas a chur ó bhail má luaitear ann gur dlí é chun slándáil an phobail a chur in áirithe agus chun an Stát a chaomhnú in aimsir chogaidh nó ceannairce faoi arm, ná chun aon ghníomh dá ndéantar nó a bheireann le tuiscint gur gníomh é a dhéantar in aimsir chogaidh nó ceannairce faoi arm de bhun aon dlí den sórt sin, a chur ar neamhní. San fho-alt seo, folaíonn "aimsir chogaidh" tráth a bheidh coinbhleacht faoi arm ar siúl nach mbeidh an Stát páirteach ann ach go mbeidh beartaithe ag gach Teach den Oireachtas ina thaobh le rún go bhfuil ann, de dheasca an choinbhleachta sin faoi arm, staid phráinne náisiúnta a dhéanann difir do bhonn beatha an Stáit agus folaíonn "aimsir chogaidh nó ceannairce faoi arm" an tréimhse aimsire sin a bheidh idir an tráth a chuirfear deireadh le haon chogadh, nó le haon choinbhleacht faoi arm den sórt sin réamhráite, nó le ceannairc faoi arm agus an tráth a bheartóidh gach Teach den Oireachtas le rún nach ann a thuilleadh don staid phráinne náisiúnta arbh é an cogadh sin, nó an coinbhleacht sin faoi arm, nó an cheannairc sin faoi arm faoi deara é.

1922 provision

The first two sub-sections of this section reproduce substantially the provision of the old Article 49, which read:

> "Save in the case of actual invasion, the Irish Free State (Saorstát Éireann) shall not be committed to active participation in any war without the assent of the Oireachtas."

It will be observed, however, that the present provisions make participation in war dependent on the assent of the Dáil alone. The Government's powers in the case of actual invasion - explicit in the present, implicit in the old Constitution - correspond with the traditional common law doctrine as to a Government's inherent right and duty to protect the population and the State under its charge.

Doubts have been expressed as to whether, because of Article 28.3.1, the Government can, acting on its own, conclude an international agreement which purported to bind Ireland to participate in a war in any prescribed circumstances in the future.[1] Casey argues, however, that unless the agreement required the State to take immediate offensive action, its constitutionality would be upheld.[2]

Emergency legislation withdrawn from judicial control

The third sub-section of this section represents the emergency power, in effect, to suspend ordinary constitutional safeguards and to withdraw Acts of the Oireachtas, passed for emergency purposes, from judicial control on the ordinary constitutional criteria.[3] The present form of the subsection is the result of the sub-section as originally enacted in 1937, plus two successive amendments contained in the First and Second Amendment of the Constitution Acts 1939 and 1941.

Extension of the meaning of "time of war"

As originally enacted, the sub-section extended only to the end of its first sentence (except that the phrase "in time of war or armed rebellion" in the closing words of the sentence was not yet there). The First Amendment of the Constitution Act 1939 (the Bill for which passed both Houses and was signed by the President on 2 September, the day after the German invasion of Poland and the day before Britain and France declared war) had only one object, namely the making available of the sub-section's cover even where the State itself was not engaged in hostilities; its s 2 added the words, "In this sub-section" down to "vital interests of the State". In 1941 the Second Amendment of the Constitution Act made a number of changes in sixteen different Articles; in Article 28.3.3 it inserted "in time of war or armed rebellion" as a clarifying repetition towards the end of the first sentence, and added to the subsection everything that comes after "vital interests of the State". As to the manner of the enactment of the First Amendment to the Constitution, see above, pp.197-8, 211.

Distinction between "war or armed rebellion" and "armed conflict in which the State is not a participant"

[1] See comments of Michael McDowell, T.D. in 371 *Dáil Debates,* col.2316, 22 April 1987.
[2] *Constitutional Law in Ireland* (2nd ed.), p.176. See generally, Farrell, "*The Government*" in Coakley and Gallagher Eds., *Politics in the Republic of Ireland* (Dublin, 1993) at 167-189.

The distinction between a "war or armed rebellion" and an "armed conflict in which the State is not a participant" has attracted judicial comment on at least two occasions. In *In re Article 26 and the Emergency Powers Bill 1976*[4] the Supreme Court held that legislation enacted for the purpose of securing public safety and the preservation of the State in time of war or armed rebellion did not have to be preceded by a resolution of each House of the Oireachtas declaring a national emergency in order to benefit from the protection of Article 28.3.3, whereas such resolutions were required in the case of legislation enacted in the context of an armed conflict in which the State is not a participant, before Article 28.3.3 could apply. Furthermore, legislation enacted in accordance with such resolutions could not then apply to a time of war or armed rebellion.

In *Russell v Fanning*[5] Hederman J, in his dissenting judgment,[6] relied on this distinction to reject the conclusion of the trial judge that persons using violence outside the State in order to achieve national unity were guilty of an attack upon the Constitution and upon the organs established thereby.

In an interesting aside in his judgment in *Finucane v McMahon*[7] Walsh J raised the question of whether the phrase "an armed conflict in which the State is not a participant" requires neutrality on the part of the State or whether or to what extent intervention of any sort by the State is permitted. In this context, one might note the remarks of the then Taoiseach, Mr. Haughey, that the granting of refuelling and transit facilities at Shannon to US forces involved in the second Gulf War could not be interpreted as making Ireland a participant in that war.[8]

Emergency legislation 1939 to date

On 2 September 1939, immediately after the passing of the First Amendment, both Houses passed the resolutions envisaged by Article 28.3.3; and on the following day an extremely comprehensive Emergency Powers Act duly expressed to be for making provision "for securing the public safety and the preservation of the State in time of war" was passed and signed.[9] This was followed in 1940-45 by several further Emergency

[3] See Morgan, "*The Emergency Powers Bill Reference II*" (1979) 14 Ir Jur (n.s.) 252, at 252-264. Though as Clarke points out in "*Emergency Legislation, Fundamental Rights and Article 28.3.3*" (1977) 12 Ir Jur (n.s.) 217, at 233: " [T]o the extent that the Irish Constitution recognises and endorses negative, moral rights as constitutional rights of a 'superior' status, it cannot at the same time consistently claim that emergency legislation can be made immune from court challenge by Article 28.3.3 or any other positive law."

[4] [1977] IR 159; (1977) 111 ILTR 29.

[5] [1988] IR 505; [1988] ILRM 333.

[6] Subsequently adopted, however, by an unanimous Supreme Court (though without express reference to the specific point considered here) in *Finucane v McMahon* [1990] 1 IR 165; [1990] ILRM 505. See p. 883.

[7] [1990] 1 IR 165; [1990] ILRM 505.

[8] 404 *Dáil Debates*, col. 645, 18 January 1991. This conclusion has been challenged - see Whelan and Heffernan, "*Ireland, the United Nations and the Gulf Conflict: Legal Aspects*" (1991) 3 Irish Studies in International Affairs 115 at 132-8.

[9] Preparation of the Bill for the Emergency Powers Act had begun in 1938, at the time of the Czechoslovak crisis and the Munich agreement: see Ronan Fanning, *The Irish Department of Finance, 1922-58*, pp. 308ff. The range of powers contained in the 1939 Act was very wide, but s 2 specifically excepted, from the things which might be done by Emergency Order, the raising of taxation, the introduction of compulsory military service, and the declaration of war without the assent of Dáil Éireann. The internment of natural-born Irish citizens without trial was also, at first, excepted, but this exception later disappeared: see below, p. 870.

Powers Acts;[10] the principal Act was continued in force until 1946, when it expired.[11] The emergency resolutions passed by both Houses in 1939, however, remained - despite the end of the world war and despite occasional protests at the absurdity of keeping the State in a condition of "emergency" - unrescinded until 1976;[12] in that year the 1939 resolutions were rescinded, only to be replaced by fresh resolutions passed in response to Northern Ireland-associated violence.[13] The 1976 resolutions were followed by a new Emergency Powers Act which made possible the detention of persons without charge for up to seven days.[14] The section containing this provision went out of force after twelve months, in 1977; but the 1976 emergency resolutions have not been rescinded by the "cessation of emergency" resolutions contemplated in the closing words of Article 28.3.3, and the Act itself requires only a Government order to bring the operative section back into force.

Challenges to the 1939-45 emergency legislation

The Emergency Powers legislation of the second world war period was attacked in *In re McGrath and Harte*[15] and *The State (Walsh) v Lennon.*[16] In the former case the applicants were under sentence of death passed by a military tribunal[17] set up under the Emergency Powers (Amendment) (No. 2) Act 1940, which consisted substantially of the provision (s 3) that the Government might order persons charged with any specified offence to be summarily tried by military officers; that the death sentence was mandatory upon conviction; and that there was to be no appeal. The prisoners' counsel raised a series of objections to different parts of the process which had ended in their conviction.

Challenges to the validity of the First Amendment

He attacked, firstly, the First Amendment of the Constitution Act itself (as this had defined "time of war" so as to include a war going on in which the State was not itself involved, the effectiveness of the emergency resolutions and the immunity of the emergency legislation obviously depended upon the amendment's validity). On this he made three points: (1) that it was not within the powers of amendment conferred on the Oireachtas (during the transitional three-year period) by Article 51; (2) that the President did not consult the Council of State before signing the Bill (with a view to a

[10] Emergency Powers (Amendment) Act 1940 (see below, pp. 866-7); Emergency Powers (Amendment) (No. 2) Act 1940 (see below, p. 650); Emergency Powers (Continuance) Act 1940; Emergency Powers (Continuance) Act 1941; Emergency Powers (Continuance and Amendment) Act 1942; Emergency Powers (Continuance) Act 1943; Emergency Powers (Continuance) Act 1944; Emergency Powers (Continuance and Amendment) Act 1945. The cover of Article 28.3.3 was also given to the General Elections (Emergency Provisions) Act 1943: see above, pp. 97, 168.

[11] When the last Act continuing the Emergency Powers Act 1939, expired in 1946, certain of the emergency powers were kept alive by being incorporated in a new measure, the Supplies and Services (Temporary Provisions) Act 1946, which however did not contain the emergency recital of Article 28.3.3. This Act was continued annually until 1958, when it was replaced by the Prices Act of that year, which is still in force.

[12] It is quite clear from Mr. de Valera's remarks in the Dáil during the passage of the Second Amendment of the Constitution Bill in 1941 that he then envisaged the period after the end of actual hostilities as being merely one of transition back to normal conditions (82 *Dáil Debates* 1203, 1886ff.). But see the replies given by Mr. de Valera as Taoiseach in 1947 (104 *Dáil Debates* 1-2); by Mr. Lemass as Taoiseach in 1960 (185 *Dáil Debates* 615-6) and 1964 (209 *Dáil Debates* 2-4); and by Mr. Lynch as Taoiseach in 1969 (242 Dáil *Debates* 1066-8) and 1971 (256 *Dáil Debates* 649) to questions about the continued state of emergency: there were always reasons for not bringing it to an end.

[13] See 292 *Dáil Debates* 2-260; 85 *Seanad Debates* 5-212 (31 August to 1 September 1976).

[14] See below, pp. 859-60.

[15] [1941] IR 68.

[16] [1942] IR 112; (1942) 76 ILTR 207.

[17] See below, p. 650.

referendum on it); and (3) that the Bill had been signed by the President "earlier than five days after the Bill had been presented to him, contrary... to Article 25.2.1".

In judgments notably terse, considering the nature of the case, both the High Court and the Supreme Court held against the prisoners on these points. On the first point, Gavan Duffy J in the High Court said the amendment was "clearly within the powers given to the Oireachtas within the first three years of the Constitution",[18] and the Supreme Court, *per* Sullivan CJ, said it was of opinion "that the meaning of this Article is too plain to admit of any ambiguity. It expressly authorises the Oireachtas to amend any provision of the Constitution save those contained in Articles 46 and 51". On the second point Gavan Duffy J said Article 51 imposed no duty on the President to consult the Council of State; the Supreme Court thought it "quite clear that the question as to whether the Council of State should be consulted was entirely a matter for the President in the exercise of his discretion". On the third point, Gavan Duffy J said:

> "[The objection] raised is that under Article 25...it is the duty of the President to wait five days before signing any Bill, that he did not wait five days before signing the Bill containing this proposal to amend the Constitution, and that this amendment is consequently invalid. But I think it quite clear that Article 25.2, dealing with the time-limit of five to seven days, does not apply to this constitutional amendment."

The Supreme Court dismissed the point even more briefly:

> "As regards Article 25.2.1, it is clearly intended to apply to Bills, other than Bills expressed to be Bills containing proposals for the amendment of the Constitution, and it has, therefore, no application to the Bill in question in this case."

It does not, however, seem that the prisoners' point was so clearly without substance.[19]

The second line of attack taken by the applicants' counsel also failed; this was essentially based on the form taken by the Emergency Powers Acts 1939 and 1940, which counsel alleged did not attract the protection of Article 28.3.3 because (1) the enacting parts of these statutes did not express them to be for the purposes set out in Article 28.3.3, and (2) these statutes did not recite the passage of the emergency resolutions by both Houses. These objections were rejected in both Courts; the recital of the Acts' purposes in their long titles was held to be a sufficient compliance, and the recital of the emergency resolutions was held to be unnecessary; the Supreme Court referred to the:

> "clear language of the Article, which, in the times and circumstances contemplated, makes it impossible to invoke other Articles of the Constitution to invalidate Acts passed by the Oireachtas and expressed to be for the purpose of securing the public safety and the preservation of the State within the terms of the Article."

Validity of Orders attacked

Lastly, several points were taken as to the validity of the Emergency Powers Orders (Nos. 41 and 41A) 1940, under which the applicants had been tried; the principal objection here was that they did not show jurisdiction on their face by stating the passage of the emergency resolutions or the Government's opinion that their provisions were nec-

[18] This formulation is incorrect. The period ran until the expiration of three years after the entry of the first President upon office, i.e. until 25 June 1941.

[19] See above, pp. 197-98. And see also p. 211 for another point which might have been taken against the First Amendment of the Constitution Act 1939.

essary or expedient for securing the public safety or the preservation of the State. The responses of the two Courts to this objection were not the same. Gavan Duffy J said:

> "I think the Statutory Orders do [show jurisdiction], whatever may be said against the form of the committal order, but, however this may be, in my opinion, the plain words of Article 28 make it impossible for this Court to invalidate either the committal order or Orders 41 and 41A on that ground."

The Supreme Court said:

> "It is sufficient to answer this argument to point out that the Orders in question are not Orders of an inferior court but are Orders made by the Government in express exercise of the powers conferred upon them by the said Acts."

In the later case, *The State (Walsh) v Lennon*[20] - applications on behalf of four prisoners for habeas corpus and for prohibition to prevent their trial by the military tribunal established under the Emergency Powers (Amendment) (No. 2) Act 1940 - most of the case was concerned with the extraordinary *ad hoc* procedure and rules of evidence specially provided for the purpose of this trial.[21] The applicants' counsel did, however, make another effort to reduce the impact of Article 28.3.3 by arguing that the phrase "nothing in this Constitution" must be given, not an unrestricted, but a "limited and defined meaning"; it could not mean the institutions actually established by the Constitution, "as that would lead to absurdity"; the phrase should be seen also as leaving intact, and cognisable by the courts, the rights of the people "over and above those conferred by the Constitution", such as the right to *habeas corpus*; this must be seen as not created, but only "affirmed" by the Constitution; if it were otherwise, and no right to habeas corpus existed separately from the Constitution, then the Supreme Court would have had to decide the appeal in *Burke's* case differently.[22] The High Court rejected this line of argument explicitly; the Supreme Court did not even advert to it in its judgment. The judgment of Gavan Duffy J in the High Court is however worth citing for his personal view of Article 28.3.3:

> "The function of the judiciary is to co-operate with the legislature and the executive in the government of the State for the people, and in the exercise of that function the judiciary may be called upon from time to time to pronounce a statute unconstitutional or to declare the act of an executive Minister illegal. But in time of war or armed rebellion the apprehension of judicial intervention may at some delicate moment hamper the legislative or the executive authority when Government needs all possible strength and freedom to steer the ship of State through the crisis, consequently the Constitution has placed in the hands of the Oireachtas, as law-giver, special authority to suspend judicial control over the other organs of government during any such emergency; that is the simple explanation of Article 28.3.3... a permanent provision, but available only in time of war or armed rebellion...
>
> I recognise, on the one hand, that an exceptional enactment, in derogation of the regular Constitution, ought not to be read as disturbing the national polity further than the language selected and the times in contemplation really require; on the other hand, an enactment expressly devised for use in a grave emergency is meant to become an efficient weapon, when the time comes for its use, and must not be so

[20] [1942] IR 112; (1942) 76 ILTR 207.

[21] See a note in 6 Journal of Criminal Law (1942) 206ff. The special Order made for the purposes of this trial (and, *inter alia*, making admissible unsigned and unsworn statements of absent persons) is reproduced in full in the reports of the case.

[22] This point was actually made by Johnston J in his dissenting judgment in *Burke's* case [1940] IR 136; (1940) 74 ILTR 36, 131.

blunted and contracted by a narrow construction as to fail in its purpose...The plain intention [of Article 28.3.3] is that the natural guardian of the citizen's constitutional guarantees, the High Court of Justice in this State, shall for the time being relinquish its guardianship...[Its] inescapable effect is to deny the protection of the High Court to the citizen, when these rights, or any of them, are invaded under the emergency law, or by, or under colour of, an executive act done in pursuance of that law, since we may not invalidate the one nor nullify the other."

A generation passed before Article 28.3.3 was again directly considered by a Court; and then somewhat different tones were heard from the Bench. When fresh emergency resolutions were passed by both Houses in 1976 and a new Emergency Powers Bill providing for seven days' detention without charge had been passed by both Houses under its cover, the President referred this Bill to the Supreme Court under Article 26: *In re Article 26 and the Emergency Powers Bill, 1976.*[23] Several new points came under discussion.

Emergency resolutions: can they be reviewed by the Courts?

First, the position of the emergency resolutions themselves was considered. It was clear, as the Court said, that they:

> "[were] not part of the Bill, although they are referred to in its long title and in section 3, and [were] not and could not be the subject of a reference to this Court under Article 26."

But could the Court, so to speak, "look behind them", and review the question whether the two Houses had been justified in passing them? (Such a proposition had never been looked at in the context of the 1939 resolutions passed at the outbreak of the Second World War, but it might be different in 1976, when the national emergency was said to arise "out of the armed conflict now taking place in Northern Ireland"). The Supreme Court let the 1976 resolutions pass, so to speak, but reserved its position in regard to reviewing future resolutions which might be based on a spurious "emergency":

> "The last matter to be considered is the question of the existence of the state of affairs necessary to permit the application of Article 28.3.3...These are the matters or statements of fact which are contained in the resolutions of the two Houses of the Oireachtas. Submissions were made as to the extent, if any, to which the Court could examine the correctness of these statements. It was submitted by the Attorney General that there is a presumption that the facts stated in the resolutions are correct. The Court accepts the existence of that presumption and the corollary that the presumption should be acted upon unless and until it is displaced. In this case it has not been displaced.
>
> The Attorney General submitted the general proposition that when the resolutions referred to in Article 28.3.3 have been passed, this Court has no jurisdiction to review the contents of them. When the consequences of this submission were pointed out to him he withdrew it, as he said it did not arise in this case. The Court expressly reserves for future consideration the question whether the Courts have jurisdiction to review such resolutions."[24]

[23] [1977] IR 159; (1977) 111 ILTR 29. See Morgan, "*The Emergency Powers Bill Reference I*" (1978) 13 Ir Jur (n.s.) 67; "*The Emergency Powers Bill Reference II*", (1979) 14 Ir Jur (n.s.) 253.

[24] Note that the European Court of Human Rights asserts a jurisdiction to review measures adopted pursuant to Article 15 of the European Convention on Human Rights which allows member states to derogate form Convention "in time of war or other public emergency threatening the life of the nation" - see *Brannigan v UK*, Series A, No.258B, 26 May 1993.

An emergency Bill can be referred to Supreme Court under the Article 26 procedure

Next, there was the question whether a Bill expressed in the terms envisaged by Article 28.3.3 could be the subject of an Article 26 reference at all; Bills of this kind were not among the categories excluded from reference by Article 26 itself, and so by inference must be capable of reference, but might it not defeat the object of Article 28.3.3 if ordinary constitutional criteria could be applied to the Bill before it had, by the President's signature, ripened into a "law"? (In this instance, the Attorney General had expressly admitted that the effect of the Bill, unless it were saved by the operation of Article 28.3.3, would be unconstitutional). The Supreme Court's answer was, essentially, that the procedural carapace of the Bill could be scrutinised on an Article 26 reference, but not its substantive content:

> "When a Bill is validly referred to the Court under Article 26 the test of its repugnancy or invalidity is what its force and effect will be if and when it becomes law. Thus in regard to a Bill which is to take effect as law under Article 28.3.3, if it is shown to the Court that the preliminary and procedural requirements for the passing of the Bill by both Houses of the Oireachtas have been complied with, it is *ipso facto,* because of the exemption granted by Article 28.3.3, incapable of being struck down on the ground of repugnancy to the Constitution or to any provision thereof."[25]

Proper mode of entitling an emergency Bill

A further point raised by counsel assigned against the Bill concerned its long title. This described the measure as "An Act for the purpose of securing the public safety and the preservation of the State in time of an armed conflict in respect of which each of the Houses of the Oireachtas has adopted a resolution on the first day of September, 1976, pursuant to s 3 sub-s (3) of Article 28 of the Constitution"; and it was argued that such a formulation, which avoided using the expression "time of war", failed to attract the protection contemplated by Article 28.3.3. In the decision of this question an important distinction emerged: between, on the one hand, a time of (actual) war or armed rebellion involving the State (in which laws expressed as contemplated by the first sentence of Article 28.3.3 would have the sub-section's protection without any necessity for resolutions of both Houses); and, on the other hand, a time of armed conflict in which the State itself is not involved but which nevertheless creates for it a condition of emergency (in which the protection of Article 28.3.3 would be available only if both Houses had so resolved). The Supreme Court said:

> "The argument is that even though it is the existence of an armed conflict that is relied on, nonetheless the expression "time of war" must be used because the latter includes the former. As against this the Attorney General has submitted that in the sub-section, particularly as amended by the Second Amendment of the Constitution, it is indicated that a time of war, an armed rebellion, and an armed conflict in which the State is not a participant are to be regarded as separate and distinct events. He relies on the fact that the expression "termination of any war, or of any such armed conflict as aforesaid, or of an armed rebellion", occurs in the latter portion of the subsection and is substantially repeated in the words "by such war, armed conflict or armed rebellion has ceased to exist" which follow a line or two later. He furthermore pointed out that the sub-section draws other distinctions between the three

[25] For criticism of this view, see *Morgan, loc.cit.* at 76-82.

types of categories mentioned. Resolutions of both Houses of the Oireachtas are necessary to declare that a national emergency exists which affects the vital interests of the State when the occasion is one of an armed conflict in which the State is not a participant and such armed conflict is actually taking place. This is to be contrasted with what may be done in "time of war or armed rebellion", when such resolutions are not required. The existence of a "time of war or armed rebellion" is sufficient to bring into operation any law which has been enacted by the Oireachtas pursuant to that sub-section and which is expressed to be for the purpose of securing the public safety and the preservation of the State. If such a law had been enacted before the occurrence of such event, it is brought into operation by the occurrence of that event.

The Attorney General submitted that the inclusion in "time of war" or "armed conflict" indicates the type of legislation which may be enacted under the sub-section. He submitted that different formalities are required for the enactment of legislation for an armed conflict in which the State is not a participant, as distinct from legislation for a time of war or armed rebellion. In the view of this Court this submission is well founded. The Court is satisfied that the purpose of the Bill, as expressed by reference to a time of an armed conflict instead of by reference to a time of war, complies with the requirements of Article 28.3.3, while at the same time restricting the area of operation of the Bill, in that the Bill would not be applicable to a "time of war or armed rebellion", as distinct from "armed conflict", because it is not expressed to be for that purpose."[26]

An emergency Act leaves general constitutional rights intact

It may, lastly, be mentioned that the Court went out of its way to limit the effect of emergency legislation, taking up a posture of jealousy towards it quite different from the perhaps over-co-operative stance of the Courts in the *McGrath and Harte* and *Walsh* decisions 35 years earlier. The Court said:

"It is important to point out that when a law is saved from invalidity by Article 28.3.3, the prohibition against invoking the Constitution in reference to it is only if the invocation is for the purpose of invalidating it. For every other purpose the Constitution may be invoked. Thus, a person detained under s 2 of the Bill may not only question the legality of his detention if there has been non-compliance with the express requirements of s 2, but may also rely on provisions of the Constitution for the purpose of construing that section and of testing the legality of what has been done in purported operation of it. A statutory provision of this nature which makes such inroads upon the liberty of the person must be strictly construed. Any arrest sought to be justified by the section must be in strict conformity with it. No such arrest may be justified by importing into the section incidents or characteristics of an arrest which are not expressly or by necessary implication authorised by the section. While it is not necessary to embark upon an exploration of all the incidents or characteristics which may not accompany the arrest and custody of a person under that section, it is nevertheless desirable, in view of the submissions made to the Court, to state that the section is not to be read as an abnegation of the arrested person's rights, constitutional or otherwise, in respect of matters such as the right of communication, the right to have legal and medical assistance, and the right of

[26] An early but important case on the necessity for the proper making and recital of a declaration required by the Constitution is *R. (O'Brien) v Military Governor, North Dublin Union* [1924] 1 IR 32.

access to the Courts. If the section were used in breach of such rights the High Court might grant an order for release under the provisions for *habeas corpus* contained in the Constitution. It is not necessary for the Court to attempt to give an exhaustive list of the matters which would render a detention under the section illegal or unconstitutional."[27]

Article 28.3.3 as background

Article 28.3.3 played a marginal role in four cases in which it itself was not in issue. In *The State (Burke) v Lennon*[28] Gavan Duffy J used it as part of the background against which he was considering the internment provisions of Part VI of the Offences Against the State Act 1939:

> "The need to provide for times of emergency was clearly foreseen and the emergencies in contemplation were defined. Besides making the declaration of war subject to the assent of Dáil Éireann, the Constitution...facilitates the enactment of a Bill declared by the Government to be urgent and immediately necessary to preserve public peace and security or by reason of a public emergency (Article 24), sanctions the establishment of special Courts...where the ordinary Courts are inadequate (Article 38), and declares that a law made expressly to secure the public safety and the preservation of the State in time of war or armed rebellion is not to be invalidated by any provision of the Constitution (Article 28); see now as to "time of war" the First Amendment (1939). There is no provision enabling the Oireachtas or the Government to disregard the Constitution in any emergency short of war or armed rebellion. And the Constitution contains no express provision for any law endowing the Executive with powers of internment without trial."

In *In re Ó Láighléis*[29] the applicant's counsel urged that the only conditions which could justify the Government in derogating from its obligations under the European Convention on Human Rights in the manner envisaged by Article 15 of the Convention, i.e. in "time of war or other public emergency threatening the life of the nation", were, in the Irish context, the conditions of Article 28.3.3 which made possible a derogation from Constitutional rights, i.e. a "time of war or armed rebellion" or a "national emergency...affecting the vital interests of the State". The Supreme Court thought it unnecessary to explore this question. The Court itself, however, instanced Article 28.3.3 later in its judgment as illustrating the proposition that:

> "When a statute provides that certain consequences follow if and when an act is done, power to do that act is given...Article 28[.3.3] does not provide that each House of the Oireachtas may pass the resolution referred to in the Article, but merely enacts that certain consequences shall follow when they do so. No one can doubt that the Houses of the Oireachtas are given power to bring the provisions of the Article into effect by passing the resolutions."

In *Ryan v Ireland*[30] the Supreme Court considered that Article 28.3.3 precluded, by implication, the operation of any common law doctrine which would prevent a member of the Defence Forces from suing the State in respect of injuries suffered while on active service. In the instant case the injuries were sustained while the plaintiff was serving with the United Nations Interim Force in Lebanon, so that considerations of defence of the State could not arise in any event. However the Supreme Court went further, holding

[27] Applied in *The State (Hoey) v Garvey* [1978] IR 1. For features of an imprisonment which can vitiate it constitutionally, see below, pp. 818-828.

[28] [1940] IR 136; (1940) 74 ILTR 36, 131.

[29] [1960] IR 93; (1961) 95 ILTR 92.

[30] [1989] IR 177; [1989] ILRM 544.

that, at common law, the State enjoyed no immunity from suit by a serving soldier in respect of injuries sustained during operations consisting of armed conflict or hostilities. Finlay CJ, with whom the other members of the Court agreed, said:

> "It is impossible, having regard to [Article 28.3.3], to accept the application of a common law doctrine arising from the necessity to ensure the safety of the State during a period of war or armed rebellion, which has the effect of abrogating constitutional rights."

As legislation equally cannot abrogate constitutional rights, this would appear to suggest that any statutory provision for such immunity would require the protection of Article 28.3.3.

The possibility that an inference of unconstitutionality might arise in relation to a provision in ordinary legislation from the fact that the authorities deemed it necessary to enact a similar provision under cover of Article 28.3.3 was considered by the Supreme Court in *People v Quilligan (No.3)*.[31] Here the appellants challenged the validity of s 30 of the Offences Against the State Act 1939, pursuant to which they had been detained for 48 hours for questioning. In support of their arguments, they pointed to the fact that the Emergency Powers Act 1976, which authorised detention for up to 7 days, had been enacted pursuant to Article 28.3.3. The Supreme Court, however, rejected any comparison between the two statutory provisions:

> "The Bill of 1976 specifically referred in its title to the resolution adopted by each House of the Oireachtas on the 1st September 1976, pursuant to [Article 28.3.3]. As such, it necessarily fell to be considered by this Court...having regard to the provisions of that Article of the Constitution. From that fact, the Court is not satisfied that any inference can be drawn as to the constitutional validity of a section empowering detention on suspicion of the commission of an offence for a lesser period than the seven days, namely, for twenty-four, extendable to forty-eight, hours."

In this instance, the two provisions were not identical. In the case of identical or very similar provisions, however, the use of Article 28.3.3 to protect the one must surely cast some shadow over the validity of the other, perhaps even to the point of rebutting the presumption of constitutionality in appropriate cases.

Statutory provisions on "national emergency" not necessarily associated with war or armed rebellion

As Article 28.3.3 contains the Constitution's only reference to a national emergency,[32] it seems appropriate to mention here a statutory provision relating to this contingency but not dependent on the Constitution or on the existence of a state of war or rebellion. This is the Protection of the Community (Special Powers) Act 1926, which provides by s 1(1) that:

> If at any time the [Government] is of opinion that a national emergency has arisen of such character that it is expedient in the public interest that extraordinary measures should be taken to ensure the due supply and distribution of the essentials of life to the community, the Government may by proclamation declare that a state of national emergency exists.

Section 1(3) provides for the early summoning of the Oireachtas if not in regular session

[31] [1993] 2 IR 305.

[32] There is a reference in Article 24.1, in the context of abridging the Seanad's time for considering a Bill, to a "public emergency, whether domestic or international", which must include "national emergency" in the sense of Article 28.3.3.

at the time of the making of the proclamation. Section 3 empowers the Government, during the period when the proclamation is in force, to make regulations, which are to have the same effect as if enacted in the Act for a variety of purposes representing different aspects of the Act's principal purpose, including the prevention of stockpiling, price control, and the:

> conferring on such persons (whether in the service or not in the service of the State) as the Government shall think proper such powers and authorities for the carrying out and enforcement of the regulations as the Government shall think proper.

No proclamation of national emergency has ever been made under this Act nor has it been litigated, so that the question of its consistency with the Constitution has not arisen.

There exists also a power - a vestige of the wartime emergency powers - for the Government to declare "an emergency affecting the supply" of a particular commodity "whenever and so often as the Government are of opinion that abnormal circumstances prevail or are likely to prevail in relation to [its] supply": s 15(1) of the Prices Act 1958. The consequence of a declaration under this section is that the Minister for Enterprise and Employment may, under s 16, fix the maximum selling price of the commodity or of any service affecting its supply or distribution. So far, however, no such declaration of a commodity emergency has ever been made.

Emergency control of wireless telegraphy

Section 10 of the Wireless Telegraphy Act 1926,[33] provides for Government control of wireless telegraphy - including principally the use of apparatus - when the Government is of opinion, and gives notice to this effect, "that a national emergency has arisen of such character that it is expedient in the public interest that the [Government] should have full control over the sending and receiving of messages, signals and other communications by means of wireless telegraphy". This provision has not so far been used.

Residual power of executive compulsion in national emergency?

A more general, and a more difficult question of theory which may be mentioned briefly by way of conclusion to the theme of national emergency is the State's rights in regard to taking *ad hoc* action, not deriving from statutory power, in some sudden or unusual contingency, local or countrywide. To what extent does the State retain a residual *coercitio*, or general power of executive compulsion, over and above what the Constitution and statute law expressly justify? The case of actual invasion is dealt with by Article 28.3.2; but other emergencies can be imagined which might require executive reaction going beyond the spheres of commodity supply and control of wireless communications, and also beyond the specialised powers of the police in regard to traffic control.[34] Common sense suggests that in the context of a natural disaster, epidemic, escape of wild animals or dangerous prisoners etc. the police, or informal auxiliaries, should not be faulted for evacuating streets, commandeering vehicles, or possibly in some cases placing persons under restraint of some kind; one could argue that there is a general right and duty in any government, by common law, to protect its people as well as its own authority. But where the frontiers of this licence might be drawn - at what point would the authorities be regarded as having abrogated constitutional rights - and what conditions would justify its exercise, is hard to say. The simplest framework in which to

[33] This section was extended by s 20(3) of the Broadcasting Authority (Amendment) Act 1976, to apply to cable systems used for transmitting visual images and/or sound.
[34] Part VIII of the Road Traffic Act 1961.

envisage the problem is that in which the State is in the defendant posture at the suit of someone aggrieved at being subjected to arbitrary compulsion, and in which the State raises the plea of necessity. Whether this is a good defence, and what would distinguish it from the illegal pretence of "act of State", are matters which have never been considered by an Irish court.[35] In *Ryan v Ireland*[36] however, the Supreme Court took the view that Article 28.3.3 precluded, by implication, the operation of common law doctrines arising from the necessity to ensure the safety of the State during a period of war or armed rebellion and which have the effect of abrogating constitutional rights. While this does not directly cover the point at issue - the existence and extent of the State's powers to act in some sudden or unusual contingency not envisaged in Article 28.3.3 - it might indicate a reluctance on the part of the judiciary to accept that the State has residual coercive powers over and beyond those provided for by constitutional and statute law.

[35] It would, for instance, be interesting to have a judicial view on the legal dimensions of the reported instruction given to the Air Corps pilots of aircraft escorting Pope John Paul II when arriving on his Irish visit at the end of September, 1979, to shoot down unauthorised aircraft approaching the Pope's plane: see *The Irish Times,* 27 September 1979. Would such intruders not have to manifest a criminal intention before such drastic use of force could be justified? And in general there is no authoritative judicial statement on the use of force by the police etc. (e.g. in pursuing fugitives, enforcing road-blocks and so on); such a statement is available only on the question of the degree of force justifiable in dispersing unlawful assemblies, below, pp. 967-8. As to this area of problems generally, see F. R. Brookfield, *Some Aspects of the Necessity Principle in Constitutional Law* (Ph.D. thesis, Oxford, 1972); and, in connection with interference with property, E. D. Brown, "*Eminent Domain in Anglo-American Law*", 18 Current Legal Problems (1965) 169. See also the Irish case of *Pedlar v Johnstone* [1920] 2 IR 450 (on the seizure by the Crown of an alien's property), in which O'Connor LJ said: "Now, it is conceded, and of course it is quite clear, that if the plaintiff in this action were a British subject, the defence of 'act of State' could not prevail....The reason is clear. The King can do no wrong. An act which is wrongful cannot, therefore, be an act which is authorised by him: or, to put it in another way, a wrongful act can never be an act of State."

[36] [1989] IR 177; [1989] ILRM 544.

Article 28.4

RESPONSIBILITY OF GOVERNMENT TO DÁIL

4. **1° The Government shall be responsible to Dáil Éireann.**
2° The Government shall meet and act as a collective authority, and shall be collectively responsible for the Departments of State administered by the members of the Government.
3° The Government shall prepare Estimates of the Receipts and Estimates of the Expenditure of the State for each financial year, and shall present them to Dáil Éireann for consideration.

4. **1° Tá an Rialtas freagrach do Dháil Éireann.**
2° I gcomhúdarás a thiocfaidh an Rialtas le chéile agus a ghníomhóid, agus táid go léir le chéile freagrach sna Ranna Stáit a riartar ag comhaltaí an Rialtais.
3° Ní foláir don Rialtas Meastacháin ar Fháltas an Stáit agus Meastacháin ar Chaitheamh Airgid an Stáit a ullmhú i gcomhair gach bliana airgeadais, agus iad a chur os comhair Dháil Éireann chun a mbreithnithe.

1922 provision

These provisions reproduce the substance of Article 54 of the 1922 Constitution.[1]

Responsibility to Dáil

The political theories to which the first two sub-sections give expression first[2] came under judicial notice in the case of *Boland v An Taoiseach*:[3] here Murnaghan J in the High Court, declining to give the plaintiff an injunction to restrain the Government from giving effect to the Sunningdale agreement, said:

> "By reason of what O'Byrne J referred to in *Buckley v Attorney General*[4] as "that respect which one great organ of State owes to another", this Court must assume, until it is clearly established to the contrary, that any declaration of policy by the Government is within the constitutional powers conferred on the Government. I must further hold that by virtue of Article 28.4.1... the Government is primarily responsible to Dáil Éireann for such a declaration of policy. In my opinion, it would not be consonant with what has been described as the "checks and balances" contained in the Constitution, in relation to the three organs of State mentioned in Artiele 6.1... that this Court should purport to usurp the functions of Dáil Éireann..."

[1] Section 5 of the Ministers and Secretaries Act 1924, provided that nothing in the Act should derogate from the collective responsibility of the Executive Council - notwithstanding that [its] members may be appointed individually to be Ministers, heads of particular Departments of State.

[2] Prior to the adoption of the present Constitution, an attempt had been made, partly in reliance on the corresponding provisions of the 1922 Constitution, to fix the then Government (sued as the President and other members of the Executive Council) with liability to pay a certain sum in compensation for the destruction of property - *Leen v President of Executive Council* [1928] IR 408, 594; (1929) 63 ILTR 24. Fitzgibbon J said in the Supreme Court:

> "As to the allegation... founded upon Article 54... it is unnecessary to do more than read the Article itself in order to see that the "collective responsibility" of the Executive Council therein provided for, is a responsibility to Dáil Éireann alone, and has no reference whatever to civil liability."

[3] [1974] IR 338; (1975) 109 ILTR 13.

[4] [1950] IR 67.

Griffin J in the Supreme Court also adverted to the Government being by the Constitution "expressly made responsible to Dáil Éireann"; in *Byrne v Ireland*[5] this was noted also by Walsh J.

Collective responsibility and Cabinet confidentiality

The issue of the confidentiality of information belonging or pertaining to the Government has come before the courts twice in recent years. In *Attorney General for England and Wales v Brandon Book Publishers Ltd.*[6] Carroll J drew a distinction between the Government and a private citizen for the purposes of the protection of confidential information, citing with approval the following passage from the judgment of Mason J in *Commonwealth of Australia v John Fairfax and Sons Ltd.*:[7]

> "The equitable principle has been fashioned to protect the personal private and proprietary rights of the citizen, not to protect the very different interests of the executive Government. It acts...not according to standards of private interest, but in the public interest...It may be a sufficient detriment to the citizen that disclosure of information relating to his affairs will expose his actions to public discussion and criticism. But it can scarcely be a relevant detriment to the Government that publication of material concerning its actions will merely expose it to public discussion and criticism. It is unacceptable in our democratic society that there should be a restraint on the publication of information relating to Government when the only vice of that information is that it enables the public to discuss, review and criticise Government action. Accordingly the Court will determine the Government's claim to confidentiality by reference to the public interest. Unless disclosure is likely to injure the public interest, it will not be protected."

Although the plaintiff here was representing a foreign government, Carroll J indicated that the same principles would apply if the Government of Ireland was seeking to restrain the publication of material. She went on to say that "there is no absolute confidentiality where the parties are a Government and a private individual."

However, where the relevant information pertains to discussions in Government, these comments have to be read in the light of the decision in *Attorney General v Hamilton (No.1)*[8] wherein a majority of the Supreme Court, relying on the principle of collective responsibility in Article 28.4.2, concluded that such discussions were confidential and consequently could not be investigated by the Houses of the Oireachtas or their agents. This issue arose out of the operation of the tribunal of inquiry, consisting of the President of the High Court, which was established by resolution of both Dáil and Seanad Éireann and charged with investigating allegations of illegal activities, fraud and malpractice in the beef processing industry. The allegations in question had included complaints that the statutory Export Credit Insurance Scheme had been abused in the manner in which insurance cover had been allocated in respect of beef exports to Iraq in the period from 1987-1988. It was against this background that the Tribunal had investigated events which had allegedly taken place on 21 October 1988. According to an official note prepared by the relevant departmental officials,[9] the Minister for Industry and Commerce had said at a meeting with his officials on that date that the question of the allocation of export credit insurance for Iraq had been discussed by the Government at its meeting on 8 June 1988 and that certain decisions confining the allocation of this

[5] [1972] IR 241.
[6] [1986] IR 597; [1987] ILRM 135.
[7] 149 CLR 39.
[8] [1993] 2 IR 250; [1993] ILRM 81.
[9] The note is scheduled to the judgment of McCarthy J.

insurance to two named companies had been taken at this meeting. The Minister was said to have been surprised to note that these decisions had not been formally recorded.

This uncertainty as to what precisely the Government had in fact decided at its meeting of 8 June 1988, was among the factual matters which the Tribunal was understandably anxious to resolve. In the course of its investigations, a question was put to a former Government minister, Mr. Ray Burke, T.D., concerning the detail of discussions which took place at the Government meetings of 8 June 1988 whereupon the competence of the tribunal to pursue this line of questioning was challenged by the Attorney General in the High Court. Following the dismissal by O'Hanlon J of the Attorney General's application for declarations that the tribunal was not legally entitled to inquire into discussions occurring during the course of a Government meeting, the case was appealed to the Supreme Court which, by a narrow majority, allowed the appeal. According to the majority - Finlay CJ, Hederman and O'Flaherty JJ - while the Government is responsible to Dáil Éireann, this was only in respect of decisions actually taken, not to the process leading up to such decisions and consequently it was not open to the Tribunal of Inquiry to inquire into the content and details of Government discussions. It is undoubtedly true that the majority judgments have an attractive symmetry to them. One can understand the approach of O'Flaherty J, who reasoned that as the Tribunal was simply an agent of the House of the Oireachtas, it could have no greater powers *vis-a-vis* the Executive than each House would have had. Likewise, it is easy to understand the reasoning of both Finlay CJ and Hederman J to the effect that absolute confidentiality is a necessary concomitant of the collective responsibility provisions of Article 28.4.2. To that extent, therefore, there is more to be said in justification of absolute confidentiality than a casual perusal of constitutional first principles might have suggested. And yet the majority reasoning ultimately fails to convince, proceeding as it does on largely artificial premises with regard to the separation of powers while omitting to take account of the anomalies which these judgments actually produce.

A number of different grounds were advanced by the members of the majority in support of their conclusions. First it was contended that confidentiality of Government discussions was a necessary corollary of the principle of collective responsibility. According to Hederman J:

> "It is clear from the very nature of the collective responsibility of the Government that discussions among its members at their formal meetings must be confidential otherwise its decisions are liable to be fatally weakened by disclosure of dissenting views...
>
> ... If it were permissible to compel in any circumstances the disclosure of the content of discussions which take place at Government meetings the Executive role of the Government as envisaged by the Constitution would be undermined perhaps even de-stabilised."

This essential premise of the majority may be contrasted with earlier authority which has consistently assumed that responsible Ministers and civil servants will not be deterred by the prospect that their confidential deliberations may ultimately be released by discovery in the course of civil litigation. The remarks of Blayney J in *PMPS Ltd v PMPA Insurance plc*[10] may be regarded as representative of this judicial view. Here the Registrar of Friendly Societies had objected to the production of a report which he had prepared in the course of the discharge of his statutory investigations. The Registrar contended that disclosure of this report would be contrary to the public interest in that the "efficiency of his office would be hampered" if those with whom he spoke "knew that they might have to answer for statements or opinions offered." Blayney J observed that:

> "The Registrar is not making the case that the contents of the memorandum are such that their disclosure would be contrary to the public interest. His objection is based on how he believes his statutory function would be affected."

(It may be noted that a similar attitude was adopted by the Supreme Court majority in the present case, since it was not contended that the revelation of the nature of the discussions at the Government meeting of 8th June 1988 would in_itself be contrary to the public interest.[11] Rather, the majority contended that the disclosure of such discussions would affect the future functioning of Government.) But in *PMPA* Blayney J rejected this argument in the context of the civil service, since he could not accept that "responsible civil servants would be any less likely to speak freely with the Registrar if this memorandum was disclosed." Indeed, in *Ambiorix Ltd v Minister for the Environment,*[12] an affidavit filed on behalf of the Taoiseach and the Ministers concerned averred that the "disclosure of [the] documents would tend to hinder the free communication necessary for Government and the running of the public service." The fact that this argument was rejected in *Ambiorix* again contrasts starkly with the essential premise underlying the absolute confidentiality rule.

While the principal purpose of the rule of collective responsibility is to protect the stability of the Government, and while, accordingly, this undoubtedly justifies a principle of confidentiality of Government discussions, it is submitted that it does not necessarily follow that such principle must be absolute. A more limited principle, rooted in the objective of maintaining Government stability, would be perfectly consistent with the rule of collective responsibility and, at the same time, could avoid some of the alarming consequences of an absolutist position.[13]

The doctrine of separation of powers was also invoked to justify the rule of confidentiality though the connection, certainly with a principle of absolute confidentiality, is hardly self-evident. Indeed Finlay CJ simply asserted, without more, that the development of the doctrine of separation of powers justified the development of the claimed confidentiality for Government discussions. The other members of the majority appear to base their reasoning on this point on a distinction between the actual decisions of the Government, for which it is collectively responsible to the Dáil pursuant to Article

[10] [1990] 1 IR 284.

[11] As McCarthy J in his dissenting judgment observed: "We are not dealing [in this instance] with pre-budget discussion or the nomination of individuals for appointments to high office [nor are] we dealing with diplomatic relations or military security..."

[12] [1992] 1 IR 277; [1992] ILRM 209.

[13] See below, pp. 256-7. Note that this was an approach which was taken by the Australian High Court in *Commonwealth v Northern Land Council* (1993) 67 Aust LJ 405 where Mason CJ said that:

> "it is only in a case where there are quite exceptional circumstances which give rise to a significant likelihood that the public interest in the proper administration of justice outweighs the very high public interest in the confidentiality of documents recording Cabinet deliberations that it will be necessary or appropriate to order production of the documents to the courts."

The Chief Justice had also said earlier:

> "Indeed, we doubt whether the disclosure of the records of Cabinet deliberations upon matters which remain current or controversial would ever be warranted in civil proceedings. The public interest in avoiding serious damage to the proper working of Government at the highest level must prevail over the interests of a litigant seeking to vindicate private rights."

28.4.1, and the manner by which such decisions are arrived at, where no such responsibility exists. However, this distinction is difficult to defend. In the instant case, the purpose of the questioning of Mr. Burke was to ascertain precisely *what* decision, if any, had been made by the Government. If the Dáil is denied the possibility of ascertaining what decisions have been made by the Government, it is difficult to see how the principle of accountability in Article 28.4.1 can be properly implemented.[14]

It is, moreover, by no means clear that the present case involved the exercise of the executive power of Government. To judge by the decision in *Murphy v Dublin Corporation*[15] it would seem that as far as discharge of the Export Credit Insurance Scheme was concerned the Minister for Industry and Commerce was merely a *persona designata* and that his functions could just as easily have been delegated to, or performed by, another entity.[16] Were it not, therefore, for the essentially fortuitous fact that the Minister had apparently elected to bring this matter before the Government there could have been no question of any doctrine of cabinet confidentiality contained in Article 28.4 precluding and inquiry into the circumstances leading up to any ministerial decision. And if the decision in question did not involve the exercise of executive powers, how can there be any justification for the reliance on Article 28.4?

This problem is also illustrated by *Lang v Government of Ireland*,[17] a case where a prison officer claimed that his dismissal by the Government pursuant to s 5 of the Civil Service Regulation Act 1956 had been in breach of natural justice. O'Hanlon J found against him on the facts, but observed that, in the light of the *Cabinet Confidentiality* case, a memorandum for Government concerning the applicant's case was now "protected and, perhaps, even precluded" from discovery. But even here it is questionable whether the Government was exercising the executive power of the State, since if these powers of dismissal had been vested in an individual Minister, there could be no question of an Article 28.4 claim of privilege.[18]

Two members of the majority - Finlay CJ and O'Flaherty J - also pointed to what they perceived as a potential anomaly involving the immunity conferred on individual members of the Oireachtas by Article 15.13, if Government discussions were not regarded as confidential. According to the Chief Justice:

> "It would be a striking constitutional anomaly if any individual member of either House of the Oireachtas would enjoy an absolute immunity from suit in the Courts

[14] Thus Egan J, dissenting, was prepared to accept that the Tribunal could hear evidence of Government deliberations but only for the specific purpose of finding out what decision had been arrived at.

[15] [1972] IR 215.

[16] As indeed they were. The evidence before the Tribunal of Inquiry demonstrated that the Scheme had been largely administered by a private insurance company as agents for the Minister.

[17] High Court, 7 July 1993.

[18] Note that in *Howard v Commissioners of Public Works* [1993] ILRM 665 O'Flaherty J (in a dissenting judgment) justified his view that the State was not bound by the operation of the Planning Acts by saying that:

> "The Minister for Local Government (now Environment) could hardly have been intended to hear appeals from his fellow Ministers. That fits ill with the idea of collective cabinet responsibility that is enshrined in the Constitution."

In other words, despite the fact that the Supreme Court had previously ruled that the Minister for Local Government was not discharging the executive power of the State in discharging appellate functions under the Planning Acts (see *Geraghty v Minister for Local Government* [1975] IR 300) there is, perhaps, a hint here that Article 28 may have some bearing on the discharge of statutory functions by a ministerial *persona designata.*

for any statement made by him in the House under any circumstances whether relevant or not and even if motivated by malice, whereas a Minister of the Government holding high office would in respect of a statement made in discussion at a Government meeting be answerable to the Courts and, if it were defamatory, would be obliged to rely on the doctrine of qualified privilege and a capacity to satisfy a jury of the absence of malice on his part."

Two points may be made here. First, as both McCarthy and Egan JJ point out, utterances in the Houses of the Oireachtas are normally made in public, so that Article 15.13 is relevant to the law of defamation only, and not to any legal requirement of confidentiality. Second, an obvious distinction between these two situations is that the immunity conferred on members of the Oireachtas is expressly provided for in the Constitution, while the principle of Government confidentiality is not. This latter principle apparently rests in part on the hitherto latent power of the Courts to infer constitutional principles in order to avoid anomalies and to enhance the efficacy of the Constitution as an instrument for the ordering of society and the governing of the nation.

One difficulty with the majority position is the fact that the Oireachtas saw fit to amend the Constitution to prohibit the disclosure of dissenting opinions of the Supreme Court in certain situations[19] but made no comparable provision relating to the Government, giving rise to the argument expressed so pithily by McCarthy J - "if it's not there, it isn't so."[20] That this may also have been the understanding of the Oireachtas can be seen from the provisions of s 71(1)(*b*) of the Ombudsman Act 1980, which provides that the Ombudsman could not have access to information or documents relating to "decisions and proceedings of the Government or of any of its committees." Finlay CJ alone addressed this argument, relying in part on the fact that the relevant constitutional amendments were enacted pursuant to Article 51 in response to a perceived danger to the authority of decisions of the Supreme Court from the formula of words used by Sullivan CJ in introducing the decision of the Court in *In re Article 26 and the Offences Against the State (Amendment) Bill 1940.*[21] The Chief Justice also claimed that, in any event, no inconsistency necessarily arose by implying a principle of Government confidentiality because the true comparison was between disclosure of government discussions and disclosure of details of judicial functions leading to the delivery of judgments which is so obviously unconstitutional that no express constitutional prohibition on the disclosure of such activity is needed.[22]

Quite apart from these difficulties with the reasoning of the majority, the precise ambit of their decision is not entirely clear. In the first place, the Court did not have to concern itself with its own powers to inquire into Government discussions. In *Murphy v Dublin Corporation*[23] Kenny J said that a claim of privilege could successfully be raised in legal proceedings in respect of the minutes of Government meetings[24] but Finlay CJ correctly classified this remark as being *obiter* and then expressly reserved the question of whether government confidentiality can prevail over the exercise of the judicial power. However, it may prove quite difficult to distinguish between the Oireachtas and the

[19] Articles 26.2.2 and 34.4.5.

[20] He continued, in characteristic fashion, "We are asked to assume that the authors of the Constitution, finding an unacceptable freedom to express unattributed dissent, secured the lock on this Court but thought it already fitted into the door of the Cabinet room where the Government met as a collective authority."

[21] [1940] IR 470.

[22] Nor did he believe that recognition of the confidentiality of Government discussions was inconsistent with the power of the Dáil to dismiss the Government.

[23] [1972] IR 215; (1973) 107 ILTR 65.

[24] Walsh J disagreed with this position in the Supreme Court.

courts on this matter - if, as is clear from *Murphy* and *Ambiorix Ltd. v Minister for the Environment,*[25] a court may reject a claim of privilege advanced by a member of the Government, should not the same rules apply where "the people, through their elected representatives, have established a tribunal of inquiry without imposing any express restriction on the scope of that inquiry in finding out the truth surrounding the matters mentioned in the resolution of both Houses"?[26] Second, while the majority sought to confine the ambit of the claim of confidentiality to Government *discussions*, the suggested distinction between discussions and documents may not be possible to sustain in the long term,[27] thus bringing the decision into possible conflict with *Murphy* and *Ambiorix* .

The very nature of the principle of confidentiality is unclear - at one point, Finlay CJ refers to the claim for confidentiality as:

> "a constitutional right which...goes to the fundamental machinery of government and is, therefore, not capable of being waived by any individual member of a government, nor...are the details and contents of discussions at meetings of the Government capable of being made public, for the purpose of this Inquiry, by a decision of any succeeding Government."

O'Flaherty and McCarthy JJ, on the other hand, appear to regard the principle as an obligation imposed on the Government. The practical significance of this debate arises in relation to whether the principle of confidentiality can be waived and if so, by whom. If the claim to confidentiality could be classified as a right vested in individual ministers, then waiver could be effected by an individual member of Government. Whatever else, however, this possibility is clearly precluded by the decision in the instant case - the former Minister in question, Mr. Ray Burke, appeared to be willing to answer questions put to him concerning Government discussions - but was prevented from doing so by the claim of privilege advanced by the Attorney General. Thus it would appear that the principle of confidentiality is a duty imposed on individual ministers, rather than a right vested in them. The question then arises as to whom the duty is owed or, conversely, in whom is the right of confidentiality vested? There would appear to be two possibilities here - the duty may be owed to the Government as a collective entity or it may be owed to the People as the sovereign power. If it is the former, then presumably the Government acting, as it must do, as a collective authority could waive the claim to confidentiality. Such a possibility seems to be ruled out by the remarks of the Chief Justice. In addition, McCarthy J considered that it was a necessary corollary of the argument for the Attorney General that an attempt by the Government to waive the claim of privilege would amount to a breach of the Constitution while O'Flaherty J spoke of the claim as an aspect of the general obligation to observe the Constitution which particularly devolves on those who hold government office. Of particular significance in this context is the fact that the Attorney General acted in this case on his own behalf, and not on behalf of the Government. This supports the view that the right of confidentiality is not vested exclusively in the Government and, consequently, cannot be waived by it. Thus we are left with the conclusion that the duty of confidentiality is one owed to the People as the sovereign power, with the implication that this duty may be waived only by constitutional referendum.

[25] [1992] 1 IR 277; [1992] ILRM 209.

[26] *Per* McCarthy J.

[27] Especially if the documents record discussions at Government meetings. Note that in *Lang v Government of Ireland*, High Court, 7 July 1993, O'Hanlon J held that a formal memorandum for Government was now protected "and, perhaps, even precluded" from disclosure in the light of the *Cabinet Confidentiality* case.

Much emphasis was also laid on the fact that the Tribunal was not discharging judicial powers and that it was simply an instrumentality of the Oireachtas, as if this characterisation should of itself greatly affect the outcome of the proceedings. In addition, there was a clear hint that the result might have been otherwise had the Tribunal been exercising such judicial powers.[28] It is hard to see why the characterisation of the powers of the Tribunal as legislative should make such a difference in this context. Once it is admitted - as it has been[29] - that the power to conduct investigations is inherent in the legislative process, then, in order to give effect to that power, the Oireachtas is surely entitled to vest in the Tribunal such powers as are as necessary, short of imposing sanctions or penalties, since to do this would invade the judicial domain. In other words, separation of powers principles allow the Oireachtas to give the Tribunal the same investigative powers as a court would enjoy - what is forbidden is the granting of powers of penalty or sanction.[30]

Finally, what is so remarkable about the majority judgments is their willingness to infer an absolute constitutional imperative (*viz.*, cabinet confidentiality) from the bare language of Article 28.[31] What is particularly striking is that the majority judgments fail to take account of the emerging "abuse of rights" doctrine, i.e., where the courts will not allow the exercise of rights in a manner which would actually subvert the Constitution itself.[32] If - to take an extreme example - Ministers were actually to plan the subversion of the Constitution at a Government meeting, it would seem to follow that - as both O'Hanlon J (in the High Court) and McCarthy J (in his dissent in the Supreme Court) pointed out - such conduct could not be inquired into by any future Tribunal of Inquiry.[33]

The very absoluteness of the rule leads to other no less unexpected results. If a Minister were to make some thoroughly objectionable comments at such a meeting, could the Taoiseach make references to such remarks when seeking to justify his decision to sack the Minister in question? By the same token, if a Minister resigns from Government because of disagreement with his or her colleagues over government policy, is he or she precluded from giving a full account of his or her motive?[34] Likewise, if a Coalition

[28] This is discussed elsewhere: see pp. 381-2.

[29] *Goodman International Ltd v Hamilton (No.1)* [1992] 2 IR 542; [1992] ILRM 145.

[30] That is why the parliamentary practice argument relied on by Finlay CJ ("The members of Dáil Éireann have never asserted...by the rules of that House, a right to obtain information from Ministers of a Government concerning discussions at meetings of Government prior to the making of decisions") cannot be regarded as persuasive. What the Chief Justice states is undoubtedly true as a matter of historical fact, but this cannot provide any answers as to what powers an investigative body such as the Tribunal can validly be granted.

[31] This is especially so given that the vast majority of the Constitution's provisions are not absolute and imply circumstances where the courts have to weigh competing rights and interests: see *Moynihan v Greensymth* [1977] IR 55.

[32] See, e.g., *Quinn v Wren* [1985] IR 322; [1985] ILRM 410.

[33] In *Sankey v Whitlam* (1978) 142 CLR 1 a former Prime Minister and three other Ministers had been charged with unlawful conspiracy to borrow a large sum of money. The Australian High Court held that certain "state papers" (not including Cabinet documents) did not enjoy immunity from discovery. Stephen J pointed out that the ordinary reasons supporting a claim for public interest immunity:

> "the need to safeguard the proper functioning of the executive arm of government and of the public service, seem curiously inappropriate when to uphold the claim is to prevent successful prosecution of the charges: inappropriate because what is charged itself is the grossly improper functioning of that very arm of government and of the public service which assist it."

Indeed, as was pointed out by the Australian High Court in the subsequent decision of that Court in *Commonwealth v Northern Land Council* (1993) 67 Aust LJ 405, it would be difficult to envisage circumstances in which such documents would not have been made available to the defence "if denial of the documents had impeded the defendants in the conduct of their defence."

[34] Thus Hederman J remarked, "There is sufficient precedent for the resignation of members who dissent and cannot accept collective responsibility but none for unauthorised disclosure of the discussions which led to that situation."

Government breaks up over some budgetary or other similar impasse, is the party leaving Government permitted to explain what had transpired at the Government meeting to justify that decision to leave?[35] May a Minister discuss what happened at a Government meeting with his civil servants? Unfortunately, in all cases the logical corollary of the Supreme Court judgments suggest a negative reply.

Another logical - if unwelcome - consequence of this decision would appear to be that records of Government meetings which reveal discussions at such meetings can no longer be released even under the thirty years' rule. These apprehensions were reinforced by the words of Finlay CJ:

> "[The constitutional right claimed] goes to the fundamental machinery of government, and is, therefore, not capable of being waived by any individual member of a Government, nor...are the details and contents of discussions at meetings of the Government capable of being made public...by a decision of any succeeding Government."

These fears almost became a reality when it was reported at the end of December 1992[36] that certain documents due for release under the thirty year rule were about to be withheld on the ground that they revealed Government discussions. The Taoiseach intervened and ordered their release, saying that the operation of the thirty year rule had not been considered by the Supreme Court in their judgments.[37] This decision, strictly speaking, would appear to infringe Article 28.4.2 as interpreted by the Supreme Court. Doubtless had the Supreme Court majority considered the point they might have been prepared to allow an exception in this instance. But by what constitutional principle could the courts fashion such an exception and not allow a similar exception to facilitate the investigation of alleged impropriety or corruption?

Such are the consequences of the majority ruling that one would hope that the Supreme Court would get an opportunity to reconsider this decision. In that event, one possible way of avoiding such consequences might be to focus on the rationale behind the principle of collective responsibility, from which the claim of confidentiality is ultimately derived. That principle is designed primarily to promote Government stability and, to a lesser extent, effective decision making. The claim of confidentiality read in the light of such purposes by a future court would not preclude the release of primary or secondary historical material relating to government meetings of a by-gone era. Nor would it necessarily prevent a former minister giving a full account of the reasons for resignation, at least where such disclosure did not further impair the stability of Government, and, by the same token, a Taoiseach could justify the dismissal of a minister. Such an approach to the claim of confidentiality might conceivably protect the minister who wished to disclose evidence of criminal behaviour though ultimately on this point it is surely preferable that disclosure of such behaviour should be regarded, in itself, as a legitimate qualification to the claim of confidentiality rather than having to be justified in terms of protecting Government stability.

Requirement to act as collective authority

The Constitution does not say which executive acts require the Government to "meet and act as a collective authority" in order to be valid; nor does it prescribe any particular

[35] Cf. The decision of the members of the Labour party to leave the Government in January 1987 following their disagreement with the health and social welfare proposals for the budget: see *The Irish Times*, 21 January 1987.

[36] *The Irish Times*, 31 December 1992.

[37] *The Irish Times*, 2 and 4 January 1993.

format for the Government's meeting and acting. There is, of course, a large number of functions which by statute are specifically attributed to the Government, so that the valid exercise of these functions must presuppose a formal consideration and decision at a Government meeting; but to what extent, in non-statutory contexts, the Government can for example become committed, in a legally relevant sense, by undertakings given by a Minister, or a number of Ministers - even including the Taoiseach - is a very uncertain question.[38]

A concise picture of how the Government works in practice, given by an official who was Secretary to the Government for twenty-three years, may be cited here:

> "As the chief executive organ of the State, the Government has a great deal of work to do besides exercising the powers and functions specifically and expressly conferred on it by the Constitution or by statute. It is its function to govern, to see that the peace is kept and the law enforced, to keep the varying needs of the community as a whole and of its different sections constantly in mind, to concert measures, so far as it can, for averting any dangers that may threaten the community and for creating conditions that will help the people to advance in welfare and prosperity. The agenda for a meeting of the Government does not, therefore, consist merely of a list of formal items, such as Orders to be made, but also includes other items relating to proposals for legislative or administrative measures recommended by Ministers as being, in their opinion, necessary or desirable in the public interest. Indeed, by a long- established practice, the Department of the Taoiseach, as the Government's secretariat, divides the items into two categories, which we call Government items and Cabinet items. Government items are those relating to the performance by the Government of specific functions devolving upon it by express provisions of the Constitution or the law - such as advising the President to make a judicial appointment or making an Imposition of Duties Order.[39] Cabinet items are the others - the miscellaneous matters which come before the Government for decision as the policy-making organ of State."[40]

On the Government's duty in regard to Estimates, see above, p. 172.

A passing reference to the doctrine of collective responsibility occurs in *McCann v An Taoiseach*[41] where Carney J, in the course of holding that the Taoiseach was both entitled and obliged to state Government policy on ratification of the Treaty on European Union in a partisan way, and that this duty could be discharged by directing the RTE Authority, pursuant to s 31(2) of the Broadcasting Act 1960, to allocate broadcasting time such a statement, said that a Taoiseach would be precluded by the terms of Article 28.4.2 from disclosing any personal reservations which he might have about government policy.

[38] See above, 226-8.

[39] A list - representative, not exhaustive - of statutory functions of the Government is given in pp. 15-17 of the work here cited: no official catalogue of these functions exists.

[40] M. Ó Muimhneacháin [Maurice Moynihan], *The Functions of the Department of the Taoiseach* (1960), p. 17. This description would apply equally today.

[41] High Court, 5 October 1992. The judge went on to hold that there was no statutory or constitutional right of reply to such ministerial broadcasts, of which there have been nineteen instances - see 424 *Dáil Debates*, cc. 1406-1408, (29 October 1992).

THE TAOISEACH AND OTHER MEMBERS OF THE GOVERNMENT

5. 1° The head of the Government, or Prime Minister, shall be called, and is in this Constitution referred to as, the Taoiseach.
2° The Taoiseach shall keep the President generally informed on matters of domestic and international policy.

6. 1° The Taoiseach shall nominate a member of the Government to be the Tánaiste.
2° The Tánaiste shall act for all purposes in the place of the Taoiseach if the Taoiseach should die, or become permanently incapacitated, until a new Taoiseach shall have been appointed.
3° The Tánaiste shall also act for or in the place of the Taoiseach during the temporary absence of the Taoiseach.

7. 1° The Taoiseach, the Tánaiste and the member of the Government who is in charge of the Department of Finance must be members of Dáil Éireann.
2° The other members of the Government must be members of Dáil Éireann or Seanad Éireann, but not more than two may be members of Seanad Éireann.

8. Every member of the Government shall have the right to attend and be heard in each House of the Oireachtas.

9. 1° The Taoiseach may resign from office at any time by placing his resignation in the hands of the President.
2° Any other member of the Government may resign from office by placing his resignation in the hands of the Taoiseach for submission to the President.
3° The President shall accept the

5. 1° An Taoiseach is teidel do cheann an Rialtais, .i. an Príomh-Aire, agus sin é a bheirtear air sa Bhunreacht seo.
2° Ní foláir don Taoiseach eolas i gcoitinne a thabhairt don Uachtarán ar nithe a bhaineas le beartas inmheánach agus le beartas idirnáisiúnta.

6. 1° Ní foláir don Taoiseach comhalta den Rialtas a ainmniú chun bheith ina Thánaiste.
2° Má éagann an Taoiseach nó má ghabhann míthreoir bhuan é, ní foláir don Tánaiste gníomhú chun gach críche in ionad an Taoisigh nó go gceaptar Taoiseach eile.
3° Ní foláir don Tánaiste, fairis sin, gníomhú thar ceann nó in ionad an Taoisigh le linn eisean a bheith as láthair go sealadach.

7. 1° Ní foláir an Taoiseach agus an Tánaiste agus an comhalta sin den Rialtas a bheas i mbun an Roinn Airgeadais a bheith ina gcomhaltaí de Dháil Éireann.
2° Ní foláir na comhaltaí eile den Rialtas a bheith ina gcomhaltaí de Dháil Éireann nó de Sheanad Éireann ach ní dleathach thar beirt acu a bheith ina gcomhaltaí de Sheanad Éireann.

8. Tá se de cheart ag gach comhalta den Rialtas bheith i lathair agus labhairt i ngach Teach den Oireachtas.

9. 1° Tig leis an Taoiseach éirí as oifig uair ar bith trína chur sin in iúl don Uachtaran.
2° Tig le haon chomhalta eile den Rialtas éirí as oifig trína chur sin in iúl don Taoiseach chun an scéal a chur faoi bhráid an Uachtaráin.
3° Ní foláir don Uachtarán

resignation of a member of the Government, other than the Taoiseach, if so advised by the Taoiseach.

4° The Taoiseach may at any time, for reasons which to him seem sufficient, request a member of the Government to resign; should the member concerned fail to comply with the request, his appointment shall be terminated by the President if the Taoiseach so advises.

10. The Taoiseach shall resign from office upon his ceasing to retain the support of a majority in Dáil Éireann unless on his advice the President dissolves Dáil Éireann and on the reassembly of Dáil Éireann after the dissolution the Taoiseach secures the support of a majority in Dáil Éireann.

11. 1° If the Taoiseach at any time resigns from office the other members of the Government shall be deemed also to have resigned from office, but the Taoiseach and the other members of the Government shall continue to carry on their duties until their successors shall have been appointed.

2° The members of the Government in office at the date of a dissolution of Dáil Éireann shall continue to hold office until their successors shall have been appointed.

12 The following matters shall be regulated in accordance with law, namely, the organisation of, and distribution of business amongst, Departments of State, the designation of members of the Government to be the Ministers in charge of the said Departments, the discharge of the functions of the office of a member of the Government during his temporary absence or incapacity, and the remuneration of the members of the Government.

glacadh le haon chomhalta den Rialtas, seachas an Taoiseach, d'éirí as oifig má chomhairlíonn an Taoiseach é sin dó.

4° Tig leis an Taoiseach uair ar bith, ar ábhair is leor leis féin, a iarraidh ar chomhalta den Rialtas éirí as oifig; mura ndéana an comhalta sin de réir na hachainí sin, ní foláir don Uachtarán an comhalta sin a chur as oifig má chomhairlíonn an Taoiseach dó é.

10. Aon uair nach leanann tromlach i nDáil Éireann de bheith i dtacaíocht leis an Taoiseach, ní foláir dosan éirí as oifig mura lánscoireann an tUachtarán Dáil Éireann ar chomhairle an Taoisigh agus go n-éiríonn leis an Taoiseach tacaíocht tromlaigh i nDáil Éireann a fháil ar ationól do Dháil Éireann i ndiaidh an lánscoir.

11. 1° Má éiríonn an Taoiseach as oifig tráth ar bith, ní foláir a mheas go n-éiríonn an chuid eile de chomhaltaí an Rialtais as oifig fairis sin; ach leanfaidh an Taoiseach agus an chuid eile de chomhaltaí an Rialtais dá ndualgais nó go gceaptar a gcomharbaí.

2° Na comhaltaí den Rialtas a bheas in oifig lá lanscortha Dháil Éireann leanfaid dá n-oifig nó go gceaptar a gcomharbaí.

12. Is de réir dlí a rialófar na nithe seo a leanas .i. Ranna Stáit a chomheagrú agus gnó a roinnt orthu, comhaltaí den Rialtas a cheapadh chun bheith ina nAirí i mbun na Ranna sin, na feidhmeanna a bhaineas le hoifig chomhalta den Rialtas a chomhlíonadh le linn an comhalta sin a bheith tamall as láthair nó ar míthreoir, agus tuarastal comhaltaí an Rialtais.

1922 provisions

Broadly similar, but not identical provisions were contained in Articles 51 - 59 of the 1922 Constitution. In particular, Ministers under the old Constitution had the same protection as judges in regard to non-reduction of their remuneration during office; and there was no provision enabling the President of the Executive Council to get rid of a Minister. Under the old Article 55, too, it was possible to appoint Ministers who were not members of the Executive Council, and who need not even be members of the Oireachtas; a number of such "extern" Ministers were in fact appointed for a few years (though all were members of the Dáil), but this experiment was not judged to be a success, and after 1927 no more were appointed.[1]

The office of Taoiseach

The office of Taoiseach replaces that of President of the Executive Council under the 1922 Constitution, and the old Department of the President of the Executive Council became, by s 3 of the Constitution (Consequential Provisions) Act 1937, the Department of the Taoiseach. Apart from the functions attributed to that Department by s 1 of the Ministers and Secretaries Act 1924, and the several further functions given the Taoiseach by subsequent legislation - and apart of course also from the many specific functions conferred upon him by the Constitution itself[2] - there is a residual area or penumbra, not defined by law, in which the political primacy reflected in the office of Taoiseach plays an important role in the State. A former Secretary to the Government described this general role as follows:

> "The Taoiseach as Head of the Government [is] the captain of the team. In this capacity, he is the central co-ordinating figure, who takes an interest in the work of all Departments, the figure to whom Ministers naturally turn for advice and guidance when faced with problems involving large questions of policy or otherwise of special difficulty and whose leadership is essential to the successful working of the Government as a collective authority, collectively responsible to Dáil Éireann, but acting through members each of whom is charged with specific Departmental tasks. He may often have to inform himself in considerable detail of particular matters with which other members of the Government are primarily concerned. He may have to make public statements on such matters, as well as on general matters of

[1] See Donal O'Sullivan, *The Irish Free State and its Senate*, pp. 88-9, 204. Kennedy CJ, who as Attorney General (and former Law Officer of the Provisional Government) had charge of the Ministers and Secretaries Bill 1923, in its passage through the Dáil, gave, in *Moore v Attorney General* ([1930] IR 471, at pp. 493-4) an account of the genesis of the office of Ministers: "It will be remembered that the first Dáil Éireann and the second Dáil Éireann [these were the pre-Constitution Dála, deliberately established to defy and ultimately replace British authority in Ireland] set up Departments of Government, and that when the Provisional Government took office, after the ratification of the Treaty, it undertook the administration of the country during the interval between the Treaty and the constitution of the Parliament and Government of the Saorstát, and that it adopted, for the carrying on of that administration, the Departments of Government which had been constituted by the Dáil at that time. By the Transfer of Functions Order, which was made on 1 April 1922, the British Government, recognising the then existing Departments as Departments of the Provisional Government, transferred to those Departments the functions in connection with the administration of public services theretofore in the hands of the Departments and officers of the British Government, including the office of the Chief Crown Solicitor, transferred to the Department of the Law Officer of the Provisional Government. Article 54 of the Constitution of the Saorstát subsequently provided for the administration of the Departments of State by Ministers, some of whom were to be members of the Executive Council, while others might be outside the Executive Council. The various Departments of State were in due course, in the case of those which had previously existed, organised and developed, and in other cases newly established and organised. The Ministers and Secretaries Act was passed in the year 1924 for the purpose of implementing the Constitution by constituting and defining the various Ministers and Departments of State, which were then actually in being, though not properly defined and regularised by law."

[2] See the Index, s.v. Taoiseach.

> broad policy, internal and external. He answers Dáil Questions where the attitude of the Government towards important matters of policy is involved. He may occasionally sponsor Bills which represent important new developments of policy, even when the legislation, when enacted, will be the particular concern of the Minister in charge of some other Department of State. His Department is the sole channel of communication between Departments generally and the President's secretariat, except in minor and routine matters. Through his Parliamentary Secretary,[3] whose office is also included in the Department of the Taoiseach, he secures the co-ordination, in a comprehensive parliamentary programme, of the proposals of the various Ministers for legislative and other measures in the Houses of the Oireachtas."[4]

The unique character of the Taoiseach's office came through in the Dáil debate on the Arts Bill, 1951, when Mr. de Valera, then in Opposition, objected to a provision which proposed that the amount of a grant should be determined by "the Taoiseach, with the concurrence of the Minister for Finance" - a formula which is common in the case of other Ministers, but had not yet been seen in the Taoiseach's case, as this was the first Bill giving him a ministerial role in the administration of a new statutory scheme. Mr. de Valera said:

> "...I think that when the Taoiseach would do anything he would be doing it in the name of the Government as a whole. I have the feeling that it has to be taken for granted that a person in the Taoiseach's position would have consulted the Minister for Finance...I am anxious to see that the Taoiseach's position as Taoiseach is maintained. I do not like to see a provision for concurrence with a colleague with whom the Taoiseach, I take it, would be in almost day-to-day consultation."

The Taoiseach (Mr. Costello) agreed to amend the provision so as to dispense with the formal requirement of the Minister for Finance's concurrence.[5] This conception of the Taoiseach's dignity has however not weathered evenly. Section 2(10) of the Prosecution of Offences Act 1974, provides that the Taoiseach may appoint, for service in the office of the Director of Public Prosecutions, "so many officers and servants as the Taoiseach shall, with the sanction of the Minister for the Public Service, from time to time determine".

Taoiseach's duty to keep President informed

The significance attached to the requirement of Article 28.5.2 in practice is hard to estimate. The matter was raised by Dáil Question in late 1976,[6] to ask the Taoiseach (Mr. Cosgrave) how often he had discharged the duty laid upon him by the sub-section; he replied:

> "Pursuant to Article 28.5.2 I visited President de Valera once, President Childers five times and President Ó Dálaigh four times."[7]

[3] Now "Minister of State at the Department of the Taoiseach": see Ministers and Secretaries (Amendment) (No.2) Act 1977, ss 1, 6.

[4] M. Ó Muimhneacháin [Maurice Moynihan], *The Functions of the Department of the Taoiseach* (Institute of Public Administration, Dublin, 1960), p. 19. The author was Secretary to the Government from 1937 until 1960.

[5] 125 *Dáil Debates* 1728-9.

[6] 294 *Dáil Debates* 429. This was shortly after the row surrounding the resignation of President Ó Dálaigh: see above, p. 95 Fn 19.

[7] Mr. Cosgrave became Taoiseach in March, 1973; Mr. de Valera's second and final term of office expired in June of that year. Mr. Childers, elected to succeed Mr. de Valera, remained in office only sixteen months before he died. President Ó Dálaigh was in office for just two years before he resigned.

A similar question was put to Mr. Haughey when Taoiseach in late 1980, and beyond saying that he had "fully and adequately discharged" this duty, he gave no details, saying that to do so would not be "in keeping with the dignity of the office of the President".[8]

Taoiseach's role in seeking dissolution of Dáil

The Taoiseach was one of the defendants named originally in *Draper v Attorney General*,[9] an action in which the plaintiff sought to have her right to vote in Dáil elections respected despite her physical inability to attend a polling-station. She sought to prevent the Taoiseach from seeking a dissolution of the Dáil until the electoral law had been changed in a manner such as to facilitate her: but the Supreme Court, without a written judgment, struck the Taoiseach out of the proceedings on the ground that no cause of action against him had been disclosed.[10]

Obligation of a defeated Taoiseach to resign

By virtue of Article 28.10, a Taoiseach who has ceased to retain the support of a majority of Dáil Éireann must resign unless the President dissolves the Dáil and the Taoiseach secures the support of a majority in the new Dáil. The interpretation of this provision gives rise to a number of interesting issues. First, when may the Taoiseach be regarded as "ceasing to retain the support of a majority in Dáil Éireann"?[11] Clearly such a situation arises where the Government loses a Dáil vote on a motion which would normally be regarded as involving an issue of confidence.[12] A similar situation arises where, following a dissolution of the Dáil where the Taoiseach had lost the support of a majority of that House, he subsequently fails to secure the support of a majority in the re-assembled Dáil.[13] A close reading of Article 28.10 indicates that the obligation to resign is only averted where the President grants a dissolution *and* the Taoiseach secures a majority in the new Dáil.[14] What is less clear is whether a Taoiseach may be regarded as having lost the support of a majority of the Dáil as a result of other developments, including perhaps, developments outside the House. A case can be made for this broader view of the phrase in Article 13.2.2 in order to preserve the President's discretion to refuse to dissolve the Dáil. For if the President could refuse a dissolution only in the case of a

[8] 325 *Dáil Debates* 563. In 1983 Dr. FitzGerald as Taoiseach also declined to be specific in this matter: 345 *Dáil Debates* 3.

[9] [1984] IR 277; [1984] ILRM 643.

[10] See *The Irish Times*, 14 May 1981.

[11] This phrase also occurs in Article 13.2.2 which gives the President an absolute discretion to refuse a dissolution of the Dáil to a Taoiseach who has ceased to retain the support of a majority of that House. Neither clause has been judicially considered to date.

[12] Apart from votes on formal motions of confidence, however, there is no definition of what might constitute an issue of confidence in the Government. A defeat on a Budget resolution is clearly one such issue. Votes on other matters may be converted into motions of confidence by a declaration from the Taoiseach that he considers the vote to be such. Defeat on issues of intermediate importance are usually cured by securing a victory on an early vote of confidence and thereby avoiding the obligation to resign. On this area generally, see Morgan, *Constitutional Law of Ireland*, (2nd ed.) pp.70-71.

[13] Thus at the first meeting of the twenty-sixth Dáil on 29 June 1989, none of the nominees for the position of Taoiseach secured a majority of the Dáil on this unprecedented occasion and, despite his initial reluctance, the outgoing Taoiseach, Mr. Haughey, was eventually prevailed upon to resign. For an account of this saga, see Hogan, "*Legal and constitutional issues arising from the 1989 General Election*" (1989) 24 Ir Jur (n.s.) 157. Note that in December 1992 this precedent was followed by the outgoing Taoiseach, Mr Reynolds T.D., when the Dáil once again failed to elect a Taoiseach on its re-assembly following a general election - see 425 *Dáil Debates*, col.73.

[14] On the other hand, the view that Article 28.10 is possibly inapplicable in such a situation - on the ground that it only applies where the Taoiseach had, and then lost, the support of a majority in the Dáil - has been aired by some commentators - see Casey, "*Constitutional Law in Ireland*" (2nd ed.,1992) pp. 139-40; editorial in *The Irish Law Times*, (1989) 7 ILT (n.s.) 177.

Taoiseach who had lost on a formal vote of confidence, a Taoiseach who did not command the support of a majority could pre-empt a Dáil vote and insist that the President grant him a dissolution in accordance with Article 13.2.1.[15] If this broader view is adopted in relation to Article 13.2.2, one would also expect it to be followed in relation to Article 28.10 in the absence of any persuasive reason for distinguishing between the situations covered by both provisions.

A further question here focuses on the period of time within which the Taoiseach must submit his resignation. Following the events of 29 June 1989 referred to above, Mr. Haughey was apparently advised that he did not have to resign immediately but that he could take several days ("anything up to a week") to consider his position. While admittedly Article 28.10 does not expressly provide for *immediate* resignation, one could argue that this is implied by the construction of the word "upon" in the first line of that section, taken in the context of a defeat on a crucial Dáil vote.[16]

Powers of a "caretaker" administration

By virtue of Article 28.11.1, the members of a Government who have resigned continue to carry on their duties until their successors have been appointed. Sub-section 2 of that Article makes similar provision in respect of the members of a Government in office at the date of a dissolution of the Dáil. While considerations of political prudence suggest that, during such interregnum, a so-called caretaker administration should be restrained in its exercise of power, the Constitution itself would appear to impose no limitations on the powers of such an administration. In particular, while the matter is not entirely clear, the principle of effectiveness lends support to the view that the Taoiseach in such a situation retains the power to request a fresh dissolution of the Dáil in order to resolve any impasse created by a failure of that House to appoint his successor.[17]

Office of Tánaiste

According to the Constitution, the Tánaiste must be a member of Dáil Éireann and must be nominated for his position by the Taoiseach. Apart from being, *ex officio*, a member of the Council of State, the only function envisaged for the Tánaiste under the Constitution is that he shall act in the place of the Taoiseach during the latter's temporary absence or, where the latter dies or becomes permanently incapacitated, pending the appointment of a new Taoiseach. The extended role conferred on the office of Tánaiste under the Programme for Government 1993 has consequently attracted criticism on the ground that it has no constitutional legitimacy.[18] It is the case that, unlike the Presidency, no provision expressly envisages the conferral of additional powers and functions on the Tánaiste.[19] On the other hand, however, neither is there any provision which expressly confines the Tánaiste's functions to those listed in the Constitution. One could argue that the allocation of responsibilities among Government ministers, including the Tánaiste, is an aspect of the exercise of the legislative power of the State, authorised by Article 28.12, and that pursuant to this power, functions and responsibilities in addition to those envisaged by the Constitution may legitimately be conferred on the Tánaiste. It follows from this argument, however, that the allocation of such addi-

[15] *Cf. Abegbenro v Akintola* [1963] 3 WLR 63.

[16] See *Hogan, loc. cit.*, pp. 169-172. See also *Morgan, op.cit.* p.268.

[17] *Hogan, loc.cit.* p. 173; *Casey, op. cit.*, pp.139-40. Though for a listing of counter arguments, see *Morgan, op.cit.*, p.269.

[18] See statement of Mr. O'Malley, T.D., *The Irish Times*, 8 February 1993; *The Irish Times*, 10 February 1993.

[19] But by the same token, nor is there any such provision referring to the office of Taoiseach which, as *Casey* puts it, "depends, not on constitutional or legal rules, but on the currents of politics." - *op. cit.*, p.130.

tional functions must rest on a proper statutory basis and to date no such provision has been made.[20]

Substitution for the Taoiseach

While the position of the Tánaiste as a substitute for the Taoiseach in temporary circumstances is clear, the Constitution makes no provision for the discharge of the Taoiseach's functions in a case where both Taoiseach and Tánaiste might be disabled from acting. There is an informal practice whereby, if both are absent, the senior member present will preside at Government meetings, and there is nothing to prevent the Government as such from acting even when Taoiseach and Tánaiste are unavailable: but as the Constitution stands, in such a case, a function specifically attributed to the Taoiseach would have to await the reappearance of one or other of them. This would appear to be a constitutional lacuna which ordinary legislation could not fill. It is true that a unique measure passed in wartime (though still in force), the Taxes and Duties (Special Circumstances) Act 1942,[21] defines in s 1 the Taoiseach as including "any person for the time being authorised by law to perform the functions of the Taoiseach", but such an authority could be valid only in respect of a mere statutory function of the Taoiseach, not one of his constitutional functions. In other words, where both Taoiseach and Tánaiste, though still in office, are disabled from acting for whatever reason, an ordinary[22] Act would not be competent to confer on some other person a function which the Constitution imputes exclusively to the Taoiseach. This lacuna may be contrasted with some constitutional provisions on the courts, which include, where the President of the Supreme Court or High Court is unavailable, provision either for a single designated substitute, or for a sequence of substitution.[23]

Individual responsibility of members of the Government as Ministers

While the responsibility of members of the Government for the Departments is collective, the individual responsibility (and mutual independence) of individual members of the Government in regard to their own Departments is established by statute, pursuant to Article 28.12. The Ministers and Secretaries Act 1924 - amended by several subsequent Acts which created new Departments and extinguished or merged old ones[24] - established by s 1 eleven Departments of State:

> "amongst which the administration and business of the public services in Saorstát Éireann shall be distributed as in the [following] sub-paragraphs is particularly mentioned, and each of which said Departments and powers, duties and functions

[20] A further question here is whether the Tánaiste can answer Dáil questions relating to his responsibilities as Tánaiste. The existing Standing Orders of the Dáil, made pursuant to Article 15.10, provide that questions addressed to a member of Government must relate to "public affairs connected with his Department or to matters of administration for which he is officially responsible" - Order 32. However, as the allocation of such functions may only be made by legislation, it would appear that an amendment to the Ministers and Secretaries Acts, identifying the additional, non-constitutional functions of the Tánaiste, is necessary before he can respond, pursuant to Order 32, to Dáil questions relating specifically to the functions of that office. Alternatively, the Dáil could presumably amend its Standing Orders to facilitate the Tánaiste in this regard.

[21] See above, p. 172.

[22] An Act passed under cover of Article 28.3.3 - and therefore, if the critical spirit shown by the Supreme Court in the *Emergency Powers Bill 1976,* reference (above, pp. 242-5) may be regarded as a fixture, only in genuine emergency conditions - would presumably be able to do it.

[23] Articles 14.2.2 (Presidential Commission); 40.4.4 (composition of High Court to determine habeas corpus applications).

[24] See the *Index to the Statutes* under "Ministers and Departments of State". By virtue of s 6 of the Ministers and Secretaries (Amendment) Act 1939, the Government may, by order, *inter alia*, alter the name of any Department of State or the title of any Minister having charge of a Department of State, and transfer the administration and business of any particular public service from one Department to another. The most recent changes in appellation and jurisdiction are contained in Statutory Instrument Nos. 10 to 22 of 1993.

> thereof shall be assigned to and administered by the Minister hereinafter named as head thereof."

(The Departments of State of Saorstát Éireann were continued as the same Departments of State after 1937 by virtue of Article 56.3.)

The Act provided also by s 7 for the appointment of subordinate office-holders (who were to be members of the Oireachtas) to be attached to the Executive Council or to Ministers as Parliamentary Secretaries; these offices, whose holders are not members of the Government, were transformed into the offices of "Ministers of State" (at this or that Department) by the Ministers and Secretaries (Amendment) (No. 2) Act 1977. The mutual independence of Ministers in regard to the running of their Departments was stated with emphasis by Kennedy CJ in *Conroy v Minister for Defence*[25] when, in the context of a suggestion that the Minister for Finance had some discretion to refuse to pay a particular person a pension granted by the Minister for Defence, he said:

> "The Minister for Finance is the administrative head of the Department of Finance, which Department of State has a sphere of activity defined by statute (the Ministers and Secretaries Act 1924). It has not authority to interfere, in matters other than financial, with the subjects by statute assigned to, or other the proper activities of, other Ministers and Departments. The granting of pensions under the [Military Service Pensions Act 1924] is a faculty of the Minister for Defence. The Minister for Finance has no legal authority or power to say to the Minister for Defence: "You shall not grant a pension to any man who has red hair", though [counsel] has made that claim."

At the same time, there is no legal principle which precludes a Minister from passing on information, properly received by him, to a colleague who requires such information for the purpose of carrying out a statutory duty - *Desmond v Glackin.*[26]

The legal liability of Ministers in respect of the exercise of their decision-making functions was considered by the Supreme Court in *Pine Valley Developments Ltd. v Minister for the Environment.*[27] Here planning permission granted by the defendant had been invalidated by the courts on an earlier occasion, with a resultant diminution in the value of the land owned by the plaintiff company. An action for damages for negligence taken by the company failed because, in the words of Finlay CJ:

> "if a Minister of State, granted as a *persona designata* a specific duty and function to make decisions under a statutory code (as occurs in this case) exercises his discretion *bona fide*, having obtained and followed the legal advice of the permanent legal advisers attached to his Department, I cannot see how he could be said to have been negligent if the law eventually proves to be otherwise than they have advised him and if by reason of that he makes an order which is invalid or *ultra vires.*"

Nor did an action for damages for breach of statutory duty lie because, according to Henchy J:

[25] [1934] IR 679; (1935) 69 ILTR 43.

[26] Supreme Court, 30 July 1992.

[27] [1987] IR 23; [1987] ILRM 747. *Pine Valley* was subsequently followed in *McMahon v Ireland,* [1988] ILRM 610; *Greene v Minister for Agriculture* [1990] 2 IR 17; [1990] ILRM 364 and *O'Donnell v Dun Laoghaire Corporation* [1991] ILRM 301. See also *C.W. Shipping Co. Ltd. v Limerick Harbour Commissioners* [1989] ILRM 416. See Hogan and Morgan, *Administrative Law in Ireland* (2nd ed.) pp. 709-716.

> "Where there has been a delegation by statute to a designated person of a power to make decisions affecting others, unless the statute provides otherwise an action for damages at the instance of a person adversely affected by an *ultra vires* decision does not lie against the decision-maker unless he acted negligently, or with malice (in the sense of spite, ill will or suchlike improper motive), or in the knowledge that the decision would be in excess of the authorised power."

Finlay CJ justified this immunity, which, though extensive, is not absolute,[28] by pointing out that its absence would lead to "an inevitable paralysis of the capacity for decisive action in the administration of public affairs." However the consequence that individuals can suffer loss as a result of State action without having any right to compensation has been criticised and compares unfavourably with practice elsewhere.[29]

One further point worth noting in this context is that the doctrine of estoppel cannot be employed to prevent the discharge by a Minister of a statutory discretion - see, e.g. *Dublin Corporation v McGrath;*[30] *Hempenstall v Minister for the Environment.*[31]

Power of courts to review ministerial decisions

A useful summary of the extent of the High Court's jurisdiction to review ministerial decisions is contained in Murphy J's judgment in *Duff v The Minister for Agriculture.*[32] He said:

> "1. [T]he legislature cannot and *a fortiori* neither can a Minister of Government take any action or do anything which would infringe the constitutional rights of any citizen.
>
> 2. Rarely, if ever, are rights, powers, duties or discretions conferred on any Minister, administrator or tribunal for the benefit of the donee. They are received by the donees effectively as trustees and exercisable for the benefit of third parties: not the donee...
>
> 3. The great range of powers conferred on executive authorities are capable of being reviewed - not appealed - by reference to what are usually described as the Wednesbury Principles set out by Lord Greene in *Associated Provincial Picture House v Wednesbury Corporation* [1948] 1 KB 223, subject to the clarification or amplification of the concept of "unreasonableness" as provided by Henchy J in *The State (Keegan) v Stardust Compensation Tribunal* [1986] IR 651.
>
> 4. Discretions conferred on a Minister do not give him an arbitrary power. [He then quoted from the judgment of Walsh J in *East Donegal Co-Operative Ltd. v Attorney General* [1970] IR 317, in which that judge stated that discretionary powers may be exercised only within the boundaries of the stated objects of the Act and

[28] It may not exist, for example, if either the Minister or his advisers act negligently - see the remarks of Murphy J in two cases - *Cotter v The Minister for Agriculture*, High Court, 15 November 1991, and *Duff v The Minister for Agriculture* [1993] 2 CMLR 969. See also *Hogan and Morgan, op.cit.*

[29] See Casey, *op. cit.*, 41-2. For the plaintiffs in *Pine Valley*, however, this saga ultimately had a happy ending, as in *Pine Valley Developments Ltd. v Ireland*, 29 November 1991, Series A, No.222, (1992) 14 EHRR 319, the European Court of Human Rights subsequently held that the non-application to the plaintiffs of legislation retrospectively validating planning permission violated their rights under Article 14 of the Convention.

[30] [1978] ILRM 208.

[31] [1993] ILRM.

[32] [1993] 2 CMLR 969. See also the remarks of McCarthy J in *Ellis v O'Dea* [1989] IR 530; [1989] ILRM 87, made in the context of the conclusion of extradition agreements, that "the role of the courts is to ensure that the statutory requirements are met and that no breach of the Constitution or constitutional rights occur."

carry with them the duty of acting fairly and judicially in accordance with principle of constitutional justice.]

5. Where...a Minister may exercise certain powers "if he is of opinion" that certain circumstances exist, the Court may be required to investigate whether the opinion in question was *bona fide* held and whether it was factually sustainable and not unreasonable. [He cited *The State (Lynch) v Cooney* [1982] IR 337 and *Desmond v Glackin*, High Court, 25 February 1992.]"

Members of Government without a portfolio

By s 4 of the Ministers and Secretaries (Amendment) Act 1939, a member of the Government who is not given charge of a Department is known as a Minister without portfolio, but may be given "a specific style or title".[33]

Senators as members of Government

The provision of Article 28.7.2, whereby up to two members of the Government (other than the Taoiseach, the Tánaiste and the Minister for Finance) may be members of Seanad Éireann has been availed of on only two occasions.[34]

Taoiseach's loss of Dáil support

As to the question of when a Taoiseach can be taken to have "ceased to retain the support of a majority in Dáil Éireann", see above, pp. 89-90.

Conflict of interest of Government members

Guidelines for determining the legitimate business and personal interests of members of the Government (and of Ministers of State, who are not members of the Government) were described to the Dáil by one Taoiseach, Dr. FitzGerald, as follows:[35]

"1. No Minister or Minister of State should engage in any activities that could reasonably be regarded as interfering, or being incompatible, with the full and proper discharge of the duties of office.

2. Ministers and Ministers of State should not hold company directorships carrying remuneration. Even if remuneration is not paid it would be regarded as undesirable that a Minister or Minister of State should hold a directorship; a resigning director can, however, enter into an agreement with a company under which the company would agree to reappointment as director on the termination of public office.

3. Ministers and Ministers of State should not carry on a professional practice while holding office but there would be no objection to making arrangements for the maintenance of a practice while holding public office and for return to the practice on ceasing to hold office.

4. In cases of doubt, the Taoiseach should be consulted."

[33] There has only been one instance so far, that of Mr. Frank Aiken, who in the 1939-45 period was "Minister for the Co-ordination of Defensive Measures".
[34] In 1957, when Senator Seán Moylan was appointed Minister for Agriculture; and in 1981, when Senator James Dooge was appointed Minister for Foreign Affairs.
[35] 369 *Dáil Debates* 3; (22 October 1986). He subsequently stated that membership of the Government was incompatible with membership of any organisation, participation in which is by policy not a matter of public knowledge - *ibid.*, cc.20-22.

INTERNATIONAL RELATIONS

International Relations	Caidreamh Idirnáisiúnta
Article 29	**Airteagal 29**
1. Ireland affirms its devotion to the ideal of peace and friendly cooperation amongst nations founded on international justice and morality.	**1. Dearbhaíonn Éire gur mian léi síocháin agus comhar, de réir an chothroim idirnáisiúnta agus na moráltachta idirnáisiúnta, a bheith ar bun idir náisiúin an domhain.**
2. Ireland affirms its adherence to the principle of the pacific settlement of international disputes by international arbitration or judicial determination.	**2. Dearbhaíonn Éire fós gur mian léi go ndéanfaí gach achrann idir náisiúin a réiteach go síochánta le headráin idirnáisiúnta nó le cinneadh breithiúnach.**
3. Ireland accepts the generally recognised principles of international law as its rule of conduct in its relations with other States.	**3. Glacann Éire le bunrialacha gnáth-admhaithe an dlí idirnáisiúnta le bheith ina dtreoir d'Éirinn ina caidreamh le Stáit eile.**

Judicial consideration of Article 29.1-2

To date, there has been only one judicial reference to these provisions. In *McGimpsey v Ireland*[1] Finlay CJ, delivering the leading judgment in the Supreme Court, took the view that the Anglo-Irish Agreement of 1985 was compatible with the obligations imposed on the State by ss 1 and 2 of Article 29, whereby Ireland affirms its devotion to the ideal of peace and friendly co-operation among nations and its adherence to the principles of the pacific settlement of international disputes.

Challenges to domestic legislation based on Article 29.3 invariably unsuccessful

Section 3 of Article 29 has been made the basis of several challenges to legislative or executive measures, mostly in the context of extradition, by way of attempts to erect what were claimed to be "generally recognised principles of international law" into domestic constitutional criteria. To date, however, such challenges have invariably been unsuccessful.[2] These cases fall into three broad categories.

No conflict presented in specific cases

In four cases,[3] the courts concluded, *inter alia*, that no conflict between the general prin-

[1] [1990] 1 IR 110; [1990] ILRM 440.

[2] In contrast, principles of international law have had the effect of restricting the jurisdiction of the courts in certain situations, in particular with regard to the enforcement of foreign revenue laws and the suing of foreign States - see below, pp. 274-6.

[3] In this context, one should also note *Hutchinson v Minister for Justice* [1993] ILRM 602, where Blayney J rejected the applicant's contention that there was an obligation under international law on the Government to ratify a Convention signed by one of its predecessors. One presumes that this part of the applicant's case was premised on Article 29.3, though no reference to this provision is made anywhere in the judgment.

ciples of international law and domestic law arose in relation to the issues presented for consideration. In *The State (Duggan) v Tapley*,[4] which concerned s 29 of the Petty Sessions (Ireland) Act 1851 (under which extraditions from the State to Britain were carried out until the decision in *The State (Quinn) v Ryan*),[5] the applicant for *habeas corpus* argued that this section was inconsistent with the Constitution inasmuch as it did not contain or respect principles of international law which he stated as follows: (a) there is no rule of international law requiring a State to deliver its citizens for trial in another State on criminal charges; (b) to entitle a State to make such a surrender there must be a statutory authority based on a treaty with the requesting State, and there must therefore first be a treaty giving reciprocal extradition rights; (c) the offence charged must be an offence in both jurisdictions, may not be one of a political character, and must be *prima facie* established by the requesting State in a judicial proceeding. The Supreme Court, *per* Maguire CJ, concluded on the first point that:

> "there is no generally recognised principle of international law which forbids the surrender in accordance with s 29 of the Petty Sessions (Ireland) Act 1851, to Great Britain of persons - whether they are Irish citizens or others - to answer a charge of a criminal offence."

On the second point, the Court noted that the applicant's counsel had cited no authority for the proposition that extradition cannot take place in the absence of a treaty; and said it was of opinion that:

> "reciprocity is not a condition of a valid law of extradition and the operation of s 29 of the Petty Sessions (Ireland) Act 1851, is not dependent on the existence of similar legislation in Great Britain."

On the third point, the Court dealt only with the question of extradition for a political offence, and said that:

> "the attempt... to establish that the non-surrender of political refugees is a generally recognised principle of international law fails. The farthest that the matter can be put is that international law permits and favours the refusal of extradition of persons accused or convicted of offences of a political character but allows it to each State to exercise its own judgment as to whether it will grant or refuse extradition in such cases and also as to the limitations which it will impose upon such provisions as exempt from extradition."[6]

The ruling on this last point was one of the grounds given by Lynch J in *Sloan, McKee and Magee v Culligan*[7] for rejecting the applicants' contention that the Extradition (European Convention on the Suppression of Terrorism) Act 1987 was contrary to international law, and consequently invalid having regard to Article 29.3, because it diminished the political offence exemption from extradition. The judge also took the view that the 1987 Act did not abolish the political offence exemption, but rather defined it in a particular way.

In *The State (Sumers Jennings) v Furlong*[8] the applicant for *habeas corpus* argued that Part III of the Extradition Act 1965 (which had replaced the extradition provisions of the

[4] [1952] IR 62; (1951) 85 ILTR 22.

[5] [1965] IR 70; (1966) 100 ILTR 105.

[6] See now s 50 of the Extradition Act 1965 and the Extradition (European Convention on the Suppression of Terrorism) Act 1987.

[7] [1992] 1 IR 223; [1992] ILRM 186, 194. This point did not feature in the subsequent appeal to the Supreme Court.

[8] [1966] IR 183.

Petty Sessions (Ireland) Act 1851, in consequence of *Quinn's* case[9]) conflicted with Article 29.3 inasmuch as it did not implement what he submitted was a generally recognised principle of international law, the "rule of speciality", which he stated as requiring that a State requesting extradition must not proceed against the person extradited for any offence other than that specified in the request (the rule was incorporated in Part II of the Act which dealt with extradition in pursuance of extradition treaties such as might thereafter be concluded with other foreign States, but not in Part III, which was a special regulation, simultaneous with reciprocal British legislation, of extradition between the State and Britain.[10]) One of the three judges in the divisional High Court hearing the case,[11] Henchy J, refused to allow that the rule which the applicant was trying to enforce was in fact the rule of speciality at all:

> "In the proceedings envisaged by Part III of the Act this state is always the extraditing state, and the rule of speciality could therefore apply only to the requesting state - the United Kingdom. What the prosecutor is seeking to assert is not the rule of speciality but a rule binding the extraditing state to ensure that the requesting state will observe the rule of speciality. In my view, this suggested rule is no part of the generally recognised principles of international law."

Finally, in *Shannon v Ireland*[12] the plaintiff, who was challenging the constitutionality of Part III of the Extradition Act 1965, argued that the absence of a provision in Part III preventing a person from being extradited where the request was made for the purpose of prosecuting or punishing him on account of his race, religion, nationality or political opinion, meant that Part III was in conflict with a generally recognised principle of international law and consequently invalid having regard to Article 29.3. He also contended that the absence of a provision in Part III making the operation of extradition under that Part conditional on a finding by the District Court that there was a *prima facie* case against the person to be extradited in regard to the offence charged in the warrant, also offended against a generally recognised principle of international law and, by extension, against Article 29.3. The Supreme Court, speaking through Henchy J , and assuming without accepting the validity of the plaintiff's first argument, ruled that there was no evidence to justify a conclusion that the extradition of the plaintiff was for the purpose of prosecuting or punishing him on account of his race, religion, nationality or political opinion. On the second point, it rejected the contention that the establishment of a *prima facie* case was a precondition to obtaining an order for extradition. All that is required is that, on a particular extradition being questioned, someone duly authorised to do so avers in good faith that a *prima facie* case exists.[13] No evidence had been offered by the plaintiff that in this or any previous case of extradition to Northern Ireland there had been any lack of good faith on the part of those seeking extradition.

While the invocation of Article 29.3 was unsuccessful in all of these cases, the implicit assumption was that the courts could test a statute on the criterion of whether its effect was contrary to generally recognised principles of international law. This assumption is called into doubt by the reasoning adopted in another cluster of cases in which Article 29.3 was invoked.

[9] [1965] IR 70; (1966) 100 ILTR 105.
[10] See below, pp. 877-8.
[11] The remaining two judges, Davitt P and Teevan J dismissed the case on the ground that Article 29.3 conferred no rights on individuals, a point with which Henchy J also agreed.
[12] [1984] IR 548; [1985] ILRM 449.
[13] See *Wyatt v McLoughlin* [1974] IR 378 at 395.

Article 29.1-3 confers no rights on individuals

In three cases, the courts took the view that Article 29.1-3 conferred no rights on individuals. The first of these was *In re Ó Láighléis*[14] (though that case was concerned principally with s 6 of Article 29): the Supreme Court, *per* Maguire CJ stated briefly that:

> "[Sections] 1 and 3 of Article 29...clearly refer only to relations between states and confer no rights on individuals:"

a view which, had it been formulated at the time, ought perhaps to have made a short end of the applicant's case in *The State (Duggan) v Tapley.*

This view surfaced in the extradition context in 1966 in *The State (Sumers Jennings) v Furlong*,[15] when it was adopted with decisive effect by the High Court. As we have already noted, the applicant for *habeas corpus* challenged the constitutionality of Part III of the Extradition Act 1965 on the ground that it conflicted with Article 29.3 inasmuch as it did not implement what he submitted was a generally recognised principle of international law, the "rule of speciality". Both Davitt P (with whom Teevan J agreed) and Henchy J relied on the *Ó Láighléis* decision in repeating that Article 29.3 conferred no rights on individuals; Henchy J pointed to the Irish version of the section as showing that Ireland was merely declared to accept "the generally recognised principles of international law as a guide (ina dtreoir) in its relations with other states". Both judges took the line also that a conflict between international law and a domestic statute could not invalidate the latter; Davitt P said the principle of speciality was "not the product of the growth of customary international law...[but] the product of "international legislation" (a distinction which appears to give a secondary role to "international legislation" as a source of "generally recognised principles of international law"[16]); and international legislation could not be accorded any primacy over domestic law:[17]

> "If we accept the submission that the rule of speciality has the effect of invalidating Part III of the Extradition Act 1965, we will be accepting the principle that a legislative authority other than the Oireachtas has the power to nullify - in effect, to repeal an enactment of the Oireachtas and in this respect to make laws for the State."

(This passage referred to the exclusive legislative power reserved to the Oireachtas by Article 15.2.1).

More recently, the view that Article 29.1-3 conferred no rights on individuals was repeated by Barrington J in *The State (Gilliland) v Governor of Mountjoy Prison*[18] when, in distinguishing between ss 1-2 of Article 29 and ss 4-6 of the same Article, he said of the former that they appear to be asserting the principles which the State will observe in its dealings with other States and:

> "are not the direct concern of the private citizen - see *Boland v An Taoiseach* [1974] IR 338. By contrast ss 4, 5 and 6 appear to deal with the exercise and control of the

[14] [1960] IR 93; (1961) 95 ILTR 92.

[15] [1966] IR 183.

[16] Principles of international law can derive from (among other sources) a pattern or trend of international treaties.

[17] In *Murphy v Asahi Synthetic Fibres (Ireland) Ltd.* [1985] IR 509; [1986] ILRM 24, however, O'Hanlon J appeared open to the argument that Article 29 could preclude the Oireachtas from subsequently enacting legislation which ran counter to an international agreement to which the State was a party and he took the view, *obiter*, that the provisions of such an agreement would prevail over inconsistent legislative provisions. However he did not advert to any of the cases considered in the present section.

[18] [1987] IR 201; [1986] ILRM 381.

executive power of the State in relation to external relations and are matters in which the citizen has a direct interest."

However there must now be some doubt as to whether this is a correct expression of the law. The seeds of such doubt were sown on a unique occasion in 1974 when the cases of *Duggan, Ó Láighléis* and *Sumers Jennings* were considered by the joint Law Enforcement Commission set up by the Irish and British Governments consequent on the Sunningdale agreement of December 1973. The Irish members included Mr. Justice Henchy and Mr. Justice Walsh, while the Northern Ireland and British judiciaries were represented by Lord Chief Justice Lowry and Lord Justice Scarman respectively. The Northern Ireland and British side took the view, on the basis of those cases, that Article 29.3 of the Irish Constitution could not prevent the Oireachtas from enacting an extradition law which would permit the extradition of politically motivated offenders to Northern Ireland; while the Irish side explained the *Duggan, Ó Láighléis* and *Sumers Jennings* cases in a way which led them to conclude that they could not advise:

> "that the Government of Ireland could legally enter into any agreement or that the legislature could validly enact any legislation affecting its relations with other states which would be in breach of the generally recognised principles of international law. For so long as these generally recognised principles forbid the extradition of persons charged with or convicted of political offences these members cannot advise that any agreement or legislation designed to produce this result would be valid."[19]

Both sides agreed that there would be no legal objection to reciprocal extra-territorial jurisdiction so as to try fugitive offenders wherever apprehended; this advice resulted in the enactment of the Criminal Law (Jurisdiction) Act 1976, and simultaneous similar British legislation.[20]

One could reasonably infer from the Irish position that, contrary to the views expressed in cases like *Sumers Jennings,* an individual threatened with extradition contrary to the general recognised principles of international law could invoke Article 29.3 in his defence. In this context, it is worth noting that in dismissing challenges, grounded on Article 29.3, to the constitutionality of Part III of the Extradition Act 1965, and the Extradition (European Convention on the Suppression of Terrorism) Act 1987 in *Shannon v Ireland*[21] and *Sloan, McKee and Magee v Culligan*[22] the Supreme Court did not refer to the question of whether an individual can rely on Article 29.3, but rather addressed the merits of the applicants' arguments. Furthermore, cases such as *Ó Láighléis* must now be read in the light of *Crotty v An Taoiseach*[23] which, according to one commentator, is authority for the proposition that there is a new constitutional right "to have government conducted in accordance with the mandates of the Constitution".[24]

Principles of international law do not prevail over domestic legislation?

As we have already noted, the members of the divisional High Court in *The State (Sumers Jennings) v Furlong*[25] took the view that principles of international law derived

[19] *Report of the Law Enforcement Commission* (1974; Prl.3832) pp.27-65.
[20] See above, pp. 20-21.
[21] [1984] IR 548; [1985] ILRM 449.
[22] [1992] 1 IR 223; [1992] ILRM 186, 194.
[23] [1987] IR 713; [1987] ILRM 400.
[24] See Casey, "*Crotty v An Taoiseach: A Comparative Perspective*" in O'Reilly ed., *Human Rights and Constitutional Law: Essays in Honour of Brian Walsh* (1992).
[25] [1966] IR 183.

from international legislation do not prevail over domestic legislation, given the terms of Article 15.2.1.[26] However in this context, Davitt P was careful to distinguish between principles of international law derived from international legislation and those derived from customary law, the implication being that the latter may have more forceful effect in Irish municipal law. Indeed one could draw this inference from the position of the Irish delegation to the Law Enforcement Commission that it could not advise that the Oireachtas could enact legislation in breach of the generally recognised principles of international law.[27]

However, as Casey points out,[28] it is unclear whether the generally recognised principles of international law are imported into the municipal legal system at the level of constitutional norms or at some lower level.[29] Comments of various members of the Supreme Court in the recent case of *The Government of Canada v Employment Appeals Tribunal and Burke*[30] do little to clarify the position. In accepting that the doctrine of state immunity was part of municipal law by virtue of Article 29.3, Hederman J noted that the Oireachtas had never sought to qualify or modify this position, which may be taken to imply that the Oireachtas is competent to modify, perhaps even annul, the impact of the generally recognised principles of international law on domestic law. In contrast, O'Flaherty J indicated that the Oireachtas could only legislate "in accordance with the Article" while McCarthy J appeared to take the view that the doctrine of state immunity had to be applied subject only to private constitutional rights.

> "Whatever the implications may be in domestic law, whatever the rights might, at first sight, arise in respect of the Unfair Dismissals Act unless it can be shown that there is a conflict with some private constitutional right, that matter is entirely governed by whatever are established to be the generally recognised principles of international law."[31]

No enforcement of another State's revenue laws

In *The State (Hully) v Hynes*,[32] decided by the (new) Supreme Court in 1961, an extradition sought under the Petty Sessions (Ireland) Act 1851, was challenged on the ground that the offence charged was not the real motive of the request, but merely a device to get the applicant within the British jurisdiction so as to charge him with fiscal offences. The Supreme Court upheld the applicant's case, saying that the Courts would not enforce or aid in the enforcement of another State's fiscal laws, it being the general international practice not to do so; but Article 29.3 and its bearing on the case were not specifically considered, and were mentioned only marginally by one member of the Court, Kingsmill Moore J.

[26] Though note O'Hanlon J 's suggestion, *obiter*, in *Murphy v Asahi Synthetic Fibres (Ireland) Ltd.* [1985] IR 509; [1986] ILRM 24, that Article 29 precluded the Oireachtas from enacting legislation inconsistent with an international agreement to which the State was a party.

[27] That common law rules have to comply with generally recognised principles of international law would seem to be implicit in the judgments of both Hederman and Egan JJ in *W. v W.* [1993] ILRM 294, though they differed on the impact of Article 29.3 on the issue of the recognition of foreign divorces. Egan J, who was one of the four majority judges, took the view that recognition of a divorce granted by a country in which either party was domiciled was consistent with the general principles of international law while Hederman J, dissenting, considered that Article 29.3 was inapplicable to the issue as it referred only to public international law.

[28] *Constitutional Law in Ireland* (2nd ed., 1992), p.159.

[29] Customary international law was traditionally regarded as part of the common law - see *The Paquette Habana* 175 US 677 (1900); *West Rand Central Gold Mining Co Ltd. v The King* [1905] 2 KB 391.

[30] [1992] 2 IR 484; [1992] ILRM 325. See *Heffernan* (1992) 14 DULJ (n.s.)160.

[31] Of course the Unfair Dismissals Acts 1977-1993 did not purport expressly to modify this doctrine and perhaps McCarthy J's remarks should be read in this context.

[32] (1966) 100 ILTR 145.

Ten years earlier, the (old) High Court and Supreme Court had refused, in *Buchanan Ltd. v McVey,*[33] to countenance proceedings the object of which was to enforce a Scots revenue claim; but while recognising the rule against enforcing foreign revenue law as an "exception to the rule arising from the comity of nations that respect is paid to the laws of foreign countries", the Supreme Court made no reference to Article 29.3.

In *In re Gibbons*[34] Walsh J referred to the "well established principle that it is contrary to the policy of our Courts to permit jurisdiction to be invoked for the purpose of enforcing the collection of foreign revenue debts or claims" and concluded, accordingly, that the High Court should, in exercising its discretionary powers under the Bankruptcy (Ireland) Amendment Act 1872, refuse to make an order in aid of a bankruptcy matter initiated for the purpose of collecting moneys due to the English revenue authorities. In *Larkins v National Union of Mineworkers*[35] Barrington J cited *Buchanan Ltd. v McVey* in support of the proposition that the courts of one country will not enforce the penal law or process of the courts of a foreign country and accordingly held that the High Court had no function in relation to British sequestration proceedings which were essentially penal in effect.

Diplomatic immunity: a principle of international law

In *Byrne v Ireland*[36] Walsh J gave, as an example of an immunity from suit which the Constitution countenanced, the granting of a diplomatic immunity under Article 29.3; his meaning presumably was that such an immunity would reflect a generally recognised principle of international law, and so could be reconciled with a Constitution which in general recognised no such privilege.

Immunity of sovereign states and their rulers

In *Saorstát and Continental Steamship Co. v de las Morenas*[37] O'Byrne J, with whom the rest of the Supreme Court agreed, said that the "immunity of sovereign States and their rulers from the jurisdiction of the Courts of other States" had "long been recognised as a principle of international law" and so by Article 29.3 "must now be accepted as a part of our municipal law".[38]

This decision must now be read in the light of *The Government of Canada v Employment Appeals Tribunal and Burke*[39] in which a majority of the Supreme Court gave a more restrictive reading to the scope of the doctrine of foreign state immunity.[40] This doctrine had been invoked, unsuccessfully, by the applicant in its defence to proceedings for unfair dismissal before the Employment Appeals Tribunal taken by one of its former employees, Mr. Burke, at its Dublin embassy. The applicant then sought an order of *certiorari* quashing the order of the E.A.T. in favour of Burke. This order was granted by the Supreme Court. However in the course of their judgments, both

[33] [1954] IR 89; (1956) 90 ILTR 121.
[34] [1960] Ir Jur Rep 60.
[35] [1985] IR 671.
[36] [1972] IR 241.
[37] [1945] IR 291; (1945) 79 ILTR 139.
[38] There seems to be a certain discordance between this view of Article 29.3, as importing principles straight into municipal law, and that of Henchy J in *Sumers Jennings's* case (above) which sees the section as a non-binding directive in the conduct of inter-State relations.
[39] [1992] 2 IR 484; [1992] ILRM 325. In *Fusco v O'Dea*, High Court, 21 April 1993, the plaintiff sought to join the UK Government as a defendant in extradition proceedings in order to obtain discovery of certain documents from them. The application was ultimately refused by Lynch J on the ground that such joinder was not necessary to enable the relevant documentation to be brought before the Court, though he also acknowledged the difficulty posed by the doctrine of state immunity.

McCarthy and O'Flaherty JJ took the view that the doctrine of foreign state immunity was no longer as extensive as it had been in 1945. Delivering the leading judgment, O'Flaherty J held that the generally recognised principles of international law are capable of developing over time and that in the instant case, the absolute state immunity doctrine recognised in *de las Morenas* had been replaced by a much more restrictive view of sovereign immunity, limited to acts within the sphere of governmental or sovereign activity and inapplicable to activities of a commercial or otherwise private law nature.[41] He considered that employment within an embassy should be presumed to be within the sphere of governmental activity and accordingly held that the new restrictive doctrine of foreign state immunity applied in this case.[42]

International treaties on aspects of private international law

In *Wadda v Ireland*[43] Keane J expressed the view that the incorporation of conventions eliminating injustices and inconveniences stemming from differences that exist between the private international law rules of different States - in the instant case, the Hague Convention on the Civil Aspects of International Child Abduction - was in accordance with Ireland's acceptance of the generally recognised principles of international law.

[40] Hederman J reserved his opinion upon the extent to which the doctrine of sovereign immunity may have been modified in respect of commercial activities.

[41] A position which had been anticipated much earlier by Hanna J in *Zarine v Owners of S.S. Ramava* [1942] IR 148.

[42] The decision in *Government of Canada* has been criticised for its failure to determine more precisely the limits within which the more restrictive doctrine of foreign state immunity applies - see *Heffernan, loc.cit.*

[43] High Court, 6 July 1993.

THE EXECUTIVE POWER IN EXTERNAL RELATIONS

4. 1° The executive power of the State in or in connection with its external relations shall in accordance with Article 28 of this Constitution be exercised by or on the authority of the Government.

2° For the purpose of the exercise of any executive function of the State in or in connection with its external relations, the Government may to such extent and subject to such conditions, if any, as may be determined by law, avail of or adopt any organ, instrument, or method of procedure used or adopted for the like purpose by the members of any group or league of nations with which the State is or becomes associated for the purpose of international co-operation in matters of common concern.

4. 1° De réir Airteagal 28 den Bhunreacht seo is é an Rialtas a oibreos, nó is le húdarás an Rialtais a oibreofar, cumhacht chomhallach an Stáit maidir lena chaidreamh eachtrach.

2° Ionas go bhféadfar aon fheidhm chomhallach leis an Stát a oibriú maidir lena chaidreamh eachtrach féadfaidh an Rialtas, sa mhéid go gcinnfear le dlí agus faoi chuimsiú cibé coinníollacha a chinnfear le dlí, má chinntear, aon organ stáit nó sás nó nós imeachta a chur chun críche nó a ghlactar chun a leithéid sin de chuspóir ag na náisiúin is comhaltaí d'aon bhuíon nó d'aon chumann de náisiúin a bhfuil nó a mbeidh an Stát i gcomhlachas leo le haghaidh comhair idirnáisiúnta i gcúrsaí a bhaineas leo uile.

The contemporary situation in 1937

As the specific reference to Article 28 suggests, sub-s 1 of this section might seem redundant if it stood alone; its presence is intended to assert emphatically the status of the Government as controlling external relations despite the contemporary situation in 1937, created by the Executive Authority (External Relations) Act 1936, which featured the British Crown still discharging a vestigial function in this area.[1] Sub-section 1 was however relied on by the Government (all of whose members were defendants) in *Boland v An Taoiseach*,[2] and was specifically cited by Griffin J in the Supreme Court.

Article 29.4.2

Sub-section 2 was designed to accommodate in the Constitution, but without saying so in so many words, the sole remaining function of the British Crown just mentioned. The "group or league of nations" was the British Commonwealth of Nations. The Executive Authority (External Relations) Act 1936, for which this sub-section provided cover, was repealed by the Republic of Ireland Act 1948, of which s 3 provides that:

> the President, on the authority and on the advice of the Government, may exercise the executive power or any executive function of the State in or in connection with its external relations.

[1] See below, under Article 49.

[2] [1974] IR 338; (1975) 109 ILTR 13.

The consequence of this section is that the President accredits diplomatic representatives and - in the class of international instruments called "head of State" agreements - executes treaties on the State's behalf.[3] Agreements of a more routine, administrative kind are made simply by the Government as such: for example the various Double Taxation Agreements in force between this and other countries. This practice of inter-Governmental agreements was in use also under the old Constitution.[4]

That Article 29.4.2 can apply to a group of nations other than the British Commonwealth was accepted by Walsh J in *Crotty v An Taoiseach*,[5] where he said, referring to Article 29.4.2:

> "The history of this particular provision is too well known to require elaboration but the wording is such that for the particular purpose of that provision the European Economic Community is in my view such a group or league of nations with which the State is associated for the purpose of international co-operation in matters of common concern. However the limitations are very clear. This provision relates solely to the exercise of the executive functions of this State in its external relations and is subject to such conditions, if any, as may be determined by law. Furthermore it simply provides for the adoption of any organ or instrument or method of procedure for the exercise of the executive functions of the State. It does not require prior consultation with any other State as to the policy itself. It also provides that there must be enabling legislation. The framers of the Constitution, and the People in enacting it, clearly foresaw the possibility of being associated with groups of nations for the purpose of international co-operation in matters of common concern and they provided for the possibility of the adoption of a common organ or instrument. Equally clearly they refrained from granting to the Government the power to bind the State by agreement with such groups of nations as to the manner or under what conditions that executive function of the State would be exercised."

Limitations on executive power in external relations

Though the presumption of constitutionality applies to the State's foreign policy, as it does to all acts of the executive, it is clear from the landmark case of *Crotty v An Taoiseach* that the power of the executive to determine such policy is not unfettered and furthermore that it is subject to judicial review.

An earlier attempt to subject the actions of the executive in external relations to judicial review failed in *Boland v An Taoiseach*[6] on the ground that what was at issue in that case was a mere statement of policy which was outside the jurisdiction of the courts to control. In *Crotty*, however, the plaintiff sought an injunction to prevent the government from ratifying an international agreement, the Single European Act on the basis that the

[3] These functions were, up to the passage of the Republic of Ireland Act 1948, discharged by the British Crown by virtue of the 1936 Act. Both the Crown and the President, while named as the contracting parties in treaties, are represented by plenipotentiaries. For examples of the pre- and post-1949 practice in this regard, see the Treaty of Commerce and Navigation between the Irish Free State and Portugal (29 October 1929: P.No.544) executed by the King through the Irish Minister for External Affairs as plenipotentiary: and the Treaty of Accession to the European Communities (22 January 1972), executed by the President through the Taoiseach and the Minister for Foreign Affairs as plenipotentiaries.

[4] See for instance the Convention for the Exchange of Money Orders between France and the Irish Free State (2 April 1929), expressed to be between the Government of the Irish Free State and the French Government.

[5] [1987] IR 713; [1987] ILRM 400.

[6] [1971] IR 371. In *The State (Gilliland) v Governor of Mountjoy Prison* [1987] IR 201; [1987] ILRM 287, the Supreme Court invalidated a statutory instrument based on an international agreement already ratified by Ireland, but not adopted in accordance with the terms of Article 29.5.2.

agreement allegedly infringed various articles of the Constitution. A majority of the Supreme Court[7] held that under the existing provisions of the Constitution, the Government was not entitled to enter into arrangements with other states which restricted its freedom to decide matters of foreign policy. After citing Article 1 of the Constitution, Henchy J said:

> "It appears to me that this affirmation [in Article 1] means that the State's right to conduct its external relations is part of what is inalienable and indefeasible in what is described in Article 5 as a "sovereign, independent, democratic state". It follows, in my view, that any attempt by the Government to make a binding commitment to alienate in whole or in part to other States the conduct of foreign relations would be inconsistent with the Government's duty to conduct those relations in accordance with the Constitution."

Walsh J, another member of the majority, said:

> "In enacting the Constitution the People conferred full freedom of action upon the Government to decide matters of foreign policy and to act as it thinks fit on any particular issue or issues so far as policy is concerned and as, in the opinion of the Government, the occasion requires. In my view, this freedom does not carry with it the power to abdicate that freedom or to enter into binding agreements with other States to exercise that power in a particular way or to refrain from exercising it save by particular procedures and so to bind the State in its freedom of action in its foreign policy. The freedom to formulate foreign policy is just as much a mark of sovereignty as the freedom to form economic policy and the freedom to legislate. The latter two have now been curtailed by the consent of the People to the amendment of the Constitution which is contained in Article 29.4.3. If it is now desired to qualify, curtail or inhibit the existing sovereign power to formulate and to pursue such foreign policies as from time to time to the Government may seem proper, it is not within the power of the Government itself to do so."

Consequently Title III of the Single European Act which committed the State, *inter alia*, to endeavour to reach a common position in matters of foreign policy with other member States of the European Communities,[8] was declared to be inconsistent with the Constitution.[9]

The reasoning in *Crotty* subsequently formed one of the grounds of attack on the constitutionality of the Anglo-Irish Agreement in *McGimpsey v Ireland*,[10] the plaintiffs arguing, *inter alia*, that that agreement fettered the power of the Government to conduct foreign relations. *Crotty* was distinguished by the Supreme Court in *McGimpsey* essentially on the ground that the Anglo-Irish Agreement did not, in fact, constitute any such fetter on the Government's powers in relation to foreign policy. Thus Finlay CJ said:

> "The Government of Ireland at any time carrying out the functions which have been agreed under the Anglo-Irish Agreement is entirely free to do so in the manner in

[7] Walsh, Henchy and Hederman JJ; Finlay CJ and Griffin J dissenting.

[8] The dissentients questioned whether, in fact the terms of the Single European Act restricted the freedom of the executive in relation to foreign affairs, a position later adopted by the Queen's Bench Divisional Court in relation to British ratification of the Treaty on European Union in *R. v Secretary of State for Foreign and Commonwealth Affairs, ex parte Rees-Mogg* [1993] 3 CMLR 101. They also differed from the majority on the extent of the judicial power to review executive action generally, as to which, see Article 28.1-2 above. On this last point, see comments of McCarthy J in *Ellis v O'Dea* [1989] IR 530; [1990] ILRM 87, which appear to side with the position of the majority in *Crotty*.

[9] As a result of the *Crotty* decision, Article 29.4.3 was amended, after a referendum held on 26 May 1987, to allow the State to ratify the Single European Act.

[10] [1990] 1 IR 110; [1990] ILRM 440.

> which it, and it alone, thinks most conducive to the achieving of the aims to which it is committed...[T]here is a vast and determining difference between the provisions of this Agreement and the provisions of the Single European Act as interpreted by this Court in *Crotty v An Taoiseach...*"

In the High Court, Barrington J, in distinguishing *Crotty*, had said:

> "We are not here dealing with a multilateral treaty conferring powers on supranational authorities. We are dealing with a bilateral treaty between two sovereign governments."

The implication that *Crotty* applied only to multilateral treaties and/or treaties conferring powers on supranational authorities has, quite properly, been criticised by academic commentators[11] and the better view is to consider the Anglo-Irish Agreement as an international agreement which, unlike the S.E.A., left intact the external sovereignty of the State. However it may not be possible to distinguish other international agreements to which Ireland is a party on the same ground and doubts have been expressed as to the compatibility of Ireland's membership of the U.N. with Article 29.4.1.[12]

Finally it is worth noting that in one case - *The State (Gilliland) v Governor of Mountjoy Prison*[13] - the Supreme Court invalidated a measure of domestic law based on an international agreement previously ratified by Ireland but not adopted in accordance with Article 29.5.2. In this context it is worth noting the terms of Article 46 of the Vienna Convention on the Law of Treaties which allows a state to invoke a breach of its internal law regarding competence to conclude treaties in order to avoid treaty obligations only where the violation is manifest and concerns a rule of internal law of fundamental importance.

No power to compel executive to ratify international agreements

While the courts may review decisions of the executive in relation to foreign affairs, the power to commit the State to binding international obligations remains vested solely in the executive. Consequently the courts have no jurisdiction to grant an order of mandamus directing the executive to ratify an international agreement - *Hutchinson v Minister for Justice*.[14]

Statutory protection of executive power in external relations

An example of statutory protection of the executive power in relation to the conduct of foreign affairs can be seen in s 5(1)(*b*) of the Ombudsman Act 1980, which precludes the Ombudsman from investigating any action taken by a person in relation to arrangements regarding participation in organisations of States or governments.

[11] See Hogan, "*The Supreme Court and the Single European Act*" (1987) 22 Ir Jur 55 (n.s.) at 68-69; Symmons, "*International Treaty Obligations and the Irish Constitution: the McGimpsey Case*" (1992) 41 ICLQ 311 at 316-7.

[12] See *Hogan, loc. cit.*, p.69; Heffernan and Whelan, "*Ireland, the United Nations and the Gulf Conflict: Legal Aspects*" (1991) Irish Studies in International Affairs 115, at 140-145.

[13] [1987] IR 201; [1987] ILRM 287.

[14] [1993] ILRM 602.

Article 29.4.3-6

THE EUROPEAN COMMUNITIES AND EUROPEAN UNION[1]

3° The State may become a member of the European Coal and Steel Community (established by Treaty signed at Paris on the 18th day of April, 1951), the European Economic Community (established by Treaty signed at Rome on the 25th day of March, 1957) and the European Atomic Energy Community (established by Treaty signed at Rome on the 25th day of March, 1957). The State may ratify the Single European Act (signed on behalf of the Member States of the Communities at Luxembourg on the 17th day of February, 1986, and at The Hague on the 28th day of February, 1986).

3° Tig leis an Stát a bheith ina chomhalta den Chomhphobal Eorpach do Ghual agus Cruach (a bunaíodh le Conradh a síníodh i bPáras an 18ú lá d'Aibreán, 1951), de Chomhphobal Eacnamaíochta na hEorpa (a bunaíodh le Conradh a síníodh sa Róimh an 25ú lá de Mhárta 1957) agus den Chomhphobal Eorpach do Fhuinneamh Adamhach (a bunaíodh le Conradh a síníodh sa Róimh an 25ú lá de Mhárta, 1957). Tig leis an Stát an Ionstraim Eorpach Aonair (do síníodh thar ceann Bhallstáit na gComhphobal i Lucsamburg an 17ú lá d'Fheabhra, 1986, agus insan Háig an 28ú lá d'Fheabhra, 1986) do dhaingniú.

4° The State may ratify the Treaty on European Union signed at Maastricht on the 7th day of February, 1992, and may become a member of that Union.

4° Tig leis an Stát an Conradh ar an Aontas Eorpach a sínigheadh i Maastricht ar an 7ú lá d'Fheabhra, 1992, do dhaingniú agus tig leis do bheith ina chomhalta den Aontas san.

5° No provision of this Constitution invalidates laws enacted, acts done or measures adopted by the State which are necessitated by the obligations of membership of the European Union or of the Communities, or prevents laws enacted, acts done or measures adopted by the European Union or by the Communities or by institutions thereof, or by bodies competent under the Treaties establishing the Communities, from having the force of law in the State.

5° Ní dhéanann aon fhoráileamh atá insan Bhunreacht seo aon dlíghthe d'achtuigh, gníomhartha do rinne nó bearta le n-ar ghlac an Stát, de bhíthin riachtanais ná n-oibleagaidí mar chomhalta den Aontas Eorpach nó de na Comhphobail do chur ó bháil dlíghidh ná cosc do chur le dlíghthe d'achtuigh, gníomhartha do rinne nó bearta le n-ar ghlac an tAontas Eorpach nó na Comhphobail nó institiúidi díobh, nó comhluchtaí atá inneamhail fá na Connarthaí ag bunú na gComhphobal, ó fheidhm dlíghidh do beith aca sa Stát.

6° The State may ratify the Agreement relating to Community Patents drawn up between the Member States of the Communities and done at Luxembourg on the 15th day of December, 1989.

6° Tig leis an Stát an Comhaontú maidir le Paitinní Comhphobail a tarrainguigheadh suas idir Ballstáit na gComhphobal agus a rinneadh i Lucsamburg ar an 15adh lá de Nollaig, 1989, do dhaingniú.

[1] Article A of the Maastricht Treaty of European Union establishes the European Union which is declared to be "founded on the European Communities". This treaty came into force on 1 November 1993.

The Third, Tenth and Eleventh Amendments

The original Article 29.4.3[2] was added to s 4 of Article 29 by the Third Amendment of the Constitution Act 1972.[3] Following the judgment of the Supreme Court in *Crotty v An Taoiseach,*[4] the Tenth Amendment of the Constitution Act 1987[5] allowed the State to ratify the Single European Act. Sub-sections 4, 5 and 6 of s 4 of Article 29 were added by the Eleventh Amendment of the Constitution Act 1992[6] which allowed the State to ratify the Maastricht Treaty on European Union and the Luxembourg Agreement on Community Patents.

Effect of the 1972, 1987 and 1992 amendments[7]

In *Crotty v An Taoiseach*[8] Barrington J described the effects of (the original) Article 29.4.3 (now Article 29.4.5) as "far-reaching":

> "The Constitution could not now be invoked to invalidate any measure which the State was directed by the institutions of the [European Communities] to take arising out of the exercise of their powers nor to invalidate any regulation or any decision of the European Court which had direct effect within this State by virtue of the provisions of the Treaties."[9]

Status of further amendments of the European Treaties: Further amendments of the Constitution necessary?

In *Crotty v An Taoiseach* [10] where the plaintiff successfully prevented the State from ratifying the Single European Act, the Supreme Court,[11] speaking by Finlay CJ in *Crotty's* case, said that the first sentence of (the original) Article 29.4.3 must be construed as;

[2] The original Article 29.4.3 comprised much of the present Article 29.4.3 and Article 29.4.5, save that there was, of course, no reference to the European Union or the institutions thereof.

[3] The referendum to make this amendment was used, in the political sense, as the issue on which the people voted for or against joining the Communities 1,041,890 votes were cast in favour of the amendment, 211,891 against: the "yes" vote was thus 82.4% of the total.

[4] [1987] IR 713; [1987] ILRM 400. The significance of this important case is considered above at pp. 278-280.

[5] The 10th amendment was carried by 755,423 votes to 324,977: the "yes" vote was just short of 70% in favour.

[6] The 11th Amendment was carried by 1,001,076 votes to 448,655: the "yes" vote was approximately 68.7%.

[7] See generally Collins and O'Reilly, "*The Application of Community Law in Ireland 1973-1989*" (1990) 27 CML Rev 315.

[8] [1987] IR 713; [1987] ILRM 400. See also the comments of McCarthy J in *Pesca Valentia Ltd. v Minister for Fisheries* [1985] IR 193; [1986] ILRM 68.

[9] As Walsh J said extra-judicially in "*Reflections on the effects of membership of the European Communities in Irish Law*" in Capotorti ed., "*Du droit international au droit de l'intergration: Liber amicorum Pierre Pescatore*" (Nomos, 1987): "For all practical purposes, [the Amendment] abrogated the Constitution to the extent to which any provisions thereof might be in conflict or inconsistent with Community law."

[10] [1987] IR 713; [1987] ILRM 400. See generally, Hogan, "*The Supreme Court and the Single European Act*" (1987) 22 Ir Jur (n.s.) 55; St. Bradley, "*The Referendum on the Single European Act*" (1987) 12 EL Rev 301 and Temple Lang, "*The Irish Court Case which delayed the Single European Act*" (1987) 24 CML Rev 709.

[11] The decision of the Supreme Court was divided into two parts. The judgment of the Court in relation to the constitutionality of the European Communities (Amendment) Act 1986 (which incorporated Title II of the Single European Act into domestic law) was delivered by Finlay CJ. Separate judgments were delivered in relation to the constitutionality of Title III (which is now superseded by Article J of the Maastricht Treaty). Walsh, Henchy and Hederman JJ found Title III to be unconstitutional, but Finlay CJ and Griffin J dissented. See generally, *Hogan, loc.cit.*; *Temple Lang, loc.cit.* and Casey, "*Crotty v An Taoiseach: A Comparative Perspective*" in O'Reilly, ed., *Human Rights and Constitutional Law: Essays in Honour of Brian Walsh* (Dublin, 1992). For further analysis of the inter-relationship between the Constitution and European Community law, see *Collins and O'Reilly, loc.cit.*; Reid, *The Impact of Community Law on the Irish Constitution* (Dublin, 1990).

> "an authorisation given to the State not only to join the Communities as they stood in 1973, but also to join in amendments of the Treaties so long as such amendments do not alter the essential scope or objectives of the Communities... To hold that the first sentence of Article 29.4.3 does not authorise any form of amendment to the Treaties after 1973 without a further amendment of the Constitution would be too narrow a construction; to construe it as an open-ended authority to agree, without further amendment of the Constitution, to any amendment of the treaties would be too broad."

While the Preamble and Article 30 of the Single Act made it clear that European political union between the member states was a "possible ultimate objective", the Court said that there was no doubt but that if that aim were ever realised:

> "it would constitute an alteration in the essential scope and objectives of the Communities to which Ireland could not agree without an amendment of the Constitution."

As Article 236 of the Treaty of Rome provides that any amendment shall enter into force "after being ratified by all the Member States in accordance with their respective constitutional requirements", domestic legislation giving effect to such amendments cannot be said to be "necessitated" by the obligations of membership. It does not follow, however, that every such amendment would be unconstitutional without the protection of (what is now) Article 29.4.5. In *Crotty's* case, the constitutionality of the European Communities (Amendment) Act 1986 (which gives effect to the various amendments of the Treaty of Rome contained in Title II of the Single European Act) was upheld by the Supreme Court, despite the fact that it was not a "necessitated" provision. The Court found that the creation of a new court of first instance attached to the European Court of Justice was not an infringement of the judicial power contained in Article 34.1 since it did not affect "in any material way the extent to which the judicial power has already been ceded to the European Court". But Title III was found to be unconstitutional without the immunity conferred by Article 29.4.3, as it trenched on the power of the Government contained in Article 29.4 to conduct foreign affairs.[12] The Supreme Court also indicated that amendments to the treaties which had the effect of altering the essential scope or objectives of the Communities would fall outside Article 29.4.3 and would be unconstitutional. It had been argued that the changes proposed in Title II such as qualified majority voting to allow for the approximation of laws concerning the provision of services, the working environment, health and safety of workers; co-operation on economic and monetary policy; and the new powers given to the Community to deal with the environment went beyond the original objectives of the Communities. This argument was rejected:

> "In many instances the Treaty of Rome provided a requirement that a decision on a particular topic should be unanimous, but would after the expiry of a particular stage or of the transitional period require only a qualified majority. The Community was thus a developing organism with diverse and changing methods for making decisions and an inbuilt and clearly expressed objective of expansion and progress, both in terms of the number of its member states and in terms of the mechanics to be used in the achievement of its agreed objectives. Having regard to these considerations, it is the opinion of the Court that neither the proposed changes from unanimity to qualified majority, nor the identification of topics which, while now separately stated, are within the original aims and objectives of the E.E.C., bring these proposed amendments outside the scope of the authorisation contained in Article 29.4.3."

[12] See pp. 278-280.

By this test it would seem that most - if not all - of the amendments of the Treaty of Rome since 1973 were validly ratified by the State, although it is equally clear that the Maastricht Treaty could not have been so ratified in the absence of the 11th Amendment of the Constitution Act. This question may yet possibly arise in the context of the scheduled review in 1996 of the European Community's defence capabilities envisaged by Article N.2 of the Maastricht Treaty. If this were to involve Community defence mechanisms - including, perhaps, the creation of a standing European army - it is difficult to see how such a treaty could be ratified by the State without a further referendum.[13] However, it is a nice question whether the courts can open up the validity of a ratification of an amendment to the Treaty once the amendment has entered into force.[14]

The extent to which Article 29.4.3-6[15] qualifies the rest of the Constitution

The question to what extent Article 29.4.3-6 may be taken to qualify another provision of the Constitution arises from the judgment of the Supreme Court in *Campus Oil Ltd. v Minister for Industry and Energy*,[16] where the issue was whether an appeal lay to the Supreme Court against a decision of the High Court to refer a question of Community law to the European Court of Justice. Walsh J concluded that no such appeal did lie, for even if a decision to refer was a "decision of the High Court" for the purposes of Article 34.4.3 of the Constitution,[17] the very existence of such an appeal procedure would run counter to the spirit and purpose of Article 177 of the Treaty of Rome.[18] Therefore, by virtue of Article 29.4.5:

> the right of appeal to [the Supreme] Court must yield to the primacy of Article 177 of the Treaty. That Article, as a part of Irish law, qualifies Article 34 in the matter in question.[19]

This case seems for several reasons to be a questionable example of harmonious interpretation of the Constitution. First, this interpretation of Article 177 of the Treaty of

[13] A referendum has been promised by the Taoiseach (Mr. A. Reynolds T.D.) on this question should it arise following the scheduled review in 1996: see his speech to the Institute of European Affairs in Dublin, *The Irish Times*, 19 May 1992.

[14] If an amendment to the Treaty of Rome has entered into force, legislation which gives effect to that amendment is arguably now "necessitated" by the obligations of membership and thus immune from constitutional challenge. On the other hand, Article 235 of the Treaty of Rome provides that an amendment to the Treaty of Rome can only enter into force if ratified by each member state "in accordance with its *own* constitutional requirements." An Irish court could, perhaps, in theory declare that domestic legislation giving effect to such an amendment was not protected by the (new) Article 29.4.5 and unconstitutional so t hat the amendment in question never properly entered into force. But all kinds of public policy - such as those advanced to justify the decision in *Murphy v Attorney General* [1982] IR 241 (see pp. 482-484) - must argue against a retroactive application of a finding of invalidity, *a fortiori* since such a retroactive invalidation would presumably disrupt the arrangements of other member states as well. On this and other similar issues arising from the *Crotty* case, see *Hogan*, *loc.cit.*.

[15] The "necessitated obligations" provisions is now part of Article 29.4.5.

[16] [1983] IR 82. See O'Keeffe, "*Preliminary Reference: The Supreme Court and Community Law*", 1983 5 DULJ (n.s.) 286; "*Appeals against an Order to refer under Article 177 of the EEC Treaty*", (1984) EL Rev 87; and *Murphy*, (1984) 1 CMLR 741.

[17] Walsh J had said in an earlier part of his judgment that the decision to refer was not a "decision" for the purposes of Article 34.4.3, as such a reference had no effects on the legal rights of the parties: see below at p. 515.

[18] Walsh J said: "The very purpose of that provision of Article 177 of the Treaty is to enable the national judge to have direct and unimpeded access to the only court which has jurisdiction to furnish him with such interpretation. To fetter that right, by making it subject to review on appeal, would be contrary to the spirit and letter of Article 177 of the Treaty."

[19] The unfettered discretion to refer only extends to the subject-matter of the reference itself. But the existence of the power to refer does not permit the judge making the reference "to avoid deciding issues in a case which must be decided and the failure to decide...may be the subject of an appeal procedure or review procedure in a higher national court" see *per* Walsh J in *Society for the Protection of Unborn Children (Ire.) Ltd. v Grogan* [1989] IR 753; [1990] ILRM 350; [1990] 1 CMLR 689.

Rome has never been laid down by the European Court of Justice, which does not consider an appeal against a decision to refer to be "contrary to the spirit and letter of Article 177".[20] Secondly, and more fundamentally, the decision proceeds on the premise that the Treaty of Rome has been incorporated by reference into the constitutional order, and that the Treaty of Rome may be invoked to qualify the language of the Constitution itself. This is a questionable premise given that Article 29.4.5 does no more than (i) allow the State to become a member of the European Community and (ii) provide a shield against constitutional attack for Community and domestic legislation and executive acts necessitated by obligations of Community membership. The *Campus Oil* case goes much further than this, and would appear to approach the radical proposition that Article 29.4.3-5 has the effect of scheduling every Article of the Treaty of Rome to the text of the Constitution.

Constitutional immunity only extends to measures "necessitated"[21]

This question arose in *Crotty's* case in the context of whether ratification of the Single European Act was "necessitated" by the obligations of Community membership. If it was so necessitated, Article 29.4.3 (now Article 29.4.5) would have conferred on it an immunity against constitutional attack. But the Supreme Court took the view that, as Article 33(1) of the Single Act provided that it would only come into force once all member states had ratified it "in accordance with their respective constitutional requirements", ratification by the State was not a *legal* obligation of membership, i.e., this presupposed that each member state had a discretion in the matter. This must in turn mean that the constitutionality of domestic legislation designed to give effect to, e.g., Community conventions and amendments to the Communities treaties may be called into question if such measures are not *necessitated* by the obligations of membership. Article 29.4.6 (as inserted by the 11th Amendment of the Constitution Act 1992) now expressly allows for legislation giving effect to the Community Patent Convention,[22] but one may fairly infer that without this express constitutional amendment, it was considered that the Convention would not be "necessitated" by the obligations of membership (as there is no legal obligation under Community law to ratify this Convention); and shorn of this constitutional immunity, such legislation would have been open to attack on the ground that it confers jurisdiction in certain types of patent cases on the German courts, thus infringing Article 34.[23]

The extent to which individual Acts of the Oireachtas, delegated legislation, administrative acts etc. which implement European Community legislation or measures can be said to be "necessitated" by Article 29.4.3 has been considered in a series of recent cases in the wake of the *Crotty* decision. The problem arises where the EC legislation or measure itself confers a discretion on the Member States: can the exercise of such discretion be

[20] (Case 166/73) *Rheinmühlen-Düsseldorf v Einführ- und Vorratstelle Getreide* [1974] ECR 33, 139.

[21] See generally, Whelan, "*Article 29.4.3 and the meaning of 'Necessity'*" (1992) 2 Irish Student Law Review 60. This is a particularly fine analysis of a difficult issue.

[22] No such legislation has as yet been enacted.

[23] See Robinson, "*The constitutional problem in ratifying the Community Patents Convention*" in Intellectual Property Robinson, ed. (Dublin, 1989). A similar constitutional objection arose in the case of the Brussels Protocol to the Rome Convention on Contractual Obligations. This Protocol gives the Court of Justice jurisdiction to rule on questions of interpretation arising from the Convention, but the Government was advised that ratification of this Protocol would not be constitutionally possible. As the Minister for Justice (Mr. R. Burke T.D.) explained (407 *Dáil Debates*, Col. 1936):

> "Since the Protocol would empower the Court of Justice to give rulings which would be binding on the courts of contracting states it is not possible under the Constitution for Ireland to ratify this Protocol. Accession to the 1980 Convention or Protocol is not necessitated by the obligations of membership of the European Communities and therefore is not covered by the terms of Article 29.4.3 of the Constitution."

said to be so necessitated? In *Lawlor v Minister for Agriculture*[24] the plaintiffs challenged the provisions of the European Communities (Milk Levy) Regulations 1985 insofar as they gave retroactive effect to the provisions of Commission Regulation (EEC) No. 1371/84 which itself established the milk quota regime throughout the Community. In effect, the plaintiff claimed that the decision of this State to apply the EC Regulations retroactively[25] interfered with his property rights[26] and was thus an unjust attack on those rights, contrary to Article 40.3. Murphy J was of the view that even if the Irish regulations infringed the plaintiff's property rights, he concluded that the "apparent infringement would fall within the exception provided by Article 29.4.3", since it seemed to him that:

> "the word 'necessitated' in that sub-section could not be limited in its construction to laws, acts or measures all of which are required in all of their parts to be enacted, done or adopted by the obligations of membership of the Community. It seems to me that the word necessitated in this context must extend to and include acts or measures which are consequent upon membership of the Community and are in general fulfilment of the obligations of such membership and even where there may be a choice of degree of discretion vested in the State as to the particular manner in which it would meet the general spirit of its obligations of membership."

Quite apart from the fact that this seems an unusually broad interpretation of the word "necessitated", it is also one which seems inconsistent with the reasoning in *Crotty's case*. If one were to apply this test then the Single Act would have been regarded by the Supreme Court as enjoying constitutional immunity under Article 29.4.3 as it was clearly a measure "consequent upon membership of the Community".[27]

In the subsequent decision of *Greene v Minister for Agriculture*[28] Murphy J seemed to acknowledge this fact. Here the plaintiffs challenged the constitutionality of the decision of the Minister to impose off-farm income limits in respect of certain headage payments for farmers in disadvantaged areas[29] and it seemed plain that this scheme would be found to violate Article 41[30] unless the ministerial decision could be said to enjoy constitutional immunity under Article 29.4.3. Murphy J found that the directive in question conferred an "almost unqualified discretion" with regard to the imposition of conditions by Member States with regard to headage payments and, qualifying somewhat the *Lawlor* test, he observed that:

> "There must be a point at which the discretion exercised by the State or the national authority is so far-reaching or so detached from the result to be achieved by the

[24] [1990] 1 IR 356.

[25] Article 5 of the EC Regulations allowed Member States a discretion as to whether to apply the milk quota regime retroactively to transfers taking place after 1 January 1983.

[26] Since the (Irish) regulations applied retroactively back to January 1983, they affected the sale of part of the plaintiff's farm in November and thus had the effect of depriving the plaintiff of part of his (very valuable) milk quota for the farm.

[27] It may be queried whether this analysis is consistent with the legislative history of Article 29.4.3. The Third Amendment of the Constitution Bill, 1971 originally employed the formula "consequent on the obligations of membership", but was amended during its passage through the Oireachtas, precisely because it was desired to retain constitutional control over all measures which were not legally required by the obligations of Community membership: see 258 *Dáil Debates* at Col. 402 and *Hogan, loc.cit.*.

[28] [1990] 2 IR 17; [1990] ILRM 364.

[29] The Ministerial scheme allowed farmers whose farm income was below a certain maximum figure to obtain headage payments, but the income of spouses was not taken into account in calculating this income limit. This in turn meant that married couples were effectively penalised *vis-à-vis* unmarried couples living together.

[30] Having regard to the decisions of the Supreme Court in *Murphy v Attorney General* [1982] IR 241 and *Muckley v Ireland* [1985] IR 472: see generally at pp. 992-994 below.

directive that it cannot be said to have been "necessitated" by it...It does seem to me that the word "necessitated" as used in Article 29.4.3 involves questions of degrees of necessity or at least limits as to discretion. In the present case...the particular provisions introduced by the defendants with regard to the income of the farmer or his spouse could not be said to have been necessitated by the obligations of the State as a member of the Communities."

Shorn of the constitutional immunity, Murphy J proceeded to invalidate the schemes as being contrary to Article 41.[31] For a discussion of the meaning of "necessitated" in the context of the implementation of Directives, see below at pp. 290-1.

Resolution of potential conflicts between the Constitution and Community Law

The potential for conflict between the precepts of Community law on the one hand and the Constitution on the other is a real one which may yet present difficulties for the Irish courts. The conventional view is, of course, that where there is a conflict between the provisions of the Constitution and Community law itself, the latter takes precedence. This is not only the view of the Court of Justice,[32] but has also been emphatically endorsed by both the High Court[33] and the Supreme Court.[34]

Interestingly, however, there have been some hints that the national courts may be reluctant to yield total supremacy in the area of fundamental rights. Thus, in *Society for the Protection of Unborn Children (Ire.) Ltd. v Grogan*[35] the defendants argued that the provisions of Article 40.3.3 had been *pro tanto* qualified by the provisions of the Treaty of Rome dealing with the right to supply services. Walsh J, for one, clearly reserved to this proposition:

> "It was sought to be argued in the present case that the effect of [Article 29.4.5]...is to qualify all rights, including fundamental rights, guaranteed by the Constitution. Any answer to the reference from the Court of Justice will have to be considered in the light of our own constitutional provisions. In the last analysis only this Court can decide finally what are the effects of the interaction of [Article 40.3.3] and [Article 29.4.5]."

[31] See pp. 993-994 below. See also *Condon v Minister for Agriculture* [1993] IJEL 151 (a case concerning the method of implementation of a ministerial discretion under a Community regulation). Lynch J said that insofar as the details of the implementation of the Regulation was reasonable, it was "necessitated" by Community obligations. If, however, it was determined that:

> "the details of implementation were unreasonable or unfair, then they could hardly be said to necessitated by the obligations of Community membership and they would be open to constitutional challenge."

This test seems questionable, inasmuch as it appears to conflate a test of reasonableness with that of legal necessity for the purposes of Article 29.4.5.

[32] See, e.g., Case 26/62 *Van Gend en Loos v Nederlandse Belastingensadministratie* [1963] ECR 1; (Case 106/77) *Simmenthal* [1978] ECR 629; (Op.1/91) *Re Draft Treaty on the European Economic Area* [1991] ECR I-6079. As the Court observed in the *Draft Treaty* opinion:

> "The EEC Treaty, albeit concluded in the form of an international agreement, none the less constitutes the constitutional charter of a Community based on the rule of law...The essential characteristics of the Community legal order which has thus been established are in particular its primacy over the law of the Member States and the direct effect of a whole range of provisions which are applicable to their nationals and to the Member States themselves."

[33] *Murphy v Bord Telecom Éireann* [1989] ILRM 63; *Lawlor v Minister for Agriculture* [1990] 1 IR 356; *Society for the Protection of Unborn Children (Ire.) Ltd. v Grogan (No. 3)* [1993] 1 CMLR 197.

[34] *Campus Oil Ltd. v Minister for Industry and Energy* [1983] IR 82.

[35] [1989] IR 753; [1990] ILRM 350.

These remarks echo a wider debate which has taken place in other Community countries (such as Germany[36] and Italy[37]), namely, whether the primacy of Community law extends even to cases where that law appears to infringe fundamental rights. While these concerns remain among some members of the judiciary of individual member states, the emerging jurisprudence of the Court of Justice stresses the protection of fundamental rights having regard to national Constitutions[38] and the European Convention of Human Rights.[39] These developments are likely to accelerate given that Article F.2 of the Maastricht Treaty on European Union declares that:

> The Union shall respect fundamental rights, as guaranteed by the European Convention for the Protection of Human Rights and Fundamental Freedom and as they result from the constitutional traditions common to the Member States, as general principles of Community law.

This does not mean that the Convention is now effective as part of Community law, for the Court has been denied jurisdiction to interpret this provision: Article L.

For the special instance of the potential inter-action of Community Law (and especially Protocol No. 17 of the Maastricht Treaty) and Article 40.3.3 of the Constitution, see p. 795-798.

General impact of European Communities membership and the Constitution

The machinery by which the European Communities and their institutions impinge on the State's institutions under the protection of this sub-section may be summarised as follows:[40]

[36] The German Constitutional Court originally took the view that it reserved the right to question the validity of Community measures which appeared to conflict with fundamental principles of German constitutional law: see *Internationale Handelsgesellschaft* [1974] 2 CMLR 540. This decision was, however, reversed by the Constitutional Court in 1986: see *Wunsche Handelsgesellschaft* [1987] 3 CMLR 225, with the Court observing that:

> "a measure of the protection of fundamental rights has been established in the meantime within the sovereign jurisdiction of the European Community which in its conception, substance and manner of implementation is essentially comparable with the standards of fundamental rights provided for in the [German] Constitution."

The developments referred to included several decision of the Court of Justice recognising the importance of fundamental rights within the Community legal order and a resolution of the European Parliament in 1977 ([1977] OJ C103/1) stressing the importance of the protection of human rights.

[37] The Italian Constitutional Court has twice hinted that it may review Community measures "in the unlikely event" that they "conflict with fundamental principles of the constitutional order or with the inalienable rights of the human being." In such circumstances, it reserved the right to hold those Community acts to have exceeded the scope of the limitations of the transfer of Italian sovereignty to the Community institutions provided for by Article 11 of the Italian Constitution (a provision comparable to Article 29.4.5 of the Irish Constitution). see *Frontini v Ministero delle Finanze* [1973] Giur. Cost. 2041 and *Spa Granital v Amministrazione finanziaria* [1984] Giur. Cost. 1098 and, more generally, La Pergola and del Duca. "*Community Law, International Law and the Italian Constitution*" (1985) 79 Amer. J Int'l. Law 598.

[38] See, e.g., (Case 4/73) *J Nold KG v Commission* [1974] ECR 491 ("the Court cannot allow measures which are incompatible with fundamental rights recognised and guaranteed by the Constitution of those States"); (Case 44/79) *Hauer v Rheinland-Pfalz* [1979] ECR 3727; (Case 63/83) *R. v Kirk* [1984] ECR 2689.

[39] See, e.g., (Case 85/87) *Dow Benelux v Commission* [1989] ECR 3137 (Article 8 of ECHR can be invoked in Community law to protect private dwellings of natural persons); (Case 5/88) *Wachauf v Germany* [1989] ECR 2609 (implementation by member states of Community law must "as far as possible" comply with the requirements of the European Convention of Human Rights); (Case C-250/89) *Elliniki Radiophonia Tileorassi* [1991] ECR 1-2925 (exercise by national authorities of discretionary powers under Treaty of Rome has to be assessed in the light of European Convention of Human Rights).

[40] See generally Henchy, "*The Irish Constitution and the EEC*" (1977) 1 DULJ 20; *Walsh, loc.cit*; *Collins and O'Reilly, loc.cit.*; *Reid, loc.cit.* and Gallagher, "*The Constitution and the Community*" (1993) 2 Irish Journal of European Law 129.

Legislative measures

The European Communities Act 1972, having by s 2 made the treaties governing the European Communities and the existing and future acts adopted by the institutions of those Communities and "by bodies competent under the said treaties"[41] part of the domestic law of the State,[42] provides by s 3 as follows:

(1) A Minister of State may make regulations for enabling section 2 of this Act to have full effect.

(2) Regulations under this section may contain such incidental, supplementary and consequential provisions as appear to the Minister making the regulations to be necessary for the purposes of the regulations (including provisions repealing, amending or applying, with or without modification, other law, exclusive of this Act).[43]

(3) Regulations under this section shall not create an indictable offence.

(4) Regulations under this section may be made before the 1st day of January, 1973, but regulations so made shall not come into operation before that day.

Section 1(1) of the European Communities (Amendment) Act 1973 (which replaced s 4 of the 1972 Act with a new section) provides as follows:

(1) (a) Regulations under this Act shall have statutory effect.

(b) If the Joint Committee [Foreign Affairs][44] recommends to the Houses of the Oireachtas that any regulations under this Act be annulled and a resolution annulling the regulations is passed by both such Houses within one year after the regulations are made, the regulations shall be annulled accordingly and shall cease to have statutory effect, but without prejudice to the validity of anything previously done thereunder.

(2) (a) If when regulations under this Act are made, or at any time within one year thereafter and while the regulations have statutory effect, Dáil Éireann stands adjourned for a period of more than ten days and if, during the adjournment, at least one-third of the members of Dáil Éireann by notice in writing to the Ceann Comhairle require Dáil Éireann to be summoned, the Ceann Comhairle shall summon Dáil Éireann to meet on a day named by him being neither more than twenty-one days after the receipt by him of the notice nor less than ten days after the issue of the summons.

[41] The words in brackets were inserted by s 2 of the European Communities (Amendment) Act 1992 and will come into force on the same day as the Maastricht Treaty of European Union.

[42] As amended by the European Communities (Amendment) Act 1986 (giving force of law to the relevant provisions of the Single European Act) by the European Communities (Amendment) Act 1992 (in respect of the relevant provisions on the Treaty of European Union) and European Communities (Amendment) Act 1993 (giving effect to the European Economic Area Agreement and any regulations made thereunder). The present meaning of the phrase "the treaties governing the European Communities" is set out in tabular form in s 2(2) of the 1993 Act.

[43] The provisions in brackets were held to be unconstitutional by Johnson J in *Meagher v Minister for Agriculture and Food*, High Court, 1 April 1993.

[44] By virtue of s 6 (1) of the European Communities (Amendment) Act 1993 the Committee is now known as the Joint Committee on Foreign Affairs instead of the Joint Committee on the Secondary Legislation of the European Communities.

(b) [Analogous provisions in regard to Seanad Éireann].

(c) Paragraphs (a) and (b) of this sub-section shall not apply to regulations in relation to which a resolution for their annulment has been refused by either House of the Oireachtas.

Up to the end of 1991, 542 sets of regulations of the kind envisaged by these provisions had been made. In addition, there have been numerous statutes or sections of statutes officially described as "necessitated" by membership of the European Communities which have been enacted by the Oireachtas.

The consequence is that there now exists a considerable body of law, wearing the vesture of domestic legislation (whether statutory, of statutory rank, or subordinate) which is *prima facie* withdrawn from judicial control on constitutional criteria: *prima facie*, because of course a mere official declaration that a measure is "necessitated" by the obligations of Community membership does not conclude the question whether in fact it is so necessitated or not. The decision of such a question, however, may not lie finally in the hands of the Irish courts as, if the result is to bring the State and the Communities, or other parties, into conflict, the jurisdiction of the European Court may be invoked.

Apart from domestic legislation necessitated by the obligations of Community membership, there is a category of Community legislation which applies here directly and automatically, without the necessity for casting in Irish legislative vesture, namely Regulations of the European Community and of Euratom (and Decisions of the European Coal and Steel Community).[45] On occasion, Irish legislation may be thought convenient in order to adapt or enforce measures in this category, but there is no necessity in principle for this in order that they should be immediately valid law here. This category also benefits from Article 29.4.5; but, unlike the measures cast in domestic legislative vesture, the very existence of the directly-applying Community legislation conflicts with both Article 6.2 (which provides that the powers of government are exercisable only by or on the authority of the organs of State established by the Constitution) and Article 15.2 (which reserves the exclusive legislative power to the Oireachtas). Accordingly, the cover of Article 29.4.5 is required whether or not the content of such measures is constitutionally exceptionable.

Constitutionality of s 3(2) of the European Communities (Amendment) Act 1973

The practice of implementing European Community directives by statutory instrument was held to be unconstitutional by Johnson J in *Meagher v Minister for Agriculture.*[46] In this case the applicant was charged with certain offences under the provisions of the European Communities (Control of Veterinary Medicinal Products and their Residues)

[45] Since Community Regulations constitute a "law enacted...by the Communities" within the meaning of Article 29.4.5 they are not open to constitutional challenge: see *per* Lynch J in *Condon v Minister for Agriculture and Food* [1993] IJEL 151. The same principle applies, of course, to Directives and decisions of the Community and (by virtue of the Maastricht Treaty) the bodies competent under those Treaties. However, the *method* of implementation of Directives under national law is not immune from challenge: see *Meagher v Minister for Agriculture and Food*, High Court, 1 April 1993 and above at p.111.

[46] High Court, 1 April 1993. This judgment is currently under appeal as of the time of writing. Section 5 (1) of the European Communities (Amendment) Act 1993 seeks to cure the potential defect identified in *Meagher's* case by providing that "without prejudice to the future exercise of powers conferred by s 3 of the 1972 Act" all existing regulations made under s 3 are confirmed "as and on the date they purported to come into operation." The Supreme Court reversed Johnson J in judgments delivered on 18 November 1993: See Addendum.

Regulations 1990 but a complaint was not made to the District Court within the six months period specified by s 10(4) of the Petty Sessions (Ireland) Act 1851. However, Article 32(8) of the 1990 Regulations purported to amend the 1851 Act and to allow prosecutions within two years after the date of the offence. The 1990 Regulations were made pursuant to s 3(2) of the 1972 Act which purports to allow the Minister to make a statutory instrument amending the law. Counsel for the State conceded that, "were it not for the European dimension" in the case, s 3(2) would be unconstitutional as involving an unlawful delegation of legislative power. The question, therefore, was whether s 3(2) of the 1972 Act could be said to be "necessitated" by the obligations of Community membership and, hence, invulnerable to constitutional attack.

Johnson J first referred to the language of Article 29.4.5 and observed that it was quite clear that:

> "for the purposes of implementing any Directive which might come from the [Community that] the Constitution contemplates a number of things which might require to be done. These are clearly set out. One is enacting law, two is doing acts and three adopting measures."

It was submitted that the Article 29.4.5 gave the Minister a discretion to choose as between implementing directives by means of an Act of the Oireachtas or a statutory instrument, but this Johnson J would not accept:

> "I view these powers granted by the Constitution for the purposes of effectively implementing obligations of membership of the Communities to be three separate individual matters. Therefore the Minister is obliged to look at the various Directives [and] ascertain what, in his view, would be the correct means to implement them and then ascertain precisely how it would be proper that these means themselves should be implemented. Quite clearly it was envisaged by the Constitution one of the means of implementation of such measures in the appropriate case would be the enactment of legislation. Indeed, it is the first of the three different means mentioned and therefore the Minister should have looked having regard to the whole of the Constitution, as to when in the implementation of the measures which he considered necessary it was required, having regard to the other Articles of the Constitution to enact laws.

He thus concluded that the power given by s 3(2) of the 1972 Act to a Minister to amend the law when implementing directives by statutory instrument was not necessitated by Article 29.4.5 and, shorn of this immunity, contravened Article 15.2.1 of the Constitution. This decision will, of course, have profound consequences as far as the implementation of directives is concerned and, henceforth, some form of omnibus legislation may be required to give effect to many such directives.[47] However, the decision does not exclude the possibility of the implementation of directives by statutory instrument, but only where this would involve the amendment of existing statutory or substantive law.

Court of Justice of the European Communities

The Court of Justice of the European Communities has jurisdiction, under Article 177 of the Treaty of Rome, to give preliminary rulings on:

[47] The original s 4 of the 1972 Act had provided that confirming legislation was necessary to give effect to such statutory instruments and one such omnibus piece of legislation was enacted: see European Communities (Confirmation of Regulations) Act 1973. Section 4 was later replaced by the alternative procedure provided for in s 1(1) of the European Communities (Amendment) Act 1973.

(a) the interpretation of [the] Treaty;

(b) the validity and interpretation of acts of the institutions of the Community and the European Central Bank;

(c) the interpretation of the statutes of bodies established by an act of the Council, where those statutes so provide.

The Article continues:

> Where such a question is raised before any court or tribunal of a Member State, that court or tribunal may, if it considers that a decision on the question is necessary to enable it to give judgment, request the Court of Justice to give a ruling thereon.
>
> Where any such question is raised in a case pending before a court or tribunal of a Member State, against whose decisions there is no judicial remedy under national law, that court or tribunal shall bring the matter before the Court of Justice.

These provisions clearly impinge both on the exclusive role of the courts in the administration of justice[48] (Article 34.1) and on the finality of the decision of the Supreme Court (Article 34.4.6), and equally require the cover of Article 29.4.5. (The provisions conferring other jurisdictions on the Court of Justice of the European Communities, for example in disputes between two Member States, or between a Member State and the Commission, or between an individual and the Communities, do not seem incompatible with Article 34.) Rulings of the Court of Justice are, of course, binding on national courts[49] and, where necessary, both national law and earlier judicial determinations at national level must yield to such rulings.

A good example of this principle is supplied by the judgment of Keane J in *Murphy v Bord Telecom Éireann.*[50] In this case the issue was whether the Anti-Discrimination (Pay) Act 1974 applied to a situation where female workers performed work of greater value than that performed by their male colleagues, but where they were actually paid less. Keane J initially ruled[51] that the 1974 Act did not provide a remedy in this situation, but the Court of Justice held, following a reference, that such a result would be incompatible with the equal pay provisions of Article 119 of the Treaty of Rome. When the matter came back again before Keane J he noted that:

> "The interpretation of [the 1974 Act] in accordance with the canons of construction normally applied in the Irish courts has in the present case yielded a result which is in conflict with Article 119 as interpreted by the Court of Justice. Where such a conflict exists, national law must yield primacy to Community law. The exclusive role of the making of laws assigned to the Oireachtas by Article 15 of the Constitution has been expressly modified by Article 29.4.3 so as to enable Community law to have the force of law in the State. Where such a conflict arises, the national law is, accordingly, inapplicable."

In other words, the Irish courts were now required to interpret the 1974 Act in the manner required by Article 119 (as interpreted by the Court of Justice), even if this meant

[48] It may be noted that in *Crotty's* case the Supreme Court saw no constitutional objection to the establishment of the Court of First Instance under the terms of the Single European Act since this "did not affect in any material way the extent to which the judicial power has already been ceded to the European Court."

[49] *Murphy v Bord Telecom Éireann* (*No.2*) [1988] ILRM 53; *Society for the Protection of Unborn Children (Ire.) Ltd. v Grogan (No.3)* [1993] 1 CMLR 197.

[50] [1988] ILRM 53.

[51] *Murphy v Bord Telecom Éireann (No.1)* [1986] ILRM 483.

departing from an earlier judicial ruling authoritatively interpreting the 1974 Act in a different fashion.

When to refer to the Court of Justice 

There have been several cases which give guidance in general terms as to when a reference should be made to the European Court of Justice under Article 177 of the Treaty of Rome, but no firm picture has yet emerged.[52] If anything, it might be said that the Irish courts have been too conservative on this question and that there is some evidence of a certain reluctance to make references.[53] The Court of Justice itself has repeatedly stated that the decision is entirely a matter for the national court,[54] but in *Irish Creamery Milk Suppliers' Association v Ireland*[55] it has hinted that no reference should be made until all the essential facts in the case have been established to the satisfaction of the national court:

> "It is.. for the national court to appraise the facts of the case and the arguments of the parties, of which it alone has a direct knowledge, with a view to defining the legal context in which the information requested should be placed. The decision when to make a reference under Article 177 in this case was thus dictated by considerations of procedural efficiency, which are not to be weighed by the Court of Justice, but solely by the national courts."

And in *Doyle v An Taoiseach*[56] Henchy J drew analogies between the general rule of avoidance of unnecessary constitutional questions, and the undesirability of a reference to the Court of Justice in cases where this was not necessary:

> "In my judgment the dispute between the parties is susceptible of a conclusive determination under the domestic law of this State. I consider that a decision on a question of Community law as envisaged by Article 177 of the Treaty of Rome is not necessary to enable this Court to give judgment in this case. Just as it is generally undesirable to decide a case by bringing provisions of the Constitution into play for the purpose of invalidating an impugned law when the case may be decided without [this], so also, in my opinion, should Community law, which also has the paramount force and effect of constitutional provisions, not be applied save where necessary for the decision in the case."

Here the Court found it could decide in favour of the plaintiffs by striking down a statutory instrument on the grounds of unreasonableness, without having to consider whether

[52] The Supreme Court has hinted that issues of Community law raising points of interpretation which were "not self evident" must be referred by that Court pursuant to Article 177(3), unless, of, course, such a determination is not necessary to enable the Court to give judgment on the appeal: *Kerry Co-Operative Creameries Ltd. v An Bord Bainne* [1991] ILRM 851. In some cases, a reasoned refusal to make a reference has been put forward. Thus, in *United States Tobacco (Ireland) Ltd. v Ireland* [1993] 1 IR 241; [1993] IJEL 157 Blayney J observed:

> "In my view the relevant law [on Articles 30 and 36 of the Treaty of Rome] has been very clearly stated in a number of decisions of the Court of Justice so that there is no doubt as to what the law is. The issue in this case is how the law should be applied to the particular facts."

[53] There are at least three recent decisions of the Supreme Court where a reference might have been made: *Attorney General (Society for the Protection of Unborn Children (Ire.) Ltd.) v Open Door Counselling Ltd.* [1988] IR 593; [1989] ILRM 19; *Attorney General v X.* [1992] 2 IR 1; [1992] ILRM 401; [1992] 2 CMLR 277. (although there would have been what Finlay CJ described as "practical time scale" difficulties with such a reference) and *Hanbridge Services Ltd. v British Aerospace*, Supreme Court, 18 March 1993.

[54] Unless, of course, it was a court of last resort. In addition, however, a national court has no jurisdiction to annul a Community measure and in cases before national courts where there is a real possibility that the measure may be invalid, the question *must* be referred to the Court of Justice: *Foto-Frost v Haupzollamt Lübeck-Ost* (Case 314/85) [1987] ECR 4199.

[55] Joined Cases 36 and 71/80 [1981] ECR 735

[56] [1986] ILRM 693.

the instrument breached Treaty obligations. A similar approach was adopted by the Supreme Court in *Attorney General v X,*[57] where the Supreme Court found it could decide the case in favour of the defendant on ordinary non-constitutional grounds, without having to refer the matter to the Court of Justice.[58]

Mandatory obligations on a "court of last resort" to refer

Article 177(3) places a general obligation to refer where a question of Community law arises before a court of last resort.[59] But to this there are some exceptions. There is no obligation to refer in cases of an *"acte clair"* (i.e., where the point of Community law is well settled);[60] where the issue has already been determined by the Court of Justice;[61] where the proceedings are merely interlocutory in nature;[62] or where a decision on Community law is not necessary for the purposes of the case.[63]

External Relations

The European Community is empowered to conclude international agreements[64] with non-member States and these agreements are binding on Member States.[65] Such a situation presents a conflict with Article 29.4.1,[66] needing the cover of Article 29.4.5.

[57] [1992] 1 IR 1; [1992] ILRM 401; [1992] CMLR 277. See also *Kerry Co-Operative v An Bord Bainne* [1991] ILRM 851.

[58] Finlay CJ noted that there was no provision in Article 177 "for the determination by that court of any question of law as a moot at the instance of a national court."

[59] In *People v Ferris* (1985) 3 Frewen 114 McCarthy J said that the "ordinary reading" of Article 177(3) suggested a "judicial remedy which does not require special leave." While the issue of whether the Court of Criminal Appeal was a court of last resort was reserved by that Court in *Ferris*, the language of McCarthy J suggests that it is, at least in those cases where no certificate has been granted (either by the Court of Criminal Appeal or the Attorney General) pursuant to s 29 of the Courts of Justice Act 1924, permitting a further appeal to the Supreme Court.

[60] (Case 238/81) *CILFIT v Ministero della Sanita* [1982] ECR 3415; [1983] 1 CMLR 472.

[61] (Cases 28-30/62) *da Costa en Schaake v Nederlandse Belastingadministratie* [1963] ECR 31; [1963] CMLR 224. This principle was applied by the Supreme Court in *Rhatigan v Textiles y Confecciones Europeas SA* [1990] 1 IR 126.

[62] (Case 107/76) *Hoffmann-La Roche v Centrafarm* [1977] ECR 957.

[63] *Doyle v An Taoiseach* [1986] ILRM 693; *Rhatigan v Textiles y Confecciones Europeas SA* [1990] 1 IR 126.

[64] This is provided for by the following provisions of the Treaty of Rome: Article 113(3) (external tariff agreements); Articles 131-136a (association agreements with certain non-European countries); Article 228 (general power to conclude agreements between the Community and other States or international organisations) and Article 238 (power to conclude association agreements with non-member States and international organisations).

[65] As the Court of Justice said in the classic *ERTA* case (Case 22/70) *Commission v Council* [1971] ECR 263: "Each time the Community, with a view to implementing a common policy envisaged by the Treaty lays down common rules, whatever form these may take, the member-states no longer have the right, acting individually or even collectively, to contract obligations towards member-states affecting these rules. To the extent that such common rules come into being, the Community alone is in a position to assume and carry out contractual obligations towards non-member States affecting the whole sphere of application of the Community legal system."

[66] Especially as interpreted by the Supreme Court in *Crotty v An Taoiseach* [1987] IR 713; [1987] ILRM 400.

INTERNATIONAL AGREEMENTS

5. 1° Every international agreement to which the State becomes a party shall be laid before Dáil Éireann.
2° The State shall not be bound by any international agreement involving a charge upon public funds unless the terms of the agreement shall have been approved by Dáil Éireann.
3° This section shall not apply to agreements or conventions of a technical and administrative character.

6. No international agreement shall be part of the domestic law of the State save as may be determined by the Oireachtas.

5. 1° Ní foláir gach conradh idirnáisiúnta ina mbeidh an Stát páirteach a leagan os comhair Dháil Éireann.
2° Aon chonradh idirnáisiunta a chuirfeadh costas ar an gciste poiblí ní bheidh sé ina cheangal ar an Stát mura dtoilí Dáil Éireann le téarmaí an chonartha.
3° Ní bhaineann an t-alt seo le conarthaí ná le comhaontuithe ar chúrsaí teicnice agus riaracháin.

6. Ní bheidh aon chonradh idirnáisiúnta ina chuid de dhlí inmheánach an Stáit ach mar a chinnfidh an tOireachtas.

Summary of constitutional schema

The judgment of Griffin J in *Crotty v An Taoiseach*[1] contains a useful description of the constitutional arrangements for entering into international agreements, other than those of a technical or administrative character. He said:

> "The constitutional scheme in respect of international agreements would appear, therefore, to be that the Government, exercising the executive power, may enter into international agreements, but such agreements must be laid before Dáil Éireann, and if the agreement involves a charge on public funds, the State is not to be bound by the agreement unless the terms of the agreement have been approved of by Dáil Éireann."

Obligation to lay international agreement before Dáil

The power to commit the State to international agreements is vested in the executive by virtue of Article 29.4. Article 29.5 provides, however, that such agreements must then be laid before the Dáil but it would appear that this obligation only exists in respect of agreements which have been ratified by the State. This appears from the judgment of Blayney J in *Hutchinson v Minister for Justice*[2] in which the applicant sought an order of *mandamus* directing the Minister to introduce the necessary legislation to enable ratification of the Convention on the Transfer of Sentenced Persons to take place.[3] The

[1] [1993] IR 713; [1987] ILRM 400.
[2] [1993] ILRM 602.
[3] It may be questioned whether legislation is necessary in order to ratify this Convention. Even if it involved a charge on public funds, the Constitution requires only the approval of the Dáil for the State to be bound by the Convention - Article 29.5.2. The consent of the Oireachtas as a whole would be required in order to *incorporate* the Convention into domestic law - Article 29.6 - and presumably this must be done by way of legislation. *Pace* Casey, *Constitutional Law in Ireland* (2nd ed. 1992) p.160, as Article 29.6 refers to "the Oireachtas", rather than the "Houses of the Oireachtas", the assent of the President is required and there does not appear to be any procedure whereby this could be obtained other than by legislation.

applicant contended, *inter alia*, that by failing to ratify the Convention, the State was in breach of Article 29.5.1. Blayney J, having held that the State was under no obligation to ratify the Convention, ruled further that there had, accordingly, been no breach of Article 29.5.1. He said:

> "[W]hat that provision relates to is "any international agreement to which the State becomes a party" but in respect of Ireland the Convention does not at the moment have the status of an agreement. It will not become an agreement until it has been ratified. It follows that it does not at present have to be laid before Dáil Éireann."

No consideration has ever been given to the consequence of a failure to comply with Article 29.5.1. As this provision applies only in respect of agreements which have already been ratified by the State, it would appear that non-compliance with its terms cannot affect the binding nature of the agreement in international law. If an agreement was subsequently incorporated into domestic law by legislation, pursuant to Article 29.6, it might appear somewhat pedantic to deprive it of legal effect in domestic law if it were the case that the authorities had omitted formally to lay it before the Dáil. The better view here might be to consider that the introduction of the appropriate legislation in the Dáil satisfied the obligation imposed by Article 29.5.1.

Classification of international agreements

In *The State (Gilliland) v Governor of Mountjoy Prison*[4] the Supreme Court classified international agreements into three categories for the purpose of Article 29.5: (i) An agreement or convention of a technical and administrative character which does not have to be laid before the Dáil and - irrespective, apparently, of whether it involves a charge on public funds - whose terms do not require the approval of the Dáil; (ii) an international agreement involving a charge upon public funds, by which the State shall not be bound unless the terms of the agreement have been approved by the Dáil; (iii) an international agreement falling into neither of the aforementioned categories, which must be laid before the Dáil, but the terms of which need not be approved by the Dáil.

International agreements not part of domestic law unless made so by the Oireachtas

Section 6 of Article 29 has been considered in a number of cases. In the first of these, *In re Ó Láighléis*,[5] the internment provisions of the Offences Against the State (Amendment) Act 1940, were challenged in reliance on the European Convention on Human Rights, which Ireland had signed in 1950 and ratified in 1953;[6] the preventive detention which internment amounted to, it was submitted, violated the provisions of Articles 5 and 6 of the Convention (bearing on personal liberty and the right to a judicial hearing in connection with any criminal charge). The Supreme Court, per Maguire CJ, said:

> "The insuperable obstacle to importing the provisions of the Convention for the Protection of Human Rights and Fundamental Freedoms into the domestic law of Ireland - if they be at variance with that law - is [Article 15.2.1 which provides] that

[4] [1987] IR 201; [1987] ILRM 278.

[5] [1960] IR 93; (1961) 95 ILTR 92.

[6] A challenge in reliance on the Constitution was excluded by the terms of Article 34.3.3, as the Bill for that Act had been referred to, and cleared by, the Supreme Court under Article 26 - *In re Article 26 and the Offences Against the State (Amendment) Bill 1940* [1940] IR 470; (1940) 74 ILTR 61.

> "the sole and exclusive power of making laws for the State is hereby vested in the Oireachtas: no other legislative authority has power to make laws for the State". Moreover, Article 29, the Article dealing with international relations, provides at s 6 that "no international agreement shall be part of the domestic law of the State save as may be determined by the Oireachtas".
>
> The Oireachtas has not determined that the Convention of Human Rights and Fundamental Freedoms is to be part of the domestic law of the State, and accordingly this Court cannot give effect to the Convention if it be contrary to domestic law or purports to grant rights or impose obligations additional to those of domestic law.
>
> No argument can prevail against the express command of s 6 of Article 29...before judges whose declared duty it is to uphold the Constitution and the laws."

Ten years later, in *Application of Woods,*[7] the applicant for *habeas corpus* challenged the legality of his detention on a number of grounds, of which one was that a sentence of "penal servitude" which had been passed on him was repugnant to the Constitution and also "contrary to Article 4(1) of the Universal Declaration of Human Rights proclaimed by the General Assembly of the United Nations on 10 December, 1948, and accepted and ratified by our Government on 25 February, 1953". The Supreme Court pointed out that "penal servitude" had nothing to do with the "servitude" or slavery which Article 4 of the Declaration prohibited; but also that the Declaration was not part of the domestic law of Ireland, citing Article 29 and the Supreme Court's judgment in *In re Ó Láighléis.*

The Oireachtas may apparently provide for the incorporation of an international agreement into domestic law even in advance of its conclusion. Thus in *The State (Gilliland) v Governor of Mountjoy Prison*[8] Barrington J ruled that, in accordance with s 8(5) of the Extradition Act 1965,[9] it was not necessary for the Oireachtas to enact a specific Act in relation to each extradition treaty entered into by the State in order to enable such treaty to be enforced in Irish domestic law. However such agreements must, by virtue of Article 29.5.1, be laid before the Dáil.

Unsuccessful invocation of judgments of European Court of Human Rights

In *Norris v Attorney General,*[10] in which the plaintiff sought to rely on a decision of the European Court of Human Rights to the effect that Northern Ireland laws penalising homosexual acts were inconsistent with the European Convention on Human Rights - saying that "since Ireland confirmed and ratified the Convention, there arises a presumption that the Constitution is compatible with [it] and that in considering a question as to inconsistency under Article 50, regard should be had to whether the laws being considered are consistent with the Convention itself" - O'Higgins CJ, with whom two other

[7] [1970] IR 154.
[8] [1986] ILRM 381.
[9] This provides that "[e]very extradition agreement...shall, subject to the provisions of this Part, have the force of law in accordance with its terms." Section 8(1) provides that government orders are required in order to bring an extradition agreement into effect in domestic law; while, by virtue of s 4, such orders may be annulled by either House of the Oireachtas. For a similar provision dealing for agreements with other states on double taxation, see s 361(1) of the Income Tax Act 1967, considered in *Murphy v Asahi Synthetic Fibres (Ireland) Ltd.* [1985] IR 509; [1986] ILRM 24.
[10] [1984] IR 36.

judges agreed (the minority did not consider the point), rejected the submission, expressly following what Maguire CJ had said in *Ó Láighléis'* case.

In *E. v E.*[11] the defendant in family law litigation had been refused legal aid, but, saying he could not pay for legal representation himself, invoked the decision of the European Court of Human Rights in *Airey v Ireland*,[12] in which the State had been found to be in breach of its Convention obligations in a similar context; he argued that this judgment bound the State and could be given effect in domestic proceedings within the State. O'Hanlon J rejected this submission; the question, he said, whether the State's legal aid scheme went far enough to satisfy the criteria of the *Airey* decision could be decided only by the Court of Human Rights itself.

In *O'B. v S*,[13] in which a challenge was made to the validity of ss 67 and 69 of the Succession Act 1965 denying any non-marital children a share in the estate of their father who had died intestate, the Supreme Court held that it was obliged to follow the provisions of the Succession Act 1965, in preference to the decision of the European Court of Human Rights in *Marckx v Belgium*.[14]

Indirect legal effect of unincorporated international agreements

While the executive cannot make an international agreement part of domestic law in the absence of authorisation from the Oireachtas, the actions of the executive may, in appropriate circumstances, result in such an agreement having indirect legal effect in domestic law. This is illustrated by the decisions of the High and Supreme Court in *Fakih v Minister for Justice*[15] and *Gutrani v Minister for Justice*.[16] Both cases arose out of decisions of the Minister to refuse applications for refugee status and for leave to remain in Ireland. Ireland is a party to the U.N. Convention on the Status of Refugees 1951, as amended by the Protocol on the Status of Refugees of 1967, but that agreement has not been incorporated into domestic law in accordance with Article 29.6. However, in a letter written on behalf of the Minister to a representative of the U.N. High Commissioner for Refugees, the Minister undertook, *inter alia*, to consider applications for asylum in accordance with the 1951 Convention and the 1967 Protocol. In *Fakih*, O'Hanlon J held that the Department would be held to the terms of this letter because of the legitimate expectation to which it gave rise, while in *Gutrani*, the Supreme Court, speaking through McCarthy J, held that the same result followed, not because of any legitimate or reasonable expectation which might have been held by the applicant, but simply as a result of the undertaking which the Minister had given.

Unincorporated international agreements may also have indirect legal effect through the operation of a presumption of compatibility of domestic legislation with international obligations In *Ó Domhnaill v Merrick*[17] Henchy J suggested, though without expressing a definitive opinion on the point, that it was arguable that the Statute of Limitations 1957, which was enacted after the State ratified the European Convention on Human Rights (in 1953), should be deemed to be in conformity with the Convention and construed and applied accordingly.

[11] [1982] ILRM 497.
[12] Series A, No.32, (1980) 2 EHRR 305.
[13] [1984] IR 316; [1985] ILRM 86.
[14] Series A, No.31, (1980) 2 EHRR 330.
[15] [1993] ILRM 274.
[16] Supreme Court, 2 July 1992. *Gutrani* was subsequently followed by Barr J in *Kajli v The Minister for Justice*, High Court, 21 August 1992.
[17] [1984] IR 151; [1985] ILRM 40.

The same judge had previously expressed the view, in *The State (Director of Public Prosecutions) v Walsh*,[18] that our laws generally are presumed to be in conformity with the European Convention on Human Rights This dictum was cited recently by O'Hanlon J in support of his view that the provisions of the European Convention on Human Rights can be considered by Irish judges when determining issues of public policy - *Desmond v Glackin (No.1)*.[19] In the instant case, the judge read the common law principles on contempt of court in the light of the guarantee of freedom of expression in Article 10 of the Convention.

International agreements not withdrawn from High Court's purview

In *The State (Burke) v Lennon*[20] Gavan Duffy J, by way of laying the ground for the main burden of his judgment, said that "the Constitution recognises in Article 29...as [an] exception from the general jurisdiction of the High Court, international agreements (unless the Oireachtas determines)..." It is hard to see exactly what he meant, if it was anything more than that an international agreement, not incorporated into domestic law by the Oireachtas, will not be enforced by the High (or any other) Court; this is not so much an "exception" from the Court's general jurisdiction, as a necessary consequence of the non-domestic-law character of such an agreement. On the other hand, it could be imagined that an Irish court might have to interpret an international agreement, even one without the character of domestic law, as a matter preliminary or ancillary to the decision of some other issue, e.g. the presence or absence of *mens rea*.

That the High Court, and on appeal, the Supreme Court, has jurisdiction to prevent the executive ratifying an international agreement was affirmed in *Crotty v An Taoiseach*[21] where the Supreme Court held, by a majority,[22] that Title III of the Single European Act was incompatible with the Constitution and therefore could not be ratified by the Government.[23] In the course of his judgment, Walsh J did indicate that post-ratification litigation would be ineffective to challenge the validity of an international agreement, reflecting the orthodox view of international law in relation to the capacity of the State to invoke its internal law as a ground for avoiding treaties.[24] However, in the subsequent case of *McGimpsey v Ireland*[25] the High and Supreme Courts reviewed the constitutionality of an international agreement in respect of which all formalities had been completed and which was thus binding on the State in international law.[26] No reference was made to the earlier comments of Walsh J in *Crotty* and this very important point appears

[18] [1981] IR 412.
[19] [1992] ILRM 490.
[20] [1940] IR 136; (1940) 74 ILTR 36, 131.
[21] [1987] IR 713; [1987] ILRM 400. See above, pp. 278-9, 282-4.
[22] Walsh, Henchy and Hederman JJ; Finlay CJ and Griffith J dissenting.
[23] Of course the actions of the executive do enjoy the benefit of the presumption of constitutionality which, in this context, is particularly strong. In *McGimpsey v Ireland* [1988] IR 567, Barrington J in the High Court said that there was a:

> "presumption that a government did not violate the Constitution in entering into a particular treaty and that unless the treaty expressly contradicts some provision of the Constitution, the onus is on the plaintiff clearly to establish that the government has violated the Constitution in entering the treaty. This onus must necessarily be a heavy one. The conduct of foreign policy of the State is not a matter which easily lends itself to judicial review and if there is any area in which judicial restraint in appropriate, that is it."

[24] Hogan, "*The Supreme Court and the Single European Act*" (1987) 22 Ir Jur (n.s.) 55 at 63. See Article 46 of the Vienna Convention on the Law of Treaties which, though not ratified by Ireland, was considered by Barrington J in *Crotty* to reflect general principles of international law and which allows a state to invoke a breach of its internal law regarding competence to conclude treaties in order to avoid treaty obligations only where the violation is manifest and concerns a rule of internal law of fundamental importance.
[25] [1990] 1 IR 110; [1990] ILRM 440.
[26] In *The State (Gilliland) v Governor of Mountjoy Prison* [1987] IR 201; [1987] ILRM 278, the Supreme Court invalidated an instrument of domestic law based on an international agreement which did not comply with Article 29.5.2.

to have been resolved *sub silentio*.[27]

The ultimate supremacy of the executive in relation to the conduct of foreign affairs is reflected in the fact that the power of the courts to review executive action in this context does not encompass a power to direct the executive to ratify an international agreement - *Hutchinson v Minister for Justice*.[28]

International agreements involving a charge upon public funds

In *The State (Gilliland) v Governor of Mountjoy Prison*[29] the Supreme Court held that, in determining what is an international agreement involving a charge upon public funds:

> "one should look first to the requirement that it be the terms of the agreement itself which involve such a charge... Purely incidental or consequential expenses which may fall on some organs of the State by reason of the adherence of the State to an international agreement but which are not created by one or other of the terms of that agreement itself, would make such agreement fit into the category of international agreements which shall be laid before Dáil Éireann (provided that they are not merely administrative or technical) but not within the category of those the terms of which require approval from Dáil Éireann."[30]

Therefore, because the 1984 Extradition Treaty with the United States required the State to bear certain expenses arising out of the translation of documents and the transportation of prisoners, it created a charge on public funds. As the terms of the Treaty - which was not of a technical or administrative character[31] - had not been approved by Dáil Éireann, the statutory instrument which purported to bring it into force was invalid.

International agreements given force as domestic law: examples

Examples of international agreements which have been made part of the domestic law of the State are the Warsaw Convention and the Guadalajara Convention (by the Air Navigation and Transport Acts 1936 and 1965, s 17(l) and s 2 respectively); the Treaties governing the European Communities (by s 2 of the European Communities Act 1972, and the European Communities (Amendment) Act 1992); the Vienna Conventions on Diplomatic and Consular Immunities (by ss 5, 6 of the Diplomatic Relations and Immunities Act 1967). Other international agreements may result, not in their being made part of the domestic law of the State, but in the Oireachtas authorising compliance with them: e.g. the Geneva Convention on Prisoners of War (1949) appears in the Prisoners of War and Enemy Aliens Act 1956, s 3, empowering the Minister for Defence to make regulations for the purpose of complying with it. Alternatively the

[27] For consideration of the implications of this development, see Symmons, "*International Treaty Obligations and the Irish Constitution: The McGimpsey Case*" (1992) 41 ICLQ 311.

[28] [1993] ILRM 602.

[29] [1987] IR 201 [1987] ILRM 278.

[30] A view anticipated by Egan J in the earlier case of *The State (Trimbole) v Governor of Mountjoy Prison* [1985] IR 550; [1985] ILRM 465, where he said, *obiter*, that the mere fact that expenses would be incurred in the administration of an international agreement did not necessarily constitute a "charge" for the purposes of Article 29.5.2. Though *cf.* the subsequent case of *The State (McCaud) v Governor of Mountjoy Prison* [1985] IR 68; [1986] ILRM 129, in which he appeared to resile somewhat from this position, inasmuch as he accepted, though again only *obiter*, that there was merit in the submission that a challenge to the validity of an international agreement in the light of Article 29.5.2 would succeed if the court could be satisfied that expense would be involved.

[31] In *Gilliland*, the Supreme Court ruled that, in accordance with Article 29.5.3, such agreements did not require Dáil approval, even where they involved charges on public funds.

Oireachtas may, instead of making an international agreement part of the law of the State, enact a law which gives effect, in Irish legislative form, to the obligations which the agreement involves; examples are the Genocide Act 1973, to give effect to the U.N. Convention on Genocide; and the Air Navigation and Transport Act 1973, which does the same with the Hague Convention on hijacking of aircraft.

Article 30

THE ATTORNEY GENERAL

The Attorney General

Article 30

1. **There shall be an Attorney General who shall be the adviser of the Government in matters of law and legal opinion, and shall exercise and perform all such powers, functions and duties as are conferred or imposed on him by this Constitution or by law.**
2. **The Attorney General shall be appointed by the President on the nomination of the Taoiseach.**
3. **All crimes and offences prosecuted in any court constituted under Article 34 of this Constitution other than a court of summary jurisdiction shall be prosecuted in the name of the People and at the suit of the Attorney General or some other person authorised in accordance with law to act for that purpose.**
4. **The Attorney General shall not be a member of the Government.**
5. **1° The Attorney General may at any time resign from office by placing his resignation in the hands of the Taoiseach for submission to the President.**
   2° The Taoiseach may, for reasons which to him seem sufficient, request the resignation of the Attorney General.
   3° In the event of failure to comply with the request, the appointment of the Attorney General shall be terminated by the President if the Taoiseach so advises.
   4° The Attorney General shall retire from office upon the resignation of the Taoiseach, but may continue to carry on his duties until the successor to the

An tArd–Aighne

Airteagal 30

1. **Beidh Ard-Aighne ann, agus is é is comhairleach don Rialtas i gcursaí dlí agus tuairimí dlí, agus ní foláir do gach cumhacht, gach feidhm agus gach dualgas dá mbronntar nó dá gcuirtear air leis an mBunreacht seo nó le dlí a oibriú agus a chomhlíonadh.**
2. **Is ag an Uachtarán a cheapfar an tArd-Aighne arna ainmniú sin ag an Taoiseach.**
3. **I gcás gach coir agus cion dá dtugtar in aon chúirt a bhunaítear faoi Airteagal 34 den Bhunreacht seo, ach amháin cúirt dlínse achomaire, is in ainm an Phobail agus ar agra an Ard-Aighne, nó ar agra dhuine éigin eile a údaraítear ina chomhair sin de réir dlí, a dhéanfar an cúiseamh.**
4. **Ní cead an tArd-Aighne a bheith ina chomhálta den Rialtas.**
5. **1° Tig leis an Ard-Aighne éirí as oifig uair ar bith trína chur sin in iúl don Taoiseach chun an scéal a chur faoi bhráid an Uachtaráin.**
   2° Tig leis an Taoiseach, ar ábhair is leor leis féin, a iarraidh ar an Ard-Aighne éirí as oifig.
   3° Mura ndéana an tArd-Aighne de réir na hachainí sin ní foláir don Uachtarán é a chur as oifig má chomhairlíonn an Taoiseach dó é.
   4° Ní foláir don Ard-Aighne dul as oifig ar éirí as oifig don Taoiseach, ach tig leis leanúint dá dhualgais nó go gceaptar comharba an Taoisigh.

Taoiseach shall have been appointed.

6. Subject to the foregoing provisions of this Article, the office of Attorney General, including the remuneration to be paid to the holder of the office, shall be regulated by law.

6. Faoi chuimsiú na bhforálacha sin romhainn den Airteagal seo is de réir dlí a rialófar oifig an Ard-Aighne, maille leis an tuarastal is iníoctha leis an té a bheas i seilbh na hoifige sin.

The Attorney General's office[1] was previously dependent on statute only

Before the coming into force of the 1937 Constitution the office of Attorney General existed not by virtue of the 1922 Constitution, which did not mention it, but by s 6 of the Ministers and Secretaries Act 1924. This provision still remains basically in force as the only statutory regulation of the Attorney General's office. Article 30, has, however, superseded it in some substantial respects.

Under that section the Attorney General used to be appointed (until 1936 by the Representative of the Crown) "on the nomination of the Executive Council"; this is now superseded by Article 30.2, which gives the power to make the nomination exclusively to the Taoiseach.[2] The section also provided that the Attorney General was to "hold office so long only as the President of the Executive Council by whom he was nominated continues to hold office": a provision different from that of Article 30.5.4, since, under that section, the appointment of an Attorney General would have automatically ended if the President of the Executive Council died in office, whereas Article 30.5.4 confines the automatic retirement of the Attorney General to the case of a Taoiseach's resignation.

It will be observed that by s 6(2) of the 1924 Act the Attorney General may be a member of the Dáil; this point is not mentioned in Article 30, no doubt because it seemed simpler to allow the sub-section to stand as the continuing law on the subject. On the other hand, Article 30.4 excludes the Attorney General from being a member of the Government; no such exclusion is to be found in the pre-1937 legislation. It seems, however, implicit in the provision of the old Article 51 that the Executive Council was to consist of Ministers, and in the structure of the 1924 Act which regulates Ministers and the Attorney General separately, clearly not envisaging (though not expressly excluding) the simultaneous appointment of a member of the Dáil as Minister and as Attorney General.

Article 59 (one of the transitory provisions) provided that "the person who [was] the Attorney General of Saorstát Éireann immediately before the coming into operation of this Constitution [should]... become and be the Attorney General" as if appointed under Article 30; even if the necessary adaptations[3] of enactments authorised by s 4 of the Constitution (Consequential Provisions) Act 1937, had not been obvious, this transitory provision would have sufficiently identified functionally the Attorney General of the

[1] See generally, Casey, *The Office of the Attorney General in Ireland* (Dublin, 1980).

[2] There is a suggestion that this change was inspired by George (later Mr. Justice) Gavan Duffy, who had been proposed for the office by Mr. de Valera when he became President of the Executive Council in 1932, but to whom, Conor Maguire (later Chief Justice) was preferred: see G.M. Golding, *George Gavan Duffy* (Dublin, 1982) at p. 51.

[3] References to "any official person" were to be construed as relating to "the official person who corresponds to or has the like function as such official person" under the old Constitution.

1937 Constitution with the former officer of that name. It also justifies the continued use of s 6(1) of the Ministers and Secretaries Act 1924 (so far as not superseded, as explained above) as defining the role of the post-1937 Attorney General,[4] as follows:

> There shall be vested in the Attorney General...the business, powers, authorities, duties and functions formerly vested in or exercised by the Attorney General for Ireland [and other pre-1922 law officers][5] and the administration and control of [some scheduled parts of the public service] and also the administration and business generally of public services in connection with the representation of the Government... and of the public in all legal proceedings for the enforcement of law, the punishment of offenders and the assertion or protection of public rights and all powers, duties and functions connected with the same respectively, together with the duty of advising the [Government] and the several Ministers in matters of law and of legal opinion.

Article 30 created the new office of Attorney General

While some parts of this sub-section are re-stated in Article 30.1 and 30.3, there was even a judicial view that Article 30 did not create a new office at all, but merely perpetuated, in constitutional vesture this time, the office created by the 1924 Act: see the comments of Kenny J to this effect in *Macauley v Minister for Posts and Telegraph.*[6] This view has now been judicially disapproved. In *The State (Collins) v Ruane*[7] Henchy J said that Article 30 "established the office of the Attorney General as a new constitutional office", but added that the powers of the pre-Constitution Attorney General passed to the post-Constitution Attorney. (This latter view is open to the rather theoretical objection that as there has been no post-Constitution legislation regulating the powers of the Attorney General in the manner envisaged by the Irish version of Article 30.6, such powers have not passed to the new office by means of statutory devolution). This point would appear to have been put beyond doubt by the comments of Walsh J in *Society for the Protection of Unborn Children (Ire.) Ltd. v Coogan,*[8] where in the course of expressly disapproving of the *dicta* of Kenny J in *Macauley's* case, he added:

> "The fact that the functions of the Attorney General may be similar or in many cases identical [to that of the office created by the 1924 Act] does not mean that the Constitution did not intend to create a new office. Just as the Supreme Court and the High Court set up under the Constitution are quite distinct and new courts different to those set up under the Constitution of Saorstat Éireann, so also is the office of the Attorney General."

Constitutional Position of the Attorney General: an independent officer

The general position of the Attorney General in the Constitution was considered in

[4] As to the question of the effect of the use of the Irish verb in the Irish version of Article 30.6 - does it imply regulation of the office by post-1937 legislation only? - see above at p. 207.

[5] In *The State (Collins) v Ruane* [1984] IR 105, counsel for the D.P.P. contended that among the rights previously enjoyed by the pre-1922 law officers was the right to take over and end a summary prosecution commenced by a private informer and that, hence, such a power should be taken by a process of statutory devolution to be exercisable by the Director. Henchy J rejected this submission, observing that there did not appear to be any "statutory source for such a power" and there was "no judicial decision in which such a power was recognised."

[6] [1966] IR 345. See also *The State (O'Callaghan) v Ó hUadhaigh* [1977] IR 42.

[7] [1984] IR 105.

[8] [1989] IR 734; [1990] ILRM 70.

[9] [1958] IR 1. See also *Kelly v Ireland* [1986] ILRM 318.

McLoughlin v Minister for Social Welfare,[9] in which the matter arose in order to determine whether the plaintiff, who was an assistant solicitor in the Chief State Solicitor's office (which was a service assigned to the Attorney General by the Ministers and Secretaries Act 1924), was or was not employed in the civil service of the Government so as to be insurable under the Social Welfare Act 1952. In the High Court Dixon J said:

> "The Attorney General is given a special position under the Constitution and under the Ministers and Secretaries Act but he is not in the position of an independent executive authority. As far as the exercise of the executive power is concerned, the Attorney General stands in an intermediate position next to the Taoiseach in the administrative control of certain services."

He held the plaintiff to be "employed in the Department of the Taoiseach in connection with one aspect of the exercise of the executive authority". This judgment was reversed on appeal. The single dissentient in the Supreme Court, Maguire CJ, said:

> "When examining Article 30...it must be borne in mind that the makers of the Constitution had in mind the provisions of the Ministers and Secretaries Act 1924... [and] the accepted interpretation of the Act in practice [according to which] the Taoiseach was responsible to Dáil Éireann for the administration of the branches of the public services placed under the control of the Attorney General...I see no difficulty in holding that [the Attorney General exercises executive power] under the authority of the Government while he retains, in the day-to-day decisions that he has to make, the independence which he has always enjoyed."

The other three judges took the opposite line. Kingsmill Moore J said:

> "it was quite clear that the Attorney General is in no way the servant of the Government but is put into an independent position. He is a great officer of State, with grave responsibilities of a quasi-judicial as well as of an executive nature. The provisions for his voluntary or forced resignation seem to recognise that it may be his business to adopt a line antagonistic to the Government, and such a difference of opinion has to be resolved by his ceasing to hold an independent position. He is specifically excluded from being a member of the Government, which again underlines his independent position...The Minister for Finance by s 9 of the Civil Service Regulation Act 1924, exercises a great measure of control over civil servants in all Departments. Those are not matters of immediate day-to-day control and direction, such as the Attorney General must be prepared to exercise over the services and the civil servants who are put under him; nor does the responsibility for those services, which is given to the Taoiseach by s 1, make the civil servants in those services into servants of the Government. The constitutional position allotted to the Attorney General by our present Constitution seems to me to make it even less possible to regard civil servants in the services controlled by him as being civil servants of the Government."

Ó Dálaigh J gave judgment in the same sense, though focusing on the prosecuting function which the Attorney General then had:[10]

> "Whatever room for debate there may be as to the position of the Attorney General prior to 1937 it can, in my opinion, no longer admit of argument since the enactment of the Constitution of Ireland that the Attorney General is not in the discharge of his functions as public prosecutor subject to the directions of the Taoiseach but is

[10] See below at pp. 307-8.

an independent constitutional officer."

The Attorney General's independent status has been affirmed in a series of cases involving Article 40.3.3 of the Constitution, where the courts have held, that, by reason of the exceptional nature of the right concerned (the right to life of the unborn), the Attorney General is "an especially appropriate person" (to use the language of Costello J in *Attorney General v X)*[11] to invoke the jurisdiction of the courts to defend the life of the unborn and who must act in this regard independently of the Government. This constitutional obligation is not confined to cases such as Article 40.3.3 (where the rights in question were expressly protected by the Constitution), but also extends to other cases where the right in question (if it exists at all) is merely implied. This emerges from the Supreme Court judgments in *Attorney General v Hamilton (No.1).*[12] Here the Attorney General had sought to prevent a Tribunal of Inquiry investigating discussions which had taken place at a particular Government meeting on the ground that such an inquiry would transgress an implied feature of the collective responsibility rule contained in Article 28.4. And although McCarthy J was in dissent on the main issue, his comments on the role of the Attorney may be taken as representative of the Court's view:

> "The nature of the office of the Attorney General charges him with the duty to enforce the Constitution, whether it be in the protection of the unprotected, as in *Attorney General v X.* or in a claim of public right or otherwise. It follows that...if the Attorney General considers that the [certain] conduct...involves a possible constitutional breach, he is entitled, in his own right, to invoke the jurisdiction of the courts. Independence of function in this context has its duties as well as its rights. "[13]

But McCarthy J added the following rider (and in respect of which the other members of the Court offered no view):

> "Because of [the Attorney General's] functions, having regard to the provisions for his resignation of the termination of his appointment under Article 30, he must be presumed to be acting with at least the tacit consent of the Government."

This latter view seems questionable and at odds with the judicially-declared independent nature of the Attorney General's office. There must have been many cases in the past - ranging from the commencement of certain types of prosecution to the seeking (as in the *X.* case) of an injunction restraining a pregnant girl from leaving the jurisdiction - where the actions of the Attorney General met with the disapproval of the Government. Moreover, it would indeed be curious if the Attorney General could be dismissed from office merely because he discharged the functions of his office in an independent man-

[11] [1992] 1 IR 1; [1992] ILRM 401. This aspect of the judgment of Costello J was affirmed by the Supreme Court. For consideration of the Attorney General's discretion in such cases, see pp. 319-321.

[12] [1993] 2 IR 250; [1993] ILRM 81.

[13] But cf. here the actions of the Attorney General during the so-called Ryan affair in December 1988, where the Attorney refused to endorse certain warrants for execution under s 2 of the Extradition (Amendment) Act 1987 on the ground that, by reason of what was perceived as unfair media coverage, the suspect's constitutional right to a fair trial would be infringed if an extradition order were to be made. (This ground of objection, incidentally, is not actually specified in the 1987 Act). The above comments of McCarthy J and the following *dictum* of Finlay CJ in *Attorney General v X.* [1992] 1 IR 1:
"It would have been quite incorrect for [the Attorney General] in this case, and in the absence of legislation providing any alternative procedure, to take it upon himself to make a decision on the facts available to him, instead of, as he did, bringing the matter before the courts."
would all seem to suggest that the Attorney General should not have decided the question at issue in the *Ryan* affair in his own right without referring this matter to the Courts. See generally, Hogan "*Some Reflections on the Role of the Attorney General and the Patrick Ryan Affair*" (1992) 2 ICLJ 128.

ner.

The prosecuting function

Section 9 of the Criminal Justice (Administration) Act 1924, reads:

> (1) All criminal charges prosecuted upon indictment in any court shall be prosecuted at the suit of the Attorney General...
>
> (2) Save where a criminal prosecution in a court of summary jurisdiction is prosecuted by a Minister, Department of State, or person (official or unofficial) authorised in that behalf by the law for the time being in force, all prosecutions in any court of summary jurisdiction shall be prosecuted at the suit of the Attorney General...

Prosecuting functions transferred to the Director of Public Prosecutions

Much of this section is obviously superseded by s 3 of Article 30, though the section is as yet unrepealed. Article 30.3, however, authorises the conferring by law of the prosecuting function even in indictable offences on some person other than the Attorney General; and in fact virtually the whole of the Attorney General's prosecuting function has now been so transferred, by s 3 of the Prosecution of Offences Act 1974, of which sub-s (1) reads:

> Subject to the provisions of this Act the Director of Public Prosecutions [an office established by the same Act] shall perform all the functions capable of being performed in relation to criminal matters...[14] by the Attorney General immediately before the commencement of this section and references to the Attorney General in any statute or statutory instrument in force immediately before such commencement shall be construed accordingly.[15]

There are certain savers of the Attorney General's function in criminal matters in subsections (3), (4) and (5);[16] and s 5(1) empowers the Government, whenever "of opinion that it is expedient in the interests of national security", to transfer functions in criminal matters back to the Attorney General.

However, the conventional understanding of the 1974 Act - namely that the Director of Public Prosecutions assumed virtually the entirety of the Attorney General's functions - was doubted by Walsh J in *The State (Collins) v Ruane:*[17]

> "The constitutional right of the Attorney General to prosecute in courts set up under Article 34 other than courts of summary jurisdiction cannot be removed by statute. The constitutional provision, however, does permit of this power also being exercisable by some other person authorised "in accordance with law to act for that purpose." In so far as criminal prosecutions which are entrusted to the Attorney General under Article 30 are concerned, the effect of s 3(1) of the Act of 1974 was

[14] Also in relation to election petitions and referendum petitions.

[15] The establishment of the office of the Director of Public Prosecutions by the 1974 Act necessarily implied among the powers of that office a power to engage solicitor and counsel "for the purposes of carrying out the constitutional duty [with regard to prosecutions] involved" see *Flynn v An Post* [1987] IR 68.

[16] These relate respectively to the Attorney General's function in upholding the constitutional validity of laws, his functions under s 29 of the Courts of Justice Act 1924 and s 34 of the Criminal Procedure Act 1967 (in relation to appeals and references of questions of law in criminal matters to the Supreme Court); and his role in authorising further proceedings under s 3 of the Geneva Conventions Act 1962 and the Genocide Act 1973.

[17] [1984] IR 105.

> to permit these functions also to be exercised by the Director of Public Prosecutions for so long as the Oireachtas saw fit."

As this suggests that the 1974 Act did not effect an outright transfer of the Attorney General's power to prosecute on indictment, this reading of Article 30.3 does not square readily with *The People (Director of Public Prosecutions) v Roddy,*[18] where the Supreme Court spoke in terms of the 1974 Act "transferring" these powers to the Director of Public Prosecutions. It is also inconsistent with the tenor of the 1974 Act; thus, s 5(1) allows the Government whenever of opinion "that it is expedient in the interests of national security" to transfer the functions back to the Attorney General. If the 1974 Act contemplated that the Attorney General and the Director of Public Prosecutions would share this task, this provision would surely be unnecessary. Nor is there any mechanism contained in the 1974 Act whereby any conflict between the law officers in relation to any particular prosecution can be resolved.

Prosecuting function vested in other authorities

There are many instances in which the prosecution of offences has been entrusted to authorities other than the Attorney General (or the Director of Public Prosecutions). Examples are the prosecuting powers given to the Minister for Posts and Telegraphs by s 13 of the Wireless Telegraphy Act 1926; to the Minister for Defence by s 7 of the Defence Act 1954; to the Minister for Industry and Commerce by s 3(5) of the Control of Exports (Temporary Provisions) Act 1956; to the Registrar of Companies by certain sections of the Companies Act 1963; to the Minister for Agriculture by s 47 of the Diseases of Animals Act 1966; to local authorities by s 27 of the Local Government (Water Pollution) (Amendment) Act 1990 and to the Central Bank under s 10 of the Central Bank Act 1989.

The position of the Attorney General in criminal proceedings

The position of the Attorney General in criminal proceedings has been considered in several cases; the principles on which these were decided are presumably now equally applicable to the office of Director of Public Prosecutions.

Discretion of the Attorney General

The sole responsibility and discretion of the Attorney General in regard to the institution of criminal proceedings was asserted, in reliance on s 9 of the Criminal Justice (Administration) Act 1924, in *Cronin v Shee*,[19] in which the High Court held that a Circuit Court judge had no right to take it upon himself, on hearing a civil action where the evidence suggested the defendant was guilty of felony, to assume that no prosecution would be brought and to go ahead and hear and decide the civil case. Hanna J said:

> "If in the course of a trial it is disclosed to the judge that a felony has been committed, if no sufficient reason is given him for omission to prosecute, or to give information of the alleged felony to the Attorney General, it is the duty of the judge who is trying the case to suspend the hearing until the plaintiff takes the requisite steps to bring the matter before the Attorney General."

Previously he had said:

> "Under the Criminal Justice (Administration) Act 1924, s 9, the entire responsibility for a prosecution under a criminal indictment lies with the Attorney General, whose function it is to determine whether a prosecution should proceed or not."

[18] [1977] IR 177.
[19] [1932] IR 23.

The question of the Attorney General's discretion first reached the Supreme Court in *The State (Killian) v Attorney General*;[20] this was an application by a prisoner, convicted of arson, for mandamus to compel the Attorney General to prosecute another person, who had confessed to the crime. The Supreme Court, per Maguire CJ, said:

> "The question in this case is whether this Court can interfere with the Attorney General in the exercise of his power of determining whether a prosecution shall go on or not...It would be unjustifiable for this Court to...interfere with the Attorney General by ordering him to prosecute, particularly when he has made it quite clear that he does not consider that he ought to do so."

This question was further examined in *The State (McCormack) v Curran.*[21] The facts of this case were unusual: the applicant was awaiting trial in Northern Ireland in respect of offences allegedly committed in the State. Under the Third Schedule to the [British] Criminal Jurisdiction Act 1975, he was entitled to a trial in this State if a warrant in respect of these offences had been duly issued by the District Court. As the applicant desired a trial in this jurisdiction, he sought an order of *mandamus* compelling the Director of Public Prosecutions to commence such a prosecution.

Barr J held that the Director's discretion was not reviewable by the courts, since to hold otherwise would be to impair his right and duty to decide such matters and would prejudice the independence specifically provided for by the Prosecution of Offences Act 1974. The Supreme Court, while dismissing the appeal, took a slightly different view on the question of review. Finlay CJ said that the Director's discretion could be reviewed if it was established that it was reached "*mala fide* or was influenced by an improper motive or improper policy." The Chief Justice also rejected the suggestion that the decision of the Director whether he should launch a prosecution in a particular case:

> "must be related exclusively to the probative value of the evidence laid before him...There are many other factors which may be appropriate and proper for him to take into consideration. I do not consider that it would be wise or helpful to seek to list them in any particular way."[22]

McCormack therefore gives no guidance on what these factors might be. Could the Director properly form a policy not to prosecute in certain types of cases, e.g., bigamy or homosexual offences?[23] (Note that in *Norris v Attorney General*[24] McCarthy J said that if there were a "positive decision" on the part of the police or the Director of Public Prosecutions not to prosecute in a case involving consenting male homosexuals, it would be "unlawful as a positive decision not to enforce the law.") Could he decline to prosecute in the case of, say, an offence committed within the State by Northern Ireland security forces who had improperly crossed the Border on the grounds that such a prose-

[20] (1958) 92 ILTR 182. The High Court has subsequently held that the decision of the Director to direct the accused persons came for trial before the Special Criminal Court was not susceptible to judicial review: see *Savage v Director of Public Prosecutions* [1982] ILRM 385 and *Judge v Director of Public Prosecutions* [1984] ILRM 224.

[21] [1987] ILRM 225. As we shall see, this case turned on the discretion of the Director of Public Prosecutions - as opposed to that of the Attorney General - but nothing turns on this fact. The Director may also be obliged to give reasons for his decision to refuse to prosecute: *Herron v DPP*, High Court, 26 July 1993.

[22] See also *O'Donnell v Director of Public Prosecutions*, *The Irish Times*, October 8, 1988. Cf. *Foley v Director of Public Prosecutions*, *Irish Times Law Reports*, September 25, 1989.

[23] Note that in *Norris v Ireland* (1991) 13 EHRR 186 the Director of Public Prosecutions informed the European Commission of Human Rights that: "[He] has no stated prosecution policy on any branch of the criminal law. He has no stated policy not to enforce any offence. Each case is treated on its own merits."

[24] [1984] IR 36.

cution would jeopardise Anglo-Irish relations, or that the accused would present a security problem if convicted? To what extent may he lawfully engage in plea bargaining, i.e., dropping one prosecution in returning a plea of guilty in another? These questions await judicial resolution.

The common informer, however, survives

The Attorney General's discretion (or that of the Director of Public Prosecutions) has however not entirely supplanted the common informer. In *The State (Ennis) v Farrell*[25] the High Court had granted an absolute order of prohibition to stop the District Court from hearing a complaint of an indictable offence brought by a common informer; on appeal, Ó Dálaigh CJ (with whom the other four judges agreed) said:

> "The argument in this Court has been confined to the single issue, whether the effect of Article 30.3...has been to bar the right of an individual...to initiate by information or summons a prosecution in respect of an indictable misdemeanour which the accused objects to being dealt with summarily and in respect of which he is unwilling to plead guilty, and further bars his right to maintain such prosecution by way of preliminary investigation of the offence charged up to the point where the District Justice either refuses informations or returns the accused for trial.
>
> Counsel for the respondent... has confined his argument to a submission that Article 30.3... contemplates that all prosecutions, except in respect of summary offences, must now be prosecuted in the name of the people and at the suit of the Attorney General and that no other person may prosecute such offences unless authorised to act for that purpose in accordance with law enacted *subsequent* to the coming into force of the Constitution...
>
> The Court, in my opinion, should require clear language to abolish the valuable right of private prosecution. Not alone is there no such language here, but the plain and ordinary meaning of s 3 is that it is leaving existing rights of private prosecution undisturbed. The English text has no future connotation; and the Irish text in the verb "údaraítear" is quite express as a present autonomous form in negativing the idea of the authorisation required being such as might be made in future. By way of contrast one may look at the language of Article 34.4.3, dealing with exceptions to the right of appeal to the Supreme Court from decisions of the High Court. There the English text is "...with such exceptions and subject to such regulations as may be prescribed by law", and the Irish text, "Taobh amuigh de cibé eisceachtaí agus faoi chuimsiú cibé rialacha a ordófar le dlí..."There in both texts the language indicates futurity. We find no such language in Article 30.3, nor is there anything elsewhere in the Article showing an intention to disturb a right which on the passing of the Constitution was not only well established but which was (and is) rightly regarded as a salutary check in the rare case of failure of wisdom on the part of such a high constitutional officer as the Attorney General...
>
> The only limitation on the right of the private prosecutor is that a prosecution *on indictment* must be conducted by the Attorney General: s 9(1) of the Act of 1924. As a consequence, the private prosecutor may conduct the prosecution thus far, i.e. up to the receiving of informations and the order for return for trial. Thereafter the Attorney General becomes *dominus litis*."[26]

[25] [1966] IR 107.

[26] *Ennis* was followed by the Supreme Court in *Cumann Luthchleas Gael Teo. v Windle*, Supreme Court, 22 June 1993, where Finlay CJ also said that, having regard to Article 30.3 "there can be no question of a private individual being entitled at common law to prefer a bill of indictment any longer in our legal system."

The (old) High Court had held in *Wedick v Osmond*,[27] and the (old) Supreme Court had affirmed in *The State (Cronin) v Circuit Court Judge of the Western Circuit*,[28] that the rights of the common informer in the prosecution of summary offences had not been taken away, but preserved, in s 9(2) of the Criminal Justice (Administration) Act 1924, under the reference to an "unofficial person". This approach is mirrored in the judgment of Gannon J in *Courtney v Well Woman Centre Ltd.*[29] Here a prosecution had been taken under the Health (Family Planning) Act 1979 by a member of the Garda Síochána in his official capacity, but it was argued that, in the absence of a ministerial order under s 96 of the Health Act 1947 authorising such a prosecution, the Minister for Health or the regional Health Boards alone were competent prosecutors. Gannon J held that these statutory provisions provided powers "in ease of and not in substitution for" those of the Garda Síochána; and he emphasised, echoing *The State (Ennis) v Farrell*[30] that legislation:

> "intended to put an end to or limit the common law rights of any member of the public, including a member of the Garda Síochána, would have to be expressed in a clear and unequivocal manner:"

a condition which s 96 of the 1947 Act did not meet.

This approach received ultimate confirmation from the Supreme Court in *Cumann Luthchleas Gael Teo. v Windle*[31] where Finlay CJ summarised the effect of the *Ennis* and *Roddy* cases by saying that:

> "the right of private prosecution, both in respect of summary offences and in respect of indictable offences up to the stage of an order for return of trial is an important common law right which...has survived the Constitution. I am satisfied that it cannot be by any form of implied provision excluded in respect of a new statutory offence and that if it were to be excluded the statute would have either expressly to exclude any form of prosecution by a private individual or confine prosecution to a specific person or body."

However, the Court concluded that since a corporation could not be regarded as an ordinary member of the public, the prosecutor in this case[32] had no standing to bring the prosecution as a statutory corporation has no power at common law[33] to prosecute as a common informer.

Police officer prosecutes as common informer

It may be added that when a police officer prosecutes, he does so not in virtue of statutory authority, but as a common informer. In *The People v Roddy*,[34] in which the Supreme Court held that summary criminal proceedings could be brought by a member of the Garda Síochána in the name of the Attorney General (or Director of Public Prosecutions) without a specific authority in that behalf in each particular case, Griffin J said:

> "From 1924 onwards, public prosecutions (i.e. those paid for out of public funds) were brought in the District Court in the name of the Attorney General or, alterna-

[27] [1935] IR 820.

[28] [1937] IR 34. See also *Murphy v Cryan* [1952] IR 225.

[29] High Court, 15 November 1985.

[30] [1966] IR 107.

[31] Supreme Court, 22 June 1993.

[32] The prosecution had been brought by Dublin Corporation, which alleged that Cumann Luthchleas Gael (the GAA) had violated the Fire Services Act 1981 by having inadequate safety precautions.

[33] The Court pointed out, however, that such a power could be readily conferred by statute.

[34] [1977] IR 177. See also *Dillane v Ireland* [1980] ILRM 167.

tively, in the name of the Attorney General and at the suit of the Superintendent of the Garda Síochána for the relevant area, or in the name of the Garda who investigated the case without doing so in the name of the Attorney General. There seems to have been no settled rule as to when such prosecutions were brought in the name of the Attorney General or at the suit of the Superintendent, or in the name of the prosecuting Garda. Where the prosecution was brought in the name of the investigating Garda, the Garda, though performing what was his duty, was in legal quality a common informer."

Police officer apparently not subject to control of the Director of Public Prosecutions

Not only has the common informer survived, but a police officer acting as such, even though doing so in pursuance of his official duty, cannot be subject to the control of the Director of Public Prosecutions: or so it appears from the judgment of the Supreme Court in *The State (Collins) v Ruane,*[35] in which the Director unsuccessfully sought to have quashed, as made without jurisdiction, the conviction resulting from a District Court prosecution brought by a member of the Garda Síochána in which the District Judge had insisted on hearing the prosecution despite intimation of the Director's wish to withdraw it. The Supreme Court upheld the decision of Gannon J in the High Court, to the effect that the Director of Public Prosecutions may not intervene to cut short a summary prosecution taken by a police officer in his own name as common informer.[36] Henchy J noted that, as Article 30.3 had no application to summary prosecutions, the rights of the Attorney General (and, consequently, those of the Director of Public Prosecutions) in relation to summary prosecutions were to be determined by reference to statute law and the common law; but the Prosecution of Offences Act 1974, conferred no such power, nor did s 6(1) of the Ministers and Secretaries Act 1924 (which transferred to the Attorney General the powers enjoyed by the former Attorney General for Ireland and which vested in him the general duty and function of enforcing the criminal law). He said:

> "[Counsel for the Director of Public Prosecutions] submitted that the wide powers of the Irish Attorney General before the Anglo-Irish Treaty in 1921 included the power to intervene in a summary prosecution for the purpose of putting an end to it, but he concedes that he is unable to find a statutory source for such a power and that he cannot point to any judicial decision in which such power was recognised. I would therefore reject the submission that the power claimed devolved on the Attorney General as part of the powers formerly vested in, or exercisable by, the Attorney General for Ireland before 1922.
>
> As for the second set of powers from s 6(1) of the Ministers and Secretaries Act 1924, the only bearing it has on criminal matters is to vest in the new office of Attorney General under the Constitution of 1922 the power, duty and function of enforcing, by prosecution, the criminal law so that offenders would be convicted and punished. That falls far short of vesting in the Attorney General the power to cut short a summary prosecution instituted by a common informer."

However, in indictable cases at least, it is permissible for a member of the Garda Síochána to consult the Director of Public Prosecutions in advance of any such prosecu-

[35] [1984] IR 105.

[36] It is, of course, otherwise where the policeman prosecutes in the name of the Director of Public Prosecutions: in that case, the Director is *dominus litis* and may discontinue the proceedings: see *The People (Director of Public Prosecutions) v Roddy* [1977] IR 177.

tion, without trenching on the mutual independence of both parties. Thus, in *The State (McCormack) v Curran,*[37] the Supreme Court held that a police officer did not, by consulting the Director of Public Prosecutions, abdicate his right to decide whether or not to prosecute.

Two special statutory functions of the Attorney General in the field of criminal prosecutions have been judicially considered on constitutional criteria.

Power of the Attorney General to send for trial by the Special Criminal Court

Under s 46(2) of the Offences Against the State Act 1939, a person charged with a non-scheduled offence and brought before the District Court may be sent for trial to the Special Criminal Court if an application is made to the District Judge:

> "grounded on the certificate of the Attorney General that the ordinary courts are, in his opinion, inadequate to secure the effective administration of justice and the preservation of public peace and order in relation to the trial of such person on such charge."

In *In re MacCurtain*[38] this was challenged as purporting to vest judicial or legislative functions in the Attorney General. Gavan Duffy J rejected this submission:

> "Now, the Attorney General is the principal legal officer of the State under Article 30... and the Legislature has declared that, if he consider that the ordinary courts are inadequate in relation to a particular trial, effect shall be given to that opinion by sending the accused person for trial to the Special Court. The scheduling of particular offences by the Act of 1939 was not essential under the Constitution and I do not follow the contention that, because an offence is not scheduled, the Attorney General is therefore required to act either in a judicial or legislative capacity. He is precisely the person to whom one would expect the Legislature to entrust consideration of such a question essentially within his domain, because he is the State authority in charge of prosecutions under an express provision of the Constitution."

The Supreme Court affirmed the judgment of Gavan Duffy J.

Forty years later, in *Savage and McOwen v Director of Public Prosecutions,*[39] the exercise of this power (now vested in the Director) in a particular case was attacked on the ground that the opinion, upon which a certificate had been issued, had been reached on unreasonable, wrong or insufficient grounds. Finlay P held in the High Court that the opinion was not subject to review by the courts, since any such review would require the Director:

> "to reveal in open court, in litigation, at the instance of the accused person himself all the information, knowledge and facts upon which he formed his opinion...The revealing of such information in open court under conditions under which persons are seeking to overthrow the established organs of the State would be a security impossibility; and to interpret s 46(2) of the Act of 1939 so as to make that necessary would be to vitiate the entire of that subsection."

This judgment was followed by Carroll J in *O'Reilly v Attorney General*[40] in the context of a challenge the decision of the Director of Public Prosecutions to transfer him from

[37] [1987] ILRM 225.
[38] [1941] IR 83.
[39] [1982] ILRM 385.
[40] [1984] ILRM 224.

the ordinary courts to the Special Criminal Court under s 48(1) of the Offences Against the State Act 1939. She rejected this argument:

> "I am of opinion, based on the terms of Article 38.3.1 and the authorities to-date, that the opinion of the Director of Public Prosecutions is not reviewable by the courts, whether in open court or as a private investigation. The Oireachtas has determined the method under Article 38.3 by which the inadequacy of the ordinary courts is to be determined, i.e., the opinion of the Director of Public Prosecutions as evidenced by his certificate. The courts do not have power to set that opinion aside, for to do so would be to substitute in a negative way their opinion as to the adequacy of the grounds on which the opinion was based."

These two judgments have rightly attracted critical comment,[41] since it is inherent in the nature of judicial review that the courts will retain the power to review the exercise of such discretionary powers on standard grounds such as vires, reasonableness etc. Furthermore, it seems wrong to interpret the legislation establishing the Special Criminal Court in such a manner as might allow the prosecuting authorities to circumvent an accused's right to jury trial.[42]

Power to send for trial notwithstanding refusal of the District Judge to do so unconstitutional

In *The State (Shanahan) v Attorney General*[43] the Supreme Court (reversing Davitt P in the High Court) held s 62 of the Courts of Justice Act 1936, constitutional; this section - attacked on the ground that it constituted an unwarrantable legislative interference with the courts' operation in a purely judicial domain - empowered the Attorney General, despite the refusal of the District Court on a preliminary investigation to send an accused person for trial for an indictable offence, to send such person for trial himself. This power became exercisable by the Director of Public Prosecutions;[44] but it did not withstand a subsequent challenge in *Costello v Director of Public Prosecutions*[45] in which the Supreme Court held it unconstitutional as an interference with the exercise of the judicial function, thus overturning the earlier decision in *Shanahan*.

Role of the Attorney General under the Extradition (Amendment) Act 1987

The Extradition (Amendment) Act 1987 was enacted as result of concerns which were expressed concerning the workings of the extradition arrangements between this State and the United Kingdom.[46] The effect of this Act is to vest in the Attorney General a new statutory role as far as the endorsement of British warrants is concerned and s 2(*a*) provides that the Attorney General must refuse to authorise the endorsement of such warrants:

[41] See Byrne, "*The Director of Public Prosecution's Power to Refer Cases to the Special Criminal Court*" [1984] 6 DULJ 177; Pye, "*Judicial Review of Discretionary Powers under Part V of the Offences Against the State Act 1939*" (1985) 3 ILT 65; Hogan and Walker, *Political Violence and the Law in Ireland* (Manchester, 1989) at 234-7. Cf. the much stronger position taken by the Supreme Court in *In re Article 26 and the Emergency Powers Bill, 1976* [1977] IR 159 where it was hinted that a declaration of emergency by the Dáil under Article 28.3.3 might be subject to review in an appropriate case.

[42] Cf. in this regard the comments of Walsh J in *McIlhenny v Special Criminal Court* [1990] 1 IR 405. Moreover, both *Savage* and *O'Reilly* might now have to be re-assessed in the light of subsequent decisions of the Supreme Court (such as *Re R. Ltd.* [1989] IR 126) which held that legislation prejudicially affecting constitutional rights (in this case the right to jury trial) must be strictly construed.

[43] [1964] IR 239.

[44] See above at pp. 307-8.

[45] [1984] IR 436.

[46] See generally Hogan, "*The Extradition (Amendment) Act 1987*" (1987) ICLSA 25/01 and Hogan, "*Reflections on the Patrick Ryan Affair*" (1992) 2 ICLJ 128.

unless the Attorney General, having considered such information as he deems appropriate, he is of opinion that -

(*a*) there is a clear intention to prosecute or, as the case may be, to continue the prosecution of, the person named or described in the warrant concerned for the offence specified therein in a place in [the United Kingdom] and

(*b*) such intention is founded on the existence of sufficient evidence.

The role of the Attorney General under the terms of the 1987 Act excited considerable public controversy in the wake of the Father Patrick Ryan affair in late 1988.[47] The British authorities had sought the extradition of Father Ryan in respect of various explosive charges. Unfortunately, however, at the same time, several prominent British politicians made prejudicial comments about the Ryan case in the House of Commons and these comments received widespread publicity. The Attorney General concluded that the British request complied with the requirements of s 2 of the 1987 Act (i.e., clear intention to prosecute and sufficiency of evidence), but declined to endorse the warrants on the ground that the extradition of Father Ryan in such circumstances would have amounted to a breach of his constitutional rights to a fair trial.

It is by no means clear that the Attorney General acted *intra vires* in reaching this conclusion. The 1987 Amendment Act specifies two grounds - sufficiency of evidence and an intention to prosecute - on which the Attorney General must satisfy himself with regard to Part III extradition warrants. As the Attorney General was so satisfied with regard to these two statutory grounds, it is accordingly not easy to see how he could refuse to endorse the warrants by reference to non-statutory criteria. The Attorney General could also be said to have exceeded his jurisdiction by in effect usurping the jurisdiction of the courts. It may well be that the courts would have arrived at precisely the same conclusion with regard to the prejudicial publicity, but they would have only done so following a full hearing, having heard the oral evidence and listened to legal argument from both sides. In taking the decision the way he did, the Attorney General unwittingly left himself open to the charge that he privately discharged judicial functions in an *ex parte* manner.

Secondly, if a non-judicial personage can refuse to perform a designated statutory function on the ground that to do so would amount to a breach of constitutional rights, where would this principle stop? It could scarcely be contended, for example, that the Garda Commissioner could have refused to perform his statutory functions under the Extradition Acts on this ground; yet the fact that the Attorney General was of this view in respect of the facts of a particular case could hardly affect the principle of the matter.

The constitutionality of this procedure was unsuccessfully challenged in *Wheeler v Culligan*.[48] It had been argued that the effect of s 2 was to confer judicial powers on the Attorney General, but Costello J would not accept this proposition:

> "In examining the information referred to in the section and arriving at the opinions which he is required to arrive at under the section, he is not, in my view, considering as a judge does, a dispute or controversy as to the existence of a legal right."[49]

[47] See generally, Hogan, "*Reflections on the Role of the Attorney General and the Patrick Ryan Affair*" [1992] 2 ICLJ 128.

[48] [1989] IR 344.

[49] Yet this is precisely what the Attorney General appears to have done in the Patrick Ryan affair: see fn 47, above. Furthermore, in *McGlinchey v Ireland (No.2)* [1990] 2 IR 220 the same judge suggested that the Attorney General would be entitled to refuse to endorse an extradition warrant in the case of some procedural

Costello J compared the functions of the Attorney General under the 1987 Act with those of a prosecuting authority such as the Director of Public Prosecutions. Both instances involved "procedural decisions" which were "necessary to be taken before justice is subsequently administered in the courts."[50]

Miscellaneous aspects of the Attorney General's prosecuting function

Various aspects of the Attorney General's function in the prosecution of offences were considered in *The State v Purcell*[51] (weight to be given to Attorney General's opposition to granting of bail); *Attorney General v Healy*[52] (Attorney General can bring summary prosecution where no one else is specifically authorised); *Attorney General v Crawford*[53] and *The State (Attorney General) v District Justice of Ballyhaunis*[54] (no jurisdiction in District Court to award costs to or against Attorney General in revenue prosecutions); *The State (Director of Public Prosecutions) v Roe*[55] (Circuit Court can award costs of criminal appeal against prosecutions); *The People (Attorney General) v Kennedy*[56] (no appeal by Attorney General against acquittal recorded by Court of Criminal Appeal); *Attorney General v O'Sullivan*[57] (Attorney General cannot be compelled to enter recognisances to prosecute appeal in customs prosecution); *The People (Attorney General) v Boggan*[58] (Attorney General not entitled to prefer indictment unless preliminary investigation first held); and *Attorney General v Dillon*[59] (Attorney General can take criminal proceedings where person authorised by statute has not done so).

The assertion of public rights: historical background

The Constitution does not formally declare the Attorney General to be the representative of the public for the assertion or defence of public rights or interests other than in the context of criminal prosecutions. But this aspect of the office, of great importance, has always been recognised; it derives from s 6(1) of the Ministers and Secretaries Act 1924, which points to the functions belonging to the law officers under the pre-1922 regime and also specifically mentions "the assertion and protection of public rights". The nature of the Attorney General's role here was expounded, with peculiar authority,[60] by Kennedy CJ in *Moore v Attorney General*:[61]

> "[The authority under which the Attorney General represents the public] is, in my opinion, to be found in the first part of the sub-section, and its extent and character,

flaw in the supporting documentation. It is difficult to see how someone who takes it upon themselves to make a determination of the character is not discharging a judicial function.

50 Yet this seems dubious, for unlike the prosecuting authorities, the Attorney General is required to meet specific statutory criteria under s 2 before deciding to endorse the warrants. In this respect, any decision of the Attorney General under s 2 seems more comparable to the functions of District Court clerks under the Petty Sessions (Ireland) Act 1851 (which were held to be judicial functions in *The State (Clarke) v Roche* [1986] IR 614) than to the functions of any prosecuting authorities.

51 [1926] IR 207; (1925) 59 ILTR 141.

52 [1928] IR 460.

53 [1940] IR 335.

54 [1940] IR 344.

55 [1985] IR 307.

56 [1946] IR 517; (1947) 81 ILTR 73.

57 [1950] Ir Jur Rep 23.

58 [1958] IR 67.

59 (1959) Ir Jur Rep 53.

60 The Chief Justice had formerly been himself the Law Officer of the Provisional Government which managed the transition of 1921-2, and the first Attorney General of Saorstát Éireann. He also had charge of the preparation of the Bill for the Ministers and Secretaries Act and (being himself a member of the House) had charge of the Bill during its passage through the Dáil.

61 [1930] IR 471.

as, for instance, whether exclusive or otherwise, is to be discovered by reference to the like authority formerly vested in the Attorney General and Solicitor General for Ireland and their successors prior to the Treaty of 1921. Accordingly, I now turn to the consideration of the position of the former Attorney General in relation to such proceedings as the present [the Attorney General was resisting, on behalf of the public, a claim to private fishery rights]; and I begin with this - that the office in Ireland was a reflection of the office of Attorney General in England, and was commonly treated in the courts as of similar status and constitution, and governed and regulated by the same rules and principles so far as capable of being applied. [By this route the Saorstát Éireann Attorney General] became, in my opinion, the legal representative of the public, that is to say, of the corporate community of the Saorstát, in all litigation in the courts of the Saorstat in which the public may be involved as a party interested, whether as plaintiff or defendant, or otherwise."

Likewise in *Attorney General and Minister for Justice v Dublin United Tramways Co.*[62] Maguire P held that the Attorney General was a proper plaintiff in an action for damages for loss of the services of a policeman injured through the defendants' negligence[63] and said:

> "The position of the Attorney General has been altered in some ways by the Constitution of Éire, but his authority to assert the rights of the public by action in the courts has not been altered. I hold that he is entitled to bring this action."

These sentiments have also received modern judicial approval. In *Campus Oil Ltd. v Minister for Industry and Energy (No.2)*[64] the plaintiffs disputed the right of the Attorney General to seek an injunction enforcing a ministerial order and contended that the traditional role of the Attorney General to assert and protect public rights not survived the enactment of the Constitution. Keane J emphatically rejected this suggestion, saying:

> "In a case such as the present, where the plaintiffs are alleged to be defying a statutory rule or order made by a Minister in what he conceives to be the public interest and not for the protection of any private interest, I am satisfied that the appropriate person to assert and defend the public interest, thus allegedly violated, is the Attorney General. This is clear from a number of decisions both prior and subsequent to the present Constitution..."

Whether the Attorney General enjoys an exclusive role in the enforcement of public rights[65]

In *Irish Permanent Building Society v Caldwell (No.1)*[66] Keane J adverted to a separate, albeit related, issue does the Attorney General enjoy an *exclusive* role as far as the asser-

[62] [1939] IR 500; (1940) 74 ILTR 46. A similar position had been taken up by the Privy Council in *Wigg and Cochrane v Attorney General* [1927] IR 285 and by Johnston J in *Attorney General v Northern Petroleum Tank Co. Ltd.* [1936] IR 450; (1936) 70 ILTR 205.

[63] The principle that the State could sue for loss of services of a State employee was ultimately rejected in *Attorney General v Ryan's Car Hire Ltd.* [1965] IR 642; (1967) 101 ILTR 57; though on grounds not material to the right of the Attorney General to represent the public or State interest.

[64] [1983] IR 88; [1984] ILRM 45.

[65] Note the controversy which surfaced in January 1992 at the Tribunal of Inquiry into the Beef Industry. When counsel for one of the parties questioned the role being played by the Attorney General at the proceedings, the Chairman (Mr Justice Hamilton) was quoted as saying that while the Attorney General continued to represent the public interest while at the same time representing the interests of the State authorities before the Tribunal, he (the Chairman) was the ultimate guardian of the public interest as far as the Tribunal's own proceedings were concerned: *The Irish Times*, 25 January 1992.

[66] [1979] ILRM 273.

tion of public rights is concerned? This was a case where the plaintiffs had alleged that the registration of a rival building society by the defendant Registrar of Building Societies was invalid. The defendants sought to have the proceedings struck out as disclosing no cause of action on the ground that, as the plaintiffs had not alleged that they would suffer individual loss and damage as a result of the registration of the rival society, they had no *locus standi* to challenge the Registrar's decision. Keane J appeared sympathetic to the defendant's argument that a claim of this kind could be asserted only by the Attorney General, whether on his own or at a relator's initiative:

> "It is at least arguable that the limitations recognised by the common law on the right of the private citizen to assert a right public in its nature without the intervention of the Attorney General were not affected by the Constitution of Saorstát Éireann (see *Moore v Attorney General*). I think that it is by no means clear that this principle was in any way affected by the enactment of the present Constitution."

However, he refused to strike out the plaintiff's case, saying that the questions raised deserved "full and unhurried consideration". It may be noted that in the earlier case of *Martin v Dublin Corporation*,[67] Costello J seemed to take a different view of the matter. The plaintiff, a professor of medieval history, had commenced proceedings seeking a declaration that part of the site at Wood Quay designated for civic offices was a national monument, and an interlocutory injunction restraining building operations on the site pending the trial of the action. The defendants contended that he lacked standing to assert public rights of this nature, but Costello J granted the relief sought, saying that the plaintiff had made out a question of substance. He thought that at the trial of the action the plaintiff would be able to establish that the general approach of the courts in constitutional cases should be followed in cases where a citizen claimed that a public body was not carrying out the law.

Whether the Attorney General enjoys an exclusive role in the enforcement of public rights

Traditionally, the Attorney General enjoyed an exclusive role as far as the enforcement of public rights was concerned and this view is reflected in the *dicta* of Keane J in the *Caldwell* case. The continued viability of this common law rule must now be viewed with reserve in view of a series of decisions which, in effect, have allowed a form of *actio popularis* as far as the enforcement of the law[68] and the Constitution[69] itself. This trend was powerfully reinforced by the Supreme Court's decision in *Society for the Protection of Unborn Children (Ire.) Ltd. v Coogan.*[70] In this case, the plaintiff sought an injunction restraining certain student organisations publishing a handbook which, it was claimed, was in breach of Article 40.3.3. The defendants contended that the plaintiff had no standing to seek the relief sought without a relator action at the instance of the Attorney General. In the High Court, Carroll J agreed with this submission, saying it was "the Attorney General who is the proper party to move in such a case." A majority of the Supreme Court took a different view, with Walsh J declaring that "every member of the public has an interest in seeing that the fundamental law of the State is not defeated." This seems to suggest that every citizen has the right to secure the enforcement of

[67] High Court, 14 November 1978.

[68] See, e.g., the *dicta* of Costello J in *Martin v Dublin Corporation*, High Court, 14 November 1978 and *The State (Sheehan) v Government of Ireland* [1987] IR 550.

[69] See, e.g., *Crotty v An Taoiseach* [1987] IR 713 and *McGimpsey v Ireland* [1990] 1 IR 110.

[70] [1989] IR 734.

the provisions of the Constitution, a proposition which, if correct, would have profound implications for the law of standing.[71] Walsh J then went on to explain why the Attorney General could not validly claim an exclusive right to enforce a public right of this kind, since a conflict of interest might well arise in certain circumstances:

> "There could well be occasions when he could legitimately be cited as a defendant in proceedings brought to defend or vindicate constitutional rights. He might well be called upon to defend the actions of the executive power of government or even the legislative power of government if protection was sought against the actions of the executive or legislative powers of government. If some department of state or some public health authority with the approval if not the encouragement of the executive power were to engage in activities which this Court in the case of *Attorney General (Society for the Protection of Unborn Children (Ire.) Ltd. v Open Door Counselling Ltd.* restrained as being a violation of the Constitution, it would be an intolerable situation if the defence of constitutional vindication of rights were to be confined to the very officer of state who had been entrusted with the task of defending such impugned activities."

And while Walsh J was speaking in the context of the enforcement of fundamental constitutional rights, there have already been broad judicial hints to the effect that private citizens can enforce other kinds of public rights in appropriate cases without the need for the intervention of the Attorney General.[72]

Role of the Attorney General as Guardian of the Constitution

One aspect of the Attorney General's role as guardian of the public interest are his functions in relation to the protection of the Constitution and the vindication of constitutional rights. This role came to the fore in 1992-3 with the decision by the Attorney General to institute proceedings in three important constitutional actions.[73] There can be no doubt but that the Attorney General enjoys such a privileged role. As Hamilton P explained in *Attorney General (Society for the Protection of the Unborn Child (Ireland) Ltd.) v Open-Door Counselling Ltd.*,[74] (where the plaintiffs sought, on the basis of Article 40.3.3, an injunction restraining the operation of abortion referral by the defendants):

> "the public interests are committed to the care of the Attorney General. He is entitled to sue to restrain the commission of an unlawful Act to protect and vindicate a right acknowledged by the Constitution, and to prevent the corruption of public morals."

In the Supreme Court, Finlay CJ described the Attorney General as "an especially appropriate person to invoke the jurisdiction of the High Court in order to vindicate and defend" the rights guaranteed by Article 40.3.3.[75]

[71] See below at p. 442.

[72] See, e.g., *Martin v Dublin Corporation*, High Court, 14 November 1978 and *Attorney General (McGarry) v Sligo Corporation* [1991] 1 IR 99.

[73] *Attorney General v X* [1992] 1 IR 1; [1992] ILRM 401; [1992] 1 CMLR 477 (application to restrain young rape victim who had sought to procure an abortion in England from leaving the State); *Attorney General v Hamilton (No.1)* [1992] 2 IR 250; [1993] ILRM 81 (judicial review proceedings seeking a declaration that the Beef Tribunal could not inquire into alleged discussions at Government meetings) and *Attorney General v Hamilton (No.2)* [1993] ILRM 821, (claim that members of the Oireachtas had waived privilege in respect of disclosure of sources by submitting statements to Beef Tribunal).

[74] [1988] IR 593; [1987] ILRM 477.

[75] Cf. also the comments of Walsh J in *Society for the Protection of Unborn Children (Ire.) Ltd. v Coogan* [1989] IR 734; [1990] ILRM 70:

This view was followed by both Costello J and the Supreme Court in *Attorney General v X*[76] where the role of the Attorney General in commencing these highly controversial injunction proceedings was expressly approved. As Finlay CJ explained:

> "It would have been quite incorrect for him in this case, and in the absence of any legislation providing any alternative procedure, to take it upon himself to make a decision on the facts available to him, instead of, as he did, bringing the matter before the courts."[77]

The question arises as to just how far this role of independent vindicator of constitutional rights might conceivably extend. A practical example arose shortly after the decision of the Supreme Court in *Attorney General v Hamilton (No.1)*[78] (where the principle of absolute cabinet confidentiality was upheld) when certain civil servants - apparently acting on their own initiative - withheld certain documents recording details of Cabinet discussions in the early 1960s from disclosure under the operation of the thirty year rule on the ground that they contained details as to discussions in cabinet. Although Finlay CJ had stressed in *Hamilton (No.1)* that this rule was a constitutional imperative and not susceptible of waiver, even by a later Government,[79] the Taoiseach nonetheless decided to make these documents available.[80] The Taoiseach's decision was itself a commendable one, but it nonetheless appeared to infringe the constitutional imperative identified by the majority in the *Cabinet Confidentiality* case. In those circumstances, should not the Attorney General have acted immediately with a view to preventing the apparent breach of the absolute confidentiality implicit in Article 28.4? Yet for the Attorney

> "It is also clear that the Attorney General by virtue of his constitutional office also has cast upon him in the appropriate case the duty of defending the Constitution and vindicating the rights conferred or guarnteed by it."

[76] [1992] 1 IR 1; [1992] ILRM 401; [1992] 2 CMLR 477. These decisions were also applied in *Attorney General v Hamilton* (No.1) [1993] 2 IR 250; [1993] ILRM 81 where the suggestion that the role of the Attorney General in such instances was confined to protecting express constitutional rights was rejected. Here the Attorney General had asserted that the right of absolute cabinet confidentiality was impliedly protected by Article 28.4 and, as Finlay CJ observed, the Attorney General "must have the clearest possible duty to intervene" to protect a right which was "fundamental to the whole operation of Government."

[77] Compare this statement of principle with the decision of the Attorney General in December 1988 in the Patrick Ryan affair to refuse to endorse extradition warrants for execution on the ground that pre-trial publicity in the requesting state had prejudiced a possible fair trial. Is it not arguable that the Attorney General should have left this issue to the courts to decide and not take it on himself? See generally, Hogan, "*Reflections on the Role of the Attorney General and the Patrick Ryan Affair*" (1992) 2 ICLJ 128.

[78] [1993] 2 IR 250; [1993] ILRM 81.

[79] The Chief Justice had said:

"It is a constitutional right which...goes to the fundamental machinery of government and is, therefore, not capable of being waived by any individual member of a government, nor, in my view, are the details and contents of discussions at meetings of the Government capable of being made public...by a decision of any succeeding Government."

[80] The documents in question were fairly innocuous in themselves, but they tended to reveal 1962 Cabinet discussions about routine matters such as judicial salaries: see *The Irish Times*, 2 January 1993 and 4 January 1993.

[81] Cf. the remarks of McCarthy J in *The State (Sheehan) v Government of Ireland* [1987] IR 550, where dealing with the argument that the applicant had no standing to seek *mandamus* to compel the Government to bring s 60 of the Civil Liability Act 1961 and that only the Attorney General could assert such a right:

"In theory, the Attorney General could assert the public right and seek the relief claimed; in practice, this has no reality. The Attorney General is legal adviser to the Government and, presumably, has advised the Government that it is not under legal obligation for which the [applicant] contends."

General to have taken such proceedings against the Taoiseach would have been somewhat incongruous.[81]

Role of the Attorney General in the enforcement of statutes

The Attorney General's role as guardian of the public interest has been held to mean that he may by virtue of his office seek an injunction to restrain breaches of that statute, even where that statute prescribes other remedies, including criminal sanctions.[82] Although this jurisdiction is exceptional and residual in character, it has been held that there is "no constitutional impropriety in the exercise of that jurisdiction as requested" since:

> "The courts are not then trying a criminal charge within the meaning of Article 38 of the Constitution, but are merely exercising a distinct and different jurisdiction in civil proceedings."[83]

Miscellaneous examples of the Attorney General's role

Further cases in which the Attorney General's role as representative of the public interest were considered are: *Attorney General v Lawless*,[84] *De Lacy Smyth v Attorney General*,[85] *Sherlock v Attorney General*,[86] *Knight v Attorney General*,[87] *Attorney General v Malone*,[88] *O'Doherty v Attorney General*,[89] *Byrne v Ireland*[90] (in the two latter cases the Attorney General's appearance was specifically justified, by Gavan Duffy J and by Walsh J respectively, by the fact that the plaintiffs' claims, if successful, would lead to a charge on public funds) and *In re Curtin*.[91]

The role of the Attorney General in asserting the public right in a particular context is acknowledged also by statute: the State Property Act 1954, refers in s 1 6(5) to "the right of the Attorney General on behalf of the State or the people to institute and carry on legal proceedings in respect of State lands".

Relator Actions

A special category of case in which the Attorney General asserts public rights is that of the so-called "relator" action, in which the Attorney General does not spontaneously, or as representative of the State, initiate proceedings, but is brought into action at the instance, or on the information *(ex relatione)* of a private individual or body who or

[82] *Attorney General (O'Duffy) v Appleton, Surgeon Dentist Ltd.* [1907] 1 IR 252; *Attorney General v Paperlink Ltd.* [1984] ILRM 383.

[83] *Attorney General v Paperlink Ltd.* [1984] ILRM 383. Here the Attorney General successfully obtained an injunction restraining further breaches of the postal monopoly, where it was established, *inter alia*, that the "penalties imposed by the [Post Office] Act 1908 were totally inadequate and that criminal sanctions would be wholly ineffective to remedy the situation."

[84] [1930] IR 247 (right of reply of counsel for Attorney General).

[85] [1932] IR 53 (proper defendant in action attacking revenue claims).

[86] (1935) Ir Jur Rep 36 (proper defendant in administration action along with next-of-kin).

[87] (1939) Ir Jur Rep 4 (proper sole defendant in administration action where no next-of-kin known).

[88] [1939] IR 590; (1940) 76 ILTR 46 (proper plaintiff in action to eject a tenant from State property). (This view may now be incorrect in view of the decision in *Byrne v Ireland* [1972] IR 241 in that there would now appear to be no impediment to an action by the State itself to eject the tenant from its own property: see now *In re Glynn* [1992] ILRM 582 where the Chief State Solicitor was appointed administrator of a will instead of the named executor (who had been convicted to the murder of the testator's sister), but where Ireland (i.e., the State) was the moving party in the application.)

[89] [1941] IR 569; (1941) 75 ILTR 171 (proper defendant in a claim for military pension).

[90] [1972] IR 241.

[91] [1991] 2 IR 562 (Attorney General entitled to represent interests of charities in probate action).

which would, alone, lack the *locus standi* for bringing proceedings which as a rule only a grievance peculiar to oneself will confer. In such cases, usually aimed at enforcing compliance with the law, the Attorney General is the nominal plaintiff; though - as happened in *Attorney General (Martin) v Dublin Corporation*[92] - may decline to take any active part in the proceedings, disclaim all liability for costs, and expressly refrain from offering an opinion on the relator's case, thus confining his own role to the mere authorising, by his fiat, of the bringing of the action. No court has yet considered whether there is any discordance with Articles 34.1, 40.1 or 40.3 in this discretion of the Attorney General to enable one litigant to by-pass the ordinary *locus standi* rules, and to refuse this facility to another (as happened in *Irish Permanent Building Society v Caldwell).*[93] In addition, it might be thought that a procedure which enabled a non-judicial personage such as the Attorney General to intervene in civil proceedings and to confer standing on a litigant (who might not otherwise have the requisite *locus standi* to maintain the proceedings)[94] amounted to an unconstitutional interference in the administration of justice.[95]

Function in constitutional litigation: role of the Attorney General in Article 26 references

The Constitution itself lays upon the Attorney General the specific function of addressing arguments (either in person or by counsel) to the Supreme Court in an Article 26 reference (Article 26.2.1). This provision does not say that the Attorney General's role here is to uphold the Bill under scrutiny, but this seems self-evident.

The Attorney General is a necessary notice party where an Act of the Oireachtas is challenged or an important constitutional point raised

It is provided by O 60 rr 1-3 of the Rules of the Superior Courts 1986, that the Attorney General must be given notice of any action or matter in which the constitutional validity of an Act of the Oireachtas is questioned or in which an important point of constitutional interpretation is raised. It would seem that the requirements of O 60 are mandatory, inasmuch as failure to serve such a notice in appropriate case "must raise significant doubts and queries" as the validity of an judicial order where such notice has not been served.[96]

Apart from this special provision, Maguire CJ said in *In re Solicitors Act 1954*,[97] that "even though the Attorney General need not attend, the Court welcomes his help when as here an issue of considerable public importance is raised".

Just as with Article 26.2.1, it seems implicit in O 60 that the Attorney General's role is

[92] [1983] ILRM 254.

[93] [1981] ILRM 242.

[94] In *Attorney General (SPUC Ltd.) v Open-Door Counselling Ltd.* [1988] IR 593; [1989] ILRM 19 the proceedings had originally commenced without the relator of the Attorney General. Once that was furnished, Hamilton P concluded that it was no longer necessary for him to determine whether the plaintiff would have had standing independently of this fact i.e., the Attorney General's intervention was sufficient in its own right to confer the necessary standing on a plaintiff suing at his relation.

[95] See generally, Hogan and Morgan, *Administrative Law in Ireland* (London, 1991) at 626-632.

[96] *Re Ellis' Application* [1990] 2 IR 291, per Finlay CJ (constitutionality of pre-1922 Act upheld by trial judge in proceedings where no O 60 notice had been served.) In this respect, the remarks of Keane J in *The State (D.C.) v Eastern Health Board*, High Court, 31 July 1986 to the effect that Order 60 only applied to post-1937 legislation (i.e., that pre-1937 legislation were not "laws" within the meaning of the rule) would appear not to have been followed by the Supreme Court in *Ellis*.

[97] [1960] IR 239. Gavan Duffy J made similar comments in *O'Doherty v Attorney General* [1941] IR 569; (1941) 75 ILTR 171.

to support the validity of the Act under challenge. In practice, the Attorney General acts as *legitimus contradictor* in such cases by instructing solicitor and counsel to defend the constitutionality of the impugned legislative measure. But this would seem to be no longer the invariable practice it once was, since there appears to be at least three modern instances where the Attorney General (either as a defendant or notice party in a constitutional action) took the (hitherto) unprecedented step of either actually challenging the validity of a statute or supporting such a challenge.[98]

Former "fiat" requirement declared unconstitutional

The former function of the Attorney General in regard to authorising by *fiat* actions against Ministers was declared unconstitutional in *Macauley v Minister for Posts and Telegraphs.* [99]

[98] See *The People (Director of Public Prosecutions) v JT* 3 Frewen 141 (supporting challenge to constitutionality of s1 of Criminal Evidence Act 1924); *Donegal Fuel and Supply Co. Ltd. v Minister for Marine*, High Court, 6 May 1992 (supporting challenge to survival of Londonderry Port and Harbour Act 1854) and *McKinley v Minister for Defence* [1992] 2 IR 333 (challenge to constitutionality of s 34 of the Civil Liability Act 1961). In *McKinley*, McCarthy J observed that: "No precedent has been cited for the Attorney General to challenge the validity of any part of a post-1937 statute; he is a necessary party to any challenge. I would not entertain the argument challenging the subsection of the Civil Liability Act."

[99] [1966] IR 345; see below at p.386.

THE COUNCIL OF STATE

The Council of State

Article 31

1. **There shall be a Council of State to aid and counsel the President on all matters on which the President may consult the said Council in relation to the exercise and performance by him of such of his powers and functions as are by this Constitution expressed to be exercisable and performable after consultation with the Council of State, and to exercise such other functions as are conferred on the said Council by this Constitution.**

2. **The Council of State shall consist of the following members:**

   i As *ex-officio* members: the Taoiseach, the Tánaiste, the Chief Justice, the President of the High Court, the Chairman of Dáil Éireann, the Chairman of Seanad Éireann, and the Attorney General.

   ii. Every person able and willing to act as a member of the Council of State who shall have held the office of President or the office of Taoiseach, or the office of Chief Justice, or the office of President of the Executive Council of Saorstát Éireann.

   iii. Such other persons, if any, as may be appointed by the President under this Article to be members of the Council of State.

3. **The President may at any time and from time to time by warrant under his hand and Seal appoint such other persons as, in his absolute discretion, he may think fit, to be members of the Council of State, but not more than seven persons so appointed shall be members of the Council of State at the same time.**

An Chomhairle Stáit

Airteagal 31

1. **Beidh Comhairle Stáit ann chun cabhair is comhairle a thabhairt don Uachtarán i dtaobh gach ní dá gcuirfidh an tUachtarán ina gcomhairle, maidir le hé d'oibriú is do chomhlíonadh na gcumhachtaí is na bhfeidhmeanna a luaitear sa Bhunreacht seo a bheith inoibrithe is inchomhlíonta aige tar éis comhairle a ghlacadh leis an gComhairle Stáit, agus fós chun aon fheidhmeanna eile a bhronntar ar an gComhairle sin leis an mBunreacht seo a chomhlíonadh.**

2. **Is iad na daoine seo a leanas a bheas ina gcomhaltaí den Chomhairle Stáit:**

   i De bhua oifige: an Taoiseach, an Tánaiste, an Príomh-Bhreitheamh, Uachtarán na hArd-Chúirte, Cathaoirleach Dháil Éireann, Cathaoirleach Sheanad Éireann, agus an tArd-Aighne.

   ii. Gach duine ar cumas dó agus ar fonn leis gníomhú ina chomhalta den Chomhairle Stáit, agus a bhí tráth ina Uachtarán nó ina Thaoiseach nó ina Phríomh-Bhreitheamh, nó ina Uachtarán ar Ard–Chomhairle Shaorstát Éireann.

   iii. Aon daoine eile a cheapfar ag an Uachtarán faoin Airteagal seo, má cheaptar aon duine, chun bheith ina gcomhaltaí den Chomhairle Stáit.

3. **Tig leis an Uachtarán uair ar bith agus ó am go ham cibé daoine eile is oiriúnach leis, as a chomhairle féin, a cheapadh le barántas faoina láimh is faoina Shéala chun bheith ina gcomhaltaí den Chomhairle Stáit, ach ní dleathach thar mórsheisear a cheaptar ar an gcuma sin a bheith ina gcomhaltaí den Chomhairle Stáit san am chéanna.**

4. Every member of the Council of State shall at the first meeting thereof which he attends as a member take and subscribe a declaration in the following form:

"In the presence of Almighty God I do solemnly and sincerely promise and declare that I will faithfully and conscientiously fulfil my duties as a member of the Council of State".

4. Ní foláir do gach comhalta den Chomhairle Stáit, an chéad uair a bheidh sé ar thionól den Chomhairle sin ina chomhalta di, an dearbhú seo a leanas a dhéanamh agus a lámh a chur leis:

"I láthair Dia na nUile-chumhacht táimse á ghealladh agus á dhearbhú go sollúnta agus go fírinneach mo dhualgais i mo chomhalta den Chomhairle Stáit a chomhlíonadh go dílis coinsiasach".

5. Every member of the Council of State appointed by the President, unless he previously dies, resigns, becomes permanently incapacitated, or is removed from office, shall hold office until the successor of the President by whom he was appointed shall have entered upon his office.

5. Gach comhalta den Chomhairle Stáit a cheapfar ag an Uachtarán beidh sé i seilbh oifige nó go dté comharba an Uachtaráin a cheap é i gcúram a oifige, is é sin mura dtarlaí roimhe sin go n-éagfaidh an comhalta sin, nó go n-éireoidh as oifig, nó go ngeobhaidh míthreoir bhuan é, nó go gcuir-fear as oifig é.

6. Any member of the Council of State appointed by the President may resign from office by placing his resignation in the hands of the President.

6. Aon chomhalta den Chomhairle Stáit dá gceapfaidh an tUachtarán tig leis éirí as oifig trína chur sin in iúl don Uachtarán.

7. The President may, for reasons which to him seem sufficient, by an order under his hand and Seal, terminate the appointment of any member of the Council of State appointed by him.

7. Tig leis an Uachtarán, ar ábhair is leor leis féin, duine ar bith dár cheap sé don Chomhairle Stáit a chur as oifig le hordú faoina láimh agus faoina Shéala.

8. Meetings of the Council of State may be convened by the President at such times and places as he shall determine.

8. Tig leis an Uachtarán an Chomhairle Stáit a chomóradh cibé áit agus am a shocróidh sé chuige.

Article 32

The President shall not exercise or perform any of the powers or functions which are by this Constitution expressed to be exercisable or performable by him after consultation with the Council of State unless, and on every occasion before so doing, he shall have convened a meeting of the Council of State and the members present at such meeting shall have been heard by him.

Airteagal 32

Cumhachtaí nó feidhmeanna ar bith a luaitear ina dtaobh sa Bhunreacht seo gur dleathach don Uachtarán iad a oibriú nó a chomhlíonadh tar éis comhairle a ghlacadh leis an gComhairle Stáit, ní cead don Uachtarán aon chumhacht ná feidhm díobh a oibriú ná a chomhlíonadh mura gcomóra sé an Chomhairle Stáit i ngach cás roimh ré, agus éisteacht leis na comhaltaí den Chomhairle sin a bheas i láthair.

Council of State an innovation

This feature of the Constitution, like the Presidency, is a 1937 innovation; strangely, it passed virtually without debate during the Dáil's consideration of the draft Constitution, and appears never to have figured in any litigation or to have received any judicial consideration.

"Majority of its members" under Article 14.4

It may be noted that the reference in Article 14.4 to the Council of State making provision, in any contingency not provided for by Article 14.1-3, for the performance of the President's functions, by "a majority of its members", was understood by the first President's Secretary as "doubtless meaning a majority of its total membership, and not of those present at a particular meeting,"[1] this interpretation, though it contains obvious inconveniences, seems the only one which accords with the words of the section. It will be noted that both the Chief Justice and President of the High Court are entitled to be present at the meeting of the Council of State, yet both may be called upon to sit should the President decide to refer the Bill under consideration to the Supreme Court. Normally such prior judicial involvement in a discussion of this kind would be regarded as undesirable, yet this procedure is constitutionally sanctioned.

[1] Michael McDunphy, *The President of Ireland*, p. 35.

Article 33

THE COMPTROLLER AND AUDITOR GENERAL

The Comptroller and Auditor General

Article 33

1. **There shall be a Comptroller and Auditor General to control on behalf of the State all disbursements and to audit all accounts of moneys administered by or under the authority of the Oireachtas.**

2. **The Comptroller and Auditor General shall be appointed by the President on the nomination of Dáil Éireann.**

3. **The Comptroller and Auditor General shall not be a member of either House of the Oireachtas and shall not hold any other office or position of emolument.**

4. **The Comptroller and Auditor General shall report to Dáil Éireann at stated periods as determined by law.**

5. **1° The Comptroller and Auditor General shall not be removed from office except for stated misbehaviour or incapacity, and then only upon resolutions passed by Dáil Éireann and by Seanad Éireann calling for his removal.**

   2° The Taoiseach shall duly notify the President of any such resolutions as aforesaid passed by Dáil Éireann and by Seanad Éireann and shall send him a copy of each such resolution certified by the Chairman of the House of the Oireachtas by which it shall have been passed.

   3° Upon receipt of such notification and of copies of such resolutions, the President shall forthwith, by an order under his hand and Seal, remove the Comptroller and Auditor General from office.

An tArd-Reachtaire Cuntas agus Ciste

Airteagal 33

1. **Beidh Ard-Reachtaire Cuntas agus Ciste ann chun gach caitheamh airgid a rialú thar ceann an Stáit, agus chun iniúchadh a dhéanamh ar gach uile chuntas ar airgead a riartar ag an Oireachtas nó faoi údarás an Oireachtais.**

2. **Is ag an Uachtarán a cheapfar an tArd-Reachtaire Cuntas agus Ciste, arna ainmniú sin ag Dáil Éireann.**

3. **Ní cead an tArd-Reachtaire Cuntas agus Ciste a bheith ina chomhalta de cheachtar de Thithe an Oireachtais, ná a bheith in aon oifig ná post sochair eile.**

4. **Ní foláir don Ard-Reachtaire Cuntas agus Ciste tuarascálacha a chur os comhair Dháil Éireann ar thrátha áirithe mar a chinnfear le dlí.**

5. **1° Ní cead an tArd-Reachtaire Cuntas agus Ciste a chur as oifig ach amháin de dheasca mí-iompair nó míthreora a luafar, ná an uair sin féin mura rithid Dáil Éireann agus Seanad Éireann rúin á éileamh é a chur as oifig.**

   2° Rúin ar bith den sórt sin a rithfid Dáil Éireann agus Seanad Éireann ní foláir don Taoiseach scéala a thabhairt don Uachtarán ina dtaobh go cuí, agus cóip de gach rún den tsamhail sin a sheoladh chuige faoi theastas Chathaoirleach an Tí den Oireachtas a rith é.

   3° Láithreach d'éis na scéala sin agus cóipeanna de na rúin sin a fháil don Uachtarán ní foláir do, le hordú faoina láimh is faoina Shéala, an tArd-Reachtaire Cuntas agus Ciste a chur as oifig.

6. Subject to the foregoing, the terms and conditions of the office of Comptroller and Auditor General shall be determined by law.

6. Faoi chuimsiú na nithe sin romhainn, is le dlí a chinnfear coinníollacha agus cúinsí oifig an Ard-Reachtaire Cuntas agus Ciste.

1922 provision

These provisions replace the substantially similar provisions of Articles 62 and 63 of the 1922 Constitution; except that the old Article 63 was amended in 1936[1] in order to give the Comptroller and Auditor General the same kind of entrenchment as was simultaneously given to the judges.[2]

Statutory provisions

Apart from a series of Acts which periodically regulated the remuneration and pension of this office, the statutory regulation of the office is contained in the Comptroller and Auditor General Acts 1923 to 1993. Section 7(3) of the 1923 Act provides:

> Unless and until it shall be otherwise provided by the Oireachtas, the Comptroller and Auditor-General shall have and exercise all such powers and perform all such duties as are prescribed by this Act or are conferred or imposed on him by any Act of the Parliament of the late United Kingdom having the force of law in Saorstát Éireann and adapted to the circumstances of Saorstat Éireann by or under the Adaptation of Enactments Act, 1922...and particularly by the Exchequer and Audit Departments Acts, 1866 and 1921.

This Act has, however, been largely superseded by the 1993 Act which consolidated much of the existing law, as well as conferring important new functions on the Controller. Sections 2 and 3 of the 1993 Act correspond with Article 33.1 in that they provide for the control of disbursements of public monies by the Controller and the audit by him of accounts of moneys administered by or under control of the Oireachtas. Section 4(2) requires the Comptroller to audit the Finance Accounts[3] as transmitted to him by the Minister for Finance. Sections 5 to 8 enable the Comptroller to audit the accounts of certain additional bodies, ranging from certain public tribunals and bodies.[4]

Section 15(6)(*a*) of the Comptroller and Auditor General (Amendment) Act 1993, prescribes a retiring age of 65 years.[5] No Comptroller and Auditor General has ever been removed from office.

[1] Constitution (Amendment No. 24) Act 1936, s 2(2) and Schedule.

[2] I.e., removal only by resolution of Dáil Éireann supported by four-sevenths of the Dáil's full membership.

[3] Defined by s 4(5) as "(*a*) an account showing the payments into and out of the Central Fund in that year and (*b*) such other, if any, accounts and statements as the Minister [for Finance] considers appropriate and specifies to the Comptroller.

[4] The bodies listed in the First Schedule include such miscellaneous bodies as An Bord Uchtála, Comhairle na nOispidéal and the National Economic and Social Council. Section 6 obliges the Comptroller to audit the accounts of health boards; s 7 imposes a similar obligation in the case of vocational education committees and s 8 empowers the Comptroller to audit the accounts of certain commercial state-sponsored bodies.

[5] By virtue of s 3(1) of the 1923 Act, the retirement age was formerly 70 years and s 15(6)(*b*) of the 1993 Act specifies that this shall continue to be the retirement age for the present holder of the office only.

Report of the Comptroller and the Auditor General

The 1993 Act requires the Comptroller to report to the Dáil in respect of a variety of matters. Section 3(11) requires the Comptroller to report to the Dáil following the completion of the audit of the appropriation accounts not later than the 30th September in the year following the financial year to which the accounts relate and a similar obligation is imposed by s 4(3) in relation to the Finance Accounts. In addition, the Comptroller is required to report to the Dáil in respect of material non-compliance with the requirements of the 1993 Act: see s 2(7) (which imposes a duty to report where the "account of the Exchequer at the Central Bank has been operated to a material extent otherwise than in accordance with this section") and s 3(3), (4) (where the Comptroller in the course of his audit discovers that certain expenditure has been improperly incurred or which was not received the authorisation of the relevant Minister).

The annual Report of the Comptroller and Auditor General is published in the form of preface to the year's Appropriation Accounts. An instance in which the Comptroller and Auditor General declared himself impeded in the discharge of his constitutional duty will be found in the Report for 1970-71, where he said he interprets the "accounts" mentioned in Article 33 as "including the accounts of any State-sponsored body, irrespective of its legal form, whose share capital is provided partly or wholly from State funds, whose loan capital is provided or guaranteed by the Government or by a Minister of State or which is in receipt of annual or periodic grants or advances from State funds to enable it to perform its functions". He said that "the exclusion of the accounts of any such body from his audit prevented him from carrying out a constitutional function in relation to the State funds administered by that body".

Article 34.1

THE COURTS

The Courts	Na Cúirteanna
Article 34	**Airteagal 34**
1. Justice shall be administered in courts established by law by judges appointed in the manner provided by this Constitution, and, save in such special and limited cases as may be prescribed by law, shall be administered in public.	**1. Is i gcúirteanna a bhunaítear le dlí agus ag breithiúna a cheaptar ar an modh atá leaghta amach sa Bhunreacht seo a riarfar ceart, agus is go poiblí a dhéanfar sin ach amháin sna cásanna speisialta teoranta sin a ordófar le dlí.**

1922 provision

These words echo the opening sentence of Article 64 of the 1922 Constitution. The principle which they express, namely that of the exclusive administration of justice by a judiciary separate from the other arms of government (and immune from interference by them), was described by Johnston J in *Lynham v Butler (No. 2)*[1] in a passage which both points to the immediate and the ultimate inspirations of the Irish constitutional article, and acknowledges the practical limits to its application:

> "This provision [Article 64], which will undoubtedly be very useful in the future as a check on encroachments by the Legislature and the Executive upon popular rights, seems to be an adaptation of Article 3 of the Constitution of the United States, namely, the provision that "the judicial power of the United States shall be vested in one Supreme Court and in such inferior courts as the Congress may from time to time ordain and establish", and that "the judicial power shall extend to all cases in law and equity arising under this Constitution, the laws of the United States and treaties made or which shall be made under their authority" and to certain other matters."

This Article of the US Constitution, he said, "did not originate in the brain of Alexander Hamilton or James Madison", but with the mid-eighteenth-century English jurist Sir William Blackstone,[2] who wrote:

> "In the distinct and separate existence of the judicial power in a peculiar body of men, nominated, indeed, but not removable at pleasure, by the Crown, consists one main preservative of the public liberty, which cannot subsist long in any State, unless the administration of common justice be in some degree separated both from the legislative and also from the executive power."

In Blackstone's words Johnston J perceived what he thought was a cautious formulation, as though Blackstone had a faint presentiment, despite the rudimentary articulation of

[1] [1933] IR 74; (1933) 67 ILTR 75.

[2] *Commentaries on the Laws of England*; Johnson J cited from the Dublin edition (1769), vol. 1, p.267. Blackstone was not the first to express the principle of a separate judiciary as a safeguard to liberty. Montesquieu had done so in his *Esprit des Lois,* published in 1748 after a long visit to England (Book XI, chapter 6, "On the English Constitution"); and rudimentary forms of the idea can be traced in John Locke, who wrote, amid the constitutional conflicts of late seventeenth-century England, against the Stuart patterns of government of which a subservient judiciary was one of the most objectionable. Both Locke and Blackstone were important influences in America at the epoch of independence: see Corwin, *The "Higher Law": Background of American Constitutional Law*, 85.

the functions of government in the age in which he wrote, of what the following ages were to bring in the way of administrative expansion. The Irish judge did not say this, but (particularly in the light of the later part of his judgment[3]) it seems likely that he was struck by the expression "*common justice*", as suggesting a reservation on Blackstone's part that to claim every adjudication whatsoever for the exclusive sphere of the courts would be to claim too much. For in fact, as Johnston J continued:

> "it has been found through universal experience that this division of governmental functions cannot, as a matter of practical polity, be carried out to its logical conclusion, and can only take place as an approximation. In no system of which I have any knowledge has it been found to be possible to confine the legislative, the executive and the judicial power each in what I may call its own watertight compartment..."

The "administration of justice" and the frontier with administrative decisions

The practical application of the principle of Article 34.1, even as modified by the recognition expressed by Johnston J, has proved full of difficulty and uncertainty. What is an "administration of justice" such that only a judge in a court can carry it out? On the other hand, where are the theoretical frontiers beyond which an executive (or "administrative", or "ministerial") authority may not go, in making decisions necessary to its functioning, without trespassing on properly judicial terrain? These questions have frequently arisen since 1922 in litigation, and a considerable body of judicial *dicta* has accumulated around them, but without, it must be said, leaving the answers much clearer. The presentation of this material, moreover, is complicated firstly by the loose and varying terminology which courts have employed at different times, and secondly by the necessity to approach it historically in order to appreciate the role of Article 37, which was a 1937 innovation and which must be considered, in some of its aspects, out of turn in dealing with Article 34.1.

Position under the 1922 Constitution

Under the 1922 Constitution the position of the administrative bodies and organs *vis-à-vis* the courts was, generally speaking, what it had been before 1922: namely, that a wide and increasing range of functions and powers - some of them of a very sweeping character, like those of the Land Commission - was entrusted by statute to authorities other than the courts notwithstanding that in the exercise of these functions and powers these authorities had to make decisions, on facts and arguments before them, which affected parties in the same way as they might have been affected by judgments of courts. The courts exercised, via *certiorari*, *mandamus* and other remedies, a supervisory jurisdiction over these authorities to prevent them from exceeding their powers or misconstruing them; but there was at first no serious suggestion that the activities of such authorities represented an encroachment on the area confided exclusively to the courts, i.e. that they were constitutionally questionable, under Article 64, as involving in fact an "administration of justice" or (in a phrase used as an apparent synonym) an exercise of "the judicial power of the State".

In 1930, however, litigation about a decision by the Commissioners of the Irish Land Commission culminated in a full assault on the constitutionality of their functions. In

[3] See pp. 333-4.

this case - *Lynham v Butler (No. 2)*[4] - the plaintiff's counsel argued that the powers of the Land Commission were affected by the Constitution, which "created a wholly new constitutional position as regards the judiciary and the exercise of judicial power...The Constituent Assembly [could not be assumed] to have intended the continuance of the anomalous position of the Land Commission..."

Definition of "judicial power" essayed

The Supreme Court upheld the constitutionality of the Land Commission's activity, but took the issue extremely seriously. Kennedy CJ observed that the question could not be decided without first arriving at a clear conception of "judicial power" such as is confided exclusively to judges in the courts; and, having noted the insufficiency of previous attempts (not, however, of Irish courts) at definition, offered his own which he stated "by way of description rather than of precise formula":

> "In the first place, the judicial power of the State is, like the legislative power and the executive power, one of the attributes of sovereignty, and a function of government... It is one of the activities of the government of a civilised State by which it fulfils its purpose of social order and peace by determining in accordance with the laws of the State all controversies of a justiciable nature arising within the territory of the State, and for that purpose exercising the authority of the State over persons and property. The controversies which fall to it for determination may be divided into two classes, criminal and civil. In relation to the former class of controversy, the judicial power is exercised in determining the guilt or innocence of persons charged with offences against the State itself and in determining the punishments to be inflicted upon persons found guilty of offences charged against them, which punishments it then becomes the obligation of the executive department of government to carry into effect.
>
> In relation to justiciable controversies of the civil class, the judicial power is exercised in determining in a final manner, by definitive adjudication according to law, rights or obligations in dispute between citizen and citizen, or between citizens and the State, or between any parties whoever they be and in binding the parties by such determination which will be enforced if necessary with the authority of the State. Its characteristic public good in its civil aspect is finality and authority, the decisive ending of disputes and quarrels, and the avoidance of private methods of violence in asserting or resisting claims alleged or denied.
>
> It follows from its nature as I have described it that the exercise of the judicial power, which is coercive and must frequently act against the will of one of the parties to enforce its decision adverse to that party, requires of necessity that the judicial department of government have compulsive authority over persons as, for instance, it must have authority to compel appearance of a party before it, to compel the attendance of witnesses, to order the execution of its judgments against persons and property."

So much towards a definition of the term "judicial power".

[4] [1933] IR 74; (1933) 67 ILTR 75. A good early example of administrative determinations made by persons other than judges for purposes ancillary to the administration of justice properly so called is provided by *Philadelphia Storage Battery Co. v Controller of Industrial and Commercial Property* [1935] IR 575. Meredith J in the High Court referred to *Lynham v Butler (No.2)* and said that, although the Controller was an official who exercised quasi-judicial functions, he should not be confused "with the judges under the Constitution in whom the judicial power is exclusively deposited". And in the Supreme Court, Kennedy CJ, having referred to several English authorities which suggested that the Controller exercised a judicial discretion by which the courts should be bound, said that these decisions could not be followed by the Irish courts as this would be "contrary to a constitutional principle."

Administrative determinations not an exercise of judicial power

The Chief Justice went on to state his opinion that the Land Commissioners were "primarily an administrative body with a great variety of ministerial duties to perform":

> "The nature of some of their ministerial duties requires that they be performed judicially, in the sense that they must be performed with fairness and impartiality and in such a way as not to offend against the canons of natural justice, which requirement however will not convert a ministerial act into a judicial act in the sense of an act which must be performed by a judge in a court of justice."

Kennedy CJ added that determinations, "adjudications", etc., performed by persons other than judges for purposes ancillary to the administration of justice properly so called were a well-known part of the machinery of the State, but were not themselves part of the exercise of the judicial power:

> "These persons even though they assume the style of tribunals or courts and sit on a dais adorned with what Lord Sankey called the "trappings of courts", so long as they do not pretend to the judicial determination of justiciable controversies and act only in subordination or as ancillary to and subject to the direction, control and correction of the courts and judges of the State, do not exercise, or indeed purport to exercise, the judicial power of the State."

Kennedy CJ's statement was followed in *Halpin v Attorney General*[5] and in *The State (McKay) v Cork Circuit Judge*;[6] in the latter case, which decided that an adjudication in bankruptcy by a county registrar (as local registrar of a bankruptcy court) was not an exercise of judicial power, but merely an ancillary administrative act, Hanna J described the challenge to the adjudication as "only another instance of the fallacy...of confusing 'acting judicially' with 'exercising the judicial power of the State'." To Kennedy CJ's description of the judicial power he said he "could add nothing as a statement of principle". The concept, however - as Kennedy CJ himself admitted - remained without precise definition.

Pragmatic approach to drawing the boundary

Of the other two judges of the Supreme Court in *Lynham's* case, Fitzgibbon J delivered a judgment to the same effect as the others, but containing no useful statement or discussion of the central problem. The third judge, Johnston J, approached the problem by what seems a more pragmatic and a more promising route. He concentrated firstly on the central purpose of the Land Commission's existence, which was essentially an administrative purpose to which quasi-judicial activity was altogether ancillary:

> "It would be a waste of public time were I to refer in detail to the numerous cases in which the Land Commission's place in the Constitution[7] has been explained and made clear...[T]he decision in *In re Maxwell's Estate*[8] made it abundantly clear that it was only where the Land Commission itself has been called upon to carry through a land purchase transaction that its quasi-judicial powers were exercisable, such powers being merely ancillary to the administrative duties which it had been constituted to carry out... [In *In re Laurence's Estate*[9] an application] for an advance of

[5] [1936] IR 266; (1935) 69 ILTR 259 (execution of distress warrants by County Registrars not unconstitutional).
[6] [1937] IR 650.
[7] I.e. in the pre-1922, British Constitution in its Irish dimension.
[8] 28 LR IR 356.
[9] [1896] 2 IR 347.

> money under the Land Purchase Acts...was refused, and that refusal, although no doubt it partook of the nature of a judicial decision, was in substance and reality an administrative act - a part of the work which the Land Commission was appointed to do - and could not have been performed by any other authority, judicial - or otherwise. The *lis* in the case *did not arise out of the relationships or rights of the parties; it was brought about by the very Act which created the Land Commission and the business which it was given to do*."[10]

He noted then that that business was being done long before the Constitution was drafted, and that its techniques, including the making of decisions of a judicial appearance, were a familiar part of the governmental landscape when the Constituent Assembly was doing its work (so that it might be assumed the intendment of Article 64 was not so extreme as to render those techniques unconstitutional):

> "The work of carrying out the land purchase code, especially since the passing of the new legislation, is an administrative task of national importance and of colossal magnitude. It was begun sixty years ago and was in active progress at the very moment when the Constitution was being framed, and in the full view of the Constitution-makers. The work could only be carried out by an administrative body consisting of men of wisdom, equipped with the most complete knowledge of the agrarian and social conditions of this country and actuated by an absolute determination that every citizen and every class of citizen should get fair play and honest treatment. As part of the procedure it was necessary that there should be some machinery for the "ascertainment" of the lands to which the Acts applied, and the Legislature has declared that this ascertainment, being part of the whole work of administration, must necessarily be left in the hands of the body or tribunal which was constituted to perform the entire task. I do not think that any other course was possible, and l am absolutely satisfied that such ascertainment of the land is not, in any sense, an exercise of judicial power within the meaning of Article 64... Any other result would have a most paralysing effect upon the whole work of the Land Commission."

Johnston J, like Kennedy CJ, drew attention to the fact that an authority such as the Land Commission, although not exercising judicial power, must still "act judicially", citing Lord Sankey in *Shell Company of Australia v Federal Commissioners of Taxation:*[11] "An administrative tribunal may act judicially, but still remain an administrative tribunal as distinguished from a court, strictly so-called"; and the US Supreme Court in *Reetz v Michigan:*[12] "Many executive officers...act judicially in the determination of facts in the performance of their official duties; and in so doing they do not exercise 'judicial power' as that phrase is commonly used and as it is used in the organic Act in conferring judicial power upon specified courts."

[10] Authors' emphasis. The "relationships or rights of the parties" must mean their relationships and rights at common, or in statute law *other* than the statutory code of which the Land Commission formed a part. This test might yet have relevance in a modern context. Section 9 of the Interception of Postal Packets and Telephone Messages (Regulation) Act 1993 creates the post of official referee whose task it is to award compensation. By conventional standards (i.e., under the five tests prescribed in *McDonald v Bord na gCon* [1965] IR 214) this would have to be regarded as an administration of justice. However, if one regards a complaint under the 1993 Act as not involving a *lis* arising "out of the relationships or rights of the parties", but as being one brought about by the 1993 Act itself, then by reference to Johnston J's test, this does not involve an administration of justice. This conclusion is, perhaps, buttressed by the fact that s 9 deliberately preserves the right of a complainant to pursue his right to sue in the courts for damages for breach of constitutional rights. This latter remedy, of course, necessarily involves an administration of justice since - in Johnston J's formulation of the test - it would concern a *lis* arising out of the relationships or rights of the parties.

[11] [1931] AC 275.

[12] 188 US 505 (1903).

No clear standard for demarcation of the area of "judicial power"

The position, accordingly, after *Lynham v Butler (No. 2)* was that the Supreme Court had confirmed that Article 64 and the principle whereby the judicial power of the State was confided exclusively to judges in regular courts were not breached by the continuing operation of administrative bodies which had to make "decisions" and "determinations" affecting the position and the rights of citizens. The case does not seem to yield a clear standard for settling the point at which such a body might stray or trespass into the properly judicial domain, since the attempt by Kennedy CJ to define the properly judicial power in the civil setting could, arguably, encompass disputes arising with an administrative authority, because he did not essay a definition of "justiciable controversy" so as to exclude such disputes. The case gives rather the impression of having been decided from back to front along the following lines: the Land Commission has an important national and social purpose and was expressly empowered by the Legislature to fulfil it; so that its very extensive task is primarily administrative and the courts would be unfitted to discharge it; therefore incidental phenomena of this administrative task - such as the making of decisions and determinations in issues which are contested - though judicial in flavour, are in their nature subordinate parts of the administrative process; and so we ought not to construe Article 64 so as to hold the process unconstitutional, particularly as it was a well-known and accepted feature of our system when the Constitution was superimposed upon it, and if it had been really felt as objectionable, the drafting hour of the new Constitution would have been the right moment to outlaw it in express terms, rather than (within a year) enacting an extension of its scope.

Article 37.1 intended as cover for quasi-judicial administrative operations

Nevertheless, although the decision must have provided cover by analogy for every other administrative process then operating, the drafting of the new Constitution in 1937 was used as an occasion to put beyond doubt the constitutional legitimacy of administrative authorities engaged in making decisions on disputed facts and arguments. Article 37.1 the inspiration of which was acknowledged to be the litigation about the Land Commission's powers[13] now reads:

> "Nothing in this Constitution shall operate to invalidate the exercise of limited functions and powers of a judicial nature, in matters other than criminal matters, by any person or body of persons duly authorised by law to exercise such functions and powers, notwithstanding that such person or such body of persons is not a judge or a court appointed or established as such under this Constitution."

The first cases which arose after the enactment of this constitutional provision in which the question of judicial power was litigated tended to show this Article as a sort of safety net which would save the liability-imposing, rights-affecting decisions of administrative authorities even if they could not be brought within whatever principle the some-

[13] Mr. de Valera had said in the debate on the draft Constitution: "There were questions about the Land Commission, as to whether their functions were of a judicial character or not...So as not to get tied in the knot that judicial powers or functions could only be exercised by the ordinary courts established here, you have to have a provision of this type" (67 *Dáil Debates* 1511-12). In *In re Loftus Bryan's Estate* [1942] IR 185, Gavan Duffy J (who in *Lynham's* case had been the advocate strenuously arguing that the Land Commission's quasi-judicial functions were unconstitutional) said: "The Oireachtas has continued the policy of committing the highly technical and intricate administration of land purchase under a wide and comprehensive code to a responsible body of specialists, with an extraordinary and unique jurisdiction: and this anomaly is carefully protected by Article 37 of the Constitution." In *Fisher v Irish Land Commission* [1948] IR 3, the same judge said Article 37 had "probably" been inserted in order to avert problems of the kind that had been debated in *Lynham's* case.

what varying judgments in *Lynham's* case might be supposed to yield. In *Fisher v Irish Land Commission*[14] Gavan Duffy J held that a Land Commission enquiry held with a view to the resumption of a holding, if it could be considered as an exercise of limited powers and functions of a judicial nature, was "not outside the pale of Article 37", though in fact he thought that functions or powers of a judicial nature were not involved at all in this instance, so that the Commissioners in his opinion had "no occasion to rely on Article 37 to validate their jurisdiction"; this too was the view of the Supreme Court. In *The State (Crowley) v Irish Land Commission*[15] - also a resumption case, but involving a subsection which had not been in issue in *Fisher's* case - the Supreme Court held that the Commission's function was quasi-judicial, but was "in accordance" with Article 37; whether it positively required the protection of Article 37 in order to survive challenge the Court did not say. Again, in *Foley v Irish Land Commission*[16] - yet another resumption case - the Supreme Court actually expressed its view on the Commission's function on the *alternative* hypothesis that it was a:

> "limited function [or power] of a judicial nature within the meaning of Article 37 or, on the other hand, [that it conferred] on the Land Commission, as an administrative body, power, by its determination within jurisdiction, to impose liability and affect rights."

(In either event it was bound to act judicially, the Court held.)

Article 37 not helpful in demarcation

The result of Article 37 and of the cases decided before and soon after its enactment could be summarised as follows. Firstly, there is an "administration of justice" in "justiciable controversies" such as must be reserved to judges in courts: Article 34 (Article 64 of the 1922 Constitution). Secondly, there is (in the Supreme Court's words in *Foley's case)* a power - such as was recognised in *Lynham's* case - of an administrative body "by its determination within jurisdiction to impose liabilities and affect rights". But thirdly, there appeared to exist a further type of power, one which the courts hesitated to ascribe to either of the two former categories, namely a "limited power or function of a judicial nature within the meaning of Article 37". This summary suggests the comment that the courts had failed, in *Lynham's* case or thereafter, to define clearly the "administration of justice" or the "judicial power" in the sense implying the exclusive competence of judges in courts, with the consequent corresponding lack of definition in the concept of an administrative determination which imposed liabilities and affected rights and the lack of a clear boundary between the two; and that this dubious situation, which the innovation of Article 37 was intended to help, led only to the emergence of a new, third category of power (the boundaries of which remained equally undefined). Indeed, in this aspect of its operation, Article 37 might seem to have increased rather then diminished uncertainty.[17] A better course might have been to accept, as Johnston J did in *Lynham's* case, that a basically administrative process with merely ancillary judicial-looking features, was not the same thing as an administration of justice in a sense which would have brought it within the very general words of Article 34.1.

[14] [1948] IR 3. Actually the earliest case after 1937 in which Article 37 was judicially mentioned was *The State (Burke) v Lennon* [1940] IR 136: this is cited in a more appropriate context below, p. 563.
[15] [1951] IR 250.
[16] [1952] IR 118.
[17] The other aspects of the operation of Article 37 - the significance of its protecting only "limited" functions and only in non-criminal matters - are considered below: pp. 561-569.

Definition of "administration of justice", "judicial power" remains elusive

In subsequent years the uncertainty created by Article 37 and reflected in the *Fisher, Crowley* and *Foley* judgments continued, as did the somewhat hand-to-mouth approach to establishing what was an "administration of justice" in the sense of Article 34.1. In *Cowan v Attorney General*[18] and in *Deaton v Attorney General*[19] it was held, respectively, by the High Court that the conduct of an election petition, and by the Supreme Court that the "selection" of a punishment, were functions forming part of the administration of justice.[20] But the definition remained elusive. The "description" given by Kennedy CJ in *Lynham's case* was several times cited with approval, e.g. in *The State (McKay) v Cork Circuit Judge*[21] by Sullivan P and Hanna J, and in *In re Solicitors Act 1954*[22] by Maguire CJ. Yet in the latter case Kingsmill Moore J showed reluctance to accept it as canonical, and gave his own view of the "judicial power" problem:

> "From none of the pronouncements as to the nature of judicial power which have been quoted can a definition at once exhaustive and precise be extracted, and probably no such definition can be framed. The varieties and combinations of powers with which the Legislature may equip a tribunal are infinite, and in each case the particular powers must be considered in their totality and separately to see if a tribunal so endowed is invested with powers of such nature and extent that their exercise is in effect administering that justice which appertains to the judicial organ, and which the Constitution indicates is entrusted only to judges."

A few years later, in *The State (Shanahan) v Attorney General,*[23] Davitt P made another effort, somewhat on the lines of that of Kennedy CJ, but cast more methodically, to grasp the nature of the judicial power of the State:

> "I have certainly no intention of rushing in where so many eminent jurists have feared to tread, and attempting a definition of judicial power; but it does seem to me that there can be gleaned from the authorities certain essential elements of that power. It would appear that they include (l) the right to decide as between parties disputed issues of law or fact, either of a civil or criminal nature or both; (2) the

[18] [1961] IR 411.
[19] [1963] IR 170; (1964) 98 ILTR 99.
[20] See also *The State (O.) v O'Brien* [1973] IR 50 (below, p. 347 and *Maher v Attorney General* [1973] IR 140 (below, p. 370), in which respectively a ministerial discretion in regard to the detention of a young convicted person, and evidentiary conclusiveness attributed to a certificate, were held to pre-empt functions which properly belonged to the courts. Under the old Constitution it was held that an exercise of the judicial power was not represented by an assessment of damages by the Master of the High Court *(Matheson v Wilson* [1929] IR 134) or by an adjudication in bankruptcy by a court registrar *(The State (McKay) v Cork Circuit Judge* [1937] IR 650). In the context of Article 34, see *Re Singer* (1963) 97 ILTR 30 (listing of cases for trial by court registrar held by Supreme Court to be purely administrative and while necessary "as a preliminary towards preparing for a sitting of a Court, is not in any sense the administration of justice referred to in Article 34.1."); *The State (Craven) v Frawley* [1980] IR 1 (the Minister for Justice, though bound to act judicially in considering whether to change the place of a prisoner's detention, is not performing a function of a kind reserved to the courts); *Magauran v Dargan* [1983] ILRM 7 (the Taxing Master performs a function ancillary to, but not part, of the judicial process and does not exercise a judicial function); *McCann v Racing Board* [1983] ILRM 67 (where Barron J held that the Racing Board's statutory power to suspend and revoke course betting permits was held to be administrative, as such powers not intended by the Constitution to be confined to the judiciary); *Stringer v Irish Times Ltd.*, High Court, 3 February 1993 (where Carney J held that the "preliminary or office stage of litigation" did not amount to an administration of justice so that a claimed immunity for libel deriving from Article 34.1 would attach to the pre-trial publication of a statement of claim or other court documents which had not yet - actually or notionally - been produced in open court).
[21] [1937] IR 650.
[22] [1960] IR 239.
[23] [1964] IR 239.

> right by such decision to determine what are the legal rights of the parties as to the matters in dispute; (3) the right, by calling in aid the executive power of the State, to compel the attendance of the necessary parties and witnesses; (4) the right to give effect to and enforce such decision, again by calling in aid the executive power of the State. Any tribunal which has and exercises such rights and powers seems to me to be exercising the judicial power of the State."

(He was not in that case concerned with Article 37, so that he did not touch the question whether a power such as he described might, in limited non-criminal matters, be exercised by persons or bodies other than judges or courts.)

A couple of years later, yet another attempt was made by Kenny J - and provisionally accepted by the Supreme Court - at stating the "characteristic features" of an administration of justice. These were:

> "(1) a dispute or controversy as to the existence of legal rights or a violation of the law;
>
> (2) the determination or ascertainment of the rights of parties or the imposition of liabilities or the infliction of a penalty;
>
> (3) the final determination (subject to appeal) of legal rights or liabilities or the imposition of penalties;[24]
>
> (4) the enforcement of those rights or liabilities or the imposition of a penalty by the court or by the executive power of the State which is called in by the court to enforce its judgment;
>
> (5) the making of an order by the court which as a matter of history is an order characteristic of courts in this country."

In the setting of the case before him - *McDonald v Bord na gCon (No.2)*[25] - Kenny J held that the making of an exclusion order by a statutory board against an individual greyhound trainer under s 47 of the Greyhound Industry Act 1956, "possessed all the characteristics [he had] mentioned of the administration of justice" and so infringed Article 34; it was not saved by Article 37, as the effect of an exclusion order was to deprive the person affected of his livelihood and so the making of the order did not represent the exercise of a "limited" function. The peculiar difficulty of isolating the concept of the "administration of justice" is well illustrated by this case, since the Supreme Court reversed the judgment of Kenny J on appeal, by way of simultaneously "accepting the characteristic features of a judicial body set out by Mr. Justice Kenny" and holding that "investigating authorities" of the kind represented by the defendant Board "did not satisfy any of these requirements".

[24] "A characteristic of the exercise of a judicial function is that by its determination within jurisdiction the tribunal, court or individual concerned imposes liabilities or affects rights", *per* Finlay CJ in *Kennedy v Hearne* [1988] IR 481; [1988] ILRM 52, 531 (determination of tax liability by Collector General does not constitute an administration of justice, since this determination did not of itself "impose a liability on the taxpayer or affect any of his rights.")

[25] [1965] IR 217; (1965) 100 ILTR 89. The last of the tests Kenny J had proposed - the making of an order "characteristic of courts in this country" - he had previously used in *Deaton v Attorney General* [1963] IR 170, having adopted it from the Australian Chief Justice Dixon in *The Queen v Davison* (1954) 90 CLR 353.

Now three categories instead of two

The Court moreover reinforced the impression that the effect of Article 37 had been to create three categories of activity in this general area where previously there had only been two:

> "The bodies or persons conducting the investigations under ss 43 and 44, while bound to act judicially, are not constituted judicial persons or bodies nor do they exercise powers of a judicial nature within the meaning of Article 37."

It followed from this formulation that the Court saw a landscape containing (1) courts; (2) non-courts exercising limited judicial functions under Article 37; (3) administrative bodies bound to act judicially. Where the theoretical or dogmatic boundaries were to be drawn between these three categories remained as uncertain as before.

In *O'Brien v Bord na Móna*[26] the Supreme Court, called upon to decide whether the compulsory acquisition functions of Bord na Móna involved activity of an administrative or of a judicial nature, eschewed all definition in the *Shanahan* or *McDonald* style, and virtually reverted to the workmanlike pragmatism of Johnston J in *Lynham v Butler (No. 2)* (though that case was not mentioned in the Court's judgment). Speaking by O'Higgins CJ the Court looked at the Turf Development Act 1946, in the light of its broad national economic objective:

> "The purpose of the statute was to make available the considerable natural resource of turf in this State in the best possible fashion for the use of the nation...The task of securing that objective was vested in Bord na Móna, a statutory corporation [and] there is no other authority of the State, executive or judicial, which should make the decision in principle as to whether, balancing the desirability of the production of turf on the one hand and the interests of an individual owner of land on the other, the production of turf or the agricultural interests of the landowner should prevail."

Against this background the Court held the Board's operations in compulsory acquisition to be administrative not judicial (so that the question whether, if judicial, they were of a "limited" nature in the sense of Article 37 did not arise).

Modern judicial thinking - much uncertainty remains

The Supreme Court has delivered three major judgments since 1986 which attempt to define the contours of the administration of justice, without, it must be said, notable success. In the first of these - *The State (Clarke) v Roche*[27] - the Supreme Court appeared to suggest that the application of prescribed statutory legal standards to the facts of a particular case constituted an administration of justice.[28] In the second - *Goodman International v Hamilton (No.1)* [29] - the Court unquestioningly applied the formulation of Kenny J in *McDonald's* case, while in the third - *Keady v Garda Commissioner*[30] - the Court raised questions about these five criteria.

[26] [1983] IR 277.

[27] [1986] IR 619.

[28] There was already a hint of this in the earlier judgment of Kenny J in *Central Dublin Development Association v Attorney General* (1975) 109 ILTR 69 where, dealing with the question whether a Minister who decided what was "development" or "exempted development" under a planning statute was exercising a function of a judicial nature, suggested a new, unitary criterion: "The answer to the question as to what is development and what is exempted development depends... upon the application of legal standards prescribed by the Act and is, therefore, an administration of justice."

[29] [1992] 2 IR 542; [1992] ILRM 145.

[30] [1992] 2 IR 197; [1992] ILRM 912. The judgment in *Keady* was delivered barely a month after the judgment in *Goodman.*

The State (Clarke) v Roche: application of legal standards constitutes an administration of justice

The present trend may be said to have begun in mid-1986 with the judgment of the Supreme Court in *The State (Lynch) v Ballagh.*[31] Here Walsh J classified the granting of bail as a judicial act because "a court has to determine the various matters which may be taken into consideration and exercise its discretion according to the law". He went on to consider s 88 of the Courts of Justice Act 1924, and s 15 of the Criminal Justice Act 1951, which confer the power of either granting bail or remanding in custody to Peace Commissioners in the case of persons charged with indictable offences. The powers of a Peace Commissioner were not at issue in the case; but he suggested, *obiter*, that these functions were judicial in character because they purport to give each Commissioner:

> "power to hear evidence, and, having heard the evidence, to exercise a discretion as to whether prisoners shall be remanded in custody or on bail. As Peace Commissioners in the exercise of these functions are not within the provisions of either Article 34 or Article 37, their position appears to be somewhat constitutionally dubious."

The Supreme Court resumed this theme in *The State (Clarke) v Roche*,[32] where the validity of a summons issued under s 10 of the Petty Sessions (Ireland) Act 1851, was in issue. By this section, a District Court clerk or Peace Commissioner (as the case may be) is required to exercise something akin to a judicial discretion before deciding whether or not to issue the summons. The Court held that a computer-based summons did not conform with the requirements of the section, as it by-passed the requirement that the District Court clerk should exercise his personal discretion as to whether or not the summons should issue. Finlay CJ added, however, that it was an "inescapable conclusion" from the terms of s 10 that the issue of a summons upon the making of a complaint "was a judicial as opposed to an administrative act"; he drew attention to the words of Walsh J in *Ballagh's* case and also doubted whether the vesting of such powers in non-judicial personages (such as District Court clerks or Peace Commissioners) was constitutionally proper.

The reasoning of the Supreme Court in these cases suggested that the Oireachtas could not invest non-judicial personages with powers in criminal cases to hear evidence and "to exercise a discretion according to law". The Courts (No. 3) Act 1986, passed in response to *Clarke's* case, provides by s 1(1) that:

> "Proceedings in the District Court in respect of an offence may be commenced by the issuing, as a matter of administrative procedure, of a [summons] by the appropriate office of the District Court."

Section 1(8) makes it clear that this procedure is entirely separate from that under s 10 of the 1851 Act (which has not been repealed). This avoids the constitutional difficulties which surfaced in *Lynch's* and *Clarke's* cases, as the summons issues automatically following an application to the appropriate District Court office; i.e., the District Court clerk is not now called upon to exercise a judicial function by deciding whether there is a *prima facie* case before issuing the summons.[33]

[31] [1986] IR 203; [1987] ILRM 65.
[32] [1986] IR 619.
[33] A fact confirmed by the Supreme Court in *Director of Public Prosecution v Nolan* [1990] 2 IR 526.

These two decisions gave rise to a series of cases, all of which, in one way or another, impugned the constitutionality of statutory provisions conferring a variety of diverse powers on non-judicial personages such as Peace Commissioners and this, in turn, gave rise to issues of characterisation as to whether the powers conferred involved the administration of justice. The dicta of Walsh J in *Lynch's* case and the principle in *Clarke's* case was taken a step further in *O'Mahoney v Melia*[34] where Keane J held that the granting of bail by a Peace Commissioner involved an administration of justice:

> "Before deciding whether the person concerned should be admitted to bail or remanded in custody, the commissioner must hear the contentions of both parties and any evidence that is put before him. He must take into account the various considerations which should be present to the mind of a judge in hearing such an application...The decision taken by the peace commissioner and the process by which it is arrived at appear clearly to have the characteristic of a judicial rather than an administrative act."

Since it was conceded that the peace commissioner had been discharging his functions in the context of criminal proceedings (so that Article 37 was inapplicable), Keane J held that s 15 of the Criminal Justice Act 1951 (as substituted by s 26 of the Criminal Justice Act 1984) was unconstitutional.

Other decisions have fallen on a different side of the line. Thus, in *Ryan v O'Callaghan*[35] Barr J held that the issue of a search warrant prior to the commencement of a prosecution was "part of the process of criminal investigation and executive rather than judicial in nature." It followed that the granting of such powers to non-judicial personages such as peace commissioners was not unconstitutional.[36] The Supreme Court took a similar view of the power to add counts to an indictment in *O'Shea v Director of Public Prosecutions:*[37] this power was, said Finlay CJ, simply "an administrative or executive function and certainly is not a judicial function."[38] Likewise, in *Wheeler v Culligan*[39] Costello J upheld the constitutionality of s 2 of the Extradition (Amendment) Act 1987 which requires the Attorney General to adjudicate on the adequacy of the evidence before endorsing British extradition warrants for execution. It might have been thought that, on the direct authority of *Clarke's* case, there was here an example of a non-judicial personage unconstitutionally applying legal standards to the facts of a criminal case, but Costello J evidently thought little of this point. Applying the five criteria laid down by Kenny J in *McDonald v Bord na gCon (No.2)*[40] the judge pointed out that the Attorney General was not "considering as a judge does, a dispute or controversy as to the existence of a legal right." Nor was he making "any final determination of any legal rights" or enforcing "any rights or liabilities" and, finally, he was "certainly not making any order which is characteristic of a court of this country." Costello J considered that in this instance the Attorney General was in no different position to that of a

[34] [1989] IR 335. This point had previously been canvassed before Gannon J in *Rederij Kennemerland NV v Attorney General* [1989] ILRM 821, but since he could find for the applicant on other grounds he did not find it necessary to decide the point.
[35] High Court, 22 July 1987.
[36] This decision was followed in a series of subsequent cases: see *Byrne v Grey* [1988] IR 31; *Farrell v Farrelly* [1988] IR 201; *Berkeley v Edwards* [1988] IR 217 (all search warrant cases).
[37] [1988] IR 655; [1989] ILRM 309.
[38] In the High Court Lardner J had essayed a useful definition of judicial power in regard to criminal cases: "The judicial power of the State is exercised and justice is administered whenever there is a determination of guilt or innocence of persons charged with an offence or a determination as to the punishment to be inflicted upon persons found guilty of offences charged against them - such determinations being of a final character, subject only to appeal."
[39] [1989] IR 344.
[40] [1965] IR 217.

prosecuting authority required to weigh up the evidence before launching a prosecution. In both cases, the decisions were "procedural" in nature and did not constitute an administration of justice.[41] These decisions are not easy to reconcile. The *McDonald* criteria were not referred to in *Clarke* and, indeed, it is by no means clear that if these principles had been applied in the latter case, the issuing of a prosecution summons would have been to be a judicial act.[42] On the other hand, *Clarke's* case was not mentioned in *Wheeler v Culligan* and since the Attorney General in the latter case was required to weigh up and consider evidence by reference to a statutory standard, it is hard to see how if the *Clarke* principles had been applied by Costello J he could have arrived at the result which he did.

The Goodman and Keady cases

In November 1991 the Supreme Court delivered two separate judgments which gave differing signals regarding the *McDonald* principles. In *Goodman International v Hamilton (No.1)*[43] the Supreme Court applied the five *McDonald* criteria in holding that the resolutions under the Tribunal of Inquiries Acts, 1921-1979 establishing the Beef Tribunal were not unconstitutional. Finlay CJ agreed that the Tribunal probably satisfied the first criterion (viz., the existence of a dispute as to the existence of legal rights or a violation of the law), but "that fact alone could alone could not conceivably make the proceedings of this Tribunal an administration of justice within the meaning of Article 34." The Chief Justice went on to stress that, on any view, the establishment of the Tribunal did not come within the fifth principle laid down by Kenny J:

> "It is no part, and never has been any part of the function of the judiciary in our system of law, to make a finding of fact, in effect, *in vacuo* and to report it to the Legislature. The courts do not even exercise a function of making, in cases between litigants, a finding of fact which does not have an effect on the determination of a right."

In the second case, *Keady v Garda Commissioner*,[44] the plaintiff challenged the statutory powers given to the Garda Commissioner to dismiss members from the police force amounted to an unconstitutional administration of justice and it was sought to apply the reasoning of the *Solicitors Act* case to members of the Garda Síochána. The Supreme Court dismissed this argument in judgments delivered by McCarthy and O'Flaherty JJ. As far as the *McDonald* tests were concerned, McCarthy J said that "to qualify as being the administration of justice, each of the five *McDonald* tests must be satisfied."[45] He added that in the present case the:

[41] Costello J said that the matter had been "put beyond doubt" by the decision of the Supreme Court in *Shannon v Ireland* [1984] IR 548 where Henchy J had said that the endorsement of an extradition warrant by the Garda Commissioner was "merely procedural." But if one strictly applies the principle in Clarke's case the analogy must be regarded as a false one, if for no other reason that the Attorney General is required to consider and apply a statutory standard (just as with the District Court clerk issuing a summons under s 10 of the 1851 Act) but *unlike* the police authorities when deciding to apply their own administrative "rules of thumb" in considering whether to prosecute. In a subsequent judgment - *McGlinchey v Ireland (No.2)* [1990] 2 IR 220 - Costello J said that the Attorney General would be under a duty not to endorse an invalid extradition warrant for execution. But if the Attorney General properly enjoys this function under s 2 of the 1987 Act this surely takes it far beyond the "purely procedural function" envisaged by Henchy J in *Shannon before* the 1987 Act had ever been enacted. See also pp. 315-317.

[42] Thus, for example, the issuing of a summons scarcely amounts - on any view - to a "final determination of any legal rights", the third criterion mentioned by Kenny J in *McDonald*.

[43] [1992] 2 IR 542; [1992] ILRM 145.

[44] [1992] 2 IR 197; [1992] ILRM 312. This case was argued some three weeks before the *Goodman* appeal and judgment was delivered approximately three weeks after judgment was given in the *Goodman* case.

[45] McCarthy J said that this followed from what Walsh J had said in the Supreme Court in *McDonald* , where he had held that Bord na gCon was not exercising judicial functions since they only satisfied one of the five tests.

"procedure under review fails the first test: there is no dispute or controversy as to the existence of legal rights or violation of the law, if violation of the law means criminal offence; tests numbers 2,3 and 4 appear to identify it as such."

As far as the general applicability of the *McDonald* tests was concerned:

"It was scarcely intended by Kenny J or by this Court to exclude from the qualifying criteria such matters as were identified by Kennedy CJ in *Lynham v Butler (No.2)* - authority to compel appearance of a party before it, to compel the attendance of witnesses, to order the execution of its judgments against persons and property."

And, echoing the words of Davitt P in *Shanahan's* case, he was reluctant to essay a definition of judicial power:

"It is easier, if intellectually less satisfying, to say in a given instance whether or not the procedure is an exercise of such power, rather than to identify a comprehensive check-list for that purpose. The requirement to act judicially is not a badge of such power."

On the other hand, O'Flaherty J thought it possible to reduce *McDonald's* five tests to just two "essential ingredients", namely, that:

"there has to be a *contest between parties* together with the infliction of some form of liability or penalty on one of the parties. Here while undoubtedly there was the infliction of a penalty - and a severe one - the other essential ingredient is not present. This was not a contest between parties; it was, as its name says, an inquiry."

There thus remains an uncertainty with regard to this issue and it seems unlikely that any comprehensive *a priori* test can now be devised. The judgments of both McCarthy and O'Flaherty JJ have this in common, namely, that they both hint that this question is henceforth likely to be resolved on a pragmatic case-by-case basis rather by reference to a pre-defined set of principles. Indeed, further evidence of this pragmatic approach is to be found in the judgment of Murphy J in *Geoghegan v Institute of Chartered Accountants in Ireland*[46] where the applicant had challenged the constitutionality of the Association's bye-laws and, in particular, those powers which the Association power to expel or suspend a member for disciplinary infractions. Although Murphy J agreed that there were "apparent similarities" between this case and the *Solicitors Act* case,[47] he stressed that a crucial difference between the two cases was that the powers in the present case rested on contract only. While it was true that the disciplinary bye-laws of the Association had been approved by the Government, nevertheless by granting such approval:

"the Government merely endorsed the bargain between the parties and did not purport to grant to the Institute or any of its constituent committees any of the executive, judicial or legislative powers of the Government."

This approach must seem questionable. It is true that Kingsmill Moore J had expressly excluded "domestic tribunals with a jurisdiction based solely on contract" from the scope of his judgment in the *Solicitors Act* case but this must be taken to mean a reference to purely *private* decisions of clubs, associations etc. and not where - as here - the

[46] High Court, 9 July 1993.

[47] The applicant in *Geoghegan* was simply facing charges of alleged misconduct, whereas, of course, the solicitors in the *Solicitors Act* case had actually been struck off the roll of solicitors. However, as Murphy J observed, the potential sanction in question was "of such severity (as Kingsmill Moore J said [in the *Solicitors Act case*] of the striking off of a solicitor from the roll) that its consequences might be more serious than a term of imprisonment."

applicant might effectively be deprived of his right to practice by means of a procedure which had received official blessing. Moreover, it is somewhat unreal to regard the relationship between the applicant and the Association as resting solely or even principally on contract.[48] The Association was incorporated by royal charter;[49] its bye-laws were approved by the Government and expulsion from the Association would be no less catastrophic for an accountant than would the act of striking off be for a solicitor. While Murphy J appeared to accept that such powers *would* be unconstitutional if they had been positively conferred by legislation, the all important distinction in his mind was that these powers had merely been assumed by the Association, albeit with the tacit consent of the Government. One wonders, however, whether this essentially formal distinction between the *Solicitors Act* case and the facts in *Geoghegan* should affect the principle of the matter. If Murphy J is correct, it would seem to follow that were the Solicitors Acts to be repealed and the power to strike off solicitors assumed by the Law Society by mutual agreement of the members, such an arrangement would be perfectly constitutional, the decision in the *Solicitors Act* case notwithstanding. It would be indeed surprising if the principles underlying the separation of powers could be circumvented by such formalistic distinctions.

Administration of justice: revenue cases may best be regarded as a special category

This entire question of what constitutes an administration of justice has also been examined in a series of challenges to the validity of revenue powers. In *The State (Calcul International Ltd.) v Revenue Commissioners*[50] the applicants had challenged powers given to the Appeal Commissioners for Income Tax (to determine the tax liability of taxpayers up to an unlimited amount) as being judicial powers which were not "limited" for the purposes of Article 37. Barron J held that the Commissioners were not exercising powers of a judicial nature; the test depended on the orders which they were entitled to make:

> "Such orders obviously impose liabilities upon the taxpayer concerned, but they do not deprive him of anything nor impose penalties nor limit his freedom of action. They declare his liability for tax upon the basis of the facts as found by them. Having declared this liability, they have no power to enforce their decision. Applying the test of the judicial power as expressed by Kingsmill Moore J in the *Solicitors Act* case, it does not seem to me that an order having such characteristics and effect can be said to be an order which, on the true intendment of the Constitution, was one reserved to judges as being properly regarded as part of the administration of justice."

[48] Cf. the comments of Farquharson LJ in *R. v Jockey Club, ex parte Aga Khan* [1993] 2 All ER 853: "[Counsel for the Aga Khan] has referred to the lack of reality of describing such a relationship as consensual. The fact is that if the applicant wished to race his horses in this country he had no choice but to submit to the Jockey Club's jurisdiction. This may be true but nobody is obliged to race his horses in this country and it does not destroy the element of consensuality." The English Court of Appeal went on to hold that the Jockey Club were therefore not a public body and, hence, not amenable to judicial review and this reasoning was approved by Murphy J in *Geoghegan*. But it is scarcely any answer to reply to the issues raised in *Geoghegan* by saying that nobody is obliged to be an accountant or, for that matter, a member of the Association when the applicant's claim was that he was facing professional ruin by reason of the application of bye-laws which he contended were unconstitutional.

[49] Which was subsequently confirmed by legislation: see Institute of Chartered Accountants in Ireland (Charter Amendment) Act 1966, s 7.

[50] High Court, 18 December 1986.

(He went on to hold that, even if he was wrong in this, the powers he was considering were limited judicial powers within the meaning of Article 37).[51]

In *Deighan v Hearne*[52] the plaintiff contended that the assessment of tax constituted a judicial function which should be discharged by the courts. Murphy J rejected his claim, saying that the assessment of tax under the Income Tax Act 1967, did not presuppose any "dispute or controversy between the taxpayer and the Inspector of Taxes". The procedure envisaged by the Act was no more than the application:

> "of established statutory provisions in relation to the imposition of personal taxation by an officer of experience and integrity which it is the statutory duty of that taxpayer to provide in a particular form and within particular time limits. Without adding to the literature on judicial functions or the administration of justice, it can be said with confidence that such a task in its essential nature is administrative and not judicial."

He also rejected the argument that the power of the County Sheriff to levy distress to enforce a tax assessment and the authentication of legal documents were judicial functions reserved to the judiciary. Referring to the judgment of Kenny J in *Deaton v Attorney General*,[53] he said that the enforcement of judgments had always been an executive function. The right of a landlord to distrain for rent without recourse to the courts had never been questioned, and he saw no reason why the public exchequer "should have any lesser rights". He described the authentication of legal and other documents as "routine matters", which could not be regarded as judicial functions. This view was endorsed on appeal by the Supreme Court, with Finlay CJ observing the "importance within a constitutional context of the revenues of the State and that has bearing upon the powers properly and necessarily vested in the Inspector of Taxes in this context." This latter point may, perhaps, be taken as a hint that the revenue cases may be regarded almost as a special category as far as the administration of justice is concerned. Some two years earlier the Supreme Court had rejected similar arguments in *Kennedy v Hearne*.[54] It was here decided that a determination by the Collector-General of tax liability did not amount to a judicial function since, first, it did not of itself affect rights or impose any liabilities and, secondly, even where the Collector-General sought to execute or levy tax on foot of that demand, it did not have the effect of ousting the jurisdiction of the courts, since the courts could intervene to restrain any ultra vires or improper or unreasonable actions on the part of the revenue authorities.

Characterisation problems

Two useful riders to this inconclusive exposition of the "judicial power" and "administration of justice" problem may be found in the judgments of the Supreme Court in *The State (O.) v O'Brien*[55] and *Re Gallagher's Application*.[56] In *O.'s* case the Court had to consider the nature of a power originally vested in "His Majesty", and devolving by

[51] See below, pp. 568-569. By way of contrast, see the dicta of McKenzie J in *Canada v Employment Appeals Tribunal* [1992] 2 IR 484 to the effect that the Employment Appeals Tribunal (which "appeared to be acting in a judicial way and to have the power to award sums of money of a very substantial manner") was exercising judicial functions which were not saved by reference to Article 37. In his view, the tribunal was probably resolving conflicts "more appropriate to and which should be reserved to the courts established by the Constitution." The Supreme Court did not address this question on appeal.
[52] [1986] IR 603 (HC); [1990] 1 IR 499 (SC).
[53] [1963] IR 170; (1963) 98 ILTR 99.
[54] [1988] IR 481.
[55] [1973] IR 50.
[56] [1991] 1 IR 31.

adaptation on the Minister, to determine the place, manner and duration of detention of a young person convicted on a capital charge; and concluded that this power appertained to the administration of justice and the domain of the courts. Walsh J said:

> "It has been submitted...that this was....in the nature of an executive power... It is true that, under the English constitutional theory which applied to Ireland at the time of the passing of the Act of 1908, the Crown was the sole and supreme executive authority of the State and all executive acts were done in the name of the King. However, that did not mean that every act done by the King was necessarily an executive act. The quality of the act *is to be determined by the* act itself not by the person who is doing the act."[57]

This approach is, of course, perfectly in keeping with the same judge's earlier characterisation analysis in *Murphy v Dublin Corporation.* [58] This problem of characterisation was also very much to the fore in *Re Gallagher's Application*. Here the question was whether s 2 of the Trial of Lunatics Act 1883 had survived the enactment of the Constitution. It was contended that this provision (which consigned to the Government the power to order the release of the criminally insane) was unconstitutional inasmuch as it conferred judicial functions in criminal matters on the executive. The Supreme Court agreed that if the powers in question constituted an administration of justice, then the section would be unconstitutional. However, McCarthy J could not agree that the procedure amounted to an administration of justice:[59]

> "The overriding circumstances is that the special verdict is a verdict of acquittal; the trial is concluded; the court does not pronounce a sentence; the role of the court is to order the detention of the person, the former accused, until the executive, armed with both the knowledge and resources to deal with the problem, decides on the future disposition of the problem....It is the carrying out of the executive's role in caring for society and the protection of the common good."

McCarthy J proceeded to compare this function with that of the executive's role in ordering the compulsory detention of the seriously mentally ill. The former Supreme Court had rejected the suggestion in *Re Philip Clarke*[60] that in so acting the executive was infringing the judicial power and in the instant case "no criticism had been levelled against" the decision in *Clarke's* case.

Difference between the "exercise of judicial power" and the "administration of justice"?

A further characterisation issue had earlier emerged in *McDonald v Bord na gCon (No.2)*[61] where it had been pointed out by Kenny J that the exercise of "judicial power" and the "administration of justice" might not in fact be coextensive:

> "Every exercise of the judicial power referred to in Article 6 is not an administration of justice, for the courts in this country have jurisdiction and powers the exer-

[57] Authors' emphasis. See generally, J.P. Casey, "*The Judicial Power under Irish Constitutional Law*" (1975) ICLQ 305; H. O'Flaherty, "*Some Aspects of the Law, the Constitution and the Courts in Ireland*" (1977) 51 ALJ 74; Barton, "*Insanity in the Supreme Court*" (1991) 13 DULJ 127.
[58] [1972] IR 215.
[59] In this respect McCarthy J differed from the earlier judgment of Keane J in *Re Neilan's Application* [1990] 2 IR 267 (who had concluded that the powers were judicial and that the section was accordingly unconstitutional). O'Hanlon J had previously adopted a different view and upheld the validity of the section in *Re Ellis's Application* [1990] 2 IR 267.
[60] [1950] IR 235; (1949) 85 ILTR 119.
[61] [1965] IR 217; (1966) 100 ILTR 89.

cise of which is not an administration of justice, and new powers and functions may be conferred on courts and judges although the exercise of these powers and functions is not an administration of justice."

He instanced the jurisdiction of the Supreme Court under Article 26, and of the High Court over wards of court. (He had previously spoken more generally to the same effect in *Deaton's* case, mentioned above.) This principle has not found favour in any of the later cases.[62] Perhaps, however, it would be more correct to say that not every power exercised by a judge necessarily amounts to an administration of justice, but whether this distinction advances our understanding of the difficult issues involved may be open to question.

Definition of "justiciable controversy"

Finally, the expression "justiciable controversy" itself requires definition. Its earliest use appears to have been in *Lynham's* case, in the judgment of Kennedy CJ, and it has been frequently used in recent years. Clearly not all controversies are "justiciable", for instance, the courts will not adjudicate on purely political issues (such as whether a particular economic programme will benefit the economy), or a controversy between a citizen and an administrative authority on an issue entirely within the authority's discretion, such as where to site a street lamp.[63] Such exclusions, even if extended into a long list, will not afford material for a definition of what *is* justiciable. Possibly the simplest refuge is to use the criterion mentioned, among others, by Kenny J in *McDonald v Bord na gCon,* and to say that a justiciable controversy is one of a type which "as a matter of history" has been capable of litigation in the courts of this country, but this test scarcely gives a complete answer to the problem. More sophisticated tests have been employed in other jurisdictions, such as whether the matters complained of affect legal or equitable rights[64] and, even if they do, whether there any "judicially discoverable and manageable standards"[65] which allow the courts to pronounce on such questions. The case-

[62] Indeed, in *Goodman International v Hamilton* [1992] 2 IR 542; [1992] ILRM 145, Finlay CJ seemed to reject the utility of such a distinction, saying that he found it "difficult to distinguish between the exercise of functions and powers of a judicial nature" and that he was satisfied "that the same considerations apply to the test to be applicable to each of these."

[63] Thus, Megarry VC could say in *Malone v Metropolitan Police Commissioner* [1979] Ch 344 that he could not believe that "the court could, or should, grant a declaration that, for instance, a referee in a football match was right (or wrong) in awarding a penalty kick."

[64] *Malone v Metropolitan Police Commissioner* [1979] Ch 344 (since European Convention of Human Rights was not incorporated into English law, it was not justiciable in an action before the English courts). There are echoes of this approach in two judgments of Blayney J in *Ahern v Minister for Industry and Commerce (No.2)* [1991] 1 IR 462 (decision to put civil servant on compulsory sick leave justiciable since it affected his right to work) and *MacPharthalain v Commissioners of Public Works* [1992] 1 IR 111 (designation of lands as constituting an area of scenic interest justiciable as it affected landowner's right to obtain certain types of grants).

[65] This phrase comes from the celebrated judgment of Brennan J in *Baker v Carr* 369 US 186 (1962). Other criteria mentioned by Brennan J included whether there was "a textually demonstrable constitutional commitment of the issue to a co-ordinate political department" and the "potentiality of embarrassment from multifarious pronouncements by various departments on one question." For leading US examples of this approach, see, e.g., *Pacific States Telegraph Co. v Oregon* 223 US 118 (1912) (courts could not examine whether Oregon's referendum procedure violated constitutional guarantee of republican form of government); *Coleman v Miller* 307 US 433 (1939) (courts could not examine whether constitutional amendment could not be validly ratified by State legislature) and *Nixon v US* 122 L Ed 21(1993) (impeachment power assigned by US Constitution to legislative branch of government, thus excluding judicial review). See also *Duff v Minister for Agriculture* [1993] 2 CMLR 969 (courts cannot review questions of Government policy, since there is no "yardstick" by which the courts could review such decisions).

law in this[66] and other jurisdictions[67] demonstrates, however, that there are really no satisfactory *a priori* answers to these difficult questions.[68]

Is it an irreducible category?

At this point, however, a further question arises. Is the category of "justiciable controversies" in any way closed or entrenched, by inference from Article 34.1 so as to inhibit the Oireachtas from abolishing causes of action which now exist? Probably the answer is "no", as the Oireachtas must have power to change the law, and most changes of law can, directly or indirectly, affect and modify rights. Thus, the former action for criminal conversation was abolished by s 1 of the Family Law Act 1981 (though without prejudice to actions commenced before the Act's passing); and in *R. D. Cox Ltd. v Owners of M.V Fritz Raabe*[69] Henchy J said, though *obiter*, that:

> "If a matter has not been made justiciable, or being justiciable has been made, either by constitutional amendment or by statute, no longer justiciable, it stands outside the range of the original jurisdiction vested in the High Court by Article 34.3.1. Examples are not wanting... of types of proceedings which are outside the jurisdiction of the High Court or any other court - either because they have never been created or have been abolished by statute...[Article 34.3.1] merely declares an amplitude of original jurisdiction in the High Court to encompass all currently justiciable matters."

In effect, therefore, it seems clear from this (admittedly dissenting) judgment that the abolition of a cause of action *cannot of itself be regarded as unconstitutional.* This cannot, however, mean that the Oireachtas has a complete free hand in the matter. The Oireachtas could not, for example, constitutionally abolish large area of the law of tort without providing for adequate and effective system of protecting and vindicating the constitutional rights of the victims of any tortfeasor.[70]

[66] See, e.g., *Macken v An Taoiseach, The Irish Times*, 26 May 1984 (held by Lynch J that question of whether US President could bring into the State any equipment necessary to launch nuclear weapons non-justiciable (semble)); *O'Reilly v Limerick Corporation* [1989] ILRM 181 (question of whether Oireachtas had adequately provided via its taxation policies of disadvantaged groups non-justiciable) and *McKenna v An Taoiseach*, High Court, 8 June 1992 (propriety of Government advertising campaign urging "yes" vote at a referendum non-justiciable, since this calls, said Costello J, for a "careful analysis and a balancing of complex political and social factors" and was thus inapt for judicial resolution).

[67] In the United Kingdom, the House of Lords has said that the judicial process is "totally inept" to deal with national security issues: see *Council of Civil Service Unions v Minister for the Civil Service* [1985] 1 AC 374. The Canadian Supreme Court (*Operation Dismantle v The Queen* (1985) 18 DLR (4th) 481) and the German Constitutional Court (*Pershing 2 and Cruise Missile* Case (1983) 66 BVerfGE 39) both rejected arguments that the deployment of cruise missiles on (respectively) Canadian and German territory would increase the chance of a hostile nuclear strike, thus jeopardising the right to life of the population. The actions were dismissed in both cases on the grounds that the alleged link between the impugned Government action and the rights in question was too speculative and uncertain. In this regard, the following remarks of the German Constitutional Court may be taken as representative: "Because the [Court] lacks legally manageable criteria [we] cannot determine whether or not German state action...has any influence on decisions of the Soviet Union which may or may not trigger the...preventive or responsive nuclear strike which the complainants fear. The federal organs responsible for the foreign and defence policy of the Federal Republic must make such evaluations."

[68] Perhaps the best explanation of all for any "political question" doctrine is that offered by Bickel, *The Least Dangerous Branch* (New Haven, 1962). In his view, the doctrine emerges from a judicial "sense of lack of capacity" compounded in unequal parts from" (a) the strangeness of the issue and its intractability to principled resolution; (b) the sheer momentousness of it, which tends to unbalance judicial judgment; (c) the anxiety, not so much that the judgment will be ignored, as that perhaps it should be but will not be; (d) finally, [the] inner vulnerability, the self doubt of an institution which is electorally irresponsible and has no earth to draw strength from."

[69] Supreme Court, 1 August 1974.

[70] This question seems bound up with the question of constitutional torts which is considered at pp. 707-708.

A further consideration might also arise, when, for instance, the abolition of the right of action for negligence in motor accident cases is canvassed it may seem that a fundamental system of commutative justice - namely, the claim to be compensated, for loss caused by the fault of another, *by that other* is being destroyed, with perhaps constitutionally questionable effect. An Irish precedent for legislation of this kind exists in the Accidental Fires Act 1943, which was passed after a disastrous fire in Athlone;[71] s 1(1) provides:

> "There any person (in this section referred to as the injured person) has suffered damage by reason of fire accidentally occurring (whether before or after the passing of this Act) in or on the building or land of another person, then, notwithstanding any rule of law, the following provisions shall have effect, that is to say:
>
> (a) no legal proceedings shall, after the passing of this Act be instituted in any court by the injured person or any person claiming through or under him or as his insurer against such other person on account of such damage;
>
> (b) if, in case the fire occurred before the passing of this Act any such legal proceedings were instituted after the 16th day of November, 1942, and before the passing of this Act and are pending at such passing, such legal proceedings shall be discharged and made void, subject to such order as to costs as the court in which such legal proceedings are pending or a judge thereof thinks fit to make."[72]

If this can validly be done in a small department of the law of tort - or in a much larger department, such as personal injuries - it is hard to see on what principle any department of the existing law can be considered immune, or why the whole legal system might not be converted into purely administrative material and so withdrawn from judicial process. What then would remain of Article 34.1 and the administration of justice?

Administrative law, principles of judicial review and the administration of justice

The scope and extent of judicial review, together with general principle of administrative law may be briefly mentioned here. A detailed consideration of these issues is more properly within the remit of a book on administrative law,[73] but we may here sketch out

[71] The reason for this Act was that the Supreme Court, in *Richardson v Athlone Woollen Mills* [1942] IR 581; (1942) 77 ILTR 27 had held that the defendants, on whose premises the fire had started, were not protected by an Irish statute of 1715, 2 Geo. I, c.5 - which also aimed at excluding actions for damage caused by accidental fires spreading from adjoining premises - on the ground that "house", the word used in that statute, meant dwelling-house and did not cover a factory; and the 1943 Bill was put to the Dáil on the basis that it would make the law what, in fact, the law had been supposed to be up to the time of the Supreme Court judgment. This background does not alter the fact that the Act took away a potential right of action.
The 1943 Act was deliberately so drawn as not to deprive the plaintiffs in the *Athlone Woollen Mills* case of the benefit of their win; and it does not appear whether any other proceedings were in being, so as to be "discharged and made void". But if so, might the Act have been constitutionally objectionable on grounds like those on which *Buckley v Attorney General* [1950] IR 67 (below, pp. 360-361) was decided? Quite possibly it was the recent passage of the Accidental Fires Act in 1943 which inspired the device of the Sinn Fein Funds Act in 1947; and State counsel in the *Sinn Féin Funds* case actually cited the Accidental Fires Act in argument.

[72] The provisions of s 1(1)(*b*) could not have withstood constitutional challenge in view of the later decision of the Supreme Court in *Buckley v Attorney General* [1950] IR 67. But this principle does not of itself affect the validity of s 1(1)(*a*), assuming such retrospective abolition of a cause of action is not otherwise deemed to be unconstitutional.

[73] For which see generally, Collins and O'Reilly, *Civil Proceedings and the State in Ireland* (Dublin, 1989) and Hogan and Morgan, *Administrative Law in Ireland* (London, 1991).

some of the newly emerging administrative law principles together with providing a brief analysis of some of the principles of long-standing.

Scope of judicial review

The Irish authorities on this point originally emerged in the context of the question of what decisions of an administrative authority were subject to review by certiorari. It was quickly established that all decisions capable of affecting legal rights and interests were amenable to review in this manner.[74] In more recent times with the introduction of the new judicial review procedure in 1986, the case-law has focused on the nature of the bodies whose decisions may be reviewed by way of judicial review. Thus, in *Murphy v Turf Club*[75] Barr J held that a decision of the respondent body to discipline a trainer was not reviewable by way of judicial review since he concluded that the relationship between the parties was governed exclusively by contract. On the other hand, in *Beirne v Garda Commissioner*[76] a majority of the Supreme Court held that the dismissal of a probationer Garda was not simply governed by contract, but derived from the Commissioner's statutory functions and was hence amenable to judicial review.

Audi alteram partem

The requirement to hear the other side - *audi alteram partem* - is one of the two common law rules of natural justice.[77] While these rules have now been given - to a greater or lesser degree - a constitutional status and protection,[78] the basic principle underlying the *audi alteram partem* remains that a person affected by, or with an interest in the outcome of, an administrative decision has the right to have adequate notice of this decision to be given an adequate opportunity to make his case before that administrative body. What the courts will regard as an "adequate opportunity" will very much depend on the circumstances, since the requirements of natural justice are not fixed and unchanging.[79]

Representative examples of application of audi alteram partem rule

Of the many cases decided on the maxim *audi alteram partem*, the following may serve as adequate representatives. In *The State (Irish Pharmaceutical Union) v Employment*

[74] See, e.g., *R. (McEvoy) v Dublin Corporation* 2 LR Ir 371 (*certiorari* lies to quash all decisions imposing liability or affecting rights of others); *R. (Wexford C.C.) v Local Government Board* [1902] 2 IR 349; (1900) 35 ILTR 87 (similar statement from Palles CB); *The State (Crowley) v Irish Land Commission* [1951] IR 250; (1950) 85 ILTR 26 (determination of Land Commission regarding land production reviewable since it was "final and affected the rights of the parties); *The State (Shannon Atlantic Fisheries Ltd.) v McPolin* [1976] IR 93 (inspectors' report held to be reviewable since it affected applicant company's reputation) and *MacPhartalain* v *Commissioners of Public Works* [1992] 1 IR 111 (designation of land by Minister as area of scientific interest reviewable as it affected right of landowners to obtain development grants under statutory scheme).

[75] [1989] IR 171. See also *Murtagh v St. Emer's National School* [1991 1 IR 482 (three day suspension from school not amenable to judicial review) and *Geoghegan v Institute of Chartered Accountants in Ireland*, High Court, 9 July 1993 (decision by chartered body to discipline member not amenable to judicial review).

[76] [1993] ILRM 1.

[77] The other rule is *nemo iudex in causa sua* : the rule against bias, considered below at pp. 353-357.

[78] This is considered below under the doctrine of "constitutional justice" at pp. 357-359.

[79] See, e.g., the comments of Henchy J in *Kiely v Minister for Social Welfare (No.2)* [1977] IR 267 and those of Costello J in *Doyle v Croke*, (1988) 7 JISLL 150, where the latter said that in considering "what procedures can properly be regarded as fair" the courts must have regard to procedures "which would be appropriate to the type of organisation or association which is to adopt them and the nature and scope of the decision to which they relate." Thus, while Hederman J could say in *Murtagh v St. Emer's National School* [1991] 1 IR 482 that a three day suspension from a national school was not a matter for judicial review, Barron J held in *Flanagan v University College, Dublin* [1988] IR 724 that the procedures required for a charge of plagiarism against a university student must "approach those of a court hearing" having regard to the consequences which an adverse decision would have for the student concerned.

Appeals Tribunal [80] the Tribunal had ordered, following an unfair dismissal hearing at which all the parties had been legally represented, that the dismissed employee should be re-engaged. The entire hearing had been directed to the circumstances of dismissal and the employee's possible entitlement to damages; neither party had raised an issue as to re-engagement. The Supreme Court held that the Tribunal had violated the principle of *audi alteram partem* in that the employer had been given no indication that the remedy of re-engagement was being considered, and had received no opportunity of making submissions as to its appropriateness. McCarthy J said:

> "Whether it be identified as a principle of natural justice derived from the common law and known as *audi alteram partem* or, preferably, as the right to fair procedures under the Constitution in all judicial or quasi-judicial proceedings, it is a fundamental requirement of justice that person or property should not be at risk without the party charged being given an adequate opportunity of meeting the claim, as identified and pursued. If the proceedings derive from statute, then, in the absence of any set or fixed procedures, the relevant authority must create and carry out the necessary procedures; if the set and fixed procedure is not comprehensive, the authority must supplement it in such a fashion as to ensure compliance with constitutional justice."[81]

Many of the leading cases have turned on the adequacy of the notice given to the person affected by the decision. Thus, in *The State (Gleeson) v Minister for Defence*[82] the Supreme Court quashed the applicant's dismissal from the Defence Forces in circumstances where he was not told of the reasons for his dismissal, nor was he given any adequate opportunity to make representations in advance of that decision.[83] On the other hand, there have been a series of other decisions where the notice to the applicant has been deemed to be sufficient. This occurred in *The State (Duffy) v Minister for Defence*[84] where the Supreme Court upheld the dismissal of a naval officer on grounds of incompetence. The officer was told by the authorities that it was proposed to discharge him on this ground and was given seven days to contest this finding. Henchy J drew a distinction between "the decision to proceed to discharge" and "the actual discharge" seven days later and held that the fact that the applicant could have made representations during this period of delay, constituted adequate compliance with the *audi alteram partem* rule. Likewise, in *Lang v Government of Ireland*,[85] where the applicant had been dismissed from the prison service on the grounds of persistent absenteeism, O'Hanlon J held that the relevant Minister had not breached natural justice in circulating a memorandum for Government[86] which contained comments adverse to the applicant and which memorandum had not been disclosed to the applicant:

> "It cannot be said that the applicant was well aware for some years before his dismissal of the matters which were causing concern to his superiors in the prison ser-

[80] [1987] ILRM 36.

[81] The requirement to fashion fair procedures had previously been articulated by the Supreme Court in *East Donegal Co-Operatives Ltd. v Attorney General* [1970] IR 317 and *O'Brien v Bord na Móna* [1983] IR 256.

[82] [1976] IR 280.

[83] Other examples include *Gallagher v Corrigan*, High Court, 2 February 1988 (where Blayney J held that prison officers who were disciplined for alleged negligence in allowing a prisoner to escape had no reason to construe a letter from the prison authorities asking them to explain their conduct as giving them notice that they would be facing disciplinary charges) and *Beirne v Garda Commissioner* [1993] ILRM 1 (where the Supreme Court held that a probationer Garda was unfairly dismissed in circumstances where he was not told of the statements made by the witnesses, so that, said Egan J, he had no opportunity "of contradicting any specific allegations or eliciting any facts of a mitigating nature from the makers of the statements).

[84] [1979] ILRM 65.

[85] High Court, 7 July 1993.

[86] The Government has power to dismiss civil servants pursuant to s 5 of the Civil Service Regulation Act 1956.

> vice; that he was given express notice of these matters on a number of occasions, and given every opportunity to put forward whatever could be said in his own defence; and that this process was repeated before the final decision was made to remove him from office."[87]

The operation of the *audi alteram partem* rule is by no means confined to such disciplinary situations. Thus, in *Frenchchurch Properties Ltd. v Wexford C.C.*[88] Lynch J quashed the refusal to grant a planning permission where the planning authority had failed to allow the applicant to make submissions on a key point. Likewise, in *TV 3 Ltd. v Independent Radio and Television Commission*[89] Blayney J set aside a decision of the Commission to withdraw the franchise for a television station where (he found) the applicants had not been given any adequate opportunity to make representations in advance of that decision.

Special circumstances where strict observance of audi alteram partem rule may be excused or overlooked

There are, however, cases presenting special circumstances which the courts will recognise as rendering literal observation of the *audi alteram partem* rule impracticable or inappropriate. Examples of such instances include *Irish Family Planning Association v Ryan*,[90] in which the Supreme Court acknowledged that, if the Censorship of Publications Board were to regard themselves as disabled from prohibiting an obscene publication until they had communicated with, and given an opportunity to be heard, to, its editor, author or publisher, in cases where such persons could not readily be traced, the whole object of the censorship legislation could be defeated; and *O'Callaghan v Commissioners of Public Works*,[91] where the plaintiff farmer had instructed an agricultural contractor to recommence ploughing which threatened the destruction of a prehistoric promontory fort. The Commissioners of Public Works placed a preservation order on it under the National Monuments Acts 1930-54, but as the plaintiff had absented himself, the Commissioners could not notify him personally. O'Higgins CJ excused any breach of *audi alteram partem* by saying that:

> "here an emergency had been created by the plaintiff's own action in defiance of his legal obligations. If the Commissioners had hesitated in acting as they did, the monument which it was their duty to preserve would have been seriously damaged or destroyed. Further, it was not possible to contact the plaintiff, because his address was not then known and did not become known to the Commissioners until some time later."

The decision of the Supreme Court in *The State (Lynch) v Cooney*[92] is in a similar vein, as the Court upheld the action of the Minister for Posts and Telegraphs in acting to prevent an election broadcast on behalf of Provisional Sinn Féin, without giving the persons affected an opportunity to make representations against his proposed order. O'Higgins CJ said:

[87] See also *Hynes v Garvey* [1978] IR 174 and *The State (Burke) v Garvey* [1979] ILRM 232.
[88] [1992] 2 IR 268.
[89] High Court, 6 May 1992. Blayney J's judgment was affirmed by the Supreme Court in a decision delivered by Egan J on October 26, 1993. See also *Madden v Minister for the Marine* [1993] 1 IR 567.
[90] [1979] IR 295.
[91] [1985] ILRM 364.
[92] [1982] IR 337.

"The time was short and a decision was urgent. There was no opportunity for debate or parley. Indeed, in the circumstances to permit or seek such opportunity might have defeated the very object and purpose of the section. There may be many cases in which justice requires that those to be affected by action of this kind should receive notice and be heard. I am quite satisfied that this was not one of such cases."

Nemo iudex in causa sua

The principle that a man should not be judge in his own cause has a certain traditional status as the most axiomatic of natural rules.[93] Its essence was stated by Kenny J in *O'Donoghue v Veterinary Council*[94] in the form of a test for determining whether or not a tribunal is impartial:

> "The test to be applied in determining whether a tribunal (be it judge or jury or disciplinary committee) is impartial is that a member is not impartial if his own interest might be affected by the verdict, or he is so connected with the complainant that a reasonable man would think that he would come to the case with prior knowledge of the facts or that he might not be impartial."[95]

Quite apart from the fact that this test may too widely stated,[96] it is, however, impossible to respect this principle universally, either in strictly judicial or in quasi-judicial administrative proceedings.

Rule of necessity

The rule against bias will generally yield to the principle of necessity, although this exception is viewed with some circumspection and will not be allowed to "defeat a real fear...of bias or injustice."[97] In *O'Byrne v Minister for Finance*,[98] in which the plaintiff was the widow of a Supreme Court judge and was making the case that deductions which had been made from his salary in respect of income tax had been unconstitutional as amounting to a reduction of his remuneration, contrary to Article 35.5. The judges of the High Court and Supreme Court who heard her case were, of course, themselves due to be affected by its outcome. In the Supreme Court this fact was not adverted to; but

[93] *Day v Savadge* (1615), Hob. 85, 87: *Per* Hobart CJ: "Even an Act of Parliament. made against natural equity, as to make a man judge in his own cause, is void in itself, for *iura naturae sunt immutabilia,* and they are *leges legum*." This however is generally agreed not to reflect the reality of English law even at that date. See C.K. Allen, *Law in the Making,* 7th ed., p. 448.

[94] [1975] IR 398.

[95] There seems to be an echo of this test in the words of Griffin J in *Connolly v McConnell* [1983] IR 172 a case about a trade union removing one of its officers. "In determining whether the tribunal is impartial any member is not to be regarded as impartial if his own interest might be affected by the decision, and this interest is not necessarily to be confined to pecuniary interest."

[96] See below at pp. 355-356.

[97] *O'Neill v Beaumont Hospital Board* [1990] ILRM 419, per Finlay CJ. In this case, the Supreme Court restrained three members of the Board - who had previously expressed strong views concerning the continued employment of the plaintiff - from adjudicating on the question of whether to dismiss him or not. However, despite the fact that these members had expressed these views at a board meeting, the Supreme Court held that it should not have the effect in the circumstances of disqualifying the entire board, since there would then be no other body which could adjudicate on the question. On the other hand, in *O'Neill v Irish Hereford Breed Society Ltd.* [1992] 1 IR 431 Murphy J refused to allow a plea of necessity to prevail in somewhat similar circumstances, since under the defendant society's rules, a quorum of members could have been convened which do not contain any members who had previously formed a provisional judgment which was hostile to the plaintiff's interests.

[98] [1959] IR 1; (1959) 94 ILTR 11.

Dixon J in the High Court, in considering a relevant American decision, pointed out that it had dealt with this problem; the US Supreme Court had held that:

> "jurisdiction could not be declined or renounced because of the individual relation of the members of the court to the question, the plaintiff being entitled by law to invoke the jurisdiction and there being no other tribunal to which under the law recourse could be had in a matter of the kind."[99]

Likewise, in *Flynn v Allen*,[100] a case where the plaintiff had sued the Benchers of King's Inns, Lynch J frankly acknowledged his difficulty:

> "I am, of course, as is every other judge of the High Court and judge of the Supreme Court, a Bencher of the King's Inns and I am conscious of the fact that in one sense I myself could be said to be a defendant in these matters. Be that as it may, the matter has to be decided by some judge of the High Court and it has come before me and I must not shirk by duty of dealing with it."

However, in *The State (Killian) v Minister for Justice*[181] where the applicant was challenging the constitutionality of the appointment of a judge before whom he had been tried, on grounds applicable in theory to all judges appointed since the enactment of the Constitution, the Supreme Court which heard his appeal was deliberately constituted of three judges whose own appointments had been of earlier date.

Differing standards for bias depending on whether judicial power is being exercised

In proceedings conducted by an administrative authority (including bodies such as professional associations with statutory powers) the position appears to be that if the power being exercised by the authority can be construed as a judicial function, such that it must depend on Article 37 for legitimacy, and that, were it not for Article 37, the function would be properly exercisable only by a judge in a court, then *nemo iudex* will apply just as it would to a judge in a court. If, however, the function being exercised by the authority is not a judicial function, but merely requires the authority to "act judicially", i.e. a function of the *Lynham v Butler (No. 2)* type, then the maxim does not apply in its full rigour, and there is no breach of natural justice if the authority fairly considers a matter in which it itself will have an interest. The authority for these statements is *O'Brien v Bord na Móna,*[102] a case in which the Board's compulsory acquisition powers were attacked on the ground *inter alia* that their exercise, to the detriment of the landowner whose interest was acquired against his will, conflicted with the *nemo iudex* principle. Speaking for the Supreme Court, O'Higgins CJ said:

[99] *Evans v Gore* (1919) 253 US 245, *per* Van Devanter J.

[100] High Court, 2 May 1988.

[101] [1954] IR 207; (1955) 89 ILTR 116.

[102] [1983] IR 255; [1983] ILRM 314. There is, however, an apparent discordance between the Supreme Court's tidy system in *O'Brien v Bord na Móna* and what the earlier Supreme Court had said, *per* Kingsmill Moore J, in *In re Solicitors Act 1954* [1960] IR 239 because in that case, although the Court found that the Disciplinary Committee of the Incorporated Law Society were "administering justice" when deciding to strike a solicitor off the rolls, it dismissed the complaints about the Committee's evident lack of impartiality as "not in point". The discordance can be resolved if it is assumed that the Court used the same phrase, "administering justice", in two different senses at different points of the judgment. At the point where Kingsmill Moore J explained why the complaints about the Disciplinary Committee's composition were not well taken (p. 272 of the report) he said: "If the Committee are not administering justice the Constitution imposes no restrictions on the composition of the body"; this may have been intended to mean "not administering justice of the kind which only a court may administer". If this surmise is wrong, then there is a discordance within the judgment itself since the whole basis of the decision was that the Committee *were* administering justice, but to a degree (because of the severity of the sanction they could inflict) beyond what Article 37 ("limited powers etc.") could warrant in a body not a court.

> "In the view of this Court it is necessary in this case to examine and consider the structure and intention of the [Turf Development Act 1946] in order to determine whether Bord na Móna in making a decision to acquire land or property rights compulsorily is exercising a function or power of a judicial nature. If it is then it cannot be a judge in its own cause. But on the other hand if it is acting in discharge of an administrative function it would have an obligation to act fairly and properly but would not necessarily be inhibited from deciding the question as to whether or not to acquire."

(The Court came to the conclusion that the Board's powers were in the latter category.) Some months before this decision, Murphy J in *Collins v Co. Cork V.E.C.*[103] had, in the context of a decision by a vocational education committee to remove a headmaster from office, frankly accepted that "some real or apparent conflict of interest may arise and must be accepted as inherent in the discharge of the duties of the statutory body".[104]

Test of bias

While a decision of an administrative authority which is infected by bias is void and is liable to set aside by the courts, this is largely to beg the question as to what degree of pre-judgment, prior involvement or interest will constitute bias. What had hitherto been regarded as a leading case - O'*Donoghue v Veterinary Council*[105] - is now, perhaps, open to question on the ground that it sets an unreasonably high standard. Here a complaint against a veterinary surgeon had been made by a colleague who subsequently sat both as a member of a group which considered the report of the committee which investigated the complaint, and also on the Council which made an order effectively suspending the first veterinary surgeon from practice for six months. The latter brought a statutory petition to the High Court seeking the cancellation of the Council's decision on the ground, *inter alia,* that the participation of the complainant in the decision amounted to a breach of "constitutional" justice. Kenny J cancelled the decision, saying:

> "It is a fundamental principle of our law that no one should act as a judge in his own cause. Although [the complainant] took no part in the preparation of the case for hearing and although he was a nominal complainant (the real complainant being the Minister for Agriculture), he must be regarded as being the complainant and, as he took part in the determination and as he voted on the resolution that the petitioner committed the acts charged and was guilty of conduct disgraceful in a professional respect, the decision of the Council must be cancelled."

[103] High Court, May 26, 1982.

[104] Similarly in *McCann v Attorney General* [1983] ILRM 67, Barron J said the composition of the Racing Board which had revoked the plaintiff's betting permit "could not be faulted...If it could have been, then all bodies entitled to exercise disciplinary powers in relation to complaints of misconduct brought before them would be acting in breach of the principles of natural justice." (By "all bodies etc." he obviously meant "all bodies with a statutory function to promote a particular interest with which such misconduct conflicts".) He distinguished *O'Donoghue's* case (see below) on the basis that there a member of the tribunal hearing the complaint was also nominally a complainant; though in the *Solicitors Act* case (see preceding note) this feature had been thought immaterial. In *O'Neill v Irish Hereford Breed Society Ltd.* [1992] 1 IR 431 Murphy J sought to reconcile these authorities by saying that while the *Solicitors Act* case and the *McCann* case made it clear that while "not every prior involvement by a member of a body exercising a quasi-judicial function with a person or conduct of a person whose affairs are under consideration by the body would necessarily disbar the member from acting in the matter, certain forms of involvement would undoubtedly have that result." Presumably Murphy J is using the phrase "quasi-judicial" advisedly, since *O'Brien v Bord na Móna* suggests that such a degree of prior involvement would not be tolerable in the case of a body discharging judicial powers.

[105] [1975] IR 398.

But later cases tend to suggest that this view is unreasonably strict. In *Corrigan v Irish Land Commission*[106] Griffin J spoke of the need to establish a "real likelihood of bias" and in *Dublin and County Broadcasting Ltd. v Independent Radio and Television Commission*[107] Murphy J said that the test must be that of "the real likelihood of prejudice" and not "on the basis of a suspicion which might dwell in the mind of a person who is ill-informed and did not seek to direct his mind properly to the facts."[108] Similarly, in *O'Neill v Beaumont Hospital Board*[109] Finlay CJ said that the test to be applied was that whether "the reasonable man" who was not "either over-sensitive or careless of his own position" would have "good grounds for a fear that he would not get [an independent hearing] in respect of the issues involved. "

Types of bias

Bias can, of course, take several forms. The first and most obvious form of bias is, of course, material or pecuniary interest. Thus, in *Doyle v Croke*[110] Costello J held that a committee decision to confine the payment of monies in a strike fund to a list of persons who were said to have adequately performed picket duty during the course of the strike constituted a breach of the rule against bias since a "reasonable person might conclude that there was a risk that an even-handed decision might not be taken by a committee all of whose members had a financial interest in its outcome.[111] Secondly, bias may take the form of personal attitudes, relationships or beliefs. *Heneghan v Western Regional Fisheries Board* [112] may be regarded as a strong case, as here Carroll J set aside the dismissal of a fisheries inspector where she found that the prime mover in the dismissal process had acted as "witness, prosecutor, judge, jury and appeal court". Thirdly, there may be a degree of institutional bias, in that administrators will often find themselves so committed to the institution which they serve that they are unable to strike a fair balance between the objectives of the institution and the contrary interests of a private claimant. Thus, Keane J could say in *The State (Comer) v Minister for Justice*[113] (a case where the prison authorities were required to adjudicate on whether a prison officer had been guilty of neglect of his duties) that the principle of *nemo iudex* "could not be literally applied" in such circumstances. Keane J was later to observe in *O'Brien v Board na Móna*:[114]

> "[A] decision is not vitiated simply because the official who made it can be said to have a natural bias in favour of advancing the interest of the authority whose interest he is there to serve, but if, in addition, he exercises an administrative discretion capriciously, partially or in a manifestly unfair manner, his action would be restrained and corrected by the courts."

[106] [1977] IR 317.
[107] High Court, May 12, 1989.
[108] The plaintiff had been the unsuccessful applicant for a radio licence and complained that a member of the Commission had a shareholding in the successful company. But on the facts, Murphy J found that there was no real likelihood of bias, since the person alleged to be affected by bias had earlier transferred his shares in the company (although unknown to him he had retained a residual legal - but not beneficial - interest in the shares). This, of course, was a private transaction - regarded by Murphy J as crucial - but with no consideration of whether the "reasonable man" would have known of these special facts.
[109] [1990] ILRM 419.
[110] High Court, 12 May 1989; (1988) 7 JISLL 150.
[111] See also *Connolly v McConnell* [1983] IR 172; *The State (Divito) v Arklow UDC* [1986] ILRM 123; *Dublin and County Broadcasting Ltd. v Independent Radio and Television Commission*, High Court, May 12, 1989.
[112] [1986] ILRM 225.
[113] High Court, 19 December 1980.
[114] [1983] IR 258.

The judgment of Costello J *The State (McEldowney) v Kelleher*[115] is in similar terms. Here the applicant had been refused a permit to collect money from the public under the Street and House to House Collections Act 1962. Section 13(4) of the Act provides that the applicant's appeal to the District Court must be dismissed if a senior police officer testifies that, in his opinion, the proceeds of the collection will be used for the benefit of an illegal organisation. In this case, the same Superintendent who had refused the initial application for a permit had also made such a sworn statement before the District Court so that the appeal was disallowed. Costello J said that the Superintendent was not in breach of the *nemo iudex* principle:

> "By making the statement on oath permitted by the [Act] the Chief Superintendent is acting as a public servant to protect the public interest as he sees it and he is not acting in a manner in which it can be said that he has a direct interest within the meaning of the rule."

The final category may be said to comprise pre-judgment and prior involvement in the case. In *O'Neill v Irish Hereford Breeders Association Ltd.*[116] Murphy J held that several members of a disciplinary committee were disqualified by reason of their prior involvement in an earlier meeting where views gravely prejudicial to the plaintiff had been expressed by them.[117]

Constitutional justice

In 1965 a new term, "constitutional justice", made its first appearance in *McDonald v Bord na gCon*,[118] when Walsh J, delivering the judgment of the Supreme Court, said that:

> "in the context of the Constitution natural justice might be more appropriately termed constitutional justice and must be understood to import more than the two well-established principles that no man shall be judge in his own cause and *audi alteram partem*."

He did not, however, hint what further principles, not already present in or implied by the concept of natural justice or other axioms of common law, this new concept might contain. In 1970, again speaking for the Supreme Court, he said in *East Donegal Co-Operative Ltd. v Attorney General*[119] when first enunciating this extension of the presumption of constitutionality - that procedures etc. provided for by statute were intended by the Oireachtas to be conducted "in accordance with the principles of constitutional justice"; but, again, the judgment afforded no catalogue of those principles. In 1972 something more concrete emerged - in the case of *Glover v BLN Ltd.*[120] - in which Kenny J had used the phrase "natural or constitutional justice" in the High Court - when Walsh J said in the Supreme Court that:

> "the dictates of constitutional justice require that statutes, regulations or agreements setting up machinery for taking decisions which may affect rights or impose liabilities should be construed as providing for fair procedures:"

[115] [1983] IR 289.
[116] [1992] 1 IR 431.
[117] See also *Corrigan v Irish Land Commission* [1977] IR 317 (where the appellant was held to be estopped from raising this point); *Turner v Pilotage Committee of Dublin Pilotage Authority*, High Court, June 14, 1988 and *O'Neill v Beaumont Hospital Board* [1990] ILRM 419.
[118] [1965] IR 217 (1965) 100 ILTR 89. For a discussion of the significance of these remarks, see Casey, "*Natural and Constitutional Justice - The Policeman's Lot Improved*" (1979-80) 2 DULJ (n.s.) 95 and Hogan, "*Natural and Constitutional Justice: Adieu to Laissez-Faire*" (1984) 19 Ir Jur (n.s.) 309.
[119] [1970] IR 317; (1969) 104 ILTR 81.
[120] [1973] IR 388.

though as the case turned on the defendants' failure to give the plaintiff (their employee under a contract of service) a chance to meet complaints against him, it is hard to see that "fair procedures" neglected by the defendants had a dimension not already comprised in the concept of natural justice. The concept of constitutional justice went into something of a decline in the mid to late 1970s following the judgment of Henchy J in *The State (Gleeson) v Minister for Defence.*[121] Referring to the words of Walsh J in *McDonald's* case he said the extended ambit of the term, by comparison with the two well-established principles of natural justice, was "unquestionable." He added, however:

> "Because of the wide scope of such constitutional guarantees, whatever value "constitutional justice" may have as a term of generic connotation, a plea of a denial of constitutional justice lacks the concreteness and particularity necessary to identify and bring into focus the precise constitutional issue that is being raised."

This rather limited analysis has been increasingly questioned in subsequent case-law. While it is true that the phrase "constitutional justice" embraces the two traditional precepts of natural justice - *audi alteram partem* and *nemo iudex in cause sua* - it also goes further by perhaps including certain substantive guarantees[122] as well as by affording greater protection against statutory encroachment.[123] Thus, the concept of "constitutional justice" probably includes the right to sue for damages for breach of the constitutional right to fair procedures;[124] the right to reasons in respect of an administrative decision;[125] the right to a decision within a reasonable time[126] and a requirement that an administrative decision is based on probative evidence.[127] Thus, in much the same way as the procedures provided for in Article 40.4.2-5 have subsumed (and are in many ways very similar to) the common law of *habeas corpus,* so it may also be said that the "two principles of natural justice as they pre-existed the Constitution are now part of the" guaran-

[121] [1976] IR 280.

[122] In *S v S* [1983] IR 68 O'Hanlon J held that a common rule which had the effect of excluding the admissibility of relevant and probative evidence was unconstitutional as inconsistent with the guarantee of fair procedures. The ordinary rules of natural justice could not, of course, have produced this result. O'Hanlon J, having referred to Articles 34.1, 34.3.1, 38.1 and 40.3, said that the "combined effect of [these] constitutional provisions appears...to guarantee...something equivalent to the concept of 'due process' under the American Constitution in relation to causes and controversies litigated before the Courts." The "out-moded" rule in question (which excluded evidence as to the true paternity of a child born to a married woman) "could not withstand constitutional challenge as it [was] repugnant to modern thinking on what constitutes fair procedures and the due administration of justice in the Courts."

[123] In *O'Brien v Bord na Móna* [1983] IR 255 Keane J said that legislation which "manifestly" departed from the rule of natural justice in circumstances "where it would have been practicable for the State to honour that guarantee by a different form of procedure" was unconstitutional. The Supreme Court did not deal with this point on appeal. In *Goodman International v Hamilton (No.2)* High Court, 18 February 1993, Geoghegan J took a similar view to that of Keane J when he tested the fairness of the procedures adopted by a Tribunal of Inquiry by reference to considerations of "practicability" under Article 40.3. It had been contended that the failure on the part of certain witnesses to give evidence rendered the proceedings unfair. In Geoghegan J's view, the procedures in question could not be constitutionally faulted so long as the Tribunal "accedes to reasonable requests for the availability of particular witnesses considered necessary for the vindication of a good name, provided that it is possible to obtain such witnesses or evidence."

[124] By analogy with cases such as *Kennedy v Ireland* [1987] IR 587.

[125] See, e.g., *International Fishing Ltd. v Minister for Marine (No.1)* [1989] IR 149.

[126] See, e.g., *Cannon v Minister for Marine* [1991] ILRM 269; *Twomey v Minister for Transport and Tourism,* Supreme Court, 12 February 1993 (semble).

[127] *M. v M.* [1979] ILRM 160 (trial judge not entitled to disregard the "corroborated and unquestioned evidence of witnesses", since to do so was not in accordance with the proper administration of justice). However, constitutional justice does not require that an employer considering allegations of professional misconduct on the part of an employee must act on the basis of the criminal standard of proof: *Georgopolous v Beaumont Hospital Board* [1994] 1 ILRM 58.

tees of fair procedures and constitutional justice.[128] To this extent, the concept of constitutional justice is not a redundant one, although it may be that in most cases the fact that this concept is now rooted in the Constitution will not materially add to the range of protection available to the person affected by an adverse administrative decision which he seeks to impugn.

Internment power an administration of justice?

The cases mentioned in the foregoing pages have generally been cases within, or on the periphery of, the category of administrative law. A special category is, however, presented by cases in which it has been alleged that the operation of a statutory power of arrest and internment is unconstitutional as representing an administration of justice. This point was argued in the infancy of the 1922 Constitution in *R. (O'Connell) v Military Governor, Hare Park Camp*,[129] in which the internment powers of the Public Safety (Powers of Arrest and Detention) Temporary Act 1924, were attacked as breaching Articles 70 and 72 (guaranteeing respectively trial in due course of law, and trial by jury). The old King's Bench Division and Court of Appeal successively rejected these submissions; Molony CJ said:

> "The power given by s 4 is not judicial power. It is a power, in its nature arbitrary, conferred by the Legislature to meet a threatened danger to the State, and limited to particular persons and for a limited time... It is in my opinion impossible to say that the Minister in making the order in the present case was acting as a court, ordinary or extraordinary..."

Fifteen years later Gavan Duffy J (who had been the applicant's counsel in *O'Connell's* case) decided *The State (Burke) v Lennon*[130] partly on the basis of the proposition which he had then unsuccessfully advanced:

> "The authority conferred on a Minister by s 55 [of the Offences Against the State Act 1939] to order arrest and detention is an authority, not *merely* to act judicially, but to administer justice, and an authority to administer criminal justice and condemn an alleged offender without charge or hearing and without the aid of a jury. The administration of justice is a peculiarly and distinctly judicial function, which from its essential nature does not fall within the executive power and is not properly incidental to the performance of the appropriate functions of the executive; consequently a law endowing a Minister of State, any Minister, with these powers is an invasion of the judicial domain and as such is repugnant to the Constitution..."

The judgment of the Supreme Court in *In re Article 26 and the Offences Against the State (Amendment) Bill, 1940*,[131] however, may be taken to have superseded this point of view, which has not since been judicially expressed although the notion that the ministerial opinion underlying the detention order could not be judicially reviewed is now in disfavour.[132]

[128] *Per* McCarthy J in *The State (Furey) v Minister for Defence* [1988] ILRM 89. See also to like effect the comments of McCarthy J in *Goodman International v Hamilton (No.1)* [1992] 2 IR 542; [1992] ILRM 145.
[129] [1924] 2 IR 104; (1923) 58 ILTR 49.
[130] [1940] IR 136.
[131] [1940] IR 470; (1940) 76 ILTR 61. See also the comments of Kenny J in *Mulloy v Sheehan* [1978] IR 438.
[132] *The State (Lynch) v Cooney* [1982] IR 337; [1983] ILRM 89. See below at p. 417.

Article 34.1 (continued)

THE INDEPENDENCE OF THE JUDICIAL FUNCTION

No complete autonomy of judicial function

The independence of the courts and their immunity from control by the Oireachtas is not absolute, and could scarcely be made so. Most of the actual court structure and of court procedure is prescribed, immediately or ultimately, by statute, which the Oireachtas can modify; there seems to be nothing to prevent the Oireachtas from changing the law retrospectively so as to nullify the effect of a court's judgment in one case or a series of cases, provided, of course, that this does not trench on the rights of parties to that litigation; and the position of the judges is not quite as impregnable as a casual reading of the relevant sections of Article 35 might suggest, as they are unprotected against a sudden arbitrary reduction in the retiring age (aimed at eliminating the senior judge or judges) or against legislation which would put the organisation of court business (and thus the manipulation of cause lists) into executive hands. In addition, the administration of criminal justice is to a certain extent under executive rather than judicial control, as the decision to institute, or not to institute, a prosecution, and the right to commute or reduce or remit a penalty imposed by a court, are in non-judicial hands (in the latter instance, by virtue of the Constitution itself: Article 13.6). What does appear to be inviolable is the actual judicial process itself while in operation; once begun, it must be allowed to run its course without interference.

INDEPENDENCE AS AGAINST LEGISLATURE

Judicial process inviolable while in actual operation

This principle was established as against the Oireachtas in the classic case of *Buckley v Attorney General* [1](often called the *Sinn Féin Funds Case).* This action began - and ended - on an ordinary summons brought to determine the ownership of about £20,000, the remains of a fund originally built up by the old Sinn Féin organisation in the years before it was fragmented by political dissension; essentially, the dispute was about whether the "rump" organisation still calling itself Sinn Féin in 1942 was entitled to money collected by and for the national organisation founded in 1905. While the action was pending in the High Court, the Oireachtas passed the Sinn Féin Funds Act 1947, of which s l0 provided that, on the passing of the Act all further proceedings in the action should, by virtue of that section, be stayed; and that the High Court, "if an application in that behalf [were] made *ex parte* by or on behalf of the Attorney General, [should] make an order dismissing the pending action without costs". By other sections the Act purported to establish a Board to administer the funds in issue (for the relief of persons who had suffered in the national struggle with which Sinn Féin was identified), and the High Court was to make an order directing the payment of these funds, which had been lodged in court, to the new Board. On 10 June 1947 counsel for the Attorney General made the application envisaged by s 10, but Gavan Duffy J refused it:

> "I am not today concerned with the merits of the plaintiffs' claim, but with their right to have it tried by a judge of the High Court...I assume the Sinn Fein Funds Act 1947,... to have been passed by the Legislature for excellent reasons...but I cannot lose sight of the constitutional separation of powers. This Court cannot, in deference to an Act of the Oireachtas, abdicate its proper jurisdiction to administer jus-

[1] [1950] IR 67. The substantive action is reported as *Buckley v Attorney General (No.2)* (1950) 84 ILTR 9.

tice in a cause whereof it is duly seized. This Court is established to administer justice and therefore it cannot dismiss the pending action without hearing the plaintiffs... Moreover, this action is not stayed unless and until it is stayed by a judicial order of the High Court of Justice; the payment out of the funds in Court requires a judicial order of this Court, and under the Constitution no other organ of State is competent to determine how the High Court of Justice shall dispose of the issues raised by the pleadings in this action."

The Attorney General appealed to the Supreme Court, but in vain. The Supreme Court (its judgment delivered by O'Byrne J) founded its decision partly on Article 43, but also on the separation of powers expressed, so far as the judicial power is concerned, by Article 34:

> "Article 6 provides that all powers of government, legislative, executive and judicial, derive, under God, from the people, and it further provides that these powers of government are exercisable only by or on the authority of the organs of State established by the Constitution. The manifest object of this Article was to recognise and ordain that, in this State, all powers of government should be exercised in accordance with the well-recognised principle of the distribution of powers between the legislative, executive and judicial organs of the State and to require that these powers should not be exercised otherwise... The effect of this Article and of Articles 34 to 37, inclusive, is to vest in the courts the exclusive right to determine justiciable controversies between citizens or between a citizen or citizens, as the case may be, and the State. In bringing these proceedings the plaintiffs were exercising a constitutional right and they were, and are, entitled to have the matter in dispute determined by the judicial organ of the State. The substantial effect of the Act is that the dispute is determined by the Oireachtas and the Court is required and directed by the Oireachtas to dismiss the plaintiffs' claim without any hearing and without forming any opinion as to the rights of the respective parties to the dispute. In our opinion this is clearly repugnant to the provisions of the Constitution, as being an unwarrantable interference by the Oireachtas with the operations of the courts in a purely judicial domain."

This is the only case in which the Oireachtas purported to interfere with the course of a judicial proceeding actually in being, but in recent times the courts have examined the constitutionality of legislative attempts to reverse with retrospective effect the consequences of a judicial decision.

The Sinn Féin Funds principle only applies to pending lis

That the *Sinn Féin Funds* principle only applies to litigation that is definitively pending at the time of the impugned legislative or executive action is a point exemplified by two Supreme Court decisions concerning gaming licences which construe this principle rather narrowly. The use of slot-machines for gaming is unlawful unless there is for the time being in force a resolution of a local authority adopting Part III of the Gaming and Lotteries Act 1956, in respect of the authority's functional area. In *The State (Divito) v Arklow U.D.C.*[2] the applicant had published the statutory notice of his intention to apply for a certificate from the District Court under the Act. The respondent local authority then rescinded an existing Part III resolution, but later re-adopted Part III for a more limited area, not including the applicant's premises. It was argued that the Council's conduct amounted to an unconstitutional invasion of the judicial domain inasmuch as it had the effect of determining an application for a gaming licence which was lawfully

[2] [1986] ILRM 123.

before the District Court. Henchy J rejected these arguments. It was true that:

> "a non-judicial intervention in the adjudicative process of a lis before any of the Courts established under the Constitution constitutes an unconstitutional invasion of a purely judicial domain...But in this case there was no *lis* before the District Court when the Council intervened. There was no pending proceeding of which the District Court was seised. All that happened was that the applicant had served and published a statutory notice of intention to make an application for a certificate in the District Court on a specified date. The District Court had not acquired jurisdiction to make any order in the matter. It could not acquire jurisdiction to make such an order until the applicant moved his application. And before that happened, the Council's resolution removed the reach of the Act from the premises. I am satisfied that the passing of that resolution did not constitute an unconstitutional invasion of the judicial process."

A similar approach was taken in *Re Camillo's Application*,[3] a case where the resolution under the 1956 Act had been rescinded while the applicant was appealing to the Circuit Court against the decision of the District Court to refuse to grant him a certificate under the 1956 Act. The applicant had sought to rely on the *Sinn Féin Funds* principle, but Griffin J thought little of the point, saying that that case was "clearly distinguishable" from the present one. He could not agree that the recession of the resolution - which had applied to the whole of the authority's functional area - had the effect of interfering with pending proceedings.

The Pine Valley saga

The power of the Oireachtas effectively to reverse a judicial decision was examined in some detail by the Supreme Court in *Pine Valley Developments Ltd. v Minister for the Environment*.[4] The plaintiffs' predecessors in title had obtained outline planning permission for industrial and office development from the Minister for Local Government (who was the statutory predecessor of the defendant) in respect of certain lands. The plaintiffs purchased these lands - which had been originally zoned for agricultural use only - in the belief that they would be able to develop them in accordance with that permission, and the purchase price reflected this fact. In fact, the grant of planning permission was held to be *ultra vires* in *The State (Pine Valley Developments Ltd.) v Dublin County Council*[5] in which the Supreme Court held that the Minister when hearing planning appeals had no power to grant a permission which contravened the development plan. Shortly afterwards, the Oireachtas sought to mend matters by enacting the Local Government (Planning and Development) Act 1982, s 6 of which provided as follows:

> (1) A permission or approval granted on appeal under Part IV of the [Local Government (Planning and Development) Act 1963] shall not be, and shall not be regarded as ever having been, invalid by reason only of the fact that the development concerned contravened, or would contravene materially the development plan relating to the area of the planning authority to whose decision the appeal related.
>
> (2) If, because of any or all of its provisions, subsection (1) of this section, would, but for this subsection, conflict with a constitutional right of any person, the provisions of that subsection shall be subject to such limitation as is necessary

[3] [1988] IR 104; [1988] ILRM 738.
[4] [1987] IR 23; [1987] ILRM 747.
[5] [1984] IR 407.

to secure that they do not so conflict but shall be otherwise of full force and effect.

Pine Valley then commenced proceedings against the respondent Minister and Ireland, claiming damages for breach of constitutional rights.[6] It was contended on their behalf that inasmuch as s 6(2) effectively excluded them from the benefits of the retrospective validation of similar planning permissions contained in s 6(1), it was unfairly discriminatory, and that the State had failed, in the case of an injustice done, by its laws to vindicate their property rights (a plea derived from Article 40.3). These arguments were rejected by the Supreme Court, both Henchy and Lardner JJ being anxious to stress the constitutional limitations on the power of the Oireachtas to rectify the consequences of the 1982 decision. Henchy J said of the unfair discrimination argument that:

> "while a discrimination has resulted, the primary and overriding purpose of [s 6(2)] was to avoid an unconstitutional invasion of the judicial domain by attempting to give validity to any permission which the Courts may have held to be lacking in validity."

Lardner J said that if s 6(1) of the 1982 Act had stood alone, it might have been held to be an unwarrantable invasion of the judicial domain, just like s 10 of the Sinn Féin Funds Act 1947:

> "Section 6(2) was included by the Oireachtas for the purpose of respecting and not interfering with the determination by the Courts of the justiciable controversy which constituted the proceedings in *The State (Pine Valley Developments Ltd.) v Dublin County Council*[7] and of respecting the constitutional rights of the parties, both plaintiffs and defendants, in that action, to have their controversy determined by the Courts rather than by the Oireachtas. It may be that there is to some extent a conflict here between the right of the parties to have their controversy judicially determined and [the plaintiffs'] property rights. That fact in itself, however, does not necessarily mean that an injustice was done to the [plaintiffs] and I am satisfied that it does not constitute an unjust attack on [their] property rights or an unlawful discrimination against them."

This was undoubtedly a curious result, especially bearing in mind that Pine Valley had been granted what ostensibly was a valid planning permission by one organ of State (viz., the Minister for Local Government). Another organ of State (Dublin County Council) successfully challenged the validity of that permission and, finally, when the Oireachtas legislated to validate all previous such planning permissions which had been tainted by a similar flaw, there was a saver in favour of the constitutional rights of an organ of State (Dublin County Council) and this saver ensured that Pine Valley's invalid permission was not retrospectively validated. It is not easy to see why Pine Valley should thus have been effectively penalised in this manner simply by reason of the happenstance of litigation.

Judgment of the European Court of Human Rights in the Pine Valley case

It was precisely this rather arbitrary factor which persuaded the European Court of Human Rights to hold[8] that the failure to validate Pine Valley's planning permission

[6] On this aspect of the case, see p. 1152.
[7] [1984] IR 407; [1982] ILRM 169.
[8] *Pine Valley Developments Ltd. v Ireland* (1992) 14 EHRR 319.

meant that the applicants had been victims of discrimination contrary to Article 14 of the European Convention on Human Rights, taken in conjunction with Article 1 of Protocol 1:[9]

> "The Government did not rely on the observations made by certain members of the Supreme Court in this connection[10] nor did it advance any other justification for the difference in treatment between the applicants and the other holders of permission in the same category as theirs."

Validation statutes and the separation of powers

A further consideration is that the Supreme Court's decision in *Pine Valley* itself seems a questionable extension of *Sinn Féin Funds* principles. It is one thing to say that the *Sinn Féin Funds* principles preclude the Oireachtas from interfering in a case which is pending before the courts,[11] but it is quite another thing to say that the Oireachtas cannot - for separation of powers reasons[12] - subsequently independently confirm and validate what the courts had previously held to be invalid.

Quite apart from the provisions of s 6 of the 1982 Act which we have just examined, there have been several validation statutes enacted in recent years, all of them containing in case of potential conflict a saver - in one form or another - in favour of the constitutional rights of any person. The first appears to have been s 1 of the Garda Síochána Act 1979 which validated the actions of a person who had been (invalidly, as it transpired) appointed as Garda Commissioner. Section 1 of the Courts (No.2) Act 1988 purported to validate the convictions, judgments and orders of a person who had acted as

[9] Article 14 of the Convention provides that:

> "The enjoyment of the rights and freedoms set forth in [the] Convention shall be secured without discrimination on any ground such as sex, race, colour, language, religion, political or other opinion, national or social origin, association with a national minority, property, birth or status."

Article 1 of Protocol No. 1 provides that:

> "Every natural or legal person is entitled to the peaceful enjoyment of his possessions. No one shall be deprived of his possessions except in the public interest and subject to the conditions provided for by law and by the general principles of international law. The preceding provisions shall not, however, in any way impair the right of a State to enforce such laws as it deems necessary to control the use of property in accordance with the general interest or to secure the payment of taxes or other contributions or penalties."

[10] These are the comments of Henchy and Lardner JJ on the reasons why s 6(2) did not have the effect of validating Pine Valley's planning permission, quoted above at p. 363. It is odd that the Government did not seek to stand over this judicial reasoning, but instead contended that, the *dicta* of Henchy and Lardner JJ notwithstanding, s 6 *did* have the effect of validating Pine Valley's planning permission. Not surprisingly, the European Court of Human Rights held that it could not go behind these judicial observations on the interpretation of national legislation, "whatever the weight of those observations in national law."

[11] Cf. the decision of the Supreme Court in *The State (O'Shea) v Minister for Defence* [1947] IR 49. In this case the applicant had succeeded in establishing that a decision of a pensions adjudicator was flawed by reason of his misapplication of the Military Service Pensions (Amendment) Act 1934 and the High Court quashed that determination. Amending legislation - the Military Service Pensions (Amendment) Act 1945 - was quickly enacted which purported (i) to allow the Minister to appeal and to the Supreme Court and (ii) to validate retrospectively the procedure which had been actually adopted by the referee in the applicant's case. When the case came on appeal, the Supreme Court simply applied the new Act to the applicant's case and allowed the appeal. The judgment of Maguire CJ (delivered two years before *Sinn Féin Funds*) contains no concession to separation of powers type considerations that would almost certainly render such legislation unconstitutional in a modern era.

[12] Of course, there may be other constitutional reasons why such validation cannot take effect: see, e.g., *Shelly v Mahon* [1990] 1 IR 36 (validation of criminal conviction would interfere with right to trial in due course of law): see p. 576.

judge at a time when he was not qualified so to act, but as the Supreme Court subsequently confirmed in two separate judgments, the saving clause means, in effect, that the section was inoperated to validate any past conviction, because this would inevitably conflict with the constitutional rights of the convicted person to trial in due course of law.[13]

Following the enactment of two separate validation statutes in the wake of both High Court and Supreme Court judgments in *Howard v Commissioners of Public Works in Ireland*[14] - the courts may yet be provided with an opportunity to re-assess the separation of powers dimension to the *Pine Valley* case. In the High Court, Costello J held that the Commissioners lacked statutory authority to build many categories of public works, including interpretative centres and the State Authorities (Development and Management) Act 1993 was enacted within a few days of that decision, conferring the requisite development powers on the Commissioners, both retrospectively and for the future. Section 2(3) contained the (by now familiar) saving clause for constitutional rights. The Supreme Court was concerned with a different point - namely whether such development required planning permission.[15] The Court having concluded that planning permission was required, s 5 of the Local Government (Planning and Development) Act 1993 now states that the planning permission shall "be deemed never to have been requires" of development by State authorities prior to the enactment of the 1993 Act.[16] The section, however, contains the following important proviso:

> Provided that if in any proceedings -
>
> (i) a court has, before the commencement of this section made a finding that permission as aforesaid was required for particular State development, or
>
> (ii) a court, after the commencement of this section, makes such a finding and the proceedings concerned were initiated before the 26th day of May, 1993,
>
> this subsection shall not have effect in relation to particular State development.

Both saving clauses were presumably drafted with an eye not to deprive the applicants in *Howard* or in any other case pending at the date of the relevant enactments of the fruits of their victory. The proper construction of these clauses would seem to require the courts to draw a distinction between past and future events if the *Sinn Féin Funds* principles are not to be taken too far. Thus, there would seem to be no constitutional impediment if the Oireachtas were to empower the Commissioners to construct the development at issue in *Howard* as and from *the date of enactment* of the State Authorities (Development and Management) Act 1993. In other words, so long as the Oireachtas recognises that any pre-1993 Act development at that site was invalid and that *Sinn Féin Funds* principles require that these actions cannot retrospectively be validated by statute, it would seem in principle to have a free hand as far as legislation for the *future is concerned.* If this analysis is correct, it would seem to follow that there

[13] *Shelly v Mahon* [1990] 1 IR 36; *Glavin v Governor of Mountjoy Prison* [1991] 2 IR 421. See also *McCarthy v Garda Commissioner* [1993] 1 IR 489.

[14] High Court, 17 February 1993; [1993] ILRM 665 (SC).

[15] See pp. 1136-1137.

[16] The other sections of the 1993 Act apply the planning permission provisions of Local Government (Planning and Development) Act 1963 to all future State development taking place after June 1994.

could have been no constitutional objection had s 6 of the Local Government (Planning and Development) Act 1982 purported to confer planning permission as and from the date of that enactment in respect of any future development at the site in question in *Pine Valley*, as opposed to any purported attempt *retrospectively* to confer such planning permission, as it was this latter construction which the Supreme Court appeared to regard as an unconstitutional attempt legislatively to reverse a decided issue. Such a - admittedly formalistic - distinction is a very fine one, but it seems necessary if the Oireachtas is to respect the *Sinn Féin* principles while at the same time preserving a very necessary freedom to legislate for future events.[17]

The Legislature may not pre-empt functions which are integral parts of the administration of justice, e.g., selection of punishment

Legislative encroachment on the judicial sphere has not only been resisted when the Oireachtas had a particular case in mind; statutory sections which tended, in a whole class of cases, to deprive the courts, in advance, of their proper function have also been held invalid. Provisions which have been invalidated for this reason have come mostly from pre-1922, i.e. British statutes in the field of criminal law, and thus the form of their invalidation is that they have been found "inconsistent" with the Constitution and hence not "carried over" from the law previously in force.

There are, first, a series of decisions which establish that the "selection of punishment" is an integral part of the administration of justice in the criminal sphere, and that the legislature is not entitled to preempt this function by conferring it on some other authority. In *Deaton v Attorney General*[18] s 186 of the Customs Consolidation Act 1876, was in issue; it purported to allow the Revenue Commissioners to "elect" which of the penalties prescribed by the section was to be imposed by the District Court on conviction of a customs offence. In the High Court Kenny J found no inconsistency with the Constitution on the ground that the Commissioners' power "is not in any sense an exercise of the judicial power or...an administration of justice." The Supreme Court thought otherwise. In delivering the Court's judgment on the appeal, Ó Dálaigh CJ said:

> "The Legislature does not prescribe the penalty to be imposed in an individual citizen's case; it states the general rule, and the application of that rule is for the courts...The individual citizen needs the safeguard of the courts in the assessment of punishment as much as on his trial for the offence. The degree of punishment which a particular citizen is to undergo for an offence is a matter vitally affecting his liberty; and it is inconceivable to my mind that a Constitution which is broadly based on the separation of powers - and in this the Constitution of Saorstát Éireann and the Constitution are at one - could have intended to place in the hands of the Executive the power to select the punishment to be undergone by citizens...The selection of punishment is an integral part of the administration of justice and, as such, cannot be committed to the hands of the Executive...
>
> The section... remains intact, but with the words "at the election of the [Revenue Commissioners]" deleted therefrom. Which of the alternative penalties prescribed

[17] Thus, if the *Pine Valley* analysis were to be taken to its logical conclusion, it would seem to mean that the Oireachtas could *never* validate the development at issue in *Howard* so that the Commissioners could never construct the interpretative centre at Mullaghmore. This would seem to be an unnecessarily wide interpretation of the *Sinn Féin Funds* principles.

[18] [1963] IR 170; (1963) 98 ILTR 99.

> by the section is proper to be imposed is, together with the issue of the guilt of the accused, a matter to be determined by the court that tries him."[19]

In *The State (Sheerin) v Kennedy*[20] the issue was on s 7 of the Prevention of Crime Act 1908; this, as adapted, purported to authorise the Minister for Justice to transfer incorrigible juvenile offenders from a Borstal institution (or St. Patrick's Institution, of which the respondent was governor) to prison, "with or without hard labour". The Court held that there was no difference in substance between St. Patrick's Institution and Mountjoy Prison (both are within the same boundary wall) - otherwise, on the principle in *Deaton's* case, the whole section would have been unconstitutional - but the power attributed to the Minister to decide whether an offender transferred under s 7 should undergo hard labour or not was invalid. The section therefore was to be understood as surviving, but with the words purporting to confer this discretion deleted. Walsh J said:

> "If there is no essential difference between a term of imprisonment and a term of detention, then I think the only portion of the section inconsistent with the provisions of the Constitution is the words "with or" following the words "term of imprisonment", the absence of which would abolish power to commute detention to a term of imprisonment with hard labour."[21]

In *The State (O.) v O'Brien*[22] the applicant for habeas corpus had been found guilty, fifteen years previously, of murder; but being only sixteen years of age at the time, he had, under s 103 of the Children Act 1908, as amended, been ordered by the trial judge to "be detained until the pleasure of the Government be made known concerning him". He now sought release on the ground of the unconstitutionality of this section; the High Court upheld his claim, and subsequently so did the Supreme Court (by a majority decision). His release was directed also on the ground that a wrong statutory formula had been used in sentencing him. On the constitutional issue, Walsh J (with whom Budd J agreed), recalling that the actual original formula of s 103 was "during His Majesty's pleasure", said that it appeared to him that:

> "the effect of the constitutional changes since 1922 [had] been to vest the exercise of all judicial power in the courts save where expressly otherwise provided for in the constitutional provisions themselves. For the reasons I have given, therefore, neither the Government nor any member of the Executive can be substituted for the words "His Majesty" in s 103 of the Act of 1908, and the power to sentence the convicted person to detention under that section and to determine the duration of the detention is vested exclusively in the courts."

[19] See also *Murphy v Wallace* [1993] 2 IR 138 (where Barron J held, following *Deaton's* case, that the provisions of s 90 of the Excise Management (Ireland) Act 1827 - which allowed the Revenue Commissioners the effective say in determining how the long the person committed on foot of a penal warrant will stay in prison - amounted to an unconstitutional usurpation of judicial power.) *Deaton's* case has provided to be an influential judgment. It was relied on by the Privy Council in both *Hinds v R.* [1977] AC 195 and *Ali v R.* [1992] 2 All ER 1 where provisions of Commonwealth legislation which allowed the prosecution a say in the selection of punishment were held to offend against entrenched separation of powers provisions in the Constitutions of Jamaica and Mauritius respectively.

[20] [1966] IR 379.

[21] This decision was applied by Gannon J in *The State (Craven) v Frawley* [1980] IR 1 in upholding the constitutionality of the power vested in the Minister for Justice by s 7 of the Prevention of Crimes Act 1908 to direct that an inmate of St. Patrick's Institution who was found to be having a bad influences on other inmates be transferred to Mountjoy Prison (on the basis that there was no difference in substance between the two institutions). However, Gannon J held that the powers given to the Minister to order that the offender undergo hard labour were unconstitutional in the light of the reasoning in *Sheerin*.

[22] [1973] IR 50.

The principle of the *Deaton* judgment was accordingly followed and reinforced. All this, however, does not necessarily prevent the Oireachtas from prescribing mandatory sentences or mandatory consequences upon conviction.

Interruption of judicial proceedings

Apart from the question of "selection of punishment", some other miscellaneous legislative interferences with the course of justice have been invalidated. Thus in *The State (C.) v Minister for Justice*[23] the Supreme Court declared inconsistent with the Constitution, as encroaching on the exclusive right of the courts to administer justice, the provisions of s 13 of the Lunatic Asylums (Ireland) Act 1875, which purported, as adapted, to empower the Minister for Justice to order "that any person who shall have been remanded by a justice...for further examination, and who during the period of such remand shall be certified...to be of unsound mind, shall be removed to the district lunatic asylum, [there to remain] until it shall be in like manner certified that such person has become of sound mind", whereupon the Minister might order the resumption of the judicial proceedings. Ó Dálaigh CJ said:

> "The preliminary investigation of indictable offences is a stage in the administration of justice...The provision of the Act of 1875 (which takes the accused away from the court's disposal, sets at nought the court's remand and adjourns the preliminary investigation *sine die*) is about as large an intrusion upon a court proceeding as one could imagine...It is for the court that has seisin of a criminal matter to determine whether or not the accused is suffering from insanity of such a character as renders him unfit to stand his trial."

On the other hand, in *Re Gallagher's Application*[24] the Supreme Court upheld the constitutionality of the Trial of Lunatics Act 1882 (which allowed the executive to determine how long a criminally insane person should be detained) on the ground that the court's role had come to an end upon conviction and sentence and that care and treatment of the criminally insane was properly a matter for the executive.

Exclusion of bail

In *In re McAllister*[25] the High Court held inconsistent with the Constitution the provisions of s 385 of the Irish Bankrupt and Insolvent Act 1857, to the effect that if a person did not fully answer a lawful question put by the court in bankruptcy proceedings, the court might commit such person to prison, "there to remain without bail" until willing to supply the information which had been refused. Kenny J said:

> "I do not think that the national parliament has power to pass legislation that the High Court shall not give bail to an accused person, and so the words "without bail" are repugnant to the Constitution and did not become part of the law of Saorstát Éireann or of the State."

It should be noted that the judge did not consider this question, or ground his decision, at any greater length than the passage cited; and that although the bankrupt, having been admitted to bail, appealed to the Supreme Court, the appeal was subsequently dismissed for want of prosecution. The question whether the Oireachtas might prescribe, for a certain class of case, that no bail should be given, has therefore not yet been considered by the Supreme Court. Kenny J's reasoning is not, however, very persuasive, since there seems no reason why the Oireachtas should not specify that certain types of remedies

[23] [1967] IR 106; (1967) 102 ILTR 177.
[24] [1991] 1 IR 31.
[25] [1973] IR 238.

(such as an injunction[26] or damages) should not be available in particular classes of cases, provided that the remedies which are available are adequate and effective to protect constitutional rights.[27] Thus, if the Oireachtas were to enact legislation restricting the availability of bail to certain classes of cases, such legislation might be found unconstitutional, but on the ground that it offended Article 40.4.1, rather than on the separation of powers principles.

Delegation of fact-finding to a body not a court

The question whether the Oireachtas might, so to speak, split an issue in such a way as to confer the finding of fact (representing an offence) on a body other than a court, while reserving the infliction of punishment for the offence to a court, was raised in *In re Haughey*[28] and was answered negatively. Here the Oireachtas had passed the Committee of Public Accounts of Dáil Éireann (Privilege and Procedure) Act 1970, of which s 3(4) provided that if any person summoned before the Dáil Committee of Public Accounts as a witness did any one of a number of things, including refusing to "answer any question to which the committee [might] legally require an answer", then the committee might "certify the offence of that person under the hand of [its] chairman to the High Court, and the High Court [might], after such inquiry as it thinks proper to make, punish or take steps for the punishment of that person in like manner as if he had been guilty of contempt of the High Court". The respondent had, in fact, refused to answer certain questions when he appeared before the committee, and the committee had duly certified that an offence under the Act had been committed by the respondent and forwarded the certificate to the High Court. Proceedings in the High Court to punish the respondent were however met by the plea that the Act was invalid under the Constitution, because, *inter alia*, it purported to confer on a body other than a court the power to administer justice. The Supreme Court agreed that on "ordinary" canons of construction, the Act would appear to confer on the Committee of Public Accounts - which was "not a court and its members are not judges" - the function of deciding that a person had committed an offence and of sending him to the High Court for punishment; and of course "under the Constitution the courts cannot be used as appendages or auxiliaries to enforce the purported convictions of other tribunals... Trial, conviction and sentence are indivisible parts of the exercise of [the power to try persons on criminal charges]." However, that was not the end of the matter; the Court found that "in this instance, the ordinary canons of construction are not applicable... The courts, in construing a statute of the Oireachtas, act on the presumption of constitutionality". This presumption the Court then applied under the form of the "double construction" test. This led the Court to understand s 3(4) as meaning, not that the committee's certificate was to be taken as a "certificate of conviction", but as "merely a step preliminary to the commencement of the trial of a criminal offence in the High Court".[29] The curious effect of this judicial reasoning was, that although the section was not struck down for repugnance to Article 34.1, the assertion of the indivisibility of the administration of criminal justice was as emphatic as if it had been.

Pre-emption of evaluation of evidence

The discretion of the courts in evaluating evidence was upheld, as being an integral part of the courts' competence to administer justice, in *Maher v Attorney General*.[30] This

[26] Cf. s 19 of the Industrial Relation Act 1990 which curbs the courts' powers to grant injunction in trade union disputes.
[27] See the comments to this effect of Henchy J in *Hanrahan v Merck, Sharpe & Dohme Ltd.* [1988] ILRM 629 and pp. 707-708.
[28] [1971] IR 217.
[29] The expression was adopted from the judgment of Henchy J in the High Court: [1971] IR at 221.
[30] [1973] IR 140.

case arose on an enactment of the Oireachtas (substantially copied, in this respect, from the corresponding British Act): s 44(2)(*a*) of the Road Traffic Act 1968, which provided that a certificate, stating that a specimen of a person's blood contained a specific concentration of alcohol, was to be "conclusive evidence that, at the time the specimen was taken or provided, the concentration of alcohol in the blood...was the specified concentration of alcohol".[31] The Supreme Court (*per* FitzGerald CJ) said:

> "[This provision] precludes the District Justice from forming any other judgment in respect of this vital ingredient of the prosecution's case: he is bound under the terms of the statutory provision to proceed and act as if this had been his own judgment on the matter. It was clearly intended by the Oireachtas that... the statutory provision was to remove this element altogether from the area of contestable facts. In effect it means that an accused person is not free to contest the determination of the concentration of alcohol set out in the certificate .
>
> The administration of justice, which in criminal matters is confined exclusively by the Constitution to the courts and judges set up under the Constitution, necessarily reserves to those courts and judges the determination of all the essential ingredients of any offence charged against an accused person. In so far as the statutory provision in question here purports to remove such determination from the judges or the courts appointed and established under the Constitution, it is an invalid infringement of the judicial power. This principle has already been clearly established by the decisions of this Court and of its predecessor in *Buckley v Attorney General, Deaton v Attorney General* and *The State (C.) v Minister for Justice.* As far as this case is concerned, the offending element of the provision is the evidential conclusiveness given to the certificate. If the word "conclusive" had not been in the paragraph, it would not be open to the objection which has now been taken. By giving the certificate this evidential quality, the Oireachtas has invalidly impinged upon the exercise of the judicial power and to that extent the statutory provision is invalid having regard to the provisions of the Constitution."[32]

Two subsequent cases have extended this principle to civil proceedings. In *The State (McEldowney) v Kelleher*[33] the Supreme Court held unconstitutional s 13(4) of the Street and House to House Collections Act 1962, because it provided, where an appeal was brought to the District Court against a refusal of a police chief superintendent to grant a collection permit, that if a police officer stated on oath that he had reasonable grounds for believing that money raised by the collection would be used for one or more of a number of listed unlawful purposes, the District Judge was to disallow the appeal; Walsh J said that "the statute created a justiciable controversy and then purported to compel the court to decide it in a particular way upon a particular statement of opinion being given upon oath". In *Cashman v Clifford*[34] the applicant sought to be heard in a

[31] Compare s 3(2) of the Offences Against the State (Amendment) Act 1972, which makes the statement of a senior police officer (as to his belief in an accused person's membership of an unlawful organisation) simply "evidence" of such membership, i.e. not conclusive evidence, but evidence capable of rebuttal, and capable of being judicially weighed: see *The People (Director of Public Prosecutions) v Ferguson*, Court of Criminal Appeal, 27 October 1975.

[32] In *Foley v Irish Land Commission* [1952] IR 118; (1952) 86 ILTR 44 Dixon J had said in the High Court that he saw nothing contrary to Article 34 in "a particular mode of proof being authorised or that mode made binding in its probative effect on the Court". This statement would now have to be viewed with some reserve.

[33] [1983] IR 289; [1985] ILRM 15.

[34] [1989] IR 121; [1990] ILRM 200.

District Court appeal which had been brought by a rival bookmaker who was appealing against a refusal to grant a licence under the Betting Act 1931. He was prevented from tendering such evidence on appeal by s 13(5)(*a*) of the 1931 Act (which provided that only the appellant, the Gardaí and the Revenue Commissioners could be heard on the appeal), but Barron J, applying the principles in *C.'s* case and *McEldowney's* case, held that the section was unconstitutional as an infringement of the judicial power. The Oireachtas, having created the justiciable issue, could not validly limit "the persons who may be heard or adduce evidence before [the courts]."

Limits to independence of the judicial function: legislation may make mandatory a particular order on establishment of particular facts

The mere fact that a statute obliges a court, once a certain state of facts has been judicially established, to make a particular order, is not an encroachment on the judicial function. This was made clear in *The State (O'Rourke) v Kelly*[35] in which the Supreme Court rejected the case made that s 62(3) of the Housing Act 1966, which provided that a District Judge, if satisfied that a demand had been duly made, "[should] issue a warrant", deprived the Judge of any real discretion and so invaded the judicial domain. The Court said:

> "It is only following the establishment of specified matters [i.e. by a judicial consideration of the relevant evidence] that the subsection operates. This is no different from many of the statutory provisions which on proof of certain matters make it mandatory on a court to make a specified order. Such legislative provisions are within the competence of the Oireachtas."

Mandatory sentences or orders, referred to in this judgment, have never been challenged on constitutional grounds. Examples are the mandatory sentence of penal servitude for life on conviction of murder (Criminal Justice Act 1964, s 2); and the consequential disqualification order which a court must make on convicting a person of certain driving offences (Road Traffic Act 1961, s 26(1)). It scarcely needs to be said that statutory consequences automatically attaching to a judicial decision but not requiring the order of a court to become effective are even less capable of being represented as inhibitions on the independence of the judicial process: examples are the twelve months' disqualification from holding a driving licence where the driver of a motor vehicle is convicted of drink driving offences (Road Traffic Act 1961, s 26); the three months' disqualification from receiving child benefit where a person is convicted of certain offences under the social welfare code (Social Welfare (Consolidation) Act 1993, s 213 (3).[36]

The Court is not entitled to disregard uncontradicted evidence

A further dimension of the role of evidence in the administration of justice is provided by *M. v M.*[37] a case which exhibits the judicial process not (as in *McEldowney's* case) constrained by statute to a particular order on the establishment of a certain state of facts, but as constrained by natural justice to accept and act on unequivocal, uncontradicted evidence rather than to act on a judge's own intuition as to its falsehood. In *M. v*

[35] [1983] IR 58.

[36] But note the comments of Flood J in *The People (Director of Public Prosecutions) v WC*, High Court, 14 July 1993: "The sentence to be imposed on the accused person in a particular case is solely a matter for the trial judge in the independent and impartial exercise of judicial discretion. To suggest otherwise would be to countenance a constitutionally impermissible invasion of judicial independence..." The logical consequence of this view would, of course, ultimately cast a shadow over the constitutionality of mandatory sentences.

[37] [1979] ILRM 160.

M. there was uncontradicted and unanimous testimony as to a husband's impotence, but the trial judge chose to regard this testimony as the product of collusion and refused the nullity decree which the evidence should have justified. The Supreme Court held that this course was not open to him. Henchy J said it was:

> "not in accordance with the proper administration of justice to cast aside the corroborated and unquestioned evidence of witnesses, still less to impute collusion or perjury to them, when they were not given any opportunity of rebutting such an accusation."

To do this, he said, would amount to condemning them unheard and so to a denial of natural justice.

Executive supersession of the court's order: return for trial on indictment

The question to what extent it may be legitimate for an authority not a court or a judge to be empowered to do that which a court has specifically refused to do has been frequently explored in the last thirty years. The first of these cases, *The State (Shanahan) v Attorney General,*[38] produced an unsatisfactory Supreme Court decision which was later reversed by the Supreme Court in *Costello v Director of Public Prosecutions.*[39] In *Shanahan* the applicant had been charged with indictable offences, but the District Judge, after hearing the depositions against her, held that they did not disclose a *prima facie* case against her, and refused to return her for trial. Thereupon the Attorney General availed of the power given him by s 62 of the Courts of Justice Act 1936, and himself ordered her return for trial to the Circuit Court on the same charges for which the District Court had refused to return her. Davitt P held that this constituted an attempt by the executive to reverse a judicial decision and, applying the principle in the *Sinn Féin Funds* case, declared the section to be unconstitutional. The Supreme Court, however, reversed the decision of the Davitt P. Walsh J said:

> "It would be within the powers of the Oireachtas to provide by legislation that persons may be put on trial on indictment preferred by the Attorney General without any preliminary investigation and sending forward for trial by the District Court. It follows that the Oireachtas can also prescribe the conditions upon which such power, when it is given to the Attorney General, is to be exercised. Section 62 imposes a condition precedent upon the exercise of the power to be sent forward for trial, etc., namely, that there shall first have been a valid preliminary investigation by the District Court and that an order refusing informations shall have been made... [It is submitted] that s 62 purports to confer upon the Attorney General the power to reverse the decision of the District Court in a matter which is within its exclusive jurisdiction. Even assuming that the refusing of informations is "exercising the judicial power of the State, and administering justice" within the meaning of the relevant articles of the Constitution... this submission would be correct only if the power given to the Attorney General was one to change or modify the order of the District Court in the matter. In my view... the submission is not well founded because the direction of the Attorney General is not an intervention in the particular controversy before the District Court which has, in the event, already been brought to an end by the refusal of informations... [but is] the initiation of a different justiciable controversy, namely, the trial upon indictment. Unlike the preliminary investigation this new justiciable controversy is one whose object is to determine the

[38] [1964] IR 239.
[39] [1984] IR 436; [1984] ILRM 413.

> guilt or innocence of the accused person. In my opinion, s 62 of the Courts of Justice Act 1936, is not inconsistent with the Constitution and it was continued in force by Article 50 of the Constitution."

This decision seems questionable. Assuming that the Oireachtas is free to extend or to reduce the boundaries of the category of "justiciable controversies", it is true that the Oireachtas could have provided that every indictable offence should be tried on the order of the Attorney General alone, and could have done away with the preliminary investigation altogether.[40] In fact the Oireachtas prescribed a sequence, beginning with the preliminary investigation and (if a *prima facie* case were disclosed) going on to the trial, which - apart from s 62 - represented throughout the exercise of the judicial power of the State. The effect of s 62 however was to enable an officer, not of judicial character, to do the very thing which the due exercise of the judicial power of the State had held unjustifiable. The distinction which the Supreme Court tried to draw between "changing or modifying" the order of the District Judge (which the Court seemed to admit would be unconstitutional) and doing something which has the effect of setting the District Justice's order at nought (which was apparently permissible) was not compelling. Neither was the Court's splitting of the prosecution into two separate "justiciable controversies"; the two courts have distinct functions, but the parties (the people and the accused) and the charge remain the same: surely only one justiciable controversy throughout.

Almost twenty years after the *Shanahan* case the same point arose again in *Costello v Director of Public Prosecutions* though in the context of the exercise of the powers of s 62 of the 1936 Act by the Director of Public Prosecutions (under s 3 of the Prosecution of Offences Act 1974). Here the Supreme Court overruled its own earlier decision and O'Higgins CJ gave three reasons for not following the *Shanahan* decision. First, the Court could not accept the reasoning of Walsh J in that case to the effect that the power conferred by s 62 was not one "to change or modify the order of the District Court in this matter"; the Chief Justice thought this was "precisely the purpose of the direction permitted by the section". The determination by the District Judge that there was not sufficient evidence to put the accused on trial for an indictable offence was a judicial one; the effect of a direction under s 62 was "to render this determination nugatory". Secondly, the Court did not accept that a direction under the section was not an intervention in the "particular controversy before the District Court which has, in any event, already been brought to an end by the refusal of informations". On this, O'Higgins CJ said:

> "The controversy which was before the District Court was one between the People and the plaintiff as to whether there was sufficient evidence to put him on trial. A power given to a non-judicial authority to come to a conclusion different from that of the District Court and to enforce that conclusion by compelling the person accused to stand trial is... an impermissible intervention in the controversy between the People and that person."

He did not accept that a direction under s 62 was merely (as Walsh J had said) "the initiation of a different justiciable controversy, namely, the trial upon indictment":

> "At all times the controversy which the law committed to judicial determination by the District Court was whether the plaintiff should stand trial upon indictment. If

[40] The Supreme Court has subsequently confirmed that there is no *constitutional* right to a preliminary examination of indictable offences: see *O'Shea v Director of Public Prosecutions* [1988] IR 655; [1989] ILRM 309 (*per* Finlay CJ) and *Glavin v Governor of Mountjoy Prison* [1991] 2 IR 421 (*per* O'Flaherty J).

> standing trial can be described as the initiation of a particular justiciable controversy "whose object is to determine the guilt or innocence of the accused person", then it was precisely whether such controversy should be initiated that the District Court was required by law to determine."

However, in *O'Shea v Director of Public Prosecutions* the Supreme Court subsequently refused to extend the *Costello* decision so as to invalidate the provisions of s 18 of the Criminal Procedure Act 1967. This provision allows the prosecution to add additional counts to an indictment *following* a return for trial, but both Lardner J in the High Court and the Supreme Court considered that the principle of *Costello's* case did not apply. While Lardner J agreed that it was the function of the District Judge to determine whether or not the accused had a case to answer in respect of the offences charged, this did not amount, in his view, to a judicial decision "that he should be put on trial for no other offence." The Supreme Court agreed with this analysis, with Finlay CJ observing that there was no question of s 18 being operated "so as to set aside or render nugatory the fundamental decision of the District Judge, which was to the effect that in regard to the facts contained in the documents and exhibits before him, the accused should be sent forward for trial."[41] While it is difficult to gainsay this analysis, the fact remains that s 18 is capable of abuse, inasmuch as the prosecution could conceivably hold back certain charges and add them to the indictment following a return for trial.[42] This point was not addressed by either Lardner J or the Supreme Court, but the judicial response would presumably have been to say (a) that the courts could intervene if such abuse were to occur and (b) the fact that s 18 is capable of abuse does not necessarily mean - having regard to the *East Donegal* principles[43] - that the section is itself unconstitutional.

Costello principles applied in other circumstances

The principles asserted in *Costello's* case have nonetheless since been applied in other cases. In *Irish Commercial Society Ltd. v Plunkett*[44] the plaintiffs brought proceedings at the behest of the Registrar of Friendly Societies against the defendant under s 14(8) of the Industrial and Provident Societies (Amendment) Act 1978, claiming damages for breach of trust and misfeasance. The plaintiff company was in liquidation, and the net point was whether the company, together with the Registrar of Friendly Societies, was entitled to bring these proceedings, in view of its insolvency. Barron J held against the company, saying that if the Registrar had a right to take such proceedings without a court order, the powers conferred by s 14(8) could be exercised in such a manner as to constitute a reversal of a court decision refusing sanction to the liquidator to institute proceedings seeking the same relief; as such a construction of the sub-section would be unconstitutional on the principle of the *Costello* decision, he concluded that s 14(8) did not empower the Registrar to take such proceedings once the plaintiff company had gone into liquidation. The Supreme Court, *per* Finlay CJ, affirmed his decision, although the judgment does not expressly deal with the constitutional point.

[41] It may be noted that in the companion case - *Walsh v President of the Circuit Court* [1989] ILRM 325 - Murphy J had declared the section unconstitutional, but was reversed on appeal. Murphy J had taken the view that "the only inference what can be drawn is that the District [Judge] has made a judicial decision to the effect that no further charge lies arising out of the material before him." It may be noted that, as we have just seen, the Supreme Court did not accept this analysis of the effect of the District Judge's decision and this was the crucial difference between the respective judgments.

[42] However, the power to add new counts is subject to express limitations. The new counts must be founded on the documents or exhibits considered by the District Judge and they must be such as may be lawfully combined in the same indictment.

[43] See pp. 459-460. See also *O'Connell v DPP*, High Court, 30 July 1993 (where Keane J held that the addition of new charges was an invalid attempt to circumvent the ruling of the District Judge discharging the accused.

[44] [1986] IR 258; [1987] ILRM 320.

However, Finlay CJ expressly endorsed a similar argument in *Director of Public Prosecutions v Olympic Amusements (Bundoran) Ltd.*[45] The District Court is empowered by statute to grant a gaming licence subject to conditions, but the holder of such a licence is also required by s 43 of the Finance Act 1975, to obtain a licence from the Revenue Commissioners in respect of any gaming machine. The Supreme Court rejected the argument that the holder of a licence from the Revenue Commissioners was entitled to disregard any conditions imposed by the District Court, Finlay CJ saying that if this contention were correct, it would render s 43 of the 1975 Act unconstitutional, as it would mean that "an act of the Revenue Commissioners could have the effect of nullifying conditions imposed by the Court". A similar question may yet arise in the context of s 50 of the Extradition Act 1965, which provides that a suspect may be released from custody should either the High Court or the Minister for Justice form the view that the offences to which the warrant relates are political offences. If the courts formed the view that the offences were not political offences, would it be then open to the Minister to form a different view? If the section does in fact envisage a situation in which the Minister could so override the courts, then the constitutionality of this feature of s 50 of the 1965 Act must very doubtful.

Direction for trial by the Special Criminal Court

In *In re Mac Curtain*[46] and *The State (Bollard) v Governor of Portlaoise Prison*[47] the powers of the Attorney General under Part V of the Offences Against the State Act 1939, in regard to directing certain trials to be held by the Special Criminal Court were attacked as being unconstitutional exercises of the judicial power by a person not a judge; but without success. An attack on the exercise of this power by the Director of Public Prosecutions also failed in *O'Reilly v Director of Public Prosecutions.*[48] A slightly different point arose in *Cox v Ireland*[49] where the plaintiff had challenged s 34 of the Offences Against the State Act 1939 on the ground that it was the actions of the Director of Public Prosecutions which effectively determined whether a person would be exposed to a greater penalty.[50] While this argument was rejected by Barr J in the High Court, it appears to have weighed heavily with the Supreme Court in its conclusion that s 34 was unconstitutional as an overbroad attack on the plaintiff's right to earn a livelihood:

> "The ultimate factor triggering the operation of s 34 in any particular case is the venue of the trial which results in the conviction for a scheduled offence. That venue is primarily selected by the fact that the offence is scheduled, and can only be avoided by a decision of the Attorney General or the Director of Public Prosecutions...."[51]

INDEPENDENCE AS AGAINST EXECUTIVE CLAIMS

The cases set out in the foregoing paragraphs have concerned the integrity of the judicial function in the face of statutory regulation. This integrity has however also been assert-

45 [1986] ILRM 123.
46 [1941] IR 83.
47 High Court, 4 December 1972. See further at pp. 647-648.
48 [1984] ILRM 224.
49 [1992] 2 IR 503.
50 Section 34 provided that public servants who were convicted of a scheduled offence before the Special Criminal Court were disqualified from office and lost their pension. If, therefore, the Director of Public Prosecutions were to have directed that a particular accused should not face trial in the Special Criminal Court for scheduled offences this would have had the effect of avoiding the operation of s 34.
51 Walsh J had anticipated this result in *The People (Director of Public Prosecutions) v Quilligan (No.1)* [1986] IR 495. The Privy Council took a similar approach in *Ali v R.* [1992] 2 All ER 1.

ed as against attempts by the Executive, in one shape or form, to reduce the area of judicial enquiry and discretion by reliance on supposed rules of common law. An early but good example is the case of *Irish Agricultural Wholesale Society v St. Enda's Co-Operative Society*[52] in which the plaintiffs had sought leave to substitute postal service, on the ground that at the time (early 1923) the country was so disturbed that summons servers were unable or unwilling to carry out their functions, and that the Minister for Home Affairs - disagreeing with the plaintiffs' view of the state of the country - had refused to supply an armed escort for the summons server in the defendants' area. In the High Court their application was refused by Dodd J who said that the Court could not "override the statement of the Minister for Home Affairs... to the effect that he did not consider that the present state of the country was such as to make it necessary to provide military protection for the service of writs." But the former Court of Appeal reversed this order. Molony CJ said:

> "The function of a judge is to decide a case according to the statutes and rules, which he is bound to observe, and no statement of a Minister can or ought to affect him in the performance of his judicial duty."

And Ronan LJ said:

> "No executive Minister has any right to limit the jurisdiction of the court unless express statutory power is given to him for that purpose: and there is no pretence that any statutory power was given to any Minister to interfere with the operation of the rule in question. That being so, I am of opinion that any point as to interfering with the discretion of the judge below is out of the case."[53]

On the other hand, the courts will probably give much greater weight to executive claims in areas within the exclusive remit of the Government. Indeed, in one (admittedly exceptional) case - *Zarine v Owners of S.S "Ramava"*[54] - the Supreme Court stated that it was bound by the replies given by the Minister for Foreign Affairs on the question of whether the annexation of one particular country by another was to be recognised in this State. But this case is probably best regarded as exceptional and the courts' deference to executive claims in this area is probably justified on separation of powers grounds, as well as the lack of manageable judicial standards[55] whereby such an issue could be objectively resolved.

Former executive privilege of the non-disclosure of documents is now much reduced

A commoner form taken by executive attempts to restrict the range of judicial cognisance is the claim of privilege in respect of documents or other official transactions. The old common rule was that the Crown could not be compelled to produce documents or to give information for the purpose of any proceedings, civil or criminal, if a Minister or permanent department head (or police officer) declared that such a disclosure would be contrary to public policy or detrimental to the public interest or service. In Ireland this

[52] [1924] 2 IR 41; (1924) 58 ILTR 14.

[53] This judgment, which appears to imply that statutory authority might validly enable a Minister to limit a court's jurisdiction. of course belongs to the infancy of the State, and to an era long before the instinct to test rules, statutory or otherwise, for conformity with the Constitution had become habitual with Bench and Bar. Article 64 of the 1922 Constitution is no less emphatic, in entrusting the judicial power of the State to the courts, than the present Article 34.1, but it was not mentioned in the case at all, so that its possible bearing on the dictum of Ronan LJ was not considered.

[54] [1942] IR 148.

[55] Indeed, for this very reason, the question of whether another State should be recognised by the Government is probably non-justiciable: see pp. 347-348.

rule was at first regarded as taken over as part of the law in force in 1922, despite complications arising from the status of the Crown.

Public policy, rather than any "regal" prerogative, was identified as the root of the rule in the first important case on the subject, *Leen v President of the Executive Council (No.1)*.[56] Here Meredith J said:

> "I can find nothing...in the authorities on this privilege in respect of discovery to suggest that the rule of law which has always been in force, and which has to be administered as heretofore under the Constitution of the Irish Free State, is dependent upon the magic of any particular nomenclature. On the contrary, it appears to me to be broad-based upon the public interest... The principle has roots in the general conception of State interests and the functions of the courts of justice, which make it independent of the particular type of constitution under which the body of law which recognises that principle is administered."

However, in a series of decisions over the following forty years or so, the courts frequently held that they could not go behind ministerial certificates withholding the production of documents.[57] In 1970-71, however, the matter was at last thoroughly explored in the High Court and then in the Supreme Court in *Murphy v Dublin Corporation*.[58] In this case the plaintiff sought a declaration that a compulsory purchase order made by the defendant corporation, and confirmed by the Minister for Local Government (who was also joined as a defendant) was invalid. The Minister objected to the production of a report made by one of his inspectors on the ground that its production would be "contrary to public policy and the public interest and service". Kenny J followed the recently decided English case of *Conway v Rimmer*[59] and said:

> "It has been assumed in many judgments that a Minister's objection to the production of a document is conclusive, but there is no decision of the Supreme Court on this matter, and assumptions by judges or counsel do not make the law. Uncontested claims to withhold production of very relevant documents have been made in cases... [where] the contention that the production of such documents would be contrary to the public interest or policy was grotesque and is evidence not of any care for the public interest but of a remarkable elasticity of conscience... A government Minister has no absolute right to withhold production of any documents, and... in every case the issue whether the documents should be made available to the other parties to the litigation should be decided by the court which has jurisdiction to require production of the documents to it for inspection."

He went on to set up two general rules by which he thought courts should be guided in exercising this discretion:

> "The first rule is that there are certain classes of documents which ought not to be produced under any circumstances: in these cases the court will not inspect them. Minutes of government meetings, documents relating to military and diplomatic matters, memoranda dealing with proposed legislation and letters between departments relating to policy formation are examples of the type of document the non-

[56] [1926] IR 456.

[57] *Kenny v Minister for Defence* (1942) Ir Jur Rep 81 (where Maguire P held that Minister entitled to claim privilege in respect of confidential documents in the context of an action arising from a contract to build Army huts); *O'Donovan v Attorney General* [1961] IR 114; (1962) 96 ILTR 121 (where a re-drawing of Dáil constituencies was under constitutional attack, Budd J upheld the claim by the Minister for Local Government to be entitled to withhold "certain advices and schemes" prepared by his advisers and officials as to the distribution of constituencies) and *O'Leary v Minister for Industry and Commerce* [1966] IR 676.

[58] [1972] IR 215.

[59] [1968] AC 910.

> disclosure of which is necessary for the proper functioning of the State... The second rule is that the claim to withhold production may be based either on the Minister's view that it is against the public interest to disclose a specified document which the Minister has considered or because it belongs to a class of document which, as a matter of policy, he thinks ought to be withheld... When a Minister... certifies that it would be against the public interest to disclose the contents of a specified document which he has considered, in my opinion the court should accept his view unless (a) it is shown not to have been formed in good faith or (b) it is one which no reasonable Minister could take or (c) it is based on a misunderstanding of the issues in the case in which its production is sought."

In this case Kenny J thought there was no evidence on which he could conclude that the Minister's view was wrong or not formed in good faith or based on a misunderstanding of the issues; accordingly, he refused the plaintiff's application for production, but added:

> "The [Minister] will, I am sure, bear in mind that the interests of justice require that documents in his possession should be made available and that a refusal to produce them will frequently result in incorrect decisions. So the claim to withhold should not be lightly made."

The plaintiffs appealed to the Supreme Court. Walsh J, with whom the four other judges agreed, hauled out into the broader constitutional waters in order to approach his decision:

> "Under the Constitution the administration of justice is committed solely to the judiciary in the exercise of their powers in the courts set up under the Constitution. Power to compel the attendance of witnesses and the production of evidence is an inherent part of the judicial power of government of the State and is the ultimate safeguard of justice in the State. The proper exercise of the functions of the three powers of government... is in the public interest. There may be occasions when the different aspects of the public interest "pull in contrary directions" - to use the words of Lord Morris of Borth-y-Gest in *Conway v Rimmer*. If the conflict arises during the exercise of the judicial power then, in my view, it is the judicial power which will decide which public interest shall prevail."

Walsh J went on to dissociate himself from the view of Kenny J that certain particularly sensitive documents ought not to be disclosed at all:

> "It is clear that, when the vital interests of the State (such as the security of the State) may be adversely affected by disclosure or production of a document, greater harm may be caused by ordering rather than by refusing disclosure or production of the document. In such a case the courts would refuse the order but would do so on their own decision. The evidence that the courts might choose to act upon to arrive at that decision would be determined by the courts, having regard to the circumstances of the case... Having regard to the nature of the powers of the courts in these matters, it seems clear to me that there can be no documents which may be withheld from production simply because they belong to a particular class of documents."

In the present instance, Walsh J considered that Kenny J was wrong in accepting the Minister's statement without examination:

> "Whatever the Minister's grounds may be, he has not disclosed them and his certificate or order simply states a conclusion. In my view, a case has not been made for the non-production of the document concerned and in that event the learned trial judge ought to have directed production of the document, at least for his own inspection, when he could then decide the matter."

The Court reversed Kenny J on the ground also that the Minister, in exercising a power to determine appeals under the Housing Act 1966, was merely a *"persona designata"*, *i.e.* conveniently given this task by the Oireachtas, which might quite easily have bestowed it on any other personage, and that the Minister was, in this activity, not exercising the executive power of the State in any sense which would entitle him to raise a claim of privilege for the purpose of withholding documents.

The principle in Murphy's case in application

The principle established by the Supreme Court in *Murphy's* case was automatically applied in the following year in *Geraghty v Minister for Local Government.*[60] Here the defendant Minister had certified that the disclosure of documents sought by the plaintiff (in an action to have a planning decision under the Local Government (Planning and Development) Act 1963, declared void) would be contrary to public policy and detrimental to the public interest and service: but it was left to the High Court to examine the documents one by one and to decide whether they should be produced to the plaintiff. Kenny J ordered the production of all but three of the documents; the latter he held to be privileged from disclosure, on the grounds (in the case of two of them) that they were in the category of legal advice to the defendant, and (in the case of the third) that it was "a document obviously intended to be confidentially written by one civil servant to another", and he thought that "the principle that confidential communications between public servants should be protected, particularly when the Minister has given a certificate, prevails over the interest of the plaintiff in seeing" them. On appeal, the Supreme Court referred to *Murphy's* case, declaring that "it was the duty and the right of the learned High Court judge and of this Court on appeal to examine each of the documents in respect of which privilege was claimed" (per Griffin J). The Court concluded that Kenny J had been right in excluding the three documents mentioned, but, in addition, the Court excluded a fourth document on the ground that there was "no difference in principle" between it and the documents constituting legal advice.[61]

Communications involving public servants are generally not privileged

In a quite a number of cases the application for discovery has been resisted on the ground that it would tend to hamper the smooth running of the public service. This is an argument which, as we have just seen in *Geraghty's* case, has met with little judicial sympathy.[62] Thus, in *Incorporated Law Society of Ireland v Minister for Justice*[63] the plaintiffs claimed that the failure of the defendant to concur in certain rules proposed by the Society in the exercise of their statutory functions was *ultra vires.* They sought discovery of the internal memoranda and correspondence relating to the Minister's decision

[60] [1975] IR 300. See also *Folens v Minister for Education*, High Court, 1 May 1981 and *Hunt v Roscommon V.E.C.* [1981] ILRM 21.

[61] Of course, a Minister or the Government or, for that matter, any public servant is entitled, like any other litigant, to rely, where appropriate, on the doctrine of legal professional privilege: see, e.g., *Silver Hill Duckling Ltd. v Minister for Agriculture* [1987] IR 289; *Bula Ltd. v Tara Ltd. (No. 5)*, High Court, 25 July 1991 and *Breathnach v Ireland* [1992] ILRM 755.

[62] Note, however, the decision of O'Hanlon J in *Cully v Northern Bank Finance Corporation Ltd.* [1984] ILRM 683, where he held that the effect of s 31 of the Central Bank Act 1942 (which requires Central Bank officials to swear an oath of secrecy in relation to all information which has come to their knowledge in the course of their employment) was to "give rise to a claim of privilege on grounds of public policy from disclosure of any information of the type referred to in the oath of secrecy." This gave rise to a "very unusual form of statutory privilege" which the officials were entitled to rely on "unless and until the validity of s 31 is successfully challenged on constitutional grounds."

[63] [1987] ILRM 42. See also, to like effect, the judgment of Costello J in *Fitzpatrick v Independent Newspapers PLC* [1988] IR 132.

and the advices given to him in relation thereto; this application was resisted on the grounds that production of the material in question would tend to hinder "the free communication necessary for the proper running of the public service". Murphy J accepted that discovery of these documents might have that effect, and he also bore in mind that the documents included correspondence passing between individual members of the Government. Nevertheless, he concluded that an order of discovery should be made:

> "as there [was] nothing in the documentation for which this particular claim of privilege [was] made which has any special potential for damage in the proper administration of the public service... To deny the plaintiffs access to the documentation for which this privilege is claimed would be to impose some measure of injustice on them and, in my view, that injustice is almost necessarily greater than the potential damage to the public service, which I regard as minimal in the present case."[64]

A similar view was expressed by Blayney J in *P.M.P.S. Ltd. v P.M.P.A. Insurance plc*[65] where he refused to accept that "responsible civil servants would be any less likely to speak freely with the Registrar [of Friendly Societies] if this memorandum were disclosed."[66] On the other hand, there may well be exceptional cases where such a claim of privilege will be upheld. In *O'Mahoney v Ireland*[67] Barrington J allowed a claim of privilege concerning a Defence Forces inquiry into an incident[68] involving the Irish contingent serving with the United Nations Forces in the Lebanon. The privilege was properly claimed having regard to the "security implications" of the Defence Forces inquiry. Similar considerations applied to a UN inquiry into the same incident. The Irish Government had received that report in confidence and could thus properly claim privilege in order to preserve the confidentiality of highly sensitive diplomatic communications.

The Ambiorix and Cabinet Confidentiality cases

The principles in *Murphy* were authoritatively re-stated by the Supreme Court in *Ambiorix Ltd. v Minister for the Environment (No.1)*,[69] in which the plaintiffs sought discovery of Government memoranda and other Cabinet documents in the course of their challenge to the decision of the Minister for the Environment to designate certain

[64] Murphy J was to express similar views in two cases decided by him in 1991: *Gormley v Ireland* [1993] 2 IR 75 and *Bula Ltd. v Tara Ltd. (No. 5)*, High Court, 25 July 1991. In *Gormley* the plaintiff had sought discovery of documentation pertaining to his internment over thirty years previously. While Murphy J accepted that much of the material involved was confidential and sensitive, it did not raise national security considerations and, hence, should be made available on discovery. In *Bula (No.5)* Murphy J said that, as a result of the decision in *Geraghty's* case "all administrators must now be conscious of the fact that no absolute privilege attaches to documents containing advice to Ministers or submissions by them and any caution or ill effects induced by that consideration must have occurred already."

[65] [1990] 1 IR 284. See also *Duff v Minister for Agriculture* [1992] 1 IR 198 (discovery of briefing notes prepared by senior civil servants to assist Minister for Agriculture and Food in preparing for his participation in the deliberations of the Council of Ministers) and *Silver Hill Duckling Ltd. v Minister for Agriculture* [1987] IR 289 (no question of public interest privilege with regard to extracts from minutes of meetings of EC Veterinary Committee); *Dublin Meatpackers Ltd. v Ireland, The Irish Times*, 13 April 1989 (no privilege for diplomatic exchanges with UK officials regarding operation of beef slaughtering scheme).

[66] The memorandum in question concerned the supervision of the defendant group. It had been prepared by the Registrar of Friendly Societies and had been sent to the Department of Industry and Commerce. Similar views had previously been expressed by Lardner J to response to an argument that discovery would "breach fundamental concepts of [civil service] confidentiality": see *Ahern v Minister for Industry and Commerce*, High Court, 4 March 1988.

[67] *The Irish Times*, 28 June 1989.

[68] The plaintiff was a soldier who had been injured in the incident and who was suing the State for negligence.

[69] [1992] 1 IR 277; [1992] ILRM 209.

building sites for the purposes of the Urban Renewal Act 1986.[70] The defendants contended that the production of these documents "could prejudice the confidentiality and the collective responsibility of the Government" and, in effect, sought to claim privilege on "class" grounds. The Supreme Court insisted that such a claim of privilege was incompatible with "the fundamental constitutional origin" of the decision in the *Murphy* case. Not only did the Court decline to overrule *Murphy* - as it had been asked to do by counsel for the Minister - but it re-affirmed the principles underlying that decision. The Court stressed that such a claim of privilege was inconsistent with *Murphy* and Finlay CJ also drew attention to the probable consequences of such a submission:

> "if [such] a privilege...were accepted as a general standard or proposition by the Court, then one of the consequences of so doing would be that the right of any individual citizen to challenge a decision made by the Government or by a Minister of Government, on the basis that it was made without material which supported it or having regard to the consideration of material which was wholly irrelevant to it, could never even be mounted."

McCarthy J put it even more pithily: any departure from the reasoning in *Murphy* "would be to lessen or impair judicial sovereignty in the administration of justice." He observed that the Constitution "guarantees fair procedures in the administration of justice; discovery of documents is part of those procedures."

Ambiorix appeared to have settled the issues with regard to public interest privilege and discovery of documents, but fresh uncertainty has been created by the subsequent decision of the Supreme Court in the *Cabinet Confidentiality* case: *Attorney General v Hamilton (No.1)*.[71] In this case, the Chairman of a Tribunal of Inquiry into the Beef Industry sought to question a former Government Minister about whether a particular decision had been taken by the Government at a certain Cabinet meeting.[72] The Attorney General objected to this line of questioning and when overruled by the Chairman, sought judicial review of this decision. A majority of the Supreme Court held that the Chairman was seeking to inquire about the discussions which had taken place at a particular Government meeting, but that this line of inquiry was absolutely precluded by the collective responsibility provisions of Article 28.4.2.[73] The majority of the Court were at pains to stress that the *Murphy* and *Ambiorix* lines of authority were concerned with the exercise of judicial power in civil proceedings and, hence, were not necessarily applicable to the principles governing the admission of evidence before such a Tribunal.[74] Finlay CJ did, however, concede that:

> "whilst some of the principles laid down in these cases with regard to the exercise of the judicial power would appear to embrace discussions between members of the Government, at meetings of the Government, that the fact that no specific claim of special confidentiality concerning those arose in either case may mean that that issue still remains to be decided in a case in which it occurs in relation to the exercise of the judicial power."

There is here a clear hint that the result might have been different if the Tribunal had been exercising judicial powers instead of being simply an instrumentality of the

[70] The plaintiffs claimed that the Minister had improperly designated the sites in questions, thus conferring an unfair fiscal advantage on the owners of the sites. When the case came on for hearing, Lynch J found that this allegation had not been made out: see *Ambiorix Ltd. v Minister for the Environment (No.2)* [1992] 2 IR 37.
[71] [1993] 2 IR 250; [1993] ILRM 81.
[72] The facts are more fully set out at pp. 250-251. See generally, Hogan, "*The Cabinet Confidentiality Case of 1992*" (1993) Irish Political Studies 131 and Farrell, "*'Cagey and Secretive': Collective Responsibility, Executive Confidentiality and the Public Interest*" in Hill and Marsh Eds., *Modern Irish Democracy: Essays in Honour of Basil Chubb* (Dublin 1993).
[73] See pp. 251-257.

Oireachtas. But why should this fact make any difference? It would be curious if such Government discussions were held not be admissible before a Tribunal of Inquiry while later held to be admissible in any subsequent civil litigation which traversed the same ground. Besides, if the proper functioning of Government were to be jeopardised by the threatened disclosure of such discussions before a Tribunal of Inquiry, it seems hardly consistent to leave open the possibility of the very same self threat of disclosure before a different forum, *viz.*, the courts.

Further anomalies resulting from the interaction of the Ambiorix and Cabinet Confidentiality cases

These are not the only anomalies which result from the inter-action of these two decisions. First, we already have a situation whereby all Government papers and documents - including, as *Ambiorix* shows, documents of a highly confidential character - can be discovered in the course of civil litigation.[75] One could readily envisage a situation whereby a Government decision is arrived at following a consideration of an extensive Memorandum for Government (which might well recite at length the views of individual Ministers) with only perfunctory discussion at the Government meeting itself. Under the *Ambiorix* principles, the documents may discovered, whereas the discussions at Government itself are inadmissible as evidence.[76] But if the declared object of the absolute confidentiality rule is to protect the workings of Government, then this objective is subverted in this (not untypical) example, since the sensitive information contained in the preparatory documentation will - in principle, at least - be available for discovery in civil proceedings.[77] Of course, it may be that, henceforth, Ministers will avoid committing their deepest thoughts to paper in advance of a Government meeting and instead express them orally at the meeting itself.[78] But such a change of practice would ill-serve the workings of Government - since other Ministers would not come sufficiently prepared for such meetings - and might well do an injustice to individual litigants, since the production on discovery of such a bland and innocuous Memorandum for Government (which did not set out the Minister's private thoughts on any given issue) might be apt to mislead.

Of course, the foregoing discussion pre-supposes that the *Ambiorix* case has, in fact, survived the *Cabinet Confidentiality* decision, and there is one subsequent High Court decision which implicitly suggests that it has not. In *Lang v Government of Ireland*[79] the applicant sought to challenge a decision of the Government to dismiss him pursuant to s 5 of the Civil Service Regulation Act 1956. It was contended that the Government had breached the rules of natural justice in not disclosing to him in advance the memorandum for Government which had been prepared for the relevant Government meeting. O'Hanlon J found against the applicant on the facts: he was fully aware of the case against him and, furthermore, found that the memorandum did not contain any new

[74] In fact, Finlay CJ later concluded that the Tribunal was "essentially an exercise of the legislative power."

[75] As McCarthy J said in dissent: "[*Ambiorix*] was concerned with documents, but I cannot identify any principle upon which one could differentiate between documents and the spoken word on an issue of disclosure or non-disclosure."

[76] It is true that this very question of admissibility in judicial proceedings (as opposed to before a Tribunal of Inquiry) was left open by the majority, and this reservation is considered above at pp. 254-255.

[77] This pre-supposes that the *Ambiorix* principle has actually survived the decision in the *Cabinet Confidentiality case*. It may be noted that there is at least one High Court decision which implicitly doubts whether the *Ambiorix* rule has survived: see *Lang v Government of Ireland*, High Court, 7 July 1993.

[78] This possible development was anticipated in *Ambiorix*, when in affidavit sworn by a senior official from the Department of an Taoiseach, it was averred (see [1992] 1 IR 277, 281) that the production of Government memoranda would not be in the public interest as "officials might tend where possible to make their comments or suggestions or recommendations orally rather in a written format, and such a tendency would not be in the interest of the public or in the interest of the efficiency of the public service."

material of which the applicant had been unaware. The memorandum had been available on discovery, but O'Hanlon J observed that, having regard to the subsequent *Cabinet Confidentiality* case, "it would now appear to be protected, and perhaps also precluded, from disclosure." But irrespective of whether O'Hanlon J is correct in this view or not, it only requires a minor variation of the facts of *Lang* to illustrate a further anomaly which flows from the *Cabinet Confidentiality* case. Suppose that a dismissed civil servant could show that in either a memorandum for Government or in the subsequent discussion of the case at a Government meeting, the relevant Government Minister had taken a wholly irrelevant consideration into account in pressing the case for dismissal. In such circumstances, fair procedures surely requires that the dismissed civil servant have access to such material, as otherwise he would not be in a position to make his case for judicial review. Indeed, as we have already seen, this very possibility was one of the reasons why in *Ambiorix* both Finlay CJ and McCarthy J rejected the State's claim for class privilege in respect of memoranda for Government. What is now left of this rationale in the light of the subsequent *Cabinet Confidentiality* case? All in all, the *Cabinet Confidentiality* decision would not seem to be compatible with *Ambiorix* and judicial consistency would seem to demand that the Supreme Court should have overruled *Ambiorix*. The fact that this step was not taken - which would have also meant overruling a long and consistent line of earlier authority dating back to the *Murphy* case in 1971 - of itself suggests a fundamental weakness in the majority's conclusions in the *Cabinet Confidentiality* case itself.

Privilege of police communications: a claim must be based on specific grounds

The Irish courts have, until lately,[80] held to the principle, taken from English practice, that communications passing between police officers are privileged from disclosure, and the possible bearing of Article 34.1 on this principle - inasmuch as its application might frustrate an accused person in making his case - has not yet been fully explored, save that it is now clear that the courts will not automatically defer to such a claim of privilege. In *Director of Public Prosecutions (Hanley) v Holly*[81] Keane J said the views expressed by the Supreme Court in *Murphy's* and *Geraghty's* cases meant that the old practice no longer represented the law: he thought privilege could be accorded by a court only where specific grounds, rather than the general "public interest", were advanced in support of the claim. Keane J confirmed this view in an elaborate judgment in *Breatnach v Ireland*.[82] In his view, the courts were required to weigh "the public interest in the proper administration of justice against the public interest "in the prevention and prosecution of crime" and that it was only where the former outweighed the latter that "an inspection should be undertaken or disclosure should be ordered." [83]

[79] High Court, 7 July 1993.

[80] In *The People (Attorney General) v Simpson* [1959] IR 105; (1959) 93 ILTR 33 the High Court held that communications between police officers were privileged and inadmissible both in civil and criminal proceedings". This principle was maintained subsequently in *The State (Quinn) v Ryan* [1965] IR 70; (1966) 100 ILTR 105 despite the submission of counsel that its application might obstruct the court's investigation of a case of alleged unlawful detention. (This point was decided in the course of argument in the High Court and does not feature in the judgments.)

[81] [1984] ILRM 149. This view had also been anticipated by the Court of Criminal Appeal in *The People (Director of Public Prosecutions) v Ferguson*, Court of Criminal Appeal, 27 October 1975, where O'Higgins CJ said that in the light of *Murphy* case, the Special Criminal Court had been correct in independently adjudicating on a claim of privilege asserted by the police, rather than simply deferring to this assertion of privilege.

[82] [1992] ILRM 755.

[83] He thought, however, that there might well be documents "the very nature of which is such that inspection is not necessary to determine on which side the scales come down. Among these he instanced:

> "information supplied in confidence to the Gardaí. [This] should not in general be disclosed, or at least not in cases like the present where the innocence of an accused person is not in issue....Again, there may be material the disclosure of which would be of assistance to criminals by revealing methods of detec-

Privilege extends to confidential security information

A similar privilege appears to attach to confidential information (i.e. that likely to have come from an informer) in at least the context of sensitive security matters. A good example of where specific grounds for a claim of privilege were successfully established is *The People (Director of Public Prosecutions) v Eccles*[84] in which the defendants had been charged with capital murder and other serious offences. They had been arrested under s 30 of the Offences Against the State Act 1939, and an extension order was made permitting their detention for a further twenty-four hours. The Chief Superintendent who had made the order claimed that he had received information from a confidential source which led him to prolong the detention period; and claimed privilege when asked to disclose the identity of his informant. In the Court of Criminal Appeal, Hederman J ruled that the Special Criminal Court had correctly allowed the claim of privilege in this case:

> "The Chief Superintendent was entitled to claim privilege in respect of both the source, and the nature of the source, of the sensitive, confidential information he received in respect of the applicant. Normally, a member of the Garda Síochána cannot claim privilege in respect of information received from a fellow member of the force simply by virtue of its being such a communication. The circumstances of this case were, however, exceptional. [The Chief Superintendent asserted privilege] on the ground that it "would be dangerous to identify whether the source was either civilian or police". This he was clearly entitled to do."

A similar point was made by Costello J in upholding a claim of privilege in *Director of Consumer Affairs v Sugar Distributors Ltd.*,[85] where the defendant sought to discover documents which would enable them to identify the complainants who had asked the Director of Consumer Affairs to carry out an investigation into alleged breaches of the Restrictive Practices Acts. Costello J said that in order to protect the "effective functioning by the Director of his statutory powers" the courts should decline to order discovery where this would reveal the identity of a complainant who had made a complaint in private. This claim of immunity was not, however, an absolute one, since the courts should examine the documentation and uphold a claim of privilege, save "where the court concludes that the documents might tend to show that the defendant had not committed the wrongful acts alleged against him."

> tion or combating crime...There may be cases involving the security of the State, where even the disclosure of the existence of the document should not be allowed. None of these factors - and there may, of course, well be other which have not occurred to me - which would remove the necessity of even inspecting the documents is present in this case."

Note that in *Gormley v Ireland* [1993] 2 IR 75, Murphy J excluded "highly confidential" Garda correspondence from the scope of his order for discovery.

84 (1985) 3 Frewen 36. The judgment of Barrington J in *The State (Comerford) v Governor of Mountjoy Prison* [1981] ILRM 86 states that the governor claimed privilege in respect of such information about a conspiracy to kidnap a warder and to break out of the prison, and implies that the Court had conceded this privilege. But not every such claim of privilege is, in fact, upheld. Thus, in *The People (Director of Public Prosecutions) v Meagher*, *The Irish Times*, 30 April 1980, the Special Criminal Court dismissed charges of membership of an illegal organisation when, in the words of Hamilton J, an Assistant Garda Commissioner who had given evidence (pursuant to s 3(2) of the Offences Against the State (Amendment) Act 1972) "was not prepared to assist the Court by disclosing confidential information on which he based his belief." Cf. the provisions of s 10 of the Interception of Postal Packets and Telecommunications Messages (Regulation) Act 1993 which provides that the courts shall not make an order for discovery of documents which would tend to show whether there had been an official authorisation in permitting the interception of an individual's mail or telephone calls.

85 [1991] 1 IR 225.

Justice frustrated by public policy

An area which has not yet been examined from a constitutional perspective is that of justice - in the sense of regular observation of rights arising from legal relationships - being frustrated by legislation or by public policy. An Irish example is *N.V de Faam v Dorset Manufacturing Co.*,[86] in which the plaintiffs (a company in Holland) sought payment of the price of goods sold to the defendants, but the defendants were prevented from making the full payment through the operation of an Emergency Powers Order aimed at controlling the export of foreign exchange. Dixon J felt that "on general principles it would be improper and contrary to public policy for the Court to give judgment for the plaintiffs on their claim as now framed" - even with an eye to allowing them to sit on their judgment until such time as the Order lapsed or was revoked - and refused also to make a declaration of their rights.

"ACCESS TO THE COURTS" AS AN ASPECT OF THEIR INDEPENDENCE

"Access to the courts": general principles

Another and most important context in which the integrity of the judicial function has been asserted is that of the "right of access to the courts". This notion has evolved over the last thirty years out of a relatively small (if increasing) number of cases, of which the first was a case just mentioned in a different connection, *The State (Quinn) v Ryan.*[87] Here the applicant for *habeas corpus* had been arrested on foot of a warrant issued in England and endorsed in Dublin in compliance with the provisions of s 29 of the Petty Sessions (Ireland) Act 1851. A patent flaw in the warrant made it clear that the prisoner would be released, so a second warrant - this time flawless - was prepared by the English police, sent to Dublin, and endorsed once more by the competent officer of the Garda Síochána. Members of the Garda Síochána sat in court equipped with the new warrant as the prisoner's release was ordered, then immediately afterwards arrested him again in the vicinity of the court and, literally while his legal advisers' backs were turned, put him in a car and drove him over the border into Northern Ireland, where they handed him over to English police officers. What the Garda Síochána had done was within the letter of the procedure set out by the 1851 Act which had on a former occasion been held by the (old) Supreme Court to be not inconsistent with the Constitution,[88] but this time the (new) Supreme Court refused to sanction the way in which the extradition machinery had been operated, because it effectively deprived the prisoner of the possibility of resorting to the courts to challenge the legality of what was being done. Ó Dálaigh CJ said:

> "From [the] survey of the evidence it becomes clear that a plan was laid by the police, Irish and British, to remove the prosecutor after his arrest on the new warrant from the area of jurisdiction of our courts with such despatch that he would have no opportunity whatever of questioning the validity of the warrant...In plain language the purpose of the police plan was to eliminate the courts and to defeat the rule of law as a factor in government... No one can with impunity set [the citizen's rights] at nought or circumvent them [by depriving him of access to the courts] and...the courts' powers in this regard are as ample as the defence of the Constitution requires."

[86] [1949] IR 203; (1949) 83 ILTR 136.
[87] [1965] IR 70.
[88] *The State (Duggan) v Tapley* [1952] IR 62; (1951) 85 ILTR 22. See above at p. 270.

Since the procedure of the 1851 Act did not explicitly rule out police action of the kind in question, its provisions were declared invalid as being inconsistent with the Constitution.[89]

In *Macauley v Minister for Posts and Telegraphs*[90] the plaintiff was trying to sue the Minister by claiming a declaration that, in breach of two agreements, the Minister had failed to provide him with a proper, reasonably efficient and effective telephone service. Section 2 of the Ministers and Secretaries Act 1924, provides that the *fiat* of the Attorney General is necessary before a Minister can be sued in that capacity; and in this case the Attorney General (very exceptionally[91]) would not grant his *fiat*. The plaintiff then asked to have this section declared invalid as being a clog on his right to litigate. Kenny J rejected one of his arguments (that the Attorney General's operation of the *fiat* amounted to an administration of justice; none of the ordinary attributes of the judicial function, he found, were present in the Attorney General's function); but he upheld the main contention that the *fiat* rule impeded free recourse to the courts, and identified a close analogy between the case and that of *The State (Quinn) v Ryan*:

> "That there is a right to have recourse to the High Court to defend and indicate a legal right and that it is one of the personal rights of the citizen included in the general guarantee in Article 40.3, seems to me to be a necessary inference from Article 34.3.1 of the Constitution which provides: "The courts of first instance shall include a High Court invested with full original jurisdiction in and power to determine all matters and questions whether of law or fact: civil or criminal." If the High Court has this full original jurisdiction..., it must follow that the citizens have a right to have recourse to that Court... The existence of this right was recognised in our courts more than eighty years ago by the Vice-Chancellor in *Massy v Rogers*[92] when he said: "Every subject of the realm is entitled to free access to those tribunals (the courts), to ascertain, establish and enforce the rights which the law gives him, whether arising upon contract, or upon testamentary disposition. In my opinion, any attempt to exclude this right is unlawful and inoperative"...The refusal of the fiat has the result that a plaintiff who wishes to sue a Minister of State in the High Court cannot validly commence his action: the refusal of it is, therefore, a denial of the right to have recourse to the High Court."

He accordingly held s 2(1) of the Ministers and Secretaries Act 1924, invalid so far as the fiat requirement was concerned. The Attorney General did not appeal to the Supreme Court, and so this *fiat* has quietly vanished from the law.

Modern re-statements of the principle

A series of important decisions has lately given the Supreme Court an opportunity to re-state the general principles concerning the right of access to the courts. In *The State*

[89] New statutory arrangements were promptly made for extradition to the United Kingdom, with provisions ensuring that the prisoner had a proper opportunity to test the lawfulness of his arrest and extradition: see Extradition Act 1965, s 48 and below pp. 878-879.

[90] [1966] IR 345.

[91] In order to obtain the *fiat*, the plaintiff had to submit a statement of facts, a copy of his draft summons or civil bill, and a certificate of counsel that the claim was proper to be allowed. A former legal assistant to the Attorney General wrote in 1954 that the fiat had been refused in only one or two cases in thirty years: O'Donoghue, "*The Citizen v The State*", Public Administration in Ireland III, p. 15. See also "*Fiat of the Attorney General*", 68 ILTSJ 75.

[92] (1883) 11 LR Ir 409.

(McCormack) v Curran[93] the applicant had been charged in Northern Ireland with certain offences under the [British] Criminal Jurisdiction Act 1975. As the offences with which he had been charged had apparently been committed in the Republic, he might have been tried in the Republic. When the Director of Public Prosecutions and the police refused to prosecute him here, he commenced mandamus proceedings seeking to compel the Director to do so. Rejecting the argument that the Director's refusal infringed the applicant's right of access to the courts, Finlay CJ said:

> "The right of access to the courts, stated in its broadest fashion, is a right to initiate litigation in the courts. There is not, in my view, any right necessary for the protection of any constitutional right to force another person to sue you [at] civil law or to prosecute you in the criminal law in the courts."[94]

This question was examined by the Supreme Court in *Murphy v Greene*[95] in the context of a statutory requirement[96] that a putative plaintiff obtain leave of the High Court before civil proceedings against a medical officer could be instituted. Finlay CJ acknowledged that these provisions constituted a *prima facie* "curtailment of the constitutional right of every individual to have access to the courts to the extent that it requires a pre-condition of leave of the court for the bringing by him of a claim for damages for an asserted wrong." Applying by analogy the reasoning of its earlier decision in *In re R. Ltd.*,[97] the Court held that any statutory curtailment of the right of access to the courts must be strictly construed. While the Supreme Court were not called to pronounce on the constitutionality of s 260 of the 1945 Act, it seems implicit in the various judgments that it would have survived constitutional challenge. Thus, Finlay CJ surmised that the object of the section was to prevent "a person who is or has been thought to be mentally ill from mounting a frivolous or vexatious action, or one based on imagined complaints", thereby implying - it may be thought - that the section constituted a reasonable regulation of the right of access to the courts. In addition, O'Flaherty J was at pains to distinguish this case from that of *Macauley's* case. Unlike the latter decision, the present involved only a "form of partial curtailment" of the right of access to the courts and he considered it significant that unlike the situation which obtained in *Macauley*, here it was "the court that decided whether the action should proceed or not." This reasoning, presumably, could be readily applied to other instances where the preliminary leave of the court was required by statute or rules of court. Thus, s 82(3B) of the Local Government (Planning and Development) Act 1963 (as inserted by s 19(3) of the Local Government (Planning and Development) Act 1992) now provides that the preliminary leave of the High Court must be obtained before any challenge to the validity of a planning decision. Any such application must be commenced within two months of the challenged decision; it must be on notice to the relevant parties and the High Court may only

[93] [1987] ILRM 225.

[94] In *Donohoe v Browne* [1986] IR 90 Gannon J held that the plaintiff could not complain of a denial of access to the High Court where his action for personal injuries had been barred as *res judicata* (because of an earlier binding determination of the Circuit Court that he was solely to blame for the traffic accident which gave rise to the proceedings).

[95] [1990] 2 IR 566; [1991] ILRM 404. See also *O'Reilly v Moroney and Mid-Western Health Board* [1992] 2 IR 145 (HC); Supreme Court, 16 November 1993.

[96] The section in question was s 260(1) of the Mental Treatment Act 1945 which provides that: "No civil proceedings shall be instituted in respect of an act purporting to have been done in pursuance of this Act save by leave of the High Court and such leave shall not be granted unless the High Court is satisfied that there are substantial grounds for contending that the person against whom the proceedings are to be brought acted in bad faith or without reasonable care."

[97] [1989] IR 126; [1989] ILRM 757. In this case the Supreme Court held (in the words of Finlay CJ in *Greene*) that any statutory provision constituting "an express legislative exception to the general provision obtained in Article 34 of the Constitution for the administration of justice in public must be strictly construed in the sense that it must not be availed of except where it was essential to do so."

grant leave where there are "substantial grounds" for contending that the decision is invalid. While these provisions constitute a very substantial restriction on the right of access to the courts, their constitutionality would presumably be upheld - applying *Murphy v Greene* reasoning - on the ground that the Oireachtas was entitled to take the view that such restrictions were desirable in the public interest, so that important planning projects could not be halted pending the outcome of lengthy litigation which was unlikely ever to succeed.

Source of right of access to the courts: Article 34 or Article 40.3?

It will be observed that in *Macauley's* case Kenny J identified a right of access to the High Court[98] (which, as he pointed out, had been asserted in the pre-written-Constitution era of *Massy v Rogers*), but then labelled this right, not as a direct product of Article 34 but rather as a latent content of Article 40.3. (In *Buckley v Attorney General*, by contrast, the Supreme Court had spoken of the plaintiffs' "constitutional right" to bring the proceedings, but had mentioned this in the immediate context of Articles 34-37; Article 40 was not mentioned.) A somewhat similar approach was adopted by the Supreme Court six years later in *O'Brien v Keogh*,[99] in which a provision of the 1957 Statute of Limitations was held invalid under the Constitution for purporting to place certain infant plaintiffs under a disability. The provision was declared invalid not, or at any rate not expressly, because it closed the doors of the courts unfairly to certain plaintiffs, but on the somewhat broader ground that it did not respect the promise of Article 40.3.2, that the State was to protect citizens as best it might from unjust attack and, in the case of injustice done, to vindicate their rights.[100] And in *Murphy v Greene*[101] McCarthy J described the right of access to the courts "as one of the unenumerated rights derived from Article 40.3.1 and its interaction with Article 34.3.1", while both Finlay CJ and Griffin J seemed to hint that the right derived from the obligation of the courts to administer justice under Article 34.[102]

Right of access to the courts means that litigants must be given an adequate opportunity of establishing their respective cases

The right of access to the courts involves affording a plaintiff an adequate opportunity of substantiating his case. In *Bula Ltd. v Tara Mines Ltd. (No.1)* [103] the plaintiffs wished to inspect the defendants' land in the course of an action for fraud described by Murphy J as raising claims which were "extremely serious and extraordinarily improbable". Nevertheless, he said the constitutional right of access to the courts meant that the plaintiffs must be given an adequate opportunity to prove their case:

[98] Although Kenny J spoke of the right of access to the High Court, this has been broadened to embrace other courts as well: see, e.g., *Vella v Morelli* [1968] IR 11 (where the effect of Article 34.4.3 was described by Walsh J as guaranteeing to litigants "the right of resort to this Court" (i.e. the Supreme Court); *The State (McEldowney) v Kelleher* [1983] IR 289 (where Costello J said that there was also "the right to have recourse in appropriate cases to the District Court to defend or vindicate a legal right").

[99] [1972] IR 144.

[100] This approach has also been taken in a number of subsequent decisions dealing with (what was claimed to be) unreasonably short or unfair limitation periods: see, e.g., *Brady v Donegal C.C.* [1989] ILRM 282; *Hegarty v O'Loughran* [1990] 1 IR 148; [1990] ILRM 403 and *Tuohy v Courtney*, High Court, September 1992.

[101] [1990] 2 IR 566.

[102] Note also the comments of McCarthy J in *Chambers v An Bord Pleanála* [1992] 1 IR 134: "Access to the courts to contest a justiciable issue is constitutionally guaranteed. It may be regulated as...in *Murphy v Greene...*"

[103] [1987] IR 85; [1988] ILRM 149.

"if... a citizen is free to institute proceedings, he must be at least equally free to invoke the procedures of the Court to present his case properly. The right of a party to seek and obtain an order for inspection (or, indeed, an order for discovery, which may be equally burdensome) is in no way dependent on the strength of the plaintiff's case... It would be impossible [in the circumstances of the present case] to vindicate the plaintiff's right to litigate if he were not afforded an adequate opportunity of inspection to attempt to substantiate the claim which he has made."

Access to the courts: stamp duty and costs

In recent years, the courts have been required to examine the operation in practice of various rules which tend to hinder the right of access to the courts. In *Re Michael Orr (Kilternan) Ltd.*[104] O'Hanlon J observed that certain stamp duty provisions "imposed extraordinarily heavy burdens" on persons engaged in litigation before the High and Supreme Courts and who wished "to avail of the administration of justice" before those courts. This is, perhaps, a hint that excessive rates of stamp duty would be inconsistent with the general right of access to the courts. Barrington J had already expressed similar views in *Re J. C.*,[105] where a destitute applicant sought an order dispensing with court fees to allow him to start a constitutional action. While he thought that the High Court might have jurisdiction to dispense with such payments, he felt that this was not required in the circumstances of the case before him, as the plaintiff had not awaited the outcome of his appeal against the refusal of a civil legal aid certificate.

The bearing of costs on the right of access to the courts was explored by Finlay P in *Henehan v Allied Irish Banks Ltd.*,[106] in which the defendants had been ordered to pay the plaintiff's costs, but the Taxing Master had disallowed his expenses in travelling from Tipperary to Dublin to prepare his case, on the authority of a decision of the old Irish Court of Appeal. Finlay P declared that he was not bound by this decision and proceeded to re-examine the principles on which it was based. This was necessary:

"due to the fact that the jurisdiction of the court to award costs and the consequences of an order providing for costs [seemed to him] to be part of the ancillary machinery associated with the access of citizens to the courts and, as such, should in [his] view be construed in the light of the constitutional origin of the right of access and the obligation of the courts to make such a constitutional right real and effective."

He felt that in view of these principles and the "patent illogicality and injustice" of refusing to allow the travelling expenses of a lay litigant, he was justified in awarding him those costs.

Security for costs rules

The potential impact on security for costs rules of the constitutional right of access to the courts has only barely been considered by the courts. In *Salih v General Accident*[107]

[104] [1986] IR 273.
[105] High Court, 25 July 1985. See also *O'Shaughnessy v Attorney General*, High Court, 12 February 1971. Note that in *MacGairbhith v Attorney General* [1991] 2 IR 412 O'Hanlon J appeared receptive to an argument that excessive court fees might amount to an unconstitutional clog on a litigants' constitutional right of access to the courts, but found that, on the facts, he was not required to rule on this question. O'Hanlon J further ruled that the right of access to the courts did not require the State to provide access to a law library for the benefit of impecunious lay litigants.
[106] High Court, 19 October 1984.
[107] [1987] IR 628.

the plaintiff had challenged the validity of O 29 of the Rules of the Superior Courts, 1986 on the ground that it infringed his right of access to the courts. O'Hanlon J evidently thought little of the point:

> "any right of access to the courts to prosecute civil claims cannot be an unfettered right and I consider that the right to apply for security for costs in the very limited category of cases where this is recognised by our law is intended to do justice between the parties, is reasonable, and is not in breach of constitutional rights..."

On the other hand, in *Fallon v An Bord Pleanála*[108] - a case concerned with the amount of security of costs - McCarthy J appeared more receptive to this argument and said that any practice with regard to the fixing of security for costs must take the constitutional right of access to the courts into account. It remains to be seen whether this isolated dictum will presage a more sophisticated analysis of the question of the compatibility of security for costs rules with access to the courts.

PROTECTION OF COURTS' INDEPENDENCE AGAINST UNLAWFUL CONDUCT

Threats to the integrity of the courts in the form of contempt

Where the administration of justice by the courts is under threat, not by way of a formal interference having some ostensible legal authority, however unfounded (as in most of the cases mentioned in the foregoing paragraphs), but by way of prejudicial or disobedient behaviour, the courts uphold their position and protect their own function through the law of contempt.[109] The principal classification of contempt is into "criminal" and "civil" contempt; these categories were described by Ó Dálaigh CJ in *Keegan v de Búrca*[110] as follows:

> "The distinction between civil and criminal contempt is not new law. Criminal contempt consists in behaviour calculated to prejudice the due course of justice, such as contempt *in facie curiae,* words written or spoken or acts calculated to prejudice the due course of justice or disobedience to a writ of *habeas corpus* by the person to whom it is directed - to give but some examples of this class of contempt. Civil contempt usually arises where there is a disobedience to an order of the court by a party to the proceedings and in which the court has generally no interest to interfere unless moved by the party for whose benefit the order was made. Criminal contempt is a common-law misdemeanour and, as such, is punishable by both imprisonment and fine at discretion, that is to say, without statutory limit, its object is punitive: see the judgment of this Court in *In re Haughey*. Civil contempt, on the other hand, is not punitive in its object but coercive in its purpose of compelling the party committed to comply with the order of the court, and the period of committal would be until such time as the order is complied with or until it is waived by the party for whose benefit the order was made. In the case of civil contempt only the court can order release but the period of committal cannot be commuted or remitted as a sentence for a term definite in a criminal matter can be commuted or remitted pursuant to Article 13.6 of the Constitution... The present case is one in which the

[108] [1992] 2 IR 380; [1991] ILRM 799.

[109] In recent times there has been some judicial unhappiness about the term "contempt of court" since it tends to give a false impression about the function of the law on contempt. As Costello J explained in *Council of the Bar of Ireland v Sunday Business Post Ltd.*, High Court, 30 March 1993, contempt of court is not "an offence against the dignity of the court. It is an interference with the administration of justice. And in punishing for contempt what the court is doing is punishing for such interference."

[110] [1973] IR 223.

> defendant stood accused of criminal contempt *in facie curiae* and could be dealt with summarily[111] by the court."

Subsequently, in *The State (Director of Public Prosecutions) v Walsh*,[112] O'Higgins CJ distinguished criminal contempt into two categories: that consisting in conduct tending to obstruct or prejudice the course of justice, whether committed inside or outside the court; and that consisting in conduct or expressions which tend to destroy public confidence in the court:

> "It is necessary to differentiate the contempt with which this appeal is concerned from other forms of contempt. Such other forms... may be contempt *in facie curiae* which consist of conduct which is obstructive or prejudicial to the course of justice, and which is committed during court proceedings; or contempts committed outside court (known as constructive contempts) where pending proceedings may be interfered with or prejudiced by what is said or done."

He did not define this "obstructive" type of contempt any more narrowly; and it may be noted that, almost fifty years previously, Johnston J had said in *In re M.M. and H.M.*:[113]

> "The tricks and turns by which justice may be obstructed or perverted are so numerous and varied, and the ingenuity of mankind is so constant, that it is impossible to define in a comprehensive way, or rather to delimit, the circumstances under which a contempt of court by the obstruction of justice may be committed, and no judge or court has ever presumed to lay down any such limitation."

Some examples of criminal contempts

In *In re M.M. and H.M.* a person had offered to influence a jury in a civil action, but as he had never in fact carried his offer into effect, an application to commit him for contempt was refused. It is also a contempt to take action which may have the effect of nullifying a court order. This emerges from *Council of the Bar of Ireland v Sunday Business Post Ltd.*[114] where a rival newspaper published details of a confidential letter written during the course of a disciplinary investigation, thus setting at nought an injunction which the plaintiffs had obtained against the defendant newspaper. Costello J said that as the earlier injunction was designed to protect the confidentiality of that letter, its publication had "constituted a most serious interference with the administration of justice." Punishable contempts were established also in *O'Brennan v Tully*[115] (refusal to answer relevant questions in cross-examination): and *In re Earle*[116] (obstruction of justice by refusal to obey habeas corpus order to produce an infant).

Prejudicial press comment on pending cases

In *Attorney General v Cooke*[117] the High Court declined to see a contempt in the publication of newspaper comment on certain activities which were the subject of pending pro-

[111] Notwithstanding the decision of the Supreme Court in *The State (Director of Public Prosecutions) v Walsh* [1981] IR 412 (which holds that an alleged contemptor may have an entitlement to jury trial on an issue of fact: see pp. 667-668), this does not affect the right of High Court to try and punish summarily a contemptor for contempt in the face of the court: see *Re Kelly and Deighan* [1984] ILRM 424.

[112] [1981] IR 412.

[113] [1933] IR 299; (1932) 67 ILTR 24, 191.

[114] High Court, 30 March 1993. See also *Re Kennedy and McCann* [1976] IR 382 (publication of details of family law case in defiance of High Court order that proceedings be held *in camera*).

[115] (1935) 69 ILTR 115.

[116] [1938] IR 485.

[117] (1924) 58 ILTR 157.

ceedings, on the ground that the comment was not intended or calculated to interfere with the course of justice; though in a somewhat comparable[198] case, *Lovell and Christmas v O'Shaughnessy: In re Crawford*[119] the High Court took a different view, Hanna J saying it was "clearly a contempt of court to write and publish during the pendency and hearing of an action comments on any of the parties calculated to affect the free course of justice."[120] In a more modern era, however, the courts have made it clear that such media comment will rarely amount to a contempt of court, unless the publication was plainly intended to have that effect or where it is likely to prejudice a jury trial. Thus, in *Weeland v RTÉ*[121] while Carroll J agreed that television coverage of a Circuit Court judgment (which was then under appeal to the High Court) was "unbalanced", she would not accept that a High Court judge would be influenced by a television programme "which was transmitted months before, rather than by the evidence given in court." Denham J took a similar view in *Wong v Minister for Justice*[122] of a newspaper article which had falsely attempted to link an applicant in judicial review proceedings with the criminal underworld: she thought that as matters set out in the article "were so clearly at variance with the facts before the High Court [that] there is no real possibility, let alone real risk of the court being influenced." A similar attitude is evident in the judgment of O'Hanlon J in *Desmond v Glackin (No.1)*,[123] a case where the public comments on radio of the Minister for Industry and Commerce concerning a matter of public controversy were said to have prejudiced judicial review proceedings which were then pending. O'Hanlon J was unimpressed with this argument, saying that he did not consider that the interview or the publicity which surrounded it "made it difficult for a judge of the High Court....to decide in an objective and unbiased manner the legal issues which arise for consideration in those proceedings."

Holding up litigants to public obliquoy

Desmond v Glackin (No.1) itself raised another aspect of the *sub judice* rule, since as O'Hanlon J put it, "it is generally considered improper to publish material which prejudges the issue for determination by the court in pending proceedings or which pillories one of the parties involved in the case." Here it was said that the Minister's comments - which tended to pour scorn on the attitude taken by the applicant in the judicial review proceedings - constituted a breach of this aspect of the *sub judice* rule. O'Hanlon J accepted the correctness of the principles underlying this submission, but felt that the present came within an exception to the rule itself. The applicant had made serious allegations against the Minister in the course of *ex parte* which had been given extensive publicity and in those circumstances, the Minister was entitled to a right of reply. While the Minister's comments had been "injudicious and indiscreet", O'Hanlon J felt that, having regard to the special circumstances of the case and the Minister's constitutional right to freedom of expression, there had been no breach of this aspect of the *sub judice*

[118] Both cases were concerned with comments published during the course of a trial which might have worked prejudicially to the accused.

[119] (1935) 69 ILTR 115.

[120] See also *McCann v An Taoiseach*, High Court, 22 June 1992 where Carney J held that a radio broadcast which had suggested that the High Court was about to take (quite extraneous) factors into account when deciding a controversial case involving the Government was a "serious contempt" of court, but that no further action was necessary since it was clear that the comments had been unintentional and a full apology had been forthcoming.

[121] [1987] IR 662. It may, perhaps, be otherwise if a litigant publicly discusses his pending action in public with a view to influencing public opinion. "It is wholly objectionable if a litigant [publicly] discusses the merits of his case and the evidence going to be produced. By doing this public opinion is turned against the defendants in advance of the trial", *per* Carroll J in *Byrne v Crowley*, High Court, 25 March 1992.

[122] High Court, 30 July 1992.

[123] [1992] ILRM 490.

rule. On the other hand, where an ordinary litigant had been gratuitously linked with a foreign underworld organisation in a newspaper account, Denham J held that the effect of this was to hold the litigant up to public obloquy in a pre-trial account which was "prejudicial to the administration of justice": see *Wong v Minister for Justice*.[124]

Refusal to give evidence

The privilege to refuse to answer relevant questions is accorded to only three categories of witnesses, viz. solicitors, religious pastors and members of the Oireachtas;[125] it is not available to others, even where they belong to professions in which the disclosure of certain kinds of information is regarded as unethical; this is clear from *In re Kevin O'Kelly*.[126] Here a journalist had refused to give evidence of an interview which he had had with an accused person, on the ground that to do so would be a breach of journalistic ethics. He was found to be in contempt of court "in the face of the court" and was given a prison sentence, against which he appealed to the Court of Criminal Appeal. This Court substituted a fine for the prison sentence, seeing grounds for leniency, but refused to regard the journalist as occupying a position of privilege - entitling him to decline to answer questions - comparable with that of a solicitor or priest.[127] Walsh J said:

> "The Court is aware that in general journalists claim the right to refuse to reveal confidences or disclose sources of confidential information. The Constitution, in Article 40.6, states that the State shall endeavour to ensure that the organs of public opinion, such as the radio and the press, while preserving their right of liberty of expression, including criticism of government policy, shall not be used to undermine public order or morality or the authority of the State. Subject to these restrictions, a journalist has the right to publish news and that right carries with it, of course, as a corollary the right to gather news. No official or governmental approval or consent is required for the gathering of news or the publishing of news. It is also understandable that newsmen may require informants to gather news. It is also obvious that not every news-gathering relationship from the journalist's point of view requires confidentiality. But even where it does, journalists or reporters are not any more constitutionally or legally immune than other citizens from disclosing information received in confidence. The fact that a communication was made under terms of express confidence or implied confidence does not create a privilege against disclosure. So far as the administration of justice is concerned the public has a right to every man's evidence except for those persons protected by a constitutional or other established and recognised privilege... It would be impossible for the judicial power... to permit any other body or power to decide for it whether or not certain evidence would be disclosed or produced."[128]

"Scandalising the court"

The other type of criminal contempt ("scandalising the courts"[129]) consists of words or conduct tending to destroy public confidence in the court against which it is directed. In

[124] High Court, 30 July 1992.

[125] This privilege only extends to members of the Oireachtas in respect of attempts - whether directly or indirectly - to make them amenable in respect of utterances in either House of the Oireachtas, contrary to Article 15: see *Attorney General v Hamilton (No.2)* [1993] ILRM 821.

[126] (1974) 108 ILTR 97.

[127] See *Cook v Carroll* [1945] IR 515; (1945) 79 ILTR 116.

[128] But Article 15 gives members of the Oireachtas a right to refuse to answer such questions where this would, directly or indirectly, render them amenable for utterances made in either House of the Oireachtas: see *Attorney General v Hamilton (No.2)* [1993] ILRM 821 and see pp. 141-145.

[129] See generally, Walker, "*Scandalising in the Eighties*" (1985) 101 LQR 359 and Law Reform Commission Consultation Paper, *Contempt of Court* (July, 1991) at Ch. 3.

The State (Director of Public Prosecutions) v Walsh, cited above, it was described as:

> "a form of contempt which falls within the archaic description "scandalising the court". This form of contempt is committed where what is said or done is of such a nature as to be calculated to endanger public confidence in the court which is attacked and, thereby, to obstruct and interfere with the administration of justice. It is not committed by mere criticism of judges as judges, or by the expression of disagreement - even emphatic disagreement - with what has been decided by a court... Such contempt occurs where wild and baseless allegations of corruption or malpractice are made against a court so as to hold the judges up "to the odium of the people as actors playing a sinister part in a caricature of justice": *per* Gavan Duffy P in *Attorney General v Connolly*."

In *Walsh's* case the defendants had said the Special Criminal Court had "no judicial independence" and had "so abused the rules of evidence as to make the Court akin to a sentencing tribunal"; this the Supreme Court took to fall indisputably within the notion of criminal contempt and to amount to a serious offence. Earlier instances of this kind of criminal contempt can be found in *Attorney General v O'Kelly*[130] (publication of insulting comments on a High Court judge's conduct of a trial); *Attorney General v Connolly*[131] (published insult to Special Criminal Court by way of imputing predictability of conviction); *In re Kennedy and McCann*[132] (insulting comments on the High Court); *In re Hibernia National Review*[133] (insulting comments on the Special Criminal Court). However, in *Attorney General v O'Ryan and Boyd*,[134] where an editor had published a letter containing insults to a Circuit Court judge, although the author of the letter was punished for contempt, the editor was said by Gavan Duffy J to have "rendered a public service to the administration of justice" (because the letter was so wild as by its absurdity to destroy the credibility of the allegations which it contained); this seems a precedent on which it would be unsafe for an editor to rely. Likewise, in *Desmond v Glackin (No.1)*[135] (where it had been alleged that the Minister for Industry and Commerce had scandalised the High Court by publicly expressing amazement at the terms of an *ex parte* injunction directed against him) O'Hanlon J agreed that the while the Minister was "unfortunate in his choice of words", this did not amount to a contempt.

"Contempt of the courts"

Even though the notion of contempt has not been exhaustively defined, striking extensions of it (as formerly understood) are possible. Thus, the conduct of the Irish and British police in the *Quinn* case[136] - their careful plan to whisk him, once the new arrest had been made, out of the Irish jurisdiction - was characterised as "contempt of the courts". Ó Dálaigh CJ said:

> "It was not the intention of the Constitution in guaranteeing the fundamental rights of the citizen that these rights should be set at nought or circumvented... As a necessary corollary it follows that no one can with impunity set these rights at nought or circumvent them, and that the courts' powers in this regard are as ample as the defence of the Constitution requires. Anyone who sets himself such a course is guilty of contempt of the courts and is punishable accordingly."

[130] [1928] IR 308; (1927) 62 ILTR 78.
[131] [1947] IR 213; (1946) 81 ILTR 92.
[132] [1976] IR 382.
[133] [1976] IR 388.
[134] [1946] IR 70; (1944) 79 ILTR 158.
[135] [1992] ILRM 490.
[136] See p. 876.

(In the event the police officers "explained" their conduct and no punishment was imposed, so that it is not clear what such punishment might have been or through what form of proceeding it might have been imposed. No similar case has since arisen.)

"Civil" contempt

Examples of civil contempt, as described by Ó Dálaigh CJ in *Keegan v de Búrca*,[137] are *Davern v Butler*,[138] a case of disobedience to an order of the Master of the High Court to lodge accounts; *Little v Cooper*[139] and *O'Conghaile v Wallace*,[140] both cases of disobedience to injunctions to restrain defendants from interfering with fishery rights, in which the plaintiffs moved for orders of attachment; *The State (Commins) v McRann*,[141] also a case of disobeying an injunction, in which Finlay P said the jurisdiction of courts of record to punish summarily for contempt had survived the enactment of the Constitution and was not inconsistent with Article 38; and *McEnroe v Leonard*,[142] a case of disobedience to a court order for the production of title deeds belonging to the plaintiff. On the other hand, while Carroll J accepted in *Society of Protection of Unborn Children (Ire.) Ltd. v Grogan*[143] that deliberate disobedience to a court order restraining the distribution of abortion information would amount to a contempt, she refused to accept that this could be established simply by reference to newspaper accounts.

It may be noted that in dealing with cases of civil contempt the High Court will exercise a prudent discretion with an eye to avoiding a course which may be futile and thus counter-productive from the point of view of upholding the Court's own authority; thus in *Ross Co. v Swan*[144] which arose out of the occupation of the plaintiffs' premises and defiance of an injunction to vacate them, O'Hanlon J said:

> "It is undesirable that the High Court should commit to prison for an indefinite period a person who has no intention of obeying the order of the Court, and who may even welcome the publicity he gains by the making of such an order as a means of furthering his own cause. If no other reasonable course is open, then the order may have to be made to vindicate the authority of the Court. If some other reasonable course is open, then it is preferable that it should be adopted."

In this case, he found that the penal provisions of the Prohibition of Forcible Entry and Occupation Act 1971, "which was passed specifically to deal with the kind of unlawful conduct here committed", offered an alternative to committal, and refused the application to commit.

Inferior courts may punish only for contempt *in facie curiae,* and in respect of other contempts must rely on the High Court for protection: see *Attorney General v O'Ryan and Boyd*[145] and *Attorney General v Connolly*.[146]

"Abuse of process" of the courts

It may be noted that the courts have an inherent jurisdiction to prevent an abuse of their process, which compliments the jurisdiction given by O 19 r 28 of the Rules of the

137 [1973] IR 223.
138 [1927] IR 182; (1927) 61 ILTR 100.
139 [1937] IR 510; (1935) 69 ILTR 108.
140 [1938] IR 526.
141 [1977] IR 78.
142 High Court, 9 December 1975.
143 [1989] IR 753; [1989] ILRM 350.
144 [1981] ILRM 416.
145 [1946] IR 70; (1945) 79 ILTR 158.
146 [1947] IR 213; (1947) 81 ILTR 92.

Superior Courts 1986, to strike out pleadings which disclose "no reasonable cause of action or answer" or for being "frivolous or vexatious".[147] The principles on which the courts will exercise this inherent jurisdiction were summarised by Costello J in *DK v AK*[148] as follows:

> "Basically the jurisdiction exists to ensure that an abuse of the Court's process does not take place. If it is established by satisfactory evidence that the proceedings are frivolous or vexatious or if it is clear that the plaintiff's claim must fail then the Court may stay the action. But it will only exercise this jurisdiction sparingly and in clear cases."[149]

This jurisdiction is illuminated by the decision of Costello J in the High Court in *Barry v Buckley*[150] and that of Blayney J for the Supreme Court in *O'Neill v Ryan.*[151] In the former case the plaintiff had offered to purchase the defendant's land; although (as the Court found) no agreement had been concluded, he issued proceedings pleading a contract and seeking specific performance, and registered a *lis pendens* against the land. Costello J said that "as considerable injustice could result if the matter was not disposed of now, it seemed that to allow the case to proceed to trial would be to permit an abuse of the Court's processes"; he ordered the proceedings to be struck out and the *lis pendens* vacated. In the *O'Neill* case the plaintiff had pleaded that the action of certain defendants had resulted in damage to a company of which he was a former shareholder, with the consequent alleged diminution in the value of that shareholding. Blayney J held that the present action did not lie, chiefly because it did not seek to recover damages on behalf of the company as such (and, hence, did not come within any of the exceptions to the rule in *Foss v Harbottle*), but also because, since the plaintiff was no longer a shareholder in the company, he had no standing to seek declaratory relief with regard to the activities which he alleged had injured the company. Against this background, since Blayney J was satisfied that the plaintiff's action "must fail", he ordered that it be struck out.

Statutory provisions on interference with justice

Special statutory provisions to deal with contempt-like behaviour are found in the Offences Against the State Acts. Section 7 of the Offences Against the State Act 1939, makes it a felony punishable by seven years' penal servitude or two years imprisonment:

> "to prevent or obstruct, by force of arms or other violent means or by any form of intimidation the carrying on of the government of the State or any branch (whether legislative, judicial, or executive) of the government of the State or the exercise or

[147] While these jurisdictions are complimentary, there is one important practice difference between them. In cases arising under O 19 r 28, the failure to disclose a reasonable cause of action must appear from the pleadings alone (see the judgment of O'Higgins CJ in *McCabe v Harding Investments Ltd.* [1984] ILRM 105 and that of Blayney J in *O'Neill v Ryan* [1993] ILRM 557.) On the other hand, in inherent jurisdiction cases, the court will look beyond the pleadings to the supporting evidence and if this establishes that the action is bound to fail, it will strike out the action on this ground.

[148] [1993] ILRM 710.

[149] Citing *Barry v Buckley* [1981] IR 306 and *Sun Fat Chan v Osseous Ltd.* [1992] 1 IR 425. In the latter case, McCarthy J said that he "inclined to the view" that if the "statement of claim admits of an amendment which might, so to speak, save it and the action founded on it, then the action should not be dismissed." Likewise, the action should not be struck out where the plaintiff's claim raises difficult questions of law deserving "full and unhurried consideration": per Keane J in *Irish Permanent Building Society v Caldwell (No.1)* [1979] ILRM 273.

[150] [1981] IR 306. See also *Dorene Ltd v Suedes Ltd.* [1981] IR 312 and *Stud Managers Ltd. v Marshall* [1985] IR 83.

[151] [1993] ILRM 557.

> performance by any member of the legislature, the judiciary, or the executive [of his functions]."

and makes it a misdemeanour punishable by two years' imprisonment to "aid or abet or conspire" towards the doing of any such thing. The section has been judicially considered only in connection with a violent demonstration not directed at the administration of justice: *The People (Director of Public Prosecutions) v Kehoe*.[152]

Section 4 of the Offences Against the State (Amendment) Act 1972, makes unlawful and punishable by fines and/or imprisonment:

> "any public statement made orally, in writing or otherwise, or any meeting, procession of demonstration in public, that constitutes an interference with the course of justice;"

and a statement, meeting, procession or demonstration is deemed to constitute such interference:

> "if it is intended, or is of such a character as to be likely, directly or indirectly to influence any court, person or authority concerned with the institution, conduct or defence of any civil or criminal proceedings (including a party or witness) as to whether or how the proceedings should be instituted, conducted, continued or defended, or as to what should be their outcome."

Sub-section 3 of the section provides that:

> Nothing in this section shall affect the law as to contempt of court.

This presumably means that the section is to be understood as supplementing and not replacing the common law of contempt.

INDEPENDENCE OF INFERIOR COURTS

For a judicial statement of the independence of the inferior courts, within the limits of their jurisdiction, from interference or direction by the superior courts, see *Clune v Director of Public Prosecutions*.[153]

[152] [1983] IR 136; [1983] ILRM 237.
[153] [1981] ILRM 17: see below at pp. 499-500.

Article 34.1 (Continued)

COURTS, JUDGES AND PUBLICITY

Courts established by law

The courts which now administer justice were established by law as recently as 1961, by the Courts (Establishment and Constitution) Act and the Courts (Supplemental Provisions) Act of that year. It was admitted by the (then) Supreme Court in *The State (Killian) v Minister for Justice*[1] that the words of Article 34 contemplated the *future* fresh establishment of courts to replace those exercising jurisdiction at the date of the Constitution's enactment: but the transitory provisions of Article 58 enabled the pre-existing courts to continue to *function* - and to have their occasional vacancies filled - for a further twenty-four years, although those who drafted and approved the Constitution scarcely intended a transition of that length.

The courts which were "established" in 1961 - and which, as Walsh J pointed out in *The State (Browne) v Feran,*[2] once established cannot be disestablished - had, however, for all practical purposes the same names,[3] personnel, jurisdictions, mutual relations, and practice as the courts which they replaced; and these in turn, despite the important effect of the Constitution itself on the general position of the courts in the Irish polity, were in fact the courts established in 1924 by the Courts of Justice Act of that year. In most substantial respects, the 1924 structure - which was strongly innovatory and reformative of the system left over from the British regime - still survives today.

However, the fresh "establishment" of the courts in 1961 had at least one very important consequence: the Supreme Court regards itself as a "new" court not identical with the pre-1961 Supreme Court (notwithstanding continuity of personnel, of practice and of jurisdiction), and, as such, as having some degree of extra latitude, not precisely defined, in the application of the doctrine of *stare decisis* in respect of decisions of the "old" Supreme Court.[4] There are, however, some divergent views on this question, since in *The State (Lynch) v Cooney*[5] Henchy J said that the doctrine of *stare decisis* applied with equal force to decisions of the previous Supreme Court and that such a conclusion was supported by the need to maintain "judicial order and continuity."
The concept of a "new" court was, however, not new in 1961; the courts set up by the Courts of Justice Act 1924, were regarded as "new" by their own judges. Kennedy CJ said in *Quinn and White v Stokes and Quirke*:[6]

> "I venture to repeat once more that the Courts of Justice of the Saorstát are not the old courts of the British regime, amended, extended, divided, or otherwise re-

[1] [1954] IR 207; (1956) ILTR 116. Here the applicant sought to impugn the validity of his conviction on the ground that the trial judge (who had been appointed in 1945) had been invalidly appointed. It was said that the transitional period for which the pre-existing Circuit Court had been continued was intended to be short, without provision for filling any vacancies which might arise in the "old' court before it was replaced. The Supreme Court rejected these arguments for the reasons considered at p. 1178.
[2] [1967] IR 147.
[3] The Courts of Justice Act 1924 set up the Supreme Court of Justice, the High Court of Justice, the Circuit Court of Justice and the District Court of Justice. These courts were commonly referred to without the words "of Justice" and the 1961 Act dropped the words also from the formal titles of the "new" Supreme, High, Circuit and District Courts The title of the Court of Criminal Appeal did not change.
[4] See *The State (Quinn) v Ryan* [1965] IR 70; (1966) 100 ILTR 105 and *Attorney General v Ryan's Car Hire* [1965] IR 642; (1967) 101 ILTR 57.
[5] [1982] IR 337.
[6] [1931] IR 558; (1931) 65 ILTR 177.

dressed, but new courts established by the Oireachtas under the authority of the Constitution of the Saorstát (in particular Articles 64 to 69 thereof)."

These words were recalled by Walsh J in *The People (Attorney General) v Bell.*[7] In *Exham v Beamish*[8] Gavan Duffy J said:

> "The traditionalism of lawyers, practising under a law of precedent, tends to obscure the fact that the High Court of Justice, established in 1924, was in simple truth, and not merely on paper, a new court under a new Constitution."

And McCarthy J spoke vigorously to the same effect in *Irish Shell Ltd. v Elm Motors Ltd.*[9]

The phrase "established by law" implies, of course, that the judge purporting to administer justice has been validly appointed and that he is entitled to hear and determine the case before him. This issue featured in two cases arising out of the continuation in office beyond the official retirement age of a retired District Judge because of an official error as to his date of birth. In the first of these cases, *Shelly v Mahon*[10] the applicant had been convicted of traffic offences by the judge at a time when he was not qualified to hold office. Blayney J had no doubt but that this constituted an infringement of Article 34.1:

> "The applicant had a constitutional right to be tried in due course of law. One of the requisites, if that right was to be respected, was that he should have been tried in a court established by law by a judge duly appointed in the manner appointed by the Constitution, since this is how Article 34 provides that justice should be administered. He was not so tried. The respondent at the time of his trial was not a judge duly appointed in the manner provided by the Constitution. He was a retired District Justice whose appointment had terminated three months and four months before. The applicant's constitutional right was accordingly infringed."

This view was endorsed by the Supreme Court on appeal.[11]

In the second case, *Glavin v Governor of Mountjoy Prison,*[12] the applicant had been returned for trial by the same retired judge and was later duly convicted by jury in the Circuit Court. While the Supreme Court agreed that there was no constitutional right to a preliminary trial. The Court, therefore, concluded that this irregularity was nonetheless fatal to the validity of the conviction. Keane J observed that:

> "For so long as the Oireachtas considers it essential that persons accused of serious crime should be afforded the important protection of a preliminary hearing, both the prosecutor and accused are entitled as a matter of constitutional right under Article 34 to a determination of the justiciable controversy between them in a court established by law by a judge appointed in the manner provided by the Constitution."

[7] [1969] IR 24; (1970) 105 ILTR 41. See also *B. v B.* [1975] IR 54 and *R.D. Cox Ltd. v Owners of M.V Fritz Raabe*, Supreme Court, 1 August 1974 (*per* Walsh J).
[8] [1939] IR 336.
[9] [1984] IR 200: see below at pp. 1165-1166 where the passage is cited. See also the judgment of Lavery J in *O'Byrne v Minister for Finance* [1959] IR 1.
[10] [1990] 1 IR 36.
[11] Indeed, the principal issue before the Supreme Court was whether this purported conviction was validated by the provisions of the Courts (No.2) Act 1988. For a consideration of the general effects of validation statutes, see pp. 364-366.
[12] [1991] 1 IR 421.

Judges appointed in the manner provided by this Constitution

The manner of judges' appointments is prescribed by the provisions of Article 35.1.

The requirement of the Constitution that justice be administered by judges, i.e. not by other persons or bodies, has frequently arisen for consideration in the context of the jurisdiction of administrative and similar authorities; see above, pp. 330-346., and below, pp. 564-569.

The requirement that justice be administered in public

The object of the publicity requirement in Article 34 was adverted to by Walsh J in *In re R Ltd*:[13]

> "The issue before this Court touches a fundamental principle of the administration of justice in a democratic state, namely the administration of justice in public....The actual presence of the public is never necessary, but the administration of justice in public does require that the doors of the courts must be open so that members of the general public may come and see for themselves that justice is done. It is in no way necessary that the members of the public to whom the courts are open should themselves have any particular interest in the cases or that they should have business in the courts, Justice is administered in public on behalf of all of the inhabitants of the State."

Relevant also, perhaps, are the views of the European Court of Human Rights on this topic in *Sutter v Switzerland*:[14]

> "The public character of proceedings before the judicial bodies referred to in Article 6(1) [of the Convention] protects litigants against the administration of justice in secret with no public secrecy: it is also one of the means whereby confidence in the courts...can be maintained. By rendering the administration of justice visible, publicity contributes to the achievement of the aim of Article 6(1), namely a fair trial, the guarantee of which is one of the fundamental principles of any democratic society."

In fact, the "special and limited cases" admitting a restriction on the publicity of the administration of justice are relatively few. It is plain, however, that such exceptions can only be "prescribed by law", i.e., by an Act of the Oireachtas. As Walsh J said in *In re R Ltd.:* "The Constitution of 1937 removed any judicial discretion to have proceedings heard other than in public save where expressly conferred by statute."[15] This would seem to suggest that the courts have no discretion to direct that particular proceedings be heard *in camera* where this power is not expressly conferred by an Act of the Oireachtas.

[13] [1989] IR 126.

[14] (1984) 6 EHRR 272. See also *Pretto v Italy* (1984) 6 EHRR 182 and *Axen v Germany* (1984) 6 EHRR 195. All of these cases concern, *inter alia*, decisions of appellate courts where the appeal was rejected without an oral hearing and without giving judgment in open court. The European Court of Human Rights, however, held that, in each of these three cases, the procedures satisfied the publicity requirements of the Convention inasmuch as the public had access to the pleadings and the judgment and the terms of the judgment were later published.

[15] See also comments of Finlay CJ in *Irish Press plc v Ingersoll Publications Ltd.* [1993] ILRM 747: "The prescription by law provided for in this constitutional provision is, of course, by enactment of the Oireachtas."

Justice administered in public, with exceptions: criminal cases

The principal exception to public trial in criminal matters is provided by s 16(2) of the Criminal Procedure Act 1967, which created a new procedure for the preliminary investigation of indictable offences:

> Where the court is satisfied, because of the nature or circumstances of the case or otherwise in the interests of justice, that it is desirable, the court may exclude the public or any particular portion of the public or any particular person or persons except *bona fide* representatives of the Press[16] from the court during the hearing.

The court envisaged by this sub-section is the District Court. All courts are however envisaged by s 20(3) and (4) of the Criminal Justice Act 1951, which empowers a court "in any criminal proceedings for an offence which is, in the opinion of the court, of an indecent or obscene nature", to exclude the general public.[17] Another important example is now provided by s 6 of the Criminal Law (Rape) Act 1981,[18] which requires the judge in all trials of sexual offences to exclude from the court during the hearing[19] all persons except officers of the court, persons directly concerned in the hearing,[20] *bona fide* representatives of the press and such other persons (if any) as the judge may in his discretion permit to remain.[21] Section 12 of the Official Secrets Act 1963, also provides that:

> "If in the course of proceedings, including proceedings on appeal, for an offence under s 9 or for an offence under Part II committed in a manner prejudicial to the safety or preservation of the State, application is made by the prosecution, on the ground that the publication of any evidence or statement to be given or made during any part of the hearing would be prejudicial to the safety or preservation of the State, that that part of the hearing should be in *camera,* the court shall make an order to that effect, but the verdict and sentence (if any) shall be announced in public."[22]

These principles were applied by the Court of Criminal Appeal in *The People (Director of Public Prosecutions) v McGinley*[23] where Hederman J held that a trial judge had been wrong to hear evidence from a probation officer in chambers before proceeding to hear evidence in open court regarding sentence. This, he said, constituted a breach of Article 34 as "the accused should always be present during all of a criminal trial or indictment which includes sentencing."

Civil matters

In civil matters, the principal exception is to be found in s 45 of the Courts (Supplemental Provisions) Act 1961, which provides that justice may be administered

[16] This does not mean that the media are free to report such proceedings: s 17 of Criminal Procedure Act 1967.

[17] Certain exceptions, intended to be beneficial to the accused person, are made by s 20(4) of the 1951 Act and the 1967 Act s 16(3).

[18] As inserted by s 11 of the Criminal Law (Rape) (Amendment) Act 1990.

[19] However, by s 6(4) it is provided that the verdict and sentence (if any) shall be pronounced in public.

[20] Which includes the parent relative of friend of the complainant or, where the accused is not of full age, the complainant.

[21] This presumably might include diverse persons such as "devilling" barristers or researchers.

[22] In one case where the accused were prosecuted for offences under ss 9 and 13 of the 1963 Act the Special Criminal Court ordered that the trial take place *in camera.* They were acquitted by direction when the prosecution refused to produce the documents to which the charges related. For the subsequent abortive attempt by the Attorney General to state a case on a point of law to the Supreme Court under s 34 of the Criminal Procedure Act 1967, see *People v Crinion* [1976] IR 29.

[23] (1989) 3 Frewen 251.

otherwise than in public in (a) applications of an urgent nature for relief by way of habeas corpus, bail, prohibition or injunction; (b) matrimonial causes and matters; (c) lunacy and matters involving minors; or (d) proceedings involving the disclosure of a secret manufacturing process. This sub-section has been judicially considered in a number of cases. In the first of these, *The State (Cremin) v Cork Circuit Judge,*[24] the Supreme Court stated that *habeas corpus* applications should be ruled in open court. In this case an application to the High Court had been made by means of an informal letter and the High Court judge merely instructed his Registrar to respond to the letter, saying that the application was refused. The Supreme Court, *per* Ó Dálaigh CJ, took exception to this procedure, saying that:

> "the broad requirement of Article 34 is that justice should be administered in public. Section 45 of the Courts (Supplemental Provisions) Act 1961, however, authorises the disposal of a *habeas corpus* application elsewhere than in open court in a case of an urgent nature. In the absence of urgency, an application is proper to be ruled in the open and not in chambers. Where an applicant is not represented by counsel and the application is made by correspondence, it is perhaps easy to overlook that the Court, should, after inquiry, rule the application orally in court and not by correspondence."

In *Agricultural Credit Corporation v Irish Business Ltd.*[25] O'Hanlon J granted an interim injunction restraining the publication of certain allegedly confidential material. The injunction was granted *in camera* pursuant to s 45(1), but O'Hanlon J also made an order restraining the media from publishing any material which would tend to inform the public that such an order was made. This would not seem to be in accordance with either s 45(1), or, indeed, the spirit of Article 34.1. The fact that s 45(1) allows such interim relief to be granted otherwise in public is designed to allow for urgent applications to be made outside of ordinary sitting hours (e.g., where a judge makes an interim order at his own home) where the exigencies of the situation might not conveniently allow for reporters to be present.[26] But while it is one thing to provide for *in camera* hearings in order to preserve the anonymity of the parties in, say, family cases,[27] it can scarcely be correct that the public remains unaware of the result of certain proceedings, or, indeed, that such proceedings have been initiated.

This issue arose in *Attorney General v X.,*[28] where, although the case was heard *in camera*, some details of the extraordinary facts of that case (but not the identity of the parties) were published by the Dublin newspapers in advance of the judgment of the High Court in the matter. The Attorney General warned that this might be a contempt of court,[29] but this, surely, would only be the case where the newspapers had tended to identify the parties as opposed to informing the public that litigation of this remarkable variety (which, after all, had been initiated by the Attorney General in its name) had been commenced. Some support for this view may be found in the judgment of Parke J

[24] Supreme Court, 8 February 1965.

[25] *The Irish Times*, August 8, 9 1985.

[26] It is of interest to note that when the application for an interlocutory injunction came before Lardner J, he refused to hear the case *in camera*, observing that s 45(1) only applied to interim applications of an urgent variety.

[27] Or the nature of the evidence at the preliminary examination stage in a criminal trial: see s 17 of the Criminal Procedure Act 1967.

[28] [1992] ILRM 401.

[29] [1992] 1 IR 1; *The Irish Times*, February 14, 1992.

in *H. v H.*[30] where he said that a statutory requirement that proceedings be heard in private does not mean that the judgment in such proceedings may not be published:

> "The decision in this appeal is being given in court rather than in chambers so that the opinion of the Court as to the correct interpretation of s 56(5)(*b*) of the Act of 1965 may be promulgated. However, in order to preserve the confidentiality inherent in the requirement of a hearing in chambers, all identifying facts and circumstances, including the names of the parties, are omitted from this judgment."

A similar approach was taken by Costello J in the *X* case. Explaining that he had heard the case *in camera* pursuant to s 45(1) in order to protect the interests of the minor, nonetheless, since the case raised issues of law, the judgment would be circulated and made public in the ordinary way, with due regard to the need to preserve the anonymity of the minor defendant.

Other miscellaneous exceptions

As a general rule, it may be said that all family law proceeding are heard otherwise than in public and this finds expression in a variety of different statutes. Thus, s 20 of the Adoption Act 1952, provides that questions of law referred by the Adoption Board to the High Court for determination may, "subject to rules of court , be heard *in camera*;" s 12(4) of the Married Women's Status Act 1957 provides that disputes as to the ownership of a family home may be heard in private if the parties so desire; ss 56 (12), 119 and 122 of the Succession Act 1965 provide respectively that disputes pertaining to the appropriation of the family home; provision for spouse and children and dispositions for the purpose of disinheriting spouse and children "shall be heard in chambers"; s 1(3)(*c*) of the Marriages Act 1972 provides that applications to the President of the High Court for permission on the part of under-16 year olds to marry "may be heard and determined in private"; s 25 of the Family Law (Maintenance of Spouses and Children) Act 1976 provides that proceedings under that Act "shall be heard otherwise than in public"; and s 14 of the Family Law (Protection of Spouses and Children) Act 1981 and s 34 of the Judicial Separation and Family Law Reform Act 1989 are in identical terms. Section 36(4) of the Status of Children Act 1987 provides that a declaration of parentage application "shall be heard otherwise than in public", unless the court otherwise directs[31] and s 3(5) of the Adoption Act 1988 requires that applications to the High Court for authorisation of the adoption of children whose parents have failed in their duty towards them "shall be heard otherwise than in public."

The Supreme Court decisions in Re R Ltd and the Irish Press Case

The other principal category of civil proceedings which may be heard *in camera* relate to proceedings involving business secrets.[32] Section 205(7) of the Companies Act 1963

[30] [1978] IR 138. This case concerned whether a family residence should be appropriated by a widow in satisfaction of her legal right share under s 115 of the Succession Act 1965. Section 56(11) requires that all such applications "be heard in chambers." See also *M.P.D. v M.D.* [1981] ILRM 179 and also the remarks of Finlay CJ in *Re R. Ltd.* [1989] IR 126.

[31] As Walsh J observed in *In re R. Ltd.* [1989] IR 126, the statutory provisions "display a varied and unexplained choice of words to describe hearings other than in public, such words as '*in camera*', 'in private' and 'in chambers'". On the other hand, in the same case, Finlay CJ seemed to hint that these phrases seem to amount to the same thing.

[32] See also s 8 of the Defamation Act 1961, which requires that any application for leave to commence a criminal prosecution against a newspaper for criminal libel must be heard *in camera*. Since it is difficult to see any evident justification for this provision - especially since the *in camera* requirement is mandatory - its constitutionality must be questionable.

provides that in the case of oppression petitions brought by minority shareholders under that section:

> If, in the opinion of the court, the hearing of proceedings under this section would involve the disclosure of information the publication of which would be seriously prejudicial to the legitimate interests of the company, the court may order that the hearing of the proceedings or any part thereof shall be *in camera*.

Section 31 of the Companies (Amendment) Act 1990 is phrased in similar terms and this also allows the court to direct that examinership proceedings shall be heard *in camera*,[33] and s 96(2) of the Patents Act 1992 provides that any appeal under that Act to the High Court against a decision of the Controller of Patents, Designs and Trade Marks which "concerns a patent application which has not been published shall be heard in private."[34]

Apart from *Re R Ltd* and *Irish Press* - which we shall examine presently - the general rule as to publicity has arisen in a number of cases. In *In re Redbreast Preserving Co. Ltd.*[35] the Supreme Court held that the examination of a witness under s 174 of the Companies (Consolidation) Act 1908, might be conducted before a judge in private, as "the collection and preparation of material upon which a judge pronounced his decision was not the administration of justice within the meaning of... Article 34.1". This reversed the decision of Budd J in the High Court, who had said that:

> "on the true construction of the Article, a judge is bound to sit in public, not merely when he is dealing with matters involving the exercise of the judicial power of the State, but also when he is administering justice in the broad sense. That means.. for example that he must sit in public when performing all the judicial functions incidental to or preliminary to the determination of actions before him."

The view of the former Supreme Court must be considered doubtful, not only on ground of first principle but also in view of the comments of Walsh J in *In re R. Ltd.*[36] when he said that if the *dicta* in the *Redbreast* case meant that:

> "the constitutional requirement that justice is to be administered in public is satisfied by the public pronouncement of a decision based on evidence taken otherwise than in public, then where that is not expressly authorised by a post-Constitution statute it is clearly incorrect and ought not to be followed. All evidence in proceedings before a court must be taken in public save where otherwise expressly permitted in accordance with the terms of Article 34 of the Constitution."

[33] Thus, the appointment of the very first examiner under the 1990 Act (in the case of the Goodman Group of companies) was made at a late night sitting of the High Court at the home of Hamilton P. Journalists were refused entry to the hearing: *The Irish Times*, August 30, 1990. On the other hand, given the circumstances of the application, s 45(1) of the 1961 Act might have provided authority for this *in camera* hearing.

[34] Note also that s 134 of the Bankruptcy Act 1988, provides that:
"The Court may direct that the whole or any part of any sitting of the Court or proceeding in any matter under this Act shall be in private."
The constitutionality of this section may be doubted, since there do not appear to be any objective factors (such as non-disclosure of business secrets, protection of minors etc.) to justify a provision of this kind. It is true that an *in camera* hearing of this kind might shield the bankrupt from unwelcome publicity, but, having regard to the Supreme Court's judgment in the *Beamish and Crawford* case, this could scarcely underpin a provision of this kind.

[35] (1957) 91 ILTR 12.

[36] [1989] IR 126.

In *In re Singer*[37] Davitt P held (and on appeal Maguire CJ agreed with him, though in a dissenting minority on the main issue in the case) that Article 34.1 did not require that the dates for trials should be fixed in open court rather than by the registrar in consultation with the judge. Maguire CJ said:

> "This work is purely administrative and, while necessary as a preliminary towards preparing for a sitting of the court, is not in any sense the administration of justice referred to in Article 34.1 of the Constitution."

In *Beamish and Crawford Ltd. v Crowley,*[38] though the nature of the proceedings was different, the Supreme Court articulated a view of the constitutional rule which suggests that it might have shared in 1969 the fundamentalist attitude of Budd J rather than its own opinion of 1957.[39] Here the plaintiffs were seeking to have their action tried in Dublin rather than in Cork (where their business was located), *inter alia* on the ground that the evidence apprehended from the defence would, if given in Cork, cause them harmful publicity:

> "But publicity, deserved or otherwise [said the Supreme Court] is inseparable from the administration of justice in public; this is a principle which, as the Constitution declares, may not be departed from except in such special and limited cases as may be prescribed by law: Article 34.1. I cannot accept that the fact that the trial will, for one of the parties, attract more undesirable publicity in one venue than in another is a matter properly to be taken into account in determining the venue."

However, this question was more fully explored in *In re R. Ltd.*[40] Here a former chief executive (and substantial shareholder) brought a petition under s 205 of the Companies Act 1963 claiming that he had been oppressed. His grounding affidavit included sensitive business information and there was evidence to the effect that he had communicated the terms of that petition to a third party before it had been served on the company. The company applied for, and was granted, an *ex parte* order [41] by Johnson J directing that the petition be heard *in camera* and this was later affirmed by Costello J. A majority of the Supreme Court concluded - *per* Walsh J - that these facts did not afford any justification for the *in camera* order:

> "It is difficult to see why the disclosure of evidence of this type must necessarily be deemed to be a failure to do justice in the case of a juristic person where it would not be such in the case of a human person or of any unincorporated body of per-

[37] (1963) 97 ILTR 130. See also *McGlinchey v Governor of Mountjoy Prison* [1988] IR 671 (decision on the part of Special Criminal Court judges as to who will sit on a criminal trial is not an administration of justice and does not require to be made in open court. Of course, by reason of Article 38.6, the publicity rule does not in any event apply to the Special Criminal Court).

[38] [1969] IR 142.

[39] The *Redbreast* case was not mentioned in the later *Beamish and Crawford* case.

[40] [1989] IR 126.

[41] Before the Supreme Court, only Finlay CJ addressed this question, saying that, given the special circumstances of the case (i.e., the apparent communication with the third party):
"I am satisfied that the making of an original or preliminary order *ex parte* to hold the hearing of the proceedings *in camera* was justified, though it is a relief which ordinarily speaking might well be inappropriate on an *ex parte* application. Any conceivable disadvantage which could arise from the making of such an order *ex parte* application which could arise from the making of an order *ex parte* is avoided by the procedure which was adopted in this case of giving an extremely early hearing to the application to set aside or remove that order. I would, therefore, reject the contention that the fact that the original order in camera was made *ex parte* vitiates the validity of the orders actually made."

> sons...A limited company is the creature of the law and by its very nature and by the provisions of the law under which it is created it is open to public scrutiny."

Walsh J went on to stress that inconvenience or practical difficulties could not of themselves justify an *in camera* hearing. Even if there were circumstances in which some or part of the proceedings should be heard *in camera*, Walsh J insisted that Article 34 required that so much of the judgment "as does not disclose particular information which has been withheld from publication should be pronounced in public."[42]

The principles in the *R* were subsequently applied by the Supreme Court in *Irish Press Plc v Ingersoll Publications Ltd.*[43] The parties were joint shareholders in two newspaper publishing companies and the question was whether an oppression petition brought by one of the shareholders against the other should be heard *in camera.* The Supreme Court was unanimously of the view that the defendant had failed to discharge the "admittedly heavy onus of proof" which rests on a litigant seeking a hearing otherwise than in public, since, quite apart from any other considerations, the evidence showed that the nature of the feuding between the parties was already public knowledge. The Chief Justice took the opportunity of elaborating on the principles of the *R* case. If the court was of opinion that the hearing of the proceedings would involve the disclosure of information "the publication of which would be seriously prejudicial to the legitimate interests of the company", then the court must go on to consider the :

> "fundamental constitutional right vested in the public, namely, the administration of justice in public, and it cannot, therefore, make an order under s 205(7) merely on the consent of all the parties concerned in the petition before it."

Finlay CJ then stressed that s 205(7) must be strictly construed in view of the provisions of Article 34.1 "bearing in mind that the entitlement of the Oireachtas pursuant to Article 34.1 to prescribe by law for the administration of justice otherwise than in public is confined to special and limited cases."[44] The Chief Justice concluded that "in most instances, at least" the court should direct an *in camera* hearing under s 205(7) only where the damage which would be done by reason of the publication to the public of evidence concerning the company would outweigh the ability of the courts to render a just remedy to the wronged petitioner (or, as the case may be, to the wrongfully sued respondent).

It may be noted that in *Long v Saorstát and Continental Steamship Co. (No. 2)*,[45] although the publicity of court proceedings was not in issue in the same sense as in the three cases just cited, the Supreme Court treated as a nullity an issue paper which had been handed by the foreman of a jury to the judge via the court registrar after both parties and counsel had left the court under the impression that the jury had disagreed. O'Byrne J said:

[42] See also the judgment of the European Court of Human Rights in *Campbell and Fell v United Kingdom* (1985) 7 EHRR 165 where the Court held that even though security reasons justified the hearing of prison disciplinary proceedings *in camera* within the prison, the failure to make public the decision of the Board of Visitors constituted a breach of the publicity requirements of Article 6 of the Convention.

[43] [1993] ILRM 747.

[44] While Finlay CJ did not refer expressly to *Murphy v Greene* [1990] 2 IR 566, a similarity of approach between the two cases with regard to the construction of a statute in the light of the Constitution is evident. The principle in *Murphy's case* was, of course, expressly derived from the earlier decision in *Re R Ltd.*

[45] (1960) 94 ILTR 134.

> "In this State justice is to be administered in open court. It is to be administered in the presence of the parties or their representatives It is important in every case, but most important in this case."

The publicity rule does not apply (because of Article 38.6) to proceedings before courts set up under Article 38.3 or Article 38.4 or Article 28.3.3.

THE HIGH COURT

2. **The courts shall comprise Courts of First Instance and a Court of Final Appeal.**
3. **1° The Courts of First Instance shall include a High Court invested with full original jurisdiction in and power to determine all matters and questions whether of law or fact, civil or criminal.**

2. **Beidh ar na cúirteanna sin Cúirteanna Céadchéime agus Cúirt Achomhairc Dheiridh.**
3. **1° Beidh ar na Cúirteanna Céadchéime sin Ard-Chúirt ag a mbeidh lándlínse bhunaidh, agus cumhacht chun breith a thabhairt, i ngach ní agus ceist dlí nó fíorais cibé sibhialta nó coiriúil iad.**

1922 provision

Virtually identical provisions were contained in Article 64 of the 1922 Constitution. The Courts of First Instance envisaged by the present Constitution were to include a High Court (Article 34.1) and also lesser courts (Article 34.3.4). The Court of Final Appeal was to be called the Supreme Court (Article 34.4.1). The phrasing of these provisions makes it clear that a new establishment of courts was intended,[1] such as has since been effected by the Courts (Establishment and Constitution) Act 1961.

The High Court

The High Court established in 1961, like its predecessor, has an unlimited civil jurisdiction (unlike the civil jurisdictions of the Circuit Court and District Court); and also, under the title of the Central Criminal Court, an unlimited criminal jurisdiction[2] (again unlike the criminal jurisdictions of the Circuit Court and District Court).[3] That is to say, no cause of action known to the law is constitutionally excluded from the jurisdiction of the High Court, nor any criminal matter; though, as will be seen, a statutory "distribution" of jurisdiction may have the effect of confining certain matters with exclusive effect to some other courts.[4]

"Full jurisdiction"

The significance of the very comprehensive formulation "full original jurisdiction in and power to determine all matters and questions whether of law or fact, civil or criminal" has been partly - but by no means - fully explored. From the (relatively) small number of judicial decisions the following points may be noted.

General capacity of the High Court to enforce rights

In the first place, the full jurisdiction of the High Court has been seen as entailing its general capacity to afford a remedy where a right is breached, even though no action, or

[1] See *The State (Killian) v Minister for Justice* [1954] IR 207; (1956) 90 ILTR 116 and see p.1178.
[2] The High Court is given this title in its criminal jurisdiction by s 11(1) of the Courts (Supplemental Provisions) Act 1961, although this nomenclature seems constitutionally doubtful: see *People (Attorney General) v Bell* [1969] IR 24; (1971) 105 ILTR 41. It has been held that the Central Criminal Court is a court of oyer and terminer (i.e., having full jurisdiction to try treasons, felonies or misdemeanours): see *R. (O'Reilly) v Attorney General* [1928] IR 83. For a very helpful discussion of the significance of Article 34.3.1, see Casey, "*The Constitution and the Legal System*" (1979) 14 Ir Jur (n.s)14.
[3] For the criminal and civil jurisdictions of the Circuit and District Courts, see principally the Courts (Supplemental Provisions) Act 1961, ss 22-27 and 33 and the Courts Act 1991, ss 2-13.
[4] See pp. 411-412 below.

other remedy in statutory vesture, appropriate to the assertion of the right is immediately obvious. This proposition has been stated with reference to the courts generally in the context of breach of constitutional rights in a number of cases;[5] but was first stated with specific reference to the High Court and to the assertion of mere statutory rights, by Gavan Duffy J in *O'Doherty v Attorney General*,[6] a case so much the stronger inasmuch as it was argued for the plaintiff that the statutory route of administrative appeal expressly provided for in his case (a claim for a military pension) must be taken to have precluded recourse to the Court. Gavan Duffy J said:

> "It would be deplorable to find that a citizen deprived of a right given to him by the Oireachtas was without redress under our polity; his obvious redress is a resort to the High Court."

Recalling that even in England it required clear statutory words to oust the jurisdiction of the court, he said he:

> "[did] not hesitate to hold that the principle applies *a fortiori* to a jurisdiction safeguarded in strong words by a written Constitution."

A similar argument as to the exclusionary effect of a statutory appeal procedure on the High Court's jurisdiction was raised in *Ormonde and Dolan v Attorney General*,[7] in which the plaintiffs, caught for time, sought to have their qualification for inclusion in the Labour Panel in a Seanad general election declared by the High Court rather than by the Judicial Referee provided by the Seanad electoral law. Pringle J held that the relevant provision:

> "did not have the effect of depriving persons in the position of the plaintiffs here who have not been nominated to any Panel, from having their qualifications for nomination to a particular Panel decided by the High Court."

(The case, however, should be looked at in its own exceptional conditions, and is not an authority for assuming a general concurrent jurisdiction of the High Court on the merits of a matter entrusted to the decision of a statutory authority.)

In *Macauley v Minister for Posts and Telegraphs*[8] Kenny J drew on the "full original jurisdiction" of the High Court mentioned in Article 34.3.1 in asserting "the right to have recourse to the High Court to defend and vindicate a legal right"; this burst through the procedural barrier represented by the requirement of a pre-Constitution statute that actions against Ministers should be authorised by the *fiat* of the Attorney General. McCarthy J agreed with this approach in *Murphy v Greene*[9] when he said that the right of access to the courts was an "unenumerated right" deriving from the "interaction" of Article 40.3.1 and Article 34.3.1. In that case, the Supreme Court appeared to suggest

[5] See, e.g., the comments of Ó Dálaigh CJ in *The State (Meads) v Governor of Limerick Prison*, Supreme Court, 26 July 1972 and see further at pp. 700-702.
[6] [1941] IR 569; (1941) 57 ILTR 171.
[7] High Court, 9 July 1969. The judgment is printed in Smyth, *The Theory and Practice of the Irish Senate*, pp. 31ff.
[8] [1966] IR 345.
[9] [1990] 2 IR 566. Note that in both *Salih v General Accident* [1987] IR 628 and *Fallon v An Bord Pleanála* [1991] ILRM 799 the courts either expressly or impliedly upheld the constitutionality of the provisions of O 29 of the Rules of the Superior Courts, 1986, which enable the High Court to order a plaintiff to provide security for costs. These decisions raise the wider issue of the constitutional right to access to the courts and are considered at pp. 386-390.

that a statutory restriction[10] on the right of access to the High Court would not be unconstitutional where there were objective reasons for such a restriction and where this restriction was not of itself unduly oppressive.[11]

Finally, the object and purpose of Article 34.3.1 was described by Gannon J in *R. v R.*[12] as ensuring that there was in existence a court to which recourse "may be had in any event or upon any occasion and in any circumstances where there may exist a wrong for which in justice a remedy may be required." As he did not consider that this requirement could be satisfied by the existence of a court with "exclusive but determinable" jurisdiction (i.e., a court whose jurisdiction was dependent upon statute), he thought it would be inconsistent with Article 34.3.1 to suppose no jurisdiction in the High Court "unless and until a jurisdiction was conferred by enactment of the Oireachtas." While the Supreme Court later appeared to take a different view on the question of whether Article 34.3.1 allowed exclusive jurisdiction to be vested in the lower courts,[13] it did not take issue. Gannon J's analysis of the object and purpose of Article 34.3.1.

Jurisdiction transcends the sum of former jurisdictions

Secondly, the High Court's jurisdiction, being "full", is not - according to a majority decision of the Supreme Court in *R. D. Cox Ltd. v Owners of M.V Fritz Raabe*[14] - to be gathered merely by adding up the jurisdictions of the old divisions of the pre-1924 High Court which, at one remove, it replaced. The question in issue here was whether the Court had jurisdiction to entertain an action *in rem* in respect of a ship mortgage not registered under the Mercantile Marine Act 1955 (the former Admiralty Court functioning under an Act of 1867 had had such jurisdiction only where the mortgage was registered under the Merchant Shipping Acts). Walsh J, with whom Griffin J agreed, took the words of Article 34.3.1 literally:

> "The fact that in former times courts of limited jurisdiction, such as the Admiralty Court, had no jurisdiction in certain types of justiciable controversies does not in any way restrict the jurisdiction of the High Court to adjudicate in any justiciable controversy... It could scarcely be argued that the High Court could not adjudicate in a claim in respect of a mortgage of a ship which was not registered simply because the old Court of Admiralty could not have done so."

[10] The restriction in question was contained in s 260 of the Mental Treatment Act 1945 which requires that no civil proceedings shall be instituted in respect of acts purporting to have been done under that Act unless the High Court is satisfied that there are "substantial grounds for contending that the person against whom the proceedings are to be brought acted in bad faith or without reasonable care." Another more recent example of such a restriction may be found in s 82(3A) of the Local Government (Planning and Development) Act 1963 (as inserted by s.19 of the Local Government (Planning and Development) (Amendment) Act 1992) which provides that any challenges to the validity of a planning decision must be brought by way of judicial review within a two months period and that leave to apply for judicial review shall not be granted unless the High Court is satisfied that "there are substantial grounds for contending that the decision is invalid or ought to be quashed."

[11] Among the justifications for this limited statutory protection in the case of s 260 of the Mental Treatment Act 1945 is the fact that, *per* McCarthy J in *Murphy v Greene*, the doctor is often required to act in cases of "urgency, the danger to others and like circumstances." In the case of s 82(3A) of the 1963 Planning Act the reason for the very short time limits is that major developments and other building projects could be held up pending drawn out challenges to the validity of a planning permission: see *Brady v Donegal County Council* [1989] ILRM 282. The constitutionality of these partial ouster clauses are considered further at pp. 387-388.

[12] [1984] IR 296.

[13] *Tormey v Ireland* [1985] IR 289.

[14] Supreme Court, 1 August 1974. See also *Geraghty v Geraghty*, High Court, 3 December 1970 (where Kenny J held that the inherent jurisdiction of the High Court pursuant to Article 34.3.1 enabled the High Court to sanction the variation of a trust even in the absence of enabling legislation).

It may be noted that Henchy J dissented, saying that Article 34.3.1:

> "created no new justiciable matters. It merely vested in the High Court original jurisdiction in all justiciable matters which are for the time being existing." Article 34.3.1 is investitive of jurisdiction, not creative of jurisdiction. It merely declares an amplitude of original jurisdiction in the High Court to encompass all currently justiciable matters.

As the admiralty action *in rem* on ship mortgages was a statutory creation, and as the relevant provisions confined it to a mortgage registered under the 1955 Act (he held), the High Court was without jurisdiction to enforce it.

Jurisdiction may, however, be distributed to other courts with an exclusive effect, provided the High Court retains an adequate power of review

Thirdly, although Article 34.3.1 speaks of "full" jurisdiction, it is not the case that the Oireachtas is incompetent to vest the adjudication of certain types of controversy exclusively in some court other than the High Court. This entire question was adverted to inconclusively by Kenny J in *Macauley v Minister for Posts and Telegraphs* when he hinted that legislation allowing the High Court to remit certain actions to the lower courts might be incompatible with Article 34.3.1.

The latter power - that of remitting actions to the Circuit Court - under s 25 of the Courts of Justice Act 1924 was challenged in *Ward v Kenehan Electrical Ltd.*,[15] in which the plaintiff argued that Article 34.3.1 entitled him to go straight to the High Court (notwithstanding that the size of his claim was within the Circuit Court's jurisdiction, to which, on the defendant's application, it had been remitted), and that he could not be compelled to resort to a court of limited and local jurisdiction such as that Court. McMahon J rejected this argument, saying that Article 34.3.1 had to be read in conjunction with Article 36.iii which entrusts to statutory regulation "the distribution of jurisdiction and business among... courts and judges". In *R. v R.*[16] Gannon J arrived a similar result, but for slightly different reasons. He took the view that the Oireachtas could not validly oust the jurisdiction of the High Court, but held nonetheless that the High Court could "in accordance with its own procedures" remit certain actions to the lower courts.

This entire question was examined in the elaborate judgment of Henchy J for the Supreme Court in *Tormey v Ireland.*[17] In this case, the plaintiff had been returned for trial to the Circuit Court but claimed an entitlement, deriving from Article 34.3.1, to trial in the Central Criminal Court (i.e., the High Court exercising its criminal jurisdiction). With the enactment of the Courts Act 1981, the High Court had lost most of its criminal jurisdiction[18] and it was said that this statutory exclusion of that jurisdiction represented an unconstitutional derogation from the Court's full original jurisdiction conferred by Article 34.3.1. Henchy J observed that this argument rested on a strictly literal interpre-

[15] [1984] IR 292.

[16] [1984] IR 296.

[17] [1985] IR 283. See generally, Hogan, "*Reflections on the Supreme Court's decision in Tormey v Attorney General*" (1986) 6 DULJ (n.s.) 31.

[18] By virtue of s 25(2) of the Courts (Supplemental Provisions) Act 1961 (as amended), the High Court has exclusive jurisdiction in treason, murder, attempt to murder, conspiracy to murder, piracy, genocide and offences under ss 6, 7 and 8 of the Offences Against the State Act 1939, including offences by an accessory, before or after the fact. In addition, s 10 of the Criminal Law (Rape) (Amendment) Act 1990 now provides that rape and other serious sexual offences are to be tried in the Central Criminal Court.

tation of Article 34.3.1 which would produce absurdity and would provoke a clash with other constitutional provisions; for example:

> "It is implicit in Article 26 that no court other than the Supreme Court shall have jurisdiction to rule on the constitutionality of a Bill referred by the President under that Article; Article 34.4.3 debars the High Court from considering the constitutionality of a statutory provision declared constitutional by the Supreme Court in a reference under Article 26; and Article 34.4.6 provides more generally that the High Court cannot entertain any question which has been determined by the Supreme Court."[19]

Moreover, Article 38.2 enabled courts of summary jurisdiction to try minor offences; special courts could try offences of the kind specified in Article 38.3.1; military courts were empowered by Article 38.4.1 to try offences against military law; and Article 37 permitted persons or bodies who were not judges to exercise limited functions and powers of a judicial nature in matters other than criminal matters. Thus, jurisdiction under Article 34.3.1 must be taken:

> "to be capable of being exercised, at least in certain instances, to the exclusion of the High Court, for the allocation of jurisdiction would otherwise be overlapping and unworkable."

In the present case, Article 34.3.1 had to be read in the light of Article 34.3.4 which obliges the Oireachtas to establish other courts of first instance with a "local and limited jurisdiction." This latter provision showed, said Henchy J, that the High Court was not expected to be a "suitable forum for hearing and determining at first instance all justiciable matters." It followed that where (as here) the Oireachtas commits certain matters to the District and Circuit Courts it may do so to the exclusion of the High Court and the exclusion of such cases from the High Court's remit could not be regarded therefore as a breach of Article 34.3.1. It would seem that inasmuch as *R. v R.* suggested that the Oireachtas may not confer exclusive jurisdiction on lower courts to the exclusion of the High Court, it has been implicitly overruled by *Tormey's* case.

The High Court's inherent power to decline jurisdiction

This power was first asserted by Gannon J in *R. v R.*[20] where he ruled that notwithstanding the jurisdiction vested in the High Court by Article 34.3.1, that Court retained an inherent power to decline jurisdiction in appropriate cases. This, where courts of local and limited jurisdiction enjoyed a concurrent jurisdiction in relation to certain justiciable matters, the High Court was not obliged:

> "to provide any person, as a matter of constitutional right, with access to [it] so as to enable him to have recourse to [it] at his choice in lieu of recourse to the court of first instance established by law and having the jurisdiction sought to be invoked."

[19] It may be thought that this particular aspect of Henchy J's reasoning is not especially convincing, in that every example given in this passage represents an instance of where there is no subsisting *lis* which could be litigated before the High Court. A litigant who, for example, attempted to challenge the constitutionality of a Bill upheld by the Supreme Court following an Article 26 reference would doubtless find that the High Court would promptly strike out his action as an abuse of process. Thus it must remain doubtful if one can extrapolate from these highly particular examples instanced by Henchy J a general principle which of necessity requires a modification of the ordinary, literal meaning of Article 34.3.1 which had been contended for by the plaintiff in *Tormey's* case.

[20] [1984] IR 90.

Thus the question whether the High Court should exercise jurisdiction in certain cases was to be decided on a case by case basis. A practice direction on this matter was issued by the Chief Registrar of the High Court subsequent to *R. v R.*[21] requiring parties in family law cases[22] to "submit such evidence or arguments as they see fit" to see whether the case was one in which it was appropriate that the High Court should exercise jurisdiction.

That the exercise of such jurisdiction by the High Court was not contingent merely on the consent of the parties was evidenced by *O'R. v O'R.*[23] This was also a family law matter in which the parties were content to have the case heard in the High Court, but Murphy J declined jurisdiction in view of the "clear intention of the Oireachtas" that applications of this kind should be made in the first instance to a court of local and limited jurisdiction. In his view, the only circumstances in which the court would be entitled to depart from the procedure envisaged by the Oireachtas would be where the High Court:

> "was satisfied that in the circumstances of a particular case there was a serious danger that justice would not be done, if that Court declined to exercise the jurisdiction vested in it by the Constitution."

In this case he could see no such danger.

Murphy J applied the same test in *Deighan v Hearne,*[24] where the plaintiff claimed a constitutional entitlement to by-pass the administrative machinery for tax assessment established by the Income Tax Act 1967, in order to have his liability determined by the High Court. While accepting that the High Court had jurisdiction to determine an inherently justiciable matter (i.e., the plaintiff's tax liability), Murphy J noted that the Court could decline to exercise it where the Oireachtas had provided "other suitable and appropriate machinery"; its jurisdiction would only come into play:

> "in the most exceptional circumstances, as long as legislation provided a constitutional procedure competently staffed and efficiently operated to carry out that unpopular but very necessary task."

Does Article 34.3.1 prevent the fettering of the powers of the High Court with regard to justiciable controversies before it?

It may be noted that *In re McAllister*[25] Kenny J used Article 34.3.1 in rejecting the notion that the Legislature could, in a certain class of case, exclude the granting of bail:

> "It was said that the prohibition on giving bail... was inconsistent with Article 34.3.1, which gives the High Court "full original jurisdiction in and power to determine all matters and questions whether of law or fact, civil or criminal". I do not think that the National Parliament has power to pass legislation that the High Court shall not give bail to an accused person and so the words "without bail" are repugnant to the Constitution."

[21] This practice direction is reported as an appendix to *O'R. v O'R.* [1985] IR at p. 368. It is also reproduced at [1984] ILRM 148.
[22] The relevant legislation had clearly evinced an intention to remove such cases from the realm of the High Court and remit them to the District and Circuit Courts.
[23] [1985] IR 367.
[24] [1986] IR 603.
[25] [1973] IR 238.

The correctness of this proposition seems dubious. Apart from the personal liberty dimension of bail, and from the presumption of innocence of an unconvicted person, which is part of the notion of "due course of law" in Article 38.1 - values which must inhibit its exclusion by statute - it does not seem obvious that the exclusion of bail in certain cases trenches on either the general area of judicial independence or the particular jurisdiction of the High Court, any more than does the prescribing of a mandatory sentence or an automatic consequence on conviction. If Kenny J's view is correct, it would mean that a wide variety of statutory provisions might be rendered unconstitutional on this account.[26] In fact, the difficulty with *McAllister's* case is that it tends to collapse the distinction between the investiture of jurisdiction in the High Court on the one hand and statutory restrictions on the availability of certain remedies on the other. It is certainly true that, if the Oireachtas were unfairly to restrict or even exclude the availability of certain remedies, this might be unconstitutional, but on the ground that it would offend against Article 40.3[27] rather than Article 34.3.1. This was suggested in passing by Gannon J in *Dublin County Council v Browne:*[28]

> "[T]he legislature has not (and constitutionally could not have) deprived the High Court of its inherent jurisdiction to grant equitable relief where justice requires by intervening in contractual relationships or where a wrong is threatened or is taking place."

Article 34.3.1 does not create any new justiciable controversies

Apart from the principle in *Tormey's* case, Article 34.3.1 and its reference to "all matters and questions" cannot be taken absolutely literally.[29] First, there must be matters and questions - even ones which are contentious and productive of grievance within their own sphere - which are not justiciable at all, for example, the exercise of authority within the family, or the exercise of discretion by an employer in recruiting employees, or by a businessman in placing contracts. Thus the glossing of the constitutional words with something like "always provided that such matters or questions arise in connection with a cause of action or an offence known to the law" seems obligatory in common sense; although in view of the innovatory temper of the modern judiciary on the larger constitutional level, perhaps "known to or latent in the law" would be better.

Secondly, Article 34.3.1 does not empower the High Court to depart from settled principles in its determination of justiciable controversies. In *M.M. v P.M.*[30] McMahon J rejected the suggestion that this provision empowered him to create a new ground of nullity:

> "Under the Constitution the jurisdiction of the High Court extends to determining all questions of nullity of marriage, but that it is a jurisdiction which clearly must be exercised upon grounds to be determined by the legislature. For the courts to add new grounds would be to engage in legislation."

[26] E.g., s 19(1) of the Industrial Relations Act 1990, severely restricts the power of the High Court to grant an *ex parte* injunction to restrain picketing by striking workers.
[27] Or some other constitutional provision guaranteeing a substantive right. The right to personal liberty in Article 40.4 presupposes, for example, that the courts will have jurisdiction to award damages for breach of that right.
[28] High Court, 6 October 1987.
[29] Note that in *McGrath and Ó Ruairc v Trustees of Maynooth College* [1979] ILRM 166 Kenny J said that the words of Article 34.3.1 though general, did not mean literally what they said, as the High Court "when reviewing the decision of an inferior court....or of a domestic tribunal does not try the case again."
[30] [1986] ILRM 515. But cf. *F v C.* [1991] ILRM 65.

Thirdly, Article 34.3.1 can have no relevance where the cause of action has been extinguished by prior litigation. In *Donohue v Browne,*[31] the defendants had obtained in the District Court an award of damages against the plaintiff for loss and damage arising from a road accident. The plaintiff then commenced High Court proceedings claiming damages for negligence arising from the same incident. When the defendants raised the plea of statutory *res judicata*, the plaintiff claimed that the relevant provisions of ss 29 and 37 of the Civil Liability Act 1961, were unconstitutional inasmuch as they were inconsistent with the High Court's full jurisdiction under Article 34.3.1. Gannon J held that, as the defendant had obtained final judgment against the plaintiff in a court of local and limited jurisdiction, the plaintiff could not now invoke the High Court's original jurisdiction in order to get the case tried again:

> "as it had been determined by a conclusive judgment binding upon him that he was solely responsible for the event giving rise to his injuries, loss and damage he is left with no cause of action, and therefore no justification for a claim of recourse to the High Court."

Fourthly, there is the body of "matters and questions" which by 1937 had long been confided to administrative regulation: a disposition which was confirmed and put beyond doubt by Article 37, but which even without the benefit of that Article, or where it does not apply, could scarcely now be called into question so as to render all administrative acts reviewable by the High Court on their merits (as distinct from recognised criteria of *vires* etc.). Gavan Duffy J - whose anti-ministerial advocacy in *Lynham v Butler*[32] may have played some part in inspiring Article 37 - seemed to go almost that distance in *In re Loftus Bryan's Estate*,[33] when he said, in relation to s 48 of the Land Law (Ireland) Act 1881, which gave the Land Commission "full power and jurisdiction to hear and determine all matters, whether of law or fact" and purported to exclude its doings from review by the courts:

> "I wish to state my emphatic opinion that no British law could continue in force under the recent [i.e. the 1922] Constitution which was so inconsistent as that enactment with the constitutional authority of the High Court to determine all matters and questions, whether of law or fact, civil or criminal; and that it is, if possible, even clearer that no such enactment now survives to fetter our High Court, on which... the like constitutional authority has been deliberately conferred by the Constitution."

In practice, however, Irish courts have not shown any tendency to invade the administrative sphere (as distinct from controlling it on vires and natural justice criteria) or to replace an administrative decision[34] with their own.[35]

[31] [1986] IR 90.

[32] [1933] IR 74; (1933) 67 ILTR 75.

[33] [1942] IR 185; (1941) 75 ILTR 82.

[34] Note the comments of O'Flaherty J in *Attorney General v Hamilton (No.1)* [1993] 2 IR 250; [1993] ILRM 81:

> "judicial restraint has been demonstrated on many occasions when the courts have declined to intervene with administrative decisions simply because a particular court might reach a different decision on the merits from that reached by an administrative body or official. This despite the fact that the High Court is invested with full original jurisdiction in all matters both civil and criminal."

[35] This is also confirmed by leading decisions such as *The State (Keegan) v Stardust Victims' Tribunal* [1986] IR 642; [1987] ILRM 401; *O'Keeffe v An Bord Pleanála* [1993] 1 IR 39; [1992] ILRM 237; *Mathews v Irish Coursing Club Ltd.* [1993] 1 IR 346; *Kiberd v Tribunal of Inquiry* [1992] ILRM 574; *Garda Representative Association v A.G.*, Supreme Court, 26 May 1993 and *Duff v Minister for Agriculture* [1993] 2 CMLR 969.

"Final and conclusive" administrative determination is not what it seems

On the other hand, the jurisdiction to control the administrative sphere on those criteria has been firmly maintained and - in the context of insisting that an administrative discretion should be exercised fairly and reasonably - has been lately extended. Where, for instance, the legislature has attempted to exclude judicial interference by the statutory device of laying down that a particular decision, or record, of an administrative authority is to be "final and conclusive" or incapable of being questioned on *certiorari,* the Irish courts have always been very reluctant to allow such a provision to oust their jurisdiction to enquire whether an administrative act or decision has been made or taken within jurisdiction.[36] In *Murren v Brennan*[37] Gavan Duffy J said that:

> "while a court of law would be slow to interfere with any decision clearly entrusted by statute to a Minister of State, the phrase "whose decision shall be final"... cannot exclude the constitutional jurisdiction of the High Court in a case deemed by the High Court to warrant interference."

Similar emphatic expressions, with reference to the status of the judicial function as entrenched by Article 34, will be found in the judgments of Gavan Duffy J in *O'Doherty v Attorney General*[38] and *In re Loftus Bryan's Estate*.[39]

At all events, the constitutionality of legislative attempts to oust the High Court's power of review must be considered doubtful in light of the decision of the Supreme Court in *Tormey v Attorney General.*[40] Here Henchy J agreed that while Article 34.3.1, when read in conjunction with Article 34.3.4 and Article 37, permitted the Oireachtas to vest lower courts or administrative tribunals with exclusive jurisdiction in respect of certain justiciable controversies, but where this had been done:

> "[The] full jurisdiction [of the High Court] is there to be invoked - in proceedings such as habeas corpus, *certiorari, prohibition, quo warranto*, injunction or declaratory action - so as to ensure that the hearing and determination will be in accordance in law. Save to the extent required under the terms of the Constitution, no justiciable matter may be excluded from the range of the original jurisdiction of the High Court."

A different judicial attitude, however, prevails in the case of partial ouster clauses which, in effect, consist of very short limitation periods within which the validity of an administrative decision may be challenged. In principle, such partial ouster clauses do not offend against Article 34.3.1, but such clauses may be vulnerable on the ground that they fail to vindicate, as required by Article 40.3, the applicant's right of access to the courts.[41]

[36] "The courts should be reluctant to surrender their inherent right to enter on a question of what are prima facie justiciable matters" *per* Henchy J in *The State (Pine Valley Developments Ltd.) v Dublin County Council* [1984] IR 417.
[37] [1942] IR 466. See also *The State (O'Duffy) v Bennett* [1935] IR 70; *The State (Hughes) v Lennon* [1935] IR 128; *The State (Horgan) v Exported Livestock Board Ltd.* [1943] IR 581; *The State (McCarthy) v O'Donnell* [1945] IR 126; *Brannigan v Keady* [1959] IR 283 and *Casey v Minister for Agriculture*, High Court, February 6, 1987. See generally Hogan and Morgan, *Administrative Law in Ireland* (London, 1991) at 374-8.
[38] [1941] IR 569; (1942) 76 ILTR 120.
[39] [1941] IR 569; (1941) 75 ILTR 171.
[40] [1985] IR 289.
[41] See, e.g., *Brady v Donegal County Council* [1989] ILRM 282. This question is best considered under the heading of "access to the courts" under Article 34.1 and Article 40.3. see pp. 387-388. See also Pye, "*The s 104 Certificate of Registration - An Impenetrable Shield No More?*" (1985) 3 ILT (n.s) 212.

Review of the exercise of administrative discretion: earlier conservative attitude

Even where the formula of a "final and conclusive" administrative determination was not employed, the courts in earlier years were not willing to review or go behind the exercise of a discretion entrusted to an administrative authority. Thus in *In re Article 26 and the Offences against the State (Amendment) Bill, 1940*[42] - admittedly a decision given in the context of a wartime emergency - the Supreme Court, in considering the proposed power of a Minister to order a person's indefinite detention if "of opinion that any particular person [was] engaged in activities which, in his opinion, [were] prejudicial to the preservation of public peace and order or to the security of the State", said that:

> "The only essential preliminary to the exercise by a Minister of the powers contained in s 4 is that he should have formed opinions on the matters specifically mentioned in the section. The validity of such opinions is not a matter that could be questioned in any court."

This view was followed by the same Court in *In re Ó Láighléis.*[43]

Now replaced by judicial willingness to scrutinise on fairness standard

In more recent times, however, the principle that a statutory discretion must be exercised fairly - and that a court can review its exercise on this standard - has come to be accepted. The newer view can be traced in *East Donegal Co-Operative Ltd. v Attorney General*,[44] in which the Supreme Court said that statutory expressions appearing to convey a discretion do not, in fact, give the recipient "an absolute or an unqualified or an arbitrary power to grant or refuse [in this instance a licence] at his will", but obliged him to act "fairly and judicially in accordance with the principles of constitutional justice". In *Loftus v Attorney General*[45] the Supreme Court said that, while the registrar of political parties was "given a discretion to register or not to register, this [was] not an unfettered discretion... If [he] exercised his discretion or his powers capriciously, partially or in a manifestly unfair manner, it would be assumed that this could not have been contemplated or intended by the Oireachtas and his action would be restrained and corrected by the courts". In *The State (Lynch) v Cooney*,[46] O'Higgins CJ plainly said that the law on this topic was now judicially perceived otherwise than at the time of the *Offences Against the State (Amendment) Bill* reference or *Ó Láighléis'* case:

> "While the opinion of the former Supreme Court, expressed in 1940 and in 1957, reflected what was then current judicial orthodoxy, judicial thinking has since then undergone a change. Decisions given in recent years show that the power of the courts to subject the exercise of administrative powers to judicial review is seen as having a wider reach than that delimited by those decisions of 1940 and 1957... The Court is satisfied that [s 31(1) of the Broadcasting Authority Act 1960, authorising the prohibition of certain broadcasts] does not exclude review by the courts and that any opinion formed by the Minister thereunder must be one which is *bona fide* held and factually sustainable and not unreasonable."

[42] [1940] IR 470; (1940) 74 ILTR 61.
[43] [1960] IR 93; (1961) 95 ILTR 92.
[44] [1970] IR 317; (1970) 104 ILTR 81.
[45] [1979] IR 221.
[46] [1982] IR 337; [1983] ILRM 89. See generally, Gearty, "*Judicial Review of Ministerial Opinion*" (1982) 4 DULJ 95.

In the last few years there has emerged what O'Flaherty J has described as:

> "A well chartered system of administrative law which requires decision-makers to render justice in the cases brought before them and sets out the procedures that should be followed, which procedures will vary from case to case and from one type of tribunal to another and which, of course, are subject to judicial review. Similarly, the rules of evidence may not necessarily be applied with the same strictness as in a court of law provided that the decision-making body keeps in the forefront of its deliberations the necessity to come to a correct and just verdict having regard to the complaints that have to be investigated; the determination to be made and the consequences such determination may have for the party or parties appearing before it."[47]

Similar principles have now been applied in a host of modern cases.[48]

Can the legislature reduce areas of justiciability?

There is also the question, forcefully raised by the words of Kenny J in *McAllister's* case cited above, whether Article 34.3.1 can really mean that the legislature is not free, even within the framework of a known type of proceeding (as, in this case, a bankruptcy proceeding) to mark off certain areas (as, in that case, the granting of bail) as being "out of bounds" to the courts. Not only the details of the courts' own structures and functioning, but a very large part of the litigious ground, on which they tread, are the creature of statute; and some definition would seem needed of the right of the courts to re-write - in reliance on Article 34.3.1- statutory provisions which regulate the exercise of judicial power.

The problem here was adverted to in a sense by the Supreme Court in *In re Haughey*,[49] when it was contended that s 3(4) of the Committee of Public Accounts of Dáil Éireann (Privilege and Procedure) Act 1970, in effect authorised the High Court to try summarily the offence of refusing to answer questions put by the Public Accounts Committee. Ó Dálaigh CJ said:

> "It is true that the High Court possesses a universal jurisdiction in matters, civil and criminal, but that does not make it a court of summary jurisdiction within the provisions of s 2 of Article 38. A court of summary jurisdiction within the meaning of that section is one whose criminal jurisdiction to try and to convict is restricted to the trial of minor offences. The term "court of summary jurisdiction" was well known prior to the enactment of the Constitution... Under our law that jurisdiction is exercised only by the District Court. In accordance with the provisions of s 5 of Article 38, the jurisdiction of the High Court to try criminal offences is a jurisdiction to try them only with a jury."

In other words, whatever the bare words of the Constitution may be - so in effect Ó Dálaigh CJ argued - they will require an interpretation modified by the known state of

[47] *Keady v Garda Commissioner* [1992] 2 IR 197; [1992] ILRM 312.

[48] See, e.g., *The State (Keegan) v Stardust Victims' Tribunal* [1986] IR 642; *The State (Creedon) v Criminal Injuries Compensation Tribunal* [1989] IR 51; *International Fishing Vessels Ltd. v Minister for Marine* [1989] IR 149; *Stroker v Doherty* [1991] 1 IR 23; *O'Keeffe v An Bord Pleanála* [1993] 1 IR 39; [1992] ILRM 237; *Mathews v Irish Coursing Club Ltd.*[1993] 1 IR 346; *McHugh v Minister for Social Welfare*, Supreme Court, 11 March 1992; *Wiley v Revenue Commissioners* [1993] ILRM 482 and *Duff v Minister for Agriculture* [1993] 2 CMLR 969.

[49] [1971] IR 217.

affairs at the time the Constitution was enacted.[50] If this is so, it might equally be argued - as against the view of Kenny J in *McAllister's* case - that the bounds to justiciability which existed in 1937, like the understanding of the phrase "court of summary jurisdiction", must be taken to have been respected by the Constitution on its enactment.

Reduction of the High Court's jurisdiction by the abolition of causes of action

Whether the category of "justiciable controversies" may constitutionally be reduced, by, e.g., the abolition of a cause of action, is a matter adverted to already in the general context of the administration of justice.[51] It may however be noted here, in the specific context of the High Court's jurisdiction, that Henchy J adverted to the abolition of causes of action in his dissenting judgment in the *Fritz Raabe* case cited above, clearly envisaging this as something which could lawfully be done and which would thus have the effect of diminishing that jurisdiction:

> "If a matter has not been made justiciable, or being justiciable has been made, either by constitutional amendment or by statute, no longer justiciable, it stands outside the range of the original jurisdiction vested in the High Court by Article 34.3.1. Examples are not wanting, on either the criminal or civil side of the law, of types of proceedings which are outside the jurisdiction of the High Court - or any other court - either because they have never been created or have been abolished by statute."

This view of Henchy J is almost certainly correct insofar as it concerns Article 34.3.1, but it is also true that the abolition or restriction of certain causes of action might infringe Article 40.3 or some other provision of the Constitution guaranteeing substantive rights.[52] The abolition of the tort of false imprisonment, for example, would not infringe Article 34.3.1 (in that the High Court would simply lack jurisdiction to entertain such a cause of action), but, in the absence of some other adequate remedy, this would almost certainly infringe Arts. 40.3 and 40.4 (inasmuch as the State would have failed by its laws to vindicate adequately the right to liberty).[53] This topic is best considered under the heading of the relationship between the Constitution and the law of torts.[54]

"Central Criminal Court"

In *The People (Attorney General) v Bell*,[55] Walsh J adverted to two points arising on the Courts (Supplemental Provisions) Act 1961, in its bearing on the jurisdiction of the High Court. Firstly the jurisdiction of the High Court which is mentioned in s 14(2) of that Act includes the jurisdiction conferred on the Court by the Constitution, and is not restricted to the jurisdiction conferred by the Act (which was additional), as a literal

[50] See pp. cix-cxi.

[51] See pp. 348-349.

[52] Note in this context that the practical effect of s 1 of the Copyright (Amendment) Act 1987, is to abolish a potential plaintiff's right of action to sue for an infringement of the copyright in an industrial design. This change represents a legislative judgment to the effect that the pre 1987 copyright law was too generous as far as the copyright owners of industrial designs were concerned. If this change is unconstitutional, it is presumably because the Oireachtas has failed - as is required by Article 40.3 - adequately to vindicate intellectual property rights. But the important point in this context is that any such challenge would have to be based on Article 40.3, as opposed to Article 34.3.1. On this point, see Hogan, "*Copyright (Amendment) Act 1987*" (1987) ICLSA 24-01.

[53] See, e.g., *Hanrahan v Merck, Sharpe & Dohme Ltd.* [1988] ILRM 629; *Sweeney v Duggan* [1991] 2 IR 274.

[54] See pp. 707-708.

[55] [1969] IR 24; (1971) 105 ILTR 41.

reading of the sub-section might suggest. Secondly, while s 14 speaks of the High Court in the exercise of its criminal jurisdiction as "The Central Criminal Court", Walsh J said it was "to say the least, extremely doubtful if an Act of the Oireachtas can alter or modify the name of the High Court whatever jurisdiction it may be exercising".

Article 34.3.2

JURISDICTION TO CONSIDER CONSTITUTIONAL VALIDITY OF LAWS: PRINCIPLES OF JUDICIAL REVIEW

2° Save as otherwise provided by this Article, the jurisdiction of the High Court shall extend to the question of the validity of any law having regard to the provisions of this Constitution, and no such question shall be raised (whether by pleading, argument or otherwise) in any Court established under this or any other Article of this Constitution other than the High Court or the Supreme Court.

2° Taobh amuigh de chás dá socraítear a mhalairt leis an Airteagal seo, beidh dlínse ag an Ard-Chúirt maidir leis an gceist sin bail a bheith nó gan a bheith ar aon dlí áirithe ag féachaint d'fhorálacha an Bhunreachta seo, agus ní cead aon cheist den sórt sin a tharraingt anuas (trí phléadáil ná argóint ná eile) i gCúirt a bith, arna bunú faoin Airteagal seo nó faoi aon Airteagal eile den Bhunreacht seo, seachas an Ard-Chúirt nó an Chúirt Uachtarach.

1922 Provision

This provision reproduces substantially the first sentence of Article 65 of the 1922 Constitution.[1] The saver refers to laws envisaged by Article 34.3.3.

(A) JURISDICTION

"Law" in this context means a post-1937 statute

The expression "law", although not accompanied by the explicit indication that what is meant is "a law enacted by the Oireachtas established by the Constitution" - i.e. a post-1937 statute[2] - is to be so understood. This is clear from the Supreme Court's view of Article 40.4.3 contained in the judgment delivered by Walsh J in *The State (Sheerin) v Kennedy*,[3] which disentangled authoritatively several expressions found in the Constitution and frequently used as though synonymous:

> "The words "invalidate" and "invalid" and "validity", when used in reference to a law, appear in a number of places in the Constitution [he recited several instances]... In Article 26... the phrase "repugnant to this Constitution" appears twice in reference to Bills which have passed both Houses of the Oireachtas but which have not yet been signed by the President and have not, therefore, become law. Article 50..., which provides for the carrying over of laws in force in Saorstát Éireann immediately prior to the date of the coming into operation of the

[1] The draft Constitution of 1937 originally envisaged that the Supreme Court alone would have jurisdiction to pronounce on the constitutionality of any law. This was later changed and the jurisdiction of the High Court was re-instated.

[2] Or statutory instrument made pursuant to such a law: *The State (Gilliland) v Governor of Mountjoy Prison* [1987] IR 201; [1987] ILRM 278. On the other hand, it seems that a statutory instrument made after 1937, but pursuant to a pre-1937 law is not a "law" for the purposes of Article 34.3.2: see *Keady v Garda Commissioner* [1992] 2 IR 197; [1992] ILRM 312 (semble).

[3] [1966] IR 379. See below at pp. 525-526 for a doubt as to whether the analysis of usage contained in *Sheerin's* case ought to be applied throughout the Constitution.

Constitution, excludes laws or the provisions thereof which are "inconsistent" with the Constitution...[4]

These different words and terms in the context in which they appear are not synonymous... So far as Article 50... is concerned it deals with laws which were actually in force and the only question was whether they should continue to be in force to the extent only to which they were not inconsistent with the Constitution. No question of validity arises in that context because the laws, if they are in force on the date in question, are dealt with on the basis that they are valid on that date. The situation which is being examined in that Article is whether a law which is valid on a certain date may cease to have effect because, notwithstanding its initial and original validity, it is inconsistent with the provisions of the Constitution.

In Article 26... where the term "repugnant" occurs, what is being dealt with is not a law but something which will only become a law if signed by the President. There the term "repugnant" is used in relation to something which is in effect a proposal in the sense that it expresses the will of Dáil Éireann and Seanad Éireann that it should be law. Unless and until it becomes law it could not be questioned as such and therefore the question of validity as a law would not yet arise.

Article 28.3.3 expressly refers to a law enacted by the Oireachtas and therefore excludes any other law, and the Oireachtas in question is the Oireachtas set up by the Constitution. What is dealt with in that section therefore is the validity of a law of the Oireachtas.

Articles 34 and 40, where the law referred to is not expressly referred to as a law of the Oireachtas, in my view must be treated as meaning that the validity in question is a validity to be determined by the provisions of the Constitution in respect of something purporting to have been done within the terms of the Constitution and within the powers conferred by the Constitution. I think it is clear from these various provisions of the Constitution that the laws referred to are statutory provisions, as distinct from non-statutory law, and the validity of any statute can only be examined in the light of the powers of the parliament which enacted it. The Oireachtas established by the Constitution is the only parliament which is, or was, subject to the provisions of the Constitution and therefore the question of determining the validity of a law having regard to the provisions of the Constitution can only refer to laws enacted by the Oireachtas established by the Constitution."

In *The State (Gilliland) v Governor of Mountjoy Prison*[5] the Supreme Court held that the word "law" in Article 40.4.3 (review of law authorising a person's detention) included statutory instruments giving effect to post-1937 statutes as well as such statutes themselves. It may be that this interpretation of the word "law" in Article 40.4.3 is peculiar to that sub-section; but if not, and if it is to be so understood throughout the Constitution, it would follow that only the High Court and Supreme Court have jurisdiction to consider the constitutionality of such statutory instruments.[6]

[4] The judge at this point referred to the corresponding distinction in the Irish text.

[5] [1987] IR 201; [1987] ILRM 278.

[6] In any event there must be some doubt as to whether the District and Circuit Courts are enabled to declare a statutory instrument invalid (even on non-constitutional grounds) in view of the jurisdictional limits imposed by s 25 of the Courts (Supplemental Provisions) Act 1961: see *Greaney v Scully* [1981] ILRM 340.

Review of pre-Constitution laws

The judicial review power which Article 34.3.2 explicitly creates applies thus only to post-1937 Acts of the Oireachtas. But judicial review can operate also in respect of pre-Constitution law, whether statute law or common law, through the joint effect of Article 50 and Article 34. Article 50 continues in force the pre-existing corpus of laws of both kinds "to the extent to which they are not inconsistent" with the Constitution; and Article 34.3.1 gives the High Court jurisdiction to "determine all matters and questions", including, necessarily, the question whether a particular pre-Constitution law is or is not inconsistent with the Constitution. Thus challenges to pre-Constitution laws, ostensibly still in force, are not infrequently mounted in the High Court.[7] As many of the working principles of judicial review are common to both pre- and post-1937 laws, these are considered here together.

An expired Act may still be subject to judicial review

The question - never before discussed - whether an Act can escape judicial review by being made to expire was answered negatively by the Supreme Court in *Condon v Minister for Labour*.[8] The plaintiffs, who represented the Irish Bank Officials Association, were challenging the constitutional validity of the Regulation of Banks (Remuneration and Conditions of Employment) (Temporary Provisions) Act 1975; but before the issue could be tried, the defendant Minister made an order by which the Act expired, and then applied for the dismissal of the plaintiff's case on the ground that it no longer disclosed a cause of action. The Supreme Court refused the dismissal; O'Higgins CJ said:

> "Serious consequences could ensue if this Court pronounced that temporary legislation of this kind should be immune from judicial review merely because it had expired before the question of its validity could be examined. All legislation passed by the Oireachtas is presumed to be valid. If the Oireachtas were free to enact temporary legislation creating offences and providing for serious penalties (as this legislation does) and if that legislation, on its expiry, escaped examination in the courts, a form of legislative intimidation could be exercised. However, a more serious aspect is that, by permitting such to happen, this Court would be failing to exercise that vigilance and care upon which constitutional rights and guarantees depend for their protection. In my view, this Court could not countenance such a development."

Bills are reviewable only in Article 26 procedure

Legislative proposals which have passed both Houses of the Oireachtas as Bills, but which have not yet received the signature of the President which will convert them into Acts (or "laws"), are subject to judicial review in the special conditions of Article 26, but *only* in those conditions. There is no jurisdiction in any court to consider the constitutionality of a Bill other than one referred to the Supreme Court by the President under that Article, nor of a Bill which is at an earlier stage of its progress through the Houses of the Oireachtas. In *Wireless Dealers Association v Fair Trade Commission*[9] the High Court and the Supreme Court refused to consider granting an injunction to restrain the Minister for Industry and Commerce from sponsoring in the Seanad a Bill which had

[7] Some examples of this jurisdiction include *Byrne v Ireland* [1972] IR 241; *King v Attorney General* [1981] IR 233; *Cashman v Clifford* [1989] IR 121; [1990] ILRM 200 and *McKinley v Minister for Defence* [1992] 2 IR 333.

[8] [1981] IR 62.

[9] Supreme Court, 14 March 1956.

passed the Dáil and whose contents were alleged by the plaintiffs to be unconstitutional. This approach has been consistently followed in the subsequent cases. In *Finn v Minister for the Environment*[10] the Supreme Court refused to entertain proceedings intended to prevent the Eighth Amendment of the Constitution Bill, 1983, which had passed both Houses of the Oireachtas, from being submitted to referendum; the plaintiff's point was apparently that the proposed amendment was of uncertain effect and thus inherently repugnant to the constitutional order. O'Higgins CJ said that, apart from Article 26 cases, the Court had no jurisdiction to construe or review any Bill, whatever its nature, and no power to interfere with the legislative process. Likewise, in *Crotty v An Taoiseach*[11] both Barrington J in the High Court and Griffin J in the Supreme Court said that the courts had no jurisdiction to review the constitutionality of a Bill, save in the context of an Article 26 reference. These views were also echoed by both Hederman and McCarthy JJ in *Slattery v An Taoiseach*[12] where the plaintiffs had sought to restrain the holding of the referendum which led to the 11th Amendment of the Constitution Act 1992, with both the former observing that the courts had no jurisdiction to restrain the "operation of legislative and constitutional procedures which are in train."

Exclusion of courts other than the High Court and the Supreme Court from judicial review of post-1937 laws

The practical importance of the *Sheerin* judgment in the context of Article 34.3.2 lies in its bearing on the latter part of this sub-section:

> "... and no such question shall be raised (whether by pleading, argument or otherwise) in any court established under this or any other Article of this Constitution other than the High Court or the Supreme Court."

This provision, which resembles the second sentence of the old Article 65, prevents the Circuit Court and the District Court - and also the Court of Criminal Appeal,[13] and the Special Criminal Court - from considering the constitutional validity of a post-1937 statute (though, by implication, they are not prevented from considering the question whether a pre-Constitution statute or rule of law is inconsistent with the Constitution).

In *Foyle Fisheries Commission v Gallen*[14] the defendant in a fisheries prosecution induced the Circuit Court to state a case for the Supreme Court on the question whether the Foyle Fisheries Act 1952, was constitutionally valid; but the Supreme Court "declined to consider such a question unless it is raised properly in proceedings appropriate for the purpose" - i.e. not only could the defendant not have the issue decided in the Circuit Court, but was not even permitted to use the Circuit Court proceedings as a base from which to bring the matter before a court which would have jurisdiction to

[10] [1983] IR 154.

[11] [1987] IR 713; [1987] ILRM 400. See also *MhicMathúna v Ireland, The Irish Times*, 10 June 1986.

[12] [1993] 1 IR 286.

[13] In *The People (Director of Public Prosecutions) v Tuite* (1983) 2 Frewen 175 McCarthy J said that Article 34.3.2 evidently precluded the Court of Criminal Appeal from entertaining questions of constitutional validity. The statute in question was the Criminal Law (Jurisdiction) Act 1976, and as the validity of that Act had been upheld by the Supreme Court following a reference under Article 26, it was in any event immune from constitutional challenge under Article 34.3.3. (See also *The People (Attorney General) v Conmey* [1975] IR 341 at pp. 460-461). On the other hand, in *The People (Director of Public Prosecutions) v JT* (1988) 3 Frewen 141, the Court of Criminal Appeal saw no jurisdictional objection to pronouncing on the constitutionality of a pre-1937 statute when it declared that s 1 of the Criminal Justice (Evidence) Act 1924, was unconstitutional.

[14] (1960) Ir Jur Rep 35.

decide the issue.[15] (Presumably the courses open to the defendant in this case might have been to institute a declaratory action against the Attorney General in the High Court, alleging the unconstitutionality of the Act; or to seek prohibition or *certiorari* against the Circuit Judge, depending on whether he was proposing to begin or had ended the hearing, which, again. would have opened the issue in the High Court.) This view was also accepted by O'Hanlon J in *Minister for Labour v Costello*[16] where he refused to allow a defendant to raise the constitutionality of a post-1937 law by way of case-stated from the District Court. This meant that a District Judge must proceed on the assumption that:

> "powers conferred on him by Act of the Oireachtas, enacted subsequent to the enactment of the Constitution of 1937 may be lawfully exercised by him unless and until that statute has been successfully impugned in proceedings appropriate for that purpose."[17]

Constitutional review of pre-1937 laws by the lower courts

Although the lower courts are, by implication, not prevented from considering the constitutional consistency of pre-Constitution laws, the mode by which this could happen is unclear. In fact, no pre-Constitution law seems yet to have been considered from the constitutional point of view by either the Circuit Court or the District Court; and, as these courts have limited and defined jurisdictions by statute, which do not include the adjudication of the constitutionality of laws of whatever kind, it seems that it would not be possible to challenge e.g. an old statute by means of a declaratory action in the Circuit Court. At the same time the judges of the lower courts take an oath to uphold the Constitution (Article 34.5.1), and, as pre-Constitution statutes naturally enjoy no presumption of consistency with a Constitution which did not exist when they were enacted, it must follow that a Circuit Court Judge or a District Judge is entitled to consider, if the point arises before him in pleading or argument, whether an old law he is being asked to apply is, in fact, consistent with the Constitution. If this proposition is correct, it would seem that words used by Carroll J in *The State (Pheasantry Ltd.) v Donnelly*[18] - she said the applicant "could not argue the constitutionality of the [Intoxicating Liquor Act 1927] in either the District Court or the Circuit Court [but] must come to the High Court in order to do so" - are too broad a statement; he could not, as a plaintiff, have taken the initiative in either of those courts to challenge the Act but as a defendant in a prosecution which rested on that Act he might have asked either court to consider its consistency with a subsequently enacted Constitution.

[15] In *In re Tivoli Cinema Ltd.* [1992] 1 IR 412; [1992] ILRM 522 Lynch J reserved the question of whether the High Court when acting exercising its appellate jurisdiction in respect of decisions of the Circuit Court could pronounce on the constitutionality of a pre-1937 law. To judge from the decisions in *Gallen* and *JT*, the answer would appear to be that there is no such bar in the case of pre-1937 laws, but Article 34.3.2 requires that, in the case of post-1937 laws, such challenges can only be commenced by means of a direct invocation of the High Court's original jurisdiction.

[16] [1988] IR 235; [1989] ILRM 485.

[17] On the other hand, in *The People (Attorney General) v McGlynn* [1967] IR 232 the Supreme Court considered the constitutionality of s 16 of the Courts of Justice Act 1947, on a case stated by the Circuit Court. This section is actually the statutory basis for the Circuit Court's power to state a case for the Supreme Court, so that it may be that the Court was considering the constitutional point in order to determine whether it had jurisdiction to determine the substantive point contained in the case stated.

[18] [1982] ILRM 512. Denham J spoke to like effect in *Coughlan v Patwell* [1993] 1 IR 31; [1992] ILRM 808, but her statement that a District Judge "cannot declare that an Act of the Oireachtas is unconstitutional" must be taken as referring to a post-1937 Act of the Oireachtas.

Constitutional duty of the lower courts to enforce constitutional rights

But even though Article 34.3.2 debars the lower courts from adjudicating upon the constitutionality of a post-1937 law, it is quite clear that the lower courts are nonetheless obliged to enforce the Constitution. Thus, in *The State (Byrne) v Frawley*[19] Henchy J said that a Circuit Court Judge should have put an end to any proceedings - irrespective of the parties' wishes - once it has been established that they have been "authoritatively declared to rest" on an unconstitutional statute. The apparent acquiescence of a party could not abrogate "the judge's duty to uphold the Constitution in his court by refusing to preside over a conclusively established unconstitutionality." Likewise, in *The People (Director of Public Prosecutions) v Lynch*[20] Walsh J ruled that District and Circuit Judges were obliged to adjudicate on the admissibility of statements said to have been obtained in violation of the accused's constitutional rights. Pointing out that judges of the District and Circuit Courts were also required to make a declaration to uphold the Constitution and the laws, Walsh J said they were:

> "not dispensed from, or expected to overlook, their constitutional obligation to uphold the Constitution in the discharge of their constitutional and legal function of administering justice."[21]

This question was authoritatively explored by Denham J in *Coughlan v Patwell*.[22] Here the District Judge had apparently refused to entertain a submission to the effect that certain evidence had been obtained in breach of the applicant's constitutional rights. While Denham J confessed that she was "unimpressed" with the merits of the applicant's case, she nonetheless held that the District Judge erred in refusing to hear the submission:

> "The District Court has a duty to act constitutionally to act in such manner as to preserve the individual's constitutional rights. If an individual as here alleges that his constitutional rights have been infringed in procedures adopted in bringing him before the court then the District Court has jurisdiction to, and indeed should, hear the submission and take such steps as it considers proper. It is not appropriate for a District Court to refuse to allow such a submission to be made to the court."

(B) PROCEDURE AND PRACTICE

The procedural machinery for testing the validity of a law (in either the restricted or the wider sense) is not prescribed by the Constitution, and the result is that a court with jurisdiction to entertain a challenge on constitutionality may do so in any procedure admissible before it in which the constitutional issue becomes relevant to the material issue.[23] Thus an application in the nature of habeas corpus can be used as the vehicle for challenging the constitutionality of a law under which the applicant is deprived of

[19] [1978] IR 326.

[20] [1982] IR 64.

[21] In *Ellis v O'Dea* [1989] IR 530 Walsh J also spoke of the "undoubted residual jurisdiction of the District Court to protect the constitutional rights of any person appearing before it." For an example of a case where the District Court enforced constitutional rights, see the report of a case where a care order was refused in one case where a five-year old child had been admitted on several occasions to hospital for illnesses and accidents because no evidence was offered to show that the parents did not offer proper guardianship and accordingly the District Judge took the view that the application was inconsistent with the constitutional guarantees of the family: see *The Irish Independent*, 3 July 1993.

[22] [1993] 1 IR 31; [1992] ILRM 808. See also *Keating v Governor of Mountjoy Prison* [1991] 1 IR 61.

[23] See especially chap. 5 (entitled "Constitutional Litigation") of Collins and O'Reilly, *Civil Proceedings and the State in Ireland: A Practitioner's Guide* (Dublin, 1989).

liberty,[24] or an application for an order of prohibition for challenging a law under which an inferior court proposes to exercise jurisdiction;[25] or an application for an injunction to restrain a course of conduct for challenging the law purporting to authorise the conduct;[26] or an application for an order of certiorari for challenging the law under which an inferior judicial or administrative authority has purported to act.[27] Moreover, anyone who finds himself in a defendant's posture in either civil or criminal proceedings in any of the superior courts can plead the unconstitutionality of a law on which the plaintiff's or prosecution's case depends.[28] In recent years the use of the declaratory action for raising constitutional challenges has grown; this is particularly appropriate and common where the challenger is trying to assert a general constitutional right, and is not more acutely affected by the challenged statute than anyone else is.[29]

Where the assertion of a constitutional right is concerned - whether or not this assertion involves challenging a statute - the courts have declared themselves ready to entertain claims even though no "statutory vesture" or specific procedure exists for raising them.[30]

Notice to the Attorney General

Order 60 r 1 of the Rules of the Superior Courts 1986, provides that the Attorney General, if not already a party, must be served with notice in any action or matter where the constitutional validity of an Act of the Oireachtas is in question, and is thereupon entitled to appear and be a party in the case,[31] so far as concerns the validity of the Act and that such notice:

> "shall state concisely the nature of the proceedings in which the question or dispute arises and the contentions of the party or parties to the proceedings."[32]

Order 60 r 2 is an innovation. It provides that in cases where *a point of constitutional interpretation* is in issue (i.e. not just cases where the constitutionality of a law has been challenged):

> "the party having carriage of the proceedings shall, if the Court so directs, serve notice upon the Attorney General."[33]

[24] See, e.g., *The State (Burke) v Lennon* [1940] IR 136; *The State (Gilliland) v Governor of Mountjoy Prison* [1987] IR 210; [1987] ILRM 287.
[25] See, e.g., *Cashman v Clifford* [1989] IR 121; [1990] ILRM 200.
[26] *Pesca Valentia Ltd. v Minister for Fisheries* [1985] IR 193.
[27] See, e.g., *The State (Lynch) v Cooney* [1982] IR 337; *The State (McEldowney) v Kelliher* [1983] IR 289 and see generally, Hogan, "*Challenging the Constitutionality of an Act of the Oireachtas by way of Certiorari*" (1982) 4 DULJ 130.
[28] See, e.g., *King v Attorney General* [1981] IR 224; *Attorney General v Paperlink Ltd.* [1984] ILRM 373; *O'Mahoney v Melia* [1989] IR 335; [1990] ILRM 14.
[29] See, e.g., *Crotty v An Taoiseach* [1987] IR 713; [1987] ILRM 400 and *McGimpsey v Ireland* [1990] 1 IR 110; [1990] ILRM 440. The question of *locus standi* in this context is considered below at pp. 438-448.
[30] See below at pp. 699-702.
[31] Curiously, the possible rights of other interested parties to be served and to appear in constitutional litigation does not appear to have been litigated in any reported case. In *O'Toole v Ireland* [1992] ILRM 218 Costello J said that Eurocontrol (an international organisation with responsibility for air safety) might have some "indirect interest" in the outcome of a challenge to the constitutionality to the Air Navigation and Transport Act 1988, but this fact did not make it a "proper party" to the proceedings:
"It seems to me that this is a constitutional action in which properly Ireland, the Attorney General and the Minister for Tourism and Transport are joined and that it is not proper to join an organisation like Eurocontrol that is not involved in the dispute in relation to the constitutionality of the Act."
[32] In *The State (Hunt) v O'Donovan* [1975] IR 39; (1973) 107 ILTR 53, however, where counsel for the prison governor told the Court that he appeared also for the Attorney General, Finlay J "did not deem it necessary to require" the service of such a notice on the Attorney General in regard to the fact that an Act of the Oireachtas was being challenged.
[33] This has occurred in a number of cases, see, e.g., *Society for the Protection of Unborn Children (Ire.) Ltd. v Coogan* [1989] IR 734.

Order 60 r 3 provides that such notice shall state concisely "the contention or respective contentions of the party or parties to the proceedings".

In *R. v R.*[34] Gannon J said of the equivalent provisions of O 60 of the 1962 Rules that they seemed to require that, before it became operative, "a dispute or question must have arisen involving an adverse contention". In *The State (D.C.) v Midland Health Board*[35] Keane J said that in view of the Supreme Court's decision in *The State (Sheerin) v Kennedy*,[36] O 60 r 1 did not apply "where the statute under attack was enacted prior to the coming into force of the Constitution". But it is questionable whether the construction of the word "law" in the *Sheerin* context should be applied here too, as the object of the rule is presumably to allow the Attorney General to appear in defence of a public statute ostensibly in force whatever its date. The view of Keane J was not shared by Carroll J in *The State (D.) v Groarke*.[37] Here the applicants - who had sought to litigate the constitutionality of the Children Act 1908 - had claimed that they were not required to serve an O 60 notice on the Attorney General. Carroll J would not accept this argument, saying that the purpose of O 60:

> "is to enable the Attorney General to argue for the constitutionality not only of post-constitution statutes, but also of pre-Constitution ones as well. A large body of our statute law dates from before the Constitution. I cannot accept that O 60 should be interpreted so that it would be possible for a pre-Constitution statute to be declared unconstitutional in an action between two private individuals without the knowledge of the Attorney General."

This view appears to have implicitly endorsed by the Supreme Court in *Re Ellis' Application*.[38] In the High Court, O'Hanlon J had upheld the constitutionality of s 2 of the Trial of Lunatics Act 1883 in proceedings where no O 60 notice had been directed. The Supreme Court doubted the propriety of this procedure, with Finlay CJ observing that the failure to serve such a notice "must raise significant doubts and queries as to the validity of the procedures leading to the making of [the] order" upholding the validity of the legislation.

A constitutional complainant need not be present in person

In *L'Henryenat v Ireland*[39] the State for some reason took the point that (as Carroll J stated it in her judgment):

> "where a plaintiff challenges an Act of the Oireachtas and alleges that his personal rights guaranteed by the Constitution are infringed, he should attend in person so as to satisfy the court that his complaints are real and that he is still alive."

The plaintiff here, although not present in person, was represented by solicitor and counsel, who presented his case "on the facts admitted and on the evidence adduced". Carroll J said:

> "He is entitled to have his case decided on that evidence. I do not know of any legal principle which requires the physical presence of a plaintiff... in prosecuting a case even when it concerns his constitutional rights. It must be assumed that when solicitor and counsel appear they do so on the express instructions of their client."

[34] [1984] IR 296.
[35] [1986] IR 273.
[36] [1966] IR 379.
[37] [1988] IR 187.
[38] [1990] 2 IR 291.
[39] [1983] IR 193.

Ordinary law of evidence applies

The ordinary law of evidence applies in the context of judicial review in the same way as elsewhere. It is, however, worth noting that in *Norris v Attorney General*,[40] in which the plaintiff challenged nineteenth-century statutory provisions penalising male homosexual behaviour, the dissenting judges in the Supreme Court (Henchy and McCarthy JJ) drew attention to the fact that the expert evidence called on the plaintiff's behalf - unanimously suggesting that these laws were needlessly oppressive - had not been contradicted by any evidence called on behalf of the Attorney General; and said that in these circumstances "the trial judge was bound in law to reject the Attorney General's defence and to uphold, at least in part, the plaintiff's case" (*per* Henchy J).[41] Similarly in *M. v M.*[42] (though here no statute was under challenge) the Supreme Court held that, where evidence given in the High Court as to a husband's impotence had been neither challenged nor contradicted, the trial judge was not free to decide in a sense adverse to the evidence because of his intuition that the evidence had been collusively mounted.

Judicial willingness to depart from ordinary court procedures where necessary to protect constitutional rights

In *Shannon v Ireland*[43] the plaintiff, who challenged the constitutionality of Part III of the Extradition Act 1965, sought to tender fresh affidavit evidence during the course of the hearing. This was prohibited by O 39 r 1 of the Rules of the Superior Courts 1962 (now reproduced in the 1986 Rules), which required a separate preliminary application to admit such evidence. Finlay P. agreed that "in any ordinary litigation between parties" such evidence could not be admitted, save by consent. But this was not any ordinary litigation; the plaintiff had claimed that his proposed extradition to Northern Ireland would be unconstitutional. Finlay P. therefore decided to admit the evidence, saying:

> "It seems to me that, on the making of such a claim, the Court has a special duty to ensure that all the material facts which can be adduced in evidence before it are adduced, and that it has all the material necessary to secure to the plaintiff his constitutional rights - even if that is inconsistent with the ordinary and desirable procedures of the Court."

Precedents not necessarily reliable?

In one case from the Supreme Court's pre-activist epoch, and not now of much authority, the Court enjoined caution in presenting, in cases of the constitutionality of a Bill or Act arguments based on the Court's finding in a previous case. In *Attorney General v Southern Industrial Trust*[44] the Court said, *per* Lavery J:

> "In the first place, it should be said that where this Court has examined the provisions of a particular Act or Bill and pronounced upon its validity or invalidity it is not always helpful to rely on the decision in another case because particular provi-

[40] [1984] IR 36.

[41] The proposition that univocal, uncontradicted evidence must always be accepted by a court is, perhaps, not so compelling where (as in *Norris's* case) the line separating hard evidence of facts from softer, though "expert" evidence of impression is not clear. McCarthy J summarised the *Norris* evidence as having been about "whether or not an act or acts prohibited by the impugned sections are, in fact, part of the make-up of an exclusively homosexual male; and are or are not required by public order and morality or any other facet" of the common good.

[42] [1979] ILRM 160.

[43] [1984] IR 268; [1984] ILRM 539.

[44] (1960) 94 ILTR 161.

sions of the law there in question may have determined the decision. Statements of principle are, of course, decisive and binding, but otherwise other decisions do not help and particularly decisions on laws impugned as violating different Articles of the Constitution."

In connection with these dicta it must be remembered that the Court in the *Southern Industrial Trust* case was at pains to distinguish its position on Article 43 from that which it had taken up in *Buckley v Attorney General.*[45] The distinction is not very successful; and the decision has been in recent years to some extent disapproved.[46]

In fact, contrary to the suggestion of Lavery J, there is every reason to suppose that the Supreme Court does regard other constitutional decisions which are *in pari materia* with the issue under consideration as helpful, relevant and, generally speaking, binding. *Desmond v Glackin (No.2)*[47] is an example of modern practice which is in point. Here the Supreme Court considered that the statutory provision under challenge was practically indistinguishable from that which had been invalidated in the earlier case of *In re Haughey* [48] and that it was bound by the *ratio decidendi* of that decision and "saw no reason to depart from that decision" and "the principles which underlined it."[49]

Persuasive authority of foreign decisions

It may be noted, finally, that the categories of judicial decision which the courts are willing to regard as persuasive authorities in reviewing legislation have recently received a very notable extension. The admission of US decisions - particularly of the US Supreme Court - has always been fairly common,[50] but up to lately neither the Bench nor the Bar have relied on cases from other foreign jurisdictions in which the principle of judicial review on constitutional criteria is known. However, in *Murphy v Attorney General,*[51] decided in October 1979, Hamilton J relied not only on US precedent in declaring unconstitutional the provisions of the Income Tax Act 1967, which taxed a married couple more heavily than a pair of single people, but also on a decision of the German Federal Constitutional Court of 1957, and a decision of the Italian Constitutional Court of 1976, each of which declared invalid similar taxation provisions as discriminating against married couples. The Supreme Court on appeal from Hamilton J in January 1980 also briefly reviewed these authorities, though it found them not relevant. There seems no reason, if language difficulties can be overcome, why the Irish courts might not receive constitutional decisions from neighbouring European democracies with comparable social and political systems as they do US decisions. In *Murphy's* case the citation

[45] [1950] IR 67.

[46] See below at pp. 1069-1073.

[47] Supreme Court, 30 July 1992.

[48] [1971] IR 217. In *Haughey* the Supreme Court had invalidated s 3(4) of the Committee of Public Accounts of Dáil Éireann (Privilege and Procedure) Act 1970 and in *Desmond (No.2)*, the Supreme Court considered that the provisions of s 10(5) of the Companies Act 1990 were for all practical purposes identical to the earlier sub-section of the 1970 Act. See further at p. 629.

[49] See also *Ambiorix Ltd. v Minister for Environment (No.1)* [1992] 1 IR 277 (where the Supreme Court considered itself bound by an earlier decision pronouncing on a question of constitutional doctrine). But for a discussion of the decline in respect for the doctrine of precedent, see pp. 534-538.

[50] Examples (by no means exhaustive) include *O'Byrne v Minister for Finance* [1959] IR 1; *Quinn's Supermarket Ltd. v Attorney General* [1972] IR 1; *McGee v Attorney General* [1974] IR 284; *The State (Healy) v Donoghue* [1976] IR 325; *The State (M.) v Attorney General* [1979] IR 73; *King v Attorney General* [1981] IR 233; *Murphy v Attorney General* [1982] IR 241; *O'B. v S* [1984] IR 316; *Clancy v Ireland* [1988] IR 326. But for reasoned refusals to follow US authority, see *The State (DPP) v Walsh* [1981] IR 412; *Ryan v Director of Public Prosecutions* [1989] IR 399; *The People (Director of Public Prosecutions) v Kenny* [1990] 2 IR 110; [1990] ILRM 569 and the judgment of Finlay CJ in *Attorney General v Hamilton (No.2)* [1993] ILRM 821.

[51] [1982] IR 241.

of German and Italian material was peculiarly apposite, as the constitutional provision here in question - Article 40.1 (the guarantee of equality before the law) - has an exact counterpart in the German and Italian Constitutions; and those two countries, along with Spain and Ireland, are the only ones in the European Communities to combine constitutional declarations of fundamental rights with a system of judicial review of legislation.[52]

Potential influence of decisions of the European Court of Human Rights and the European Court of Justice

With the ever-increasing importance of the decisions of the European Court of Human Rights, together with the pronouncements of the European Court of Justice in areas touching on human rights and civil liberties, it is not surprising that the Irish courts have begun to be influenced by the jurisprudence of both European Courts.[53] In *Norris v Attorney General*[54] Henchy J, for one, was willing to admit of the "persuasive influence" of the European Court of Human Rights. Likewise in *Desmond v Glackin (No.1)*[55] O'Hanlon J followed an earlier judgment of the European Court of Human Rights, saying that while:

> "The Convention itself is not a code of legal principles which are enforceable in the domestic courts.....but this does not prevent the judgment of the European Court [of Human Rights] from having a persuasive effect when considering the common law regarding contempt of court in the light of constitutional guarantees of freedom of expression contained in our Constitution of 1937."

And while O'Hanlon J spoke only in terms of freedom of expression, it would seem that there is no reason why decisions of the Court of Human Rights in other areas of the Convention with similar or analogous guarantees to those contained in the Constitution - such as the right to life, personal liberty, respect for family life - should not be a source of influence for the Irish courts.

(C) Availability of Interim Relief

The circumstances in which a plaintiff can obtain interim relief restraining the enforcement of an allegedly unconstitutional statute or an invalid administrative decisions are somewhat unclear, although such relief would appear to be available, at least in principle.

This problem appears to have surfaced first in *The State (Attorney General) v Mangan*[56] where a District Judge adjourned summonses under the Customs Consolidation Act 1876, pending the determination of a High Court action[57] on the constitutionality of that Act. On appeal against orders of *certiorari* and *mandamus* obtained by the Attorney General against the Judge, the Supreme Court held that this adjournment was properly within his discretion, and that he was entitled to take notice of the fact that proceedings were pending which questioned the constitutionality of the law he was required to

[52] It may also be noted that there is now a small body of academic writings drawing attention to the potential utility for an Irish audience of continental constitutional decisions, see, e.g., Kelly, "*Equality before the Law in Three European Jurisdictions*" (1983) 18 Ir Jur 259

[53] Decisions of the Court of Justice of the European Communities are, of course, in any event absolutely binding on the Irish courts. The same is not true of the European Convention on Human Rights, the legal status of which in domestic law is considered at pp. 296-298.

[54] [1984] IR 36.

[55] [1992] ILRM 490.

[56] (1961) Ir Jur Rep 35.

[57] The constitutional action was *Melling v Ó Mathghamhna* [1962] IR 1.

enforce. The law here in issue was a pre-1937 statute and it might be argued that the principle admitted by the Supreme Court here would not be applicable to a case involving an Act of the Oireachtas and that a District Judge would be obliged to treat the latter in all respects as valid until such time as declared invalid by a superior court; yet in *The State (Llewellyn) v Ua Donnchadha*,[58] in which not an adjournment but an insistence on going ahead with a summons under an impugned (post-1937) Act was in issue, the Supreme Court attached no visible significance to the distinction. Walsh J said:

> "*Mangan's* case does not deal with the situation which has arisen in this case where the District Justice has elected to proceed rather than to adjourn, but it is authority for the proposition that this is a matter in which the District Justice has a discretion and that an order of *mandamus* will not be made unless it can be shown that, in the exercise of that discretion, he has acted outside his jurisdiction by taking into account considerations which he is not entitled to take into account or has exceeded his jurisdiction in some other way. The corollary would appear to be that an order of prohibition would not be made against him either if he elected to proceed, provided that he had not exceeded his jurisdiction.
>
> However, insofar as this may be taken as indicating that the question of whether or not to adjourn proceedings pending the outcome of a challenge to the validity of legislation is a matter entirely for the discretion of the lower court in question, it would seem that, for reasons to be discussed presently, this passage does not fully represent the modern law."

The matter was more fully exposed by Murphy J in *Nova Media Services Ltd. v Minister for Posts & Telegraphs*,[59] a case where the plaintiff company had operated an unlicensed radio station. Following the seizure of radio equipment, they initiated proceedings to challenge the constitutionality of that Act but also sought an interlocutory injunction restraining the defendants from any further seizure. Murphy J accepted that they had made out a stateable case on their constitutional arguments,[60] but refused the relief sought on the ground that the balance of convenience did not lie in their favour. Although he accepted that they might suffer considerable loss if no injunction was granted, this was outweighed by the:

> "considerable damage which might be caused to the common good by the interference with statutory controls and regulations [which might] be very considerable indeed and, certainly... could never be assessed in monetary terms."

It would only be:

> "in the most extraordinary circumstances that the courts would intervene to prevent the Minister or Government agencies from exercising a function conferred upon him or them by the express terms of a statute made for the control of a public resource and for the benefit of the public good."[61]

[58] [1973] IR 151; (1974) 108 ILTR 49.

[59] [1984] ILRM 161.

[60] I.e., that the Act interfered with constitutional rights of property and free speech and that the seizure of goods without a court order was incompatible with the guarantee of trial in due course of law contained in Article 38.1

[61] See also the companion case, *Sunshine Radio Productions Ltd. v Attorney General* [1984] ILRM 170, where the facts and relief sought were similar. Murphy J refused to grant an interlocutory injunction, saying it was impossible to see how the court could direct "a Government Minister to return equipment to a plaintiff to enable that plaintiff to commit what is on the face of it a criminal offence." Likewise in *Hand v Dublin Corporation*, *The Irish Times*, 11 December 1986, Murphy J refused to grant restraining the operation of the Casual Trading Act 1980, pending a challenge to its validity. The judge added that it was only in the most exceptional circumstances that the courts would restrain a Minister from carrying out his statutory duty and that, in any event, the plaintiff would be entitled to damages if they were successful at the trial of the action.

Interlocutory injunction pending the outcome of constitutional challenge

This issue was taken a step further by the Supreme Court in *Pesca Valentia Ltd. v Minister for Fisheries*.[62] The plaintiffs had been granted licences in respect of their fishing fleet under s 222B of the Fisheries (Consolidation) Act 1959, as inserted by s 2 of the Fisheries (Amendment) Act 1983. These licences were subject to the condition that 75% of the crew were either Irish nationals or nationals of another member state of the European Community. The plaintiffs pleaded inability to comply with this condition,[63] and, pending a challenge to the constitutionality of the Act[64] sought interlocutory relief. The Supreme Court rejected the submission that its earlier decision in *The State (Llewellyn) v Ua Donnchadha* precluded the granting of interim relief in constitutional actions. Finlay CJ said:

> "It is... the duty of the courts to protect persons against the invasion of their constitutional rights or against unconstitutional action. It would seem wholly inconsistent with that duty if the Court were to be without power in an appropriate case to restrain by injunction an action against a person which found its authority in a statutory provision which might eventually be found to be invalid having regard to the Constitution. In particular, it seems to me that this power must exist in an appropriate case where the form of action is under a penal section and involves conviction and the imposition of a penalty for the commission of a criminal offence."

Here the balance of convenience clearly favoured the plaintiffs,[65] as it was not clear that they could recover damages for the losses which they would suffer by being convicted and penalised under an unconstitutional statute[66] and, secondly, by being effectively pre-

[62] [1985] IR 93; [1986] ILRM 68. This is the first *written* judgment in which the issue of the availability of interim relief in a constitutional context appears to have been squarely addressed. But cf. *Attorney General v Paperlink Ltd., The Irish Times*, 15 February 1983 where the defendants had attempted to operate a postal service, despite the existence of a post monopoly which had been statutorily conferred on the Department of Posts and Telegraphs by the Post Office Act 1908. Although the defendants were then challenging the constitutionality of that monopoly, the Attorney General nonetheless sought an injunction restraining them from infringing the Act. The Supreme Court refused to grant such an injunction, as O'Higgins CJ said that if the application were to have been granted, the defendants' business would have been destroyed, even if they succeeded at the trial of the action. In this case the consequence of not granting the injunction were not as serious as far as the Minister was concerned and the balance of convenience clearly lay with the defendants. The defendants' action ultimately failed: see [1984] ILRM 383.

[63] The company engaged in deep-sea fishing and Irish fishermen were, apparently, unwilling to be away for the lengthy periods which this involved. See also *Beara Fisheries Ltd. v Minister for Marine* [1987] IR 413.

[64] This challenge was abandoned at the trial of the action and the plaintiffs' arguments instead concentrated on the contention that the nationality requirements were incompatible with European Community law. This challenge ultimately failed: see *Pesca Valentia Ltd. v Minister for Fisheries (No.2)* [1990] 2 IR 305.

[65] Other plaintiffs have not been as fortunate. In *Cooke v Minister for Communications*, *The Irish Times Law Report*, February 20, 1989 the Supreme Court (in an *ex tempore* judgment) refused to grant interim relief restraining interference by the authorities with the activities of an illegal radio operator. Although Walsh J recognised that the plaintiff had made out an arguable case and the inconvenience manifest (the Minister had made an order under the Radio and Television Act 1988 directing that the plaintiff's electricity supply be terminated), interim relief was refused. In *Grange Developments Ltd. v Dublin County Council (No.4)* [1989] IR 377 Murphy J recognised that there was some "apparent discrepancy" between *Pesca Valentia* and *Cooke*, but nevertheless, applying "ordinary grounds of balance of convenience, stateable case and irreparable damage", refused to grant an interlocutory injunction in a case where the defendants wished to challenge the constitutionality of legislation requiring them to pay compensation to the plaintiff. See also *Staunton v Voluntary Health Insurance Co.*, High Court, 22 February 1989.

[66] This is a point which is sometimes overlooked, since it is by no means certain that a person who has suffered loss by reason of the operation of an unconstitutional statute is entitled to damages: see, e.g., *Pine Valley Developments Ltd. v Minister for Environment* [1987] IR 23; [1987] ILRM 747.

vented from carrying on fishing with their existing crews pending the determination of the action.[67]

Executive restrained in Crotty's case from ratifying the Single European Act pending the outcome of a referendum.

The most spectacular example of an injunction of this kind is to be found in *Crotty v An Taoiseach*,[68] where Barrington J restrained the Government from ratifying the Single European Act.[69] The plaintiff had attacked the constitutionality of the European Communities (Amendment) Act 1986 - which gives effect in domestic law to Titles I and II of the Single European Act - on the ground, inter alia, that it was not "necessitated" by Treaty obligations and so not protected by the provisions of Article 29.4.3. Barrington J agreed that a stateable case had been made out by the plaintiff, but the issue of the balance of convenience presented him with much greater difficulty. On the one hand, the Government had agreed with the other Governments of the Community that the Act should be ratified by 1 January 1987, and the Government's failure to ratify by that date would cause serious embarrassment.[70] Yet if the Government was to be allowed to ratify (the other member states all having already done so), the Single European Act would enter into force as an amendment to the Treaty of Rome and would now become, by virtue of Article 29.4.3, thereafter unassailable. He referred to *Acciaierie San Michele SpA v High Authority*[71] where the European Court of Justice ruled that it could not go behind the instrument of ratification of a Member State;[72] thus this might mean that it would be no use to plead unconstitutionality before either the Irish courts or the Court of Justice. In these unusual circumstances - and not withstanding the presumption of constitutionality attaching to the European Communities (Amendment) Act 1986, and to the exercise of executive functions by the Government - he felt obliged to preserve the status quo by granting the injunction sought.[73]

(D) LOCUS STANDI

The question of *locus standi* of a party wishing to challenge the validity of an Act of the Oireachtas (or the constitutionality of a pre-Constitution statute) has received much con-

[67] However, the terms of the injunction were varied by the Supreme Court in order to permit the authorities to inspect the boats in order to determine whether any breaches of the licences had occurred (with a view to possible prosecution afterwards if the substantive action failed). As to whether an injunction can be granted against Ireland, see p. 1153.

[68] [1987] IR 713; [1987] ILRM 400.

[69] On this see above at pp. 282-284.

[70] The case was not finally disposed of until April 1987, with the result that the Government failed to ratify the Single Act by the deadline of 1 January 1987. Final ratification took place on 24 June 1987 following a referendum.

[71] [1967] ECR 1.

[72] The Court of Justice said:

> "It is clear from the instruments of ratification whereby all the Member States bound themselves in an identical manner, that all the States have adhered to the Treaty on the same conditions definitively, and without any reservations other than those set out in the supplementary protocols, and that therefore any claim by a national of a Member State questioning such adherence would be contrary to the system of Community law."

[73] The Court of Justice has ruled that, as a matter of Community law, the national procedural law of each Member State must allow for the granting of such interim relief in cases where this is necessary to protect Community law rights: see *R. v Transport Secretary, ex parte Factortame Ltd.* [1990] ECR I-2433; [1990] 3 WLR 852. It may be observed that some Constitutions expressly provide for the granting of interim relief in such circumstances: see, e.g., Article 32 of the German Constitution. For example, in the *Federal Abortions Laws* decision of 4th August 1992, the German Constitutional Court utilised *Factortame* -type principles in order to stay the coming into force of a contentious law pending a full challenge as to its constitutionality.

sideration in a series of recent decisions. Although the law in this area is still evolving and lacks precision, the following principles seem to emerge. First, the courts will only entertain a constitutional challenge where it is demonstrated that the litigants' rights have either been infringed or are threatened.[74] Secondly, the courts will only listen to arguments based on the plaintiff's own personal situation and will generally not allow arguments based on a *jus tertii*.[75] However, since "every member of the public has an interest in seeing that the fundamental law of the State is not defeated"[76] the courts will permit a citizen to challenge an actual or threatened breach of a constitutional norm where there is no other suitable plaintiff or where the threatened breach is likely to affect all citizens in general.[77] However, before pursuing these issues, it is first necessary to consider the position of non-citizens and juristic persons.

Non-citizens

It is possible that a distinction may be drawn, in this connection, between citizens and non-citizens. In *The State (Nicolaou) v An Bord Uchtála*[78] a British subject was challenging the constitutionality of the Adoption Act 1952, via an application for *certiorari* against the Adoption Board based on the alleged failure of the Act to respect the rights of a natural father (himself); and the Supreme Court, while it fully considered his case on its merits (even though rejecting it), said it "expressly reserved for another and more appropriate case consideration of the effect of non-citizenship upon the interpretation of [Articles 40,41 and 42] and also the right of a non-citizen to challenge the validity of an Act of the Oireachtas having regard to the provisions of the Constitution". The question had been dealt with somewhat inconclusively in the High Court, as the Attorney General, as a matter of policy, had expressly refrained from arguing that the applicant, as a non-citizen, had lesser rights under the Constitution than a citizen. The judges seemed to lean against the proposition that citizenship or the lack of it was immaterial. Teevan J said:

> "In my view it is one for discernment according to the particular circumstances. Circumstances may exist by reason of which it would be no more than impertinent for a non-citizen to attack the constitutionality of one of our statutes, or by reason of which it would otherwise be necessary or prudent to take the point. In the present case the Attorney General did not consider it necessary or politic to do so, and, with respect to the opposite opinion, I think this should be accepted and that the issues might be determined without reference to the prosecutor's non-citizenship."

Henchy J referred to Articles 40.1 and 40.3 - which assert rights of the "citizen" but upon which Nicolaou had relied, claiming that for the purpose of these sections "citizen" was equivalent to "person" - and holding that he was not a citizen for that purpose, said:

> "I hold that neither Article 40.1 nor Article 40.3 confers on the prosecutor any constitutional rights, and that accordingly it is not open to him to show that the Act or any part of it is repugnant to Article 40.1 or Article 40.3."

[74] *Cahill v Sutton* [1980] IR 269.

[75] *Norris v Attorney General* [1984] IR 36; *Madigan v Attorney General* [1986] ILRM 136.

[76] Per Walsh J in *Society for the Protection of Unborn Children (Ire.) Ltd. v Coogan* [1989] IR 734.

[77] *Crotty v An Taoiseach* [1987] IR 713; [1987] ILRM 400; *Society for the Protection of Unborn Children (Ire.) Ltd. v Coogan* [1989] IR 734; [1990] ILRM] 70; *McGimpsey v Ireland* [1990] 1 IR 110; [1990] ILRM 440.

[78] [1966] IR 567; (1968) 102 ILTR 1. For a discussion of the potential interaction of the Constitution and the conflict of laws, see pp. 487-493 and the entitlement of non-citizens to rely on the personal rights provisions of the Constitution, pp. 679-682.

He did, however, consider on its merits the claim of Nicolaou based on Articles 41 and 42, the assertions of which do not specify "citizens" as the beneficiaries of the rights asserted.

On the other hand, in *Kostan v Ireland*[79] a Bulgarian national, master of a Bulgarian fishing vessel which had breached Irish exclusive fishery limits, successfully sued for a declaration that the section making possible summary trial for this offence was constitutionally invalid; the judgment of McWilliam J does not disclose that any point was taken as to the plaintiffs right to bring such an action. And in *L'Henryenat v Ireland*,[80] a similar case, the French master of a French trawler succeeded in having provisions of the Fisheries (Consolidation) Act 1959, declared invalid for infringing Articles 38.1, 40.3 and 40.4.1, again without any point apparently having been taken as to the relevance of his alien status to his *locus standi* for bringing such proceedings.[81]

The courts now appear to lean against drawing any distinction based on citizenship for the purpose of *locus standi*, at least in cases involving individual rights. In *In re Article 26 and the Electoral (Amendment) Bill 1983*,[82] the Supreme Court drew a distinction between Articles 12, 16 and 47 which provide the mechanism "by which the people may choose their rulers and their legislators", on the one hand; and Articles such as Articles 40 to 44 "which grant to individuals particular rights within society and in relation to the organs of State", on the other. This suggests that aliens will have standing to rely on the provisions of Articles such as Articles 38 and 40 to 44.[83] This distinction was also implicitly drawn by McCarthy J in his concurring judgment in *McGimpsey v Ireland*[84] where he appeared to suggest that only citizens had standing to seek enforce a constitutional imperative, the non-observance of which did not affect their own personal circumstances in any special or injurious fashion.[85] The corollary of this view is that non-citizens prejudicially affected by the operation of legislation (such as in *Kostan's* case) will have standing to attack its constitutionality.[86] The following passage from the judgment of Gannon J in *Rederij Kennemerland v Attorney General*[87] thus accurately reflects this emerging distinction:

> "[Non-citizens entering the State are] entitled to expect and to insist that those laws will be applied and administered in accordance with the Constitution...To the extent that the laws are not so applied...in relation to them, their persons and property they are entitled to call upon the courts to uphold the Constitution...But I do not think they have any right or standing to challenge the legislation of this country...for any purpose other than that of affording to them a remedy...for a wrong, harm or disadvantage suffered by such alleged failure to uphold the Constitution."

[79] [1978] ILRM 12; (1968) 102 ILTR 1.
[80] [1983] IR 193; [1984] ILRM 249.
[81] The Supreme Court reversed the decision of Carroll J (who in the High Court had found the legislation to be unconstitutional), but this does not affect the point under discussion.
[82] [1984] IR 548; [1985] ILRM 449.
[83] For further discussion of this point, see pp. 488-489.
[84] [1990] 1 IR 110; [1990] ILRM 440.
[85] He observed that: "In *Crotty v An Taoiseach* [1987] IR 713 a successful challenge was made by an undoubted citizen against the ratification of part of the Single European Act. It seems very unlikely that a non-citizen would have been allowed to maintain such proceedings. The citizens of the United Kingdom in Britain have a very real interest in the Anglo-Irish Agreement: is each one of them to be heard to challenge its validity as being repugnant to the Constitution of Ireland? I think not."
[86] Note, however, that in *Osheku v Ireland* [1986] IR 733; [1987] ILRM 330 Gannon J said that the plaintiff had no standing to challenge the constitutionality of the Irish Nationality and Citizenship Act 1956, because he was an illegal immigrant.
[87] [1989] ILRM 821.

Juristic persons

Questions of nationality aside, there is no clear authority on whether any distinction is to be drawn, for purposes of *locus standi* to challenge Acts, between citizens as natural persons on the one hand, and artificial or juristic persons on the other. Such a distinction has been drawn, in the constitutional context, so far only in the area of Article 40.1 and the guarantee of equality before the law, and there seems no reason whatever to extend it to the sphere of judicial review of legislation generally. However, in *East Donegal Co-Operative v Attorney General*[88] O'Keeffe P adverted inconclusively to the idea when he said that "artificial persons may possibly not be entitled to rely on the constitutional guarantees [for the purpose of challenging Acts] (although they have been held to be so entitled in the United States)..." In *Private Motorists Provident Society Ltd. v Attorney General*[89] the Supreme Court reserved the question whether an artificial legal person could rely on individual constitutional guarantees (such as the right to private property or free association), but this question may not be of much practical importance, as O'Higgins CJ pointed out that an individual shareholder is entitled to complain "if the impugned legislation interferes with any of his personal rights".[90] In many ways, this is curious reasoning. If the Oireachtas elects to vest artificial persons with legal personality to sue and be sued, it is not easy to see why - at least as a general rule[91] - such corporate entities should not have standing to rely on the Constitution in an appropriate case. Moreover, it would run wholly counter to fundamental company law principles if an individual shareholder was to be allowed to be put forward as an ersatz plaintiff instead of the company, bearing in mind that a shareholder has no legal or equitable interest in the property of a company.[92] Perhaps the decision in *Society for the Protection of Unborn Children (Ire.) Ltd. v Coogan*[93] will presage a more relaxed judicial attitude to this question. Here the Supreme Court held that a corporate entity could sue to enforce Article 40.3.3, provided it could show that it had a genuine "bona fide concern and interest", subject always to the reservation expressed by Finlay CJ to the effect that a corporate body could not acquire the necessary standing to sue "merely by reason of its articles and memorandum of association."

What kind of interest will give locus standi?

The question of *locus standi*, as it arises in the majority of cases, i.e. where individual citizens challenge legislation, has received close judicial attention only in the last fifteen years or so . When constitutional litigation first began to be fairly common in the early 1960s, the State does not seem to have taken any point as to *locus standi* against plaintiffs such as *O'Donovan*[94] and *Ryan*,[95] who were not more acutely affected than anyone

[88] [1970] IR 317; (1970) 104 ILTR 81.

[89] [1983] IR 339; [1984] ILRM 88. See also *Pine Valley Developments Ltd. v Minister for Environment* [1987] IR 28 (shareholders had property rights which were protected by Article 40.3).

[90] "Ordinarily when this problem arises it is overcome by joining as a plaintiff a shareholder of the corporate plaintiff who is an Irish citizen...In the [present] case the absence of an individual Irish citizen asserting his own constitutional rights is fatal to the argument based on the constitutionality of the [Companies Act 1990]": *Chestvale Properties Ltd. v Glackin* [1992] ILRM 221 *per* Murphy J. See also *Attorney General v Paperlink Ltd.* [1984] ILRM 373.

[91] There may be cases - such as where a putative plaintiff is seeking to enforce a constitutional imperative quite independently of his own personal circumstances (e.g., as in *Crotty v An Taoiseach* [1987] IR 713; [1987] ILRM 400) - where it might be inappropriate to allow an artificial person to sue. But cf. *Society for the Protection of Unborn Children (Ire.) Ltd. v Coogan* [1989] IR 734; [1990] ILRM 70, where a corporate entity was afforded standing to sue in such a case.

[92] See, e.g., *Kerry Co-Operative Creameries Ltd. v An Bord Bainne Co-Operative Ltd.* [1991] ILRM 851; *O'Neill v Ryan (No.3)* [1993] ILRM 557.

[93] [1989] IR 734; [1990] ILRM 70.

[94] *O'Donovan v Attorney General* [1961] IR 114; (1962) 96 ILTR 121.

[95] *Ryan v Attorney General* [1965] IR 294.

else by the Acts which they challenged; in the *East Donegal Co-Operative* case the Attorney General justified the earlier cases by saying (as summarised by O'Keeffe P. in his judgment in the High Court) that:

> "each of those plaintiffs had a demonstrable right to bring the proceedings; the first had such right as a person directly interested in the re-framing of electoral constituencies effected by the questioned statute, and the second had such right as a person whose constitutional right to a supply of water would clearly be subjected to some limitation by the provisions of the statute;"

but this seems a frail position. The former had indeed once been (and was afterwards to become again) a member of Dáil Éireann, and at the time of the action was a member of Seanad Éireann, but it can hardly be the law that his personal successful interest in politics could give him a standing not possessed by any other citizen who might simply object to being governed by a Dáil elected on a seat-distribution contrived to suit the Government which had sponsored the redistribution Bill.[96] The latter was the mother of a family, which obviously gave an extra edge to her apprehensions about a dangerous water supply, but scarcely an interest different in kind from that of any other citizen equally dependent on water. The *O'Donovan* and *Ryan* pattern was repeated in *McMahon's* case,[97] in which the plaintiff had no peculiar interest of his own to assert.

Nevertheless, during this period, caution was being expressed in the courts about the conception of the constitutional challenging of statutes as a free-for-all. Already in the *East Donegal Co-Operative* case the Supreme Court had said, *per* Walsh J:

> "With regard to the *locus standi* of the plaintiffs the question raised has been determined in different ways in countries which have constitutional provisions similar to our own... At one end of the spectrum of opinions on this topic one finds the contention that there exists a right of action akin to an *actio popularis* which will entitle any person, whether he is directly affected by the Act or not, to maintain proceedings and challenge the validity of any Act passed by the parliament of the country of which he is a citizen or to whose laws he is subject by residing in that country. At the other end of the spectrum is the contention that no-one can maintain such an action unless he can show that not merely do the provisions of the Act in question apply to activities in which he is currently engaged but that their application has actually affected his activities adversely. The Court rejects the latter contention and does not find it necessary in the circumstances of this case to express any view upon the former."

The decision in Cahill v Sutton

Shortly afterwards, in *The State (Llewellyn) v Ua Donnchadha*,[98] Henchy J expressed apprehension as to the mischief that could be caused by "nominal plaintiffs" seeking declarations of unconstitutionality. And seven years later the same judge delivered the

[96] This was the political kernel of the plaintiff's case against the Act. In *Dillon-Leetch v Calleary*, Supreme Court 31 July 1974, the Supreme Court, *per* Henchy J, permitted an unsuccessful election candidate to challenge the election even though the only person who could possibly have benefited was another candidate who had been defeated (unlike the petitioner) by a very small margin: the Court recognised his interest, as a voter. in seeing that the correct person was elected.

[97] [1972] IR 69; (1972) 106 ILTR 89. Mr. McMahon was not even on the electoral register, and had no visible interest greater than that of any other citizen in genuinely free elections and in the principle of the secret ballot to this end. See also *Boland v An Taoiseach* [1974] IR 338; (1975) 109 ILTR 13 (where a citizen was permitted to challenge the constitutionality of an executive agreement).

[98] [1973] IR 151; (1974) 108 ILTR 49.

principal judgment in *Cahill v Sutton*,[99] which apart from exceptional cases definitively limited *locus standi* to persons who could point to a detriment, actual or apprehended, to themselves resulting from the Act's operation. The issue arose here in a very unusual way. The plaintiff had brought an action for personal injuries against her doctor, based on what she said was his negligence in treating her in 1968. She did not commence her action until 1972. But s 11(2)(*b*) of the Statute of Limitations 1957, prescribed a three-year limitation period for such actions; and the defendant successfully pleaded this limitation against her. She thereupon challenged the constitutionality of that provision, but failed in the High Court, where Finlay P refused to declare it invalid. In the Supreme Court, on her appeal, she argued that the sub-section failed to respect the personal rights of plaintiffs who did not become aware of the facts on which their claims might be based until after the expiry of the limitation period, in that it made no exception in their favour. The point was taken against her that, as *she herself had admittedly been aware of the facts of her own case since immediately after the allegedly negligent treatment in 1968*, she could not have benefited even had such an exception been in the sub-section; and that she should not be permitted to seek to eliminate the sub-section - thus freeing herself from the limitation it imposed - by advancing the case of a hypothetical plaintiff. The Supreme Court accepted this objection. Henchy J said:

> "The plaintiff is seeking to be allowed to conjure up, invoke and champion the putative constitutional rights of a hypothetical third party, so that the provisions of s 11(2)(*b*) may be declared unconstitutional on the basis of that constitutional *jus tertii* - thus allowing the plaintiff to march through the resulting gap in the statute.
>
> ... The primary rule as to standing in constitutional matters is that the person challenging the constitutionality of the statute, or some other person for whom he is deemed by the court to be entitled to speak, must be able to assert that, because of the alleged unconstitutionality, his or that other person's interests have been adversely affected, or stand in real or imminent danger of being adversely affected by the operation of the statute.
>
> On that test the plaintiff must be held to be disentitled to raise the allegation of unconstitutionality on which she relies."

Both Henchy J and O'Higgins CJ pointed out that, were the Court to decide otherwise, it would throw the process of judicial review open to cranks and busy-bodies; Henchy J added that it would raise the undesirable possibility, "contrary to the spirit of the Constitution", that political opposition to a measure might simply be switched, after its enactment, from the Oireachtas to the courts. (He adverted too to the danger that, if the Court held with the plaintiff, it would have the effect of "reviving all other claims of a like nature"; though, of course, this effect would presumably have followed even if the sub-section had been struck down at the instance of a meritorious plaintiff.)[100]

[99] [1980] IR 269. See Whyte, "*Nominal Plaintiffs and the Irish Constitution*" 74 Gazette of the Incorporated Law Society of Ireland 299; Sherlock, "*Understanding Standing: Locus Standi in Irish Constitutional Law*" (1987) Public Law 245 and Humphreys and O'Dowd, "*Locus Standi to Enforce the Constitution*" (1990) 8 ILT (n.s.) 14.

[100] This needs however to be read in conjunction with what the same judge had said a few months previously, in *Murphy v Attorney General* [1982] IR 241, as to public policy preventing the courts from allowing excessive disruption through giving retrospective effect to constitutional decisions as to a law's invalidity: see below, p. 483.

Rules on locus standi should however not be too restrictive

Judicial reaction to *Cahill v Sutton* has been somewhat inconsistent, but, in general, the requirements as to interest and apprehended injury have been generously interpreted and, indeed, as the Supreme Court has subsequently reminded us, the decision in *Cahill* "is not of such sweeping application as it is sometimes thought."[101] On the other hand, as we shall presently see, the *jus tertii* aspect of *Cahill v Sutton* has been fairly rigorously applied.[102]

Cahill v Sutton applied

In *The State (Lynch) v Cooney*[103] Walsh J - although he was the judge who had first questioned the idea of a constitutional *actio popularis*, in the *East Donegal Co-Operative* case - said he thought the concept of a "person aggrieved" should be "generously interpreted", and, applying by analogy an observation on administrative law to the area of judicial review of statutes, seemed to adopt the view that restrictive rules about standing would be inimical to a healthy legal system. In *Norris v Attorney General*[104] the Supreme Court applied *Cahill v Sutton* by not permitting the plaintiff, a declared homosexual, to raise the right of marital privacy against a law which, in its incidental application to married couples, might well breach that right, but which the plaintiff (as someone neither married nor likely to be married) had no standing to attack on that ground. He was, however, permitted to challenge the law on grounds which were in fact relevant to his own situation: and the mere fact that he had never been prosecuted or molested under that law did not (as the Attorney General had contended it should) take away his standing to challenge it. O'Higgins CJ said:

> "In my view, as long as the legislation stands and continues to proclaim as criminal the conduct which the plaintiff asserts he has a right to engage in, such right, if it exists, is threatened, and the plaintiff has standing to seek the protection of the Court."[105]

It is worth noting that McCarthy J dissented from the other four members of the Court by his willingness to allow the plaintiff to rely on the right of marital privacy, on the ground of the absurdity and inequality which he thought their application of *Cahill v Sutton* in this area would produce.

Exceptional relaxation of the locus standi rule

The Court in *Cahill v Sutton* did not attempt an exhaustive list of cases in which it thought it would be proper to relax the strictness of the interest rule which it there laid down; but clearly it recognised that occasions for exceptional relaxation could exist. Henchy J said:

> "This rule, however, being but a rule of practice must, like all such rules, be subject to expansion, exception or qualification when the justice of the case so requires... For example, while the challenger may lack the personal standing normally required, those prejudicially affected by the impugned statute may not be in a position to assert adequately, or in time, their constitutional rights. In such a case the

[101] *Society for the Protection of Unborn Children (Ire.) Ltd. v Coogan* [1989] IR 734; [1990] ILRM 70, *per* Walsh J.
[102] See pp. 443-444.
[103] [1982] IR 337; [1983] ILRM 89.
[104] [1984] IR 36.
[105] See also *O'Mahony v Melia* [1989] IR 335 (where Keane J held, following *Cahill v Sutton* that "it could not conceivably be suggested that no rights" of the plaintiffs "were 'broken, endangered or threatened' if the legislation" which purported to authorise their overnight detention was invalid.)

court might decide to ignore the want of normal personal standing on the part of the litigant before it. Likewise, the absence of a prejudice or injury peculiar to the challenger might be overlooked, in the discretion of the court, if the impugned provision is directed at, or operable against a grouping which includes the challenger, or with whom the challenger may be said to have a common interest - particularly in cases where, because of the nature of the subject matter, it is difficult to segregate those affected from those not affected by the challenged provisions."

The application of exceptions of his first class is illustrated by *L'Henryenat v Ireland*[106] and by *Society for the Protection of Unborn Children (Ire.) Ltd. v Coogan.*[107] In the former case the master of a French trawler who was being prosecuted for fishery offences challenged the constitutionality of provisions of the relevant Fisheries Acts, on grounds which related partly to himself, partly to the owner of the vessel (who was not a party to the action). Carroll J would not permit him to argue the constitutionality of these provisions as they affected the owner; the countervailing considerations to which Henchy J adverted in *Cahill v Sutton* as justifying an exceptional departure from the rule were not present here, as "there was no question of the owner of the boat not being in a position to assert adequately or in time his constitutional rights". Conversely, an exception was allowed by the Supreme Court in *Coogan* - a case where a corporate entity with a bona fide interest in seeking the enforcement of Article 40.3.3 - since, as Finlay CJ noted, in respect of a threat to the unborn child there could never "be a victim or potential victim who can sue."

It is possible to say that the substance of the second class of exception envisaged by Henchy J had in fact already been admitted in the cases of *O'Donovan, Ryan* and *McMahon*, mentioned above where the respective plaintiffs were asserting a breach of what would nowadays be described as a constitutional imperative. In this particular context, a more generous approach to the issue of *locus standi* may now be discerned in a trilogy of major cases, commencing with *Crotty v An Taoiseach.*[108] In *Crotty's* case the plaintiff had sought an injunction to prevent the Government from ratifying the Single European Act; Barrington J adverted to what Henchy J had said in *Cahill's* case about the dangers of allowing political opposition to a measure to be simply switched from the Oireachtas to the courts, but said that while the case involved the constitutionality of a controversial political measure it was also an issue dealing with the powers of Government and with constitutional rights which are matters of law and in which a responsible citizen by his attitude to them, right or wrong, could take a legitimate interest, and:

> "in so much as it is a matter which affects the whole constitutional and political structure of the society in which he lives it is a matter in which the individual citizen might have a legitimate interest which might be accepted in a court of law... The plaintiff clearly has *locus standi* because his contention is that what is being done [amounts to an] amendment of the Constitution which should be submitted to

[106] [1983] IR 193.

[107] [1989] IR 734; [1990] ILRM 70.

[108] [1987] IR 713; [1987] ILRM 400. See also *The State (Sheehan) v Government of Ireland* [1987] IR 550, where Costello J held that the applicant had sufficient interest to seek an order of *mandamus* bringing an important section of the Civil Liability Act 1961, into force, even though he would not personally benefit from this change. The judge denied that the applicant's interest was merely academic, as he was an aggrieved citizen "who may have suffered the loss of a substantial amount of money due to the Government's failure to carry out its duty"; he thought the applicant had therefore sufficient interest in the proceedings to maintain the application. The Supreme Court did not find it necessary to decide this issue, although with Henchy J observing that the applicant was "lacking in the special interest in the outcome of the *mandamus* proceedings", there was here, perhaps, a hint that he had no such standing.

a referendum, and that he as a citizen has the right to be consulted in such a referendum and that his right is being infringed."

In the Supreme Court, Finlay CJ said that, since if the European Communities (Amendment) Act 1986, and the Single European Act entered into force, they would affect every citizen, the plaintiff had *locus standi* for his challenge "notwithstanding his failure to prove the threat of any special injury or prejudice to him, as distinct from any other citizen, arising from this Act". This trend was continued by the decision of the Supreme Court in *Society for the Protection of Unborn Children (Ire.) Ltd. v Coogan*,[109] where the Court stressed that the Attorney General did not enjoy a monopoly with regard to the vindication of a public right and that a *bona fide* (albeit, in this case, a corporate) plaintiff had sufficient standing to secure the enforcement of Article 40.3.3. Walsh J observed that he thought that *Cahill v Sutton* had been mis-interpreted and added that every citizen had a right to ensure "that the fundamental law of the State was observed." This *dictum* may yet have profound implications for the law of standing to challenge a breach by the State of a constitutional imperative, even though that litigant may have suffered no actual or tangible injury. The third case in this series is *McGimpsey v Ireland*[110] where the Supreme Court agreed that a citizen, irrespective of a showing of actual injury, would have standing to enforce Articles 2 and 3.

And yet even this generous approach to the question of standing has its limits as evidence by the Supreme Court's later decision in *McDaid v Sheehy*.[111] While this decision is essentially turns on the question of judicial "self-restraint" in the context of constitutional adjudication[112] - since the Court stressed that the applicant's conviction would be nonetheless valid even if his challenge to the constitutionality of the Imposition of Duties Act 1957 were to have succeeded - Finlay CJ did point out that as the applicant's interests "had not been prejudiced or damaged by the operation of the [1957] Act...or of any statutory order made pursuant to it " he could have "no conceivable interest in further pursuing his challenge to the constitutional validity" of that Act. What is of interest is that - unlike cases such as *Crotty* or *McGimpsey* - there is here no suggestion that the applicant should have been accorded standing in view of the fact that the 1957 Act affected the interests of taxpayers in general. One can only assume that the Court was unwilling in such circumstances to depart from the normal *Cahill v Sutton* rules because (a) the 1957 Act potentially affected the individual constitutional rights and interests of taxpayers (unlike the possible abstract breach of a constitutional norm disclosed in cases such as *Crotty* or *McGimpsey*) and (b) it was inherently probable in the nature of things that some suitably qualified applicant who was actually affected by the operation of the 1957 Act would come forward to challenge its operation in an actual concrete case.

Infant plaintiffs

It may be briefly noted that an infant, who normally could sue only by his parent or "next friend", has *locus standi* to challenge an Act if the parent's interest in the challenge may be adverse to his own: *O'Brien v Keogh*,[113] where an infant's right to challenge the Statute of Limitations, which his parent had raised against him, was upheld by the Supreme Court.

[109] [1989] IR 734.
[110] [1990] 1 IR 110; [1990] ILRM 440.
[111] [1991] 1 IR 1; [1991] ILRM 250. See also *Duggan v An Taoiseach* [1989] ILRM 710.
[112] Discussed below at pp. 450-451.
[113] [1972] IR 144.

Jus tertii rule strictly applied

As mentioned above, one aspect of the decision in *Cahill v Sutton* which has been strictly applied is the *jus tertii* rule. In practice what this means is that the plaintiff cannot, as it were, seek a general review of the legislation which is under attack, but may only rely on such arguments as bear on his or own personal circumstances.[114] This, indeed, is illustrated by the facts and decision in *Cahill v Sutton* itself. The plaintiff was, indeed, affected by the operation of the Statute of Limitation 1957 (in that s 11(2)(*b*) of that Act prevented her from suing the defendant), and so in one limited sense she might, in fact, have been judged to have the necessary standing to sue. However, her claim failed, since the Supreme Court would not allow her - for the reasons already canvassed above - to advance the case of hypothetical plaintiffs, since the personal circumstances of those putative plaintiffs were very different from her own. In *King v Attorney General*,[115] where the plaintiff succeeded in having portion of s 4 of the Vagrancy Act 1824, declared inconsistent with the Constitution and, so to speak, "excised", so as to invalidate his conviction under that section, the Supreme Court denied his *locus standi to* attack the section as a whole, or any portion of it save that which had been used in prosecuting him. In *McCann v Attorney General*,[116] in which the plaintiff complained that provisions of the Racing Board and Race Courses Act 1945, were unconstitutional in not expressly prescribing fair procedures in the exercise of the Racing Board's disciplinary powers, Barron J said that, even if those provisions could not be rescued by the presumption of constitutional behaviour in favour of statutory bodies, since the plaintiff in this case had in fact received fair procedure, he had no *locus standi* to challenge them. *Norris v Attorney General*[117] provides a particularly good example of the operation of this doctrine. Here, since it was inherent in the plaintiff's case that he was a congenital homosexual for whom marriage was not an option, he had no standing to challenge the constitutionality of anti-sodomy statute on the ground that it invaded the privacy of married couples. Likewise, in *Madigan v Attorney General*[118] the plaintiffs (who were both Irish residents and who had challenged the constitutionality of the residential property tax created by Part VI of the Finance Act 1983) were confined to making such arguments as bore on their own personal circumstances and were not permitted to canvass, for example, arguments based on the possible impact of the legislation on non-resident citizens. Indeed, the Supreme Court drew attention to what is a logical corollary of the *jus tertii* rule, namely, that just because the plaintiffs (as it happened) had failed in their constitutional challenge that "another plaintiff with sufficient *locus standi* [sc. to raise these other arguments] might not successfully attack its validity."

[114] In *O'Brien v Keogh* [1972] IR 144 Ó Dálaigh CJ had said that the court's duty in constitutional actions the courts' duty: "is to examine it in as wide a manner as if the provision is to examine it in as wide a manner as if the provision had been the subject of a reference under Article 26 of the Constitution: that is to say, the court must advert as best it can to the full scope of the provision away and beyond the problem presented by the circumstances of the particular case before the court." But, as O'Hanlon J noted in *Madigan v Attorney General* [1986] ILRM 136, this statement appears to have superseded by later developments, including *Cahill v Sutton* itself.

[115] [1981] IR 233.

[116] [1983] ILRM 67. See also *MacGairbhith v Attorney General* [1991] 1 IR 412 (plaintiff had no *locus standi* to challenge the imposition of court fees, since he had in fact exercised his right of access to the courts "on a number of occasions and there is no evidence to suggest that he has prevented from exercising that right or caused undue hardship in the process of exercising it by having to pay the levies of which he complains.")

[117] [1984] IR 36.

[118] [1986] ILRM 123. See also *MhicMhathúna v Attorney General* [1989] IR 504 (High Court in considering challenge to constitutionality of social welfare payments being paid to unmarried mothers cannot, in the words of Carroll J, "take into account arguments based on assumptions or hypotheses outside the facts and circumstances of the action before the court").

A slightly discordant note may have been struck by the Supreme Court in *Cox v Ireland*,[119] where the Court invalidated s 34 of the Offences Against the State Act 1939 on the ground that it was a disproportionate attack on the property rights of a person convicted of a scheduled offence. As Humphreys has perceptively noted,[120] the Court invalidated the section "essentially from the perspective of a person convicted of a non-serious, non-subversive offence." Yet since there is reason to suppose that the offences in question were serious,[121] the question as to how s 34 was disproportionate when applied to the factual circumstances of the plaintiff's own case would necessarily arise. *Cox*, however, is possibly best viewed as an example of where the *jus tertii* rule was not too stringently applied, rather than presaging any major departure from the manner in which the rule has heretofore been consistently applied.

The plaintiff must exhaust all other remedies

In *E. v E.*,[122] (not a challenge to an Act but eliciting a criterion probably applicable equally to such a challenge) where the plaintiff complained that the provision made for a case such as his by the Scheme of Civil Legal Aid and Advice, 1979, was inadequate (he had been ruled ineligible for legal aid, but said he could not afford to pay for it himself), O'Hanlon J held that, as he had not "exhausted the procedure which was open to him under the Legal Aid Scheme for obtaining free legal aid, before coming to court to assert his rights", he had no *locus standi* to challenge it. Similar principles were applied in *Re J.C.*,[123] where the applicant challenged the constitutionality of the Civil Legal Aid scheme and the Social Welfare (Consolidation) Act 1981, claiming that he was debarred from pursuing his substantive action because of lack of means. Barrington J found that, as he had not waited for the outcome of his appeal against the refusal of a legal aid certificate before commencing proceedings, he had no standing to raise these constitutional issues.

The plaintiff may bring a challenge based on an apprehended injury

Does *locus standi* for challenging an Act depend on one's having already sustained injury by its operation, or is it enough to have a reasonable apprehension of injury? This question was answered decisively in the sense of the latter alternative in the *East Donegal Co-Operative* case.[124] O'Keeffe P said in the High Court that he thought:

> "a citizen of Ireland, who may possibly be prejudicially affected by the operation of a statute which is unconstitutional, need not wait until what he apprehends may happen has in fact happened before bringing proceedings to have the statute declared repugnant to the Constitution."

119 [1992] 2 IR 503.

120 (1991) 13 DULJ (n.s) 118.

121 The plaintiff had been convicted of the possession of firearms.

122 [1982] ILRM 497. The principle of exhaustion of other remedies was also implicitly accepted by Barrington J in *Brennan v Attorney General* [1983] ILRM 449, though he found that the plaintiff here had in fact no effective remedy open to him under existing law.

123 High Court, 25 July 1985.

124 [1970] IR 317; (1970) 104 ILTR 81. Walsh J adverted to US precedents which had been advanced to the effect that hypothetical, "advisory" opinions would not be given on Acts from which no infringement had yet been suffered, and emphasised that the Constitution of Ireland, unlike the US Constitution, did in fact provide for advisory opinions (Article 26) and did not impose, in the context of challenging Acts, the condition that "there must be in existence a dispute or conflict as to legal rights between the parties and peculiar to the parties". Note that the US Supreme Court has held that "Article III judicial power exists only to redress or otherwise to protect against injury to the complaining party.": *Warth v Seldin* 422 US 490 (1975).

The Supreme Court agreed with him:

> "Rights which are guaranteed by the Constitution are intended to be protected by the provisions of the Constitution. To afford proper protection, the provisions must enable the person invoking them not merely to redress a wrong resulting from an infringement of the guarantees but also to prevent the threatened or impending infringement of the guarantees and to put to the test an apprehended infringement of these guarantees."

This approach is also visible in a number of subsequent decisions. Thus, in *Curtis v Attorney General*[125] the plaintiff, who had been charged with various customs offences, challenged the constitutionality of s 34 of the Finance Act 1963. This section enables the District Judge conducting the preliminary examination to determine conclusively the value of the goods in question; if convicted on indictment, the plaintiff would have been liable to a fine representing treble the value of the goods. Carroll J rejected the argument that the action was premature in that the District Court had yet to determine the value of the goods and might ultimately accept the plaintiff's own valuation. She said that while the determination of the District Court might be in the plaintiff's favour:

> "he is nevertheless in imminent danger of a determination affecting his rights. It is not necessary that a determination adversely affecting rights must first be made before a constitutional challenge can be started. It is enough if there is a reasonable apprehension of such a determination: see *Cahill v Sutton*."[126]

An equally generous approach to the question of what constituted such an "imminent danger" of invasion of constitutional rights may be discerned in the judgment of Finlay CJ for the Supreme Court in *Desmond v Glackin (No.2)*.[127] In this case, the principal respondent had been appointed an inspector under the Companies Act 1990 to investigate the ownership of certain companies. The applicant had disputed the entitlement of the inspector to question him about certain matters and the inspector had certified the applicant's refusal to attend before him to the High Court under s 10(5) of the 1990 Act.[128] That application had been adjourned on the applicant's undertaking to co-operate with the inquiry and it was contended that the applicant could not show that he stood in danger of further certification and that his challenge was therefore premature. The Supreme Court disagreed, saying that once it was clear that the inspector was free to make such inquiries[129] the likelihood was that a further certificate would issue from the inspector, so that, in the words of Finlay CJ, the applicant was a person "with an immediate and direct interest in the question of constitutional validity" and therefore had the requisite *locus standi*. This seems a generous approach, inasmuch as an essential premise of the Court's judgment appears to be largely based on surmise as to what the

[125] [1985] IR 458; [1986] ILRM 428.

[126] This was also the approach taken in *Norris v Attorney General* [1984] IR 36: see p. 440.

[127] Supreme Court, 30 July 1992. See also the *McGlinchey v Ireland (No.2)* [1990] 2 IR 220 where "not without considerable hesitation" Costello J permitted a plaintiff (who had been previously extradited to Northern Ireland and who feared that another such application might be in the offing) to challenge the constitutionality of the Extradition Act 1965. The judge said that he had concluded that in the "particular and highly exceptional circumstances of the case the plaintiff's apprehensions that his liberty may be curtailed by a request for extradition to Northern Ireland give him at the present time a standing to challenge the constitutionality of the statute by which that request would be implemented."

[128] A sub-section which the Supreme Court found to be practically identical to s 3(4) of the Committee of Public Accounts of Dáil Éireann (Privilege and Procedure) Act 1970 and, following the decision in *Re Haughey* [1971] IR 217, held the section to be unconstitutional in that it allowed for the summary trial by the High Court of a non-minor offence, contrary to Article 38: see p. 629.

[129] As the Court made clear in a separate judgment on that issue which was delivered on the same day by McCarthy J.

likely course of particular events might be. Nor is the case really comparable with *Norris*, since in the latter case the plaintiff claimed that he had a constitutional right to engage in conduct which (as the law then was) was criminalised by statute, thus exposing him to an ever constant threat of prosecution.

An interesting nuance may be discerned in the judgment of O'Hanlon J in *O'Donoghue v Minister for Health.*[130] In this case the parents of a young handicapped boy had sought to compel the State to provide a special course of education for him and invoked the provisions of Article 42 of the Constitution for this purpose. The State contended that the constitutional point was now moot, inasmuch as the boy was now receiving the education in question. O'Hanlon J rejected this submission, saying that the education had been provided only as a matter of grace and favour and this fact did not take from the right of the parents to have the question of their constitutional entitlements under Article 42 judicially determined.

Locus standi and pre-Constitution laws

The question whether for the purpose of *locus standi* there is a distinction between Acts of the Oireachtas and pre-Constitution laws has not so far arisen. Even though a difference between those two types of law, in a sense which a court operating judicial review would think relevant, can be seen - and is in fact seen for the purpose of the presumption of constitutionality, the "double construction" rule, the *intra vires* test etc. - it is hard to suggest what practical consequences, for *locus standi* purposes, might logically flow from that difference. If the public policy behind the *locus standi* hurdle is that settled patterns of law are in the public interest and that private interests ought not to be permitted to disturb them unless an injustice would be the result of insulating them against attack, then in spite of the fact that Article 50 accords only provisional countenance to pre-Constitution laws - the same considerations ought to justify imposing conditions of the *Cahill v Sutton* type whatever the date of the legislation being complained of.

The function and purpose of the locus standi rules: a re-assessment

It remains to re-assess the function and purpose of the *locus standi* rules having regard to the divergent (and not always consistent) judicial views that have been expressed on this subject.

The first question which arose is whether the *Cahill v Sutton* type *locus standi* rules are constitutionally required or are they simply judicially created rules of prudence which may be relaxed or expanded as occasion requires. This question has implications far beyond the law of standing, since it contains the answer to a more fundamental question, namely, whether the courts are prepared to see that the executive and legislature observe each and every provision of the Constitution, even in cases (such as Articles 2 and 3, where it is unlikely that there will ever be a plaintiff who can point to real and tangible injury as a result of a breach of a constitutional norm). In this connection it may be observed that the US courts have firmly set their face against expanded standing rules of this kind. The "case and controversies" provisions of Article III of the US Constitution have been held to imply a minimum standing threshold which is not satisfied by "abstract injury in non-observance of the Constitution....asserted by citizens".[131] In this

[130] High Court, 27 May 1993.

[131] *Schlesinger v Reservists Committee to Stop the War* 418 US 208 (1974), *per* Burger CJ. In addition to these constitutionally required standing rules, the US judiciary have "also adhered to a set of prudential principles that bear on the question of standing": *Valley Forge Christian College v Americans United for Separation of Church and State, Inc.* 454 US 464 (1982), *per* Rehnquist J (he instanced the *jus tertii* rule as an example of such a "prudential" - i.e., not constitutionally mandated - standing requirement.)

connection, the US courts have been unimpressed by the argument that every citizen has an interest in ensuring that the Constitution is observed.[132]

This approach appears to have been decisively rejected by the Irish courts. Even the language of Henchy J in *Cahill v Sutton* ("this rule...being but a rule of practice") strongly suggests that Article 34.1 does not *require or impose* minimum standing requirements, although separation of powers-type considerations did feature prominently in his judgment. Secondly, cases such as *Crotty, Society for the Protection of Unborn Children (Ire.) Ltd. v Coogan* and *McGimpsey* all recognise the right of interested citizens to see that the Constitution is observed. All of this implies that the *Cahill v Sutton locus standi* rules are purely prudential, judicially-created rules designed to safeguard the proper administration of justice by ensuring, for example, that the courts are not required to pronounce on a moot; that the case will not be decided in the abstract and that one litigant will not be permitted to argue what, in effect, is another litigant's case. Viewed in this light, the *Cahill v Sutton* rules have a close affinity with the "rule of avoidance" articulated in cases such as *McDaid v Sheehy.*[133]

But if prudential requirements such as those just mentioned mean that the courts will deny standing in cases such as *Cahill v Sutton*, why it may be asked, are these rules relaxed in cases such as *Crotty* and *Coogan*? The answer would appear to be two-fold. First, cases such as *Cahill v Sutton* present constitutional challenges based on the personal rights provisions of the Constitution (right of access to the courts, property rights etc.). In such cases there is, generally speaking, no need for the courts to entertain a suit based on a supposed infringement of the rights of third parties or an abstract infringement of the Constitution itself since if these personal rights have, in fact, been infringed there will be usually be no shortage of litigants asserting such a breach. In other words, the supposed constitutional infringement in this type of case can wait until a suitably qualified litigant comes forward and the administration of justice is generally thought to be best served by waiting for such a plaintiff to emerge. Secondly, however, the case of an abstract breach of a constitutional norm - such as, for example, where justice was not administered in public, contrary to Article 34.1[134] or where the State was to fail in its duty under Article 41 to safeguard the institution of marriage[135] or where the State was to endow a religion contrary to Article 44 by, e.g., gifting property to a religious institution[136] - such a "better plaintiff" is unlikely to emerge, since in the nature of things it is

[132] "The proposition that all constitutional provisions are enforceable by any citizen simply because citizens are the ultimate beneficiaries of those provisions has no boundaries....Any other conclusion would mean that the Founding Fathers intended to set up something in the nature of an Athenian democracy...to oversee the conduct of the National Government by means of lawsuits in the courts", *per* Burger CJ in *United States v Richardson* 418 US 166 (1974).

[133] [1991] 1 IR 1.

[134] There is a clear hint in *Irish Press Plc. v Ingersoll Irish Publications Ltd.* [1993] ILRM 747, - where Finlay CJ spoke of the "fundamental constitutional right *vested in the public*, namely, the administration of justice in public" (authors' emphasis) - that Article 34.1 confers an enforceable right of this kind in a *bona fide* plaintiff (such as, perhaps, a newspaper journalist) to enforce this constitutional norm, even though they might not have any personal stake or interest in the litigant which it was proposed to hold *in camera*. But cf. *Attorney General v X.* [1992] 1 IR 1; [1992] ILRM 401; [1992] 2 CMLR 277, where an argument of this kind was summarily rejected.

[135] In *Greene v Minister for Agriculture* [1990] 2 IR 17 Murphy J characterised Article 41 as not conferring any personal constitutional right, the breach of which sounded in damages. He held that the plaintiffs had nonetheless standing to ensure that the State abided by this constitutional duty. While Murphy J's characterisation of Article 41 may be open to question, the distinction which he drew seems to be correct as a general principle which could be applied to other provisions of the Constitution.

[136] This was the gravamen of the plaintiffs' complaint in the leading case of *Valley Forge Christian College v Americans United for the Separation of Church and State, Inc.* 454 US 464 (1982), but the US Supreme Court held that they had no standing to challenge the constitutionality of this voluntary conveyance since it was at best an abstract breach of a constitutional norm which had not personally caused them any tangible injury.

unlikely that one *bona fide* plaintiff will be better qualified than another to assert a breach of this kind. In these circumstances the courts - rather than see a breach of the Constitution go unremedied - appear to be prepared to deem such a plaintiff to have the necessary *locus standi* to take an action of this kind. At all events, it will have been seen from the foregoing discussion that the precise doctrinal rationale for the present *locus standi* remains to be fully explored.

(E) CANONS OF REVIEW: PRESUMPTION OF CONSTITUTIONALITY

While the Constitution prescribes no special rules for its own application in the testing of statutes, such rules have evolved. In 1939, in the first case in which a statute was challenged under the new Constitution - *Pigs Marketing Board v Donnelly*[137] - Hanna J said:

> "When the Court has to consider the constitutionality of a law it must, in the first place, be accepted as an axiom that a law passed by the Oireachtas, the elected representatives of the people, is presumed to be constitutional unless and until the contrary is clearly established."

This principle was affirmed in the following year by the Supreme Court in *In re Article 26 and the Offences Against the State (Amendment) Bill 1940*:[138]

> "Where any particular law is not expressly prohibited and it is sought to establish that it is repugnant to the Constitution by reason of some implied prohibition or repugnancy, we are of opinion, as a matter of construction, that such repugnancy must be clearly established."[139]

This principle has been repeatedly re-stated;[140] and was, in *Buckley v Attorney General*,[141] rationalised by the Supreme Court as follows:

> "In our opinion, [it] springs from, and is necessitated by, that respect which one great organ of the State owes to another."

This explanation of the "presumption of constitutionality" has, in its turn, been re-stated in later cases.[142]

137 [1939] IR 413.

138 [1940] IR 470; (1940) 76 ILTR 61.

139 The presumption is evidently equally applicable to Acts of the Oireachtas, to Bills which passed both Houses and then referred to the Supreme Court under Article 26. The presumption also applies to resolutions of both Houses: see *Goodman International v Hamilton (No.1)* [1992] 2 IR 545.

140 Prominent (but random) examples include *In re Article 26 and the School Attendance Bill, 1942,* [1943] IR 334; (1943) 77 ILTR 96; *McDonald v Bord na gCon* [1965] IR 217; (1966) 100 ILTR 89; *East Donegal Co-Operative Ltd. v Attorney General* [1970] IR 317; (1970) 104 ILTR 81; *In re Haughey* [1971] IR 217; *Boland v An Taoiseach* [1974] IR 338; (1974) 109 ILTR 13; *R. v R.* [1984] IR 296; *McMahon v Leahy* [1984] IR 525; [1985] ILRM 423; *Harvey v Minister for Social Welfare* [1990] 2 IR 232; [1990] ILRM 185; *McDaid v Sheehy* [1991] 1 IR 1; [1991] ILRM 250; *Goodman International v Hamilton (No.1)* [1992] 2 IR 542; [1992] ILRM 145.

141 [1950] IR 67.

142 "It seems to me inescapable that having regard to the fact that the presumption of constitutional validity which attaches to both statutes and bills derives...from the respect shown by one organ of State to another, and by the necessary comity between the different organs of State, that it must apply in precisely the same way to a resolution of both Houses of the Oireachtas, even though it does not constitute legislation.": *Goodman International v Hamilton* [1992] 2 IR 542, *per* Finlay CJ. The "presumption of constitutionality" as understood in the US Supreme Court was mentioned by Mr. de Valera during the Dáil Debate on the draft Constitution: "Even where there is a Supreme Court, as there is in the United States of America, some of the best judges of those courts, when asked to decide as constitutional court, have said, and put it as the foreground of their work and interpretation, that, ordinarily, the view of the Legislature in interpreting their Constitution should be their guide: that there is presumption, and should be a presumption, that they are doing

"Self-restraint" in judicial review of legislation

The courts have also articulated the principle of "self-restraint" with regard to judicial review of legislation, which in general limits the exercise of judicial review to cases where it is necessary for the decision of the issue. The principle that the constitutional validity of a law will be considered by a court only where this is unavoidable is to some extent a product of "the comity that ought to exist between the great organs of States"[143] and is simply an aspect of the presumption of constitutionality. It is, however, also a product, as Henchy J put it in *The State (P. Woods) v Attorney General*, of "the inherent limitations of the judicial process": a court could invalidate a statute, and thus leave a gap in the law, but could not create a new Act to plug the gap:

> "It unmakes what was put forth as a law by the legislature, but, unlike the legislature, it cannot enact a law in its place. It is clear that if this power, which may seem abrogative and quasi-legislative, were used indiscriminately it would tend to upset the structure of government... Because of the constitutional proprieties involved in the judicial review of legislation and the inherent limitations of the judicial process, the rule has been evolved[144] that a court should not enter upon a question of constitutionality unless it is necessary for the determination of the case before it."

In the case before him, where both the warrant of the Court of Criminal Appeal, and the constitutionality of the Court itself, were being challenged, he found that the warrant was bad on ordinary legal grounds, and declined therefore to enter on the constitutional question.

The same approach was adopted by the Supreme Court (though without restatement of the principle) in *Roche v Minister for Industry and Commerce*:[145] and again in *M. v An Bord Uchtála*,[146] in which an adoption order was challenged both on the ground of the alleged unconstitutionality of sections of the Adoption Act 1952, and on that of the alleged failure of the Board to conform with statutory requirements in making its order. O'Higgins, CJ said:

> "Where the relief which a plaintiff seeks rests on two such distinct grounds, as a general rule the Court should consider first whether the relief sought can be granted on the ground which does not raise a question of constitutional validity. If it can, then the Court ought not to rule on the larger question of the constitutional validity of the law in question. Normally, such a law as a statute of the Oireachtas will enjoy a presumption of constitutionality which ought not to be put to the test unnecessarily."[147]

their work reasonably and fairly, and that it is only in cases where there is clearly and definitely a departure, not merely from the letter of the Constitution, but from the spirit of the Constitution, that they should hold differently" *(67 Dáil Debates* 427).

[143] *Per* Henchy J in *The State (P. Woods) v Attorney General* [1969] IR 385, quoting O'Byrne J in *Buckley v Attorney General* [1950] IR 67. This passage was also quoted by Finlay CJ in *McDaid v Sheehy* [1991] 1 IR 1; [1991] ILRM 250 who said that it was a corollary of this principle that "the Courts should not engage in the question of the possible invalidity of an Act of the Oireachtas unless it is necessary for the decision to do so."

[144] "Has been evolved": sc. in American constitutional law, from which he cited several cases, among them the classic judgment of Brandeis J in *Ashwander v Tennessee Valley Authority* 297 US 288 (1936). This decision was later to be cited with approval by Finlay CJ in *McDaid v Sheehy* [1991] 1 IR 1; [1991] ILRM 250.

[145] [1978] IR 149.

[146] [1977] IR 287.

[147] The rule was re-stated in the following form by O'Higgins CJ in *Cooke v Walsh* [1984] IR 710: "It is well settled that the consideration of any question involving the validity of a statute or a section thereof should, in appropriate circumstances, be postponed to the consideration of any other question, the resolution of which will determine the issue between the parties."

There might, however, be special cases:

> "However, there may be circumstances of an exceptional nature where the requirements of justice and the protection of constitutional rights make the larger enquiry necessary."

This was not so in the case before the Court here.[148] But such a case arose in the following month, in *The State (Kenny) v Ó hUadhaigh*,[149] in which the order of a District Judge was attacked partly on the ground that he had omitted a necessary inquiry as to age before convicting a young person, partly on the ground of the alleged inconsistency of a section of the Children Act 1908, with the Constitution. As Finlay P was able to decide the issue and quash the conviction on the former ground, he might have declined - on the principle outlined above - to enter on the constitutional question:

> "The ordinary rule of practice [is] that the Court should not decide upon the constitutionality of an enactment by way of *obiter* or as a moot, but should so decide only in a case where it is necessary for the decision of the Court. This general proposition is one with which I would concur."

But here was a special case of the kind envisaged by the Chief Justice in *M.'s* case:

> "However, in this case, where the question of the constitutionality of s 123 of the Act of 1908 was argued fully in front of me, and where it affects the rights of young persons and is, as far as I know, one that may well be used frequently in the courts, it seems to me that if I came to the conclusion that the section is unconstitutional I would have an obligation to say so, and thus discharge my general duty not only to protect citizens against an invasion of their constitutional rights but to be alert in enforcing them on their behalf.

But, as we shall presently see, it must be doubtful if this reasoning is compatible with some of the most modern re-statements of the "self-restraint" formula."

Recent re-statements of the rule of self-restraint

In two important decisions the Supreme Court has re-stated the rule of self-restraint in constitutional actions. In *Murphy v Roche*[150] the plaintiff wished to sue the unincorporated club of which he was a member for damages for personal injuries. Two preliminary questions arose: (i) was the plaintiff at common law estopped from suing the defendants? and (ii) if so, was this common law rule carried over by Article 50? Finlay CJ said that the Court ought to decline to decide any constitutional questions which "arise in the form of a moot" and which "were not necessary for the determination of the rights of the parties before it":

> "Where the issues between the parties can be determined and finally disposed of by resolution of an issue of law other than constitutional law, the court should proceed to determine that other issue first, and, if it determines the case, should refrain from expressing any view on the constitutional issue that may have been raised."

[148] But the Supreme Court's conclusion that there were no such exceptional circumstances is itself questionable. The Court's refusal to adjudicate on this issue cast a shadow over the validity of thousands of adoption orders and indirectly led to a special constitutional amendment in 1979 which was designed to safeguard the validity of such adoption orders.

[149] [1979] IR 1.

[150] [1987] IR 106. See also *Brady v Donegal Co. Council* [1989] ILRM 282 (where the Supreme Court ruled that the applicants must first establish the invalidity of the planning permission under challenge before they were permitted to attack the constitutionality of a two months' limitation period restricting the time limit for such challenges.)

These principles were, however, subject "to the overriding consideration of doing justice between the parties". In this case, the court directed a preliminary trial on the issue of the estoppel only, as, depending on the result of that determination, the constitutional law issue might become unnecessary to decide. In the second case, *McDaid v Sheehy*,[151] the Supreme Court actually took the opportunity of overruling of an earlier decision of its own which "constitute[d] a break in what appears to be a relatively consistent attitude of [the] Court to this question."[152] Here the applicant had challenged the validity of a 1975 statutory instrument which had been made pursuant to s 1 of the Imposition of Duties Act 1957 on the ground that the latter Act infringed Article 15.2.1.[153] Although that order had been subsequently confirmed by the Finance Act 1976 - so that any initial invalidity or unconstitutionality which had attached to that order had been subsequently cured - in the High Court, Blayney J had nonetheless held that s 1 of the 1957 Act was unconstitutional. The Supreme Court set aside this finding on the ground that it had not been necessary for Blayney J to have adjudicated on this issue, since it was clear in view of the 1976 confirming legislation that the applicant had not been "prejudiced or damaged by the operation of any provision of the Act of 1957 or of any statutory order made pursuant to it." Finlay CJ added that not only was the "settled jurisprudence" of the Supreme Court against deciding the issue of constitutional validity in such circumstances, but there were also practical considerations which strongly supported that view. In any inquiry as to whether an order made under s 1 of the 1957 Act constituted an impermissibly wide piece of delegated legislation:

> "consideration would have to be given to its precise terms, to its intended duration and to the actual effect it had on the interests of the citizen who challenged it. These and cognate questions which would be raised in a consideration challenge...underline the necessity for this Court to abstain from deciding that issue in this case where the validity of this section is no longer of importance to and where it has no effect in law on the interests of the applicant."[154]

It may be observed that there is here no concession at all to the suggestion which the Chief Justice had made when sitting over a decade previously as President of the High Court in *Kenny*, namely, that because the statute was frequently used (over three hundred orders had been made pursuant to the Imposition of Duties Act 1957), the court should pronounce on its constitutionality - even if not strictly required by the facts of the case before it - and thus discharge a duty to vindicate the constitutional rights of the citizenry in general. To that extent, Finlay P's *dictum* in *Kenny* seems at odds with the Supreme Court's later decision in *McDaid* and the former decision of the High Court must be taken as having been tacitly overruled.

It will have been noted that the general principle of not unnecessarily adjudicating on a statute's constitutional validity or consistency was stated by Finlay P in *Kenny's* case as applicable to both pre- and post-Constitution statutes, even if he was not quite so sure

[151] [1991] 1 IR 1; [1990] ILRM 250.

[152] Finlay CJ was here referring to *McDonald v Bord na gCon (No.1)* [1964] IR 350 where the Supreme Court had allowed the plaintiff to challenge the constitutionality of Greyhound Industry Act 1958 and to have this tried as a preliminary issue, i.e., without any necessary formal proof that the resolution of this issue was either necessary or essential to the plaintiff's case. Note however that O'Higgins CJ said in *The State (Rollinson) v Kelly* [1984] IR 248; [1984] ILRM 625 that he thought s 25(2) of the Finance Act 1926, unconstitutional, even though it was not necessary to decide this issue as the applicant's convictions had already been held to be bad in law

[153] See pp. 110-111.

[154] For other recent examples of this approach, see, e.g., *Phillips v The Medical Council* [1991] 2 IR 115; *Re Tivoli Cinema Ltd.* [1992] 1 IR 412; [1992] ILRM 552.

about the former type; and that the Act issue in that case was a pre-Constitution statute. If the principle is accepted as applicable to all statutes ostensibly in force, whatever their date, it will be seen that the rationale related to the presumption of constitutionality - the comity, or mutual respect, of the great organs of State - drops away: as an Irish court scarcely exists in comity with the parliament which enacted the Children Act of 1908, and cannot presume conformity of such an Act with an Irish Constitution enacted twenty-nine years later. Of the two reasons stated by Henchy J in *P. Woods'* case, therefore, there would remain valid only that related to the inability of the judicial arm to replace any gap which it might tear in the structure of statute law.

Is the presumption of constitutionality sometimes particularly strong?

There have been judicial suggestions that the presumption of constitutionality may actually operate with variable intensity, depending on the type of legislation under challenge. In *Ryan v Attorney General*[155] Kenny J said, in connection with the function of the Oireachtas in reconciling the exercise of personal rights with the claims of the common good (the context was the obligatory fluoridation of water), that the presumption "applies with particular force to this type of legislation". A few months earlier he had said, in *McDonald v Bord na gCon*,[156] that:

> "While the Court has power to declare an Act to be unconstitutional because it does not defend and vindicate the personal rights of the citizen, it is a jurisdiction to be exercised with extreme care and caution, particularly having regard to the now accepted extensive role of the State in economic and social matters."

This presumption appears to operate with particular intensity in the case of challenges to revenue statutes. This point was graphically made by O'Hanlon J in *Madigan v Attorney General*[157] in relation to a challenge to the residential property tax created by Part VI of the Finance Act 1983:

> "In challenging the validity of a taxation statute enacted by the Oireachtas, it appears to me that a plaintiff faces a very uphill battle. In the first place [there is the general presumption of constitutionality]. Secondly, it has been recognised that tax laws are in a category of their own and that very considerable latitude must be allowed to the legislature in the enormously complex task of organising and directing the financial affairs of the State."

A similarly strong presumption would also seem to apply in the case of constitutional challenges to social welfare legislation[158] and to the validity of executive acts in the conduct of foreign affairs.[159]

155 [1965] IR 294.

156 [1965] IR 217; (1966) 100 ILTR 89.

157 [1986] ILRM 123.

158 See the comments of Barrington J in *Hyland v Minister for Social Welfare* [1989] IR 624; [1990] ILRM 213. And while this is not explicitly stated, this seems implicit in the judgment of Carroll J in *MhicMhathúna v Ireland* [1989] IR 504 and that of Costello J in *O'Reilly v Limerick Corporation* [1989] ILRM 181.

159 This seems implicit in a trilogy of Supreme Court decisions in this area: *Boland v An Taoiseach* [1974] IR 338; (1974) 109 ILTR 13; *Crotty v An Taoiseach* [1987] IR 713; [1987] ILRM 400 and *McGimpsey v Ireland* [1990] 1 IR 110; [1990] ILRM 440. In *McGimpsey's* case, Barrington J in the High Court had expressly articulated a presumption of constitutionality of executive acts based on the words of O'Byrne J in the *Sinn Féin Funds* case. Barrington J also stressed that the onus in such cases was a "heavy one": "The conduct of the foreign policy of the State is not a matter which easily lends itself to judicial review and if there is any area in which judicial restraint is appropriate, that is it."

Is the presumption sometimes weak?

On the other hand, could it be argued that a Consolidation Act (since the Oireachtas does not debate the content of its sections) ought to enjoy only a diminished presumption? Perhaps a rational basis could also be established for according only a token presumption of constitutionality to Acts of the Oireachtas which (as is often the case) have been substantially, and sometimes literally copied from current British legislation.[160] Here the "comity of the great organs of State" and the respect which the courts consequently owe the executive ought not to obscure the reality that a Department which prepares a Bill by looking at a British precedent is likely to be less alert for elements which should not pass an Irish constitutional scrutiny than if it had undertaken to construct a Bill for its purpose from scratch, and out of original materials.[161]

No presumption of for Acts of the pre-1937 Oireachtas

The presumption of constitutionality is available only to Acts of the (post-1937) Oireachtas: in *The State (Sheerin) v Kennedy*[162] the Supreme Court was unanimous with the judgment of Walsh J:

> "All laws in force on the date immediately prior to the coming into operation of the Constitution are presumed not to be in conflict with the Constitution in force at the date of their enactment or in excess of the powers of the parliament which enacted them, but they enjoy no such presumption in respect of the provisions of the present Constitution and fall to be examined under the provisions of Article 50 of the Constitution - not as to their validity but, even assuming they were valid, as to whether or not they are inconsistent with the provisions of the present Constitution."

In *McMahon v Attorney General*[163] Ó Dálaigh CJ said tersely, in connection with the Electoral Act 1923, that:

> "The Constitution of Ireland, 1937, does not offer any presumption of constitutionality to the statute roll of Saorstát Éireann."

But should there be a qualified presumption in their favour?

On the other hand, Kenny J seemed to think in *Macauley v Minister for Posts and Telegraphs*[164] that statutes of the pre-1937 Oireachtas might get the benefit of some sort of presumption of consistency with the 1937 Constitution. He said, referring to a British statute of 1651, that no presumption of being constitutional applied to it. But:

[160] A practice which McWilliam J once described as "the scissors and paste penchant of our Legislature": *Breatnach v McC.* [1984] IR 340. Thus - to take a representative example of this practice - s 8 of the Defamation Act 1961 is a virtual reproduction of s 8 of the Law of Libel Amendment Act 1888. Section 8 requires that any application to commence a criminal libel prosecution must be heard *in camera* . This section gives all the appearance of having been copied virtually verbatim from the earlier British statute, but without anybody having given much thought to the compatibility with Article 34.1 of this mandatory *in camera* requirement: see p. 401.

[161] There is a hint of this in *O'Brien v Keogh* [1972] IR 144 where Ó Dálaigh CJ said of s 49(2)(*a*)(ii) of the Statute of Limitations 1957 (which was found to be unconstitutional) that "it would appear that the impugned provision is a transcription of the British Act of three years earlier...It does not bear any evidence of having been considered in the light of Article 40.3 of the Constitution..."

[162] [1966] IR 379. Note that Barrington J spoke to the same effect (on the subject of the nineteenth century Valuation Acts) in *Brennan v Attorney General* [1983] ILRM 449.

[163] [1972] IR 69; (1972) 106 ILTR 89. See also the comments of O'Higgins CJ to like effect in *de Búrca v Attorney General* [1976] IR 38; (1977) 111 ILTR 37.

[164] [1966] IR 345.

> "the [Minister and Secretaries] Act of 1924 has that presumption in its favour and should, if possible, be construed in such a manner that it will be consistent with the Constitution."

It may be recalled also that in the very first case in which the presumption of constitutionality was stated, *Pigs Marketing Board v Donnelly,*[165] the statutes under challenge were Acts of the pre-Constitution Oireachtas (the Pigs and Bacon Acts 1935 and 1937); Hanna J appeared to relate the presumption to the fact that they had been enacted by "the elected representatives of the people".

As *Sheerin's* and *McMahon's* cases were decided by the Supreme Court subsequent to *Macauley's* case (which was decided by Kenny J in the High Court) the view that an Act of 1924 could enjoy the full presumption of constitutionality under the 1937 Constitution must be regarded as overruled,[166] but value remains in the constructional proposition that a pre-1937 Act should, if possible, be construed so that it will be consistent with the Constitution. The functional, political and personal continuity between the Oireachtas of the 1922 Constitution and the post-1937 Oireachtas - and between the courts of Saorstát Éireann and the courts of the 1937 Constitution - suggests the wisdom of according a qualified presumption, a presumption of courtesy, to enactments of the old Oireachtas,[167] even though the strict logical basis for such a presumption is lacking; perhaps on the basis that the method of global continuance of laws (subject to possible inconsistency) implies that the 1922 constituent assembly, and in 1937 the people, thought the corpus of existing law in general acceptable within the new Constitution.

No presumption for pre-independence statutes

The presumption of constitutionality is, *a fortiori,* not applicable to pre-1922, British statutes, for the reason simply stated by Budd J in *Educational Co. v Fitzpatrick (No. 2)*:[168]

> "It is suggested that there is some presumption that [the Trade Disputes Act 1906] is constitutional. Such a presumption may well apply to Acts of the Oireachtas, since the legislative body must be deemed to legislate with a knowledge of the Constitution and presumably does not intend by its measures to infringe it. There is no logical basis for such a presumption in the case of Acts of the late United Kingdom Parliament. The legislature then had no knowledge of the Constitution to be and could never be said to have legislated with any regard to it."

But it may be noted that in 1930 two judges of the High Court, while not speaking in terms of any "presumption", were in favour of an approach even to pre-1922 British statutes which would be slow to find them inconsistent with the 1922 Constitution, for reasons of practical utility: in *The State (Kennedy) v Little*[169] O'Byrne J said:

> "It seems to me to have been intended to set up the new State with the least possible change in the previously existing law, and that Article 73 [which continued the pre-

[165] [1939] IR 413.

[166] This is also borne out by the later *obiter* observations of O'Flaherty J in *MF v Superintendent, Ballymun Garda Station* [1991] 1 IR 189; [1990] ILRM 767 where he re-iterated that pre-Constitution legislation enjoyed no presumption of constitutionality, i.e., not distinguishing here between pre-1922 British legislation and legislation enacted by the old Oireachtas between 1922 and 1937.

[167] There is rough analogy in this argument between the enactments of the "old" and "new" Oireachtas and decisions of the former and present Supreme Court. Decisions of the former Supreme Court are nonetheless binding on the present Court: see the comments of Henchy J in *The State (Lynch) v Cooney* [1982] IR 337 and pp. 535-536.

[168] [1961] IR 345.

[169] [1931] IR 39; (1931) 65 ILTR 9.

1922 laws in force unless inconsistent with the Constitution] should be so construed as to effectuate this intention."

Johnston J said:

"I think... that we should be very slow to do anything that would have the effect of depriving the Saorstát of the benefit of the vast body of useful statutory law which regulated hundreds and thousands of necessary matters in the body politic at the date of the coming into operation of the Constitution."

There is more than a hint of this approach in the judgment of O'Higgins CJ in *Norris v Attorney General*[170] when he said that the whole purpose of Article 50.1 was "to continue in force the laws which had previously operated in Saorstát Éireann, with as few exceptions as possible." Nevertheless, the Supreme Court confirmed in *Norris* that while pre-22 legislation enjoyed no (it might almost be said) *formal* presumption of constitutionality, the onus of establishing inconsistency rests with the person who "challenges [its] continued validity."[171] One would be hard put to identify a real distinction between this requirement and the presumption of constitutionality itself.

Test of consistency with Irish common sense and public policy in the case of pre-1922 law?

On the other hand, there are several judicial decisions which suggest that not only must a pre-1922 law survive the test of consistency with the Constitution, but it must also not conflict with what might be called the common sense or public policy of the people which may be supposed to underlie the Constitution's text. In *Exham v Beamish*[172] Gavan Duffy J refused to apply the old English rule which, for the purpose of void perpetuities, did not regard the age of child-bearing as having any natural limit: he said the Court was:

"bound to decline to treat any such absurdity in the machinery of administration as having been imposed on it as part of the law of the land: nothing is law here which is inconsistent with derivation from the people."

In recent times, O'Hanlon J took a somewhat similar line in *S v S*[173] when asked to apply the old rule which did not permit a spouse to rebut the presumption of legitimacy in favour of all issue born to a wife during the subsistence of a marriage. Although he did not describe the rule as absurd, and did measure it against the constitutional value, elaborated only in recent years, of "fair procedures", he appeared to disapprove it on the more general ground of its "running counter to that paramount public policy (of ascertaining truth and doing justice" in holding that it "ceased to have legal effect in the State after the enactment of the Constitution of 1937".[174] Both of these cases involved judge-made rules and not statute law, but the idea informing them would seem equally applicable to a pre-1922 (or perhaps even a post-1922 but pre-1938) statutory provision which offended the relatively non-specific values which these judges expressed. But *Vone*

170 [1984] IR 36.

171 Note also that in *Cowan v Attorney General* [1961] IR 411, in which provisions of electoral laws of 1882 and 1884 were under challenge, Haugh J cited the presumption doctrine, as enunciated by the Supreme Court in earlier cases, to declare the burden of proof of unconstitutionality carried by the plaintiff.

172 [1939] IR 336.

173 [1983] IR 68; [1984] ILRM 66.

174 There are also elements of this approach to be found in the judgment of Barr J in *CM v TM (No.2)* [1990] 2 IR 52; [1991] ILRM 268 and those of Blayney and Egan JJ in *W. v W.* [1993] ILRM 294. Both cases concerned the non-survival of the dependent domicile rule and while the rule was ultimately found to offend against specific provisions of Article 40, a sense of judicial unease with the anomalous operation of such an arbitrary rule is not far from the surface of these judgments.

Securities Ltd. v Cooke[175] shows that there are definite limits to what the courts are prepared to do under this rubric. This case concerned the meaning of the word "month" as it appeared in a lease. At common law, the word "month" was taken to mean a lunar month unless the contrary intention appeared. The plaintiffs argued that this common law rule was so archaic and so out of touch with modern usage that it should be "rejected as outmoded and unworthy of recognition or application in the courts". The Supreme Court refused to adopt this line, because it would mean (as Henchy J put it) the retroactive abrogation of the rule in its application to existing situations, with consequent injustice to vested property rights. Yet in *S v S* O'Hanlon J treated as invalid the former irrebuttable presumption of legitimacy, despite the fact that this, too, would affect property rights already acquired by its operation.

Pre-1922 statutes and the doctrine of desuetude

This issue is also relevant in the context of whether pre-1922 and other older statutes can fall into desuetude. In *Nova Media Services Ltd. v Minister for Posts and Telegraphs*[176] Murphy J said (albeit in the context of post-1922 legislation, the Wireless Telegraphy Act 1926) that a statute cannot "wither away from lack of use, and... cannot be repealed, waived or abandoned by the express decision or agreement of the executive". Yet in *The State (Feeley) v O'Dea*[177] Keane J said that the provisions of s 8(1) of the Petty Sessions (Ireland) Act 1851 (which, as adapted, prevented the District Court from sitting in a building where "spirituous or fermented liquors" are sold) had fallen into a "limbo of desuetude"[178] and were inoperative, as they belonged to the "vanished world of grand juries, county cess and presentment sessions". These views of two judges of co-ordinate jurisdiction seem irreconcilable; the former would seem to be more in harmony with traditional doctrine on statute law.

Amendment of old law a sign that the Oireachtas considers it constitutional

An interesting nuance in the ostensible contrast between post-1937 laws (which enjoy a presumption of constitutionality) and pre-1937 laws (which do not) emerged in the judgment of Pringle J in *O'Brien v Manufacturing Engineering Co. Ltd.*,[179] where what was in issue was s 60 of the Workmen's Compensation Act 1934, as amended by s 6 of the Workmen's Compensation (Amendment) Act 1953. With regard to the argument that the latter Act alone enjoyed the presumption, he said nevertheless:

> "I would have thought that the Oireachtas should be presumed to have regarded the section which it purported to amend as not being repugnant to the Constitution in force at the time when the amending Act was passed."

Subsequently, in *The People (Attorney General) v Conmey*,[180] Walsh J took the view, in regard to the express re-enactment of s 29 of the Courts of Justice Act 1924, by s 48 of the Courts (Supplemental Provisions) Act 1961, that the earlier section was entitled to the benefit of the presumption that the Oireachtas in 1961 did not intend to violate the Constitution unless the re-enactment led "to no other possible conclusion". A similar approach was taken (though in a very clear case, as the old provision had been expressly re-applied by the new one) by Finlay P in *The State (Walshe) v Murphy*.[181] And Murphy

[175] [1979] IR 59.
[176] [1984] ILRM 161.
[177] [1986] IR 687. See generally, Hogan, "*The Doctrine of Desuetude*" (1987) 9 DULJ (n.s.)136.
[178] The phrase is borrowed from the judgment of Henchy J in *Waterford Harbour Commissioners v British Railway Board* [1979] ILRM 296.
[179] [1973] IR 334; (1972) 108 ILTR 105.
[180] [1975] IR 341.
[181] [1981] IR 275.

J appeared to hint (though did not say expressly) something of the same kind in *Nova Media Services Ltd. v Minister for Posts and Telegraphs*,[182] when he noted that the Wireless Telegraphy Act 1926 (which was in issue), had been amended by several post-1937 Acts, and that the Wireless Telegraphy Act 1972, provided that it should, together with the 1926 Act and intervening Acts, be construed as one Act. And in *E.S.B. v Gormley*[183] the Supreme Court sought to tackle this question by saying:

> "Where Acts passed since the coming into force of the Constitution expressly re-enact pre-Constitution statutes...such re-enactment gives to them the status of having been passed since the coming into force of the Constitution, thus applying the presumption to them. It is equally clear that the mere fact of an amendment of a pre-Constitution statute contained in a statute passed after the coming into force of the Constitution does not of itself give to that pre-Constitution statute a presumption of validity."

Finlay CJ went on to examine the amendment of s 53 the Electricity (Supply) Act 1927 by the Electricity (Supply)(Amendment) Act 1945. The Chief Justice concluded that, having regard to "the nature and terms of that amendment, which extends and expands the nature of the work to which s 53 originally applied", this amendment "effectively re-enacted s 53 [of the 1927 Act] as part of a post-Constitution statute."

Gormley's case thus provides an example of where a pre-1937 statute attracted the presumption of constitutionality an the same manner as if it had been enacted after 1937. The logical difficulty with this, however. was pointed out by Barrington J in *Brennan v Attorney General*:[184]

> "The issue is whether the statute, bearing the meaning it then had, is or is not consistent with the Constitution of 1937 and was or was not carried forward by Article 50... If the statute, as so interpreted, was not carried forward by Article 50 it is immaterial that the Oireachtas later tried to amend or adapt it because there was nothing for them to amend or adapt."

Probably the right way to look at the matter is this: as the whole doctrine of presumption of constitutionality rests on the presumed intention of the Oireachtas to respect the Constitution, then, even though a pre-1937 provision is now discovered for the first time to have been inconsistent with the Constitution and so not carried over, the Oireachtas by re-enacting it (as in *Conmey's* case) can be taken to have breathed into a dead text both new life and the presumption of constitutionality as well; or by merely amending it (as in *O'Brien's* case) can be taken to have done the same thing implicitly if not expressly. The matter awaits final settling.

No presumption where unconstitutionality is patent

Again on the authority of Pringle J, the presumption of constitutionality does not operate where the unconstitutional nature of the statutory provision is patent. In *M. v An Bord Uchtála*,[185] where s 12(2) of the Adoption Act 1952, was in issue, he said:

> "I have approached this case, as I must, on the basis that the provisions of the Act of 1952 must be presumed to be constitutional and that, in the ordinary case, the onus would be on the plaintiffs to rebut this presumption. I agree, however, with the

[182] [1984] ILRM 161.
[183] [1985] IR 129.
[184] [1983] ILRM 449. The Supreme Court was not required to address this question on appeal: see [1984] ILRM 355.
[185] [1975] IR 81; (1975) 109 ILTR 62.

statement of Taft CJ in *Bailey v Drexel Furniture Co.*[186] where he said: "But, in the Act before us, the presumption of validity cannot prevail, because proof to the contrary is found on the very face of its provisions." I consider that that is the position here. The provisions of s 12(2) of the Act of 1952 on their face are clearly in contravention of Article 44.2.3... for the reasons advanced by counsel for the plaintiffs."

In *Loftus v Attorney General*[187] the judgment of the Supreme Court contains a phrase which indicates that that Court, too, accepted that the presumption of constitutionality has no place in a case where the unconstitutionality shows plainly on the face of the Act.

(E) Canons of review: (II) Corollaries of presumption of constitutionality

The "double construction" rule

The presumption of constitutionality in favour of post-1937 Acts has thrown up a corollary which, like the presumption itself, is probably attributable to American example: this at any rate is suggested by the words of Henchy J in *The State (P. Woods) v Attorney General.*[188] He called it a "refinement" of the presumption and drew attention to its concordance with the practice of the American Supreme Court, citing *US v Delaware & Hudson Co.*[189] and *US v Witkovich.*[190] This corollary was stated as such for the first time in the judgment of the Supreme Court in *McDonald v Bord na gCon (No.2)*,[191] delivered by Walsh J, and is conveniently spoken of as the "double construction" rule; but it appears in a rudimentary form - i.e., not expressly related to the presumption of constitutionality - in *Grimes v Owners of S.S Bangor Bay*[192] decided by the old Supreme Court seventeen years earlier, when O'Byrne J said, in interpreting sections of the Courts of Justice Act 1924, that:

> "if a statute purported to confer upon any court of first instance, other than the High Court, (an unlimited jurisdiction, it would in my opinion, contravene the clear intendment of the Constitution and would, for that reason, be outside the powers conferred upon the Oireachtas and invalid. Such a result should if possible be avoided. Accordingly, I take the view that if the statute can reasonably be so construed as to comply with the powers of the Constitution [sc. that of 1922], such construction should be placed upon it."

In *McDonald's* case Walsh J said:

> "The Greyhound Industry Act 1958, being an Act of the Oireachtas, is presumed to be constitutional until the contrary is clearly established. One practical effect of this presumption is that if in respect of any provision or provisions of the Act two or more constructions are reasonably open, one of which is constitutional and the other or others are unconstitutional, it must be presumed that the Oireachtas intended only the constitutional construction and a court called upon to adjudicate upon the constitutionality of the statutory provision should uphold the constitutional con-

[186] 259 US 20 (1922).
[187] [1979] IR 221.
[188] [1969] IR 385.
[189] 213 US 366 (1909).
[190] 353 US 194 (1957).
[191] [1965] IR 217; (1966) 100 ILTR 89.
[192] [1948] IR 350.

struction. It is only when there is no construction reasonably open which is not repugnant to the Constitution that the provision should be held to be repugnant."

In that case this "double construction" test was applied in such a way as to read into the provision of a section enabling exclusion orders to be made, the requirement that an investigation with due regard for natural (or "constitutional") justice should precede the proposal to make an exclusion order:

> "While the Board may determine the manner in which the investigation shall be carried out, the clear words or necessary implication which would be required to exclude the principles of natural justice from such investigation are not present in the sections."

In other words, while one construction - the unconstitutional one - suggested that the Board might formulate its proposal without, at that stage, having held an investigation or given the person affected any indication of the charge against him, another construction - not explicitly excluded by the words of the Act - would envisage a due investigation being held, even though the exclusion order section did not say so, in which event the whole proceeding would be unobjectionable. This - the constitutional construction - was preferred, on the basis that the Oireachtas must be "presumed" to have intended it rather than the unconstitutional one.

This notion took on more definition in the same judge's words the following year in *The State (Quinn) v Ryan*:[193]

> "In the exercise of powers conferred by an Act of the Oireachtas any Act inconsistent with the provisions of the Constitution is probably *ultra vires* the statute unless expressly authorised by the statute or authorised by necessary implication, because it may be presumed until the contrary be clearly shown that the Oireachtas did not intend to give legislative authority for acts inconsistent with the Constitution to which the Oireachtas itself is subject."

Only if the words of the statute admit no course of events other than a constitutionally objectionable one - so one might paraphrase the foregoing statement - is the presumption in favour of the Act so to speak, disappointed; the Oireachtas is seen to have failed to respect the limitations laid on it, and (since it is forbidden to exceed these limitations) the Act itself is *ultra vires* the Oireachtas and invalid.

Extent of application of the presumption

Six years later Walsh J delivered the judgment of the Supreme Court in *East Donegal Co-Operative Ltd. v Attorney General*[194] and once again added some features to the presumption:

> "An Act of the Oireachtas, or any provision thereof, will not be declared to be invalid where it is possible to construe it in accordance with the Constitution; and it is not only a question of preferring a constitutional construction to one which would be unconstitutional where they both may appear to be open, but it also means that an interpretation favouring the validity of an Act should be given in cases of doubt."

The Act then, must get the benefit of a doubt. Moreover, official actions envisaged by the Act even if their modes of performance are not specified in the Act must be per-

[193] [1965] IR 70; (1966) 100 ILTR 105.
[194] [1970] IR 317; (1970) 104 ILTR 81.

formed in such a way as to respect the Constitution (because the Oireachtas must have intended them so to be performed):

> "At the same time... the presumption of constitutionality carries with it not only the presumption that the constitutional interpretation or construction is the one intended by the Oireachtas but also that the Oireachtas intended that proceedings, procedures, discretions and adjudications which are permitted, provided for or prescribed by an Act of the Oireachtas are to be conducted in accordance with the principles of constitutional justice. In such a case any departure from those principles would be restrained and corrected by the courts."

The presumption has been subsequently extended to include executive acts[195] and resolutions of the Oireachtas[196] and in both instances the courts relied expressly on the principle of the "respect which one great organ of the State owes to another" which O'Byrne J had enunciated in the *Sinn Féin Funds* case. There are, however, limits to the doctrine. It does not, for instance, apply to the interpretation of an international treaty, since such a treaty "has only one meaning and that is its meaning in international law" and its interpretation "cannot be coloured by reference to the Constitution.[197] Moreover, the presumption of constitutionality does not extend to official acts and statutory discretions to be performed outside of the State, since as the Supreme Court said in the Criminal Law (Jurisdiction) Bill 1975, reference[198] that it was:

> "not prepared to hold that such a presumption can be applied to proceedings, procedures, discretions and adjudications required by the legislation to be performed outside the State by persons having no obligation to uphold the Constitution."

"Double construction" test in application

The subsequent case law amply demonstrates that more then mere judicial lip service is paid to the "double construction" rule, since its application will often serve to rescue what on first impression might seem to be a constitutionally dubious statute. *The People (Attorney General) v Conmey*[199] provides a good illustration of this. Here it was argued that the provisions of s 29 of the Courts of Justice Act 1924, continued expressly by ss 12, 48 of the Courts (Supplemental Provisions) Act 1961, inasmuch as they excluded generally further appeals to the Supreme Court from decisions of the Court of Criminal Appeal, were unconstitutional under Article 34.4.4 for purporting thereby to exclude, *inter alia*, appeals on cases involving questions as to the constitutional validity of laws; but by operating the "double construction" rule Walsh J in the Supreme Court was able to absolve the section from unconstitutionality:

> "The effect of this is that it must be assumed that the Oireachtas in 1961 did not intend to violate the constitutional provisions referred to unless the statutory provision leads to no other possible conclusion. As the Constitution does not allow the Court of Criminal Appeal to decide, on appeal or otherwise, any question as to the validity of any law having regard to the provisions of the Constitution, the question of an appeal to the Supreme Court in such a case cannot be said to have been within

[195] *McGimpsey v Ireland* [1988] IR 567 (HC).
[196] *Goodman International v Hamilton (No.1)* [1992] 2 IR 542; [1992] ILRM 145.
[197] *McGimpsey v Ireland* [1988] IR 567 (HC), per Barrington J.
[198] [1977] IR 129; (1976) 110 ILTR 69.
[199] [1975] IR 341. There is a similar presumption that the Oireachtas has not legislated "in a manner which is in breach of rights protected under Community law": *Murphy v Bord Telecom Éireann (No.2)* [1988] ILRM 53.

the contemplation of the provisions of s 29 of the Act of 1924 as re-enacted by s 48 of the Courts (Supplemental Provisions) Act 1961."

This doctrine has been since re-enunciated in a number of cases, of which *Loftus v Attorney General,*[200] *Doyle v An Taoiseach*[201] and *Hegarty v O'Loughran* [202] may serve as illustrations. In *Loftus* the plaintiffs alleged that the powers vested by s 13 of the Electoral Act 1963, in the Registrar of Political Parties (in regard to registering, or refusing to register a party) were arbitrary and unconstitutional; the Supreme Court recalled that it had on a number of occasions held that:

> "a statutory provision which has been enacted by the parliament established under the Constitution will, unless it plainly shows on its face a repugnancy to the Constitution, be entitled, not only to a presumption of constitutionality, but also to a presumption that what is required, or allowed to be done, for the purpose of its implementation, will take place without breaching any of the requirements, express or implied, of the Constitution... No standard or objective test or criterion is provided either in the section or elsewhere in the Act in accordance with which [the Registrar's] opinion is to be formed... [But s 13] does not confer on the Registrar of Political Parties an arbitrary power... While he is given a discretion to register or not to register, this is not an unfettered discretion. He is bound to act fairly and judicially in accordance with the Constitution. Accordingly he must consider every application on its merits . . . If the Registrar exercised his discretion or his powers capriciously, partially or in a manifestly unfair manner it would be assumed that this could not have been contemplated or intended by the Oireachtas and his action would be restrained and corrected by the courts."

The presumption of constitutionality will sometimes require the courts to give an artificial meaning to a statute in order to save it from successful challenge, if this can be achieved without doing violence for the language of the statute itself. An example is supplied by *Doyle v An Taoiseach*, where the natural meaning of s 79 of the Finance Act 1980 suggested that it was intended to confirm the validity of certain orders which were expressed to operate between May and December 1979. However, the Supreme Court, *per* Henchy J, observed that as such a construction of the section would be unconstitutional having regard to Article 15.5,[203] and "there was nothing in the 1980 Act which would justify the attribution to Parliament of an intention that the section was to operate unconstitutionally, the Court treated the section as having only prospective effect." In effect, therefore, the Court - in order to preserve the constitutionality of the section - stripped it of its primary meaning so that, as thus interpreted, the section was little more than an empty shell, devoid of its original purpose.

An interesting application of the possible limits to the double construction test may also be found in *Hegarty v O'Loughran*. This case turned in part on whether s 11(2)(*b*) of the Statute of Limitations 1957 prescribed an absolute time bar in respect of all personal injury actions,[204] irrespective of whether the facts giving rise to the cause of action could reasonably have been discovered within that period. The Supreme Court construed the section as prescribing an absolute time-bar, even though there was reason to suppose that this interpretation might be unconstitutional.[205] Carroll J had previously said in

[200] [1979] IR 211.
[201] [1986] ILRM 693.
[202] [1990] 1 IR 148; [1990] ILRM 403.
[203] See p. 128.
[204] Subject to certain statutory exceptions (fraud etc.) which were not relevant to the case.
[205] The Supreme Court had previously hinted at this possible flaw in the statute in *Cahill v Sutton* [1980] IR 269.

Morgan v Park Developments Ltd.[206] that such an interpretation of the section would be unconstitutional and therefore, applying the presumption of constitutionality, she favoured a more open-ended interpretation of the section in order to avoid (what she perceived as) an unconstitutional interpretation of the section. In *Hegarty*, however, Finlay CJ said that this analysis could only apply where two or more constructions of the statute were reasonably open. In the present case, he thought that the section only admitted of one construction, namely, that the section did create an absolute time-bar. The Chief Justice was at pains to say that such a strict interpretation[207] of the section was not necessarily unconstitutional and he drew attention to the potential hardships to the defendants which might be caused by an open-ended time limit. Finlay CJ then concluded by saying that he would reserve his position "on the question of its constitutional validity" pending any possible constitutional challenge, other than "to presume it constitutional, as I must do." This case highlights a potential dilemma for the courts when it comes to construing a statute where (as in *Hegarty*) there had been no direct challenge to the constitutionality of the section, but where a certain interpretation of the statute might render it vulnerable to attack. There is here, of course, a clear indication - despite the Chief Justice's formal reservation of his position - that the section as thus construed is not unconstitutional. But if the situation had been otherwise - and the Supreme Court had found itself coerced by ordinary principles of statutory interpretation to arrive at an interpretation that was probably unconstitutional - could the Court have avoided pronouncing on that constitutional question, even in the absence of a formal challenge to the statute's validity. Or does the presumption of constitutionality oblige the courts to carrying on applying a statute which, thus construed, is almost certainly unconstitutional pending a formal pronouncement of that invalidity?

It was probably with such considerations in mind that Gannon J formulated the double construction test in the following terms:

> "If the statutes and sections are not capable of interpretation, sensible construction and effective implementation consistent with the Constitution, only then may they be declared invalid to the extent that they are found inconsistent with the Constitution."[208]

Presumption extends to official acts authorised by law

Most of the cases which have now accumulated on the presumption as to official acts authorised by Act of the Oireachtas being performed in a constitutional manner centre around "constitutional justice" and fair procedures. Thus, Henchy J could elaborate on this theme in *The State (Lynch) v Cooney*[209] in the special context of an administrative function depending on the formation of an opinion by the person exercising the function:

> "The presumption of constitutional regularity of official acts means, amongst other things, not only that the power must be exercised in good faith, but that the opinion or other subjective conclusion set as a precondition for the valid exercise of the power must be reached by a route that does not make the exercise unlawful such as by misinterpreting the law, or by misapplying it through taking into consideration

[206] [1983] ILRM 156.

[207] The potential harshness of which has since been ameliorated - as far as personal injuries are concerned - by the enactment of the Statute of Limitations (Amendment) Act 1991.

[208] *R v R.* [1984] IR 296.

[209] [1982] IR 337. Henchy J had earlier spoken along the same lines in *Burke v Minister for Labour* [1979] IR 354. See also the judgment of Finlay P in *Killiney and Ballybrack Development Association Limited v Minister for Local Government* (1978) 112 ILTR 69.

irrelevant matters of fact or through ignoring relevant matters. Otherwise, the exercise of the power will be held to be invalid for being *ultra vires*."

Viewed in this way, the extension of the presumption of constitutionality to official acts under statute, first enunciated in the *East Donegal* case, seems to be a simple presumption of legality on principles already recognised in the common law.

Yet the presumption of constitutionality can carry the courts a good deal further, a point illustrated by the judgment of Henchy J himself in *McMahon v Leahy*.[210] In this case Henchy J held that, in the special circumstances of the case, to permit the extradition of the plaintiff would violate Article 40.1. He rejected the argument that, once it had been shown that none of the statutory exemptions from extradition applied, the court had no discretion but to make the extradition order in view of the apparently mandatory language of Extradition Act 1965:

> "Where... a post-Constitution statute authorises the making of an order in stated circumstances, the legislative intent must be held to comprehend that the authorised order will not be made, even though the stated circumstances are shown to exist, if it is shown that the order would necessarily infringe the constitutional right of the party against whom it would operate. The [presumption of constitutionality] carries with it not only the normal presumption that laws enacted by the National Parliament are not repugnant to the Constitution but also the presumption that the provisions of such laws will not be administered or applied in a way that will infringe constitutional rights. The presumption of constitutionality extends to both the substance and the operation of a statute: it is a presumption that admits of rebuttal only by a contrary intention appearing in the terms of the statute itself."

A similar line was taken by the Supreme Court in *Eccles v Ireland*.[211] The plaintiffs in this case attacked the validity of convictions imposed by the Special Criminal Court, alleging that the members of the Court were not impartial. It was said that s 39 of the Offences against the State Act 1939 (which provides that members of the Court shall hold office at the pleasure of the Government and that the Minister for Finance shall pay such remuneration to members of the Court as he shall think fit) was unconstitutional in that it conferred an unfettered discretion on the authorities to influence the course of proceedings before the Court (e.g., by terminating the appointment of individual members of the Court whose decisions did not suit the Government). This submission was rejected by Finlay CJ for the Supreme Court. Recalling the language of Walsh J in the *East Donegal Co-Operative* case, he said that there was a presumption that administrative discretions would be exercised in accordance with constitutional principles:

> "If [the] authorities were to seek to exercise their power in a manner capable of interfering with the judicial independence of the [Special Criminal] Court, in the trial of persons charged before it, it would be attempting to frustrate the constitutional right of persons accused before that Court to trial in due course of law. Any such attempt would be prevented and corrected by the courts established under the Constitution."

In *Crotty v An Taoiseach*[212] Barrington J accepted that there was a presumption that the Government was acting within constitutional limitations in ratifying an international treaty; this echoed what had already been said by the Supreme Court in *Boland v An*

[210] [1984] IR 548; [1985] ILRM 449.
[211] [1985] IR 289; [1986] ILRM 343.
[212] [1987] IR 713; [1987] ILRM 400. See also *McGimpsey v Ireland* [1990] 1 IR 110; [1990] ILRM 440.

Taoiseach,[213] where the Court presumed that the executive had not intended to infringe Articles 2 and 3 by signing the Sunningdale Agreement.

Limits to the presumption of constitutionality

In 1971 the Supreme Court gave a demonstration of how far it would go in applying this extension of the presumption of constitutionality. In *In re Haughey*[214] s 3(4) of the Committee of Public Accounts of Dáil Éireann (Privilege and Procedure) Act 1970, was in issue; it purported to empower the Dáil Committee of Public Accounts, where a witness had refused to answer a question which he was legally required to answer, to:

> "certify the offence of that person under the hand of the chairman of the committee to the High Court and the High Court may, after such enquiry as it thinks proper to make, punish or take steps for the punishment of that person in like manner as if he had been guilty of contempt of the High Court."

Mr. Haughey contended that this purported to empower a committee - which was not a court, nor were its members judges - to try and to convict him of a criminal offence, leaving only the imposition of punishment to the High Court. This would violate Article 38 and so would be invalid. The Court said:

> "If the Court [were] to apply the ordinary canons of construction of statute law, the Court would affirm the construction of the subsection first contended for on behalf of Mr. Haughey and in such case... the subsection thus construed would offend against the Constitution... But, in this instance, the ordinary canons of construction are not applicable. Here the constitutionality of an Act of the Oireachtas established by the Constitution is questioned; in such case the Court must apply different canons of construction."

The Court then recalled the principles enunciated by Walsh J in the *East Donegal Co-Operative* case just cited, and said:

> "Applying this doctrine in the present case, the Court is of opinion that it is its duty to reject the construction which the ordinary canons of construction recommend and to treat the committee's certificate, not as a certificate of conviction, but as "merely a step preliminary to the commencement of the trial of a criminal offence in the High Court", as Mr. Justice Henchy expressed it in his judgment in the High Court. This construction saves the sub-section from the constitutional infirmity from which, in the first instance, Mr. Haughey's counsel had urged the sub-section suffers."

In the High Court, Henchy J had used the *East Donegal Co-Operative* principles in order to interpret the High Court's power under the sub-section as including the power to have the recalcitrant witness tried by jury; but the Supreme Court refused to go this distance:

> "For the Attorney General it was urged that the principle of presumption of constitutionality warranted such a construction. In the opinion of this Court the formula "after such inquiry as it (the High Court) thinks proper to make" can be stretched, by presumption of constitutionality, to contemplate a trial in the High Court by a High Court judge or judges but, as has been pointed out, the presumption of constitutionality is not to be applied where it would do violence to the plain meaning of the words. It is, in the opinion of this Court, beyond the reach of the presumption of

[213] [1974] IR 338; (1975) 109 ILTR 13.
[214] [1971] IR 217.

constitutionality to read into the simple inquiry formula of the sub-section an intention to authorise trial by Jury."

The previous occasion here alluded to, on which the limits of the presumption were outlined by the Court, was the East *Donegal Co-Operative* case; the Court had said:

> "It must be added, of course, that interpretation or construction of an Act or any provision thereof in conformity with the Constitution cannot be pushed to the point where the interpretation would result in the substitution of the legislative provision by another provision with a different context, as that would be to usurp the functions of the Oireachtas. In seeking to reach an interpretation or construction in accordance with the Constitution, a statutory provision which is clear and unambiguous cannot be given an opposite meaning."[215]

The "intra vires" test used in pre-Constitution statutes

A different kind of test - the "*intra vires* test" - is applied in construing a pre-Constitution statute: it was first formulated in *The State (Quinn) v Ryan*.[216] Police officers, acting under the Petty Sessions (Ireland) Act 1851, had arrested and extradited Quinn so precipitately that he had no opportunity to consider and, if lie wished, to challenge the legality of the arrest. This course. though deliberately planned by the police, was entirely within the powers conferred by the words of the Act; and so, since those powers could be exercised in such a way as to defeat the prisoner's constitutional right of recourse to the courts (as happened here), the Supreme Court found the Act itself inconsistent with the Constitution. Walsh J said:

> "The true test is to discover what is *intra vires* the statute. At the time the statute was passed and at all times up to the enactment and coming into force of the Constitution of Saorstát Éireann a prisoner could under these sections be instantly removed from this jurisdiction to the jurisdiction from whence the warrant came. If an act is *intra vires* a statute but at the same time inconsistent with the Constitution it is clear that the statute cannot stand."[217]

A canon of construction (if it may be so called) referable to pre-1937 legislation was suggested by Kingsmill Moore J in *Educational Co. v Fitzpatrick (No. 2)*.[218] He called attention to Article 15.4.2, which declares invalid "every law... which is in any respect repugnant to the Constitution or to any provision thereof", and said:

> "As I cannot conceive that the Constitution laid down a more stringent test for the validity of laws passed by the Oireachtas than it did for the continued validity of statutes or law carried forward into our *corpus iuris* by Article 50, I must interpret the words in Article 50, "Subject to this Constitution and to the extent to which they are not inconsistent therewith", as negativing the carrying forward of any statute or law which is "in any respect repugnant to the Constitution or to any provision thereof" to the extent of such repugnancy."

[215] See also *Hegarty v O'Loughran* [1990] 1 IR 148; [1990] ILRM 403.

[216] [1965] IR 70; (1966) 100 ILTR 105. It had, however, been foreshadowed in *Cowan v Attorney General* [1961] IR 411 in which Haugh J found that the functions attributable by 19th century legislation to a barrister hearing an election petition could exceed the limits imposed by Article 37 on the exercise of judicial powers by persons other than judges, and so the statutory provisions on which those functions depended were unconstitutional.

[217] This test was adopted and applied the following year by Kenny J in *Macauley v Minister for Posts and Telegraphs* [1966] IR 345 where the Ministers and Secretaries Act 1924, was in issue; and it was adverted to by Walsh J himself in the *East Donegal Co-Operative* case in delivering the judgment of the Supreme Court.

[218] [1961] IR 345.

(E) Canons of Review: (iii) Incipient Collapse of Scheme Based on Presumption of Constitutionality?

Scheme based on presumption of constitutionality under strain

The foregoing sections of this chapter have described how the presumption of constitutionality, first enunciated in the *Pigs Marketing Board* case, and there applied to pre-Constitution Acts by a judge hearing a post-Constitution action, has sprouted a number of corollaries amounting to an entire constructional scheme under the influence of a fastidiously literal approach to the Constitution's text. Thus the presumption is seen as availing only post-1937 Acts on the very logical ground that an Oireachtas (or pre-1922 Parliament) functioning under a different constitution cannot rationally be presumed to have intended to respect a Constitution which had not yet emerged; consequently there is no room for the "double construction" test in the case of pre-1938 Acts: and these, since they continue to be in force only so far as not inconsistent with the Constitution, must be able to survive the "*intra vires* test", which means since there is equally no room in a pre-Constitution Act for a presumption of constitutional procedures that if some official process is authorised by a pre-Constitution Act in words which do not exclude its being carried out - whether expressly or by necessary implication - in a constitutionally objectionable way, that Act itself must fall, in whole or in part. It was submitted above that, despite the impeccable logic of this scheme, some kind of qualified presumption might be extended in favour of at least the Acts of the 1922-37 Oireachtas: and that the acknowledged public policy of maximum continuity and minimum disruption might fairly raise some kind of judicial screen to protect even pre-1922 legislation. But now there seem to be signs that the scheme is beginning to crack under its own weight. The few cases which may be mentioned to support this conjecture are perhaps not enough to justify it; but should the number of such cases increase, it will be time for a complete reappraisal by the Supreme Court of this area of the principles of judicial review.

Is there any real difference in the onus of proof in challenges to pre- and post-Constitution laws?

The presumption of constitutionality itself, once pre-Constitution Acts were expressly declared excluded from its benefit, developed a certain unreality. Even without that exclusion, it amounted only to the rule that a party attacking a statute carried the onus of demonstrating its unconstitutionality; but, as the majority of such parties are in the plaintiff posture, it never became clear that the burden they were made to carry was greater than that carried by every plaintiff anyway (*semper necessitas probandi incumbit illi qui agit*). Once the pre-1938 Acts were removed from the reach of the presumption, difficulty was certain to appear: there was no presumption in their favour, but surely this did not mean that anyone challenging such an Act did not even carry the usual burden of proving his assertion? and if it was, in fact, decided that an assault on a pre-Constitution Act entailed a burden of proof, was there any concrete quality in the difference between that burden and the burden implied by the "presumption" enjoyed by a post-1937 law? In the event, the judicial decisions over the last decade or so have, at last, all but acknowledged the purely verbal nature of the distinction. In *Norris v Attorney General*[219] O'Higgins CJ leading the Supreme Court majority, said that "the onus of establishing the inconsistency of an Act of 1861 with the Constitution is placed on the person who challenges [its] continued validity". He stated the familiar formula denying any presumption of constitutionality to such an Act but repeated that, "to achieve the result [of

[219] [1984] IR 36.

having the Act declared not to have been continued under Article 50.1] the plaintiff must show that such inconsistencies exist". Here we are very near, if not at, the point of a distinction without a difference. Later in the same year (1983), Costello J followed this approach in *Attorney General v Paperlink Ltd.*,[220] in which the constitutionality of an Act of 1908 was challenged not by the plaintiff, but by the counter-claiming defendants; the judge said the onus of showing the inconsistency of the Act with the Constitution lay on them, not on the plaintiff; and it is impossible to detect any difference in the severity with which their efforts to discharge this onus were judged, and that which would have been applied had the target of challenge been a post-1937 Act enjoying a "presumption of constitutionality".

"Double construction test" applied to pre-Constitution laws.

The "double construction" test logically emerging from the presumption also seems to be breaking out of its logically exclusive setting of post-1937 laws. In *Ó Monacháin v An Taoiseach*[221] the plaintiff alleged a breach of duty by the Government under s 71 of the Courts of Justice Act 1924 (in not appointing an Irish-speaking justice to the District Court of a Gaeltacht area): and, in approaching this claim, Henchy J in the Supreme Court first considered the status of this pre-Constitution provision. Noting that it continued in force under Article 50 only to the extent of its non-inconsistency with the Constitution, he said "it follows from that, that if the section has two meanings, one of them inconsistent with the Constitution and the other one not inconsistent, effect should be given to the sense which is not inconsistent".[222] This seems for several reasons a sensible approach; but the logical basis for it (the presumption that the legislature intended only the constitutional sense) is of course missing.

Thirdly, the *"intra vires"* test articulated in *The State (Quinn) v Ryan*[223] as appropriate to pre-Constitution laws is not being consistently so applied. In *Quinn's* case Walsh J had said that "if an act [i.e. an official proceeding] is *intra vires* a statute but at the same time inconsistent with the Constitution it is clear that the statute cannot stand". This referred to an Act of 1851. But in *Garvey v Ireland*,[224] where the effect of the Police Forces Amalgamation Act 1925, was being considered from the point of view of whether the arbitrary removal of the Commissioner of the Garda Síochána was authorised by it although not expressly prohibited, the Supreme Court did not apply the *Quinn* principle, but on the contrary retreated to a presumption of constitutional procedures related, naturally, to the Constitution enacted twelve years later than the Act under scrutiny. O'Higgins CJ said:

> "The Act of 1925 is a pre-Constitution statute. However, regard must be had to the fact that this statute falls to be administered under different circumstances and under an entirely different Constitution. Today the Government. the Oireachtas, the Courts and the State itself may only act in conformity with the Constitution. The Act of 1925 and all other laws in force in Saorstát Éireann...continue in force not only merely to the extent to which they are not inconsistent with the Constitution but also subject to the Constitution. The Constitution incorporates into our laws and their administration the requirements of natural justice, and by Article 40.3 there is guaranteed to every citizen whose rights may be affected by decisions taken by others the right to fair and just procedures."

[220] [1984] ILRM 373.
[221] [1986] ILRM 660.
[222] "Leanann sé uaidh sin, má tá dhá bhrí leis an alt, ceann acu ar aimhréir leis an mBunreacht agus ceann eile nach bhfuil ar aimhréir leis, ba cheart éifeacht a thabhairt don bhrí nach bhfuil ar aimhréir."
[223] [1965] IR 70; (1966) 100 ILTR 105.
[224] [1981] IR 75.

Likewise, in *Osheku v Ireland*[225] - which concerned challenge to the Aliens Act 1935, and the validity of a deportation order which was about to be made thereunder - Gannon J said:

> "If the course taken by the Minister in exercising his discretion should be found on review by the courts to be inconsistent with the provisions of the Constitution, it does not follow that the statute and the statutory orders which confer the discretion on the Minister are themselves inconsistent with the Constitution."

Yet, the Aliens Act 1935, being pre-Constitution in date, is supposedly regulated by the *intra vires* test, rather than by the presumption of constitutionality. Had this line been taken by the Court in *Quinn's* case, it might have rescued the Petty Sessions Act 1851.

(F) CANONS OF INTERPRETATION OF STATUTES

The general approach of the courts to the question of statutory interpretation in a constitutional context is best exemplified by the judgment of Walsh J in *O'Brien v Manufacturing Engineering Co. Ltd.*[226] who made it clear on the other hand that an Act is not to be tested by reference to some outside possibility, but by considering its ordinary practical effect. In this case the validity of a special period of limitation was in issue, and the Court said:

> "It is, of course, conceivable that occasions may arise when some particular prospective litigant or injured party may have no knowledge whatever of any statutory period of limitation, whether under this Act or any other Act and may thereby be unable to maintain his action; but the reasonableness or otherwise of a statutory provision which depends for its validity upon its reasonableness is not to be determined by the possibility that such a hypothetical case may arise but is to be examined in the general circumstances of the ordinary life of this country prevailing at the time the enactment comes into force."

Bad administration of an Act does not affect its validity

The judgment of Barrington J in *The State (Boyle) v Governor of Curragh Military Detention Barracks*[227] is authority for the proposition that a statute does not become unconstitutional because of the way in which it is administered. This, of course, is no more than the corollary of the presumption of constitutionality, since it is inherent in any such a presumption that the Act will be administered in the manner that bests protects constitutional rights. Here a *habeas corpus* applicant attacked the Prisons Act 1972, which authorised the transfer of convicted prisoners from civil to military custody (because of administrative problems of accommodation), saying that, since the actual conditions of military custody were more onerous, the order transferring him from a civil prison was in effect a punishment additional to that which had been inflicted by the court which convicted him. Barrington J said:

> "The Act he alleges, is coloured by the way in which it is administered. I cannot accept this submission. The Act was either valid or invalid on the day on which it was enacted by the Oireachtas and its constitutional validity cannot be affected by the manner in which it is administered." [228]

[225] [1986] IR 733; [1987] ILRM 330. See also *Pok Sun Shum v Ireland* [1986] ILRM 593.

[226] [1973] IR 334.

[227] [1980] ILRM 242.

[228] If the Act in question had been a pre-Constitution statute and if had turned out that treatment which was constitutionally objectionable was within the Act's ostensible powers, presumably - on the *intra vires* test first formulated in *The State (Quinn) v Ryan* [1965] IR 70; (1966) 100 ILTR 105 - the Act itself would have to fall.

Perhaps the right way to look at this statement is to regard it as related to the presumption of constitutional behaviour on the part of persons invested with a statutory authority. In other words, if the Act (not being *per* se unconstitutional) did not specify how prisoners transferred to military custody were to be treated, neither did it authorise treatment of them so oppressive as to amount to an attack on their personal rights, and both the Minister making the order to transfer, and those acting in pursuance of it are presumed to respect those rights. If they fail to do so, the remedy lies in appropriate proceedings against the authority concerned, not in a challenge to the Act. Precisely this approach was taken by the Supreme Court in *O'Callaghan v Ireland* [229] in rejecting a challenge to the constitutionality of s 23 of the Misuse of Drugs Act 1977. It had been suggested that because the search warrant powers thereby conferred had not expressly excluded the possibility of abuse, this somehow rendered the section unconstitutional. The Court simply drew attention to the presumption of constitutionality and added that:

> "If any member of the [Gardaí] should in purported exercise of the powers conferred on him by [the section] expose any person to unnecessary harassment, distress or embarrassment, it would be abuse of [those] powers and an unconstitutional violation of that person's rights, for which that person would have the appropriate and correct remedies."

Legislation of a technical character falls into a special category

A distinction was drawn by Ó Dálaigh CJ, in delivering the Supreme Court's judgment in *Ryan v Attorney General*,[230] in regard to the Court's function in adjudicating on the constitutionality of legislation, between legislation of a technical character and legislation for the appraisal of which no technical data would be necessary:

> "The constitutionality of a statute is, in many instances, determinable by a consideration and interpretation of the terms of the statute itself without reference to evidence as to their meaning or effect. Any matters necessary to elucidate its scope in such cases are matters of which the Court can take judicial notice. In the case of this Act however, the Court is considering a statute which uses scientific terminology, deals with a scientific procedure and required scientific knowledge to comprehend the effect of its provisions. These are not matters which are presumed to be within the knowledge of the Court, and, accordingly, the unconstitutionality of the Act if it be unconstitutional, cannot be determined except by reference to the particular evidence which is furnished in the case. Since evidence may differ from case to case and as scientific knowledge may increase and the views of scientists alter, the Court's determination cannot amount to more than a decision that on the evidence produced the plaintiff has, or has not, discharged the onus of demonstrating that the Act is unconstitutional."

The implication of these words seems to be that in cases of the latter type, the principle of *stare decisis* would have only a feeble application if the balance of evidence were to shift; perhaps also that the doctrine of *res judicata* might not apply, so that it would be open to a new (or the same) plaintiff, armed with evidence of different quality, to challenge afresh a technical statute previously held constitutional.

Taxation statutes fall into a special category

Taxation statutes are also in a special category. In *Madigan v Attorney General*[231] O'Hanlon J said that, while Article 40.3 can be invoked against a tax law which amounts to an "unjust attack" on property rights:

229 Supreme Court, 24 May 1993.
230 [1965] IR 294.
231 [1986] ILRM 136.

> "it has been recognised, both in our own jurisdiction and in the United States that tax laws are in a category of their own, and that very considerable latitude must be allowed to the legislature in the enormously complex task of organising and directing the financial affairs of the State."

"Parliamentary history" of Acts

In connection with the construction of Acts in the process of testing their constitutionality there is, finally, the question of their "parliamentary history", which in the setting of constitutional litigation might seem particularly important. No case has yet arisen in which the courts have faced this question in this setting, but in several fairly recent non-constitutional cases they have generally applied the traditional rule of common law against admitting material from a statute's "parliamentary history" as an aid to its interpretation. In considering this general question, we may examine the admissibility in turn of (i) official memoranda; (ii) the Long Title to an Act and (iii) parliamentary debates.

Official memoranda

In *McCarthy v Walsh*[232] the intention of the Oireachtas in connection with damages for mental distress through bereavement under the Civil Liability Act 1961, was in issue; Murnaghan J said:

> "An explanatory memorandum on the Civil Liability Bill, 1960, was published by the Stationery Office for, it would seem, the Department of Justice. The practice of publishing similar explanatory memoranda is one of comparatively recent origin. If the purpose of these publications is to indicate the evils intended to be remedied by a particular statute, I imagine they might be looked at to see what the purpose of the Legislature was in enacting a particular statute, but as the law stands at the moment the courts cannot interpret an Act by reference to such an explanatory memorandum."[233]

In 1970, however, the Supreme Court made extensive use of the "travaux preparatoires" for the European Convention on Extradition, on which s 50 of the Extradition Act 1965, is based, in order to elucidate the expression "offence connected with a political offence"; Ó Dálaigh CJ said in *Bourke v Attorney General*[234] that this was "a valid and proper approach". In 1972, in *McMahon v Attorney General,*[235] the Supreme Court took note of the Report of the Special Parliamentary Committee on electoral systems which preceded the introduction of the Ballot Bill 1872; this had been the origin of the ballot secrecy provisions of the Electoral Act 1923, which were under constitutional attack in that case. In 1973, in *Maher v Attorney General,*[236] the Supreme Court used the *Report of the Commission on Driving under the influence of Drink or a Drug* [237] in interpreting the will of the Oireachtas in the setting of s 44 of the Road Traffic Act 1968. The Supreme Court has now apparently sanctioned the use of the official explanatory memorandum to a Bill as an aid to statutory interpretation. In *McLoughlin v Minister for the*

[232] [1965] IR 246.

[233] Still, this explanatory memorandum explained that the proposal of s 49 of the Bill was to import into Irish law "what in Scots law is known as *solatium* or *solatium doloris*", and Murnaghan J went on to consider, at some length, what this term meant in Scotland.

[234] [1972] IR 36; (1973) 107 ILTR 33.

[235] [1972] IR 69; (1972) 106 ILTR 89.

[236] [1973] IR 140; (1974) 108 ILTR 41.

[237] 1963, Prl. 7165.

Public Service[238] the Court made use of the explanatory memorandum to the Garda Síochána Compensation Act 1941, and rejected an interpretation of the Act which was inconsistent with its purpose as declared in the memorandum. Henchy J did not, however, elaborate on the limits (if any) of the use that might be made of such an official memorandum.

One issue which has arisen from time to time is whether reference may be made to post-1922 British parliamentary papers or official reports as an aid to construction in the case of Acts of the Oireachtas owing their inspiration to British legislation. In *Fitzpatrick v Fitzpatrick's Footwear Ltd.*[239] Kenny J declared himself in favour of the idea, saying that "it is permissible to look at the reports of committees on the reform of company law to see what was the object the draftsman of the Act had in mind". However, in *Breathnach v McC.*[240] McWilliam J refused to consider a report of the (British) Royal Commission on Income Tax as an aid to the construction of the (Irish) Income Tax Act 1967:

> "Although I am aware of what Black J once described as "the scissors-and-paste penchant of our legislature", I am of opinion that I am not entitled, nor should I make any attempt, to interpret a statute of the Oireachtas by reference to the report of an English Royal Commission which led to a similar English statute. I leave open the question of whether I would be entitled to consider a report by a similar Irish commission or not."

Exceptionally, the Oireachtas itself may determine what *travaux preparatoires* may be taken into account. Thus, s 4 the Jurisdiction of Courts and Enforcement of Judgments (European Communities) Act 1988 enables the Irish courts to take judicial notice of two official Community reports and of the Judgments Convention; and such reports "may be considered by any Court when interpreting any provision of those Conventions and that Protocol" and shall be given "such weight as is appropriate in the circumstances".[241]

Long title

The question whether the long title of an Act may be invoked as a guide to statutory interpretation has featured in a number of Supreme Court decisions. In *The State (Aer Lingus Teo.) v Labour Court*[242] Hederman J said that the long title could be invoked in order to resolve any ambiguity in a statute, but that it could not be looked at "to modify the interpretation of plain language". A majority of the Supreme Court took the same view in *The People (Director of Public Prosecutions) v Quilligan (No.1)*[243] in which Barr J in the High Court had directed the acquittal of the defendants on the grounds that their arrests under s 30 of the Offences Against the State Act 1939, were unlawful. He had invoked the long title to the Act - which refers, *inter alia*, to "conduct calculated to undermine public order and the authority of the State" - in order to qualify the apparent-

238 [1985] IR 631; [1986] ILRM 28. Note that in *C.K. v C.K.* [1993] ILRM 534, where the construction of the Child Abduction and Enforcement of Custody Orders Act 1991 (which gives effect in Irish law to the Hague and Luxembourg Conventions on Child Abduction and Custody) Denham J appeared to hint that while she could have regard to the *travaux preparatoires* of such a Convention in view of the decision in *Bourke's* case, it would be inappropriate to have regard to the Dáil debates, since the words in question were those of the Hague Convention which "were not drafted in or for the Dáil." See also the similar comments of Keane J in *Wadda v Ireland*, High Court, 6 July 1993.

239 High Court, 18 November 1970.

240 [1984] IR 340; [1984] ILRM 679.

241 Similar provisions are to be found in s 3 of the Contractual Obligations (Applicable Law) Act 1991 and s 10(2) of the Jurisdiction of Courts and Enforcement of Judgments Act 1993.

242 [1987] ILRM 373.

243 [1986] IR 495; [1987] ILRM 606.

ly unambiguous language of s 30[244] so as to confine its powers of arrest to "political" or "subversive"-type cases (categories not, in fact, recognised as such by the Act). He was unanimously reversed by the Supreme Court following an appeal by the Director of Public Prosecutions. Henchy J agreed that the long title indicated an intention to deal with acts and conduct tending to undermine the authority of the State, but said it did not follow that the Act drew a clear line between "subversive" and "ordinary" offences:

> "I find the sweep of these provisions to be so unequivocal as to negative the conclusion that the operation of the Act is confined to subversive offences."

Griffin J agreed, saying that he found the language of s 30 so "clear and unequivocal that the long title may not be looked at or used for the purpose of limiting or modifying that language". McCarthy J dissented in part on this point (although he concurred in the result), saying that reference could be made to the long title for the purpose of giving a schematic interpretation to the Act.[245]

Parliamentary debates

The traditional rule was - and, indeed, still is - that it is not permissible for the courts to have regard to what has been said in the Oireachtas as an aid to the construction of statutes. Thus, in *Minister for Industry and Commerce v Hales*[246] the Supreme Court was asked to construe the Holidays (Employees) Act 1961, having regard to evidence about the intentions of the Minister who had introduced the Bill and, in particular, had introduced a sub-section at Committee Stage with the specific object of making the Bill applicable to the issue which subsequently arose in this case. The High Court refused to go beyond the words of the Act itself; McLoughlin J said:

> "What has to be interpreted is not the intention of the Minister but the intention of the legislature as expressed in the Act."

However, the trend of looking at other extraneous material - such as travaux preparatoires and official memoranda - which had become evident during the 1970s had evidently emboldened the courts to take a more adventurous view of this question since in 1981 Costello J actually took the step of actually looking at what had happened in the Oireachtas during the passage of legislation it was called on to construe in *Beecham Group Ltd. v Bristol Myers Co.*[247] when, referring only to *Bourke's* case as authority, he briefly said he "believed he was entitled' to look at the Dáil debate on the Bill for the Patents Act 1964. Two months later in *Wavin Pipes Ltd. v Hepworth Iron Co. Ltd.*[248] - a case arising on interpretation of the same Act - he explained more fully why he was

[244] Which provides that a member of the Garda Síochána "may arrest a person whom he suspects of having committed or being about to commit or being or having been concerned in the commission" of a scheduled offence.

[245] Cf. the comments of Walsh J in *East Donegal Co-Operative Ltd. v Attorney General* [1970] IR 317: "Words or phrases which at first sight might appear to be wide and general may be cut down in their construction when examined against the objects of the Act which are to be derived from a study of the Act as a whole including the long title. Until each part of the Act is examined in relation to the whole it would not be possible to say that any particular part of the Act was either clear or unambiguous". Note also that in *Rowe v Law* [1978] IR 55 O'Higgins CJ referred to the marginal note in order to construe s 90 of the Succession Act 1965. This would appear to be an impermissible aid to statutory construction in view of s 11(*g*) of the Interpretation Act 1937, which provides that no "marginal note shall be taken to be part of the Act or instrument or to be considered or judicially noticed in relation to the construction or interpretation of the Act or instrument or any portion thereof".

[246] [1967] IR 50; (1968) 102 ILTR 109. See also *Irish Amusements Ltd. v Casey* [1968] IR 121; (1970) 104 ILTR 17 for a brief re-statement of the traditional rule.

[247] High Court, 13 March 1981.

[248] High Court, 8 May 1981. See the perceptive note by *Casey*, (1981) 3 DULJ 110.

innovating in this way. He mentioned *McMahon's* and *Maher's* cases, but in particular *Bourke's* case, saying that:

> "if the courts can properly look at the history of the adoption of an international convention for the purpose of ascertaining the meaning of the words used in it, there would appear to be no reason in principle why in appropriate cases they should not be free when construing the words of a statute to obtain assistance from the history of its enactment by parliament."

In the case before him, one of the parties was contending for a construction of words in the Patents Act in a sense for the express recognition of which an amendment had been moved at the Committee Stage of the Bill in the Dáil[249] and rejected, the Minister having clearly explained why such an understanding of the words would be unacceptable. Costello J said:

> "It would be difficult to find a clearer case than this to demonstrate how the parliamentary history of an enactment can assist in ascertaining the legislative intent... The evidence relating to (a) the fact of the rejected amendment and (b) the reasons given for its rejection assists therefore in establishing that the words used in the statute should not be interpreted as the defendants suggest."

In *F.F. v C.F.*[250] Barr J referred to the Dáil debates as an aid to the construction of s 2 of the Statute Law Revision (Pre-Union Irish Statutes) Act 1962. He concluded that, notwithstanding the repeal of the Act for Joint Tenants 1542, by that Act the Court still has power to sever a joint tenancy, as the then Minister for Justice had informed the Dáil that s 2 was intended to preserve:

> "any legal right or principle of law which might have been created by or derived from any of the statutes which it was decided to repeal."

However, two recent decisions of the Supreme Court appear to rule out this approach. In *The People (Director of Public Prosecutions) v Quilligan (No.1)* [251] on the other hand, Walsh J was against the admission of parliamentary debates; "whatever may have been in the minds of the members of the Oireachtas when the legislation was passed", their intention could only be deduced "from the words of the statute". And in *Howard v Commissioners of Public Works in Ireland*[252] the Supreme Court strongly implied that contemporary materials of this kind could not be used as a means of statutory interpretation. This case turned in part on whether the Oireachtas when enacting s 84 of the Local Government (Planning and Development) Act 1963 (which provided for a consultation procedure short of a formal application for planning permission) had intended to exempt the State from the application of statute. In the High Court, Costello J concluded that it had not, in part because he suggested that the Oireachtas had wrongly assumed that the former prerogative rule that the State was not bound by the application of statute was still in force. On appeal, however, the Supreme Court stressed that the courts could not (as Blayney J put it) "speculate as to the intention of the legislature in enacting s 84". Finlay CJ was even more emphatic, saying that it would not be permissible to interpret a statute:

> "upon the basis of either speculation, or indeed, even of actual information obtained with regard to the belief of individuals who either drafted the statute or took part as

249 Costello J was himself in the best position to take this point, as it was he who, when a member of the Dáil seventeen years previously, had moved this amendment. See 207 *Dáil Debates* 1644ff.

250 [1987] ILRM 1.

251 [1986] IR 496; [1987] ILRM 606.

252 [1993] ILRM 665.

> legislators in its enactment with regard to the question of the appropriate legal principles applicable to matters being dealt with in the statute,"

This approach would appear, by implication, at least, to exclude the possibility of any reliance on the legislative history of a domestic enactment.[253] This, in turn, would seem to have important implications for constitutional interpretation, since reference to parliamentary debates would have seemed to offer a rational preliminary to the application of anything like the "double construction" test. The exclusion of such parliamentary material would also appear to rule out the "original intent" method of approach to constitutional interpretation, since this by definition is very heavily dependent on contemporary sources - such as parliamentary debates on the Constitution - as an aid to constitutional construction.[254]

(G) PARTIAL UNCONSTITUTIONALITY, SEVERANCE AND JUDICIAL REVIEW OF CONSTITUTIONAL LACUNAE

Partial unconstitutionality: principles of "severability"

Problems of statutory interpretation arise in connection with a finding that a challenged statutory provision is unconstitutional only in part. As Article 15.4 limits the invalidity of a successfully challenged law to "the extent only of such repugnancy", and Article 50 limits the non-continuance of a previously existing law to the extent of its inconsistency with the Constitution, the courts are obliged to keep the operation of declaring either sort of law unconstitutional within a minimum extent. This means that, in some cases, only portion of a particular section is treated (so to speak) as "deleted", on its being found unconstitutional, while the rest of the section is permitted to stand.[255] However, these partial "deletions" are only carried out when this can be done cleanly and without violence to the presumed legislative will; the courts will not patch or mend a provision which a simple excision would render futile, or turn into something which the legislature had never envisaged.

Thus in *Maher v Attorney General*[256] it was made clear that the constitutional flaw in an Act may be such that the courts will not undertake a patching operation more properly the business of the legislature. In this case the plaintiff succeeded in having the provisions of s 44(2)(*a*) of the Road Traffic Act 1968, declared unconstitutional on the ground that, by making a certificate of blood alcohol content "conclusive evidence" as to the matter certified, the judicial function was pre-empted and infringed; the Supreme Court, however, refused to accept the submission that the paragraph should be regarded as surviving minus the word "conclusive". FitzGerald CJ in giving the Court's judgment said:

[253] Different considerations may possibly arise in the context of statutes such as, for example, the Child Abduction and Enforcement of Custody Orders Act 1991, which give effect in domestic law to such an approach in *Bourke v Attorney General* [1972] IR 36; (1973) 107 ILTR 33, *C.K. v C.K.* [1973] ILRM 534 and *Wadda v Ireland*, High Court, 6 July 1993, for which see p. 471. It may be noted that the House of Lords has recently sanctioned a far-reaching change in what had hitherto been a common-law practice of song-standing by permitting reference to *Hansard* in certain cases as an aid to statutory construction: see *Pepper v Hart* [1993] 1 All ER 42.

[254] See pp. cxvi-cxvii.

[255] Examples include *Deaton v Attorney General* [1963] IR 170; (1964) 98 ILTR 99; *The State (Sheerin) v Kennedy* [1966] IR 379; *The State (C.) v Minister for Justice* [1967] IR 106; (1968) 102 ILTR 177; *In re McAllister* [1973] IR 238; *King v Attorney General* [1981] IR 233; *O'G. v An Bord Uchtála* [1985] ILRM 61; *Cashman v Clifford* [1989] IR 121; [1990] ILRM 200 and *Desmond v Glackin (No.2)*, Supreme Court, 30 July 1992.

[256] [1973] IR 140; (1974) 108 ILTR 41.

> "The submission means that it is within the jurisdiction of the Court to sever or separate the word "conclusive" so as to give the paragraph, with that word removed, constitutional validity. The application of the doctrine of severability or separability in the judicial review of legislation has the effect that if a particular provision is held to be unconstitutional, and that provision is independent of and severable from the rest, only the offending provision will be declared invalid. The question is one of interpretation of the legislative intent. Article 15.4.2... lays down that every law enacted by the Oireachtas which is in any respect repugnant to the Constitution or to any provision thereof shall, but to the extent only of such repugnancy, be invalid; therefore there is a presumption that a statute or a statutory provision is not intended to be constitutionally operative only as an entirety. This presumption, however, may be rebutted if it can be shown that, after a part has been held unconstitutional, the remainder may be held to stand independently and legally operable as representing the will of the legislature. But if what remains is so inextricably bound up with the part held invalid that the remainder cannot survive independently, or if the remainder would not represent the legislative intent, the remaining part will not be severed and given constitutional validity. It is essentially a matter of interpreting the will of the legislature in the light of the relevant constitutional provisions, and it must be borne in mind in all cases that Article 15.2.1... provides that "the sole and exclusive power of making laws for the State is hereby vested in the Oireachtas: no other legislative authority has power to make laws for the State". If, therefore, the courts were to sever part of a statutory provision as unconstitutional and seek to give validity to what is left *so as to produce an effect at variance with legislative policy,*[257] the court would be invading a domain exclusive to the legislature and thus exceeding the court's competency. In other words, it would be seeking to correct one form of unconstitutionality by engaging in another. The usurpation by the judiciary of an exclusively legislative function is no less unconstitutional than the usurpation by the legislature of an exclusively judicial function..."

The Court reviewed the relevant part of the Road Traffic Act 1968, and concluded that:

> "the legislature, in opting to make the certificate conclusive evidence of the analysis, had not directed its attention to what would happen if the certificate were not conclusive and that, if it had, it would not have allowed s 44(2)(*a*) to go forth merely with the word "conclusive" omitted... To hold that the paragraph could survive with the word "conclusive" omitted would amount to an amendment rather than an interpretation, thus requiring the Court to act in a legislative rather than a judicial role. The Court accepts as correct the argument on behalf of the Attorney General that if the paragraph is invalid it is totally invalid."[258]

Thus, in *O'Brien v Keogh*[259] the Supreme Court said, in regard to the Statute of Limitations, 1957, s 49(2)(*a*)(ii):

> "It is not possible to save by deletion some part of the impugned paragraph. The provision has no purpose without the words that establish the date of the running of the statute. It must therefore for its constitutional frailty fall in its entirety."

[257] This would have been the case here, as the Oireachtas had specifically rejected the recommendation of the *Commission on Driving while under the Influence of Drink or a Drug* (1963: Prl. 7165) that the blood or urine analysis should be merely *prima facie* evidence.

[258] See also the comments of Ó Dálaigh J in *Melling v Ó Mathghamhna* [1962] IR 1 (courts cannot take on "restorative functions" where "the framework of a section collapses from constitutional infirmity").

[259] [1972] IR 144.

Similarly in the earlier case in *The State (Doyle) v Minister for Education*[260] the old Supreme Court had said, in declaring invalid most of s 10(1)(*d*), (*e*) of the Children Act 1941:

> "It is unfortunate that this declaration involves the invalidation of provisions which if they stood alone are quite in accord with the Constitution. They are however so inextricably entangled with the portion which we find repugnant to the Constitution that there is no way of avoiding this result."[261]

Other instances where the courts have declined to make an excision, for the purpose of rescuing the rest of a section, on the grounds that the section as so pruned would be turned into a provision which could not be imputed to the intentions of the legislature which enacted it, are *The State (Attorney General) v Shaw*,[262] in which Finlay P refused to delete merely the words "at the suit of the Crown" from a section of an Act of 1877 about the award of costs in customs prosecutions, since the exclusion of these words "would leave the remainder of the section in a condition which does not represent the legislative intent, because a section limiting a Crown privilege would have been thereby converted into a section giving a jurisdiction to award costs in all customs cases" (the expression "at the suit of the Crown" had not been adapted by any post-1922 statute and so had failed to survive the enactment of the Constitution); *Murphy v Wallace*[263] where Barron J held that he could not sever any of the penal warrant provisions of s 90 of the Excise Management Act 1827, because to delete only the part which he found to confer an unconstitutional discretion on the Revenue Commissioners would be to leave a power which had not been intended by the legislature. Nor will the courts engage in severance where the result would be to expose the Exchequer to an unanticipated financial burden as a result of the excision of a condition restricting eligibility under the scheme: see *Greene v Minister for Agriculture*.[264] And in *King v Attorney General*, cited above, in which the majority of the Supreme Court (O'Higgins CJ dissenting) "deleted" the portion of s 4 of the Vagrancy Act 1824, under which the plaintiff had been convicted, and declined to save that portion by excising from It some words in which the constitutionally objectionable element resided. Henchy J explained the majority view by referring to an American case, *Lynch v US*,[265] from which he cited words of Brandeis J:

> "It is true that a statute bad in part is not necessarily void in its entirety. A provision within the legislative power may be allowed to stand if it is separable from the bad. But no provision, however unobjectionable in itself, can stand unless it appears both

260 Decided in 1955, but belatedly reported at [1989] ILRM 277.

261 These instances are only cases of the application to a special circumstance (i.e. the invalidation of legislative provisions through judicial review on constitutional criteria) of the general refusal of courts to do the job of the Legislature. The courts will not. for example, attempt to supply a *casus omissus* in a statute: see the many authorities cited with approval, and followed, by Fitzgibbon J in *O'Donoghue v Roche* [1927] IR 152: he said: "I hold that neither this Court nor any other has jurisdiction to supply an omission in the Act." The Supreme Court has likewise confirmed that it cannot undo an evident mistake contained in a statute: *The State (Murphy) v Johnston* [1983] IR 235; *Howard v Commissioners of Public Works in Ireland* [1993] ILRM 665.

262 [1979] IR 136.

263 [1993] 2 IR 138.

264 [1990] 2 IR 17; [1990] ILRM 364. This the concerned the invalidation of a ministerial scheme for breach of Article 41 of the Constitution (see pp. 993-994). Murphy J stressed that: "The ministerial schemes not being laws enacted by the Oireachtas are not invalidated by virtue of Article 15.4 of the Constitution. Again, that Article would have no application and would provide no direct assistance in determining the extent to which the schemes would be invalidated or the date from which they would cease to have operative effect. The ministerial schemes are defective and must be condemned "because they failed to protect constitutional rights".

265 292 US 571 (1934).

> that, standing alone, the provision can be given legal effect and that the legislature intended the unobjectionable provision to stand in case other provisions held bad should fall."[266]

The most elaborate application of the doctrine of severance is now to be found in the judgment of the Supreme Court in *Desmond v Glackin (No.2)*.[267] This case concerned the inter-action of s 10(5) and 10(6) of the Companies Act 1990. Section 10(5) allowed a court-appointed inspector to certify to the High Court that a witness had failed to answer questions and the High Court was given a discretion to punish an offender as if he had been guilty of contempt of court. Section 10(6) (which was stated to be without prejudice to the court's power under the preceding sub-section) is a complimentary provision which, in effect, allows the inspector to apply for the High Court to direct that a witness answer certain questions or produce certain documents. The High Court might, upon inquiry, either give such a direction or absolve the witness from such an obligation and the Supreme Court was satisfied that this sub-section "does not contain any constitutional flaw." However, the Supreme Court, confirming its reasoning in the earlier *Haughey* case,[268] held that the power granted to the High Court by s 10(5) to punish an offender "in like manner as if he had been guilty of contempt of court" was unconstitutional.[269] Finlay CJ then continued by observing:

> "The Court is satisfied that the proper interpretation of these two sub-sections leads to a conclusion that the Legislature intended not only the provision for punishment which is held to be inconsistent with the Constitution, but as a separate discretionary jurisdiction in the [High] Court the powers contained in s 10(6). If, in addition, to the words deleted from s 10(5) by the order of the High Court,[270] there is added a consequential deletion of the words contained in s10(6): "Without prejudice to its power under s 10(5), the court may after a hearing under that subsection", then there remains in the combined provisions of the two subsections one of the original intentions of the Legislature, and such a severance in the view of the Court would be permissible, having regard to the applicable principles which have been set out."

In other words, the Supreme Court, having examined the two sub-sections in conjunction, concluded that they embodied two separate legislative objectives - one constitutional and the other unconstitutional. The Court excised so much of both sub-sections as contained the constitutional flaw, thus leaving intact the remainder of the sub-sections which embodied the constitutionally acceptable legislative objective. It remains to be seen whether other statutory provisions in need of severance will so readily lend themselves to this form of sophisticated analysis.

Different rule for pre-Constitution statutes?

It is worth noting, however, that O'Higgins CJ in his dissenting judgment in *King's* case expressed the view that, while the problem of severability might arise in any statute whether of pre-or post-Constitution date, the question of "legislative intent" was proper to be considered only in relation to enactments of the Oireachtas. Pre-Constitution laws derived their validity not from the Oireachtas, but from Article 50 of the Constitution

[266] See also *Blake v Attorney General* [1982] IR 117. See generally, McCormack, "*The Doctrine of Severability in the Judicial Review of Legislation*" 78 Gazette of the Incorporated Law Society of Ireland 5.
[267] Supreme Court, 30 July 1992.
[268] [1971] IR 217 and pp. 629, 630.
[269] Since it exposed the offender to the possibility of "severe penalties appropriate only to the commission of major offences by a trial held otherwise than with a jury": see p. 630.
[270] In his judgment delivered on 25 February 1992, O'Hanlon J had deleted the words "punish the offender in like manner as if he had been guilty of contempt of court" from s 10(5) of the 1990 Act.

and only to the extent of their objective non-inconsistency with the Constitution; so that the question of possibly "distorting the legislative intent" by an excision was not relevant (or so it appears his words should be paraphrased).

Judicial review of constitutional lacuna in Act?

An area not yet properly explored is that of what might be called a constitutional lacuna in some statutory provision or scheme, i.e. where the constitutional weakness consists not in what the Act provides, but in what it fails to provide. This problem was within view in *Reynolds v Attorney General*,[271] in which the plaintiff complained that, although he had reached the age of 18, he was not permitted to vote at the 1973 General Election because (like many other young citizens) his name was not on the annually-compiled register which had been drawn up before he obtained the franchise through the constitutional amendment of 1972. Kenny J held against him on the ground that the right to vote at Dáil elections was conditional on one's "complying with the law relating to Dáil elections" (Article 16.1.2); but said that in any case "there was no way in which the Court could devise the machinery by which those between the ages of 18 and 21 could vote" in other words, even if the Court had found his inability to vote to be unconstitutional, it could not assume the essentially legislative function of making an appropriate new provision for the registration of electors. It was avoided in *Crowley v Ireland*[272] a case not involving a statute by a reading of Article 40.3 which is scarcely persuasive. But in *The State (Walshe) v Murphy*[273] Finlay P drew attention to the frequent provisions of the Constitution "where the Oireachtas is actively obliged to regulate certain matters by law; in other words, to enact statutory provisions to provide for them". If, in such an instance, the Oireachtas neglects to make appropriate provision, or makes a provision which by an omission offends a constitutional value; or, more generally, if the Oireachtas constructs a statutory scheme in the course of its general legislative discretion (i.e. without specific direction in a constitutional Article to do so) but, again, offends a constitutional value by an omission, is there any form in which the power of judicial review can be invoked?

Revival of old scheme to fill the void?

A point which seems dubious was made obiter by Walsh J in *O'B. v S.*[274] Rejecting a challenge to the Succession Act 1965 based on its allegedly unconstitutional exclusion of illegitimate children from intestate succession, he said that, even if the Court were to strike down the Act. it would avail the challenger nothing, since, the Act having repealed all pre-existing rules of succession, "the resultant absence of any rules would leave her without any claimable share". But - apart from the special case of succession - if a statute introduces a new scheme by way of repealing and replacing an old one, and is then found unconstitutional, might it not be said that the repealing provision as well as the replacing provisions (both being components of the overall legislative act) is invalid, so that the old scheme will revive?

[271] High Court, 16 February 1973.
[272] [1980] IR 102.
[273] [1981] IR 275. See also the judgment of McMahon J in *Draper v Attorney General* [1984] IR 277.
[274] [1984] IR 316. See also the judgment of Keane J in *Somjee v Minister for Justice* [1981] ILRM 324 for a similar approach.

In one exceptional case, *McKinley v Minister for Defence*,[275] the Supreme Court remedied an unconstitutional omission in a common law rule[276] by extending its ambit to all spouses so as to cure the unconstitutionality. This, however, was in the context of a common law rule: such a novel remedy might not be possible in the case of a similarly drawn statute-based rule, since this would seem to involve the courts in legislation. But, despite what Keane J said in *Somjee v Minister for Justice*,[277] there would seem to be no reason why the courts should not deliver a form of German-style admonitory decision[278] drawing attention to the constitutional *lacuna* and inviting the Oireachtas to remedy the situation. Indeed, something of the kind happened in *Blake v Attorney General*[279] where the Supreme Court, having invalidated the operative portions of the Rent Restrictions Acts, effectively ordered the lower courts to stay any consequential ejectment application brought on foot of that decision pending the enactment by the Oireachtas of suitable legislation. It would be strange if the courts had no such role, they would find themselves otherwise powerless to remedy underinclusive - and otherwise unconstitutional - statutory provisions.

(H) Effects of finding of unconstitutionality

Operative time and effect of a finding of invalidity or inconsistency

The question of the time from which a law, which has been declared inconsistent with or invalid under the Constitution, is to be considered a nullity, and the closely-related question of the retroactive potential of such a declaration, are matters which for many years escaped scrutiny altogether and in the last twenty years or so have only been even partially explored. How this could have been so is puzzling.[280] Many persons must have been in British prisons, having been extradited under s 29 of the Petty Sessions (Ireland) Act 1851, at the date of *The State (Quinn) v Ryan*;[281] did the Supreme Court's decision affect their position or give them any rights? Conceivably some motorists may have endured the consequences of conviction under s 44(2)(*a*) of the Road Traffic Act 1961, purely through the "conclusiveness" attributed to the certificate there provided for, at the date of *Maher v Attorney General*;[282] were they now entitled to have their licence suspensions lifted and fines repaid? Possibly it could be argued that the State in all its branches is entitled to treat as valid all pre-1937 law until such time as it may be found inconsistent with the Constitution - particularly where, as in the matter of extradition, these very provisions had previously been challenged and found unobjectionable by the courts[283] - but this could scarcely be said in relation to post-1937 legislation, since here,

[275] [1992] 2 IR 333. See pp.119-120. This problem was also in view in *AD v Ireland*, High Court, 29 July 1992, but the plaintiffs claim that the State's failure to provide for an adequate system of criminal injuries' compensation violated Article 40.3 failed on the facts.

[276] The rule in question had provided that only husbands could sue in respect of a loss of spousal consortium. All members of the Court were agreed that the rule as it originally stood offended against Article 40.1, but divided on the remedy. The majority favoured the extension of the rule on a gender-neutral basis, whereas the minority held that this was not possible and favoured the invalidation of the rule.

[277] [1981] ILRM 324.

[278] For which see, Rupp-von Brünnick, "*The Admonitory Functions of the German Constitutional Court*" (1972) 20 AJCL 387.

[279] [1982] IR 117.

[280] After the decision in *The State (Burke) v Lennon* [1940] IR 136; (1940) 76 ILTR 36, 131 the Government released a number of other persons who had been detained under the invalidated provisions of the Offences Against the State Act 1939, but it does not appear that any of them sued for false imprisonment.

[281] [1965] IR 70; (1966) 100 ILTR 105. See above at p.876.

[282] [1973] IR 140; (1974) 108 ILTR 41. See above at pp. 369-370.

[283] *The State (Duggan) v Tapley* [1952] IR 62; (1951) 85 ILTR 22.

in theory, an objectionable provision is the product of the Oireachtas having enacted that which Article 15.4.1 forbade it to enact.

The aftermath of *O'Brien v Keogh*[284] provides a good example of some the problems that arise in this context. In this case, the Supreme Court held that s 49(2)(*a*)(iii) of the Statute of Limitations 1957 (which provided a three-year limitation period in the case of personal injuries, where the infant plaintiff was in the custody of its parents) was unconstitutional. In *Ó Domhnaill v Merrick*[285] it was judicially assumed that this had the effect of:

> "making the period of limitation under the Act of 1957 for the [infant] plaintiff's claim the period expiring three years after the date on which she became of full age."

This would seem to imply (ignoring questions of retrospectivity) that a declaration of unconstitutionality is tantamount to a statutory repeal of the condemned provisions. But - ignoring the fact that this sub-section was repealed by the Statute of Limitations (Amendment) Act 1991 - what if *O'Brien's* case were to be overruled? Would this have the effect of reviving s 49(2)(*a*)(iii) of the 1957 Act or would fresh legislation be necessary in order to effect this result? Principle seems to suggest the latter result - especially, perhaps, in view of the express powers of judicial review conferred by Article 34.3.2 - although there is also much to be said for the former view.[286]

Consequences of invalidity

The theory of the situation is not very clear, as is demonstrated by a series of cases, which touch on what has the makings of an embarrassing problem (as the US Supreme Court has found).[287] In *McMahon v Attorney General*[288] the Supreme Court, by a 3-2 majority, found that the law on ballot papers which had been followed in Dáil elections since 1923 was unconstitutional in not ensuring a complete secrecy of the ballot, as Article 16.1.4 requires. Fitzgerald J, one of the two dissentients, noted that:

> "The plaintiff has not advanced any argument on the possible consequences of a finding of the procedure being unconstitutional. It appears to me that such a finding raises or could raise the issue as to whether all elections and by-elections since 1923 were unconstitutional. It certainly creates the situation in which a citizen might be encouraged to raise such an issue."[289]

Yundecided

[284] [1972] IR 144.
[285] [1984] IR 151; [1985] ILRM 40.
[286] In 1923 the US Supreme Court had held that a minimum wage law was unconstitutional, but this decision was formally overruled in 1937. The US Attorney General then advised the President that the 1923 ruling had simply "suspended enforcement" of the legislation and that the legislation was now once again válid and enforceable in the light of the 1937 ruling: "The decisions are practically in accord in holding that the courts have no power to repeal or abolish a statute, and that notwithstanding a decision holding it unconstitutional a statute continues to remain on the statute books." 39 Ops. Atty. Gen. 22 (1937). But despite the persuasiveness of this reasoning, these words would have to be treated with caution in an Irish context, since unlike the United States (where the power of judicial review has been held simply to arise by implication following the seminal decision in *Marbury v Madison* (1803) 1 Cranch 137) it could be contended that Article 34.3.2 does, in fact, give our courts the power "to abolish or repeal" a statutory provision which is found to be unconstitutional. In this regard, one must note the words of Henchy J in *Murphy v Attorney General* [1982] IR 241, where he said that a declaration of unconstitutionality amounted to a "judicial death certificate."
[287] See, e.g., the leading decision of the US Supreme Court in *Linkletter v Walker* 381 US 618 (1965), where the Court held - in what has proved to be a very controversial judgment - that it could withhold retroactive effect for its rulings. The Court found that the US Constitution "neither prohibits nor requires retrospective effect", so that it was the judicial task "to weigh the merits and demerits" of retroactivity for the rule in question "by looking to the prior history", to the "purpose and effect" of the new constitutional rule and to whether "retrospective operation will further or retard its operation."
[288] [1972] IR 69; (1972) 106 ILTR 89.
[289] The majority avoided the issue, with Ó Dálaigh CJ merely noting that it had been no part of the plaintiff's case that the validity of any past election had been or could have been affected by this constitutional irregularity.

These words do not disclose his own view, even if perhaps they hint at it. The point, although clearly visible from the terrain over which *McMahon's* case was fought, remained therefore undecided. It emerged again, however, a few years later, and in a very similar kind of setting, in *de Búrca v Attorney General,*[290] where the plaintiff impugned the provisions of the Juries Act 1927, relating to the preparation of lists of jurors. The Supreme Court unanimously gave judgment in her favour; but O'Higgins CJ said:

> "If, then, the property qualification is not in accordance with Article 40.1, and is not saved by any inference to be drawn from Article 38.5, what is to be said of the thousands of criminal jury trials which have been held since the enactment of the Constitution and which have resulted in convictions? Were these trials invalid? I confess that this matter did cause me some concern during the hearing. I have come to the conclusion that, in so far as these trials were held before juries and each jury was fairly drawn from a panel, there could be no infringement of Article 38.5. The fact may have been that the panel was wrongly restricted, or could have been challenged. However, this does not alter the fact that the trial was a trial by jury and that no person served on such juries who was not eligible... In *McMahon's* case the courts were not asked to entertain any suggestion that such irregularity invalidated previous elections nor, in my view, could such a submission have been successfully made. The overriding requirements of an ordered society would invalidate such an argument. In this instance, the same considerations apply."

Walsh J boldly declared his willingness to hold previous jury verdicts invalid if logically compelled to do so, and did not attach any status to "the overriding requirements of an ordered society". However, he too thought the problem was avoided since:

> "...nobody served on any of these juries who was not entitled by law to do so. Therefore, no verdict was rendered by any jury composed wholly or in part of persons who were not entitled to be on that jury."

The line of escape thus adopted by O'Higgins CJ and Walsh J seems very dubious. It was reiterated by O'Higgins CJ in *The State (Byrne) v Frawley*[291] but was in that case severely criticised by Henchy J (with whom Griffin J agreed). Henchy J said:

> "But even if it could be said that only duly qualified persons served on such juries, that would not detract from the fact that jury lists compiled under the Juries Act 1927, were unrepresentative beyond the level of constitutionality... The extent to which juries drawn from those lists were incapable of presenting a genuine reflection of community values and standards is shown when it is pointed out that the combined effect of the rating qualification and the exclusion of women meant that some 80% of the adult citizens in a jury district were shut out from jury service. I find the proposition that juries drawn from the remaining 20% were valid - because no ineligible persons served on them - no more supportable than a proposition that an election would be valid when 80% of those who should have had an opportunity of voting were barred from the polls. The essential spuriousness of such an election would not be overcome by an assertion that no ineligible persons voted."[292]

[290] [1976] IR 38; (1977) 111 ILTR 37.
[291] [1978] IR 326.
[292] But here again the majority deftly avoided the logical consequences of their decision by holding that the applicant - who had raised no objection at the time of his trial - was now estopped by his conduct from raising the point.

The decision in Murphy v Attorney General

The problem arose at last in a form from which there was no escape, when in *Murphy v Attorney General*[293] a married couple, having succeeded in getting those provisions of the Income Tax Act 1967, declared unconstitutional which had the effect of taxing them more heavily than an unmarried couple, sought the refund of all the money they had overpaid on demands made under these provisions; this claim naturally opened up the question of the status of over- payments made by many other married couples over the preceding twelve years or so, thus raising the prospect of claims so enormous as to disrupt the State's finances. O'Higgins CJ took the line that, since Article 25.4.1 prescribed that every Bill was to become law on signature by the President, invalidity subsequently established could not relate back to the moment of enactment; the latent defect, so to speak, incubated into full invalidity only at the date of the Court's finding. The other four judges, on the other hand, thought that a declaration of invalidity meant that, as the Oireachtas was now seen to have exceeded its powers by enacting something repugnant to the Constitution (which Article 15.4.1 forbade it to do) the Act or provision in question had been a nullity at all times. Henchy J, who spoke also for Parke J and, on this point, to the same effect as Griffin and Kenny JJ, said the argument that invalidity attached only from the moment of the Court's finding failed for three main reasons:

> "(1) It fails to recognise the true nature of the constitutional limitation of the legislative power vested in the Oireachtas; (2) it distorts the meaning that must be given to "invalid" in its constitutional context; and (3) it flies in the face of an unbroken line of judicial decisions which, expressly or by necessary implication, point to the date of enactment as the date from which invalidity is to attach to the measure which has been struck down because of its unconstitutionality."

Similarly, although *obiter* as such legislation was not in issue in this case, he said he thought a pre-Constitution law subsequently found inconsistent with the Constitution must be seen as having ceased to operate with the coming into force of the Constitution:

> "Such a declaration under Article 50.1 amounts to a judicial death certificate, with the date of death stated as the date when the Constitution came into operation."

There is no doubt but that this approach is consistent with general principles of judicial review, but one may query whether this analysis will apply to each and every case in which a law has been invalidated.[294]

Henchy J then articulated what he termed as "the primary rule" of redress:

> "Once it has been judicially established that a statutory provision is invalid, the condemned provision will normally provide no legal justification for any acts done or left undone or for transactions undertaken in pursuance of it; and the persons damnified by the operation of the invalid provision will normally be accorded by the Courts all permitted and necessary redress."

[293] [1982] IR 241.

[294] In this context, particular problems may yet arise in the case of statutes which *were* constitutional at the date of their enactment, but which *have become* unconstitutional by reason of changing circumstances, such as inflation or population movements. Thus, the Rent Restrictions Acts were probably not unconstitutional when originally enacted, but it was principally the failure of the Oireachtas to revise the maximum rents payable in line with inflation which ultimately caused their invalidation for breach of Article 40.3 in *Blake v Attorney General* [1982] IR 117. The same might possibly have said of the Electoral Act 1959 struck down by reason of shifting population movements in *O'Donovan v Attorney General* [1961] IR 114; (1962) 96 ILTR 121. Murphy J first drew attention to this problem in *Browne v Attorney General* [1991] 2 IR 58. It was not necessary for him to resolve it, although he said that if the legislation "was constitutional at the time of its enactment it would seem impossible to contend that it was ever *ultra vires* the Oireachtas...to enact the legislation."

However, whether a pre- or post-Constitution statute was struck down, it did not follow that the legal order could or should undertake to repair all or any of the loss, or amend the grievance which had been caused by the operation of what now turned out to be an illegal measure. This "primary rule" of redress was subject to exceptions, especially where public policy factors or the need to avoid injustice to third parties who had changed their position in good faith in reliance on the validity of the (now condemned) rule:

> "While it is central to the due administration of justice in an ordered society that one of the primary concerns of the courts should be to see that prejudice suffered at the hands of those who act without legal justification, where legal justification is required, shall not stand beyond the reach of corrective legal proceedings, the law has to recognise that there may be transcendent considerations which make such a course undesirable, impractical or impossible. Over the centuries the law has come to recognise, in one degree or another, that factors such as prescription (negative or positive), waiver, estoppel, laches, a statute of limitation, *res judicata*, or other matters (most of which may be grouped under the heading of public policy) may debar a person from obtaining redress in the courts for injury, pecuniary or otherwise, which would be justifiable and redressable if such considerations had not intervened.
>
> For a variety of reasons, the law recognises that in certain circumstances, no matter how unfounded in law certain conduct may have been, no matter how unwarranted its operation in a particular case, what has happened has happened, and cannot or should not be undone. The irreversible progressions and by-products of time, the compulsion of public order and of the common good, the aversion of the law from giving a hearing to those who have slept on their rights, the quality of legality - even irreversibility - that tends to attach to what has become inveterate or has been widely accepted or acted upon, the recognition that even in the short term the accomplished fact may sometimes acquire an inviolable sacredness, these and other factors may convert what has been done under an unconstitutional, or otherwise void, law into an acceptable part of the *corpus juris*."

Muckley v Ireland: The sequel to Murphy

In the immediate aftermath of this decision the Oireachtas enacted s 21 of the Finance Act 1980 which sought to impose the same burden of taxation on married couples for the tax years prior to the date of that decision. The justification for this was a desire to maintain tax equity as between persons who had been assessed for tax under the old rule, but who had not yet paid the sums that were previously due and other taxpayers who had paid such sums under the (now) unconstitutional regime but, who, in the light of the Supreme Court decision, could not now recover such sums. This section was, however, held to be unconstitutional by both Barrington J in the High Court and by the Supreme Court in *Muckley v Ireland.*[295] Barrington J based his decision on Article 40.3, saying that in *Murphy*:

> "It was found to be impractical to vindicate the personal rights of the married couples who paid an invalid tax because directing the State to refund taxes unconstitutionally collected would have caused financial and administrative chaos."

The same public policy concerns were not present in the present case, as the taxes were merely assessed, but not collected: "There is no impracticality in defending the citizen

[295] [1985] IR 472.

against exactions which the State has no authority to impose." This decision was subsequently confirmed by the Supreme Court and *Muckley* would seem to be a good example of Henchy J's "primary rule" of redress.

Delay, acquiescence, laches or other conduct affecting third party rights may defeat a claim to be redressed

Just as in *Murphy's* case - where the State was held to be entitled to be defeat the vast majority of claims for repayment of taxes by reason of change of position and reliance in good faith on the validity of the sections in question - the courts have held in a series of cases that, by reason of delay, acquiescence or otherwise, some litigants have been debarred from their conduct from relying on a finding of invalidity. Thus, in *W. v W.*[296] (where a husband claimed that his re-marriage was invalid on the ground that his wife's earlier foreign divorce would not now be recognised within this jurisdiction in the wake of the invalidation of the domicile of dependency rule) Egan J referred to what Henchy J had said in *Murphy* and concluded that the husband was now in any event estopped by his conduct from arguing that his wife lacked capacity to contract a second marriage.

Can the courts limit the temporal effect of a judicial ruling?

A related question is whether the courts are empowered to place a temporal limit on the retroactive effect of a judicial ruling. Thus, when the Supreme Court clearly indicated in *The State (Clarke) v Roche*[297] that the hitherto long-standing practice whereby certain types of summonses issued by District Court clerks was unconstitutional (but where, unlike *Murphy's* case, there was no formal declaration of unconstitutionality) the question arose as to whether this decision had retrospective effect. In *White v Hussey*[298] Barr J ruled that it did not:

> "If the Supreme Court [had] intended that its finding as to the invalidity of the erstwhile practice...was to be regarded as having retrospective effect, then that conclusion would have been specifically stated in the *Roche* judgment...It seems to me that it would be a matter for that court."

While courts in other jurisdictions have assumed the power to limit the temporal effect of their judgments, this has always been done expressly and, generally speaking, as part of the original judgment itself.[299] Nevertheless, the approach of Barr J seems, for several reasons, dubious. First, it is inconsistent with the general principle underlying a judicial

[296] [1993] ILRM 294. See also the comments of Barr J. in *C.M. v T.M. (No.2)* [1990] 2 IR 52

[297] [1986] IR 619.

[298] [1989] ILRM 109. See also the judgment of Lynch J in *Connors v Delap* [1989] ILRM 93 and that of Barr J in *CM v TM (No.2)* [1990] 2 IR 52.

[299] Thus, the European Court of Justice has held that it alone has power to limit the temporal effect of its judgments and that any such limitation must be stated expressly in the original jurisdiction itself: see *Barra v Belgium* (Case 309/85) [1988] ECR 355; [1988] 2 CMLR 409. The European Court has emphasised that it will require exceptional circumstances before the Court will countenance the non-retroactive effect of its rulings: see *Defrenne v SABENA (No.2)* (Case 43/75) [1976] ECR 455; *Pinna v Craisse d'Allocations Familiares de la Savoie* [1986] ECR 1; *Blaizot v University of Liege* (Case 42/86) [1988] ECR 379; *Barber v Guardian Royal Exchange Group* (Case C-262/88) [1990] ECR I-1889; [1990] 2 CMLR 513 and *Ten Oever v Stichting Bedrijfspensionenfonds voor het Glazenwassers-en Schoonmaakbedrijf* (Case C-109/91), Court of Justice, 6 October 1993. The Court of Justice will generally only permit non-retroactivity where not to do so would be to interfere with third-party vested rights or where to undo past transactions would cause administrative chaos. It was precisely for these reasons that the Court in *Defrenne* (equal pay); *Blaizot* (differential fees in university education) and *Barber* and *Ten Oever* (discriminatory pension schemes) refused to apply its rulings retroactively.

decision, namely, that the court is deemed to be deciding what the law is.[300] More importantly, all the members of the Supreme Court in *Murphy* rejected the argument that the retrospective consequences of a decision should depend on some judicially imposed arbitrary cut-off date and Henchy J spoke of the:

> "[A]rbitrariness and inequality, in breach of Article 40.1, that would result in a citizen's constitutional right depending on the fortuity of when a court's decision would be pronounced."

Finally, it would be indeed remarkable if a court could be permitted to impose such a cut-off date in respect of a judicial decision which invalidated some practice or rule, but where no such formal limitation could be imposed where the court had actually invalidated a statutory provision. For these reasons it would seem - the decision in *White v Hussey* notwithstanding - that a judicial decision of this kind falls into the same category as a case in which a statutory provision has been invalidated, namely, that in both cases the courts cannot impose a formal temporal limitation on the retrospective effects of their judgments.

Fiat justitia dum maneat coelum?

In *Murphy's* case Henchy J had said he was deliberately avoiding "any general consideration of the broad question as to when, and to what extent, acts done on foot of an unconstitutional law may be immune from suit in the courts", as this was unnecessary for the concrete case before him. In this case, along with three other members of the Court, his view was that as tax payments are quickly absorbed into the State's financial bloodstream, and as taxpayers must be taken to understand that and accept it, however grudgingly they may pay up, they cannot afterwards be allowed to claim the very disruptive disgorgement of those payments even when the legal basis for exacting them is void. This reasoning does not seem applicable, by any kind of plausible analogy, to many other cases where a law now declared unconstitutional may leave other people, who were caught by it earlier, anxious for redress - for example, people whose cases might have been covered by the *Quinn* or *McGee* decisions - and there would remain, so far as the judgment of Henchy J is concerned, only the very general exposition of the water-under-the-bridge principle cited above (which, although he disclaimed such a proposition, pretty well amounts to an overall argument for non-retroactivity in any case where a declaration of unconstitutionality leaves persons other than the plaintiff potentially aggrieved by past events now revealed as illegal). Perhaps the right course would be to accept the somewhat more modest proposition implicit in the rhetorical expression of O'Higgins CJ, (who in the *Murphy* case did not need to deal with the problem, as he dated invalidity from the moment of judgment) when he said in *Byrne's* case, in regard to the convulsion which would be caused by overturning innumerable jury convictions: "Could organised society accept such a conclusion?" This rather pragmatic view was given a more theoretical and constitutionally based justification by Barrington J in *Muckley* when he said that while Article 40.3 obliges the State to defend and vindicate constitutional rights, the guarantee is qualified by considerations of practicability and in some cases it would be impractical and impossible to vindicate the constitutional rights of litigants by reason of the financial and administrative chaos this would cause. If, therefore, one regards the duty to provide redress as stemming from Article 40.3, the

[300] See, e.g., *Finucane v McMahon* [1990] 1 IR 165; [1990] ILRM 505, where Hamilton P rejected an argument that the court should apply the "old" law regarding the political offence doctrine to the applicant's case, simply because the offences in question were committed in 1981 before a series of a judicial decisions (see pp. 879-880) limiting the scope of that exception. In effect, Hamilton P. was here rejecting an argument that the courts could place a temporal limitation on the scope of a judicial decision.

courts could, in appropriate cases, quite legitimately invoke public policy considerations of this kind as qualifying the State's duty to vindicate the constitutional rights that have been so infringed.[301]

The courts should perhaps be slow to set up a list of reasons why doing full, including retroactive justice, would be inconvenient or impracticable, and draw the line rather at the point where really serious embarrassment of the State - the chaos which the State's existence is supposed to counteract and exclude - would be the result of accepting claims flowing from the operation of a statute always illegal.[302]

Breach of constitutional procedure

A further question, related to the foregoing, is that of a finding of unconstitutionality not in relation to a law, but in relation to some process for which the Constitution prescribes rules for the carrying out of it: an example might be the exceeding of a time-limit laid down by the Constitution for the holding of an election; or the neglect by the Oireachtas to revise Dáil constituencies at least once every twelve years, as Article 16.2.4 requires. In the latter case there is at least the authority of the Supreme Court in *In re Article 26 and the Electoral (Amendment) Bill 1961*[303] (where the twelve-year period was perforce exceeded in consequence of the 1959 Electoral (Amendment) Act being found invalid[304]) that:

> "while the subsection makes it obligatory on the Oireachtas to carry out the revision of constituencies at least once in every twelve years, if this period has been allowed to elapse without a revision being carried out the obligation remains to carry it out as soon as possible. There is, of course, a satisfactory explanation in this case."

The Court, in other words, treated the constitutional requirement as though it contained an implied term permitting, so to speak, a cy-près interpretation of itself; though this, it should be noted, was in the context of an impossibility (that of observing a time-limit which had already passed) for which there was a "satisfactory explanation". Even if the explanation had been unsatisfactory, and if the time-limit had been wilfully neglected, could the Court have taken any other course but to stand over an Electoral Act subsequently passed? The alternative here, since the Dáil then sitting had been validly elected under the 1947 Electoral Act might have been simple enough: a referendum to make the appropriate amendment in the Constitution to cure, or to allow for the irregularity. But suppose the 1959 Electoral Act had been invalidated not during the term of the Dáil which had taken part in its enactment, but during the term of the subsequent Dáil (elected in 1961). Would there have been any alternative to holding the 1961 General Election void, and all the proceedings of the Oireachtas elected in that year a nullity? Note that in this event, a constitutional amendment to cure the situation would not be possible, since

[301] There are analogies here with other decisions concerning the ambit of Article 40.3: see, e.g., *Moynihan v Greensmyth* [1977] IR 56 (rights protected by Article 40.3 not absolute and Oireachtas may have to balance competing interests) and *The State (Trimbole) v Governor of Mountjoy Prison* [1985] IR 550 (where Finlay CJ held that, where an invasion of constitutional rights had occurred, the courts had a positive duty "to restore *as far as possible* the person so damaged to the position in which he would have been if his rights had not been invaded) (italics supplied). Nor will the State be allowed to set up or rely upon an unconstitutionality against a private citizen where to do would be oppressive: *McCarthy v Garda Commissioner* [1993] 1 IR 489. Here Flood J gave further evidence of this pragmatic approach when he refused to allow the State to contest the validity of an acquittal which had followed an (admittedly invalid) return for trial but for which the applicant had no responsibility.

[302] There are analogies here with the courts' attitude to discretionary relief following the invalidation of an administrative decision: see Hogan and Morgan, *Administrative Law in Ireland* (London, 1991) at 383-385 and 595-611.

[303] [1961] IR 169.

[304] See above at pp. 162-163.

there would be no Dáil or Seanad to pass the amending Bill prior to its submission to the people. And if this is so, then arguably the same problem would arise if a Dáil election were held in constituencies not drawn in conformity with the population distribution disclosed at the last preceding census (a requirement quite independent of the twelve-year maximum).[305] In this jurisdiction[306] no judicial authority on this range of problems appears yet to exist.[307]

(I) THE CONSTITUTION AND THE CONFLICT OF LAWS

The inter-action between the Constitution and the conflict of law rules presents potentially difficult questions which to date have been only imperfectly explored. While the question of whether and in what circumstances non-citizens may invoke the Constitution has already been considered,[308] more problematic questions arise in the case of temporary residence, a problem that has already arisen in a number of cases involving child abduction.[309] The possibilities that suggest themselves in this context are almost endless, especially as far as the potential extra-territorial effect of the Constitution is concerned. Could, for example, an Irish soldier serving with the United Nations in the Lebanon rely on Article 38.1 while he was stationed in that country to set aside a decision of a court-martial which disciplined him?[310] Could a non resident and non-EC national invoke Article 40.6.1 to challenge a decision of the Minister for Foreign Affairs to refuse him an entry visa to Ireland where the basis for that refusal was that the Minister took exception to the applicant's (peaceful) criticism of Irish Government policy? Would it make any difference if the Government was acting in furtherance of United Nations resolutions which were designed to impose sanctions on the

[305] *O'Malley v An Taoiseach* [1990] ILRM 461 and see pp. 164-165.

[306] This problem has, however, been touched on other countries. In *Simpson v Attorney General* [1955] NZLR 271 the New Zealand Court of Appeal was asked to annul a general election where the prescribed statutory procedures concerning the dissolution of Parliament had not been complied with by the Governor-General. The Court of Appeal - which freely admitted its anxiety not to cause serious public inconvenience - held (but not very persuasively) that these procedures were directory only and, hence, that the non-compliance had not nullified the ensuing general election. The German Constitutional Court similarly baulked from following the logical consequences of invalidity when it was asked to annul the results of the 1961 federal election following population shifts which had taken place since a 1949 apportionment statute. The Court avoided the major question by claiming (again, not very persuasively) that the inequalities caused by the operation of the 1949 law had not become evident at the time of the 1961 election and held that while the results of that election could not be therefore upset, the 1949 law could not serve as the basis for future elections now that these inequalities had become apparent. This problem also surfaced in Australia in the wake of the constitutional crisis of the mid-1970s when it became apparent following a series of decisions that the Governor-General had not complied with the terms of the Australian Constitution when he authorised a dissolution of both Houses of the Australian Parliament. Again, the Australian courts preferred pragmatism to strict logic. As Barwick CJ said in *Victoria v Commonwealth* (1975) 134 CLR 81: "The dissolution itself is a fact which can neither be void nor undone. If, without having power to do so, the Governor-General did dissolve both Houses, there would be no basis for setting aside the dissolution or for treating it as not having occurred." In *Western Australia v Commonwealth* (1975) 134 CLR 201 Jacobs J put it even more pithily: "The people's expression [in the general election] cures any formal defect which may previously have existed."

[307] There is, however, some judicial and academic authority on the related but more general problem of legality after a revolution; see above, p. 3. In this context a suggestion has been made which might be helpful here too, namely the notion of an "implied term" or a series of "implied terms", in a Constitution. By this theory one could say the people intended - even if they did not say so explicitly - that where the exact observance of the Constitution has become impossible, some *ad hoc* remedy, provided it is in the general spirit of the Constitution, must be taken to have their implied approval.

[308] See above at pp. 435-436.

[309] See pp. 488-489 and generally, Binchy, *The Irish Conflict of Laws* (Dublin, 1987) at 334-339. See also Binchy, "*Constitutional Remedies and the Law of Torts*" in O'Reilly ed., *Human Rights and Constitutional law: Essays in Honour of Brian Walsh* (Dublin, 1990); Lobel, "*The Constitution Abroad*" (1989) 83 AJIL 871 and Neuman, "*Whose Constitution*" (1990) 100 Yale LJ 909.

[310] See, e.g., *Reid v Covert* 354 US 1 (1957) (legislation authorising the trial in Germany by US military tribunal of the wives of US servicemen stationed there held to be unconstitutional.)

foreign states in question? As the case-law on these difficult questions is still in its infancy, the following rather is a tentative analysis is of some of the issues which have already arisen or which may yet do so.

Temporary residence and the Constitution

Some of the cases touching on this topic indirectly raised choice of law questions involving the Constitution. Two child abduction cases neatly illustrate this problem. In the first case, *Northampton County Council v ABF*,[311] an English local authority sought the return of a child who had been taken to Ireland by her father because he did not want her put up for adoption. Hamilton J, having adverted to the natural law provenance of Article 41, went on to observe that:

> "It seems to me that non-citizenship can have no effect on the interpretation of Article 41 or the entitlement to protection afforded by it...The natural law is of universal application and applies to all human persons, be they citizens of this state or not, and in my opinion it would be inconceivable that the father of the infant child would not be entitled to rely on the recognition of the Family contained in Article 41 for the purpose of enforcing his rights as the lawful father of the infant...or that he should lose such entitlement merely because he removed the child to this jurisdiction..."[312]

This might be characterised as the "universalist" approach, which reflecting its natural law underpinning, applies the fundamental rights provisions of the Constitution to all persons within the jurisdiction of the courts.[313] Yet the subsequent decision of the Supreme Court in *Saunders v Mid-Western Health Board*[314] demonstrates judicial unease at the prospect of such an expansive approach. In this case an English couple who had no Irish connection brought their children to Ireland appears to have regarded their rather fortuitous and temporary presence within the jurisdiction as not having conferred on them constitutional rights *vis-à-vis* their children. In other words, despite the "inalienable and imprescriptible rights" language of Article 41 - which, on one view, might be thought - to follow the logic of Hamilton J in *ABF* - to represent a command to all organs of the State (including the judicial arm) to apply these rights to persons within the jurisdiction - the Court appears to have applied what amounts to a form of choice of law analysis in holding that English law applied. By way of contrast, however, O'Flaherty J had no difficulty in holding that Article 41 applied to an Indian child who had been living in Ireland for several years with Irish family: see *Eastern Health Board v An Bord Uchtála*.[314a] This differing approach seems to have based not so much on a literal, textual egegisis[315] of the language of the Constitution, but rather on either the

[311] [1982] ILRM 550.

[312] Hamilton J declined automatically to make an order enforcing the English custody decree and ordered a plenary hearing as to what would be in the child's own best interests. For a somewhat similar approach, see *Kent County Council v CS* [1984] ILRM 292.

[313] The approach of Brennan J in his dissenting opinion in *US v Verdugo-Urquidez* 494 US 259 (1990) (see fn. 315 infra,) is also very similar to that of Hamilton J: "The Framers of the Bill of Rights did not purport to "create" rights...Bestowing rights and delineating protected groups would have been inconsistent with the drafter's fundamental conception of a Bill of Rights as a limitation on the Government's conduct with respect to all whom it seeks to govern."

[314] *The Irish Times*, 24 April 1987. This was an *ex tempore* and not a reserved judgment.

[314a] [1993] ILRM 577.

[315] This is not say that such an approach would be without merit in some contexts, e.g., issues connected with citizenship, diplomatic protection and voting rights and in this regard it is difficult to take issue with the approach of the Supreme Court in *Re Article 26 of the Constitution and the Electoral (Amendment) Bill* [1984] IR 268. Indeed, it may be noted that there are elements of the Hobbesian "social contract" approach to this question in both this decision and in *Saunders*. In other words, *certain* constitutional rights and entitlements (perhaps those especially bound up with political citizenship rights) are confined to those members of the

connections which the plaintiffs in each case had with Ireland or the nature of the right in question. Thus, in some contexts - such as the right to liberty - it may be appropriate to allow an alien to rely on constitutional protections, even on the basis of temporary presence.[316] This point had been well made by O'Flaherty J in the *Eastern Health Board* case, where he said that it would be "remarkable" if Article 42.5 could not be invoked "to protect any child in the State who is left, in effect, parentless," stressing that the fights of the child in Article 42 "are surely of universal application."

Extra-territorial effects of the Constitution

The first case in which the potential extra-territorial effects of the Constitution appears to have been touched on is *Re Article 26 and the Criminal Law (Jurisdiction) Bill*[317] where the Court stressed that the doctrine of constitutional justice did not apply to courts or tribunals outside the State by persons who have no obligation to uphold the Constitution.[318] This theme was taken up by the Court of Criminal Appeal in *The People (Director of Public Prosecutions) v Campbell*[319] where the validity of the accused's detention in a prison in Northern Ireland was at issue.[320] Hederman J rejected the contention that the legality of this detention was to be judged by reference to the constitutional standards of this State:

> "As to the rights which Irish citizens are granted by the Constitution, the judgment of the Supreme Court in [in the *Criminal Law (Jurisdiction) Bill* case makes it clear that the right to obtain constitutional justice from tribunals...is a right which does not extend to tribunals established outside of the jurisdiction of the State. The lawfulness of the custody in Northern Ireland of an Irish citizen cannot therefore be impugned by reference to a non-existent right. The conclusions of the Supreme Court with regard to the right to constitutional justice apply with equal force to any other of the unspecified personal rights which an accused person may enjoy by virtue of Article 40.3....in relation to criminal proceedings in this State."[321]

Yet while the orthodox approach of Hederman J - which confines the application of the Constitution to the territorial ambit of the State - is in itself unexceptional, it cannot be accepted without qualification. Thus, the potential extra-territorial application of the

community who owe positive obligations of loyalty to the State. This particular analysis is especially evident in McCarthy J's concurring judgment in *McGimpsey v Ireland* [1990] 1 IR 110; [1990] ILRM 70. See also the statement of Rehnquist CJ in *US v Verdugo-Urquidez* 494 US 245 (1990) to the effect that most constitutional rights are confined to that class of persons "who are part of a national community or who have otherwise sufficient connection with this country to be considered part of that community." It may be noted, however, that in the *Eastern Health Board* case O'Flaherty J briefly analysed the text of Article 42 in support of his conclusion that the rights mentioned therein were of "universal application."

316 For a particularly good example, see *The State (Trimbole) v Governor of Mountjoy Prison* [1985] IR 550. See also the differing views expressed on this subject by Finlay CJ and Walsh J in *Fajujona v Minister for Justice* [1990] 2 IR 151.

317 [1977] IR 129.

318 A slightly different point is whether the Constitution applies to foreign entities who might - in one sense - be said to be acting as agents of the State (such as where, for example, a foreign Government take steps to detain an Irish citizen abroad at the specific request of the Irish Government). This point was raised in an oblique way in *Moyne v Londonderry Harbour Commissioners* [1986] IR 286, where Costello J said that Article 40 did not apply to a foreign corporation performing statutory duties within the State.

319 (1983) 2 Frewen 131.

320 The accused had been charged with offences under s 3(1)(*a*) of the Criminal Law (Jurisdiction) Act 1976 which makes it an offence for persons in Northern Ireland charged with or, convicted of, certain offences to escape form lawful custody.

321 The decision in this case may be compared in some respects with the decision of the US Supreme Court in *US v Verdugo-Urquidez* 494 US 259 (1990) where the Court ruled that the "search and seizure" provisions of the 4th Amendment of the US Constitution did not apply to search of a non-citizen's dwelling conducted in Mexico by agents of the US Government.

Constitution was never far from the surface in the abortion cases, where the courts either granted or envisaged the treating of injunctions restraining either the giving of information or assistance to women travelling to the United Kingdom for the purpose of procuring an abortion or actually restraining such women from leaving the jurisdiction.[322] While in all of these cases the courts were dealing with Irish citizens (or Irish corporate entities) resident in Ireland,[323] nevertheless the decisions of the courts with regard to Article 40.3.3 had some (if only *de facto)* extra territorial element.[324]

Extradition, Deportation and Human Rights Standards Abroad

The problem of the extra-territoriality becomes particularly acute if it is contended that the deportation or extradition of a person to another country may result in the infringement of his constitutional rights. This problem was directly in view in a series of extradition cases decided by the Supreme Court in March 1990. The cases concerned the aftermath of the escape in September 1983 of thirty eight IRA prisoners form the Maze Prison in Northern Ireland. The escape had been a violent one: several prisoner officers were stabbed; others were kicked and beaten and one was stabbed and died from a heart attack. Following the break-out, it appears that a great number of the remaining IRA prisoners were assaulted by prison officers who were enraged by the death of their colleague and these attacks included assaults by dogs handled by prison officers. The prison officers then refused to co-operate with every form of enquiry into allegations of assault and "clearly at an early stage entered into a widespread conspiracy to deny absolutely all accusations of assault or ill-treatment and also to deny the refusal of requests for medical assistance."[325] The falsity of these denials was only subsequently uncovered in November 1988 following a civil action taken by one of the prisoners[326] where certain new documents came to light which showed that, not only had the requests for medical treatment been ignored, but that serious assaults had, in fact, taken place following the escape. But despite these developments, no action of any kind - whether criminal or disciplinary - appears to have been taken against the prison officers concerned, many of whom were still serving in the Maze Prison.

By the time that *Finucane v McMahon*[327] came before the Supreme Court in March 1990 the facts of *Pettigrew* had by then become known. While the Court was divided on the political offence question,[328] all of the judges were agreed that the applicant had shown that there was sufficient risk of ill-treatment were he to be returned to the Maze Prison in Northern Ireland. Because of this, the Court held that it was required to order the release of the applicant in order to ensure that his constitutional rights were not so violated. Finlay CJ put it thus:

> "It was submitted by the respondents that the very fact that so many of the prisoners have now successfully brought their claims before the courts in Northern Ireland indicated that there was no ground for the applicant's fear of invasion of his consti-

[322] *Attorney General (Society for the Protection of Unborn Children (Ire.) Ltd. v Open Door Counselling Ltd* [1988] IR 593; [1989] ILRM 19; *Attorney General v X* [1992] 1 IR 1; [1992] ILRM 401; [1992] 2CMLR 277 and pp. 792-803.

[323] And, hence, the cases could be said to concern "the application in Ireland of Article 40.3.3" within the meaning of Protocol No.17 of Maastricht Treaty": see p. 798.

[324] This was especially true of the facts of the *X.* case where the defendant in question was actually in England at the time when the original interim injunction was granted.

[325] *Finucane v McMahon* [1990] 1 IR 165; [1990] ILRM 505 *per* Finlay CJ.

[326] *Pettigrew v Northern Ireland Office* (1989) 3 BNIL 83.

[327] [1990] 1 IR 165; [1990] ILRM 505. This approach had earlier been signalled by the Supreme Court in the earlier extradition case arising out of the same facts: *Russell v Fanning* [1988] IR 505. The plaintiff's claim of probable ill-treatment failed on the facts, but this was before the revelations in the *Pettigrew* case.

[328] See pp. 881-886.

tutional rights. I have no difficulty in accepting that if ill-treatment of any of the prisoners in the Maze Prison is brought to the notice of the courts in Northern Ireland it will be condemned and remedied.....The Court has, however, as its primary obligation, the duty to prevent such invasions of the applicant's rights and it is not a sufficient discharge of that duty for it to rely upon the vindication of those rights by compensation after they have been invaded.....I have come to the conclusion that there is a probable risk, if the applicant were returned to the Maze Prison in Northern Ireland, that he would be assaulted or injured by the illegal actions of the prison staff....[T]he total absence of any repercussions on the staff as a result of the ill-treatment of prisoners in the aftermath of the escape, and from that point of view, the success of their conspiracy to cover up their conduct would appear to make the applicant, in my view, a probable target for ill-treatment."

The decision in *Finucane* may be usefully contrasted with the celebrated decision of the European Court of Human Rights in *Soering v United Kingdom.*[329] Here the applicant sought to resist his extradition from the United Kingdom to the United States where he was sought to face a charge of murder. It was said that, as there was a real risk that Mr Soering would face the death penalty if convicted on this charge, compliance with this request would involve a breach by the United Kingdom of Article 3 of the Convention.[330]

While it was conceded that the death penalty was not, of itself, contrary to the provisions of the Convention, it was argued that to extradite Soering in circumstances where he might experience the so-called "death row phenomenon"[331] would be to violate the guarantees contained in Article 3. At this point, the Court of Human Rights said:

> "[H]aving regard to the very long period of time spent on death row in such extreme conditions, with the ever present and mounting anguish of awaiting execution of the death penalty, and to the personal circumstances of the applicant, especially his age and mental state at the time of the offence, the applicant's extradition to the United States would expose him to a real risk of treatment going beyond the threshold set by Article 3."

What is at once both interesting and remarkable about these cases is that in both *Finucane* and *Soering*, the courts seemed willing to test the conditions operating in foreign prisons by reference to their own legal standards. This approach is undoubtedly innovative and it carries its own attendant dangers in that the courts are required, in effect, to pronounce on the state of affairs prevailing *within* the jurisdiction of the requesting state. If that assessment proves to be unfavourable - as it was in both *Finucane* and *Soering* - the requesting state is likely to be offended. In addition, such findings by a foreign court will probably be regarded as unjustifiable intrusion into its own internal affairs. At a wider level, the human rights dimension to the extradition question is still fraught with difficulties and uncertainties. The reasoning employed in these cases is all very well, but a refusal to extradite suspects on the ground of apprehended ill-treatment at the hands of a requesting state could be said to give rise to undesirable political consequences. This would seem especially to be so given that it involves the Irish courts - implicitly, at least - investigating conduct that has taken place or may take place out of the State. This in turn might be said to be an example of an attempt by the Irish courts "to police the Constitution" by giving the Constitution a form

[329] (1989) 11 EHRR 439.

[330] This provides that: "No one shall be subjected to torture or to inhuman or degrading treatment or punishment."

[331] I.e., spend a very long time in prison on "death row" awaiting the outcome of various appeal and *habeas corpus* applications

of extra-territorial dimension. Nevertheless, these decisions may yet have important implications in the deportation and immigration areas, especially where the detainee claims that his constitutional rights will be infringed if he is returned to his country of origin.[332]

Possibility that the suspect will not get a fair trial abroad if extradited

The other possibility opened up by the recent decisions is the suggestion that a suspect will not be delivered up for extradition purposes if there is a real risk that he will not get a fair trial abroad. This question first received judicial consideration in *Clarke v McMahon.*[333] The applicant in this case had been sentenced at Belfast Crown Court in 1979 to a term of imprisonment following conviction for attempted murder and related offences arising out of an armed attack in which certain civilians had been injured. While the applicant was ultimately to succeed before the Supreme Court on the ground of probable ill-treatment,[334] the other argument - namely, that the Irish courts should decline to order extradition because the foreign conviction was flawed - is also of considerable interest. The Supreme Court agreed that, in exceptional circumstances, the Irish courts could go behind a foreign conviction where this was necessary to protect the constitutional rights of the requested person. Finlay CJ said that:

> "The statement that the court cannot in an extradition case properly undertake an investigation into the validity of a conviction recorded in a requesting state must be understood as being subject to this inherent power. The facts of this case, in my view, go nowhere near establishing a situation in which this inherent power might be invoked and it is, therefore, not necessary for me to speculate on what might constitute, in any other case, such a situation."

This appears to suggest that the Irish courts will, where necessary, apply their own constitutional standards when reviewing the validity and propriety of foreign convictions. Nevertheless, this jurisdiction is quite exceptional and will only be invoked where there is compelling evidence to suggest that the suspect's constitutional rights would be infringed if he were to be extradited to face trial (or, as the case may be, to serve a sentence in respect of a foreign conviction). The reluctance of the courts to widen the grounds in which the plea will be entertained is evidenced by the judgment of the Supreme Court in *Ellis v O'Dea (No.2).*[335] The applicant in this case was wanted in England for serious explosives charges and the case had already attracted considerable attention in the British media. It was said that, given the now notorious miscarriages of justice involving Irish defendants, there was a real risk that the applicant would not get a fair trial but this was not accepted by the Supreme Court. Finlay CJ said:

> "Particular emphasis was laid by counsel in this Court...details of....cases which have become notorious in relation to the quashing of convictions obtained through forensic evidence which appears to have been wholly unreliable. Having carefully considered these cases and the information contained in the affidavit concerning them, they do not, in my view, establish a risk that the plaintiff will be tried or pros-

[332] Cf. *Gutrani v Governor of Mountjoy Prison*, Supreme Court, 2 July 1992 (where McCarthy J made passing reference to the *Finucane* principles in the context of an illegal alien - who claimed to be a political refugee - seeking to resist deportation to Libya). See also the decisions of the European Court of Human Rights in *Cruz Varas v Sweden* (1992) 14 EHRR 1 and *Vilarajah v United Kingdom* (1992) 14 EHRR 248.

[333] [1990] 1 IR 228; [1990] ILRM 648.

[334] Clarke had participated in the mass escape from the Maze prison and his case was thus governed by the decision in *Finucane.*

[335] [1991] 1 IR 251. In an earlier judicial review application the Supreme Court had seemed more sympathetic to this ground: see *Ellis v O'Dea (No.1)* [1989] IR 530; [1990] ILRM 87.

> ecuted or that investigations will be conducted in an manner which would be inconsistent with the reasonable standards of fair trial required by our Constitution."

In view of the admitted miscarriages of justice involving Irish defendants charged with terrorist offences, might it not be said that, empirically, at least, there was as much a chance that Ellis would not get a fair trial as there was that Finucane would be ill-treated if he were to be returned to the Maze Prison? At all events the failure by the Supreme Court to intervene in a case such as this case demonstrates that this jurisdiction is truly exceptional one to be reserved for cases with especially compelling facts.

FINALITY OF FINDING OF VALIDITY UNDER ARTICLE 26

3° No Court whatever shall have jurisdiction to question the validity of a law, or any provision of a law, the Bill for which shall have been referred to the Supreme Court by the President under Article 26 of this Constitution, or to question the validity of a provision of a law where the corresponding provision in the Bill for such law shall have been referred to the Supreme Court by the President under the said Article 26.

3° Ní bheidh dlínse ag Cúirt ar bith chun baíliocht dhlí nó fhorála ar bith de dhlí a chur in amhras is dlí a ndearna an tUachtarán an Bille lena aghaidh a chur faoi bhreith na Cúirte Uachtaraí faoi Airteagal 26 den Bhunracht seo, ná chun bailíocht fhorála de dhlí a chur in amhras má rinne an tUachtarán an fhoráil chomhréire sa Bhille le haghaidh an dlí sin a chur faoi bhreith na Cúirte Uachtaraí faoin Airteagal sin 26.

Rule not yet circumvented

No attempt seems ever to have been made to circumvent the rule contained in this sub-section. There have been five statutes to which the sub-section applied: the Offences against the State (Amendment) Act 1940; the Electoral (Amendment) Act 1961; the Criminal Law (Jurisdiction) Act 1976; the Emergency Powers Act 1976 and the Adoption Act 1988; all of these, except the Electoral (Amendment) Act 1961, are still in force.[1] In 1957 the internment powers of the Offences against the State (Amendment) Act 1940, were attacked in *In re Ó Láighléis;*[2] the Supreme Court, after reciting the history of the Act and Article 34.3.3, said (*per* Maguire CJ):

> "The Court is therefore bound to approach the consideration of this appeal on the basis that the Act is valid and incapable of being challenged as repugnant to the Constitution in these or any other proceedings. This is accepted by [counsel for the appellant]."[3]

Is the Article 34.3.3 rule of questionable value?

It is questionable whether the rule of Article 34.3.3 is a good one, as a reference under Article 26 can lead only to the Bill being debated in terms of hypotheses which may occur to counsel or to the court, whereas when enacted it may prove to have quite different and unforeseen qualities in practice, by which time it will be immune from challenge as a result of this provision.

[1] The Emergency Powers Act 1976 has not been repealed, but it has not been in force since October 1977. It may be re-activated, however, at any time by Government order.

[2] [1960] IR 93; (1961) 95 ILTR 92. Note that in the course of delivering the judgment of the Court of Criminal Appeal in *People v Tuite* (1983) 2 Frewen 175, McCarthy J observed that as the constitutionality of the Criminal Law (Jurisdiction) Act 1976 had been upheld by the Supreme Court following an Article 26 reference, "this Court is precluded from any consideration as to whether or not the Act or any section of it is so repugnant."

[3] And yet this might prove possible in the special case of the Offences Against the State (Amendment) Act 1940. Since there are now substantial doubts as to whether that reference was a valid one (see p. 1178), might it not be argued that as (i) the "old" Supreme Court had no jurisdiction to entertain that reference; (ii) therefore Article 34.3.3 has no application to the "old" Supreme Court's pronouncement on the constitutionality of the 1940 Act and (iii) that the present Supreme Court is now free - should it so elect - to depart from the reasoning of the "old" Supreme Court and pronounce the 1940 Act to be unconstitutional?

But perhaps the Article 26 finding is not a binding precedent

The rigour of this sub-section would seem somewhat mitigated if there is substance in the view (expressed by Kenny J in *Ryan v Attorney General*[4]) that the Supreme Court's opinion on an Article 26 reference does not bind the High Court in the same way as would a judgment *inter partes*. This would mean that, while the Act cleared under Article 26 remains invulnerable, the reasoning on which the Article 26 judgment was based does not necessarily apply to any similar enactment. There are, however, judicial dicta to the contrary: see Davitt P in *In re Ó Láighléis*[5] and Henchy J in *The State (Lynch) v Cooney.*[6] On the other hand, Article 34.3.3 does not prevent the Supreme Court overruling part of the reasoning contained in an earlier Article 26 reference and, indeed, this has already happened on at least one occasion: in *McGimpsey v Ireland*[7] the Supreme Court overruled part of the reasoning of the earlier *Criminal Law (Jurisdiction) Bill* reference.

Does the Article 34.3.3 rule apply where an Act which has previously been upheld under an Article 26 reference is later amended?

Another interesting question which does not yet appear to have surfaced is whether the rule contained in this sub-section continues to have application in the case of legislation which has been previously upheld under an Article 26 reference, but which has been more latterly amended by subsequent legislation. For example, certain provisions of the Criminal Law (Jurisdiction) Act 1976, have now been repealed and other provisions therein substituted by s 14(4) of the Criminal Damage Act 1991. First principles strongly suggest that these new added provisions do not enjoy the benefit of immunity from constitutional challenge. But can the matter be taken any further? As it happens, the amendments effected by the 1991 Act are relatively minor and self-contained in character, so that there is no obvious reason to suppose that the rest of the 1976 Act should not continue to attract the protection of Article 34.3.3. Suppose, however, the amendments were of a radical variety which transformed the entire Act (including, perhaps, provisions which, although not expressly amended by the later legislation, took on a new meaning in the light of these amendments). In such circumstances, it would seem that there must come a point where, by reason of the radical character of later amendments, the Act has been transformed to such an extent that it can no longer be regarded as the Act that had been cleared on a previous Article 26 reference. This would then appear to open the door to a later constitutional challenge where the Act would, perhaps, have lost entirely the immunity it previously enjoyed under the rubric of Article 34.3.3.

Analogous reasoning might well apply in the case of a Bill which had been upheld following a reference where the Constitution itself had been subsequently amended. In these changed circumstances would the immunity from challenge still apply ? Perhaps the best solution would be to say that the Act retains its immunity so far as the unamended constitutional provisions are concerned, but that it might be contested solely on the basis that it conflicts with the subsequent constitutional amendment.

4 [1965] IR 294.

5 [1960] IR 93; (1961) 95 ILTR 92.

6 [1982] IR 337; [1983] ILRM 89. For citation from these two judgments see above at p. 216.

7 [1990] 1 IR 110; [1990] ILRM 440. It should be noted that certain dicta of Sullivan CJ in the *Offences Against the State Bill* reference were disapproved of in *The State (Lynch) v Cooney* [1982] IR 337.

COURTS OF LOCAL AND LIMITED JURISDICTION

4° The Courts of First Instance shall also include Courts of local and limited jurisdiction with a right of appeal as determined by law.

4° Beidh ar na Cúirteanna Céadchéime, fairis sin, Cúirteanna ag a mbeidh dlínse theoranta áitiúil maille le ceart achomhairc ina n-aghaidh faoi mar a chinnfear le dlí.

1922 provision

This reproduces part of Article 64 of the 1922 Constitution.

"New" courts

The courts mentioned in this provision were equally to be "new" courts, but when they ultimately came to be established they did not differ materially in name, functions, mutual relations, or personnel from the courts of local and limited jurisdiction which, established in the 1924 reorganisation, were still working in 1961.[1] In *The People (Attorney General) v Conmey*[2] the Supreme Court held that the Court of Criminal Appeal, although not mentioned in the Constitution, was validly established under the cover of this subsection, since the expression "right of appeal as determined by law" might be taken to authorise the establishment of a special appellate instance such as (in the case of decisions of the Circuit Court) the Court of Criminal Appeal represents *vis-á-vis* a court of local and limited jurisdiction. Equally there is nothing in the Constitution to rule out the endowing of this court with an appellate function *vis-á-vis* the High Court in its criminal function (as the Central Criminal Court).[3]

Courts of first instance are not necessarily of limited and local jurisdiction

As the wording of Article 34.3.4 makes clear, the Oireachtas may establish courts of first instance, other than the High Court, which are not courts of local and limited jurisdiction. This point was made by Walsh J in *The State (Boyle) v Neylon*[4] when he said:

> "The Oireachtas is free to set up as many courts of first instance as it sees fit, but it is not free to bestow on them, or any statutory appellate court, the constitutional review functions of the High Court or the Supreme Court...Therefore, the Circuit Court as an institution can be set up without breaching any provision of Article 34 even if it is not a court of local and limited jurisdiction."

However, this passage cannot be taken as an acknowledgement of the fact that the Circuit Court is not a court of local and limited jurisdiction, since the case was argued on the assumption that the Circuit Court was such a court of local and limited jurisdiction.

[1] See below pp. 1178-1179.
[2] [1975] IR 341.
[3] This is a paraphrase of a judgment which does not expressly deal with the question whether, as the appellate instance appears in connection with courts of jurisdiction *both local and limited* (as the Irish "theoranta áitiúil" makes plain), that sub-section can cover an appellate jurisdiction from a court with a jurisdiction such as that of the High Court in its Central Criminal Court guise, which is neither local nor limited. The Court of Criminal Appeal exists by virtue of the Courts (Establishment and Constitution) Act 1961, s 3.
[4] [1986] IR 551.

"Right of appeal as determined by law"

There are conflicting views on whether Article 34.3.4 requires the Oireachtas to provide a right of appeal in all cases from decisions of courts of local and limited jurisdiction. In *The State (Hunt) v O'Donovan*[5] the applicant, having pleaded guilty to an offence in the District Court, had been sent forward for sentence to the Circuit Court, and duly sentenced there without having been indicted (in conformity with s 13 of the Criminal Procedure Act 1967, and with practice); and now found himself unable to appeal against the severity of the sentence, as s 63 of the Courts of Justice Act 1924, had the effect of giving an appeal only where the case had been dealt with in the Circuit Court on indictment. He argued that Article 34.3.4 gave him an appeal from the Circuit Court which was a court of local and limited jurisdiction. But Finlay J interpreted Article 34.3.4:

> "as prohibiting the constitution of a court of local and limited jurisdiction from which there was no appeal at all; but there is a very large gap between that interpretation and one which excludes the right of the law to determine from which precise decision an appeal will lie."

The "law" he interpreted here as meaning statute law:

> "it cannot be suggested that there was ever a common-law right of appeal from such a court of local and limited jurisdiction."[6]

But the *obiter* remarks of O'Higgins CJ in the subsequent case of *Murphy v Bayliss*[7] tend to cast doubt on this decision. Here a District Judge, who had refused to make an extradition order, stated a case for the opinion of the High Court. The defendant resisted this, claiming that the District Judge had no power to state a case in view of the provisions of s 47(5) of the Extradition Act 1965, which, it was said, had the effect of making a decision of the District Court "final and unappealable." This argument was rejected by the Supreme Court, which pointed out that the effect of the sub-section was merely to prevent an appeal being taken to the Circuit Court, leaving unaffected the power to state a case. O'Higgins CJ said that he doubted whether, in view of the provisions of Article 34.3.4, any statute could have the effect of rendering a decision of the District Court final and unappealable.

The "local and limited" requirement

The mandatory nature of the description "of local and limited jurisdiction" came through in *Grimes v Owners of SS Bangor Bay*,[8] an admiralty action, in which, on an issue of costs, the Supreme Court had to decide whether the case might have been brought in the Circuit Court. The provisions which determined the jurisdiction of the "old" Circuit Court were ss 48 and 52 of the Courts of Justice Act 1924, but as these sections said nothing about admiralty cases the defendants argued that in such matters an unlimited jurisdiction of the Circuit Court had to be implied. Black J agreed with

[5] [1975] IR 39; (1973) 107 ILTR 53.

[6] But - to quote from an admittedly later judgment of the Supreme Court - such a "law" must not "ignore the fundamental norms of the legal order postulated by the Constitution" (to quote Henchy J in *King v Attorney General* [1981] IR 233) and it might well be argued that a law which, without obvious justification, deprived a convicted person of a right to appeal against sentence merely because he happened to plead guilty in the District Court and was returned for sentence to the Circuit Court, violated such fundamental norms inasmuch as it was anomalous, haphazard and discriminatory. The anomaly disclosed in *Hunt's* case was cured by the Criminal Procedure (Amendment) Act 1973, s 1.

[7] Supreme Court, 22 July 1976.

[8] [1948] IR 350. See also J.P. Casey, "*The Constitution and the Legal System*" (1979) 14 Ir Jur (n.s.) 14.

them; but the majority thought otherwise. O'Byrne J considered that the old Article 64, part of which Article 34.3.4 reproduces:

> "enjoine[d] and require[d] that [the Circuit Court] should be local and limited in its jurisdiction...[Though one Court] its jurisdiction is to be exercised locally by the judges of that court in the manner specified by [s 52] and this section was intended, in my opinion, to satisfy the constitutional requirement that the jurisdiction of courts of first instance, other than the High Court, should be local...If a statute purported to confer upon any court of first instance, other than the High Court, such unlimited jurisdiction, it would, in my opinion, contravene the clear intendment of the Constitution."

In recent times, however, the courts have tended to take a less literal approach to the construction of Article 34.3.4.

In *Tormey v Ireland*[9] the plaintiff attacked the constitutionality of s 32 of the Courts Act 1981, which vests in the Circuit Court an exclusive jurisdiction in respect of most indictable crimes, with the exception of certain very serious offences such as murder and treason. Henchy J said that, reading Articles 34.3.1 (which vests the High Court with "full original jurisdiction") and 34.3.4 in conjunction, it was clear that:

> "the jurisdiction to try thus vested by the Constitution in courts tribunals, persons or bodies other than the High Court must be taken to be capable of being exercised, at least in certain instances, to the exclusion of the High Court, for the allocation of jurisdiction would otherwise be overlapping and unworkable."

Article 34.3.4 amounted to a recognition of the fact that the High Court was "not expected to be a suitable forum for hearing and determining at first instance all justiciable matters"; where such exclusive jurisdiction was given to the lower courts by statute the full original jurisdiction of the High Court could still be invoked "so as to ensure that justice will be done in that matter or question." This decision appears to give the Oireachtas considerable latitude as to the jurisdiction which it may confer on the District and Circuit Courts.[10]

The "local" nature of the Circuit Court's jurisdiction was examined in *The State (Boyle) v Neylon.*[11] Here the applicant had pleaded guilty to certain indictable offences and was sent forward, pursuant to s 31 of the Courts Act 1981, from the Circuit Court at Wicklow to the Dublin Circuit Court for sentence. He subsequently challenged the validity of this procedure on the ground that the Circuit Court at Dublin could not pass sentence in respect of a court with which it had no geographical connection. Walsh J, speaking for the Supreme Court, rejected this argument:

> "The ability to transfer the trial of a case from one locality to another does not alter the essential local exercise of a jurisdiction of the Circuit Court. The constitutional provision in referring to 'local...jurisdiction' does not mean that it must be local in the sense of being particularly connected with the place of residence of one party or

[9] [1985] IR 289; [1985] ILRM 375.

[10] For the question of the duty of the District and Circuit Courts to consider constitutional issues, see the judgment of Walsh J in *Ellis v O'Dea* [1989] IR 530; [1990] ILRM 87, and that of Denham J in *Coughlan v Patwell* [1993] 1 IR 31; [1992] ILRM 808.

[11] [1986] IR 551; [1987] ILRM 535.

another. But even where the place of the tort or the contract - that would be the local jurisdiction referred to in the Constitution."

The limited nature of the lower courts' jurisdiction was interpreted by Gannon J in *The State (O'Reilly) v Delap*[12] as requiring that the orders of such courts show jurisdiction on their face:

> "The District Court is a court of limited and local jurisdiction, pursuant to the provisions of Article 34.3.4. The orders of the District Court as a matter of record should be seen to be in accordance with the jurisdiction of the Court. If one of the limitations of jurisdiction relate to the range of punishment within limits prescribed by statute, the order of the Court prescribing such a punishment must be seen to be within such limit."

The same judge had earlier said in *R. v R.*[13] that in the case of courts of local and limited jurisdiction there was no distinction between "having jurisdiction and exercising jurisdiction." Only the High Court could validly decline jurisdiction on the ground that there were other courts to which recourse might be had in accordance with law.

Independence of the local courts

An important point was made by Gannon J in *Clune v Director of Public Prosecutions*[14] in regard to the status in the Constitution enjoyed by courts of limited jurisdiction, or "inferior courts", as the Circuit Court and District Court are sometimes called. The case was an attempt by accused persons to prevent the Director from prosecuting them in the District Court for offences which, though indictable, they apprehended the District Judge might consider fit to be tried summarily.[15] Gannon J refused to anticipate the decision on this matter which the District Judge would have to make, after due and proper consideration of the relevant factors, or to act on the assumption that the District Judge would go wrong. He said:

> "The concept of guiding, directing, controlling, supervising or correcting lay magistrates which might have been inferred from proceedings of certiorari and prohibition and mandamus prior to the establishment of the State is not appropriate to courts established under our Constitution. The courts of limited jurisdiction established by legislation pursuant to constitutional authority in that behalf are not in any sense subject to direction, control or supervision by the superior courts established by the Constitution. The statutory courts are "inferior courts" in the sense only that the range of their jurisdiction is limited and defined by legislation... Our District Courts are now administered by fully competent and qualified lawyers, whose independence as judges, not only from the executive but even from their judicial colleagues, must be respected. The Justice sitting in the District Court has the sole and exclusive authority to control and supervise the conduct of proceedings in his own Court within the limits of the jurisdiction conferred upon him. His independence and authority are secured in his freedom not only from pressures of political or

[12] High Court, 20 December 1985.
[13] [1984] IR 296.
[14] [1981] ILRM 17.
[15] See pp. 624-625.

> executive nature but also from purported intervention, direction or control by any superior court."[16]

Morris J spoke to the same effect in *KM v Director of Public Prosecutions*[17] when, rejecting the contention that the High Court could give directions as to the manner in which a Circuit Court Judge should deal with a pending criminal matter, he said:

> "for this court to prescribe procedures for that judge would...be an unconstitutional breach of the judicial independence of [that] judge and be an unconstitutional usurpation of his powers and functions."

Prosecution's right of appeal from decisions of the District Court

There are a variety of statutory provisions which in effect enable the prosecution to appeal against a dismissal of a prosecution in the District Court.[18] In *Considine v Shannon Regional Fisheries Board*[19] the respondents had sought to appeal a dismiss of a District Court prosecution to the Circuit Court as permitted by s 310 of the Fisheries (Consolidation) Act 1959. Costello J rejected the applicant's challenge to the constitutionality of this provision, holding that, as counsel had put it "the Oireachtas carried out a legislative act which was permitted and, indeed, contemplated by Article 34.3.4." And, as Costello J observed, the Supreme Court's decision in *People v O'Shea*[20] was authority for the proposition that Article 38.1 could not be prayed in aid to qualify the plain language of such an appellate provision. It was true that *O'Shea* had concerned Article 34.4.3 (the appellate jurisdiction of the Supreme Court), but the "principle of law established by the Supreme Court must apply with equal force" to Article 34.3.4.

[16] Similar observations were made by Davitt P in *The State (Attorney General) v Durcan* [1964] IR 279 by way of explanation of the reluctance of the High Court since 1924 "to interfere on certiorari with the decisions of the District Court and the Circuit Court" in comparison with the relative willingness of the pre-1922 King's Bench Division "to correct the legal errors of the justices at Petty or Quarter Sessions." This difference in approach he ascribed in part to the fact that since 1924 the District Court has been manned by full-time professional judges.

[17] High Court, 21 June 1993.

[18] The principal provision is s 2 of the Summary Jurisdiction Act 1857 (as amended by s 51 of the Courts (Supplemental Provisions) Act 1961): see the discussion at p. 580.

[19] High Court, 18 November 1993.

[20] [1982] IR 384. For further discussion, see pp. 505-509, 578-580.

THE SUPREME COURT

4. 1° The Court of Final Appeal shall be called the Supreme Court.
2° The president of the Supreme Court shall be called the Chief Justice.

4. 1° An Chúirt Uachtarach is teideal don Chúirt Achomhairc Dheiridh.
2° An Príomh-Bhreitheamh is teideal d'uachtarán na Cúirte Uachtaraí.

No point seems ever to have arisen on the nomenclature of the Supreme Court or of the Chief Justice. When the courts were reconstituted in 1961, however, the old name "Supreme Court of Justice" was replaced by the simple "Supreme Court" (similar changes were made with the High Court, the Circuit Court, and the District Court).

The Supreme Court is the only court of final appeal, but it also has other functions

In *The State (Browne) v Feran*[1] Walsh J, with whom the four other judges agreed, said that in his view the former provision meant "that the only court of final appeal shall be the Supreme Court, not that the Supreme Court shall be only a court of final appeal". He said that the effect of Article 36.iii was that the Oireachtas could confer an original jurisdiction on the Supreme Court, "though in that case the Court would be a court of first and final instance", and pointed out that already the Supreme Court had jurisdictions which were not appellate, under Article 12.3.1 (establishment of the President's incapacity) and Article 26 (consideration of constitutionality of a Bill referred to it by the President).[2]

Membership of the Supreme Court

The Supreme Court contains four ordinary judges in addition to the Chief Justice and President of the High Court[3] (Courts (Supplemental Provisions) Act 1961, s 4). Section 7(*a*) of the same Act requires that the full Court of five judges to sit only in cases arising under Articles 12 or 26 of the Constitution, or in cases involving the question of the constitutional validity of a (post-1937) law; in other cases, while a full Court is common (particularly for important cases), the Chief Justice may determine that the Court is to consist of three judges.[4] This provision was invoked by the Court in *The State*

[1] [1967] IR 147.

[2] But cf. now the comments of Finlay CJ. in *Attorney General (Society for the Protection of Unborn Children (Ire.) Ltd.) v Open-Door Counselling Ltd. (No.2)*, Supreme Court, 20 July 1993:

> "Under the terms of Article 34 of the Constitution this Court is a Court of Appeal only, and has not got any originating jurisdiction of any kind, other than the following.."

[He then listed Articles 12.3 and 26 and some statutory examples].

[3] The President of the High Court is *ex offico* a judge of the Supreme Court: Courts (Establishment and Constitution) Act 1961, s 1(3). In addition, if a Supreme Court judge is serving in the Law Reform Commission, his place in the Court may be filled by an extra appointment (Law Reform Commission Act 1975, s 14, as amended by the Courts Act 1979, s 2.)

[4] It may be noted that where "owing to the illness of a judge of the Supreme Court or for any other reason", a sufficient number of judges of the Supreme Court "is not available for the transaction of the business of that Court", the Chief Justice may request any ordinary judge of judges of the High Court to sit for the purposes "of any appeal to or other matter cognisable by the Supreme Court" and any judge so requested shall sit and be "an additional judge of the Supreme Court for such appeal or other matter": Courts (Establishment and Constitution) Act 1961, s 1(4). Owing to pressure of business and other factors, this provision is nowadays frequently invoked and thus, for example, two High Court judges formed the requisite court of five in hearing a constitutional challenge in *Tormey v Ireland* [1985] IR 289.

(Williams) v Kelly[5] in rejecting the submission that the respondent in a *habeas corpus* application was entitled to have the appeal heard by a full Court of five judges.

[5] [1970] IR 259. See also *Peilow v French O'Carroll* (1971) 105 ILTR 21. One commentator has suggested that s 7(4) may be unconstitutional inasmuch the constitutional guarantees of judicial independence and removal from office "imply that a judge of the Supreme Court cannot be excluded by statute from sitting on that court in any case": see Humphreys, "*Reflection on the Role and Functioning of the Supreme Court*" (1990) 12 DULJ (n.s) 127.

APPELLATE JURISDICTION OF THE SUPREME COURT

3° The Supreme Court shall, with such exceptions and subject to such regulations as may be proscribed by law, have appellate jurisdiction from all decisions of the High Court, and shall also have appellate jurisdiction from such decisions of other courts as may be prescribed by law.

3° Taobh amuigh de cibé eisceachtaí agus faoi chuimsiú cibé rialacha a ordófar le dlí, beidh dlínse achomhairc ag an gCúirt Uachtarach ar bhreitheanna uile na hArd-Chúirte agus, fairis sin, ar na breitheanna sin ó chúirteanna eile a ordófar le dlí.

1922 position

This provision reproduce part of Article 66 of the 1922 Constitution so far as concerns the Supreme Court's general appellate jurisdiction in regard to decisions of the High Court. In *Warner v Minister for Industry and Commerce*[1] the Supreme Court held that the "exceptions" envisaged by Article 66 were such exceptions as might *subsequently* (i.e. after the enactment of the Constitution) be established by legislation, so that a pre-1922 statutory provision to the effect that a decision of the High Court was to be final could not operate to oust the Supreme Court's appellate jurisdiction in respect of that decision; this interpretation of Article 66 was also adopted in *In re Domville's Estate,*[2] and was expressly followed in *Attorney General (Fahy) v Bruen,*[3] in which the Supreme Court held that, while a decision of the High Court on a case stated by a District Judge was not appealable to the Supreme Court because the relevant statutory provision, s 83 of the Courts of Justice Act 1924, made this decision "final and conclusive", a decision of the High Court on a case stated under s 6 of the Summary Jurisdiction Act 1857, was so appealable notwithstanding that the 1857 Act made this also "final and conclusive".

But the rule only applies to "new" courts

In *Sullivan v Robinson*[4] an attempt was made to bring an appeal to the Supreme Court against a High Court decision on a case stated; by s 56 of the Courts of Justice Act 1936, an appeal was permissible only with leave of the High Court, and this had not been given. The appellant relied nevertheless on Article 34.4.3, arguing that the "regulations" there envisaged for limiting or excluding appeals meant, on the *Warner* and *Bruen* principle, laws enacted after the date of the (1937) Constitution, and no such regulating laws had in fact been enacted. The Supreme Court held, however, that the provisions of Article 34.4.3 referred to the *future* Supreme Court and the *future* High Court yet to be established; that until these courts were established, the "old" Supreme Court and High Court continued to operate, under the transitional provisions of Article 58; and that the jurisdiction of these courts were still governed by s 56 of the Courts of Justice Act 1936, as expounded by the Supreme Court in *Minister for Industry and Commerce v Healy*[5] - i.e., no appeal without leave. Similarly in *Dillon-Leetch v Calleary (No. 1)*[6] the Supreme Court held that, in spite of s 2 of the Electoral Act 1960, which continued in force the Parliamentary Elections Act 1868, whereby the determination of an election

[1] [1929] IR 582.
[2] [1930] IR 640.
[3] [1936] IR 750; (1936) 70 ILTR 247.
[4] [1954] IR 161; (1954) 88 ILTR 169.
[5] [1941] IR 545.
[6] Supreme Court, 25 July 1973.

petition was to be "final to all intents and purposes", this exclusion of appeal could not oust the constitutional appellate jurisdiction of the new Supreme Court established in 1961; any such ouster would require specific enactment *subsequent to* the Court's establishment.

New appellate jurisdiction

In 1961, however, the Courts (Establishment and Constitution) Act set up the courts contemplated by the Constitution, and in a series of three important decisions the Supreme Court has since declared its own appellate jurisdiction, resulting from Article 34.4.3, in areas where formerly no appellate jurisdiction was thought to exist. Two of these decisions are of major constitutional significance, as they reverse long-recognised rules of practice favourable to the liberty of the individual.

Habeas Corpus

In 1939 the Supreme Court had held, in *The State (Burke) v Lennon*,[7] that an appeal did not lie against the granting of an order of *habeas corpus*, notwithstanding the general language of Article 34.4.3. This decision relied on the 1890 decision of the House of Lords in *Cox v Hakes*,[8] in which it was held that the general words of the Judicature Act 1873, providing that the Court of Appeal was to have power to "hear and determine appeals from any judgment or order... of [the] High Court of Justice", would not suffice to abrogate a rule so important to the subject's liberty as that by which the grant of *habeas corpus* was final. But in 1967, in *The State (Browne) v Feran*,[9] the Supreme Court went back over this ground and decided not to follow the view which the 1939 Supreme Court had taken. Walsh J, with whom the other four judges agreed, said:

> "It is important to bear in mind... that what was being construed in *Cox v Hakes* was a statute, and it cannot be suggested that the canons of construction applicable to a statute are equally applicable to the construction of a written Constitution...in which words, which in their ordinary meaning import inclusion or exclusion, cannot be given a meaning other than their ordinary literal meaning save where the authority for so doing can be found within the Constitution itself...If the law in force prior to the coming into force of the Constitution provided that there were some matters in which no appeal lay and the Constitution states (as it does) that an appeal lies in all matters save where excepted, then since the establishment of this Court there is, on the face of it, a clear inconsistency and the constitutional provision must prevail."

Arguments based on an implicit exception - in the *Cox v Hakes* direction - said to be latent in Article 40.4 were rejected, and the Court decided that an appeal against the granting of an order of *habeas corpus* did, in fact, lie to it.

Orders for costs

In the following year a probate action, *In bonis Morelli: Vella v Morelli*,[10] gave the Supreme Court an opportunity to re-emphasise the absolute effect of Article 34.4.3. The

[7] [1940] IR 136; (1940) 74 ILTR 36, 161.
[8] (1890) 15 App Cas 506.
[9] [1967] IR 147.
[10] [1968] IR 11. See also *Jack O'Toole Ltd. v MacEoin Kelly Associates* [1986] IR 281 and *S.E.E. Co. Ltd. v Public Lighting Services* [1987] ILRM 256 (full right of appeal available against High Court order in security for costs matters, although Supreme Court will give due weight to the manner in which High Court judge exercised his discretion). On the Supreme Court's general power to order the provision of security for costs in the context of a pending appeal, see p. 518.

President of the High Court, who heard the action, made no order as to the plaintiff's costs; and the plaintiff, on appealing to the Supreme Court on the issue of costs, was met by the argument on the part of the defendant that the long-standing practice of the courts was not to entertain appeals against a judge's decision on costs, this being a discretionary matter, unless he had gone wrong in principle. The Supreme Court however held with the plaintiff. Walsh J said:

> "[The defendant's] submission, if accepted, would restrict the appellate jurisdiction of this Court which by the terms of the Constitution can only be restricted, within the limits permitted by the Constitution, by a law enacted subsequent to the coming into force of the Constitution; and no practice could be permitted to restrict litigants from exercising the right of resort to this Court guaranteed to them by the Constitution."

Shortly afterwards, in *The People (Attorney General) v Bell,*[11] the Supreme Court affirmed its conclusions in *The State (Browne) v Feran* and *In bonis Morelli; Vella v Morelli.* Here a judge of the High Court had relied on s 52 of the Supreme Court of Judicature (Ireland) Act 1877, in purporting to give leave to appeal to the Supreme Court against his award of costs to defendants in criminal proceedings; the Supreme Court held that that section, being inconsistent with the general appeal assured by Article 34.4.3, had not survived the enactment of the Constitution. Walsh J said:

> "In my view the right of the Attorney General to bring the present appeal is one which can be invoked by virtue of the provisions of the Constitution and does not depend upon the provisions of s 52 of the Act of 1877."

Appeals against an acquittal

Finally, in 1982, in *The People (Director of Public Prosecutions) v O'Shea,*[12] the words of Article 34.4.3 were used by the Supreme Court in establishing that - at any rate until such time as it might be excluded by law - an appeal lay to that Court against all decisions of the High Court *even including acquittals* by the Central Criminal Court (which, by s 11 of the Courts (Supplemental Provisions) Act 1961, is simply the High Court exercising its criminal jurisdiction); this was a revolutionary decision, as the previous law of long standing leaned against appeals against acquittal. In *R. (Kane) v Tyrone Justices*[13] Palles CB had said it was an "elementary principle" that:

> "an acquittal made by a court of competent jurisdiction and made within its jurisdiction, although erroneous in point of fact, cannot as a rule be questioned and brought before any other court."

There might be an exceptional, statutory appeal against certain acquittals, but:

> "before you can appeal against an acquittal, the words of the statute must be clear, express, and free from any ambiguity."

[11] [1969] IR 24; (1971) 105 ILTR 41. See also *Dawson v Hamill (No.2)* [1991] 2 IR 213 (in view of *Vella's* case, the Supreme Court is entitled to reconsider the exercise of High Court's discretion in judicial review matters.)
[12] [1982] IR 384.
[13] (1906) 40 ILTR 181.

This had been followed by the former Supreme Court in *The People (Attorney General) v Kennedy*,[14] in which Murnaghan J said:

> "Have the people, at the suit of the Attorney General, an appealable interest against the decision of a court entering an acquittal on a criminal charge, where an appeal is given in general words and the Attorney General is not specifically named? In my opinion this point has been decided in several cases in accordance with a long-established course of practice [he referred to the principle enunciated by Palles CB in *Kane's* case]."

The traditional finality of an acquittal was reiterated - though not in the context of an appeal to the Supreme Court, but of *certiorari* to quash a jury's verdict of not guilty entered by the mistaken direction of a Circuit Court judge - in *The State (Attorney General) v Judge Binchy*;[15] the Supreme Court, per Ó Dálaigh J, said it was "entirely without precedent to go behind [a "not guilty"] verdict, and it [was] now too late to create one". Fourteen years on, however, in *The People (Attorney General) v Conmey*,[16] the Court signalled a change, based entirely on the clear, general words of Article 34.4.3. What was in issue was whether a person convicted by the Central Criminal Court and who had appealed unsuccessfully to the Court of Criminal Appeal could, in reliance on those general words, bring yet another appeal to the Supreme Court (a further appeal from the Court of Criminal Appeal to the Supreme Court was provided for in fact by s 29 of the Courts of Justice Act 1924, where either the Court of Criminal Appeal itself or the Attorney General certified that a point of exceptional public importance was involved, but this precondition was missing here). The Supreme Court held that a person in this situation has a choice of appealing straight to the Supreme Court, or of appealing to the limited concurrent jurisdiction of the Court of Criminal Appeal, but not both. This direct appeal to the Supreme Court, never contemplated or regulated by statute law, arose from the general words of Article 34.4.3; and those general words admitted an appeal equally by an accused person against conviction, and by the People against his acquittal. O'Higgins CJ said:

> "The Supreme Court was given, by Article 34.4.3, full appellate jurisdiction over all determinations and decisions of the Central Criminal Court, and this includes a jurisdiction to hear and determine an appeal from a verdict of not guilty."

And Walsh J said:

> "An acquittal or a conviction and/or sentence by the High Court is a decision of the High Court which is within the appellate jurisdiction of this Court unless it has been excepted from the appellate jurisdiction of this Court by an Act of the Oireachtas in respect of decisions of the High Court in the exercise of its criminal jurisdiction."

However, as the question of an appeal against acquittal was not an issue in *Conmey's* case, those statements were mere *obiter dicta*, but after some conflicting judicial *dicta*,[17] the right of direct prosecution appeal against an acquittal in the High Court was upheld in *The People (Director of Public Prosecutions) v O'Shea*.[18]

[14] [1946] IR 517; (1947) 81 ILTR 73.

[15] [1964] IR 395. *Dicta* of Ó Dálaigh J about the normal finality (in the context of the plea of *autrefois acquit*) will also be found in *The People (Attorney General) v Marchel O'Brien* [1963] IR 92.

[16] [1975] IR 341. See generally, Casey, "*Confusion in Criminal Appeals: the Legacy of Conmey*" (1975) 10 Ir Jur (n.s.) 300.

[17] In *People v Shaw* [1982] IR 1 and *People v Lynch* [1982] IR 64. See Casey, "*Criminal Appeals: the Confusion Persists*" (1981) 16 Ir Jur (n.s.) 271.

[18] [1982] IR 384. See Hogan, "*Criminal Appeals - A New Departure*" (1983) 5 DULJ 254.

In this case, O'Higgins CJ, with whom Walsh and Hederman JJ agreed in separate judgments, took the view that whatever the common law may have been before the enactment of the Constitution, it could not have the effect of modifying the Constitution's plain words, in this case by making "all decisions" mean "some decisions" or "nearly all decisions":

> "The Constitution brought into existence a new State, subject to its own particular and unique basic law, but absorbing into its jurisprudence such laws as were then in force to the extent to which these conformed with that basic law. It follows that existing laws or formerly accepted legal principles or practices cannot be invoked to alter, restrict or qualify the plain words used in the Constitution unless the authority for so doing derives from the Constitution itself. Indeed the very existence of an inconsistency between what was formerly the law and what the words of the Constitution, according to their literal meaning, declare, repeals and abrogates what had been the law...[The respondent] cannot rely solely on the legal principles which prevailed prior to the establishment of Saorstát Éireann. He must go much further than this. He must establish that there is something in the Constitution itself which qualifies the plain words of Article 34.4.3 so as to restrict the appellate jurisdiction thereby given to the Supreme Court in criminal cases to appeals against convictions. Or he must show that a statutory provision made subsequent to the Constitution has such an effect."

The first of those alternative obstacles the respondent tried to surmount by arguing that the jury trial provided for by Article 38.5 is trial by a jury whose verdict, if of acquittal, is inherently unappealable; but this argument was rejected by O'Higgins CJ as being a misunderstanding of the true pre-1922 jurisprudence, which was:

> "not that an acquittal recorded by a criminal jury may not be appealed, but rather that no acquittal, apparently on the merits, on any criminal charge, whether it be tried by a jury or summarily, could be so appealed."

There was, therefore, nothing special about Article 38.5 which could qualify Article 34.4.3. As for the respondent's alternative argument that s 34 of the Criminal Procedure Act 1967, by providing for a reference by the Attorney General to the Supreme Court of a question of law arising on a verdict of acquittal by direction (though without prejudice to the acquittal itself), had impliedly limited the Court's appellate jurisdiction in such cases to references of this kind, the Chief Justice said:

> A law which regulates by subtraction from the Supreme Court's appellate jurisdiction must do so expressly[19] and must, in particular, conform to the stipulation contained in Article 34.4.4 that it shall not extend to cases involving questions of constitutional validity... The section relied on does not purport to be a regulation, as envisaged by Article 34.4.3, nor does it refer to the appellate jurisdiction which it is supposed to curtail. I regard it as a section of general application conferring on the Supreme Court an additional consultative jurisdiction in relation to questions of law arising on directions given by trial judges in both the Central Criminal Court and the Circuit Court. It is in no way inconsistent with the continuation of the Supreme Court's full appellate jurisdiction under Article 34.4.3."

[19] In practice, however, it seems that the Supreme Court will not insists on the necessity for express subtraction where such exclusion from its appellate jurisdiction is necessarily to be implied from the surrounding statutory context: see *Beecham Group Ltd. v Bristol Meyers* [1983] IR 325 and *Minister for Justice (Clarke) v Jie* [1993] 1 IR 425; [1991] ILRM 823: see pp. 520-521.

He concluded his judgment by marking out a narrow scope for the Court in entertaining appeals against acquittal; such appeals ought, he thought, to be treated in a manner similar to appeals from jury verdicts in civil cases:

> "Verdicts, properly arrived at and supported by evidence, while in theory appealable, would not be disturbed. This Court would be bound by findings of fact made at the trial. A conviction would be open to challenge on the sufficiency of the evidence relied on to support it or on the trial judge's directions or rulings of law. An acquittal duly recorded by a jury on a consideration of the evidence would be immune. Where, however... the acquittal resulted from a direction given by the judge, so that the verdict was recorded as a result of the judge's decision and not that of the jury, the Court would consider the appeal in the same manner as a similar appeal in a civil action."

From the majority view, thus led by the Chief Justice,[20] Finlay P and Henchy J strongly dissented. The former took the view that the non-appealability of an acquittal was an inherent ingredient of jury trial: that the Oireachtas, by making statutory provision for appeals only from jury *convictions* to the Court of Criminal Appeal (by ss 31 and 63 of the Courts of Justice Act 1924, and s 48 of the Courts (Supplemental Provisions) Act 1961), and for reference of a point of law to the Supreme Court without prejudice to an acquittal itself (by s 34 of the Criminal Procedure Act 1967), had "clearly indicate[d] an entire and continuing acceptance by the legislature of the immunity of a verdict in favour of an accused by a jury acting within its jurisdiction"; and that this special and particular element of a criminal trial "must take precedence over the general right of appeal" provided by Article 34.4.3. Henchy J, in a very elaborate contradiction of the majority view, began by a scathing denial of any authority to the views expressed by the Chief Justice and Walsh J in *Conmey's* case ("peripheral observations deserving of course of all due respect but not binding on this or any other court"). Addressing himself to the problem *de novo,* he asked whether an appeal lies to the Supreme Court from literally every decision of the High Court save those excepted by post-1937 statute, and said Article 34.4.3 could not be looked at in isolation from the rest of the Constitution in order to answer that question. Moreover, in practice a large number of "decisions" of the High Court - mostly in the quasi-administrative or procedural areas - were not appealable. Thus he felt able to paraphrase the words of Article 34.4.3 "all decisions of the High Court" as "all *appealable* decisions of the High Court". Like Finlay P, he felt that decisions of acquittal were not in the appealable category and went on to the presumed attitude of the people in 1937:

> "I venture to think that if one were to scrutinise the debates in parliament and the records of the written and spoken arguments for and against the draft Constitution in 1937, one would not find the hint of an opinion, either from the proponents or opponents of the Constitution, that a verdict of not guilty emanating from a jury trial as mandated by Article 38.5 could be reopened by appeal or otherwise. Indeed, it is to be arguably contended that if such opinion had been expressed by any reputable person or body [sc. as a view of the meaning of Article 34.4.3] the Constitution would never have been enacted by the people."

[20] O'Higgins CJ, however, both in this case and previously in *Lynch's* case, used forms of words which seemed to hint at an opinion that the coexistence of alternative appeals was an oversight (and perhaps that the newly acknowledged right of appeal against an acquittal as well); and that it was time that the Oireachtas took appropriate action to limit appeals from the Central Criminal Court to the Court of Criminal Appeal alone. In *Lynch's* case he said that the alternative appeals "would continue to exist until such time as appropriate legislation is passed delimiting the Supreme Court's appellate jurisdiction in accordance with Article 34.4.3"; in *O'Shea's* case he said that the Court's jurisdiction existed "pending appropriate changes prescribed by law".

He added further considerations based on equality before the law and on personal rights which are mentioned under Articles 40.1 and 40.3 respectively.[21]

Power to order a re-trial following a prosecution appeal

In the wake of *O'Shea's* case, this new appellate jurisdiction was given official recognition by O 87 of the Rules of the Superior Courts 1986 which regulates the form and scope of appeals from decision of the Central Criminal Court to the Supreme Court. O 87 r 9 purports to allow the Court to order a re-trial, even (apparently) in the case of a successful appeal by the prosecution, but the precise status and practical efficacy of this rule seems somewhat questionable in the light of the decision of the Supreme Court in *People v Quilligan (No. 2)*.[22]

In *People v Quilligan (No.1)* [23] in 1986 the Supreme Court allowed an appeal by the prosecution following the acquittal of the accused by direction of the trial judge, Barr J. He had ruled that the incriminating evidence had been obtained while the accused were in unlawful custody following their arrest under s 30 of the Offences Against the State Act 1939. The Supreme Court allowed the appeal by the prosecution, holding that the arrests were, in fact, lawful. The question then arose as to whether the Court had power to order the re-trial of the accused and in *People v Quilligan (No.2)* the Supreme Court found itself unable to agree on this issue. Two judges, Henchy and Griffin JJ, took the view that the constitutional right of appeal under Article 34.4.3 did not carry with it "a concomitant or ancillary jurisdiction to order a re-trial." Such a power could only be legislatively conferred and even then they doubted whether this would be constitutionally valid since it might be thought to be incompatible with "what is inherent in the constitutional guarantee of trial by jury". Moreover, if the legislation only applied to persons acquitted by direction of the High Court (as opposed to persons acquitted by other trial courts), this would be tantamount to a form of unconstitutional discrimination. On the other hand, both Walsh and McCarthy JJ stressed that the constitutional right of appeal carried with it the necessary inherent jurisdiction to give effect to that right of appeal and this extended to the right to order a re-trial where this was necessary in the interests of justice. Hederman J reserved his position on the wider issue of principle, but agreed with Henchy and Griffin JJ that no re-trial should be made on the facts of the present case.

Thus, although *O'Shea's* case has settled, for the moment, the issue in favour of the applicability of the general words of Article 34.4.3 to appeals against acquittals in the High Court, it will be seen that the sentiments as expressed in *Quilligan (No.2)* reflect some continuing unhappiness with this jurisdiction, so that it may be unsafe to regard the matter as being completely settled. The entire question of the Court's power to order a re-trial following a successful appeal against acquittal has thus been left open by *Quilligan (No.2)*, but both principle and logic would seem to dictate that if Article 34.4.3 confers such a right of appeal on the prosecution, this must also extend to give effect to such right of appeal by conferring a jurisdiction to order, where appropriate, a right of re-trial. And while the Supreme Court has entertained some half-dozen such prosecution appeals since *O'Shea's* case (and has ruled on many important substantive

[21] See p. 740 and pp. 1080-1081 respectively. See also *Considine v Shannon Regional Fisheries Board*, High Court, 18 November 1993 and above at p. 500.
[22] [1989] IR 46.
[23] [1986] IR 495.

issues of law in the process[24]), the actual result of *Quilligan (No. 2)* (which suggests the absence of a right to order a re-trial even if this proposition was not assented to by an actual majority of the Court[25]) may mean that the right of appeal will decline in terms of practical importance. In any event, it is high time that the matter was settled one way or another through legislation and it should be noted that it is now proposed at the time of writing to abolish entirely the right of appeal - both by the prosecution and the defence - from the Central Criminal Court to the Supreme Court: see s 11 of the Criminal Procedure Bill 1993.

Form and scope of appeals to the Supreme Court

Article 34.4.3 prescribes neither the form nor the scope of appeals from High Court decisions to the Supreme Court. Clearly if the Oireachtas is entitled to cut down the material area within which such appeals can be brought, it is entitled also to restrict the scope or the form of an appeal (provided that basic constitutional values of justice are respected), e.g. by confining appeals in certain matters to questions of law, or by prescribing that appeals shall be heard on transcripts of the earlier trial rather than by taking all the evidence afresh. There is, however, no such general regulation of this appellate jurisdiction by Act of the Oireachtas. Instead, appeals to the Supreme Court are governed by O 58 of the Rules of the Superior Courts 1986 (made in virtue of a number of statutory provisions). Order 58 r 1 states that: "All appeals to the Supreme Court shall be by way of re-hearing"; but whereas the expression "rehearing" when used in reference to appeals taken from the Circuit Court to the High Court (Courts of Justice Act 1936, s 37(2)) has the effect that the whole case is tried again, with evidence given afresh, this does not happen in appeals from the High Court to the Supreme Court. Whether O 58 r 1 is *intra vires* the Rules Committee, and whether, if so, actual Supreme Court practice can be said to be in accordance with it, are questions which have not yet been judicially considered. However, as McCarthy J observed in *Hay v O'Grady*[26] the Court in its own decisions has, in effect, limited the untrammelled nature of its appellate jurisdiction.

Thus, although O 58 r 1 states that: "All appeals to the Supreme Court shall be by way of re-hearing", this rule has, on the whole, been construed in such a manner as restricts the form and scope of the appellate jurisdiction. A good example is provided by *Northern Bank Finance Ltd. v Charlton.*[27] Here the Supreme Court drew attention to the fact that this rule did not mean that the High Court proceedings "are completely re-heard or re-enacted" on appeal. Henchy J observed that the expression "rehearing" was a term of art in this context:

> "The Court will normally be precluded from hearing or seeing the witnesses whose oral testimony was the core of the hearing in the High Court. So the appeal will be "by way of re-hearing" only to the extent that that will be possible by examining documentary material, particularly a written version or report of the evidence, save for those exceptional cases when fresh or represented evidence is received."

[24] See, e.g., *People v Byrne* [1987] IR 363 (concerning aspects of the arrest powers under s 30 of the Offences Against the State Act 1939) and *People v Healy* [1990] 2 IR 73 (holding that a suspect has a constitutional right of access to a solicitor during the course of his detention).

[25] Order 87 r 9 of the Rules of the Superior Courts, 1986 purports to give the Supreme Court the power to order such a re-trial, but the *vires* of this Rule seems questionable in the light of the comments of Henchy J in *Quilligan (No.2).*

[26] [1992] 1 IR 210; [1992] ILRM 689.

[27] [1979] IR 149.

It was not quite accurate to say that the Court's appellate jurisdiction was confined to issues of law:

> "Save for exceptional cases where a statutory provision may limit the Court's jurisdiction to questions of law, in civil cases this Court may exercise appellate jurisdiction from decisions of the High Court on both questions of law and questions of fact. But the exercise of that jurisdiction in regard to questions of fact is necessarily limited in practice as a result of the requirements of the Rules of the Superior Courts [which state] that the oral hearing is to be transposed into written form for the purposes of the appeal."[28]

Although there was a "formidably voluminous record" of what took place in the High Court it was necessarily imperfect:

> "It cannot recapture the mood of the trial, the demeanour of witnesses, the essential nuances of particular responses, and other features of the trial which, although they may have been crucially determinative in the judicial ascertainment of the facts, may have become blurred or lost when the oral evidence was reduced to writing. Herein lies the source of this Court's restricted jurisdiction in regard to matters of fact. It cannot put itself in the position of the trial judge. He has had opportunities of judicial assessment which are denied to this Court."

He thus concluded (as did the rest of the Court) that the Supreme Court should be slow to interfere with findings of fact arrived at in the High Court, unless the version of the evidence which was acted on (whether by judge or jury) "could not reasonably be correct."[29]

These principles are well established and there is by now a large corpus of jurisprudence in which they have been applied, which, in particular distinguishes between the "primary or basic facts" (which findings can only be set aside in exceptional circumstances) and "secondary or inferred facts." As Henchy J explained in *JM and GM v An Bord Uchtála*,[30] "secondary facts" are those:

> "which do not follow directly from an assessment or evaluation of the credibility of witnesses or the weight to be attached to their evidence, but derive from facts have been established *viva voce*, their consequences or implications for the purpose of the matters in issue must be found by a process of deduction from the facts found or admitted, rather than by an assessment of the witnesses or of the weight or the correctness of the evidence. In regard to such secondary facts, the advantage of the High Court judge who saw and heard the witnesses is of such minor importance that this Court will feel free to draw its own inferences if it considers that the inference

[28] This seems questionable, as the Superior Court Rules Committee could scarcely foreclose the Supreme Court's own decision as to the proper scope of the appeal.

[29] See, e.g., the comments of O'Flaherty J in *Kennedy v Galway VEC*, Supreme Court, 1 July 1992: "While this Court has repeatedly said that it will not interfere with findings of primary fact made by a trial judge, there must be exceptional cases where the evidence is so clearly the one way as to require the intervention of this Court to say that the verdict entered by the trial judge cannot stand." Here the Court reversed certain primary facts as found by the trial judge (together with the finding of liability in favour of the plaintiff) where, having regard to all the evidence, the Court concluded that "it was impossible to say that the plaintiff had made out her case" and where her evidence had been "comprehensively disproved." See also *Maguire v Keane* [1986] ILRM 326.

[30] [1987] IR 510; [1988] ILRM 203.

> drawn by the judge in the High Court were not correct. Such secondary facts include all matters which are evaluative of the primary facts."[31]

It suffices to add the cautionary comments of McCarthy J in *Hay v O'Grady*.[32] Stressing the somewhat limited nature of the Court's appellate jurisdiction with regard to findings of fact, he added that:

> "If the findings of fact made by the trial judge are supported by credible evidence, this Court is bound by those findings, however voluminous and, apparently, weighty the testimony against them. The truth is not the monopoly of the majority."

The Supreme Court will not generally entertain a legal issue which was not addressed by the High Court

While by virtue of O 58 r 6 of the Rules of the Superior Courts 1986, any notice of appeal to the Supreme Court may be amended at any time "on such terms as the Supreme Court may think fit", the Court will not generally make such an order if it would have the effect of deciding a newly raised point of law as at first instance. This point was made by Henchy J in *Movie News Ltd. v Galway County Council*,[33] where the defendants had appealed against a decision of the High Court quashing a compulsory purchase order. When the appeal came on for hearing, the defendants sought leave to amend their notice of appeal in order to rely on an entirely new ground. Henchy J noted that their counsel had expressly disclaimed reliance on this ground before the High Court, and that if the Court were to accede to "this last-minute and informal application for leave to rely on this new ground", the Court would be unjustifiably ignoring the earlier proceedings:

> "It would in effect be deciding this case as of first instance. However, save for matters committed to it by the Constitution or by statute, this Court has only an appellate jurisdiction. It should not - except for exceptional reasons which do not exist in this case - under the guise of an appeal, enter on the trial of a matter as of first instance and thereby deprive the party aggrieved with its decision of the constitutional right of appeal which he would have had if that matter had been decided in the High Court."

And as Finlay CJ said in *Attorney General (Society for the Protection of Unborn Children (Ire.) Ltd. v Open Door Counselling Ltd (No.2)*,[34] the Supreme Court has "consistently declined, otherwise than in the most exceptional of circumstances, dictated by the necessity of justice, to consider an issue of constitutional law which, though arising in a case not yet determined by it, has not been fully argued and decided in the High Court."[35] *K.D.(C.) v M.C.*[36] provides an another example of this practice: here the Supreme Court refused to allow the respondent in a nullity petition to raise an entirely new argument. The respondent had sought to argue in the High Court that the divorce

[31] These principles were applied by the Supreme Court in *Hanrahan v Merck, Sharp & Dohme Ltd.* [1988] ILRM 629 and *Best v Wellcome Foundation Ltd.* [1992] ILRM 609.

[32] [1992] 1 IR 210; [1992] ILRM 689.

[33] Supreme Court, 25 July 1973.

[34] Supreme Court, 20 July 1993.

[35] Note, however, that in *Goulding Chemicals Ltd. v Bolger* [1977] IR 211 the Supreme Court permitted the respondents to raise the constitutionality of s 11 of the Trade Union Act 1941, even though, this matter had not been argued before the High Court. O'Higgins CJ described this procedure as unusual, and one not to be regarded as a precedent, saying that it had been permitted only with considerable misgivings, and because there was no procedure under which the appropriate arguments could then be initiated in the High Court.

[36] [1985] IR 697.

should be recognised on the basis that he was domiciled in England at the time; but he abandoned this argument on appeal, contending instead that the test should be whether he had a "real and substantial connection" with England at the time when the divorce was granted. The Supreme Court refused to entertain this argument. Finlay CJ said the Court was being asked to decide this point of law "as a moot... in advance of the hearing of any evidence" as to whether the respondent could satisfy this test, even if it were applicable.

The Supreme Court has no inherent supplementary original jurisdiction

A closely related question which has arisen in a number of cases is whether the Supreme Court enjoys an inherent original jurisdiction to hear and determine an issue which is either pending before the High Court or which the Supreme Court itself has previously decided. This problem first surfaced in *Murphy v Attorney General* [37] in which the Supreme Court had declared invalid certain sections of the Income Tax Act 1967, the Court's judgment had not dealt with the question of the moment from which the declaration of invalidity was to be considered to operate, nor with the extent of repayment which the plaintiffs (or others) could claim. The Attorney General (according to the account given by Henchy J) "indicated that the import of the Court's judgment... was not clear to him, so he applied to have the appeal re-entered for the purpose of 'speaking to the minutes of the order'". This was for the purpose of eliciting rulings on those matters. Henchy J, as a lone dissentient, thought that:

> "this Court had not the necessary jurisdiction to determine the point; that the constitutional and statutory jurisdiction of this Court in this case was entirely appellate; that this point was outside the scope of the appeal; that the High Court's "full original jurisdiction in and power to determine all matters and questions whether of law or fact, civil or criminal" (Article 34.3.1) had been invoked by the plaintiffs and had been exercised by the High Court to the extent that it reserved liberty to apply to it on this point; that this was a matter that was required to be decided at first instance in the High Court, upon due determination of the necessary facts (which facts had not yet been fully investigated); and that this Court could exercise the necessary jurisdiction only if an appeal had been taken from the decision of the High Court that the matter stood properly reserved for its "own determination."

The rest of the Court, however, did not consider the Court debarred from ruling on these questions consequential on its main judgment, and supplementary opinions were accordingly delivered, in an unprecedented proceeding, three months after the declaration of invalidity.[38] But here, at least, the *lis* was still in being and no final order of the Court had been perfected. However, two subsequent decisions of the Supreme Court - *Belville Holdings Ltd. v Cronin*[39] and *Attorney General (Society for the Protection of Unborn Children (Ire.) Ltd. v Open-Door Counselling Ltd. (No.2)*[40] - demonstrate that different considerations will apply where an appellant seeks to vary or discharge a *final* court order. In *Belville Holdings* the issue was whether a High Court judge was correct when she made an order which supplemented and varied a final High Court order which had been made some three years previously. The Supreme Court set aside the variation of the original order. While Finlay CJ agreed that the court had an inherent jurisdiction to

[37] [1982] IR 241.
[38] See pp. 482-483.
[39] Supreme Court, 8 February 1993.
[40] Supreme Court, 20 July 1993.

amend a final order,[41] he stressed that this jurisdiction should only be exercised in "special or unusual circumstances":

> "The finality of proceedings both at the level of the trial and, possibly more particularly, at the level of ultimate appeal is of fundamental importance to the certainty of the administration of the law and should not lightly be breached."

These considerations were very much to the fore in the Chief Justice's subsequent judgment for the majority of the Supreme Court in *Open-Door Counselling (No.2)*. The circumstances in which this case arose were exceptional. Following the entry into force of the Fourteenth Amendment of the Constitution Act 1992 in December 1992[42] the defendants sought to vary or discharge a perpetual injunction granted by the Supreme Court in March 1988[43] which had restrained them from providing information within the State about abortion services in another jurisdiction. The Chief Justice held that it would be inconsistent with the appellate nature of the Supreme Court's jurisdiction it if it were now:

> "to consider a question of the interpretation of the Constitution by way of motion to vary an order previously made in appeal finally determined by it, which, by inevitable necessity has never been decided by the High Court and, furthermore, is in the instant case a provision of the Constitution which was not in force or enacted at the time when the appeal was determined."

From this judgment Denham J was the sole dissentient. In her view, the Court had an inherent jurisdiction to ensure that "the Constitution is not, and rights thereunder are not, circumvented." While conceding that any such jurisdiction should be sparingly exercised "as the fabric of the administration of justice and the system of the courts is best served by a clear hierarchical structure concluding in the Supreme Court", she thought that the present case came within one of the rare exceptions[44] when the Court should exercise its implied non-appellate jurisdiction to protect constitutional rights.[45]

What is a "decision" of the High Court?

The question of what may be regarded as a "decision" of the High Court for the purpose of claiming a right of appeal (in cases not excluded by statute) under Article 34.4.3 has arisen on a few occasions. While the test appears to be one of substance rather than form, although there are two important judgments of the Supreme Court which appear perhaps to have been unduly influenced by questions of form. One such case is *The*

[41] The Chief Justice considered that this jurisdiction was wider than that conferred by O 28 r 11 of the Rules of the Superior Courts 1986 (this "slip rule" gives the courts power to correct clerical errors), and, approving the judgment of Romer J in *Ainsworth v Wilding* [1896] 1 Ch 673, he also said that the court could amend a final order where the order did not accurately reflect "what the court actually decided and intended."

[42] The amendment entered into force on December 23, 1992. This amendment guarantees the right to provide abortion information "subject to such conditions as may be laid down by law": see p. 790.

[43] *Attorney General (Society for the Protection of Unborn Children (Ire.) Ltd.) v Open Door Counselling Ltd.* [1988] IR 593; [1989] ILRM 19.

[44] Denham J pointed to cases such as *Murphy* as a previous example of this jurisdiction. However, that was a case where the Supreme Court assumed jurisdiction in the matter *before* a final order had been made, although it is questionable whether such a technical distinction should make any difference to the principle involved. It does seem clear, however, that in the light of *Open Door (No.2)*, the majority in *Murphy* were probably wrong to assume jurisdiction to decide the ancillary questions arising from the main judgment of the Court when these questions had not been dealt with by the High Court.

[45] Denham J was particularly swayed by the fact that the facts were not in dispute and that the "old" injunctions were now plainly inconsistent with Article 40.3.3 as amended by the Thirteenth and Fourteenth Amendments of the Constitution Acts 1992.

People (Attorney General) v Fennell (No. 2),[46] where the Supreme Court held that a finding by a jury, empanelled to try an accused person's sanity, that the person was sane, was not a "decision" in this sense:

> "there was no obligation on the Court to record that finding, and no jurisdiction in the Court to make any order consequent on the finding."

The presumption of sanity had not been displaced and there was no reason why the trial should not proceed as if no question of insanity had been raised. (The Court, however, said that "if he had been found to be insane, it would have been the duty of the Court to direct the finding to be recorded and to make an order for his custody", thus implying that a finding of *insanity* as distinct from sanity would result in an appealable decision in the sense of Article 34.4.3.) It is doubtful, however, if this decision would be followed today, since it appears to be based on an unduly formalistic analysis of the nature of the jury's verdict and without sufficient regard to the importance of the substantive rights under appeal.

This matter was fully explored by the Supreme Court in *Campus Oil Ltd. v Minister for Industry and Energy*.[47] In this case the plaintiffs challenged the validity of the Fuels (Control of Supplies) Order 1982, which required oil companies to buy a certain percentage of their petroleum requirements from the state-owned refinery at Whitegate. The High Court referred certain questions under Article 177 of the Treaty of Rome to the European Court of Justice, seeking guidance as to whether this ministerial order was compatible with Articles 30 and 31 of the Treaty (which guarantee free movement of goods). The Supreme Court ruled that no appeal lay against this decision, Walsh J saying that a decision of this kind was not a "decision of the High Court" within the meaning of Article 34.4.3, for in his view the High Court had made no order "having legal effect upon the parties to the litigation".[48] Nevertheless, he thought that if and when the High Court judge came to apply the Treaty provisions to the case before him, he would then have made a decision which was susceptible to appeal. Once again, this approach seems unduly formalistic since it fails to take account of the realities (such as the considerable delay and additional expense) of a reference to the Court of Justice.

Campus Oil was distinguished in *Society for the Protection of Unborn Children (Ireland) Ltd. v Grogan*.[49] In this case, Carroll J had adjourned the plaintiff's application for an interlocutory injunction pending a reference of certain issues of law to the European Court of Justice under Article 177 of the Treaty of Rome. When the plaintiffs sought to appeal this adjournment they were met with the objection that this did not constitute "a decision" of the High Court. However, the Supreme Court ruled that the test was one of substance rather than form, with Finlay CJ saying that:

> "no mere absence of formal words from a High Court order could be permitted to remove from the appellate jurisdiction of this Court a determination of a High Court judge which affects one of the parties involved and has all the characteristics of a decision."

[46] [1940] IR 453.
[47] [1983] IR 82; [1984] 1 CMLR 479. For commentary on this case, see O'Keefe, "*Preliminary Deference: The Supreme Court and Community Law*" (1983) 5 DULJ (n.s.) 286; O'Keefe, "*Appeals against an Order under Article 177 of the EEC Treaty*" (1984) 9 ELRev 87 and *Murphy*, (1984) 9 ELRev 741.
[48] This "legal effects" test would appear too erect too formal a distinction between various forms of judicial order. A reference to the European Court of Justice generally involves litigants in considerable delay, expense and general inconvenience, as well as putting in jeopardy the interpretation of the Treaty for which one or other of the parties was contending.
[49] [1989] IR 753; [1990] ILRM 350.

Judged by this standard, the reality was that Carroll J had declined to grant an interlocutory injunction and that the plaintiff was entitled (successfully as it happened) to appeal against that refusal.

The comments of McCarthy J in *The State (Hughes) v O'Hanrahan*[50] and in *Minister for Justice v Wang Zhu Jie*[51] are also worth noting. In the former case, the respondents had been given, in the High Court, *ex parte*, an extension of time within which to show cause to a conditional order of certiorari. Henchy and Hederman JJ were content merely to dismiss the appeal against this order, but McCarthy J said that orders of this nature which were properly made *ex parte* could not be made the subject of an appeal, save at the behest of the party applying for such an order. In *Wang Zhu Jie* Costello J had refused the appellant leave to appeal to the Supreme Court under s 52(2) of the Courts (Supplemental Provisions) Act 1961 and it was sought to bring an appeal against the refusal to grant leave. While the Supreme Court ruled that s 52(2) constituted a "regulation" of its appellate jurisdiction, it is of interest to note that McCarthy J reserved the question of whether the refusal to grant leave was, itself, a "decision" of the High Court, thereby suggesting, perhaps, that it was not such a "decision." Yet this very reservation seems unduly cautious, since, to judge by the standard articulated by Finlay CJ in *Grogan*, such a refusal had legal consequences for the parties involved and had all the characteristics of a judicial decision.[52]

The inherent jurisdiction of the Supreme Court

The Supreme Court has held on several occasions that it has an inherent jurisdiction derived from Article 34.4.3 which enables it to regulate and give effect to its appellate jurisdiction, For example, in *Dhand v McCrabbe,*[53] Ó Dálaigh J held that the Supreme Court had an inherent jurisdiction to dismiss an appeal for want of prosecution, although the Rules of Court made no such express provision. In *The People (Director of Public Prosecutions) v O'Shea*[54] O'Higgins CJ said that:

> "if the Constitution confers on this Court a particular appellate jurisdiction it may be assumed that it also confers the necessary powers to make that jurisdiction effective to remedy what is complained of."

McCarthy J made a similar point in *Hughes v O'Rourke*[55] in the context of the Court's inherent power to extend the time for lodging appeals from the High Court; it was:

> "beyond question that the Supreme Court has an inherent power to regulate the exercise of its own jurisdiction. This power derives from the Constitution which, whilst expressly creating this Court and specifying its jurisdiction, of necessity cloaks it with all powers required properly to exercise that jurisdiction."

[50] [1986] ILRM 538.
[51] [1993] 1 IR 426; [1991] ILRM 823.
[52] See also *Green v Blake* [1948] IR 242 (where the Supreme Court entertained an interlocutory appeal against a ruling of the trial judge in a civil action in the High Court); *In re McGovern* [1971] IR 149; (where the Supreme Court said it was "questionable" whether an administrative direction given by a judge of the High Court to an officer attached to the Court qualified as a "decision" of the High Court capable of appeal under Article 34.4.3 and *Dillon-Leetch v Calleary (No.1)*, Supreme Court, July 25, 1973 (where the Supreme Court held that the judicial findings on the hearing of an election petition constituted a "decision" of the High Court).
[53] (1958) 92 ILTR 196. Compare this approach with that of Henchy and Griffin JJ in *People v Quilligan (No.2)* [1989] IR 45: see p. 509.
[54] [1982] IR 384; [1983] ILRM 549.
[55] [1986] ILRM 538.

This principle was applied in *Holohan v Donohoe*,[56] where a majority of the Supreme Court decided that the Court possessed an inherent power to assess damages in lieu of ordering a retrial in the High Court. A different view was, however, taken by a sharply divided Court in *People v Quilligan (No.2)*,[57] where the Court could not agree on whether it had an inherent right to order a re-trial following a successful prosecution appeal. Henchy and Griffin JJ considered that the right to order a re-trial was a substantive jurisdiction which could only be conferred (if at all) by the Oireachtas. On the other hand, Walsh and McCarthy JJ argued persuasively that such a right was - in the words of McCarthy J - "an essential part of the jurisdiction of this Court to hear and determine an appeal from a verdict of acquittal of the trial judge."

But there are inherent limitations to the Court's appellate jurisdiction. This was recognised by Finlay CJ in *Holohan v Donohoe*[58] (with whom Hederman J concurred) who said (echoing the approach of Henchy J in *Northern Bank Finance Co. v Charlton*)[59] he agreed with the view:

> "that the appellate jurisdiction, even when untrammelled by legislation, has other inherent limitations, and, in particular, this court may not substitute for findings of fact made by a court of trial (whether consisting of a judge sitting without a jury or with a jury) which are supported by evidence, its own findings of fact."

This point was re-iterated by McCarthy J in *Hay v O'Grady*[60] where he observed that in a series of decisions the Supreme Court had, in effect, apparently limited its own jurisdiction under Article 34.4.3. This meant that even in the case of an appeal from a decision of a High Court judge sitting alone, the Supreme Court would:

> "ordinarily refrain from substituting its own view of appropriate decision for that of those charged with making such decision and appropriately qualified to do so. That is not to say that, where appropriate, a Court might not conclude that the decision-maker had failed adequately to inform himself or to apply appropriate standards."

Power to stay an order of the High Court

Order 58 r 18 of the Rules of the Superior Courts 1986, provides that an appeal to the Supreme Court "shall not operate as a stay of execution or of proceedings under the decision appealed from", except so far as the High Court or the Supreme Court shall order. However, the Supreme Court will normally grant a stay where "if the order stands without any stay of execution, then the compliance by the [appellant] with its provisions will end that case as a reality."[61] In personal injuries cases, factors such as whether a stay was applied for before the High Court; the reality of a successful appeal on liability and whether there is a real risk that monies paid on foot on a High Court decree will prove to be irrecoverable in the event of a successful appeal will all be regarded as especially important in considering whether to grant a stay of the High Court order.[62]

[56] [1986] IR 45; [1986] ILRM 268.
[57] [1989] IR 46.
[58] [1986] IR 45; [1986] ILRM 268.
[59] [1979] IR 149.
[60] [1992] 1 IR 210; [1992] ILRM 689.
[61] *Megaleasing UK Ltd. v Barrett* [1992] 1 IR 219; [1993] ILRM 497, *per* McCarthy J (stay placed on High Court to make immediate discovery, since this would do no more "than allow for the possibility of the appeal being successful on the procedural issue"). See also *O'Toole v RTÉ (No 1)* [1993] ILRM 454 and *Emerald Meats Ltd. v Minister for Agriculture*, [1993] 2 IR 443.
[62] *Corish v Hogan,* Supreme Court, 1 December 1990; *Redmond v Ireland* [1992] 2 IR 362.

Security for costs

Order 58 r 17 of the Rules of the Superior Courts 1986, provides that the Supreme Court may direct "under special circumstances" that "such deposit or other security for costs" to be occasioned by any appeal be lodged by an appellant. The Court will only make an order where there are special circumstances and the following have been held to amount to special circumstances: the fact that the appellant lived abroad and had no obvious assets;[63] where there was undue delay in bringing on the appeal[64] and where the appellant had been deliberately chosen as a nominal plaintiff because of his lack of means.[65] On the other hand, the Supreme Court will not order provision of security for costs where the appeal raises a point of law of exceptional public importance[66] or where this effectively would frustrate the appellant's constitutional right of access to the courts.[67]

Non-appellate jurisdiction of the Supreme Court

In the *The People (Attorney General) v McGlynn*[68] the Supreme Court itself raised and decided the question whether the words of Article 34.4.3 implied that the Supreme Court had a purely appellate jurisdiction (such as to render, accordingly, s 16 of the Courts of Justice Act 1947, invalid, as this section gave the Court a consultative jurisdiction in cases stated, prior to decision, by the Circuit Court). The Court held that the section was not invalid, for the reason given in *The State (Browne) v Feran*,[69] that while no subtraction of jurisdiction from that provided by the Constitution was possible, the addition of other kinds of jurisdiction was permissible.

Appellate jurisdiction of the Supreme Court from courts other than **the** *High Court*

Article 34.4.3 makes it clear, that unlike appeals from the High Court, the appellate jurisdiction of the Supreme Court in respect of appeals from other courts is entirely dependent on statute. The Supreme Court enjoys a limited appellate jurisdiction from decisions of the Court of Criminal Appeal under s 29 of the Courts of Justice Act 1924 and by s 3 of the Criminal Justice Act 1993;[70] and by s 14 of the Courts-Martial Appeals Act 1983, from the Courts-Martial Appeal Court. The Supreme Court also formerly enjoyed an appellate jurisdiction from decisions of the Circuit Court by virtue of s 36(2) of the Workmen's Compensation Act 1934, prior to the repeal of this Act by the Social Welfare (Occupational Injuries) Act 1966.

[63] *The State (Hempenstall) v Shannon (No.2)* [1936] IR 334; *Midland Bank Ltd. v Crossley-Cooke* [1969] IR 56.

[64] *Somers v Erskine (No.3)* [1945] IR 308.

[65] *Fallon v An Bord Pleanála* [1992] 2 IR 380.

[66] *Moore v Attorney General (No.2)* [1929] IR 544; *Fallon v An Bord Pleanála* [1992] 2 IR 380.

[67] *Fallon v An Bord Pleanála* [1992] 2 IR 380.

[68] [1967] IR 232.

[69] [1967] IR 147.

[70] A novel and interesting constitutional argument might yet arise with regard to the operation of the appeal certificate procedure provided for in s 3 of the 1993 Act. By s 2, the Director of Public Prosecutions is given power to appeal an unduly lenient sentence to the Court of Criminal Appeal. Section 3 allows for an appeal (with leave) in respect of a point of law of exceptional public importance by either the convicted person or the DPP to the Supreme Court. However, it is provided that such leave may be granted only by either the Court of Criminal Appeal, the Attorney General or the Director of Public Prosecutions. The constitutionality of this procedure would surely be called into question if the Director were to purport to give leave to himself to appeal on such a point of law, since the evident lack of mutuality in the leave procedure might render it vulnerable to challenge on grounds ranging from the fair administration of justice under Article 34.1 to equality before the law under Article 40.1.

Exceptions from the general right of appeal to the Supreme Court

Several statutory exceptions from the generality of Article 34.4.3 exist and, indeed, there has been a increasing tendency in recent years to curtail this appellate jurisdiction, especially in cases where the High Court is itself exercising an appellate - as opposed to an original - jurisdiction. Legislation "excepting" or "regulating" this appellate jurisdiction can, broadly speaking, be divided into three categories. The first category can properly be regarded as an "exception" in that it does not admit of any possibility of appeal in any circumstances. Thus, for example, s 86(6) of the Central Bank Act 1989 states quite simply that:

> "An appeal against a decision of the [High] Court under this section shall not lie to the Supreme Court."[71]

In the second example we may include instances where the right of appeal is made conditional or contingent in some way or another, such as the necessity to obtain leave to appeal from the High Court itself. Thus s 52(2) of the Courts (Supplemental Provisions) Act 1961 provides that:

> "An appeal shall lie by leave of the High Court to the Supreme Court from every determination of the High Court [under s 52(1).]"

Another variant of this may be found in s 108(7) of the Patents Act 1992 which provides that a decision of the High Court on an appeal from a decision of the Controller of Patents, Designs and Trade Marks with regard to the removal or suspension of a patent agent:

> "shall be final, save that, by leave of [High] Court or the Supreme Court, an appeal, by the Controller or the person concerned from the decision shall lie to the Supreme Court on a specified question of law."

The most elaborate version of such a regulation may now be found in s 82(3B)(*b*)(i) of the Local Government (Planning and Development) Act 1963 (as inserted by s 19 of the Local Government (Planning and Development) Act 1992) which provides that a decision of the High Court in respect of an application to quash a decision of a planning authority or An Bord Pleanála shall be final and:

> "no appeal shall lie from the decision of the High Court to the Supreme Court in either case save with the leave of the High Court which leave shall only be granted where the High Court certifies that its decision involves a point of exceptional public importance and that it is desirable in the public interest that an appeal should be taken to the Supreme Court."[72]

Finally, there are instances in which the form and scope of the Supreme Court's appellate jurisdiction is curtailed or excepted in some fashion and this is generally done by confining the scope of the appeal to an appeal on a specified point of law. An example of this is provided by s 96(7) of the Patents Act 1992 which provides that:

[71] See also Monopolies, Mergers and Take-Overs (Control) Act 1978, s 12 and the Fisheries Act 1980, s 54(7) for other miscellaneous examples of such statutory ouster of appellate jurisdiction.

[72] There is a saver (necessary in view of Article 34.4.4) in s 82(3A)(*b*)(ii) for determinations of the High Court "in so far as it involves a question as to the validity of any law having regard to the provisions of the Constitution."

> "An appeal to the Supreme Court from a decision of the [High] Court under this section shall lie only on a question of law."[73]

The second and third categories can more properly be regarded as "regulating" (as opposed to "excepting") the Supreme Court's jurisdiction, in that they admit of a form of appeal to that Court, albeit one which has been qualified by legislation.

Presumption against ouster of jurisdiction

The general principle is that any law excepting or regulating the Supreme Court's appellate jurisdiction must be clear and unambiguous. As Walsh J stated in *People v Conmey*:[74]

> "any statutory provision which had as its object the excepting of some decisions of the High Court from the appellate jurisdiction of this [i.e. the Supreme] Court, or any particular provision seeking to confine the scope of such appeals within particular limits, would of necessity have to be clear and unambiguous."

Nevertheless, as we shall see, there have been several examples of statutory provisions which have been found to meet this test.

In *Eamonn Andrews Productions v Gaiety Theatre*[75] the Supreme Court was asked to admit an appeal from a decision of the High Court on appeal from the Circuit Court, in reliance of the general words of Article 34.4.3; it was argued that s 39 of the Courts of Justice Act 1936, which excluded such further appeals in the case of the "old" Supreme Court, ceased to be operative on the passing of the 1937 Constitution. The Court rejected this view, and decided that the 1936 provisions were validly re-enacted, with application to the "new" Supreme Court, by s 48 of the Courts (Supplemental Provisions) Act 1961; the 1936 provisions were therefore to be read and construed as if [they were] a post-Constitution enactment excluding from the appellate jurisdiction of this Court the decisions of the High Court in appeals from the Circuit Court. The Court re-emphasised that only post-Constitution enactments could effect a valid exception. Similar reasoning was applied in *W.J. Prendergast & Son Ltd. v Carlow County Council*.[76]

On the other hand, despite some judicial *dicta* to the contrary, the exclusion of jurisdiction need not necessarily be express: it will, it seems, suffice where the exclusion is to be necessarily implied. Thus, in *Beecham Group Ltd. v Bristol Meyers Ltd.*[77] the question arose as to whether s 75(7) of the Patents Act 1964 (which was the statutory forerunner to what is now s 96(7) of the Patents Act 1992) allowed for an appeal on a point of law in all cases except in relation to High Court decisions under the sections set out between the brackets in that sub-section (where no appeal would lie); or, alternatively, whether the sub-section allowed for a general right of appeal, save that the right of appeal was confined in some instances to specified points of law. O'Higgins CJ accepted the former interpretation and appears to have regarded s 75(7) as having excluded the Court's appellate jurisdiction by necessary implication. This reasoning also appears to

[73] Similar provisions are to be found in the Trade Marks Act 1963, s 57(5); Article 41 of the Brussels Convention (as scheduled to the Jurisdiction of Courts and Enforcement of Judgments (European Communities) Act 1988) and the Electoral Act 1992 , s 132(6).
[74] [1975] IR 341.
[75] [1973] IR 295.
[76] [1990] 2 IR 482.
[77] [1983] IR 325.

underlie the judgment of the Supreme Court in *Minister for Justice v Wang Zhu Jie*,[78] where the appellant sought to appeal against the refusal of Costello J to grant leave to appeal under s 52(2) of the Courts (Supplemental Provisions) Act 1961. The appellant had argued that there was no express statutory bar forbidding an appeal against refusal to grant leave to appeal, but the Supreme Court appears to have taken the view that this right was impliedly barred by the statutory language. Finlay CJ said that s 52(2) should be construed as:

> "effecting an exception from the absolute right of appeal provided for in Article 34.4.3...from decisions of the High Court to the Supreme Court, and substituting therefor a regulated right of appeal which is subject to the final discretion of the judge of the High Court [to grant or refuse leave to appeal]."

Nevertheless, the general presumption against the statutory ouster of the Supreme Court's appellate jurisdiction was emphatically restated in *Holohan v Donohoe*.[79] At issue here was whether the Supreme Court enjoyed the right to substitute its own assessment of damages for those awarded by a civil jury in the High Court; and if so, whether that right had been regulated by the provisions of s 96 of the Courts of Justice Act 1924 (as re-enacted and applied to the present High and Supreme Courts by s 48 of the Courts (Supplemental Provisions) Act 1961). A majority of the Supreme Court[80] concluded that the Court possessed such an inherent jurisdiction, for, as Henchy J put it:

> "The true position is that the court's jurisdiction to make such an order [to assess damages] has a constitutional and not a statutory basis... s 96 [of the 1924 Act] is relevant only if it could be said to have cut down (under Article 34.4.3), by exception or regulation, the full right of appeal and, hence, the court's appurtenant right to make an order necessary for the purpose of doing justice in the appeal."

He noted that s 96 of the 1924 Act merely empowers the Court to set aside the judgment appealed against and to enter such judgment as it considers proper in lieu of ordering a new trial; also citing the dicta in *The People (Attorney General) v Conmey*[81] and *The People (Director of Public Prosecutions) v O'Shea*[82] to the effect that any exception from or regulation of the Court's appellate jurisdiction must be "clearly and unambiguously" expressed, a test which the section clearly did not meet.

However, *Campus Oil Ltd. v Minister for Industry and Energy*[83] shows that the constitutional right of appeal contained in Article 34.4.3 must yield to another constitutional provision, namely, Article 29.4.3 (now Article 29.4.5). In this case Murphy J had referred certain question to the European Court of Justice under Article 177 of the Treaty of Rome. The Supreme Court ruled that no appeal lay against this decision. Even if (contrary to his own view)[84] it was a "decision of the High Court" for the purposes of

[78] [1993] 1 IR 426; [1991] ILRM 829.

[79] [1986] IR 45; [1986] ILRM 250.

[80] Finlay CJ, Henchy, Griffin and Hederman JJ. McCarthy J dissented on the grounds that in his view the quantum of damages and their assessment were issues of fact reserved to the jury which fell outside the Supreme Court's inherent jurisdiction under Article 34.4.3

[81] [1975] IR 341.

[82] [1982] IR 384.

[83] [1983] IR 82.

[84] This seems questionable. First, the European Court of Justice has never ruled that national appeals against decisions to refer are incompatible with Article 177: see *Rheinmühlen-Düsseldorf* v *Einfuhr- und Vorratsstelle Getreide (No. 2)* [1974] ECR 139. Secondly, as Article 29.4.3 is merely an enabling provision in that it allows the State to join the European Communities and it seems a dubious course to qualify an express provision of the Constitution by reference to a provision not even expressed by, but only perhaps implicit in, an extraneous document, whatever its special status under Article 29.4.3.

Article 34.4.3, the right of appeal was, according to Walsh J, superseded by Article 29.4.3, which had, in effect, incorporated Article 177 of the Treaty of Rome; and to permit an appeal against a decision to refer would be contrary to the "spirit and letter" of Article 177 and thus also contrary to Article 29.4.3.

In *Hughes v O'Rourke*[85] Hederman J said that Rules of Court could amount to a "regulation by law" of the Supreme Court's appellate jurisdiction for the purposes of Article 34.4.3.[86] It is questionable whether "law" in Article 34.4.3 can encompass a rule made by a Committee; if it can, might it not do so elsewhere in the Constitution, e.g., in Article 40.4.?[87]

Hearing of new evidence on appeal

In *B. v B.*[88] it was held that the constitutional nature of the Supreme Court's appellate function did not prevent that Court from hearing new evidence in the course of an appeal, even if (as in this case) such evidence bore on an issue which had not been raised in the court of first instance.

However, in the nature of things, given the Supreme Court's function as an appellate court of last resort, it is unlikely that this right will be exercised, save in unusual cases. This is reflected in the terms of O 58 r 8 which requires that any such evidence shall only be admitted on "special grounds" and then with leave of the Supreme Court. However, any such evidence must have been in existence at the time of the hearing in the High Court. This point was emphasised by Finlay CJ in *Dalton v Minister for Finance,*[89] where the plaintiff sought to introduce new evidence on appeal demonstrating that her medical condition had deteriorated since the date her personal injuries action had been heard by the High Court. The Court would not permit her to do this, with the Chief Justice observing that, as the High Court could not possibly have considered or assessed this evidence, to permit it to be admitted would be "wholly inconsistent" with the appellate nature of the Supreme Court's jurisdiction. On the other hand, where the new evidence was available at the time of the hearing in the High Court, the Supreme Court will only permits its use for appellate purposes where (i) it could not have been obtained with reasonable diligence at the time of trial;[90] (ii) it must have an important bearing (although not necessarily decisive) on the outcome of the trial and (iii) it must be *prima facie* credible.

Exclusion of appeal possible if aimed at an individual case?

A point which has never yet arisen in practice may be mentioned here hypothetically: would it be competent for the Oireachtas under Article 34.4.3 to enact a law excluding from appeal to the Supreme Court a class of cases, or even an individual case, in which judgment had been given by the High Court but no appeal yet taken? Instinct suggests

[85] [1986] ILRM 538.

[86] Does this mean, for example, that the security for costs rules contained in O 58 r 17 constitute a "regulation" of the Supreme Court's appellate jurisdiction inasmuch as requirement to provide security constitutes an impediment to the otherwise untrammelled constitutional right of an appellant to appeal to the Supreme Court against a decision of the High Court?

[87] However, some support for this view of "law" may be found in the majority judgments in *The State (Gilliland) v Governor of Mountjoy Prison* [1987] IR 213; [1987] ILRM 278.

[88] [1975] IR 34.

[89] [1989] IR 269.

[90] See *Murphy v Minister for Defence* [1991] 1 IR 161 (army circular relevant to personal injuries claim admitted by Supreme Court on appeal since document could not have been discovered with reasonable diligence prior to trial). See also *Lynagh v Mackin* [1970] IR 180 and *Smyth v Tunney*, Supreme Court, 26 June 1992.

the objectionability of such a law and since "the judicial process, once commenced, is inviolable",[91] the principle of judicial independence would seem to argue against the constitutionality of such a law.[92]

[91] *Per* Henchy J in *Hamilton v Hamilton* [1982] IR 466.

[92] As against this, the US Supreme Court has upheld legislation designed to oust a particular case from the appellate jurisdiction of that Court: see the (much criticised) decision in *Ex parte McCardle* 7 Wall. 506 (1869). There Chase CJ said: "We are not at liberty to inquire into the motives of the legislature. We can only examine into its power under the Constitution; and the power to make exceptions to the appellate jurisdiction of this Court is given by express words...Without jurisdiction the Court cannot proceed at all in any cause..." It may be noted that McCardle had challenged the validity of certain federal legislation and, of course, in an Irish context Article 34.4.4 would now preclude the enactment of any law ousting the jurisdiction of the Supreme Court in a case which involved the validity of any Act of the Oireachtas.

SUPREME COURT'S JURISDICTION ENTRENCHED IN CASES OF CHALLENGE TO LAWS

4° No law shall be enacted excepting from the appellate jurisdiction of the Supreme Court cases which involve questions as to the validity of any law having regard to the provisions of this Constitution.

4° Ní cead aon dlí a achtú a chuirfeadh ar an taobh amuigh de dhlínse achomhairc na Cúirte Uachtaraí cásanna ina mbeadh ceisteanna le réiteach i dtaobh baíl a bheith nó gan a bheith ar aon dlí, ag féachaint d'fhorálacha an Bhunreachta seo.

1922 provision

This provision, which reproduces the substance of a parenthetical provision of Article 66 of the 1922 Constitution, was considered by Walsh J in *The State (Browne) v Feran.*[1]

Implications of this entrenchment of jurisdiction

In reinforcing his view (with which the rest of the Supreme Court agreed) as to the equal appealability of orders granting *habeas corpus* and orders refusing it, Walsh J pointed to this clause as meaning that, if *habeas corpus* appeals involving the validity of a law cannot be excluded from the Supreme Court by statute, so much the less can they be excluded by a mere practice such as that resting on *Cox v Hakes.*[2] He did not say in so many words, but clearly intended to take for granted, that the State has an interest in pursuing such an appeal just as valid as a prisoner's interest in doing so:

> "The words "which involve questions as to the validity of any law" are very wide and are not to be construed simply as meaning cases brought seeking a declaration as to the validity of any law. A case may involve a question as to the validity of any law even if the point is raised not by pleading but arises in argument or otherwise, and there have been many instances of this occurring, particularly in matters concerning habeas corpus. Subsection 4 expressly invalidates any law enacted to except such cases from the appellate jurisdiction of this Court. *A fortiori* this constitutional provision would exclude any practice or procedure or law, existing before the coming into force of the Constitution and importing such an exception from appeal to this Court, from being carried over by virtue of the provisions of Article 50 of the Constitution. A similar provision appeared in Article 66 of the Constitution of Saorstát Éireann and in my view it also operated to exclude any such practice, procedure or law from being carried over by virtue of Article 73, of that Constitution. The judgments in *The State (Burke) v Lennon,*[3] while mentioning the existence of Article 34, section 4, sub-section 4, do not appear to have considered the effect of it in relation to any question of the carrying over of any procedure, legal principles or laws in force prior to the coming into operation of the Constitution. In my view the decision in *The State (Burke) v Lennon* ought not to be followed as I consider the

[1] [1967] IR 147 In *Attorney General (Society for the Protection of Unborn Children (Ire.) Ltd.) v Open Door Counselling Ltd. (No. 2)*, Supreme Court, 20 July 1993, Denham J said that one of the effects of Article 34.4.4 was to foster the Supreme Court's "special role in regard to the Constitution."

[2] 15 AC 506.

[3] [1940] IR 136; (1940) 74 ILTR 36, 131. *Burke's* case contains only mention - but no discussion - of Article 34.4.4.

effect of following it would be completely contrary to the ordinance of Article 34, section 4, sub-section 4."

In regard to the scope of this sub-section, Walsh J said in *The People (AG) v Conmey*:[4]

> "It is to be noted that the term employed is "cases" which is wider than "decisions" but necessarily includes decisions. I mention this because, in the course of the arguments before this Court, one of the points canvassed was that a judge's decision on the question of the validity of a law having regard to the provisions of the Constitution could be appealed as such ruling without necessarily involving the decision of the trial itself. In my view, the use of the word "cases" in this provision of the Constitution excludes that possibility, and the whole case in which the ruling was made, or the question as to the validity of a law was decided, falls within the appellate jurisdiction of this Court."

Saver of entrenched appellate jurisdiction under the Planning Acts

While there have been relatively few legislative attempts[5] to oust the appellate jurisdiction of the Supreme Court, one recent example is afforded by s 82(3B)(*b*)(i) of the Local Government (Planning and Development) Act 1963 (as inserted by s 19 of the Local Government (Planning and Development) (Amendment) Act 1992). This provides that in applications for judicial review of planning decisions, the decision of the High Court shall be final and that an appeal to the Supreme Court may only be taken with leave of the High Court. Leave is only to be granted in cases presenting a point of law of exceptional public importance where it is desirable in the public interest that such an appeal should be taken. However, in order to avoid a potential clash with Article 34.4.4, s 3(B)(*b*)(ii) provides:

> This paragraph shall not apply to a decision of the High Court insofar as it involves a question as to the validity of any law having regard to the provisions of the Constitution.[6]

Entrenchment confined to post-1937 laws?

In *The State (Sheerin) v Kennedy*[7] the Supreme Court, speaking by Walsh J, analysed the varying usage of the Constitution (in regard to the judicial review of statutes or Bills) in such a way as to relate the expression "validity of a law having regard to the provisions of the Constitution" exclusively to the enactments of the Oireachtas created by the Constitution, i.e. to post-1937 statutes. If this interpretation is observed in Article 34.4.4 as well as in Article 40.4.3 (which was in issue in *Sheerin's* case) it will follow that it would be within the competence of the Oireachtas to exclude from appeal to the Supreme Court cases on the constitutionality of a pre-1937 law. As Article 34.4.4 is merely an expanded form of a parenthesis in the old Article 66, and as it would be hard to impute to those who framed the 1922 Constitution the intent to differentiate, in this context which was then wholly novel in Ireland, between existing and future statute law, it may be that the *Sheerin* analysis ought to be confined to Article 40.4.3, where it origi-

[4] [1975] IR 341.
[5] See pp. 519-520.
[6] There does not appear to be any other example of such a saving clause, or, at least, one drafted so obviously with Article 34.4.4 in mind.
[7] [1966] IR 379. See generally pp. 421-422.

nated, and which, unlike Article 34.4.4, had no counterpart in the 1922 Constitution (it was actually an afterthought, inserted by the Second Amendment of the Constitution Act 1941).

Entrenchment not confined to post-1937 statutes, but includes statutory instruments

In view of the majority decision in *The State (Gilliland) v Governor of Mountjoy Prison*[8] it would now appear that the expression "validity of any law having regard to the provisions of the Constitution" includes not only post-1937 statutes, but also statutory instruments made pursuant to such Acts.[9] Although the *Gilliland* decision was given in the context of Article 40.4.3, its reasoning would appear equally applicable to Article 34.4.4.[10]

[8] [1987] IR 201; [1987] ILRM 278.

[9] To judge by the fact that a plurality of judgments were delivered in *Keady v Garda Commissioner* [1992] 2 IR 197; [1992] ILRM 312 (where the validity of a 1971 statutory instrument made pursuant to a pre-1937 Act was at issue) one may, perhaps, infer that only statutory instruments made pursuant to post-1937 Acts will be regarded as "laws" within the meaning of Articles 34.4.4 and 34.4.5.

[10] But see the comments of Ó Dálaigh CJ in *The State (McKeever) v Governor of Mountjoy Prison* (Supreme Court, 19 December 1966) where he said that the case-stated procedure only applied to "an Act of the Oireachtas passed since the coming into force of the Constitution."

Article 34.4.5

ONE JUDGMENT ONLY IN CASES ON VALIDITY OF A LAW

5° The decision of the Supreme Court on a question as to the validity of a law having regard to the provisions of this Constitution shall be pronounced by such one of the judges of that Court as that Court shall direct, and no other opinion on such question, whether assenting or dissenting, shall be pronounced, nor shall the existence of any such other opinion be disclosed.

5° Is é a chraolfas breith na Cúirte Uachtaraí ar cheist i dtaobh bail a bheith nó gan a bheith ar dhlí ag féachaint d'fhorálacha an Bhunreachta seo ná an duine sin de bhreithiúna na Cúirte sin a cheapfaidh an Chúirt sin chuige sin, agus ní cead tuairim ar bith eile ar an gceist sin, ag aontú nó ag easaontú leis an mbreith sin, a chraoladh ná ní cead a nochtadh tuairim ar bith eile den sórt sin a bheith ann.

Historical background to Article 34.4.5

This provision - inserted in the Constitution by the Second Amendment of the Constitution Act 1941[1] - is similar to the provision of Article 26.2.2 for the Court's decisions on Bills referred to the Court by the President. Both provisions seem to have been inserted as a direct result of the judgment of the Supreme Court in *Re Article 26 and the Offences Against the State (Amendment) Bill 1940.*[2] Here Chief Justice Sullivan commenced the judgment of the Court by announcing that it was the "decision of the majority of the judges." As Finlay CJ explained in *Attorney General v Hamilton (No. 1*:.[3]

> "This was apparently seen to indicate a dissenting opinion which, it was felt, could greatly reduce the authority of the decision of the Court and, we are informed, and it is commonly believed, led directly to the insertion of the additional clauses by the Act of 1941 in both Article 26 and Article 34."

The Chief Justice was here examining the historical background of Article 34.4. in order to demonstrate that such was the exceptional nature of these constitutional provisions that they did not provide a safe guide in respect of the interpretation of other provisions of the Constitution. It had been suggested that, since the Constitution made express pro-

[1] This amendment, enacted by the Oireachtas alone just before the expiry of the three-year transitional period during which, under Article 51, the Constitution could be so amended (i.e. without a referendum) contained a number of miscellaneous amendments. In the debate on the one-judgment proposal, Mr. de Valera acknowledged that it had been inspired by the practice of the Court of Criminal Appeal. He added: "From an educational point of view, the proposal [for separate judgments] would, no doubt, be valuable, but, after all, what do we want? We want to get a decision....The more definite the position is the better, and, from the point of definitiveness, it is desirable that only one judgment be pronounced....[and] that it should not be bandied about from mouth to mouth that, in fact, the decision was only come to by a majority of the Supreme Court. Then you would have added on, perhaps, the number of judges who dealt with the matter in the High Court before it came to the Supreme Court, as might happen in some cases You would then have an adding up of judges, and people saying: 'They were five on this side and three on the other, and therefore the law is the other way'. That would be altogether undesirable" (82 *Dáil Debates* 1857-9). For an amusing and wry analysis of the merits of the one-judgment rule, see McCarthy, "*Una Voce Poco Fa*" in O'Reilly, ed., *Human Rights and Constitutional Law; Essays in Honour of Brian Walsh* (Dublin, 1992) at 163. See also Whyte, "*The One Judgment Rule in Action*" (1983) 5 DULJ (n.s.) 273.

[2] [1940] IR 376.

[3] [1993] 2 IR 250; [1993] ILRM 81.

vision for the one-judgment rule in Article 34.4.4, but had made no such provision in respect of the confidentiality of discussions at Government meetings, the *exclusio unius* rule would seem to argue against the absolute confidentiality which, it was claimed, attached to such meetings. Finlay CJ did not think that it would be safe to conclude from Article 34.4.4 "an inconsistency in implying a necessary confidentiality to the discussions of Government meetings."

The one judgment rule applies only in cases on post-1937 laws

This "one judgment" rule applies only to adjudications on post-Constitution statutes, as was made clear by Walsh J in *The State (Sheerin) v Kennedy*:[4]

> "While the scope of the phrase "validity...having regard to the provisions of this Constitution" has not previously been the subject of any decision directed expressly to that point, it has by implication on a number of occasions been interpreted by this Court and by the former Supreme Court as referring only to laws enacted by the Oireachtas set up under the present Constitution. On occasions in both Courts opinions by more than one judge have been pronounced in cases dealing with the question of whether or not certain provisions of Acts of the Oireachtas of Saorstát Éireann and of the parliament of the former United Kingdom of Great Britain and Ireland were inconsistent with the provisions of the Constitution... [He gave examples]. In each of these cases it is clear that the Court was of opinion that the provisions of Article 34.4.5...did not apply in cases dealing with [such statutes]. In contrast, decisions concerning the validity of an Act of the Oireachtas have always been pronounced in accordance with the provisions of Article 34.4.5."

Pre-1937 legislation which has been "effectively re-enacted" by subsequent legislation will attract the one-judgment rule: see *Costello v Director of Public Prosecutions*[5] and *Gormley v Electricity Supply Board.*[6] In *Costello* the plaintiff had challenged the constitutionality of s 62 of the Courts of Justice Act 1936. But as this section was re-enacted by s 48(3) of the Courts (Supplemental Provisions) Act 1961, and later applied to the courts established by the Courts (Supplemental Provisions) Act 1961, and later amended by the deletion of certain words by the Criminal Procedure Act 1967, O'Higgins CJ said that it must be treated as if it were "a section of a statute of the Oireachtas." In *Gormley*, the validity of s 53 of the Electricity (Supply) Act 1927, was under challenge and it had been substantially amended by s 46 of the Electricity (Supply) (Amendment) Act 1945. Finlay CJ held that this amounted to an "effective re-enactment" of the original section, with the result that it acquired the "status of having been passed since the coming into force of the Constitution". The one-judgment rule was observed in both cases.

The rule does not apply to ancillary rulings

In *Murphy v Attorney General*,[7] in which provisions of the Income Tax Act 1967, were under challenge, the substantive decision was delivered as one judgment: but, when the Court dealt later with ancillary questions as to the extent, if any, to which its finding of unconstitutionality was to be retroactive, separate opinions were pronounced.

[4] [1966] IR 379.
[5] [1984] IR 436; [1984] ILRM 413.
[6] [1985] IR 129; [1985] ILRM 484.
[7] [1982] IR 241.

The rule does not apply to questions simultaneously in issue along with constitutional validity of law

Similarly where, in the same case, issues other than the constitutional validity of a law are decided by the Court, the single decision on the validity of the law may be followed by separate judgments on the other matters: notable examples are *In re Haughey,*[8] *The People (Attorney General) v Conmey,*[9] *The State (Lynch) v Cooney,*[10] *Crotty v An Taoiseach*[11] and *Desmond v Glackin.*[12]

The rule does not apply to cases where post-1937 Acts only indirectly affected

Note also that in *McMahon v Attorney General,*[13] where the Electoral Act 1963, was indirectly affected by a judgment of unconstitutionality bearing mainly on the Electoral Act 1923; the Court evidently did not consider that the "one judgment" rule applied. Walsh and Budd JJ agreed with Ó Dálaigh CJ: FitzGerald and McLoughlin JJ pronounced dissents.

But the rule also applies to sub-ordinate legislation

It had previously been thought that the one judgment rule did not apply to decisions on the constitutionality of subordinate legislation (statutory instruments, by-laws etc.), since in *Quinn's Supermarket v Attorney General,*[14] where Articles 2 and 4 of the Victuallers' Shops (Hours of Trading on Weekdays) (Dublin, Dun Laoghaire and Bray) Order 1948, were under challenge, separate judgments were delivered. A different view was, however, taken by the Supreme Court in *The State (Gilliland) v Governor of Mountjoy Prison*[15] where the validity of the Extradition Act 1965 (Part II) (No.20) Order 1984 was at issue. In the High Court, Barrington J thought it unconstitutional and stated a case for the opinion of the Supreme Court pursuant to Article 40.4.3. Finlay CJ, delivering the judgment of the Supreme Court majority, held that the phrase "validity of a law" contained in Article 40.4.3 included:

> "not only the statutory provision expressly enacted by the Oireachtas in this case, namely, the Extradition Act 1965, but also...the machinery expressly created in that Act for the application of Part II of it by Government Order."

As the statutory instrument in question was therefore a "law" for the purposes of Article 40.4.3, it followed that it was also a "law" for the purposes of Article 34.4.5, so as to render the one-judgment rule applicable.

Both Hederman and McCarthy JJ dissented in persuasively argued judgments; the latter referred to the fact that several judgments had been given in *Quinn's Supermarket Ltd. v Attorney General*[16] (where the constitutional validity of an order made under the Shops (Hours of Trading) Act 1938 had been under challenge), and could not accept that the then Court was not alive to the "constitutional obligation of a single judgment" in any case involving the validity of any post-1937 law. However, a further refinement in this

[8] [1971] IR 217.
[9] [1975] IR 341.
[10] [1982] IR 341.
[11] [1987] IR 713; [1987] ILRM 400.
[12] Supreme Court, 30 July 1992.
[13] [1972] IR 69; (1971) 106 ILTR 89.
[14] [1972] IR 1.
[15] [1987] IR 213.
[16] [1972] IR 1.

position may be discerned in *Keady v Garda Commissioner*[17] where several judgments were delivered by the Supreme Court in the course of upholding the constitutionality of a 1971 statutory instrument made pursuant to the Police Forces (Amalgamation) Act 1925. While no member of the Court adverted to the possible significance of Article 34.4.5, the inference to be drawn here, perhaps, is that the *Gilliland* reasoning will only apply where the statutory order is made on foot of a post-1937 Act of the Oireachtas.

Decision is that of the majority

The fact that, while Article 26.2.2 provides that "the decision of the majority of the judges of the Supreme Court shall, for the purposes of this Article, be the decision of the Court", no analogous provision exists in Article 34.4.5 is evidently due to its being understood that the ordinary common law rules on the decisions of an appellate court apply in the latter case, whereas the Supreme Court is performing under Article 26 not an appellate, but a unique consultative function to which a common law rule is not automatically applicable.

Utility of the one-judgment rule?

The value and utility of the one-judgment rule would appear to be questionable. While it must be conceded that this rule tends to produce certain definitiveness in the Supreme Court's pronouncements, this may well be a false consensus which masks the real differences in views on the part of the Court's members.[18] The one-judgment rule may also tend to compel the judges to engage in a search for the lowest common denominator, often resulting in judgments containing very general statements.[19]

[17] [1992] 2 IR 197; [1992] ILRM 312.

[18] For example, had the one-judgment rule applied in *Norris v Attorney General* [1984] IR 36 it would have meant that the public would have been deprived of the benefit of hearing two lively dissents advancing a contrary view.

[19] *The State (Hunt) v O'Donovan* [1975] IR 39 would appear to be an example of where Article 34.4.5 prevented the Court giving a reasoned judgment for its conclusions, presumably because no three judges could agree on a particular ratio.

Article 34.4.6

FINALITY OF SUPREME COURT'S DECISION

6° The decision of the Supreme Court shall in all cases be final and conclusive.	**6° Ní bheidh dul thar breith na Cúirte Uachtaraí i gcás ar bith.**

1922 provision

Article 66 of the 1922 Constitution contained a similar provision.

Conflict with Community law

Article 34.4.6 was in potential conflict with Article 177 of the 1957 Treaty of Rome establishing the European Community, to which Ireland acceded in 1972. The Article (from s 4 of the Treaty, on the Court of Justice of the Communities) reads:

> The Court of Justice shall have jurisdiction to give preliminary rulings concerning:
>
> (a) the interpretation of this Treaty;
> (b) the validity and interpretation of acts of the institutions of the Community and the European Central Bank;[1]
> (c) the interpretation of the statutes of bodies established by an act of the Council, where those statutes so provide.
>
> Where such a question is raised before any court or tribunal of a Member State, that court or tribunal may, if it considers that a decision on the question is necessary to enable it to give judgment, request the Court of Justice to give a ruling thereon.
>
> Where any such question is raised in a case pending before a court or tribunal of a Member State, against whose decisions there is no judicial remedy under national law, that court or tribunal shall bring the matter before the Court of Justice.

Article 177(3) clearly impinges on the "finality" normally attached by Article 34.4.6 to the decision of the Supreme Court, not in the sense that a further appeal against the Court's decision is envisaged, but in the sense (to which the Irish text of the Constitution does more justice) that the "finality" in cases to which Article 177 of the Treaty applies is not a sovereign but a dependent finality; it must await the ruling of the Court of Justice of the Communities on the issue referred to it. This impairment of the Supreme Court's position is legitimated by the Third Amendment of the Constitution, which added an appropriate clause to Article 29.

The obligation to refer under Article 177(3) is not absolute

Despite the apparently mandatory language contained in Article 177(3), the Supreme Court, as a court of last resort is not obliged (although it may still do so) to refer a question of Community law to the Court of Justice where the answer to the issue raised is either obvious (*"acte clair"*) or where a reference is not necessary for the disposition of the case because of a previous preliminary reference.[2] In the leading case on the matter,

[1] The reference to the European Central Bank was inserted by Article G of the Maastricht Treaty.

[2] *Da Costa v Nederlandse Balastingsadministratie* (Cases 28-30/62) [1963] ECR 31; [1963] CMLR 224. A preliminary reference is not required where an issue of Community law arises in the course of interlocutory proceedings: *Hoffmann La Roche v Centrafarm* (Case 107/76) [1977] ECR 957; [1977] 2 CMLR 334.

Cilfit Srl. v Ministero della Sanita,[3] the Court ruled that national courts of last resort were not obliged to make a reference:

> "where the correct application of Community law [is] so obvious as to leave no scope for any reasonable doubt as to the manner in which the question raised is to be resolved."

These principles have been applied by the Supreme Court on a number of occasions and references have been refused on the ground that either no point of Community law arose on the facts[4] or that the determination of the Community law question was not necessary in the circumstances.[5] The Supreme Court's attitude to this general issue was succinctly stated by Finlay CJ in *Kerry Co-Operative Creameries Ltd. v An Bord Bainne*:[6]

> "If [the Supreme Court] decides that the resolution of such questions [of Community law] is not necessary to enable it to give judgment in the case, then no reference is made. [In such a case] it would not be appropriate for this Court to express any view on the issues of European Community law arising in this manner, except for the particular instance where it may conclude that what was alleged to be an issue of EC law is in fact incapable of any but one resolution and has so clearly been determined."

Stare decisis: rule diluted

An aspect of the "finality" of the Supreme Court's decisions worth mentioning particularly is the degree to which the Court respects the maxim *stare decisis*. Until 1964 it had been tacitly assumed that the Supreme Court, like the House of Lords in England, considered itself bound by its own former decisions; but two cases in that year gave the Court occasions to declare that it did not. It must, however, be emphasised firstly, that the Court of 1964 exploited the fact that it had been set up, technically, as a "new" Court in 1961,[7] so that decisions of the former Supreme Court were not, strictly speaking, "its own" decisions - and that in the two cases in point, as well as in two subsequent cases, it was pre-1961 judgments that were departed from; secondly, that the Court made it clear that to reject the rigid application of stare decisis did not mean it would depart from earlier rulings for any but compelling reasons.

In the first of these cases, *The State (Quinn) v Ryan*,[8] where the Court departed from a decision of the former Supreme Court[9] on the constitutionality of s 29 of the Petty Sessions (Ireland) Act 1851, Walsh J rejected any supposed adoption by the Supreme Court of the working rules of the British House of Lords, and said the US Supreme

[3] (Case 283/81) [1982] ECR 3415; [1983] 1 CMLR 472. See generally Lasok & Bridge, *Law and Institutions of the European Communities* (London, 1991) at 356-370.

[4] See, e.g., *Attorney General (Society for the Protection of Unborn Children (Ire.) Ltd.) v Open Door Counselling Ltd.* [1988] IR 593; [1989] ILRM 19; *Rhatigan v Textiles y Confecciones Europeas SA* [1990] 1 IR 126 and *Kerry Co-Operative Creameries Ltd. v An Bord Bainne* [1991] ILRM 851 (no issue as to Article 85 of the Treaty of Rome arose on the facts, but a reference was made under Article 86).

[5] *Doyle v An Taoiseach* [1986] ILRM 693; *Attorney General v X.* [1992] 1 IR 1; [1992] ILRM 401. In *Doyle* Henchy J observed that, by analogy with the rule of avoidance in domestic constitutional cases, Community law "should not be applied save where necessary for the decision in the case." These views were approved by Finlay CJ in *X.* when he remarked that there was no provision in Article 177 for the determination by the Court of Justice "of any question of law as a moot at the instance of a national court."

[6] [1991] ILRM 851. Collins and O'Reilly, "*The Application of Community Law in Ireland 1973-1989*" (1990) 27 CMLRev 315 say that the Supreme Court had made only five Article 177 references up to date up to that date. Since then there has been at least one further reference - the *Kerry Co-Op* case in May 1991.

[7] See p. 398.

[8] [1965] IR 70; (1966) 100 ILTR 105.

[9] In *The State (Duggan) v Tapley* [1952] IR 62; (1951) ILTR 22.

Court, if any court was to be "held up as an example", would be more appropriate in this context.[10] But:

> "This is not to say... that the Court would depart from an earlier decision for any but the most compelling reasons. The advantages of *stare decisis* are many and obvious so long as it is remembered that it is a policy and not a binding, unalterable rule."

A week later the Court gave judgment in *Attorney General v Ryan's Car Hire Ltd.*[11] and overturned a line of authority, including a Supreme Court decision of 1956, on the question whether the State could sue for loss of services of a State servant injured through another's negligence. Kingsmill Moore J said:

> "The law which we have taken over is based on the following of precedents and there can be no question of abandoning the principle of following precedent as the normal, indeed almost universal, procedure. To do so would be to introduce into our law an intolerable uncertainty. But where the Supreme Court is of the opinion that there is a compelling reason why it should not follow an earlier decision of its own, or of the courts of ultimate jurisdiction which preceded it, where it appears to be clearly wrong, is it to be bound to perpetuate the error?"
>
> In my opinion the rigid rule of *stare decisis* must in a court of ultimate resort give place to a more elastic formula. Where such a court is clearly of opinion that an earlier decision was erroneous it should be at liberty to refuse to follow it, at all events in exceptional cases".

In 1967, in *The State (Browne) v Feran,*[12] the Supreme Court, without going into any rationalisation of its rejection of *stare decisis* as a rigid formula, simply refused to follow the Supreme Court's 1939 decision in *The State (Burke) v Lennon*[13] that no appeal lay against the granting of an order of *habeas corpus*, saying that to do so would be "completely contrary to the ordinance of Article 34.4.4".

In 1972, in *O'Brien v Manufacturing Engineering Co. Ltd.*,[14] the Supreme Court departed from several decisions of the former Supreme Court on s 60(2) of the Workmen's Compensation Act 1934, Walsh J recalling that the Court had already decided in a number of cases that it was "free not to follow decisions of the former Supreme Court of Justice where this Court considers they were not correct - or even decisions of its own in similar circumstances". In 1977 the Court expressly reserved, in *Moynihan v Greensmyth*,[15] the question whether it had correctly decided in *O'Brien v Keogh*[16] less than five years earlier that part of the Statute of Limitations 1957 was constitutionally

[10] A similar note had previously been struck by Lavery J in *O'Byrne v Minister for Finance* [1959] IR 1 and similar sentiments were subsequently expressed by McCarthy J in *Irish Shell Ltd. v Elm Motors Ltd.* [1984] IR 200. McCarthy J said:

> "In no sense are our Courts a continuation of, or successors to, the British courts. They derive their powers from a Constitution enacted by the people and would, in my view, find more appropriate guidance in the decisions of courts in other countries based upon a similar constitutional framework than in what, at times, appears to be an uncritical adherence to English precedent..."

[11] [1965] IR 642; (1966) 101 ILTR 57.

[12] [1967] IR 147.

[13] [1940] IR 136; (1939) ILTR 36, 131.

[14] [1973] IR 334; (1972) 108 ILTR 105.

[15] [1977] IR 55.

[16] [1972] IR 144.

invalid. In 1981, in *Blake v Attorney General,*[17] the Supreme Court simply said it was "unable to accept the view" of the former Supreme Court in *Attorney General v Southern Industrial Trust*[18] that the property rights mentioned in Article 40.3 were the same as those guaranteed in Article 43. In 1982, in *The State (Lynch) v Cooney,*[19] the Supreme Court departed from the principle of the former Supreme Court, that a ministerial "option" formed for a statutory purpose could not be reviewed, O'Higgins CJ relying on the "shift in judicial thinking" in such matters since the 1940s and 1950s, and Henchy J simply saying he thought the earlier rulings should be "overruled". And in 1984, in *Costello v Director of Public Prosecutions,*[20] the Supreme Court departed from its earlier view[21] that s 62 of the Courts of Justice Act 1936, did not violate the Constitution in permitting the Director of Public Prosecutions to order the return for trial on indictment of a person whom the District Court, after a preliminary investigation, had refused to return.

The pace at which stare decisis is diluted accelerates

The pace at which the *stare decisis* rule is diluted in practice appears, if anything, to be accelerating. Since 1985 there have been at least seven instances of where the Supreme Court has either expressly departed from earlier judgments of its own in constitutional cases or treated earlier observations of individual judges as non-binding *dicta.* In *Re J.H.*[22] the Supreme Court refused to follow earlier comments of O'Higgins CJ in *J. v D.*[23] which had appeared to suggest that the relevant test in child custody cases was to be found in s 3 of the Guardianship of Infants Act 1964. Since this test made no reference to Articles 41 and 42, Finlay CJ felt that he could not follow it. Likewise in *People v Conroy*[24] a majority of the Supreme Court refused to follow earlier suggestions in *People v Lynch*[25] to the effect that the jury should rule on issues of fact arising from a *voir dire* since such a procedure was, said Henchy J, "so capable of undue prejudice as to be incompatible with a fair trial." In *The State (Gilliland) v Governor of Mountjoy Prison*[26] the Supreme Court refused to follow earlier *dicta* in *The State (Browne) v Feran*[27] which would confined the application of Article 40.4.3 to statutes (as opposed to statutory instruments) enacted by the Oireachtas. Finally in three major decisions in early 1990 the Supreme Court expressly overruled earlier decisions of its own in areas of supreme constitutional importance.

In the first of these, *McGimpsey v Ireland*[28] the Supreme Court overruled earlier dicta of the Court in *Re Article 26 and the Criminal Law (Jurisdiction) Bill*[29] which had suggested that Articles 2 and 3 did not constitute a claim of legal right in respect of the territory of Northern Ireland. Next, in *People v Kenny*[30] the Supreme Court decided "after very careful consideration" to overrule the test as to the admissibility of unconstitutionally obtained evidence set out by Griffin J in *People v Shaw.*[31] Finally, in *Finucane v*

[17] [1982] IR 117.
[18] (1960) 94 ILTR 161.
[19] [1982] IR 337.
[20] [1984] IR 436.
[21] As expressed in *The State (Shanahan) v Attorney General* [1964] IR 239.
[22] [1985] IR 375; [1985] ILRM 302.
[23] Supreme Court, 22 June 1977.
[24] [1986] IR 460.
[25] [1982] IR 64.
[26] [1987] IR 201.
[27] [1967] IR 147.
[28] [1990] 1 IR 110; [1990] ILRM 440.
[29] [1977] IR 129.
[30] [1990] 2 IR 110; [1990] ILRM 569.
[31] [1982] IR 1.

McMahon[32] (where the applicant claimed to be entitled to the benefit of the political offence exception contained in s 50 of the Succession Act 1965) a majority of the Supreme Court overruled a decision of a differently composed majority of the Court delivered just two years earlier in *Russell v Fanning*.[33] The individual members of the Supreme Court gave various reasons for arriving at this decision to overrule *Russell*. Walsh J said there was no valid basis for that decision and McCarthy J, stressing that *Russell* itself had dealt somewhat inadequately with the earlier decisions of the Court on the political offence question, added:

> "The Court is now asked to review the decision in *Russell v Fanning* and, if necessary, to overrule it. I have re-read the judgments in that case; because of the challenge made to it I am free to differ from its conclusions. I affirm the views I expressed, and the reasons I stated."

The two dissenting judges, Finlay CJ and Griffin J, adhered to the *Finucane* reasoning, but the Chief Justice added that he would accept the majority view in future cases "so that the basic principles underlying it may clearly represent the decision of this Court."[34]

Some restraint recognised

In 1975 the Court had drawn some restraining boundaries around its own freedom in regard to departing from precedents of its own or of the old Supreme Court. In *Mogul of Ireland v Tipperary (N.R.) County Council*[35] it was asked, despite a line of earlier Supreme Court decisions to the contrary, to rule that malicious damage claims might extend to compensation for consequential loss. The Court appeared to be tempted to do this; but refrained because of the earlier authority. O'Higgins CJ said:

> "When a court does pronounce on the meaning of a statute and thereby defines the law, a court of review ought not to pronounce this definition incorrect merely because a contrary view as to the statute's meaning is also possible."

And Henchy J said, after citing the words of Kingsmill Moore J quoted above:

> "Therefore, the primary consideration is whether this Court is clearly of opinion that the decision in *Smith's* case[36] was erroneous. If the point were *res integra*, one might reach the opposite conclusion, but I do not think it is possible to assert a *clear* opinion that *Smith's* case was wrongly decided...A decision of the full Supreme Court (be it the pre-1961 or the post-1961 Court), given in a fully-argued case and on a consideration of all the relevant materials, should not normally be overruled merely because a later Court inclines to a different conclusion. Of course, if possible, error should not be reinforced by repetition or affirmation, and the desirability of achieving certainty, stability and predictability should yield to the demands of justice. However, a balance has to be struck between rigidity and vacillation, and to

[32] [1990] 1 IR 165; [1990] ILRM 505.

[33] [1988] IR 505; [1988] ILRM 333.

[34] Thus, in *Carron v McMahon* [1990] 1 IR 239; [1990] ILRM 802 decided a few weeks after *Finucane* the Supreme Court unanimously applied the *Finucane* reasoning. See generally, Humphreys, "*Reflections on the Role and Functioning of the Supreme Court*" (1990) 12 DULJ (n.s.)127. Note that in *McDaid v Sheehy* [1991] 1 IR 1; [1991] ILRM 250 the Supreme Court overruled *McDonald v Bord na gCon (No 1)* [1964] IR 350, since that decision constituted "a break in what otherwise appears to be a relatively consistent attitude" by the Court to the question of mootness.

[35] [1976] IR 260.

[36] *Smith v Cavan and Monaghan Co. Councils* [1949] IR 322.

achieve that balance the later Court must, at the least, be *clearly* of opinion that the earlier decision was erroneous.

Even if the later Court is clearly of opinion that the earlier decision was wrong, it may decide in the interests of justice not to overrule it if it has become inveterate and if, in a widespread or fundamental way, people have acted on the basis of its correctness to such an extent that greater harm would result from overruling it than from allowing it to stand. In such cases the maxim *communis error facit ius* applies."

But even this principle has been unevenly applied, since in *Doyle v Hearne (No.1)*[37] a majority of the Supreme Court overruled two earlier decisions[38] which involved pure questions of statutory interpretation. Griffin J, in a persuasive dissent, pointed out that this was the first case in which a previous decision of the Supreme Court had been overruled "by other than a unanimous decision of a Court of five." He added that there did not seem to him to be "any compelling reason" why the earlier decisions should be overruled.

A similar unwillingness to be unduly restricted by precedent is evidenced in family cases, where the courts prefer to pay great attention to the individual facts of each case. In *S v S*,[39] a custody case where the wife had an on-going sexual relationship with another man, reference had been made to previous decisions of the Court involving roughly analogous facts. The Court was, however, unwilling to approach the case in this manner, stressing the limits to the doctrine of precedent in cases of this kind. McCarthy J said:

"Save for a clear expression of general principle, little assistance is to be gained in resolving any one case of child custody by reference to the facts of others. Whilst there may be similarities between many cases, no two cases can be identical and the courts should be slow to decide one such case by reference to the facts of another."

State decisis: flexibility versus consistency?

What is still not clear from these latest decisions - the 1975 decision in *Mogul* notwithstanding - is the extent to which the Supreme Court will consider itself free to depart from its earlier decisions, especially as far as constitutional matters are concerned. Speaking at the broadest level of generality, the decisions of the Supreme Court fall into three broad categories: (a) decisions concerning common law principles; (b) decisions on questions of statutory interpretation and (c) constitutional decisions.

As far as the first category is concerned, it is plain that whereas the courts have a traditional role in extending and developing the common law (and, thus, where necessary, overruling earlier Supreme Court decisions[40]), there are recognised boundaries beyond

[37] [1987] IR 601; [1988] ILRM 318. See generally, Hogan, "*Precedent and Statutory Interpretation*" (1989) 11 DULJ (n.s.) 196.

[38] *Dolan v Corn Exchange Ltd.* [1975] IR 315; *Corley v Gill* [1975] IR 313. Finlay CJ did refer to *Mogul* , but added that have reached "a clear view of the interpretation of this section", he felt it his duty "to express it."

[39] [1992] ILRM 732.

[40] A good example of this is supplied by *McNamara v ESB* [1975] IR 1. See also the judgment of Henchy J in *Kelly v Board of Governors of St. Laurence's Hospital* [1988] IR 402 and that of Finlay CJ in *Dunne v National Maternity Hospital* [1989] IR 91. See also *Boyle v Lee* [1992] 1 IR 555 (where the Supreme Court departed from two earlier decisions in order to restore certainty to an important aspect of conveyancing law).

which the courts cannot go.[41] In other words, while the Supreme Court has latitude to relax the *stare decisis* rule where to do otherwise would be to re-inforce an earlier decision which is erroneous or not in harmony with modern legal values, nevertheless considerations of judicial continuity together with the maxim *communis error facit jus* place real restraints on that freedom where the Court is asked to overrule a decision of long-standing or up-root a rule which has become embedded in the fabric of the common law. An example here may be found in the judgment of Henchy J in *Hynes-O'Sullivan v O'Driscoll*[42] where he refused to overrule pre-1961 Supreme Court judgments dealing with qualified privilege. This was partly because the point had not been fully argued, but also because this was an area of the law where any "radical change" should more properly be effected by statute:

> "The public policy which a new formulation of the law would represent should more properly be found by the Law Reform Commission or by those others who are in a position to take a broad perspective as distinct from what is discernible in the tunnelled vision imposed by the facts of a single case. That is particularly so in a case such as this where the law as to qualified privilege must reflect a duel balancing of the constitutional protection of every citizen's good name. The articulation of public policy on a matter such as this would seem to be primarily a matter for the legislature."

As far as the second category is concerned, principle suggests that the Supreme Court should be particularly reluctant to overrule earlier decisions raising questions of "pure" statutory interpretation. The reasons for this are two-fold. First, questions of statutory interpretation rarely raise very wide issues of principle (such as are raised by, for example, common law rules dealing with recovery for economic loss or the assessment of damages) and so the Court in abiding by its earlier decision is usually not giving new life to a common law or constitutional principle now considered to be erroneous. Secondly, if the Oireachtas is dissatisfied with the interpretation placed on the statute, it can always act by introducing amending legislation.

However, the extent to which the Supreme Court should have freedom to overrule earlier constitutional decisions is quite problematic. On the one hand, given the importance of constitutional adjudication, arguments emphasising the need for judicial consistency in this area are very powerful, especially since the frequent overruling of earlier decisions might tend to undermine public confidence. In addition, there has also emerged a body of constitutional jurisprudence which is now so well established that to overrule it now might lead to a great disruption of institutional arrangements or to the manner in which sections of the public have arranged their affairs.[43] On the other hand, having

[41] These issues are canvassed in cases such as *Vone Securities Ltd. v Cooke* [1979] IR 59; *UF v JC* [1991] 2 IR 330; *L v L* [1992] 2 IR 77; [1992] ILRM 115 and *McKinley v Minister for Defence* [1992] 2 IR 333. In this regard, the comments of Egan J in *L. v L.* [1992] 2 IR 77 - where a wife had claimed a proprietary interest in the family by virtue of Article 41.2.2 (for which see pp. 1010-1012) - are instructive:
"Present case law is based on long-standing equitable principles as a result of which trusts are implied in favour of a contributing spouse. These principles have been extended to their permissible limit."

[42] [1988] IR 436.

[43] It is, for example, probably too late now for the Supreme Court to overrule the decision in *Ryan v Attorney General* [1965] IR 294 since that decision has formed the basis for practically every constitutional decision of note since the mid-1960s. c.f. the judgment of O'Connor J in *Planned Parenthood v Casey* (1992) 120 L. Ed. 2d. 683 where she advanced four "prudential and pragmatic" considerations which the courts might employ in considering whether to overrule previous decisions raising questions of constitutional law:
(1) that the rule has proved to be practically unenforceable;
(2) that it has not fostered any form of "reliance" which would make reversal inequitable;
(3) that it merely a remnant of abandoned doctrine;
(4) that it has been rendered obselete by changing factual circumstances.

regard to the difficulty in actually amending the Constitution, it would, perhaps, be wrong for the Supreme Court to perpetuate constitutional error, especially perhaps where the decision in question was out of line with other judicial pronouncements on this issue[44] or where the earlier decisions insufficiently protected or even threatened important constitutional rights.[45] In these respects, therefore, it would seem that the Supreme Court's power to relax the *stare decisis* rule in constitutional cases is at least at great as it is in the case of ordinary common law principles and certainly wider than in the case of "pure" issues of statutory interpretation.[46]

Decisions given per incuriam are overruled

To be distinguished from cases in which the Supreme Court consciously turns its back on deliberate, fully considered decisions previously made are the (rare) cases in which the Court disregards an earlier decision on the ground that it was given with some element of inadvertence, e.g. in unawareness of some decisive statutory provision which ought to have settled the matter in a different sense. Examples are *The State (Harkin) v O'Malley*[47] in which *The People (Attorney General) v Doyle*[48] was disregarded; *Brown v Donegal Co. Council*[49] in which *Smyth v Dun Laoghaire Borough Corporation*[50] was similarly not applied; and *McHugh v Minister for Social Welfare*[51] in which certain aspects of *Harvey v Minister for Social Welfare*[52] were not followed as having been given *per incuriam.*

Dictum not integral to ratio decidendi is not a precedent

The Supreme Court follows general common law doctrine in not recognising as a binding precedent at all (even as qualified by its power to depart from former rulings) a statement in a former case which was not integral to the *ratio decidendi*: see the words of Walsh J in *The State (Abenglen Properties Ltd.) v Dublin Corporation*[53] and of Henchy J in *The State (Lynch) v Cooney* [54] and *People v Quilligan (No. 2).*[55]

The Supreme Court decision, even if dubious, still binds other courts

It may be noted that, even where the Supreme Court has strongly hinted disapproval of one of its own earlier decisions, for so long as it has not yet departed from it by substi-

[44] The overruling of *The State (Shanahan) v Attorney General* [1964] IR 239 in *Costello v Director of Public Prosecutions* [1984] IR 436 provides a good example of this. See also *McDaid v Sheehy* [1992] 1 IR 1; [1991] ILRM 250, (overruling earlier decision which represented "a break in what otherwise [was] a relatively consistent attitude" by the Supreme Court to the question).

[45] See, e.g., the reasoning in *People v Conroy* [1986] IR 460 and *People v Kenny* [1990] 2 IR 110; [1990] ILRM 569.

[46] There are, of course, other considerations which may come into the reckoning and these include: whether the judgment was *ex tempore* or reserved (see the comments of Henchy J in *The State (Harkin) v O'Malley* [1978] IR 269); whether the Supreme Court consisted of a court of three or five judges (see *per* McCarthy J in *Doyle v Hearne (No.1)* [1987] IR 601; [1990] ILRM 318) and whether the decision to overrule an earlier decision represents the unanimous view of the Supreme Court (see the comments of Griffin J in *Finucane v McMahon* [1990] 1 IR 165; [1990] ILRM 505).

[47] [1978] IR 269.

[48] (1967) 101 ILTR 136.

[49] [1980] IR 132.

[50] (1960) Ir Jur Rep 45. In *Doyle v Hearne (No.1)* [1987] IR 601; [1988] ILRM 318, McCarthy J appeared to suggest that the earlier decision of the Supreme Court in *Corley v Gill* [1975] IR 313 had been given *per incuriam* because a particular argument which might have been advanced in the earlier case was not so advanced. But this view would seem to represent a considerable extension of the *per incuriam* doctrine.

[51] Supreme Court, 11 March 1992.

[52] [1990] 2 IR 232; [1990] ILRM 185.

[53] [1984] IR 436.

[54] [1982] IR 237.

[55] [1989] IR 45.

tuting a different ruling, the other courts, including the High Court, will consider themselves still bound by the earlier one. Thus although in *Moynihan v Greensmyth*, cited above, the Court said it appeared that *O'Brien v Keogh* seemed incompatible with the (old) Supreme Court's decisions in *Foley v Irish Land Commission*[56] and *Attorney General v Southern Industrial Trust,*[57] and "reserved for a case in which the point has been duly raised and argued the question whether *O'Brien v Keogh* was correctly decided)", yet in *Campbell v Ward,*[58] when Carroll J was asked to treat as valid the provision which *O'Brien v Keogh* had struck down, she refused, saying she "did not consider that those words gave her liberty to hear any arguments as to whether the case of *O'Brien v Keogh* was correctly decided"; she considered herself "bound by the existing decision of the Supreme Court in that case until such time as the Supreme Court reviews its decision".

In a personal injuries case, *McDonnell v Byrne Engineering Co. Ltd.,*[59] a High Court judge indicated that he did not propose to follow an earlier decision of the Supreme Court in *Carroll v Clare County Council.*[60] The resulting jury award was set aside on the ground that it had not been obtained in accordance with due course of law. O'Higgins CJ said that following the "clear and concise statement of the law" in *Carroll*, "it became the duty of all judges trying such cases to follow this directive"; the Supreme Court, which was designated by the Constitution as the final court of appeal:

> "had the duty, when necessary, to declare what legal principles should apply to cases that were reviewed by the Court. Where necessary, it had the duty to lay down guidelines for all courts and all judges as to the manner in which such cases should be tried. It was equally the duty of all other courts and judges to follow directions as to law and procedure as given by the Supreme Court."

Res judicata does not apply to habeas corpus

An important qualification was read by the Supreme Court into Article 34.4.6 in *Application of Woods*,[61] namely, that in cases where the Constitution places a special duty on the courts to investigate a question of lawfulness - i.e. specifically in *habeas corpus* cases under Article 40.4 - the mere fact that the Supreme Court has previously ruled a detention to be lawful will not prevent it from examining the matter again, at the instance of the same prisoner, where new considerations or new arguments are presented to it. In this case a *habeas corpus* application had previously failed in both the High Court and the Supreme Court, but on a renewed application, in which the applicant raised fresh grounds of complaint, and in which the High Court held that by reason of the Supreme Court's former decision it had no jurisdiction (because of Article 34.4.6) to entertain the complaint, the Supreme Court held that Article 34.4.6 did not have a final and conclusive effect in this sense. Ó Dálaigh CJ said:

[56] [1952] IR 118; (1952) 86 ILTR 44.
[57] (1960) 94 ILTR 161.
[58] [1981] ILRM 60. See also *Lynch v Burke* [1990] 1 IR 1 where O'Hanlon J expressed unhappiness with a decision of the "old" Supreme Court in *Owens v Greene* [1932] IR 225. O'Hanlon J said that he was bound to follow that decision but that "having regard to the fact that it is a decision which appears to conflict with the interpretation of this branch of the law in so many other common law jurisdictions", it might well be a case "where the Supreme Court would be disposed to review again the correctness of that decision, if a suitable opportunity for doing so."
[59] *The Irish Times*, 4 October 1978. This report is reproduced as an appendix to R. Byrne and P. McCutcheon, *The Irish Legal System* (Dublin, 1989), p. 123.
[60] [1975] IR 230.
[61] [1970] IR 154.

> "Article 34.4.6... says that "The decision of the Supreme Court shall in all cases be final and conclusive." The President of the High Court has interpreted the Article as prohibiting a person who is detained from seeking *habeas corpus* if he has made an earlier application which has been rejected by the Supreme Court...
>
> The duty of the courts, to see that no one is deprived of his personal liberty save in accordance with law, overrides considerations which are valid in litigation *inter partes* If, therefore, the applicant raised matters before the President on this application which had not been ruled on a previous application... the duty of the High Court under the Constitution was to examine such grounds and say whether or not it was satisfied that the applicant was being detained in accordance with law."

Res judicata does not apply to judgment obtained by fraud

The rigour of Article 34.4.6 is tempered by the fact that it has now been established that the *res judicata* rule does not apply to a judgment of the Supreme Court which has been obtained by fraud, since such a decision would in fact be a nullity and, presumably, not a "decision" in the sense envisaged by Article 34.4.6.[62] Nevertheless a very heavy onus will rest on the party seeking to impeach that judgment and to judge from the judgment of Murphy J in *Din v Banco Ambrosiano SPA,*[63] it will not suffice to show that new evidence has since become available or even that the Supreme Court might have misunderstood certain issues of foreign law.

[62] *Waite v House of Spring Gardens Ltd.*, High Court, 26 June 1985; *Din v Banco Ambrosiano SPA* [1991] 1 IR 569.

[63] [1991] 1 IR 569. See also *Belville Holdings Ltd. v Cronin*, Supreme Court, 8 February 1993 (in which Finlay CJ expressly envisaged the possibility of a final order being set aside in the case of fraud).

Article 34.5

JUDGES' DECLARATION UPON APPOINTMENT

1° Every person appointed a judge under this Constitution shall make and subscribe the following declaration:

"In the presence of Almighty God I... do solemnly and sincerely promise and declare that I will duly and faithfully and to the best of my knowledge and power execute the office of Chief Justice (*or as the case be*) without fear or favour, affection or ill-will towards any man, and that I will uphold the Constitution and the laws. May God direct and sustain me."

2° This declaration shall be made and subscribed by the Chief Justice in the presence of the President, and by each of the other judges of the Supreme Court, the judges of the High Court and the judges of every other Court in the presence of the Chief Justice or the senior available judge of the Supreme Court in open court.

3° The declaration shall be made and subscribed by every judge before entering upon his duties as such judge, and in any case not later than ten days after the date of his appointment or such later date as may be determined by the President.

4° Any judge who declines or neglects to make such declaration as aforesaid shall be deemed to have vacated his office.

5. 1° Gach duine a cheapfar chun bheith ina bhreitheamh faoin mBunreacht seo ní foláir dó an dearbhú seo a leanas a dhéanamh agus a lámh a chur leis:

"I láthair Dia na nUilechumhacht táimse,... á ghealladh agus á dhearbhú go sollúnta agus go fírinneach go gcomhlíonfad go cuí agus go dílis, chomh maith agus is eol agus is cumas dom, oifig an Phríomh-Bhreithimh (*nó de réir mar a oireas*) gan eagla gan claonadh, gan bá gan drochaigne chun duine ar bith, agus go gcumhdód Bunreacht agus dlíthe Éireann. Dia do mo stiúradh agus do mo chumhdach."

2° Is i láthair an Uachtaráin a dhéanfaidh an Príomh-Bhreitheamh an dearbhú sin agus a chuirfidh a lámh leis, agus is sa chúirt go poiblí agus i láthair an Phríomh-Bhreithimh nó an bhreithimh den Chúirt Uachtarach is sinsearaí dá mbeidh ar fáil a dhéanfaidh gach breitheamh eile den Chúirt Uachtarach agus gach breitheamh den Ard-Chúirt agus de gach Cúirt eile an dearbhú sin agus a chuirfidh lámh leis.

3° Ní foláir do gach breitheamh an dearbhú a dhéanamh agus a lámh a chur leis sula dté i gcúram dualgas a oifige, agus cibé scéal é, ar dháta nach déanaí ná deich lá tar éis lae a cheaptha, nó dáta is déanaí ná sin mar a chinnfidh an tUachtarán.

4° Aon bhreitheamh a dhiúltós nó a fhailleos an dearbhú réamhráite a dhéanamh ní foláir a mheas go bhfuil scartha aige lena oifig.

Declaration under the former Constitution

Provision for a similar declaration had previously existed not in the 1922 Constitution, but in s 99 of the Courts of Justice Act 1924 (repealed by s 3 of the Courts (Supplemental Provisions) Act 1961).

Rhetorical allusions to the declaration

The declaration of Article 34.5 has been adverted to, in a more or less rhetorical way, in a few cases, though the provision which requires it has never been considered or interpreted.

In *In re Tilson, Infants*[1] Black J said, in regard to the idea that the Constitution might discriminate between different religions in the matter of ante-nuptial agreements:

> "If I had thought it did, I never could have made a public declaration that I would uphold it."

In *In re Ó Láighléis*[2] Maguire CJ said, in regard to the European Human Rights Convention which had been pleaded against the internment provisions of the Offences against the State (Amendment) Act 1940, and to Article 29.6 which provides that international agreements are not part of the law of the State unless the Oireachtas makes them so:

> "No argument can prevail against the express command of Article 29.6 before judges whose declared duty it is to uphold the Constitution and the laws."

In *Keegan v de Búrca*,[3] in which the defendant was held guilty of contempt of court, McLoughlin J said:

> "I admire the defendant for her humanity and compassionate concern for the underprivileged and I admire her for her courage in sacrificing her liberty on their behalf, but the declaration I made on attaining office does not permit me to show favour for the defendant on this account."

In *The State (Trimbole) v Governor of Mountjoy Prison*[4] McCarthy J remarked that:

> "other than the President, no holder of an office under the Constitution save the members of the judiciary is required to make a declaration to uphold the Constitution and the laws. There are analogous provisions in the Police Forces Amalgamation Act 1925, and the Defence Act 1954. In particular, no member of either House of the Oireachtas or the Executive at any level is required by the

[1] [1951] IR 1; (1952) 86 ILTR 49.

[2] [1960] IR 93; (1961) 95 ILTR 92.

[3] [1973] IR 223.

[4] [1985] IR 550; [1985] ILTR 465. See also the comments of the same judge in *Conway v Irish National Teachers' Organisation* [1991] 1 IR 305; [1991] ILRM 497, a case where exemplary damages were awarded for breach of constitutional rights. As McCarthy observed:

> "Every member of the judiciary has made a public declaration to uphold the Constitution; it would be a singular failure to do so if the courts did not, in appropriate cases such as this, award such damages as to make an example of those who set at nought constitutional rights of others."

> Constitution itself to make such a declaration. This circumstances emphasises, if emphasis were needed, the high responsibility that lies upon the judiciary to ensure that constitutional rights are not flouted with impunity."

In *Crotty v An Taoiseach*[5] Finlay CJ said that the right of the courts to intervene to protect the constitutional rights of individuals against interference by actions of the executive was expressly vested in the High and Supreme Courts by Articles 34.3.1. and 34.4.3, and impliedly arose from the form of the judicial oath contained in Article 34.5.1.

Finally, it may be noted that in *Society for the Protection of Unborn Children (Ire.) Ltd. v Grogan*[6] Carroll J alluded briefly to the judicial oath when she excused herself from hearing an Article 40.3.3 case following an objection from the plaintiffs. The plaintiffs had objected on the ground that Carroll J was Chairman of the Commission of the Status of Women which - according to the plaintiffs - had issued a controversial statement in the aftermath of the *X* case. Carroll J was reported as having said that she "would not dream" of hearing the case unless both parties were satisfied. She expressed regret that the plaintiffs had not got confidence in her ability to deal with the case impartially in accordance with law as "she had taken an oath to uphold the Constitution."

Relevance of judicial declaration to the judicial conduct of proceedings

One consequence of the judicial oath is that the judge appears to be under a duty to give practical effect to the Constitution's requirements, irrespective of the wishes of the parties. In *The State (Byrne) v Frawley*[7] Henchy J said it was a judge's duty - irrespective of the wishes of the parties - to put an end to any civil or criminal proceedings before the court once it has been established that they have been "authoritatively declared to rest" on an unconstitutional statute:

> "As is required by the Constitution, every judge, on being appointed, makes a solemn declaration in open court that he will uphold the Constitution and the laws...The silence or acquiescence of a party...cannot abrogate the judge's duty to uphold the Constitution in his court by refusing to preside over a conclusively established unconstitutionality."

Relevance of judicial declaration to the discretion of judges of inferior courts

The fact that all judges are required to take an oath to uphold the Constitution is sometimes rhetorically prayed in aid of the proposition that all member of the judiciary have jurisdiction to - and must adjudicate on - claims based on the Constitution.[8] In *The People (Director of Public Prosecutions) v Lynch*[9] Walsh J said that judges of the District and Circuit Courts should be permitted to rule on the question of the admissibility of the statements said to have been obtained in violation of the accused's constitutional rights; judges of the District and Circuit Courts were also required to make a declaration to uphold the Constitution and the laws, and they were:

[5] [1987] IR 713; [1987} ILRM 400.
[6] *The Irish Times,* 18 July 1992.
[7] [1978] IR 326.
[8] Subject always to the restriction that only the High Court and Supreme Court can declare a post-1937 law to be unconstitutional.
[9] [1982] IR 64.

> "not dispensed from, or expected to overlook, their constitutional obligation to uphold the Constitution in the discharge of their constitutional and legal function of administering justice."

And in *Coughlan v Patwell*[10] Denham J stressed that the District Court was under a duty "to act in such manner as to preserve the individual's constitutional rights." While she did not expressly invoke the judicial oath for this purpose, it seems implicit in her judgment that a judicial refusal to refuse to entertain a submission based on an alleged infringement of the individual's constitutional rights was incompatible with such a declaration.

[10] [1993] 1 IR 31; [1992] ILRM 808.

JUDGES APPOINTED BY THE PRESIDENT

Article 35

1. The judges of the Supreme Court, the High Court and all other Courts established in pursuance of Article 34 hereof shall be appointed by the President.

Airteagal 35

1. Is ag an Uachtarán a cheapfar breithiúna na Cúirte Uachtaraí, na hArd-Chúirte agus an uile Chúirte eile a bhunaítear de bhun Airteagal 34 den Bhunreacht seo.

Appointments on the advice of the Government

This function of appointing judges is not one of Presidential discretion, but is a function which, in conformity with Article 13.9, is to be performed "only on the advice of the Government". The appointment of a judge, as Finlay P said in *The State (Walshe) v. Murphy*[1] is an act "requiring the President's intervention for its effectiveness in law, [but] in fact [it is] the decision and act of the Executive". This means that any attempt to change the system of appointment by ordinary legislation - by, e.g., requiring the consent of both Houses of the Oireachtas - would probably be unconstitutional inasmuch as it trenched on a constitutional right of the Executive.[2]

In *The State (Killian) v Minister for Justice*[3] the Supreme Court accepted that the judges whose appointment was envisaged by this section were judges of the courts contemplated by Article 34, i.e. courts which in 1937 were yet to be established.

When these were eventually set up in 1961, by the Courts (Establishment and Constitution) Act of that year, the courts established by the Courts of Justice Act, 1924, and continued in their jurisdictions by the transitory provisions of Article 58, were extinguished. The judges of the old courts, however, were maintained in the equivalent "new" judicial offices, by virtue of the special provisions of ss 5, 17 and 29 of the Courts (Supplemental Provisions) Act 1961. As these were technically fresh appointments, fresh declarations under Article 34.5 had to be made.

[1] [1981] IR 275.

[2] The reasoning of the majority in *Attorney General v Hamilton (No.1)* [1993] 2 IR 250; [1993] ILRM 81 might be thought to provide some support - on general separation of powers principles - for this particular argument.

[3] [1954] IR 207: (1956) 90 ILTR 116.

INDEPENDENCE OF JUDGES

Article 35.2-5

2. **All judges shall be independent in the exercise of their judicial functions and subject only to this Constitution and the law.**

3. **No judge shall be eligible to be a member of either House of the Oireachtas or to hold any other office or position of emolument.**

4. **1° A judge of the Supreme Court or the High Court shall not be removed from office except for stated misbehaviour or incapacity, and then only on resolutions passed by Dáil Éireann and by Seanad Éireann calling for his removal.**
2° The Taoiseach shall duly notify the President of any such resolutions passed by Dáil Éireann and by Seanad Éireann, and shall send him a copy of every such resolution certified by the Chairman of the House of the Oireachtas by which it shall have been passed.
3° Upon receipt of such notification and of copies of such resolutions, the President shall forthwith, by an order under his hand and Seal, remove from office the judge to whom they relate.

5. **The remuneration of a judge shall not be reduced during his continuance in office.**

Airteagal 35.2-5

2. **Beidh gach breitheamh saor neamhspleách maidir lena fheidhmeanna breithimh a oibriú, gan de smacht air ach an Bunreacht seo agus an dlí.**

3. **Ní cead aon bhreitheamh a bheith ina chomhalta de cheachtar de Thithe an Oireachtais, ná bheith in aon oifig ná post sochair eile.**

4. **1° Ní cead breitheamh den Chúirt Uachtarach ná den Ard-Chúirt a chur as oifig ach amháin de dheasca mí-iompair nó míthreorach a luafar, ná an uair sin féin mura rithid Dáil Éireann agus Seanad Éireann rúin á éileamh é a chur as oifig.**
2° Rúin ar bith den sórt sin a rithfidh Dáil Éireann agus Seanad Éireann ní foláir don Taoiseach scéala a thabhairt don Uachtarán ina dtaobh go cuí agus cóip de gach rún díobh a sheoladh chuige faoi theastas Chathaoirleach an Tí den Oireachtas a rith é.
3° Láithreach d'éis na scéala sin agus cóipeanna de na rúin sin a fháil don Uachtarán ní foláir dó, le hordú faoina láimh is faoina Shéala, an breitheamh lena mbainind a chur as oifig.

5. **Ní cead laghdú a dhéanamh ar thuarastal breithimh an fad is bheidh in oifig.**

1922 provision

These sections reproduce in substance Article 69 and part of Article 68 of the 1922 Constitution.

Other provisions tending to judicial independence

The principle of judicial independence, stated here, is given further strength by the provisions of Articles 35.4 and 35.5,[1] and also by the rule of common law that acts done or

[1] Note that despite the fact that Article 38.6 withdraws from the Special Criminal Court the specific guarantees of judicial independence contained in Article 35, the Supreme Court ruled that the members of that Court enjoyed a constitutional guarantee of independence: see *Eccles v Ireland* [1985] IR 545; [1986] ILRM 343.

words spoken by a judge in his judicial capacity are absolutely privileged.[2] This rule is usually justified on grounds of public policy, for, as Murnaghan J observed in *Byrne v Ireland*:[3]

> "It would be very invidious if the High Court had to entertain an action against the State based on an allegation against the Supreme Court."

Moreover, the desirability of maintaining public confidence in the judiciary, considerations of judicial esteem and independence and, indeed, the very propriety of stigmatising another judicial decision as negligent all tend to re-inforce the continued vitality of this common law rule in the much changed constitutional environment.[4] In other words, the citizen's right of action to sue and recover damages in respect of a justiciable controversy[5] will probably have to yield to the State's constitutional duty to safeguard the independence of the judiciary.

This view is suggested by the Supreme Court's decisions in *Pine Valley Developments Ltd. v Minister for Environment*[6] and by a broad judicial hint in *McIlwraith v Fawsitt.*[7] In *Pine Valley* the plaintiff company had sued the Minister for the Environment for loss it had incurred as result of the invalidation by the Supreme Court[8] of a planning permission granted by the Minister. Finlay CJ held that the State's obligation under Article 40.3.2 to protect individual property rights was not absolute.[9] The requirements of the common good demanded that an immunity be given:

> "to persons in whom are vested statutory powers of decision from claims for compensation where they act without negligence and bona fide. Such an immunity would contribute to the efficient and decisive exercise of statutory powers and would...tend to avoid indecisiveness and delay, which might otherwise be avoided."

The *Pine Valley* decision thus establishes that persons exercising quasi-judicial powers enjoy a qualified immunity in respect of acts done in the exercise of their powers; it follows, *a fortiori*, that judges must enjoy at least a similar privilege in the exercise of their judicial functions.

In *McIlwraith*, the Supreme Court re-affirmed a traditional rule to the effect that in judicial review or analogous proceedings there should be no order for costs against members of the judiciary where they had acted *bona fide* and where they had not sought to defend the decision which was now impugned. Finlay CJ, however, raised the issue of whether

[2] *Tughan v Craig* [1918] 1 IR 245; *Macauley v Wyse-Power* (1943) 77 ILTR 61; *Coyle v Roe, The Irish Times*, 26 June 1984 and see generally, Hogan & Morgan, *Administrative Law in Ireland* (London, 1991) at 716-7.

[3] [1972] IR 241. See also the comments of Lord Salmon in *Sutcliffe v Thackrah* [1974] AC 727: "The law recognises that, on balance of convenience, public policy demands that [the judiciary] shall have an immunity. It is of great public importance that they shall all perform their functions free from fear that disgruntled and possibly impecunious persons who have lost their cause or been convicted may subsequently harass them with litigation."

[4] In *Attorney General v Hamilton (No.1)* [1993] 2 IR 250; [1993] ILRM 81 McCarthy J commented that: "At common law acts done or words spoken by a judge in his judicial capacity are absolutely privileged. That common law rule has never been tested within the constitutional framework, although the common law rule has been enforced: see *Macaulay & Co. Ltd. v Wyse-Power* (1943) 77 ILTR 61".

[5] As recognised in *O'Brien v Keogh* [1972] IR 241 and see p. 771.

[6] [1987] IR 23; [1989] ILRM 747.

[7] [1990] 1 IR 343.

[8] *The State (Pine Valley Developments Ltd.) v Dublin County Council* [1984] IR 407; [1982] ILRM 169.

[9] Finlay CJ relied on *Moynihan v Greensmyth* [1977] IR 56 as authority for this proposition.

the guarantee of judicial independence might not mean that the State was, in any event, obliged to indemnify members of the judiciary in the cases of costs properly awarded against them:

> "Considerations of the obligation owed by the executive under the Constitution to support the judiciary in the carrying out of its separate duties under the Constitution may well lead in appropriate cases to an obligation which the courts could enforce against the executive to indemnify members of the judiciary in regard to costs which are properly awarded against them..."

The Chief Justice expressed no concluded view on this issue, since the matter had not been canvassed in argument. Nevertheless, the logic of this view (if it were to be judicially adopted) suggests that the requirements of judicial independence demand that a judge is not exposed to any possible financial burden (such as an order for costs or damages) as a result of any decision he should make. [10]

Special position of judges

The special position of judges and the relationship between this and the maintenance of public confidence in their impartiality and integrity was well brought out by Kennedy CJ in *In re the Solicitors Act and Sir James O'Connor*,[11] a case in which a former Lord Justice of Appeal (in the pre-1924 courts) was applying for leave to be admitted as a solicitor. Convention leaned against him; Kennedy CJ said:

> "There is good and powerful reason in support of such a rule, for it is beyond doubt that if a man should step down from the privileged position of the Bench and throw off what is a sacred office to engage in the rough-and-tumble of litigious contest, and compete with the practitioners for the feed business of the court, perhaps challenge the decisions which he pronounced, or even fail to support them in argument, he will shake the authority of the judicial limb of government, and mar the prestige and dignity of the courts of justice upon which the whole structure of the State must always lean. Moreover, a new way of scandal and corruption would be opened up to any who would pursue it...[He decided in favour of Sir James O'Connor's admission, but said he felt] that, in the interests of justice, Sir James O'Connor should not exercise the personal right of audience in the courts...He would still be regarded as laying down the law with judicial authority, and he would tend to overbear inferior courts, while it would be a scandal were he to explain his own judgments for the purpose of advancing a client's cause."

This case was referred to by Lavery J in *O'Byrne v Minister for Finance*[12] in the context of the protection of judicial independence. In the course of his (dissenting) judgment, he said:

> "One idea emerges [from Articles 65-69 of the 1922 Constitution] - that the judicial power of the State should be vested in judges set apart in many important ways

[10] Note that in *Maharaj v Attorney General of Trinidad* [1978] 2 All ER 670 the Privy Council held that an alleged contemtnor who had been wrongly deprived of his liberty by order of the trial judge could obtain damages against the State of Trinidad. Lord Diplock denied that this amounted to vicarious liability, rather "it was a liability of the State itself...in public law."

[11] [1930] IR 623; (1930) 64 ILTR 25. For the background to this case, see Hogan, "*Chief Justice Kennedy and Sir James O'Connor's Application*" (1988) 23 Ir Jur (n.s.) 144.

[12] [1959] IR 1; (1960) 94 ILTR 11.

from the life of the community and denied important civil rights in order that they should be independent in the exercise of their functions.

> Apart from specific prohibitions barring a judge from participating in the ordinary activities of a citizen, judges have to recognise many limitations both in their public and private lives. For example, they have effectively to surrender the right to practise their profession should they cease to be judges, either by removal or retirement: see [*Sir James O'Connor's* case].
>
> What forces might be anticipated as likely to threaten judicial independence?... The danger of interference with independence is obviously from the executive and legislative organs of government...
>
> As the independence is declared, it is to be expected that it would be secured and protected. As has been said, the judicial power is the weakest of the three organs of government, as it holds neither the sword nor the purse."

This question also arose in an indirect way in April 1992, when Mr. Justice O'Hanlon made certain controversial remarks concerning the abortion debate.[13] It was reported that the judge had been "summoned" to a meeting with the Taoiseach (Mr. Reynolds) and the Attorney General (Mr. Whelehan) so that he might "explain his position."[14] Mr. Justice O'Hanlon publicly repudiated this summons, saying:

> "I think it is important to point out, in the interests of preserving the status and independence of the judiciary in the exercise of its functions under the Constitution, that there is no power whatever conferred on the Executive to 'summon' a Judge of the High Court to attend a meeting with the Taoiseach, or to require him to 'explain his position' about anything."[15]

Judges' right to protect independence by summary punishment of contempt

The relevance of the law of criminal contempt of court to the independence of the judiciary declared by Article 35.2 was emphasised by the Supreme Court in *The State (Director of Public Prosecutions) v Walsh*,[16] which decided that criminal contempt, although a serious and not a minor offence, was a necessary exception from the rule of Article 38.5 as to trial by jury in such cases, save where there were outstanding issues of fact which required a jury determination. The Court took the view that judicial independence could be upheld in the face of this sort of conduct only if judges of their own motion and in their own discretion could punish it, without having to rely on the executive arm to institute a trial on indictment. O'Higgins CJ said:

> "Article 35.2 is a solemn recognition by the people in enacting the Constitution that the judiciary, as the custodians of the rights of citizens, shall be free to act as justice requires, and shall be guaranteed independence from all other organs of State in discharging judicial functions. How could such a guarantee be honoured if judges, when attacked and derided in the discharge of their functions, had to look for protection elsewhere?...I am of the opinion that implicit in the guarantee under Article 35.2 of independence to judges in the discharge of their judicial functions is a

[13] This was immediately in the wake of the Supreme Court judgments in *Attorney General v X* [1992] 1 IR 1; [1992] ILRM 401; [1992] 2 CMLR 277.
[14] *The Irish Times*, 8 April 1992.
[15] *The Irish Times*, 9 April 1992.
[16] [1981] IR 412.

recognition that such judges must be free and independent to act summarily, if necessary, to protect their judicial proceedings against criminal acts which are designed to interfere with the course of justice."

Henchy J added:

> "By their verdict the jury [which he thought an inherently unsuitable tribunal for judging issues of criminal contempt] may put a wrongful acquittal beyond correction; [and] such an incorrigible acquittal may leave a contemned judge in a state of odium and rejection in the minds of the public, to the detriment of his independence."

In *Re Kelly and Deighnan*[17] O'Higgins CJ said that the High Court enjoyed a jurisdiction to deal summarily with cases of contempt in the face of the Court, where this was necessary "to protect the administration of justice." In the light of these two decisions, therefore, the position, would appear to be as follows:

> "(a) There is no constitutional right to jury trial in the case of contempt in the face of the court or, in other criminal contempt cases, where there are no outstanding issues of fact, since in both cases, the *prima facie* right to jury trial must yield to the superior constitutional interest of protecting the independence of the judiciary;
>
> (b) In criminal contempt cases - not being cases of contempt in the face of the court - the accused is entitled to a jury trial on a disputed issue of fact."

Ineligibility for election to the Oireachtas

The first part of Article 35.3 means that if a person, being a member of Dáil or Seanad, is appointed a judge, he is taken to have automatically vacated his parliamentary seat; and, presumably, that a person, being a judge, may not, if elected to either House, take his seat unless he resigns from his office as judge. The provision does not appear to prevent a judge from standing as a candidate for Dáil or Seanad (though no such instance has ever arisen, and would be open to serious objection apart from the possibility of election); there seems to be certain discordance between the Irish and English texts, as the former prevents a judge from "being a member" ("bheith ina chomhalta") of either House, while the latter makes him "ineligible", i.e., arguably, incapable of going through the election process.

No objection to honorary appointments

The second part of Article 35.3 is regarded, in practice, as preventing a judge from taking on any other *paid appointment*. There is no objection to his writing books and receiving royalties; nor to his holding honorary offices, still less to acting as a Chairman or member of a Tribunal of Inquiry.[18] Judges have also been candidates in elections other than to Dáil or Seanad, for example, to the Governing Body of University College, Dublin, or to the Senate of the National University of Ireland, where the electorates have been large bodies of university graduates.

[17] [1984] ILRM 424.

[18] Judges have also acted as President of the Law Reform Commission, university visitors and have also been made Chairman of bodies such as An Bord Pleanála.

Removal of judges from office

Although Article 35.4 refers specifically only to judges of the Supreme Court and High Court, the same procedure would have to be followed in order to remove a judge of the Circuit Court or the District Court, as these judges are declared to "hold office by the same tenure as the judges of the Supreme Court and the High Court" by, respectively, s 39 of the Courts of Justice Act 1924, and s 20 of the Courts of Justice (District Court) Act 1946. An ordinary statute could substitute a different procedure for removing Circuit Court judges and District Judges, since, as Finlay CJ observed in *Magee v Culligan* [19] the Constitution does not contain any guarantee, save in the case of judges of the Supreme Court and High Court, "of the particular method by which they can be removed from office." Nevertheless, any such statute would risk invalidation if its operation tended to impinge on the independence of the courts.

Temporary judges

A related question is whether the appointment of judges for a fixed, temporary period is incompatible with the guarantee of judicial independence. The Supreme Court has recently taken the view in *Magee v Culligan* that this system of appointing temporary judges to the Circuit Court and District Court is not unconstitutional in that the appointment of judges for a fixed period of time is merely a regulation of the terms of appointment of judges of those courts within the meaning of Article 36.ii and that for the duration of such a fixed-term appointment the judges in question enjoys all the constitutional guarantees buttressing his independence. As Finlay CJ said:

> "The fact that the provisions of s 20 of the 1946 Act as a legislative regulation of the terms and conditions of judges of the District Court applies that particular protection to judges of the District Court who are permanent, as distinct from temporary, does not, the court is satisfied, in any way render the appointment of judges of the District Court for fixed short periods inconsistent with any provision of the Constitution, nor does it in any way interfere with or limit their constitutionally guaranteed independence."

On the other hand, it might be said that this view is somewhat formalistic in that the failure to re-appoint a judge who had served out his fixed term appointment might be said to amount in substance to a "removal" of that judge in circumstances where the prescribed procedures of Dáil and Seanad resolutions etc. were not followed. Moreover, if such a procedure were ever to be applied in the case of the judges of the High Court and the Supreme Court, this would seem to run squarely against the guarantee contained in Article 35.4.1.

"Stated misbehaviour or incapacity"

Article 35.4.1 guarantees that judges of the Supreme Court and High Court can only be removed for "stated misbehaviour or incapacity" and then only following resolutions of the Dáil and Seanad calling for removal. This phrase has never been judicially interpreted, but "incapacity" would seem to suggest physical unfitness for office. "Stated misbehaviour" is a more problematic phrase. In essence, the question reduces itself to this:

[19] [1992] 1 IR 223; [1992] ILRM 186.

does "misbehaviour" imply simply criminal misconduct?[20] Or does it extend more widely and include possible infractions of the accepted (but un-written) judicial code of behaviour?[21] If, for example, a judge were publicly to endorse a stated party political position or behave in a manner which was universally regarded as unseemly by his judicial colleagues would this be regarded as "misbehaviour" within the meaning of Article 35.4.1?

Enquiry into behaviour of District Judges

In the case of District Judges, there are statutory mechanisms less drastic than removal for calling them to order: s 21 of the Courts of Justice (District Court) Act 1946, provides for a judicial enquiry into the conduct or condition of health of a District Judge[22] and s 10(4) of the Courts (Supplemental Provisions) Act 1961, provides that:

> "where the Chief Justice is of opinion that the conduct of a justice of the District Court has been such as to bring the administration of justice into disrepute, the Chief Justice may interview the justice privately and inform him of such opinion."

There are no corresponding provisions for judges of any of the courts higher than the District Court.

"Vacation" of judicial office

Section 6 of the Courts (Establishment and Constitution) Act 1961, provides for the "vacation" of judicial offices otherwise than by removal or retirement. Sub.-section 1 defines "judicial office" (that held by judges of the Supreme Court, High Court, or Circuit Court, or justices of the District Court, or by the President of any of these Courts); the following sub-sections provide:

> (2) A judicial office held by any person may be vacated by resignation in writing under his hand addressed to the President and transmitted to the Taoiseach.
> (3) A judicial office held by any person shall be vacated by his being appointed, with his consent, to another judicial office.

Income taxation not an unconstitutional reduction

The effect of Article 35.5 was fully considered by the Supreme Court in 1958 in *O'Byrne v Minister for Finance*[23] in which the widow of a deceased judge of the Supreme Court, who throughout his period in office as a judge had paid income tax by deduction from his salary under Schedule E of the Income Tax Act 1918, sought a declaration that the salary her husband had received was exempt from income tax (and super-tax and sur-tax) and that the deductions which had been made in respect of such

[20] One must, assume, however, that the criminal misconduct must be relatively serious. A judge could scarcely be removed following conviction for minor traffic offences (although it might be otherwise in the case of, say, a series of drunk driving offences). On the other hand, an actual conviction might not be necessary to establish misbehaviour where - to take an admittedly extreme case - a judge was acquitted of a very serious indictable offence by reason of some technical failure on the part of the prosecution with regard to proofs.
[21] In April 1992 the President of the Law Reform Commission (Mr. Justice O'Hanlon) reportedly made a number of public comments on the question of abortion in the light of the judgment of the Supreme Court in *Attorney General v X* [1992] 1 IR 1; [1992] ILRM 401; [1992] 2 CMLR 277: see *The Sunday Tribune*, 5 April 1992. Shortly afterwards, the Taoiseach wrote to him to object to him making public comments on a matter of public controversy and purportedly terminating his appointment as President of the Law Reform Commission. Mr. Justice O'Hanlon then announced that he would withdraw from the Presidency of the Commission, although he felt under no legal compulsion to do so: see *The Irish Times*, 13 April 1992.
[22] Such an enquiry was held in early 1957.
[23] [1959] IR 1; (1960) 94 ILTR 11.

tax were unconstitutional reductions of his remuneration in the sense of Article 35.5. This action was dismissed by Dixon J in the High Court. He reviewed exhaustively the history of the constitutional principle and relatively modern American, Australian and South African cases on the subject, concluding that "the whole trend of judicial opinion" had been against the immunity contended for by the plaintiff. Also:

> "The framers of the [1922] Constitution must have been more familiar with the position previously obtaining as to the judiciary in Great Britain and Ireland than with that elsewhere; and the safeguards of judicial independence inserted in Article 68 were most probably suggested by the British constitutional theory and practice, under which, as has been seen, the taxation of judicial remuneration was not thought of as any inroad or attack on the independence of the judges or as any interference with the guaranteed amount of their remuneration...
>
> The obligation of contributing rateably according to one's means to the expenses of maintaining the organised society in which one lives, and to which one necessarily belongs, must, I think, in the case of a judge, be regarded as an incident of his remuneration rather than, in any real sense, a diminution of it."

On appeal to the Supreme Court this decision was upheld.[24] Maguire CJ said:

> "The purpose of the Article is to safeguard the independence of judges. To require a judge to pay taxes on his income on the same basis as other citizens and thus to contribute to the expenses of government cannot be said to be an attack on his independence."

Kingsmill Moore J said:

> "If the object of the constitutional provision is to safeguard the independence of the Judiciary from pressure or interference by the Executive, this object is attained so long as the tax is not used to discriminate against the judges as such."

With these two judgments Haugh J agreed, thus forming a majority of the Court; central to their view, and that of Dixon J, was the idea that the purpose of the constitutional provision (and of similar provisions in other common law jurisdictions) was to prevent discriminatory penalising of judges in order to bend them to the Government's will. Lavery J (with whom Maguire J agreed) dissented:

> "There is nothing in the provision of the Constitution raising the question of discrimination. The provision is simply that the remuneration is not to be diminished and diminished it is and I cannot find anything to restrict the generality of the provision."

Extreme example of executive and legislative respect for principle

The degree to which the principle of non-reduction of judges' salaries is respected by executive and legislature may appear from a speech of the Minister for the Public Service (Deputy John Boland) in the Dáil in 1983 when introducing the Oireachtas (Allowances to Members) and Ministerial, Parliamentary and Judicial Offices (Amendment) Bill, 1983. This made provision for changes in the remuneration of

[24] In the course of his judgment in this case, Maguire CJ revealed that he himself had put forward this claim to the Government on the judges' behalf in 1950, but that having heard the arguments he was now satisfied that it was baseless.

Oireachtas members and members of the judiciary, arising from cases other than general public service remuneration changes, being made by ministerial order having immediate effect;

> "either increasing or decreasing such remuneration, and such an order would be capable of being annulled by resolution of the Dáil within twenty-one sitting days but without prejudice to anything already done thereunder. However, in the case of the judiciary the order will simply be presented to both Houses but would not, for constitutional reasons, be capable of annulment."[25]

This seems an extreme reading of the constitutional safeguard, which, on another view, is scarcely breached by the general, non-discriminatory application of a common mode of subordinate legislation whereby (in theory)[26] the order is made expressly conditional on its not being annulled within that time-limit.

[25] 345 *Dáil Debates* 1381.

[26] Such ministerial orders are virtually never annulled, as the authority of the Government will normally command a Dáil or Seanad majority in its defence. The hypothesis of a *reduction* in remuneration being the subject of the order itself is, at any rate on past experience, entirely fanciful; though here, of course, the protection of judicial remuneration would operate.

Article 36

ORGANISATION OF THE COURTS

Article 36

Subject to the foregoing provisions of this Constitution relating to the Courts, the following matters shall be regulated in accordance with law, that is to say:-

i. the number of judges of the Supreme Court, and of the High Court, the remuneration, age of retirement and pensions of such judges,

ii. the number of the judges of all other Courts, and their terms of appointment, and

iii. the constitution and organisation of the said Courts, the distribution of jurisdiction and business among the said Courts and judges, and all matters of procedure.

Airteagal 36

Faoi chuimsiú na bhforálacha sin romhainn den Bhunreacht seo a bhaineas leis na Cúirteanna is de réir dlí a rialófar na nithe seo a leanas .i.

i. líon breithiúna na Cúirte Uachtaraí, agus na hArd-Chúirte, tuarastal, aois scortha agus pinsin na mbreithiúna sin,

ii. líon breithiúna gach Cúirte eile, agus na coinníollacha faoina gceaptar iad, agus

iii. comhdhéanamh agus comheagraíocht na gCúirteanna sin, roinnt na dlínse agus na hoibre ar na Cúirteanna sin agus ar na breithiúna sin, agus gach ní a bhaineas le nós imeachta.

1922 Provision

These provisions substantially reproduce Article 57 of the Constitution of 1922.

General effect of Article 36

This Article was incidentally considered by the Supreme Court in *The State (Browne) v Feran*;[1] Walsh J said:

> "By Article 36... all courts other than the Supreme Court and the High Court derive their existence and their jurisdiction only from Acts of the Oireachtas. Counsel... relied upon the provisions of Article 36, and particularly paragraph (iii) thereof, in support of his arguments that the Constitution sought to retain in the hands of the Oireachtas the constitution and organisation of the courts and the distribution of jurisdiction among the courts. Article 36 expressly states that such matters which may fall to be regulated in accordance with law are "subject to the foregoing provisions" of the Constitution. So far as the Supreme Court and the High Court are concerned the provisions of Article 36, while not permitting any restriction of the jurisdiction of those courts not already permitted in the foregoing Articles, may add jurisdictions to those jurisdictions already derived from the Constitution. Examples of such statutorily conferred jurisdictions would be an appellate jurisdiction in the High Court, and a consultative jurisdiction in the High Court. In the case of the Supreme Court such conferred jurisdictions could include a consultative jurisdiction in the Supreme Court and an appellate jurisdiction from decisions of courts other than the High Court. In several instances such jurisdictions have already been conferred."

[1] [1967] IR 147.

Undesirable possibilities of Article 36?

On the face of it, this Article would apparently permit the "flooding" of the Supreme Court (by a statutory increase in the number of its judges sufficient to overbear an existing majority of a tendency unwelcome to a Government), the elimination of senior judges (by a statutory reduction in the existing age of retirement), and the insulation of certain classes of business, or even of a single case, from the activity of a particular judge, by a statutory transfer of the task of distributing court business away from the courts themselves; at present, s 10(3) of the Courts (Supplemental Provisions) Act 1961, declares that "it shall be the function of the President of the High Court...to arrange the distribution and allocation of the business of the High Court", but there is no obvious constitutional bar to this statutory provision being replaced with another which would transfer this function to a non judicial authority. Judges of the Circuit Court are permanently assigned to particular circuits not by the President of the Circuit Court but by the Government, under s 20 of the Courts (Supplemental Provisions) Act 1961, and the Courts Act 1964, s 4; and Judges of the District Court are also permanently assigned to particular districts by the Government (though there may be a temporary change of assignment made by the Minister for Justice with the consent of the District Judge concerned): Courts (Supplemental Provisions) Act 1961, s 31 and Schedule VI.

It is likely, however, that any such potential encroachment on the independence of the judiciary would run into constitutional objections, the apparently wide and permissive language of Article 36 notwithstanding. For example, any reduction in the statutory retirement age for members of the judiciary could presumably not apply to *existing* members of that Court, since this would presumably be regarded as an unjustified infringement of their terms of appointment, and, hence, a violation of the guarantee of independence provided by Article 35.2. Likewise, any attempt on the part of the Executive to influence the composition of a particular court for their own purposes would be likely to be restrained. As Lynch J observed in *Magee v Culligan*[2] (where the possibility that the power to appoint temporary District Judges might be used for this very purpose had been canvassed):

> "The power to appoint a temporary District Judge must be exercised *bona fide* for the purposes mentioned therein[3] and any attempt to exercise such power [to appoint a temporary District Judge for a particular case or a series of cases in the expectation of a particular decision would be contrary to the whole constitutional concept of the administration of justice and would have to be restrained.]"

Present provisions of the law on numbers of judges

The present provision by law for the number of judges of the Supreme Court is four in addition to the Chief Justice and the President of the High Court: Courts (Supplemental Provisions) Act 1961, s 4(1); and the number of ordinary judges of the High Court (i.e. other than the President of the High Court) is fixed at not more than sixteen by the Courts Act 1991, s 17. However, the Law Reform Commission Act 1975, provides by s 14 (as amended by s 17(2) of the Courts Act 1991) that if a Supreme Court or High Court judge is appointed a Commissioner, the number of judges of the Court concerned may be increased so as to make good his absence. Judges of the Circuit Court may num-

[2] [1992] 1 IR 223; [1992] ILRM 186.
[3] Section 51 of the Courts of Justice Act 1936 (as applied by s 48 of the Courts (Supplemental Provisions) Act 1961. This allows the Government to appoint temporary judges where "there is a temporary absence from duty" on the part of any judge or there is an "unusual and temporary increase in business in the District Court."

ber not more than seventeen (in addition to the President of the Court): Courts Act 1991, s 18; and there may be, in addition to the President, not more than forty-five judges of the District Court: Courts Act 1977, s 1(3) (as amended by s 19 of the Courts Act 1991). Provision for temporary appointments[4] to the Circuit Court and District Court is made by the Courts of Justice Act 1936, ss. 14. 51: the Courts of Justice Act 1947, s 4 and Schedule; and the Courts (Supplemental Provisions) Act 1961, s 48(8).

Qualification for judicial appointment

The Constitution does not prescribe any necessary qualification for appointment as a judge; it does not even say that judges must have been professional lawyers on appointment. However, substantial experience in the practice of the barrister's (or, in the case of the District Court, of the solicitor's) profession is made requisite by ss 5, 17, 29 of the Courts (Supplemental Provisions) Act 1961, which to some extent replaces, but mainly merely supplements or adapts the earlier Courts of Justice Acts. In *The State (Walshe) v Murphy,*[5] in which the validity of a temporary District Judge's appointment was challenged on the ground that he did not have the requisite standing as a practising barrister before appointment, the respondent's multiple defence included the argument that the Oireachtas was not authorised by Article 36 to lay down such qualifications as requisite, since such legislation was not covered by the words describing what might be "regulated in accordance with law". A Divisional High Court rejected this contention. Finlay P, with whom Gannon and Hamilton JJ agreed, conceded the respondent's point that the phrase "terms of appointment" must be understood in its ordinary sense and did not include necessary qualifications:

> "Terms of appointment must, it seems, mean the period for which the appointment is made, the remuneration applicable thereto, the date of retirement, the pension attachable to the post and, possibly, other terms applicable to the discharge of the duties involved, such as the locality in which they will be carried out and the provision of staff or assistance and the provision for expenses connected with the discharge of those duties. However, by any ordinary interpretation of the words, it does not appear to me that the phrase includes the qualifications required for a person seeking appointment to the post. In relation to the advertising of posts in the public service and in the world of private commerce, one is accustomed to advertisements which delineate separately the conditions or terms of appointment and the qualifications for appointment."

However, having refused to read an authority to prescribe qualifications out of Article 36.ii, he found it in Article 36.iii, latent in the expression "constitution of the courts". He found a route in the *Oxford English Dictionary* which led from "constitution" through "composition" (supported here by the Irish "comhdhéanamh" = make-up) to "forming"; and also to a sense of "constitute" as meaning "set up, ordain, appoint, establish". He concluded:

> "It seems to me that, since the word "constitution" in Article 36.iii involves the concept of appointment, formation or making up, it would appear to follow that the determination of the qualifications of any person to be appointed as a judge of any court is clearly within the provisions of Article 36.iii."

[4] The constitutionality of this procedure was upheld by the Supreme Court in *Magee v Culligan* [1992] 1 IR 223; [1992] ILRM 186. See p. 551.

[5] [1981] IR 275.

From this starting-point the Court concluded that the temporary District Judge had not, in fact, been qualified[6] for appointment.[7]

This point was taken a step further by Finlay CJ in *Magee v Culligan* where he held that the statutory power to appoint temporary District Judges constituted an exercise by the Oireachtas of its powers under Article 36.ii, inasmuch as it was a "regulation of the terms of appointment of judges of the District Court, and a regulation of the constitution and organisation of those courts."[8]

"Distribution of jurisdiction and business"

Article 36.iii was used by McMahon J in *Ward v Kenehan Electrical Ltd.*[9] to justify s 25 of the Courts of Justice Act 1924, which permits the High Court to remit to the Circuit Court a matter which, though initiated in the High Court, is within the other's jurisdiction. The plaintiff contended that this provision was inconsistent with the "full and original jurisdiction" of the High Court, to which he wished to resort directly, saying he could not be compelled to go to a court of limited and local jurisdiction; but McMahon J pointed to Article 36.iii as qualifying Article 34.3.1: it:

> "enable[d] laws to be made for the distribution of jurisdiction and business among all the courts which may be established under the Constitution including courts of first instance other than the High Court. It follows therefore that business which falls within the full original jurisdiction of the High Court may within the limits express and implied in the Constitution be assigned to some other court."

However, insofar as *Ward* is regarded as an authority for the proposition that Article 36 may be used to derogate from, or qualify the provisions of, Article 34.3.1, it can no longer be supported in view of *R. v R.*[10] and the Supreme Court's decision in *Tormey v Ireland.*[11] In the former case, Gannon J said that Article 36.iii could not be invoked to justify a diminution of the High Court's jurisdiction as it must be read subject to the provisions of Article 34.[12] This view was endorsed by Henchy J, who delivered the judgment of the Supreme Court in *Tormey*:

[6] The Court did not consider what would be the effect of its findings on all the other orders (apart from the conviction of the applicant, which was quashed) made by the invalidly appointed judge. However, in two later cases arising out of criminal convictions purportedly made by an invalidly appointed judge, the Supreme Court had little difficulty in holding that the convictions were invalid and that the defects in the appointment could not be retrospectively cured (as the Oireachtas had attempted to do via the Courts (No. 2) Act 1988): see *Shelly v Mahon* [1990] 1 IR 36; *Glavin v Governor of Mountjoy Prison* [1991] 2 IR 421; [1991] ILRM 478.

[7] But it does not follow that all acquittals are likewise flawed: *McCarthy v Garda Commissioner* [1993] 1 IR 489; [1992] ILRM 186.

[8] In this connection, it is interesting to note that s 1(4) of the Courts (Establishment and Constitution) Act 1961 allows a judge of the High Court to sit at the request of the Chief Justice as a judge of the Supreme Court "on the hearing of an appeal to or other matter cognisable by the Supreme Court." This request may be made where "owing to the illness of a judge of the Supreme Court or for any other reason" a "sufficient number of judges of the Supreme Court is not available for the transaction of the business of that Court." In the light of *Magee's* case, this is, presumably, a valid regulation - by virtue of Article 36.ii - of the constitution and organisation of the business of the Supreme Court.

[9] [1984] IR 289.

[10] [1984] IR 296. See generally, Hogan, "*Constitutional Aspects of the Distribution and Organisation of Court Business*" (1984) 4 DULJ (n.s.) 40.

[11] [1985] IR 289; [1985] ILRM 375. Henchy J nevertheless held that Article 34.3.1 did not prevent jurisdiction being given to lower courts to the exclusion of the High Court: see pp. 411-412. (Costello J had also said at first instance in *Tormey* [1984] ILRM 657 that Article 36 justified legislation conferring exclusive jurisdiction on the lower courts.)

[12] However, he said that the High Court enjoyed an inherent jurisdiction - quite independently of Article 36 - to decline jurisdiction "in accordance with its own procedures" in appropriate cases: see pp. 412-413.

"The question whether any particular statutory vesting of jurisdiction in the District Court or the Circuit Court to the exclusion of the High Court is constitutionally valid cannot be determined by reliance on the provisions of Article 36...While "the said Courts" must be taken in the context to comprehend courts such as the District Court established under Article 34.2.1 as well as the Supreme Court and the High Court, the powers given by Article 36 to Parliament are made expressly "subject to the foregoing provisions of the Constitution relating to the Courts." Among those foregoing provisions of Article 34. Article 36, therefore, cannot be operated or relied on in derogation of the provisions of Article 34."

Article 36 invoked to justify new arrangements for the distribution of court business in lower courts

In *O'R v O'R.*[13] Murphy J invoked Article 36 to justify his refusal to hear a routine family law case, despite the fact that both parties were willing to have the case determined in the High Court. In his view, the Oireachtas had evinced a clear intention that cases arising under the Family Law (Maintenance of Spouses and Children) Act 1981, should be heard in the District or Circuit Courts. Accordingly, the High Court - in the absence of compelling circumstances - should give effect to those wishes:

"It must be recognised that in accordance with Article 36 the Oireachtas is bound to enact legislation regulating in accordance with law (among other things) the constitution and organisation of the courts and the distribution of jurisdiction and business among the courts."

[He then listed reasons why the Circuit Court might seem the best forum for these cases.]:

"The only circumstances in which the [High Court might justifiably intervene would be where it] was satisfied that in the circumstances of a particular case there was a serious danger that justice would not be done if that court declined to exercise the jurisdiction vested in it by the Constitution in relation to that particular case."

[13] [1985] IR 367. See also *The State (Boyle) v Neylon* [1986] ILRM 337 where Gannon J held that the place in which the Circuit Court exercised jurisdiction was a matter for the Oireachtas to legislate on in accordance with Article 36.iii.

EXERCISE OF LIMITED JUDICIAL FUNCTIONS

Article 37

1. **Nothing in this Constitution shall operate to invalidate the exercise of limited functions and powers of a judicial nature, in matters other than criminal matters, by any person or body of persons duly authorised by law to exercise such functions and powers, notwithstanding that such person or such body of persons is not a judge or a court appointed or established as such under this Constitution.**

2. **No adoption of a person taking effect or expressed to take effect at any time after the coming into operation of this Constitution under laws enacted by the Oireachtas and being an adoption pursuant to an order made or an authorisation given by any person or body of persons designated by those laws to exercise such functions and powers was or shall be invalid by reason only of the fact that such person or body of persons was not a judge or a court appointed or established as such under this Constitution.**

Airteagal 37

1. **Aon duine nó aon dream a n-údaraítear go cuí dóibh le dlí feidhmeanna agus cumhachtaí teoranta breithiúnais a oibriú i gcúrsaí nach cúrsaí coireachta, má oibríd na feidhmeanna agus na cumhachtaí sin ní bheidh an t-oibriú sin gan bhail dlí de bhíthin aon ní sa Bhunreacht seo, siúd is nach breitheamh ná cúirt a ceapadh nó a bunaíodh mar bhreitheamh nó mar chúirt faoin mBunreacht seo an duine nó an dream sin.**

2. **Ní raibh ná ní bheidh aon uchtáil ar dhuine a ghlac éifeacht nó a bhfuil sé sainráite gur ghlac sí éifeacht aon tráth tar éis don Bhunreacht seo do theacht i ngníomh faoi dhlíthe a d'achtaigh an tOireachtas agus is uchtáil de bhun ordú do rinne nó údarú do thug aon duine nó aon dream a bhí sonraithe leis na dlíthe sin chun na feadhmeanna agus na cumhachtaí sin da oibriú ó bhail dlí de bhíthin amháin nár bhreitheamh ná cúirt do ceapadh nó do bunaíodh mar bhreitheamh nó mar chúirt faoin mBunreacht seo an duine nó an dream sin.**

Article 37 an innovation

This Article in its original form, which consisted only of its present s 1, and to which nothing in the 1922 Constitution had corresponded, was inserted in the draft Constitution as a response to litigation which had arisen under that Constitution as to the proper boundary between the judicial power of the State properly so called (which under the old Article 64 was to be administered in courts by judges, as the present Article 34.1 similarly requires), and the exercise of powers of a judicial kind by administrative authorities in the setting of their own statutory objects, which had been an increasingly frequent feature of government since the previous century. That litigation took the form of making, and contesting, the case that this exercise of a judicial-type power by administrative authorities - notably the former Land Commission - represented in the Irish setting an unconstitutional usurpation of the judicial power of the State, reserved to courts and judges; and the bearing of Article 37 on this area of problems and on the demarcation of the judicial power generally is discussed in the context of Article 34.1, above, p.

336ff. It is there suggested that the Article may have confused rather than clarified these matters.

Where Article 37 has played an important role has been in confining the quasi-judicial activity of persons or bodies other than judges or courts to matters which the courts regard as *limited* and *non-criminal*. In testing the constitutionality of powers of a judicial nature being entrusted to persons other than judges, therefore, two possibilities must be eliminated before a power of this kind can be considered legitimate: (i) the possibility that the power is exercised in a "criminal matter"; (ii) the possibility that it is not "limited" in its nature.

(I) IS THE POWER TO BE EXERCISED IN A CRIMINAL MATTER?

The first judicial definition of "criminal matter" in the context of Article 37 was provided as recently as 1976, when, in *The State (Murray) v McRann*,[1] a Divisional High Court had to consider in the light of that Article the status of punishments imposed by prison governors, under the Rules for the Government of Prisons 1947, for breaches of prison discipline. Finlay P, with whom Murnaghan and Gannon JJ agreed, found that applying discipline, even to the point of ordering punishment, in the course of prison administration (and presumably of any other analogous specialised system, to which the same reasoning would apply) did not amount to exercising jurisdiction in a criminal matter, even where the act constituting the breach of discipline was (as in this case) also a criminal offence. He said:

> "A crime or criminal charge must be defined...as an offence against the State itself or as a public offence. A criminal matter within the meaning of Article 37 can be construed as a procedure associated with the prosecution of a person for a crime. It may be the preliminary investigation of such a charge, it may be the trial itself, it could be an appeal from the trial or, presumably, an application for bail pending trial or appeal. The essential ingredient of a criminal matter must be its association with the determination of the question as to whether a crime against the State or against the public has been committed.
>
> At no stage is the governor of a prison who operates rules 68 and 69 concerned with the determination of whether the prisoner has committed a crime against the State or against the public. The governor is solely concerned with whether a breach of prison discipline has occurred and, if so, which of the permitted penalties should be imposed. The fact that an act or piece of conduct may constitute both a breach of prison discipline and an offence against the State and the public does not make the investigation an investigation of a criminal matter."

This passage was approved by O'Flaherty J in *Keady v Garda Commissioner*[2] where the Supreme Court rejected a challenge to the validity of a Garda disciplinary inquiry which had found the plaintiff guilty of disciplinary breaches. It was argued that, as the plaintiff had been acquitted of criminal charges arising from the same incidents, the holding of the inquiry had transgressed Article 37 in that the breaches of discipline constituted "criminal matters" within the meaning of Article 37 and, hence, that they could not

[1] [1976] IR 133.
[2] [1992] 2 IR 197; [1992] ILRM 312.

properly be dealt with before such a tribunal. But O'Flaherty J could not accede to this argument:

> "The reference in Article 37....excepting "criminal matters" must mean that there can be no trial of a person on a criminal charge save as provided for in Article 38. This cannot be held to exclude allegations of criminal conduct in other circumstances. Clearly many cases taken in the courts on the civil side may involve allegations of criminality: allegations of dangerous driving, fraud and perjury are random examples. There is no constitutional basis for saying that such allegations cannot be aired before administrative tribunals or before inquiries which have a statutory basis or at other domestic tribunals or inquiries."

This approach is also evident in *Goodman International v Hamilton (No.1)*[3] where the plaintiffs had claimed that the terms of reference of a Tribunal of Inquiry[4] established by resolution of the Dáil and Seanad had usurped the role of the judiciary in the administration of justice. The Supreme Court held that, in investigating these matters, the Tribunal was not conducting an administration of justice, so that the possible application of Article 37 did not arise. Hederman J, however, said that Article 37 could only apply where "there is of necessity some form of trial or adjudication" and McCarthy J added that the determination of the truth or falsity of allegations was not the sole prerogative of the judiciary, since the "critical factor is trial and adjudication, not inquiry."

In an earlier case, *Cowan v Attorney General,*[5] Haugh J heard a challenge to legislation under which an election petition to have the plaintiff declared disqualified (for bankruptcy) from candidature for the Dublin City Council was assigned to be tried by a practising barrister. Examining the powers envisaged for the election court by the nineteenth-century Acts governing it, he concluded that:

> "an election court, even if only exercising limited functions and powers of a judicial nature, must of necessity be ready at all times to exercise its powers in the criminal matters assigned to it [which included the trial of charges of corrupt or illegal practices, and the infliction of fines or imprisonment by way of punishment] either of its own volition or at the request of the Attorney General -a function that is expressly prohibited by the Constitution. For these reasons I must hold that the election court when it sits to hear any matter is unconstitutional."

No appeal was taken from his finding to the Supreme Court; but, if his view was correct, it would mean that Article 37 forbids the exercise of a judicial function by a person not a judge even where, in a particular case, no question of trying a criminal charge arises, if the function inherently contains such a power, provided that the non-judicial personage has the power to try and adjudicate.[6]

Internment without trial an exercise of criminal justice?

In *The State (Burke) v Lennon,*[7] in which Gavan Duffy J held that a Minister in ordering

[3] [1992] 2 IR 542; [1992] ILRM 145. See generally, Ní Raifeartáigh, "*Goodman and the Beef Tribunal*" (1992) 2 ICLJ 141.

[4] These concerned allegations "concerning illegal activities, fraud and malpractice in or connection with the beef processing industry made or referred to (a) Dáil Éireann and (b) on a television programme transmitted on 13 May 1991."

[5] [1961] IR 411.

[6] This rider is necessary in view of the comments of McCarthy J in the *Goodman* case to the effect that the critical and - to his mind, the key distinguishing feature - between that case and the *Cowan* case, was that in the latter case there was "trial and adjudication" and not simply a mere "inquiry", as in the *Goodman* case.

[7] [1940] IR 136; (1940) 74 ILTR 36, 131.

an internment under Part VI of the Offences Against the State Act 1939, was purporting to administer justice, the judge thought his conclusion that this was unconstitutional was:

> "fortified by Article 37...expressly authorising a law to empower an officer who is not a judge to exercise limited functions and powers of a judicial nature in non-criminal matters; the Article must imply that no such jurisdiction can be conferred by law in a criminal matter, so that criminal justice is exercisable only by a person who is a judge under the Constitution."[8]

This position seems unsound. The proceeding authorised by that Act (and, since 1940 by the Offences against the State (Amendment) Act of that year) cannot be described as a criminal matter: the opinion which the Minister must form (that the person concerned "is engaged in activities which, in his opinion, are prejudicial to the preservation of public peace and order or to the security of the State") does not amount to a criminal charge or even to an opinion imputing criminal conduct, nor does internment purport to be a punishment.

Are the functions of the Peace Commissioners and the District Court clerks in criminal proceedings constitutionally suspect?

In *The State (Lynch) v Ballagh*[9] the constitutionality of certain functions exercised by Peace Commissioners under s 15 of the Criminal Justice Act 1951 (as inserted by s 26 of the Criminal Justice Act 1984) was called (*obiter*) into question. These provisions enable a Peace Commissioner, having heard evidence, to exercise a discretion as to whether the prisoner shall be remanded in custody or on bail. Walsh J said in the Supreme Court:

> "These are functions which when carried out by the District Court are clearly judicial functions. As Peace Commissioners in the exercise of these functions are not within the provisions of either Article 34 or Article 37... their position appears to be constitutionally somewhat dubious."

Finlay CJ also adverted to this problem some months later in *The State (Clarke) v Roche*.[10] This case concerned the compatibility of computer-issued summonses with ss 10 and 11 of the Petty Sessions (Ireland) Act 1851, which require that the complaint shall have been personally communicated to the District Court clerk prior to the issue of the summons. The Supreme Court held that the computer summons procedure did not comply with this requirement, Finlay CJ saying that it was an "inescapable conclusion" from the terms of s 10 of the 1851 Act that the issue of a summons following a com-

[8] The view which Gavan Duffy J took of internment as a judge he had previously advanced as an advocate: see *R. (O'Connell) v Military Governor, Hare Park Camp* [1924] 2 IR 104. As to the possibility that he inspired the inclusion of Article 37 in the draft Constitution of 1937, see above, p. 335. In *Mulloy v Sheehan* [1978] IR 438 Kenny J specifically differed from what Gavan Duffy J had said in *Burke's* case: "My present view is that the use of the word "satisfied" does not have the consequence that the person who has to be satisfied is exercising the judicial power of the State." Nor is there even a trace of this suggestion of Gavan Duffy J's in any of the later cases involving such statutory formulae: see, e.g., *The State (Lynch) v Cooney* [1982] IR 337; *Kiberd v Tribunal of Inquiry* [1992] ILRM 574.

[9] [1986] IR 203; [1987] ILRM 65. There is, however, no constitutional impediment to the issue of search warrants by a Peace Commissioner under s 42 of the Larceny Act 1916, as this has been held not to involve a judicial function: see *Ryan v O'Callaghan*, High Court, 22 July 1987, *Berkeley v Edwards* [1988] IR 217; *Byrne v Grey* [1988] IR 31 and *Farrell v Farrelly* [1988] IR 201.

[10] [1986] IR 619; [1987] ILRM 309. This problem was also present in *Rainey v Delap* [1988] IR 470; [1988] ILRM 620.

plaint was a judicial as distinct from an administrative act. He drew attention to the words of Walsh J in *Lynch's* case, and, while reserving his position, appeared to imply that the issuing of summonses by a non-judicial personage by virtue of this procedure was the administration of criminal justice and, therefore, outside Article 37.

Section 1(1) of the Courts (No.3) Act 1986, attempts to circumvent these difficulties by providing that District Court proceeding may be commenced "by the issuing, as a matter of administrative procedure", of a summons by the appropriate District Court office. At first sight the constitutionality of this provision might seem doubtful, given that it is not open to the Oireachtas to make what is in fact a judicial act an administrative one by merely declaring it to be so. However, as s 1(8) of the Act makes clear, s 1(1) creates an entirely new administrative procedure for issuing summonses, which is altogether outside the scope of the Petty Sessions (Ireland) Act 1851. Whereas s 10(4) of the 1851 Act required the District Court clerk to decide whether the complainant had established that there was a *prima facie* case before he issued the summons against the defendant (which, of course, led Finlay CJ to conclude in *Clarke's* case that this was the administration of criminal justice), these difficulties seem to be avoided by the solution of the 1986 Act which simply excises altogether from the criminal process the exercise of a vestigial preliminary discretion not, apparently, constitutionally essential to it. [11]

This entire issue was also considered by Keane J in *O'Mahony v Melia,*[12] where the plaintiffs had been remanded in custody overnight by a Peace Commissioner. The decision to remand the plaintiffs in custody was held to be a judicial function, and one which, in this instance, could not be saved by reference to Article 37 since the function in question had been discharged in relation to a criminal matter.[13]

Functions of the Employment Appeals Tribunal constitutionally suspect?

The Employment Appeals Tribunal (which is not composed of judges) was established by the Employment Equality Act 1977. The Tribunal is empowered to award compensation to dismissed employees up to a maximum sum of an amount representing two years' salary. The Tribunal would appear to be administering justice and it must be an open question as to whether its powers are "limited" within the meaning of Article 37. While the constitutionality of the 1977 has never directly been impugned, in *Government of Canada v Employment Appeals Tribunal*[14] McKenzie J drew attention to these potential constitutional difficulties.

(II) IS THE POWER NOT A LIMITED ONE?

Any statutory power, whether of a judicial or any other nature, is in one sense necessarily "limited", since it can be exercised only within the four corners of the area, great or small, which the statute marks out and "delimits". It is not, however, in this sense that the courts have understood the word in the Article 37 context, but rather in the senses of "modest", "not far-reaching", "confined to special situations"; in other words, in senses

[11] This seems implicit in the judgment of the Supreme Court in *Director of Public Prosecutions v Nolan* [1990] 2 IR 526. As Blayney J said in *Toss Ltd. v Dublin Metropolitan District Justice*, High Court, 24 November 1987, the 1986 Act "does make the issue of a summons an administrative act."

[12] [1989] IR 335; [1990] ILRM 14.

[13] Keane J accordingly held that s 15 of the Criminal Justice Act 1951 (as substituted by s 24 of the Criminal Justice Act 1984) - which purported to confer such powers of remand on Peace Commissioners - was unconstitutional.

[14] [1991] ELR 57. On appeal ([1992] ILRM 325), the Supreme Court did not address these issues.

which leave much room for subjective judicial appraisal, since there appears to be no objective criterion for any of these notions.

The first full consideration of Article 37[15] and of the question of "limited" powers was in *In re Solicitors Act 1954*,[16] when the appellants, who had been struck off the roll of solicitors by order of the Disciplinary Committee of the Incorporated Law Society, contended that this function was unconstitutional since the Committee was not a court nor were its members judges, and that the function of striking-off was not a "limited" one. The Supreme Court held with them, declaring the relevant parts of the Solicitors Act 1954, invalid. Kingsmill Moore J said:

> "There is no question here of a domestic tribunal with a jurisdiction based solely on contract... Here we are dealing with a tribunal which depends for its existence and its powers on a legislative act of the State. If the effect of such legislation is to confer the power to administer justice on persons who are not regularly appointed as judges it is by Article 34 unconstitutional, unless it can be brought within some of the saving provisions of the Constitution."[17]

Could the process of striking a solicitor off the rolls be brought within the saving provision of Article 37 as a "limited function or power"? The Supreme Court thought not:

> "A tribunal having but a few powers and functions but those of far-reaching effect and importance could not properly be regarded as exercising "limited" powers and functions...If the exercise of the assigned powers and functions is calculated ordinarily to affect in the most profound and far-reaching way the lives, liberties, fortunes or reputations of those against whom they are exercised they cannot properly be described as "limited"...The power to strike a solicitor off the rolls is a "disciplinary" and "punitive" power...It is a sanction of such severity that in its consequences it may be much more serious than a term of imprisonment...The powers and functions conferred by the Act...are of such a far-reaching nature that their exercise amounts to an administration of justice, nor...can they be described as merely limited powers and functions of a judicial nature within Article 37. Their exercise is unconstitutional. It follows that the two appellants were not validly struck off the roll of solicitors."

In a slightly later case, however - *In re Solicitors Act 1954, and D., a Solicitor*[18] - Maguire CJ distinguished the Supreme Court's earlier decision on that Act. Here the solicitor concerned had not been struck off the rolls, but merely denied a practising certificate for a period of a year, in other words his right to practise had merely been temporarily suspended; and the decision to deny him the certificate had been made in a procedure which provided for an appeal to the Chief Justice, so that it was not final as the decision of the Disciplinary Committee in the earlier case was intended to be. Maguire CJ held that the Society's direction was not an administration of justice, and appeared to imply also that, even if it was, the nature of the sanction made the function a limited one

[15] Article 37 had been mentioned in passing in earlier cases such as *The State (Burke) v Lennon* [1940] IR 136; (1940) 74 ILTR 36, 131: *In re Loftus Bryan's Estate* [1942] IR 185; (1941) 75 ILTR 82 and *Fisher v Irish Land Commission* [1948] IR 3; (1948) 82 ILTR 50: see p. 336.
[16] [1960] IR 239.
[17] In *Geoghegan v Institute of Chartered Accountants in Ireland*, High Court, 9 July 1993, Murphy J referred to this passage and said that it demonstrated that the Supreme Court was considering "not merely activities which had in their appearances and consequences (however severe) the hallmarks of the administration of justice, but also the source of the power to engage in such activities."
[18] (1961) 95 ILTR 60.

in the sense of Article 37. The Supreme Court reversed his order on appeal, but on the merits of the actual case, and the Court did not consider its constitutional aspect.

Another case in which an objection based on Article 37 failed - inasmuch as the function being exercised did not go as far as the *Solicitors Act* case test - was *Central Dublin Development Association v Attorney General.*[19] Kenny J held in the High Court that the power of a Minister under the Local Government (Planning and Development) Act 1963, to decide what was "development" and what was "exempted development", although an "administration of justice", was a limited power. He noted that there was an appeal from the Minister's decision to the High Court, and said:

> "I do not think that the decision as to what is or is not development or exempted development affects the fortunes of citizens in a profound way because the result of the Minister's decision is that planning permission has to be obtained. The Minister's decision does not decide finally that a particular development cannot be carried out; it decides only that permission is or is not required."

(He observed, it may be noted, that he thought it:

> "impossible...to formulate a test by which limited functions and powers of a judicial nature can be distinguished from those which are unlimited because the scope and effect of the functions and powers must be considered in each case.)"

Three years after the first *Solicitors Act* case the High Court followed it in *Cowan v Attorney General.*[20] Haugh J said:

> "If the plaintiff can establish that the defendant... when sitting as commissioner on an election court, is doing more than exercising limited functions or powers of a judicial nature, or is exercising any functions or powers in matters that are criminal, then the statutes that create such office are clearly repugnant to both Articles 34 and 37... since he is not a judge appointed in the manner provided by the Constitution acting in courts established by law."

The judge then expressly applied a test formulated in the first *Solicitors Act* case:

> "An election court when commencing the hearing of an election petition may know what it is about to try, but if and when, in any petition, the court should, of its own volition, order the attendance of a new witness or witnesses, entirely new issues may arise that may involve findings by the court that could well affect, in the most profound and far-reaching way, the lives, liberties, fortunes or reputations of those against whom they are exercised; and I am of opinion that the [election] court, availing of all the powers and duties conferred upon it in its ordinary day-to-day exercise of its powers and functions, is in fact not exercising the limited functions and powers allowable by Article 37, and is therefore unconstitutional."

(He found also, as has been seen, that it was illicit for its potential exercise of functions in criminal matters.)

[19] (1975) 109 ILTR 69.

[20] [1961] IR 411. In *Goodman International v Hamilton (No.1)* [1992] 2 IR 542; [1992] ILRM 145 McCarthy J appears to have implicitly approved of the tests of far-reaching effect laid down in both *Cowan* and *Central Dublin Development*, but found them inapplicable in the context of a challenge to the establishment of a Tribunal of Inquiry which, by definition, could make no adjudication or decision.

In *McDonald v Bord na gCon (No. 2)*[21] Kenny J followed the *Solicitors Act* principle in the High Court, finding, in regard to the function of making exclusion orders against persons associated with the greyhound industry, that:

> "the power to make such an order is calculated ordinarily to affect in a most profound and far-reaching way the fortunes and reputations of owners and trainers... In my opinion the powers and functions conferred on the Board by s 47 of the Act are not limited in the sense which that word has been given by the decision of the Supreme Court in *In re Solicitors Act 1954*."

(The Supreme Court, however, took the view that the Board was not exercising judicial powers within the meaning of Article 37 at all - "an essential difference between the judgment of this Court and the judgment of Mr. Justice Kenny".)

The test laid down by the former Supreme Court in *Solicitors Act* case was applied by Finlay P in *M. v Medical Council*[22] where the plaintiff had challenged the constitutionality of ss 45 - 48 of the Medical Practitioners Act 1978, on the ground that these provisions purported to give the defendants judicial powers of a non-limited nature in relation to certain disciplinary matters. Finlay P said that there was a "very striking difference" between the extent and nature of the powers conferred on the disciplinary committee of the Law Society in the *Solicitors Act* case and those conferred on the defendants here:

> "Neither the Committee nor the [Medical] Council has any power to erase the name of a practitioner from the register, to suspend him from his practice, to attach conditions to the continuation of his practice, to make him pay compensation or to award costs against him. The only power vested in them in regard to any of these matters (other than payment of compensation - which is not provided in the Act at all) is to initiate proceedings in the High Court which may lead to an order being made by the High Court in respect of any of those matters."

Finlay P concluded that the powers vested in the defendants were not, in fact, judicial powers at all, and that even if they were, they were clearly "limited" in nature:

> "The only powers of the Committee or the Council which could be said to be final and, in a sense, binding are the publication of a finding by the Committee of misconduct or unfitness to practise and the Council's power to advise, admonish or censure a practitioner. Even if it could be said that the publication to the public of a finding by a committee of enquiry of misconduct or unfitness was something affecting the rights of a practitioner...or if the same could be said of advising, admonishing or censuring...these would be functions so clearly limited in their effect and consequence that they would be within the exception provided by Article 37...even if they constituted the administration of justice."

Similar statutory safeguards are to be found in other recent legislation: see the Dentists Act 1985, Part V and the Nurses Act 1985, Part V and the necessity for such elaborate procedures was probably prompted by official apprehensions as to the implications of the *Solicitors Act* case. That such fears were probably well founded is attested to by the judgment of Finlay CJ in *K v An Bord Altranais.*[23] Having observed that, under the pro-

[21] [1965] IR 217; (1966) 100 ILTR 89.
[22] [1984] IR 485.
[23] [1990] 2 IR 396.

visions of the Nurses Act 1985, the High Court alone retained the power to suspend or de-bar nurses from the register, the Chief Justice explained that:

> "The necessity for that procedure to vest that power unequivocally in the courts, in my view arises from the constitutional frailty that would attach to the delegation of any such power to a body which was not a court established under the Constitution having regard to the decision of the former Supreme Court in *In re Solicitors Act...*"

Some judicial unhappiness with the Solicitors Act test now evident

Recently, however, there is clear evidence of judicial unhappiness with the logical implications of the *Solicitors Act* case[24] and nearly all the recent cases show a tendency either to confine that case to its special facts or to refuse to apply the principle by analogy. A good example of this recent trend is provided by the judgment of Barron J in relation to the powers of the Appeal Commissioners under Part XXVI of the Income Tax Act 1967, in *The State (Calcul International Ltd. and Solatrex International Ltd) v Appeal Commissioners*,[25] holding that the powers of the Appeal Commissioners were confined to deciding whether:

> "the assessment raised by the tax inspector should be reduced or increased. They do not have power to enforce their decisions nor to impose liabilities. Essentially, their decisions are enforced by the institution of legal proceedings to recover the amount of tax determined by them as being payable."

He said that, applying the test of Kingsmill Moore J in the *Solicitors Act* case, the making of an order having such characteristics and effect could not be regarded as an administration of justice. But, even if he was wrong on this point, he was nonetheless prepared to hold that the powers in question were "limited" judicial powers for the purposes of Article 37. The applicants had argued that the Act purported to entitle the Appeal Commissioners to decide any issue of fact of whatever kind and to exercise a jurisdiction unlimited in amount; the judge, however, thought the test was:

> "the effect of the assigned power when exercised. So the nature of a power as opposed to its effect when exercised is immaterial...In reality, the decision has no effect on the fortune of the taxpayer, since the Appeal Commissioners do no more than decide the amount for which the taxpayer was always liable. Their decision may well affect the particular taxpayer adversely since he may be found liable to pay a sum for which he believes he was not liable. But this does not have far-reaching effects. The payment of customs duty or value-added tax is related proportionately to the relevant taxable income. Such payments cannot have far-reaching effects on the fortune of the taxpayer...since in each case the liability is relative, being proportionate either to his income or to his turnover, as the case may be.""

[24] This trend was forecast by Casey, "*The Judicial Power under Irish Constitutional Law*" (1975) 24 ICLQ 305.

[25] High Court, 18 December 1986. Another example may be found the judgment of McMahon J in *Madden v Ireland*, High Court, May 22, 1980 where he held that the fixing by the Land Commission of the price of lands to be compulsorily acquired by it. Starting from the perception that modern government requires a large range of regulatory agencies which cannot be accommodated under a rigid separation of powers, McMahon J said that he thought this price-fixing function was of a kind which Article 37 was intended to cover and, by this route, arrived at the conclusion that the function was of a limited nature. It will be observed that the sequence of reasoning here is the reverse of that used in the *Solicitors Act* case, although the judge specifically referred to that case in his judgment.

This reasoning seems very questionable. If the Appeal Commissioners err in their method of assessing a taxpayer's income, the effect of the resulting tax bill could well be far-reaching.

This trend continued in *Keady v Garda Commissioner*[26] in which O'Flaherty J described the *Solicitors Act* case as "anomalous" and hinted that the ambit of this decision should be strictly limited, if not, indeed, curtailed. Here a member of the Garda Síochána who had been dismissed from the force claimed that the Garda Síochána (Discipline) Regulations 1971,[27](which allowed the Garda Commissioner to authorise such dismissal) were constitutionally objectionable in view of the principle of the *Solicitors Act* case. Both McCarthy and O'Flaherty JJ stressed that the *Solicitors Act* decision concerned - as the former put it - the right of an individual:

> "to work in an occupation for which he has been trained over a period of and achieved an expertise and certified qualification. If he loses that certificate and holds himself out as being so qualified, he commits a criminal offence."

O'Flaherty J added that the *Solicitor's Act* case was to be distinguished from the present case because while a Garda "who is dismissed loses his immediate employment he does not lose any qualification by virtue of his dismissal."[28]

Exclusive jurisdiction over justiciable controversies may be given under the cover of Article 37

Some other miscellaneous aspects of Article 37 may now be mentioned. In *Tormey v Ireland*[29] Henchy J said that it was implicit in Article 37 that, despite the general grant of full original jurisdiction to the High Court by Article 34.3.1, the jurisdiction thus vested:

> "in courts, tribunals, persons or bodies other than the High Court must be taken to be capable of being exercised, at least in certain cases, to the exclusion of the High Court, for the allocation of jurisdiction would otherwise be overlapping and unworkable."

Exercise of the Article 37-type function does not preclude review by the High Court

Henchy J also noted in *Tormey's* case that, where such exclusive jurisdiction had been devolved on a tribunal under cover of Article 37, the High Court would not hear and determine the matter or question but:

> "its full jurisdiction is there to be invoked - in proceedings such as *habeas corpus, certiorari, prohibition, mandamus, quo warranto*, injunction or a declaratory action - so as to ensure that the hearing and determination will be in accordance with law. Save to the extent required by the terms of the Constitution itself, no justiciable matter may be excluded from the range of the original jurisdiction of the High Court."[30]

[26] [1992] 1 IR 197; [1992] ILRM 312.
[27] Which have now been superseded by the Garda Síochána (Discipline) Regulations 1989.
[28] A similar approach was taken by Murphy J in *Geoghegan v Institute of Chartered Accountants in Ireland*, High Court 9 July 1993.
[29] [1985] IR 289; [1985] ILRM 375.
[30] Gavan Duffy J had previously arrived at the same conclusion in *O'Doherty v Attorney General* [1941] IR 569; (1941) 75 ILTR 171.

This means that statutory ouster clauses designed to prevent judicial review of administrative decisions cannot constitutionally preclude such review, at least in cases where the tribunal has been invested with an exclusive jurisdiction in respect of a particular category of justiciable controversy under cover of Article 37.

Uncertainty resolved in the adoption context by amendment

The uncertainty of this whole area had the result that in the course of the hearing of *M. v An Bord Uchtála*[31] misgivings began to arise as to whether the function of making adoption orders might not be capable of accommodation within the notion of "limited" functions and powers. As any such finding - although not claimed in that particular case - would automatically threaten the stability of thousands of families and their adoptive children, the Sixth Amendment of the Constitution was promoted in order to add to Article 37 the provision which now constitutes the Article's second section.

Whether such a technique of *ad hoc* amendment of Article 37 is advisable may be doubted. Over and above its immediate object it may have unsuspected constructional implications in the future. It may be argued, in a context not foreseen in 1979, that the people, by specifically protecting the function of making adoption orders from attack under Article 37, impliedly admit that this function is not a "limited" one, and that similarly some other function now in administrative hands, of importance comparable with the function of the Adoption Board, must be deemed illicit under Article 37. [32]

Article 37.2 was considered for the first time by Barron J in *J.M. and M.M. v An Bord Uchtála*,[33] where the issue was whether it lay within the competence of the Board to determine whether a child was illegitimate. He thought it did, and said the effect of Article 37.2 was that:

> "not only can the adoption order itself not be impugned... but equally any step taken by the Adoption Board to enable it to make such an order is likewise incapable of being impugned."

Whether Article 37.2 will bear such a construction is doubtful, as the language of the sub-Article prevents any adoption being invalid "by reason only of the fact" that the members of An Bord Uchtála were not constituted as judges or a court established under the provisions of the Constitution.

Determination covered by Article 37 gets benefit of the res judicata rule

One statement of Gavan Duffy J on aspects of proceedings protected by Article 37 may, finally, be briefly noted. In *Athlone Woollen Mills v Athlone U.D.C.*[34] he suggested that a function under Article 37 sufficiently partook of the nature of a judicial decision to attract the benefit of the *res judicata* rule; he said the grant of a planning permission:

[31] [1977] IR 287.

[32] On the other hand, the judgment of Finlay CJ in *Attorney General v Hamilton* (*No.1*)[1993] 2 IR 250;[1993] ILRM 81 strongly suggests that a later amendment of the Constitution enacted for a particular purpose cannot be used as an aid to the construction of other provisions of the Constitution.

[33] High Court, 15 April 1986. This question was not addressed by the Supreme Court on appeal: see [1988] ILRM 203.

[34] [1950] IR 1.

"involves the exercise of limited powers of a judicial nature, so that the decision is properly described as a judicial decision pronounced by a judicial tribunal, as those terms are understood in relation to the doctrine of *res judicata*. I am of opinion that the doctrine of *res judicata* with the consequent estoppel applies."

TRIAL OF OFFENCES IN DUE COURSE OF LAW

Trial of Offences

Article 38

1. No person shall be tried on any criminal charge save in due course of law.

Triail i gCionta

Airteagal 38

1. Ní cead aon duine a thriail in aon chúis choiriúil ach mar is cuí de réir dlí.

1922 provision echoes earlier history

This sentence corresponds with the opening words of Article 70 of the 1922 Constitution, but longer pedigree was established by Kenny J in *Conroy v Attorney General*;[1]

> "I think that s 1 of the Article is an echo of a clause in the Great Charter of Ireland granted in 1216...[The] phrase "due process of law" was adopted by those who drafted the Fifth Amendment to the Constitution of the United States of America which prevents any person being deprived of life, liberty or property without due process of law. I think that s 1 of the Article gives a constitutional right to every person to be tried in accordance with the law and in accordance with due course or due process of law."

Similar sentiments were expressed by McCarthy J in *Goodman International v Hamilton (No.1)*[2] when he said that the language of Article 38.1 was "an echo of the phrase 'due process of law' in the Fifth Amendment of the US Constitution" and that for this reason the jurisprudence of the US Supreme Court on this topic was particularly relevant.[3]

"Shall be tried...": nature of a criminal trial

Article 38.1 is plainly referable to the *trial* of offences, but the novel question of whether the Oireachtas is free to establish parallel procedures providing for the investigation of alleged criminal (or potentially criminal) conduct was examined by the Supreme Court in *Goodman International v Hamilton (No.1)*[4]. In this case, the Oireachtas had established a Tribunal of Inquiry pursuant to the Tribunals of Inquiry Acts, 1921-1979 to investigate allegations of illegal activities, fraud and malpractice in the beef industry which had been made both in the Oireachtas and on a television programme. The applicants (who were the subject-matter of many of the allegations) claimed, *inter alia,* that the adoption of these procedures violated Article 38.1 inasmuch as they provided for an *ersatz* and constitutionally irregular form of criminal trial. The Supreme Court rejected these submissions, saying that even the investigation of whether criminal acts had been committed by a named person and the reporting to the Oireachtas of the truth or falsity of such an allegation could not "under any circumstances" be regarded as amounting to a trial on a criminal charge. As Finlay CJ explained:

> "The essential ingredient of a trial of a criminal offence in our law...is that it is had before a court or judge which has got the power to punish in the event of a verdict

[1] [1965] IR 411.

[2] [1992] 2 IR 542; [1992] ILRM 145.

[3] Although he conceded that the actual prescription of the Fifth Amendment - not to be deprived of life, liberty or property without due process of law - might have a "wider scope" than that of Article 38.1.

[4] [1992] 2 IR 542; [1992] ILRM 145.

of guilty. It is of the essence of a trial on a criminal charge or a trial on a criminal offence that the proceedings are accusatorial, involving a prosecutor and an accused, and that the sole object and purpose of the verdict, be it one of acquittal or of conviction, is to form the basis for either a discharge of the accused from the jeopardy in which he stood, in the case of an acquittal, or for his punishment for the crime which he has committed, in the case of a conviction."

The Chief Justice went on to point out that the Tribunal had "none of those features": it had no jurisdiction to impose a punishment or penalty. Its findings could not form the basis of either an acquittal or conviction of a person on a criminal charge: the Tribunal was a simple "fact-finding operation" which reported to the Oireachtas. This approach seems unduly formalistic. It is certainly true that one could scarcely raise a constitutional objection just because a tribunal or other administrative body is required to consider allegations of criminal impropriety, but it is surely a different matter where the Tribunal is empowered to bringing in specific findings of criminal wrong-doing. In such circumstances, it is surely cold comfort to the citizen concerned to be told that no specific *penalty* had been or could be imposed if he has nonetheless been stigmatised by a public finding that he has engaged in (possibly very serious) criminal wrong-doing.[5]

"DUE COURSE OF LAW": ELEMENTS OF THIS STANDARD

"Due course of law" not defined

The precise extent, or content, of the concept "due course of law" is not specified in Kenny J's judgment in *Conroy's* case or elsewhere; in *The State (Healy) v Donoghue*[6] Gannon J called it:

> "a phrase of very wide import which includes in its scope not merely matters of constitutional and statutory jurisdiction, the range of legislation with respect to criminal offences, and matters of practice and procedure, but also the application of basic principles of justice which are inherent in the proper course of the exercise of the judicial function."

Judicially expounded

Notwithstanding the imprecision which must necessarily attend a phrase such as "trial in due course of law", there have nonetheless been several judicial attempts to expand on its meaning. Kenny J had said in 1966 in *McDonald v Bord na gCon (No. 3)*[7] that the requirement of "due course of law" meant that a lower court (though obviously the dic-

[5] Such concerns were powerfully expressed by Murphy J in his dissenting judgment in *Victoria v Australian Building Construction Employees' and Builders Labourers' Federation* (1981-2) 152 CLR 25. The majority of Australian High Court upheld the validity of an inquiry into an alleged bribery scandal, but Murphy J held that the establishment of the tribunal violated the separation of powers:

> "It is a fine point to answer that the finding is not binding and does not of itself make the person liable to punitive consequences. It is by fine points such as this that human freedom is whittled away...If a government chooses not to prosecute, the fact that the finding is not binding on any court is of little comfort to the person found guilty; there is no legal proceeding which he can institute to establish his innocence. If he is prosecuted, the investigations and findings may have created ineradicable prejudice..."

Hederman J referred to this passage and commented - rather complacently, it may be thought - that it identified "a danger that such powers [of inquiry] might be abused. If this were to happen the courts would restrain it." See generally, Ní Raifeartáigh, "*Goodman v Beef Tribunal*" (1992) 2 ICLJ 141.

[6] [1976] IR 325; (1976) 110 ILTR 9.

[7] High Court, 21 January 1966.

tum must apply to a superior court also) "should have *some* evidence before it on which in a criminal case it may legitimately decide that the citizen is guilty of the offence charged against him". In the *Criminal Law (Jurisdiction) Bill 1975*[8] (a reference to the Supreme Court under Article 26) O'Higgins CJ in delivering the Court's opinion said that Article 38.1 required:

> "fair and just treatment for the person so charged, having due regard to the rights of the State to prosecute for the offence charged and to ensure that the person so charged will stand his trial. The phrase "due course of law" requires a fair and just balance between the exercise of individual freedoms and the requirements of an ordered society." [9]

In *Eccles v Ireland*,[10] the Supreme Court appeared to suggest that Article 38.1 prescribes - quite apart from the special guarantees in Articles 34 and 35 - a minimum standard for any administration of justice. The plaintiffs, who had been convicted by the Special Criminal Court of capital murder, attacked the constitutionality of s 39 of the Offences Against the State Act 1939, on the ground that it allowed the Government to terminate the appointment of individual members of that Court for the reason only that their decisions did not suit the executive. Finlay CJ rejected that construction of the Act on the ground that any such interference would constitute an attempt:

> "to frustrate the constitutional right of persons accused before that Court to a trial in due course of law... Whilst the Special Criminal Court does not attract the express guarantees of judicial independence contained in Article 35, it does have, derived [from the rights of the accused person under Article 38.1] a guarantee of independence in the carrying out of its functions."

It has also been suggested that long-established principles of criminal justice are protected by Article 38.1. Thus, in *O'Leary v Attorney General*[11] Costello J said that since the presumption of innocence "had long been an integral part of the common law tradition" and a "fundamental postulate" of every criminal trial, a statutory provision which permitted a trial otherwise than in accordance with that presumption would prima facie conflict with Article 38.1. And yet this historical analysis will not always be decisive. For example, the rule which barred a prosecution appeal against a jury verdict of not guilty was just as much a "fundamental postulate" of our criminal justice system even though this rule has not survived in the face of constitutional challenge.[12] In this context, just as with Article 40.3, the courts are faced with profound difficulties in identifying criteria which will allow them to give effect to general principles latent in these provisions.[13]

Perhaps because of the very lack of particularity in the phrase, it seems to be used in constitutional proceedings to mean fairness in any form not easily defined or not falling into some familiar category. Nevertheless, it seems plain that the guarantee in Article

[8] [1977] IR 129; (1976) 110 ILTR 69.

[9] This is a very frequently cited passage: see, e.g., the comments of Murphy J in *The State (O'Connell) v Fawsitt* [1986] IR 362; [1986] ILRM 639.

[10] [1985] IR 545.

[11] [1993] 1 IR 102; [1991] ILRM 454.

[12] *People (Director of Public Prosecutions) v O'Shea* [1982] IR 384.

[13] See generally at pp. 671-678. Note that in *O'Leary v AG* [1993] 1 IR 102; [1991] ILRM 454, Costello J was prepared to look at international conventions and instruments (including the UN Universal Declaration of Human Rights and the European Convention on Human Rights and Fundamental Freedoms in order to ascertain whether the right in question enjoyed constitutional protection.

38.1 is not confined to procedural matters only (as the words "save in due course of law" might be thought to imply), but also embraces important substantive rights.

In *The State (Vozza) v Ó' Floinn*,[14] where the applicant had been convicted by a District Judge after a summary trial on a charge of robbery, not having been informed of his right to be tried by jury for a non-minor offence like this, the Supreme Court held that he had been tried by the judge without jurisdiction, and so (Kingsmill Moore J said) had not been "tried in due course of law"; the same was said by Gannon J in *The State (McDonagh) v Barry*[15] of a process in the District Court, culminating in the imposition of a sentence of imprisonment, which was irregular in several respects. In *The State (Kenny) v Ó hÚadhaigh*[16] the applicant attacked s 123 of the Children Act 1908, on the ground that by potentially removing the benefit of s 102 (no imprisonment for a child under fifteen) from a child who mis-states his age as over fifteen, a trial in which the section was applied was not a trial in due course of law: presumably, though the judgment of Finlay P. does not say so, the point was that this rule, in effect a kind of penal estoppel, struck one as oppressive and unfair.[17] In *King v Attorney General*,[18] in which the Supreme Court ruled inconsistent with the Constitution s 4 of the Vagrancy Act 1824, which made certain conduct an offence if committed by a "suspected person or reputed thief" Henchy J, - the rest of the Court either agreed with him or spoke to similar effect - first made a long list of the section's objectionable features, and then listed four constitutional provisions which the section as a whole offended; but without specifying which constitutional provision related to which objectionable feature. However, Article 38.1 and trial in due course of law were among his list of constitutional rules; and the way he listed the 1824 section's blemishes suggests that they all contributed to a conflict with that Article:

> "In my opinion, the ingredients of the offence and the mode by which its commission may be proved are so arbitrary, so vague, so difficult to rebut, so related to rumour or ill-repute or past conduct, so ambiguous in failing to distinguish between apparent and real behaviour of a criminal nature, so prone to make a man's lawful occasions become unlawful and criminal by the breadth and arbitrariness of the discretion that is vested in both the prosecutor and the judge, so indiscriminately contrived to mark as criminal conduct committed by one person in certain circumstances when the same conduct, when engaged in by another person in similar circumstances, would be free of the taint of criminality, so out of keeping with the basic concept inherent in our legal system that a man may walk abroad in the secure knowledge that he will not be singled out from his fellow-citizens and branded and punished as a criminal unless it has been established beyond reasonable doubt that he has deviated from a clearly prescribed standard of conduct, and generally so singularly at variance with both the explicit and implicit characteristics and limitations of the criminal law as to the onus of proof and mode of proof, that it is not so much a question of ruling unconstitutional the type of offence we are now considering as identifying the particular constitutional provisions with which such an offence is at variance."

[14] [1957] IR 227.

[15] Unreported, High Court, 22 November 1982.

[16] [1979] IR 1.

[17] Note, however, that in *Hickey v Governor of St. Patrick's Institution*, Supreme Court, 7 May 1993 the Supreme Court, *per* O'Flaherty J ruled in a case where the young person falsely stated that he was more than fifteen years old that s 123 of the 1908 Act "could not possibly make lawful something that would not otherwise be authorised by the legislation" and that the section at best provided a form of "limited protection" for those persons who had, for example, acted on foot of the warrant committing the juvenile to prison.

[18] [1981] IR 233. See Cooney, "*Due Process and a Crime of Condition*" (1980) 15 Ir Jur (n.s.) 289.

In *Curtis v Attorney General*[19] the plaintiff attacked a (penal) customs provision which allowed the District Court to determine conclusively the value of the goods in question; this finding was binding on the higher court (before which the accused person might be tried on indictment); and also on the Court of Criminal Appeal. Carroll J held that these provisions were unconstitutional, in that the power to determine the value of the goods (and, consequentially, the amount of the potential fine) was in the hands of a court which had no jurisdiction to try the charge. She considered that it was an "integral" feature of the administration of justice that "the relevant facts on which the prescribed punishment depends should be decided by the court of trial". Finally, in *Shelly v Mahon*[20] the Supreme Court had occasion to apply Article 38.1 in unusual circumstances. Here the applicant had been convicted by a person who at the time was not a judge appointed under the Constitution.[21] The Courts (No.2) Act 1988 sought to confer retrospective validity on the orders which had purportedly been made by the respondent. A majority of the Supreme Court concluded that the 1988 Act could not retrospectively cure the absence of a proper trial in due course of law, since, as Walsh J observed, any other conclusion "would make nonsense" of the provisions of Article 38.1.[22]

Accepted principles of criminal justice

The phrase "due course of law" may therefore best be regarded as conveying a bundle of principles and maxims more or less generally accepted in the common law world, most of them ancient, some of them of modern origin. Some of these principles are so well established and so much taken for granted that it is not easy to illustrate them by reference to recent instances in which Irish courts have found it necessary to affirm them.

Nullum crimen sine lege

The principle that no one may be tried or punished except for an offence known to the law is a fundamental element of the Irish and common-law system and an essential security against arbitrary prosecution. It was stated in *Attorney General v Cunningham*[23] as follows (by O'Byrne J, giving the judgment of the Court of Criminal Appeal):

> "The offence as charged in the indictment is one of maliciously firing into [a] dwelling-house... and it seems to us that the proper question for our determination is whether that is, at common law, an indictable offence. In considering that question the Court must have regard to the fundamental doctrine recognised in these courts that the criminal law must be certain and specific, and that no person is to be punished unless and until he has been convicted of an offence recognised by law as a crime and punishable as such."[24]

[19] [1985] IR 458.

[20] [1990] 1 IR 36.

[21] The difficulties had been caused by the fact that due to an apparent oversight, the District Judge in question had actually reached his retirement age at the date of the trial of the applicant.

[22] See also *Glavin v Governor of Mountjoy Prison* [1991] 2 IR 421; [1991] ILRM 478, where the Supreme Court relied on Article 38.1 to quash a conviction in circumstances where the return for trial (as opposed to the conviction itself) had been made by a person who was no longer a District Judge. It had been argued that since there is no *constitutional* right to a preliminary examination (see *O'Shea v Director of Public Prosecutions* [1988] IR 655), the ratio in *Shelly's* case did not apply. Griffin J disposed of this argument by saying:

> "I am quite satisfied that a trial in due course of law must necessarily mean a trial in compliance with the law as it existed at the time when the trial took place and that this extends, not only to trial on indictment in the Circuit Court or the Central Criminal Court, but also to all examinations or other steps required by legislation to take place preliminary to the trial on indictment."

[23] [1932] IR 28.

[24] See also *Doolan v Director of Public Prosecutions* [1992] 2 IR 399 (where O'Hanlon J rejected the argument that the offence of "indecent assault" was not one known to the law).

This principle was re-affirmed in *The People (Attorney General) v Edge*,[25] in which it was held by the Supreme Court that the offence charge - "kidnapping" - was not an offence at common law. Both these cases were mentioned by Kenny J in his judgment in *King v Attorney General*[26] as "authority for the proposition that a person may be convicted of a criminal offence only if the ingredients of, and the acts constituting the offence are specified with precision and clarity". He said:

> "It is a fundamental feature of our system of government by law (and not by decree or diktat) that citizens may be convicted only of offences which have been specified with precision by the judges who made the common law, or of offences which, created by statute, are expressed without ambiguity... In my opinion, both governing phrases [in s 4 of the Vagrancy Act 1824] "suspected person" and "reputed thief" are so uncertain that they cannot form the foundation for a criminal offence."

While the principle that no one may be tried or punished except for an offence known to the law is a fundamental principle of the Irish and common law systems, Hamilton P said in *Attorney General (Society for the Protection of the Unborn Child (Ireland) Ltd.) v Open-Door Counselling Ltd.*[27] that this principle may have to give way, as occasion requires, to the courts' constitutional obligation to create new criminal offences in order adequately to protect fundamental rights:

> "Though ordinarily it is no function of the courts to extend the criminal law, it may well be that where there is a breach of, or interference with, a fundamental personal or human right, they are under a constitutional obligation so to do in order to respect, and, as far as practicable, to defend and vindicate that right."[28]

No retroactive penal sanction

While Article 15.5 specifically forbids the Oireachtas to "declare acts to be infringements of the law which were not so at the date of their commission", it does not mention the bringing of prosecutions, based on a new criminal statute, in respect of acts committed before the statute made them criminal. Nevertheless it is certain that the courts would not entertain such a prosecution if it were ever brought. In *Attorney General v McBride*,[29] while the arguments based on this principle were not successful, the judgment of Hanna J clearly accepted that this principle existed. The courts have not yet had to consider the position where the Oireachtas has sought retroactively to increase the maximum sentence which the accused may serve. It seems probable, however, that this would be regarded as an infringement of Article 38.1.[30]

[25] [1943] IR 115; (1944) 78 ILTR 125.
[26] [1981] IR 223.
[27] [1988] IR 593; [1987] ILRM 477.
[28] Note that Hamilton P held that he could not decide in civil proceedings whether the defendants, activities amounted to a conspiracy to corrupt public morals, since to do so would be to usurp the function of the jury in respect of an indictable offence.
[29] [1928] IR 451; (1928) 62 ILTR 125. See also *The State (Ryan) v Lennon* [1935] IR 170; (1935) 69 ILTR 125; *Minister for Agriculture v McConnell* [1942] IR 600 and *Doyle v An Taoiseach* [1986] ILRM 693 and pp. 127-129.
[30] Note that Article 7(1) of the European Convention of Human Rights caters precisely for this point by providing that "Nor shall a heavier penalty be imposed than the one that was applicable at the time the criminal offence was committed."

No second trial on the same charge

This principle is not as absolute as its statement, whether in English or in Latin, would suggest.[31] Its essence, as stated by Blackstone[32] and cited by O'Higgins CJ in *The People (Director of Public Prosecutions) v O'Shea*,[33] is this:

> "When a man is once fairly found not guilty upon any indictment, or other prosecution, before any court having competent jurisdiction of the offence he may plead such acquittal in bar of any subsequent accusation for the same crime."

The passage was paraphrased by Ó Dálaigh J in *The People (Attorney General) v Marchel O'Brien*[34] as:

> "indicat[ing,] as two necessary ingredients in the plea of *autrefois acquit*, that there has been a fair trial, that is to say, a trial on the merits, and that the court which acquitted had jurisdiction to try the charge."

Shortly afterwards, in *The State (Attorney General) v Judge Binchy*,[35] the Supreme Court took the view that, where an accused person has been acquitted by the judge's direction, due to the judge's (in this case mistaken) impression that jurisdiction to try the accused was lacking, the accused has never been "in jeopardy" - since the case was never let go to the jury - and that, had the directed verdict disclosed that the acquittal was due to this mistaken impression, it could have been quashed.[36] O'Higgins CJ, having cited both *Marchel O'Brien's* and *Judge Binchy's* cases in his *O'Shea* judgment, arrived at the general conclusion that:

> "[a directed] acquittal results in no trial because it is not in fact the verdict of the jury. It follows therefore that the person accused has not been in jeopardy."

The accused might therefore in such circumstances - the majority of the Supreme Court held - be put on trial again. *O'Shea's* case, however, turned not merely on the power to subject to a second trial someone who has "not been in jeopardy", but on the far more general proposition that Article 34.4.3 means literally what it says, and that the "decisions of the High Court" which may be appealed against to the Supreme Court include acquittals by juries in the Central Criminal Court; and although O'Higgins CJ, who led the majority in accepting this proposition, emphasised that a very sparing use would be made of the Court's power to order a second trial of an acquitted person, two members of the Court (Finlay P and Henchy J) dissented strongly from the whole idea that a jury acquittal might not be final. The latter judge said he was:

> "satisfied, for a variety of reasons, that a quintessential feature of the jury trial required under Article 38.5 is the consequence that when that trial properly takes

[31] Furthermore, the dismissal of criminal charges is not a bar to subsequent disciplinary proceedings: see, e.g. *Flynn v An Post* [1987] IR 68; *Myers v Garda Commissioners,* High Court, 22 January 1988 and *Keady v Garda Commissioner* [1992] 2 IR 197; [1992] ILRM 312. But the State cannot proceed with disciplinary measures where (said Hederman J) "the object of the disciplinary proceedings is to establish that he was guilty of the same acts as those in respect of which he was acquitted"; *McGrath v Garda Commissioner (No.1)* [1991] 1 IR 69: [1990] ILRM 817: *McCarthy v Garda Commissioner* [1993] 1 IR 489.

[32] *Commentaries on the Laws of England,* book 4, chap 27.

[33] [1982] IR 241.

[34] [1963] IR 92; (1964) 98 ILTR 107.

[35] [1964] IR 395.

[36] The verdict, however, was recorded as "not guilty" *simpliciter*, and the Court declined to interfere with it, saying there was no precedent for doing so.

place within jurisdiction and results in the jury's verdict of not guilty, *whether directed by the judge or not*,[37] that verdict can never again be questioned in any court by way of appeal or otherwise."

This question was addressed again in *The People (Director of Public Prosecutions) v Quilligan.*[38] In the first *Quilligan* case, the Supreme Court allowed an appeal from a directed acquittal in the Central Criminal Court and the issue then arose as to whether the Supreme Court in such circumstances had power to order a re-trial. A majority[39] of the Court ruled that no order should be made in the instant case, but two of that majority - Henchy and Griffin JJ - went further and ruled that the Court had no jurisdiction to make such an order:

> "The rule of *autrefois acquit* means that if an accused duly and successfully raises the plea that he has already been trial in a court of competent jurisdiction, acting within jurisdiction, for the offence now charged, and that he was acquitted of that charge in that court, for the second trial for that offence may not take place. This rule is but an aspect of the canon of fundamental fairness of legal procedures inherent in our Constitution, which is expressed in the maxim *nemo debet bis vexari pro eadem causa.*"

And in *McCarthy v Garda Commissioner*[40] Flood J trenchantly spoke of the unimpeachability of a jury verdict of acquittal in terms which echo those of Henchy J in *O'Shea* and *Quilligan (No.2).* Here the accused has been returned for trial (and subsequently acquitted) by a person who (by reason of a clerical error as to his age) was not at the time a duly constituted District Judge. When the applicant sought to restrain the Garda Commissioner from re-opening (via disciplinary proceedings) the precise allegations covered by the acquittal, the State riposted by pleading that the acquittal was a nullity. Flood J referred to the acquittal as a "certificate of the person's uninterrupted innocence" and continued:

> "it seems to me that to rip the certificate of innocence...from the applicant and metaphorically to shred it and declare it a total nullity...all by reason of a clerical error made in 1977 as to the age of a District Judge would be wholly inequitable [and] oppressive"

Autrefois acquit in summary jurisdiction cases

A few cases on *autrefois acquit* in connection with the summary criminal jurisdiction of the District Court may be mentioned at this juncture. In *Attorney General (Ó Maonaigh) v Fitzgerald,*[41] the plea was successfully raised where the State, having failed to secure a conviction for dangerous driving causing serious bodily harm, tried to prosecute for the separate statutory offence of dangerous driving (simpliciter) in respect of the same incident. In *O'Leary v Cunningham,*[42] where a District Judge wrongly convicted the defendant on a charge of receiving stolen goods when the evidence showed that he had been a principal in the robbery, and made no order at all on the robbery charge which had also

[37] O'Higgins CJ did indicate that the Supreme Court could not - save in exceptional circumstances - interfere with a jury verdict of not guilty.

[38] [1986] IR 495 (*Quilligan (No.1)*) and [1989] IR 45 (*Quilligan (No.2)*).

[39] Henchy, Griffin and Hederman JJ; Walsh and McCarthy JJ dissenting.

[40] [1993] 1 IR 489.

[41] [1964] IR 458.

[42] [1980] IR 367.

been brought against him, the Supreme Court held that the conviction for receiving could not be upheld, but also that the District Judge's failure to make an order on the robbery charge amounted to an acquittal, which the Circuit Court (on appeal from the District Court) could not set aside. On the other hand, in *Director of Public Prosecutions v Gill*,[43] where a defendant had attended in the District Court to answer a summons, but the prosecution had failed to turn up (the judge however making no order), and a second summons was issued, the Supreme Court held that the judge had not conducted a hearing or made a determination of anything, and the issuing of a new summons was valid.

There is a statutory process which (as it is available to the State which has failed to secure a conviction in the District Court) represents a mechanism whereby a person thus acquitted can be again subjected to summary trial on the same charge. This is contained in s 2 of the Summary Jurisdiction Act 1857, as amended by s 51 of the Courts (Supplemental Provisions) Act 1961: "any party to any proceedings whatsoever heard and determined by a District Judge [other than those related to an indictable offence not dealt with summarily by him] if dissatisfied with such determination as being erroneous on a point of law", can apply in writing to the Judge asking him to state a case for the High Court's opinion, and the Judge, unless of the view that the request is frivolous, must then state a case accordingly. As the question whether there was any evidence on which the Judge could have based his decision is itself a question of law[44] this clearly opens up a wide power to review District Court dismissals of summonses. The jurisdiction seems nowadays to be more frequently invoked by the State than heretofore[45] and two decisions may be mentioned to illustrate it. In *Director of Public Prosecutions v O'Connor*,[46] where a District Judge had dismissed a charge of an electoral offence on what seemed a mistaken view of the law, the Director's attempt to have the matter reopened by this route failed for the technical reason that the High Court considered the sending of a letter to the respondents, accompanying a copy of the case stated, was not a compliance with the requirement to give notice of the appeal; the Court thus saw itself as not having been given jurisdiction to hear it. In *Director of Public Prosecutions v Nangle*,[47] on the other hand, the High Court held that the District Judge had in fact had grounds, on the evidence before him, to entertain a doubt to the benefit of which the defendant was entitled. Finlay P said:

> "I am satisfied... that it would constitute an unwarranted interference by me in a proceeding which is exclusively confined to correcting errors of law by an inferior court in the determination of proceedings before it, to hold that evidence [as summarised by him] could not have raised a doubt in the mind of the District Justice."

The status of a nolle prosequi

The status of a trial discontinued on the entry by the State of a *nolle prosequi*, rather than concluded by an acquittal, will depend on the circumstances. On the one hand, in the wartime case of *The State (Walsh) v Lennon*[48] (a prosecution before the Emergency

[43] [1980] IR 263.
[44] *The State (Turley) v ÓFloinn* [1968] IR 245.
[45] This seems particularly true in the case of road traffic prosecutions which fail on technical grounds before the District Court where prosecution appeals under s 2 of the 1857 Act seem fairly common: see, e.g., *Director of Public Prosecutions v Lynch* [1991] 1 IR 43 and *Director of Public Prosecutions v Brady* [1991] 1 IR 337. For a discussion of the constitutionality of such appellate procedures, see p. 500.
[46] High Court, 9 May 1983.
[47] [1984] ILRM 171.
[48] [1942] IR 112; (1942) 76 ILTR 207.

Powers (Amendment) (No. 2) Act 1940, military court), where the State had interrupted a trial by entering a *nolle prosequi* and then recommenced the prosecution (under changed rules of evidence), the Supreme Court held that the *nolle prosequi* was not equivalent to an acquittal. On the other hand, in *The State (O'Callaghan) v Ó hUadhaigh*[49] Finlay P made absolute an order of prohibition to prevent the trial of a person on charges in respect of which a *nolle prosequi* had formerly been entered; in the later case of *The State (Coveney) v Members of the Special Criminal Court*[50] he said that in *O'Callaghan's* case "in effect, the Director of Public Prosecutions by the entry of a *nolle prosequi* [had] sought to avoid a ruling made at the trial of an accused person", but that, in general, he accepted the position taken by the Supreme Court in *Walsh's* case.

No abuse of process

There have been several subsequent cases where applicants have sought to apply the principle of O'*Callaghan's* case to circumstances - it was contended - amounted to an abuse of process. Most of them turn on their individual facts, but a number may be mentioned here. In *Hamill v Director of Public Prosecutions*[51] Barrington J refused to prevent the Director from preferring fresh charges against the accused, following the allowing of his appeal by the Court of Criminal Appeal against conviction by the Special Criminal Court. Barrington J said that as the proceedings before the Special Criminal Court were a nullity, they formed no bar to a further prosecution. He was troubled by the fact that the plaintiff had already served eleven months in prison on foot of the invalid sentence imposed by the Special Criminal Court, but assumed that any court of trial subsequently dealing with him would, in the event of his being convicted on the new charges, "give such weight to this aspect of the matter as is appropriate and just". Barrington J also agreed that it would be "a serious matter" if the Director had deliberately kept fresh charges in reserve for use against the defendant in a subsequent prosecution should that prove necessary; the plaintiff, however, had not established that this had actually occurred. This question was also further considered by Barron J in the important case of *Ryan v Director of Public Prosecutions*[52] where the first trial of the applicant on rape charges had collapsed.[53] At that trial certain statements had been ruled to be inadmissible and the applicant then sought an injunction restraining the introduction of such evidence at the subsequent re-trial. Barron J refused the relief sought on the ground that to tender such evidence at a re-trial would not be in itself an abuse of process. He agreed that the principle in O'*Callaghan's* case would apply if the "re-trial had been engineered for the purpose of overcoming the adverse ruling", but here this had happened through the fault of neither party and hence that principle had no application.

Other examples of cases raising the issue of *nemo debet bis vexari* include *O'Connor v Director of Public Prosecutions*[54] (where the mounting of a second prosecution following an abortive mistrial was held by Lardner J to be unfair) and *The State (O'Keeffe) v McMenamin*[55] (where Carroll J refused to prohibit the respondent District Judge from

[49] [1977] IR 42. *The State (Walsh) v Lennon* was not adverted to either by Finlay P or by counsel.
[50] [1982] ILRM 284.
[51] High Court, 16 May 1983.
[52] [1988] IR 232; [1989] ILRM 466.
[53] The jury had inadvertently been given certain inadmissible evidence. See also *Claffey v Director of Public Prosecutions*, High Court, 27 November 1992 where the accused had given some indication of a line of defence in the first abortive mistrial. Murphy J refused to restrain a re-trial, saying that this information "would be of such marginal value" to the prosecution that "this Court exercising the utmost care to protect the constitutional right...to fair proceedings could not attach any significance to it."
[54] High Court, 21 March 1986.
[55] [1986] ILRM 653.

hearing a fresh prosecution after the first charges had been struck out, saying that there was no "cat and mouse situation", as the prosecution had said that the charges were unlikely to be re-entered). It may be taken for granted, however, that today's courts will not countenance any unfair or cat-and-mouse proceeding involving *nolle prosequi.*

Furthermore, the High Court will not permit the continuation of a prosecution which is doomed to failure. This important point was made by Morris J in *K.M. v Director of Public Prosecutions*[56] where the accused had been charged with the sexual offence of a minor. The victim unequivocally contended that she had been penetrated by the applicant, whereas the prosecution themselves contended that this had not occurred and that there had been merely improper sexual contact between the victim and the applicant. There was, however, no other evidence of sexual assault (apart from the alleged acts of penetration) and Morris J held that on these special facts there was no evidence on which reasonable jury could properly convict in respect of the charge of sexual assault and granted an order restraining the prosecution. Morris J himself recognised that this jurisdiction was itself exceptional and that it would require "strong and convincing evidence" to displace the presumption that both the prosecution and the trial judge were acting in accordance with fair procedures.

Statutory recognition of the principle of the finality of an acquittal

The principle of the finality of an acquittal is recognised by statute in several contexts: e.g. ss 110, 185 of the Defence Act 1954 (in connection with trials by court-martial); s 17 of the Extradition Act 1965 (no extradition if there has been final judgment here or in a third country in respect of the offence for which extradition is sought: the section carries the side-note *Non bis in idem*); s 34(1) of the Criminal Procedure Act 1967 (reference of question of law, arising on acquittal by direction, to the Supreme Court by the Attorney General or Director of Public Prosecutions but without prejudice to the verdict in favour of the accused); s 15 of the Criminal Law (Jurisdiction) Act 1976 (an acquittal or a conviction in Northern Ireland can be pleaded in bar of a prosecution for the same offence here). The two latter provisions were cited by Henchy J in support of his view of the fundamental nature of *non bis in idem,* in *The People (Director of Public Prosecutions) v O'Shea.*[57]

Autrefois convict

Autrefois convict was recognised as a good plea in *The State (Attorney General) v Judge Deale*;[58] and, by the Supreme Court, in *The State (Tynan) v Keane*,[59] though not effective in this case because the first conviction, later quashed, had been made without jurisdiction. *Tynan's* case raised in concrete form the question of whether the quashing of a conviction entitles the successful applicant to raise a plea in bar so as to preclude any retrial. In *Tynan* Walsh J held that a plea in bar could not be raised if it was based on an excess or want of jurisdiction, since such an adjudication was in reality no adjudication at all. The present case fell into that category since the conviction had been imposed in the absence of the applicant. Yet Walsh J considered that there was "something essentially different" in the quashing by *certiorari* of an improper conviction by a tribunal competent jurisdiction:

[56] High Court, 21 June 1993.
[57] [1982] IR 383.
[58] [1973] IR 180.
[59] [1968] IR 348. See also *O'Donnell v Hegarty* [1941] IR 538; *The State (de Búrca) v Ó hUadhaigh* [1976] IR 85; *The State (McMorrow) v Barry*, High Court, 17 June 1980.

> "Such a quashing would amount to an acquittal. Similarly, an improper acquittal by a Court of competent jurisdiction would not be subject to being quashed on *certiorari*. In both these latter instances the accused person would have been in peril in that he was before a tribunal which might have subjected him to lawful imprisonment...The impropriety which would ground such an order of *certiorari* would be one referable to the conduct of the hearing of the tribunal, and not one referable to a matter vitiating the jurisdiction of the tribunal.

While this distinction permitted the re-trial of the applicant in the present case, nonetheless justice and fairness required that any period of imprisonment served by the applicant pursuant to his "*valid*" conviction would have to be taken into account by trial judge on the re-trial, assuming, of course, that this re-trial led to a further conviction. Yet, the distinction drawn by Walsh J is not always self-evident and sits uneasily with the later statement of Henchy J in *The State (Holland) v Kennedy*[60] to the effect that all errors of law affecting the jurisdiction of the lower court render void any resulting conviction. Nevertheless, in *Sweeney v Brophy*[61] Hederman J denied that there was any inconsistency between the two decisions. In this case there had been fundamental irregularities in the manner in which the accused had been convicted in the District Court and it was common case that the conviction must be quashed. Despite the fact that the conviction was held to be void, Hederman J ruled that the applicant had, in fact, been in peril and could thus plead in bar:

> "If there is a breach of the fundamental tenets of constitutional justice in the hearing or the failure to hear the evidence in the case the trial can properly be regarded as one that has not been held in due course of law and any conviction arising therefrom should be quashed so as to entitle the defendant to plead *autrefois acquit*."

This may be contrasted with the earlier decision in *Tynan* where the conviction was quashed since it had been imposed in the defendant's absence - plainly "a breach of the fundamental tenets of constitutional justice" - yet this was found to be no bar to a trial. The above passage also seems not to accord taken by Finlay CJ in a judgment delivered on the very same day as *Sweeney: Sheehan v Reilly.*[62] Here the Supreme Court quashed a conviction where the sentence imposed exceeded the statutory maximum. Finlay CJ said that the conviction and sentence were "null and void *ab initio*" so that the applicant might be put on trial again for the same charge. He concluded, however, that having regard to the fact that the applicant had already spent considerable time in prison, considerations of fairness and due procedure made it inappropriate to direct a further consideration of this charge." This seems a logically more coherent method of dealing with this issue - and one which is more in harmony with the doctrine of *ultra vires* - then the approach taken in *Tynan* and *Sweeney*, especially as the latter involves the wholly artificial - and retrospective - characterisation of whether or not the applicant had ever truly been in peril at the time of his conviction.

Statutory encroachment on principle of autrefois convict

There is, however, provision in s 5 of the Courts of Justice Act 1928, whereby the Court of Criminal Appeal, or, on appeal from it, the Supreme Court, when it reverses a conviction in whole, may order the person concerned to be re-tried for the same offence. (As the Court of Criminal Appeal exercises its jurisdiction only in cases in which original

[60] [1977] IR 193.
[61] [1993] ILRM 449.
[62] [1993] 1 IR 368; [1993] ILRM 427.

jurisdiction has been exercised by the Central Criminal Court, the Circuit Court or the Special Criminal Court, this process does not apply to convictions by the District Court; the Circuit Court, to which appeals lie from the District Court, has no equivalent jurisdiction.) This section appears itself to recognise its exceptional character as an encroachment on the *autrefois convict* principle: sub-s 2 says that the person ordered to be re-tried may be again indicted, tried, and (if found guilty) sentenced "notwithstanding any rule of law".[63]

No trial in absentia.

In *The People (Attorney General) v Messitt*[64] an accused person had behaved in such a disorderly way - as the evidence suggested, possibly in consequence of psychopathy - that the trial judge had ordered his removal from the court; his counsel had also asked leave to withdraw, apparently finding his task impossible. In the absence of the accused, the trial proceeded, and some evidence highly prejudicial to him was heard. The Court of Criminal Appeal set aside his conviction and sentence, Kenny J saying:

> "While the judge had authority to order that the accused should be removed from the courtroom because of his disorderly conduct, this Court is of opinion that this evidence... should not have been received in his absence and when he had no legal representation, without an opportunity being given to him to adduce medical evidence in support of his complaint that he was unable, because of physical illness, to conduct his defence, and without testimony that his violent conduct was not caused by mental illness."

There is, however, no absolute rule - provided that the essentials of justice are observed - prescribing the presence of the accused throughout the trial. Thus in *The People (Director of Public Prosecutions) v Kelly*[65] the defendant, who had absconded on the forty-first day of his trial, after giving direct evidence but before being cross-examined, was convicted and sentenced in his absence. Where a summary trial takes place in the District Court, a summons stating the complaint having been served on the defendant, then, "if he disregards the requirement of attendance, [he] may be tried in his absence:

[63] The provisions of the Criminal Justice Act 1993 - which allow the prosecution to appeal to the Court of Criminal Appeal against the imposition of an unduly lenient sentence following conviction on indictment - may also be regarded as an encroachment on the principle of *autrefois convict.* Note, however, the comments of Blackmun J delivering the majority judgment of the US Supreme Court in *United States v Di Francesco* 449 US 117 (1980), where he said that a sentence "does not have the qualities of constitutional finality that attend an acquittal." The Court upheld the constitutionality of a prosecution appeal against a lenient sentence, with Blackmun J commenting:

> "The basic design of the double jeopardy provision...is, as a bar against repeated attempts to convict, with consequent subjection of defendant to embarrassment, expense and insecurity, and the possibility that he may be found guilty even though innocent. These considerations...have no significant application to the prosecution's statutorily granted right to review a sentence."

See generally O'Malley, "*Prosecution Appeals against Sentence*" (1993) ILT 121, which provides an authoritative analysis of the relevant issues.

[64] [1972] IR 204. See also *Re Dolphin* (High Court, 27 January 1972) where Kenny J held that a District Judge had exceeded his jurisdiction in deciding in the absence of the accused that he was not fit to plead. The judge said this was:

> "such a serious issue that it should not be decided in the absence of the accused unless his behaviour in Court makes it necessary to have him removed. It certainly should not be decided in his absence when he is in custody."

[65] [1982] IR 1. See also *The People (Attorney General) v Jasinski* 1 Frewen 283 (1963) (trial judge entitled to order the removal of disruptive defendant from Court). But note *The People (Director of Public Prosecutions v McGinley* (1989) 3 Frewen 251 where Hederman J ruled that it was impermissible for a trial judge to hear evidence regarding sentence in chambers: Article 34 demanded that such evidence be heard in public and in the presence of the accused.

see r 64 of the [District Court] Rules of 1948": *per* Henchy J in *Director of Public Prosecutions v Gill.*[66]

The fullest treatment of this question is now to be found in the judgment of Murphy J in *Lawlor v Hogan.*[67] Here the applicant had been charged with robbery before the District Court and consented to summary trial. He did not, however, turn up at his trial,[68] but was there represented by a solicitor who conducted the proceedings on his behalf. The applicant claimed that his conviction was invalidated by reason of his absence and Murphy J took the opportunity to articulate three general propositions:

> "1 That in so far as the judicial process in criminal matters expressly requires matters to be dealt with by or in relation to the individual accused, clearly he must be present to enable those functions to be performed.
>
> 2 The right of an accused to be present and to follow the proceedings against him is a fundamental right of the accused which every Court would be bound to protect and vindicate.
>
> 3 If a trial judge is satisfied that the accused has consciously decided to absent himself from the trial (at a time when his presence is not essential to enable some particular procedure to be complied with) then the trial judge would be entitled in his discretion to proceed with the trial in the absence of the accused."

Murphy J agreed that in this case the physical presence of the accused would have been "essential to enable the Court to inform him of his right to be tried by a jury and to enable him to form a view as to whether he would object to being tried summarily". Here, however, the applicant had been physically present to exercise that right and Murphy J held that, in the circumstances, the trial judge had properly exercised his discretion to deciding to proceed with the trial.

Sentence to be pronounced in public

In *The State (Kiernan) v de Búrca*[69] the old Supreme Court said it was a "fundamental rule that the pronouncement of a sentence following a conviction was an essential part of the administration of justice in the case". In *Molloy v Sheehan*[70] the new Supreme Court, referring to *Kiernan's* case, re-stated the fundamental rule (*per* Kenny J) as being "that the sentence must be spoken in court".

Duration of sentence to be precise and certain

In *The State (Keating) v Ó hUadhaigh*[71] Finlay P quashed a conviction and sentence where there was some doubt as to when the sentence would commence; he described this ambiguity as a "fatal flaw". This principle was accepted (though with a different result) by Barron J in *The State (Gleeson) v Martin,*[72] where the applicants' sentences were expressed to run consecutively from the date of the "legal expiration" of earlier sentences. He refused the relief sought, as he considered that this expression was sufficiently precise and clear; "legal expiration" meant "upon the actual determination of the sentence, whenever that legally occurs".

[66] [1980] IR 253.
[67] [1993] ILRM 606.
[68] The reason why the applicant absented himself from his trial is not disclosed in the judgment.
[69] [1963] IR 348.
[70] [1978] IR 438. See also *Campbell and Fell v United Kingdom* (1985) 7 EHRR 165.
[71] High Court, 11 May 1984.
[72] [1985] ILRM 577. See also *The State (Dixon) v Martin* [1985] ILRM 240.

Sentence not to be arbitrary or disproportionate

This principle was first expressly admitted by the Supreme Court in *Cox v Ireland*[73] in the course of invalidating s 34 of the Offences Against the State Act 1939. This section provided for the mandatory loss of office, pension and other emoluments in respect of all public servants convicted of scheduled offences in the Special Criminal Court. While Finlay CJ acknowledged that the State was entitled "for the protection of public peace and order" by its laws "to provide onerous and far-reaching penalties and forfeitures imposed as a major deterrent to the commission of crimes threatening such peace and order and State authority", the State's obligation to protect and vindicate constitutional rights meant that such penalties must be neither arbitrary nor disproportionate in their operation. Having regard the varying gravity of the range of scheduled offences and the fact that the operation of s 34 is triggered by the venue of the trial (i.e., the Special Criminal Court) which in turn is primarily selected by the fact that the offence is scheduled, the Court concluded that the section was invalid as "impermissibly wide and indiscriminate." It remains to be seen whether this principle might be applied in other contexts.[74] However, Flood J took up this theme in *The People (Director of Public Prosecutions) v WC*[75] where, referring to *Cox's* case he said that the Constitution required the courts "impose a sentence which is appropriate to the degree of guilt, taking into account all relevant circumstances as they arise in that case." He added that selection of a particular punishment to be imposed on a particular offender was subject to the "constitutional principle of proportionality", which in turn required that:

> "the imposition of a particular sentence must strike a balance between the particular circumstances of the commission of a relevant offence and the relevant circumstances of the person sentenced. It is not open to a judge in a criminal case, whether for a particular type of offence, or in respect of a particular class of offender, to fetter the exercise of his judicial discretion through the operation of a fixed policy, or to otherwise pre-determine the issue."

The logical consequence of such a principle, however, must be to cast some shadow over the constitutionality of fixed mandatory sentences and one may question whether the courts will be adventurous enough to go this far and actually invalidate, for example, s 4(*a*) of the Criminal Justice Act 1990 which prescribes a minimum of forty year sentence for treason and certain forms of murder.

Burden of proof

The inter-action of the constitutional requirements as to trial in due course of law and the evidential rules as to burden of proof is a matter which has only recently explored by the courts in recent times and even then imperfectly. As Costello J confirmed in *O'Leary v Attorney General*,[76] Article 38.1 requires that all criminal trials be conducted in accordance with the presumption of innocence. While it is clear that the courts will

[73] [1992] 2 IR 503.

[74] One possibility might be in relation to the director disqualification provisions of Part VII of the Companies Act 1990. This imposes a mandatory disqualification on all directors convicted on indictment of offences "related to a company". As Murray observes in "*Director Disqualification and the Criminal Law*" (1992) 2 ICLJ 165, some of the offences created by the Companies Act 1990 have only a peripheral connection with a company *per se* (e.g., obstructing a right of entry or search under the Companies Acts) and, hence, it may be said that the legislation is similarly overbroad and indiscriminate in that such a far-reaching disqualification order does not necessarily advance the legislative policy (*viz*., to disqualify directors who have engaged in fraud or dishonesty).

[75] High Court, 14 July 1993.

[76] [1993] 1 IR 102; [1991] ILRM 454.

not accept a standard of proof less than the common law standard of proof beyond reasonable doubt, legislation which reverses the *evidential* burden of proof (the *legal* burden of proving guilt remaining at all times on the prosecution) is not necessarily unconstitutional.

In *O'Leary*, the plaintiff challenged the constitutionality of s 24 of the Offences Against the State Act 1939. This section creates a rebuttable presumption that a person found in possession of incriminating documents[77] is a member of an illegal organisation. Costello J stressed first that the section did not affect the legal burden which at all times remained on the prosecution. However, he concluded that such a "reverse-onus" presumption was not necessarily unconstitutional as:

> "the Constitution should not be construed as absolutely prohibiting the Oireachtas from restricting the exercise of the right to the presumption of innocence. The right is to be implied from Article 38, which provides that trials are to be held 'in accordance with law' and it seems to me that the Oireachtas is permitted in certain circumstances to restrict the exercise of the right because it is not be regarded as an absolute right whose enjoyment can never be abridged."

Costello J referred with approval to a decision of the European Commission of Human Rights in *X. v United Kingdom* [78] where a similar presumption[79] was held not necessarily to infringe the provisions of Article 6 of the European Convention on Human Rights:

> "The Commission recognises, however, that this form of provision could, if widely or unreasonably worded, have the same effect as a presumption of guilt. It is not, therefore, sufficient to examine only the form in which the presumption is drafted. It is necessary to examine the substance and effect."

Costello J thus upheld the constitutionality of the section.

This question was further analysed by the Supreme Court in *Hardy v Ireland* [80] where the constitutionality of s 4(1) of the Explosive Substances Act 1883 was upheld. This sub-section provides that any person who makes or knowingly has control or possession of an explosive substance "under such circumstances as to give to a reasonable suspicion that he is not making it or does not have it under his control for a lawful object" is guilty of a felony "unless he can show" that this was done for a lawful purpose. While the Supreme Court accepted that the effect of this provision could be to shift the persuasive burden to the accused, such a provision was not regarded by the members of the Court as, in Egan J's words, "inevitably offend[ing against] the requirement of due process." Murphy J could not see any inconsistency between Article 38.1 and a statutory provision which he characterised as affording the accused a "a particular defence of which he can avail if...he proves the material facts on the balance of probabilities."

[77] The plaintiff had been found guilty by the Special Criminal Court (and his conviction affirmed by the Court of Criminal Appeal: see 3 Frewen 163) in circumstances where he was found in possession of 37 posters showing a man in para-military uniform brandishing a rifle and bearing the legend 'IRA calls the shots'. As for the meaning of the phrase "incriminating documents", see s 2 of the Offences Against the State Act 1939 and p. 972.

[78] *Collection of Decisions*, 42, 135.

[79] The statutory provision presumed that a man living with or habitually in the company of a prostitute is presumed to be knowingly living on the earnings of a prostitute.

[80] Supreme Court, 18 March 1993. See also *Ó Broin v Ruane* [1989] ILRM 732 (where Lynch rejected a claim to the constitutionality of s 21 of the Road Traffic (Amendment) Act 1978 - which created a presumption that certain procedures had been followed by the Gardaí - saying that this challenge had "no substance.").

Beyond affirming that Article 38.1 requires that (a) the legal burden must at all times rest with the prosecution and (b) that reverse-onus provisions are not necessarily unconstitutional, neither O'*Leary* or *Hardy* offer much further guidance on these difficult questions. If one proceeds, however, from the statement of O'Higgins CJ in the *Criminal Jurisdiction Bill* case[81] to the effect that Article 38.1 requires a "fair and just balance" between individual rights and the requirements of an ordered society, then it seems plain that statutory provisions which cast either an evidential or persuasive burden on the accused are not *of themselves* necessarily unconstitutional. Thus, the requirements of an ordered society would seem to suggest that it is unreasonable to expect the prosecution to carry "an impossible burden of proof".[82] This in turn means that the peculiar difficulties associated with, for example, proof of mental state would seem to afford constitutional justification to presumptions such as that the accused intended the natural and probable consequences of his act[83] and the presumption of sanity.[84] In each case there is likewise a rational co-relationship between the basic fact proved and the fact to be presumed, since as a general rule, most persons are sane and it is also to be assumed that an accused intended the natural and probable consequences of his act.

Judged by such standards, it is easy to see why the presumption in *Hardy's* case was deemed constitutionally acceptable by the Supreme Court. First, the presumption can only operate where the prosecution establish that there are circumstances giving rise to a reasonable suspicion that the accused has unlawful possession or control of the explosives, thus avoiding any potentially unfair burden that might otherwise be placed on a person who is, *prima facie*, lawfully in possession of the explosives. Secondly, a requirement that the prosecution prove what is essentially a negative (i.e., that the accused did not have such possession or control for a lawful purpose) might seem unduly onerous.[85] Finally, as a matter of practical experience, persons who are found in possession of explosives in the circumstances envisaged in s 4 of the 1883 Act generally do not have a lawful purpose in mind.[86] In contrast, this does not seem true of the section challenged in *O'Leary's* case, since there does not seem any necessary or perhaps even general co-relation between possession of seditious literature and membership of an illegal organisation.[87]

[81] [1977] IR 152.

[82] *Per* Lamer CJ delivering the judgment of the Canadian Supreme Court in *R. v Chaulk* (1990) 3 SCR 1303. This objective was said to be "sufficiently important" to warrant limiting constitutionally protected rights.

[83] Note, however, that the US Supreme Court has taken a different view on the ground that the mental capacity of the accused must be proved by the prosecution, where that mental element is an essential ingredient of the offence. The Court, has accordingly condemned as unconstitutional presumptions to the effect that the accused intended the natural and probable consequences of his acts: see *United States v US Gysum Co* 438 US 422 (1978) and *Sandstrom v Montana* 442 US 510 (1979).

[84] See in this regard the very perceptive article by O'Higgins and Ó Braonáin, "*Section 4 of the Criminal Justice Act 1964*" (1992) 2 ICLJ 179.

[85] Thus, the US Supreme Court has held that it is not unconstitutional if the burden of proof with regard to "affirmative defences" (e.g. issues, such as provocation, which do not *of themselves* negative any of the facts of the crime which the prosecution must prove) rests on the defence: see *Patterson v New York* 432 US 197 (1977). The "lawful purpose" requirement of s 4 of the 1883 Act would seem to be an "affirmative defence" in this sense.

[86] The Canadian Supreme Court reached a similar conclusion in *R v Schwartz* (1988) 2 SCR 443 (onus requiring person found in possession of a restricted weapon to produce firearms acquisition certificate not unconstitutional.)

[87] It may be noted that s 21 of the 1939 Act would almost certainly not survive constitutional challenge in either the United States or Canada. As Powell J said in *Patterson v New York* (1977) 432 US 197:

> "A State must prove every ingredient of an offence beyond a reasonable doubt, and that it may not shift the burden of proof to the defendant by presuming that ingredient upon proof of other elements of the offence."

Rules of natural justice

These, in their application to criminal proceedings, require that a person charged with an offence should be clearly told what it is that is alleged against him, and that he should have a proper opportunity to make his defence. In *The State (Howard) v Donnelly*[88] Davitt P said that the conviction in question:

> "[could] not stand [if] the Justice erroneously refused to hear evidence which was presumably relevant and might possibly have influenced him to acquit. In such an event he can be considered to have disregarded an essential of justice and to have acted without or in excess of his jurisdiction...[But if what had happened was that] the Justice [had] heard fully and fairly so much of the (defendant's] case as he, represented by his counsel, wanted him to hear, it could not reasonably be said that there was any failure to abide by the maxim *audi alteram partem*, or that the Justice had acted without or in excess of his jurisdiction."

The principle was upheld also in *The State (Gleeson) v Minister for Defence*[89] and *Beirne v Garda Commissioner*[90] which, although not criminal matters (they concerned the discharge of men from the Defence Forces and Gardaí respectively) were analogous inasmuch as the men concerned were not given details of the complaints against them nor an opportunity of answering the complaints. The right to an opportunity to defend oneself and meet a charge or complaint includes the right to test those making the charge or complaint, or substantiating it, by cross-examination: *In re Haughey*,[91] in which the "tribunal" in question had been the Dáil's Public Accounts Committee, but in which the point established by the defendant must be valid *a fortiori* in criminal proceedings. Thus, in *Gill v Connellan*[92] Lynch J quashed the applicant's conviction in circumstances where the latter's legal advisers had not been allowed to conduct an effective cross-examination of the prosecution witness by reason of rulings of the District Judge. It has, however, yet to be decided whether the right to cross-examine embraces the right to confront the witnesses in person. Part III of the Criminal Evidence Act 1992 now sanctions a major departure from standard criminal procedure in that it allows for evidence to be given by video-link by witnesses[93] in sexual offence cases, but provided that the right to cross-examination is preserved, it does not seem that Article 38.1 requires the actual presence of witnesses.

Section 21 effects precisely this result. The charge is that of membership of an unlawful organisation and the prosecution may prove that by proving possession of incriminating documents. See also the decision of the Canadian Supreme Court in *R v Whyte* (1988) 2 SCR 3 (presumption that person found in the driver's seat of a motor vehicle had care and control of the vehicle held to be unconstitutional, since the result of such a presumption was that the accused could be convicted in spite of reasonable doubt as to his guilt.)

[88] [1966] IR 51.

[89] [1976] IR 280.

[90] [1993] ILRM 1.

[91] [1971] IR 217.

[92] [1987] IR 541. See also *Ó Broin v Ruane* [1989] IR 214 (District Judge wrong to stop cross-examination of Garda witnesses as to whether statutory procedures followed, although Lynch J observed that the judge "must be entitled to control cross-examination and keep it within reasonable bounds."

[93] Section 13(1) provides that such evidence may be tendered in this manner by a person under 17 years "unless the court sees good reason to the contrary" and in any other case with the leave of the court. Note that in *Maryland v Craig* 497 US 836 (1990) the US Supreme Court upheld a challenge to the constitutionality of such a law. O'Connor J said that she considered that the use of such special procedures were "necessary to further the important [goal] of preventing trauma to child witnesses in child abuse cases [while] adequately ensur[ing] the accuracy of the testimony and preserves the adversary nature of the trial."

Sufficient time to prepare one's defence

Natural justice also embraces the right to sufficient time to prepare one's defence: *Curran v Attorney General*,[94](in which Gavan Duffy J admitted the principle, though said the five days here allowed for the preparation of a court-martial defence, while "very short", was not necessarily unjust in the context) and *O'Callaghan v Clifford*[95] (where Denham J held that the refusal of the District Judge to accede to a defence application for an adjournment meant the accused had insufficient time to consult with counsel, thus infringing his rights to due process).

The accused must have an effective opportunity to meet the case against him

Natural justice in this context means that the accused must have an effective opportunity of meeting the case against him. In *The State (Walshe) v Murphy*[96] the defendant in a prosecution for drunken driving had not been supplied with a copy of the statutory certificate stating the concentration of alcohol found in his urine sample until almost two years after the sample had been taken, and over a year from the date of the original request for a copy. Finlay P quashed the conviction, saying that natural justice required that a person charged with such an offence should be supplied with a copy of the certificate in sufficiently good time:

> "to provide him with a realistic opportunity to have the specimen which he has retained analysed and to contest the validity or correctness of the certificate."

The rule of natural justice and fair procedures will continue to apply even after conviction. The accused has a right to be heard separately on the question of penalty[97] and if evidence is tendered on the issue of penalty, the accused must be given an effective opportunity of dealing with this evidence.[98]

Whether fair procedures require that an accused be given advance notice of the evidence against him?

A question which arises both in the context of trial on indictment and (perhaps more especially) summary trial is whether fair procedures requires the prosecution to furnish the defence with advance notice of evidence which it is proposed to tender against the accused. In the case of trial on indictment, s 6(1) of the Criminal Procedure Act 1967 requires that the accused be furnished with a "book of evidence" containing all relevant documentary evidence, including the statements of the evidence of the prosecution witnesses. This statutory requirement was described by Henchy J in *The State (Williams) v Kelliher*[99] as coming "within the range of the basic fairness of procedures which is constitutionally implicit in the administration of justice."

[94] High Court, 27 February 1941.

[95] Supreme Court, 1 April 1993.

[96] [1981] IR 275. See also the judgment of Gannon J in *The State (O'Regan) v Plunkett* [1984] ILRM 347 (drunk driving conviction quashed where statutory certificate of alcohol level handed to defence on the morning of the hearing.)

[97] *Grahame v Racing Board*, High Court, 22 November 1983.

[98] *The State (Stanbridge) v Mahon* [1979] IR 214 (accused not given opportunity of dealing with prosecution evidence of his previous bad character); *The State (Slattery) v Roe* [1986] IR 769 (where Supreme Court quashed a conviction where the respondent judge, when sentencing the applicant for drugs offences, acted on the basis of probation reports which had become dated and Henchy J stressed that the accused had no adequate opportunity to adduce evidence of present circumstances which would have been relevant to sentence).

[99] [1983] IR 112.

There is no equivalent statutory provision in the case of summary trial and the question arises as to whether constitutional justice requires that the accused person be furnished with advance notice of the case against him. In *Clune v Director of Public Prosecutions*[100] Gannon J said that this was not required as a general rule, since he thought that a case in which such a procedure might be required was not fit for summary trial. However, he clearly hinted that there might nonetheless be cases where the District Judge would make arrangements to allow the defence have advance notice of the case against them. This question was taken a stage further by Barr J in *Cowzer v Kirby* [101] where the applicant - who had been charged with an indictable offence in the District Court - sought a copy of a statement of the evidence which a key prosecution witness proposed to tender. Barr J was impressed by the fact that had the applicant elected for summary trial he would be entitled to such evidence by virtue of the Criminal Procedure Act 1967 and he did not think that there was "any logic" in the proposition that a person charged with an indictable offence should lose such rights "merely because he elects to have the charge dealt with summarily." While he did not suggest that the applicant would be entitled to a formal book of evidence, Barr J nevertheless concluded that:

> "However, where he elects to be tried summarily, constitutional justice and fair procedures require that at the very least the accused should be furnished prior to trial with copies of the statements of all witnesses whose evidence is crucial to the prosecution case against him. This ought not to present any significant administrative difficulty or impede the objectives of summary trial in the District Court."

This question was re-considered by Geoghegan J in *Director of Public Prosecutions v Doyle*[102] where he indicated that he preferred the approach of Gannon J in *Clune*. Unlike Barr J, he did not consider it illogical that a person opting for summary trial would lose some of the rights which he would have had if the trial was being heard upon indictment, since this seemed to him "to be a natural consequence of the accused's own election to go for summary trial." He then summed up the position as follows:

> "The Constitution guarantees fair procedures in all trials whether summary or upon indictment. Therefore, if in any given case fair procedures dictate that an accused in a summary trial should be given advance notice of the material evidence against him then the judge should not embark on the trial unless that is done."

This intermediate position would seem to mean that the accused would be entitled to advance notice of such prosecution evidence in cases where by reason of its particular circumstances the case "would be unreasonably difficult to defend without advance notice of the crucial evidence."

The State is entitled to the benefit of fair procedures

Not only the accused person, but also the State, is entitled to the benefit of the *audi alteram partem* maxim: *The State (Hayden) v Good*;[103] *The State (Aherne) v Cotter*[104] (*per* Henchy J) and *Director of Public Prosecutions v Brennan.*[105]

[100] [1981] ILRM 17.
[101] High Court, 11 February 1991.
[102] High Court, 25 May 1993.
[103] [1972] IR 351.
[104] [1982] IR 188.
[105] [1992] 2 IR 233 (District Judge acceded to defence submission that accused had been in unlawful custody and dismissed charges; held by Barron J, quashing the acquittals, that the failure to enter on an adjudication of the prosecution charges amounted to a denial of fair procedures).

The case against the accused must be in a language which he understands

It is obviously part of the concept of natural justice that a party affected by criminal (or other legal) proceedings should be told of the case against him in a language which he understands. This was specifically established in *The State (Buchan) v Coyne*,[106] in which a District Judge had refused to order the interpretation into English, for the benefit of a defendant who knew only English, of police evidence tendered in Irish. The High Court quashed the resulting conviction, Sullivan CJ saying:

> "It is quite obvious that in this case one of the fundamental principles of the administration of criminal justice has been disregarded and the conviction obtained in it could not possibly stand in any court of law."[107]

No one is to be a judge in his own cause

The maxim *nemo iudex in causa sua* in its application to criminal proceedings was tacitly exemplified in *The People (Attorney General) v Singer*.[108] Here a person accused of a complex fraud was tried by a jury containing as foreman one of the victims of the alleged fraud, who was a claimant against the accused's company, now in liquidation, in respect of his lost investment. The Court of Criminal Appeal set the conviction aside for this reason (and others). Ó Dálaigh J, delivering the Court's judgment, said:

> "The whole purpose of jury-trial is third-party judgment, judgment by indifferent persons... The victim is not to be thought of as indifferent, and his presence on the jury manifestly offends against the concept of fair trial - the essence of which is third-party judgment - however honestly he should strive to discharge his duty as juror. A victim of a crime is, by the crime itself, set apart from those who may be called upon to try the accused. The crime must be looked upon as disabling the victim from acting as a juror on the trial of the offence. In the opinion of the Court it effects a disqualification.
>
> It is true that the foreman was associated as an alleged victim only with count 4 of the indictment which is the general deficiency charge. But the infirmity of the foreman's presence in the jury room is communicated to the entire case in all its counts. It is not conceivable that the jury's verdict could be severed."

This principle is also reflected in Article 6(1) of the European Convention of Human Rights which requires that "in the determination of...any criminal charge against him,

[106] (1936) 70 ILTR 185. This decision was mentioned by Gannon J in *The State (Healy) v Donoghue* [1976] IR 325 as "an example of a breach of a fundamental right going to the root of the decision of the court." See also *R. (Ó Cóilean) v Crotty* (1937) 61 ILTR 81; *Attorney General v Joyce* [1929] IR 526 (all mentioned in connection with Article 8, above, pp. 53-54). Note that Article 6 of the European Convention on Human Rights and Fundamental Freedoms mentions, as one of the "minimum rights" of an accused person, that he be informed of the nature and cause of the accusation "in a language which he understands."

[107] Cp. the decision of the Court of Criminal Appeal in *The People (Attorney General) v Jasinski* 1 Frewen 283 (1963) where the Court of Criminal Appeal held that "inasmuch as [the accused] had a good knowledge of English and was [legally represented] he was not entitled as of right to have [the prosecution's closing speeches] translated into Polish."

[108] [1975] IR 408 (decided in 1963). For a discussion of bias in the wider context of administrative law, see generally Hogan and Morgan, *Administrative Law in Ireland* (London, 1991) at 420-439. In the important case of *R. v Gough* [1993] 2 All ER 724 the House of Lords ruled that the test of bias is whether, having regard to all the relevant circumstances, there was a "real danger of bias" on the part of the relevant member of the tribunal concerned. However, in cases of "direct pecuniary interest" in the outcome of the proceedings, the courts would assume bias and automatically disqualify the person concerned from adjudication. *Singer's* case would presumably come within the latter category.

everyone is entitled to a fair...hearing by an impartial tribunal." This has been held by the European Court of Human Rights as meaning that:

> "it must be determined whether, quite apart from the judge's personal conduct, there are ascertainable facts which may raise doubts as to his impartiality. In this respect, even appearances may be of a certain importance. What is at stake is the confidence which the courts in a democratic society must inspire to the public and above all, as far as the criminal proceedings are concerned, in the accused. Accordingly, any judge in respect of whom there is a legitimate reason to fear a lack of impartiality must withdraw."[109]

Privilege against self-incrimination

This rule - expressed also in the maxim *nemo tenetur se ipsum accusare* - which is incorporated in the Fifth Amendment of the US Constitution, was in issue in *The State (McCarthy) v Lennon.*[110] In this case, the applicant had been convicted on a confession made by way of reply to questions which, under s 15 of Article 2A of the 1922 Constitution, it was an offence to refuse to answer. His case was unsuccessful, as the Supreme Court held that it was bound to give effect to Article 2A; but all three judges made it plain that, apart from the special situation under Article 2A, the rule whereby no one could be obliged to incriminate himself was valid. Fitzgibbon J said:

> "By the common law, which existed for centuries before the Free State was constituted, statements or confessions obtained from an accused party by threats or inducements held out by persons in authority could not be given in evidence against him, and the maxim *Nemo tenetur se ipsum accusare* was rigidly enforced by the judges. When the Constitution of the Free State was framed that law was continued in force here by Article 73."

What remained unclear, however, was whether the Supreme Court was here deciding that the privilege of self-incrimination enjoyed the status of a constitutional right (albeit one which had been temporarily suspended by virtue of Article 2A) or whether (as seems more likely) Fitzgibbon J was simply referring to a fundamental *common law* right whose existence had simply been continued in force by Article 73 of the 1922 Constitution.[111] The proposition that a statutory provision requiring information to be given under penalty for refusal will override the common law privilege against self-incrimination has been accepted - with express assent to what the old Supreme Court had said in *McCarthy's* case - by the Court of Criminal Appeal in The *People v*

[109] *Hauschildt v Denmark* (1990) 12 EHRR 266. In this case, the Court held that the impartiality of the trail judge was open to doubt, since he had previously declined to allow the accused bail pursuant to a special statutory provision which required the judge to be convinced that there was a "very high degree of clarity" on the issue of guilt before bail could be refused. See also the interesting decision in *Demicoli v Malta* (1992) 14 EHRR 47 (where the European Court held that Article 6(1) was infringed in circumstances where two members of Parliament who had been satirised in an article written by a journalist later participated in a parliamentary decision to punish and fine the journalist in question for breach of parliamentary privilege.)

[110] [1936] IR 485. See generally, O'Connor and Cooney, "*Criminal Due Process, the Pre-Trial Stage and Self-Incrimination*" (1980) 15 Ir Jur (n.s.) 219 and Redmond, "*The Privilege against Self-Incrimination*" (1992) 2 ICLJ 118.

[111] In *In re McAllister* [1973] IR 238 (a bankruptcy matter) Kenny J said that he reserved the question "as to whether the Constitution confers a right against self-incrimination." Note that s 21 of the Bankruptcy Act 1988 now expressly abolishes the right against self-incrimination in the context of a judicial examination of the assets etc. of the bankrupt, while providing that any answers given pursuant to this statutory demand shall not be admissible in evidence. The Attorney General advised that the removal of the right of self-incrimination in this context was not unconstitutional: see *D.25 Joint Committee on Legislation: Sub-Committee on the Bankruptcy Bill, 1982, No. 6.*

McGowan,[112] where what was in issue was s 52 of the Offences Against the State Act 1939, a provision very similar to s 15 of the old Article 2A. The Court of Criminal Appeal did not, however, consider - and would have had no jurisdiction to consider[113] - how this section assorts with the Constitution. This question was also touched by Finlay CJ when delivering the judgment of the Supreme Court in *The People (Director of Public Prosecutions) v Quilligan (No.3).*[114] In this case the accused had made incriminatory statements following their arrest under s 30 of the Offences Against the State Act 1939. They then challenged the constitutionality of this provision on a variety of grounds, including that the powers of interrogation[115] thereby conferred infringed the right to silence. The Supreme Court was content merely to list the protections afforded to persons detained in custody[116] and concluded that it had not been shown that the interrogation powers conferred by s 30 constituted "an invasion or failure to protect the right to silence of the citizen." This rather curious remark can only be interpreted as meaning that the powers of interrogation under s 30 do not extend so far as requiring the suspect under pain of penalty to incriminate himself.[117] The Court added the following rider:

> "The Court does not find it necessary, therefore, to express any view on the question as to whether in what circumstances or subject to what qualifications, if any, a right of silence or self-incrimination is an unenumerated right pursuant to the Constitution."

The Supreme Court was plainly here reserving its position on this question, even if the authorities to date tend to lean against - rather than favour - the existence of a constitutional right protecting the privilege against self-incrimination. But clearly, if the general principle that one cannot be forced to incriminate oneself is perceived as a dimension of the due course of law prescribed by Article 38.1, the question must ultimately arise whether it is competent for the Oireachtas to abridge it by statute; and whether, if this can be permitted in the conditions of the Offences Against the State Act 1939, there is any reason why the privilege could not be dismantled by statute over the whole range of the criminal law.

Legislation prescribing penalties for failure to answer

A distinction must also be made between legislation which provides that it is a criminal offence for the suspect not to answer the questions posed and legislation which goes further and allows for the *use* of such information against the accused in subsequent criminal proceedings. Here again, there appears to be no consistent judicial view. In *The*

[112] [1979] IR 45. Note also the comments of Ó Dálaigh CJ in *The State (O'Connor) v Larkin* [1968] IR 255 where he said that the right of an accused person "not to offer any evidence in his defence is basic to an accusatorial system of criminal justice."
[113] By virtue of Article 34.3.2: see pp. 421-422.
[114] Supreme Court, 14 July 1992.
[115] It should be stressed that the Court here was concerned with the ordinary common law powers of interrogation enjoyed by members of the police in respect of suspects detained under s 30 and not the special statutory powers conferred by s 52 of the 1939 Act. The Court of Criminal Appeal had previously concluded that these powers were mutually exclusive: see *The People (Director of Public Prosecutions) v Kelly (No.2)* [1983] IR 1.
[116] Considered below at pp. 856-857.
[117] This despite the provisions of s 30(5), (6) which make it an offence to refuse to give one's name and address or to give false information in respect of such a demand. This, of course, is in contrast to s 52 of the same Act which enables the Gardaí to demand that the suspect give an account of his movements. Finlay CJ said that the s 52 powers "had not been invoked" in the present case and hence the Court was not required to consider any constitutional issue which might arise in relation to that provision. Note, however, that the report of the first *Quilligan* case states that the admissions of the defendants had been procured following a demand under s 52: see *The People (Director of Public Prosecutions) v Quilligan (No.1)* [1986] IR 495,497.

People (Attorney General) v Gilbert[118] the accused had been indicted for the larceny of a motor vehicle. A policeman had demanded that he should give information under s 107 of the Road Traffic Act 1961, as to who was driving the vehicle at a particular time. The accused could not legally have refused to answer the question by invoking the privilege against self-incrimination without incurring the penalties prescribed by the section. The Court of Criminal Appeal held that this rendered the statement inadmissible; it had not been made voluntarily since the accused had been told that a failure to answer would involve serious penalties. But a differently composed Court of Criminal Appeal apparently took another view in *The People (Director of Public Prosecutions) v Doyle*,[119] where O'Higgins CJ said of s 52 of the Offences Against the State Act 1939 (which empowers the police to require a person detained under s 30 of that Act to give, on pain of incurring a penalty, an account of his movements) that, were it not for its provisions:

> "evidence obtained as result of informing a person in detention that, if he did not give an account of his movements, he would be liable to imprisonment would be clearly inadmissible as a statement obtained under threat."

Sections 15(1) of the Criminal Justice Act 1984, provides that where a policeman finds a person in possession of any firearm or ammunition, has reasonable grounds for believing that the possession is in contravention of the criminal law, and informs that person of that belief, then:

> "he may require that person to give him any information which is in his possession, or which he can obtain by taking reasonable steps, as to how he came by the firearm or ammunition and as to any previous dealings with it, whether by himself or by any other person."

Section 15(3) provides that the person concerned must be told in ordinary language that his failure or refusal without reasonable cause to give such information, or the giving of misleading information, is an offence; though any information so given shall not be used in evidence against him in any other proceedings. Somewhat similar provisions are made, in the context of offences of dishonesty and of various suspicious circumstances, by ss 16, 18 and 19. As ss 15 and 16 merely require the person arrested to answer the questions asked but do not permit such answers to be used in evidence *against him*, these new provisions do not, as such, infringe the privilege against self-incrimination, though they look like a move in this direction.

The right to counsel

Until 1976 the existence of any such general right had not been acknowledged.[120] A limited system of publicly-provided legal aid was provided by the Criminal Justice (Legal Aid) Act 1962, extended by the Criminal Procedure (Amendment) Act 1973. In 1976, however, in *The State (Healy) v Donoghue*,[121] the Supreme Court formally elevated the right to legal assistance to being part of the concept of due course of law and fair trial. The applicant was almost totally illiterate, had left school at the age of thirteen, and while he was qualified by lack of means to receive free legal aid, he was not at first informed by the court before which he was charged of his right to apply for it; and subsequently, when a solicitor was ultimately assigned to him, that solicitor left the legal

[118] [1973] IR 383.
[119] [1977] IR 317.
[120] See *Attorney General v McGann* [1927] IR 503 where the lack of professional aid was said by the Court of Criminal Appeal "was not a legal ground of appeal."
[121] [1976] IR 325.

aid scheme with the result that he remained unrepresented professionally during his trial. The Supreme Court quashed his conviction. O'Higgins CJ said:

> "If the right to be represented is now an acknowledged right of an accused person, justice requires something more when, because of a lack of means, a person facing a serious criminal charge cannot provide a lawyer for his own defence. In my view the concept of justice under the Constitution... requires that in such circumstances the person charged must be afforded the opportunity of being represented.
>
> No one can be compelled to accept legal aid, and a person charged is entitled to waive his right in this respect and to defend himself... However, if a person who is ignorant of his right fails to apply and on that account is not given legal aid, then, in my view, his constitutional right is violated. For this reason it seems to me that when a person faces a possible prison sentence and has no lawyer, and cannot provide for one, he ought to be informed of his right to legal aid. If the person charged does not know of his right, he cannot exercise it; if he cannot exercise it, his right is violated."[122]

Henchy J added:

> "A person who has been convicted and deprived of his liberty as a result of a prosecution which, because of his poverty, he has had to bear without legal aid has reason to complain that he has been meted out less than his constitutional due. This is particularly true if the absence of legal aid is compounded by factors such as a grave or complex charge; or ignorance, illiteracy, immaturity or other conditions rendering the accused incompetent to cope properly wish the prosecution; or an inability, because of detentional restraint, to find and produce witnesses; or simply the fumbling incompetence that may occur when an accused is precipitated into the public glare and alien complexity of courtroom procedures, and is confronted with the might of a prosecution backed by the State."

In *O'Neill v Butler*[123] McMahon J said, in relation to the "exceptional circumstances" which s 2 of the Criminal Justice (Legal Aid) Act 1962, mentions as an alternative ground (along with "the gravity of the charge") for granting legal aid to poor persons, that:

> "it would not be proper to leave the onus of establishing such exceptional circumstances upon a defendant who may be ignorant or inarticulate and the Justice should enquire into the matter himself...Where the interests of justice require that the defendant should have legal aid the Constitution requires that he be afforded the opportunity of being legally represented. and it is the duty of the Justice on behalf of the State to see that this opportunity is afforded."

The implications of *Healy* were further considered by Denham J in *Cahill v Reilly*[124] where, following conviction, evidence of previous convictions were tendered in evidence, thus rending a custodial sentence more likely. The judge held that "when a custodial sentence becomes probable or likely after conviction" even though this might not have been likely before that stage, fair procedures required that the District Judge

[122] This passage was construed by O'Flaherty J in *Rock v Governor of St. Patrick's Institution*, Supreme Court, 22 March 1993 as meaning that the courts must afford "every *reasonable* opportunity to a defendant to make his defence and equip himself to make his defence."
[123] [1979] ILRM 243.
[124] High Court, 24 March 1992.

"should inform the accused...of his right to be legally represented or his right to apply for legal aid" in relation to the sentencing matter. But where legal aid is clearly waived by "an experienced adult", its absence will not entitle him to complain afterwards about his trial: *The State (Sharkey) v McArdle*.[125] And even where the accused is "young, uneducated and indigent" and receives a custodial sentence, he cannot later complain if through his own contumelious acts the District Judge is not in a position to adjudicate on his application for free legal aid: *Rock v Governor of St. Patrick's Institution.*[126]

It is, however, important to realise that legal aid is not necessarily available in every instance where the accused's liberty is at stake. Thus, in *Cahill v Reilly*[127] Denham J reserved the question of whether legal aid was to be made available in every case where the accused faced a possible sentence of imprisonment. This point had previously been made even more graphically by the Supreme Court in *The State (O.) v Daly*[128] the applicant, a detainee in a district mental hospital, had been charged with assault. The District Judge formed the view that there was *prima facie* evidence that he had committed the assault but that if he were placed on trial, he would be unfit to plead. On the District Judge's certificate to this effect the applicant was transferred to the Central Mental Hospital by ministerial order under s 207 of the Mental Treatment Act 1945. The Supreme Court held that this detention was not vitiated by the fact that he had not been legally represented. O'Higgins CJ said that the principle in *Healy*'s case applied only to "the trial of persons charged with criminal offences and not to the earlier or ancillary stages of criminal proceedings" and stressed that the transfer procedure was "very much ancillary and preparatory" to that of a criminal trial.

In the case of persons facing criminal charges in the usual way, the courts should be slow to refuse to assign them the solicitor of their choice. This emerges from the decision of Barr J in *The State (Freeman) v Connellan*,[129] where the District Judge had refused to assign the solicitor chosen by the applicant. The judge granted an order of prohibition, saying that"

> "in the light of the applicant's constitutional rights...where the court has any reservation about the assignment to the applicant of a solicitor nominated by him, the judge should ask the defendant why he wishes to have the services of that particular solicitor...The court should.. refuse to nominate the applicant's choice of solicitor... only if, in the view of the judge, there is good and sufficient reason why the applicant should be deprived of the services of the solicitor nominated by him."

Barr J said that the approach which had been taken by the District Judge - that the onus was on the applicant to establish why he wanted a particular solicitor - was "unnecessarily and unreasonably restrictive". The principle in *Healy's* case also applies to circumstances where the accused has been misled in respect of the availability of counsel of his choice.[130]

[125] Supreme Court, 4 June 1981.
[126] Supreme Court, 22 March 1993.
[127] High Court, 24 March 1992.
[128] [1976] IR 325.
[129] [1986] IR 433.
[130] See *The State (Collins) v Ruane* [1984] IR 105 (where the Supreme Court quashed a conviction in circumstances where, through no fault of his own, the accused was left, in the words of McCarthy J, "without legal help to deal with a prosecution which he had reason to think would either be withdrawn or be defended on his behalf by a professional lawyer") and *Dawson v Hamill* [1989] IR 275 (where Lynch J quashed a conviction in circumstances where the prosecution was allowed to tender new evidence in the absence of the applicant's counsel and where that counsel had been led to believe that his attendance on that particular day had been specifically excused).

Apart from the special position of persons whose lack of means qualifies them for legal aid, the right to counsel does not mean a right to counsel at the State's expense. In *K Security v Ireland*,[131] where the plaintiffs sought to have recouped to them the costs of their legal representation at a tribunal of enquiry, Gannon J said:

> "None of the judgments [in *Healy's* case] goes so far as to declare that every person charged with a criminal offence has a constitutional right to have the expense of his defence paid out of State funds. Neither can it be logically or rationally deduced from any of these judgments that every person who has incurred the expense necessary to secure, with the aid of solicitor and counsel, a fair and just trial has a constitutional right to be recouped such expense out of State funds."

The right to an early trial

This feature of "due course of law" was suggested by Gannon J in *The State (Healy) v Donoghue*[132] under the name "the right to reasonable expedition". The matter arose in a concrete way in *In re Singer*,[133] in which the applicant had been returned for trial by the District Court to "the next Circuit Criminal Court" on a number of charges of complicated fraud. The next sittings of the Circuit Court for criminal cases came and went, but the applicant had not been brought to trial. The judgments in his (successful) *habeas corpus* application contain *dicta* on the importance of avoiding delay. Maguire CJ (who dissented on the main issue) said:

> "The rule that an accused person should be returned for trial to the first competent tribunal is in accordance with the fundamental and well recognised principle that justice should not be delayed. There seems to be no clearer illustration of the truth of the maxim that justice delayed is justice denied than the case of an accused person who is not given an opportunity of establishing his innocence at the earliest opportunity."

Lavery J said:

> "I cannot believe that the framers of the Constitution or the Oireachtas when enacting the Courts of Justice Act 1924, and the many amending Acts contemplated that the right of an accused person to be brought before the first available court - a right enjoyed for centuries - should be abridged."

The ground on which the Court by a majority ordered the release of the applicant was that the committal warrant under which he had been held was now spent; on being released, however, he was immediately re-arrested, and a further period of months elapsed during which further charges were preferred against him. He again sought habeas corpus, on the ground *inter alia* of excessive delay; but this time the Supreme Court was unanimous against him *(In re Singer (No. 2))*.[134] Lavery J said:

> "The delay was great but it must be judged in the circumstances of the case. It is clear that the charges are numerous and complicated."

[131] High Court, 15 June 1977. For details of the Attorney General's scheme (whereby legal aid is provided in certain meritorious cases to indigent applicants for habeas corpus and judicial review remedies in criminal cases) see Collins and O'Reilly, *Civil Proceedings and the State in Ireland: A Practitioner's Guide* (Dublin, 1989) at 53-4.[132] [1976] IR 325.
[133] (1963) 97 ILTR 130.
[134] (1964) 98 ILTR 112.

Ó Dálaigh J said:

> "The detention has indeed been long and very burdensome for the appellant. But assuming, without here asserting, that circumstances might be envisaged in which an order of *habeas corpus* would go in respect of excessive delay in the taking of depositions, in this case no grounds have in my opinion been furnished by the appellant to warrant its being said that the delay and detention associated with it were here excessive. I have moreover to bear in mind that the appellant was allowed bail; and, while he has asserted that the amount of the bail was such as to be unprocurable, the appellant did not carry any appeal to this Court against the amount of such bail."

The constitutional status of the right to early trial was authoritatively examined in *The State (O'Connell) v Fawsitt.*[135] Here the applicant for prohibition had been charged with assault arising out of an incident in January 1981. He was returned for trial in July 1982, but his case was regularly adjourned until a date was fixed for July 1984. However, a jury could not then be empanelled, and the trial was put back until October 1984. By this stage the applicant had obtained employment in England, but returned for the trial in late October. The case was put back for another week, but he could not stay without putting his employment at risk. He returned for a trial again at the end of January 1985, but the case was again adjourned until early February. The case was then still further adjourned, as several vital witnesses, who had been present at prior adjournments of the case, were not then available. In the High Court, Murphy J refused prohibition mainly because he thought the question of undue delay was essentially one for the trial judge. The Supreme Court, however, reversed his decision, holding that there had, in fact, been undue delay. Moreover, this delay was prejudicial to the accused as it resulted in the non-availability of an important defence witness. Finlay CJ said that the remedy of prohibition was the appropriate one to vindicate the accused's right to a fair trial:

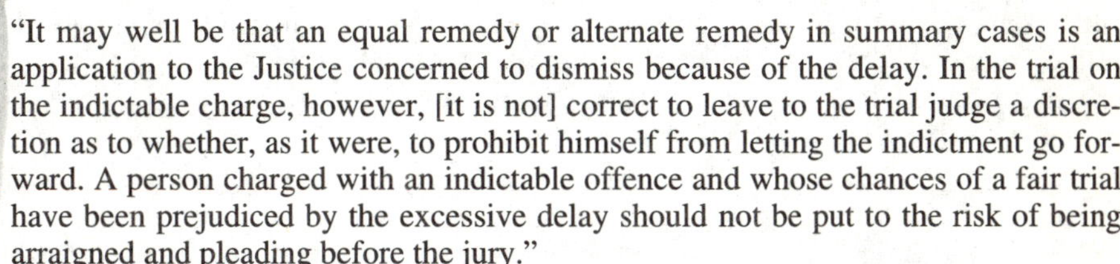

> "It may well be that an equal remedy or alternate remedy in summary cases is an application to the Justice concerned to dismiss because of the delay. In the trial on the indictable charge, however, [it is not] correct to leave to the trial judge a discretion as to whether, as it were, to prohibit himself from letting the indictment go forward. A person charged with an indictable offence and whose chances of a fair trial have been prejudiced by the excessive delay should not be put to the risk of being arraigned and pleading before the jury."

The subsequent decisions show that the issue of undue delay will largely turn on whether this has prejudiced the defence. In *N.C. v Director of Public Prosecutions*[136] Barr J found that an unexplained delay of upwards of nine years' in making a complaint about alleged sexual abuse of a minor was "unreasonably long in all the circumstances." This delay had hampered the accused in the preparation of his defence and thus "deprived him of his constitutional right to fair procedures and a fair trial." On the other hand, a delay of eighteen months was excused by the Supreme Court in *O'Flynn v Clifford,*[137] as there was, said Walsh J, "no evidence that the prosecuting authorities were in a position to institute their prosecution before they did so" or that the delay had caused actual prejudice. The question of actual prejudice also featured prominently in *The People (Director of Public Prosecutions) v Quilligan (No.3)*[138] where there had

[135] [1986] IR 362; [1986] ILRM 639.

[136] [1991] 1 IR 471.

[137] [1989] IR 524. In *Cahalane v Murphy*, High Court, 13 August 1993, Carney J said that the DPP was under an onus to justify a delay of over 5½ years.

[138] [1993] 2 IR 305.

been a four year delay between the date of the original trial and the re-trial, which delay was not in any way attributable to the conduct of the parties.[139] This delay meant that an alibi witness who had given evidence at the first trial had died shortly before the second trial and this key defence evidence was now unavailable. A majority of the Supreme Court concluded that this delay had infringed the accused's constitutional right to an early trial, with Finlay CJ observing:

> "Having regard to the general right of an accused person to a trial with reasonable expedition....and having regard to the prejudice that, undoubtedly, potentially exists from the non-availability of the [alibi] witness in the interests of justice this [re-trial] should have been prevented..."

Yet it is hard to escape the impression that what happened was, as McCarthy J pointed out in dissent, "pure misfortune" largely unrelated to delay *as such*. Would the decision in *Quilligan (No.3)* have been the same if the key witness had died immediately after the accused had been charged? It is difficult to see why not, since in both cases the potential prejudice to the accused would be the same. If this is so, it may be that *Quilligan (No.3)* should be regarded as an example of where to permit the trial to proceed would work an injustice to the accused rather than a decision concerned with the issue of delay as such.

Undue delay in summary prosecutions

Most of the undue delay cases turn on compliance with the six month time limit prescribed by s 10(4) of the Petty Sessions (Ireland) Act 1851.[140] However, there appears to be a tendency in more recent legislation to extend this statutory time limit.[141] One may start by considering the judgment of Blayney J in *Maher v Carroll*[142] where the defendant had been charged with road traffic offences arising out of an incident in January 1985, the complaint had been made just within the six months time limit prescribed by s 10(4) of the 1851 Act but the summons was not actually issued until November 1985, with a return date for January 1986. Blayney J held that there had not been undue delay. In the absence of "very special circumstances", a complaint made within the statutory time-limit could not be said to have been unreasonably delayed:

[139] The delays were largely caused by two intervening appeals to the Supreme Court. See also *Cahalane v Murphy*, High Court, 13 August 1993.

[140] It suffices that the complaint is made *within* the six months period, provided that the subsequent hearing is heard with reasonable expedition thereafter: see *Director of Public Prosecutions v Gill* [1980] IR 263; *Director of Public Prosecutions v Nolan* [1990] 2 IR 526; *Director of Public Prosecutions v McKillen* [1991] 2 IR 508. In *Gill's* case, Henchy J said that provided the complaint was made within the statutory six months limit, the issue of the summons after six months was not necessarily invalid. He did add, however, that if "because of undue delay in issuing the summons or in bringing it to a hearing, the defendant is unfairly prejudiced in making his defence, natural justice may require that the summons be dismissed."

[141] Examples include Animal Remedies Act 1993, s 22(2) (two year limit) and European Communities (Amendment) Act 1993, s 5(4) (two year limit in respect of all offences created by regulations made under the European Communities Act 1972). A more elaborate provision in respect of all summary prosecutions under the Road Traffic Acts is now proposed to be enacted in the Road Traffic Bill of 1993, s 42 of which provides that, subject to an absolute limit of three years, all prosecutions must be commenced either within the six months time limit or any later time within three months on which evidence sufficient "in the opinion of the person by whom the proceedings are instituted, to justify proceedings comes to such person's knowledge."

[142] High Court, 8 August 1986. But cf. *The State (Cuddy) v Mangan* [1988] ILRM 720 where a complaint had been made within the six months time limit, but the summons was not issued and served until some two and a half years later. D'Arcy J held that the applicant was prejudiced by the delay and that his right to fair procedures was thereby denied. This, however, is an exceptional case "where the overall lapse of time from offence to trial is such as to be unconscionable and unreasonable *per se*": see *per* Carroll J in *Director of Public Prosecutions (Finn) v Bouchier Hayes*, High Court, 19 December 1992.

"The legislature has prescribed a relatively short period for making the complaint, and once it has been made within that period, I consider that a defendant's right to reasonable expedition has not been infringed. Were this not the case, one would be introducing a second time limit in regard to the making of complaints, a wholly undefined one based on the defendant's right to reasonable expedition, which would create a serious element of uncertainty in the prosecution of summary offences."[143]

In this case the District Court clerk had also expressed doubts about the validity of the summons, and had consulted the complainant before deciding to issue it; and the defendant had offered "no evidence from which an inference of prejudice could be drawn". The subsequent authorities demonstrate that the delay cases tend to fall into two distinct categories: (a) a delay which in fact produces prejudice and (b) a delay which by its very length alone is unfair and prejudicial. Morris J has explained that in the former case "the onus of proving prejudice is on the defendant and in the latter the onus is on the State to justify the delay."[144]

While the courts have jurisdiction to dismiss a summary prosecution on the ground of unconscionable or excessive delay, the period alleged to be excessive "must be measured against the limitation period provided for the making of the complaint."[145] Thus, delays of up to eight months have generally been held not to be excessive or unreasonable (assuming, of course, that prejudice cannot be shown)[146], especially where the delay can be satisfactorily explained. For example, in *Director of Public Prosecutions (Finn) v Bouchier Hayes*[147] Carroll J hinted that a delay of eleven months might be excused if it were shown that this was due to an industrial dispute and assuming that the defendant could not show prejudice. *Director of Public Prosecutions (Deery) v Byrne*[148] was a case on the other side of the line and Geoghegan J held that the District Judge was entitled to dismiss a summons where no explanation had been forthcoming in respect of a delay of six months.

All of these cases were, of course, decided in the context of the six months time limit prescribed by s 10(4) of the Petty Sessions (Ireland) Act 1851. It remains to be seen how the courts would react to similar delays when measured in the context of the two year limitation period prescribed by some recent legislation, e.g., by s 4(5) of the European Communities (Amendment) Act 1993. Judged in that new statutory context, a delay of just over two years between the date of the offence and the hearing could scarcely be regarded as unconscionable in itself, although, of course, it might be easier for an accused to show prejudice by reason of the delay. And if the accused could show prejudice by reason of the delay even where the summons was applied for well within the extended statutory time limit, the courts might find themselves coerced to strike out

143 But note the comments of Geoghegan J in *Director of Public Prosecutions (Deery) v Byrne*, High Court, 5 February 1993 where he said that it was "bad practice" for the prosecution "deliberately or negligently to delay unreasonably the commencement of the prosecution, irrespective of the statutory limitation period of the statutory limitation period", although he reserved the question of whether summary proceedings commenced within the six month period could be dismissed on the ground of delay.

144 *Director of Public Prosecutions v Carlton* [1993] 1 IR 81.

145 *Director of Public Prosecutions v Carlton* [1993] 1 IR 81.

146 *Director of Public Prosecutions v Carlton* [1993] 1 IR 81; *Director of Public Prosecutions v Corbett (No.1)* [1991] 2 IR 1; *Director of Public Prosecutions v Corbett (No.2)* [1992] ILRM 674; *Director of Public Prosecutions (Finn) v Bouchier Hayes*, High Court, 19 December 1992 (eleven months delay).

147 High Court, 19 December 1992.

148 High Court, 5 February 1993. See also the companion case decided by Geoghegan J on the same day: *Director of Public Prosecutions (Deery) v Carroll*, High Court, 5 February 1993. See also *Director of Public Prosecutions v Burnby*, High Court, 24 January 1989 (unexplained delay of over six months; held by Barr J that the District Judge was entitled to dismiss summons).

such summonses in order to vindicate the accused's constitutional right to an early trial.[149]

Evidence of previous convictions not to be introduced

This rule was most recently stated by McWilliam J in *King v Director of Public Prosecutions*,[150] in which what was mainly in issue was the discriminatory effect of s 4 of the Vagrancy Act 1824, penalising "loitering" in the case of "suspected persons or reputed thieves". The judge said:

> "It is one of the concepts of justice which the courts have always accepted that on a criminal trial evidence of character or previous convictions shall not be given except at the instigation of the accused, as this could prejudice the fair trial of the issue of the guilt or innocence of the accused. [He cited Ó Dálaigh CJ in *The People v O'Callaghan*[151] "The courts owe more than verbal respect to the principle that punishment begins after conviction, and that every man is deemed to be innocent until he is proved guilty."]...The provisions that evidence may be given of known character of the accused and that no evidence need be given of any act showing or tending to show intent are contrary to the concept of justice which is implicit in the Constitution."[152]

"Prejudicial" evidence not admissible

The courts will exclude as inconsistent with standards of fairness in criminal trials any evidence whose prejudicial effect outweighs its probative value. In *The People (Director of Public Prosecutions) v Marley*[153] the Court of Criminal Appeal quashed a conviction for fraud where one of the prosecution witnesses inadvertently disclosed that the accused had previously been acquitted on a murder charge. Although the trial judge had instructed the jury to regard the accused as a completely innocent man, Keane J said that a verdict of guilty arrived at by a jury which had heard that the accused had been wanted for murder was one "which could not safely be allowed to stand". Similar considerations underlay the majority Supreme Court decision in *The People (Director of Public Prosecutions) v Conroy*,[154] where one of the reasons given as to why the jury should not be present during a "trial within a trial" to determine the admissibility of statements was that the jury might be exposed to highly prejudicial - but inadmissible - evidence, which would thereby put their impartiality in jeopardy. Finlay CJ said Article 38.1 implied a right to a trial with a jury "from whose knowledge there is excluded any evidence which is inadmissible at law"; Henchy J added that the presence of the jury at

[149] The statement to the contrary of Blayney J in *Maher v Carroll*, High Court, 8 August 1986 would presumably have to be re-assessed in the light of this very much extended statutory time limit.

[150] [1981] IR 233.

[151] [1966] IR 501; (1970) 104 ILTR 53.

[152] See also *The State (O'Reilly) v Windle* , High Court, 4 November 1986 (where Blayney J quashed a conviction where he found that the intervention of the District Judge "opened the door to let in evidence of previous convictions"). Note that s 43(1) of the Larceny Act 1916 which allowed for the admission of evidence of prior convictions in order establish to guilty knowledge was repealed by s 5 of the Larceny Act 1990. This repeal was probably prompted by official doubts as to the constitutionality of the section: see Law Reform Commission Report No. 23, *Report on Receiving Stolen Property* (1987), para. 23.

[153] [1985] ILRM 17. But cf. *The People (Director of Public Prosecutions) v McMahon* [1984] ILRM 461 (Special Criminal Court consisting of professional judges capable of disregarding in admissible prejudicial evidence given inadvertently by police witness). On the other hand, in *The People (Director of Public Prosecutions) v Hardy, The Irish Times*, December 6, 1989, Barr J is reported as having said that as the Special Criminal Court which had heard the accused's bail application had been exposed to prejudicial evidence concerning the accused, a differently composed Court should preside over the prosecution of the case.)

[154] [1986] IR 460.

the trial within a trial was such that it would frequently make the jury trying the preliminary issue of admissibility:

> "unfit to try the general issue of guilt or innocence. This would be particularly so where the jury's special verdict ruled out the questioned statement and there was other evidence which might justify a conviction. A jury thus informed of the circumstances and contents of the rejected statement would lack the characteristics of an impartial jury for the trial of the issue of guilt or innocence."

Similar principles are also evident in the judgment of the Court of Criminal Appeal in *The People (Director of Public Prosecutions) v McGrail.*[155] Here Hederman J stressed that an accused could only be asked questions concerning previous bad character in circumstances where he had gratuitously impugned the character of a prosecution witness. For the trial judge to rule otherwise would involve a procedure which inhibited the accused "from challenging the veracity of the evidence against him at the risk of having his own previous character put in evidence" and something which was patently unfair.

(B) "DUE COURSE OF LAW": EVIDENCE WRONGFULLY OBTAINED

General principles

Since 1964 the courts have evolved the doctrine that, while evidence obtained illegally or in breach of the Judges' Rules may be admissible, if the illegality amounts to a deliberate and conscious breach of the accused person's constitutional rights the evidence thus obtained will be inadmissible.[156] The general rule may now be stated as follows: evidence obtained as a result of a deliberate breach of a constitutional right should be excluded, unless there are extraordinary excusing circumstances which justify its admission. In this regard, the test as to whether the violation of constitutional right was deliberate and conscious is an objective one. However, if the evidence has been obtained as a result of a mere illegality (i.e., an irregularity not amounting to a breach of any constitutional right) then such evidence is admissible, but the court has a discretion to exclude, and will, in general, exclude the evidence if it is satisfied that the illegal act was the result of a settled or deliberate policy.

This doctrine was first formulated in *The People (Attorney General) v O'Brien*,[157] in which stolen property was found in the course of a search of a private house in reliance on a warrant which, because of an accidental naming of a different house from that searched, was in fact not a lawful authority for the search; the evidence represented by the property was objected to on the ground that it was procured via a breach of the defendant's constitutional right to inviolability of the dwelling. In that instance the Supreme Court held the evidence admissible, but only because the error was purely formal and accidental; but as Kingsmill Moore J said (agreeing with Walsh J):

> "where there has been such a deliberate and conscious violation of constitutional rights by the State or its agents evidence obtained by such violation should in general be excluded;"

[155] [1990] 1 IR 38.
[156] This doctrine is invariably confined in its application to criminal cases. But there is no reason why it might not apply in a civil action so as to exclude evidence (obtained as a result of, say, the illegal interception of telephone communications). See *A.C. v D.C.*, High Court, 8 December 1981 where, in the context of a family law action, McMahon J excluded evidence improperly obtained by one spouse following an unlawful search - contrary to Article 40.5 - of the other's dwelling.
[157] [1965] IR 142.

(though both judges also agreed that there might be "extraordinary excusing circumstances such as the imminent destruction of vital evidence or the need to rescue a victim in peril"[158] which even then might justify admitting the evidence).

The principle thus enunciated has since been followed in cases where the police detained persons for longer than allowed by law and then sought to put in evidence statements made after the expiry of the lawful period. In *The People (Director of Public Prosecutions) v Madden*[159] the defendant had been arrested under s 30 of the Offences Against the State Act 1939, but had been detained for some hours beyond the maximum period allowed by statute.

The Court of Criminal Appeal considered that, although the police might have acted "for the best of motives and in the interests of the due investigation of [a murder]", the deliberate holding of the defendant beyond the expiry of the 48 hours could not be excused. O'Higgins CJ said:

> "This statement was taken by a senior Garda officer who must have been aware of the lawful period of detention which applied in this defendant's case and in circumstances which suggest that he deliberately and consciously regarded the taking and completion of the statement as being of more importance than the according to the defendant of his right to liberty, should he, the defendant, desire to exercise such right... Although the statement made by the defendant was a voluntary one made after caution, nevertheless by reason of the fact that it may have been taken under circumstances which involved a deliberate and conscious breach of the defendant's constitutional rights the statement ought to have been excluded."

O'Brien's case and *Madden's* case were followed also in *The People (Director of Public Prosecutions) v O'Loughlin*,[160] in which the defendant, having at first voluntarily accompanied Garda officers and voluntarily remained at a Garda station while investigations in one case were being completed, was subsequently - without having been charged - taken by the police to a different station and questioned about a quite different series of offences, and finally made an inculpatory statement. The Court of Criminal Appeal took the view that this statement should have been ruled inadmissible in evidence by the trial judge, as the circumstances, ultimately amounting to constraint, in which he had been questioned represented a conscious and deliberate violation of his constitutional rights. The Court said (*per* O'Higgins CJ):

> "Our law does not contemplate or permit the holding of a person for questioning...[That this happened] could only have been the result of a deliberate decision by these officers who were aware of the applicant's rights. These rights were disregarded and swept aside because of the concern to continue the investigation into cattle-stealing. This was not such a special circumstance...as could excuse the violation of constitutional rights which took place."

The rationale for this doctrine was explained in *The State (Trimbole) v Governor of Mountjoy Prison*.[161] Here the extradition of the applicant had been sought by the

[158] See below at p. 613.
[159] [1977] IR 336; (1977) 111 ILTR 117. See also *The People (Director of Public Prosecutions) v Stenson*, Special Criminal Court, 28 January 1977.
[160] [1979] IR 85. The principle of these cases was again stated (but in this instance not applied) in *The People (Director of Public Prosecutions) v Walsh* [1980] IR 294. Walsh J, who dissented from the rest of the Supreme Court in this case, would have applied it so as to rule out the admission of a fingerprint in evidence.
[161] [1985] IR 550; [1985] ILRM 465.

Australian authorities. As the Irish police were awaiting the making of an order by the Government applying the Extradition Act 1965, to the Commonwealth of Australia, it was decided to arrest Trimbole under s 30 of the Offences Against the State Act 1939, ostensibly on the ground that he was illegally in possession of firearms (a scheduled offence), but in reality in order to ensure that he would available for extradition as soon as the order was made, which was the day after the arrest, and following the extension of the detention period for another twenty-four hours. Trimbole challenged the validity of his detention, and Egan J held it was tainted by a conscious and deliberate infringement of his constitutional right to liberty, as there never had been any genuine suspicion that he had committed, or was about to commit, the firearms offence. The authorities on the exclusion of evidence obtained by unconstitutional means stood on a principle which was not confined to questions of admissibility of evidence:

> "Courts have no higher duty to perform than that involving the protection of constitutional rights and if at any time the protection of those rights should delay, or even defeat, the ends of justice in a particular case, it is better for the public good that this should happen rather than that constitutional rights should be nullified."

He concluded that the applicant's detention was unlawful as it resulted from a deliberate infringement of constitutional rights for which there was no justification. This finding was upheld by the Supreme Court, where Finlay CJ deduced the following principles from the earlier authorities:

> "The courts not only have an inherent jurisdiction but a positive duty: (i) to protect persons against invasion of their constitutional rights; (ii) if such invasion has occurred, to restore as far as possible the person damaged to the position in which he would be if his rights had not been so invaded; and (iii) to ensure as far as possible that persons acting on behalf of the executive who consciously and deliberately violate the constitutional rights of citizens do not for themselves or their superiors obtain the planned results of that invasion."

The principle was not confined either to the "question of the admissibility of evidence or to the question of the punishment of persons for contempt of court"; it was comparable with the inherent jurisdiction enjoyed by the courts at common law to prevent an abuse of their own processes. As the original arrest was "part and parcel" of a planned operation prompted by the delay in bringing into operation the reciprocal extradition arrangements, it followed that the subsequent arrest and all other orders for his detention were tainted with illegality. This is an example of the application of the second and third principles mentioned by the Chief Justice: Trimbole was restored to the position in which he would have been were it not for the unlawful arrest, and the agents of the executive were denied the "planned results" of their invasion of his constitutional rights.

Confusion as to existence of the good faith exception

A series of cases in the 1980s revealed an uncertainty as to whether the "conscious and deliberate" requirement was an objective or subjective test. In *The People (Director of Public Prosecutions) v Shaw*[162] Griffin J, speaking for the majority of the Supreme Court, said that a person's statement cannot be ruled out as evidence "obtained in deliberate and conscious breach of constitutional rights, even though the taker of the statement may not have known that what he was doing was either illegal or unconstitution-

[162] [1982] IR 1.

al." Likewise in *The People (Director of Public Prosecutions) v Lawless*[163] the police had conducted a search of a house using a search warrant which turned out to be defective. The Court of Criminal Appeal held that, even if there had been a breach of the applicant's constitutional right to inviolability of the dwelling, there had been no conscious breach. McCarthy J agreed that the actions of the search party were deliberate, but said that the irregularity resulted from "a pure oversight; there was no evidence of deliberate deceit or illegality, no policy to disregard the provisions of the Constitution or to conduct a search without a warrant". This appeared not to accord with the approach of the courts since *Madden's* and *O'Loughlin's* cases, namely, that if the act infringing constitutional rights has been deliberate (i.e., not accidental), then one did not have to go any further in order to secure the exclusion of the evidence; it was not necessary to show that there has been something approaching *mala fides*, or a deliberate policy to disregard the Constitution. A series of subsequent decisions of the Supreme Court - *The People (Director of Public Prosecutions) v Quilligan (No.1)*[164] and *Director of Public Prosecutions v Gaffney*[165] - seemed to suggest a different view to that taken by Griffin J in *Shaw*. In *Quilligan's* case, a majority of the Court did not subscribe to the view that an element of *mala fides* was necessary before unconstitutionally obtained evidence should be excluded.[166] In *Gaffney's* case, the Supreme Court excluded evidence which had been obtained following an unlawful arrest of the defendant in his home, in breach of Article 40.5, there being here no suggestion that the good faith on the part of the arresting Gardaí could have prevented the exclusion of the evidence.

Uncertainty resolved by the Supreme Court in Healy's and Kenny's cases

This lingering uncertainty was finally resolved by the Supreme Court by two decisions delivered in late 1989 and early 1990: *The People (Director of Public Prosecutions) v Healy*[167] and *The People (Director of Public Prosecutions) v Kenny.*[168] In the former case, Gardaí taking a statement from the accused - who had been detained under s 30 of the Offences Against the State Act 1939 - had refused to allow him access to a solicitor. This was held by the Supreme Court to constitute a deliberate and conscious breach of his constitutional rights. Both Finlay CJ and McCarthy J rejected the "good faith" submission, with the Chief Justice observing that the fact that the Gardaí may not have realised that the breach was a refusal of the defendant's constitutional rights "was immaterial." McCarthy J put it even more starkly:

> "A violation of constitutional rights is not to be excused by the ignorance of the violator no more than ignorance of the law can ensure to the benefit of a person who...is presumed to have intended the natural and probable consequences of his conduct. If it were otherwise, there would be a premium on ignorance."

This question arose in even more concrete form in *Kenny's* case. Here Gardaí searched a private dwelling pursuant to a search warrant which, it later transpired, was invalid.[169]

[163] (1985) 3 Frewen 30.
[164] [1986] IR 495; [1987] ILRM 606.
[165] [1987] IR 173.
[166] Although in his concurring judgment Henchy J stressed that because the "arresting gardaí were acting in good faith", therefore regardless "of any unconstitutionality in the arrest, the statements were admissible in evidence." See also *The People (Director of Public Prosecutions) v Lawless* 3 Frewen 30 (1985) where McCarthy J, speaking for the Court of Criminal Appeal, appeared to require evidence of something approaching *mala fides* or a deliberate breach of the Constitution in order to bring the exclusionary rule into play.
[167] [1990] 2 IR 73; [1990] ILRM 313.
[168] [1990] 2 IR 110; [1990] ILRM 569.
[169] It was shown that the Peace Commission who issued the warrant had not inquired into the basis of the Garda's suspicion and failed to exercise the requisite judicial discretion. There was no question, however, but that both the Peace Commissioner and the Garda believed that the warrant was valid.

Was the evidence obtained as a result of the search to be excluded on the basis that it in fringed the accused's constitutional rights? On this question, the Supreme Court divided three to two[170] in favour of exclusion of the evidence.

For the majority, Finlay CJ rationalised the test in terms of the State's duty to vindicate the accused's personal rights under Article 40.3.1, so that the courts were under an obligation to choose the principle "which is likely to provide a stronger and more effective defence and vindication of the right concerned." It was true that a subjective good faith test would have the effect of imposing a "negative deterrent", but:

> "to apply, on the other hand, the absolute protection rule of exclusion whilst providing also that negative deterrent, incorporates as well a positive encouragement to those in authority over the crime prevention and detection services of the State to consider in detail the personal rights of the citizens as set out in the Constitution, and the effect of their powers of arrest, detention, search and questioning in relation to such rights. It seems to me an inescapable conclusion that a principle of exclusion which contains both negative and positive force is likely to protect constitutional rights in more instances than is a principle with negative consequences only."

On the other hand, the dissenting judgment of Lynch J has much force. He explained cases such as *Healy* on the basis that "there was a deliberate disregard of the accused's rights" and expressed the view that evidence obtained in breach of constitutional rights:

> "must be rejected if there is any element of blame or culpability or unfairness (including any such element to be inferred by the reasonable application of the doctrine *ignorantia juris haud excusat*) in relation to the breach of the right on the part of those who obtained the evidence unless there are adequate excusing circumstances."

The dissent has the merit that it is not as absolute in its terms as the rule espoused by the majority, while at the same time not placing the "premium on ignorance" - to use the words of McCarthy J in *Healy* - which some feared might result from the adoption of a purely subjective test.

There must be a causative link between the breach of constitutional rights and obtaining the evidence in question

It is, of course, implicit in the case-law that there must be causative link between the breach of constitutional rights complained of and the evidence which is sought to be explained of. The necessity for this causal relationship was stressed by Finlay CJ in *Healy's* case[171] and was further explored by Blayney J in *Walsh v Ó Buachalla.*[172] In this case the applicant had been arrested on a charge of drunk driving but the Gardaí refused to permit him seek the presence of a solicitor at a time when a doctor arrived to take a blood sample. Blayney J held that, even assuming the refusal amounted to a breach of applicant's constitutional rights,[173] the evidence objected to - namely the blood sample - was obtained after - *but not as a result of* - the violation:

[170] Finlay CJ, Walsh and Hederman JJ; Griffin and Lynch JJ dissenting.

[171] "The vital issue which arises, therefore, if a breach of the right of access to a solicitor has occurred as a result of the conscious and deliberate act of a member of the Garda Síochána, is as to whether there is a *causative link between that breach and the obtaining of an admission.*" (Authors' emphasis).

[172] [1991] 1 IR 56.

[173] The Gardaí had considered that the request was not genuine.

> "The applicant was required by statute to give a specimen of his blood or urine. No advice from a solicitor could have altered that. So his being refused access to a solicitor did not in any way lead to a specimen of blood being obtained.

This approach is also evident in the judgment of Finlay CJ for the Court of Criminal Appeal in *The People (Director of Public Prosecutions) v Cullen.*[174] In this case the accused contended that the Gardaí had falsely alleged that he made certain verbal admissions in their presence. The Gardaí had been unable to locate the solicitor requested by the accused and it was suggested that the latter's absence[175] had contributed to the making of this alleged verbal admission. The Court could not accept this: there was nothing to suggest that the accused had been coerced by improper questions to make the statement in question (something a solicitor might have advised him on) and, hence, no causative link between the alleged admission and the absence of a solicitor.[176]

Breach of the constitutional right to liberty: other miscellaneous examples

Some other miscellaneous examples of cases involving breaches of the constitutional right to liberty may now be mentioned. In *The People (Director of Public Prosecutions) v Coffey*[177] the accused had voluntarily accompanied the police to the police station, but had not been informed that he was at all times free to leave. Hamilton J found that this detention was unlawful, and, in the absence of any excusing circumstances, excluded the statement which the accused had made while in custody. A similar principle was applied by the Supreme Court in *Director of Public Prosecutions v Joyce,*[178] where the defendant had been arrested on suspicion of drunken driving. Hederman J held that as he had not been arrested in a public place (as is required by statute), but in the yard adjacent to his house, the arrest was unlawful. It followed that the evidence had been improperly obtained, and that it should be excluded. In *The People (Director of Public Prosecutions) v Higgins*[179] the Supreme Court excluded a statement which had been obtained from the defendant in a police station where he had been detained, not for the purpose of being charged or brought before a court, but (as the police admitted) for the purpose of being interrogated. Finlay CJ said he had been detained unlawfully to the knowledge of the police officers concerned, and, consequently, in deliberate and conscious violation of his constitutional rights. Finally, in *The People (Director of Public Prosecutions) v Byrne*[180] the Supreme Court excluded a statement obtained by the accused following his arrest under s 30 of the Offences Against the State Act 1939 in circumstances where the prosecution were unable to prove that the order extending the period of accused's detention had been validly made.[181]

[174] Court of Criminal Appeal, 30 March 1993.

[175] The accused contended that *Healy's* case gave him an absolute entitlement to the presence of a solicitor, but the Court did not find it necessary to rule on this submission.

[176] It was also suggested that had a solicitor been present, the accused might have earlier admitted guilt and obtained a more lenient sentence. This was also rejected, since there was "a fundamental, logical difficulty in having as a ground for setting aside a conviction, a failure of the applicant to get advice to avail of an opportunity to admit guilt".

[177] [1987] ILRM 727. For a similar approach, see the judgment of O'Higgins CJ for the Court of Criminal Appeal in *The People (Director of Public Prosecutions) v Farrell* [1978] IR 13.

[178] [1984] ILRM 206.

[179] Supreme Court, 22 November 1985.

[180] [1987] IR 363

[181] Note, however, that the decision to exclude the evidence can be made only by the trial judge and not in any collateral proceedings, such as judicial review. Thus, even where some illegality or unconstitutionality is established in judicial review proceedings, the decision on the admissibility of any evidence tainted by such illegality or unconstitutionality will remain that of the trial judge in the criminal case: see *Farrell v Farrelly* [1988] IR 201; *Byrne v Grey* [1988] IR 31 and *O'Mahoney v Melia* [1989] IR 335; [1990] ILRM 14.

Denial of access to legal advisers

In *The People (Director of Public Prosecutions) v Madden*[182] a defendant sought to have the statement made by him excluded from evidence on two grounds: firstly, that when he was under arrest under s 30 of the Offences Against the State Act 1939, the:

> "failure on the part of the Garda Síochána to provide for [him] a legal adviser at the time of, or prior to, the making of this statement, whether he asked for one or not, was a deprivation of his constitutional right."

The Court of Criminal Appeal said it was satisfied that:

> "a person held in detention by the Garda Síochána whether under the provisions of the Offences Against the State Act 1939, or otherwise has got a right of reasonable access to his legal advisers and that a refusal upon request to give such reasonable access would render his detention illegal. Reasonable in this context must of course be construed having regard to all the circumstances of each individual case, particularly as to the time at which access is requested and the availability of the legal adviser or advisers sought."

This important statement of principle was of no benefit to the defendant in the present case, as the Court said it was not satisfied that:

> "there was any obligation on the Garda Síochána when detaining a person...to proffer to such person the assistance of a legal adviser without his request...The finding of fact in this case made by the Special Criminal Court was that the defendant did not at any time during his detention request the assistance of a legal adviser or the presence of a legal adviser...This Court is therefore satisfied that he was not deprived in that context of any constitutional or other lawful right."

On the other hand, in *The People (Director of Public Prosecutions) v Kelly*,[183] where the defendant had been detained, under s 30 of the Offences Against the State Act 1939, in three successive police stations, the Supreme Court, finding that this procedure was not *per se* unlawful, said however that if the prisoner had been moved around for the purpose of "harassment or of isolating him from assistance or access to which he could properly be entitled, then that fact itself would clearly render his detention unlawful".

In a series of subsequent cases different judicial views were heard on this question. In *The People (Director of Public Prosecutions) v Farrell*[184] O'Higgins CJ for the Court of Criminal Appeal denied that an accused must be told of his right to consult a legal adviser prior to making a statement; and he followed this judgment in the same Court in *The People (Director of Public Prosecutions) v Pringle*,[185] adding that:

[182] [1977] IR 336; (1977) 111 ILTR 117.

[183] [1982] IR Cf. also the judgment of Lynch J in *Director of Public Prosecutions v Sheehy* [1987] ILRM 138 where he held that the mere fact that the defendant, who had been arrested on suspicion of drunken driving, had been transferred from one Garda station to another did not of itself render the detention unlawful. However, while there was here no evidence of *mala fides*, he accepted that if the defendant had been transferred in order "to defeat his rights to consult a solicitor or communicate with a relative or a doctor of his choice, then the detention would become unlawful."

[184] [1978] IR 13.

[185] (1981) 2 Frewen 57.

> "if a person has not got a constitutional right to have the services of a solicitor before being questioned by an investigating Garda, neither has he got a constitutional right to the presence of a solicitor while any investigation is being carried out."

The Chief Justice did, however, say that a person in lawful custody was "entitled to reasonable access to his lawyer".

This question was finally authoritatively resolved by the Supreme Court[186] in *The People (Director of Public Prosecutions) v Healy*[187] where the accused - who had been arrested under s 30 of the Offences Against the State Act 1939 - had been denied access to his solicitor pending the completion of a statement. Having reviewed the authorities, Finlay CJ observed:

> "The undoubted right of reasonable access to a solicitor enjoyed by a person who is in detention must be interpreted as being directed towards the vital function of ensuring that such person is aware of his rights and has the independent advice which would be appropriate in order to permit him to reach a truly free decision as to his attitude to interrogation or to the making of any statement, be it exculpatory or inculpatory. The availability of advice from a lawyer must, in my view, be seen as a contribution, at least, towards some measure of equality in the position of the detained person and his interrogators."

The Chief Justice accordingly concluded that such "an important and fundamental standard of fairness in the administration of justice as the right of access to a lawyer" must rank as constitutional - and not merely legal - in origin. Finlay CJ went on to hold that, on the facts, the defendant's right of access had been violated, since the Gardaí had deliberately postponed such access until such time as the accused had made an incriminating statement. The suspect had a right to be told immediately of the arrival of his legal advisers and, should the suspect request it, immediate access. Finlay CJ further explained that:

> "The only thing that could justify the postponement of informing the detained person of...immediately complying with a request made by a detained person...for access to [his solicitor] would be reasons which objectively viewed from the point of view of the interest or the welfare of the detailed person, would be viewed by a court as being valid."[188]

Practical significance of Healy's case in view of s 5 of the Criminal Justice Act 1984

The practical significance of this decision is no longer as great as it might otherwise have been, given that s 5(1) of the Criminal Justice Act 1984 imposes a legal duty on the Garda Síochána to inform a person arrested pursuant to either s 4 of the 1984 or s 30 of

[186] In *The People (Director of Public Prosecutions) v Conroy* [1986] IR 460; [1988] ILRM 4 both Walsh and Henchy JJ had expressed conflicting views on whether a suspect had a constitutional right to a solicitor, while the other members of the Court reserved their position.

[187] [1990] 2 IR 73; [1990] ILRM 313.

[188] The statement made by O'Higgins CJ for the Court of Criminal Appeal in *The People (Director of Public Prosecutions) v Pringle* (1981) 2 Frewen 57 to the effect that the police were entitled to postpone the granting of access to a solicitor must no longer be regarded as good law in view of the decision in *Healy*. Note also the comments of Lynch J in *Director of Public Prosecutions v Sheehy* [1987] ILRM 138. See p. 609, supra.

the Offences Against the State Act 1939[189] of his right to consult a solicitor. This legislative development notwithstanding, *Healy's* case is nonetheless of importance in two particular respects. First, it imposes a duty to inform the suspect in all cases, and not simply where he has been arrested pursuant to either s 4 of the 1984 Act or s 30 of the 1939. Secondly, it elevates that obligation to the status of a constitutional right and this may prove to be significant in the context of the operation of the exclusionary rule if this constitutional right is violated by the police during the course of detention.

Oppressive interrogation

The defendant in *The People (Director of Public Prosecutions) v Madden*[190] also argued that persistent police questioning was "an abuse of and in excess of the powers conferred by s 52 of the Offences Against the State Act 1939,[191] and tainted therefore with illegality his detention...thus making the obtaining of evidence a breach of his constitutional rights". The Court however held that the fact that he was:

> "on repeated occasions requested to give an account of his movements by different members of the Garda Síochána did not constitute illegal action towards him nor the deprivation of any right on his part."

But if questioning crosses the line into oppressive interrogation, any statement resulting from it must be excluded from evidence by the trial judge. This appears clearly from *The People (Director of Public Prosecutions) v McNally*,[192] in which the Court of Criminal Appeal set aside the convictions of two persons on foot of statements obtained after lengthy night-and-day interrogation over periods exceeding 40 hours. The Court adopted two English descriptions of oppressive interrogation, that of Sachs J in *R. v Priestly*[193] - "something which tends to sap and has sapped that free will which must exist before a confession is voluntary" - and that of McDermott LJ in *R. v Prager*[194] - "Questioning which by its nature, duration or other intended circumstances (including the fact of custody) excites hopes (such as the hope of release) or fears, or so affects the mind of the subject that his will crumbles and he speaks when otherwise he would have stayed silent"; and cited also what Griffin J had lately said in *The People v Shaw*:[195]

> "A statement will be excluded as being involuntary if it was wrung from its maker by physical or psychological pressures, by threats or promises made by persons in authority, by the use of drugs, hypnosis, intoxicating drink, by prolonged interrogation or excessive questioning, or by any one of a diversity of methods which have in common the result or the risk that what is tendered as a voluntary statement is not the natural emanation of a rational intellect and a free will."

[189] Section 9 of the Criminal Justice Act 1984 provides that the provisions of s 5 shall apply "with the necessary modifications" to the exercise of the arrest powers under s 30 of the 1939 Act.

[190] [1977] IR 336; (1977) 111 ILTR 117.

[191] The section provides that a person detained under Part IV of the Act may be required to give a full account of his movements and actions during a specified period; failure to do so is an offence. The constitutionality of this provision is considered above at pp. 593-594.

[192] (1981) 2 Frewen 43.

[193] 51 Cr App Rep 1.

[194] 56 Cr App Rep 151.

[195] [1982] IR 1.

The question of when persistent police interrogation becomes oppressive must, however, depend on the particular circumstances of each case. In *Pringle's* case[196] the accused had been subjected to lengthy, although not continuous, interrogation over a forty-eight hour period. O'Higgins CJ, speaking for the Court of Criminal Appeal, said that in considering the question whether there had been oppressive interrogation, "the physical, mental and emotional characteristics" of the person whose will has been said to have been undermined must be considered. In rejecting the plea of oppressive questioning, he noted that the accused had received five visits from his solicitor over the forty-eight hour period, which must have "strengthened his resolve and assisted in counteracting any weakness of will" which the conditions of his custody may have produced; and thought it also relevant that the accused, who was a former fisherman, was "an experienced man of the world not unused to conditions of physical hardship". In contrast, however, the Supreme Court held in *The People (Director of Public Prosecutions) v Lynch*[197] that the sustained questioning of the accused over a 22 hour period, coupled with the denial of access to his family or the opportunity for rest or sleep all amounted "to such circumstances of harassment and oppression as to make it unjust and unfair" to admit any incriminating statements.

Worth mentioning also are the words of Kingsmill Moore J in *The People (Attorney General) v O'Brien*[198] in the hypothetical context of evidence obtained by physical violence:

> "The Attorney General has refused to argue for this rule in its unqualified form that relevant evidence can never be excluded however illegal the action which obtained it, conceding that evidence obtained by methods of gross personal violence or other methods offending against the essential dignity of the human person should not be received. Such a concession would appear to be entirely consistent with the spirit of our Constitution as shown in Article 40.3.1, 2."

Earlier he had said in the same hypothetical context:

> "To countenance the use of evidence extracted or discovered by gross personal violence would, in my opinion, involve the State in moral defilement."

A relatively trivial physical interference not justified by law (the taking of fingerprints without either warrant or the consent of the prisoner on remand) was (in 1960) held by the High Court insufficient to rule out the evidence so obtained: *The People (Attorney General) v McGrath.*[199]

[196] 2 Frewen 57. A similar objection was rejected by the Court of Criminal Appeal in *The People (Director of Public Prosecutions) v McGing* (1985) 3 Frewen 18 where the accused, who had been arrested under s 30 of the Offences Against the State Act 1939, claimed that the absence of any policewoman during her interrogation was a denial of her constitutional right to fair procedures. While Hederman J agreed that the physical presence of a policewoman during interrogation was "obviously desirable", the fact that these procedures were not followed did not of itself make the interrogation oppressive. The accused had received three visits from her solicitor during that period and had not complained of her treatment to him. In these circumstances her interrogation had not been unfair.

[197] [1982] IR 64.

[198] [1965] IR 142.

[199] (1965) 99 ILTR 59. See also *The People (Director of Public Prosecutions) v O'Shea* (1981) 2 Frewen 57 where the Court of Criminal Appeal upheld the admission as evidence of blood samples illegally taken from the accused while he was ill in hospital (this forms part of the judgment in *Pringle's* case).

"Extraordinary excusing circumstances"

Other possible breaches of constitutional rights which can vitiate evidence have been discussed in a few cases. An instance of the "extraordinary excusing circumstances" (hypothetically admitted in *O'Brien's* case) which would render evidence admissible notwithstanding the breach of constitutional rights accompanying its collection is provided by *The People v Shaw.*[200] Here a man suspected of abducting and possibly murdering a girl who had disappeared was in police custody for three days before being brought before a District Court, although he might have been brought before a District Judge the morning after his arrest. After being in custody for about 30 hours he made a statement and subsequently accompanied the police on a journey in which he pointed out the places where he had killed the girl, disposed of her body and burned her clothes. His counsel sought to have this evidence ruled out on the ground that it was obtained through the deliberate and conscious breach of the accused's rights involved in his extended custody without production in court. The Supreme Court, however, accepted that the trial judge had been entitled to find (as he did) that the police motive had been the anxiety to save this girl in the remotely possible event that she was still alive, and that this had predominated over any concern to formulate charges against their prisoner; this motive, the Court found, amounted to an "extraordinary excusing circumstance" (in fact not unlike one of the hypothetical examples given by Walsh J in *O'Brien's* case) which would justify the admission of the evidence obtained during a custody technically illegal. Mere eagerness on the part of the police to extend their investigations into offences other than that in connection with which a person originally submitted to questioning does not amount to an extraordinary excusing circumstance sufficient to justify detention: The *People (Director of Public Prosecutions) v O'Loughlin.*[201] Another example of extraordinary excusing circumstances is provided by *The People (Director of Public Prosecutions) v Lawless*,[202] in which the Court of Criminal Appeal, *per* McCarthy J (who referred with approval to what Kingsmill Moore J had said on this issue in *O'Brien's* case) suggested that the prevention of the destruction of vital evidence would amount to an extraordinary excusing circumstance.[283]

Illegality not amounting to a breach of constitutional rights: discretion to exclude evidence

The courts have said on several occasions that where the illegality does not amount to a deliberate and conscious breach of constitutional rights, the evidence obtained as a result of that breach will not necessarily be excluded. The courts will, however, take into account factors such as the gravity of the breach; whether it is the result of deliberate and settled policy; and the general public interest in suppressing crime: see the comments of Kingsmill Moore J in *The People (Attorney General) v O'Brien*[204] and Finlay CJ in *Director of Public Prosecutions v McMahon.*[205] A good recent indication of the general approach to this question was provided by Henchy J in *The People (Director of Public Prosecutions) v Quilligan (No.1)*[206] when he said that:

[200] [1982] IR 1.

[201] [1979] IR 85.

[202] (1985) 3 Frewen 30.

[203] Seventeen packets of diamorphine (heroin) were found by the police in a manhole beside the flat. These packets had apparently been flushed down the lavatory as police were entering the house. This evidence was ruled to be admissible.

[204] [1965] IR 142.

[205] [1986] IR 393; [1987] ILRM 87. See also *Director of Public Prosecutions v McCutcheon*, High Court, 15 November 1985.

[206] [1986] IR 495; [1987] ILRM 606.

> "mere illegality in the mode of arrest does not make subsequent incriminating statements inadmissible. They may be ruled inadmissible only if they fall into one of the recognised grounds for rejecting incriminating statements, such as that they were not voluntary, or that they were taken in breach of the Judges' Rules or that their prejudicial effect outweighs their probative capacity or that they were obtained by fundamentally unfair means."

In *The People (Director of Public Prosecutions) v O'Shea*[207] swabs and blood samples were taken from the accused while he was in hospital, and so ill as not to be in a position to consent. The Court of Criminal Appeal agreed that this was illegal, but thought it did not amount to a breach of his constitutional rights; O'Higgins CJ said the public interest was best served by the admission of the evidence, despite the illegality. In *Director of Public Prosecutions v McMahon*[208] Finlay CJ followed *O'Brien's* case and said that illegally (as opposed to unconstitutionally) obtained evidence was admissible, unless the court, in its discretion, decided to exclude it. Here a number of police officers had committed a trespass in the course of a search of licensed premises; the Chief Justice held that the evidence which they obtained by inspecting the use of gaming machines, though illegally acquired, did not amount to a breach of any constitutional right. The question of the exercise of discretion was a matter for the trial judge; but

> "in balancing the public interest that crime should be detected against the undesirability of using improper methods, particular importance may attach to the fact that the Gardaí in entering the public houses to view the machines were trespassers only, not involved in any criminal or opprobrious conduct, and that the offence of permitting gaming on licensed premises may be considered as one with grave social consequences."[209]

(C) "DUE COURSE OF LAW": FAIR PROCEDURES

The foregoing pages have attempted to list some more or less concrete and specific rules and principles which could be seen as requiring to be observed in order that a criminal trial should be "in due course of law". Several of these, as has been seen, have undergone notable evolution in the Irish courts in recent years. Side by side with those specific principles, however, there has developed since the late 1970s, and with great rapidity, the more general notion of "fair procedures": a phrase which is a little difficult to explain. In some contexts it looks almost like another way of saying "due course of law"; in others, a synonym for natural justice; but since it would be plainly redundant if it meant something as well established in their own right as these ideas, it is perhaps best to look at it as a sort of fine-mesh catch-all notion, intended to fill with the general instinct of fair play whatever interstices may be left between more traditional rules and principles of criminal justice such as those mentioned above.

The notion seems to have first taken verbal shape in *In re Haughey*,[210] in which the fairness of the procedures of the Dáil Public Accounts Committee was in issue; the analogy,

[207] 2 Frewen 57 (1981). See also *The People (Director of Public Prosecutions v Ryan*, Court of Criminal Appeal, 30 November 1992 (taking of fingerprints by prison officer without having complied with prior statutory requirement requiring prior authority by superior officers and where Lynch J appeared to suggest that trial judge could only have exercised his discretion so as to admit the evidence.)

[208] [1986] IR 393; [1987] ILRM 87.

[209] McCarthy J said that if the evidence established that, having regard to the "multiplicity of searches and the rank of the searching officers", there was a policy to conduct the searches without a warrant, then the "discretion could only properly be exercised so as to exclude the evidence."

[210] [1971] IR 217.

in the circumstances of that case, to a criminal proceeding was close, and the Supreme Court *dicta* are certainly applicable *a fortiori* to the subject-matter of Article 38.1. The applicant maintained, and the Supreme Court majority accepted, that he was entitled to be afforded "reasonable means of defending himself" before the Committee, to which serious accusations about the applicant had been made; these he enumerated as (a) the provision of a copy of the evidence reflecting on his good name; (b) leave to cross-examine, by counsel, his accuser or accusers; (c) permission to give rebutting evidence; (d) leave to address the Committee by counsel. The Committee's procedures ruled out (b) and (d); and Ó Dálaigh CJ said:

> "Without [these] two rights, no accused...could hope to make any adequate defence of his good name. To deny such rights is, in an ancestral adage, a classic case of *clocha ceangailte agus madraí scaoilte*.[211] Article 40.3...Is a guarantee to the citizen of basic fairness of procedures...The provisions of Article 38.1...apply only to trials of criminal charges in accordance with Article 38; but in proceedings before any tribunal where a party to the proceedings is on risk of having his good name, or his person or property, or any of his personal rights jeopardised, the proceedings may be correctly classed as proceedings which may affect his rights, and in compliance with the Constitution the State, either by its enactments or through the courts, must outlaw any procedures which will restrict or prevent the party concerned from vindicating these rights."

Subsequently, in *The State (Royle) v Kelly*,[212] Walsh J said of "due course of law", with obvious reference to the interstitial function on which the "fair procedures" label has now solidified with usage, that

> "what amounts to such a breach of the constitutional guarantee, apart from breaches of specific statutory provisions etc., may in most cases be a question of degree."

Whereas Ó Dálaigh CJ in *Haughey's* case had read the "fair procedures" principle out of Article 40.3 and the citizen's personal rights, O'Higgins CJ in *The State (Healy) v Donoghue*[213] saw it as given effect through Articles 34 and 38:

> "It is justice which is to be administered in the courts, and this concept of justice must import not only fairness, and fair procedures, but also regard to the dignity of the individual... [Considered in the light of Articles 34 and 40.3] it is clear that the words "due course of law" in Article 38 make it mandatory that every criminal trial shall be conducted in accordance with the concept of justice, that the procedures applied shall be fair, and that the person accused will be afforded every opportunity to defend himself. If this were not so, the dignity of the individual would be ignored and the State would have failed to vindicate his personal rights."

"Fair procedures" also represented an evolving value:

> "The general view of what is fair and proper in relation to criminal trials has always been the subject of change and development. Rules of evidence and rules of procedure gradually evolved as notions of fairness developed."

Yet he enunciated a useful standard:

[211] Stones tied down and dogs on the loose.
[212] [1974] IR 259.
[213] [1976] IR 325; (1976) 110 ILTR 9.

> "There are thousands of trivial charges prosecuted in the District Courts throughout the State every day. In respect of all these there must be fairness and fair procedures, but there may be other cases in which more is required and where justice may be a more exacting task-master. The requirements of fairness and of justice must be considered in relation to the seriousness of the charge brought against the person and the consequences involved for him."

He also cited with approval words used by Gannon J in the High Court in the same case:

> Among the natural rights of an individual whose conduct is impugned and whose freedom is put in jeopardy are the rights to be adequately informed of the nature and substance of the accusation, to have the matter tried in his presence by an impartial and independent court or arbitrator, to hear and test by examination the evidence offered by or on behalf of his accuser, to be allowed to give or call evidence in his defence, and to be heard in argument or submission before judgment be given. By mentioning these I am not to be taken as giving a complete summary, or as excluding other rights such as the right to reasonable expedition and the right to have an opportunity for preparation of the defence. The rights I have mentioned are such as would necessarily have a bearing on the result of a trial. In my view, they are rights which are anterior to and do not merely derive from the Constitution, but the duty to protect them is cast upon the courts by the Constitution.

The facts in *Healy's* case arose from the disadvantaged condition of the accused, who was nearly illiterate, was not at first informed of his right to legal aid, and in the event remained unrepresented professionally during his trial. In a subsequent case, *The State (Glover) v McCarthy*,[214] where a frightened woman agreed to plead guilty to shop-lifting, Gannon J said she "may have been in fact in the sort of position of disadvantage indicated" in *Healy's* case; he said "the clear message from the judgments of the Supreme Court in that case is that a District Justice should be ever on the alert for indications of such sort of circumstances".

No unfair pre-trial publicity

It is plain that adverse and prejudicial pre-trial publicity may make it difficult, if not altogether impossible, for an accused to obtain a fair trial. In the relatively few cases to date the question has principally arisen in the context of whether it would be now safe to permit the accused's trial to proceed by reason of the adverse pre-trial publicity and related issues - such as a possible conflict between the right to a trial on one hand and freedom of expression on the other have only been fleetingly explored. It is also worth stressing that much has turned on the special facts of each case.

Rather curiously, the first case in which this issue squarely arose concerned a decision of the Attorney General under s 2 of the Extradition (Amendment) Act 1987 which never progressed to the judicial arena. In November 1988, the Belgian authorities had refused to extradite one Father Patrick Ryan to the United Kingdom where he was sought on various conspiracy charges.[215] He was then deported to Ireland and the British authorities then sought his extradition to the United Kingdom. There then followed a barrage of publicity in the British media which sought in "extravagantly worded head-

[214] [1981] ILRM 47.

[215] See generally, Hogan, "*Some reflections on the role of the Attorney General and the Patrick Ryan Affair*" (1992) 2 ICLJ 128

lines"[216] to attack the character of the suspect and indeed, went to far as to assert guilt. There were also prejudicial comments in the House of Commons, some of which also directly attributed guilt. While the Attorney General agreed that the statutory requirements contained in s 2 of the 1987 Act had been satisfied, he nonetheless refused to sanction the execution of the extradition warrants, saying that he was satisfied that this would imperil the suspect's constitutional rights. The right to trial in due course of law included a right to protection "against the creation of a prejudice or animosity in the minds of jurors such as would effectively deprive a person of the right to a non-biased trial". The Attorney concluded that, having regard to "the extreme nature and extent of the prejudicial material published", the prejudice was "irredeemable" and could not be cured by a jury direction.

This question was later examined by Carney J in *Doherty v Director of Public Prosecutions.*[217] In this case there had been extensive newspaper publicity concerning the circumstances in which a jury had been discharged following a mis-trial. The newspaper reportage had highlighted some of the very unusual facts of the case and had strongly hinted that the applicant was guilty of the offences charged. Carney J felt that as against this background it would be unsafe to allow a re-trial to proceed and granted an order of prohibition sought. On the other hand, in *Cullen v Toibín*[218] the Supreme Court refused to grant an injunction restraining publication of an exceptionally detailed and graphic account of the background to a murder pending the outcome of the accused's appeal against conviction to the Court of Criminal Appeal. The Court considered that in this case the right of freedom of expression should take precedence, stressing that the dangers of prejudice in the context of an appeal on a point of law to a court composed of professional judges were minimal.[219]

Right to inspect forensic evidence

In some circumstances fair procedures will require that the accused be given an opportunity to inspect the forensic evidence. In *Murphy v Director of Public Prosecutions*[220] Lynch J found that the failure by the prosecuting authorities to allow the applicant's legal representatives to inspect the wreck of a stolen car before disposing of it was a breach of fair procedures, since in the circumstances[221] it meant that the applicant would now be denied the opportunity of providing possible corroborative evidence with regard to his denial. This is not a universal rule, however, and thus the courts will not restrain a prosecution where the Gardaí themselves have carried out a forensic inspection and where the applicant has delayed in duly in seeking such an inspection.[222]

Miscellaneous examples

A few other cases may be briefly mentioned. In *The State (McGlinchey) v Governor of Portlaoise Prison*,[223]where two separate prosecutions, ultimately resulting in two suc-

[216] The quotations are taken from a lengthy statement of the Attorney General which was read into the Dáil record by the Taoiseach (Mr. C. Haughey T.D.): see 385 *Dáil Debates* at Col. 1199-1214.
[217] High Court, 6 February 1993.
[218] [1984] ILRM 577.
[219] See to like effect the comments of McCarthy J in *The People (Director of Public Prosecutions) v Ferris* (1986) 3 Frewen . But note the comments of Finlay CJ about the dangers of such prejudice even in the cases of professional judges: see *The People (Director of Public Prosecutions) v Conroy* [1988] IR 460.
[220] [1989] ILRM 71.
[221] The applicant had been charged with driving the stolen car.
[222] *Rogers v Director of Public Prosecutions* [1992] ILRM 695.
[223] [1982] ILRM 187. Note also the comments of Walsh J to like effect in *O'Flynn v Clifford* [1989] IR 524: "It would be improper to simply defer the making of charges against a suspected person already undergoing a prison sentence if the object or effect of deferring the bringing of charges until the expiration, or after the expiration, of a sentence was to make him serve consecutive terms of imprisonment, and the matter could have been dealt with at the date of his original trial or during his imprisonment."

cessive rather than concurrent terms of imprisonment, were brought, Finlay P said that:

> "if he had been satisfied that this was a case in which the prosecuting authorities had purposely or consciously delayed the bringing of a charge against the applicant so as to harass him and to increase the eventual periods of detention served by him in respect of two separate offences, then undoubtedly it would be an unfair procedure and one which the courts must and will condemn."

(He was not, however, so satisfied in this case.) In *The State (Hughes) v Neylon*[224] Finlay P said that an accused person returned for trial must be told where and when he is to be tried; otherwise he "could not adequately prepare for his defence". In *L'Henryenat v Ireland*[225] Carroll J had found in the High Court that the statutory power making possible the detention of a fishing boat arrested for a fishery offence pending trial of the ship's master, subject to a very large sum for security, amounted to a bail which was (in the words of the Supreme Court) "oppressive and contrary to fair procedures as implicitly required by the Constitution"; the Supreme Court reversed her, finding that (as the security had to be found not by the accused person, but by the ship's owner) it was not a bail, but did not disagree with her view of how an oppressive bail must be looked at from the constitutional perspective. In *The State (McKeown) v Magee*[226] O'Hanlon J held that a District Judge was not in breach of the principle of fair procedures in refusing to order the disclosure, to an accused person, of the names of other persons who had taken part in an identification parade. In *Corporation of Dublin v Flynn*[227] the Supreme Court held that there must be, in every criminal trial, a determination of every point constituting the offence charged against the accused: a point which had been decided against him in an earlier, separate proceeding was not *res judicata* for the purpose of later criminal proceedings; any inhibition on the accused in contesting the point from the start would be contrary to the principles of criminal justice. (The "fair procedures" concept was not mentioned, but the decision seems best classified under this head.) In *The People (Director of Public Prosecutions) v Mulligan*[228] (where Griffin J, speaking for the Court of Criminal Appeal, said that the principle of fair procedures did not entitle that Court to form a subjective opinion, unrelated to the record of the evidence or the legal merits of the appeal, that the conviction under appeal was unsafe or unsatisfactory); in *The People (Director of Public Prosecutions) v Cull*[229] (the Court of Criminal Appeal allowed an appeal against conviction for membership of an illegal organisation where the accused had been cross-examined before the Special Criminal Court about his alleged membership of the I.R.A. at times other than those specified in the indictment,

[224] [1982] ILRM 108.

[225] [1983] IR 193.

[226] High Court, 18 March 1983.

[227] [1980] IR 357.

[228] (1980) 2 Frewen 16. This judgment was expressly approved by both McCarthy and O'Flaherty JJ in *The People (Director of Public Prosecutions) v Egan* [1990] ILRM 780 (where the Supreme Court ruled that it could not interfere with a jury verdict on the basis of a "lurking doubt": it could only interfere where the jury verdict was perverse).

[229] (1980) 2 Frewen 36. But cf. *The People (Director of Public Prosecutions) v O'Leary* (1989) 3 Frewen 30 (where the Court of Criminal Appeal refused to quash a conviction where the accused was found guilty of membership of an unlawful organisation having been cross-examined about prejudicial matters which were not the subject of a specific charge). Note also the comments of Lynch J in *The People (Director of Public Prosecutions) v Ryan*, Court of Criminal Appeal, 30 November 1992, to the effect that *Cull's* case is not authority for the proposition that the prosecution are under any general duty to forewarn the accused or defence witnesses of any line of cross-examination, although the courts "will always be astute to ensure that no unfairness occurs."

as the introduction of such matters for the first time during the cross-examination was so prejudicial to the defendant's interests as to be inconsistent with the guarantee of fair procedures); in *Flynn v Director of Public Prosecutions*[230] Finlay CJ said that any act done by the Director of Public Prosecutions in the course of a criminal prosecution "which contributed to or was likely to contribute to an unfair or unjust proceeding is restrainable by the courts." In *Curtis v Attorney General*[231] Carroll J said that the exclusion from a criminal trial of a "disputed issue of fact concerning a material issue" was contrary to fair procedures. In *The State (Lynch) v Ballagh*[232] Henchy J said that the prosecution "may not procure the attendance in court of an accused person by means of a deliberate and conscious violation of his constitutional rights".

The Interest of the State in an Effective Criminal Process

Although Article 38 and the concept of "due course of law" come into view mostly in the context of a defendant's rights, the State (or, more properly, the People) has a clear and legitimate duty and right to maintain an effective criminal process, and is entitled to invoke "due course of law" in its defence. Cases have generally not turned on this principle; but it is worth noting the judicial decisions and dicta which it silently underlies.

A good general statement, whose validity is not affected by the doubts which must surround the decision of the actual issue here involved, is that of O'Higgins CJ in *The People v O'Shea:*[233]

> "The Constitution is concerned with justice and, in the context of this case, with criminal trials being fairly conducted in due course of law. While these considerations provide safeguards for the person accused, they also guarantee to the State which accuses him, and which has a duty to detect and suppress crime, that he will be tried fairly and properly on the evidence adduced against him and in accordance with law. If, as a result of an error made by the trial judge, the jury is not permitted to consider the evidence or the charge brought against an accused or to pronounce on his guilt or innocence, can it be said that justice has been accorded to the State and to society? In my view, it cannot; and, if this be so, a situation would exist which the Constitution prohibits."

This dimension was also present in the partially dissenting judgments of Walsh and McCarthy JJ in *The People (Director of Public Prosecutions) v Quilligan (No.2).*[234] Here the question was whether the Supreme Court had power to order the re-trial of the accused on a murder charge following the successful appeal by the Director of Public Prosecutions against the directed acquittal which the trial judge had ordered. Walsh J concluded that the Supreme Court had such an inherent jurisdiction and observed:

> "[The accused] are entitled as of right to a fair trial, but the People, who in the Director of Public Prosecutions have brought this prosecution, are also entitled to

[230] [1986] ILRM 290. In *Murphy v Director of Public Prosecutions* [1989] ILRM 71 Lynch J referred to the decision in *Flynn* and said that it showed that "in effect any act of the DPP in relation to the prosecution of an offence contributing to an unfair result is restrainable."
[231] [1985] IR 458; [1986] ILRM 428.
[232] [1986] IR 203; [1987] ILRM 65.
[233] [1982] IR 384.
[234] [1989] IR 46.

> have the matter tried and fairly tried in accordance with law. So far this has not been afforded to them."[235]

Similar considerations of the State's legitimate interest are probably visible in *The State (Coveney) v Members of the Special Criminal Court*,[236] in which Finlay P said that "one of the known objectives is the speedy dispatch of criminal proceedings" and in the (partially dissenting) judgment of McCarthy J in *The People (Director of Public Prosecutions) v Quilligan (No.3)*,[237] where speaking in the context of alleged undue delay, he observed that: "As the accused is entitled to a fair trial, so also is the State." The duty of those charged with the prosecution of crime was given emphasis by McCarthy J in *Norris v Attorney General*,[238] when he said (in connection with the fact that the plaintiff had never been prosecuted under the law which he was challenging) that that law still remained in force, and:

> "if there were a positive decision made by the Gardaí or the Director of Public Prosecutions never to prosecute in any such case, it would... be unlawful, as a positive decision not to enforce the law."

Somewhat more dubious is the approach of Lynch J in *Connors v Delap*[239] where he refused to quash a conviction on technical grounds where it was apparent that the applicant had no defence on the merits, since if he were now to do so, it "would clearly deprive the people of Ireland of the just retribution to which they are entitled in respect of the crime committed by the applicant." This is questionable, inasmuch as discretionary factors such as this have never been regarded as sufficient to justify the High Court quashing an admittedly bad conviction.[240]

The State's right to the benefit of the *audi alteram partem* rule in criminal (as in other) contexts has also been acknowledged, both generally *(The State (Hayden) v Good*[241]) and in the special area of *habeas corpus (Application of Zwann*[242] and *The State (Rogers) v Galvin).*[243]

Is mutuality of criminal procedures required as between the prosecution and the defence?

An interesting question which has not yet been satisfactorily resolved is the extent to which fairness of procedures can be said to require mutuality or equality of procedures as between the prosecution and defence. An example here is the approach of Lynch J in *Dawson v Hamill*[244] where the issue was whether the prosecution should be allowed to introduce new evidence which had just come to light at a time when the prosecution's case had closed. Lynch J observed that had the situation been reversed, the court would undoubtedly allow the defence to re-open the case and adduce further evidence. This

[235] McCarthy J spoke to similar effect, saying that "unless a fresh trial is held it would appear that the error at the first trial will be perpetuated."
[236] [1982] ILRM 384.
[237] Supreme Court, 14 July 1992.
[238] [1984] IR 36.
[239] [1989] ILRM 93.
[240] See generally, Hogan and Morgan, *Administrative Law In Ireland* (London, 1991) at 600-603 and Collins, "*Ex Debito Justitiae*?" (1988) 10 DULJ (n.s.)130.
[241] [1972] IR 351.
[242] [1981] IR 395; [1981] ILRM 395.
[243] [1983] IR 249; [1983] ILRM 149.
[244] [1989] IR 275.

being so, the mutuality of fair procedures required that the prosecution be allowed to introduce such fresh evidence. This approach is also evident in a number of other cases which recognise the State's interest in an effective criminal process.[235]

But there are well-recognised limits to this sense of mutuality of procedures. Just because the accused is, for example, entitled to appeal his conviction it does not necessarily follow that the prosecution must enjoy similar rights.[236] Nor does the fact that the trial judge may not constitutionally direct a jury to bring in a particular guilty verdict mean that a similar principle must operate in a reverse, since - as the Supreme Court recognised in *The People (Director of Public Prosecutions) v Davis*[237] - the absence of such a power might work a serious injustice to an accused person and justifies the lack of mutuality or reciprocity in procedures as between prosecution and defence.

What is a "criminal charge"?

The question of what constitutes an offence the subject of a "criminal charge" has not received any final, exhaustive theoretical treatment; though a certain area of doubt has now been cleared. An earlier line of cases, centring round customs and revenue prosecutions, seemed to locate these outside the criminal sphere despite their obviously penal dimension; thus in *Attorney General v Casey*[238] and *Ó Cróinín v Brennan*[239] the old Supreme Court had held that a proceeding for a revenue penalty, as it did not require proof of fraud or *mens rea*, was in the nature of a civil, not a criminal proceeding; and in *The State (Attorney General) v Mangan*[240] the High Court had held that customs offences "are something between criminal offences and civil wrongs, and may fairly be described as quasi-criminal" (*per* Davitt P). The President saw s 186 of the Customs Consolidation Act 1876 (applicable here to the "keeping" of butter imported without a licence) as not creating a criminal offence because of its failure expressly to prohibit this act; although the statute used the expressions "offence" and "offender", although forfeitures were provided for by way of penalty, although it was in this case necessary to prove *mens rea*, although suspects might be detained, and although there was provision for imprisonment in default of payment of the penalty.

This line of authority was however superseded by *Melling v Mathghamhna*,[241] where Ó Dálaigh J described (though not in reference to any other specific judge or case) the perception that a proceeding involving arrest, a penalty, and imprisonment in default could be non-criminal as "Kafka-esque"; and Lavery J said:

[235] See p. 620.

[236] As Henchy J remarked in (an admittedly dissenting judgment) *The People (Director of Public Prosecutions) v O'Shea* [1982] IR 384: "The lack of reciprocity, residing in the fact that the accused is allowed to appeal a conviction while the prosecution is debarred from appealing an acquittal, is accepted and justified on the ground that it is part of the price that has to be paid for the independent verdicts of lay people sitting as jurors and applying community standards."

[237] [1993] ILRM 407. Likewise the fact that a convicted person can successfully contest the invalidity of a return for trial made by a person who was not entitled at that time to exercise judicial powers (*Glavin v Governor of Mountjoy Training Unit* [1991] 2 IR 421; [1991] ILRM 478) does not mean that the State can rely on the self-same invalidity in order to impeach an acquittal: *McCarthy v Garda Commissioner* [1993] 1 IR 489.

[238] [1930] IR 163. In *McLoughlin v Tuite* [1989] IR 82 the Supreme Court observed that the reasoning in *Casey's* case was "primarily based on the origin and nature of an information on behalf of the Crown as a method of suit for the recovery of money due to the Crown and its apparently accepted survival into the law of Saorstát Éireann" and hence that it was not a "safe decision" on which to decide the constitutionality of ss 500 and 508 of the Income Tax Act 1967 which provided for the provision of revenue penalties.

[239] [1939] IR 274; (1938) 82 ILTR 198.

[240] (1961) Ir Jur Rep 17.

[241] [1962] IR 1; (1963) 97 ILTR 60.

> "It seems to me clear that a proceeding, the course of which permits the detention of the person concerned, the bringing of him in custody to a Garda station, the entry of a charge in all respects in the terms appropriate to the charge of a criminal offence, the searching of the person detained and the examination of papers and other things found upon him, the bringing of him before a District Justice in custody, the admission to bail to stand his trial and the detention in custody if bail be not granted or is not forthcoming, the imposition of a pecuniary penalty with the liability to imprisonment if the penalty is not paid has all the *indicia* of a criminal charge. The penalty is clearly punitive in character, being £100 or treble the duty-paid value of the goods."[242]

A more theoretical approach was disclosed by Kingsmill Moore J, who held that the *indicia* of a criminal offence were (i) its character as an offence against the community at large rather than an individual; (ii) the punitive nature of the sanction, (iii) the requirement of *mens rea*.[243] These tests were applied by Carroll J (and, on appeal, by the Supreme Court) in *McLoughlin v Tuite*[244] in holding that the imposition of a penalty under s 500 of the Income Tax Act 1967, in revenue cases was a civil matter and did not amount to the administration of criminal justice by the Revenue Commissioners. Both Carroll J and the Supreme Court concluded that not all of these *indicia* of criminal proceedings were present in this instance. For example, although s 500 "was devoid of all phraseology with criminal overtones", Carroll J thought the first test was satisfied in that the penalty was payable to the Central Fund (i.e., the community at large). But the other two tests were not satisfied: while the sanction was punitive, there was no provision for imprisonment if the penalty was not paid; furthermore, the fact that liability to pay the penalty did not cease on death but continued against the estate of the deceased indicated that *mens rea* was not an essential ingredient.[245] In addition, the *indicia* mentioned by Ó Dálaigh J in *Melling's* case as not being features of civil proceedings (such as the power of arrest, detention, entry and search, and imprisonment in default of payment) were all absent from the sections in issue.

This analysis has been followed in a series of subsequent decisions, which again all involve the characterisation of revenue penalties as either civil or criminal. In *Director of Public Prosecutions v Downes*[246] Barr J held that a fixed mandatory revenue penalty "created a non-criminal liability for payment of a fixed sum to the Exchequer where there has been a failure to comply with the [statutory] requirements."[247] Contrariwise, in

[242] See, however, the judgment of Costello J in *Attorney General v Paperlink Ltd.* [1984] IR 384 for a trace of the old opinion that a proceeding to recover a statutory forfeiture is civil, not criminal. The approach of Keane J in *Pesca Valentia Ltd. v Minister for Fisheries (No.2)* [1990] 2 IR 305 seems preferable. Here the State sought to recover on foot of an undertaking as to damages which the plaintiffs had tendered following the grant of an interlocutory injunction in their favour restraining the enforcement of fishing legislation. Keane J said: "It is wholly unrealistic to measure the damage to the defendants by reference to the penalties which would have been imposed had the criminal prosecutions proceeded....If I were to award damages to the defendants in the form suggested...I would in effect be imposing a penalty on the plaintiff rather than compensating the defendants. Since the plaintiff has never been tried before a judge and jury on any of these charges, such a procedure would seem to be constitutionally suspect in the highest degree."

[243] This appears to have been in the mind of Finlay P in *The State (Murray) v McCrann* [1979] IR 133; (1978) 112 ILTR 33 when he said that *Melling's* case had "defined a crime or criminal charge as an offence against the State itself or as a public offence."

[244] [1986] IR 235 (HC); [1989] IR 82 (SC).

[245] As Finlay CJ observed: "The provision for the recovery of this penalty against the estate of a deceased taxpayer...is quite inconsistent with its existence as a criminal offence."

[246] [1987] IR 139; [1987] ILRM 665.

[247] Barr J pointed out that (i) the language of the section differed fundamentally from other statutory provisions creating revenue penalties which used the words "guilty, "conviction on indictment" etc.; (ii) the fact that the court had power in other cases to impose a range of fines or periods of imprisonment and (iii) the fact that the obligation to pay devolved on death to the deceased's estate.

Director of Public Prosecutions v Boyle[248] Murphy J held that the provisions of ss 24 and 25 of the Finance Act 1926 created a criminal offence. He attached "considerable importance to the vocabulary used in the section of the Act under consideration" and concluded (i) that the reference in the sections to "excise penalties" was intended as "punitive" and not merely coercive and (ii) that the use of phrases such as "offence" and "summary conviction" were inconsistent with the contention that the section created a civil liability only.

Murphy J took a similar approach in *O'Keeffe v Ferris*[249] where he rejected the argument that the fraudulent trading provisions of s 297 of the Companies Act 1963 created a criminal offence. While it was true that this section did not conform "to the popular notion of the compensation or reparation ordinarily directed in civil proceedings", it lacked the requisite indicia of a criminal offence. There was, for example, no power to terminate the proceedings by nolle prosequi and the parties injured was not the State, but rather the creditors of the company. Finally, the s 297 proceedings could only be invoked in the course of a liquidation and Murphy J concluded that it would seem "extraordinary" that an "act which constituted a criminal offence or a wrong against the public generally would be punishable only in such an event."

[248] [1993] ILRM 128.
[249] [1993] 3 IR 165.

Article 38.2

MINOR OFFENCES

2.	**Minor offences may be tried by courts of summary jurisdiction.**	**2.**	**Féadfar mionchionta a thriail ag cúirteanna dlínse achomaire.**

1922 provision

The substance of this provision was contained in Article 72 of the 1922 Constitution; though the wording was somewhat different. The Article prescribed trial by jury "save in the case of charges in respect of minor offences triable by law before a Court of Summary Jurisdiction" (and military offences). The provision of Article 38.2 must be similarly read together with Article 38.5, which provides that, with the same exceptions plus trials by "special courts", "no one shall be tried on any criminal charge without a jury".

District Court

The only court of summary jurisdiction is the District Court. Its criminal jurisdiction is prescribed by s 33(1) of the Courts (Supplemental Provisions) Act 1961, by reference to the jurisdiction vested in the "old" District Court, substantially described in s 77 of the Courts of Justice Act 1924. Appeals against conviction or sentence by the District Court are brought to the Circuit Court by way of rehearing by the Circuit Court judge sitting without a jury; Courts of Justice Act 1928, s 18.

SUMMARY JURISDICTION

The nature of summary jurisdiction was authoritatively stated by O'Higgins CJ in *The State (McEvitt) v Delap*.[1] The Chief Justice noted that "considerable confusion" appeared to exist with regard to its exercise, and thought it would be "helpful to look briefly at its development and history", which he did thus:

> "The jurisdiction to try offences in a summary manner is a jurisdiction which depends entirely on statute. According to O'Connor's *Justice of the Peace* (1915 ed., vol. 1, p. 3) it was first given to Justices of the Peace by the statute 11 Hen. 7, c. 3, in relation to a number of statutory offences. That statute was followed by 33 Hen. 8, c. 6, which provided for summary conviction in relation to the offence of carrying dags or short guns. In ensuing years the statutory extension of the summary jurisdiction of Justices spread to a large variety of offences - both common law and statutory. In the last century the Petty Sessions (Ireland) Act 1851, and the Fines Act (Ireland) 1851, Amendment Act 1874, and other statutes in relation to Dublin, regulated and prescribed the procedure for the exercise of summary jurisdiction by Justices. These various statutes became known collectively as the Summary Jurisdiction Acts. In relation to particular statutes which created an offence and/or provided for summary trial, it was sometimes enacted that the defendant should have an option to be tried by indictment, or that the Justices could so opt (e.g., s 2 of the Merchandise Marks Act 1887, and s 46 of the Offences Against the Person Act 1861). In the absence of such a provision, no right to trial by jury existed where summary trial was directed. Where an offence was created by statute

[1] [1981] IR 125.

and was not expressly or by necessary implication *(Cullen v Trimble*, (1872) LR 7 QB 416) made subject to summary jurisdiction, it could only be tried by a jury as an indictable misdemeanour *(Russell on Crime*, 7th ed., p. 11; *R. v Hall*, (1891)1 QB 747).

On the establishment of the State, the District Court of Justice became (inter alia) the court of summary jurisdiction in relation to criminal matters. By s 77A of the Courts of Justice Act 1924, it was given all the jurisdiction which had been vested "by statute or otherwise in Justices or a Justice of the Peace sitting at Petty Sessions". This effectively transferred to the District Court of Justice the criminal jurisdiction formerly exercisable by Justices of the Peace under the Summary Jurisdiction Acts. In addition, s 77B of the Act of 1924 gave that court summary jurisdiction in relation to specified indictable offences if the Justice was of the opinion that the offence was a minor one and the accused (on enquiry having been made of him) did not object. This latter provision was repealed by the Criminal Justice Act 1951, and was replaced by s 2 of that Act which empowers the District Court to try summarily twenty-one scheduled and indictable offences if the District Court be of the opinion that the facts alleged or proved constitute a minor offence, and if the accused, "on being informed by the Court of his right to be tried with a jury", does not object. Special provision is made for the Attorney General's consent also in relation to certain specified types of offence.

Apart from the transferred jurisdiction of the former Justices of the Peace and the prescribed jurisdiction in relation to scheduled indictable offences under the Act of 1951, other statutes create particular offences and provide for summary trial; these statutes, in so providing, confer additional jurisdiction on the District Court in relation to the new offences which are thereby created. When one of these statutes provides only[2] for summary trial, the offence created by the statute is not indictable and cannot be tried by a jury."

When a summary trial is provided by statute, there is no right to a jury trial - unless a constitutional challenge shows the offence not to be minor

The final paragraph of this passage covered the central point in *McEvitt's* case; this applicant, although charged with an offence which was admittedly minor in nature, still sought to be tried by a jury. It was true that the statute in question provided the alternative of trial on indictment, but this meant that where the act constituting the offence had been serious, the prosecution could opt to have the defendant indicted before a jury - or that the District Judge, if he realised in the course of what started as a summary trial that the offence was not in fact "minor", could decline jurisdiction and proceed instead with a preliminary investigation leading to a trial on indictment[3] - not that the accused could himself opt for a jury trial. The only way an accused person can have jury trial for the offence for which the Act provides only summary trial, is (as the Chief Justice said in *McEvitt's* case) to "undertake the heavy onus of showing that the statute in question offends Article 38.5 by providing for the summary trial of an offence which is not a minor offence"; this he can only do in the High Court (at least, if the statute in question is an Act of the post-1937 Oireachtas).[4]

[2] The report says "only provides", but this seems to be a misprint.

[3] See below at p.628.

[4] See above at pp. 424-425.

Summary disposal of indictable offences

It should be noted that while there is no *constitutional* right to jury trial in the case of non-minor offences, this right is conferred by *statute* in the case of certain specified offences and in certain circumstances. The principal statute in question is the Criminal Justice Act 1951[5] which allows for summary trial of certain scheduled offences.[6] Section 2(2) of the 1951 Act provides that:

> (a) The District Court may try summarily a person charged with a scheduled offence if-
>
> (i) the Court is of opinion that the facts proved or alleged constitute or offence fit to be so tried , and
> (ii) the accused, on being informed by the Court of his right to be tried with a jury, does not object to being tried summarily.
>
> (b) A person shall not be tried summarily for [public mischief, indictable offences concerning the administration of justice and perjury] or for an attempt to commit such an offence unless the Director of Public Prosecutions has consented to his being so tried.

Potential constitutional difficulties with this mode of procedure?

Two possible objections may be raised to the constitutionality of the mode of procedure prescribed by the 1951 Act. First, the right to jury trial is clearly mandatory in the case of all[7] non-minor offences,[8] but it may be queried whether Article 38.5 creates, in effect, an implicitly closed constitutional category[9] which serves to preclude the Oireachtas from extending the right to jury trial to cases where this mode of trial is not constitutionally required. The answer is almost certainly in the negative, since the right to jury trial is probably best regarded as an essential protection for the accused person and one which the Oireachtas is free to extend by legislation to certain categories of minor offences. Besides, the language of Article 38.2 itself ("Minor offences may be tried by courts of summary jurisdiction") points to this conclusion, inasmuch as it suggests that while the Oireachtas may elect to allow such cases to be tried summarily, this is not obligatory and that the right to jury trial in such cases may be statutorily conferred.

A related question is, assuming the right to jury trial for minor offences rests on statute only (and not on Article 38.5), whether the Oireachtas would be free to construct a different type of jury to hear such cases. Would there be any constitutional objection if, for example, the Oireachtas were to decide (perhaps for reasons of cost and administrative convenience) to provide for a six person jury to hear certain *minor* offences, even if such a scheme would be regarded as unconstitutional if applied in the case of *non-minor* offences?[10] There would seem to be no such constitutional bar - assuming the hypotheti-

[5] As amended by the Criminal Procedure Act 1967, s 19; the Criminal Law (Jurisdiction) Act 1976, ss 21(6), 22.
[6] Among them public mischief, perjury, gross indecency, attempted unlawful carnal knowledge of young girls, offences under Larceny Acts, 1916-1990, the Forgery Act 1913 and any attempt to commit an indictable offence triable summarily.
[7] With the exception, of course, of cases expressly authorised by Articles 38.3 and 38.4 respectively: see p. 639.
[8] See generally at pp. 657-658.
[9] See, e.g., *Re Article 26 and the Electoral (Amendment) Bill 1983* [1984] IR 268 and pp. 22A-24A.
[10] See p. 660.

cal six-person jury provision did not violate the requirements of Article 38.1[11] - since in such a case the accused could scarcely rely on Article 38.5, given that his rights in that regard derived entirely from statute.

The other point concerns the constitutionality of s 2(2)(*b*) which requires the consent of the Director of Public Prosecutions before certain offences can be tried summarily. In effect, therefore, it is a non-judicial personage who has the final say in deciding whether the accused should be returned for trial on indictment, thereby exposing him to a range of more serious penalties. In this respect, it stands comparison with s 34 of the Offences Against the State Act 1939, which was found unconstitutional precisely because, as a result of a trial in the Special Criminal Court which "can only have be avoided by a decision of the Attorney General or the Director of Public Prosecutions", the accused stood exposed to a range of higher penalties.[12]

The public policy of summary jurisdiction

The reasons of policy which underlie the institution of summary jurisdiction were stated by Gannon J in *Clune v Director of Public Prosecutions*[13] as follows:

> "A summary trial is a trial which could be undertaken with some degree of expedition and informality without departing from the principles of justice. The purpose of summary procedures for minor offences is to ensure that such offences are charged and tried as soon as reasonably possible after their alleged commission so that the recollection of witnesses may still be reasonably clear, that the attendance of witnesses and presentation of evidence may be procured and presented without great difficulty or complexity, and that there should be minimal delay in the disposal of the work-load of minor offences."

Some of these reasons are less compelling than others. It might be said that the more serious the offence, the more important would be the fresh recollection of witnesses; and their marshalling is not inherently (though it may be conventionally) more troublesome in one kind of trial than in the other. It would be a sufficient reason for summary trial to say that the multiple disruption of jurors' private affairs, the expense, the delay, and the general panoply of a jury trial render this form of justice completely impractical for the mass of minor offences with which the State has to deal, and that the defendant's interest, where only a minor punishment can be imposed, is insufficient to outweigh those public considerations.

"MINOR OFFENCE"

The Constitution nowhere defines a minor offence. In the first twenty years or so of the Constitution's existence the matter does not seem to have attracted judicial attention, apparently on the assumption that the provisions of the 1922 and 1937 Constitutions in regard to minor offences did not intend to effect any change in the pre-existing pattern. In *The State (Attorney General) v Mangan*[14] Davitt P took the line in the High Court that the Constitution of 1922, not having been "unnecessarily radical or needlessly revolutionary", had "changed what had to be changed, but left much as it was", including, in

[11] There would seem to be no reason why a six-person jury might be thought to offend against the requirements of Article 38.1. It might be otherwise if the Oireachtas were to sanction even further departures from the traditional method of jury trial, e.g., where the jury were given special fact-finding roles on a "trial within a trial": see, e.g., *People v Conroy* [1986] IR 486.

[12] *Cox v Ireland* [1992] 2 IR 503.

[13] [1981] ILRM 17.

[14] (1961) Ir Jur Rep 17.

his opinion, the pre-1922 frontier between summarily triable and indictable offences: and the 1937 Constitution had, he thought, taken over the same system.

But in the last thirty years there has been a series of cases challenging statutory provisions which assigned this or that offence to summary trial, and therefore obliging the courts to consider the nature of a "minor offence" on principle. In the first of these cases, *Melling v Ó Mathghamhna,*[15] a set of criteria were elaborated which are substantially still accepted; though their application seems both to leave room for highly subjective judicial appraisals, and to lead, in some cases, to results which must be felt as unsatisfactory. It is hard to repress the suspicion that, in those latter cases, the considerations of public policy mentioned above as underlying all summary jurisdiction have played an inarticulate part, no doubt a subconscious one, in the evasion of some of the consequences to which those criteria would naturally lead. Perhaps the same suspicion was in the mind of Kingsmill Moore J when he found himself one of the dissenting minority of the Supreme Court in *Melling's* case; he said:

> "As the intention clearly was to safeguard the citizen, so the question of what is a "minor" offence must be considered primarily from the point of view of the person to be safeguarded and not from the point of view of executive convenience. That does not, however, mean that the general interest of the State is to be ignored."

Severity of punishment is the principal criterion

In *Melling's* case the appellant had been charged with fifteen smuggling offences under s 186 of the Customs Consolidation Act 1876, which, as adapted, purported to empower the Revenue Commissioners to proceed summarily, at their election, either for a penalty of treble the value of the goods involved in an offence, or for a penalty of £100; here the Revenue Commissioners had elected to proceed for a penalty of £100 in respect of each offence. When Melling sought a declaration that s 186 was inconsistent with the Constitution on the ground that the offences with which he was charged were not "minor" and so could not be tried summarily, the Supreme Court, by a majority, dismissed his appeal, but was unanimous in giving priority to the severity of punishment which an offence might attract as a criterion in deciding whether or not an offence is "minor". Lavery J, who spoke for the majority in considering that this particular instance, in which a penalty of £100 was claimed, was one capable of summary trial as a charge of a "minor offence", still emphasised that offences under s 186 were not *necessarily* minor - he instanced a claim for a penalty of £1,000, when he said "it would be open for the Justice to decline jurisdiction" - and specifically disagreed with a dictum of Molony CJ in *R. (Eustace) v District Justice of Co. Tipperary*[16] the only existing authority in this area, which had arisen on the corresponding provision of Article 72 of the 1922 Constitution that "the mere fact of the penalty having been increased does not alter the character of the offence", and also cited American authorities for his own view that "the severity of the sentence is the most important factor for consideration".

Kingsmill Moore J, though ultimately dissenting, thought the same on this point:

> "Regarded from the point of view of the citizen offender the difference between a minor offence and a major offence depends chiefly on the punishment which is meted out to the convicted criminal. It is this which stamps an offence as serious or not in his eyes."

[15] [1962] IR 1; (1963) 97 ILTR 60.
[16] [1924] 2 IR 69; (1924) 58 ILTR 17.

Ó Dálaigh J, who also dissented on the result, said that:

> "if one is to have regard to the reality of the guarantee of trial by jury the amount of the penalty must in every case be a very important factor - if not the most important factor - in determining whether or not an offence is minor."

Similar statements continued to be made in subsequent cases. In *Conroy v Attorney General*[17] the Supreme Court, speaking by Walsh J, said "the primary consideration in determining whether an offence be a minor one or not is the punishment which it may attract"; here the Court held that the offence of drunken driving was "minor" as the maximum "primary" punishment it could attract was six months' imprisonment, or a fine of £100, or both. In *The State (Sheerin) v Kennedy*,[18] the Supreme Court, repeating that the main test of a minor offence was the severity of punishment, held that an offence punishable (under a pre-1922 statute) by detention for up to three years in St. Patrick's Institution (for young offenders, formerly a Borstal institution) was not a minor offence, and accordingly that s 2 of the Prevention of Crime Act 1908, which enabled such a sentence to be imposed on summary trial, was inconsistent with the Constitution; the mere fact that this institution was intended to reform and rehabilitate offenders did not change matters, as "the deprivation of liberty is the real punishment" (*per* Walsh J, with whom the other four members of the Court agreed). The "severity of penalty" test was applied again in *In re Haughey*,[19] so as to take a statutory offence (that of refusing to answer a question put by a Dáil committee, punishable "as if, it were a contempt of the High Court) out of the minor offence category, since it attracted, because of the assimilation to contempt, "imprisonment and fine at discretion, i.e. without statutory limit" (*per* Ó Dálaigh CJ, giving the judgment of the Supreme Court).[20]

The test was again applied by Hamilton J in *Cullen v Attorney General*,[21] in which the plaintiff challenged s 57 of the Road Traffic Act 1961, whereby the District Court was empowered, in a case of injury to person or property resulting from negligent driving, to fine the defendant the probable amount of a civil award of damages (the section specifying no limit) and to pay the amount of the fine to the injured party; in the view of Hamilton J, this provision purported to increase the penalty to an extent which took the offence out of the minor category. Section 57(1), (2) were accordingly invalid. In *Kostan v Ireland*[22] McWilliam J applied the "severity of punishment" test so as to declare invalid s 221 of the Fisheries (Consolidation) Act 1959, as amended; the section authorised the summary trial of a fishery offence, on conviction of which the plaintiff had had fish and fishing gear to the value of £102,040 forfeited by the District Court. The judge said "no one can deny that a punishment involving the loss of property to the value of anything in the region of £100,000 is severe". In *The State (Clancy) v Wine*,[23]

[17] [1965] IR 411.
[18] [1966] IR 379.
[19] [1971] IR 217
[20] This was stated by Finlay CJ in *Desmond v Glackin (No. 2)*, Supreme Court, 30 July 1992 to be the essential *ratio* of *Haughey*. The Court saw no reason to depart from this aspect of *Haughey* - despite having been invited to so - since that decision "provided a freedom and protection concerning the possible or conceivable imposition of severe penalties appropriate only to the commission of major offences by a trial held otherwise than with a jury." The Court held that s 10(5) of the Companies Act 1990 was unconstitutional for precisely this reason.
[21] [1979] IR 394.
[22] [1978] ILRM 12. See J.P. Casey, "*Minor Offences*" (1978) DULJ (n.s.) 50.
[23] [1980] IR 228.

The State (Pheasantry Ltd.) v Donnelly,[24] *L'Henryenat v Ireland*[25] the status of the severity of punishment was again affirmed as the main test as to the character of an offence, and this must now be regarded as well settled.

Some ancillary judicial statements provide some further touches to this picture. First, the severity of the punishment is to be appraised from the standpoint of an ordinary citizen. In *Melling's* case Ó Dálaigh J said that:

> "regard has to be had to the burden which a fine of a particular amount would impose upon the ordinary or average citizen, with, if anything, as I incline to think, a leaning in the direction of people of humbler circumstances; and this should certainly be so when, as in this case, the penalty or fine is a fixed one and unrelated to the offender's ability to pay."[26]

Secondly, it was emphasised by the Supreme Court in *In re Haughey*[27] (but subsequently doubted) that the test relates to the severity of the penalty authorised by law, not to that of the penalty actually imposed in a particular case:

> "To apply the test of the penalty actually imposed would, in effect, be to deny to an accused the substance of the right to trial by jury guaranteed by Article 38.5:"

presumably, because by the time penalty was imposed he would already have undergone summary trial and conviction.[28] However, where the penalty is stated by the law in indefinite terms, as for example in the case of forfeiture of fishing gear, the mere fact that in a given case (such as *Kostan's*) the loss caused by forfeiture would be huge does not automatically make the offence non-minor and unfit for summary trial; in *L'Henryenat v Ireland*[29] Carroll J said it would be a matter for the District Judge to decide, having regard to the facts of the case, whether the offence was a minor one, in which case he could try it summarily, or non-minor, in which case he must decline jurisdiction.[30]

Mixed views were expressed on this very issue by the Supreme Court in *The State (Rollinson) v Kelly*[31] where the applicant had been convicted of 56 separate betting offences. The District Judge imposed the maximum penalty of £500 in respect of each offence, but, pursuant to s 78 of the Excise Management Act 1827, he mitigated each penalty to £125. This raised the question of whether the Court was obliged to look at the maximum penalty available in respect of each offence (i.e., £500) or the penalty actually imposed (i.e., £125). O'Higgins CJ took the view that it was "the penalty prescribed by legislation which must be considered"; Henchy and Griffin JJ were of opinion that the test was the "penalty actually imposed on conviction", while Hederman J pointed out that both of these tests lacked precision:

[24] [1982] ILRM 512.
[25] [1983] IR 193.
[26] Cited with approval by Gannon J in *Clune v Director of Public Prosecutions* [1981] ILRM 17.
[27] [1971] IR 217.
[28] Note that this aspect of *Haughey* was approved by the Supreme Court in *Desmond v Glackin (No. 2)*, Supreme Court, 30 July 1992 (where s 10(5) of the Companies Act 1990 was invalidated for this very reason) with Finlay CJ stressing that Article 38.2 provided a protection "against the possible or conceivable imposition of severe penalties" which were appropriate only in the case of the trial of major offences with a jury.
[29] [1983] IR 193.
[30] A similar view had previously been taken by Lavery J in *Melling*.
[31] [1984] IR 248.

"The test is not the maximum penalty which the statute (if the offence be a statutory one) authorises provided that the accused is tried before a court which has constitutional competence to impose such a sentence, but it is the sentence that the offence can attract before the tribunal that does in fact try him."

This approach has much to commend it. If, for example, the maximum penalty for larceny following trial on indictment is prescribed as five years, it is not a minor offence *if so tried in that manner* for that very reason. On the other hand, where the maximum penalty for the same offence following summary trial is twelve months, it does not by reason of this fact alone cease to be a minor offence.[32]

Thirdly, there is no judicial statement from which one could deduce the precise quantum of punishment that would remove an offence from the "minor" category. In *Sheerin's* case Walsh J observed that in *Melling's* case and *Conroy's* case the Supreme Court had been willing to see offences carrying up to six months' imprisonment as minor offences; but said that:

"it is unnecessary to determine what precise period in excess of the period of six months would constitute the boundary line between minor offences and other offences. However, I have no doubt that an offence which attracts as a punishment the deprivation of liberty for a period of up to three years cannot be regarded as a minor offence."

This view was echoed by Barr J in *J. v Delap*[33] where counsel for the Attorney General conceded that "an offence punishable by imprisonment or detention for a period of three years or more cannot be regarded as minor in nature." This concession notwithstanding, the provisions of ss 57(1) and 65 of the Children Act 1908 (which allow the District Court to order the detention of a young offender at a reformatory school for up to four years) were found by Barr J not to be unconstitutional on the ground that such detention was principally educational - and not punitive - in character.[34] Finally, it may be noted that in *Melling's* case the dissentient judges (Kingsmill Moore and Ó Dálaigh JJ) had taken the view that the possible imprisonment of the offender, in default of paying the fine, for up to nine months took offences under s 186 of the Customs Consolidation Act 1876, out of the minor category.

Fourthly, where a money penalty is provided by a pre-Constitution statute, whether as a fixed sum or as an upper limit, the severity of the penalty is to be appraised by reference to the present value of money and not to its value at the time of the Constitution's enactment. The contrary view was first stated in *Melling's* case by the two dissentient judges

[32] Thus, where an accused is charged with an offence carrying a maximum penalty of twelve months imprisonment following summary conviction, it does not assist him to point to the fact that conviction on indictment carries much heavier potential penalties.

[33] [1989] IR 167.

[34] Barr J said: "An obligation to remain at a place for the education and training of young offenders does not...convert a school into a penal institution analogous to a prison, nor ought the period of education and training which a young offender spends there be regarded as a period of imprisonment in the penal sense of that term. I accept that such detention has in it an element of punishment, but its primary purpose is educational and, most importantly, the period of detention is in the main related to the function of the school as a place of instruction and correction. The duration of a prison sentence on the other hand is primarily related to the gravity of the offence which gave rise to it and the character of the convict."
This seems a questionable conclusion, since the fact remains that the convicted young offender is sentenced to a period of *compulsory detention* of up to four years. It is hard to see how a sentence involving compulsory detention for such a lengthy period could be other than a non-minor offence.

- considering, however, the question whether the enactment under review had survived the 1922 Constitution. It was re-stated, and applied, by Gannon J in the High Court in *The State (Rollinson) v Kelly*,[35] when, in trying to decide whether a revenue offence created in 1926 and carrying a penalty of £500 should be regarded as minor (although the penalty actually imposed was but £125), he compared this sum with what the annual salary of most District Judges had been in that year and in 1937 (£l ,000) and with the salary at that time of the President of the Executive Council (£2,500). On the basis of this comparison he had no difficulty in finding the offence non-minor, thus entitling the accused to trial by jury.[36] A majority of the Supreme Court took a different view, stressing that where the penalty imposed was a monetary fine, it must, said Henchy J, "be assessed by reference to the standards or values current at the time of the imposition of the penalty." [37] He went on to compare the fine of £125 with that imposed in *Melling*:

> "In the year 1960 (when £100 represented approximately £900 in today's money) the then Supreme Court held in *Melling v Ó Mathghamhna* that a conviction for smuggling which carried a penalty of £100 represented a minor offence. In the present case the primary financial penalty is in real terms considerably less, and the secondary or alternative penalty of imprisonment in default is at least no greater, then those applicable in *Melling's* case."

To judge from a miscellaneous variety of recently enacted legislation, the Oireachtas appears to be of the view that a fine of £1,000 is the maximum which may be imposed following summary conviction.[38]

Fifthly, an important point relating to penalty arose in *O'Sullivan v Hartnett*,[39] a prosecution for being in possession of 900 unlawfully captured salmon. First, the defendant argued that, as conviction would involve forfeiture, and as the value of 900 salmon was very considerable, the offence could not be considered minor on the punishment criterion. McWilliam J in the High Court rejected this plea, holding that the forfeiture of fish of which the defendant had never been lawfully in possession could not be considered a penalty. This view does not seem compelling: if one of the very issues which the trial is to determine is whether or not the defendant was lawfully in possession of that which (if his possession is found unlawful) he must forfeit, then, seen from the moment when the prosecution is initiated, the potential loss, or prejudice, which the defendant is at peril of suffering if the trial goes against him has a fair claim to be regarded as punishment for the purpose of deciding whether he is to be tried by the more or the less weighty tribunal. (The Supreme Court did not deal expressly with this point.)

[35] [1982] ILRM 249. A majority of the Supreme Court took a different view: see [1984] IR 248.

[36] Similarly in *Charlton v Ireland* [1984] ILRM 39 Murphy J held an offence to be non-minor because it attracted an excise penalty of £500 which, in 1937, "would have represented a very significant amount."

[37] Henchy J added:

> "With due respect to dicta to the contrary in some of the decided cases, I do not consider that the state of the law when the Constitution was enacted in 1937 or public opinion at the time of that enactment are crucial considerations. It seems to me that the matter depends on the situation at the time when the sentence was imposed."

This approach seems correct and is borne out by analogy with other cases where plaintiffs complained that their property rights or some licence or privilege was eroded or defeated by the effects of inflation: see *Brennan v Attorney General* [1984] IR 355; *Cafolla v Attorney General* [1985] IR 486 and *Browne v Attorney General* [1991] 2 IR 58.

[38] See, e.g., s 15(5)(*a*) of the Merchant Shipping Act 1992; the Table to the Environmental Protection Agency Act 1992 and s 9(2) of the Control of Dogs (Amendment) Act 1992. For a discussion of the possibility of automatic indexation of fines and how this might affect minor offence categorisation, see Law Reform Commission Report, *The Indexation of Fines* (LRC - 37) (Dublin, 1991)

[39] [1983] ILRM 79.

Sixthly, in the same case, although the fine and forfeiture penalty in respect of a single salmon in unlawful possession were trivial, the Supreme Court had regard rather to the cumulative effect of fine and forfeiture in respect of such a multitude of fish: the potential fines were reckoned as nearly £10,000 in value, and so, bearing in mind also the possible sentence of up to six months' imprisonment, "by any level or order or criteria neither of the offences charged could be held to be a minor offence". This must be contrasted with the view of Murphy J in *Charlton v Ireland* [40] where, in relation to a total of sixty-four offences charged, he thought that the punishment attached to each, and not the cumulative total of sixty-four potential fines, should be the basis for the application of the severity criterion. The matter also arose in *The State (Rollinson) v Kelly* . While Henchy J expressly reserved his position,[41] Hederman J had no doubt that the prescribed penalties for each offence must be considered separately for this purpose:

> "The fact that when all these offences are added together the total amount of the penalties is a considerable amount of money which, if it were the penalty imposed for one of those convictions, would be sufficient to carry it out of the minor [offence] category does not, in my view, change the essential character of each of the offences whose combined penalties reach such a sum. Each offence must be regarded as a separate offence. They might well have been tried on different days or even [in] different months. The fact that they were all on the same day does not alter their individual character."

This passage was quoted with approval by Carroll J in *The State (Wilson) v Neilan*[42] when she said that:

> "in determining whether an offence is or is not a minor offence, each one must be looked at separately...[An] offence which is a minor offence cannot change into a non-minor offence merely because an accused is charged with a number of similar minor offences."

Nevertheless, the line taken in *O'Sullivan* v *Hartnett* has not been expressly disavowed by the Supreme Court. Indeed, the *O'Sullivan* view seems the more correct, as it seems to accord better with the spirit of Article 38.1 where a number of charges are to be dealt with *in a single proceeding*.[43]

"Primary" and "secondary' punishment

Finally, in a development which must seem one of the less convincing exercises of the Supreme Court since the era of judicial activism began about 1960, the Court drew a distinction, new to Irish law, between "primary" and "secondary" punishment in the context of deciding whether an offence was to be regarded as minor or not. This was in *Conroy v Attorney General*,[44] in which the plaintiff had submitted that the Court should have regard not only to the fine and/or imprisonment which a conviction under s 49 of

[40] [1984] ILRM 39.

[41] But in a manner which - it may be thought - cast doubt on the validity of such a procedure: "I express no opinion on whether it was constitutionally permissible for the District Justice, notwithstanding that each offence was a minor one, to make with one stroke, as it were, 56 convictions bearing an aggregate penalty of £6,750."

[42] [1985] IR 89.

[43] Note the formula employed by s 2(9) of the Copyright (Amendment) Act 1987 which prescribed amended fines for offences tried summarily under s 27 of the Copyright Act 1963, "provided, however, that a fine so imposed...shall not exceed £1,000 in respect of articles comprised in the same transaction."

[44] [1965] IR 411.

the Road Traffic Act 1961, would entail, but also to the disqualification from driving (for a minimum of twelve months for a first offence, or three years for a subsequent offence) which accompanied it. This disqualification might, in the case of many individuals, amount to disabling them from continuing to earn their livelihood; and Kenny J, in the High Court, had accepted readily that this dimension of conviction was material to the question whether the offence of drunken driving was minor. He said:

> "In one of the cases in the United States of America it was said that disqualification from driving is not a punishment, but this view is so contrary to common sense that its acceptance would bring the law into ridicule."

The Supreme Court thought otherwise:

> "So far as punishment is concerned, the punishment which must be examined for the purpose of gauging the seriousness of an offence is what may be referred to as "primary punishment" [loss of liberty or deprivation of property]. Any conviction may result in many other unpleasant and even punitive consequences for the convicted person... These unfortunate consequences are too remote in character to be taken into account in weighing the seriousness of an offence by the punishment it may attract... [Disqualification] in so far as it may be classed as a punishment at all is not a primary or direct punishment but rather an order which may, according to the circumstances of the particular individual concerned, assume, though remotely, a punitive character... Undoubtedly disqualification may have a deterrent quality but that does not make it a punishment. It is a regulation of the exercise of a statutory right in the interest of public order and safety."

This view of disqualification as not representing "primarily" a punishment was stated again by the Court of Criminal Appeal in *The People (Attorney General) v Poyning*;[45] and, in connection with the potential revocation of a betting licence under s 15 of the Betting Act 1931, it was assented to by Gannon J (and later by the Supreme Court) in *The State (Rollinson) v Kelly*:[46]

> "The power to suspend or revoke a licence under s 15 appears to be a regulation of the statutory control of betting and not primarily, though perhaps incidentally, a punishment in its consequences."

In *Charlton v Ireland*[47] Murphy J too accepted that the revocation of a bookmaker's licence would not count as a "primary punishment". In *The State (Pheasantry Ltd.) v Donnelly*[48] the idea of "primary" and "secondary" punishment was again employed by Carroll J, in a case in which the forfeiture of a restaurant wine licence, in consequence of a licensing infringement, was proved to have the effect (because the premises could, under s 28(2) of the Intoxicating Liquor Act 1927, never again be licensed) of reducing the estimated market value of the premises from £40,000 or £50,000 to about £7,500. She adopted the *Conroy* principle, and described the disqualification in issue in that case, and the forfeiture in issue in the *Pheasantry* case, as "withdrawals of rights granted by Acts" (much as Gannon J had seen the revocation of a betting licence in *Rollinson's* case). Murphy J again accepted this principle in *Cartmill v Ireland*[49] where he held that

[45] [1972] IR 402.
[46] [1982] ILRM 249 (HC); [1984] IR 248 (SC).
[47] [1984] ILRM 39.
[48] [1982] ILRM 512.
[49] [1987] IR 192.

the forfeiture of gaming equipment following a conviction under the Gaming and Lotteries Act 1956 was a secondary punishment not to be taken into account in deciding whether an offence was a minor one. He said it was recognised in *Conroy's* case that:

> "there may be good executive and administrative reasons for depriving a citizen of the right to use equipment or exercise functions which are in themselves valid and proper because the citizen has displayed an incapacity or unwillingness to use the equipment or discharge the functions in a proper manner. How much more should there be an administrative or executive power to deprive a citizen of equipment [such as] gaming instruments which are inherently designed for the commission of a criminal offence."

Even if one remains within the parameters of the *Conroy* decision, this reasoning seems highly questionable. The essence of the *Conroy* case (and the decisions which followed it) all concerned the circumstances in which a statutory right or licence (such as the right to use a motor vehicle) might be withdrawn, but the penal deprivation of property (such as the forfeiture of a motor vehicle) has always been regarded as punishment in the "strict" or "primary" sense of that term. The difficulty with the judgment in *Cartmill* is that Murphy J has here collapsed the distinction between "the right to *use equipment or exercise* functions" on the one hand and the *deprivation* of equipment (in this case valuable and costly gaming machines) on the other.[50]

Apart from the instinct which must protest against admitting - at any rate in the context of identifying a minor offence - any distinction between "primary" and "secondary" punishment, it seems wrong to present a forfeiture, revocation or disqualification as a "regulation" or "withdrawal" of a statutory right. The truth, historically, in this State or in any other, must be that once upon a time everyone was free to sell drink, lay bets or travel in a vehicle; only when the State perceived a potential public injury in this uncontrolled liberty (in the case of the mechanically propelled vehicle, no doubt almost immediately after its emergence) was it proposed to avert this injury, or reduce the risk of it, by a regime of licensing. This was, if from the best of motives, a general though conditional curtailment of freedom, though not a punishment. To make, however, in the case of an individual infringing one of the terms on which limited freedom was still allowed him, a conditional liberty into an absolute deprivation of liberty in the sphere concerned, is a real punishment. This is how the Legislature which creates such disqualifying rules regards them, and how it marks as serious the infraction for which they are invoked. Measured against this fact, the superficial distinction between the modalities of punishment which underlies the words "primary" and "secondary" does not seem significant in the context of appraising the gravity of the offence.[51]

"Moral quality of the act criterion"

The second criterion stated by the Supreme Court in *Melling's* case for determining whether or not an offence is minor was "the moral quality of the act". Lavery J said:

[50] Authors' italics. Had, for example, the Road Traffic Acts provided for the forfeiture of the motor vehicles which drunk drivers were found driving, it would not have occurred to anyone to argue that the forfeiture of such vehicles was other than primary punishment, still less that because such vehicles were "inherently designed for the commission of a criminal offence", this punishment should only be regarded as "secondary" in character and, hence, not to be taken into account in deciding whether the offence was minor. Cf. the comments of McWilliam J in *Kostan v Ireland* [1978] ILRM 12 where he said that the forfeiture of fishing gear was "intended to be a penalty" as it was "a direct consequence of a conviction" under the Fisheries (Consolidation) Act 1959. See also *Cox v Ireland* [1992] 2 IR 503.

[51] In *Hand v Dublin Corporation* [1991] 1 IR 409 the Supreme Court was asked expressly to overrule *Conroy's* case, but it ruled that the issue did not arise directly on the facts of the appellant's case.

> "Opinions based on legal and moral considerations as to the seriousness of offences against the Customs Acts vary greatly but I think it cannot be doubted that an element of moral blame should be imputed to those who, on a commercial scale, violate the Revenue Acts."

Kingsmill Moore J spoke more graphically to the same effect:

> "From a moral point of view the offence of smuggling varies enormously. The importation of a pair of silk stockings for personal use would not be too sternly reprobated even by strict moralists; but large-scale smuggling of valuable articles, organised and conducted as a profitable business, has not only been reprobated in severe terms by judges but would be regarded by most people as involving moral delinquency."

A similar moral distinction was drawn by McWilliam J in the concrete case of *O'Sullivan v Hartnett*[52] as between the offence of catching a single salmon unlawfully, and being (as the defendant was alleged to be) in possession of a huge haul of 900 unlawfully captured salmon.

However, once the courts venture beyond generalities of this kind a certain scholastic unreality seems to invade the question. In *The State (Rollinson) v Kelly*[53] Henchy J observed that, while the gravity of the penalty was still the principal criterion, there were:

> "certain offences (random examples of which are treason, genocide, murder, rape)[54] which, because of the moral heinousness or the grave social evil inherent in them, can never be accounted minor no matter what penalty is attached to them."

Ó Dálaigh J had previously said in *Melling's* case, that:

> "an offence of great moral obliquity even if punishable by a small penalty and made triable only summarily nevertheless should, probably, not be considered minor."

Should this mean that the theft of a small sum from a destitute man calls for trial by jury?[55] In *Conroy v Attorney General*[56] Walsh J delivering the Supreme Court's judgment, said:

> "The moral aspect of an offence can only be judged or stated in relation to minimum legal requirements necessary to establish that offence in law as distinct from pronouncing upon the facts of any particular instance of that offence... The offence in s 49 [of the Road Traffic Act 1961] drunken driving may be established in circumstances where there is only a minimal moral guilt... The fact that in many or

[52] [1983] ILRM 79.

[53] [1984] IR 248.

[54] In both *Conroy v Attorney General* [1965] IR 411 and *The People (Director of Public Prosecutions) v Tiernan* [1988] IR 250; [1989] ILRM 149, the Supreme Court confirmed that the nature of the offence was such that rape could never be regarded as a minor offence.

[55] In *O'Leary v Cunningham* [1980] IR 367 Griffin J in the Supreme Court had expressed surprise that a charge of robbery, in a case where the sum taken was only £47, should for that purely fortuitous reason have been considered a charge of a minor offence by a District Judge. This, however, is a somewhat different point.

[56] [1965] IR 411.

even most cases the circumstances under which the offence is committed are of a character to create a considerable moral guilt is not relevant when those aggravating circumstances are not the necessary ingredients of the offence."

This sounds reasonable; and yet, as the moral quality of every act is a function of factors in the actor's will, and operating on his will, which other people cannot judge, does it make sense anyway to speak of the moral quality of an offence rather than of the offender? In *Conroy's* case Kenny J had said in the High Court that, according to the natural moral law, it is the nature and quality of an act and not its consequences which bring it into, or leave it outside the category of a morally culpable act: and in *The State (Clancy) v Wine*[57] Finlay P adopting this principle, held that an assault which had caused a serious injury (in this instance, severe damage to the victim's eye) was not for that reason alone "a morally reprehensible act which could not constitute a minor offence". Would it then be constitutionally acceptable, had the assailant unintentionally caused the victim's death, to make manslaughter in this form summarily triable? Perhaps the right way out of these problems is to accept that the legislature, in prescribing penalties, has made its own rough estimate of the relative moral obliquity of the typical case, which the courts will not review, save in unusual and exceptional circumstances. In this way the criterion of the moral quality of the act would be fused in the severity criterion; the actual culpability of the offender (though never really measurable), to the extent that the evidence permits it to be appraised, can be matched to the appropriate penalty, up to the statutory limit, by the court dealing with him.

"State of the law and public opinion" in 1937

The third criterion set up in *Melling's* case was the state of the law at the time of the Constitution's enactment; and the fourth criterion was the state of public opinion at that time. In the form in which these last two criteria have been applied, they are difficult to keep distinct, and perhaps indeed they are, in this context, only different aspects of the same criterion. Moreover, they are clearly less important considerations than the first two criteria of severity of punishment and the moral quality of the act.[58] In *Melling's* case Lavery J, speaking for the Supreme Court majority, mentioned a number of pre-Constitution statutes which provided for the summary trial of offences carrying penalties comparable in severity with those under s 186 of the Customs Consolidation Act 1876; and, though frankly stating that "it is a matter of first impression whether a particular offence is of a minor character or not", thought that s 186 did not depart from a general pattern which the Constitution showed no intention of changing radically. Ó Dálaigh J was willing to agree that at least the pattern exhibited by the laws enacted since independence were a guide for what the new Constitution intended in 1937:

> "One can have little doubt that the framers of the Constitution of Ireland, when in Article 38 they spoke of a minor offence, meant the kind of thing that had been generally understood to be such under the laws of Saorstát Éireann."

In *Conroy's* case the Supreme Court took the same line again:

[57] [1980] IR 228.

[58] In *Conroy's* case, Walsh J described them as but "secondary considerations." Cf. the comments of Henchy J in *The State (Rollinson) v Kelly* [1984] IR 248: "With due respect to dicta to the contrary in some of the decided cases, I do not consider that the state of the law when the Constitution was enacted in 1937 or public opinion at the time of that enactment are crucial considerations."

The Constitution of Saorstát Éireann may be considered to have accepted the existing pattern of distinction between offences to be tried in a court of summary jurisdiction and offences to be tried on indictment by a jury. In 1937 the people with full knowledge of the existing structure of the courts and the modes of trial gave themselves the present Constitution... The procedure for prosecuting offences of drunken driving prescribed by [the Road Traffic Act 1933] was part of the procedural pattern in existence and was widely known in 1937. Its creation by Act of the Oireachtas sufficiently indicates that it reflected public opinion. The procedure prescribed by s 49 of the Act of 1961 in form corresponds to the pattern in existence in 1937 and the offence thereby created does not, by reason of the punishment prescribed, differ in character from the corresponding offence in the Act of 1933."

While there does appear to be general acceptance of the pre-1937 position as a rough guide to what the Constitution meant by a minor offence, the somewhat limited value of the criterion is borne out by the judgment of the Supreme Court in *The State (Rollinson) v Kelly*,[59] where the majority refused to endorse the approach of Gannon J (described above) where he had valued in real contemporary terms the amounts of fines prescribed by pre-1937 Acts. Though in that case Gannon J had not pronounced on the constitutional validity of a pre-1937 enactment (since the Act in that case left open the option of trial by indictment) this line of appraisal must have led, had only summary trial been provided for by the pre-Constitution Act to a finding of unconstitutionality where a fine seemed extremely heavy in 1937 terms. With the abandonment of that approach by the Supreme Court, the state of the law and public opinion in 1937 must have scarcely negligible value when it comes to an assessment of whether the monetary fines prescribed by pre-1937 legislation are minor offences or not. It may be noted, also, that this latest approach goes back to *Melling's* case and the Supreme Court's dissenting minority. Kingsmill Moore J said:

> "I am unable to get any assistance as to what is a minor offence by considering the severity of punishments which could be imposed summarily in 1922. It appears to me that Article 72 [of the 1922 Constitution] was directed expressly to removing from the jurisdiction of District Justices offences which by their severity of punishment could not be regarded as being minor."

Ó Dálaigh J (though, as has been seen, willing to admit the legislation of 1922- 37 as a guide) thought the same in regard to pre-1922 laws:

> "The framers of the Constitution of Saorstát Éireann had no particular reason to look with reverence or respect to the British statute roll in Ireland as affording them an example of standards which they would wish to enshrine in their new Constitution - and least of all in the matter of norms of imprisonment related to summary jurisdiction. If Ireland had a complaint, it is that that jurisdiction was exercised too summarily."

[59] [1984] IR 248.

SPECIAL COURTS AND MILITARY COURTS

3. **1° Special courts may be established by law for the trial of offences in cases where it may be determined in accordance with such law that the ordinary courts are inadequate to secure the effective administration of justice, and the preservation of public peace and order.**
2° The constitution, powers, jurisdiction and procedure of such special courts shall be prescribed by law.

4. **1° Military tribunals may be established for the trial of offences against military law alleged to have been committed by persons while subject to military law and also to deal with a state of war or armed rebellion.**
2° A member of the Defence Forces not on active service shall not be tried by any court-martial or other military tribunal for an offence cognisable by the civil courts unless such offence is within the jurisdiction of any court-martial or other military tribunal under law for the enforcement of military discipline.

5. **[Trial by jury]***

6. **The provisions of Articles 34 and 35 of this Constitution shall not apply to any court or tribunal set up under section 3 or section 4 of this Article.**

3. **1° Féadfar cúirteanna faoi leith a bhunú le dlí chun cionta a thriail i gcásanna a gcinnfear ina dtaobh, de réir an dlí sin, nach leor na gnáthchúirteanna chun riaradh cirt a chur i bhfeidhm le héifeacht agus chun síocháin agus ord poiblí a chaomhnú.**
2° Is le dlí a shocrófar comhdhéanamh, cumhachtaí, dlínse agus nós imeachta na gcúirteanna faoi leith sin.

4. **1° Féadfar binsí míleata a bhunú chun daoine a thriail i gcionta in aghaidh dlí mhíleata a deirtear a rinneadar le linn a mbeith faoi dhlí mhíleata, agus fós chun broic le heisíth nó le ceannairc faoi arm.**
2° Duine de na Fórsaí Cosanta nach bhfuil ar fianas ní cead é a thriail i láthair aon armchúirte ná binse míleata eile i gcion is intriailte sna cúirteanna sibhialta, mura cion é atá faoi dhlínse aon armchúirte nó binse míleata eile faoi aon dlí chun smacht míleata a chur i bhfeidhm.

5. **[Triail le coiste tiomanta]***

6. **Ní bhainfidh forálacha Airteagal 34 ná Airteagal 35 den Bhunreacht seo le haon chúirt ná le haon bhinse a bhunófar faoi alt 3 nó alt 4 den Airteagal seo.**

1922 Constitution

The 1922 Constitution had not only contained no explicit provision for "special" courts, but in Article 70, after providing that "no one shall be tried save in due course of law", it had expressly said that "extraordinary courts shall not be established".[1] However, the Article went on:

[* Article 38.5 is dealt with separately in the next chapter (below, pp. 657-658). The arrangement of Article 38 seems awkward, as s 6 of the Article relates not to s 5 but only to ss 3 and 4.]

[1]For further general accounts of the special courts, see Robinson, *The Special Criminal Court* (Dublin, 1974) and Hogan and Walker, *Political Violence and the Law in Ireland* (Manchester, 1989) at 227-244.

> "...save only such military tribunals as may be authorised by law for dealing with military offenders against military law. The jurisdiction of military tribunals shall not be extended to or exercised over the civil population save in time of war, or armed rebellion, and for acts committed in time of war or armed rebellion, and in accordance with the regulations to be prescribed by law. Such jurisdiction shall not be exercised in any area in which all civil courts are open or capable of being held, and no person shall be removed from one area to another for the purpose of creating such jurisdiction."

The courts and tribunals contemplated by Article 36.3-4 can appear in a variety of forms, as the history of the State since 1922 demonstrates. Apart from the simple case of military tribunals trying offences against military law charged against persons subject to military law,[2] these institutions are perhaps best classified as (1) extraordinary criminal tribunals with a basis in statute: and (2) extraordinary criminal tribunals with no basis in statute. A classification such as military/non-military may be confusing, as the statutory provision for "special courts" in the sense of Article 36.3.1 may envisage such courts being composed of military personnel; this is in fact the case with Part V of the Offences Against the State Act 1939, under which Special Criminal Courts may be established; the Special Criminal Courts which operated in the 1939-46 and 1961-62 periods were actually so composed.

EXTRAORDINARY CRIMINAL TRIBUNALS WITH BASIS IN STATUTE

Public Safety Act 1927: "special courts"

Two such tribunals were at different times provided for in the statute law of Saorstát Éireann. Consequent upon the murder of Kevin O'Higgins, the Minister for Justice, in 1927, a Public Safety Act was passed which by s 3 provided that in the event of any conflict between itself and the Constitution, it should operate as an amendment to the Constitution; and s 20(1) of the Act provided that:

> "Whenever the Executive Council is of opinion that it is necessary in order to secure the due administration of justice and the sure punishment of crime that persons charged with any of the offences mentioned in the Schedule to this Act these were, broadly, offences of or associated with political violence and subversion should be brought before and tried by special courts established under this Act in lieu of the ordinary courts, the Executive Council may by proclamation declare that Part IV of this Act shall come into operation."

Section 22(1) envisaged that the members of the Tribunal would be officers of the Defence Forces. The special courts provided for by this Act were, however, never in fact set up; and the Act though given by s 1(2) a duration of five years, was repealed at the end of 1928 by the Public Safety Act of that year.

1931: Constitution (Special Powers) Tribunal

In 1931 a much more far reaching provision for an extraordinary criminal jurisdiction was made (following a new outbreak of political violence that year, including several murders and widespread intimidation of jurors), and the provision itself was inserted

[2] See below at pp. 657-658.

into the Constitution, in the form of Article 2A, by the Constitution (Amendment No. 17) Act. Section 2 of the interpolated Article 2A provided that:

> Article 3 and every subsequent Article of this Constitution shall be read and construed subject to the provisions of this Article, and in the case of any inconsistency between this Article and the said Article 3 or any subsequent Article, this Article shall prevail.

Article 2A provided for a wide range of supplementary powers for the State in the repression of political violence and subversion, but in particular it provided for the establishment of a tribunal called "the Constitution (Special Powers) Tribunal"; by s 4(2) this was to:

> consist of five members, all of whom shall be officers of the Defence Forces of Saorstát Éireann not below the rank of commandant and [who] shall be appointed and removable at will by the... Executive Council.

Section 5(1) required three members of the Tribunal were to be present at every sitting of the Tribunal, and were to constitute the Tribunal for the purpose of the sitting; and the Tribunal was to act by those three members or a majority of them. By s 5(2) the Tribunal had "full and absolute control of its own procedure in all respects". By s 6(5) there was to be no appeal from its "order, conviction, sentence or other act", and:

> the Tribunal shall not be restrained or interfered with in the execution of its jurisdiction or powers under this Article by any court nor shall any proceedings before the Tribunal be removed by *certiorari* to any court.

By s 7 the Tribunal, on finding a person guilty of any one of a number of offences specified in the Appendix to the Article, might:

> in lieu of the punishment provided by law (other than this Article) for such offence, sentence such person to suffer any greater punishment (including the penalty of death) if in the opinion of the Tribunal such greater punishment is necessary or expedient.

The Appendix specified several offences of a politically violent or subversive kind, but also:

> any offence whatsoever (whether committed before or after this Article was inserted in this Constitution...) in respect of which an Executive Minister certifies in writing under his hand that to the best of his belief the act constituting such offence was done with the object of impairing or impeding the machinery of government or the administration of justice.

The Tribunal was set up at once on the passing of the Act and functioned - with an interruption in 1932-33[3] - until 1937, when it disappeared along with the 1922 Constitution

[3] The operation of Article 2A was suspended by Mr. de Valera's Government after he reached office in 1932 (Fianna Fáil had strongly opposed its enactment the previous year; but by 1933 the resurgence of political violence had seen it brought back into operation: see O'Sullivan, *The Irish Free State and its Senate* (London, 1940), ch. 19). In the course of his cruelly sardonic judgment in *The State (Ryan) v Lennon* [1935] IR 170, Fitzgibbon J with this background in mind said: "But the fact that the Constitutions of other countries prohibit

in which it had been anchored. It was the subject of several important decisions in the year 1934, in particular in the case of *The State (Ryan) v Lennon*.[4]

This case, notable for a dissenting judgment of Kennedy CJ which vigorously stated the classical natural law position which denies a sovereign parliament's right to legislate in violation of natural law and holds any purported legislation of this kind to be void, arose from the arrest of four men and their placing on trial, on various charges, before the Tribunal. Their counsel launched an attack on Article 2A along the whole front, arguing that it was not a valid amendment of the Constitution. They failed in the High Court; and again in the Supreme Court, though Kennedy CJ was on their side. Of the effect of the provisions concerning the Tribunal he said:

> "The net effect, then, is that the Oireachtas has taken judicial power from the Judiciary and handed it to the Executive, and has surrendered its own trust as a legislature to the Executive Council, in respect of the extensive area of matters covered by the Appendix to the Article. Remembering that the "Tribunal" is to consist of five persons holding commissions as commandants (or higher ranks) issued to them by, and held at the pleasure of, the Executive Council, and holding membership of the "Tribunal" at the will of the Executive Council, the result of the Article clearly is that whenever any Executive Council thinks it expedient to use the Article, that Council itself prosecutes (in pursuance of its proper function) a person charged by it with an offence (which may be an offence brought within the scope of the Article by an Executive Minister's certificate) and conducts the prosecution before itself, "trying" the charge by its own removable nominees, and itself convicts the accused person, by the same convenient and decorous machinery, and prescribes any sentence for the individual case it chooses through the same convenient and decorous machinery. Every Act from the arrest of the individual and the charging him with an "offence" to the sentence and its execution, is, therefore, in naked reality, the act of the Executive Council."

The other two judges of the Supreme Court, however, held otherwise in regard to the validity of Article 2A, though both of them made their feelings about it clear; Murnaghan J saying that "the extreme rigour of the [Constitution (Amendment No. 17) Act which introduced Article 2A] is such that its provisions pass far beyond anything having the semblance of legal procedure, and the judicial mind is staggered at the very complete departure from legal methods in use in these courts." But, as they held that the amendment, extreme though it was, was within the powers of the Oireachtas, the Tribunal survived this challenge.[5]

1939: Special Criminal Court

Between the coming into force of the new Constitution at the end of 1937 and the enactment of the Offences Against the State Act in June, 1939, no statutory provision existed for extraordinary criminal tribunals; but this Act contained, in Part V, provisions for the

such invasions of the rights of liberty and property, and such extraordinary innovations in the methods of administering justice in criminal cases as have been introduced [by Article 2A] affords no grounds for condemning as unconstitutional in *this* country, or as contrary to any inalienable rights of an Irish citizen, an enactment which appears to have received the almost unanimous support of the Oireachtas, for we have been told that those of our legislators by whom it was opposed most vehemently as unconstitutional and oppressive, when it was first introduced, have since completely changed their opinions, and now accord it their unqualified approval."

4 [1935] IR 170; (1935) 69 ILTR 125.

5 The attempted exclusion by s 6(5) of Article 2A of all judicial review of the Tribunal did not, however, succeed: *The State (O'Duffy) v Bennett* [1935] IR 70; *The State (Hughes) v Lennon* [1935] IR 128.

establishment of special criminal courts. Section 35(1), reproducing the formula of Article 38.3.1, provides that:

> if and whenever and so often as the Government is satisfied that the ordinary courts are inadequate to secure the effective administration of justice and the preservation of public peace and order and that it is therefore necessary that this Part of this Act should come into force, the Government may make and publish a proclamation declaring that the Government is satisfied as aforesaid and ordering that this Part of this Act shall come into force.

In *People v Quilligan (No. 1),*[6] Walsh J referred to the constitutional provisions establishing the institutions of government and observed that the enactment of the Offences Against the State Act 1939 was designed to protect the integrity of those institutions and to guard them against attack:

> "While it may be may be that some of these constitutional provisions are self-executing in the sense that they do not require legislation to implement them, nevertheless the legislation embodied [in the 1939 Act] must be seen as a legislative intervention designed to secure and make effective the rights guaranteed by the Constitution and to provide punishment for and otherwise deal with the breaches of the Constitution envisaged in Articles [6,15, 28, 34, 35 and 40]."

In an important passage, Walsh J went on to explain that the power of the Government to issue the requisite proclamation under Part V did not necessarily apply only to the type of offences created by Parts II and III of that Act.[7] He observed that the Special Criminal Court was very frequently engaged in trying "black market" cases during, and for some time after, the Second World War and he continued:

> "It is common knowledge, and, indeed, was discussed in the debates in the Oireachtas leading to the enactment of the 1939 Act that what was envisaged were cases or situations of a political nature where juries could be open to intimidation or threats of various types. However, a similar situation could well arise in types of cases far removed from what one could call "political type" offences. There could well be a grave situation in dealing with ordinary gangsterism or well financed.....drug dealing or other situations where it might be believed or established that juries were for some corrupt reason, or by virtue of threats, or illegal interference, being prevented from doing justice."

In view of these considerations as articulated by Walsh J it would seem that a resolution establishing the Special Criminal Court, or for that matter, specifying that certain offences were to be regarded as scheduled offences, would enjoy a particularly strong presumption of validity. In addition, s 35(5) of the 1939 Act provides that Dáil Éireann may by resolution annul such a proclamation. Section 36(1) provides that the Government may, while Part V of the Act is in force, declare specified offences to be scheduled offences for the purposes of that Part of the Act.

Establishment, composition and independence of the Special Criminal Court

Section 38(1) proves that as soon as may be after that Part of the Act is brought into force, a Special Criminal Court is to be established; by s 38(2) further Special Criminal

[6] [1986] IR 485

[7] For which see pp. 970-973.

Courts may be established at need. In *McGlinchey v Governor of Portlaoise Prison*[8] it was suggested that whereas the Government was expressly given power by s 38(2) to establish a second Special Criminal Court, no person or body is nominated by s 38(1) to establish the first Special Criminal Court. It was thus contended that this statutory lacuna rendered invalid the establishment of the Special Criminal Court. Speaking for a Divisional High Court, Lynch J was not unduly troubled by this apparent omission. Observing that this construction would have left Part V of the 1939 Act wholly ineffectual, he applied the presumption *ut res magis valeat quam pereat* :

> "There is no doubt that s 38(1) could have been more felicitously drafted so as to declare expressly by whom was to be established the Special Criminal Court which the sub-section declares should be established. I have no doubt at all, however, that a necessary inference arises that the Government is given the power to establish the first special criminal court following the making of the proclamation, having regard to the terms of [s 38(1) and (2) and s 39(2)]."

Section 39(1) requires that every Special Criminal Court is to consist of an uneven number of members (not less than three), each of whom, by s 39(2), is to be appointed, and be removable at will, by the Government. Section 39(3) provides that:

> "No person shall be appointed to be a member of a Special Criminal Court unless he is a judge of the High Court or the Circuit Court, or a justice of the District Court, or a barrister of not less than seven years standing, or a solicitor of not less than seven years standing, or an officer of the Defence Forces not below the rank of commandant."

The eligibility requirements prescribed by s 39(3) were considered in *The State (Gallagher) v Governor of Portlaoise Prison*[9] where the applicant had claimed that his conviction by the Special Criminal Court was invalidated by the presence of a retired High Court judge as president of that Court. This contention was rejected by Henchy J, who observed that as a High Court judge reverts to the status of a barrister upon retirement, the retired judge in question satisfied the requirements of s 39(3) inasmuch as he was a barrister of more than seven years' standing at the time he presided over the court. This view was later endorsed (although without explicit reference to the *Gallagher* case) by the Supreme Court in *McGlinchey v Governor of Portlaoise Prison,*[10] where Finlay CJ drew attention to the fact that, unlike many other statutory provisions dealing with eligibility for judicial appointment, s 39(3) made no mention of the fact that the barrister or solicitor in question be a *practising* barrister or solicitor.[11]

Section 39(4) allows the Minister for Finance to fix the remuneration and allowances to be paid to the members of the Special Criminal Court. In *Eccles v Ireland*[12] the plaintiffs (who had been convicted of capital murder by the Special Criminal Court) claimed that s 39 was unconstitutional in that it allowed the Government to remove the judges of that Court at will and thus deprive the Court of the benefit of guarantees of judicial indepen-

[8] [1988] IR 671.
[9] *The Irish Times*, July 27, 1983.
[10] [1988] IR 671.
[11] Cf. *The State (Walshe) v Murphy* [1981] IR 275 and see pp.557-558. It may be noted that since 1986 all members of the Special Criminal Court have been serving members of the judiciary. This appears to reflect official concern lest the membership of the Special Criminal Court be seen to consist of persons who might not otherwise enjoy the security of tenure and guarantee of independence guaranteed by Articles 34 and 35 of the Constitution to serving members of the judiciary in their other capacities (e.g., as judge of the High Court).
[12] [1985] IR 545; [1986] ILRM 343.

dence. Barrington J rejected this argument on the ground that the provisions of Articles 34 and 35 are specifically excluded by Article 38.6 from applying to the Special Criminal Court. The Supreme Court rejected the appeal, but for slightly different reasons. Finlay CJ, relying on the presumption of constitutionality, said that it was incorrect in law to say, for example, that the power of the Minister for Finance to fix the remuneration of the members of the Court extended to power to refuse to pay such remuneration for the reason only that their decisions did not suit the executive. He continued:

> "If [the executive were] to seek to exercise its power in a manner capable of interfering with the judicial independence of the court in the trial of persons charged before it would be attempting to frustrate the constitutional right of persons charged before that court to a trial in due course of law. Any such attempt would be prevented and corrected by the courts established under the Constitution. Whilst, therefore, the Special Criminal Court does not attract the express guarantees of judicial independence contained in Article 35, it does have, derived from the Constitution, a guarantee of independence in the carrying out of its function."

While this reasoning may - especially in view of the express exclusion contained in Article 38.6 - strike some as contrived, it has the welcome consequence that the Special Criminal Court is shielded from executive interference and is rendered invulnerable to challenge before the Court of Human Rights on the ground that its establishment and procedures violate Article 6 of the European Convention of Human Rights.[13]

Characteristics of the Special Criminal Court

Under s 40 the majority decision is to be the decision of the Special Criminal Court, and the existence or content of individual opinions, whether assenting or dissenting, is not to be disclosed.[14] By s 41(1) every Special Criminal Court has control of its own procedure in all respects. By s 44 convictions or sentences of a Special Criminal Court are subject to appeal to the Court of Criminal Appeal in the same way as convictions or sentences of the Central Criminal Court. Section 41(4) provides that, subject to the provisions of the Act "the practice and procedure applicable to the trial of a person on indictment in the Central Criminal Court shall, as far as practicable, apply to the trial of a person by a Special Criminal Court" and this provision has been considered in a number of cases.

In *The People (Director of Public Prosecutions) v Rice*[15] it was held by the Court of Criminal Appeal that the power given by s 44(1) of the Larceny Act 1916, to a jury, on acquitting a person on a charge of robbery, to convict him instead of assault with intent to rob, was not a matter of "practice and procedure", but a substantive power, and so could not be exercised by the Special Criminal Court in reliance on that provision. In *The People (Director of Public Prosecutions) v McGowan*[16] the defence had contested

[13] Article 6(1) requires that the accused in a criminal trial be tried by "an independent and impartial tribunal established by law." See, e.g., *Belilos v Switzerland* (1988) 10 EHRR 466 where the court held that a Swiss Cantonal law which permitted the trial of an accused charged with a minor crime by a member of a police board breached Article 6(1), since the defendant in such a case could "legitimately have doubts as to the independence and organisational impartiality of the Police Board."

[14] This fact was used by Henchy J in *The State (Littlejohn) v Governor of Mountjoy Prison*, Supreme Court, 18 March 1976, in rejecting the argument that an order returning the applicant for trial by the Special Criminal Court on the ground of the inadequacy of the ordinary courts was "incongruous" when the Special Criminal Court was in fact composed of ordinary judges. The special one-judgment rule, he said, gave those individual judges the protection of a measure of secrecy as to their individual judgments.

[15] [1979] IR 15.

[16] [1979] IR 45.

the admissibility of certain statements, but these were ruled to be admissible followed a "trial within a trial". Each of the witnesses who had given evidence as to the taking of the statements re-affirmed their original evidence and counsel for the defence did not avail of the opportunity for cross-examination. The Court of Criminal Appeal ruled that this constituted sufficient compliance with the requirements of s 41(4) of the 1939 Act. And in *People (Director of Public Prosecutions) v McMahon*[17] the Special Criminal Court had refused to disqualify itself in circumstances where highly prejudicial - but inadmissible - evidence had been given on behalf of the prosecution. In the Court of Criminal Appeal, Hederman J rejected this argument, observing that the obligation to follow the practice of the Central Criminal Court was only "so far as practicable":

> "Clearly it is impractical - indeed impossible - to import a role, however valuable, governing the conduct of jury trial [into the sphere of] a non-jury court. This analogy is not valid. In the present case the Special Criminal Court was made of experienced judges who clearly recognised the highly prejudicial nature of the evidence, and they asserted in open court that they were capable of excluding such evidence from their minds."[18]

Adaptation of the practice and procedure of the Central Criminal Court to the operation of the Special Criminal Court is in some measure (but not completely) effected by the Special Criminal Court Rules, 1972-1975.[19] Like the Constitution (Special Powers) Tribunal, the Special Criminal Court ranks as an inferior court and is thus amenable to judicial review.[20] Thus, in *The State (Director of Public Prosecutions) v Special Criminal Court*[21] Barrington J held that the Special Criminal Court had no jurisdiction to accept amendments to rectify errors in the indictment and that the Director should have preferred fresh charges and served a new book of evidence in relation to them. Barrington J made the important point that the Court was a creature of statute and that "the conditions of its statutes, on which its jurisdiction depended, must be rigorously and meticulously observed."[22]

These provisions, in several important respects far less drastic than those of the old Article 2A in regard to the Constitution (Special Powers) Tribunal, have been operated in the years 1939-46, 1961-2, and 1972 to date; during the two earlier periods the members of the Special Criminal Court were all officers of the Defence Forces, while in the latter period the members have all been either judges or former judges of the ordinary courts. Moreover, since 1986, all members of the Court have been actually *serving judges.*

[17] [1984] ILRM 461.

[18] But cf. the comments of Finlay CJ in *The People (Director of Public Prosecutions) v Conroy* [1986] IR 460: "Experience as a judges indicates that even as a trained lawyer that there is a very significant difficulty in excluding from one's mind incriminating evidence on the trial of a criminal case which is inadmissible".

[19] In *McGlinchey v Governor of Portlaoise Prison* [1988] IR 671, Lynch J said that the provisions of the Rules requiring public sittings only referred to "trials and applications for trials and such like matters" and did not refer to such administrative minutiae as the selection of which judges should sit to hear a particular case.

[20] See, e.g., *The State (Coveney) v Special Criminal Court* [1982] ILRM 284 and *The State (Director of Public Prosecutions) v Special Criminal Court*, High Court, 19 May 1983.

[21] High Court, 19 May 1983. Similar views were expressed by Henchy J for the Court of Criminal Appeal in *People (Director of Public Prosecutions) v Rice* [1979] IR 45.

[22] In *McElhinney v Special Criminal Court* [1990] 1 IR 405 Walsh J agreed that the provisions of the Offences Against the State Acts "relating to the procedure of the Special Criminal Court must be construed strictly because among other things they deprive a person of the constitutional obligation of a trial by jury in indictable offences of a non-minor character which although an obligation can also be construed as being a right conferred upon an accused person."

In its first period of operation the Special Criminal Court and its parent legislation were considered in relation to the Constitution in *In re MacCurtain*.[23] In this case counsel for the applicant argued, firstly, that his trial by the Special Criminal Court was unconstitutional, as that Court had consisted entirely of Army officers and was therefore in reality a military tribunal of the sort contemplated by Article 38.4 as permissible only in time of war or armed rebellion. This argument was rejected by Gavan Duffy J in the High Court and subsequently also by the Supreme Court, with Sullivan CJ saying:

> "Reliance was placed on the facts that the Court was composed of military officers and sat in a military barracks, and that the accused was in military custody. But Article 38.3.2 empowers the Legislature to prescribe the constitution, powers, jurisdiction and procedure of the Special Courts. The Legislature has prescribed the constitution of Special Courts in s 39 of the Act...it has not been suggested that any member of the Court by which the appellant was tried was not duly qualified under that section. The Special Criminal Court in this case, although it was constituted entirely of officers of the Defence Forces, was, in our opinion, a tribunal quite distinct from the military tribunal contemplated by Article 38.4."

Secondly, it was contended that it was unconstitutional for the Oireachtas to purport to confer discretion on the Government as to when Part V of the Act might be brought into force. Gavan Duffy J said:

> "The Oireachtas clearly considered the Government to be the authority best situated, from its position and the information at its disposal, to determine whether or not special tribunals were necessary in the circumstances set out in the section. In my opinion the provision that the Government may make such a proclamation when satisfied that the ordinary courts are inadequate is clearly meant to be an essentially executive decision of the highest executive authority in the State. In my opinion, the Government, in declaring itself satisfied within the section of the inadequacy of the ordinary courts and of the necessity to set up special courts, cannot be said to be acting either in a judicial or in a legislative capacity. Nor is there any need under the Act for the Government to give its reasons..."

A similar view was taken by the Supreme Court. Thirdly, it was argued that the provision of s 46(2) of the Act empowering the Attorney General to require the sending for trial by the Special Criminal Court of a person charged with any indictable offence, even one not scheduled, was unconstitutional as vesting judicial or legislative functions in the Attorney General; both Courts rejected this submission also.

Thirty years later, in *The State (Bollard) v Governor of Portlaoise Prison*,[24] a similar attack on Part V of the 1939 Act also failed. Kenny J rejected submissions that the power of the Attorney General under s 45 (to request that the District Judge send forward to the Special Criminal Court for trial a person charged with a scheduled offence which is triable summarily) was an exercise of judicial power; and that the power of the Attorney General under s 46 to request trial by the Special Criminal Court of a non-scheduled offence if he certifies:

> "that the ordinary courts are, in his opinion, inadequate to secure the effective administration of justice and the preservation of public peace and order in relation to the trial of such person on such charge"

[23] [1941] IR 83.
[24] High Court, 4 December 1972.

amounted to an exercise of judicial power. In the latter connection he held that the object of this section was specifically contemplated by Article 38.3.1. (It may be noted, however, that in dealing with the applicant's unspecific complaints under Article 40 he emphasised that the Court as currently constituted consisted entirely of judges.) In *Savage v Director of Public Prosecutions*[25] the same point was again taken (though with reference to the Director) and again rejected; Finlay P added a further independent rationalisation for the non-reviewability of the prosecuting authority's certificate: commonsense considerations of security made it impracticable to require this authority to give its reasons for coming to the opinion on which the certificate was based. Similar arguments were employed by Carroll J in *O'Reilly v Director of Public Prosecutions*[26] where the plaintiffs challenged the constitutionality of s 48 of the 1939 Act. This provides for the automatic transfer of an accused from the Central Criminal Court (i.e., the criminal division of the High Court) to the Special Criminal Court and it was said that this thereby trenched on the full exclusive jurisdiction of the High Court under Article 34.3.1.[27] Carroll J could not accept this, saying that in her view:

> "[The] constitutional jurisdiction of the High Court is limited by the operation of Article 38.3 and the mandatory order sending the accused persons forward for trial to the Special Criminal Court is not an unwarranted intrusion of the powers of the High Court. On the contrary, it is constitutionally justified under Article 38.3."

On the question of judicial review, she felt that "no analogy could be drawn" between the opinion of the Director authorised by the 1939 Act and Article 38.3 respectively and the exercise of a power by a Minister under an ordinary Act of the Oireachtas. She continued:

> "The courts do not have power to set the Director's opinion aside, for to do so would be to substitute in a negative way their opinion as to the adequacy of grounds on which the opinion was based."

This is a surprising argument, as it is well-established that judicial review for vires is not in any way concerned with the merits.[28]

This entire matter was further considered by Lynch J in *Foley v Director of Public Prosecutions,*[29] yet another case in which the propriety of the plaintiff's transfer to the Special Criminal Court had been called into question. Having referred to *Savage* and *The State (McCormack) v Curran,*[30] Lynch J agreed that while might appear to be a "slight conflict" between the decisions:

> "The net result of the judgments in these cases was that the decision of the Director of Public Prosecutions in issuing certificates under the Offences Against the State

[25] [1982] ILRM 385.

[26] [1984] ILRM 224. These cases have come in for considerable academic criticism: see Byrne, "*Judicial Reviewability of a Prosecutorial Discretion*" (1981) 16 Ir Jur (n.s.) 86; Byrne, "*The Director of Public Prosecution's Power to refer cases to the Special Court*" (1984) 6 DULJ (n.s.) 177; and Pye, "*Judicial Review of discretionary powers under Part V of the Offences Against the State Act 1939*" (1985) 3 ILT (n.s.) 65.

[27] For which see pp.408-415.

[28] See generally, Hogan and Morgan, *Administrative Law in Ireland* (London, 1991) at 328-330.

[29] *The Irish Times Law Reports*, September 25, 1989.

[30] This case concerned the reviewability of a decision of the Director not to prosecute in a particular case and this is considered at p. 309. Finlay CJ said that this decision could be reviewed if there was "*mala fides* or improper motive or improper policy."

Act 1939, was not reviewable unless the applicant had established a prima facie case of some irregularity of a serious nature such as to amount to some impropriety of some sort or another."

Special Criminal Court as venue

In some recent cases, there have been suggestions to the effect that the selection of the Special Criminal Court as a venue may not operate (the absence of the right to jury trial aside) so as to prejudice the accused by, e.g., exposing him to further penalties. This was first hinted by Walsh J in *The People (Director of Public Prosecutions) v Quilligan*[31] where he doubted the constitutionality of s 34 of the Offences Against the State Act 1939 inasmuch as it provided for severer penalties[32] on public servants convicted of scheduled offences before the Special Criminal Court:

> "It is the Attorney General or the Director of Public Prosecutions who basically has power to decide whether, upon conviction of such [scheduled] offence, disqualification and forfeiture shall be incurred because the question of whether the case is tried in the ordinary courts or in the Special Courts is his decision. Effectively then it is his decision which determines whether or not a conviction will carry with it forfeiture or disqualifications."[33]

However, when the constitutionality of s 34 was actually challenged in *Cox v Ireland,*[34] Barr J refused to invalidate the section on this ground, saying that, by reason of s 46(1) and (2) and its certificate procedure, the selection of the trial venue had been determined by "the Oireachtas and not [by] the Director."[35] The Supreme Court, however, found the section unconstitutional on the ground that it was "impermissibly wide and indiscriminate", stressing that:

> "The ultimate factor triggering the operation of s 34 in any particular case is the venue of the trial which results in the conviction for a scheduled offence. That venue is primarily selected by the fact that the offence is scheduled and can only be avoided by a decision of the Attorney General or of the DPP in respect of which the accused person has no right of representation."

[31] [1986] IR 495.

[32] The penalties included automatic forfeiture of office or employment; forfeiture of pension rights and the imposition of a seven year ban on the resumption of public service employment. The word "provided" is used advisedly, inasmuch as s 34 was declared unconstitutional in its entirety in *Cox v Ireland* [1992] 2 IR 545.

[33] While Walsh J did not expressly say so, the inference to be drawn from this passage is that because it is the actions of either the Attorney General or Director of Public Prosecutions which effectively determines whether the accused come before the Special Criminal Court, this, in s 34 type cases, effectively allowed a non-judicial personage to have a role in the selection of a criminal penalty, thereby offending against Article 34 and general separation of powers principles.

[34] [1992] IR 545. See generally, *Humphreys,* (1991) 13 DULJ (n.s.) 118.

[35] However, Barr J found the section unconstitutional on equality and personal rights grounds (for which see pp.733-734). Given that, as we have already seen (at pp. 313-314), the Director has virtually an unfettered say in whether a particular accused comes before the Special Criminal Court, the approach of Barr J seems unduly formalistic. Compare this reasoning with that of the Privy Council in *Ali v R.* [1992] 2 All ER 1, where the impugned legislation enabled the Mauritius Director of Public Prosecution to prosecute drug offences *either* before a court which could *only* impose the death penalty upon conviction *or* before a court which could only impose a fine and imprisonment. Lord Keith held, approving the reasoning of Ó Dálaigh CJ in *Deaton v Attorney General* [1963] IR 170, that such legislation infringed the separation of powers principles contained in the Constitution of Mauritius inasmuch as it enabled the Director "in substance to select the penalty to be imposed in a particular case."

1940: summary trial, only-one-penalty military court

A further exceptional criminal jurisdiction created by statute - though under cover of Article 28.3.3, not Article 38.4 - may conveniently be dealt with here. In June 1940 the Oireachtas enacted[36] the Emergency Powers (Amendment) (No. 2) Act. The principal Emergency Powers Act 1939, while giving extremely wide powers of all kinds to the Government, had nevertheless provided by s 2(5) that "nothing in this section shall authorise...the making of provision for the trial by courts-martial of persons not being persons subject to military law"- thus alluding, by the use of the concluding words, to Article 38.4.1 and the "military tribunals" there envisaged (although these would appear to be essentially military tribunals or courts-martial of an informal or drumhead kind, not based on statute). But the Emergency Powers (Amendment) (No. 2) Act 1940, deleted from that sub-section the words "or the making of provision for the trial by courts-martial of persons not being persons subject to military law", and went on to provide (s 3):

> "The Government may, by an Order under s 2 of the Principal Act make provision for the trial, in a summary manner, by commissioned officers of the Defence Forces, of any person alleged to have committed any offence specified in such order, and, in case of the conviction of such person of such offence, for the imposition and the carrying out of the sentence of death, and no appeal shall lie in respect of such conviction or sentence."

A court - consisting, in fact, of senior officers who were already members of the Special Criminal Court - was set up in pursuance of this Act and several persons were tried and sentenced by it.[37] This court and the Acts and Orders which produced and regulated it were considered in *In re McGrath and Harte*[38] and *The State (Walsh) v Lennon*.[39] Most of the substance of these two cases concerned the effect of Article 28.3.3 and no interpretation of Article 38 was involved. However, it may be noted that in the former case the validity of the Order for the trial of the applicants was attacked on the grounds that it did not contain any provision as to how the members of the military court were to be selected, or how an accused person should be brought before it; and that, as the applicants were charged with murder committed before the making of the Order which set up the military court, the effect was to give the Order a retrospective operation not authorised by the Act (though envisaged by the Order itself, which defined a "Specified Offence" as one set out in the Schedule and committed after the passing of the Act but either before or after the making of the Order). The Supreme Court said, in regard to the composition and procedure of the military court:

> "In our opinion no such provisions were necessary. Any three persons having the qualifications specified in clause 3 of the Order would, in our opinion, constitute such a court, and would have jurisdiction to try an accused person charged with a specified offence and brought before them for trial."

And in regard to the argument on retrospective effect:

[36] The Bill passed the Dáil in a few minutes on 19 June 1940 (the time of fall of France): 80 *Dáil Debates* 1739-41.

[37] For statistics, see 102 *Dáil Debates* 609-10. For a frank comment by the Minister for Justice of the day (Deputy Gerald Boland TD) on the court's terrifying competence: see 101 *Dáil Debates* 116.

[38] [1941] IR 68. See further at pp.239-242.

[39] [1942] IR 112; (1942) ILTR 207.

"Section 3 of the Act provides that the Government may, by such an Order, make provision for the trial in a summary manner of any person alleged to have committed any offence specified in such Order. In our opinion these words, taken in conjunction with the provisions of s 2(1) of the Principal Act are sufficiently wide to enable the Government by Order, made under these Acts, to provide for the trial and punishment of persons alleged to have committed offences whether before or after the making of such Order."

The extremely drastic character of the military court - as compared even with the Constitution (Special Powers) Tribunal - was reinforced by further Emergency Powers Orders at the end of 1941; these came under attack in *The State (Walsh) v Lennon,*[40] in which the four applicants had originally been charged before the Special Criminal Court. The proceedings there were discontinued after the Attorney General had entered a *nolle prosequi* in the case of each accused; they were then charged with the same offence before the military court, being sent for trial there under Emergency Powers Orders Nos. 41F and 139 of 1941. The former Order directed that the four accused should be tried together rather than separately; this, it was argued for the accused, was *ultra vires* as it purported to preclude the military court from exercising discretion and control over its own proceedings. The latter Order made huge inroads on the ordinary laws of evidence; unsigned statements, by persons who were not called to give evidence in court, were to be admissible, and the court, if it considered it "proper that it should not be bound by any rule of evidence, whether statutory or at common law", was not to be bound by such rule. In regard to this it was contended that the Order constituted such a fundamental change in the law of evidence as to deprive the court of the attributes of a judicial tribunal, and prevented it from carrying out such a trial as was contemplated by s 3 of the Act. All of these arguments failed in the High Court and Supreme Court. In the High Court Maguire P adverted to the fact that the applicants were trying to get round the protection of Article 28.3.3 by appealing to what might be termed paraconstitutional rights, existing independently of the written Constitution, and rejected this approach; Gavan Duffy J said:

"In my opinion, the applicants have come for relief to a Court which has no power to give them relief. Their right to resort to the High Court springs from the constitutional guarantees, entrusted to the protection of the High Court, and that right is suspended. The right to *habeas corpus* in this State is now very carefully defined by the Constitution, and the right to a trial in due course of law is enshrined in the Constitution...[But so] long as the jurisdiction of this Court to enforce those constitutional rights remains in abeyance in pursuance of an Article in the Constitution, persons in the position of the applicants cannot justify an application to this Court by reference to the guarantees in the Constitution."

In the Supreme Court, Sullivan CJ took the same view of Article 28.3.3. Of Order No. 139 he said:

"If, as is conceded, the Government had power to set up a special tribunal to try specified offences, and to invest it with special powers for this purpose, it is, in our opinion, quite impossible to hold that that tribunal is deprived of its jurisdiction and powers by reason of alterations in the laws of evidence to be recognised by such tribunal."

[40] [1942] IR 112. The whole proceeding in this case is very severely criticised in a note in (1942) 6 Journal of Criminal Law.

He pointed out also that it had never been decided that the entering of a *nolle prosequi* was a bar to a fresh indictment for the same offence, as it was well established that a discharge of an accused person in consequence of a *nolle prosequi* did not amount to an acquittal.[41]

EXTRAORDINARY CRIMINAL TRIBUNALS WITH NO BASIS IN STATUTE

"Military tribunals" in Article 38.4.1 appears to envisage, not so much courts of the type established under the Emergency Powers (Amendment) (No.2) Act 1940 - although, as has been seen, the Act seemed to refer itself to that part of Article 38[42] - but rather informal, "drumhead" courts-martial with no statutory basis. This is to be inferred from the wording of the section: "Military tribunals may be established", not (as in the case of the special courts envisaged in Article 38.3.1) "may be established *by law*". This deviation from a formula which is common in the Constitution is scarcely an oversight, and it must imply that the Constitution contemplates, in the case of offences against military law, or for use against civilians in time of war or armed rebellion, a jurisdiction set up ad hoc by or through the Defence Forces but not specifically authorised or regulated by the Oireachtas. Courts of this kind have not been known since the enactment of this Constitution, but relatively recent pre-constitutional precedents exist in the years of the armed struggle for independence and the subsequent civil war (1920-23). This principles applied by the Irish courts in approaching the operations of courts-martial of this type were, in turn, based on principles established by the English courts in the Boer War period.

These principles may be summarised as follows: (1) the executive is entitled to repel force by force, either in war or in armed rebellion; (2) for this purpose the military arm of the executive may exert repression on civil populations in the areas affected; (3) this repression may be exerted through the mode of "courts" of military personnel informally established; (4) the ordinary courts have no jurisdiction to interfere with or review the operations of such court martial. In *Ex parte Marais*[43] Halsbury LC said:

> "The truth is that no doubt has ever existed that where war actually prevails the ordinary courts have no jurisdiction over the action of the military authorities. Doubtless cases of difficulty arise when the fact of a state of rebellion or insurrection is not clearly established. It may often be a question whether a mere riot, or disturbance neither so serious nor so extensive as really to amount to a war at all, has not been treated with an excessive severity, and whether the intervention of the military force was necessary; but once let the fact of actual war be established, and there is a universal consensus of opinion that the civil courts have no jurisdiction to call in question the propriety of the action of military authorities."

In *Tilonko v Attorney General of Natal*[44] this doctrine received further elaboration with specific reference to courts-martial used against persons not subject to military law. Lord Halsbury said:

[41] But see above at pp. 580-582 and *The State (O'Callaghan) v Ó hÚadhaigh* [1977] IR 42.
[42] See p. 650.
[43] [1902] AC 109.
[44] [1907] AC 93.

> "If there is war, there is the right to repel force by force, but it is found convenient and decorous, from time to time, to authorise what are called "courts" to administer punishments, and to restrain by acts of repression the violence that is committed in time of war, instead of leaving such punishments and repression to the casual action of persons acting without sufficient consultation, or without sufficient order or regularity in the procedure in which things alleged to have been done are proved. But to attempt to make these proceedings by so-called "courts-martial", administering summary justice under the supervision of a military commander, analogous to the regular proceedings of courts of justice is quite illusory."

In 1921 the immunity of the military, acting through the "decorous" agency of informal "courts", from control by the ordinary courts in time of war was upheld in *R v Allen*.[45] The notable feature of this case, in which the applicant had been sentenced to death by a military court for the unlawful possession of arms, was that a statute specifically directed to the conditions of the time - the Restoration of Order in Ireland Act 1920 - was in force, and under this Act the death penalty could not have been imposed, by the statutory courts-martial which it authorised, for this offence. The British Commander-in-Chief deposed that war was actually raging, and the King's Bench Division accepted this as a fact ousting its jurisdiction to interfere. Similar decisions were given in the cases of *R. (Garde and Others) v Strickland*[46] and *R. (Ronayne and Mulcahy) v Strickland*;[47] in these cases, unlike *Allen's* case, the military assertion that war was raging was in fact contradicted by affidavits to the effect, *inter alia*, that all the ordinary courts sat regularly and discharged their business. The King's Bench Division would not accept this criterion as valid for disproving the existence of a state of war; though Molony C .J in *Garde* did uphold the right of the Court to decide for itself whether war was raging, rather than a duty to accept blindly the military statement on the point. He said:

> "This contention [that the courts must accept the military view] is absolutely opposed to our judgment in *Allen's* case and is destitute of authority, and we desire to state, in the clearest possible language, that this Court has the power and the duty to decide whether a state of war exists which justifies the application of martial law."[48]

In a single case, *Egan v Macready*,[49] a decision which conflicted with that in *Allen's, Garde's* and *Ronayne's* cases was reached in a different Division of the then High Court. The applicant had been sentenced to death by an informal military court for an offence for which the courts-martial of the Restoration of Order in Ireland Act could not have imposed this penalty. O'Connor MR held in the Chancery Division that, since the state of war existed at the date of the Act's passing, the powers of the military authorities were in fact limited by it, and that the offence charged against Egan could only be tried by a court-martial under the Act.

When British rule was replaced by that of the Provisional Government, and that Government in turn found itself having to put down rebellion, its Army, acting on a resolution of Dáil Éireann,[50] set up military courts for the trial of civilians charged with cer-

[45] [1921] 2 IR 241; (1921) 55 ILTR 107.
[46] [1921] 2 IR 317.
[47] [1921] 2 IR 333.
[48] Molony CJ reiterated this view (in the context of internment by the military authorities) in *R. (O'Brien) v Military Governor, North Dublin Union* [1924] 1 IR 32.
[49] [1921] 1 IR 265; (1921) 55 ILTR 197.
[50] 28 September 1922. This was still the pre-Constitution Dáil; and the Government was still the Provisional Government.

tain specified offences. In *R. (Childers) v Adjutant General of Provisional Forces*[51] the applicant was refused *habeas corpus* by O'Connor MR, having been tried for unlawful possession of arms by a military court which was expected to impose a sentence of death. O'Connor MR. readily accepted that war was raging;[52] and refused to follow his own decision in *Egan's* case on the ground that there was no statute now in force, analogous to the Restoration of Order in Ireland Act that could be seen as delimiting and regulating the actions of the Army in putting down rebellion; the plenary powers of the executive in this regard again held full sway.[53]

The fact that this executive was still in an inchoate stage of constitutional regulation made no difference to the principle. In *R. (Johnstone) v O'Sullivan*,[54] where two ladies had been arrested and were awaiting a military trial for possession of arms, *habeas corpus* was refused them, on the grounds now familiar from *Allen's* case and its successors, by the King's Bench Division and by the Court of Appeal; when it was argued in the latter Court that the Provisional Government had no power to create an Army, Pim J said that there was:

> "an inherent right at common law in every government that may be attacked to defend itself [and to] form an army... for the protection of itself and of the people committed to its charge."

And O'Connor MR formulated a concise test for determining whether or not a state of war existed sufficient to justify "martial law". After describing the state of the country at the time (October 1922) he said:

> "The test that I apply to determine whether war exists or not is this: Is the forcible resistance to authority so widespread, so continuous, so formidable, of such duration that the help of an army must be invoked, not merely in one or two instances, but habitually or constantly, lest the State shall perish? Tested in that way, there is no doubt that, in point of law, a state of war exists."

On 6 December 1922 the Constitution of the Irish Free State came into force, and had the effect of imposing permanent limitations on the scope of "martial law" and military courts. Article 6 (on personal liberty) provided that:

> "nothing in this Article contained shall be invoked to prohibit control or interfere with any act of the military forces of the Irish Free State...during the existence of a State of war or armed rebellion."

[51] [1923] 1 IR 5; (1922) 56 ILTR 183.

[52] He said: "I am sitting here in this temporary makeshift for a Court of Justice. Why? Because one of the noblest buildings in this country, which was erected for the accommodation of the King's Courts and was the home of justice for more than a hundred years, is now a mass of crumbling ruins, the work of revolutionaries, who proclaim themselves the soldiers of an Irish Republic. I also know that the Public Record Office (a building that might well have spared by even the most extreme of irreconcilables) has been reduced to ashes, with its treasures which can never be replaced. I know also that railways have been torn up, railway stations destroyed, the noblest mansions burned down, roads made impassable, bridges blown up, and life and property attacked in almost every county in Southern Ireland. If this is not a state of war, I would like to know what is."

[53] The prisoner in this case (Erskine Childers) was actually executed while his appeal against the order of O'Connor MR was pending. See Dorothy McArdle, *The Irish Republic*, pp. 810ff.

[54] [1923] 2 IR 13; (1923) 57 ILTR 17.

Article 70, moreover (cited already), provided exceptionally for the functioning of military tribunals in time of war or armed rebellion. The military courts continued to operate until the end of the civil war in mid-1923.[55] Their acts were formally validated by s 3 of the Indemnity Act 1923.[56]

It may be noted that - in contrast, for instance, to the Constitution (Special Powers) Tribunal or, in general, special courts with a statutory basis defining their jurisdiction - there is authority for the view that informal military courts are not subject to judicial review. In *Re Clifford and O'Sullivan*[57] prisoners sought a writ of prohibition against a military court and, having been turned down by the Irish King's Bench Division and Court of Appeal, appealed to the House of Lords, where they failed again. Lord Cave said:

> "The so-called "military court"...was not and did not claim to be a court or judicial tribunal in any legal sense of those terms...They sat, not as a tribunal for hearing charges of crime, but as a military committee for considering a matter arising under the Proclamation[58] and advising the commanding officer thereon; and, although in the interest of the prisoners brought before them they followed the formula of law, their proceedings were in no sense criminal proceedings...There is no precedent for the issue of the writ against a body which has no statutory or common law authority to [try cases and pass judgments] and which claims no such authority...Those officers did not purport to act as a court in any legal sense. If so, however wide a view may be taken of the power of the courts to grant prohibition, prohibition will not lie in this case."

The principle in *Clifford and O'Sullivan's* case was applied and brought a stage further in *R..(Johnstone) v O'Sullivan*,[59]in which a preliminary issue was whether an appeal lay against the refusal of *habeas corpus*. This turned on whether the case involved a "criminal cause or matter", since in such matters appeal was excluded by s 50 of the Supreme Court of Judicature Act (Ireland), 1877. The old King's Bench Division and Court of Appeal held that the case was not a "criminal cause or matter", as the military tribunal which was due to try the applicants was not a "court", and the subject-matter of its proceedings was not a "charge" or "crime" in any of the regular senses of those words. However, given modern developments in the law of judicial review - by which the courts look primarily not so much to the source of the tribunal's power but rather to its practical operation on the applicant[60] - it may be that this precedential value of this authority has been thereby weakened.

Jurisdiction over Persons Subject to Military Law

The exercise of jurisdiction by military tribunals over persons subject to military law - in this context called courts-martial - is provided for by the Defence Act 1954. Sections

[55] After the decision in *R. (O'Brien) v Military Governor, North Dublin Union* [1924] 1 IR 32 (delivered by the Court of Appeal on 1 August 1923) to the effect that there was "no doubt, a certain amount of disorder" in the city of Dublin, but no proven state of war or armed rebellion, these courts could not have lawfully operated.

[56] Enacted 3 August 1923, two days after the judgment in *O'Brien* mentioned in the preceding note. On the constitutional validity of such an Indemnity Act see below at p. 787 and *R. (Cooney) v Clinton* [1935] IR 245.

[57] [1921] 2 AC 570; (1921) 55 ILTR 153.

[58] The Proclamation of the Lord Lieutenant, 10 December 1920, placing the counties of Cork, Limerick, Tipperary and Kerry under martial law (under the Restoration of Order in Ireland Act 1920).

[59] [1923] 2 IR 13; (1923) 57 ILTR 17.

[60] See generally, Hogan and Morgan, *Administrative Law in Ireland* (London, 1991) at 572-579.

118 and 119 of the Act define the categories of persons subject to military law,[61] and the remainder of Part V of the Act is devoted to the application of military law. Sections 185-226 deal with the composition and functioning of courts-martial; ss 124-169 with offences against military law. Section 240 empowers the Minister for Defence is empowered to make rules of procedure for courts-martial; these were made in the same year (Rules of Procedure (Defence Forces), 1954). By s 169 of the Act (as amended) a court-martial may try, as offences against military law, if committed by a person subject to military law, a large number of offences at ordinary criminal law; though by Regulations made by virtue of s 192 - the Defence (Civil Authority with Respect to Courts-Martial) Regulations 1954 - this jurisdiction "in the case of an offence relating to the person or property of a person not subject to military law, depend[s] on the consent of the Superintendent of the Garda Síochána within whose district the offence is committed". Appeals (to an appeal court of ordinary judges) against the findings of court-martial are provided for by the Courts-Martial Appeals Act 1983. Persons subject to military law are of course in no way immune from the operation of the ordinary criminal law.

Effect of Article 38.6

The effect of Article 38.6 is clearly very sweeping. The courts and tribunals envisaged by Article 38.3 and 38.4 need not be composed of judges; their proceedings need not be public;[62] they are not necessarily subject to appeal;[63] and the members of these courts do not benefit from the provisions of Article 35 tending towards judicial independence.[64] On the other hand, in *Attorney General v Connolly*[65] Gavan Duffy P said that Article 38.6 did not take away the High Court's power to exercise a "superintendence" of those courts, or its "correlative right" to protect them.

[61] Note that the expression "persons subject to military law" is not given any constitutional definition. Would it then be competent for the Oireachtas to extend the jurisdiction of courts martial via extensions of the classes of persons subject to military law? These already include limited categories of civilians: see ss 18 and 119 of the Defence Act 1954.

[62] The Special Criminal Court constituted since 1972 has been composed of judges (or, prior to 1986) of former judges and has, in fact, sat in public.

[63] The Special Criminal Court's convictions and sentences may in fact be appealed to the Court of Criminal Appeal: s 44 of the Offences Against the State Act 1939. Appeals from the convictions and sentences of courts-martial now lie to a special court: Courts Martial Appeal Act 1983.

[64] This exclusion has now, in practice, been heavily qualified by the decision of the Supreme Court in *Eccles v Ireland* [1985] IR 545; [1986] ILRM 343.

[65] [1947] IR 213; (1947) 81 ILTR 92. There is a strong hint of a similar approach in the judgment of Henchy J in *Tormey v Ireland* [1985] IR 289.

Article 38.5

TRIAL BY JURY

5. Save in the case of the trial of offences under section 2, section 3 or section 4 of this Article no person shall be tried on any criminal charge without a jury.	**5. Ní cead duine a thriail in aon chúis choiriúil ach i láthair choiste tiomanta, ach amháin i gcás cionta a thriail faoi alt 2, alt 3 nó alt 4 den Airteagal seo.**

1922 provision

Article 72 of the 1922 Constitution contained a corresponding provision.

"Jury" is not defined

"Jury" is one of the terms which the Constitution uses without defining, and the question accordingly arises whether the effect of the section is to give constitutional entrenchment to juries in the sense in which their composition and function were understood in 1937. At the very least, there must be some irreducible component of jury trial, as then understood, which is so entrenched, as it seems certain that if the function and mode of operation of juries were substantially changed, the intent of Article 38.5 would not be respected. This question has never been globally considered; but it is possible to report a number of judicial statements on different aspects of it.

General rule of jury trial

It may be noted first that Article 38.5 is more properly regarded as a "constitutional imperative" rather than a personal "right", inasmuch as trial by jury for non-minor offences[1] is "not only preferred but made mandatory".[2] This would seem to mean, for example, that it is not open to an accused charged with a non-minor offence to waive this right to jury trial.[3] General appraisals of the constitutional value represented by jury trial can be found in several cases. In *Melling v Ó Mathghamhna*[4] Ó Dálaigh J said:

> "The alternative tribunal which the law allows the citizen in the case of a criminal charge which is not a minor offence is a jury, whose members are wholly independent of executive or legislative disciplines or displeasure and who necessarily by their very numbers bring to the administration of justice the commoner touch. The safeguard of trial by jury is against an improbable but not-to-be-overlooked future; and it is for this reason the Constitution enshrines it."

And in the same case Kingsmill Moore J said:

> "Rightly or not, trial by jury had for centuries been regarded popularly as a most important safeguard for the individual, a protection alike against the zeal of an enthusiastic Executive or the rigidity of an ultra-conservative Judiciary. Especially was this so in the history of Ireland. It seems to me reasonably clear that the Saorstát Éireann Constitution meant to preserve and extend this right."

[1] Excepting, of course, cases coming before the Special Criminal Court.

[2] *Holohan v Donohue* [1986] IR 45; [1986] ILRM 250 *per* Henchy J.

[3] This does not, of course, extend to minor offences where there may be a *statutory* right to jury trial, as under the Criminal Justice Act 1951.

[4] [1962] IR 1; (1963) 97 ILTR 60.

A more rhetorically forceful statement on the same lines came from Henchy J in *The People (Director of Public Prosecutions) v O'Shea*,[5] in the special context of what he (as one of the Supreme Court minority) believed was the inherent non-appealability of jury acquittals:

> "I am convinced that the indissoluble attachment, to trial by jury, of the right after acquittal to raise the plea of *autrefois acquit was* one of the prime reasons why the Constitution of 1937 (like that of 1922) mandated trial with a jury as the normal mode of trying major offences. The bitter Irish race- memory of politically appointed and Executive-oriented judges, of the suspension of jury trial in times of popular revolt, of the substitution therefor of summary trial or detention without trial, of cat-and-mouse releases from such detention, of packed juries and sometimes corrupt judges and prosecutors, had long implanted in the consciousness of the people, and therefore in the minds of their political representatives, the conviction that the best way of preventing an individual from suffering a wrong conviction for an offence was to allow him to "put himself upon his country", that is to say, to allow him to be tried for that offence by a fair, impartial and representative jury, sitting in a court presided over by an impartial and independent judge appointed under the Constitution, who would see that all the requirements for a fair and proper jury trial would be observed, so that, amongst other things, if the jury's verdict were one of not guilty, the accused could leave court with the absolute assurance that he would never again "be vexed" for the same charge."

In *O'Callaghan v Attorney General*[6] Blayney J said that these authorities showed that:

> "There appears to emerge a fairly clear consensus that the essence of trial by jury is that the decision as to the guilt or innocence of the accused is made by a group of his fellow citizens and not by a judge or a number of judges."

And the Supreme Court's decision in *People v Davis*[7] shows that these dicta were not merely rhetorical. Here the trial judge had directed that the jury return a murder verdict, but the Supreme Court ruled that this judicial direction constituted an unconstitutional usurpation of the jury's function. Having referred to the passages from the judgments of Ó Dálaigh J in *Melling* and Henchy J in *O'Shea* already quoted above, Finlay CJ went on to add:

> "I am satisfied that these expressions of opinion lead inevitably to a conclusion that the constitutional right to trial with a jury contained in Article 38.5...has a fundamental and absolutely essential characteristic the right of the jury to deliver a verdict."

The Chief Justice added that this did not mean that a trial judge could not "express an opinion that a particular verdict of guilty" was the only one which "would be reasonable or proper on the evidence", but this "must of necessity fall short of the right to direct a verdict of guilty."

[5] [1982] IR 384.
[6] [1992] 1 IR 538; [1993] ILRM 267 (HC).
[7] [1993] ILRM 407.

Is the unanimity of the twelve jurors constitutionally entrenched?

Does the constitutional term "jury" in the criminal context mean a group of twelve jurors whose unanimous verdict of guilty is necessary for conviction, as was the case in 1937 (though the Juries (Protection) Act 1929, enacted at a time of widespread intimidation of jurors, and continued in force until 1931, provided for verdicts on a majority of nine of twelve jurors)? The unanimity rule was abrogated by s 25 of the Criminal Justice Act 1984 which by sub-s (1):

> "The verdict of a jury in criminal proceedings[8] need not be unanimous in a case where there are not fewer than eleven jurors if ten of them agree on the verdict."

Under sub-s (2) it is further provided that a majority guilty verdict must be pronounced in open court, whereas in the case of sub-s (4) it is provided that the court must cause the jury verdict to be taken "in such a way" that it shall not be indicated "whether the verdict was unanimous or by a majority." An important safeguard is further supplied by s 25(3) which provides that the court may not accept a majority verdict unless it appears that "the jury have had such period of time for deliberation as the court thinks reasonable having regard to the nature and complexity of the case" and the court shall not in any event "accept such verdict unless it appears to the court that the jury have had at least two hours for deliberation."[9]

On this point there is, first, the view of Walsh J in *de Búrca v Attorney General*,[10] which - since the issue was the formation of the panels from which juries are drawn, not the number of jurors or their mode of finding a verdict - must be regarded as an *obiter dictum*:

> "It is undoubtedly true that jury trial, as we know it, has certain incidents such as the unanimity of verdict in criminal cases and the majority verdict in civil cases, and that juries consist of twelve persons. In my view such matters, however, are not the essential ingredients of trial by jury. The constitutional provision of trial with a jury is not a guarantee that juries must always consist of twelve persons, neither more nor less, or that the verdict must be unanimous. Looking at the essence of trial with a jury, I am of opinion that it does presuppose that the trial should be in the presence, and under the authority, of a presiding judge having power to instruct the jury as to the law and to advise them as to the facts, and the jury should be free to consider their verdict alone without the intervention or presence of the judge or any other person during their deliberations. I think it also imports an element of secrecy.
>
> In my view, it was not the intention of the Constitution to impose a standard and uniform procedure upon all legislation relating to trial by jury or upon all forms of trial with a jury... While saying that I do not think that a jury may not consist of more or less than twelve members, I am not offering any view as to what figure would constitute the minimum below which a jury would lose its essential character.

[8] Section 25(5) provides that the majority verdicts rule does not affect "the trial of any offence for which the court is required, upon conviction of the accused, to sentence him to death..." This sub-section is now redundant in view of the abolition of the death penalty by the Criminal Justice Act 1990.
[9] The two hour requirement is mandatory: see *People v Kelly* [1989] ILRM 370.
[10] [1976] IR 38; (1977) 111 ILTR 37.

> I am also of the view that the Constitution does not preclude the Oireachtas from enacting that prospective jurors should have certain minimum standards of ability or personal competence without which jury trial might fail to serve as an essential part of the administration of the criminal law..."

The point nevertheless remains that in 1937 the necessity of securing all twelve jurors' votes for a conviction was reckoned central to the system of criminal justice and a vital security to a person unjustly accused. It might well be thought that any dilution of the jury, as it was in 1937, should require the authority of a referendum to amend the Constitution, but this argument found little favour with the Supreme Court in *O'Callaghan v Attorney General*[11] where the constitutionality of s 25 of the 1984 Act was upheld. Delivering the judgment of the Court, O'Flaherty J concluded that:

> "The essential feature of a jury trial is to interpose between the accused and the prosecution people who will bring their experience and common sense to bear on resolving the guilt or innocence of the accused. A requirement of unanimity is not essential to this purpose."

And yet this is not necessarily so, in that the very fact that there may be as many as two dissentients may suggest a lack of consensus on the part of the jury, sufficient perhaps to raise a doubt concerning the guilt of the accused.[12] This would certainly be true if the level of majority required were to be "substantially lowered", a fact recognised by the Supreme Court itself.[13]

Mode of jury's functioning

The question of the exact delimitation of the criminal jury's role, and whether it would be constitutionally permissible to reduce, qualify or dilute it (by, for example, permitting the judge to lead or participate in the jury's deliberations) has also not been settled, although several recent decisions have served to clarify this question. Here, again, only *obiter dicta* can be offered. In *O'Shea's* case, mentioned above, Henchy J (dissenting on the principal issue) said:

> "This important personal right, commonly referred to as the right to trial by jury, is indicated in Article 38.5 to be a right to a "trial with a jury", presumably to make clear (as did Article 72 of the 1922 Constitution) that what was being delineated was essentially a right to the evolved and evolving common- law trial by jury, that is to say, a trial before a judge and jury, in which the judge would preside, ensure that all conditions necessary for a fair and proper trial of that nature are complied with, decide all matters deemed to be matters of law, and direct the jury as to the legal principles and rules they are to observe and apply; and in which the jury, constituted in a manner calculated to ensure the achievement of the proper exercise of their functions, would, under the governance of the judge, be the arbiters of all disputed issues of fact and, in particular, the issue of guilt or innocence."

[11] [1993] 2 IR 17; [1993] ILRM 764.

[12] On the other hand, O'Flaherty J correctly observed that one advantage of a majority verdict was to ensure that "the aim of the zealot who glories in dissent and who may make his or her way on to a jury from time to time is defeated."

[13] In *Burch v Louisiana* 441 US 130 (1974) the US Supreme Court held that a conviction by a non-unanimous jury of six persons did not comply with the constitutional requirement of jury trial. But where is the line to be drawn? Presumably the Supreme Court would not accept a simple majority of 7-5, but would the 9-3 majority rule contemplated by the Juries (Protection) Act 1929 survive challenge in a modern era?

Whether, however, the elements to which the judge pointed are to be looked at as not merely traditional and conventional, but constitutionally entrenched, so as to resist change by ordinary legislation, is not clear. Finlay P, the other dissenting judge said;

> "The question necessarily arises as to what are the essential constituent factors of trial with a jury. Can it be satisfied by any intervention of any description by a jury in the process of trial on the criminal charge concerned? If the Legislature were to purport to enact a statute relating to particular charges not coming within the exceptions which I have already outlined [envisaged in Article 38.5 itself] providing that a portion only of the facts necessary to determine the question of guilt or innocence should be determined by the judge would such legislation be consistent with Article 38.5? If legislation purported to provide that a jury should be, in respect of certain offences, drawn from those eligible for jury service by a selective method operated by a State authority, would this be consistent with the sub-Article? If in respect of certain offences the Legislature purported to provide that, as happens in some of the other legal systems, the jury should sit with and consider its verdict with the presiding judge, would such legislation be consistent?"

Finlay P said that decisions of the Court itself provided answers to those hypothetical questions; but the answers which he adduced are (with the exception of the principle of indiscriminate jury selection established in *de Búrca's* case) merely *obiter dicta*.

Preservations of secrecy and confidentiality of jury deliberations is essential

In *de Búrca's* case Walsh J expressed the view that the requirements of jury trial imported an element of secrecy into the jury's deliberations, a fact re-emphasised by the Supreme Court in *O'Callaghan's* case.[14] In the latter case it had been argued that the majority verdicts rule trenched on the right of jury secrecy inasmuch as the existence of a majority verdict is publicly announced.[15] O'Flaherty J agreed that the "deliberations of a jury should always be regarded as completely confidential" and that the "deliberations of a jury should not be published after a trial". This did not, however, affect the Court's view of the validity of the sub-section, since it did not breach the confidentiality of the *deliberations* - as opposed to the *verdict* - of a jury.

Jury decides all relevant issues of fact

As a general rule, all relevant issues of fact must be left to the jury for their consideration and the shadow of unconstitutionality will hang over legislation which seeks to deprive the jury of any portion of their fact-finding role. In *Curtis v Attorney General*[16] the plaintiff had been charged with various smuggling offences, and had elected for trial on indictment. However, s 34(4)(*d*) of the Finance Act 1963, provided that the District Judge's determination of the value of the goods was final and conclusive (i.e. even for the purposes of the trial on indictment). If convicted, the plaintiff was liable to a fine equal to treble the value of the goods. Carroll J held that the relevant portions of the 1963 Act which purported to commit this matter to the determination of the District

[14] In *People (Director of Public Prosecutions) v Courtney*, *The Irish Times*, 28 January 1993, Lynch J is reported as having expressed concern that one of the jurors who had sat on the jury which had convicted an accused of murder had been interviewed by a newspaper and had given an account of the jury's deliberations. Lynch J requested that the matter be investigated by the Director of Public Prosecutions.

[15] However, in the case of majority verdicts of not guilty, the fact that they have been arrived at by a majority is not announced: see s 25(4) of the 1984 Act.

[16] [1985] IR 458; [1986] ILRM 428.

Judge to the exclusion of the jury were unconstitutional.[17] She felt that *The People (Director of Public Prosecutions) v Lynch*[18] was authority for the plaintiff's contention that all "relevant issues of fact should be left to a jury to decide in a criminal case"; and here:

> "the value of the goods is a disputed issue of fact concerning a material issue. A jury would have to determine, in relation to the first offence charged, whether there was a fraudulent intent to evade customs duty, or, in relation to the alternative offence, whether the plaintiff was knowingly concerned in dealing in uncustomed goods. Both offences involve a particular *mens rea*, but...a jury would be entitled to take into account the value of the goods in deciding if there were such *mens rea*. Only the jury have the right to resolve the disputed facts. Therefore, the statutory exclusion of a material issue of fact from the jury is...repugnant to Article 38.1 and Article 38.5."

To this general rule there are some important exceptions, chief among them the requirement that, in the case of disputed evidence, the issue of admissibility will be for the trial judge - and not the jury - even though this may involve the judge resolving contentious issues of fact.

Jury does not decide on the admissibility of disputed evidence

The nature of the jury's role in determining the admissibility of disputed evidence first arose in a constitutional context[19] in *The People (Director of Public Prosecutions) v Lynch.*[20] Here Walsh J (with whom O'Higgins CJ concurred)[21] held that whether an inculpatory statement had been made in circumstances vitiated by a breach of the accused's constitutional rights depended on a disputed issue of fact, and that question should be resolved by a jury and not a judge. This decision was regarded as heralding a novel departure from previously accepted practice and the question was considered again some four years later by a full Supreme Court in *The People (Director of Public Prosecutions) v Conroy*.[22] In this case the appellant had been convicted of murder on the strength of the admission of an inculpatory statement made during the course of an interrogation while in police custody; he claimed that he had been detained involuntarily (as he had not been formally arrested) and denied access to a solicitor. The trial judge had ruled on these disputed issues of fact and had refused to leave them to the jury in the manner apparently required by *Lynch's* case. A majority of the Supreme Court upheld the trial judge's ruling.[23] Finlay CJ said that *Lynch's* case had involved a fundamental departure from previously accepted practice, and he adverted to the grave dangers in exposing the jury to evidence which was subsequently found to be inadmissible in law:

> "The constitutional right to a trial in due course of law [requires] the right to trial with a jury from whose knowledge there is excluded any evidence of guilt which is inadmissible at law."

[17] In the course of his dissenting judgment in O'*Shea's* case (see p. 508), Finlay P had already hinted that this type of legislation would be unconstitutional.

[18] [1982] IR 64; [1983] ILRM 428. This case is considered below, but note that much of the reasoning of this aspect of the *Lynch* was not followed in *The People (Director of Public Prosecutions) v Conroy* [1986] IR 460.

[19] The issue, had, of course, previously arisen on several occasions (see, e.g., *State v Treanor* [1924] 2 IR 193) but in circumstances where the constitutional dimensions of the problem had not been argued.

[20] [1982] IR 64.

[21] The third member of the Court - Kenny J - did not address this question.

[22] [1986] IR 460.

[23] However, the Court ordered a re-trial on other grounds.

Henchy J agreed, saying that while the general principle underlying *Lynch's* case was correct (*viz*., that all issues of fact must be decided by the jury rather than by the judge), the well-established exceptions to that principle rendered inappropriate its invocation for purposes like the present. Its application here:

> "would frequently make the jury trying the particular issue governing admissibility unfit to try the general issue of guilt or innocence. This would be particularly so where the jury's special verdict ruled out the questioned statement and there was other evidence which might justify a conviction. A jury thus informed of the circumstances and contents of the rejected statement would lack the characteristics of an impartial jury for the trial of the issue of guilt or innocence. The alternative to such a mistrial would be, after the trial within a trial was over, to try the issue of guilt or innocence before another jury. This, however, would be inconsistent with the unitary and unbroken trial with a jury which is necessarily postulated by the constitutional right to trial with a jury. What Article 38.5 guarantees is a single trial with a jury, not a succession of trials: see *The People (Attorney General) v McGlynn*."[24]

Walsh J dissented, saying that it was the constitutional function of the jury to decide questions of fact. Where the prosecution's case depended on the admissibility of a statement by an accused person, he thought it would seem:

> "incongruous if the most vital facts of the case, namely, those which will govern the admissibility of the evidence... should be taken away from the jury."

Despite the apparently unequivocal nature of the ruling in *Conroy's* case - which had overruled the novel change heralded in *Lynch's* case and restored the previous long-standing practice - some judicial unhappiness still remains. This emerged in *The People (Director of Public Prosecutions) v Quilligan (No. 3)*[25] where the trial judge had ruled following a *voir dire* that certain confession evidence should go before the jury. McCarthy and Egan JJ were of the view that *Conroy* should not be followed, since as the former judge put it:

> "To exclude the jury from a consideration of whether or not a statement was voluntarily made is to deny the accused the constitutional right to trial by jury. That right is not ensured by limiting the jury's function to a determination of whether or not the statement is true even while directing the jury that the determination of truth or otherwise may depend upon their view as to the various allegations against...the Gardaí."

On this aspect of this multi-faceted case, the majority of the Court,[26] was, however, unwilling - in O'Flaherty J's words - "to take away from the regime which was so definitively established" in *Conroy's* case. They stressed that the trial judge's ruling was only - in the words of Hederman J - "for the specific question of the admissibility of the evidence" and that it did not have the effect:

[24] [1967] IR 232. Ó Dálaigh CJ had said in this case that the nature of a criminal trial by jury was that "once it starts, it continues right through until discharge or verdict. It has the unity and continuity of a play."
[25] Supreme Court, 14 July 1992.
[26] Finlay CJ, Hederman and O'Flaherty JJ. As for the issue of undue delay, see pp. 598-602 and for the question of the constitutionality of s 30 of the Offences Against the State Act 1939, see pp. 856-857.

> "of removing from the jury the right to determine the truth of the disputed facts and in consequence to give such weight as they thought proper to the evidence admitted by the trial judge."

It follows that, even though it now seems settled law that the issue of admissibility is for the trial judge alone, the jury must be instructed as to their duty in the event that they are not satisfied that the confession evidence is not true or that the statement was not obtained voluntarily.[27]

Representative character essential to a constitutional jury

The character of a jury as a representative cross-section of a community - even of a community in a particular locality - was explored in *de Búrca v Attorney General*[28] and was the subject of further dicta in *The State (Byrne) v Frawley*.[29] In *de Búrca's* case the provisions of the Juries Act 1927 (which excluded from jury service all citizens who were without a minimum rating qualification in respect of a house or land, and exempted women from service subject to an individual woman's right to apply to serve), were successfully challenged; two of the judges of the Supreme Court (Henchy and Griffin JJ) based their finding on Article 38.5.[30] Henchy J said:

> "Of course, the jury must be drawn from a pool broadly representative of the community so that its verdict will be stamped with the fairness and acceptability of a genuinely diffused community decision. The particular breadth of choice necessary to satisfy this requirement cannot be laid down in advance. It is left to the discretion of the Legislature to formulate a system for the compilation of jury lists and panels from which will be recruited juries which will be competent, impartial and representative... Where a system of jury recruitment is assailed for being exclusionary to the point of unconstitutionality, the test is whether, by intent or operation, there is an exclusion of any class or group of citizens (other than those excluded for reasons based on capacity or social function) who, if included, might be expected to carry out their duties as jurors according to beliefs, standards, or attitudes not represented by those included. If such a class or group is excluded it cannot be said that a resulting jury will be representative of the community. The exclusion will leave untapped a reservoir of potential jurors without whom the jurors' lists will lack constitutional completeness.
>
> The minimum rating qualification, in my opinion, produces that result...It excludes a range of mental attitudes which, because they will be absent from the jury-box and the jury-room, will leave an accused with no hope of the contribution they might make in the determination of guilt or innocence. This is particularly so in the trial of offences involving damage to property... A jury which is so selective and exclusionary is not stamped with the genuine community representativeness necessary to classify it as the jury guaranteed by s 5 of Article 38. It is, therefore, unconstitutional."

He reached a similar conclusion in regard to the virtual exclusion of women:

[27] It follows that, as O'Flaherty J observed: "No doubt, the accused is entitled to traverse again all the ground that was traversed before the trial judge...In a sense, the trial judge's function is but a preliminary step enabling the jury to enter on what is their function, which is to weigh the evidence."

[28] [1976] IR 38; (1977) 111 ILTR 37.

[29] [1978] IR 326.

[30] The other judgments were based on Article 40.1 ("equality before the law").

> "First, it fails the test of representativeness because it means that some 50% of the adult population will never be included in the jury lists...Secondly, and of even greater importance, that narrowed choice means that a woman's experience, understanding, and general attitude will form no part in the jury processes leading to a verdict. Whatever may have been the position at common law or under statute up to recent times, it is incompatible with the necessary diffusion of rights and duties in a modern democratic society that important public decisions such as voting, or jury verdicts involving life or liberty, should be made by male citizens only. What is missing in decisions so made is not easy to define; but reason and experience show that such decisions are not calculated to lead to a sense of general acceptability, or to carry an acceptable degree of representativeness, or to have the necessary stamp of responsibility and involvement on the part of the community as a whole."

Griffin J cited American decisions[31] in support of his own similar conclusion. He said:

> "The purpose of a jury is to interpose between the State and the accused person an impartial body of the accused's fellow citizens to try the issue joined between the prosecution and the accused. Therefore, in my opinion, the jury should be a body which is truly representative, and a fair cross-section, of the community."

He emphasised, however, that this did not entitle an accused person to:

> "a jury which is tailored to the circumstances of the particular case, whether relating to the sex or other condition of the defendant or to the nature of the charges to be tried, provided that the jury be indiscriminately drawn from those eligible in the community for jury service: see *Hoyt v Florida*.[32] It might happen that a jury drawn by lot would include no women or, indeed, no men; but that would not invalidate the jury."

It may be queried whether the Juries Act 1976 (which was enacted to regularise the situation in the wake of the *de Búrca* itself) itself complies with this criterion of representativeness. For example, s 20 allows the prosecution to challenge seven jurors "without cause shown" (i.e., for no stated reason)[33] and Part II of the First Schedule provides for a wide category of persons "excusable as of right"[34] including members of religious orders, doctors, dentists, nurses, veterinary surgeons, pharmaceutical chemists, students, persons aged between 65 and 70 years (and, in some circumstances) teachers and members of the civil service. In addition, persons aged 70 years are ineligible for jury service.[35] Doubtless such exclusions[36] are inserted for the convenience of the individuals concerned, but might it not be argued that the convenience of some provides no constitutional justification for the large scale exclusion of relatively large and important sections of the community?

[31] *Thiel v Southern Pacific Co.* 328 US 217 (1946); *Hoyt v Florida* 368 US 57 (1961); *Taylor v Louisiana* 419 US 522 (1975).

[32] 368 US 57 (1961).

[33] This right of challenge is also granted to the accused.

[34] Part 1 of the First Schedule of the 1976 Act provides that certain persons (e.g., Gardaí, barristers, solicitors, holders of former holders of judicial office, the Director of Public Prosecutions and members of his staff) are ineligible for jury service. But this ineligibility is understandable and, presumably, constitutionally excusable on the ground that such persons have or had connections with the administration of justice.

[35] Section 6.

[36] Persons belonging to these categories are excusable as of right - in other words, they need only claim the exclusion to be then excluded from jury service. In practice, such persons tend to claim the exclusion.

The judge should not proceed with the trial before an unconstitutional jury; but an accused person can acquiesce (and is then estopped from complaining)

Some further touches were added to this picture by Henchy J in *The State (Byrne) v Frawley*,[37] in which the applicant failed to have his trial treated as a nullity because the jury had been drawn from a pre-*de Búrca* panel; the majority of the Supreme Court held that, having allowed his trial (and appeal) to proceed though he and his counsel knew of the *de Búrca* decision, he was debarred from now complaining.[38] Henchy J - having said however that once a trial judge realises a jury is wrongly constituted he should not proceed with the trial - pointed out, in regard to the effect of the *de Búrca case,* that once the minimum rating qualification had been found unconstitutional:

> "there was no locational qualification of any kind for jury service...There must, for a constitutional jury, be a valid nexus between juror and jury district. This is needed to ensure that the jury's verdict will have the quality of a community decision, for a jury so constituted will reach its verdict in the knowledge that, in a real and special sense, its members will have to live with that decision...
>
> The gravamen of the complaint made in the *de Búrca* case [was]...that such jury lists were so artificially shrunken and selective that an accused person was denied the representative jury source which is vital for the jury guaranteed by Article 38.5...The extent to which juries drawn from those lists were incapable of presenting a genuine reflection of community values and standards is shown when it is pointed out that the combined effect of the rating qualification and the exclusion of women meant that some 80% of the adult citizens in a jury district were shut out from jury service."

In this pair of cases a divergence of view emerged - as between O'Higgins CJ, Walsh and Kenny JJ on the one hand, and Henchy and Griffin JJ on the other hand as to the status of all the verdicts reached by all the juries (in the pre-*de Búrca* era) which now turned out to have been selected from unconstitutionally constructed panels. Walsh J in *de Búrca's* case, followed by O'Higgins CJ (with whom Kenny J agreed) in the *Byrne* case, took the view that, as it could not be said that anyone unqualified had served on those juries, they were unobjectionable despite the basis on which they had been selected. Henchy J (with whom Griffin J agreed) said however in *Byrne's* case that this proposition was "no more supportable than a proposition that an election would be valid when 80% of those who should have had an opportunity of voting were barred from the polls".[39]

[37] [1978] IR 326.

[38] The minority judges - O'Higgins CJ and Kenny J - took the view that the jury had not been objectionable. Contrast the views of the majority in this case with the dissenting opinion of Kenny J in *Corrigan v Irish Land Commission* [1977] IR 317 in connection with acquiescence in objections being adjudicated by the same persons who had made the determination which was the subject of objections.

[39] They took the line, however, that since the *de Búrca* decision no convicted persons (other than the applicant in the case before them) had instituted proceedings set a side on the ground that the jury had been invalid "such retrospective acquiescence in the mode of trial and in the conviction and its legal consequences would appear to raise an insuperable barrier against a successful challenge at this stage to the validity of a conviction or sentence. O'Higgins CJ had regarded the possibility of a mass of such challenges as something which "organised society" could not accept. This issue is, perhaps, best considered under the heading of "Effects of Finding of Unconstitutionality" at pp. 480-486.

The accused has no right to a jury from a particular locality

Although Henchy J had spoken *obiter* in *Byrne's* case about the constitutional necessity for "a valid nexus between juror and jury district", an expression which in the context of an accused person's rights seems to demand a locality-nexus between the accused and those who are to try him, the decided cases point in the contrary direction. In *The State (Hughes) v Neylon*[40] Finlay P, in disposing of a complaint about a trial transferred from the Circuit Court to the Central Criminal Court (sitting in Dublin), said that *de Búrca's* case did not "in any way recognise or acknowledge a right of an accused person to be tried by a jury drawn from any particular locality". This issue also featured in *The State (Boyle) v Neylon*[41] where the applicant had challenged the constitutionality of s 31 of the Courts Act 1981, inasmuch as it had allowed for the transfer of his pending trial from the Wicklow Circuit Court to the Dublin Circuit Court. As the offences had been committed in Wicklow, the applicant had contended that a trial in Dublin had deprived him of the necessary nexus between the locality in which the offences had been committed and the court and jury[42] which eventually tried him. However, the Supreme Court, speaking through Walsh J, rejected this contention:

> "Experience itself has shown that justice itself would require a provision of this kind to avoid the risk of an injustice to one party or another by reason of local circumstances or conditions. The constitutional provision in referring to "local ...jurisdiction" does not mean that it must be local in the sense of being particularly connected with the place of residence of one party or another."

Limited right to a jury trial in contempt cases

It was argued in *Attorney General v Connolly*[43] that the provisions of Article 38.5 entitled a person charged with criminal contempt of court to trial by a jury; the High Court - relying on the decision of the High Court in *Attorney General v O'Kelly*[44] held that this constitutional provision had not taken away the jurisdiction always formerly held by the Court and its predecessors to punish summarily for criminal contempt, and that it would have required clear language to effect such a deprivation of the Court's power to protect itself and inferior courts. In *The State (Commins) v McRann,*[45] although a case of civil contempt, Finlay P said that Article 38.5 had to be regarded in this context as qualified by Article 34.1 with the effect that summary trial and punishment of criminal contempt was permissible and indeed necessary to the courts' maintenance of their own authority.

But a different perspective emerged in *The State (Director of Public Prosecutions) v Walsh*[46] where the question was settled by that Court: criminal contempt of court, even when a serious offence,[47] is a necessary exception from the generality of Article 38.5,

[40] [1982] ILRM 108.

[41] [1986] IR 551.

[42] The accused had pleaded guilty, so the question of nexus with the local jury did not, strictly speaking, arise for consideration.

[43] [1947] IR 21; (1947) 81 ILTR 92.

[44] [1928] IR 308; (1928) 62 ILTR 78.

[45] [1977] IR 78. The question had been regarded by the Supreme Court in 1972 as still open: in *Keegan v de Búrca* [1973] IR 223 Ó Dálaigh CJ (with whom Walsh J agreed) said it was unnecessary in that case "to deal with the question of when a person charged with criminal contempt shall be tried with by jury pursuant to Article 38.5."

[46] [1981] IR 412.

[47] As in this case: Henchy J said the offence (of scandalising the Special Criminal Court) "could not be accounted a minor one"

save that an alleged contemptor is entitled to jury trial on a disputed issue of fact. Explaining the necessity for the general exception from the application of Article 38.5, O'Higgins CJ said that:

> "[Article 38] and in particular s 5 thereof, refers to offences against the body of *substantive*[48] criminal law which exists in this and every other country and which requires for its enforcement the action of the Executive...The offence of criminal contempt is peculiarly within the control and summary jurisdiction of the courts."

Henchy J (with whom Griffin and Kenny JJ agreed) added some reflections on the inherent unsuitability of jury trial for the punishment of contempt of court. He was concerned in particular that a perverse - but unimpeachable - jury verdict might "set at nought the constitutional guarantee that basic fairness of procedures will be observed" and "could at the same time undermine the independence of the judiciary." Henchy J modified these views, however, by provisionally admitting that had there been controverted issues of fact in regard to the imputability of a criminal contempt to these defendants (there were no such issues in this case) "it would not seem to be compatible with...fundamental fairness of procedures, [or] equality before the law" if those issues were exempt from determination by a jury.[49]

The correctness of this analysis - involving as it does a possible bi-furcated jury role in contempt cases - seems questionable. First, a jury is just as capable of delivering a perverse verdict on an issue of fact as on the ultimate issue of guilt. Secondly, the *Walsh* decision involves the jury delivering a special verdict on an issue other than guilt or innocence. Yet this very same procedure insofar as it involved a special verdict on the admissibility of confession evidence was condemned as unconstitutional in *The People (Director of Public Prosecutions) v Conroy.*[50]

Miscellaneous aspects of the right to a jury trial

On the problem of a finding of unconstitutionality impliedly invalidating past proceedings, see above, pp. 480-486. On the application to a jury of the maxim *nemo iudex in causa sua*, see *The People (Attorney General) v Singer.*[51] On the necessity for a jury's deliberations to be free from the possibility of outside interference, see *The People (Attorney General) v Heffernan (No. 2)*[52] and *O'Callaghan v Attorney General*[53] or prejudice, see *The People (Attorney General) v Quinn.*[54] On the practice of the police in making enquiries about prospective jurors - so as to inform the prosecution for the purpose of allowing it to exercise its right of challenge - see answers to a Dáil question on 22 November 1978.[55] On the desirability that the trial judge should warn the jury that they must not talk about the case of hearing to anybody who is not one of their number: see *The People (Director of Public Prosecutions) v McKeever.*[56]

[48] Authors' emphasis. The word suggests that criminal contempt falls into a category of its own as "adjectival", or ancillary criminal law necessary to support the processes of law.

[49] In a supplementary judgment delivered after the defendants had spoken to the minutes of the Court's order, the Court adhered to its original view that the case presented no disputed issue of fact which would warrant a direction of trial by jury on that issue: see [1981] IR 445.

[50] Although it could be contended that *Conroy* did not condemn all bi-furcated jury verdicts, but only those which exposed the jury to the risk of hearing inadmissible and prejudicial evidence.

[51] [1975] IR 408.

[52] [1951] IR 206; (1951) 85 ILTR 54.

[53] [1993] 2 IR 17; [1993] ILRM 764.

[54] [1965] IR 366.

[55] 309 *Dáil Debates* 1538.

[56] Court of Criminal Appeal, 16 July 1992.

Article 39

TREASON

Article 39
Treason shall consist only in levying war against the State, or assisting any State or person or inciting or conspiring with any person to levy war against the State, or attempting by force of arms or other violent means to overthrow the organs of government established by this Constitution, or taking part or being concerned in or inciting or conspiring with any person to make or to take part or be concerned in any such attempt.

Airteagal 39
Is é amháin is tréas ann cogadh a chur ar an Stát, nó cabhrú le stát nó le duine ar bith, nó saighdeadh faoi dhuine, nó bheith i gcomhcheilg le duine, chun cogadh a chur ar an Stát, nó iarracht a dhéanamh le harm nó ar mhodh fhoréigneach eile ar na horgain rialtais a bhunaítear leis an mBunreacht so a threascairt, nó páirt nó baint do bheith ag neach lena leitheid sin d'iarracht, nó éinne do shaighdeadh nó bheith i gcomhcheilg leis chun a déanta nó chun páirt nó baint do bheith aige léi.

Innovation based on US model

This Article, to which nothing in the 1922 Constitution corresponded, is evidently inspired by the first sentence of Article III, s 3, of the United States Constitution, which provides that "Treason against the United States shall consist only in levying War against them, or in adhering to their Enemies, giving them Aid and Comfort".[1]

Statutory provisions

The Treason Act 1939 (passed in May of that year) originally provided for the death penalty for treason committed within the State, or (in the case of a person who is "an Irish citizen or ordinarily resident within the State") outside the State (s 1(1), (2)). Section 2 of the Criminal Justice Act 1990, now provides that "a person convicted or treason...shall be sentenced to imprisonment for life"[2] and s 4 further directs that in such a case, the court, in passing sentence, shall specify that the accused shall serve a minimum of forty years' imprisonment.[3] Section 1(4) of the 1939 Act mirroring a further provision of Article III of the US Constitution, provides that "No person shall be convicted of treason on the uncorroborated evidence of one witness". Section 2 creates the offence (punishable by up to twenty years' penal servitude) of "encouraging, harbouring or comforting persons guilty of treason", and s 3 makes guilty of misprision of treason, and punishable with up to five years' penal servitude:

> "every person who, knowing that any act the commission of which would be treason is intended or proposed to be, or is being, or has been committed, does not forthwith disclose the same, together with all particulars thereof known to him, to a Justice of the District Court, or an officer of the Garda Síochána, or some other person lawfully engaged on duties relating to the preservation of peace and order."

[1] For an authoritative exposition of the meaning of this clause, see *Cramer v United States* 325 US 1 (1944).

[2] Similar provision is made in the case of persons who, while subject to military law, are found guilty of treason by court-martial: see s 169 of the Defence Act 1954 (as amended by the First Schedule to the Criminal Justice Act 1990.)

[3] This does not apply to children or young persons. Section 5 imposes certain restrictions on the power of commutation or remission and on the power to grant temporary release to persons convicted of treason (and certain other types of murder).

No prosecution has been brought under this Act since its enactment, nor have the terms of the Act come under judicial scrutiny.[4]

Attempted overthrow of the State is a treasonable activity

Article 39 was adverted to judicially for the first time in *Quinn v Wren.*[5] This was an extradition case where the plaintiff claimed that, as the offences allegedly committed by him were done under the aegis of the "Irish National Liberation Army", he was entitled to the benefit of the political offence exception provided for by s 50 of the Extradition Act 1965. The Supreme Court dismissed the claim on several grounds, among them the fact that the "Irish National Liberation Army" was a treasonable organisation. Finlay CJ said that as the admitted objective of this organisation was the overthrow of the Government by force of arms, this:

> "necessarily and inevitably involved the destruction and setting aside of the Constitution by means expressly and impliedly prohibited by it: see Articles 15.6 and 39."

Hederman J added that the organisation's objectives were clearly in violation of Article 39, and that the law of the State, in order to remain in conformity with the Constitution, cannot give immunity to persons engaged in such activities.

This ruling was briefly extended by the Supreme Court in *Russell v Fanning*[6] to cover the actions of illegal organisations outside the State, on the ground that, by engaging in such para-military activities outside the State, they were unconstitutionally usurping the functions of the Government.[7] This rather artificial reasoning was not, however, followed in the subsequent decision of *Finucane v McMahon.*[8] While Walsh J agreed that the statement of principle in *Quinn v Wren* was "manifestly correct", this principle could not be extended further to cover acts of politically motivated violence committed outside the jurisdiction:

> "The fact that the policy or activities followed by persons acting outside the jurisdiction of the State is opposed to or contrary to the policy adopted by the Government of Ireland in relation to the unity of the country is not...sufficient to equate to a policy to overthrow this State or to subvert the Constitution of this State."

While a full discussion of these decisions more properly belongs to section dealing with personal liberty,[9] the *Finucane* case is authority for a rather self-evident proposition, namely, that Article 39 only applies to activities designed to subvert the State or Constitution by force of arms and cannot embrace activities (however reprehensible) which encompass the destruction or de-stabilisation of any other State.

[4] Provisions similar to those of the Treason Act 1939, were contained (along with others) in the Treasonable Offences Act 1925; this Act was repealed in its entirety by s 5 of the Offences Against the State Act 1939.
[5] [1985] IR 322; [1985] ILRM 411.
[6] [1988] IR 505; [1998] ILRM 333.
[7] Finlay CJ explained that "for a group of persons...to seek to take-over the carrying of a policy of re-integration [of the national territory] decided by himself or themselves upon the authority of the organs of State established by the Constitution is to subvert the Constitution and to usurp the function of Government."
[8] [1990] 1 IR 165; [1980] ILRM 505. See generally, Humphreys, "*Reflections on the Role and Functioning of the Supreme Court*" (1990) 12 DULJ (n.s.)127.
[9] For which see pp. 880-883.

FUNDAMENTAL RIGHTS

BUNCHEARTA

Statements of fundamental rights are more extensive than those of 1922

Articles 40-44, which contain a large body of provisions collectively entitled "Fundamental Rights", represent one of the most conspicuous novelties of the 1937 Constitution by comparison with that of 1922, which devoted relatively little space (Articles 6-10) to the subject, and which, because of the general helplessness of the Constitution when confronted with ordinary legislation,[1] played almost no part in the maintenance of those rights. When the draft Articles 40-44 were published, no great importance was attached to them and nothing very much was expected from them - possibly because the framers of the 1937 Constitution expressly intended them as mere "headlines to the legislature" rather than as an essential part of the mechanism of a vigorous judicial review[2] - but in practice they have been the basis of many very significant decisions, and are invoked with steadily increasing frequency.

Some general questions about fundamental rights in the courts require consideration before the individual Articles are dealt with.

Source of fundamental rights: the Constitution itself or a higher source?

There is first of all the problem of the derivation of fundamental rights. On this question there are, broadly speaking, two opinions. One opinion sees Articles 40-44 as merely stating, and stating not necessarily very exactly or completely, rights which, quite apart from their statement, are inherent in the person by natural law, or in the citizen because of the nature of the Irish state. It seems to be a corollary of this view that some rights, not explicitly mentioned in the Constitution, are nevertheless latent in general expressions such as "the personal rights of the citizen"; and a further corollary, not without

[1] See below, under Article 51.

[2] Mr. de Valera said on 3 June 1937 during the Dáil debate on the draft Constitution: "In future the Legislature will have to look after the public interest, as it is doing today. Are we going to shackle the Legislature in the future in a way in which it is not shackled today, and in which it would be most unwise to shackle it? We are providing for that freedom of action to work in the public interest and to safeguard the public interest in the future which the Legislature has today - that and no more...I think the Legislature ought to be enabled in its own judgment to decide [what the public interest consists in] and not the courts. The courts have to interpret the laws. The courts have not placed upon them the responsibility that the Legislature has. The Legislature has the responsibility of working in the public interest and of seeing, in the passing of its laws, that the rights of the individual, as an individual, and the rights of the community, as a community, do not conflict and are properly co-ordinated. That is the duty of the Legislature; and what we want to see is that in future the Legislature will not be so restricted that it will not be able to function properly" (67 *Dáil Debates* 1784 - 6). The next week the following exchange took place: *Mr. de Valera*: "You must give to the Legislature the power of regulating the exercise of these rights in such a manner as to ensure that the exercise of these rights will not be contrary to the public good. That is absolutely necessary; you cannot avoid it, and you cannot tie yourself up by precluding the Legislature from doing it. The Deputy [Patrick McGilligan] may say: Then what is the good of your phrase here at all - this phrase about the right of the citizens to assemble peaceably? He may ask, what is its value? I say that it is of value, and that it is a general headline to the Legislature." *Mr. McGilligan*: "Which they can neglect." *Mr. De Valera:* "Yes, unfortunately, they can." *Mr. McGilligan*: "And the courts cannot interfere?" *Mr. de Valera*: "Unfortunately - and the Deputy knows it quite well - we cannot provide by any Constitution against the possible abuse of its powers by the Legislature in future. It is vain to attempt to do so. All we can do is to set headlines for the Legislature, as we are doing here - headlines with regard to the things the Legislature should aim at" (68 *Dáil Debates* 2167).

important adherents, is that even when recourse to the protection of the Constitution is excluded by virtue of the Constitution itself e.g. under Article 28.3.3 - recourse is still possible to a range of eternal, natural rights existing independently of the Constitution.[3] The other opinion is to the effect that the only guarantees which courts operating under the Constitution can enforce are the guarantees to which the Constitution gives expression; though this view would not of course prevent a very liberal understanding of the guarantees contained in it.

Positivist view formerly in ascendant

This more conservative opinion received, in the context of the 1922 Constitution, emphatic statement from the majority of the Supreme Court in *The State (Ryan) v Lennon*,[4] in which it was argued that certain rights were so fundamental as to be beyond the power of the Oireachtas to abridge by way of amendment of the written Constitution. This was, indeed, accepted by Kennedy CJ,[5] but the other two judges of the Court outvoted him. Fitzgibbon J said:

> "There is, however, a broader ground upon which [counsel for the applicants] have endeavoured to found an argument. They assert that there are certain rights, inherent in every individual, which are so sacred that no Legislature has authority to deprive him of them. It is useless to speculate upon the origin of this doctrine...as we are concerned, not with the principles which might or ought to have been adopted by the framers of our Constitution, but with the powers which have actually been entrusted by it to the Legislature and Executive which it set up. "The Declaration of the Rights of Man and of Citizens" by the National Assembly of France on October 5th, 1789, that "liberty, property, security, and resistance to oppression are the natural and imprescriptible rights of man", cannot be invoked to overrule the provisions of a statute enacted in accordance with the provisions of a written Constitution. When a written Constitution declares that "the liberty of the person is inviolable", but goes on to provide that "no person shall be deprived of his liberty except in accordance with the law", then, if a law is passed that a citizen may be imprisoned indefinitely upon a *lettre de cachet* signed by a Minister or, as we have seen, even by a Minister's clerk: *The State (Quinlan) v Kavanagh*,[6] the citizen *may* be deprived of his "inviolable" liberty, but, as the deprivation will have been "in accordance with law", he will be as devoid of redress as he would have been under the regime of a French or Neapolitan Bourbon...
>
> Unless, therefore, these rights appear plainly from the express provisions of our Constitution to be inalienable, and incapable of being modified or taken away by any legislative Act I cannot accede to the argument that the Oireachtas cannot alter, modify, or repeal them. The framers of our Constitution may have intended "to bind man down from mischief by the chains of the Constitution"[7] but if they did, they defeated their object by handing him the key of the padlock in Article 50."[8]

[3] For further discussion of this point, see Clarke, "*Emergency Legislation, Fundamental Rights and Article 28.3.3 of the Irish Constitution*" (1977) 12 Ir Jur (n.s) 217.
[4] [1935] IR 170; (1935) 69 ILTR 125.
[5] See below, pp. 673-684.
[6] [1935] IR 249.
[7] A phrase of Thomas Jefferson cited earlier in the same judgment.
[8] These views were cited by Sullivan CJ in *In re Article 26 and the Offences Against the State (Amendment) Bill 1940* [1940] IR 470; (1940) 74 ILTR 61; and *In re Article 26 and the School Attendance Bill 1942* [1943] IR 334; (1943) 77 ILTR 96; and by Dixon J in *Foley v Irish Land Commission* [1952] IR 118; (1952) 86 ILTR 44.

Murnaghan J said:

> "In reference to...Articles which are alleged to be fundamental, the only criteria which the appellants can suggest is that the Court should undertake the responsibility of deciding in any set of circumstances which Articles should be held to be fundamental. Before the Court should seek to assume such a power it is, in my opinion, necessary that the Court should find a very stable foundation for such an exercise of jurisdiction."

This foundation he was unable to find; adding that, if the arguments on "fundamentality" were correct, even an amendment made by plebiscite (after the expiry of the period in which an amendment might be made by ordinary legislation) could not validly alter certain Articles - an extreme view, he thought.

It may be added that a couple of years later, and perhaps with the issues in *The State (Ryan) v Lennon* still in his mind, Murnaghan J dealt another blow to the notion that any fundamental law should be invoked by the courts in order to permit them to condemn acts of the legislature; on this occasion his view, although briefly expressed, and on a subordinate aspect of the case before him, was even more openly positivist, as the statute under attack was not an Act of the Oireachtas (which was in practice immune from challenge on constitutional grounds[9]) but a pre-1922 Act carried over by Article 73 of the 1922 Constitution only conditionally, to the extent that it was not inconsistent with the Constitution. In *The State (McKay) v Cork Circuit Judge*,[10] he noted that the applicants had:

> "attacked the making of an adjudication in bankruptcy by the Registrar, which, they contended, could only be made after a hearing *inter partes*. I have already stated my opinion that the Legislature is competent to determine in what circumstances an order of adjudication may be made without notice to the party intended to be affected, and I hesitate to conjecture what would be the result upon a legal system if the courts pretended to have a better knowledge of natural justice than the Legislature, and on that ground assumed to set aside Acts of Parliament adopted by the Constitution. In the history of English law such an idea was entertained by Coke, but has ever since been rejected."

The natural law view: Chief Justice Kennedy's lone stand (1934)

On the other side of the argument, the first landmark in the modern Irish history of the view that a natural law of divine origin is above human law, however positively expressed, is the judgment of Kennedy CJ, dissenting from his two colleagues, in *The State (Ryan) v Lennon*.[11] What was in issue was the validity of the provisions imported into the 1922 Constitution, as Article 2A, by an amendment effected by ordinary legislation;[12] these provisions contained extremely drastic changes in what had previously been fundamental principles of criminal law and procedure. When Article 2A was attacked on the ground that its enactment breached immutable rules of natural law, the Chief Justice assented to the argument:

[9] See below, under Article 51.
[10] [1937] IR 650.
[11] [1935] IR 170; (1935) 69 ILTR 125.
[12] See below, under Article 51.

> "The Constituent Assembly [conferred] on the Oireachtas [an amending] power...but that power is limited and circumscribed by a number of restrictions...In the first place, what I may describe as an over-all limitation arises in this way. The Constituent Assembly declared in the forefront of the Constitution Act (an Act which it is not within the power of the Oireachtas to alter, or amend, or repeal), that all lawful authority comes from God to the people, and it is declared by Article 2 of the Constitution that "all powers of government and all authority, legislative, executive, and judicial, in Ireland are derived from the people of Ireland". It follows that every Act whether legislative, executive or judicial, in order to be lawful under the Constitution, must be capable of being justified under the authority thereby declared to be derived from God. From this it seems clear that, if any legislation of the Oireachtas (including any purported amendment of the Constitution) were to offend against that acknowledged ultimate Source from which the legislative authority has come through the people to the Oireachtas, as, for example, if it were repugnant to the Natural Law, such legislation would be necessarily unconstitutional and invalid, and it would be, therefore, absolutely null and void and inoperative.
>
> I find it very difficult to reconcile with the Natural Law actions and conduct which would appear to be within the legalising intendment of the provisions of the new Article 2A relating to interrogation. I find it impossible to reconcile as compatible with the Natural Law the vesting, in three military servants of the Executive, power to impose as punishment for any offence within the indefinite, but certainly extensive, ambit of the Appendix, the penalty of death, whenever these three persons are of opinion that it is *expedient*. Finally, the judicial power has been acknowledged and declared (and the acknowledgement and declaration remain) to have come from God through the people to its appointed depositary, the judiciary and courts of the State. While they can fulfil that trust, dare any one say that the Natural Law permits it, or any part of it, to be transferred to the Executive or their military or other servants?"

He concluded that:

> "parts of the amendment (the new "Article 2A") are incapable of being validly enacted under the Constitution, some as repugnant to the Natural Law and therefore repugnant to the Source of power acknowledged and declared by the Constituent Assembly, others as repugnant to some of the principles postulated by the Constituent Assembly as fundamental."

The 1939 judgment of Gavan Duffy J in *The State (Burke) v Lennon*,[13] while it did not mention or even hint at natural law, did suggest that higher principles lay behind the Constitution, which the Constitution "enshrined" but did not necessarily replace:

> "In my opinion, the right to personal liberty and the other principles which we are accustomed to summarise as the rule of law were most deliberately enshrined in a national Constitution, drawn up with the utmost care for a free people, and the power to intern on suspicion or without trial is fundamentally inconsistent with the rule of law and with the rule of law as expressed in the terms of our Constitution."

[13] [1940] IR 136; (1940) 74 ILTR 36, 131.

He also rejected the crude positivism of Fitzgibbon J in *Ryan's* case:

> "In my opinion, the saving words in the declaration that "No citizen shall be deprived of his liberty save in accordance with law" cannot be used to validate an enactment conflicting with the constitutional guarantees. The opinion of Mr. Justice Fitzgibbon in *Ryan's* case is relied upon by counsel for the Attorney General but it does not apply, in my judgment, to a Constitution in which fundamental rights and constitutional guarantees effectively fill the lacunae disclosed in the polity of 1922. The Constitution, with its most impressive Preamble, is the Charter of the Irish People, and I will not whittle it away."

During the 1940s and 1950s no more was heard from the Bench about higher law (though some academic legal views in its favour were warmly voiced),[14] but in the 1960s, with the arrival of a new generation of judges in the superior courts, some new tones were heard. Mr. Justice Henchy wrote in 1962:

> "From the point of view of jurisprudence, the most striking change effected by the present Constitution is the break with the positivist character of the common law which had been developed in comparatively modern times... The Irish Constitution rejects such a basis for law. Its Preamble makes clear that the Constitution and the laws which owe their force to the Constitution derive, under God, from the people and are directed to the promotion of the common good. If a judicial decision rejects the divine law or has not as its object the common good, it has not the character of law. This idea is no strange addition to the common law; it is as old as Coke."[15]

1963: The tide turns: Ryan v Attorney General

The following year Kenny J heard the case of *Ryan v Attorney General*[16] (the water fluoridation case) and accepted the plaintiff's submission that there was such a thing as a "right of bodily integrity", even though not specifically mentioned in the Constitution; it was, he held, one of a residue of personal rights tacitly contemplated by Article 40.3.1. The question of where authority might be found for identifying, one by one, such residual personal rights he answered as follows:

> "I think that the personal rights which may be invoked[17] to invalidate legislation are not confined to those specified in Article 40 but include all those rights which result from the Christian and democratic nature of the State...There are many personal rights of the citizen which follow from the Christian and democratic nature of the State which are not mentioned in Article 40 at all - the right to free movement within the State and the right to marry are examples of this...The conclusion, that there is a right of bodily integrity, gets support from a passage in the Encyclical Letter "Peace on Earth": "Beginning our discussion of the rights of man, we see that every man has the right to life, to bodily integrity and to the means which are necessary and suitable for the proper development of life; these are primarily food, clothing, shelter, rest, medical care, and finally the necessary social services."

[14] See J.M. Kelly, *Fundamental Rights in the Irish Law and Constitution*, 2nd ed., pp.62 *et seq.*
[15] (1962) 25 MLR 544, 557. This article was written shortly before its author was appointed a judge of the High Court, and published shortly afterwards.
[16] [1965] IR 294.
[17] The report reads "involved", not "invoked", but this looks like a misprint.

Apart from the implications of this judgment for the expansion of strictly constitutional rights from the explicit into the latent, the reference to the nature of the State as "Christian and democratic" unmistakably suggests a "higher law" approach. The State is, indeed, described expressly as "democratic" in Article 5; but it would be hard to argue - on any understanding of the word "democratic" - that the right to marry is a consequence of this. It seems to be more a consequence, in Mr. Justice Kenny's view, of the "Christian" nature of the State; and this is the point at which a belief in a range of para-constitutional rights seems to emerge, since, on the one hand, the State is nowhere in the Constitution described as Christian, and, on the other hand, the right to marry is plainly and necessarily implied by the terms of Article 41, but Mr. Justice Kenny did not choose to base it on this Article.

In *The State (Nicolaou) v An Bord Uchtála*[18] the applicant based his claim partly on what he said was the "natural right" of the father of an illegitimate child to have a say in its upbringing; the Supreme Court (*per* Walsh J) said it "had not been satisfied that any such right has ever been recognised as part of the natural law", a formulation which seems to hint that, had the Court in fact been so satisfied, it might have conceded the applicant's case.

Fundamental personal rights antecedent to Constitution, not derived from it

Some years later, the case of *McGee v Attorney General*[19] elicited in the Supreme Court statements on higher law, antecedent to the Constitution, of a kind that had not been heard since the judgment of Kennedy CJ in *The State (Ryan) v Lennon*. Asked by the plaintiff to invalidate a law penalising the importation of contraceptives on the ground that it infringed her personal right of privacy within her marriage, four of the five judges held with her; and Walsh J said:

> "In this country it falls finally upon the judges to interpret the Constitution and in doing so *to determine, where necessary, the rights which are superior or antecedent to positive law*, or which are imprescriptible or inalienable [these phrases come from Articles 41 and 42]...The very structure and content of the Articles dealing with fundamental rights clearly indicate that justice is not subordinate to the law. In particular, the terms of Article 40.3 *expressly subordinate the law to justice*. [Earlier in his judgment he had said:] Articles 41, 42 and 43 emphatically reject the theory that there are no rights without laws, no rights contrary to the law and no rights anterior to the law. They indicate that justice is placed above the law and acknowledge that natural rights, or human rights, are not created by law but that the Constitution confirms their existence and gives them protection."[20]

There is, admittedly, the difference between this approach and that of Kennedy CJ that the latter had to pull his antecedent principles out of the air, so to speak; while Walsh J was able to point to the Constitution itself as conceding their existence. Nevertheless there is a substantial difference between the tenor of this judgment and those of Maguire P and Johnston and Maguire JJ in 1939 and 1942, mentioned above.

[18] [1966] IR 567; (1968) 102 ILTR 1.
[19] [1974] IR 284; (1975) 109 ILTR 29.
[20] Emphasis added. See also, by the same judge, "*Existence and Meaning of Fundamental Rights in Ireland*" (1980) 1 Human Rights Law Journal 171.

Not long after *McGee's* case, Gannon J had to consider, in *The State (Healy) v Donoghue*,[21] the bearing of Article 38 and "due course of law" from the perspective of the rights of an accused person; he spoke unambiguously of such a person's "natural rights", cited what Walsh J had said in *McGee's* case, and said:

> "The sense of justice is fundamental in human nature and from it derive essential rights which do not require any positive law for their enunciation... [He mentioned several "natural rights of an individual whose conduct is impugned and whose freedom is put in jeopardy", amounting to a paraphrase of "due course of law", and added:] In my view, they are rights which are anterior to and do not merely derive from the Constitution..."[22]

One of the strongest statements of the significance of the natural law in recent times can be found in *Murphy v P.M.P.A. Insurance Co.*[23] Here Doyle J held that a contract *uberrimae fidei* conferred a cloak of confidentiality on information provided pursuant to its terms and that an apparent statutory obligation to furnish the information to a third party constituted "an encroachment to a greater or lesser degree on natural liberty or natural rights." Some natural law rights existed independently of the Constitution:

> "The encroachment on what are claimed to be natural rights in this case and which is sought to be justified by the complainant is not such as stems from the Articles of the Constitution dealing with the rights of the individual. At one time it was thought that the Constitution had provided a comprehensive code of personal rights and that all pre-existing common law personal or natural rights had been subsumed in it. It is now, however, well established that certain natural and personal rights may exist side by side with the Constitution although not specifically referred to or comprehended in the Articles of the Constitution which give personal guarantees."

Natural law and the Constitution: multiple meaning of "natural" rights

A feature of most of the judicial references to "natural law" or "natural rights" under the Constitution is that they assume that there is a general consensus about the identity of the natural law. In fact, the concept of "natural rights" has a variety of meanings. A basic distinction possible in this context is that between natural law standards as understood in the common law tradition[24] - manifested in concepts such as equity, the notion of the reasonable man, a reasonable price, etc. - and the now dominant conception of natural law as antecedent to the Constitution. Natural rights in the former sense are latent and vulnerable to statutory encroachment in the ordinary law, whereas in the latter sense they are patent and accorded primacy in the Constitution. Seen in this light, the only novelty of Irish constitutional doctrine is the specific assignment of priority over statute law, including the Constitution itself, to a range of natural values; whereas the common law, also recognising those values, holds itself powerless to protect them from abridgement by the legislature. What practical effect the identification of this distinction

[21] [1976] IR 325; (1976) 110 ILTR 9.

[22] For more recent judicial affirmations of the proposition that the individual's personal rights are antecedent to the Constitution, see the remarks of Gannon J in *O'Flynn v Clifford* [1988] IR 740 and of McCarthy J in *Murray v Ireland* [1991] ILRM 465.

[23] [1978] ILRM 25.

[24] Thus in *G. v An Bord Uchtála* [1980] IR 32; (1979) 113 ILTR 25, Parke J remarked that "The emotional and physical bonds between a woman and the child which she has borne give to her rights which spring from the law of nature and which have been recognised at common law long antecedent to the adoption of the Constitution."

may have in Irish constitutional law is not easy to say. Probably it means that (a) while large "natural" values to which the Constitution points as antecedent to positive law (including itself as an item of positive law) may be invoked before an Irish court independently of the words of the Constitution, and (*quaere*) even to supersede them, still (b) the mere fact that a rule of law can plausibly be labelled "natural" does not raise it to a constitutional power, or immunise a right flowing from it against curtailment.

Moving on from this distinction between natural rights protected by the common law and those protected by the Constitution, a more sophisticated analysis of natural rights has been advanced in which it has been argued that the term "natural" can be understood, in the context of the Scholastic tradition of natural law, which would seem to be the one most relevant to Irish jurisprudence,[25] in as many as five different ways.[26] First, it could refer to those rights which are contingent on various natural facts, events or relations - such as the existence of a blood-tie between adult and child - but the validity or justification of which rights is derived from some independent constitutional, legal or moral source.[27] Second, it might mean those rights which some natural law theories claim to belong to any person, merely on the basis of his/her being a human person.[28] Third, it might denote a sub-class of basic rights identified by the interaction of the two previous meanings - i.e. certain basic rights enforceable against persons in a natural relationship (e.g. parent/child) with the claimant of the right. Fourth, it could be understood as referring to those rights derived from the nature of, or definition of, justice.[29] Finally, the phrase could describe those rights derived from, or which conform with, God's agency as recognised in the natural teleology of physical events. For the most part, references to natural law in Irish caselaw do not advert to these distinctions,[30] nor do they indicate in which sense the term is being used by the particular judge. Judicial invocation of such an undistilled concept of natural law in the context of review of legislation presents the obvious danger that invalidation of such legislation might not always be seen to be based on objective, ascertainable criteria.

[25] In *McGee v AG* [1974] IR 284; 109 ILTR 29, Walsh J inferred from the Preamble and Article 6 that natural law, as understood in the Constitution, was "the law of God promulgated by reason and the ultimate governor of all the laws of men." Writing extra-judicially, he said that, "It can be correctly asserted that the Constitution of Ireland has opted for the theological origin of natural law", having earlier referred to the claim of St. Thomas Aquinas that "natural law was that part of the law of God which was discovered by human reason" - "*The Constitution and Constitutional Rights*" in Litton, ed., *The Constitution of Ireland: 1937-1987* (Dublin, 1988), 86 at 94. See also the similar views of O'Hanlon J in "Natural Rights and the Irish Constitution" (1993) ILT 8, and of Costello J in "*Natural Law, the Constitution and the Courts*" in *Essays in Memory of Alexis Fitzgerald* (Dublin, 1987)

[26] See Clarke, "*The Role of Natural Law in Irish Constitutional Law*" (1982) 17 Ir Jur (n.s.) 187.

[27] See Kenny J in *G. v An Bord Uchtála*, [1980] IR 32. See also a reference in the judgment of Finlay CJ in *J.K. v V.W.* [1990] 2 IR 437; [1990] ILRM 121, to the rights of interest or concern of a natural father arising from the blood link between father and child.

[28] See, *e.g.* the remarks of Kenny J in *Conroy v AG* [1965] IR 411, wherein, having heard evidence from a moral theologian as to the moral gravity of the offence of drunken driving, he referred to that evidence as being "derived from and measured by the natural law or natural ethics...[The witness] said that from the ethical standpoint, every individual as an individual has certain inherent rights of which the right to life is the most fundamental; after it comes the right to bodily integrity. These inherent rights of the individual impose on everyone an obligation to respect them." Similar descriptions of fundamental rights may be found in the judgments of Henchy J in *McGee v AG* [1974] IR 284, Barrington J in *Finn v AG* [1983] IR 154, and McCarthy J in *Murray v Ireland* [1991] ILRM 465.

[29] See, e.g. *The State (Healy) v Donoghue* [1976] IR 325, discussed above, p. 677

[30] Though in *G. v An Bord Uchtála* [1980] IR 32; (1979) 113 ILTR 25, Kenny J recognises a distinction between "natural rights" in the first sense outlined above, and "natural rights" in the sense of some superior norms upon which much of the Constitution is based.

Corollaries of natural law theory: fundamental rights can be invoked by persons who are not citizens

In each version of natural law theory described above, the condition of citizenship is irrelevant, so that it would seem to follow that non-citizens should be able to rely on the fundamental rights provisions of the Constitution, or at the very least, those which explicitly acknowledge a natural law origin.[31] The caselaw, however, contains a range of views on this issue.

The question whether the Constitution confers fundamental rights on non-citizens as well as citizens arises only because of the variable usage, as between different Articles, whereby some rights are expressed to be those of citizens (personal liberty, inviolability of the dwelling, the unspecified personal rights of Article 40.3, and the rights of free expression, assembly and association); while others, such as rights in regard to family, education, private property, and religion, as well as the rights which can be read out of Articles 34 and 38, are stated in general or "higher-law" terms without specific reference to citizens.

A number of decisions and *dicta* deny or cast doubt on the proposition that aliens can rely on the fundamental rights provisions of the Constitution. An early example of this may be seen in the decision of Henchy J in the divisional High Court decision in *The State (Nicolaou) v An Bord Uchtála*[32] in which he held that non-citizens could not invoke ss 1 and 3 of Article 40.[33] Those provisions admittedly stated the rights protected therein in terms of the citizen. However Finlay CJ has also denied that aliens can rely on Articles 41 and 42 of the Constitution, provisions which are clearly derived from natural law theory. Thus in *Kent Co. Council v C.S.*[34] where an Irish father who had lived in England since 1956 brought his child to Ireland in order to avoid the wardship jurisdiction of the English courts, he held that the father's rights under Articles 41 and 42 had not been infringed and ordered the return of the child to the UK. He took a similar view in *Saunders v Mid-Western Health Board*[35] when, delivering the *ex tempore* judgment of the Supreme Court, he said:

> "Where...parents having no connection with Ireland bring their children unlawfully from the country in which they are, into the jurisdiction of this court, in breach of an order made by the court in the jurisdiction in which they were domiciled and in which the children were being reared, I do not accept that they can by that act alone confer on themselves and their children constitutional rights under Articles 41 and 42 of the Constitution."

Consistently with that viewpoint, he later held that alien parents of Irish citizens could not assert any constitutional right to reside in Ireland: see *Fajujonu v Minister for*

[31] Assertion of constitutional rights which takes the form of a challenge to an Act of the Oireachtas involves, or may involve, other considerations; as to this special context, see above, pp. 435-436.
[32] [1966] IR 567.
[33] One of his colleagues on the High Court, Teevan J, disagreed with this conclusion and in the Supreme Court, the question was "expressly reserved for another and more appropriate occasion." It is worth noting in passing that Gavan Duffy J seemed to doubt whether non-citizens could invoke the constitutional guarantees for private property in *Fisher v Irish Land Commission* [1948] IR 3; (1949) 82 ILTR 50.
[34] [1984] ILRM 292.
[35] Supreme Court, 23 June 1987.

Justice.[36] In another recent case, *Minister for Justice v Wang Zhu Jie*[37] Costello J implied that aliens did not enjoy the same rights as citizens when he said, referring to the Aliens Act 1935, that it gave considerable powers to the authorities over aliens, "powers which perhaps might not be thought to be desirable or necessary or legal against citizens."

In a second group of cases, all concerning personal liberty, the courts assume, without so deciding, that aliens can invoke the fundamental rights protected by the Constitution - see *The People v Shaw*;[38] *Nantharatnam v Minister for Justice*;[39] *Ji Yoa Lau v Minister for Justice.*[40] This approach is hardly surprising as habeas corpus proceedings, although designed to assert the liberty which Article 40.4.1 proclaims for the citizen, are in a special category, because the procedure outlined in Article 40.4.2 - 5 speaks of a "person" alleged to be unlawfully detained.

Finally there are those cases in which the courts have affirmed that the fundamental rights provisions of the Constitution can be invoked by non-citizens. Thus, in *Northants Co. Council v A.B.F.*,[41] Hamilton J said:

> "The natural law is of universal application and applies to all human persons, be they citizens of this State or not, and in my opinion it would be inconceivable that the father of the infant child [the father was not an Irish citizen] would not be entitled to rely on the recognition of the family contained in Article 41...These rights are recognised by [the Constitution] and the courts created under it as antecedent and superior to all positive law: they are not so recognised by the law or the courts of the jurisdiction to which it is sought to have the infant returned."

In the earlier case of *The State (McFadden) v Governor of Mountjoy Prison*[42] Barrington J accepted, *obiter*, that non-citizens could enjoy the benefit of the constitutional guarantee of basic fairness of procedures in the administration of justice. He said:

> "The substantive rights and liabilities of an alien may be different to those of a citizen. The alien, for instance, may not have the right to vote or may be liable to deportation. But when the Constitution prescribes basic fairness of procedures in the administration of law it does so, not only because citizens have rights, but also because the courts in the administration of justice are expected to observe certain forms of due process enshrined in the Constitution. Once the courts have seisin of a dispute, it is difficult to see how the standards they should apply in investigating it should, in fairness, be any different in the case of an alien than those to be applied in the case of a citizen."

[36] [1990] 2 IR 151; [1990] ILRM 234. In one respect his views in *Fajujonu* go beyond his earlier position in the *Kent Co. Co.* and *Saunders'* cases in that the plaintiffs in the latter cases had no significant contemporary connection with the State whereas the Fajujonus had been resident in the country for eight years.
[37] [1993] 1 IR 426; [1991] ILRM 823.
[38] [1982] IR 1.
[39] *The Irish Times*, 4 October 1983.
[40] [1993] 1 IR 116; [1993] ILRM 64.
[41] [1982] ILRM 164. Similar views were expressed by Costello J in *Oxfordshire Co. Co. v J.H.*, High Court, 19 May 1988 and in *Wong v The Minister for Justice*, High Court, 30 July 1992, Denham J commented that counsel had "quite rightly pressed no argument on the ground that Mr. Wong as an alien has any limitation on rights in this jurisdiction .
[42] [1981] ILRM 113. See also *Kajli v The Minister for Justice*, High Court, 21 August 1992, where counsel for the Minister conceded that immigration officers had a constitutional duty to give a deportee the benefit of fair procedures in relation to his deportation,

The same judge considered the effect of the use of the word "citizen" in Articles 40 - 44 in a *dictum* in *Finn v Attorney General*.[43] In the context of considering whether these provisions could protect persons other than citizens, he said:

> "It is arguable that these rights derive not from a man's citizenship but from his nature as a human being. The State does not create these rights, it recognises them, and promises to protect them. The French Declaration of Rights, 1789, is entitled "Declaration of the Rights of Man and the Citizen". Sometimes the citizen is referred to in the text, but Article 1 opens with the statement "Men are born and remain free and equal..."A similar switching of gear can be discovered in Articles 40 - 44 of the Constitution. Articles 41, 42 and 43 recognise that man has certain rights which are antecedent and superior to positive law. By doing so, the Constitution accepts that these rights derive not from the law but from the nature of man and society, and guarantees to protect them accordingly...The fact that the wording of Article 40.3 commits the State to protect and vindicate the life of "every citizen" does not justify the inference that it relieves the State of the obligation to defend and vindicate the lives of persons who are not citizens. This is because the whole scheme of moral and political values which are clearly accepted by the Constitution indicates otherwise."

In *The State (Trimbole) v Governor of Mountjoy Prison*,[44] which arose out of attempts by the executive to extradite the applicant, an Australian, back to Australia, McCarthy J, after referring to the obligation on the courts to defend "the Constitution and the constitutional rights of every person within the jurisdiction of the courts", said:

> "It is important... to emphasise that the application of such legal principles must be the same for an Australian citizen on a temporary visit to Ireland as they would be for an Irish citizen, permanently resident in Ireland, when either of them is sought by a requesting State with which State Ireland has an extradition treaty or arrangement."

Similarly, in *The State (Kugan) v O'Rourke*[45] Egan J rejected the respondent's contention that the remedy of *habeas corpus* under Article 40.4.2 was not available to non-citizens, pointing out that under the terms of that provision, such relief can be sought by "any person". In *The State (Bouzagou) v Station Sergeant, Fitzgibbon St. Garda Station*[46] Barrington J accepted that non-citizens could rely on Articles 41 and 42, a view shared by O'Flaherty J in *Eastern Health Board and T.M. and A.M. v An Bord Uchtála*.[47] In *The People (Attorney General) v Gilliland*[48] Henchy J, delivering the judgment of the Supreme Court, indicated that aliens were entitled to bail in the same circumstances as citizens while in *Kennedy and Arnold v Ireland*,[49] Hamilton P accepted that the second-named plaintiff, who was not a citizen of Ireland, was entitled to the same personal rights as if he were.

[43] [1983] IR 154.
[44] [1985] IR 550; [1985] ILRM 465.
[45] [1985] IR 658; [1986] ILRM 95.
[46] [1985] IR 426; [1986] ILRM 98.
[47] [1993] ILRM 577. The other members of the Supreme Court did not comment on this point, which arose in the context of deciding whether the Adoption Act 1988 permitted the adoption of non-citizens.
[48] [1985] IR 643; [1986] ILRM 357.
[49] [1987] IR 587; [1988] ILRM 472.

In none of the above cases did the non-citizen have to establish a significant connection with the State, such as a period of residence of reasonable duration, in order to qualify for constitutional protection. However such a condition could be seen as implicit in the remarks of Walsh J in *Fajujonu* in which, in contrast to the Chief Justice, he extended the protection of Articles 41 and 42 to an entire family consisting of adults who were non-citizens and children who were born in the State. He said:

> "[The parents] and their three children constitute a family within the meaning of the Constitution and the children are entitled to the care, protection and the society of their parents in this family group which is resident within the State. There is no doubt that the family has made its home and residence in Ireland."

An implication of that last sentence is that a family which is in the State for a very brief period might not be able to avail of Articles 41 and 42.

Finally, it is worth noting the comments of Gannon J in *Rederij Kennemerland B.V. v Attorney General*[50] in which Dutch nationals, *inter alia*, challenged the constitutional propriety of the powers vested in Peace Commissioners under s 233A of the Fisheries (Consolidation) Act 1959, as amended by s 12 of the Fisheries (Amendment) Act 1978. He said:

> "The vessels involved in these proceedings are Dutch owned and operated, and the masters are Dutch nationals and, I infer, are neither citizens of Ireland nor have property nor place of business nor residence in Ireland. By entering and making use of the waters within the fishery limits of the State they become amenable to the laws of this country. Thereupon they are entitled to expect and insist that those laws will be applied and administered in accordance with the Constitution of the State. To the extent that the laws are not so applied or administered in relation to them, their persons and property they are entitled to call upon the Superior Courts to uphold the Constitution and to provide a remedy against breach of the provisions of the Constitution."[51]

The significance of this approach is that it allows for the application of the fundamental rights provisions of the Constitution to non-citizens without having to invoke any natural law theory.

Are such rights immune from legislation enacted pursuant to Article 28.3.3 and Article 29.4.5?

Constitutional recognition of rights which are "antecedent and superior to all positive law" - Article 41.1.1 - would appear to be inconsistent with those constitutional provisions which seek to protect certain types of legislation and State actions from judicial invalidation on grounds of incompatibility with the Constitution - Article 28.3.3 in relation to emergency legislation and Article 29.4.5 in relation to legislation and other State actions necessitated by membership of the EC.[52] This inconsistency does not appear to

[50] [1989] ILRM 821.

[51] He went on to suggest that their right to challenge the constitutionality of legislation is limited to the purpose of affording to them a remedy or relief for any wrong, harm or disadvantage suffered by a failure to uphold the Constitution.

[52] See *Clarke, loc. cit.* at footnote 3 above.

have been adverted to in the caselaw to date and, given the constitutional recognition of the "higher law", can presumably be resolved only by qualifying the immunities from judicial review conferred by the sub-sections cited.

Immutability of aspects of the Constitution?

More radically again, a further corollary of some variants of natural law theory would seem to be that the power to amend the Constitution, conferred by Article 46, is implicitly limited to making amendments compatible with such theory. This position was recently argued for by Mr. Justice O'Hanlon, in the course of an article questioning the compatibility of the 1992 amendments to Article 40.3.3 with natural law.[53] If one accepts that the Constitution acknowledges a concept of natural rights which are superior to positive norms, the logic of this reasoning appears unassailable.[54] However its practical application gives rise to difficulties of a most profound nature. Chief among these is that this reasoning conflicts with the constitutional value of democratic decision-making and it clearly elevates the "anti-majoritarian" problem associated with judicial review onto a new plane inasmuch as it makes the judiciary the ultimate arbiters of the validity of legal norms by precluding any recourse to constitutional amendment to reverse a judicial decision invalidating legislation.[55] Furthermore the O'Hanlon thesis also overlooks the epistemological difficulties inherent in natural law theory and the absence of any consensus as to what natural law might require in a given situation[56] presents a profound practical difficulty in applying this doctrine. One suspects that these factors may ultimately lead to some reluctance on the part of the judiciary to adopt this particular corollary of natural law theory.[57]

The explicit enunciation of this corollary of natural law theory may, perhaps, be a reaction to the growing dominance of competing ideologies in the other branches of government and among the electorate generally. It remains to be seen how the dominance of

[53] *Loc. cit.* He also argued that the State's power to bind itself by international agreement was similarly limited. An analogous argument, based not on any explicit concept of natural law but rather on the idea of human dignity, has been advanced by an American academic, Walter Murphy who contends that popular consent cannot legitimate constitutional change which would destroy or damage human dignity - see "*Consent and Constitutional Change*" in O'Reilly, ed., *Human Rights and Constitutional Law: Essays in Honour of Brian Walsh* (1992), p.123.

[54] A not dissimilar position was arrived at, though without any reliance on natural law theory, by a majority of the Supreme Court of India in *Kesavananda's* case (1973) ASC 1461. Here the majority held that the power of Parliament to amend the Indian Constitution was subject to an implicit limitation that it could not be used to amend the "basic structure of the Constitution". The amending power, contained in Article 368 of the Indian Constitution (which appears to have been modelled on Article 46 of the Irish Constitution), provides, *inter alia*, that "Notwithstanding anything in this Constitution Parliament may, in the exercise of its constituent power amend by way of addition, variation or repeal any provision of this Constitution in accordance with the procedure laid down in this Article." The position of the majority in *Kesavananda's* case was subsequently reaffirmed in *Gandhi v Raj Narain* (1975) ASC 2299.

[55] It seems somewhat ironic that Article 40.3.3, which was ostensibly designed to prevent judicial usurpation of the role of the electorate in relation to abortion policy, should provide the context for the argument that the judiciary must, in certain circumstances, ignore the will of that electorate as expressed in a referendum.

[56] In *McGee v AG* [1974] IR 284, for example, Walsh J, who based his decision partly on natural law theory, concluded that the plaintiff had a legal right of access to artificial contraception while the teaching of the Roman Catholic Church has continually maintained that such contraception is contrary to natural law.

[57] Though Whelan argues that the version of democratic theory espoused by Irish judges has much in common with natural law theory and therefore may not be a very compelling check on judicial review of alterations to the constitutional text - "*Constitutional amendments in Ireland: the competing claims of democracy*" in *Justice and Legal Theory: Proceedings of the First Annual Conference of Law and Philosophy in Ireland*, Quinn ed., (forthcoming).

such views will affect the judicial perception of the role of the natural law in constitutional adjudication though already there are signs of a more critical approach from academic quarters.[58]

Are there unwritten fundamental rights which qualify the express words of the Constitution?

A different problem from that of natural law to which constitutional statements of fundamental rights merely give imperfect expression, is that of the exhaustiveness, or otherwise, of constitutional rules; in other words, the question whether the plain words of an Article are to be understood as modified by long-established principles of ordinary law, which a literal reading of the Article would defeat. This question is of course not confined to the field of fundamental rights (although it surfaces most acutely in that context); and division of judicial opinion on it by no means coincides with division of opinion on the claims of natural law. Judges who all seem to assent to these claims will be found on both sides of the issue whether there exists a range of what might be called paraconstitutional rules which can operate to qualify, indeed in some cases to negative, what the Constitution actually says. Those who accept this idea tend to express it in the form of refusing to impute to the draftsmen, the members of the Dáil, or the people in 1937, the intention to do away, by general words, with some principle, friendly to liberty, which the law up to that year contained.

This problem emerged first in 1939, in *The State (Burke) v Lennon*[59] in the form of the question whether Articles 40-44 must be regarded as having totally subsumed fundamental rights and the modes by which they could be enforced. Here the Supreme Court refused to entertain an appeal against the granting by the High Court of an order of *habeas corpus*; despite the provision of Article 34.4.3 that the Supreme Court was generally to have "appellate jurisdiction from all decisions of the High Court", the Court felt that this was not enough to uproot the former well-established rule of no appeal against the granting of such an order.[60] Sullivan CJ said:

> "Certain constitutional principles are stated in the Constitution, but many other important constitutional principles have been adopted as existing in the law in force."

This view, which might seem capable of giving the Court a route back from the strict positivist position of *Ryan's* case, was dissented from by Johnston J:

> "The terms of Articles 34 and 40 of the new Constitution are clear and comprehensive, and they do not at all suggest that, in regard to cases like the present, an appeal does not lie to the Supreme Court. The Constitution of 1937 represents a fresh start in respect of the fundamental principles that are to be the guide of this country for the future, and I do not think that a further Constitution - an unwritten one - was

[58] Mr. Justice O'Hanlon's article has already provoked replies from Murphy - "*Democracy, Natural Law and the Irish Constitution*" (1993) ILT 81, (to which the judge in turn replied in "*The Judiciary and the Moral Law*" (1993) ILT 129) - and Clarke - "*The Constitution and Natural Law: A Reply to Mr. Justice O'Hanlon*" (1993) ILT 177. See also the earlier articles by Clarke, cited above, fn 3 and fn 26, and by Quinn, "*The Nature and Significance of Critical Legal Studies*" (1989) ILT 282 and "*Reflections on the Legitimacy of Judicial Activism in the field of Constitutional Law*" (Winter, 1991) Dlí 29.

[59] [1940] IR 136; (1940) 74 ILTR 36, 131.

[60] See below, pp. 907-909.

> intended by the people of Éire to exist side by side with this written Constitution or even - perhaps it would be more correct to say - outside and beyond the present Constitution. I think that the practical effect of our decision in this case will be to add to Article 34.4 half a dozen words making a further reservation from the jurisdiction of the Supreme Court..."[61]

In 1942 it was argued for the prisoners in *The State (Walsh) v Lennon*[62] that there existed common law rights, independent of the Constitution, which were breached by certain Emergency Powers Orders, and that these Orders, to the extent that they breached common law rights rather than those specified in the Constitution, were not protected by the operation of Article 28.3.3. This argument failed, Maguire P saying:

> "The contention is that the constitutional principles which assure to a citizen his personal liberty, his right to resort to this Court for an order or habeas corpus, his right that he shall not be tried on a criminal charge save in due course of law, have as their source the common law, and exist side by side with these rights in the written Constitution...I do not find in the judgment of Murnaghan J or elsewhere in the judgments in [*Burke's*] case any basis for the contention that these rights are to be found in a body of principles which exist side by side with the written Constitution, having their source in the common law, and of equal validity with the principles stated in the Constitution, and which, on the argument here, would have the added virtue that they are uncontrolled by Article 28.3.3. The constitutional rights relied upon in this case find clear expression in Articles 40 and 38 of the Constitution. In my view they cannot be found elsewhere than in the Constitution."

Gavan Duffy J said:

> "The particular common law principles here invoked must both, in my opinion, of necessity have merged in the express provisions declaring how the two corresponding rights are to be in force under the new polity established by An Bunreacht."

And Martin Maguire J said:

> "[The argument for the prisoners] involves the propositions that the State has two Constitutions, the one enacted by the people, written and defined; the other unwritten and undefined, and that the latter may be invoked, or called in aid, to the extent even of defeating the clear terms of the Constitution where a conflict real or apparent is alleged between them. There is no authority for these propositions. I am unable to accept this argument. The mischief and inconvenience to which it would lead are obvious."

Yet the idea that certain principles, not stated in the Constitution and even (in some contexts) conflicting with its clear language, ought to be seen as of constitutional rank, so to speak, so as to modify that clear language, still has important adherents today. After a period in the 1960s and 1970s in which construction of the Constitution was perhaps excessively literal, a reaction seems to be taking place, at least where the effect of literal

[61] The opinion of Johnston J was subsequently vindicated by the (new) Supreme Court in *The State (Browne) v Feran* [1967] IR 147: see below, pp. 908-909.
[62] [1942] IR 112; (1942) 76 ILTR 207.

construction is inimical to traditional liberal values. Thus in *The People (Director of Public Prosecutions) v O'Shea*[63] an issue rather similar to that in *Burke's* case arose, inasmuch as the literal words of Article 34.4.3 were used by the Supreme Court in order to hold permissible an appeal to the Court from an *acquittal* in the Central Criminal Court - thus reversing what had always been supposed to be the rule attributing finality to an acquittal - but the Court's decision was by a mere 3-2 majority, the dissenting judges (Finlay P and Henchy J) strongly and plausibly arguing for admitting the traditional rule of no appeal against acquittal as a tacit constitutional value co-ordinate with Article 34.4.3 and capable of modifying it.[64]

No such thing as an absolute and unqualified fundamental right

An important problem is the extent to which fundamental rights are absolute or admit of qualification and cutting-down;[65] and the related question whether the beneficiary of a constitutional right can waive or divest himself of it.

The short answer to the former question is that scarcely any constitutional right is or can be absolute and unlimited.[66] Kenny J said in *Ryan v Attorney General*[67] (with reference to the "personal rights" of Article 40, though the same must be true in some measure of the rights mentioned in later Articles):

> "None of the personal rights of the citizen are unlimited; their exercise may be regulated by the Oireachtas when the common good requires this. When dealing with controversial social, economic and medical matters on which it is notorious views change from generation to generation, the Oireachtas has to reconcile the exercise of personal rights with the claims of the common good and its decision on the reconciliation should prevail unless it was oppressive to all or some of the citizens or unless there is no reasonable proportion between the benefits which the legislation will confer on the citizens or a substantial body of them and the interference with the personal rights of the citizen."

The wording of Articles 40-44 themselves - particularly Articles 40 and 42 - support this kind of view. Personal liberty can be divested "in accordance with law";[68] the citizen's dwelling, though generally "inviolable", may be entered "in accordance with law";[69] the rights of free expression, assembly and association are guaranteed "subject to public order and morality";[70] freedom of conscience and of religious practice is subject to the same qualification.[71] The State may "as occasion requires delimit by law" the exercise of the right of private property "with a view to reconciling [it] with the exigencies of the common good".[72] Only family rights and rights in regard to education seem to be expressed less equivocally; the family is "a moral institution possessing inalienable and imprescriptible rights, antecedent and superior to all positive law";[73] and the right (and

[63] [1982] IR 384.
[64] See above, pp. 505-509.
[65] See Costello, "*Limiting Rights Constitutionally*" in O'Reilly, ed., *Human Rights and Constitutional Law: Essays in Honour of Brian Walsh* (Dublin, 1992), p.179.
[66] The European Convention on Human Rights recognises two absolute rights, the right not to be tortured (Article 3) and the right not to be held in slavery (Article 4), both of which must surely qualify for protection under the Irish Constitution also.
[67] [1965] IR 294.
[68] Article 40.4.1.
[69] Article 40.5.
[70] Article 40.6.1.
[71] Article 44.2.1.
[72] Article 43.2.2.
[73] Article 41.1.1.

duty) of parents to educate their children is also "inalienable".[74] But even the latter Article envisages circumstances in which the State may see itself obliged to "supply the place of parents".[75] Moreover in *Murray v Ireland*[76] Costello J, arguing for a purposive interpretation of the Constitution, indicated that the State's power to regulate the exercise of constitutional rights did not depend on any express affirmation of such power in the Constitution and used as an example of this the rights of the family under Article 41. He said:

> "The power of the State to delimit the exercise of constitutionally protected rights is expressly given in some Articles and not referred to at all in others, but this cannot mean that where absent the power does not exist. For example, no reference is made in Article 41 to any restrictive power, but it is clear that the exercise by the Family of its imprescriptible and inalienable right to integrity as a unit group can be severely and validly restricted by the State when for example its laws permit a father to be banned from a family home or allow for the imprisonment of both parents of young children."

A further important point worth noting in this context is that only post-1937 legislation can give effect to a permitted statutory qualification upon any right guaranteed or granted by the Constitution.[77] Moreover such legislation must be strictly construed.[78]

Waiver of constitutional rights

The question to what extent the beneficiary of a fundamental or natural personal right can waive it is one on which the courts have displayed some hesitancy. This is surprising, as ordinary life contains many instances, which can scarcely be all unconstitutional, in which the exercise of such rights is foregone for certain purposes or periods: thus a State servant accepts a discipline which will cut down his rights of assembly or association; a soldier or police officer accepts limitations of personal freedom even more severe; and a range of free contractual arrangements can obviously cut down the exercise of various kinds of property right. But it was only during the 1980s that the Supreme Court started to delineate waiver as a legitimate operation in the field of constitutional rights.

Thus in *Murphy v Stewart*[79] Murnaghan J said he thought a person *sui iuris* could, with full knowledge, surrender or waive his rights under Article 40.6.1.iii; but when the case reached the Supreme Court on appeal, Walsh J, with whom the other judges agreed, seemed slower to commit the Court:

[74] Article 42.1.
[75] Article 42.5.
[76] [1985] IR 532; [1985] ILRM 542. In the subsequent Supreme Court appeal - [1991] ILRM 465 - counsel for the plaintiffs expressly conceded that the rights they were claiming could be validly restricted by the State.
[77] *Aughey v AG* [1989] ILRM 87.
[78] See *e.g., Murphy v Greene* [1990] 2 IR 566; [1991] ILRM 404; *N.U.J. v Sisk* [1992] 2 IR 171; [1992] ILRM 96; *Irish Press plc v Irish Ingersoll Publications* [1993] ILRM 747.
[79] [1973] IR 97; (1973) 107 ILTR 117.

> "For the purposes of this appeal it is unnecessary to say how or to what extent, if any, a person may agree to surrender or waive a right guaranteed by the Constitution but, on the assumption that it could be done, I agree with the learned trial judge [that it would have to be on the basis of full knowledge and free consent]."

In three other cases decided by the Supreme Court at that time,[80] *Becton Dickinson Ltd. v Lee*,[81] *Glover v B.L.N. Ltd.*[82] and *Meskell v C.I.É.*,[83] the Court or its majority (*per* Walsh J in all three cases) again found it unnecessary to decide this question (though it arose marginally in all of them); in *Meskell's* case however - by speaking of a person's "refusal to waive his right to dissociate" - appearing to countenance such a thing provisionally. Also, in *McMahon v Attorney General*[84] Ó Dálaigh CJ said - admittedly in connection with the right to vote at Dáil elections resulting from Article 16 and not any of the fundamental or "natural personal" rights - that, in the case of a blind voter who got a friend to mark his ballot paper for him, he did not look on this reduced secrecy of the ballot "being based on the principle of waiver by the voter": a *dictum* formulated so as to suggest he thought a waiver of this sort might be possible, but not definitely holding it to be so. And in *Cotter v Ahern*[85] Finlay P held that four of the defendants had attempted to coerce the plaintiff into "abandoning or waiving his constitutional right to dissociate".

The first five of these cases were decided by the Supreme Court in the 1971-2 period, and, as has been seen, add up to at most a very tentative agreement that constitutional rights might be waived. All the time, however, a decision of the Supreme Court was on record - from the very different field of parents' rights - in which, in 1966, the Court had clearly said that a right of the category protected by Article 40.3, at least, might be surrendered. This was *The State (Nicolaou) v An Bord Uchtála*,[86] in which the Court had held that the rights of the mother of a non-marital child did not arise from Articles 41 and 42 (which related only to the family based on marriage) but were natural personal rights of the kind latent in the general language of Article 40.3; and - in the context of the mother's having parted with her child for the purpose of its adoption, her right to do which was disputed - the Court had pointed out that:

> "there [was] no provision in Article 40 which prohibits or restricts the surrender, abdication, or transfer of any of the rights guaranteed in that Article by the person entitled to them."

It is not clear why this was not cited to the Court in the 1971-2 cases, as the generality of this observation would seem to put an end to any reason for the hesitancy which those cases display. In 1978, however, the matter surfaced again, in the context of adoption of a non-marital child with the consent of the child's mother, in *G. v An Bord Uchtála,*[87] and this time the Court was explicit in interpreting this consent as a waiver of the moth-

[80] Judgments in all four cases were given on 18 and 19 December 1972.
[81] [1973] IR 1.
[82] [1973] IR 388.
[83] [1973] IR 121.
[84] [1972] IR 69; (1972)106 ILTR 89.
[85] [1976-7] ILRM 248.
[86] [1966] IR 567; (1968) 102 ILTR 1.
[87] [1980] IR 32; (1979) 113 ILTR 25. See note by *Redmond*, (1979 - 80) DULJ 104.

er's natural personal right to the child's custody, a right which the Constitution in the absence of this waiver would have protected. O'Higgins CJ said that, in agreeing to place her child for adoption, the mother had "dispensed with her constitutional right to insist on the custody of her child"; and Walsh J, after citing what he had said in speaking for the Court in *Nicolaou's* case, now generalised the admissibility of waiver:

> "Natural rights may be waived or surrendered by the persons who enjoy them provided such waiver is not prohibited either by natural law or by positive law."

Waiver must rest on full knowledge and consent

He emphasised however (as foreshadowed in *Murphy v Stewart*, cited above) that this must, in the case of the mother parting with her non-marital child, be on the basis of full knowledge and consent. Moreover, "a consent motivated by fear, stress, anxiety, or consent or conduct dictated by poverty or other deprivations cannot constitute a valid consent."[88] The necessity of full knowledge and consent in this kind of case was asserted again by Finlay P in *S v Eastern Health Board*:[89] and in *E.M. v E.M. and M.M.*[90] Murphy J added that, while the surrender or abandonment of the right to custody of a non-marital child might be established by conduct, the conduct must be "such as to warrant the clear and unambiguous inference that such was [the mother's] fully informed, free and willing intention".[91] Whether these stringent conditions of waiver, laid down in so sensitive an area in which a wrong decision can have irremediable human effects, are to be generalised over the whole field of fundamental rights, has not yet been judicially discussed; though in *The State (Rogers) v Galvin*[92] Henchy J, speaking for the Supreme Court, said, in the context of Article 40.4.2 which specifically entitles a habeas corpus respondent to certify in writing the grounds of the detention, that this entitlement could be waived by a respondent police officer only with "full authority, knowledge and intention".[93]

No waiver of inalienable family rights

Rights excluded from the possibility of waiver are those of Articles 41 and 42 (which relate to the family based on marriage). Article 42 speaks of the "inalienable right and duty" of parents to educate their children, a formulation which speaks clearly against

[88] In *McF. v G.* [1983] ILRM 228, McWilliam J qualified this somewhat by saying that "if absolute rules as to fear, stress, anxiety or poverty were to be applied, there could hardly be a case found in which one or other of them would not be present, so that it could be argued that a consent was not valid."
[89] High Court, 28 February 1979. See *O'Connor* (1981) 16 Ir Jur (n.s.) 275.
[90] High Court, 2 December 1982.
[91] For a case illustrating the need for consent to be fully informed, see *In re D.G., an infant, O'G. v An Bord Uchtála* [1991] 1 IR 491; [1991] ILRM 514.
[92] [1983] ILRM 149.
[93] The issue of waiver has recently been considered by the courts again, though in the context of parliamentary privileges under ss 12 and 13 of Article 15, rather than in relation to fundamental rights. In *Attorney General v Hamilton (No.2)*, High Court [1993] ILRM 821, Geoghegan J adopted the formula used by the US Supreme Court in *US v Helstoski*, 442 US 477 (1972), that effective waiver of these parliamentary privileges would require "explicit and unequivocal renunciation of the protection" and that that standard - which he considered to be higher than the standard set in *G. v An Bord Uchtála* [1980] IR 32 - had not been met in the instant case. Accordingly he did not have to decide the further issue whether the privileges could be waived only by the particular House and not by individual members, though he did signal a preference for the former view. While the issue was not pursued in the Supreme Court, Finlay CJ indicated his approval, *obiter*, of Geoghegan J's conclusions (though he assumed that the immunity could be waived by individual members of the Oireachtas) and Blayney J opined that "voluntary conscious deliberate repetition" outside the Dáil of utterances made therein would amount to waiver of the immunity under Article 15.13.

waiver; and Article 41 asserts the "inalienable and imprescriptible rights" of the family, a phrase with which Kenny J came to grips in *Ryan v Attorney General*[94] in a way which seems to rule waiver out:

> "Inalienable" means that which cannot be transferred or given away while "imprescriptible" means that which cannot be lost by the passage of time or abandoned by non-exercise."[95]

In the particular matter of parents' purporting to deprive themselves of the right to custody of children, the Supreme Court held in 1955 in *The State (Doyle) v Minister for Education*[96] that this was constitutionally impossible. Maguire CJ reviewed the old common law which did not recognise that a parent could deprive himself or herself of the right and duty to take care of the child, and said:

> "Had s 10 of the Children Act 1941 which purported to permit a parent to surrender this right been passed before the making of the Constitution it would appear in that portion of it which is here impugned to conflict with the common law principle that parents not alone have the right to control the education of their children but that they cannot surrender this right. The common law however would have had to yield before such a statutory enactment. It seems however to this Court that the makers of the Constitution by the provisions of Article 42 and particularly by [ss 1 and 3.1] of that Article deliberately preserved this common law principle and have put it beyond the reach of ordinary legislation."

Right to jury trial waived by "guilty" plea?

The question whether a plea of guilty to the charge of an indictable offence represents a waiver of the right to a jury trial has occasionally been canvassed. It seems most simply answered by saying that a criminal trial is the trial of an *issue* between the people and the accused; and that as the plea of guilty has disposed of any issue, no room remains for a "trial", by jury or otherwise.[97] The question of whether an accused who has pleaded not guilty in such circumstances may waive his right to jury trial seems more problematic. Perhaps the best solution is to regard the right to jury trial not merely as a right which is simply personal to the accused, but rather as a mandatory constitutional rule ("a

[94] [1965] IR 294.

[95] But see above, pp. 210-211 as to meaning of "imprescriptible". In *G. v An Bord Uchtála* [1980] IR 32, Walsh J attempted, somewhat unconvincingly, to introduce into this area a distinction between those rights which are absolutely inalienable and those which are relatively inalienable. Nothing further has been heard of this distinction since.

[96] Supreme Court, 21 December 1955; now reported in [1989] ILRM 277 and also in O'Reilly and Redmond, *Cases and Materials on the Irish Constitution* (1980) at p.632.

[97] However, in *The State (Meads) v Governor of Limerick Prison*, Supreme Court, 26 July 1972, Ó Dálaigh CJ, delivering the Court's judgment, said: "The word 'tried' in the warrant is, in my opinion, sufficiently apt to cover the operations of the Circuit Court or the Central Criminal Court in the case of a prisoner who is sent forward on signing a plea of guilty." And in *The State (Littlejohn) v Governor of Mountjoy Prison*, Supreme Court, 18 March 1976, the power of sending forward for "trial" to the Special Criminal Court was held by the Supreme Court to have been properly exercised even where the accused had pleaded guilty and only the sentence remained to be determined.

constitutional imperative") which is not susceptible of waiver by the accused. Article 38.5 may in this respect be analogous to the publicity rule in Article 34.1: see *Irish Press Plc v Irish Ingersoll Publications Ltd.*[98]

Impairment of rights by unreasonable time (or other) limitation

On the question whether a constitutional right is infringed by the provision of an unreasonably short time, or otherwise unreasonably restricted opportunity for its exercise, the Supreme Court said in *O'Brien v Manufacturing Engineering Co.*[99] (*per* Walsh J) that:

> "Rights conferred by the Constitution, or rights guaranteed by the Constitution, are of little value unless there is adequate opportunity for availing of them: any legislation which would create such a situation must necessarily be invalid, as would any legislation which would authorise the creation of such a situation: see the decision of this Court in *The State (Quinn) v Ryan*."[100]

Collision of constitutional rights

The question of collision of constitutional rights[101] has arisen in a number of cases since the early 1970s.[102] In the first of these, *Quinn's Supermarket v Attorney General*,[103] the validity of an Order which exempted Jewish shops from closing-hour regulations (so as to enable Jews to buy meat ahead of the Sabbath, on which their religion forbids trading) was in issue, by reference to Article 44.2.3 which forbids "any discrimination on the ground of religious profession, belief or status". The Supreme Court saw here a conflict between the right to practise religion, guaranteed by Article 44.2.2 (which the exemption in favour of Jews was intended to facilitate) and the guarantee against discrimination; and the Court resolved it - in heavy reliance on US authorities, notably *Abington School District v Schempp*[104] - by saying that a discrimination, provided it went no further than was necessary, did not infringe the guarantee if *its object* was to further the right of religious practice. Walsh J said:

> "Therefore, there arises a conflict between the constitutional guarantee of the free profession and practice of religion and the constitutional guarantee against discrimination on the ground of religious profession, belief or status. [He reviewed the American cases.] It appears to me...that the primary object and aim of Article 44, and in particular the provisions of s 2 of that Article, was to secure and guarantee freedom of conscience and the free profession and practice of religion subject to

[98] [1993] ILRM 747. See also *Attorney General v Hamilton (No.1)* [1993] 2 IR 250; [1993] ILRM 81 (Government could not agree to waive the absolute confidentiality rule which a majority of the Supreme Court found to be implicit in Article 28.4).

[99] [1973] IR 334; (1974) 108 ILTR 105.

[100] [1965] IR 70; (1966) 100 ILTR 105.

[101] In *A.G. v Hamilton (No.2)* [1993] ILRM 821, Geoghegan J classified the conflict between the parliamentary privilege enjoyed by members of the Oireachtas under ss 12 and 13 of Article 15 and the right to their good name of persons against whom certain members of the Dáil had made allegations as a clash of constitutional rights, which had to be resolved in favour of the parliamentary privilege as "the privilege...is absolute and intended by the Constitution to be absolute in the sense even that it cannot be sacrificed to protect other constitutional rights." However it is probably more accurate to characterise this situation as one in which a privilege marks the boundary to a right, rather than as the collision of two constitutional rights. The debate on the necessity to resolve a clash of constitutional rights was not pursued in the subsequent Supreme Court appeal.

[102] It does, however, emerge in a rudimentary form much earlier, in *Cooper v Millea* [1938] IR 749, in which Gavan Duffy J saw a conflict between the constitutionally recognised rights of trade unions, and the right, recognised in Article 45, of the individual to an adequate means of livelihood. This conflict, he said, would have to be resolved "on principle".

[103] [1972] IR 1.

[104] (1963) 374 US 203.

> public order and morality...If, however, the implementation of [this guarantee] requires that a distinction should be made to make possible for the persons professing or practising a particular religion their guaranteed right to do so, then such a distinction is not invalid having regard to the provisions of the Constitution. It would be completely contrary to the spirit and intendment of [Article 44.2] to permit the guarantee against discrimination on the ground of religious profession or belief to be made the very means of restricting or preventing the free profession or practice of religion."

The same kind of point surfaced in *McMahon v Attorney General*,[105] in which the Supreme Court, while enforcing the terms of Article 16.1.4 by declaring unconstitutional an arrangement relating to ballot papers which in theory would have permitted the discovery of how a citizen had voted in a Dáil election, had to deal with the objection that perfect secrecy of the ballot was in any case unobtainable if one were to allow a blind citizen to vote, as this vote could only be recorded by another hand and eye to which the blind voter's wishes had been disclosed. Ó Dálaigh CJ saw the situation of the blind voter as one of conflict or collision, and referred to the principle stated in the *Quinn's Supermarket* case:

> "The right to vote of the incapacitated person has to be reconciled with the general right to vote by secret ballot. The latter right, which by its very nature is a guarantee of the free exercise of the right to vote, cannot be made the means of preventing the exercise of the right to vote simply because the incapacity of some electors renders absolute secrecy impossible. A law which contained provisions which enabled such a person to vote with the maximum degree of secrecy compatible with his incapacity would not only be desirable but would be necessary to implement the right to vote conferred on such person by the Constitution. I do not look upon the exercise, with less than full secrecy, of the incapacitated voter's franchise as being based on the principle of waiver by the voter; willy-nilly and of necessity his vote cannot be cast otherwise."

Here, too, it appears that what is paramount is the individual's right to achieve the central object of this part of the Constitution: to vote, as it was to practise his religion unimpeded in the *Quinn's Supermarket* case. If in special instances this collides with an essentially subsidiary feature of the constitutional value in question (no religious discrimination: a secret ballot) the subsidiary feature can validly be encroached on to the extent of the necessity but no further.

"Hierarchy of Constitutional rights"

A collision of rights also occurred in *The People (Director of Public Prosecutions) v Shaw*,[106] where the Supreme Court had to consider, on the one hand, the status of a prisoner's custody by the police (did it amount to a violation of his constitutional rights, so as to vitiate and render inadmissible evidence which emerged as a result of it?) and, on the other hand, the life of a girl whom the prisoner had abducted and, in fact, murdered, but the slim chance of still finding whom alive had prompted the police, as the trial judge found, to hold the prisoner in the hope that he would lead them to her. Here, for the first time, the suggestion was heard in the Supreme Court (from Kenny J) that there was such a thing as a "hierarchy of rights". He said:

[105] [1972] IR 69; (1972) 106 ILTR 89.
[106] [1982] IR 1.

> "There is a hierarchy of constitutional rights and, when a conflict arises between them, that which ranks higher must prevail...The decision on the priority of constitutional rights is to be made by the High Court and, on appeal, by this Court. When a conflict of constitutional rights arises, it must be resolved by having regard to (a) the terms of the Constitution, (b) the ethical values which all Christians living in the State acknowledge and accept and (c) the main tenets of our system of constitutional parliamentary democracy...I have no doubt that the decision made by Detective Superintendent Reynolds to regard M's right to life as ranking higher than the appellant's right to personal liberty for three days was the correct one... It was not a question of the end justifying the means - a doctrine which most ethical teachers since Aristotle have repudiated. It was a question of vindicating a higher-ranking constitutional right."

In the same case, Griffin J, with whom Henchy and Parke JJ agreed, gave preference to the notion of a harmonious interpretation of the Constitution over the idea of a hierarchy of rights, though at the same time accepting that in certain situations, the courts would be compelled to give a priority to one right over another:

> "If possible, fundamental rights under a Constitution should be given a mutually harmonious application, but when that is not possible, the hierarchy or priority of the conflicting rights must be examined both as between themselves and in relation to the general welfare of the society. This may involve the toning down or even the putting into temporary abeyance of a particular guaranteed right so that, in a fair and objective way, the more pertinent and important right in a given set of circumstances may be preferred and given application."

Kenny J's formulation was subsequently criticised by McCarthy J for a "possible lack of objectivity"[107] but the idea of a hierarchy of rights has since been accepted, albeit, perhaps, with some reluctance.

In *Murray v Ireland*[108] Costello J cautioned against over-reliance on the literal text of the Constitution in determining the relative importance of conflicting constitutional rights and argued instead that any conflict should be resolved by having regard to the intrinsic nature of the rights involved. He was responding to the plaintiffs' contention that their constitutional right to beget children was protected by Article 41.1 rather than by Article 40, and as such ranked very high in the scale of values protected by the Constitution. He said:

> "As I suggested in *AG v Paperlink Ltd*...in construing the Constitution the courts should bear in mind that the document is a political one as well as a legal one; and, whilst not ignoring the express text of the Constitution, a purposive approach to interpretation which would look at the whole text of the Constitution and identify its purpose and objectives in protecting human rights is frequently a desirable one."

107 See his judgment in *Attorney General v X* [1992] 1 IR 1; [1992] ILRM 401; [1992] 2 CMLR 277. Presumably he had in mind the references to the Christian ethical values and the main tenets of constitutional parliamentary democracy as factors to be taken into account in determining the priority of rights *inter se*.
108 [1985] IR 532; [1985] ILRM 542.

After citing the judgment of Henchy J in *Tormey v Ireland*[109] in support of his views, he continued:

> "It does not follow therefore that because the Constitution ascribes to only some human rights characteristics of inalienability and imprescriptibility [it] should be construed as implying that other fundamental human rights lack these qualities, or that only those rights are superior to positive law which are so expressly described in the Constitution. The right to life, for example, is one of the personal rights expressly referred to in Article 40.3.2 and the right not to be tortured is one of the personal rights protected but not expressly enumerated in Article 40.3.1. Both these rights must surely be reckoned as amongst the most important basic human rights, and the Constitution should be interpreted to give effect to this view, even though neither is expressly described as being inalienable and imprescriptible or as being superior to positive law. So if the court is required to make a valuation between two constitutionally protected human rights (as it was required to do in *D.P.P. v Shaw*) it should have particular regard to the intrinsic nature of the rights concerned, a view consistent with the views of Mr. Justice Griffin (p.56) and Mr. Justice Kenny (p.63) in [*Shaw's* case]. If this view is correct then it would follow that should it become necessary for the purposes of deciding any of the issues in this case to evaluate the right asserted by the plaintiffs this should be done by considering its innate qualities and nature, and the plaintiffs' right to beget children should not be devalued merely because it happens to be a "personal" right protected by Article 40.3.1 without the benefit of the more expressive and explicit language employed in Article 41.1.1."

In this case, Costello J concluded that the State could lawfully prevent the plaintiffs from exercising their right to procreate.[110]

Costello J's opinion that the right to life is one of the most important basic human rights was shared by the Supreme Court in *The Attorney General (The Society for the Protection of Unborn Children (Ireland) Ltd.) v Open Door Counselling Ltd.*[111] when it held, *per* Finlay CJ, that there was no constitutional right to obtain information the purpose of the obtaining of which was to defeat the right to life of the foetus.[112] In *The Attorney General v X*,[113] however, the Supreme Court was presented with the unenviable task of accommodating conflicting rights to life within the constitutional hierarchy of rights, when the Attorney General sought an injunction to prevent a young girl, pregnant as a result of an alleged rape, from having an abortion in the UK. The dramatic facts of this case presented two conflicts of rights - a conflict between the right to life of the foetus and that of the mother and a conflict between the former right and the mother's right to travel. In their treatment of these conflicts, some members of the Supreme Court

[109] [1985] IR 289; [1985] ILRM 375.

[110] In the subsequent Supreme Court appeal, McCarthy J, (with whom Hamilton P, O'Flaherty and Keane JJ concurred), while accepting that there was a hierarchy of constitutional norms, held that it was unnecessary and, indeed, undesirable, to identify such a hierarchy in the instant case - [1991] ILRM 465.

[111] [1988] IR 593; [1989] ILRM 19.

[112] In the High Court, Hamilton P had held that the right to privacy, the rights of association and freedom of expression and the right to disseminate information could not be invoked to interfere with this right to life.

[113] [1992] 1 IR 1; [1992] ILRM 401; [1992] CMLR 277. It is also implicit in the decision of Finlay CJ in *Conway v I.N.T.O.* [1991] 2 IR 305; [1991] ILRM 497 in which he identified as a factor in determining when it was appropriate to award punitive damages for a breach of constitutional rights that the right breached was one of "supreme and fundamental importance".

endorsed the approach enunciated by Griffin J in *Shaw,* which saw the doctrine of the hierarchy of rights as something to be invoked only where a harmonisation of rights was not possible. Thus in relation to the second of the two conflicts presented by the case, Finlay CJ said:

> "I accept that where there exists an interaction of constitutional rights the first objective of the courts in interpreting the Constitution and resolving any problem thus arising should be to seek to harmonise such interacting rights. There are instances, however, I am satisfied, where such harmonisation may not be possible and in those instances I am satisfied, as the authorities appear to establish, that there is a necessity to apply a priority of rights."

In similar vein, McCarthy J said that "I would prefer to seek harmony between the various rights guaranteed and to reconcile them to each other rather than to rank one higher than another." In relation to the conflict between the rights to life and to travel, two members of the Court - Finlay CJ and Egan J - indicated, *obiter*, that the right to life of the unborn should take priority over the right to travel of the mother, implicitly taking the view that reconciliation of these rights was not possible in the instant case.[114] However in what can only be regarded as an exercise in sophistry, two of the judges - Finlay CJ and McCarthy J - purported to resolve the conflict between the rights to life of the mother and the foetus though a harmonious interpretation of the Constitution, the end result of which was to recognise the mother's right to terminate her pregnancy in order to avert a real and substantial risk to her own life.[115] Thus McCarthy J said:

> "It is not a question of setting one[right] above the other but rather of vindicating, as far as practicable, the right to life of the girl/mother (Article 40, s 3, sub-s 2), whilst with due regard to the equal right to life of the girl/mother, vindicating, as far as practicable, the right to life of the unborn...
>
> It is not a question of balancing the life of the unborn against the life of the mother; if it were, the life of the mother would virtually always have to be preserved, since the termination of pregnancy means the death of the unborn; there is no certainty, however high the probability, that the mother will die if there is not a termination of pregnancy. In my view, the true construction of the Amendment, bearing in mind the other provisions of Article 40 and the fundamental rights of the family guaranteed by Article 41, is that, paying due regard to the equal right to life of the mother, when there is a real and substantial risk attached to her survival not merely at the time of application but in contemplation at least throughout the pregnancy, then it may not be practicable to vindicate the right to life of the unborn."

Perhaps such casuistry was required because the text of the Constitution expressly equated two rights which, in fact, cannot be reconciled on those rare occasions in which they come into conflict. Whatever the reason, it is difficult to avoid the conclusion that the decision of the majority produced a result which, in the circumstances of this case, ranked the right to life of the mother over that of the foetus.[116]

[114] The sole dissenting judge, Hederman J, was also of this opinion, while O'Flaherty J did not advert to this point at all in his judgment. McCarthy J disagreed with his colleagues on this matter, taking the view that the right to travel did not admit of any limitation because of the intent of the traveller.

[115] The remaining members of the majority, O'Flaherty and Egan JJ, did not attempt explicitly to balance these conflicting rights but rather approached the matter on the basis of identifying those circumstances in which the right to life of the foetus could lawfully be terminated.

[116] Equally the practice of permitting "indirect" abortions produces the same result.

A constitutional right implies a duty in others; and vice versa

There are important *dicta* to the effect that the existence of a constitutional right in one person implies a duty in others to respect it and that such rights are enforceable, not only as against the State, but also as against private individuals. In *Educational Co. of Ireland v Fitzpatrick (No. 1)*[117] Ó Dálaigh J said:

> "Liberty to exercise a right, it seems to me, *prima facie* implies a correlative duty on others to abstain from interfering with the exercise of such right."

In the second phase of the same case[118] Budd J echoed this:

> "Obedience to the law is required of every citizen, and it follows that if one citizen has a right under the Constitution there exists a correlative duty on the part of other citizens to respect that right and not to interfere with it."

This proposition was implicitly re-affirmed by Hamilton P in *Attorney General (Society for the Protection of the Unborn Child (Ireland) Ltd.) v Open-Door Counselling Ltd.*[119] when he said:

> "The Court is under a duty to act so as not to permit any body of citizens to deprive another of his constitutional right, to see that such rights are protected and to regard as unlawful any infringement or attempted infringement of such constitutional right as constituting a violation of the fundamental law of the State."[120]

That one individual may sue another individual in order to protect constitutional rights was made clear by Costello J in *Hosford v Murphy (John) and Sons Ltd.*[121] who said:

> "Uniquely, the Irish Constitution confers a right of action for breach of constitutionally protected rights against persons other than the State and its officials."

The existence of a constitutional duty laid upon the State may imply a right on the part of the individual. Thus in *Crowley v Ireland*,[122] a case in which the plaintiff was relying on Article 42.4 ("The State shall provide for free primary education"), McMahon J said:

> "It is not seriously disputed that the constitutional duty of the State to provide for free primary education creates a corresponding right to receive primary education on the part of those for whom it is designed."

In the Supreme Court in this case O'Higgins CJ (though in the minority on the outcome of the case) said:

[117] [1961] IR 323.

[118] [1961] IR 345. This was cited by Walsh J, speaking for the Supreme Court in *Meskell v C.I.É.* [1973] IR 121.

[119] [1988] IR 593; [1987] ILRM 477. This proposition would also be an implied premise of the Supreme Court decision on the subsequent appeal - [1989] IR 593; [1989] ILRM 19.

[120] See also the comments of McCarthy J in *Conway v I.N.T.O.* [1991] 2 IR 305; [1991] ILRM 497.

[121] [1987] IR 621; [1988] ILRM 300. For a consideration of this *Drittwirkung* ("third party effect") of the fundamental rights provisions of the Constitution, see von Prondsynski, "*The Protection of Constitutional Rights: Comparisons between Ireland and Germany*" (1979 - 80) DULJ 14, at pp.20 - 23.

[122] [1980] IR 102.

"The imposition of the duty under Article 42.4 creates a corresponding right in those in whose behalf it is imposed to receive what must be provided. It cannot be doubted, therefore, in my view, that citizens have the right to receive what it is the State's duty to provide for under Article 42.4."

More recently, in *Hosford* [123] Costello J argued that it would be possible to derive the rights of the family under both sub-ss 1 and 2 of Article 41, s 1, from the duties imposed on the State by sub-s 2, proceeding on the premise that the rights protected by both sub-sections are co-extensive.[124]

Analysis of jural relationships surrounding fundamental rights

Some commentators have argued for a more precise analysis, based on the writings of *W.N. Hohfeld*,[125] of the jural relationships arising out of the guarantees of fundamental rights and freedoms.[126] In this context, important distinctions are drawn between, *inter alia*, rights and freedoms, and rights and powers. The identifying characteristic of a right is said to be that it has a duty as an invariable correlative,[127] whereas a freedom refers to the benefit derived from the absence of a legal duty imposed on the person enjoying the freedom. A power is regarded as the opposite of legal disability and the correlative of legal liability. It is possible to discern apparent allusions to these sophisticated distinctions in some judgments of Costello J. Thus in *Attorney General v Paperlink Ltd.*[128] he referred to:

"the distinction between a personal right guaranteed by the Constitution and the freedom to exercise a constitutionally guaranteed personal right, a distinction which is to be found throughout the entire Constitution and which is made explicit, for example, in Article 40.6.1."[129]

Later in the same judgment, he said that "A Constitution which guarantees personal rights imposes co-relative constitutional duties on the State."

In *Murray v Ireland*[130] the same judge distinguished between a right and a power. Here the plaintiffs, who were both serving sentences of life imprisonment, argued that they had a constitutional right to beget children and that the State had to facilitate them in the exercise of this right. The State countered by arguing that any right which the plaintiffs might have in this context had to be balanced against the right of the State to imprison them. Costello J regarded this argument as conceptually unsound, saying:

[123] [1987] IR 621; [1988] ILRM 300.

[124] The judgment of Murphy J in *Greene v Minister for Agriculture* [1990] 2 IR 15; [1990] ILRM 364, however, suggests that not every constitutional duty imposed on the State creates a corresponding personal right on the part of the citizen. In that case, the judge held that the State's breach of its obligation to guard with special care the institution of marriage - Article 41.3 - did not create a corresponding right in the individual citizen so that a breach of the duty would necessarily constitute an infringement of any right of his and accordingly he restricted the plaintiffs to declaratory relief only, dismissing their claim for damages. However this decision is not easy to reconcile with other cases in which plaintiffs recovered damages because of the State's breach of Article 41.3, such as *Murphy v AG* [1982] IR 241, and *Hyland v Minister for Social Welfare* [1989] IR 624; [1990] ILRM 213.

[125] W.N. Hohfeld (W. Cook ed.) *Fundamental Legal Conceptions as Applied in Legal Reasoning* (Yale, 1923), ch.1.

[126] See Redmond, "*Towards an Hohfeldian View of the Rights and Freedoms in the Irish Constitution*" (1979 - 80) DULJ 52.

[127] This characteristic of a right has certainly been recognised by the Irish judiciary - see preceding section, pp. 696-697.

[128] [1984] ILRM 373.

[129] However he did not indicate what the practical consequences, if any, of this distinction might be.

[130] [1985] IR 532; [1985] ILRM 542.

> "It is common enough in everyday discussion on human and political rights to refer to the "right" of the State to punish, or to take life, or to expropriate property, etc. But the indiscriminate ascription of "rights" to the State can lead to confusion and is not appropriate when what is in issue is the exercise by one of the organs of government of a power conferred by law. This is the position in the present case. The Governor of Limerick Prison is detaining the plaintiffs in custody by virtue of a warrant issued by a court of law after a finding of guilt in a criminal trial. The State (through the Governor) is thus exercising a legal power to deprive the plaintiffs of their constitutional right to liberty. The court is therefore being asked to adjudicate on the validity of the exercise of a legal power and not on a conflict between the exercise of two competing rights. This distinction between the exercise of a power and the exercise of a right (a point emphasised by some legal theorists) is a useful one to bear in mind in the context of constitutional disputes. The Constitution in protecting and guaranteeing the citizen's rights has imposed very clear and specific correlative duties on the State to protect and vindicate them but it has also designated the State the guardian of the common good and has empowered it to restrict those rights in certain circumstances. So this is not a case in which the court should balance the so-called "right" of the State to imprison wrongdoers against the plaintiffs' right to beget children. The issue is whether the restrictions on the plaintiffs' rights caused by the exercise of the State's power to imprison the plaintiffs are constitutionally permissible."[131]

A difficulty with the Hohfeldian distinction between rights and freedoms in the present context is Hohfeld's insistence that a duty exists as a correlative only to a right and never to a freedom. However as the State is always bound to operate in accordance with the Constitution - see *Crotty v An Taoiseach*[132] - and in particular has a duty not to interfere with those concepts described as "freedoms" therein, such as freedom of conscience (Article 44.2), it would seem that the Hohfeldian distinction between rights and freedoms does not correspond to the distinction between these terms drawn in the text of the Constitution.[133]

The State's overriding duty to prevent the infringement of personal rights

The possible existence of a common law remedy does not absolve the State from its duty, imposed by Article 40.3.1, to prevent an infringement of personal rights. In *E.S.B. v Gormley*,[134] in which the validity of statutory provisions authorising the plaintiff company to enter and work on the defendant's land was in issue, the Supreme Court said:

[131] This analysis of the relationship between the State and the individual would appear to be preferable to that advanced by Gannon J in *Osheku v Ireland* [1986] IR 733; [1986] ILRM 330. Here an illegal immigrant sought to establish a right to remain in this country by relying, *inter alia*, on the fact that he had married an Irish citizen and thus enjoyed the protection of Articles 41 and 42. Gannon J rejected this contention, holding that the rights of the plaintiff had to be read in the light of the "fundamental rights" of the State to preserve the integrity of the State and to maintain social order. Arguably what should have been debated here was the legality of the State's power in the particular case to act in the interests of the common good, rather than, as happened, the identification of the "rights" of the State and a consequent balancing of those rights against the rights of the individual.

[132] [1987] IR 713.

[133] Of course this does not preclude the use of Hohfeld's analysis to reclassify as rights, in the Hohfeldian sense, concepts which are actually referred to as freedoms in the text of the Constitution.

[134] [1985] IR 129; [1985] ILRM 494.

"Whilst it is clear from the decision of this Court in *Meskell v C.I.É.* that where a person's constitutional rights have been violated he is entitled to sue for and obtain damages, such a cause of action cannot give aid to those who contend for the validity of this section. For such a cause of action to arise by virtue of the exercise by the plaintiff of this statutory power presupposes the violation of the defendant's rights by means of an unjust attack on her property rights in these lands. The duty of the State under Article 40.3.2 by its laws to protect the defendant from that attack must be considered antecedent to its duty after the happening of such an attack to vindicate her rights."

A similar view was taken by Finlay CJ in the Supreme Court in *Finucane v McMahon*[135] where, in the context of refusing to order the appellant's extradition because of fear that his constitutional rights would be infringed by prison staff in Northern Ireland, he said:

"This Court has... as its primary obligation, the duty to prevent such invasions of the applicant's rights and it is not a sufficient discharge of that duty for it to rely upon the vindication of those rights by compensation after they have been invaded."

No specific procedure required for assertion of constitutional right

The question of the procedure whereby constitutional rights can be asserted before the courts has been noticed in some cases. As a general rule no problem will arise, as an appropriate procedure will be evident; there may, however, be situations in which no procedure seems to offer itself as appropriate, and in these situations a principle first enunciated by Walsh J in *Byrne v Ireland*[136] will come into play:

"Where the people by the Constitution create rights against the State or impose duties upon the State, a remedy to enforce these must be deemed to be also available."[137]

This, he said, was so even if a wrong or breach of obligation on the part of the State "might not be within the recognised field of wrongs in the law of tort": he instanced the right to free primary education recognised by Article 42 (and previously by the old Article 10), this being only one of several obligations undertaken by the State towards the citizens:

"It is not the case that these are justiciable only when some law is being passed which directly infringes these rights or when some law is passed to implement them. They are justiciable when there has been a failure on the part of the State to discharge the obligations..."

[135] [1990] 1 IR 165; [1990] ILRM 505.
[136] [1972] IR 241.
[137] In the earlier case of *The State (Quinn) v Ryan* [1965] IR 70, Ó Dálaigh CJ said, "It was not the intention of the Constitution in guaranteeing the fundamental rights of the citizens that these rights should be set at nought or circumvented. The intention was that rights of substance were being assured to the individual and that the courts were the custodians of these rights. As a necessary corollary, it follows that no one can with impunity set these rights at nought or circumvent them, and that the courts' powers in this regard are as ample as the defence of the Constitution requires."

While these words in *Byrne's* case applied to enforcing a right as against the State, the same judge (with the agreement of Ó Dálaigh CJ and Budd J) generalised them in *Meskell v C.I.É.*:[138]

> "A right guaranteed by the Constitution or granted by the Constitution can be protected by action or enforced by action even though such action may not fit into any of the ordinary forms of action in either common law or equity and... the constitutional right carried within it its own right to a remedy or for the enforcement of it. Therefore, if a person has suffered damage by virtue of a breach of a constitutional right or the infringement of a constitutional right, that person is entitled to seek redress against the person or persons who have infringed that right."

In *The State (Shatter, Gallagher & Co.) v de Valera (No.2)*[139] Barrington J agreed that "it may be more usual to raise a constitutional issue in plenary proceedings" but at the same time clearly accepted that this is not inevitably so, pointing out that:

> "the great issues decided in the *Sinn Féin Funds* case were first raised in that most humble of all applications - an *ex parte* application for the payment of money out of court."

Where a constitutional right is being asserted, the courts occasionally relax the normal rules of procedure. In *Shannon v Ireland*[140] Finlay P said:

> "It seems to me that the Court has a special duty to ensure on the making of such a claim [for the protection of constitutional rights] that all material facts which can be adduced in evidence before it are adduced and that it has all the material necessary before it to secure to the plaintiff his constitutional rights even if that is inconsistent with the ordinary and desirable procedures of the Court."

Accordingly he admitted evidence on affidavit during the course of the trial notwithstanding the absence of agreement between the parties.

"Statutory vesture" of right not necessary for enforcement

In two cases in the early 1970s, the principle was also established that a statutory vesture of constitutional rights was not necessary to the court's power to enforce them - *The State (Murphy) v Governor of Portlaoise Prison*[141] and *The State (Meads) v Governor of Limerick Prison*.[142] These were both cases in which the applicants, having pleaded guilty to indictable offences on being charged in the District Court, were sent forward for sentence to the Circuit Court; but then found themselves without a statutory route of appeal, as the relevant provisions of the Criminal Procedure Act 1967, mentioned appeal from the Circuit Court to the Court of Criminal Appeal only in cases where persons had been "convicted on indictment", and said nothing about appeal (against sentence) in cases of

[138] [1973] IR 121.
[139] High Court, 16 January 1987.
[140] [1984] IR 548; [1985] ILRM 449.
[141] High Court, 23 November 1971.
[142] Supreme Court, 26 July 1972. In *The State (Hunt) v O'Donovan* [1975] IR 39; (1973) 107 ILTR 53, Finlay J cited both *Murphy* and *Meads* with evident acceptance of the principle that "statutory vesture" is not required for the enforcement of a constitutional right.

sentence on plea on guilty. Habeas corpus proceedings in both cases were grounded upon, *inter alia*, the contention that the applicants were being denied a constitutional right of appeal by the implication of the silence of the 1967 Act as to cases like theirs. In the earlier case, *(Murphy's)*, Butler J in the High Court noted that in *Byrne's* case, Walsh J had pointed out, (as Butler J paraphrased it), that:

> "the existence of a constitutional right and the power of the courts to enforce it do not depend on legislation recognising the right or providing machinery to enforce it... All that could be said against the impugned sections is that they do not provide a machinery for the exercise of the alleged right but they do not take [it] away nor in themselves interfere with its exercise."

In *Mead's* case the Supreme Court (*per* Ó Dálaigh CJ) said:

> "If Article 40... has the meaning contended for by the applicant, then so be it: let him claim and enforce his right. The 1967 Act does not purport to restrict any such right, if it exists. The High Court is the appropriate forum for the declaration of constitutional rights. Constitutional rights, for enforcement, do not require statutory vesture unless the Constitution itself were to express such a limitation."[143]

In *The People v Shaw*[144] Kenny J, referring to Article 40.3, said,

> "The obligation to implement this guarantee is imposed not on the Oireachtas only, but on each branch of the State which exercises the powers of legislating, executing and giving judgment on those laws: Article 6. The word 'laws' in Article 40, s 3, is not confined to laws which have been enacted by the Oireachtas, but comprehends the laws made by judges and by ministers of State when they make statutory instruments or regulations."

The principle that constitutional rights do not require statutory vesture has been re-stated in more recent times in relation to the right to life of the unborn. In *The Attorney General v X*[145] Finlay CJ, after citing *The State (Quinn) v Ryan,*[146] *The People v Shaw,*[147] and *The Attorney General (Society for the Protection of Unborn Children (Ireland) Ltd.) v Open Door Counselling Ltd.*[148] said:

[143] The nature of some constitutional rights is such that they do require statutory vesture before they can be enforced. In *O'B. v S* [1984] IR 316, [1985] ILRM 86, for example, the Supreme Court recognised that, in the context of intestate succession, the right to inherit property referred to in Article 43.1.2 could only be effective where there were legal rules determining succession on intestacy. The Court held that no constitutional right to inherit property was vested in the defendant in this case but also said, *obiter*, "If the defendant has a vested right to property under the terms of the Succession Act then, of course, it would be a right falling to be defended and vindicated under Article 40.3."

[144] [1982] IR 1. This would appear to contradict his earlier views in *Crowley v Ireland* [1980] IR 102, as to which, see below, pp. 787-789.

[145] [1992] 1 IR 1; [1992] ILRM 401; [1992] 2 CMLR 277.

[146] [1965] IR 70.

[147] [1982] IR 1.

[148] [1988] IR 593; [1989] ILRM 19.

> "Having regard to these statements of the law expressed by this Court and to the principles underlining them, I have no doubt that the submission that the courts are in any way inhibited from exercising a function to vindicate and defend the right to life of the unborn which is identified and guaranteed by Article 40, s 3, sub-s 3 of the Constitution by reason of a want of legislation is incorrect ..."[149]

Remedies for breach of constitutional rights

Neither the Constitution itself nor any other law prescribes any particular procedure as appropriate for remedying a breach of constitutional rights (just as no special procedure is laid down for challenging the constitutionality of statutes). The ordinary range of actions and orders are open here to the aggrieved person, and the circumstances of his case will suggest the most appropriate. Issues of personal liberty are most commonly litigated in the *habeas corpus* procedure under Article 40.4; though the injunction procedure is also known, as in *O'Boyle and Rodgers v Attorney General*;[150] and in *Dunne v Clinton*[151] the plaintiff recovered damages against police defendants for false imprisonment. Actions claiming declarations are increasingly common - obvious examples are *Ryan v Attorney General*,[152] and *McGee v Attorney General*[153] - while injunctions are not infrequently granted to restrain a breach of constitutional rights - see, *e.g.*, *Murtagh Properties Ltd. v Cleary;*[154] *Parsons v Kavanagh.*[155] In one case, *Attorney General v X,*[156] an injunction was initially obtained in the High Court to restrain an apprehended, as opposed to actual, breach of a constitutional right - the injunction was designed to prevent the first defendant obtaining an abortion in England - though it was subsequently discharged by a majority of the Supreme Court who took the view that, under the circumstances, the injunction failed to vindicate the right to life of the mother.[157]

Claims for damages

There have also been successful claims for damages for breach of constitutional rights[158] though in most cases, the damages were calculated in accordance with common law principles and, in particular, the breach of constitutional rights did not, *per se*, result in

[149] His judgment in the earlier *Open Door* case also contained an indirect reference to the "function of the courts ... [not being] dependent on the existence of legislation, when their jurisdiction to defend and vindicate a constitutionally guaranteed right has been invoked ..."

[150] [1929] IR 558; (1929) 63 ILTR 33.

[151] [1930] IR 366; (1930) 64 ILTR 136.

[152] [1965] IR 294.

[153] [1974] IR 284; (1975) 109 ILTR 29.

[154] [1972] IR 330.

[155] [1990] ILRM 560.

[156] [1992] 1 IR 1; [1992] ILRM 401; [1992] 2 CMLR 277. See below, pp. 796-803.

[157] In *Weeland v RTÉ* [1987] IR 662, the plaintiff sought an injunction to prevent the broadcast of a programme on the ground, *inter alia*, that it would prejudice his right to a fair trial in a civil matter. However Carroll J refused to grant the injunction because, *inter alia*, the plaintiff failed to establish this aspect of the case on the facts.

[158] *E.g. Meskell v C.I.É.* [1973] IR 121; *Cotter v Ahern,* [1976-7] ILRM 248; *Kearney v Minister for Justice*, [1986] IR 116; [1987] ILRM 52. In this last case, where the plaintiff complained of a violation of his right to communicate because of the failure of prison staff to deliver his mail to him, he obtained nominal damages only because he had suffered no pecuniary loss nor was he able to show that the wrongful actions were oppressive or vindictive. In *Crowley v Ireland* [1980] IR 102, the Supreme Court left open "the difficult question whether damages may be awarded against a Minister of State or Ireland for failure to perform a duty imposed by the Constitution" (*per* Kenny J): but there would seem to be no reason to place the State in this context on a footing of privilege. On the issue of damages for breach of constitutional rights, see Cooney and Kerr, "*Constitutional Aspects of Irish Tort Law*" (1981) DULJ 1.

the award of punitive damages.[159] However where a person's constitutional rights have been infringed deliberately, consciously and without justification by the State, exemplary damages are appropriate. In *Kennedy v Ireland,*[160] where the plaintiffs brought an action arising out of the unjustified tapping of their telephones, Hamilton P said:

> "In determining the damages to which the plaintiffs are entitled, I must have regard not only to the distress which was suffered by the plaintiffs as a result of the infringement of their constitutional right to privacy, the implications thereof and the publicity consequent thereto, but also to the fact that the infringement was carried out deliberately, consciously and without justification by the executive organ of the State which is under a constitutional obligation to respect, vindicate and defend that right.
>
> The plaintiffs are in my opinion entitled to substantial damages and it is, in the circumstances of this case, irrelevant whether they be described as "aggravated" or as "exemplary" damages."[161]

In *Kennedy*, Hamilton P had maintained a distinction between exemplary damages for serious invasion of the right to privacy and punitive damages, holding that the latter would have been awarded had the defendants also brought the good name of the plaintiffs into disrepute. However this distinction has subsequently been rejected by the Supreme Court in a case which establishes that exemplary damages may be awarded, in appropriate circumstances, against private individuals who violate constitutional rights - *Conway v I.N.T.O.*[162] This case arose out of the interruption of primary schooling in certain schools in Co. Cork because of an industrial dispute.[163] In the High Court, Barron J had awarded damages of £11,500 to the plaintiff, a pupil at one of the schools, of which £1,500 came under the heading of exemplary damages. The defendants appealed on the grounds, *inter alia*, that exemplary damages should not have been awarded at all or, that if awarded, the assessment in the instant case was excessive. As Finlay CJ's judgment[164] contains a comprehensive statement of the various headings under which damages for breach of constitutional rights (which, for this purpose, he equates with an action in tort) may be awarded, it is worth quoting *in extenso*:

[159] See, *e.g. Cosgrove v Ireland*, High Court, 9 June 1981. For criticism of this position, see *Cooney and Kerr, loc. cit.*

[160] [1987] IR 587; [1988] ILRM 472.

[161] He awarded £20,000 to each of the first two plaintiffs and £10,000 to the third plaintiff.

[162] [1991] 2 IR 305; [1990] ILRM 497.

[163] For the history of these events, see *Crowley v Ireland* [1980] IR 102, discussed below pp. 1057-1058. In an earlier case arising out of the same events - *Hayes v Ireland* [1987] ILRM 651, the plaintiff was awarded general damages of £4,000. Dismissing the defendants' contention that a minimal award of damages should be made because of the *bona fide* motives behind the withdrawal of labour by the teachers, Carroll J said, "The defendants arguments... could only be relevant in deciding whether exemplary or punitive damages should be awarded and the plaintiff does not seek punitive damages. In my opinion no acknowledgement can be made of the difficult position in which the teachers found themselves. The plaintiff is entitled to recover in full such damages as he can prove to have been sustained by him."

[164] Concurring judgments were delivered by Griffin and McCarthy JJ. In the course of his judgment, Griffin J endorsed the views of O'Flaherty J in *McIntyre v Lewis* [1991] 1 IR 121 that in assessing exemplary damages, the judge should have regard to, *inter alia*, the means of both parties. However his application of this principle to actions involving breach of constitutional rights has been criticised on the ground that the means of the plaintiff should play no part in the assessment of exemplary damages in such cases - see Byrne and Binchy, *Annual Review of Irish Law 1991*, (Dublin, 1993), pp.451-2.

"In respect of damages for tort or for breach of constitutional right, three headings of damage in Irish law are, in my view, potentially relevant to any particular case. They are:

(1) ordinary compensatory damages being sums calculated to recompense a wronged plaintiff for physical injury, mental distress, anxiety, deprivation of convenience, or other harmful effects of a wrongful act and/or for monies lost or to be lost and/or expenses incurred or to be incurred by reason of the commission of the wrongful act.

(2) Aggravated damages, being compensatory damages increased by reason of:

(a) the manner in which the wrong was committed, involving such elements as oppressiveness, arrogance or outrage, or

(b) the conduct of the wrongdoer after the commission of the wrong, such as a refusal to apologise or to ameliorate the harm done or the making of threats to repeat the wrong, or

(c) conduct of the wrongdoer and/or his representatives in the defence of the claim of the wronged plaintiff, up to and including the trial of the action.

Such a list of the circumstances which may aggravate compensatory damages until they can properly be classified as aggravated damages is not intended to be in any way finite or complete. Furthermore the circumstances which may properly form an aggravating feature in the measurement of compensatory damages must, in many instances, be in part a recognition of the added hurt or insult to a plaintiff who has been wronged, and in part also a recognition of the cavalier or outrageous conduct of the defendant.

(3) Punitive or exemplary damages arising from the nature of the wrong which has been committed and/or the manner of its commission which are intended to mark the court's particular disapproval of the defendant's conduct in all the circumstances of the case and its decision that it should publicly be seen to have punished the defendant for such conduct by awarding such damages, quite apart from its obligation, where it may exist in the same case, to compensate the plaintiff for the damage which he or she has suffered."

The Chief Justice held that it was not possible to maintain any real distinction between punitive and exemplary damages because it was impossible to award damages for the purpose of making an example of a person without punishing that person and *vice versa*. He then turned to consider whether a judge could assess exemplary damages for breach of constitutional rights and, after citing the passage from the judgment of Ó Dálaigh CJ in *The State (Quinn) v Ryan*[165] quoted above,[166] said:

165 [1965] IR 70.
166 Fn. 137.

> "It seems clear to me that the court could not be availing of powers as ample as the defence of the Constitution and of constitutional rights requires unless, in the case of the breach of those rights, it held itself entitled to avail of one of the most effective deterrent powers which a civil court has, the awarding of exemplary or punitive damages."

He continued:

> "This does not mean that every wrong which constitutes the breach of a constitutional right in any sense automatically attracts exemplary damages. It does not, in my view, even mean that in every such case, irrespective of the facts or circumstances surrounding it, the court should specifically concern itself with the question of exemplary damages...
>
> In this particular case, however, it is clear that the circumstance as found by McMahon J in *Crowley v Ireland* that the intended consequence of the defendants' acts was the direct deprivation of the plaintiff of her constitutional right to free primary education, coupled with the special relationship which the defendants consisting of both the organisation and the individuals bore to the general rights of children to free primary education make it a case in which the question of whether or not exemplary damages should be awarded, necessarily arose."

Having regard to the facts that, in the instant case, the right which was breached was one vested in a child; that it was one of supreme and fundamental importance, having regard to the education and training of a child,[167] that the defendants were aware of that importance; and that the breach was an intended, as distinct from inadvertent, consequence of the defendants' conduct, the Chief Justice held that this was an appropriate case in which to award exemplary damages.[168]

Punitive sanctions

A number of cases have drawn attention to the possible use of punitive sanctions to vindicate constitutional rights.[169] In *The State (Quinn) v Ryan*[170] the Supreme Court adverted to the possibility that a person engaged in a course of action deliberately intended to eliminate the courts and thereby set at nought the constitutional rights of another could be guilty of "contempt of the courts" and punished accordingly. This point was amplified by Finlay CJ in *The State (Trimbole) v Governor of Mountjoy Prison.*[171] Here the Supreme Court dismissed an appeal against an order of the High Court, made pursuant to Article 40.4.2, directing that the applicant be released forthwith from detention. In the High Court, Egan J had held that the arrest of the applicant under s 30 of the Offences Against the State Act 1939, was made simply for the purpose of allowing the police to

[167] For criticism of the reasoning of the Chief Justice on this point - on the ground that the seriousness of an infringement of a constitutional right can vary from trivial to serious and that a grave violation of a lesser right should not, in principle, result in a less generous award of damages than in the case of a trivial breach of a superior right - see Binchy, "*Constitutional Remedies and the Law of Torts*" in O'Reilly ed. *Human Rights and Constitutional Law: Essays in honour of Brian Walsh* (Dublin 1992).

[168] He also held that, bearing in mind the rationale behind exemplary damages, the trial judge was entitled to have regard to the fact that the defendants faced multiple actions arising from this industrial dispute, when calculating the amount of such damages.

[169] In *The People (D.P.P.) v Tiernan* [1988] IR 250; [1989] ILRM 149, Finlay CJ described the crime of rape as a "gross attack upon the human dignity and the bodily integrity of a woman and a violation of her human and constitutional rights. As such it must attract very severe legal sanctions." Despite the fact that other crimes also violate constitutional rights, this appears to be the only occasion on which the courts have suggested that this dimension of criminal behaviour might result in the imposition of particularly onerous sanctions.

[170] [1965] IR 70; (1966) 100 ILTR 105.

[171] [1985] IR 550; [1985] ILRM 465.

hold him pending the finalisation of arrangements for his extradition to Australia. After referring to *The State (Quinn) v Ryan, The People (Attorney General) v O'Brien,*[172] *The People (Director of Public Prosecutions) v Madden*[173] and *The People (Director of Public Prosecutions) v Lynch,*[174] the Chief Justice said:

> "I am satisfied that from these decisions certain general principles can be deduced. They are: (a) The Courts have not only an inherent jurisdiction but a positive duty (i) to protect persons against the invasion of their constitutional rights; (ii) if invasion has occurred, to restore as far as possible the person so damaged to the position in which he would be if his rights had not been invaded; and (iii) to ensure as far as possible that persons acting on behalf of the executive who consciously and deliberately violate the constitutional right of citizens do not for themselves or their superiors obtain the planned results of that invasion.[175] Notwithstanding the fact, therefore, that of the four cases to which I have referred, three are concerned with the admissibility of evidence in criminal trials and the fourth was concerned with the punishment of persons acting in breach of the Constitution where neither protection nor reparation of the party injured was practical, I am satisfied that this principle of our law is of wider application than merely to either the question of the admissibility of evidence or to the question of the punishment of persons for contempt by unconstitutional action. This jurisdiction and direct duty arising from the Constitution and the position of the courts created by it is in some ways similar to, though more ample and dominant than what I am satisfied was an inherent jurisdiction recognised by the common law in courts to prevent an abuse of their own processes."

In *Attorney General (Society for the Protection of the Unborn Child (Ireland) Ltd.) v Open-Door Counselling Ltd.*[176] Hamilton P went even further, though speaking *obiter*:

> "Though ordinarily it is no function of the courts to extend the criminal law, it may well be that where there is a breach of or interference with a fundamental personal or human right, they may be under a constitutional obligation so to do in order to respect, and, as far as practicable, to defend and vindicate that right."

The reverse side of this coin is that, provided no challenge to a post-1937 Act is involved,[177] there is no reason why a breach of constitutional right cannot be pleaded in criminal or other proceedings before inferior courts, special courts, or the Court of Criminal Appeal, as happened in, for example, *Madden's, Stenson's, O'Loughlin's* and *Farrell's* cases.[178]

[172] [1965] IR 142.
[173] [1977] IR 336; (1977) 111 ILTR 117.
[174] [1982] IR 64.
[175] The Supreme Court has subsequently clarified that this principle applies even where the agents of the executive are not themselves aware that they are violating constitutional rights, once it can be shown that they were acting consciously and deliberately - *The People (D.P.P.) v Kenny* [1990] 2 IR 110; [1990] ILRM 569. See above, pp. 606-607.
[176] [1988] IR 593; [1987] ILRM 477. The Supreme Court did not advert to this point in the subsequent appeal - [1988] IR 593; [1989] ILRM 19.
[177] See above, pp. 426-427.
[178] See above, pp. 603-604, 609.

The role of the law of tort in the protection of constitutional rights

In the aftermath of *Meskell v C.I.É.*[179] and in particular, Walsh J's remark therein that constitutional rights can be protected or enforced by action "even though such action may not fit into any of the ordinary forms of action in either common law or equity", it was speculated that nominate torts such as assault, battery, libel and false imprisonment might disappear, to be replaced by an "innominate claim for infringement of personal rights."[180] In fact nothing so dramatic has occurred; instead the courts have tended to take the view that the law of tort generally provides adequate protection for personal rights and that it is only in those cases where common law remedies are inadequate or non-existent that an action based directly on the Constitution would arise. Thus in *Hanrahan v Merck Sharp & Dohme (Ireland) Ltd.*[181] - a case in which the plaintiffs sought damages for injuries and loss suffered as a result of emissions from the defendant's factory - Henchy J said:

> "I agree that the tort of nuisance relied on in this case may be said to be an implementation of the State's duties under [Article 40.3.1-2] as to the personal rights and property rights of the plaintiffs as citizens."

Rejecting the plaintiffs' contention that vindication of their constitutional rights required a shifting of the burden of proof in relation to the tort of nuisance, so that it would be for the defendants to show that the emissions did not cause the injuries and damage alleged, he said:

> "So far as I am aware, [Article 40.3.1-2] have never been used in the courts to shape the form of any existing tort or to change the normal onus of proof. The implementation of those constitutional rights is primarily a matter for the State[182] and the courts are entitled to intervene only when there has been a failure to implement or, where the implementation relied on is plainly inadequate, to effectuate the constitutional guarantee in question...A person may of course, in the absence of a common law or statutory cause of action, sue directly for breach of a constitutional right [here he cites *Meskell*]; but when he founds his action on an existing tort he is normally confined to the limitations of that tort. It might be different if it could be shown that the tort in question is basically ineffective to protect his constitutional rights."[183]

In *Hynes-O'Sullivan v O'Driscoll*[184] the same judge invoked the constitutional right to one's good name to buttress an existing element of the tort of defamation - namely, that

[179] [1973] IR 121.
[180] Heuston, "*Personal Rights under the Irish Constitution*" (1976) 11 Ir Jur (n.s.) 205. See also the discussion by Cooney and Kerr, *loc. cit.*
[181] [1988] ILRM 629.
[182] The reference to the State in this context is not entirely clear; perhaps Henchy J was using the term as a synonym for the legislature.
[183] A similar view was taken in *Sweeney v Duggan* [1991] 2 IR 274, where Barron J rejected the claim that an employer had a duty under Article 40.3 to ensure that his employee would be duly compensated for any injury arising out of or in the course of the employment. According to the judge, Article 40.3.2 gave the plaintiff no more than a guarantee of a just law of negligence, which in the circumstances existed.
[184] [1988] IR 436; [1989] ILRM 349.

the defence of qualified privilege does not exist if the person making the communication honestly, but mistakenly, believes that the person receiving it has a duty or interest in receiving it.[185]

Where an existing tort is ineffective to protect constitutional rights, the courts may either modify the definition of the tort or permit the plaintiff to sue directly for infringement of constitutional rights. It has been argued that this choice has significant implications, as the criteria for determining liability for infringement of constitutional rights may not necessarily be identical with those appropriate to tort law.[186] There would appear to be only one example of where the courts took the former action - in *McKinley v The Minister for Defence*[187] a majority of the Supreme Court extended the action for loss of consortium to plaintiff wives in order to avoid difficulties with the constitutional guarantee of equality.

Finally it must be said that judicial analysis of the use of the law of tort to protect constitutional rights is as yet at a somewhat primitive stage and it may be that the courts too readily assume that constitutional rights may be adequately vindicated in this way. However it has been persuasively argued that tort law, with its focus on wrongs, may be basically ineffective to protect rights and that the Constitution may not be an appropriate environment for the operation of principles of tort law dealing with such concepts as remoteness of damage and vicarious liability.[188] These difficult and complex issues have yet to be addressed by the courts.

Locus standi to defend constitutional rights

Until quite recently, it was believed that a plaintiff must show actual or probable injury to himself through breach of his constitutional right;[189] this subject of *locus standi* has been mostly considered in relation to challenges to Acts, but in *Lennon v Ganly*[190] it surfaced where the plaintiff tried to stop the Irish Rugby Football Union from going on a tour to South Africa, saying his personal rights would be infringed by the tour inasmuch as its effects would injure the common good. O'Hanlon J dismissed his action because, *inter alia*, he was:

[185] A similar view was taken by McCarthy J in the same case. In *Walsh v Family Planning Services Ltd.* [1992] 1 IR 498, McCarthy J cautioned against using the personal rights guarantees in Article 40 to "elevate the status of a trifling cause of action", (here, a technical assault), again implicitly saying that the plaintiff should be left to his remedy in tort.

[186] See *Binchy, loc. cit.* A further implication here is that an action for breach of constitutional rights, unlike an action in tort, would not be subject to the limitation periods in the Statute of Limitations 1957. (Note that in *Hayes v Ireland* [1987] ILRM 651, Carroll J held that such an action was not a tortious action for the purpose of the (then) sweeping statutory immunity from such actions afforded to trade unions by s 4 of the Trade Disputes Act 1906.) This is not to say, however, that a plaintiff suing for breach of constitutional rights can afford to sit on his hands indefinitely, for at least one judge, Henchy J accepted that failure to exercise a constitutional right in good time led to forfeiture of that particular right - see below, p. 710.

[187] [1992] 2 IR 333. See below, pp. 713-715.

[188] Binchy, *loc. cit.* The author does suggest, however, that "areas of *immunity* from tortious liability ... are more presumptively close to the parameters of the *Meskell* principle than are principles of *positive* tortious liability", suggesting as a possible explanation for this paradox the fact that public policy tends to feature more strongly in the assessment of immunity issues in contrast to those of liability.

[189] Though this point appears to have been overlooked in a number of cases involving trade unions, where employers obtained injunctions to prevent infringements of the constitutional rights of their employees - see, e.g., *Educational Company of Ireland Ltd. v Fitzpatrick (No.2)* [1961] IR 345; *Murtagh Properties Ltd. v Cleary* [1972] IR 330.

[190] [1981] ILRM 84.

> "not satisfied that the plaintiff has made out a *prima facie* case that any particular damage to his own rights or interests will take place as a result of the tour, over and above the damage which he says it will cause to the good name of Ireland in the international community and to her trading links with some other countries. He does not contend that he has any economic interests personal to himself [or any travel plans which might be endangered]."

However the majority decision of the Supreme Court in *The Society for the Protection of Unborn Children (Ireland) Ltd. v Coogan*[191] sets down a more liberal test of standing for persons seeking to restrain an infringement of constitutional rights, at least in certain circumstances. In that case the plaintiff society sought an injunction to restrain the defendants from publishing information about abortion services in the UK but had their action dismissed by Carroll J in the High Court on the ground that the Attorney General was the proper party to move in the case. A majority of the Supreme Court, however, allowed an appeal, taking the view that *locus standi* was established where the plaintiff had a *bona fide* interest in seeking to vindicate the constitutional right in question - the right to life of the unborn. After distinguishing this case, where the plaintiff sought to restrain a threatened breach of the Constitution by the defendants, from actions challenging the constitutionality of legislation, Finlay CJ said:

> "In such a case [as the present one] I am satisfied that the test is that of a *bona fide* concern and interest, interest being used in the sense of proximity or an objective interest."

Similar language was used by Walsh J who said that the essential question was whether the plaintiff had a "*bona fide* interest to invoke the protection of the courts to vindicate the constitutional right in question."[192] In the instant case, the majority held that the involvement of the plaintiff society in earlier litigation seeking to protect the right to life of the unborn, coupled with the importance and nature of that right which, by definition, could not be invoked by the person in whom it was vested, constituted sufficient ground for holding that the society had the necessary legal standing to bring the action.

The ruling in *Coogan* potentially applies to situations involving persons other than the unborn child, such as infants or persons suffering from mental or physical illness, where the individual is not in a position directly to defend his or her own constitutional rights.[193] However in the vast majority of cases, of course, the victim of the threatened breach of constitutional rights will be in a position to take action to defend his or her interests and in such situations, one expects that the courts may continue to insist that the plaintiff establish actual or likely injury to his or her own rights or interests before allowing an action to proceed.

[191] [1989] IR 734; [1990] ILRM 70. The entire question of *locus standi* is more fully discussed at pp. 434-448.

[192] Of the remaining members of the majority, Hederman J concurred with both the Chief Justice and Walsh J, while Griffin J agreed that in the circumstances of the instant case, the plaintiff society had standing to sue, but refrained from deciding the larger question of what test of standing should be used in relation to the enforcement of constitutional rights generally. The sole dissentient, McCarthy J, held that the Attorney General was the only person who could seek to restrain a breach of constitutional rights by private individuals and that the refusal, by the plaintiff society, of the Attorney General's offer to consider favourably a request for his consent to a relator action disqualified it from having the necessary standing to maintain the proceedings in the instant case.

[193] Article 40.4.2 similarly recognises that an application for an order for release from unlawful detention may be made on behalf of the person detained.

Suspension and forfeiture of constitutional rights

For the position in regard to the suspension of some of the constitutional rights of a person imprisoned on conviction, or otherwise in detention authorised by law, see below, pp. 819-820. That constitutional rights could be forfeited in contexts other than that of imprisonment on conviction was accepted by Henchy J in a number of cases in which he held that failure to exercise a constitutional right in good time led to forfeiture of that right in the particular circumstances of the case.[194]

Exercise of constitutional rights by infants

The constitutional rights of a child under the age of reason are exercised by the choice of its parents or legally recognised guardian, subject, however, to the power of the courts by appropriate proceedings to overrule that choice in the dominant interest of the welfare of the child.[195]

Exercise of constitutional rights by artificial persons

Whether artificial legal persons, such as companies, can rely on the fundamental rights provisions of the Constitution has never been authoritatively decided by the courts. In a number of cases, this issue has been decided *sub silentio* in favour of the company having standing: see, *e.g. Educational Company of Ireland Ltd. v Fitzpatrick*,[196] (freedom of association), *Attorney General for England and Wales v Brandon Book Publishers Ltd.*,[197] (freedom of expression) and *The Attorney General v Hamilton (No.1)*[198] and *(No.2)*[199](right to good name).[200] In one recent case - *Kerry Co-Operative Creameries Ltd. v An Bord Bainne*[201] - an argument advanced on behalf of the plaintiff company based on Article 40.1 was dealt with by Costello J on its merits, though he expressly declined to consider whether bodies corporate could claim the benefit of the guarantee of equality. However in a number of other cases, the view has been taken that certain fundamental rights at least cannot be invoked by corporate bodies. Thus in *Attorney General v Paperlink Ltd.*[202] the parties accepted that the personal rights of Article 40.3 could not be invoked by a company while three High Court judges have held that property rights may be asserted only by humans.[203] One way of resolving the apparent con-

[194] See his decisions in *The State (Byrne) v Frawley* [1978] IR 326, *M v An Bord Uchtála* [1977] IR 287; and *Murphy v AG* [1982] IR 241.

[195] *The State (M.) v Attorney General* [1979] IR 73; *Fajujonu v Minister for Justice* [1990] 2 IR 151, [1990] ILRM 234.

[196] [1961] IR 345

[197] [1986] IR 597; [1987] ILRM 135.

[198] [1992] 2 IR 542; [1992] ILRM 145.

[199] [1993] ILRM 821.

[200] In *A.G. (S.P.U.C. (Ireland) v Open Door Counselling Ltd.* [1988] IR 593; [1989] ILRM 19, an action initiated by a company for the purpose of enforcing the right to life of the unborn was converted into a relator action by the Attorney General, thereby precluding any discussion of the company's *locus standi*. The same company brought a number of other actions in the Irish courts for the same purpose - see *S.P.U.C. (Ireland) Ltd v Coogan*, [1989] IR 734; [1990] ILRM 70; *S.P.U.C. (Ireland) Ltd. v Grogan* [1989] IR 753; [1990] ILRM 350; *S.P.U.C. (Ireland) Ltd. v Grogan (No.2)* [1992] 2 IR 471; *S.P.U.C. (Ireland) Ltd. v Grogan* [1993] 1 CMLR 197. A challenge to the company's *locus standi* in the first *Grogan* case was limited, however, to the question of whether it had a sufficient *bona fide* concern and interest to maintain the suit; no point appears to have been made in relation to its standing *as a body corporate*, though of course in this context the company was not seeking to enforce a fundamental right directly for its own benefit.

[201] [1990] ILRM 664.

[202] [1984] ILRM 373.

[203] Carroll J in *Private Motorists' Provident Society v A.G.* [1983] IR 339; [1984] ILRM 88 (in the subsequent appeal, the Supreme Court decided not to offer any opinion on this issue); Costello J in *Kerry Co-Operative Creameries Ltd. v An Bord Bainne* [1990] ILRM 664; Murphy J in *Chestvale Properties Ltd. v Glackin* [1992] ILRM 221.

tradiction of artificial persons being permitted to rely on the fundamental personal rights of the individual would be to regard the company as agent for its human shareholders. Thus in *Pine Valley Developments Ltd. v Minister for the Environment*[204] Henchy J noted that:

> "when the lands were then purchased, the shareholders in Pine Valley had in the eyes of the law as then understood acquired through their company valuable property rights in the lands."[205]

Of course, an obvious stratagem for avoiding any difficulties in this regard, and one which is invariably followed, is to join an individual shareholder as a co-plaintiff for the purpose of invoking the fundamental rights provisions.

[204] [1987] IR 23; [1987] ILRM 747.

[205] For an interesting discussion of this issue, see Ussher, *Company Law in Ireland* (London, 1986), at pp.53 - 56, in which he argues that, in order to avoid difficulties of double indemnity and of quantification of damages, an action akin to the derivative action should be used to permit a corporation to act as proper plaintiff in respect of unconstitutional conduct adversely affecting other persons in a legal relationship with it.

Article 40.1

EQUALITY BEFORE THE LAW

Personal Rights
Article 40

1. All citizens shall, as human per sons, be held equal before the law. This shall not be held to mean that the State shall not in its enactments have due regard to differences of capacity, physical and moral, and of social function.

Cearta Pearsanta
Airteagal 40

1. Áirítear gurb ionann ina bpearsain daonna na saoránaigh uile i láthair an dlí.
Ach ní intuigthe as sin nach bhféachfaidh an Stát go cuí, ina chuid achtachán, don difríocht atá idir daoine ina mbuanna corpartha agus ina mbuanna morálta agus ina bhfeidhm chomhdhaonnach.

New constitutional provision

The concept of "equality before the law", although a familiar tag in legal and political debate,[1] had not figured before 1937 in the Irish Constitution. In the 1937 Draft Constitution debate, Opposition Deputies had pointed out the small value of a maxim which resisted exact analysis; in replying to them, Mr. de Valera outlined two different meanings attributed to the phrase: firstly, the impartiality of judicial behaviour; secondly, the principle that legislation should not be discriminatory as between classes. He seemed to say that the former value was universally accepted; but that the latter, if badly stated, imposed an impossible standard: differences of capacity and of social function often compelled differing treatment by the law, and the qualification contained in the second sentence of Article 40.1 was intended to recognise this necessity.[2] As the impartiality of the judicial function seems specifically aimed at by Article 34.5 (the declaration required of judges on taking office) and perhaps also Article 35.2, the "equality before the law" prescribed by Article 40.1 has not been considered by the courts in this context, but generally only in the other, i.e. that of legislation.[3]

The second sentence of Article 40.1 makes it plain that the precept expressed by the first is intended to apply to the process of enacting law, and does not merely become operative in the process of applying law already enacted (although the traditional formula "equality before the law" considered purely in its grammatical dimension would suggest

[1] In modern times the precept "equality before the law" appears to go back to the French Declaration of the Rights of Man of 1793: "Tous les hommes sont égaux par la nature et devant la loi." Contemporary commentary on the concept of equality before the law under the Irish Constitution can be found in Temple Lang, "*Private Law Aspects of the Constitution*", (1971) 6 Ir Jur (n.s.) 237; Forde, "*Equality and the Constitution*", (1982) 17 Ir Jur (n.s.) 295; Beytagh, "*Equality under the Irish and American Constitutions: A Comparative Analysis*", (1983) 18 Ir Jur (n.s.) 56, 219; J M. Kelly. "*Equality before the law in three European jurisdictions*", (1983) 18 Ir Jur (n.s.) 259; Curtin, *Irish Employment Equality Law*, (Dublin, 1989) chap 1. Specifically in relation to women and the Constitution, see Scannell, "*The Constitution and the Role of Women*" in *De Valera's Constitution and Ours*, ed. Farrell, (1988), p.123 and Connolly, "The Constitution" in *Gender and the Law in Ireland*, ed. Connolly, (1993), p.4.

[2] 67 *Dáil Debates* 1590ff.

[3] For a statement as to how excessive judicial intervention in the questioning of witnesses may affect the perception of judicial neutrality, see the remarks of McCarthy J in his dissenting judgment in *Donnelly v Timber Factors Ltd.* [1991] 1 IR 553. See also *per* Morris J in *Dineen v Delap*, High Court, 21 October 1993.

that the maxim envisaged "law" as a datum as something already in position - before the equality principle could be deployed, and therefore as something whose own genesis, being chronologically prior, was not to be reviewed on that standard).[4]

Other relevant constitutional articles

Other constitutional articles enjoin the State from discriminatory action in certain specific contexts. Thus Article 40.6.2 provides that laws regulating the manner in which the rights of association and free assembly may be exercised shall contain no political, religious or class discrimination; Article 44.2.3 prohibits the State from imposing any disabilities or making any discrimination on the ground of religious profession, belief or status; while Article 44.2.4 provides that legislation providing State aid for schools shall not, *inter alia*, discriminate between schools under the management of different religious denominations.

The courts have also identified a principle of equality of spouses within marriage implicit in Articles 41 and 42 of the Constitution which has sounded the death-knell for a number of common law rules reflecting a dominant role for the husband. Thus the paternal rule giving the father a permanent right to custody and control of the children's upbringing was declared to be inconsistent with the Constitution as early as the 1950s in *In re Tilson, infants*.[5] In 1981 the common law defence of marital coercion available to a wife who had committed an offence in the presence of her husband suffered a similar fate - *The State (Director of Public Prosecutions) v Walsh*[6] - as did the rule of dependent domicile a decade later - *W. v W.*[7] Two common law rules of evidence have also been affected by this principle - in *S. v S.*[8] the rule that a wife could not give evidence that her husband was not the father of her child was declared to be inconsistent with the Constitution, while in *The People (Director of Public Prosecutions) v T.*[9] the Court of Criminal Appeal held that the rule preventing one spouse from being a competent witness against the other - the origins of which lay partly in the traditional view that, upon marriage, the legal existence of the wife was incorporated and consolidated into that of her husband - could not prevail against the right of an individual to be protected against attack by another family member.[10]

In all of the foregoing cases on marital equality, equality was achieved through the abolition or restriction of the discriminatory rule in question. However in a recent case, *McKinley v The Minister for Defence*,[11] a majority of the Supreme Court held that the

[4] This question received some notice in Germany, where Article 3 of the Constitution ("Basic Law") of 1949 contains the principle of equality before the law in a grammatical vesture identical with that employed in Article 40.1. The consensus has been that the principle applies to the law-making process, partly because the Constitution specifically commands the legislature to respect fundamental rights (of which the equality precept forms part), but partly because the principle is seen as a "supra-positive principle of law", something that in Ireland might have been called "antecedent and superior to positive law". See J M. Kelly, *loc. cit.* wherein he compared the positions reached by the courts in interpreting the principle in Ireland, Germany and Italy (where, again, it appears in the Constitution of 1947 in the traditional grammatical shape). This study was inspired by the appearance in *Murphy v Attorney General* [1982] IR 241, apparently for the first time in Irish constitutional litigation, of citations of German and Italian decisions.

[5] [1951] IR 1; (1952) 86 ILTR 49. See below, pp. 1041-1042.

[6] [1981] IR 412.

[7] [1993] 2 IR 476; [1993] ILRM 294. See below, pp. 1018-1020. This decision had been anticipated by Barr J in *M.(C). v M.(T.)* [1988] ILRM 456 and [1990] 2 IR 52; [1991] ILRM 268.

[8] [1983] IR 68.

[9] (1988) 3 Frewen 141. See *C. Jackson*, (1989) 11 DULJ (n.s.) 149.

[10] The presumption of advancement, whereby property advanced by a husband to his wife is presumed to have been given as a gift, free from any resulting trusts, must also be constitutionally dubious, given that it, too, is based on the common law understanding of marriage.

[11] [1992] 2 IR 333. See *Hogan*, (1992) 14 DULJ (n.s.) 115.

effect of the principle of equality of spouses was to extend the benefit of the common law rule to the wife. The plaintiff's husband suffered serious injuries in an explosion, one of the consequences of which was that he was rendered impotent. In a claim taken by the plaintiff against her husband's employer, the Minister for Defence, she claimed compensation for, *inter alia*, loss of consortium. At common law, this action was available only to the husband, a position which the Supreme Court unanimously agreed was inconsistent with the guarantee of equality in Article 40.1. However the Court divided on the question of how to respond to this inconsistency. A majority - Hederman, McCarthy and O'Flaherty JJ. - took the view that the defect should be remedied in a positive manner, by extending the action to wives, while the minority - Finlay CJ and Egan J - thought that the solution was to abolish the action entirely.

The reasoning of two members of the majority - Hederman and O'Flaherty JJ - was somewhat generalised and, indeed, verged on the rhetorical. Hederman J concluded that the status afforded to marriage and to married women in particular by Article 41, read in the light of the declaration in the Preamble that one of the objectives of the Constitution was to assure "the dignity and freedom of the individual", compelled the Court to accept the extension of the action to wives, while O'Flaherty J came to the same conclusion, based on the guarantee of equality, the special recognition afforded to marriage by the Constitution and the constitutional prohibition on divorce. The invocation of such amorphous concepts as the status of marriage or the dignity and freedom of the individual does not lend itself to particularly compelling reasoning and it is difficult to discern its limits. If the dignity, freedom and constitutional status of married women warrants the recognition of their right to sue for loss of consortium, why does it not also guarantee wives a share in the matrimonial home?[12] At the end of the day, one is left with the impression of rhetoric disguising judicial policy-making.

The third member of the majority, McCarthy J, attempted to formulate a general proposition justifying the decision to extend the scope of the action for loss of consortium. He said:

> "[W]here a common law rule offends against the principle of equality in a marriage relationship, the solution is to identify and declare the equality by positive rather than negative action. Whatever the origin of a particular common law right, however artificial its base as viewed from a modern standpoint, if, as here, such a right is so firmly established as part of the common law, equality among equals requires a Court declaration to that effect, rather than what would be judicial legislation by denying such a claim to the husband."

This proposition is not without its difficulties. In the first place, the fact that a rule is firmly established as part of the common law has not prevented the courts from declaring it to be unconstitutional, nor should it. This is so, even where the rule offends against the principle of equality in marriage and indeed it has been pointed out that, in relation to some of those rules at least, such as the rule of dependent domicile, "positive" judicial action would be impossible.[13] Second, it is not easy to see why the courts should have the luxury of engaging in positive action to remedy inequalities within marriage created by common law rules when they have eschewed such an approach in relation to legislative inequalities.[14] Finally, McCarthy J in common with the other members

[12] *L. v L.* [1992] 2 IR 77; [1992] ILRM 115. See below, pp. 1010-1012.
[13] *Hogan, loc. cit.*
[14] See *Somjee v Minister for Justice* [1981] ILRM 324; *Mhic Mhathúna v Ireland* [1989] IR 504. In some other jurisdictions, the courts are content to identify the inequality and then leave it to the legislature to decide how to remedy the situation - see, e.g. the decision of the German Constitutional Court in the *Judicial Salaries*

of the majority, fails to deal adequately with the argument that Article 50 ties the hands of the courts in this context, by directing them to declare a common law rule which is admittedly unconstitutional, to be null and void, rather than allowing it to be saved through a process of judicial legislation.[15]

This last point, in fact, formed the basis for the dissenting opinion of Finlay CJ. After quoting Article 50.1, he said:

> "That provision cannot, in my view, be construed as imposing...upon the Court an obligation as far as possible to amend or alter common law rights existing and in force in Saorstát Éireann at the date of the passing of the Constitution so as to make them comply with the Constitution."

This certainly seems to accord with the meaning of Article 50.1 which saves those laws already in existence at the date of the coming into operation of the Constitution which are consistent with the Constitution. It is difficult to see how the original common law action for loss of consortium could have passed this test.

The remaining judge - Egan J - did not share the views of the Chief Justice as to the effect of Article 50 inasmuch as he refused to rule out the possibility that the courts could create a right of action in order to protect the constitutionality of another law, but he took the view that such action was inappropriate in respect of loss of consortium which he characterised as anomalous and grounded on a concept of the wife which would be regarded as anathema in the present day.

The rather amorphous reasoning of the majority, coupled with the failure to address the argument based on Article 50 are, it is submitted, significant flaws in this decision and it remains to be seen whether *McKinley* will survive future judicial scrutiny to become the harbinger of a more robust judicial attitude to the matter of remedies available to rectify constitutional inequalities.

In one further case, *O'G. v Attorney General*[16] a statutory provision, s 5 of the Adoption Act 1974, which prevented childless widowers from adopting while imposing no similar disability on widows, was declared to be unconstitutional in the face of evidence indicating that no rational basis underpinned this distinction.

The principle of equality of spouses within marriage has its limitations, however - in *L. v L.*[17] the Supreme Court rejected the contention that the principle of community property within marriage was mandated by Article 41.2, invoking in support of this conclusion the doctrine of separation of powers.

Finally, the recent judgment of Denham J in *Howard v The Commission of Public Works in Ireland*[18] implies that the guarantee of equality in Article 40.1 is only part

case, BVerfGE 26, 100 (1969) where, having held that the disparity in the salaries payable to the judges of the Labour Court in contrast to those of the judges of the Administrative Court was contrary to the equality provisions of Article 3 of the Basic Law, the Court left it to the Bundestag to decide whether the higher salaries should be reduced or the lower salaries increased.

[15] Neither McCarthy nor O'Flaherty JJ addressed this issue at all, while Hederman J simply declared, without elaboration, that Article 50 was not of relevance to the case.

[16] [1985] ILRM 61. See below, p. 1029.

[17] [1992] 2 IR 77; [1992] ILRM 115. See below, pp. 1010-1012.

[18] [1993] ILRM 665.

(albeit a significant part) of a general constitutional concept of equality, the origins of which she did not identify, but whose content may be informed by doctrine of separation of powers. She said:

> "On the one hand this concept [of equality] means that all citizens as human persons are equal before the law, though the State may, in its enactments, have due regard to differences of capacity, physical and moral, and of social function. This right to equality is one of the personal rights of citizens.
>
> In addition to recognising the right to equality of citizens, the concept of equality includes the concept that, in the execution of their power, the organs of government shall act with due regard to the concept of equality. Thus, while accepting that there may be specific exceptions, in general the position of a citizen, as a person, should not be lesser than a "person" in the form of a body corporate, of whatever status."

She went on to hold that the presumption against the application of legislation to the State was contrary to this notion of equality.

Addressees of the equality principle

The question of who are the intended addressees of the equality principle has so far escaped specific consideration by the courts. Litigation on the section, so far, shows that it is primarily conceived of as a precept addressed to the State, and that individuals in their private business relationships etc. are not thought of as affected by it (though they may, of course, be affected by legislation specifically aimed at excluding certain kinds of discrimination, such as the Employment Equality Act 1977, forbidding sex discrimination in the treatment of employees[19]). Any overall requirement that individuals should treat one another equally would be unworkable as well as an encroachment on personal liberty.[20] Yet the question is worthy of authoritative judicial treatment, however predictable its result might be. In the only two cases in which an attempt was made to deploy the constitutional equality principle against activities other than those of the State - against trade union officials, in *Murtagh Properties v Cleary*[21] and against a co-operative in *Kerry Co-Operative Creameries Ltd. v An Bord Bainne Co-Operative Ltd.*[22] - the question whether Article 40.1 had any role in such a context was not noticed.[23] Certainly in the former type of case, even if not in private relationships generally, there is something to be said for extending the reach of the equality precept beyond the organs of the State; and there is a clear precedent in *Meskell v C.I.É.*[24] for imputing to trade unions the duty to respect the constitutional rights of others. If, for instance, the right to work is a "personal right" in the sense of Article 40.3, as the courts have held it to be, it could be said that the courts are bound to vindicate it whoever infringes it, so that if it is infringed through a discriminatory trade union practice, the State could be seen as obliged, through its judicial arm, to repress the discrimination. And it is worth noting that in

[19] As to which, see *Curtin, op.cit.*

[20] In Germany the general view is that the equality guarantee can bind only the State, and that any attempt to force its application as between private or non-State interests (i.e. its so-called *Drittwirkung*, or operation on third parties) would fatally conflict with the prime constitutional value of individuals' liberty. See *Kelly, loc. cit.*

[21] [1972] IR 330.

[22] [1990] ILRM 664 (HC); [1991] ILRM 851 (SC).

[23] Except insofar as Costello J in the *Kerry Co-Op.* case reserved his opinion as to whether bodies corporate could claim the benefit of Article 40.1 - [1990] ILRM 664 at 717.

[24] [1973] IR 121: see below, pp. 980-981. Of course this proposition could be got on its feet only if the Courts changed their minds about the significance of the phrase "as human persons as restricting the application of the equality principle; see below, pp. 719-724.

The State (Lynch) v Cooney[25] Henchy J suggested, *obiter*, that if Radio Telefís Éireann were to discriminate unfairly in the allotment of broadcasting time for party political broadcasts, it would be in breach of Article 40.1.

Does the guarantee bind all arms of the State in the same way? - the judiciary

Another problem is this: does the equality precept, in its application to the State, bind all the arms of the State in the same way? It is quite clear that the principle does bind the judiciary - indeed the essence of the principle is impossible to detach from the general notion of justice, the administration of which is envisaged by Article 34 - and this has been expressly acknowledged by the courts on at least three occasions.[26] In *The People (Attorney General) v O'Driscoll*,[27] which arose from an allegation by defendants in a criminal trial that they had been discriminated against because they were travellers, Walsh J in the Court of Criminal Appeal said:

> "A complaint made about the conduct of the trial was that the judge in some way permitted the fact that the applicants were itinerants to creep into the evidence or to colour the case in a way which has caused them to be the objects of discrimination at the trial. Needless to say, if any such position were disclosed in the transcript or otherwise established to the satisfaction of this Court, the conviction would be quashed without hesitation on the grounds that the trial violated the provisions of Article 40.1".

(Nothing of the kind was, however, disclosed.) An application of the equality precept in the context of legal proceedings may be seen in *McMahon v Leahy*,[28] where, in proceedings arising from an extradition request, the State attempted to contest a prisoner's claim that he was entitled to the benefit of the "political offence" exemption, despite not having contested similar claims earlier made by other prisoners wanted for extradition for exactly the same offence (a mass jail-break). The Supreme Court refused to allow the State to controvert his plea, O'Higgins CJ saying:

> "If the State succeeded, four citizens whose arrest had been sought by the Northern Ireland authorities, and who had been involved in the same escape as a fifth person, would have been held by the Courts, in interpreting the law, to be politically exempt, while the fifth person, in respect of whom no different considerations applied, would have been held not to be exempt. In such circumstances, could it be said that all these five citizens had been held equal before the law? This obligation to provide equal treatment for citizens of the State is ordained by Article 40. It is the clear duty of the Court to see that this obligation is discharged."

The principle here was later stated summarily by Henchy J in *The State (Keegan) v Stardust Victims Compensation Tribunal*[29] when, referring to *McMahon's* case, he said:

[25] [1982] IR 337; [1983] ILRM 89.

[26] See further below, FN 55. To the extent to which Article 40.1 has been applied to common law rules, this might be seen as the courts enforcing the equality precept on themselves, by way of notionally directing themselves to disregard rules the application of which would infringe the principle. In one recent case, *The Society for the Protection of Unborn Children (Ireland) Ltd. v Grogan (No.3)* [1993] 1 CMLR 197, it was argued, unsuccessfully, that a judicial ban on the dissemination of information about abortion services abroad infringed Article 40.1 inasmuch as, under EC law, it could not apply to persons formally associated with foreign clinics providing such services. Morris J dismissed the claim on the ground that the Supreme Court decision in this area - *A.G. (S.P.U.C.(Ireland) Ltd.) v Open Door Counselling Ltd.* [1988] IR 593; [1989] ILRM 19 - admitted of no such distinction. He did not deal with the question of whether or to what extent the courts are bound by Article 40.1.

[27] 1 Frewen 351.

[28] [1984] IR 525; [1984] ILRM 423.

[29] [1986] IR 642; [1987] ILRM 202.

> "I would accept that Article 40.1 of the Constitution requires that people who appear before the Courts in essentially the same circumstances should be dealt with in essentially the same manner." [30]

A shared characteristic of all of these cases is that the application of the principle of equality has been accepted without any consideration of whether the "essential attributes of the human person"[31] are affected by the particular discrimination complained of.

The executive

The application of the principle of equality to the legislature is also clear; but what about executive authorities, or authorities which, whether primarily executive or not, are authorised by the legislature to lay down general rules, i.e. to create "subordinate legislation"? In *East Donegal Co-Operative v Attorney General*[32] the Supreme Court, *per* Walsh J, fastened on the second sentence of Article 40.1 as indicating that the whole section was aimed only at the Oireachtas. Confronted with a provision of the Livestock Marts Act 1967, which purported to enable the Minister for Agriculture, if he thought fit, to "grant exemption from the provisions of this Act in respect of the carrying on of any particular business or business of any particular class or kind", the Court said:

> "The constitutional right of the Oireachtas in its legislation to take account of difference of social function and difference of capacity, physical and moral, does not extend to delegating that power to members of the Executive, to the exclusion of the Oireachtas, in order to decide as between individuals (all of whom are, by the terms of an Act bound by it) which of them shall be exempted from the application of the Act..."

This view rests on regarding the words "the State in its enactments" in Article 40.1 as equivalent to "the Oireachtas".[33] Although the word "enact" (and the corresponding "achtú", from which "achtachán" in the Irish version of Article 40.1 derives) are used in the forefront of Acts of the Oireachtas, and although these words are not officially used of the making of subordinate legislation, the words "the State in its enactments" should have been understood more broadly. The Constitution frequently speaks specifically of the "Oireachtas", and of "law" or "laws" rather than the State's "enactments", when contemplating legislative elaboration or qualification of constitutional provisions by the National Parliament, and its avoidance of this usage here might seem to intend to include, within the field of application of Article 40.1, the making of ministerial etc. rules and orders as well as of statutes in the proper sense. The Supreme Court's interpretation here would also logically mean that a subordinate authority, when engaged in making regulations etc., would not be covered by the concession in the second sentence of Article 40.1 as to the legitimacy of differentiating in response to differences of capacity and social function; yet in *Dillane v Ireland*[34] the Court, speaking by Henchy J,

[30] In *The People (D.P.P.) v O'Shea* [1982] IR 384, the same judge, in his dissenting opinion, thought that a law which had the effect that acquittals in the Central Criminal Court were appealable by the prosecution and acquittals in the Circuit Court non-appealable, would breach Article 40.1. He followed this up with a remark in *The People (D.P.P.) v Quilligan (No.2)* [1989] IR 46, that a statutory jurisdiction to order a retrial in a case of acquittal on indictment would be of questionable constitutionality - having regard to the principle of equality before the law - if it unequally and selectively applied only to appeals from the Central Criminal Court. (See now s 11 of the Criminal Procedure Bill 1993, which proposes to abolish the right of appeal against acquittals by the Central Criminal Court.)

[31] See below, pp. 719-722.

[32] [1970] IR 317; (1970) 104 ILTR 81.

[33] A similar view would appear to be implicit in the unanimous decision of the Supreme Court in *McGimpsey v Ireland* [1990] 1 IR 110; [1990] ILRM 440, that the Anglo-Irish Agreement was not a "law" within the meaning of Article 40.1.

[34] [1980] ILRM 167. The German and Italian equality guarantees are taken to bind all the arms of the State: see *Kelly, loc. cit.*

recognised that the District Court Rules Committee had been "well within the law-making discretion allowed by Article 40.1" in differentiating (on a basis which the Court held to be one of "social function") between an ordinary common informer and a member of the Garda Síochána in the matter of an award of costs.[35]

The only authority to date in which the application of the concept of equality (though not necessarily Article 40.1) to the executive appears to have been fully considered is that of *Howard v Commissioners of Public Works in Ireland.*[36] In the Supreme Court, Denham J said that, in arriving at her conclusion that the presumption against the application of statutes to the State had not survived the enactment of the Constitution, she had had regard to the concept of equality. She continued:

> "On the one hand this concept means that all citizens as human persons are equal before the law, though the State may, in its enactments, have due regard to differences of capacity, physical and moral and of social function. This right to equality is one of the personal rights of citizens.
>
> In addition to recognising the right to equality of citizens, the concept of equality includes the concept that, in the execution of their power, the organs of government shall act with due regard to the concept of equality. Thus, while accepting that there may be specific exceptions, in general the position of a citizen, as a person, should not be lesser than a "person" in the form of a body corporate, of whatever status.
>
> This concept of equality, allied to the doctrine of the separation of powers, and to the absence of any specific provision in the Constitution to give the executive a special position in relation to the legislature, convinces me that the executive has no special position. Thus, in legislating in accordance with the Constitution, the Oireachtas legislates for all, and that includes the executive."[37]

Beneficiaries of the guarantee - "essential attributes of the human personality"

The question of who are the intended beneficiaries of the equality guarantee - unlike the foregoing question about its addressees - has been expressly considered by the courts, with what must seem a very unsatisfactory result.[38] The courts have seized on the phrase "as human persons", and have used it in order to limit the range of the equality precept to contexts in which the discrimination, or alleged discrimination, relates to what the courts seem to view as essential rather than contingent features of a citizen's existence. This conception of equality as bearing only on the rudimentary human personality emerged for the first time in *Macauley v Minister for Posts and Telegraphs*,[39] in which the plaintiff, though successful on another ground, failed to persuade Kenny J that Article 40.1 was infringed by the provision of s 2 of the Ministers and Secretaries Act 1924, requiring the *fiat* of the Attorney General before a Minister could be sued. The judge said

[35] In *McHugh v Commissioner of the Garda Síochána* [1985] ILRM 606, while the Supreme Court did not mention Article 40.1, the judgment of Costello J in the High Court proceeded on the basis that the section did apply to the Garda Síochána (Discipline) Regulations, 1971, thus suggesting - with *Dillane's* case but unlike the *East Donegal Co-Operative* case - that subordinate legislation as well as Acts of the Oireachtas are comprehended in the word "law" in the section. See also *Devaney v Minister for Agriculture*, High Court, 22 March 1979.

[36] [1993] ILRM 665.

[37] A similar view was expressed by Finlay CJ, who cited the Indian case of *State of West Bengal v Corporation of Calcutta* [1967] ALL IR 997 in support of this view.

[38] Though for evidence of a possible judicial re-appraisal of this development, see below, pp. 723-24.

[39] [1966] IR 345.

"The answer to the plaintiff's complaint in relation to equality before the law is that the guarantee in the Constitution of equality before the law relates to the position of the citizen as a human person. The fiat is required only when a Minister is being sued as a Minister, not when he is being sued as a human person. The Act of 1924 deals with actions taken against a Minister as a corporation sole...It follows, I think, that the necessity... to get the fiat is not an infringement of the guarantee..."

In 1970, in *East Donegal Co-Operative v Attorney General,*[40] the Supreme Court, speaking by Walsh J, held invalid a provision of the Livestock Marts Act 1967, which purported to enable the Minister for Agriculture to exempt from the Act's application "any particular business", seeing this as a potential discrimination between individuals; but held valid a similar power in respect of "businesses of any particular class or kind", saying that:

"this primarily does not involve the making of a distinction between citizens but rather permits the making of a distinction which would benefit or otherwise affect all businesses of the particular class or kind involved."

The reasoning of the Court here seems rather muddled, since an exemption affecting a particular class or kind of business might be just as unfair and injurious to the individuals owning businesses outside the exempted class as if the exemption were constructed as benefiting individual businesses; but, apart from this weakness, the judgment can be seen as another stage on the road towards the present restrictive understanding of Article 40.1 inasmuch as the Court appeared to say it could avail only individuals.[41]

This process was virtually completed by the Court in *Quinn's Supermarket v Attorney General*.[42] This case mainly turned on the prohibition of Article 44.2.3 against religious discrimination; but the plaintiffs had also pleaded Article 40.1. The Court held this section inapplicable to the case. Walsh J, with whom Ó Dálaigh CJ and Budd and FitzGerald JJ agreed, said:

"This provision is not a guarantee of absolute equality for all citizens in all circumstances but it is a guarantee of equality as human persons and (as the Irish text of the Constitution makes quite clear) is a guarantee related to their dignity as human beings and a guarantee against any inequalities grounded upon an assumption, or indeed a belief, that some individual or individuals or classes of individuals, by reason of their human attributes or their ethnic or racial, social or religious background, are to be treated as the inferior or superior of other individuals in the community. This list does not pretend to be complete,[43] but it is merely intended to illustrate the view that this guarantee refers to human persons for what they are in themselves rather than to any lawful activities, trades or pursuits which they may engage in or follow. Furthermore, it need scarcely be pointed out that under no possible construction of the constitutional guarantee could a body corporate or any entity but a human being be considered to be a human person for the purpose of this provision. In my view this provision has no bearing whatsoever upon the point to be considered in the present case, as no question of human equality or inequality aris-

[40] [1970] IR 317; (1970) 104 ILTR 81.

[41] Though see now the decision of Costello J in *Kerry Co-Operative Creameries Ltd. v An Bord Bainne*, [1990] ILRM 664, which left open the possibility that bodies corporate might be able to invoke the guarantee.

[42] [1972] IR 1.

[43] In both *O'Donovan v A.G.* [1961] IR 114 and *McKenna v An Taoiseach*, High Court, 8 June 1992, Budd and Costello JJ respectively understood Article 40.1 to guarantee equality in the exercise of the franchise, though in neither case is there any reference to the concept of the human personality. (The earlier of these two cases, of course, pre-dated the emergence of the relevance of this concept to Article 40.1 in *Macauley*.)

es. It is also quite clear that the provision cannot be invoked to support the terms of the Order of 1948 [which was under challenge] by reference to differences of capacity, physical or moral, and of social function.[44]

The idea that a body corporate could not invoke Article 40.1 reappears, though in a much weaker form, in *Abbey Films Ltd. v Attorney General*,[45] in which Kenny J, speaking for the Supreme Court, said, on the question whether it was an unconstitutional discrimination to provide that a company must appear, in certain proceedings, by a solicitor, while a citizen might appear in person:

> "Even if Article 40.1 were to be held to be applicable to a company (which the Court refrains from deciding), the nature of a company and its difference of capacity from that of an individual are such as would justify [the differing treatment]."[46]

Soon after the *Quinn's Supermarket* case Kenny J tried *Murtagh Properties v Cleary*,[47] in which the plaintiffs submitted that the defendant trade unionists (who were picketing their premises to induce them to dismiss female bar attendants) were aiming, in effect, to infringe what they said was an equal right to earn one's livelihood irrespective of sex. Kenny J held against them on this submission (though in favour of them on others), saying that Article 40.1 was

> "not a guarantee that all citizens shall be treated by the law as equal for all purposes, but it means that they shall, as human persons, be held equal before the law. It relates to their essential attributes as persons, those features which make them human beings. It has, in my opinion, nothing to do with their trading activities or with the conditions on which they are employed.

This approach was again endorsed by Pringle J in the High Court in *de Búrca v Attorney General*[48] (he was of course bound to follow the Supreme Court's line, but showed no reluctance to do so); and by the Supreme Court itself, again speaking by Kenny J, in *Murphy v Attorney General*.[49] The only evidence to date of any judicial discomfort in this matter is provided by some oblique expressions used by Barrington J in the High Court in *Brennan v Attorney General*,[50] when he pointed out that Article 40.1 is concerned with human beings in society, and delicately said that he understood the Supreme Court to have tacitly acknowledged this in *de Búrca's* case by finding the 1927 Juries Act unconstitutional for discrimination although the basis of the discrimination had no connection with the essential human nature of citizens excluded from jury service. However this judicial hint that too much might be read out of the words "as human persons" was overlaid later by the Supreme Court on appeal.[51] O'Higgins CJ, speaking for the Court, re-stated and re-affirmed the restrictive doctrine enunciated in the *Quinn's Supermarket* case:

[44] Kenny J (sitting as a member of the Supreme Court) spoke to the same effect, saying the guarantee of Article 40.1 "does not relate to trading activities or to the hours during which persons may carry on business for neither of these is connected with the essentials of the concept of human personality."

[45] [1981] IR 158.

[46] See the similar approach of Costello J in *Kerry Co-Operative Creameries Ltd. v An Bord Bainne*, [1990] ILRM 664, where he explicitly put to one side the question as to whether bodies corporate could invoke Article 40.1, holding on the facts of that case that no invidious discrimination had been made out.

[47] [1972] IR 330.

[48] [1976] IR 38; (1977) 111 ILTR 37.

[49] [1982] IR 241. See also *Condon v Minister for Labour*, unreported, High Court, 11 June 1980, in which McWilliam J said an Act preventing excessive wage increases for bank officials was not "based on any facet of human personality", but on the legislature's view that it was necessary for the common good.

[50] [1983] ILRM 449.

[51] [1984] ILRM 355.

> "In the view of the Court, a complaint that a system of taxation imposed on occupiers of land... has proved to be unfair, even arbitrary or unjust, is not cognisable under the provisions of Article 40.1. This section deals, and deals only, with the citizen as a human person; and requires for each citizen, as a human person, equality before the law...The inequality...in this case does not concern [the plaintiffs'] treatment as human persons. It concerns the manner in which as occupiers and owners of land their property is rated and taxed. Each person who owns or occupies the land in question will be treated in exactly the same way because the tax is related not to the person but to the land which, irrespective of who he may be, he occupies."[52]

The difficulty with the dominant view is, firstly, that it seems to attribute to human personality an unrealistically small ambit, and, secondly, that it involves in turn a discrimination between a human person acting independently of any juristic personality, and a human person or a number of human persons, who for a particular purpose have availed of a facility offered by the law, namely, the formation of a juristic personality which he or they sustain and which could not exist without them (or without succeeding further human personalities). On the first point it could be plausibly said that if (as the courts have held) rights such as the right to work, to earn a livelihood, to choose and follow a profession or career, are natural personal rights, they are such because the ordinary conditions of the world, in which the human personality has to exist, impose necessities on that personality to which working, earning a livelihood, following a career etc. are a response; the same can be said, with only a very slight expansion of these rights, of engaging in business, acquiring property (the "external goods" which Article 43 recognises man has a natural right to own) and negotiating ancillary trading and working conditions. If all such matters are subtracted from the concept of "human person", not much remains; so that it seems more satisfactory to understand that expression in Article 40.1 as visualising the complex of activities which human existence for most people involves On the second point, it is enough to contrast one citizen who (say) trades under his own name, as an individual, with another who trades through a corporate personality. There may be several contexts in which this difference will amount to a difference of capacity or function such as to explain a statutory regulation which treats them variously; but to declare the constitutional guarantee of equality generally ousted in such a case seems to give it too limited a value. The restriction of its application to "man" qualified only by race, religion, social position and not much else seems to put a constitutional premium on his remaining so far as possible in a state of nature.[53]

[52] This reasoning was subsequently followed by the Supreme Court again in *Madigan v A.G.* [1986] ILRM 136, and by Murphy J in *Greene v Minister for Agriculture* [1990] 2 IR 117; [1990] ILRM 364, and *Browne v A.G.* [1991] 2 IR 58.

[53] The position reached in Ireland, on the mere strength of a narrow interpretation of the phrase "as human persons", should be contrasted with that reached in Germany and Italy in respect of the "equality before the law" guarantee in the Constitutions of those countries. In both jurisdictions it has been for many years clear that juristic as well as natural persons are entitled to the benefit of the rule: and (in Germany) that even groups with no legal personality, such as political parties, may rely on it. The concise reasoning of the Italian Constitutional Court in a case about associations for the assistance of disabled persons may be cited: "An unjustified discrimination between the different associations must inevitably have repercussions on the legal sphere of the members, and so must amount, even if only indirectly, to a violation of the equality of the citizen" (Corte constituzionale 1966/25). It is true that this conclusion is facilitated by Article 2 of the Constitution, which guarantees the inviolable rights of man "whether as an individual, or in the social formations in which his personality unfolds": but this is simply a handsome pleonasm. The very word "citizen" carries within it the recognition that the subjects of the legal system exist within a society. See *Kelly, loc. cit.*

Decline of the "human personality" doctrine?

While the judiciary have never expressly re-acted to this criticism of the "human personality" doctrine,[54] there is some evidence to suggest that it may be falling out of favour, though at this point it is too early to predict its demise with confidence. In the first place, it is worth noting that the doctrine has never been applied in cases touching on the administration of justice.[55] Second, in a series of cases concerning spouses, the principle of equality, admittedly derived in part from Article 41 rather than Article 40.1,[56] has been applied in a variety of contexts without any judicial consideration of whether the essential attributes of the human person are implicated.[57] Third, notwithstanding earlier cases like *Macauley v Minister for Post and Telegraphs*,[58] *Quinn's Supermarket v Attorney General*[59] and *Murtagh Properties Ltd. v Cleary*,[60] there is some evidence, admittedly still slight, that equality arguments will be entertained where the impugned classification affects a constitutional right - see, in particular, the Supreme Court decisions in *Cox. v Ireland*,[61] concerning the right to earn a livelihood and the right to private property, and *The People (Director of Public Prosecutions) v Quilligan (No.3)*,[62] concerning personal liberty. Finally, and perhaps most significantly, there would appear to be a growing tendency on the part of some judges to deal with equality issues on their merits, as it were, rather than side-stepping them through reliance on the "human personality" doctrine. So, for example, while the doctrine has been relied on to neutralise equality arguments in the context of fiscal policy in cases such as *Brennan v Attorney General*;[63] *Greene v Minister for Agriculture*;[64] and *Browne v Attorney General*[65] - in the last two cases, by the same judge, Murphy J - in other cases arising in the same context, such as *Dennehy v Minister for Social Welfare*[66] and *MhicMhathúna v Ireland*,[67] the judges involved faced up squarely to the equality issues presented to them.[68] In the light

[54] Except Murphy J who, in *Greene v Minister for Agriculture* [1990] 2 IR 17; [1990] ILRM 364, declined an invitation to adopt the wider interpretation of Article 40.1 contended for in the second edition of this work on the ground that he was precluded from doing so by *Murphy v A.G.* [1982] IR 241 (though he also implied that the wider interpretation would present unspecified difficulties for the courts).

[55] In addition to the cases listed above, pp. 717-718, see also *de Búrca v A.G.* [1976] IR 38; (1977) 111 ILTR 37; *Dillane v Ireland* [1980] ILRM 167; *The State (D.P.P.) v Walsh* [1981] IR 412; *O'Shea v D.P.P.* [1988] IR 655 and *Mapp v Gilhooley* [1991] 2 IR 253, in each of which arguments grounded on Article 40.1 and relating to various aspects of the forensic system were entertained by the courts without any advertence to the "human personality" doctrine.

[56] Though Hederman J in *W. v W.* [1993] 2 IR 476;[1993] ILRM 294, based his decision that the rule of dependent domicile of a married woman did not survive the enactment of the Constitution squarely on Article 40.1.

[57] See above, pp. 713-715.

[58] [1966] IR 345.

[59] [1972] IR 1.

[60] [1972] IR 330.

[61] [1992] 2 IR 503.

[62] Supreme Court, 14 July 1992.

[63] [1984] ILRM 355.

[64] [1990] 2 IR 17; [1990] ILRM 364.

[65] [1991] 2 IR 58.

[66] High Court, 26 July 1984.

[67] [1989] IR 504.

[68] Indeed in one case arising in the context of commercial transactions, Costello J entertained a complaint of unlawful discrimination advanced on behalf of two companies, while reserving his opinion as to whether corporate personalities could enjoy the benefit of Article 40.1 - see *Kerry Co-Operative Creameries Ltd. v An Bord Bainne* [1990] ILRM 664. The Supreme Court did not explicitly deal with this point in the subsequent appeal - [1991] ILRM 851.

of these developments, an authoritative re-appraisal of the human personality doctrine may not be far off.[69]

THE CRITERION OF EQUALITY BEFORE THE LAW

The interpretation of the criterion of equality before the law, as it is applied by the courts in judicial review of legislation, is peculiarly difficult; as Barrington J said in *Brennan v Attorney General*,[70] it is "probably the most difficult and elusive concept contained in the Constitution". It is proposed, not simply to present the Irish case material - which, as the courts have not yet elaborated a clear set of working principles, offers a curiously disorganised picture of largely instinctive judgments, scarcely classifiable except in relation to their outcome, whether upholding or invalidating the impugned legislation - but to put forward dogmatically a number of such working principles (some of them suggested by continental European practice) for which either some support can be found in elements of the Irish decisions, or good reasons appear to offer justification, whether the Irish courts have been silent so far on the point, or have even gone in an opposite direction.

(a) Equality does not mean uniformity; laws may legitimately differentiate, and in some situations justice requires that they must do so

The courts have several times said that Article 40.1 does not mean that any legislative scheme must present identical features to all citizens: such a mechanical uniformity, in failing to appreciate the existence of categories naturally different (in the senses relevant to the purpose of the legislation) would work inequality in its result, rather than equality. Thus in *The State (Nicolaou) v An Bord Uchtála*[71] Walsh J, speaking for the Supreme Court, said:

> "In the opinion of the Court Article 40.1 is not to be read as a guarantee or undertaking that all citizens shall be treated by the law as equal for all purposes, but rather as an acknowledgement of the human equality of all citizens and that such equality will be recognised in the laws of the State. The section itself in its [second sentence recognises] that inequality may or must result from some special abilities or from some deficiency or from some special need and it is clear that the Article does not either envisage or guarantee equal measure in all things to all citizens. To do so regardless of the factors mentioned would be inequality..."

Two other cases in which the Supreme Court again emphasised that equality before the law does not mean uniformity may be mentioned. In *The State (Hartley) v Governor of Mountjoy Prison*[72] the Supreme Court refused to condemn the provisions of the Extradition Act 1965, which set up distinct regimes of extradition depending on whether it was sought to the United Kingdom or to some other country; the part of the Act governing extradition elsewhere than to the UK afforded the person concerned, as the Supreme Court agreed, "more extensive privileges or safeguards". But the Court said (*per* Ó Dálaigh CJ):

[69] Note that in *Howard v Commissioners of Public Works in Ireland* [1993] ILRM 665, Denham J took the view that the concept of equality encompassed more than what she described as the personal right of citizens to be treated equally before the law; that it included the principle that, in the execution of their power the organs of government shall act with due regard to the concept of equality. This parallel concept of equality is not, by definition, troubled by the "human personality" doctrine.

[70] [1983] ILRM 449.

[71] [1966] IR 567; (1968) 102 ILTR 1.

[72] Supreme Court, 21 December 1967.

> "It is the appellant's contention that this difference in our extradition arrangements is discriminatory and a violation of the principle of equality before the law. In my opinion this is not an acceptable construction of Article 40. The Article does not require the State to make the same extradition arrangements with all States. A diversity of arrangements does not effect discrimination between citizens in their legal rights Their legal rights are the same in the same circumstances. This in fact is equality before the law and not inequality, as the appellant submits"

Hartley's case was followed in 1972 by *O'Brien v Keogh*,[73] in which one of the points was the alleged breach of Article 40.1 by the provision of s 49 of the Statute of Limitations, 1957, to the effect that an infant in the custody of a parent at the date of accrual of a right of action in respect of personal injuries caused by negligence would have three years within which to bring this action (dating from the accrual of the right of action), whereas an infant not in such custody at that time would have three years dating from the cessation of the disability of infancy - i.e. a longer period within which he could sue. The answer made to this was (as stated in the judgment of the Supreme Court) that "the distinction between infants in the custody of a parent and those who are not in such custody is a distinction related to moral capacity and social function" and thus within the saver in Article 40.1; but the Court, in deciding the issue, said nothing about capacity or function, and would not even admit that inequality existed here at all. Ó Dálaigh CJ said:

> "The essential difference is between being in the custody of a person who is either a parent or is, in effect, *in loco parentis* on the one hand and not being in such custody on the other hand. Far from effecting inequality, the purpose of the provision would appear to attempt to establish equality between the two groups [He then cited *Hartley's* case.] Article 40 does not require identical treatment of all persons without recognition of differences in relevant circumstances. It only forbids invidious discrimination."[74]

It will be noted that in both *Nicolaou's* case and *O'Brien v Keogh* the Supreme Court considered the hypothesis of legislation which might treat situations alike although the objective differences between the situations called in justice for a treatment which would represent a differentiated response to the dissimilarity. With these *dicta* the Court seems to have accepted, if only *obiter*, the proposition familiar in continental equality jurisprudence: namely, that the principle of equality before the law is breached not only by the unlike treatment of like situations, but also by the converse, the like treatment of unlike situations.[75] Indeed the doctrine, as so stated, appears to have explicit support from Walsh J, who said in *de Búrca v Attorney General*[76] that Article 40.1 "imports the Aristotelian concept that justice demands that we treat equals equally and unequals unequally".[77]

Some further cases illustrating the range of discretion which can legitimately be exercised by the State in its laws, or by its subordinate organs in their regulating and executing functions, may be mentioned. In 1971, in *O'Shaughnessy v Attorney General*,[78] the validity of the Criminal Justice (Legal Aid) Act 1962, was challenged by a would-be

[73] [1972] IR 144.

[74] As to "invidious discrimination", see below, pp. 737-738.

[75] See *Kelly, loc. cit.*

[76] [1976] IR 38; (1977) 111 ILTR 37.

[77] Aristotle, *Politics*, iii, 9. For an example of a case where legislation was struck down because it failed to take account of material differences in two situations, see *Cox v Ireland* [1992] 2 IR 503, considered below, pp. 733-734.

[78] High Court, 16 February 1971.

civil plaintiff who could not afford to sue, and who alleged that the Act in providing for assistance only for persons charged with criminal offences but not for civil litigants, unfairly discriminated in breach of Article 40.1. O'Keeffe P thought that:

> "it is for the legislature to determine how the personal rights of the citizen are to be vindicated[79]...[The Act] is not to be held [invalid] on the ground either that the Courts consider that the priorities should be different, or that in providing assistance to those charged with criminal offences the State has elected not to provide any assistance to persons whose civil rights have been affected. I do not consider that legislation of this kind fails to accept or acknowledge the equality of all citizens before the law."

In *Devaney v Minister for Agriculture*,[80] the argument that a State department ran a discriminatory system of making appointments in requiring that a field officer should own a car was rejected by McWilliam J - "carried to its logical conclusion, [this contention] would mean that no employer could select, from several applicants for a job in which travelling was involved, the applicant who had a car, although this might be of mutual advantage to both"; and in *McHugh v Commissioner of the Garda Síochána*,[81] in which the plaintiff complained that a police disciplinary enquiry had focused on his behaviour rather than on that of the other officer involved in an incident, Costello J held that the relevant regulations permitted the exercise of such a discretion. They entitled the investigating officer:

> "to form a preliminary opinion that one member rather than another member may have been guilty of breach of discipline. This opinion is founded on factual information then in his possession, and he does not base his decision on any ethnic, racial, social or religious grounds. He cannot therefore be said to be discriminating in a constitutionally invidious way.
>
> The fact that this discretionary power may be abused, which certainly did not happen in this case, is not a ground for invalidating the regulations"

This judgment was affirmed by the Supreme Court, though without specific reference to Article 40.1.[82]

(b) A discrimination is prima facie legitimate if it corresponds with a difference of capacity or of social function

This proposition derives very simply from the second sentence of Article 40.1; it corresponds with the idea, visible in continental equality jurisprudence, that common sense or the realities of society may justify or even positively require a certain form of legislative differentiation.[83] In Ireland the principle can be illustrated by six cases, four of them from the area of tutelage of specially vulnerable persons. The earliest of these - and the earliest of all the cases on Article 40.1, which was rarely invoked before the late 1960s - was *In re Philip Clarke*,[84] in which the applicant raised, *inter alia*, Article 40.1 against

[79] Whatever about O'Keeffe P's conclusion in *O'Shaughnessy*, this premise would appear to be somewhat outdated, even by 1971.
[80] High Court, 22 March 1979.
[81] [1985] ILRM 606.
[82] [1986] IR 228; [1987] ILRM 181.
[83] See *Kelly, loc. cit.* The second sentence of Article 40.1.2 applies only to enactments, so that common law rules do not enjoy the protection of this proviso to the guarantee of equality - see the comment of Hederman J in *W. v W.* [1993] 2 IR 476; [1993] ILRM 294.
[84] [1950] IR 235; 85 ILTR 119.

the provisions of the Mental Treatment Act 1945, under which he had been detained; but the Supreme Court refused to see an unconstitutional discrimination in this law. The Court said (*per* O'Byrne J):

> "The impugned legislation is of a paternal character, clearly intended for the care and custody of persons suspected to be suffering from mental infirmity and for the safety and well-being of the public generally. The existence of mental infirmity is too widespread to be overlooked, and was, no doubt, present to the minds of the draughtsmen when it was proclaimed in Article 40.1...that, though all citizens, as human beings, are to be held equal before the law, the State may, nevertheless, in its enactments, have due regard to differences of capacity, physical and moral, and of social function. We do not see how the common good would be promoted or the dignity and freedom of the individual assured[85] by allowing persons, alleged to be suffering from such infirmity, to remain at large to the possible danger of themselves or others."

Again, in *The State (Nicolaou) v An Bord Uchtála*,[86] where the essence of the applicant's case against the Adoption Act 1952, was that it prevented the natural father of a non-marital child from having any role in consenting or refusing to consent to its adoption, Walsh J, delivering the judgment of the Supreme Court, based it in part on the Court's perception of the common realities attending a out of wedlock birth:

> "In the opinion of the Court each of the persons described as having rights under s 14(1) and s 16(1) can be regarded as having, or capable of having, in relation to the adoption of a child a moral capacity or social function which differentiates him from persons who are not given such rights [e.g. the natural father]. When it is considered that an illegitimate child may be begotten by an act of rape, by a callous seduction or by an act of casual commerce by a man with a woman, as well as by the association of a man with a woman in making a common home without marriage, and that, except in the latter instance, it is rare for a natural father to take any interest in his offspring, it is not difficult to appreciate the difference in moral capacity and social function between the natural father and the several persons described in the sub-sections in question."[87]

Next, in *Landers v Attorney General*,[88] where the provisions of the Prevention of Cruelty to Children Act 1904 (which prevented a child from giving singing performances on licensed premises at night), were under challenge as allegedly effecting a discrimination contrary to Article 40.1, Finlay J in the High Court said:

[85] These phrases come from the Preamble to the Constitution.

[86] [1966] IR 567; (1968) 102 ILTR 1.

[87] That the natural father has no constitutional rights to the guardianship of his child was re-affirmed by a majority of the Supreme Court in *J.K. v V.W.* [1990] 2 IR 437; [1990] ILRM 121, though without any reference to Article 40.1 or indeed, to *Nicolaou's* case. In the sequel to this decision - *K. v W. (No.2)* [1990] ILRM 791 - Barron J took the view that, in custody cases, difference between the two competing homes which spring solely from socio-economic causes should not be taken into account by the judge because, "[t]o do otherwise would be to favour the affluent as against the less well-off which does not accord with the constitutional obligation to hold all citizens as human persons equal before the law." *Pace* Barron J however, it is submitted that the courts can have regard to the differences in economic resources as between competing households as this factor could be quite significant in deciding how best to protect the welfare of the child. Any resulting discrimination would arguably be justified on the ground that it subserves the constitutional value of safeguarding the welfare of the child. See also Byrne and Binchy, *Annual Review of Irish Law 1990*, (Dublin, 1991) pp.320-2.

[88] (1975) 109 ILTR 1.

> "I cannot be persuaded that to prevent even a boy of unusual musical talent from singing in a dance hall or similar place of public entertainment until he has reached the age of fourteen years could fairly or reasonably be described as invidious discrimination."

In *The State (M.) v Attorney General*,[89] another provision of the Adoption Act 1952, was challenged. Here the parents of a non-marital child both wished to send the child to live with the father's parents in Nigeria (as the child had inherited its father's racial characteristics and seemed more assured of a stable future in that country), but the Minister for Foreign Affairs refused to authorise a passport for the child, considering himself bound by s 40 of the Adoption Act which permitted the removal of a child born within marriage from the State with its parents consent, but of a non-marital child irrespective of its parents' wishes only if it was in order that it should reside abroad with its mother (as was not the case here). Finlay P held the provision unconstitutional on other grounds, but not on the ground of alleged invidious and unfair discrimination against non-marital children. He said:

> "I am satisfied that for an illegitimate child and a legitimate child there is a difference of moral capacity and social function, at least in the context of the removal of the child out of the State. A legitimate child is part of a family unit; the rights and, in a sense, the duties of the family being specially provided for in the Constitution. In the generality of cases the legitimate child has the protection of a joint decision by its parents. On the other hand, an illegitimate child has not the benefit of being a member of a family unit...Further, in my view there is much weight in the submissions to the effect that in the generality of cases the mother of an illegitimate child may be subjected to strains, stresses and pressures arising from economic and social conditions which fully justify the Legislature in making special provisions with regard to the welfare of that child, which provisions are not considered necessary for the welfare of a legitimate child."

In *Abbey Films Ltd. v Attorney General*[90] the Supreme Court held justified, under the "difference of capacity or social function" criterion, a provision of the Restrictive Practices Act 1972, which required a company to have a solicitor to act for it in certain proceedings, while an individual might appear in person.

In *Murphy v Attorney General*[91] the Supreme Court had to review an income tax law which, aggregating the incomes of married couples, left them (because of progressive tax bands) together worse off than if they were unmarried couples living together (whose incomes would not have been aggregated). The Court struck down this law on other grounds, but not because of breach of Article 40.1; the Court said the inequality was:

> "justified by the particular social function under the Constitution of married couples living together...Numerous examples could be given from the income tax code of types of income tax payers who are treated differently, either favourably or unfavourably, because of their social functions. This particular unfavourable tax treatment of married couples living together, set against the many favourable discriminations made by the law in favour of married couples, does not, in the opinion of the Court, constitute an unequal treatment forbidden by Article 40.1, particularly having regard to the vital roles under the Constitution of married couples as parents, or potential parents, and as heads of a family."

[89] [1979] IR 73.
[90] [1981] IR 158.
[91] [1982] IR 241. Followed in *Greene v Minister for Agriculture* [1990] 2 IR 17; [1990] ILRM 364.

MURPHY V. AG

Here, again, the second sentence of Article 40.1 was used as a route of escape; though it must be said that to use a difference in social function, where the quality of the difference is acknowledged to be one expressly supported by the State, as the basis for less rather than more favourable treatment, verges on the eccentric.

In *Dillane v Ireland*[92] the Supreme Court upheld a distinction, made by Rule 67 of the District Court Rules, in regard to a District Judge's power to award costs against a party to proceedings: among those against whom, exceptionally, no such award can be made is a member of the Garda Síochána acting in discharge of his duties as a police officer. A police officer who brings a prosecution is, in the eye of the law, a common informer; but this Rule has the effect of differentiating between, so to speak, the official common informer in the shape of a police officer, and an ordinary common informer. The Court, *per* Henchy J, thought that:

> "for a variety of reasons - among them the desirability that members of the Garda Síochána should be encouraged to discharge their police duties assiduously by being given immunity from liability for costs or witnesses' expenses in the District Court - this discrimination could reasonably be thought a justifiable concomitant of the social function of the members of the Garda Síochána when carrying out their duties as police officers"

He stressed that "whether the Court supports or approves of that distinction is irrelevant":

> "what matters is whether it could reasonably have been arrived at as a matter of policy by those to whom the elected representatives of the people delegated the power of laying down the principles upon which costs are to be awarded."

And he offered also a statement of the Court's approach to distinctions evidently related to social function, a statement simple enough to deserve to become canonical:

> "When the State, whether directly by statute or immediately through the exercise of a delegated power of subordinate legislation, makes a discrimination in favour of, or against, a person or a category of persons, on the express or implied ground of a difference of social function, the courts will not condemn such discrimination as being in breach of Article 40.1 if it is not arbitrary, capricious, or otherwise not reasonably capable, when objectively viewed in the light of the social function involved, of supporting the selection or classification complained of."

In *Norris v Attorney General*,[93] the Supreme Court by a majority rejected a challenge to nineteenth-century legislation penalising homosexual conduct between males (while leaving female homosexual practice untouched). On the point that this distinction as between men and women was an unconstitutional discrimination, the Court's majority, *per* O'Higgins CJ, said that the Legislature was:

> "perfectly entitled to have regard to the difference between the sexes and to treat sexual conduct or gross indecency between males as requiring prohibition because of the social problem which it creates, while at the same time looking at sexual conduct between females as being not only different but as posing no such social problem."

[92] [1980] ILRM 167.
[93] [1984] IR 36.

This judgment did not refer to the second sentence of Article 40.1, but clearly the different social dimensions of male and female homosexuality can be classed as differences in social function.[94]

More recently, in *MhicMhathúna v Ireland*[95] Carroll J held that the position of a single parent is different to that of two parents living together and that such state of affairs justified the restriction of certain tax and welfare benefits to single parents only. This might be regarded as a case of discrimination being justified by difference in capacity.

The case of *O'G. v Attorney General*,[96] demonstrates that the Courts have jurisdiction to review a discriminating measure based on the view taken by the Oireachtas as to a difference in capacity or social function, and to invalidate it if they consider the legislative appraisal to be ill-founded and the difference illusory. Here an infant had been given into the custody of a couple who proposed to adopt it; before the adoption was finalised, the wife was killed in an accident, leaving her husband a childless widower. By s 5(1) of the Adoption Act 1974, however, widowers in this position (unlike widows) were prevented from adopting. The widower attacked this provision as discriminatory, and produced expert evidence to show that the difference in sex did not affect the development of the emotional bonding necessary to an infant with a parent. As between the widower and the infant's natural mother, its welfare was also clearly best served by staying with the former. McMahon J was

> "satisfied that the proviso to s 5 is founded on an idea of difference in capacity between men and women which has no foundation in fact and the proviso is therefore an unwarranted denial of human equality and repugnant to Article 40.1."

It may be added that, as we have already noted, the Courts have invalidated various rules, mainly inherited from the common law, which were based on illusory differences of capacity or of social function as between husband and wife.[97]

(c) A discrimination is prima facie legitimate if it subserves some value which the Constitution expressly or implicitly upholds

This proposition could be said to be suggested by the reference made by the Supreme Court to the Preamble in *In re Philip Clarke*, cited above, in which the restraints on personal liberty provided by the Mental Treatment Act 1945, were related to the "common good" and the "dignity and freedom of the individual" held up by the Preamble as the State's objectives. A clearer instance is afforded, albeit in a minority opinion, by the judgment of O'Higgins CJ in *de Búrca v Attorney General*:[98]

[94] These dimensions were very fully explored by the German Federal Constitutional Court in 1957: it reached the same conclusion, for the same reasons, as the Supreme Court in *Norris's* case: see *Kelly. loc. cit.* Henchy J, who dissented from the majority on the principal point in the case (see below, pp. 768-769), nevertheless thought, on the argument based on Article 40.1, that "the proviso contained in its second sentence... makes constitutionally acceptable under that Article the line of demarcation between the acts made criminal and those here complained of for being left unprescribed by the criminal law". The same judge also adverted, *obiter*, to the potential rescue effect of the second sentence in *The State (Cussen) v Brennan* [1981] IR 181. (The Court of Human Rights subsequently ruled that the legislation criminalising homosexuality violated Norris' right to respect for private life, contrary to Article 8 of the Convention - Series A, No.142 (1989) 13 EHRR 186 - and it was eventually repealed by s 2 of the Criminal Law (Sexual Offences) Act 1993.)

[95] [1989] IR 504.

[96] [1985] ILRM 61.

[97] See above, pp. 713-715.

[98] [1976] IR 38; (1977) 111 ILTR 37.

> "Article 40 permits the State to have regard in its laws to differences of capacity, physical and moral, and of social function. It does not seem incongruous or inappropriate for the State, under this Article, to temper or cushion obligations generally imposed in so far as they affect women. In particular, one would expect this to be done under a Constitution which expressly recognises that by her life within the home, woman gives to the State a support without which the common good cannot be achieved: see Article 41.2. Where, therefore, as in the case of jury service, the State imposes on all citizens an obligation to serve, the discharge of which necessarily takes the citizen concerned away from his occupation and his home, special provision must obviously be made in respect of women. In my view, such special provision is permissible under the second sentence of Article 40.1 and is almost mandatory under Article 41.2...I cannot see how this can be regarded as an invidious discrimination."

Later in his judgment he added:

> "When one considers the special recognition of women and mothers in Article 41 of our Constitution, it does not appear inappropriate that the State in its laws should give some preference to woman; particularly when the exercise of her right in relation to jury service also involves the acceptance of a burden. As I have stated, this is a discrimination which is not invidious because it does not amount to an exclusion and because some preferential treatment of women citizens seems to be contemplated by the Constitution."

Again, in *The State (Nicolaou) v An Bord Uchtála*[99] the Supreme Court justified the regime contained in the Adoption Act 1952 - notwithstanding that it denied to natural fathers of non-marital children the status enjoyed by the fathers of children born within marriage - as being directed to securing for the non-marital child its "natural and imprescriptible rights", referred to in Article 42.5; the purpose and effect of the Act was "to redress the inequalities imposed by circumstances on orphans and illegitimate children". And in *The State (Cussen) v Brennan*[100] Henchy J seemed to say that - provided a knowledge of Irish was relevant to the discharge of the duties of a particular office - the status accorded to Irish by Article 8 would entitle an authority to prescribe a knowledge of Irish as a necessary qualification for that office, though this would necessarily exclude non-Irish speakers; a *dictum* not entirely satisfactory, since in the hypothesis he gave, the requirement of a knowledge of Irish could be justified even if Article 8 did not exist.

A decision which at last states the principle here proposed is *O'B. v S.*[101] in which the non-marital child of a deceased intestate challenged the provisions of the Succession Act 1965, which restricted entitlement on succession to intestates' estates to offspring born within marriage. The Supreme Court admitted the first step of the argument based on discrimination: there was, indeed, no difference of physical or moral capacity or social function which could justify treating non-marital children less favourably than legitimate offspring. But, assuming the legislature to have devised these provisions with an eye to the principal value stated by Article 41 - the protection of marriage and of the family based on marriage - the differentiating provision could be dispensed from the necessity of finding cover under the "capacity or function" proviso of Article 40.1. The Court said, *per* Walsh J:

[99] [1966] IR 567; (1968) 102 ILTR 1.
[100] [1981] IR 181.
[101] [1984] IR 316; [1985] ILRM 86. The same idea seems latent in the Court's judgment in *Quinn's Supermarket v Attorney General* [1972] IR 1; this case turned however on the specific prohibition of religious discrimination in Article 44.2.3.

> "Legislation which differentiates citizens or which discriminates between them does not need to be justified under the proviso of justification for it can be found in other provisions of the Constitution."

In *Dennehy v Minister for Social Welfare*[102] legislation which provided for social welfare payments to deserted wives but not to deserted husbands was challenged as discriminatory. The plaintiff, a deserted husband, was able to show that in his own case, and similar cases, there were many features of hardship which were objectively indistinguishable from the situation of a deserted wife; but Barron J refused to hold the legislative scheme impermissible. He drew attention to Article 41.2, in which the State particularly recognises the importance to the common good of "women's life with the home"; having regard to this provision, it did not seem to him:

> "that as a matter of policy it would be unreasonable, unjust or arbitrary for the Oireachtas to protect financially deserted wives who are mothers who have dependent children residing with them, or to recognise that mothers who have had to care for children will have lost out in the labour market and so are likely to need similar protection when similarly deserted."[103]

An unusual case also falling into this category is *Pine Valley Developments Ltd. v Minister for the Environment*,[104] in which a legislative provision passed specifically in order to validate retrospectively a number of planning decisions after proceedings brought by the plaintiff company to challenge one of those decisions (affecting itself) had disclosed a fatal flaw in all of them, had contained a specific saver, excepting from the section's effect the very decision which the plaintiffs had successfully attacked. This meant an obvious discrimination to the prejudice of the plaintiffs; but the Supreme Court found that the object of the saver was to respect the judicial process by refraining from legislatively reversing a judicial decision; the upholding of this constitutional value was an adequate excuse for the discrimination which then unavoidably followed.[105]

(d) A distinction, though in its nature capable of justification, is unconstitutional if it is excessive in its measure

This principle,[106] cognate with other rules of law which impose on a particular act the stipulation that it does not exceed in degree the measure of what is necessary, appears from *Quinn's Supermarket v Attorney General* cited at Fn 101. The point about the trading hours regulations here challenged was that, in general, the regulations prevented victuallers' shops from opening after 6.30 p.m. on Saturdays; but as this hour more or less coincided with the end of the Jewish Sabbath (which began at sunset on Friday), and as, during the Sabbath, Jewish shops could not open for religious reasons, the

[102] High Court, 26 July 1984.

[103] Note however that the statutory classification complained of was not a precise match for the distinction implicitly drawn by Article 41.2 for the welfare schemes covered deserted wives who were not necessarily mothers.

[104] [1987] IR 23; [1987] ILRM 747.

[105] The discrimination alleged here by the plaintiffs was presented as an unjust attack on property rights rather than as a violation of Article 40.1 (from whose benefit, on the prevailing doctrine, a commercial company would in any case have been excluded); but the ratio of the decision seems equally available in the Article 40.1 context. The plaintiffs fared better in Europe where the European Court of Human Rights subsequently ruled that the legislation discriminated against them in the exercise of their property rights, contrary to Article 14 of the Convention, read with Article 1 of the First Protocol thereto - Series A, No.222, (1992) 14 EHRR 319.

[106] A similar principle, known as the principle of proportionality, operates under Article 14 of the European Convention on Human Rights - see the *Belgian Linguistics* case Series A, No.6, (1979) 1 EHRR 252, *James v UK* Series A, No.98, (1986) 8 EHRR 123 and *Lithgow v UK* Series A, No.102, (1986) 8 EHRR 326.

exemption was made so as to permit Jews to buy kosher meat at an hour later than 6.30 on Saturday, thus avoiding offending either their religion or the law. But the terms of the exemption were not confined to Saturday - since they exempted kosher shops generally from an order which regulated weekday opening generally - and so the discriminating exemption went too far, i.e. further than was necessary for the protection of religious observance. Accordingly, the exemption was invalid.

The same principle appears in the words of the Supreme Court in *O'Brien v Manufacturing Engineering Co.*,[107] where the Court considered whether a special limitation period of twelve or (exceptionally) twenty-four months for the bringing of a common law action by an injured workman who had accepted statutory weekly payments under the Workmen's Compensation Acts, as distinct from the normal three years for the bringing of such an action where no such payments had been accepted, was an objectionable discrimination. The Court held that in principle an abridged limitation period was not objectionable; but considered, as a separate issue, the question whether the period in question was unreasonably short. The Court's view was that:

> "a period of twelve months or, where there are substantial grounds for not initiating within twelve months, a period of twenty-four months is not unreasonably short to enable a person not suffering from any disability to ascertain whether or not he has a common-law action and to institute that action. In the opinion of the Court, the provision in question has not been shown to be invalid having regard to the provisions of Article 40.1."

A very recent application of this principle may be seen in *Cox v Ireland*.[108] At issue here was the constitutionality of s 34 of the Offences Against the State Act 1939 which provides that any person convicted of a scheduled offence by the Special Criminal Court shall forfeit any office or employment remunerated from public monies, be disqualified for a period of seven years after the date of conviction for eligibility to hold any such office or employment and, finally, be disqualified for receipt of any pension or superannuation allowance payable from public monies. The plaintiff, a teacher in a community school, had been so convicted and accordingly under s 34 could not be re-employed in his former position for a period of seven years after the date of conviction. He contended, *inter alia*, that s 34 infringed Article 40.1 insofar as it discriminated between persons convicted of an offence in the Special Criminal Court and persons convicted of the same offence in an ordinary court; between persons convicted of scheduled offences before the Special Criminal Court and those convicted of non-scheduled offences, possibly of equal seriousness, before the same court; and between persons convicted of scheduled offences before the Special Criminal Court whose office or employment is funded out of State funds and those convicted of the same offences whose office or employment was otherwise funded. The Court held that s 34 constituted a potential infringement on the right to earn a livelihood and on the right to property but also accepted that the State was entitled, in the interest of protecting public peace and order and the authority of the State, to provide for the imposition of penalties contained in s 34 and also to ensure that among those involved in carrying out the functions of the State, there was not included persons who commit crimes against public peace and order and State authority. However in pursuing such objectives, the State was still obliged to continue to protect as far as practicable the constitutional rights of the citizen. In the instant case, the Court concluded that the objectives of s 34 did not justify the extent to which it trenched on constitutional rights, pointing out that such was the breadth of offences listed as scheduled offences under the 1939 Act that the mandatory penalties in s 34 could attach to

[107] [1973] IR 334; (1974) 108 ILTR 105.
[108] [1992] 2 IR 503.

someone convicted of a relatively minor offence in circumstances which bore no relation at all to any question of the maintenance of public peace and order or the authority of the State.[109] The Court also noted that the ultimate factor triggering the operation of s 34 was the venue of the trial; that that venue is primarily selected by the fact that the offence is scheduled and that it can only be avoided by a decision of the Attorney General or of the Director of Public Prosecutions in respect of which the accused had no right of representation. For these reasons, the Court held that s 34 failed, as far as practicable, to protect the constitutional rights of the citizen and accordingly, was impermissibly wide and indiscriminate. So while a distinction could justifiably be drawn between persons in public employment convicted of offences threatening public peace and order and State authority and other defendants, in this case the distinction was excessive in its measure - it went further than was necessary for the protection of the State - and thus was unconstitutional.[110]

(e) A statutory scheme based on classification is not necessarily invalid for discrimination merely because it results in unequal treatment of two individuals whose situations are similar

This proposition has not yet been accepted or articulated by the Irish courts, but it seems a likely candidate for early expression. The point - recognised in continental equality jurisprudence - is that every statutory scheme must generalise, in other words, that in certain contexts it may be administratively impossible to have regard to each individual situation, notwithstanding that some individual situations within a particular class may diverge considerably from the norm taken as typical for the creation of that class. A typical member of one class may in his situation more closely resemble the typical member of another class than other members of his own; but this ought not to upset the scheme's validity, unless, indeed, the incidence of such divergence is frequent enough, or its degree injurious enough, to suggest that the legislature ought to have made special provision for it.[111] A similar set of answers can be used for grievances arising from the use of statutory time-limits, dates, ages, distances, sizes etc.; there may be as little objective reason to include in some statutory category a case falling narrowly on one side of the statutory line, as there is to exclude a case falling just as narrowly on the other side of it; but, if the legitimacy of any line is conceded, and the statutory choice of line fairly made, these "borderline" grievances cannot be avoided and their existence ought not to invalidate the distinction.[112]

[109] For criticism of the breadth of the scheduled offences under the 1939 Act, see Robinson, *The Special Criminal Court* (Dublin, 1974) at pp.9-10.

[110] One might have thought that this reasoning, *mutatis mutandis*, would also condemn the exceptional powers of detention provided for by s 30 of the 1939 Act whose parameters are also defined by the category of scheduled offences under that Act. However in *The People (D.P.P.) v Quilligan (No.3)* [1993] 2 IR 305, the Supreme Court, without referring to *Cox*, employed a less exacting standard of review under Article 40.1 in upholding that section, ruling that the fact that a law discriminates as between one group of persons and another does not, *per se*, render it constitutionally invalid and that in the instant case it had not been established that s 30 amounted to invidious discrimination.

[111] In *Purcell v AG* [1990] 2 IR 405, the plaintiff made a case which, in the terms of the proposition under consideration, could be formulated as saying that a system of farm tax had exceeded the level of generalisation tolerable under the principle of equality. He was one of a number of farmers with a holding of a certain size who had been made liable to farm tax. Because of administrative difficulties, not every farmer with holdings of this size had been added to the list of taxpayers under the scheme when the Minister for Finance announced in a budget speech that the farm tax was to be abolished. The plaintiff objected to having to pay the tax already assessed on him when a significant number of farmers with similar holdings were not made so liable, arguing that the tax scheme resulted in unequal treatment of individuals whose situations were similar. In the event, Barron J eschewed any reliance on the principle of equality in ruling for the plaintiff, holding that when the Minister unlawfully interfered with the farm tax scheme by announcing its abolition in the absence of amending legislation, the scheme ceased to be enforceable not only for the future but also for the past.

[112] This difficulty has been recognised by the US Supreme Court on numerous occasions: see, e.g. *Metropolis Theatre Co. v Chicago* 228 US 61 (1913) ("the problems of government are practical ones and may justify, if

The only Irish case which seems to come near an expression of the status of generalisation in legislation is *The State (Nicolaou) v An Bord Uchtála,*[113] where the Supreme Court, in upholding provisions of the Adoption Act 1952, which implicitly excluded the natural father of a non-marital child from any influence on decisions in relation to the child's adoption, based its judgment in part on its view of the common or typical part played by a natural father in such a situation - except in the case of the so-called common-law marriage, it was "rare for a natural father to take any interest in his offspring". This pattern, the Court thought, justified the Oireachtas in seeing a "difference of moral capacity and social function" as between natural fathers and persons given a status by the Act in relation to adoption decisions; notwithstanding that the particular applicant in this case was not, on the Court's perceived standard, a typical natural father.

(f) On the other hand, the creation of a statutory class must itself be justifiable; the equal treatment of all the members within it is not enough

This proposition does not seem to have been explicitly admitted yet. On the contrary, there are five or six judicial suggestions that, if all members of a class are treated equally, that concludes the question of possible discrimination. Thus Pringle J in the High Court in *O'Brien v Manufacturing Engineering Co.*[194] adverted to the second sentence of Article 40.1:

> "which envisages that citizens may be divided into different classes. Therefore, it would appear that there is no unfair discrimination provided that every person in the same class is treated in the same way."

Again, in *The State (Hartley) v Governor of Mountjoy Prison,*[195] where the applicant had attacked the regime established by the Extradition Act 1965, under which a person whose extradition to the United Kingdom was sought enjoyed (as the Supreme Court agreed) "more extensive privileges or safeguards" than a person whose extradition was sought to some other State, the Court said:

> "The Article [40.1] does not require the State to make the same extradition arrangements with all States...A diversity of arrangements does not effect discrimination between citizens in their legal rights. Their legal rights are the same in the same circumstances This in fact is equality before the law and not inequality, as the appellant submits."

One could admit that, in the particular context of extradition with its usual basis in reciprocal arrangements, identical rules governing extradition to all countries might be impossible, and yet feel that the general statements in the passage cited, like the words of Pringle J quoted above, fail to state an important point: the question whether the *creation* of classes for differing statutory treatment is legitimate ought to be logically prior to the question whether, in the event, all members within one such class were treated equally. The same might be said of the Supreme Court's approach, in *East Donegal Co-Operative v Attorney General,*[116] to the power given to the Minister for Agriculture to

they do not require, rough accommodations."); *Califano v Jobst* 437 US 47 (1977) ("General rules are essential if a [social welfare] fund of this magnitude is to be administered with a modicum of efficiency, even though such rules inevitably produce seemingly arbitrary consequences in some individual cases.")

[113] [1966] IR 567; (1968) 102 ILTR 1.

[114] [1973] IR 334; (1974) 108 ILTR 105.

[115] Supreme Court, 21 December 1967.

[116] [1970] IR 317; (1970) 104 ILTR 81.

exempt businesses of a particular class from the provisions of the Livestock Marts Act 1967; this power the Court held valid, as:

> "the benefits or otherwise of such exemption would apply equally then to all persons engaged in the designated class or kind of business."

The Court did, of course, say that the presumption as to constitutional procedures etc. would apply to the ministerial function of making such an exemption, and this naturally would disqualify any failure in natural justice or good faith on the Minister's part; but even in the absence of such a failure, it might still be possible to show that an exemption, by having distinguished on insufficient grounds between two classes of business objectively similar, had breached the equality principle. Again, in *The State (Kenny) v Ó hÚadhaigh,*[117] Finlay P rejected the submission that s 123 of the Children Act 1908, discriminated against young persons, on the simple ground that "every young person or child is treated in exactly the same fashion"; in *Norris v Attorney General*[118] Henchy J (although dissenting on the main issue) said, in dealing with the submission that laws penalising homosexual behaviour only when committed by males were discriminatory, that "it was and is a matter of legislative policy to decide whether a compulsion of the common good is capable of justifying the distinction drawn"; in *Cooke v Walsh,*[119] in which the defendant alleged an unconstitutional discrimination in Article 6(3) of the Health Service Regulations 1971, which excluded from free health service treatment persons who had received awards of damages in respect of road accident injuries, Hamilton P said that "as the power given to the Minister for Health is the power to differentiate between classes of the persons eligible for the services and not as between individuals, it appears to me that the provisions of Article 40.1 have no application";[120] in *Doyle v Hearne (No.2),*[121] referring to the differential treatment of persons converting from a six-day licence to a seven-day licence pursuant to s 27 of the Intoxicating Liquor Act 1960 - they could not invoke s 20 of the Intoxicating Liquor Act 1962 to prevent the granting of a licence in respect of premises situated less than one mile from their own - the Supreme Court, *per* Finlay CJ, said that s 27 was not invidiously discriminatory because "all persons who converted from a six to a seven-day licence, pursuant to [s 27 of the 1960 Act] are being treated alike and...whilst it can be said that the section is discriminatory as between them and persons who did not convert, it is not invidiously discriminating for this reason." Most recently, in *The People (Director of Public Prosecutions) v Quilligan (No.3)*[122] the Supreme Court used the same reasoning in rejecting an argument that s 30 of the Offences Against the State Act 1939 infringed Article 40.1 by discriminating between persons arrested pursuant to its provisions and persons arrested other than pursuant to s 30. Delivering the judgment of the Court, Finlay CJ said:

> "Every person who is suspected of the commission of an offence under the 1939 Act or an offence scheduled for the purposes of that Act is subject in law to the same rights and obligations and to the possibility of detention for the same period or periods. Similarly, every person arrested on suspicion of the commission of a crimi-

[117] [1979] IR 1.
[118] [1984] IR 36.
[119] [1983] ILRM 429.
[120] The applicability or otherwise of Article 40.1 did not feature in the subsequent Supreme Court decision as the Court held that the 1971 Regulations were *ultra vires* the Minister's powers under the Health Act 1970.
[121] [1988] IR 317.
[122] Supreme Court, 14 July 1992.

nal offence which is not an offence against the Act of 1939 and is not scheduled for the purposes of that Act is subject to the same powers of detention on the part of the Garda Síochána and to the same rights, though such powers of detention and rights are different from those applicable to persons arrested under section 30.

The mere fact that a law discriminates as between one group or category of persons and another does not, of itself, render it constitutionally invalid. What is necessary to establish such invalidity is the existence of invidious discrimination, and the court is satisfied that that has not been established with regard to section 30 in this case."

The only explicit[123] judicial suggestion so far as to the necessity to justify the creation of a class in the context of judicial review (independent of the question whether all members of the class are treated equally) - and it is a rather tentatively expressed one - has come not from the Supreme Court, but from Barrington J in the High Court in the case of *Brennan v Attorney General*, cited above, when, politely referring to the sentence of Pringle J cited above from *O'Brien v Manufacturing Engineering Co.*, he said:

"No doubt this is true, but it might be prudent to express, what is perhaps implied in it, that the classification must be for a legitimate legislative purpose, that it must be relevant to that purpose, and that each class must be treated fairly."

(g) A differentiation becomes an unconstitutional discrimination if its quality bears no reasonable relation to the quality of the difference between the situations which it is to regulate

This formula, like any other formula in this area, will not exclude the element of subjective judicial appraisal with which courts must necessarily work in applying a standard so objectively elusive as that of equality. But it is perhaps more satisfactory than the mere word "invidious" as the test of unconstitutionality, which, first surfacing in 1972 in *O'Brien v Keogh*[124] and since then becoming canonical through use in many Article 40.1 cases, represents the Supreme Court's only attempt so far to modify the notion of equality *via* its opposite, discrimination, so as to express the essence of the precept. The phrase "invidious discrimination" makes the word "invidious" bear a meaning, in this context, by no means familiar in ordinary usage, and seems to have an American origin: at any rate, a line of American cases, of pedigree apparently no more ancient than 1959, use this expression in the context of infringements of the "equal protection of the laws" guaranteed by the post-Civil War Fourteenth Amendment.[125] The phrase seems an unsat-

[123] This proposition might be taken to be implicit in cases like *O'G. v Attorney General* [1985] ILRM 61, and *MhicMhathúna v Ireland* [1989] IR 504, where statutory classifications are scrutinised to see if they reasonably relate to ideas of difference in capacity which are factually based. In the former case, a distinction between widows and widowers in the Adoption Act 1974 was declared unconstitutional because it was based on what McMahon J decided was an illusory idea that women are innately better at bonding with infants than men. In contrast, discrimination in favour of single parents in the tax and welfare systems was upheld by Carroll J in *MhicMhathúna*, who held that it was justified by the different factual situations of single parent families and two parent families. See also *Mapp v Gilhooley* [1991] 2 IR 253 where, though not dealing with a classification as such but rather with an argument that the rule requiring evidence to be given on oath was overbroad, the Supreme Court took the view that the rule was not unlawfully discriminatory after (briefly) considering its purpose.

[124] [1972] IR 144.

[125] In *Allied Store of Ohio v Bowers* 358 US 522 (1959) the phrase was used as a synonym (which in ordinary speech it is certainly not) for "palpably arbitrary": and in *San Antonio School District v Rodriguez* 411 US 1, 60 (1973) it was used to mean "wholly arbitrary or capricious". In *Harper v Virginia Board of Elections*, 383 US 663 (1966) the Supreme Court gave it the status of a criterion: "The test is whether the difference in treatment is an invidious discrimination." See also *Lehnhausen v Lake Shore Auto Parts Co.* 410 US 356, 359 (1973).

isfactory addition to the Irish constitutional lexicon, since, apart from the fact that it fails to deliver a concrete and objective standard, which perhaps is too much to hope for, it also - as one might expect in a phrase emerging from the landscape of racial discrimination - suggests the element of deliberately creating distinctions as expressions of a tacit prejudice. The Supreme Court itself seems to wish to discard the formula;[126] the Court said (*per* Kenny J) in *Murphy v Attorney General*:[127]

> "Throughout the argument of the present case the phrase "invidious discrimination" was used to indicate the type of inequality which is prohibited by Article 40.1. According to the 1979 edition of Collins English Dictionary "invidious" means "l. incurring or tending to arouse resentment, unpopularity; 2. (of comparisons or distinctions) unfairly or offensively discriminatory". While the second meaning can be used to describe the inequality prohibited by Article 40.1, the primary meaning of the word is the first, and its use in discussing Article 40.1 is more likely to mislead than to help."

Since then the Supreme Court has not attempted to expand the word "invidious" into more comprehensible standard, or to substitute other words for it.[128] The only attempt has come from Barrington J in the High Court in *Brennan v Attorney General*;[129] when he said:

> "It may be that all discrimination between citizens not relevant to a legitimate legislative purpose is invidious."

Even this does not seem to go far enough, as a differentiation might be relevant to a legitimate legislative purpose, but the *mode or quality* of the differentiation, i.e. its end effect on parties, might be one not rationally suggested by the quality in the difference of the situations which it should be the law's object to bring, so to speak, into an equilibrium.

Three cases may be mentioned here, not as supporting the standard just proposed, but as illustrating it by their apparent failure to recognise it. The first of these was *O'Brien v Manufacturing Engineering Co.*,[130] in which a provision of the Workmen's Compensation (Amendment) Act 1953, was challenged; this provision distinguished, for the purpose of bringing common-law proceedings for personal injuries caused by an

[126] Though it has re-surfaced in a number of recent judgments, none of which, it might be added, clarify the meaning of the term. In *McGimpsey v Ireland* [1990] 1 IR 110; [1990] ILRM 440, Finlay CJ, delivering the leading judgment, remarked that there were no grounds "for suggesting that there has been an invidious or any discrimination between the two communities in Northern Ireland by virtue of the terms of the Anglo-Irish Agreement". In *The People (D.P.P.) v Quilligan (No.3)* [1993] 2 IR 305, the Supreme Court also held that s 30 of the Offences Against the State Act 1939 did not create any invidious discrimination while a similar view was taken of s 27 of the Intoxicating Liquor Act 1960 in *Doyle v Hearne (No.2)* [1988] IR 317. In the earlier case of *Kerry Co-Operative Creameries Ltd. v An Bord Bainne* [1990] ILRM 664, Costello J held that a rule of an industrial and provident society permitting the allocation of bonus shares on the basis of a member's current trading with the society was not "invidiously discriminating". In the Supreme Court, McCarthy J held that the rule, though it might produce inequality, was not "unfair" and that it did not constitute an oppression of the minority shareholders - [1991] ILRM 851 at 869.

[127] [1982] IR 241.

[128] Though in *O'Shea v D.P.P.* [1988] IR 655, a contention that the power of the D.P.P., after the conclusion of the preliminary examination, to substitute counts in respect of offences not charged in the District Court was unconstitutional because unfairly discriminatory was dismissed by the Supreme Court who found that there was nothing "unfair" in such a power. See also the brief comment of McCarthy J in *Kerry Co-Operative Creameries Ltd. v An Bord Bainne* [1991] ILRM 851 upholding a rule of the defendant society on the ground that it was not "unfair".

[129] [1983] ILRM 449. The Supreme Court did not address this issue in the subsequent appeal, holding that Article 40.1 was inapplicable to a system of taxation imposed on occupiers of land - the subject matter of the complaint in *Brennan* - [1984] ILRM 355.

[130] [1973] IR 334; (1974) 108 ILTR 105.

employer's fault, between workmen who had and those who had not accepted the statutory weekly payment for disability (irrespective of fault): those who had accepted had only one year (or, exceptionally, two years) for bringing their actions, those who had not had the normal three years for this purpose. The Supreme Court drew attention to the advantages which the Workmen's Compensation code represented for an injured workman, and considered that when those advantages were "coupled" with the shorter limitation period no breach of his rights had taken place. But the Court did not ask whether the quality of the difference between the two categories of injured workmen bore a rational relation to the quality of the difference in how they were treated for limitation purposes; and in fact there is no visible nexus between, or rational need to create, a legislative equilibrium by relating the quality of having accepted statutory payments and the quality of being subject to a shortened limitation period. Why should the potential defendant, by having paid the statutory compensation unrelated to fault, earn a right to be put out of risk of being sued at common law for fault earlier than if he had not paid it (seeing that the sum of such payments would in any case have been credited against the amount of a future common-law award)?

A similar sense that the discrimination, instead of aiming at an equilibrium, or balancing-out of interests, *via* a rational matching of quality-of-objective-difference with quality-of-different-treatment, resulted from a fairly casual piece of legislative officiousness, is conveyed by the law which was questionably upheld in *The State (Hunt) v O'Donovan*.[131] What was in issue here - and had previously been in issue in *The State (Murphy) v Governor of Portlaoise Prison*[132] and *The State (Meads) v Governor of Limerick Prison*,[133] though in those cases the point on Article 40.1 was not decided - was s 13 of the Criminal Procedure Act 1967, the effect of which was that a person who signed a plea of guilty to an indictable offence on being charged with it in the District Court, and, on being sent forward for sentence to the Circuit Court, was there sentenced, had no right of appeal against the sentence to the Court of Criminal Appeal, unlike - and here lay the alleged discrimination - a person who waited until indicted in the Circuit Court before pleading guilty. Instead, however, of seeking to find this distinction objectively "reasonable", Finlay J based his rejection of the attack on s 13 essentially on the element of free will, which the applicant might have exercised otherwise:

> "A person can never be dealt with under that section unless he so wishes. There is no moral or legal duty on a person, when charged with an indictable offence before the District Court, to signify his desire to plead guilty to that charge. Unless he does so, the provisions of s 13 of the Act of 1967 never come into operation. Even after he has been sent forward by the District Court on a plea of guilty (if he makes one), the accused, before being sentenced by the Circuit Court, must be asked if he wishes to withdraw that plea; if he does withdraw his plea he is indicted, and to that indictment he may plead either guilty or not guilty and, if sentenced, he has a statutory right of appeal against that sentence. However, to take a hypothetical case, each of two persons might be charged with the same type of crime but one of them might be sent forward for sentence on his plea of guilty which he does not withdraw, while the other might be convicted, or plead guilty, on indictment; in such circumstances it is undoubtedly true that one has a right of appeal against the severity of sentence while the other has not that right. I must ask myself whether this result, on the principles laid down in the cases to which I have referred, constitutes...an invidious discrimination... The person who has been sent forward for sentence on his plea has the opportunity to withdraw that plea up to the very last

131 [1975] IR 39; (1973) 107 ILTR 53.
132 High Court, 23 November 1971.
133 Supreme Court, 26 July 1972.

> moment; in addition such person is sentenced, after due submission and evidence, by a constitutional court with an independent judge subject to legal maximum standards as to the penalty he may impose. In these circumstances I do not consider that these provisions are repugnant to [Article 40.1]...It is of importance to note that the choice to which I have referred is not illusory. Practitioners are well accustomed to using an early and unequivocal admission of an offence as a plea in leniency, and it often succeeds. Furthermore, there is a brevity and speed in the procedure...which may constitute an advantage to an accused person."

The Supreme Court, in upholding the refusal of Finlay J to hold with the applicant, gave no reasons in its five-line judgment, from which it may be concluded that it saw no reason to distance itself from the criterion he erected. It is, however, perfectly possible for a discrimination to be accepted to his disadvantage by a person on the basis of his own free choice, while no "reason" supports the existence of the discrimination itself so as to make it "reasonable"; and in this case the adequacy of the qualitative nexus between the distinction in the two objective situations of accused persons exercising different choices, and the distinction in their treatment, is not evident. The State, it is true, has an interest in the rapid and inexpensive disposal of criminal prosecutions; but, seen from the perspective of the individual defendant whose personal liberty is very likely in issue, this interest does not seem of sufficient weight to justify forcing on him so dangerous an option. Here there is the impression that a distinction was made almost for the sake of making one, by a busybody legislator; and it may be noted that the provision in question has since been repealed.[134]

By way of appendix to *Hunt's* case, mention may be made of a point which arose in *The People (Director of Public Prosecutions) v O'Shea*,[135] in which an issue of inequality arose not from a statute but from the new interpretation of Article 34.4.3 according to which the Supreme Court majority held that the general words of the subsection, prescribing appeal to the Supreme Court from all decisions of the High Court unless excepted by a post-1937 law, admitted such an appeal even against an acquittal by the High Court exercising its criminal jurisdiction as the Central Criminal Court. No such appeal against acquittal existed where the trial had taken place in the Circuit Court; and Henchy J, one of the two Supreme Court dissentients, pointed to the conflict which this disparity of treatment represented with the equality principle of Article 40.1. Walsh J, one of the majority, said that this conflict necessarily arose from the Constitution itself, one provision of which could not be invoked to neutralise another: but the doctrine of harmonious interpretation, on which the whole judgment of Henchy J rested, would have met this argument. Given that what he called the "basic requirements of justice" are an underlying constitutional value, the existence of Article 40.1 ought to have weighed something in the scale against the literal interpretation of Article 34.4.3.[136]

The third case in this category is *Loftus v Attorney General*,[137] in which a provision of the Electoral Act 1963, was under attack; on the ground, *inter alia*, that it differentiated, for the purpose of the newly-introduced "registration" of political parties, between those

[134] Criminal Procedure (Amendment) Act 1973, s 1.
[135] [1982] IR 384.
[136] Henchy J raised this argument once more in his judgment in *The People (D.P.P.) v Quilligan No.2)*, [1989] IR 46, where he was part of a majority which refused an application for the re-trial of the 2 accused, whose previous acquittal by the Central Criminal Court had been overturned by the Supreme Court, exercising the jurisdiction first identified in *O'Shea* (on this occasion Walsh J was in the minority.) (Note that s 11 of the Criminal Procedure Bill 1993 now proposes to abolish this right of appeal.)
[137] [1979] IR 221.

already represented in the Dáil, which were entitled to automatic registration, and others, which had to go through an application process The act of registration was in no sense a licensing operation, nor did it carry any implication or certificate as to the constitutional respectability of a party; but the Act provided that Dáil election candidates were entitled to have the name of their party included on the ballot paper only if their party was registered (this was the sole practical effect of the whole registration machinery). As the criteria for registration could not be met by the plaintiff's party (which was not yet represented in the Dáil) he alleged that the differentiation was unfair and contrary to Article 40.1. The Supreme Court, holding against him, said:

> "In enacting the legislation it was proper for the Oireachtas to have regard to the existing distinction between political parties which were then represented in the Dáil and those which were not. The very fact of being represented in the Dáil satisfied in respect of each such party the statutory requirements that the party be genuinely political and that it be organised to contest elections. To require existing parties, not then represented, or newly-formed parties to apply and to satisfy these requirements. is a treatment of such parties in a manner necessarily different but not invidious and unfair."

Here, again, the difference of legislative treatment corresponds with a genuine objective difference in the situation of two categories of political party. But it is not clear that the *quality of that difference* can be rationally related to the quality of the difference in treatment; and the Supreme Court, by looking at the criteria for registration rather than at its only practical effect, did not give enough weight to this point. When the criterion here applied (in the Dáil already, or not?) is part of a process the sole result of which is to give one group the right to call attention to itself on the ballot paper, while potentially denying it to the other, the reasonableness of the distinction is not evident, and it appears merely officious again the work of a legislative busybody, and not serving any serious constitutional value or legitimate public purpose (thus falling foul of the standard of "invidiousness" proposed tentatively by Barrington J in *Brennan's* case).

Unlike the preceding cases, one might consider that the proposition being contended for implicitly underpins the reasoning of Carroll J in *MhicMhathúna v Ireland*.[138] What was at issue here was the preferential treatment, under the tax and social welfare codes, of single parent families in comparison with two parent families. Rejecting the plaintiff's contention that this discrimination offended against Article 40.1, Carroll J said:

> "The position of a single parent is different to the position of two parents living together. The parent on his or her own has a more difficult task in bringing the children up single handedly because two parents living together can give each other mutual support and assistance. I have no doubt that the role of a single parent is more difficult than that of two parents and that in giving a tax-free allowance to a single parent, the Oireachtas recognised that and attempted to alleviate it...Therefore a state of facts exists as between single parents and married couples living together with children which justifies an additional tax-free allowance for the single parent.
>
> Since the tax-free allowance is only available to a person who is earning, the State also had to make provision for child support for a woman on her own where there were no earnings. This the State did by means of [various welfare schemes directed to one-parent families headed by women]...[139]

[138] [1989] IR 504.

[139] Though such families headed by men now also qualify for similar welfare payments - see the Social Welfare (Consolidation) Act 1993, ss 157 - 158.

> In giving an allowance to an unmarried mother, the State has to bear in mind the needs of the child in respect of whom the allowance is payable and the desirability of having that child brought up by its own mother.
>
> I am satisfied therefore that a state of affairs exists which reasonably justifies the difference in allowances for an unmarried mother in comparison with the plaintiffs."

This is a very good example of where the quality of the differentiation - the provision of additional financial assistance to single parent families - bore a reasonable relation to the quality of the difference between the situations which it regulated - the additional financial and emotional strain endured by such families in comparison with two parent families - and so the legislation could be upheld. By implication from Carroll J's reasoning, if no such relationship existed, the differentiation would have been unconstitutional.

Miscellaneous cases

It remains, finally, only to mention a few miscellaneous cases in which Article 40.1 was invoked, with or without success, against statutory provisions, but in which the judgments disclose no statement of principle or approach additional to what has been cited above from other cases. *The State (McIlhagga) v Governor of Portlaoise Prison*,[140] arose from a sentence of imprisonment imposed subject to the condition that it should be lifted on repayment of money, the obtaining of which on false pretences was the offence of which the applicant had been convicted; the Supreme Court rejected the argument that this condition discriminated between persons with means and those without, as it aimed merely at the restoration of what had been wrongfully got. Article 40.1 was also unsuccessfully raised in *The State (H.) v Daly*,[141] in which Finlay P upheld provisions of the Mental Treatment Act 1945, which differentiated between the matters on which an inspector of mental hospitals was to report when a person was confined in an ordinary district mental hospital, and those on which he was to report where the person was confined in the Central Mental Hospital; in *Cullen v Attorney General*,[142] in which Hamilton J invalidated s 57 of the Road Traffic Act 1961,[143] which, where a person has been convicted by a District Judge of driving without insurance, permits the imposition of an additional fine, to represent the probable amount of an award of damages, and payable to a person injured on that occasion by the defendant's negligence; in *Finnegan v An Bord Pleanála*,[144] in which the Supreme Court rejected the submission that the exaction of a deposit of £10 to accompany a planning appeal was a discrimination between "those who have money and those who have not"; and *Draper v Attorney General*,[145] in which the Court held that Article 40.1 was not violated by the non-existence of special provision enabling physically incapacitated persons to vote in Dáil elections. In addition, Article 40.1 was invoked in *Dooley v Attorney General*,[146] a case about the Prohibition of Forcible Entry and Occupation Act 1971, but the Supreme Court held, in effect, that the plaintiff had misunderstood the provision on which the challenge was based. In *Heaney v Minister for Finance*[147] Murphy J rejected a challenge based on the alleged discrimination in the Prize Bond scheme, supposed to exist in the fact that the

[140] Supreme Court, 29 July 1971.
[141] [1977] IR 90.
[142] [1979] IR 394.
[143] Not because of any infringement of Article 40.1, but because the section was regarded as providing for the summary trial of a non-minor offence, contrary to Article 38.5.
[144] [1979] ILRM 134.
[145] [1984] IR 277; [1984] ILRM 643.
[146] [1977] IR 205.230
[147] [1986] ILRM 164.

plaintiff, who had bought a bond 20 years previously for £5, had no more than the same chance, in a current draw, as the holder of a bond bought yesterday, also for £5, but in real terms for much less (due to inflation); the apparent inequality, he held, was illusory, as the plaintiff's long-standing bond had already enjoyed many chances of winning. In *The State (Keegan) v Stardust Victims Compensation Tribunal*[148] the Supreme Court refused to see any inequality in the Tribunal's treatment of the applicant in regard to awards of different amounts for nervous shock, there being no evidence as to the facts put before the Tribunal on which it had reached its conclusions. On the other side of the line is *King v Attorney General*,[149] in which the Supreme Court held s 4 of the Vagrancy Act 1824 to be inconsistent with, *inter alia*, Article 40.1 for discriminating against a constitutionally impossible category, "suspected persons or reputed thieves".[150]

[148] [1986] IR 642; [1987] ILRM 202.
[149] [1981] IR 233.
[150] See above, p. 575.

Article 40.2

CONTROL OF TITLES

2. 1° Titles of nobility shall not be conferred by the State.

2° No title of nobility or of hon- our may be accepted by any citizen except with the prior approval of the Government.

2. 1° Ní cead don Stát gairm uaisleachta a bhronnadh ar aon duine.

2° Ní cead d'aon saoránach gairm uaisleachta ná gairm onóra a ghlacadh ach le haontú roimh ré ón Rialtas.

1922 provision

The 1922 Constitution contained a corresponding provision in Article 5, which read:

> "No title of honour in respect of any services rendered in or in relation to the Irish Free State (Saorstát Éireann) may be conferred on any citizen of the Irish Free State (Saorstát Éireann) except with the approval or upon the advice of the Executive Council of the State."

This formulation clearly envisaged that the British might expect to continue the bestowal of royal honours here, and was obviously designed to subject any such thing to the control of the Irish Government. (In the event it did not arise.) In the original form of the draft Article 40.2 there was a second sentence in the first sub-section which read: "Orders of Merit may, however, be created"; but this provision was dropped at the Recommittal.[1] The debate in the Dáil reveals that Article 40.2 was intended as a qualification to Article 40.1.[2]

Official practice

The current practice is that "titles of nobility or of honour" are interpreted officially as being honours conferred by or on behalf of a sovereign authority, the recipients of which become entitled, by the law or custom of the other country, to use prefixes to their names; where it arises, permission is normally given. Article 40.2.2 is not taken to relate to mere "letters after one's name", medals, ribbons, or academic honours.

Article 40.2 does not appear ever to have been judicially considered.

[1] 68 *Dáil Debates* 183. The discussion on orders of merit is at 67 *Dáil Debates* 1617 ff.

[2] Mr. de Valera said that "it is only in the context of 'all citizens as human persons shall be held equal', as a rule, that you have this question of whether you shall or shall not have titles of nobility, and so on" (67 *Dáil Debates* 1622). It may be that both the old Article 5 and the present Article 40.2 were suggested by Article 109 of the German Constitution (of the Weimar Republic) of 1919. For an interesting note on Article 40.2, see "*The Constitution and the Acceptance of Honours*" (1946) 80 ILTSJ 165.

PERSONAL RIGHTS

3. **1° The State guarantees in its laws to respect, and, as far as practicable, by its laws to defend and vindicate the personal rights of the citizen.**

2° The State shall, in particular, by its laws protect as best it may from unjust attack and, in the case of injustice done, vindicate the life, person, good name, and property rights of every citizen.

3. **1° Ráthaíonn an Stát gan cur isteach lena dhlíthe ar chearta pearsanta aon saoránaigh, agus ráthaíonn fós na cearta sin a chosaint is a shuíomh lena dhlíthe sa mhéid gur féidir é.**

2° Déanfaidh an Stát, go sonrach, lena dhlíthe, beatha agus pearsa agus dea-chlú agus maoinchearta an uile shaoránaigh a chosaint ar ionsaí éagórach chomh fada lena chumas, agus iad a shuíomh i gcás éagóra.

Innovation

These sub-sections had no precedent in the 1922 Constitution.

Sub-sections formerly regarded as containing no firm criteria

In the earlier life of the Constitution these sub-sections were treated by the courts, when they adverted to them at all, as a general statement with no very specific content; references to them tended to be marginal to the other constitutional provisions on which the courts or counsel relied. Thus in *The State (Burke) v Lennon*[1] Gavan Duffy J cited the contents of this "significant clause" of Article 40 in laying the ground for his finding against internment; but in the very same context the Supreme Court, in *In re Article 26 and the Offences Against the State (Amendment) Bill, 1940*,[2] found it "impossible to accede" to the argument that internment provisions were repugnant to the clause:

> "The guarantee in the clause is not in respect of any particular citizen, or class of citizens, but extends to all the citizens of the State, and the duty of determining the extent to which the rights of any particular citizen, or class of citizens, can properly be harmonised with the rights of the citizens as a whole seems to us to be a matter which is peculiarly within the province of the Oireachtas, and any attempt by this Court to control the Oireachtas in the exercise of this function would, in our opinion, be a usurpation of its authority."

The Court thus saw no serious criterion for judicial review in the sub-sections; nor did it deepen its analysis of them in the next case in which they were invoked, *In re Philip Clarke*,[3] when provisions of the Mental Treatment Act 1945, permitting the police to detain a mentally infirm person, were challenged:

> "The [impugned] section cannot, in our opinion, be construed as an attack upon the personal rights of the citizen. On the contrary it seems to us to be designed for the protection of the citizen and for the promotion of the common good."

[1] [1940] IR 136; (1940) 74 ILTR 36,131.
[2] [1940] IR 470; (1940) 74 ILTR 61.
[3] [1950] IR 235; (1951) 85 ILTR 119.

In particular, in the first twenty-five years of the Constitution's existence there was almost[4] no exploration of the general phrase "personal rights" in the first sub-section: no one could have said whether it was or was not coextensive with the specific rights, collectively labelled "Fundamental Rights", set out in Articles 40-44; or whether it was meant to summarise the curious parallel set of rights referred to in the second sub-section; or whether it had some meaning transcending both of those categories. It was, of course, not so much that the drafters of the Constitution had had clear notions about these matters in their minds which the courts had somehow failed to perceive and to marshal for practical purposes, as that in 1937, when no one guessed at or intended the active engine which judicial review was later to become, there seemed no need to organise, as a set of neat and clear legal norms, statements which were to be mere "headlines to the legislature".[5] Hence much overlapping, duplication, minor verbal distinctions, from which in recent times much judicial ingenuity has sought to extract results which cannot be realistically imputed to the drafters' intentions. On the other side of the balance, however, the very imprecision of Article 40.3 has made possible, since the landmark case of *Ryan v Attorney General*[6] in 1963, an important and beneficial strain of judicial activism in the doctrine of "unspecified personal rights".[7]

Period of closer analysis

During the 1980s, the courts subjected Article 40.3 to close scrutiny, leading to the emergence of a number of conflicting analyses which focus, in particular, on the differences between sub-sections 1 and 2. One analysis distinguished between unspecified personal rights, which are protected by sub-section 1, and specified personal rights protected by sub-section 2. Thus, in *Attorney General v Paperlink Ltd.*[8] Costello J took the view that the right to earn a livelihood fell within the scope of Article 40.3.1, rather than Article 40.3.2, as it was not derived from the citizen's property rights, one of the specified rights mentioned in the latter provision. Conversely, in *Brennan v Attorney General,*[9] where the plaintiffs argued that the system of county rates authorised by s 11 of the Local Government Act 1946, amounted to an unjust attack on property rights, the Supreme Court held that the complaints of the aggrieved parties should be considered primarily under Article 40.3.2. However, in *Cafolla v O'Malley*,[10] Costello J modified his earlier views, moving now to the position that, as the Constitution is a political as well as a legal document, no significance should be attached to the fact that the State's duty towards the citizen's unspecified personal rights in Article 40.3.1 is phrased in somewhat different language from that describing its duty towards specified personal rights, set out in Article 40.3.2:

> "Whilst it is true that the language of the two sub-paragraphs is not identical, I do not think that, in the ambit of the protection afforded and the State's duty to the citizen which arises, I should regard these differences as being of any significance. I believe...that the Court should not in interpreting the Constitution employ the same literal approach as it would, for example, when construing a Finance Act; and that as a political as well as a legal document it should not too strictly parse the phraseology employed but rather consider the broad intentions of the instrument as a

[4] But not quite: see Mr. Justice Budd's reference to the right to work and earn a livelihood, made in 1954; below, pp. 756-757.
[5] See above, p. 671, Fn. 2.
[6] [1965] IR 294.
[7] See R.F.V Heuston, "*Personal Rights under the Irish Constitution*" (1976) 11 Ir Jur (n.s.) 205; W.N. Osborough, "*Constitutional Law - A Waning of Judicial Activism?*" (1979-80) DULJ 101.
[8] [1984] ILRM 373. See *McCormack*, (1984) 6 DULJ (n.s.) 144.
[9] [1984] ILRM 355.
[10] [1985] IR 486.

whole. If, then, I find that there has been an "unjust attack" on the exercise by the plaintiff of his right to earn a livelihood it will follow that an infringement of the rights conferred by both subparagraphs has been established."[11]

This approach does not have universal support, and instances can still be found where a more literal approach has been taken, most evident in the judgment of Henchy J in *Pine Valley Developments Ltd. v Minister for the Environment*:[12]

"Article 40.3.1 is not relevant to a case such as the present where the complaint is essentially not of a failure to defend and vindicate a personal right but of an injustice alleged to have been actually done to a personal right. Such a complaint falls to be decided under Article 40.3.2."

In his analysis of Article 40.3.2, Henchy J drew a distinction between the first part of the sub-section, detailing the State's duty to protect personal rights from unjust attack, which he noted is qualified by the phrase "as best it may",[13] and the remainder of the provision imposing an unqualified obligation on the State to vindicate the life, person, good name and property rights of every citizen where an injustice has actually occurred.[14] Article 40.3.2 was analysed also in *E.S.B. v Gormley*,[15] where the Supreme Court held that the State's duty to protect the citizen's personal rights from unjust attack must be considered to be antecedent to its duty to vindicate such rights in the case of injustice done. Therefore it was no answer to a challenge to s 53 of the Electricity (Supply) Act 1927, which allowed the E.S.B. to place electricity lines on private property without paying compensation to the owners, to say that if constitutional rights were infringed, the owner could sue the E.S.B. for damages.

Contemporary decisions containing no firm criteria

Such close analysis of the text of Article 40.3 remains the exception rather than the rule. Indeed the rather large terms of the provision occasionally tempts judges to invoke it, mantra-like and without any elaboration, in support of implied rights. A good example of this is the decision of Barr J in *C.M. v T.M.*[16] in which he identified as personal rights warranting the protection of Article 40.3, the right to an independent domicile and the right to continue to receive maintenance after a foreign domicile-based divorce has been obtained. In relation to the former case, he simply asserted that "a married woman's right to an independent domicile, now specifically recognised by statute, is a fundamental personal right within the ambit of Article 40.3.1 which the state has an obligation by its laws to respect, defend and vindicate." Recognition of the second right was preceded by nothing more than the premise that failure to protect it would cause hardship:

"It seems to me that if s 5 of the [Family Law (Maintenance of Spouses and Children) Act 1976] was construed as meaning that a maintenance order made during the subsistence of a marriage for the benefit of a spouse and/or children thereof

[11] On appeal, the Supreme Court proceeded on the basis that the plaintiff's property rights were at risk, without adverting to Costello J's analysis in the High Court.

[12] [1987] IR 23; [1987] ILRM 747.

[13] In *Moynihan v Greensmyth* [1977] IR 55, the Supreme Court deduced from this phrase that there could be circumstances in which the State would have to balance protection of a personal right against other obligations arising from regard to the common good. *Pine Valley* itself could be regarded as a good example of such a balancing exercise.

[14] The unqualified obligation arises only where the prior condition of proving an injustice done has been satisfied and the burden of proof here rests on the person seeking to enforce the obligation - see the judgment of Henchy J (Finlay CJ and Hederman J concurring) in *Hanrahan v Merck Sharp and Dohme* [1988] ILRM 629.

[15] [1985] IR 129; [1985] ILRM 494.

[16] [1991] ILRM 268.

> would automatically lapse if a foreign decree of divorce entitled to recognition in Irish law is obtained by the debtor spouse, it might result in unjust hardship for those in whose interest the order was made...In my view such a narrow construction would be incompatible with the Constitution in that it may have the effect of depriving a spouse and/or children of maintenance benefit to which our courts have found them to be entitled, even in circumstances where no alternative or comparable maintenance has been awarded to them in lieu thereof by any other court...A statutory provision which could bring about that result would seem to me to be incompatible with Article 40.1 and Article 40.3.1 and Article 41 of the Constitution."[17]

A similar temptation obviously exists for counsel as the provision has been invoked (unsuccessfully) to challenge the alleged failure of the State to have regard to the interests of the majority community in Northern Ireland[18] and in support of a right not to be extradited in respect of political offences[19] and a right to oblige the Government to act in accordance with the Constitution.[20]

A more restrained approach to the identification of implied personal rights may be seen in the judgment of Costello J in *McKenna v An Taoiseach*[21] where, rejecting the plaintiff's claim that she had a right that the decision of the electorate on the ratification of the Treaty on European Union should be arrived at by fair procedures and scrupulously in accordance with the Constitution, he said:

> "I cannot agree that it is a permissible mode of constitutional construction to fashion a constitutionally protected fundamental right in the manner implied by this part of the plaintiff's claim. What has been done is (a) to predicate the manner in which some or all of the organs of government should act to comply with their constitutional obligations and then (b) to assume that the Constitution conferred a protected fundamental right on each citizen that the organs of government would so act. But such an assumption cannot validly be made. As the right asserted in this part of the claim is not a personal right protected by Article 40.3.1, and as it is not one which can reasonably be implied from any of those expressly protected in the constitutional text, no infringement of a constitutional right has occurred."

The specific values protected by Article 40.3.2

Before passing to a consideration of the "unspecified personal rights" something may be said about the values expressly mentioned in Article 40.3.2 - life, person, good name and property rights.

[17] Another example of this type of reasoning can be seen in *Ryan v Ireland* [1989] IR 126; [1989] ILRM 544, where Finlay CJ's conclusion that the State enjoyed no common-law immunity from suit in respect of operations consisting of armed conflict or hostilities was followed by the remark that, even if such an immunity did exist at common law, "in the blanket form which has been contended for it would be inconsistent with the guarantees by the State to respect, defend and vindicate the rights of the citizens contained in Article 40, s 3 sub-ss 2 of the Constitution." Henchy J used Article 40.3.1 in similar fashion in support of his conclusion that the defence to a defamation action of qualified privilege did not cover a person making a communication who honestly but mistakenly believed that the person receiving such communication had a duty or interest in receiving it - *Hynes-O'Sullivan v O'Driscoll* [1988] IR 436; [1989] ILRM 349.

[18] *McGimpsey v Ireland* [1990] ILRM 460; [1990] 1 IR 110.

[19] *Magee v Culligan* [1992] 1 IR 223; [1992] ILRM 186. See also *Shannon v Ireland* [1984] IR 548.

[20] *McKenna v An Taoiseach*, High Court, 8 June 1992. Though *cp. Crotty v An Taoiseach* [1987] IR 713; [1987] ILRM 400, and Casey, "*Crotty v An Taoiseach: A Comparative Perspective*" in O'Reilly, ed., *Human Rights and Constitutional Law: Essays in Honour of Brian Walsh* (Dublin, 1992).

[21] High Court, 8 June 1992.

(i) The right to life

The right to life expressed in Article 40.3.2 does not seem ever to have been invoked - never, for example, against the infliction of capital punishment - or even mentioned in an Irish court until *Ryan v Attorney General*.[22] It was not central to that case, which turned rather on the "right to bodily integrity"; but Kenny J, in admitting that the latter right existed, seemed to connect it closely with the right to life, although both in this case and in the slightly later case of *Conroy v Attorney General*[23] he buttressed his conclusion not so much with the explicit constitutional right to life, as with that flowing from Christian moral theology.[24] In *McGee v Attorney General*[25] the constitutional right to life began for the first time to develop a profile independent of this, when Walsh J derived from it the right of a woman, whose condition of health made pregnancy hazardous for her, not to have her life put at risk in consequence of the laws of the State:

> "One of the personal rights of a woman in the plaintiff's state of health would be a right to be assisted in her efforts to avoid putting her life in jeopardy. I am of opinion also that not only has the State the right to do so, but, by virtue of the terms of the proviso to s 1 and the terms of s 3 of Article 40, the State has the positive obligation to ensure by its laws as far as is possible (and in the use of the word "possible" I am relying on the Irish text of the Constitution) that there would be made available to a married woman in the condition of health of the plaintiff the means whereby a conception which was likely to put her life in jeopardy might be avoided when it is a risk over and above the ordinary risks inherent in pregnancy."

But in the same case the same judge went further, by mentioning, for the first time in an Irish court, the right to life in the context of an unborn child:

> "Any action on the part of either the husband and wife or of the State to limit family sizes by endangering or destroying human life must necessarily not only be an offence against the common good but also against the guaranteed personal rights of the human life in question."

He became fully explicit on this point in *G. v An Bord Uchtála*:[26]

> "[A child] has the right to life itself and the right to be guarded against all threats directed to its existence whether before or after birth... The right to life necessarily implies the right to be born, the right to preserve and defend, and to have preserved and defended, that life..."

In spite of these *dicta*, *McGee's* case, which had the effect of demolishing one of the criminal inhibitions to contraception, was the first chapter in the history of the enactment of the third sub-section of Article 40.3.[27]

[22] [1965] IR 294.
[23] [1965] IR 411.
[24] In *Ryan's* case he had cited a papal encyclical, "*Peace on Earth*" (John XXIII, 1963) "Beginning our discussion of the rights of man, we see that every man has the right to life, to bodily integrity and to the means which are necessary and suitable for the proper development of life: these are primarily food, clothing, shelter, rest, medical care. and finally the necessary social services." In *Conroy's* case, having heard evidence from a former professor of moral theology on the subject of the moral gravity of drunken driving, he summarised this evidence as being to the effect that "from the ethical standpoint, every individual as an individual has certain inherent rights of which the right to life is the most fundamental; after it comes the right to bodily integrity..."
[25] [1974] IR 284; (1975) 109 ILTR 29.
[26] [1980] IR 32; (1979) 113 ILTR 25.
[27] Considered below, pp. 790 *et seq*.

The right to life, together with the rights to bodily integrity and property, was recently invoked in an unsuccessful attempt by the Director of Public Prosecutions to persuade the Supreme Court to reverse its decision in *The People (Attorney General) v O'Callaghan*[28] and allow a propensity to criminal behaviour to be taken into account in refusing bail - *Ryan v The Director of Public Prosecutions.*[29]

To date, the Irish courts have not yet been asked to consider whether there is a correlative right to die, particularly in the context of a terminally-ill patient refusing life-prolonging treatment. Mr. Justice Costello, writing extra-judicially, has suggested that a doctor who turned off a terminally ill patient's life-support machine might not be guilty of murder under Irish law; and that the right of privacy might evolve so as to include the right of such a patient, if competent to make a rational choice, to have life-prolonging treatment discontinued.[30]

(ii) The right of the person to protection

The appearance of the word "person" as one of the objects of the verbs "protect" and "vindicate" conveys no clear idea over and above the other obligations which Article 40 and the other "fundamental rights" Articles impose upon the State. Although this word, featuring in this recital, might have been plausibly made into the immediate root of some of the "unspecified personal rights" derived from Article 40.3.1, it has in fact played no independent part at all, apart from an isolated passage in *The State (Burke) v Lennon*[31] in which Gavan Duffy J said that a law providing for internment without trial "does unjustly attack the person" of the prisoner. It could, for example, be argued that protection of the person means protection of the person in all normal dimensions which human existence in society entails, and thus carries in itself the right to privacy, the right to earn a livelihood, and so on; but in the various cases in which the right to earn a livelihood was invoked, it was presented usually in the form of an aspect of property rights; and when, as in *Norris v Attorney General*,[32] a claim was raised in defence of an expression of human personality, albeit by an abnormal and to some people repugnant mode, the right of privacy for an individual's actions was deduced from the general post-*Ryan* cornucopia of "personal rights" rather than from the specific reference in Article 40.3.2 to the State's duty to protect the rights of *the person.*

In archaic usage, "person" signified "character" and an illustration of this meaning of the term may be inferred from the decision of Blayney J in *J.G. v Governor of Mountjoy Prison.*[33] At issue here was the constitutionality of s 102 of the Children's Act 1908 which authorised the detention of young offenders between the age of 14 and 16 in an adult prison where the Court certified that the offender was of so unruly a character that he could not be detained in a juvenile detention centre or that he was of so depraved a character that he was not a fit person to be so detained. Dismissing counsel's argument that this provision was inconsistent with Article 40.3 and in particular with justice, prudence and charity. Blayney J held that it defended the plaintiff's rights by prohibiting their imprisonment except in certain specified circumstances. Moreover, it also protected the other young offenders in the place of detention against persons of depraved char-

[28] [1966] IR 501. See below, pp. 843-846.
[29] [1989] IR 399.
[30] "*The Terminally Ill - The Law's Concerns*" (1986) 21 Ir Jur (n.s.) 35.
[31] [1940] IR 136; (1940) 74 ILTR 36, 131.
[32] [1984] IR 36.
[33] [1991] 1 IR 373.

acter. Though the judge himself did not employ the term, one could argue that this latter concern for the moral, as distinct from physical, well-being of the young offenders, implicit in his remarks, may capture the essence of the State's obligation to vindicate the "person" of every citizen.

(iii) The right to one's good name

This was the right which, of all those stated or latent in Article 40.3, seems to have been the first used to ground a judgment. In *The State (Vozza) v Floinn*[34] the applicant had been tried without jurisdiction, as he had been tried summarily on a charge for which he might have had a jury, but had not been informed of his rights in this regard; it was put to the Supreme Court that it should exercise its discretion not to grant *certiorari*, but Maguire CJ said it would be a serious matter for the applicant if the stigma of his conviction remained on the record, and Kingsmill Moore J, taking the same view, said:

> "The Constitution by Article 40.3.2 provides that the State "shall, in particular, by its laws protect as best it may from unjust attack and, in the case of injustice done, vindicate the life, person, good name and property rights of every citizen". Here we have a wrong continuing, character at issue, and a defective order operating as a blot on character. Injustice has been done, and if the words of the Constitution are to have any effect, an order for *certiorari* should issue *ex debito justitiae*."

The citizen's right to his good name was again asserted, fifteen years later, by the Supreme Court in *In re Haughey*,[35] together with a corollary, namely the right to *defend* one's good name by appropriate means when it is impugned (presumably, whether in a legal proceeding or in any other setting). The applicant here had not been allowed by the Dáil Public Accounts Committee to cross-examine witnesses who had offered evidence prejudicial to him, or to address the committee in his own defence; he was admittedly not formally in the position of a defendant, as the committee was merely enquiring into the fate of public funds, but in the course of the enquiry material so damaging to him was adduced that the Supreme Court thought the guarantee of fair procedures which it saw in Article 40.3 was not respected by the committee. Ó Dálaigh CJ speaking for the majority identified four minimum protections which the State must afford to a person whose good name is under attack at an Inquiry in which witnesses enjoy statutory immunity -

a) the person accused should be furnished with a copy of the evidence which reflected on his good name;

b) he should be allowed to cross-examine, by counsel, his accuser;

c) he should be allowed to give rebutting evidence; and

d) he should be permitted to address the tribunal, again by counsel in his own defence.

He said:

[34] [1957] IR 227.
[35] [1971] IR 217.

> "Without the two rights [of cross-examining and of addressing the committee] which the committee's procedures have purported to exclude, no accused - I speak within the context of the terms of the inquiry - could hope to make any adequate defence of his good name."

However, in *K Security v Ireland*,[36] Gannon J rejected an attempt to extend the implications of the right to good name (and the other values protected by Article 40.3.2) when involved in judicial or analogous proceedings. Here the plaintiff had felt obliged to be represented at a Tribunal of Inquiry set up to investigate a television programme in the making of which his firm had become involved; and he now sought to recover from the State the cost of his representation, even though the Act governing the Tribunal's working made no provision for an award of costs. Using the *Haughey* case as a basis, he argued (in the paraphrase of Gannon J) that:

> "[the Tribunal] was established by the State to conduct publicly an investigation for State purposes, which of its nature threatened [his] good name, reputation, business connection and property rights... The nature and purpose of the enquiry was such as to put [him] in a position more analogous to that of a person accused of a criminal offence than to that of a witness to facts. The principles of justice require that in such circumstances [he] is entitled as of right to be legally represented before the Tribunal. The right to be legally represented before the Tribunal involves the necessary ancillary right to be indemnified by the State against the expense incurred for such legal representation."

Gannon J retorted upon him the very words of Article 40.3.2:

> "The purpose of the enquiry, stated in simplest form, appears to have been to ascertain whether or not the good name and property rights of some citizens had been subjected to unjust attack or required to be defended or vindicated... Seen in this light the appointment of the Tribunal and the holding of the enquiry was a vigilant exercise by the State of its constitutional duties imposed by Article 40.3."

He refused to regard the plaintiff as being in a position more vulnerable than that of a mere witness, or analogous to that of the plaintiff in *Re Haughey* (though he did not explain what he saw as the difference between the two positions); and held that, even if he were incorrect in that view, the State was not obliged to pay the costs of the plaintiff's legal representation.[37]

An attempt to rely on the right to one's good name in order to restrict the activities of a tribunal of inquiry established by resolutions of the Dáil and Seanad failed in *Goodman International v Hamilton (No.1)*.[38] The applicants contended, *inter alia*, that the publicity attendant on the proceedings of the tribunal could make them incapable of having a fair trial by jury in a criminal charge, if such charge were brought against them, and that they would therefore be deprived of the possibility of obtaining an acquittal on such a trial which would clear their good name. Dismissing this contention, Finlay CJ, with whom O'Flaherty and Egan JJ concurred, pointed out that if a person charged with a criminal offence can establish that due to pre-trial publicity a fair trial is impossible, the courts have jurisdiction to prevent an injustice occurring (presumably by granting an

[36] High Court, 15 July 1977.

[37] See also *Condon v C.I.É.*, High Court, 16 November 1984, where a submission that the plaintiff's constitutional right to his good name and property rights obliged the State to pay the legal costs incurred by him in defending such rights before an inquiry was rejected by Barrington J.

[38] [1992] 2 IR 542; [1992] ILRM 145.

order of prohibition to restrain any prosecution) and that, given the manifest public importance of the inquiry, a very clear breach of an unambiguous constitutional provision would be required before the courts would consider impeding such inquiry. In his judgment, Hederman J, (O'Flaherty and Egan JJ concurring) took the view that the procedures to be adopted by the tribunal were such as to vindicate the applicants' right to their good name, as "every opportunity will be afforded to anyone in respect of whom any allegation of impropriety is levelled to establish his version of events."

At a later stage in the Tribunal's proceedings, the same plaintiffs were back in court again, seeking further protection for their right to their good name:- *Goodman International v Hamilton (No.2).*[39] The immediate background to this litigation was a ruling of the Chairman of the Tribunal, Hamilton P, that three members of Dáil Éireann could not be compelled, because of Article 15.12-13, to explain statements made by them in the Dáil, nor could they be required to furnish to the Tribunal the source of the information on which the statements were based. In *Attorney General v Hamilton (No.2)*[40] Geoghegan J held, *inter alia*, that the rights of privilege and non-amenability conferred on members of the Oireachtas by Article 15.12-13 were absolute even in the sense that they could not be sacrificed to protect constitutional rights such as the right to a good name.[41] Facing the possibility that the three Dáil Deputies could refuse to answer questions in the Tribunal relating to the matters under investigation, the plaintiffs had argued, again before Geoghegan J that vindication of their right to a good name entitled them to an immediate ruling by the Tribunal clearing them in respect of the allegations made. They had also argued that the Deputies should not be entitled to give hearsay evidence or to participate further in respect of any allegations made by them and that such allegations should not have considered further by the Tribunal.

Dismissing these arguments, Geoghegan J held that the Tribunal would discharge its obligation to respect and vindicate the right to a good name by ensuring that there is a fair hearing in which, where appropriate, the protections identified by Ó Dálaigh CJ in *Re Haughey*[42] were provided and reflected in the ultimate report of the Tribunal. More specifically, he rejected the contention that the Tribunal was obliged to make interim and definitive reports or recommendations ahead of the official ultimate report. After noting two important differences between the position of the plaintiffs and that of the plaintiff in *Re Haughey* - in the earlier case, there had been a real and appreciable danger of the good name of Mr Haughey being destroyed on foot of hearsay or purely speculative evidence, while in the instant case, Hamilton P had made it clear that he would rely only on direct evidence; secondly, unlike Mr Haughey, the plaintiffs here had been granted the rights of parties to the hearing and were allowed to appear by counsel to cross-examine witnesses and to address the Tribunal - he concluded:

[39] High Court, 18 February 1993.
[40] [1993] ILRM 821, decided the same day as *Goodman International v Hamilton (No.2).*
[41] He went on to hold, however, that having regard to the rights protected by the Constitution, the right to refuse to answer questions arising under Article 15.13 could apply only to "utterances made in either House of the Oireachtas or at a meeting of a Committee of either House of the Oireachtas involved in the legislative process" and that, in the instant case, it did not apply in respect of any matter contained in the statements of the Dáil Deputies delivered to the Tribunal. On this point he was subsequently overruled by a majority of the Supreme Court who held that the immunity also applied where (*per* Finlay CJ) "there was a dual speaking of the words concerned, one inside and one outside the House of the Oireachtas concerned". (On the facts of the case, there was no question that the repetition by the Deputies of their Dáil statements in their statements to the Tribunal constituted a waiver by them of their protection under Article 15). By the time the Supreme Court had delivered its decision on the appeal, Geoghegan J had himself decided that the Deputies were entitled, at common law, to refuse to answer questions arising out of confidential communications with members of the public - *Goodman International v Hamilton (No.3)*, High Court, 27 May 1993. For a further discussion of fair procedures in the context of this Tribunal, see *Boylan v Beef Tribunal* [1993] 1 IR 210.
[42] [1971] IR 217.

"[M]y view is that the Tribunal is carrying out its obligation to vindicate the applicants' good name if it does not permit hearsay evidence to impugn that good name and if it accedes to reasonable requests for the availability of particular witnesses considered necessary for the vindication of a good name provided that it is possible to obtain such witnesses or evidence."

This litigious odyssey also illustrates a constitutional limitation on the right to one's good name, *viz.*, that it cannot prevail against the privileges and immunities conferred by Article 15.12-13.[43]

The right to one's good name was also invoked by Carney J in *Stringer v The Irish Times*[44] when dismissing an argument that in the context of ongoing litigation, privilege attached to documents which had not been - either actually or notionally - opened in court. According to the judge, this contention involved the logical consequence that "anybody could be defamed with impunity by the expenditure of the current price of the stamp duty on a plenary summons", a situation which was not consistent with the State's obligation to vindicate the good name of every citizen.

In the context of criminal and disciplinary proceedings

The right to one's good name has been considered in the context of criminal and disciplinary proceedings in a number of cases. In *The State (O'Rourke and White) v Martin*[45] Gannon J expressed the view that every person tried on a criminal charge had:

"in the protection of his good name and his livelihood the benefits of the presumption of innocence [and other features of due course of law]."

In *M. v Medical Council*[46] the plaintiff argued that the failure of the Medical Practitioners Act 1978, to prohibit the publication of the findings of a Fitness to Practice Committee, in the event of their being of opinion that a practitioner was guilty of professional misconduct or unfit to practice medicine, constituted a failure to vindicate and defend his good name. Finlay P held, however, that Article 40.3.2 cannot constitute an obligation on the State by its laws to protect any person from every statement or publication which might damage his good name. Pointing out that the public has a clear and identifiable interest in the case of a person practising medicine to be informed of a responsible view reached by his colleagues with regard to his standard of conduct or fitness, he declined to regard the Act's procedures as a failure to protect the good name of a practitioner from an unjust attack. Furthermore, as the Act enabled a person such as the plaintiff to have a full hearing in public before the High Court in which, if he was successful, the verdict would necessarily and completely vindicate his reputation, there was in fact a sufficient protection of his good name to make the entire statutory scheme consistent with the Constitution.

The law of defamation

The connection between the general law of defamation and the constitutional right to one's good name has been made in a number of cases. Brief references to the State's obligation to vindicate the good name of every citizen in the case of injustice done occur in the judgment of McCarthy J in *Barrett v Independent Newspapers Ltd.*[47] - where, dissenting on this point, he held that a trial judge could direct a jury to find that a person

[43] See above, pp. 140-144.
[44] High Court, 3 February 1993.
[45] [1984] ILRM 331.
[46] [1984] IR 485.
[47] [1986] IR 13; [1986] ILRM 601.

had been defamed - and in *Kennedy v Hearne*[48] where Murphy J expressly acknowledged the role of the law of defamation in vindicating the citizen's right to his good name. The impact of the Constitution on the law of defamation featured more prominently in *Hynes-O'Sullivan v O'Driscoll*[49] where two members of the Supreme Court - Henchy and McCarthy JJ - invoked the right to one's good name in dismissing the defendant's contentions that the defence of qualified privilege to an action for defamation exists if the speaker honestly, or alternatively, honestly and reasonably, believes that the person receiving the communication has a duty or interest in receiving it.

Given that the law of defamation may be regarded as protection for the constitutional right to one's good name, doubts may exist as the constitutionality of the exclusion of defamation from the range of actions in respect of which the State is willing to provide civil legal aid.[50] The obligation on the State to vindicate the right to the citizen's good name, where injustice has been done, is unqualified.[51] Even if one took the view that this obligation did not give rise to a duty to provide legal aid to an impoverished, defamed plaintiff, it must surely be the case that once the State decides to provide such aid, any exclusion from the scheme, particularly one which affects constitutional rights, must be justifiable. However, the exclusion of defamation actions from the Scheme of Civil Legal Aid and Advice would appear to be based on an assumption, for which no supporting evidence has ever been offered, that its inclusion would either result in a flood of litigation or encourage vexatious litigation.

(iv) Property rights

The guarantee of property rights in Article 40.3.2 is but one of two references in the Constitution to the rights of private property - the other being Article 43. As these two constitutional provisions tend to be invoked together in litigation, it seems best to combine the discussion of this dimension of Article 40.3 with discussion of the later Article.[52]

THE "UNSPECIFIED PERSONAL RIGHTS" OF ARTICLE 40.3

The expansion of the reach of Article 40.3, which is one of the most conspicuous features of contemporary constitutional jurisprudence, began in the 1950s, but became rapid only after 1964. This trend has taken the form of judicial willingness to identify further rights as ancillary or corollary to those stated in the second sub-section; or to acknowledge them as latent in the general expression "personal rights" in the first: a trend which has had many positive results, but which has also been marked - unfortunately from the point of view of one attempting a systematic exposition of an organic law - by a certain blurring of definition, a certain bursting of conceptual banks, rather as though legal rivers finding their confluence in the estuary of liberty and justice, had had

48 [1988] IR 481; [1988] ILRM 52, 531.

49 [1988] IR 436; [1989] ILRM 349. This decision has been criticised, however, on the ground that the references to the Constitution contained therein are essentially rhetorical and that the Court did not engage in a proper analysis of the impact of the Constitution on the law of defamation - see McDonald, "*Towards a Constitutional Analysis of Non-Media Qualified Privilege*" (1989) 11 DULJ (n.s.) 94; see also O'Dell, "*Does Defamation Value Free Expression?*" (1990) 12 DULJ (n.s.) 50.

50 See *Scheme of Legal Aid and Advice* (Pl. 4197), Sch.A, para. A1.

51 See Henchy J in *Pine Valley Developments Ltd. v Minister for the Environment* [1987] IR 23; [1987] ILRM 747.

52 See below, pp. 1061 *et seq.*

their courses confused by flooding further upstream, leaving a somewhat trackless delta for the constitutional geographer. Thus the "right of access to the courts" was identified by Kenny J in *Macauley v Minister for Posts and Telegraphs*[53] as "a necessary inference from Article 34.3.1" (the plenary jurisdiction of the High Court), but in the form of "one of the personal rights of the citizen included in the general guarantee of Article 40.3"; if it is, in fact, something necessarily implied by Article 34.3.1 (or 34.1), where is the need to squeeze it in under the umbrella of another constitutional provision as well? The same judge said in *Ryan v Attorney General*[54] that the right to marry must be regarded as protected by Article 40.3, as it flowed from what was for him the same source, *viz.* the Christian and democratic nature of the State; but is it not already implicit in Article 41 which specifically enthrones "marriage, on which the family is founded"? In *Haughey's* case and in *The State (Healy) v Donoghue*[55] the right to fair procedures, although presumably the justice which the State administers through the courts would not be justice if procedures could be unfair, was related not to Article 34 but to Article 40.3. Arguably, too, the right to travel which Kenny J and Finlay P. acknowledged in *Ryan's* case and *The State (M.) v Attorney General*[56] respectively could be more simply derived from the guarantee of personal liberty in Article 40.4.1 than from the general recognition of "personal rights" in Article 40.3.1. In *Draper v Attorney General*[57] the Supreme Court "reserved its opinion" as to whether the right to vote in Dáil elections (although already conferred on citizens by Article 16.1.2) could claim the benefit of Article 40.3 as well. And so on.

However, it must be acknowledged that the context of the milestone *Ryan* case was one from which a cause of constitutional action could not have been extracted unless by the invocation of a general penumbra of rights other than those specified, and not readily deducible as corollaries of those specified. The criticism contained in the foregoing paragraph is intended merely to suggest that, where a new form of right is asserted for the first time, it would seem more orderly to build it, if possible, into the environment of a well-understood specific right; and to reserve Article 40.3.1 as a safety-net for sustaining newly-invoked rights which cannot reasonably be otherwise accommodated.

That Article 40.3 contained "unspecified personal rights" was first openly declared in *Ryan's* case; but two or three precursors may be mentioned, all of which were interpretations of "property rights" which made the phrase encompass rights about work and livelihood, and labour (and its withholding). In 1954, in *Tierney v Amalgamated Society of Woodworkers*,[58] Budd J had cited Article 40.3.1 and referred to the plaintiff's counsel:[59]

> "[saying] with some force that the right to work and earn one's livelihood is just as important a personal right of the citizen and just as much entitled to vindication, as a right of property. Lord Justice Denning says as much in *Lee v The Showmans' Guild of Great Britain*,[60] and with respect I agree."

[53] [1966] IR 345.
[54] [1965] IR 294.
[55] [1976] IR 325; (1976) 110 ILTR 9.
[56] [1979] IR 73.
[57] [1984] IR 277; [1984] ILRM 539.
[58] [1959] IR 254.
[59] Mr. T. J Connolly, S.C., who was also counsel for the parties relying on Article 40.3 in *Educational Co. v Fitzpatrick (No. 2)* and later in *Ryan v Attorney General* and who was described as "the father of modern Irish constitutional law" by Barrington J writing extra-judicially, in "*The Constitution in the Courts*", in Litton (ed.) *The Constitution of Ireland 1937-1987* (I.P.A. 1988), 110 at p.114.
[60] [1952] 2 QB 329, 343.

In 1957, in *Brendan Dunne Ltd. v Fitzpatrick*,[61] the same judge adverted to Article 40.3 as one of a number of constitutional provisions which bolstered:

> "[the rights of] the employer and worker respectively to deal with and dispose of their property and labour as they will without interference unless such interference be made legitimate by law."

And in *Educational Co. v Fitzpatrick (No. 2)*[62] Kingsmill Moore J said in the Supreme Court:

> "The undertaking in Article 40.3.2 to protect the property rights of every citizen may perhaps include an undertaking to protect his right to dispose of his labour as he wills, and would include impliedly a right not to be forced against his will into a union or association which exacts from him a regular payment."

In both statements of Budd J, and in that just cited of Kingsmill Moore J, there seems to be a perception of the rights surrounding labour and livelihood as mere deductions from, or aspects of, the explicitly mentioned "property rights" of Article 40.3.2; though what Budd J said in *Tierney's* case might also mean that he saw the right to work as having a status independent of property. And this idea emerged also in a later part of the judgment of Kingsmill Moore J in the *Educational Co.* case:

> The right to dispose of one's labour and to withdraw it seems to me a fundamental personal right which, though not specifically mentioned in the Constitution as being guaranteed, is a right of a nature which I cannot conceive to have been adversely affected by anything within the intendment of the Constitution. But the matter does not arise for decision in this case.

First declaration of a latent, "unspecified" right

The matter of unspecified personal rights of constitutional rank did, however, arise two years later in *Ryan v Attorney General,* and received a treatment in the High Court from Kenny J, subsequently endorsed by the Supreme Court, which makes the case a constitutional milestone of enormous importance.[63] The plaintiff sought to have provisions of the Health (Fluoridation of Water Supplies) Act 1960, declared unconstitutional on the ground (*inter alia*) that fluoride was dangerous to health, and that to oblige her and her family to accept fluoridated water through the public water supply (to which they had no practical alternative) was an infringement of their personal rights guaranteed by Article 40.3 - which, she said, implicitly included a "right of bodily integrity". This was the first time that anyone had claimed a specific right as latent in the general expression "personal rights" and not deduced from any of the rights actually enumerated in the section - life, property, etc.

Kenny J held against her on the objective question of the properties of fluoride, but agreed with her contention that:

> "the personal rights which may be invoked to invalidate legislation are not confined to those specified in Article 40 but include all those rights which result from the Christian and democratic nature of the State."

[61] [1958] IR 29.

[62] [1961] IR 345.

[63] [1965] IR 294. Fifteen years after his *Ryan* judgment, Mr. Justice Kenny acknowledged in the course of a lecture the significance of the epoch which he had inaugurated, when he said, in connection with Article 40.3: "Judges have become legislators, and have the advantage that they do not have to face an opposition": see (1979) NILQ 189, at p. 196. The explanation which he gives, in the immediately succeeding passage, of the strictly legal justification for the *Ryan* innovation is not very satisfactory.

The judge went on:

> "If [the general guarantee of Article 40.3] extends to personal rights other than those specified in Article 40, the High Court and the Supreme Court have the difficult and responsible duty of ascertaining and declaring what are the personal rights of the citizens which are guaranteed by the Constitution. In modern times this would seem to be a function of the legislative rather than of the judicial power; but it was done by the courts in the formative period of the common law and there is no reason why they should not do it now.
>
> A number of factors indicate that the guarantee is not confined to the rights specified in Article 40 but extends to other personal rights of the citizen. Firstly, there is sub-s 2 of s 3 of Article 40. [He cited this.] The words "in particular" shows that sub-s 2 is a detailed statement of something which is already contained in sub-s 1 of the general guarantee. But sub-s 2 refers to rights in connection with life and good name and there are no rights in connection with these two matters specified in Article 40. It follows, I think, that the general guarantee in sub-s 1 must extend to rights not specified in Article 40.
>
> Secondly, there are many personal rights of the citizen which follow from the Christian and democratic nature of the State which are not mentioned in Article 40 at all - the right to free movement within the State and the right to marry are examples of this. This also leads to the conclusion that the general guarantee extends to rights not specified in Article 40.
>
> In my opinion, one of the personal rights of the citizen protected by the general guarantee is the right to bodily integrity. I understand the right to bodily integrity to mean that no mutilation of the body or any of its members may be carried out on any citizen under the authority of the law except for the good of the whole body and that no process which is or may, as a matter of probability, be dangerous or harmful to the life or health of the citizens or any of them may be imposed (in the sense of being made compulsory) by an Act of the Oireachtas. [He cited a papal encyclical in support of the right to bodily integrity.] If then the Act of 1960 imposes the consumption of fluoridated water on the citizens and if that is or may, as a matter of probability, be dangerous or harmful to the life or health of any of the citizens, the plaintiff's right to bodily integrity would be infringed and the legislation would be unconstitutional."

With this statement of principle the Supreme Court agreed (while also finding against the plaintiff on the facts):

> "The Court agrees with Mr. Justice Kenny that the "personal rights" mentioned in s 3.1 are not exhausted by the enumeration of "life, person, good name, and property rights" in s 3.2 as is shown by the use of the words "in particular"; nor by the more detached treatment of specific rights in the subsequent sections of the Article. To attempt to make a list of all the rights which may properly fall within the category of "personal rights" would be difficult and, fortunately, is unnecessary in this present case.
>
> It [was contended] that among the personal rights of the individual is to be included a right to what [counsel] called "bodily integrity", and this the Attorney General intimated he was prepared to concede in the words "a right to the integrity of the person". Neither counsel offered the Court any assistance as to what the limits of

> this right to bodily integrity were. [The Court cited Mr. Justice Kenny's definition.] [Counsel for the plaintiff] says that the judge's definition is too narrow and he contends that any interference with bodily constitution is a violation of the right. However, for the reasons which hereinafter appear[64] it is unnecessary to define "bodily integrity" or the "right to the integrity of the person" or to consider to what degree and in what circumstances the State might interfere with the right, whether for the benefit of the individual concerned, the common good, or by way of punishment. The Court is not pronouncing upon Mr. Justice Kenny's definition."

The right of bodily integrity and the right not to have health endangered by the State

The right of bodily integrity once established, it broadened, in later cases involving the treatment of prisoners serving sentences, into a more general right not to have one's health endangered by the actions of the State: though, given the very special circumstances of penal imprisonment, it is not clear that the right, as so stated, can be relied on in every other set of circumstances as well, e.g. so as to catch the State for some form of general non-feasance like failure to ensure proper housing conditions for all citizens.

In the first of these cases, *The State (C.) v Frawley*,[65] the applicant for habeas corpus was suffering from a severe sociopathic disorder which led him to commit violent acts injurious in the main to himself, this in turn causing the prison authorities to subject him to an extremely rigorous regime in the interest (as the Court found) of his own safety. One of his objections to this was that he was not being given the kind of medical attention he desired (which expert evidence had shown to be very highly specialised, and, if it was to be appropriate to the prisoner's rare condition, not available in Ireland). Finlay P said he did not think the State's obligation included "a duty to build, equip and staff the very specialised unit" which the prisoner, and a very few other similar sufferers, might need; but accepted as a general proposition that the principle in *Ryan's* case could apply by analogy here too:

> "I see no reason why the principle [of bodily integrity as an unspecified personal right] should not also operate to prevent an act or omission of the Executive which, without justification, would expose the health of a person to risk or danger... [To state that] the Executive has a duty to protect the health of persons held in custody as well as is reasonably possible in all the circumstances of the case seems to me no more than to state in a positive manner the negative proposition which I have above accepted. Therefore, I am satisfied that such a proposition is sound in law."

The case of *The State (McDonagh) v Frawley*[66] does not add much to *C.'s* case: it was one in which a convicted prisoner who complained of backache for which he said he was not receiving proper treatment sought habeas corpus on the ground of alleged breach of his right of bodily integrity. The High Court and Supreme Court did not question that lack of medical attention might amount to such a breach, but found that his complaint had not been substantiated (no medical opinion was produced to support it). The Chief Justice, speaking for the Supreme Court, said the prisoner:

[64] The Court found that the ingestion of water fluoridated to the extent proposed was harmless and so could not injure bodily integrity.

[65] [1976] IR 365. See *Cooney* at (1977) 12 Ir Jur (n.s.) 103.

[66] [1978] IR 131. See *Byrne* (1979) 14 Ir Jur (n.s.) 109.

> "must accept prison discipline and accommodate himself to the reasonable organisation of prison life as laid down in the prison regulations. He cannot demand the medical treatment he thinks he should get, but he will be given such medical treatment as the medical officer of the prison thinks appropriate."

However, in *The State (Richardson) v The Governor of Mountjoy Prison*[67] Barrington J, referring to the right not to have one's health endangered which Finlay P had stated in *C.'s* case, accepted the evidence brought on behalf of the applicant, a woman prisoner, as to the disgusting sanitary conditions then prevailing in the women's section of the prison as amounting to a threat to her health. He noted that the prison rules accepted the State's responsibility here by way of prescribing exercise, the duties of the medical officer, and standards of hygiene, and said that:

> "the State has failed in its duty under the Constitution and the Rules to protect the applicant's health, and to provide her with appropriate facilities to maintain proper standards of hygiene and cleanliness."[68]

An obvious corollary of the right to bodily integrity is the right to freedom from torture, or inhuman or degrading treatment. This was recognised also in *The State (C) v Frawley,* cited above, in which the applicant also alleged that the severe regime of constraint to which he was subjected amounted to this. Finlay P said:

> "If the unspecified personal rights guaranteed by Article 40 follow in part or in whole from the Christian and democratic nature of the State, it is surely beyond argument that they include freedom from torture, and from inhuman or degrading treatment and punishment."[69]

(Twelve years earlier, Kingsmill Moore J in *The People (Attorney General) v O'Brien*[70] had said the infliction of torture to extract evidence would "involve the State in moral defilement.") However, Finlay P held that the character of "torture" or "inhuman and degrading treatment" was to be gathered partly from its purpose; and as the purpose of the restraint imposed on the prisoner here was to prevent self-injury or self-destruction, the restraint could not be thus described.[71]

Right to bodily integrity to be respected by private individuals

The right to bodily integrity must be respected, not only by the State, but also by private individuals. In both *The People (Director of Public Prosecutions) v Tiernan*[72] and *The People (Director of Public Prosecutions) v J.T.*[73] sexual assaults were characterised as an infringement of the victim's right to bodily integrity, raising the possibility that the victim could sue the attacker for damages for, *inter alia*, infringement of constitutional rights.

[67] [1980] ILRM 82.

[68] He deferred making an appropriate order on the basis of his findings in order to give the authorities an opportunity to improve the situation.

[69] See also *Murray v Ireland* [1985] IR 532; [1985] ILRM 542, where Costello J referred, *obiter*, to "the right not to be tortured [as] one of the personal rights protected but not expressly enumerated in Article 40.3.1."

[70] [1965] IR 142.

[71] The State's obligation to prevent the ill-treatment of a detainee has recently emerged as a factor which could defeat an application for extradition - see below, pp. 886-867.

[72] [1988] IR 250; [1989] ILRM 149.

[73] (1988) 3 Frewen 141.

Unsuccessful invocation of the right to bodily integrity

The right to bodily integrity has been unsuccessfully invoked in four cases. An imaginative attempt to displace the burden of proof in tort cases through reliance on this right failed in *Hanrahan v Merck Sharp and Dohme.*[74] This was an action for an injunction and damages arising out of the alleged pollution of the plaintiff's farm by emissions from the defendants' factory, in which the plaintiff submitted that a legal system which required him to discharge the onus of establishing that the air had been altered to a harmful degree as a result of emissions from the factory did not respect, *inter alia*, his right to bodily integrity. In the Supreme Court, Henchy J, with whom Finlay CJ and Hederman J concurred, dismissed this submission, saying:

> "[T]he guarantee to respect and defend personal rights given in Article 40.3.1 applies only 'as far as practicable' and the guarantee to vindicate property rights given in Article 40.3.2 refers only to cases of 'injustice done'. The guarantees, therefore, are not unqualified or absolute. I find it impossible to hold that Article 40.3.1 means that a plaintiff in an action for nuisance is to be relieved of the onus of proving the necessary ingredients of that tort. Neither, in my view, does Article 40.3.2 warrant such a dispensation, for the guarantee of vindication there given arises only 'in the case of injustice done', so it is for the plaintiff to prove that the injustice relied on was actually suffered by him and that it was caused by the defendant."

In *Sweeney v Duggan*[75] an equally imaginative use of the right to protect a victim of an industrial accident in the face of his employer's insolvency failed when Barron J rejected the claim that the employer had a duty under Article 40.3 to ensure that the employee would be duly compensated for any injury sustained arising out of or in the course of the employment. According to the judge, Article 40.3.2 gave the plaintiff no more than a guarantee of a just law of negligence, which in the circumstances existed.

In *A.D. v Ireland*,[76] Carroll J rejected the plaintiff's contention that the right to bodily integrity encompassed a constitutional right to be compensated by the State in respect of criminal injuries sustained by her, holding that the question of compensation for criminal injuries was a matter of policy for the Government and the Oireachtas.

Finally, in *The Society for the Protection of Unborn Children (Ireland) Ltd. v Grogan*[77] Morris J considered that an argument that women who travel to the UK for an abortion are deprived of post-operative care in Ireland, to the extent that the State could then be regarded as having failed to vindicate their right to bodily integrity, was not supported by the evidence adduced before him. Moreover the defendants failed to show how their activities - disseminating information about abortion clinics in the UK - could remedy the alleged problem of deprivation of post-operative care.

The right to work and to earn a livelihood

Another "personal right" which has been identified in several cases as latent in the guarantees of Article 40.3 is the right to work or the right to earn a livelihood. It has been seen that this was the context in which some early (i.e. pre-*Ryan v Attorney General*) cases had touched on Article 40.3 by way of interpreting the right to work, or to dispose of one's labour, as a kind of property right. In the first post-*Ryan* case in the same area, however, the status of the right to work as an unspecified personal right deriving from

[74] [1988] ILRM 629.
[75] [1991] 2 IR 274.
[76] High Court, 29 July 1992.
[77] [1993] 1 CMLR 197.

Article 40.3 is somewhat clouded, firstly, by the fact that the element of sex discrimination played a part in the case, secondly by the role played by Article 45, and thirdly by the fact that the judge (Kenny J) did not articulate the right as an ingredient of Article 40.3 in so many words in the way he had articulated the right of bodily integrity in *Ryan's* case.

Murtagh Properties v Cleary[78] was an action in which the plaintiffs sought to restrain the picketing of their premises by members of a trade union who objected to the employment of female staff; they pleaded, *inter alia*, that the Constitution recognised a right to earn a livelihood without discrimination of sex, and that the right was infringed when an employer who was willing to employ a woman was prevented from doing so by persons objecting solely on the grounds of sex. The most notable feature of the plaintiffs' case was their novel reliance on Article 45 - the "Directive Principles of Social Policy" - as being, even though not itself "cognisable" by the courts, still capable of acting as a course of guidance as to the personal rights latent in Article 40.3. Kenny J held with them on this point.[79] Citing Article 45.2, he said:

> "The parenthesis ["(all of whom, men and women equally, have the right to an adequate means of livelihood)"] recognises the right to an adequate means of livelihood and, while this is not enforceable against the State, its existence logically involves that each citizen has the right to earn a livelihood...Its purpose was to emphasise that, in so far as the right to an adequate means of livelihood was involved, men and women were to be regarded as equal. It follows that a policy or general rule under which anyone seeks to prevent an employer from employing men or women on the ground of sex only is prohibited by the Constitution."

The right to work or earn a livelihood took on clearer shape, as a right latent in Article 40.3, at the end of the same year (1972) in *Murphy v Stewart*,[80] when Walsh J (with whom Ó Dálaigh CJ and Budd J agreed) said in the Supreme Court, though *obiter* as the point was not squarely in issue:

> "It has been submitted in this Court on behalf of the plaintiff, and not really contested by the defendants, that among the unspecified personal rights guaranteed by the Constitution is the right to work; I accept that proposition. The question of whether that right is being infringed or not must depend upon the particular circumstances of any given case; if the right to work was reserved exclusively to members of a trade union which held a monopoly in this field and the trade union was abusing the monopoly in such a way as to effectively prevent the exercise of a person's constitutional right to work, the question of compelling that union to accept the person concerned into membership (or, indeed, of breaking the monopoly) would fall to be considered for the purpose of vindicating the right to work."

The right to earn a livelihood was successfully invoked in two further cases. In *Parsons v Kavanagh*[81] the plaintiff sought an injunction to restrain a competitor operating a passenger bus service in breach of the Road Transport Acts 1932-33. O'Hanlon J held that the right to earn a livelihood carried with it the entitlement to be protected against any unlawful activity on the part of any other person which materially impairs or infringes that right and as the defendants had been shown to have engaged in unlawful activity which impaired the plaintiff's constitutional right, he affirmed the order of the Circuit

78 [1972] IR 330.

79 But against them on others, see above, p. 721.

80 [1973] IR 97; (1973) 107 ILTR 117.

81 [1990] ILRM 560.

Court granting an injunction. In *Cox v Ireland*[82] the Supreme Court declared s 34 of the Offences Against the State Act 1939 to be unconstitutional on the ground, *inter alia*, that it infringed the right to earn a livelihood. That section, *inter alia*, disqualified a person convicted by the Special Criminal Court of a scheduled offence for holding any office or employment remunerated out of public monies for a period of seven years from the date of the conviction. The Court accepted that the State was entitled, in the interest of public peace and order and the protection of its own authority, to provide onerous and far-reaching penalties and forfeitures on persons convicted of crimes threatening such peace and order and State authority, and that it was also entitled to ensure that such persons were not involved in carrying out the functions of the State. However the range of offences covered by the mandatory disqualification in s 34 was so broad as to render that disqualification disproportionate, for it affected persons whose motive or intention in committing a scheduled offence bore no relation at all to any question of the maintenance of public peace and order or the authority of the State. Accordingly, s 34 failed as far as practicable to protect, *inter alia*, the individual's right to earn a livelihood and so was unconstitutional.

In a number of other cases the right to earn a livelihood, while recognised to exist as an unspecified personal right under Article 40.3, has been invoked without success. Thus in *Landers v Attorney General*,[83] the provisions of the Prevention of Cruelty to Children Act 1904, which prevented a juvenile from giving singing performances in licensed premises in the evening, were challenged as breaching the child's personal right to take up a career at any age. Finlay J held against this contention, though without deciding whether the right was a property right or a right "following from the Christian and democratic nature of the State". He said:

> "The plaintiff, now aged eight-and-a-half, can prepare for a career which he can commence as a professional singer with relatively minor restrictions when he reaches the age of ten years and with minimal restrictions when he reaches the age of eleven years. Balancing the restrictions imposed by the sub-sections with the liberties still remaining to [him] in the general context of his personal right to prepare for and follow a chosen career, which I would consider to be the real personal right relevant to the issues in this case, which is guaranteed by Article 40.3, I find no unconstitutionality in the sub-sections arising from the provisions of this Article."

A similar "balancing" was evident in *Rogers v I.T.G.W.U.*[84] The plaintiff had been a foreman docker, but was compulsorily retired at the age of sixty-five in consequence of a resolution of the union that this should be the age of compulsory retirement. Finlay P said it seemed to him that:

> "the provision of such compulsory retirement coupled with pension rights was in accordance with, and not in conflict with, the directive principles of social policy of Article 45 recognising and acknowledging the right of persons to earn a livelihood. [The plaintiff's] exclusion from working in the docks in Cork undoubtedly cut down his chance of obtaining alternative employment, but it did not...entirely exclude it. The opportunity for younger persons to commence upon, and continue upon obtaining, the job of casual docker in Cork, or elsewhere, must depend upon some turnover in those ordinarily employed. The achievement of that turnover in an orderly fashion providing a universal compulsory retiring age, coupled with pension provision, [was] a proper and bona fide objective for a trade union to pursue."

[82] [1992] 2 IR 503. See *Humphreys*, (1991) 13 DULJ (n.s.) 118.
[83] (1975) 109 ILTR 1.
[84] [1978] ILRM 51. See *Kerr*, (1978) DULJ 61.

In another case decided at about this time, *Yeates v Minister for Posts and Telegraphs*,[85] Kenny J recognised the existence of the "constitutional right to earn a livelihood", though the defendant, by giving the plaintiff a service direction which he was entitled to give him, had not infringed this right even though obedience to the direction would have entailed actions on the plaintiff's part which were unacceptable to his industrial ethos. In *Gannon v Duffy*,[86] where the plaintiffs sought an injunction to restrain a breach of their constitutional right to work and their "right not to be compelled to lose their employment" because they did not belong to the defendants' union (which had a closed shop agreement with the employers), McWilliam J implicitly accepted that this right existed, though he had "very considerable doubts as to whether [it could] be held to be infringed so as to give a cause of action against a person...lawfully trying to enforce his own rights", and therefore refused an injunction, saying a full oral hearing of the issue was necessary. In *Egan v The Minister for Defence*[87] the applicant, a commandant in the Air Corps, challenged the constitutionality of s 47(6) of the Defence Act 1954 which empowered the Minister for Defence to refuse his request for permission to take early retirement from the defence forces in order to take up civilian employment. According to the applicant, this infringed his constitutional right to use his labour as he sees fit. The claim was rejected by Barr J for two reasons. First, on the assumption that such a right existed, the applicant had waived this right by entering into a voluntary contract to serve in the defence forces until the retirement age applicable to his ultimate rank. Second, (apparently denying implicitly that the right as contended for by the applicant did exist), he had not sought to resign from the defence forces but to retire prematurely and this was not a right, but a concession. A challenge by sales representatives to the constitutionality of s 4 of the Finance Act 1982, which provided for the taxation as a benefit in kind of the provision of a car to an employee, on the ground, *inter alia*, that this infringed the plaintiffs' right to earn a livelihood was dismissed by Murphy J who held, *inter alia*, that the tax was not imposed on the car, or on its business or private use, but rather on its availability for private use- *Browne v Attorney General.*[88]

That statutory restrictions on the right to earn a livelihood must be clearly provided for is evident from the Supreme Court decision in *Hand v Dublin Corporation.*[89] The plaintiffs, who were street traders, challenged the constitutionality of s 4(6) of the Casual Trading Act 1980, whereby persons convicted of two or more offences under the Act would be disqualified for being granted a casual trading licence required in order to engage in casual trading. Delivering the judgment of the Court, Griffin J pointed out that the right to trade and earn a livelihood is not unqualified and that it was open to the Oireachtas to provide for strict control and regulation of casual trading in public places, having regard to the exigencies of the common good. Referring specifically to s 4(6), he said that this provision:

> "makes perfectly clear the circumstances in which the licence granted in pursuance of that section may be lost, and those engaged in casual trading can be under no misapprehension as to the consequences of failure to comply with the provisions of the Act and of conviction of two or more offences under the Act...

[85] [1978] ILRM 22.
[86] High Court, 4 March 1983. See *Kerr and Whyte* (1984) 6 DULJ (n.s.) 187.
[87] High Court, 24 November 1988.
[88] [1991] 2 IR 58.
[89] [1991] 1 IR 409.

In the opinion of the Court, where a person engaged in casual trading has been convicted of an offence under the Act of 1980, it is neither unjust nor unreasonable to deprive that person of the right to obtain a licence under the Act by reason of his having been convicted of a second or further offences under the Act."

The right to a livelihood is not an unqualified right to any particular livelihood

In *Attorney General v Paperlink Ltd.*,[90] the defence offered by a firm operating a courier service to proceedings to enforce the postal monopoly of the Minister for Posts and Telegraphs included the plea that the enforcement of the monopoly infringed the right of the firm's proprietors to a livelihood; Costello J held against them, saying:

> "It seems to me to be inaccurate and potentially confusing to state without qualification that each citizen has the constitutional right to carry on the occupation in which he is actually earning his living. The defendants like all citizens have a constitutional right to earn a living; they may choose to exercise that right by doing manual work or non-manual work, by entering a profession or by entering employment, by engaging in commerce (either alone or with others), by manufacturing goods, providing a service, or engaging in agriculture. Their freedom to exercise this constitutional right is not an absolute one, however, and it may be subject to legitimate legal restraints."

Such a legitimate restraint he found in the Post Office Act 1908. The case is not as instructive as it might have been, since part of the defendants' argument - that the monopoly as actually exercised was wasteful and inefficient and could be more effectively organised while still leaving them freedom to operate their courier service - never got on its feet; the judge declined to admit evidence on these matters, saying that it would involve the Court in passing judgment on things which, even if it found the facts to be as the defendants said, still would not mean that the monopoly was unconstitutional.[91]

Nature of the right to earn a livelihood

Costello J also took the opportunity to comment on the nature of the right to earn a livelihood, taking the view that, whereas at one time this right was regarded as a property right, in the light of more recent constitutional development it seemed more proper to regard it as being one of the unspecified personal rights derived from Article 40.3.1. However he subsequently modified this position in *Cafolla v O'Malley*,[92] holding that the right was derived from two different sources:

> Generally speaking, the right to earn a livelihood can properly be regarded as an unspecified personal right first protected by Article 40.3.1. But this right may also exist as one of the bundle of rights arising from the ownership of private property capable of being commercially used, and so receive the protection of Article 40.3.2.[93]

[90] [1984] ILRM 373. See *McCormack*, (1984) 6 DULJ (n.s.) 144.

[91] Costello J thus did not take the point that, if the monopoly were shown to be inefficient and the public interest therefore was not served by it, the only constitutional basis on which a monopoly might be allowed to exclude private initiative would have disappeared.

[92] [1985] IR 486; [1986] ILRM 177.

[93] In *Hand v Dublin Corporation* [1991] 1 IR 409, the Supreme Court was prepared to assume, though without deciding, that the right to earn a livelihood is a property right protected by Article 40.3.2.

He threw further light on the substance of the right itself in *Moyne v Londonderry Port and Harbour Commissioners,*[94] holding that the infliction of a pecuniary loss does not, of itself, establish that an infringement of the right to earn a livelihood has taken place.

The right to earn a livelihood does not ground the right to legal aid

Though the right to earn a livelihood arguably includes the right to go to court in defence of that livelihood, it would appear that it does not include the right to demand that the State provide financial assistance for such litigation. Thus in *O'Shaughnessy v Attorney General,*[95] O'Keeffe P dismissed the plaintiff's claim that the State was obliged to provide him with legal aid in order to vindicate his rights under Article 40.3 even though he was prepared to assume that the plaintiff had sustained a loss in his business as a result of the matters giving rise to the action. The President reasoned that it was for the legislature, and not the courts, to determine how the personal rights of the citizen are to be vindicated.[96]

Miscellaneous references to right to earn a livelihood

A few other cases in which the right to earn a livelihood figured marginally may be briefly mentioned. It was recognised as an unspecified personal right protected by Article 40.3 in *Moran v Attorney General*[97] and *The State (Gleeson) v Minister for Finance,*[98] though only parenthetically, as those cases were essentially concerned with failure to observe natural justice (in carrying out acts which had the effect of depriving the aggrieved parties of their right to earn a livelihood). In *Gleeson's* case the right was expressed also as including (in the case of a soldier) the right to be given a satisfactory discharge, inasmuch as this would affect future employment prospects. In *Murphy v Attorney General*[99] Hamilton J emphasised that "by entering the married state, a woman does not surrender her right to work". A fleeting reference to the right to earn a livelihood also occurs in *Barry v South Eastern Health Board,*[100] where McKenzie J, in rejecting the suggestion that doctors in the General Medical Services Scheme must obtain the consent of the relevant Health Board before opening a private surgery, said:

> "A doctor has a constitutional right to earn his living, and I see here an attempt by the hand of the State to squeeze the freedom of the medical profession."

In *Ahern v Minister for Industry and Commerce,*[101] Blayney J accepted that a decision to put the applicant on compulsory sick leave was justiciable because it affected his right to work, though ultimately, in the exercise of his discretion, the judge refused to grant an order of *certiorari* quashing the decision.

For a reference to the protection of the individual's right to earn his livelihood as warranting the operation of the presumption of innocence and other aspects of due process in the context of criminal proceedings, see *The State (O'Rourke and White) v Martin.*[102]

[94] [1986] IR 299.
[95] High Court, 16 February 1971.
[96] This is a rather old-fashioned view, however, and one inconsistent with *Ryan v AG* [1965] IR 294. See further below, pp. 773-775.
[97] [1976] IR 400; (1976) 110 ILTR 85.
[98] [1976] IR 280.
[99] [1982] IR 241.
[100] High Court, 18 December 1986.
[101] High Court, 6 July 1990.
[102] [1984] ILRM 333.

The right to marital privacy

The right of marital privacy was first recognised in *McGee v Attorney General*,[103] where what was in issue was the constitutionality of a statutory provision which had the effect of depriving the plaintiff, a married woman, of access to contraceptive preparations for the purpose of limiting her family, which, in view of her medical condition, she and her husband had agreed to do. Budd J said in the Supreme Court:

> "Whilst the "personal rights" are not described specifically, it is scarcely to be doubted in our society that the right to privacy is universally recognised and accepted with possibly the rarest of exceptions, and that the matter of marital relationships must rank as one of the most important of matters in the realm of privacy."

Henchy J held that the section under challenge "violated the plaintiff's personal right to privacy in regard to her marital relations"; and Griffin J that "the right of marital privacy is one of the personal rights guaranteed by Article 40.3.1." (Walsh J, who gave judgment to the same effect, based the right of marital privacy on Article 41 rather than on Article 40.3.[104]) However, in *Murphy v Attorney General*[105] Hamilton J refused to extend the right of marital privacy to the point claimed by the plaintiffs (in the context of an attack on income tax legislation), and would not admit what they said was "a constitutional right of spouses to privacy in respect of his or her income" such that neither should be obliged to disclose this to the other.

The right to individual privacy

A further fourteen years were to elapse before a general right to privacy was successfully invoked by a litigant.[106] One notable earlier attempt failed when, in *Norris v Attorney General*[107] the plaintiff contended, *inter alia*, that the laws[108] penalising homosexual acts between males were inconsistent with the Constitution; the "core of his challenge", as O'Higgins CJ put it, was:

[103] [1974] IR 284; (1975) 109 ILTR 29. See an article by Mr. Justice Walsh, "*The Judicial Power and the Protection of the Right of Privacy*" (1977) DULJ 3.

[104] However both Hamilton P in *Kennedy v Ireland* [1987] IR 587; [1988] ILRM 472, and Costello J in *Murray v Ireland* [1985] IR 532; [1985] ILRM 542, have taken the view that the right to marital privacy is grounded more properly in Article 40.3 than in Article 41.

[105] [1982] IR 241. This issue was not addressed by the Supreme Court in the subsequent appeal.

[106] Though in *Murphy v P.M.P.A. Insurance Co. Ltd.* [1978] ILRM 25, Doyle J recognised an unspecified natural right, which appears to be akin to the right to privacy, in relation to the obligation of insurers to preserve the confidentiality of information furnished to them by the insured. See also *Desmond v Glackin (No.2)*, Supreme Court, 30 July 1992. For consideration of the potential impact of the right to privacy on freedom of expression, see *O'Dell, loc.cit.*, at pp.70-75.

[107] [1984] IR 36. See *Gearty* in (1983) 5 DULJ (n.s.) 264. The right to privacy was also unsuccessfully invoked in *Madigan v Attorney General* [1986] ILRM 136, where one of the plaintiffs contended that it would be an invasion of his privacy to require him to disclose his income to the owner/occupier of his house, for the purposes of determining whether the latter was liable for residential property tax pursuant to the Finance Act 1983, as liability only existed where the combined yearly income of the household exceeded £20,000. The Supreme Court did not advert specifically to this point in its judgment upholding the validity of the tax, though it did say, in relation to this aggregated income provision, that it was based "on the common experience in society that members of families and households, to the extent that they can do so, contribute to the expenses and outgoings of the family home." In *A G (Society for the Protection of the Unborn Child (Ireland) Ltd.) v Open-Door Counselling Ltd.* [1988] IR 593; [1987] ILRM 477, Hamilton P held that the right to privacy could not be invoked to interfere with such a fundamental right as the right to life of the unborn. This point did not feature in the subsequent appeal, though there can hardly be any doubt that the Supreme Court would have affirmed Hamilton P's ruling if it had.

[108] Sections 61 and 62 of the Offences Against the Person Act 1861 and s 11 of the Criminal Law (Amendment) Act 1885.

> "the assertion that the State has no business in the field of private morality and has no right to legislate in relation to the private sexual conduct of consenting adults [and that] for the State to attempt to do so is to exceed the limits of permissible interference and to shatter that area of privacy which the dignity and liberty of human persons require to be kept apart as a haven for each citizen."

O'Higgins CJ, (with whom Finlay P and Griffin J concurred) traced the provenance of this position, *via* the Report of the Wolfenden Committee in Britain in 1957, to the teaching of John Stuart Mill; but contrasted with it the expressions in the Constitution's Preamble which stamped the ethical character of Christianity on the State, and, noting both the immemorial hostility of Christian teaching to homosexual behaviour and the purely human and social evils which its practice tended to promote, said he could not accept that:

> "in the very act of [adopting a Constitution consistent with religious conviction and Christian beliefs] the people rendered inoperative laws which had existed for hundreds of years prohibiting unnatural sexual conduct which Christian teaching held to be gravely sinful."

On the relation of this position to the right of privacy asserted by the plaintiff, he appeared to accept - though not very categorically - that such a thing as a right of individual privacy did exist; but dealt firmly with the plaintiff's claim of:

> "a "no go area" in so far as the law and the State are concerned in the field of private morality. I do not accept this view, either as a general philosophical proposition concerning the purpose of law, or as having particular reference to a right of privacy under our Constitution. I regard the State as having an interest in the general moral well-being of the community and being entitled, where it is practicable to do so, to discourage conduct which is morally wrong and harmful to a way of life and to values which the State wishes to protect. A right of privacy or, as it has been put, a right "to be let alone", can never be absolute."

Two of the five judges of the Court strongly dissented from the majority. Henchy J said it was "well attested by previous decisions of the Court" - though this seemed too much to claim, apart from the special context of marriage - that:

> "a right of privacy inheres in each citizen by virtue of his human personality, and that such right is constitutionally guaranteed as one of the unspecified personal rights comprehended by Article 40.3."

The "right of privacy", as he saw it, compendiously expressed:

> "a complex of rights, varying in nature, purpose and range, each necessarily a facet of the citizen's core of individuality within the constitutional order. [He gave instances recognised by the State: the secret ballot, and the marital privacy recognised in *McGee's* case.] There are many other aspects of the right of privacy, some yet to be given judicial recognition. It is unnecessary for the purpose of this case to explore them. It is sufficient to say that they would all appear to fall within a secluded area of activity or non-activity which may be claimed as necessary for the expression of an individual personality, for purposes not always necessarily moral or commendable, but meriting recognition in circumstances which do not endanger considerations such as State security, public order or morality, or other essential components of the common good."

Was the substance of the plaintiff's claim outweighed by considerations of those kinds? The evidence given in the High Court compelled the answer No: and accordingly Henchy J was for holding the impugned sections inconsistent with the Constitution. McCarthy J took a very similar line. He referred to the definition of the right of privacy given in the US Supreme Court as "the right to be let alone"; but admitted he "could not delimit the area in which the State may constitutionally intervene so as to restrict the right of privacy". The evidence in fact adduced, however, was all against the proposition that the State had any sound reason to intervene in the manner of which the plaintiff complained, so he agreed with Henchy J in considering himself bound to hold the sections unconstitutional.[109]

Eventually, in 1987, a general right to privacy was successfully invoked before the High Court. The case was that of *Kennedy v Ireland*,[110] in which the plaintiffs complained of unjustifiable tapping of their telephones by the State and, in particular, sought damages for this breach of their right to privacy. Hamilton P held for the plaintiffs, saying:

> "The right to privacy is not an issue, the issue is the extent of that right or the extent of the right "to be let alone". Though not specifically guaranteed by the Constitution, the right of privacy is one of the fundamental personal rights of the citizen which flow from the Christian and democratic nature of the State. It is not an unqualified right. Its exercise may be restricted by the constitutional rights of others, or by the requirements of the common good, and it is subject to the requirements of public order and morality... The nature of the right to privacy must be such as to ensure the dignity and freedom of an individual in the type of society envisaged by the Constitution, namely, a sovereign, independent and democratic society. The dignity and freedom of an individual in a democratic society cannot be ensured if his communications of a private nature, be they written or telephonic, are deliberately, consciously and unjustifiably intruded upon and interfered with. I emphasise the words "deliberately, consciously and unjustifiably" because an individual must accept the risk of accidental interference with his communications and the fact that in certain circumstances the exigencies of the common good may require and justify such intrusion and interference. No such circumstances exist in this case."[111]

In *Kane v The Governor of Mountjoy Prison*[112] Finlay CJ, with whom Henchy and Griffin JJ concurred, was prepared to assume for the purpose of the argument that a right of privacy might exist in an individual, even while travelling in the public streets. However overt police surveillance which was justifiable under the circumstances of the case - the gardaí anticipated having to execute an extradition warrant on the person under surveillance[113] - was not unlawful. Similarly, the right of privacy is not breached

[109] As predicted by Henchy J at the time, the European Court of Human Rights subsequently held that these provisions breached Article 8 of the European Convention on Human Rights - *Norris v Ireland* Series A, No.142 (1991) 13 EHRR 186 and they were eventually repealed by s 14 of the Criminal Law (Sexual Offences) Act 1993.

[110] [1987] IR 587; [1988] ILRM 472.

[111] In appropriate circumstances, the authorities may legitimately intercept telephone conversations and postal communications pursuant to the Interception of Postal Packets and Telecommunications Messages (Regulation) Act 1993 - see below, pp. 950-952.

[112] [1988] IR 757; [1988] ILRM 724.

[113] McCarthy J, with whom Hederman J concurred, dissented on this point, taking the view that mere anticipation of the warrant would not justify overt surveillance, but pointing out that in the instant case, the procedure under the Extradition Act 1965 had not merely been set in motion, it was reaching finality.

when a person in police custody is kept under observation by persons who are lawfully required to deal with him while in custody - *The Director of Public Prosecutions v Kenny.*[114]

The right of privacy featured again in *Desmond v Glackin (No.2)*[115] in which the applicant sought an order of prohibition restraining an inspector, appointed by the Minister for Industry and Commerce to investigate the membership of two named companies involved in a controversial purchase of property by Telecom Éireann, from using information obtained indirectly through the Central Bank,[116] which use, it was alleged, breached a duty of confidentiality imposed, *inter alia*, by the Constitution. In the High Court, O'Hanlon J considered the constitutional right to privacy and confidentiality to be co-extensive with the common law right to confidentiality[117] in the context of the instant case but held that the public interest justified the provision to the inspector of the information in question. The applicants' subsequent appeal to the Supreme Court was dismissed,[118] McCarthy J, with whom the other members of the Court concurred, saying that there was no principle of law, nor of common sense, which would prohibit a Minister of State who properly has obtained information from an agent acting on his behalf, from transmitting such information to another Minister of State where such information could assist that Minister in carrying out a statutory duty.

Personal rights corollary to explicit constitutional values

It could perhaps be said of the unspecified personal rights so far described - bodily integrity and the right not to have one's health put at risk by the State, the right to work and earn a livelihood, and the right to privacy, whether marital or individual - that they are not absolutely obvious corollaries of any of the rights expressly specified in the Constitution, whether in Article 40.3.2, or elsewhere in the Fundamental Rights section of the Constitution, or in some different part of the Constitution; and that if they are to be set up with constitutional rank at all, they require the cover of Article 40.3.1. An account must now be given of a number of other rights which the courts have seen as expressions of the same constitutional guarantee, but which might (as was said above) have been just as easily got on their feet in reliance on other constitutional statements, which statements are indeed sometimes also invoked in asserting them, thus rendering the role of Article 40.3 less clear.

The right to litigate or to have access to the courts

The earliest of these to appear was the right to litigate, or the right to have "recourse" or "access" to the courts. This was the basis of the decision of Kenny J in *Macauley v Minister for Posts and Telegraphs*,[119] decided in 1966; here he held that the subjection of actions against Ministers to the necessity of getting the *fiat* of the Attorney General was an infringement of "the personal right of the citizen", in the sense of Article 40.3, to have recourse to the courts:

[114] [1992] 2 IR 141.
[115] High Court, 25 February 1992.
[116] The information in question had been obtained by the Minister for Finance from the Central Bank, acting as his agent under the Exchange Control Acts 1954 to 1962.
[117] Considered by the Court of Appeal in *Marcel v Commissioner of Police of the Metropolis* [1992] 1 All ER 72.
[118] Supreme Court, 30 July 1992.
[119] [1966] IR 345.

"That there is a right to have recourse to the High Court to defend and vindicate a legal right and that it is one of the personal rights of the citizen included in the general guarantee of Article 40.3 seems to me to be a necessary inference from Article 34.3.1[120]...If the High Court has this full original jurisdiction to determine all matters and questions (and this includes the validity of any law having regard to the provisions of the Constitution), it must follow that the citizens have a right to have recourse to that Court to question the validity of any law having regard to the provisions of the Constitution or for the purpose of asserting or defending a right given by the Constitution, for if it did not exist, the guarantees and rights in the Constitution would be worthless."

This view was reiterated by Budd J - though in partial reliance on Article 34 as well as on Article 40.3 - in *Byrne v Ireland*,[121] in the setting of the citizen's right to sue the State in tort. However, in *O'Brien v Keogh*[122] the Supreme Court, *per* Ó Dálaigh CJ, while holding that "the right to litigate claims was a personal right of the citizen within Article 40", took the right to litigate to be a form of property right. In this case, the Supreme Court held that the right to litigate was violated by s 49(2)(*a*)(ii) of the Statute of Limitations which required infants in the custody of their parents to bring an action within three years of the cause of action accruing and which compared unfavourably with the more generous limitation period of six years for other infant litigants.[123] In *O'Brien v Manufacturing Engineering Co.*[124] the Court again treated a right of action as a property right within Article 40.3, though in this case a two year limitation period for the initiation of an action for personal injuries by an employee against his or her employer was held not to be unreasonable. The view that the right to litigate is a property right, and the decision in *O'Brien v Keogh*, while not expressly disapproved, was however regarded as doubtful by the Supreme Court in the subsequent case of *Moynihan v Greensmyth*.[125] Nevertheless in *Brady v Donegal County Council*[126] the view was again taken, this time by Costello J, that the right to litigate was a property right protected by Article 40.3.2.[127] He went on to hold that a two-month limitation period without any saving clause enabling the court to extend the period in favour of a plaintiff whose

[120] Notwithstanding this reliance on Article 34.3.1 which refers specifically to the High Court, it seems clear that the right of access to the courts applies in respect of all of the courts - see the remarks of Costello J in *The State (McEldowney) v Kelleher* [1983] IR 289 at 297 in respect of the District Court and of McCarthy J in *Fallon v An Bord Pleanála* [1991] ILRM 799 at 811 in respect of the Supreme Court.

[121] [1972] IR 241.

[122] [1972] IR 144.

[123] The current position is now provided for by s 5 of the Statute of Limitations (Amendment) Act 1991 which, *inter alia*, permits an infant to bring an action within three years of attaining his/her eighteenth birthday.

[124] [1973] IR 334; (1974) 108 ILTR 105.

[125] [1977] IR 55. See *Osborough*, (1979-80) DULJ 101. Less than five years separate this case from the two *O'Brien* cases; but there had been a complete change in personnel of the Supreme Court. None of the judges who were on the Court in July 1972 were on the Court which decided *Moynihan v Greensmyth* in June 1977. In *Campbell v Ward* [1981] ILRM 60, Carroll J held that, notwithstanding the comments in *Moynihan v Greensmyth*, she was obliged to follow *O'Brien v Keogh* until such time as it was overruled.

[126] [1989] ILRM 282.

[127] In the subsequent Supreme Court appeal, the Attorney General challenged, *inter alia*, the view that the right to litigate was a property right but the issue was not reached by the Court who held that, until certain issues of fact were determined in a particular way, the plaintiffs had no *locus standi* to challenge the constitutionality of the limitation period.

ignorance of the existence of the cause of action was caused or contributed to by the defendant was so unreasonable as to be unconstitutional.[128]

In *Society for the Protection of Unborn Children (Ireland) Ltd. v Coogan*[129] Walsh J commented that, in an appropriate case, the right of access to the courts includes:

> "not only access in defence of [the citizen's] own personal and direct rights which are being threatened by the executive, or by... fellow citizens, but also the right to seek to restrain the acts of the executive or other persons from breaching the constraints imposed by the Constitution if the public interest requires that such breaches should be restrained."

Generally speaking, the citizen's right of access to the courts does not encompass a right to represent another litigant,[130] though in *In re G.J. Mannix Ltd*[131] the Court of Appeal in New Zealand considered that such representation could be permitted in exceptional cases.[132]

The citizen's right of access to the courts must be read subject to the judicial power to strike out an action so as to prevent an abuse of the judicial process. If it is established that proceedings are frivolous or vexations or if it is clear that the plaintiff's claim must fail, the court may stay the action, though this jurisdiction must be exercised sparingly and only in clear cases: *D.K. v A.K.*[133]

To date, judicial defence of the right to litigate has been mainly limited to preventing the State - acting through statutory, common law or even judicial rules - impeding access to the courts. As we have seen above, the courts have invalidated legislative provisions requiring the Attorney General's permission before Government Ministers may be sued or prescribing unjust limitation periods. Moreover statutory provisions limiting access to the courts must be strictly construed[134] and it has been suggested that the State may not

[128] The issue of the reasonableness or otherwise of particular limitation periods has been before the courts on two more recent occasions, though neither case resolves the debate as to the nature of the right to litigate. In *Hegarty v O'Loughran* [1990] 1 IR 148; [1990] ILRM 403, the Supreme Court held that the three year limitation period in personal injuries cases, provided for by s 11(2)(*b*) of the Statute of Limitations 1957, started to run when the injury occurred to a plaintiff, rather than when such injury was discovered. McCarthy J railed against "the unfairness, the harshness, the obscurantism that underlies this rule"; however no challenge had been made by the plaintiff to the constitutionality of the sub-section. (In contrast to McCarthy J, Finlay CJ indicated that he did not accept that the interpretation put on s 11(2)(*b*) by the Court necessarily meant that it was unconstitutional. Note, however, that more relaxed provisions are now contained in ss 2, 3 of the Statute of Limitations (Amendment) Act 1991.) In *Tuohy v Courtney*, High Court, 3 September 1992, Lynch J upheld the constitutionality of sub-ss (1)(*a*) and (2)(*a*) of s 11 of the Statute of Limitations 1957 which prescribe a six year time limit on, respectively, contractual actions and tortious actions other than those in respect of personal or fatal injuries. The judge expressly commented that it was not necessary for him to express any views on the question of whether a cause of action is a personal right and/or a property right.

[129] [1989] IR 734; [1990] ILRM 70.

[130] See *Battle v Irish Art Promotion Centre Ltd.* [1968] IR 252.

[131] (1984) 1 NZLR 309.

[132] *Mannix* was considered by Budd J in *P.M.L.B. v P.H.J*, High Court 5 May 1992, but he concluded that the case before him was not "exceptional" in this context.

[133] [1993] ILRM 710. See also *O'Neill v Ryan* [1993] ILRM 557.

[134] *In re R. Ltd* [1989] IR 126, [1989] ILRM 757 (concerning *in camera* hearings under s 205(7) of the Companies Act 1963); *Murphy v Greene* [1990] 2 IR 566; [1991] ILRM 404 (concerning s 260 of the Mental Treatment Act 1945 which prevented civil proceedings being instituted in respect of action taken under the Act unless the High Court was satisfied that there were substantial grounds for alleging bad faith or lack of reasonable care), followed in *O'Reilly v Moroney and Mid-Western Health Board* [1992] 2 IR 145.

impose excessive rates of stamp duty on litigants.[135] Common law immunities from suit must also be read in the light of the right to litigate; in *Ryan v Ireland*[136] the Supreme Court indicated that an immunity from suit enjoyed by the State in respect of negligence occurring during armed conflict or in a theatre of war would be inconsistent with both sub-sections of Article 40.3.[137] Judicial decisions are not exempt from this scrutiny and in *Henehan v Allied Irish Banks Ltd.*[138] the High Court refused to follow a judicial decision unduly restricting the jurisdiction of the courts to award costs.[139]

A constitutional right to civil legal aid?

However attempts to establish that the State has a positive constitutional duty to assist a civil litigant who is denied effective access to the courts because of factors such as poverty, for which the State is not directly and immediately responsible, have almost invariably failed.[140] Thus in *O'Shaughnessy v Attorney General*[141] O'Keeffe P dismissed a challenge to the constitutionality of the Criminal Justice (Legal Aid) Act 1962 because it failed to make any provision for legal aid in civil cases on the ground that it was for the legislature to determine how the personal rights of the citizen were to be vindicated. Legislation affording assistance to one class of persons - those charged with criminal offences - could not be held to be unconstitutional on the ground either that the Court considered that the priorities should be different or that in providing such assistance, the State had elected not to assist civil litigants. In *Application of J.C.*[142] the plaintiff's claim that he was denied access to the courts because of his poverty was not sufficiently well developed to allow Barrington J rule authoritatively on the point, while in *MacGairbhith v Attorney General*[143] O'Hanlon J dismissed the rather hopeful claim that personal litigants had a constitutional right to be provided with a law library by the State.

Unlike the plaintiffs in the three aforementioned cases, the applicant in *M.C. v The Legal Aid Board*[144] was legally represented which, no doubt, accounts for the more thor-

[135] See the *dicta* in *Re Michael Orr (Kilternan) Ltd.* [1986] IR 273; *Application of J.C.*, High Court, 25 July 1985, and *MacGairbhith v Attorney General* [1991] IR 412. See also the extra-judicial comments of O'Flaherty J in "*The Independent Bar as the Defender of Human Rights*" in O'Reilly, ed., *Human Rights and Constitutional Law: Essays in Honour of Brian Walsh* (Dublin, 1992) in which he refers to the clog on access to the courts by reason of the charging of stamp duty as a "vexed question". *Cp. The State (Commissioner of Valuation) v O'Malley*, High Court, 27 January 1984, where McWilliam J concluded that a requirement to enter into a recognisance of £5 before pursuing an appeal under the Valuation (Ireland) Act 1852 did not infringe the right of access to the courts.

[136] [1989] IR 177.

[137] Of course not every immunity from suit is necessarily unconstitutional, as the right to litigate is not absolute. Thus the courts have recognised that where a person is obliged, in the discharge of a public duty, to make a decision affecting the liberty and property of others, and he does so honestly and in good faith, he cannot be sued because of the consequences of that decision to others - see *Pine Valley Developments Ltd. v Minister for the Environment* [1987] IR 23; [1987] ILRM 747; *McMahon v Ireland* [1988] ILRM 610.

[138] High Court, 19 October 1984.

[139] On the other hand, it is worth noting that the High Court has an inherent power to restrain a person from instituting legal proceedings without first obtaining the consent of the court - see *The State (M.C.) v Eastern Health Board*, High Court, 29 July 1986.

[140] That the State is constitutionally obliged to provide legal representation to indigent defendants in criminal proceedings is well established - see *The State (Healy) v Donoghue* [1976] IR 325, discussed above, pp. 595-596 - and the courts now also take the view that persons detained in Garda custody are constitutionally entitled to have access to a solicitor, though at their own expense - see *The People (D.P.P.) v Healy* [1990] 2 IR 73, discussed above, p. 610. However in *Incorporated Law Society v Minister for Justice*, [1978] ILRM 112, McWilliam J rejected the contention that the citizen's right of access to the courts entitled a convicted prisoner to consult the solicitor of his choice and held, accordingly, that the Minister could lawfully order that particular solicitors be excluded from specific prisons.

[141] High Court, 16 February 1971.

[142] High Court, 25 July 1985.

[143] [1991] 2 IR 412.

[144] [1991] 2 IR 43.

ough manner in which her claim to civil legal aid was presented. A respondent in nullity proceedings, she had applied for civil legal aid under the Scheme of Civil Legal Aid and Advice but because of the build up of arrears of applications, caused by inadequate staffing levels, the Legal Aid Board had to defer consideration of her application. She argued, *inter alia*, that the Scheme of Civil Legal Aid and Advice was a purported compliance by the State with its constitutional duty of affording the applicant access to the courts and that the continuing unreasonable delay in processing her application for legal aid amounted to a deprivation of her right of access to the courts. Dismissing these arguments, Gannon J said:

> "The existence of [the nullity proceedings] does not confer any duty on the State nor on any of the Respondents to either of the parties thereto either under the Constitution or at law. The duty of administering justice and adjudicating by due process does not create any obligation on the State to intervene in any private civil litigation so as to ensure that one party is as well equipped for their dispute as is the other. The fact that the existence of fundamental personal rights is expressly recognised by the Constitution does not impose on the State any duty to intervene in aid of a party involved in any private civil dispute in relation to any such personal rights...I am not convinced that there is any provision in the Constitution which imposes a duty on the State to provide any form of support for civil litigation among citizens. In the absence of such duty I can find no express or implied right in any citizen to require the State to provide financial support for, or to afford free facilities for, civil litigation of a dispute with another citizen."[145]

It is arguable, however, that this somewhat peremptory dismissal of the applicant's claim does not do full justice to the case that the State has a constitutional obligation to provide civil legal aid to needy litigants. A limited version of such an obligation, grounded on the courts' obligation to administer justice under Article 34.1, was recognised by Lardner J in *Stevenson v Landy and others*[146] in the context of wardship proceedings taken by the Eastern Health Board. Here the Legal Aid Board had refused to grant legal aid to the mother of the child involved to contest the proceedings because she had failed to show that she was reasonably likely to be successful in the proceedings - paragraph 3.2.3.4 of the Scheme of Civil Legal Aid and Advice. Lardner J quoted from the judgment of O'Higgins CJ in *The State (Healy) v Donoghue*[147] wherein he had said:

> "The requirements of fairness and justice must be considered in relation to the seriousness of the charge brought against the person and the consequences involved for him. Where a man's liberty is at stake, or where he faces a very severe penalty which may affect his welfare or his livelihood, justice may require more than the application of normal and fair procedures in relation to his trial. Facing, as he does, the power of the State which is his accuser, the person charged may be unable to defend himself adequately because of ignorance, lack of education, youth or other incapacity. In such circumstances his plight may require, if justice is to be done, that he should have legal assistance. In such circumstances, if he cannot provide such assistance by reason of lack of means, does justice under the Constitution also require that he be aided in his defence? In my view it does."

[145] In *Corcoran v Minister for Social Welfare* [1992] ILRM 133, Murphy J similarly held that there was no constitutional right to legal aid for persons appearing before administrative tribunals.

[146] High Court, 10 February 1993. The same judge subsequently held that persons seeking release from detention under the Trial of Lunatics Act 1883 had a similar right to legal aid - *Kirwan v The Minister for Justice*, High Court, 29 July 1993.

[147] [1976] IR 325.

Lardner J then continued:

> "That statement was made in relation to a criminal prosecution. The present case is of a different nature. Having considered the circumstances of the applicant and in which the application for legal aid to be represented in the wardship proceedings is made, I have come to the conclusion that the dicta which I have quoted are applicable, *mutatis mutandis*, to the wardship proceedings."

He went on to construe paragraph 3.2.3.4 of the Scheme of Civil Legal Aid and Advice as being satisfied wherever an applicant for legal aid has a "worthwhile contribution" to make to the hearing of the case, commenting that "this approach is more in accordance with the requirements of the Constitution in regard to the administration of justice".

Stevenson clearly does not establish a right to civil legal aid for all indigent litigants as it applies only where the State is a party to the proceedings. However there is, at least, an arguable case that the State's obligation to provide civil legal aid may be wider than that recognised in *Stevenson.* One could argue, *pace* Gannon J in *M.C.*, that a right to civil legal aid may be derived from the individual's right of access to the courts. In *Airey v Ireland,*[148] which arose out of an attempt by the plaintiff to initiate matrimonial proceedings, the European Court of Human Rights held that the right of access to the courts guaranteed by Article 6(1) of the European Convention on Human Rights could oblige the State, in certain circumstances, to provide impoverished litigants with the assistance of a lawyer. No suggestion was made by the European Court that this obligation was limited to cases where the State itself was a party to the proceedings. On the face of it, the right of access to the courts secured by Article 6(1) would appear to be the same in substance as that guaranteed by Article 40.3 and thus *Airey* may be persuasive authority for a judge construing the latter provision.[149] The guarantee of equality in Article 40.1 may also lend support to this position insofar as it requires that citizens be treated equally when involved in the legal process. It is hardly fanciful to suggest that this might oblige the State to remedy the imbalance in a dispute between a litigant who is legally represented and his opponent who cannot afford such representation. Even if such a right to legal aid is not free-standing, it could arise as an aspect of the State's constitutional obligation to defend "as far as practicable" other constitutional rights such as the right to property, the right to one's good name or, as in *M.C.*, the right to protect one's status as a member of a family based on marriage.

Implications of right of access to courts for court practice and procedure

In a number of cases, the courts have had to consider the implications of the individual's right of access to the courts for aspects of court practice and procedure.

Order 29 r 6 of the Rules of the Superior Courts 1986 empowers the High Court to make an order requiring a potential plaintiff to provide security for costs. The constitutionality of this power was upheld in *Salih v General Accident*[150] where, after pointing out that the right of access to the courts is not unfettered, O'Hanlon J concluded that the right to apply for security for costs was intended to do justice between the parties, was reasonable and was not in breach of the plaintiff's constitutional rights. In *Fallon v An Bord*

[148] Series A, No.32; (1979) 2 EHRR 305. See Cousins, "*Access to the Courts*" (1992) 14 DULJ (n.s.) 51.
[149] *Airey* was cited to Gannon J in *M.C. v Legal Aid Board* [1991] 2 IR 43, but is not specifically addressed in his judgment. It also featured in the earlier case of *E. v E.* [1982] ILRM 497, in which O'Hanlon J held that he had no jurisdiction to decide whether its demands on the State were fully met in the Scheme of Civil Legal Aid and Advice.
[150] [1987] IR 628.

Pleanála[151] a majority of the Supreme Court held that, in fixing the amount of the security required, a court should always bear in mind that no litigant with an arguable case should be effectively denied access to the courts solely because of poverty. More specifically, a court should not depart from the general practice of requiring one third of the estimated costs to be incurred unless the interests of justice could only be served by requiring a sum substantially in excess of that figure.

In *Bula Ltd. v Tara Mines Ltd.*[152] the plaintiffs wished to inspect the defendants' land in the course of an action for fraud. Murphy J considered that the right of access to the courts necessarily gave rise to such a right of inspection, without the plaintiff having to establish a *prima facie* case:

> "If, then, a citizen is free to institute proceedings, he must be at least equally free to invoke the procedures of the court to present his case properly. In my view the right of a party to seek and obtain an order for inspection (or indeed an order for discovery which may be equally burdensome) is in no way dependent upon the court being satisfied as to the strength of the plaintiff's case ..."
>
> In these circumstances it seems to me that it would be impossible to vindicate the plaintiff's right to litigate if he were not afforded an appropriate opportunity of inspection to attempt to substantiate the claim which he has made.

As the above quote makes abundantly clear, this principle applies equally to an order for discovery of documents.[153]

In *In re D. and Midland Health Board,*[154] Finlay CJ, with whom the other members of the Supreme Court agreed, held that the High Court's wardship jurisdiction in lunacy matters was not limited to persons of unsound mind whose person requires protection and management *and* who were also entitled to any property requiring protection or management. Invoking Article 40.3.2 in support of this conclusion, he said:

> "Such a construction of the jurisdiction in lunacy matters vested by the [Courts (Supplemental Provisions) Act 1961] in the High Court seems to me to obtain significant support from a consideration of the provisions of Article 40.3.2 of the Constitution where the obligation imposed on the State by its laws as best it may from unjust attack and in the case of injustice done to vindicate the life and person of every citizen is put in equal place with the obligation to protect and vindicate the property rights of every citizen."

Finally, in *Mapp v Gilhooley*[155] the Supreme Court rejected the contention of an infant plaintiff that the requirement to give *viva voce* evidence in a trial of a civil action on oath or affirmation amounted to, *inter alia*, an impermissible restriction of his right of access to the court. According to Finlay CJ, the broad purpose of this requirement was to ensure as far as possible that such evidence was true by the provision of a moral or

[151] [1992] 2 IR 380; [1991] ILRM 799.
[152] [1987] IR 85; [1988] ILRM 149.
[153] A similar argument was advanced in *Ellis v O'Dea* [1989] IR 530; [1990] ILRM 87, where the applicant, invoking both his right of access to the courts and his right to fair procedures, sought to prevent the District Judge proceeding with an extradition hearing until such time as the applicant was furnished with copies of the informations grounding the extradition warrants. The Supreme Court held that, while in appropriate cases it might be necessary to secure the production of the informations, no such occasion had arisen in the instant case where the matter had not yet been fully heard by the District Court.
[154] [1987] IR 449; [1988] ILRM 251.
[155] [1991] 2 IR 253; [1991] ILRM 672.

religious and legal sanction against deliberate untruth and as such, it could not be inconsistent with the Constitution, either as discriminatory or as an infringement of the right of access to the courts.

The right to justice and fair procedures

Another right connected with - one would have said, inseparable from - the administration of justice, namely the right to fair procedures, has frequently been regarded as part of the latent content of Article 40.3, in relation to both civil and criminal proceedings and is considered in more detail elsewhere.[156]

The right to travel within the State

The right to personal liberty, guaranteed generally by Article 40.4, must include the right to move around, whether inside the country or (so far as this State's power to interfere is concerned) outside it; a deprivation of liberty, although instinctively pictured in the form of imprisonment or being locked up, is essentially a deprivation of mobility. Yet when the right to travel was first enunciated, it was not as a corollary of Article 40.4, but as an unspecified right under Article 40.3. It surfaced first as a mere *dictum* in *Ryan v Attorney General*,[157] when, in the form of the "right to free movement within the State", it was given by Kenny J as an instance of "the many personal rights of the citizen which follow from the Christian and democratic nature of the State which are not mentioned in Article 40 at all" but are latent in Article 40.3.

The right to travel outside the State

It was, however, directly in issue in *The State (M.) v Attorney General*[158] in the form of the right to travel outside the State and the ancillary right to a passport. Finlay P said in the High Court that:

> "one of the hallmarks which are commonly accepted as dividing States which are categorised as authoritarian from those which are categorised as free and democratic is the inability of the citizens of, or residents in, the former to travel outside their country except at what is usually considered to be the whim of the executive power. Therefore, I have no doubt that a right to travel outside the State in the limited form in which I have already defined it (that is to say, a right to avail of such facilities as apply to the holder of an Irish passport at any given time) is a personal right of each citizen... subject to the guarantees provided by Article 40 although not enumerated."

This right - this time in the form of the right to "travel and play rugby abroad" - was again recognised, by O'Hanlon J, in *Lennon v Ganly*,[159] a case brought in an unsuccessful effort to stop the Irish Rugby Football Union from going ahead with a proposed tour of South Africa which was officially discouraged because of the racial segregation enforced on the playing of games in that country.[160]

In *The State (M.) v Attorney General*[161] Finlay P did accept that the right to travel could be subjected to:

[156] As to civil proceedings, see pp. 350-359; as to criminal proceedings, see pp. 589-593.
[157] [1965] IR 294.
[158] [1979] IR 73.
[159] [1981] ILRM 84.
[160] Control of travel, whether within or outside the State, was in fact envisaged by s 212)(*j*) of the Emergency Powers Act 1939: the same paragraph also permitted restriction of entry to the State in terms which would have covered even Irish citizens. The Act expired in 1946.
[161] [1979] IR 73.

> "obvious and clearly justified restrictions, the most common in practice being the existence of some undischarged obligation, by the person seeking a passport or seeking to use his passport, to the State such as his having entered into a recognisance to appear before a Criminal Court for the trial of an offence."[162]

In relation to children, in particular, the right to travel must be construed:

> "as a right which can be exercised not by [the child's] own choice which it is incapable of forming but by the choice of its parent, parents or legally recognised guardians, subject always to the right of the Courts by appropriate proceedings to deny that choice in the dominant interest of the welfare of the child."

More recently, and not without controversy, the recognition of restrictions on the right to travel derived from the State's obligation to defend and vindicate the right to life of the unborn, contained in Article 40.3.3, led to the enactment of the Thirteenth Amendment to the Constitution, guaranteeing freedom to travel abroad.[163] This explicit recognition of freedom to travel arguably renders Article 40.3 superfluous as a source of constitutional protection in this context.

The family and Article 40.3

While one article of the Constitution is devoted exclusively to "the Family" - Article 41 - this is not the sole repository of constitutional rights for family members as such and a number of cases derive such rights from Article 40.3.

The right to marry

The whole constellation of rights expressed or clearly implied by Articles 41 and 42 in the field of the family and the upbringing and education of children must, one would have thought, necessarily include the right to marry, since Article 41 specifically commits the State to guarding "with special care the institution of marriage [and protecting] it against attack". Nevertheless in *Ryan's* case Kenny J mentioned the right to marry as an example of the personal rights latent in Article 40.3; and FitzGerald CJ in his dissenting judgment in *McGee v Attorney General*[164] also related the right to marry to Article 40.3, saying it was a right which had existed in "most, if not all, civilised countries for many centuries" and had not been "conferred" in this country by the Constitution.

In the earlier case of *Donovan v Minister for Justice*[165] Kingsmill Moore J recognised the limited nature of this right when he said that there was nothing unconstitutional or improper in a provision of the General Orders and Regulations of the Garda Síochána requiring members of the force to obtain the prior permission of the Commissioner before they married. One must doubt, however, whether a contemporary judge would take the same tolerant view of such intrusive legislation.

The right to procreate

Though one might also have thought that this right could be derived from Article 41, this possibility was rejected by Costello J in *Murray v Ireland*,[166] where he held that Article 41.1.1 protected only those rights which can properly be said to belong to the

[162] An example of such a restriction can be seen in *Lombard v O'Shea* (reported in *The Irish Times*, 5 May 1987), where Murphy J continued an order impounding the passport of the defendant in liquidation proceedings. There does not, however, appear to be any statutory basis for this practice. See above, pp. 66-69.
[163] For further discussion of this, see below, pp. 809-810.
[164] [1974] IR 284; (1975) 109 ILTR 29.
[165] (1951) 85 ILTR 134.
[166] [1985] IR 532; [1985] ILRM 542.

institution of the Family itself, as distinct from the personal rights which each individual member might enjoy by virtue of membership of the Family. Thus the right to beget children, which he stressed was distinct from the constitutional right to marital privacy established in *McGee v Attorney General*,[167] was one of the unspecified rights protected by Article 40.3. The right was not, however, for that reason less valuable than if it had come under the protection of Article 41.1.1; in evaluating the respective strengths of different constitutional rights, one had to have regard to the purpose and objective of the Constitution, and not merely the literal wording used. However, in common with all other personal rights, the right to beget children was not absolute, and the State was lawfully empowered to restrict this right in the case of the plaintiffs, who were serving sentences of life imprisonment. This analysis was also adopted by the Supreme Court in the subsequent appeal.[168]

The right to independent domicile

An interesting feature of constitutional jurisprudence on the family is its policy of equality of the spouses within marriage and a number of common law rules reflecting the former dominant position of the husband have been declared to be inconsistent with the Constitution. In *C.M. v T.M.*[169] Barr J declared one such rule, whereby the domicile of the wife was determined by that of her husband, to be contrary to the fundamental personal right to an independent domicile, guaranteed by Article 40.3.1.[170]

The right to maintenance

In the same case, Barr J invoked, *inter alia*, Article 40.3.1 in rejecting the view that the recognition of a foreign divorce automatically precluded a person from continuing to receive maintenance from her former spouse under the Family Law (Maintenance of Spouses and Children) Act 1976.

The personal rights of unmarried mother in regard to her child

The same group of rights surrounding the family - since they are clearly recognised as natural rights and so, in this context, spring from the biological, emotional, social, and spiritual relationships which parenthood in monogamy involves - would have required no great contortions of reasoning to be extended by analogy, or a sort of cy-près operation, to an unmarried mother and her child, perhaps even, in appropriate cases, to an unmarried father also. But the courts have not taken this course, for the reason that the family enthroned by Article 41 is that founded on marriage (Article 41.3.1). This became first apparent in *The State (Nicolaou) v An Bord Uchtála*,[171] in which the Adoption Act 1952, was under attack on a number of grounds, one of them being that the Act infringed the guarantees of Article 41 relating to the family. The Supreme Court however held that Article 41 had no relevance to the situation of a non-marital child and its mother, who did not form a "family" for the purpose of Article 41. Walsh J in giving

[167] [1974] IR 284; (1975) 109 ILTR 29.

[168] [1991] ILRM 465.

[169] [1991] ILRM 268. At an earlier stage in these proceedings, Barr J had indicated, *obiter*, that the rule of dependent domicile "was swept away by principles of equality before the law and equal rights in marriage as between men and women which are enshrined in the Constitution - see in particular [Article 40.1 and 40.3 and Article 41]." - [1990] 2 IR 52; [1988] ILRM 456 at 470. See *Turner*, (1989) 11 DULJ (n.s.) 180.

[170] In a subsequent case, *W. v W.* [1993] ILRM 294, the Supreme Court approved this position, relying, however, on Article 40.1 rather than Article 40.3. See below, pp. 1081-1020.

[171] [1966] IR 567; (1968) 102 ILTR 1.

the Court's judgment said that the mother's "natural right to the custody and care of her child" fell rather to be protected by Article 40.3 (he mentioned also "such other natural personal rights as she may have" but refrained from pronouncing on their extent). That an unmarried mother must look to Article 40.3 (rather than Article 41 or 42) for her rights was reaffirmed in *G.* v *An Bord Uchtála*;[172] in this case O'Higgins CJ rationalised the source of the unmarried mother's natural rights as follows:

> "This right is clearly based on the natural relationship which exists between a mother and child. It arises in my view from the infant's total dependency and helplessness and from the mother's natural determination to protect and sustain her child. How far and to what extent it survives as the child grows up is not a matter of concern in the present case."

He said that the provisions of the Guardianship of Infants Act 1964, which make the mother guardian of a non-marital child and give her statutory rights to sue for its custody "constitute a compliance by the State with its obligation, in relation to the mother of an illegitimate child, to defend and vindicate in its laws this right to custody". Walsh J in his judgment spoke in the same sense.

Since the 1970s, the State has provided concrete assistance to unmarried mothers in the form of specific social welfare and tax-free allowances. A challenge to the constitutionality of these arrangements, taken by a married couple who received no equivalent assistance, was dismissed by Carroll J on the ground, *inter alia*, that a state of facts existed which reasonably justified the preferential treatment afforded to unmarried mothers and accordingly the State could not be said to have failed in its duties to the plaintiffs under Article 40.3: *MhicMhathúna v Ireland.*[173] Implicit in this holding would appear to be the view, no doubt influenced by Article 40.1, that action taken by the State in discharge of its duties under Article 40.3 must be based on reasonable classifications and should not discriminate between persons in similarly situated categories.

Has the father of non-marital child any "natural personal rights"? -

In *The State (Nicolaou) v An Bord Uchtála*[174] an attempt was made to establish that the father of a non-marital child had a natural personal right in relation to the child; this claim was rejected by the Supreme Court:

> "It has not been shown... that the father of an illegitimate child has any natural right, as distinct from legal rights, to either the custody or society of that child and the Court has not been satisfied that any such right has ever been recognised as part of the natural law. If an illegitimate child has a natural right to look to his father for support that would impose a duty on the father but it would not of itself confer any right upon the father. The appellant has therefore failed to establish that any personal right he may have guaranteed to him by Article 40.3 [this conditional formulation was due to his not being an Irish citizen] has been in any way violated by the Adoption Act of 1952."

In *In re S.W., an infant, K. v W.*[175] a majority of the Supreme Court held that the natural father had no constitutional right to the guardianship of his child, although (*per* Finlay CJ) "there may be rights of interest or concern arising from the blood link between the father and the child". Though the Court did not clarify the juridical nature of these

[172] [1980] IR 32; (1979) 113 ILTR 25.
[173] [1989] IR 504. See below, p. 1123.
[174] [1966] IR 567; (1968) 102 ILTR 1.
[175] [1990] 2 IR 437; [1990] ILRM 121. See below, pp. 1037-1039.

"rights of interest or concern", perhaps in an appropriate case they might flower into constitutional rights? Certainly this question cannot be dealt with in isolation from the rights of the child, in whose interest it might not necessarily be that his natural father should be permitted to interfere in the adoption process or in any decision about his future, but it seems wrong to close the door on principle against a natural father. Suppose a case in which the custody of a child is disputed between its natural father (its mother having died or gone away) and another party, in circumstances where the child's welfare seemed equally assured with either, and no complications of religion or of disturbing a settled habitat existed. Would not most judges prefer the father's claim? and would they not do so by reference to nature in some guise or other?[176] and would an emerging pattern of similar judgments not amount to recognising a "natural personal right", even if a highly contingent and easily defeasible one, on the father's part?

The rights of a non-marital child

The judgments in *G. v An Bord Uchtála* also emphasised the rights of the child born out of wedlock and related them to Article 40.3 (though these rights must be also the rights of children in a marital family). O'Higgins CJ said:

> "The child also has natural rights. Normally these will be safe under the care and protection of the mother. Having been born the child has the right to be fed and to live, to be reared and educated, to have the opportunity of working and of realising his or her full personality and dignity as a human being. These rights of the child and others which I have not enumerated must equally be protected and vindicated by the State. The State, under the provisions of Article 42.5... in exceptional cases is given the duty as guardian of the common good to provide for a child born into a family where the parents for physical or moral reasons fail in their duty towards that child. In the same way, in my view, in special circumstances, in relation to a child born outside the family, the State may have an equal obligation to protect that child even against its mother, if her natural rights are used in such a way as to endanger the health or life of the child or to deprive him of his rights. In my view this obligation stems from the provisions of Article 40.3 of the Constitution."

Walsh J added that there was in his view:

> "no difference between the obligations of the unmarried parent to the child and those of the married parent. These obligations of the parent or parents amount to natural rights of the child and they exist for the benefit of the child... Not only has the child born out of lawful wedlock the natural right to have its welfare and health guarded no less well than that of a child born in lawful wedlock, but *a fortiori* it has the right to life itself and the right to be guarded against all threats directed to its existence whether before or after birth."

The rights of children generally

By virtue of Article 42.5, the State must, in those exceptional cases where the parents have failed for physical or moral reasons in their duty towards their children, endeavour to supply the place of the parents, but always with due regard for the rights of the child. In *Re Article 26 and the Adoption (No.2) Bill 1987*[177] the Supreme Court indicated that a

[176] See e.g. the English case of *In re C.(M.A.), an Infant* [1966] 1 WLR 646, decided a few months before *Nicolaou's* case, in which two of the three judges of the Court of Appeal gave weight to the instinctual bond connecting a natural father with his child. The facts of the case were, however, different.

[177] [1989] IR 656; [1989] ILRM 266. See also *M.F. v Superintendent, Ballymun Garda Station* [1991] 1 IR 189; [1990] ILRM 767.

co-extensive duty arose under Article 40.3 and that the rights of a child who is a member of a family are not confined to those identified in Articles 41 and 42 but also include, *inter alia*, unenumerated rights under Article 40.3.

In the earlier case of *P.W. v A.W.*[178] Ellis J held that a child has the personal right, under Article 40.3, to have its welfare regarded as the paramount consideration in any dispute as to its custody, a right which additionally arises from "the Christian and democratic nature of the State".

The right to communicate

Another unspecified personal right protected by Article 40.3[179] and which has been identified in recent decisions is the right to communicate. The idea of such a right had previously surfaced (though without specific reference to Article 40.3) in *The State (Murray) v Governor of Limerick Prison,*[180] where D'Arcy J held that an interference with the applicant's right to communicate with her husband and to receive communications from him either by visits or letters, imposed in accordance with prison regulations, did not render her detention unlawful. The right to communicate received more comprehensive examination in *Attorney General v Paperlink Ltd.*,[181] in which the Attorney General sought an injunction to restrain the defendants from conveying letters in breach of the Post Office Acts, 1908-1969. One of the defendants' arguments was that the 1908 Act infringed the right of citizens to communicate freely with each other. On this point, Costello J said:

> "As the act of communication is the exercise of such a basic human faculty... a right to communicate must inhere in the citizen by virtue of his human personality and must be guaranteed by the Constitution. But in what Article? The exercise of the right to communicate can take many forms and the right to express freely convictions and opinions is expressly provided for in Article 40.6.1.i. But the activity which the defendants say is inhibited in this case is that of communication by letter, and as this act may involve the communication of information and not merely the expression of convictions and opinions, I do not think that the constitutional provision dealing with the right to express convictions and opinions is the source of the citizen's right to communicate. I conclude that the very general and basic human right to communicate which I am considering must be one of those personal unspecified rights of the citizen protected by Article 40.3.1."

He went on to hold, however, that the right was not absolute and was not infringed by the 1908 Act as that Act did not prohibit the defendants from delivering a letter themselves, and, in fact, by making provision for a nation-wide service for the delivery of letters, facilitated the exercise of this right. Furthermore, there was no right "to communicate freely without being obliged to have recourse to the State as the vehicle of such communication".

In *Kearney v Minister for Justice*[182] Costello J held that Rule 63 of the Rules for the Government of Prisons, 1947, requiring letters to and from prisoners to be read by

[178] High Court, 21 April 1980. Regrettably subsequent decisions have been less responsive to the needs of children embroiled in custody disputes.

[179] Though there is some disagreement as to whether this right is not also protected by Article 40.6.1.i. A specific incident of this generic right is now protected by para 3 of Article 40.3.3 which guarantees freedom to disseminate information relating to services lawfully available in another state.

[180] High Court, 23 August 1978.

[181] [1984] ILRM 343. See *McCormack*, (1984) 6 DULJ (n.s) 144.

[182] [1986] IR 116; [1987] ILRM 52.

prison staff, was a justifiable restriction on the plaintiff's right to communicate. However, the non-delivery of mail to the plaintiff as a result of unauthorised action taken by prison officers did constitute a breach of that right, in respect of which he awarded nominal damages of £25.

The same judge concluded, in *McKenna v An Taoiseach*[183] that the plaintiff's right to communicate was not infringed by a partisan governmental campaign supporting ratification of the Treaty on European Union. He pointed out that, even if it could be established that the governmental campaign rendered less effective the communications which the plaintiff wished to make to her fellow citizens, it did not prevent her from communicating those opinions and, accordingly, there was no violation of her right.

A right to take industrial action?

Whether Article 40.3 protects the right to take industrial action has never been conclusively decided by the courts, though there are a number of persuasive *dicta* which support that proposition[184] and such a right might possibly be inferred from the guarantee of the freedom of citizens to form unions in Article 40.6.1.iii. However, it is well settled that industrial action may be restricted by reference to the legal and constitutional rights of parties affected.[185] In *Talbot (Ireland) Ltd. v Merrigan*,[186] in which the company sought an interlocutory injunction restraining the defendants from imposing an embargo on company products, Henchy J is reported as saying:

> "Whether there was a trade dispute or not, a body or bodies must operate within the constitutional framework and the constitutional guarantees in Article 40, and it would have to be borne in mind that innocent persons could not be damnified... [Such innocent persons included] persons such as dealers who had no dispute with anybody, or the owners of vehicles who had no dispute with anybody but who, because of this embargo, could not get their vehicles serviced - a service they were entitled to under contract."

It has been suggested[187] that a distinction should be drawn between those forms of industrial action which are within the law - specifically striking and picketing - and all other forms of industrial action, to which the principle in *Talbot* would be restricted. Proponents of this view point out that Henchy J is reported to have referred, albeit indirectly, to striking and picketing as "legitimate industrial action". It may be that this distinction also underlies another decision in this area, *Crowley v Ireland*,[188] in which McMahon J held that the refusal of the defendants to enrol the plaintiffs in their school was an unlawful interference with their constitutional rights and therefore actionable. This case arose out of a trade dispute in the primary schools of a Co. Cork parish, concerning the appointment of a teacher as school principal in an alleged breach of the Rules for National Schools, during the course of which the teachers' union, the I.N.T.O., instructed its members in neighbouring parishes not to enrol any pupils from the affect-

[183] High Court, 8 June 1992.

[184] See, e.g., Budd J in *Brendan Dunne Ltd. v Fitzpatrick* [1958] IR 29; Kingsmill Moore J in *Educational Co. v Fitzpatrick (No. 2)* [1961] IR 345. See also Kerr and Whyte, *Irish Trade Union Law* (1985), at pp.246-248; Kerr, "*Trade Disputes, Economic Torts and the Constitution: the Legacy of Talbot*", (1981) 16 Ir Jur (n.s.) 241; Wilkinson, "*Workers, Constitutions and the Irish Judiciary: a Jurisprudence of Labour Liberty*" (1989) 24 Ir Jur (n.s.) 198.

[185] See *Educational Co. v Fitzpatrick (No. 2)* [1961] IR 345; *Meskell v C.I.É.* [1973] IR 121.

[186] *Ex tempore* judgment of the Supreme Court, 30 April 1981. A summary of the judgment, which appeared in *The Irish Times* of 1 May 1981, is reproduced in McMahon and Binchy, *Cases and Materials on the Law of Torts* (2nd ed., 1992), p.484.

[187] See *Kerr, loc. cit.*, pp.253-258.

[188] [1980] IR 102.

ed schools. Significantly, counsel for the plaintiffs had conceded that they did not challenge the right of the teachers to withdraw their labour but rather limited their claim to a contention that the directive from the union was an unlawful interference with the constitutional rights of the plaintiffs to free primary education. In the High Court, McMahon J held that the union was liable because, even if the teachers in the neighbouring parishes could be said to be exercising a constitutional right in refusing to enrol students from the affected schools, their purpose in so acting was to deprive those children of primary education in order to exert pressure on the school management:

> "The character of an act depends on the circumstances in which it is done and the exercise of a constitutional right for the purpose of infringing the constitutional rights of others is an abuse of that right which, in my opinion, can be restrained by the Courts. The teachers who refused to enrol the Drimoleague schoolchildren in adjoining schools did not act primarily for the purpose of exercising a right to work or not to work, or to choose the conditions under which they would work. In my view their purpose was to deprive the Drimoleague children of primary education in order to exert pressure on [the school manager]; what was done amounted to the use of unlawful means to deprive the Drimoleague children of their constitutional right. Therefore it is actionable at the suit of the children who can show that they have been deprived of their constitutional right by the action of the teachers."[189]

The difficulty with this view is that it appears to conflate purpose with foreseeability, as McMahon J was surely wrong when he said that the purpose behind the directive was to deprive the schoolchildren of their education. That such deprivation was foreseeable cannot be doubted but the purpose, or motive, of the teachers and their union was, surely, to be able to determine the conditions under which they would work, specifically the conditions of eligibility for promotion to school principal.[190] Even allowing for this confusion, McMahon J's ruling has serious implications for the right to take industrial action as it implies that such action must always be injuncted whenever it affects the constitutional rights of other parties. If one adds to this the reported comments of Henchy J in *Talbot* that the Constitution protects the rights of consumers or users of products affected by industrial action, the scope for legitimate industrial action virtually disappears, a result which is scarcely consistent with the constitutional guarantee of the right of citizens to form unions.

As it happens, McMahon J's judgment contains within itself the seeds of an alternative analysis of the situation in *Crowley*. While he was prepared to assume that the action of refusing to enrol students might be considered to be the exercise of a constitutional right, at an earlier point in his judgment he doubted whether this was in fact the case. If the issue of the union directive prohibiting such enrolment did not involve the exercise of a constitutional right, then it inevitably followed that the union was liable because "as Mr. Justice Walsh pointed out in *Meskell v Córas Iompair Éireann*[191] it is no answer to a claim based on an infringement of a constitutional right to say that the defendant was

[189] The subsequent Supreme Court appeal was concerned solely with McMahon J's finding of liability on the part of Ireland and the Minister for Education and accordingly the Court did not have to consider that part of the High Court decision dealing with the liability of the union. However in a sequel to the *Crowley* case, *Conway v I.N.T.O.* [1991] 2 IR 305; [1991] ILRM 497, the passage quoted above was referred to, with apparent approval, by both Finlay CJ and Griffin J.

[190] O'Higgins CJ in the Supreme Court pointed out that the directive issued only after the appointment of the principal in a permanent capacity and hinted that it may have been motivated by feelings of anger and resentment. However it does not follow from the fact that the appointment had been made permanent that the industrial action had necessarily failed and one could equally argue that the issue of the directive was intended to increase the pressure on the school management so as to secure ultimate victory for the union.

[191] [1973] IR 121.

exercising a common-law right." This analysis would appear to have been adopted implicitly by Carroll J in a sequel to *Crowley - Hayes v Ireland*[192]- when she suggested that if the teachers' union had chosen the wider, non-discriminatory weapon of a countrywide strike, (involving the exercise of constitutional rights), no liability might have been incurred. The significance of this approach to the issue is that it removes the emphasis from the concepts of motive and foreseeability and focuses attention more on the nature of the industrial action taken. Thus if there is a constitutional right to withdraw labour, protected by Article 40.3, and a constitutional right to picket, protected by Article 40.6.1.ii, then in the ordinary course of events the exercise of those rights cannot be restrained even where interference with the constitutional rights of others is foreseen, unless, of course, the sole motivation behind the industrial action is a desire to infringe the constitutional rights of others or the industrial action threatens a constitutional right of a higher order, such as, for example, the right to life in the case of a dispute at a hospital. This affords a measure of protection to the rights of organised labour and yet would not protect such activities as the issue of the directive in *Crowley* or the "blacking" of products in *Talbot.*

May non-citizens rely on Article 40.3?[193]

The question whether non-citizens may rely on the personal rights of Article 40.3 has not been expressly decided, though it arose in *Nicolaou's* case, where the applicant (a British subject) argued, *inter alia*, that as the equality of citizens before the law was based on their being "human persons", he being also a human person ought to share the same rights as a citizen. On this issue, in the High Court Henchy J held against the applicant, Teevan J in his favour; but in the Supreme Court the question was "expressly reserved for another and more appropriate case". If, however, the view is taken that the personal rights of Article 40.3 are "natural", in the sense of inherent in the individual and antecedent to the Constitution, it is hard to see how non-citizens can be prevented from relying on them. Another case in which a court adverted to the possibility that fundamental rights expressed as pertaining to "the citizen" might not be available to a non-citizen seems to be *Fisher v Irish Land Commission*,[194] in which Gavan Duffy J said, somewhat inconclusively:

> "It occurred to me that the plaintiff might have complained that he was entitled to better protection than s 39 [of the Land Act 1939] affords him, by virtue of the constitutional guarantees for private property - see in particular Article 40.3 and Article 43 - though I doubt whether he is a citizen."

This doubt can, at most, refer to Article 40.3, as Article 43 acknowledges not the citizen's right, but man's, in virtue of his rational being, to the private ownership of external goods.

In *McGee's* case Walsh J took up a position which must logically weigh against the restriction of the benefit of Article 40.3 to citizens, when he said the right to life "necessarily implies the right to be born". This clearly imputes the natural personal rights of Article 40.3 to human beings generally (leaving aside all disputes about the moment when a "human being" comes into existence), as presumably the attribution of citizenship to an embryo is impossible.

[192] [1987] ILRM 651.

[193] As to whether non-citizens may rely on the fundamental rights sections of the Constitution generally, see above, pp. 679-682.

[194] [1948] IR 3; (1948) 82 ILTR 50.

A different question is the challenging of an Act of the Oireachtas on constitutional grounds by a non-citizen: see above, pp. 435-436.

Artificial persons

In *P.M.P.S v Attorney General*[195] the Supreme Court "expressed no opinion" on whether a society (under the Industrial and Provident Societies Acts) had rights under Article 40.3. In *Attorney General v Paperlink Ltd.*[196] Costello J said it had been accepted by the parties that the personal rights of Article 40.3 could not be invoked by a company and a similar view was recently expressed by Murphy J in *Chestvale Properties Ltd. v Glackin.*[197] This of course leaves untouched the rights of the persons interested in a society or company and affected by its treatment; accordingly, in cases involving companies in which it is sought to rely on constitutional rights, individual shareholders are invariably joined as plaintiffs. It may be briefly added that, in the *Paperlink* case, Costello J accepted that the right to earn a livelihood can be exercised by means of a company, and that this format for earning a livelihood does not oust the right to invoke this "personal" right.

Origin of the personal rights of Article 40.3

The natural law view of the origin of the undefined personal rights of Article 40.3 first surfaced in *Nicolaou's* case, both in the judgment of Teevan J and in that of the Supreme Court, which considered it:

> "abundantly clear that the rights referred to in Article 40.3 are those which may be called the natural personal rights and the very words of sub-s 1, by the reference therein to "laws" exclude such rights as are dependent only upon law. [s 3] cannot therefore in any sense be read as a constitutional guarantee of personal rights which were simply the creation of the law and in existence on the date of coming into operation of the Constitution."

The point of this was to show that rights merely created by statute - unlike "natural personal rights" - could be modified without infringing Article 40.3.

Distinction between the "personal right" and the right merely conferred by law

This distinction between a personal right in the sense of Article 40.3 and a right merely conferred by law emerged again in *Loftus v Attorney General,*[198] in which the plaintiffs made the case that the prejudicial effect (as they saw it) of s 13 of the Electoral Act 1963, which empowered the Registrar of Political Parties to refuse (on defined criteria) to register their party, represented a failure by the State to defend and vindicate their personal rights. The Supreme Court, observing that this statutory power must be exercised in a constitutional manner, said the right to registration:

> "is a right which is created by law and which depends for its exercise and enjoyment on the conditions laid down by law being complied with. It is not one of the personal rights referred to in Article 40.3, and no contravention of this Article has taken place."

[195] [1983] IR 339; [1984] ILRM 88. Carroll J in the High Court had taken the view that the guarantee of private property in Article 40.3 could be invoked only by human persons.
[196] [1984] ILRM 373. See also his remarks to the same effect in *Kerry Co-Operative Creameries Ltd. v An Bord Bainne* [1990] ILRM 664.
[197] [1992] ILRM 221.
[198] [1979] IR 221.

This view seems open to the objection that a right given statutory vesture may easily be a natural right by origin, so that a court willing to consider natural law principles, wherever these are to be gathered, ought to examine an asserted right against that permanent background, whether a statutory formulation has intervened or not. It will be recalled, in this connection, that a right of recourse or access to the courts - accepted as a "personal right" in the sense of Article 40.3 in *Macauley's* case[199] and subsequently - was identified as such originally not in consequence of natural law considerations, but of Article 34 and its establishment of the High Court with its "full original jurisdiction".

Walsh J subsequently said, in *McGee v Attorney General*[200] that Articles 41-3:

> "emphatically reject the theory that there are no rights without laws, no rights contrary to the law and no rights anterior to the law. They indicate that justice is placed above the law and acknowledge that natural rights, or human rights, are not created by law but that the Constitution confirms their existence and gives them protection."

These words were cited and expressly applied by Gannon J, in *The State (Healy) v Donoghue,*[201] to the (unspecified) right to fair procedures which he saw as latent in Article 40.3. He said that in his view the rights collectively so described:

> "are anterior to and do not merely derive from the Constitution, but the duty to protect them is cast upon the courts by the Constitution."

"Injustice done" and Acts of Indemnity

The constitutionality of legislation of the type of the Indemnity Act 1923 - which had the effect of depriving persons of their potential actions in respect of a certain range of wrongs - has never been tested.[202] It must seem that an Act which operates to deprive a person of the right to litigate is constitutionally questionable since Article 40.3, so far from permitting the retrospective legalisation of that which is illegal, specifically commits the State to vindicating the citizen's rights "in the case of injustice done". In recognition of this risk, the Garda Síochána Act 1979 (which is intended to validate the acts of a person purportedly appointed to the office of Commissioner during a period in which the office was in fact still held by another person) contains, as sub-s 2 of s 1, this provision:

> If, because of any validation expressed to be effected by sub-section (1) of this section, that sub-section would, but for this sub-section, conflict with a constitutional right of any person, the validation shall be subject to such limitation as is necessary to secure that it does not so conflict but shall be otherwise of full force and effect.[203]

Does Article 40.3 apply only to laws, not to omissions to legislate?

In *Crowley v Ireland,*[204] in which it was alleged that the Minister for Education had failed to defend and vindicate the right of children (under Article 42.4) to free primary

[199] [1966] IR 345.
[200] [1974] IR 284; (1975) 109 ILTR 29.
[201] [1976] IR 325.
[202] The matter did arise in 1923, in connection with that Act before the old Court of Appeal in *R. (Cooney) v Clinton* [1935] IR 245, (a belated report), but the Court, while admitting that a "grave constitutional question" was potentially involved, treated the Act as an implicit amendment of the 1922 Constitution: see below. under Article 51. A more recent example of this kind of legislation is the Mental Treatment (Detention in Approved Institutions) Act 1961, which declared that "no damages were to be recoverable" in respect of certain detentions for which no lawful authority had existed.
[203] See above, pp. 365-367.
[204] [1980] IR 102.

education (in the circumstances of a teachers' strike which had closed three local schools), the Supreme Court majority, *per* Kenny J, emphasised that this particular obligation imposed by Article 40.3 relates only to the State's legislative activity:

> "The obligation imposed on the State by both sub-sections of Article 40.3 is as far as practicable by its *laws* to defend and vindicate the personal rights of the citizen. It is not a general obligation to defend and vindicate the personal rights of the citizen. It is a duty to do so by its laws, for it is through laws and by-laws that the State expresses the will of the people who are the ultimate authority."[205]

An earlier attempt to challenge a legislative omission in reliance on Article 40.3 also failed in *O'Shaughnessy v Attorney General*[206] where the plaintiff claimed that the State had failed to vindicate his rights because it did not provide for legal aid for needy litigants in civil matters. Dismissing the claim, O'Keeffe P said that it was for the legislature to determine how the personal rights of the citizen were to be vindicated and that where, as here in the Criminal Justice (Legal Aid) Act 1962, legislation provided assistance to one class of persons but not to another, it was not to be held repugnant to the Constitution on the ground either that the Courts considered that the priorities should be different, or that in providing assistance to those charged with criminal offences the State had elected not to provide any assistance to persons whose civil rights had been affected.

However there are a number of difficulties with Kenny J's restricted view of the duty of the State under Article 40.3. In the first place, the courts have accepted on at least two occasions that the State's duty to defend and vindicate the personal rights of the individual may be discharged through the law of torts. Thus in *Hanrahan v Merck Sharp and Dohme*[207] Henchy J, with whom Finlay CJ and Hederman J agreed, took the view that in the instant case, where the plaintiffs complained of emission of dangerous substances from a nearby pharmaceutical plant, the tort of nuisance could be said to be an implementation of the State's duty in regard to the personal and property rights of the plaintiffs. Similarly in *Sweeney v Duggan,*[208] in which the plaintiff alleged that his employer had a duty, *inter alia*, to safeguard the plaintiff's right to bodily integrity in and about his employment by ensuring that he would be duly compensated for any occupational injuries suffered, Barron J held that Article 40.3.2 gave the plaintiff no more than a guarantee of a just law of negligence, which in the circumstances existed.[209]

[205] In *Igoe v Ireland* [1989] IR 386, Blayney J followed *Crowley v Ireland* in holding that Article 40.3 did not impose a general obligation on the State, in the absence of legislation, to defend and vindicate the personal right of the applicant to the custody of his child. Accordingly he refused to grant an order of *mandamus* directing the Minister for Foreign Affairs to withdraw his estranged wife's passport in so far as it related to his child. The Supreme Court dismissed the subsequent appeal, but it may be significant that it chose to do so on the narrower ground that the granting of such an order would be ineffective, given the facts of the case, to secure custody of his son for the applicant and it expressly reserved for a future occasion the question as to whether the courts could, in any circumstances, direct the Minister for Foreign Affairs to cancel a passport.

[206] High Court, 16 February 1971.

[207] [1988] ILRM 629. Kenny J himself accepted, in *The People v Shaw* [1982] IR 1, that the word "laws" in Article 40.3 included judge-made laws, a proposition subsequently endorsed by the Supreme Court in *AG. v X* [1992] 1 IR 1; [1992] ILRM 401; [1992] 2 CMLR 277. See also the remarks of Finlay CJ in *A.G. (S.P.U.C. (Ireland) Ltd.) v Open Door Counselling Ltd.* [1988] IR 593; [1989] ILRM 19.

[208] [1991] 2 IR 274.

[209] The view that the personal rights of the citizen can be vindicated through the law of torts is not without its difficulties for, as Binchy points out, "tort law simply was not designed to do this task. The medieval English judges who fashioned the contours of trespass to the person, chattels and land exercised no prophetic role in seeking to anticipate the Irish Constitution's protection of citizens' rights to life, bodily integrity, health and property." See "*Constitutional Remedies and the Law of Torts*" in O'Reilly, *op. cit.*

Second, a number of personal rights have been successfully asserted against the State in non-statutory contexts. The most obvious example of this would be the right to fair procedures but one can also point to the right to privacy in *Kennedy v Ireland.*[210]

Third, the position adopted by Kenny J in *Crowley* would seem to imply that Article 40.3 could not be invoked by one individual as against another, whereas again there are numerous examples of the use of this provision in private law disputes.[211]

Finally, some judicial authority suggests that "laws" is not to be interpreted to mean only such legislation as already exists and that the State may have a constitutional duty under Article 40.3 to remedy legislative omissions where such omissions threaten personal rights. In *Brennan v Attorney General*[212] the plaintiffs had challenged the imposition of county rates based on a system of valuation of lands which, according to Barrington J in the High Court, was "shot through with unnecessary anomalies and inconsistencies", a finding also accepted by the Supreme Court. In its judgment, that court held that s 11 of the Local Government Act 1946, which authorised the use of such a system as the basis for assessing agricultural rates, was an unjust attack on the property rights of the plaintiffs and that Article 40.3.2 imposed a duty on the State to take action in protection of their rights. The failure of the State to take such action led to the invalidation of s 11 to the extent that it authorised the collection of the county rate on land independently of buildings.[213] In *A.D. v Ireland*[214] Carroll J rejected the plaintiff's contention that the right to bodily integrity encompassed a right to be compensated by the State for criminal injuries sustained by her. In 1986 the State had effectively terminated a scheme of *ex gratia* compensatory payments to victims of crime for personal injuries sustained and, as the plaintiff's injuries were inflicted in 1988, she was effectively complaining about a legislative failure to provide for criminal injuries compensation. In holding against the plaintiff, the judge ruled that the question of compensation was a matter of policy for the Government and the Oireachtas. Far from relying on the distinction between legislative actions and omissions drawn in *O'Shaughnessy* and *Crowley,* Carroll J accepted the point that "if the Courts find there is a constitutional right which is being ignored by the State, the Court will also find a remedy in the absence of the State undertaking to observe that right."

[210] [1987] IR 587; [1988] ILRM 472. See above, p. 769.

[211] E.g. *Educational Co. of Ireland Ltd. v Fitzpatrick (No.2)* [1961] IR 345; *Murtagh Properties Ltd. v Cleary* [1972] IR 330; *Murphy v Stewart* [1973] IR 97; (1973) 107 ILTR 117; *Rodgers v ITGWU* [1978] ILRM 51.

[212] [1984] ILRM 355.

[213] In *Browne v Attorney General* [1991] 2 IR 58, the plaintiffs had essentially argued that a failure to amend ss 117-120 of the Income Tax Act 1967 to take account of inflation resulted in those provisions becoming unconstitutional, though it is not clear from the judgment whether they were relying on Article 40.1 or Article 40.3 or both, in this context. In the event, Murphy J held that this issue did not arise for decision in the instant case.

[214] High Court, 29 July 1992.

RIGHT TO LIFE OF UNBORN

3° The State acknowledges the right to life of the unborn and, with due regard to the equal right to life of the mother, guarantees in its laws to respect, and, as far as practicable, by its laws to defend and vindicate that right.[1]

This subsection shall not limit freedom to travel between the State and another state.

This subsection shall not limit freedom to obtain or make available, in the State, subject to such conditions as may be laid down by law, information relating to services lawfully available in another state.

3° Admhaíonn an Stát ceart na mbeo gan breith chun a mbeatha agus, ag féachaint go cuí do chomhcheart na máthar chun a beatha, ráthaíonn sé gan cur isteach lena dhlíthe ar an gceart sin agus ráthaíonn fós an ceart sin a chosaint is a shuíomh lena dhlíthe sa mhéid gur féidir é.

Ní theorannóidh an fo-alt seo saoirse chun taisteal idir an Stát and stát eile.

Ní theorannóidh an fo-alt seo saoirse chun faisnéis a fháil nó a chur ar fáil sa Stát maidir le seirbhísí atá ar fáil go dleathach i stát eile ach sin faoi chuimsiú cibé coinníollacha a fhéadfar a leagan síos le dlí.

Innovation

These provisions had no precedent in the 1922 Constitution.

Historical background

Prior to 1983, abortion in Ireland was prohibited by ss 58 and 59 of the Offences Against the Person Act 1861.[2] The former provision made it an offence for a pregnant woman unlawfully to attempt to procure a miscarriage, while the latter provision criminalised the supply of any poison or instrument to a woman, knowing that she intends to use such poison or instrument with intent to procure the miscarriage of any woman.[3] In *R. v Bourne*[4] Macnaghten J directed a jury that, in relation to a criminal prosecution taken under s 58 of the 1861 Act, the prosecution had to prove beyond reasonable doubt that the abortion had not been carried out in good faith in order to preserve the life of the mother. Moreover, he said that a surgeon would be obliged to carry out an abortion where the consequences of the pregnancy would make the mother a physical and mental

[1] On 25 November 1992, the electorate rejected a proposal to insert the following clause into this subsection - "It shall be unlawful to terminate the life of an unborn unless such termination is necessary to save the life, as distinct from the health, of the mother where there is an illness or disorder of the mother giving rise to a real and substantial risk to her life, not being a risk of self-destruction." For analysis of the terms of this clause, see Hogan, "*Law, Liberty and the Abortion Controversy*" in Whelan, ed. *Law and Liberty in Ireland* (1993), p.113. For the background to Article 40.3.3 generally, see Sherlock, "*The Right to Life of the Unborn and the Irish Constitution*" (1989) 24 Ir Jur (n.s.) 13.

[2] Section 10 of the Health (Family Planning) Act 1979 - which Act dealt with the provision of family planning services - expressly saved ss 58 and 59.

[3] For further discussion of these provisions, see Charleton, "*Judicial Discretion in Abortion: the Irish Perspective*" (1992) 6 International Journal of Law and the Family 349 at pp.358-362.

[4] [1939] 1 KB 687; [1938] 3 All ER 615.

wreck.[5] One of the more obscure aspects of the debate on abortion is to what extent, if at all, this direction represented the law in Ireland.[6] It is clear, however, that it did not affect medical practice in this country, whereby a pregnancy would be terminated only where such result was the indirect consequence of an attempt to save the mother's life.[7]

In the event, the progenitor of the first paragraph of Article 40.3.3 was not *Bourne*, but rather the Supreme Court decision in *McGee v Attorney General*[8] to the effect that the married family enjoyed a constitutional right to privacy which encompassed the right to obtain contraceptives. That such a decision could lead to a constitutional amendment intended to copperfasten the existing prohibition on abortion might seem surprising, particularly given that the ruling in *McGee* contained a number of judicially imposed limitations. In the first place, it did not necessarily apply to single people.[9] More pertinent to the present discussion, the majority had been very careful to point out that their decision did not touch on the related issue of abortion, Walsh J commenting that "this case is not in any way concerned with instruments, preparations, drugs or appliances, etc., which take effect after conception" and, later:

> "Any action on the part of either the husband and wife or of the State to limit family sizes by endangering or destroying human life must necessarily not only be an offence against the common good but also against the guaranteed personal rights of the life in question."

Indeed on different occasions before 1983, various members of the Supreme Court had indicated, without any dissent, that the Constitution as it then stood did not encompass a right to have an abortion.[10]

The key to the link between *McGee* and the debate on abortion arguably lies in the experience of the US Supreme Court which had used the concept of privacy, identified in the context of the practice of contraception,[11] to legalise abortion in certain circumstances.[12] Some Irish commentators argued that *McGee* had similar potential and that a constitutional amendment was necessary in order to prevent an undemocratic usurpation by a future generation of Irish judges of the right of the electorate to determine abortion poli-

[5] In the instant case, a girl of fourteen had become pregnant as a result of multiple rape and the jury acquitted the defendant who performed an abortion.

[6] In *Attorney General v X* [1992] 1 IR 1; [1992] ILRM 401; [1992] 2 CMLR 277, Mr. Justice O'Flaherty stated that the enactment of Article 40.3.3 did not bring about any fundamental change in the law without, however, indicating whether *Bourne* correctly represented the pre-1983 position in Ireland while Egan J seemed to regard *Bourne* as good law. On the other hand, Mr. Justice McCarthy appeared to consider that s 58 constituted an absolute ban on abortion while the Chief Justice, Mr. Justice Finlay, emphasised in his test for lawful abortions that there had to be a real and substantial risk to the life, as distinct from the health, of the mother. By implication, this would appear to reject the broader interpretation of *Bourne.* Counsel for the defendants had contended that, prior to 1983, abortion was permitted if there was, as a matter of probability, a real and substantial risk to the life of the mother, a test narrower than that in *Bourne* which permitted abortion wherever continuance of the pregnancy would result in the mother becoming a "physical or mental wreck". This debate is somewhat academic now as there is no prospect of *Bourne* being regarded as good law today.

[7] This practice reflected the distinction drawn in Roman Catholic moral theology between medical interventions procuring the death of the foetus directly and those which have as a secondary and undesired consequence the termination of the pregnancy. Such a distinction, however, has never been expressly made in Irish law.

[8] [1974] IR 284; (1975) 109 ILTR 29. See above p. 767.

[9] See *Norris v Attorney General* [1984] IR 36.

[10] See Walsh J in *G. v An Bord Uchtála* [1980] IR 32; McCarthy J in *Norris v Attorney General* [1984] IR 36.

[11] *Griswold v Connecticut* 381 US 79 (1965).

[12] *Roe v Wade* 410 US 113 (1973). See also the decision of the Supreme Court of Canada in *Margentaler, Smoling and Scott v The Queen* (1988) 37 CCC (3d) 449 that the prohibition of abortion in the Canadian Criminal Code was not in accordance with the principles of fundamental justice guaranteed by the Canadian Constitution because it deprived women of the "security of the person".

cy.[13] Apparently persuaded by such arguments, a majority of the electorate gave its approval to the first paragraph of Article 40.3.3 on 7 September 1983.[14] The enactment of this paragraph was a unique example, in the Irish experience, of a constitutional amendment being proposed and pioneered outside the party political system and to that extent, came close to resembling the old device of the initiative in the Constitution of the Irish Free State, which was designed to allow the electorate to promote proposals for legislative and constitutional change.

From the People to the courts: 1983 to 1989

Having secured victory in the 1983 referendum, the supporters of the resultant amendment then turned to the courts in a series of cases designed to prevent the operation, in this jurisdiction, of abortion referral services. This strategy, in turn, opened the door to European law, as the unsuccessful defendants in one case appealed to the European Court of Human Rights while, in a further case, the High Court sought the advice of the Court of Justice as to the applicability of EC law.

Initially the anti-abortion campaigners had reason to be satisfied with this litigation strategy. In 1988, the Supreme Court, relying on the 1983 amendment, granted an injunction restraining the defendants, two counselling agencies, from assisting pregnant women "to travel abroad to obtain abortions by referral to a clinic, by the making of their travel arrangements or by informing them of the identity and location and method of communication with a specified clinic or clinics" - *The Attorney General (Society for the Protection of Unborn Children (Ireland) Ltd.) v Open Door Counselling Ltd.*.[15] Delivering the leading judgment, Finlay CJ said:

> "The essential issue in this case, having regard to the nature of the guarantees contained in Article 40, s 3, sub-s 3 of the Constitution is the issue as to whether the defendants' admitted activities were assisting pregnant women within the jurisdiction to travel outside that jurisdiction in order to have an abortion. To put the matter in another way, the issue and the question of fact to be determined is: were they thus assisting in the destruction of the life of the unborn?
>
> I am satisfied beyond doubt that having regard to the admitted facts the defendants were assisting in the ultimate destruction of the life of the unborn by abortion in that they were helping the pregnant woman who had decided upon that option to get in touch with a clinic in Great Britain which would provide the service of abortion."

The Court also held that there was no constitutional right to information about the availability of a service of abortion outside the State which, "if availed of, would have the direct consequence of destroying the expressly guaranteed constitutional right to life of the unborn."

At one level, this case might be regarded as having been decided *in vacuo*, in the sense that the court had to consider the activities of the defendants generally, rather than in

[13] See, e.g., the following articles by William Binchy, "*Marital Privacy and Family Law*" (1977) 65 Studies 330; "*Marital Privacy and Family Law: A Reply to Mr O'Reilly*" (1977) 65 Studies 330; and "*The Need for a Constitutional Amendment*" in Flannery, ed. *Abortion and the Law* (1983). *Cp.* O'Reilly "*Marital Privacy and Family Law*", (1977) 65 Studies 8 and Treacy, "*The Constitution and the Right to Life*" in Flannery, *op. cit.* p.74.

[14] For an account of the political campaign leading to the approval of this constitutional amendment, see Hesketh, *The Second Partitioning of Ireland?* (1990).

[15] [1988] IR 593; [1988] ILRM 19.

relation to a specific case, and this may have contributed to the somewhat absolutist position adopted by Supreme Court, from which it was subsequently forced, implicitly, to resile when confronted with the harsh realities of *Attorney General v X.*[16]

One year later, in *The Society for the Protection of Unborn Children (Ireland) Ltd. v Coogan*,[17] a majority of the Supreme Court held that the plaintiff society had sufficient legal standing to bring an action enforcing compliance with Article 40.3.3.[18] This decision was presaged by the remarks of Finlay CJ in the *Open Door* case where, dealing with the defendants' contention that the Attorney General had no *locus standi* to maintain the action as it did not concern any specific pregnant woman, he said:

> "If, therefore, the jurisdiction of the courts is invoked by a party who has a *bona fide* concern and interest for the protection of the constitutionally guaranteed right to life of the unborn, the courts, as the judicial organ of government of the State, would be failing in their duty as far as practicable to vindicate and defend that right if they were to refuse relief upon the grounds that no particular pregnant woman who might be affected by the making of an order was represented before the courts."

In *Coogan*, the Chief Justice, with whom Walsh, Griffin and Hederman JJ agreed, concluded that the plaintiff society did have such *bona fide* concern and interest:

> "On the evidence adduced in the High Court, there can be no question of the plaintiff being an officious or meddlesome intervenient in this matter. I would accept the contention that it could not acquire a *locus standi* to seek this injunction merely by reason of the terms of its articles and memorandum of association. The part, however, which the plaintiff has taken in [the *Open Door* proceedings] which were successfully brought to conclusion by the Attorney General at its relation, and the particular right which it seeks to protect with its importance to the whole nature of our society, constitute sufficient grounds for holding that it is a person with a *bona fide* concern and interest and accordingly has the necessary legal standing to bring the action."

McCarthy J dissented, commenting:

> "I confess to a feeling of great unease at the prospect of any person or group of persons, however well intentioned, being held at law competent to maintain an action of this kind without the intervention of the Attorney General, despite his offer of assistance.[19] Of far greater import is the claim by the Society, as a preliminary to such action, to demand and receive an undertaking from a citizen or a group of citizens as to their future conduct. The implications to a free society of such a claim are alarming. Success in earlier proceedings against other defendants gives no licence for such a practice and the refusal of the Attorney General's offer, in my judgment, disqualifies the Society from having the necessary standing to maintain these proceedings."

[16] [1992] 1 IR 1; [1992] ILRM 401; [1992] 2 CMLR 277. See below, pp. 796-803.

[17] [1989] IR 734; [1990] ILRM 70. The plaintiff society was seeking an injunction to restrain a students' union from publishing a booklet containing information about abortion services provided in the UK.

[18] No challenge appears to have been made to the plaintiff society's standing on the ground of its status as a body corporate - as to which, see above, pp. 710-711.

[19] The Attorney General had indicated that he was prepared to deal favourably with a request from the plaintiff society for his consent to a relator action, but the plaintiff society expressly declined to make such a request.

In a subsequent action, *The Society for the Protection of Unborn Children (Ireland) Ltd. v Grogan,*[20] the society had sought an injunction restraining members of three students' unions from distributing certain information in relation to abortion services available outside the State. Carroll J, in the High Court, exercised her discretion, pursuant to Article 177 of the Treaty of Rome, to refer the case to the Court of Justice of the European Community for a preliminary ruling on certain aspects of EC law before coming to a final conclusion.[21] In the interim, she made no express order refusing or adjourning the application for the injunction. The plaintiff appealed to the Supreme Court against this failure of the High Court to grant an injunction pending receipt of the opinion from the Court of Justice which, it was agreed, would take a minimum of 18 months. A unanimous Supreme Court ruled, *inter alia*, that the fact that the case had been referred to the Court of Justice did not automatically have the effect of postponing a decision on whether or not to grant an interlocutory injunction. The Court decided to grant such an injunction, in the process formulating a new approach to the granting of such injunctions in cases involving the protection of constitutional rights. Finlay CJ said:

> "This application for an interlocutory injunction, therefore, consists of an application to restrain an activity which has been clearly declared by this Court to be unconstitutional and therefore unlawful and which could assist and is intended to assist in the destruction of the right to life of an unborn child, a right acknowledged and protected under the Constitution. That constitutionally guaranteed right must be fully and effectively protected by the courts.
>
> If and when a decision of the Court of Justice of the European Communities rules that some aspect of European Community law affects the activities of the defendants impugned in this case, the consequence of that decision on these constitutionally guaranteed rights and their protection by the courts will then fall to be considered by these courts.
>
> Having regard to that duty of the Court, it is clearly quite inappropriate to approach the exercise of the discretion to grant or refuse an interlocutory injunction upon the basis of a supposed *status quo ante* consisting of activities which are constitutionally forbidden acts. The true principle which falls to be considered in this case in relation to the exercise of that discretion is the unqualified existence of the relevant provisions of the Constitution at the time of the application for an injunction which, in my view, having regard to the constitutional law applicable, replaces the ordinary concept of *status quo ante* arising in interlocutory injunction cases.
>
> With regard to the issue of the balance of convenience, I am satisfied that where an injunction is sought to protect a constitutional right, the only matter which could properly be capable of being weighed in a balance against the granting of such protection would be another competing constitutional right.
>
> I am quite satisfied that in the instant case where the right sought to be protected is that of a life, there can be no question of a possible or putative right which might exist in European law as a corollary to a right to travel so as to avail of services, counterbalancing as a matter of convenience the necessity for an interlocutory injunction."

[20] [1989] IR 753; [1990] ILRM 350.

[21] See further below, p. 795.

Reverses in Europe: rulings of the European Commission on Human Rights

The successes obtained by the anti-abortion lobby before the Irish courts were in large part reversed in Europe. The defendants in the *Open Door* case had instituted proceedings under the European Convention on Human Rights and in the initial stage of this procedure, completed on 7 March 1991, the European Commission on Human Rights held, by a majority of 8 to 5, that the injunction granted by the Supreme Court violated Article 10 of the Convention, guaranteeing freedom of expression. Six of the Commissioners took the view that the Supreme Court order did not come within the scope of Article 10(2), which permits certain restrictions on freedom of expression, because the activities of the defendants were not proscribed by law, the terms of Article 40.3.3 being insufficiently precise for this purpose.[22] Three of the majority Commissioners also took the view that the Irish measures went beyond what was necessary in a democratic society because they were disproportionate. In this context, it was noted that a ban on information was ineffective in protecting the right to life of the unborn in the absence of a ban on travel.

Rulings of the European Court of Justice

The preliminary ruling of the Court of Justice in *Grogan*,[23] some seven months later, handed the anti-abortion lobby what could only be described as a pyrrhic victory. Most damaging from their point of view was the ruling of the Court that termination of pregnancy, performed in accordance with the law of the State in which it is carried out, constituted a service within the meaning of Article 60 of the Treaty of Rome. The Court did go on to hold that it was not contrary to EC law for Ireland to prohibit the defendants from distributing information about abortion clinics in other jurisdictions where those clinics have no involvement in the distribution of the said information. However the clear implication of this ruling was that agencies having a commercial relationship with foreign abortion clinics, and indeed the clinics themselves, were entitled, under EC law, to disseminate information in Ireland about the services provided.

From the courts to the politicians - Protocol No.17 to the Maastricht Treaty

Apparently as a result of this decision, the Government was persuaded to lobby its European partners for the adoption of what eventually became Protocol No.17 to the Treaty on European Union, signed at Maastricht on 7 February 1992. This states:

> "Nothing in the Treaty on the European Union or in the Treaties establishing the European Communities or in the Treaties or Acts modifying or supplementing those Treaties shall affect the application in Ireland of Article 40.3.3 of the Constitution of Ireland."

Some doubt has been expressed as to the validity of this Protocol.[24] However, assuming its validity it would appear to insulate any domestic prohibition on abortion from the

[22] (1992) 14 EHRR 131.

[23] [1991] 3 CMLR 849; [1992] ILRM 461. See Phelan, " *Right to Life of the Unborn v Promotion of Trade in Services: the European Court of Justice and the Normative Shaping of the European Union*" (1992) 55 MLR 670; *Colvin*, (1991-2) 15 Fordham International Law Journal 476; *Curtin*, (1992) CML Rev 585.

[24] Thus Curtin has suggested that the Court of Justice might yet find that the Protocol was not a valid exercise of inter-governmental rights because it trenched on fundamental rights and freedoms under EC law - see *The Irish Times*, 7 March 1992.

effects of EC law after 1 November 1993, when the Treaty on European Union came into force.[25]

The impact of the Protocol in other areas is less clear and, in particular, two diametrically opposed views emerged as to its effect on the right to travel.[26] On the one hand, it was argued that the Protocol did not protect from EC law any activity having a transborder dimension and that consequently it did not affect the right to travel to another member State in the EC. On the other hand, it was contended that Article 40.3.3, as it was then formulated, arguably permitted the State to restrict a woman from travelling abroad and that this position would be copperfastened if the Protocol became law. As we shall see presently, the subsequent amendments to Article 40.3.3 guaranteeing, *inter alia*, the right to travel would appear to have made this particular debate redundant.

Clearly the Protocol does not restrict Ireland's power unilaterally to amend Article 40.3.3. However it is by no means clear that such unilateral amendment would automatically obtain the benefit of the immunity from EC law provided by the Protocol as it is arguable that the reference to Article 40.3.3 in the Protocol is a reference to that provision as it stood on 7 February 1992, the date on which the Treaty on European Union was signed.[27]

One can only deduce from the chronological sequence of events that this Protocol was designed to preserve intact the existing domestic prohibition on abortion and on the dissemination of information on abortion services abroad.[28] However before very long, it became clear, in a most remarkable way, that Protocol No.17 had implications which had never been foreseen by the Government when it negotiated for its inclusion in the Treaty on European Union.

A dilemma for the Supreme Court - Attorney General v X

Ten days after the signing of the Treaty on European Union at Maastricht, in what must surely qualify as the most controversial case ever to come before an Irish court,[29] Costello J granted, *inter alia*, an injunction which had the effect of preventing a 14 year old girl, pregnant as a result of an alleged rape, from travelling to the UK in order to procure an abortion - *Attorney General v X. and others*.[30] In relation to the defendants'

[25] In fact, despite a popular perception to the contrary, there is not a scintilla of evidence that the European Community wishes to harmonise national abortion laws throughout the Community. Following a careful and very thorough analysis of the possible legal bases in the Treaty of Rome or the jurisprudence of the Court of Justice for any such putative harmonisation policy, Kingston and Whelan conclude that the development of such a policy is "perhaps possible, but not at all probable." - See "*The Protection of the Unborn in Three Legal Orders - Part II*" (1992) ILT 104 at 107. Curtin states, even more strongly, that, "[T]here is no possibility whatsoever of the Community legislature (or indeed the Court of Justice in Luxembourg) acting to legalise abortion itself *in Ireland.* The question of whether abortion should be legal or otherwise in a given member state is a moral value judgment outside the scope of Community law and within the sphere of sovereign decision-making by member states." - *The Irish Times,* 2 March 1992.

[26] See further below, p. 798.

[27] In fact this issue is addressed by the Solemn Declaration, as to which, see below, pp. 803–806.

[28] Though see the Solemn Declaration, below, pp. 803-805.

[29] Such was the intense interest in this case that within weeks of the Supreme Court decision, the Incorporated Council of Law Reporting for Ireland published in a separate volume the judgments of the High and Supreme Court, together with the submissions made to the Supreme Court, a move which is without precedent in the history of Irish law reporting - *The Attorney General v X and others*, ed. McDonagh, (Incorporated Council of Law Reporting for Ireland, 1992). Extensive legal comment on the *X* case and subsequent developments was carried in the national newspapers for a number of weeks afterwards.

[30] [1992] 1 IR 1; [1992] ILRM 401; [1992] 2 CMLR 277. The injunction actually restrained the defendant from leaving the jurisdiction for a period of nine months from the date of the court order, with no limitation as to destination or purpose of travel.

claim that the injunction should not be granted as this would prejudice the mother's right to life because of the very real danger that the mother would commit suicide if she was unable to procure an abortion, Costello J said:

> "The situation which has arisen in this case is not one of those which may arise in the practice of medicine, namely, a situation in which surgical intervention, necessary to save the life of the unborn, may involve risk to the mother's life, or in which the surgical intervention necessary to save the life of the mother may involve risk to the life of the unborn. This is a case in which the risk to the mother's life comes from herself. What the court is asked to do is not to make an order because if it did the mother may take her own life.
>
> I think that in a case such as this, involving a young girl in a highly distressing and deeply disturbing situation, the court has a duty to protect her life not just from the actions of others but from actions she may herself perform.
>
> What the court, therefore, is required to do is to assess by reference to the evidence the danger to the life of the child and the danger that exists to the life of the mother. I am quite satisfied that there is a real and imminent danger to the life of the unborn and that if the court does not step in to protect it by means of the injunction sought, its life will be terminated. The evidence also establishes that if the court grants the injunction sought there is a risk that the defendant may take her own life. But the risk that the defendant may take her own life if an order is made is much less and is of a different order of magnitude than the certainty that the life of the unborn will be terminated if the order is not made. I am strengthened in this view by the knowledge that the young girl has the benefit of the love and care and support of devoted parents who will help her through the difficult months ahead. It seems to me, therefore, that having had regard to the rights of the mother in this case, the court's duty to protect the life of the unborn requires it to make the order sought."[31]

The subsequent unprecedented public reaction, both domestic and international, was in the main hostile and the case brought the abortion question firmly back onto the Irish agenda. The case also set in motion a train of events, the pace of which was, at times, bewildering and which sometimes left the Government open to charges of inconsistency in its argumentation.

[31] In relation to the other arguments advanced by the defendants, Costello J held that, in the absence of legislative regulation of the manner in which the right to life of the unborn and that of the mother could be reconciled, the courts had the jurisdiction to achieve such reconciliation in individual cases. He also ruled that the court could restrain the first defendant's constitutional right to liberty if that was necessary in order to prevent her doing an unlawful act, specifically, procuring an abortion. Finally, he concluded that the first defendant's right under EC law to travel to another member state in order to obtain an abortion had to be read subject to public policy and that the 1983 Amendment to the Constitution was, accordingly, a permissible derogation from EC law on this point. This last ruling has been criticised on the ground that under EC law, public policy considerations could be used solely to justify restrictions on persons coming *into* a country and never to restrict the freedom of a person who wishes to *leave* a jurisdiction - see the separate comments by *Curtin* and *Hogan* in *The Irish Times*, 19 February 1992 and Hogan, "*Protocol 17*" in Keating ed., *Maastricht and Ireland* (1992), 109 at p.112. For a rebuttal of this argument, however, see Kingston and Whelan, "*The Protection of the Unborn in Three Legal Orders - Part III*" (1992) ILT 166 at 166-7. However the two authors go on to suggest - as does *Hogan* in *The Irish Times*, 24 February 1992 - that Costello J did not adequately deal with the requirement under EC law that, *inter alia*, the restrictions on intra-Community trade must not be out of proportion to the aim sought by or the result brought about by the national rule - see the opinion of Advocate General van Gerven in *The Society for the Protection of Unborn Children (Ireland) Ltd. v Grogan* [1991] 3 CMLR 849 at 874-5 wherein he took the view that a travel ban would be disproportionate in this context.

To begin with, it quickly became apparent that Costello J's decision not only raised important issues in relation to constitutional policy on abortion, it also had implications for the ratification by the Irish electorate of the Treaty on European Union because of the existence of Protocol No.17. A right to travel to obtain services, grounded on EC law, was seen as a possible counterbalance to the requirements of the 1983 amendment as interpreted by Costello J. The Protocol, however, purported to take EC law out of the equation and, as we have seen, two conflicting views emerged as to the effect of this on this right to travel. On the one hand, it was argued that the words "in Ireland" meant that the Protocol did not protect from EC law any activity having a transborder dimension. On this view, the existing right to travel to another member State in the EC was not affected by the Protocol.[32] On the other hand, it was contended that Article 40.3.3 appeared to permit the State to restrict a woman from travelling abroad; that this was an interpretation of the "application in Ireland" of that provision and that, consequently, this position would be copperfastened if the Protocol became law.[33] If this latter view was correct, then someone like X would not be able to invoke a right to travel under EC law if the Protocol was ever ratified. Thus ratification of the Treaty on European Union by the Irish electorate became embroiled in what was always going to be a controversial debate on abortion policy.

The case was appealed to the Supreme Court[34] which was thus presented with the profound dilemma of trying to reconcile, in the absence of any legislative guidance, the constitutional right to life of the mother with that of the unborn, a dilemma which, as we have just noted, was greatly exacerbated by the possible implications of its decision for the ratification of the Treaty on European Union. Moreover the pressing nature of the case effectively precluded the Court from relying on principles of EC law in resolving this dilemma because, had it done so, it would have been required by Article 177 of the Treaty of Rome to seek the advice of the Court of Justice as to the proper interpretation of those principles, a process which would have delayed final resolution of the issues by as much as eighteen months.[35]

In an *ex tempore* ruling handed down on 26 February, a majority of the Court held that the injunction should be lifted; the full judgments of the five judges were subsequently delivered on 5 March.

Finlay CJ began by affirming the right of the Attorney General to institute the proceedings in the instant case and the right of the court to protect the right to life of the unborn, even in the absence of legislative guidance on the matter. He then turned to consider the meaning of the 1983 amendment; in particular whether it allowed for any lawful abortion and, if so, under what circumstances - the so-called "substantive issue". Reading this provision in the light of earlier judicial comments on the impact of the Preamble on judicial interpretation of the Constitution,[36] he said:

[32] See *Binchy, The Irish Times,* 25 February 1992 and 27 February 1992; *Curtin, The Irish Times,* 2 March 1992, 7 March 1992 and 24 April 1992. See also the reported views of "senior legal experts" at the Court of Justice in Luxembourg in *The Irish Times,* 25 February 1992.

[33] See *Hogan, The Irish Times,* 24 February 1992, 6 March 1992, 17-18 April 1992, 25 April 1992; *McDowell, The Irish Times,* 6 March 1992.

[34] In an unprecedented move, the State offered to pay the costs of the defendants' appeal to the Supreme Court.

[35] The Court did, in fact, hear argument on the applicability of EC law from counsel for the defendants but subsequently ruled (*per* Finlay CJ) that it was not necessary to address those issues in order to resolve the case.

[36] The comments of Walsh J and O'Higgins CJ in *McGee v Attorney General* [1974] IR 284, at 318, and *The State (Healy) v Donoghue* [1976] IR 326, at 347, respectively. See above, pp. 4-5.

> "Such a harmonious interpretation of the Constitution carried out in accordance with concepts of prudence, justice and charity...leads me to the conclusion that in vindicating and defending as far as practicable the right of the unborn to life but at the same time giving due regard to the right to the mother to life, the Court must, amongst the matters to be so regarded, concern itself with the position of the mother within the family group, with persons on whom she is dependent, with, in other instances, persons who are dependent upon her and her interaction with other citizens and members of society in the areas in which her activities occur. Having regard to that conclusion, I am satisfied that the test proposed on behalf of the Attorney General that the life of the unborn could only be terminated if it were established that an inevitable or immediate risk to the life of the mother existed, for the avoidance of which a termination of the pregnancy was necessary, insufficiently vindicates the mother's right to life.
>
> I, therefore, conclude that the proper test to be applied is that if it is established as a matter of probability that there is a real and substantial risk to the life, as distinct from the health, of the mother, which can only be avoided by the termination of her pregnancy, such termination is permissible, having regard to the true interpretation of Article 40, s 3, sub-s 3 of the Constitution."

As to whether the risk of suicide in the instant case constituted a "real and substantial risk" to the life of the mother warranting the performance of an abortion, the Chief Justice accepted that this was a risk which, as would be appropriate in any other form of risk to the life of the unborn, should be taken into account in reconciling the right of the unborn to life and the right of the mother to life. He continued:

> "If a physical condition emanating from a pregnancy occurs in a mother, it may be that a decision to terminate the pregnancy in order to save her life can be postponed for a significant period in order to monitor the progress of the physical condition, and that there are diagnostic warning signs which can readily be relied upon during such postponement.
>
> In my view, it is common sense that a threat of self-destruction such as is outlined in the evidence in this case, which the psychologist clearly believes to be a very real threat, cannot be monitored in that sense and that it is almost impossible to prevent self-destruction in a young girl in the situation in which this defendant is if she were to decide to carry out her threat of suicide.
>
> I am, therefore, satisfied that on the evidence before Costello J, which was in no way contested, and on the findings which he has made, that the defendants have satisfied the test which I have laid down as being appropriate and have established, as a matter of probability, that there is a real and substantial risk to the life of the mother by self-destruction which can only be avoided by termination of her pregnancy."

This conclusion was sufficient to dispose of the appeal but because other issues relating to the defendant's right to travel had been fully argued before the Court and were of considerable public interest, Finlay CJ went on to offer his views on them, albeit as *obiter dicta*. Rejecting the contention that the mother had an absolute right to travel[37]

[37] The right to travel was first recognised as an implied constitutional right by Finlay P (as he then was) in *The State (M.) v Attorney General* [1979] IR 73. By virtue of Article 2(2) of the Fourth Protocol to the European Convention on Human Rights, an individual has the right to leave his/her own country. This right may, however, be restricted on the grounds, *inter alia*, of public order or policy, of protecting health and morals, or of

which could not be restricted by any vindication or defence of the right of the unborn child to life, he said:

> "I accept that where there exists an interaction of constitutional rights the first objective of the courts in interpreting the Constitution and resolving any problem thus arising should be to seek to harmonise such interacting rights. There are instances, however, I am satisfied, where such harmonisation may not be possible and in those instances I am satisfied...that there is a necessity to apply a priority of rights.
>
> Notwithstanding the very fundamental nature of the right to travel and its particular importance in relation to the characteristics of a free society, I would be forced to conclude that if there were a stark conflict between the right of a mother of an unborn child to travel and the right to life of the unborn child, the right to life would necessarily have to take precedence over the right to travel."

Nor did he accept that the power of the Court to interfere with the mother's right to travel was in any way limited or restricted by the absence of legislation. As for the argument that it would be impossible to police an order restraining the right to travel, he did not consider that it could be said that:

> "a mere expectation that a significant number of people may be unwilling to obey the orders of a court could deprive that court from attempting, at least, in appropriate cases to discharge its constitutional duty by the making of an injunction restricting, to some extent, the right to travel of an individual."[38]

Similar judgments in respect of the substantive issue were delivered by the three other judges in the majority. After quoting the concluding paragraph in the quotation from the judgment of Costello J cited above,[39] McCarthy J said:

> "In my judgment, this was an incorrect approach to the problem raised by the terms of the Eighth Amendment. It is not a question of balancing the life of the unborn against the life of the mother; if it were, the life of the unborn would virtually always have to be preserved, since the termination of pregnancy means the death of the unborn; there is no certainty, however high the probability, that the mother will die if there is not a termination of pregnancy. In my view, the true construction of the Amendment, bearing in mind the other provisions of Article 40 and the fundamental rights of the family guaranteed by Article 41, is that, paying due regard to the equal right to life of the mother, when there is a real and substantial risk attached to her survival not merely at the time of application but in contemplation at least throughout the pregnancy, then it may not be practicable to vindicate the right to life of the unborn. It is not a question of a risk of a different order of magnitude; it can never be otherwise than a risk of a different order of magnitude.

protecting the rights and freedom of others. There is very little case-law on this aspect of the Convention and it has been suggested that the right to leave is quite a weak one - van Dijk and van Hoof, *Theory and Practice of the European Convention on Human Rights* (2nd ed. 1990) p.491. As we shall see presently, a pregnant woman has a right under EC law to travel to another member State in order to avail of abortion services lawfully provided in that State.

[38] An implication here would seem to be that if, in a specific case, it was going to be impossible to monitor the behaviour of a defendant to ensure that she did not breach an injunction restraining her from travelling abroad, the court would not grant such an injunction. Certainly in the course of hearing submissions from counsel, Finlay CJ is reported as agreeing that the court would not issue an order which is futile - [1992] 1 IR 1 at 40; *McDonagh, op. cit.*, p.45.

[39] At p. 797.

On the facts of the case, which are not in contest, I am wholly satisfied that a real and substantial risk that the girl might take her own life was established; it follows that she should not be prevented from having a medical termination of pregnancy."

He disagreed with the Chief Justice on the matter of the State's power to restrict travel, holding that the courts had no jurisdiction to make an order interfering with the right to travel:

> "In my view, it is not a question of balancing the right to travel against the right to life; it is a question as to whether or not an individual has a right to travel - which she has. It cannot, in my view, be curtailed because of a particular intent. If one travels from the jurisdiction of this State to another, one, temporarily, becomes subject to the laws of the other State. An agreement, commonly called a conspiracy, to go to another State to do something lawfully done there cannot, in my opinion, permit of a restraining order...I go further. Even if it were a crime in the other country, if I proclaim my intent to explode a bomb or shoot an individual in another country, I cannot lawfully be prevented from leaving my own country for that purpose.
>
> The reality is that each nation governs itself and enforces its own criminal law. A Court in one state cannot enjoin an individual leaving it from wrongdoing outside it in another state or states. It follows that, insofar as it interferes with the right to travel, there is no jurisdiction to make such an order."[40]

Earlier McCarthy J's deep sense of frustration with the legislature had manifested itself in an excoriating criticism of legislative inertia:

> "In the context of the eight years that have passed since the Amendment was adopted and the two years since *Grogan's* case the failure by the legislature to enact the appropriate legislation is no longer just unfortunate; it is inexcusable. What are pregnant women to do? What are the parents of a pregnant girl under age to do? What are the medical profession to do? They have no guidelines save what may be gleaned from the judgments in this case. What additional considerations are there? Is the victim of rape, statutory or otherwise, or the victim of incest, finding herself pregnant, to be assessed in a manner different from others? The Amendment, born of public disquiet, historically divisive of our people, guaranteeing in its laws to respect and by its laws to defend the right to life of the unborn, remains bare of legislative direction."

The remaining two judges in the majority - O'Flaherty and Egan JJ - agreed that the 1983 Amendment permitted abortion where there was a "real and substantial risk to the life of the mother". They disagreed with each other on the matter of whether the State could interfere with the right to travel, O'Flaherty J siding with McCarthy J, while Egan J agreed with the Chief Justice that the right to travel could not take precedence over the right to life of the unborn.

The sole dissenting judge, Hederman J, implicitly rejected the majority opinion that a risk of self-destruction could be equated with medical risks to the life of the mother for the purpose of justifying an abortion:

[40] *Pace* McCarthy J, surely the argument here is not that the court should attempt to give extra-territorial effect to the principles of Irish criminal law on abortion, but rather that it should vindicate the constitutional right to life of the unborn in this jurisdiction.

"In the present case neither this Court nor the High Court has heard or seen the mother of the unborn child. There has been no evidence whatever of an obstetrical or indeed of any other medical nature. There has been no evidence upon which the Court could conclude that there are any obstetrical problems, much less serious threats to the life of the mother of a medical nature. What has been offered is the evidence of a psychologist based on his own encounter with the first defendant and on what he heard about her attitude and behaviour from other persons, namely, the Garda Síochána and her parents. This led him to the opinion that there is a serious threat to the life of the first defendant by an act of self-destruction by reason of the fact of being pregnant. This is a very extreme reaction to pregnancy, even to an unwanted pregnancy. But as was pointed out in this Court in *S.P.U.C. v Grogan* [1989] IR 734, the fact that a pregnancy is unwanted was no justification for terminating it or attempting to terminate it. If there is a suicidal tendency then this is something which has to be guarded against. If this young person without being pregnant had suicidal tendencies due to some other cause then nobody would doubt that the proper course would be to put her in such care and under such supervision as would counteract such tendency and do everything possible to prevent suicide. I do not think the terms of the Eighth Amendment or indeed the terms of the Constitution before the Amendment would absolve the State from its obligation to vindicate and protect the life of a person who had expressed the intention of self-destruction. This young girl clearly requires loving and sympathetic care and professional counselling and all the protection which the State agencies can provide or furnish.

There could be no question whatsoever of permitting another life to be taken to deal with the situation even if the intent to self-destruct could be traced directly to the activities or the existence of another person."

Unlike the Chief Justice, Hederman J opined that it should not be impossible to guard the mother against self-destruction and preserve the life of the unborn child at the same time:

"Suicide threats can be contained. The duration of the pregnancy is a matter of months and it should not be impossible to guard the girl against self-destruction and preserve the life of the unborn child at the same time. The choice is between the certain death of the unborn life and a feared substantial danger of death but no degree of certainty of the mother by way of self-destruction."

The facts of the *X* case presented, for all involved, a dreadful dilemma in human terms. For the Supreme Court judges called finally to resolve this dilemma, the terms of the first paragraph of Article 40.3.3 afforded very little assistance for the text tried to achieve the impossible - it expressly equated two rights which, on those rare occasions when they come into conflict, cannot be reconciled.[41] In reality, of course, there are only two options available in this situation - to prefer the life of the mother over that of the foetus or to give priority to the foetus. While debate may rage as to when a conflict of rights exists in this context, neither side of the debate has ever suggested giving priority to the foetus once such a conflict has materialised. To that extent, the decision of the majority to give preference to the right of the mother is not surprising. What is surprising about the majority judgments, however, is the manner in which they equate the threat of suicide with life-threatening medical conditions of a physical nature as a real

[41] Perhaps it was a reluctance to confront this ultimate absurdity of the text which led some members of the majority, notably Finlay CJ and McCarthy J, to reason somewhat casuistically, that they were not engaged in the ranking of the respective rights of the mother and the foetus.

and substantial risk to the life of the mother. Regrettably none of the majority judgments go into any detail in defending this equation.[42] An apparent difference between the threat of suicide and that of physical illness lies in the possibility of averting the former without necessarily terminating the pregnancy and indeed this was a central plank in Hederman J's dissent. However, the State is obliged to defend and vindicate the right to life of the unborn only "as far as practicable". Accordingly, if one takes the view that the all-pervasive control measures necessary to prevent the mother committing suicide are not practicable, the distinction between the risk posed by suicide and that posed by life-threatening illnesses would seem to disappear. Finlay CJ invoked common sense in support of the proposition that it would be "almost impossible" to prevent the defendant committing suicide. If he had elaborated on this position, he might have pointed to the fact that, *pace* Hederman J, the threat of suicide would have to be contained even after the pregnancy was over, perhaps for many months afterwards, and that, unlike cases of conventional illnesses, the medical authorities would not be able to rely on the patient's co-operation. Moreover, the reality of prison suicides indicates that a very high degree of supervision of the patient - perhaps round-the-clock supervision - would be required in order to avert the risk of suicide. However, even if one considered that such steps were practicable - as Hederman J did, though the Court does not appear to have heard any evidence as to the nature or extent of the measures actually required - one could not easily equate the position of the pregnant woman threatening suicide with that of the pregnant woman emperilled by life-threatening illnesses. The failure of the various judges to tease out these issues - perhaps a by-product of the extraordinary circumstances in which the case was decided - does leave the impression that, in some respects at least, the foundations for the majority decision could have been dug more deeply.

Be that as it may, the ruling in *X* eased the dreadful predicament in which the young defendant found herself and stemmed the tide of international criticism of Irish abortion law but otherwise appears to have pleased no one. Those who had campaigned for the introduction of Article 40.3.3 in 1983 were dismayed at the latitude given to the mother's right to life as a factor qualifying the right to life of the unborn. Their opponents, meanwhile, were concerned about the possibility that, if Protocol No.17 was ratified, pregnant women seeking abortions abroad, whose lives were not endangered by the pregnancy, could be prevented from travelling by the State, given that three members of the Court envisaged that the constitutional right to travel could be restrained in order to protect the right to life of the unborn. The decision in *X* also had implications for the existing constitutional ban on the dissemination of information about abortion services abroad as it seemed to follow from the Supreme Court ruling that women whose lives were at risk could not lawfully be denied such information.[43]

Back to the Politicians: The Solemn Declaration-

After some initial hesitation, the Government decided to seek an amendment to Protocol No.17 which would ensure that EC law rights to travel and information would continue

[42] Thus Patrick Riordan S.J has commented:
"It seems that the Supreme Court accepts the phenomenon and the threat of suicide as given, without reference to the sociological analysis of suicide or of their own action. What about the impact of the Supreme Court's recognition of a threat of suicide as justifying life-taking measures on the web of norms and values whereby people are restrained form the ultimate alienation of suicide? Although taken in the name of protecting women's lives, this decision may have the effect of increasing the threat to their lives through *anomie*" - "*Abortion: The Aftermath of the Supreme Court's Decision*" (1992) 81 Studies 293.

[43] Indeed, on 24 March 1992, counsel for the State expressly conceded that such was the case in argument before the European Court of Human Rights in the *Open Door Counselling Ltd.* case.

to be available to Irish citizens after ratification of the Treaty on European Union. The other member States refused to re-open debate on the Protocol for fear that this might set a precedent for the re-negotiation of other aspects of the Treaty. Consequently, the Government had to settle for a Solemn Declaration of the intentions of the High Contracting Parties on the matter of the Protocol.[44] This provides:

> "The High Contracting Parties to the Treaty on European Union signed at Maastricht on the 7th day of February 1992
>
> Having considered the terms of Protocol No.17 to the said Treaty on European Union which is annexed to that Treaty and to the Treaties establishing the European Communities
>
> Hereby give the following legal interpretation:
>
> that it was and is their intention that the Protocol shall not limit freedom either to travel between member States or, in accordance with conditions which may be laid down in conformity with Community law, by Irish legislation, to obtain or make available in Ireland information relating to services lawfully available in member States.
>
> At the same time the High Contracting Parties solemnly declare that, in the event of a future constitutional amendment in Ireland which concerns the subject matter of Article 40.3.3 of the Constitution of Ireland and which does not conflict with the intention of the High Contracting Parties hereinbefore expressed, they will, following the entry into force of the Treaty on European Union, be favourably disposed to amending the said Protocol so as to extend its application to such constitutional amendment if Ireland so requests."

In fact it would appear to be impossible to reconcile the terms of the Solemn Declaration with the actual history of events which clearly implies that the Protocol was designed to *protect* the existing constitutional ban on the dissemination of information. The point has also been well made that if the Solemn Declaration was an accurate account of the intention of the Government when it signed the Treaty on European Union, encompassing Protocol No.17, on 7 February 1992, then the action of the Attorney General on the previous day in commencing High Court proceedings for an injunction to prevent a pregnant young girl travelling to the UK in order to procure an abortion flew in the face of this understanding of the Protocol.[45]

Quite apart from this difficulty, there is some uncertainty as to the legal status of the Declaration though it is quite clear that neither the Solemn Declaration nor Protocol No.17 could have had any legal effect prior to the coming into effect of the Treaty on European Union.[46] Even with the coming into force of that Treaty on 1 November 1993,

[44] This Solemn Declaration was formally adopted by the EC foreign ministers on 1 May 1992.

[45] See *McDowell, The Irish Times,* 17-18 April 1992. See also the reported comments of *Hogan* in *The Irish Times,* 2 May 1992.

[46] A position confirmed by Morris J in *The Society for the Protection of Unborn Children (Ireland) Ltd. v Grogan* [1993] 1 CMLR 197. On 23 April 1992, the Taoiseach, Mr. Albert Reynolds, T.D., had said that if the Maastricht Treaty (including the Protocol) was approved in the June referendum, the Attorney General would seek no further injunctions to stop women from travelling abroad. This, apparently, was based on the Attorney General's "practical interpretation" of the Solemn Declaration that the Irish people would, in approving the Maastricht Treaty, have voted in favour of a right to travel. However this argument was implicitly rejected by Morris J in *Grogan* when he held that the courts could not have regard to the terms of the Solemn Declaration until such time as the Treaty on European Union had come into effect.

the status of the Solemn Declaration remains unclear. The preponderance of opinion suggests that it is not legally binding and that it can, at most, amount only to a statement of political intent.[47] On the other hand, it has been argued that, having regard to Article 31(3) of the Vienna Convention on the Law of Treaties 1969, the Court of Justice must take the Solemn Declaration into account if it is ever called on to interpret the Protocol.[48] However, as Kingston and Whelan remark:

> "[I]t is a matter for speculation whether [this] argument is undermined by the characterisation of the Solemn Declaration as a "retrospective claim", at odds with the evident intention of the parties. Arguably, the argument must turn on whether the Court of Justice would favour (should a case arise) the *imputed* or the *actual* intention of the parties to the Treaty."[49]

Whether it takes effect in the political or legal arena, the Solemn Declaration implies two points. First, that a future amendment to the Constitution will not be covered by the terms of the Protocol, and thus immune from the effect of EC law, unless the other member States agree to amend the Protocol. Second, that that approval will only be forthcoming for an amendment which does not conflict with freedom to travel or to receive and disseminate information under EC law. So any future constitutional amendment seeking to modify *X* will come within the scope of the Protocol only if it respects EC law on the issues of travel and information.

-To the courts-

Meanwhile the litigation - both at home and in Europe, continued. In August 1992, following the procedures envisaged by Article 177 of the Treaty of Rome, Morris J handed down a decision in which he applied the principles stated by the Court of Justice in *Grogan* to the facts of that case.[50] The defendants had contended, *inter alia*, that the right under EC law to travel to the UK to obtain an abortion had a collateral right to receive information relating to the clinics where such service is provided and, accordingly, the defendants had a right to provide pregnant women with this information. According to Morris J, this contention completely ignored the finding of the Court of Justice that a prohibition on students' associations disseminating information about abortion services abroad was not contrary to EC law where the clinics providing such services had no involvement in the distribution of this information. The defendants also submitted that, having regard to the Supreme Court decision in *X*, it was now permissible to communicate information about abortion services to persons covered by that ruling. However this argument was dismissed on the ground that the defendants had not limited the provision of information to persons coming within the scope of the *X* case. Significantly, inasmuch as he did not reject the contention that it was permissible to communicate information about abortion services to persons covered by the Supreme Court ruling in *X*, Morris J would appear to imply that that judgment qualified the earli-

[47] Robinson argues that there is no binding authority on the legal status of Declarations appended to Community Treaties and that the case law of the Court of Justice - specifically *R. v Immigration Appeal Tribunal, ex parte Antonissen*, case [1991] 1 ECR 745; [1991] 2 CMLR 373 - indicates that declarations passed contemporaneously to secondary EC legislation are of no legal effect - "*European Dimensions of the Abortion Debate*" in *Abortion, Law and Conscience* (Dublin, 1992) 273, at pp.279-80. See also *Hogan, The Irish Times*, 17-18 April 1992; *Callan, The Sunday Tribune*, 19 April 1992; *Curtin, The Irish Times*, 24 April 1992; *Gwynn-Morgan, The Irish Times*, 27 April 1992.

[48] *Fitzsimons, The Irish Times*, 6 May 1992.

[49] "*The Protection of the Unborn in Three Legal Orders - Part III*" (1992) ILT 166 at 169-70. In fact the likelihood of such a case arising is now remote in the light of the subsequent amendments to Article 40.3.3 which appear to have removed the potential for conflict between domestic and EC law on the matters of travel and information - see below, pp. 809-810.

[50] [1993] 1 CMLR 197.

er decision in *The Attorney General (The Society for the Protection of Unborn Children (Ireland) Ltd.) v Open Door Counselling Ltd.*[51] Counsel for the defendants also invoked the terms of the Solemn Declaration which, he said, encapsulated public policy in this matter and which, accordingly, should inform the court's decision. Dismissing this contention, Morris J pointed out that, at the date of judgment, the Solemn Declaration had not yet entered into force and, citing *The State (Llewellyn) v Ua Donnchadha*[52] for the proposition that issues must be determined in accordance with existing law, he held that he could not have regard to the terms of the Solemn Declaration. The plaintiff society having indicated that it would seek to enforce any injunction obtained by way of application for committal, Morris J also rejected the defendants' contention that relief should be confined to a declaration of rights.[53] As for a challenge by the defendants to the *locus standi* of the plaintiff society, Morris J held that this argument had been fully considered and rejected by the Supreme Court in *The Attorney General (The Society for the Protection of Unborn Children (Ireland) Ltd.) v Open Door Counselling Ltd.*[54]

A little more than two months after Morris J had delivered his judgment in *Grogan,* the European Court of Human Rights handed down its decision in the appeal taken by the Open Door and Dublin Well Woman clinics - *Open Door Counselling Ltd. and Dublin Well Woman Ltd. v Ireland*[55] in which the applicants contended, *inter alia*, that their right to freedom of expression under Article 10 of the European Convention on Human Rights was infringed by the Supreme Court injunction. A majority of the Court ruled, *inter alia*, that the restriction on the freedom of the applicants to impart information was "prescribed by law" within the meaning of the proviso to the guarantee contained in Article 10(2).[56] The majority also accepted that the restriction pursued the legitimate aim of the protection of morals of which the protection in Ireland of the right to life of the unborn is one aspect. However the Court, again by a majority, also held that the restriction was disproportionate to the aims pursued and that consequently it violated Article 10. In support of this conclusion, the majority pointed to the fact that the Government had conceded that the sweeping nature of the Supreme Court injunction could no longer be defended in the light of the *X* case, insofar as women entitled to an abortion in Ireland were now also entitled to information about such services. Moreover the link between the provision of information and the destruction of unborn life was not as definite as had been contended, given that some women who receive non-directive counselling decide against having an abortion. Furthermore the Government did not seriously contest the fact that information concerning abortion facilities abroad could be obtained from other sources such as magazines or telephone directories and the injunction appeared to have been largely ineffective in protecting unborn life in that it did not prevent large numbers of Irish women from continuing to obtain abortions in the UK. Finally, the undisputed evidence before the Court was that the injunction created a risk to the health of those women seeking abortions at a later stage in their pregnancy due to the lack of proper counselling.[57]

[51] [1988] IR 593; [1989] ILRM 19.

[52] [1973] IR 151.

[53] *Charleton* records that a motion seeking committal of the defendants for contempt failed because the plaintiff relied, for its proofs, on newspaper reports apparently quoting some of the defendants as defying the court order. However the trial judge apparently held such evidence to be inadmissible as being an infringement of the rule against hearsay - *loc. cit.* at pp.367-8.

[54] [1988] IR 593; [1989] ILRM 19. Additional arguments advanced by the defendants, grounded on Articles 40.1 and 40.3, were also dismissed by Morris J and are considered elsewhere at p. 717, Fn. 26 and p. 761 respectively.

[55] Series A, No. 246; (1993) 15 EHRR 244.

[56] The European Commission on Human Rights had taken a different view on this point - see above, p. 795.

[57] A subsequent application by the applicants to the Supreme Court, following the enactment of the Fourteenth Amendment of the Constitution Act 1992, to overturn its injunction was dismissed by a majority of the Court, Denham J dissenting, on the ground that the Supreme Court had no original jurisdiction to entertain the application - Supreme Court, 20 July 1993. See below, p. 810.

-and to the People: the 1992 amendments

Less than one month after the European Court of Human Rights delivered its judgment in the *Open Door* case, the electorate was given an opportunity to amend constitutional policy on abortion.[58] As part of the campaign to secure approval for the Treaty on European Union, commitments had been given by the Government that constitutional amendments addressing the issues raised by the *X* case, and in particular safeguarding rights derived from EC law, would be put before the people. Accordingly three separate proposed constitutional amendments were put before the electorate on 25 November 1992. Two of the proposals, inserting new paragraphs guaranteeing freedom to travel and freedom of information into Article 40.3.3, were adopted, thereby removing the potential for any conflict between that Article and Ireland's international obligations in relation to both freedoms. A further proposal to permit abortion where such was necessary to save the life, as distinct from the health, of the mother where such life was at risk from an illness or disorder of the mother, other than a risk of suicide, was defeated by an unlikely coalition of interests. Many supporters of the original 1983 amendment were opposed to any provision permitting "direct" abortion, while their opponents refused to countenance any dilution of the principle established in *X*, namely that a real and substantial risk to the life of the mother, including one posed by risk of suicide, justified the performance of an abortion.

The present state of the law : the so-called 'substantive issue'-

The litmus test for determining when abortions may lawfully be carried out in Ireland is contained in the majority judgments in *Attorney General v X*[59] which, as we have seen, essentially hold that abortion is permissible only where continuance of the pregnancy constitutes a real and substantial risk to the life of the mother.[60] For these purposes, a threat of suicide constitutes a real and substantial risk to the mother's life.[61] This obvi-

[58] Though O'Hanlon J, writing extra-judicially, has argued that, as the right to life of the unborn is grounded in natural law, it is not open to the People to amend the Constitution in any way which would adversely affect such right - "*Natural Rights and the Irish Constitution*" (1993) ILT 8. For further discussion of this point, see above, pp. 683-684.

[59] [1992] 1 IR 1; [1992] ILRM 401; [1992] 2 CMLR 277. As we have already noted - above, p. 796 fn 25 - it is extremely unlikely that domestic law on abortion will ever be affected by EC law. Moreover, adoption of Protocol No. 17 has removed even this remote possibility as its effect in this context is to restrict the availability of abortions in Ireland to those permitted under Article 40.3.3. As for the European Convention on Human Rights, the issue of abortion has come before the European Commission of Human Rights on only two occasions and it has yet to come before the Court of Human Rights. Thus far, the decisions of the Commission would appear to be characterised by a desire to avoid hard and fast rulings on this complicated question. In *Bruggeman and Scheuten v Germany*, Ap. 6959/75, Report of 12 July 1977, the Commission left open the question as to whether the foetus was covered by Article 2 of the Convention which protects the right to life. In *X v UK*, Ap. 8416/78, Report of 13 May 1980, the Commission agreed that the foetus did not have an unqualified right to life under Article 2 but did not feel it necessary to decide whether the foetus was totally excluded from the scope of that Article or whether it had rights which must be balanced against those of the mother in a reasonable manner. As for arguments predicated on the mother's right to privacy, in *Bruggeman and Scheuten* the Commission held that laws of what was then West Germany, which permitted abortion only in the case of danger to the mother's life, health (physical or mental) or on eugenic grounds, did not infringe the guarantee of privacy in Article 8. It should be noted that, while these laws permit abortion on broader grounds than are allowed in *X*, it does not follow that the more restrictive Irish policy is necessarily contrary to the Convention. See generally on this topic, *van Dijk and van Hoof, op.cit.* at pp.218-220.

[60] While the formulation of the test varies slightly from judge to judge, nothing of significance turns on these variations.

[61] Though Walsh J is reported to have argued that, as the Attorney General did not contest the assertion that a threat of suicide constituted a threat to the life of the mother for the purposes of Article 40.3.3, the Court's acceptance of this point in *X* cannot be regarded as conclusive and that this aspect of the case is not necessarily binding on a later court - see extract from a paper delivered to the UCG Law Society on 11 November 1992 and quoted in O'Hanlon J, *loc. cit.*, p.11.

ously implies that a risk to the *health*, as opposed to the *life* of the mother is insufficient to justify an abortion. Furthermore, the risk to the mother's life cannot be slight or theoretical; it must be real and substantial if the abortion is to be lawful.

Though none of the judges in the Supreme Court adverted to this point, it cannot be imagined that the ruling in *X* would permit abortion at any stage in the pregnancy, no matter how late. Clearly if the foetus had developed to the point where it was, or would soon be, viable outside the womb, it would be possible to vindicate both the life of the mother and that of the foetus by inducing labour or performing a caesarian section and it is disingenuous to suggest that *X* permits an abortion at that point.[62]

The judgments in *X* offer no direct guidance as to the liability, under the Constitution,[63] of medical personnel who perform a direct abortion in circumstances in which it is not absolutely clear that the mother's life is at risk or, alternatively, whose decision not to perform such an abortion results in the death of the mother. Two preliminary points are worth noting here. First, given the complexity of the medical issues involved, the courts will be extremely reluctant to substitute their judgment as to what action should have been taken for that of medical personnel. Second, in a life-threatening situation, if the mother chooses to disregard her doctor's advice to have an abortion, which is her prerogative, no liability can attach to the doctor should the mother subsequently die.

The legal position on liability for infringing the constitutional rights of the foetus or mother, as the case may be, is not entirely clear, as the courts have rarely considered the impact of the defendant's mental attitude on his liability for infringing a constitutional right. As a matter of policy, one could argue that, given that constitutional rights are deserving of the greatest possible protection, a doctrine of strict liability should operate so that liability would be imposed once it was established that the right had been infringed and irrespective of the defendant's mental attitude.[64] However a number of authorities suggest that liability for infringing a constitutional right may not arise where the act which amounts to the infringement was committed unintentionally or accidentally.[65] So if a doctor negligently performed an operation which resulted in the death of the foetus, it is arguable that no liability for breach of constitutional rights would arise. The doctor who, through negligence, fails to appreciate that an abortion is necessary in order to save the mother's life would presumably be in the same position.

Apart from the matter of the liability of medical personnel, a number of other issues were not addressed by the judges in *X* and require statutory regulation. The matter of determining at what point in the pregnancy a woman may no longer seek an abortion,

[62] Thus McCarthy J said, "[T]he right of the unborn is to a life contingent; contingent on survival in the womb until successful delivery."

[63] Apart from liability under the Constitution, a person performing an abortion may be criminally liable under ss 58 and 59 of the Offences Against the Person Act 1861 unless s/he has a *bona fide* belief that the mother's life is threatened by continuation of the pregnancy. While it is undoubtedly difficult for a prosecutor to establish the subjective intention of a defendant, ultimately it is for the jury, having considered all the evidence, to decide whether the defendant had a *bona fide* belief that an abortion was necessary to save the mother's life. A refusal to perform an abortion, resulting in the death of the mother, could, theoretically, give rise to criminal liability if it could be shown that the doctor's decision was so grossly negligent as to constitute voluntary manslaughter (unless, of course, the mother had given explicit instructions that the pregnancy was not to be terminated.) In addition to criminal liability, civil liability could also arise in this area under the law of tort, especially in respect of medical negligence.

[64] By analogy, say, with the Supreme Court decision in *The People v Kenny* [1990] 2 IR 110; [1990] ILRM 569, on the exclusion of evidence obtained in violation of constitutional rights. See above, pp. 606-607.

[65] See, e.g. *People (Attorney General) v O'Brien* [1965] IR 142; *The People v Walsh* [1980] IR 294; *The People v Shaw* [1982] IR 1; *Hosford v John Murphy & Sons* [1987] IR 621; [1988] ILRM 300.

even where her life is at risk, is a very obvious and important issue in this category. Some statutory guidance as to the cogency of evidence necessary to justify an abortion is also necessary as is statutory protection for the rights of those hospital personnel who do not wish, for religious or moral reasons, to assist in the termination of a pregnancy.

-Freedom to travel-

The second paragraph of Article 40.3.3 is intended to ensure that a pregnant woman cannot be prevented from travelling abroad[66] to obtain an abortion. Already, however, it has been argued that the amendment is ineffective to achieve this goal because, given that the proposed new paragraph refers only to Article 40.3.3 guaranteeing the right to life of the unborn, injunctions to prevent a pregnant woman travelling abroad could still be sought based on other constitutional articles, such as, *e.g.,* Article 41 referring to the rights of the family.[67] While this is certainly a plausible argument, one could equally argue that if the constitutional right to life of the unborn may not be invoked to restrict freedom to travel, then, in accordance with the interpretative doctrine of harmonious interpretation, other constitutional rights should not be construed to achieve a different result.

It has also been suggested that, while it may no longer be possible to get an injunction to prevent a woman travelling abroad in order to obtain an abortion, one can still seek an injunction from the Irish courts to prevent her having an abortion abroad. There are two difficulties with this argument, however. First, it assumes that Article 40.3.3 has extra-territorial effect, an assumption for which there is no evidence. Second, it is clear, in view of the decision of the Court of Justice in *Society for the Protection of Unborn Children (Ireland) Ltd. v Grogan,*[68] that a pregnant woman has a right under EC law to travel to another member State of the EC in order to avail of abortion services lawfully provided in that other country. *A fortiori,* once she has arrived at her destination, she is entitled under EC law to obtain an abortion and therefore it is difficult to see how an Irish court could injunct her from having such an abortion.

Penultimately, it is arguable that this paragraph protects, not only the pregnant woman travelling abroad for an abortion, but also anyone providing assistance to such a woman, at least in a case where the provision of such assistance was necessary for the effective exercise of the freedom to travel.

Finally, it is worth noting that this paragraph refers to a *freedom,* rather than a *right,* to travel. A possible implication of this wording is that while the State and, for that matter, anybody else, cannot prevent a woman from travelling, it may not necessarily be under any duty positively to assist her in going abroad by, *e.g.*, providing travel information.[69] It remains to be seen whether this distinction will have any practical consequences in relation to the granting of an interlocutory injunction seeking to prevent a pregnant woman travelling abroad in order to have an abortion. It will be recalled that, in *Grogan*, Finlay CJ reformulated the law applicable to the grant of interlocutory injunctions seek-

[66] The paragraph guarantees freedom to travel to all countries, not just to other member States of the EC.

[67] See *O'Rourke* in *The Irish Times,* 29 October 1992; see also the statement of the Labour Party in *The Irish Times,* 15 October 1992.

[68] [1991] 3 CMLR 849; [1992] ILRM 461.

[69] This speculative argument is based on a modification of the Hohfeldian distinction between rights and freedoms. W.N. Hohfeld argued, in *Fundamental Legal Conceptions as Applied in Judicial Reasoning (1919)*, that a right differs from a freedom in that a right always entails, as a correlative, the existence of a duty on someone else, whereas a freedom consists of the absence of a duty or restraint on the individual. See Redmond, "*Towards an Hohfeldian View of the Rights and Freedoms in the Irish Constitution*" (1979-80) DULJ 52. See above, pp.697-698.

ing to protect constitutional rights, stating that, in assessing the balance of convenience, the only matter which could properly be capable of being weighed in a balance against the granting of such protection would be another competing constitutional right. However it seems clear that the second paragraph of Article 40.3.3 precludes the granting of any type of injunction seeking to prevent a pregnant woman travelling abroad for an abortion and accordingly it would seem that constitutional freedoms, as well as rights, should be taken into account by the courts when assessing the balance of convenience in such cases.

-Freedom to obtain or disseminate information

The third paragraph of Article 40.3.3 is designed to reverse the Supreme Court's decisions in *The Attorney General (Society for the Protection of Unborn Children (Ireland) Ltd. v Open Door Counselling Ltd.*[70] and *Society for the Protection of Unborn Children (Ireland) Ltd. v Grogan*[71] preventing the dissemination of information about abortion services lawfully provided in other states. While this amendment is, itself, self executing it does empower the Oireachtas to enact legislation regulating the manner in which such information will be disseminated and the government's explanatory publication on the referenda stated that such legislation would permit non-directive counselling, where abortion would be but one of a number of options discussed, but not counselling which promotes abortion or encourages the woman to select it in preference to other options or which amounts to direct abortion referral.[72] Again, as in the amendment on travel, this amendment refers to a *freedom* to obtain or make available information, with the possible implication that the State has no duty positively to assist anyone in obtaining or disseminating this information.

The meaning of this paragraph did feature in argument before the Supreme Court in *The Attorney General (Society for the Protection of Unborn Children (Ireland) Ltd. v Open Door Counselling Ltd.*[73] in which the applicants sought the discharge of the injunction granted by the Supreme Court in 1988 restraining them from, *inter alia*, disseminating information about abortion clinics in the UK. The applicants contended that, in the absence of the statutory regulation referred to in the third paragraph of Article 40.3.3, the freedom to disseminate such information was unconditional. The majority of the Supreme Court did not address this point - having taken the view that the Court had no original jurisdiction to entertain the application in the first place - but Denham J, who dissented on the jurisdictional point, took the view that the right to make information available was not dependent on the enactment of appropriate legislation. This would appear to be the better view as a reading of the third paragraph makes it plain that the freedom to obtain and disseminate information is not made conditional on the introduction of legislation, but rather that the Oireachtas is empowered to impose restrictions on such freedom by way of legislation.

[70] [1988] IR 593; 1989] ILRM 19.
[71] [1989] IR 753; [1990] ILRM 350.
[72] *The Referendums on The Right to Life, Travel and Information: Key Questions and Answers*, pp.6 and 13. Perhaps one should infer that this distinction will not be applied to the doctor/patient relationship for the ruling in *X* surely requires that a doctor should be free to recommend to a woman, whose life is in danger because of a pregnancy, that she should have an abortion.
[73] Supreme Court, 20 July 1993.

Article 40.4.1

PERSONAL LIBERTY

4. 1° No citizen shall be deprived of his personal liberty save in accordance with law.

4. 1° Ní cead a shaoirse phearsanta a bhaint d'aon saoránach ach amháin de réir dlí.

"In accordance with law" - does "law" mean ordinary legislation, or something higher?

The saver built in to the general guarantee of personal liberty - and the corresponding formulation in Article 6 of the 1922 Constitution[1] - have been the focus of much litigation and also of much debate, of an academic kind, as to whether the word "law" in a constitutional setting like this means just "ordinary legislation" or has some higher sense. On the former construction, personal liberty is no better established than the legislature will allow it to be.

The "ordinary legislation" view

The simple positivist interpretation of "law" as something capable of abridging personal liberty first appeared in the Irish courts after independence in *R. (O'Connell) v Military Governor of Hare Park Camp*,[2] in which the applicant for *habeas corpus* challenged the constitutionality of the Public Safety (Powers of Arrest and Detention) Temporary Act 1924, under which he had been interned without trial. It was argued on his behalf that the Oireachtas had no power to authorise the detention of any person "except he should be first tried in due course of law",[3] but the King's Bench Division (subsequently upheld by the Court of Appeal) held that nothing in the Treaty or Constitution limited the power of the Oireachtas in this respect. Molony CJ said:

> "The phrase "in due course of law" simply means in accordance with the law then in force: see *King v Halliday*.[4] I am of opinion that the order made in the present case was made "in due course of law", because it was authorised by the statute, and that statute was within the powers of the Legislature."

Dodd J added:

> "In a land of settled government the liberty of the subject is the prevailing note. In a land unsettled and turbulent, the duty of the Legislature is to continue as far as may be to reconcile personal liberty with safety to the persons and property of the citizens."

Pim J said:

> "The argument... seemed to be based on the assumption that the words "in accordance with law" in Article 6 meant "in accordance with the normal and constant law". Such an argument, if sound, would have the effect of preventing the Free State Legislature from ever strengthening the criminal law dealing with the liberty of the person - that is, it would prevent it from legislating for the peace, order, and good government of Ireland in a very essential particular. This would be a strange interpretation of the Article.

[1] "The liberty of the person is inviolable, and no person shall be deprived of his liberty except in accordance with law."
[2] [1924] 2 IR 104; (1924) 58 ILTR 49; [1935] IR 243.
[3] The phrase echoes Article 70 of the 1922 Constitution.
[4] *R. (Zadig) v Halliday* [1917] AC 260.

It would be possible, I think, to argue successfully that a permanent law giving the Executive power to deprive any citizen of his liberty without trial was contrary to the spirit of Article 6, and therefore a violation of the Constitution; but that is a very different thing from a temporary law made in abnormal times and for a temporary purpose."

It will be noticed that, while the effect of the decision was to equate "law" in Article 6 with "ordinary legislation", two of the three judges - in particular Pim J - seemed clearly to be influenced by the notorious circumstances of the Act's passing, i.e. the aftermath of the Civil War; and seemed to leave open the possibility of a more generous construction of Article 6 when the times allowed it.

Relatively disturbed conditions were again the background in *In re O'Duffy*,[5] in which the constitutionality of arrest and detention under Article 2A[6] was questioned; O'Byrne J said:

"I think that there is nothing inconsistent between that Article and Article 6 of the Constitution. Under Article 6 a person may be detained in accordance with law, and once the court is satisfied that a person is so detained it has no power to interfere either by way of *habeas corpus* or otherwise. Article 2A of the Constitution undoubtedly enlarges the methods whereby a person may be lawfully detained. Apart from that there is no inconsistency between the two Articles."

It was of course provided in Article 2A that in the case of any inconsistency between it and any subsequent Article, Article 2A should prevail, so that no real issue arose on that level in this case. But on the other hand it is clear that the Court did not think of reading any higher meaning into "law" in Article 6 than "ordinary legislation", since Article 2A was itself the creature of ordinary legislation - the Constitution (Amendment No. 17) Act 1931.

Dissent of Kennedy CJ -

In *The State (Ryan) v Lennon*[7] the dissenting judge, Kennedy CJ, tried to reverse this trend; in his judgment, which was based on natural law postulates, he said in regard to the parts of Article 2A which trenched on personal liberty by way of arrest and detention:

"In the Constitution...the Constituent Assembly also enunciated certain propositions, containing statements of fundamental principle in the constitutional sphere so expressed as to convey clearly the intention that they are to be accepted for the purposes of the Constitution as immutable and absolute, subject only to the specific qualifications expressed in certain cases...[Such a] declaration of principle is contained in Article 6, which lays it down that the liberty of the person is inviolable, flowing from which there follows the concrete case, "no person shall be deprived of his liberty" with the specific qualification "except in accordance with law". An enactment to the general effect that a citizen may be taken and detained in custody, without being charged with any offence known to the law but just whenever or for as long as a soldier or policeman deems it expedient, would conflict with the principle laid down in Article 6, and, in my opinion, whether purporting to be an ordinary law, or an amendment of the Constitution, would be invalid and void and could not be sustained under the power of amendment. On the other hand, ordinary laws may

[5] [1934] IR 550; (1935) 69 ILTR 82.

[6] See below, p. 855.

[7] [1935] IR 170; (1935) 69 ILTR 125.

be enacted validly specifying the cases in which, the causes for which, the times during which, and the persons by whom, a person may in accordance with the ordinary law be deprived of his liberty."

- outvoted

But the other two judges of the Supreme Court took a more traditional view of "law". Fitzgibbon J said:

> "In Article 6 it is declared that "the liberty of the person is inviolable", but that is not a law of universal application, for the Article proceeds: "and no person shall be deprived of his liberty *except in accordance with law"*. The law may, therefore, make provisions in accordance with which a person may be deprived of his liberty. It is for the Legislature to prescribe those provisions, and for the courts to enforce them, and even if, under Amendment No. 17, a person has been deprived of his liberty by the mere caprice of an Executive Minister...or the unfounded suspicion of [a member of the Garda Síochána or the Defence Forces] such a deprivation would be "in accordance with law", and the prisoner would have no redress."

Murnaghan J's approach was to refuse to attempt to decide that some Articles of the Constitution were more "fundamental" than others, so as to place them beyond the amending power.

Dissent of Gavan Duffy J -

An attitude implicitly similar to that of Kennedy CJ was however taken up by Gavan Duffy J in the High Court in *The State (Burke) v Lennon,*[8] in which the internment powers of Part VI of the Offences against the State Act 1939, were under challenge. In granting an absolute order of *habeas corpus*, he adverted principally to the ministerial function under the Act of ordering a person's detention which, he thought, was an encroachment on the judicial sphere and so unconstitutional; but also to what he held was the Act's violation of the guarantee of personal liberty in Article 40.4.1:

> "Article 40, if I understand it, guarantees that no citizen shall be deprived of liberty, save in accordance with a law which respects his fundamental right to personal liberty, and defends and vindicates it, as far as practicable, and protects his person from unjust attack;[9] the Constitution clearly intends that he shall be liable to forfeit that right under the criminal law on being duly tried and found guilty of an offence. In my opinion, a law for the internment of a citizen, without charge or hearing, outside the great protection of our criminal jurisprudence and outside even the special courts, for activities calculated to prejudice the State, does not respect his *right* to personal liberty and does unjustly attack his person...
>
> In my opinion, the saving words in the declaration that "No citizen shall be deprived of his liberty save in accordance with law" cannot be used to validate an enactment conflicting with the constitutional guarantees. The opinion of Mr. Justice Fitzgibbon in *Ryan's* case is relied upon by State counsel, but it does not apply, in my judgment, to a Constitution in which fundamental rights and constitutional guarantees effectively fill the lacunae disclosed in the polity of 1922. The Constitution, with its most impressive Preamble, is the charter of the Irish people and I will not whittle it away."[10]

[8] [1940] IR 136; (1940) 74 ILTR 36, 131.

[9] These phrases are cited from Article 40.3.

[10] The phrase "whittle away" in the context of constitutional principles had been used by Kennedy CJ in *Lynham v Butler (No. 2)*, [1933] IR 74, in which Gavan Duffy had appeared as plaintiff's counsel.

- overruled

However, just as the voice of Kennedy CJ was outvoted by his colleagues in *Ryan's* case in 1934, so the view of Gavan Duffy J was effectively overruled in 1940 by the Supreme Court in the case under Article 26 on the constitutionality of the Bill passed to replace the invalidated Part VI of the 1939 Act: *In re Article 26 and the Offences Against the State (Amendment) Bill, 1940.*[11] Sullivan CJ, delivering the Court's judgment on provisions substantially identical with those found unconstitutional by Gavan Duffy J, said:

> "The phrase "in accordance with law" is used in several Articles of the Constitution, and we are of opinion that it means in accordance with the law as it exists at the time when the particular Article is invoked and sought to be applied. In this Article, it means the law as it exists at the time when the legality of the detention arises for determination. A person in custody is detained in accordance with law if he is detained in accordance with the provisions of a statute duly passed by the Oireachtas; subject always to the qualification that such provisions are not repugnant to the Constitution or to any provision thereof."

Any apparent circularity introduced into this statement of principle by its closing qualification was resolved in the Chief Justice's next sentence, in which he said that any such repugnancy must be established "by reference to some *other* provision of the Constitution" - i.e. other than Article 40.4.1. There could scarcely be a more emphatic denial of any "higher law" content in the word "law" in that section, or a more flatly positivist interpretation of it; and the Court did not even betray - except for a most general reference to the common good[12] - the anxiety shown by earlier courts such as those in O'*Connell's* and *Ryan's* cases to justify decisions, similar in concrete result, by adverting to the disturbed condition of the times or the exceptional circumstances of the enactment under review.

Retreat from "ordinary legislation" view begins

However, nine years later the Supreme Court - still containing three of the five judges who decided the *Offences Against the State (Amendment) Bill* case - seemed to retreat a little from the extreme positivism of that decision. In *In re Philip Clarke*[13] the applicant for *habeas corpus* had been detained under s 165(1) of the Mental Treatment Act 1945, which empowered a member of the Garda Síochána to take a person "believed to be of unsound mind" into custody if of opinion that it was necessary "for the public safety or the safety of the person himself" that he be placed "under care and control". The Supreme Court rejected an attack on the constitutionality of this provision, but did not confine itself to saying that, as it was part of the "law", it fell within the saving qualification of Article 40.4.1; instead, an objective justification of the provision was delivered:

> "The impugned legislation is of a paternal character, clearly intended for the care and custody of persons suspected to be suffering from mental infirmity and for the safety and well-being of the public generally. The existence of mental infirmity is

[11] [1940] IR 470; (1940) 74 ILTR 61.

[12] Cited above in connection with the Preamble, p. 5.

[13] [1950] IR 235; (1951) 85 ILTR 119. Article 40.4.1 was relied on by counsel for the applicant, but was not specifically mentioned in the Supreme Court's judgment.

too widespread to be overlooked, and was, no doubt, present to the minds of the draftsmen when it was proclaimed in Article 40.1...that, though all citizens, as human beings, are to be held equal before the law, the State may, nevertheless, in its enactments, have due regard to differences of capacity, physical and moral, and of social function. We do not see how the common good would be promoted or the dignity and freedom of the individual assured by allowing persons, alleged to be suffering from such infirmity, to remain at large to the possible danger of themselves and others... The section cannot, in our opinion, be construed as an attack upon the personal rights of the citizen. On the contrary it seems to us to be designed for the protection of the citizen and for the promotion of the common good."[14]

Shift towards "higher law" accelerates

In 1966 the case of *The People (Attorney General) v O'Callaghan*[15] - which established a spectacular liberal bridgehead on the territory of the State's claim to have accused persons remanded in custody pending trial - gave the Supreme Court, on appeal from Murnaghan J, an opportunity to reinforce the suggestion of *Philip Clarke's* case that statutes cutting down personal liberty would be scrutinised on general constitutional principles rather than accepted as automatically validating their contents as being "in accordance with law". In stating the unacceptability of traditional reasons for refusing bail, in particular the alleged likelihood of the accused person committing further offences if left at large, Ó Dálaigh CJ looked critically at the provisions of the Offences Against the State (Amendment) Act 1940, in order to show up a contrast between even this drastic internment system and the old bail law:

> "[These 1940 provisions] allow of preventive detention. But a number of conditions have to be satisfied before the provisions can be operated. First, there must be a Government proclamation declaring that the powers conferred by Part II of the Act are necessary to secure the preservation of public peace and order...Furthermore, even under this most stringent Act a Minister of State is empowered to detain a person only if of opinion that he *is engaged* in activities which are prejudicial to the preservation of the public peace and order...The Minister is not empowered to act because he is of opinion that a person if not detained *will engage* in such activities. I cite these provisions to contrast them with the powers which, it was suggested, should be exercised in respect of the applicant in this case. The answer to the submission we have heard is, no such power exists under the law or the Constitution."

Walsh J even outlined criteria by which a statute abridging the liberty of an unconvicted person would be tested:

> "In this country it would be quite contrary to the concept of personal liberty enshrined in the Constitution that any person should be punished in respect of any matter upon which he has not been convicted or that in any circumstances he should be deprived of his liberty upon only the belief that he will commit offences if left at liberty, save in the most extraordinary circumstances carefully spelled out by the Oireachtas and then only to secure the preservation of public peace and order or the public safety and the preservation of the State in a time of national emergency or in some situation akin to that."

[14] These, again, are allusions to the Preamble.
[15] [1966] IR 501; (1968) 102 ILTR 45.

Becomes headlong

The discrediting of the positivist view of "law" in Article 40.4.1 appears since then to have become total: in *In re Article 26 and the Emergency Powers Bill 1976*,[16] the Attorney General specifically asked the Supreme Court to judge the Bill on the basis (with which the Court expressed no disagreement) that the seven-day arrest without trial, provided by the Bill, was unconstitutional unless saved by the emergency recital provided for by Article 28.3.3.

Four years later, the Supreme Court struck down, for manifold repugnancy to the Constitution, part of s 4 of the Vagrancy Act 1824, which attached heightened criminal liability to a "suspected person or reputed thief"; in this case, *King v Attorney General,*[17] Henchy J listed a number of constitutional provisions against which the section offended, including Article 40.4. He said:

> "It violates the guarantee...that no citizen shall be deprived of personal liberty save in accordance with law - which means without stooping to methods which ignore the fundamental norms of the legal order postulated by the Constitution.

This sentence condenses, and tellingly presents, the final evolution of half a century of constitutional jurisprudence since the old *Ryan* decision.[18]

"In accordance with law": conditions of form or of fact which will negative this requirement

(a) Conditions of form: legal irregularity: not every irregularity entitles to habeas corpus

Not every departure from legal correctness will render a detention unlawful so as to attract an order of *habeas corpus*. In *The State (McDonagh) v Frawley*[19] O'Higgins CJ, delivering the judgment of the Supreme Court, said:

> "The stipulation in Article 40.1...that a citizen may not be deprived of his liberty save "in accordance with law" does not mean that a convicted person must be released on *habeas corpus* merely because some defect or illegality attaches to his detention. The phrase means that there must be such a default of fundamental requirements that the detention may be said to be wanting in due process of law.[20]

[16] [1977] IR 159; (1977) 111 ILTR 29.

[17] [1981] IR 233. See *Cooney*, (1980) 15 Ir Jur (n.s) 289.

[18] This formula was subsequently invoked by Barr J in *Ryan v O'Callaghan*, High Court, 22 July 1987, where, in the context of considering the legitimacy of the power of a Peace Commissioner to issue a search warrant, he rejected the contention that the phrase "save in accordance with law" in Article 40.5 - dealing with the inviolability of the dwelling - meant "save in accordance with the order of a court established under the Constitution".

[19] [1978] IR 131, followed in *McGlinchey v The Governor of Portlaoise Prison* [1988] IR 671, and more recently cited with approval by the Supreme Court - *per* O'Flaherty J - in *Rock v Governor of St. Patrick's Institution*, 22 March 1993, where it was held that the imposition of a sentence of imprisonment *in absentia* did not entitle the applicant to an order for release under Article 40.4.

[20] In the earlier case of *The State (Rossi and Blythe) v Bell* [1957] IR 281, (1956) 90 ILTR 143 - an extradition case under the Petty Sessions (Ireland) Act 1851 - habeas corpus was granted because of a fundamental flaw in the English warrant which, having been endorsed here, was used to arrest the applicants: it did not name the wanted persons, but merely gave physical descriptions of them. The use of the wrong name in a similar warrant was the basis for the applicant's first arrest in *The State (Quinn) v Ryan* [1965] IR 70, (1966) 100 ILTR 105; here, too, an absolute order of *habeas corpus* was made - see above, pp. 385-386.

> For *habeas corpus* purposes, therefore, it is insufficient for the prisoner to show that there has been a legal error or impropriety, or even that jurisdiction has been inadvertently exceeded."

The Chief Justice gave an instance:

> "For example, if the judge at a murder trial in which the accused was convicted were to impose a sentence of imprisonment for life, instead of penal servitude for life as required by the statute, the resulting detention would be imposed technically without jurisdiction. But the prisoner would not be released under Article 40.4, for it could not be said that the detention was not "in accordance with the law" in the sense indicated. In such a case the court would leave the matter of sentence to be rectified by the Court of Criminal Appeal; or it could remit the case to the court of trial for the imposition of the correct sentence."[21]

Another authority in the same direction is *The State (McKeever) v Governor of Mountjoy Prison*[22] in which Ó Dálaigh CJ (with whom the rest of the Supreme Court agreed) said:

> "It could not be said that the [applicant] was detained in accordance with the law if the irregularities or the procedural deficiencies complained of were shown to be such as would invalidate any essential step in the proceedings leading ultimately to his detention."

But (the case concerned imprisonment resulting from default on an instalment order for debt) "mere pleading irregularities could not assist the [applicant]".

Moreover, an application for *habeas corpus* cannot be used as an informal means of obtaining the resolution of disputed questions of fact or law previously ruled upon or pending determination under regular court procedure. In such a case, recourse must be had to the regular legal process, such as appeals or applications for judicial review - *per* Gannon J in the Divisional High Court decision in *McGlinchey v The Governor of Portlaoise Prison*.[23]

Habeas corpus in the case of convicted prisoner

In the case of persons detained in consequence of conviction and sentence there is, firstly, the statement of Maguire P (delivering the judgment of the High Court) in *The State (Cannon) v Kavanagh*[24] that a convicted prisoner is:

> "*prima facie* detained according to law, and it would require most exceptional circumstances for this Court to grant even a conditional order of *habeas corpus* to a prisoner so convicted."

[21] In similar vein, the Supreme Court had previously held, in *The State (Dillon) v Kelly* [1970] IR 174, that where the High Court orders the release of a convicted prisoner on the ground that the place (as distinct from the fact) of his detention is not in accordance with the law, the Court should order his rearrest and committal to the correct place of detention to serve the rest of his sentence. See also *The State (Dickenson) v Kelly* [1964] IR 73, and *The State (Holden) v Governor of Portlaoise Prison* [1964] IR 80.

[22] Supreme Court, 19 December 1966. This decision was later cited in *The State (Wilson) v Governor of Portlaoise Prison*, Supreme Court, 29 July 1969, and both *McKeever's* and *Wilson's* cases were cited by Gannon and Griffin JJ in *The State (Healy) v Donoghue* [1976] IR 325, (1976) 110 ILTR 9.

[23] [1988] IR 671. The Supreme Court subsequently upheld the High Court's dismissal of the application for *habeas corpus*, though without referring to this specific point.

[24] [1937] IR 428; (1937) 71 ILTR 249.

This was cited with approval by O'Higgins CJ in *McDonagh's* case just mentioned,[25] but on the other hand, in *The State (Royle) v Kelly*[26] Henchy J said something more about the circumstances in which *habeas corpus* might be granted to a convicted prisoner:

> "Where, as in the present case, the prisoner has been convicted and sentenced by a court established by law under the Constitution, and the jurisdiction of that court to try the offence and impose the sentence has not been challenged, it would be necessary to show that the procedure has been so flawed by basic defect as to make the conviction a nullity before it could be held that the detention was not in accordance with law."[27]

In *The State (Aherne) v Cotter*[28] the same judge said:

> "Before a convicted person who is serving his sentence may be released under our constitutional provisions relating to *habeas corpus*, it has to be shown not that the detention resulted from an illegality or a mere lapse from jurisdictional propriety but that it derives from a departure from the fundamental rules of natural justice, according as those rules require to be recognised under the Constitution in the fullness of their evolution at a given time and in relation to the particular circumstances of the case. Deviations from legality short of that are outside the range of *habeas corpus*."[29]

(b) Conditions of fact: breach of prisoner's rights

The detention of a person, though in itself or initially lawful, may become unlawful because of the way the prisoner is treated. This principle has three aspects which may be briefly distinguished.

(i) There is first of all the principle that a person in custody still retains all his constitutional rights save to the extent that the exercise of some of them is necessarily suspended or curtailed by the fact of imprisonment itself; and if he is treated in a way which infringes his (so to speak) surviving rights, this may vitiate his detention or "taint it with illegality". This principle coexists with, or shades into other dimensions of the law of imprisonment, such as the necessity to observe the rules, whether of statute or of subordinate regulation, as to how a person is to be taken into, or kept in custody.

(ii) The foregoing statements are, however, modified by the fact that, while the courts will act to remedy illegalities attaching to an imprisonment, not every illegality - even where treatment has amounted to a breach of constitutional rights - will entitle a prisoner to the *habeas corpus* remedy, i.e. to be set free.

[25] Both *Kavanagh's* case and *McDonagh's* case were subsequently cited with approval by O'Hanlon J in *McGlinchey v Ireland* [1990] 2 IR 215, in which he rejected the contention that findings of fact, allegedly prejudicial to the applicant, which had been made by the Special Criminal Court at an earlier trial of two other accused persons, thereafter disqualified a differently constituted Court from trying the applicant. An appeal to the Supreme Court was subsequently dismissed on 21 December 1989.

[26] [1974] IR 249.

[27] An unsatisfactory element in the trial proceedings falling short of such a "basic defect" would be material for an appeal to the Court of Criminal Appeal, but not for *habeas corpus*. The same point of view seems to underlie the terse judgment of Lavery J in *The State (Woods) v Governor of Mountjoy Prison* [1962] IR 248.

[28] [1982] IR 188; [1981] ILRM 169; [1983] ILRM 17.

[29] See also the comments of Ó Dálaigh CJ in the earlier case of *Application of Lucey* [1972] IR 347, in which he said, "A person undergoing a lawful sentence cannot be released on *habeas corpus* unless there has been something such as a fundamental failure of natural justice in the course of the trial".

(iii) Treatment of a person in custody amounting to a conscious and deliberate breach of his constitutional rights will vitiate and render inadmissible any evidence elicited through the breach, unless there has been a conflict of competing constitutional rights, leading to preference being given to the "higher" right. As this principle, however, is only a statement of the more general principle with special application to custody cases, and as the more general principle applies even where no custody is involved (and was indeed first enunciated in such a case), this matter is dealt with in the context of the prosecution of offences and "due course of law".[30]

This section, accordingly, deals with the question of detention which becomes tainted with illegality because of the manner of the prisoner's treatment and of the criteria by which the courts will grant or refuse *habeas corpus* in such cases.

Distinction between unconvicted and convicted persons?

The first matter to dispose of in this connection is the question whether any distinction is to be drawn between persons in custody who have not been convicted, and such persons who are serving sentences of imprisonment after conviction. In theory such a distinction must exist, and indeed it is reflected in the prison rules which apply a different regime to convicted prisoners from that prescribed for prisoners on remand awaiting trial. In the *Emergency Powers Bill, 1976*,[31] reference - the case which opened up this whole area - the Supreme Court had said that:

> "[s 2 of the Bill] is not to be read as an abrogation of the arrested person's rights (constitutional or otherwise) in respect of matters such as the right of communication, the right to have legal and medical assistance, and the right of access to the courts. If the section were used in breach of such rights the High Court might grant an order for release under the provisions for *habeas corpus* contained in the Constitution. It is not necessary for the Court to attempt to give an exhaustive list of the matters which would render a detention under the section illegal or unconstitutional."

Necessary suspension of some of a prisoner's constitutional rights

However, two years later the Court felt obliged, in *The State (McDonagh) v Frawley*,[32] to "clear up some misunderstandings which obviously exist in matters of this kind". Emphasising that the passage cited above was to be understood as applying only to unconvicted detainees under that emergency measure, the Court said that the "status and rights" of a convicted person were "quite different":

> "while so held as a prisoner pursuant to a lawful warrant, many of the [applicant's] normal constitutional rights are abrogated or suspended. He must accept prison discipline and accommodate himself to the reasonable organisation of prison life as laid down in the prison regulations."[33]

[30] See above, pp. 603-614.

[31] [1977] IR 159; (1977) 111 ILTR 29.

[32] [1978] IR 131.

[33] Another contemporary indication that the exercise of some of a prisoner's constitutional rights could be suspended as a necessary practical consequence of prison existence is to be seen in *The State (Fagan) v Governor of Mountjoy Prison*, High Court, 6 March 1978, where McMahon J said, "The prisoner retains his right of access to the courts and he can complain of any interference with his constitutional rights which is not necessary in order to give effect to the sentence of the court in the institution in which it must be served." In *The State (Richardson) v Governor of Mountjoy Prison* [1980] ILRM 82, Barrington J gave a useful exposition of *McDonagh's* case on the "suspension of rights" question. That imprisonment necessarily results in the suspension of some constitutional rights was re-affirmed in *Murray v Ireland* [1991] ILRM 465, discussed below, p. 1006, though curiously without any reference to *McDonagh*.

Moreover, the Court said:

> "applications under Article 40.4 are not suitable for the judicial investigation of complaints as to conviction, sentence or conditions of detention which fall short of that requirement [viz. that the detention is not in accordance with law]."

Whether the theoretical distinction between a person held under an exceptional preventive measure, and a convicted prisoner, has much practical reality - so far as the suspension of his rights is concerned - may be doubted. On the one hand, the rights instanced by the Court as surviving in the case of the emergency detainee (communication,[34] access to legal and medical assistance and to the courts) are exercisable also by a convicted prisoner. On the other hand, it cannot be the case that a detainee under the Emergency Powers Act 1976, would have retained the capacity to exercise during the seven-day arrest period literally *all* his constitutional rights save that to liberty, i.e. not to be physically confined; even this form of detention, if it is to be effective, must necessarily inhibit the exercise of rights of assembly and association, and is scarcely reconcilable with the continued exercise of an array of further rights explicit or implicit in Articles 40.3, 41, 42 and 43.

Vitiation of custody by infringement of surviving rights

The second part of the citation above from *McDonagh's* case opens up the question whether, and in what conditions, an infringement of a prisoner's rights will so taint his detention with illegality as to deprive it of the character of detention "in accordance with law" so as to lead the High Court to set him at liberty.

Very shortly after the Supreme Court's decision in the *Emergency Powers Bill* reference, when the Bill had become law, Hamilton J in *The State (McCann) v Herlihy*[35] said, where a prisoner alleged that he was confined in a cell such as to endanger his health, that:

> "any detention under [the Act] must be in accordance with the provisions of the Constitution and must have regard to the rights of arrested persons as citizens and as human beings."

Subsequently, in *The State (Harrington) v Garvey*,[36] in which a prisoner sought *habeas corpus* on the ground, *inter alia*, that he had been beaten up while in custody under the same Act. Finlay P found his allegations unfounded, but said that:

> "if he was assaulted, that would in law constitute an illegal Act making his entire detention unlawful and entitling him to be released."

In *The State (Greene) v Governor of Portlaoise Prison*,[37] a *habeas corpus* application was brought by a convicted prisoner, grounded on allegations that the prison regime of body searches, close supervision etc. (applied to certain prisoners in the light of experience of smuggling in of explosives, break-outs etc.) amounted to a breach of his constitutional rights to human dignity, health and bodily integrity and family privacy; and to inhuman and degrading treatment. The application failed, as Hamilton J took the view that the common good required that sentences be carried out and that discipline and security be maintained in prisons, and that in the special circumstances the applicant's

[34] However the right to communicate of the detainee may be more extensive than that of the convicted person inasmuch as it is not subject to the interests of prison security - see below, pp. 826-827.

[35] High Court, 29 October 1976.

[36] High Court, 14 December 1976.

[37] High Court, 20 May 1977.

constitutional rights had not been breached; but nonetheless he was prepared to examine the case on the basis that such a breach, if established, would have rendered the applicant's detention unlawful. The Supreme Court's judgment in the *Emergency Powers Bill* reference, he noted, was directed to s 2 of that Bill; but, he said:

> "it applies equally in all cases where a detention, otherwise legal, may be rendered illegal or unconstitutional because of the manner or conditions of detention."

He mentioned English cases:

> "which suggest that *habeas corpus* cannot be used for the purpose of testing the legality of conditions of a confinement...This is a view with which I do not agree particularly where the conditions of confinement are alleged to constitute a breach of constitutional rights."

Then came *The State (McDonagh) v Frawley*[38] in which, although the Supreme Court (as has been noted above) appeared to reject the idea that *habeas corpus* could be used as a remedy for ill-treatment in custody, and to restrict the words used in the *Emergency Powers Bill* judgment to the special conditions of that Bill, it did so none too conclusively, since it left open the possibility that the conditions in which a prisoner was detained might be such as to deprive the detention itself of legality: a proposition which renders the *McDonagh* decision somewhat circular, since ill-treatment amounting to breach of a prisoner's rights is obviously possible in the context of any kind of detention, and if this breach renders the whole detention no longer "in accordance with law", Article 40.4 must necessarily find application. This seems to be the view which the courts themselves take of the *McDonagh* judgment. Thus in two judgments delivered the same day, Barrington J accepted in one - *The State (Boyle) v Governor of the Curragh Military Detention Barracks*[39] - that *McDonagh* meant *habeas corpus* should not issue to correct a fault in the detention which could be remedied otherwise, while in the other - *The State (Richardson) v Governor of Mountjoy Prison*[40] - he unambiguously contemplated the release by *habeas corpus* of a prisoner suffering ill-treatment in at least some cases:

> "It would clearly not be possible to enumerate in advance what are the conditions which would invalidate a detention otherwise legal. If a court were convinced that the authorities were taking advantage of the fact that a person was detained, consciously and deliberately to violate his constitutional rights or to subject him to inhuman or degrading treatment, the court must order his release. Likewise, if the court were convinced that the conditions of a prisoner's detention were such as seriously to endanger his life or health, and that the authorities intended to do nothing to rectify these conditions, the court might release him...The position would be similar if the conditions of the prisoner's detention were such as seriously to threaten his life or health, but the authorities were, for some reason, unable to rectify the conditions."

In that particular case the prisoner complained of the disgusting sanitary conditions in the women's section of the prison as being a danger to her health, but as the authorities satisfied the judge as to their willingness to improve matters at once, the case did not come within the area he described, and he refused *habeas corpus*. His judgment is, however, notable for a judicial rarity, a tabulation in textbook form of the relation of *habeas corpus* to convicted prisoners' rights:

[38] [1978] IR 131. See *Byrne*, (1979) 14 Ir Jur (n.s.) 109.
[39] [1980] ILRM 242.
[40] [1980] ILRM 82.

(1) Convicted prisoners, as human beings and citizens, have rights under the Constitution, including a right of access to the Court.
(2) Many of these rights are abrogated, suspended or limited by reason of the prisoner's conviction and sentence.
(3) A prisoner lawfully convicted and sentenced has lost his right to personal liberty for the period of his sentence. Therefore, *habeas corpus* is not an appropriate procedure in which to investigate his complaints.
(4) Exceptionally, however, the conditions under which a prisoner is detained may be such as to make his detention unlawful, notwithstanding the existence of a valid warrant. In such case, *habeas corpus* will lie.
(5) Lesser legitimate complaints of prisoners fall to be investigated in other forms of legal proceedings.
(6) The prisoner's subsisting rights can often be ascertained from the Prison Rules themselves, read in the light of the Constitution.

Later in the same year Finlay P adopted a similar approach in *Cahill v Governor of the Curragh Military Detention Barracks*,[41] where the applicant complained of ill-treatment which in fact appeared to the Court to consist of necessary disciplinary measures for dealing with a concerted disorderly protest among the prisoners. He said that the "systematic assaults and ill-treatment" which the prisoner alleged would, if established, "affect the legality of his detention"; but the fact that the prisoner had been soaked during the hosing out, by prison personnel, of the cell which the prisoner himself had deliberately fouled did not amount to any such ill-treatment. He found, however, that the regime in the military detention barracks did not conform, in several respects, with what the Rules for the Government of Prisons, 1946, required; on the other hand, those breaches of legality:

> "did not constitute according to the standard set by the Supreme Court in [*McDonagh's* case] such a default of fundamental requirements that the detention of the applicant could be said to be wanting in due process of law."

Barrington J took a similar line in *The State (Comerford) v Governor of Mountjoy Prison*,[42] where a prisoner on remand awaiting trial had been transferred to a high security part of the convict section of the prison; this was done, as the judge found, because it was feared the prisoner might be a party to an escape conspiracy, and so for security rather than for punitive reasons. It was, however, irregular because s 13 of the Prisons (Ireland) Act 1877, required a clear difference in the treatment of remand prisoners as compared with the treatment of convicted prisoners, and this was reflected in provisions of the prison rules. But he "[did] not think that the irregularity was such as to make the...detention unlawful or to entitle [the prisoner] to an absolute order of *habeas corpus*".[43]

Two more recent cases may briefly be mentioned - in *The State (Murray) v Governor of*

[41] [1980] ILRM 191.
[42] [1981] ILRM 86.
[43] The right of a convicted prisoner to some form of relief arising from the non-compliance of his detention with the Prison Rules also featured in *J.G. v Governor of Mountjoy Prison* [1991] 1 IR 373. In that case, two young offenders lodged in Mountjoy Prison were not segregated from the other prisoners, contrary to rules 223-4 of the Prison Rules. Counsel for the applicants had not sought their release on this ground but as the issue of whether they might be entitled to any other form of relief was not fully argued before Blayney J, he re-entered this aspect of the case for further hearing, by which time the prison authorities had moved to comply with the Prison Rules
[44] High Court, 23 August 1978.
[45] [1978] IR 131.

Limerick Prison[44] D'Arcy J held, following *The State (McDonagh) v Frawley*,[45] that an interference with the applicant's right to receive and send letters or visit her husband, occasioned by the withdrawal of his privileges in accordance with prison regulations, did not render her detention unlawful, while in *The State (Tyndall) v Governor of Mountjoy Prison*[46] Murphy J held that the transfer of the prosecutor to the special AIDS unit of Mountjoy prison did not render his imprisonment unlawful, as this had been done in the interests of the prisoner and was not a punitive measure.

All that can be said by way of summary of these cases is that lesser, or easily remediable, breaches of legality in the manner of a detention will not entitle to *habeas corpus*; but a serious breach - a conscious and deliberate violation of the prisoner's rights such as systematic physical ill-treatment - will do so. It does not seem possible, on the strength of the case-law, to establish with greater exactness the frontier between these two categories of illegality with their varying effects on the issue whether a person is deprived of his liberty "in accordance with law".

Miscellaneous rights of prisoners: no oppressive interrogation

A few cases which supplement this general picture in regard to the rights of prisoners may be mentioned.[47] The same area of constitutional rights which excludes active ill-treatment would also exclude oppressively prolonged interrogation: in *The People (Director of Public Prosecutions) v Doyle*[48] the Court of Criminal Appeal said that:

> "obviously it would be possible for a protracted period of detention coupled with persistent interviewing or interrogation to constitute oppression even without physical violence or threats of violence."

In *The People (Director of Public Prosecutions) v Breathnach*[49] the Court of Criminal Appeal adopted with approval the definitions of "oppressive questioning" in *R. v Prager*:[50] "questioning which by its nature, duration or other attendant circumstances (including the fact of custody) excites hopes (such as the hope of release) or fears,[51] or so affects the mind of the subject that his will crumbles and he speaks when otherwise he would have stayed silent"; and *R. v Priestly*:[52] "something which tends to sap and has sapped the free will which must exist before a confession is voluntary." The same court subsequently held, in *The People (Director of Public Prosecutions) v Pringle*,[53] that in determining whether questioning is oppressive, the physical, mental and emotional characteristics of the person being interrogated must be considered.

Reference was also made to a detainee's right not to be subject to oppressive interrogation in *The People (Director of Public Prosecutions) v Quilligan*,[54] Walsh J describing oppressive interrogation as:

[46] *The Irish Times*, 6 September 1986.

[47] For a judicial listing of the rights of a person detained pursuant to s 30 of the Offences Against the State Act 1939, see *The People (D.P.P.) v Quilligan (No.3)* [1993] 2 IR 305, discussed below, pp. 856-857.

[48] [1977] IR 336.

[49] 2 Frewen 43.

[50] (1972) 56 Cr App R 151.

[51] In *The People (D.P.P.) v Boylan* [1991] 1 IR 477, the Court of Criminal Appeal hinted that a threat of going to the detainee's home and making life unpleasant for his wife and family could vitiate any confession subsequently made. The Supreme Court had previously excluded a confession where this had occurred: *People (D.P.P.) v Hoey* [1987] IR 837.

[52] (1967) 51 Cr App R 1.

[53] 2 Frewen 57.

[54] [1986] IR 495. See also *The People (D.P.P.) v Quilligan (No.3)* [1993] 2 IR 305.

> "any form of questioning which the courts would regard as unfair or oppressive either by reason of its nature, the manner in which it is conducted, its duration or the time of day, or of its persistence into the point of harassment where it is not shown that the arrested person has indicated clearly that he is willing to continue to be further questioned."

In the earlier case of *The People (Director of Public Prosecutions) v McGing*[55] the Court of Criminal Appeal had commented that it was undesirable for persons detained under s 30 of the Offences Against the State Act 1939, to be interviewed for lengthy periods by a single member of the Garda Síochána and, furthermore, that where a woman is being interrogated, a Ban-Garda should be present where practicable. However, the Court refused to hold that the interrogation of the defendant did not conform with the constitutional requirements of fair procedures as, during the period of interrogation, she had been visited on three occasions by her solicitor and had made no complaint about the nature of her treatment. The Court reserved its opinion as to whether an interrogation which did not conform to constitutional requirements of fair procedures gave rise to a judicial discretion to exclude the fruits of such interrogation analogous to the discretion to exclude admissions obtained in breach of the Judges' Rules.

Right to medical attention

The right to medical attention, stated hypothetically in the *Emergency Powers Bill* reference, was acknowledged again by the Supreme Court in *McDonagh's* case;[56] though the Court did not accept that the prisoner, who complained of back-ache, was entitled to choose his own medical adviser rather than be attended by the prison doctor.[57]

Access to legal advisers -

The issue of access to a solicitor has been referred to in various decisions dating from the mid-1970s, though its status as a constitutional right has been authoritatively confirmed only in the very recent past. It first surfaced in the *Emergency Powers Bill* judgment which mentioned the right to communicate with, and have access to legal advisers; this figured the following month in *The People (Director of Public Prosecutions) v Doyle*,[58] when the Court of Criminal Appeal said that a person in detention:

> "has got a right of reasonable access to his legal advisers and that a refusal upon request to give such reasonable access would render his detention illegal,"

a view subsequently endorsed by Walsh J in both *The People v Shaw*[59] and *The People (Director of Public Prosecutions) v Conroy.*[60]

One month after the decision in *Doyle*, Finlay P added the dimension of privacy: "where a detained person is entitled to access to his legal adviser, this must be achieved in privacy and out of the hearing of any member of the Garda Síochána" - *The State (Harrington) v Garvey*.[61] He re-stated the principle in mid-1977 in the case of a prisoner

[55] 3 Frewen 18.
[56] [1978] IR 131. And more recently in *The People (D.P.P.) v Quilligan (No.3)* [1993] 2 IR 305.
[57] However Hederman J has accepted that a person detained by the Gardaí prior to being brought before the courts has the right to the presence of a medical practitioner of his own choice - *The People (D.P.P.) v Quilligan (No.3)* [1993] 2 IR 305.
[58] [1977] IR 336.
[59] [1982] IR 1.
[60] [1986] IR 460; [1988] ILRM 4.
[61] High Court, 14 December 1976.

called *Lynch,*[62] adding that, while prison authorities may examine papers brought in by a legal adviser, this must be only for the purpose of ensuring that they conceal nothing, not in order to read them. In early 1978 - a few months before the *McDonagh* judgment seemed to limit *habeas corpus* relief to very serious (though undefined) cases of illegal treatment - D'Arcy J went so far, in *The State (Gallagher) v Governor of Portlaoise Prison,*[63] as to suggest that, "depending on the circumstances", the illegality arising through the seizure by the authorities of a prisoner's letter to his solicitor might render the prisoner "immediately entitled to his liberty".

That the right of a person arrested and detained in custody to have access, during his detention, to a solicitor whose attendance he has requested or whose attendance has been requested by other persons *bona fide* acting on his behalf is constitutional in origin was eventually confirmed by the Supreme Court in *The People (Director of Public Prosecutions) v Healy.*[64] Finlay CJ, with whom Walsh, Hederman and McCarthy JJ agreed,[65] said:

> "The undoubted right of reasonable access to a solicitor enjoyed by a person who is in detention must be interpreted as being directed towards the vital function of ensuring that such person is aware of his rights and has the independent advice which would be appropriate in order to permit him to reach a truly free decision as to his attitude to interrogation or to the making of any statement, be it exculpatory or inculpatory. The availability of advice from a lawyer must, in my view, be seen as a contribution, at least, towards some measure of equality in the position of the detained person and his interrogators.
>
> Viewed in that light, I am driven to the conclusion that such an important and fundamental standard of fairness in the administration of justice as the right of access to a lawyer must be deemed to be constitutional in its origin, and that to classify it as merely legal would be to undermine its importance and the completeness of the protection of it which the courts are obliged to give...
>
> A right of reasonable access to a solicitor by a detained person, I am satisfied, means, in the event of the arrival of a solicitor at the garda station in which a person is detained, an immediate right of that person to be told of the arrival and, if he requests it, immediate access. The only thing that could justify the postponement of informing the detained person of the arrival of the solicitor or of immediately complying with a request made by the detained person when so informed, for access to him, would be reasons which objectively viewed from the point of view of the interest or welfare of the detained person, would be viewed by the court as being valid. I reject completely the submission made on behalf of the Director of Public Prosecutions that the test to be applied to the question of reasonable access is a sub-

[62] High Court, 17 June 1977.

[63] High Court, 6 March 1978.

[64] [1990] 2 IR 73; [1990] ILRM 313. See above, p. 606. See also *Walsh v Ó Buachalla* [1991] 1 IR 56, a case under the Road Traffic Acts where it had not been established that there was a causative link between the alleged breach of the detained person's right of access to his solicitor and the obtaining of evidence - a blood sample - and accordingly Blayney J held that the evidence was admissible. See also *The People (D.P.P.) v Quilligan (No.3)* [1993] 2 IR 305 and *The People (D.P.P.) v Cullen*, Court of Criminal Appeal, 30 March 1993. *Cullen* is another instance where no causative link was found between the alleged breach of the right of access to a solicitor and the obtaining of evidence.

[65] The remaining judge, Griffin J, felt that it was not necessary, in the instant case, to decide whether the right of access to a solicitor was constitutional in origin, though he did add that he would have little difficulty in accepting that it was a constitutional right.

jective test in the mind of the jailer of the detained person. The test is whether the superintendent's refusal of access was a conscious and deliberate act as it clearly was. The fact that he may not have appreciated that his refusal was a breach of the defendant's constitutional right is immaterial. Furthermore, I would also reject the submission made on behalf of the Director that the fact that a detained person was in the course of making a statement, whether it was exculpatory or incriminatory, at the time of the arrival of the solicitor could possibly be an objectively valid reason for postponing informing him of that arrival, and asking him whether he wished to suspend the making of that statement in order to have access to the solicitor."

The Chief Justice expressly reserved for a future occasion whether a detained person is entitled to be informed of his right of access to a solicitor by the gardaí who are detaining him,[66] or whether a detained person is entitled to have a solicitor present while he is being interrogated. The existence of both rights have been previously denied by the Court of Criminal Appeal in *The People (Director of Public Prosecutions) v Madden*[67] and *The People (Director of Public Prosecutions) v Pringle*[68] respectively.[69]

Right to privacy

In *The Director of Public Prosecutions v Kenny*[70] Barron J accepted that a person in Garda custody had a right to privacy but that it was not breached by observation of the detainee by persons who are lawfully required to deal with him while in custody. He reserved his opinion as to whether the right might be breached by observation of the detainee by persons with no legal duty to deal with him.

Right to communicate

While a convicted prisoner may have a right to communicate, it would appear to be extremely limited. Thus in *The State (Gallagher) v Governor of Portlaoise Prison*,[71] McMahon J heard a *habeas corpus* application based on the complaint, *inter alia,* that the prisoner's letters (to persons other than legal advisers, though no special point was taken on this) had been withheld by the governor; he said that "even if these complaints were correct, that would clearly not constitute such a default of fundamental requirements that the detention could be said to be wanting in due process of law". He added that the prison rules, to which he clearly saw no constitutional objection, did not entitle a prisoner "to write letters to bank managers about opening a company account or to conduct a business while serving a sentence".

In similar fashion, Costello J, in *Kearney v Minister for Justice*[72] held that a prisoner's right to communicate could be restricted in the interests of prison security, and consequently Rule 63 of the Rules for the Government of Prisons 1947, which authorised

[66] By virtue of ss 5 and 9 of the Criminal Justice Act 1984, persons detained under s 4 of the 1984 Act or s 30 of the Offences Against the State Act 1939 must be informed, without delay, of their entitlement, *inter alia*, to consult a solicitor and the Garda in charge of the station must, on request, contact the solicitor "as soon as practicable."

[67] [1977] IR 336. See also *The People (D.P.P.) v Doyle* [1977] IR 336, and *The People (D.P.P.) v Farrell* [1978] IR 13.

[68] (1981) 2 Frewen 57.

[69] Though the contrary view appears to have been taken by Hederman J in *The People (D.P.P.) v Quilligan (No.3)* [1993] 2 IR 305.

[70] [1992] 2 IR 141.

[71] High Court, 25 April 1983.

[72] [1986] IR 116; [1987] ILRM 52.

prison staff to read letters to and from prisoners, was not unconstitutional. However, the non-delivery of mail to the plaintiff as a result of unauthorised action taken by prison staff did constitute a breach of his constitutional rights, for which he was awarded £25 damages.[73]

Unconvicted persons detained in a Garda station would appear to have better protection in this regard.[74] In *In re Emergency Powers Bill 1976,*[75] Walsh J listed the right to communicate as one of the rights retained by persons detained under such emergency legislation while in *The People (Director of Public Prosecutions) v Kelly,*[76] Finlay P said that the removal of a person detained under s 30 of the Act of 1939 from one Garda station to another, done for the purpose either of harassment or of isolating him from assistance or access to which he was entitled, would clearly render his detention unlawful, a position subsequently endorsed by O'Higgins CJ in the Supreme Court. In *Director of Public Prosecutions v Sheehy*[77] Lynch J held that a member of the Garda Síochána, acting *bona fide*, may bring a person to a succession of Garda stations for the purpose of carrying out all the statutory procedures under the Road Traffic (Amendment) Act 1978, at one of such stations. However:

> "if the defendant had been brought from one Garda station to another in order to defeat his rights to consult a solicitor or communicate with a relative or a doctor of his choice, then the detention would become unlawful having regard to the decision of the Supreme Court in the *Emergency Powers Bill*, 1976 [reference]."

More recently, in *The People (Director of Public Prosecutions) v Healy*[78] McCarthy J said that the right of communication is not one-sided: "as the prisoner has the right to communicate with his relatives so have they the right to communicate with him."

Right to silence?

It is not yet clear whether there is a constitutional privilege against self-incrimination, popularly referred to as a right to silence. Such a privilege did exist at common law[79] but has been subject to a number of statutory incursions.[80] This matter is discussed further above.[81]

[73] See also two *ex tempore* judgments of the Supreme Court - *Hutchinson v Minister for Justice*, 16 October 1992, and *Holland v Minister for Justice*, 9 July 1993 - in which the Court indicated that a corollary of a prisoner's right to communicate is that he is entitled to be told when his correspondence is being stopped pursuant to Rule 63 and to be given some "very short reason" for such decision.

[74] By ss 5 and 9 of the Criminal Justice Act 1984, a person detained under s 4 of the 1984 Act or s 30 of the Offences Against the State Act 1939, must be informed of his right to have notification of the fact and place of his detention communicated to a person reasonably named by him and, on request, the officer in charge of the station must notify that person accordingly as soon as practicable. Where the detained person is under the age of seventeen years, his parent or guardian must be informed of the fact and place of detention as soon as practicable.

[75] [1977] IR 159. In *The People (D.P.P.) v Quilligan (No.3)* [1993] 2 IR 305, Hederman J held that a person arrested under s 30 of the 1939 Act cannot be held incommunicado.

[76] [1983] IR 1.

[77] [1987] ILRM 138.

[78] [1990] 2 IR 73.

[79] See *The State (McCarthy) v Lennon* [1936] IR 485.

[80] E.g. s 52 of the Offences Against the State Act 1939, requiring a person to give an account of his movement; ss 15 and 16 of the Criminal Justice Act 1984 which create offences of withholding information regarding firearms or ammunition, and stolen property, respectively.

[81] At pp. 593-594.

Statutory regulation of persons in Garda custody

Pursuant to s 7 of the Criminal Justice Act 1984, the Minister for Justice made the Criminal Justice Act 1984 (Treatment of Persons in Custody in Garda Síochána Stations) Regulations, 1987 (S.I. No. 119 of 1987) which regulate the treatment of persons in police custody. However, by virtue of s 7(3) of the Act a failure on the part of any member of the Garda Síochána to observe any provision of such regulations shall not of itself render that person liable to any criminal or civil proceedings or of itself affect the lawfulness of the custody of the detained person or the admissibility in evidence of any statement made by him.

No justification of illegal detention possible

Finally, it is worth noting Walsh J's comments, in *The People (Director of Public Prosecutions) v Howley*[82] that it not possible to justify an illegal detention by reference to ulterior motives. Referring to the detention of the accused in that case under s 30 of the Offences Against the State Act 1939, he said:

> "Either his detention is lawful or it is not. There is no intermediate position. There can be no question of competing or predominant issues which can determine that question. If an arrest is not lawful it is not rendered so by the seriousness or importance of the offence being investigated...It is not legally possible to justify an illegal detention even though where extraordinary excusing circumstances can be proved to exist it may be excused so far as the admissibility of evidence is concerned. Where a person is suffering illegal detention the High Court and this Court is bound by the Constitution to order his release and there can be no question of any consideration being given to permitting the detention to continue because of some dominant motive. But as was also pointed out by this Court in *Trimbole's* case the necessary release from illegal detention does not carry with it any immunity from the proper enforcement of the due process of the law to make such person amenable to answer criminal offences in the courts."

DEPRIVATION OR CURTAILMENT OF PERSONAL LIBERTY IN CRIMINAL PROCEEDINGS OR BY JUDICIAL ORDER

(i) Police powers to investigate and prevent crimes

That the Gardaí, in carrying out their duties to investigate and prevent crimes, are entitled to approach and, in certain circumstances, stop members of the general public has been affirmed in two recent cases. In *The Director of Public Prosecutions v Cowman*[83] a District Judge had dismissed charges against the accused, apparently on the basis that the arresting Garda was not entitled to approach him without having already formed an opinion that grounds existed for suspecting that the accused had committed an offence or was planning to commit a breach of the peace. Declaring the decision to be wrong in law, O'Hanlon J took the view that no such restriction was imposed by law on the right of a member of the Garda Síochána to approach members of the public from time to time as they think fit for the purpose of speaking to them on an informal basis. A similar approach was taken by Carney J to the practice of operating random road traffic checks

[82] [1989] ILRM 629. See also *The People (D.P.P.) v Walsh*, 3 Frewen 260.
[83] [1993] 1 IR 335.

involving the stopping of vehicles in *The Director of Public Prosecutions (Stratford) v Fagan.*[84] According to the judge, the Gardaí had a common law power, arising out of their duty to detect and prevent crime, to operate random road traffic checks including checks in relation to drunken driving which involve the stopping of vehicles even where there is no immediate suspicion that an offence has been committed. He also concluded that such a power was implicit in s 109(1) of the Road Traffic Act 1961, as amended by the Schedule to the Road Traffic Act 1968, obliging a member of the public to stop his vehicle on being so required by a member of the Gardaí and to keep it stationary for such period as is reasonably necessary in order to enable such member to discharge his duties.

If a member of the Gardaí wishes to exercise a statutory power to search an individual, that individual must be informed of the nature and description of the statutory power which is being invoked - *The Director of Public Prosecutions v Rooney.*[85] In the same case, O'Hanlon J also held that it was not necessary to arrest the individual prior to exercising the power of search under s 29 of the Dublin Police Act 1842. A similar approach was taken by the Supreme Court to the power of search conferred by s 23 of the Misuse of Drugs Act 1977, as amended by s 12 of the Misuse of Drugs Act 1984, in *O'Callaghan v Ireland.*[86] Dismissing the plaintiff's claim that a power of search and detention which was independent of any decision of the Garda concerned to arrest the person searched was oppressive and therefore unconstitutional, the Court, *per* Finlay CJ, said that the potential damage to society from the use and distribution and, therefore, possession of controlled drugs, was so great and constituted such a pernicious evil that the legislature was clearly justified in providing for the power of search contained in s 23. The Court also confirmed that a person detained for the purpose of being searched has the same rights concerning access to legal advice, freedom from harassment, interrogation or assault, etc., as a person under arrest. Finally, in answer to the plaintiff's claim that s 23 was unconstitutional because it failed to provide directions as to how the power of search conferred by the section was to be exercised, leading to the possibility that it could be used in a manner which was embarrassing and inappropriate and therefore oppressive, the Court held that an exercise of the power in such manner would amount to an abuse of power and a violation of constitutional rights for which appropriate remedies were available.

(ii) Institution of criminal proceedings by arrest[87]: arrest as start of criminal proceedings: with warrant

Criminal proceedings may be instituted by summons or by arrest,[88] with or without warrant. A certain discretion exists as to which means is to be employed in a particular case; s 11 of the Petty Sessions (Ireland) Act 1851, provides:

[84] [1993] 2 IR 95.
[85] [1992] 2 IR 7; [1993] ILRM 61.
[86] Supreme Court, 24 May 1993.
[87] A useful definition of arrest is to be found in *D.P.P. v McCreesh* [1992] 2 IR 239, where Hederman J said, "An arrest consists in or involves the seizure or touching of a person's body accompanied by a form of words which indicate to that person that he is under restraint. Whilst the older cases held that words alone would not suffice to constitute an arrest, nowadays words alone *may* amount to an arrest if, in the circumstances, they are calculated to bring, and do bring, to the person's notice that he was under restraint and he submitted to the compulsion." However, not every restraint will amount to an arrest - in *The People (D.P.P.) v Kehoe* [1985] IR 44, the Court of Criminal Appeal considered that the placing of handcuffs on the accused during the course of a shoot-out between Gardaí and armed raiders did not constitute an arrest.
[88] Though express statutory authority is required before a Garda may enter on private property against the will of the owner in order to effect an arrest - *D.P.P. v McCreesh* [1992] 2 IR 239. Consent to enter property may, however, be given by implication: *Minister for Justice v Wang Zhu Jie* [1993] 1 IR 426; [1991] ILRM 823, and *D.P.P. v Forbes* [1993] ILRM 817.

(1) In all cases of indictable crimes and offences...the justice[89] shall issue a warrant to arrest and bring [a person against whom an information has been sworn] before him...; or if he shall think that the ends of justice would be thereby sufficiently answered, it shall be lawful for him, instead of issuing such warrant, to issue a summons in the first instance to such a person, requiring him to appear and answer to the said complaint; but nothing herein contained shall prevent any justice from issuing a warrant for the arrest of such person at any time before or after the time mentioned in such summons for his appearance;...

(2) In all cases of summary jurisdiction the justice may issue his summons directed to such person, requiring him to appear and answer to the complaint...; and in all cases of offences where such persons shall not appear at the required time and place, and it shall be proved on oath, either that he was personally served with such summons or that he is keeping out of the way of such service... the justice may issue a warrant to arrest and bring such person before him...

These provisions may be roughly summarised as follows: a person accused of an indictable offence may be arrested on warrant, unless thought likely to appear in answer to a summons (though the District Judge or Peace Commissioner choosing this more delicate method may change his mind and have him arrested after all); while a person accused of an offence triable summarily can be proceeded against only by summons, unless he disobeys or avoids the summons, in which case he may be arrested on warrant.[90]

Arrest without a warrant

In a large number of cases an arrest can be made even without warrant. An ordinary citizen may arrest without warrant a person whom he suspects of committing a felony (though only if a felony has in fact been committed) or sees committing a breach of the peace; or whom he reasonably suspects of being in the act of committing, or having committed, any offence scheduled in the Criminal Law (Jurisdiction) Act 1976 (these are offences of a kind associated with terrorism) if committed in Northern Ireland. A member of the Garda Síochána may at common law arrest without warrant a person whom he reasonably suspects of committing a felony (whether in fact a felony has been committed or not) or sees committing a breach of the peace; and by s 19 of the Criminal Law (Jurisdiction) Act 1976, he may arrest someone whom he suspects with reasonable cause of being about to commit one of the Act's scheduled offences in Northern Ireland. In addition, important powers of arrest without warrant are conferred on the Garda Síochána by ss 29, 30 and 32 of the Offences Against the State Act 1939; and a large variety of other statutes (mostly of no political relevance) empower members of the Garda Síochána to arrest without warrant in special circumstances relevant to the purposes of such Acts: simple instances are, s 13 of the Criminal Law (Sexual Offences) Act 1993 (on suspicion of having committed an offence under various provisions of that Act) and s 14 of the Animal Remedies Act 1993 (empowering a Garda to arrest "with reasonable cause" where he suspects that the person concerned has committed certain offences pertaining to the sale or possession of illegal growth hormones.) A power of arrest without warrant is also contained in the proposed Criminal Justice (Public Order) Bill 1993. Sections 49 and 50 of the Road Traffic Act 1961 (on suspicion of driving or being in charge of a mechanically propelled vehicle while under the influence of an

[89] Now a District Judge or a Peace Commissioner: Courts of Justice Act 1924, ss 78, 88.
[90] Rules of the District Court 1948, Rule 34 (vol. XXXVI of the bound S.R.O., p.929).

intoxicating liquor or drug).[91] A member of the Defence Forces is given, in special circumstances,[92] a power of arrest without warrant by s 15(4) of the Criminal Law Act 1976; though this section (by sub-s 8) has effect only whenever the Emergency Powers Act 1976, is in force.

By s 4 of the Criminal Justice Act 1984, where a person has been arrested without a warrant on suspicion of having committed, or having attempted to commit, an offence punishable by a term of imprisonment for a term of 5 years or by a more severe penalty, he may be detained for up to 12 hours before being charged. However, where enough evidence is available to prefer a charge, this must be done without delay unless he is suspected of another offence to which s 4 applies.

No distinction between "detention" and "arrest"

Some rules relating to arrest have been clearly affirmed by the courts. In *Attorney General v Cox*[93] the Court of Criminal Appeal rejected the suggestion that the law might recognise some form of restraint not amounting to arrest; Kennedy CJ said:

> "According to [Cox's] counsel he was *under arrest*, according to the police, *merely detained*...This Court does not accept the distinction sought to be made between "detained", when a person is not a free agent and no longer the master of his own movements, and "arrest" as the term is understood in law. They are in effect one and the same."[94]

This case received the confirmation of the High Court in *Dunne v Clinton*,[95] in which the plaintiffs had been "detained" during the further investigation of an offence. Hanna J said:

> "In law there can be no half-way house between the liberty of the subject, unfettered by restraint, and an arrest. If a person under suspicion voluntarily agrees to go to a police station to be questioned, his liberty is not interfered with, as he can change his mind at any time. If, having been examined, he is asked, and voluntarily agrees, to remain in the barracks until some investigation is made, he is still a free subject, and can leave at any time. But a practice has grown up of "detention", as distinct from arrest. It is, in effect, keeping a suspect in custody, perhaps under as comfortable circumstances as the barracks will permit, without making any definite charge against him, and with the intimation in some form of words or gesture that he is under restraint, and will not be allowed to leave. As, in my opinion, there could be no such thing as notional liberty, this so-called detention amounts to arrest, and the suspect has in law been arrested and in custody during the period of his detention. The expression "detention" has no justification in law in this connection, and the use of it has in a sense helped to nurture the idea that it is something differ-

[91] A list of other such Acts will be found in Ryan and Magee, *The Irish Criminal Process*, (Cork, 1983) Appendix G.

[92] A police officer not below the rank of superintendent must have requested an officer of the Defence Forces to provide military assistance in order that the powers of sub-s (3) and (4) of s 15 may be exercised. Sub-section (3) relates to the stopping of vehicles. Both sub-sections contain powers of search.

[93] Court of Criminal Appeal, 9 April 1929.

[94] See also *Melling v Ó Mathghamhna*, [1962] IR 1; (1963) 97 ILTR 60, where Lavery J rejected as "over-subtle" an attempted distinction between detention and arrest, saying, "Arrest is, in fact, only the act of taking into custody and is followed by detention in every criminal charge."

[95] [1930] IR 366; (1930) 64 ILTR 136.

> ent from arrest, and that it relieves the [Garda Síochána] from the obligation to have the question of the liberty of the suspected person determined by a peace commissioner or the court."[96]

In *The People (Director of Public Prosecutions) v Coffey*[97] Hamilton J directed the jury that the defendant had been detained in circumstances in which, having gone voluntarily to the Garda Station, he was subject to the "care and attention" of members of the Garda Síochána at all times; was constantly interviewed and questioned about a murder; was asked to surrender his car keys; and was not informed that he was free to leave.[98]

Despite these various judicial affirmations of the synonymity of "arrest" and "detention", some recent authorities appear to accept that one can be stopped for the purposes of being searched without necessarily being under arrest.[99]

"Holding for questioning" etc. euphemism for illegality

In *The People (Director of Public Prosecutions) v O'Loughlin*[100] the Court of Criminal Appeal, speaking by O'Higgins CJ, said:

> "Apart from [the provision of s 30 of] the Offences Against the State Act 1939,[181] there is no procedure under our law whereby a person may be held in a Garda station without charge. In particular, our law does not contemplate or permit the holding of a person for questioning... "Holding for questioning" and "taking into custody" and "detaining" are merely different ways of describing the act of depriving a man of his liberty. To do such without lawful authority is an open defiance of Article 40.4.1 of the Constitution."[102]

Thus in *The People (Director of Public Prosecutions) v Higgins*[103] the accused had been arrested in connection with a road traffic offence but was subsequently held for questioning in connection with other offences before being brought before a District Justice. A statement, allegedly made by the accused and incriminating him in those other offences, was declared inadmissible by the Supreme Court on the ground that his continued detention was unlawful and a conscious and deliberate violation of his constitutional rights.

At common law, the power of arrest is only justified if it is exercised for the purpose of bringing an arrested person to justice before a court - *The People (Director of Public*

[96] In a similar case, however *(Doherty v Liddane* (1940) Ir Jur Rep 58), the plaintiff failed, as the twenty-six hours during which he had been in custody were spent by the police in efforts, of which he knew and approved, to find someone to go bail for him.

[97] [1987] ILRM 727.

[98] In *The People (D.P.P.) v Conroy* [1986] IR 460; [1988] ILRM 4, some members of the Supreme Court, notably Finlay CJ, Walsh and Henchy JJ, hinted that a person who was assisting the police in their enquiries was detained where he was not informed of his right freely to leave the Garda station; had his clothes taken from him; and was always in the presence of a police officer, except when he was put in a cell which could only be opened from the outside.

[99] See *D.P.P. v Rooney* [1992] 2 IR 7; [1993] ILRM 61; *O'Callaghan v Ireland*, Supreme Court, 24 May 1993.

[100] [1979] IR 85.

[101] See now also s 4 of the Criminal Justice Act 1984 which authorises detention for up to twelve hours without charge.

[102] See also *The People (D.P.P.) v Shaw* [1982] IR 1, where Walsh J said in the Supreme Court that "if there exists a practice of arresting persons for the purpose of 'assisting the police in their enquiries', it is unlawful. In such circumstances the phrase is no more than a euphemism for false imprisonment." The same point is also made in *The People (D.P.P.) v Walsh* [1980] IR 294.

[103] Supreme Court, 22 November 1985.

Prosecutions) v Walsh.[104] Accordingly, where a suspect in an assault case was arrested by a Garda for the purpose of securing evidence - in the hope of securing identification, he brought her to court at a time when the victim was likely to be present - the arrest was declared unlawful by the Court of Criminal Appeal - *The People (Director of Public Prosecutions) v Donaghy.*[105]

Overt surveillance not detention

In *The People (Director of Public Prosecutions) v Pringle*[106] the Court of Criminal Appeal held that an accused was not in police custody even though the evidence established that at all times while he was in hospital - he had been wounded in a shoot-out and was brought directly to hospital by the arresting police - his room was under armed guard; persons entering the room were searched; his solicitor was kept under observation during his consultation; and the accused had no other clothing than his pyjamas. According to the Court:

> "the Gardaí...have a duty to arrest a person whom they suspect has committed a felony, but they are entitled to postpone that duty as they did in the present case. If they do so, it is in accordance with their duty to bring a suspected felon to justice that they take proper steps to ensure that the suspect does not escape...The Court rejects the submission that a suspect under close surveillance, as the applicant was in this case, must necessarily be in Garda custody."[107]

A similar view was taken, albeit in somewhat different circumstances, in *Kane v The Governor of Mountjoy Prison.*[108] The applicant had been detained for forty eight hours in Granard garda station pursuant to s 30 of the Offences Against the State Act 1939. After his release from custody, members of the Gardaí and the Army, aware that an application for an extradition warrant was to be made in respect of the applicant, kept him under intense overt surveillance for a period of some five hours before he was eventually arrested for assault. Dismissing the applicant's contention that this level of surveillance amounted to unlawful detention vitiating the subsequent arrest, Finlay CJ, with whom Henchy and Griffin JJ agreed, said:

> "The essential feature of detention in this legal context is that the detainee is effectively prevented from going or being where he wants to go or be and instead is forced to remain or go where his jailer wishes him to remain. When the applicant left Granard garda station, the evidence clearly establishes that what he wanted to do was to go to Cavan. He was free to do so and he achieved his purpose."

The Chief Justice also held that, while such surveillance would be unlawful if there was no specific adequate justification for it, such was not the case here. The Gardaí, aware of the intended issue and backing of an extradition warrant had a clear duty to take reasonable steps to ascertain where it could be speedily executed, once obtained. They had a

[104] [1980] IR 294. See also *The People (D.P.P.) v Shaw* [1982] IR 1.
[105] 3 Frewen 138.
[106] (1981) 2 Frewen 57.
[107] In *The People (D.P.P.) v Arthurs, The Irish Times*, 30 January 1987, the Special Criminal Court held that a man being treated in hospital was not in Garda custody although armed detectives "supervised" him around the clock for several days.
[108] [1988] IR 757; [1988] ILRM 724. See *Humphreys*, (1988) 11 DULJ (n.s.) 138.

strong suspicion that the applicant was a member of the I.R.A. who was likely to go into hiding, receiving support and assistance from sympathisers and these factors justified the extent and nature of the surveillance carried out.[109]

Arrest with warrant lawful only if on charge for which warrant issued

The case of *The People (Attorney General) v White*[110] affirmed the rule that an arrest is lawful only if made on the charge for which a warrant has issued, or for an offence, present to the mind of the arresting officer, for which arrest without warrant is permitted by law, and the person being arrested is told the reason for his arrest; no one is obliged to submit to an arrest made otherwise, and even if a death is inflicted in resisting such an arrest, it will not be murder, but at most manslaughter. Here, in the summary given by Gavan Duffy P:

> "a party of Detective Gardaí, armed with revolvers, surrounded [a] house...where they knew two men to be lodging whom they determined to arrest; of one of them...the ground of arrest without a warrant was his membership of an illegal organisation; the other man was in fact [White, the appellant] but the police did not know his identity. It is a singular and highly important feature of this prosecution that, from beginning to end of the trial, no cause for the arrest of Henry White was alleged by any witness, though a lawful cause of arrest for some misdemeanour might, quite possibly, have been found in the emergency legislation in force during the year 1942."

One of the police was killed in the subsequent shooting affray, and White was convicted of his murder by the Special Criminal Court. On appeal this conviction was replaced, under the power given the Court of Criminal Appeal by s 34 of the Courts of Justice Act 1924, by one of manslaughter; Gavan Duffy P. said:

> "Arrest, it was insisted [in *Leachinsky v Christie*] is not a right; it is a power, conferred for the protection of society; the essence of the law of arrest (apart from the exceptional law of internment on suspicion), is that arrest is a first step towards an intended prosecution and the police cannot, for reasons of convenience, take the law into their own hands. This principle of freedom is of "supreme importance"...White, against whom on the evidence the police had nothing, was trapped by an armed force, determined on his arrest, and he killed a police officer while still hard pressed to find a way out. That was a criminal homicide, but it was manslaughter, not murder, since there was no lawful authority for the intended arrest...White does not lose the benefit of that law concerning unlawful arrest by any knowledge that he was firing at a police officer. It is idle to invoke ss 15 and 22 of the Firearms Act 1925...to show that White was liable to arrest for the felony of carrying a firearm with intent to endanger life; the Gardaí were not attempting to arrest him for that offence."

[109] In the course of his judgment, Finlay CJ had expressed the opinion that no distinction existed in the present context between the duty of investigating crime and executing an extradition warrant. While agreeing with the overall result, McCarthy J, with whom Hederman J agreed, dissented from this view, arguing that in relation to the detection of crime, "the combination of interference with privacy and the impairment of freedom of choice of movement would be to provide for a circumstance that may never happen."

[110] [1947] IR 247. This judgment expressly followed the contemporaneous case of *Leachinsky v Christie* in England - [1947] AC 573.

Reason for arrest must not be withheld from person arrested

In *In re Ó Láighléis*[111] - where it was alleged that the applicant had not been told the reason for his arrest (under s 4 of the Offences Against the State (Amendment) Act 1940) - the Supreme Court recognised that:

> "arrest must be for a lawful purpose; and since no one is obliged to submit to an unlawful arrest the citizen has a right before acquiescing in his arrest to know why he is being arrested. The Court sees nothing in s 4...which manifests an intention on the part of the Oireachtas to modify this wholesome rule of law; and accordingly the Court is of opinion that a person arrested under a Minister's warrant must be told that such a warrant exists and that he is being arrested and will be detained under it."[112]

However, the Court, in refusing *habeas corpus*, pointed out that the applicant had not established that he did not know why he was being arrested; and in *The People (Director of Public Prosecutions) v Walsh*[113] the Supreme Court interpreted its predecessor in *Ó Láighléis'* case as saying that "the onus was placed on the person arrested to establish that he did not know why he was arrested" (*per* O'Higgins CJ); "the appellant's right to be informed was not questioned. It simply was not exercised by him." In *The People (Director of Public Prosecutions) v Shaw*[114] Walsh J stated the rule as follows:

> "To effect a lawful arrest, the person arrested must be told by the person effecting the arrest the charge upon which he is being arrested, unless he otherwise knows the reason for the arrest."[115]

The formulation based on the "onus" placed on the person arrested was repeated by the Court of Criminal Appeal in *The People (Director of Public Prosecutions) v Campbell*,[116] in which the arresting Garda had told his prisoner only that he was arresting him under s 30 of the Offences Against the State Act 1939; the Court held that, even though the person concerned then resisted arrest, it was clear that this resistance did not take place because of the inadequacy of the information given. The Court did, however, say:

> "The situation might be different (but the Court expressly refrains from stating any view on the point) had the applicant asked [the police officer] what was the scheduled offence [he] suspected him of having committed and had the officer refused to tell him."[117]

The Court also relied on part of the *Ó Láighléis* judgment in stating that "even if the arrest was invalid the subsequent detention was lawful when he was given information

[111] [1960] IR 93; (1961) 95 ILTR 92.

[112] This principle applies equally to persons arrested under s 30 of the Offences Against the State Act 1939 - see *The People (D.P.P.) v Quilligan* [1986] IR 495; *The People (D.P.P.) v Ferris* (1986) 3 Frewen 114 and *The People (D.P.P.) v Quilligan (No.3)* [1993] 2 IR 305. By virtue of Article 5(2) of the European Convention on Human Rights, everyone who is arrested is entitled to be informed promptly, in a language which he understands, of the reasons for his arrest and of any charge against him.

[113] [1980] IR 294. See *O'Connor* in (1981) 16 Ir Jur (n.s.) 281.

[114] [1982] IR 1.

[115] Though it is not necessary to use technical or precise language - *D.P.P. (Cloughley) v Mooney*, High Court, 24 June 1992. In that case Blayney J held that telling the accused that he was being arrested for "drunk driving" was a sufficient communication of the reason for his arrest pursuant to s 49(3) of the Road Traffic Act 1961. See also *The People (D.P.P.) v Ferris* (1986) 3 Frewen 114.

[116] (1983) 3 Frewen 131.

[117] See now *The People (D.P.P.) v Byrne* [1987] IR 363; [1989] ILRM 613.

which made it clear to him why he had been arrested": though this statement seems to go a long way towards devitalising the basic principle that arrest must be accompanied by the reason for it.

Use of force in effecting an arrest

An arresting officer is only entitled to use such force as is reasonably necessary to effect and maintain an arrest. Where force is used for any other purpose, the officer is not acting in the execution of his duty and may be liable for injuries sustained by his prisoner: *Dowman v Ireland*.[118]

Burden of proof in establishing legality of detention

In *The People (Director of Public Prosecutions) v Conroy*[119] the Supreme Court unanimously rejected the trial judge's view that the accused person must make out a *prima facie* case of illegality before the court should consider the lawfulness of the detention. Finlay CJ said:

> "Upon an issue being raised by counsel on behalf of the accused as to whether his client was, at and prior to the time of the making of a confession, in custody, it seems to me that the onus of proof is on the State to establish either that his custody was legal, or that he was not in custody, and that the judge should ordinarily permit evidence to be adduced of that issue."[120]

On a related point, in *The People (Director of Public Prosecutions) v Farrell*[121] the Court of Criminal Appeal held that the maxim *omnia praesumuntur rite esse acta* could not cover the activities of a police officer invoking statutory powers which interfered with the normal rights and liberties of citizens.

McCarthy J expressed a similar view in *The People (Director of Public Prosecutions) v Byrne*,[122] where he said:

> "*Omnia praesumuntur rite esse acta* - that an individual who has acted in a public capacity was duly appointed and has properly discharged official duties - is common to criminal and civil proceedings. This presumption, however, is limited; there is a wide gap between a presumption in favour of the regularity of acts...and that degree of proof required not merely in every criminal trial, as such, but, also, in every instance of what is, on its face, a breach of the constitutional right to personal liberty."

Accordingly, the failure of the State to establish the state of mind of a police officer who had made an extension order under s 30 of the Offences Against the State Act 1939, meant that it had not proved the accused was lawfully detained.

[118] [1986] ILRM 111.

[119] [1986] IR 460; [1988] ILRM 4.

[120] See also *MacIntyre's* case (*The Irish Times*, 8 May 1987) where Gannon J is reported as saying that where doubts are raised in the mind of the District Judge about the validity of an extension order made pursuant to s 30, those doubts were, in law, required to be dispelled by the police, rather than to be proved by the detained person.

[121] [1978] IR 13.

[122] [1987] IR 363; [1989] ILRM 613.

Forum for challenging legality of detention by Gardaí

In *Keating v The Governor of Mountjoy Prison*[123] the Supreme Court ruled that a challenge to the legality of detention by the Gardaí must ordinarily be taken in the High Court by way of an application under Article 40.4.2. In the instant case, a challenge had been made to the detention of the applicant pursuant to the Criminal Justice Act 1984 at the remand hearing before the District Judge. He refused to enter into this issue and remanded the applicant in custody. This approach was endorsed by the Supreme Court who said (*per* McCarthy J):

> "Article 40, s 4, sub-s 2 expressly contemplates the complaint of unlawful detention being made to the High Court or any judge thereof;...it would clearly be an unwarrantable and unlawful usurpation of the constitutional role of the High Court if an inferior court were to embark on such an enquiry, with a view to holding that a person was being unlawfully detained and ordering his release. The District Court has no such function."[124]

However McCarthy J also appeared to accept that, in extreme cases, the District Judge could, at a remand hearing, discharge an accused:

> "[T]here may be cases in which a District Justice in pursuance of his constitutional duty, having regard to some outrage committed upon a person brought before a District Court, would refuse to proceed as prescribed by the Criminal Procedure Act 1967...If cases arise where the circumstances of arrest are such as to amount to an affront to the constitutional role of the courts, then the District Justice will refuse to proceed with the matter and will discharge the person before him."

Later validation of arrest; re-arrest

A person who was unlawfully arrested or whose detention became unlawful acquires no immunity against subsequent (lawful) re-arrest. In a number of cases decided during the 1960s, the Supreme Court had taken the view that orders of *habeas corpus*, granted to prisoners detained in a prison not authorised by law, could be coupled with an order for re-arrest so that the prosecutor could serve out the balance of his sentence in a lawful place of detention.[125] Some doubt was cast on these decisions by a passage in *The State (McDonagh) v Frawley*[126] wherein O'Higgins CJ said:

> "[I]n cases in which it has not been shown to the satisfaction of the court that the detention is "in accordance with law" in the sense indicated, the release of the detained person must be ordered and, notwithstanding judicial dicta to the contrary, the order of release may not be coupled with an order of re-arrest. The protection of personal liberty, which Article 40.4 is intended to ensure, would be hollow and ineffectual if the order of release was not unqualified and unconditional."

123 [1991] 1 IR 61; [1990] ILRM 850.

124 In a concurring judgment, O'Flaherty J expressed the view that an argument that there has been a breach of procedures provided by the section authorising arrest should be dealt with in the course of the trial proceedings in deciding what evidence is admissible and what is not. A difficulty with this view, however, is that some cases which might be disposed of at a preliminary stage will be required to continue to full hearing - see Byrne and Binchy, *Annual Review of Irish Law 1990* (Dublin 1991) at p.263.

125 See, e.g., *The State (Brien) v Kelly* [1970] IR 69; *The State (Dillon) v Kelly* [1970] IR 175.

126 [1978] IR 131.

However in the later case of *The People (Director of Public Prosecutions) v Pringle*[127] the Court of Criminal Appeal observed that:

> "it is well established that a detention which may initially have been illegal can, in certain circumstances, be legalised (*In re Ó Láighléis*) and there are circumstances in which a valid arrest at law can be made immediately after the release of a person from a custody which had been, for one reason or another, illegal."

(iii) Custody pending trial; bail, prompt production before court

Section 15 of the Criminal Justice Act 1951, as inserted by s 26 of the Criminal Justice Act 1984, provides as follows:

> (1) A person arrested pursuant to a warrant shall on arrest be brought before a justice of the District Court having jurisdiction to deal with the offence concerned or, if a justice is not immediately available, before a peace commissioner in the district of such a justice as soon as practicable.[128]
>
> (2) [This makes similar provision for persons arrested without a warrant and charged with an offence.]
>
> (3) Where a person is arrested pursuant to a warrant later than the hour of 10 o'clock on any evening or, having been arrested without warrant, is charged after that hour and a justice is due to sit in the District Court district in which the person was arrested not later than noon on the following day, it shall be sufficient compliance with subsection 1 or 2, as the case may be, if he is brought before a justice at the commencement of the sitting.
>
> (4) If he is brought before a peace commissioner, the commissioner, having heard the evidence offered, shall remand him, either in custody or on such bail as the commissioner thinks fit, and remit the case for hearing before a justice of the District Court having jurisdiction to deal with it.[129]
>
> (5) If the accused is remanded on bail and there and then finds bail, the case shall be remitted to the next sitting of the Court.
>
> (6) In any other event, the case shall be remitted to a sitting of the Court at a named place to be held within eight days after the arrest.
>
> (7) This section is without prejudice to the provisions of any enactment relating to proceedings after arrest or charge in particular cases.

[127]2 Frewen 57. Remarks of the Court of Criminal Appeal in *The People v Kehoe* [1985] IR 444; [1986] ILRM 690, suggest that where a common law arrest has been made, a garda who then discovers grounds for arrest under s 30 of the Offences Against the State Act 1939 may be entitled to effect a further arrest without going through the "colourable manoeuvre" of an apparent release from custody.

[128] Section 4 of the Criminal Justice Act 1984 provides that a person arrested under that Act must be brought to a garda station "as soon as reasonably possible". In *The People (D.P.P.) v Boylan* [1991] 1 IR 477, a delay of two hours in bringing the accused to the garda station meant that his initial detention was unlawful. See also *Rederij Kennemerland BV v Attorney General* [1989] ILRM 821, where a failure to bring the applicants before the District Court "as soon as may be", as required by s 234 of the Fisheries (Consolidation) Act 1959, invalidated their detention under that Act.

[129] Sub-section 4 was declared invalid in *O'Mahony v Melia* [1989] IR 355; [1990] ILRM 14.

These provisions reproduce the common law position[130] and are supplemented by the District Court Rules, 1948.[131]

Appearance in court cures defect in process for procuring attendance

A defect in the process for procuring the attendance of an accused in court is normally cured if the accused appears in court, provided, of course, that attendance has not been procured by means of a deliberate and conscious violation of the accused's constitutional rights.[132] In *Farrell v Farrelly*[133] O'Hanlon J considered that such appearance would resolve any difficulty which might arise should it be held that a peace commissioner cannot lawfully issue a warrant for arrest. According to the judge, an application to a peace commissioner for such a warrant could not be regarded as a deliberate and conscious violation of constitutional rights since it would have been made "pursuant to statutory procedures which have been followed, without challenge, within living memory." However this conclusion would appear to be doubtful in view of the more recent decision of the Supreme Court in *The People (The Director of Public Prosecutions) v Kenny*[134] that in deciding whether a violation of constitutional rights was carried out consciously and deliberately, it was immaterial whether or not the actor knew that what he was doing was in breach of the constitutional rights of the accused.

Remand in custody

In *O'Mahony v Melia*[135] Keane J held that the power to remand a person in custody, or alternatively, to grant bail, conferred by s 15(4) of the 1951 Act (as amended by s 26 of the Criminal Justice Act 1984) constituted an administration of justice and accordingly could not be exercised by a peace commissioner.[136] By virtue of s 24(1) of the Criminal Procedure Act 1967, a District Judge is given a general power to remand in custody. The general principle is that such remand cannot exceed eight days; however s 24(3) of the 1967 Act provides:

> "Where the Court remands a person in custody (other than on the occasion of his first appearance before the Court) it may remand him for a period exceeding eight days but not exceeding thirty days if he and the prosecutor consent."

[130] See above, pp. 832-833.

[131] *Cp.* Article 5(3) of the European Convention on Human Rights which provides: "Everyone arrested or detained in accordance with the provisions of paragraph 1(c) of this Article shall be brought promptly before a judge or other officer authorised by law to exercise judicial power and shall be entitled to trial within a reasonable time or to release pending trial. Release may be conditioned by guarantees to appear for trial." While the word 'promptly' is not necessarily to be understood literally, the scope for flexibility in applying the notion of promptness is limited and in *Brogan v UK* Series A, No. 145B; [1989] 11 EHRR 117, the Court held that a delay of four days and six hours in bringing the accused before a judge infringed Article 5(3). The UK subsequently derogated form the Convention in order to permit continued use of statutory powers of arrest and extended detention, a derogation which the European Court held to be justified under Article 15 of the Convention in *Brannigan v UK* Series A, No 2588, 26 May 1993.

[132] See *Attorney General v Burke* [1955] IR 30; *Application of Tynan*, [1969] IR 1; *D.P.P. v Clein*, [1983] ILRM 76; *State (Lynch) v Ballagh* [1986] IR 203; [1987] ILRM 65; *Egan v Johnson*, High Court, 19 March 1993.

[133] [1988] IR 201.

[134] [1990] 2 IR 110; [1990] ILRM 569.

[135] [1989] IR 335. This would also appear to sound the death-knell for the power of a peace commissioner to order the continued detention of a boat and its crew, pursuant to s 233A of the Fisheries (Consolidation) Act 1959, an issue which surfaced, but was not necessary to resolve, in *Rederij Kennemerland BV v Attorney General* [1989] ILRM 821.

[136] In *Farrell v Farrelly* [1988] IR 201 O'Hanlon J found it unnecessary to rule whether the peace commissioner's power to issue warrants for arrest was similarly unconstitutional.

The usual eight-day remand may also, by sub-ss 4 and 5 respectively, be extended in case of illness or accident, or if there is no Court sitting due on the day to which a person has been remanded. Repeated remands, totalling much more than eight days, are possible under s 21 of the Act:

> "Where an accused person is before the District Court in connection with an offence the Court may, subject to the provisions of this Part, remand the accused from time to time as occasion requires."

The attitude of the courts to the remanding of an accused (but still untried) person in custody is illustrated by the case of *The State (O'Flaherty) v Ó Floinn*[137] (which antedated the passing of the Criminal Procedure Act 1967). What was in issue here was the construction of the Courts of Justice Act 1924, of which s 91 provided for the making of rules for the District Court by a rule-making authority; these rules might, *inter alia*, take the form of "adaptation or modification of any statute that may be necessary" for their purpose. Rule 55(4) of the District Court Rules, 1948, in purported exercise of this power, provided a maximum remand period in custody of fifteen days, although the statute in force in this regard - the Indictable Offences (Ireland) Act 1849, s 21 - provided only for a maximum eight-day custody remand. The Supreme Court held the rule *ultra vires* the rule-making authority; Kingsmill Moore J said:

> "This rule, if valid, is a very serious encroachment on the liberty of the individual. The safeguards provided by s 21 of [the Act of 1849] are swept away, and the period of remand in custody is almost doubled. It is not a matter of imprisoning a person against whom, although he must be presumed innocent till he has been found guilty, a *prima facie* case has already been established by a preliminary investigation judicially conducted. A person who is merely under suspicion, against whom no evidence other than evidence of arrest and charge is offered, and who may be perfectly innocent, can be incarcerated for fifteen days without any chance of proving his innocence, or of knowing what facts are alleged against him. It is true that even under the provisions of the earlier section an accused person could be remanded from time to time and so be kept in custody for a total period far exceeding fifteen days; but he had the valuable right to have his case examined by a judicial personage every eight days and the remand could only be ordered where the justice was judicially satisfied that for a reasonable cause it was necessary or advisable to defer the examination."

Ó Dálaigh J added:

> "The subject-matter of the change being the liberty of the individual I must begin by regarding any curtailment of that liberty as serious. That is not merely a personal view: it is one that the Constitution enjoins. Next, I have it that the Legislature had, in 1849, thought right to regulate the common law requirements of reasonableness by fixing an upper limit of eight days...With these matters present to my mind I think it is my duty to say that the alteration effected...is radical in character and something more than the mere modification permitted by s 91 of the Act of 1924, and is therefore *ultra vires*."[138]

[137] [1954] IR 295; (1956) 90 ILTR 179.

[138] Gavan Duffy J in the High Court had reached the same conclusion about the similar provision of the earlier District Court Rules in *The People v Cadden and O'Grady* (1939) Ir Jur Rep 35.

The tone of these judgments suggest that the area concerned - that of personal liberty - made the Court more jealous in construing the "modifying" power of the rule-making authority than it might have been in a constitutionally less sensitive area.[139]

Unreasonable delay in proceeding with trial

A prisoner returned by the District Court for trial on indictment may be held in custody (a) until his appearance before the next sitting of the trial court, by warrant of the District Judge; (b) after his appearance before the trial court, if an adjournment should be necessary, by warrant of that court; or he may be released on bail by either of these courts. If he is not released on bail, but held in custody, the lapse of an unreasonable time before his trial is proceeded with may conceivably be grounds for granting him, not bail, but an absolute order of *habeas corpus* under Article 40.4 of the Constitution, as appears from *In re Singer (No. 2)*.[140] In this case, the prisoner, having been in custody before and during the preliminary investigation since 30 May 1959 and having been returned for trial, had still not been arraigned by the end of July 1960: he was not, in the event, granted an absolute order, but this was because the Supreme Court considered that, having regard to the complexity of the charges against him (multiple fraud), the delay in going ahead with the trial was not unreasonable: it is clear from the judgments that had the Court thought otherwise, an unconditional release would have been possible. Lavery J said:

> "The delay was great, but it must be judged in the circumstances of the case. It is clear that the charges are numerous and complicated."

And Ó Dálaigh J said:

> "This delay has indeed been long and very burdensome for the appellant. But assuming without here asserting, that circumstances might be envisaged in which an order of *habeas corpus* would go in respect of excessive delay in the taking of depositions, in this case no grounds have in my opinion been furnished by the appellant to warrant it being said that the delay and detention associated with it were here excessive. I have, moreover, to bear in mind that the appellant was allowed bail; and, while he has asserted that the amount of the bail was such as to be unprocurable, the appellant did not carry any appeal to this Court against the amount of such bail."[141]

Bail

An accused or convicted person awaiting trial or the hearing of an appeal[142] may be admitted to bail, i.e. he may be released in consideration of the placing by him, or by another or others, or both, of a sum of money at the court's disposal, to be forfeited

[139] Though it is arguable now that any statutory provision, irrespective of the context in which it operates, purporting to allow an agency other than the Oireachtas to modify or amend legislation is unconstitutional, having regard to Article 15.2 - see above, pp. 107-112.

[140] (1964) 98 ILTR 112.

[141] It is now quite clear that unreasonable delay prejudicial to the defendant affords good grounds for preventing a trial going ahead. This matter is discussed in more detail above, pp. 598-602.

[142] The criteria for granting bail are the same in the case of a person detained in custody for extradition purposes as in the case of a person facing criminal charges. This was decided by the Supreme Court in *The People (Attorney General) v Gilliland* [1985] IR 643; [1985] ILRM 357, in which the Attorney General had argued that in an extradition case the prisoner should not be granted bail unless he satisfied the court that there was "no real or reasonable possibility" that if granted bail he would not be available for extradition. Henchy J said, "In an extradition case the State's duty is to take all reasonable steps to ensure that the prisoner will ultimately

("estreated") should the accused person not "answer to his bail" by appearing for his trial or for his appeal.[143] In addition to the power of the courts to grant bail, the person in charge of a garda station may also admit a person brought in custody to such station to what is known as "station bail". This is provided for by s 31 of the Criminal Procedure Act 1967 and was considered by the Supreme Court in *The State (Lynch) v Ballagh*.[144]In this case, the station sergeant acted pursuant to the District Court (Criminal Procedure Act 1967) Rules, 1985, in making the recognisance returnable to a time and place other than the earliest possible sitting of the District Court after the arrest. A majority of the Court held that the 1985 Rules were *ultra vires* the Rules Committee of the District Court as, in the words of Walsh J:

> "the members of the Garda Síochána are part of the executive branch of government; and the performance of the functions assigned to them by statute cannot be regulated by a rules-making committee whose function is to make rules to enable the District Court to function, to carry out its duties and exercise its jurisdiction, and to regulate its practice and procedure."

He pointed out that the object of s 15 of the Criminal Justice Act 1951 (as inserted by s 26 of the Criminal Justice Act 1984) was to ensure "that an accused person is brought promptly before a court if he is in custody, and if he is on bail, to the next sitting of the Court".[145] Walsh J also cast doubt on the constitutionality of a peace commissioner's power, under that section, to grant bail. In *O'Mahony v Melia*[146] Keane J held that such a power was an aspect of the administration and accordingly could be exercised only by members of the judiciary.

The jurisdictions of different courts in regard to the granting of bail, and the objects and principles of the bail system, are stated by Walsh J in *The People (Attorney General) v O'Callaghan*,[147] a case of fundamental and controversial character, in which the Supreme Court identified and condemned certain criteria as being improper considerations in making the decision to refuse to admit an accused person to bail.

Criteria for granting or refusing bail

The criteria on which the courts operated for forty years up to *O'Callaghan's* case were essentially those listed by Hanna J in *The State v Purcell*[148] as having been "from time to time laid down by courts of high authority". The fundamental test on bail motions, he said, was the probability of the accused person's evading justice; and the matters which a court might take into consideration in arriving at a view on this question of probability were: "(1) the seriousness of the crime charged; (2) the severity of the punishment provided by the law for the offence; (3) the strength of the case as it appears against the

be available for extradition. In an ordinary criminal case the State's duty is to ensure that the prisoner will be available for his trial. In either case the State's duty must operate in a way that will not conflict with the fundamental right to personal liberty of a person who stands unconvicted of an offence under the law of the State." In *The State (Dunne) v Martin* [1982] IR 229, the Supreme Court held that the granting of bail to the prosecutor in judicial review proceedings was not warranted where he was serving sentences of imprisonment on foot of a judicial order which was good on its face.

[143] A person released on bail who fails to appear before a court in accordance with his recognisances is guilty of an offence under s 13 of the Criminal Justice Act 1984.

[144] [1986] IR 203; [1987] ILRM 65.

[145] In *The State (D.P.P.) v Ruane*, High Court, 6 February 1987, Blayney J reconciled s 31(1) of the 1967 Act with s 15 of the 1951 Act by holding that s 15 applied only where station bail had been refused.

[146] [1989] IR 335.

[147] [1966] IR 501; (1968) 102 ILTR 45.

[148] [1926] IR 207; (1925) 59 ILTR 141.

accused on the depositions; (4) the prospect of a reasonably speedy trial; (5) the opposition of the Attorney General for the State".

In 1942, in *Attorney General v Duffy*,[149] a bail motion in the High Court gave Hanna J the occasion to add a further criterion to the list he had made in *Purcell's* case, namely:

> "if the evidence is that the accused is likely to interfere with the course of justice, the Court is entitled to consider it as a material ground against bail being granted."

The authority of the criteria laid down by Hanna J in *Purcell's* and *Duffy's* cases was reinforced by the Supreme Court in 1965 in *The People (Attorney General) v Crosbie*[150] in which Ó Dálaigh CJ tersely summoned up the position of the bail applicants as follows:

> "These applicants are charged with non-capital murder and counsel for the Attorney General has given an unqualified "No" in answer to the Court's question: "Is it apprehended that the applicants will abscond if bailed?" Nor, moreover, is it apprehended that there will be any interference with witnesses. In these circumstances it is the Court's duty to admit these untried prisoners to bail."

He also cited, as setting out the basic law of bail "with accuracy and clarity", a passage from Sandes, *Criminal Law and Procedure in the Republic of Ireland*.[151]

> "Bail is based on the principle that an accused person should not be kept unnecessarily in custody, so, whenever it is possible, and can with safety be done, an untried prisoner ought to be released on bail... Bail is not to be withheld merely as a punishment."

The following year the Supreme Court heard the case of *The People (Attorney General) v O'Callaghan*.[152] This was a bail motion which had been refused in the High Court, where Murnaghan J had erected, without referring to *Purcell's* or *Duffy's* cases, a new and more extensive set of "matters which may be, and should be where appropriate, taken into account by the Court in considering whether or not it is likely that the prisoner may attempt to evade justice" (which he still acknowledged as the fundamental test). These matters he enumerated as follows:

> "1. *The nature of the accusation or in other words the seriousness of the charge*. It stands to reason that the more serious the charge, the greater is the likelihood that the prisoner would not appear to answer it.
>
> 2. *The nature of the evidence in support of the charge*. The more cogent the evidence, the greater the likelihood of conviction and consequently the greater the likelihood of the prisoner attempting to evade justice.
>
> 3. *The likely sentence to be imposed on conviction*. The greater the sentence is likely to be, the greater the likelihood of the prisoner trying to avoid it. The prisoner's previous record has a bearing on the probable sentence and consequently must be before this Court.

[149] [1942] IR 529.
[150] [1966] IR 426.
[151] Second edition, London, 1951.
[152] [1966] IR 501; (1968) 102 ILTR 45.

4. *The likelihood of the commission of further offences while on bail.* In this connection, a prisoner facing a heavy sentence has little to lose if he commits further offences. A prisoner may consider that he has to go to prison in any event and in an effort to get money to support his family may commit further offences.

5. *The possibility of the disposal of illegally acquired property.* Stolen property may be stored or cached away.

6. *The possibility of interference with prospective witnesses and jurors.*

7. *The prisoner's failure to answer to bail on a previous occasion.*

8. *The fact that the prisoner was caught red-handed.*

9. *The objection of the Attorney General or of the police authorities.*

10. *The substance and reliability of the bailsmen offered.* (This is primarily a matter for the District Justice.)

11. *The possibility of a speedy trial.*"

He added that:

> "In certain cases the likelihood of personal danger to the prisoner - from the hands of persons injured or incensed by the crime - may in itself be a ground for refusing bail."

Criteria for refusing bail made more stringent

In the Supreme Court on appeal, Walsh J recognised the propriety (though with certain important reservations) of considering the matters which Murnaghan J had numbered 1, 2, 3, 5, 6, 7 and 8; but virtually tore up, with the agreement of Budd J, the rest of the scheme. He said:

> "Ground number 4 of the learned Judge, that is to say, the likelihood of the commission of further offences while on bail, is a matter which is in my view quite inadmissible. This is a form of preventative justice which has no place in our legal system and is quite alien to the true purposes of bail...
>
> In this country it would be quite contrary to the concept of personal liberty enshrined in the Constitution that any person should be punished in respect of any matter upon which he has not been convicted or that in any circumstances he should be deprived of his liberty upon only the belief that he will commit offences if left at liberty, save in the most extraordinary circumstances carefully spelled out by the Oireachtas and then only to secure the preservation of public peace and order or the public safety and the preservation of the State in a time of national emergency or in some situation akin to that."

On this point Ó Dálaigh CJ had been equally explicit:

> "[I take the submission for the Attorney General] to mean that he should be detained in custody because, if granted bail, it is feared he may commit other offences.

The reasoning underlying this submission is, in my opinion, a denial of the whole basis of our system of law. It transcends respect for the requirement that a man shall be considered innocent until he is found guilty and seeks to punish him in respect of offences neither completed nor attempted. I say "punish", for deprivation of liberty must be considered a punishment unless it can be required to ensure that an accused person will stand his trial when called upon."

Walsh J went on to deal with Mr. Justice Murnaghan's ground number 9:

"Naturally a court must pay attention to the objections of the Attorney General, or other prosecuting authority, or the police authorities, when considering an application for bail. The fact that any of these authorities objects is not of itself a ground for refusing bail, and indeed to do so for that reason only would be, as Mr. Justice Hanna pointed out in *The State v Purcell*, to violate the constitutional guarantees of personal liberty."

On Mr. Justice Murnaghan's ground number 11, he said:

"The possibility of a speedy trial is relevant to the extent that if there is no prospect of a speedy trial a court may very well allow bail where it might not otherwise have allowed it. It cannot be too strongly emphasised, however, that the prospect of a speedy trial is not a ground for refusing bail where it ought otherwise to be granted."

Without rejecting what Murnaghan J had said about the substance of bailsmen (ground number 10), he qualified it very heavily, referring to the common law principle (in England enshrined in the Bill of Rights in 1688) that the amount of bail must not be so high as to be, in the particular economic circumstances of the accused person and his friends, effectively unprocurable.[153] He also adverted to Mr. Justice Murnaghan's closing suggestion that bail might be refused in order to protect the accused:

"This proposition is quite unsustainable. If an accused wants protective custody he need not ask for bail or accept it. A bail motion cannot be used as a vehicle to import into the law the concept of protective custody for an unwilling recipient. An accused person on bail is entitled to as much protection from the law as may be required."[154]

Finally, he adverted to a submission evidently make by counsel for the Attorney General:

"In conclusion I wish to state that I completely reject for being without foundation in law, history or reason the submission made to this Court that bail is a privilege only."

The practical result of *O'Callaghan's* case was to increase sharply the proportion of accused persons granted bail. This has been alleged to have had effects serious enough to lead to an amendment of the Constitution (so as to incorporate a less liberal set of bail criteria) being officially considered.[155] In *Ryan v The Director of Public Prosecutions,*[156] nonetheless, an attempt to persuade the Supreme Court to overrule *O'Callaghan* was

[153] See also the decision of the European Court of Human Rights in *Neumeister v Austria*, Series A, No.8 (1979) 1 EHRR 91.

[154] Though in *In re Dolan*, High Court, 5 November 1973, bail was refused where the court accepted, as a matter of probability, that the accused would not stand trial, not of his own volition, but because he would be prevented by violence or threats of violence.

[155] See 300 *Dáil Debates* 132.

[156] [1989] IR 399.

firmly rebuffed. The respondent had argued that a discretion existed at common law to refuse bail on the ground that the applicant was likely to commit criminal offences before his trial. He also contended that such a discretion arose from the court's constitutional duty to protect the right to life, bodily integrity and property. In the leading judgment, Finlay CJ held that the existence of the alleged common law discretion was not supported by any authorities to which the Court had been referred but rather was negatived by them.[157]

> "What is, however, clear from these decisions [on bail cited by the respondent] is, as has been emphasised in both of the judgments in *The People (Attorney General) v O'Callaghan*... that the established reasons for the refusal of bail all come within the broad category of preventing the evasion of justice, either by the accused absconding; by the accused interfering with witnesses; or by the accused destroying, concealing or otherwise interfering with physical evidence. Quite apart from the constitutional objection to any form of preventive detention and to an invasion of the presumption of innocence which is set out in the judgments in *O'Callaghan* which I have quoted and with which I fully agree, if the discretion vested in the courts in relation to granting bail were to be exercised in an attempt to prevent the apprehended commission of a crime, it would, in my view, constitute an abuse of a power, namely, the exercise of it for a purpose which was outside its scope."

He then considered the constitutional dimension to the problem, in the process setting out a series of difficult issues which would arise if *O'Callaghan* was to be overruled:

> "An intention to commit a crime, even of the most serious type, is not in our criminal law a crime itself unless it is furthered by overt acts of preparation or converted by an agreement with another into a conspiracy. The courts cannot create offences or crimes, though the Oireachtas may. Are they, however, to be permitted to detain a person because he is suspected of an intention, which even if proved in a full criminal trial, could not lead to his punishment? If such a power did exist in the courts, why should its exercise be confined to cases where the suspect is an applicant for bail? Why should the courts' prevention of the apprehended harm cease in the event of the determination without a sentence of imprisonment of the original charge, which charge may in its character and seriousness bear no resemblance at all to the feared offence? How can such an intention be proved, and by what standard of proof must it be established? Could there be any grounds on which an accused person suspected of such an intention would be afforded less comprehensive notice of the evidence to be offered against him of the grounds for such suspicion and less opportunity to prepare and be represented to contest such allegations than he is afforded in relation to the presenting of a criminal charge against him? Would every application for bail accordingly, in which this ground was advanced as the substantial ground of opposition, take on the nature and necessary requisites of a criminal trial? These queries not only indicate practical problems but more importantly highlight the nature of the jurisdiction which it is sought to invoke without legislation.
>
> The criminalising of mere intention has been usually a badge of an oppressive or unjust legal system. The proper methods of preventing crime are the long-established combination of police surveillance, speedy trial and deterrent sentences."

[157] In his concurring opinion, McCarthy J held that such a discretion would offend against a fundamental principle of the common law - the presumption of innocence.

Two more recent *ex tempore* decisions of the Supreme Court continue to reflect this reluctance to restrict the availability of bail. In *The People (Director of Public Prosecutions) v Doherty*[158] where the prosecutor sought to have the accused, who had previously been granted bail, remanded in custody on the ground that he was likely to abscond, Finlay CJ, with whom O'Flaherty and Egan JJ agreed, held that a statement of opinion by a Garda based entirely on information whose source was not revealed, could not outweigh uncontested evidence of an actual and factual compliance by the applicant over a period with the bail conditions which had been imposed on him. In *The Director of Public Prosecutions v Brophy*[159] the Court held that the evidence did not establish a sufficient link between the applicant and a threat made to a witness to justify a refusal of bail. Any possibility that he might abscond to the U.S.A. - he had a visa to enter that country - could be dealt with by his giving up his passport to the Garda authorities.

(iv) Deprivation of liberty as a punishment: imprisonment etc. as punishment

Deprivation of liberty by way of punishment imposed by a court on conviction of an offence takes in theory two forms: imprisonment (or, in the case of juveniles, "detention" in a special institution[160]) and penal servitude. The latter expression has a purely historical explanation; as Finlay J put it in *The State (Jones) v O'Donovan*,[161] "the sentence of penal servitude is the creation of statute and is a direct substitution for the sentence of transportation". The attachment of penal servitude to a crime marks it, however, as serious, as the shortest term of penal servitude that can be imposed is three years; and a verbal imputation of criminal conduct in another is a slander actionable without proof of special damage only if the crime imputed is punishable with penal servitude, not mere imprisonment. Imprisonment imposed by virtue of statute, on the other hand, is limited to two years at most (though if imprisonment is allowed as a punishment at common law, there is no upper limit to its term).

"Penal servitude" as special category now obsolete

The practical difference - in terms of the prison regime - between imprisonment and penal servitude is now non-existent. In the *Application of Woods*[162] Ó Dálaigh CJ pointed out that the Rules for the Government of Prisons, 1947, contain "no special or exceptional provisions for prisoners serving sentences of penal servitude"; in rebutting an argument of the applicant's, he said:

> "The Constitution contains no provision which could be considered as rendering a sentence of penal servitude unconstitutional...A sentence of penal servitude in our law, it may be pointed out, has nothing to do with the "servitude" referred to in Article 4 of the United Nations' Universal Declaration of Human Rights. A sentence of penal servitude is no more and no less than a sentence of imprisonment. The word "servitude" in Article 4 means the condition of being a slave or serf; slavery and serfdom are in another world entirely."

A sentence of imprisonment may however be made more rigorous by the addition of "hard labour",[163] though only where the statute concerned specifically so provides.

[158] 26 February 1993.
[159] 2 April 1993.
[160] St. Patrick's Institution: Criminal Justice Act 1960, s 13.
[161] [1973] IR 329.
[162] [1970] IR 154.
[163] This is obsolete as a special category of punishment.

Irregularities in the imposition or enforcement of sentences of deprivation of liberty are not infrequently made the grounds for *habeas corpus* proceedings and are best exemplified in that context. Some special principles affirmed in regard to such sentences by the courts in recent years may however be noticed here.

It was held in *The State (Woods) v Governor of Mountjoy Prison*[164] that no one could be required to serve a continuous period of imprisonment with hard labour of more than two years, whether composed of sentences in respect of separate convictions or not. In *The State (Jones) v O'Donovan*[165] it was held that a sentence of three years' penal servitude, to commence on the expiry of a prior and separate sentence of six months' imprisonment, was in order; though in *The People (Attorney General) v Poyning*[166] it was held that a sentence of penal servitude should not be expressed to commence any earlier than the date of the conviction. In *The State (O.) v O'Brien*[167] a sentence of (juvenile's) detention "until the pleasure of the Government be made known" was an incorrect adoption of s 103 of the Children Act 1908; the power to determine the length of any sentence being vested exclusively in the courts. The Children Act 1908 also featured in *J.G. and D. McD. v The Governor of Mountjoy Prison*[168] in which Blayney J held that s 102(3) - which authorises the imprisonment of a young offender in an adult prison where the court certifies either that the young person is of so unruly a character that he cannot be kept in a place of detention for young offenders or that he is of so depraved a character that he is not a fit person to be detained in such place - did not infringe the rights of such an offender under Article 40.3. According to the judge, s 102(3) was a perfectly fair provision as it protected the other young persons in the place of detention against anyone who was of so depraved a character as to be not fit to be detained there. Moreover the person to whom the sub-section was applied had the protection that an order for his imprisonment in an adult prison could not be made unless the court issued an appropriate certificate under the sub-section. In *Black v The Governor of Cork Prison*[169] Carney J held that pre-trial detention does not necessarily have to be taken into account by a District Judge when imposing sentence under the Criminal Justice Act 1984, though he did agree that, whenever possible, regard should be had to such detention and he cautioned counsel and solicitors to ensure that it is brought to the judge's attention. Finally it is worth noting that a sentence of imprisonment may be imposed *in absentia*[170] and that the judicial power to imprison includes the power to suspend the sentence in whole or in part.[171]

Temporary release

Where a prisoner is granted "full temporary release" under s 2 of the Criminal Justice Act 1960, the sentence of imprisonment may be re-activated after its original currency has expired where the prisoner is in breach of the conditions of the release. In this situation, however, the prisoner may rely on the guarantee of fair procedures. Thus in *Cunningham v Governor of Mountjoy Prison*[172] excessive delay in re-activating the

164 [1962] IR 248.
165 [1973] IR 329.
166 [1972] IR 402.
167 [1973] IR 50.
168 [1991] 1 IR 373.
169 High Court, 1 February 1993.
170 See *The People (D.P.P.) v Kelly* [1982] ILRM 1; *D.P.P. v Gill* [1980] IR 253; *Lawlor v Hogan* [1993] ILRM 606; and *Rock v The Governor of St. Patrick's Institution*, Supreme Court, 22 March 1993.
171 *The People (D.P.P.) v Aylmer*, Supreme Court, 18 December 1986.
172 [1987] ILRM 33.
173 [1984] IR 458; [1985] ILRM 141.

order meant that the procedures adopted were unfair, and so the order to re-activate was quashed. Similarly in *The State (Murphy) v Kielt*[173] a failure to give the prisoner an opportunity to refute allegations that he had breached a condition of his release invalidated the decision to revoke the temporary release order.

Following on this last decision, it would appear that a new policy evolved of granting temporary release for short periods so that prison governors would no longer have to decide whether to terminate an existing temporary release - which decision attracts the rules of constitutional justice - but rather would have the task of deciding whether to grant a fresh release. The constitutionality of this practice was upheld by Murphy J in *Ryan v The Governor of Limerick Prison*[174] on the ground that "the temporary release is a privilege or concession to which a person in custody has no right and indeed it has never been argued...that he should be heard in relation to any consideration given to the exercise of such a concession in his favour." That the doctrine of legitimate expectation might, however, operate to give a prisoner a right to be heard in relation to the granting of temporary release is clear from *Sherlock v The Governor of Mountjoy Prison.*[175] Here the applicant had been granted temporary release on at least 15 occasions over a twelve year period, giving rise, according to Johnston J, to a legitimate expectation that he would get a renewal of his temporary release and, if that was not done, that he would be given an explanation as to why it was not being done and an opportunity to be heard in that regard.

Suspension of constitutional rights

In *The State (McDonagh) v Frawley*[176] the Supreme Court indicated, *per* O'Higgins CJ, that while a convicted prisoner is held pursuant to a lawful warrant, many of his normal constitutional rights are abrogated or suspended as the prisoner must "accept prison discipline and accommodate himself to the reasonable organisation of prison life as laid down in the prison regulations."[177] This was subsequently confirmed in *Murray v Ireland,*[178] in which the plaintiffs, a husband and wife who were both serving sentences of penal servitude for life, sought a declaration that would oblige the prison authorities to provide facilities to enable them to exercise, within the confines of prison, the right to beget children. Recognising that the State may delimit the exercise of constitutionally protected rights, Costello J in the High Court[179] considered the effect of the State's legal power to deprive the plaintiffs of their constitutional right to liberty:

> "Prisoners have liberty to exercise certain constitutionally protected rights (and enjoy other negative rights such as the right not to be tortured) not because they are in some way superior in a scale of values to the right to liberty...Those rights which may be exercised by a prisoner are those (a) which do not depend on the continuance of his personal liberty (so a prisoner cannot exercise his constitutional right to earn a livelihood) or (b) which are compatible with the reasonable requirements of the place in which he is imprisoned or... do not impose unreasonable demands on it."

[174] [1988] IR 198.
[175] [1991] 1 IR 451.
[176] [1978] IR 131.
[177] See also *The State (Fagan) v The Governor of Mountjoy Prison*, High Court, 6 March 1978, where McMahon J said, "The prisoner retains his right of access to the courts and he can complain of any interference with his constitutional rights *which is not necessary in order to give effect to the sentence of the court in the institution in which it must be served.*" (Emphasis added.)
[178] [1991] ILRM 465.
[179] [1985] IR 532; [1985] ILRM 542.
[180] Applying these principles in *Kearney v Minister for Justice* [1986] IR 116; [1987] ILRM 52, the same

In the instant case, he concluded that the reasonable requirements of the prison service would not permit the exercise by all married prisoners of their right to beget children.[180] This analysis was subsequently endorsed by the Supreme Court where Finlay CJ, having referred to marital rights protected by the Constitution, said:

> "[I]t is possible to say that only a right of communication, and that without privacy, and a right by communication to take some part in the education of children of the marriage would ordinarily survive a sentence of imprisonment as a convicted prisoner."

Detention may also lawfully affect the constitutional rights of persons other than the prisoner. In *The State (Gallagher) v Governor of Portlaoise Prison*[181] Lynch J held that the fact that the Rules for the Government of Prisons, 1947, adversely affected the rights of the prosecutor's family to associate with him did not render the Rules unconstitutional, as this was clearly envisaged by the Constitution and in particular by Article 38.

(v) Loss of liberty in the course of the administration of civil justice: imprisonment for refusal to pay debt

Imprisonment for debt exists only in cases where a wilful refusal, not inability, to pay may be presumed.[182] The Enforcement of Court Orders Act 1926, ss 15-20, as amended by s 6 of the Enforcement of Court Orders Act 1940, contains a procedure whereby a debtor against whom judgment has been given, and who has no goods that could be taken in execution, may be "examined" by a District Judge as to his means, and, if the Judge is not satisfied of his inability to pay, he may make an instalment order against him. Then:

> "where a debtor is liable, by virtue of an instalment order, to pay a debt and costs either in one payment or by instalments and such debtor fails to make such payment or fails to pay any one or more of such instalments accruing due while such order is in force at the time or times appointed in that behalf by such order, the creditor may, at any time while such order is in force or within twelve months after it has ceased to be in force, apply to a Justice of the District Court for the arrest and imprisonment of such debtor."[183]

The maximum term of this imprisonment is three months; and the Judge is not to order such arrest and imprisonment if the debtor satisfies the court that "his failure to pay was due neither to his wilful refusal nor to his culpable neglect".[184] Section 8 of the 1940 Act

judge held that the restrictions on the plaintiff's right to communicate imposed by r 63 of the Prison Rules, 1947, which requires that letters to and from prisoners be read by prison staff, were not unconstitutional as they were justifiable in terms of prison security. On the prisoner's right to communicate, see the *ex tempore* judgments of the Supreme Court in *Hutchinson v Minister for Justice*, 16 October 1992, and *Holland v Minister for Justice*, 9 July 1993, cited above, p. 827, Fn. 75.

[181] [1987] ILRM 45.

[182] The Fourth Protocol to the European Convention on Human Rights and Fundamental Freedoms guarantees, in its Article 1, freedom from imprisonment merely on the ground of inability to fulfil a contractual obligation. It has been suggested that the word "merely" implies that where a debtor has acted in a fraudulent or malicious way, Article 1 will not bar his detention, even where it has been established that he is unable to pay the debt - see van Dijk and van Hoof, *Theory and Practice of the European Convention on Human Rights* (1990), pp.488-9.

[183] Whether a District Judge generally has jurisdiction to re-issue a warrant for the arrest and imprisonment of a debtor for the purpose of rendering effective the original order was expressly left undecided by Blayney J in *Credit Finance Bank Ltd. v Healy*, High Court, 29 January 1987.

[184] It follows that an application for the committal of a debtor must be made on notice to the debtor - see *Berryman v The Governor of Loughan House*, High Court, 16 November 1992.

[185] Members of the Permanent Defence Force or reservists on permanent service are exempted from these

as amended by s 29 of the Family Law (Maintenance of Spouses and Children) Act 1976 and s 28 of the Judicial Separation and Family Law Reform Act 1989, provides a similar procedure in the case of defaulters on payments ordered pursuant to ss 8 and 9 of the 1976 Act and ss 13 and 14 of the 1989 Act; and s 19 of the Land Act 1939, assimilates to judgments under s 15 of the 1926 Act a "warrant issued by the Land Commission under s 28 of the Land Act 1933".[185] By s 9 of the 1940 Act the Minister for Justice may "at any time and for any reason which appears to him sufficient" direct the release of a person who is "in prison in pursuance of an order of a court made on account of the failure of such person to pay a sum of money", either forthwith "or after payment of a specified part of the said sum of money", but must first (unless this is impracticable) consult the judge by whom the order was made. In *The State (Ring) v Governor of Mountjoy Prison*[186] an imprisoned defaulter sought *habeas corpus* unsuccessfully on the ground of having made a part payment subsequent to his committal, which payment however his creditor appropriated to instalments falling due subsequent to the committal.

(vi) Loss of liberty in the course of fiscal administration: (formerly) imprisonment for default in paying tax

A series of enactments (culminating in the consolidating s 490 of the Income Tax Act 1967) provided for the execution of a judgment for the recovery of taxes and duties, and appurtenant fines and forfeitures, by way of levy on the debtor's goods in the first instance; failing satisfaction, the Garda Síochána on the certificate of the Sheriff or County Registrar was directed to:

> "take and convey the debtor to the nearest prison and there deliver him to the Governor of such prison there to remain and be kept by such Governor until satisfaction be made...or until the expiration of the period of six months, whichever shall be the shorter."

A few months later this provision was repealed by s 25 of the Finance Act 1967.

An even more drastic provision, whereby not even the judgment of a court was needed to precede the imprisonment of a revenue debtor, was contained in s 483(1) of the Income Tax Act 1967 (re-enacting s 165 of the Income Tax Act 1918):

> "If a person neglects or refuses to pay tax charged upon him by virtue of this Act within ten clear days after demand as aforesaid, and no sufficient distress can be found whereby the same may be levied, the Special Commissioners may, by warrant under their hands and seals, commit him to prison, there to be kept without bail until payment be made of that sum or security given to their satisfaction for payment thereof, together with such further sum, as the Commissioners shall adjudge to be reasonable, for the costs and expenses of apprehending and conveying him to prison; and every such person shall be detained and kept in prison according to the tenor and effect of the warrant."

The following sub-section empowered the Minister for Finance or the Revenue Commissioners to have the defaulter released. In the course of the proceedings of the Standing Joint Committee on Consolidation Bills, doubts were expressed as to the con-

processes by s 107 of the Defence Act 1954. (The powers and duties of the Land Commission were subsequently vested in the Minister for Food and Agriculture by the Irish Land Commission (Dissolution) Act 1992.)

186 (1971) 105 ILTR 113.

187 Money Bills are excluded from the Article 26 procedure. As a purely consolidating measure this Bill would

stitutionality of this provision, but as a Consolidation Bill cannot omit anything of an Act which it is proposed to embrace, the section in question had to stand. On its passing both Houses and being presented to the President for signature, the President convened the Council of State to consider an Article 26 reference (the Bill had not been certified as a Money Bill).[187] The Government however thereupon introduced the short Income Tax (Amendment) Bill, 1967, which came into force as an Act simultaneously with the main Bill, and provided that:

> "If the Bill referred to in the Preamble becomes law as the Income Tax Act 1967, sections 480(2)(3)[188] and 483 of the Act shall immediately stand repealed."

(vii) Imprisonment for contempt of court

For contempt of court as behaviour prejudicial to the position of the courts, see above, pp. 390-396; for contempt of court as an offence which may be dealt with summarily, though by the imposition of a definite, not an indefinite sentence, see above, pp.667-668; for contempt of court as a concept necessarily limiting freedom of expression, see below, pp. 933-937.

A person may be deprived of liberty by order of a court in consequence of contempt in two ways: by a sentence of imprisonment for a definite period in cases of "criminal" contempt,[189] or by an order of indefinite committal in cases of "civil" (or "procedural") contempt.[190] This distinction, so far as concerns the contrast between a definite and an indefinite period of imprisonment, is based on the differing objectives of the court in each type of case, and was explained by Finlay P. in *The State (Commins) v McRann*,[191] in which an applicant for *habeas corpus* had disobeyed an order of the Circuit Court restraining him from interfering with another person in her use and enjoyment of certain lands. On being committed for contempt, he argued that the Court should have imposed a fixed term, rather than an indefinite period, of imprisonment. Finlay P said:

> "The major distinction which has been established over a long period and by a long series of authority between criminal and civil contempt of court appears to be that criminal contempt of court brings into play the right of the court to protect its own dignity, independence and processes, and that accordingly in such cases, where the court does impose sentences of imprisonment, its intention is primarily punitive. Furthermore, in such cases of criminal contempt the court moves of its own volition or may do so at any time. In civil contempt, on the other hand, the court only moves at the instance of the party whose rights are being infringed and who has, in the first instance, obtained from the court the order which he now seeks to have enforced. The purpose of the imposition of imprisonment in such cases is clearly primarily coercive, and for that reason it must of necessity be in the form of an indefinite imprisonment, which may be terminated either at any time when the court, upon application on the part of the person imprisoned, is satisfied that he is prepared to abide by its order and that the coercion has, in fact, worked, or at any time when the party seeking to enforce his order shall for any reason waive his rights and agree or consent to the release of the imprisoned party."

not have fallen within the definition of Money Bill in Article 22.1.1.
[188] These sub-sections dealt with distraint on goods.
[189] See above, pp. 390-395.
[190] See above, p. 395.
[191] [1977] IR 78.
[192] [1973] IR 223.

The judge cited, in support, words of Ó Dálaigh CJ in *Keegan v de Búrca*:[192]

> "Civil contempt...is not punitive in its object but coercive in its purpose of compelling the party committed to comply with the order of the court, and the period of committal would be until such time as the order is compiled with or until it is waived by the party for whose benefit the order was made."

These considerations, he found, were "a complete answer to the challenge made to the validity of the [committal] order... based on its indeterminate nature".

In *The State (H.) v Daly*[193] the Supreme Court approved the *Commins'* case, holding that a civil contempt did not require to be found by a trial jury.[194]

An order for committal is discretionary, Lavery J said in *Gore Booth v Gore Booth*.[195] In *Ross Co. v Swan*[196] O'Hanlon J said that the jurisdiction to imprison indefinitely for civil contempt was "exercised sparingly", and cited with approval an English case in which Denning MR had said it should not be exercised where it was unlikely to produce the desired result or where there was some reasonable alternative course open; in the instance before him, the contempt had taken the form of a "sit-in" and appeared to come within the range of the Prohibition of Forcible Entry and Occupation Act 1971; and as proceedings under that Act could effectually deal with the situation, he declined to order the defendants' committal.

An application to discharge from prison a person indefinitely committed for contempt must be accompanied by evidence that he has purged,[197] or is ready to purge, his contempt.

Inferior courts can commit to prison only for a contempt "in the face of the court", and in respect of other contempts must rely on the High Court for protection.[198]

"POLICE" MEASURES CURTAILING LIBERTY IN THE INTEREST OF STATE SECURITY, PUBLIC ORDER OR HEALTH, ETC.

(i) Extended arrest

A person arrested on a criminal charge must normally be brought at the first opportunity before a District Judge for the purpose of determining the further course of proceedings against him. However, a series of statutes since 1922 have contained provisions for an extended arrest, not accompanied by a charge, and going beyond the minimum period necessary for bringing the arrested person before a District Judge (or Peace Commissioner), but also not amounting to indefinite detention or internment. The pur-

[193] [1977] IR 90.

[194] In this case the question of mental illness and the possible negativing of *mens rea* in contempt was considered.

[195] (1962) 96 ILTR 32, 40.

[196] [1981] ILRM 416.

[197] I.e., is willing to apologise for and desist from the course of conduct which amounted to contempt.

[198] See *Attorney General v Connolly* [1947] IR 213; (1947) 81 ILTR 92; *Attorney General v O'Ryan and Boyd* [1946] IR 70; (1945) 79 ILTR 158. Though in *Kelly v Brady, The Irish Times*, 20 May 1993, Lardner J in the High Court took the view that an application to have an editor and journalist attached for contempt in connection with an article written about a man awaiting sentencing by the Circuit Court should be dealt with in the lower court. (The defendants were subsequently fined £5,000 by the Circuit Court judge - *The Irish Times*, 25 May 1993.)

[199] Hanna J said in *Attorney General v McBride* [1928] IR 451; (1928) 62 ILTR 145, that the Judge "must be

pose of this kind of extended, though not unlimited arrest has been to permit a more thorough investigation of an offence or of a suspicion entertained against the person arrested. It will be seen that while the earlier judges did not seem much disturbed about this sort of measure, in recent times the State has appeared to admit its inconsistency with the constitutional guarantee of personal liberty.

1923

The Public Safety (Emergency Powers) (No. 2) Act 1923, provided by s 2(1) that:

> "It shall be lawful for a responsible officer to arrest and to detain in custody for any period not exceeding one week any person found committing or attempting to commit or whom such officer suspects of having committed any of the offences mentioned in Part II of the Schedule to this Act."

By s 2(3) any such person, if not charged with an offence within the week, had then to be released. Section 16 defined a "responsible officer" as an Army officer not below the rank of commandant or a police officer not below that of superintendent.

1924 and 1926

These provisions were in substance repeated (though with a wider definition of "responsible officer") in the Public Safety (Powers of Arrest and Detention) Temporary Act 1924, which replaced the 1923 Act and itself expired in early 1925; and again in the Public Safety (Emergency Powers) Act 1926, which remained in force until 1939.

1927

Following the murder of the Minister for Justice, Kevin O'Higgins, in July 1927, the Public Safety Act 1927, was passed. This provided for a much tougher form of extended arrest, though with at least some minimal interposition of a judicial function.[199] Section 16 provided that a District Justice might order the detention of a person for seven days where a superintendent of the Garda Síochána was of opinion that there was:

> "ground for suspecting such person of being or having been engaged or concerned in the commission of [a scheduled offence]...and that his detention [was] necessary or desirable for the proper investigation of such offence, or any other like offence."

By sub-s 3 an Executive Minister could extend this period of seven days by a further two months; but sub-s 4 contained the same kind of safeguard as the Acts of 1923, 1924 and 1926: if the prisoner had not been charged by the expiry of three months from his arrest, he was to be released.

In *Attorney General v McBride*[200] the constitutionality of this provision was unsuccessfully attacked (it was argued, in vain, that s 3 of the Act which provided that if the Act were in contravention of the Constitution it should *pro tanto* operate as an amendment thereof, did not in fact validly amend it.[201]) Hanna J said it was "not disputed that s 16 is an alteration or amendment of Article 6 of the Constitution", i.e. its inconsistency with Article 6 was admitted; but he held the section to have operated as a valid amendment of the Article. The whole Act was repealed at the end of 1928.

judicially satisfied by evidence as to the facts which must be established under the section".

[200] [1928] IR 451; (1928) 62 ILTR 145.

[201] See below, under Article 51.

1931

In 1931 the Constitution (Amendment No. 17) Act imported Article 2A into the Constitution; by s 14(1) of this Article a mild form of extended arrest was provided:

> A person who has been apprehended and removed to a station of the Garda Síochána under this Article may, on the direction of a member of the Garda Síochána not below the rank of inspector given within thirty-six hours after such removal, be detained in custody...until whichever of the following events first happens, that is to say:
>
> (a) such person is informed in writing by a member of the Garda Síochána that he will be brought before the Constitution (Special Powers) Tribunal;[202] or
>
> (b) the expiration of seventy-two hours from the said apprehension of such person.

By sub-s 3 any reference in the whole Action to "detention on suspicion" under the Article was to be construed as meaning the detention in custody provided for by this section.

In *In re O'Duffy*[203] O'Byrne J said that Article 2A "undoubtedly enlarges the methods whereby a person may be lawfully detained". However, in construing the extended-arrest power of s 14, he held that it operated only when the original arrest had been lawful, which was not so in the case before him.[204] The whole of Article 2A disappeared on the replacement of the 1922 Constitution with that of 1937.

1939

The Offences Against the State Act 1939, provided by s 30(1) that a member of the Garda Síochána may arrest a person "whom he suspects of having committed or being about to commit or being or having been concerned in the commission" of one of the offences envisaged by the sub-section, or of having certain documents or information; and, by sub-s 3:

> Whenever a person is arrested under this section, he may be removed to and detained in custody in the Garda Síochána station, a prison, or some other convenient place for a period of twenty-four hours from the time of his arrest and may, if an officer of the Garda Síochána not below the rank of chief superintendent so directs,[205] be so detained for a further period of twenty-four hours.[206]

By sub-s 4 a person neither released nor charged before the expiry of this cumulative period of forty-eight hours must be released on its expiry.

[202] See above, pp. 640-642.

[203] [1934] IR 550; (1935) 69 ILTR 82. There is an article on this case (in which it is called after another applicant, Sullivan) in 68 ILTSJ 1.

[204] He held that the arrests had not been for any offence mentioned in s 13, and that the provisions of s 13(3) (as to informing a superior officer of the arrests) had not been complied with.

[205] In *The People (D.P.P.) v Kehoe* [1985] IR 444, the Court of Criminal Appeal said that the record of this direction should simply state that the arrested person was to be detained for a further 24 hour period commencing at the expiry of the original 24 hour period of detention, and should not state the exact time of the commencement and expiry of the additional period of detention, lest some *bona fide* error should occur.

[206] An essential proof of the validity of an extension of the original period of detention is that the authorising officer entertained the same suspicions as the arresting officer. Thus in *The People (D.P.P.) v Byrne* [1987] IR 363; [1989] ILRM 613 where the Chief Superintendent in question had died before the trial of the person detained, the further detention was held to be unlawful because of failure to establish this essential proof.

[207] [1993] 2 IR 305. See *Humpheys*, (1992) 14 DULJ (n.s.) 105.

Section 30: constitutionality

The constitutionality of s 30 was challenged in *The People (Director of Public Prosecutions) v Quilligan (No.3)*[207] on three different grounds. First, it was contended that the difference in treatment meted out to persons arrested on suspicion of having committed a scheduled offence, who are subject to the rigours of s 30, by comparison with that of persons arrested in connection with non-scheduled offences, who are entitled to be brought before a court as soon as practicable,[208] was an invidious discrimination contrary to Article 40.1. This argument was dismissed, somewhat tersely, by the Supreme Court who said, *per* Finlay CJ:

> "The mere fact that a law discriminates as between one group or category of persons and another does not, of itself, render it constitutionally invalid. What is necessary to establish such invalidity is the existence of invidious discrimination, and the court is satisfied that that has not been established with regard to section 30 in this case."

This conclusion is, with respect, less than convincing, for it would certainly appear that s 30 can work some arbitrary distinctions. It is scarcely possible to defend a situation in which a person who omits to renew an annual licence for a sporting gun could be liable to interrogation over a period of 48 hours without being charged, while a murderer would not necessarily be subject to the same statutory regime.[209]

The defendants also submitted that the personal right to liberty was insufficiently respected and defended by a law which permitted detention for twenty-four or forty-eight hours. In support of this contention, they pointed out that in *Re Article 26 and the Emergency Powers Bill 1976*[210] the Attorney General had had recourse to Article 28.3 in defending the seven-day detention period provided for by that Bill, inferring that the detention authorised by s 30 would be unconstitutional in the absence of the protection of Article 28.3. However given the difference in detention periods authorised by these two pieces of legislation, the Court did not believe that any such inference could be drawn. As for s 30 itself, the Court noted that a person detained under that section had the following rights - the right to be released if the arresting Garda did not have a *bona fide* suspicion based on reason of one or other of the matters provided for in the section; at the time of arrest, the right to be informed, if he did not already know, of the offence of which he was suspected; the right to legal and medical assistance and of access to the courts; the right to remain silent; the right to the protection of the Judges' Rules in regard to the giving of cautions and the abstention from cross-examination of a prisoner and the right not to be subject to oppressive questioning. Moreover the original period of detention could be extended only where a Chief Superintendent had the necessary *bona fide* suspicion which justified the original arrest and was satisfied that further detention was necessary for the purposes provided for in the section. In view of these protections, the Court concluded that the defendants had failed to establish that s 30 violated their personal right to liberty.

[208] Unless they have been arrested pursuant to s 4 of the Criminal Justice Act 1984, as to which, see below, pp. 860-862.
[209] Note that in *Cox v Ireland* [1992] 2 IR 503, decided a year earlier, the Supreme Court itself had drawn attention to the potentially arbitrary classifications involved in the scheduled offences.
[210] [1977] IR 159; (1977) 111 ILTR 29.
[211] Special Criminal Court, 24 May 1974.

Finally, the defendants argued that the possibility of being interrogated over a period of forty-eight hours infringed their implied right to silence. The Court held that, in view of the rights enjoyed by a person detained under s 30 which it had earlier adumbrated, no invasion of any right to silence occurred, though it did not find it necessary to decide whether or to what extent a right to silence is constitutionally protected.

Section 30: reasons for arrest

In *The People (Attorney General) v McDermott*[211] Finlay J had held that the rule requiring a person to be informed of the reason for his arrest at the time of the arrest was sufficiently observed, in the case of an arrest under this section, if the arresting Garda told his prisoner that the arrest was in virtue of the section.[212] However some doubt was cast on the correctness of *McDermott* by Walsh J in *The People (Director of Public Prosecutions) v Quilligan*[213] in which, citing *The People (Director of Public Prosecutions) v Walsh*,[214] he said that a person arrested under s 30 must be informed of which of the many possible offences he is suspected unless he already has that information.[215] This approach was subsequently followed by the Court of Criminal Appeal in *The People (Director of Public Prosecutions) v Ferris*[216] in which the accused had been arrested on board a ship carrying firearms, ammunition and explosive substances. In that context, informing them that they were being arrested for possession of firearms was sufficient notification of the reason for their arrest. The matter would now appear to be authoritatively settled in favour of Walsh J's view by the Supreme Court decision in *The People (Director of Public Prosecutions) v Quilligan (No.3)*[217] wherein the Court said, *per* Finlay CJ, that a person arrested pursuant to s 30 must be informed, if he does not already know, of the offence of which he is suspected.

Section 30: Garda's bona fide suspicion

For an arrest under s 30 to be valid, the arresting officer must have a *bona fide* suspicion that a scheduled offence has been committed or is about to be committed.[218] Thus in *The State (Trimbole) v The Governor of Mountjoy Prison,*[219] the arrest of the applicant under s 30 ostensibly on the ground that he was in possession of firearms but in reality to ensure that he would be available for extradition, was an abuse of power by the Gardaí which was restrained by the courts through the granting of an order of *habeas corpus*. However the Court of Criminal Appeal has held that it is not necessary for the arresting officer to have formed the suspicion himself - the communication to such officer of the suspicion of a superior officer will be sufficient for this purpose - *The People (Director of Public Prosecutions) v McCaffrey.*[220]

[212] In *The People (Director of Public Prosecutions) v Campbell*, (1983) 2 Frewen 131, the Court of Criminal Appeal noted that the *McDermott* judgment had, since its date (1974), been consistently followed by the Courts, but found it unnecessary to consider whether the case had been wrongly decided.

[213] [1986] IR 495; [1987] ILRM 606.

[214] [1980] IR 294.

[215] See also his *obiter* remarks to the same effect in *The People (D.P.P.) v Byrne* [1987] IR 363; [1989] ILRM 613.

[216] (1986) 3 Frewen 114.

[217] [1993] 2 IR 305.

[218] Moreover, in *The People (D.P.P.) v Quilligan (No.3)* [1993] 2 IR 305, the Supreme Court indicated that the suspicion must be "based on reason", implying that the existence of a *bona fide* suspicion will be determined on an objective, rather than subjective, basis.

[219] [1985] IR 550; [1985] ILRM 65. See also the remarks of Walsh J in *The People (D.P.P.) v Quilligan* [1986] IR 495; [1987] ILRM 606.

[220] [1986] ILRM 687.

[221] [1985] ILT 83.

The courts are generally reluctant to compel an arresting officer to disclose the source of any information which lad him or her to form the requisite suspicion and this is certainly the case where disclosure would expose an informant to the risk of injury or worst - see *The Director of Public Prosecutions v Connolly*;[221] *The People (The Director of Public Prosecutions) v Eccles*.[222] However privilege will not be granted merely because disclosure could, in a general way, be said to be contrary to the public interest - *The Director of Public Prosecutions (Hanley) v Holly*.[223]

Section 30: questioning about non-scheduled offence

A person arrested under s 30 on suspicion of having committed or being about to commit a scheduled offence may be questioned about other offences during the period of detention, provided the Gardaí are genuinely pursuing the scheduled offences and are not using the arrest in respect of the scheduled as a colourable device to enable them to question the accused about a non-scheduled offence.[224] Thus in *The People (Director of Public Prosecutions) v Walsh*,[225] where a woman had been killed during the course of a break-in at her home, the Gardaí arrested the accused on suspicion of having committed a scheduled offence - malicious damage to a pane of glass broken in order to gain entry and to a heavy metal pot which had probably been used to kill the victim - but also questioned him about the killing. The Court of Criminal Appeal, *per* Finlay CJ, held that where the scheduled and non-scheduled offences formed part of the same transaction, the Gardaí were not prohibited from interrogating the accused about both offences, a position subsequently confirmed by the Supreme Court on appeal. In *The People (Director of Public Prosecutions) v Howley*[226] the Supreme Court held that it was not necessary that the predominant or primary motive for the arrest must be to investigate the scheduled offence; all that is required is that the Gardaí must have a genuine desire to pursue the scheduled offence. Referring to the defendant's submission, citing *Walsh* and *Quilligan* in support, that a person arrested under s 30 in connection with a relatively minor scheduled offence could be interrogated about a serious non-scheduled offence only where both offences were inextricably mixed, Walsh J said:

> "[T]he submission made is to misunderstand the decisions. What these decisions were concerned with was whether the Garda Síochána were genuinely pursuing the scheduled offences, even though they were comparatively trivial. The courts concerned were satisfied that the Garda Síochána were genuinely pursuing these offences, and that the genuineness of the pursuit was evidenced by the fact that these offences were inextricably mixed with the murder offences because it was clear in each case that whoever had been guilty of the lesser offences was quite obviously involved in the murder offences.[227] Therefore what the cases established is that when an arrest for a scheduled offence [is] effected under s 30..., not only must the arresting Garda have the necessary reasonable suspicion concerning the

[222] 3 Frewen 46.
[223] [1984] ILRM 149.
[224] See *The State (Bowes) v Fitzpatrick* [1978] ILRM 195.
[225] [1986] IR 722; [1988] ILRM 137. See also *The People (D.P.P.) v Quilligan* [1986] IR 495 and the earlier decision of the Court of Criminal Appeal in *The People (D.P.P.) v Towson* [1978] ILRM 122. See also McCutcheon, "*Arrest, Investigation and Section 30*" (1987) 9 DULJ (n.s.) 46.
[226] [1989] ILRM 629. See *McCutcheon*, (1988) 10 DULJ (n.s.) 158.
[227] For an example of a case where Walsh J, delivering an *ex tempore* judgment on behalf of the Court of Criminal Appeal, held that no such genuine investigation of a scheduled offence existed, see *The People (D.P.P.) v Walsh*, 3 Frewen 260, in which the accused was arrested pursuant to s 30 in connection with the stabbing of two women. The scheduled offence involved was the malicious damage to the clothing of the women caused by the stabbings.
[228] [1986] IR 495; [1987] ILRM 606.

particular offence in question, but that in fact there must be a genuine desire and intent to pursue the investigation of that offence or suspected offence and the arrest must not simply be a colourable device to enable a person to be detained in pursuit of some other alleged offence. The decisions do not provide any basis for asserting that where a person is genuinely arrested for the purpose of investigating a scheduled offence, and when the arrest itself is not otherwise flawed, it must be established that there is a link between the two offences to maintain the lawfulness of the detention if in the course of the detention the detained person is questioned in respect of the other suspected offence whether it be a scheduled offence or not."

Section 30: not confined to "political" offences

In *The People (Director of Public Prosecutions) v Quilligan*[228] the Supreme Court held that s 30 was not limited to political or subversive offences. In the High Court, Barr J had taken the contrary view, invoking the long title to the 1939 Act which refers to, *inter alia*, "conduct calculated to undermine public order and the authority of the State". However a majority of the Supreme Court[229] took the view that the language of s 30 was clear and unambiguous and admitted of no distinction between subversive and "ordinary" offences.

Section 30: miscellaneous

Two other cases on s 30 are *The State (Walsh) v Maguire*[230] (the detention is not interrupted by bringing the prisoner to a District Court, and the section is satisfied if he is charged there though he may already have been charged in the Garda station); and *The People (Director of Public Prosecutions) v Kelly (No.2)*[231] (the reference in the section to "a" Garda station does not exclude detention in a number of successive stations).

1976

In 1976 a more substantial extended arrest - in temporary substitution for, not in addition to, that under s 30 of the Offences against the State Act 1939, which remained in force, but in abeyance - was provided for by the Emergency Powers Act which enjoys the protection of Article 28.3.3 and of Article 34.3.3 as well.[232] By s 2(1) of the Act a member of the Garda Síochána may arrest a person "if he suspects with reasonable cause that that person has committed, is committing or is about to commit" an offence envisaged by the sub-section, or has a document or article or information relating to such an offence. Then, by sub-s 3:

> "Whenever a person is arrested under this section, he may be removed to and kept in custody in a Garda Station, prison, or other convenient place for a period of forty-eight hours from the time of his arrest and may, if a member of the Garda Síochána not below the rank of chief superintendent so directs, be kept in such custody for a further period not exceeding five days."

229 McCarthy J concurred in the result, though he dissented from the majority view that the long title could not modify the clear language of the Act.
230 [1979] IR 372.
231 [1983] IR 1; [1983] ILRM 271.
232 See above, pp. 215, 216, 218.
233 [1977] IR 159; 111 ILTR 29. See Gwynn Morgan, "*The Emergency Powers Bill Reference*" (1978) 13 Ir

By sub-s 4, if neither released nor charged within those seven days, he must be released on their expiry. On the hearing of the reference to the Supreme Court of the Bill for this Act under Article 26[233] the Attorney General asked the Court to decide the case on the basis that s 2 would be repugnant to the Constitution if it were not saved by Article 28.3.3; the Court said:

> "As the matter has not been discussed further, the Court does not find it necessary to express an opinion on the question whether s 2 of the Bill or any part of it would be repugnant if it were not saved by Article 28.3.3."

The Court however added:

> "A statutory provision of this nature which makes such inroads upon the liberty of the person must be strictly construed. Any arrest sought to be justified by the section must be in strict conformity with it. No such arrest may be justified by importing into the section incidents or characteristics of an arrest which are not expressly or by necessary implication authorised by the section."

The Act went out of operation after one year, but its provisions could be reactivated by order of the Government. In *The State (Hoey) v Garvey*[234] Finlay P. held that the Act did not authorise the arrest and detention of a person on a second occasion if the second arrest was grounded upon the same suspicion as had justified the first arrest, even though the police had acquired further information between the dates of the two arrests.

1984

By virtue of s 4 of the Criminal Justice Act 1984, a person suspected of having committed, or having attempted to commit, an offence for which a person of full age and capacity and not previously convicted may be punished by imprisonment for a term of five years or more, may be detained in a Garda station for up to six hours where the member of the Garda Síochána in charge of the station has reasonable grounds for believing that his detention is necessary for the proper investigation of the offence. The period of detention may be extended by a further six hours by direction of an officer of the Garda Síochána not below the rank of superintendent if such officer has reasonable grounds for believing that the further detention is necessary for the proper investigation of the offence.[235]

Once there are no longer reasonable grounds for suspecting that the person has committed an offence to which s 4 applies, he must be released forthwith. On the other hand, where enough evidence has been amassed to support a charge for an offence, the suspect must be charged without delay, unless he is suspected of having committed another offence to which s 4 applies and the Garda in charge of the station has reasonable grounds for believing that continuance of his detention is necessary for the proper investigation of that offence.

Jur (n.s.) 67; (1979) 14 Ir Jur (n.s.) 252.

[234] [1978] IR 1.

[235] Provision is made for suspending interrogation of the suspect where he is being detained between midnight and 8.00 a.m. in order to afford him reasonable time to rest, in which case the period of suspension is excluded in reckoning the period of detention authorised by the Act - s 4(6).

[236] Where a person under the age of seventeen is detained under the section, he must be notified of his right to

Where a person not below the age of seventeen[236] is detained pursuant to s 4, he must be informed without delay of his right to consult a solicitor and to have notification of his detention and place of detention sent to one other person reasonably named by him - s 5. Where the person so requests, the Garda in charge of the station is obliged to notify the solicitor and the named person accordingly as soon as practicable.

Section 6 provides that where a person is detained under s 4, a police officer may demand of him his name and address; search him; photograph him; take his fingerprints; retain for testing anything he has in his possession; or make any test for determining whether he had been in contact with firearms or explosives. By s 10, where a person detained under s 4 is subsequently released without being charged, he cannot be arrested again for the same offence or any other offence of which he ought reasonably to have been suspected at the time of the first arrest, except on the authority of a District Judge.

(ii) Internment: indefinite

Internment, or the indefinite detention without trial of citizens or others[237] on grounds of security, has been possible under several successive enactments since the foundation of the State. The civil war period, in which persons were held in custody by the Army under non-statutory, martial law powers,[238] ended for legal purposes on 31 July 1923, when O'Connor MR. granted writs of *habeas corpus* to two prisoners of the Army on the ground that a state of war no longer existed; three days later[239] the first Irish internment law appeared in the form of the Public Safety (Emergency Powers) (No. 2) Act 1923.

1923

This Act - expressed to be temporary, and with a built-in expiry date of six months after its coming into operation - provided by s 1 that an Executive Minister might order the arrest and detention of any person upon certifying in writing that he was satisfied that there was reasonable ground for suspecting that such person was concerned in the commission of some scheduled offence, or on receiving a report from the military authorities that the person's detention was "a matter of military necessity arising out of the existence of a state of war or armed rebellion, whether local or general", or on certifying in writing that he was satisfied that the public safety was endangered by the person's being allowed to remain at liberty. Section 3 provided for the continuing custody of persons in military custody at the passing of the Act; and s 4 for the establishment of "Appeal Councils" to enquire into detentions at the request of prisoners. Some hundreds of persons were held under this Act.

consult a solicitor and his parent or guardian (or spouse, if he is married) must be informed, as soon as practicable, of his detention, the place of detention and his entitlement to consult a solicitor - s 5(2). If the Garda in charge of the station is unable to communicate with the parent, guardian or spouse, as the case may be, the provisions applicable to persons not below the age of 17 apply.

[237] The internment of aliens (whether combatant or not) was authorised by the Emergency Powers Act 1939, s 2(2)(*k*). Aliens were originally the main target of this provision, as is seen by the parenthesis "(other than natural-born Irish citizens)". This parenthesis was removed by s 2(1) of the Emergency Powers (Amendment) Act 1940, in order to plug the gap in internment legislation left by Gavan Duffy J in his judgment in *The State (Burke) v Lennon* [1940] IR 136; (1940) 74 ILTR 36, 131, pending the passage and clearance of the Offences Against the State (Amendment) Act 1940.

[238] See *R. (Johnstone) v O'Sullivan* [1923] 2 IR 13; (1923) 57 ILTR 17.

[239] See *R. (O'Brien) v Military Governor, North Dublin Union* [1924] 1 IR 32, for the background to this No. 2 Act; the original, in its operative part identical, Act was held ineffectual to justify the applicant's detention because it lacked the recital (required by Article 47) that both Houses had declared it "necessary for the immediate preservation of the public peace, health or safety".

[240] [1924] 2 IR 104; (1924) 58 ILTR 49; [1935] IR 247.

1924

At the end of January 1924, shortly before it was due to expire, some of its provisions were replaced (and in effect continued) by the Public Safety (Powers of Arrest and Detention) Temporary Act 1924. Section 1 provided that:

> "It shall be lawful for an Executive Minister to cause the arrest and, subject to the provisions of this Act to order the detention in custody in any place in Saorstát Éireann of any person in respect of whom such Minister shall certify in writing that he is satisfied that there is reasonable ground for suspecting such person of being or having been engaged or concerned in the commission of any of the offences mentioned in the schedule to this Act."

Section 4 provided for the continuing detention of persons in military custody at the passing of the Act; s 10(2) that the Act was to come into force on 1 February 1924 and remain in force for one year and then expire.

In *R. (O'Connell) v Military Governor of Hare Park Camp*[240] the applicant for *habeas corpus* had been held under s 4 of this Act; an Executive Minister had certified, as the section required, that he was of opinion that "the public safety would be endangered by" the applicant's being set at liberty. It was argued for him that this section was "an attempt to deprive the High Court of its power to order the issue of a writ of *habeas corpus*"; but this argument was rejected, and the reasoning behind a similar rejection in the English case of *R. (Zadig) v Halliday*[241] was approved by the King's Bench Division.[242] The old Court of Appeal affirmed the order of the King's Bench Division, O'Connor MR saying:

> "This is no doubt drastic legislation but its meaning is quite clear...As in *Cooney's* case,[243] the validity of the Act has been challenged but, for the same reasons as were given in the judgments just pronounced [in that case], we must hold that the Act is *intra vires* and binding in this Court."

1926

This Act expired on 31 January 1925 but late in the following year the Public Safety (Emergency Powers) Act 1926, was passed. The new Act was intended to be permanent, though its internment provisions were designed to lie in abeyance unless Part II of the Act which contained them, was brought into force by a specific proclamation of a state of emergency by the Executive Council. That Part empowered a Minister to order the arrest and indefinite[244] detention of any person:

> "in respect of whom such Minister shall certify in writing that he is satisfied that there is reasonable ground for suspecting such person of being or having been engaged or concerned in the commission of any of the offences mentioned in the schedule to this Act."

[241] [1917] AC 260.

[242] See above, pp. 811-812. Moloney CJ emphasised that the Act did not take away the right to *habeas corpus*, but merely provided an extra legal circumstance in which it could be refused.

[243] *R. (Cooney) v Clinton* [1935] IR 245; a report published twelve years late, by way of appendix to *The State (Ryan) v Lennon* [1935] IR 170.

[244] Subject however to what an Appeals Council (provided for by s 6) might recommend.

Section 6 provided for Appeal Councils to review the detention of particular individuals and to make recommendations thereon. The proclamation of emergency, however, on which these provisions depended, was to remain in force for only three months; though it could be repeated or renewed at the discretion of the Executive Council (s 1(2)). In fact no proclamation of an emergency was ever made under this Act though it was in force for nearly thirteen years, so that no internments took place under it either.

1939 and thereafter

It was repealed and replaced (shortly before the outbreak of the second world war, and on the occasion of an I.R.A. bombing campaign in Britain) by the Offences against the State Act 1939. This Act provided, *inter alia*, powers of internment, contained in Part VI. By s 54 that Part might be brought into force:

> "if and whenever and so often as the Government makes and publishes a proclamation declaring that the powers conferred by this Part of this Act are necessary to secure the preservation of public peace and order and that this Part of this Act should come into force immediately."

By s 55(1) and (3) respectively it was provided that:

> "Whenever a Minister of State is satisfied that any particular person is engaged in activities calculated to prejudice the preservation of the peace, order, or security of the State, such Minister may by warrant under his hand order the arrest and detention of such person under this section...
>
> Every person arrested under...this section shall be detained in a prison or other place prescribed in that behalf by regulations...until this Part of this Act ceases to be in force or until he is released under the subsequent provisions of this Part of this Act whichever first happens."

By s 59 provision was made for a Commission to enquire into individual cases of detention, like the Appeal Councils of the earlier Acts. On 22 August 1939 a proclamation in the terms of s 54 was made by the Government, and a number of persons were then taken into custody and held without charge.

One of these, James Burke, was the subject of a *habeas corpus* application brought by his brother and heard by Gavan Duffy J in November: *The State (Burke) v Lennon*.[245] Much of the case turned on the question whether the Minister for Justice (who had signed the warrant ordering Burke's arrest and detention under the Act) was, in effect, purporting to administer justice and whether the Act in purporting to empower him to do so, was unconstitutional for that reason,[246] but Gavan Duffy J, in granting the application, also adverted to the status of Part VI of the Act as an encroachment upon personal liberty:

> "As to personal liberty, it is one of the cardinal principles of the Constitution, proclaimed in the Preamble itself... In my opinion, the saving words in the declaration that "No citizen shall be deprived of his liberty save in accordance with law" cannot be used to validate an enactment conflicting with the constitutional guarantees.[247]

[245] [1940] IR 136; (1940) 74 ILTR 36, 131.

[246] As to this, see above, p. 359.

[247] For the significance of this passage in the history of "higher law", see above, p. 813.

[248] See below, p. 907. A number of persons detained under Part VI of the 1939 Act were then set at liberty.

> The power to intern on suspicion or without trial is fundamentally inconsistent with the rule of law and with the rule of law as expressed in the terms of our Constitution."

The Supreme Court refused to entertain the State's appeal against the granting of *habeas corpus* by Gavan Duffy J,[248] so that in consequence of his judgment the State was obliged to assume that the whole of Part VI of the Act was invalid having regard to the provisions of the Constitution (though the Court, in this earliest phase of judicial review, did not so declare in specific terms).

The Government then introduced, and both Houses of the Oireachtas passed, the Offences Against the State (Amendment) Bill 1940; and, on its being presented to him for signature, the President first referred it to the Supreme Court under Article 26.[249] As it was virtually identical with the disapproved Part VII of the 1939 Act - the main change was that the words "Whenever a Minister...is *satisfied* etc." of the original s 55 were now replaced by "Whenever a Minister is *of opinion* that any particular person is engaged in activities which, *in his opinion*, are prejudicial etc." - the Article 26 procedure here in effect operated as a substitute for an appeal against the *Burke* decision, so far as getting the Supreme Court's view on the constitutionality of internment was concerned.

The Supreme Court upheld the Bill (which the President then signed). In delivering the Court's judgment, Sullivan CJ drew attention to the fact that although several pre-1937 Acts had provided for internment without trial, and the framers of the Constitution must be taken to have realised this, yet the Constitution did not specifically forbid it. He referred to arguments based on the Preamble to the Constitution (which mentioned as one of the State's objectives "the dignity and freedom of the individual") and said:

> "There is nothing in this clause of the Preamble which could be invoked to necessitate the sacrifice of the common good in the interests of the freedom of the individual."

The internment provided for by the Bill the Court considered to be "a precautionary measure taken for the purpose of preserving the public peace and order and the security of the State"; *R. (Zadig) v Halliday*[250] and *O'Connell's* case[251] were cited with approval. The Court's treatment of the phrase "in accordance with law" in Article 40.4 has already been described (above, p. 814).

The Offences Against the State (Amendment) Act 1940, now attracted the protection of Article 34.3.3 and was immune from further challenge on grounds of infringing the Constitution; but it was attacked, in *In re Ó Láighléis*,[252] on the grounds of alleged repugnancy to Articles 5 and 6 of the Convention for the Protection of Human Rights and Fundamental Freedoms, adopted by the Council of Europe in 1950 and ratified by Ireland in 1953. The Supreme Court rejected this argument on the ground that:

[249] *In re Article 26 and the Offences Against the State (Amendment) Bill 1940* [1940] IR 470; (1940) 74 ILTR 61.
[250] [1917] AC 260.
[251] [1924] 2 IR 104; (1924) 58 ILTR 49; [1935] IR 247.
[252] [1960] IR 93; (1961) 95 ILTR 92.
[253] See above, p. 835.

"The Oireachtas has not determined that the Convention...is to be part of the domestic law of the State, and accordingly this Court cannot give effect to the Convention if it be contrary to domestic law or purports to grant rights or impose obligations additional to those of domestic law.

No argument can prevail against the express command of s 6 of Article 29...before judges whose declared duty it is to uphold the Constitution and the laws."

Of the six other grounds relied on by the applicant, one concerned the lawfulness of his arrest.[253] Of the remaining five, the first was that s 3(2) of the Act contemplated the making of a proclamation (that the powers of internment were necessary) only obliquely, and did not expressly confer the power to make such a proclamation. The Court found this submission "wholly unsustainable":

"When a statute provided that certain consequences follow if and when an act is done, power to do that act is given. Many parallels could be quoted. One is the provision of Article 28.3.3...Article 28 does not provide that each House of the Oireachtas may pass the resolution referred to in the Article, but merely enacts that certain consequences shall follow when they do so. No one can doubt that the Houses of the Oireachtas are given power to bring the provisions of the Article into effect by passing the resolutions."

The second ground was that, as the applicant had originally been arrested under s 30 of the 1939 Act (which provided for an extended arrest of a maximum two days), he should have been released on the expiry of the two days, not held further under a new and different power, viz. that of detention under the warrant of a Minister under the 1940 Act. The Court held that the Minister's warrant, which became effective before the expiry of the two days, was an immediately effective authority for his detention, taking over, as it were, from the s 30 extended arrest, and continuing after the maximum period of extended arrest had expired.

The third ground was that the power of detention contained in s 4 of the 1940 Act related only to persons arrested under that section, not to persons arrested under s 30 of the 1939 Act. The Court said the power to arrest and detain in s 4 was:

"to be read distributively. There is a power to arrest and a power to detain. Where a person is already in custody under a conviction or other authority an arrest - save in a formal sense - may not be possible. But the power to detain is not therefore done away with. On the contrary, the power to detain is the substantive power; the power to arrest is ancillary."

A further ground was that the applicant's affidavit had so challenged the basis for the Minister's "opinion" (under s 4) that the Minister should have made an affidavit to prove that he did in fact hold the opinion, set out in the warrant, that the applicant was engaged in activities which in the Minister's opinion were prejudicial to the security of the State; an enquiry into the truth of the respondent's return was called for under s 3 of the Habeas Corpus Act 1816. The Court said this provision was "enabling, not mandatory"; the Court might indeed have enquired as to whether this Ministerial opinion existed. But as the applicant's counsel had specifically admitted that he did not question the Minister's *bona fides*, such an enquiry would have no point. Counsel's "real purpose", the Court said, appeared to be "to question the validity of the Minister's opinion" - a different thing altogether. The Court recalled that:

[254] [1942] AC 206.

"In the course of its consideration of the Offences Against the State (Amendment) Bill, 1940, before it became law, this Court had occasion to consider the meaning of s 4. Chief Justice Sullivan, delivering the judgment of the Court, said: "The only essential preliminary to the exercise by the Minister of the powers contained in s 4 is that he should have formed opinions on the matters specifically mentioned in the section. The validity of such opinions cannot be questioned in any Court." [Counsel for the applicant] wishes to do precisely what in 1940 the Court said cannot be done."

The Court went on to distinguish the position in which it found itself - faced with a power depending on mere "opinion" - from that faced by the House of Lords, in *Liversidge v Anderson,*[254] in the internment power of Regulation 18B of the Defence (General) Regulations 1939, which depended on a Minister's having "reasonable cause to believe" a person to be of hostile associations:

"Lord Atkin regarded "reasonable cause" for a belief as an objective fact, examinable and triable like any other fact. The contrast he drew was between "reasonable cause" for a belief and "mere belief" that a fact exists. His difference with his brethren was as to the construction of Regulation 18B. The Act of 1940 does not require a Minister of State to have "reasonable cause" for his belief: he is authorised to act on his opinion. "Mere belief" is enough. Lord Atkin clearly regarded "mere belief" as a subjective state which was not examinable or triable by a Court."[255]

The last argument for the applicant was that, the Commission set up under s 8 of the 1940 Act having failed to discharge its functions properly in his regard, he was deprived of his only safeguard against indeterminate imprisonment and so should be set free. The Court rejected this argument too, saying that the section contemplated an enquiry which was entirely of an administrative character - its "only duty [was] to enquire into the grounds of detention and to report thereon to the Government" - and the applicant's submissions had proceeded on the wrong basis that the Commission was a court.

Emergency provisions

Almost contemporary with the enactment of the Offences Against the State Act 1939, was the Emergency Powers Act 1939, which in its long title recited the words necessary to secure for it the protection of Article 28.3.3. This Act contained a very large range of powers designed to deal with the exigencies of wartime,[256] including a power of the Government conferred by s 2(2), by means of an emergency order, to:

"(*k*) authorise and provide for the detention of persons (other than natural-born Irish citizens) where such detention is, in the opinion of a Minister, necessary or expedient in the interests of public safety or the preservation of the State;

(*l*) authorise the arrest without warrant of persons (other than natural-born Irish citizens) whose detention had been ordered or directed by a Minister."

Section 2 of the Emergency Powers (Amendment) Act 1940, amended these provisions by deleting the qualifications in favour of natural-born Irish citizens. (This was a reaction to the judgment of Gavan Duffy J in *The State (Burke) v Lennon*, which, by invali-

[255] It may be noted that the Court's view as to the non-reviewability of a Minister's opinion was reversed in *The State (Lynch) v Cooney* [1982] IR 337: see above, p.417.

[256] It was signed by the President after passing both Houses on 3 September 1939, the day Britain and France declared war on Germany.

[257] [1960] IR 93; (1961) 95 ILTR 92.

dating Part VI of the Offences Against the State Act 1939, had left the Government without any internment powers except in respect of aliens. Once the Offences against the State (Amendment) Bill had been cleared by the Supreme Court, the need to use the Emergency Powers Act in this connection disappeared, and it was used thereafter only for its original purpose, the internment of alien combatants - mainly airmen forced to land and ship-wrecked sailors - and spies.) The Emergency Powers Act 1939, finally expired in 1946.

Reason for arrest

In *In re Ó Láighléis*[257] the Supreme Court said that the law in regard to giving a person being arrested the reason for his arrest applied as much to an arrest for the purpose of internment under the Offences Against the State (Amendment) Act 1940, as to an arrest for the purpose of bringing criminal proceedings.[258]

A warrant for arrest for internment (as for any other purpose) must "show jurisdiction on its face" by reciting the statutory authority under which it is made: *The State (Hughes) v Lennon; The State (Burke) v Lennon.*[259]

(iii) Detention of persons a probable source of infection: infectious diseases

Under s 38(1) of the Health Act 1947:

> Where a chief medical officer is of opinion, either consequent on his own inspection of a person in the area for which such medical officer acts or consequent upon information furnished to him by a registered medical practitioner who has inspected such person, that such person is a probable source of infection with an infectious disease[260] and that his isolation is necessary as a safeguard against the spread of infection, and that such person cannot be effectively isolated in his home, such medical officer may order in writing the detention and isolation of such person in a specified hospital or other place until such medical officer gives a certificate...that such person is no longer a probable source of infection.[261]

On such a person's being detained, he must by sub-s 2 be given a copy of the medical officer's order (or, as the case may be, it must be shown to the person's parent or other person in charge of him) together with a statement in writing of his right under that sub-section to appeal against his detention to the Minister for Health. The section contains further detailed regulations as to correct behaviour towards the person so detained.

(iv) Detention under the Mental Treatment Act 1945

Persons of unsound mind

Section 165(1) of the Mental Treatment Act 1945,[262] provides that:

[258] See above, p. 835.

[259] [1935] IR 128; and [1940] IR 136, (1940) 74 ILTR 36, 131, respectively.

[260] By s 29 the Minister is empowered by regulation to specify the diseases which are infectious diseases. Note also s 48 which empowers a medical officer of health to prohibit the attendance of a verminous child at school.

[261] *Cp.* Article 5(1)(e) of the European Convention on Human Rights which also permits the detention of persons suffering from, *inter alia*, infectious diseases.

[262] The greater part of the Mental Treatment Act 1945 has existed on a legislative version of "Death Row" since 1981, as s 50 of the Health (Mental Services) Act 1981 provided for the repeal of all but Part VIII of the 1945 Act. However a ministerial order is required in order to bring the 1981 Act into effect and no such order has ever been made. Nor it is likely that the 1981 Act will ever be activated as a *Green Paper on Mental Health* (pl.8918) was published in 1992 in anticipation of fresh legislation in this area.

[263] In *X v UK*, Series A, No.46, (1981) 4 EHRR 188, the European Court of Human Rights held that a person

> Where a member of the Garda Síochána is of opinion that it is necessary that a person believed to be of unsound mind should, for the public safety or the safety of the person himself, be placed forthwith under care and control, he may take the person into custody and remove him to a Garda Síochána station.[263]

Sub-s 2 authorises such a person to be then detained in a mental hospital on the application of the member of the Garda Síochána who took him into custody. The constitutionality of this procedure was attacked in *In re Philip Clarke*,[264] but was upheld; in the Supreme Court O'Byrne J described the provision as being legislation of a "paternal character". He said:

> "The section cannot, in our opinion, be construed as an attack upon the personal rights of the citizen. On the contrary, it seems to us to be designed for the protection of the citizen and for the promotion of the common good."[265]

Provisions more usually invoked for the detention of mentally ill persons are contained elsewhere in Parts XIV-XVI of this Act whereby a "reception order" can be applied for, by or at the request of a husband or wife or relative[266] (or, with special conditions, by another person); these orders have the effect of authorising the confinement of mentally ill persons in a district mental hospital.[267]

By s 260 of the Act no civil proceedings may be brought:

> "in respect of an act purporting to have been done in pursuance of this Act...unless the High Court is satisfied that there are substantial grounds for contending that the [proposed defendant] acted in bad faith or without reasonable care."

This inhibition on access to the courts was in issue in *O'Dowd v North-Western Health Board*,[268] when the Supreme Court divided two to one against permitting the plaintiff to proceed with an action for false imprisonment.[269] The dissenting judge, Henchy J, said:

detained because of mental illness was entitled, under Article 5(4) of the Convention, to automatic periodic review of a judicial character of the legality of the ongoing detention. To the extent to which Irish law fails to provide for such review, it would appear to be contrary to the Convention.

[264] [1950] IR 235; (1951) 85 ILTR 119.

[265] A similar phrase was used by McCarthy J in *Application of Gallagher* [1991] 1 IR 31; [1991] ILRM 339, when upholding s 2(3) of the Trial of Lunatics Act 1883 which authorises the detention of accused persons found to be "guilty but insane" - according to the judge, this provided for "the carrying out of the executive's role in caring for society and the protection of the common good."

[266] The relative's consent to the detention of a mentally ill person may not necessarily protect the State from an action for unlawful detention - *cp.* the decision of the European Court of Human Rights in *Nielsen v Denmark*, Series A, No.144, (1989) 11 EHRR 175.

[267] Persons in remand custody may, if certified insane, be transferred to a mental hospital by virtue of s 13 of the Lunatic Asylums (Ireland) Act 1875, as extended by the Criminal Justice Act 1960, s 8. Persons certified while undergoing a sentence of imprisonment are so transferred by virtue of the Central Criminal Lunatic Asylum (Ireland) Act 1845, as adapted (see *Index to the Statutes*). The verdict of "guilty but insane" returned in accordance with s 2(2) of the Trial of Lunatics Act 1883 is a verdict of acquittal but s 2(3) obliges the court to order the detention of the accused until the executive decides the question of his continued detention or release - *Application of Gallagher* [1991] 1 IR 31; [1991] ILRM 339.

[268] [1983] ILRM 186.

[269] See also *Lyons v Southern Health Board, The Irish Times,* 7 April 1987 where McKenzie J refused an application for leave to take proceedings against the defendants arising out of the detention of the plaintiffs under the Mental Treatment Act 1945, on the ground that there was no evidence that the defendants had acted in bad faith.

[270] [1990] 2 IR 566; [1991] ILRM 757. See also *O'Reilly v Moroney and Mid-Western Health Board*, Supreme

> "If what happened in this case had happened in *Clarke's* case, *habeas corpus* would not have been refused [this was a reference to failure to conform with procedures required by the Act]... It was the implementation of [the personal rights guarantees of Article 40.3] that caused the Legislature to hedge around the making of a chargeable patient reception order with the [safeguards in the Act. Some of these are designed] in particular to ensure that, not even for a short period, will a citizen be unnecessarily deprived of his liberty and condemned to the tragic and degrading status of a compulsory inmate of a mental hospital, with the dire social consequences that such a fate is likely to have on his future and on that of his relations."

In *Murphy v Greene*[270] the Supreme Court held that, as s 260 imposed a limitation on the individual's constitutional right of access to the courts, it must be strictly construed. Nonetheless an intending plaintiff is required to prove, as a matter of probability, the existence of facts establishing substantial grounds for contending that the proposed defendant acted in bad faith or without reasonable care, though it is not necessary for the court to conclude whether, as a matter of probability, he is likely to succeed in the proposed action.

A case in which *habeas corpus* was granted because a reception order under the Act had not been signed (as required) by the "person in charge" of the hospital is *In re J.*[271]

The Mental Treatment (Detention in Approved Institutions) Act 1961, was a short indemnifying Act in respect of detentions which were irregular at the date of the Act's passing.

(v) Detention under the Children Act 1908

Pursuant to s 20 of the Children Act 1908,[272] a child or young person in respect of whom a specified offence[273] has been, or there is reason to believe has been, committed, may be taken to a place of safety by a member of the Garda Síochána or any person authorised by a District Judge and there detained until s/he can be brought before a court of summary jurisdiction. Section 24 provides that a District Judge, who has heard information on oath that such an offence has been or is being committed in respect of the child or young person or that such child or young person has been or is being assaulted, ill-treated or neglected in such a way as to cause unnecessary suffering or to be injurious to the health of the child, may authorise a member of the Garda Síochána to search for the child and, if the information proves correct, to detain him or her in a place of safety until s/he can be brought before a court of summary jurisdiction. This section also empowers a District Judge to issue a warrant authorising a member of the Garda Síochána to remove the child or young person, with or without a search, to a place of safety, there to be detained until s/he is brought before a court of summary jurisdiction.

Court, 16 November 1993.

[271] (1954) 88 ILTR 120.

[272] Parts III and IV of the Child Care Act 1991 update and improve the procedures for removing children at risk to a place of safety but to date these have not yet been brought into operation. See pp. 1048-1050.

[273] These are any offence under Part II of the 1908 Act or under ss 5, 27, 42, 43, 52, 55 or 56 of the Offences Against the Person Act 1861 or under the Criminal Law Amendment Act 1885 or the Dangerous Performance Acts 1879 and 1897 or any other offence involving bodily injury to a child or young person.

[274] For instances of such lawful detention, see *M.F. v Superintendent, Ballymun Garda Station* [1991] 1 IR

Such lawful detention, which is clearly intended for the benefit and protection of the child involved, can last only until such time as the child can be brought before the court for the purpose of having an order, providing for his and her care and detention made pursuant to s 20(3) of the Act.[274]

(vi) Internment of aliens in wartime

Ireland signed in 1949 the Geneva Convention on Prisoners of War and on the Protection of Civilians in Time of War, and the Prisoners of War and Enemy Aliens Act 1956, regulates, in the light of these Conventions, the internment of prisoners of war and of enemy aliens. (Previously the Emergency Powers Act 1939, had by s 2(2)(*k*) and (*l*), authorised the arrest and detention of persons "other than natural-born Irish citizens" where a Minister thought this necessary or expedient in the interests of public safety or the preservation of the State, thus obviously envisaging the internment of aliens and citizens of alien origin; but s 2 of the Emergency Powers (Amendment) Act 1940, deleted from these paragraphs the qualifications in favour of natural-born Irish citizens, thus making their effect general. The Emergency Powers Act 1939, expired in 1946.)

(vii) Protective custody

The law does not recognise any right to deprive persons of their liberty for their own protection, except in the transient circumstances of an imminent breach of the peace or in the special circumstances envisaged by the Children Act 1908. In *Connors v Pearson*[275] a boy had been kept in police custody for two months as the police thought it necessary to safeguard a potential witness against apprehended violence or intimidation. The old King's Bench Division and Court of Appeal successively held this to be unjustifiable. Molony CJ said:

> "Police officers...may be justified in temporarily restraining the action of an individual in order to avert a menace to the public peace; but this is a power which is confined to cases where it is manifest that a breach of the peace is imminent."[276]

Gibson J added:

> "Imprisonment of a possible witness *quia timet* to protect him without his consent from unknown malefactors or intimidation is not within any common law principle of justification, and must be authorised, if at all, by statute."

In more recent times D'Arcy J has ruled to the same effect. In a bail application of *Teelin*[277] the police opposed bail "in the interests of the accused man's own safety", saying "there was a distinct probability what he would be interfered with" by relatives of his wife (with whose murder he was charged). D'Arcy J said "the notion of custodial security was unknown to the law...this man was entitled to bail. The law must be upheld and it was the duty of the Gardaí to do so. He had grave doubts if he was [even] entitled to place any restriction on where this man should reside when on bail."

189; [1990] ILRM 767; *Herron v District Judge of Mallow District Court*, High Court, 12 June 1992.

[275] [1921] 2 IR 51.

[276] See below, pp 966-967.

[277] See *The Irish Times*, 4 November 1978. See also the passage from the judgment of Walsh J (contradicting the view of Murnaghan J in the High Court) in *The People (Attorney General) v O'Callaghan*, [1966] IR 501; (1968) 102 ILTR 45, cited above, pp. 844-845. *Cp.* the High Court decision in *In re Dolan*, 5 November 1973, where bail was refused when the court accepted, as a matter of probability, that the accused would be prevented from standing trial by violence or threats of violence.

[278] [1965] IR 294. See above, pp. 777-778.

MISCELLANEOUS MATTERS CONCERNING PERSONAL LIBERTY

(i) Limitation of movement into, within or out of the state

Mr. Justice Kenny said *obiter* in *Ryan v Attorney General*[278] that the "right to free movement within the State" was one of the unexpressed personal rights latent in Article 40.3 and following from the "Christian and democratic nature of the State"; and since that time it has again been asserted, by McWilliam J, in *King v Attorney General.*[279] The right to travel out of the State was also asserted by Finlay P. in *The State (M.) v Attorney General*;[280] and reiterated by O'Hanlon J in *Lennon v Ganly*.[281] Following on *Attorney General v X*,[282] in which a majority of the Supreme Court had indicated that the right to travel could be restrained in the interests of protecting the right to life of the unborn, Article 40.3.3 was amended to provide that it shall not limit freedom to travel between this State and another state.[283] Note also the Fourth Protocol to the European Convention on Human Rights which provides by Article 2, though with predictable qualifications, that:

(1) Everyone lawfully within the territory of a State shall, within that territory, have the right to liberty of movement and freedom to choose his residence.

(2) Everyone shall be free to leave any country, including his own.

Section 2(2)(*j*) of the Emergency Powers Act 1939, empowered the Government by Emergency Order to authorise and provide for the prohibition, restriction, or control of the entry or departure of persons into or out of the State and the movements of persons within the State. The Act expired in 1946.

Limitation of the movement of persons (as well as of animals) is envisaged by s 15(*b*) of the Diseases of Animals Act 1966, under which the Minister for Agriculture may make orders prohibiting or regulating movement into, within or out of an infected place or area.

Aliens

Aliens are subject to a special regime. The Aliens Act 1935, by s 5(1), empowers the Minister for Justice to make an order prohibiting any class of aliens from entering or from leaving the State, or requiring them or forbidding them to "reside or remain in particular districts or places" in the State. The Act is given effect to by the very comprehensive Aliens Order, 1946, and the Aliens (Amendment) Order 1962. Article 5(4) of the 1946 Order[284] (inserted by Article 3 of the Aliens (Amendment) Order 1975 empowers an immigration officer to order the detention of an alien who has been refused permission to land until such time as he is removed from the State and the maximum time per-

[279] [1981] IR 233.
[280] [1979] IR 73.
[281] [1981] ILRM 84.
[282] [1992] 1 IR 1; [1992] ILRM 401.
[283] See above, pp. 809-810.
[284] Article 5, as amended, deals with the position of aliens coming from a place outside the State "other than Great Britain or Northern Ireland." In *Fakih v Minister for Justice* [1993] 2 IR 406; [1993] ILRM 274, O'Hanlon J held that this applied to aliens who had been detained for some days by immigration officials in the UK before being sent back to this country (from whence they had tried to gain admission to England).
[285] [1993] ILRM 64.

missible for such detention is two months. Accordingly in *Ji Yoa Lau v Minister for Justice*[285] Hamilton P held that the detention of an alien until such time as his application for refugee status could be determined was unlawful and he directed his release.[286]

"Asylum"

The number of aliens with no automatic right to enter or remain in the country but who are seeking political asylum has increased significantly in recent years. There is no "right of asylum" in international law or in Irish law in the sense of an obligation on the State to admit any alien; however in 1985 a written commitment was given to the United Nations High Commissioner for Refugees, on behalf of the Minister for Justice, that applications for asylum would be considered in accordance with a procedure proposed by the Commissioner and both the High and Supreme Courts have recently held that the Minister is bound by this undertaking.[287] That procedure envisages, *inter alia*, that an alien will not be refused entry or removed until he has been given an opportunity to present his case fully, his application has been properly examined and a decision reached on it and that the application will be examined in accordance with the United Nations Convention on the Status of Refugees 1951, as amended by the Protocol on the Status of Refugees of 1967.[288]

(ii) Deportation

Deportations of citizens were carried out during the Civil War (1922-23) by order of the military courts operating under the Provisional Government and thereafter.[289] Subsequently, the Public Safety Act 1927, provided by s 13 that the Minister for Justice might make an "expulsion order" to:

> "require any person who in the opinion of the said Minister has been associated with any of the activities of an unlawful association whether as a member thereof or otherwise or has been associated with or concerned in any [scheduled offence] or any offence of a treasonable or seditious nature or any murder or other crime of violence and whose continued presence in Saorstát Éireann is in the opinion of the said Minister prejudicial to the public safety or the maintenance of law and order to depart from Saorstát Éireann within a specified time after the date of such order and not to return to Saorstát Éireann so long as such order remains in force."

[286] In an earlier case, *Nantharatnam v Minister for Justice, The Irish Times,* 4 October 1983, the same judge had directed the release of a Tamil student who had been refused permission to land on the ground that he was not in possession of a valid passport - some pages had been torn out of the passport. According to Hamilton J, the removal of the pages did not affect the validity of the passport.

[287] See *Fakih v Minister for Justice* [1993] 2 IR 406; [1993] ILRM 274, where O'Hanlon J considered that aliens had a legitimate expectation that the Minister would process applications for refugee status in accordance with his undertaking, and *Gutrani v Governor of the Training Unit, Mountjoy Prison* [1993] 1 IR 427, where McCarthy J came to the same conclusion, though for a different reason, saying, "It does not appear to me to depend upon any principle of legitimate or reasonable expectation; it is, simply, the procedure which the Minister has undertaken to enforce." *Gutrani* was followed in *Kajli v Minister for Justice*, High Court, 21 August 1992, in which Barr J held that the Minister had failed to consider adequately the applicants' request for asylum, contrary to para 4 of the Departmental letter - the Minister made his decision without waiting for final submissions from the applicants - and accordingly quashed his decision refusing asylum. Moreover, by not giving any reasons for his decision, the Minister additionally failed to comply with para 10 of the letter.

[288] The full text of the letter, which details ten different points in relation to the processing of applications for refugee status, is set out in the judgments in both the *Fakih* and *Gutrani* cases. Also relevant in this context is Article 5(4) of the European Convention on Human Rights which entitles, *inter alia*, persons detained pending deportation to have the legality of their detention judicially reviewed.

[289] See the *General Regulations for the Trial of Civilians by Military Courts* (2 October 1922, i.e. before the coming into force of the 1922 Constitution and so resting on the authority of the Provisional Government); vol. XIX of the bound S.R.O., p. 515.

[290] Moreover Article 3 of Protocol No.4 to the European Convention on Human Rights prohibits the expulsion

Disobedience of the expulsion order was made an offence punishable by six months' imprisonment with hard labour. The Act itself, however, was repealed in late 1928; and no other statutory provision for the deportation of citizens has since been made.[290]

Deportations of aliens are possible under the Aliens Act 1935,[291] which empowers the Minister for Justice, by s 5(1)(*e*), to:

> "make provision for the exclusion or the deportation and exclusion of such aliens[292] from [the State] and provide for and authorise the making by the Minister of orders for that purpose."[293]

Section 5(5) provides that an alien "ordinarily resident" in the State for five years or more, and employed, must be given three months' notice of deportation; in *The State (Goertz) v Minister for Justice*[294] the Supreme Court held that an alien who had entered the country by parachute in 1940, been arrested and interned (under s 2(2)(*k*) of the Emergency Powers Act 1939) in 1941, released in 1946, and ordered to be deported in 1947 under s 5(1)(*e*) of the Aliens Act 1935, was not "ordinarily resident" in the State for five years so as to be entitled to three months' notice. Maguire CJ said:

> "In my view the provision that an alien who is ordinarily resident here for five years and who fulfils the other requirements of the section, should be given a breathing space before being compelled to leave, is designed to help an alien who has come to the country legally and is taking part in the normal life of the community, as a businessman or in the practice of a profession, and upon whom, accordingly, it would be an undue hardship to be forced, summarily, to uproot himself and break business or professional ties. It cannot be said in this case that the appellant was resident here in that sense."[295]

The power of the Minister to deport aliens with family members who are Irish citizens was recently considered by the Supreme Court in *Fajujonu v Minister for Justice*[296] where the plaintiffs sought, *inter alia*, an order restraining the defendant from prohibiting them continuing to reside in the State or from taking any further action against them under the 1935 Act and a declaration that they were entitled to reside within the State. The family consisted of the two parents, both of whom were illegal aliens, and three

of nationals.

[291] See Costello, "*The Irish Deportation Power*" (1990) 12 DULJ (n.s.) 81. A special regime for nationals of other E.C. countries is contained in the European Communities (Aliens) Regulations, 1972 (S.I. 333 of 1972). In *Minister for Justice v Wang Zhu Jie* [1993] 1 IR 426; [1991] ILRM 823, Costello J in the High Court remarked that the 1935 Act gave considerable powers to the authorities over aliens, "powers which perhaps might not be thought to be desirable or necessary or legal against citizens" but that "in relation to aliens, the situation ... is very different". In the instant case, the judge held that one such power was a power to arrest without a warrant. This issue did not feature in the subsequent Supreme Court appeal which was confined to the question of that Court's jurisdiction to hear an appeal from Costello J's decision.

[292] I.e. as are specified - whether by reference to their nationality, or membership of some other kind of class, or individually - by the Minister in an Aliens Order. The Act defines "alien" as one who is not a citizen of Saorstát Éireann (now, citizen of Ireland).

[293] The constitutionality of this provision has been questioned on the basis that it amounts to an unrestricted delegation of legislative power to the executive, contrary to Article 15.2 as interpreted in *Cityview Press Ltd. v An Chomhairle Oiliúna* [1980] IR 381. See *Costello, loc. cit.*, p.90-1.

[294] [1948] IR 45; (1948) 82 ILTR 34, 111.

[295] The applicant in this case subsequently committed suicide in the Aliens Office at Dublin Castle just before he was due to be deported.

[296] [1990] 2 IR 151; [1990] ILRM 234. See also the decision of the European Court of Human Rights in *Berrehab v The Netherlands*, Series A, No.138, (1989) 11 EHRR 322, in which the Court held that the deportation of the Moroccan father of a young child was an unjustified infringement of the right to respect for private and family life, guaranteed by Article 8 of the Convention.

[297] The other members of the Court - Griffin, Hederman and McCarthy JJ - concurred with both judgments.

children, all of whom were Irish citizens, having been born in the State. In the Supreme Court it was contended on behalf of the third-named plaintiff, the eldest child, that among her constitutional rights under Articles 40, 41 and 42 was a right to remain resident within the State and to have preserved the family of which she was a member as a unit of society within the State and to be parented by her parents within the State. Finlay CJ held that while the parents, as aliens, had no constitutional right to remain in Ireland, the children, as citizens, had a constitutional right to the company, care and parentage of their parents within a family unit. Moreover the parents were entitled to assert a choice of residence on behalf of their infant children in the interest of those children. Accordingly the Minister could order the deportation of the family under the 1935 Act only if, after due and proper consideration, he was satisfied that deportation was justified in the interests of the common good and by the need to protect the State and its society. A slightly different emphasis may be found in the judgment of Walsh J[297] who reached the same conclusion as the Chief Justice, though grounded on the constitutional rights of the family as a unit, rather than specifically on the rights of the children. This approach could potentially protect the alien married to an Irish citizen, whereas Finlay CJ's line of reasoning does not necessarily go that far. Insofar as both approaches may accept, by implication, that the child citizen of alien parents could be deported where the interests of the common good and the need to protect the State and society so requires, they would appear to be incorrect. In the first place, there is no statutory power to deport citizens. Second, deportation of nationals is prohibited by Article 3 of Protocol No.4 to the European Convention on Human Rights.

The decision in *Fajujonu* was considerably less deferential towards the State's interest in controlling immigration than a number of earlier High Court cases[298] and may signal a more rigorous judicial scrutiny of decisions made under the immigration code.[299] The legality of some aspects of that code has recently been called into question. As we have already noted,[300] it has been suggested that s 5 of the 1935 Act may infringe Article 15.2 by providing for an unrestricted delegation of legislative power to the executive. In addition, doubts have been raised about the delegation of the power to issue work permits and visas to Departments of State other than the Department of Justice; and about Article 3 of the Aliens Order 1975 which has been interpreted[301] as conferring on immigration officers an "overriding discretion" to admit or decline entry outside the strict terms of the Order.[302]

(iii) Extradition: the position up to 1965[303]

Until 1965 the extradition of persons wanted for trial in other countries was governed, in the case of Britain, by s 29 of the Petty Sessions (Ireland) Act 1851; in the case of what formerly were called British Dominions, by s 3 of the Fugitive Offenders Act 1881; and in the case of other countries, by the Extradition Acts 1870-1906.

298 See *Pok Sum Shun v Ireland* [1986] ILRM 593; *Osheku v Ireland* [1986] IR 733; [1987] ILRM 330.
299 See discussion by Costello, *loc. cit.*, pp.82-3.
300 See p. 873, Fn 293.
301 In *The State (Kugan) v O'Rourke* [1985] IR 658.
302 See *Costello, loc.cit.* pp.83-86, 90-1.
303 See generally, Forde, *Extradition Law in Ireland* (Dublin, 1987) and Hogan and Walker, *Political Violence and the Law in Ireland* (Manchester, 1989). There is a burgeoning body of periodical literature on this topic - see O'Higgins, "*The Irish Extradition Act 1965*" (1966) 15 ICLQ 369; McCall, Smith and Magee, "*The Anglo-Irish Law Enforcement Report in a Historical and Political Context*" [1975] Crim LR 205; Cantrall, "*The Political Offence Exception in international extradition: a comparison of the United States, Great Britain and the Republic of Ireland*" (1977) 60 Marq L Rev 777; Connelly, "*Non-extradition for Political Offenders: A Matter of Legal Obligation or Simply a Policy Choice?*" (1982) 17 Ir Jur (n.s.) 59; McGrath, "*Extradition: Another Irish Problem*" (1983) 34 NILQ 292; Connolly, "*Ireland and the Political Offence*

To Britain

The procedure for extradition to Britain contained in s 29 of the Petty Sessions (Ireland) Act 1851 (based on a system of "backing", or endorsement, by Irish police officers of warrants issued in Britain) was declared by the High Court in *The State (Dowling) v Brennan and Kingston*[304] to have been continued in force in Saorstát Éireann by virtue of Article 73 of the Constitution. Hanna J said:

> "I am satisfied that s 29 of the Petty Sessions (Ireland) Act 1851, was, and is, in force in the Saorstát under Article 73 as one of the laws taken over. In my opinion it does not in any way conflict with the Constitution nor is it inconsistent with any of the provision of the Constitution."

The applicant for *habeas corpus* in the case was, however, set at liberty on another ground. He was then rearrested under a second warrant, and this time the High Court refused an order of *habeas corpus*; though Gavan Duffy J dissented from his two colleagues, holding that s 29 had not survived 1922:

> "The emergence of an Irish State, bound to protect its citizens, has created a radically different position, a position incompatible with s 29 of the Act of 1851, as it stands."

On appeal to the Supreme Court, the order of the High Court was affirmed, Fitzgibbon J said:

> "If it would be, as I do not think can be disputed, within the competence of the Dáil to enact s 29 today with the adaptations make in 1923,[305] I can see no ground for holding that this could not be done by Dáil Éireann sitting as a Constituent Assembly, and if they could, I think they did it by Article 73."

Meredith J said:

> "I am of opinion that s 29 is not repugnant to the Constitution, and that to hold otherwise would mean that Saorstát Éireann, despite its status, has no power to pass any extradition law whatever, and no matter what the safeguards. If that were the position then it seems to me that our Constitution would put us outside the pale so far as international relations and the comity of nations are concerned."

In 1950 the continuance of s 29 under the 1937 Constitution was established in *The State (Duggan) v Tapley*[306] - being accepted in the High Court by Gavan Duffy J, who in *Dowling's* case had denied its survival under the Constitution of 1922; his reasoning was that *Dowling's* case had called "public attention" to s 29 in the very months (May and June 1937) in which the draft Constitution was under debate inside and outside the Dáil, and that Article 29 of the new Constitution (dealing with the international relations) would therefore have been "couched in language clearly abolishing the established procedure of s 29 of the Act of 1851, if that abolition was intended". The judgment of the High Court was upheld on appeal to the Supreme Court; Maguire CJ said the section "was taken over by the Constitution as part of the law in force".[307]

Exception to Extradition" (1985) 12 JL. & Soc. 152; Campbell, "*Extradition to Northern Ireland: Prospects and Problems*" (1989) 52 MLR 585; Gilbert, "*The Irish Interpretation of the Political Offence Exception*" (1992) 41 ICLQ 66; Delany and Hogan, "*Anglo-Irish Extradition Viewed from an Irish Perspective*" (1993) Public Law 93.

[304] [1937] IR 483; (1937) 71 ILTR 90, 131.

[305] He presumably meant the Adaptation of Enactments Act 1922.

[306] [1952] IR 62; (1951) 85 ILTR 22.

[307] I.e. under Article 73 of the old, and Article 50 of the new Constitution.

[308] [1957] IR 281; (1956) 90 ILTR 143.

The 1851 procedure was in issue in *The State (Rossi and Blythe) v Bell*[308] - in which Murnaghan J held that a British warrant must meet the requirements of a valid Irish warrant, in order to make lawful an arrest in Ireland - and *The State (Griffin) v Bell*[309] - in which the Supreme Court held that, in cases where the courts could not take judicial notice of the laws of another country, a police authority endorsing a warrant must have evidence that the act charged against the person sought constituted an offence within the country where the warrant originated. In neither case, however, was the constitutionality of the 1851 procedure impugned; and in *The State (Hully) v Hynes*[310] the High Court held itself bound by the Supreme Court's decision in *Duggan's* case to hold s 29 consistent with the Constitution.

In 1964, however, a case arrived in the Supreme Court which moved the Court to reverse the earlier authorities; it did so in reliance partly on the view that *stare decisis* was a policy, not a rigidly binding rule, and partly on the basis that it was itself a "new" Court (since the Courts (Establishment and Constitution) Act 1961) and thus not strictly bound by the decisions of the "old" Supreme Court. In *The State (Quinn) v Ryan*[311] the applicant had been arrested on an English warrant endorsed in Dublin, released by *habeas corpus* because of a flaw in the warrant, at once rearrested on a second, flawless warrant, and rushed over the Border into Northern Ireland before he had an opportunity of considering his position or consulting his legal advisers on it. Nothing that had been done was clearly forbidden by s 29; therefore, said the Supreme Court, as his right of access to the courts could be thus frustrated and denied him within the powers of s 29, that section was unconstitutional.[312] The position created by this decision was that there was now no lawful machinery for the extradition of alleged offenders to Britain.

The position in regard to Northern Ireland had been irregular even before the *Quinn* case, as the 1851 procedure naturally had envisaged Britain and Ireland as a single political entity, and no adaptation of that procedure authorised, or had ever attempted professedly to authorise, the handing over of persons arrested in the Republic of Ireland to authorities in Northern Ireland. In *O'Boyle and Rodgers v Attorney General*[313] this point was successfully made in the High Court in a case where the two plaintiffs were sought by the Northern Ireland police and warrants had been issued under the 1851 Act and endorsed by the Commissioner of the Garda Síochána; while the judgment of Meredith J merely described the tenor of the injunction which he agreed to make, restraining the arrest of the plaintiffs, the burden of their counsel's argument was that there was no power under the 1851 Act once Saorstát Éireann had emerged, to enable one police authority in Dublin to execute a warrant issued by a quite different police authority in Belfast, and this was clearly the decisive point. Thereafter, up to the decision in *Quinn's* case, extradition across the Irish border in both directions appears to have been carried on reciprocally and informally by the respective police authorities without any lawful authority, or even ostensible authority, at all.[314]

309 [1962] IR 355.
310 (1966) 100 ILTR 145.
311 [1965] IR 70; (1966) 100 ILTR 105.
312 This was the first occasion on which the Supreme Court expressly departed from an earlier Supreme Court decision.
313 [1929] IR 558; (1929) 63 ILTR 33.
314 This arrangement was criticised by P. O'Higgins in 1958 *British Yearbook of International Law* 274.
315 [1931] IR 39; (1931) 65 ILTR 9.

To other countries

The procedure of s 3 of the Fugitive Offenders Act 1881, governing the backing of warrants for arrest and extradition to the former British Dominions, was held consistent with the 1922 Constitution in *The State (Kennedy) v Little,*[315] but the question of its consistency with the 1937 Constitution was never litigated. Unlike the procedure of s 29 of the Petty Sessions (Ireland) Act 1851, however, this Act contained safeguards to give an arrested person a chance to test the legality of the arrest, so that it did not implicitly fall with the *Quinn* judgment.

Extradition to countries other than Britain or former British Dominions was rarely sought in the pre-*Quinn* period; it was evidently governed by the Extradition Acts, 1870-1906, to the extent (never judicially determined) to which they remained in force within the State.

Extradition Act 1965

After the *Quinn* decision, extradition generally was placed on a completely new statutory basis with the Extradition Act 1965 (the British enacted simultaneously the Backing of Warrants (Republic of Ireland) Act with the effect of making the new system reciprocal as between Britain and Northern Ireland, on the one hand, and Ireland, on the other). The main features of the Act are: (a) s 6(1) and the Schedule repealed s 29 of the Petty Sessions (Ireland) Acts, 1851, the Fugitive Offenders Act 1881, and the Extradition Acts, 1870-1906; (b) s 8 makes extradition generally (i.e. apart from the special arrangements for the United Kingdom) dependent on extradition agreements entered into by the State with other countries; (c) s 10 allows extradition only for an offence which is punishable in the State by "imprisonment for a maximum period of at least one year or by a more severe penalty"; (d) there is no extradition for an offence which is a "political offence or an offence connected with a political offence" (s 11),[316] a purely military offence (s 12), revenue offences (s 13),[317] or an offence carrying the death penalty, unless the requesting country gives a sufficient assurance that it will not be carried out (s 19); (e) s 20 applies the "rule of speciality" which means that the person extradited is not to be proceeded against for any offence but that in respect of which he has been extradited,[318] (f) a request for extradition must be accompanied by particulars of the offence alleged and of the relevant law of the requesting country; (g) ss 31 and 48 provide that, unless the person concerned gives his consent before a judge of the District Court, he is not to be surrendered for fifteen days after his arrest, or until the conclusion of *habeas corpus* proceedings, whichever is the later: this provision is designed to meet the constitutional weakness disclosed in the 1851 procedure by the *Quinn* case; (h) by s 14, an Irish citizen cannot be extradited "unless the relevant provisions [i.e. of the extradition treaty in question] otherwise provide", but this saver does not apply to persons wanted on British warrants (separately governed by Part III of the Act); (i) by s 17, the rule *non bis in idem* is applied; and (j) a warrant for extradition cannot be endorsed for execution if the Minister for Justice, or the High Court, on the question being referred to that Court by the Minister, directs in accordance with s 44 that it shall not be so endorsed.[319]

[316] As to the meaning of "political offence", see below, pp. 880-886.

[317] See *Rey v Fleming,* High Court, 29 January 1980. In *McDonald v McMahon*, High Court, 13 January 1989, Lardner J held that revenue offences refer to offences under the tax code of another country and that, in any event, the charging of fees for the issue or renewal of Irish passports by Irish embassies abroad was not a revenue raising device.

[318] Pursuant to s 3(1) of the Extradition (Amendment) Act 1987, the Minister may "with such adaptations and modifications as he considers necessary or expedient", by order apply the provisions of, *inter alia*, s 20 in relation to the delivery of a person under Part III of the 1965 Act. There is at least an arguable case that, by virtue of the passage in quotation marks above, s 3(1) is contrary to Article 15.2 of the Constitution - see above, pp. 107-110.

[319] The Minister, or the Court, as the case may be, may so direct if the warrant relates to a political offence or an offence connected with a political offence, an offence under military law which is not an offence under ordinary criminal law, or a revenue offence, or where there are substantial reasons for believing that the person

The Extradition (Amendment) Act 1987

Section 2 of the Extradition (Amendment) Act 1987 confers a power to prevent extradition, analogous to that of the Minister for Justice under s 44 of the 1965 Act on the Attorney General. Before a warrant for extradition can be endorsed for execution, the Attorney General must be satisfied that there is a clear intention to prosecute the person named in the warrant for the offence specified therein in a place in relation to which Part III of the 1965 Act applies and that such intention is founded on the existence of sufficient evidence.[320] A challenge to the constitutionality of this Act, on the ground that it involved the Attorney General in the administration of justice, failed in *Wheeler v Culligan*.[321]

Constitutionality of the Extradition Act 1965

The constitutionality of the Extradition Act 1965, has been challenged in four cases: *The State (Sumers Jennings) v Furlong,*[322] where the argument turned on Article 29;[323] *The State (Hartley) v Governor of Mountjoy Prison*,[324] which involved a consideration of the guarantee of equality;[325] *Shannon v Ireland*[326] where the plaintiff unsuccessfully invoked Article 29.3, Article 34.1 and Article 40.3;[327] and *McGlinchey v Ireland (No.2).*[328] The last case was the only one in which an argument grounded on the guarantee of personal liberty was advanced. The plaintiff contended, *inter alia*, that the Act was unconstitutional in that it failed to protect him from the consequences of proceedings rendered illegal by virtue of the fact that they were taken on foot of an illegal warrant for arrest issued by the requesting state.[329] Costello J dismissed this claim, holding that on the

named in the warrant will be prosecuted or detained for a political offence or an offence connected with a political offence or an offence under military law which is not an offence under ordinary law. In *Kane v McMahon*, [1990] 1 IR 239, a divisional High Court held that s 44 did not oblige the Minister to consider each and every warrant for extradition before such warrant is endorsed by the Garda Commissioner.

[320] In a controversial exercise of this power, the then Attorney General, Mr. John Murray S.C., directed that a warrant for the extradition of Fr. Patrick Ryan to England not be executed because media coverage of the case in that country had irrevocably prejudiced the possibility of a fair trial. In a published statement of his reasons, the Attorney General acknowledged that this factor was not referred to in the 1987 Act but referred to the fact that, as a constitutional officer under Article 30, he was obliged to take into account all potential violations of Fr. Ryan's constitutional rights - *The Irish Times,* 14 December 1988. See Hogan, "*Some reflections on the role of the Attorney General and the Patrick Ryan affair*" (1992) ICLJ 128. A similar view of the Attorney General's functions under this Act would appear to have been taken by Costello J in *McGlinchey v Ireland (No.2)* [1990] 2 IR 220, insofar as he suggested that the Attorney General would be constitutionally obliged to ensure that an invalid warrant for extradition was not endorsed for execution, even though being satisfied as to the validity of the warrant is not listed as a basis for not issuing a direction preventing extradition under the 1987 Act.

[321] [1989] IR 344. See above, pp. 361-362.

[322] [1966] IR 183.

[323] See above, pp. 270-271.

[324] Supreme Court, 21 December 1957

[325] See above, pp. 724-725.

[326] [1984] IR 548; [1985] ILRM 449.

[327] In relation to the first two arguments, see pp. 271, 362, fn 41 respectively. Article 40.3 was invoked in support of a right to fair procedures, which is considered generally at pp. 350-359 and 589-593.

[328] [1990] 2 IR 220.

[329] In addition to this argument, the plaintiff had also contended that the 1965 Act was unconstitutional because, by virtue of Articles 2 and 3 of the Constitution, the Constitution did not permit the Oireachtas to recognise by its laws the legal efficacy of laws enacted for Northern Ireland which had not been enacted by the Oireachtas and therefore the Garda Commissioner could not endorse a warrant for the arrest of an Irish citizen issued at the request of a member of the R.U.C., a police force which had not been established by Act of the Oireachtas. Dismissing this claim, Costello J held that the Constitution did not prohibit the Oireachtas from recognising laws enacted for Northern Ireland by the UK or Northern Ireland parliaments. See above, p. 16.

[330] [1976] IR 233.

authority of *Gillespie v Attorney General,*[330] and contrary to the plaintiff's premise, a person arrested in the State on foot of a warrant which he alleges is not valid according to the law of the requesting State can adduce evidence of foreign law and ask the court to condemn the foreign warrant. The judge also noted, *obiter*, that an additional safeguard was now provided by the Extradition (Amendment) Act 1987 inasmuch as if it came to the attention of the Attorney General that the warrant from the requesting State was invalid, he would be constitutionally obliged to ensure that the warrant was not endorsed for execution.

Political offences

Since the recrudescence of political violence in Northern Ireland, or connected with the troubles there, in the early 1970s the question of extradition to Northern Ireland, or to Britain, had become politically sensitive because of the exception made by s 50 of the Act[331] in favour of a "political offence or an offence connected with a political offence": an exception which only reflected common international practice and doctrine in the area of extradition, based in part on English case-law going back to the last century; though in *The State (Duggan) v Tapley*[332] the Supreme Court had held that this practice did not amount to a "generally accepted principle of international law", in the sense of Article 29.3, sufficient to forbid the surrender of politically motivated offenders whose extradition was sought under the 1851 Act. The Court said:

> "The farthest that the matter can be put is that international law permits and favours the refusal of extradition of persons accused or convicted of offences of a political character but allows it to each State to exercise its own judgment as to whether it will grant or refuse extradition in such cases."

In the first case which turned on the section, *Bourke v Attorney General*,[333] Irish affairs were in no way involved; the plaintiff, whose extradition was sought to Britain, had assisted a prisoner to escape from a British prison where he was serving a long sentence for spying in Britain for the former Soviet Union. The Supreme Court gave a generous interpretation to the section when the plaintiff invoked it: his own alleged offence was not a political offence, but the spy's act in escaping was a political offence, and so the plaintiff's act in facilitating his escape was "an offence connected with a political offence". Ó Dálaigh CJ, with whom three other members of the Court agreed, reviewed the earlier foreign doctrine on political offences, and, noting that the fugitive spy's object was not merely to break jail but to get to Russia and "continue in the service of his Soviet master", considered that his escape was a political offence:

> "as much as in substance, though not in form, as his original [spying offences]. In a world divided by ideological differences, Blake's [the spy's] offence was as political as if in war time he had deserted to the enemy lines and changed his uniform. Therefore ...the plaintiff's offence in assisting that escape was connected with Blake's offence [and therefore] the plaintiff may not be extradited."

When, in pursuance of the Sunningdale agreement of 1973, a joint Law Enforcement

[331] This section is in the special Part of the Act dealing with extradition between this country and Northern Ireland and Britain. There is a similar section (s 11) dealing with extradition generally, i.e. between this country and countries other than Britain.
[332] [1952] IR 62; (1951) 85 ILTR 22.
[333] [1972] IR 36; (1973) 107 ILTR 33.
[334] *Law Enforcement Commission: Report to the Minister for Justice of Ireland and the Secretary of State for Northern Ireland* (Prl. 3832); Dublin, 1974.

Commission was set up to consider, mainly, the problems created by the principle of non-extradition for political offences in the context of Northern Ireland-associated terrorism, its Report[334] disclosed a difference of opinion, as between the Irish representatives on the one hand and the British and Northern Ireland representatives on the other, as to whether this principle was part of the "generally recognised principles of international law" so as to inhibit the State, because of Article 29.3, from departing from it; the Irish side thought it was, and the Northern Ireland and British side thought it was not (and were able, embarrassingly, to derive support for their view from the old Supreme Court's decision in *The State (Duggan) v Tapley*). In the event, the exception remained; and cross-Border extradition to the North on charges of, or connected with terrorism was for several years regularly refused through the operation of s 50. During those years, however, the courts seem never to have concentrated on the question of what constitutes a political offence such as to be entitled to immunity from extradition,[335]the words of Ó Dálaigh CJ, in *Bourke's* case cited above not offering any serviceable standard. However during the 1980s, the Supreme Court addressed this issue on no fewer than five occasions during the course of which it had, at one point, virtually abolished the concept of the political offence exception in relation to subversive crimes arising out of the situation in Northern Ireland.

Judicial definition

This process began in *McGlinchey v Wren*[336] at the end of 1982, in a case where the plaintiff's extradition to Northern Ireland was sought on a charge of murder. He resisted extradition on the ground that, if extradited and prosecuted for this offence, he would be prosecuted for a political offence or an offence connected with a political offence; that the murder had been "claimed" by the I.R.A.; and that he had at the time of the murder been active in the I.R.A. The Supreme Court, speaking by O'Higgins CJ, said:

> "The judicial authorities on the scope of [political offences and offences connected with political offences] have in many respects been rendered obsolete by the fact that modern terrorist violence, whether undertaken by military or paramilitary organisations, or by individuals of groups of individuals, is often the antithesis of what could reasonably be regarded as political, either in itself or in its connections. All that can be said with authority in this case is that, with or without the concession made on behalf of the plaintiff, this offence could not be said to be either a political offence or an offence connected with a political offence. Whether a contrary conclusion would be reached in different circumstances must depend on the particular circumstances, and on whether those particular circumstances showed that the person charged was at the relevant time engaged, either directly or indirectly, in *what reasonable, civilised people would regard as political activity.*[337]...This Court is invited to assume that because of the existence of widespread violence organised by paramilitary groups in Northern Ireland, any charge associated with

[335] In *Hanlon v Fleming* [1981] IR 489, [1982] ILRM 69, Henchy J treated the definition of a political offence for the purpose of s 50 as being still (in October 1981) an open question: "Even if it had been found as a fact that the explosive material mentioned in the charge specified in the warrant had been intended for transmission to the I.R.A., it would not necessarily follow that the accused would be exempt from extradition on the ground that the offence charged is a political offence, or an offence connected with a political offence. There has been no decision of this Court on such a point. It must be left open for an appropriate case."

[336] [1982] IR 154; [1983] ILRM 169. See Sutherland, "*The Development of the International Law of Extradition*" (1984) 28 St. Louis University Law Journal 33. The case, as described by the Chief Justice, was one in which "a deliberate attack was made by men with Armalite rifles on the house of two very old people and their daughter, in which the elderly woman was riddled with bullets and died".

[337] Authors' emphasis.

[338] [1984] IR 569; [1985] ILRM 385.

terrorist activity should be regarded as a charge [covered by s 50]. I am not prepared to make any such assumption. The excusing *per se* of murder, and of offences involving violence and the infliction of human suffering, done by or at the behest of self-appointed arbiters, is the very antithesis of the ordinances of Christianity and civilisation and of the basic requirements of political activity. [The onus of satisfying the conditions of s 50 is on the person invoking it.] In my view the plaintiff has singularly failed to discharge that onus."

To this powerful statement excluding acts of terrorism from the category of political offences, the Court might perhaps have added that to interpret an Act of the Oireachtas in such a way as to privilege offences of the kind described by the Court could not accord with the ideals expressed in the Preamble to, and elsewhere in, the Constitution.

A little more than 18 months after its decision in *McGlinchey*, the Supreme Court was again asked to consider the meaning of "political offence" in *Shannon v Fanning*.[338] Though the members of the Court were unanimous in their view that the plaintiff had failed to establish that he was being extradited in respect of a political offence,[339] differing views emerged as to the appropriate tests for defining such an offence. O'Higgins CJ applied the rather open-ended test used in *McGlinchey's* case, *viz*., whether a person is sought for a political offence depends on whether the circumstances show that he was, at the relevant time, engaged, either directly or indirectly, in what reasonable, civilised people would regard as political activity. Hederman J, however, rejected this approach as leading to uncertainty. After adverting to the distinction drawn in *Bourke v Attorney General*[340] between "purely political offences" and "relative political offences", he said:

"The decisive criterion to determine whether an ordinary criminal offence becomes a relative political offence is whether the perpetrator acted with a political motive or for a political purpose."

In his opinion, it followed that the Court had to be satisfied that the requested person did the act complained of, because in the absence of such evidence "one cannot assign actual motives to a hypothetical guilt"; where, therefore, the Court had no such evidence, it could not hold that the offences charged were political offences. A third approach was advanced by McCarthy J; he was not satisfied that at any time there had been an accepted definition of a political offence, but thought:

"the objective determination of whether or not an offence charged is a political offence or an offence connected with a political offence within the meaning of the Act should primarily rest upon an assessment of three factors:

1. The true motivation of the individual or individuals committing the offence. I do not share the view that, in order to assess motive, the individual charged must admit his involvement in the crime.

2. The true nature of the offence itself.

3. The identity of the victim or victims.

In assessing all or any of these factors, the proximity of each to the alleged political aim is critically important and is capable of objective assessment.

[339] His extradition had been sought so that he could stand trial for the murder of two retired politicians.
[340] [1972] IR 36; (1973) 107 ILTR 33.
[341] [1985] IR 322; [1985] ILRM 411.

In the third case in this series to come before the Supreme Court - *Quinn v Wren*[341] - a new line of reasoning emerged to restrict the scope of the "political offence" defence. Here the plaintiff had relied on s 50 in resisting his extradition in respect of an alleged fraud, arguing that the offence had been committed on behalf of the Irish National Liberation Army, a proscribed organisation whose objective was the establishment of a "thirty-two county workers' republic" by force of arms. Dismissing the claim, Finlay CJ considered the overall relation of constitutional values to s 50, concluding that the section could not be construed so as to protect persons seeking to overthrow the Constitution and the State:

> "To interpret the words "political offence" contained in s 50... so as to grant immunity or protection to a person charged with an offence directly intended to further that objective would be to give to the section a patently unconstitutional construction. This Court can not, it seems to me, interpret an Act of the Oireachtas as having the intention to grant immunity from extradition to a person charged with an offence the admitted purpose of which is to further or facilitate the overthrow by violence of the Constitution and of the organs of State established thereby."[342]

The reasoning in *Quinn v Wren* was applied and extended in *Russell v Fanning*[343] so that the political offence defence could never be raised in respect of an offence committed on behalf of an organisation whose objectives included the overthrow of the Constitution and the State, irrespective of the circumstances of the particular crime or of the motivation of the particular individual involved. Here the plaintiff, who was a member of the I.R.A. and whose extradition was sought in connection with offences committed during the course of a mass escape of republican prisoners from a prison in Northern Ireland, had expressly disclaimed any desire on his own part to overthrow the Constitution. However a majority of the Supreme Court[344] held that where the extradition of a person is sought in respect of a crime alleged to have been committed outside the State as part of the activities of an organisation committed to overthrowing the organs of State established by the Constitution, that person cannot escape extradition on the ground of the political exception by relying on personal aims or objectives which are less extensive than those of the organisation. Strong dissents were entered by Hederman and McCarthy JJ, both of whom distinguished *Quinn v Wren* on the facts. According to Hederman J:

> "There is an essential difference in the facts which were established in *Quinn v Wren* ... and the facts established in the present case. Nowhere is there any evidence that the offences with which the plaintiff in the present case is charged were directed or intended to be directed against any of the institutions of this State or directed towards overthrowing the institutions of this State."

For his part, McCarthy J considered the extension of the reasoning in *Quinn's* case to amount to a judicial repeal of s 50(2)(*a*)(i) providing for the political offence exemption.

[342]As Hogan and Walker have pointed out, this effectively stood the reasoning of the Irish members of the Law Enforcement Commission on its head. The Irish side said in 1974 that it would be unconstitutional to extradite persons charged with terrorist offences arising out of the Northern Ireland conflict, yet the Supreme Court was now saying in 1985 that it would be unconstitutional to exempt such offenders - *Political Violence and the Law in Ireland* (Manchester 1989) at p.289.

[343] [1988] IR 505; [1988] ILRM 333.

[344] Finlay CJ, Henchy and Griffin JJ.

[345] [1990] 1 IR 165; [1990] ILRM 505. See note by *Humphreys*, (1990) 12 DULJ (n.s.) 127.

Two years later, a differently composed Supreme Court endorsed the minority position in *Russell*. This occurred in the case of *Finucane v McMahon*,[345] where the extradition of the plaintiff was sought in respect of crimes arising out of the same incident as had led to the extradition of Russell. In his judgment, Walsh J affirmed the decision in *Quinn v Wren*, saying that as a statement of principle it could not be questioned and was manifestly correct. However he continued:

> "[I]t is well established that every extradition case must be decided in the light of its own particular facts and circumstances, and so the question must arise whether the particular activity for which the applicant was convicted in Northern Ireland and the escape subsequently made can legitimately be construed as subverting the Constitution and usurping or endeavouring to usurp the function of the Government under the Constitution."

He then engaged in an extensive analysis of the political and historical background to the Irish extradition legislation, during the course of which he endorsed the distinction, first drawn in *McGlinchey*, between a political offence and terrorism, before concluding that:

> "the Court cannot draw an inference that it was the intention of the Oireachtas that the provisions relating to the political exemption in the Act of 1965 should not apply to persons charged with politically motivated offences of violence when the objective of such offences was to secure the ultimate unity of the country."

Hederman and McCarthy JJ, not surprisingly, agreed with Walsh J while the two remaining members of the Court - Finlay CJ and Griffin J, who had constituted part of the majority in *Russell* - somewhat reluctantly agreed that in the interest of securing certainty in the law, the views of their three colleagues should henceforth govern those extradition cases in which the political exemption was raised.

This aspect of the decision in *Finucane* was subsequently confirmed in a later Supreme Court decision, *Carron v McMahon*,[346] where again the opportunity was taken to affirm both *Quinn v Wren* and *McGlinchey v Wren*.[347]

The Extradition (European Convention on the Suppression of Terrorism) Act 1987

This Act was designed to give effect to the European Convention on the Suppression of Terrorism, which was effectively aimed at reducing the scope of the political offence exemption. Section 3 provides that certain designated offences are not to be regarded as political offences, while s 4 empowers the courts or the Minister to rule that any serious offence involving an act of violence against the life, physical integrity or liberty of a person, or involving an act against property if the act created a collective danger for persons, and any offence of attempting to commit any of the foregoing offences, shall not be regarded as a political offence or an offence connected with a political offence. This

[346] [1990] 1 IR 239; [1990] ILRM 802.

[347] In *Clarke v McMahon* [1990] 1 IR 228; [1990] ILRM 648, counsel for the plaintiff had expressly abandoned any claim based on s 50 of the 1965 Act and Finlay CJ speculated that this may have been because the offence upon which the political exemption defence would ultimately have rested was more in the nature of terrorist activity, involving indiscriminate shooting at civilians.

[348] 370 *Dáil Debates* cols. 2695-2708.

is without prejudice to the right of the courts to declare, for reasons other than those specified in the 1987 Act that an offence is not a political offence or connected with a political offence: s 11.

Serious criticism was directed at this legislation during its passage through the Oireachtas.[348] In particular, s 3 was criticised on the ground that it failed to include within its ambit, *possession* as opposed to *use* of firearms and, in addition, that it was not clear whether offences involving the use of explosives or automatic firearms came within the scope of the section where such use endangered a single person as opposed to persons generally. Section 4 was also criticised on the ground that, by conferring a discretion to exclude offences from the category of political offences, it failed to give adequate effect to Article 2 of the Convention which gave signatory states the option of providing that certain serious offences, such as murder and manslaughter, could not be regarded as political in nature.

The 1987 Act has been considered by the courts on two occasions to date. In *Ellis v O'Dea (No.2)* [349] the applicant, in respect of whom extradition orders had been made by the District Court, sought orders for his release pursuant to the Extradition Acts 1965 to 1987 and also pursuant to Article 40. His extradition had been sought to answer charges of (a) conspiracy to cause an explosion likely to endanger life or cause serious injury to property and (b) possession of explosives contrary to the Explosive Substances Act 1883 and the Criminal Law Jurisdiction Act 1975. The British authorities claimed that some of the explosive substances referred to in the charges alleged against the applicant had been used in a number of bomb attacks in England in which innocent civilians had been killed. On that basis, Hamilton P in the High Court concluded, following *McGlinchey v Wren,*[350] that the offences set forth in the warrants could not be regarded as political offences.[351] He then went on, however, to hold that the offences in question did not come within the scope of s 3(3)(*a*)(v) of the 1987 Act as that provision did not cover the use of explosives which endangered "only one person or property". Though no appeal was taken against this part of the High Court decision to the Supreme Court, Finlay CJ commented that Hamilton P had ruled that, having regard to s 4 of the 1987 Act the offences in question could not be regarded as political offences. On the meaning of s 3(3)(*a*)(v), he indicated that the effect of s 11 of the Interpretation Act 1937, whereby the use of the singular imports the plural also, unless a contrary intention appears, would have to be considered in an appropriate case.[352]

In the cases of *Sloan v Culligan, McKee v Culligan* and *Magee v Culligan*[353] the plaintiffs had escaped from prison in Northern Ireland and had subsequently been convicted *in absentia* of various offences, including possession of firearms, unlawful imprisonment and murder and attempted murder of British soldiers. They were subsequently arrested, tried and convicted in this jurisdiction in relation to offences arising out of their escape from custody and as their prison sentences here were about to expire, the Northern authorities sought their extradition in respect of the convictions and sentences imposed in Northern Ireland. The plaintiffs sought their release under s 50 of the 1965 Act arguing, *inter alia*, that the 1987 Act was unconstitutional insofar as it sought to

349 [1991] 1 IR 251; [1991] ILRM 346.

350 [1982] IR 154; [1983] ILRM 169.

351 He also held that the conditions for the application of s 4 of the 1987 Act were satisfied, but pointed out that that section could not apply to offences which fell within the ambit of s 3.

352 McCarthy J concluded, on the basis of s 11, that the word "persons" did import the singular "person".

353 [1992] 1 IR 223; [1992] ILRM 194.

354 In December 1991, the Irish Government gave a commitment to introduce new legislation remedying this

restrict their implied constitutional right under Article 40.3 not to be extradited in respect of political offences. In the High Court, Lynch J dismissed the constitutional challenge on the grounds that the 1987 Act did not abolish the political offence exemption from extradition, but merely defined political offence in a negative way so as to exclude certain offences which might otherwise by argued to be political offences. Nor did the Act retrospectively deprive the plaintiffs of a vested right to liberty as they had already lost that right on being convicted and sentenced to imprisonment and the protection against having to fulfil this liability to imprisonment afforded to the plaintiffs by the Extradition Acts was not a personal right of the sort envisaged by Article 40.3. Turning then to consider the applicability of the political exemption, Lynch J concluded that the offences in question could be regarded as political, having regard to *Finucane's* case and that regard would then have to be had to the 1987 Act. He held that the offence of false imprisonment - of which the first plaintiff had been convicted - came within the meaning of s 3(3)(*a*)(iv) of the Act and therefore could not be regarded as a political offence. The circumstances of the firearms offences of which the first and second plaintiffs had been convicted related to possession with intent only and not to the use of such firearms, as required by s 3(3)(*a*)(v). Accordingly these offences continued to be regarded as political offences. Finally the offences of murder and attempted murder, of which the third plaintiff had been convicted, were excluded from the category of political offences by s 3(3)(*a*)(v) as in the particular circumstances of the case they had involved the use of an automatic firearm.

On appeal, Lynch J's interpretation of s 3(3)(*a*)(v) was upheld, Finlay CJ saying that in so far as s 3 imposed a liability on an individual to be delivered out of the jurisdiction for the purpose of standing trial or serving a sentence where, were it not for the provisions of the section, no such liability might exist, the section should be strictly construed. In relation to the distinction drawn between use and possession of automatic firearms for the purposes of s 3(3)(*a*)(v), he said:

> "There is, in ordinary language, a difference between possession and use, but more importantly still, the phrase contained in subclause (v): "if such use endangers persons" being a present tense, makes it impossible to construe the section as including not only a present use, with a present danger to persons, but also a possession with an intention for future use endangering persons."

Thus possession of firearms, whether automatic or otherwise, is not excluded by the 1987 Act from the category of political offences in respect of which an order under s 50 of the 1965 Act may be sought.[354]

The third plaintiff had also sought, *inter alia*, a declaration that s 1(4) of the 1987 Act was invalid, having regard to Article 15.5 and Article 40.3, on the ground that the subsection constituted a retrospective interference with personal liberty and unfair deprivation of a vested right not to be extradited in respect of an offence which was political in nature. Dismissing this claim, the Supreme Court held that s 1(4) did not infringe Article 15.5 as it did not declare any act to be an infringement of the law. The Court also rejected the contention that the plaintiff had any vested right under Article 40.3 not to be extradited in relation to political offences:

defect in the 1987 Act - see *The Irish Times*, 12 December 1991.

[355] [1971] IR 205.

> "The right of the plaintiff...concerning the question of his delivery into another State for the purpose of serving a sentence lawfully imposed on him in that State was...a right at any given time to proper, due and fair procedures concerning an investigation of the validity of the warrant in respect of which he is delivered, and to a fair, proper and due inquiry into the protections applicable in law, within the State at the time of the application for his delivery, which may afford him a protection arising from the concept of a political offence or from any other of the concepts appropriate to prevent such a delivery."

Two cases may be briefly mentioned as footnotes to the question of the political offence. In *The State (Magee) v O'Rourke*[355] sub-s 2(*b*) of s 50 was in issue; this provides that, even where a person's extradition is sought for a non-political offence, if there appear to the Court to be "substantial grounds for believing" that the person, if extradited, will be "prosecuted or detained for a political offence or an offence connected with a political offence", the Court may direct that he be not extradited. Here the applicant alleged that this was likely in his own case; and produced evidence in support of his belief, which the respondent did not contradict with other evidence, but sought merely to discredit by cross-examination and argument. This situation, the Supreme Court held, amounted to the "substantial grounds" mentioned in the sub-section, and extradition was refused. In *Hanlon v Fleming*[356] the Supreme Court held that, as the finding of the High Court judge, that the offence charged against the plaintiff was not a political offence or connected with a political offence, was supported by evidence, it could not be disturbed.

Refusal of extradition where suspect's fundamental rights at risk

An interesting trend in recent Irish extradition law is that, just as the application of the "political offence" exception has been narrowed both by statutory curtailment and judicial interpretation, a new ground for refusing extradition appears to be opening up, namely that the courts will refuse extradition where there is a real risk that the suspect's fundamental rights will be breached or, at least, will not be adequately protected.[357] This issue has arisen in two contexts to date - first, where there is a probability of ill-treatment of the detained person if he is returned to the requesting State; second, where there is a likelihood that he will not get a fair trial if extradited.

The issue of ill-treatment was relied on by the courts for the first time in *Finucane v McMahon*,[358] where the appellant claimed that there was a real risk that he would be ill-treated if he were extradited to Northern Ireland. Following the break-out of prisoners from the Maze Prison, in which he was involved, and during the course of which a prison officer died of a heart attack, it appears that a great number of the remaining IRA prisoners were assaulted by prison officers who were enraged by the death of their colleague. The prison officers then refused to co-operate with every form of enquiry into

[356] [1981] IR 489.

[357] This trend reflects developments taking place under the European Convention on Human Rights - see *Soering v UK*, Series A, No.161, (1989) 11 EHRR 439; *Cruz Varas v Sweden* Series A, No.201, (1992) 14 EHRR 1. See generally, Van den Wyngaert, "*Applying the European Convention on Human Rights to Extradition: Opening Pandora's Box*" (1990) 39 ICLQ 757.

[358] [1990] 1 IR 165; [1990] ILRM 505.

[359] *Ibid. per* Finlay CJ at 204-5. The falsity of these denials was only subsequently uncovered in November

the allegations of assault and "clearly at an early stage entered into a widespread conspiracy to deny absolutely all accusations of assault or ill-treatment and also to deny the refusal of requests for medical assistance."[359]
The Supreme Court unanimously agreed that the applicant had shown that there was a probable risk of ill-treatment were he to be returned to the Maze Prison in Northern Ireland. Because of this, the Court held that it was required to order the release of the applicant in order to ensure that his constitutional rights were not so violated. Finlay CJ said:

> "It was submitted by the respondents that the very fact that so many of the prisoners have now successfully brought their claims before the courts in Northern Ireland indicated that there was no ground for the applicant's fear of invasion of his constitutional rights. I have no difficulty in accepting that if ill-treatment of any of the prisoners in the Maze Prison is brought to the notice of the courts in Northern Ireland it will be condemned and remedied...This Court has, however, as its primary obligation, the duty to prevent such invasions of the applicant's rights and it is not a sufficient discharge of that duty for it to rely upon the vindication of those rights by compensation after they have been invaded...I have come to the conclusion that there is a probable risk, if the applicant were returned to the Maze Prison in Northern Ireland, that he would be assaulted or injured by the illegal actions of the prison staff...[T]he total absence of any repercussions on the staff as a result of the ill-treatment of prisoners in the aftermath of the escape, and from that point of view, the success of their conspiracy to cover up their conduct would appear to make the applicant, in my view, a probable target for ill-treatment."

This reasoning was applied, *mutatis mutandis*, in the companion case of *Clarke v McMahon.*[360]

The cogency of the evidence supporting the Court's conclusions in these two cases that there was a probable risk of ill-treatment if extradition went ahead has been questioned - in particular it has been pointed out that there were no grave disciplinary breaches by the prison staff since 1983 and that none of the returned escapees had been subjected to ill-treatment since that time - and it has been suggested that the true ratio in *Finucane* and *Clarke* is that the Irish courts will in effect penalise the requesting state by refusing to order extradition where that state has failed "to keep its house in order" by allowing serious disciplinary infractions to go unremedied.[361]

The second limb of this ground - that extradition should be refused because of the likelihood that the accused will not get a fair trial - was judicially considered in two recent cases - *Clarke v McMahon*[362] and *Ellis v O'Dea (No.2)*[363] though on both occasions the

1988 following a civil action taken by one of the prisoners where certain new documents came to light which showed that, not only had the requests for medical treatment been ignored, but that serious assaults had, in facts, taken place following the escape - *Pettigrew v Northern Ireland Office* (1989) 3 BNIL 83. In the earlier case of *Russell v Fanning* [1988] IR 505; [1988] ILRM 333, which grew out of the same events as *Finucane*, the plaintiff had made a similar claim about the possibility of ill-treatment as part of his attempt to resist extradition. However at that time, before the decision in *Pettigrew*, the Supreme Court accepted the High Court's decision that the evidence did not establish the existence of a practice of ill-treatment or the use of unlawful violence by prison staff against prisoners.

360 [1990] 1 IR 228; [1990] ILRM 648.

361 *Delany and Hogan, loc. cit.*, pp.113-114.

362 [1990] 1 IR 228; [1990] ILRM 648.

363 [1991] 1 IR 251.

364 When the UK sought the extradition of Fr. Patrick Ryan, the Attorney General exercised his power under

courts refused to accept that any such likelihood existed.[364] In *Clarke* the applicant had been sentenced at Belfast Crown Court in 1979 to a term of 18 years imprisonment. He had been convicted on ten counts of attempted murder and related offences arising out of an armed attack on a farmhouse in County Tyrone in which certain civilians had been injured. Like Finucane, he had also participated in the mass break-out from the Maze prison in September 1983 and had escaped to the Republic. When he was later apprehended in the Republic, he sought to resist an order for his extradition on the ground that (a) his conviction at Belfast Crown Court was flawed and (b) there a real risk that he would be subjected to ill-treatment were he now to be returned to the Maze Prison.

While the applicant was ultimately to succeed before the Supreme Court on the ground of probable ill-treatment, the other argument is also of considerable interest. When the applicant had been initially arrested in March 1978, he was taken in turn to two separate R.U.C. police stations where he made inculpatory statements. Although he had made formal complaints of ill-treatment to both his solicitor and doctor during the period of his custody, he did not challenge the admissibility of these inculpatory statements at his trial, not did give or call any evidence at that trial. In addition, the applicant sought to introduce new alibi evidence detailing his whereabouts on the night of the incidents in question.

The Supreme Court agreed that, in exceptional circumstances, the Irish courts could go behind a foreign conviction, where this was necessary to protect the constitutional rights of the requested person. Finlay CJ said that:

> "The statement that the court cannot in an extradition case properly undertake an investigation into the validity of a conviction recorded in a requesting state must be understood as being subject to this inherent power. The facts of this case, in my view, go nowhere near establishing a situation in which this inherent power might be invoked and it is, therefore, not necessary for me to speculate on what might constitute, in any other case, such a situation."

This appears to suggest that the Irish courts will, where necessary, apply their own constitutional standards when reviewing the validity and propriety of foreign convictions. Nevertheless, this jurisdiction is quite exceptional and will only be invoked where there is compelling evidence to suggest that the suspect's constitutional rights would be infringed if he were to be extradited to face trial (or, as the case may be, to serve a sentence in respect of a foreign conviction).

The reluctance of the Irish courts to widen the grounds in which this plea will be entertained is evidenced by the judgment of the Supreme Court in *Ellis*. The applicant in this case was wanted in England on serious explosives charges and the case had already attracted considerable attention in the British media. It was said that, given a series of notorious miscarriages of justice involving Irish defendants, there was a real risk that the applicant would not get a fair trial but this was not accepted by the Supreme Court. Finlay CJ said:

the Extradition (Amendment) Act 1987 to prevent extradition on the ground that the accused could not receive a fair trial in the UK. See fn.320 above.

[365] If this is so, this tends to show that the real reason behind the decision in *Finucane* was that the Supreme

> "Particular emphasis was laid by counsel in this Court...[on] cases which have become notorious in relation to the quashing of convictions obtained through forensic evidence which appears to have been wholly unreliable. Having carefully considered these cases and the information contained in the affidavit concerning them, they do not, in my view, establish a risk that the plaintiff will be tried or prosecuted or that investigations will be conducted in a manner which would be inconsistent with the reasonable standards of fair trial required by our Constitution."

This conclusion is, perhaps, surprising, given that, in view of the admitted miscarriages of justice involving Irish defendants charged with terrorist offences - ranging from the Birmingham Six, the Guildford Four and the Maguire family - there was at least as much empirical evidence, if indeed not more so, that Ellis would not get a fair trial as there was that Finucane would be ill-treated if he were to be returned to the Maze Prison. Perhaps a significant distinction between the two cases is that in relation to the miscarriages of justice - and in contradistinction to the aftermath of the Maze Prison escape - the British authorities had clearly sought to investigate and ascertain the truth and to take steps to ensure that this would not be repeated.[365]

Clarke and *Ellis* thus demonstrate quite clearly that it will require quite exceptional circumstances before the Irish courts will be prepared to invoke their residual jurisdiction to protect the constitutional rights of suspects by refusing to make an extradition order on the ground that the suspect will not receive a fair trial.[366]

Both limbs of this new ground for refusing extradition are not without their difficulties. In particular, they involve the Irish courts - implicitly at least - investigating conduct that has taken place or may take place outside the jurisdiction, so giving the Constitution an extra-territorial dimension. The first ground, moreover, may present more specific problems, given the apparent inevitability of illegal assaults by fellow prisoners in prison regimes, for while the facts in *Finucane* and *Clarke* focused on ill-treatment by prison staff, the logic of the judicial reasoning therein does not appear to admit of any distinction between "official" ill-treatment, so to speak, and the more common instances of ill-treatment at the hands of fellow inmates.

"Corresponding" offence

Another problem to which the law on extradition between this country and Britain has given rise is that presented by the requirement of s 47(2) that an order for extradition shall not be made by the District Court:

> "if it appears to the Court that the offence specified in the warrant does not correspond with any offence under the law of the State which is an indictable offence or is punishable on summary conviction by imprisonment for a maximum period of at least six months."

In *The State (Furlong) v Kelly*,[367] in which the Supreme Court said that before making an order for extradition, the District Justice must have evidence that this condition of correspondence has been fulfilled, Ó Dálaigh CJ gave what he called an "algebraical" explanation of the conditions:

Court was unhappy that no disciplinary action had been taken against the prison officers who had ill-treated the prisoners following the mass escape - see above, p. 887.

[366] Though note the judicial hint from Walsh J in *Ellis* that the joinder of a charge of conspiracy to a charge for the substantive offence may infringe the constitutional guarantee of fair procedures.

[367] [1971] IR 132.

[368] [1974] IR 378.

> "If the English offence consists of, say, four essential elements a+b+c+d, then a corresponding Irish offence exists only if it contains either precisely these same four essential elements or a lesser number thereof. If the only Irish offence that can be pointed to has an essential additional ingredient (that is to say, if the Irish offence may be defined as a+b+c+d+e), then there is no corresponding Irish offence to satisfy [s 47(2)] for the simple reason that, *ex hypothesi*, conduct a+b+c+d falls short of being an offence under Irish law or, in plainer words, is not an offence."

He added the general principle:

> "It is fundamental to extradition that no-one shall be extradited for acts or omissions (the offence alleged in the warrant) which, if repeated within the State, would not offend against our law."

Three years later, in *Wyatt v McLoughlin*,[368] the Court developed this by pointing out that the "ingredients" which the District Court must check against the existing Irish criminal code are not evidenced by the recital in the warrant of legal terms which, in the context of an English statute, may connote a situation of fact quite different from that connoted by a term which is verbally identical in a statute forming part of the Irish system. Walsh J said:

> "The courts of this State, when dealing with warrants endorsed for execution [under Part III of the Act] much be satisfied that the acts constituting the particular offence for which extradition is sought are acts which, if committed within this jurisdiction, would constitute a criminal offence...It cannot be sufficient simply to use the name by which the crime is known, or alleged to be known, in the requesting country even though that same name may be used in this country as the name of a crime, because the acts complained of, although having identical names, may constitute quite different criminal offences in different countries or, indeed, no offence at all in one of them. For example, what constitutes embezzlement in one country may be larceny in another, and acts which would constitute the offence of abortion or unlawful homosexual behaviour in one country may not constitute any offence in the other."

The principle so stated was applied by Finlay P in *Whyte v Sheehan*,[369] in which he ordered the release of a person whose extradition had been ordered by the District Judge on the strength of a warrant reciting that he had "assaulted [X] with intent to rob him contrary to s 8 of the Theft Act 1968" (this was the English Act which had largely replaced the Larceny Act 1916, which was in substance still in force in Ireland). He cited the words of Walsh J in *Wyatt's* case and said:

> "To say as the warrant does that the plaintiff assaulted some person is to describe a crime and not to give information as to an act committed by him; to say that he did so with intent to rob is simply to again describe an intention to commit another crime and not to give particulars or information with regard to a further act or acts which [it] was alleged he intended to carry out...No evidence was offered to the District Justice or to me of English law which would permit me to ascertain what meaning the words assault and rob respectively have within the criminal law of England."

[369] High Court, 26 May 1977.
[370] [1979] IR 423.

In *Wilson v Sheehan*[370] the same principle was applied in considering another English warrant which mentioned s 8 of the Theft Act 1968; this reference, the Supreme Court found again, could not satisfy the requirements of s 47(2); but in this case the warrant did contain, in addition, a sufficient recital of the facts underlying the charge to enable the Court to conclude that the English offence did in fact correspond with an Irish one of the kind which s 47(2) contemplated. Similarly in *Hanlon v Fleming*[371] the Court again found a sufficient correspondence - in this case, indeed, an instance where, to revert to the algebraical formulation of Ó Dálaigh CJ in *Furlong's* case, the English offence actually contained an ingredient additional to that which the corresponding Irish offence would require. Henchy J, however, pointed out that with the continuing statutory reform of English criminal law since 1965, "with the absence of any corresponding range of reform in this State", the number of clearly corresponding offences had been much reduced:

> "the result is that the envisaged system of extradition has shrunk to the extent that it now operates only vestigially:"

and he thought it "high time" that new extradition arrangements were negotiated, preferably on the basis of specifying extraditable offences rather than on the "shifting and uncertain foundation of corresponding offences".

The general position reached in this sequence of cases received slight modification in *Harris v Wren*,[372] a case which arose in the area of offences not against property but against the person. Extradition was sought for indecent assault under an English Act of 1956; and the particular acts on which the charge was based were recited. For the plaintiff it was argued that certain incidents attached to the English offence which were absent in the offence called indecent assault under analogous Irish law; these incidents, however, could not have been called "ingredients" in the sense of elements necessary to the constitution of the offence itself, but it was submitted that they sufficed to prevent the authorities from showing a "corresponding" offence in Irish law. Finlay P rejected this argument:

> "I am satisfied that the particulars of the acts committed and the nature of the general allegation contained in the warrant constitutes the offence of indecent assault in this country. Even if it were established by proper proof to my satisfaction that upon being tried on this charge the plaintiff would, in the event of the offence being established as having occurred whilst the injured party was under sixteen years of age, be deprived of a defence which he would have in this country on the same set of facts, it would not in my view have led me to the conclusion that this was not a corresponding offence. The word contained in [s 47(2)] is "corresponding" and it is not necessary to establish total identity."

In *Molloy v Sheehan*[373] the Supreme Court, *per* Kenny J, had made two points which may briefly be added to the picture: where the offence for which extradition is sought was created by a pre-1922 Act applying to the then entire United Kingdom and still in force both here and in Britain, this knowledge will justify a District Judge in regarding the condition of s 47(2) as satisfied; and, where several offences are specified in a warrant, extradition can be ordered (so far as the correspondence test is concerned) if any one of them satisfies the test.

[371] [1981] IR 489. See also *Rey v Fleming*, High Court, 29 January 1980, where Hamilton J held that even if a correspondence is incorrectly stated in the District Court this can be cured in the High Court.
[372] [1984] ILRM 120.
[373] [1978] IR 438.
[374] High Court, 13 January 1989.

Attempts to argue that the offence under English law of criminal conspiracy did not correspond with any Irish offence failed in two recent cases. In *McDonald v McMahon,*[374] the plaintiff argued that where evidence justified a prosecution for the substantive offence, to bring an additional charge of conspiracy would constitute unfair procedures, in breach of the constitutional guarantee of fair procedures, and an abuse of the process of the Court. Accordingly he contended that no correspondence existed between the offences of conspiracy specified in the warrant and any offence under Irish law. Lardner J, however, was not satisfied that the bringing of conspiracy charges in such circumstances constituted unfair procedures[375] and held that correspondence did exist. In *Ellis v O'Dea (No.2)*[376] the plaintiff submitted that the English law on conspiracy contained two principles which had no counterpart on this side of the Irish Sea, namely, that a person who conspires with another and is at that time situated outside the jurisdiction of the UK courts is amenable to trial in those courts if one of his co-conspirators does an act within the UK in furtherance of the criminal conspiracy, and that where two or more persons are engaged in a joint venture constituting a criminal offence, each is responsible for the acts of the others, so that any person so engaged is amenable to trial in the courts of the UK if one of his accomplices does an act in furtherance of the crime within the UK. However the Supreme Court held unanimously, *per* Finlay CJ, that both principles did exist in Irish law so that correspondence was established.

Extradition: miscellaneous

Other cases decided on the Extradition Act are: *Jennings v Quinn*[377] (in the right of the police to seize goods as evidence, or as being reasonably believed to be stolen property, at the time of executing a warrant under Part III of the Act); *The State (Holmes) v Furlong*[378] (on an order being bad for non-compliance with s 47(1) of the Act in that the "point of departure from the State" was not sufficiently specified); *Gillespie v Attorney General*[379] (on the admissibility of evidence to disprove the authenticity of the foreign warrant); *The State (Barry) v Governor of Mountjoy Prison*[380] (the offence charged must correspond with an offence under the law of this State); *The State (Whelan) v Governor of Mountjoy Prison*[381] (the rule of speciality does not apply as between Ireland and Britain).

In *McMahon v Leahy*[382] the Supreme Court held that where it had previously been decided, in the context of extradition proceedings brought against a number of individuals, that a particular offence was a political offence, the constitutional guarantee of equality precluded the State from subsequently challenging that finding in relation to the extradition of another member of the group. Henchy J made the further point that the courts have a limited discretion to refuse an extradition order, even where none of the statutory exemptions from extradition apply. He said:

[375] Though see the subsequent decision of the Supreme Court in *Ellis v O'Dea* [1989] IR 530; [1990] ILRM 87, where Walsh J raised the possibility that such a practice might fall foul of the constitutional guarantee of fair procedures.
[376] [1991] 1 IR 251.
[377] [1968] IR 305.
[378] [1967] IR 210.
[379] [1976] IR 233.
[380] (1974) 108 ILTR 49.
[381] High Court, 9 February 1976. Though both countries have recently agreed to apply the speciality rule to extradition arrangements between the two countries - see *The Irish Times*, 12 December 1991.
[382] [1984] IR 525; [1985] ILRM 423.
[383] [1988] ILRM 70.

"When a statute authorises the making of a particular order in stated circumstances, proof that such circumstances exist will normally lead to the making of the authorised order. But where - as is the case here - a post-Constitution statute authorises the making of an order in stated circumstances, the legislative intent must be held to comprehend that the authorised order will not be made, even though the stated circumstances are shown to exist, if it is shown that the order would necessarily infringe a constitutional right of the party against whom it would operate."

In *Harte v Fanning*[383] Carroll J cited *Hanlon v Fleming*[384] in support of the proposition that delay in requesting extradition is not a ground for refusing it. She also noted that the fact that the person against whom the order would operate had recently married was irrelevant to the proceedings seeking to prevent his extradition.

In *McGlinchey v The Governor of Portlaoise Prison*[385] Lynch J in a divisional High Court held that where an individual had been lawfully arrested under s 30 of the Offences Against the State Act 1939, the authorities could elect to proceed upon an extradition order which was not available at the time of arrest, rather than laying appropriate charges themselves.

(iv) Seizure of goods at time of arrest: seizure of goods as evidence

The law on the question of goods seized from an arrested person at the time of his arrest received an authoritative statement from the Supreme Court in *Jennings v Quinn*.[386] The prisoner had been arrested in response to a warrant issued in England and endorsed under Part III of the Extradition Act 1965; after being extradited he began an action against two police officers claiming the return of goods which had been in his possession but were taken from him at the time of his arrest. O'Keeffe J (with whom Ó Dálaigh CJ and Walsh J agreed) recalled that in the old Irish case of *Dillon v O'Brien and Davis*:[387]

"it was held by the Exchequer Division (Palles CB, Dowse B. and Andrews J) that, when a person is lawfully arrested to be brought before a court on a criminal charge, property seized at the time of the arrest and which is to be used as evidence on that charge may lawfully be retained for that purpose by the police."

He stated his own view of the law as follows:

"In my opinion the public interest requires that the police, when effecting a lawful arrest, may seize, without a search warrant, property in the possession or custody of the person arrested when they believe it necessary to do so to avoid the abstraction or destruction of that property and when that property is:

(a) evidence in support of the criminal charge upon which the arrest is made, or

(b) evidence in support of any other criminal charge against that person then in contemplation, or

(c) reasonably believed to be stolen property or to be property unlawfully in the possession of that person;

[384] [1981] IR 489; [1982] ILRM 69.
[385] [1988] IR 671. The Supreme Court subsequently affirmed the High Court decision on this, and on a myriad of other technical points raised by the applicant.
[386] [1968] IR 305.
[387] 20 LR Ir 300.

> and that they may retain such property for use at the trial of the person arrested, or of any other person or persons, on any criminal charge in which the property is to be used as evidence in support of the charge or charges; and that thereafter they should return the property to the person from whom it was seized, unless the disposal of the property otherwise has been directed by a court of competent jurisdiction."

He held also that the same conditions would justify sending property out of the jurisdiction, if there was evidence that it was required for the trial of the person extradited, but not otherwise.

HABEAS CORPUS PROCEDURE

2° Upon complaint being made by or on behalf of any person to the High Court or any judge thereof alleging that such person is being unlawfully detained, the High Court and any and every judge thereof to whom such complaint is made shall forthwith enquire into the said complaint and may order the person in whose custody such person is detained to produce the body of such person before the High Court on a named day and to certify in writing the grounds of his detention, and the High Court shall, upon the body of such person being produced before that Court and after giving the person in whose custody he is detained an opportunity of justifying the detention, order the release of such person from such detention unless satisfied that he is being detained in accordance with the law.

2° Nuair a dhéanann duine ar bith gearán, nó a dhéantar gearán thar ceann duine ar bith, leis an Ard-Chúirt nó le breitheamh ar bith di á rá go bhfuil an duine sin á choinneáil ina bhrá go haindleathach, ní foláir don Ard-Chúirt agus d'aon bhreitheamh agus do gach breitheamh di chun a ndéanfar an gearán sin fiosrú a dhéanamh láithreach i dtaobh an ghearáin sin agus féadfaidh a ordú do neach coinnithe an duine sin ina bhrá an duine sin a thabhairt ina phearsain i láthair na hArd-Chúirte lá a ainmnítear agus a dheimhniú i scríbhinn cad is forais dá bhraighdeanas, agus ní foláir don Ard-Chúirt, nuair a bheirtear an duine sin ina phearsain i láthair na Cúirte sin agus tar éis caoi a thabhairt do neach a choinnithe ina bhrá ar a chruthú gur braighdeanas cóir an braighdeanas, a ordú an duine sin a scaoileadh as an mbraighdeanas sin mura deimhin leis an gCúirt sin gur de réir an dlí atáthar á choinneáil.

3° Where the body of a person alleged to be unlawfully detained is produced before the High Court in pursuance of an order in that behalf made under this section and that Court is satisfied that such person is being detained in accordance with a law but that such law is invalid having regard to the provisions of this Constitution, the High Court shall refer the question of the validity of such law to the Supreme Court by way of case stated and may, at the time of such reference or at any time thereafter, allow the said person to be at liberty on such bail and subject to such conditions as the High Court shall fix until the Supreme Court has determined the question so referred to it.

3° I gcás duine a deirtear a bheith á choinneáil ina bhrá go haindleathach a thabhairt ina phearsain i láthair na hArd-Chúirte de bhun ordaithe chuige sin arna dhéanamh faoin alt seo agus gur deimhin leis an gCúirt sin an duine sin a bheith á choinneáil ina bhrá de réir dlí áirithe ach an dlí sin a bheith neamhbhailí ag féachaint d'fhorálacha an Bhunreachta seo, ní foláir don Ard-Chúirt an cheist sin bail a bheith nó gan a bheith ar an dlí sin a chur faoi bhreith na Cúirte Uachtaraí i bhfoirm chaís ríofa agus féadfaidh, le linn an cheist a chur faoi bhreith amhlaidh nó tráth ar bith ina dhiaidh sin, ligean don duine sin a shaoirse a bheith aige, faoi réir na mbannaí agus na gcoinníollacha sin a cheapfaidh an Ard-Chúirt go dtí go dtabharfaidh an Chúirt Uachtarach breith ar an gceist a chuirfear faoina breith amhlaidh.

4° The High Court before which the body of a person alleged to be unlawfully detained is to be produced in pursuance of an order in that behalf made under this section shall, if the President of the High Court or, if he is not available, the senior judge of that Court who is available so directs in respect of any particular case, consist of three judges and shall, in every other case, consist of one judge only.

4° Is triúr breitheamh is Ard-Chúirt in aon chás áirithe, ina ndéantar duine a deirtear a bheith á choinneáil ina bhrá go haindleathach a thabhairt ina phearsain i láthair na hArd-Chúirte de bhun ordaithe chuige sin arna dhéanamh faoin alt seo, má dhéanann Uachtarán na hArd-Chúirte nó, mura mbeidh seisean ar fáil, an breitheamh is sinsearaí den Chúirt sin dá mbeidh ar fáil a ordú, i dtaobh an cháis sin, an líon sin a bheith inti agus is breitheamh amháin is Ard-Chúirt i ngach cás eile den sórt sin.

5° Where an order is made under this section by the High Court or a judge thereof for the production of the body of a person who is under sentence of death, the High Court or such judge thereof shall further order that the execution of the said sentence of death shall be deferred until after the body of such person has been produced before the High Court and the lawfulness of his detention has been determined and if, after such deferment, the detention of such person is determined to be lawful, the High Court shall appoint a day for the execution of the said sentence of death and that sentence shall have effect with the substitution of the day so appointed for the day originally fixed for the execution thereof.

5° I gcás an Ard-Chúirt nó breitheamh di do dhéanamh ordaithe faoin alt so á ordú duine faoi bhreith bháis a thabhairt i láthair ina phearsain, ní foláir don Ard-Chúirt nó don bhreitheamh sin di a ordú freisin feidhmiú na breithe báis sin a mhoilliú go dtí go dtabharfar an duine sin ina phearsain i láthair na hArd-Chúirte agus go gcinnfear an dleathach an duine sin a choinneáil ina bhrá nó nach dleathach agus má chinntear, tar éis an fheidhmithe sin a mhoilliú, gur dleathach an duine sin a choinneáil ina bhrá, ceapfaidh an Ard-Chúirt lá chun an bhreith bháis sin a fheidhmiú agus beidh éifeacht ag an mbreith bháis sin faoi réir an lá a cheapfar amhlaidh a chur in ionad an lae a socraíodh i dtosach chun an bhreith bháis sin a fheidhmiú.

Habeas corpus procedure

These four sub-sections were enacted as part of the Second Amendment of the Constitution in May 1941 and replaced there the original, sub-s 2, which was a simpler version of the new sub-section 2 and was virtually identical with the corresponding part of Article 6 of the 1922 Constitution. Sub-section 2 contains the essence of the principle and practice known as *habeas corpus*[1] and familiar in Ireland (though with interrup-

[1] This expression is traditional and is generally used throughout this chapter. However, it does not appear in the Constitution; and the practice of the courts in recent years has often been to refer to "relief under Article 40.4" or to an "order under Article 40.4.2" rather than to *habeas corpus*.

tions) since the seventeenth century. It is the mechanism whereby the legality of a detention is most frequently challenged, and a flaw or irregularity in a detention established, with the consequent setting at liberty of the person proved to be in wrongful detention; it was also the mechanism conventionally used even in the fairly recent past in disputes concerning the custody of (and the ancillary right to bring up and educate) a child.[2] The form taken by the procedure is, briefly, that the party complaining of unlawful detention applies ex parte for, and as a rule automatically[3] gets, a initial order directed to the person alleged to be detaining him - typically, the governor of a prison - and calling on that person to appear and justify the detention. If, on that appearance, that person fails to justify the detention, the initial order is made absolute and the person the subject of the application is ordered to be released. If on the other hand the lawfulness of the detention is established to the Court's satisfaction, the initial order is "discharged". In recent years, following the introduction of the judicial review procedure contained in O 84 of the Rules of the Superior Courts 1986, a practice has emerged[4] whereby in some instances the High Court will make no order under Article 40.4.2 but will instead grant the applicant leave to apply for judicial review (so that, for example, the warrant of imprisonment can be quashed) and directs that the application proceed as if commenced by way of an application for judicial review. Whether this procedure is actually compatible with Article 40.4.2 - which pre-supposes a self-contained procedure whereby the legality of the detention may be expeditiously determined - must be regarded as extremely doubtful, especially in view of recent developments which will be considered presently.[5]

Present practice does not conform with the procedure established by Article 40.4.2

The fact that the procedure in actual use does not square with the words of Article 40.4.2 - which makes no mention of conditional orders - has been judicially adverted to on occasion, most recently by Walsh J in *The State (Aherne) v Cotter,* [6] when he said, in reference to O 84 of the Rules of the Superior Courts, 1962 (which, unlike the Constitution, use the phrase *habeas corpus* and provides for procedure by way of conditional order, thus reflecting traditional practice):

> "The application to challenge the legality of the deprivation of someone's personal liberty is enshrined as a constitutional right in respect of which the whole procedure is set out in the Constitution itself. It is outside the competence of any rule-making authority to make any rules whatever to regulate this procedure. Indeed it is questionable, as it has been previously questioned, whether the method of a conditional order followed by the procedure of an order absolute is the appropriate procedure however convenient it may appear to be. The rules of the Superior Courts which refer to *habeas corpus* do not refer to the constitutional procedure and are not applicable thereto but would refer to such provisions as are still operative of the Habeas Corpus Acts and the procedures thereunder."

[2] For example, *In re Tilson, Infants* [1951] IR 1 (see pp. 1041-1042) was a *habeas corpus* application.
[3] Though in *The State (Cannon) v Kavanagh* [1937] IR 428 Maguire P said it would require "most exceptional circumstances for [the High Court] to grant even a conditional order of habeas corpus" to a person undergoing sentence after conviction on indictment: this was cited with approval by the Supreme Court in *The State (McDonagh) v Frawley* [1978] IR 131 and *McGlinchey v Governor of Portlaoise Prison* [1988] IR 671 and also by O'Hanlon J in *McGlinchey v Ireland* [1990] 2 IR 215.
[4] See Collins and O'Reilly, *Civil Proceedings and the State in Ireland: A Practitioner's Guide* (Dublin, 1989) at p.48.
[5] See below at p. 898
[6] [1982] IR 188. See also the comments of Lavery J in *Re Singer* (1963) 97 ILTR 130. See generally, Hogan, "*Procedural Aspects of an Inquiry under Article 40.4.*" (1983) DULJ 84.

It may be noted that O 84 of the Rules of the Superior Courts 1986 now distinguishes between the traditional *habeas corpus* procedure (conditional order; cause shown, motion to make absolute etc.) and the procedure established by Article 40.4.2. While O 84 rr 2-13 continue in force the traditional procedures under the Habeas Corpus Act 1782, O 84 r 1(2) makes it clear that this procedure is not applicable in the case of applications under Article 40.4.2:

> "The expression "order of *habeas corpus*" does not include an order made pursuant to Article 40, section 4 of the Constitution."[7]

An application under Article 40 must not be converted into other form of procedure

As we have seen, following the introduction of the new judicial review procedure by O 84 of the Rules of the Superior Courts, 1986, a practice emerged whereby applications for release under Article 40 were often treated by the High Court as applications for judicial review and leave to apply for such relief was often granted in lieu of an inquiry under Article 40. This happened in *Sheehan v Reilly*[8] where the High Court had declined to order an inquiry under Article 40 and instead granted leave to apply for judicial review. This practice was held to be wrong by the Supreme Court, with Finlay CJ observing that:

> "Such an application in its urgency and importance must necessarily transcend any procedural form of application for judicial review or otherwise. Applications which clearly, in fact, raise an issue as to the legality of the detention of a person must be treated as an application under Article 40, no matter how they are described."

The Chief Justice went on to point out that, in the present case, the procedure by way of judicial review (with "its consequential procedural delays") had meant that the applicant in this case was released at a later stage that might have occurred had there been a direct hearing on an Article 40 inquiry. In these circumstances, it was "quite inappropriate to convert the application under Article 40 into a judicial review proceeding which foreseeably might cause delay." Despite its special facts, *Sheehan's* case would seem to rule out any judicial attempts - no matter how well intentioned - to convert applications for an inquiry under Article 40 into the legality of the detention of a person into any other or alternative form of procedure.

Survival of old Habeas Corpus Acts doubtful?

To what extent the old Habeas Corpus Acts survive - indeed, whether their survival is compatible with the express provision of Article 40.4 which might be thought to supersede and replace them - is not at all clear. It may be recalled that in *The State (Walsh) v Lennon*[9] the view of the old High Court (Maguire P, Gavan Duffy and Martin Maguire JJ) was that no common law right to *habeas corpus* existed side by side with the

[7] Cf. the comments of Costello, "*A Constitutional Antiquity? - The Habeas Corpus (Ireland) Act 1782 Revisited*" (1988) 23 Ir Jur 240:

> "In 1986 the Superior Court Rules Committee ceased to regulate the procedure for an order under Article 40.4.2. This development reflected the influence of a doctrinaire view which holds that the sole source of institutions, offences or procedures institutionalised in the Constitution being the Constitution itself, any elaboration by legislation in these areas is illegal."

[8] [1993] 2 IR 81; [1993] ILRM 927.

[9] [1942] IR 112.

Constitution; the same approach would presumably equally exclude the coexistence with it of a statutory right. Yet in *Application of Zwann,*[10] where a judge of the High Court had released the applicants without giving an opportunity (as Article 40.4.2 requires) to certify the grounds of their detention in writing - a procedure which however O 84 of the 1962 Rules countenanced[11] - he did so under the Habeas Corpus Act 1781 (an Act of the old Irish Parliament): the Supreme Court merely expressed doubt as to the continued validity of this Act and of O 84 r 9. The matter awaits full exploration and settlement.[12]

Several important aspects of *habeas corpus* procedure have been considered by the courts over the last fifty years, though one or two significant decisions are older.

Repeated applications

In 1937 the High Court had to deal, in *The State (Dowling)* v *Kingston (No. 2),*[13] with an important matter concerning the extent of the right to *habeas corpus*: if an applicant, having obtained a conditional order, failed in his application to have it made absolute, could he (as distinct from appealing to the Supreme Court) renew his application before a different judge, and, if necessary, go from judge to judge until he either found one willing to give him an absolute order, or had exhausted the whole list of judges of the High Court? There were historical reasons for thinking that this might be so; and relatively recent English authority appeared to support the proposition.

In *Dowling's* case the applicant (who was relying on Article 6 of the 1922 Constitution, still in force) was refused an absolute order by a Court of three judges who decided against him by a majority. He then applied to the dissenting judge (Gavan Duffy J, who had thought him entitled to the absolute order) and asked him, alone, to order his release, relying on the expression in Article 6 "the High Court and any and every judge thereof" Gavan Duffy J however demurred; and on appeal the Supreme Court unanimously rejected the notion that the right to *habeas corpus* meant the right to be set free if any High Court judge could be found who was of the opinion that the imprisonment complained of was not in accordance with law. Sullivan CJ said:

> "In the present case the application to make absolute the conditional order was made to a Court constituted of three judges, it was heard and determined by that Court, and the order that was made expressed the decision of the majority of the members of that Court. The contention that the order of the Court should have been in conformity with the decision of the dissenting judge is unsupported by any authority and is in my opinion quite unsustainable."

Murnaghan J placed the matter in the clearest light by distinguishing between, on the one hand, a refusal by a judge to grant even a conditional order on an *ex parte* application (which would be a relatively rare occurrence) and, on the other hand, a refusal by a Court (which might or might not be composed of a single judge) to make a conditional order absolute - such refusal being consequential on a determination by that Court that the detention complained of was in accordance with the law:

[10] [1981] IR 395. See also *Kent County Council v CS* [1984] ILRM 292, where Finlay P treated an application under the Habeas Corpus Act 1782 as an application under Article 40.4.2.
[11] As does O 84 rr 2-13 of the Rules of the Superior Courts 1986.
[12] See generally, Costello, loc. cit.
[13] [1937] IR 699.

"It seems to me that the use of the words "and any and every judge thereof" is explained by the aim of Article 6 to give jurisdiction to each individual judge who may be approached outside of Court and to impose on him the duty of dealing with the complaint made *ex parte*. The Article thus secures a speedy and convenient hearing of the complaint at the instance of any person detained...

I am of opinion that when the Constitution spoke of detention in accordance with law, it contemplated a fixed and settled law and not the varying opinions of individual judges. When the High Court has pronounced that the detention is in accordance with law, did the Constitution contemplate a succession of applications to individual judges, any one of whom might declare the contrary?...In my opinion there is no right to apply to a judge after the High Court has pronounced the detention to be legal. It is quite a different matter (which however does not arise for discussion in this appeal) to say that the refusal of a judge to grant the first *ex parte* application prevents an application to another judge. In such a case the detention has not been declared to be in accordance with law it is only a view that there is no case to inquire into at all. In my opinion the right to make an ex parte application after a refusal by another judge has been confused with a hearing by the Court or judge at which the detention has been declared to be legal."[14]

Thirty years later, in the *Application of Woods*[15] the Supreme Court added a dimension to this clear ruling that, although an unsuccessful *ex parte* application for a conditional order might be repeated, there was a right to only one "determination" by the High Court (whether consisting of one judge or of three) on the lawfulness of a detention. This new dimension which emerged primarily in the context of Article 34.4.6 and the "finality" of the judgment of the Supreme Court - amounts to the rule that an application for *habeas corpus* may be renewed, and a second "determination" sought, if the application rests on new grounds which were not advanced (even if they might have been) on the first occasion. Ó Dálaigh CJ said:

"The High Court, on receipt of a complaint under Article 40.4.2...is required to order the release of the person detained unless satisfied that he is being detained in accordance with the law. The same duty rests on the Supreme Court. This means that both Courts are not confined to an examination of the illegality complained of by the applicant but are required to be alert for other grounds which could render the detention unlawful. But neither the High Court nor the Supreme Court warrants, by its decision in an application for *habeas corpus*, that every possible ground of complaint has been considered and ruled. This would cast on the Court an impossible burden. Such matters as are considered by the Supreme Court in its judgment are finally decided for the High Court. But this will not preclude an applicant from later raising a new ground even though that ground might have been, but was not, put forward on the first application.

The principles which apply in litigation inter partes are not applicable in *habeas corpus*. The duty which the Court has under the Constitution of ordering the release of a person, unless satisfied that he is lawfully detained, requires that the Court should entertain a complaint which bears on the question of the legality of the

[14] Note that in *The State (Richardson) v Governor of Mountjoy Prison* [1980] ILRM 82 Barrington J made an order ("after considerable argument") for an inquiry under Article 40 in circumstances where the original application had been refused by Keane J.

[15] [1970] IR 154.

[16] High Court, 24 November 1969. See generally, Kenny, "*Informality in Modern Irish Habeas Corpus Procedure*" (1974) 9 Ir Jur 67.

detention - even though in earlier proceedings the applicant might have raised the matter but did not do so. The duty of the Courts, to see that no-one is deprived of his personal liberty save in accordance with law, overrides considerations which are valid in litigation inter partes."

There must be some limits

However, some signs have emerged which would seem to qualify what was said on this point in *Woods*. Shortly before the decision in *Woods*, Henchy J had said in *Re McDonagh*[16] which was "the ninth time [since the applicant's conviction and sentence] that a Court order has been made disposing of an application by him to escape the consequences of his conviction", that there had to be some limit to repeated applications:

> "While it is understandable, because of the special nature and purpose of *habeas corpus*, that more than one application may be made in respect of a particular detention, and that failure to state a particular complaint of unlawful detention in an earlier application should not, ipso facto, be a bar to raising it in a subsequent application, I should have thought that where a person has been convicted and sentenced to imprisonment, it could not be said that he will never, during his imprisonment, be debarred from applying for *habeas corpus* notwithstanding how many previous applications he has already made...The result would be litigiousness and the processes of the Court would be abused."

These sentiments have begun to find judicial favour. In *McGlinchey v Ireland*[17] the Supreme Court held that Egan J had been correct to refuse an application on the ground that an identical application had already been refused by Johnson J. Nevertheless, Finlay CJ went on to say that the courts had a duty, in such a fundamental matter, to investigate the complaint to see if there were any grounds for an inquiry and to conduct such an inquiry under Article 40.4 "if any of the grounds should appear arguable." It is also of interest to note that, in a subsequent application by the same applicant, *McGlinchey v Ireland,*[18] O'Hanlon J said that the applicant was "debarred from presenting further applications to the court unless it could be shown that further grounds can be put forward which have not been considered in the course of earlier applications to the High Court and Supreme Court." While the present situation concerning repeated applications is accordingly somewhat unclear, it seems that while the fact that an applicant has repeatedly applied for relief will not, *ipso facto*, exclude the present application from full consideration, nevertheless the courts will be reluctant to put the full Article 40.4 procedure in train in the absence of fresh evidence or new grounds not previously advanced.

Application on another's behalf

While Article 40.4.2 envisages expressly a complaint made "by or on behalf of any person",[19] it does not necessarily mean that an uncontrolled option exists. In *The State*

[17] *The Irish Times*, 28 July 1987.

[18] [1990] 2 IR 215. See also *McGlinchey v Governor of Portlaoise Prison* [1988] IR 671 where Gannon J said that Article 40.4.2 "cannot properly be used as an informal means of obtaining...the resolution of disputed questions of fact or law previously ruled upon or pending determination under regular court procedures."

[19] Of course, relief under Article 40.4.2 is not confined to citizens. For some reason, this point had been taken in *The State (Kugan) v O'Rourke* [1985] IR 658 where two Sri Lankan citizens (who had been refused leave to enter the State) sought to challenge the validity of their detention, Egan J said that the wording of Article 40.4.2 clearly showed that it was open to any person, irrespective of status or citizenship, to make such an application.

(Burke) v Lennon,[20] in which the application in respect of the prisoner was in fact made by his brother, Gavan Duffy J said:

> "I shall speak throughout of Seamus Burke [the prisoner] as the applicant; he has made an affidavit and is the applicant in effect, but in form the applicant is his brother; no objection has been made on this score, but I am not to be taken as construing Article 40 of the Constitution to sanction an application by a third party where the person detained can make the application himself."

However, in the *Application of Woods*[21] the Supreme Court consented to entertain an application brought on the prisoner's behalf by another person (actually a fellow-prisoner whom Woods wished to act for him, and also - though the Court would not permit this[22] - to conduct his case before the Court). Ó Dálaigh CJ said:

> "It should be clear that it is not questioned that under Article 40.4.2 a person has the right to complain to the High Court on behalf of another person that that other person is being unlawfully detained. This right includes a right to state the grounds which are put forward for alleging that such other person is being unlawfully detained."[23]

It is not clear whether the Court recognised this right as absolute - so as to include e.g. an officious volunteer acting against the prisoner's wishes - or whether some practical limitations, such as Gavan Duffy J evidently was willing to envisage, might be imposed. It is however certain that any such limitations would have to be consistent with the Courts' duty to protect the liberty of the citizen and to investigate alleged unlawful infringements of it.

In *The State (Quinn) v Ryan* [24] the Supreme Court entertained a *habeas corpus* application in the prisoner's own name, but in circumstances in which it was obvious that his authority to the solicitor who had been acting for him could not have been given in respect of this particular application (indeed this was the gist of the case, inasmuch as he had been whisked by Irish and British police out of the jurisdiction without having had a chance to consult his legal advisers). Ó Dálaigh CJ said:

> "Mr. Justice Teevan [in the High Court] refused a conditional order because he considered that the solicitor for the [applicant] had not his client's authority to make an application for a conditional order of *habeas corpus* and because it was not shown that he was in custody. It might be, the judge thought, that the [applicant] had vanished of his own volition. This is possible, but the probabilities on the information available to this Court are otherwise: they point to an arrest.
>
> As to the authority of the [applicant's] solicitor the Court is of opinion in the circumstances of this case that there is sufficient shown to entitle the solicitor to main-

[20] [1940] IR 136.

[21] [1970] IR 154. See, to like effect, the judgment of Kenny J in *The State (Egan) v Governor of Central Mental Hospital*, High Court, 27 January 1972.

[22] See also *McGlinchey v Ireland, The Irish Times*, July 27, 1987, where Finlay CJ said that it was not possible for one person to represent for the purposes of argument, the case of another, "even on an application under Article 40 in regard to the legality of the detention." This latter remarks must be understood in the context of third parties presenting arguments on the substantive issue of the legality of the detention where cause has been shown by the detainer, as opposed to third party applications to the High Court for an initial inquiry.

[23] See also the comments of O'Higgins CJ in *The People v Pringle* 2 Frewen 57 to the effect that any such application can be made by a solicitor or counsel "without any express instructions and even without the consent of the person concerned." See also *In re D.* [1987] IR 449 where the Article 40.4.2 application was brought by the parents of a mentally retarded applicant on her behalf.

[24] [1965] IR 170.

tain this application. The indications are that the [applicant] was prevented from consulting with his legal advisers and the Court cannot permit an Article of the Constitution to be set at nought with impunity."

While the essence - and the effectiveness of *habeas corpus* lies in the fact that the Court's order to produce a prisoner and to justify his detention is directed normally to the person in immediate physical control of the prisoner, there have been cases in which a merely indirect, or assumed, control has sufficed to make someone answerable to the Court. An English case with an Irish background will illustrate this well: *Secretary of State for Home Affairs v O'Brien,*[25] in which the British Home Secretary had had the applicant arrested and deported to Dublin, where on arrival he had been interned. The Home Secretary had no legal standing in the new Irish State which had just come into being, but the Court of Appeal took the view that, though he had parted with legal control of the prisoner, he might still have some de facto influence on what became of him and might be in a position to procure his release; he was accordingly treated as being a proper respondent and was ordered to make a return to a writ of *habeas corpus*.

On the other hand, in *The State (Quinn) v Ryan*[26] in 1964 the Supreme Court refrained from making absolute conditional orders of *habeas corpus* against Irish police officers who had co-operated with British officers in removing a prisoner from the State and into Britain, as the Irish officers no longer had custody of the prisoner (but they were held to have committed "contempt of the courts" by their conduct).[27] In the High Court, Teevan J said:

"The probability...that, under the pressure of the Court process, the defendant might secure the return of the person formerly held by him...[is not present here]. It would be absolutely impossible for Inspector Ryan to resume custody or otherwise secure production in Court of the [applicant]...Furthermore, that impossibility appears to be recognised as such by the [applicant's] counsel in that, in their written submission, they requested this Court to use its endeavours towards procuring governmental intervention with the British authorities for the return of the applicant. As I read this submission it implies the concession that Inspector Ryan is powerless to produce, or to arrange for the production of, the [applicant]. This is not a case where the facts throw doubt on whether the respondent has truly ceased to have control over the [applicant]."

However, in *Application of Zwann,*[28] in which the applicants (a Dutch trawler crew detained under a fisheries statute) had immediately left the jurisdiction when the High Court made an absolute order of *habeas corpus*, the Supreme Court entertained the State's appeal and discharged the High Court's order despite the apparent futility of the process. O'Higgins CJ said the departure of the applicant was not:

"any bar or obstacle to the prosecution of this appeal. It is true that this Court will not entertain questions which are purely hypothetical or academic, and will not hear complaints made by persons who lack a real interest or locus standi in the question raised. However, this is not such a case. Here the matter raised on appeal is of real concern to the Attorney General and to those charged with the duty of initiating prosecutions under the Fisheries (Consolidation) Acts. It is of no significance that

[25] [1923] AC 603.
[26] [1965] IR 70.
[27] See pp. 394-395.
[28] [1981] IR 395.

> the success of the appeal can now have no practical effect. If this Court is satisfied for any reason that the orders in question ought not to have been made then these orders must be set aside."

He added that to decline to do so merely because of the "practical difficulties" (of proceeding further against the absent Dutchmen) would be for the Court to decline to exercise its proper appellate jurisdiction; and said the principle of entertaining an appeal against habeas corpus, even where re-arrest was not possible, had been implicitly accepted in *The State (Browne) v Feran* [29] and *The State (Dillon) v Kelly*.[30]

The purely technical "custody" of bailsmen was held insufficient to justify the making of an order of *habeas corpus* against them in *In re Attorney General v Blennerhassett*.[31]

Production of the body

In *The State (M. Woods) v Kelly*[32] an applicant for *habeas corpus*, in appealing to the Supreme Court against the High Court's refusal to make the order, was allowed to add a new ground of appeal based on the reference in Article 40.4.2 to "producing the body" of a person whose detention is to be inquired into. Ó Dálaigh CJ , with whom the other members of the Court agreed, said:

> "Counsel submitted that Article 40 requires that a judge who makes a conditional order of *habeas corpus* must, at the same time, order the production in Court of the body of the relevant [applicant]. The [applicant] in this particular case was represented by counsel; he did not ask to be present at the argument in Court, nor did the order of Mr. Justice Kenny direct that his body should be brought into Court. The power conferred by Article 40 to order the production in Court of the body of the [applicant] is, in my opinion, an enabling power. The submission made on behalf of the [applicant] is two-edged. The corollary of the submission is that the Court cannot make an order setting the [applicant] at liberty unless he is present in Court. It is, in my view, clear on the wording of Article 40 that the President was not disabled from making the order allowing the cause shown by reason of the absence of the body of the prosecutor in Court."

That the power to order the production of the prisoner in person is a mere enabling power was repeated by the Court in *The State (Rogers) v Galvin,*[33] when Henchy J, speaking for the Court, said such an order was superfluous in a case where the prisoner making the application was actually already present in Court (as had happened here).

The provision of Article 40.4.2 about the Court's power to order a *habeas corpus* respondent to "certify in writing the grounds of [the prisoner's] detention is - unlike the power to order the production of the prisoner in person - not merely enabling but mandatory. This appeared in clear terms first in *Application of Zwann*,[34] where Barrington J, having quashed by *certiorari* a detention order made under a fisheries statute, made at the same time what seemed to him the necessarily consequential absolute order of *habeas corpus*. This order was recited as having been made in virtue of Article 40; but the Supreme Court discharged it on appeal, O'Higgins CJ saying that the recital could not be correct:

[29] [1967] IR 417.
[30] [1970] IR 174.
[31] (1933) 67 ILTR 136.
[32] [1969] IR 269.
[33] [1983] IR 249.
[34] [1981] IR 395.

"since it is implicit in Article 40.4.2 that before such an order can be made an opportunity must be afforded to the detaining person to justify such detention [and no such opportunity had been given]."

This point was made even more emphatically in *The State (Rogers) v Galvin,*[35] in which an absolute order had been made by a High Court judge who was at the time presiding over the Special Criminal Court before which the applicant had been brought and charged. This judge heard the application and heard evidence also from the police officer in whose custody the prisoner was; but that officer had no opportunity to arrange separate legal representation or to "certify in writing the grounds of the detention". Nevertheless the judge made an absolute order. On appeal the Supreme Court reversed him, Henchy J saying:

"This opportunity of justifying the detention [provided for by Article 40.4.21 is always treated as including an opportunity of justifying the detention by means of a certificate in writing. [Unlike the power to order production of the prisoner's body] it cannot be treated as a merely enabling or dispensable preliminary. It is mandatory. It lies at the heart of the jurisdiction to grant a release by *habeas corpus*. It is a constitutional recognition of the rule of natural justice expressed in the maxim *audi alteram partem*. It guards against the risk that, on an *ex parte* application, or on an application in which the detainer has not had a proper opportunity of countering the detainee's complaint, an unjustified order of release from custody may be made. It gives constitutional form and shape to what had been for centuries an essential prelude to release by means of the writ of *habeas corpus*."[36]

Significance of "forthwith enquire"

The question whether the immediate enquiry prescribed by Article 40.4.2 implies an instant, uninterrupted proceeding with a determination on the spot was raised by the applicant in *The State (Whelan) v Governor of Mountjoy Prison*.[37] His grievance was, that when his application was first heard the High Court had been told that an earlier decision of the President of the High Court on a point which was now again in issue - and which, if applied in his own case, would have led to his being set at liberty - was under appeal to the Supreme Court: and the High Court thereupon adjourned his application, setting him free on bail for the time being. The Supreme Court then reversed the earlier decision, thus depriving him of the precedent which might have availed him had it been followed when his application was first entertained. Even though his counsel had acquiesced in the adjournment on bail, he now said that the High Court judge who had adjourned the hearing had acted unconstitutionally inasmuch as the words "forthwith enquire" in Article 40.4.2, together with the special exception made by Article 40.4.3 for cases where a law was under challenge, showed that apart from that exception there was no jurisdiction to interrupt the *habeas corpus* hearing by an adjournment. Barrington J rejected this submission; the exceptional provision of Article 40.4.3 he said "should not be over-emphasised" (sc. to the point of bringing the *expressio unius exclu-*

[35] [1983] IR 249.

[36] These comments may now have to be read in the light of the comments of Finlay CJ in *Sheehan v Reilly* [1993] 2 IR 81; [1993] ILRM 427 where it was apparently suggested that, in certain exceptional circumstances, the High Court might order the immediate release of the applicant following informal inquiries by the judge of the detainer, but without, apparently, having given the detainer an opportunity of justifying the detention in writing or appearing through solicitor and counsel to defend the legality of the detention.

[37] [1983] ILRM 52. See also *In re D.* [1987] IR 449 (High Court wrong to adjourn Article 40.4.2 application pending outcome of wardship petition).

sio alterius rule into play), as it had been inserted in the Constitution by amendment in 1941 in response to a special (and, as it turned out, transient) necessity; and, in general,[38] he said:

> "it appears to me also that, on an application for *habeas corpus*, the duty of the High Court is forthwith to enquire into the legality of the [applicant's] detention, but that once the enquiry is entered on, and provided the urgency and importance of the proceedings are kept in mind, the Court is entitled...to conduct the enquiry in the manner which the Court thinks best calculated to resolve the issues of law and fact raised in the proceedings, and to achieve the interest of justice. If the application raises difficult issues of law or fact the Court may have to consider whether the [applicant] should be admitted to bail until these issues are resolved. The duty of the High Court "forthwith" to enquire into the legality of the...detention stresses the importance and the urgency of *habeas corpus* proceedings. But it does not mean that the High Court should skimp its enquiry or proceed on an inadequate understanding of the law or the facts. The reference in the same sub-section to a "named day", he held similarly, did not mean that the enquiry was to be completed on that day."

Nonetheless, the Supreme Court has recently emphasised the importance of speed and urgency which must of necessity attach to applications under Article 40. In *Sheehan v O'Reilly*[39] the Court held that the High Court should not have concerted an Article 40 inquiry into an application for judicial review where this "foreseeably might cause delay." Finlay CJ also pointed out that, upon an application under Article 40.4.2, the High Court judge:

> "has got a jurisdiction and discretion...even prior to reaching a conclusion that a sufficient doubt as the legality of the detention of the applicant has been raised to warrant calling upon the jailor or detainer to show cause, to make inquiries of a speedy and, if necessary, informal nature to try and ascertain the facts."

This meant that, in the instant case, had the High Court ascertained the material facts concerning the various sentences imposed by the District Court by "simple immediate request" to the prison authorities and to the authorities of the District Court, the applicant might even have been released on the date of the initial Article 40 application.[40] The facts of the *Sheehan* case were undoubtedly special, so that it may be difficult to extract a general principle from this judgment as to when, and in what circumstances, the High Court should exercise, of its own motion, as it were, the rather novel[41] quasi-inquisitorial jurisdiction apparently contemplated by the language of Article 40.4.2 ("forthwith enquire"). At the same time, this case does strongly suggest that there may well be cases where it is incumbent on the High Court judge to make immediate inquiries of his own motion following an Article 40 application.

[38] A similar argument is to be found in the judgment of Finlay CJ in *Attorney General v Hamilton (No.1)* [1993] 2 IR 250; [1993] ILRM 81 with regard to the amendments effected to the Article 26 procedure by the special provisions of the Second Amendment of the Constitution Act 1941.

[39] [1993] ILRM 427.

[40] There is a hint here in the judgment of Finlay CJ that had the High Court been satisfied following such immediate inquiries with the appropriate authorities that the detention was unlawful, the judge might have ordered the release of the applicant there and then. How such a procedure could be reconciled with the obligation to give the detainer an opportunity to justify the detention in writing (for which see pp. 904-905), is not clear.

[41] There does not appear to have any previous recorded instance where the Supreme Court directed that the High Court should have made enquiries of its own motion upon an Article 40 application. Hitherto, the invariable practice of the High Court had been to approach the hearing of such applications in the ordinary way, viz., that the establishment of the facts was a matter for the parties.

Appeals

While Article 34.4.3 gives the Supreme Court "with such exceptions and subject to such regulations as may be prescribed by law...appellate jurisdiction from all decisions of the High Court", and while no law has been enacted which excepts any class of *habeas corpus* case from this appellate jurisdiction, it was for a long time the general view that the jurisdiction existed only for the benefit of an unsuccessful applicant, not for the benefit of an unsuccessful respondent.[42] This amounted to continuing, notwithstanding the general words of Article 34.4.3, to observe the principle of the nineteenth-century English case of *Cox v Hakes*:[43] an appeal could be brought by a prisoner against the refusal of a writ, but no appeal could be brought by a gaoler against the granting of one.

This liberal rider was judicially affixed to the Constitution by the Supreme Court in *The State (Burke) v Lennon*.[44] Here Gavan Duffy J had made absolute a conditional order of *habeas corpus* in favour of a person interned under Part VI of the Offences against the State Act 1939, at the same time declaring this Part to be unconstitutional. The constitutional issue being of grave importance to the Government, the respondents, relying on the general words of Article 34.4.3, sought to appeal against the *habeas corpus* order to the Supreme Court, but failed. Sullivan CJ said that, apart from the meaning of Article 34, it was necessary to consider what the former law had been:

> "As to the rights of such a person [alleged to be unlawfully detained] prior to the Constitution of the Irish Free State there is no controversy; he could apply to any of the High Courts for a writ of *habeas corpus*, and if, on the return to that writ, the Court was satisfied that his detention was unlawful, it made an order for his immediate release, and when he had been discharged from custody pursuant to that order the legality of his discharge could never be questioned by an appeal. That was decided in *Cox v Hakes*...The law as declared in *Cox v Hakes* was by [Article 73 of] the 1922 Constitution continued in force in the Irish Free State unless it was inconsistent with any Article of that Constitution. At no time while that Constitution continued was that law questioned in any court of the Free State."

The case was, however, now being made that in fact *Cox v Hakes* had not overridden Article 66 of the 1922 Constitution or the similar Article 34.4.3 of that of 1937. But in construing the latter, Sullivan CJ said he was:

> "entitled to have regard to the provisions of Article 40.4, and in considering that Article I am entitled to consider the principles formerly applicable in *habeas corpus* cases...The latter Article contemplates summary application, upon the hearing of which the right to release will be summarily determined. I think that in accordance with settled principles and established practice that determination is, and was intended to be, final. It follows that in my opinion an appeal does not lie to this Court from an order of the High Court made under Article 40.4 discharging a person from illegal custody."

With this statement of principle, Murnaghan, Meredith and Geoghegan JJ agreed the only dissent came from Johnston J, who thought that Article 34.4.3 ought to be literally construed.[45]

[42] See *R. (Johnstone) v O'Sullivan* [1923] 2 IR 13.
[43] 15 App Cas 506.
[44] [1940] IR 136.
[45] See pp. 684-685.

In 1967 the misgivings of Johnston J in *Burke's* case were vindicated by the Supreme Court in *The State (Browne) v Feran*,[46] in which the Court refused to follow the line taken by the "old" Supreme Court in 1939. Walsh J, with whom the four other judges agreed, noted that some pre-1922 law surrounding habeas corpus - the rule prohibiting an appeal by an unsuccessful applicant if the matter were "criminal"[47] had been regarded as abrogated by the general words of Article 66, while other pre-1922 law - *Cox v Hakes* - had been regarded as surviving those general words; and said "such a selective interpretation of the constitutional provisions finds no support in those provisions". He went on:

> "I do not consider that there is anything in the wording of either Article 6 of the Constitution of Saorstát Éireann or Article 40.4 of the Constitution of Ireland which amounts to an express exclusion, or to an exclusion to be necessarily implied, from the words "all decisions" in Article 34 of the Constitution, or in Article 66 of the Constitution of Saorstát Éireann, of the right of appeal from decisions of the High Court granting an order of *habeas corpus*."

The difficulty which the "old" Supreme Court had seen in what it thought was its lack of jurisdiction to reverse an order for the release of a prisoner did not seem serious to him:

> "The submission is that, in as much as Article 40...directs the High Court to order the release of the person detained unless it is satisfied that the detention is lawful, there is an absolute discharge and there is no method by which he may be retaken. It is undoubtedly true that an order for release must be made and that nothing in the nature of a stay can be put upon it for the purpose of an appeal. That, however, does not determine the matter. If this Court, on appeal, is satisfied that the detention was lawful it means, first of all, that the order of the High Court is to be set aside. The question of how the former prisoner may be retaken may depend upon the precise circumstances of each case. A prisoner who is released from an unlawful detention in which he was held while on remand remains still subject to the further order of the Court dealing with his case, and he may be remanded in custody in so far as that is permitted by law. In the case of a convicted prisoner, a fresh warrant of execution could be issued if it were to be held that the original warrant, which was held in the High Court to be unlawful or insufficient to warrant the detention complained of, is spent by its initial execution. I do not see why this Court, in the exercise of its inherent jurisdiction in reversing the order of the High Court, should not direct a warrant for the apprehension of the former prisoner for the purpose of his recommittal to a place of detention...It may well be that while the appeal is being determined the former prisoner is no longer available for apprehension but that cannot affect the jurisdiction of the Court to hear and determine the appeal."[48]

The difficulty caused by *Burke's* case in the fact that the constitutionality of the legislation under which he had been held could not be decided in the Supreme Court if that Court would not entertain an appeal against his release, was resolved in 1941 by the enactment, as part of the Second Amendment of the Constitution, of sub-s 3 of Article 40.4 Walsh J, expounded it as follows:

[46] [1967] IR 147.

[47] Supreme Court of Judicature (Ireland) Act 1877, s 50. See, e.g., *Re Clifford and O'Sullivan* [1921] AC 570 and *R. (Johnstone) v O'Sullivan* [1923] 2 IR 13. Walsh J observed that, in any event, the enforcement of the constitutional right to liberty *via* Article 40.4. was a civil - and not a criminal - matter.

[48] As was to happen in later cases such as *Application of Zwann* [1981] IR 395 and *The State (Trimbole) v Governor of Mountjoy Prison* [1985] IR 550.

> "Subsection 3 of s 4 of Article 40 is confined specifically to cases where the High Court is satisfied that a person is detained in accordance with a law enacted since the 27th December 1937 - see the decision of this Court in *The State (Sheerin) v Kennedy* [49] - and that such law is invalid having regard to the provisions of the Constitution... In those circumstances the case does not fall to be determined under Article 40.4.2, and the right to release from the detention under that sub-section becomes dependent upon the operation of sub-section 3. Those circumstances also determine the nature of the jurisdiction of this Court by substituting a consultative case stated for the ordinary appellate jurisdiction conferred by Article 34.4.3 in respect of the validity of the law in accordance with which the person is detained, but not in respect of any other matters decided in the High Court in the same case, including the question of the validity of any other law."

(In *Sheerin's* case, to which Walsh J adverted, Kenny J in the High Court had, in reliance on Article 40.4.3, stated a case for the opinion of the Supreme Court on the constitutionality of s 2 of the Prevention of Crime Act 1908, being himself of the view that it was unconstitutional. Walsh J, with whom the rest of the Court agreed, said that the question of the constitutionality of a pre-1937 law was one to be determined by reference to Article 50 - was it, or was it not, "consistent" with the Constitution so as to have been continued in force? - and such a law could not be the subject of the special appeal in the form of case stated under Article 40.4.3, which related purely to post-1937 laws.[50])

No power to place a stay an order for release

While the Supreme Court does have jurisdiction to order the re-arrest of an applicant, it is plain since the decision in *The State (Trimbole) v Governor of Mountjoy Prison*[51] that this jurisdiction will be exercised only if the Supreme Court has decided that the order of release made by the High Court was incorrect. It follows that that Court has no power to place a stay on an order for release pending an appeal by the respondents against the order of the High Court.

Judicial attitudes to habeas corpus

There are essentially three governing principles underlying much of the case-law on Article 40.4.2 procedure. The first is that since the object of this remedy is to provide a speedy and efficacious remedy whereby the legality of a person's detention may be determined, it is wrong to use this procedure for other purposes. This was illustrated by *In re D.*,[52] where Hamilton P adjourned an application under Article 40.4.2 to enable a health board bring a wardship petition in respect a mentally retarded person under their care. The Supreme Court felt that an adjournment for this purpose - although perfectly understandable in the circumstances - was inappropriate, since, according to Finlay CJ:

[49] [1966] IR 379.

[50] For another example of this (rare) case-stated procedure, see *The State (Gilliland) v Governor of Mountjoy Prison* [1987] IR 201. For a discussion of the jurisdiction issued raised both in this case and in *Sheerin*, see generally pp. 421-422 and pp. 529-530 respectively.

[51] [1985] IR 550.

[52] [1987] IR 449. See also *Cahill v Governor of the Military Detention Barracks, Curragh Camp* [1980] ILRM 191 (wrong to invoke Article 40.4.2 procedure when in reality some other remedy is desired).

> "The High Court on hearing an application [under Article 40.4.2] must reach a single decision, namely, whether the detention of the person is or is not in accordance with law....Such a procedure does not...admit of any supervision or monitoring of the interests of the person concerned, even allowing for a condition of mental retardation or other want of capacity."[53]

Allied to this is the judicial view that the Article 40.4 procedure should only be employed in *post-conviction* inquiries[54] where, in the words of O'Higgins CJ in *The State (McDonagh) v Frawley,*[55] there has been "such a default of fundamental requirements that the detention may be said to be wanting in due process of law" and that other legal defects attaching to conviction, sentence or conditions of detention fall to be investigated "under other forms of proceedings." [56]

The third principle from which the courts start in questions of personal liberty is that statutes restrictive of personal liberty will be very strictly and narrowly construed. In *Attorney General v McBride*,[57] where the extended arrest provisions of the Public Safety Act 1927, were in issue, Hanna J said:

> "It is the first duty of the courts to show the greatest solicitude in protecting the liberty of the subject from anything but a strict application of a statute of this nature, even though such statute be essential to the public safety."

A good modern example of this approach may be found in a striking judgment of McCarthy J in *McMahon v Leahy.*[58] In this case affidavits grounding an extradition warrant had not been properly sworn and the judge said that he could not overlook this carelessness on the part of the Northern Irish authorities:

> "Narrow though this approach may appear to be, the insistence on strict compliance with all the requirements of the exercise of statutory powers is a fundamental feature of our jurisprudence; it is the duty of the superior courts to exercise vigilance necessary to ensure such compliance."

And in *Russell v Fanning*,[59] Barr J said that, in an application for *habeas corpus*, the High Court could investigate all errors of law and fact, even if such errors would normally be regarded as having been made within jurisdiction.

[53] See also *McGlinchey v Governor of Portlaoise Prison* [1988] IR 671 where Gannon J said in the High Court that an Article 40 application could not be employed to resolve "disputed questions of law or fact previously ruled on or pending determination under regular court procedure. The Supreme Court agreed with him, with Finlay CJ saying that Article 40.4.2 was a "simple and uncomplicated procedure" because it deals with an "essential and vital matter, the liberty of the individual. It is therefore important that it should not be debased by using it for purposes for which it was not intended." See also the same judge's comments on the need for speed and urgency in the determination of Article 40 applications in *Sheehan v Reilly* [1993] 2 IR 81; [1993] ILRM 427.

[54] "It should be re-iterated...that post-trial inquiries under Article 40.4...cannot be concerned with some [mere] alleged legal error or impropriety": see per Hederman J in *Hardy v Ireland*, Supreme Court, 18 March 1993. The situation is, of course, otherwise in the case of pre-trial detainees: see pp. 819-823.

[55] [1978] IR 131.

[56] These principles have been endorsed by the Supreme Court on many subsequent occasions: see, e.g., *McGlinchey v Governor of Portlaoise Prison* [1988] IR 671; *Rock v Governor of St. Patrick's Institution*, Supreme Court, 22 March 1993.

[57] [1928] IR 451. See also *In re Duffy* [1934] IR 550.

[58] [1984] IR 525. See also the comments of O'Higgins CJ in *People v Farrell* [1978] IR 13 and those of McCarthy J in *People v Byrne* [1987] IR 363 and Hamilton P in *Byrne v Grey* [1988] IR 31.

[59] [1988] IR 565.

On the other hand, there is no established catalogue of factors which will render a detention unlawful; and in *The State (Royle) v Kelly*[60] Henchy J expressed himself against any attempt to draw up such a catalogue. Dealing with the phrase "in accordance with law" in Article 40.4.2 he said:

> "The expression is a compendious one and is designed to cover these basic legal principles and procedures which are so essential for the preservation of personal liberty under our Constitution that departure from them renders a detention unjustifiable in the eyes of the law. To enumerate them in advance would not be feasible and, in any case, an attempt to do so would only tend to diminish the constitutional guarantee."

No simultaneous re-arrest

In *The State (McDonagh) v Frawley*[61] the Supreme Court said (*per* O'Higgins CJ):

> "In cases where it has not been shown to the satisfaction of the Court that the detention is "in accordance with law", in the sense indicated, the release of the detained person must be ordered and, notwithstanding judicial dicta to the contrary, the order of release may not be coupled with an order of re-arrest. The protection of personal liberty, which Article 40.4 is intended to ensure, would be hollow and ineffectual if the order of release was not unqualified and unconditional."

This appears to conform with the requirements of s 5 of the Habeas Corpus (Ireland) Act 1781 which (assuming it has survived the enactment of the Constitution) provides:

> That no person...who shall be delivered or set at large upon any *habeas corpus*, shall at any time hereafter be again imprisoned, or committed for the same offence by any person or persons whatsoever, other than by the legal order or process of such court wherein he or they shall be bound by recognisance to appear, or other court having jurisdiction of the cause..."[62]

On the other hand, the release on *habeas corpus* of a prisoner awaiting trial, due to some defect in the legality of his detention, is not a bar to his subsequent rearrest on the original charge. This was established in *In re Singer (No. 2).*[63] Walsh J (taking the same view as the other judges of the High Court and subsequently of the Supreme Court) said:

> "The applicant submits that because of the order for his release...he could not again be either arrested or detained in custody in respect of the charges upon which he was being detained at the time of his release. Such a claim, which does not take into account the reasons for the order for his release, really amounts to a claim that once a person has been released on *habeas corpus* no matter what the reason he can never again be apprehended or detained in custody in respect of the charges which were pending against him at the time of his release. Such a proposition, if it were correct, would lead to absurd results."

[60] [1974] IR 259.

[61] [1978] IR 131. See also *The State (McFadden) v Governor of Mountjoy Prison* [1981] ILRM 113.

[62] The object of this section appears to have been originally intended only for the protection of a person released on bail: see *Re Singer* (1964) 98 ILTR 112 and *Costello, loc.cit.*

[63] (1964) 98 ILTR 112.

However, it seems that the better interpretation of section 5 is that it prevents the re-arrest of the applicant in respect of the same offence[64] or where it would involve the re-litigation of the same jurisdictional point."[65]

[64] See *The State (Dowling) v Kingston (No.2)* [1937] IR 699 (where both Maguire P and Hanna J held that section 5 did not apply because "the offence charged was not that upon which the [applicant] was first arrested.") and *The State (Bowes) v Fitzpatrick* [1978] ILRM 195 (applicant could be arrested and charged with murder following order of High Court releasing him from custody following his unlawful detention in respect of malicious damage offence).

[65] *The State (McFadden) v Governor of Mountjoy Prison (No.2)* [1981] ILRM 120 (*semble*).

Article 40.4.6

DEFENCE FORCES NOT AMENABLE TO *HABEAS CORPUS* IN TIME OF WAR OR ARMED REBELLION

6° Nothing in this section, however, shall be invoked to prohibit, control, or interfere with any act of the Defence Forces during the existence of a state of war or armed rebellion.

6° Ach aon ghníomh de ghníomhartha na bhFórsaí Cosanta le linn eisíthe nó ceannairce faoi arm, ní cead aon ní dá bhfuil san alt seo a agairt chun an gníomh sin a thoirmeasc nó a rialú nó a bhac.

This provision corresponds with the second clause of Article 6 of the 1922 Constitution: this, in turn, reproduced formerly recognised rules of common law, chiefly relevant in the Irish setting to military "courts" applying "martial law".[1] Note that the artificial meaning given to the expression "time of war" in Article 28.3.3 has no counterpart in this sub-section.

As there has been no state of war or armed rebellion in the country since the civil war of 1922-23, this sub-section has not been judicially considered. The corresponding provision of the 1922 Constitution was relied on unsuccessfully in *R. (O'Brien) v Military Governor, North Dublin Union*;[2] the old Court of Appeal held that on that day (1 August 1923) a state of war did not exist in Dublin, though there was "a certain amount of disorder".

[1] See pp. 652-655 and see also *R. (Johnstone) v O'Sullivan* [1923] 2 IR 13.
[2] [1924] 1 IR 32.

Article 40.5

INVIOLABILITY OF THE DWELLING

5. The dwelling of every citizen is inviolable and shall not be forcibly entered save in accordance with law.	**5. Is slán do gach saoránach a ionad cónaithe, agus ní cead dul isteach ann go foréigneach ach de réir dlí.**

1922 provision

This provision, which is substantially identical with Article 7 of the 1992 Constitution,[1] has received relatively little judicial attention, though the first case in which it was considered provided the occasion for *dicta* which have had an important effect in the law of evidence.[2]

Entry forbidden unless authorised by law

This was *The People (Attorney General) v O'Brien*.[3] In this case an accused person had been convicted of receiving stolen property, the items concerned having been found by the police during a search of his home. The search warrant which they held, however, contained in consequence of a clerical error an address which was not the address of the accused man's home, so that in effect the warrant was not authority for the search which had taken place, and the search itself was thus not in accordance with law. It was argued unsuccessfully for the accused that evidence obtained in consequence of such an irregular search - which amounted to a violation of the accused's dwelling, constitutionally protected by Article 40.5 - should have been excluded; but the Court of Criminal Appeal, while rejecting the point, gave leave for it to be taken by way of further appeal to the Supreme Court under s 29 of the Courts of Justice Act 1924. The Supreme Court dismissed the appeal as the error had clearly been innocent; but reserved the position as regards evidence which might be obtained via a deliberate infraction of a constitutional right. Walsh J also expounded the meaning of Article 40.5:

> "[These words do] not mean that the guarantee is against forcible entry only. In my view, the reference to forcible entry is an intimation that forcible entry may be permitted by law but that in any event the dwelling of every citizen is inviolable save where entry is permitted by law and that, if necessary, such law may permit forcible entry."

Meaning of "dwelling"

The expression "dwelling" also received some interpretation:

> "In a case where members of a family live together in the family house, the house as a whole is for the purpose of the Constitution the dwelling of each member of the family. If a member of a family occupies a clearly defined portion of the house apart from the other members of the family, then it may well be that the part not so

[1] It has been surmised that the expression "inviolable" was suggested to the drafters of the 1922 Constitution by the equivalent expression in the corresponding Article 115 of the 1919 Constitution of the Weimar Republic (G.J. Hand, "A Reconsideration of a German Study (1927-1932) of the Irish Constitution of 1922" [Leo Kohn, *The Constitution of the Irish Free State*], *Das Europa der zweiten Generation*, 855).

[2] See above, pp. 603-604. The effect of the guarantee of the inviolability of the dwelling on the admissibility of evidence is usually considered in the context of the criminal law. However for an example of its operation in a civil action, see *O.C. v T.C.*, High Court, 8 December 1981, in which McMahon J refused to admit, as evidence in a matrimonial case, letters and photographs unlawfully removed by the wife from her estranged husband's residence.

[3] [1965] IR 142.

occupied is no longer his dwelling, as would be the case where a person not a member of the family occupied or was in possession of a clearly defined portion of the house."

The guarantee extends only to that part of a building which constitutes a dwelling, so that in *Director of Public Prosecutions v McMahon*,[4] the Supreme Court held that:

> "the act of entering, as a trespasser, the public portion of a licensed premises which is open for trade does not...constitute any invasion or infringement of any constitutional right of the owner of those premises."

Thus evidence obtained when members of the Garda Síochána, dressed in plain clothes, entered the defendant's licensed premises for the specific purpose of ascertaining whether offences against the Gaming and Lotteries Act 1956, were being committed, was regarded as having been obtained by an unlawful or illegal method, but without infringement of a constitutional right.

The People (Director of Public Prosecutions) v Lawless[5] is authority for the proposition that the guarantee of inviolability of the dwelling may be invoked only by a person whose home is in the dwelling in question. Here the accused had been convicted of a number of offences under the Misuse of Drugs Act 1977, on the basis of, *inter alia*, evidence obtained on foot of what turned out to be a technically deficient search warrant for the premises on which he was arrested, which was not his home but another's. The Court of Criminal Appeal rejected his contention that this evidence should be excluded as having been obtained in breach of a constitutional right to the inviolability of the dwelling. McCarthy J pointed out, *inter alia*, that if there had been a violation of the constitutional right to inviolability of the dwelling in this case, the appropriate complainant would be the tenant of the flat in question and not the applicant. Of course it is not necessary to be the legal or beneficial owner of the title to the premises in question, as it is quite clear from the remarks of Walsh J in *O'Brien* that family members may also rely on the guarantee. Nor is it likely that the family must necessarily be in occupation of the dwelling at the time of the intrusion for the Article to apply, for otherwise second residences like holiday homes would not be protected.[6]

Implicit in Walsh J's judgment in *O'Brien* is the view that Article 40.5 extends only to the structure of the house and does not cover the surrounding area, such as a garden or driveway. This point was made explicit by Blayney J in *Director of Public Prosecutions v Corrigan*[7] where the accused challenged the validity of his arrest under s.49(6) of the Road Traffic Act 1961, on the grounds that, at the time of his arrest, the arresting police officer was trespassing on his property. (The District Judge had found as a fact that the arrest had taken place in the driveway to the accused's house.) In the High Court, Blayney J said:

[4] [1986] IR 393; [1986] ILRM 871. A similar distinction has been drawn by the European Court of Justice in two cases, *Dow Benelux N.V. v Commission of the European Communities* [1989] ECR 3137 and *Dow Chemical Iberica SA v Commission of the European Communities* [1989] ECR 3165, wherein it held that, while the right to the inviolability of the dwelling was part of Community law, it applied only to the private dwellings of natural persons and not to business premises as there were not inconsiderable divergences between the legal systems of the Member States in regard to the nature and degree of protection afforded to business premises against intervention by public authorities. In *Niemitz v Germany*, Series A, No.251B, 16 December 1992, on the other hand, the European Court of Human Rights held that Article 8 of the Convention, guaranteeing, *inter alia*, the right to respect for one's home, applied equally to the applicant's offices.

[5] (1985) 3 Frewen 30. See also, to similar effect, the Supreme Court decision in *D.P.P. v Forbes* [1993] ILRM 817, dealing with the common law protection relating to the forecourt of a dwelling.

[6] See *Gillow v UK*, Series A, No.109, (1989) 11 EHRR 335.

[7] [1986] IR 290; 1987] ILRM 575.

> ""Dwelling" in the section means a house, or part of a house, and...the protection [of Article 40.5] would not extend accordingly to a garden surrounding the dwelling, or leading to it, and so would not...extend to the driveway of the defendant's house where he was arrested."

However in relation to areas outside a house and in relation to premises other than dwellings, such as office premises,[8] the common law offers comparable protection, outlined in the leading English case of *Morris v Beardmore.*[9] Here a unanimous House of Lords ruled that a power to go onto property against the owner's will would not be implied into a statutory provision empowering a policeman to require an individual to provide a specimen of breath. In *Director of Public Prosecution v McCreesh*[10] Hederman J, with whom Griffin J agreed,[11] quoted extracts from some of the speeches in *Morris* which emphasised the need for express statutory authorisation of the entry onto the premises and said that they were in line with the law of this State.[12] Accordingly, as s.49 of the Road Traffic Act 1961 did not expressly authorise the Gardaí to go onto private property in order to effect an arrest pursuant to that section, the arrest of the defendant by the Gardaí in the driveway to his house, after he had told the Gardaí that they were trespassing and should leave immediately, was invalid.[13]

"Save in accordance with law"

In *Ryan v O'Callaghan*[14] Barr J ruled, applying the remarks of Henchy J in *King v Attorney General,*[15] that the phrase "save in accordance with law" in Article 40.5 meant "without stooping to methods which ignore the fundamental norms of the legal order postulated by the Constitution". In his opinion the common good required that there be a simple procedure readily available to the police whereby they may obtain search warrants relating to premises so as to facilitate them in the investigation of crime. Here the procedures for obtaining a search warrant from a Peace Commissioner, set out in s 42 of the Larceny Act 1916, did not ignore these "fundamental norms" because it:

> "contains important elements for the protection of the public...The investigating police officer must swear an information that he has reasonable cause for suspecting that stolen property is to be found at the premises to be searched and he must satisfy a Peace Commissioner, who is an independent person unconnected with criminal investigation per se, that it is right and proper to issue the warrant."

Barr J's approach in *Ryan* may be contrasted with that of Lardner J in *O'Mahoney v Shields*[16] in which, having applied s 8 of the Wireless Telegraphy Act 1926 which

[8] For an example of where both the constitutional and common law guarantees applied to different parts of the same premises, see *O'Mahony v Shields*, High Court, 22 February 1988.

[9] [1981] AC 446; [1980] 2 All ER 753. This protection is available only to the owners or occupiers of the property in question - see *D.P.P. v Forbes* [1993] ILRM 817.

[10] [1992] 2 IR 239.

[11] The third member of the Court, McCarthy J, delivered a similar judgment, though without expressly concurring with his brethern.

[12] See also *Minister for Social Welfare v Bracken*, High Court, 29 July 1992, where the power of entry onto premises conferred on a departmental inspector pursuant to s 114 of the Social Welfare (Consolidation) Act 1981 was read subject to these common law principles so as to require the inspector to seek permission to enter before exercising this power. (However an occupier who unreasonably refused permission for the purpose of frustrating a proper inquiry was guilty of an offence under s 114(4).) See now s 212(3)(a) of the Social Welfare (Consolidation) Act 1993 which empowers the inspector to enter "without prior notification" and at all reasonable times, any premises or place liable to inspection under the Act.

[13] See now s 39 of the proposed Road Traffic Bill 1993, which purports to confer such authority on the Gardaí. See Addendum below.

[14] High Court, 22 July 1987. Followed in *Farrell v Farrelly* [1988] IR 201.

[15] [1981] IR 233.

[16] High Court, 22 February 1988.

authorises a District Judge to grant a search warrant upon receiving sworn information that the informant has reasonable grounds for believing that apparatus for wireless telegraphy is being kept or used at that place, he contented himself with saying that, in the light of Article 40.5, the Oireachtas might consider it desirable to amend s 8 so as to require more substantive evidence to be laid before the District Judge.[17]

Implied permission to enter

Clearly where express permission to enter a dwelling has been given, there can be no breach of Article 40.5. In some situations, the owner of a premises may be regarded as having given implied permission to come on to his property (which, of course, may be revoked). Thus in *Director of Public Prosecutions v Gaffney*[18] Walsh J, with whom Finlay CJ and Hederman J concurred, suggested that the police could be held to have had a licence to proceed from the defendant's gateway to his front door, though permission would be needed before they could proceed any further. Furthermore, he indicated that, while this is not an invariable rule and has to be considered in the light of the circumstances of each case, the absence of an express refusal or of an express order to leave cannot be construed as an implied invitation or permission to enter[19] and to that extent cast doubt on the decision of O'Hanlon J in *Director of Public Prosecution v Closkey.*[20] In *Minister for Justice v Wang Zhu Jie*[21] Costello J said that property owners impliedly permit members of the Gardaí to come onto their property to make inquiries and that the Gardaí are entitled to assume this in the ordinary course of their duties as law enforcement officers. A similar view was expressed by O'Flaherty J, delivering the judgment of the Supreme Court in *Director of Public Prosecutions v Forbes,*[22] when he said:

> "It must be regarded as axiomatic that any householder gives an implied authority to a member of the Garda to come onto the forecourt of his premises to see to the enforcement of the law or to prevent a breach thereof."

However this would not apply where the Gardaí were involved in a covert operation against the owner of the property which they entered with a view to ascertaining whether there was any evidence on the premises with which they could charge the owner with a criminal offence - *Director of Public Prosecutions v McMahon*[23] - nor where the owner is in fact trying to escape arrest - *Director of Public Prosecutions v Corrigan.*[24]

[17] This advice was not taken, however, when s 8 of the 1926 Act was amended in 1988 - see s 17 of the Broadcasting and Wireless Telegraphy Act 1988. See also s 14(1) of the Broadcasting Act 1990 which is very similar to s 8 of the 1926 Act. In relation to the search of a business premises, note that in *Chappell v UK,* Series A, No.152, (1990) 12 EHRR 1, the European Court of Human Rights held that a search of the applicant's business premises, part of which he occupied as a dwelling, pursuant to an Anton Pillar order designed to protect the plaintiffs' copyright did not amount to a breach of Article 8 of the Convention.

[18] [1987] IR 173; [1988] ILRM 39.

[19] A similar view was taken by McCarthy J who argued that the various relationships commonly identified in issues of occupiers' liability in tort were not relevant to a criminal law issue such as the present.

[20] High Court, 6 February 1984. Here the Gardaí had initially been admitted to the home by the defendant's sister but when they arrested the defendant, the sister sought to oppose and prevent the arrest. Notwithstanding this apparent revocation of the permission to enter, O'Hanlon J upheld the validity of the arrest.

[21] [1993] 1 IR 426; [1991] ILRM 823.

[22] Supreme Court, 26 May 1993.

[23] [1986] IR 393; [1986] ILRM 871.

[24] [1986] IR 290; [1987] ILRM 575.

Entry on dwelling: at common law

The entry of a dwelling against the will of the owner is authorised by law in a number of situations. At common law a search warrant can be issued by a District Judge (or Peace Commissioner) only where the Gardaí state the belief that stolen goods are on the premises; otherwise the principle of *Entick v Carrington*[25] applies, so as to prevent the executive from claiming a "general warrant" to look through private premises. In the absence of a warrant, the Gardaí can only effect a lawful arrest in a person's home where (a) they have reasonable grounds for suspecting that he has committed a felony, in which case the Court of Criminal Appeal has held that they have authority to enter the dwelling to make an arrest: *The People (Attorney General) v Hogan*;[26] or (b) they have been given permission by an appropriate person to enter the premises: *Director of Public Prosecutions v Closkey*;[27] *Director of Public Prosecutions v Gaffney*.[28] In the latter case, McCarthy J suggested that a revocation of permission to enter, before any arrest had been made, would render any subsequent arrest on the premises, made without a warrant, unlawful. However a Garda who is trying to effect an arrest, either with or without a warrant, may use reasonable force to gain entry, provided s/he has unsuccessfully sought prior admission.[29]

By statute, with and without warrant

A large number of statutory powers of entry and search have been created, by no means all dependent on the issue of a warrant in each case by a judicial authority. Thus, to give only a few examples, by s 8 of the Wireless Telegraphy Act 1926, a District Judge may issue a warrant to search premises believed to contain unlawfully operated wireless apparatus;[30] by s 17 of the Censorship of Publications Act 1946, a District Judge can issue to a police officer a warrant to search premises which are reasonably suspected to contain prohibited publications being kept for sale or distribution; and by s 26 (1) of the Misuse of Drugs Acts, 1977 and 1984, a warrant can be issued by a District Judge or Peace Commissioner where there is information on oath of reasonable ground for suspecting that controlled drugs etc. are on the premises. But no warrants are required by s 94 of the Health Act 1947, which empowers an authorised officer to enter and inspect premises to see whether there has been a contravention of the Act and, if unable to gain admittance otherwise, to break in; or by s 26 of the Finance Act 1926, which authorises an officer of customs and excise to enter premises used for bookmaking and to search for and inspect documents; or by s 24 of the Firearms Act 1925, by which the police may search premises suspected of being, or being about to be, the scene of an offence under the Act; or by s 212 of the Social Welfare (Consolidation) Act 1993 which empowers inspectors to enter premises and inspect records to see whether the social insurance law (in regard to contributions and benefits) is being complied with. The validity of statutory provisions permitting authorised officers to enter dwelling houses

[25] (1765) 16 State Trials 1030; 2 Wils 275.

[26] 1 Frewen 360.

[27] High Court, 6 February 1984.

[28] [1987] IR 173; [1988] ILRM 39.

[29] *D.P.P. v Corrigan* [1986] IR 290; [1987] ILRM 575; *McMahon v McDonald*, High Court, 3 May 1988; Supreme Court, *The Irish Times*, 27 July 1988.

[30] See *O'Mahony v Shields*, High Court, 22 February 1988, in which Lardner J upheld the validity of a warrant granted pursuant to this section but commented that it might be desirable for the Oireachtas to amend s 8 to require more substantive evidence to be considered by the District Judge before granting a warrant. (But note fn 17 above.) This decision has been criticised on the ground that its acceptance of the validity of the warrant reflected a deference to the powers of the Oireachtas not evident in *Ryan v O'Callaghan*, High Court, July 22, 1987 - see Byrne and Binchy, *Annual Review of Irish Law 1988*, (Dublin) pp.192-4.

without warrants was accepted by Murphy J in *Deighan v Hearne*[31] where he cited *Abbey Films Ltd. v Attorney General*[32] in support of the proposition that:

> "a statutory provision could confer the power on an authorised officer (without the intervention of the judicial process) to enter into a dwelling house and inspect documents there where such action was warranted by the "exigencies of the common good"."[33]

Thus the judge dismissed the plaintiff's argument that the power of the County Sheriff under s.485 of the Income Tax Act 1967, to break and enter into a citizen's dwelling, as part of the process of recovering amounts due in unpaid taxes by distress, offended against the Constitution. Of course, opinions may differ as to whether the "exigencies of the common good" justify a specific statutory power - thus conflicting views have been expressed as to the constitutionality of s 23 of the Enforcement of Court Orders Act 1926 which empowers a sheriff, *inter alia*, forcibly to enter premises of a third party without a warrant where he has reasonable grounds for believing that there are goods of the judgment creditor on the premises.[34]

A very extensive statutory power of entry and search is conferred by s 29 of the Offences Against the State Act 1939, (as amended by s 5 of the Criminal Law Act 1976). This authorises a member of the Garda Síochána, not below the rank of superintendent, to issue a search warrant in respect of any place where that officer is satisfied that there is reasonable ground for believing that evidence of or relating to the commission or intended commission of an offence under the 1939 Act or the Criminal Law Act 1976, or a scheduled offence under the 1976 Act or treason, may be found in such place. The range of this power is quite broad in that it may apply in respect of hundreds of offences; furthermore, this is an executive warrant not requiring the imprimatur of any judicial authority. In *The People (Director Of Public Prosecutions) v O'Leary*[35] the applicant argued that such a warrant had too broad a sweep and that it was a warrant "at large".[36] However the Court of Criminal Appeal ruled, without any detailed analysis of the possible impact of Article 40.5 - and especially of the "fundamental norms of the legal order" referred to in *Ryan v O'Callaghan*[37] - that the warrant in the instant case complied with s 29 and that the entry of the dwelling was in accordance with law, as required by the Constitution.[38]

[31] [1986] IR 603. In the subsequent Supreme Court appeal - [1990] 1 IR 499 - the Court rejected the claim that s 485 amounted to a failure by the State, in breach of Article 40, to protect the taxpayer's property rights. In coming to this conclusion, the Court had regard to the rights of the taxpayer, at various stages prior to the issue of the certificate authorising the sheriff to seize the property, to challenge in tribunals and courts the decisions made against him. No explicit reference was made to Article 40.5.

[32] [1981] IR 158.

[33] Note, however, that in *Funke v France*, Series A, No.256A, 25 February 1993, and *Miailhe v France*, Series A, No. 256C, 25 February 1993, the Court of Human Rights held that search and seizure powers conferred on the French custom authorities breached Article 8 because:

> "in the absence of any requirement of a judicial warrant, the restrictions and conditions [imposed on such powers and] provided for by law...appear too lax and full of loopholes for the interferences with the applicant's rights to have been strictly proportionate to the legitimate aim pursued."

[34] The constitutionality of the provision was doubted by the Bankruptcy Law Committee, which recommended that such a right of entry should be based on a search warrant - see Report of the Committee on Reform of Bankruptcy Law and Procedure (1973) and see now ss 27 and 28 of the Bankruptcy Act 1988 - but defended by the Law Reform Commission in its *Report on Sheriffs* (1988). For discussion, see *Byrne and Binchy, op.cit.*, pp.324-8.

[35] (1988) 3 Frewen 163.

[36] Implicitly invoking *Entick v Carrington* (1765) State Trials 1030 2 Wils 275.

[37] High Court, 22 July 1987.

[38] For criticism of this aspect of the decision, see *Byrne and Binchy, op.cit.*, pp.190-191.

In *Byrne v Grey*[39] Hamilton P adopted the remarks of Lord Diplock in *R. v I.R.C. ex parte Rossminster Ltd.*[40] to the effect that statutory provisions authorising the entry into and search of houses or office premises should be construed in a manner that is least restrictive of the individual's common law (and in this jurisdiction) constitutional rights.[41] Thus in the instant case, the judge held that a search warrant granted pursuant to s 26 of the Misuse of Drugs Acts 1977 and 1984, was invalid because of non-compliance with the Act - instead of satisfying himself that facts existed constituting reasonable grounds for suspecting that an offence had been or was being committed, the peace commissioner who issued the warrant relied instead on a statement by a Garda that he, the Garda, had reasonable grounds for this suspicion.[42]

Adopting this approach, it may be doubted whether provisions such as s 6(4) of the Anti-Discrimination (Pay) Act 1974 or s 19(6) of the Employment Equality Act 1977, which empower equality officers to enter "premises" in pursuit of investigations under the equality legislation, protect entry into dwellings, in the absence of any definition of the word "premises".

Statutory protection of the inviolability of the dwelling

In contrast to the statutory provisions in the preceding section, which purport to authorise entry into dwellings and premises, the Prohibition of Forcible Entry and Occupation Act 1971 offers a measure of statutory protection for, *inter alia*, the inviolability of the dwelling. This Act, in s 2 criminalises the forcible entry onto land (including houses) by someone other than the owner or a person acting in pursuance of a *bona fide* claim of right, where the trespass interferes with the use and enjoyment of the land in question and the trespasser fails to respond to a request by the owner or by a member of the Garda Síochána to leave with all reasonable speed and in a peaceful manner. Forcible occupation of land is also an offence under s 3. Section 13 of the proposed Criminal Justice (Public Order) Bill 1993 provides for an additional measure of protection in this area by criminalising trespass on any dwelling or its curtilage in circumstances where the trespass is done without reasonable excuse and causes, or is likely to cause, fear in another.

Article 40.5 as a complement to certain existing tortious remedies?

In all of the cases considered to date by the Irish courts under this heading, Article 40.5 has been invoked in the context of the physical entry of individuals into a dwelling place. However, it is possible that, this provision might also be relevant where occupancy of the dwelling is disturbed by phenomena such as air or noise pollution.[43]

[39] [1988] IR 31.

[40] [1980] AC 952.

[41] See similar remarks by Henchy J in *D.P.P. v Gaffney* [1987] IR 173; [1988] ILRM 39, and also the remarks of Lardner J in *O'Mahoney v Shields*, High Court, 22 February 1988, to the effect that the limits of the statutory power must be respected and strictly adhered to.

[42] Applied by the Court of Criminal Appeal and approved by the Supreme Court, independently of the D.P.P.'s concession of the point, in the subsequent appeal in *The People (D.P.P.) v Kenny* [1990] 2 IR 110; [1990] ILRM 569. (Griffin and Lynch JJ dissented on the matter of whether this automatically rendered inadmissible evidence obtained pursuant to the warrant - see above, pp. 606-607.) In *Byrne,* Hamilton P refused to grant an order of *certiorari* on the ground that the issue in the application - whether the evidence obtained as a result of the search should be declared inadmissible - should be dealt with in the course of the applicant's trial.

[43] See, in the context of Article 8 of the European Convention on Human Rights, *Powell and Rayner v UK*, Series A, No.172, (1990) 12 EHRR 355.

CERTAIN RIGHTS GUARANTEED SUBJECT TO PUBLIC ORDER AND MORALITY

6. 1° The State guarantees liberty for the exercise of the following rights, subject to public order and morality:-

6. 1° Ráthaíonn an Stát saoirse chun na cearta seo a leanas a oibriú ach sin a bheith faoi réir oird is moráltachta poiblí:-

1922 provisions

The clauses which follow relate to freedom of expression, of assembly, and of association; they all take the form of a statement of the liberty, followed by substantial qualification of it. In the Constitution of 1922 all these rights were expressed briefly in Article 9; the only explicit qualification was that they were guaranteed "for the purposes not opposed to public morality", though the enactment of laws "regulating the manner in which the right of forming associations and the right of free assembly may be exercised" was envisaged inasmuch as any such laws were to contain "no political, religious or class distinctions".

Application by the Supreme Court

These opening words of Article 40.6.1 have been considered by the Supreme Court on two occasions. They were paraphrased by the Court in *The State (Lynch) v Cooney*[1] as follows:

> "This provision enables the State in certain instances to control these rights and freedoms. The basis for any attempt at control must be, according to the Constitution, the overriding considerations of public order and public morality."

The Court set out from this position to consider, and uphold, a statutory power which had been used to prohibit broadcasts on behalf of a subversive political organisation.[2]

In the subsequent case of *Aughey v Ireland*[3] dealing with freedom of association, Walsh J., with whom the other members of the Court agreed, noted that considerations of public order or morality could justify a complete prohibition on that freedom, unlike considerations of the public interest - referred to specifically in Article 40.6.1.iii - which, on the authority of *N.U.R. v Sullivan,*[4] authorised only regulation of that freedom falling short of outright prohibition.

"Public order and morality" refers to conditions in this State only?

In *Attorney General for England and Wales v Brandon Book Publishers Ltd.*,[5] where the plaintiff sought an interlocutory injunction to prevent the publication in this jurisdiction of the memoirs of a deceased member of the British secret service, Carroll J held that a reference to public order and morality in Article 40.6.1.i could not be used to restrict the defendant's right to publish a book which might affect the public order or morality in another State. She said:

[1] [1982] IR 337; [1983] ILRM 89.
[2] See below, pp. 955-956.
[3] [1989] ILRM 87.
[4] [1947] IR 77.
[5] [1986] IR 597; [1987] ILRM 135.

> "Article 40.6.1 guarantees liberty for the exercise of the right of citizens to express freely their convictions and opinions subject to public order and morality. In the expansion of that, the article refers to the organs of public opinion preserving their rightful liberty of expression provided it is not used to undermine public order or morality or the authority of the State. There is no question of public order or morality or the authority of the State being undermined here. Therefore in my opinion there is, *prima facie*, a constitutional right to publish information and the onus rests on the plaintiff to establish, in the context of an interlocutory application, that the constitutional right of the defendant should not be exercised."

It is a nice question as to whether the reference to public order and morality in the opening words of Article 40.6.1 should be interpreted in a similar fashion. On the one hand, one would ordinarily understand references to public order and morality to refer to conditions in this State, as opposed to elsewhere; furthermore, one is reluctant to construe two similar phrases in a provision in two different ways. On the other hand, the reference to public order and morality in Article 40.6.1.i comes in the context of a guarantee of the right of organs of public opinion (as opposed to individuals), *inter alia*, to criticise Government policy and is coupled with a reference to the authority of the State, factors which are missing from the opening words of Article 40.6.1. One may speculate as to whether these differences are sufficient to justify the State restraining an individual from, say, broadcasting subversive or immoral material into a neighbouring State.[6]

[6] In a case dealing with the converse of this scenario, the European Court of Human Rights held that, under Article 10 of the Convention, the Swiss authorities were entitled to control, by means of a licensing system, radio broadcasts originating in Italy and re-transmitted in Switzerland - *Groppera Radio AG v Switzerland*, Series A, No. 173, (1990) 12 EHRR 321.

Article 40.6.1.i

FREEDOM OF EXPRESSION

[The State guarantees liberty for the exercise, subject to public order and morality, of]

i. The right of the citizens to express freely their convictions and opinions.

The education of public opinion being, however, a matter of such grave import to the common good, the State shall endeavour to ensure that organs of public opinion, such as the radio, the press, the cinema, while preserving their rightful liberty of expression, including criticism of Government policy, shall not be used to undermine public order or morality or the authority of the State.

The publication or utterance of blasphemous, seditious, or indecent matter is an offence which shall be punishable in accordance with law.

[Ráithaíonn an Stát, faoi réir oird is moráltachta poiblí, saoirse chun a oibriú]

i. Ceart na saoránach chun a ndeimhní is a dtuairimí a nochtadh gan bac.

Ach toisc oiliúint aigne an phobail a bheith chomh tábhachtach sin do leas an phobail, féachfaidh an Stát lena chur in áirithe nach ndéanfar orgain aigne an phobail, mar shampla, an raidió is an preas is an cineama, a úsáid chun an t-ord nó an mhoráltacht phoiblí nó údarás an Stáit a bhonn-bhriseadh. San am chéanna coimeádfaidh na horgain sin an tsaoirse is dleacht dóibh chun tuairimí a nochtadh agus orthu sin tuairimí léirmheasa ar bheartas an Rialtais.

Aon ní diamhaslach nó ceannairceach nó graosta a fhoilsiú nó a aithris is cion inphionóis é de réir dlí.

1922 provision

This provision corresponds to part of Article 9 of the old Constitution, though that provision does not appear ever to have been judicially considered in any detail.

Range of the guarantee uncertain

The range of this guarantee is uncertain in certain respects and, in particular, it is not entirely clear whether it is restricted to the expression of convictions and opinions or whether it also extends to the dissemination of factual information.[1] The former approach has been taken by Costello J in two cases - *Attorney General v Paperlink Ltd.*[2] and *Kearney v Minister for Justice.*[3] In *Paperlink*, the defendants (a private courier firm)

[1] See the discussion of this issue by the Law Reform Commission in its *Report on the Civil Law of Defamation* (1991) pp.111-116. For an insight into the implications of this distinction for the law on defamation, see O'Dell, "*Does Defamation Value Free Expression?*" (1990) 12 DULJ 50, in which he argues that Article 40.6.1.i protects speech based on the speaker's subjective perception of facts and requires, accordingly, that liability for defamatory remarks should be fault-based, a view not shared by the Commission, *op. cit.* p.124. For criticism of the Commission's Report on this point (and others), see McDonald, "*Defamation Report - A Response to the LRC Report*" (1992) ILT 270. For a response to the Commission's earlier consultation paper, see O'Dell, "*Reflection on a Revolution in Libel*" (1991) ILT 181, 214.

[2] [1984] ILRM 373. See *McCormack*, (1984) 6 DULJ (n.s.) 144. *Paperlink* was recently followed on this point by Keane J in *Oblique Financial Services Ltd. v The Promise Production Co. Ltd.*, High Court, 24 February 1993.

[3] [1986] IR 116; [1987] ILRM 52.

said the legislation under which the Attorney General was trying to assert the monopoly of the Minister for Posts and Telegraphs against them represented an inhibition on the constitutional right of communication. But (said Costello J):

> "the activity which the defendants say is inhibited in this case is that of communication by letter, and as this act may involve the communication of information and not merely the expression of convictions and opinions, I do not think that the constitutional provision dealing with the right to express convictions and opinions is the source of the citizen's right to communicate."[4]

In *Kearney* the same judge held that Article 40.6.1.i did not cover all matters capable of expression and in particular did not protect the mere transmission of information.[5] On the other hand, in *Attorney General for England and Wales v Brandon Books Publishers Ltd.*[6] where the plaintiff had sought to prevent the publication of the memoirs of a deceased member of the British secret services, Carroll J held that the defendants had a constitutional right under Article 40.6.1.i to publish information which does not involve any breach of copyright provided that the public interest in this jurisdiction is not affected by the publication and there was no breach of confidentiality in a private or commercial setting.[7] Furthermore the attempt to restrict Article 40.6.1.i to the expression of convictions and opinions has been criticised because it gives rise to a number of anomalies.[8] In particular it would mean that different parts of the same publication would be covered by different constitutional provisions. Moreover, the last paragraph of Article 40.6.1.i, criminalising the publication of blasphemous, seditious or indecent matter, clearly covers factual material.

Should the courts ultimately take the view that Article 40.6.1.i does not extend to the dissemination of information, it should be noted that the Fourteenth Amendment to the Constitution expressly recognises the freedom to obtain or disseminate information relating to services available in another State,[9] while Costello J considered that Article 40.3 protected a general right to communicate.

Quite apart from the uncertainty as to whether Article 40.6.1.i applies to the dissemination of factual information, other problems remain. Does the provision protect the expression of an opinion which is indissolubly coupled with, or merely subserves, some impulse or emotion, or must anything of this kind find shelter under the general "personal rights" umbrella of Article 40.3?

[4] He considered that the right to communicate was protected by Article 40.3. See also his decisions in *Kearney v Minister for Justice* [1986] IR 116; [1987] ILRM 52 and *McKenna v An Taoiseach*, High Court, 8 June 1992. *Cp.* Article 10(1) of the European Convention on Human Rights which provides that the right to freedom of expression "shall include freedom to hold opinions and to receive and *impart information* and ideas..." (emphasis added). See *Markt Intern v Germany* Series A, No.164, (1990) 12 EHRR 161.

[5] This rather strict approach to the interpretation of Article 40.6.1.i contrasts with the same judge's rejection of a literal interpretation of Article 40.6.1.iii in *Doyle v Croke* (1988) 7 JISLL 170. See below, pp. 982-983.

[6] [1986] IR 597; [1987] ILRM 135.

[7] Carroll J also held that there was no absolute confidentiality where the parties were a Government agency and a private individual (though obviously she was not referring to Official Secrets legislation).

[8] See Fennelly, "*The Irish Constitution and Freedom of Expression*" in Curtin and O'Keeffe, eds., *Constitutional Adjudication in European Community and National Law* (Dublin 1992). See also Russell, "*Contempt of Court*" (1968) 3 Ir Jur (n.s.) 1, p.17 and *McDonald, loc. cit.*

[9] Thus reversing the Supreme Court decision in *A.G (S.P.U.C. (Ireland) Ltd.) v Open Door Counselling Ltd.* [1988] IR 593; [1989] ILRM 19, wherein Finlay CJ, with whom the other members of the Court agreed, held that Article 40.6.1.i did not protect a right to obtain information about the availability of abortion services outside the State. As Friedman points out - "*On the Dangers of Moral Certainty and Sacred Trust*" (1988) 10 DULJ (n.s.) 71 - this conclusion was arrived at without any textual analysis of Article 40.6.1.i. On the Fourteenth Amendment, see above, p. 810.

The latter question, indeed, might have been answered when the Supreme Court was considering *Norris v Attorney General*,[10] in which the plaintiff challenged the laws against male homosexual behaviour, including a section which penalised the "procuring" of an act of gross indecency, the latter on the ground that it infringed his rights under Article 40.6.1.i (as well as his right of free association under Article 40.6.1.iii). But the majority of the Court rejected this submission without considering the question whether Article 40.6.1.i ought to be relevant to the plaintiff's case at all. The Chief Justice said:

> "Freedom of expression and freedom of association are not guaranteed as absolute rights. They are protected by the Constitution subject to public order and morality. Accordingly, if the impugned legislation is otherwise valid and consistent with the Constitution, the mere fact that it prohibits the plaintiff from advocating conduct which it prohibits or from encouraging others to engage in such conduct or associating with others for the purpose of so doing, cannot constitute a breach of the Constitution."

The reference in the second paragraph of Article 40.6.1.i to the State's powers in relation to the organs of public opinion is also not without its difficulties. Is the "liberty of expression" referred to in that paragraph equivalent to the right to express freely convictions and opinions referred to in the first paragraph? One might consider it excessively sophisticated to distinguish between these two concepts. However if Costello J's understanding of the first paragraph prevails - that it does not encompass factual material - then no doubt it would be very desirable to regard the phrase "liberty of expression" as having a broader scope so as to protect the liberty of the media to report factual material. Apart from this issue, does the media enjoy greater or lesser protection than individuals in this context? Three possible answers to this question were canvassed by the Law Reform Commission in its *Report on the Civil Law of Defamation*.[11] First, that this reference requires wider protection to be given to media organs; second, that it simply confirms that the media organs are beneficiaries of the guarantee of freedom of expression; and finally, that it authorises the State to impose greater restrictions on the media than on citizens. The Commission concluded that the first interpretation was neither desirable nor warranted having regard to the constitutional text.[12] However the contrary view has been advanced by McDonald who argues that media speech and individual speech are intrinsically different activities inasmuch as media speech is invariably public, whereas individual speech is not necessarily so and that "the specific reference to Article 40.6.1.i to media liberty of expression must mean that appropriate and balanced legal protections which recognise the unique features of media speech activities are mandated by the Constitution." [13] As for the second and third interpretations, the Commission considered that the choice as between these two depended on whether or not corporate bodies are covered by the word "citizen" in the first paragraph.[14] If they were so covered, the second paragraph could be regarded as imposing additional restrictions on the freedom of expression of media organs. If, however, corporate bodies were not included in the concept of "citizen", the second paragraph could be seen simply as confirmation that media organs enjoy the benefit of the guarantee of freedom of expression. On the face of it, however, it would seem that, if the liberty of expression enjoyed by the media is in essence the same as the citizen's right to express convictions and opinions,[15] the scope

[10] [1984] IR 36.

[11] *Op. cit.*, pp.116-120.

[12] A view shared by Casey, *Constitutional Law in Ireland* (2nd ed., 1992) p.437.

[13] *Loc. cit.* p.274.

[14] For further discussion of this, see above, pp. 710-711.

[15] In that they are both restricted to expression of opinions, or alternatively, both cover opinion and factual material - see above, pp. 923-924.

of that freedom of expression is narrower than that enjoyed by citizens generally because it may be curtailed in the interests of the authority of the State, whereas the right of citizens is subject to no such restriction.

Other relevant constitutional provisions

As we have already noted, the Fourteenth Amendment to the Constitution recognises a limited freedom to obtain and disseminate information about services lawfully available in another country, while Article 40.3 is regarded by some judges as protecting a general right to communicate. Further constitutional protection for freedom of expression may be found in Article 15, ss 10, 12 and 13, concerning parliamentary debates.[16]

LIMITATIONS ON FREEDOM OF EXPRESSION

The boundaries of freedom of expression are delineated by limitations on that freedom, derived from the Constitution, legislation and the common law, which serve various interests.

LIMITATION IN THE INTEREST OF STATE SECURITY

In common with the other freedoms guaranteed by Article 40.6.1, freedom of expression is expressly made subject to, *inter alia*, public order by the opening words of the article.[17] The reference to public order is repeated - with a further reference to the authority of the State[18] - in the more specific context of the State's powers in respect of the media.

In *Attorney General for England and Wales v Brandon Book Publishers Ltd.*[19] Carroll J held that the constitutional restriction on freedom of expression in the interests of public order or morality or State security - contained in the second paragraph of Article 40.6.1.i[20] - applied in respect of the interests of this State only, and that, in any other case, the onus rested on those seeking to restrict this freedom to establish their case. Furthermore, citing *Commonwealth of Australia v John Fairfax and Sons Ltd.*[21] in support, she held that, unless disclosure is likely to injure the public interest, the Government's claim to confidentiality will not be protected.[22]

State security

That the Constitution offers no protection to seditious speech or writing is clear from the second clause of Article 40.6.1.i, which declares it to be an offence; this declaration merely confirms the existence of sedition as the gist of offences already known at com-

[16] See above, pp. 141-147.

[17] In *Aughey v Ireland* [1989] ILRM 87 Walsh J took the view that considerations of public order and morality could justify a complete prohibition on the exercise of freedom of association; furthermore restrictions on freedom of association in the interests of public order and morality must be provided for by post-1937 legislation which is clear and unambiguous. Presumably the same reasoning applies in the present context.

[18] It would seem that statements which insult the Government cannot be regarded as an attack on the authority of the State. In *Castells v Spain* Series A, No.236, (1992) 14 EHRR 445, the European Court of Human Rights held that the prosecution and conviction of the applicant for insulting the Spanish government interfered with his freedom of expression under Article 10 of the Convention. At the same time, the Court accepted that criticism of the Government may be restricted in the interest of preserving public order to enable the Government to react appropriately to defamatory, false and bad faith accusations.

[19] [1986] IR 597; [1987] ILRM 135.

[20] *Quaere* whether the opening words of Article 40.6.1 should receive the same interpretation - see above, pp. 921-922.

[21] (1980) 147 CLR 39.

[22] Moreover, if the material in question is published in another jurisdiction, it would become difficult, if not impossible, for the Government to maintain a ban on publication in the interest of State security - see the decisions of the European Court of Human Rights in *The Observer v UK* Series A, No.216, (1992) 14 EHRR 153, and *The Sunday Times v UK (No.2)* Series A, No.213, (1992) 14 EHRR 229.

mon law. These offences - seditious libel[23] and seditious conspiracy - are however in practice only very rarely the subject of prosecutions,[24] no doubt because much of the same ground is covered by statutory offences which are more easily prosecuted.[25]

Publications connected with illegal organisations

Control of free expression in the Irish State in the interest of its own security goes back to its beginnings, when a military censorship of publications was operated for a time during the civil war of 1922-23.[26] Subsequently the Public Safety Act of 1927 (passed in consequence of the murder of the Minister for Justice, Kevin O'Higgins) provided by s 9 that it should not be lawful to:

> "print, publish, distribute, sell or offer or expose for sale without the previous permission of the Minister for Justice any book, newspaper, magazine, periodical, pamphlet, leaflet, circular or other document containing any statement by or on behalf of or emanating from or purporting to be made by or on behalf of or to emanate from an unlawful association or any statement aiding or abetting or calculated to aid or abet an unlawful association."[27]

Infringement of this prohibition was punishable by fine and/or imprisonment, as well as forfeiture of the offending material and, in the case of a printing offence, forfeiture of all printing machinery as well. By s 10 a judge of the High Court might make an order declaring the Minister for Justice "to be at liberty" to suppress a seditious or similar periodical; s 11 gave the Executive Council power to prohibit the importation of such periodicals. The whole Act was however repealed at the end of the following year.

In 1931 a recrudescence of political violence was the occasion for the far-reaching Constitution (Amendment No. 17) Act which interpolated its operative part into the Constitution as a new Article (numbered 2A). Section 23 of the Article made it unlawful to:

> "print, publish, distribute, sell or offer or expose for sale any book, newspaper, magazine, periodical, pamphlet, leaflet, circular or other document which is issued or published on behalf of an unlawful association."[28]

This was a more modest version of s 9 of the 1927 Public Safety Act; though in the case of conviction by the Constitution (Special Powers) Tribunal established by Article 2A there was no limit to the punishment which the Tribunal could inflict. By s 26 the Tribunal might declare any publication to be seditious. Article 2A was in suspension for some time in 1932-33 and disappeared, with the rest of the 1922 Constitution, in 1937.

The Offences Against the State Act 1939, contained new provisions about unlawful organisations and documents; these provisions are still in force. Section 10 (1) makes it unlawful to:

[23] The current law on seditious libel was examined by the Law Reform Commission in its *Consultation Paper on the Crime of Libel* (1991), pp.56-62. The Commission concluded that the offence was incompatible with Article 40.6.1.i and for this, and other reasons, recommended its abolition - para.217. See also the subsequent *Report on the Crime of Libel* (1991), pp.10-11.

[24] The Digests of reported decisions since 1919 contain no reference to either of these offences.

[25] Thus in *The People (D.P.P.) v O'Leary*, (1988) 3 Frewen 163, possession of an incriminating document was used, pursuant to s 24 of the Offences Against the State Act 1939, as evidence in a prosecution for membership of an unlawful organisation contrary to s 21 of that Act.

[26] See *Official Notice of Military Censorship of Newspapers and Publications* and *Official Notice of Military Censorship of Reports of Military Operations* (both of date 2 July 1922).

[27] For "unlawful association" under the Public Safety Act 1927, see below, pp. 969-970.

[28] For "unlawful association" under Article 2A, see below, p. 970.

"set up in type, print, publish, send through the post, distribute, sell, or offer for sale any document

(*a*) which is or contains or includes an incriminating document;

(*b*) which is or contains or includes a treasonable document; or

(*c*) which is or contains or includes a seditious document."

Section 2 provides that:

"the expression "incriminating document" means a document of whatsoever date, or bearing no date, issued by or emanating from an unlawful organisation or appearing to be issued or so to emanate or purporting or appearing to aid or abet any such organisation or calculated to promote the formation of an unlawful organisation;[29]

the expression "treasonable document" includes a document which relates directly or indirectly to the commission of treason;

the expression "seditious document" includes:

(a) a document consisting of or containing matter calculated or tending to undermine the public order or the authority of the State, and

(b) a document which alleges, implies or suggests or is calculated to suggest that the Government functioning under the Constitution is not the lawful Government of the State or that there is in existence in the State any body or organisation not functioning under the Constitution which is entitled to be recognised as being the government of the country, and

(c) a document which alleges, implies or suggests or is calculated to suggest that the military forces maintained under the Constitution are not the lawful military forces of the State, or that there is in existence in the State a body or organisation not established and maintained by virtue of the Constitution which is entitled to be recognised as a military force, and

(*d*) a document in which words, abbreviations, or symbols referable to a military body are used in referring to an unlawful organisation."

Section 10 also provides that it shall not be lawful:

"for any person to send or contribute to any newspaper or other periodical publication or for the proprietor of any newspaper or other periodical publication to publish in such newspaper or publication any letter, article or communication which is sent or contributed or purports to be sent or contributed by or on behalf of an unlawful organisation or which is of such nature or character that the printing of it would be a contravention of [sub-s 1 cited above]."

[29] In *The People (D.P.P.) v O'Leary*, (1988) 3 Frewen 163, a poster of a man in a paramilitary uniform holding a rifle, with the words "IRA calls the shots" alongside the picture, was regarded as an incriminating document for the purposes of s 24 of the 1939 Act.

Section 11 contains provisions aimed against the importation of newspapers or periodicals containing seditious matter; s 12 makes it an offence merely to be in possession of a treasonable, seditious or incriminating document; and s 13, which exempts from application only periodicals which are "printed by the proprietor thereof on his own premises", obliges "every person who shall print for reward any document" to do all the following things, namely:

(*a*) at the time of or within twenty-four hours after printing such document, print or write on at least one copy of such document the name and address of the person for whom or on whose instructions such document was printed;

(*b*) retain, for six months from the date on which such document was printed, a copy of such document on which the said name and address is printed or written as aforesaid;

(*c*) on the request of a member of the Garda Síochána at any time during the said period of six months, produce for the inspection of such member the said copy of such document so retained as aforesaid.

Section 14 obliges printers to print their names and addresses on all documents (other than certain excepted categories, mostly official documents) printed for reward and which they know or have reason to believe are intended for sale, distribution, or display, whether general or limited.

Statements interfering with justice

These provisions have been supplemented by s 4(1) of the Offences Against the State (Amendment) Act 1972, which reads:

(*a*) Any public statement made orally, in writing or otherwise...that constitutes an interference with the course of justice shall be unlawful.

(*b*) A statement...shall be deemed to constitute an interference with the course of justice if it is intended, or is of such a character as to be likely, directly or indirectly to influence any court, person or authority concerned with the institution, conduct or defence of any civil or criminal proceedings (including a party or witness) as to whether or how the proceedings should be instituted, conducted, continued or defended, or as to what should be their outcome.

Offences against the section are punishable by fine or imprisonment or both.

Emergency provisions

It may be noted that s 2(2) of the Emergency Powers Act 1939, empowered the Government by Emergency Order, *inter alia*, to:

(*h*) authorise and provide for the censorship, restriction, control, or partial or complete suspension of communication by means of all or one or more of the services maintained or controlled by the Minister for Posts and Telegraphs or by any other means, whether public or private, specified or indicated in such emergency order;

(*i*) make provision for...prohibiting the publication or spreading of subversive statements and propaganda, and authorise and provide for the control and censorship of newspapers and periodicals.

These provisions, under which a censorship of the mails and of the press was maintained throughout the second world war,[30] ceased to be in force with the expiry of the Act in 1946. So, too, did s 7, under which the publication or disclosure of court proceedings under the Act could be prohibited or restricted.

For special provisions to prohibit broadcasting of subversive material, see below, pp. 954-957.

For unlawful acts prejudicial to State security and relating to official information and secrets, see the next section.

LIMITATION IN THE INTEREST OF OFFICIAL PRIVACY

Official secrets

The statutory protection of the privacy of official secrets was to be found until 1963 in the Official Secrets Acts 1911 and 1920, together with, during the second world war, s 2(2)(i) of the Emergency Powers Act 1939, which empowered the Government by Emergency Order to "make provision for preserving and safeguarding the secrecy of official documents and information and for controlling the publication of official information". The Emergency Powers Act expired in 1946; and the Acts of 1911 and 1920 were repealed and replaced by the Official Secrets Act 1963.[31]

By s 4(1) of this Act:

> "A person shall not communicate any official information to any other person unless he is duly authorised to do so or does so in the course of and in accordance with his duties as the holder of a public office or when it is his duty in the interest of the State to communicate it."[32]

By s 51(1):

> A person who is or has been
>
> (*a*) a party to a contract with a Minister or State authority or with any person on behalf of a Minister or State authority, or
>
> (*b*) employed by such party,
>
> shall not communicate to any third party any information relating to the contract and expressed therein to be confidential.

[30] The press censorship was occasionally raised in the Dáil. For a list of these occasions, see *General Index to Dáil Debates*, vols. 81-109 (1940 to 1947), pp. 183-4.

[31] Prosecutions under this Act are rare: but an instance is reported in the Dublin newspapers of 8 February 1984 (the editor and owners of the *Irish Independent* were fined for publishing material from an internal police bulletin).

[32] This obligation of secrecy has been relaxed to allow the Revenue Commissioners publish annual lists of tax defaulters - see s 23(3) of the Finance Act 1983. Furthermore, by virtue of s 10 of the National Archives Act 1986, departmental records more than 30 years old may be made available for inspection by members of the public, unless that would be contrary to the public interest.

Section 9 deals with acts relating to official information and contrary to State security, and provides as follows:

> (1) A person shall not, in any manner prejudicial to the safety or preservation of the State
>
> (*a*) obtain, record, communicate to any other person or publish, or
>
> (*b*) have in his possession or under his control any document containing, or other record whatsoever of, information relating to
>
> (i) the number, description, armament, equipment, disposition, movement or condition of any of the Defence Forces or of any of the vessels or aircraft belonging to the State,
>
> (ii) any operations or projected operations of any of the Defence Forces or of the Garda Síochána or of any of the vessels or aircraft belonging to the State,
>
> (iii) any measures for the defence or fortification of any place on behalf of the State,
>
> (iv) munitions of war, or
>
> (v) any other matter whatsoever information as to which would or might be prejudicial to the safety or preservation of the State.
>
> (2) Where a person is charged with a contravention of this section it shall be a good defence to prove that the act in respect of which he is charged was authorised by a Minister or by some person authorised in that behalf by a Minister or was done in the course of and in accordance with his duties as the holder of a public office.

By s 10, where a person is charged with a contravention of s 9:

> the fact that he has (whether within or outside the State) been in communication with or attempted to communicate with a foreign agent or with a member of an unlawful organisation shall be evidence that the act in respect of which he is charged has been done in a manner prejudicial to the safety or preservation of the State.

There follow, in the same section, provisions to explain and define elements of this presumption.

LIMITATION IN THE INTEREST OF THE PUBLIC PEACE AND ORDER

Under this head may be listed various forms of spoken and written words - some of them perhaps not easily regarded as an exercise of the power of "expression" in the sense of Article 40.6.1.i - which may be penalised as being prejudicial to public peace and order.

(a) *Insults and threats*. Insulting or threatening words and behaviour may amount to a breach of the peace;[33] while the sending of threatening letters is unlawful under s 16 of

[33] See examples in O'Connor, *The Irish Justice of the Peace*, 2nd ed., Part I, pp.67ff.

the Offences Against the Person Act 1861. By virtue of the Prohibition of Incitement to Hatred Act 1989, it is an offence to publish or distribute written material or to use words, behave or display written material, or to distribute, show or play a recording of visual images or sounds if such material or actions are threatening, abusive or insulting and intended, or likely, to stir up hatred on account of race, colour, nationality, religion, ethnic or national origins, membership of the travelling community or sexual orientation, while s 3 of the Criminal Damage Act 1991 makes it an offence, in certain circumstances, to threaten to damage property.[34]

Section 6 of the Criminal Justice (Public Order) Bill 1993 proposes to criminalise, *inter alia*, the use of threatening, abusive or insulting words in a public place" with intent to provoke a breach of the peace or whereby a breach of the peace may be occasioned" while s 5 proposes to make it an offence for any person to engage in any "shouting, singing or boisterous conduct" in a public place between midnight and 7.00 a.m. or at any other time having been requested by a Garda to desist "in circumstances likely to give reasonable cause for annoyance to any other person in any place in the vicinity."

Statutory provisions criminalising the use of abusive or insulting language would appear, *prima facie*, to infringe Article 40.6.1.i and arguably may only withstand constitutional scrutiny if they can be shown to be necessary to prevent a breach of the peace. Accordingly, there must be considerable doubt as to the constitutionality of s 5 of the 1993 Bill which appears to subject the speaker's right of expression to the listener's right not to be annoyed.[35]

(b) *Criminal libel.* A criminal libel is "a public offence, as tending to a breach of the peace by provoking the person libelled to break it";[36] unlike civil defamation, it is not necessary that it should be published to a third party - its communication to the party libelled alone will suffice - and the truth of the libel is by itself no defence.[37] Provisions in regard to criminal libel are contained in Part II of the Defamation Act 1961. In its *Consultation Paper on the Crime of Libel*[38] the Law Reform Commission expressed concern about the vagueness of certain aspects of the current law and about the provision of statutory defences to newspapers but not to other defendants, concluding that the current position threatens freedom of speech to a high degree. Accordingly it called for reformulation of the offence which would confine its scope.

(c) *False information.* Section 12 of the Criminal Law Act 1976, provides that a person is guilty of an offence if he:

(*a*) knowingly makes a false report or statement tending to show that an offence has been committed, whether by himself or another person, or tending to give rise to apprehension for the safety of persons or property, or

(*b*) knowingly makes a false report or statement tending to show that he has information material to any inquiries by the Garda Síochána and thereby causes the time of the Garda Síochána to be wastefully employed.

[34] This does not apply to reports of proceedings in the Houses of the Oireachtas or to judicial proceedings - s 5 of the 1989 Act.

[35] See further below, pp. 963-964 and the Addendum.

[36] Halsbury, *Laws of England* (1911 edition), vol.18, p.605.

[37] It is necessary to go further and prove that publication was for the public benefit - s 6 of the Defamation Act 1961.

[38] Published in 1991 and followed by the subsequent *Report on the Crime of Libel*, published in 1992.

(d) *Incitement to commit an offence.* At common law, it is a misdemeanour to incite another to commit an offence, even where the substantive offence is not committed.[39] In addition, various statutory provisions make it an offence to encourage or advocate the commission of specific offences.[40]

LIMITATION IN THE INTEREST OF THE AUTHORITY OF THE COURTS

Considerations of public order or morality or the authority of the State also justify some restriction on freedom of expression in the interest of protecting the authority of the courts.[41]

Criticism of the courts is permissible

In *Attorney General v O'Ryan and Boyd*[42] Maguire P said:

> "Judges and others in authority are open to criticism. Fair and free criticism is allowable and should be welcomed. We must safeguard the rights of the citizen and the rights of newspaper editors. The last thing I would wish is that citizens should feel that the courts are too ready to use against legitimate criticism this powerful weapon of attachment for contempt of court. I would rather err on the other side."

Criticism of the courts must stop short of contempt[43]

Gavan Duffy J spoke in the same case about its being "essential to preserve to the public the right of fair criticism of the courts". There are, however, limits to this right, as several cases since 1922 make clear; these are imposed not out of any ceremonial reverence towards the courts or judges, but in order to protect their independence and capacity to function properly, for which the confidence of the public is necessary. As Gavan Duffy P said in *Attorney General v Connolly*:[44]

> "The defendant asserts his right of free speech but the right to free speech is not a licence to undermine public order...This court will always, I trust, be vigilant to protect the constitutional right of fair criticism...but a political opponent cannot be allowed, under cover of an attack on the Executive, to present a court to public obloquy as a mischievous and wicked sham."

While it is contempt of court to comment on a case still at hearing, or pending,[45] or capable of appeal, in such a way as to purport to tell a court what it should do,[46] most cases of criminal contempt[47] arise from abusive criticism of judgments or of a series or

[39] *The People (A.G) v Capaldi* (1949) 1 *Frewen* 95.

[40] See, e.g., s 4(1) of the Prohibition of Forcible Entry and Occupation Act 1971 and s 5 of the Misuse of Drugs Act 1984.

[41] See comment of O'Hanlon J to that effect at p.32 of his judgment in *Desmond v Glackin (No.1)* [1992] ILRM 490.

[42] [1946] IR 70; (1945) 79 ILTR 158.

[43] For a detailed analysis of the law on contempt, see the Law Reform Commission *Consultation Paper on Contempt of Court* (1991) and above, pp. 390-395.

[44] [1947] IR 213; (1947) 81 ILTR 92.

[45] It is not sufficient that the institution of proceedings is imminent - a court must have seisin of the case in respect of which the contempt is alleged - see *The State (D.P.P.) v Independent Newspapers Ltd.* [1985] ILRM 183. Though note the recommendation of the Law Reform Commission that in certain limited circumstances, the law of contempt should be extended to cover situations in which proceedings are imminent - *op. cit.*, pp.320-321.

[46] See below, pp. 391-392.

[47] See above, pp. 393-394. On the law of criminal contempt, see Mr. Justice Henchy, "*Contempt of Court and Freedom of Expression*", (1982) 33 NILQ 326.

trend of judgments, commonly referred to as "scandalising the court".[48] Allegations of both forms of contempt surfaced in *Weeland v R.T.É.*[49] and *Desmond v Glackin (No.1)*.[50] In *Weeland*, the plaintiff sought an interlocutory injunction to restrain R.T.É. from broadcasting a programme concerning land transactions to which he was a party, which transactions were the subject matter of an appeal to the High Court from a decision of Judge Gleeson in the Circuit Court. He alleged that references made to certain aspects of Judge Gleeson's judgment in the course of the programme amounted to contempt of court because, *inter alia*, the tenor and manner of presentation suggested criticism of the judgment and the programme was a deliberate interference with the High Court appeal. In a judgment containing a strong affirmation of the right of fair criticism of the courts, Carroll J refused to grant the injunction. She pointed out that the plaintiff was not entitled to an injunction simply because there were legal proceedings in being but that he must prove contempt of court. Neither head was made out in the instant case. In relation to the contention that the programme purported to tell the High Court how it should deal with the appeal, Carroll J said:

> "[T]o allege that a High Court judge would be influenced by a T.V. programme which was transmitted months before, rather than by the evidence given in court, I find to be unbelievable."

Nor did the programme amount to abusive criticism of the Circuit Court decision. While the programme failed to advert at all to the reasons given by Judge Gleeson for the view he took of the evidence, and while the person producing the programme did not agree with the judgment, there was no suggestion that the judge had acted from improper motives "or anything of that nature". Carroll J continued:

> "I do not see why a judgment cannot be criticised, provided it is not done in a manner calculated to bring the court or the judge into contempt. If that element is not present there is no reason why judgments should not be criticised. Nor does the criticism have to be confined to scholarly articles in legal journals. The mass media are entitled to have their say as well. The public take a great interest in court cases and it is only natural that discussion should concentrate on the result of cases."

In *Desmond v Glackin (No.1)*, the plaintiff brought an application to attach one of the defendants, the Minister for Industry and Commerce, Mr. O'Malley, T.D. for contempt on the ground, *inter alia*, that he was guilty of scandalising the court.[51] The grounds for this particular allegation were that, in an interview with RTÉ, the defendant had expressed amazement that the High Court had granted an *ex parte* injunction restraining his inspector from continuing an investigation into certain aspects of the plaintiff's affairs; that he had referred to the High Court as having "facilitated [the plaintiff] in blocking the enquiry;" and that he had criticised the Court for having apparently accepted at face value an allegation made on oath that he, the Minister, had acted illegally. O'Hanlon J rejected this contention, taking the view that the expression of surprise at

[48] It is possible to infer from a statement of O'Hanlon J in *Desmond v Glackin (No.1)* [1992] ILRM 490 at 503, that somewhat greater latitude is given to a speaker charged with scandalising the courts than to a person accused of obstructing or prejudicing the course of justice.
[49] [1987] IR 662.
[50] [1992] ILRM 490.
[51] The plaintiff also alleged that the defendant had infringed the *sub judice* rule. This is discussed below, pp. 937-940.

the High Court order did not exceed the bounds of fair and permissible criticism and that the reference to the Court facilitating the blocking of the enquiry was to the speed with which the *ex parte* order had been granted, rather than to the effect of the order itself. As for the criticism of the Court that it had apparently accepted the truth of an allegation that the Minister had acted unlawfully, the judge considered this to be "fairly innocuous" speculation by the Minister as to what had happened at the hearing.

Insulting statements about courts

In addition to the older cases mentioned in the context of Article 34, three cases may be mentioned here where the offence of scandalising the court was made out; all three were first before the courts in the month of July 1976.

In the first of these, *The State (Director of Public Prosecutions) v Walsh (No. 3)*,[52] the complaint arose from an article in *The Irish Times* citing the views of an association which had said, in relation to a trial before the Special Criminal Court for capital murder, in which the accused persons were convicted, that the Court "had no judicial independence" and "had so abused the rules of evidence as to make it akin to a sentencing tribunal". The newspaper's owners, its editor and the journalist who had reported the association's statement were originally charged with this contempt, along with the two authors of the quoted statement, but had been discharged from the proceedings[53] by Finlay P, who said:

> "that the offence of contempt of court consisting of scandalisation of the court was an offence which implied intention or involved, as they described it in a criminal case, *mens rea*. In the absence of that intention, he did not think it would be proper to impose any penalty, notwithstanding the seriousness of what was said."[54]

The authors of the contempt, after the complaint had been tried by Finlay P without a jury,[55] were given suspended (in one case provisionally suspended) sentences of eighteen and twelve months' imprisonment. The President noted what the Supreme Court had said about the words they had used, in the course of its judgment on the issue whether they might be punished summarily - O'Higgins CJ said the words fell into the category of "wild and baseless allegations of corruption or malpractice... so as to hold the judges up 'to the odium of the people as actors playing a sinister part in a caricature of justice'"[56] and amounted to a serious crime - and said he regarded this view as a precedent he was ready to follow, although *obiter* to the issue of summary punishment; he commented also, in justifying the imposition of prison sentences, on the "tardiness and ambiguity" of the apology which these two defendants had offered.

In a similar case, *In re Hibernia National Review Ltd*,[57] the owners and editor of *Hibernia* had been proceeded against for publishing a letter in which a murder trial before the Special Criminal Court was referred to with inverted commas as a "trial" and in which other similar insinuations were visible. Kenny J, delivering the Supreme

[52] High Court, 21 October 1981.
[53] This stage of the proceedings is also unreported: see *The Irish Times*, 15 July 1976.
[54] See also *McCann v An Taoiseach*, High Court, 22 June 1992, where Carney J held that a radio broadcast which had suggested that the High Court was about to take extraneous factors into account when deciding a controversial case was a serious contempt of court but that no further action was necessary since the comments were unintentional and a full apology had been forthcoming.
[55] This issue is reported: *The State (D.P.P.) v Walsh* [1981] IR 412.
[56] The phrase cited by the Chief Justice had been used by Gavan Duffy J in *Attorney General v Connolly* [1947] IR 213.
[57] [1976] IR 388.

Court's judgment in granting a conditional order of attachment, said:

> "This letter suggested that the members of the Special Criminal Court, all of whom were members of the judiciary, conducted a travesty of a trial to procure a false verdict of guilty. It is difficult to think of a more serious charge against the Court... [He cited Lord Russell of Killowen's dictum that] any act done or written, calculated to bring a court or a judge of the court into contempt, was contempt of court."

He went on to say that the Supreme Court wished to emphasise:

> "that criticism of the existence of the death penalty or the establishment of the Special Criminal Court was not a contempt of court. These were matters which might validly be criticised in public and be the subjects of letters to newspapers. Reasonable criticism of courts or a system of law they operated, or penalties they imposed, was not contempt of court. What is contempt is the publication of a statement which brings a court or a judge of the court into contempt and in each case the distinction has to be drawn by the court between the criticism, be it informed or uninformed, and remarks which have as their purpose the bringing of the court into contempt."

In *In re Kennedy and McCann*[58] the editor of *The Sunday World* and one of the paper's columnists were proceeded against for imputations against the courts in a dispute under the Guardianship of Infants Act 1964; the article in question had alleged that the criterion established by that Act as paramount - the welfare of the children - had been disregarded, and said "it seems that money and the lifestyle it could buy was regarded by the courts as by far the most important consideration". It suggested also that justice could not be obtained in Irish courts, in which context Ireland was said to have a "sick society" which was "hypocritical about motherhood, morality and the family". Both editor and journalist were fined by the Supreme Court;[59] O'Higgins CJ said:

> "The right of free speech and the free expression of opinion are valued rights. Their preservation, however, depends on the observance of the acceptable limit that they must not be used to undermine public order or morality, or the authority of the State. Contempt of court of this nature carries the exercise of these rights beyond this acceptable limit, because it tends to bring the administration of justice into disrepute and to undermine the confidence which the people should have in judges appointed under the Constitution to administer justice in our courts...
>
> [He cited Lord Russell of Killowen's dictum on contempt.] Lord Russell added that judges and courts were alike open to criticism; and if reasonable argument or expostulation was offered against any judicial act as contrary to law or to the public good, no court could, or would, treat that as contempt of court...In this instance there has been a contempt of a serious nature. Not only was the article in breach of an order prohibiting publication, but it was a distortion of the facts, and was calculated to scandalise the members of the court...for it imputed to them base and unworthy motives which, if they were actuated by them, would render them unfit for their office...

[58] [1976] IR 382.

[59] They had apologised, and the Court said it would be unjust not to give their apology "considerable weight". Nevertheless, there had to be punishment for this serious offence: "It must not go forth from this Court that a contempt of this nature can be met by an expression of regret and an apology."

[60] [1981] IR 412.

> The offence of contempt by scandalising the court was committed when, as here, a false publication was made which intentionally, or recklessly, imputed base or improper motives or conduct to the judge or judges in question."

For another instance of contempt proceedings for "scandalising" a court, see *The State (Director of Public Prosecutions) v Walsh*[60] (cited above in the context of the exceptional power to punish a serious offence summarily, pp. 667-668).

LIMITATION IN THE INTEREST OF A FAIR TRIAL

The concept of "due process of law" - described by Gannon J as "the application of basic principles of justice which are inherent in the proper course of the exercise of the judicial function"[61] - justifies certain restrictions on freedom of expression in the interest of a fair trial.[62]

"Sub judice" principle

As we have already noted, one variant of criminal contempt is conduct tending to obstruct or prejudice the course of justice. In particular, it is accepted that the courts will act to inhibit the making and publication of statements tending to influence the decision of a pending issue, particularly a trial by jury or holding a litigant up to public obloquy for exercising his right of access to the courts - the so-called "*sub judice*" rule.[63] This recognition of the necessity to protect the integrity of criminal justice was visible in the judgment of Costello J in *Application of MacArthur*,[64] in which the applicant, accused of murder in a case with sensational though accidental features, sought the attachment of the then Taoiseach (Mr. Haughey) and the owners and editors of newspapers for, respectively, expressions inadvertently used at a press conference, an indication of an item of evidence likely to be used at the trial, and publication of a photograph of the accused. The judgment is not very illuminating, as the judge, in order not to give enhanced currency to the matters of which the applicant complained, expressly avoided specifying them; but he did envisage the punishment of a person for contempt taking the form of words "calculated to prejudice the due course of justice",[65] even though in the case

[61] *The State (Healy) v Donoghue* [1976] IR 325; (1976) 110 ILTR 9.

[62] Though for the view that statutory restrictions on the reporting of court proceedings infringe Article 40.6.1.i, see Russell, "*Contempt of Court*" (1968) 3 Ir Jur (n.s.) 1 at p.17.

[63] In its *Consultation Paper on Contempt of Court* (1991), the Law Reform Commission concluded that, on balance, the *sub judice* rule does not offend against the guarantee of freedom of expression - p.291. For further discussion of the *sub judice* rule in the context of free speech, see O'Dell, "*Speech in a Cold Climate: The 'Chilling Effect' of the Contempt Jurisdiction*" in Heffernan ed. *Human Rights: A European Perspective*, (forthcoming).

[64] [1983] ILRM 355.

[65] He referred to *Keegan v de Búrca* [1973] IR 223. In the absence of an intention to prejudice the course of justice, no liability exists - *A.G. v Cooke* (1924) 58 ILTR 157. Thus in *Murphy v Byrne*, *The Irish Times*, 26 June 1993, the broadcaster Gay Byrne was acquitted of a charge of contempt after Morris J held that it had not been established to his satisfaction beyond all reasonable doubt that an interview which he conducted with the plaintiff in proceedings pending before the High Court was calculated to prejudice a jury. (This would appear to cast doubt on the correctness of the decision in *Kelly v Brady*, *The Irish Times*, 25 May 1993, where an editor and journalist were fined £5,000 by the Circuit Court for contempt in circumstances in which it seems quite clear that they had not intended to influence the course of justice.) In *The Council of the Bar of Ireland v Sunday Business Post Ltd.*, High Court, 30 March 1993, Costello J held that that owners of the "The Sun", its editor and one of the paper's journalist were guilty of contempt for publishing material in respect of which the plaintiff body had previously obtained a temporary order restraining publication by the "Sunday Business Post" and any person having notice of the order. The editor and journalist were aware of the existence of the order, leading Costello J to comment:

> "[C]ontempt may occur through a reckless failure to ascertain the legal consequences of a court's order just as much as from a deliberate flouting of it and I think that such recklessness would have occurred in this case if the respondents had failed to take legal advice on the significance of an order the contents of which they were aware of."

before him, where the words were inadvertent and steps had been taken by the defendant to prevent their publication, he thought the Court's powers should not be exercised, and refused a conditional order of attachment. In the case of the newspapers, he said he "could not emphasise too strongly the undesirability of publishing matter relating to the evidence to be adduced at a forthcoming criminal trial". Against one of the papers he said no prima facie case for the exercise of the Court's powers had been made out; in the case of the other, however - which by publishing a photograph of the accused had prejudiced the question of visual identification - a case had been established, though, as he said such motions should normally be brought by the State's law officer, he made no order pending an indication of his intentions by the Director of Public Prosecutions.

Common sense suggests that, in this area, the same degree of suggestibility cannot be attributed to a court composed of judges as might be imputed to a court containing a jury. In *Cullen v Toibín*[66] the plaintiff, who had been convicted of murder, sought an injunction to restrain the defendants from publishing an article, based on material supplied by a witness whose evidence had led to his conviction, in the interval between his trial and the hearing of his appeal. This was granted in the High Court (Barrington J saying that, having read the text of the article, he would have felt obliged to get himself replaced had he been a member of the Court of Criminal Appeal); but the Supreme Court reversed his order. O'Higgins CJ said the appeal court would be considering pure questions of law in the appeal, and that such a publication could not have any effect on the Court's consideration of those questions. He said he did not approve the publication of such an article - "better taste might indicate that articles of this kind should not be published during the currency of legal proceedings involving a citizen" - but:

> "there was the matter of the freedom of the press guaranteed by the Constitution and that should not be lightly interfered with... [It] should only be interfered with by the courts where it was necessary in the administration of justice, but certainly not in a case of [this] kind."

Hederman and McCarthy JJ agreed, the latter saying he thought that:

> "[for the Court to accept] that that Court or any other court on reading the article would lose its objectivity in determining a pure issue of law... would be more damaging than the possible conclusion of some misguided reader of the article that it could prejudice the Court of Criminal Appeal in determining a pure issue of law."[67]

In *Wong v The Minister for Justice*[68] Denham J accepted that the risk of a judge sitting alone, as opposed to a jury, being influenced by a newspaper article was minimal, though she did not rule it out completely, citing remarks of Barrington J in *Cullen v*

[66] [1984] ILRM 577.

[67] In a similar vein, see the comment of Carroll J in *Weeland v RTÉ* [1987] IR 662 that "to allege that a High Court judge would be influenced by a television programme which was transmitted months before, rather than by the evidence given in court, I find to be unbelievable." Though note the comments of the Law Reform Commission in its *Consultation Paper on Contempt of Court* (1991), at pp.97-99. In *Kelly v Brady*, *The Irish Times*, 25 May 1993, a journalist and editor of *The Irish Times* were fined £5,000 for contempt for publishing an article which profiled an individual who had been convicted of drugs offences by a jury but who was still awaiting sentencing by a trial judge. The Circuit Court judge is reported as saying that he himself was incorruptible but that he was concerned about the possibility that the article might influence expert witnesses yet to give evidence.

[68] High Court, 30 July 1992.

Toibín and Finlay CJ in *The People (Director of Public Prosecutions) v Conroy*[69] in support. However in the instant case:

> "where the article in question came mid-trial, in a civil matter, and where facts set out in the article are admitted to be false, and where they are so clearly at variance with the facts before the High Court in judicial review, there is no real possibility, let alone real risk, of the Court being influenced."

It may be noted that in *Director of Public Prosecutions v Irish Press Ltd.*[70] Finlay P. said the test of a contempt consisting of expressions tending to influence a court's decision was not whether in fact they did "interfere with the due and proper and fair trial of any legal proceeding, whether criminal or civil", but whether, when uttered or published, they were likely to have done so.

Acting pursuant to the *"sub judice"* rule, a court may inhibit, not only statements tending to influence a judge or jury in the outcome of their deliberations, but also "conduct which was calculated so to abuse or pillory a party to litigation or to subject him to such obloquy as to shame or dissuade him from obtaining the adjudication of a court to which he was entitled." An allegation that the defendant, the then Minister for Industry and Commerce, Mr. O'Malley, had so pilloried the plaintiff in the course of an interview with RTÉ formed one of the grounds for the plaintiff's application for attachment for contempt in *Desmond v Glackin*.[71] Applying the presumption that Irish public policy is in accord with the Convention on Human Rights, and more specifically, that the law on contempt conforms with Article 5 and 10(2) of the Convention,[72] O'Hanlon J decided the issues in the case in the light of the decision of the European Court of Human Rights in *Sunday Times v UK*.[73] In that case, a majority of the Court held that an injunction, granted by the House of Lords on the ground of contempt of court, restraining a newspaper from publishing material was contrary to the guarantee of freedom of expression in Article 10 of the Convention as it was not necessary in a democratic society for maintaining the authority of the judiciary. According to the Court, the particular formulation of the law of contempt adopted by the House of Lords - that it was not permissible to prejudge issues in pending cases - was too absolute and failed to achieve a proper balance between freedom of expression and protection of judicial proceedings. In the instant case, O'Hanlon J noted that the plaintiff had made serious allegations of *mala fides* against the defendant in a grounding affidavit for an *ex parte* injunction and concluded that the Minister should have some right of reply. Accordingly he held that, although the Minister's remarks were injudicious and indiscreet, they did not amount to contempt of court.

Contempt of court on this ground was established in *Wong v The Minister for Justice*[74] where a newspaper had incorrectly linked the applicant, an alien who had instituted proceedings challenging a ministerial decision not to permit him to remain in Ireland, with the Chinese criminal underworld. According to Denham. J:

> "The basis of this ground is wider than solely the concern that the Court will be biased as a result of the report. The basis is that the administration of justice suffers as a result of a litigant mid-trial being held up to such public obloquy. If such false reporting were to be the norm the administration of justice would suffer."

[69] [1986] IR 460. Finlay CJ was actually addressing the question of the effect of hearing inadmissible evidence on a judge in a criminal case.

[70] High Court, 15 December 1976. See also *Kelly v Brady*, *The Irish Times*, 25 May 1993.

[71] [1992] ILRM 490.

[72] See statement of Henchy J to that effect in *The State (D.P.P.) v Walsh* [1981] IR 412 at 440.

[73] Series A, No.30, (1979) 2 EHRR 245.

[74] High Court, 30 July 1992.

In the instant case, however, the tendering of apologies to the court adequately purged the contempt.

By virtue of Article 15.13, the courts have no jurisdiction to punish any member of the Oireachtas for a statement made in the course of parliamentary debate on litigation pending in the courts. However for almost seventy years, the Dáil operated a self-imposed *sub judice* rule in order to avoid the risk of prejudicing judicial proceedings. Until relatively recently, the operation of this convention was perhaps overly cautious as it precluded debate on any issue once a writ had issued. In 1993 the convention was relaxed somewhat so that now an issue may be raised in the House, notwithstanding the existence of court proceedings, provided that, in the terms of the relevant Dáil motion:[75]

1. The matter raised must be clearly related to public policy;

2. A matter may not be raised where it relates to a case where notice[76] has been served, that is to be heard before a jury or is then being heard before a jury;

3. A matter should not be raised in such an overt manner so that it appears to be an attempt by the Oireachtas to enroach on the functions of the courts or judicial tribunals;

4. Members may only raise matters in a substantive manner, that is by way of Parliamentary Question, debate on the adjournment and Motion and so forth, where due notice is required; and

5. When permission to raise a matter has been granted, there continues to be an onus on Members to avoid, if at all possible, comment which might in effect prejudice the outcome of the proceedings.

Statutory restriction of press reports

Section 20 of the Criminal Justice Act 1951, formerly provided by sub-s 1 that the court concerned might exclude the public and restrict press reports where, on the preliminary investigation of an indictable offence, the court was satisfied that this was "expedient for the purpose of ensuring that the accused [would] not be prejudiced in his trial". The latter provision was repealed by the Criminal Procedure Act 1967, which replaced it with a new provision making no specific reference to the object of not prejudicing the accused person, though it may be assumed that this object underlies the 1967 provision also. This provision (s 17) reads:

(1) No person shall publish or cause to be published any information as to any particular preliminary examination other than a statement of the fact that such

[75] See *Dáil Debates,* Vol.430, cols 354-355.

[76] This should, perhaps, read "notice of trial" - see comments of Michael McDowell TD to this effect, *ibid.*, col.363.

[77] Section 17 does not apply to press reports appearing before charges are brought, and in *The State (D.P.P.) v Independent Newspapers Ltd.* [1985] ILRM 183 O'Hanlon J refused to extend the laws on contempt of court to cover such publications, having regard to the "countervailing importance of preserving the freedom of the Press".

[78] For the suggestion that this sub-section may be unconstitutional, having regard to the decision in *Re Haughey* [1971] IR 217 - examined above, pp. 464-465 - see Casey, *Constitutional Law in Ireland* (2nd ed., 1992).

examination in relation to a named person on a specified charge has been held and of the decision thereon.[77]

(2) If it appears to a justice of the District Court, on the application of the Attorney General, that any person has contravened sub-section (1), he may certify to that effect under his hand to the High Court and the Court may thereupon inquire into the alleged offence and after hearing any witnesses who may be produced against or on behalf of that person, and after hearing any statement that may be offered in defence, punish or take steps for the punishment of that person in the like manner as if he had been guilty of contempt of the Court.[78]

(3) Sub-section (1) shall not apply to the publication of such information as the justice by whom the preliminary examination was conducted permits to be published at the request of the accused.

Sub-section (3) of this provision clearly shows that its main beneficiary is envisaged as the accused person.

Other statutory provisions worth noting in this context are s 4 of the Offences Against the State (Amendment) Act 1972, cited above p. 929, and s 14(2) of the Censorship of Publications Act 1929, which prohibits the publication of evidence - though not the court's decision, which may be published - given in proceedings for divorce, annulments or judicial separations.[79]

Limitation in the Interest of Individuals' Privacy

Certain restrictions are placed on the reporting of court proceedings in the interest of the privacy of individuals' lives and affairs: thus s 45(1) of the Courts (Supplemental Provisions) Act 1961 provides for the hearing *in camera*, matrimonial causes and matters, lunacy matters and matters involving minors, and proceedings involving the disclosure of a secret manufacturing process while s 205(7) of the Companies Act 1963 authorises the court to direct that all or part of a hearing of a petition under that section be held *in camera.*[80] Inasmuch as these provisions envisage the absence of reporters from such proceedings, they represent limitations on freedom of expression or reportage only to the extent that a breach of the court's privacy may be a contempt.[81] In *In re Kennedy and McCann,*[82] while the main issue was the publication of remarks which scandalised the courts, O'Higgins CJ drew attention to the fact that the case which had been commented on (one under the Guardianship of Infants Act 1964) had been heard *in camera* in both High Court and Supreme Court:

> "Orders providing for the hearing of such cases *in camera* were made in order to preserve, for the sake of the children and their welfare, a decent privacy in relation to the disputes which had arisen between their parents...As a result of [the article

[79] For a discussion of the constitutionality of this provision, see *Casey, op. cit.* p.446-7.
[80] Considered in *In re R. Ltd.* [1989] IR 126, [1989] ILRM 757, and *Irish Press plc v Ingersoll Irish Publications Ltd.* [1993] ILRM 747. See above, pp. 405-406
[81] Thus where a journalist and editor were unaware of the fact that proceedings had been held *in camera*, the publication of a report relating to those proceedings was not an offence, as the defendants lacked the necessary *mens rea* for contempt - *Crindle Investments Ltd v Browne, The Irish Times*, 27 May 1993.
[82] [1976] IR 382.

> complained of] the privacy of the hearing had been at least partly destroyed...[It] tore away the shield of privacy which the courts had erected, and exposed the children to a glare of publicity which could affect very seriously their ordinary lives, companionship at school, and their relationship with their parents."[83]

Under this general heading there may be mentioned also s 25 of the Prices Act 1958, which (in the interest of the privacy of the affairs of commercial concerns) makes it an offence to disclose information gained by virtue of the powers of obtaining information created by the Act; ss 7 and 8 of the Criminal Law (Rape) Acts 1981 and 1990 which prohibit the publication of material likely to identify either the complainant or the accused in a prosecution of a sexual assault offence; para 9(1) of the First Schedule to the Competition Act 1991, which prohibits a person disclosing information available to him by virtue of the powers of obtaining information conferred by the Act or by any other enactment conferring functions on the Competition Authority or through being present at a meeting of the Authority held in private; and s 18(1B) of the Broadcasting Act 1960 (inserted by s 3 of the Broadcasting (Amendment) Act 1976) and s 9(1)(*e*) of the Radio and Television Act 1988 which place an obligation of the RTÉ Authority and independent sound broadcasters respectively not to encroach unreasonably upon the privacy of any individual.

The courts have also a statutory discretion to exclude members of the public - but not *bona fide* representatives of the press - from criminal trials in specified circumstances.[84] By virtue of s 5 of the Punishment of Incest Act 1908, even the press are excluded from the hearing of cases taken under that Act which must be heard *in camera*. The constitutionality of this provision has, however, been questioned.[85]

Limitation in the Interest of Private Reputations

Freedom of expression may also be restricted in the interest of an individual's right to his or her good name, protected by Article 40.3.2. This is invariably achieved through the law of defamation which is similar to that of England, though parts of the common law of defamation were modified by the Defamation Act 1961, and some of the Civil Liability Act 1961 - specifically s 11(4) and (5) - is also relevant.[86] Many decisions of the High Court and Supreme Court on questions of libel and slander will be found listed in the *Irish Digests*, 1919 to 1988.

Subject only to the defence of privilege, a person is liable under current law for any

[83] It has been argued that restrictions on the reporting of *in camera* hearings are only legitimate to the extent to which they are necessary to preserve the privacy and secrecy of identity of the parties involved and that a blanket ban on discussion of *in camera* hearings is not necessarily justifiable - see article by *O'Dell*, cited at Fn. 63 above.

[84] Children Act 1908, ss 114 and 131, as amended by the Children Act 1941, s 29; Criminal Justice Act 1951, s 20(3); Criminal Procedure Act 1967, s 16(2); Criminal Law (Rape) Act 1981, s 6 inserted by s 11 of the Criminal Law (Rape) (Amendment) Act 1990.

[85] *Casey, op. cit.* pp.441-2.

[86] See generally, McDonald, *Irish Law of Defamation* (2nd ed., 1989); McMahon and Binchy, *Irish Law of Torts* (2nd ed., 1990), ch.34. See also the law on criminal libel, discussed above, p. 932.

[87] Thus mirroring a similar development in US constitutional law in the celebrated case of *New York Times v Sullivan* 376 US 225 (1964).

[88] See O'Dell, "*Does Defamation Value Free Expression?*" (1990) 12 DULJ (n.s.) 50 at 59-60.

[89] *Report on the Civil Law of Defamation* (1991), pp.122-4. The Commission did accept that if the Oireachtas wished to legislate for fault-based liability in this area, there was nothing in the Constitution to inhibit such a development. Note that in *Barford v Denmark* Series A, No.149, (1991) 13 EHRR 493, the European Court of Human Rights accepted that the State could legitimately restrict freedom of expression in the interests of protecting the reputation of two lay judges from defamatory statements. At the same time, such restrictions must be proportionate to the aim of protecting reputations: *Thorgeirson v Iceland* Series A, No.239, (1992) 14 EHRR 843.

untrue statement of fact which tends to lower another in the eyes of the average right-thinking person. Liability is strict inasmuch as a mistaken belief as to the validity of the statement is no defence. It has been argued that the guarantee of freedom of expression requires a move from this position to one of fault-based liability,[87] in that fear of having to prove objective fact - the defence of justification - "imposes veritable self-censorship, the very antithesis of free expression of *conviction*...The effect of the Constitution is to de-emphasise an enquiry into the truth of the facts, and instead to concentrate on the state of mind of the speaker...If no fault underpins the perception on which the opinion or conviction is based, then to impose liability would conflict with the constitutional guarantee."[88] This argument did not find favour with the Law Reform Commission who took the view that the task of balancing the competing rights of the citizen to his or her good name and of freedom of expression rests with the Oireachtas which has a wide area of discretion in this regard.[89]

Judicial references to the Constitution in the context of defamation have tended to be to the plaintiff's right to his or her good name, protected by Article 40.3.2,[90] rather than to the defendant's freedom of expression.[91] In *Hynes-O'Sullivan v O'Driscoll,*[92] two members of the Supreme Court referred to both concepts in rejecting the defendant's contentions that qualified privilege exists if the speaker honestly, or honestly *and reasonably,* believes that the person receiving the communication has a duty or interest in receiving it. Dismissing the first of these contentions, Henchy J said:

> "An occasion of qualified privilege is to be given recognition only to the extent that it is necessary under Article 40, s 6, sub-s 1 to recognise, on an objective basis, the right to express freely convictions and opinions. The constitutional priorities would be ignored if the law considered an occasion of qualified privilege to depend only on the honest opinion of the communicator as to the existence of a right or duty in the other person to receive the communication. The constitutional right to one's reputation would be of little value if a person defamed were to be deprived of redress because the defamer honestly but unjustifiably believed that the person to whom the words were published had a right to receive the communication."

Similar reasoning was employed by McCarthy J in dismissing the alternative contention that honest and reasonable belief could support the defence of qualified privilege.[93] This decision has been criticised on the ground that the references to the Constitution are essentially rhetorical and that the Court did not engage in a proper analysis of the impact of the Constitution in this area.[94]

[90] As to which, see above, pp. 751-755.

[91] Though in *X v RTÉ,* an *ex tempore* decision of the Supreme Court, 27 March 1990, reported in *The Irish Times,* 28 March 1990 and reviewed by Byrne and Binchy, *Annual Review of Irish Law 1990,* pp.534-7, McCarthy J invoked the guarantee of freedom of expression in order to refuse the plaintiff's application for an *ex parte* injunction restraining RTÉ from broadcasting a programme which identified him as a person involved in the Birmingham bombings of 1974.

[92] [1988] IR 436; [1989] ILRM 349.

[93] Note that the Law Reform Commission has since called for the defence of qualified privilege to be extended to cover this situation - *op. cit.,* para.4.27.

[94] See McDonald, "*Towards a Constitutional Analysis of Non-Media Qualified Privilege*" (1989) 11 DULJ (n.s.) 94; see also *O'Dell, loc. cit.*

[95] But Paul O'Higgins, writing in 1960 ("*Blasphemy in Irish Law*", 23 MLR 151) gives no instance of a prosecution for blasphemy by words or behaviour later than the year 1909 and even this one is very doubtful. O'Higgins also records that Mr. de Valera was of the view that no new offence had been created by Article 40.6.1.i and that the provision simply referred to the common law offence - p.153. In *D.P.P. v Draper, The Irish Times*, 24 March 1988, the accused, who had damaged some religious statues, was charged with causing malicious damage to property rather than blasphemy.

Limitation in the Interest of Public Morality

Blasphemy

While Article 40.6.1.i declares that the "publication or utterance" of blasphemy is an offence, spoken blasphemy remains an offence at common law,[95] and only blasphemous libel (i.e. in written form) has received statutory regulation. Section 13(1) of the Defamation Act 1961, provides that:

> "Every person who composes, prints or publishes any blasphemous or obscene libel shall, on conviction thereof on indictment, be liable to a fine not exceeding five hundred pounds or to imprisonment for a term not exceeding two years or to both such fine and imprisonment or to penal servitude for a term not exceeding seven years."

The following sub-section deals with disposal of the blasphemous or obscene material. The Censorship of Films Act 1923, s 7(2), provides for the withholding of a certificate from a film of blasphemous content. In addition to being guilty of blasphemous libel, a blasphemer may also, depending on the circumstances, be guilty of an offence under s 2 of the Prohibition of Incitement to Hatred Act 1989, which criminalises actions likely to stir up hatred against a group of persons on account of their, *inter alia*, religion. This provision may also be relevant in relation to spoken blasphemy.

In 1991, the Law Reform Commission considered the impact of the Constitution on the law of blasphemy[96] and concluded that it was likely that the law protected religious beliefs in the Judaeo-Christian tradition only.[97] However the Commission also took the view that it was unlikely that the offence would extend to a denial of the truth of the doctrines of Christianity, but rather would have to consist of an insulting and outrageous attack upon such doctrines. The Commission concluded that there is no place for the offence of blasphemous libel in a society which respects free speech and recommended that the reference to blasphemy in Article 40.6.1.i be deleted as part of any extensive revision of anachronistic or anomalous constitutional provisions.[98]

Indecent or obscene material

Article 40.6.1.i criminalises the publication or utterance of, *inter alia*, indecent matter,

[96] *Consultation Paper on the Crime of Libel* (1991), pp.80-84.

[97] In *R. v Chief Magistrate, ex parte Choudhury* [1991] 1 All ER 306, the English High Court held that the common law of blasphemy was confined to protecting only the Christian religion and that, accordingly, the publication of a book, "*The Satanic Verses*", considered by Muslims to be blasphemous, did not constitute a blasphemous libel.

[98] See also the Commission's *Report on the Crime of Libel* (1991), pp.12-13. Pending such a constitutional amendment, the Commission recommended that the offence be re-defined by legislation so as to clarify its constituent elements - the Commission suggesting that the uncertainty of the present law may be contrary to the European Convention on Human Rights, having regard to the decision of the Court of Human Rights in *Sunday Times v UK,* Series A, No.30, (1979) 2 EHRR 245 and the views of the European Commission of Human Rights in *Gay News Ltd. v UK*, Ap. 8710/79, (1983) 5 EHRR 123 - and to extend protection to non-Christian religions.

[99] *R. v Hicklin* (1868) LR 3 QB 360. *Cp.* the formula used by the European Court of Human Rights in *Müller v Switzerland*, Series A, No.1333, (1991) 13 EHRR 212, where, in the course of holding that the conviction of the applicants for displaying obscene paintings did not offend against Article 10 of the Convention, the Court agreed with the national court that the paintings were "liable grossly to offend the sense of sexual propriety of persons of ordinary sensitivity". This formula would appear to be less subjective than its common law equivalent.

[100] *Knuller (Publishing Printing and Promotions) Ltd. v D.P.P.* [1973] AC 435; [1972] 2 All ER 898; *R. v Gibson* [1991] 1 All ER 439.

though without providing any definition of indecency. Composing, printing or publishing an obscene libel is an indictable offence - s 13 of the Defamation Act 1961 - though again there is no constitutional or statutory definition of obscenity; at common law, the test is "whether the tendency of the matter charged as obscene was to deprave and corrupt those whose minds are open to such immoral influences and into whose hands a publication of this sort may fall."[99] The common law also recognises an offence of outraging public decency consisting of the deliberate display of material which, in fact, outrages public decency. For this offence, it is not necessary to prove that the defendant intended to outrage or that the material had a tendency to corrupt those who saw it.[100] Other statutes (some of them amended or extended by subsequent legislation) under which persons may be prosecuted for various offences connected with indecent or obscene publications or displays are: the Vagrancy Acts 1824-1988, s 4; the Dublin Police Act 1842, s 14; the Towns Improvement (Ireland) Act 1854, s 72; the Customs Consolidation Act 1876, s 42; the Indecent Advertisements Act 1889; and the Post Office Act 1908, s 63.[101] Holding an obscene or indecent performance is an offence at common law,[102] though, as Casey notes, private possession of obscene or indecent material is not an offence.[103]

Censorship of films and videos

A censorship of films is exercised under the Censorship of Films Act 1923 to 1992. The 1923 Act establishes the office of Official Censor of Films and a Censorship of Films Appeal Board.[104] By s 5(1):

> "No picture shall be exhibited in public by means of a cinematograph or similar apparatus unless and until the Official Censor has certified that the whole of such picture is fit for exhibition in public."

Section 8 provides an appeal against refusal by the Censor to grant a certificate; if the Appeal Board upholds the appeal, the Censor must grant the certificate. Section 7 provides both for the issue of certificates with special restrictions, and for the issue of a certificate if the applicant makes cuts which the Censor indicates. The criterion on which the Censor may refuse a certificate is given by s 7(2) as his opinion that:

> "such picture or some part thereof is unfit for general exhibition in public by reason of its being indecent, obscene or blasphemous or because the exhibition thereof in public would tend to inculcate principles contrary to public morality or would be otherwise subversive of public morality."

[101] An attempt to invoke the 1908 Act and regulations made thereunder in order to deny free postage facilities to a candidate in Dáil elections on the ground that his brochure was "grossly offensive" failed in *Dillon v Minister for Post and Telegraphs*, Supreme Court, 3 June 1981. The Supreme Court, *per* Henchy J, doubted whether an assertion in the brochure that "Today's politicians are dishonest because they are being political and must please the largest number of people" could be considered grossly offensive. In any event, the 1908 Act prohibited the posting of material which was "indecent, obscene or grossly offensive" and the statement certainly did not come within this more restrictive meaning of "grossly offensive."

[102] For which prosecutions are extremely rare. A celebrated instance was the prosecution of the producer of Tennessee Williams's *Rose Tattoo* in Dublin in 1957, he was charged with "showing for gain an indecent and profane performance". On the criminal issue it went no further than the District Court, where District Justice Ó Floinn dismissed it, delivering a careful judgment in which he approved the address of the English Mr. Justice Stable to the jury in the (then) recent case of *R. v Secker and Warburg* [1954] 2 All ER 683 (the *Philanderer* case): see *The People (Attorney General) v Simpson* (1959) 93 ILTR 33.

[103] *Op. cit.*, p.458. Custom authorities may, however, seize such material pursuant to s 42 of the Customs Consolidation Act 1876.

[104] The Censorship of Films (Amendment) Act 1992 now provides for the appointment of Assistant Censors to assist the Official Censor in the performance of his functions under this legislation.

The amending Acts of 1925 and 1930 are relatively unimportant;[105] but the Censorship of Films (Amendment) Act 1970, clearly signalled a liberalisation of this area. By s 2 it permits a (fresh) application to be entertained in respect of pictures on which decisions had been made before 18 January 1965, or not less than seven years before the date of the application. It is thus to some extent a counterpart of the Censorship of Publications Act 1967.

Censorship of videos[106] is provided for under the Video Recordings Acts 1989 and 1992. Section 3(3) of the 1989 Act empowers the Censor to make a prohibition order in respect of any video which, in the opinion of the Censor, is unfit for viewing. Where such an order is made, it is an offence to possess such a video for purpose of supplying it to another; to supply or offer to supply such a video; to exhibit it elsewhere than in a private dwelling; or to import it into the State without a permit. By virtue of s 3(1), a video is unfit for viewing if:

(*a*) the viewing of it -

(i) would be likely to cause persons to commit crimes, whether by inciting or encouraging them to do so or by indicating or suggesting ways of doing so or avoiding detection, or

(ii) would be likely to stir up hatred against a group of persons in the State or elsewhere on account of their race, colour, nationality, religion, ethnic or national origins, membership of the travelling community or sexual orientation, or

(iii) would tend, by reason of the inclusion in it of obscene or indecent matter, to deprave or corrupt persons who might view it, or

(*b*) it depicts acts of gross violence or cruelty (including mutilation or torture) towards humans or animals.

Section 10 of the Act provides for an appeal against, *inter alia*, a prohibition order to the Censorship of Films Appeal Board.

Censorship of publications

Censorship of publications exists by virtue of the Censorship of Publications Acts 1929 to 1967. Of the first of these Acts, the only provisions still remaining in force are those restricting the publication of reports on judicial proceedings and of material advocating abortion, and prohibiting the sale of indecent pictures. Section 14 makes it unlawful to

[105] They brought trailers and advertisements, and soundtrack, within the censorship net respectively.

[106] "Video work" is defined as any series of visual images (whether with or without sound) - (a) produced, whether electronically or by other means, by the use of information contained on any disc or magnetic tape and (b) shown as a moving picture" - s 1. This would appear to encompass computer games, in addition to what are commonly called "videos".

print or publish, in relation to any judicial proceedings:

(*a*) any indecent matter the publication of which would be calculated to injure public morals, or

(*b*) any indecent medical, surgical or physiological details the publication of which would be calculated to injure public morals.

An exception is made in the case of *bona fide* technical publications for the legal or medical professions. Section 16, as amended by s 12(i) of the Health (Family Planning) Act 1979, generally prohibits the printing, publishing, sale or distribution of:

> "any book or periodical publication...which advocates or which might reasonably be supposed to advocate the procurement of abortion or miscarriage or any method, treatment, or appliance to be used for the purpose of such procurement."

The constitutionality of this provision must be open to question. In the first place, it must be read subject to the Fourteenth Amendment to the Constitution which guarantees freedom to obtain and disseminate information relating to services lawfully available in another State, and which clearly encompasses abortion services in such State. Furthermore, it would seem to be a logical corollary of the Supreme Court decision in *The Attorney General v X*[107] that, should abortion services ever be provided in this jurisdiction, pregnant women would be entitled to receive information about such services, at least where the pregnancy posed a risk to the life of the mother. Quite apart from the foregoing, one wonders whether the blanket ban on any publication advocating abortion is not a disproportionate restriction on freedom of expression, accepting the legitimacy of the State's interest in protecting the right to life of the unborn.

The censorship of publications properly so called was originally provided for in Part II of the 1929 Act but this Part was repealed and replaced by the Censorship of Publications Act 1946, which provides (s 2) for a Censorship of Publications Board of five persons appointed by the Minister for Justice and (s 3) for a similarly appointed Censorship of Publications Appeals Board, whose chairman is to be a judge or a practising barrister or solicitor. By s 6 the Board:

> "shall examine every book duly referred to them by an officer of customs and excise and every book in respect of which a complaint is made to them in the prescribed manner by any other person and may examine any book on their own initiative."

The Board, in examining a book, is to have regard to:

(*a*) the literary, artistic, scientific or historic merit or importance, and the general tenor of the book;

(*b*) the language in which it is written;

[107] [1992] 1 IR 1; [1992] ILRM 401; [1992] 2 CMLR 277.

(*c*) the nature and extent of the circulation which, in their opinion, it is likely to have;

(*d*) the class of reader which, in their opinion, may reasonably be expected to read it;

(*e*) any other matter relating to the book which appears to them to be relevant.

When examining a book under this section, the Board may "communicate with" its author, editor or publisher, and may take his representations into account. But if the Board:

> "having duly examined a book, are of opinion
>
> (*a*) that it is indecent[108] or obscene,[109] or
>
> (*b*) that it advocates the procurement of abortion or miscarriage or the use of any method, treatment or appliance for the purpose of such procurement,[110] and that for any of the said reasons its sale and distribution in the State should be prohibited, they shall by order prohibit such sale and distribution."[111]

By s 9, as amended by s 12(4) of the Health (Family Planning) Act 1979, the Board is to examine recent issues of periodicals about which a complaint is made by anyone, and if they are of opinion that these issues:

(*a*) have usually or frequently been indecent or obscene, or

(*b*) have advocated the procurement of abortion or miscarriage or the use of any method, treatment or appliance for the purpose of such procurement,[112] or

(*c*) have devoted an unduly large proportion of space to the publication of matter relating to crime,

the Board may prohibit the sale and distribution of future issues of the periodical. By ss 8 and 10 it is provided that appeals may be brought to the Appeal Board in respect of books or periodicals prohibited under ss 7 and 9. By s 14 it is made an offence to sell, distribute, etc., a prohibited book or publication. By s 16 the Board is to prepare and keep a Register of Prohibited Publications.

The censorship system contained in the two Acts of 1929 and 1946 proved extremely controversial,[113] and in 1967 a new Censorship of Publications Act mitigated the severi-

[108] Defined in s 1 as "suggestive of, or inciting to, sexual immorality or unnatural vice or likely in any other similar way to corrupt or deprave."

[109] For a definition of "obscenity", see above, pp. 944-945. The 1929 Act had, in place of the phrase "indecent or obscene", used the expression "in its general tendency indecent or obscene", and the 1946 standard, by dropping the reference to general tendency, was understood to be less liberal insofar as evidently permitting a prohibition order on the strength of merely occasional passages. However in *Irish Family Planning Association Ltd. v Ryan* [1979] IR 295, Kenny J took the view that the formula in the 1946 Act had the same meaning as its predecessor in the 1929 Act, a view endorsed by Casey, *op. cit.*, p.457.

[110] But see comments above, on p. 947, in relation to s 16.

[111] Section 7 as amended by s 12(3) of the Health (Family Planning) Act 1979. It is questionable whether such a power - described by Kenny J as a judicial power in *Irish Family Planning Association Ltd. v Ryan* [1979] IR 295 - can properly be regarded as limited in terms of Article 37.1 - see *Casey, op. cit.*, p.459.

[112] But see above, p. 947 in relation to a similar provision in s 16.

[113] See N. St John Stevas, *Obscenity and the Law* (London, 1956), chapter 8 ("The Irish Censorship, an Experiment"); and an address by Rev Peter Connolly (Professor of English at St. Patrick's College, Maynooth) reported in *The Irish Times*, 19 February 1959; also an article by the same author in XIII *Christus Rex*, vol. 3 (July 1959), pp. 151ff.: Michael Adams, *Censorship: The Irish Experience* (Dublin, 1968); and A.

ty of the code by placing what may be shortly called a twelve-year limit on the life of any prohibition order, past or future, made on a book on the ground that it was indecent or obscene; this had the effect of automatically "unbanning" nearly all the books banned before mid-1955, a date which roughly marks the period at which the operations of the Censorship Board began a more liberal course.[114]

The censorship of publications has apparently been challenged on grounds relevant to the freedom of expression of Article 40.6.1.i only once. In *Irish Family Planning Association v Ryan*[115] the statutory sections and consequent orders by which one of the Association's publications had been banned were challenged on the ground, *inter alia*, that they failed to respect citizens' rights "to express their convictions and opinions" and to "impart information and ideas without interference by public authority subject to public order and morality". The High Court and Supreme Court did not find it necessary to explore these themes, as they held against the Board on the narrower ground that, in a case (as O'Higgins CJ put it) "where fair questions or points of view arise in relation to the matters to be regarded under s 6(2)" the Board ought to have communicated with the Association (which it had not done) so as to give it a chance to put its case in defence of the booklet. The Court said the Board might have reasonably exercised a discretion not to communicate with the publishers in a case involving patent pornography,[116] a category into which this purely factual and informative publication clearly did not fall.

THE FORMATION OF PUBLIC OPINION AND JOURNALISTS' PROBLEMS

The conflict which can arise between values such as the due administration of justice, on the one hand, and the claims of the journalist's profession, on the other, has received notice not only in the context of inordinate comment amounting to contempt of court but also in that of the right asserted by journalists to "protect their sources". This, too, will result in a contempt of court if it takes the form of refusing to answer questions properly put in the course of a legal proceeding. The matter arose in *In re Kevin O'Kelly*,[117] when a journalist refused to identify a person whose interview had been recorded by him on tape, or to give evidence about the circumstances of the interview, saying that as a journalist he had:

> "a duty also to the community, as all my other colleagues have, to foster the free exchange of ideas, and if confidence between journalists and their clients were even to [seem] to be breached then it would put the exercise of journalism in jeopardy; maybe, perhaps, in such a state as to make it impossible to foster the free exchange of ideas again."

The Special Criminal Court sentenced him to three months' imprisonment for contempt; on appeal, the Court of Criminal Appeal maintained the same view of his conduct (though substituting a fine for the imprisonment). Walsh J said:

> "The Court is aware that in general journalists claim the right to refuse to reveal confidences or disclose sources of confidential information. [He cited Article 40.6.1.i] Subject to these restrictions [i.e. no undermining of public order or morali-

F. Comyn, "*Censorship in Ireland*", Studies, Spring 1969, pp. 42ff.

114 It seems unlikely that the modern courts could have failed to invalidate, on grounds of unreasonableness, the very many absurd orders made by the Board in its earlier existence, if these were still in force.

115 [1979] IR 295.

116 As Kenny J pointed out, anonymous pornography could never be prohibited if the Board in every case was obliged to communicate with the publisher.

117 (1974) 108 ILTR 97. See also *Burke v Central Independent Television Plc.*, High Court, 21 October 1993.

ty or the authority of the State] a journalist has the right to publish news and that right carries with it, of course, as a corollary the right to gather news. No official or governmental approval or consent is required for the gathering of news or the publishing of news. It is also understandable that newsmen may require informants to gather news. It is also obvious that not every news-gathering relationship from the journalist's point of view requires confidentiality. But even where it does, journalists or reporters are not any more constitutionally or legally immune than other citizens from disclosing information received in confidence...So far as the administration of justice is concerned the public has a right to every man's evidence except for those persons protected by a constitutional or other established and recognised privilege...The exercise of the judicial power carries with it the power to compel the attendance of witnesses and the production of evidence and, *a fortiori*, the answering of questions by witnesses."[118]

LIMITATION IN THE INTEREST OF PROTECTING COPYRIGHT OR CONFIDENTIAL INFORMATION

In *Attorney General for England and Wales v Brandon Book Publishers Ltd.*[119] Carroll J accepted that freedom of expression could be restricted in the interests of protecting copyright or confidential information.[120] Here, however, where the plaintiff was seeking to prevent publication of the memoirs of a deceased member of the British secret service, there was no breach of copyright nor of confidentiality in a private or commercial setting. Furthermore there is no absolute confidentiality where the parties are a Government and a private individual and in such a situation confidentiality would only be protected where disclosure would be likely to injure the public interest. Consequently, as the interest of the Irish State was not at risk in the instant case, Carroll J refused to grant the injunction.

In *A.C.C. Ltd. v Irish Business,*[121] however, the plaintiff obtained an injunction restraining publication of articles based on confidential material belonging to the plaintiff on the grounds of breach of confidence and copyright. Similarly, in *Oblique Financial Services Ltd. v The Promise Production Co. Ltd.*[122] Keane J granted an interlocutory injunction to

[118] A similar power is conferred on tribunals by s 4 of the Tribunals of Inquiry (Evidence) (Amendment) Act 1979, considered in *Kiberd v Hamilton* [1992] 2 IR 257. The compatibility of powers of this nature with Article 10 of the European Convention on Human Rights may yet have to be considered by the European Court of Human Rights, for in September 1993, a complaint by a journalist that his prosecution under the UK Contempt of Court Act 1981 for refusing to disclose his sources violated the Convention was declared admissible by the European Commission of Human Rights - *The Irish Times*, 8 September 1993.

[119] [1986] IR 597; [1987] ILRM 135.

[120] Publication of confidential information may be justifiable in the public interest - see *A.G. v Jonathan Cope Ltd.* [1976] QB 752. See also North, "*Public or Private? A Paradox for 1984*" (1984) 7 DULJ (n.s.) 90.

[121] *The Irish Times*, 8 August 1985. In *The Council of the Bar of Ireland v Sunday Business Post Ltd.*, High Court, 30 March 1993, reference is made to proceedings in which a temporary injunction restraining publication of an article was obtained on the ground of breach of confidence.

[122] High Court, 24 February 1993.

restrain the defendants from publishing confidential information. He took the view that the defendants' freedom of expression under Article 40.6.1 was not in issue, as that freedom did not apply to the dissemination of factual information,[123] and that their right to communicate under Article 40.3 had to be read subject to the plaintiffs' right to confidentiality.

GENERAL CONTROL OF CERTAIN MEANS OF COMMUNICATION

Interception and censorship of postal and telephone etc. communications

(a) *Telephones telegrams, telexes.* Section 98 of the Postal and Telecommunications Services Act 1983, prohibits the interception, or disclosure of the contents of telecommunications messages,[124] except where a person is acting (i) for the purpose of an investigation by a member of the Garda Síochána of a suspected offence under s 13 of the Post Office (Amendment) Act 1951[125] or (ii) pursuant to a direction issued by the Minister for Communications under s 110 of the 1983 Act or (iii) under some "other lawful authority", the latter presumably a reference to what was originally a common law power[126] exercised by the Minister for Justice, extrapolated from the long-standing practice in regard to letters, but which now has a statutory basis in the Interception of Postal Packets and Telecommunications Messages (Regulation) Act 1993.[127] Pursuant to this legislation, the Minister for Justice may only authorise interceptions for the purpose of criminal investigation or in the interests of the security of the State - s 2(1).[128] Moreover, by virtue of s 3 of the 1993 Act, a direction under s 110 of the Act of 1983 shall not be issued unless there is in force an authorisation under s 2 of the later Act or the direction is a general one requiring an interception if and so long as an authorisation is in force.

In *Malone v UK*[129] the European Court of Human Rights held that the absence of adequate safeguards and review procedures in relation to ministerial warrants authorising the tapping of telephones infringed Article 8 of the European Convention on Human Rights guaranteeing the right to privacy. Partly as a result of this decision, s 9 of the 1993 Act entitles a person who believes that his communications have been improperly intercepted to have his complaint investigated by a Complaints Referee who is empow-

[123] See discussion above, pp. 923-924.

[124] This phrase is not defined in the Act but ordinarily refers to communications by electronic transmission of impulses and hence covers telephone messages, telegrams and telexes.

[125] Relating to telephone calls of an obscene or menacing character.

[126] See H. W. R. Wade, "*Telephone Tapping: Law and Practice*", a broadcast talk printed in *The Listener*, 12 June 1958. He pointed out that a provision authorising this is found in an Act of 1710, and that the General Post Office, so far from being intended to ensure the privacy of mails from interception, was described by the Ordinance of 1657 which created it as "the best means to discover and prevent many dangerous and wicked designs...against the peace and welfare of the Commonwealth". See also replies to Dáil questions on this matter: 17 February 1972 (258 *Dáil Debates* 2136ff.); 28 February 1980 (318 *Dáil Debates* 1009); 1 May 1980 (320 Dáil Debates 504); and (with reference to the practice whereby the Minister for Defence, in the sphere of the military intelligence service, requests an interception which however is authorised by the Minister for Justice) 26 April 1983 (341 *Dáil Debates* 1752) and 7 July 1983 (344 *Dáil Debates* 2316). See also, for a picture of official practice in this connection, the diaries of Mr. Peter Berry, formerly Secretary of the Department of Justice, cited in *Magill* magazine, June 1980: and, for a controversial episode concerning the improper use of interception facilities, *Kennedy v Ireland* [1987] IR 587.

[127] In what is possibly the only prosecution to date under s 98 of the 1983 Act, two newspaper editors, two newspaper reporters and two radio journalists were each convicted and fined after publishing and broadcasting taped telephone conversations between Mr John Bruton, T.D., leader of Fine Gael, and other members of that party - see *The Irish Times*, 29 July 1993.

[128] The conditions justifying interception for either such purpose are detailed in ss 4 and 5 of the Act respectively. On 5 May 1993, the Minister of State at the Department of Justice, Mr O'Dea, told the Dáil that "forty official interceptions [were currently] authorised by the security forces"- 430 *Dáil Debates*, cols.491.

[129] Series A, No.82, (1984) 7 EHRR 14. See also *Klass v Germany* Series A, No.28, (1980) 2 EHRR 214.

ered, if s/he upholds the complaint, to quash the authorisation and make a recommendation for the award of compensation to the complainant. In addition, s 8 of the Act provides for ongoing review of the operation of the legislation by a serving High Court judge, to ascertain whether its provisions are being complied with. This judge may investigate any case in which an authorisation has been given and may also direct the Minister for Justice to cancel such an authorisation. The remedies provided by the 1993 Act are without prejudice to the individual's right to pursue a constitutional action - s 9(1). Such an action was taken - prior to the enactment of the 1993 Act - in *Kennedy v Ireland*[130] where the plaintiffs were awarded aggravated damages when their telephones were unjustifiably tapped by servants of the State. The judgment of Hamilton P, however, focuses on the intrusion on their right to privacy rather than on any interference with their freedom of expression.

(b) *The postal service*. While ss 66 and 84 of the Postal and Telecommunications Services Act 1983, respectively declare the inviolability of the mails in general terms, and prohibit the opening, delaying or detaining of a postal packet,[131] this is subject to exceptions where, *inter alia*, a person is acting in pursuance of a direction issued by the Minister for Communications under s 110 of the Act[132] "or under other lawful authority" - s 84(2). The latter is presumably a reference to the long-standing executive power to intercept and inspect the mails,[133] formerly recognised by s 56 of the Post Office Act 1908, which the 1983 Act repealed, and which is now regulated by the Interception of Postal Packets and Telecommunications Messages (Regulation) Act 1993. As we have already noted, this Act authorises interceptions[134] by the Minister for Justice solely for the purpose of investigating crime or in the interests of State security - s 2(1).[135] During the second world war the Emergency Powers Act, 1939, also empowered the Government by s 2(2)(*h*) to:

> "authorise and provide for the censorship, restriction, control, or partial or complete suspension of communication by means of all or one or more of the services maintained or controlled by the Minister for Posts and Telegraphs."

This Act expired in 1946.

In relation to the prison population, r 63 of the Rules for the Government of Prisons 1947 empowers the authorities to intercept and, if necessary, censor every letter to or from a prisoner. The constitutionality of this power was upheld by Costello J in *Kearney v Minister for Justice*.[136]

(c) *Wireless broadcasting*. The Wireless Telegraphy Act 1926, deals with reception and transmission of matter broadcast by sound radio or by television. Part I provides that no person may keep any apparatus for wireless telegraphy except by licence of the Minister for Communications; the consistency of this provision with the Constitution was challenged in *Nova Media Ltd. v Minister for Posts and Telegraphs*[137] both on the ground

[130] [1987] IR 587.

[131] For consideration of the legal and political problems arising from a postal workers' boycott of South African mail, see 368 *Dáil Debates* col.515 (27 June 1986).

[132] Which must now be read subject to s 3 of the 1993 Act, see above, p. 951.

[133] See *H. W. R. Wade, loc. cit.*

[134] The definition of "interception", in this context, is an act which, *inter alia*, if done otherwise than in pursuance of a direction under s 110 of the 1983 Act would constitute an offence under s 84 of that Act. The opening of an undeliverable letter does not, therefore, come within the scope of the 1993 Act.

[135] The review and complaints procedures provided for by the 1993 Act in relation to telephone tapping - discussed above in the preceding paragraph above.

[136] [1986] IR 116; [1987] ILRM S2. See above, pp. 826-827.

[137] [1984] ILRM 161. See also the companion case of *Sunshine Radio Productions Ltd. v Minister for Posts*

that it represented an unjustified inhibition on freedom of expression and on the ground that it was a business monopoly such as the Constitution does not countenance;[138] in the application for an interlocutory injunction to restrain the Minister from interfering with the plaintiffs' installations, Murphy J said that "a stateable case had been made out" and noted that the defendants had virtually conceded this; however he refused to grant the relief sought, invoking the balance of convenience.

Section 10 of the Act provides, *inter alia*, that if the Government is of opinion that a "national emergency" has arisen requiring such a measure, it may exercise "full control" over wireless messages.[139]

Section 11 of the 1926 Act makes it an offence to transmit:

(*a*) any message or communication of an indecent, obscene or offensive character;

(*b*) any message or communication subversive of public order;

(*c*) any false or misleading signal of distress;

(*d*) any false or misleading message, signal or communication to a ship or other vessel or an aircraft in distress.

Independence of RTE

Until the Broadcasting Authority Act 1960, was enacted, the national broadcasting system (up to that year, in sound only) was run directly by the Minister for Posts and Telegraphs,[140] but under that Act and the Broadcasting Authority (Amendment) Acts of 1964, 1966 and 1976 the national radio and television service (Radio Telefís Éireann) is under the control of an Authority[141] whose members are appointed by the Government, but enjoy a considerable independence, as s 2 of the 1976 Act provides that:

> "A member of the Authority may be removed by the Government from office for stated reasons, if, and only if, resolutions are passed by both Houses of the Oireachtas calling for his removal."

Impartiality of RTÉ

The impartiality of RTÉ broadcasting is the object of s 3 of the 1976 Act which imports into the 1960 Act in substitution for its s 18(1), the following sub sections:

(1) Subject to sub-section (1A) of this section, it shall be the duty of the authority to ensure that:

(*a*) all news broadcast by it is reported and presented in an objective and impar-

and Telegraphs [1984] ILRM 170.

138 See J.M. Kelly, "*The Constitutional Position of RTÉ*" in Administration, Autumn 1967, vol. 15, p.205; and below, pp. 1090-1091. However in *Attorney General v Paperlink Ltd.* [1984] ILRM 373, Costello J upheld the constitutionality of a similar monopoly in relation to the postal services.

139 Section 20(3) of the Broadcasting Authority (Amendment) Act 1976 makes provision for the extension to cable systems of the Minister's power to make regulations with respect to the possession, sale, purchase, construction or use of apparatus for wireless telegraphy in the event of such emergency.

140 Under Part II of the Wireless Telegraphy Act 1926. By s 34 of the 1960 Act the Minister (now titled the Minister for Communications) may not exercise the powers given him by that Part of the 1926 Act; but the Part is not repealed.

141 The name of the Authority is, by s 3 of the 1966 amending Act "Radio Telefís Éireann", though this (or the abbreviation RTÉ) is colloquially used as the name of the whole service.

tial manner and without any expression of the Authority's own views,

(*b*) the broadcast treatment of current affairs, including matters which are either of public controversy or the subject of current public debate, is fair to all interests concerned and that the broadcast matter is presented in an objective and impartial manner and without any expression of the Authority's own views,[142]

(*c*) any matter, whether written, aural or visual, and which relates to news or current affairs, including matters which are either of public controversy or the subject of current public debate, which pursuant to section 16 of this Act is published, distributed or sold by the Authority is presented by it in an objective and impartial manner.

Paragraph (*b*) of this sub-section, in so far as it requires the Authority not to express its own views, shall not apply to any broadcast in so far as the broadcast relates to any proposal, being a proposal concerning policy as regards broadcasting, which is of public controversy or the subject of current public debate and which is being considered by the Government or the Minister.

Should it prove impracticable in a single programme to apply paragraph (*b*) of this sub-section, two or more related broadcasts may be considered as a whole; provided that the broadcasts are transmitted within a reasonable period.

(1A) The Authority is hereby prohibited from including in any of its broadcasts or in any matter referred to in paragraph (c) of sub-section (1) of this section anything which may reasonably be regarded as being likely to promote, or incite to, crime or as tending to undermine the authority of the State.

(1B) The Authority shall not, in its programmes and in the means employed to make such programmes, unreasonably encroach on the privacy of an individual.

Section 31 of the 1960 Act provides by sub-s 2 that the Minister:

"may direct the Authority in writing to allocate broadcasting time for any announcements by or on behalf of any Minister of State in connection with the functions of that Minister of State, and the Authority shall comply with the direction."

Section 20(4) of the Broadcasting Act 1960 prohibits the Authority from accepting any advertisement "which is directed towards any religious or political end or has any relation to any industrial dispute." It is not easy to point to any legitimate state interest which could legitimate such a ban;[143] moreover the specific ban on religious advertising may also offend against Article 44.2.3, prohibiting discrimination on grounds of religious profession, belief or status.

[142] The prohibition on the expression of the Authority's own views raises a *prima facie* case of conflict with Article 40.6.1.i. During the course of debate on a comparable provision in the Radio and Television Act 1988 - s 9 - the Minister for Communications, Mr Burke T.D., told the Dáil that the Attorney General's office had advised that the risk of unconstitutionality was "very small indeed" - 381 *Dáil Debates*, cols.1155-6. Though see below, p. 957 Fn. 152.

[143] See Hogan , "*Federal Republic of Germany, Ireland and the United Kingdom: Three European Approaches to Political Campaign Regulation*" (1992) 21 Capital University Law Review 501.

Control of broadcasting of subversive material

Sub-s 1 of s 31 has however proved controversial. As amended by s 16 of the 1976 Act[144] it now consists of three sub-sections as follows:

(1) Where the Minister[145] is of the opinion that the broadcasting of a particular matter or any matter of a particular class would be likely to promote, or incite to, crime or would tend to undermine the authority of the State, he may by order direct the Authority to refrain from broadcasting the matter, or any matter of the particular class, and the Authority shall comply with the order.

(1A) An order under sub-section (1) of this section shall remain in force for such period not exceeding twelve months as is specified in the order and the period for which the order is to remain in force may be extended or further extended by an order made by the Minister or by a resolution passed by both Houses of the Oireachtas providing for its extension; provided that the period for which an order under the said sub-section (1) is extended or further extended by an order or resolution under this sub-section shall not exceed a period of twelve months.

(1B) Every order made by the Minister under this section shall be laid before each House of the Oireachtas as soon as may be after it is made and, if a resolution annulling the order is passed by either such House within the next twenty-one days on which that House has sat after the order is laid before it, the order shall be annulled accordingly but without prejudice to its validity prior to the annulment.

The constitutionality of the powers of this section was challenged on one occasion. In *The State (Lynch) v Cooney*,[146] where the defendant (who was the Minister) had used the section to prohibit the making of election broadcasts on behalf of Provisional Sinn Féin because of that organisation's association with and support of the Provisional I.R.A., the applicant submitted, *inter alia*, that the section conflicted with Article 40.6.1.i and the guarantee of freedom of expression. After succeeding in the High Court before O'Hanlon J, he was decisively rebuffed by the Supreme Court. O'Higgins CJ, having recited that by Article 40.6.1 (opening words) the control of this freedom had to be based on the need to uphold public order and public morality, said (for the Court):

> "The constitutional provision in question refers to organs of public opinion and these must be held to include television as well as radio. It places upon the State the obligation to ensure that these organs of public opinion shall not be used to undermine public order or public morality or the authority of the State. It follows that the use of such organs of opinion for the purpose of securing or advocating support for organisations which seek by violence to overthrow the State or its institutions is a use which is prohibited by the Constitution. Therefore it is clearly the duty of the State to intervene to prevent broadcasts on radio or television which are aimed at such a result or which in any way would be likely to have the effect of promoting or inciting to crime or endangering the authority of the State. These, however, are objective determinations and obviously the fundamental rights of citizens to express

[144] The amendment liberalised the section, as it defined narrowly the purposes for which this power could be used. Up to 1976 the purposes were left undefined.

[145] The relevant Minister is currently the Minister for Arts, Culture and the Gaeltacht.

[146] [1982] IR 33; [1983] ILRM 89. See *Gearty*, (1982) 4 DULJ (n.s.) 95. An attempt to challenge s 31 under the European Convention on Human Rights failed when the Commission declared the application manifestly ill-founded - *Purcell v Ireland*, decision of 16 April 1991(1991) 12 HRLJ 254.

had written, was not reviewable by the courts. The defendants had argued that, irrespective of the topic under discussion, Gerry Adams could not be divorced in the public mind from advancing the cause of Sinn Féin because of his prominent position in that organisation. The judge took the view that this was not such an unreasonable decision, having regard to the principles in *The State (Keegan) v Stardust Victims' Compensation Tribunal*,[150] to warrant judicial interference. The effect of this decision would appear to be to introduce a distinction between rank and file members of Sinn Féin and more prominent members of that organisation, the latter being absolutely precluded from broadcasting on the airwaves irrespective of the topic under discussion, whereas a more limited ban applies in respect of the former.

Regulation of independent radio and television

The Radio and Television Act 1988 provides for the establishment of Independent Radio and Television Commission whose primary function is to arrange for the provision of sound broadcasting services and one television programme service in addition to those provided by RTÉ - s 4(1). This function is discharged by entering into sound broadcasting contracts and a television programme service contract with contractors. The criteria for selecting the most suitable applicants to be awarded such contracts are detailed in s 6. In addition to having to obtain a contract from the Commission, sound broadcasters must also hold a licence from the Minister in respect of the transmitter to which the contract relates - s 4(3) - and the Minister is empowered to vary any term or condition of such a licence on a wide range of grounds - s 7. Section 9 imposes restrictions on broadcasting comparable to those imposed on the RTÉ Authority by s 18 of the Broadcasting Act 1960, with the additional restriction that the independent broadcaster may not broadcast "anything which may reasonably be regarded as offending against good taste or decency."[151] By virtue of s 9(1)(*a*), the independent broadcaster, in common with the RTÉ Authority, may not express his own views in the course of news broadcasts. During the passage of this legislation through the Dáil, the Minister reported that the Attorney General's office had advised that the risk of this aspect of s 9 being unconstitutional was "very small indeed".[152] Section 10 regulates advertising on independent radio and provides, *inter alia*, that no advertisements may be broadcast which are directed towards any religious or political end or which have any relation to any industrial dispute. This is equivalent to s 20(4) of the Broadcasting Act 1960, the constitutionality of which is doubted above.[153] Section 11 provides, *inter alia*, that the Minister may direct, by regulation, that complaints form members of the public be investigated by the Broadcasting Complaints Commission, while s 31 of the Broadcasting Act 1960 is extended to independent broadcasters by s 12 of the 1988 Act.

[150] [1986] IR 642; [1987] ILRM 202.

[151] In order to save this potentially wide-ranging restriction from constitutional attack, perhaps the concept of "good taste or decency" should be related to that of obscenity, discussed above, pp. 944-945.

[152] 381 *Dáil Debates*, cols. 1155-6. A similar view is expressed by Byrne and Binchy in *Annual Review of Irish Law 1988*, (Dublin 1989) at p.402-3. For a less sanguine view of the constitutionality of this provision, see the commentary on the Act in (1988) ICLSA, No.20 at p.14.

[153] See p. 954.

> freely their convictions and opinions cannot be curtailed or prevented on any irrational or capricious ground. It must be presumed that when the Oireachtas conferred these powers on the Minister it intended that they be exercised only in conformity with the Constitution."

Having thus cleared the section, the Court then (in separate judgments) upheld the ministerial exercise of the power in this instance.[147] The Chief Justice, with whom Griffin and Hederman JJ concurred, went into the statements and the record of Provisional Sinn Féin, including words and behaviour indicating an intention to subvert the State, and said:

> "A democratic State has a clear and binding duty to protect its citizens and its institutions from those who seek to replace law and order by force and anarchy, and the democratic process by the dictates of the few. In my view, it is abundantly clear that the Minister was not only justified in forming the opinion that he did form, but, also, that he could not have formed any other."

Pursuant to their power under s 31, successive Ministers have prohibited RTÉ for broadcasting, *inter alia*, interviews with spokesmen for Sinn Féin; broadcasts made by or on behalf of, or inviting support for, that organisation; or broadcasts by a person representing that organisations. In its interpretation of this prohibition, RTÉ issued directions to its staff banning any interviews with members of, *inter alia*, Sinn Féin, irrespective of the topic under discussion. The legality of this directive was successfully challenged in *O'Toole v RTÉ*[148] when in accordance with this policy, RTÉ refused to broadcast a number of interviews with the applicant, a member of Sinn Féin, concerning an industrial dispute in which he was spokesman of the strike committee. The Supreme Court, *per* Finlay CJ, considered that RTÉ's blanket ban on broadcasting interviews with members of Sinn Féin constituted an addition to or amendment of the terms of the Ministerial order, rather than its implementation and that the broadcasts in the instant case did not come within the scope of that order. RTÉ had sought to justify the complete prohibition of interviews with members of Sinn Féin on the ground that, having regard to the number of persons conducting interviews on behalf of RTÉ and the possibility of their diverse, subjective views concerning implementation of the Ministerial order, this was the only totally safe, practical way to implement the prohibition. Moreover, the fear was also expressed that members of Sinn Féin who were being interviewed on live broadcasts in connection with matters not covered by the terms of the order could spontaneously introduce statements of support for their organisations. The Court concluded that the first difficulty could be circumvented by a system of monitoring of broadcasts. As for the second point, if RTÉ apprehended that a member of Sinn Féin was likely spontaneously to include a prohibited matter in a broadcast, it was entitled to insist that he or she should broadcast other then live.

O'Toole was subsequently distinguished, however, on the ground that it did not involve the exercise of any judgment or broadcasting expertise, concerning as it did, a blanket exclusion on Sinn Féin members from broadcasting. In *Brandon Book Publishers Ltd. v RTÉ*[149] Carney J in the High Court held that a decision by RTÉ not to carry an advertisement by the President of Sinn Féin, Gerry Adams, for a book of short stories which he

[147] In the circumstances of this particular case, no obligation was imposed on the Minister to give any hearing to the persons affected by his order. Fennelly notes the interesting comparison between this aspect of *Lynch* and the Supreme Court decision in *Irish Family Planning Association Ltd. v Ryan* [1979] IR 295 - *loc. cit.* pp.190-1.

[148] [1993] ILRM 458.

[149] [1993] ILRM 806. See also a companion case taken against the Independent Radio and Television Commission, reported in *The Irish Times*, 30 October 1993

Sections 17 and 18 of the 1988 Act deal with television. The former section obliges the Independent Radio and Television Commission to invite applicants for a third television channel (in addition to the two existing channels run by RTÉ), while the latter section applies to this new service most of the provisions attaching to sound broadcasters under the 1988 Act.

The Radio and Television Act 1988 should be read in conjunction with the Broadcasting and Wireless Telegraphy Act 1988, s 3 of which provided that a broadcast is not to be made from any premises or vehicle.[154]

Broadcasting Complaints Commission

Section 4 of the 1976 Act inserted new sections in the 1960 Act providing for a Broadcasting Complaints Commission, the members of which can be removed only by the same means as are prescribed for the members of the Authority itself.

The main function of this Commission is to deal with complaints relating to the obligations laid upon RTÉ by ss 18(1) and 31(1) of the 1960 Act as amended by ss 3 and 16 of the 1976 Act respectively.[155]

[154] By virtue of s 6 of this Act a vehicle from which an unauthorised broadcast is made may be forfeited, following conviction on indictment of a person of an offence under ss 3 and 5 of the Act at the discretion of the court. No such penalty applies in respect of Premises and the constitutionality of this distinction has been questioned - *Byrne and Binchy, op.cit.*, p.406.

[155] Hall and McGovern contend, citing *R. v Broadcasting Complaints Commission, ex parte Owen* [1985] QB 1153 as a persuasive authority, that the Commission's jurisdiction does not extend to hearing general complaints about the editorial policy of broadcasting authorities - "*Regulations of the Media: Irish and European Community Dimensions*" (1986) 8 DULJ (n.s.) 1 at p.14.

Article 40.6.1.ii

FREEDOM OF ASSEMBLY

[The State guarantees liberty for the exercise, subject to public order and morality, of]

ii. The right of the citizens to assemble peaceably and without arms.

Provision may be made by law to prevent or control meetings which are determined in accordance with law to be calculated to cause a breach of the peace or to be a danger or nuisance to the general public and to prevent or control meetings in the vicinity of either House of the Oireachtas.

[Ráthaíonn an Stát, faoi réir oird is moráltachta poiblí, saoirse chun a oibriú]

ii. Ceart na saoránach chun teacht ar tionól go sítheoilte gan arm.

Féadfar socrú a dhéanamh de réir dlí chun cosc a chur nó rialú a dhéanamh ar thionóil a gcinnfear de réir dlí gur baol briseadh síochána a theacht díobh nó gur contúirt nó cránas don phobal i gcoitinne iad, agus fós ar thionóil i gcóngar do cheachtar de Thithe an Oireachtais.

1922 provision

Article 9 of the 1922 Constitution declared that:

> "The right... to assemble peaceably and without arms... is guaranteed for purposes not opposed to public morality."

Neither of these provisions has ever been judicially construed, or, with two exceptions,[1] even mentioned. It is clear that limitations over and above those envisaged in the second clause of Article 40.6.1.ii do in fact exist to restrict an absolute right of assembly; these, along with other statutory and common law limitations, may be listed.

LIMITATION IN THE INTEREST OF PRIVATE RIGHT

Trespass

An assembly held on private property and without the owner's permission is a trespass,[2] and it has never been suggested that the private right to exclude trespassers is overridden by a general right of assembly. It might equally amount to a nuisance to nearby occupiers to hold an assembly whether on public or on private land. Each participant in either kind of assembly is potentially liable in tort to parties injured; a result which illuminates Dicey's perspective,[3] that the common law does not recognise a "right" of assembly, but that such a right may be constructed out of whatever free areas are left after enumeration of the things which the law prohibits.

[1] *Brendan Dunne Ltd. v Fitzpatrick* [1958] IR 29; *The People (D.P.P.) v Kehoe* [1983] IR 136; [1983] ILRM 237. In *Browne v Dundalk Urban District Council* [1993] 2 IR 512; [1993] ILRM 328, the guarantee of freedom of assembly was invoked by the plaintiffs, members of Sinn Féin, who complained of a decision of the defendant council to revoke a booking of the town hall for the Sinn Féin Árd Fhéis. In the event, O'Hanlon J did not have to address this constitutional dimension to their case.

[2] Section 13 of the Criminal Justice (Public Order) Bill 1993 proposes to criminalise trespass on any dwelling or its curtilage in circumstances where the trespass is done without reasonable excuse and causes, or is likely to cause, fear in another.

[3] A.V Dicey, *The Law of the Constitution* (10th ed.), ch. VII.

LIMITATION IN THE INTEREST OF PUBLIC UTILITY

Public roads

The same is true of the relation of the common law on public roadways to the "right" of assembly. The common law permits on public highways only the activity for which they were made and thrown open, i.e. "passing and repassing", using them for getting from one place to another.[4] There is no right to hold a stationary meeting or demonstration on a roadway; this principle is unaffected by the fact that such meetings are frequently held.[5]

LIMITATION IN THE INTEREST OF PEACE AND ORDER

Non-peaceable meetings

Article 40.6.1.ii. itself accords only the right to assemble "peaceably". Thus McCarthy J., speaking for the Court of Criminal Appeal in *The People (Director of Public Prosecutions) v Kehoe*[6] (a case which arose out of a violent demonstration in which many police officers and others were injured), said that:

> "clearly, a very large proportion of those taking part in the march were there for the purpose of exercising their constitutional right to express peacefully their social or political opinions - a right guaranteed by Article 40.6.1.ii in the following terms, subject to public order and morality - the right of the citizens to assemble peaceably and without arms. [But many were there with offensive implements.] These, as the Court found, were not the accoutrements of peaceful protest."

Meetings which are not of a peaceable nature may fall foul of the common law of unlawful assembly, rout and riot. In *Barrett v Tipperary (N.R.) Co. Council*[7] (a malicious injury case) the definition of unlawful assembly contained in *Archbold, Criminal Pleading, Evidence and Practice* (33rd ed., 1954) was adopted by McLoughlin J:

> "an unlawful assembly at common law is an assembly of three or more persons (a) for purposes forbidden by law, such as that of committing a crime by open force; or (b) with intent to carry out any common purpose, lawful or unlawful, in such a manner as to endanger the public peace, or to give firm and courageous persons in the neighbourhood of such assembly reasonable grounds to apprehend a breach of the peace in consequence of it...I have never come across a case in which unlawful assembly was held to exist where there was not some evidence of force or violence in the commission of an offence or of some show of force or violence or of some breach of the peace or of some conduct tending to excite alarm in the mind of a person of firm and reasonable courage."

In *R. v McNaghten*[8] it was held that persons assembling to obstruct officers of the law are all guilty of an unlawful assembly whether a riot develops or not. An unlawful

[4] Section 9 of the Criminal Justice (Public Order) Bill 1993 proposes to criminalise wilful obstruction of the right of free passage of any person or vehicle in a public place. (See Addendum).

[5] Wade and Bradley (*Constitutional and Administration Law*, 10th ed.) cite a dictum from *Ex parte Lewis*, (1888) 21 QBD 191, 197: "Things are done every day in every part of the Kingdom, without let or hindrance, which there is not and cannot be a right to do, and not infrequently are submitted to with a good grace because they are in their nature incapable by whatever amount of user, of growing into a right."

[6] [1983] IR 136; [1983] ILRM 237.

[7] [1964] IR 22.

[8] 14 Cox CC 576; an Irish land war case of 1881.

assembly becomes a rout "so soon as the assembled persons do any act towards carrying out the illegal purpose which has made their assembly unlawful", such as setting out for the place where the purpose is to be carried into effect. The rout becomes a riot "so soon as this illegal purpose is put into effect forcibly" by persons "mutually intending to resist any opposition". The common law on these subjects has, however, been in practice largely overshadowed by statutory provisions.[9]

These provisions had a forerunner in Article 2A of the 1922 Constitution, inserted in 1931, of which s 24 provided as follows:

> (1) Whenever it appears to the Executive Council that the holding of public meetings in or in the vicinity of any particular building or any particular road or street is likely to lead to a breach of the peace or to be prejudicial to the maintenance of law and order, the Executive Council may issue a proclamation prohibiting the holding in or within a specified area (including such building, road, or street and not extending more than one mile therefrom) during a specified period (not exceeding three months) from the date of the proclamation of either (as the Executive Council shall think proper to specify) any public meeting whatsoever or any public meeting held otherwise than under specified conditions or for specified objects.
>
> (2) Whenever it appears to an Executive Minister that any proposed public meeting is likely to promote or incite to the commission of acts of violence or intimidation or to interfere with the administration of the law or the maintenance of law and order, such Executive Minister may issue a proclamation prohibiting the holding of such meeting at the place and time at which it was proposed to be held or at any other place within three days before or after such time.

By sub-s 3 disobedience to such prohibitions was an offence (punishable by the Constitution (Special Powers) Tribunal).[10] These provisions went out of force when the whole Constitution was replaced in 1937.

Meetings in support of unlawful organisations

Less than two years later new provisions - more stringent in that the discretion to operate them is vested in the police rather than in the Government or in a Minister - were enacted as part of the Offences Against the State Act 1939. Section 27 provides as follows:

> (1) It shall not be lawful to hold a public meeting which is held or purports to be held by or on behalf of or by arrangement or in concert with an unlawful organisation or which is held or purports to be held for the purpose of supporting, aiding, abetting, or encouraging an unlawful organisation or of advocating the support of an unlawful organisation.
>
> (2) Whenever an officer of the Garda Síochána not below the rank of chief superintendent is of opinion that the holding of a particular public meeting about to be or proposed to be held would be a contravention of the next preceding sub-section of this section, it shall be lawful for such officer by notice given to a person concerned in the holding or organisation of such meeting or published in a manner reasonably calculated to come to the knowledge of the persons so concerned, to prohibit the holding of such meeting, and thereupon the holding of such meeting shall become and be unlawful.

[9] See below, pp. 961-964, and also Addendum.
[10] See above, pp. 640-642.

Sub-section 3 provides for an appeal to the High Court against the making of a prohibition; sub-s 4 prescribes penalties for contraventions; and sub-s 5 defines "public meeting" so as to include a meeting held "in a building or on enclosed land to which the public are admitted, whether with or without payment". It will be noticed that whereas the weight of the provisions of Article 2A had been against meetings which threatened the peace and law and order, the provisions of the Offences Against the State Act 1939, s 27, are associated with the "unlawful organisations" which are the prime target of the Act.[11]

Again, while s 24 of Article 2A had spoken generally in sub-s 1 about meetings in the vicinity "of any particular building", the 1937 Constitution specifically mentions meetings "in the vicinity of either House of the Oireachtas", and s 28 of the 1939 Offences against the State Act takes up this idea:

(1) It shall not be lawful for any public meeting to be held in, or any procession to pass along or through, any public street or unenclosed place which or any part of which is situate within one-half of a mile from any building in which both Houses or either House of the Oireachtas are or is sitting or about to sit if either -

(a) an officer of the Garda Síochána not below the rank of Chief Superintendent has, by notice given to a person concerned in the holding or organisation of such meeting or procession or published in a manner reasonably calculated to come to the knowledge of the persons so concerned, prohibited the holding of such meeting in or the passing of such procession along or through any such public street or unenclosed place as aforesaid, or

(b) a member of the Garda Síochána calls on the persons taking part in such meeting or procession to disperse.

Sub-s 2 provides penalties for contraventions.[12]

Tending to obstruct justice

The Offences Against the State (Amendment) Act 1972, contains a special provision on meetings (or utterances) tending to obstruct justice. By s 4(1):

(a) Any public statement made orally, in writing or otherwise, or any meeting, procession or demonstration in public, that constitutes an interference with the course of justice shall be unlawful.

(b) A statement, meeting, procession or demonstration shall be deemed to constitute an interference with the course of justice if it is intended, or is of such a character as to be likely, directly or indirectly to influence any court, person or authority concerned with the institution, conduct or defence of any civil or criminal proceedings (including a party or witness) as to whether or how the proceedings should be instituted, conducted, continued or defended, or as to what should be their outcome.

Sub-section 2 provides penalties for contraventions; and sub-s 3 provides that nothing in the section is to affect the law as to contempt of court. (It may be noted that the terms of s 7(1) of the 1939 Act would already catch, as felony, a meeting or demonstration that

[11] See below, pp. 970-973.

[12] Maxima: £50 fine, or three months' imprisonment, or both.

amounted to an attempt to obstruct justice (or any other branch of government) or the performance of their functions by any "member of the legislature" or any State officials or employees.)

Public order legislation

In addition to the foregoing legislation dealing with meetings which support unlawful organisations or which obstruct justice, statutory regulation of public meetings and assemblies generally is proposed in the Criminal Justice (Public Order) Bill 1993. This Bill proposes, *inter alia*, to replace the common law offences of riot, rout, unlawful assembly and affray with three statutory offences or riot, violent disorder and affray. Section 14(1) provides that where 12 or more persons present together at any place (whether public or private) use or threaten to use unlawful violence for a common purpose and their conduct, taken together, would cause a person of reasonable firmness present at that place to fear for his or another person's safety, then each person using unlawful violence shall be guilty of riot. The offence of violent disorder will apply where three or more persons use or threaten to use unlawful violence in such circumstances - s 15 - while s 16 provides that the proposed offence of affray shall consist of the use or threatened use of unlawful violence by two or more persons towards each other where, again, the conduct of such persons taken together is such as would cause a person of reasonable firmness present to fear for his or another person's safety.

The Bill also proposes to criminalise the following activities in public places - intoxication;[13] disorderly conduct;[14] engaging in any threatening, abusive or insulting words or behaviour with intent to provoke a breach of the peace or whereby a breach of the peace may be occasioned;[15] the distribution or display in a public place of any threatening,

[13] Section 4. The accused must be intoxicated in a public place "to such an extent as would give rise to a reasonable apprehension that he might endanger himself or any other person in his vicinity." For subsequent amendments to the 1993 Bill, see Addendum.

[14] Section 5 proposes to make it an offence for any person to engage in any "shouting, singing or boisterous conduct" in a public place between the hours of 12 o'clock midnight and 7 o'clock in the following morning or at any other time having been requested by a member of the Garda Síochána to desist "in circumstances likely to give a reasonable cause for annoyance to any other person in any place in the vicinity."

[15] Section 6. The constitutionality of this proposed clause - together with that of s 5 - must be questionable, although the "fighting words" problem has yet directly to be addressed by Irish courts. It is true that in other jurisdictions "fighting words" have not enjoyed a great measure of constitutional protection: see, e.g. *Chaplinsky v New Hampshire* 315 US 568 (1942) (upholding conviction for breach of the peace where a speaker had provoked violence having denounced a city marshall as "a damned Fascist"). At the same time - and despite the qualifying language of Article 40.6.1.ii - the decision of the US Supreme Court in *Terminiello v Chicago* 337 US 1 (1949) could well have application in this context. Here a breach of the peace conviction was set aside where the speaker had not engaged in or provoked actual violence, although he had denounced the crowd in hostile language ("snakes", "slimy scum"). As Douglas J said:

> "[A] function of free speech under our system of government is to invite dispute. It may indeed best serve its high purpose when it induces a condition of unrest, creates dissatisfaction with conditions as they are, or even stirs people to anger. Speech is often provocative and challenging. It may strike at prejudices and preconceptions and have profound unsettling effects as it presses for acceptance of an idea. That is why freedom of speech, though not absolute...is nevertheless protected against censorship or punishment unless shown likely to produce a clear and present danger of a serious substantive evil that rises far above public inconvenience, annoyance or unrest."

The foregoing discussion applies *a fortiori* to section 5, the contents of which must be - in certain respects at least - highly suspect. While several American authorities recognise the right "to be left alone" from unwanted speech or communication (see e.g. *Rowan v Post Office Department* 397 US 728 (1970)), nevertheless a provision which allows a member of the Gardaí to order a member of the public to refrain from shouting or singing - a common feature of many peaceful protest marches - *simply* because it is likely to give reasonable cause for *annoyance* to any other person in the vicinity seems a manifest breach of Article 40.6.1.ii: see *Cox v Louisiana* 379 US 536 (1965). The inherent vagueness of the proposed criminal offences (what sort of shouting is likely to annoy persons in the vicinity?) seems additionally calculated to present Article 38.1 difficulties.

abusive or obscene writing, sign or visible representation with intent to provoke a breach of the peace or whereby a breach of the peace may be occasioned.[16] It will also be an offence wilfully to obstruct the free passage of any person or vehicle.[17]

Failure, without lawful authority or reasonable excuse, to comply with the directions of a Garda who suspects that a person (a) is or has been acting in a manner contrary to ss 4, 5 or 6 or (b) is, without lawful authority or reasonable excuse, acting in a manner which consists of loitering in a public place in circumstances that give rise to a reasonable apprehension for the safety of persons or the safety of property or for the maintenance of public peace,[18] is also an offence - s 8. For the purpose of this offence, the Garda can direct that the person desist from the conduct in question and leave immediately the vicinity of the place concerned in a peaceable or orderly manner.

Finally, Part III of the Bill empowers the Gardaí to control access to events attracting, or likely to attract, a large assembly of persons through the erection of barriers on the means of access to such events. In addition, the Gardaí may search persons or vehicles going to such events for intoxicating liquor, disposable containers or any article which could be used to cause injury and may refuse to allow a person to proceed to the event unless he surrenders permanently such liquor, container or article.

PICKETING

What is colloquially called "picketing", i.e. the application of moral pressure by several persons maintaining a conspicuous presence in the vicinity of a particular premises (in practice often, though not necessarily, accompanied by placards to indicate the object of the pressure) is in law a "watching and besetting". As such it is generally regarded as unlawful under the Conspiracy and Protection of Property Act 1875,[19] unless it can be justified as something done in furtherance of a trade dispute under s 11 of the Industrial Relations Act 1990.[20] It was in this connection that the constitutional right of assembly and Article 40.6.1.ii received one of their rare judicial mentions, in *Brendan Dunne Ltd. v Fitzpatrick.*[21]

In this case the plaintiffs successfully sought an injunction to restrain the defendants from picketing their premises by way of protest against late opening hours on one evening a week (an arrangement which had been agreed between the plaintiffs and their employees). The defendants relied both on s 2 of the Trade Disputes Act 1906 - the predecessor to s 11 of the 1990 Act - and on Article 40.6.1.ii; but Budd J held against them

[16] Section 7.

[17] Section 9.

[18] Unlike the offence of loitering declared to be inconsistent with the Constitution in *King v Attorney General* [1981] IR 233, this new offence is not restricted to conduct by a "suspected person or reputed thief" nor does it consist of the act of loitering itself, but rather a failure to comply with a direction from a Garda to desist from such conduct, in circumstances where the Garda had a reasonable apprehension for the safety of persons or property or for the maintenance of the public peace.

[19] It is arguable, however, that picketing *per se* is not unlawful at common law and only becomes so if it entails the commission of a tort such as nuisance or trespass to the highway - see Kerr and Whyte, *Irish Trade Union Law* (1985), ch.10. As Casey points out, in *Constitutional Law in Ireland* (2nd ed., 1992), p.477, the logic of the contrary view is that trade union pickets only are protected in law and that pickets in any other context are unlawful, notwithstanding the terms of Article 40.6.1.ii.

[20] Which replaced s 2 of the Trade Disputes Act 1906, as amended by s 11 of the Trade Union Act 1941 and the Trade Disputes (Amendment) Act 1982. On s 11, see Kerr, *The Trade Union and Industrial Relations Acts of Ireland* (1991), pp.189-193 and also *Westman Holdings Ltd. v McCormack* [1992] 1 IR 151.

[21] [1958] IR 29.

on the grounds that the numbers engaged in the picketing were excessive, and that some of the picketers' placards invited the public to support concerns other than the plaintiffs'. He said:

> "The existence of a trade dispute involves the right to picket, but it still remains to be decided whether or not the particular form of picketing adopted by the defendants was justified under the provisions of the Act. [This] entitles a person acting on behalf of himself or of a trade union in furtherance of a trade dispute to attend at or near a place where a person works or carries on business "if they so attend merely for the purpose of peacefully obtaining or communicating information, or of peacefully persuading any person to work or abstain from working".

As the defendants' behaviour exceeded the concession of the Act, he held that the plaintiffs' rights had been infringed. On the defendants' case based on Article 40.6.1.ii, he said:

> "The right of the citizens to assemble peaceably and to express their opinions freely are guaranteed only subject to public order and morality. As I read Article 40 the rights guaranteed are subject to the overriding proviso that in the exercise of such rights public order is not to be disturbed... To my mind, if citizens in the course of an assembly commit a breach of the peace or some other breach of the law, they thereby disturb public order and their actions are not protected by the Constitution in respect of the breach of the law committed.
>
> Prior to the coming into operation of the Constitution the picketing or watching and besetting of premises was unlawful unless justified by the Trade Disputes Act 1906... I am unable to find that the law as it stood is in any way inconsistent with the terms of the Constitution..."

In *Becton, Dickinson Ltd. v Lee*[22] FitzGerald J criticised the "ultra-liberal interpretation of the Trades Disputes Act 1906", which, he said:

> "coupled with the failure of the authorities to enforce the law, has led to a public misconception and belief that a right to protest carries with it a right to picket. This is not the law."[23]

He emphasised that the immunity conferred by s 2 of the 1906 Act was dependent on two factors: a trade dispute in existence, and the picketing being carried on solely for the purpose of peacefully obtaining or communicating information or of peacefully persuading any person to work or to abstain from working.

In *Ferguson v O'Gorman*[24] the Supreme Court held that picketing, if otherwise lawful, was a reasonable use of the highway in view of s 2 of the 1906 Act.

Some cases in which the legitimacy of a particular picket was considered, having regard to the question whether there in fact existed a genuine "trade dispute", are: *Ryan v*

[22] [1973] IR 1.
[23] The reference in this passage to the failure of the authorities to enforce the law should now be read in the light of *Bayzana Ltd. v Galligan* [1987] IR 241; (1987) 6 JISLL 121 where the plaintiff, which was seeking an interlocutory injunction to restrain picketing, was required by the Supreme Court to give an undertaking that it would enforce the injunction.
[24] [1937] IR 620.

Cooke and Quinn;[25] *Quigley v Beirne*;[26] *Esplanade Pharmacy Ltd. v Larkin*;[27] and *E.I.Co. v Kennedy*.[28] In the latter case a further feature was the conduct of the picket, in which connection Walsh J said:

> "The use of words such as "scab" or "blackleg" are historically so associated with social ostracism and physical violence as to be far beyond anything which might be described as mere rudeness or impoliteness and go beyond what is permitted by law. In the present context the references made to the race or nationality of the employers could produce the same disorderly response and also go beyond what is permitted by law. Excessive numbers in pickets may also go beyond what is reasonably permissible for the communication of information or for the obtaining of information and may amount to obstruction or nuisance or give rise to a reasonable apprehension of a breach of the peace."

In *Goulding Chemicals Ltd. v Bolgers*[29] the Supreme Court repeated that picketing was not lawful if designed by its manner or the number of participants to intimidate; and that the privileges of ss 2 - 4 of the Trade Disputes Act 1906, were (because of s 11 of the Trade Union Act 1941[30]) confined to members and officials of authorised trade unions holding negotiation licences.[31]

In *Ryan v Cooke and Quinn*[32] Johnston J held that placards which "disseminated a falsehood" did not represent a peaceful "communication of information".

The right of picketing even within the limits of the Trade Disputes Act 1906, was further cut down by statute for a particular industry in the Electricity (Special Provisions) Act 1966, s 6.[33]

Police Interference with Assembly which is in itself Lawful

Control of lawful assemblies

This subject gave rise to some not entirely unanimous case-law in the nineteenth century, intertwined perhaps unavoidably with the question whether the police, as distinct from actually dispersing a meeting, may put some restraint on an individual whose own conduct is lawful but where the circumstances give reason to fear a breach of the peace in consequence of that conduct. In *Humphries v Connor*[34] a police officer was found to be justified in removing from a person an emblem in itself lawful but in the actual circumstances dangerously provocative. In *O'Kelly v Harvey*[35] a police officer was held

25 [1938] IR 512.
26 [1955] IR 62.
27 [1957] IR 285; (1958) 92 ILTR 149.
28 [1968] IR 69.
29 [1977] IR 211.
30 See now, s 9(1) of the Industrial Relations Act 1990.
31 The Court also ruled, however, that such privileges were not restricted to persons engaged in official trade disputes. This ruling has effectively been reversed by ss 14 and 17 of the Industrial Relations Act 1990.
32 [1938] IR 512.
33 This provided that it should "not be lawful for a person, wrongfully and without legal authority and in contemplation or furtherance of a strike to which this Act applies [defined in s 2] to watch or beset the house or other place where any person resides or works or carries on business... with a view to compelling or inducing that person to abstain from doing or to do any act which that person has a legal right to do or abstain from doing." The Act was brought into operation only briefly and proved ineffectual.
34 17 Ir CLR 1.
35 10 LR Ir 285; 14 LR Ir 105.

justified in dispersing an assembly, even if lawful, where he had reasonable grounds for fearing that it would lead to a breach of the peace. In *R. (Orr) v Justices of Londonderry*[36] the Irish Queen's Bench Division retreated somewhat from the position of the Court of Criminal Appeal in *O'Kelly v Harvey*; but in *Coyne v Tweedy*[37] (a case primarily about the arrest of an individual, but with an immediate background of two assemblages in potential confrontation and breach of the peace) the position of the earlier two cases was re-established. Fitzgibbon LJ said:

> "It is too late, at least in Ireland, to question the power of a constable, as a reasonable exercise of his duty to preserve the peace, to put a person into a safe place, who is not himself a wrongdoer, but who, if not removed, will become the subject of a breach of the peace."

This principle, in its corollary application to meetings, seems to be tacitly acknowledged by the Constitution itself (though in the context of a statutory regulation which has in fact never been made) when it speaks of preventing or controlling meetings "which are determined in accordance with law to be calculated to cause a breach of the peace or to be a danger or nuisance to the general public"; the "determination" might be the reasonable belief of a police officer, and the language of the clause does not imply the unlawfulness of the assembly itself, as it might, without being itself unlawful, be still "calculated to cause" the various evils listed. This reading seems strengthened by the Irish text, which speaks, in regard to such meetings, of a "baol briseadh síochána a theacht díobh", the fear or danger of a breach of the peace "coming from them", an expression which seems to make it clear that unlawfulness in the meeting itself is not a necessary condition of police interference. If a meeting, though lawful, is likely to provoke others, that may suffice to bring it within range of prevention or control.

Degree of Force Permissible in Dispersing an Unlawful Assembly

Forcible dispersal of assembly

In dispersing an unlawful assembly the police (and, if they are called in, the military[38]) are bound to use no more force than the purpose necessitates. The law on this subject was authoritatively restated by Hanna J in 1937 in *Lynch v Fitzgerald and Others (No. 2)*,[39] a case which was brought under the Fatal Accidents Act 1846, by the father of a youth killed by a bullet fired by one of a group of detectives in repressing an attempt to disrupt a cattle sale. The disrupters, armed with sticks, had broken through a police cordon into the sale yard, being followed by a few onlookers including the deceased; the police cordon had reformed at once, so that the invading party was effectively trapped; nevertheless, the evidence showed that the detectives inside the yard had deliberately fired on the intruders. Hanna J cited with approval the words of Bowen LJ[40] a generation earlier:

> "By the law of this country every one is bound to aid in the suppression of riotous assemblages. The degree of force, however, which may be used in their suppression depends on the nature of each riot, for the force used must always be moderate and proportioned to the circumstances of the case and to the end to be attained.

[36] 28 LR Ir 440.
[37] [1898] 2 IR 167.
[38] On military force being used "in aid of the civil power", see above, p. 134.
[39] [1938] IR 382; (1937) 71 ILTR 212. This civil action was tried without a jury, under s 28 of Article 2A of the old Constitution; see *Lynch v Fitzgerald (No. 1)* [1937] IR 77.
[40] In the Report of the Select Committee on the Featherstone Riot, 1893 (Parliamentary Papers, 1893-4).

> The taking of life can only be justified by the necessity for protecting persons or property against various forms of violent crime or by the necessity of dispersing a riotous crowd which is dangerous unless dispersed, or in the case of persons whose conduct had become felonious through disobedience to the provisions of the Riot Act and who resist the attempt to disperse or apprehend them... Officers and soldiers are under no special privileges and subject to no special responsibilities as regards this principle of law. A soldier for the purpose of establishing civil order is only a citizen armed in a particular manner. He cannot, because he is a soldier, excuse himself if, without necessity, he takes human life."

He also cited, as "a correct statement of the law and a perfect instruction to those of the [police] force who are authorised to use arms", an instruction issued by the Commissioner of the Garda Síochána a few years earlier:

> "It is an invariable rule that the degree of force to be used must always be moderated and proportioned to the circumstances of the case, and the end to be attained. Hence it is that arms... must be used with the greatest of care, and the greatest pains must be exercised to avoid the infliction of fatal injuries...A gun should never be used, or used with any specified degree of force, if there is any doubt as to the necessity."

In finding that, on these principles, the three detectives involved could not be justified in their action, Hanna J recalled that they went back "to the common law principle that it is lawful to use only a reasonable degree of force for the protection of oneself or any other person against the unlawful use of force, and that such repelling force is not reasonable if it is either greater than is requisite for the purpose or disproportionate to the evil to be prevented". The facts, he said, disclosed a *prima facie* case of manslaughter, and he reported accordingly to the Attorney General.[41]

[41] The three detectives were not prosecuted; two were promoted shortly afterwards to sergeant.

FREEDOM OF ASSOCIATION

[The State guarantees liberty for the exercise, subject to public order and morality, of]

iii. The right of the citizens to form associations and unions.
Laws, however, may be enacted for the regulation and control in the public interest of the exercise of the foregoing right.

[Rathaíonn an Stát, faoi réir oird is moráltachta poiblí, saoirse chun a oibriú]

iii. Ceart na saoránach chun comhlachais agus cumainn a bhunú.
Ach is cead dlíthe a achtú chun oibriú an chirt réamhráite a rialú agus a stiúradh ar mhaithe leis an bpobal.

1922 provision

The 1922 Constitution likewise had stated in Article 9 that:

> "The right... to form associations or unions is guaranteed for purposes not opposed to public morality."

As with the other rights guaranteed in Article 40.6, the extent of the right of association will best appear from a survey of the express limitations placed on its exercise.[1] These fall into three categories - limitation in the interest of public order; limitation in the interest of public morality; and limitation in the public interest generally. The first two of these are provided for in the opening words of Article 40.6.1 while the third is specifically provided for in sub-para.iii. In *Aughey v Ireland*[2] Walsh J noted that the legislature could proscribe an association or union in the interest of protecting public order or morality but not, on the authority of *N.U.R. v Sullivan*,[3] pursuant to sub-para.iii.[4]

A full treatment of the guarantee of freedom of association also requires that something be said about the way in which the right has been invoked in the special contexts of trade unions and of political parties.

LIMITATION IN THE INTEREST OF THE STATE'S SECURITY

Earlier laws against subversive organisations

Several statutes, passed between 1925 and 1931 but now no longer in force, contained provisions aimed at subversive associations. The Treasonable Offences Act 1925, penalised the formation or furtherance of "secret societies" in the army or police force; a "secret society" was defined by s 8(2) as one whose members were bound not to disclose its proceedings. (The Act was repealed by the Offences against the State Act 1939, and the provision against secret societies in army or police was replaced by s 1 of the latter Act cited below.) The Public Safety Act 1927, empowered by s 4 the Executive

[1] See the remarks on freedom of assembly, above, p. 959. Quite apart from these express limitations, this freedom may also be qualified where such action is necessary in order to vindicate the constitutional right of another. Thus in *Attorney General (S.P.U.C. (Ireland) Ltd.) v Open-Door Counselling Ltd.* [1988] IR 593; [1987] ILRM 477, Hamilton P in the High Court held that the defendants' right to associate could not be invoked to interfere with the right to life of the unborn. (This point was not adverted to by the Supreme Court in the subsequent appeal.)
[2] [1989] ILRM 87.
[3] [1947] IR 77. See below, pp. 974-976.
[4] This distinction may also be regarded as implicit in the concluding comment of Murnaghan J in *N.U.R. v Sullivan* [1947] IR 77 that "a law which takes away the right of citizens, at their choice, to form associations and unions, *not contrary to public order or morality*, is not a law which can validly be made under the Constitution." (Emphasis added).

Council to declare certain associations to be unlawful and by s 5 penalised membership of such associations; the Act was repealed the following year. The Constitution (Amendment No. 17) Act 1931, imported a whole new Article (2A) into the Constitution, of which s 19 recreated, in virtually identical terms, the category of unlawful associations which the 1927 Public Safety Act had contained; membership was punishable by the Constitution (Special Powers) Tribunal.[5] These provisions disappeared with the rest of the 1922 Constitution in 1937.

Law now in force: 1939 and thereafter

The statutory provisions currently in force on this subject are contained in the Offences against the State Act 1939; the Offences Against the State (Amendment) Act 1972; and the Criminal Law Act 1976. The basic provisions are those of the 1939 Act. Section 16 deals with secret societies in army or police as follows:

> (1) Every person who shall -
>
> (a) form, organise, promote, or maintain any secret society amongst or consisting of or including members of any military or police force lawfully maintained by the Government, or
>
> (b) attempt to form, organise, promote, or maintain any such secret society, or
>
> (c) take part, assist, or be concerned in any way in the formation, organisation, promotion, management, or maintenance of any such society, or
>
> (d) induce, solicit, or assist any member of a military or police force lawfully maintained by the Government to join any secret society whatsoever,
>
> shall be guilty of a misdemeanour and shall be liable on conviction thereof to suffer penal servitude for any term not exceeding five years or imprisonment for any term not exceeding two years.
>
> (2) In this section the expression "secret society" means an association, society, or other body the members of which are required by the regulations thereof to take or enter into, or do in fact take or enter into, an oath, affirmation, declaration or agreement not to disclose the proceedings or some part of the proceedings of the association, society or body.

Section 18 in its opening words echoes, and thus claims authority from, Article 40.6.1.iii, and is the foundation on which much of the law against subversion rests:

> In order to regulate and control in the public interest the exercise of the constitutional
>
> right of citizens to form associations, it is hereby declared that any organisation which

[5] In *Blythe v Attorney General (No. 2)* [1936] IR 549; (1936) 70 ILTR 166, the plaintiffs sought a declaration from the High Court that the association they were in the process of forming was not unlawful (being apprehensive, because of their experiences with earlier associations which had been proscribed, that the same thing would happen to this). Johnston J however refused to make any such anticipatory declaration. Previously ([1934] IR 266; (1934) 68 ILTR 47; (1934) LJ Ir 66) he had however refused an application to strike the action out as frivolous and vexatious.

(a) engages in, promotes, encourages, or advocates the commission of treason or any activity of a treasonable nature, or

(b) advocates, encourages, or attempts the procuring by force, violence, or other unconstitutional means of an alteration of the Constitution, or

(c) raises or maintains or attempts to raise or maintain a military or armed force in contravention of the Constitution or without constitutional authority, or

(d) engages in, promotes, encourages, or advocates the commission of any criminal offence or the obstruction of or interference with the administration of justice or the enforcement of the law, or

(e) engages in, promotes, encourages, or advocates the attainment of any particular object, lawful or unlawful, by violent, criminal, or other unlawful means, or

(f) promotes, encourages, or advocates the non-payment of moneys payable to the Central Fund or any other public fund or the non-payment of local taxation,

shall be an unlawful organisation within the meaning and for the purposes of this Act and this Act shall apply and have effect in relation to such organisation accordingly.

Section 19 gives the Government power "if and whenever the Government are of opinion that any particular organisation is an unlawful organisation", to declare it to be such and that it "ought, in the public interest, to be suppressed" while sub-s 4 provides that such suppression order shall be conclusive evidence for all purposes that the organisation to which the order relates is an unlawful organisation other than in respect of an application under s 20. By s 20 a suppression order may be challenged by applying to the High Court for a declaration that the organisation concerned is not an unlawful organisation, and the section contains conditions in regard to the exercise by the High Court of this jurisdiction.

The constitutionality of s 19(4) was challenged in *Sloan v Special Criminal Court*[6] on the ground that it was an impermissible invasion by the Oireachtas into the judicial domain. Rejecting this contention, Costello J said:

> "It seems to me the Oireachtas, by the 1939 Act established procedures by which an organisation could be declared an illegal organisation. Instead of declaring that membership of named organisations would be illegal, the Oireachtas provided that membership of an organisation which had been designated by the Government to be illegal would be illegal. This provision of the Act is not, in my judgment, an impermissible infringement of the judicial power. If an order is made under the section, then the justiciable dispute which may be before the Court is whether an accused is a member of an illegal organisation and not whether the organisation itself is illegal."

[6] High Court, 12 July 1989.

Membership of unlawful organisation

By s 21 membership of an unlawful organisation is made an offence; the section also provides two special defences to a charge of membership. Membership can, by s 24, be proved by the possession of an "incriminating document";[7] but s 3 of the Offences Against the State (Amendment) Act 1972, introduced a radical extension of the method of proof of membership, particularly sub-s 2 of the section:

(1) (a) Any statement made orally, in writing or otherwise, or any conduct, by an accused person implying or leading to a reasonable inference that he was at a material time a member of an unlawful organisation shall, in proceedings under section 21 of the Act of 1939, be evidence that he was then such a member.

(b) In paragraph (a) of this sub-section "conduct" includes omission by the accused person to deny published reports that he was a member of an unlawful organisation, but the fact of such denial shall not by itself be conclusive.

(2) Where an officer of the Garda Síochána, not below the rank of chief superintendent, in giving evidence in proceedings relating to an offence under the said section 2l, states that he believes that the accused as at a material time a member of an unlawful organisation, the statement shall be evidence that he was then such a member.

(3) Sub-section (2) of this section shall be in force whenever and for so long only as Part V of the Act of 1939 is in force.[8]

The constitutionality of both s 24 of the 1939 Act and s 3(2) of the 1972 Act was challenged in *O'Leary v Attorney General*[9] on the ground that they removed the burden from the prosecution of having to prove the guilt of the accused by requiring the accused to establish that he is not a member of an illegal organisation and that this shifting of the burden of proof deprived the accused of the benefit of the presumption of innocence. While accepting that the plaintiff had a constitutionality protected right to the presumption of innocence, Costello J held that it had not been infringed in the instant case. According to the judge, s 33(2) of the 1972 Act merely made admissible in evidence in certain trials statements of belief which would otherwise be inadmissible; the court remained free to evaluate such evidence and was not required to convict in the absence of exculpatory evidence, so that the presumption of innocence still operated in this situation. As for s 24, while it shifted the evidential burden of proof to adduce sufficient evidence to raise a *prima facie* case, it did not affect the legal burden of proof which is imposed on the prosecution of having to establish the case against the accused beyond all reasonable doubt. Again the court was free to evaluate and assess the significance of the evidence and if a reasonable doubt remained as to the accused's guilt, it must dismiss the charge, even in the absence of exculpatory evidence.

By s 21(2) of the 1939 Act the maximum imprisonment on summary conviction of membership is three months, but the maximum imprisonment on conviction on indictment - two years under that section - was increased to seven years by s 2 of the Criminal Law Act 1976. Section 3 of the 1976 Act moreover, provides that:

[7] This is defined in s 2 as a document "issued by or emanating from an unlawful organisation or appearing to be so issued or so to emanate or purporting or appearing to aid or abet any such organisation or calculated to promote the formation of an unlawful organisation".

[8] Part V has been in force during the periods 1939-46, 1961-2 and 1972 to date.

[9] [1993] 1 IR 102; [1991] ILRM 454.

> "Any person who recruits another person for an unlawful organisation or who incites or invites another person (or other persons generally) to join an unlawful organisation or to take part in, support or assist its activities shall be guilty of an offence and shall be liable on conviction on indictment to imprisonment for a term not exceeding ten years."

Section 22 of the 1939 Act provides for the forfeiture of the property of an unlawful organisation while s 25(1), as amended by s 4 of the Criminal Law Act 1976, empowers a Chief Superintendent to order the closure of a building for a period of twelve months where he is satisfied that it is, or was being, used for the purposes, direct or indirect, of an unlawful organisation.[10] This provision would appear to have been considered on only one occasion - *Ó Brádaigh v Fleming*[11] in which the lessee of a building which was the subject of a closing order applied to the High Court under s 25(3) to have the order quashed. There was evidence that the premises had been used by persons convicted, in 1957 and 1961, of membership of illegal organisations and by others who had been convicted, more recently, of firearms offences. Under these circumstances, Kenny J held that the Chief Superintendent could reasonably conclude that the premises were being used, directly or indirectly, for the purposes of an illegal organisation as such purposes included meetings and the exchange of information. The judge also indicated, *obiter*, that a closing order would be set aside if it was unreasonable as, for example, where the illegal use of the premises had ceased or where a few rooms of a large building had been used by an illegal organisation.

By virtue of s 1(1)(*b*)(iii) of the Criminal Justice Act 1964, "murder done...in the course or furtherance of the activities of an unlawful organisation within the meaning of s 18 (other than paragraph (*f*))" of the Offences Against the State Act 1939, was a capital offence. This provision has since been repealed by s 9 of the Criminal Justice Act 1990.

LIMITATION IN THE INTEREST OF PUBLIC MORALITY

A limitation of freedom of association in the interest of public morality may be seen in the case of *Norris v Attorney General*,[12] in which the plaintiff attacked the statute law penalising homosexual conduct between males. His challenge was founded mainly on his invocation of a right of personal privacy, but he also pleaded Article 40.6.1.iii, saying that this part of the criminal law in effect impaired his right to freedom of association. The Supreme Court majority, speaking by O'Higgins CJ, rejected his claim on all points; his argument based on freedom of association was dealt with as follows:

> "Freedom of expression and freedom of association are not guaranteed as absolute rights. They are protected by the Constitution subject to public order and morality. Accordingly, if the impugned legislation is otherwise valid and consistent with the Constitution, the mere fact that it prohibits the plaintiff from advocating conduct which it prohibits or from encouraging others to engage in such conduct or associating with others for the purpose of so doing, cannot constitute a breach of the Constitution."

[10] While such orders can be extended, s 25(6), as inserted by s 4(*b*) of the 1976 Act, provides that a closing order shall not operate for more than three years.
[11] *The Irish Times*, 25 November 1972.
[12] [1984] IR 36.

LIMITATION IN THE PUBLIC INTEREST GENERALLY

(a) Generally - Statutory regulation of activity in which an association may engage, if it is not objectionable on some other ground, does not *per se* breach the right of free association. This fairly evident proposition, which seems to result clearly from the second sentence of Article 40.6.11.iii, was stated in *P.M.P.S v Attorney General*,[13] in which the plaintiffs challenged the provision of the Industrial and Provident Societies (Amendment) Act 1978, which prohibited them from accepting or holding deposits after a date five years from the passing of the Act. This, they argued, would, *inter alia*, frustrate a purpose for which their association had been formed. The Supreme Court, however, said:

> "Mr. Moore's [the second plaintiff's] right to associate with others has not been interfered with. The exercise of such a right is not prevented by a law limiting and controlling in the public interest what such an association may do...[T]his is not an infringement of Article 40.6.1.iii."

b) In the interests of industrial relations[14] - Apart from special provisions dealing with members of the Garda Síochána and the Defence Forces,[15] only one attempt has been made by statute to place any limitation on the exercise of the right of association in the context of industrial relations and trade unions.[16] This was Part III of the Trade Union Act 1941, which provided for the setting up of a "Trade Union Tribunal" with the function of granting or refusing determinations, both in respect of "trade unions of masters" and in respect of trade unions of workmen, that a particular union had the sole right to organise masters or workmen of a particular class. Section 26(1) read:

> "Subject to the provisions of this section, where application is made to the Tribunal by a trade union which claims to have organised for the purpose of the carrying on of negotiations for the fixing of wages and other conditions of employment a majority of workmen of any particular class for a determination that such trade union alone shall have the right to so organise workmen of that class, the Tribunal, after hearing such application and having considered all the circumstances of the case, shall, as they consider proper in the public interest, either -
>
> (a) grant such determination, or
>
> (b) refuse to grant such determination, or
>
> (c) determine that two or more specified trade unions alone shall have the right to so organise workmen of that class."

By s 34(3), a determination in favour of one union operated to prohibit any other union from accepting as new members workmen of the class concerned. These provisions were attacked as being unconstitutional in *N.U.R v Sullivan*,[17] an action brought by the plaintiffs against the Irish Transport and General Workers Union, which had applied for

[13] [1983] IR 339; [1984] ILRM 88. See *Whyte*, (1983) 5 DULJ (n.s.) 273.

[14] On this area, see Kerr and Whyte, *Irish Trade Union Law* (1985), ch.1; Von Prondzynski, *Freedom of Association and Industrial Relations: A Comparative Study* (1987); Forde, *Industrial Relations Law* (1991), ch.3.

[15] See s 13 of the Garda Síochána Act 1924, as amended by the Garda Síochána (Amendment) Act 1977, and the Defence (Amendment) Act 1990, respectively.

[16] Various other pieces of legislation restrict the taking of industrial action by specified categories of worker, while the right to engage in collective bargaining with more than one employer is restricted to authorised trade unions and excepted bodies by virtue of Part II of the Trade Union Act 1941 Act as amended.

[17] [1947] IR 77; (1947) 81 ILTR 55.

a determination that it alone should have the right to organise workers in the road passenger service of Córas Iompair Éireann. The N.U.R. argued that Part III of the Trade Union Act 1941, interfered with the right of citizens to form associations and unions (and also that the Act countenanced political discrimination[18]). This case failed before Gavan Duffy J in the High Court, who found that the Act was within the "regulation and control in the public interest" envisaged by Article 40.6.1.iii. He said:

> "The complete answer to the plaintiffs seems to me to be that the Act is a law regulating the exercise of that right, in the public interest, as understood by the Oireachtas. If that is, as I hold it to be, the character of the Act the fact that it may incidentally deplete the membership of unprivileged unions cannot have the effect of making its provisions unconstitutional; and a regulating law does not cease to be a regulating law, authorised by our Constitution, because it is designed to make some trade unions stronger than others and therefore more attractive to workers who are citizens.
>
> The claim is that regulations or control in the context cannot, as a matter of law, extend to prohibition.. Assuming the enactment to be prohibitive of the citizens' right, though I should rather term it restrictive, I find impressive authority in *United States v Hill*[19].. for the opinion that a constitutional power of regulation may be broad enough in law to carry a veto...
>
> Now one of the standard meanings of the word "regulate" is "to subject to guidance and restrictions"; the Act itself claims to be restrictive, and I am really being asked to find that the restriction goes too far. That would be to narrow a term ("regulation and control") of very wide connotation in the organic law, and to do so after the need for the measure has been declared by the appropriate organ of government, far better equipped than the judiciary to know the need. I could not so decide upon a personal view (if I held it) of so indeterminate a phrase, without importing a misplaced legal pedantry into the interpretation of the national charter against a quite reasonable view of its real meaning."

He refused the declarations sought, and the N.U.R. appealed to the Supreme Court. This Court, without any serious exploration of the concept of "regulation" of the right of association by law, reversed Gavan Duffy J and declared Part III of the Act "in its main principles repugnant to the Constitution". The Court said (*per* Murnaghan J):

> "[The Act] does not prohibit all association, but it purports to limit the right of the citizen to join one or more prescribed associations i.e. the union or unions in respect of which a determination has been made. Any such limitation does undoubtedly deprive the citizen of a free choice of the persons with whom he shall associate. Both logically and practically, to deprive a person of the choice of the persons with whom he will associate, is not a control of the exercise of the right of association, but a denial of the right altogether. It was stressed, in argument, that control, in the public interest, was given to the Oireachtas and that such control might extend to depriving the citizen of all freedom of choice of his associates, provided he could join a prescribed association for the particular object. The Constitution states the right of the citizens to form associations or unions in an emphatic way, and it seems

[18] The plaintiffs claimed that if the defendants (the Irish Transport and General Workers Union) were granted a determination of sole right to organise in their class of employment, they would be forced to associate themselves with the National Labour Party which the defendants had been instrumental in establishing: see below, p. 988.

[19] 248 US 420.

> impossible to harmonise this language with a law which prohibits the forming of associations or unions and allows the citizen only to join prescribed associations and unions.
>
> In the opinion of this Court, a law which takes away the right of the citizens, at their choice, to form associations and unions, not contrary to public order or morality, is not a law which can validly be made under the Constitution."

This was the first occasion in which the Supreme Court set aside a piece of legislation which had been duly enacted by the Oireachtas.[20] However it is questionable whether the Court did not unduly restrict the regulatory power conferred on the Oireachtas by Article 40.6.1.iii[21] and it is notable that its decision has never been applied in any subsequent case. In *Aughey v Ireland*,[22] in which the plaintiffs challenged the validity of s 1 of the Garda Síochána Act 1977 limiting the number of associations which could seek to control or influence the pay, pensions or conditions of service of members of the Gardaí, *N.U.R. v Sullivan* was distinguished on the basis that s 1 did not amount to an outright prohibition on members of the Gardaí forming or becoming members of a trade union but was merely a restriction on the activities in which such a union could engage. However the artificial nature of this distinction between complete prohibition on joining an association and restriction of its activities is well illustrated by the earlier case of *P.M.P.S v Attorney General.*[23] Here the plaintiff company unsuccessfully challenged the validity of the Industrial and Provident Societies (Amendment) Act 1978, whose effect was to make it impossible for the company to carry on a banking business, on the ground, *inter alia*, that the legislation violated the shareholders' freedom of association. The legislation was upheld by the Supreme Court who took the view that "the exercise of [the right to associate] is not prevented by a law limiting and controlling in the public interest what such an association may do." Yet in this case, the evidence before the Supreme Court was that the company would have to go into liquidation if the legislation was upheld, while the legislation in *N.U.R. v Sullivan* simply prevented the plaintiff union from recruiting new members but did not threaten to drive it completely out of existence.

Any regulation of freedom of association, which may be effected only by post-1937 legislation,[24] must be done explicitly. Thus in *N.U.J. and I.P.U. v Sisk*[25] the Supreme Court rejected the contention that the Trade Union Act 1975 did not permit members of an Irish union (the I.P.U.) to merge, by way of a transfer of engagements, with a foreign-based union (the N.U.J.) operating in this jurisdiction. On the face of it, the N.U.J. came within the statutory definition of trade union contained in the Trade Union Acts 1871-1990 but in the High Court, Keane J had construed this definition in the light of what he considered to be the absurdities and inconveniences which would otherwise arise so as to exclude foreign-based unions which were neither registered nor certified under the Irish legislation. Reversing him on appeal, Finlay CJ, who delivered the leading judg-

[20] The Court had previously advised the President that the School Attendance Bill 1942 was repugnant to the Constitution and so that Bill was never enacted into law.

[21] What might be regarded as judicial unease with this decision manifested itself as early as 1956 when Davitt P, in *Attorney General v Southern Industrial Trust* ((1960) 94 ILTR 161), drew attention to the logical consequence of the Supreme Court's ruling in *N.U.R. v Sullivan* by drawing an analogy between Article 40.6.1.iii and Article 43. Citing the sentence in the judgment beginning "Both logically and practically" he said: "It could be reasoned similarly that to deprive a person of any part of his property, is not a delimitation of the exercise of his rights over his property, but a denial of those rights altogether."

[22] [1989] ILRM 87.

[23] [1983] IR 339; [1984] ILRM 88. See *Whyte,* (1983) 5 DULJ 273.

[24] See the remarks of Walsh J in *Aughey v Ireland* [1989] ILRM 87.

[25] [1992] 2 IR 171; [1992] ILRM 96.

ment of the Court, held that the right of members of a trade union to vote in favour of a transfer of engagements by their union to another union was a "necessary and valuable expansion of the general right to form trade unions and belong to them" and continued:

> "It does not seem to me, therefore, appropriate that the legislature should be interpreted as having by some form of implication, as distinct from a very express provision, regulated, controlled or restricted this particular right.
>
> I am, therefore, driven to the conclusion that the terms of the provisions of s 9 of the Act of 1975 could not properly be said to be a clear or unambiguous indication by the legislature of an intention to exclude from the terms of ss 2, 3 and 4 of the Act a trade union operating with a negotiation licence and with members within the State though not registered in it."

Statutory protection of right to belong to union

It is worth mentioning that the Unfair Dismissals Act 1977, contains an express protection of an employee's right to belong to a union. By s 6(2) of the Act the dismissal of an employee is:

> "deemed, for the purposes of this Act to be an unfair dismissal if it results wholly or mainly from [*inter alia*]
>
> (a) the employee's membership, or proposal that he or another person become a member of, or his engaging in activities on behalf of, a trade union or excepted body under the Trade Union Acts, 1941 and 1971."

where his trade union activities do not encroach on working hours as agreed with his employer.[26]

Trade unions and the right of association

The right of association has been upheld by the courts in a series of decisions not related to any statutory provision, but to various litigation involving trade unions and employers. While one could reasonably regard the guarantee as having been intended, in the context of industrial relations, for the protection of trade unionism and the right of workers to organise against potentially hostile employers and/or State policy, it has never been applied by the courts in this way. Instead litigation on the guarantee has almost invariably been directed against trade unions. From these decisions a number of broad principles emerge as corollaries of Article 40.6.1.iii.

No compulsion to accept members

(a) The right of existing associations not to have members forced upon them. In *Tierney v Amalgamated Society of Woodworkers*[27] the plaintiff sought a declaration that he was qualified for membership of the defendant union, and an order directing the union to accept his application for membership; the union had previously refused to do so on the grounds that he was "not a genuine carpenter". Budd J (with whom on appeal the Supreme Court unanimously agreed) held that the Constitution offered no support for the plaintiff's case. The constitutional right of free association was not expressly mentioned - the plaintiff placed his case on the right to work - but must be latent in the

[26] See *Kerr and Whyte, op. cit.*, pp.33-37; *Forde, op. cit.*, pp.63-64 and 65-66.
[27] [1959] IR 254.

judge's remarks on the plaintiff's contention that the union was bound to accept him as a member once his qualification for membership was established, as he said it ought to be:

> "The right contended for here... is altogether revolutionary. It has heretofore been of the essence of a voluntary organisation that the members, and they alone, should decide who should be their fellow-members. Otherwise, the element of "voluntariness" ceases to exist. A social club, for example, could scarcely exist if the association of members ceased to be voluntary... I do, of course, see that there are in modern times many differences between trade unions and other voluntary organisations, such as social clubs, and that a somewhat different legal concept has come to be applied to trade unions. In the particular matter which I am considering, however - the voluntary nature of the organisation - I do not see that a trade union stands at present on a different footing from any other voluntary organisation as regards the free choice of new members."

In *Murphy v Stewart*[28] the Supreme Court reached a similar conclusion to that in *Tierney*, on this occasion, however, after giving explicit consideration to Article 40.6.1.iii. The plaintiff's desire to change union was thwarted by the ultimate refusal of the second union to take him into membership without the consent of the union of which he was originally a member.[29] The plaintiff then brought an action in which he claimed that the refusal of the defendant union to give its consent to the transfer of membership amounted to an infringement of his constitutional rights. This claim was rejected by a unanimous Supreme Court which held, *inter alia*, that Article 40.6.1.iii did not guarantee citizens the right to join unions or associations, merely a right to form them. However Walsh J (with whom the other members of the Supreme Court agreed) added a most important rider, though *obiter*, to the principle in *Tierney's* case:

> "It has been submitted... that among the unspecified personal rights guaranteed by the Constitution is the right to work; I accept that proposition. The question of whether that right is being infringed or not must depend upon the particular circumstances of any given case; if the right to work was reserved exclusively to members of a trade union which held a monopoly in this field and the trade union was abusing the monopoly in such a way as to effectively prevent the exercise of a person's constitutional right to work, the question of compelling that union to accept the person concerned into membership (or, indeed, of breaking the monopoly) would fall to be considered for the purpose of vindicating the right to work."

In *Tierney's* case Budd J, in holding that s 13(1) of the Trade Union Act 1941, could not be construed as obliging the defendant union to accept a particular person as member, expressly envisaged[30] that a statutory provision *might* have such an effect, without considering whether such a provision would infringe Article 60.6.1.iii; the *dictum* of Walsh J about abuse of a hypothetical union monopoly, however, suggests that statutory provisions to combat such abuse or monopoly, even if they took the form of compelling acceptance of qualified persons as members, would be upheld, presumably as a form of "regulation or control in the public interest" of the right of association.[31]

[28] [1973] IR 97; (1973) 107 ILTR 117.

[29] By virtue of cl. 47(d) of the Constitution of the Irish Congress of Trade Unions, Congress unions have restricted their freedom to recruit new members from among the membership of another union without that other union's consent.

[30] He said: "If the Oireachtas had intended to create any statutory right in a member of the public to have his candidature for admission to a trade union brought before a meeting, and. as might reasonably be thought to follow logically, to have his candidature accepted provided he fulfilled the conditions, it is inconceivable to me that the Legislature would not have conferred such an important and revolutionary right in clear and express terms..."

[31] While there is, as yet, no statutory right to join a trade union, the power of a union to determine applications for membership is subject to certain statutory regulation - see s 3(1)(*b*) of the Trade Union Act 1913 and s 4 of

Right of "dissociation"

(b) The right of an individual to abstain from membership of an association and the duty of others not to induce compulsion of such membership. Several cases decided since 1960 have established these principles in the context of existing employees resisting attempts to coerce them into union membership.[32] In the earliest of them, *Educational Co. of Ireland v Fitzpatrick (No. 2)*,[33] the plaintiffs were being subjected to picketing by a number of their employees, who were members of a trade union, in order to get them to force other employees, who were not members of the union, to join it. The plaintiffs successfully brought proceedings for an injunction to restrain the picketing, for although Budd J and the Supreme Court in affirming him, held that there was a trade dispute within the Trade Disputes Act 1906,[34] such as would normally legitimise picketing, they held also that, in the words of Kingsmill Moore J,

> "the Trade Disputes Act 1906, can no longer be relied upon to justify picketing in aid of a trade dispute, where that dispute is concerned with an attempt to deprive persons of the right of free association or free dissociation guaranteed by the Constitution. The definition of trade dispute must be read as if there were attached thereto the words "Provided that a dispute between employers and workmen or between workmen and workmen as to whether a person shall or shall not become or remain a member of a trade union, or having as its object a frustration of the right of any person to choose with whom he will or will not be associated in any form of union or association shall not be deemed to be a trade dispute for the purposes of this Act."

Budd J had said:

> "I hold...that under the Constitution a citizen is free to join or not to join an association or union as he pleases. Further, that he cannot be deprived of the right to join or not to join such association or union as he pleases (subject always to the limitations in the Constitution, not relevant to this case) and that is tantamount to saying that he may not be compelled to join any association or union against his will...
>
> I am satisfied that...pressure is being brought to bear on the employers to force them to coerce the nine non-union men to join the union against their constitutional right to refuse to do so.

the Employment Equality Act 1977. See also EC Regulations 1612/68 and 312/76 prohibiting discrimination against nationals of other EC countries in relation to admission to membership, and participation in the administration, of unions.

[32] The court have yet to consider the constitutionality of arrangements whereby *prospective* employees are offered employment on condition that they join and remain members of a specified union. In *Becton Dickinson and Co. Ltd. v Lee* [1973] IR 1, Henchy J suggested, *obiter*, that such arrangements could be regarded as a valid waiver by the prospective employee of the right to dissociate.

[33] [1961] IR 345: in the earlier injunction proceedings between the same parties ([1961] IR 323) Ó Dálaigh J had already foreshadowed the result of the substantive action. In 1938, in *Cooper v Millea*, [1938] IR 749; (1938) 72 ILTR 209, Gavan Duffy J had held unlawful the acts of the defendants, who, by threatening a strike, had secured the dismissal of the plaintiff, who had left the defendants' union and joined another one: he referred in passing to "the right to form unions [being] expressly recognised by the Constitution" but did not base his judgment on the Constitution. *Cooper v Millea* was followed by O'Byrne J in the similar case of *Riordan v Butler* [1940] IR 347; (1940) 74 ILTR 152, but without any reference to the Constitution. Workers enjoy a similar right to abstain from union membership under the European Convention on Human Rights - see *Young, James and Webster v U.K* Series A, No. 44, (1982) 4 EHRR. 38.

[34] See now s 8 of the Industrial Relations Act 1990.

> The plaintiffs, in my view, have the positive duty of abstaining from interfering with their employees' constitutional rights. Therefore, again, the action of the defendants is an attempt to compel the plaintiffs to interfere with the constitutional rights of others in a practical fashion and as such cannot be supported by the Trade Disputes Act 1906, or any other legislation which is subordinate to the Constitution, which grants the positive right of free association to the nine non-union men."[35]

The reasoning of the majority which led to this judicial recognition of the right to dissociate has been criticised on the grounds that it is at variance with a perspective of the guarantee of freedom of association which sees that freedom as a protection against the State and employers of the right of unions to exist[36] and that it confuses the concepts of freedom and right.[37] However subsequent decisions have re-affirmed the proposition that Article 40.6.1.iii guarantees the right of existing employees not to join trade unions.

Thus *Educational Co.* was followed by McLoughlin J in *Crowley v Cleary*,[38] a case which the judge found distinguishable from the earlier authority only to the extent that the union involved did not overtly require the non-union employee to become a member, nor overtly require the plaintiff employer to dismiss him if he did not do so; but, said the judge, "its action and intentions [in threatening a picket] constituted a subterfuge to bring about the same result". He accordingly granted the injunction sought. It was followed also in *Murtagh Properties v Cleary*;[39] a case which Kenny J found presented a "compelling analogy" to it, though it concerned the right to a livelihood, not to freedom of association.

Lastly, in *Meskell v Córas Iompair Éireann*,[40] the Supreme Court held that an agreement between the defendant company and a trade union, whereby the company bound itself to employ only union members in a particular employment grade - and tried to give effect to its undertaking by dismissing all employees in this grade with an offer of instant re-employment provided that they signed an undertaking to be and remain members of the union while in that employment - amounted to a conspiracy to deprive the plaintiff of his constitutional right to abstain from joining a particular association, which had been recognised in the *Educational Co.* case as correlative to his right of association. Walsh J said:

> "To exercise what may be loosely called a common-law right of dismissal as a method of compelling a person to abandon a constitutional right, or as a penalty for not doing so, must necessarily be regarded as an abuse of the common-law right because it is an infringement, and an abuse, of the Constitution which is superior to the common law and which must prevail if there is a conflict between the two. The

[35] Maguire CJ, who was one of the dissenting minority in this case, said he did not believe the object and effect of the Constitution was by a side-wind to deprive trade unions of rights which they had had in 1937: "I must say that it came as a surprise to me that it should be contended that our Constitution had by implication withdrawn from the protection [of the Trade Disputes Act. 1906] a dispute of this nature to the extent that peaceful picketing could not be employed to further it...To my mind it would require clear and unambiguous language to bring about [the] result that recognised trade union activities should be subject to any restraints to which they were not then subject." See also the decision of a Circuit Court judge (O'Connor) in *Buckley v Rooney* (1950) Ir Jur Rep 5, to the effect that a closed shop agreement between union and employers did not infringe Article 40.6.1.iii. For further critical analysis of the reasoning in the *Educational Company* case, see Casey, "*Freedom of Association in Labour Law*" (1972) 21 ICLQ 699 at p.707-8; *Kerr and Whyte*, *op. cit.*, pp.7-15; Redmond, "*Towards an Hohfeldian View of the Rights and Freedoms in the Irish Constitution*" (1979-80) DULJ 52 at p.55. Smartt, "*The Right to Associate: Hohfeld Revisited*" (1993) 3 ISLR 116.

[36] Kahn-Freund, *Labour and the Law* (3rd ed.,1983), pp.200-270; *Casey*, *loc. cit.*

[37] *Redmond*, *loc. cit.* See above, pp. 697-698.

[38] [1968] IR 261.

[39] [1972] IR 330.

[40] [1973] IR 121.

same considerations apply to cases where a person is dismissed or penalised because of his insistence upon, or his refusal to waive, his right to dissociate. In each of these cases the injured party is entitled, in my view, to recover damages for any damage he may have suffered by reason of, the dismissal or penalty resulting from his insistence upon exercising his constitutional right, or his refusal to abandon it or waive it."

The agreement between the trade unions concerned and the defendants to procure or cause [the plaintiff's] dismissal was an actionable conspiracy because the means employed constituted a breach or infringement of the plaintiff's constitutional rights.

Damages for breach of right of dissociation

The principle established in *Meskell's* case was afterwards applied by Finlay P in *Cotter v Ahern*,[41] in which the plaintiff, having had a dispute with the Irish National Teachers Organisation and having left it, had nevertheless been appointed principal of a national school; some of the defendants (members of the I.N.T.O.) had thereupon prevailed on the school manager to cancel this appointment, and had also succeeded in preventing his appointment as principal in other schools in the area. When eventually he secured an equivalent appointment, it was so far away that he had to sell his house, buy another one and move his family. The I.N.T.O. defendants were held guilty of an actionable conspiracy, having combined:

> "to prevent the appointment or promotion of a national teacher as part of a general campaign or objective to try to ensure that he and all other national teachers in any particular area or in the whole country will become and remain a member of a trade union and thus to seek to coerce or penalise that person into abandoning or waiving his constitutional right to dissociate."

Damages were awarded against them (both for this actionable conspiracy and for the separate tort of procuring a breach of contract) representing the expenses of removal and the professional fees incurred in the sale and purchase of the houses; and they were moreover ordered to indemnify the school manager for the damages awarded against him for breach of contract, representing a year's difference in salary between the plaintiff's existing post and the principalship of which he had been disappointed. (In *Meskell's* case damages were ultimately agreed between the parties.) No damages were awarded, however, for breach of constitutional rights *per se*.

Finally in this context, it is worth noting that non-unionists have no constitutional right to refuse to meet with trade union members during the course of their employment - *Collins v Cork V.E.C.*[42]

The right to participate in union's decision - making processes

(c) The right of union members to participate in the decision-making processes within the union. This right was recognised for the first time in *Rodgers v I.T.G.W.U.*[43] in which Finlay P, as he them was said that it was:

> "a necessary corollary to the right to join and become a member of a trade union that the right must extend to taking part in the democratic processes provided by [the union] and in particular to taking part in the decision-making processes within the rules of the trade union."

[41] [1976-7] ILRM 248.
[42] Supreme Court, 8 March 1983.
[43] [1978] ILRM 51.

Thus the action of the union in adopting a policy of compulsory retirement at 65 without affording the plaintiff an opportunity to vote on the resolution amounted to an infringement of his freedom of association.[44] A curious feature of Finlay P.'s decision was that he went on to suggest that the right to participate in the decision-making processes of the union could be restricted by the terms of the union rule book:

> "It would clearly be open to a trade union so to formulate its rules so that in regard to certain matters, or even in regard to all matters, that decision making would be in the hands of the delegates or elected officers and specified members of the union and a person who joined under those terms could not complain of being excluded in accordance with the rules of the union which he joined from the making of any particular decision."

That a constitutional right might be limited by the unilateral imposition of restrictions by another party is surprising,[45] to say the least, but arguably a more serious flaw in the reasoning of Finlay P is his reliance on the right to join a union as the basis for the right to participate in its decision-making processes. As we have already seen, the suggestion that the Constitution might protect a right to join a trade union was rejected by the Supreme Court on two previous occasions[46] and in one of these cases - *Murphy v Stewart* - Walsh J specifically drew attention to the fact that the constitutional guarantee is a guarantee to form, rather than to join, associations or unions. If one does not have a constitutional right to join a union then, *a fortiori*, one does not have a *constitutional* right to participate in the decision-making processes of the union. Such a right could exist as a *contractual* right on the part of an individual accepted into membership by a union.

Previous criticism[47] of *Rodgers v I.T.G.W.U.* on this ground was, however, rejected by Costello J in *Doyle v Croke* [48] because:

> "if the constitutional right of citizens to form associations and unions is to be effective the Article in which it is to be found should not be construed restrictively as the right would be of limited value if it did not protect individual members against procedures which might be unfair to them. I have no difficulty, therefore, in respectfully following [*Rodgers*] and in holding that the plaintiffs and all the members of their union had a constitutional right by virtue of Article 40.6.1.iii to fair procedures in the conduct of the strike and the negotiations leading to its settlement."

[44] However Finlay P held on the facts that the plaintiff failed deliberately to avail of a second opportunity which was afforded him to participate in the union's decision-making processes in relation to this policy and consequently dismissed his claim. The plaintiff's arguments grounded on his right to work fared no better. See below, p. 763

[45] This could only be explained away as an implied waiver of rights, as suggested by *Kerr*, (1978) DULJ 61, if one takes the view that constitutional rights may validly be waived through entering into a contract of adhesion and it must be doubtful whether this complies with the demanding conditions for valid waiver set by the Supreme Court in *G v An Bord Úchtála* [1980] IR 32.

[46] *Tierney v A.S.W.* [1959] IR 254 and *Murphy v Stewart* [1973] IR 97. In the latter case, Walsh J did suggest, *obiter*, that the Constitution might compel a union to accept a person into membership if that was necessary in order to vindicate that person's right to work.

[47] See *Kerr and Whyte, op. cit.* pp.24-26.

[48] (1988) 7 JISLL 170. See also his extra-judicial comments in "*Fair Procedures, the Constitution and Trade Unions*" (1989) 8 JISLL 1, in the course of which he advocates a purposive approach to the interpretation of Article 40.6.1.iii. Applied in a different context, such an approach could lead to the recognition of a constitutional right to take industrial action as an aspect of freedom of association - see above, pp. 783-785 - as happened in the decision of the Ontario High Court of Justice in *Re Service Employees' International Union and Broadway Manor Nursing Home* (1984) 4 DLR (4th) 231. However for rejection of this proposition, see *Collymore v Attorney General of Trinidad and Tobago* [1970] AC 538; *Public Service Alliance of Canada v The Queen in right of Canada* (1984) 11 DLR (4th) 337; *Reference re Public Service Employee Relations Act (Alberta)* (1989) 38 DLR (4th) 161.

Thus a resolution passed at a meeting of striking workers which purported to exclude those workers who had failed to attend for picket duty from the benefits of any settlement of the trade dispute negotiated by the union was held to be invalid because of the union's failure to notify all of the workers in dispute of the holding of the meeting or to give any prior notice of the proposed resolution. While Costello J followed *Rodgers* on this point, he did not address the difficulty posed by Finlay P's acceptance that the member's right to participate in the decision-making process could be restricted, to the point of extinction, by appropriately drafted provisions in the rule-book, nor did he advert to the rejection of any constitutional right to join a trade union - the premise on which *Rodgers* was based - in *Tierney* and *Murphy*. In view of these difficulties, one wonders whether a surer foundation for the outcomes in both *Rodgers* and *Doyle* would not be the decision of the Supreme Court in *Glover v BLN Ltd.*[49] implying a right to fair procedures under Article 40.3 into, *inter alia*, any agreement setting up machinery for taking decisions which may affect rights or impose liabilities.

Employer not bound to negotiate with any particular union

The right of association of employees does not imply any duty on the employer beyond respecting that right in itself, and of course discharging his side of any agreement with employees. In particular, it does not oblige him to negotiate with any association which employees may form.[50] Thus in *Dublin Colleges A.S.A. v City of Dublin V.E.C.*,[51] where a number of teachers had formed a new union of their own and sought formal recognition from the Vocational Education Committee, Hamilton J said the plaintiffs naturally had a constitutional right of association:

> "but [there is] no corresponding obligation on any body or person, such as the defendants herein, to recognise that association for the purpose of negotiating the terms and conditions of employment of its members, or for any purpose."

Similarly in *Abbot and Whelan v I.T.G.W.U.*,[52] which arose out of a contest between two unions for members among the employees in a hospital, McWilliam J said:

> "The suggestion... that there is a constitutional right to be represented by a union in the conduct of negotiations with employers... in my opinion could not be sustained. There is no duty placed on any employer to negotiate with any particular citizen or body of citizens."

To force the Health Board running the hospital to deal with the plaintiffs would, he said, be a "great extension of the principle that a citizen must not be coerced into joining an association or union against his will".

Other cases in this general area have centred on the personal right to work and earn a livelihood, rather than on the right of association: see above, pp. 761-766.

[49] [1973] IR 388.

[50] Though under the European Convention on Human Rights, a union member may be entitled to have his/her union make representations on his/her behalf to an employer - *National Belgian Police Union v Belgium* Series A, No.19, (1979) 1 EHRR 578; *Swedish Engine Drivers Union v Sweden* Series A, No. 20, (1979) 1 EHRR. 617; *Schmidt and Dahlstrom v Sweden* Series A, No. 21, ([1979) 1 EHRR 637.

[51] Unreported, High Court, 31 July 1981.

[52] (1982) 1 JISLL 56, followed by Murphy J in *Inspector of Taxes v Minister of Public Services*, High Court, 24 March 1983. This conclusion was anticipated by Walsh J in *E.I. Co. Ltd. v Kennedy* [1968] IR 69, wherein he said: "In law an employer is not obliged to meet anybody as the representative of his workers, nor indeed is he obliged to meet the worker himself for the purpose of discussing any demand which the worker may make." A similar approach was also taken by the Jamaican courts in *Banton v Alcoa Minerals of Jamaica Ltd.* (1971) 17 WIR 275. See also Casey in "*Reform of Collective Bargaining Law*" (1972) 7 Ir Jur (n.s.) 1.

POLITICAL PARTIES

Political parties as such are not mentioned in the Constitution - the right to form and join political parties is taken for granted as simply a normal product of the right of association, or, in the terms of the older common law, as part of the range of activity which, not being unlawful, was therefore inferentially lawful - and political parties figure only in the most marginal way in ordinary legislation and even in the Standing Orders of Dáil and Seanad. Thus, apart from the provisions of the Electoral Act 1992, which will be mentioned in the remainder of this section, the only explicit references to parties in legislation seem to be in the provisions granting allowances to the leaders of parties represented in the Dáil (by way of assistance towards secretarial and research expenses, etc.) contained in the Ministerial and Parliamentary Offices Acts 1938 to 1992.[53] Similarly the only express reference to parties in the Standing Orders of Dáil Éireann (1986 edition) is contained in Order 89, which regulates the order in which private members' motions and bills are to be taken.

The Electoral Act 1992, makes provision for a "Register of Political Parties" (s 25). This provides that the Clerk of Dáil Éireann ("Registrar of Political Parties" for the purposes of the section) is to keep this register, in which he is to enter any political party which applies to him, and which, in his opinion, is "(i) a genuine political party, and (ii) organised in the State or a part thereof to contest a Dáil election or a European election or a local election". Sub-s 9 constitutes an appeal board to settle "any doubt, dispute or question" arising in connection with the register; it consists of a judge of the High Court, together with the Chairman (or Deputy Chairman) of the Dáil and of the Seanad. The only consequence of substance attaching to being registered, as distinct from having one's registration refused, is that candidates at Dáil and European elections[54] who are members of registered parties may add their parties' names to their own names on the ballot paper; other candidates may not (s 88 of the 1992 Act and Fourth Schedule thereto; s 11 of the European Assembly Elections Act 1977 and First Schedule thereto). (Formerly all candidates, whether of a party allegiance or none, were entered on the ballot paper without any indication of party.) In no way does the 1992 provision purport to "licence" or "recognise" parties or their activities, or to withhold licence or recognition from them, or to regulate their formation.

In *Loftus v Attorney General*[55] the forerunner to the 1992 Act - the Electoral Act 1963 - was challenged in on a number of grounds;[56] those relevant to the constitutional right of association, as summarised in the judgment of the Supreme Court, were that the Act:

> "impose[d] a curb on the freedom of political action which is contrary to the Constitution. This submission was also put in another way by contending that once the electoral law of the State enables a candidate's party affiliations to be stated on the ballot paper then the denial of this advantage to a candidate representing a bona fide political party is an unwarranted and invalid interference with his constitutional

[53] The most recent such provision is in ss 12 - 14 of the Oireachtas (Allowances to Members) and Ministerial and Parliamentary Offices (Amendment) Act 1973, as amended by s 2(5) of the Oireachtas (Allowances to Members) and Ministerial, Parliamentary and Judicial Offices (Amendment) Act 1983.

[54] In the case of European elections, the name of the European political grouping to which the candidate's party belongs, if any, is also included on the ballot paper - s 11 of the European Assembly Elections Act 1977 and the First Schedule thereto.

[55] [1979] IR 221.

[56] The plaintiffs also relied, unsuccessfully, on Article 40.1 and Article 40.6.1-2 to challenge a provision in the 1963 Act since repealed, providing for the automatic registration of political parties already represented in the Dáil at the date of establishment of the Register of Political Parties under the 1963 Act.

> right of free association which is guaranteed to him, as a citizen, by Article 40.6.1. This denial cannot be excused on the ground that the restrictions imposed on an unregistered party are a regulation of the right of association in the public interest because no public interest is thereby served."

O'Higgins CJ, delivering the judgment of the Supreme Court, referred to the new form of ballot paper which was to contain party names, and said:

> "In order to avail of this facility the political party must be registered as such. It seems reasonable that the requirement for registration should be that the applicant party be "a genuine political party" and also should be "organised to contest a Dáil election or a local election". The word "genuine" is here used to distinguish the real from the feigned, the authentic from the spurious, and to ensure that merely by calling itself a political party an organisation which is in no true sense political will not qualify for registration. Again, since registration is concerned with elections a political party which is not organised to contest such is excluded from registration. Here the words "organised to contest a Dáil election or a local election" refer not to the degree of perfection of the organisation but to the fact of its organisation for that object and purpose.
>
> This being the purpose and effect of the sub-section and the ancillary provisions mentioned, no interference with the rights of bona fide political parties in respect of elections is effected. It seems proper and in the public interest to regulate such statutory rights and facilities as are given by this legislation. If some control and regulation were not provided, genuine political action might be destroyed by a proliferation of bogus front organisations calling themselves political parties but with aims and objects far removed from the political sphere."

On this part of the judgment it might be observed (1) that the pre-1963 total exclusion of reference to parties from the ballot paper was practically if not entirely unique in Western Europe, most of whose people are accustomed to vote primarily for parties; (2) that a reference to a candidate's party allegiance, if any, could be plausibly called a corollary of the rights implicit in free elections, in order to help voters to record a sequence of preference throughout perhaps fifteen or so candidates, not all of whom might be known to them as individuals; (3) that when the "no party label" fetish was abandoned in 1963, the possibility of now showing one's party allegiance should have been regarded as a normalisation of electoral mechanisms rather than as the according of a "right" or "facility"; (4) that no serious public interest is capable of being served by the ponderous machinery of a "Register" of parties just to control and restrict the use of party labels on ballot papers. A restriction such as to exclude labels that are confusing, offensive or prolix could easily be defended as being in the interest of order; but what business is it of the State's if a candidate, being a member of a tiny localised group of eccentrics, or even of a "bogus front organisation", chooses to offer himself for election - and hazard a deposit - under a grandiloquent party title? The Supreme Court's apprehension that without such control "genuine political action might be destroyed" seems a small compliment to the discernment of the electorate, and to overestimate its susceptibility to fine words.

In relation to the obligation imposed on parties "operating in relation to a particular part only of the State" to include a reference to such part in its name,[57] the Court said:

[57] Section 13(3)(c) of the 1963 Act - see now s 25(6)(*c*) of the 1992 Act.

"This sub-section refers to political parties which seek to operate in and for one particular area only. It does not refer to parties which have or claim a national aim or objective but which by reason of actual strength are restricted in activity to one particular area; such parties are not local parties as envisaged by sub-s 5(*c*) but small national parties."

The 1963 Act was attacked also on the ground that the appeal board could not be constituted in the period following a dissolution of the Dáil as there could then be no "Chairman" (or "Deputy Chairman") of Dáil Éireann; thus, as the Court summarised it:

"in the crucial period leading to the election of a new Dáil there could be no appeal from a decision of the Registrar and the rights of citizens concerned with a political party which had been refused registration were on that account not respected, nor defended nor vindicated."

The Court held, however, that although the Dáil was dissolved the intention of the Constitution must be deemed to have been that the Chairman and Deputy Chairman of the outgoing Dáil would retain a vestigial existence for certain purposes,[58] so that the appeal board could in fact be validly constituted at such a time.

A further attack on the Act - based on the alleged arbitrary power which it gave the Registrar of Political Parties - is mentioned in connection with interpretation of the Constitution.[59]

On the same day that the Supreme Court gave judgment on the constitutional challenge to the validity of the Act judgment was also given (by Finlay P, as he then was, with whom the other judges of the Supreme Court agreed) on the plaintiffs' concurrent complaint against the actual determination of the appeal board against their party. Here their claim for declarations succeeded, as the Court took the view that their application for registration had been rejected on a wrong basis. Firstly, the appeal board had adopted as a test a criterion used in an earlier case[60] of what was meant by "a genuine political party":

"The words... offer some difficulties of definition but we take the view that the words mean that the application must be made by an existing party or group which has a sizeable public image and which has a visible organisation."

Finlay P said on this

"As already appears from the judgment of the Court [on the constitutional challenge] the true construction of the words "genuine political party" does not depend on the extent to which the group or body in question has established itself in the public consciousness, or on the range or effectiveness of its organisation. It must be adjudged to be a "genuine political party" if it is bound together by the cohesion of common political beliefs or aims and by being organised for electoral purposes into an entity to such an extent and with such distinctiveness as to justify its claim to be truly a political party in its own right. In so far as the Registrar and the appeal board applied a standard based on the extent to which the plaintiffs' political party had established a public image, I am of opinion that the application was rejected on a wrong principle. A party may be a genuine political party before it has succeeded in

[58] The purposes of Article14 (the Presidential Commission).

[59] See above, p. 461.

[60] The application of Pádraic Kelly to register the "Republican Party" on 19 June 1964. The judgment of the appeal board in that case is cited by Finlay P in *Loftus'* case.

> acquiring either a "sizeable public image" or a "visible organisation". The fact that a party may be obscure or ineffectual or have little impact on the public consciousness will be irrelevant if, on the application of the tests already set out, it may fairly be said to be a genuine political party."

In the present case the appeal board had refused the plaintiffs' application also on the ground that it was not organised "to a degree of organisation in the constituency of a type which is usual for contesting a Dáil election"; Finlay P referred to what the Court had said in its single judgment on the constitutional issue, i.e. that "organised" referred not to the degree of perfection of the organisation "but to the fact of its organisation for that object and purpose"; the appeal board had accordingly gone wrong in principle here too. Finally - for reasons which also appeared in the single judgment - the appeal board's understanding of the "particular part only of the State" criterion was also wrong. The Court thus, in *Loftus'* case, could be said to have upheld the principle of registration of political parties on less than convincing grounds, but to have sketched out generous criteria for the working of the system.

Article 40.6.2

NO DISCRIMINATION IN REGULATORY LAWS

2° Laws regulating the manner in which the right of forming associations and unions and the right of free assembly may be exercised shall contain no political, religious or class discrimination.

2° Ní cead aon idirdhealú, maidir le polaitíocht nó creideamh nó aicmí, a bheith i ndlíthe a rialaíos modh oibrithe an chirt chun comhlachais agus cumainn a bhunú agus an chirt chun teacht le chéile ar saorthionól.

1922 provision

Article 9 of the 1922 Constitution contained the same prohibition; it will be noted that both the 1922 and 1937 Constitutions avoided giving the benefit of this prohibition to the right of expression, although the latter is dealt with otherwise side by side with the rights of assembly and association.[1] As *Casey* points out,[2] the prohibition of religious discrimination seems somewhat superfluous, having regard to Article 44.2.3.

Non-discrimination

One of the plaintiff union's contentions in *N.U.R. v Sullivan*[3] was that Part III of the Trade Union Act 1941, enabled discrimination to be made of a kind forbidden by Article 40.6.2, because (as the argument was summarised by Gavan Duffy J) "a trade union obtaining an organising monopoly for a class may lawfully apply part of its general funds to the furtherance of its political objects" (this apprehension was concrete to the extent that the defendant union which had applied for this monopoly was associated with the National Labour Party which had been set up in competition with the Irish Labour Party). In what might be regarded as a forerunner to the later decision of the Supreme Court in *East Donegal Cooperative v Attorney General*[4] on the operation of the presumption of constitutionality, Gavan Duffy J said:

> "In forbidding political discrimination here, the Constitution has in view, not politics in the original sense as the science of government, but politics in the more popular sense in which we talk of a political party; the veto is on "taking sides" in State affairs. A particular trade union may or may not have a political object in this sense; a political object may be one of its actual aims, or it may only figure as a pious aspiration in a picturesque jumble of objects ill defined... Indeed, evidence before the Tribunal that a trade union has a political object in its rules may, when all the circumstances are known, fail to disqualify it as a candidate for the organising monopoly of its class under the Act... But no court can turn a good Act into a bad one by reading it in collocation with vague extraneous matter of doubtful relevance. No court can invalidate a measure, in advance, because an objector is minded to anticipate an impropriety, which he calls an infraction of the Constitution, in the course of its administration. In my judgment there is no trace of political discrimination in the enactment. I have not today to consider what precise Article in the Constitution an aggrieved citizen should invoke or what general law, if a determination of the Tribunal were to thrust upon him, against his convictions, a real, and not a fanciful, political domination, but in that improbable event I do not think his legal advisers would have much difficulty in finding the appropriate remedy."

[1] The reason for this is obscure. Perhaps it is simply a drafting oversight, though this seems unlikely.
[2] *Constitutional Law in Ireland* (2nd ed., 1992).
[3] [1947] IR 77.
[4] [1970] IR 317; 104 ILTR 81.

THE FAMILY AND EDUCATION

The Family

Article 41

1. 1° The State recognises the Family as the natural primary and fundamental unit group of Society, and as a moral institution possessing inalienable and imprescriptible rights, antecedent and superior to all positive law.
   2° The State, therefore, guarantees to protect the Family in its constitution and authority, as the necessary basis of social order and as indispensable to the welfare of the Nation and the State.

2. 1° In particular, the State recognises that by her life within the home, woman gives to the State a support without which the common good cannot be achieved.
   2° The State shall, therefore, endeavour to ensure that mothers shall not be obliged by economic necessity to engage in labour to the neglect of their duties in the home.

3. 1° The State pledges itself to guard with special care the institution of Marriage, on which the Family is founded and to protect it against attack.
   2° No law shall be enacted providing for the grant of a dissolution of marriage.
   3° No person whose marriage has been dissolved under the civil law of any other State but is a subsisting valid marriage under the law for the time being in force within the jurisdiction of the Government and Parliament established by this Constitution shall be capable of contracting a valid marriage within that jurisdiction during the lifetime of the other party to the marriage so dissolved.

An Teaghlach

Airteagal 41

1. 1° Admhaíonn an Stát gurb é an Teaghlach is buíon-aonad príomha bunaidh don chomhdhaonnacht de réir nádúir, agus gur foras morálta é ag a bhfuil cearta doshannta dochloíte is ársa agus is airde ná aon reacht daonna.
   2° Ós é an Teaghlach is fotha riachtanach don ord chomhdhaonnach agus ós éigentach é do leas an Náisiúin agus an Stáit, ráthaíonn an Stát comhshuíomh agus údarás an Teaghlaigh a chaomhnú.

2. 1° Go sonrach, admhaíonn an Stát go dtugann an bhean don Stát, trína saol sa teaghlach, cúnamh nach bhféadfaí leas an phobail a ghnóthú dá éagmais.
   2° Uime sin, féachfaidh an Stát lena chur in áirithe nach mbeidh ar mháithreacha clainne, de dheasca uireasa, dul le saothar agus faillí a thabhairt dá chionn sin ina ndualgais sa teaghlach.

3. 1° Ós ar an bPósadh atá an Teaghlach bunaithe gabhann an Stát air féin coimirce faoi leith a dhéanamh ar ord an phósta agus é a chosaint ar ionsaí.
   2° Ní cead dlí ar bith a achtú a bhéarfadh cumhacht chun pósadh a scaoileadh.
   3° I gcás pósadh duine ar bith a scaoileadh faoi dhlí shibhialta aon Stáit eile agus an pósadh sin, agus bail dlí air, a bheith ann fós faoin dlí a bheas i bhfeidhm in alt na huaire taobh istigh de dhlínse an Rialtais agus na Parlaiminte a bhunaítear leis an mBunreacht seo, ní fhéadfaidh an duine sin pósadh ar a mbeadh bail dlí a dhéanamh taobh istigh den dlínse sin an fad is beo don duine eile a bhí sa chuing phósta a scaoileadh amhlaidh.

Education

Article 42

1. **The State acknowledges that the primary and natural educator of the child is the Family and guarantees to respect the inalienable right and duty of parents to provide, according to their means, for the religious and moral, intellectual, physical and social education of their children.**

2. **Parents shall be free to provide this education in their homes or in private schools or in schools recognised or established by the State.**

3. **1° The State shall not oblige parents in violation of their conscience and lawful preference to send their children to schools established by the State, or to any particular type of school designated by the State.**
   2° The State shall, however, as guardian of the common good, require in view of actual conditions that the children receive a certain minimum education, moral, intellectual and social.

4. **The State shall provide for free primary education and shall endeavour to supplement and give reasonable aid to private and corporate educational initiative, and, when the public good requires it, provide other educational facilities or institutions with due regard, however, for the rights of parents, especially in the matter of religious and moral formation.**

5. **In exceptional cases, where the parents for physical or moral reasons fail in their duty towards their children, the State as guardian of the common good, by appropriate means shall**

Oideachas

Airteagal 42

1. **Admhaíonn an Stát gurb é an Teaghlach is múinteoir príomha dúchasach don leanbh, agus ráthaíonn gan cur isteach ar cheart doshannta ná ar dhualgas doshannta tuistí chun oideachas de réir a n-acmhainne a chur ar fáil dá gclainn i gcúrsaí creidimh, moráltachta, intleachta, coirp agus comhdhaonnachta.**

2. **Tig le tuistí an t-oideachas sin a chur ar fáil dá gclainn ag baile nó i scoileanna príobháideacha nó i scoileanna a admhaítear nó a bhunaítear ag an Stát.**

3. **1° Ní cead don Stát a chur d'fhiacha ar thuistí, in aghaidh a gcoinsiasa nó a rogha dleathaí, a gclann a chur ar scoileanna a bhunaítear ag an Stát nó ar aon chineál áirithe scoile a ainmnítear ag an Stát.**
   2° Ach ós é an Stát caomhnóir leasa an phobail ní foláir dó, toisc cor an lae, é a dhéanamh éigeantach minimum áirithe oideachais a thabhairt do na leanaí i gcúrsaí moráltachta, intleachta agus comhdhaonnachta.

4. **Ní foláir don Stát socrú a dhéanamh chun bunoideachas a bheith ar fáil in aisce, agus iarracht a dhéanamh chun cabhrú go réasúnta agus chun cur le tionscnamh oideachais idir phríobháideach agus chumannta agus, nuair is riachtanas chun leasa an phobail é, áiseanna nó fundúireachtaí eile oideachais a chur ar fáil, ag féachaint go cuí, áfach, do chearta tuistí, go mór mór maidir le múnlú na haigne i gcúrsaí creidimh is moráltachta.**

5. **I gcásanna neamhchoiteanna nuair a tharlaíonn, ar chúiseanna corpartha nó ar chúiseanna morálta, nach ndéanaid na tuistí a ndualgais dá gclainn, ní foláir don Stát, ós é an Stát caomhnóir**

endeavour to supply the place of the parents, but always with due regard for the natural and imprescriptible rights of the child.

leasa an phobail, iarracht a dhéanamh le beart oiriúnach chun ionad na dtuistí a ghlacadh, ag féachaint go cuí i gcónaí, áfach, do chearta nádúrtha dochlóite an linbh.

Articles an innovation

These Articles are among the most innovatory in the entire Constitution: the Constitution of 1922 contained nothing at all about the family and marriage, and its references to education were confined to Article 8 (which conformed with Article 16 of the Treaty of 1921 and corresponded with the present Article 44.2.4-6) and Article 10 (which corresponded with the present Article 42.4 to the extent only that it proclaimed a right to free elementary education). The Articles are generally thought to have been inspired by papal encyclicals and by Catholic teaching; there was, however, a declaration in the German Constitution of 1919 of the special status, and the State's special protection, of marriage and motherhood, as well as of parents' rights and duties (Article 119).

Articles 41 and 42 were taken seriously by the judiciary at a relatively early date: thus in the *School Attendance Bill* reference[1] in 1943 the Supreme Court used Article 42 in declaring portion of the Bill repugnant to the Constitution: and two years later, in *In re M., an Infant,*[2] Gavan Duffy P used the same Article in equating the rights of a non-marital child, in regard to education and upbringing, with those of a legitimate one. The same judge in 1946, in *In re O'Connor, minors*,[3] where money had been deposited in a bank, before the entry into force of the Constitution, in the joint names of a mother and her infant children, said in regard to "the traditional, judge-made theory of a resulting trust for the mother's estate in the absence of rebutting evidence", that:

> "justice is being administered under our own Constitution, wherein very definitely the family is recognised as a fundamental unit of society and as a moral institution with imprescriptible rights... [This theory] will have to be reconsidered under that new light, because no inconsistent doctrines of the old Courts of Equity can prevail against the principles of the Constitution...Under a radically different polity, equity was shy of acknowledging all the natural obligations of a mother, while the law in the same spirit boggled at finding any enforceable obligation for parents to support their children...
>
> Where our children are concerned, we shall have to re-examine this and certain other of our problems with great care under the guidance of the Constitution of Ireland."

The case-law surrounding Articles 41 and 42 frequently rests on both Articles, because of the close mutual connection of their subject-matter; accordingly, their effect will be considered not section by section, but within certain topics to which one or both Articles have been material in litigation.

[1] [1943] IR 334; (1943) 77 ILTR 96.

[2] [1946] IR 334: (1946) 80 ILTR 130.

[3] Unreported: High Court (Gavan Duffy P), 31 July 1946. The excerpts from the judgment here reproduced were cited by G. M. Golding in his LL.M. thesis at University College, Dublin, in 1979 ("Mr. Justice Gavan Duffy: A Judicial Biography and Study in Legal Philosophy"), p.445: though this and other unpublished judgments are not included in the published version *George Gavan Duffy, 1882-1951*, Irish Academic Press, 1982.

The Rights of Marriage

Definition of marriage

The meaning of "marriage" in a constitutional context was considered by Costello J in *Murray and Ireland*[4] in which he derived it from the Christian notion of "a partnership based on an irrevocable personal consent given by both spouses which establishes a unique and very special life-long relationship."[5] This approach to the concept of marriage would appear to close off a line of argument which sought to extend the protection of Articles 41 and 42 to "natural families".[6]

Costello J's definition was cited in *N. (K.) v K.*[7] by McCarthy J who, together with Finlay CJ and Griffin J, referred to the constitutional status of the family based on marriage and the constitutional prohibition of divorce in support of the view that, for a valid marriage to exist, the consent of the parties must be "full and free".

That the civil definition of marriage does not necessarily equate with that used in the canon law of the Roman Catholic Church may be seen in the case of *Ussher v Ussher*,[8] which, though decided long before the enactment of the Constitution, is a clear authority for the mutual independence of the State and canon law; also by *The People (Attorney General) v Ballins*,[9] in which a woman who had first married in a registry office (and so in a form not valid by the law of the Church, though valid in the State's eyes) and had then been married by a priest to another person was convicted of bigamy.[10]

Right to protection against legislative attack[11]

In recent times, growing attention has been given to the rights of marriage. The first occasion on which the status of marriage as an institution was specifically and successfully relied on was *Murphy v Attorney General*.[12] Here the plaintiffs, a married couple

[4] [1985] IR 532; [1985] ILRM 542. This point was not adverted to in the subsequent Supreme Court appeal - [1991] ILRM 465.

[5] The Christian view of marriage also informs the common law understanding of the concept. Thus in *Conlon v Mohamed* [1987] ILRM 172, Barron J held that Irish law could not recognise an Islamic marriage which did not comply with the *lex loci celebrationis* - in this case, South Africa - because it was potentially polygamous. On appeal, the Supreme Court upheld Barron J's conclusion that the marriage was potentially polygamous - [1989] ILRM 523. (It was not contested that a polygamous marriage cannot be recognised as valid under Irish law.)

[6] See Staines, "*The Concept of 'The Family' under the Irish Constitution*" (1976) 11 Ir Jur (n.s.) 223. Though note that there is some support for the view that Article 41.2 applies to unmarried mothers - see below, p. 1012. Note also that under the European Convention on Human Rights, the concept of the family encompasses the non-marital family: see *Johnston v Ireland*, Series A, No.112, (1987) 9 EHRR 203 and *Berrehab v Netherlands*, Series A, No.138, (1989) 11 EHRR 322.

[7] [1985] IR 733; [1986] ILRM 75.

[8] [1912] 2 IR 445; (1912) 46 ILTR 109.

[9] (1964) Ir Jur Rep 14.

[10] See also *The People (A.G.) v Hunt* (1946) 80 ILTSJ 19. However in a later case, where a marriage had been annulled canonically, and where the man had remarried, his former wife had sought to have him prosecuted for bigamy; the Director of Public Prosecutions was reported to have written to her that "he did not consider that the evidence warranted any prosecution" - see *The Irish Times*, 9 July 1979. Bigamy prosecutions are very rare: see reply of Minister for Justice on 15 November 1979 (316 *Dáil Debates* 1843ff.).

[11] Protection of the married family against legislative or other attack may also be a function of Article 12 of the European Convention on Human Rights - see van Dijk and van Hoof, *Theory and Practice of the European Convention on Human Rights* (1990) at p.446.

[12] [1982] IR 241. This guarantee was also cited by Henchy J in *Hamilton v Hamilton* [1982] IR 466 and by McCarthy J in *W v Somers* [1983] IR 122 as the constitutional backdrop to the Family Home Protection Act 1976 which limits the power of a person to alienate the matrimonial home without the prior written consent of his/her spouse.

each of whom earned an income, complained of the provisions of the Income Tax Act 1967, which treated their two incomes as a single income (thus pushing the joint income into higher tax-bands and so costing them, as a couple, more than if they had been unmarried and their incomes separately assessed and charged). The Supreme Court, upholding in this respect the judgment of Hamilton J in the High Court, said that:

> "the pledge [of Article 41.3.1] to guard with special care the institution of marriage is a guarantee that this institution in all its constitutional connotations, including the pledge given in Article 41.2.2 as to the position of the mother in the home, will be given special protection so that it will continue to fulfil its function as the basis of the family and as a permanent, indissoluble union of man and woman."

Despite the many advantages which other parts of the law accorded to married people, which the Court was pressed to admit as counter-balancing this particular taxation disadvantage, the Court said:

> "the nature and potentially progressive extent of the burden created by s 192 of the Act of 1967 is such that, in the opinion of the Court, it is a breach of the pledge by the State to guard with special care the institution of marriage and to protect it against attack. Such a breach is, in the view of the Court, not compensated for or justified by such advantages and privileges."

The obligation on the State to protect the institution of marriage against attack was reaffirmed in *Muckley v Ireland*,[13] in which the Supreme Court rejected an attempt to restrict the principle in *Murphy v Attorney General* to situations where the effect of State policy would be to induce men and women to cohabit without entering a contract of marriage or, if married, to separate. At issue in this case was the constitutionality of s 21 of the Finance Act 1980, which required married persons, who in past years had not paid all or some of the tax levied on them pursuant to those provisions of the Income Tax Act 1967, declared to be invalid in *Murphy's* case, to pay the same amount as if those provisions had not been invalid during those years. Although such retrospective provisions could not be regarded as constituting an inducement to people to behave in a particular way in the future, the Supreme Court declared them to be invalid because they penalised the married state.

In a number of subsequent cases, the courts have had to consider the implications of the constitutional protection for marriage in contexts other than that of tax law. Thus in *Hyland v Minister for Social Welfare*[14] the Supreme Court applied this principle to invalidate a provision in the social welfare code - s 12(4) of the Social Welfare (No.2) Act 1985 - which reduced the amount of unemployment assistance payable to a married claimant whose spouse was in receipt of some other form of welfare.[15] In *Greene v Minister for Agriculture*[16] Murphy J granted a declaration that administrative schemes designed to provided compensatory payments to persons farming in disadvantaged areas were invalid because the means test provided for the aggregation of certain income of

[13] [1985] IR 472; [1986] ILRM 364.

[14] [1989] IR 624; [1990] ILRM 213.

[15] In contrast to the response to *Murphy*, where the more favourable treatment enjoyed by cohabiting taxpayers was extended to their married counterparts, the immediate legislative response to *Hyland* was to extend the restriction on the payment of unemployment assistance to both married and cohabiting claimants - see the Social Welfare (No. 2) Act 1989, see now s 122 of the Social Welfare (Consolidation) Act 1993. See also ss 3(12), 3(13), 177(2) and 197 of the 1993 Act.

[16] [1990] 2 IR 17; [1990] ILRM 364. The defendants lodged an appeal to the Supreme Court but subsequently withdrew it after implementing fresh schemes which satisfied the plaintiffs.

[17] However he dismissed the plaintiffs' claim for damages on the ground that "the duty cast on the State [to

married, but not cohabiting, claimants.[17] In contrast, Keane J said, *obiter*, in the earlier case of *H. v Eastern Health Board*[18] that, in the context of the means-testing of welfare claimants:

> "it is perfectly legitimate for the Oireachtas to distinguish between the income of a husband (other than social welfare allowances payable for his own support) and the income of a man with whom a woman happens to be cohabiting. In the former case, the husband is obliged both at common law and by statute to devote the appropriate part of that income to the support of his wife. No such obligation exists in the case of the unmarried cohabitee."[19]

The decision of Carroll J in *Mhic Mhathúna v Ireland*[20] may have revived, in limited circumstances, the inducement test rejected by the Supreme Court in *Muckley*. In *Mhic Mhathúna*, the plaintiffs sought to impugn aspects of both the tax and welfare codes which discriminated in favour of unmarried parents when compared with their married counterparts on the ground, *inter alia*, that such policies infringed Article 41. Dismissing the claim, Carroll J said, in respect of this particular argument, that the policies in question - the payment of a social welfare allowance to unmarried mothers and the allocation of a special tax-free allowance to single parents - did not constitute inducements not to marry. Furthermore, "the extra support directed by the State to single parents...is child centred and cannot in my opinion be designated as an attack on the institution of marriage." In her judgment, Carroll J did not refer to *Muckley* and consequently offered no justification for the resurrection of the inducement test. It is submitted, however, that such justification may indeed exist. In *Murphy, Muckley* and *Hyland*, the comparisons drawn were not the same as that made in *Mhic Mhathúna*. In the former cases, the courts were asked to compare the treatment of married persons with single persons in the same situation, the only pertinent difference between the two groups being the marital status of the parties concerned. Consequently there would appear to be no justification in social policy terms for any difference in treatment which discriminated against married persons, in which case the 'penalty' test of *Muckley* would seem quite appropriate. In the instant case, however, the court was invited to compare the treatment of *married parents living together* with that of an *unmarried parent living alone*. There are considerable factual differences here, particularly as far as the children are concerned, and such differences arguably justify a legislative policy designed to minimise the disadvantage suffered by children of one-parent families. At the same time, it can be argued that there must be limits to how far such a policy may go and it can hardly be doubted that a legislative policy designed to persuade parents not to marry or, if married, to separate would be contrary to Article 41. Thus a test is needed which will allow the State to mitigate the difficulties faced by one-parent families while at the same time ensuring respect for the institution of marriage. Carroll J's inducement test arguably fits the bill as it allows the State to provide rudimentary support for one-parent families while implying that there are limits to the extent of such support.

guard with special care the institution of marriage] does not create a corresponding right in the individual citizen so that a breach of the duty would necessarily constitute an infringement of any right of his." It is submitted, with respect, that there does not appear to be any good reason in principle why damages should not be recoverable by family members affected by a breach of this constitutional duty and, indeed, this was accepted by Costello J in *Hosford v J. Murphy and Sons Ltd.* [1987] IR 621; [1988] ILRM 300. See also below, p. 697, Fn. 124.

[18] [1988] IR 747.

[19] In actual fact, the various means tests in the Social Welfare (Consolidation) Act 1993 now provide for the aggregation of the resources of both married and cohabiting couples - see the Third Schedule to the Act.

[20] [1989] IR 504.

[21] [1981] ILRM 125. See also *P.K. v M.B.*, High Court, 27 November 1992.

Right to protection in other contexts

The constitutional protection afforded to the married state has also been considered in contexts other than that of legislative attack. Thus in *E.R. v J.R.*[21] Carroll J held that communications between a marriage counsellor and a married couple were privileged, saying:

> "The Constitution guarantees that the State will protect the family. The provision of confidential marriage counselling which may help a married couple over a difficulty in their marriage is protection of the most practical kind for the family and should be fostered."

In *Attorney General for England and Wales v Brandon Book Publishers Ltd.*[22] the same judge accepted, *obiter*, that communications between husband and wife would be protected in accordance with the principle in *Argyle v Argyle*,[23] namely, that all confidential communications, and not merely those relating to business matters, between husband and wife will be protected against breaches of confidence by either party or by third parties.

In *The People (Director of Public Prosecutions) v T.*[24] Walsh J, delivering the judgment of the Court of Criminal Appeal, considered that the constitutional obligation placed on the courts to enforce the protection afforded to the family and to family life by Article 41 necessarily included an obligation to enforce those provisions against family members guilty of injuring other members of the family. Accordingly he held that the evidence of the wife of a man accused of various sexual offences against his daughter was admissible and that the common law rule that a wife was not a competent or compellable witness against her husband did not survive the enactment of the Constitution.[25]

More recently, in *Murray v Ireland*[26] Finlay CJ, with whom Hamilton P, O'Flaherty and Keane JJ concurred, stated that the guarantee of the institution of marriage necessarily involved constitutional protection of certain marital rights such as the right of cohabitation; the right to take responsibility for and actively participate in the education of any children born of the marriage; the right to beget children or further children of the marriage; and the right to privacy within the marriage, privacy of communication and of association.

Protecting discrimination in favour of marital family

Article 41, and in particular the State's obligation to safeguard the family based on marriage, affords obvious protection to legislative or other policies which discriminate in favour of the marital family. This is evident from the Supreme Court decision in *O'B. v S*[27] that ss 67 and 69 of the Succession Act 1965, which precluded a non-marital child from succeeding on intestacy to her father's estate,[28] were not contrary to the guarantee of equality in Article 40.1. The Court said:

[22] [1986] IR 597; [1987] ILRM 135.
[23] [1967] 1 Ch 302.
[24] (1988) 3 Frewen 141.
[25] He also pointed out that such a rule did not apply to a common law marriage and that, in the light of *Murphy v A.G.*, [1982] IR 214, the family based on marriage should not be placed in a less advantageous position.
[26] [1991] ILRM 465.
[27] [1984] IR 316; [1985] ILRM 86.
[28] See now s 29 of the Status of Children Act 1987 which effectively abolished this particular discrimination in respect of intestacies arising after the commencement of Part V of the 1987 Act.
[29] [1984] ILRM 138.

"It can scarcely be doubted that the Act of 1965 was designed to strengthen the protection of the family as required by the Constitution and, for that purpose, to place members of a family based upon marriage in a more favourable position than other persons in relation to succession to property, whether by testamentary disposition or intestate succession. In doing so, the Act of 1965 provided that, in the event of intestate succession, children of the deceased born outside marriage would not stand in the line of succession, although they could succeed to property by bequest - subject to the particular provisions for the benefit of a spouse of the deceased or his children born within marriage. Having regard to the constitutional guarantees relating to the family, the Court cannot find that the differences created by the Act of 1965 are necessarily unreasonable, unjust or arbitrary."

The Court also noted that:

"The provisions of Article 41 create not merely a State interest but a State obligation to protect the family."

Thus it would seem that, in order to fulfil its obligations to guard with special care the institution of marriage, the State must at least ensure parity of treatment as between marital and non-marital families and may, if it so wishes, discriminate positively in favour of the former.

Limits to constitutional privileges of marriage

However there are limits to the privileges which the Constitution implies for marriage. In *Abdelkefi v Minister for Justice*[29] Barron J was very dismissive of the argument that an Irish citizen, normally resident abroad, had a constitutional right to the company of her husband, a Tunisian citizen, whenever she came to visit Ireland

"I can see nothing in the refusal by the Aliens Registration Office which could be said to weaken the family as an institution or to weaken its position in our society, nor is there anything in such refusal which can be said to undermine the status of marriage."[30]

Right to marry

The constitutional right to marry was adverted to by Kingsmill Moore J in 1951 in *Donovan v Minister for Justice*[31] when he stated that there was nothing unconstitutional or improper in a provision of the Garda Síochána code which required members of the force to obtain the permission of the Garda Commissioner before marrying. Apart from *Donovan*, there is no judicial decision on the right to marry, as distinct from rights arising from marriage once contracted. Proceedings were brought in 1976-7 against the State by a male and a female prisoner, confined in different prisons serving long sentences, seeking a declaration of their right to marry one another (their already born child was a third plaintiff), and a declaration that the prevention of their marriage by the State was a violation of their constitutional rights: but before the action came to hearing the State relented and permitted them to have their marriage ceremony performed.[32]

[30] This case, because of its special circumstances, was perhaps relatively easy to decide. Different considerations apply where the alien's family is resident in the State and contains Irish citizens - see *Fajujonu v Minister for Justice* [1990] 2 IR 151; [1990] ILRM 234, discussed below, pp. 1001-1003.
[31] (1951) 85 ILTR 134.
[32] See *The Irish Times,* 25 January 1978.

Nowadays this right, although it would seem a necessary derivative from the recognition accorded to the institution of marriage, is likely to be related to Article 40.3 rather than to Article 41.[33]

The Rights of the Family

"Family" is that founded on marriage

In *The State (Nicolaou) v An Bord Uchtála*[34] one of the arguments raised by the applicant (the natural father of a child who had been given in adoption against his wishes) was that the Adoption Act 1952, which permitted adoption by consent of the mother alone and made no provision for consulting the father of an non-marital child, "violated the rights guaranteed to the family under Article 41". This submission was rejected in both the High Court and the Supreme Court. In the former, Murnaghan J said the applicant's proposition was "fundamentally unsound because the Constitution recognises only 'the family' founded on the institution of marriage". Henchy J said:

> "For the State to award equal constitutional protection to the family founded on marriage and the "family" founded on an extra-marital union would in effect be a disregard of the pledge which the State gives in Article 41.3.1, to guard with special care the institution of marriage..."

The Supreme Court, speaking by Walsh J, said it was:

> "quite clear... that the family referred to in [Article 41] is the family which is founded on the institution of marriage and, in the context of the Article, marriage means valid marriage under the law for the time being in force in the State..."[35]

In *In re J. an Infant*[36] a father and mother who, by their subsequent marriage, had legitimated their child (under s 1 of the Legitimacy Act 1931) were held by the High Court to constitute a family in the sense of Article 41; Henchy J said the section "operated to endow the child...with membership of a family founded on the institution of marriage". And in *G. v An Bord Uchtála*,[37] while the Supreme Court re-emphasised the point made in *Nicolaou's* case, that an unmarried mother and her child were not a family in the sense of Article 41, Walsh J said he had no doubt that:

[33] The right to marry and found a family is expressly recognised by Article 12 of the European Convention on Human Rights and in *F. v Switzerland*, Series A No.128, (1988) 10 EHRR 41 the European Court of Human Rights held that the right had been violated by a temporary restriction placed on the applicant's right to remarry, in accordance with the Swiss Civil Code, because he had been held to be primarily at fault in respect of the dissolution of an earlier marriage. Article 12 does not give rise to a right to divorce - *Johnston v Ireland*, Series A, No.112, (1987) 9 EHRR 203 - nor to a right to marry a person of the same sex - *Rees v UK*, Series A, No.106, (1987) 9 EHRR 56; *Cossey v UK*, Series A, No.184, (1991) 13 EHRR 622;*Van Osterwijck v Belgium*, Series A, No.40, (1981) 3 EHRR 557.

[34] [1966] IR 567; (1968) 102 ILTR 1. See also below, pp. 1036-1037.

[35] In *McGee v Attorney General* [1974] IR 284; (1975) 109 ILTR 29, Griffin J in the Supreme Court noted that the Constitution did not define "family" but said that in that case it necessarily included the plaintiff, her husband and their children. In *Jordan v O'Brien* [1960] IR 363; (1961) 95 ILTR 115, Lavery J said in the Supreme Court that he would "accept, without deciding, that the word "family" as used in the Constitution, does mean parents and children". But in this case, which turned on the Rent Restrictions Act 1946, the Supreme Court - overruling an earlier decision of Murnaghan J in *McCombe v Sheehan* [1954] IR 183; (1954) 88 ILTR 114 - gave a wider meaning to "family" for the purpose of giving the statutory protection of the Act to a dwelling occupied by the sister of a deceased tenant. In *The People (D.P.P.) v J.T. (*1988) 3 Frewen 141, Walsh J re-affirmed that families not based on marriage do not come within Article 41.

[36] [1966] IR 295. A case following (in respect of the definition of a family for the purposes of Articles 41-42) *Nicolaou's* case, and distinguishing *J.'s* case, is *McN. v L.*, unreported: High Court (Kenny J), 12 January 1970.

[37] [1980] IR 32; (1979) 113 ILTR 25.

[38] Also of interest in this specific context are words of Butler J in *The People (Director of Public*

"orphaned children who are members of a family whose parents have died continue to be a family for the purpose of the Constitution... The family is recognised as the fundamental unit group of society founded on marriage and the fact that the married parents of the children have died does not alter the character of the unit."[38]

Equality of spouses within marriage

While at common law, marriage resulted in the incorporation of the legal existence of the wife into that of the husband during the marriage, the Constitution, in contrast, regards marriage as a union of equals.[39] The earliest indication of this change may be seen in *In re Tilson, infants*[40] in which a majority of the Supreme Court held that the old common law paternal rule, giving the father a permanent right to custody and to control of the children's upbringing, had been replaced by a constitutional policy of joint parental rights. In more recent times, a number of other common law rules reflecting the former inequality of spouses within marriage have been declared to be inconsistent with the Constitution. Thus in *The State (Director Of Public Prosecutions) v Walsh*[41] the Supreme Court held that the common law defence of marital coercion available to a wife who had committed an offence in the presence of her husband was not carried over in 1937; in *S v S*[42] the rule that a wife could not give evidence that her husband was not the father of her child suffered a similar fate while in *W. v W.*[43] the Supreme Court finally interred the remains of the common law rule whereby the wife's domicile was determined by that of her husband. Though the rule that one spouse was not a competent witness against the other applied equally to both husbands and wives, its origins lay at least partly in the common law view of marriage and it certainly cannot prevail against the right of an individual to be protected against attack by another family member - *The People (Director Of Public Prosecutions) v T.*[44] In one further case, *O'G. v Attorney General*[45] a statutory provision discriminating against widowers in the context of adoption - a childless widower could not adopt whereas no such restriction was placed on widows - was declared unconstitutional in the face of evidence indicating that no rational basis underpinned the distinction drawn between widows and widowers.

Prosecutions) v Coughlan, The Irish Times, 30 May 1979 a case in which a young married woman had been brutally assaulted by her husband while in labour and had then killed him. She pleaded guilty to manslaughter and received a suspended sentence of five years' penal servitude; the judge said that, "In considering what penalty to impose, I must remember she is the surviving parent, and the Constitution confers rights on the family, and rights on the children."

[39] Subject, perhaps, to Article 41.2, (as to which, see below, pp. 1009-1012), which admittedly, gives special recognition to the contribution to the common good which woman is considered to provide by her life within the home and, by virtue of sub-s 2 thereof, imposes some indeterminate obligation on the State to ensure that mothers (not wives) are not obliged by economic necessity to engage in labour to the neglect of their duties in the home. In *McKinley v The Minister for Defence* [1992] 2 IR 333, Hederman J referred to the constitutional status of marriage as "attaching to the woman by virtue of Article 41.2 perhaps to a greater extent than it attaches to the man." In contrast, Article 5 of Protocol No.7 to the European Convention on Human Rights provides that "[s]pouses shall enjoy equality of rights and responsibilities of a private law character between them, and in their relations with their children, as to marriage, during marriage and in the event of its dissolution. This Article shall not prevent States from taking such measures as are necessary in the interests of the children."

[40] [1951] IR 1; (1952) 86 ILTR 49. See below, pp. 1041-1042.

[41] [1981] IR 412.

[42] [1983] IR 68.

[43] [1993] 2 IR 476; [1993] ILRM 294. See below, pp. 1015-1020.

[44] (1988) 3 Frewen 141. See C. Jackson, (1989) 11 DULJ (n.s.) 149.

[45] [1985] ILRM 61. See below, p. 1029.

[46] [1992] 2 IR 333.

In all of the foregoing cases, the doctrine of equality of spouses has resulted in the abolition or restriction of discriminatory rules or provisions. In *McKinley v Ireland,*[46] however, equality was secured by extending the common law action for loss of consortium to cover loss of a husband's consortium.

Childless couples

If authority was ever needed for the proposition that a childless couple constituted a family for the purposes of Articles 41 and 42, it may be found in the decision of Costello J in *Murray v Ireland,*[47] wherein he held that a married couple without children were entitled to the same constitutional protection as a married couple with children, though the rights and duties of the latter would be more varied than those of the former.

Adoptive and legitimate children

In *The State (Nicolaou) v An Bord Uchtála*[48] one of the arguments on behalf of the applicant, who was alleging the unconstitutionality of the Adoption Act 1952, was that the Act by enabling an adoptive child to be placed on the same footing as natural legitimate children in the adopting family, infringed Article 41 by encroaching on the rights of that family and its members. The Supreme Court rejected this submission:

> "The adoption of a child by the parents of a family in no way diminishes for the other members of that family the rights guaranteed by the Constitution. Rights of succession, rights to compensation for the death of a parent and such matters may properly be the subject of legislation and the extension of such legal rights by legislation to benefit an adopted child does not encroach upon any of the inalienable and imprescriptible rights of children referred to in Article 42.5."

Family rights and non-citizens : international child abduction -

The issue of whether non-citizens in the jurisdiction may invoke the protection of Articles 41 and 42 has arisen in three different contexts, international child abduction, the residency rights of aliens and, most recently, adoption. Given that the rights declared by Articles 41 and 42 are not conferred by the Constitution but merely recognised by it, they themselves being (in the view of the courts) rooted in natural law,[49] it would seem to follow that such rights cannot be restricted to citizens. Thus in *Northants Co. Council v A.B.F.,*[50] when an English father, who had removed his (legitimate) child to Ireland to avoid the consequence of an adoption order which in English law could be made even without his consent, encountered the objection that he could not rely on Articles 41 and 42 because he was not a citizen, Hamilton J said:

> "The natural law is of universal application and applies to all human persons, be they citizens of this State or not, and it would be inconceivable that the father of the infant child would not be entitled to rely on the recognition of the family contained in Article 41 for the purpose of enforcing his rights as the lawful father of the

[47] [1985] IR 532; [1985] ILRM 542.
[48] [1966] IR 567; (1968) 102 ILTR 1.
[49] See above, pp. 679-682.
[50] [1982] ILRM 164. See also the decision of Barrington J in *The State (Bouzagou) v Station Sergeant, Fitzgibbon St. Garda Station* [1985] IR 426; [1986] ILRM 98.
[51] As Irish law now provides, albeit in very limited circumstances, for the adoption of legitimate children with-

> infant... These rights are recognised by [the Constitution] and the courts created under it as antecedent and superior to all positive law; they are not so recognised by the law or the courts of the jurisdiction to which it is sought to have the infant returned."[51]

A similar view was advanced by Costello J in *Oxfordshire Co. Council v J.H. and V.H.*[52] though he was prepared to accept, on the facts of that case, that there were compelling reasons for refusing to award custody to the parents who had unlawfully removed their children from the care of the plaintiff council.

However, in *Kent Co. Council v C.S*,[53] where an Irish father (living since 1956 in England) had removed his legitimate child to Ireland out of the jurisdiction of the English courts to avoid their wardship jurisdiction (the child's mother, having departed, was not in the picture), his pleading of Articles 41 and 42 was in vain. Finlay P (as he then was) found that the father's rights had not been infringed, and, in observance of the general rule of comity of courts, ordered the infant's return to the jurisdiction from which he had been removed. The same judge, delivering the *ex tempore* judgment of the Supreme Court in *Sanders v Mid-Western Health Board*,[54] said:

> "Where ... parents having no connection with Ireland bring their children unlawfully from the country in which they are, into the jurisdiction of this court, in breach of an order made by the court in the jurisdiction in which they were domiciled and in which the children were being reared, I do not accept that they can by that act alone confer on themselves and their children constitutional rights under Articles 41 and 42 of the Constitution."

- residency rights -

In the context of the residency rights of an alien married to an Irish citizen, or whose children are Irish citizens, the courts have accepted the premise that Articles 41 and 42 are applicable, though with varying views as to the extent of the State's power to curtail such rights. Thus in *Pok Sun Shum v Ireland*[55] the plaintiff, who was married to an Irish citizen, argued that, by virtue of Articles 41 and 42, the Minister for Justice could not control the duration of the plaintiff's stay within, or his departure from and re-entry to, the State. This was rejected by Costello J on the grounds that the rights of the family are not absolute and, in particular, must be read subject to the provisions of the Aliens Act 1935. The plaintiff's wife's claim for a declaration that she had a right to reside within the State with her husband was also dismissed on the grounds that such a right must be read subject to the Minister for Justice's power to deport aliens.[56] A similar decision was

out the consent of the parents, it may be that the Irish courts would now come to a different conclusion on these facts.

[52] High Court, 19 May 1988.

[53] [1984] ILRM 292.

[54] 23 June 1987.

[55] [1986] ILRM 593.

[56] A similar claim in *Abdelkefi v Minister for Justice* [1984] ILRM 138, that the Irish wife of a Tunisian had a constitutional right "to the company of her husband whenever she comes to and remains within the State" - the couple normally lived abroad - received short shrift from Barron J who said that he could see nothing in the refusal by the Aliens Registration Office to give the plaintiff permission to reside in this country which weakened the family as an institution or which undermined the status of marriage.

[57] [1986] ILRM 330.

handed down in *Osheku v Ireland,*[57] where Gannon J held that, given the fundamental right of the State to maintain social order by controlling the movements of aliens, the deportation of the plaintiff would not constitute an infringement of any of the constitutional provisions for the protection of the family.

These cases now have to be read in the light of *Fajujonu v The Minister for Justice.*[58] The parents in this case, both of whom were residing illegally in the State, had three children, all of whom were Irish citizens. Because he was an illegal immigrant, the husband was refused a work permit by the Department of Labour. Furthermore, because he was consequently unable to support his family without State assistance, he was requested by officials of the Department of Justice to make arrangements to leave the country. Fearing that the defendant intended to deport the parents, the parents and one of the children[59] sought, *inter alia*, an order restraining the defendants from prohibiting the plaintiffs from continuing to reside in the State or from taking any further action against them pursuant to the Aliens' Act 1935 and a declaration that the plaintiff were entitled to reside within the State. Having failed in the High Court, the plaintiffs appealed to the Supreme Court where they contended that the third-named plaintiff, as a citizen of Ireland, was entitled to the protection of the constitutional rights guaranteed by Articles 40, 41 and 42 and that among those rights was a right to remain resident within the State and have preserved for her the family of which she was a member as a unit of society within the State and to be parented by her parents within the State. This, it was argued, was a constitutional right of great importance which could only be restricted or infringed for compelling reasons. Both Finlay CJ and Walsh J delivered judgments in the Supreme Court (Griffin, Hederman and McCarthy JJ concurring with both judgments). The Chief Justice took the view that, while the parents, as aliens, had no constitutional right to remain in Ireland,[60] the position of the children was different.:

> "[W]here, as occurs in this case, an alien has in fact resided for an appreciable time in the State and has become a member of a family unit within the State containing children who are citizens...there can be no question but that those children, as citizens, have got a constitutional right to the company, care and parentage of their parents within a family unit. I am also satisfied that *prima facie* and subject to the exigencies of the common good that that is a right which these citizens would be entitled to exercise within the State.
>
> I am also satisfied that whereas the parents who are not citizens and who are aliens cannot, by reason of their having as members of their family, children born in Ireland who are citizens, claim any constitutional right of a particular kind to remain in Ireland, they are entitled to assert a choice of residence on behalf of their infant children, in the interest of those infant children."

The existence of such a constitutional right on the part of the children meant that the Minister could order the deportation of the family under the 1935 Act only if, after due and proper consideration, he was satisfied that deportation was justified in the interests of the common good and by the need to protect the State and its society. However as there was no evidence that the Minister and his officers would carry out their functions under the 1935 other than in accordance with fair procedures and having regard to the constitutional rights of the children, the Chief Justice dismissed the plaintiffs' appeal.

While the Chief Justice was careful to draw a distinction between the constitutional position of the children and that of their parents, Walsh J, in contrast, based his decision on the rights of the family as a unit. According to the judge:

[58] [1990] 2 IR 151; [1990] ILRM 234. See also the decision of the European Court of Human Rights in

> "the first two-named plaintiffs and their three children constitute a family within the meaning of the Constitution and the children are entitled to the care, protection and the society of their parents in this family group which is resident within the State. There is no doubt that the family has made its home and residence in Ireland."

In the absence of any evidence that the parents were in any way unfit to look after the children or that there was any ground upon which the State could lawfully separate them either temporarily or permanently from their children, the issue for the court was whether a family, the majority of whose members are Irish citizens, can effectively be put out of the country on grounds of poverty. Walsh J answered this question in the negative:

> "In view of the fact that these are children of tender age, who require the society of their parents and when the parents have not been shown to have been in anyway unfit or guilty of any matter which make them unsuitable custodians to their children, to move to expel the parents in the particular circumstances of this case would, in my view, be inconsistent with the provisions of Article 41 of the Constitution guaranteeing the integrity of the family....
>
> ...[The Minister for Justice] would have to be satisfied, for stated reasons, that the interests of the common good of the people of Ireland and of the protection of the State and its society are so predominant and so overwhelming in the circumstances of the case that an action which can have the effect of breaking up this family is not so disproportionate to the aim sought to be achieved as to be unsustainable."

However as there was no indication that the Minister intended to decide the case on any other basis, Walsh J also agreed that the plaintiffs' appeal should be dismissed.

There is evidence in the passages quoted from both judgments that the judges were influenced by the fact that the plaintiffs had resided in Ireland for quite some time and that the family had made its home here. An obvious implication is that an alien family, one of whose children is fortuitously born in the country, thereby acquiring citizenship, might not be in the same fortunate position as the Fajujonus when it comes to the matter of deportation. However it is submitted that, as the rights of the child derive from its citizenship, the length of time which the family has a unit has resided in the State would appear to be irrelevant in this context. For once the child, as a citizen, is entitled to reside in the State, it is difficult to see how its right to the company, care and parentage of its parents, derived from Articles 41 and 42,[61] can depend on the length of this period of residence. Furthermore, in policy terms, the desirability of promoting and protecting

Berrehab v Netherlands, Series A, No.138, (1989) 11 EHRR 322, in which the Court ruled that the deportation of the father of an under-age child amounted to an infringement of Article 8 of the Convention guaranteeing respect for private and family life. In the instant case, the father, though divorced from the child's mother, had maintained close contact with the child and the Court concluded that a proper balance had not been achieved between the interests of the Netherlands in controlling immigration and the applicants' right to respect for their family life.

[59] The other children were born after the proceedings had been instituted.

[60] While on two occasions the Chief Justice referred in a general way to the rights of the family as a relevant factor in this context, on a further occasion he made specific reference to "important family rights *in the children of this marriage*", (emphasis added) thus reinforcing his view that the parents, as aliens, had no constitutional right of residence. In *Fajujonu*, Finlay CJ appears to be going beyond his earlier decisions in *Kent Co. Co. v C.S* and in *Sanders v Mid-Western Health Board* inasmuch as the plaintiffs in those cases had no significant recent connection with the State whereas in *Fajujonu* the Chief Justice was prepared to deny the protection of Articles 41 and 42 to non-citizens already resident in the State for eight years.

[61] See *In re J.H.* [1985] IR 375; [1985] ILRM 302.

[62] To the extent to which this decision implies that the child citizen of alien parents could be deported in the

the psychological bond between parent and child must also call into question any linkage between the child's right to the company of its parents and the length of time which the family has resided in the State.[62]

Finally, it is arguable that the reasoning in *Fajujonu* is also applicable to the childless marriage of an alien and a citizen unless one is prepared to accept that a spouse is not constitutionally entitled to the society of his/her partner.

- and adoption

An opportunity to return to this debate presented itself in *Eastern Health Board and T.M. and A.M. v An Bord Uchtála*[63] in which the Supreme Court was asked to consider whether the provisions of the Adoption Acts 1952-88 applied to a child of alien parents. In the High Court, Carroll J had held that alien parents not within the jurisdiction could not have constitutional duties under the Constitution and that there was no common good involved in the State supplying the place of such parents. Accordingly she concluded that the Adoption Act 1988 did not apply to the case of a foundling born abroad, whether Irish citizenship had been conferred on the child or not. Finlay CJ, delivering the leading judgment in the Supreme Court, did not expressly deal with the issue of the constitutional position of aliens, contenting himself with the ruling that the Adoption Act 1988 applied to any child within the jurisdiction who would otherwise qualify for adoption, irrespective of that child's nationality, citizenship or place of birth.[64] Alone of the Supreme Court judges, O'Flaherty J adverted to the constitutional point, saying:

> "The reference to "parents" and "children" in Article 42, section 5 is not confined to citizens of this State. Indeed it would be remarkable if this section could not be invoked to protect any child in the State who is left, in effect, parentless."

After listing the minimum requirements necessary to satisfy Article 42.5, he described these as being of "universal application".

At the end of the day, there would appear to be no fewer than three positions articulated in the caselaw on the position of aliens under Articles 41 and 42. At one end of the spectrum is the argument that, given that the rights protected by these Articles are rooted in the natural law, they apply to citizen and alien alike.[65] An intermediate position appears to make the application of those Articles to aliens contingent on the latter having established roots in this country[66] while, finally, support can be found for the view that aliens have no rights whatsoever under Articles 41 and 42.[67] The logic of that natural law understanding of fundamental rights which sees them as inherent in each individual and

interests of the common good and of the need to protect the State and society, it would appear to be incorrect - see pp. 873-874.

[63] [1993] ILRM 577.

[64] In the instant case, the child had been completely abandoned within days of its birth and so there would have been no difficulty in finding that the natural parents had failed in their duty towards the child for the purposes of the 1988 Act. However, as Finlay CJ himself hinted, a different result might obtain where the natural parents contested the application to have the child adopted on the grounds that their particular conduct towards the child was in accordance with accepted standards of their duty in their own society.

[65] See Hamilton J in *Northants. Co. Co. v A.B.F.* [1982] ILRM 164; O'Flaherty J in *Eastern Health Board and T.M. and A.M. v An Bord Uchtála*, Supreme Court, 8 March 1993.

[66] See Walsh J in *Fajujonu, The Minister for Justice* [1990] 2 IR 151; [1990] ILRM 234.

[67] See Finlay CJ in *Fajujonu v The Minister for Justice* [1990] 2 IR 151; [1990] ILRM 234; *Sanders v Mid-Western Health Board*, Supreme Court, 23 June 1987 and, as President of the High Court, in *Kent Co. Co. v C.S*, High Court, 9 June 1983.

[68] See above, pp. 678-682.

which arguably informs these Articles,[68] suggests that the first view is the correct one, though clearly this may have significant implications for immigration policy.

Collective rights of family and personal rights of individual members of family

In *Murray v Ireland,*[69] Costello J drew a distinction between the collective rights of the family as an institution, which rights may usually be exercised on behalf of the family by any of its members, and the personal rights of the individual members of the family, acquired by virtue of their membership of that social unit. He said:

> "The rights in Article 41.1.1 are those which can properly be said to belong to the institution itself as distinct from the personal rights which each individual member might enjoy by virtue of membership of the family. No doubt if the rights of the unit group were threatened or infringed any member of the family could move the court to uphold them, but the cause of action would then be the threat to the rights granted to the unit, and not to those of its individual member."

While the Supreme Court decision in the subsequent appeal[70] was silent on this particular aspect of Costello J's decision, Finlay CJ made a similar, albeit not identical, point in *L. v L.*[71] when he said:

> "Neither Article 41.1.1 or 2 purports to create any particular right within the family, or to grant to any individual member of the family rights, whether or property or otherwise, against other members of the family, but rather deals with the protection of the family from external forces."

A similar approach to that of Costello J in *Murray* can be seen in *The State (Bouzagou) v Station Sergeant, Fitzgibbon St. Garda Station*[72] where Barrington J held that where the parents have separated, neither party can automatically rely on Articles 41 and 42 as against the other, and that, in the absence of agreement between husband and wife, the task of reconciling the rights of individual members of the family is one for the courts.

While there would thus appear to be some judicial support for this distinction, it must be said that it is difficult to see what practical implications the distinction may have, other than in relation to standing to enforce such rights.

Effect of marital breakdown on rights of family

The break-up of a marriage does not affect the constitutional rights of the family,[73] though it may affect a person's standing to assert such rights. Thus in *In re Doyle, An Infant*: *State (Doyle) v Minister for Education*[74] Maguire CJ, speaking for the Supreme Court, said:

> "Mere recital of [Article 42] is enough to demonstrate that desertion on the part of a mother without just cause leaves the authority of the family unimpaired and in no way diminishes the parental right with regard to the education of the children."

[69] [1985] IR 532; [1985] ILRM 542.
[70] [1991] ILRM 465.
[71] [1992] 2 IR 77; [1992] ILRM 115.
[72] [1985] IR 426; [1986] ILRM 593.
[73] Though in *Dennehy v Minister for Social Welfare*, High Court, 26 July 1984, Barron J held that the failure of the State to provide financial support for a family headed by a deserted husband was not *per se* an attack on the family, as the family had already been broken up by the desertion of the wife.
[74] [1956] IR 217 (High Court): Supreme Court, 21 December 1955, now reproduced in O'Reilly and Redmond, *Cases and Materials on The Irish Constitution* (1980), 632 and [1989] ILRM 277.
[75] [1985] IR 426; [1986] ILRM 98.

In *The State (Bouzagou) v Station Sergeant, Fitzgibbon St. Garda Station*[75] Barrington J indicated that the fact of marital breakdown has a bearing on which party can act on behalf of the family in protecting its constitutional rights. Here the wife and children were living as a separate unit and the wife had indicated that she did not want to readmit the husband to the family; she had indeed obtained a barring order against him. In those circumstances, where "it is not a question of asserting the rights of a family, or even of the parents, as against the outside world but of reconciling the rights of individual members of the family when the family itself is divided", Barrington J held that the husband could not automatically claim the rights guaranteed to the family under Article 41.

The courts have yet to consider whether, and if so, how, the granting of a decree of nullity or the recognition of a foreign divorce decree affects the rights of the family under Articles 41 and 42.[76] Insofar as the rights recognised by Articles 41 and 42 vest only in valid marriages, it would seem to follow that such rights never vest in void marriages. Greater conceptual difficulties have been identified in relation to voidable marriages subsequently set aside by a decree of nullity.[77] Such marriages are valid unless a nullity decree is obtained, in which case the marriage is regarded retrospectively as never having been valid. Consequently it would seem that the effect of such a decree is retrospectively to extinguish the rights which the family previously enjoyed under Articles 41 and 42, though it seems impossible to reconcile this result with the description of those rights as being "inalienable and imprescriptible". The alternative view, that the family continues to enjoy such rights even after the granting of the nullity decree, does not, on the other hand, accord with the common law fiction that the marriage never was valid. Clearly there is a complex conceptual dilemma here. Perhaps one way of resolving this dilemma would be to focus on the nature of the rights provided for in Articles 41 and 42. Such rights are clearly contingent on the coming into existence of a valid marriage. Perhaps therefore one could argue that, in the case of the voidable marriage subsequently annulled by judicial decree, the court has recognised that the contingency does not exist, so that the rights do not vest, but that prior to such judicial declaration, there is a presumption in favour of the validity of the marriage which obliges society to treat the unit as deserving of constitutional protection? While this reasoning is admittedly somewhat jesuitical, it may have the merit of being able to explain how a family could appear to lose rights which are declared to be "inalienable and imprescriptible". Finally, in relation to marriages dissolved by foreign divorces which are recognised in this jurisdiction, there would not appear to be any reason why such a unit could not continue to enjoy the benefits of the rights acknowledged in Articles 41 and 42, the divorce notwithstanding. While such rights are contingent on the creation of a valid marriage, nothing in the Constitution suggests that they are coterminous with such marriage[78] and consequently they are not necessarily affected by the divorce, though, of course, the divorce may have some bearing on the standing of a party to assert the rights of the family.[79]

[76] In *C.M. v .T.M* [1991] ILRM 268, Barr J did consider the effect of a foreign divorce on statutory rights of maintenance. See below, pp. 1021-1022.
[77] See Duncan and Scully, *Marriage Breakdown in Ireland: Law and Practice* (1990), pp. 70-1. See below, p. 1024.
[78] Thus the ending of a marriage through the death of one spouse does not affect the parental rights and duties of the remaining spouse under Articles 41 and 42.
[79] See further below, pp. 1022.
[80] [1985] IR 532; [1985] ILRM 542. In the Supreme Court, counsel for the Murrays expressly conceded that

Rights of the family not absolute

In *Murray v Ireland*[80] Costello J affirmed that, notwithstanding the particular terminology used to describe the rights of the family under the Constitution, such rights may be validly restricted by the State.[81] The plaintiffs, who were both serving sentences of penal servitude for life, contended that they had a basic human right to beget children; that this right was protected by Article 41; and that they were entitled to have facilities provided by the prison authorities for its exercise. Costello J held that the right to beget children was, in fact, protected by Article 40.3 and that it had to be read subject to the State's power to imprison the plaintiffs,[82] but his conclusion would have been the same even if he had taken the view that the right was guaranteed by Article 41. He said:

> "It is now well established that the Constitution does not *confer* on citizens of the State fundamental human rights but *recognises* their existence as being antecedent and superior to positive law and protects them accordingly...but the rights so recognised are not only those limited few which are so expressly described in the Constitution. Similarly, the power of the State to delimit the exercise of constitutionally protected rights is expressly given in some Articles and not referred to at all in others, but this cannot mean that where absent the power does not exist. For example, no reference is made in Article 41 to any restrictive power but it is clear that the exercise by the Family of its imprescriptible and inalienable right to integrity as a unit group can be severely and validly restricted by the State when, for example, its laws permit a father to be banned from a family home or allows for the imprisonment of both parents of young children."

This analysis was accepted by the Supreme Court on appeal, Finlay CJ saying:

> "It is quite clear that as an inevitable practical and legal consequence of imprisonment as a convicted person that (*sic*) a great many of these constitutional rights arising from the married status are for the period of imprisonment suspended or placed in abeyance.
>
> Of the [marital] rights which I have outlined it is possible to say that only a right of communication, and that without privacy, and a right by communication to take some part in the education of children of the marriage would ordinarily survive a sentence of imprisonment as a convicted prisoner."

Family rights not defined

The Constitution, while guaranteeing the family's rights, does not say what these are, and the courts in consequence have had to rely largely on their instinct. This instinct

the rights claimed by the plaintiffs may be validly restricted by the State in certain circumstances - [1991] ILRM 465.

[81] A similar view was taken in *Osheku v Ireland* [1986] IR 733; [1987] ILRM 330, in which Gannon J held that the rights of the family must be read subject to the interests of social order and the common good. However his conclusion that the prosecution of the (married) plaintiff for his violation of the Aliens Act 1935, or his deportation by the Minister for Justice would not infringe any of the constitutional provisions for the protection of marriage and the family must now be read subject to the Supreme Court's decision in *Fajujonu v Minister for Justice* [1990] 2 IR 151; [1990] ILRM 234, as to which, see above, pp. 1001-1003.

[82] See also *The State (Gallagher) v Governor of Portlaoise Prison* [1987] ILRM 45, where Lynch J upheld the power of the State to restrict the constitutional rights of a family by imprisoning one of its members, on the grounds that such a restriction is clearly envisaged by Article 38.

[83] Unreported, Supreme Court, 23 July 1980.

comes through, even if not with dogmatic clarity, in a case such as *McDonald v Dublin Co. Council*,[83] in which the plaintiff, the mother of a travelling family, was being threatened with forcible removal from the site, belonging to the defendant Council, on which they lived in a mobile home as trespassers. She claimed that the formal resolution by the Council that they should be removed was "an interference with the constitutional rights of [herself] and her family". The rights of the Council in law were plain; but the Supreme Court, speaking by O'Higgins CJ, said that bulldozing the family off the site could not be a proper course for a housing authority. The injunction which the Court granted to restrain this operation was lifted only when alternative accommodation (even though not in every respect suitable) was offered. The Chief Justice said:

> "Nothing is solved merely by moving such families from place to place. By doing so, not only is the problem perpetuated, but the claims and rights of the children to any possibility of education and a settled life and future are ignored."

In *Ryan v Attorney General*[84] the plaintiff alleged, *inter alia*, that to force her and her family (by leaving them no choice but) to use fluoridated water was a violation of the rights guaranteed to the family by Article 41. In the High Court Kenny J said:

> "Not one of the counsel in this case has attempted to state what the inalienable and imprescriptible rights of the family are and, as the Constitution gives little help on this, I am in some difficulty in dealing with this argument. "Inalienable" means that which cannot be transferred or given away while "imprescriptible" means that which cannot be lost by the passage of time or abandoned by non-exercise.[85] The right of the family to educate the children of that family is, I think, one of the rights which any moral philosophy would recognise but this right cannot, in my opinion, be one of the rights referred to in Article 41 for there is a separate Article (Article 42) dealing with education and it is highly unlikely that the Constitution gives the family two separate rights to educate... Some clue to the ambit of the rights of the family referred to in Article 41 is to be found in sub-s 2 of s 1 where there is a reference to a guarantee by the State to protect the family in its constitution and authority. It seems, therefore, that the rights referred to in s 1.1 of Article 41 relate to the constitution and authority of the family. It was argued by the plaintiff's counsel that the addition of the fluoride into drinking water affected the authority of the family to decide what drink and food the members of the family should consume and that the Act of 1960 was, therefore, an attack on the authority of the family. If it be assumed for the purposes of this argument that fluoridation of water is capable of being a violation of any right, it does not seem to me that it in any way affects the authority of the family. [He referred to long-standing legislation on food standards etc.] In my opinion, legislation dealing with the contents of food or drink does not in any way affect the authority of the family and the Act of 1960 is not an interference with the rights guaranteed to the family by Article 41."

An interesting approach to the task of identifying the constitutional rights of the family can be found in *Hosford v J Murphy and Sons Ltd*.[86] Here the plaintiffs' father had been very seriously injured in an industrial accident as a result of the defendants' negligence, and the plaintiffs sought damages for the alleged infringement of their constitutional rights under Articles 41 and 42. After noting that "uniquely, the Irish Constitution confers a right of action for breach of constitutionally protected rights against persons other than the State and its officials", Costello J said:

[84] [1965] IR 294.
[85] On this understanding of "imprescriptible", see above, pp. 210-211
[86] [1987] IR 621; [1988] ILRM 300.
[87] See above, pp. 697-698.

> "In this case the basis for such a claim should be sought in Article 41.1.1 rather than in Article 41.1.2 which relates to *the State's* obligations towards the family. But the undefined rights which obtain constitutional protection by virtue of [Article 41.1.1] must be the same as those which obtain protection under Article 41.1.2 for it would be an unreasonable construction of the Constitution to suggest that the rights which obtain protection from the State's "recognition" in Article 41.1.1 are either more extensive or more restricted than those which the State "guarantees to protect" in Article 41.1.2."

Implicitly using an Hohfeldian analysis of rights,[87] he then argued that it would be possible to derive the rights of the family under both sub-sections from the duties imposed on the State by Article 41.1.2. An examination of these duties led him to dismiss the action against the defendants, saying:

> "It must be remembered that the Court is construing a constitutional document whose primary purpose in the field of fundamental rights is to protect them from unjust laws enacted by the legislature and from arbitrary acts committed by State officials It would require very clear words to construe the State's constitutional obligations (as distinct from its common law obligations) as including a duty to ensure that its officials would not drive carelessly. I do not think that the words employed in Article 41 are apt to do, and the State's guarantee of protection does not, in my judgment, include a guarantee that its officials will drive State vehicles without negligence.
>
> It follows that the rights which are conferred by Article 41.1.2 are (a) the right to protection from legislation which attacks or impairs the constitution or the authority of the family and (b) the right to protection from the *deliberate* act of State officials which attacks or impairs the constitution or authority of the family. It would also follow that a private person whose *negligent* act so seriously injured the head of a family that the constitution of the family unit was fatally impaired had not thereby infringed any constitutional right enjoyed by members of the affected family under either paragraph of Article 41.1."

For the same reason he concluded that the defendants had not infringed the plaintiffs' right under Article 42 to be educated by their father. While the plaintiffs in the instant case were unsuccessful, it has been suggested that Costello J's decision may result in the recognition of new heads of liability where a person commits adultery or otherwise entices a spouse away from his or her family.[88]

"Family authority"

In *Ryan*, the Supreme Court read the plaintiff's arguments on Article 41 as referring to an interference with parental authority. Speaking by Ó Dálaigh CJ the Court said:

> "The aspect of that authority which is in question is the authority of the family or the parents to provide for the health of its members in the way it thinks best. It is sought to establish, as a corollary, that parents are entitled to omit to provide for the health of their children if they so think fit. One of the duties of parents is certainly to ward off dangers to the health of their children, and in the Court's view there is

[88] See Byrne and Binchy, *Annual Review of Irish Law 1987,* (Dublin, 1988) p.88.
[89] [1974] IR 284; (1975) 109 ILTR 29.

nothing in the Constitution which recognises the right of a parent to refuse to allow the provision of measures designed to secure the health of his child... There is nothing in the Act which can be said to be a violation of the guarantee on the part of the State to protect the family in its constitution and authority."

Family planning and marital privacy

In *McGee v Attorney General*[89] the plaintiff was a married woman, who, in agreement with her husband and because she wished for strong medical reasons to avoid another pregnancy, wanted to import contraceptives for her own use, and, as the import of contraceptives was prohibited by s 17(3) of the Criminal Law Amendment Act 1935, sought a declaration that this provision was inconsistent with the Constitution, *inter alia*, because it "deliberately frustrated a decision made by the appropriate authority in the family on behalf of the family and touching a matter of vital importance to the family" and so "attacked the family in its constitution and authority"; the rights of the family under Article 41, she asserted, "must include the right to make the kind of decision" that she and her husband had made. She won in the Supreme Court, though of the four judges who decided for her, three based their judgment on Article 40.3. The fourth, Walsh J, went extensively into the argument based on Article 41:

> "It is a matter exclusively for the husband and wife to decide how many children they wish to have; it would be quite outside the competence of the State to dictate or prescribe the number of children which they might have or should have. In my view, the husband and wife have a correlative right to agree to have no children.
>
> ... It is a fundamental point...that the rights of a married couple to decide how many children, if any, they will have are matters outside the reach of positive law where the means employed to implement such decisions do not impinge upon the common good or destroy or endanger human life...It is outside the authority of the State to endeavour to intrude into the privacy of the husband and wife relationship for the sake of imposing a code of private morality upon that husband and wife which they do not desire.
>
> In my view, Article 41... guarantees the husband and wife against any such invasion of their privacy by the State. It follows that the use of contraceptives by them within that marital privacy is equally guaranteed against such invasion and... that it cannot be frustrated by the State taking measures to ensure that the exercise of that right is rendered impossible."

WOMAN'S LIFE WITHIN THE HOME

Cited in defence of discriminatory legislation

Article 41.2, referring to woman's life within the home and obliging the State to endeavour to ensure that mothers shall not be compelled by economic necessity to work outside

[90] Evidence of some judicial unease with this provision may perhaps be seen in Barrington J's classification of

the home, is one of the more dated provisions of the Constitution and, until recently, had received relatively little attention from the judiciary.[90] On three occasions, the provision was cited - once successfully - in support of legislation which discriminated on grounds of sex. Thus in *de Búrca v Attorney General*[91] O'Higgins CJ, dissenting, invoked the provision to justify the recognition of a difference in capacity and social function (under Article 40.1) on the part of women, so as to permit their exemption from automatic jury service. In *O'G. v Attorney General*[92] the Attorney General unsuccessfully relied on Article 41.2.1 as a justification for s 5(1) of the Adoption Act 1974, which prohibited a widower from adopting a child unless he already had another child in his custody, but did not impose any similar restriction on widows. McMahon J said:

> "The Article recognises the social value of a mother's services in the home but that does not involve a denial of the capacity of widowers as a class to be considered on their merits as suitable adopters."

The provision was invoked with greater success in *Dennehy v Minister for Social Welfare*,[93] where Barron J used it to support his conclusion that the failure of the State to treat deserted husbands in the same way as deserted wives for the purposes of social security was justified by the proviso to Article 40.1.[94]

Does not entitle wife to share of matrimonial property

In *L. v L.*[95] a somewhat ambitious attempt was made by Barr J to use Article 41.2 as a basis for providing home makers with a share in the matrimonial property. From the time of the marriage, the wife in the instant case had made no direct or indirect contribution in money or money's worth towards the acquisition of the family home; she had, however, adopted the full-time role of wife and mother in the home. Barr J held that, on existing authority, she was not entitled to a beneficial interest in the family home. However, he considered that Article 41.2 required the courts to have regard to her work as home maker and in caring for the family when calculating her contribution to the acquisition of the family home and accordingly he made an order declaring that she was entitled to a 50% beneficial interest in that property.

the duty imposed on the State by Article 41.2.2 as one of "imperfect obligation" - see *Hyland v Minister for Social Welfare* [1989] IR 624; [1990] ILRM 213. Casey has suggested that the issues presented by Article 41.2.2 are not justiciable - *Constitutional Law in Ireland* (2nd ed., 1992) at p.495. However one could argue in response that if this provision was not intended to be justiciable, it would have been quite easy to preface it with a formula such as that found at the beginning of Article 45. Furthermore, in *L. v L.* [1992] 2 IR 77; [1992] ILRM 115, Finlay CJ accepted (at 121) that this provision imposed an obligation on the judiciary as well as on the legislature and executive and a similar view would appear to be implicit in Hederman J's decision in *McKinley v Minister for Defence* [1992] 2 IR 333, as he cited Article 41.2 as part of the constitutional background to his conclusion that the action for loss of consortium should apply to plaintiff wives.

[91] [1976] IR 38; (1977) 111 ILTR 37.

[92] [1985] ILRM 61.

[93] High Court, 26 July 1984. *Cp. The State (Kenny) v Minister for Social Welfare* [1986] IR 693, where Egan J concluded that it would be unreasonable for the Minister to exclude one category of mother from receipt of a particular rate of social welfare payment while granting it to three other categories. However, no express reference was made to Article 41.2.

[94] However a difficulty with this reasoning is that Article 41.2 refers to the position of *mothers* within the home, whereas the relevant social welfare provisions concerned deserted *wives*, not all of whom would be mothers.

[95] [1989] ILRM 528. See comment by *Jackson* at (1989) 11 DULJ (n.s.) 158. See also the *ex tempore* judgment of Barrington J in *H. v H.*, High Court, 20 June 1989, which contains *dicta* supportive of Barr J's approach.

[96] See the very careful analysis of the decision by Byrne and Binchy, *Annual Review of Irish Law 1988*, (Dublin 1988) pp.213-21.

[97] Barr J explicitly ruled that the property right conferred on a woman by Article 41 was "limited to a benefi-

Unfortunately, this laudable attempt to improve the economic security of the home maker was so beset with problems and anomalies that it was fated not to succeed.[96] It arguably failed to protect certain classes of women - those who worked outside the home, those living in rented accommodation[97] and those who had no children - and discriminated against men. The judgment also failed to address important issues such as the possible effect of spousal misconduct or repudiation of marriage on this constitutional interest, or the date of vesting of the home maker's interest - does such an interest come into existence only with the court order or can it pre-date such order? And if the latter, what implications does this have for third parties, such as banks and building societies, dealing with the couple?

Accordingly it was not surprising that the Supreme Court should reject this approach.[98] According to each member of the Court, judicial recognition of a share in the matrimonial home based on Article 41.2 would amount to a usurpation of the legislative role.[99] Thus Finlay CJ said:

> "I conclude that to identify this right in the circumstances set out in this case is not to develop any known principle of the common law, but is rather to identify a brand new right and to secure it to the plaintiff. Unless that is something clearly and unambiguously warranted by the Constitution or made necessary for the protection of either a specified or unspecified right under it, it must constitute legislation and be a usurpation by the courts of the function of the legislature."

Dealing specifically with Article 41.2, the Chief Justice suggested that the provision would affect the judicial determination of an alimony or maintenance application by a wife who is also a mother:

> "If a court is assessing the alimony or maintenance payable by a husband to a wife and mother, either pursuant to a petition for separation or to a claim under the Family Law (Maintenance of Spouses and Children) Act 1976, it should, in my view, have regard to and exercise its duty under [Article 41.2] in a case where the husband was capable of making proper provision for his wife within the home by refusing to have any regard to a capacity of the wife to earn herself, if she was in addition to a wife a mother also, and if the obligation so to earn could lead to the neglect of her duties in the home. In other words, maintenance or alimony could and must be set by a court so as to avoid forcing by an economic necessity the wife and mother to labour out of the home to the neglect of her duties in it. Beyond that capacity of the judiciary to take part in the endeavour to comply with the provisions of Article 41.2.2..., I do not consider that the transfer of any particular property right could be a general jurisdiction capable of being exercised in pursuance of that sub-article of the Constitution."

cial interest in the family dwelling and its contents". This presupposes that the husband is the beneficial owner, or part-owner, of the dwelling, which is not the case where the couple rent their accommodation.

98 [1992] 2 IR 77; [1992] ILRM 115. See the comment by *Jackson* in (1992) 14 DULJ (n.s.) 153 and the analysis by Byrne and Binchy, *Annual Review of Irish Law 1991*, (Dublin 1992) pp.216-222. Two High Court judges had already refused to follow Barr J's decision - see Lardner J in *J.F. v B.F.*, High Court, 21 December 1988 and Barron J in *E.N. v R.N.* [1990] 1 IR 383. Barron J's decision on this point was upheld by the Supreme Court - [1992] 2 IR 116; [1992] ILRM 127 - though it varied his calculation of the wife's share of the matrimonial home, made in accordance with the existing doctrines of resulting or constructive trusts.

99 Though McCarthy J left open the possibility that "in another instance circumstances may arise whereby, on the true interpretation of the relevant article, it would prove necessary to accord to the mother some proprietary interest in the home." See also on this, *Byrne and Binchy*, *op. cit.* at 217-8, arguing the case, based on Article 41.2, for the courts to be able to order a husband to make lump sum payments as maintenance to a wife other than in the context of separation proceedings.

100 See *Jackson*, *loc. cit.* .pp. 156-8; *Byrne and Binchy*, *op. cit.* pp.218-9.

It has been commented that a potential difficulty with this approach to maintenance and alimony applications is that it may corral women into a particular role within the family.[100]

Finally, it is worth noting that two members of the Court - Finlay CJ and Egan J - expressly endorsed, albeit in *dicta*, the constitutional propriety of the Judicial Separation and Family Law Reform Act 1989 which empowers the courts to declare a right in a spouse to a beneficial interest in the family home as part of the general jurisdiction of the court when granting a separation.[101] This may augur well for the constitutionality of the more radical Matrimonial Home Bill 1993, s 4 of which is designed to provide every spouse with equal rights of ownership in the matrimonial home and household effects unless they already have these rights or agree otherwise.[102] The equal rights of ownership will be held by way of joint tenancy, so that when one spouse dies, the other automatically becomes sole owner of the joint interest. The interest vested pursuant to the legislation will be an equitable interest only and one commentator has speculated that this may be an attempt to minimise the risk of constitutional challenge based on property rights.[103]

Guarantee confined exclusively to married mothers?

Writing extra-judicially,[104] Walsh J hinted at the possibility that Article 41.2 might not be confined exclusively to married mothers - he observed that the word "family" does not occur in that provision - and in *L. v L.*, McCarthy J cautioned that he was not to be taken as holding that the section was restricted to mothers of families based on marriage.[105] Should Article 41.2 have the broader application, then it would provide additional protection for social policies such as the Lone Parent's Allowance scheme against the type of argument raised by the plaintiffs in *Mhic Mhathúna v Ireland*.[106]

THE PROHIBITION OF DIVORCE

Article 41.3.2.

The Irish courts both before and since 1922 have exercised jurisdiction to pronounce decrees of nullity of marriage - where a missing prerequisite for marriage enables it to be said that no true marriage exists - and decrees of "divorce *a mensa et thoro*", where on foot of a matrimonial offence such as adultery or cruelty the parties are released from marriage obligations towards each other, but are not free to remarry, the marriage itself being considered to be still subsisting.[107] The law also recognises the validity of separa-

[101] Section 20(2)(*f*) of the 1989 Act specifically directs the court, when deciding whether, and if so, how, to exercise its statutory powers to award maintenance and make property adjustment orders, to have regard to, *inter alia*, any contribution to the welfare of the family by looking after the home or caring for the family.
[102] Of further relevance in this context is the comment of Finlay CJ in *L. v L.* that "anything that would help to encourage that basis of full sharing in property values as well as in every other way between the partners of a marriage, must directly contribute to the stability of the marriage, the institution of the family, and the common good." - [1992] 2 IR 77 at 107; [1992] ILRM 115 at 120.
[103] Buckley, "*Reform of Family Property Law*", paper delivered at a conference in Trinity College, 10 July 1993.
[104] See "*The Constitution and Constitutional Rights*" in Litton ed., *The Constitution of Ireland 1937-1987* (Dublin 1988),
[105] See also O'Flaherty J's statement of his belief that "Article 41 is not confined exclusively to the family" - [1992] 2 IR 77 at 112; [1992] ILRM 115 at 124. *Cf.* the views of *Byrne and Binchy*, *op. cit.*, p.220.
[106] [1989] IR 504.
[107] Three Bills for divorce were lodged with the Examiner of Private Bills in 1924 but were withdrawn because of the controversy they aroused: see Donal O'Sullivan, *The Irish Free State and its Senate*. pp. 161ff. See also the attempt to exclude such Bills by changing Standing Orders, above, p. 141.
[108] [1985] IR 532; [1985] ILRM 542. This point was not considered in the subsequent Supreme Court appeal,

tion deeds, whereby the parties to a marriage agree to live apart. Such deeds may contain provision for maintenance, custody of children, etc. But the Irish courts never exercised a divorce jurisdiction in the usual sense, i.e. a jurisdiction to dissolve a marriage and leave the parties free to remarry. The Matrimonial Causes Act 1857, which created such a jurisdiction in England, did not extend to Ireland; and persons domiciled in Ireland could become divorced after (as before) 1857 only by a private Act of Parliament. The Oireachtas created by the Constitution of 1922 certainly inherited the power of dissolving marriages by Act but never exercised it, nor did it legislate in this area at all. (Northern Ireland was also for a time without a judicial divorce jurisdiction, but this was created by the Matrimonial Causes Act (N.I.), 1939.) Article 41.3.2 has a clear meaning: it deprived the Oireachtas of the (unused) power which the former Oireachtas had possessed. The meaning of this provision was considered in one case - *Murray v Ireland*[108] - in which the plaintiffs contended that the State's refusal to allow them to consummate their marriage was contrary to Article 41.3.2, as constituting in effect a dissolution of the marriage. This argument was dismissed by Costello J who said that that provision was concerned only with the prohibition of legislation whose effect would be to dissolve an existing marriage.

In *Johnston v Ireland*[109] an attempt to have Article 41.3.2 declared incompatible with various provisions of the European Convention on Human Rights failed when the Court of Human Rights held that the guarantee of the right to marry in Article 12 of the Convention did not encompass a right to divorce. Nor did the State's obligations, under Article 8, to respect family life require the introduction of divorce. The Court went on to rule that the recognition of certain foreign divorces was not contrary to the prohibition on discrimination in the enjoyment of the rights and freedoms protected by the Convention, contained in Article 14 (taken in conjunction with Article 8), as the situations of persons domiciled abroad, whose divorces are recognised, and persons not so domiciled, whose divorces are not, are not analogous.

An attempt to set aside the prohibition on divorce by more direct political means failed when the Tenth Amendment to the Constitution Bill, 1986, which proposed to delete Article 41.3.2, was rejected in a referendum held on 26 June 1986, by 935,843 votes to 538,279.

Enforcement of foreign divorces

Problems have arisen on the interpretation of Article 41.3.3 as well as on the "public policy" of the whole section in regard to foreign divorces.

The first case in which public policy, in regard to foreign divorces, was read out of Article 41.3 was *Mayo-Perrott v Mayo-Perrott*,[110] which was an action brought by a successful divorce petitioner in England to recover, in Ireland, the costs of the petition which the English court had awarded to her. The ordinary rule of private international law - as the Irish courts recognised - is that a valid foreign judgment, if for a liquidated

reported at [1991] ILRM 465. Casey records a case - *Draper v Attorney General, The Irish Times*, November 25, 1986 - in which the plaintiff claimed that, as the New Testament and Mosaic Law provided divorce for the Christian, the State must consequently make provision "for the public order of same". O'Hanlon J struck out the action on the ground that the pleadings failed to disclose a reasonable cause of action with some prospect of success - *op. cit.*, p.501. In *McKinley v Minister for Defence* [1992] 2 IR 333, the constitutional prohibition on divorce was invoked, though without elaboration, by O'Flaherty J in support of his conclusion that the action for loss of consortium should extend to plaintiff wives.

[109] Series A, No.112, (1987) 9 EHRR 203.

[110] [1958] IR 336; (1959) 93 ILTR 185.

[111] 1955, unreported.

sum and final and conclusive, will be enforced. There is, however, the qualification that a foreign judgment will not be enforced if the cause of action, on which the judgment was given, is not recognised in the country where enforcement is sought; and obviously, apart from other obstacles of principle, the divorce decree itself could not have been enforced by order of an Irish court. The plaintiff however was asking only for enforcement of the ancillary judgment for costs; but she failed in both the High Court and the Supreme Court, which held unanimously that it could not enforce any part of the English court's order, and refused to treat the order for costs as severable from the rest. Kingsmill Moore J said:

> "Our law will [not] give active assistance to facilitate in any way the effecting of a dissolution of marriage in another country where the parties are domiciled...The law... would fail to carry out public policy if by a decree of its own courts it gave effect to the process of divorce by entertaining a suit for the costs of such proceedings."

The judge who had heard the case in the High Court (Murnaghan J) said after dismissing it that similar considerations would apply to an application then before him *(Heffernan v Heffernan*[111]) upon letters of request for an order directing the examination, within the jurisdiction, of a witness for the purposes of a divorce suit then pending before a German court.

Relaxation of judicial hostility to enforcement of foreign divorce

The *Mayo-Perrott* case belongs to the period just before the 1960s brought, with a new establishment of courts, the entry of new blood to the judiciary and a generally more liberal atmosphere, a period of independence and activism which is still continuing. Even in the sensitive area of marriage and divorce the reasoning in *Mayo-Perrott* was never extended beyond the issue of recovery of costs and a gradual relaxation of judicial hostility to the enforcement of foreign divorces began to emerge, although for as long as Article 41.3.2 remains part of the Constitution, the disfavour in which divorce is held must remain part of public policy. But only seven years after *Heffernan v Heffernan*, when in an exactly similar instance - *Hovells v Hovells*[112] - the High Court having again refused to order the examination of a witness, the Minister for External Affairs[113] appealed to the Supreme Court, and submitted that the "former practice" of the courts had been to give effect to such requests, in conformity with international practice. The Supreme Court - though without argument or consideration, as the respondent did not seek to have the order discharged - granted the application. In *Cohane v Cohane*[114] there seems to be a further slight move away from the rigorous *Mayo-Perrott* position: the Supreme Court gave (in connection with the practice as to security for costs) a judgment favourable to a divorced wife seeking to enforce the terms of a separation agreement incorporated in the divorce decree.

This distinction between the divorce decree, *strictu sensu*, and judicial remedies addressing the consequences of the break-up of the marriage is an important feature of the more recent judicial policy towards the enforcement of foreign divorce decrees. Thus, in *Mahon v Mahon*,[115] where a woman divorced in Britain in 1967 was seeking the enforcement of a maintenance order made by an English court in 1973, Hamilton J

[112] 1962, unreported.
[113] The practice is that foreign courts address such requests in the first instance to the Minister for Foreign (formerly "External") Affairs.
[114] [1968] IR 176.
[115] Unreported, High Court, 11 July 1978.
[116] [1984] IR 368.

said he accepted the principle of *Mayo-Perrott's* case in regard to Irish public policy, but that as the maintenance order was:

> "merely providing for the maintenance of spouses and as such cannot be regarded as contrary to public policy, [it could] not be said that such enforcement or recognition is giving active or any assistance to facilitate in any way the effecting of a dissolution of marriage or is giving assistance to the process of divorce."

A similar approach was taken by Finlay P (as he then was) in *G. v G.*[116] when he held that the plaintiff was entitled to the unpaid balance of a sum owed to her by the defendant in respect of the maintenance of their child, provided for in a separation agreement subsequently incorporated into a divorce decree in Massachusetts.

In *Cohane, McMahon* and *G*, the foreign order or agreement sought to be enforced had originally been made separately from the divorce decree. However in *Sachs v Standard Chartered Bank (Ireland) Ltd.*,[117] the Supreme Court enforced an order for maintenance of the wife which had been made as a consequential order in an English divorce petition. In the course of his judgment, Finlay CJ, with whom Hederman and McCarthy JJ agreed, accepted the distinction, drawn by Barrington J in the High Court, between orders addressing problems attendant on marital breakdown, which orders are enforceable, and orders relating strictly to divorce proceedings, which are not. He said

> "A major distinguishing feature between the order sought now to be enforced and the order for costs which was in question in the decision in *Mayo-Perrott v Mayo-Perrott* is that the award in question in this case arose from the obligations which according to the law of England were imposed upon the former husband by the fact of marriage and by his apparent desertion of his wife and his having ceased to support her. In the *Mayo-Perrott* case the order for costs arose directly and was inextricable from the order dissolving the marriage...The provision of maintenance arising from the obligation of a spouse in a marriage to a dependent spouse is something recoverable within the law of this country and something for which ample provision has been made by relatively modern legislation. In these circumstances, it seems to me that not only should public policy not be deemed to prevent enforcement of this judgment, but that the requirements of public policy seem clearly to favour it."

It is worth mentioning - perhaps as a further sign that the Irish courts are now reluctant to take up strongly conservative attitudes towards divorce - the case of *L. v L.*[118] Here there was a contest between the children of the testator's first marriage and the children of the marriage which, after becoming divorced from his first wife in England, he had there contracted. His will had disregarded the issue of the first marriage, and these children raised a case under s 117 of the Succession Act 1965. This potentially involved, on one construction of the case, an enquiry as to whether Irish law would recognise the divorce and the validity of the second marriage for the purpose of diminishing or destroying the plaintiff's claim; but Costello J avoided this question altogether, by holding that - irrespective of the status in Irish law of the second marriage and the issue of it - the testator could, even in respect of an irregular union and non-marital offspring, incur a "moral duty" towards them (the expression used in s 117(1)) which might justify provision for them to the detriment of legitimate offspring.[119]

[117] [1987] ILRM 297. See also *T.N. v P.J.N.*, High Court, 29 July 1987.
[118] [1978] IR 288.
[119] See now s 29 of the Statute of Children Act 1987 which extends the benefit of the Succession Act 1965 to non-marital children.
[120] [1982] ILRM 418.

In clear cases, the public policy forbidding the supporting of the principle of treating marriage as dissoluble still stands. Thus in *Dalton v Dalton*,[120] in which the court had to consider a separation agreement containing a clause providing for a divorce *a vinculo* between parties domiciled here, O'Hanlon J said:

> "It appears to me that considerations of public policy require that the Court shall not lend its support to an agreement providing for the obtaining of a divorce *a vinculo* by a husband and wife, and this may well be the position even if the parties are domiciled elsewhere than in Ireland when the application is made, or propose to take up such foreign domicile in the future."

Relying on the *Mayo-Perrott* precedent, he refused to make the separation agreement a rule of Court, saying that to ask the Court to do so was "to ask the Court to lend its support to a course of conduct which is contrary to public policy within this jurisdiction".

Recognition of validity of foreign divorces [121]

A separate question is whether Irish law *recognises the validity* of a divorce obtained abroad, an issue which has recently been authoritatively concluded by the Supreme Court.[122] This question was originally canvassed in the *Mayo-Perrott* case, and here the judges were not unanimous; though as their decision rested on the separate issue of enforcement of an order for costs, the views expressed on the effect of Article 41.3.3 may be regarded as *obiter dicta*. Three of the five judges did not give views on the matter; of the remaining two, Maguire CJ offered an extremely restrictive reading of the sub-section, which would have the effect of denying validity in Irish law to any divorce whatsoever obtained and between parties of whatever nationality or domicile.

Kingsmill Moore J took an opposite view. Reviewing earlier Irish and English decisions which established that before 1921 both Irish and English courts had recognised as valid, divorces granted abroad where both spouses were domiciled in the divorce jurisdiction, even where the English courts would not have recognised the grounds of such divorces as sufficient, he said there was nothing in the Constitution of 1937 to abrogate this "practically universal rule of private international law":[123]

[121] The recognition of foreign divorces under the Irish Constitution has given rise to a considerable amount of academic discussion. See Jones, "*The Non-Recognition of Foreign Divorces in Ireland*" (1968) 3 Ir Jur (n.s.) 299; O'Reilly, "*Recognition of Foreign Divorce Decrees*" (1971) 6 Ir Jur (n.s.) 293; Kerr, "*The need for a Recognition of Divorces Act*" (1976) 1 DULJ 11; O'Connor, "*The Recognition of Foreign Divorce Decrees*" (1986) 4 ILT (n.s.) 45; *Report of the Law Reform Commission on Recognition of Foreign Divorces and Legal Separations*: LRC 10 (1985); and the following articles by W. Duncan: "*The Future of Divorce Recognition in Ireland*" (1970) 2 DULR. 2; "*Foreign Divorces obtained on the basis of Residence and the Doctrine of Estoppel*" (1974) 9 Ir Jur (n.s.) 59; and "*Collusive Foreign Divorces - How to have your cake and eat it*" (1981) DULJ 17.

[122] *W. v W.* [1993] ILRM 294 - see below, pp. 1018-1020. On the recognition of foreign divorces generally, see *Duncan and Scully, op.cit.* ch.17.

[123] Two points are worth noting in this context. First, in deciding whether the foreign court had jurisdiction to grant the divorce, the test of jurisdiction is that laid down by Irish law, which is currently that of domicile, and not that of the divorce jurisdiction. Second, domicile is defined in accordance with Irish law, not the law of the divorce jurisdiction. (For a statement of the legal principles governing the determination of domicile, see *Re Adams Deceased* [1967] IR 424; *In bonis Rowan, decd., Rowan v Rowan* [1988] ILRM 65; *M.(C) v M.(T)* [1988] ILRM 456 (judgment of Barr J at 462, dealing with change of domicile.) See also *Duncan and Scully, op. cit.* pp.455-7.)

[124] *Breen v Breen* [1961] 3 WLR 900.

"The general policy of the Article seems to me clear. The Constitution does not favour dissolution of marriage. No laws can be enacted to provide for a grant of dissolution of marriage in this country. No person whose divorced status is not recognised by the law of this country for the time being can contract in this country a valid second marriage. But it does not purport to interfere with the present law, that dissolutions of marriage by foreign courts, where the parties are domiciled within the jurisdiction of those courts, will be recognised as effective here. Nor does it in any way invalidate the remarriage of such persons...

It must be noted that the prohibition [of Article 41.3.3] is *not* applicable to all cases of dissolution of marriage, but only to cases where, under the law for the time being in force within our jurisdiction, the original marriage is regarded as valid and subsisting or in other words where, by that law, the divorce is regarded as not being effectual to put an end to the original valid marriage. No doubt the Oireachtas could pass a law that no dissolution of marriage, wherever effected, even where the parties were domiciled in the country of the Court pronouncing the decree, was to be effective to annul the pre-existing valid marriage. If it did so, then, by the law for the time being in force, the first marriage would still be valid and subsisting within our jurisdiction. But the Oireachtas has not done so, and the law as existing when the Constitution was passed was that a divorce effected by a foreign court of persons domiciled within its jurisdiction was regarded as valid in our jurisdiction. Such law was preserved unless inconsistent with the new Constitution, and, in the absence of any statement in the Constitution altering such law, inconsistency cannot be spelled out from the words now being interpreted, for they are perfectly consistent with the preservation of the pre-existing law, which was the "law for the time being in force"."

Surprisingly - in view particularly of problems in intestate succession and under the Succession Act 1965, to which the question was very germane - the law on this matter received no authoritative statement (the views just cited being, as has been said, mere *dicta*) until 1971; though an English judge, Karminski J considered the matter in 1961 and opted very decidedly for the interpretation of Kingsmill Moore J and against that of Maguire CJ.[124] In 1971 Kenny J heard the case of *Bank of Ireland v Caffin*[125] and stated the law, also on the Kingsmill Moore lines. Thus, in the instant case, where the husband had been domiciled in England,[126] a divorce obtained in that jurisdiction was recognised in Irish law so that the husband's second wife was the "spouse" for the purposes of the Succession Act 1965.

The correctness of the judgment of Kenny J was implicitly accepted in 1975 by the Supreme Court in *Gaffney v Gaffney*,[127] which was a case in which a divorce had been obtained from an English court by a couple actually domiciled in Ireland who had falsely given an English address in the divorce proceedings. The Court held that the English divorce decree had, in consequence of this deception, been made without jurisdiction, as divorce jurisdiction must be founded on domicile, and refused to recognise it, so that the

[125] [1971] IR 123. See also his judgment in *C. v C.*, High Court, 27 July 1973, which contains a similar statement of the law, but where recognition was withheld because the husband was domiciled in Ireland.
[126] Which was also deemed to be the domicile of his wife, by virtue of the rule of dependent domicile.
[127] [1975] IR 133. See also *N.W. v J.S (otherwise W)*, High Court, 19 June 1987, where again it was assumed that a foreign domicile-based divorce would be recognised by the Irish courts. (In the instant case, O'Hanlon J held that the couple were domiciled in Ireland at the date of institution of the English divorce proceedings and accordingly refused to recognise the divorce.)
[128] Including one Supreme Court decision - *K.D. (C) v M.C.* [1985] IR 697, [1987] ILRM 189. See also *L.B. v*

plaintiff (a first wife who had been bullied into both the divorce and the deception) was to be regarded as still married to her husband at the time of his death (the background was that after the divorce decree the husband had married again, so that the case arose from a dispute as to which survivor was the widow for the purposes of the Succession Act 1965). Griffin J said:

> "As the decree of divorce *a vinculo* was granted without jurisdiction, our courts will and must treat the decree as invalid and the marriage of the plaintiff and her husband as subsisting at the date of his death. Accordingly, the plaintiff is the person entitled to claim as wife under the provisions of the Succession Act 1965."

However, the same judge - alone of the five members of the Court - gave a reminder that *Caffin's* case still remained to be expressly affirmed by the Supreme Court; *Gaffney's* case having been decided on the simple issue of domicile. He said:

> "For the purpose of the present case, it is not necessary to decide whether and to what extent, if at all, the recognition of a decree of divorce *a vinculo* made by a foreign court is inconsistent with or repugnant to any of the Articles of the Constitution, and I express no view on this question."

Recent judicial modification of recognition rules (dependant domicile)

Notwithstanding this cautionary note, a number of subsequent cases[128] proceeded on the assumption that divorce decrees granted in the common domicile of both spouses were recognised in this jurisdiction, to the point where this came to be regarded as well settled law.[129] Given that, at common law, the domicile of the wife was deemed to be that of the husband, this recognition rule effectively meant that a divorce granted by the court where the husband was domiciled would be recognised by the Irish courts. The inequality as between husband and wife inherent in this approach eventually led to significant judicial modification of the common-law position, in relation to both the notion of the dependent domicile of the wife and the rule of recognition for foreign divorces, in the case of *W. v W.*[130] In opposing the plaintiff's application for various remedies under the Judicial Separation and Family Law Reform Act 1989, the defendant contended that he was not legally married to her because Irish law did not recognise her English divorce from her first husband. The High Court had held that, at the time of this divorce in 1972, in which the plaintiff had been the petitioner, she was domiciled in this jurisdiction. The defendant contended that the rule of dependent domicile did not survive the enactment of the Constitution and that, accordingly, the divorce should not be recognised in this jurisdiction as both parties were not domiciled in the divorce jurisdiction. At all material times, the domicile of the plaintiff's first husband was English and, as the Domicile and Recognition of Foreign Divorces Act 1986 did not apply - the divorce having been granted before 2 October 1986, the date of commencement of that Act - the case raised squarely the issue of whether the common law rule of dependent domicile

L.B. [1980] ILRM 257; *T. v T.* [1983] IR 29, [1982] ILRM 217; *Sexton v Looney*, High Court, 8 July 1985; *Sachs v Standard Chartered Bank (Ireland) Ltd.* [1987] ILRM 297; *M.(C) v M.(T.)* [1988] ILRM 456 (judgment of Barr J at 465).

129 This position was endorsed by the Oireachtas in the Domicile and Recognition of Foreign Divorces Act 1986, s 5(1) of which described as a "rule of law", the proposition that a divorce is recognised if granted in a country where both spouses are domiciled.

130 [1993] 2 IR 476; [1993] ILRM 294. These common law rules had been modified prospectively with effect form 2 October 1986 by the Domicile and Recognition of Foreign Divorces Act 1986 - see below, pp. 1020-1021. The judicial modification in *W. v W.* operated *retrospectively* to cover the period before the date of commencement of the 1986 Act.

131 Thus in *Gaffney v Gaffney* [1975] IR 133, Walsh J had adverted to the possibility that this rule might be

had been carried over into Irish law by Article 50 of the Constitution. Doubts as to the constitutionality of this rule had been expressed from time to time[131] and in his judgments in *C.M. v T.M. (No.2)*[132] and *C.M. v T.M.*[133] Barr J had held that the rule offended against Articles 40.1, 40.3 and 41 and was accordingly invalid even before its legislative repeal in 1986. His position was approved by a unanimous Supreme Court in *W* on the ground that the rule of dependent domicile was contrary to the guarantee of equality.[134]

Having declared that this rule did not survive the enactment of the Constitution, the Court then had to consider what rules should govern the recognition of foreign divorces granted before 2 October 1986. Two options presented themselves. On the one hand, the requirement of common domicile of both spouses in the divorce jurisdiction could be retained, though with the domicile of the wife now to be determined factually, rather than fictionally as was previously the case. On the other hand, the common law recognition rules could be modified to permit recognition where *either* spouse was domiciled in the divorce jurisdiction, thus achieving by way of judicial legislation in respect of the period prior to 2 October 1986 what had been put in place by the 1986 Act in respect of the period after that date. Hederman J, dissenting from the majority, took the former position on the ground that the courts had no authority to give retroactive effect to the legislative changes contained in the 1986 Act. He also advanced a substantive objection to the more liberal alternative, saying:

> "To extend the principle of recognition of a foreign divorce to embrace divorces obtained in any part of the world, so long as one of the parties was 'domiciled' or 'resident' there or elsewhere, would lead to unimaginable confusion and injustice, as for example would be the case in respect of divorces obtained in such varied jurisdictions as those of Haiti, Mexico, New York and Nevada in the United States of America and countries where the Muslim form of divorce is accepted. I am not aware of any country which affords such wide recognition."

With respect to Hederman J, these fears would appear to be somewhat overstated. In the first place, the majority decision in *W* does not lend any support to arguments for the recognition of residence-based divorces and, indeed, such arguments were rejected by the Supreme Court as recently as 1985 in *K.D. (C) v M.C.* [135] Furthermore, in relation to the recognition of domicile-based divorces, it must be borne in mind that 'domicile' is determined in accordance with the Irish definition of that term and so there is a common criterion for recognition irrespective of the particular divorce jurisdiction in question.

The majority judgments delivered by Blayney and Egan JJ - Finlay CJ and O'Flaherty J concurring - opted to replace the requirement of common domicile with a requirement that either party be domiciled in the divorce jurisdiction. After explaining that the object of the recognition rules was to avoid limping marriages, Blayney J deduced from a reading of English authorities[136] that the common law rule of recognition is judge-made law and not immutable and that the question of whether a foreign divorce should be recognised should be answered by the court in the light of its present policy, regardless of

challenged where the wife had never physically left her domicile of origin while her husband had established a domicile of choice in another jurisdiction. In *K.D.(C) v M.C.* [1985] IR 697, [1987] ILRM 189, McCarthy J said that he was not to be taken as accepting that the rule had survived the enactment of the Constitution. See also the comments of O'Hanlon J in *N.W. v J.S (W.)*, High Court, 19 June 1987.

132 [1990] 2 IR 52; [1988] ILRM 456.

133 [1991] ILRM 268. (Both cases involved the same litigants.)

134 See above, p. 713.

135 [1985] IR 697, [1987] ILRM 189.

136 *Travers v Holley* [1953] P. 246; *Indyka v Indyka* [1967] 2 All ER 689.

137 [1992] 2 IR 77; [1992] ILRM 115. See pp. 1010-1012.

when the decree was granted. In opting to recognise the divorce granted in the instant case, where the husband was domiciled in the divorce jurisdiction, the judge pointed out that the same result would have obtained under the former rule but that, given the demands of equality, the rule of recognition would have to be re-formulated in order to cover divorces granted in the country in which either spouse was domiciled. Furthermore, this re-formulated rule had the merit of being consistent with the legislative policy contained in the Domicile and Recognition of Foreign Divorces Act 1986, outlined below. For his part, Egan J invoked, without further specification, the Constitution and the general principles of international law in support of this more liberal basis for recognising foreign divorces.

While the majority decision may provoke unease among those who dislike the notion of judicial legislation - given the very nebulous distinction between such activity eschewed by the Supreme Court in cases like *L. v L.*[137] and the more acceptable judicial refinement of common law rules such as in the instant case - it does have the merit of introducing a uniform rule for the recognition of foreign divorces, so that one's marital status is not affected one way or the other by the mere happenstance of the date of a foreign divorce.

Domicile and Recognition of the Foreign Divorces Act 1986

In 1986, the Oireachtas exercised the power, which both Kingsmill Moore and Kenny JJ had recognised was implicit in Article 41.3.3, to legislate for the recognition of foreign divorces. The common law rule requiring common domicile of both spouses in the divorce jurisdiction before the divorce is recognised has been relaxed somewhat by s 5 of the Domicile and Recognition of Foreign Divorces Act 1986 which provides, *inter alia*, that a divorce granted after the commencement of the Act - 2 October 1986 - shall be recognised if granted in the country where either spouse is domiciled, or, where neither spouse is domiciled in this State, if it is recognised in the country or countries where the spouses are domiciled.[138] Section 5(3) deals specifically with divorces granted within the UK, providing that a divorce granted in any of the jurisdictions listed therein - England and Wales, Scotland, Northern Ireland, the Isle of Man and, lastly, the Channel Islands - shall be recognised if either spouse is domiciled in any of those jurisdictions.[139]

The opportunity was also taken, in s 1 of the Act to abolish the rule of dependent domicile for wives with effect from 2 October 1986,[140] though this provision is somewhat

[138] Duncan and Scully argue that pre-1986 divorces recognised, though not granted, by the country of the parties' common domicile should be recognised here on the basis of the principle that the country of domicile should determine matters of personal status - *op. cit.*, p.457.

[139] In *W. v W.* [1993] 2 IR 476; [1993] ILRM 294 Hederman J stated that the statutory rule of recognition applied to divorces granted within these jurisdictions only. This, with respect, would appear to be incorrect as s 5(1), which replaces the requirement of common domicile with that of the domicile of either spouse, is subject to no such territorial limitation. The correct view of s 5(3) would appear to be that a divorce granted in any one of the five jurisdictions listed therein will be recognised if either spouse is domiciled in that jurisdiction or in any one of the remaining four.

[140] Section 2 of the Act provides that the domicile that a person had at any time before 2 October 1986 shall be determined as if the Act had not been passed and in *W. v W.* [1993] 2 IR 476; [1993] ILRM 294, Hederman J concluded that s 2 was invalid on the assumption that it amounted to a statutory endorsement of operation of the rule of dependent domicile in respect of the period prior to 2 October 1986. While that might have been regarded as an obvious implication of s 2 at the time of its enactment, it should be noted that that section does not expressly save the rule of dependent domicile for wives; that it can be interpreted consistently with the Constitution by reading it to save only pre-1986 rules which survived the enactment of the Constitution, and that the rules determining the domicile of minors, altered by s 4 of the Act may fall into this category. (Though for an analysis suggesting that both the common law and statutory rules on the domicile of minors are unconstitutional, see Byrne and Binchy, *Annual Review of Irish Law 1988*, (Dublin, 1989) pp.75-7.)

[141] [1993] ILRM 294.

redundant now in the light of the Supreme Court ruling in *W. v W.*[141] that the rule of dependent domicile did not survive the enactment of the Constitution.

Northern Ireland divorces

In *Caffin's* case Kenny J reserved his position on what he described as the "difficult question" of whether a divorce granted by the courts in Northern Ireland to a person domiciled there will be recognised by Irish law. This question appears to have arisen from the possibility that Articles 2 and 3 might have a bearing on it, and the desire to reserve a matter which had not been argued; but there does not seem to be any basis for supposing that a Northern Ireland divorce would be viewed by the courts on any different basis from a divorce validly decreed in any other jurisdiction. The matter is now put beyond any doubt in respect of divorces granted after 2 October 1986 by s 5(3) of the 1986 Act which provides, *inter alia*, for the recognition of divorces granted in Northern Ireland if either spouse is domiciled there.

Grounds for refusing recognition

Even where a foreign divorce ostensibly satisfies the recognition requirements of the common law or of the 1986 Act recognition may be refused if the parties deliberately mislead the foreign court in relation to that court's jurisdictional requirements[142] or if they have colluded together in establishing the grounds for their divorce in such a way as to procure a "substantial defeat of justice."[143] In *Gaffney v Gaffney* Kenny J said that the courts would not recognise a divorce obtained under duress[144] and English authority exists for the proposition that fraud between the parties justifies non-recognition of foreign divorce decrees.[145]

Decisions on recognition of foreign divorces are unaffected by the doctrine of estoppel by conduct which may not be invoked to determine a matter of marital status.[146] Indeed Irish judges appear reluctant to allow the doctrine of estoppel to defeat claims - quite apart from the issue of marital status - which would follow from non-recognition of such divorces.[147]

Effect of recognition

Where a foreign divorce decree is recognised in this jurisdiction, the parties cease to have the status of spouses and are free to re-marry. However it is not quite clear to what extent the statutory entitlements of the former spouses, *qua* spouse, are affected by the divorce. Clearly they cannot assert claims under the Succession Act 1965.[148] However in *C.M. v T.M.*[149] Barr J held that a maintenance order already granted under the Family

[142] *Gaffney v Gaffney* [1975] IR 133.
[143] *L.B. v H.B.* [1980] ILRM 257.
[144] [1975] IR 133. In the Supreme Court, however, Walsh J suggested that the victim of the duress would have to have the divorce set aside in the divorce jurisdiction before s/he could successfully assert the status of spouse.
[145] *Kendall v Kendall* [1977] Fam. 208.
[146] *C. v C.*, High Court, 27 July 1973; *Gaffney v Gaffney* [1975] IR 133. In *W. v W.* [1993] 2 IR 478; [1993] ILRM 294, Egan J said, *obiter*, that the defendant had participated in a solemn ceremony with the plaintiff which "quite clearly they treated as being a valid marriage" and that he ought not be entitled to argue that the marriage was a nullity. However this application of the doctrine of estoppel was made without any consideration of the conflicting authorities and must be regarded with some caution.
[147] See *L.B. v H.B.* [1980] ILRM 257.
[148] *Bank of Ireland v Caffin* [1971] IR 123.
[149] [1991] ILRM 268.
[150] *Duncan and Scully* consider that the existence of such a doctrine in Irish law is "unlikely" - *op. cit.* p.462.

Law (Maintenance of Spouses and Children) Act 1976 was not dependent on the subsistence of the marriage and consequently remained enforceable notwithstanding the subsequent dissolution of the marriage in England. Furthermore if the doctrine of "divisible divorce" exists in Irish law, then a spouse who takes no part in foreign *ex parte* divorce proceedings may retain separable personal rights despite the recognition of the divorce.[150]

The courts have yet to consider whether a foreign divorce can affect the constitutional rights of the family. If such rights were coterminous with a valid marriage, then clearly the divorce decree would have some impact. However there does not appear to be any reason why the rights protected by Articles 41 and 42 should necessarily be limited in that way and one can argue that constitutional rights which come into existence on the creation of a valid marriage may continue to exist notwithstanding the subsequent dissolution of that marriage. This accords with the description of those rights as inalienable and imprescriptible and while it implies that an individual may simultaneously enjoy certain of those rights - such as the right to marital privacy and the right to protection against legislative attack[151] - in respect of two or more families, such a conclusion does not appear to present any theoretical or practical difficulties.

Limits on further legislative and judicial development?

It is quite clear from the terms of Article 41.3.3 that the Oireachtas may, from time to time as it sees fit, amend the law on the recognition of foreign divorces. The Supreme Court has also asserted a jurisdiction to modify the common law rules on recognition in the light of contemporaneous public policy.[152] At the same time, in view of the prohibition on the enactment of domestic divorce legislation, it is arguable that the power of the Oireachtas to legislate for the recognition of foreign divorces is not completely unfettered. A very liberal policy of recognising foreign divorces of the Haitian variety, for example, would certainly offend against the spirit of Article 41.3.2 and to that extent could be constitutionally suspect. This reasoning, together with considerations born of the doctrine of separation of powers, may also explain the reluctance of the courts to liberalise the recognition rules in any significant way.[153]

THE LAW ON NULLITY

Though the Constitution does not expressly refer to nullity law, it has a bearing on this area of the law in two different respects. First, the State's obligation to protect the institution of marriage may have implications for the burden of proof required of a petitioner seeking to have a marriage declared null and void. Second, the constitutional prohibition of divorce forms an important part of the backdrop to recent decisions extending the grounds on which a nullity decree may be granted.

[151] In contrast, where an individual was a member of two or more families simultaneously entitled to constitutional protection under Articles 41 and 42, constitutional rights in respect of custody might presumably apply only where there was a biological or adoptive relationship between the parent and child.

[152] See the majority decision in *W. v W.* [1993] 2 IR 476; [1993] ILRM 294. Judicial development of the rules of recognition had been implicitly anticipated in *Caffin's* case, where Kenny J reserved his position as to whether a residence-based foreign divorce would have any effect in this jurisdiction and also in *Gaffney*, where Walsh J commented that the common law principles on recognition were not frozen in their pre-1922 condition by either the 1922 or the 1937 Constitutions.

[153] Indeed, apart from *W. v W.* [1993] 2 IR 476; [1993] ILRM 294, the courts have not, in fact, availed of any opportunity significantly to expand the rules on recognition. See *C. v C.* , High Court, 27 July 1973, where Kenny J refused to recognise a residence-based divorce decree and *K.D. (C) v M.C.* [1985] IR 697, [1987] ILRM 189 where the Supreme Court refused to adopt a more flexible test allowing recognition whenever the party had a "real and substantial connection" with the country granting the divorce decree.

[154] [1976-77] ILRM 156.

Burden of proof

In *S v S,*[154] having surveyed the historical origin of the High Court's jurisdiction to grant civil annulments, Kenny J indicated that the petitioner had to establish his or her case beyond all reasonable doubt[155] and in *F.(otherwise C) v C.*[156] Keane J in the High Court rejected the proposition that this position had been in any way abridged or eroded by the Constitution. In the Supreme Court, however, McCarthy J[157] referred to his comments in the earlier case of *N (otherwise K.) v K.*[158] in which he indicated that the case for nullity had to be established upon the balance of probabilities, and continued, *obiter*:

> "If the observations of Kenny J in *S v S*...mean, as apparently in the instant case Keane J thought, that there is a greater onus imposed upon a petitioner, then, in my view, this was an incorrect statement of the law applicable in this jurisdiction. There may have been a misunderstanding of the reference to the Constitution contained in *N. v K.*; the guarantee protects the institution of marriage but it does not presuppose the existence of a valid marriage in any given case so as to increase the burden of proof where a petitioner calls in aid s 13 of the [Marriage Law (Ireland) Amendment Act 1870]. It begs the question to say that the constitutional guarantee endorses, for instance, the citation from Lord Birkenhead in *C. (otherwise H.) v C.* [1921] P. 399.[159] The burden of proof point only arises where there is an issue of fact. There is no such issue here. The point is irrelevant to the issue as to what constitutes incapacity."

In *S v K.*[160] Denham J commented that in view of the constitutional protection of the institution of marriage, there was a heavy burden of proof on a petitioner which she described as "a severe and heavy burden...of a quasi-criminal trial nature." That she did not consider this to be equivalent to establishing the case beyond reasonable doubt may be taken from her earlier comment that "[i]n practice the courts have been requiring a high but less demanding burden than that in criminal cases."[161]

Extended grounds for nullity

In *N. (K.) v K.*[162] Henchy J noted a connection between the constitutional prohibition on divorce and contemporary judicial decisions extending the grounds for granting a decree of nullity. He said:

> "In relation to the contract of marriage, it is to be said that the courts, at least in this jurisdiction, have given a more liberal scope to the doctrine of duress as a nullifying element than would be applied in the construction of certain other kinds of contract. This is probably because, the dissolution of marriage being prohibited by the Constitution, certain marriages which at no stage were viable have been declared null on a liberal and humane interpretation of the doctrine of duress in relation to the contract of marriage."

[155] A similar view was taken by Hanna J in *McM v McM and McK v McK* [1936] IR 177 in relation to petitions based on impotence, though his remarks were subsequently described by Denham J in *S v K.*, High Court, 2 July 1992, as "the high water mark of the law on the burden of proof in this type of case."
[156] [1991] ILRM 65.
[157] Three other members of the Court, Griffin, Hederman and O'Flaherty JJ, concurred with Finlay CJ who, on this point, expressly reserved the matter for determination in a case in which it was necessary for the decision.
[158] [1986] ILRM 75.
[159] In which Lord Birkenhead indicated that the petitioner 'must remove all reasonable doubt'.
[160] High Court, 2 July 1992. See also Budd J in *A.B. v E.B.*, High Court, 14 October 1993.
[161] In *P.K. v M.B. (otherwise M.K.)*, High Court, 27 November 1992, Costello J accepted that the petitioner had in fact made out his case beyond any reasonable doubt but expressly reserved his decision as to whether this is the necessary burden of proof in nullity cases.
[162] [1985] IR 733; [1986] ILRM 75.
[163] *U.F. (orse U.C.) v J.C.* [1991] 2 IR 330; [1991] ILRM 65.

This judicial liberalisation of nullity law has continued apace, the courts now recognising incapacity to form a caring or considerate relationship, due to illness or to some involuntary characteristic of a person's personality, as a ground for ruling that a marriage is voidable.[163]

Status of voidable marriage under the Constitution

In nullity law, an important distinction exists between a void marriage which never had legal effect and a voidable marriage which is regarded as valid until a decree annulling it has been pronounced by the courts. However the annulment of a voidable marriage does give rise to constitutional difficulties, as Duncan and Scully point out:

> "If it is true that the members of a family based on a voidable marriage enjoy these various constitutional guarantees [for members of marriage-based families], it follows that the effect of a decree of nullity is retrospectively to extinguish them..
>
> ...[A]n alternative view is possible. This is that a voidable marriage, because it has once been valid, has full constitutional protection, and that once the various constitutional rights have vested in the members of the family, they cannot, because they are variously described as imprescriptible and inalienable, be removed by judicial decree. The difficulty with this theory is that the decree of nullity in respect of a voidable marriage maintains the fiction that the marriage was never valid and therefore, presumably, that it never attracted constitutional rights. To hold otherwise would be to accept that the decree effectively dissolves, rather than annuls, the marriage. What emerges is an impossible dilemma. If a decree in respect of a voidable marriage is genuinely an annulment, then it is difficult to see how the constitutional guarantees for the family can survive it; if some constitutional rights do survive, this can only be based on a recognition that the marriage did in fact exist, and hence the annulment begins to look more like a dissolution."[164]

Obviously there are difficult problems here. However one way of accommodating the concept of the voidable marriage within the Constitution might be to focus on the nature of the rights provided for in Articles 41 and 42. Such rights are clearly contingent on the coming into existence of a valid marriage.[165] Might it not be argued that, in the case of the voidable marriage annulled by the courts, the courts have recognised that the contingency does not exist, so that the rights do not vest, but that prior to such judicial declaration, there is a presumption in favour of the validity of the marriage which obliges society to treat the unit as deserving of constitutional protection? Thus one could argue that the nullity decree does not, in theory, retrospectively extinguish vested constitutional rights though admittedly the net effect would be the same as if it did.[166]

PUBLIC POLICY AND SEPARATION DEEDS

Separation agreements; No implication of dum casta clause

There have been three cases in which the courts have considered - with mixed results - the alleged effect of the public policy represented by Article 41.3 on separation deeds (whereby the parties to a marriage agree, without recourse to a court, to live apart).

164 *Op.cit.* pp.70-71.
165 Though one could argue that they are not necessarily dependent on the *continued* existence of such marriage - see above, p. 1022.
166 This argument cannot be used in relation to marriages recognised as valid in Irish law but subsequently dissolved by foreign divorces recognised in this jurisdiction as a premise for such decrees would be that the marriage was valid, consequently attracting the inalienable and imprescriptible rights referred to in Articles 41 and

In the first of these cases, *Lewis v Lewis*,[167] husband and wife had separated under a deed whereby a maintenance allowance was payable by the husband to the wife, and in which there was no *dum casta* clause on which this payment was to be dependent. The allowance fell into arrears; the wife sued for the arrears, and the husband pleaded that his wife was now living in adultery (he then sued for, and obtained, a decree of divorce a *mensa et thoro* on that ground). It was argued for him on the hearing of the claim for maintenance arrears that, even though the separation deed contained no *dum casta* clause, it was "contrary to public policy in Éire" that the deed should be implemented in view of the misconduct of the wife. Hanna J said:

> "To distinguish the public policy in Éire from that in England, reliance has been placed upon the provisions of Article 41 of our present Constitution wherein the State recognises the family as a moral institution, and pledges itself to guard with special care the institution of marriage, and prohibiting the enactment of any law providing for the grant of a dissolution of marriage. The effect of these provisions is that, notwithstanding any kind of matrimonial offence, the marriage tie still continues, as it does in this case, even after a divorce a *mensa et thoro.*
>
> In my judgment, the provisions of our Constitution do not help on the question of public policy in Ireland, which I have to decide, as regards a separation deed without a *dum casta* clause. I can find no public policy that I could legally rely upon as a guide upon this matter."[168]

In a later case, *Ormsby v Ormsby*,[169] the situation was similar except that the roles of husband and wife were reversed. Haugh J stated a case for the Supreme Court, on the husband's claim for arrears of maintenance under a deed with no *dum castus* clause, as to whether it was contrary to public policy to enforce payment to the husband, who was maintaining another household. For the defendant wife it was argued that the Constitution implied a *dum castus*, even if not a *dum casta*, clause in separation deeds: it was "difficult to conceive any more serious attack on marriage or the family than to permit an adulterous household in opposition to [the husband's] lawful family". The Supreme Court decided unanimously against this submission; Sullivan CJ said:

> "Article 41 of the Constitution has satisfied me as being the law of this country as it existed prior to the Constitution."

Murnaghan J said the pre-1937 law was "binding on the courts under Article 50"; Black J added that he could not see how Article 41 altered the public policy in any way, except in s 2.2-3.

42. For consideration of how such decrees might be accommodated within the constitutional framework, see above, p. 1022.

[167] [1940] IR 42; (1940) 74 ILTR 170. It may be noted that in this case counsel on both sides had based arguments on Article 41. For the plaintiff wife it was submitted that "Article 41... in reaffirming the indissolubility of the marriage tie, strengthens the wife's claim"; for the defendant husband it was said that "more particularly in view of Article 41... judgment for a guilty wife in such a case is a licence to commit adultery... [An English court had] held that a deed of separation, even without a *dum casta* clause, must be construed as an agreement that the parties should live in chastity. The decision in that case was reversed on appeal, but it is submitted that [it]... states the law in such a way as to be more in keeping with public policy in this country."

[168] While Hanna J was not prepared to imply a *dum casta* clause in this case, he did suggest that it might be inequitable to enforce an obligation to maintain where the dependent spouse was cohabiting with, and being supported by, another partner.

[169] (1945) 79 ILTR 97.

[170] [1982] ILRM 418.

[171] On this topic generally, see O'Halloran, *Adoption: Law and Practice* (Dublin 1992). See also the *Report of the Review Committee on Adoption Service* (1984).

Non-enforceability of agreement to seek divorce a vinculo

These cases on adultery clauses may be contrasted with *Dalton v Dalton*[170] in which O'Hanlon J refused to make a separation agreement a rule of court, pursuant to s 8 of the Family Law (Maintenance of Spouses and Children) Act 1976, because it contained a clause whereby the parties agreed to obtain a *divorce a vinculo* abroad. According to the judge, to make such an agreement a rule of court would be "to lend [the court's] support to a course of conduct which is contrary to public policy."

ADOPTION

Legal adoption possible since 1952

Legal adoption, as distinct from informal adoption or fosterage, has existed only since 1953.[171] The Adoption Act 1952 provided for the setting-up of an adoption board (An Bord Uchtála) with power to make adoption orders on the application of persons wishing to adopt a child; this Act together with further Acts of 1964, 1974, 1976, 1988 and 1991, contains the procedure, conditions and safeguards for adoption. The essence of the system originally was that a child born out of wedlock[172] became by operation of law integrated into the same relationship with the adoptive parents as if he had been born their own legitimate child.[173] In *G. v An Bord Uchtála*[174] O'Higgins CJ said:

> "At common law an illegitimate child was termed "filius nullius" and regarded as being no more than the "unfortunate offspring of the common failing of a man and woman", a burden on the locality and a person to be shunned. In this unchristian treatment of a human being natural rights were, of course, forgotten and a lonely life was ordained merely because of the accident of birth. Not only is this not so now under the Constitution, but the State has the added obligation to defend and vindicate in its laws all natural rights of all citizens. In relation to illegitimate children and certain others the State has by the Adoption Acts endeavoured to discharge this obligation. The purpose of these Acts is to give to these children the opportunity of becoming members of a family and to have the status and protection which such membership entails."[175]

In *M. v An Bord Uchtála*[176] Henchy J (who dissented from the majority of the Supreme Court on what the result of the case should be) emphasised the normally final and irrevocable nature of an adoption order as follows:

> "When the adoptive parents agreed to adopt this child five years ago, the State, for its part, underwrote the confidentiality of the adoption and the sanctity and security of the family resulting from the adoption. The State, speaking through the legislature, stipulated to this effect in the Adoption Act 1952. This solemn and far-reaching undertaking could, of course, be held by the courts to be nugatory in a particular

[172] Or both of whose (legitimate) parents were dead.
[173] Though in *Re Stamp, Stamp v Redmond* [1993] ILRM 383, Lardner J held that adopted children did not fall within the meaning of the word "issue" used in a will.
[174] [1980] IR 32; 113 ILTR 25.
[175] And without diminishing the rights of the other marital children in the adopting family - see remarks of Walsh J to this effect in *The State (Nicolaou) v An Bord Uchtála* [1966] IR 567.
[176] [1977] IR 287.
[177] [1977] IR 287.
[178] In *In re M., M.(J.) and M.(G.) v An Bord Uchtála* [1987] IR 510, Barron J said that, as a result of the enact-

case if a valid challenge to the jurisdiction to make the adoption order followed hard on the adoption order. But not if years are allowed to pass. Otherwise, the familial stability and security aimed at by adoption would be defeated."

In the course of the hearing of this case,[177] doubts arose as to whether the function of making adoption orders could be regarded as a "limited" function for the purposes of Article 37 (which permits non-judicial personnel to exercise limited functions and powers of a judicial nature). Accordingly Article 37 was amended by the Sixth Amendment of the Constitution which provided for an additional section expressly safeguarding decisions of the Adoption Board in this context.[178]

Recent changes in adoption policy

While adoption law was originally designed to bolster the constitutional model of the family based on marriage, insofar as it took children from family units which did not conform to this model and delivered them to units which did, recent legislative changes[179] may signal a departure from this approach. Thus O'Halloran says:

> "[In 1952] it may have seemed provident that the adoption process could accept from those defined out of the constitutionally approved marital family unit and deliver to those that conformed to it. Legal loose ends were thus neatly tied up. It was unthinkable that adoption orders could be granted on a non-consensual basis or in respect of the child of married and living parents. Now it seems doubtful that the eligibility for adoption of a child whose upbringing has been jeopardised by family breakdown, due to parental incompatibility or parental abuse, should be dependent on whether or not that breakdown occurs in the context of non-marital family relationships. Faced with providing permanent care-taking arrangements for the rapidly growing numbers of children removed from defaulting parents and the realisation that their welfare needs might well be met by the increasing numbers of prospective adopters now forced to search overseas for available children, the State has to some extent compromised its initial principles. Adoption orders may now occasionally be granted in respect of legitimate children and notwithstanding the lack of parental consent. The introduction of statutory provisions for an adoption service and for post-adoption payments also indicates the steady encroachment of a public service dimension into what was originally an area of private family law."[180]

While such developments clearly carry the potential for conflict with the Constitution, to date the courts have managed to accommodate them by relying on Article 42.5.[181]

Challenges to Adoption Act 1952

The constitutionality of the Adoption Act 1952 has been challenged in four cases. In one of these, *M. v An Bord Uchtála*,[182] the Supreme Court, finding itself able to decide the

ment of Article 37.2, not only can an adoption order not be impugned on the ground that members of the Adoption Board are not judges appointed under the Constitution, but any step taken by the Board to enable it to make such an order is likewise incapable of being impugned. This statement may be overbroad, however, as the protection here referred to is restricted to constitutional arguments based on the status of the members of the Adoption Board and does not preclude any challenge to a decision of the Board based on any other aspect of the Constitution. This point was not addressed in the subsequent Supreme Court appeal - [1987] IR 510; [1988] ILRM 203.

[179] Especially the Adoption Act 1988 and the Child Care Act 1991.

[180] *Op. cit.*, pp.31-2.

[181] See below, pp. 1029-1032.

[182] [1977] IR 287.

[183] [1975] IR 81; (1975) 109 ILTR 62.

issue on the simple ground of the non-observance by the Board of statutory requirements for a valid adoption order - the Board had not satisfied itself that the mother understood the revocable nature of the consent which she had given - did not consider the constitutional arguments. A different case with a similar title, *M. v An Bord Uchtála,*[183] hinged on the prohibition of religious discrimination of Article 44.2.3 and is dealt with under that sub-section of the Constitution; the result of the case was to invalidate the requirement of s 12 of the 1952 Act to the effect that the adoptive parents must be of the same religion as the adoptive child - thus ruling out, by definition, adoption by the parties to a "mixed" marriage who, not being of the same religion as one another, could not both be of the same religion as any third person: the invalidated provision was replaced by s 4 of the Adoption Act 1974, which provided that:

> "An adoption order shall not be made in any case where the applicants, the child and his parents, or, if the child is illegitimate, his mother, are not all of the same religion, unless every person whose consent to the making of the order is required by s 14 of the 1952 Act or by s 2 of the Adoption Act 1964, knows the religion (if any) of each of the applicants when he gives his consent."

The third case was that of *The State (Nicolaou) v An Bord Uchtála*, the only case in which the principle of adoption itself was attacked as unconstitutional: it is dealt with below, in connection with illegitimacy of children and the rights of natural parents.[184]

Lastly, there was the case of *The State (M.) v Attorney General*,[185] in which both the unmarried parents wished their child to go to Nigeria to be brought up by the father's (Nigerian) parents, but were refused a passport for the child by the Minister who felt himself bound to respect the provisions of s 40 of the Adoption Act 1952. The relevant parts of this section read:

> (1) No person shall remove out of the State a child under seven years of age who is an Irish citizen or cause or permit such removal.
>
> (2) Sub-section (1) shall not apply to the removal of an illegitimate child under one year of age by or with the approval of the mother, or, if the mother is dead, of a relative for the purpose of residing with the mother or a relative outside the State.
>
> (3) Sub-section (1) shall not apply to the removal of a child (not being an illegitimate child under one year of age) by or with the approval of a parent, guardian or relative of the child.

As the Act defined "relative" in such a way as to exclude the family of the unmarried father, and as the child at the time in question was only seven months old, the course which the parents wished for the child was excluded by the terms of the section. Finlay P took the view that the child had a natural personal right (under Article 40.3) to travel outside the State, that the child was of an age when it could form no will of its own to exercise this right, but that its choice could be formed on its behalf by its legally recognised guardian - i.e. in this instance, the mother - "in the dominant interest of the welfare of the child"; he saw an "important and vital advantage" to the child's welfare in its being permitted, as quickly as possible, to enjoy a stable home life in Nigeria; and held the 1952 Act unconstitutional insofar as its effect was to prevent this:

[184] At pp. 1036-1037.
[185] [1979] IR 73.
[186] [1985] ILRM 61.

"I take the view that by reason of the absence in it of any discretion vested in a court or otherwise for exceptional cases which would permit the removal out of the State of an illegitimate child within the first year of its birth other than for the purpose of residing with its mother or a relative as defined, the provisions of this section are unconstitutional because they fail to defend and vindicate the personal right of the child to travel in the manner in which I have defined it."

Accordingly, saying his duty was to "set aside only so much of the section as is necessary to render it constitutional", he declared unconstitutional the whole of sub-s 2 and the words in parentheses in sub-s 3. The section as so pruned he thought would be:

"a sufficient vindication and protection by the State of the right of an illegitimate child to travel in the manner in which I have defined that as a constitutional right, and as such would be a constitutional section."

Adoption by widowers

In *O'G. v Attorney General*[186] a successful challenge was made to the constitutionality of s 5(1) of the Adoption Act 1974 which empowered the Adoption Board to grant an application by a widower for an adoption order provided that, *inter alia*, the widower already had, at the date of his application, another child in his custody. No such condition was imposed on widows and, after hearing expert evidence which showed that the sex of the parent did not affect the development of the emotional relationship between infant and parent, McMahon J said that he was:

"satisfied that [this condition] is founded on an idea of difference in capacity between men and women which has no foundation in fact and ... is therefore an unwarranted denial of human equality and repugnant to Article 40.1."[187]

Adoption of legitimate children

Clearly one of the most significant developments in adoption law in recent times has been the enactment of the Adoption Act 1988, extending the category of legitimate children who can be adopted.[188] This is striking evidence that, in certain limited cases, adoption can no longer be regarded as being exclusively a private family transaction but that it has also a public service, or welfare, dimension.[189] The central principle of this legislation is contained in s 3(1) which provides, in relevant part, that:

if... it is shown to the satisfaction of the [High] Court -

(I) that

(a) for a continuous period of not less than 12 months immediately preceding the time of the making of the application, the parents of the child ... for physical or moral reasons, have failed in their duty towards the child,

[187] See now s 10(1)(*c*) of the Adoption Act 1991 which permits applications by a widow or widower without drawing any distinction between the two.

[188] Prior to 1988, a legitimate child could be adopted only where s/he was legitimated by virtue of the Legitimacy Act 1931 but whose birth had not been re-registered under that Act - s 2 of the Adoption Act 1964. See below, p. 1032, Fn. 197.

[189] See *O'Halloran, op. cit.*, ch.1.

[190] [1989] IR 656; [1989] ILRM 266.

(b) it is likely that such failure will continue without interruption until the child attains the age of 18 years,

(c) such failure constitutes an abandonment on the part of the parents of all parental rights, whether under the Constitution or otherwise, with respect to the child, and

(d) by reason of such failure, the State, as guardian of the common good, should supply the place of the parents,

(II) that the child -

(a) at the time of the making of the application, is in custody of and has a home with the applicants, and

(b) for a continuous period of not less than 12 months immediately preceding that time, has been in the custody of and has had a home with the applicants, and

(III) that the adoption of the child by the applicants is an appropriate means by which to supply the place of the parents,

the Court may, if it so thinks fit and is satisfied, having had due regard for the rights, whether under the Constitution or otherwise, of the persons concerned (including the natural and imprescriptible rights of the child), that it would be in the best interests of the child to do so, make an order authorising the Board to make an adoption order in relation to the child in favour of the applicants.

Before this legislation was signed, its constitutionality was upheld by the Supreme Court in *In re Article 26 and the Adoption (No.2) Bill 1987*.[190] The major difficulty facing the Bill was the argument that it amounted to an attack on the inalienable and imprescriptible rights of the original family. The Court dismissed this argument, somewhat unconvincingly, saying:

> "The Court rejects the submission that the nature of the family as a unit group possessing inalienable and imprescriptible rights makes it constitutionally impermissible for a statute to restore to any member of an individual family constitutional rights of which he has been deprived by a method which disturbs or alters the constitution of that family if that method is necessary to achieve that purpose. The guarantees afforded to the institution of the family by the Constitution, with their consequent benefit to the children of a family, should not be construed so that upon the failure of that benefit it cannot be replaced where the circumstances demand it, by incorporation of the child into an alternative family."

While one might welcome this conclusion, it fails to deal adequately with the problem posed by the description of the rights of the family based on marriage as being "inalienable and imprescriptible"[191] except, perhaps, that there is a shadow of a suggestion that this description may apply only to the concept of the Family as a social institution, rather than to individual families.[192] Such a distinction, if it was intended by the Court, is

[191] In *G. v An Bord Uchtála* [1980] IR 32 Walsh J made an equally unconvincing attempt to tackle this problem by classifying these rights into those which are "absolutely inalienable" and those which are "relatively inalienable".

[192] See the analogous treatment of private property, below, pp. 1072-1073.

[193] According to the Court, the rights of a child who is a member of a family are not confined to those identi-

certainly novel and at variance with the existing jurisprudence on Articles 41 and 42, though it might be important in facilitating an expansion in the welfare role of the State necessitated by the disappearance, especially in larger urban areas, of traditional supports for the family unit.

Referring to Article 42.5, the Court held that that provision should not be construed as being confined to the parents' duty of providing education for their children and that the State could intervene to supply, not only the parental duty to educate, but also the duty to cater for the other personal rights of the child.[193] At the same time, children protected pursuant to Article 42.5 did not become the children of the State. In addition to its duty and right under Article 42.5 to intervene to protect a child whose parents have failed in their duty towards it, the State had a similar obligation to vindicate the personal rights of the child under Article 40.3. Before proceeding under either provision, the State was obliged to have due regard for the natural and imprescriptible rights of the child.

Turning to the provisions of the legislation under consideration, the Court pointed out that the matters detailed in sub-clauses I(A) to II(B) were essential proofs which must be separately established before the court could exercise its discretion to make an authorising order. Sub-clause I(A) required proof that, for not less than twelve months, the sole parent or each of the parents had, for physical or moral reasons, failed in their duty towards the child. Failure had to be total, and accordingly the Court indicated that a mere inadequacy of standard in the discharge of the parental duty would not satisfy this requirement. Furthermore, the failure had to be for physical or moral reasons, leading the Court to conclude that failure due to externally originating circumstances such as poverty would not constitute a failure within the meaning of the sub-clause. One should also note that, in a two parent family, the failure must be on the part of *both* parents, so that in the case of a family terrorised by a violent father, adoption of the children is not an option unless it can also be shown that the mother has failed in her duties. However the Court also said that the failure need not necessarily be blameworthy[194] and perhaps this would allow the State to intervene to protect children in a family where the will of one parent is so overborne by that of a dominant, violent partner that he or she does nothing to protect the children from physical or emotional abuse. By virtue of subclause I(B), unless there was excluded the likelihood that, before the child reaches the age of eighteen, the parent or parents or either of them could resume the discharge of their duties towards it, an authorising order could not be made. Sub-clause I(C) required that, in addition to proof of failure of parental duty, it must also be shown that the parents have abandoned their rights, indicating a special regard for the constitutionally protected parental rights. The comments of the Court on the concept of abandonment of rights in this context are not especially illuminating. According to the Court, abandonment could be established by evidence of the conduct of the parent or parents concerned which would in certain cases include statements made by them and/or the nature and type of the failure in duty which had been established. However failure of parental duty established under either of the preceding sub-clauses was not of itself evidence of abandonment; on the other hand, while a mere statement by the parents that they wished to abandon a child would not necessarily constitute proof of abandonment, it could do so in an appropriate case.[195] Sub-clause I(D) required the court to consider whether the

fied in Articles 41 and 42 but also include rights referred to in Articles 40, 43 and 44.

[194] *Byrne* and *Binchy* argue that this statement should be understood as referring to the behaviour of mentally ill or addicted parents - see *Annual Review of Irish Law 1988*, (Dublin, 1989) p.248.

[195] *Byrne* and *Binchy* argue that, in addition, abandonment can arise only where the parents wish to abandon their rights - *ibid.* p.250.

[196] See, in particular, *In re Doyle, an Infant; State (Doyle) v Minister for Education*, Supreme Court, 21

place of the parents is required to be supplied - the Supreme Court giving as an example of where this might not arise, the situation of a sixteen year old child of sufficient maturity - and, if so, whether it was appropriate for the State to supply their place. Penultimately, where all of the above matters had been established to the satisfaction of the court, it then had to consider whether adoption was an appropriate means to supply the place of the parents - sub-clause III. Finally, the court could make an authorising order if it was satisfied that such would be in the best interests of the child, having had due regard for the rights of the persons concerned, including the natural and imprescriptible rights of the child. According to the Supreme Court, the "persons concerned" mean all those who in the opinion of the High Court judge have an interest in or are likely to be affected by the application. Furthermore the best interests of the child are not to be ascertained on some simple material test but necessarily involve proper consideration of all the consequences, from the point of view of the child, of bringing it by adoption out of the family into which it was born and into an alternative family.

The Supreme Court's acceptance of the constitutionality of this legislation does mark a shift from some of its earlier, more restrictive rulings on the scope of Article 42.5.[196] At the same time, the scope for State intervention pursuant to the 1988 Act - which itself provides for adoption only - is extremely limited[197] and further judicial reinterpretation of Article 42.5 may be required in order to deal adequately with the growing problem of child abuse.

Adoption of foreign children

One of the striking features of contemporary social practice in relation to adoption is the increasing demand for the adoption of foreign children, due to the very significant decline in the number of adoptable Irish children.[198] The question of whether the child of alien parents could be adopted under the Adoption Acts was considered by the Supreme Court in *In re A.N.M., an infant, Eastern Health Board v An Bord Uchtála.*[199] In the High Court, Carroll J held that alien parents not within the jurisdiction had no duties under the Constitution and that there was no common good involved in the State supplying the place of alien parents. Accordingly she held that the Oireachtas did not intend, in the Adoption Acts, to take away the rights of alien parents. However this interpretation of the legislation was rejected by a unanimous Supreme Court. Delivering the lead judgment, Finlay CJ concluded that the Adoption Act 1988 was a significant step forward in the capacity of society to care and provide for children in need of care and protection and that it should not be construed as unavailable to any child within the jurisdiction who would otherwise qualify for adoption. In particular, he rejected exclusion based on nationality, citizenship or place of birth. Delivering a concurring judgment, O'Flaherty J referred to the constitutional dimension of the case, saying:

December 1955; O'Reilly and Redmond, *op.cit.* at p.632; [1989] ILRM 277.

197 When one considers that comparable safeguards do not exist in relation to s 2 of the Adoption Act 1964, permitting the adoption of a child legitimated by virtue of the Legitimacy Act 1931 but whose birth has not been re-registered under that Act, doubts must exist as to the validity of that section. See Staines, "*The Concept of 'The Family' under the Irish Constitution*" (1976) 11 Ir Jur (n.s.) 223; Shatter, *Family Law in Ireland* (3rd ed.), p.329.

198 This decline is, in turn, largely due to the introduction of the Unmarried Mother's Allowance (now Lone Parent's Allowance) in 1973. Thus Shatter records that in 1967, almost 97% of all non-marital children born in this country were adopted, whereas by 1985, the comparable figure was just under 17% - *op.cit.* p.1.

199 [1993] ILRM 577. The recognition of foreign adoption orders is now regulated by the Adoption Act 1991. In a case decided before the enactment of this legislation - *M.F. v An Bord Uchtála*, [1991] ILRM 399 - McKenzie J held that the Adoption Board had jurisdiction to recognise such adoption orders in accordance with the common law principle recognising such orders if they were valid according to the law of the foreign jurisdiction and if, at the time of the adoption, the adopter was domiciled in that jurisdiction.

200 He invoked Article 25 of the Universal Declaration of Human Rights, 1948, in support of this conclusion.

> "The reference to "parents" and "children" in Article 42, section 5 is not confined to citizens of this State. Indeed, it would be remarkable if this section could not be invoked to protect any child in the State who is left, in effect, parentless. The minimum requirements to satisfy this constitutional provision are that the child should have adequate shelter; food, clothing and care, including especially medical care as well as a basic education. These requirements which, in turn, constitute the rights of the child, whether to be provided by a parent or the State, are surely of universal application."[200]

In the instant case, where the child in question had been abandoned at birth and had lawfully entered the jurisdiction in the company of the adoptive parents, the Supreme Court gave a very strong signal that the High Court should grant an order pursuant to s 3 of the Adoption Act 1974, dispensing with the consent of the natural parents for adoption and enabling the Adoption Board to make an order for adoption if, as was very likely, that Board saw fit.

Consent to adoption

The Adoption Act 1974, provides by s 3 that where the mother of a non-marital child has agreed "to the placing of the child for adoption" but subsequently fails, neglects or refuses to consent to the making of an adoption order, or withdraws a consent already given, the applicant for the order can apply to the High Court for an order authorising the Board to dispense with her consent. This happened in *G. v An Bord Uchtála*,[201] where the mother had been influenced at first to seek the adoption of her child because she feared her own parents' reaction to the discovery that she had a baby; but then found that her parents' reaction was not hostile, but friendly. The Supreme Court held that, in deciding whether to dispense with a mother's consent in such cases, the High Court must have regard solely to what is in the "best interests of the child".[202] O'Higgins CJ said:

> "This will involve a consideration of the circumstances of the mother, her reasons for refusing or withdrawing her consent, and the prospects of how the child's future will be served by refusing the order sought."

On the question of the consent (which in this case the mother had given and then withdrawn) Walsh J said it:

> "must be such as to amount to a fully informed, free and willing surrender or abandonment of these rights...In my view a consent motivated by fear, stress or anxiety, or consent or conduct dictated by poverty or other deprivations cannot constitute a valid consent."

In *S v Eastern Health Board*[203] Finlay P held that agreements to place for adoption must have been made freely with full knowledge of their consequences, where neither the advice of persons engaged in the transaction nor the surrounding circumstances deprive the mother of the capacity to make a full informed, free decision. In *M. v M.*[204] Murphy J said he thought *G.*'s case was authority for the propositions (*inter alia*) that:

201 [1980] IR 32; (1979) 113 ILTR 25.
202 See also *E.F. v An Bord Uchtála*, High Court, 23 February 1993.
203 High Court, 28 February 1979. See *O'Connor*, (1981) 16 Ir Jur (n.s.) 275. See also *P.M. and G.M. v An Bord Uchtála*, High Court, 27 November 1984.
204 High Court, 2 December 1982.
205 High Court, 28 July 1981. See also *E.F. v An Bord Uchtála*, High Court, 23 February 1993.

> "the constitutional right of a parent (and *a fortiori* the legislative right) to custody of a legitimate or illegitimate child may be lost by surrender or abandonment of those rights;"

and that:

> "a surrender or abandonment of such rights may be established by conduct, but only where (as [Finlay P] pointed out in *S v Eastern Health Board*) "it is such as to warrant the clear and unambiguous inference that such was her fully informed, free and willing intention".

However, in *McC. v An Bord Uchtála*,[205] McWilliam J held that, once it could be said that such a consent had in fact been given, a change of mind on the mother's part thereafter would not undo its effect.

The question of "consent", though apparently authoritatively disposed of by these decisions, has proved difficult in practice. There are two elements in a valid consent - a) it must be fully informed and b) freely given.

For a consent to be fully informed, the natural mother must "be put in possession of all the information necessary to make the decision, helped to appreciate the consequences that will flow from it, and be given a full account of the alternatives available."[206] In particular, the mother must be advised of the possible effect of s 3 of the Adoption Act 1974. Thus, in *In re D.G., an infant, O'G. v An Bord Uchtála*[207] Finlay CJ said that:

> "a mother agreeing to place her child for adoption could not be said to reach a fully informed decision so to agree, unless at the time she made the agreement she was aware that the right which she undoubtedly has to withdraw that consent or to refuse to consent further to adoption, is subject to the possibility that, upon application by the prospective adopting parents, the court could conclude that it was in the best interests of the child to dispense with the mother's consent, and if following upon such a decision the board decided that it was appropriate to order the adoption of the child, she (the mother) could lose, forever, the custody of the child."[208]

Whether consent has been freely given may be difficult to determine in practice. According to Henchy J in *In re M.,M.(J) and M.(G.) v An Bord Uchtála*:[209]

> "this test must be applied in the light, not only of what happened on the occasion of the signing, but also in the context of the proximate relevant circumstances before and after the event."

[206] O'Halloran, *op. cit.*, p.71. See his useful discussion of this area at pp.71-73.
[207] [1991] 1 IR 491; [1991] ILRM 514. On the basis of this case, it would appear that it is not strictly necessary for the adoption society which is arranging the adoption to provide the necessary information and advice pursuant to s 39 of the Adoption Act 1952, provided the society is satisfied that such information and advice has been furnished to the mother by an appropriate person.
[208] *Byrne* and *Binchy* argue that it may be necessary to advise the mother, not only of the possibility that the court might dispense with her consent, but also of the actual likelihood of this occurring - *Annual Review of Irish Law 1990,* (Dublin, 1991) pp.290-1.
[209] [1987] IR 510; [1988] ILRM 203.
[210] [1983] ILRM 228. See also *R.C. and P.C. v An Bord Uchtála and St. Louise Adoption Society*, High Court, 8 February 1985.
[211] [1977] IR 287.

In *McF. v G.*[210] McWilliam J, citing *G.'s* case and *S v E.H.B.* to support the view that:

> "consent must be a free consent given in the full knowledge of the consequences which follow on the placing of the child for adoption, and is not valid if motivated by fear, stress or anxiety or dictated by poverty or other deprivations,"

added the very important practical qualification that:

> "if absolute rules as to fear, stress, anxiety or poverty were to be applied, there could hardly be a case found in which one or other of them would not be present, so that it could be argued that a consent was not valid...The fact that [the plaintiff here] might have made a different decision had she come from a differently orientated family, been wealthy or proposing to marry the father of the child does not seem to me to alter the position that, under the circumstances in which she found herself, she gave her consent freely and fully appreciating what she was doing."

Judicial review of adoption orders

Adoption orders can naturally be reviewed on the familiar criteria of vires, natural justice, *etc.*: see *M. v An Bord Uchtála*[211] (where the order was made without jurisdiction in the absence of a necessary precondition, *viz.* the Board's satisfying itself that the mother understood the nature of her consent), and also *The State (Attorney General) v An Bord Uchtála.*[212] By s 20 of the 1952 Act the Board may refer questions of law to the High Court for determination; two instances are *S W., Applicant,*[213] and *M.F. v An Bord Uchtála.*[214]

CONSTITUTIONAL POSITION OF NON-MARITAL CHILDREN AND NATURAL PARENTS

Rights of non-marital children

While the Supreme Court has held that legislative discrimination in favour of marital families is constitutionally permissible,[215] the view has also been expressed on a number of occasions that non-marital children have the same constitutional rights as children born in wedlock. Thus in *In re M., an Infant*[216] Gavan Duffy P said of a non-marital child the subject of a custody dispute that he regarded:

> "the innocent little girl as having the same "natural and imprescriptible rights" (under Article 42) as a child born in wedlock to religious and moral, intellectual, physical and social education."

[212] (1957) Ir Jur Rep 35.
[213] [1957] IR 178.
[214] [1991] ILRM 399.
[215] *O'B. v S* [1984] IR 316. See also the earlier case of *Wilson v Attorney General*, unreported, High Court, 29 May 1979, in which McWilliam J held that the common law rule denying succession rights to the blood relations of a deceased person who was himself born out of wedlock was not unconstitutional.
[216] [1946] IR 334; (1946) 80 ILTR 130.
[217] [1966] IR 567; (1968) 102 ILTR 1.

The same view was expressed by the Supreme Court in *Nicolaou's* case[217] and reiterated in *The State (G.) v An Bord Uchtála*.[218] The doctrine of the latter case was summarised by Murphy J in *M. v M.*[219] as authority for the proposition:

> "that the illegitimate child has an equal right with legitimate children to the constitutional protection of its personal rights to life, to be fed, to be protected, to be reared and educated."

Legislative discrimination against non-marital families is constitutionally permissible, but not mandated, and discrimination against non-marital children was abolished by the Status of Children Act 1987,[220] thus bringing our law into line with our obligations under the European Convention on Human Rights.[221]

Natural parents without rights under Articles 41-42

The position of the parents of non-marital children, and the question whether they have any rights under Articles 41 and 42, has arisen in a small number of cases. In *M., an Infants* case, mentioned above, Gavan Duffy P said that:

> "Under Irish law...I do not think that the constitutional guarantee for the family (Article 41 of the Constitution) avails the mother of an illegitimate child
>
> [However,] it is as true in Irish law as in English law that the claim of a father to his child normally prevails... And by analogy I think the Court should go a long way towards recognising the force of the natural claim of a mother to her child born out of wedlock, even though her legal right be less coercive."

The matter arose in acute form - because rights were asserted for a natural father as well as for a natural mother - in *The State (Nicolaou) v An Bord Uchtála*.[222] Here the natural father of a non-marital child which had been adopted on foot of an adoption order made by the Board was seeking to have the adoption order quashed, on the grounds, *inter alia*, that the Adoption Act 1952, under which the order was made, infringed his own natural right as the child's father by permitting its adoption without his consent, and that Article 42 was also infringed inasmuch as the Act violated that Article by "purporting to allow the natural mother to surrender a right which the Constitution declares to be inalienable", and "takes away one of the imprescriptible rights of an illegitimate child in that it allows him or her to be deprived of the society and support of a willing parent". (The argument based on the father's natural right is dealt with under the "personal rights" of Article 40.3.) So far as the argument involved a claim of parental right in the sense of Articles 41 and 42 for the applicant or for the natural mother, it was rejected.[223] In the High Court Henchy J said:

[218] [1980] IR 32. O'Higgins CJ referred to the old common law treatment of a non-marital child as "unchristian": under the Constitution, he said, the State had a duty to protect all natural rights of its citizens, and had endeavoured, in relation to non-marital children and some others, to discharge this obligation by the Adoption Acts.

[219] Unreported, High Court, 2 December 1982.

[220] As to which, see Byrne and Binchy, *Annual Review of Irish Law 1987*, (Dublin, 1988) pp.178-191.

[221] See *Johnston v Ireland* Series A, No.112, (1987) 9 EHRR 203.

[222] [1966] IR 567; (1968) 102 ILTR 1.

[223] *Cp.* Article 8 of the European Convention on Human Rights guaranteeing, *inter alia*, a right of respect for family life, which guarantee applies equally to marital and non-marital families - *Marckx v Belgium*, Series A, No.31, (1980) EHRR 330.

[224] The same judge subsequently expressed the view, in *G. v An Bord Uchtála* [1980] IR 32; (1979) 113 ILTR

"It is clear that the rights guaranteed to parents by Article 42.1 arise only in cases where the parents and the child are members of the same family; and the only family recognised by the Constitution is the family which Article 41.3.1 recognises as being founded on marriage. In my opinion the [applicant] is given no rights over his illegitimate child by Article 42.1."[224]

But mother has rights under Article 40.3

The Supreme Court, *per* Walsh J, said:

> For the same reason [i.e. the family of Articles 41-42 being that founded on marriage] the mother of an illegitimate child does not come within the ambit of Articles 41 and 42...Her natural right to the custody and care of her child, and such other natural personal rights as she may have (and this Court does not in this case find it necessary to pronounce upon the extent of such rights), fall to be protected under Article 40.3, and are not affected by Article 41 or Article 42...There is no provision in Article 40 which prohibits or restricts the surrender, abdication, or transfer of any of the rights guaranteed in that Article by the person entitled to them. The Court therefore rejects the submission that the [Act] is invalid in as much as it permits the mother of an illegitimate child to consent to the legal adoption of her child, and lose, under... s 24(b) of the Act all parental rights and be freed from all parental duties in respect of the child... It is the opinion of the Court that the parent referred to in Article 42.1 is a parent of a family founded upon marriage and this of itself disqualifies the appellant as a parent within the meaning of that term in Article 42.1...[225]

Similarly in *The State (M.) v Attorney General*[226] Finlay P said that the provisions of the Guardianship of Infants Act 1964:

> "do not appear to permit of the father of an illegitimate child being a plaintiff before the Court who is entitled to seek the directions of the Court with regard to the welfare of the child."

The Supreme Court returned to this matter in *In re S.W., an infant, K v W,*[227] in the process introducing an element of uncertainty into the law through a troublesome reference to rights arising from the blood link between father and child. Here the natural father had applied for guardianship and custody of his child pursuant to s 6A of the Guardianship of Infants Act 1964.[228] In the High Court, Barron J interpreted s 6A to mean that the applicant should be appointed guardian if he was a fit person to be so appointed and provided that there were no circumstances involving the welfare of the child which required that he should not be so appointed. On appeal, this approach was rejected by a majority of the Supreme Court. Delivering the majority judgment,[229] Finlay CJ said that Barron J's interpretation of s 6A was apparently inspired by a submission

25, that, as parents of non-marital children do not fall within the ambit of Article 42.1, neither do they have inalienable duties.

[2255] In *G. v An Bord Uchtála* [1980] IR 32, two members of the Supreme Court - Henchy and Kenny JJ - expressed the view that the natural mother had a legal, but not constitutional, right to custody. However the majority - O'Higgins CJ, Walsh and Parke JJ - considered that her right to custody was constitutionally protected, a view held by Finlay P in *S v Eastern Health Board*, High Court, 28 February 1979.

[226] [1979] IR 73.

[227] [1990] 2 IR 437.

[228] Inserted by s 12 of the Status of Children Act 1987.

[229] Walsh, Griffin and Hederman JJ concurring; McCarthy J dissented on the grounds that the test stated in the High Court was correct provided the trial judge made the welfare of the infant the paramount consideration.

[230] For criticism of this particular conclusion, see Byrne and Binchy, *Annual Review of Irish Law 1990*,

made on behalf of the applicant that he had a constitutional right, "or a natural right identified by the Constitution" to the guardianship of the child and that s 6A simply declared or acknowledged that right. He continued:

> "I am satisfied that this submission is not correct and that although there may be rights of interest or concern arising from the blood link between the father and the child, no constitutional right to guardianship in the father of the child exists. This conclusion does not, of course, in any way infringe on such considerations appropriate to the welfare of the child in different circumstances as may make it desirable for the child to enjoy the society, protection and guardianship of its father, even though its father and mother are not married.
>
> The extent and character of the rights which accrue arising from the relationship of a father to a child to whose mother he is not married must vary very greatly indeed, depending on the circumstances of each individual case.
>
> The range of variation would, I am satisfied, extend from the situation of the father of a child conceived as a result of a casual intercourse, where the rights might well be so minimal as practically to be non-existent, to the situation of a child born as the result of a stable and established relationship and nurtured at the commencement of his life by his father and mother in a situation bearing nearly all the characteristics of a constitutionally protected family, when the rights would be very extensive indeed."

In the light of this understanding of the father's rights, and as s 6A only conferred on the father the right to apply to be appointed guardian, as distinct from a right to be guardian, the majority concluded that where the father's application for appointment as guardian is linked to an application for custody, the court should only consider the wishes of the father where it has first concluded that the quality of welfare which would probably be achieved for the infant with the prospective adoptive parents is not to an important extent better than that which would probably be achieved by custody with the father. When the matter was referred back to him in the High Court, Barron J ruled that he was precluded by Article 40.1 from taking into account the socio-economic differences between the two competing homes[230] and that he must apply the Supreme Court's test in the light of the dangers to the psychological health of the infant occasioned by a change of custody. These dangers were such that he could not hold that the quality of welfare likely to be achieved with the prospective adoptive parents would not be to an important extent better than that likely to be achieved by custody with the applicant. Accordingly, he could not take account of the latter's wish to be involved in the guardianship of his child.

An unhappy feature of the Supreme Court decision in this case is that it fails to clarify the juridical nature of the natural father's rights in respect of his child. It is quite clear that the father has neither a constitutional nor a statutory right to guardianship.[231] However the majority acknowledge that there may be rights of interest or concern aris-

(Dublin, 1991) pp.320-322.

[231] Note that in *Johnston v Ireland*, the European Commission on Human Rights took the view that Article 8 of the Convention does not oblige the State to grant a right to custody to the natural father of a child born out of wedlock where the parents were free to marry but had chosen not to do so - Report of Commission, 5 March 1985.

[232] The reference to "blood link" in the majority judgment is perhaps unfortunate, as it suggests that rights

ing from the blood link between parent and child.[232] Could such rights warrant constitutional protection or is this a reference to statutory or common law rights only? In the instant case, the context in which both the Supreme and High Courts considered the father's rights was that of his statutory rights under the 1964 Act. Furthermore in *Nicolaou* the Supreme Court had rejected the view that the natural father had any constitutional rights under Article 41 or any right under Article 40.3 to the custody or society of his child and while this decision was not mentioned in the majority judgment in *K v W,* it is very unlikely that such silence implies disapproval. Even so, however, one cannot rule out the possibility that, in appropriate circumstances, a natural father might enjoy certain other constitutional rights in respect of his child. For example, could it not be argued that a natural father who has obtained custody by agreement and who has developed a stable, caring relationship with his child, has constitutional rights, coextensive with those enjoyed by married parents under Article 42, in respect of the education of that child?

The decision of the Supreme Court in *K v W* may not be the last word on this issue, for on 17 February 1993, the European Commission on Human Rights declared admissible a complaint by the plaintiff in that case that Ireland had failed to respect his family life under Article 8 of the Convention. The Commission held, unanimously, that there had been a breach of Article 8 because the child could be adopted without the natural father's knowledge or consent. Furthermore, the test applied by the Supreme Court as regards the weight to be placed on his right to guardianship - that his wishes should be considered only where a court has first concluded that the quality of welfare which would be achieved with the father - failed adequately to protect the father's relationship with his child as it posed a formidable, if not insuperable, obstacle to a successful application by the father where, as in the instant case, it would inevitably cause the child some psychological trauma to be moved from the adopters. The Commission also held that the fact that the father had no standing in the adoption procedure meant that there was a violation of Article 6(1).[233]

Right of natural parent with regard to child's upbringing after parent's death

Worth noting is the only case which seems an authority on the rights of an unmarried parent in regard to the upbringing of a child after the parent's death: *In re Connor*,[234] in which the Court of Appeal refused to allow the deceased mother's dying wish in regard to the religious upbringing of her non-marital daughter to prevail over the Court's view of what was in the interest of the child's welfare. O'Connor LJ in a strong dissent thought the wishes of the dead unmarried mother were as much entitled to respect as those of the dead father of a legitimate child.

could arise automatically on mere proof of paternity. However it is clear from the passage in the judgment quoted above that the nature of the social, as distinct from biological, relationship between father and child will have a crucial impact on the extent of the father's rights.

[233] In the context of this decision on admissibility, it is worth noting that in *Johnston v Ireland*, Series A No.112, (1987) 9 EHRR 203, the European Court of Human Rights listed the impossibility of a natural father to be appointed joint guardian of his non-marital child and his lack of parental rights in relation to her as some of the aspects of Irish law which led the Court to conclude that the child's right to respect for her family life under Article 8 had been violated. (The couple here wished to marry but were unable to do so because of the prohibition on divorce, the father having previously been married.)

[234] [1919] IR 361.

[235] The word "welfare" is defined in s 2, in terms taken straight from the Constitution, as comprising, in rela-

CUSTODY OF CHILDREN

Welfare of child paramount consideration

Disputes over the custody of children - whether as between parents and outsiders, or as between one parent and the other - have frequently had constitutional dimensions arising from Articles 41 and 42. Apart from these Articles, the main statutory regulation of this matter is s 3 of the Guardianship of Infants Act 1964:

> Where in any proceedings before any court the custody, guardianship or upbringing of an infant, or the administration of any property belonging to or held on trust for an infant, or the application of the income thereof, is in question, the court, in deciding that question, shall regard the welfare of the infant as the first and paramount consideration.[235]

This provision gives statutory force to a rule elaborated in many judicial decisions both before and after the enactment of the Constitution (or that of 1922).

The impact of the Constitution on custody disputes has not been without controversy. In particular, it has engendered a judicial approach which tends to emphasise the rights of the adults, on some occasions to the detriment of the rights of the child.[236] This is especially true of disputes between parents and outsiders or "strangers", for in relation to custody disputes *inter parentes*, the constitutional rights of the adults cancel each other out, as it were, leaving the court to resolve the matter of custody by reference to the statutory guidelines contained in the 1964 Act in particular, to the welfare of the child.[237]

Disputes between parents over children's custody and education.

The impact of the Constitution on custody disputes *inter parentes* was settled relatively early on in its history. Essentially, the old common law rule of paternal supremacy, whereby the wishes of the father determined the child's custody and education, was replaced by a constitutional policy of joint parental rights, which is now reflected in s 6(1) of the Guardianship of Infants Act 1964,[238] which provides that:

> "The father and mother of an infant shall be guardians of the infant jointly."[239]

tion to an infant, the religious and moral, intellectual, physical and social welfare of the infant.

[236] The *Report on the Kilkenny Incest Investigation* (pl.9812) observed that "the very high emphasis on the rights of the family in the Constitution may consciously or unconsciously (sic) be interpreted as giving a higher value to the rights of parents than to the rights of children" and went on to recommend the amendment of the Constitution to include a "specific and overt declaration of the rights of born children" - p.96. See also O'Reilly, "*Custody Disputes in the Irish Republic: the Uncertain Search for the Child's Welfare?*" (1977) 12 Ir Jur (n.s.) 37. For an insightful discussion of the philosophical, political and social justifications advanced in the Irish context for protecting parents' rights, and of the advantages and disadvantages which follow from the constitutional protection of such rights, see Duncan, "*The Constitutional Protection of Parental Rights*" in Eekelaar and Sarcevic, *Parenthood in Modern Society*, (1993), p.431.

[237] For detailed discussion on the law regulating custody disputes *inter parentes*, see Duncan and Scully, *op. cit.*, ch.14. Since publication of that book, the problem of international child abduction has been tackled, in the Irish context, by the enactment of the Child Abduction and Enforcement of Custody Orders Act 1991 which incorporates into Irish law both the Hague Convention on the Civil Aspects of International Child Abduction of 1980 and the Council of Europe Convention on Recognition and Enforcement of Decisions concerning Custody of Children and on Restoration of Custody of Children of 1980. This Act is discussed below, pp. 1050-1051

[238] In *B. v B.* [1975] IR 54, Ó Dálaigh CJ said that this was "no more than a reiteration of the principle enunciated in [Article 42.1]."

[239] Section 6(4) provides that the mother of a non-marital infant shall be its guardian; and s 2, the definitions section, provides that while "father" and "mother" include adoptive parents, "father" does not include the natural father of a non-marital infant.

[240] IR 5 Eq 98.

The old rule giving the father a permanent right to custody and to the direction of children's upbringing, which only very strong considerations could displace, was taken by the courts up to 1950 as being unaffected, in the eye of the law, by the ante-nuptial agreements as to the religion in which children were to be educated, very common in cases of "mixed" marriages; the father's right was absolute, and entitled him in law to disregard even the most solemn ante-nuptial undertaking. Old cases on this point are *In re Meades, Minors*[240] and *In re Story, Infants.*[241]

The continued validity of this rule in the context of the 1937 Constitution was assumed even as late as 1945 in *In re Frost, Infants*,[242] in which a Catholic mother failed to recover the custody of her children who had (originally with her consent, but contrary to an ante-nuptial agreement) been placed by their Protestant father, since deceased, in a Protestant institution. In the Supreme Court, Sullivan CJ considered that it was not necessary to consider the question whether the provisions of the Constitution affected what had been the established law as to the validity and effect of ante-nuptial agreements in respect of the religion of children, in view of the fact that subsequent to their marriage the parents agreed that their children should be educated in a different religion from that stated in the ante-nuptial agreement.

Five years later, however, in the controversial case of *In re Tilson, Infants*,[243] the issue of ante-nuptial agreements arose squarely when a Protestant father, having agreed before marriage, in writing, to the Catholic upbringing of such children as he and his Catholic wife should have, afterwards removed from the family home three of their four children and placed them in a Protestant institution. On the mother's habeas corpus application to recover them, Gavan Duffy P held that the old principle of paternal supremacy, incapable of binding itself by ante-nuptial agreement, could not live under the Constitution:

> "The plea implies that the paternal trust is more sacred in the eye of the law than a man's sacred ante-nuptial agreement...I have the temerity to prefer a principle of public policy that would imperatively require a man to keep faith with the mother whom he has induced to wed him by his categorical engagement to respect her convictions in the supernatural domain of her children's creed, at least when that promise is shown to have been of grave importance to her, as it must be to a Catholic. But, if the Constitution is found to have superseded the former judge-made law, saved in England by the rule of *stare decisis* when it became an anachronism with the decay of religion, the public policy of other days will have no significance for us.
>
> Articles 41 and 42, redolent as they are of the great papal encyclicals *in pari materia*, formulate first principles with conspicuous power and clarity...
>
> For religion, for marriage, for the family and the children, we have laid down our own foundations. Much of the resultant polity is both remote from British precedent and alien to the English way of life, and, when the powerful torch of transmarine legal authority is flashed across our path to show us the way we should go, that disconformity may point decisively another way...

[241] [1916] 2 IR 328; (1916) 50 ILTR 123.
[242] [1947] IR 3; (1948) 82 ILTR 24; followed in *In re Keenan, Infants* (1950) 84 ILTR 169.
[243] [1951] IR 1; (1952) 86 ILTR 49.
[244] [1954] IR 74; (1958) 92 ILTR 1.

> Quite apart from Canon Law, the doctrine of Articles 41, 42 and 44 of the Constitution appears to me to present the ante-nuptial agreement of the parties upon the creed to be imparted to their future children in a new setting and, subject to the welfare of the particular infants concerned, to invite recognition of the agreement in our courts as a compact that serves the social order in Ireland, because the agreement, far from conflicting in any way with those Articles, is consonant with their spirit and purpose and tends directly (1) to safeguard a marriage which cannot be dissolved; (2) to safeguard the harmony of the projected family; and (3) to safeguard the innate and imprescriptible right of the child to religious education, its most precious inheritance in the eyes of a Christian State. I apprehend that this Court is bound under the Constitution to cherish that inheritance of helpless citizens. Consequently, however wide the unfettered *patria potestas may* be, a judicial theory which, under cover of public policy, would freely allow a father to spoil his children's birthright by uprooting their creed at his pleasure in plain defiance of his gravest express obligations undertaken as husband and father, can find no place in a jurisprudence moulded to fit the Constitution of Ireland, whether the agreement be held to give them a moral claim before the Court or a legal right."

He made the order sought; and was upheld on appeal to the Supreme Court by a majority of four to one. The dissenting judge, Black J, said he thought the old rule "an archaic law and a relic of barbarism"; but had to ask himself whether the Constitution had put an end to it:

> "If it has, it is a great mercy. If it has not, then I have no power to prevent its baneful operation. The question is one of pure law."

He concluded, in fact, that Article 42 did not have the effect claimed for it by Gavan Duffy P But the other judges, speaking by Murnaghan J, thought otherwise:

> "In my opinion the true principle under our Constitution is this. The parents - father and mother - have a *joint* power and duty in respect of the religious education of their children. If they together make a decision and put it into practice it is not in the power of the father nor is it in the power of the mother to revoke such decision against the will of the other party. Such an exercise of their power may be made after marriage when the occasion arises; but an agreement made before marriage dealing with matters which will arise during the marriage and put into force after the marriage is equally effective and of as binding force in law."

He emphasised that this decision was based on Article 42 alone, and that the Court did not therefore need to consider submissions based on Articles 41 and 44.

Parents' agreement as to upbringing may be implied

The principle established in the *Tilson* case produced a corollary in 1957 in *In re May, Minors*,[244] in which a couple, both originally Catholic (so that no question of an ante-nuptial agreement had arisen), had had five children, who were being brought up as Catholics when the father joined the Witnesses of Jehovah and then tried to change his children's religious upbringing. The mother applied to have them made wards of court and herself appointed guardian. Davitt P granted the application and, in giving judgment on the central issue between the parents, said that, having regard to the history of this couple, including the Catholic upbringing of their children up to the time of the husband's conversion:

[245] See *In re J.H., an infant* [1985] IR 375; [1985] ILRM 302. In *M. v M.*, High Court, 2 December 1982,

"an agreement between the parents to have the children brought up and educated as Catholics must be implied. There is no other inference which can be reasonably drawn.

In accordance therefore with the provisions of Article 42.1...as interpreted in the *Tilson* case, neither parent has the right to depart in any way from the terms of such agreement. So long as Mrs. May objects, Mr. May has no right to attempt to teach the children, or to have them educated, otherwise than in strict accordance with such agreement; or adversely to influence, or in any way to interfere with, their religious beliefs."

The principles which emerged from the *Tilson* and *May* cases are reinforced by s 17(1) of the Guardianship of Infants Act 1964, which reads:

"Upon any application by a parent for the production or custody of an infant, if the court is of opinion that that parent ought not to have the custody of the infant, the court shall have power to make such order as it thinks fit to secure that the infant be brought up in the religion in which the parents, or a parent, have or has a legal right to require that the infant should be brought up."

Disputes between parents and strangers

While the judicial approach to custody disputes *inter parentes* was essentially adult-orientated, the equal constitutional rights of both parents neutralised the impact of the Constitution, permitting the application of the legislative policy of determining such disputes by taking the welfare of the child as the first and paramount consideration. However in custody disputes between parents and strangers, the rights of the adults are not equally weighted and the constitutional rights of the former have almost invariably trumped the interests of the stranger. Furthermore, the courts have developed a strong presumption that the rights and interests of the child are best served by giving custody to the parent.[245] Unfortunately this approach has, on a number of occasions, led to decisions which arguably did not best serve the welfare of the child.[246]

One of the earliest cases in which this emphasis on the rights of the parent is manifest is that of *In re O'Brien, an Infant*.[247] Here it was submitted that a father who, through long-term illness, had been unable to look after his child (the mother having died and the child being in the care of a grandparent) should fail in his application for the child's custody, now that he was restored in health and able to care for it, on the grounds (1) that the declaration of family rights in Article 41 would not avail a father who had been long absent, and (2) that the father had failed in his duty towards the child in the sense of Article 42.5 and of s 3 of the Custody of Children Act 1891. These contentions were rejected by the Supreme Court. O'Byrne J, with whom the four other judges agreed, said:

Murphy J formulated a similar presumption that the welfare of the child is best served by placing it with its natural mother.

[246] Articles 41 and 42 played no part in a number of post-1937 parent-stranger disputes, where as a result the courts were able to give some weight to the principle of the welfare of the child - see *The State (Williams) v Markey* [1940] IR 421; (1940) 74 ILTR 237; *In re Tamburrini* [1944] IR 508; *In re M., an Infant* [1946] IR 334, (1946) 80 ILTR 130; and *In re Cullinane, an Infant* [1954] IR 270.

[247] [1954] IR 1; (1953) 87 ILTR 156.

[248] Supreme Court, 22 June 1977. See *Duncan*, (1978) DULJ 67.

> "I cannot, and do not, accept the contention... that this declaration and guarantee is confined to the family as actually constituted when the Article is sought to be applied and that it does not embrace a member of the family who has been separated from the family home for some pressing and temporary necessity.
>
> [Article 42.1] seems to contemplate and require that the children should be members of the family and attached to the parental home. The sanctity of the family and the enduring existence of parental authority seem to me to be guaranteed by these provisions and I consider that I am entitled to say that the framers of the Constitution considered, and enacted, that the best interests and happiness of the child would be served by its being a member of the parental household. The Constitution, however, made provision in Article 42.5 for what it regarded as exceptional cases... but the appellant has failed to show that the father has failed in his duty to his child within the meaning of Article 42.5."

Constitutionality of Guardianship of Infants Act 1964

The judicial emphasis on the rights of the parents has occasionally led to suggestions that statutory provisions setting different priorities may be unconstitutional. In *O'Brien*, O'Byrne J said he was "assuming, but without deciding", that s 3 of the Custody of Children Act 1891 (in substance re-enacted by s 16 of the Guardianship of Infants Act 1964) was consistent with the Constitution. Section 16 of the 1964 Act provides that:

> Where a parent has
>
> (a) abandoned or deserted an infant, or
>
> (b) allowed an infant to be brought up by another person at that person's expense, or to be provided with assistance by a health authority under s 55 of the Health Act 1953, for such a length of time and under such circumstances as to satisfy the court that the parent was unmindful of his parental duties,
>
> the court shall not make an order for the delivery of the infant to the parent unless the parent has satisfied the court that he is a fit person to have the custody of the infant.

Presumably, any question-mark that hung over s 3 of the 1891 Act in the minds of the Supreme Court as to its consistency with the Constitution must also hang over s 16 of the 1964 Act. That something like a question-mark is in fact present in the mind of the Court on this matter is suggested by the case of *J v D.*,[248] in which a father, who had deserted his wife and children, sought after his wife's death to recover custody of them from the maternal aunts in whose homes they were being brought up; the Supreme Court refused his application, but O'Higgins CJ observed that no arguments had been offered to the Court on the "difficult problems" which could arise if the 1964 Act were said to conflict with Article 41. However, Kenny J said that the right of a parent to custody was a rule of prudence rather than an absolute rule; in his view, Article 41 had not changed the law as stated at the end of the last century by Holmes LJ in *O'Hara's* case.[249]

[249] [1900] 2 IR 232; (1900) 34 ILTR 17.
[250] [1966] IR 295.

Some years earlier, in *In re J, an Infant*,[250] the High Court had given custody of a child who had been born out of wedlock, but legitimated by its parents' subsequent marriage, to the parents as against a couple who were trying to adopt the child; Henchy J said he wished (as it did not arise in the case) to reserve the question whether the "welfare of the child" consideration of s 3 of the 1964 Act could override the constitutional right and duty of the parents to provide for its education.[251]

Judicial emphasis on rights of adults

The dangers in the adult-orientated approach of the Courts arguably became manifest in two decisions of the Supreme Court dealing with custody disputes arising from, respectively, defective and abortive adoption proceedings. In *M. v An Bord Uchtála*[252] a child had been placed for adoption when he was six weeks old. His natural parents subsequently married, one year after the adoption order had been made and two years after the initial placement. However, due to a defect in the process leading up to the making of the adoption order,[253] the Supreme Court held that the adoption order was itself invalid. Consequently the marriage of the boy's natural parents had the effect, under the Legitimacy Act 1931, of legitimising him as part of their family. Four years after the child had been placed with his adoptive parents, the natural parents commenced legal proceedings seeking his return and when the case came before the Supreme Court two years later, a majority ruled in favour of the plaintiffs. Thus the adult-orientated approach to custody disputes was pursued to the point where the majority was prepared to order that a child of six years of age be taken from the home in which he had grown up and handed over to total strangers simply because this second unit constituted a family for the purposes of the Constitution, enjoying inalienable and imprescriptible rights.[254]

The underlying assumption in *M* that the integrity of the marital family should be protected in all but the most exceptional of cases was reaffirmed by the Supreme Court in *In re J.H., an infant*.[255] Here a three week old child had been placed for adoption but before the adoption was finalised, the natural parents married and the mother withdrew her consent. Litigation ensued between the natural and putative adoptive parents over the child's custody and by the time this reached the Supreme Court, the child was two years old, having spent all this time with the putative adoptive parents. Nonetheless the Court ruled in favour of the natural parents. Delivering the leading judgment, Finlay CJ held that s 3 of the Guardianship of Infants Act 1964, must be construed as involving a constitutional presumption that the welfare of such a child is to be found within the family unless the court is satisfied that there are compelling reasons why this cannot be

[251] Another statutory provision which makes possible the withholding from a father of what would normally be his right is s 1(4) of the Punishment of Incest Act 1908, by which the Court is empowered, where a male person is convicted of incest with a female under twenty-one, "to divest the offender of all authority over such female, and, if the offender is the guardian of such female, to remove the offender from such guardianship, and in any such case to appoint another guardian or other guardians." The question whether this provision is consistent with the Constitution has not been litigated; but at first sight the situation envisaged would seem to be an example of the failure in parental duty for physical or moral reasons envisaged by Article 42.5 as permitting the State to supply the parent's place.

[252] [1977] IR 287.

[253] The Supreme Court held that the natural mother had not been properly advised of her right to withdraw her consent at any time prior to the making of the adoption order.

[254] A subsequent action commenced by the adoptive parents in which they sought to challenge the Supreme Court order on the ground that they had not been afforded an opportunity of being heard during the original proceedings was settled by the parties on terms which made the child a ward of court and permitted him to remain in the custody of the adoptive parents. See *The Irish Times*, 24 July and 7 October 1976.

[255] [1985] IR 375; [1985] ILRM 302. See *Duncan*, (1986) 8 DULJ (n.s.) 76.

[256] In his judgment, McCarthy J indicated that such compelling reasons must be "clearly established." In

achieved,[256] or the evidence establishes an exceptional case where the parents have, for moral or physical reasons, failed, and continue to fail, to provide education for the child.[257] Consequently the welfare of the child could not be the sole criterion for the determination by the court of the issue as to the custody of the child. While this judgment might appear to have broadened the grounds for defeating a claim for custody by parents - inasmuch as the Court held that, in addition to the grounds stipulated in Article 42.5, custody could also be refused for "compelling reasons" - the actual outcome reaffirms the adult-orientated approach of earlier cases. Thus, in his first judgment, Lynch J awarded custody to the putative adoptive parents because of the risk of long term psychological harm to the child from any change in custody, but when the Supreme Court referred the matter back to him for reconsideration in the light of the principles stated in its judgment, he awarded custody to the natural parents.[258] By implication, an appreciable but uncertain risk of long term psychological harm to the child would not appear to be a "compelling reason" for rebutting the presumption that the child's welfare is best served within the marital family.

Protecting the interests of the child

While the courts have generally resolved custody disputes between parents and strangers by focusing on the rights of the adults involved, it is submitted that such an approach is not necessarily mandated by the Constitution and that a more balanced approach which takes proper account of the rights of the child is open under the Constitution. In the first place, Article 42.5 provides that the State, acting as guardian of the common good, may supply the place of parents who, in exceptional cases, have failed in their duty towards their children for physical or moral reasons.[259] This provision was considered by the Supreme Court in *The State (Doyle) v Minister for Education*[260] in which the constitutional validity of s 10 of the Children Act 1941 was at issue. This section, amending s 58 of the Children Act 1908, provided that a child under fifteen years found destitute, and not an orphan, but whom its parents were unable to support, might by order of a district justice be sent to an industrial school for "such time as to the court may seem proper for the teaching and training of such child", though not beyond the age of sixteen. In this case the infant's mother had deserted the child, and at the father's request a district justice had used the section to send the child to an industrial school. Subsequently the father found himself in a better position to support the child and asked for her return, but was refused custody of her by the Minister for Education. On the father's application for habeas corpus, Ó Dálaigh J stated a case for the Supreme Court on the constitutional

Oxfordshire Co. Co. v J.H. and V.H., High Court, 19 May 1988, Costello J held that, in the light of evidence before him and of orders made by courts in England, there were compelling reasons for refusing to return two children to the custody of their parents. (The children had been made wards of court by an English court and placed in the custody of a local authority, but were subsequently taken, unlawfully, by their parents to Ireland). This decision was subsequently upheld by the Supreme Court, though no written judgment is available.

[257] Finlay CJ indicated that a finding that a parent was guilty of conduct which would disentitle him or her to custody, having regard to ss 14 and 16 of the Guardianship of Infants Act 1964, virtually amounted to a finding of an exceptional case where, for moral or physical reasons, the parent has failed in his or her duty to provide for the education of the child and in which the State could accordingly intervene.

[258] [1985] IR 397; [1986] ILRM 65.

[259] In *In re A.N.M., an infant, Eastern Health Board v An Bord Uchtála* [1993] ILRM 577, 8 March 1993, O'Flaherty J stated that the reference to "parents" and "children" in Article 42.5 was not confined to citizens of this State and that the minimum requirements necessary to satisfy the provision were that the child should have adequate shelter, food, clothing and care, including medical care as well as a basic education.

[260] [1956] IR 217 (High Court): Supreme Court 21 December 1955 and reproduced in *O'Reilly and Redmond, op.cit* at pp.632-635 and [1989] ILRM 277.

[261] [1989] IR 656; [1989] ILRM 266. See above, pp. 1030-1032.

validity of s 10, being himself of the opinion that it was invalid. The Supreme Court, speaking by Maguire CJ, agreed with this opinion. On the argument that this was one of the "exceptional cases" envisaged by Article 42.5, the Court said:

> "While it may well be that the provisions of s 10, insofar as they permit the State to supply the place of the parents because of lack of means, are protected by that sub-Article, it cannot be that the mere fact that parents are at a given time unable to support their child would entitle the parents to surrender, and the State to accept a surrender of the parents' rights, or would enable the parents by agreement with the State to rid themselves of the duty so plainly stated in Article 42.1. It seems that where such a surrender is sanctioned, it can only be for a period limited by the parents' inability to provide for the education of a child. It is submitted that once the detention of a child in an industrial school is permitted it may well be that its detention over a lengthy period is essential in order to enable it to be properly educated. In the view of this Court, however, sub-Article 5 does not enable the Legislature to take away the right of a parent who is in a position to do so to control the education of his child, where there is nothing culpable on the part of either parent or child."

This very restrictive reading of Article 42.5 must now be read in the light of *Re Article 26 and the Adoption (No.2) Bill 1987*[261] where the Supreme Court's interpretation of this constitutional provision differs from that in *Doyle* in at least two respects. First, in the later case, the Court accepted that Article 42.5 protected legislation which provided for a *permanent* surrender of the rights of the married parents, a proposition which was not accepted in *Doyle*. Second, in *Doyle* the Court interpreted Article 42.5 primarily in terms of how and to what extent it facilitated the surrender of the parents' duty to educate, whereas in the *Adoption (No.2) Bill* reference, the Court viewed Article 42.5 from the perspective of the State's duty to protect the personal rights of the child, the emphasis shifting from parent's duties to children's rights.

As we have already noted, the decision of the Supreme Court in *In re J.H., an infant*[262] indicates that Article 42.5 does not state exhaustively the grounds on which the State may intervene to provide for the welfare of a legitimate child and that such intervention may also be permitted where there are "compelling reasons" why the child's welfare cannot be achieved within the marital family. Furthermore in the *Adoption (No.2) Bill 1987* reference, the Court referred to the fact that the State had a duty, both under Article 42.5 and Article 40.3, to protect the rights of the child.[263] This duty falls as much on the judiciary as it does on the executive and legislature and thus it is submitted that, quite apart from the exceptional cases envisaged by Article 42.5, there is adequate constitutional justification for a judicial approach to custody disputes which gives priority to the rights and interests of the child. A striking example of such an approach may be seen in the case of *P.W. v A.W.*[264] in which Ellis J refused to grant custody of a young girl to her mother who was suffering from a psychiatric illness. Instead he confirmed an earlier High Court order giving custody to the child's aunt, who was supported in this by the father. Ellis J's decision was rooted in a child-centred approach to the issue. He said:

[262] [1985] IR 375; [1985] ILRM 302.

[263] A point re-iterated in *M.F. v Superintendent, Ballymun Garda Station* [1991] 1 IR 189; [1990] ILRM 767.

[264] High Court, 21 April 1980. See also *J. v D.*, Supreme Court, 22 June 1977, where one of the three Supreme Court judges, Kenny J, denied that "there is any natural or *prima facie* right of a parent to the custody of his children" and offered the view that Article 41 did not affect the principle of making the child's welfare paramount. The remaining judges, O'Higgins CJ and Parke J, decided this custody dispute between a father and two maternal aunts without reference to the custody. See *Duncan*, (1978) DULJ 67.

[265] Goldstein, Freud and Solnit argue persuasively that in custody disputes it is in society's best interests that

> "If, however, there is a conflict between the constitutional rights of a legitimate child and the prima facie constitutional right of its mother to its custody, I am of opinion that the infants' rights, which are to be determined by regard to what is required for its welfare, should prevail, even if its welfare is to be found in the custody of a 'stranger', if for good and justifiable reason...valid objection can be taken to the mother's inability to provide for her child's welfare, either emanating from the mother herself or for reasons connected with the child's welfare, and not necessarily confined to failure by the parents (here [the father]) of their duty towards their children for physical and moral reasons, whereby the parents', or as here the mother's, custody would or could not vindicate, protect or be compatible with the child's constitutional rights including its welfare...
>
> ...In my opinion, the inalienable and imprescriptible rights of the family under Article 41 of the Constitution attach to each member of the family including the children. Therefore in my view the only way the 'inalienable and imprescriptible' and 'natural and imprescriptible' rights of the child can be protected is by the Courts treating the welfare of the child as the paramount consideration in all disputes as to its custody, including disputes between a parent and a stranger. I take the view also that the child has the personal right to have its welfare regarded as the paramount consideration in any such dispute as to its custody under Article 40.3 and that this right of the infant can additionally arise from 'the Christian and democratic nature of the State'."

W. v W. predates the Supreme Court decision in *In re J.H., an infant* and clearly has to be read in the light of that later decision. However the principal value of Ellis J's decision in the present context is that it indicates how a more balanced approach to the complex area of custody disputes - an approach which pays greater emphasis on the rights of children and which is more protective of the important psychological relationships which the young child establishes with a caring adult[265] - can be achieved by rearguing the constitutional principles involved and without the necessity of a constitutional amendment.[266]

Power of State to take children into care

The legitimacy of the power of the State, acting through the regional Health Boards, to take children into care pursuant to s 24 of the Children's Act 1908, was conceded by counsel for the parents in *The State (M. C.) v Eastern Health Board*[267] but Barron J held that such a power was a "serious abridgement" of the rights of parents and consequently

the law should make the child's needs paramount and that this demands protection of the psychological - not the biological - parent-child relationship - *Beyond the Best Interests of the Child* (1973).

[266] Another example of the rights of children being used to counterbalance the rights of their parents occurs in *The State (D.C.) v Midland Health Board*, High Court, 31 July 1986, in which Keane J refused to grant an absolute order of habeas corpus to a child's parents because there was a possibility that the granting of such an order, before the District Court could adjudicate on the application for a fit person order in respect of the child under the Children's Act 1908, would affect the welfare of the child "whose natural and imprescriptible rights are also guaranteed by Article 42.5."

[267] High Court, 29 July 1986. See also the similar decision of Keane J in *The State (D.C.) v Midland Health Board*, High Court, 31 July 1986.

[268] A care order was recently refused in the case of a five-year old child who had been admitted to hospital on

must be exercised in such a way as to keep to a minimum the interval of time between the removal of the child from its parents and the determination of its future custody by the District Court.[268] He accepted that the Children's Act 1908, envisaged a procedure which was as expeditious as possible and held that it was not inconsistent with the Constitution.[269]

Parts III and IV of the Child Care Act 1991 contain new provisions, which have not yet been activated, detailing the State's power to take children into care. By virtue of s 12, where a Garda has reasonable grounds for believing that there is an immediate and serious risk to the health or safety of a child and that it would not be sufficient for the protection of the child from that risk to await the application for an emergency care order by a health board under s13, s/he may remove the child to safety, delivering it as soon as possible to the custody of the regional health board. If that health board does not return the child to its parents or to a person acting *in loco parentis*, it must seek an emergency care order from the District Court pursuant to s 13, which will be granted if the Court is of opinion that there is reasonable cause to believe that there is an immediate and serious risk to the health or welfare of the child which necessitates his being placed in the care of the health board or there is likely to be such a risk if the child is removed from the place where he is for the time being. The effect of such an order is to place the child under the care of the health board for a period of not more than eight days. If it is sought to keep the child in the custody of the health board for any longer period, an application must be made to the District Court for a care order pursuant to s 18 of the Act. Such an order will be granted if the court is satisfied that (a) the child has been or is being assaulted, ill-treated, neglected or seriously abused, or the child's health, development or welfare has been, is being or is likely to be, avoidably impaired or neglected and (b) that the child requires care or protection which he is unlikely to receive unless the court makes an order under the section. Section 24 provides that in any proceedings under the Act in relation to the care and protection of a child, the court, having regard to the rights and duties of the parents, whether under the Constitution or otherwise, shall (a) regard the welfare of the child as the first and paramount consideration and (b) in so far as is practicable, give due consideration, having regard to its age and understanding, to the wishes of the child. Where a care order has been made, the health board may place him/her in foster care or in residential care. The board may also make such other suitable arrangements as it thinks proper, including placement with a relative. If the child is eligible for adoption, the board may also place him/her with a suitable person with a view to adoption.

Procedures under this Act must conform to the rules of natural justice, so that the parents or their advisers would be entitled to have access to any evidence and reports which would be relied on by the health boards in applying for care orders,[270] though in pro-

several occasions for illnesses and accidents because no evidence was offered to show the parents did not offer proper guardianship. Accordingly the District Judge took the view that the application was inconsistent with the constitutional guarantees of the family - *The Irish Independent*, 3 July 1993.

[269] A challenge to the constitutionality of this power failed in *The State (D.) v Groarke and the Midland Health Board* [1988] IR 187 when Carroll J refused to entertain argument on the point because the prosecutors had failed to notify the Attorney General, pursuant to O 60 r 1 of the Superior Court Rules 1986, that their action involved a challenge to the constitutionality of this provision.

[270] See the Supreme Court decision in *The State (D.) v Groarke* [1990] 1 IR 305; [1990] ILRM 10,131 in relation to proceedings taken under the 1908 Act. Section 27(3) of the 1991 Act obliges the court to furnish any report sought by it on any question affecting the welfare of the child to each party to the proceedings.

[271] *The State (F.) v Superintendent Ballymun Garda Station* [1991] IR 189; [1990] ILRM 767.

ceedings taken under the Children's Act 1908, the Supreme Court did accept that natural justice did not always require that parents be informed of the identity and location of foster parents to whom the children have been entrusted.[271]

International child abduction

On a number of occasions, the Irish court have had to deal with cases in which children have been brought to this country either in defiance of a custody order made by a foreign court or where one parent is acting without the consent of the other. The general approach of the Irish courts has been to order the return of the child to the jurisdiction in which s/he ordinarily resides and, in those cases in which a foreign order as to custody exists, the doctrine of comity of the Courts has often been invoked.[272] In one case, however, *D.A.D. v P.J.D.*[273] Blayney J refused to make a peremptory order for the return of the child. Instead he took the view that the welfare of the child remained the paramount consideration in such cases and that, accordingly, there would have to be a full investigation of every aspect of the case before a final order could be made.[274] This decision, however, must now be read in the light of the Child Abduction and Enforcement of Custody Orders Act 1991.

This Act incorporates into Irish law both the Hague Convention on the Civil Aspects of International Child Abduction (1980) and the Council of Europe (Luxembourg) Convention on Recognition and Enforcement of Decisions concerning Custody of Children and on Restoration of Custody of Children (1980). Though they differ in certain respects,[275] both Conventions seek to ensure the speedy return of the abducted child to the country from which s/he was taken. However by virtue of Article 20 of the Hague Convention, the return of the child may be refused if it would not be permitted by the fundamental principles of the requested State relating to the protection of human rights and fundamental freedoms. Article 10(1)(a) of the Luxembourg Convention contains a similar provision, permitting the requested State to refuse to recognise and enforce a foreign custody order "if it is found that the effects of the decision are manifestly incompatible with the fundamental principles of the law relating to the family and children in the State addressed." In the Irish context, these provisions would appear to allow the High Court[276] to refuse to return the child where such return would infringe Articles 41 and 42 of the Constitution. In *J. v R.*[277] Finlay CJ, speaking for the Supreme Court, said that the word "manifestly" indicates a standard of proof, to be discharged by the person objecting to the return of the child, which is something more than the probability appropriate for ordinary proof in civil actions, though not as onerous as proving the matter as a certainty or beyond a reasonable doubt. The incompatibility would have to be estab-

[272] See, e.g. *Kent County Council v C.S* [1984] ILRM 292; *Sanders v Mid-Western Health Board*, Supreme Court, 23 June 1987; *Oxfordshire County Council v J.H. and VH.*, High Court, 19 May 1988.

[273] High Court, 7 February 1986. Though see the decision of Denham J in *C.K. v C.K.* [1993] ILRM 534, discussed below.

[274] In this case, however, the child had been resident in Ireland for a period of thirteen months and this may be a basis for distinguishing the case from other authorities, where the children would have been in the jurisdiction for much shorter periods of time.

[275] Most notably, the Luxembourg Convention applies only where the applicant spouse is seeking to enforce a foreign custody order whereas the Hague Convention applies even if no such foreign custody order exists, where one parent removes the children without the consent of the other parent.

[276] By virtue of ss 7 and 23 of the 1991 Act the High Court is given jurisdiction to hear and determine applications under both Conventions.

[277] Supreme Court, 17 February 1993.

[278] The phrase "manifestly incompatible" does not appear in Article 20 of the Hague Convention; nonetheless

lished as a matter of "high probability".[278] In the instant case, the Court concluded that no case had been made out that granting the (unmarried) father limited access to his child was something which was incompatible with the fundamental principles of the law relating to the family and children in Ireland, having regard to s 13 of the Status of Children Act 1987.

The effect of Article 20 of the Hague Convention has recently been considered on two occasions. In *C.K. v C.K.*[279] the defendant sought to oppose the return of his children to his wife, resident in Australia, on the ground, *inter alia*, that Article 20 and the Constitution required the High Court, before making an order under the 1991 Act to satisfy itself that the welfare of the children would be best served by ordering their return. However Denham J rejected the suggestion that the High Court must, in every case, inquire into the welfare of the child before making an order under the 1991 Act. According to the judge, any excessive delay or inquiry into the process by which children are returned to their habitual residence would only serve to defeat the objective of the legislation, which is to secure the speedy return of children who have been unlawfully removed from their habitual residence. If evidence had been adduced which established that the return of the children would result in a breach of any of their constitutional rights,[280] then no order for their return would be made. However no such evidence had been presented in the instant case and the Court could not assume that the Australian courts would not adequately inquire into the welfare of the children before making any custody order. Thus an inquiry into the welfare of the child is not an automatic part of the process provided for by the 1991 Act and, to that extent, it would seem that Blayney J's decision in *D.A.D. v P.J.D.* may no longer be good law.[281]

C.K. v C.K. was cited with approval by Keane J in *Wadda v Ireland*[282] in which the constitutionality of the 1991 Act was challenged on the grounds that, *inter alia*, it failed to respect various constitutional rights of the plaintiffs - a child and her Irish mother who was contesting the father's application to have the child returned to him in the UK pursuant to the 1991 Act. The judge dismissed the case on the ground, *inter alia*, that Article 20 of the Convention afforded adequate protection to the fundamental rights and freedoms set out in Articles 40 to 44 of the Constitution.

Age up to which child subject to parents' right of custody

The possible bearing of the Constitution on the age up to which a child is subject to his parent's right of custody irrespective of his own wishes was inconclusively canvassed by the Supreme Court in *The People (Attorney General) v Edge*,[283] a case in which a fourteen-and-a-half-year-old boy was taken from the boarding school, to which his

it would seem to be somewhat anomalous if a different standard of proof was to operate in cases taken under that Convention.

[279] [1993] ILRM 534.

[280] Throughout this part of her judgment, Denham J continually referred to a breach of the constitutional rights of the *children* as the basis for refusing to make an order under the 1991 Act. However it seems quite clear from the terms of Article 20 of the Hague Convention that an infringement of the rights and freedoms of the parent would also afford a defence to proceedings under this legislation.

[281] After Denham J had delivered her judgment, counsel for the father immediately applied to the Supreme Court for a stay on the order. However in an *ex tempore* judgment delivered the same day, the Supreme Court refused the application, Finlay CJ pointing out that a delay of at least five or six weeks would occur before any appeal could be heard. Bearing this in mind, and also the facts that the children had been unlawfully removed from Australia in the first place and that the father would have full access to the Australian courts dealing with the custody issue, the Court concluded that in the interests of justice and in the interest of the children, it should not grant a stay.

[282] High Court, 6 July 1993.

[283] [1943] IR 115; (1944) 78 ILTR 125.

[284] [1919] 1 IR 361.

father had sent him, by an (unrelated) adult friend with whom he was apparently willing to reside. On the one hand, O'Byrne J mentioned *In re Connor*[284] in which it had been held that at fourteen a boy had reached the discretion entitling him to select his own abode, and agreed with the Court of Criminal Appeal which had said:

> "If, as is urged, *In re Connor* lays down [such a rule] the result would indeed be startling in view of the provisions of Articles 41 and 42 of the Constitution."

Black J also said he doubted whether, if there were no law against taking by persuasion a boy of fourteen-and-a-half from his parents against their will:

> "the State can be said to have fulfilled its own express and solemn guarantee enshrined in Article 41.1.2 of our Constitution."

On the other hand, Gavan Duffy J pointed out that:

> "the constitutional status of the family is not yet buttressed upon any penal enactment, designed to safeguard a father's claim to the custody of his boy up to an age determined by the Oireachtas, nor have we here an indictment for an offence against the Constitution itself, if, merely to complete the argument, I may assume that some such charge would lie...I should be slow to hold that the old law is actually inconsistent with the Constitution; if the Oireachtas were to pass a...Bill recognising the common law age of discretion for boys and its legal consequences, I do not think it probable that the resultant statute would be held *ultra vires*...[Counsel for the Attorney General] suggested that the Constitution must be taken to embody the common law, as it stood here in 1937; but I find nothing in the text to support, and much to negative, this novel elucidation of our charter."

The Guardianship of Infants Act 1964, has not settled this matter, since, while an "infant" is a person under eighteen,[285] and while the Act speaks (s 14) of a parent's "right to custody", nevertheless by s 17(2):

> "Nothing in this Act shall interfere with or affect the power of the court to consult the wishes of the infant... or diminish the right which any infant now possesses to the exercise of his own free choice."

EDUCATION OF CHILDREN (INDEPENDENT OF CUSTODY QUESTION)

Potential for ideological conflict

The matter of education generally is addressed in Article 42 and in a number of the provisions of Article 44. The former Article clearly reflects Roman Catholic social teaching[286] inasmuch as it explicitly recognises, *inter alia*, the constitutional right and duty of parents to provide for the education of their children and the freedom to provide such education in private schools.[287] Section 4 of this Article further obliges the State to "endeavour to supplement and give reasonable aid to private and corporate educational

[285] Section 2 of the 1964 Act as amended by s 2 of the Age of Majority Act 1985.

[286] For a clear statement of this teaching in the context of education, see the memorandum by Eoin MacNeill, Minister for Education, 1922-25, published in (1979) 14 Ir Jur (n.s.) 378.

[287] While parents have a constitutional freedom to send their children to any school they wish, this does not mean that they may compel a particular school to enrol their children. This issue forms the backdrop to a recent case, *Carmody v Meehan, The Irish Times*, 15 September 1993, in which Morris J granted an interim injunction to a school manager preventing two families from leaving their children at a school where they had not been enrolled.

[288] Cp. Article 2 of Protocol No.1 to the European Convention on Human Rights which provides, *inter alia*,

initiative", while always having due regard to the rights of parents, especially in the matter of religious and moral formation.[288] It follows that parents are constitutionally free to send their children to denominational schools and, should they do so, the State may assist such educational initiative.[289] That provisions of this nature endorsed denominationally controlled education was accepted by the Supreme Court in *Crowley v Ireland*[290] where every member of the Court subscribed to the view that the existing arrangements for the management of primary education along denominational lines were constitutionally valid.[291] In contrast, the ideological ancestry of Article 44, which, *inter alia,* prohibits discrimination on denominational grounds in the provision of State assistance for schools, safeguards the rights of those children who do not wish to receive religious instruction at school and proscribes State endowment of religion generally, lies in nineteenth century liberalism. The potential conflict between these ideologies did not emerge for many years because of the dominant position of the Roman Catholic church in Irish society. However with the growing secularisation of Irish society, the first signs of actual conflict are beginning to emerge and litigation has been instituted challenging the public funding of school chaplains and the "integrated curriculum".[292]

Outsiders or State not entitled to influence or dictate mode of education

There have been a number of cases in which the rights of parents to educate their children as they see fit - including educating them in a particular religion - have been considered in settings where the custody of the children was not an issue either as between the parents and outsiders, or as between the parents *inter se.* This matter is equally within s 3 of the Guardianship of Infants Act since "education" must be a part of "upbringing" (to which the section applies), so that the welfare of the child is the paramount consideration, as of course it was in judicial practice long before the Act was passed.

that in the exercise of any functions which it assumes in relation to education and teaching, "the State shall respect the right of parents to ensure such education and teaching in conformity with their own religious and philosophical convictions." In *Kjeldsen, Madsen and Pedersen v Denmark* Series A, No.23, (1979) 1 EHRR 711 the European Court of Human Rights ruled that while this provision prohibited the State from pursuing an aim of indoctrination that might be considered as not respecting parents' religious and philosophical convictions, a programme of compulsory sex education did not amount to such indoctrination. Nor does this provision require the State to respect the parents' linguistic preferences - *Belgian Linguistic* case, Series A, No. 6, (1979) 1 EHRR 252. On the other hand, a parent's views on corporal punishment could amount to philosophical convictions for the purposes of the article - *Campbell and Cosans v UK,* Series A, No.48, (1982) 4 EHRR 293. For the view that the integrated curriculum - whereby religious values infuse the entire curriculum - may infringe this provision of the Convention, see Clarke, "*Freedom of Thought and Educational Rights in the European Convention*" (1987) 22 Ir Jur (n.s.) 28.

[289] In providing such assistance, however, the State may not make any distinction on the ground of religious profession, belief or status - Article 44.2.3.

[290] [1980] IR 102.

[291] In his book, *Church and State: Essays in Political Philosophy* (Cork, 1984), Professor Desmond Clarke has argued that a system in which religious schools have a monopoly on the provision of education is unconstitutional because it infringes the constitutional right of a child to freedom of conscience; because it frustrates the constitutional rights of non-believers who do not wish to avail of denominational schools; and because it offends against the principle of non-endowment of religion. It is submitted, however, that Clarke's first argument fails to take proper account of the constitutional role of parents in respect of the education of their children, especially their religious and moral formation. His second argument does not logically lead to an outright condemnation of denominational education, but rather requires State support for non-denominational schools on the same terms as is currently provided for denominational schools. Finally, given the terms of provisions such as Article 42.2, Article 42.4 and Article 44.4, it is extremely unlikely that the principle of non-endowment of religion completely proscribes State funding for denominational schools, though it may affect certain types of current expenditure, as to which, see below, pp. 1103-5. See Whyte, "*Education and the Constitution*" in Lane, ed. *Religion, Education and the Constitution* (Dublin 1992).

[292] For further discussion of this topic, see Article 44 below, pp. 1104-1105, 1113-1114. See also *Whyte, loc. cit.* and "*Education and the Constitution: Convergence of Paradigm and Praxis*" in Vol.25 Ir Jur (forthcoming)

[293] [1934] IR 311.

Examples of litigation in respect of education, the question of custody or religion not being involved, are *In re Westby, Minors (No.2)*[293] and *In re Kindersley*;[294] in those two cases no constitutional issue was raised, though it may be noted that in the former (decided in 1934) Murnaghan J gave his opinion in a form which foreshadowed Article 42:

> "I am of opinion that this Court should not on an assumption of national policy force children to be educated in a way which the parents do not approve."

There have been, in addition, four rather miscellaneous cases in which parents' rights in regard to education under Article 42 have been expressly considered. Two of these concerned the validity of testamentary dispositions made in connection with directions as to the religious upbringing of children other than the testators'. In the earlier of the two, *Burke and O'Reilly v Burke and Quail*,[295] the testatrix had left property on trust for a minor to whom she was not related, the income to be used for bringing him up a Catholic in Ireland, and the selection of a Catholic school to be in the absolute discretion of the trustees. On a construction summons Gavan Duffy P held that:

> "the will at this point would override the sacred parental authority and defy the parental right and duty of education under Article 42 of the Constitution. Consequently, this clause in the will, however well-meaning from the standpoint of an anxious benefactor, is inoperative and must be ignored."

Similarly in the later case, *In re Blake, deceased*,[296] a testator had bequeathed a legacy to trustees in trust for the education of his grandchildren, provided that they were brought up as Catholics. On a construction summons. Dixon J followed *Burke and O'Reilly v Burke and Quail*. He was referred to older English cases to the same effect, based there on public policy, and said, in regard to Article 42:

> "This Article puts the matter on a different and higher plane in this country, as the parental right and duty is declared and guaranteed by our fundamental law...It is clear that any attempt to restrict or fetter that right would be contrary to the solemnly declared policy and conceptions of the community as a whole and therefore such as the courts established under that Constitution could not and would not lend their aid to. The provision in the will that the children to benefit should have been brought up in the Roman Catholic faith is, therefore, void as against public policy and cannot be given effect to. It is hardly necessary to add that this principle applies and must be applied irrespective of the particular religion involved."

The parental rights in regard to purely scholastic, as distinct from religious, education were considered and defended by the Supreme Court in *In re Article 26 and the School Attendance Bill 1942*.[297] Section 4, the provision referred for scrutiny by the President, provided by sub-s 1 that a child between the ages of six and fourteen:

[294] [1944] IR 111; (1944) 78 ILTR 159.
[295] [1951] IR 216; (1950) 84 ILTR 70.
[296] [1955] IR 89.
[297] [1943] IR 334; (1943) 77 ILTR 96. On the background to this case, see Osborough, "*Education in the Irish Law and Constitution*" (1978) 13 Ir Jur (n.s.) 145.
[298] "Recognised school" was defined by s 2 as "a school for the benefit of which grants are...made from public

> "shall not be deemed for the purposes of this Act to be receiving suitable education in a manner other than by attending a national school, a suitable school, or a recognised school[298] unless such education and the manner in which such child is receiving it, have been certified...by the Minister [for Education] to be suitable."

The Court considered the State's powers under Article 42.3.2 - its right to require a "certain minimum education" - and said:

> "What is the meaning and extent of this provision? What is referred to as "a certain minimum education" has not been defined by the Constitution and accordingly, we are of opinion that the State, acting in its legislative capacity through the Oireachtas, has power to define it. It should, in our opinion, be defined in such a way as to effectuate the general provisions of the clause without contravening any of the other provisions of the Constitution. Subject to these restrictions, it seems to us that the State is free to Act so long as it does not require more than a "certain minimum education" which expression, in the opinion of this Court, indicates a minimum standard of elementary education of general application."

On this basis, the Court found the section repugnant in three respects. First, the Court thought that a Minister, even if acting on a reasonable construction of the section:

> "might require a higher standard of education than could properly be prescribed as a minimum standard under Article 42.3.2...We are further of opinion that the standard contemplated by the section might vary from child to child, and, accordingly, that it is not such a standard of general application as the Constitution contemplates."

Secondly, the Court thought it repugnant that parents might be exposed to penalties in respect of such period as might elapse between a child's sixth birthday and such time as the Minister gave a certificate that its education at home was suitable, since by s 4(1) the education was not "suitable" until it *had been* so certified. Thirdly, and perhaps the most important objection:

> "Under sub-s 1 not only the education, but also *the manner in which such child is receiving it* must be certified by the Minister. We do not consider that this is warranted by the Constitution. The State is entitled to require that children shall receive a certain minimum education. So long as parents supply this general standard of education we are of opinion that the manner in which it is being given and received is entirely a matter for the parents and is not a matter in respect of which the State under the Constitution is entitled to interfere."

This last point has been criticised on the ground that content and manner of education are not separable in the way suggested by the Court. Furthermore the point is well made that the subsequent development of the presumption of constitutionality would afford adequate protection for such a provision today.[299]

A further objection was raised to the Bill, but directed against s 3 (which was not the subject of the reference). The Court accordingly expressed no opinion on this objection, but still saw fit to recite it in its judgment. It was that:

moneys and which is recognised by the Minister as a school at which education suitable for children to whom the [School Attendance Act. 1926] applies is given". "Suitable school" was defined by s 1 of that Act as "a school for the time being certified by the Minister...to be a suitable school".

299 See *Osborough, loc. cit.*, p.173; *Casey, op. cit.*, p.527. However pending judicial reappraisal of this matter, the decision in the *School Attendance Bill* reference casts a shadow over proposals for legislative regulation of school managements contained in the Green Paper, *Education for a Changing World*, (Pl.8969, 1992).

300 It has been surmised - by the late Dr. Alfred O'Rahilly, *The Constitutional Position of Education in the*

> "One of the excuses under s 3 is that there is not a national school, a suitable school, or a recognised school accessible to the child which the child can attend and to which the parent of the child does not object on religious grounds to send the child. It is contended that the grounds of objection should not be restricted to religious grounds in view of the provisions of Article 42.3.1...that the State shall not oblige parents in violation of their *conscience and lawful preference* to send their children to the schools named therein."[300]

"Certain minimum education"

In the *School Attendance Bill* case, the Supreme Court's attempt at defining the "certain minimum education" which, under Article 42.3.2, the State could require children to receive, was not very helpful. Counsel opposing the Bill had suggested that the minimum must be "certain and precise"[301] and that it "must be such as can be provided by parents according to their means."[302] Both formulae were ignored by the Court which suggested instead that the phrase indicated "a minimum standard of elementary education of general application", a proposition which is scarcely enlightening. This question was tackled by John Kelly in a paper delivered in the late 1960s[303] in which he argued that, having regard to the terms of Article 42.3.2, the standard and content of the "certain minimum education" must be determined by reference to the actual conditions of society:

> "...[S]ince nothing but actual conditions can justify the State in prescribing compulsory education, the State is only justified in prescribing such minimum compulsory education as these conditions require...
>
> ...[T]he requirements of actual conditions are the only standard by which not merely the level, but also the *kind* of compulsory education can, in reason or in law, be determined. Just as actual conditions do not require, and the State would therefore have absolutely no right to enforce, university education for all, so too actual conditions do not require, and the State has consequently no right to enforce, the learning of subjects which cannot reasonably be thought to belong to a minimum moral, intellectual and social education."[304]

"Education" has a limited meaning

The meaning of "education" in the context of Article 42 was canvassed in *Ryan v Attorney General*,[305] when the plaintiff contended that the fluoridation of public water

Republic of Ireland (Cork U.P., 1952), p. 9 - that one of the purposes of the Bill was to enable the Minister to prevent parents from sending their children to schools in England.

[301] [1943] IR 334 at 337.

[302] *Ibid.*, p.338

[303] Published now as an appendix to Whyte, "*Education and the Constitution: Convergence of Paradigm and Praxis*" in Vol.25 Ir Jur (forthcoming).

[304] Arguing from this premise, he went on to raise doubts about the constitutionality of the policy of including Irish as a compulsory subject in the primary school curriculum, though to the extent to which he failed to take account of Article 8, there may be more to be said for that policy from a constitutional perspective than Kelly allowed. Note, in this context, *Groener v Minister for Education* [1990] ILRM 335, in which the Court of Justice held that national rules making appointment to a permanent full-time post as a lecturer in public vocational education institutions conditional upon proof of an adequate knowledge of Irish were permitted under Article 3 of Regulation 1612/68 on free movement of workers.

[305] [1965] IR 294. See also *Osborough, loc. cit.*, pp.169-171.

[306] One preferred by O'Hanlon J in *O'Donoghue v Minister for Health*, High Court, 27 May 1993.

[307] [1972] IR 241.

supplies violated that Article too, inasmuch as it interfered with parents' rights to educate (in the broadest sense of physically rearing and nurturing) their children as they saw fit. In the High Court Kenny J said:

> "The word "education" undoubtedly had this wide meaning at one time, but in 1937, when the Constitution was enacted, it had become obsolete. Moreover, it seems to me that the terms of the Article show that the word "education" was not used in this wide sense in the Constitution. Section 1 of the Article recognises the "right and duty of parents to provide, according to their means, for the religious and moral, intellectual, physical and social education of their children", but in s2 it is provided that the parents are free to provide *this* education in their homes or in schools recognised or established by the State. The education referred to in s 1 must, therefore, be one of a scholastic nature. It seems to me, therefore, that the fluoridation of the public water supply (even if it be harmful) does not interfere with or violate the rights given to the family and to the parents by Article 42 of the Constitution."

(He noted in passing - as being not relevant to any of the issues in the case - what he called "the puzzling contrast between the family and the parents in s 1 of Article 42".) The Supreme Court took a somewhat different view of "education",[306] as including training not necessarily "scholastic" in the ordinary sense, but agreed with him that Article 42 did not help the plaintiff:

> "[Counsel for the plaintiff] contends that the provision of suitable food and drink for children is physical education. In the Court's view this is nurture, not education. Education essentially is the teaching and training of a child to make the best possible use of his inherent and potential capacities, physical, mental and moral. To teach a child to minimise the dangers of dental caries by adequate brushing of his teeth is physical education for it induces him to use his own resources. To give him water of a nature calculated to minimise the danger of dental caries is in no way to educate him, physically or otherwise, for it does not develop his resources."

Right to free elementary education

The right to free elementary education declared by Article 42.4 was first judicially mentioned in the context of enforceability in *Byrne v Ireland*.[307] which was concerned with the question whether the State had inherited the sovereign immunity from suit formerly enjoyed by the Crown. Walsh J held that no such immunity had survived even for the benefit of Saorstát Éireann, not to speak of the post-1937 State; and he pointed to Article 10 of the 1922 Constitution which gave all citizens the right to free elementary education. He said:

> "In my view, that was clearly enforceable against Saorstát Éireann if no provision had been made to implement that Article of its Constitution."

The applicability of the same view to Article 42.4 of the present Constitution was established some years later in *Crowley v Ireland*,[308] a case which arose out of a dispute involving the Irish National Teachers Organisation and a school manager about the appointment of a principal teacher, and leading to the closure through strike action of three national schools in Drimoleague parish. Action was brought on behalf of five of the 180 children who were without schooling for many months, claiming a declaration that, *inter alia*, the Minister was in breach of his duty under Article 42.4 in permitting

[308] [1980] IR 102.

[309] A subsidiary point made on the children's behalf - that the free elementary education must be provided in

these children to remain in this situation; an injunction was ultimately obtained from the High Court (and affirmed by the Supreme Court) ordering the Minister to provide transport for these pupils to schools in other districts, and, from the moment that this was done, McMahon J held that the Minister was discharging his obligations under the Constitution,[309] but that up to that time he had been in breach of them.

This finding was however reversed by the Supreme Court (by a majority); Kenny J, with whom Henchy and Griffin JJ agreed, emphasised that the duty laid upon the State by Article 42.4 was not to "provide", but to "provide for" free primary education - a distinction which he thought was brought out by the Irish version. One significant implication of this distinction was that the Constitution endorsed the existing system of primary school management. Having regard to this distinction, and to the history of education in Ireland in the nineteenth century, Kenny J noted that:

> "the enormous power which the control of education gives was denied to the State; there was interposed between the State and the child the manager or the committee or board of management."

He found that, in the circumstances of the case (in which the Minister might, by taking direct action, have precipitated a general school strike and so made matters far worse) the Minister had not been shown to be at fault or to have caused a breach by the State of its constitutional duty.[310]

In the same action the plaintiffs sued members of the I.N.T.O. for having contrived to get teachers in adjoining schools to refuse to accept these children on their rolls during the dispute; this they had done, McMahon J held:

> "not primarily for the purpose of exercising a right to work or not to work, or to choose the conditions under which they would work...Their purpose was to deprive the Drimoleague children of primary education in order to exert pressure on the parish priest, the school manager; and what was done amounted to the use of unlawful means to deprive the Drimoleague children of their constitutional right. It is therefore actionable at the suit of the children, who can show that they have been deprived of their constitutional right by the action of the teachers."[311]

On this basis he reserved the question whether the children were entitled to damages (as he had heard no evidence directed towards this point). The I.N.T.O. defendants did not appeal against this decision on the issue of principle.[312]

More recently, the High Court has had to consider the effect of Article 42.4 in relation to the education of severely and profoundly mentally handicapped children. In *O'Donoghue v The Minister for Health*[313] the plaintiff, suing through his mother, was an

their own locality - he rejected: "I do not think the Constitution required that it should be given within the parish where the pupils live. If the plaintiffs' case were well founded, it would be constitutionally impossible to have an amalgamation of schools of several parishes."

[310] It was on this point that the minority dissented, O'Higgins CJ, with whom Parke J concurred, taking the view that, even prior to the introduction of the transport system in January 1978, the Minister had an obligation to try to help the children locally in Drimoleague itself.

[311] For consideration of this case in relation to the right to take industrial action, see above, pp. 783-785.

[312] In the Supreme Court, the plaintiffs' claim for damages against the I.N.T.O. for interference with constitutional rights was held to have been made out and this led to a number of subsequent cases against the union - see *Hayes v Ireland* [1987] ILRM 651; *Conway v I.N.T.O.* [1991] 2 IR 305; [1991] ILRM 497; *Hurley v I.N.T.O.*, Supreme Court, 14 February 1991; *Sheehan v I.N.T.O.* Supreme Court, 14 February 1991. See above, pp. 703-705.

[313] High Court, 27 May 1993.

[314]Pl. 1969.

eight year old mentally handicapped boy who sued the Ministers for Health and Education on the ground that, in failing to provide free primary education for him, they had deprived him of his rights under Article 42. In acceding to the claim, O'Hanlon J demonstrated a readiness to review the respondents' decision as to what constituted an appropriate level of primary education for the plaintiff and, perhaps more significantly, as to the level of resources required to discharge the State's obligations under Article 42.4. The respondents had argued that arrangements made to place the plaintiff in a pilot scheme for the education of children suffering from severe mental and physical handicap satisfied any claim arising under the Constitution. However this was rejected by the judge who said that he was far from convinced that these arrangements could be regarded as meeting the specific obligation imposed on the State by Article 42.4 to provide for free primary education for the plaintiff. On the evidence, the provision of free primary education for children severely or profoundly handicapped mentally and/or physically required a much greater deployment of resources than was thought appropriate even as recently as 1983 when the Report of a Working Party on *The Education and Training of Severely and Profoundly Mentally Handicapped Children in Ireland*[314] was completed. He said that to ask a single teacher to undertake the primary education of 12 severely or profoundly handicapped children far exceeded the workload deemed appropriate for a teacher in the ordinary primary school where pupils did not suffer from mental or physical handicap. Furthermore, if primary education was to meet the special needs of such children, a new approach was required and the teaching process should, as far as practicable, be continuous throughout the year. Accordingly he granted a declaration that the respondents had deprived the plaintiff of his rights under Article 42 and he also gave the plaintiff's mother liberty to apply to the court in future should the State fail to respond by taking whatever action was appropriate to vindicate her son's constitutional rights.

O'Hanlon J's approach contrasts with that of the Supreme Court in *Crowley* which was much more deferential towards Departmental decisions, though of course it could be argued that in the latter case, the stakes were much higher as the Department of Education feared a complete breakdown in the provision of primary education if it had intervened in the industrial dispute in Drimoleague. His approach also contrasts with that of Costello J who, in a different context, disclaimed any function, as a judge, to adjudicate on the fairness or otherwise of the manner in which other organs of State had administered public resources.[315] The case is currently under appeal.

Constitutional position of teachers

The Constitution makes no explicit reference to the constitutional position of teachers. Commenting extra-judicially on the teaching of religion in schools, Walsh J suggested that some accommodation must be made for the teacher who has a conscientious objection to teaching a particular religion but noted that:

> "it is doubtful if any teacher can be permitted to refuse to teach [religion] simply because he or she does not believe it, as distinct from having a conscientious objection to teaching it."[316]

In *Flynn v Power*[317] Costello J held that a teacher could be lawfully dismissed by a denominational school if her lifestyle was openly in conflict with the values which the

[315] *O'Reilly v Limerick Corporation* [1989] ILRM 181. See above, pp. 44-46.
[316] "*The Constitution and Constitutional Rights*" in Litton, ed. *The Constitution of Ireland 1937-1987*, (Dublin, 1988), p.100.
[317] [1985] ILRM 336.
[318] *Cityview Press Ltd. v An Chomhairle Oiliúna* [1980] IR 381, discussed above, pp. 107-108.

school sought to promote. However there was no discussion of any constitutional dimension to this case.

Prohibition of school attendance

A unique but eminently reasonable provision authorises a State official to prevent (presumably only temporarily) a child from receiving education: s 48 of the Health Act 1947 (as amended by s 37 of the Health Act 1953) empowers a medical officer of health to prohibit the attendance of a verminous child at school. A parent permitting the prohibition to be disobeyed may be fined £5.

Need for legislation

Educational policy in Ireland is characterised by a dearth of legislation - particularly in regard to primary education and comprehensive and community schools - and a consequent reliance on administrative circulars emanating from the Department of Education. This practice may very well infringe Article 15.2.1, which has been interpreted by the Supreme Court to mean that the Oireachtas may only delegate parliamentary power for the purpose of implementing principles and policies previously adopted by the Oireachtas itself.[318]

More specifically, it is also arguable that, having regard to the terms of Article 44.2.4, State aid for schools can be provided for only by way of legislation.[319]

In this context it should be noted that a Green Paper on Education, *Education for a Changing World,*[320] was published in 1992 and that a White Paper outlining a statutory framework for education is expected to appear in 1994.

[319] See below, p. 1114.
[320] Pl. 8969.

Article 43

PRIVATE PROPERTY

Private Property

Article 43

1. **1° The State acknowledges that man, in virtue of his rational being, has the natural right, antecedent to positive law, to the private ownership of external goods.**

2° The State accordingly guarantees to pass no law attempting to abolish the right of private ownership or the general right to transfer, bequeath, and inherit property.

2. **1° The State recognises, however, that the exercise of the rights mentioned in the foregoing provisions of this Article ought, in civil society, to be regulated by the principles of social justice.**

2° The State, accordingly, may as occasion requires delimit by law the exercise of the said rights with a view to reconciling their exercise with the exigencies of the common good.

Maoin Phíobháideach

Airteagal 43

1. **1° Admhaíonn an Stát, toisc bua an réasúin a bheith ag an duine, go bhfuil sé de cheart nádúrtha aige maoin shaolta a bheith aige dá chuid féin go príobháideach, ceart is ársa ná reacht daonna.**

2° Uime sin, ráthaíonn an Stát gan aon dlí a achtú d'iarraidh an ceart sin, ná gnáthcheart an duine chun maoin a shannadh agus a thiomnú agus a ghlacadh ina hoidhreacht, a chur ar ceal.

2. **1° Ach admhaíonn an Stát gur cuí, sa chomhdhaonnacht shibhialta, oibriú na gceart atá luaite sna forálacha sin romhainn den Airteagal seo a rialú de réir bunrialacha an chirt chomhdhaonnaigh.**

2° Uime sin, tig leis an Stát, de réir mar a bheas riachtanach, teorainn a chur le hoibriú na gceart réamhráite d'fhonn an t-oibriú sin agus leas an phobail a thabhairt dá chéile.

Article an innovation

The Constitution of 1922 contained nothing corresponding either to the law or to the philosophy of this Article.[1] Until the early 1980's it played a relatively small part in constitutional jurisprudence, no doubt because of the substantial qualifications which it attaches to private rights in favour of the common good.[2] Moreover, the interpretation of the Article has been embarrassed by uncertainty as to its standing *vis-à-vis* the concurrent guarantee of Article 40.3, which commits the State:

> "by its laws [to] protect as best it may from unjust attack and, in the case of injustice done, [to] vindicate the... property rights of every citizen."

A striking feature of the jurisprudence in this area is the apparent inability of the courts to clarify the relationship between this provision and Article 43. As we shall see presently, the older cases looked to Article 43 as the principal guarantee of specific items of property. Then, for a brief period during the 1980s, that provision was relegated to the role of protecting the *institution* of private property, while Article 40.3 protected the rights of the individual to particular items of property. More recently, however, this dis-

[1] The inspiration of Article 43 is generally supposed to be the encyclical *Quadragesimo Anno* of Pope Pius XI (1931).

[2] K.C. Wheare said that in this respect it compared with the Constitution of the former Yugoslavia - *Modern Constitutions*, (2nd ed., 1966), p.43.

tinction appears to have broken down and complaints about interference with specific property rights are again being considered by the courts in the light of the provisions of Article 43.

In addition to this uncertainty about the proper relationship between Article 43 and Article 40.3, there is also a lack of consistency on the part of the courts to the question of the role of compensation in the constitutional regime guaranteeing private property. These issues will be addressed presently, but initially we will consider the scope of the constitutional guarantee of private property.

Scope of the guarantee: definition of property

Most obviously of all, the constitutional guarantee applies to land and to rights arising from land ownership.[3] It also applies to moveable property[4] and money.[5] Intangible rights are also protected[6] - Article 43.1.2 itself refers to a "general right to transfer, bequeath and inherit property", while the guarantee has been invoked in relation to intangible rights created by legislation,[7] such as licences,[8] and by contract.[9]

In *Kerry Co-Operative Creameries Ltd. v An Bord Bainne*[10] Costello J had occasion to consider the relationship between one important type of contractual interest, namely shareholding in a company or in an industrial and provident society,[11] and the constitutional guarantee of property. The plaintiffs complained of changes in the rules of the defendant organisation which, they alleged, amounted, *inter alia*, to an expropriation of their property. In particular it was claimed that the power of expulsion conferred on the defendant organisation permitted it to repay to the expelled member only the amount which such member had paid up on its shares; as a consequence the expelled member was deprived of the "substantial assets constituted by its ownership of the shares and in

[3] See, e.g. *Central Dublin Development Association v Attorney General* (1975) 109 ILTR 69, involving restrictions on the use of land in the interests of proper planning; *O' Callaghan v Commissioner for Public Works* [1985] ILRM 364, concerning restrictions on land user in the interest of preserving the national heritage, and *Whelan v Cork Corporation* [1991] ILRM 19, concerning statutory abolition of restrictive covenants.

[4] E.g. *Attorney General v Southern Industrial Trust* (1960) 94 ILTR 161, concerning forfeiture of a car.

[5] *Buckley v Attorney General* [1950] IR 67; *Clancy v Ireland* [1988] IR 326; [1989] ILRM 670.

[6] Though in *Tuohy v Courtney*, High Court, 3 September 1992, the Attorney General argued that Article 43, and by association, the reference to property rights in Article 40.3.2, envisaged tangible or corporeal property only. Lynch J did not feel it necessary to decide this point.

[7] *Shanley v Commissioner of Public Works in Ireland* [1992] 2 IR 477, proceeds on the assumption that a statutory right to renewal of a tenancy is a property right for the purposes of the Constitution. In the instant case, however, Carroll J held that the plaintiff, who leased premises from the State, was not covered by the Landlord and Tenant Act 1931 and accordingly never acquired a statutory right to renewal of his tenancy.

[8] E.g. *Hempenstall v Minister for Environment*, [1993] ILRM 318, concerning taxi licences. In *Hand v Dublin Corporation*, [1991] 1 IR 409, the Supreme Court was prepared to assume, though without deciding, that the constitutional right to earn a livelihood, was a property right. The context here was a provision in the Casual Trading Act 1980 disqualifying the plaintiffs from holding casual trading licences.

[9] See, e.g. *Chestvale Properties Ltd. v Glackin* [1992] ILRM 221, where Murphy J accepted, *obiter*, that mutual contractual obligations between the applicants and their bankers and solicitors respectively constituted property for the purposes of the constitutional guarantee. See also *Cox v Ireland* [1992] 2 IR 503, the Supreme Court referred to the right to a pension, gratuity or emolument already earned and to the advantages of a subsisting contract of employment as property rights protected by the Constitution. See also *McCormack*, (1982) 17 Ir Jur (n.s.) 340.

[10] [1990] ILRM 664; the decision of the Supreme Court on appeal is reported at [1991] ILRM 851.

[11] Though the organisations in the instant case were of the latter variety, Costello J took the view that, as far as the rights of shareholders were concerned, basic principles of company law were equally applicable. A similar view was taken by McCarthy J in the Supreme Court though O'Flaherty J left open the possibility that the plaintiffs' arguments might have been more appropriately addressed to the Court if it had been dealing with a limited liability company.

particular of its just and rightful share in the accumulated value of the first-named defendant." In the same way, it was argued that new rules for the allocation of bonus shares would diminish the plaintiffs' percentage share of the defendant's overall shareholding, thereby reducing the plaintiffs' share in the accumulated value of the defendant. Finally it was contended that the funding of bonus shares from profits of the defendant's foreign subsidiaries, and the proposed manner of allocation of such shares which was disadvantageous to the plaintiffs, deprived the latter of their rightful share of the income derived by the defendant from assets acquired by past contributions made by the plaintiffs. Thus the underlying premise for the constitutional claim grounded on property rights was that, in addition to having a contractual right as shareholders to be repaid the amount they subscribed for their shares and to share in the distribution of any surplus assets in the event of the board being wound-up, their status as shareholders also entitled the plaintiffs to a share in the net value of the board's underlying assets and those of its subsidiaries. This premise was rejected by Costello J who pointed out that the assets acquired by a company are in the legal ownership of the company and that no shareholder has a legal right to any specific portion of the company's assets. He cited the following passage from the judgment of Kenny J in *Attorney General v Jameson*[12] as an accurate description of the rights of a shareholder in relation to the assets of the company:

> "The assets of the company, its premises, stock in trade, etc. are all capable of being disposed of without limitation or fetter of any sort. No shareholder has a right to any specific portion of the company's property, and save by, and to the extent of, his voting power at a general meeting of the company, cannot curtail the free and proper disposition of it. He is entitled to a share of the company's capital and profits, the former...being measured by a sum of money which is taken as the standard for the ascertainment of his share of the profits. If the company disposes of its assets, or if the latter be realised in a liquidation, he has a right to a proportion of the amount received after the discharge of the company's debts and liabilities. In acquiring these rights - that is, in becoming a member of the company - he is deemed to have simultaneously entered into a contract under seal to conform to the regulations contained in the articles of association...There is no interest in the land, legal or equitable, vested in the defendants by reason of their testator's membership in their company. His property in the company was represented by contractual rights that created no such interest."

Costello J continued:

> "These same principles apply in relation to the rights of a shareholder in a registered society. The shareholder has rights which can properly be regarded as property rights (*Private Motorists' Provident Society Ltd. v Moore* [1984] ILRM 88) but their nature and extent are to be ascertained by reference to the contract it has entered into with the society whose terms are contained in the society's rules."

The judge found in particular that there is no implied term in that contract that the fractional interest held by the shareholder in the company's issued share capital would remain constant and would not be altered by the issuing of additional shares. As the plaintiffs did not have property rights such as they alleged, it followed that no question of an infringement of the constitutional guarantee of private property arose. This analysis was subsequently accepted by the Supreme Court, McCarthy J commenting that he found it "wholly convincing".[13]

[12] [1904] 2 IR 644.
[13] [1991] ILRM 851, at 862.

This view of the nature of a shareholding surfaced more recently in *O'Neill v Ryan*,[14] when the Supreme Court rejected the proposition that a shareholder may bring a personal action in respect of the reduction in value of his shareholding resulting from damage to the company against the party who caused such damage. This is because the shares are merely a right of participation in the company on the terms of the articles of association and while the monetary value of the shares can be reduced as a result of loss suffered by the company, the right of participation remains unaffected.[15]

The logical implication of this position would seem to be that, absent an attempt directly to expropriate an individual's shareholdings, legislative or other interference with a company's business which affects the market price of the shares can never offend against the guarantee of private property, because, on the one hand, the shareholders' contractual interest - in the sense of participation rights - is unaffected while, on the other, a body corporate may not be able to invoke Article 40.3 of the Constitution.[16] However, that proposition was implicitly rejected - at least as far as legislative interference is concerned - in the earlier Supreme Court decisions in *Private Motorists Provident Society v Attorney General*[17] and *Pine Valley Developments Ltd. v Minister for the Environment*[18] where the shareholders were considered to have property rights protected by Article 40.3 against unjust legislative attack.[19] The authorities are not, therefore, readily reconcilable and we may not have heard the last word on this issue.

The constitutional guarantee may also apply to intangible rights created other than by way of legislation or contract.[20] An issue yet to be resolved in this context is whether the guarantee applies to a cause of action. The Supreme Court initially took the view - in *O'Brien v Keogh*[21] and *O'Brien v Manufacturing Engineering Co. Ltd.*[22] - that the guarantee did apply to a cause of action but later cast doubt on this proposition in *Moynihan v Greensmyth.*[23] However this issue may be somewhat academic because, if not covered by the constitutional guarantee of private property, the right to sue would certainly be protected as an unenumerated personal right under Article 40.3, where similar limitations to those tolerated in relation to property rights apply.

[14] [1993] ILRM 557.

[15] The Court adopted this analysis from the Court of Appeal decision in *Prudential Assurance Company Ltd. v Newman Industries Ltd.* [1982] 1 Ch 204.

[16] See *Chestvale Properties Ltd. v Glackin* [1992] ILRM 221. See above, p. 786.

[17] [1983] IR 339; [1984] ILRM 88

[18] [1987] IR 23; [1987] ILRM 747.

[19] In neither case did the Court have to consider whether the shareholders could rely on the constitutional guarantee of private property as against the company or other shareholders.

[20] In *Falcon Travel Ltd. v Owners Abroad Group plc* [1991] 1 IR 175, Murphy J accepted, albeit without adverting to the Constitution, that a reputation was a property right in the context of an action for passing off. *Cp.* the decision of the European Court of Human Rights in *Van Marle*, Series A, No.101, (1986) 8 EHRR 483, to the effect that the goodwill of an accountancy practice was a "possession" within the meaning of Article 1 of Protocol No.1 to the European Convention on Human Rights.

[21] [1972] IR 144.

[22] [1973] IR 334.

[23] [1977] IR 55. In *Brady v Donegal County Council* [1989] ILRM 282, Costello J proceeded on the assumption that a right to challenge, by way of legal proceedings, the validity of the defendant's decision on a planning matter was a property right, the Attorney General having failed to contest that view. The Attorney General did subsequently challenge this assumption in the Supreme Court but the issue was not resolved there as the Court held that certain issues of fact still had to be determined before the constitutional issues could be reached. The conflicting views on this point were also canvassed in *Tuohy v Courtney*, High Court, 3 September 1992, but at the end of the day, Lynch J did not find it necessary to decide the issue.

Inapplicable to property of bodies corporate

Before leaving this discussion of the scope of the constitutional guarantee of private property, it is worth noting that, on a number of occasions, the courts have taken the view that it may be invoked only by humans.[24] Accordingly, in cases involving property held by companies, individual shareholders are invariably joined as plaintiffs.

We turn now to consider the development, since 1937, of judicial attitudes to the constitutional guarantee of private property.

Evolution of judicial attitudes to the guarantee of private property - "days of laissez faire at an end"

Article 43 was first invoked against two Acts of the Oireachtas of Saorstát Éireann, the Pigs and Bacon Acts 1935 and 1937. In *Pigs Marketing Board v Donnelly (Dublin) Ltd.*[25] the plaintiffs sought to recover from the defendants sums of money due to them under both these Acts by virtue of the price-controlling mechanism they contained; the defendants pleaded, *inter alia*, that the Acts were inconsistent with Article 43. Hanna J in the High Court dealt first with the argument that the Acts were not for the "peace, order, and good government of the State" as envisaged for all legislation by Article 12 of the old Constitution, and baulked at being asked to interpret this phrase so as to render it a useful standard for judicial review: there was "no rule of law to guide the Court"; it was "a question entirely of practical political science", a "kind of political shibboleth, the meaning and application of which has changed and will continue to change from one generation to another". He then went on:

> "These remarks apply with more force to the submission that the laws passed must be consistent with social justice, assuming that the use of that phrase in Article 43 is to apply to legislation. I cannot define that phrase as a matter of law. It cannot be the old standard of the greatest good of the greatest number, for, at the present day, it may be considered proper that the claim of a minority be made paramount on some topic. As to the meaning of social justice, opinions will differ even more acutely than on the question of "good government". I cannot conceive social justice as being a constant quality, either with individuals or in different States. What is social justice in one State may be the negation of what is considered social justice in another State. In a court of law it seems to me to be a nebulous phrase, involving no question of law for the courts, but questions of ethics, morals, economics, and sociology, which are, in my opinion, beyond the determination of a court of law, but which may be, in their various aspects, within the consideration of the Oireachtas, as representing the people, when framing the law."

The judge, however, unbent somewhat from this fairly negative posture later in his judgment. Emphasising the "axiom" that an Act of the Oireachtas must be presumed constitutional[26] unless clearly established to be otherwise, he said it had been:

> "frankly argued on behalf of the defendants that any law passed by the State which interferes with the free operation of competition in trade or interferes with the contractual or proprietorial rights of citizens, is unconstitutional. In my opinion it is too

[24] See Carroll J in the High Court in *Private Motorists' Provident Society v Attorney General* [1983] IR 339; (in the subsequent appeal, the Supreme Court concluded that it was not necessary to decide this issue in the instant case) Costello J in *Kerry Co-Operative Creameries Ltd. v An Bord Bainne* [1990] ILRM 664; Murphy J in *Chestvale Properties Ltd. v Glackin* [1992] ILRM 221.

[25] [1939] IR 413.

[26] The first statement of this presumption, which has become established (see above, p. 450 *et seq*).

late in the day to have that view accepted. The days of laissez faire are at an end, and this is recognised in paragraph 2 of clause 2, which enacts that the State can "as occasion requires delimit by law the exercise of the said right with a view to reconciling their exercise with the exigencies of the common good". I am of opinion that the Oireachtas must be the judge of whatever limitation is to be enacted. This law does not abolish private ownership in pigs or bacon, it only delimits the exercise of these rights by the persons in whom they are vested, and if the law is contrary to the common good, whatever that may mean, it must be clearly proved...I have gone through our own statutes from the year 1932, and I find almost fifty statutes that seem to me to delimit the exercise of the rights of private property and of contract, not to mention the Land Acts. Accordingly, in my view, this point is also unsustainable."

This perspective of the relationship of the Legislature to private property was shared in 1945 by Gavan Duffy J in *Fisher v Irish Land Commission*,[27] a case involving primarily the question of the frontier between administrative and judicial functions. On the issue whether persons such as the Land Commission could constitutionally make determinations affecting the plaintiff's property rights, the judge said:

"[The question] is whether our Legislature is competent to make the expropriation of private property in land depend in the main on the opinion as to public policy of a non-judicial organ of government...To dub [the process of expropriation] "justiciable" because it may result in the suppression of a private right is to ignore the paramount importance of the fact that the expropriatory measure has been deliberately ascribed by the Legislature to the politico-economic sphere. The Constitution in Article 43.2 subjects private ownership to the claims of social justice, but it does not assign public policy specially to the judiciary. Therefore the power here conferred, not being peculiarly and distinctively judicial, is a power which the Oireachtas is competent to vest wherever it thinks proper."

The Supreme Court affirmed Gavan Duffy J (in a judgment delivered the day before its judgment in *Buckley v Attorney General*). Maguire CJ said:

"It is not contested that the Legislature has the power to expropriate owners so as to make land available for public purposes."

It will be noted that the point of grievance in *Fisher's* case arose out of the Land Act 1939, part of the very code that Hanna J had mentioned as something taken for granted as permissible under the Constitution, even though expropriatory in its operation, in his judgment in the *Pigs Marketing Board* case. For Gavan Duffy J the days of laissez faire were, evidently, equally at an end.

Conflicting judicial trends visible in 1947-57

However, two years later, although in a very special case, the Supreme Court repelled a legislative encroachment in the property field with a very strong reading of Article 43. This case, *Buckley and Others (Sinn Féin) v Attorney General*[28] (usually called simply the *Sinn Féin Funds* case) arose from an Act of the Oireachtas, the Sinn Féin Funds Act 1947. This Act was passed with the object of stopping litigation about entitlement to the remnants of a fund collected by the old, pre-Civil War Sinn Féin organisation (of which only an insignificant rump remained in existence under the old name), and diverting the money to a board which was to administer it in a charitable manner judged appropriate

[27] [1948] IR 3; (1948) 82 ILTR 50.
[28] [1950] IR 67.

to the nature of the original organisation. By s 10 of the Act, on the application *ex parte* of the Attorney General, the High Court was to dismiss, without costs, the action which had already begun, and was to pay out the sums lodged in Court in a manner prescribed by the Act. When the Attorney General made this application it was refused with some high words by Gavan Duffy P (as he had become since *Fisher's* case); his refusal was however based on the Act's being an invasion of the judicial sphere, not on its expropriatory character or on Article 43. But when the Attorney General appealed to the Supreme Court, the decision of Gavan Duffy P was affirmed not only on this ground, but also on the ground that the Act breached constitutional property rights. O'Byrne J said:

> "We do not feel called upon to enter upon an inquiry as to the foundation of natural rights or as to their nature and extent. They have been the subject-matter of philosophical discussion for many centuries. It is sufficient for us to say that this State, by its Constitution, acknowledges that the right to private property is such a right and that this right is antecedent to all positive law. This, in our opinion, means that man by virtue, and as an attribute, of his human personality is so entitled to such a right that no positive law is competent to deprive him of it and we are of opinion that the entire Article is informed by, and should be construed in the light of, this fundamental conception. Consistently with, and as an adjunct to, this recognition, the Constitution proclaims (1) that in a civil society, such as ours, the exercise of such rights should be regulated by principles of social justice, and (2) that, for this purpose, the State may pass laws delimiting the exercise of such rights so as to reconcile their exercise with the requirements of the common good.
>
> It was contended by counsel for the Attorney General that the intendment and effect of Article 43.1.2 was merely to prevent the total abolition of private property in the State and that, consistently with that clause, it is quite competent for the Oireachtas to take away the property rights of any individual citizen or citizens. We are unable to accept that proposition. It seems to us that the Article was intended to enshrine and protect the property rights of the individual citizen of the State and that the rights of the individual *are* thereby protected, subject to the right of the State, as declared in clause 2, to regulate the exercise of such rights in accordance with the principles of social justice and to delimit the exercise of such rights so as to reconcile the exercise with the exigencies of the common good.
>
> In particular cases this may give rise to great difficulties. It is claimed that the question of the exigencies of the common good is peculiarly a matter for the Legislature and that the decision of the Legislature on such a question is absolute and not subject to, or capable of, being reviewed by the courts. We are unable to give our assent to this far-reaching proposition. If it were intended to remove this matter entirely from the cognisance of the courts, we are of opinion that it would have been done in express terms as it was done in Article 45 with reference to the directive principles of social policy, which are inserted for the guidance of the Oireachtas, and are expressly removed from the cognisance of the courts.
>
> ... In the present case there is no suggestion that any conflict had arisen or was likely to arise,[29] between the exercise by the plaintiffs of their rights of property in the trust moneys and the exigencies of the common good, and, in our opinion, it is only

[29] But such a case could plausibly have been made. The known object of the Act was to prevent a modest fund of about £21,000 from being largely dissipated in litigation, which is what ultimately happened. The action as tried is reported as *Buckley v Attorney General and Power (No. 2)* (1950) 84 ILTR 9; the judgment of Kingsmill Moore J is interesting.

the existence of such a conflict and an attempt by the Legislature to reconcile such conflicting claims that could justify the enactment of the statute under review.

In the opinion of this Court, the Sinn Féin Funds Act 1947, is repugnant to the solemn declarations as to the rights to private property contained in Article 43...and, accordingly, we are of opinion that it was not within the power of the Oireachtas to pass such an Act."

This decision, undoubtedly a very powerful statement of the right of private property, received some implicit toning-down - though hardly enough to be called a modification - four years later in *Foley v Irish Land Commission,*[30] where one of the issues was whether the power given to the Land Commission by s 2 of the Land Act 1946, to resume possession of a holding previously allotted was an infraction of Article 43. This time the Court - again speaking by O'Byrne J - upheld the legislation under challenge:

"The argument put before this Court on behalf of the appellant, when reduced to its logical conclusion, seems to involve the proposition that any limitation placed by the Oireachtas on private property, which may result in the loss of that property by the owner, is repugnant to the Constitution and, accordingly, void. If this argument be sound, the Constitution has certainly placed serious fetters upon the Legislature in dealing with property rights and the Court is not prepared to accept such a far-reaching proposition.

The Land Purchase Acts, of which the Act of 1946 forms part, constitute a very important branch of our social legislation. As has been pointed out in this Court,[31] the object of these Acts is to create a peasant proprietorship of a certain standard...

Bearing in mind the general object of the Land Purchase Acts and the manner in which these Acts are financed we are of opinion that the imposition of the condition as to residence, with the statutory sanction for failure to comply therewith, is not an abolition of the right of private ownership within the meaning of Article 43.1.2... and we are further of opinion that this limitation of the rights of the appellant is sanctioned by clause 2.2 of the said Article as a delimitation of his rights, as allotted, with a view to reconciling their exercise with the exigencies of the common good and in accordance with the principles of social justice."

This judgment is of course in perfect harmony with the *Sinn Féin Funds* judgment, and reinforces it implicitly, as against the *Pig Marketing Board* case, in refusing to concede sole discretion to the Oireachtas in the field of property; but it will be noted that its emphasis is in the opposite direction, even to the use of the same turn of speech ("the Court is not prepared to accept such a far-reaching proposition"). In the earlier case the Court overruled the Oireachtas as it could find no "conflict" which required "reconciliation" *via* an interference with individual property rights; in the latter case, the social purpose of the Land Acts[32] was enough to justify the fairly radical mechanisms they contained, which served the "exigencies of the common good" even though at the individual's expense.[33]

[30] [1952] IR 118; (1952) 86 ILTR 44.

[31] In *Fisher v Irish Land Commission* the previous day: [1948] IR 3, at p.26.

[32] Compare the words of Dixon J in the High Court: "The nature and character of this work has often been described in terms which leave no doubt of its social and public import."

[33] In *McGee v Attorney General* [1974] IR 284; (1975) 109 ILTR 29, Walsh J expressly approved what O'Byrne J had said in the *Sinn Féin Funds* case about the non-exclusive discretion of the Oireachtas on the "common good".

Article 40.3 enters the scene

In 1957 the case of *Attorney General v Southern Industrial Trust*[34] led to the first recognition of the concurrence of Article 40.3.2 and Article 43. The case arose from the forfeiture of a car, the property of the first-named defendants (a hire-purchase company), which had been the subject of an offence, under the Customs (Temporary Provisions) Act 1945, committed by the second defendant. The company contended that the relevant provisions were invalid in that the forfeiture (which affected only them, although they were quite innocent of any offence) breached their rights under Article 43. In the High Court Davitt P considered the character of the customs enactment and its claim to be regarded as a "delimitation" of property rights in the interest of the common good: he noted the deterrent effect of the forfeiture penalty; the importance to the economy of effective customs laws; and observed that if forfeiture were to be excluded where the smuggled goods actually belonged to an innocent party, the effectiveness of the law would be much diminished. Whether this reasoning would prevail today in the light of modern conceptions of due process of law, fair procedures, etc., may be doubted; but at least the judge came to close grips with the policy of the Act (which the Supreme Court did not) and also stated his view of the relation of the two constitutional provisions in terms which were not accepted by the Supreme Court of the day but which found favour with another Supreme Court a quarter of a century later:

> "There is a clear distinction to be drawn between (1) the general and natural right of man to own property; (2) the right of the individual to the property which he does own; and (3) his right to make what use he likes of that property; and I think this distinction is to be observed in these Articles. Article 40.3 seems to me to be the only provision in the Constitution which protects the individual's rights to the property which he does own. By it the State guarantees to respect this right and by its laws, as far as practicable, to defend it and as best it may to protect it from unjust attack, and where injustice has been done to vindicate it. This is no absolute guarantee but is qualified in more than one respect. It *impliedly* guarantees that the State itself will not by its laws *unjustly* attack the right; and I think that the justice or otherwise of any legislative interference with the right has to be considered in relation, *inter alia*, to the proclaimed objects with which the Constitution was enacted, including the promotion of the common good."

The Supreme Court judgment in this case did not repeat the analysis undertaken by Davitt, J, but merely said that "the property rights guaranteed are to be found in Article 43 and not elsewhere and the rights guaranteed by Article 40 are those stated in Article 43". The substance of the Court's decision was simply that the delimitation of private property rights, and the assessment of what the common good required, were "matters primarily for the consideration of the Oireachtas", and even a divesting of individual items of property - something which the State had for many years claimed the right to do[35] - did not infringe Article 43.

The whole tone and effect of the *Southern Industrial Trust* case did not seem easily reconciled with the Supreme Court's strong words in the *Sinn Féin Funds* case; and for the following twelve years it was not possible to state clearly what exactly the property guarantees of the Constitution amounted to. In 1969, in *East Donegal Co-Operative v Attorney General*,[36] O'Keeffe P in the High Court took much the same line as to the pri-

[34] (1960) 94 ILTR 161.
[35] Lavery J, speaking for the Court cited ten such statutes (mostly of pre-1922 origin), saying these examples were by no means exhaustive.
[36] [1970] IR 317.

mary discretion of the Oireachtas in delimiting property rights as had been taken in the *Southern Industrial Trust* case. But in the same year a start was made towards rationalising the position by Kenny J. In *Central Dublin Development Association v Attorney General*,[37] the plaintiffs attacked powers given to planning authorities by the Local Government (Planning and Development) Act 1963, as infringements of both Article 40.3.2 and Article 43. Kenny J declared the two earlier cases mutually contradictory; but he also unearthed the judgment of Davitt P in the *Southern Industrial Trust* case and approved his analysis of the relationship between the two provisions guaranteeing property rights. He said that an analysis of the text of the Constitution and of the decisions on it lead to these conclusions:

> "(1) The right of private property is a personal right;
>
> (2) In virtue of his rational being, man has a natural right to individual or private ownership of worldly wealth;
>
> (3) This constitutional right consists of a bundle of rights most of which are founded in contract;
>
> (4) The State cannot pass any law which abolishes all the bundle of rights which we call ownership or the general right to transfer, bequeath and inherit property;
>
> (5) The exercise of these rights ought to be regulated by the principles of social justice and the State accordingly may by law restrict their exercise with a view to reconciling this with the demands of the common good;
>
> (6) The courts have jurisdiction to inquire whether the restriction is in accordance with the principles of social justice and whether the legislation is necessary to reconcile this exercise with the demands of the common good;
>
> (7) If any of the rights which together constitute our conception of ownership are abolished or restricted (as distinct from the abolition of all the rights), the absence of compensation for this restriction or abolition will make the Act which does this invalid if it is an unjust attack on the property rights."

"Unjust attack" on personal rights of property

Against the background of this analysis Kenny J considered the plaintiffs' arguments against, firstly, the power of a planning authority to make a development plan. He said:

> "I do not think that the giving of power to a planning authority to make a development plan after they have considered and heard objections to the draft is an unjust attack on property rights. A plan of development for each city and town is necessary for the common good... The making of a plan will necessarily decrease the value of some property but I do not think that the Constitution requires that compensation should be paid for this as it is not an unjust attack on property rights. If this argument were correct, many owners of houses would have been entitled to be paid compensation when the Rent Restrictions Act 1946, was passed."

[37] (1975) 109 ILTR 69, (the case was decided in 1970.)

He similarly rejected arguments that the authority's power to acquire land in an "obsolete area" for development, and the vague criteria on which an "obsolete area" could be so declared; the absence of provision for reinstatement of the original owners in their premises in an "obsolete area"; the authority's power to require discontinuance of a specified user of land; and the whole system requiring planning permission for the development of land or the retention of unauthorised structures represented unjust attacks on property rights. In the last connection he said:

> "Article 43.2.1 does not require that the exercise of the rights of property must in all cases be regulated by the principles of social justice. It recognises that the exercise of these rights ought to be regulated by these principles and that the State *accordingly* may delimit (which I think means restrict) by law the exercise of the said rights with a view to reconciling it with the exigencies of the common good...Town and regional planning is an attempt to reconcile to exercise of property rights with the demands of the common good, and Part IV of the 1963 Act defends and vindicates as far as practicable the rights of the citizens and is not an unjust attack on their property rights."

This case followed Davitt P in the *Southern Industrial Trust* case in focusing on the notion of "unjust attack" on property rights, a notion which invites highly subjective interpretation. For example it is clear from a passage cited above that Kenny J would have regarded the Rent Restrictions Act 1960, as constitutionally defensible notwithstanding that its effect, and that of later rent restriction legislation, was to reduce drastically (and in some respects arbitrarily) the value of house property to its owner, and without compensation. But - as will shortly be seen - the Supreme Court subsequently took exactly the opposite view of this very legislation.

The position reached after the *Central Dublin* case was that - though on the authority of the High not the Supreme Court - Articles 40.3.2 and 43 were being seen as distinct from one another, with the citizen's rights to items of his own property being protected only against "unjust" attack, the criterion for which might be adjusted, depending on circumstances, so as to justify the non-payment of compensation in certain cases of expropriation.[38] But in 1972, in two cases decided on the same day, the Supreme Court considered the property rights of two plaintiffs within Article 40.3.2 without adverting to the *Foley* and *Southern Industrial Trust* decisions, i.e. without giving the weight that the earlier Supreme Court had given to the discretion which Article 43 accords to the Oireachtas in this area. These cases - *O'Brien v Keogh*[39] and *O'Brien v Manufacturing Engineering Co.*[40] - concerned the effect of statutory limitations on the bringing of actions, and hence of abridgements of the citizen's "personal right to sue for personal injuries", which was, the Court found, a form of property right under Article 40.3.2; in the former case the Court held that the State by this enactment had failed to protect a property right of the plaintiff against unjust attack, in the latter the allegation of a similar failure was rejected. A few years later, in *Moynihan v Greensmyth*,[41] the Court, noting its own inadvertence in the *O'Brien* cases, said:

[38] Though *cp. Condon v Minister for Labour (No.2)*, High Court, 11 June 1980, where McWilliam J held that an Act regulating bank officials' wage increases was not an unjust attack if it was reasonable for the legislature to think it necessary for the common good. See *McCormack*, (1982) 17 Ir Jur (n.s.) 340.
[39] [1972] IR 144.
[40] [1973] IR 334; (1974) 108 ILTR 105. The recurrence of the name O'Brien is a coincidence; they were separate litigants.
[41] [1977] IR 55.

> "In both [*O'Brien* cases] the Court acted on the assumption that a right to litigate a particular claim was a property right and that as such its protection was guaranteed by Article 40.3.2 of the Constitution. In neither of those cases does it seen that the Court's attention was directed to the [decisions of the pre-1961 Supreme Court] in *Foley v Irish Land Commission*[42] and *Attorney General v Southern Industrial Trust*.[43] In these cases it was held in effect that the property rights guaranteed by Article 40.3.2 are not rights over particular items of property but are the property rights guaranteed by Article 43, namely the "natural right to the private ownership of external goods" and the "general right to transfer, bequeath, and inherit property". To divest a citizen of the ownership of a particular item of property in certain circumstances was held to be permissible under Article 43.2.
>
> If this opinion were to be adhered to, the reasoning underlying the decisions in the two *O'Brien* cases would seem to be incompatible with the Court's ruling in [*Foley's* case and the *Southern Industrial Trust* case]. Accordingly, in order to give a comprehensive answer to the question posed by the present case, it would be necessary for the Court to give a considered ruling as to whether the right claimed by the plaintiff is a property right and, if so, whether it is one of the property rights guaranteed by Article 40.3.2. For that purpose it would be necessary to review the Court's decisions in [all four earlier cases as well as the *Sinn Féin Funds* case]."

As the Court was asked by both sides to decide this case on the basis that the right of action was a property right within Article 40.3.2, this review was not undertaken, but the Court said it "wished to make it clear" that it "did not necessarily accept" as well founded the assumption on which its decision was to be based: and reserved for an appropriate occasion the question whether *O'Brien v Keogh* had been properly decided. (The issue whether there had been a failure by the State to defend this plaintiff's property right against unjust attack was decided against the plaintiff.)

Such an occasion arose in *Blake v Attorney General*,[44] which was a challenge to the Rent Restrictions Act 1960, as amended. This Act was part of a code going back to the period immediately after the first world war, and related originally to the social need to ensure reasonably modest rents and security of occupation for tenants; but the end effect, despite periodical amendments, was that a large number of dwellings, falling within the ambit of statutory control, produced rents representing a very small proportion of prevailing market rates, and turning controlled premises into a wholly uneconomic asset for their owners. In essence, the State had purported to achieve a social objective, cheap housing, at the expense of a fairly arbitrarily selected class of house owners: and without the payment of any compensation for their loss, the houses being of course deprived of their inherent market value because of the fixity of tenure of "sitting" tenants paying very low rents. The Supreme Court now moved to disentangle the sphere of Article 43 ("private property") from that of Article 40.3.2 (in its bearing on the "property rights of the citizen"):

[42] [1952] IR 118; (1952) 86 ILTR 44.

[43] (1960) 94 ILTR 161.

[44] [1982] IR 117. See McCormack, "*Blake - Madigan and its Aftermath*" (1983) 5 DULJ (n.s.) 205. For a sequel to *Blake* raising the question of whether the Rent Restrictions Acts could affect the assessment of compensation for compulsory acquisition of property which took place before those Acts were declared unconstitutional, see *Reid v Limerick Corporation* [1987] ILRM 83.

"Article 43 is headed by the words "Private Property". It defines the attitude of the State to the concept of the private ownership of external goods and contains the State's acknowledgement that a natural right to such exists, antecedent to positive law, and that the State will not attempt to abolish this right or the associated right to transfer, bequeath and inherit property. The Article does, however, recognise that the State "may as occasion requires delimit by law the exercise of the said rights with a view to reconciling their exercise with the exigencies of the common good". It is an Article which prohibits the abolition of private property *as an institution*, but at the same time permits, in particular circumstances, the regulation of the exercise of that right and of the general right to transfer, bequeath and inherit property. In short, it is an Article directed to the State and to its attitude to these rights, which are declared to be antecedent to positive law. It does not deal with a citizen's *right to a particular item of property* such as [a house affected by the rent control legislation]. Such rights are dealt with in Article 40 under the heading "Personal Rights" and are specifically designated among the personal rights of citizens. Under this Article the State is bound, in its laws, to respect and as far as practicable to defend and vindicate the personal rights of citizens.

There exists, therefore, a double protection for the property rights of a citizen. As far as he is concerned, the State cannot abolish or attempt to abolish the right of private ownership *as an institution* or the general right to transfer, bequeath and inherit property. In addition he has the further protection under Article 40 as to the exercise by him of his own property rights *in particular items of property*."[45]

Thus the question raised in this case - since the rent control legislation plainly did not purport to abolish private property, in any of its dimensions, *as an institution* - was whether the legislation was an unjust attack on the plaintiffs' property rights in the sense of Article 40.3.2; and the Court found that it was, since the effective reduction of the value of the landlords' interest was achieved arbitrarily (many rented premises were outside the controls) and without compensation. The Bill which the Houses of the Oireachtas then passed, in order to plug the gap left by the Supreme Court in its *Blake* judgment, which provided (briefly speaking) for a phasing-out of rent control, but again at the landlords' expense, was also held repugnant to the Constitution; In *re Article 26 and the Housing (Private Rented Dwellings) Bill, 1981*.[46] Speaking by O'Higgins CJ the Court said:

"The effect of the rebates permitted by s 9 is that, for a period of five years after the passing of the Bill, landlords are to receive an amount which will be substantially less than the just and proper rent payable in respect of their property. In the absence of any constitutionally permitted justification, this clearly constitutes an unjust attack upon their property rights. The Bill offers no such justification for depriving the landlord of part of his or her just rent for the period specified in the Bill. This Court has already held that the pre-existing rent control constituted an unjust attack upon property rights. In such circumstances to impose different but no less unjust deprivations upon landlords cannot but be unjust having regard to the provisions of the Constitution."

[45] The italicised phrases in this excerpt are the authors' emphasis. In *O'B. v S* [1984] IR 316; [1985] ILRM 86, the Court emphasised that Article 43 guarantees only the general right of inheritance, not any specific rights of individuals in this connection.

[46] [1983] IR 181; [1983] ILRM 246.

Article 43: reprise

However, less than two years after isolating Article 43 as a guarantee of the institution of private property, the genie was out of the bottle again. In both *P.M.P.S v Attorney General*[47] and *O'Brien v Bord na Móna*[48] the Supreme Court implicitly relied on Article 43 when holding that the respective pieces of legislation did not infringe the constitutional guarantee of private property because they promoted the common good. The connection between the concept of "unjust attack" on property rights, proscribed by Article 40.3, and the values contained in Article 43 was made explicit in *Dreher v Irish Land Commission*[49] where Walsh J said:

> "I think it is clear that any State action that is authorised by Article 43 and conforms to that Article cannot by definition be unjust for the purpose of Article 40.3.2."[50]

In four subsequent cases, the Supreme Court again drew on the qualifications to the right to private property contained in Article 43.2 - the concepts of social justice and the exigencies of the common good[51] - in determining whether an "unjust attack" on property rights has taken place. Thus in *Cafolla v O'Malley*[52] Costello J in the High Court had expressed the view that restrictions reasonably required by the exigencies of the common good could not amount to an unjust attack on property rights, and listed as examples of such legitimate restrictions, laws prohibiting fishermen from fishing at certain times and limiting the nature and size of the catch; restrictions on the hours of trading in licensed premises; and laws regulating the prices at which goods could be sold or services remunerated. His general proposition appears to have been accepted by the Supreme Court when, in upholding restrictions on the use of gaming machines, it said that:

> "such restrictions would not be an unjust attack on the plaintiff's property rights when they were so clearly imposed with due regard to the exigencies of the common good."

In *O'Callaghan v Commissioners of Public Works*[53] the Supreme Court quoted from the judgment of Walsh J in *Dreher* to emphasise the continued close relationship between Article 40.3 and Article 43. According to the Court, Article 43 did more than merely institutionalise private property; it also authorised the State in certain circumstances to regulate the exercise of property rights and had to be read in conjunction with Article 40.3, when the question of unjust attack on the property rights of the citizen was in issue, so as to give effect, so far as possible, to both provisions. In this case, the National Monuments Act 1930, as amended, was held to be justified in terms of the common good; and furthermore, as it was neither arbitrary nor selective, it did not constitute an unjust attack on the plaintiff's property-rights.

In *Madigan v Attorney General*[54] O'Higgins CJ, delivering the judgment of the Court, said that tax measures which necessarily interfere with citizens' property rights:

[47] [1983] IR 355; [1984] ILRM 88. See *Whyte*, (1983) 5 DULJ (n.s.) 273.
[48] [1983] ILRM 314.
[49] [1984] ILRM 94.
[50] Subsequently cited with approval by O'Higgins CJ in *O'Callaghan v Commissioner for Public Works* [1985] ILRM 364, and by Finlay CJ in *Electricity Supply Board v Gormley* [1985] IR 129; [1985] ILRM 494, and applied by Murphy J in *Lawlor v Minister for Agriculture* [1990] 1 IR 356.
[51] For an argument that the governing criterion here should be that of social justice, rather than the exigencies of the common good, see Barrington, "*Private Property under the Irish Constitution*" (1973) 8 Ir Jur (n.s.) 1.
[52] [1985] IR 486.
[53] [1985] ILRM 364.
[54] [1986] ILRM 136.

> "cannot be challenged as being unjust on that account, if what has been done can be regarded as action by the State in accordance with the principles of social justice and having regard to the exigencies of the common good as envisaged by Article 43.2."

In the instant case, the Court agreed with O'Hanlon J in the High Court that the imposition of a tax on the owner-occupiers of residential property was not "offensive to principles of justice or fair play''.

Finally, in *E.S.B. v Gormley*[55] the Supreme Court had to consider the constitutionality of ss 53 and 98 of the Electricity (Supply) Act 1927, as amended, which empowered the plaintiffs to lay electricity lines over land and to lop trees and hedges obstructing or interfering with such lines. In this case, the Court arguably inverted the previous relationship between Article 40.3 and Article 43, so that instead of using the latter provision to inform its understanding of "unjust attack" in Article 40.3, it relied on Article 40.3 to elucidate the meaning of social justice and the requirements of the common good referred to in the later article. Thus the Court concluded that the imposition of a statutory obligation on the plaintiffs to pay compensation when exercising their powers under s 53 would not be inconsistent with social justice or the requirements of the common good, nor would it be impractical. The absence of such an obligation, therefore, rendered s 53 unconstitutional. However, there did not appear to be any injustice in the imposition of the relatively minor burden on land-owners of lopping trees so as to protect a major electricity transmission line, and so the Court upheld s 98.

More recently, Walsh J's remarks in *Dreher* were cited with approval in two High Court cases. In *Clancy v Ireland*[56] Barrington J used them as a preface to his somewhat terse conclusion that:

> "[i]n all the circumstances it appears to me that the [Offences Against the State (Amendment) Act 1985][57] amounts to a permissible delimitation of property rights in the interests of the common good."

In *Lawlor v Minister for Agriculture,*[58] Murphy J, again having invoked *Dreher*, held that the European Community (Milk Levy) Regulations 1985, which imposed restrictions on the amount of milk produced by dairy farmers, were made with a view to reconciling the exercise of ownership rights with the exigencies of the common good. Moreover:

> "[t]he interference with the property rights of dairy farmers in general and Mr. Lawlor, the plaintiff, in particular, having conformed with Article 43 of the Constitution, does not require to be examined by reference to Article 40, section 3. Furthermore if the matter did fall to be considered under that Article, I am quite satisfied that the careful balance which was made between the rights of vendors and purchasers subsequent to the commencement of the base period and the solution applied - that is to say the retrospective operation of the regulations - were in no sense unjust. They were neither capricious nor arbitrary. They considered and weighed fairly and, in my view, correctly the interests of all the parties whose rights were bound to be affected once it was accepted that there would be an overall limitation on milk production."

[55] [1985] IR 129; [1985] ILRM 494.
[56] [1988] IR 326. See *de Búrca*, (1989) 11 DULJ (n.s.) 132.
[57] Which provided for the freezing of accounts held on behalf of organisations declared to be unlawful under the Offences Against the State Act 1939 and for the payment of such monies to the Exchequer.
[58] [1990] 1 IR 356.

In the second edition of this work, the remarks of Walsh J in *Dreher* were seen as giving cause for concern -

> "in other words, a law delimiting property rights and subserving the exigencies of the common good cannot be challenged by individuals as an unjust attack on their property rights no matter how injuriously it may affect them. This seems (if the paraphrase is fair) an extreme position, and altogether it might accord better with the Constitution's spirit if it were stated the other way round, viz. that a law cannot be taken to subserve the common good if it represents an unjust attack on individuals' property rights."[59]

It would appear, however, that these fears were misplaced and that instead of Article 43 providing protection for what would otherwise be an unjust attack proscribed by Article 40.3, the Articles mutually inform each other. Thus a restriction on private property will not amount to an unjust attack on property rights if such restriction is socially just and subserves the exigencies of the common good. At the same time, a restriction on an individual's property rights which is unjust will not be regarded as consistent with social justice nor as warranted by the requirements of the common good. Indeed in retrospect it would seem that the debate as to which Article applied may have been "much sound and fury, signifying nothing". Circumstantial evidence supporting this conclusion may be seen in the fact that in both *O'Brien v Bord na Móna*[60] and *P.M.P.S v Attorney General,*[61] the Supreme Court upheld both High Court decisions, notwithstanding the handing down of the decision in *Blake v Attorney General*[62] in the interval between the respective High and Supreme Court decisions. Moreover in *Pine Valley Developments Ltd. v Minister for the Environment*[63] Finlay CJ imported the concept of the common good into his reading of Article 40.3.2, quoting in support the following passage from the Supreme Court decision in *Moynihan v Greensmyth*:[64]

> "It is noted that the guarantee of protection given by Article 40.3.2. is qualified by the words "as best it may". This implies circumstances in which the State may have to balance its protection of the right as against other obligations arising from regard for the common good."

In summary, therefore, it would appear that the courts have to read the notion of "unjust attack" in the light of their understanding of the demands of social justice and the exigencies of the common good, bearing in mind that the latter concepts can never justify what would otherwise be an unjust attack on property rights.

What is an "unjust attack"?

In deciding whether a limitation on property rights offends against the Constitution, it is submitted that the courts should consider two distinct points. First, is the objective giving rise to the restriction justified in terms of social justice and the exigencies of the common good?[65] Second, are the means for securing that objective compatible with the Constitution? By way of an illustration of the latter point, one can point to *Clancy v*

[59] P.654.
[60] [1983] ILRM 314.
[61] [1983] IR 355; [1984] ILRM 88.
[62] [1982] IR 117.
[63] [1987] IR 23.
[64] [1977] IR 55.
[65] *Cp.* Article 1 of Protocol No.1 to the European Convention on Human Rights which qualifies the right to the peaceful enjoyment of possessions by reference to the concept of public or general interest, a concept given a broad interpretation by the European Court of Human Rights - see *James v UK* , Series A, No. 98, (1986) 8 EHRR 123, and *Lithgow v UK,* Series A, No. 102, (1986) 8 EHRR 329.

Ireland[66] where one of the circumstances leading Barrington J to uphold legislation providing ultimately for the confiscation of monies in bank accounts was the fact that the legislation provided for a fair hearing. Similarly, in *Deighan v Hearne*[67] the Supreme Court held that, having regard to the right of the taxpayer to appeal against an assessment and his right to challenge such assessment by way of judicial review, legislation empowering an Inspector of Taxes to make an assessment and providing that, in the absence of any appeal, the assessment should then become final and conclusive did not vest in the Inspector powers which could be considered unjustly harsh. This consideration also protected the power of the Revenue Commissioners to certify sums in default and the power of the county registrar or sheriff to levy the sum so certified by seizing goods, animals and other chattels belonging to the taxpayer.[68]

In relation to the first, or substantive, question posed above, the case-law provides relatively little guidance of a general nature, though a few pointers may be sketched out.

The Constitution may provide guidance on "unjust" criterion

Apart from Article 43, other provisions of the Constitution have the potential to inform our understanding of what is "unjust" in the context of restrictions on property rights.[69] Thus in *Pine Valley Developments Ltd. v Minister for the Environment*[70] legislation giving retrospective validation to planning permissions expressly provided that it would not apply where such validation conflicted with a constitutional right of any person. Consequently the plaintiff company did not get the benefit of the legislation as it had exercised its constitutional right to challenge the validity of the planning permission in the courts. This exclusion of the plaintiff company from the scope of the legislation did not amount to an unjust attack on property rights, because this limitation on the application of the legislation was necessary in order to avoid an interference by the Oireachtas with the judicial process.[71]

In the earlier case of *Dillane v Ireland*[72] the Supreme Court identified a useful criterion in Article 40.1. The point at issue was whether a rule of court, putting police officers in a privileged position in regard to orders for costs, breached the equality precept of Article 40.1 and also represented an unjust attack on the plaintiff's personal property rights under Article 40.3.2; the Court held that the case based on Article 40.1 must fail, as there was a clear difference of "social function", as between the police and others, which could justify the rule about costs; and, as the discrimination could be thus justified, it was not an "unjust attack" on the plaintiff's rights. Henchy J said:

[66] [1988] IR 326; [1989] ILRM 670.
[67] [1990] 1 IR 499.
[68] See also *Madden v Minster for Marine*, [1993] 1 IR 567, where Johnson J quashed a decision of the defendant granting a licence to engage in fish farming because this interference with the rights of other citizens had taken place without notice to them and without affording them any right of appeal.
[69] In *O'Callaghan v Commissioners of Public Works* [1985] ILRM 364, O'Higgins CJ, delivering the judgment of the Supreme Court, said: "The term "unjust attack"... contemplates an interference with the property right or rights concerned, which endangers or which is injurious to those rights, and which is not, and cannot be, justified under other provisions of the Constitution."
[70] [1987] IR 23; [1987] ILRM 747..
[71] The European Court of Human Rights subsequently held that this situation violated the plaintiffs' rights under Article 14 of the Convention which, taken with Article 1 of Protocol No.1 to the Convention, guarantees that, *inter alia*, the right to the peaceful enjoyment of possessions shall be protected without discrimination on any ground such as sex, race, colour, language, religion, political or other opinion, national or social origin, association with a national minority, property, birth or other status - Series A, No. 222, (1992) 14 EHRR 319.
[72] [1980] ILRM 167.

> "What happened when the plaintiff was denied his costs under the rule was categorically permitted by Article 40.1, so it cannot be part of the injustice which Article 40.3.2 was designed to prevent."

In this type of situation, the classification permitted by Article 40.1 directly affected the plaintiff's property rights. In the absence of such a direct connection, however, compliance with the guarantee of equality in the classification of restrictions on property rights cannot automatically dispose of arguments challenging the validity of such restrictions as being, in the first place, an unjust attack on property rights. To take an extreme example, legislation which, say, impounded unlicensed motor vehicles, but which exempted on grounds of social function cars owned by medical personnel, would not offend Article 40.1. However, this feature of the legislation, of itself, does not mean that the original power to impound is a justified restriction on property rights,

What is irrational, absurd, or excessive is unjust

A good instance of the free-floating concept of "unjust attack" is provided by a case in which the "injustice" resulted from the sheer irrationality, in modern conditions, of an antique system of taxation. This was *Brennan v Attorney General*,[73] in which the system of levying rates on agricultural land based on a valuation mechanism over a century old was attacked by a group of farmers. In the High Court,[74] Barrington J exhaustively reviewed the history of the system, and the anomalies which it involved in modern times, and said that:

> "If the Oireachtas were today to introduce legislation providing for the valuation of the lands of Ireland, such legislation, if enacted, would enjoy the benefit of the presumption of constitutionality. But if such legislation were to provide that the lands of Ireland were to be valued by reference to crops grown, and the scale of agricultural prices obtained, in the years 1849 to 1852 [this had been the basis of the valuation still in force] such provision would be so eccentric and ludicrous that the courts would have, I suggest, no difficulty in holding that it failed to respect the property rights of individual farmers...These Acts are not consistent with the Constitution in that they do not respect the plaintiffs' property rights or respect the plaintiffs' right to equality before the law in relation to their property rights."

On appeal, the Supreme Court upheld the substance of Barrington J's decision. Taking the view that the valuation of the land was in itself entirely neutral as far as the Constitution was concerned - what mattered was the use to which the valuation was put - it varied his declaration, setting aside that portion declaring the Valuation Acts to be unconstitutional. However, the Court had allowed the plaintiffs to amend their pleadings to include a claim that s 11 of the Local Government Act 1946, which provided for the raising of money by means of the poor rate on land, calculated in accordance with the Valuation Acts, was unconstitutional, and it ruled for them on this point. Delivering the judgment of the Court, O'Higgins CJ said:

[73] [1984] ILRM 355.
[74] [1983] ILRM 449.

> "In the assessment of a tax such as a county rate reasonable uniformity of valuation appears essential to justice. If such reasonable uniformity is lacking the inevitable result will be that some ratepayer is required to pay more than his fair share ought to be. This necessarily involves an attack upon his property rights which by definition becomes unjust."[75]

Other cases of "unjust attack"

Retrospectively changing the rules governing property rights is, *prima facie*, an unjust attack on those rights. Thus in *Vone Securities Ltd. v Cooke*[76] the Supreme Court upheld the common law rule that "month" in a legal document normally means a lunar month of 28 days. Dealing with the contention that the common law rule should be replaced with a presumption that the parties intended to mean "calendar month", Henchy J said that to do so would "fly in the face of property rights already acquired in compliance with, or by the operation of, the [common law] rule" and that it would not be proper for the Court to invalidate the rule retrospectively, "particularly having regard to the guarantees in the Constitution as to property rights." Statutory provisions affecting property rights are, similarly, presumed not to have retrospective effect though such a presumption may be rebutted where the legislation expresses a clear and unambiguous intention to rebut the presumption, where the circumstances are such that the inevitable conclusion is that the Act can operate retrospectively or, finally, where the change effected by the statute is purely procedural.[77] While legislative rebuttal of the presumption against retrospectivity must be "clear and unambiguous", it need not, apparently, be explicit - in *Chestvale Properties Ltd. v Glackin*[78] Murphy J inferred that inspectors appointed pursuant to the Companies Act 1990 could investigate matters which pre-dated the coming into operation of the Act from the fact that s 6 of the 1990 Act repealed all provisions of the earlier Companies Act 1963 dealing with inspectors.

A further example of an "unjust attack" on property rights occurred in *McHugh v Commissioner of the Garda Síochána*,[79] where Finlay CJ, with whom the other members of the Supreme Court agreed, said that the defendant and, vicariously, Ireland owed a duty to the plaintiff, in the protection of his property rights, not to initiate an inquiry which might result in being a nullity and put him to entirely unnecessary expense or, in the alternative, if they had decided for good reason to initiate such an inquiry, owed him an obligation to recoup to him the expense to which he was unnecessarily put.

[75] This case cannot be regarded as marking any departure from the traditionally cautious attitude of the courts in relation to matters of taxation. The facts here presented an extreme case, the Court having accepted Barrington J's finding that the valuation system was "shot through with unnecessary anomalies and inconsistencies", and the Court expressly left open whether the rate would have been invalidated if the Attorney General had been able to establish a "significant relationship" between the valuation of the land and its market value. *Cp. Browne v Attorney General* [1991] 2 IR 58, where Murphy J held that taxation as a benefit in kind of the use of motor cars provided to employees by their employers was not "shot through with unnecessary anomalies and inconsistencies" and accordingly was not unconstitutional.

[76] [1979] IR 59.

[77] On the presumption of prospectivity in the construction of legislation, see *Gardner v Lucas* (1878) 3 App Cas 582; *In re Athlumney, ex parte Wilson* [1898] 2 QB 547; more recently, the words of O'Higgins CJ in *Hamilton v Hamilton* [1982] IR 466; [1982] ILRM 290 - he thought that to give a provision of the Family Home Protection Act 1976, an injuriously retrospective operation would be an "unjust attack" on the property rights affected - and the decisions of Blayney and Murphy JJ in *Dublin County Council v Grealy* [1990] 1 IR 77 and *Dublin Heating Co. Ltd. v Hefferon* [1992] ILRM 51, respectively.

[78] [1992] ILRM 221.

[79] [1986] IR 228; [1987] ILRM 181.

Worth mentioning also is *Director of Public Prosecutions (Long) v McDonald*,[80] in which what was in issue was s 92 of the Road Traffic Act 1961, under which bye-laws might be made which could have the effect of interfering with a fair or market held on a public road (*i.e.* with a form of property right). The Supreme Court, speaking by Henchy J, said this property right was:

> "required by Article 40.3 to be protected as far as practicable by the laws of the State. The legislature...obviously considered that the common good warranted that a fair or market held on a public road could be encroached on by bye-laws made under that section, but only to the extent of securing the free passage of [traffic]. Such an inroad on the property right was obviously deemed by the legislature to be constitutional."

But if these prohibitions applied in such a way as to put a fair or market out of business without compensation, that, he said, "could be unconstitutional".[81]

In *Webb v Ireland*[82] Walsh J said that to allow a landowner to claim ownership of mislaid or unremembered chattels previously placed on his land for safe keeping, simply by reason of his being the owner of the land, would be to fail to vindicate the property rights of the true owners of the chattels, contrary to Article 40.3.

In *ESB v Gormley*[83] the Supreme Court invalidated s 53 of the Electricity (Supply) Act 1927, as amended, which authorised the plaintiffs to lay electricity lines, requiring the construction of three electricity masks, across the defendant's land. This amounted to a permanent interference with the use of land affected and consequently the failure of the legislation to provide for compensation rendered it unconstitutional.

In *Brady v Donegal County Council*[84] Costello J held that a statutory limitation period of two months containing no saver in favour of plaintiffs whose ignorance of their rights during this limitation period was caused by the defendant's wrong-doing was unreasonable and consequently unconstitutional.[85]

The most recent case in which a substantive unjust attack on property rights was identified by the courts[86] is *Cox v Ireland*.[87] Here the Supreme Court had to consider the constitutionality of s 34 of the Offences Against the State Act 1939. That section provided, *inter alia,* that State employees convicted of a scheduled offence before the Special Criminal Court should forfeit any pension, superannuation allowance or gratuity earned in respect of any service rendered before the date of conviction. According to the Court, the State was entitled, in the interest of protecting public peace and order and its own authority, to stipulate onerous penalties for persons convicted of offences threatening such peace, order and authority and in particular to ensure that State employees were not

[80] [1983] ILRM 213.

[81] This seems an unlikely phrase for Henchy J to have used. Is "could" (in the typescript judgment) a misprint for "would"?

[82] [1988] IR 353; [1988] ILRM 565.

[83] [1985] IR 129; [1985] ILRM 494.

[84] [1989] ILRM 282.

[85] The assumption in Costello J's judgment that a right to litigate was a property right was challenged by the Attorney General in the subsequent Supreme Court appeal but the matter was not decided as the Supreme Court held that certain issues of fact had to be determined by the High Court before the constitutional issues could be reached.

[86] *Madden v Minister for the Marine* [1993] 1 IR 567 having been decided on the question of procedures - see above, p. 1077, Fn. 68.

[87] [1992] 2 IR 503. See *Humphreys,* (1991) 13 DULJ (n.s.) 118.

involved in such activities. However, s 34 was overbroad because it affected persons whose motive or intention in committing a scheduled offence bore no relation at all to any question of the maintenance of public peace and order or the authority of the State. Accordingly that section failed, as far as practicable, to protect the property rights of the citizen in his pension and therefore was unconstitutional.

Cases of no "unjust attack"

On the other side of the line, and very much in the preponderance, are those cases where the interference or regulation complained of did not, in the Court's view, amount to an "unjust attack". In five cases - *Abbey Films Ltd. v Ireland,*[88] *Dublin County Co. v Grealy;*[89] *Kerry Co-Operative Creameries Ltd. v An Bord Bainne;*[90] *Shanley v Commissioner of Public Works;*[91] and *Hempenstall v Minister for the Environment*[92] the courts held that, on the facts of each case, there was no attack on property rights in the first place, while a sixth, *Pine Valley Development Ltd. v Minister for the Environment*[93] is authority for the proposition that where the State attempts to enhance property rights, any inadvertent diminution of those rights does not constitute an unjust attack. In the instant case, the Supreme Court unanimously held that a ministerial decision to grant outline planning permission was not a form of delimitation or invasion of the rights of the landowner, but rather was intended as an enlargement and enhancement of those rights. Consequently, when the plaintiffs lost money because, as it subsequently transpired, the ministerial decision was invalid, it was not open to them to argue that their

[88] Here the provisions of s 15 of the Restrictive Practices Act 1972, were attacked on the ground, *inter alia*, that the section gave the Examiner of Restrictive Practices powers of investigation (including entry on premises and inspection of books) which amounted to "an unjust attack upon private property". The Supreme Court dismissed this plea in a short paragraph, saying, "None of these powers affect "the right of private ownership or the general right to transfer, bequeath, and inherit property" referred to in Article 43.1.1. The powers of entry and inspection given by the section do not in any way infringe these constitutional rights."

[89] [1990] 1 IR 77; [1990] ILRM 641. Blayney J held that s 25 of the Local Government (Planning and Development) Act 1976, which empowered the local authority to make an order vesting lands in itself where a developer had failed to carry out instructions to maintain, in a specified manner, part of a development as an open space, had prospective effect only and accordingly did not apply to the plaintiff's development which had been completed before the Act came into force.

[90] [1991] ILRM 851. The Supreme Court held that shareholders in a provident and industrial society had no right to a share in the underlying assets of the society so that rule changes which, *inter alia*, increased the number of shares did not amount to an infringement of the plaintiffs' property rights. See above, pp. 1062-1063.

[91] [1992] 2 IR 477. Carroll J held that the plaintiff, as a tenant in State property, was never entitled to a statutory renewal of his lease under s 19 of the Landlord and Tenant Act 1931 and accordingly could not complain about s 4 of the Landlord and Tenant (Amendment) Act 1980 which provided that, *inter alia*, the legislative successor to ss 19 - 16 of the 1980 Act - did not bind a State authority in its capacity as lessor or immediate lessor.

[92] [1993] ILRM 318. The applicants, six taxi owners, had failed to satisfy the court that the Minister's action in repealing a prohibition on the issue of new licences to hackney owners would result in a diminution in the value of their taxi licences. As part of his reasoning in this case, Costello J indicated that property rights arising in licences created by law are subject to the conditions created by law and to an implied condition that the law may change those conditions; accordingly an amendment of the law which, by changing the conditions under which the licence is held, reduces the commercial value of the licence cannot be regarded as an attack on the property right in the licence. He also said that a change in the law which has the effect of reducing property values cannot be impugned simply because of the property value diminution, giving as examples new zoning regulations in the planning code and new legislation relating to the issue of intoxicating liquor licences. See his remarks to the same effect, in the context of a diminution in the value of shareholdings, in the earlier case of *Kerry Co-Operative Creameries Ltd. v An Bord Bainne* [1990] ILRM 664 at 717.

[93] [1987] IR 23; [1987] ILRM 747.

property rights had been unjustly attacked.[94] In a further case, *Hanrahan v Merck Sharp & Dohme (Ireland) Ltd.*[95] the Supreme Court, after noting the guarantee to vindicate property rights in Article 40.3.2 was not absolute, as it applied only in cases of "injustice done", held that the fact that the burden of proof rested on the plaintiffs to establish the tort of nuisance - they complained of the effect of emissions from the defendants' factory on their own health and on their farm - did not amount to a failure by the State to vindicate their property rights.

In numerous other cases where some limitation on property rights has been imposed, the exigencies of the common good have been cited, on occasions like a mantra, to defeat any constitutional challenge. In this way the courts have justified restrictions on the use of gaming machines;[96] limitations on land user in the interests of protecting national monuments;[97] the compulsory acquisition of bogland;[98] the regulation and control of banking business;[99] residential property tax;[100] the freezing of bank accounts operated on behalf of unlawful organisations;[101] the superlevy regime on milk production;[102] restrictions on the granting of casual trading licences;[103] statutory powers to investigate the control of companies;[104] and an extra-statutory scheme of compensation for owners of diseased cattle.[105] In *Webb v Ireland*[106] Walsh J invoked the common good to justify State ownership, as against all persons other than the true owner,[107] of all objects which constitute antiquities of importance and which have no known owner. The "interests of society" were invoked by Lynch J in *Tuohy v Courtney*[108] in defence of statutory limitation periods while in *Whelan v Cork Corporation*[109] Murphy J raised the possibility that principles of social justice might justify the statutory abolition of a restrictive covenant hitherto enjoyed by the plaintiff.

[94] The Supreme Court also held that the exclusion of the plaintiffs from the scope of legislation conferring retrospective validity on such ministerial decisions did not amount to an unjust attack on their property rights, as such exclusion was necessary in order to avoid legislative interference with the judicial process. The European Court of Human Rights, however, subsequently ruled that this state of affairs infringed Article 14 of the Convention which read with Article 1 of Protocol No.1 of the Convention guarantees, *inter alia*, that the right to the peaceful enjoyment of possessions shall be protected without discrimination on any ground such as, *inter alia*, property status - Series A, No.222, (1992) 14 EHRR 319.

[95] [1988] ILRM 629.

[96] *Cafolla v O'Malley* [1985] IR 486.

[97] *O'Callaghan v Commissioner of Public Works* [1985] ILRM 364.

[98] *O'Brien v Bord na Móna* [1983] ILRM 314. See *Coffey*, (1984) DULJ (n.s.) 152. In the High Court, Keane J held that the exigencies of the common good justified the *permanent* acquisition of such bogland, extending even beyond the time when the bogland would have been completely stripped of turf. While the Supreme Court upheld the legislation in question - the Turf Development Act 1946 - it did not specifically deal with this point and it is surely arguable that an interference with property rights, even when in essence warranted by the common good, must not exceed the measure of that exigency.

[99] *P.M.P.S. v Attorney General* [1983] IR 355; [1984] ILRM 88. See *Whyte*, (1983) 5 DULJ (n.s.) 273.

[100] *Madigan v Attorney General* [1986] ILRM 136.

[101] *Clancy v Ireland* [1988] IR 326; [1989] ILRM 670.

[102] *Lawlor v Minister for Agriculture* [1990] 1 IR 356.

[104] *Hand v Dublin Corporation* [1991] 1 IR 409. In this case the Supreme court assumed, without deciding, that the right to earn a livelihood, affected by the restrictions on the grant of casual trading licences contained in the Casual Trading Act 1980, was a property right.

[104] *Chestvale Properties Ltd. v Glackin* [1992] ILRM 221.

[105] *Rooney v Minister for Agriculture and Food* [1991] 2 IR 539.

[106] [1988] IR 353; [1988] ILRM 565. He also hinted that the Oireachtas could vest ownership of such antiquities, even as against the true owner, subject to the payment of just compensation, "if in the circumstances justice required the payment of any compensation".

[107] He hinted that the common good might even justify legislation divesting the true owner of his rights in such antiquities in favour of the State.

[108] High Court, 3 September 1992.

[109] [1991] ILRM 19.

In *Grange Developments Ltd. v Dublin County Council (No.3)*[110] the constitutionality of s 55 of the Local Government (Planning and Development) Act 1963 was upheld by a process of creative statutory interpretation. This section provided for the payment of compensation where a developer is refused planning permission for a particular site. Such a claim for compensation could be defeated, however, if the local authority gave an undertaking to grant planning permission in respect of that land - s 57(3). In this epic saga, the claimant had been refused planning permission by the respondents and had made a claim for compensation. For the respondents, it was a case of "third time lucky" as two earlier undertakings which they had given to the claimant were invalidated by the courts.[111] However in upholding the validity of the third undertaking, Murphy J referred to the fact that the *bona fide* intention of the respondent to grant permission in accordance with the undertaking might be frustrated or defeated at the behest of other interested parties. He held that the Constitution required the legislation to be so construed that, if such undertaking was frustrated, the planning authority which had taken credit for the supposed value of the permission in defeating the original claim for compensation would be bound to pay to the applicant the balance of the amount assessed, together with an appropriate sum for interest:

> "The court would be failing in its duty to vindicate the property rights of citizens and indeed their right to constitutional justice if it failed to provide machinery to ensure that the Act of 1963 and in particular s 55 thereof could be implemented in accordance with the construction I have put on it. The absence of appropriate regulatory machinery to enable a property owner to recover the amount of a credit which he was required to allow in anticipation of events which did not occur should not be permitted to defeat the right of the local authority to invoke the undertaking procedures or to prevent the property owner from recovering the balance of compensation payable to him."[112]

Finally, the courts are particularly reluctant to hold that tax laws amount to an unjust attack on property rights. Such laws enjoy the benefit of a very strong presumption of constitutionality[113] and will only fall foul of the constitutional guarantee of property rights if they are discriminatory or arbitrary in their operation. So in *Browne v Attorney General*[114] Murphy J held that the taxation of the use of a motor car as a benefit in kind was not "shot through with unnecessary anomalies and inconsistencies" and accordingly did not infringe the taxpayers' property rights under Article 40.3. In *Deighan v Hearne*[115] the power of the State to levy income tax was evidently so acceptable to the plaintiff that he confined his constitutional challenge to the questions of which arm of government should be employed to levy such tax and what procedures should be used. He failed on both counts.[116]

[110] [1989] IR 367.

[111] See *Grange Developments Ltd. v Dublin County Council* [1986] IR 246; [1989] ILRM 145 and *Grange Developments Ltd. v Dublin County Council (No.2)* [1989] IR 296.

[112] In a subsequent case in this saga, Murphy J acceded to an application by the claimant to have the arbitrator's award granting it compensation enforced pursuant to s 41 of the Arbitration Act 1954, dismissing the respondents' defence that such order should be refused because they had initiated legal proceedings challenging the constitutionality of the provision - s 55 of the 1963 Act - pursuant to which the arbitrator had made his award - *Grange Developments Ltd. v Dublin County Council (No.4)* [1989] IR 377.

[113] See, e.g., the remarks of O'Hanlon J in the High Court in *Madigan v Attorney General* [1986] ILRM 136.

[114] [1991] 2 IR 58.

[115] [1990] 1 IR 499.

[116] See pp. 345, 1077.

Status and measure of compensation

It will have been noticed that the cases presented so far occasionally refer to compensation as an element which may validate or make acceptable constitutionally what otherwise would be an objectionable inroad on private property, or to absence of compensation as an element confirming the injustice of the interference. Yet there is no settled doctrine on the constitutional status of compensation.[117] The cases disclose *dicta* which appear to admit a range of possibilities, varying from simple expropriation, through partial compensation at less than market value, to full market value, and even (where because of a temporary fluctuation the current market value might not be a just compensation) something more than it, though in this latter context, it is worth noting the possibility, raised by McCarthy J in *X.J.S Investments Ltd. v Dun Laoghaire Corporation,*[118] that legislation authorising the use of public funds to pay what might be excessive compensation could be unconstitutional.

In any event a right to compensation can arise only where there would otherwise be an unjust attack on property rights; and so there is no obligation on the State to provide compensation for loss incurred in the course of a speculative commercial enterprise (even where, as in *Pine Valley Developments Ltd. v Minister for the Environment*[119] an invalid ministerial decision to grant outline planning permission was the major reason for the loss).

Earlier leanings against expropriation without compensation

The *Central Dublin Development Association* case was the first in which the role of compensation, as a factor mitigating expropriation, was considered. But a few earlier cases had shown the inclination of the courts, where the terms of a law left them any room for doing so, to lean against confiscation (i.e. expropriation without compensation): thus in *Rooney v Department of Agriculture*[120] Powell J declared a right of compensation for the compulsory acquisition of land even though the enabling regulation did not expressly provide for this; and in *Rafter v Dublin Corporation*[121] Casey J applied the ordinary law of vendor and purchaser to a compulsory purchase so as to oblige a local authority to pay interest on an unpaid balance of a compensation award. But Article 43 itself is silent on the subject (unlike s 5(1) of the Government of Ireland Act 1920, the former constitution of Northern Ireland),[122] though in *Cassels v Dublin Corporation*[123] Budd J raised (but refrained from giving a view on) the question whether

[117] The failure of Swedish law to provide compensation to property-owners whose land use was restricted by the issue of expropriation permits was one reason why that law was held to violate Article 1 of Protocol No.1 to the European Convention on Human Rights - *Spörrong and Lonnroth*, Series A, No. 52, (1993) 5 EHRR 35. The European Commission on Human Rights subsequently regarded that case as deciding that "a right to compensation for interference with property rights [is] an inherent feature of the right of property set forth in Article 1 in so far as it might form a necessary ingredient in a fair balance between public and private rights." - Report of Commission in *Lithgow and others v UK*, 7 March 1984. See also the decision of the Court in *Papamichalopoulos v Greece*, Series A, No. 260, 24 June 1993.

[118] [1986] IR 750; [1987] ILRM 659. See now the Local Government (Planning and Development) Act 1990 which restricts the right to claim compensation in respect of planning decisions.

[119] [1987] IR 23; [1987] ILRM 747.

[120] [1920] 1 IR 176. Powell J said: "In order to secure the public safety and the defence of the realm [the acquisition had been made under the Defence of the Realm Act 1914] it may be necessary to obtain immediate possession of the lands and buildings, but neither the public safety nor the defence of the realm requires that the value of the subject's land or the temporary possession of it should be confiscated."

[121] [1953] IR 36.

[122] This forbids the "taking of any property without compensation". For Northern Ireland cases on this, see the *Report of the Committee on the Price of Building Land* (1973; Prl. 3632), paragraph 103.

[123] [1963] IR 193.

the loss involved in a demolition order without compensation under s 23 of the Housing (Miscellaneous Provisions) Act 1931, might make the Act inconsistent with the Constitution.

In the *Central Dublin Development Association* case it was argued for the Attorney General that, as Article 44.2.6 specifically forbids the taking of the property of religious denominations *without compensation*, and as Article 43 contains no such qualification, confiscatory acquisition of property (other than that of religious denominations) is not unconstitutional;[124] but Kenny J refused to accept this, saying:

> "The State has pledged itself by Article 40.3.2 by its laws to protect as best it may from unjust attack the property rights of every citizen; and while some restrictions on the exercise of some of the rights which together constitute ownership do not call for compensation because the restriction is not an unjust attack, the acquisition by the State of all the rights which together make up ownership without compensation would in almost all cases be such an attack."

Though "justice" of this depends on circumstances

Part VI of the Act under challenge in the *Central Dublin Development Association* case provided that in several different sets of circumstances no compensation was to be payable in respect of interferences by the planning authority with what (apart from the Act) would be property rights in their normal full extent; and Kenny J held all these exclusions of compensation to be constitutional. One example may be given, the exclusion of compensation for refusal of planning permission where the development in prospect was the putting up of a structure on land which had not been developed; he simply said it seemed to him "reasonable" to exclude compensation if the refusal was based on the fact that the water and sewerage facilities were inadequate.

E.g. in control of land prices

Two years later Mr. Justice Kenny was appointed Chairman of a Committee on the Price of Building Land set up by the Minister for Local Government, and the Committee's Report (March 1973) contains a discussion of the constitutional problem of controlling the price of land which, because of the public provision of services, has acquired a value far beyond its original agricultural value; as Mr. Justice Kenny was one of the only two legal, and the only judicial member of the Committee, it is probably fair to attribute this discussion, and the Committee's views, to him. The Report, having reviewed the *Sinn Féin Funds* case and the *Central Dublin Development Association* case, said:

> "Our proposal is not that a local authority should have power to acquire land anywhere at a price below its market price. It is that a court should be authorised to operate a form of price control in designated areas. In that sense the proposal involves a delimitation of property rights but one which is no more restrictive than other forms of price control. We believe that this delimitation is not unjust because

[124] An echo of this argument occurs in *Rooney v Minister for Agriculture and Food* [1991] 2 IR 539, a case concerning rights to compensation where diseased cattle are slaughtered on the orders of the Minister, in which O'Flaherty J commented that, "it is not necessary to enquire into whether there is any constitutional requirement to provide compensation for herd owners who have diseased animals except to note that the only explicit mention of compensation in the Constitution of Ireland, 1937, is in Article 44, s 2, sub-s 6 regarding the taking of property of religious denominations or educational institutions." (O'Flaherty J was a junior counsel in the *Central Dublin Development Association* case.)

> the landowners in question have done nothing to give the land its enhanced value and the community which has brought about this increased value [by the provision of services nearby] should get the benefit of it."

The proposal, however, has not been taken up by any of the Governments which have been in office since the date of the Report; and the official view, strengthened certainly by the outcome of the litigation about rent control legislation, is that statutory restriction of the free market price in such a context would be constitutionally fragile.[125] The same point of view underlies the official resistance to agitation to have ground rents abolished.[126]

In *Dreher v Irish Land Commission*,[127] the Supreme Court was led by Walsh J in expressing views less sensitive than those of successive administrations to the claims of private ownership. Here the plaintiff had attacked the provisions of the Land Acts which had the effect that, on compulsory acquisition of his lands, he was paid in Land Bonds with the nominal value at which his land had been assessed (£30,000), but an actual cash value of only £29,400; legislation which thus deprived him of some of the admitted value of his land was, he said, unconstitutional. The Supreme Court speaking by Walsh J took the view that "the provision is not patently inconsistent with the Constitution", and that, as the relevant section required the Land Bonds to be issued at a rate which made them "as near as could be reasonably achieved, equal in actual value to the price fixed", it "could not be read as creating any reasonably avoidable injustice or indeed any real injustice". Walsh J had prefaced this with some observations - *obiter*, as he expressly said the present case did not fall within any of the categories he mentioned - on the role of compensation relative to compulsory acquisition:

> "It may well be that in some particular cases social justice may not require the payment of any compensation upon a compulsory acquisition that can be justified by the State as being required by the exigencies of the common good.[128] It is not suggested that the present case is one such, nor is it in dispute that in the present case the appellant was entitled to just compensation for the land compulsorily acquired from him. It does not necessarily follow that the market value of lands at any given time is the equivalent of just compensation as there may be circumstances where it could be considerably less than just compensation and others where it might in fact be greater than just compensation. The market value of any property whether it be land or chattels or bonds may be affected in one way or another by current economic trends or other transient conditions of society."

The first sentence in this passage seems the most significant one, and looks as though it supports the view expressed by the Committee on the Price of Building Land cited above.

[125] A view supported by Keane J, writing extra-judicially in "*Land Use, Compensation and the Community*" (1983) 18 Ir Jur (n.s.) 23.

[126] See the speech by the Minister for Justice (Deputy Michael Noonan) in reply to a Private Member's motion, 345 *Dáil Debates* 666ff. (25 October 1983).

[127] [1984] ILRM 94.

[128] See also his remark in *Webb v Ireland* [1988] IR 353; [1988] ILRM 565, that the common good might justify legislation divesting a person of his title to antiquities of importance in favour of the State, "subject to the payment of just compensation, *if in the circumstances justice required the payment of any compensation.*" (Emphasis added.)

Acquisition without compensation

In a number of cases the courts have upheld statutory provisions which restrict property rights without providing compensation. In *O'Callaghan v Commissioners of Public Works*[129] the Supreme Court held that the absence of a provision for compensation in respect of a limitation on the use of land imposed by the National Monuments Act 1930, did not amount to an unjust attack on the plaintiff's property rights. It should be noted, however, that in this case the plaintiff had been substantially on notice of the limitation before the purchase of the lands in question, and the limitation itself was regarded as deriving from the common duty and interest of all citizens in regard to the preservation of national monuments.

That compensation is not always constitutionally required is also, perhaps, hinted at by the Supreme Court's decision in *Cafolla v O'Malley*[130] in which the plaintiff had argued that the introduction of legislative restrictions on the use of gaming machines constituted an expropriation of business without compensation and was therefore contrary to Article 40.3. The Court did not deal expressly with this argument but did suggest that an absolute prohibition on the use of these machines would not be unconstitutional, and did not qualify this with any reference to any obligation on the part of the State to provide compensation: this being probably related to a negative view on the Court's part as to the social effects of gaming facilities and also, perhaps, the fact that the 1956 Act conferred a privilege to engage in activities which are, *prima facie*, unlawful. A similar hint is contained in O'Flaherty J's judgment in *Rooney v Minister for Agriculture and Food*[131] where he specifically noted that the only explicit mention of compensation in the Constitution is in Article 44.2.6 dealing with the taking of property of religious denominations or educational institutions.

In *Lawlor v Minister for Agriculture*[132] Murphy J held, without elaboration, that the general limitation or curbing on the right to enter into or expand dairy production in all of the circumstances is not a limitation on ownership rights such as calls for monetary compensation. As Murphy J was also of the view that the interference with property rights in the instant case conformed with Article 43, perhaps he may have considered this case to fall within the category identified by Walsh J in *Dreher*, namely those cases where social justice does not require the payment of any compensation upon a compulsory acquisition that can be justified by the State as being required by the exigencies of the common good.

[129] [1985] ILRM 364.
[130] [1985] IR 486.
[131] [1991] 2 IR 539.
[132] [1990] 1 IR 356. In *Whelan v Cork Corporation* [1991] ILRM 19 the same judge, having held that the effect of s 28 of the Landlord and Tenant (Ground Rents) (No.2) Act 1978 was to extinguish restrictive covenants in favour of third parties, and not merely such covenants between lessor and lessee, speculated that the Attorney General might attempt to justify such statutory termination of a covenant without compensation on the ground that it did not constitute an unjust attack on the property rights of the covenantees because their rights were "more effectively and more justly protected and vindicated under the Local Government (Planning and Development) Acts 1963 to 1982 and by the evolution and general acceptance of environmental planning which regulates property rights of this nature in accordance with the principles of social justice."

Contemporary statements against expropriation without compensation

Other decisions and *dicta* are more solicitous of the rights of property owners. Thus one may deduce from the Supreme Court decision in *E.S.B. v Gormley*[133] the principle that compensation should be provided in all cases where it is not inconsistent with social justice or the requirements of the common good and is "clearly practicable". In this case it was noted that the plaintiffs' power of compulsory acquisition of land or rights over land was accompanied by an express statutory right to compensation and that the plaintiffs had, in fact, paid compensation calculated in accordance with guidelines agreed with the Irish Farmers' Association.[134] The Court held, therefore, that the imposition of a statutory obligation to pay compensation, which in the absence of agreement would be independently assessed, would not be inconsistent with social justice or with the requirements of the common good. It followed that it was clearly practicable to protect the defendant against an unjust attack on her property rights where the attack consisted of the acquisition of those rights without compensation.

Strict construction of the statutory provisions excluding compensation

In a similar vein, the courts sometimes show themselves to be very chary of statutory provisions excluding compensation. Thus in *In re Viscount Securities*[135] Finlay P formulated a proposition reflecting concern about expropriation without compensation when he held that:

> "if the legislature intended that an invasion, restriction or reduction of property rights should be enacted without providing compensation, in the event of a reduction in value for damage suffered, it is a necessary principle of the construction of statutes in accordance with the Constitution that they should have expressly and unambiguously so provided."

Accordingly, s 56(1)(*a*) of the Local Government (Planning and Development) Act 1963, was interpreted strictly so as to exclude from the right to compensation only those developments consisting of or including a material change in the use of a structure or land, other than the carrying out of works on the land.[136]

Similarly, in *Grange Developments Ltd. v Dublin Co. Council*[137] the Supreme Court construed s 57 of the 1963 Act in such a way as to protect the plaintiff's right to seek compensation. McCarthy J said:

[133] [1985] IR 129; [1985] ILRM 494. See also *In re Ranks Ltd.* [1988] ILRM 751 in which Murphy J held that s 290 of the Companies Act 1963, which allows a company in liquidation to disclaim continuing onerous contractual obligations, preserved the right of the other party to the contract to prove for the resultant injury to his valuable contractual rights, on the ground that any other interpretation might well be unconstitutional.

[134] In *Clancy v Ireland* [1988] IR 326; [1989] ILRM 670, counsel for the State argued that a similar right to compensation contained in The Offences Against the State (Amendment) Act 1985 (which provides for the forfeiture to the Minister for Justice of monies in a bank account which, in the Minister's opinion, is the property of an unlawful organisation) rebutted any suggestion of an unjust attack on private property. While Barrington J did not specifically comment on this aspect of the case, the provision for compensation must surely have been a material factor in his conclusion that, in all the circumstances, the 1985 Act was a permissible delimitation of property rights in the interests of the common good. See also *O'Mahony v Shields*, High Court, 22 February 1988, in which the plaintiff had argued that s 8 of the Wireless Telegraphy Act 1926 was unconstitutional because, by permitting the seizure of broadcasting equipment found on premises, it authorised forfeiture of property without trial. Lardner J, however, held that the section did not go that far and that a defendant acquitted in any prosecution resulting from the search and seizure would be entitled to reclaim possession of the items seized.

[135] (1978) 112 ILTR 17.

[136] See now Parts II, III, IV of the Local Government (Planning and Development) Act 1990, in particular s12.

[137] [1986] IR 246; [1987] ILRM 245.

> "Since the Act of 1963 effects an interference with a personal right, it must be strictly construed; so much the more, where the interference is being lessened or ameliorated by compensation, must any exclusion or qualification of the right to compensation be, itself, so construed."[138]

Independent assessment of compensation

The principle of independent assessment of compensation was affirmed by the Supreme Court in *E.S.B. v Gormley*[139] in which it rejected the contention that the payment *ex gratia* of an amount of compensation determined by the E.S.B. respected a right to compensation:

> "lacking as it does the essential ingredient of the ultimate right to have the amount assessed by an independent arbiter or tribunal."

However this point appears to have been overlooked in the later case of *Rooney v Minister for Agriculture and Food*[140] where the Supreme Court, speaking through O'Flaherty J, indicated that, if there was a constitutional obligation to compensate herd owners whose diseased cattle were slaughtered pursuant to the Bovine Tuberculosis (Attestation of the State and General Provisions) Order 1978, this obligation had been well met by the terms of an extra-statutory scheme authorising the Minister to make grants to affected farmers. Though O'Flaherty J noted, with apparent approval, O'Hanlon J's classification of such payments as contractual - in *McKerring v Minister for Agriculture*[141] - he failed to address the essence of the plaintiff's complaint that the extra-statutory scheme dealt less favourably with the herd owner than a statutory scheme of compensation anticipated by s 58 of the Diseases of Animals Act 1966 because the former scheme involved a unilateral element whereby the herd owner might have to take or leave what was on offer by way of grants as opposed to the more beneficial regime that would be in operation if there was a process of dialogue in seeking agreement between the parties and, ultimately, the possibility of resort to arbitration. This last sounds much more like the type of arrangement envisaged in *Gormley*, a case not cited to the Court.

The right to inherit property

Article 43.1.2 refers to, *inter alia*, the right to "inherit property", a phrase which received close scrutiny in *O'B v S.*[142] The defendant, who was the deceased's non-marital daughter, challenged the plaintiff's right to administer the estate in accordance with the Succession Act 1965, which did not permit non-marital children to succeed to their father's estate on intestacy, on the ground, *inter alia*, that this infringed her right to inherit property under Article 43. Delivering the judgment of the Supreme Court, Walsh J noted that the right to transfer property under Article 43.1.2 could be effected by transfer *inter vivos* or by testamentary disposition. The issue here was whether the expression "and inherit property" in subsection 2 conferred a constitutional right on the defendant to inherit her father's estate on intestacy. According to the Court, however, that left untouched a very important question, as succession on intestacy has to be determined by rules which have always been fixed by law. It appeared, therefore, that the phrase "and inherit property" was necessarily related to the exercise of the power to transfer property

[138] See also the decision of Murphy J in *In re Ranks (Ireland) Ltd.* [1988] ILRM 751, referred to above, p. 1088, Fn 133.

[139] [1985] IR 129; [1985] ILRM 494.

[140] [1991] 2 IR 539.

[141] [1989] ILRM 82.

[142] [1984] IR 316; [1985] ILRM 86.

by bequest and that the State had merely guaranteed in Article 43.1.2 not to pass any law attempting to abolish the general right to inherit property so bequeathed. At the same time it was recognised that the State might, in appropriate cases, prevent succession to property, and in this context the Court drew attention to Part X of the Succession Act[143] though without offering any view as to its validity.

It followed from these general principles that the Succession Act 1965 was not contrary to Article 43.1.2. Furthermore, as the defendant had no right to inherit her father's property under Article 43, her claim under Article 40.3 also failed. The Court observed that if the plaintiff had a vested right to property under the Succession Act it would be a right attracting the protection of Article 40.3; but as she had no such statutory right, Article 40.3 could not be invoked. The Court subsequently reserved its opinion as to what limitations might exist in relation to the ability of the Oireachtas to allow intestate succession by non-marital children to their parents' estates.[144]

The condition on the right to alienate should not be oppressive

Cognate with the theme that the demands of justice, in regard to compensation for expropriation, may vary with circumstances, is the idea that a condition attached to the exercise of a particular right in relation to property ought not to be oppressive, but ought to have some reasonable relation to the circumstances. This has been visible in some of the cases mentioned above, where private and public interests have been in competition. It comes through well in *Meade v Attorney General*,[145] in which Murnaghan J rejected the claim that s 98 of the Housing Act 1966 (which provided that a local authority's consent to subdivision of a plot vested under the Labourers Acts might be subject to a payment) infringed the plaintiff's rights under Article 40.3 and Article 43; he thought the sum required by the authority was "not unreasonable or oppressive given the market value of the plot", which the plaintiff had contracted to sell off as a building site for more than three times that sum. The point which presumably gave substance to the statutory power was that the plot had originally been provided at public expense, and vested in a tenant in pursuit of a social purpose, to provide a dwelling for a person in the qualifying category, not to enable him to dispose of it for gain.

A State-created monopoly as a limitation on the property right to do business

A monopoly created by the State for itself or for some designated State-sponsored body - such as the postal, telecommunications and transport monopolies - represents a total pre-emption of this area of economic activity and thus an exclusion from it of private business activity. Viewed in relation to property rights (though of course other perspectives will also be relevant depending on the case, such as the personal right to earn a livelihood or the right to freedom of expression) this phenomenon would require to be constitutionally justified. There is no doubt, on the one hand, that the right of private property under Article 43, i.e. as an institution, includes the right to do business; as early as 1936 Hanna J accepted, in the *Pigs Marketing Board* case, that the "free operation of competition in trade" and the "contractual rights of citizens" were aspects of the value which Article 43 was designed to protect; and, in 1969, Kenny J said in the *Central*

143 In this Part, s 120 precludes various categories of persons, described as unworthy to succeed, from shares in the deceased's estate, while s 121 gives the courts wide powers to deal with dispositions made for the purpose of defeating the legal right share of the deceased's spouse and/or children.

144 Part V of the Status of Children Act 1987 now provides that, for the purpose of, *inter alia,* testate and intestate succession occurring after 14 June 1988, references to relationships between persons shall be construed in accordance with s 3 of the Act i.e. without regard to the marital status of anyone's parents.

Dublin Development Association case that the right of private property consisted of "a bundle of rights, most of which are founded in contract", i.e. in business, speaking broadly, of one kind or another. On top of this, Article 45 seems to disclose, in its Directive Principles of Social Policy, a firm hostility to monopoly if it injures the public interest, and envisages a role for the State in this area only to "supplement" private initiative "where necessary".[146] In *Attorney General v Paperlink Ltd.*,[147] in which the Attorney General was proceeding against the defendants (a courier firm) for breaches of the postal monopoly, the defendants raised this point among others; unsuccessfully, because Costello J would not permit them to call evidence as to the inefficiency of the State postal monopoly, as he thought it irrelevant: "even if it was shown that the Post Office was not being administered in an efficient manner it would not follow from this that any of the defendants' rights were being infringed". What, however, would be the position if (as happened in 1979) the postal service ceased altogether to operate (in that instance because of an industrial dispute) for a long period? Here the existence of a statutory monopoly becomes clearly and seriously injurious to the public interest if its consequence is that others are not permitted to provide the important services which it was once thought the public interest required a State monopoly to administer properly. An authoritative judicial survey of this whole stretch of country is needed.

Statutory recitals of the Article 43 value

Statutes which effect a limitation of the exercise of property rights occasionally contain an express reference to the "exigencies of the common good", the value mentioned in Article 43.2.2: e.g. the Fuels (Control of Supplies) Act 1971, s 2(1); and the Housing (Private Rented Dwellings) Act 1982 (long title).

[145] High Court, 20 October 1972.

[146] See also in Article 45 the disfavour shown to any "concentration of the control of essential commodities in a few individuals": a public-interest principle as applicable to a State monopoly of a utility as to any private monopoly.

Article 44.1

RESPECT FOR RELIGION

Religion	Creideamh
Article 44	**Airteagal 44**
1. The State acknowledges that the homage of public worship is due to Almighty God. It shall hold His Name in reverence, and shall respect and honour religion.	**1. Admhaíonn an Stát go bhfuil ag dul do Dhia na nUilechumhacht é a adhradh le hómós go poiblí. Beidh urraim ag an Stát dá ainm, agus bhéarfaidh oirmhidin agus onóir do Chreideamh.**

Article 44.1 an innovation

Nothing in the 1922 Constitution corresponded to the present Article 44.1 - indeed, apart from the guarantees of freedom of religious conscience and practice and the prohibition of religious discrimination, the 1922 Constitution contained no reference whatever to religion, whether general or specific.[1]

"Religion" not necessarily Christian

Article 44.1, however, together with the Preamble, underlies now the view of Walsh J in the Supreme Court in *Quinn's Supermarket v Attorney General*[2] that the Constitution "reflects a firm conviction that we are a religious people". He pointed out also that Article 44.1:

> "acknowledges that the homage of public worship is due to Almighty God but it does so in terms which do not confine the benefit of that acknowledgement to members of the Christian faith."

Judicial decisions protecting religion

This section has had very little impact on the interpretation of law, if one excepts the highly individual and independent judgments of Gavan Duffy J, for whom the constitutional enshrinement of religion, the Irish tradition of Christianity, and the special position of the Catholic Church under Article 44.1.2-3 were so closely associated that his *dicta* in this area are best recorded under the latter subsections.[3] More recently, there have been a small number judicial decisions protecting religious interests, though none explicitly refers to Article 44.1. In *E.R. v J.R.*[4] Carroll J held that communications between a married couple and a marriage counsellor were privileged, primarily on the basis that this was warranted by the State's obligation, under Article 41, to protect the family. However she also commented that the fact that the counsellor in this case was a clergyman bolstered her conclusion:

[1] For an account of the development of Church-State relations in Ireland since 1922, written from a legal perspective, see Hogan, "*Law and Religion: Church-State Relations in Ireland from Independence to the Present Day*" (1987) 35 AJCL 47. The standard work in this area is the late Professor John Whyte's, *Church and State in Modern Ireland* (2nd ed. 1980). See also, by the same author, "*Recent Developments in Church-State Relations*" (1985) 6 Seirbhís Phoiblí 4.

[2] [1972] IR 1. This was repeated by Walsh J in *McGee v Attorney General* [1974] IR 284; (1975) 109 ILTR 29 and by O'Higgins CJ in *Norris v Attorney General* [1984] IR 36.

[3] See below, pp. 1095-1098.

[4] [1981] ILRM 125. Followed by Costello J in *P.K. v M.B.*, High Court, 27 November 1992.

> "The Article (now repealed) concerning the special position of the Catholic Church, while it may have influenced the decision of Gavan Duffy J in *Cook v Carroll*,[5] is neither relevant nor essential to deciding whether the relationship in question should be fostered, even though it is a priest who is claiming privilege.[6] The fact that the marriage counsellor is also a minister of religion adds weight to the proposition that a confidential relationship between such marriage counsellor and the married couple should be fostered. When I refer to a priest, I am including ministers of religion in general. Advice given by a minister of religion has an added dimension which is not present between lay people."

In the recent case of *M.M. v C.M.*[7] O'Hanlon J held that the proceedings an ecclesiastical tribunal was similarly privileged. Rejecting the plaintiff's contention that the tribunal could be required to produce documentation supporting his allegation of an improper relationship between his wife and a priest, O'Hanlon J said:

> "In my opinion there exists an urgent public interest in the preservation of the confidentiality of such proceedings. The Canon Law provisions themselves provide an elaborate code of secrecy. If a priest is suspected of conduct rendering him unfit to continue in pastoral care, it is most important that any allegation made against him should be investigated as soon as possible and as comprehensively as possible. If innocent he is entitled to have his good name in the eyes of the Church and of his flock vindicated without delay, and if guilty, then any failure to ascertain the truth of the matter may result in serious spiritual and moral harm to those entrusted to his care as well as harming the Church itself in its moral authority over those who profess allegiance to it. Unless the veil of secrecy and confidentiality can be drawn over such proceedings, as envisaged by Canon Law itself, then it appears to me that much greater difficulty would be experienced in procuring the necessary witness evidence for the determination of the issue, and the whole inquiry procedure would be hampered and perhaps rendered ineffective."

In *Tara Prospecting Ltd. v Minister for Energy*[8] Costello J referred to the Preamble and Article 1 in upholding the Minister's power to exclude Croagh Patrick, a place of pilgrimage associated with St. Patrick, from a prospecting licence. According to the judge, if the Minister decided that a proposed operation would be offensive to many people on religious grounds, he was entitled to take that conclusion into consideration in deciding whether it would be in the public interest to allow mining.

[5] [1945] IR 515. See below, pp. 1096-1097.

[6] A view shared by Geoghegan J in *Goodman International v Hamilton (No.3)*, High Court, 27 May 1993, in which he pointed out that the basis for Gavan Duffy J's decision in *Cook v Carroll* was that the priest/parishioner privilege fell within the four conditions for the establishment of a privilege set out in Wigmore's, *Treatise on the Anglo-American System of Evidence* (3rd ed., 1940).

[7] High Court, 26 July 1993.

[8] [1993] ILRM 771.

THE DELETED PROVISIONS OF ARTICLE 44

The first section of Article 44 had, until 1972 when they were deleted by referendum,[1] two further clauses, originally sub-ss 2 and 3.[2] They read:

2° The State recognises the special position of the Holy Catholic Apostolic and Roman Church as the guardian of the Faith professed by the great majority of the citizens.
3° The State also recognises the Church of Ireland, the Presbyterian Church in Ireland, the Methodist Church in Ireland, the Religious Society of Friends in Ireland, as well as the Jewish Congregations and the other religious denominations existing in Ireland at the date of the coming into operation of this Constitution.

2° Admhaíonn an Stát an chéim faoi leith atá ag an Naomh-Eaglais Chaitliceach Aspalda Rómhánach ós í is caomhnóir don Chreideamh atá ag ard-fhormhór na saoránach.
3° Admhaíonn an Stát, fairis sin, Eaglais na Éireann, an Eaglais Phreispitéireach in Éirinn, Eaglais Mheitidisteach in Éirinn, Creideamh-Chumann na gCairde in Éirinn, maraon leis na Pobail Ghiúdacha agus na haicmí eile creidimh atá in Éirinn lá an Bunreacht seo a theacht i ngníomh.

Provisions a (temporary) innovation

While these provisions - which had no counterpart in the Constitution of 1922 - are no longer part of the Constitution, they played a certain part in a small number of cases which are still part of the law. Moreover, although repealed, they may perhaps still be looked at for guidance on the intended sense of other provisions, or of the Constitution as a whole.

At least three references to these repealed provisions survive in statutory provisions which are ostensibly still in force. Section 128(4)(*c*) of the Companies Act 1963, dispensed from the requirement to file audited accounts along with its annual return:

> "a company, not having a share capital, which is formed for an object that is charitable and is under the control of a religion recognised by the State under Article 44 of the Constitution, and which exercises its functions in accordance with the laws, canons and ordinances of the religion concerned."

Section 2(1)(*b*) of the Companies (Amendment) Act 1986 continues this exemption in force in relation to the new filing requirements imposed by that Act.

Section 2(5) of the Street and House to House Collections Act 1962, purports to exempt from the application of that Act, house to house collections that are:

[1] The Fifth Amendment of the Constitution Bill (containing this change) was approved by the people by 721,003 votes to 133,430.

[2] For the history behind the drafting of these clauses, see Keogh, "*The Irish Constitutional Revolution: An Analysis of the Making of the Constitution*" in *The Constitution of Ireland 1937-1987*, ed. Litton (1988). Article 44.1.2 may have been inspired by Article 114 of the Constitution of Poland 1921 which, read, in relevant part: "The Roman Catholic Faith, being that of the majority of the nation, occupies in the State a preponderant position among religions which all receive equal treatment."

(*a*) for the benefit of an object that is charitable and is under the control of a religion recognised by the State under Article 44 of the Constitution, and

(*b*) held in accordance with the laws, canons and ordinances of the religion concerned, while section 23(5) of the same Act uses the same formula to describe collections which are exempt from the obligation to provide specified information about the proceeds of the collection.

It may be a question whether these provisions, even if the relevant part of Article 44 had not been repealed, could have survived a challenge based on Article 44.2.3, which prohibits discrimination on grounds of religious status; and it might also be a question how a "religion" - rather than a religious body or organisation - could "control" anything. But apart from these issues, what is the status of these provisions since the repeal of Article 44.1.3? Clearly, in the first place, if in the context of particular litigation the non-recognised status of a religious denomination emerging only after 1937 were material, the provisions are unconstitutional. But even as between a charity operated by well-established religious interests, such as organs of the Catholic Church or the Church of Ireland, on the one hand, and a charity not so operated, on the other, its constitutionality must be suspect. A court would have to consider whether the legislative intent was being distorted if the respective provisions were "deleted" from the word "charitable" onwards; if so, the whole of both clauses would fall.

Perspective of Mr. Justice Gavan Duffy: effect of sections on charities

It is in connection with these provisions that the unique adventurousness of Gavan Duffy J[3] is best described. In *In re Howley*[4] he had to decide, shortly after the enactment of the Constitution, whether the Chapter of the (Catholic) diocese of Killala was an ecclesiastical or foreign corporation; and disclosed, first of all, that he envisaged the Reformation as having merely interrupted and distorted the Catholic common law, which an Irish court could rediscover and apply:

> "The great stream of the common law rolls on from generation to generation, remaining through all vicissitudes (subject to statute law) the same stream, so that interruptions to its normal flow during three centuries must be regarded as temporary pollutions, the removal of which leaves the common[5] law under our Constitution today the same vigorous current."

On the specific question before him he said:

> "The Treaty of the Lateran of 11 February 1929, coupled with our diplomatic representation at the Vatican and its diplomatic representation in Ireland, may strengthen the argument for recognition in our courts of corporations established by the Church, whose special position, as the guardian of the Faith professed by the great majority of the citizens, is formally recognised by the State under the Constitution."

[3] Though he was not the only judge to rely on these provisions - in *Bank of Ireland Trustee Co. Ltd. v A.G.* [1957] IR 257, Dixon J said that it was "implicit in the terms of [the deleted provision] that adherence to and practice of any of the religions there recognised may be presumed to be of public benefit." Accordingly he held that a bequest to a Roman Catholic contemplative order was for a charitable purpose.
[4] [1940] IR 119; (1940) 74 ILTR 197.
[5] The judgment reads "canon" but this seems like a misprint for "common".

In *Walsh v Walsh*[6] he observed that the Christian conception of the family was rooted in Ireland long before the Constitution. In *Maguire v Attorney General*[7] he departed from earlier clear authority in holding valid as a charitable bequest a gift for prayer and worship alone:

> "In my judgment, a testamentary gift to found a convent for the perpetual adoration of the Blessed Sacrament is, beyond all doubt, a gift charitable at common law, because it is a gift to God, a gift directly intended to perpetuate the worship of God.
>
> And that conclusion is in harmony with the Constitution enacted by the Irish people "In the name of the Most Holy Trinity... to Whom, as our final end, all actions both of men and States must be referred."

Effect on judicial notice

In *Burke and O'Reilly v Burke and Quail*,[8] in which a testamentary gift was made conditional on the beneficiary's not "ceasing to practise the Catholic religion", he said that:

> "under a Constitution which "recognises the special position of the Holy Catholic Apostolic and Roman Church as the guardian of the Faith professed by the great majority of the citizens" this Court requires no formal proof of the ordinary obligations of a Catholic:

i.e. the Court would take judicial notice of Catholic practice. And in *In re Tilson, Infants,*[9] after summarising Article 44, he paraphrased it so as to convert the special position of the Catholic Church into a "right" (though he did not make the concrete effect of his judgment depend on this):

> "Thus religion holds in the Constitution the place of honour which the community has always accorded to it in public opinion. The right of the Catholic Church to guard the faith of its children, the great majority, is registered in our fundamental document, while non-Catholics are assured that their principles shall be respected."

Effect on privilege of witnesses

Perhaps the most striking of the innovatory judgments which he based on his conceptions of the place of the Christian and Catholic faith in the Irish tradition and the Irish Constitution is the judgment which added a new category to the communications which a witness is privileged from being obliged to disclose. In *Cook v Carroll*[10] a Catholic parish priest had refused to disclose, on being called as a witness in an action of seduction, the content of a conversation between himself, in his pastoral capacity, and the girl concerned. Conversations of this kind had not formerly been considered privileged (so as to permit a witness to refuse to answer); indeed in England it had been held that even disclosures made in the confessional box to a priest did not enjoy the privilege attaching to conversations between solicitor and client. Gavan Duffy J refused to follow English precedent in this matter and to hold the witness guilty of contempt. He said:

6 [1942] IR 403; (1942) 76 ILTR 149.
7 [1943] IR 238; (1943) 77 ILTR 139.
8 [1951] IR 216; (1950) 84 ILTR 70.
9 [1951] IR 1; (1952) 86 ILTR 49.
10 [1945] IR 515; (1945) 79 ILTR 116. *Cp.* the recent majority decision of the Supreme Court of Canada in *R. v Gruenke* (1991) 67 CCC (3d) 289 rejecting the contention that a blanket privilege attached to religious advisor-advisee communications. However the majority also accepted that there was a rebuttable presumption that such communications were not privileged, so that privilege could be established on a case-by-case basis. Note also the recent decision of O'Hanlon J in *M.M v C.M.*, High Court, 26 July 1993, holding that proceedings of an ecclesiastical tribunal are privileged. See above, p. 1093.

"The issue here is governed by common law, not by any Act of Parliament, and, while common law in Ireland and England may generally coincide, it is now recognised that they are not necessarily the same; in particular, the customs and public opinion of the two countries diverge on matters touching religion, and the common law in force must harmonise with our Constitution.

I have to determine the issue raised in this case on principle and in conformity with the Constitution of Ireland. That Constitution in express terms recognises the special position among us of the Holy Catholic Apostolic and Roman Church as the guardian of the Faith professed by the great majority of the citizens; and that special recognition is solemn and deliberate. The same Constitution affirms the indefeasible right of the Irish people to develop its life in accordance with its own genius and traditions.

In a State where nine out of every ten citizens today are Catholic and on a matter closely touching the religious outlook of the people, it would be intolerable that the common law, as expounded after the Reformation in a Protestant land, should be taken to bind a nation which persistently repudiated the Reformation as heresy. When, as a measure of necessary convenience, we allowed the common law generally to continue in force, we meant to include all the common law in harmony with the national spirit; we never contemplated the maintenance of any construction of the common law affected by the sectarian background...

I hold that the emergence of the national Constitution is a complete and conclusive answer to the objection that I have no judicial precedent in favour of the parish priest. I hold that I am free to give judgment, in the light of the Constitutions on principle, and that I am bound to do so."

This judgment privileges private conversations with priests (and must equally apply to pastors of other religious denominations in similar conditions) which take place in the context of their pastoral work, and must *a fortiori* privilege disclosures in the confessional. It does not appear that the repeal of the original sub-s 2 would withdraw any authority from the decision.[11] In a later Circuit Court case, *Forristal v Forristal*,[12] (a libel action), the scope of this privilege was limited to communications between a clergyman and his parishioners, so that the privilege did not apply in respect of a letter written by the defendant to a priest asking his help in composing a family quarrel because the defendant was not one of the priest's parishioners. However this restriction does not apply where the clergyman acts as a marriage counsellor - see the decision of Carroll J in *E.R. v J.R.*.[13]

Effect on the law on the upbringing of children

In the controversial case of *In re Tilson, Infants*[14] arguments based on the original Article 44.1.2 were addressed to the Supreme Court on behalf of the Catholic mother

[11] In *E.R. v J.R* [1981] ILRM 125, Carroll J explicitly stated that the deleted provisions were neither relevant nor essential to her decision that communications between a married couple and a clergyman acting as a marriage counsellor were privileged, an opinion shared by Geoghegan J in *Goodman v Hamilton (No.3)*, High Court, 27 May 1993.

[12] (1966) 100 ILTR 182.

[13] [1981] ILRM 125. See also s 7(7) of the Judicial Separation and Family Law Reform Act 1989, which provides that communications between either spouse and a third party made for the purpose of achieving reconciliation or separation by agreement shall, in certain circumstances, not be admissible as evidence in any court.

[14] [1951] IR 1; (1952) 86 ILTR 49.

seeking to regain the custody (and therewith control of the education and religious formation) of her children from the institution in which her Protestant husband had placed them. The sub-section played no part in the decision of the case - which turned on the effect of ante-nuptial agreements as to the upbringing of children - but Murnaghan J, delivering the judgment of the Supreme Court majority, used a turn of speech which aroused the suspicion of the dissenting Black J. Murnaghan J said:

> "It is right, however, to say that the Court, in arriving at its decision, is not now holding that the last-mentioned Articles [41, 44] confer any privileged position before the law upon members of the Roman Catholic Church, and during the argument counsel for the respondent expressly disclaimed any such privileged position."

Black J,[15] who dissented on strictly legal grounds,[16] dealt first with the judgment of Gavan Duffy P in the court below, and said he was not at all sure whether Gavan Duffy P thought that:

> "in regard to these ante-nuptial agreements, the Constitution was discriminatory as between different religions or whether he thought that it was not. Ever since this Constitution was enacted, I was firmly convinced, as I am still, that in respect of all legal rights and privileges it admitted of no discrimination as between persons of different religions. If I had thought it did, I never could have made a public declaration that I would uphold it; and if in fact it did, I imagine it would gain for us an unenviable distinction among the democratic peoples of the world."

He then dealt with what Murnaghan J had said:

> "It is not, in my view, enough to say that we are not now holding that the last-mentioned Articles confer any privileged position, etc.; for that might be read as admitting of a mental reservation that these Articles do confer such a privileged position, and that although not now held to do so, they may at some future time be held to do so. I think it would be in the national interest and in that of our jurisprudence that we should here and now unequivocally declare that our Constitution does not confer any such privileged position before the law upon members of any religious denomination whatsoever. For my part I declare that such is my opinion. Further, [counsel for the respondent] while making the disclaimer alluded to, seemed reluctant to answer my query as to whether the non-discrimination in the matter of ante-nuptial contracts was confined to those whose religion is Christian. This leads me to add that in my opinion it is not so confined."

Article 44.1.2-3 and a "pluralist" society

Apart from the continuing importance of *Cook v Carroll* (in which the Court clearly relied, in part, on Article 44.1.2) and of the *Tilson* case (in which there did appear, as Black J hinted, to be a certain inarticulate regard to that subsection) the deleted portion of Article 44 may apparently even now be of importance in buttressing an impression of the kind of Constitution that the people gave themselves in 1937 and therefore still have; though the context in which the deleted portion has been invoked had a purpose the opposite of what might have been expected from *Cook v Carroll* and the *Tilson* case, namely, to demonstrate that Ireland has a "pluralist" society. In *McGee v Attorney General*[17] Walsh J, by way of implicitly rejecting the notion that the Irish courts should

[15] The only non-Catholic member of the Court.

[16] See above, p. 1042.

[17] [1974] IR 284; (1975) 109 ILTR 29.

follow the view of one religion rather than of others in interpreting natural law and natural rights, said:

> "The judgment in [the *Quinn's Supermarket case*[18]] pointed out that the Constitution recognises and reflects a firm conviction that the people of this State are a religious people and that, as it then stood, the Constitution referred specifically to a number of religious denominations which coexisted within the State, thereby acknowledging the fact that while we are a religious people we also live in a pluralist society from the religious point of view. In my view, the subsequent deletion of sub-ss. 2 and 3 of s 1 of Article 44 by the fifth amendment to the Constitution has done nothing to alter this acknowledgement that, religiously speaking, the society we live in is a pluralist one .
>
> In a pluralist society such as ours, the courts cannot as a matter of constitutional law be asked to choose between the differing views, where they exist, of experts on the interpretation by the different religious denominations of either the nature or extent of these natural rights as they are to be found in the natural law. The same considerations apply also to the question of ascertaining the nature and extent of the duties which flow from natural law."

[18] [1972] IR 1; see below, pp. 1106-1109.

FREEDOM OF RELIGIOUS CONSCIENCE AND PRACTICE

2. 1° Freedom of conscience and the free profession and practice of religion are, subject to public order and morality, guaranteed to every citizen.

2. 1° Ráthaítear do gach saoránach saoirse choinsiasa is saorchead admhála is cleachta creidimh, ach gan san a dhul chun dochair don ord phoiblí ná don mhoráltacht phoiblí.

1922 provision

Section 2.1 is identical with the opening words of Article 8 of the 1922 Constitution, but those words were never judicially considered in the 1922-37 period, and s 2.1 has been considered on only one occasion.

Limited interpretation of "conscience"

In *McGee v Attorney General*[1] the plaintiff relied on this sub-section (among other provisions of the Constitution) in seeking a declaration that s 17 of the Criminal Law Amendment Act 1935, was inconsistent with the Constitution; her point in this connection was that her freedom of conscience (in exercise of which she wished to limit her family by means of a chemical contraceptive) was violated by the provision, which forbade the importation of such preparations. On this issue she was not successful; both the High Court and the Supreme Court took a narrower view of "freedom of conscience" than that for which she contended. In the High Court O'Keefe P said:

> "Freedom of conscience, according to [plaintiff's] counsel, means freedom to decide on a course of action and to act accordingly. In the context of this case, according to counsel, it means freedom to decide what is best in the interests of one's family, and to act accordingly. One must accept that in the serious predicament[2] in which she finds herself, the plaintiff has decided that the correct course for her to adopt, in the interests of herself and her family, is to take effective steps to ensure that she will not again conceive a child and so put her life in jeopardy; at the same time she does not wish to deny to her husband, or to herself, the natural life of a married couple. This I do accept, I believe that the plaintiff considered the courses open to her fully before coming to a decision, and that her decision was what she considered to be the best decision open to her in the circumstances. The fact that the decision of the plainfiff was a serious and conscientious one made in the interest of her family does not, in my view, make the matter one of conscience in the context of Article 44 of the Constitution. Freedom of conscience in that context means freedom to choose a religion and to act in accordance with its percepts; it does not mean freedom to arrive at decisions on matters of one's private welfare and to act accordingly. I consider that Article 44 has no relevance to the present action."

In the Supreme Court, although she won on other grounds, her arguments on Article 44 were again rejected. FitzGerald CJ said:

> "In my opinion the freedom of conscience referred to in that sub-section relates to the choice and profession of a religion, and to it alone; the word "conscience" can

1 [1974] IR 284; (1975) 109 ILTR 29.

2 A medical condition making further child-bearing dangerous.

of Article 44. I do not think that is so. The whole context in which the question of conscience appears in Article 44 is one dealing with the exercise of religion and the free profession and practice of religion. Within that context, the meaning of Article 44.2.1 is that no person shall directly or indirectly be cocreed or compelled to act contrary to his conscience in so far as the practice of religion is concerned and, subject to public order and morality, is free to profess and practise the religion of his choice in accordance with his conscience. Correlatively, he is free to have no religious beliefs or to abstain from the practice or profession of any religion. Because a person feels free, or even obliged, in conscience to pursue some particular activity which is not in itself a religious practice, it does not follow that such activity is guaranteed protection by Article 44. It is not correct to say, as was submitted, that the Article is a constitutional guarantee of a right to live in accordance with one's conscience subject to public order and morality. What the Article guarantees is the right not to be compelled or coerced into living in a way which is contrary to one's conscience and, in the context of the Article, that means contrary to one's conscience so far as the exercise, practice or profession of religion is concerned."

Budd, Henchy and Griffin JJ did not find it necessary to consider Article 44 for the purpose of their decisions. The unanimity of the other judges in both Courts, however - though they differed on other aspects of Mrs. McGee's case - makes it seem ceertain that "freedom of conscience" here means "freedom of conscience in practising, or in not practising a *religious* belief".

Writing extra-judicially,[3] Walsh J has offered a further insight into the extent of the protection afforded by this provision. Commenting on the position of the teacher asked to teach religion class, he said:

“If [the teacher] has a conscientious objection to teaching a particular religion, some accomodation must be made for that; but it is doubtful if any teacher can be permitted to refuse to teach it simply because he or she does not believe it, as distinct from having a conscientious objection to teaching it”.[4]

Obligation on the State actively to assist practice of religion?

In the majority of cases, it is likely the State's obligations under this provision would be discharged through a policy of non-interference with religious views and practices. However, it is arguable that in cases involving persons who, left to their own accord, would not be able to practice their religion and in respect of whom the State has a special responsibility, a more active policy of providing religious services may be required. Obvious examples here are prisoners[5] and patients in hospitals or homes maintained by the State. In this context, it is worth noting s 39 of the Health Act 1970 which, *inter alia*,

[3]"*The Constitution and Constitutional Rights*" in Litton cd. *The Constitution of Ireland 1937-1987* (Dublin, 1988).

[4]*Ibid.*, p.100. *In Merriman v St. James' Hospital, The Irish Times,* 25 November 1986, a Circuit Court judge ordered the re-engagement of a hospital worker who had been dismissed for refusing, on grounds of conscience, to bring a crucifix and candle to a dying patient. While Judge Clarke stated that the religious views of the employee must be respected, he does not appear to have explicitly considered the terms of Article 44.2.1, rather basing his decision on s 6 of the Unfair Dismissals Act 1977 which provides that a person cannot be dismissed on account of religious or political beliefs.

[5]See *O'Lone v Shabazz* 482 US 342 (1987). See also the comments of Brennan J in *Abington School District v Schempp* 373 US 203 (1963) on the provision of places of worship in military establishments and the employment of prison chaplains.

obliges each health board to make arrangements for the performance of religious services in each hospital, sanatorium and home maintained by it.

Freedom of conscience and practice subject to public order and morality

Unlike Article 9 of the European Convention on Human Rights, which guarantees freedom of thought, conscience and religion without qualification and permits restrictions only with regard to *expression* of belief, Article 44.2.1 qualifies freedom of conscience and the free profession and practice of religion by reference to public order and morality. However, in what appears to be the only case to date in which these qualifications were considered in this jurisdiction, the court was concerned with the expression of belief, rather then with the nature of the belief itself, In *Director of Public Prosecutions v Draper,*[6] the Court of Criminal Appeal dismissed an appeal against conviction in the case of a man convicted on two counts of malicious damage to religious statues. Referring to the man's motivation - he believed that he had been sent by God - McCarthy J said that the court was not questioning the sincerity of his beliefs. However the guarantee of freedom of conscience and the free profession and practice of religion was expressly subject to public order and morality. In the instant case, there was no question of morality but rather one of public order. There was a requirement that the property of citizens must be protected. The defendant had damaged property and the law said that this was an offence.[7]

Statutory vindication of the freedom of religious conscience

For an example of statutory vindication of freedom of religious conscience, see s 4(2) of the Health Act 1953 which provides, in the context of providing medical services pursuant to the Act that:

"Any person who avails himself of any service provided under this Act shall not be under any obligation to submit himself or any person for whom he is responsible to a health examination or treatment which is contrary to the teaching of his religion."

[6]*The Irish Times*, 24 March 1988.

[7]The court did suspend the remaining four months of the six month sentence when the defendant gave an undertaking not to damage or interfere with such property again.

NO RELIGIOUS ENDOWMENT OR DISCRIMINATION

2° The State guarantees not to endow any religion.
3° The State shall not impose any disabilities or make any discrimination on the ground of religious profession, belief or status.

2° Rathaíonn an Stát gan aon chóras creidimh a mhaoiniú.
3° Ní cead don Stát neach a chur faoi mhíchumas ar bith ná aon idirdhealú a dhéanamh mar gheall ar chreidimh nó admháil chreidimh nó céim i gcúrsaí creidimh.

1922 provision

These provisions echo similar provisions within Article 8 of the 1922 Constitution (which reproduced provisions of Article 16 of the Treaty of 1921 which in turn echoed provisions of the Government of Ireland Bills of 1886 and 1893 and the Government of Ireland Act 1920).

Prohibition of religious endowment

The prohibition on endowment of religion contained in Article 44.2.2 appears to have arisen in litigation on only one occasion, namely the case of *McGrath and Ó Ruairc v Trustees of Maynooth College*.[1] The question whether the subvention paid by the State to the college was unconstitutional was briefly dealt with by Kenny J, who took the view that as Maynooth College, in addition to its status as a seminary, was also a college of a university (being a recognised college of the National University of Ireland), subvention of it was not constitutionally objectionable.

In an opinion[2] on the effect of s 5 of the Government of Ireland Act 1920 which contains a prohibition of religious endowment identical to that in Article 44.2.2, the then Attorney General for Northern Ireland, J.C. McDermott K.C.[3] wrote that the word "endow" meant "to enrich with property; to provide a permanent income for a person, society or institution".[4] Thus the notion of endowment would seem to be limited to the provision of property,[5] income or a source of income and so it is arguable that Article 44.2.2 does not preclude the State from making occasional financial contributions in money or money's worth to religious bodies.[6] McDermott himself did not believe that every benefit connected in some way with a right or privilege over property would constitute an endowment, giving as an example, the use of a publicly-funded school for the

[1] [1979] ILRM 166. *Morgan* ((1986) 21 Ir Jur (n.s.) 146) refers to another case - *Moloney v Southern Health Board, The Cork Examiner*, 14 July 1987 - in which the plaintiff complained of the building by the Southern Health Board of a religious statue (an image of Padre Pio). This case settled, however, on terms favourably to the plaintiff, though it might be questioned whether the erection of a statue can constitute an endowment of religion.

[2] This opinion is set out in full in the appendix to an article by Graham, "*Religion and Education - The Constitutional Problem*" (1982) 33 NILQ 20.

[3] Subsequently Lord Chief Justice of Northern Ireland.

[4] The Oxford English Dictionary contains a virtually identical definition - see 2nd ed., (1989) p. 234.

[5] Writing extra-judicially, Mr Justice Keane has pointed out that the prohibition against endowment of religion appears to have been included in the Government of Ireland Act 1920 and in the Home Rule Bills of 1886 and 1893 because of fears that the Church of Ireland might otherwise lose its medieval cathedrals under the new regime - "*Fundamental Rights in Irish Law - A Note on the Historical Background*" in O'Reilly, ed., *Human Rights and Constitutional Law: Essays in Honour of Brian Walsh* (1992).

[6] Such as, for example, one-off grants to religious charities to be spent directly on the objectives of the charity, or the provision of a military guard of honour on occasion of religious ceremonies.

purposes of religious instruction provided such religious user remained ancillary to the main purpose of the building. On the other hand, he did suggest that the payment of a teacher out of public funds for religious teaching would constitute indirect endowment of religion insofar as it would amount to providing regular income for the purpose of advancing religious education and thus some particular religion. However, an extra-judicial comment of Walsh J directly contradicts that last proposition. He argues that it is a corollary of Article 42 that:

> "there seems to be no objection to the state providing religious education, if the parents wish it for their children, and to the state providing the type of religious education requested by the parents. As taxpayers, parents should be free to require that some of their tax be devoted to the teaching of what they wish their children to learn. This is not a contravention of the provision in Article 44 whereby the state guarantees not "to endow any religion". The teaching of religion, or of any particular religion, as a subject in education is not to be confused with the endowment of a religion."[7]

McDermott also offered some views as to the meaning of the word "religion" in this context. In his opinion, it covered the major world religions but also religions one within the other, e.g. the different denominations within Christianity.

Writing about s 5 of the 1920 Act and comparing it with the First Amendment to the US Constitution, which prohibits any "law respecting an establishment of religion", Graham argued that s 5 is directed against discriminatory endowment of particular religions, rather than endowment of religion *simpliciter*. It is unlikely that the Irish courts would take a similar view of Article 44.2.2, if only because of the inherent practical difficulties - how would one define "religion" and "discrimination" for the purpose of prohibiting discriminatory endowment of religion? - and it is submitted that the better view is that Article 44.2.2 prohibits endowment of all religion.

Of course, Article 44.2.2 cannot be read in isolation and must be interpreted in the light of other constitutional provisions such as Article 42.4 and sub-s 3 and 4 of Article 44.2. Read in this way, the prohibition of endowment would not affect State financing of the educational activities of a religious body - and probably other secular activities of such bodies - provided there is no discrimination on ground of religious profession, belief or status. Indeed, if one takes the historical approach to the interpretation of Article 44.2.2, it may not prohibit the teaching of religion as part of an overall education, provided that the right of students to withdraw from such instruction while still attending school is respected.[8]

Doubts exist as to the constitutionality of at least two aspects of current educational policy[9] in the light of the principle of non-endowment - the funding of chaplains and the "integrated curriculum" - the permeation of religious values throughout the primary curriculum. Apart from possibly infringing the principle of non-endowment, the financing of chaplains may also offend against the State's obligation not to discriminate on ground of religious profession, belief or status - inasmuch as publicly-funded employment is

[7] "*The Constitution and Constitutional Rights*" in Litton ed. *The Constitution of Ireland 1937-1987* (Dublin 1988), p.99.
[8] See the extra-judicial remarks of Walsh J. cited above - *ibid.* See also Whyte, "*Education and the Constitution*" in Lane ed. *Religion, Education and the Constitution* (Dublin, 1992), pp.98-108.
[9] Casey also questions the constitutionality of the funding of Maynooth College - *Constitutional Law in Ireland* (2nd ed., 1992) at p.566. But see *Whyte, loc. cit.* p.105.

being reserved for persons with particular religious beliefs or positions[10] - while the integrated curriculum, on the face of it, appears to infringe the right of students to withdraw from religious instruction while continuing to attend publicly-funded schools.[11] It is understood that challenges to the constitutionality of both of these arrangements are currently before the courts.

Despite the somewhat absolute nature of the prohibition on endowment of religion, an argument could be made that, in certain limited situations, the State may be entitled to provide an income to religious personnel. As has already been mentioned above,[12] the State's obligation to guarantee free profession and practice of religion under Article 44.2.1 could possibly involve the taking of active measures in relation to groups particularly dependent on the State, such as prisoners or persons resident in hospitals or homes maintained by State agencies. In such situations, the payment of fees to persons providing religious services, though on the face of it an apparent breach of the principle of non-endowment, might possibly be justifiable under Article 44.2.1.[13] Such a situation is provided for by s 39 of the Health Act 1970 which obliges each health board to make arrangements for the performance of religious services in each hospital, sanatorium and home maintained by it and which further provides that the amount of any payment made by a health board pursuant to such arrangement shall be subject to the approval of the Minister for Health.

The prohibition of religious discrimination

The prohibition of discrimination has been relied on in six cases, on three of these occasions with success.

In *Schlegel v Corcoran and Gross*[14] Gavan Duffy J refused to hold unreasonable the refusal of a landlord to consent to the assignment by a tenant of his interest to a Jewish assignee.[15] He disposed of one of the proposed assignee's arguments by saying he failed to see "the supposed connection between the problem before the landlord and the constitutional veto upon any discrimination by the State on the ground of religious belief"; it seems clear from the tenor of his judgment[16] that he saw the plaintiff's anti-Semitism as not directed against a form of religious belief so much as against a race, and accordingly saw the Court's protection of her and of her "honest effort to defend the amenities of her residence" as not infringing the rule against religious discrimination.[17]

[10] For consideration of the argument that such discriminatory practices might be protected by Article 44.2.5, see below, p. 1115.
[11] Though see below, pp. 1113-1114.
[12] See above, p. 1101.
[13] See the analogous reasoning in *Quinn's Supermarket v AG* [1972] IR 1, where the prohibition on religious discrimination in Article 44.2.3 was read subject to the guarantee of the free profession and practice of religion in Article 44.2.1.
[14] [1942] IR 19; (1942) 76 ILTR 46.
[15] Section 56 of the Landlord and Tenant Act 1931 (see now s 66 of the Landlord and Tenant (Amendment) Act 1980) provided that such consent should not be unreasonably withheld.
[16] "The plaintiff's objection has been characterised as a caprice and as mere prejudice; but caprice is not the right word for an anti-Semitism which, far from being a peculiar crotchet, is notoriously shared by a number of other citizens; and if prejudice be the right word, the antagonism between Christian and Jew has its roots in nearly two thousand years of history, and is too prevalent as a habit of mind to be dismissed offhand, in a country where religion matters, as the eccentric extravagance of a bigot, without regard to the actual conditions under which consent was withheld." This is the dark side of a remarkable judge.
[17] *Casey* argues, quite convincingly, that it is very unlikely that this decision would be followed today - *op. cit.* p.568. *Pace* Gavan Duffy J, it is arguable that judicial endorsement of *Schlegel* is contrary to Article 44.2.3, if we accept that that provision precludes the State, acting through its judicial arm, from lending its weight to religious or racial discrimination between private parties. Furthermore, the presumption of constitutionality surely precludes the view that religious discrimination is "reasonable" for the purposes of s 66 of the Landlord and Tenant (Amendment) Act 1980.

In *The State (O'Connor) v Ó Caomhánaigh*[18] the applicant had been convicted, under s 3 of the Tumultuous Risings (Ireland) Act 1831, of sending threatening letters, but now claimed that this Act, since it was part of a series commonly known as the Whiteboys Acts, had an inherent element of religious discrimination and so had not been carried over as part of the law in force by the continuation provisions of the Constitutions of 1922 and 1937, as it was contrary to Articles 8 and 44, respectively, of these Constitutions. The Supreme Court took judicial notice of the historical fact that Whiteboys were mainly Papists, and acknowledged that s 15 of the first of the Whiteboy Acts gave power to justices and others to search the premises of "Papists and reputed Papists" for arms. Lavery J said:

> "If this Court was dealing with the Act of 1776 alone there might be something to be said for the argument, though I would not myself accede to it, that there was a religious discrimination sufficient to invalidate the section under the constitutional law."

But the Court would not read all the Whiteboy Acts together; the provision under which the applicant had been convicted had to be looked at by itself; and that provision contained nothing to suggest that any of the religious prejudice or discrimination of the 1776 Act had infected the Act of 1831 - which had, in fact, repealed s 15 of the earlier Act. He found that s 3 of the 1831 Act was:

> "perfectly general and has no internal indication of discrimination against Papists or reputed Papists or any other class... Many statutes - and indeed many of the principles of the common law - were conditioned by the political, economic, religious and social sentiments of the time of their enactment or establishment, but it is the provisions themselves which are now to be looked at and examined, not the motives of those who enacted [or established] them."

Instances of discrimination - Ministerial order on shop trading hours

In recent years three important cases have provided occasions for exploring more thoroughly the rule against religious discrimination. The first of these, *Quinn's Supermarket v Attorney General*,[19] arose from an Order made by the Minister for Industry and Commerce in 1948 under s 25 of the Shops (Hours of Trading) Act 1938; this Order laid down restricted hours of opening for meat shops in the Dublin area on weekdays, but specifically excluded from its operation "any shop in which the only business carried on therein is that of selling meat killed and prepared by the Jewish ritual method", i.e. such shops were free to open at times other than those generally in force. The plaintiff supermarket was prosecuted for a breach of the restricted hours, and thereupon commenced an action seeking a declaration that the Order, inasmuch as it discriminated on religious grounds (in favour of kosher shops), was unconstitutional. The Order was held invalid by the High Court and, on appeal, by the Supreme Court, though on narrower grounds than those on which the plaintiff's main case rested. Walsh J (with whom Ó Dálaigh CJ and Budd and FitzGerald JJ agreed) began by sorting out the sense of "disabilities":

> "The plaintiffs have certainly suffered a disability in the sense that they are legally disqualified from, and are deprived of the power of, carrying on the business of selling meat after the hours set out in the statutory instrument. This is a deprivation but in my view, where the provision speaks of disabilities, the disability must be one

[18] [1963] IR 112.
[19] [1972] IR 1.

which is suffered and imposed on the ground of the religious profession, belief or status of the person so disabled... If an imposed disability is to be examined, and the grounds upon which it is imposed are to be examined, clearly the grounds must relate to the person or body upon whom the disability is imposed."

There was no evidence here that the disability imposed on the plaintiff supermarket and its shareholders related to their religious profession, belief or status. Accordingly the plaintiff's case, so far as it was based on the "disabilities" part of Article 44.2.3, could not succeed.

It was a different matter with the "discrimination" part of the sub-section. Walsh J continued:

"It was submitted on behalf of the defendants here that "discrimination" should be construed as if it read "discrimination against". In my view the learned High Court judge was quite correct in rejecting that submission. If the provision had read "discrimination against" - meaning distinguishing unfavourably on the grounds of religious profession, belief or status - it would also mean that the test would have been related to the religious profession, belief or status of the person discriminated against. It is the omission of the word "against" which confirms me in my view that this portion of the constitutional provision should be construed as meaning that the State shall not make any "distinction" on the ground of religious profession, belief or status. This is confirmed by the Irish text which says "ná aon idirdhealú do dhéanamh..." To discriminate, in that sense, is to create a difference between persons or bodies or to distinguish between them on the ground of religious profession, belief or status; it follows, therefore, that the religious profession, belief or status does not have to be that of the person who feels he has suffered by reason of the distinction created -"

i.e. the sub-section equally forbade a distinction intended as favourable to, or in ease of, certain persons on grounds of their religion. As it was common case that the motive of the 1948 Order's exemption of kosher shops was to compensate the Jewish community for the fact that their law of Sabbath observance ruled out one of the ordinary shopping days for them, Walsh J concluded that:

"the exception made in relation to the sale of meat killed according to the Jewish ritual is a discrimination on the ground of religious profession, belief or status within the meaning of Article 44.2.3 and that it is, *prima facie* at least, unconstitutional."

But the matter did not end there. There was, he found, a conflict between Article 44.2.1 and Article 44.2.3 in a case, such as the present, where a literal application of the non-discrimination rule would tend to work against the free profession and practice of religion - members of the Jewish community unable to buy meat on the Sabbath would either have to go without, or break the strict dietary laws of their religion. This conflict he resolved in favour of religious practice, calling attention to the opening words of Article 44 and its acknowledgement that:

"the homage of public worship is due to Almighty God but...in terms which do not confine the benefit of that acknowledgement to members of the Christian faith;"

as well as to the specific recognition of Article 44.1.3 (this was before its deletion by referendum)[20] of the Jewish congregations. He said:

[20] See above, p. 1094 *et seq.*

> "It would be completely contrary to the spirit and intendment of the provisions of Article 44.2 to permit the guarantee against discrimination on the ground of religious profession or belief to be made the very means of restricting or preventing the free profession or practice of religion. The primary purpose of the guarantee against discrimination is to ensure the freedom of practice of religion. Any law which by virtue of the generality of its application would by its effect restrict or prevent the free profession and practice of religion by any person or persons would be invalid having regard to the provisions of the Constitution, unless it contained provisions which saved from such restriction or prevention the practice of religion or persons who would otherwise be so restricted or prevented...s 25 of the Shops (Hours of Trading) Act 1938, under which the Order complained of had been made did not require... that no provision could be made to exempt the person or persons whose practice of religion would be restricted or prevented without such exemption. In my view, the section, if it had so intended, would itself have been invalid."

It will be seen that Walsh J (and the three judges who agreed with him) in getting thus far, paid a certain price for establishing that "discrimination" meant a distinction whether favourable or unfavourable in its effect on the party whose religion was in contemplation: namely that a conflict within the Constitution itself was disclosed, and that in order to resolve it in what is obviously the right direction, they were driven to state what amounts to this, that a perfectly general law may be invalid because of its effect on a sectional religious interest, i.e. because it has *omitted* to make an appropriate discrimination. This seems a very large proposition.

Walsh J now went on to consider the separate complaint of the plaintiffs that:

> "the discrimination is more than is necessary as it results in shops in which the only business carried on is the sale of kosher meat being open without restriction as to hours on every weekday as well as on Sundays...In my opinion the plaintiffs are justified in their complaint that the discrimination is more than is necessary in so far as it relates to weekdays other than Saturdays. There is no evidence whatsoever to suggest that the free practice of the Jewish religion would be hampered in any way by the application of the fixed hours to the kosher-meat shops on those days, and no such ground has been advanced... For the reasons I have already given, a discrimination on Saturdays would be invalid. However, the words of the exemption in Article 2 of the Order of 1948 give exemption for every day, and by its terms [it] is incapable of being modified by deletion so as to confine it to Saturdays. Therefore, in my view it is invalid although an exemption from the trading hours on Saturday would not be invalid even if in practice such an exemption was not availed of. Such an exemption would avoid the possibility of a member of the Jewish community having to choose between the practice of his religion and the sale or purchase of meat on that day."

[21] The plaintiff's counsel made it clear that his clients were not attacking the privilege of Jewish shops as such, merely seeking to get the same facility made available to themselves. It may be noted that in this case the Court depended heavily on US precedents, notably *McGowan v Maryland* 366 US 420 (1961); *Sherbert v Verner* 374 US 398 (1963): *Braunfeld v Brown* 366 US 599 (1961); *Abington School District v Schempp* 374 US 203 (1963).

The fifth member of the Court, Kenny J, reached the same conclusion on the issue of "justifiable discrimination":

> "It seems to me that the prohibition on discrimination on the ground of religious profession or belief...does not apply to legislation passed to secure or encourage the free profession and practice of religion."

But he differed on the issue of "discrimination more than is necessary", taking the view that the exemption in favour of late trading hours on all weekdays, not just Saturdays, was a "compensation" for the trading loss incurred through the observance of the Sabbath on Saturday.[21]

Department of Education rules

The *Quinn's Supermarket* case was followed in 1974-75 by two others, in which the concept of religious discrimination was further explored. In the first of these, *Mulloy v Minister for Education,*[22] what was in issue was a set of Rules for the Payment of Incremental Salary to Secondary Teachers, made by the Minister in 1958, under which the Minister might allow incremental credit in respect of service under an approved arrangement "in certain under-developed countries on the continent of Africa", but this credit was available in respect of such service only to "a recognised lay teacher", and when the plaintiff, who had given such service but was also a priest of the Holy Ghost Congregation, was refused credit for his service in Nigeria by the Department of Education, he brought an action for a declaration that the rule in question was unconstitutional. The High Court and Supreme Court unanimously held with him. In the High Court Butler J said:

> "It seems to me to be clear beyond argument that the terms of the scheme confining it to lay teachers do create a difference and do distinguish between them and teachers of a different religious status, namely, clerics such as the plaintiff. It is also clear that the ground of such discrimination is the difference in religious status."

This view was affirmed by the whole Supreme Court. Walsh J cleared out of the way one possible source of misunderstanding:

> "[Article 44.2.3] in my opinion, does not refer to "profession" in the sense that somebody is a religious in the religious life as a profession, and the Irish text of the Constitution makes quite clear that what comes under the heading of "religious profession" is the particular religious faith which is professed by the person in question."

He referred to the principle elaborated in the *Quinn's Supermarket* case, and said:

> "The present case concerns the disposition of public funds on a basis which, if sustainable, enables a person who is not a religious to obtain greater financial reward than a person who is a religious and is otherwise doing the same work and is of equal status and length of service...If that were constitutionally possible it would enable the State to prefer religious to lay people, or vice versa, in a matter which is

[22] [1975] IR 88.

in no way concerned with the safeguarding or maintenance of the constitutional right to free practice of religion...In my view, the State is not permitted by the Constitution to do this. The reference to religious status, in both the Irish text and the English text of the Constitution, relates clearly to the position or rank of a person in terms of religion in relation to others either of the same religion or of another religion or to those of no religion at all. Thus it ensures that, no matter what is one's religious profession or belief or status, the State shall not impose any disabilities upon or make any discrimination between persons because one happens to be a clergyman or a nun or a brother or a person holding rank or position in some religion which distinguishes him from other persons, whether or not they hold corresponding ranks in other religions or whether or not they profess any religion or have any religious belief, save where it is necessary to do so to implement the guarantee of freedom of religion and conscience already mentioned."

Adoption Act 1952

Shortly after Butler J had heard *Mulloy's* case, Pringle J heard the case of *M. v An Bord Uchtála.*[23] This action was brought to challenge s 12 of the Adoption Act 1952, of which sub-s 1 provided that an adoption order was not to be made unless the conditions contained in the section in regard to religion were fulfilled; and sub-s 2 provided that:

> "The applicant or applicants shall be of the same religion as the child and his parents or, if the child is illegitimate, his mother."

This of course had the effect of ruling out immediately any adoption by a couple who were parties to a "mixed" marriage; even in a case such as the present case, in which one of the applicants was the natural mother of the child whom the applicants now sought to adopt. Pringle J had no difficulty in finding s 12(2) to be "on its face" in contravention of Article 44.2.3; and for the reasons advanced by counsel for the plaintiffs. These, as summarised by himself, were:

> "The effect of [sub-s 2] is both to impose a disability and to make a discrimination in respect of (a) the plaintiffs as a group, (b) the plaintiffs individually, and (c) the child, on the ground of religious profession or belief. In regard to the plaintiffs as a group, as husband and wife, it was contended that there is a disability imposed and a discrimination caused on the ground of their religious profession or belief between a husband and wife who are of the same religion and a husband and wife, like the plaintiffs, who are of different religions. In regard to the plaintiffs as individuals, it was submitted that each of the plaintiffs is under a disability and is discriminated against because they happen to have married a person of a different religion; in addition it was said that the second plaintiff is under a disability and is discriminated against as the mother of a child whom she cannot adopt because they are not of the same religion. As regards the child, the contention is that he is under a disability and is discriminated against because he is not of the same religion as both the plaintiffs and because he is not of the same religion as his mother."

[23] [1975] IR 81; (1975) 109 ILTR 2.

[24] *Per* Walsh J, delivering the majority judgment in *Quinn's Supermarket v AG* [1972] IR 1.

[25] Part II of the First Schedule to the Juries Act 1976.

The judge was evidently willing to accede to all these arguments individually. It may be noted that the State brought no appeal from his judgment to the Supreme Court; instead, the Adoption Act 1974, was enacted, which replaced s 12 of the 1952 Act with a provision (s 4) that permits adoption irrespective of the religion(s) of adoptive parents provided that the situation in this regard is known to the person whose consent to the adoption is required.

Other possible instances of discrimination

Religious discrimination by the State is not invalid where "the implementation of the guarantee of free profession and practice of religion requires that a distinction should be made to make possible for the persons professing or practising a particular religion their guaranteed right to do so."[24] It is not clear, however, that all instances of legislative discrimination on grounds of religious profession, belief or status this test. One could imagine that the exemption of members of the clergy from jury service[25] satisfies this requirement insofar as the absence of this exemption would prevent, albeit temporarily, such a person from ministering to his or her flock. However, it is difficult to see how the preferential treatment afforded to certain religious under the Companies Acts and the Street and House to House Collections Act 1962[26] is necessary to facilitate the free profession and practice of religion. The statutory regulation of the formalities of marriage may also be vulnerable on this count, as the formalities for the various denominations are not uniform.[27] It has also been suggested that ancient statutory provisions forbidding the election to Parliament of certain types of clergymen are contrary to this provision.[28] Finally, could the prohibition on the acceptance by RTÉ of, *inter alia*, religious advertising[29] not be regarded as discrimination on grounds of the religious belief of the advertiser, which, again, is hardly defensible in terms of Article 44.2.1.

The prohibition of religious discrimination affects only the State

In *McGrath and Ó Ruairc v Trustees of Maynooth College*[30] the plaintiffs had been, while priests, appointed as professors in the College, but on becoming laicised were (for that and other reasons) dismissed. It was argued for them, *inter alia*, that this represented a "discrimination on the ground of religious status", within Article 44.2.3; but the Supreme Court unanimously rejected this submission, all the judges pointing out that the prohibition applied to the State, not to other persons or bodies; the fact that the College received a subvention from the State did not alter this. Henchy J interpreted the constitutional provision as follows:

[26] As to which, see above, pp. 1094-1095. In addition to these instances of discrimination, which in turn discriminate between religions recognised under the former Article 44.1.2-3 and religions not so recognised, s 2 of the 1962 Act also exempts church-gate collections generally from the scope of that Act. The *Report of the Committee on Fund-raising Activities for Charitable and other Purposes,* (1990, Pl.7028) recommended the exemption from registration under proposed legislation regulating fund-raising activities of charitable companies established by religious bodies, referred to in s 2 of the Companies (Amendment) Act 1986, as well as of ministers of religion who raise funds for the purposes of religion, though without considering whether such exemptions were constitutionally permissible.

[27] See the discussion in the *Report of the Committee on the Constitution* (1967), pp.47-48. The best account of the law as to the formalities of marriage, which he describes as "complex and obscure, being contained in a labyrinth of statutes stretching from 1844 to 1972", is to be found in Shatter, *Family Law in the Republic of Ireland* (3rd ed., 1986), pp.82-96. In *I.E. v W.E.*[1985] ILRM 691, the court was informed that a challenge was being mounted to the constitutionality of the Marriages (Ireland) Acts 1844 to 1871, though nothing further appears to have come of this.

[28] Casey, "*The Development of Electoral Law in the Republic of Ireland*" (1977) 28 NILQ 357.

[29] See s 20(4) of the Broadcasting Authority Act 1960.

[30] [1979] ILRM 166.

> "In proscribing disabilities and discriminations at the hands of the State on the ground of religious profession, belief or status, the primary aim of the constitutional guarantee is to give vitality, independence and freedom to religion...Far from eschewing the internal disabilities and discriminations which flow from the tenets of a particular religion, the State must on occasion recognise and buttress them. For such disabilities and discriminations do not derive from the State; it cannot be said that it is the State that imposed or made them; they are part of the texture and essence of the particular religion; so the State, in order to comply with the spirit and purpose inherent in this constitutional guarantee, may justifiably lend its weight to what may be thought to be disabilities and discriminations deriving from within a particular religion."

This passage relates to "disabilities and discriminations deriving from within a particular religion"; it is not clear, therefore, whether the courts can enforce a discrimination derived from a freely expressed private choice (e.g. a testamentary gift requiring that the donee must assume a particular religion before the gift can take effect).

RELIGION AND SCHOOLS: RELIGIOUS PROPERTY

4° Legislation providing State aid for schools shall not discriminate between schools under the management of different religious denominations, nor be such as to affect prejudicially the right of any child to attend a school receiving public money without attending religious instruction at that school.

4° Reachtaíocht lena gcuirtear cúnamh Stáit ar fáil do scoileanna ní cead idirdhealú a dhéanamh inti idir scoileanna atá faoi bhainistí aicmí creidimh seachas a chéile ná í do dhéanamh dochair do cheart aon linbh chun scoil a gheibheann airgead poiblí a fhreastal gan teagasc creidimh sa scoil sin a fhreastal.

5° Every religious denomination shall have the right to manage its own affairs, own, acquire and administer property, movable and immovable, and maintain institutions for religious or charitable purposes.

5° Tá sé de cheart ag gach aicme chreidimh a ngnóthaí féin a bhainistí, agus maoin, idir shoaistrithe agus do-aistrithe, a bheith dá gcuid féin acu, agus í a fháil agus a riaradh, agus fundúireachtaí chun críocha creidimh is carthanachta a chothabháil.

6° The property of any religious denomination or any educational institution shall not be diverted save for necessary works of public utility and on payment of compensation.

6° Ní cead maoin aon aicme creidimh ná aon fhundúireachtaí oideachais a bhaint díobh ach amháin le haghaidh oibreacha riachtanacha chun áise poiblí, agus sin tar éis cúiteamh a íoc leo.

1922 and earlier provisions

These sub-sections reproduce the substance of s 5 of the Government of Ireland Act 1920 (which in turn echoed s 7 of the Intermediate Education (Ireland) Act 1878, the Government of Ireland Act 1914 and the Home Rule Bills of 1886 and 1893) and of Article 16 of the Treaty of 1921 (the only element of that Treaty which survives in the Constitution). In the Constitution of 1922 Article 8 contained provisions virtually identical with sub-ss 4 and 6. Despite the apparent sensitiveness of this area, none of these provisions has been in issue in any case of importance either under the old or under the present Constitution; though in Northern Ireland, where the Government of Ireland Act 1920, represented the constitution until 1972, there have been several cases on the "diversion" or taking of property and compensation.[1]

Article 44.2.4

The guarantee of the right of a child to attend a school receiving public money without having to attend religious instruction at that school can be traced back to the Intermediate Education (Ireland) Act 1878. In the past, this right was respected by providing specific periods for religious instruction on the school timetable and permitting students to withdraw from such classes. At the same time, there was never any strict separation between the religious and the secular in the rest of the curriculum with the result that, for example, students could encounter literature of a religious or spiritual

[1] See e.g. *Ulster Transport Authority v Brown* [1953] NI 79; *O.D. Cars Ltd. v Belfast Corporation* [1960] NI 60; *R (Secretary of State for N.Ireland) v The Recorder of Belfast* [1973] NI 112.

nature in language classes and religious artefacts were present in most, if not all, schools. Since 1971, the teacher's handbook for the primary school curriculum has endorsed the so-called "integrated curriculum", whereby religious values permeate the entire curriculum. The constitutional status of these arrangements is unclear. On the one hand, it could be argued that the failure of publicly-funded schools to maintain a rigid separation between religious and secular instruction infringes Article 44.2.4 insofar as it deprives a student attending such a school of the freedom not to receive religious instruction. Moreover, State funding of the integrated curriculum might fall foul of the prohibition on endowment of religion in Article 44.2.2 and might also infringe the obligation imposed on the State to have due regard for the rights of parents, especially in relation to religious and moral formation in the provision of primary education.[2] On the other hand, it could be contended, applying the historical approach to constitutional interpretation, that Article 44.2.4 does not demand a rigid separation of religious and secular and that the phrase "religious instruction" must be understood as referring only to classes expressly designated for that purpose.

Article 44.2.4 arguably implies that State funding for schools must be provided by legislation.[3] Apart from any difficulties created by Article 15.2,[4] the argument that the State has the choice of disbursing such aid otherwise than by way of Act of the Oireachtas carries with it the unacceptable implication that non-statutory aid could discriminate between schools of different religious denominations or ignore the right of a student to withdraw from religious instruction.

Article 44.2.5

In *Mulloy v Minister for Education*[5] Walsh J said, though without developing the theme, that sub-s 3 of Article 44 (forbidding discrimination) must be read "in conjunction with the provisions of sub-s 5 of the same section of Article 44"; presumably, though this is not clear, to underline the interest of the plaintiff (a member of the Holy Ghost Congregation) in sharing the material benefits of the Rules which purported to exclude him from their benefit on grounds of his being a cleric.

In *McGrath and Ó Ruairc v Trustees of Maynooth College*[6] some of the judges of the Supreme Court adverted to Article 44.2.5 and its guarantee of the right of every religious denomination to manage its own affairs, in upholding the right of Maynooth College to enforce the discipline of its statutes.

In *O'Dea v O'Brien*[7] Murphy J refused to grant an interlocutory injunction to the plaintiff, a nun, who was challenging a decision of her religious superior to have her transferred from one congregation to another. According to the judge, the rules of constitutional justice did not apply to a decision made by a religious superior in relation to a member of his or her community. Article 44.2.5 would also seem to lend support to this conclusion, though it is not adverted to in the judgment.

[2] See Whyte, "*Education and the Constitution*" in Lane, ed., *Religion, Education and The Constitution* (1992) at pp. 107-108. It has also been suggested that the integrated curriculum may infringe the right to freedom of thought, conscience and religion in Article 9 of the European Convention on Human Rights - see Clarke "*Freedom of Thought and Educational Rights in the European Convention*" (1987) 22 Ir Jur (n.s.) 28.

[3] At present, virtually the entire educational policy of the State lacks statutory authority, a situation which is constitutionally suspect - see *Whyte, loc. cit.* pp.109-110.

[4] See above, pp. 107-108.

[5] [1975] IR 88.

[6] [1979] ILRM 166.

[7] [1992] ILRM 364.

Casey argues that Article 44.2.5 would seem to allow religious denominations to use public monies in support of policies which, if adopted by the State itself, would offend against the principle of non-discrimination in Article 44.2.3, a situation which he describes as "Kafka-esque".[8] For example, the State clearly cannot legislate to allow employers discriminate on grounds of religion in the recruitment of staff. However, if a religious denomination discriminates on grounds of religion in the recruitment of persons to positions which are publicly funded, such as teaching posts, can this be regarded as an exercise by the denomination of its "right to manage its own affairs"? Admittedly the prohibition on religious discrimination in Article 44.2.3 is addressed to the State and not to private individuals or organisations. On the other hand, it certainly seems contrary to the spirit of that provision for the State to be able to finance a discriminatory policy of a religious organisation and one might argue that the allocation of public monies for such a purpose is *ultra vires* the State, having regard to Article 44.2.3. In addition, it is arguable that Article 44.2.5 is designed to prevent State interference in the private affairs of a religious denomination but that where public monies are involved, the matter is no longer "private" in that sense so that the State is entitled to ensure that the monies are not spent in a manner contrary to any relevant constitutional provision, such as Article 44.2.3. Accordingly, religious denominations would be free to discriminate on grounds of religion in the use of their own resources but when using public monies, could do so only where the non-discrimination rule would work against the free profession and practice of religion.[9]

Property rights of religious denominations

Crichton v Land Commission and Gault[10] is indexed as being a case decided on Article 44.6; but, apart from being a case decided in a lower court (the Circuit Court), its status as a constitutional case seems spurious. The Land Commission had purported to acquire lands belonging to the (Church of Ireland) diocese of Kilmore and including a schoolhouse used as such and also for the general purposes of the diocese; but the Land Commission had also stated that the land was not required by them for the purposes of the Land Acts, which were the only purposes entitling them to acquire land at all. The successful challenge by the diocesan trustees could evidently have succeeded on simple grounds of vires; but Judge Sheehy went further, reciting Article 44.6, and said:

> This schoolhouse was held by a religious body for educational and religious purposes, and therefore the attempted acquisition by the Land Commission was unconstitutional and void.

Report of the Committee on the Price of Building Land

An analysis of Article 44.2.6 may be found in the *Report of the Committee on the Price of Building Land*.[11] Three difficult issues arising from this provision were identified. First, what is the meaning of the phrase, "the property of any religious denomination"? Construed literally, this phrase might not include property held on trust for a parish or a religious order. Casey suggests, however, that a purposive interpretation of this phrase is more appropriate, so that it covers "property which, directly or indirectly, comes under the aegis of a religious denomination."[12] Another difficulty with this phrase is that, on a

[8] *Constitutional Law in Ireland* (2nd ed.), p.571-2.
[9] By analogy with the position of the State in *Quinn's Supermarket v A.G.* [1972] IR 1.
[10] (1950) 84 ILTR 87.
[11] 1973, Prl. 3632. The Chairman of the Committee was Mr. Justice Kenny, to whom discussion of the constitutional issues in the Report may be ascribed.
[12] *Op. cit.*, p.573.

narrow construction, the protection of Article 44.2.6 would extend only to property held on behalf of, e.g., the Catholic Church as such and would not cover property held by bishops, religious orders or institutions sharing the Catholic faith and obedience. Writing extra-judicially, Walsh J suggested that the phrase probably does not extend to religious orders as such, on the ground that a religious order is a group of individuals which is free to change its religion as often as it likes or indeed to cease being a religious order altogether and that the property is always the property of the individuals who make up the order.[13]

Second, what is the meaning of "diverted"? Any suggestion that "diverted" amounts to something less than "taken" was discounted by the Report, having regard to the Irish text of the provision, which uses the phrase "a bhaint díobh".

Finally, what are "necessary works of public utility"? The Report did not exhaustively consider the meaning of this phrase but did conclude that a proposal to acquire land for the purpose of letting it to private builders would not come within its scope. Some assistance as to what is meant by "works of public utility" is afforded by the old Article 8, which forbade the diversion of the property envisaged "except for the purpose of roads, railways, lighting, water or drainage works or other works of public utility". This suggests that "public utility" could not be construed so as to privilege some grander function, in pursuit of which a Government might wish to take over an existing religious or educational establishment.[14]

[13] "*The Constitution and Constitutional Rights*" in Litton ed., *The Constitution of Ireland 1937-1987* (Dublin 1988) at p.103.

[14] A question which has not yet arisen is this: can it be said that the property of a religious order or institution is the property of a "religious denomination"? On a narrow construction of that phrase, the protection of Article 44.2.6 would extend only to the property e.g. of the Catholic Church as such, but this is not a legal person: its "property" is normally held by its bishops or by orders or institutions sharing the Catholic faith and obedience.

Article 45

DIRECTIVE PRINCIPLES OF SOCIAL POLICY

DIRECTIVE PRINCIPLES OF SOCIAL POLICY

Article 45

The principles of social policy set forth in this Article are intended for the general guidance of the Oireachtas. The application of those principles in the making of laws shall be the care of the Oireachtas exclusively, and shall not be cognisable by any Court under any of the provisions of this Constitution.

1. The State shall strive to promote the welfare of the whole people by securing and protecting as effectively as it may a social order in which justice and charity shall inform all the institutions of the national life.

2. The State shall, in particular, direct its policy towards securing:-

i. That the citizens (all of whom, men and women equally, have the right to an adequate means of livelihood) may through their occupations find the means of making reasonable provision for their domestic needs.

ii. That the ownership and control of the material resources of the community may be so distributed amongst private individuals and the various classes as best to subserve the common good.

iii.That, especially, the operation of free competition shall not be allowed so to develop as to result in the concentration of the ownership or control of essential commodities in a few individuals to the common detriment.

iv. That in what pertains to the control of credit the constant and

BUNTREORACHA DO BHEARTAS CHOMHDHAON-NACH

Airteagal 45

Is mar ghnáth-threoir don Oireachtas a ceapadh na bunrialacha do bheartas chomhdhaonnach atá leagtha amach san Airteagal seo. Is ar an Oireachtas amháin a bheidh sé de chúram na bunrialacha sin a fheidhmiú i ndéanamh dlíthe, agus ní intriailte ag Cúirt ar bith ceist i dtaobh an fheidhmithe sin faoi aon fhoráil d'fhorálacha an Bhunreachta seo.

1. Déanfaidh an Stát a dhícheall chun leas an phobail uile a chur chun cinn trí ord chomhdhaonnach, ina mbeidh ceart agus carthanacht ag rialú gach forais a bhaineas leis an saol náisiúnta, a chur in áirithe agus a chaomhnú chomh fada lena chumas.

2. Déanfaidh an Stát, go sonrach, a bheartas a stiúradh i slí go gcuirfear in áirithe:-

i. Go bhfaighidh na saoránaigh (agus tá ceart acu uile, idir fhear is bean, chun leorshlí bheatha), trína ngairmeacha beatha, caoi chun soláthar réasúnta a dhéanamh do riachtanais a dteaghlach.

ii. Go roinnfear dílse agus urlámhas gustail shaolta an phobail ar phearsana príobháideacha agus ar na haicmí éagsúla sa chuma is fearr a rachas chun leasa an phobail.

iii. Go sonrach, nach ligfear d'oibriú na saoriomaíochta dul chun cinn i slí go dtiocfadh de an dílse nó an t-urlámhas ar earraí riachtanacha a bheith ina lámha féin ag beagán daoine chun dochair don phobal.

iv. Gurb é leas an phobail uile is buanchuspóir agus is

predominant aim shall be the welfare of the people as a whole.

príomhchuspóir a rialós ina mbaineann le hurlámhas creidmheasa.

v. That there may be established on the land in economic security as many families as in the circumstances shall be practicable.

v. Go mbunófar ar an talamh faoi shlándáil gheilleagrach an oiread teaghlach agus is féidir de réir chor an tsaoil.

3. 1° The State shall favour and, where necessary, supplement private initiative in industry and commerce.

3. 1° Féachfaidh an Stát le fonn ar thionscnamh príobháideach i gcúrsaí tionscail is tráchtála agus cuirfidh leis nuair is gá sin.

2° The State shall endeavour to secure that private enterprise shall be so conducted as to ensure reasonable efficiency in the production and distribution of goods and as to protect the public against unjust exploitation.

2° Déanfaidh an Stát iarracht chun a chur in áirithe go stiúrfar fiontraíocht phríobháideach i slí gur deimhin go ndéanfar earraí a tháirgeadh agus a imdháil le hiniúlacht réasúnta agus go gcosnófar an pobal ar bhrabús éagórach.

4. 1° The State pledges itself to safeguard with especial care the economic interests of the weaker sections of the community and, where necessary, to contribute to the support of the infirm, the widow, the orphan, and the aged.

4. 1° Gabhann an Stát air féin cosaint sonrach a dhéanamh ar leas gheilleagrach na n-aicmí is lú cumhacht den phobal agus, nuair a bheas riachtanas leis, cabhair maireachtála a thabhairt don easlán, don bhaintreach, don dílleacht agus don sean.

2° The State shall endeavour to ensure that the strength and health of workers, men and women, and the tender age of children shall not be abused and that citizens shall not be forced by economic necessity to enter avocations unsuited to their sex, age or strength.

2° Déanfaidh an Stát iarracht chun a chur in áirithe nach ndéanfar neart agus sláinte lucht oibre, idir fheara is mná, ná maoth-óige leanaí a éagóradh, agus nach mbeidh ar shaoránaigh, de dheasca uireasa, dul le gairmeacha nach n-oireann dá ngné nó dá n-aois nó dá neart.

Influence on Indian Constitution

The influence of Article 45 has spread beyond these shores as it is clearly the inspiration for Articles 37 to 39 and 46 of the Indian Constitution[1] and Articles 32, 35 and 37 of the Constitution of the Union of Burma, 1947.

[1] See O'Normain, "*The Influence of Irish Political Thought on the Indian Constitution*" (1952) 1 Ind. YBIA 156. The provisions were not carried over verbatim - in particular, Article 37 of the Indian Constitution, while providing that the Directives Principles of State Policy are not enforceable by the courts, stated that "it shall be the duty of the State to apply these principles in making law." The Indian courts have taken the view that judicial interpretation of legislation falls within the meaning of the phrase "making law" and accordingly construe legislation in the light of these Directive Principles - see, e.g. *Balwant Raj v Union* (1968) AA 14; *UPSE Board v Hari Shankar* (1979) ASC 65.

Article 45 formerly ignored by the courts

During the first decades of the Constitution's operation it was generally assumed that the introductory words of Article 45 were to be taken literally, and that the principles expressed in the Article were completely outside the range of judicial consideration.[2] Thus, in the *Sinn Féin Funds Case*,[3] the Supreme Court, in rejecting the State's argument that the exigencies of the common good (a phrase of Article 43) were "peculiarly a matter for the Legislature", whose decisions were "absolute and not subject to, or capable of, being reviewed by the courts", said:

> "We are unable to give our assent to this far-reaching proposition. If it were intended to remove this matter entirely from the cognisance of the courts, we are of opinion that it would have been done in express terms, as it was done in Article 45 with reference to the directive principles of social policy, which are inserted for the guidance of the Oireachtas, and are expressly removed from the cognisance of the courts."

Much the same line was taken by Walsh J in *Byrne v Ireland*,[4] when he used the not-cognisable rule even more forcefully in order to assert the courts' power to enforce the performance by the State of its obligations under other Articles, on the principle *exclusio unius expressio alterius*:

> "It is also to be noted that Article 45 of the Constitution...contains an express provision that the application of those principles "shall not be cognisable by any court under any of the provisions of this Constitution". This express exclusion from cognisance by the courts of these particular provisions reinforces the view that the provisions of the Constitution obliging the State to act in a particular manner may be enforced in the courts against the State as such."

This point had previously been made in *Comyn v Attorney General*[5] when Kingsmill Moore J said that Article 45:

> "puts the State under certain duties, but they are duties of imperfect obligation since they cannot be enforced or regarded by any court of law, and are only directions for the guidance of the Oireachtas."

At the same time the Article had a significant function:

> [Its] importance, for the lawyer, lies in the implication that the duties referred to in Articles 40 to [44] are real duties enforceable by the courts at least to the extent that any law which neglects or nullifies them can be declared invalid - as has been done.

And in *O'Brien v Manufacturing Engineering Co. Ltd.*[6] Pringle J, when asked to hold that a provision of the Workmen's Compensation Act 1934, was inconsistent with the Constitution because it failed to "safeguard the economic interests of the weaker sections of the community", i.e. did not correspond with the principle of Article 45.4, said he was:

[2] The "right to an adequate means of livelihood" of Article 45.2.i was however adverted to incidentally by Gavan Duffy J in *Cooper v Millea* [1938] IR 749.
[3] *Buckley v Attorney General* [1950] IR 57.
[4] [1972] IR 241.
[5] [1950] IR 142; (1949) 83 ILTR 146.
[6] [1973] IR 334; (1974) 108 ILTR 105.

> "satisfied that by reason of the wording of the first paragraph of Article 45, whether one looks at the Irish or the English version thereof, the courts cannot enquire into the question as to whether the Oireachtas[7] has implemented what are described as the "fundamental rules for social policy" (according to the Irish version) or the "principles of social policy" (as in the English version) set forth in that Article."

In late years used as an interpretative instrument: in the context of the right to livelihood

But a somewhat different line of opinion has grown up in late years. It may be that this opinion can be traced back as far as the judgment of Budd J in 1953 when, in *Tierney v Amalgamated Society of Woodworkers*,[8] he accepted that there existed a constitutional personal right (in the sense of Article 40.3) to work; although Article 45 is nowhere mentioned in the course of his judgment or that of the Supreme Court, it is listed among the matters in issue in the headnote to the report and in the note on counsel's arguments, and Budd J referred to "the right to work and earn one's livelihood", the latter part of the phrase possibly an echo of the "right to an adequate means of livelihood" in Article 45.2.1. But the new opinion surfaced definitively in *Murtagh Properties v Cleary*[9] in 1972, when, as it happened, the right to work was again involved, in this case the right of a woman who was effectively being excluded from employment because the union concerned objected to non-male labour being used. She stated her right as "the right to earn a livelihood without discrimination of sex" and associated it with the implicit personal rights of Article 40.3; and Kenny J, in elaborating further the doctrine which he had first stated in *Ryan v Attorney General*,[10] recurred to that case for the principle on which such personal rights might be identified; they might be:

> "derived from other clauses in the Constitution or from the Christian and democratic nature of the State. The right relied on in this case is derived, it was said, from Article 45... However, the defendants argued that the Court cannot have regard to this Article because it is expressed to be for the guidance of the Oireachtas...[but the opening] passage does not mean that the courts may not have regard to the terms of the Article, but that they have no jurisdiction to consider the application of the principles in it in the making of laws. This does not involve the conclusion that the courts may not take it into consideration when deciding whether a claimed constitutional right exists."

He then went on to consider Article 45.2.1 in detail in its bearing on the plaintiff's affirmation of a right to work without sex discrimination.[11] In *Rogers v I.T.G.W.U.*,[12] where the plaintiff alleged a breach of his personal right under Article 40.3 to earn a livelihood because of the decision of the union to enforce a compulsory retirement age, Finlay P said that:

[7] The Oireachtas which enacted the 1934 Act however, was the creature of a Constitution which did not contain these "Directive Principles of Social Policy".
[8] [1959] IR 254.
[9] [1972] IR 330. Followed by Costello J in *Attorney General v Paperlink Ltd.* [1984] ILRM 373 - see below, p. 1121.
[10] [1965] IR 294.
[11] See above, p. 762.
[12] [1978] ILRM 51.

> "he provision of such compulsory retirement coupled with pension rights was in accordance with, and not in conflict with, the directive principles of social policy of Article 45 requiring and acknowledging the right of persons to earn a livelihood."

Protection of children

Similarly in *Landers v Attorney General*,[13] a challenge to a statutory provision which had the effect of prohibiting the plaintiff (a child aged eight-and-a-half) from giving singing performances on licensed premises at night, Finlay P considered himself not prevented:

> "from having some regard to the directive principles of social policy laid down in Article 45 when considering the constitutionality of a pre-Constitution statute. In particular I take the view that I am entitled to look at Article 45.4.2 which imposes upon the State the obligation of endeavouring to ensure that the strength and health of workers, men and women, and the tender age of children shall not be abused, for the purpose of reaching a general conclusion as to what may fairly be embraced by the expression "the exigencies of the common good".

On this basis he held that "the prevention of the public performance of children under ten years of age in specified types of places of entertainment could properly be considered by the legislature to be part of the common good".

Private enterprise and State monopoly

In two more recent cases, *Nova Media Services v Minister for Posts and Telegraphs*[14] and *Attorney General v Paperlink Ltd.*[15] two other judges of the High Court (Murphy J and Costello J respectively) took the presentation of arguments based on Article 45 in their stride. In the first of those cases (both of which raised the question of the State's entitlement to a monopoly) the immediate issue was whether an interlocutory injunction should be granted, so that the substantive issue was not fully explored; Murphy J merely said that the plaintiffs had "made out a stateable case" in regard to several submissions, including the submission that:

> "Article 45 - setting out as it does the directive principles of social policy - and in particular sub-paragraph 3 thereof recognises an ideological preference for private enterprise over State monopoly so that *prima facie* any *de jure* or *de facto* monopoly for the State in respect of radio broadcasting is - or so the argument goes - contrary to the Constitution."

In the latter case, which was a plenary hearing of a complaint against a courier service for breach of the Post Office monopoly, Costello J referred to a similar argument, and said:

> "This guideline [Article 45.3.1] is couched in most general language. Undoubtedly it demonstrates a view, found in other Articles of the Constitution, that the social order should not be based on a system in which all the means of production are owned by the State, and a preference for one in which, in the main, industry and commerce are carried on by private citizens rather than by State agencies. But it does not follow from this very general guideline that the Oireachtas could not pass laws establishing State trading corporations or public utilities and I do not consider

[13] (1975) 109 ILTR 1.
[14] [1984] ILRM 161.

that it is proper to infer from its provisions that the State is called upon in legal proceedings to justify the existence of a State monopoly either in the form of a public utility or a trading corporation."

Doctrine of restraint of trade

In *Kerry Co-Operative Creameries Ltd. v An Bord Bainne*[16] McCarthy J held that the doctrine of restraint of trade should be read in the light of Article 45. He said:

> "The doctrine of restraint of trade is a classic instance of the application of public policy; it has been part of the common law since the 16th century. It is desirable from the standpoint of the public good, to protect the right to work of weaker parties from abuse and to gain the economic benefits of preventing such abuses": [He then cites Article 45.2].

A little later in his judgment, he indicated that the introductory words of Article 45 did not preclude the courts from considering that Article in the construction of the common law:

> "[T]he construction of the doctrine [if restraint of trade] should be informed by the application of Article 45 of the Constitution; some decisions have excluded the application of Article 45, others have applied the Article.[17] In my view, the exclusion of the application of the Article by any court in respect of the making of laws, does not exclude their (sic) consideration in the construction of the common law."

No Supreme Court ruling yet on the status of Article 45

Apart from McCarthy J's remarks in the *Kerry Co-Op* case, this progressive minimisation of the effect of the exclusion in the introduction to Article 45 has, however, not been considered by the Supreme Court and is perhaps not yet canonical in the High Court. In 1972, some months after Kenny J had decided *Murtagh Properties v Cleary*, O'Keeffe P gave his judgment in *McGee v Attorney General*,[18] in which the plaintiff claimed that the provisions of s 17(3) of the Criminal Law Amendment Act 1935, were inconsistent with the Constitution, including Article 45. He said:

> "The Irish version of this provision differs somewhat from the English, and under the provisions of the Constitution the Irish text prevails. The difference is in the final part of the paragraph, where the Irish text reads: "agus ní hintriailte ag cúirt ar bith ceist i dtaobh an fheidhmithe sin fá aon fhoráileamh d'fhoráiltíbh an Bhunreachta seo". This appears to exclude from the cognisance of the courts only questions as to the attempts of the Oireachtas to have regard to the principles laid down in the course of framing legislation, and it may be argued that it does not preclude the consideration of these principles by the courts when a statute of the Oireachtas is not under review. Section 4 of Article 45 appears to be the section to which the plaintiff's advisers draw particular attention. In relation to Article 45, let me say at once that I do not consider that it has any relevance to the problem involved in this case. Even if it should be thought that the directive principles in

[15] [1984] ILRM 373.
[16] [1991] ILRM 851.
[17] He cited *Buckley, Byrne, Comyn, O'Brien* and *McGee* in the former category, and *Murtagh Properties, Ryan, Rodgers, Landers, Nova and Paperlink* in the latter.
[18] [1974] IR 284; 109 ILTR 29.

> Article 45 may be taken into account by the courts, and I consider that in a case such as this they cannot be, I do not consider that the principles enunciated have any bearing on the question posed. Therefore, I must leave Article 45 out of consideration."

This very cautious approach to the question of admitting the very large criteria to the machinery of much constitutional litigation was seen also in the Supreme Court when this case was under appeal; four of the five judges did not consider Article 45 at all (one of them saying he did not find it necessary to do so), while the fifth judge (FitzGerald CJ, who dissented on the main issue) curtly restated the older, conservative view on Article 45:

> "Article 45 refers to principles of social policy which are intended for the general guidance of the Oireachtas in its making of laws and which are declared to be exclusively its province and not cognisable by any court. In my opinion, the intervention by this, or any other court, with the function of the Oireachtas is expressly prohibited under this Article. To hold otherwise would be an invalid usurpation of legislative authority."

Perhaps not inconsistent with the admission of a certain background role for Article 45, but worth citing, is the dictum of Henchy J in the Supreme Court in *The People (Director of Public Prosecutions) v O'Shea*,[19] that "if any person were to institute proceedings in the High Court seeking to compel the State to give effect to any of the specified directives, the High Court would be bound to strike out those proceedings for want of jurisdiction."

Re-statement of the limited jurisdiction of the courts to consider Article 45

In *MhicMhathúna v Ireland*[20] the plaintiffs' reliance on Article 45 fell on the wrong side of the dividing line drawn in *Murtagh Properties* between judicial review of legislation and judicial identification of constitutional rights. The plaintiffs contended, *inter alia*, that a legislative policy of replacing tax-free allowances in respect of children with increased social welfare children's allowances infringed their personal right, derived from Article 45.2.1, to be allowed provide for their family from their own means as distinct from having to rely on social welfare payments. Carroll J dismissed this claim on the ground that the court could not adjudge legislation to be unconstitutional in the light of Article 45. For good measure, she went on to hold that the constitutional right claimed by the plaintiffs was not well founded.[21]

Legislature's express recognition of directive principle

An early instance of the legislature expressly recognising the Directive Principles of Article 45 is afforded by s 6(1) of the Central Bank Act 1942, which repeats the intent imputed by Article 45.2.iv to the State, namely, "that in what pertains to the control of credit the constant and predominant aim shall be the welfare of the people as a whole".

[19] [1982] IR 384.
[20] [1989] IR 504.
[21] See above, p. 780. [Article 40.3]

Article 46

AMENDMENT OF THE CONSTITUTION

AMENDMENT OF THE CONSTITUTION

Article 46

1. **Any provision of this Constitution may be amended, whether by way of variation, addition, or repeal, in the manner provided by this Article.**

2. **Every proposal for an amendment of this Constitution shall be initiated in Dáil Éireann as a Bill, and shall upon having been passed or deemed to have been passed by both Houses of the Oireachtas, be submitted by Referendum to the decision of the people in accordance with the law for the time being in force relating to the Referendum.**

3. **Every such Bill shall be expressed to be "An Act to amend the Constitution".**

4. **A Bill containing a proposal or proposals for the amendment of this Constitution shall not contain any other proposal.**

5. **A Bill containing a proposal for the amendment of this Constitution shall be signed by the President forthwith upon his being satisfied that the provisions of this Article have been complied with in respect thereof and that such proposal has been duly approved by the people in accordance with the provisions of section 1 of Article 47 of this Constitution and shall be duly promulgated by the President as a law.**

AN BUNREACHT A LEASÚ

Airteagal 46

1. **Is cead foráil ar bith den Bhunreacht seo a leasú, le hathrú nó le breisiú nó le haisghairm, ar an modh a shocraítear leis an Airteagal seo.**

2. **Gach togra chun an Bunreacht seo a leasú ní foláir é a thionscnamh i nDáil Éireann ina Bhille, agus nuair a ritear nó a mheastar a ritheadh é ag dhá Theach an Oireachtais ní foláir é a chur faoi bhreith an phobail le Reifreann de réir an dlí a bheas i bhfeidhm i dtaobh an Reifrinn in alt na huaire.**

3. **Ní foláir a lua i ngach Bille den sórt sin é a bheith ina "Acht chun an Bunreacht a leasú".**

4. **Aon Bhille ina mbeidh togra nó tograí chun an Bunreacht seo a leasú ní cead togra ar bith eile a bheith ann.**

5. **Aon Bhille ina mbeidh togra chun an Bunreacht seo a leasú ní foláir don Uachtarán a lámh a chur leis láithreach, ar mbeith sásta dó gur comhlíonadh forálacha an Airteagail seo ina thaobh agus gur thoiligh an pobal go cuí leis an togra sin de réir forálacha alt 1 d'Airteagal 47 den Bhunreacht seo, agus ní foláir don Uachtarán é a fhógairt go cuí ina dhlí.**

Amendments of the Constitution to date

There have been eleven amendments of the Constitution under the provisions of this Article (two Acts to amend the Constitution had previously been passed under the transitory provisions of Article 51). The Articles affected were: Article 16 (Fourth Amendment of the Constitution Act 1972 and Ninth Amendment of the Constitution Act

1984); Article 18 (Seventh Amendment of the Constitution (Election of Members of Seanad Éireann by Institutions of Higher Education) Act 1979); Article 29 (Third Amendment of the Constitution Act 1972, Tenth Amendment of the Constitution Act 1987 and Eleventh Amendment of the Constitution Act 1992); Article 37 (Sixth Amendment of the Constitution (Adoption) Act 1979); Article 40 (Eighth Amendment of the Constitution Act, 1983, Thirteenth Amendment of the Constitution Act 1992, Fourteenth Amendment of the Constitution Act 1992); and Article 44 (Fifth Amendment of the Constitution Act 1972). Five further Bills to amend the Constitution were passed or deemed passed by the Oireachtas, but were rejected by the people on being submitted to them by referendum.[1]

The provisions of Article 46 mean that the Constitution cannot be altered by the Oireachtas alone and that it is therefore comparatively "rigid". The 1922 Constitution was also designed to be ultimately rigid, as its Article 50 provided a similar referendum requirement for amendments after the expiry of the transitional period; but this period was extended in such a way that the Constitution remained flexible - i.e. capable of amendment by the Oireachtas alone - during its entire life. The lengths to which this flexibility was carried are described under Article 51.

No review of a Bill to amend the Constitution

There is no jurisdiction in the courts to review in any way a Bill to amend the Constitution, any more than any other Bill except in the Article 26 procedure activated by a reference from the President. This seems self-evident, but two litigants in 1983 tried to stop the progress of the Eighth Amendment of the Constitution Bill, 1982, to referendum after its passage by both Houses. One of these cases, *Roche v Ireland*,[2] is noted under Article 47. In the other, *Finn v Minister for the Environment*,[3] in which the plaintiff sought a declaration that the proposal contained in the Bill was repugnant to the Constitution and of no legal effect, the Supreme Court curtly dismissed his action in a few words, saying:

> The judicial power to review legislation on the ground of constitutionality is confined (save in cases to which Article 26 applies) to enacted laws. Save in these excepted cases there is no jurisdiction to construe or review the constitutionality of a Bill, whatever its nature. The courts have no power to interfere with the legislative process. For this reason the plaintiff lacks standing to maintain these proceedings and has no cause of action.

This case, however, received a detailed judgment from Barrington J in the High Court which is worth citing because of his interpretation of sub-s 1 of Article 46. The plaintiff's point was that the referendum proposal was superfluous, since the "right to life" of the unborn which it purported to guarantee was already implicit in the Constitution; and, since Article 46.1 permitted amendment only "by way of variation, addition, or repeal", an amendment which merely re-stated something already present was not within the Article. Barrington J traced the probable history of the formula "variation, addition, or repeal" to the point which had been argued in *The State (Ryan) v Lennon*[4] in 1934 that the power of "amendment" in Article 50 of the [1922] Constitution did not extend to a power of repeal but meant merely a power to improve, to vary in detail or to remedy defects. While this submission was rejected by the Supreme Court the case and the prob-

[1] See pp. 166, 790 and 1013.
[2] High Court, June 17, 1983.
[3] [1983] IR 154.
[4] [1935] IR 170.

lem would have been present to the minds of the drafters of the present Constitution and probably account for the wording of Article 46.1.

He said he was:

> "satisfied that by Article 46.1 the people intended to give themselves full power to amend any provision of the Constitution and that this power includes a power to clarify or make more explicit anything already in the Constitution."

There arose also in this case, in the context of the question whether a Bill expressed to be an amendment of the Constitution could be scrutinised by the courts in any form whatsoever, the hypothesis that such a Bill might, in contravention of sub-s 4 of the Article, contain some other proposal as well. Barrington J said that, in this unlikely event, the President would apparently be justified in refusing to sign it; but conceded also provisionally that the jurisdiction of the courts, however, might be invoked against the unlawful action of the Oireachtas:

> "subject to this possible exception I accept [the] submission that the High Court has no function in relation to the content of a proposal to amend the Constitution."

Similar considerations would presumably apply if the injunction of Article 46.3 (requiring an amending Bill to declare itself as such) were disobeyed.

The decisions in *Finn* and *Roche* notwithstanding, further unsuccessful attempts were made to stop referenda in 1986[5] and in 1992. In this latter case, *Slattery v An Taoiseach,*[6] the plaintiffs sought to restrain the holding of a referendum on the Eleventh Amendment of the Constitution Bill 1992 on the ground, *inter alia*, that the Government had (according to them) failed to supply the public with adequate information concerning the import of the Maastricht Treaty on European Union. This the Supreme Court was unwilling to do, saying that such intervention would be an unwarranted invasion of the judicial power. Hederman J referred extensively to the decision of the former Supreme Court in *Wireless Dealers' Association v Free Trade Commission*[7] and concluded that since the process was still in the legislative stage, there could be "no injunction against the Government to prevent them from carrying out the directions of the Oireachtas."

The Committee on the Constitution 1966-1967

Apart from the actual amendments so far made, and from the attempted amendments alluded to above, official consideration has been given from time to time to more thorough-going amendment. An all-party Committee of members of the Oireachtas, set up informally in August 1966 to consider possible changes in the Constitution, reported at the end of 1967;[8] but, apart from the Committee's unanimous recommendation in regard

[5] *MhicMathúna v Ireland, The Irish Times,* 10 June 1986 (unsuccessful attempt to stop divorce referendum).

[6] [1993] 1 IR 286.

[7] Supreme Court, 14 March 1956 (where the Court had held that, the Article 26 reference procedure aside, the courts had no power to interfere in the legislative process).

[8] *Report of the Committee on the Constitution* (December, 1967) (Pr. 9817).

to deleting Article 44.1.2-3 (which was done in 1972 by the Fifth Amendment), none of its views have been put into effect. A number of specifically legal problems arising on the interpretation and working of the Constitution were submitted to the Attorney General by the Committee, for consideration by a special legal committee under his chairmanship with a view to recommending amendments where thought desirable; this legal committee completed its work, and its report was virtually in final form, in August 1968, but this report was never published nor, indeed, does it appear that it was ever formally submitted to anyone, as the all-party Committee had by then completed its work and dispersed.

Amendment of the Preamble

As to whether the amending power of Article 46 extends to the Preamble to the Constitution, see above, p. 9.

Article 47

THE REFERENDUM

THE REFERENDUM

Article 47

1. **Every proposal for an amendment of this Constitution which is submitted by referendum to the decision of the people shall, for the purpose of Article 46 of this Constitution, be held to have been approved by the people, if, upon having been so submitted, a majority of the votes cast at such referendum shall have been cast in favour of its enactment into law.**

2. **1° Every proposal, other than a proposal to amend the Constitution, which is submitted by referendum to the decision of the people shall be held to have been vetoed by the people if a majority of the votes cast at such referendum shall have been cast against its enactment into law and if the votes so cast against its enactment into law shall have amounted to not less than thirty-three and on-third per cent. of the voters on the register.**

   2° Every proposal, other than a proposal to amend the Constitution, which is submitted by referendum to the decision of the people shall for the purposes of Article 27 hereof be held to have been approved by the people unless vetoed by them in accordance with the provisions of the foregoing subsection of this section.

3. **Every citizen who has the right to vote at an election for members of Dáil Éireann shall have the right to vote at a referendum.**

4. **Subject as aforesaid, the referendum shall be regulated by law.**

AN REIFREANN

Airteagal 47

1. **Gach togra a dhéantar chun an Bunreacht seo a leasú agus a chuirtear faoi bhreith an phobail le reifreann, ní foláir a mheas, chun críche Airteagal 46 den Bhunreacht seo, go dtoilíonn an pobal leis an togra sin má tharlaíonn, tar éis é a chur mar sin faoi bhreith an phobail, gur ar thaobh é a achtú ina dhlí a thugtar tromlach na vótaí a thugtar sa reifreann sin.**

2. **1° Gach togra, nach togra chun leasaithe an Bhunreachta, a chuirtear faoi bhreith an phobail le reifreann ní foláir a mheas go ndiúltaíonn an pobal dó más in aghaidh é a achtú ina dhlí a thugtar sa reifrinn sin, agus nach lú an méid votaí a thugtar tromlach na vótaí a thugtar amhlaidh in aghaidh é a achtú ina dhlí ná cion trí tríochad is trian faoin gcéad de líon na dtoghthóirí atá ar an rolla.**

   2° Gach togra, nach togra chun leasaithe an Bhunreachta, a chuirtear faoi bhreith an phobail le reifreann ní foláir a mheas, chun críocha Airteagal 27 den Bhunreacht seo, go dtoilíonn an pobal leis mura ndiúltaíd dó de réir forálacha an fho-ailt sin romhainn den alt seo.

3. **Gach saoránach ag a bhfuil sé de cheart vótáil i dtogchán do chomhaltaí de Dháil Éireann tá sé de cheart aige vótáil i reifreann.**

4. **Faoi chuimsiú na nithe réamhráite is le dlí a rialófar an reifreann.**

Regulation by law

Regulation of the referendum by law has been effected by the Referendum Act 1942; the Referendum (Amendment) Act, 1946; the Referendum (Amendment) Act, 1959; the Electoral Act 1960 (Part IV); the Electoral Act 1963 (Part V); the Referendum (Amendment) Act 1968; the Electoral (Amendment) Act 1972; the Referendum (Amendment) Act 1972; the Referendum (Amendment) Act 1979; the Referendum (Amendment) Act, 1983; Referendum (Amendment) Act 1984; the Electoral (Amendment) Act 1986; the Referendum (Amendment) Act 1987; Referendum (Amendment) Act 1992 and Referendum (Amendment) (No.2) Act 1992. Since 1979, every Referendum Act has provided that the ballot papers were to contain concise statements in simple language of the purpose of these Amendments and s 2 of the Referendum (Amendment) Act 1992 now provides that such statements may be provided for future referenda by simple resolution of both Houses of the Oireachtas.

Oddly enough, Article 47 does not specify any time within which a Bill to amend the Constitution is to be submitted to referendum after passing both Houses. So far as the letter of the Article goes, it would be open to the Minister for the Environment (whom s 8 of the Referendum Act 1942, authorises to appoint the polling day) to delay this indefinitely. Clearly this would be contrary to the sense of Article 47.1, but it is not so clear how a breach of that section could be established, nor by what kind of proceedings the Minister could be compelled to appoint a polling day within any particular time.[1]

In *Roche v Ireland*[2] a plaintiff attempted to stop the Eighth Amendment of the Constitution Bill 1982, being put to referendum, on the ground that, as the wording of the proposed amendment was unclear, he could not rationally decide how to vote and was thus deprived of his constitutional right to vote guaranteed by Article 47.3. Carroll J - pointing out *obiter* that he was not deprived of his vote, since if uncertain of the amendment's meaning he could simply vote against it - dismissed his action, saying that "the wording of the amendment could not be the subject of scrutiny by the courts at this stage", and that the courts had no jurisdiction to interfere with the legislative process.[3]

Duty on the part of the Government to provide information and funding for opposition groups during course of a referendum?

Two separate actions taken during the course of the referendum campaign on the Eleventh Amendment of the Constitution Bill 1992 raised the questions of whether the Government could be said to be under a duty to provide information about the Maastricht Treaty on European Union, or, indeed, to provide funding to disparate groups opposing its ratification. In essence, the plaintiffs in both cases argued that the underlying spirit of Article 47 pre-supposed a public debate in which both sides of the argument were put fairly and that these conditions were not complied with where the Government conducted a "partisan" campaign (such as placing advertisements in the media) with the aid of public funds, while denying the same benefits to the opposition groups. In the first of these cases, *McKenna v An Taoiseach*[4] Costello J said that, while he could understand the sense of grievance felt by the plaintiff, the complaint was essentially one of political misconduct which was not justiciable by the courts:

[1] For example, the Eight Amendment of the Constitution Bill 1982, passed both Houses finally on 26 May 1983, but was not put to referendum until 7 September 1983; the delay was generally understood to relate to the undesirability of a poll during the summer holiday period.

[2] High Court, 17 June 1983.

[3] See also *Finn v Minister for Environment* [1983] IR 154.

[4] High Court, 8 June 1992.

> "But not every grievance can be remedied by the courts. And judges must not allow themselves to be led, or, indeed, voluntarily wander into areas calling for adjudication on political and non-justiciable issues. They are charged by the Constitution with exercising the judicial power of government and it would both weaken their important constitutional role as well as amount to an unconstitutional act for judges to adjudicate on such issues."[5]

These are undoubtedly noble sentiments, but one still has the lingering feeling that this judgment did less than justice to the plaintiffs' contentions. By a parity of reasoning, for example, it would seem to follow that there would be no constitutional objection to the political party or parties in power availing of public funds to fund their election campaign while thereby disadvantaging the opposition parties. If one regards one of the important functions of the courts in constitutional matters as ensuring fairness in the political process,[6] then it would seem that the courts should, after all, have some role in ensuring the fair allocation of public funds for political purposes. This was certainly the view of the German Constitutional Court in the *Official Propaganda Case*[7] where the provision of public moneys to fund advertisements[8] supporting the then Government was held unconstitutional on the ground that this violated constitutional principles of equality and guarantees for free and equal elections. In the Court's view:

> "[The Basic Law] bars the State from taking sides during an election campaign in order to influence the competitive relations among political powers. Organs of the State must serve everyone and remain neutral during an election campaign."

In *Slattery v An Taoiseach,*[9] however, the Supreme Court substantially endorsed the approach of Costello J, saying that it had no role in the referendum process and it could not compel the Government to provide opposition groups with public funds to assist their campaign.

[5] Costello J also refused to grant an injunction restraining the dissemination of a guide to the Maastricht Treaty published by the Government. The plaintiffs had claimed that it was misleading and lacked objectivity. But whether this was actually so or not was a matter "for others" and was "entirely inappropriate" for judicial resolution.

[6] Cf. the re-apportionment decision in *O'Donovan v Attorney General* [1961] IR 114.

[7] (1977) 46 BVerf GE 125.

[8] Some of the advertisements contained merely factual information concerning recent legislation, but others were quite nakedly partisan in their content. The then opposition Christian Democrats took particular exception to a long-running advertisement in *Der Spiegel* which announced that: "All in all, this Government has brought you more freedom."

[9] [1993] 1 IR 286.

REPEAL OF 1922 CONSTITUTION

REPEAL OF CONSTITUTION OF SAORSTÁT ÉIREANN AND CONTINUANCE OF LAWS

BUNREACHT SHAORSTÁT ÉIREANN A AISGNAIRM AGUS DLÍTHE A BHUANÚ

[This heading refers to the next three Articles, 48-50 inclusive]

Article 48
The Constitution of Saorstát Éireann in force immediately prior to the date of the coming into operation of this Constitution and the Constitution of the Irish Free State (Saorstát Éireann) Act, 1922, in so far as that Act or any provision thereof is then in force shall be and are hereby repealed as on and from that date.

Airteagal 48
An Bunreacht a bheas i bhfeidhm do Shaorstát Éireann díreach roimh lá an Bunreacht seo a theacht i ngníomh agus an tAcht um Bunreacht Shaorstáit Éireann, 1922, sa mhéid go mbeidh an tAcht sin nó aon fhoraíl de i bhfeidhm an uair sin, aisghairtear leis seo iad agus beid aisghairthe an lá sin agus as sin amach.

Novel mode of repeal of the old Constitution

At the moment of the enactment of the Constitution, the existing legal provision governing amendment of the 1922 Constitution of Saorstát Éireann and, *a fortiori*, amendment amounting to total repeal and replacement was Article 50 of that Constitution. This provided that during the transitional period which was still running[1] amendments could be made by ordinary legislation; amendment by way of plebiscite was not mentioned. The question which here arises in connection with the mode of enactment of the 1937 Constitution in general, and Article 48 in particular, is considered above[2] in connection with the words of enactment in the Preamble.

[1] See below, p. 1168.
[2] See at p. 3.

Article 49

SUCCESSION TO THE PREROGATIVE

Article 49

1. **All powers, functions, rights and prerogatives whatsoever exercisable in or in respect of Saorstát Éireann immediately before the 11th day of December, 1936, whether in virtue of the Constitution then in force or otherwise, by the authority in which the executive power of Saorstát Éireann was then vested are hereby declared to belong to the people.**

2. **It is hereby enacted that, save to the extent to which provision is made by this Constitution or may hereafter be made by law for the exercise of any such power, function, right or prerogative by any of the organs established by this Constitution, the said powers, functions, rights and prerogatives shall not be exercised or be capable of being exercised in or in respect of the State save only by or on the authority of the Government.**

3. **The Government shall be the successors of the Government of Saorstát Éireann as regards all property, assets, rights and liabilities.**

Airteagal 49

1. **Gach uile chumhacht, feidhm, ceart agus sainchumas a bhí inoibrithe i Saorstát Éireann nó i dtaobh Shaorstát Éireann díreach roimh an 11ú lá de Mhí Nollag, 1936, cibé acu de bhua an Bhunreachta a bhí i bhfeidhm an uair sin é nó nach ea, ag an údarás ag a raibh cumhacht chomhallach Shaorstát Éireann an uair sin, dearbhaítear leis seo gur leis an bpobal iad uile.**

2. **Ach amháin sa mhéid go ndéantar socrú leis an mBunreacht seo, nó go ndéanfar socrú ina dhiaidh seo le dlí, chun go n-oibreofar, le haon organ dá mbunaítear leis an mBunreacht seo, aon chumhacht, feidhm, ceart nó sainchumas díobh sin, achtaítear leis seo nach dleathach agus nach féidir na cumhachtaí, na feidhmeanna, na cearta, agus na sainchumais sin a oibriú sa Stát nó i dtaobh an Stáit ach amháin ag an Rialtas nó le húdarás an Rialtais.**

3. **Is é an Rialtas is comharba ar Rialtas Shaorstát Éireann i gcás gach maoine, sócmhainne, cirt agus féichiúnais.**

Transfer to the people of the former Crown prerogative

The purpose of this Article is to transfer to the people (but for exercise by the Government) the position and prerogative of the British Crown, and to transfer to the Government the position of the previous Government. The drafters of the Constitution evidently considered that at least some such prerogatives had survived the enactment of the 1922 Constitution, but as a result of three major Supreme Court decisions,[1] it now transpires that this view was mistaken and that no such prerogatives have survived. As a consequence, it would seem that there is nothing left on which Article 49 can operate and that its presence in the Constitution is now somewhat redundant. As against this, the

[1] *Byrne v Ireland* [1972] IR 241; *Webb v Ireland* [1988] IR 353; [1988] ILRM 565 and *Howard v Commissioners of Public Works* [1993] ILRM 665. See generally, Kelly, "*Hidden Treasure and the Constitution*" (1988) 10 DULJ 5.

Supreme Court's decision in *Webb v Ireland*[2] seems to suggest that certain common law rules - which had hitherto been considered only as aspects of the prerogative - may, perhaps, have survived in re-constructed constitutional form if otherwise compatible with the democratic and republican character of the State. These larger questions will be considered presently. First, however, it is necessary to explain the background to Article 49 itself.

The opening sentence of Article 51 of the 1922 Constitution, as it was until amended on 11 December 1936, read:

> "The Executive Authority of the Irish Free State (Saorstát Éireann) is hereby declared to be vested in the King, and shall be exercisable, in accordance with the law, practice and constitutional usage governing the exercise of the Executive Authority in the case of the Dominion of Canada, by the Representative of the Crown."

The Article went on to envisage the Executive Council (i.e. what corresponded to the Government in the 1937 Constitution) which was to "aid and advise" in the exercise of this executive authority. Because of the surrounding "constitutional usage", enjoyed through its representative (the Governor-General) a purely symbolic and ceremonial position, the effective executive power resting with the Executive Council. These arrangements reflected Article 2 of the 1921 Treaty and, not surprisingly perhaps, it was assumed that so much of the regal prerogative rights as were not otherwise unconstitutional had survived for the benefit of the Executive Council. This seems implicit in the authoritative exposition of post-1922 constitutional theory and practice contained in the judgment of Kennedy CJ in *In re Reade.*[3] Having explained that the constitutional status of the Free State had been assimilated by Article 2 of the 1922 Constitution to that of a dominion, Kennedy CJ went on:

> "The Crown is in each Dominion the permanent symbol of executive government, but the actual executive government is in fact an unconstitutional reality in the hands of national Ministers responsible to, and changeable at the will of, the national Parliament."

Fading out of the Crown

In 1936 the Government of the day, which had already announced its intention to promote a new Constitution from which all trace of the Crown would have disappeared, anticipated this event by making the abdication of King Edward VIII (on 10 December) the occasion for a radical amendment of the old Constitution.[4] The day after the abdication the Dáil (the only House of the Oireachtas[5]) passed the Constitution (Amendment No. 27) Act which removed the Governor-General from the Constitution, and with him virtually all trace of the King, the opening sentence of Article 51, cited above, being repealed in its entirety. The King survived only in a hidden form - like a face camouflaged by foliage in a children's puzzle - namely in a new sentence interpolated into the same Article:

> "Provided that it shall be lawful for the Executive Council, to the extent and subject to any conditions which may be determined by law to avail, for the purposes of the appointment of diplomatic and consular agents and conclusion of international

[2] [1988] IR 353.
[3] [1927] IR 31.
[4] See O'Sullivan, *The Irish Free State and its Senate* (London, 1940), pp. 480ff. and Sexton, *Ireland and the Crown, 1922-1936* (Dublin, 1989) at pp. 163ff.
[5] The Senate had been abolished in 1936 by the Constitution (Amendment No. 24) Act.

> agreements, of any organ used as a constitutional organ for the like purposes by any of the nations referred to in Article 1 of this Constitution [viz. "the Community of Nations forming the British Commonwealth of Nations".]

This "organ used as a constitutional organ" turned out to be, under s 3(1) of the Executive Authority (External Relations) Act passed the next day, "the king recognised by [Australia, Canada, Great Britain, New Zealand, and South Africa] as the symbol of their co-operation". The arrangement thus made for external relations continued in force until the Executive Authority (External Relations) Act was repealed by the Republic of Ireland Act 1948, which transferred external executive functions to the President (to be exercised on the authority of the Government), and therewith cut the last institutional link between the State and the United Kingdom.

The disappearance of the Crown was considered in *The State (Attorney General) v Shaw.*[6] In this case, Finlay P held that s 5 of the Customs, Inland Revenue and Savings Bank Act 1877, which provided that in all prosecutions or proceedings "at the suit of the Crown" under the Customs Acts the same rules as to costs should apply "as shall be observed in proceedings as between subject and subject", was inconsistent with the Constitution, even though the object of the provision was to remove a privilege or immunity which would otherwise have attached to the Crown:

> "Since it has no function of any description under the Constitution of Ireland, the Crown can have no privilege or immunity in our law. It follows that a statutory provision which limits, or makes an exception to, the privileges or immunity of the Crown must be inconsistent, in its entirety, with the Constitution."

Non-survival of the prerogative

While the present status of individual prerogative rights[7] is considered below, it seems here convenient to consider the broader questions which pertain to the present applicability and utility of Article 49 itself. These questions were first addressed by Walsh J in *Byrne v Ireland*:[8]

> "The position and power granted to the King in [the 1922 Constitution owed] everything to the express provisions to that effect in that Constitution. In Saorstát Éireann he was not the personification of the State and, therefore, the common-law immunities or prerogatives of the King which were personal to him did not exist in Saorstát Éireann because any such claim postulated, of necessity, the acceptance in the Constitution of Saorstát Éireann of the King as the personification of the State. All royal prerogatives to be found in the common law of England and the common law of Ireland prior to the enactment of the Constitution of Saorstát Éireann, 1922, ceased to be part of the law of Saorstát Éireann because they were based on concepts expressly repudiated by Article 2 of that Constitution and, therefore, were inconsistent with the provisions of that Constitution and were not carried over by Article 73 thereof."

Walsh J went on to hold that for this and other reasons[9] the common law rule that the State was immune from suit had not survived the enactment of the Constitution.

[6] [1979] IR 36.

[7] This term is used for convenience purposes only and is, in fact, something of a misnomer, since none of these rights have, in fact, survived in their traditional, common law guise. Insofar as they exist at all today, they survive having gone through a form of constitutional reconstruction and metamorphosis, as happened to the former prerogative of treasure trove in *Webb v Ireland* [1988] IR 353; [1988] ILRM 565.

[8] [1972] IR 241.

[9] Considered below at pp. 1150-1151.

However, the potential significance of the wider ratio - that none of the erstwhile prerogative rights had survived beyond 1922 - did not become fully apparent until the decision of the High Court and Supreme Court in *Webb v Ireland*[10] some fifteen or more years later. In this case the plaintiffs had brought an action in detinue against the National Museum claiming the return of the Derrynaflan Chalice.[11] When the defendants set up the defence of treasure trove, the plaintiffs claimed that the prerogative of treasure trove had not survived the enactment of the Constitution of the Irish Free State. Blayney J quoted from the judgment of Walsh J in *Byrne v Ireland* and held that this reasoning was equally applicable to the prerogative of treasure trove:

> "[It was argued] that *Byrne v Ireland* decided no more than that the royal prerogative of immunity from suit had not been carried over into our law and that it did not determine what the position is in regard to the other prerogatives of the Crown. This is no doubt correct, but the reasoning on which the decision was based was that none of the prerogatives had survived under the 1922 Constitution. It was because of this that the prerogative in contention in the action, namely, immunity from suit, had not survived. The finding that none of the prerogatives of the Crown had been carried over into the law of Saorstát Éireann by the 1922 Constitution was, accordingly, part of the *ratio decidendi* in *Byrne v Ireland.*"

Accordingly, Blayney J held that the prerogative right of treasure trove had not been carried over by Article 50, and the plaintiffs were entitled to the chalice.

The Supreme Court agreed with the views of Blayney J on the question of the non-survivability of prerogative rights (and expressly approved of the reasoning of Walsh J in *Byrne*), but nonetheless found for the State on other grounds. On the broader question, Finlay CJ added:

> "It was contended...that it was possible to distinguish between a prerogative of immunity from suit...and which could be traced to the royal dignity of the King and a prerogative of treasure trove which it was stated could be traced or related not to the dignity of his person but to his position as sovereign or ruler. Such a distinction does not later the view which I have expressed with regard to the effect of the provisions of the Constitution of 1922, and appears to me to ignore the essential point which is that by virtue of the provisions of the Constitution of 1922 what w as being created position of the King in that sovereign State was such only as was vested in him by that Constitution and by the State created by it."

Some questions would seem to arise on this view, if it is to be understood as meaning that no dimension whatever of the ancient prerogative survives for the public benefit. For instance, by what authority could the Government - in the absence of specific legislative authority - establish an extra-statutory scheme such as the Criminal Injuries Compensation Tribunal, or the Civil Legal Aid Board?[12A] What about the State's power to create corporations by letters patent? Did the prerogative power to grant such letters patent; the power to grant patents of precedence for counsel[12] or, indeed, the right to

[10] [1988] IR 353; [1988] ILRM 565.

[11] The plaintiffs were amateur treasure-hunters who had found a hoard of early Christian objects at Derrynaflan (Co. Tipperary). The hoard was described by Blayney J as "one of the most significant discoveries of early Christian art ever made."

[12] As Lord Watson said in *Attorney General for Canada v Attorney General for Ontario* [1898] AC 247:

> "In England the [appointment of counsel for the Crown] has always been a matter of prerogative in this sense, that it has been personally exercised by the Sovereign with the advice of the Lord Chancellor, the appointment being made by letters patent under the sign-manual."

[12A] Note that in *MF* v *Legal Aid Board* [1993] ILRM 797 Finlay CJ said that the Board was constituted "by executive act" of the Minister, i.e., perhaps implying that Article 28 provided constitutional Authority for this decision.

grant passports[13] vanish with the enactment of the Constitution of 1922? One might argue, perhaps, that the Government could discharge such powers by virtue of the executive powers granted to it by Article 28. The fact remains, however, that were it not for the very existence of the prerogative in the first place - and its supposed survival after 1922 - no one would have ever sought to argue that the Government could have discharged such functions in the absence of appropriate enabling legislation. It is also difficult to reconcile this view with cases such as *In re Irish Mutual Insurance Association Ltd.*[14] and *Cork County Council and Burke v Commissioners of Public Works*[15] which suggested that only the specifically regal dimensions of the prerogative (i.e., those incompatible with the general republican character of the State) were assumed not to have passed over in 1922, while other parts of the prerogative - those founded on the general public interest - did so pass.

However, the radical character of both *Byrne* and *Webb* was further illustrated by the Supreme Court's decision in *Howard v Commissioners of Public Works.*[16] Here the question was whether the building of interpretative centres[17] by the Commissioners of Public Works required a prior grant of planning permission. This, in turn, raised the question of whether the Commissioners - as an emanation of the State - could avail of the supposed rule whereby the State was exempt from the application of statute. A majority of the Supreme Court declined to follow the dicta of O'Byrne and Black JJ in the *Cork County Council* case and as Finlay CJ was to point out, both of these judges had "unequivocally accepted the then accepted succession of the State to the former....Crown prerogative. Finlay CJ then led a majority[18] of the Court in holding that this supposed rule had not survived the enactment of the Constitution. Having reviewed the relevant English authorities[19] he concluded that:

> "Neither of these...decisions can be viewed as in any way declaring a principle of common law which is freed from the particular position of the Crown in English Constitutional theory, or which has by any means been divested of its association with the entire doctrine and history of the Crown prerogative."

Denham J spoke in similar terms:

> "I am satisfied that this...rule [of construction] is, in fact, so rooted in the prerogative and the Crown as the personification of the State that it is, in fact, inseparable from that concept and this is not a new rule of construction."

Note that in *Geoghegan v Institute of Chartered Accountants*, High Court, 9 July 1993 counsel for the State actually claimed that *Webb's* case notwithstanding, some regal prerogatives had survived and instanced the granting of patents of precedence as an example. It was also suggested that these powers might be exercised by the President. Murphy J said he did not have to rule on these "interesting" questions.

[13] As Finlay P said in *State (M.) v Minister for Foreign Affairs* [1979] IR 13 "the granting or withholding of a passport does not appear to be of statutory origin but would appear to have derived originally from the Crown prerogative."

[14] [1955] IR 176.

[15] [1945] IR 561.

[16] [1993] ILRM 665.

[17] The Commissioners proposed to build interpretative centres at two sites of outstanding natural beauty: Mullaghmore in County Clare and Luggala in Roundwood, County Wicklow. These proposals proved to be very controversial and evoked strong feelings on both sides of the argument.

[18] Finlay CJ, Egan, Blayney and Denham JJ; O'Flaherty J dissenting. Although Egan J agreed that the old prerogative rule had not survived, he joined O'Flaherty J (who was of the view that it had) in holding that even if one had regard only to terms of Local Government (Planning and Development) Act 1963 the Commissioners were impliedly absolved from the necessity to apply for planning permission.

[19] *B.B.C. v Johns* [1965] Ch 32; *Lord Advocate v Dumbarton D.C.* [1990] 2 AC 580.

She later added that "the absence of a presumption in favour of the executive is a natural corollary of a democratic State." Thus, with *Howard's* case the rule that the state was not bound by the application of statute disappeared and with it any lingering expectation that the specifically non-regal dimensions of the prerogative had survived the enactment of the Constitution.[20]

The consequence of this trilogy of cases - *Byrne*, *Webb* and *Howard* - is to render Article 49 quite ineffectual and redundant. By any standards, this is a remarkable interpretation to arrive at with regard to a provision of the Constitution. This principle of effectiveness - *ut res magis valeat quam pereat* - would seem no less applicable to a provision of the Constitution than it does to a statute. Moreover, it seems somewhat disingenuous to have arrive at such a conclusion without having regard to the constitutional history of the Irish Free State itself:

> "the statutory usage of the Irish Free State, positive and negative, together with the opinions of judges who played a role in drafting its Constitution, together with the record of what was actually done in those years in matters such as pardons, passports and precedence of counsel, suggest that the Crown and its prerogative were understood to have survived into the newly independent State, as far as such survival was not, in letter or in spirit, inconsistent with some specific dimension of the new Constitution. I think that for us today, 50 or 60 years later, to take the line that our fathers and grandfathers in legal, political and official life quite misunderstood the nature of the machine they were not only operating but also in fact constructed, is to adopt an unreal and intellectually unamiable position."[21]

However, the significance of the *Webb* judgment does not end there, for the Supreme Court was willing to admit of the existence of the right of treasure trove, albeit not one based on notions of the Crown prerogative, but rather transmuted via a constitutional reconstruction. As Finlay CJ explained:

> "The existence of such a general ingredient of sovereignty of the State [as recognised by Article 5] does, however, seem to me to lead to the conclusion that the much more limited right of the prerogative of treasure trove known to the common law should be upheld, not as a right derived from the Crown, but rather as an inherent attribute of sovereignty of the State which was recognised and declared by Article 11 of the 1922 Constitution."

This, it may be said, seems a pragmatic - even if intellectually unappealing - response to a problem which had been created by a certain degree of constitutional dogmatism exhibited in *Byrne*. On this view, therefore, the decision to grant a passport could, for example, be said to represent a prerogative right necessary to give effect to the democratic principles contained in Article 5 and the right to travel impliedly protected by Article 40.3. On the other hand, since there is self-evidently no constitutional provision which could, for example, justify the creation of a corporation by letters patent, this prerogative right would seem to have failed on either view of the tests established by *Byrne* and *Webb*.

With this background in mind, we may now proceed to examine some of the more important dimensions of the prerogative.

[20] Unless, of course, as happened in *Webb's* case, the former prerogative rule survives in a different constitutional guise: see fn. 7, supra.
[21] *Kelly, loc.cit.* See also Lenihan, "*Royal Prerogatives and the Constitution*", (1989) 24 Ir Jur 1.

Prior payment of debts due to the State

The prerogative of the Crown included, in 1922, the right to prior payment of Crown debts on the administration of an insolvent estate. Prior to 1922 the traditional common law priority of Crown debts had been somewhat disturbed by statute, in that certain types of debt were given priority even over some Crown debts, and some Crown debts were given a priority over others; Kennedy CJ in *In re K., an Arranging Debtor*[22] called this an "abrogation" of the prerogative priority in favour of a statutory priority. At the moment of the coming into operation of the 1922 Constitution, therefore, some part of the "Crown debts" category had been subsumed in and regulated by statute; other Crown debts however had been held by Palles CB in In *re Galvin*[23] to retain their old priority over ordinary debts.

At first it was assumed that this position had survived into the-new State. In 1926 Johnston J said *In re K., an Arranging Debtor*[24] he "had been referred to nothing in the Constitution of the Free State which abrogated or limited that principle" (of prerogative priority). Moreover, in regard to a sweeping new statutory priority created by s 38(2) of the Finance Act 1924:

> "Moneys due or payable to or for the benefit of the Central Fund shall have and be deemed always to have had attached to them all such rights, privileges, and priorities as have heretofore attached to debts due to the Crown..."

Johnston J described it as having "expressly recognised" the principle; and in the Supreme Court, although the prerogative claim in this particular case was rejected, it is clear that the Court did not envisage the 1922 Constitution as having disturbed so much of the prerogative priority as had not been superceded by a statutory one. In 1931 in *In re Hennessy,*[25]the Supreme Court expressly recognised and enforced a right of prior payment for Crown debts; Murnaghan J, who delivered the Court's judgment, said it had been argued "that no priority could exist for Crown debts since the passing of the Constitution", but dismissed this in a sentence.[26]

However, in 1938 Gavan Duffy J had to consider, in *In re Irish Aero Club*,[27] the scope of s 38(2) of the Finance Act 1924. This he held to be limited (despite its general mention of "moneys") to taxes and duties under the care of the Revenue Commissioners, and not to extend to other forms of revenue - a view with which Kingsmill Moore J and the Supreme Court afterwards agreed.[28] But, within its area of application, he said the intended priority was clear:

> "even if the assumed continuance of the royal prerogative under the then existing Constitution be open to question."

[22] [1927] IR 260; (1927) 61 ILTR 25.

[23] [1897] 1 IR 520; (1897) 31 ILTR 27.

[24] [1927] IR 260; (1927) 61 ILTR 27. The same judge was later to observe in *Cooper v Attorney General* [1935] IR 425 that "the prerogative rights of the Crown were carried over as part of the law of the Irish Free State by Article 72 of the [1922] Constitution." This case concerned a claim to prerogative rights of fishery in tidal waters Johnston J. found that the existence of such a prerogative right had never existed at common law and rejected as unsustainable the Attorney General's plea that such a prerogative right was vested in the Crown in trust for the public generally.

[25] [1932] IR 11.

[26] This decision was later followed in a series of contemporary decisions: see *In re W., an arranging debtor* [1933] IR 202; (1933) 67 ILTR 70; *In re A & B Taxis* [1931] IR 87 and *McIntosh v Thompson* [1932] IR 45.

[27] [1939] IR 204.

[28] In *In re Irish Employers' Mutual Insurance Association Ltd.* [1955] IR 176.

A few months later Gavan Duffy J had occasion to go more fully into this assumption. In *In re P.C. an Arranging Debtor*[29] a priority, not based on statute but on the alleged survival of prerogative rights, was claimed by the Minister for Posts and Telegraphs against an insolvent debtor in respect of telephone charges; and in rejecting this he constructed an elaborate comparison between the British Exchequer and the form taken by British Finance and Consolidated Fund Acts, on the one hand, and Irish Finance and Appropriation Acts ever since 1922 on the other:

> "Telephone charges were (and still are) fixed by regulations under the Telegraph Acts and the proceeds of the telephone business were paid into the British Exchequer to the account of the Consolidated Fund, or else they were applied as an appropriation in aid of moneys provided by Parliament for the service, and deemed by statute to be moneys provided by Parliament for that purpose. Now, the British Finance and Consolidated Fund Acts (unlike ordinary British statutes) opened with these words: "Most Gracious Sovereign We, Your Majesty's most dutiful and loyal subjects, the Commons of the United Kingdom of Great Britain and Ireland in Parliament assembled, towards raising the necessary supplies to defray Your Majesty's public expenses and making an addition to the public revenue, have freely and voluntarily resolved (*or* towards making good the supply which we have cheerfully granted to Your Majesty in this session of Parliament, have resolved) to (give and) grant unto Your Majesty..." The grants of public money were thus made to the King for *his* public expenses to be defrayed out of *his* exchequer. It was well established that, whenever the King's claims and those of his subjects came into competition, the King's claims must be preferred, not because he was the executive authority, but by reason of the pre-eminence which he enjoyed at common law over all persons, on the principle expressed in the phrase *detur digniori*. Any priority that the Postmaster-General may have enjoyed was, therefore, in no sense his priority; it was the prerogative of his sovereign lord, the King, to whom the moneys in question belonged in law.
>
> That was not the position under the Constitution of Saorstát Éireann, nor is it the position today. There was, and there is, a Central Fund for the revenues of the State and that Fund was not, and is not, a royal exchequer. The Finance and Appropriation Acts since 1922 contain no trace of any formula resembling those which I have cited from British money Acts...
>
> The... view that the claim of the Post Office may be sustained at common law seems to me untenable. Such a claim at common law must be a prerogative claim, properly so-called, which, if admissible under the law of Saorstát Éireann, postulates, of necessity in order to carry the prerogative, the existence (apart from the Central Fund) of some royal fund or exchequer, entitled by law to the proceeds of the telephone undertaking; I need not consider whether or not Article 49 of the new Constitution would hit a claim made on behalf of such a fund nor how the claim could be formulated under a kingless Constitution, for there is no evidence whatever of the existence of such a fund..."

(It may be added that at the outset of his judgment Gavan Duffy J took the point that Article 49.2 declares that prerogatives are to be exercised only "by or on the authority of the Government"; and in this case there was:

> "no evidence of any authority from the Government for the assertion of any of the claims which I am now considering.)"

[29] [1939] IR 306; (1939) 73 ILTR 84.

The non-survival of the prerogative right of prior payment under the Constitution of 1922, let alone that of 1937, was put beyond doubt in 1953 in *In re Irish Employers Mutual Insurance Association Ltd*.[30] Here the Commissioners of Public Works had entered into contracts of insurance with a mutual company; the company became insolvent, and the Commissioners, purporting to rely on a prerogative right, sought payment from the liquidator of sums representing compensations which the Commissioners had been compelled to make, but which their contract with the company entitled them to be indemnified for. The liquidator applied to the High Court for directions, and Kingsmill Moore J, after an exhaustive scrutiny of the history of this branch of the royal prerogative, and of the contrasting Irish and British constitutions, came to the conclusion (he was not strictly bound to follow him) that Gavan Duffy J had been correct in *P.C.'s* case. He summarised his own view thus:

> "From this survey of the Constitution, the subsequent legislation, and the forms adopted in the financial procedure I have come to the conclusion that the Central Fund of Saorstát Éireann did not possess the characteristics of a royal exchequer, that the king owned no property in Ireland, and that, therefore, the prerogative of priority payment which is dependent on the existence of a royal property, claim, or title had ceased to exist by the critical date."

That the legislature itself in 1924 had taken this view he deduced from s 38 of the Finance Act of that year; among other reasons, he said:

> "the phrase "as have heretofore attached to debts due to the Crown" is not apt to suggest that such priorities were still in existence at the passing of the Act. "Heretofore" means "formally", "before now", "in times past", and does not naturally connote a time continuing right up to the present.[31] For the latter meaning the more correct word is "hitherto". If the Legislature considered that the priorities of crown debts were still in existence the proper phraseology would be either "as now attach" or "as have hitherto attached".

The issue then went to the Supreme Court on appeal; the decision of Kingsmill Moore J was affirmed; though two of the four judges affirmed it on a ground not here relevant, the other two did so on the ground of the view tersely stated by Murnaghan J after approving Kingsmill Moore J's reasoning:

> "In my opinion there is no room for that part of the prerogative which gave Crown debts priority of demand."[32]

It will be seen, therefore, that the former prerogative of the right to prior payment of Crown debts was the first such former prerogative whose non-survival was judicially confirmed as being incompatible with the democratic and republican character of the State and, as such, was inherently not susceptible to constitutional re-construction in another form as, for example, was the case with treasure trove.[33]

[30] [1955] IR 176.

[31] On an earlier occasion "heretofore" had already been glossed as "formerly": *O'Neill v Bradley* [1929] IR 422.

[32] When Mr. Justice Kingsmill Moore died in early 1979, Mr. Justice Walsh in a tribute to him from the bench referred particularly to his judgment in this case.

[33] This, of course, is not to suggest that the present statutory provisions allowing for priority of payments in respect of, e.g., revenue debts are necessarily unconstitutional.

EXEMPTION OF STATE FROM APPLICATION OF STATUTES

It was well settled, in the pre-1922 view of the royal prerogative, that it included the right of the Crown not to be bound by statute unless expressly or implicitly referred to in the statute concerned; and two decisions of the High Court of Saorstát Éireann showed that it was taken for granted that this aspect of the prerogative had survived into and for the benefit of the new State. In *In re Maloney, a Bankrupt*[34] the Irish Land Commission succeeded in establishing a priority (next after the statutory priorities of s 4(l) of the Preferential Payments in Bankruptcy (Ireland) Act 1889) for a debt due to it from the bankrupt's estate. It is clear that the Land Commission was regarded by Johnston J as equivalent, in this case, to the Crown; he was satisfied that:

> "that branch of the prerogative on which the present claim is based - namely, that the Crown, as representing the Government and people of the country, is not bound by a statute unless it is expressly or by necessary implication referred to therein - can be resorted to... by the Land Commission acting...for and on behalf of the Minister for Finance."[35]

In 1938 the case of *Irish Land Commission v Ruane*[36] shows the High Court (in an appeal from the Circuit Court heard by Johnston and Gavan Duffy JJ) again accepting - though in the case of Gavan Duffy J, evidently with some inner reservation - that the prerogative right of exemption from statute existed in favour of the Irish State. Johnston J ruled that the tenor of s 4(1) of the Increase of Rent and Mortgage Interest (Restriction) Act 1923 was such as to indicate that the Oireachtas had intended that the 1923 Act should apply to the State and its administrative agencies, such as the Land Commission. Gavan Duffy J decided to the same effect, though on slightly different grounds. But those grounds being simple, he said he thought it "would be a pity to burden this small case" with the Land Commission's claim that:

> "because it is an organ of State, [it] is entitled as such to the benefit of some equivalent or survival under our Constitution of the prerogative whereby the British Crown was immune from the provisions of any statute which did not include it either expressly or by necessary implication. The necessary implications of this claim involve some highly interesting questions of constitutional law..."

In 1945, in *Cork County Council and Burke v Commissioners of Public Works*[37] a claim for rates on houses which were formerly Crown property and exempt was resisted on the ground that general rating enactments did not bind the State. The Supreme Court upheld this defence; O'Byrne J cited the continuation provisions of Article 73 of the 1922 Constitution and said he could:

> "see no reason for holding that the prerogative, with which I am dealing, was not transferred to the Irish Free State. It was part of the common law, which was applied to the Irish Free State by Article 73... [And in view of Articles 49 and 50 of the 1937 Constitution] it seems to me clear that the State is now entitled to the benefit of the prerogative in question."

However, the Court was the first to scrutinise objectively the whole question of whether, so to speak, such a prerogative right could live in the atmosphere of a republican

[34] [1926] IR 202.

[35] See also to the same effect the judgment of Johnston J in *Galway County Council v Minister for Finance* [1931] IR 148.

[36] [1938] IR 148; (1938) 72 ILTR 119.

[37] [1945] IR 561.

Constitution; both O'Byrne and Black JJ went beyond a mere finding of survival, and attempted to rationalise the prerogative of exemption from statute in terms which would tend to free it from any necessary connection (such as in the case of priority of payment of debt) with a royal personality and the doctrines which it might generate. O'Byrne J cited an early consideration of the issue under another republican Constitution, that of the United States of America, in the 1821 case of *United States v Hoar*,[38] in which Story J said:

> "Where the Government is not expressly, or by necessary implication included, it ought to be clear from the nature of the mischiefs to be redressed or the language used that the Government itself was in contemplation of the legislature before a court of law would be authorised to put such an interpretation upon any statute. In general, Acts of the Legislature are meant to regulate and direct the acts and rights of citizens and in most cases the reasoning applicable to them applied with very different and often contrary force to the Government itself.
>
> It appears to me, therefore, to be a safe rule, founded in the principles of the common law, that the general words of a statute ought not to include the Government, or affect its rights, unless that construction be clear and indisputable upon the text of the Act."

Black J gave judgment to the same effect. He said:

> "Much time was devoted to discussing the true nature of this right and to combating the supposition that so far as it still exists, it is inseparable from the institution of kingship. If that were so, one would not expect to find such a right recognised for over a century by the courts of the United States of America where the institution of kingship has no existence. Yet it seems that when the various States... took over the common law, they took over this prerogative right as part of it, and it has been treated as vested in their Governments."

He called attention also to other early American cases:

> "in one of which the ancient prerogative right of the king to be exempt from statutes which did not name him, was declared to have been vested in him solely as *parens patriae* and universal trustee;"

and to points in English constitutional history which lent "some support to the theory that every part of the prerogative was long conceived of as enjoyed in a fiduciary capacity". It will be seen, therefore, that both judges were anxious to anchor the prerogative of exemption from statute in a reason which would be as applicable to a republican form of government as to a monarchy.

This approach was strongly approved by Walsh J in laying the ground for his decision in *Byrne v Ireland*[39] on the supposed immunity of the State from actions of tort. In his judgment (with which Ó Dálaigh CJ agreed) he went back to *US v Hoar*, and cited from the judgment of Story J a sentence which O'Byrne J had omitted to cite:

> "But, independently of any doctrine founded on the notion of prerogative, the same construction of statutes of this sort ought to prevail, founded upon the legislative intention."

[38] (1821) 2 Mason 311; 26 Fed Cas 329. This case has a slightly unusual provenance. It is not, in fact, a decision of the US Supreme Court, but rather a decision of Story J. sitting alone as a Federal Circuit judge. The fact that it is a decision of Story J - who with the possible exception of Marshall CJ must rank as the greatest US judge of the nineteenth century - tends to give this case a peculiar authority.

[39] [1972] IR 241.

He went on to call this "a most vital sentence because it rationalises the principle expressed by Story J". A further sentence which O'Byrne J had not cited he also quoted:

> "And though this is sometimes called a prerogative right, it is in fact nothing more than a reservation, or exception, introduced for the public benefit, and equally applicable to all governments."

This approach was not to find favour with the Supreme Court in *Howard v Commissioners of Public Works*[40] where, as we have seen,[41] it was held that as the rule of exemption was inseparable from its prerogative origins, it had not survived the enactment of the Constitution. Both Finlay CJ and Denham J quoted from recent British authorities to make this point, including the following passage from the judgment of Diplock LJ in *B.B.C. v Johns*:[42]

> "The question is, thus, one of construction of a statute. Since laws are made by rulers for subjects, a general expression in a statute such as "any person", is descriptive of those upon whom the statute imposes obligations or restraints is not to be read as including the ruler himself."

Denham J thought that the "enlightening phrase" in this passage was the reference to "since laws are made by rulers for subjects..." and she went on to conclude that the British authorities demonstrated that the rule was so deeply rooted in the prerogative "and the Crown as the personification of the State that it is, in fact, inseparable from that concept". It is, of course, true that the English courts have restated the rule in these terms, but this of itself should come as no surprise especially as those courts are not concerned to engage in a form of constitutional purification exercise whereby the specifically regal dimensions of the prerogative are to be distilled separately form such portion of the prerogative that might be exercisable in the general public interest. It is also true that the general authority of the *Cork County Council* case was weakened by the fact that - as both Finlay CJ and Denham J were quick to point out - that decision "was grounded on the belief that the prerogative of the Crown survived into the new State." But the essential point made by both O'Byrne and Black JJ in that case - namely, that certain rights, formerly regarded as prerogative rights, can survive in a democratic republic and that such rights are not (to use the words of Black J) "inseparable from the institution of kingship" - remains a valid one.

This very point was well made by Stone J delivering the judgment of the US Supreme Court in *Guaranty Trust Co v United States.*[43] In deciding that the principle *quod nullum tempus occurrit regi* - that the sovereign is exempt from the consequences of its laches and from the operation of statutes of limitation - applied to the Federal Government, Stone J agreed that this rule appeared to be a "vestigial survival of the prerogative of the Crown". But this fact was of historical interest only:

> "Whether or not that alone accounts for its origin, the source of its continuing vitality where the royal prerogative no longer exists is to be found in the public policy now underlying the rule even though it may in the beginning have had a different policy basis...Regardless of the form of Government and independently of the royal prerogative once thought sufficient to justify it, the rule is supportable now because its benefit and advantage extend to every citizen and its uniform survival in the United States has been generally accounted for and justified on grounds of policy rather than upon any inherited notions of the personal privilege of the King."

[40] [1993] ILRM 665.
[41] See at pp. 1136-1137.
[42] [1965] Ch 32.
[43] 304 US 126 (1937).

Indeed, the rule that the State is not generally bound by statute has survived in the United States, albeit in a slightly modified form designed to reflect the public interest - as opposed to specifically regal character - of the rule. Thus, in *Nardone v United States*[44] Roberts J said that the rule generally applied to two distinct categories of cases. The first was where an act, if not so limited, would deprive the sovereign of a recognised or established prerogative, title or interest.[45] The second class was where the application of the statute would result in an obvious absurdity as, for example, "the application of a speed law to a policeman pursuing a criminal or the driver of a fire engine responding to an alarm.[46] It will, thus, be seen that the US Supreme Court could readily engage in this constitutional purification exercise with regard to the continued application of the rule and it is, perhaps, somewhat surprising that its Irish counterpart elected not to do likewise.

Application of the Planning Acts to State authorities

In the wake of *Howard's* case, the Oireachtas quickly stepped in to regularise the situation. The Local Government (Planning and Development) Act 1993 now provides that development by State authorities[47] will henceforth[48] be required in the case of all such developments taking place one year after the coming into force of the Act. By s 2(1)(*a*) the Minister for the Environment is empowered to provide by regulation that the Acts will not apply to specified classes of development which in the opinion of the Minister, is in connection with, or for the purposes of "public safety or order, the administration of justice or national security or defence.[49]

Whether the Oireachtas can legislate to exempt the State from the application of statute?

A question which, of course, directly arises in the wake of the 1993 Act is whether it is competent for the Oireachtas to exempt the State - whether generally or in particular classes of cases - from the application of statute. The answer would seem to be, in gen-

[44] 308 US 338 (1939).

[45] He instanced Statutes of Limitation as a "classic instance" of this and referred, approvingly, to the decision of Story J in *US v Hoar*.

[46] There is an element of this approach in the dissenting judgment of O'Flaherty J in *Howard*. He pointed out that at the time the 1963 Act was enacted, the Minister for Local Government (now Environment) enjoyed the appellate role (which was subsequently given to An Bord Pleanála) and continued:

> "It is clear that the Minister was not bound by the legislation. He could not, for example, have done anything as absurd as appeal to himself..."

[47] Defined by s 1(1) as meaning "any authority being (a) a Minister of the Government or (b) the Commissioners [of Public Works in Ireland]." This definition does *not* include local authorities and the 1993 Act now provides for a new consultation procedure by local authorities with regard to any proposed development by them: see Local Government (Planning and Development) Act 1963, s 78 (as inserted by s 3 of the 1993 Act). It is, perhaps, surprising, that the Oireachtas did not avail of the opportunity to declare expressly that the requirements as to planning permission etc. did not apply to proposed developments by local authorities. By direct analogy with *Howard's* case, it might now be argued that local authorities are caught by the application of statute (unless expressly exempted) and that this is not negatived by the presence of this new consultation procedure, much in the same way as the Supreme Court found that the presence of s 84 did not relieve State authorities from the obligation to apply for planning permission.

[48] As a transitional measure, s 4(1) exempts all post developments undertaken by State authorities prior to the coming into force of the 1993 Act save that this section does not apply to litigation pending at the date of the *Howard* decision.

[49] This allows for the exemption of prisons, court buildings, military aerodromes etc. from the application of the 1993 Act.

[50] Finlay CJ quoted with approval from the judgment of Subba Rao CJ in *State of West Bengal v Corporation of Calcutta* (1967) AIR 997 where the latter said:

> "The State can make an Act if it chooses, providing for its exemption from its operation...such an Act provided it does not infringe fundamental rights, will give the necessary relief to the State."

eral terms, yes. Both Finlay CJ[50] and Denham J[51] expressly contemplated the enactment of such legislative exemptions and, clearly, the exemption in favour of prisons, military installations etc. contemplated by s 2(1)(*a*)(i) of the 1993 Act is constitutionally defensible under Article 40.1.[52] On the other hand there are, presumably, limits to this power of exemption. This was most clearly signalled by Denham J when she said:

> "The concept of equality [in Article 40.1] includes the concept that, in the execution of their power, the organs of Government shall act with due regard to the concept of equality. Thus, while accepting that there may be specific exceptions, in general, the position of a citizen, as a person, should not be lesser that a "person" in the form of a corporate body, of whatever status."

Thus, if a statute without little self-evident justification were to exempt the State from legislating regulating ordinary private rights and duties - such as, for example, the landlord and tenant Acts - then its constitutionality would surely thus be open to question in the light of the specific reservation to this effect contained in Denham J's judgment.

Immunity from Suit

The State's immunity from suit was at first taken for granted, then circumvented

In 1922 it was beyond dispute that the Crown could not be sued. This immunity, which was treated as an aspect of the prerogative, was variously referred to the principle that the sovereign could not be made answerable in his own courts, or (so far as a pretended tortious liability was concerned) that the king can do no wrong. The general assumption, in the years after 1922, was, that this immunity from suit had survived into and for the benefit of Saorstát Éireann,[53] although strangely enough this assumption was never seriously examined, in the light of the question whether it was compatible with the 1922 or with the 1937 Constitution, until 1971.

Several cases in which the attempt was made to sue the State in the form of a Minister succeeded only in establishing subsidiary principles as valid within Saorstát Éireann, without either affirming or denying, or even questioning, the notion of what in the US was called "sovereign immunity".

[51] On this point Denham J said:

> "The Oireachtas may legislate including or including the application of an Act to the executive in accordance with constitutional parameters"

[52] See, e.g., the comments of Henchy J in *Dillane v Ireland* [1980] ILRM 167 with regard to the exemption of Gardaí from the possible exposure to costs following an unsucessful prosecution.

[53] It appears from the Dáil debate on the Bill for the Ministers and Secretaries Act 1924 that the Attorney General who promoted it (Hugh Kennedy, subsequently Chief Justice) intended s 2(1) not merely to constitute a Minister a corporation sole with perpetual succession for the purpose of being sued on *causes of action for which a Minister might already be sued* (the restrictive interpretation which was later placed on the section in *Carolan v, Minister for Defence* [1927] IR 62; (1927) 61 ILTR 27) but actually to do away with the old sovereign immunity of the Crown in the new Irish State. He said (5 *Dáil Debates* 1498, 6 December 1923): "Might I point out that this section makes a tremendous advance in this regard upon the previous[ly] existing position. In England no action can be brought against a Minister first of all without a *fiat*, and, secondly, certain kinds of action are excluded altogether: that is to say, one can only proceed by petition of right, and can only proceed in actions raised in contract. No action in respect of wrong can be brought against a Minister with or without a fiat in England. This section has advanced to the far more democratic position of permitting actions to be brought against Ministers, as such..." It would seem that, had this intention been made explicit by a specific creation of vicarious liability in Ministers for the wrongs of their subordinates in the service, the result of *Byrne v Ireland* (below, pp. 1150-1151) would have been reached nearly a half a century sooner. See generally, Osborough, "*The Demise of the State's Immunity in Tort*" (1973) 8 Ir Jur 274.

Thus, on the tort side, *Carolan v Minister for Defence*[54] was an action for damages received through the negligence of a soldier driving an Army lorry; the Minister was sued as having an alleged vicarious liability for the acts of his subordinate. The plaintiff relied on s 2(1) of the Ministers and Secretaries Act 1924, which provided that:

> "Each of the Ministers, heads of the respective Departments of State mentioned in Section 1 of this Act shall be a corporation sole under his style or name aforesaid... and may sue and (subject to the flat of the Attorney General having been in each case first granted) be sued under his style or name aforesaid, and may acquire, hold and dispose of land for the purposes of the functions, powers or duties of the Department of State of which he is head or of any branch thereof."

This action was dismissed on appeal by the High Court. Sullivan P followed the English case of *Bainbridge v Postmaster General*[55] in holding that there was no relation of master and servant (such as would ground vicarious liability) between a subordinate, such as the Army driver, and the Minister:

> "Members of the armed forces of the State are servants of the public in the employment of the Government, and, as such, fellow-servants of the Minister for Defence, for whose neglect or default he would not prima facie be liable."

As to the effect of s 2(1) of the Ministers and Secretaries Act 1924, he said:

> "I think it is reasonable to suppose that the Oireachtas intended by the above section: 1, to secure continuity of title, and obviate the necessity for the transfer of State property, rights, and obligations from a Minister to his successor; 2, to secure that persons contracting with the Government through any of its Departments should have the ordinary remedy by action available in case of breach of contract; 3, to enable a Minister to be sued in his corporate capacity for a wrongful act done by him as such Minister, or by his orders and directions. I cannot think that the Legislature intended to go further, and create by this section a liability in each Minister for ail the wrongful acts or defaults of all the persons employed in his Department."

The section therefore in effect merely replaced the former petition of right with an ordinary action, in cases of contract, and (evidently) recognised a tort liability only in respect of wrongs actually authorised by a Minister, not those committed by his subordinates. (In the particular case of injury caused through the negligent driving of a State-owned vehicle, a special statutory liability was created not long afterwards by s 170 of the Road Traffic Act 1933 - replaced by s 59 of the Civil Liability Act 1961 - whereby the Minister for Finance can be sued for damages.)

The effect of s 2(1) of the Ministers and Secretaries Act 1924, in contract cases had been seen, though only implicitly, a short time before *Carolan's* case, in *Grenham v Minister for Defence*,[56] in which the plaintiff sought to recover for the alleged hire of cars to the Army in the period 1922-24. The claim failed, but on the grounds that there was no evidence that the acts alleged were not covered by the Indemnity Act 1923, and (as Hanna J said):

> "no evidence on which [the jury] could find a contract of hire between the plaintiff and the defendant, or between the plaintiff and anyone else who was the defendant's agent *ad hoc*."

[54] [1927] IR 62; (1927) 61 ILTR 27.
[55] [1906] 1 KB 178.
[56] [1926] IR 54.

It was however clearly assumed by both counsel and the Court that an action so constituted on a contract, if established and not barred, could be maintained.

A further element entered the situation two months after the hearing of *Grenham's* case, at the end of 1925: in *Leyden v Attorney General*[57] a teacher brought an action against several parties, including the Minister for Education, seeking declarations of his salary rights, and it was argued for the defendants in the Supreme Court, in reliance on the English case of *Churchward v The Queen*,[58] that, as Murnaghan J put it, "a contract with a Government Department, which depended for its fulfilment upon a grant by the Oireachtas, [could] not in any form be made the subject of proceedings, or treated as an enforceable contract". Murnaghan J said:

> "It is not necessary, in my opinion, to give a decision upon the issues raised by such a contention: they do not preclude the Court from making a declaration in the present case as to the construction of the plaintiff's contract with the National Education Commissioners. I say only this much, that such a doctrine will require a careful scrutiny before it is given such a wide application as was here contended for."

Johnston J added:

> "*Churchward v The Queen* was an action for damages for an alleged breach of contract by the Admiralty. In the present action, however, the plaintiff claims merely a declaration as to his rights as against a public department, and it has been well settled within the last twenty years that the courts will entertain such an action... Farwell LJ said in *Eastern Trust Co. v McKenzie, Mann & Co. Ltd.*:[59] "There is a well-established practice in England in certain cases where no petition of right will lie, under which the Crown can be sued by the Attorney General, and a declaratory order obtained... It is the duty of the Crown, and of every branch of the Executive, to abide by and obey the law. If there is any difficulty in ascertaining it, the courts are open to the Crown to sue, and it is the duty of the Executive in cases of doubt to ascertain the law, in order to obey it, not to disregard it."

The following year, in *Kenny v Cosgrave*,[60] the Supreme Court gave judgment in an action brought by a builder against the President of the Executive Council on an alleged promise, and an alleged warranty of authority to promise, to indemnify the plaintiff for any loss he might sustain in refusing to compromise with striking workers. The doctrine that the Executive cannot validly contract to pay public money without the authority of Parliament was re-stated by Fitzgibbon J in terms which raise the question why he did not advert to the possibility of avoiding the consequences of the doctrine by means of a declaratory action, as in *Leyden's* case the year before (Fitzgibbon J had not been a member of the Court which decided the latter):

> "It would be wholly illegal for the Executive Council or any member of it to make a binding contract to pay public money without the authority of the Oireachtas; and the plaintiff must be assumed to know this...

57 [1926] IR 334; (1925) 59 ILTR 19.
58 (1865) LR 1 QB 173.
59 [1915] AC 750.
60 [1926] IR 517.

> The contract alleged would not have been enforceable against the Executive Council. The Executive Council could not promise to pay the plaintiff an indemnity out of public funds without the sanction of the Oireachtas, and no contract to do so would be enforceable against them nor would it be enforceable by petition of right or any analogous proceedings."

He cited in support of his position *Churchward v The Queen,*[61] *Rederiaktiebolaget Amphitrite v The King,*[62]*Auckland Harbour Board v The King*[63] and *Commercial Cable Co. v Government of Newfoundland,*[64] though the *Rederiaktiebolaget Amphitrite* case contains, in the passage cited, an apparent distinction between a "commercial contract" and an "assurance" by the Government as to "what its executive action would be in the future", the latter being the unenforceable element and of course different from the executive's situation in *Leyden's* case. The "safeguards and restrictions upon the expenditure of public money" reflected in the *Auckland Harbour Board* case, Fitzgibbon J said, were "enshrined, in a manner if anything more sacrosanct, in the Constitution of Saorstát Éireann".[65]

Kenny v Cosgrave, apart from appearing to throw some doubt on the position established in *Leyden's* case, yielded the corollary that a Minister could not be made personally liable on a contract made by him in his public capacity, nor upon an implied warranty given by him in his public capacity, that he had authority to make the contract; and that as the assumed principal could not have been made liable on the contract, no damages were recoverable from him for the absence of such an assumed authority.

In *Leen v President of the Executive Council (No. 2)*[66] the plaintiff sought to recover, by way of a declaratory action, money which he said the Oireachtas had envisaged the payment of to him when by the Appropriation Act 1924, it appropriated over £7m. to payments of compensation for malicious injury to property; again, the question of the position of the State or its Government as defendants in claims for money alleged to be due did not squarely arise, as the plaintiff failed mainly because he could not prove that the sum corresponding to the malicious injuries award made in his favour had actually been included in this £7m. But Kennedy CJ said that he wished:

> "in the fullest manner to reserve for future consideration the legal position, as to rights and remedies, of a person claiming the payment of a specific sum, payable to him, and proved to be included in the moneys which the Minister for Finance is authorised by a particular Appropriation Act to issue out of the Central Fund for the service of a particular year, if hereafter such a case should arise."

And Murnaghan J, who dissented from the other judges on the principal issue and thought the Court should declare that the Minister for Finance had no right to withhold the payment claimed, cited the words of Farwell LJ, which had been quoted by Johnston J in *Leyden's* case, about the courts' power to declare rights and the Executive's duty to respect them, adding:

> "These observations apply with even greater force in the Irish Free State...The High Court has full original jurisdiction to determine all matters and questions, whether of law or fact: Article 64."

[61] (1865) LR 1 QB 173.
[62] [1921] 3 KB 500.
[63] [1924] AC 318.
[64] [1916] 2 AC 610.
[65] See above, pp. 170-176. For a modern instance of an action in contract against a Minister, see *McKerring v Minister for Agriculture* [1989] ILRM 82.
[66] [1928] IR 408, 594.

In *Latchford v Minister for Industry and Commerce*[67] the plaintiffs succeeded in establishing their claim to the payment of a bread subsidy by means of an action for declarations; and in *Maunsell v Minister for Education*,[68] in which a teacher sued for a declaration of his rights to salary, Gavan Duffy J said:

> "I cannot entertain any suggestion that a public servant, the conditions of whose remuneration are in dispute, is precluded from invoking the jurisdiction of the High Court to declare his rights, until an Appropriation Act has been enacted providing his Department with money to pay him, however necessary it may be to prove that such an Act has been passed before an order for payment is made."

It will be noted that in all these cases, whether taking the form of actions in tort, in contract, or in a kind of statutory debt, the question of the liability of the State as such, or of the People, was never squarely raised in the context of any possible prerogative immunity inherited from the Crown; and during these years it would almost appear that the legal profession wished to avoid confronting the issue. Claims of a contractual nature against the State continued to be brought by the oblique mechanism of the declaratory action; claims of a tortious nature, so far as they failed to be met by *ex gratia* payments, were brought against the individual State servant immediately to blame, in the expectation that the State would indemnify him against an unfavourable judgment.

Signs of change hinted at in Macauley's case

The first real straw in the judicial wind came in 1965 by *Macauley v Minister for Posts and Telegraphs*,[69] in which Kenny J, in laying the ground for his finding as to the *fiat*,[70] described the nature and history of the petition of right as a mode of redress in cases where claims in contract and debt could not be brought against the Crown, and said:

> "For reasons which have never been satisfactorily explained, a petition of right could not be brought when the complaint related to a legal wrong (classified as a tort) committed by an official in the public service: in such a case an action lay against the official personally, but neither the Crown nor a Minister of State could be made liable. This absurd rule has been adopted in this country
>
> The subsequent cases in our courts (*Comyn v Attorney General*[71] and *Commissioners of Public Works v Kavanagh*[72]) have however established an entirely new concept... These two cases establish that the Republic of Ireland (or the People) is, and that Saorstát Éireann was, a legally recognised juristic person capable of holding property. In my view, the State may now be sued in the courts whenever this is necessary to vindicate or assert the rights of a citizen."

It made no difference, from the perspective of this standpoint, whether a right so asserted arose in a contractual, quasi-contractual, proprietary or tortious setting. For the first time, the High Court, even if *obiter*, had indicated that the State or People enjoyed no prerogative immunity from the assertion of an individual's right by litigation.

[67] [1950] IR 33.
[68] [1940] IR 213; (1939) 73 ILTR 36.
[69] [1966] IR 345.
[70] See pp. 770-771.
[71] [1950] IR 142; (1949) 83 ILTR 146.
[72] [1962] IR 216; (1963) ILTR 180.

The development foreshadowed in *Macauley's* case was completed in 1971 in the case of *Byrne v Ireland*.[73] Here the plaintiff was a woman who had been injured by falling into a trench which had been dug by State employees in the Department of Posts and Telegraphs and negligently refilled; her claim against the State (not the People[74]) was resisted on the ground that Ireland had inherited the former prerogative of the Crown making it immune from suit ("sovereign immunity"), the Supreme Court, in holding with the plaintiff by a majority of four to one, finally disposed of any surviving belief in this doctrine. Indeed it was held not to have survived even the enactment of the Constitution of 1922: Walsh J said:

> "[The King] was but the executive organ of Saorstát Éireann, and if he had a personal immunity that did not relieve the principal, Saorstát Éireann, from making good the damage caused by the executive organ in carrying out the executive powers of government of the principal, Saorstát Éireann, which was itself the creation of the People...
>
> I have already stated the reasons for my opinion that the King had no place in the Irish legal system after 1922, save that which was expressly provided by the terms of the Constitution of Saorstát Éireann. The power and position granted to him by Article 51 of that Constitution did not purport to grant immunity from suit in exercise of the executive authority of the Irish Free State thereby declared to be vested in him. In my view... no such immunity was available in Saorstát Éireann by virtue of any inherent quality in the royal person. If immunity from suit could have been claimed for the State, it could only have been on the basis of a rationalisation such as that enunciated in *United States v Hoar*:[75] and adopted by O'Byrne J in *Cork County Council v Commissioners of Public Works*;[76] that immunity, if it existed, would have been enjoyed by Saorstát Éireann and not by the King."

But such a rationalisation was missing in this case:

> "There is no basis, theoretical or otherwise, for a claim that the State can do no wrong or, in the particular context, that Saorstát Éireann could do no wrong; and there is no basis, in theory or otherwise, for a submission that the State cannot be made vicariously liable for a wrong committed by its officers, employees and servants in the course of the service of the State. Earlier in this judgment I have given my reasons for holding that immunity from suit is not a necessary ingredient of State sovereignty.
>
> In my view, the whole tenor of our Constitution is to the effect that there is no power, institution, or person in the land free of the law save where such immunity is expressed, or provided for, in the Constitution itself. [He gave instances of immunities of different kinds which the Constitution did contain.] But there is nothing in the Constitution envisaging the writing into it of a theory of immunity from suit of the State...stemming from or based upon the immunity of a personal sovereign who was the key-stone of a feudal edifice. English common-law practices, doctrines, or immunities cannot qualify or dilute the provisions of the Constitution ."

He went on to consider the wording and background of Article 49.1 and the Constitution (Amendment No. 27) Act and Executive Authority (External Relations) Act 1936:[77]

[73] [1972] IR 241.

[74] She had originally sued the "People of Ireland", but the High Court amended the title of proceedings (by consent) so that the defendant became "Ireland: see [1972] IR at 244.

[75] (1821) 2 Mason 311; 26 Fed Cas 329.

[76] [1945] IR 561.

[77] See pp. 1133-1134.

> "It is to be noted that neither of these Acts made any reference whatsoever to the immunities or prerogatives of the King, if any, which existed in Saorstát Éireann on the 10th December, 1936; these Acts made no reference whatsoever to any question of succession to or transmission of these prerogatives or immunities, if any. It is unnecessary to enquire what powers, functions, rights or prerogatives were exercisable by the King on the l0th December, 1936, in or in respect of Saorstát Éireann as, for the reasons I have already given, they did not include a right of immunity from suit in the courts of Saorstát Éireann. Therefore, the provisions of Article 49.1...did not carry over or set up an immunity from suit. It was quite within the competence of the People in enacting the Constitution of 1937 to provide for an immunity from suit which did not exist prior to the coming into operation of the Constitution, but no such provision was made."

He went on to point out that, even if such an immunity did exist, it would belong to the People "as distinct from the State"; and that if it were attempted to set up this People's immunity for the benefit of the State, it could, under s 2 of Article 49, only be done "by or on the authority of the Government", and - as had previously been noted in an analogous instance by Gavan Duffy J in *In re P.C., an arranging debtor*[78] there was no evidence of any such authority having been given. Budd J gave judgment to the same effect as Walsh J, saying that, so far as Article 49 was concerned, he wished only to add:

> "some observations which, in my view, indicate in a different way that immunity from suit was not carried over by this Article to the State...
>
> It is at least questionable whether a right of immunity from suit is properly describable as a right that can be "exercised", which is a word that imports the notion of something positive having to be done. It would seem more correct to say that a right of immunity from suit is something which an authority such as a State has in itself - something of a passive nature reposing in it without the right having to be set in motion in a positive sense. It can at least be said that, by reason of the nature of the wording of the Article, there are some reasonable grounds for thinking that this particular type of immunity was not intended to be included in the provisions of the Article..."

He agreed with Walsh J that immunity from suit did not exist in Saorstát Éireann, so that no problem of whether it had been carried over by Article 50 would arise; but even if it had existed in Saorstát Éireann, he thought its nature so inconsistent with both the general tenor of the 1937 Constitution and some of its individual provisions that Article 50 would not have saved it. This line of argument, however, seems relevant only if one has finally decided that immunity from suit is not envisaged at all by Article 49 (which in its own way is a "carrying-over" Article just as much as Article 50 is), and that such a privilege is to be construed as a right at common law of a species different from the sort of "prerogative" that is "exercisable" in the sense of Article 49.

Half a century after the State's foundation, accordingly, *Byrne v Ireland* has clearly established - in terms no less applicable to contract than to tort - that the State can be sued on the same basis as an individual. A result has thus been tardily achieved by judicial policy which seems originally - in 1923 - to have been a political intention.[79]

[78] [1939] IR 306; (1939) 73 ILTR 84.
[79] See p. 1145.

Constitutionality of other immunities and quasi-immunities

The question, however, remains whether it is competent for the Oireachtas to confer either a complete or a limited immunity from suit on some subordinate body which it has created, in other words for the State to create by ordinary law an immunity which it would not itself enjoy. This problem may arise for adjudication in the context of ss 64 and 88 of the Postal and Telecommunications Services Act 1983. As a result of these provisions, An Post and Bord Telecom Éireann are purportedly freed from civil liability in respect of loss caused by certain failures, delays etc. in their (monopoly) services.[80]

It is not clear how the provision would this stand up to the principles declared in *Byrne's* case, but, in principle, it would seem that such an immunity is inconsistent with the State's obligation under Article 40.3 to defend and vindicate the citizen's personal rights.[81] Different considerations may well arise in other types of immunities or quasi-immunities. For example, considerations based on the need to protect judicial independence may justify the absolute immunity from liability enjoyed by judges in respect of all judicial acts.[82] Likewise, a perceived need to avoid such "indecisiveness or delay" that might be caused if the holder of public office were to be liable in damages for all ultra vires acts means that such persons enjoy a quasi-immunity from suit and are only liable were it is established that they did not act bona fide: *Pine Valley Developments Ltd. v Minister for Environment.*[83]

Remedies available against the State

The *Byrne* decision throws up several ancillary questions touching on the range of remedies potentially available against the State. One important such question, *viz.*, the execution of judgment against the State, did not seem to cause the Supreme Court any difficulty; Walsh J said:

> "It is unnecessary at this juncture to consider how such a decree [a judgment against the State and not against the Attorney General] would be executed or enforced but it is sufficient to say that an order for mandamus to compel compliance with the judgment would be an appropriate step and not without precedent."

Budd J said he took it for granted that "the necessary moneys to meet the decree" would be voted:

> "That would only be what would be normally expected in a State governed according to the rule of law, and there would seem to be no reason to believe that the State would not honour its legal obligations... It is unnecessary to come to a final decision on the ways and means of enforcing such a decree beyond remarking that prima facie the ordinary procedure of execution by way of levy or enforcement by mandamus would both seem to be appropriate."

[80] See also s 36 of the Fire Services Act 1981 (which clothes fire and sanitary authorities with a complete immunity from suit in respect of alleged negligence in the discharge of their statutory functions), s 61 of the Safety, Health and Welfare at Work Act 1989 (which confers a complete immunity on the National Authority for Occupational Safety and Health).

[81] Cf. *Ryan v Ireland* [1989] IR 177 (where the Supreme Court held that such common law immunities as existed which relieved the Defence Forces from liability in respect of injuries to soldiers engaged on active service were unconstitutional).

[82] See Hogan and Morgan, *Administrative Law in Ireland* (London, 1991) at 716-7.

[83] [1987] IR 23. See also *McMahon v Ireland* [1988] ILRM 610.

In *The State (King) v Minister for Justice*[84] Doyle J granted an order of mandamus against Minister for Justice to provide (as was his statutory duty) proper courthouse accommodation at Waterford. The case would have passed unremarked but that the former immunity of the Crown's Ministers from such orders was raised by the respondent. Doyle J said the 1922 Constitution had altered radically the concept of royal or even of parliamentary sovereignty, reciting in Article 2 "a formal declaration that all powers of government and all authority...are derived from the people of Ireland." This in turn meant that no such common law immunity had survived the enactment of the 1922 Constitution. [85]

In one important case, however, something of a discordant note was struck when the Supreme Court stated - albeit without giving reasons - that it did not seem appropriate ever to grant an injunction against Ireland: *Pesca Valentia Ltd. v Minister for Fisheries.*[86] Instead, the practice is to grant the injunction against some agent of the State - such as a Minister, or the Director of Public Prosecutions or even, perhaps, the Government.[87] As has been noted, this immunity would seem difficult to justify:

> "If Ireland can be liable for damages, why should it enjoy an immunity for another form of remedy, such as an injunction? This is especially so, given that it now seems that mandamus (a very similar form of remedy to an injunction) will lie against Ireland."[88]

Damages against the State for breach of constitutional duty

The question of whether the State can be liable for breach of constitutional duty has not been finally settled. In *Crowley v Ireland*[89]Kenny J, speaking for the Supreme Court majority, expressly refrained from giving an opinion on "the difficult question whether damages may be awarded against a Minister of State or Ireland for failure to perform a duty imposed by the Constitution". What is clear, however, is that such an action , if it lies at all, will only lie in respect a breach of a *personal* constitutional right. This emerges from the judgment of Murphy J in *Greene v Minister for Agriculture.*[90] Here the plaintiffs established that a headage payments scheme implemented by the Minister had infringed Article 41.3.1 (which provides that the State "pledges to protect the institution of marriage, on which the family is founded and to protect it against attack") in that it discriminated against married persons.[91] While Murphy J accepted that Article 41.3.1 imposed a duty which was enforceable against the State - he might almost have said that it was a constitutional imperative - it did not amount to a personal constitutional right (such as the right to liberty or the right to property) and, hence, the plaintiffs could not recover damages in respect of such breach:

[84] [1984] IR 169. Judgment was in fact delivered in 1975.

[85] Costello J later rejected a similar submission in *The State (Sheehan) v Government of Ireland* [1987] IR 550, where it had been argued that mandamus could not lie against the Government. This submission had been apparently based on the proposition that "in English law since a prerogative order emanates from the Crown it cannot lie against the Crown." But, as Costello J observed, there was here "no analogy" between "the law of Ireland and England on this topic", since under the Constitution:

> "the Government which it establishes is not the successor to the Crown. There is no constitutional reason, therefor, which would prohibit the making of an order of mandamus against the Government."

[86] [1985] IR 193.

[87] In *Crotty v An Taoiseach* [1987] IR 713 both Barrington J and the Supreme Court granted the plaintiff an interlocutory injunction restraining the Government from ratifying the Single European Act.

[88] *Hogan and Morgan, op.cit.* 723.

[89] [1980] IR 102. Note also that in *Pine Valley Developments Ltd. v Minister for the Environment* [1987] IR 23 Finlay CJ also reserved the question of whether an action might lie against the State for failure "on the part of the Oireachtas to legislate in protection of personal rights".

[90] [1990] 2 IR 17.

[91] See below at pp. 993-994.

> "Whilst I accept that citizens are entitled to ensure that [Article 41.3.1] is honoured, the duty cast on the State does not create a corresponding right in the individual citizen so that a breach of duty would necessarily constitute an infringement of any right of his."[92]

If this view is correct, then it would seem to follow that a private citizen cannot recover for breach by the State of a constitutional imperatives - such as, for example, the duty of absolute Government confidentiality created by Article 28.4 or the non-establishment of religion provisions contained in Article 44.2.3. But even on this analysis a breach of what would normally be regarded as a personal constitutional right may not give rise to liability on the part of the State. Suppose, for example, that parts of the Censorship of Publications Acts were declared unconstitutional on the ground that their provisions were overbroad. Could the author of a book whose publication was wrongly enjoined by the Censorship Board recover damages for breach of his constitutional right of free expression?

Damages for breach of constitutional rights

It is, however, now plain that damages may be awarded against the State[93] for breach of constitutional rights. In practice, such liability will be awarded on a vicarious basis, as happened in what appears to have been the first case where such damages were awarded: *Kearney v Minister for Justice.*[94] Here a prisoner was awarded a small sum of damages for breach of his constitutional right to communicate following the wrongful refusal of certain prison officers to deliver some items of personal correspondence. Likewise, in *Kennedy v Ireland,*[95] the State was made vicariously liable for actions of a former Minister for Justice and certain police officers in respect of the unlawful interference with the plaintiffs' constitutional rights to privacy.[96]

Aspects of the State as a litigant

It may be briefly noted that in *Byrne v Ireland* Walsh J emphasised the role of the Government in respect of actions against the State, and envisaged in theory a situation in which the Government might decline to have the State defended in litigation:

> "There can be no doubt that when the State is sued it is entitled to defend itself; this power or right to defend itself is one which can be exercised in respect of the State only by or on the authority of the Government by virtue of the provisions of Article 49.2...If in such a case it is the Attorney General's opinion that the Government should authorise the defence by the State of the claim brought against it, the defence is a matter of public interest and is properly financed out of public moneys. If the Government does not wish to authorise the defence by the State, then the Attorney General would not defend the case either."

[92] At first sight, this holding seems incompatible with the decision in *Murphy v Attorney General* [1982] IR 241, where the plaintiffs recovered taxes found to have been levied unconstitutionally following the invalidation of certain sections of the Income Tax Act 1967 on the ground that it breached the pledge contained in Article 41: see pp. 992-993. It might be argued that this relief was simply restitutionary, and ancillary to the main finding of unconstitutionality and did not amount - as such - to an award of damages for breach of Article 41.3.1. This, however, seems a very fine point of distinction.

[93] Of course, damages may be awarded where another private citizen has infringed the constitutional rights of another: see *Meskell v C.I.E.* [1973] IR 121; *P.H. v John Murphy & Sons Ltd.* [1987] IR 621; [1988] ILRM 300 and *Conway v I.N.T.O.* [1991] 2 IR 305.

[94] [1986] IR 116.

[95] [1987] IR 587.

[96] Their telephones conversations had been unlawfully intercepted.

In *Murphy v Attorney General*[97] the Supreme Court observed that in a case where the plaintiff claimed unliquidated damages against the State, it was not sufficient merely to join the Attorney General. As Walsh J had observed in *Byrne's* case, if such a claim was to succeed, judgment would be against the State and not against the Attorney General, since the latter would only have been joined in a representative capacity.

In addition, there seems to be no reason why the State should not sue as plaintiff in its own right and there appears to be at least two instances of where this has occurred.[98]

Rights and prerogatives relating to property

The State Property Act 1954, makes provision in its Part III for "rights and prerogatives belonging to the People in relation to property, escheat and *bona vacantia*". The first section in this Part (s 27) provides that:

> "Every right and every prerogative which, by virtue of Article 49 of the Constitution, belong to the People and relate to any property (including choices-in action) shall be exercised by the Government through and by the Minister for Finance."

In view of the reasoning in *Webb v Ireland* this provision would now seem to be redundant, as no such Article 49 type prerogatives have survived the enactment of the Constitution.[99]

Note also s 19 of the 1954 Act which deals with "gifts to a State authority, the Nation or the People"; and s 18 which gives the same priority as is conferred on certain debts by s 38(2) of the Finance Act 1924, to:

> "moneys due or payable to a State authority by way of former crown rent or rent, rent-charge, royalty or other profits of State land or by way of fees in respect of State land."

[97] [1982] IR 241.

[98] *Ireland v Mulvey*, *The Irish Times*, November 11, 1989 (claim by the State to ownership of an eight-century cross by virtue of Article 5 of the Constitution); *Ireland v Kelly* [1992] ILRM 582 (claim by the State that Chief State Solicitor should be appointed executor of particular will).

[99] A similar fate would seem to have befallen s 377(4) of the Companies Act 1963 which states that nothing in s 377 (which imposes certain requirements on unregistered companies, including those created by charter) "shall...restrict the power of the Government to grant a charter in lieu of or supplementary to any such charter as aforesaid..." However, if this prerogative has not survived the enactment of the Constitution s 377(4) would appear to be redundant, there being nothing on which it can operate. Charters granted before 1922 are not, it seems, affected by the subsequent constitutional changes and have been carried over by Article 50 of the Constitution: see *Geoghegan v Institute of Chartered Accountants in Ireland*, High Court, 9 July 1993. Note that the Government are empowered by s 5(2) of the Executive Powers (Consequential Provisions) Act 1937 to adapt any such existing charters, letters patent etc. by providing that any references to the Crown shall be read as referring to the Government.

CONTINUANCE OF LAWS

Article 50

1. **Subject to this Constitution and to the extent to which they are not inconsistent therewith, the laws in force in Saorstát Éireann immediately prior to the date of the coming into operation of this Constitution shall continue to be of full force and effect until the same or any of them shall have been repealed or amended by enactment of the Oireachtas.**
2. **Laws enacted before, but expressed to come into force after, the coming into operation of this Constitution, shall, unless otherwise enacted by the Oireachtas, come into force in accordance with the terms thereof.**

Airteagal 50

1. **Na dlíthe a bheas i bhfeidhm i Saorstát Éireann díreach roimh lá an Bhunreacht seo a theacht i ngníomh leanfaid de bheith i lánfheidhm agus i lánéifeacht, faoi chuimsiú an Bhunreacht seo agus sa mhéid nach bhfuilid ina choinne, go dtí go n-aisghairtear nó go leasaítear iad nó aon chuid díobh le hachtú ón Oireachtas.**
2. **Dlíthe a bheas achtaithe roimh an mBunreacht seo a theacht i ngníomh agus a mbeidh luaite iontu iad do theacht i bhfeidhm dá éis sin, tiocfaid i bhfeidhm de réir mar a luaitear iontu mura n-achtaí an tOireachtas a mhalairt.**

1922 Provision

When the Irish Free State came into being in 1922 its Constitution contained, in Article 73, a provision practically identical with s 1 of the present Article 50. The old Article 73 was generally taken to be the vehicle on which the whole *corpus* of law used in Ireland was carried across the constitutional divide and formally continued in force in the new State, except to the extent that inconsistencies between it and the new Constitution itself might emerge. Similarly in 1937 the present Article 50 was taken to have the same function of perpetuating generally the pre-1922 *corpus* plus whatever accretions the 1922-1937 period had brought to it.

The "inconsistency" test, of course, does not refer merely to conflicts between old Acts and new constitutional rights; an old statutory provision may fail to survive simply because it does not make sense in the context of the legislative separation of 1922 and the emergence of independence. Thus in *I.T.G.W.U. v T.G.W.U.*[1] Meredith J held that s 6 of the Trade Union Act Amendment Act 1876, which provided for mutual registrations of unions between England, Scotland, and Ireland, was inconsistent with the Constitution:

> "The whole basis of the section is a legislative union, and it provides for recognitions and reciprocal obligations for which a section applicable only to, and in, Saorstát Éireann could not possibly provide. That being so, it is unnecessary to point out the inconsistencies with our Constitution, by reason of the vesting of important jurisdictions in external authorities, that would result from a partial or one-sided application - entire application being quite impossible - of the section in Saorstát Éireann."

[1] [1936] IR 471.

Scope of Article 73

A potentially important question (albeit one with decreasing significance as the date 1922 recedes further) relates to the scope of Article 73. Did it capture, subject to constitutional inconsistency, only those items of legislation which might properly be described as "domestic" in character (i.e., legislation relating directly or indirectly to matters bearing on the Irish Free State)[2] or did it also operate to bring over into our law *all* items of pre-1922 legislation enacted by the Westminster Parliament, even though some of this legislation (such as that bearing on Great Britain or the colonies) would have had no relationship with Ireland. To put the question another way, did Article 73 capture legislation such as that dealing with private railways in Yorkshire or colonial solicitors?[3] If the answer is in the affirmative, this would suggest that Article 73 captured the entirety (subject, of course, to possible constitutional inconsistency) of the pre-1922 Westminster statute roll, but that virtually all of this "non-domestic" legislation is redundant or spent.

The possible dimensions of this problem first surfaced in *Performing Rights Society Ltd. v Bray UDC,*[4] where the case turned on whether the Copyright Act 1911 was carried over by Article 73. The Supreme Court, reversing Johnston J, held that the 1911 Act no longer had any application in the Irish Free State[5] and that Article 73 had no application, since the Act had ceased to have efficacy in the Free State upon its establishment. The Privy Council[6] restored the reasoning of Johnston J, with Lord Sankey LC offering this view on the effect of Article 73:

> "It is not a question of what laws "came over" at the critical moment, but that the right view to take is that by virtue of Article 73 all such laws as were in force immediately before the 6th December 1922, continued and remained in force except so far as they were inconsistent with the Constitution, and [I] cannot hold that the Copyright Act 1911, and its provisions were in any way inconsistent with the Constitution."

This would suggest that Article 73 captured all legislation then existing in 1922, subject only to possible constitutional inconsistency. The matter was considered again by a Divisional High Court in *The State (Kennedy) v Little,*[7] where it had been suggested that the Fugitive Offenders Act 1881, was not "domestic" or "municipal" legislation (in the sense that it did not appertain to the Irish Free State). This analysis of the 1881 Act was not accepted by Johnston J, but he did, however, observe that:

[2] This was the argument of Mr. Gavan Duffy K.C. (as he then was) in *The State (Kennedy) v Little* [1931] IR 39.

[3] The usage of statute would seem to suggest a negative answer to this question, since a perusal of the latest *Index to Statutes* (Dublin, 1985) demonstrates that the Oireachtas has seen fit to amend only local and personal Acts affecting persons or entities within its jurisdiction such as - to take purely random examples - Limerick Corporation Gas Act 1878 and the Rathmines and Rathgar Water Act 1880. Note also that s 17 of the Adaptation of Enactments Act 1922 provides that the expression "British statute" shall include "Local and Personal Acts *having effect in Saorstát Éireann.*" (authors' italics). This is further evidence for the proposition that the Oireachtas was of the view that pre-1922 local and personal Acts which did not have effect within this jurisdiction were not captured by Article 73. Any such parliamentary practice cannot, however, be conclusive on the point.

[4] [1928] IR 506. The decision of the Privy Council is reported at [1930] IR 509.

[5] Because s 25(1) of that Act had restricted its application to the United Kingdom, but not to any "self-governing dominion unless declared by the Legislature of that dominion to be in force therein." The Irish Free State was no longer part of the United Kingdom and the Oireachtas had never expressly adopted the provisions of the 1911 Act.

[6] This was one of the very few cases in which the Privy Council had granted leave to appeal pursuant to Article 66 of the 1922 Constitution prior to the abolition of the right to apply for leave to appeal in 1933.

[7] [1931] IR 39; (1931) 65 ILTR 9.

"It is obvious that different considerations apply to each of these classes of legislation, and no useful result can be achieved by bulking them together as 'Imperial' or 'Colonial' or 'reciprocal' or 'non-municipal.' When they come to be considered in the Irish courts, each must be viewed in the light of its own object and provisions."

Here, at least, there is a suggestion that certain types of pre-1922 legislation were not in any sense carried over by Article 73.

This question was squarely addressed by Costello J in *Donegal Fuel and Supply Co. Ltd. v Londonderry Port and Harbour Commissioners*[8] which concerned the survival of the 19th century private legislation which had imposed a statutory duty on a Northern Irish statutory body to maintain and repair a pier in Donegal. This anomalous situation resulted from the failure on the part of the Oireachtas to enact the appropriate legislation after 1922, but Costello J held that this legislation was unconstitutional. He thought that the test for Article 73 purposes was whether such legislation could have been enacted by the Oireachtas immediately after the enactment of the Constitution:

"The legislative powers conferred by Article 12 of the [1922] Constitution [meant] that the power of the Oireachtas to [legislate] did not include a power to legislate for matters which were within the exclusive jurisdiction of other sovereign States. "

Costello J concluded that legislation such as this could not have been constitutionally enacted by the Oireachtas, since it purported to impose financial and other burdens on a foreign corporation and "would have constituted and amounted to an unjustified interference in the internal affairs of the United Kingdom." For these reasons, he felt that such legislation had not survived the enactment of the Constitution. On this analysis, therefore, it follows that only such pre-1922 "domestic" legislation - i.e., that legislation which, when adapted, deals with matters properly within the provenance of the Oireachtas - has actually been carried over by Article 73. This, in turn, serves to place a rather narrower construction on the scope of Article 73 than had previously been envisaged.

Article 72 (and Article 50) concerned "with the content of the law and not its source"

Another question relating to both Article 73 of the 1992 Constitution and the present Article 50 arises following the demise of the prerogative in the light of a series of Supreme Court decisions,[9] namely, whether certain powers previously exercised by virtue of the prerogative power in the pre-1922 United Kingdom have survived the enactment of the Constitution. This question arose in *Geoghegan v Institute of Chartered Accountants in Ireland,*[10] where the respondent body had been incorporated by royal charter in 1888. While it seems implicit in the judgment of Murphy J that he

[8] High Court, 6 May 1992. But cf. *Waterford Harbour Commissioners v British Railways Board* [1979] ILRM 296 which concerned somewhat analogous 19th century legislation which imposed a statutory duty on the defendants to maintain a daily steamer service between Waterford and Fishguard. Although the legislation had been repealed in the United Kingdom, it remained unrepealed by the Oireachtas. Costello J held that the 1898 Act became part of Irish law by virtue first of Article 73 of the 1922 Constitution and by Article 50 of the present Constitution and that the plaintiffs could recover damages for breach of that duty. But while this case was distinguished by Costello J in *Donegal Fuel*, the distinction between the two cases is not self-evident. Both cases would seemed to have involved the imposition of an onerous statutory duty on a foreign corporation and, to judge by the reasoning in the later case, the 1898 Act at issue in the *Waterford Harbour Commissioners* case would seem to have been equally open to constitutional objection.

[9] *Byrne v Ireland* [1972 IR 241; *Webb v Ireland* [1988] IR 353; [1988] ILRM 565 and *Howard v Commissioners of Public Works* [1993] ILRM 665.

[10] High Court, 9 July 1993.

accepted that such prerogative power could not now be exercised, he rejected the argument that a body which had been validly incorporated prior to 1922 "in pursuance of a charter granted in accordance with royal prerogative withered away or ceased to have the right to exercise the powers conferred upon it by Charter" on the coming into force of the Constitution. He continued that he could see no reason in principle why:

> "a law enacted in Great Britain in medieval times by the Monarch himself in pursuance of the legislative which (as well as judicial and executive powers) vested in him not merely as a theoretical concept but as a practical reality could not have passed into the laws of the Irish Free State. The filtering process provided by Article 73 of the 1922 Constitution (like the comparable provision in the 1937 Constitution) related to the content of the law and not its source."

While one may detect an element of judicial pragmatism in this approach - and Murphy J frankly admitted that "any other result would be chaotic in the extreme" - it does present some theoretical difficulties. If, indeed, Article 50 is only concerned with "the content of the law and its source", then it would seem to follow that legislation enacted, powers exercised etc. prior to the 1937 could not be challenged on the ground that the procedures which were followed then would now be regarded as constitutionally flawed. It seems to follow from this that legislation enacted by the Oireachtas of Saorstát Éireann between 1922 and 1937 cannot be challenged on separation of powers grounds. It would also seem to mean that whereas the Government cannot *now* seek to exercise any prerogative powers in relation to , say, charter bodies, the actual establishment of such bodies - provided it was done prior to 1922 - cannot now be challenged on the ground that the original prerogative power in question has since disappeared. The dimensions of this particular distinction remain to be fully explored.

Judicial review of pre-1937 law

Many cases in which pre-1937 law has been under consideration in the courts in a constitutional setting contain a formal reference to Article 50 (or the old Article 73, or both) as being the route by which such law still retains validity.[11] Conversely, findings of unconstitutionality in respect of pre-1937 law take the formal shape of findings of "inconsistency" with the Constitution (not, properly speaking,[12] of "repugnancy" or "invalidity") so as not, therefore, to get the benefit of the continuance provision of Article 50.1.[13] Findings of unconstitutionality in respect of pre-1922 law have sometimes led the courts to declare that the law was already inconsistent with the 1922 Constitution, so as not even to have been continued into Saorstát Éireann by the old Article 73 (so that the formal question of its further continuance under the 1937 Constitution would not arise);[14] and at other times the courts, in finding a pre-1922 law

[11] E.g., *Western Australian Insurance Co. v Attorney General* [1926] IR 57; (1925) 59 ILTR 109; *In re Reilly, a bankrupt* [1942] IR 416; (1943) 77 ILTR 38; *Waterford Harbour Commissioners v British Railways Board* [1979] ILRM 296.

[12] See *The State (Sheerin) v Kennedy* [1966] IR 379; above pp. 421-422.

[13] E.g., *The State (Quinn) v Ryan* [1965] IR 70; (1966) 100 ILTR 105 (s 29 of the Petty Sessions (Ireland) Act 1851); *The State (Sheerin) v Kennedy* [1966] IR 379 (s 7 of the Prevention of Crime Act. 1908); *King v Attorney General* [1981] IR 224 (s 4 of the Vagrancy Act 1824); *Cashman v Clifford* [1989] IR 121 (s 13(5)(*a*) of the Betting Act 1931); *Murphy v Wallace* [1993] 2 IR 138 (s 90 of Excise Management Act 1827); *People (Director of Public Prosecutions) v JT* 3 Frewen 141 (s 1(*c*) of Criminal Evidence (Amendment Act 1924).

[14] See, e.g. *Byrne v Ireland* [1972] IR 241; *Webb v Ireland* [1988] IR 353; [1986] ILRM 565 (non-survival of Crown prerogatives); *Donegal Fuel and Supply Co. Ltd. v Londonderry Port and Harbour Commissioners*, High Court, 6 May 1992.

inconsistent with the 1937 Constitution, have not bothered to say whether it was already inconsistent with that of 1922.[15] The criteria on which, and the techniques by which, the consistency of pre-1937 law with the Constitution is tested have been described above, under Article 34.3.2.[16]

"Least possible change" principle

The general purpose of the old Article 73, to which that of the present Article 50 is obviously analogous, was stated briefly by O'Byrne J (who had served on the committee which drafted the 1922 Constitution) in *The State (Kennedy) v Little:*[17]

> "It seems to me to have been intended to set up the new State with the least possible change in the previously existing law, and that Article 73 should be so construed as to effectuate this intention...[Pending any legislation that might amend what was carried over] I am of opinion that the fullest possible effect should be given to Article 73, and that the previously existing laws should be regarded as still subsisting unless they are clearly inconsistent with the Constitution."

This particular case turned on whether the Fugitive Offenders Act 1881 was still in force, so the matter of carrying-over statute law was in the front of the Court's mind; Johnston J said he thought the Court:

> "should be very slow to do anything that would have the effect of depriving the Saorstát of the benefit of the vast body of statutory law which regulated hundreds and thousands of necessary matters in the body politic at the date of the coming into operation of the Constitution."[18]

In *The State (Hully) v Hynes*[19] Davitt P referred with approval to what O'Byrne J had said in *The State (Kennedy) v Little,* and added that the mere fact that a pre-1922 statute required adaptation in post-1922 conditions was no proof of an inconsistency with the Constitution.

Applicable to non-statutory as well as to statutory law

But the equal applicability of Article 73 to non-statutory, common or judge-made law seemed taken for granted, not only in the words of O'Byrne J ("least possible change") and the rationalisation of Johnston J ("slow to deprive ourselves of the benefit" being a principle which bore just as clearly on common law); Ronan LJ had said in the old Court of Appeal in *R. (Armstrong) v County Court Judge of Wicklow*[20] in a terse *dictum*

[15] E.g., *The State (C.) v Minister for Justice* [1967] IR 106; (1968) 102 ILTR 177, in which Ó Dálaigh CJ said: "If [s 13 of the Lunatic Asylums (Ireland) Act 1875] is inconsistent with the Constitution, it will not be necessary to go further back [to the Constitution of 1922]."

[16] The only possible differences between post and pre-1937 laws in this regard appear to relate to the doctrines of severance and the presumption of constitutionality.

[17] [1931] IR 39; (1931) 65 ILTR 9.

[18] Cf. also the words of Johnston J in *Performing Right Society Ltd. v Bray UDC* [1930] IR 506:

> "I cannot believe that this great constitutional change [of 1922] brought with it, or was intended to bring with it, a juristic vacuum in any department of national activity. On the contrary, it is plain beyond controversy that the Constitution is based upon the assumption of the existence in the Irish Free State of a fully developed body of law, regulating all rights and duties within that territory."

And while the Supreme Court reversed Johnston J on the very special facts of this case, this statement of principle would seem nonetheless applicable.

[19] (1966) 100 ILTR 145.

[20] [1924] 2 IR 139; (1924) 58 ILTR 33, 121. This judgment of Ronan LJ was recalled by Black J in *In re Reilly, a Bankrupt* [1942] IR 416; (1943) 77 ILTR 38.

with a demotic ring: "But for that Article there would be no law at all in the country".[21] The survival (if consistent with the Constitution) of common law was later recognised by Murnaghan J in *Fogarty v O'Donoghue*[22] when he said:

> "The web of life cannot...easily be broken, and the Constitution adopted, as Dáil Éireann had previously adopted, the existing laws and statutes...This adoption...was made by Article 73 of the Constitution."

The same view was expressed by Fitzgibbon J in *The State (McCarthy) v Lennon*[23] when he said the common law privilege against self-incrimination was continued in force by the old Article 73; and under the 1937 Constitution by Gavan Duffy J in *Exham v Beamish*,[24] when he said, in an unambiguous context of judge-made rules:

> "In my opinion, when Saorstát Éireann, and afterwards Éire, continued the laws in force, they did not make binding on their courts anything short of law."

In *Cork Co. Council and Burke v Commissioners of Public Works*[25] O'Byrne J said that the former royal prerogative "was part of the common law, which was applied to the Irish Free State by Article 73".[26] In *Mayo-Perrott v Mayo-Perrott*[27] Kingsmill Moore J held that the former rule recognising the validity of divorces granted in other jurisdictions had been carried over by Article 50 unless inconsistent; and in *Educational Co. v Fitzpatrick (No. 2)*[28] he spoke of Article 50 "carrying forward statutes *or law* into our *corpus iuris*".

Dissent of Mr. Justice Walsh

The only dissent from this general view of Article 50 is the *dictum* of Walsh J (with whom O'Higgins CJ agreed) in *Gaffney v Gaffney*.[29]He said:

> "Contrary to what appears to have been the view of Kingsmill Moore J in the *Mayo-Perrott* case] I do not think that Article 50...refers to any law other than statute law, and in my view the text of Article 50 makes that clear. The reference is not to "law" or to "the law" but to "the laws" in a context which deals with repeal or amendment by enactment of the Oireachtas. It will be noted that [Article 40.4.1] uses the phrase "in accordance with law" and [Article 40.4.2] speaks of somebody being detained "in accordance with the law". Our law contains a great deal more than statute law; many of the doctrines of the common law, which are regarded as part of our law, were created by judges and in due course came to be modified, if not entirely abandoned, by judges."

[21] Cf. O'Casey, *The Shadow of a Gunman* (1923) Act 1: *Seamas*: Just you be careful what you're saying', Mr. Mulligan. There's law in the land still. *The landlord:* Be me sowl there is, an' you're goin' to get a little of it now (*serves notice to quit*).

[22] [1926] IR 531.

[23] [1936] IR 485.

[24] [1939] IR 336.

[25] [1945] IR 561. See also the comments of Murnaghan J, in *Ormsby v Ormsby* (1945) 79 ILTR 97; those of Gavan Duffy P and Black J in *In re Tilson, Infants* [1951] IR 1; (1952) 86 ILTR 49. Likewise, in *The State (Lavelle) v Carroll*, High Court, 25 October 1963 Davitt P held that the common law presumption that the law in a foreign jurisdiction was the same as here until the contrary was proved was so "sufficiently well established" as to have become part of our law by virtue of Article 73 of the 1922 Constitution and Article 50.

[26] The statement by O'Byrne J to the effect that the prerogative had survived is, of course, no longer good law. See, e.g. *Howard v Commissioners of Public Works in Ireland* [1993] ILRM 665 and pp. 1143-1144.

[27] [1958] IR 336.

[28] [1961] IR 345: "Statutes *or* law"; authors' emphasis.

[29] [1975] IR 133.

He went on to make the point that, if it were otherwise - i.e. if non-statutory, judge-made law were to be regarded as caught by Article 50 - the organic growth (and decay) of principles of judge-made law would stop, as Article 50.1 itself appears to confine all amending power to the Oireachtas; and such an interpretation of Article 50 must be unacceptable:

> "Neither Article 73 of the Constitution of Saorstát Éireann nor Article 50 of the present Constitution could be construed as freezing our common law, or other non-statutory law, in the condition in which it was found at the coming into force of the Constitution of 1922 so that it could never be departed from save by enactment of the Oireachtas."

The view of Walsh J contains difficulties and has not been followed

Apart from the question whether this position taken up by Walsh J is the product of an over-minute exegesis of the Constitution's text, already adverted to in another context,[30] it seems to involve the problem of the source of validity of non-statutory law of pre-1922 origin, if this body of law cannot rely for its survival on the continuance provisions of the old Article 73 and the present Article 50; and this would seem to be the inevitable conclusion to be drawn from the interpretation placed on Article 50 by Walsh J, since by expressly mentioning and preserving statute law (when it might, if this were so intended, have just as easily mentioned and preserved all forms of law) it must be taken to disclaim sponsorship of the non-statutory rules.

Perhaps the best way to approach this matter is, firstly, to admit that the expression "repealed or amended" does suggest the changing of legislative measures; but to say, secondly, that "amendment" is not an inappropriate expression to denote the statutory alteration of rules of common law. It might then be said that the remaining question is only the old problem, essentially a verbal one, whether judges "make" law, or merely "declare" it by processes of analogy, distinction, and so on. The point which it seemed to Walsh J important to uphold, namely the traditional area of freedom of the judges, is in jeopardy only if it is insisted that this is a "law-making" function; this is of course reserved to the Oireachtas by Article 15.2.1 in explicit, and by Article 50.1 in implicit, terms.

But the very same judicial freedom seems rescued if it is presented as a function essentially interpretative; so seen, it does not collide with the exclusive *amending* power given by Article 50.1 to the Oireachtas.[31] Indeed it could be argued also that the interpretative power, from which whole new structures of law have emerged, is itself part of the common law, and just as much carried over by the old Article 73 and the present Article 50 as any other part.

[30] See pp. xcviii-xcix.

[31] Cf. the comments of Lardner J. in *R.T. v V.P. (orse. V.T.)* [1990] 1 IR 545:

> "Historically, the common law has developed at least in part by the application of established principles to new cases - to novel facts and circumstances. It has undoubtedly involved the development of the law and novel judicial decisions are not uncommonly referred to as judge-made law. It is a judicial activity which had occurred in Ireland for centuries and has contained in the superior courts prior to the enactment of the Constitution of Ireland, 1937. In my view it is not in its proper exercise an impermissible exercise of the legislative function."

In fact the suggestion of Walsh J has not been endorsed in any subsequent case. In *Vone Securities Ltd. v Cooke* [32] Costello J said the common law rule, that the word "month" meant "lunar month" unless a contrary intention appeared was part of the law in 1922 and was carried over by virtue of the old Article 73 and Article 50. And in *McKinley v Minister for Defence*[33] Hederman J was terse in his opposition to this suggestion:

> "I do not accept that the words "laws" in Article 50 restrict common law procedures or remedies only to those current in 1937."[34]

Indeed, Walsh J appears to have rejected this suggestion when delivering the judgment of the Court of Criminal Appeal in *People (Director of Public Prosecutions) v JT*[35] when he said that the effect of the Supreme Court's decision in *The State (Browne) v Feran*[36] was to hold that Article 50 "encompasses not merely all prior statutory rules, but also all prior common law rules."

Finally, in *W. v W.*[37] the Supreme Court held that the common law rule which had been at issue in *Gaffney's* case - namely, a wife's domicile of dependency - was itself unconstitutional[38] and, by virtue of Article 50, had not survived the enactment of the Constitution. This again is implicit acknowledgement of the fact that, had the rule not been unconstitutional, it would have been brought over by Article 50, thus scotching the suggestion that Article 50 only had application in respect of statute law.

Status of pre-1922 judgments of the House of Lords and the old Irish Court of Appeal

In regard to judge-made law, an important question arises on the joint operation of the old Article 73 and the present Article 50, namely, to what extent pre-1922 judgments of the House of Lords are binding on the Irish courts, *apart* from the possibility of inconsistency with the Constitution. This arose in an acute form in *Exham v Beamish*,[39] in which Gavan Duffy J rebelled against the suggestion that the English rule (established before 1922) which measured the question of a void perpetuity from what might happen, seen from the date of a settlement, irrespective of what actually did then happen, and which refused to regard the age of child-bearing as having any natural limits, ought to be regarded as law here too. He said:

> "As a matter of practice, we constantly refer to judgments in the English courts and such judgments, as every lawyer will recognise, have often proved to be of great service to us; but let us be clear. In my opinion when Saorstát Éireann, and afterwards Éire, continued the laws in force, they did not make binding on their courts anything short of law. In my opinion, judicial decisions in Ireland before the Treaty,[40] and English decisions which were followed here, are binding upon this

[32] [1979] IR 59. In *S v S* [1983] IR 68 O'Hanlon J. accepted that the common law rule in *Russell v Russell* formed part of the common law as it existed prior to 1937, but that, as the rule itself was unconstitutional, it was not carried over by Article 50.
[33] [1992] 2 IR 333.
[34] Here a majority of the Supreme Court took the novel step of extending the common law action for loss of consortium by allowing a wife to sue in respect of her husband's injuries.
[35] (1988) 3 Frewen 141.
[36] [1967] IR 147.
[37] [1993] ILRM 294.
[38] In that it offended against the equality guarantee in Article 40.1: see p. 713.
[39] [1939] IR 336.
[40] This is presumably a slip for "before the coming into force of the Constitution of Saorstát Éireann", the date material to the old Article 73. The signing of the Treaty a year earlier is not a date of materiality to the continuance or non-continuance of laws.

> Court only when they represent a law so well settled or pronounced by so weighty a juristic authority that they may fairly be regarded, in a system built up upon the principle of *stare decisis*, as having become established as part of the law of the land before the Treaty; and to bind, they must, of course, not be inconsistent with the Constitution.
>
> ... In my opinion, this Court cannot be fettered in the exercise of the judicial power by opinions of very different courts under the old regime, unless those opinions must reasonably be considered to have had the force of law in Ireland, so that they formed part of the code expressly retained...If, before the Treaty, a particular law was administered in a way so repugnant to the common sense of our citizens as to make the law look ridiculous, it is not in the public interest that we should repeat the mistake. Our new High Court must mould its own *cursus curiae*; in so doing I hold that it is free, indeed bound, to decline to treat any such absurdity in the machinery of administration as having been imposed on it as part of the law of the land; nothing is law here which is inconsistent with derivation from the people."

This view appeared to recognise not one but two hurdles which the pre-1922 common law had to cross in order to remain law in the new State: not only had it to harmonise with the express terms of the Constitution, but it had to pass the test of non-repugnance to the people's common sense as well. The innovatory spirit of Gavan Duffy J - seen also in such cases as *Cook v Carroll*,[41] *Maguire v Attorney General*[42] and *In re Tilson, Infants*[43] - did not in this instance spread to the other judges; his decision in *Exham v Beamish* remains largely isolated. In *Boylan v Dublin Corporation*,[44] decided by the Supreme Court ten years later, Maguire CJ said that a decision of the House of Lords given a month before the 1922 Constitution came into force "would appear to be binding on this Court"; and Black J (who differed from Maguire CJ as to the actual result in the case before the Court) took the same view of the English precedent:

> "In view of the date of this decision - November 1922 - I regard myself as bound by whatever it decided and by every logical corollary thereof."

Six months later, in *Minister for Finance v O'Brien*,[45] Murnaghan J said:

> "Decisions - or, rather, the advice - of the Privy Council are not of binding authority here, but as I understand the position, decisions of the House of Lords upon law common to England and Ireland given before the coming into operation of the Constitution of 1922 are of binding force in the courts until their effect has been altered by our Legislature."

Shortly afterwards, in *Corry v National Union of Vintners, Grocers and Allied Trades Assistants*[46] Maguire CJ described a 1914 House of Lords decision as "binding upon the [Supreme] Court."

41 [1945] IR 515; (1945) 79 ILTR 116.
42 [1943] IR 238; (1943) 77 ILTR 139.
43 [1951] IR 1; (1952) 86 ILTR 49.
44 [1949] IR 60.
45 [1949] IR 91; (1950) 84 ILTR 95.
46 [1950] IR 315. Cf. also the judgment of O'Hanlon J in *S. v S.* [1983] IR 68 where the "narrow and outmoded" nature of the rule in *Russell v Russell* seems to have assisted the judge to his conclusion that the rule itself was unconstitutional and not carried over by Article 50. Note also the comments of Kenny J in *Spa Estates v Ó hArgáin*, High Court, 20 June 1975, where he described a decision of the Court of Appeal for Southern Ireland as "plainly wrong", yet reserved the question of whether he was bound by a decision of that Court.

In more recent times, less deference has been paid to pre-1922 decisions. Thus, in *Henehan v Allied Irish Banks Ltd.*,[47] Finlay P said - in language which echoed that of Gavan Duffy J in *Exham v Beamish* - that he was not bound by a decision of the old Irish Court of Appeal that a personal litigant could not recover the costs of his travelling expenses to and from court. He said there was a "patent illogicality and injustice" in such a rule, and that, in order to give effect to the constitutional right of access to the courts:

> "the order for costs when made within the discretion of the Court should include properly incurred and vouched travelling expenses for the purpose of presenting the case."

But this approach is less likely to be adopted where property or other vested rights are at stake. This was made clear by the Supreme Court in *Vone Securities Ltd. v Cooke*,[48] where the court applied the common law rule whereby the word "month" when used in a lease means "lunar month" unless the contrary intention appears. Henchy J rejected the submission that the court had power to modify the application of a rule which he conceded was an "unjustifiable archaism", as this:

> "would involve the retroactive abrogation of the rule in its application to existing circumstances. That, however, would fly in the face of property rights already acquired in compliance with, or by the operation of, the rule... It would not be proper for this Court to give the rule the retroactive rejection asked for, particularly having regard to the guarantees in the Constitution as to property rights."

This would seem to suggest that the operation of the principle contained in *Exham v Beamish* should be confined within strict limits; even, perhaps, that *Exham v Beamish* itself was wrongly decided, in that it, too, sanctioned the retrospective abrogation of a vested property right.

In more recent times the matter arose in *Irish Shell Ltd. v Elm Motors Ltd.*,[49] and McCarthy J in the Supreme Court said that the pre-1922 decisions of the House of Lords, the Court of Appeal (in England) and the Judicial Committee of the Privy Council were:

> "part of the *corpus* of jurisprudence and law that was taken over on the foundation of Saorstát Éireann being the laws in force...at the date of the coming into operation of the 1922 Constitution: and were thence carried past 1937 by Article 50;"

but (apart from all question of consistency with the Constitutions of 1922 and 1937) while *dicta* in the *Boylan* and *O'Brien* cases:

[47] High Court, 19 October 1984.

[48] [1979] IR 59. The views expressed by Henchy J in the *Vone Securities* case echo those contained in an article of his written some seventeen years earlier ("Precedent in the Irish Court" (1962) 25 MLR 544) where, explaining the rationale behind the court's reluctance to disturb pre-1922 precedent constituting a settled body of common law doctrine, he said:

> "The earlier decision may be of long standing and have become the basis of property right, contracts, disbursements, exemptions or otherwise have become such an essential part of the fabric of the law that to expunge it would cause the greater damage."

[49] [1984] IR 200.

> "appeared to support the view that decisions of the House of Lords upon law common to England and Ireland given before...independence are a binding force in our courts, in my view the decision of this Court in *Attorney General v Ryan's Car Hire Ltd.*[50] and *The State (Quinn) v Ryan*,[51] wherein the rigidity of the principle of *stare decisis* was denied, must now call into question the binding force of any such pre-1922 decision."

In other words, if the Supreme Court now feels free in a proper case to depart from an earlier decision of its own, *a fortiori* it must be free to depart from earlier English authority.

As the date 1922 recedes, the practical importance of the point diminishes, though it is obviously still capable of coming into issue. On the one hand, it could be said that, as the House of Lords was the apex of the judicial system of which the pre-1922 Irish courts formed part, and as those courts would have recognised themselves as bound by a decision of that House, pre-1922 decisions of the House of Lords, even if they never fell to be applied here before independence, were still an immanent, or contingent, part of the "laws in force" so as to be borne across on Article 73. On the other hand, the spirit of Gavan Duffy J is much more marked among the modern judiciary, to whom the *Exham v Beamish* option would be likely to appeal; and, as has been seen, there is the view of McCarthy J that the mere fact of having been carried over successively by Article 73 of the old and Article 50 of the present Constitution does not solidify pre-1922 judicial authority into the condition of a statute, or immunise it against judicial reversal.

Legislation of late 1937

The provision of the second section of Article 50 refers to the Constitution (Consequential Provisions) Act 1937; the Defence Forces Act 1937; the Electoral (Chairman of Dáil Éireann) Act 1937; the Interpretation Act 1937; the Local Government (Nomination of Presidential Candidates) Act 1937; the Presidential Elections Act 1937; the Presidential Seal Act 1937; the Seanad Electoral (Panel Members) Act 1937; and the Seanad Electoral (University Members) Act 1937.

[50] [1965] IR 642.
[51] [1965] IR 70; (1966) 100 ILTR 105.

Article 51

TRANSITIONAL AMENDMENT OF THE CONSTITUTION

TRANSITORY PROVISIONS[1]

FORÁILTÍ SEALADACHA[1]

[This heading refers to the final thirteen Articles, 51-63 inclusive]

Article 51

1. **Notwithstanding anything contained in Article 46 hereof, any of the provisions of this Constitution, except the provisions of the said Article 46 and this Article may, subject as hereinafter provided, be amended by the Oireachtas, whether by way of variation, addition or repeal, within a period of three years after the date on which the first President shall have entered upon his office.**

2. **A proposal for the amendment of this Constitution under this Article shall not be enacted into law, if, prior to such enactment, the President, after consultation with the Council of State, shall have signified in a message under his hand and Seal addressed to the Chairman of each of the Houses of the Oireachtas that the proposal is in his opinion a proposal to effect an amendment of such a character and importance that the will of the people thereon ought to be ascertained by Referendum before its enactment into law.**

3. **The foregoing provisions of this Article shall cease to have the force of law immediately upon the expiration of the period of three years referred to in section 1 hereof.**

4. **This Article shall be omitted from every official text of this Constitution published after the expiration of the said period.**

Airteagal 51

1. **D'ainneoin aon ní dá bhfuil in Airteagal 46 den Bhunreacht seo, tig leis an Oireachtas, taobh istigh de thrí bliana taréis an lae rachas an chéad Uachtarán i gcúram a oifige agus fá chuimsiú na nithe atá leagtha amach annso in ar ndiaidh, leasú a dhéanamh, le hathrú nó le breisiú nó le haisghairm, ar aon fhoráiltí den Bhunreacht seo taobh amuigh d'fhoráiltí Airteagail 46 agus foráiltí an Airteagail seo féin.**

2. **Aon togra déantar chun an Bunreacht seo do leasú faoin Airteagal so ní cead é achtú ina dhlí nó chuireann an tUachtarán, roimh an achtú sin agus d'éis comhairle do ghlacadh leis an gComhairle Stáit, teachtairacht faoina láimh is faoina Shéala go dtí Cathaoirleach gach Tí faoi leith den Oireachtas dá chur in iúl dóibh gurb é a thuairim gur togra é chun a leithéid sin de leasú thábhachtach do dhéanamh go mba chóir breith an phobail d'fháil air le Reifreann sula n-achtófaí ina dhlí é.**

3. **Beidh deireadh le feidhm dlí na bhforailtí sin romhainn den Airteagal so láithreach ar gcaitheamh na dtrí mblian a luaitear in alt 1 den Airteagal seo.**

4. **Ní foláir an tAirteagal seo d'fhágáil as gach téacs oifigiúil den Bhunreacht seo dá bhfoilseofar d'éis na tréimhse réamhráite.**

[1] In conformity with the provisions of Article 51.4 and Article 52, the Transitory Provisions (Articles 51 to 63) are not printed in the texts of the Constitution published since the times there specified (i.e. the last complete text including all the transitory provisions was published in 1938). As Articles 52 to 63 continue to have the force of law (Article 52.2), and as Article 51, although spent, may still arise for interpretation in regard to amending Acts passed under its cover, this omission is very inconvenient. (The Transitory Provisions have once again been recently officially published, though of course in a format separate from the body of the

Transitory period of the 1922 and 1937 Constitutions

This Article empowered the Oireachtas to amend the Constitution without a referendum for a limited period[2] which - unlike the corresponding though longer period provided in Article 50 of the 1922 Constitution[3] - could not be extended by operation of this Article itself. It was availed of to pass two amending Acts: the First Amendment of the Constitution Act 1939, which had the single purpose of giving a special, artificial meaning to the expression "time of war" in Article 28.3.3;[4] and the Second Amendment of the Constitution Act 1941, which contained a large number of amendments, some very minor, but including a still wider artificial meaning for "time of war".[5]

In *In re McGrath and Harte*[6] it was argued for the applicants (who were under sentence of death passed by a military court whose jurisdiction depended on a chain of events of which one was the passage of the First Amendment of the Constitution Act) that s 2 of Article 51 impliedly required the President to consult the Council of State before signing the Bill for the Act which he had not done. Gavan Duffy J held that the Article "imposed no obligation on the President to do so"; on appeal, the Supreme Court, *per* Sullivan CJ, said it seemed to them clear that the question as to whether the Council of State should be consulted was entirely a matter for the President in the exercise of his discretion.[7]

"Blanket" or implicit amendment

The question of whether a constitutional amendment made by ordinary legislation during a transitional period such as Article 51 (and Article 50 of the 1922 Constitution) envisaged must be specific, or whether "blanket" or implicit amendment is necessary, has arisen on several occasions, going back to the earliest days of the State. No problem has arisen in regard to the transitory period under the 1937 Constitution, as the amendments contained in the two amending Acts of 1939 and 1941 were all specific. Under the 1922 Constitution, interpretation of which is still necessary from time to time, the matter came up in two ways apart from specific amendments.

Firstly, there were instances in which an enactment was declared, in the event of its conflicting with the Constitution, to amend the Constitution to the extent of the conflict, but in which the precise points of conflict were not identified. Thus s 3 of the Public Safety Act 1927, provided that:

Constitution.) In the 1938 edition of the Constitution the Irish version of Articles 51-63 is printed in "Gaelic" type and according to old spelling conventions: no official edition of these Articles in standardised Irish spelling exists, but the authors have for the sake of uniformity reproduced them here in standardised form.

[2] The first President (Dr. Douglas Hyde) entered upon office on 25 June 1938, so that the transitory period ended on 25 June 1941.

[3] Eight years, extended by the Constitution (Amendment No.16) Act 1929, to sixteen years by virtue of Article 50 itself.

[4] See above, pp. 237-238.

[5] *Id.* For a discussion of the historical background to aspects of the First Amendment, see the judgment of Finlay CJ in *Attorney General v Hamilton (No.1)* [1993] 2 IR 250; [1993] ILRM 83.

[6] [1941] IR 68.

[7] As to whether the First Amendment of the Constitution Act was properly and effectively enacted having regard to the provisions of Article 25.2 and Article 25.5, see above, pp. 197-198 and pp. 239-240.

> Every provision of this Act which is in contravention of any provision of the Constitution shall to the extent of such contravention operate and have effect as an amendment for so long only as this Act continues in force of such provision of the Constitution.

In *Attorney General v McBride*,[8] Hanna J said:

> "This clause purports to be a discharge of the obligation thrown upon the Oireachtas by Article 50. The question arises: is it a sufficient compliance in law with Article 50 to insert in an Act of Parliament, in vague and general terms, a clause such as this a drag-net - without specifying either any Article, or part of an Article, of the Constitution that is to be amended or whether in fact any amendment is made? The Constitution is a sacred charter, not to be lightly, vaguely, or equivocally tampered with. But this s 3 leaves the subjects of the State, who have rights under the Constitution and rights to exercise against amendments of the Constitution, in the dark as to what is really altered in the Constitution, instead of enlightening them as to any change in their status. An "omnibus" amendment of this kind is contrary to the spirit of Article 50, if not to the letter. The rights of the people should not be obscured by the facile pen of the parliamentary draftsman."

However, having regard to the wording of Article 50, which permitted amendment in the transitory period "by way of ordinary legislation", he felt:

> "compelled, but with great hesitation, to come to the conclusion that this s 3 comes within that term; but it is a precedent that should not be followed."

A few years later the same device was nevertheless again adopted, though with the difference that the amending enactment - the Constitution (Amendment No. 17) Act 1931 - had the effect of building its operative part into the Constitution itself as a new Article (numbered 2A). Section 2 of that new Article 2A provided that:

> "Article 3 and every subsequent Article of this Constitution shall be read and construed subject to the provisions of this Article, and in the case of any inconsistency between this Article and the said Article 3 or any subsequent Article, this Article shall prevail."

1922 Constitution automatically defeasible by any legislation

This provision, although deplored, was held by the Supreme Court majority to be a valid amendment of the Constitution in *The State (Ryan) v Lennon*,[9] and recently, in *McMahon v Attorney General*,[10] Ó Dálaigh CJ accepted that the "omnibus" technique had validly amended the 1922 Constitution:

> "This was not the limit of the 1922 Constitution's debility. An even more extreme proposition was judicially admitted: that any Act at all, even one in which no potential conflict with the Constitution was contemplated or mentioned in any way, and in which therefore no intention to amend it was expressed, would still operate to amend it (i.e. would be valid in spite of it) during the transitional period."

In *R. (Cooney) v Clinton*,[11] the constitutionality of the Indemnity Act 1923, was in issue, and O'Connor MR said:

[8] [1928] IR 451; (1928) 62 ILTR 145.
[9] [1935] IR 170; (1935) 69 ILTR 125.
[10] [1972] IR 69; (1972) 106 ILTR 89.
[11] [1935] IR 245 (but decided in 1923).

> "It is difficult to see how, during the period of eight years, any Act passed by the Oireachtas can be impeached as *ultra vires* so long as it is within the terms of the Scheduled Treaty. It was urged that any Act of Parliament purporting to amend the Constitution should declare that it was so intended, but I cannot accede to the argument in view of the express provision that any amendment made within the period may be made by ordinary legislation."

Eight years later the doctrine of automatic amendment was again accepted, by Fitzgibbon J, in *Lynham v Butler (No.2)*.[12] However, in *The State (Burke) v Lennon*,[13] Gavan Duffy J drew attention to the fact that although the Offences against the State Act 1939, had been passed within the transitory period of the 1937 Constitution, and although the constitutionality of part of the Act was now in issue, counsel for the State had not argued that the Act operated to amend the Constitution even in the absence of any expression of intent to do so; this forbearance, Gavan Duffy J said, was "quite right". In *Conroy v Attorney General*[14] the Supreme Court appeared to extend its non-acceptance of the notion of automatic or implicit amendment even back to the 1922 Constitution;[15] it rejected (though without giving reasons) the submission that that Constitution must be taken to have been automatically amended by any provision of the Road Traffic Act 1933, which was in conflict with it.[16]

[12] [1933] IR 74; (1933) ILTR 75; (1932) LJ Ir 172.

[13] [1940] IR 136; (1940) 74 ILTR 131.

[14] [1965] IR 411.

[15] However, note that in *Shanley v Commissioners of Public Works* [1992] 2 IR 477 Carroll J accepted that insofar as the Landlord and Tenant Act 1931 was inconsistent with Article 11 of the 1922 Constitution, it had *pro tanto* amended the Constitution, since a "statute purporting to amend the [1922] Constitution did not have to declare that it was so intending."

[16] Hugh Kennedy, the first Attorney General and the first Chief Justice, had been the legal adviser of the Provisional Government and had been an important force in the committee which drafted the 1922 Constitution (see Brian Farrell, "*The Drafting of the Irish Free State Constitution*", a study in four parts contained in the Ir Jur, vols. 5 and 6 (1970-71)). His account of how the old Article 50 came to have that form, and his view of the use to which it was put, is contained in his introduction to Leo Kohn's *Constitution of the Irish Free State* (1932): "It was originally intended, as appears by the draft, that amendment of the Constitution should not be possible without the consideration due to so important a matter affecting the fundamental law and framework of the State, and the draft provided that the process of amendment should be such as to require full and general consideration. At the last moment, however, it was agreed that a provision be added to Article 50, allowing amendment by way of ordinary legislation during a limited period so that drafting or verbal amendments, not altogether unlikely to appear necessary in a much debated text, might be made without the more elaborate process proper for the purpose of more important amendments. This clause was, however, afterwards used for effecting alterations of a radical and far-reaching character, some of them far removed in principle from the ideas and ideals before the minds of the first authors of the instrument." His powerful dissent in *The State (Ryan) v Lennon* (see above, pp. 673-674.) may be read against the background of his feelings thus disclosed two years earlier.

Article 52

PERMANENT OFFICIAL TEXT OF THE CONSTITUTION: OMISSION OF TRANSITORY ARTICLES

Article 52

1. **This Article and the subsequent Articles shall be omitted from every official text of this Constitution published after the date on which the first President shall have entered upon his office.**
2. **Every Article of this Constitution which is hereafter omitted in accordance with the foregoing provisions of this Article from the official text of this Constitution shall notwithstanding such omission continue to have the force of law.**

Airteagal 52

1. **Ní foláir an tAirteagal seo agus na hAirteagail atá ina dhiaidh d'fhágáil as gach téacs oifigiúil den Bhunreacht seo dá bhfoilseofar d'éis an lae rachas an chéad Uachtarán i gcúram a oifige.**
2. **Gach Airteagal den Bhunreacht seo a fágfar dá éis seo as téacs oifigiúil an Bhunreachta so do réir na bhforáiltí sin romhainn den Airteagal so, leanfaidh sé d'fheidhm dlí do bheith aige d'aínneoin é bheith fágtha ar lár amhlaidh.**

Inconvenient results

The very inconvenient result of the provision of Article 52.1 (and of Article 51.4) is that the text of the Transitory Provisions can be found printed with the rest of the Constitution only in very early editions of the Constitution. However, the text of all the Transitory Provisions, in a format separate from the main text of the Constitution, has recently been published in official form.[1]

Henchy J said in *Eamonn Andrews Productions v Gaiety Theatre*[2] that Article 58.1 was "a transitory provision that has now lapsed"; but as it enjoys the force of law by Article 52.2, this must be regarded as a loose expression for "a provision to regulate a transition which is now complete".

[1] As the Transitory Provisions of the Constitution of Ireland (Foráiltí Sealadacha de Bhunreacht na hÉireann).
[2] [1973] IR 295.

TRANSITION AND RECONSTITUTION OF HOUSES OF OIREACHTAS AND OF GOVERNMENT; CONTINUANCE OF CIVIL SERVICE; ENTRY UPON OFFICE OF FIRST PRESIDENT

Article 53

1. On the coming into operation of this Constitution a general election for Seanad Éireann shall be held in accordance with the relevant Articles of this Constitution as if a dissolution of Dáil Éireann had taken place on the date of the coming into operation of this Constitution.
2. For the purposes of this Article references in the relevant provisions of this Constitution to a dissolution of Dáil Éireann shall be construed as referring to the coming into operation of this Constitution, and in those provisions the expression "Dáil Éireann" shall include the Chamber of Deputies (Dáil Éireann) established by the Constitution hereby repealed.
3. The first assembly of Seanad Éireann shall take place not later than one hundred and eighty days after the coming into operation of this Constitution.

Airteagal 53

1. Ar dteacht i ngníomh don Bhunreacht so, ní foláir olltoghchán do Sheanad Éireann do dhéanamh do réir na nAirteagal iomchuí den Bhunreacht so, amhail is go ndéanfaí Dáil Éireann do lán-scor lá an Bunreacht so do theacht i ngníomh.
2. Tagartha insna foráiltí iomchuí den Bhunreacht so do Dháil Éireann do lán-scor ní foláir, chun crícheanna an Airteagail seo, iad do léiriú ina dtagartha don Bhunreacht so do theacht i ngníomh, agus áireofar faoin bhfocal "Dáil Éireann" insna foráiltí sin an Teach Teachtaí (Dáil Éireann) a bunaíodh leis an mBunreacht a aisghairmthear leis seo.
3. Beidh céad-thionól Sheanad Éireann ann lá nach déanaí ná naoi bhfichid lá taréis teacht i ngníomh don Bhunreacht so.

Article 54

1. The Chamber of Deputies (Dáil Éireann) established by the Constitution hereby repealed and existing immediately before that repeal shall, on the coming into operation of this Constitution, become and be Dáil Éireann for all the purposes of this Constitution.
2. Every person who is a member of the said Chamber of Deputies (Dáil Éireann) immediately before the said repeal shall, on the coming into operation of this Constitution, become and be a member of Dáil Éireann as if he had been elected to be such member at an election held under this Constitution.

Airteagal 54

1. An Teach Teachtaí (Dáil Éireann) a bunaíodh leis an mBunreacht a aisghairmthear leis an mBunreacht so, agus a bheas ann díreach roimh an aisghairm sin, is é Dáil Éireann chun crícheanna uile an Bhunreachta so ar dteacht i ngníomh don Bhunreacht so.
2. Gach uile dhuine is comhalta den Teach Teachtaí sin (Dáil Éireann) díreach roimh an aishairm sin is comhalta de Dháil Éireann é ar dteacht i ngníomh don Bhunreacht so, amhail is go dtoghfaí ina chomhalta de Dháil Éireann é i dtoghchán a bheadh ann faoin mBunreacht so.

3. The member of the said Chamber of Deputies (Dáil Éireann) who is immediately before the said repeal Ceann Comhairle shall upon the coming into operation of this Constitution become and be the Chairman of Dáil Éireann.

3. An comhalta den Teach Teachtaí sin (Dáil Éireann) is Ceann Comhairle díreach roimh an ais-ghairm sin, is é is Cathaoirleach ar Dháil Éireann ar dteacht i ngníomh don Bhunreacht seo.

Article 55

1. After the coming into operation of this Constitution and until the first assembly of Seanad Éireann, the Oireachtas shall consist of one House only.

2. The House forming the Oireachtas under this Article shall be Dáil Éireann.

3. Until the first President enters upon his office, the Oireachtas shall be complete and capable of functioning notwithstanding that there is no President.

4. Until the first President enters upon his office, Bills passed or deemed to have been passed by the House or by both Houses of the Oireachtas shall be signed and promulgated by the Commission hereinafter mentioned instead of by the President.

Airteagal 55

1. Taréis teacht i ngníomh don Bhunreacht so agus go dtí go mbeidh céad-thionól Sheanad Éireann ann ní bheidh san Oireachtas ach aon Teach amháin.

2. Is é Dáil Éireann an Teach is Oireachtas faoin Airteagal so.

3. Go dtí go dtéidh an chéad Uachtarán i gcúram a oifige beidh an tOireachtas iomlán agus in acmhainn feidhme bíodh gan Uachtarán do bheith ann.

4. Go dtí go dtéidh an chéad Uachtarán i gcúram a oifige, aon Bhillí a rithfear nó a measfar a ritheadh ag aon Teach nó ag an dá Theach den Oireachtas is iad an Coimisiún a luaitear annso in ar ndiaidh a chuirfeas lámh leo agus fhogrós iad, in ionad an Uachtaráin.

Article 56

1. On the coming into operation of this Constitution, the Government in office immediately before the coming into operation of this Constitution shall become and be the Government for the purposes of this Constitution and the members of that Government shall without any appointment under Article 13 hereof, continue to hold their respective offices as if they had been appointed thereto under the said Article 13.

Airteagal 56

1. Ar dteacht i ngníomh don Bhunreacht so is é an Rialtas a bheas in oifig díreach roimh theacht i ngníomh don Bhunreacht so is Rialtas chun críocheanna an Bhunreachta so, agus leanfaídh comhaltaí an Rialtais sin dá n-oifigí faoi seach gan iad do cheapadh faoi Airteagal 13 den Bhunreacht so amhail is go gceapfaí chun na n-oifigí sin iad faoi Airteagal sin a 13.

2. The members of the Government in office on the date on which the first President shall enter upon his office shall receive official appointments from the President as soon as may be after the said date.

3. The Departments of State of Saorstát Éireann shall as on and from the date of the coming into operation of this Constitution and until otherwise determined by law become and be the Departments of State.

4. On the coming into operation of this Constitution, the Civil Service of the Government of Saorstát Éireann shall become and be the Civil Service of the Government.

5. 1° Nothing in this Constitution shall prejudice or affect the terms and conditions of service, or the tenure of office or the remuneration of any person who was in any Governmental employment immediately prior to the coming into operation of this Constitution.

2° Nothing in this Article shall operate to invalidate or restrict any legislation whatsoever which has been enacted or may be enacted hereafter applying to or prejudicing or affecting all or any of the matters contained in the next preceding sub section.

2. Na comhaltaí den Rialtas a bheas in oifig an lá rachas an chéad Uachtarán i gcuram a oifige, ceapfaidh an tUachtarán go hoifigiúil iad chomh luath agus is feidir é tar éis an lae sin.

3. Is iad Ranna Stáit Shaorstát Éireann is Ranna Stáit lá an Bunreacht so do theacht i ngníomh agus ón lá sin amach agus go dtí go gcinntear a mhalairt le dlí.

4. Is í Stát-sheirbhís Rialtas Shaorstát Éireann Stát-sheirbhís an Rialtais ar dteacht i ngníomh don Bhunreacht so.

5. 1° Ní dhéanfaidh aon ní dá bhfuil insan Bhunreacht so dochar ná difir do théarmaí agus coinníollacha seirbhíse, ná do shealbhachas oifige, ná do thuarastal aon duine dá raibh in aon fhostaíocht Rialtais díreach roimh theacht i ngníomh don Bhunreacht seo.

2° Ní oibreoidh aon ní atá san Airteagal seo chun aon reachtaíocht ar bith atá achtaithe nó a hachtófar ina dhiaidh seo do chur ó bhail ná do shrianadh is reachtaíocht a bhaineann nó a bhainfeas le gach ní nó le haon ní nó nithe, nó dhéanann nó dhéanfas dochar nó difir do gach ní nó d'aon ní nó nithe, dá bhfuil insan bhfo-alt deiridh sin roimhe seo.

Article 57

1. The first President shall enter upon his office not later than one hundred and eighty days after the date of the coming into operation of this Constitution.

2. After the date of the coming into operation of this Constitution and pending the entry of the first President upon his office the powers and functions of the President under this

Airteagal 57

1. Ní foláir an chéad Uachtarán do dhul i gcúram a oifige lá nach déanaí ná naoi bhfichid lá taréis lá an Bunreacht so do theacht i ngníomh.

2. Taréis lá an Bunreacht so do theacht i ngníomh agus go dtí go dtéidh an chéad Uachtarán i gcúram a oifige is iad oibreos cumhachta agus feidhmeanna an Uachtaráin faoin mBunreacht so

Constitution shall be exercised by a Commission consisting of the following persons, namely, the Chief Justice, the President of the High Court, and the Chairman of Dáil Éireann.

3. Whenever the Commission is incomplete by reason of a vacancy in an office the holder of which is a member of the Commission, the Commission shall, during such vacancy, be completed by the substitution of the senior judge of the Supreme Court who is not already a member of the Commission in the place of the holder of such office, and likewise in the event of any member of the Commission being, on any occasion, unable to act, his place shall be taken on that occasion by the senior judge of the Supreme Court who is available and is not already a member, or acting in the place of a member, of the Commission.

4. The Commission may act by any two of their number.

5. The provisions of this Constitution which relate to the exercise and performance by the President of the powers and functions conferred on him by this Constitution shall apply to the exercise and performance of the said powers and functions by the said Commission in like manner as those provisions apply to the exercise and performance of the said powers and functions by the President.

ná Coimisiún dena daoine seo leanas .i. an Príomh-Bhreitheamh, Uachtarán na hArd-Chúirte agus Cathaoirleach Dháil Éireann.

3. Aon uair a bheidh an Coimisiún neamh-iomlán toisc oifig gur comhalta den Choimisiún a sealbhóir do bheith folamh, ní foláir an Coimisiún d'iomlánú, an fhaid a bheidh an oifig sin folamh, tríd an mbreitheamh sinsir den Chúirt Uachtarach nach comhalta den Choimisiún cheana do chur ar an gCoimisiún in ionad an té a bhí i seilbh na hoifige sin, agus fós má bhíonn comhalta den Choimisiún ar aon ócáid gan bheith i gcumas feidhme ní foláir an breitheamh sinsir den Chúirt Uachtarach a bheas ar fáil, agus ná beidh ina chomhalta den Choimisiún cheana ná ag gníomhú in ionad chomhalta dhe, do ghabháil ionaid an chomhalta éagumasaigh sin ar an ócáid sin.

4. Is dleathach don Chomisiún gníomhú trí bheirt ar bith dá líon.

5. Na foráiltí den Bhunreacht so bhaineas leis an Uachtarán d'oibriú agus do chomhlíonadh na gcumhachta agus na bhfeidhmeanna a bronntar air leis an mBunreacht so, bainfid leis an gCoimisiún sin d'oibriú agus do chomhlíonadh na gcumhachta agus na bhfeidhmeanna sin faoi mar bhainid na foráilti sin leis an Uachtarán d'oibriú agus do chomhlíonadh na gcumhachta agus na bhfeidhmeanna sin.

By the Second Amendment of the Constitution Act 1941, the final section of Article 56 was added to the original Article; and the words "terms and conditions of service, or the tenure of office or the remuneration" were substituted for the original words "terms, conditions, remuneration or tenure" in s 5.1.

Article 56.3 was briefly referred to in passing by Gavan Duffy J in *Maunsell v Minister for Education*[1] as having continued the Department of Education of Saorstát Éireann as the corresponding Department of State under the 1937 Constitution; and in *Irish Land Commission v Ruane,*[2] where he said a Department of State" (under the Ministers and Secretaries (Amendment) Act, 1928) "could, no doubt, claim the privilege of `Government Department'" under the Land Act 1923).

The first President, Dr. Douglas Hyde, entered upon his office on 25 June 1938.[3]

[1] [1940] IR 213; (1939) 73 ILTR 36.
[2] [1938] IR 148; (1938) 72 ILTR 119.
[3] For an account of the ceremonial attending this occasion, see two articles by the first President's former aide-de-camp, Captain Basil Peterson, in *The Irish Times*, 1-2 July 1980.

Article 58

TEMPORARY CONTINUANCE OF COURTS

Article 58

1. On and after the coming into operation of this Constitution and until otherwise determined by law, the Supreme Court of Justice, the High Court of Justice, the Circuit Court of Justice and the District Court of Justice in existence immediately before the coming into operation of this Constitution shall, subject to the provisions of this Constitution relating to the determination of questions as to the validity of any law, continue to exercise the same jurisdictions respectively as theretofore, and any judge or justice being a member of such Court shall, subject to compliance with the subsequent provisions of this Article, continue to be a member thereof and shall hold office by the like tenure and on the like terms as theretofore unless he signifies to the Taoiseach his desire to resign.

2. Every such judge and justice who shall not have so signified his desire to resign shall make and subscribe the declaration set forth in section 5 of Article 34 of this Constitution.

3. This declaration shall be made and subscribed by the Chief Justice in the presence of the Taoiseach, and by each of the other judges of the said Supreme Court, the judges of the said High Court and the judges of the aid Circuit Court in the presence of the Chief Justice in open court.

4. In the case of the justices of the said District Court the declara-

Airteagal 58

1. Ar dteacht i ngníomh don Bhunreacht so agus dá éis sin agus go dtí go gcinntear a mhalairt le dlí, ní foláir don Chúirt Uachtarach, don Ard-Chúirt, don Chúirt Chuarda agus don Chúirt Dúiche a bheas ann díreach roimh theacht i ngníomh don Bhunreacht so leanúint, fá chuimsiú na bhforáiltí den Bhunreacht so a bhaineas le breith do thabhairt ar cheisteanna i dtaobh bail do bheith ar aon dlí, de na dlínsí céanna faoi seach d'oibriú do bhí dá n-oibriú acu go nuige seo agus, ar an gcoinníoll go gcomhlíonfaidh sé na foráiltí seo in ar ndiaidh den Airteagal so, leanfaidh aon breitheamh is comhalta d'aon Chúirt díobh sin de bheith ina chomhalta den Chúirt sin, agus beidh sé i seilbh oifige ar an sealbhachas is ar na coinníollacha céanna ar a raibh sé go nuige sin, mura gcuirfidh in iúl don Taoiseach gur mian leis éirí as.

2. Gach breitheamh díobh sin ná cuirfidh in iúl ar an gcuma sin gur mian leis éirí as oifig, ní foláir dó an dearbhú atá in alt 5 d'Airteagal 34 den Bhunreacht so do dhéanamh agus a lámh do chur leis.

3. Is i láthair an Taoisigh a dhéanfaidh an Príomh-Bhreitheamh an dearbhú sin agus a chuirfidh a lámh leis, agus is i láthair an Phrímh-Bhreithimh insan chúirt go poiblí a dhéanfaidh gach breitheamh de bhreithiúna eile na Cúirte Uachtaraí sin, de bhreithiúna na hArd-Chúirte sin agus de bhreithiúna na Cúirte Cuarda sin, an dearbhú sin agus a chuirfidh a lámh leis.

4. Is insan chúirt go poiblí a dhéanfaidh breithimh na Cúirte

tion shall be made and subscribed in open court.

5. Every such declaration shall be made immediately upon the coming into operation of this Constitution, or as soon as may be thereafter.

6. Any such judge or justice who declines or neglects to make such declaration in the manner aforesaid shall be deemed to have vacated his office.

Dúiche sin an dearbhú agus a chuirfidh a lámh leis.

5. Láithreach ar dteacht i ngníomh don Bhunreacht so nó chomh luath agus is féidir é dá éis sin is eadh déanfar gach dearbhú díobh sin.

6. Aon bhreitheamh díobh sin a dhiultós nó a fhailleos an dearbhú sin do dhéanamh ar an modh réamhráite ní foláir a mheas go bhfuil scartha aige lena oifig.

Delay in establishing new courts made the subject of a challenge

In *The State (Killian) v Minister for Justice*[1] attention was called to the fact that the provisions of Article 58, although among those expressly labelled "transitory" by the Constitution itself, were still being relied on to justify, in the year 1951, the continued jurisdiction of the pre-1937 courts (established by the Courts of Justice Act 1924), the "new" courts contemplated by Article 34 never in fact having been set up. In *Killian's* case an attempt was made to challenge the order of a Circuit Court judge on the ground that the judge's own appointment (in 1945) was void, as Article 58 did not authorise or envisage the making of any fresh appointments to fill such vacancies as might arise in the "old" courts which were leading a merely transitory existence pending their replacement; this, it was pointed out, was in sharp contrast to the provision of Article 75 of the 1922 Constitution, which in its corresponding transitory provisions regarding the courts, had specifically permitted the filling of casual vacancies in the transitional period. The Supreme Court, *per* Murnaghan J, made (it may be thought) undeservedly little of this acute point; the Court said "it must...be remembered that the circumstances are vastly different in the two cases", but without explaining where exactly the vast difference lay; and considered also that the filling of casual vacancies was positively required by s 45 of the Courts of Justice Act 1924, which "was a law in force in Saorstát Éireann immediately prior to the date of the coming into operation of the Constitution and under Article 50...continues to be of full force and effect", but did not consider whether, in the context presented by the applicant's argument, the continuance of that particular provision and its use for an indefinite period after 1937 was consistent with Article 34 (as it would have to be, in order to attract the carryover effect of Article 50).

Some years later an effort was made, in *Foyle Fisheries Commission v Gallen*[2] to raise the question whether the District Court, which was still the "old" District Court carrying on by virtue of Article 58, could exercise a criminal jurisdiction in respect of an act committed in an area (*viz.* part of Northern Ireland) where that Court, as originally constituted, had no jurisdiction at all. The Supreme Court however declined to consider the point, as it had been raised by way of case stated from the Circuit Court, and, as it impliedly impugned the constitutionality of the Foyle Fisheries Act 1952, that Court should not, under Article 34.3.2, have entertained the question in any shape or form.[3]

[1] [1954] IR 207; (1956) ILTR 116. In *Attorney General v Connolly* [1947] IR 213; (1947) 81 ILTR 92 Gavan Duffy P had said that "Article 58.1 expressly continues the jurisdiction of the former High Court, until the law determines otherwise."

[2] (1960) Ir Jur Rep 35.

[3] See above, pp. 424-425.

During the period of the transition - which actually lasted until 1961[4] - the courts, while recognising that they were not the courts contemplated by Article 34, treated references in the Constitution to the "High Court" and the "Supreme Court" as being applicable to the "old" High and Supreme Courts for as long as they had not been replaced. Thus the "old" Supreme Court heard three references of Bills under Article 26; in *Sullivan v Robinson*[5] O'Byrne J, in delivering the judgment of that Court, said that the phrase in Article 58 "subject to the provisions of this Constitution relating to the determination of questions as to the validity of any law" meant that:

> "the reference of Bills to the Supreme Court was contemplated as something that might be done during the transition period before courts were set up under the Constitution."[6]

He pointed out that, otherwise, the *habeas corpus* provisions of Article 40, which centre on the High Court, would have lapsed, in effect, during the transitional period:

> "It was contemplated that some period of time must necessarily elapse before the new courts could be established and it could not, in our opinion, be successfully argued that the framers of the Constitution contemplated that, in the intervening period, the right to *habeas corpus* should disappear. In our opinion this right was jealously guarded both by Article 58.1 and by the express provisions of Article 40.4."

However, apart from this, the Court held that the statutory rules governing the "old" courts still applied and had not been replaced by such rules obviously intended to govern the "new" courts once created - as that of Article 34.4.3; and this view was re-stated by the "new" Supreme Court in *Eamonn Andrews v Gaiety Theatre,*[7] in which Walsh J said:

> "All the pre-existing statutory restrictions which affected the appellate jurisdiction of the former Supreme Court of Justice continued in force so long as that Court existed or until such statutory provision had been repealed or amended: see the decision of the former Supreme Court of Justice in *Sullivan v Robinson.*[8] The provisions of Article 34.4.3 of the Constitution dealing with the appellate jurisdiction of the Supreme Court did not in any way relate to the courts carried on by virtue of Article 58."

Provision analogous to that of Article 58 had been made (in respect of the courts of the old regime) by Article 75 of the 1922 Constitution; this was referred to in *The State (Attorney General) v Judge Roe*,[9] as well as in *The State (Killian) v Minister for Justice.*[10]

[4] The new courts were set up by the Courts (Establishment and Constitution) Act, of that year.
[5] [1954] IR 161; (1954) 88 ILTR 169.
[6] This argument could not have been made consistently with the analysis of constitutional terminology subsequently undertaken by Walsh J in *The State (Sheerin) v Kennedy* [1966] IR 379, as the reference to "validity" of a "law" is not, according to that analysis) apposite for an Article 26 situation. As to the reality of the *Sheerin* position, see the Preface to this book.
[7] [1973] IR 295.
[8] [1954] IR 161; (1954) 88 ILTR 169.
[9] [1951] IR 172; (1952) 86 ILTR 91.
[10] [1954] IR 207; (1956) 90 ILTR 116.

CONTINUANCE OF ATTORNEY GENERAL, COMPTROLLER AND AUDITOR GENERAL, DEFENCE AND POLICE FORCES; COMING INTO FORCE OF THE CONSTITUTION; THE TEXT OF THE CONSTITUTION

Article 59

On the coming into operation of this Constitution, the person who is the Attorney General of Saorstát Éireann immediately before the coming into operation of this Constitution shall, without any appointment under Article 30 of this Constitution, become and be the Attorney General as if he had been appointed to that office under the said Article 30.

Airteagal 59

An té is Príomh-Aturnae Shaorstát Éireann direach roimh theacht i ngníomh don Bhunreacht so is é is Ard-Aighne ar theacht i ngníomh don Bhunreacht so amhail is go gceapfaí chun na hoifige sin é faoi Airteagal 30 den Bhunreacht so, agus sin gan é cheapadh faoi Airteagal sin 30.

Article 60

On the coming into operation of this Constitution the person who is the Comptroller and Auditor General of Saorstát Éireann immediately before the coming into operation of this Constitution shall, without any appointment under Article 33 of this Constitution, become and be the Comptroller and Auditor General as if he had been appointed to that office under the said Article 33.

Airteagal 60

An té is Ard-Scrudóir Shaorstát Éireann direach roimh theacht i ngniomh don Bhunreacht so is é is Ard-Reachtaire Cuntas is Ciste ar theacht i ngníomh don Bhunreacht so amhail is go gceapfaí chun na hoifige sin é faoi Airteagal 33 den Bhunreacht so, agus sin gan é cheapadh faoi Airteagal sin 33.

Article 61

1. **On the coming into operation of this Constitution, the Defence Forces and the Police Forces of Saorstát Éireann in existence immediately before the coming into operation of this Constitution shall become and be respectively the Defence Forces and the Police Forces of the State.**
2. **1° Every commissioned officer of the Defence Forces of Saorstát Éireann immediately before the coming into operation of this Constitution shall become and be a commissioned officer of corresponding rank of the Defence Forces of the State as if he had**

Airteagal 61

1. **Na Fórsaí Cosanta agus an Póilíos a bheas ag Saorstát Éireann díreach roimh theacht i ngníomh don Bhunreacht so is iad is Fórsaí Cosanta agus is Póilíos faoi seach don Stát ar theacht i ngníomh don Bhunreacht so.**
2. **1° Gach oifigeach gairme dá mbeidh i bhFórsaí Cosanta Shaorstát Éireann díreach roimh theacht i ngníomh don Bhunreacht so is oifigeach gairme é ar an gcéim chéanna i bhFórsaí Cosanta an Stáit, amhail is go bhfaigheadh sé**

received a commission therein under Article 13 of this Constitution.
2° Every officer of the Defence Forces of the State at the date on which the first President enters upon his office shall receive a commission from the President as soon as may be after that date.

gairm insna Fórsaí sin faoi Airteagal 13 den Bhunreacht so.
2° Gach oifigeach a bheas i bhFórsaí Cosanta an Stáit an lá rachas an chéad Uachtarán i gcúram a oifige, gheobhaidh sé gairm oifigigh ón Uachtarán chomh luath agus is féidir é ina dhiaidh sin.

Article 62
This Constitution shall come into operation
i. on the day following the expiration of a period of one hundred and eighty days after its approval by the people signified by a majority of the votes cast at a plebiscite thereon had in accordance with law, or,
ii. on such earlier day after such approval as may be fixed by a resolution of Dáil Éireann elected at the general election the polling for which shall have taken place on the same day as the said plebiscite.

Airteagal 62
Tiocfaidh an Bunreacht so i ngníomh
i. an chéad lá d'éis tréimhse naoi bhfichid lá taréis an pobal do thoiliú leis agus dá chur san in iúl le tromlach de na vótaí a bhéarfar ar phobal-bhreith a déanfar ina thaobh do réir dlí, nó
ii. lá is luaithe taréis an toilithe sin, má socraítear amhlaidh le rún ón Dáil Éireann a toghfar insan olltoghchán dá ndéanfar vótáil lá na pobal-bhreithe sin.

Article 63
A copy of this Constitution signed by the Taoiseach, the Chief Justice, and the Chairman of Dáil Éireann shall be enrolled for record in the office of the Registrar of the Supreme Court, and such signed copy shall be conclusive evidence of the provisions of this Constitution. In case of conflict between the Irish and the English texts, the Irish text shall prevail.

Airteagal 63
Ní fólair cóip den Bhunreacht so faoi láimh an Taoisigh, an Phrímh-Bhreithimh, agus Chathaoirleach Dháil Éireann do chur isteach ina hiris in oifig Iriseoir na Cúirte Uachtaraí agus is fianaise do-chloíte an chóip shínithe sin ar fhoráiltí an Bhunreachta so. I gcás gan an téacs Gaeilge agus an téacs Sacs-Bhéarla do bheith do réir a chéile is ag an téacs Gaeilge a bheidh an forlámhas.

The Constitution came into operation by virtue of Article 62.i on 27 December 1937, i.e. 180 days after the date of the plebiscite (1 July 1937).[1] No laws were enacted in the last days of 1937, so that all Acts of 1937 or earlier date were enacted under the old, all Acts of 1938 or later date under the new, Constitution.

The provision of the last sentence in Article 63 - although by Article 52.3 it still has the force of law - was repeated in Article 25.5 in extended form by the Second Amendment of the Constitution Act 1941.

[1] No resolution pursuant to Article 62.ii having been passed by Dáil Éireann.

ADDENDUM

Such is the pace of contemporary judicial and legislative developments that it is necessary for us to note very briefly some additional material which came to hand after this book went to press and which effected material changes to our discussion in the main text.

Articles 1-3

On Wednesday, 15 December 1993, the Taoiseach, Mr. Reynolds, and the British Prime Minister, Mr. Major, signed a Joint Declaration in which, *inter alia*, the Irish Government re-affirmed Northern Ireland's statutory constitutional guarantee and accepted that "the democratic right of self-determination by the people of Ireland as a whole must be achieved and exercised with and subject to the agreement and consent of a majority of the people of Northern Ireland and must, consistent with justice and equity, respect the democratic dignity and the civil rights and religious liberties of both communities." As part of an effort to build up trust between the two communities, the Government undertook to examine "any elements in the democratic life and organisation of the Irish State that can be represented to the Irish Government in the course of political dialogue as a real and substantial threat to [the Unionist] way of life and ethos, or that can be represented as not being fully consistent with a modern democratic and pluralist society and ... any possible ways of removing such obstacles." Moreover, the Government also committed itself, in the event of an overall settlement and as part of a balanced constitutional accommodation, to "put forward and support proposals for change in the Irish Constitution which would fully reflect the principle of consent in Northern Ireland." This last committment clearly covers the territorial claim to Northern Ireland in Articles 2 and 3, while pursuant to the earlier undertaking, the Government might be required to consider, *inter alia*, aspects of the Preamble and the prohibition on divorce.

The acceptance by the Irish Government that the right of self-determination of the Irish people could be exercised only with the consent of a majority of the people of Northern Ireland was preceded by a statement that the lessons of Irish history demonstrate that stability and well-being cannot be found under any political system which is refused allegiance or rejected on grounds of identity by a significant minority of those governed by it. This suggests that these comments are best regarded as a statement of the *de facto* position and as such, compatible with the Constitution, having regard to *Boland* v *An Taoiseach*[1].

Article 26

This procedure was invoked for the ninth time on 3 December 1993, when President Robinson referred the Matrimonial Home Bill 1993 to the Supreme Court for an advisory opinion as to its constitutionality.

Article 29.4.5

In *Meagher v Minister for Agriculture and Food*[2] the Supreme Court reversed the decision of Johnson J (pp. 145-146; 252-255) and upheld the constitutionality of s 3(2) of the European Communities Act 1972. The Court reasoned, *per* Finlay CJ, that having regard to the large number of Community laws which have to be implemented "by appropriate action" into the law of the State:

> "the obligation of membership would necessitate facilitating of these activities...by the making of ministerial regulation rather than legislation of the Oireachtas. The

[1] [1974] IR 338; (1975) 109 ILTR 13.

[2] [1994] ILRM 1.

> Court is accordingly satisfied that the power to make regulations in the form in which it is contained in s 3(2) of the Act of 1972 is necessitated by the obligations of membership by the State of the Communities and now of the Union and is therefore by virtue of Article 29.4.5 immune from constitutional challenge."

In other words, the Supreme Court appears to have seen the "necessitated obligations" test as embracing not only matters which are required as a matter of strict law as a condition of Union or Community membership, but also methods or procedures which are considered necessary or appropriate in order to give effect to Community law.

In separate judgments delivered by Blayney and Denham JJ, the Court upheld the validity of a statutory instrument which extended the time limit for a summary prosecution beyond that specified in the Petty Sessions (Ireland) Act 1851, even though the question of such time limits was not mentioned in the relevant directives. The evidence demonstrated that the Minister believed that the existing time limit contained in the 1851 Act was too short to allow for effective prosecution of the offences. Blayney J thus considered that:

> "the implementation of the directive required that the regulation should provide for an adequate time for the preparation of the prosecutions. It was not necessary that the directive should itself fix a time. It was a matter for the State to decide on the length of time required to enable the prosecution to be brought ...."

Blayney J continued by saying that the State was bound by Community law to introduce effective sanctions and:

> "if this necessitated a measure which impliedly amended an existing statute, that measure would prevail over a statute because it was in substance a measure of Community law. It is only in form that it is part of the domestic law. It derives its force from the directive which is binding on the State as to the result to be achieved."

Yet this conclusion is not necessarily self-evident, since in this case it was the member-State which judged that the extended time limit for the prosecution was necessary. To characterise such an implementing measure "as in substance a measure of Community law" is not immediately persuasive and seems almost to conflate the distinction - purposefully drawn by Article 189(3) of the Treaty of Rome - between a regulation and a directive. If Blayney J is correct, the consequences would appear to be far-reaching. If a Minister judged that the imposition of draconian penalties was necessary to provide for the effective summary prosecution of certain offences provided for in a directive, would this then be immune from constitutional scrutiny on the ground that the implementing measure was "in substance a measure of Community law", even though the imposition of such penalties following summary conviction would otherwise (i.e., in the context of a domestic statute) breach Article 38.2.

Article 34.1

In *Z v Director of Public Prosecutions*[3] Hamilton P refused an application (which had been supported by both the applicant and the respondent) that judicial review proceedings to restrain a criminal trial on the ground of alleged unfair pre-trial publicity be heard *in camera*. In his view, Article 34.1 required that the case be heard in public and the present application did not come within the terms of s 45(1) of the Courts

[3] High Court, 30 November 1993.

(Supplemental Provisions) Act 1961 (see pp. 401-403). Hamilton P said that the phrase "urgent applications" referred only to those "which are because of their nature so urgent that they must be made to a judge in his home or some place to which the public do not directly have access."

Article 38.1

In *D v Director of Public Prosecutions*[4] a majority of the Supreme Court reversed the decision of Carney J (see p. 617) whereby he had restrained the re-trial of the applicant on the grounds of adverse pre-trial publicity. And while Finlay CJ and Egan J dissented on the principal issue, all members of the Court were in agreement with the following test enunciated by the Chief Justice:

> "The fundamental nature of the constitutional right involved and the incapacity of the Court further to intervene to defend it leads, in my view, to the conclusion that the standard of proof which the Court should require from the applicant in this case concerning his allegation of the likelihood of an unfair trial is that he should be required to establish that there was a real or serious risk of that occurring. Such an approach is consistent with the view taken by this Court in the different context of extradition proceedings in the case of *Finucane v McMahon*[5]"

The majority judgments of Blayney and Denham JJ stressed that because of the isolated nature of the reportage in question (in one newspaper article), the applicant had not established that there was a "real risk" of an unfair trial by reason of this publicity. Blayney J agreed that there was a "slight risk" of this, but he considered that there was no more than there would be "in any other case where there is room for sympathy for the complainant." In her judgment Denham J stressed that this was not a case of "massive national coverage [or] of media saturation", clearly implying that in such a case an applicant might have better prospects of establishing the risk of an unfair trial.

However, in *Z v Director of Public Prosecutions* (a case which did involve enormous - and adverse - pre-trial publicity), the applicant failed in his bid to restrain the holding of a trial. Hamilton P said that there was a risk that "the administration of the criminal law in notorious cases could be brought to a halt by adverse media publicity." In the present case, the adverse publicity notwithstanding, if the jurors were to have regard to extraneous factors, this would be to disregard their judicial oaths and "the clear directions given to them by the trial judge." Hamilton P expressed confidence that any such jury "would act with responsibility in accordance with the terms of their oaths [and] would follow the directions given by the trial judge and give a true verdict in accordance with the evidence."

Article 40.5

The Road Traffic Bill 1993 (which, *inter alia*, reversed *Director of Public Prosecutions v McCreesh*[6] and which is referred to at p. 916) was modified at Report Stage in the Dáil to restrict the power of Gardaí forcibly to enter a dwelling house to cases in which they are in "hot pursuit" of a suspect seen at the scene of an accident in which a person

[4] Supreme Court, 17 November 1993.
[5] [1990] 1 IR 165.
[6] [1992] 2 IR 239.

has been injured. In order to effect an arrest under ss 49(8) or 50(10) of the Road Traffic Act 1961, the Gardaí may enter without a warrant onto the curtilage of the home, but not the dwelling itself: see s 39 of the Bill.

Article 40.6.1.i.

During the passage of the Criminal Justice (Public Order) Bill 1993 through the Dáil, significant changes were made to s 5, considered at p. 932, which reduce the risk of it being declared unconstitutional. The offence of engaging in disorderly conduct in a public place is now restricted to engaging in *offensive* conduct (as opposed to "shouting, singing or boisterous conduct") which, moreover, is defined as "unreasonable behaviour ... likely to cause serious offence or annoyance..." (as opposed to mere "annoyance".) The breadth of s 6 has also been restricted somewhat inasmuch as now, in order to establish liability for engaging in threatening, abusive or insulting behaviour in a public place, contrary to that section, it is necessary to show that the defendant was at least reckless as to whether his conduct would occasion a breach of the peace.

On 11 January 1994, the Government announced that the Ministerial order banning television and radio interviews with members of certain prescribed organisations, made pursuant to s 31(1) of the Broadcasting Act 1960, would not be renewed when it lapsed on 19 January 1994.

Article 40.6.1.ii.

A number of other provisions of the Criminal Justice (Public Order) Bill 1993 considered at pp. 963-4, were also amended, generally in a restrictive manner, before the Bill left the Dáil. The offence of displaying in public material which is threatening, abusive, insulting or obscene, provided for in s 7, now requires the prosecution to show that the defendant was at least reckless as to whether his conduct would occasion a breach of the peace, while, on the other hand, the offence of failing to comply with the directions of a member of the Garda Síochána in s 8 has been extended to cover a person acting contrary to s 7. Wilful obstruction of the free passage of any person or vehicle in a public place will now be an offence only if done "without lawful authority or reasonable excuse" - s 9 - while, by virtue of amendments to s 16, a person cannot be convicted of the proposed new offence of affray unless he intends to use or threatens to use violence or is aware that his conduct may be violent or threaten violence.

SUBJECT INDEX

(*Note*: Page references in *italics* indicate where the text of an Article is set out.)